10-1-74

The
USED BOOK PRICE GUIDE

1972-73
Pt. 2

An Aid In Ascertaining Current Prices

Compiled by

Mildred S. Mandeville

RETAIL PRICES OF RARE, SCARCE, USED
and OUT-OF-PRINT BOOKS
(Dealer-Code Identification page 363 - 368)

5 YEAR EDITION

Vol. L - Z

From May, 1968 to May, 1973 Catalogs

PRICE GUIDE PUBLISHERS
525 Kenmore Station, Kenmore, Washington 98028

1973

Send check to: PRICE GUIDE PUBLISHERS
525 Kenmore Station
Kenmore, Washington 98028

LA BAR,GEO-Reminiscences of-Phila-1870-port-1st ed-scarce-
ABBurrell,ed (4a1) 12.50

LABAREE,BENJ W.-Local Hist Contributions & Techniques in Study
of 2 Colonial Cities-n.p.-1959-wrps (5j4) 4.00

LA BARRE,A J LE FEBURE DE-Description de la France
Equinoctiale-Paris-1666-Ribou-4to-calf-lg fldng map-1st ed-
rare (5n9,map reprd) 750.00

LABARRE,WESTON-The Aymara Indians of Lake Titicaca Plateau,
Polivia-Amer Anthro Assn-1948 (5qq5) 9.00

LABATUT,J,ed-Highways in Our National Life-1950 (5L7) 7.50

LABAUME,EUGENE-Circumstantial Narrative of Campaign in
Russia-Lond-1815-Sam'l Leigh-8vo-2nd Engl ed-2 fldg battle
plans (5i8,rbkd,lacks lg map) 12.00

--Narrative of campaign in Russia, in 1812-Lond-1815-12mo-
orig blu bds-prntd papr labl-1st ed in Engl-prntd by TChaplin
(5i8,vg,label rub) 15.00

L'ABBERTON,J M-Marine Engineering-NY-1943-illus-1st ed-
439p (5s1,ex-libr) 5.00

LA BEDOYERE,MICHAEL DE-Geo Washington-Lond-1935-illus-
1st ed (5q8) 6.00

LABISKY,WALLACE R-Waterfowl Shooting-NY-(1954)-Leidl,illus-
(4a1) 7.50

LABORATOIRE DE FLORE-ou chymie champetre vegetale-Paris-
1773-384p-calf-12mo (5w1) 25.00

LA BORDE,M-Hist of the So Carolina College-Columbia-1859-
cl-463p (5h6,sl loose) 20. (5h0,rub) 22.50

LABOUCHERE,NORNA-Ladies' Bookplates-Lond-1845-358p-
illus hndbk (5t7,chip) 12.50

LABOUNOUX,P-Le Cidre-Paris-(1910)-12mo-199p-illus-wrps
(5w1) 4.50

LABOUREUR,SUZANNE-Petits & Grands Plats ou le tresor des
amateurs de vraie cuisine-Paris-(1928)-382p-bds-scarce (5g9) 5.00

LA BREE,BEN,ed-Confederate Soldier in the Civil War-Louisville-
1897-frontis-photos-2nd ed (5zz5,sl wn) 75.00

--same-Paterson-1959-elephant folio-480p-photos (4j4) 25.00

LACE & EMBROIDERY REVIEW-NY-1909 to 11-Vol 1,#4 thru
Vol 7,#2-bnd in 3 vols-illus-4to (5ii2) 40.00

LACE DICTIONARY-NY-1913-12mo-cl-illus-1st ed (5p5) 12.50

LACERDA,JOHN-Conqueror Comes to Tea-New Brunswk-Rutgers
Univ-1946-224p (5x9) 2.00

LACH,ALMA S-A Child's 1st Cook Book-NY-(1950)-96p-illus
(5c5) 2.00

LACKINGTON,JOHN-The Confessions of..late Bookseller at Temple
of the Muses-NY-1806-Cooper&Wilson-sm12mo-orig calf-
189p-1st Amer ed (5L1) 45.00

LACKLAND,WM-5 Weeks in a Balloon-NY-1869-345,9p-illus
(5t7,libr label) 15.00

LA CLAVIERE,R de MAULDE-Women of Renaissance-NY-1905-
port-510p (5q0) 12.00

LACLOS,CHODERLOS DE-Dangerous Acquaintances: Les Liaisons
Dangereuses-Lond-1940-Nonesuch Pr-Englished by Dowson
(5b0,edges browned) 7.50 (5t5) 11.50

LACOIN,LOUIS-Construction et Reglage du Moteur a Explosions-
Paris-(191-?)-474p-illus (5y2,ex-libr) 15.50

LA CONDAMINE,CHAS MARIE DE-Journal du Voyage fait par
ordre du Roi, a l'Equateur-Paris-1751-6 fldg plts-fldg map
(4e1,rub,crack) 150.00

--A Succinct Abridgement of a Voyage made within the inland parts
of South America-1747-fldg map-8vo-half calf-108p (4e1) 85.00

LACOSTE,P J-La Route du Vin en Gironde-Bordeaux-(1948)-
361p,(1)-photos-wrps-2 col maps,1 fldg (5w1) 10.00

--Le Vin de Bordeaux-Bordeaux-(1947)-77p,(1)-map-sq8vo-
wrps (5w1) 4.50

LACOUR,PIERRE-The Manufacture of Liquors, Wines & Cordials-
NY-(1863)-(2)p,iv,312p (5w1) 18.50

LACROIX,ARDA-Billy the Kid-NY-(1907)-128p-wrps-front photo
of BHaswell (5h2) 20.00

LACROIX,PAUL-Arts in Middle Ages, & at period of Renaissance-
Lond-1875-Chapman&Hall-19 plts-416 blk&white illus(t.p.
calls for 400)-4to-4th thous-a.e.g. (5b0,ex-libr) 75.00

--XVIIIme Siecle,Institutions Usages & Costumes,France 1700 to
1789-Paris-1875-illus-hf mor-col engrs-in French
(5t7,bndg wn) 25.00

--The 18th Century,its Institutions, Customs & Costumes,France,
1700 to 1789-NY-1876-illus in col & b/w-mor-a.e.g.
(5j3,rub) 15.00

--Military & Religious Life in Middle Ages & at period of
Renaissance-Lond-n.d.-504p-illus (5t4,rbnd) 17.50

--Science & Literature in Middle Ages & at period of Renaissance-
NY-1878-DApplton&Co-4to-mor-13 plts-418 b/w illus,(t.p.
calls for 400)-a.e.g. (5b0,ex-libr,bkplt) 75.00

--Vie Militaire et Religieuse au Moyen Age et a l'epoque de La
Renaissance-Paris-1873-hf mor-571p-illus-g.e. (5t7) 25.00

LA CROSS & MILWAUKEE RR CO-4th Annual Report,Jan 1856-
Milw-1856-Dail Wisc Book & Job Steam Pr-8vo-orig wrps
(5i9,vg) 25.00

LA CROSSE COOK BOOK,THE-LaCrosse,Wis-1923-Ladies Soc of
1st Presby Church-2nd ed-327p (5g9,rprd) 5.00

LA CUISINE CREOLE-(Lafcadio Hearn)-NewOrl-(1885)-268p-
frontis-2nd ed (5c4) 17.50

LA CUISINE RAISONEE-Quebec-1949-721,53p-frontis-illus-
sm4to (5g9) 6.50

LACY,G H-Anglers'Handbook for India-Calcutta-1905-illus-332p-
4th ed-fldg map (5t7) 7.00

LACY,MARY-The Female Shipwright-Hull-1805-2nd ed-rare
(5c1,rbnd) 75.00

LACY,CAPT R-The Modern Shooter-Lond-1846-illus-pt mor (5j3) 10.00

LA DAGE,JOHN-Modern Ships-Camb-1953-377p-illus (5s1,dj) 5.00

LADD,ANNA COLEMAN-The Candid Adventurer-Bost-1913-
HoughtonMiff-8vo-pic cl (5b2) 4.00

LADD,G T-Introduction to Philosophy-1890 (5L7) 4.50

--Philosophy of Mind-1895 (5L7) 4.50

LADD,GEO TRUMBULL-In Korea wi Marquis Ito-NY-1908-Scrib-
477p-illus (5p7) 6.00

LADD,HORATIO-Hist of the War wi Mexico-NY-1883-328p
(5n4,fox) 15.00

--The Story of New Mexico-Bost-1891-473p-plts-fldg map-1st ed
(5g5) 42.50

LADD,ILETA KERR-Seeing Texas,Children's Travelogue of Texas-
Dallas-1943-photos (5a8,pres) 15.00

LADD,RICHARD S-Maps showing Explorers' Routes, Trails & Early
Roads in US-Wash-1962-137p-wrps (5j4) 6.00

LADER,L-Bold Brahmins-1961-plts (5L7) 7.50

LADIES AID COOK BOOK OF BAPTIST CHURCH-Lanesboro-n.d.-
(?1913)-76p-ads-wrps (5c4,loose) 4.00

LADIES & GENTLEMENS' LETTER WRITER -& Guide to Polite
Behavior..bnd wi Ladies & Gentlemen's Amer Etiquette-
Bost-n.d.(ca1859)-col hf t.-128to 256p (5w7,chip) 7.50

LADIES BOOK OF KNITTING,THE-Bost-1886-illus (5n7) 2.00

LADIES CABINET OF FASHION, MUSIC & ROMANCE,THE-
Lond-Vol 2,Jul to Dec 1833-12mo-19(of 24)col costume plts,
viip-(3),424p (5w7,rbkd) 8.50

--same-Vol 9,Jan to June 1836-26 col costume plts-hf calf-
434p,(2)p (5w7,cov wn) 14.50

--same-Vol 9,Jan to June 1837-26 col costume plts-hf calf-
(5)p,440p,(3)p (5w7,cov wn) 14.50

--same-Vol 4,1840-26 col costume plts-14 engrs-hf calf-
(4),442p,(6)p (5w7,cov wn) 14.50

LADIES' DELIGHT COOK BOOK #1-GAR Fair-Bost-1886-32p-illus-
12mo-APOrdway&Co (5c5) 3.50

LADIES GUIDE TO BEAUTY,THE-People's Hand Book Ser-NY-
(?1849)-49p-wrps (5n7,fade) 3.50

LADIES'HANDBOOK & HOUSEHOLD ASST-Lebanon-(1886)-
(2),76p,(6)ads (5c4,fox) 6.50

LADIES HOME JOURNAL-Book of Inter Decoration-GarCty-(1959)-
col photos-224p-4to (5w7) 7.50

LADIES'HOME JOURNAL-Cookbook-NY-(1960)-col photos-727p-
4to (5c0) 4.50

LADIES'INDISPENSABLE ASSISTANT-wi Ladies'Cooking Assistant
& Family Friend-NY-1850-72p,48,(121),136-FJDow,publ
(5c0,lacks wrps,2 pgs torn) 14.50

LADIES INDISPENSABLE COMPANION & HOUSEKEEPERS' GUIDE-
NY-1859-vii,136p-Lincoln #471a-(by Mrs Prism)
(5c0,cov wn) 15.00

LADIES MODEL FANCY WORK MANUAL-NY-(1893)-64p-illus
(5n7,brown) 1.50

LADIES'WREATH,THE-An Illus Annual,Mrs S T Martyn,ed-NY-1851-
ii,(313)-452,(7)-292p-extra col title-11 col flower plts-
hf calf (5w7,sig loose) 4.50

LADREY,C-L'Art de Faire le Vin-Paris-1863-xxiv,26l,(2)p-12mo-
calf bk-bds (5w6) 12.50

--same-Paris-(1871)-xi,346,(1)p-12mo-bds-3rd ed (5w1) 8.50

LADREY,M C-Chimie Appliquee a la Viticulture & a L'Oenologie-
Paris-1857-viii,639p-fldg map & table-wrps (5w1,name on cov)9.50

LADY'S ALMANAC FOR 1858,THE-Bost-1858-123p-ads-32mo-
illus (5w7) 3.50

--same-1865-128p-ads-32mo (5w7) 5.00

LADY'S ANNUAL,THE-Christmas & New Year Gift-NY-n.d.-lea-
264p-(1860?)-Sartain plts (5ff7) 8.50

LADY'S HOME MAGAZINE,THE-(Arthur's Home Mag)-Vol 13 & 14-
Jan to Dec 1859-Phila-1859-half lea-12 col fashion plts & dec-
(5w7) 6.50

LADY'S MAGAZINE,THE-& Respository of Entertaining Knowlege
for 1792-Phila-(Jun) 1792-frontis-303p-orig lea bk bds-
(June thru Nov) (5tt6,f) 150.00

USED BOOK PRICE GUIDE

LADY'S POCKET COMPANION-& Indispensable Friend-NY-
n.d.-(ca185-)-64p,64,64,64,64,63 (2)   (5w7)   12.50
LADY'S POCKET LIBRARY-Phila-1794-prntd by RFolwell for
Matthew Carey-12mo-sheep-2nd ed   (5i0,rub)   27.50
LADYS'S POETICAL MAGAZINE-or Beauties of British Poetry-
Lond-Vol 1,1781, Vol 4,1782-illus-pub Harrison&Co -
2 vols   (5p6,lacks bkstrp)   30.00
LADY'S RANCHE LIFE, A-in Montana-Lond-1887-170p-7x4"-
R1(McMay)   (5s4,shake)   8.00
LADY'S WREATH, THE-NY-1852-illus annual-Helen Irving,ed-
432p-9 col floral plts &other illus   (5t4)   15.00
LA FARGE, HENRY-Lost Treasures of Europe-NY-1946-(Pantheon)-
sm4to-427 photos   (4a1)   10.00
--same-NY-1947-   blue cl-427 photos   (5t5)   6.00
LA FARGE, J-No Postponement-NY-1950-1st ed   (5x2,dj)   8.50
LA FARGE, JOHN-The Higher Life in Art-NY-1908-hf mor-illus-
t.e.g.   (4a0)   25.00
LA FARGE, O-The Race Question & the Negro-NY-1943 (5x2)   12.50
LA FARGE, OLIVER-Intro to Amer Indian Art-NY-1931-33 plts-cl
(4a5)   12.50
--Laughing Boy-Cambr-1929-1st ed of auth's 1st book
(5ss3,dj) 15. (5gg6,dj) 10. (4b4,5a5,5kk9) 17.50
--Long Pennant-Cambr-1933-305p-dec cov
(5s1,ex-libr) 3.50   (5F1,f)   4.50
--A Pictorial Hist of the Amer Indian-(1956)-Crown-4to-autg-
(5t3,mint,dj,5k4,mint,dj)   7.50
--same-NY-1957-Crown-272p-4to   (5p0)   7.50
--Raw Material-Bost-1945-HoughtonMiff (5b2,pres) 5. (4b4)   6.00
--Sparks Fly Upward-Bost-1931-322p-1st ed (5dd9) 7. (4b2)   6.00
LA FAYETTE'S, PROF EUGENE-French Family Cook Book-Lond&NY-
1885-160p   (5c5,chip)   4.50
LA FAYETTE, GEN-Memoirs of-Hartf-Barber&Robinson-1825-455p-
12mo-lea   (5iL,lt fox) 18. (5L3)   20.00
LAFAYETTE PTA-What's Cookin'-(Lafayette)-n.d.-spiral-256p
(4g9)   4.50
LAFENSTRE, GEORGES-La Fontaine-Paris-1895-Hachette-16mo-
208p-frontis   (5p1)   4.00
LAFFERTY, MAUDE W-The Lure of Kentucky-Louisvlle-1939-8vo-
1st ed   (5m6)   8.50
LAFFON, F G-Situation Viticole de La Haute-Garonne-Toulouse-
1900-203p-wrps-fldg map & chart   (5w1,wrps tn)   6.50
LAFFORGUE, GERMAIN-Le Vignoble Girondin-Paris-(1947)-
4to-wrps-24 illus-col map-Tome 1-319p(3)   (5w1)   16.50
LAFITTE OR THE BARATARIAN CHIEF, A TALE-NY-1828-16mo-
bds-lea back-106p-uncut-rare   (5j5,v wn,crude rebkd)   125.00
LAFITTE THE PIRATE OF THE GULF-NY-1836-Harper-2 vols-
12mo-orig cl-prntd papr labls-1st ed   (5x1)   80.00
LAFITTE, JEAN-The Journal of Jean LaFitte-NY-1958 (5a8,dj)   4.00
LAFLER, HEN ANDERSON-Alameda County,the ideal place for
your Calif home-(Alameda Co,1915)-illus-maps-charts (5dd4) 15.00
LA FLESCHE, FRANCIS-War Ceremony & Peace Ceremony of the
Osage Indians-Wash-1939-BAE bul 101-8vo-plts-280p-wrps
(5t7,libr stmp)   7.50
LAFLIN, L E-Genealogy wi additions by ALHolman-1930-
3p,142p   (5mm3)   12.50
LA FOLLETTE, ROBT H-8 Notches & other stories-1950-45p-illus-
orig stiff wrps   (5hh3)   7.50
LA FOLLETTE, ROBT M-LaFollette's Autobiog-Madison-c1913-
807p   (5w4)   6.50
--same-Madison-(1918)-illus-2nd ed   (5q8)   10.00
LA FOND, GEORGES-L'Amerique du Sud-Paris-1927-illus & maps-
hf lea-wrps   (5r7)   12.50
LA FONTAINE, JEAN DE-Cent Fables Choisies-Paris-(ca1890)-
illus de Henry Morin-intro de MLTarsot-4to-g.cl-pastel
(5c8,soil)   8.50
--Contes et Nouvelles en vers-Amsterdam-1762-calf-8vo-2 vols-
2 ports-80p engravs   (4L1,box) 1,850.00
--Fables-Paris-1813-PDidot-2 vols-qtr calf (5c8,rub,lt fox)   15.00
--Fables-Nouvelle ed,dans laquelle on apercoit d'un coup d'oeil
la moralite de la fable-Paris-1834-calf-checkerbd panel-
12mo-g. floral design-g. lea labl   (5c8,fine bndg)   15.00
--Fables de-Limoges-1836-360p-illus-calf   (5v0,wn)   10.00
--Fables-Paris-1868-illus par Grandville-667p-thkimp8vo-
extra g. sp-hf crushed mor   (5c8,f bndg,lt fox)   27.50
--Fables, The-NY-1930-Limited Editions Club-8vo-2 vols-cl-t.e.g.-
ltd to 1500c, box   (5p1)   35.00
--The Fables of-Phila-n.d.(c1880)-Wm T Amies-thk4to-733p-cl-
Dore,illus   (5rr2)   25.00
--The Fables of-Lond-1933-Heinemann-8vo-469p plus 12 plts-
transl by EdwMarsh-12 engrvs by Gooden-mor-a.e.g.-g.sp
(5p1,f bndg)   40.00
--Fables,avec les commentaires de Coste-Paris-(1802)-Billois,
An X-2 vols-12mo-25 plts-orig calf
(5c8,rub,sl shake,lacks e.p.)   35.00

LA FONTAINE, JEAN DE (continued) -
--Fables,avec notes-Paris-1830-Crapelet-2 vols-75 wdcut vignts-
16mo   (5c8,spots)   15.00
--Fables Choisies, mises en vers-La Haye,HvanBulderen,
1688 to 94- 5 vols in 1-Causse,illus-prntd wi textual corrs-
calf labl   (5c8)   250.00
--same-Paris-1824-ABoulland&Cie-edition ornee de 54 figures-
full pg plts-obl8vo-qtr lea   (5c8,rub)   65.00
--Fables Choises Pour Les Enfants-Paris-n.d.-4to-48p-a.e.red-
prntd cl-DeMonvel,illus-Plon Nourrit   (5p1,lacks ties)   22.50
--Fables de la Fontaine mise en action par Victor Cholet-Paris-
n.d.-(ca1840)-48mo-128p-frontis-prntd bds-Lavigne,APouilleux-
(5p1,misbnd)   15.00
--La Fontaine en Estampes-ou nouvelle edition des fables-Paris-
1821-Nepveu-4to-462p-110 hf pg engrvs-hf g.mor (5c8)   125.00
--La Fontaine's Fables-Paris, 1806-Chenu-4 vols in 1-Thomson,transl-
hf t.-orig bds-v rare (5rr2,wn,cov dtchd) 75. (4c3,cov dtchd) 125.00
--La Fontaine's Tales-Lond-1814-Chappel-8vo-2 vols-orig bds-
papr labls (5rr2,chip) 35.   (4c3,f)   75.00
--Selected Fables-NY-1948-Quadrangle Pr-8vo-91p-pic bds-
illus   (5p1,dj)   8.50
--The Tales and Novels of-NY-1929-2 vols-priv prntd-scarce (5a6)25.00
--Tales & Novels of-Nijmegen,Holland-1929-GJThieme-2 vols-
12 etchings-bds-ltd to 990c   (5i4,chip)   27.50
LAFUENTE, ENRIQUE-Velazquez-Lond-1943-Phaidon-34p text &
cat wi 14 illus & 6 tip in col plts-folio-cl   (5m5,sl soil)   24.00
LAGANKE, FLORENCE-Patty Pans-Bost-1930-illus-268p (5c7)   3.50
LAGER, JOHN G-Napoleon's Visitors & Captives 1801 to 1815-
NY-1904-   lev-g. designs on sp   (5d2,f bndg)   15.00
LAGER, MILDRED-The Useful Soybean-NY-1945-McGrawHill-
295p-1st ed   (5c9)   4.00
LAGERLOF, SELMA-The Girl from the Marsh Croft-Bost-1910
(5v0,f)   5.00
--Invisible Links-Bost-1899-1st Amer ed   (5v2,vf)   7.50
LAGOA, VISCONDE DE-Joao Rodrigues Cabrilho-Lisboa-1957-
8vo-cl-60p-illus-ltd to 1000c-scarce   (5h4,f)   10.00
LA GORCE, JOHN OLIVER-Florida,the Fountain of Youth-
(Wash,1930)-t8vo-bds-illus-93p-Reprnt from Natl Geogr
(5j5,autg)   10.00
LA GRANGE, HELEN-Clipper Ships of Amer & GrBritain 1833 to
1869-NY-(1936)-4to-37 col plts   (5L7) 15.   (5t4)   17.50
LAHEE, HEN C-Annals of Music in Amer-Bost-1922-298p-
Marshall Jones   (5p7)   4.00
--Famous Violinists of Today & Yesterday-Bost-(1899)-384p-illus
(5t4)   5.00
LA HONTAN, BARON DE-New Voyage to NoAmer-Lond-1703-
2 vols-hf mor-4 maps(2 fldg)-20 plts (3 fldg)-1st Engl ed-
HBonwicke   (5w8)   460.00
--same-Lond-1703-2 vols-22 maps & plts(some fldg)-hf mor
(5s9,lacks frontis Vol 2)   325.00
--Nouveaux Voyages dans l'Amerique Septentrionale-LaHaye-
1704-Les Freres l'Honore-2 vols-calf-24 maps & plts (some fldg)
(5w8,sl brown)   250.00
--Viaggi-Milan-1831-Truffi-2 vols in 1-16mo-sheep bkd bds-
1st Ital ed   (5n9)   75.00
--Voyages dans l'Amerique Septentrionale-Amsterdam-1728-
Honore-12mo-2 vols-sheep-24 maps & 109 plts (mostly fldg)
(5n9)   325.00
--Voyages au Canada-Paris-1900-hf mor   (5w8)   15.00
--New Voyages to NoAmer-Chig-1905-buck-2 vols-maps-illus-
Thwaites,ed   (5jj7)   75.00
LAIDACKER, SAM-Anglo Amer China-Bristol,Pa-1951-8vo-cl-
illus-13p, 144p-Part 2 (complete in itself)   (5t2)   15.00
LAIGHTON, OSCAR-90 Yrs at the Isles of Shoals-Andover-1929-
167p-illus-priv prntd   (5t7)   10.00
LAIGNEL, G-Barbarie du Ministere de la Marine-Paris-1821-
Chez l'Auteur-8vo-116p, 4p-disbnd   (5ss2)   17.50
LAIN, J-Brooklyn City Directory for Yr Ending May 1, 1860-
Brklyn-(1859)-Lain-8vo-442p, 35p-prntd bds-roan bk
(5j5, bndg shabby)   30.00
LAING, ALEX-Amer Sail-NY-(1961)-346p-500 illus-1st ed
(5s1,dj,f)   11.00
--Clipper Ship Men-NY-(1944)-279p-illus (5e8,dj) 5.75 (5t4)   7.50
--Sea Witch-1933   (5L7)   5.00
--same-NY-1944-illus-487p   (5s1,pres,ex-libr)   4.50
LAING, PAUL L-Hist of Otisville,Mich-Flint-1956-129p-cl (5h2) 8.50
LAING, R M-Plants of NewZealand-Auckland-1927-8vo-cl-
175 photos-3rd ed rev & enlgd   (5z9)   5.00
LAING, S-Human Origins-Lond-1897-422p plus index-illus-
pt lea   (5t3,f)   5.00
--Problems of the future and essays-Lond-1889-Chapman&Hall-
409p   (5v6)   5.00

LAIRD, JOHN A-Hist of the 12th Engineers US Army, Mobilized
StL June 1917-n.p.-1919-307p-illus-fldg maps-fldg chart-
1st ed   (5w9)   10.00

LAIRD, MARY A B DuPONT-D'Andelot & Berlin Families-n.p.-
1935-60p-fldg chart   (5m2) 10. (5t9,5h9)   8.50

LAKE, ALEXANDER-Killers in Africa-NY-1953-8vo-290p-photos
                             (4a6, tn dj)   3.50

LAKE CHAMPLAIN TERCENTENARY COMM-Tercentenary
Celebration of Discovery of Lk Champlain & Vermont-
(Montpelier, Vt)-1910-167p-illus-royal   (5t7,dj)   10.00

LAKE CO, ILLINOIS-History of-(Chig)-1912-4to-fab-872p-map
                             (5jj7,f)   60.00

LAKE, DEVEREUX-Some branches of Lake Family in Amer-1937-
256p   (5mm3)   12.50

LAKE ERIE-Register guide book to islands-Sandusky-1872-16mo-
wrps   (5g3)   7.50

LAKE GEORGE & LAKE CHAMPLAIN-Maps & Illus, wi sketches
descriptive of-Glens Falls, NY-1887-173p (5t4)   7.50

LAKE GEORGE CAMP & CANOE CHATS-NY-(ca 1885)-134p-
folio   (5xx7,autog) 12.50

LAKE, KIRSOPP-Christman Festival-NY-1937-frontis-ltd to 500c-
F Warde,prnt   (4a1)   7.50

LAKE MOHONK CONF-of Friends of Indian etc-Proceeds of 23rd
Annual Meeting-1905   (5xx7)   15.00

LAKE MOHONK, NEW PLATZ, ULSTER CO-Guide book to Prov-
1875-sm4to-illus-(mounted photos) (5g3) 10.00

LAKE, NANCY-Daily Dinners, A collection of 366 Distinct Menus
in Engl & French-Lond-1892-184p (5c5)   4.50

LAKE SHORE & MICH SOUTHERN RWY REPORTS-in 1 Vol for
1870 thru 1880-Clev-calf-2" thk inc maps (5s4, wn, rprd) 40.00

LAKE, SIMON-The Submarine in War & Peace-Phila-1918-
71 illus   (5c1)   40.00

LAKE, STUART N-Wyatt Earp, frontier marshall-1931-HoughtonMif-
illus-1st issue with "elby" for belly on p.54
(5yy7) 10. (4b3,flake) 12.50 (5k4,dj f,5ee3 f) 15.00

LAKE WINNEAPESAUKEE-Armstrong Dining Room & News Co, publ
(1909)-32p-10x8-illus-stiff wrps (5e8)   3.75

LAKES, ARTHUR-Prospecting for Gold & Silver in NoAmer-Scra-
1896-2nd ed-287p-cl-maps-illus (5jj9)   10.00

LAKESIDE CLASSICS, THE-Vols 1 thru 62-Chig-1903 to 65-
maps & illus-16mo-orig blu, grn & red cl-g.t.-other edges
uncut-scarce   (5m3)   775.00

LAKLAN, CARLI-Gifts From your Kitchen-NY-(1955)-256p-
illus   (5c0) 3.95 (5c9)   3.50

LAKY, J J-Study of Geo Berkeley's Philosophy-1950-sewn (5L7) 4.50

LALANDE, J J de-Astronomie-Paris-1764-Desaint & Saillant-calf-
mor labls-4to-2 vols-36 fldg plts-1st ed (5h0,f) 250.00

LALANNE, MAXIME-A Treatise on Etching-Lond-n.d. (Pref.1880)-
105p-   orig etchngs-4to-cl-t.e.g. (5m5) 20.00

LALIERE, A-Le Cafe Dans L'Etat De StPaul (Bresil)-Paris-1909-
417p-illus   (5w1,pres, lacks wrps) 12.50

LALOU, RENE-Contemporary French Literature-NY-Knopf-1924-
lg8vo-Bradley, transl-1st US ed (5m2)   6.00

LA MANCE, L S-House of Waltman & Allied Families-(1928)-278p
                             (5mm3)   9.00

LAMAR, CLARINDA P-Life of Jos Rucker Lamar 1857 to 1916-NY-
1926-284p-cl   (5h7)   7.50

LAMAR, MIRABEAU BUONAPARTE-Papers of-Austin-1922 to 1927-
Vols 2 thru 6-Gulick,ed -in 6 vols (5yy3) 40.00
--same-Austin-v.d.-1st ed-6 Vol bound in 7-orig wrps
(5hh4,autg by Gulick)   115.00

LAMARCK, J B-Recherches sur les causes des principaux phenomenes
physiques-Paris-Maradan-Vol 2 (only)-412p (5v6,bndg v poor) 6.00
--Zoological philosophy-Lond-1914-MacM-410p (5v6) 10.00

LaMAZIERE, PIERRE-The Brothel-NY-1930-illus-ltd to 750c-
(1 of 50 bnd in 3/4 mor)   (5i4)   15.00

LAMB, ARTHUR H-The Osage People-Pawhuska, Okla-n.d.-
(ca 193-)-32p-illus-stiff wrps-scarce pamph (5t3,f) 3. (5h0) 5.00
--Tragedies of Osage Hills, as told by "sage" of the Osage-Pawhuska-
1935-pic wrps-illus-203p   (5jj7,f)   12.50

LAMB, CHAS-Adventures of Ulysses-Lond-1808-12mo-203p-1st ed-
frontis-engrvd t.p. & prntd t.p.-cl (5v2,f,rbnd) 135.00
--same-Lond-1839-WmSmith-16mo-120p-cl-urn on cov-a.e.g.
(5p1, cor wn)   7.50
--Album Verses, with a Few Others-Lond-1830-Moxon-part mor-
1st ed   (5z7, f bndg) 65.00
--All Tales from Shakespeare-Heinemann-1912-2 vols-lge sq8vo-
dec cl-44 col plts   (4d0)   7.50
--Beauty and the Beast-Lond-1886-GeoRedway-16mo-vel-
1st rprnt from orig ed of 1811-ltd to 100c (5r9, spots,5ss9,dust) 15.00
--same-Lond-(1887)-Leadenhall Pr-Tuer,ed-illus-blk bds (5c8) 12.50
--Book of Ranks & Dignities of Brit Society, Chiefly intended for
Instr of Young Persons-Lond-(1805)-Tabart&Co-24 col engrvs-
orig bds-1st ed-with 25th plt (4c3,rbkd,box) 125.00

LAMB, CHAS (continued)
--same-Lond-1809-2nd ed-List of Plates error-orig lea bk bds-
(5v2, lt rub)   135.00
--Dream Children & The Child Angel-Lond&Tor-(1929)-Dent-12mo-
30p-col wrp-illus-Aldine Chapbooks-1st ed (5p1, fade) 7.50
--Elia-Lond-1823-orig bds-papr labl on sp-1st ed-hf t.
(5d2, box)   150.00
--Essays of Elia-Bost-1860-frontis-8vo-cl-466p (5t2)   4.00
--The letters, wi sketch by ThosNoonTalfourd-Lond-1837-EdwMoxon-
2 vols-12mo-ports-hf calf-1st ed (5x3, lacks hf t.) 25.00
--Letters of -(Lond)-(1935)-Dent-3 vols-ELucas,ed (4b5,vg) 40.00
--Letters of-Bost-n.d.-Ainger,ed-Brainard, publ-illus-2 vols-
275p & 293p-deluxe ed   (5p9)   12.50
--Mrs. Leicester's School-Lond-(1899)-Dent-pic bds-WGreen, illus-
obl 8vo-20 col plts   (4c3,vg)   20.00
--Prince Dorus-Lond-1889-Leadenhall Pr-sq8vo-9 col plts-part vel-
facs ed ltd to 500 proof cpys, autg by publ (5v2) 20. (5c8) 15.00
--Specimens of English Dramatic Poets who lived about time of
Shakespeare-Lond-1808-calf   (5d2, hng rprd) 17.50
--Tales from Shakespeare-Lond-1844-JosSmith-Cruikshank, illus-
slim 12mo-328p-orig dec cl, small def to frontis margin-
cheap ed   (5c8)   7.50
--same-Bickers-1876-12 illus from Boydell Gallery-t8vo-pic cl-
a.e.g.-386p   (4d2)   12.50
--same-Lond-1877-CrosbyLockwood-red mor-20 engrs by Harvey-
(5c8)   15.00
--same-Phila-1895-g.t.-155 illus-Romeo&Juliet on cov (5kk9,f) 8.50
--same-Lond-1901-RaphaelTuck-2 vol ed-plts, Harold Copping-
pic cl-orig buck d.j.   (5c8,f,dj)   15.00
--same-Lond-(1901)-ENister-6 col plts & 70 illus by WPaget
(5c8, lf loose)   6.00
--same-Lond-1909-t8vo-11 col plts by ArtRackham-wht cl-
g.designs on cov-dec e.p.   (5t8)   30.00
--same-Lond-1899-Temple Classics for Young People-limp lea-
12 illus, ArtRackham-reissued 1909 (5c8,sl rub) 17.50
--same-Lond-1909-Dent-304p-pic cl-11 illus by Rackham (5t0) 17.50
--same-Lond-n.d.(ca 1910)-g.t.-20p col illus by NormanPrice-
8vo-dec cl   (5p6,f)   12.00
--Works-Lond-1818-C&JOllier-2 vols-8vo-calf-g.-1st coll ed
(5x3, rprd)   50.00
--Works of-Moxon, Lond-1855-4 vols-tooled lea (5e8, f bndg) 25.00

LAMB, D S-Howard Univ Medical Dept-Wash-1900-sm4to-illus-
souvenir   (5x2,rbkd)   35.00

LAMB, DANA-Enchanted Vagabonds-NY-1938-Harper&Bros-
1st ed   (5x5)   7.50

LAMB, EDW-The Planned Economy in Soviet Russia-Phila-c1934
(5x7)   3.50

LAMB, F W-Gen Sketch of Some of Desc of Robt Savory of Newbury-
1904-16p   (5mm3)   3.50

LAMB, FRED W-Lamb Family Record-1900-5p, 24p-wrps (5mm3) 4.00

LAMB, MARTHA J-Hist of City of NY-1896-3 vols-Barnes&Co-
maps-illus-t.e.g.   (5u3)   20.00

LAMB, PATRICK-Royal Cookery, or the Compleat Court Cook-
Lond-1716-8vo-40 fldg plts-illus-18th cent calf -2nd ed
(5b0, sp rub, pgs sl wtrstnd) 125.00

LAMB, R-Orig & Authentic Journal of Occurrences During Late
Amer War-Dublin-1809-Wilkinson&Courtney-8vo-calf & mbld
bds-1st ed-16p list of subscribers (4h0,f) 100.00

LAMB, RUTH deF-Amer Chamber of Horrors-NY-1936-8vo-cl-
illus-1st ed-scarce   (5p5,dj)   10.00

LAMB, TOM-Jolly Kid Alphabet-Joliet-(ca 1920s)-PFVolland Co-
animated lettrs-heavy bd in col-obl4to-14p (5c8,sl cov scrape) 12.50

LAMB, WALLACE E-Lake Champlain & Lake George Valleys-1940-
3 vols   (5zz0)   37.50

LAMB, WINIFRED-Greek & Roman Bronzes-Lond-1929-Methuen-
Methuen's Handbks of Arch-NY-1929 reprnt-lg8vo-cl
(5m5,shake)   18.50

LAMBERT, MRS ALMEDA-Guide for Nut Cookery-BattleCrk-1899-
451p-col frontis   (5c0)   30.00

LAMBERT, ARTHUR W, JR-Modern Archery-NY-1929-illus-295p
(5ss8,autg)   10.00

LAMBERT, AYLMER B-Description of the Genus Pinus-Lond-1832-
col plts-lg4to-2 vols-lev-g. (5z9, f bndg, lib stmp) 1,000.00

LAMBERT, JAS H-Pennsylvania at the Jamestown Expos, Hampton
Roads, Va, 1907-Phila-1908   (5p0)   6.00

LAMBERT, JOS I-100 Yrs wi the Second Cavalry-FtRiley, Kans-1939-
maps-illus   (5k4,f)   60.00

LAMBERT, MARCUS B-A Dictionary of the Non Engl Words of the
Penn German Dialect-(Lancaster 1924) (5m2) 12.50

LAMBERT, MISS-The Hand Book of Needlework-NY-1842-263p-
illus-a.e.a.   (5w0, fade) 15.00

LAMSON, DAVID R-2 Yrs Experience among the Shakers-
WestBoylston-1848-8vo-orig cl-1st ed (5i0, rubber stamp) 65.00

LAMSON, J-Round Cape Horn-Bangor-1878-156p-1st ed (5L3) 22.50

LANCASTER, JOS-Improvements in Education-NY-1807-lea
(4F3,wn) 15.00

LANCASTER, ROBT A-Historic Virginia Homes & Churches-
Phila-1915-316 illus-ltd ed 37.50
(5m2,cov spots)

LANCASTER, SAML C-The Columbia-Portl-1915-140p-cl plts-
col fldg panorama-illus (4a8) 7.50

--same-Portl-1926-photos-147p-3rd ed
(5s4,stnd) 5. (5s4,dj) 7.50 (5jj1,f,dj) 7.00

LANCASTER'S KITCHEN SECRETS-Woman's Soc of Christian Serv
of Methodist Church-Lanc-(1951)-42p,(20)-spiral bnd wrps
(5c4) 3.00

LANCOUR, A HAROLD-Passenger Lists of Ships coming to NoAmer,
1607 to 1825-NY-1938-26p-wrps (5n4) 3.50

"LAND FOR THE LANDLESS"-Record of Parties on Homestead
Principle-n.p.-n.d.- (1860)-7p-unbnd as issued (5h1) 3.00

LAND GRANTS TO RRs-Letter from Auditor of RR Accts to
Robt McLane-n.p.-Govt pub Feb. 1881-46th Cong-28p pamph-
stitchd (5s4,lacks cov) 6.50

LAND, MARY-Louisiana Cookery-BatonR-(1954)-illus-376p (5c4) 5.00

LAND OF THE MAMMOTH,THE - By author of "Realm of the Ice
King"-Lond-n.d.-(ca1882)-Religious Tract Soc-16mo-
160p(16(cat)-illus-wire stitchd (5p1) 15.00

LANDA, DIEGO DE-Yucatan, Before & After the Conquest-Balt-
1937-(Maya Soc)-2nd ed-illus-maps-unbnd (5jj3) 15.00

LANDACRE, PAUL-Calif Hills & Other Wood Engravings-LosAng-
1931-folio-bds-autog-ltd to 500c,nbrd (5h4,sl rub) 22.50

LANDAUER, BELLA C-"Chalking the Hat",etc-NY-1930-Harbor Pr-
28p-priv prntd-ltd to 60c,nbrd-thin 4to (5j5) 45.00

--Some Alcoholic Americana from the Collection of-NY-1932-
26 plts-7p text-priv prntd-Harbor Pr-ltd to 60c, nbrd (5j5) 35.00

LANDCASTER INDIAN TREATY-wi Indians of the Six Nations-Phila-
1744-BFranklin-folio-disbnd-1st ed-rare (5n6,f,box) 2,500.00

LANDER, RICH-Journal of Exped to Explore Course & Termination
of Niger-NY-1837/36-12mo-2 vols-port-fldg map-illus-
calf,bds (4a6,rub) 20.00

LANDERHOLM, CARL-Notices & Voyages of Famed Quebec Mission
to NW-1956-ltd ed 1000c (5ii1,f) 20.00

LANDES, R-The City of Women-NY-1947-1st ed
(5x2,dj) 6.00

LANDHEER, BART-The Netherlands in a Changing World-NY-
c1947 (5x7,autg) 4.50

LANDHORNE, JOHN-Fables of Flora-Lond-1794-73p-illus
(5aa3,rbkd) 12.50

LANDING FORCE MANUAL-US Navy, 1918-Annap-1918-553p-
illus-24mo-g.stmpd cov (5s1,ex-libr) 3.00

--same-US Navy-Wash-1927-Govt pub-703p-illus-addenda
clipped in (5s1) 3.50

LANDING OF FRENCH ATLANTIC CABLE AT DUXBURY,July,1869-
Bost-1869-8vo-photos-1st ed (5ss5,ex-libr) 9.00

LANDIS, C S-.22 Caliber Rifle Shooting-Marines,NoCar-(c1932)-
8vo-419p-illus (4a6) 15. (5ss8) 7.50

--Woodchucks & Woodchuck Rifles-NY-(1951)-401p-illus (5t7) 25.00

LANE, CARL D-Amer Paddle Steamboats-NY-1943 (4a9,fade) 25.00

LANDIS, CHAS K-Rails Over the Horizon-Harrisb-1938-cl-
171p-illus (5y2,sl soil) 5.95

LANDON, E C-Anc & Desc of Robt Pepper of Roxbury,Mass-1932-
94p (5mm3) 6.00

LANDON, FRED-Lake Huron-Indpls-1944-Amer Lakes-398p-illus
(5p9) 5. (5h9) 6.00

LANDON, MELVILLE D-30 Yrs of Wit-NY-1899-orig pict cl (5m1) 6.50

LANDON, PERCIVAL-The Opening of Tibet-NY-1905-illus-4to-
484p (5t4) 10. (5x7) 12.50

LANDOR, WALTER SAVAGE-Gebir, Count Julian & Other Poems-
Lond-1831-EdwMoxon-hf calf-8vo (5b0,sl rub) 12.50

--Imaginary Conservations-(Verona)-1936-RHBoothroyd, ed-8vo-cl-
ltd to 1500c,nbrd-autg by prntr (5b0,dj,box) 20.00

--same-Lond-1891-wi bibliog by CGCrump-6 vols-8vo-g.-t.e.g.-
crushed mor (5b0,f bndg) 125.00

--A poet's dream-Edinb-1928-8vo-orig blu prntd wrps-ltd to 35c-
1st ed (5x3,f) 30.00

LANDRUM, DR J B O-Hist of Spartenburg Co,SoCar-1900(reprnt 1960)-
543p (5mm3) 15.00

LANDRY, S O-The Cult of Equality-NOrl-1945 (5x2) 20.00

LANDS AND PEOPLE-1967 edition-7 vols (4e7) 30.00

LANDSCAPE WONDERS OF THE WESTERN WORLD-Chig-1888-
Passenger Dept, Burlington Rte,CB&W RR-12mo-72p-illus-
timetabls-orig pict wrps (5g0) 15.00

LANDSEER, SIR EDW-Engravings From-Bost-1876-24 illus-folio
(5ww3) 15.00

LANE, A-Italian Porcelain-NY-n.d.-4 col,96 mono plts-79p (5w7) 8.50

LANE, ALLEN STANLEY-Emperor Norton-Caldwell-1939-8vo-
1st ed (5h5,tn dj) 12.50

LANE, ARTHUR-Guide to the Collection of Tiles-Lond-1939-75p-
49 plts-V&A Museum (5w7) 12.50

LANE, ARTHUR-Italian Porcelain-Lond-1954-plts-79p-8vo(5ww3)12.50

LANE, CARL-Fleet in the Forest-NY-(1943)-369p (5s1,ex-libr) 3.00

LANE, CARL D-The Cruiser's Manual-NY-(1949)-432p-illus
(5t4,e.p. tn) 7.50

LANE, E H-Soldiers' Record of Jericho,Vt-1868-47p (5mm3) 5.00

LANE, E W,ed-Thousand & One Nights...Arranged for Family
Reading-NY-1848-Harper&Bros-8vo-2 vols-cl-g.-illum titles-
wdcts by Harvey (5rr2,f) 25.00

--Thousand & One Nights'commonly called Arabian Nights
Entertainment-NY&Phila-1913-8vo-cl-8 vols-illus-
"Aldus Ed de luxe" (5t2) 20.00

LANE, ELIZ FERRIER-Thos Ferrier & some desc-1906-56p (5t9) 6.00

LANE, DR FERDINAND C-The Story of Mountains-GarCty-1951-
Dblday-488p-illus-cl (5t7) 7.50

LANE, FRANKLIN K-His Letters,Personal & Political-Bost-(1923)-
Anne W Lane,ed-t.g.-crushed lev mor (5d2,f bndg) 10.00

--Letters of,Personal & Political-Anne Lane,ed-Bost-1922-illus
(5q8) 5.00

--same-Bost-(1924)-HM-AWLane,ed-illus (5p9) 4.50

LANE, HON HENRY S-Reconstruction & Amendments of Constitution,
Speech-n.p.-n.d.-(Wash-1866)-16p-unbnd as issued (5h2) 5.00

LANE, MRS J C-Key & Allied Families-1931-495p (5t9) 20.00

LANE, JOHN J,comp-Trolley Way Finder-Bost-1910-maps-obl 12mo-
fldg to 16mo-papr-159p-NE St Rwy Club (5q0) 7.50

LANE, MARGARET-The Tale of Beatrix Potter,a Biog-Lond-1946-
4 col & 16 b&w plts (5v0,f) 8.50

LANE, ROSE WILDER-The Peaks of Shala-Lond-1922-224p-cl-
Chapman&Dodd (5d7) 4.50

LANE, SAML A-50 Yrs & Over of Akron & Summit County-Akron-
1892-1167p-cl (5h2) 35.00

LANE, GEN WALTER P-Adventures and Recoll of-Marshall,Tex-
(1928)-12mo-180p (4a7,mint) 12.50

LANE, WHEATON J-Commodore Vanderbilt,an Epic of the Steam
Age-NY-1942-illus-1st prntg (5w5) 10. (5m2,dj) 6.00

LANE, WM-Portrait Index-Wash-1906-1600p (5j4) 40.00

LANE, WM CARR-Letters of-SantaFe-Apr, 1928-Hist Soc of NM-
8vo-wrps-ElPalacio Pr (5g5) 7.50

LANG, ANDRES-Angling Sketches-NY-1891-12mo-cl-176p-illus
(5t0) 4.00

LANG, ANDREW-Ballads & Lyrics of Old France,wi Other Poems-
Lond-1872-12mo-orig white cl (bkstrip darkened)-1st ed of
auth's 1st book (5gg6,review copy,fade) 25.00

--The Arabian Nights Entertainment-Lond-1898-1st ed
(4c3,mint) 32.50

--Aucassin & Nicolete-Lond-c1910-12 drwngs by Gilbert James-
scarlet calf,onlays on sp (5d2) 10.00

--Ban & Arriere Ban-Lond-1894-erratum slip-1st ed (4c3,f) 17.50

--The Blue Fairy Book-Lond-1889-1st ed-rare
(5v0,vg) 125. (5v2,cov fair) 37.50

--same-Lond-1892-5th ed-gilt cl (5c8,lt soil) 8.50

--The Blue Poetry Book-Lond-1891-illus-1st ed (4c3,vg) 12.50

--Book of Princes & Princesses-Lond-1908-8 col plts-1st ed
(5c8,sl crack) 10.00

--The Book of Romance-Lond-1902-1st ed-illus
(5v0,shake) 7.50 (4c3,mint) 32.50

--Cock Lane & Common Sense-Lond-1894-357,24p (5w0) 7.50

--The Gold of Fairnilee-NY-1888-4to-15 col plts-1st Amer ed-
scarce (4c3,f) 20.00

--Grass of Parnassus, Rhymes Old & New-Lond-1888-124p-8vo-bds-
lrg papr,(dec e.)-ltd to 113c (5t7) 6.00

--Green Fairy Book-Lond-1892-Longmans, Green-4to-366p-orig bds-
HJFord,illus-lrg papr issue-ltd 150c-1st ed (5c8,rbkd) 45.00

--Johnny Nut & the Golden Goose-Lond-1887-Longmans,Green-lrg
8vo-illus, Lynen (4c3,vg) 30. (5c8,vg) 32.50

--Letters on Literature-Lond-1889-200p-bds-deckled edges-
ltd to 113c (5t7) 15.00

--Letters to Dead Authors-Lond-1892-t8vo-lrg papr issue-2 toned bds-
ltd to 113c,nbrd (5r9) 12.50

--Lilac Fairy Book-Lond-1910-6 col plts-1st ed
(4c3,soil) 10. (5c8,vg) 12.50

--The Mark of Cain-Bristol-1886-JWArrowsmith-hf calf-sp g.-
1st ed-ltd ed (5xx6,pres,vel wrps bnd in) 27.50

--The Pink Fairy Book-NY-1897-a.e.g.-illus (5v2,mint) 10.00

--Prince Prigio-Bristol-1889-JWArrowsmith-27 illus, Browne-
orig dec cl-1st ed (5c8) 15.00

--Prince Ricardo of Pantouflia-Bristol&Lond-(1893)-illus, Browne-
orig g. cl (5c8,t.p.cut) 10. (4c3,chip) 15.00

--The Red Book of Heroes-Lond-1909-1st ed (4c3,vg) 7.50

--Red Fairy Book-NY-(ca1896)-ALBurt-cl (5c8) 7.50

--Red True Story Book-Lond-1895-illus-1st ed (5c8,sl fox) 10.00

--True Story Book-Longmans-1893-1st ed-8vo-dec cl-a.e.g.-plts-
338p (4a8) 6.50 (5c8) 10.00

LANG, ANDREW (continued)
--same-Lond-1893-lg papr issue-ltd to 150c,nbrd-imp 8vo-
calf by Morrell   (5c8)   40.00
--The Yellow Fairy Book-Lond-1894-Longmans, Green-1st ed
                                                 (5ss9,sl fox) 20.00
LANG, MRS ANDREW-Book of Princes & Princesses-Longmans-1908-
Ford, illus-cl-8vo-a.e.g.-361p-8 col plts   (4d2,vf)   12.50
LANG, MRS EDWIN-Basketry Weaving & Design-NY-1925-93p-
photos-1st ed   (5t3,ex-libr) 5.   (5n7)   4.50
LANG, GEORGES EMMANUEL-Biblioteque de M-Paris-1925-
in 2 parts-text & illus   (5t5)   15.00
LANG, GLADYS T-The Complete Menu Book-Bost-1939-4to-
399p   (5c0)   3.00
LANG, H JACK-The Wit & Wisdom of Abr Lincoln as Reflected in
his Briefer Letters & Speeches-Clev&NY-(1943)-265p (5t7,dj)   6.50
LANG, HERBERT O-History of Tuolumne Co,Calif-SanF-1882-
BFAlley-509 & 48p-ports-sheep   (5tt0)   200.00
LANG, JOHN D-Report of Visit to Some of Tribes of Indians located
West of Mississippi Riv-NY-1843-prntd wrps
(5n9,sl stn,mor rbnd) 55. (5m3,sl dmpstn) 45.   (4a5,f)   65.00
LANG, L J,ed-The Autobiog of...Thos C Platt-NY-1910-Dodge-
556p-illus   (5p7)   7.50
LANG, LINCOLN A-Ranching wi Roosevelt-Phila-1926-8vo-cl-
254p-24p photos-1st ed   (5g6) 10.   (5jj1,vf)   8.50
LANG, MRS-The Red Book of Heroes-Lond-1909-illus-pict g. cl-
1st ed   (5r9,vf,d)   15.00
LANG, OLGA-Chinese Family & Society-Yale Univ Pr-1946-
395p   (5p0)   7.50
LANG, OSSIAN, ed-Robinson Crusoe, His Life on a Desert Island-
NY-1907-ASBarnes-illus, GCruikshank-8vo-pict cl-196p-
frontis   (5aa2)   4.50
LANG, RUTH HODGSON,comp-Zeta Tau Alpha Cook Book-
Evanston-n.d.-(?192-)-286p-2nd ed-Brown #613   (5c4)   4.50
LANG, W-History of Seneca Co-Springfield-1880-cl-691p-
errata pg   (5jj9,wn) 37.50   (5zz5)   50.00
LANG, WALTER B-The First Overland Mail,Butterfield Trail-
1940,1945-2 vols bnd in 1-illus-wrps   (5k4,f)   25.00
LANG, COL WM W-Paper on the Resources & Capabilities of Tex
read before Farmers Club of Amer Insti,Cooper Union, NY,
Mar 8, 1881-Austin-1881-frontis-wrps-62p   (5t4)   25.00
LANGDON, AMELIE-Just for Two-Minnpls-1903-224p-1st ed
                                                 (5g9)   4.50
--same-Minnpls-1907-(8)p, 223p   (5c0)   3.00
LANGDON, MRS EMMA F-The Cripple Creek Strike-Victor,Colo-
1904-248p-photos-1st ed-scarce   (5zz5)   27.50
--same-Denver, Colo-1904 to 1905-463p-photos-fldg facs
                                                 (5t3, rbnd)   22.50
LANGDON, JOHN E-Canadian Silversmiths, 1700 to 1900-Tor-1966-
76 plts-272p-ltd to 1000c   (5w8)   30.00
--Canadian Silversmiths & Their Marks, 1667 to 1867-Lunenberg, Vt-
1960-Stinehour Pr-illus-ltd to 500c   (5w8)   40.00
LANGDON, SAML-Gov Corrupted by Vice & Recovered by
Righteousness,a Sermon-Watertwn, Mass-1775-Benj Edes-12mo-
mor   (5L1,f)   75.00
LANGDON, WM C-Everyday Things in Amer Life 1607 to 1776-
Scribner-193/-illus   (5e8)   12.75
--same-NY-1943-illus   (5t2)   10.00
LANGDON, WM R,transl-Viscount Kikujiro Ishill, Diplomatic
Commentaries, Apr 1931-Balt-1936-351p-unbnd   (5t0)   7.50
LANGE, ALGOT-In the Amazon Jungle-NY-1912-Putnam-405p-
map   (5p7) 6.   (5L7)   8.50
--Lower Amazon-1914-plts   (5L7)   5.00
LANGE, HOWARD F-Catering-NY-(1955)-illus-128p   (5c5)   4.50
LANGER, SUZANNE K-Feeling & Form-1953   (5L7)   4.00
--Philosophy in New Key-Cambr-1942-8vo-313p-cl
                              (5L7,ex-libr) 3.50 (5t0,dj)   5.00
LANGER-Encyclopedia of World History-1968   (4e7)   15.00
LANGEVIN, HECTOR L-Le Canada-Que-1855-wrps-166p (5ss5)   10.00
LANGFORD, GERALD-Alias O. Henry-NY-1957-Macm-294p
                                                 (5p0)   5.00
LANGFORD, JOHN-The tourist's guide to City of Montreal-Montr-
1866-16mo-wrps-2nd ed, rev   (5g3)   7.50
LANGFORD, N P-Diary of Washburn Exped to Yellowstone &
Firehole Rivers 1870-n.p.-(1905)-1st ed-illus-122p
(5s4) 12.50 (5x5) 20. (5k4,f,pres,4a5,f,5i3)   15.00
--Vigilante Days & Ways-NY-1912-frontis-554p-cl
(5k4, fleck) 7.50 (5h7, bkpt) 8.50 (5r8, cov wn) 10.50 (5rr9)15.00
--same-Bost-1890-1st ed-2 vols-dec cl-beveled edges-illus
                                                 (5k4,pres)   65.00
--same-Bost-1893-2nd ed-2 vols   (5yy7,ex-libr)   30.00
--same-Missoula-1957-reprnt-456p-illus-new intr by Dorothy
Johnson & autg by her-buckskin-ltd ed 200c   (5k2)   50.00

LANGHORNE, JOHN-Fables of Flora-Lond-1804-81p-hf calf-
12mo-22 vignts   (5c8, chip)   17.50
LANGHORNE, JOHN-The origin of the veil, a poem-Lond-1773-
for TBecket-4to-wrps-1st ed   (5x3)   50.00
LANGLEY, HENRY G-SanFran Directory for Yr commencing
Sept 1862-SanFran-1862-8vo-639p (5hh4, sp rprd, rub)100.00
--same for 1868-SanFran-1868-8vo-bds-lea bkstrp-788, 95p-
                                 (5hh4, cov rub & soil) 65.00
--The State Register & Book of Facts for Yr 1857-SanFran-1857-
12mo-384p-buck-scarce   (5F5, rbnd)   27.50
LANGLEY, SAML PIERPONT-Langley Memoir on Mechanical Flight-
1911   (5zz4)   45.00
--The New Astronomy-Bost-1888-t8vo-illus (5m6, shake, rub) 9.00
LANGLOIS, L P-Prosper, ou le Petit Peureux Corrige par des
exemples naturels et frappans-Paris-1822-sm4to-orig pict bds-
14 hand col plts, incl hf titl (dated 1823) (5c8, rub) 50.00
LANGNER, LAWRENCE-The Magic Curtain-NY-1951-Dutton-
498p   (5p0)   7.50
LANGSAM, WALTER-The World Since 1914-NY-1933 (5x7)   5.00
LANGSDORFF, GEO H VON-Bemerkungen aus einer Reise um die
Welt-Frankfurt-1812-Wilmans-lg4to-2 vols in 1-2 frontis-
44 plts(2 fldg)-calf bkd bds-1st ed(wi 1st view of SanFran)
                                 (5n9)   850.00
LANGSTAFF, JOHN BRETT-Dr Bard of Hyde Park-NY-1942
                      (5p0) 5.   (5w0, dj)   7.50
LANGSTAFF, JOHN BRETT-David Copperfield's Library-Lond-
(1924)-Allen&Unwin-16mo-157p-illus-frontis & 1 plt-1st ed
                                 (5p1)   17.50
LANGSTROTH, L L-The Hive & the Honey Bee-Medina-1914-cl-
sm8vo-378p-illus   (5t2)   4.00
LANGSTROTH ON THE HIVE & HONEY BEE-Hamilton-1896-
illus-521p, 13p-rev by Chas Dadant & Son (5t0, hng crk) 5.00
LANGTON, H H-James Douglas A Memoir-Tor-1940-U Pr-130p-
illus-500c prntd   (5dd7)   7.00
--Jas Loudon & Univ of Toronto-Tor-1927-32p-port-wrps (5a1) 4.50
LANGTON, MARY B-How to Know Oriental Rugs-NY-1904-244p-
20pg illus-12mo-pic cl-1st ed   (5t0)   7.50
LANGTON, ROBT-Childhood & Youth of Chas Dickens-Lond-1891-
rev & enlgd ed-260p-82 plts   (5v0) 7.50 (4a8) 6.50
LANGTRY, JOHN-Come Home-Tor-1903-400p (5dd7)   7.50
LANGUAGE OF FLOWERS, THE-Poetically Expressed-NY-(1847)-
16mo-128p-5 hand col flower plts (5v0, vf)   10.00
LANGUEPIN, J J-To Kiss High Heaven, Nada Devi-Lond-(1956)-
WmKimber-199p-illus-cl   (5d7, foxing)   6.00
LANGWORTHY, FRANKLIN-Scenery of Plains, Mntns & Mines-
Ogdensburg-1855-324p-1st ed-rare (5r8, rbnd)   62.50
--same-Princeton-1932-PaulCPhillips, ed-plts
                      (5j5, fade) 15. (5r8, 5g6, f)   20.00
LANHAM, EDWIN-The Stricklands-Bost-1939-Little, Brown-8vo-
cl   (5b2, fade)   3.50
LANIER, HENRY W-The Book of Bravery-Scribner-1927-thk8vo-
illus   (5k4)   4.50
LANIER, HENRY W ed-Players Book-NY-1938-illus-1st ed (5qq7)15.00
LANIER, HENRY WYSHAM-First English Acresses-NY-1930-
The Players-illus-prints-1st ed (5qq7)   15.00
LANIER, HENRY WYSHAM-The Romance of Piscator-NY-1904-
Holt-8vo-dec cl-frontis   (5b2)   5.00
LANIER, J F D-Sketch of the Life of-NY-1871-cl-62p-prntd for
use of family only   (5a0, photo tip in) 15.00
LANIER, SIDNEY-The Boy's King Arthur-NY-1880-beaut illus cl-
1st ed   (5v0, f)   20.00
--same-NY-1925-sm4to-pic cl-321p-9 col plts-NCWyeth, illus
                                 (5t2)   7.50
--same-NY-1933-4to-cl-321p-9 col plts by NCWyeth (5t0) 6.50
--The Boy's Mabinogian-NY-1881-1st ed (4c3)   17.50
LANJUINAIS, J D-Appreciation du projet de loi relatif aux trois
concordats-1817-bds   (5L7, wn)   15.00
LANKESTER, MRS-Wild Flowers Worth Notice-Lond-1861-illus-
138p-12mo   (5s7)   7.50
LANKS, HERBERT C-Highway to Alaska-NY-1944-plts-200p
                                 (4a8, pres)   8.50
LANMAN, CHAS-Dictionary of the US Congress-Phila-1859-cl-
534p, 159p   (4h2)   20.00
LANMAN, CHAS-Farthest North-NY-1885-illus (5ss1, shake) 6.50
--Haw Ho Noo, Records of a Tourist-Wash-1850-266p-rare
                                 (4b2, lacks cov) 10.00
--The Private Life of Daniel Webster-NY-1852-illus-1st ed (5F0) 5.00
--Summer in the Wilderness, Embracing a canoe voyage up the
Mississ & around Lk Superior-NY-1847-208p & ads (5t4) 25.00
LANMAN, JAS H-History of Michigan-NY-1841-270p-12mo
                                 (5dd4, fox)   25.00
LANNING, JOHN TATE-The Spanish Missions of Georgia-ChaplHill-
c1935-321p-illus-fldg map   (5h9)   8.50

LANSBURGH, RICH H-Industrial Management-NY-1940-Wiley-
666p-3rd ed   (5p0)   5.00
LANSDALE, M T-Chateaux of Touraine-NY-1907-363p-61 plts-
4to-cl-photos   (5m5, wn)   8.00
LANSING, ROBT-The Peace Negotiations-Bost-1921-illus
(5ww4, dj) 6.   (5m2)   7.50
--War Memoirs of-Indpls-c1935-383p-frontis   (5w0, dj)   5.00
LANT, J H-Bridgeton, Millville & Vineland Directory for 1869 to
1870-Millville-1869-orig prntd bds-136p-illus-ads-scarce
(5ii8, rbkd)   30.00
LANTERI, ED-Modelling-Lond-n.d.-plts-3 vols-4to-cl (4a2)   12.00
LANTOW, J L-Assimilations of Calcium & Phosphorus from Different
Mineral Compounds & Their Effect on Range Cattle-NM Col of
Agri Bul #214, Jun 1933-30p-photos-wrps   (5L5)   4.00
LANTZ, DAVID E-Coyotes in Their Economic Relations-Wash-1905-
28p-wrps   (4a5)   6.00
--Raising Deer & Other Large Game Animals in the US-Wash-
1910-62p-wrps   (5n4)   2.50
LANTZ, JACOB W-Lantz Family Record-1931-265p-scarce (5mm3)35.00
LANZA, CLARA-Horace Everett-NY-1897-1st ed   (5ee3, vg)   7.50
LANZA, GAETANO-Strength of Wooden Columns-Bost-1882-50p-
illus-wrps   (5hh7, libr stmp)   5.75
--Transverse Strength of Large Spruce Beams-Bost-1882-8p-illus-
wrps   (5hh7, libr stmp)   5.00
LAPE, REV THOS-The Mourner Comforted-NY-1849-32mo-187p
(5w7)   3.00
LA PEROUSE, JEAN-Atlas du Voyage de La Perouse-(Paris)-
hf lea-port-69 nbrd plts & maps-plus 2 plts laid in (5tt0, stns) 100.00
--Viaggio di La Perouse intorno al Mondo-Milan, Sonzogno-1815-
12mo-4 vols-hf mor-lea labls-map-16 col plts-1st Italian ed
(5n9, lacks 4 lvs) 100.00
--Voyage de La Perouse Autour du Monde-Paris-1797 (-1798)-
4 vols plus atlas-69 plts & maps-orig bds-1st ed text-
2nd ed atlas   (5z9, rub) 550.00
--same-Paie-1798-text & folio atlas-plts-hf lea-2nd French ed-
4 vols   (5tt0, lacks 6 plts) 100.00
LAPHAM, CLAUDE-Scoring for the Modern Dance Band-Lond-
1937-164p   (5p7)   5.00
LAPHAM, I A-Wisconsin: Its Geogr & Topogr Hist, Geology &
Mineralogy, etc-Milw-1846-202p-papr cov as issued-2nd ed
(4c1, rbnd, rprd) 35.   (5h6, lacks bk cov & map) 12.50
--Geographical & Topographical Descrip of Wisc-Milwk-1844-
col fldg map-256p-hf mor-12mo-1st ed   (4c1, rbnd) 125.00
LAPHAM, W B-Robt & John Hazelton, their Desc-1892-352p
(5mm3)   40.00
--Thos (Nock) Knox of Dover, NH in 1652 & Some of his Desc-
1890-34p-wrps   (5mm3)   12.50
LAPHAM, WM B-Bradbury Memorial-1890-320p   (5mm3)   25.00
--History of Bethel 1768 to 1890-1891-455p-illus
(5e8, lacks cov, v poor)   37.75
--History of Rumford-1890-432p-cl   (5e8, rbnd)   37.50
LAPICK, GAETAN J-Scientific Fur Servicing-NY-1952-117p
plus plts   (5h8)   4.00
LAPLACE, PIERRE S-Mecanique Celeste-Bost-1829 to 39-Butts, prntr-
4 vols-4to-papr labl-orig cl-1st Eng ed-ports
(4h0, sp wn, labl chip) 850.00
LA PRADE, MALCOLM-That Man in the Kitchen-Bost-1946-244p-
illus   (5c5, 5c9)   3.00
LARCOM, LUCY-Beckonings for Every Day-Bost-1886-1st ed (5ee3) 5.00
--Landscape & Amer Poetry-NY-(1879)-sm4to-orig pic cl-illus
(5mm2, sl wn)   8.50
--A New England Girlhood-NY-1892-1st ed   (5v0, f)   7.50
--Similtudes-Bost-1854-16mo-cl-1st ed of auth's 1st book
(5gg6, f)   27.50
LARDEN, W-Argentine Plains & Andine Glaciers-1911
(5L7, cov stnd)   6.50
LARDEN, WALTER-Recoll of an Old Mountaineer-Lond-1910-
EdwArnold-320p-illus-cl   (5d7)   7.50
LARDNER, D-Elementary Treatise on Differential & Integral
Calculus-1825-buck   (5L7, rbnd)   15.00
--Popular lectures on the steam engine, wi additions by Renwick-
NY-1828-13 plts (3 fldg)-orig bds-cl bk-papr labl (5g3, fox) 35.00
--Steam Engine Familiarly Explained & Illustrated, with
historical sketch by Renwick-1852-illus   (5L7)   25.00
--A Treatise on hydrostatics & pneumatics, wi notes by Joslin-
Phila-1832-273p-bds-cl bk-papr labl-1st Amer ed
(5g4, libr release) 10.   (5b8)   14.50
LARDNER, RING W-Bib Ballads-NY&Tor, Chig-(c1915)-PFVolland-
8vo-63p, unnbrd-pic cl-t.e.g.-1st ed of auth's first book-rare
(5v2, mint) 75.   (5p1, pg lt smudged)   37.50
--How to Write Short Stories-NY-1924-Scribner's Sons-1st ed
(5ss3, dj, chip)   25.00
--The Love Nest & Other Stories-NY-1926-1st ed (5r9)   15.00

LARDNER, RING W (continued)
--My 4 Weeks in France-Indpls-(1918)-12mo-illus-orig cl(5r9) 10.00
--Round Up-NY-1929-Scribner's Sons-1st ed (5ss3, chip dj)   25.00
--The Story of a Wonder Man-NY-1927-8vo-orig cl-illus-1st ed
(5p5)   10.00
--Treat Em Rough-Indpls-(1918)-160p-illus-cl (4b5) 10. (5ee3) 7.50
LARDNER'S-1000 & Ten Things Worth Knowing-Phila-n.d.-
(ca 186-)-143p-wrps   (5c0)   10.00
LARGE, E C-The Advance of the Fungi-NY-1940-Holt-488p-
illus   (5p7)   5.00
LARGE, R G-The Skeena, River of Destiny-Vanc-1957-plts-180p
(4d2)   5.00
LARIMER COUNTY STOCKGROWERS ASSOC 1884 to 1956-
(Ft Collins, 1956)-108p-photos-4p of brands-fldg map-stiff wrps-
spiral bndng   (5L5)   12.50
LARIMER, SARAH L-The Capture & Escape, or, Life among the Sioux-
Phila-1871-2nd-ed-252p-illus-scarce   (5t3, fade)   25.00
LARK, THE-SanFran-1895 to 1897-Doxey-24 nbrs bnd in 2 vols-
dec cl   (5yy3)   50.00
LARKE, JULIAN K-Genl Grant & His Campaign-NY-1864-469, 40p
plus ad   (5j6)   5.00
--Genl US Grant, His Early Life & Milit Career-NY-1885-572p
(5j6)   4.50
LARKIN, JOHN A-Amer Public Men-NY-(1906)-Dodd, Mead-
102p-cl & bds   (5tt8)   10.00
LARKIN, LEW-Bingham, Fighting Artist-KansCty-(1954)-358p-
photos-1st ed   (5t3, autg, dj)   7.50
LARKIN, OLIVER W-Art & Life in Amer-NY-(1956)-551p-illus
(5t4)   7.50
LARKIN, PASCHAL-Property in 18th Century-Cork UP-1930-
252p-   (5aa0)   12.50
LARKIN, THOS O-California in 1846, described in letters from...-
SanFran-1934-Grabhorn Pr-550c prntd-illus   (5jj1)   20.00
--Map of Valley of Sacramento including Gold Region-Bost-(1848)-
17x22" map-TWiley, Jr-fldg-rare   (5tt0) 1,500.00
LARNED, E D-Hist of Windham Co, Conn, 1600 to 1880-1880-
2 vols   (5t9)   22.50
--Historic Gleanings in Windham Co-1899-254p   (5t9)   15.00
LARNED, J N-History for Ready Reference etc-Springfield-1901-
6 vols-lg4to-maps   (5xx7) 30.   (5w5)   27.50
--1894-5 vols   (4e2)   25.00
--Literature of Amer History-Columbus-1953-588p   (4a5)   30.00
--70 Centuries of Life of Mankind-Springfield-1912-2 vols-illus
(4a1)   10.00
LARNED, LINDA H-The Hostess of Today-NY-1906-303p-
orig ed   (5c0)   5.00
--The New Hostess of Today-NY-1917-428p-illus   (5c0)   4.50
--100 Cold Desserts-NY-1914-109p-bds-16mo   (5g9)   3.50
LA ROCHEFOUCAULD, F A F-Des prisons de Philadelphie-1819-
4th ed   (5L7, sl stn)   12.50
LA ROCHEFOUCAULT, FRANCOIS-Maxims & Moral Reflections-
Phila-1778-prntd according to new ed, rev-prntd by RobtBell
(5mm2, rbnd)   12.50
LAROCQUE, FRANCOIS ANTOINE-Journal de Larocque de la
Riviere Assinboine Jusqu'a La Riviere "Aux Roches Jaunes"
1805-Ottawa-1911-LJBurpee, ed- v scarce   (5dd9)   45.00
LAROUSSE-Encyclopedia of Art-Preshistoric & Ancient (4e7) 12.50
--Same-Medieval & Byzantine   (4e7)   12.50
LAROUSSE-Encyclopedia of World Geography   (4e8)   15.00
LAROUSSE GASTRONOMIQUE-Par Prosper Montagne-Paris-
1938-Libr Larousse-1850 engrvs-1087p-4to   (5x0)   30.00
LARPENTEUR, CHAS-40 Yrs a fur trader on the Upper Missouri,
personal narrative-NY-1898-2 vols-Coues, ed-maps-illus-
950c prntd-rare   (4c1) 60.   (5s9)   42.50
--40 Yrs a Fur Trader-Chig-1933-Lakeside Pr-360p plus index-
illus-fldg map (4g4, f) 7.50 (5r8) 15. (5w8) 12. (5a9, vf) 12.50
LARRABEE, WM-The Railroad Question-Chig-1895-488p-cl
(5ee3, dj, mint)   20.00
LARRABEE, WM C-Wesley & His Coadjutors-Cinn-1851-Tefft, ed-
12mo-2 vols-cl-frontis   (5t2)   6.50
LARSEN, HANNA A-Told in Norway-NY-1927-1st ed
(5ss9, sl stn)   7.50
LARSEN, N-156 Recettes de Boissons Americaines-Paris-n.d.-
12mo-wrps-96p(6)   (5w1, wrps stnd, wn)   3.50
LARSON, C A-Who, 60 Yrs of Amer Eminence-1958   (5L7)   5.00
LARSON, LAURENCE M-The Changing West & Other Essays-
Northfield-1937-170p plus index-illus   (5t3, dj)   4.00
LARSON, MEL-Skidrow Stopgap, the Memphis Story-Wheaton-
1950   (5h6)   4.00
L'ART POUR TOUS-Paris-1894-P.Gelis-Didot, Director-folio-
96 plts   (5t7)   15.00
LARWOOD, JACOB-History of Signboards-Lond-1875-536p-
illus   (5xx7, pg loose)   12.50

LARWOOD, JACOB (continued)
--same-Lond-1866-3rd ed-illus   (5c3) 5. (5L7)   8.50
--same-Lond-1900-11th ed-8vo-facs   (5m6)   10.00
LA SALLE, J B de-Les Regles de la Bienseance et de la Civilite
   divisees en deux parties-Charleville-1806-Chez Raucourt-
   new ed-bnd in part of vel manuscript-286p-24mo   (5p1)   45.00
LA SALLE, NICOLAS de-Relation of discovery of Mississippi Riv-
   Chig-1898-bds-269c prntd-orig French wi transl by Anderson
                                    (5g3, unopnd)   35.00
LAS CASAS, BARTHOLOME de-Relation des voyages et des
   decouvertes que les Espagnols ont fait dans les Indes Occidentales-
   1698-bnd in: L'art de voyager utilement-calf   (5L7, crack)   75.00
LASERSON, MAX M-The Amer Impact on Russia-NY-1950-Macm
                                          (5p7)   6.00
LASHER, M H-Logging Chance-Phila-(1944)-245p-illus-1st ed
                                    (5s4, sp rprd)   5.00
LASKI, HAROLD J-The Amer Democracy-NY-1948
   (5t0) 4.   (5q8, 5x0)   6.50
--The Amer Presidency-NY-c1940
       (5hh3) 4. (5x7) 5. (5t0) 4.50 (4e2)   8.00
LASKI, MARGHANITA, ed-The Patchwork Book-Lond-1946-8vo-
   illus-g.t.-456p-Pilot Pr   (5aa2)   4.50
LASSAIGNE, JACQUES-Toulouse Lautrec-Lond-1939-(Hyperion Pr)-
   4to-1st ed-blk&w&col plts   (5jj3, f, dj)   25.00
LASSEN COUNTY-Fairfield's Pioneer History of Lassen Co, Calif-
   SanFran-(1916)-HSCrocker Co-506p-map-cl   (5tt0)   30.00
LASSITER, W L-Shaker Recipes for Cooks & Homemakers-NY-(1959)-
   302p-illus   (5c0)   6.50
LASSWELL, MARY-I'll Take Texas-Bost-1958-376p-1st ed (5k0,dj) 5.00
LASSWELL, MARY-Mrs Rasmussen's Book of One Arm Cookery-
   Bost-1946-101p-illus   (5c0, autg) 5.   (4g9)   4.00
LAST MAN, THE-Lond-1826-Colburn-3 vols-12mo-hf calf-1st ed-
   lf of ads   (5xx6, vg)   325.00
LAST OF THE BUFFALO, THE-buffalo herd of Flathead Reservation-
   (Winnipeg)-1908-narrow obl folio-photos-pic wrps (5k4)   20.00
--same-Cinn-1909-(6p) text-23p photos-oblong-tied-wrps-
   in envelope   (5L2)   20.00
LAST OF THE MEDICI, THE-(1930)-Harold Action-priv prntd:
   G. Orioli-8vo-cl-medallion on cov-No. 2 of Lungarno Series-
   ltd to 365c   (5dd8)   15.00
LAST RUN, THE-Kay Co, Okla, 1893-PoncaCty-1939-Ponca Cty
   Chapter, DAR-352p plus index-cl-(1967 reprnt)   (5h0)   15.00
LATE OCCURRENCES, THE-in NoAmer & Policy of GrBritain
   considered-Lond-1766-JAlmon-8vo-hf mor-42p   (5L1)   75.00
LATE REGULATIONS-respecting Brit Colonies on Continent of
   Amer Considered in Letter from Gentleman in Phila-Lond-
   1766-reprntd for JAlmon-8vo-hf mor-hf t., t., & 39p-
   2nd Lond reprnt-(John Dickinson)   (5L1) 50. (5n2)   85.00
LATEST MAP-of Mining Dist & Bay of SanFrancisco-SanFran-1851-
   Zakresk&Hartmann, litho-litho map, 13x10"-ex rare-Wheat 211
                                    (5hh0, creased)   750.00
LATHAM, CHAS-In Engl homes-Lond-1908, 1909-2 vols (of 3)-
   857p-4to-cl-photos   (5m5)   15.00
--Gardens of Italy-Lond-(1905)-2 vols-138 plts-folio-cl-g.e.-
   1st ed   (5z9, rub)   60.00
LATHAM, RONALD-In Quest of Civilization-Lond-(1946)-illus
                                       (4a1)   10.00
LATHERN, J-Hon Judge Wilmot-Tor-1881-rev ed-165p
                                    (5dd0, autg)   6.50
LATHERS, RICH-Reminis of 60 Yrs of a Busy Life in SoCar, Mass,
   & NY-NY-1907-AFSanborn, ed-425p-illus-ltd to 500c, nbrd
                                       (5r7)   25.00
LATHROP, AMY-Tales of Western Kansas-(Norton, Kans, 1948)-
   photos-map-1st ed   (5k4, f) 12.50   (5yy7)   7.50
LATHROP, BARNES F-Migration into East Texas, 1835 to 1860-
   Austin-1949   (4a5)   7.50
LATHROP, CORNELIA P-Black Rock, Seaport of Old Fairfield, Conn,
   1644 to 1870-NewHav-1930-Tuttle, Morehouse&Taylor-t8vo-
   cl-illus-214p   (5j5)   20.00
LATHROP, DOROTHY P-The Fairy Circus-NY-1931-col plts-1st ed-
                                  (4c3, mint, dj)   35.00
--Hide & Go Seek-NY-1938-Macm-8vo-(40p)-pic cl-1st ed
                                   (5p1, fray dj)   7.50
--The Little White Goat-NY-1933-15 plts-1st ed of her 2nd bk
   (5v2, mint, dj, pres) 20.   (4c3, f, dj)   15.00
LATHROP, ELISE-Early Amer Inns & Taverns-NY-1926-McBride-
   365p-cl-1st ed-illus   (5h9) 15. (5w1) 12.50 (5j5)   17.50
--same-NY-1936-365p   (5zz0) 10. (5p0)   8.50
LATHROP, GEO-Some Pioneer Recoll-Phila-1927-reprnt-photos-
   32&75p   (5t3)   30.00
LATHROP, GEO P-Somebody else-Bost-1878-Roberts-sm8vo-1st ed
                                    (5m2, sl wn)   5.00

LATHROP, JOHN-Innocent Blood Crying to God from Streets
   of Boston, a Sermon, 5th of Mar, 1770-Bost-1771-Edes&Gill-
   sm4to-hf mor-1st Amer ed-rare-Howes 122 (5n2)   475.00
LATHROP, JOHN-Synopsis of a course of lectures on natural
   philosophy-Bost-1811-16mo-disbnd-15p, (1)   (5g3)   10.00
LATHROP, JOS-Sermons Delivered on Various Occasions-Bost-
   Jun, 1812-IsaiahThomas-392p-calf-red labl (5ee3, vf)   15.00
LATIMER, MISS E-Idyls of Gettysburg-Phila-1872-126p-illus (5t4) 5.00
LATIMER, E W-Europe in Africa in the 19th Century-Chig-1895-
   illus-451p   (5ii3)   12.50
LATIMER, J B-Tables of Tonnage of Ships-Edinb-n.d.-(ca 1840)-
   (ca 300p)-pkt size-hf lea   (5s1, ex-libr, wn)   10.00
LATOUR, AMY-Kings of Fashion-Lond-1958-t8vo-cl-26 plts-
   1st ed   (5p5)   10.00
LATOURETTE, K S-The Chinese, their hist & culture-NY-1934-
   Macm-2 vols-1st ed   (5x9)   5.00
--Hist of Expansion of Christianity-1937-7 vols-maps (5L7)   50.00
LATROBE, BENJ H B-Impressions Respecting NewOrleans-NY-
   1951-(Wilson, ed)-4to-bds-autg by editor (5m8, dj soiled) 10.00
LATROBE, C I-Journal of Visit to SoAfrica in 1815 & 1816-NY-
   1818-1st Amer ed-395p-hf lea   (5i3, libr mark, rub)   25.00
--same-Lond-1818-col plts-4to-406p   (5q1, pres box)   175.00
LATROBE, CHAS-The Rambler in NoAmer-Lond (1836)-2 vols-
   map-2nd ed-cl-lea labls   (5a8, rbnd)   100.00
LATROBE, F C-Iron Men & Their Dogs-Balt-1941-illus-225p (4e4) 7.50
LATROBE, J H B-The First Steamboat Voyage on Western Waters,
   the "NEW ORLEANS"-Balt-1871-wrps   (5c1)   12.50
--Lost Chapter in Hist of Steamboat-Balt-1871-Md Hist Soc Fund
   Pub-44p-cl   (5y2, ex-libr)   7.50
LATSHA, C B-Adam Good Family-1914-150p   (5t9)   7.50
LATTA, F F-Black Gold in the Joaquin-Caldwell-1949-344p-illus-
   8vo-1st ed-scarce   (5h5)   17.50
--San Joaquin Primeval-Tulare-(1929)-88p-Tulare Times
                                 (5tt0, autg letter)   50.00
LATTA, JAS W-Was Secession Taught at West Point-n.p.-1909-
   40p-orig prnt wrps   (5w0)   10.00
LATTA, M L-Hist of My Life & Work-Raleigh, NoCar-1903-illus-
   R8vo-priv publ   (5x2)   75.00
LATTA, ROBT-Reminis of Pioneer Life-KansCty-1912-1st ed-
   186p-illus   (5i3)   15.00
LATTER DAY SAINTS MILLENIAL STAR-(Liverpool)-Jan-Dec 1852-
   Vol 14 complete-lea   (5dd6, lacks bk)   18.50
LATTIMORE, OWEN-The Situation in Asia-Bost-1949-1st ed
   (5x7) 3.   (5F0, dj)   3.50
LATZKE, PAUL-A Fight wi an Octopus-Chig-(1906)-8vo-illus-116p-
   orig prntd wrps-1st ed   (5ss5)   12.50
LATZO, ANDREAS-Lafayette, a Life-NY-1936-402p-frontis-
   1st ed   (5w9)   5.00
LAUBIN, REGINALD-The Indian Tipi-Univ of Okla-1957-illus
                                       (5m2)   3.00
LAUBREAUX, A-L'Amateur de Cuisines-Paris-1931-219p-illus-wrps
                                    (5c5, sp tn)   4.00
LAUBREAUX, ALIN-The Happy Glutton-Lond-1931-205p-illus-
   sq4to   (5c7)   7.50
--Mulatto Johnny, transl from the French-1931   (5L7)   3.50
LAUCK, W JETT-Political & Industrial Democracy-NY-1926-
   1st ed   (5q8, libr bkplt)   9.50
LAUDE, G A-Kansas Shorthorns-Iola-1920-634p plus index-illus-
   1st ed   (5t3)   4.00
LAUDER, HARRY-A Minstrel in France-NY-1918-338p-illus-
   1st Amer ed   (5w0, autg)   7.50
LAUDIER, CHAS P J-Calif Golden Treasures, Mother Lode Country-
   n.p.-(Toyahvale)-1962-(Chas Peters)-158p-wrps   (5h1)   3.50
LAUFE, ABE, ed-An Army Doctor's Wife on Frontier-Pitts-1962-
   352p-cl   (5t3, f, 5h7, f, dj) 6. (5ee3, dj)   8.50
LAUFER, BERTHOLD-Archaic Chinese Jades- NY -1927-sm4to-51p-
   plts-catalog-Field Mus of Natural Hist, Chig -priv prntd for Bahr-
   stiff bds-cl ≤p   (5m5)   35.00
--Chinese Baskets-Chig-1925-2p intro & 38p plts, loose as issued-
   4to-wrps-Field Mus of Nat Hist, Chig, Anthro Design Series, #3-
   protective slip case   (5t0)   15.00
--Jade-Chig-1912-68 plts-370p-Field Mus of Nat Hist Publ #154
                                       (5x0)   40.00
LAUGEL, AUGUSTE-US During the War-NY-1866-Bailliere Bros-
   313p-ads   (5mm8)   10.00
LAUGHING HORSE, THE-SantaFe-Apr, 1926-DHLawrence Number-
   prntd wrps   (5r9)   25.00
LAUGHLIN, CLARA-The Death of Lincoln-NY-1909-336p-illus
                                   (5ee3, 5t4)   5.00
LAUGHLIN, CLARA E-The Martyred Towns of France-NY-1919-
   469p-t.e.g.   (5w9)   5.00
--Reminis of Jas Whitcomb Riley-NY-(1916)-port   (5m1)   5.00

LAUGHLIN, J LAURENCE-Hist of Bimetallism in the US-NY-
1886-8vo   (5ss5)   8.50

LAUGHLIN, J LAWRENCE, ed-Banking Reform-Chig-1912-428p-
Pub by Natl Citizens League for Sound Banking System (5y2)   5.50

LAUGHLIN, JAS, ed-New Directions in Prose & Poetry, 1937-
Norfolk, Conn-(1937)-New Directions-dec ppr bds (4k3, box)   17.50

LAUGHLIN, JAS-Some Natural Things-(Norfolk, 1945)-cl-16mo-
auth's 1st book   (5c2, f, dj)   15.00

LAUGHTON, L G-Old Ship Figure Heads & Sterns-Lond-1925-
279p-56 plts (8 col)-sm folio-cl   (5ss2, rub)   95.00

LAUGHLIN, L I-Jos Ledlie & Wm Moody, early Pittsb residents,
their background & des-1961   (5L7)   12.50

LAUGHLIN, LEDLIE I-Pewter in Amer, Its Makers & Their Marks-
Bost-1940-2 vols-4to-cl-illus-v scarce-1st ed
                      (5t2, vf, cl dj)   250.00

LAUGHLIN, RUTH-Caballeros-Caldwell-1945-illus (5m9, dj)   6.50

LAUGHING PHILOSOPHER, THE-Ride si Sapis, Mart-Dublin-1777-
244p-calf-prntd for Jas Williams   (5t7)   10.00

LAUGHTON, CATHERINE C, ed-Mary Cullen's Northwest Cook Book-
Portl-(1946)-Binfords&Mort, pub-340p   (4g9)   6.00

LAUGHTON, CHAS-Tell Me a Story, An Anthology-NY-1937-
392p   (5p7)   5.00

LAUGHTON, CHAS E-Message of...to Legislature of 1891-
Olympia-1891-68p-g.e.-OCWhite, State Prntr (5r0, pres, rub)   10.00

LAUMONIER, PAUL-Ronsard, poet lyrique-Paris-1923-4to-hf mor-
806p-orig wrps bnd in-(12th ed, rev)   (5p6, libr stmp)   18.00

LAUREL, THE-a gift for all seasons-by Amer authors-Balt-1837-
Bayly&Burns12mo-orig gr cl-reprnt   (5i0, fox)   12.50

LAURENCE, C A-Pioneers Days in Cedar Rapids, 1860 to 1880-
1936-170p-(only 500c printed)   (5mm3)   25.00

LAURENT, DR EMILE-Magica Sexualis-NY-c1934   (5x7)   7.50

LAURENT, M L'ABBE-Galerie en Action de la Vie des Enfants-
Paris-1853-t8vo-272p-15 plts-polychrome bndg   (5v2)   27.50

LAURIDSEN, PETER-Russian Explorations, 1725 to 1743-Chig-1889-
2 fldg maps   (5g8)   15.00

LAURIE, ALEX-Chrysanthemums-NY-1930-110p-illus   (5s7)   3.00

LAURIE, B, ed-The Newgate Calendar-NY-1932-illus   (5x7)   6.50

LAURISTON, VICTOR-Inglorious Milton, an Unconventional Biog-
Chatham, Ont-1954-8vo-cl-408p-ltd to 1000c, autg (5t2)   10.00

--Lambton's 100 Years-Sarnia, Ont-(1949)-illus-335p (5kk4, f)   20.00

LAURITZEN, JONREED-Arrows Into the Sun-NY-1944-314p-12mo-
                (5dd6, pres)   6.00

--Song Before Sunrise-GarCty-1948-314p-end sheet maps
                (5dd6, pres)   9.00

LAUT, AGNES C-Blazed Trail of Old Frontier-NY-1926-McBride-
1st ed-illus by Chas Russell (5L2, box, f) 35. (5i3, 5jj7, vf)   20.00

--same-NY-1926-RobtMcBride-271p-fldg map-cl-Russell, illus-
ltd to 200c, autg, box   (4c1) 50.00   (5yy3)   60.00

--Cadillac, Knight Errant of Wilderness-Indpls-(1931)-298p-cl-
1st ed   (5h1, dj, f) 8.50   (5jj7, f)   15.00

--Canada, Empire of the North-Bost-1909-26p, 446p   (5t0)   4.00

--same-Toronto-1909-Briggs   (4b9) 5.00 (5i6)   5.00

--The Canadian Commonwealth-Indpls-(1915)-334p-cl-1st ed (5t2)   5.00

--The Conquest of the Great NorWest-NY-1911-2 vols in 1-
409p, 415p-frontis-fldg maps   (5h9)   15.00

--same-Tor-(Musson)-c1918   (5h9)   12.50

--same-NY-(1918)-2 vols in 1-824p-3 maps   (5ss1)   10.00

--Conquest of Our Western Empire-NY-1927-363p-illus-1st ed
       (5dd5) 10.   (5ee3) 6.50   (5s4, rprd)   8.00

--same-NY-1932-363p-plts   (5s6)   7.50

--Enchanted Trails of Glacier Park-NY-1926-251p-photos-
1st ed   (5s4, pres) 9.   (5d7) 4.50   (5L2)   7.50

--The Fur Trade of Amer-NY-1921-8vo-341p-cl-illus-1st ed (5F5)10.00

--Heralds of Empire-NY-1902-372p-1st ed (5ee3) 4.   (5r6)   5.00

--The Overland Trail-NY-1929-358p-illus-2 maps-1st ed
   (5s4, rprd) 11.   (5t3) 8.50 (5L3, mint, dj)   9.50

--Pathfinders of the West-NY-1907-380p-illus(5b9) 5. (5s6)   8.50

--same-NY-1904-380p-illus-1st ed   (5ee3, autg)   12.50

--Pilgrims of the Santa Fe-NY-1931-illus-363p   (5ee3, f)   10.00

--The Romance of the Rails-NY-1929-2 vols-illus (4e4, 5y2)   27.50

--same-NY-1936-Tudor Pub Co   (5x5)   7.50

--Story of the Trapper-NY-1919-12mo-284p-illus   (5dd5)   5.00

--Through our Unknown SoWest-NY-1915-271p-illus-8vo-cl (5t2)   5.00

--same-NY-1925-271p-illus   (5i3, dj)   8.50

LAVAL, ANTOINE F de-Voyage de la Louisiane-Paris-1728-
Mariette-lg4to-buck-lea labl-31maps, diagrams &tables,
(some fldg)-1st ed   (5n9)   250.00

LAVAL, PIERRE-The Diary of-NY-1948-240p-illus   (5w5)   3.50

LAVALLE, M J-Histoire et Statistique de la Vigne & Des Grands
Vins-Paris-1855-244p-prntd wrps   (5w6, lacks plts)   8.50

LAVALLEE, JOS-Travels in Istria & Dalmatia-Lond-1805-
RichPhillips-8vo-hf cl-fldg map-fldg tinted engrs, 6-
1st ed in English   (5i8)   25.00

LAVATER, J C -Physiognomy-Lond-n.d.-12mo-calf-illus
              (5j2, rbkd)   10.00

LAVATER, JOHANN CASPAR-Aphorisms on Man-Phila-1790-
Spotswood-100p-16mo-cl-1st Amer ed-ex scarce   (5L1)   50.00

--Whole Works of Lavater on Physiognomy-Lond-c1798-hf calf-
4 vols-illus   (5z7)   75.00

LA VAULX, PAUL-L'Aeronautique des Origines a 1922-Paris-
HFloury-lg4to-ltd to 500c, nbrd   (5b0, fldg box, unopnd)   275.00

LAVELEYE, EMILE de-The Socialism of Today-Lond-n.d.-8vo-cl-
331p   (5t2, libr bkplt)   5.00

LAVELLE, P-Irish Landlord since the Revolution-1870   (5L7)   5.00

LAVENDER, DAVID-Bent's Fort-NY-1954-450p
       (5ee3, 5a8, 5k4) 6.   (5t7)   6.50

--The Big Divide-GarCty-1948-photos-1st ed   (5yy7)   7.50

--Land of Giants-NY-1958-6 maps-468p   (5s0)   8.50

--One Man's West-NY-1943-Smith   (5x5)   12.50

LAVENDER, WM, comp-Centennial Tales-(RockIsl)-1941-59, (26)p-
cl   (5h7)   5.00

LAVER, JAS-French Painting & the 19th Century-Lond-1937-
Batsford-4to-cl-plts   (5m7, crack)   24.00

--Ladies' Mistakes-1933-Nonesuch Pr-thin 8vo-cl-9 illus
            (5t5, sl scuff)   5.50

--Love's Progress-Bloomsbury-1929-Nonesuch Pr-R8vo-bds-1st ed
              (5t5)   5.00

--Macrocosmos, a Poem-NY-1930-Alfred A Knopf-ltd to 500c,
autg, box   (5i4, box dmgd)   20.00

--same-Lond-1929-4to-bds-papr labls-1st ed-ltd to 775c
             (5t5, autg)   10.00

--A Stitch in Time-Lond-1927-Nonesuch Pr-bds-ltd ed
             (5a9, mint)   15.00

--Style in Costume-Lond-1949-63p-32 plts-pict bds   (5w9)   5.00

--Whistler-Lond-(1930)- calf-red lea labls-a.e.g.
            (5j2, vg, f bndg)   40.00

LAVERGNE, A-La Verite sur La Question Scolaire Du Nord Ouest-
Montreal-1907-63p-scarce (4b9, libr labl) 30. (4e6, f)   40.00

LAVERTY'S, MAURA-Cookbook-NY-1947-illus-149p   (5c0)   3.00

LAVINE, EMANUEL-The 3rd Degree-NY-1930-248p   (5t4)   6.00

LAVOISIER, ANTOINE L-Traite Elementaire de Chimie-Paris-
Chez Cuchet-1789-2 vol-8vo-13 fldg plts-2 fldg tables-calf-
1st ed-2nd issue-322p & 653p   (5hh0, vf)   950.00

--Elements of Chemistry, in a New Systematic Order-Edinb-1790-
illus-13 plts-hf calf   (5m4, f)   175.00

LAVRIN, JANKO-Dostoevsky-Lond-(1943)-Methuen-158p-
2nd ed   (5p9)   5.00

--same-NY-1947-161p-frontis   (5t0)   4.00

--Dostoevsky & His Creation-Lond-(1920)-Collins-190p (5p9)   5.00

LAW AND ORDER-(Chig, 1920)-12mo-port-59p-orig limp mor-
scarce   (5m6)   17.50

LAW, JOHN-Money & Trade Considered-1760-16mo
          (5L7, wn, ex-libr)   7.50

LAW, JUDGE JOHN-The colonial history of Vincennes-Vincennes-
1858-Harvey, Mason-157p-8vo-orig cl
     (5jj7, f) 25.   (5t9, libr mrks) 20.   (5i0, f)   35.00

LAW OF WOMAN LIFE-n.d.-8vo-20p-wrps   (5t7)   3.50

LAW QUARTERLY REVIEW-(Lond)-Vols 1 to 70-(1885 to 1955)
            (5rr4, rbnd) 1,000.00

--same-single bound vols   (5rr4)   20.00

LAW, WM-Characters & Characteristics of...Non juror & Mystic-
Lond-1898-H&S-328p   (5p7)   10.00

LA WALL, C H-4,000 Yrs of Pharmacy-Phila-1927-8vo-illus-
665p-cl   (5t2, dj, f) 7.50   (5L7)   12.50

LAWES, EDW-Elementary Treatise on Pleading in Civil Actions-
Portsmouth, NY-1806-8vo-lea-246p-1st Amer Ed   (5t2)   5.00

LAWES, LEWIS E-Invisible Stripes-NY-c1938-315p   (5w9)   3.00

--20,000 Yrs in Sing Sing-NY-1932-412p   (5p9)   4.00

LAWING, NELLIE N-Alaska Nellie-Seattle-(1940)-201p-photos-
e.p. maps   (5ss1, autg)   8.50

--same-Seattle-1948-201p-plts   (5s0)   6.50

LAWLESS, EMILY-Grania, Story of an Island-NY-1892-355p-
cl   (5h2)   5.00

LAWLESS, RAY M-Folksingers & Folksongs in Amer-NY-1960 (5p0)7.50

LAWLEY, F-Manuale del Vignaiuolo-Firenze-1865-illus-
(4)p, 240p   (5w1)   18.50

LAWRENCE, REV A B-A Hist of Texas, or, the Emigrant's Guide
to the New Republic-NY-1844-275p-frontis-calf
(4c7, lacks frontis, rbnd)67.50(5a8, crack) 125. (5n4, fox)   100.00

LAWRENCE, A W-Later Greek Sculpture & Its Influence on East
& West-NY-1927-Chamberlin&Lucas-illus-158p-8vo (5ww3)   25.00

LAWRENCE, A W-Narr of the Discovery of Amer-NY-c1931-300p-
maps   (5h9)   7.50

LAWRENCE, A W-Oriental Assembly-Lond-(1939)-8vo-cl-photos-
1st ed   (5d9, dj)   25.00

LAWRENCE, ABBOT-Remarks of Mr Lawrence on duty of Congr
to continue protection of Amer labor-Bost-1832-wrps (5g4) 10.00
--Letters to the Hon WmCRives of Virg-Bost-1846-wrps (5g4) 7.50
LAWRENCE, ADA-Young Lorenzo-Florence-1931-Orioli-illus-
12mo-illus-vel-ltd to 740c
(5t7, warp) 15. (4b5, f, dj, unopnd) 37.50
LAWRENCE, ALEX A-Jas Moore Wayne, Southern Unionist-
Univ NoCar-1943-250p-illus (5mm8, dj, vf) 5.00
LAWRENCE, AMOS-Extracts from the diary & correspondence-
Bost-1855-illus-mor-WmRLawrence, ed (5q8) 7.50 (5g3, sl wn) 6.00
--same-Bost-1856-frontis (5t0) 5. (5L7, rbnd) 8.50
LAWRENCE, CHAS-History of Phila Almshouses & Hospitals-n.p.-
1905-illus-398p (4m2) 15.00
LAWRENCE CITY-Mission Cook Book-Lawrence, Mass-n.d.(ca 1921)-
164p (4g9) 5.00
LAWRENCE, D H-Aaron's Rod-NY-1922-ThosSeltzer-1st Amer ed
(5ss9, vg) 15.00
--Amores-Lond-(1916)-8vo-orig blu cl-1st ed (5dd8) 45.00
--same-NY-1916-113p-1st Amer ed (5w9) 8.50
--Assorted Articles-NY-1930-Knopf-1st Amer ed (4b5, dj, mint) 25.00
--same-Lond-1930-Secker-1st ed (4c2) 15.(4b5, mint, fray dj) 17.50
--Birds, Beasts & Flowers-Lond-(1923)-Martin Secker-1st ed-
cl bk bds (4b5, f, dj, unopnd) 50.00
--Collected Poems of-NY-1929-1st Amer ed-2 vols (5hh1, vg) 25.00
--England, My England-NY-1922-1st Amer ed (5hh1, vg) 15.00
--same-Lond-(1924)-Secker-1st ed (4b5, vg) 15.00
--The Escaped Cock-Paris-1929-(Black Sun Pr)-4to-dec-
orig prnt wrps-1st ed-ltd to 450c (5ii3, box) 95.00
--Etruscan Places-NY-1932-Viking-1st Amer ed(5hh1, dj, vg) 15.00
--Fire & Other Poems-SanFran-1930-lg12mo-lin-1st ed-ltd to 300c
(5ss7, dj, vf, advance prospectus laid in) 125.00
--Kangaroo-Lond-(1923)-Martin Secker-1st Engl ed
(5hh1, f, rprd dj) 35.00
--Lady Chatterley's Lover-1928-priv prntd-pirated ed-ltd to 500c,
nbrd (5ss9, tn) 20.00
--same-n.p.-1930-priv prntd-auth's unabrdg popular ed
(4b5, pres Frieda L., dj, crude rbkd) 35.00
--same-NY-1932-318p-frontis (5t4) 12.00
--Lasca's Story of Dottor Manente-Florence-n.d.(c1929)-Orioli-
1st ed-ltd to 1000c (4b5, vg, dj) 35.00
--Last Poems-NY-1933-1st Amer Ed (5ii3) 15.00
--Little Novels of Sicily-NY-1925-Seltzer-8vo-blu cl-1st ed
(5d3) 10.00
--The Lost Girl-Lond-(1920)-12mo-1st ed, 1st issue-orig dk brn cl,
bottom edge untrmd (5cc9, hng crk) 150.00
--same-Lond-(1920)-8vo-cl-3rd issue wi altered text-1st ed(5dd8) 15.00
--same-NY-1921-ThosSeltzer-8vo-blu cl-1st Amer ed (5d3) 25.00
--The Lovely Lady-Lond-1927-MSecker-1st ed (4b5, mint, dj) 35.00
--The Man Who Died-Lond-1931-MSecker-1st ed
(5hh1, vg, dj) 25. (5ss3, sp fade) 20.00
--same-Lond-1935-WmHeinemann-4to (5hh1, vg, dj) 12.50
--A Modern Lover-NY-1934-Viking-1st ed (publ same time as
Engl ed) (5ss9, f, dj, bkpt) 30.00
--Mornings in Mexico-Lond-1927-Secker-1st ed (4b5, mint, dj) 35.00
--Movements in European History-Oxford Univ Pr-1925-354p-
maps (5p9) 5.00
--The Paintings of-Lond-(1929)-Mandrake Pr-priv prntd-col illus-
folio-grn cl-red lea bkstrp-t.e.g.-ltd to 500c (5d8) 175.00
--Pansies-Lond-1929-MSecker-8vo-bds&cl-1st trade ed
(5ee9, 5F9, f dj) 15.00
--same-(Lond, 1929)-8vo-orig prntd wrps in slipcase-definitive ed-
Colophon-ltd to 500c, autg, nbrd (5ee9) 75.00
--same-Lond-(1929)-Secker-dec bds-white vel papr bkstrp-
ltd to 250c, autg-1st ed (5ee9) 75.00
--The Plumed Serpent, (Quetzalcoatl)-Lond-(1926)-M Secker-
1st ed (4c2, sl stn) 20. (4b5, mint, dj) 35.00
--same-NY-1926-Knopf-445p (5p9, 4b5, cov stnd) 5.00
--Pornography & Obscenity-Lond-(1929)-Faber&Faber Ltd-cl-
12mo-1st Engl ed (4b5, mint) 12.50
--same-Lond-(1929)-Faber&Faber-wrps (4b5, 4c 2) 10. (5hh1, f) 12.50
--same-NY-1930-Knopf-1st Amer ed
(4b5, rub, sl chip, bkpt) 6. (5ss9, sl chip, bkpt) 7.50 (4b5, f) 10.00
--The Prussian Officer-Lond-1914-8vo-cl-wi 16p catalogue-
1st ed (5dd8) 37.50
--same-Lond-(1914)-Duckworth&Co-8vo-orig blu cl-g.stmpd wi
20p catalogue-1st bndg, 1st issue-1st ed (5d8, ex f) 75.00
--same-Lond-(1914)-1st issue (5j3, cov wn, sl dmpstn) 20.00
--Psychoanalysis & the Unconscious-NY-1921-1st ed
(5b9, cov stnd, sl tn) 12.50
--The Rainbow-NY-1916-Huebsch-1st Amer ed (5b9, vg) 12.50
--same-NY-1921-Huebsch (5p9) 4.00
--Rawdon's Roof-Lond-1928-Elkin Mathews & Marrot-1st ed-
orig bds-ltd to 530c, autg (4b5, unopnd, vg, dj) 75.00

LAWRENCE, D H (continued)
--Reflections on the Death of a Porcupine & Other Essays-1925-
Centaur Pr-1st ed-ltd to 925c
(5ss3, cl dj) 45. (5d8) 30. (5hh1, f) 25.00
--St Mawr-NY-1925-Knopf-1st Amer ed (5hh1, vg) 7.50
--same-Lond-(1925)-Secker-1st ed (4c2) 15.00 (4b5, vg) 15.00
--Story of Doctor Manente being 10th & Last Story from Suppers
of AFGrazzini-Florence-(1929)-8vo-papr bds-1st ed-
ltd to 1000c (5ee9, dj) 25.00
--Tortoises-NY-Thos Seltzer-1921-orig pic bds-papr labl-8vo-
1st ed (5i8, unopnd, sp sl wn) 20.00
--Touch & Go, #2 of Plays for a People's Theatre-Lond-1920-
CWDaniel-12mo-1st Engl ed
(4b5, unopnd, vg, dj) 30. (5hh1, vg, dj) 25.00
--same-NY-1920-Seltzer-1st Amer ed-bds (4b5, f, dj tn) 20.00
--The Virgin & the Gipsy-Lond (1930)-Martin Secker-(6), 191, (1)-
cl-1st ed (4b5, mint, dj) 35. (5z7, f) 25.00
--We Need One Another-NY-1933-Equinox-1st ed
(4b5, mint, dj) 35.00
--The White Peacock-NY-1911-12mo-cl-1st ed of auth's 1st book,
publ a day earlier than Engl-copyr dated 1910-ex scarce
(5gg6, fade, wn) 250.00
--same-Lond-1911-12mo-cl-1st Engl ed (5gg6) 25.00
--The Widowing of Mrs. Holroyd-NY-1914-Kennerley-1st Amer ed-
(4b5, vg) 20.00
--Women in Love-NY-1920-priv prntd-1st ed-t8vo-ltd to 1250c
(4b5, mint) 75.00
--same-Lond-(1921)-Martin Secker-508p (5t7) 10.00
--same-NY-1922-TSeltzer-548p (5p9) 3.75
--The Woman Who Rode Away & other Stories-Lond-1928-
Martin Secker-292p-1st ed (4c2, fade) 12.50 (5F9, f, dj) 20.00
LAWRENCE, DANIEL-Account of Convincement & Call to Ministry
of Margaret Lucas-Stanford, NY-1803-12mo-hf mor-111p, (1)
(5L1) 20.00
LAWRENCE, DAVID-Who Were the 11 Million-NY-1937-79p
(5w4, 5x7) 3.00
LAWRENCE, EDW A-Colver Passage-Caldwell-1954-260p-photos
(5ss1, dj) 6.00
LAWRENCE, FREDK-The Life of Henry Fielding-Lond-1855-hf mor
(5ss9) 10.00
LAWRENCE, FRIEDA-Not I, But the Wind-New Mex-(1934)-Rydal Pr-
1st ed-ltd, autg (5hh1, dj, lacks fly) 25. (4b5, mint, dj) 45.00
LAWRENCE, GRACE L-Nettleton Cook Bk-KansCty-1909-160p-ads
(5c4, shaken) 5.00
LAWRENCE, HENRY W-The Not Quite Puritans-Bost-1928-228p-
illus-1st ed (5w5) 5.00
LAWRENCE, JOHN-The Hist of the Church of the United Brethren
in Christ-Dayton-1860-2 vols (5w9, wn) 8.50
LAWRENCE, JOS STAGG-Wall St & Washington-Princeton-1929-
1st ed (5ss5) 10.00
LAWRENCE, KANSAS-Lawrence-1905-40p-pict wrps (5n4) 8.50
LAWRENCE, MASS-Quarter Centennial Hist of-1878-174p-ports
(5t9) 6.00
LAWRENCE, PHILIP HENRY-Lithology-Lond-1865-1st ed
(5ss5, ex-libr, rbnd) 10.00
LAWRENCE, R M-Historical Sketches of Lawrence Family-1888-
215p (5t9) 6.00
LAWRENCE, R MEANS-Desc of Maj Sam'l of Groton, Mass-1904-
344p (5mm3) 8.50
LAWRENCE, RICH HOE-History of Soc of Iconophiles of City of NY-
NY-1930-illus-sm4to-290p (5t4) 25.00
LAWRENCE, RUTH-Colonial Families of Amer-NY-(n.d.)-c 1920-
thk4to-dec mor-a.e.g. (5x5, f bndg, hng crack) 85.00
--Genealogical Histories of Prentiss & Allied Families-1930-
folio-69p-lea (5t9) 10.00
LAWRENCE, T E-Birds, Beasts & Flowers-Lond-1930-Cresset Pr-
folio-bds-prchment bk-1st illus ed-ltd to 500c (5dd8) 50.00
--Crusader Castles-(Lond)-1936-Golden Cockerel Pr-t.e.g.-
ports-photos-4to-3/4 mor-2 vols-1 of 1000c-only ed (5ee9) 375.00
--Letters of T.E.Lawrence-Garnet, ed-Lond-(1938)-thk8vo-cl-
896p-illus-maps-1st ed (5dd8) 15. (5nn2) 17.50
--The Man Who Died-Lond-1935-4to-dec papr bds-cl bk-illus
by Farleigh-1st illus ed-ltd to 2000c (5dd8) 10.00
--The Mint-Lond-(1955)-JonathanCape-1st trade ed (5ss3, dj) 10.00
--Oriental Assembly-Lond-(1939)-photos-1st ed (5hh1, f, dj) 45.00
--Revolt in the Desert-Lond-1927-JonathanCape-1st ed
(5ss3, dj rprd) 35. (4b5) 25.00
--same-NY-1927-illus-335p (4a6) 5. (5t7) 8.50
--Secret Dispatches from Arabia-(n.d.)-Golden Cockerel Pr-
ltd to 1000c-lg8vo-hf niger (5ss9, f) 150.00
--Seven Pillars of Wisdom-Lond-(1935)-lg papr iss 1st publ ed,
ltd to 750c-thk sq8vo-bevelled edges-Cape (5dd8, 5hh1) 125.00
--same-Lond-1935-Cape-1st trade ed (4b5, vg) 25.00

LAWRENCE, T E (continued)
--same-GarCty-1935-illus-cl-1st Amer Trade ed (5ss3,sp stn,dj) 25.00
--same-NY-1938-deluxe ed   (5b9,fade) 6.00
--same-NY-1939-672p-illus-8vo-cl-unabridgd ed (5t0,dj) 7.50
--same-Lond-(1939)-Reprint Soc-2 vols   (4b5,sp sl spot) 10.00
--Letters to H S Ede 1927 to 1935-(Lond,1942)-Golden Cockerel Pr-
   4to-ltd to 500c-1st ed   (5dd8) 37.50
--The Wilderness of Zin, Palestine Exploration Fund, 1914-
   (Lond,1915)-orig gray bds-map-4to-photos-1st ed (5d8) 125.00
LAWRENCE, SIR WALTER R-The India We Served-Lond-1928-8vo-
   cl-317p-1st ed   (5t0) 5.00
LAWRENCE, WM-Phillips Brooks, a Biography-NY-1930-port (5p5) 7.50
LAWRENCE, WM R, ed-Extracts from Diary & Corres of late Amos
   Lawrence-Bost-1859-359p-illus   (5w5,wn) 10.00
LAWS & LIBERTIES OF MASSACHUSETTS-Reprnt of 1648 ed-
   Cambr-1929-59p-lg folio size-facs   (5a9,f,dj) 15.00
LAWS, BERNARD-Stability & Equilibrium of Floating Bodies-NY-
   1914-251p   (5s1) 7.50
LAWS FOR THE ARMY & NAVY OF THE CONFEDERATE STATES-
   Richmond-1861-98p-prntd wrps   (5g4,wn,wtrstnd) 25.00
LAWS FOR REGULATING & GOVERNING MILITIA OF COMMON-
   WEALTH OF MASS-Bost-1807-Thomas&Andrews-48p-orig plain
   wrps   (5m3) 15.00
LAWS OF US RELATING TO NAVIGA & MERCHANT MARINE-
   Part 2, 1903-Govt pub-Wash-1903-531p   (5s1,ex-libr) 5.00
LAWSON, SIR CHAS-Private Life of Warren Hastings-Lond-1911-
   254p-plts-3rd ed   (5a1) 6.50
LAWSON, H M-Desc of Clement Corbin of Muddy Riv(Brookline),
   Mass, & Woodstock, Conn-1905-378p   (5mm3) 27.50
LAWSON, J MURRAY-Yarmouth Past & Present, a Book of Remin-
   Yarmouth-1902-plts (sm fldg)-647p (4i6) 25. (4d2) 15.00
LAWSON, JOHN-History of Carolina-Raleigh-1860-scarce
                                       (4a1,rebnd) 52.50
LAWSON, LADY-Highways & Homes of Japan-Lond-1910-352p-
   t.e.g.   (5x9) 4.00
LAWSON, LIZZIE-Old Proverbs wi New Pictures-Lond-c1890-4to-
   64p-Cassell&Co-plts-pic bds   (5v0,f) 15.00
LAWSON, MARIE-Hail, Columbia-NY-1931-387p-col plts-
   1st ed, deluxe-juvenile   (5s4) 5.00
LAWSON, MARIA-History & Geography of Brit Col-Tor-1906-
   Gage-148p-illus   (5dd7) 6.50
LAWSON, PUBLIUS V-The Story of Oshkosh-n.p.-n.d.-8vo-
   orig wrps-20p   (5ss5) 5.00
LAWSON, ROBT-Rabbit Hill-NY-1944-illus-1st ed-scarce (4c3) 25.00
LAWSON, W T-Literature of the Mexican War-NY-1882-
   prntd wrps-rare   (4a5) 45.00
LAWSON, WM P-Log of a Timber Cruiser-NY-1915-illus-214p
                                        (5ss8,autg) 15.00
--same-NY-1926-illus   (5m9) 5.00
LAWTON, LANCELOT-Empires of the Far East-Lond-1912-
   GrantRichards-Vol 2 (of 2 vols)-pkt map   (5x9) 6.50
LAWTON, MARY-The Last of the Titans-NY-1929-390p-illus (5p0) 5.00
LAWTON, MARY-A Lifetime wi Mark Twain-NY-(1925)-illus
                                   (5p9) 6. (5mm2) 10.00
LAWTON, MARY-The Queen of Cooks & some Kings-NY-1925-
   208p-photos   (5c9) 6.00
LAWYER, J P, Jr-History of Ohio-Columbus-1905-388p-illus-12mo
                                            (5h9) 6.50
LAWYER, SARAH R-Jonathan & Hannah Steelman Family-
   (Elkton-1952)-106p-cl   (5h1) 8.50
LAY, W A-Experimental Pedagogy-NY-1936-371p-8vo (5p1) 10.00
LAYARD, AUSTEN H-Discoveries among Ruins of Nineveh & Babylon-
   NY-1854-illus-8vo-cl-549p   (5t2, lt stnd) 6.00
--Nineveh & Its Remains-NY-1849-illus-fldg map-plts-2 vols-
   scarce   (4e1) 25.00
LAYARD, AUSTEN HENRY-The Italian Schools of Painting-Lond-
   1902-2 vols-illus   (5j3) 10.00
LAYARD, GEO SOAMES-Suppressed Plates-Lond-1907-Black-g.t.-
   65 wd engrs-sq8vo-scarce   (5t8) 17.50
LAYCOCK, EDW P-Canada's Most Western Cathedral-Lond-(1931)-
   wrps-45p   (5s6) 4.50
LAYNE, J GREGG-Annals of LosAng from arrival of 1st white men
   to the Civil War-SanFran-1935-Calif Hist Soc-97p-cl-
   Spec Publ #9   (5d6) 50.00
--Western Wayfaring- LosAng-1954-maps-4to-bds-Auto Club of
   SoCalif   (5h5, cor jammed) 6.00
LAYS OF THE MINNESINGERS-Lond-1825-326p-plates-hf lea
                                        (5c3, rub) 6.00
LAYTHA, EDGAR-North Again for Gold-NY-1939-54 illus (5w8) 9.00
LAYTON, MARK-Forest Ranger-NY-1945-245p   (5s4) 2.50
LAYTON, T A - Choose Your Wine-Lond-(rev 1949)-188p
                                     (4g9) 6. (5w1) 6.50
--Five to a Feast-Lond-(1948)-219p   (5c7) 4.50 (5g9) 5.00

LAYTON, T A (continued)
--Wine's My Line-Lond-1955-256p-photo illus   (5w1) 6.50
--Wines of Italy-Lond-1961-photos-221p   (5w1) 5.00
LAZARSFELD, P F-How the Voter Makes Up His Mind in a
   Presidential Campaign-NY-c1944-Publ #B3   (5w4) 6.50
LAZELL, J ARTHUR-Alaskan Apostle-NY-(1900)-218p-photos
                                         (5ss1,dj) 6.00
LAZELL, T S-John Lazell of Hingham & Some of His Desc-Reprnt-
   1936-130p   (5t9) 22.50
--Nathaniel Whiting of Dedham, Mass, 1641, & 5 Generations of
   his Desc-1902-80p   (5mm3) 13.50
LEA, ALBERT M-The Book that Gave to Iowa Its Name-IowaCty-
   1935-53p-col fldg map   (5L3, f) 15.00
--A Pacific Railway-(Knoxville, Tenn, 1858)-16p-prntd wrps-
   caption titl only
                                             (5m3) 60.00
LEA, ELIZ E-Domestic Cookery-Balt-1853-310p-5th ed (5c0) 16.50
LEA, HENRY C-Historical Sketch of Sacerdotal Celibacy etc-Phila-
   1867-601p   (5xx7) 12.50
--same-Bost-1884-lg8vo-cl-682p-2nd ed, enlrgd (5t2) 7.50
--History of Auricular Confession etc-Phil-1896-3 vols (5xx7) 20.00
--same-Phila-LeaBros-in 2 vols -1896   (5p9) 20.00
--A History of the Inquisition in Spain-NY-1908-4 vols-t.g.-
   crushed mor   (5d2, fine bndg) 55.00
--History of Inquisition of Middle Ages-NY&Lond-1904-3 vols
                                             (5q0) 20.00
--History of Sacerdotal Celibacy in the Christian Church-NY-1907-
   3rd rev ed-2 vols-3/4 maroon crushed mor-sp g.
                                    (5d2, f bndg, mint) 30.00
--same-Lond-1932-4th ed, rev-611p   (5p9) 7.50
LEA, HENRY CHAS, comp-Materials Toward a History of Witchcraft-
   NY-1957-3 vols   (5x7, box) 20.00
LEA, HOMER-The Vermilion Pencil-NY-1908-12mo-cl-1st ed of
   auth's 1st book   (5gg6, dj) 50.00
LEA, J HENRY-Ancestry of A Lincoln-HM-1909-ports-4to (5kk4) 17.50
LEA, JAS H-Ancestry & Posterity of John Lea of Christian Malford,
   Wiltshire, Eng & of Penna-Phila-1906-4to-611p-illus
                            (4m2, rbnd) 42.50 (5mm3) 40.00
LEA, LUKE-Report...Re Debts Contracted by Indian Agents in Calif-
   Wash-1852-SED 61- 26p   (4a5) 4.50
LEA, TOM-The Brave Bulls-Bost-1949-270p-1st ed
                  (4c7, autg, dj) 15. (5n4, autg) 15. (4a5) 6.50
--Bullfight Manual for Spectators-SanCarlos-(1949)-24p-illus-
   stiff wrps-1st ed   (5dd6) 5.00
--Calendar of Twelve Travelers Through the Pass of the North-El Paso-
   1947-Hertzog-illus-wrps   (4a5) 10.00
--same-(ElPaso-Hertzog)-1946-sm folio-cl-12 pg drwngs by
   Tom Lea-ltd to 365c, autg   (5ee9, dj, extra pres) 75.00
--The Hands of Cantu-Bost-1964-244p-1st ed
                  (5n4, autg) 13.50 (5n4) 8.50 (5g2, f, dj) 15.00
--The King Ranch-Bost&Tor-(1957)-maps-drwngs-2 vols(bxd)
                           (5r0) 25. (5dd9) 16. (5t7, box) 30.00
--The King Ranch-Kingsville-1957-prntd for King Ranch-2 vols-
   -ltd Saddle Blanket ed-spec all rag papr-designed by Hertzog
          (4c7, bo x) 385.00 (4a5, pres, box, mint) 325.00
--The Land of the Mustang-Austin-1965-28p-buck-col illus-
   ltd ed   (5n4) 10.00
--Portfolio of 6 Paintings wi Intro by JFrank Dobie-Austin-1953-
   1st ed-folio   (4a5) 85.00
--The Primal Yoke-Bost-1960-336p-1st ed   (5n4) 6.00
--Twelve Travelers-Through the Pass of the North-ElPaso-1947-
   from orig-Carl Hertzog   (5g6) 10.00
--Western Beef Cattle, Series of 11 Paintings-Dallas-1950-illus-wrps
                            (4a5, mint) 10. (5g0) 12.00
--The Wonderful Country-(1952)-illus-1st ed
                  (5dd6) 8. (5g2) 6. (5ee3, dj, f) 7.50
LEA, ZILLA R-The Ornamented Chair-Rutland-(1960)-photos-173p-
   4to   (5w7, box) 10.00
LEACH, F P-Lawrence Leach of Salem, Mass & Desc-1924 to 1926-
   3 vols   (5mm3) 15.00
--Thos Hungerford of Hartford & New London, Conn & Some Desc-
   1932-113p   (5mm3) 10.00
LEACH, FRANK A-Recollections of a Newspaperman-SanFran-1917-
                           (5x5, dj) 10. (5dd6) 12.50
LEACH, GEO E-War Diary-1923-205p   (5ss1, pres) 10.00
LEACH, J-Rough Sketches of Life of an Old Soldier-Lond-1831-
   411p-lea & mrbld bds   (5xx7, rub) 10.00
LEACH, J A-Australian Bird Book-Melbourne-1939-rev-8th ed-illus-
   200p   (4d2) 6.50
LEACH, J G-History of Girard Natl Bank of Phila-1902-plts (5L7) 7.50
--Memoranda Relating to Anc & Family of Levi Parsons Morton-
   1894-191p   (5mm3) 12.50
--Penrose Family in Phila-1903-163p   (5mm3) 17.50

LEACH, JACK F–Conscription in US Historical Background–
Tokyo–(1952)–10p, 501p–o.p.–8vo–cl–1st ed   (5t0, f)   10.00
LEACH, JOS–The Typical Texan–Dallas–1952–169p plus index–
illus, Carl Hertzog–1st ed   (5t3, dj)   5.00
LEACH, JOS GRANVILLE–Some Acct of the Pawling Family of
NY & Penn–Lancaster–1918–25p–orig wrps   (5w4)   4.00
LEACH, M L–Hist of Grand Traverse Region–TravCty–1883–
(MtPl–n.d.)–162p–wrps–facs rptn–ltd to 1000c   (5h2)   5.00
LEACH, PAUL R–That Man Dawes–Chig–c1930–349p–illus
(5w5, soil)   5.00
LEACOCK, STEPHEN–Back to Prosperity–Tor–1932   (5w8)   10.00
--The British Empire–NY–1940   (5x7)   4.50
--Canada, the Foundations of Its Future–Montr–1941–Seagram–
illus–10 col plts–sm4to–pict cl (5jj1,f) 15. (5t2,f,box)   7.50
--Canada's War at Sea–Montr–1944–Beatty–2 vols in 1–illus–
orig wrps–sm4to–1st ed–ads (5qq8,vf) 10. (5hh9)   12.50
--Chas Dickens, His Life & Work–NY–1936–DDoran–315p–illus
(5x0)   4.50
--Elements of Political Science–Bost–1906–12mo–cl–1st ed of
auth's 1st book   (5gg6, autg of Ben A Williams)   15.00
--Lincoln Frees the Slaves–NY–1934–1st ed   (5x2, dj)   12.00
--Literary Lapses–Montr–1910–Gazette Pr   (5w8)   15.00
--Moonbeams from Larger Lunacy–NY, Lond&Tor–1915–282p–
1st ed   (5aa0)   4.50
--Montreal, Seaport & City–Tor–(1948)–illus–cl–340p–1st ed (5t2) 7.50
--The Unsolved Riddle of Social Justice–NY–1920   (5x7)   4.00
LEAD DAILY CALL–Souvenir Ed, Historical & Biogr illustrating
Black Hills–Lead, SD–1905–photos–tall–no pagination–wrps
(5L2)   25.00
LEADENHALL PRESS– 1,000 Quaint Cuts from Books of Other Days–
Lond–c1900–dec bds–sm4to–170p–rare ltd ed, prntd 1 side only
(5v2)   65.00
LEADER, ALFRED–Through Jamaica with a Kodak–Bristol–1907–
JnWright–8vo–col pic wrps–photos–map–208p   (5j5)   22.50
LEAF, EARL–Isles of Rhythm–NY–(1948)–photos–211p   (5c3)   5.00
LEAF, MUNRO–Aesop's Fables–NY–(1941)–Heritage Pr–4to–
pic cl   (5p1, box)   10.00
--Fair Play–NY–1939–Stokes–4to–96p–1st ed (5p1, dj, autg)   15.00
--John Henry Davis–NY–1940–Stokes–sq8vo–1st ed–dec cl–56p–
col plts   (5dd0)   7.50
--The Story of Ferdinand–NY–1936–Viking–RobtLawson, illus–8vo–
pic e.p.–cl bkd pic bds–1st ed (5v0) 60. (5p1)   65.00
--same–1937–8th prntng   (5p1, dj, autg)   12.50
--Wee Gillis–NY–1938–Viking–RobtLawson, illus–4to–(72p)–
cl bk pic bds–1st ed   (5p1, dj)   35.00
LEAGUE ISLAND, ADVANTAGES OF–for a Naval Station, dockyard,
etc...answered by a NewEngl Man–Phila–1866–74p–fldg map–
orig wrps   (5w4)   6.50
LEAGUE OF AMER WHEELMEN–Handbook of Ohio Division–(Cinn)–
1892–184p–cl   (5h1)   8.50
LEAGUE OF NATION, FINANCIAL & ECON INTELL SVC–Taxation
of Foreign & Nat'l Enterprises–1932, 1933–5 vols   (5rr4)   45.00
LEAHY, ADM WM D–I Was There–NY–(1950)–illus (5F0) 3. (5k0) 5.00
LEAKEY, L S B–Animals in Africa–NY–n.d.–photos–144p
(5ss8, dj)   10.00
LEAMING, T–Phila Lawyer in the London Courts–1911–plts (5L7) 5.00
LEAMY, EDMUND–The Golden Spears & other fairy tales–NY–
(c1911)–DesmondFitzGerald–180p–8vo–illus, Corinne Turner–
frontis–6 plts–pic cl–1st Amer ed   (5p1)   15.00
LEANDER, C–Scuola, Del Lavorio All Uncinetto–Milan–1845–160p–
obl 16mo–bds   (5n7, bds creased)   5.00
LEAR, EDW–Book of Nonsense–NY–(ca 1870)–from 10th Lond ed–
Jas Miller–110 leaves–col–orig pic cl–rare
(5c8, cov wn, stnd) 45. (4c3)   75.00
--same–Lond, NY–c1880–4to–Toy Book format–pic wrps–12 leaves–
col illus   (5v2, f)   20.00
--same–Lond–1893–29th ed–illus–obl–cl   (5c8, vg)   17.50
--same–Lond&NY–1901–thk obl 4to–pic cl–10 illus (5v0, rub) 7.50
--same–NY–1919–Stokes–miniature ed–reprnt–cl–112p–illus (5s0) 4.50
--More Nonsense–Warne–1888–1st separate ed–lg obl 8vo–dec cl–
4p intro–104p–illus   (4d2, vg)   15.00
--same–Lond&NY–1889–Warne–3rd ed–108p–obl 4to–blu g. cl
(5c8, lacks 2 lvs pref & 1 lf)   8.00
--A Nonsense Birthday Book–Lond–(ca 1888)–n.d.–from Bk of
Nonsense & More Nonsense–1st ed–illus on alternate leafs–sm8vo–
383p–g.l
(5v0) 15. (5j2, few names) 15. (5c8, few names)   15.00
--Nonsense Book–Bost–1888–1st collected ed–wi all 4 bks,
ea wi t.p.–illus–cl   (4c3)   25.00
--Nonsense Song, Stories, Botany & Alphabets–Bost–1871–illus–
Jas R Osgood–orig dec bds–rare   (4c3, lacks fly)   85.00
--Nonsense Songs & Stories–Lond–n.d.–Warne–9th ed–illus–
illus cl   (5v2, vf)   20.00

LEAR, EDW (continued)
--Owl & the Pussy Cat & Duck & the Kangaroo–Lond–1892–
Fred Warne&Co–orig illus by Foster–Sepia–thin 8vo–
pic bds   (5c8, lt soil, rbkd)   15.00
--Owl & the Pussy Cat–Lond–n.d.–Warne–illus–32mo–
early ed in pic wrps   (4a1)   7.50
--Pelican Chorus & Other Nonsense Verses–Lond–Warne–(1899)–
sq8vo–62p–Brooke illus–col t.– 7 col plts–pict bds   (5a1)   8.50
--Teapots & Quails & Other New Nonsenses–Cambr–1953–
Harvard   (4c3, f, dj)   10.00
LEARNED, MARION–Life of Francis Dan'l Pastorius–Phila–1908–
324p–illus   (5w4)   10.00
--Philipp Waldeck's Diary of Amer Revolution–Phila–1907–illus
(5jj3)   10.00
LEARY & GETZ–Philadelphia, Valuable Historical, Theological &
Misc Books–Phila–n.d. (ca 1850)–(31p) (5ii4, lacks wrps) 5.50
LEARY, JAS C–DDT & the Insect Problem–NY–1946–175p (5s7) 4.50
LEARY, JOHN J, JR–Talks with T R–Bost–c1920–334p–illus (5w5) 6.00
LEARY'S RECKONER & COIN BOOK–Phila–(1864)–240p–prntd bds
(5h2, bnd upside dn)   5.00
LEASE, REX–What Actors Eat, When They Eat–LosAng–(1939)–241p–
232 photos wi recipes–4to (4g9, chip) 9.50 (4g9, f)   12.50
LEASOR, JAS–The Clock with 4 Hands–NY–c1959   (5x7)   4.00
--The Red Fort–NY–1957–Reynal–383p   (5x9)   4.00
LEATHAM, A E–Sport in 5 Continents–Edinb–1912–333p–plts (5a1) 6.50
LEATHER STOCKING AND SILK–or, hunter John Myers and his
times–NY–1854–Harper–12mo–orig cl–1st ed of auth's 1st book
(5i0, sl rub)   90.00
LEATHERBEE, E B–Anc & Desc of Luke Rogers & Sarah(Wright Brown)–
1907–71p   (5mm3)   6.00
LEAVEN FOR DOUGHFACES–By a Former Resident of the South
(Lyman, Darius auth)–Cinn–1856–1st ed–332p–scarce (5ii8) 37.50
LEAVENWORTH, E W–Leavenworth Family in US–1873–376p (5t9)17.50
LEAVENWORTH, DOUGLAS & FRANKLIN CO, KANS–Portrait &
Biographical Record of–Chig–1899–1st ed (Chapman Publ Co)–
842p plus index–illus–lea   (5t3, rub)   45.00
LEAVES OF GRASS–(W Whitman)–NY–1867–3/4 blk lea–4th ed
(5d2)   20.00
--same–Bost–(1860, 1)–3rd ed, 1st issue   (5ss9, lacks fly)   50.00
LEAVITT, C H–Crook, An Amer Family 1698 to 1955–1956–354p
(5mm3)   15.00
LEAVITT, E W–Blair Family of N E–1900–198p   (5mm3)   30.00
--Starkeys of N E & Allied Families–1910–16p, 149p (5mm3) 15.00
LEAVITT, EMILY W–Genealogy Warren Family 1637 to 1890 &
Conant 1581 to 1890–1890–59, p, 18p   (5mm3)   17.50
LEAVITT, JOHN McDOWELL–Kings of Capital & Knights of Labor–
NY–(1885)–Wiley–613p–1st ed   (5x4)   20.00
--same–NY–c1886–engrs(tissue guards)–681p   (5w5, wn)   10.00
LEAVITT, JOSHUA–Cheap postage–Bost–1848–wrps   (5g8)   15.00
LEAVITT, ROBT KEITH–Noah's Ark, New Engl Yankees & the Endless
Quest–Springfield–1947–106p–sm4to–wrps (5v0) 6. (5j4) 7.50
--Prologue to Tomorrow–Phila–1950–100p–illus   (5e4)   4.00
LEAVITT, STURGIS E–Hispano Amer Literature in U S–Cambr–1932–
Harvard U Pr–8vo–54p–wrps   (4a3)   15.00
LEBANON, MAINE–Vital Records to 1892–3 vols   (5t9)   12.00
LEBANON, OHIO, CITY BEAUTIFUL–n.p.–n.d.–(Cinn–ca1910?)–
18p–wrps–Ideal Location For Homes (wrp title)   (5h1)   2.50
LE BARON, GRACE–The Children of BedfordCourt–Bost–1905–1st ed
(5b9, f)   7.50
LE BAS, SIR HEDLEY–The Lord Kitchener Memorial Book–Lond–n.d.–
sm4to–illus   (5x7)   7.50
LE BEAU MONDE–Lond–1806, 1807–bnd vol magazine–hf calf–
rare   (5b9, crack)   50.00
LEBHAR, GODFREY M–Chain Stores in Amer–NY–1952–Chain
Store Publ–362p   (5p0)   7.50
LE BLANC, VINCENT–Les Voyages Fameux–Paris–1658–Clousier–
4to–limp vel–2nd ed, corr   (5n9)   125.00
LE BLOND, MRS AUBREY–Adventures on the Roof of the World–
Lond–1904–Unwin–333p–illus–cl   (5d7)   7.50
--Day In, Day Out–Lond–(1928)–JnLane–264p–illus (5d7, wn) 6.00
--Mountaineering in Land of the Midnight Sun–Lond–1908–Unwin–
304p–illus–cl   (5d7, wn)   7.50
--The Old Gardens of Italy–Lond–1912–photos–173p   (5s7)   6.50
--True Tales of Mountain Adven for non climbers young & old–
Lond–1906–3rd impress–299p–illus–cl–Unwin   (5d7)   5.00
LE BON, GUSTAVE–Les Civilisations de L'Inde–Paris–1887–4to–
dec bds–a.e.g.   (5j3)   10.00
LE BOSQUET, OLIVIA KATE–Chafee & Le Bosquet Families–
Honolulu–1955–228p–illus–8vo (5mm3) 7.50 (5hh4)   10.00
LeBOURDAIS, D M–Canada's Century–Tor–1951–214p–19 plts (5s0) 5.00
--Northward on the New Frontier–Ottawa–(1931)–311p–photos–
scarce   (5ss1)   8.00

LE BRASSEUR, GABRIELLE-Hints on Cookery & Management of
the Table (Ma Cuisine)-Lond-1891-180p (31p) (5c5,ex-libr) 4.50

LECHFORD, THOS-Plain Dealing, Or, Newes from New England-
Lond-1642-Butter-sm4to-mor extra-1st ed
(5a3) 1,250. (5n2) 1,500.00

--same-Bost-1867-R4to-211p-ltd to 285c (35 are R4to) (5qq8) 35.00

--same-Bost-1867-211p-lea & mrbld bds-ltd to 285c-1642 Lond
reprnt (5h2,underline) 12.50

LECKENBY, CHAS H-The Tread of the Pioneers-Steamboat Springs-
1945-illus-1st ed (5k4,vf,autg) 75.00

LECKY, ELIZ-Auntie's Rhymes-Lond-(ca 1890)-RaphaelTuck-lg8vo-
8 illus-bds (5c8,lt soil) 5.00

LECKY, PETER-Peter Lecky, By Himself-Lond-(1935)-349p (5s6) 8.50

LECKY, CMNDR S T S -"Wrinkles" in Practical Navigation-Lond-
1891-474p;16p-illus-g.stmpd cov (5s1,wn) 6.50

--same-1917-822p-plts (5s1,lacks 1 plt,rprd) 6.50

LECKY, WM E H-The Amer Revolution 1763 to 1783-NY-1908-
518p-cl (5h1) 5.00

--same-NY-1912-518p (5t4) 4.50

--Democracy & Liberty-1896-2 vols (5L7) 7.50

--Hist of Rise & Influence of Spirit of Rationalism in Europe-1925-
2 vols (5L7) 9.50

--Hist of Ireland in the 18th Century-Lond-1913-(Cabinet Ed)-
5 vols (5j2) 20.00

--Map of Life, conduct & character-1899 (5L7,sl spot) 3.50

LECLERC, FREDERIC-Texas & Its Revolution-Houston-1950-4to-
fldg map-ltd to 500c, nbrd-cl (5h5,vf) 25.00

LE CLERQ, CHRISTIAN-First Establishment of the Faith in New
France-NY-1881-map-plts-part mor-2 vols-1st ed in Engl-
Shea, ed (5jj7,f) 125.00

--New Relation of Gaspesia-Tor-1910-Champlain Soc-maps-452p
(5yy9) 35.00

LECOCQ, M-Notes de Linguistique Comparee (Ancien et Nouveau
Monde)-Paris-1897-2 vols-prntd wrps-scarce (5r7,ex-libr) 20.00

LECOMTE, HENRI-Le Cafe-Paris-1899-341p-lea bk (5w1,ex-libr) 6.50

LECONTE, CARRIE E-Yosemite 1878-1964-Mallette Dean-sm4to-
port-bds-lin bkstrp-ltd to 450c (5hh4,vf) 30.00

LE CONTE, JOS- A Journal of Ramblings thru the High Sierra of
Calif-SanFran-1930-wrps-ltd to 1500c (5x5) 10.00

LE CONTE, J-'Ware Sherman-Berkeley-1938-port-maps-146p
(5r0,5t7) 7.50

LE COQ, ALBERT VON-Buried Treasures of Chinese Turkestan-
Lond-(1926)-180p-52 plts-1st ed (5t4) 17.50

LE CORBUSIER-Marseilles Block-Lond-1953-illus-72p-4to (5ww3) 22.50

LECORNU, J-La Navigation Aerienne-Paris-n.d.-Vuibert & Nony-
8vo-cl-363 illus-2nd ed, rev-orig wrps bnd in (5b0) 95.00

LECOUNT, J M-Holy Hill, its history-Hartford, Wis-1891-illus
(5jj7) 15.00

LECOUVREUR, FRANK-From East Prussia to the Golden Gate-
NY & LosAng-1906 (5h5,pres) 12.50 (5x5) 10.00

LECTURES D'UN PERE A SON FILS-Paris-1828-262p-orig calf-labl-
frontis-hf title(dated 1827) (5c8) 10.00

LECTURES INSTRUCTIVES ET AMUSANTES-Tours & Paris-1867-
38 essays-plts-12mo-120p-bds-par F P B (5c8, cov wn) 22.50

LECUNA, V, comp-Selected Writings of Bolivar-NY-1951-2 vols-
822p (5L7) 7.50 (5w0) 8.50

LEDERER, NORBERT-Tropical Fish & their care-NY-1934-Knopf-
229p-illus (5x0) 3.75

LEDERMAN, MARTIN-The Slim Gourmet-NY-1955-239p (5c5) 3.50

LEDUC, GILBERT F-Washington & "The Murder of Jumonville"-Bost-
1943-235, (3)p-cl (5h7,f,dj soil) 10.00

LE DUC, W G-Minnesota Yr Book for 1851-StPaul-(1851)-fldg map-
prntd wrps-10p ads at end (5g3,rprd) 50.00

--same for 1852-StPaul-(1852)-98p plus 12 pg adverts-orig prntd bds-
sheep bk-frontis-1st ed (5m3,fldg map tip in) 65.00

--same for 1853-StPaul-(1853)-fldg map-prntd wrps (5g3,rprd) 50.00

LEE, A E-Hist of Columbus, Ohio-Vol 1 only-1892-921p (5mm3) 10.00

LEE, A M-Race Riot-NY-1943-Dryden Pr-1st ed (5x2) 15.00

LEE, AARON-From Atlantic to the Pacific-Seattle-(1915)-190p-illus-
port-dec cov-v scarce (5s4,rprd) 15.00

LEE, ALFRED P-Bibliography of Christopher Morley-NY-1935-277p-
1st ed (5mm1,dj) 10.00

LEE, ALFREDA-Table Decorations & Party Plans-Pelham-(1936)-
128p (5w7) 3.50

LEE, ANNA MARIA-Memoirs of Eminent Female Writers of All Ages
& Countries-Phila-1827-sm12mo-183p-calf-1st ed (5v0) 10.00

LEE, ARTHUR-A Speech in support of the Petition from Gen'l Congress
at Phila-Lond-1755-Almon-sm4to-half mor-1st ed (5n2) 150.00

LEE, ARTHUR T-Army Ballads & Other Poems-n.p.-1871-160p-
12mo-illus (5s4,fade) 6.00

LEE, BOURKE-Death Valley-NY-1930-Macm-210p-illus-cl (5d6) 15.00

--same-NY-1932-319p (5yy7,dj) 10.00

LEE, C A-Edith, a novel-Lond-1871-TinsleyBros-2 vols in 1-8vo-
orig dec cl-1st ed (5xx6) 25.00

LEE, CALVIN-Chinese Cooking for Amer Kitchens-NY-(1958)-
190p (5c9) 5.00

LEE, CHAS-Snow, Ice & Penguins-NY-(1950)-417p (5ss1,wn) 4.00

LEE, CHAS A-Aleutian Indian & Engl Dictionary-Sea-1896-23p-
wrps (5c9) 17.50

LEE, CHAUNCEY-The Amer Accomptant;being a plain, practical
& systematic Compendium of Fed Arith in 3 parts-Lansingburgh,
(NY)-1797-WmWWands-297p, (15)-8vo-calf-1st ed
(5L1,lacks plate, fade, wn) 20.00

LEE, CLARK-They Call it Pacific-NY-1943-dec cov (5s1) 4.00

LEE, COUNTY, ILL-Portrait & Biographical Record of-Chig-1892-
850, (4)p-mor (5y0) 60.00

LEE, COUNTY, IOWA-History of-Chig-1879-illus-887p-8vo-
part mor (5kk4,chip) 55.00

LEE, CUTHBERT-Contemporary Amer Portrait Painters-Rudge, NY-
1929-deluxe ed-ltd to 500c (5ww4) 25.00

LEE, DANIEL-Ten Years in Oregon-NY-1844-344p-fldg map-cl
(5tt0) 30. (5s2,f,lea) 35.00

LEE, DORIS-Painting for Enjoyment-NY-(1947)-4to-illus (5jj3) 7.50

LEE, DOROTHY ELLIS-History of Arlington Co, Virg-Richmond-1946-
illus-1st ed (4a1,artist pres) 15.00

LEE, E MARKHAM-Johannes Brahms-Lond-n.d.-SampsonLow-185p
(5p0) 5.00

LEE, ELIZA BUCKMINSTER-Naomi, or, Boston 200 yrs ago-Bost-
1848-Crosby & Nichols-8vo-orig cl-1st ed
(5b2, sp crude rprd) 8.50 (5i9) 20.00

LEE, F B-Hist of New Jersey from most Remote Period to Close of
19th Century-Newark-1905-illus-475p-4to (5ii8,rbnd) 35.00

LEE, FRANCIS BAZLEY-New Jersey as a Colony & as a State-NY-
1903-Soc of N J-4 vols-illus (5p9) 20.00

LEE, GUY C-History of NoAmer-Phila-(1904)-20 vols-thk8vo-illus-
Subscribers Only-Barrie-mor raised bands-US coat of arms tooled
on cov-"Ed of the Presidents" (5t0,Taft,autg,f bndg) 300.00

LEE, MRS HANNAH F-Historical sketches of the old painters-Phila-
1852-Hazard-Reprnt-Family Libr ser (5m2,sl wn) 7.50

LEE, HENRY-How Dry We Were-Englewood Cliffs-(1963)-244p-
photos (5ss1,dj) 5.00

LEE, HENRY-Letters & journals with other family letters-
Bost-1926-RMorse, ed-illus-cl & bds (5g4) 7.50

LEE, HENRY-Memoirs of the War in Southern Dept of the US etc-
Wash-1827-Force-orig calf-new ed wi corr (5tt6) 35.00

--same-NY-1869-Univ Publ-illus-maps-plans-mor-rev (5mm8) 15.00

--Observ on Writings of Thos Jefferson-NY-1832-calf-237p (4j4) 22.50

--True History of Civil War-Phila-1908-421p (4j4) 4.00

LEE, IRVING J, ed-The Language of Wisdom & Folly-NY-1949-
Harper (5p0) 4.00

LEE, J F-Octavia the Octoroon-NY-1900 (5x2) 25.00

LEE, J N-Memoranda of Lees & Cognate Families-1898-47p (5mm3)7.50

LEE, JACK "Powder River"-The Stampede-Greenburg-n.d.-154p-
port-illus (5r8) 8.25 (5jj1,autg) 10.00

--West of Powder River-1933-1st ed-203p (5r1) 8.50

LEE, JAS-The Family Robinson of Italy-Bost-(c1916)-Small, Maynard-
sq8vo-dec cl-g.t.-197p-plts (5aa2) 5.00

LEE, JAS-Silesian Tolk Tales-NY-(1915)-illus-12mo (4a1) 6.00

LEE, JENNETTE-Simeon Tetlow's Shadow-NY-1909-1st ed-frontis
(5ee3) 4.50

LEE, JOHN-Reunion of Desc of John Lee of Farmington, Conn, 1896-
1896-65p (5t9) 7.50

LEE, JOHN D-A Mormon Chronicle, the Diaries of John D. Lee-
SanMarino-1955-2 vols-illus (5t3,dj,5F5) 35.00

--The Mormon Menace-NY-(1905)-368p-illus
(5dd6,f) 13.50 (5t3,f) 7.50

--Mormonism Unveiled-StL-1877-calf (5x5) 20.00

--same-Lewisburgh-1882-413p-cl-col plts (5jj9) 25.00

--same-StL-1891-413p-lea-col plts (5k0,chip,wn) 15.00

LEE, JOHN H-Origin & Progress of the Amer Party in Politics-
Phila-1855-orig cl-264p-1st ed (4m2,soil) 25.00

LEE, JOS-Report of the Capitol Building Comm to Gov of Texas-
Austin-EWSwindells-1885-48p, 108p-illus-3 maps
(5g0,maps loose) 25.00

LEE, KATHERINE-Love or money-Lond-1891-Bentley-3 vols-8vo-
orig cl-1st ed (5xx6, sp wn, crack) 17.50

LEE, L-John Lee of Farmington, Conn & His Desc, 1897-527p-2nd ed-
also, Reunion of Desc of John, at Farmington, 1896-1896-65p
(5t9) 40.00

--Supplement-1900-ports-176p (5t9) 7.50

LEE, LAURIE-The Edge of Day-NY-1960-Morrow-8vo-illus-276p
(5p1) 3.00

LEE, MABEL BARBEE-Cripple Creek Days-NY-(1958)-270p (5t7) 5.00

LEE, MRS MARGUERITE DuPONT-Virginia Ghosts & Others-Richmnd-
1932-Byrd Pr-287p-66 plts-8vo-cl-1st ed (5ee3,pres,f) 27.50

LEE,MARY CATHERINE-A Quaker girl of Nantucket-Bost-1889-
Houghton-pict cl-1st ed   (5m2,sl wn)   5.00
LEE,MASS-Records of the Town to 1801-1900-374p   (5t9)   10.00
LEE,MINNIE M-Hubert's Wife,a Story for You-Balt-1875-246p-
cl-scarce   (5h7)   15.00
--Strayed from the fold-Balt-1878-1st ed   (5p6)   6.00
LEE,MRS-The African Crusoes-NY-n.d.-(ca1860)-Dick&Fitzgerald-
8vo-454p-cl-frontis-3 plts   (5rr2)   15.00
LEE,NATHANIEL-The Rival Queens-Bost-1807-WPBlake-16mo-
48p-sewed   (5j5)   50.00
LEE,NELSON-Life of a Fairy-Lond-(1850)-Crowquill, illus-Darling-
orig pic wrps-1st ed   (5c8,rub) 17.50
LEE,NELSON-3 Years Among the Camanches-Albany-1859-Taylor-
8vo-orig cl-wi added pic t.pg-1st ed-v rare (5n9,sl stn) 450.00
LEE,NORMAN-The Journal of Norman Lee,1898-Vancouver-1959-
R&F Reid,pr-Gordon R Elliott,ed-dec bds-mor bk-illus & tip ons-
ltd to 100c   (5w8,f bndg) 37.50
LEE,ROBT E-Lee's Dispatches-NY-1915-Putnam's-400p-illus-
fldg map-g.t.   (5mm8,pres) 25.00
--Reports of Operations of Army of NoVirg from June,1862 to &
including Battle at Fredericksburg,Dec 13,1862-Richmnd-1864-
RMSmith-2 vols-part calf   (5j6)   85.00
LEE,ROBT E, Jr-Recoll & Letters of Gen'l Robt E Lee-NY-1904-
461p   (5L7) 5. (5j6) 8.   (5p0)   7.50
--same-NY-1904-deluxe ed-ports   (5h6)   10.00
LEE,ROBT W-An Illustrated Hist of Fort Bliss-ElPaso-n.d.-16p-
wrps   (5n4)   3.00
LEE,RUTH WEBB-Antique Fakes & Reproductions-Framingham Centre-
(1938)-224p-illus   (5t7,autg)   7.50
--Early Amer Pressed Glass-Mass-(1933)-368p-190 plts-enlgd &rev-
                     (5w7) 10. (5v3)   11.50
--Handbook of Early Amer Pressed Glass-Mass-1946-illus-wrps
                     (5qq7,wn sp)   5.00
--A Hist of Valentines-Wellesley Hill-(1952)-239p-illus-1st ed
                     (5t7,dj)   10.00
--Sandwich Glass-Mass-(1939)-204 plts,(1 col)-526p (5w7)   10.00
--Sandwich Glass,the Hist of the Boston & Sandwich Glass Co-
Northborough-1947-590p-illus   (5k0,dj)   10.00
--Victorian Glass Handbook-Wellesley Hills-1946-illus-259 plts-
wrps   (5p0)   3.00
LEE,S P-Report & Charts of Cruise of US Brig Dolphin-Wash-
1854-SD59-fldg maps   (5n4,pres,f) 20. (5s1,wn) 13.00
LEE,SARAH B-12 Stories of Sayings & Doings of Animals-Lond-
1853-4 illus-cl   (5c8)   12.50
LEE,SARAH W B-Juvenile Album-T Holmes-(1846)-illus-obl 8vo-
dec cl-g.t.-67p-plts   (5yy9)   12.50
LEE,SIDNEY-A Life of Shakespeare-NY-1909-Macm-495p-
new&rev ed   (5p0)   7.50
--The Passionate Pilgrim-Oxford-1905-Clarendon Pr-vel-sm4to
                     (5mm2)   12.50
--Shakespeare & The Modern Stage-NY-1906   (5mm2)   7.50
LEE,SUSAN E-These Also Served-LosLunas-1960-1st ed
                     (5g5,f,dj) 10.00
LEE,TINA-Fun with Paper Dolls-GarCty-(1949)-64p-4to-illus-
charts   (5n7)   3.00
LEE,VERNON-Essay on Art & Life-East Aurora-1896-Roycroft Shop-
ltd to 352c,initialled by EHubbard (5i4)   10.00
--Studies of 18th Century in Italy-Lond-1907-sm4to-450p-plts-ports-
hf calf-2nd ed   (5a1,uncut) 12.50
LEE,W-John Leigh of Agawam(Ipswich),Mass & Desc-1888-499p
                     (5mm3)   27.50
LEE,W STORRS-Father Went to College-1936-245p (5e8,dj)   10.00
--Stagecoach North-NY-1941-Macm-8vo-cl-illus-210p-1st ed
                     (5j5)   6.50
--The Yankees of Connecticut-NY-1957-301p-1st ed
                     (5h9) 5.   (5t2)   4.50
LEE,WM-Junkie-NY-n.d.-(1953)-Ace Books-12mo-orig pic wrps-
1st ed of auth's 1st book   (5i8)   8.00
LEE,WM-Letters of Wm Lee,Sheriff & Alderman of London-Brooklyn-
1891-Ford,ed-3 vols-8vo-unbnd, in orig sheets-ltd to 250c
                     (5ss5)   25.00
LEE,WILLIS-Guide Book of Western US,Part B,Overland Rte,
Yellowstone-Wash-1916-Bul #612,US Geolog Sur-25 maps,fldg-
251p-photos   (5s4,ex-libr) 12.50
LEECH,MARGARET-Reveille in Washington 1860 to 1865-NY-(1941)-
8vo-483p-map   (4a7) 7.50 (5ss1) 4.50 (5w9) 6.00
LEECH,SAM'L-30 Years from Home-Bost-1844-12mo-illus-305p
                     (5m4)   25.00
LEECH,W L-Calendar of the Papers of Franklin Pierce-Wash-1917-
102p   (5j4)   8.50
LEECHMAN,DOUGLAS-Native Tribes of Canada-Tor-n.d.-
348p plus index-maps   (5t3,f)   8.50

LEEDS,DAN'L-Amer Almanack for Yr of Christian Account-(NY-
1713-Bradford)-24p in 3 fld 4to sheets-ex rare almanac-
"Sold by Elkana Pembrook in Newport,1713"
                     (5L1,cl fldg case) 100.00
LEEKEY,WM-A discouse on the use of the pen-Lond-n.d.-(c1733)-
8vo-disbnd-for RWare   (5x3)   30.00
LEEMING,JOHN F-The Book of the Delphinium-Lond-1932-76p-
col plts   (5s7)   3.00
LEEMING,JOS-Brave Ships of Engl,Amer-NY-1941-illus-344p
                     (5s1,ex-libr)   4.00
--Ships & Cargoes-NY-1926-285p-photos-1st ed (5s1,ex-libr)   4.50
LEEPA,ALLEN-Challenge of Modern Art-NY-1957-256p-illus
                     (5t4)   5.00
LEEPER,DAVID ROHRER-The Argonauts of '49-SoBend-1894-
JBStoll-146p,16p-cl-errata slip at end (5n9) 55. (5d6) 45.00
LEES,DR F R-Condensed Argument for Legislative Prohibition of
Liquor Traffic-Lond-1866-160p   (5w1,chip)   5.00
LEES,FREDK R-Temperance Bible Commentary-NY-1870-469p-
cl-1st Amer ed   (5h7,lt fox)   8.50
LEE'S MAP-of Industries of Western Penn, No.1-NY-1884-
lg fldg map,34 x 30 inches   (5m6,sl tn) 12.50
LEESON,MICHAEL-Hist of Saginaw County-1881-960p-illus-
pt lea-Chapman&Co   (5mm7,bkstrp wn) 30.00
LEETE,E L-Family of Wm Leete-1884-168p   (5t9)   13.50
LEEUWENHOEK,DOBELL C-Antony van Leeuwenhoek & His "Little
Animals"-1932-orig ed   (5L7)   15.00
LE FABLIER DU PREMIER AGE-Paris-1817-LePrieur-12mo-213p-
16 plts-calf-4th ed-rare   (5c2,wn)   22.50
LE FANU,JAS S-The Purcell Papers-Lond-1880-Bentley-3 vols-
8vo-cl-1st ed   (4i8)   125.00
LEFAR,SERGE-Serge Lifar a l'Opera-Paris-Thibault de Champrosay-
(1943)-4to-bds-cl sp-ltd to 950c   (5b0,cor chip) 27.50
LEFEVRE,FELICITE-Soldier Boy-(NY,Greenberg)-c1926-8vo-
pic cl-(63p)-1st ed   (5p1,dj)   15.00
LE FEVRE,GEO N-Pennsylvania Le Fevres-Strasburg-1952-illus
                     (5j3,ink)   15.00
LE FEVRE,P-Les Chemins de Fer-Paris-(1888)-illus (5r7)   7.50
LEFFEL'S-Illus Catalogue & Price List of Leffel's Amer Double
Turbine Water Wheel-Springfield-1868-79p (5e4,lacks wrps) 25.00
LEFFINGWELL,A-Leffingwell Record,Desc of Lt Thos Leffingwell
of Norwich,Conn-1897-256p   (5t9)   40.00
LEFFINGWELL,WM B-The Vale of Minnekahta-Hot Springs-(ca 1893)-
38p plus fldg map inside bk-photos-wrps
                     (5L0,map tn,underline)   4.00
--Wild Fowl Shooting-Chig-1888-373p-illus   (5t7)   10.00
LE FILS,CREBILLON-Lady of Quality-NY-Sheridan Soc-1928-201p-
illus-ltd to 1000c-1st ed   (5i1,cov wn)   6.00
LE FORS,JOE-Wyoming Peace Officer,an Autobiogr-Laramie-
(1953)-illus-1st ed   (5kk4,mint,dj) 25.00
LEFROY,A H F-Canada's Federal System-Tor-1939 (5r4,rbnd)   10.00
LEFTWICH,BILL-Tracks Along the Pecos-Pecos-1957-8vo-70p-
photos-prntd wrps-1st ed   (5g0)   7.50
LE GAL,EUGENE-School of the guides,designed for use of milita
of US-NY-1860-24mo-illus-limp cl   (5g8)   20.00
LE GALLIENNE,RICHARD-From a Paris Garret-NY-1936-329p
                     (5q0)   7.50
--My Ladies' Sonnets-(Liverpool)-1887-priv prntd-16mo-bds-
papr labl-1st ed of auth's first book (5gg6)   10.00
--same-(Liverpool)-1887-priv prntd-sm4to-bds-papr labl-
ltd to 50c,autg   (5gg6)   50.00
--An Old Country House-NY-1905-4to-(144p)-illus (5w7)   8.50
--Pieces of Eight-GarCty-1918-illus   (5p6)   5.00
--Prose Fancies-Lond&NY-1894-8vo-port-bds-203p-ltd to 200c
                     (5t7)   15.00
--Romance of Perfume-NY&Paris-1928-1st ed-sm4to-illus-46p-
bds-Hudnut   (5t4) 5. (5tt5) 8.50 (5w3)   6.50
--Romance of Zion Chapel-Lond-1898-1st ed   (5mm1)   4.50
--The Romantic '90s-NY-1925   (5p9)   5.00
--Sleeping Beauty & other Prose Fancies-NY-1900 (5p9)   4.00
LEGEND OF WONALANSET,THE-Bost-1914-8vo-28p-orig wrps
                     (5m6)   4.00
LEGENDS OF THE RHINE & OF LOW COUNTRIES-Lond-1832-
Colburn&Bentley-3 vols-12mo-hf calf-1st ed (5i8,scuff) 12.50
LEGG,EVELYN-Country Baskets-Lond-1960-photos-107p (5n7)   3.25
LEGGE,JAS-Religions of China,The,Confucianism & Taoism-NY-
1881-308p   (5t7)   10.50
LEGGETT,WM-Naval stories-NY-1834-Carvill-16mo-orig cl-
1st ed-scarce   (5x1)   75.00
LEGGETT,WM F-The Story of Silk-NY-1949-361p-cl (5y2,dj,5n7) 5.00
LEGLER,HENRY E-Leading Events of Wisc History-Milwkee-1898-
illus-322p   (5jj7,fray)
--A Moses of the Mormons; Strang's City of Refuge & Island Kingdom-
Milwkee-1897-Parkman Club Publs Nos 15,16-wrps-ex scarce-
                     (5zz5)   20.00

LEGMAN, G-Love & death, a study in censorship-n.p.-(NY)-1949-
Breaking Point-95p-orig stiff wrps-1st ed   (5m2)   6.00
LE GOLIF, LOUIS-Memoirs of a Buccaneer-NY-1954
                           (4a9,dj) 5.   (5c1)   5.50
LE GRAND, JOHN C-Minority Reprt of Comm on Internal
Improvements, Chesapeake &Ohio Canal-House of Delegates
Doc No. 17, March 1, 1841-38p   (5h8,ink)   12.50
LE GRAND, LEWIS-The Military Hand Book & Soldier's Manual of
Info wi Dictionary of Military Terms-NY-(1861)-Beadle & Co,
141 Williams St-141p-orig prntd wrps-rare-1st ed   (5m3)   47.50
LE GRAND, M-Fabliaux or Tales-Lond-1796 to 1800-2 vols in 1-
lg8vo-620p-illus-mor-raised bands-1st ed   (5v0,lt rub)   40.00
--General Hist of Quadrupeds-Newcastle-1811-8vo-525p-wdcuts-
buck-scarce   (5v0,rbnd) 27.50
LEHIGH COAL & NAVIGATION CO-A history of-Phila-1840-
2 fldg maps-wrp titl   (5g8,wrps cut)   12.50
LEHIGH RIVER-Incidents of the Freshet on the...6th Month, 4th &
5th, 1862-Phila-1863-56p-orig prntd wrps   (5w0,wn)   7.50
LEHMANN, ERNST A-The Zeppelins-NY-1927-Sears-329p
                                     (5p0)   15.00
LEHMANN, HERMAN-Nine Yrs Among the Indians, 1870 to 1879-
Austin-1927-235p   (4a5,mint) 27.50   (5zz5,dj) 20.00
LEHMANN, KARL-Thos Jefferson, Amer Humanist-NY-1947-
273p-illus-1st prntg   (5h9)   4.50
LEHMANN, JOHN-The Noise of History-Lond-1934-R8vo-cl-
1st ed-ltd to 75c, nbrd, autg   (5ss7,dj)   15.00
LEHMANN, R C, ed-Chas Dickens as Editor-NY-1912-illus
                                    (5mm2)   6.50
LEHMANN, ROSAMOND, ed-Orion-Lond-1945-Vol 2-illus-8vo-
cl   (5t2)   7.50
LEHMANN HAUPT, HELLMUT-Peter Schoeffer of Gernsheim &
Mainz-Rochester-1950-LeoHart-8vo-cl-20 plts (5j4) 10. (5d5) 7.50
LEHNER, JOS CHAS-World's Fair Menu & Recipe Book, Pan Pacific
Int'l Expo-SanFran-1915-144p-lg4to-frontis-port
                      (5c0,hng brok) 9.50   (4g9)   15.00
LEHR, ELIZ DREXEL-King Lehr & the Gilded Age-Phila-1935-Lipncott-
8vo-cl-32 illus-332p   (5j5)   7.50
LEIB, CHAS-9 Mo in Quartermaster's Dept-Cinn-1862-200p-mor-
scarce   (5h2)   35.00
LEIBOWITZ, ADOLPHE-Japanese Prints & their Creators-n.p.-1935-
(Shoreline Pr)-illus-12mo-1 col plt-scarce   (5j3)   10.00
LEIDESDORFF PAPERS-Manuscript List of 1023 lettrs & documents-
SanFran-(1894?)-cl   (5d6,pencil note by Cowan)   50.00
LEIDING, HARRIETTE K-Charleston Historic & Romantic-Phila-1931-
293p-80 illus-1st ed   (5h9) 7.50   (5ee3,f,dj)   8.50
LEIGH, BENJ WATKINS-Speech of on the Expunging Resolution,
April 4, 1836-WashCty-1836-35p-wrps-Browning
                             (5q8, lacks wrps)   12.50
LEIGH, OLIVER-Edgar Allan Poe-Chig-1906-8vo-illus-cl-
Dilettante Ser, 1   (5b2)   12.50
LEIGH, ROBT-Public Library in the US-NY-1950-272p-hf mor(5j4) 9.50
LEIGH, W R-Frontiers of Enchantment-NY-1938-8vo-300p-illus
                         (4a6) 10.   (5x2,dj)   7.50
LEIGHT, HERMANN-History of the World's Art-Lond-(1952)-illus
                                    (5m2)   10.00
LEIGHTON, ALEX H-The Governing of Men at a Japanese Relocation
Camp in Ariz-1945-Princeton Univ Pr-404p-illus   (5x0)   7.50
LEIGHTON, CAROLINE C-Life at Puget Sound-Bost-1884-258p-
1st ed   (5ee3)   8.50
LEIGHTON, CLARE-Country Matters-NY-1937-160p-8vo-73 illus
                                   (5ww3)   12.50
--The Farmer's Year-Lond-1933-obl folio-cl-12p illus (5d1) 20.00
--Four Hedges, a Gardners Chronicle-NY-1935-1st ed-illus
                              (5qq7,fade,5w0)   10.00
--Southern Harvest-NY-1942-4to-1st prntng   (5h6)   5.00
--The Wood that Came Back-Poughkeepsie-c1935-Artists & Writers
Guild-4to-(30p)-wrps   (5p1,chip)   4.00
LEIGHTON, GEO R-Five Cities, the Story of their Youth & Old Age-
NY&Lond-1939-plts   (5h6)   5.00
LEIGHTON, ISABEL-The Aspirin Age 1919 to 1941-NY-1941(5m2)5.00
LEIGHTON, J A-Man & the Cosmos-1922   (5L7)   7.50
LEIGHTON, MARGARET-Comance of the 7th-NY-(1957)-1st ed-
illus   (5k4,dj,autg)   6.00
LEIGHTON, WM-Florentine Sonnets-Florence-1911-4to-photos-
orig vel-priv prntd   (5p5)   7.50
LEINSTEIN, MME-Rudiments of Grammar, in verse, or a Party to the
Fair-Lond-(c 1828)-Dean&Murray-12mo-32p in prntd wrps-
13 hand col wdcuts   (5c8,t.p.tn)   60.00
LEIP, HANS-The River in the Sea-NY-(1957)-222p-illus-cl&bds
                                   (5t7,dj)   5.00
LEIPNIK, F L-History of French Etching from 16th Century to Present
Day-Lond&NY-(1924)-4to-106 illus-frontis   (5m2)   25.00
LEIPZIG, F P-Extension in Oregon-StBenedict-n.d.-122p-wrps(4a5)3.50

LEISING, WM-Arctic Wings-NY-1959-335p-plts (5dd0) 5. (5ss1) 3.50
LEISURE MOMENTS IMPROVED-Phila-1848-213p-cl-14p col plts
                                    (5ff7)   15.00
LEISY, ERNEST-The Amer Historical Novel-Univ of Okla-(1952)-
280p-cl   (5t0)   4.50
LEITER, MRS H, comp-Flower City Cook Book-Rochester-1911-188p-
                                    (4g9)   5.50
LEITH, ALICIA AMY-Birthday Book of Flower & Song-Lond-(1877)-
Routledge-sm4to-white cl-12 flower designs   (5i4)   10.00
LEITH, C K-World Minerals & World Politics-NY-1931-213p
                                (5p0,pencil)   4.50
LEITH, JAS-Memoirs of the Late Lt Gen'l Sir Jas Leith-Lond-1848-
163p, 22p-12mo-cl-lea   (5t7,wn)   10.00
LEITHAUSER, J G-Worlds Beyond the Horizon-NY-1955-412p-illus-
maps   (5h9)   7.50
LELAND, CHAS G-The Algonquin Legends of New Engl-Bost-1885-
8vo-illus-2nd ed   (5ss5,sl rub)   15.00
--The Art of Conversation-NY-1864-Carleton-scarce 1st ed (5m2) 6.50
--The Egyptian Sketch Book-Lond-1873- calf-g.-1st ed-
errata slip   (5d2)   12.50
--same-NY-1874-Hurd&Houghton-pic cl   (5m2)   5.00
--Flaxius, lvs from life of an immortal-Lond-1902-Wellby-pic cl-
1st ed   (5m2)   5.00
--Hans Breitmann's Ballads-Bost-1914-Riverside Pr-ltd 59 350c, nbrd
                                    (5r9)   10.00
--Johnnykin & The Goblins-NY-Macm-1876-illus-1st US ed (5m2) 6.50
--Legends of Florence-NY-1895-Macm-dec cl-g.t.-bevelled edges-
1st series-8vo-   (5b2,sl tn)   5.00
--same-NY-1896-Macm-2nd series-8vo-dec cl (5b2,soil)   6.00
--Meister Karl's Sketch Book-Phila-1855-12mo-cl-1st ed of
auth's first book   (5gg6)   25.00
--same-Phila-(1872)-rev ed   (5m2,sl wn)   5.00
--Memoirs-NY-1893-439p   (5j6)   6.00
--The Music Lesson of Confucius & Other Poems-Bost-1872-Osgood-
1st ed   (5m2)   5.00
--Ohnngkin & the Goblins-NY-1876-illus   (5r7)   7.50
--The Poetry & Mystery of Dreams-Phila-1856-1st ed (5mm2)   12.50
--Songs of the Sea & Lays of the Land-Lond-1895 (5m2)   5.00
--Sunshine in Thought-NY-1863-Evans-197p-2nd ed (5x4)   15.00
--Wood Carving-Lond-1901-162p-6 plts-4th ed rev by Holtzapffel-
                                    (5n7)   7.50
LELAND, G-Abraham Lincoln & the Abolition of Slavery-1879
                              (5x2,fair)   10.00
L'ELOGE DE L'YVRESSE-A La Haye-1714-216p(2)-frontis-
12mo-calf   (5w1,crack)   200.00
LELONG, B M-The Olive in Calif-Sacr-1889-19p-14 plts-wrps
                                    (4a5)   7.50
LE MAIR, H WILLEBEEK, artist-A Child's Garden of Verses-Phila-
(1926)-12 col plts-1st ed   (5v2,f)   10.00
--Little Songs of Long Ago-Lond-(1912)-   (5v2, libr mrks)   15.00
--Our Old Nursery Rhymes-Lond-(1911)   (5v2, libr mrks)   15.00
LE MAITRE, JULES-On the Margins of Old Books-NY-1929-322p
                                    (5n4)   4.00
LEMCKE, GESINE-European & Amer Cuisine-NY-1911-(c1903)-
614p-frontis   (5c0,hng broke)   5.00
--same-NY-1924-(c1914)-618p   (5c0)   5.00
LEMERY, LOUISE-Treatise of All Sorts of Foods-Lond-1745-Osborne-
12mo-calf-g.sp-lea labl-2nd Engl ed   (4h0,lf tn)   125.00
LEMERY, M L-A Treatise of All Sorts of Foods-Lond-1745-
372p(12)   (5w1,hng rprd)   125.00
LE MESURIER, LT COL H G-The Engl Ancestors of Epes Sargent-
n.p.-n.d.-priv prntd-cl&bds   (5w5)   5.00
LEMLEY, JOHN-Autobiogr & Personal Recoll-Rockfrd-1875-port-
8vo-2nd ed   (5m6,rub)   9.00
--same-Rockford-1875-cl-400p-1st ed   (4h1)   15.00
--Personal Recoll of-Albany-1893, 4-illus-12mo-cl-453p (5t2) 4.50
LEMMON, ROB S-Wildflowers of NoAmer-GarCty-1961-Hanover-
280p-col   (5p7)   6.50
LEMOINE, J M-Explorations of Jonathan Oldbuck-Que-1889-
qtr mor   (5r5, f, front wrps bnd in)   75.00
--Historic Canadian Ground-Montr-1892-Witness Prnt House-30p-
illus   (5aa1)   6.50
--Maple Leaves-Quebec-1863, 1864, 1865-Vol 1 to 3 in 1 vol-
photos   (5w8)   75.00
--Quebec Past & Present-Quebec-1876-cl-illus (5w8,shake)   10.00
--The Scot in New France-Montr-1881-Dawson-83p (5aa1)   10.00
LEMON, SISTER ADELE M-Hawaii, Lei of Islands-Honolulu-1956-
Tongg Pub-1st ed   (5x5,dj)   6.00
LEMON, MARK-Fairy Tales-Lond-(1868)-JnSlark-illus by Doyle &
Bennett   (5c8,f)   30.00
LEMMONIER, PIERRE C-Histoire Celeste, ou Recueil de Toutes les
Observations Astronomiques-Paris-1741-Briasson-4to-calf-frontis-
6 fldg plts-1st ed of auth's 1st work   (4h0,vf)   250.00

LEMOS, PEDRO J-Indian Arts, Pueblo & Navajo-Worcester-1932-
Davis Pr-4to portfolio-27 plts(3 col)-scarce
     (5g6)   5.00
LEMP, WM J BREWING CO-StL Souvenir of Columbian Expo, Chig,
1893-StL-(1893)-obl 16mo-45 plts-8p-wrps (5w1) 10.00
LEMPRIERE'S-Classical Dictionary-1788 (4e2) 10.00
LEMUS, MANUEL-Breve Noticia sobre Honduras-Teguicilgalpa-1897-
Nacional-lg8vo-46p-wrps-scarce (4a3, chip) 17.50
LE NAIL, E-Le Chateau de Blois-Paris-1875-lg folio-mor bk-t.e.g.-
Libraire Generale de l'Architecture-1st ed-plts (4h0, sl wtrstn) 50.00
LENAWEE CO, MICH-Atlas-1874 (5mm7, lacks pt t.p.) 35.00
LENAWEE CO, MICH-Portrait & Biographical Album of-1888-1217p-
lea   (5rr6 , loose chip) 35.00
LENDRUM, JOHN-History of the Amer Revolution-Exeter-1836-
2 vols-new, rev & corr ed (5s2) 15.00
LENDY, CAPT A F-Elements of Fortification, field & permanent-
Lond-1857-Parker-222p-illus (5mm8) 8.50
LENG, C W -Staten Island & its People-1930-3 vols-hf lea (5t9) 45.00
LENGLET DU FRESNOY, NICHOLAS-Geography for Children-Lond-
1795-12mo-144p-lin-fldg frontis-18th ed (5v0) 35.00
LENGYEL, C-4 Days in July-1958 (5L7) 6.00
LENIN, V I-Marx, Engels, Marxism-NY-(1935)Hnt'l Publ-226p (5p0)4.00
LENNON, FLORENCE B-Victoria thru the Looking Glass-NY-1945-
Simon&Schuster-1st ed (5hh1) 6.00
LENNOXVILLE MINING & SMELTING CO-Geological surveys &
reports on property of, Twnship of Ascot, Canada East-Bost-
1864-fldg map-wrps (5g4) 7.50
LENOIR, B A-Traite de la Culture de la Vigne & de la Vinification-
Paris-n.d.-8 plts-618p-lea bk (5w6, hng split) 18.50
LENOX, DAVID F-Personal Memoirs of a Missouri Confed Soldier
& His Commentaries on Race & Liquor Question-Texarkana-
(1906)-58p-wrps-rare-1st ed (5t3, chip) 75.00
LENROOT, CLARA-Will you Walk into My Garden-NY-1936-
Derrydale Pr-illus-12mo-ltd ed (4a1) 15.00
--Long, Long, Ago-n.p.-1929 (5jj1, f) 7.00
LENSKI, LOIS-NY-1928-sm4to-104p-col plts (5v0, f) 12.50
LENT, HENRY B-Bombardier-NY-1944-171p (5v6) 2.00
--The Waldorf Astoria-(NY)-1934-126p-photos-bds (5c5, split) 3.00
LENTZ, HAROLD-Jack the Giant Killer-NY-(1933)-pop up illus
in col-moveable book (5v2, f) 7.50
--Little Red Riding Hood-NY-(1934)-Blue Ribbon Pr-sq8vo-pic bds-
illus by Cloud-pop up ed wi 3 plts (5c8, plts dmgd) 5.00
--Mother Goose-NY-(1934)-Blue Ribbon Pr-sq8vo-pic bds-
pop up illus in col-3 mechanical plts (5c8, plts sl dmg) 7.50
--Pinocchio, being life & adven of a wooden puppet who finally
became a real boy-NY-(1932)-pop up illus in col-Blue Ribbon
Books-thk8vo-96p-stiff bds-4 dbl pg animations (5c8, vg) 25.00
LENWOOD, FRANK-Pastels from the Pacific-Lond-1917-224p-
illus   (5j3, vg) 10. (5p7) 6.00
LENYGON, FRANCIS-Decoration in England from 1640 to 1760-
Lond-1927-Batsford-Vol 2 in series-276p-plts-folio-cl-
2nd ed, rev (5m5, wn, crack) 40.00
LENZ, ELLIS CHRISTIAN-Muzzle Flashes-Huntington-(c1944)-
Standard Publ-8vo-823p (4a6, dj) 17.50
LENZ, F K-History of the Amer Branch of Lenz Family-1937-187p
    (5mm3) 5.00
LENZ, T W-Reise nach Saint Louis am Mississippi-Weimar-1838-
Voigt-16mo-pt cl-1st ed (4h0, wrps bnd in, ink) 200.00
LEO, ALAN-Casting the Horoscope-Lond-1927-illus-1st ed (5p5) 12.50
LEOLIN-Resistance to Laws of the US; considered in 4 letters to
Harrison Gray Otis-Bost-1811-uncut-stitchd (5g8) 10.00
LEON AND BROTHER-Catalogue of 1st Editions of Amer Authors-
NY-1885-8vo-orig hf mor (5gg6) 15.00
LEON, FRANCISCO DE P-Los Esmaltes De Uruapan-Mexico-1939-
123p plus 52p col plts-lg8vo-orig wrps (5x5, f) 20.00
LEON GAUTHIER, PIERRE-Les Clos de Bourgogne-Beaune-(1931)-
219p, (1)-ltd ed (5w1) 10.00
LEON PINELO, ANTONIO DE-Question Moral Si el Chocolate que
branta el ayuno Eclesiastico-Madrid-1636-Goncalez-8vo-
hf calf-g.stmpd-1st ed-v rare (5n2) 850.00
LEON PONTIFEX-Bost-(1890)-DeWolfe, Fiske-232p-1st ed (5x4) 10.00
LEONARD, REV B A-Report on Indian Missions in States of NY,
Mich & Wisc-NY-1890-Hunt&Eaton-16p-wrps (5t1) 25.00
LEONARD, DAN'L-Massachusettensis, or a Series of Letters of
Present Troubles in Prov of the Massachusetts Bay-Lond-1776-
Mathews-8vo-hf mor-1st Engl ed (5n2) 125.00
LEONARD, ELIZ J-Buffalo Bill, king of the Old West-NY-1955-
illus (5k4, 5zz7, dj, mint) 5. (5t7, 5L7) 7.50
--Call of the Western Prairie-NY-(1952)-339p-illus-cl
    (5dd5) 15. (5r0) 7.50
LEONARD, ERMINA N-Newton Genealogy-1915-872p-scarce
    (5t9) 60.00
LEONARD, FREDA P-Marietta Practical Home Cook Book-Marietta-
1903-219, (2)p-cl (5h7, lack fly) 4.00

LEONARD, HENRY A-Pigeon Cove & Vicinity, (Cape Ann)-Bost-
1873-193p-illus (5e8) 14.75
LEONARD, HUGH F-Hand Book of Wrestling-NY-1897-4to-267p-
plts-cl-ltd to 300c (5xx7) 17.50
LEONARD, I A-Books of the Brave-1949-plts (5L7) 6.00
LEONARD, IRVING A-Don Carlos de Siguenza Y Gongora-
Univ of Calif-1929-287p-(UC Publ, Vol 18)-t8vo-cl-scarce(5F5)22.50
--Ensayo Bibliografico de Don Carlos de Siguenza Y Gongora-
Mexico-1929-69p-wrps (5n4) 12.50
--Mercurio Volante de Don Carles de Seguenza Y Gongora-LosAng-
1932-Quivira Soc Vol3-128p plus index-illus-map-ltd to 665c
    (5zz5) 40.00
--Spanish Approach to Pensacola, 1689 to 1693-Albuqu-1939-
Quivira Soc-322p-ltd to 550c (4j4) 30.00
LEONARD, JOHN W-History of City of NY, 1609 to 1909 wi Brief
Biographies-NY-1910-4to-954p-illus (5t9) 20. (5r7,4n2) 22.50
--Story of the US Marines-(Phila)-n.d.-(ca1920)-illus (5w9, rprd) 7.50
LEONARD, L W-Hist of Dublin, N Hamp wi a register of Families-
1920-1018p (5mm3) 15.00
LEONARD, LAURA K-The Garland Cookbook-NY-(1946)-148p-
photos & chart (5c0) 3.00
LEONARD, LEAH W-Jewish Cookery-NY-1949-497p (5g9) 3.00
LEONARD, LEVI O-A Railroad to the Sea-IowaCty-1939-12mo-
cl-277p-illus-1st ed-scarce (5h4, f) 10.00
LEONARD, LEVI W-History of Dublin, (NH)-1920-1018p-illus-
enlrgd by Seward (5ss5, labl rmvd) 20. (5e8) 18.75
--Literary & Scientific Class Book-Keene, NH-1828-318p-sm8vo-
7 plts-orig sheep (5L1, crack) 35.00
LEONARD, P-The West Coast of Africa-Phila-1833-12mo
    (5x2, fox) 40.00
LEONARD, WM-Discourse on Order & Propriety of Divine Inspiration
& Revelation & Discourse etc-Harvard-1853-United Soc-88p-
12mo-cl-rare (5r7, fray) 25. (5m3, f) 27.50
LEONARD, WM E-A Man Against Time-NY-1945-8vo-cl-78p
    (5m8, dj) 4.50
--Red Bird-NY-1923 (5F1, f, dj) 5.00
--A Son of Earth-NY-1928-1st ed (5ss3, box, autg) 25. (5b9, fade) 10.00
LEONARD, ZENAS-Narrative of Adventures of Zenas Leonard-
Chig-1934-Lakeside Classic-264p plus index-fldg map
    (5a9) 10. (5t3) 7.50
LEONARDO DA VINCI-Leonardo da Vinci on the Human Body-
NY-(1952)-thk4to-cl-506p-215 plts (5d5) 30.00
LEONHART, RUDOLPH-Treasure of Montezuma-Canton, Ohio-1888-
cl-279p (4h1) 15.00
LEONI, A LEGEND OF ITALY-Lond-1868-8vo-orig prntd wrps-
JR-(a wise forgery of Ruskin) (5xx6, chip) 35.00
LEONIDAS, A POEM-Lond-1737-for RDodsley-4to-hf calf-1st ed
of auth's 1st book-(R Glover) (5x3) 40.00
LEONIDAS, PROF-Stage Hypnotism-Chig-1901 (5ww4) 5.00
LEONOWENS, MRS ANNA H-The Romance of the Harem-Bost-
1873-277p-illus (5t4) 10.00
--Siamese Harem Life-Lond-1952-illus-cl-228p (5x9) 4. (5t2, dj, f) 3.00
LEOPARD, JOHN C-History of Daviess & Gentry Co, Mo-Topeka-
1922-Hist Publ Co-1039p-illus-part lea-rare (5zz5) 65.00
LEOPOLD, ALDO-Game Management-NY-(1933)-481p-illus
    (5xx7) 10.00
LEOPOLD, NATHAN F-Life plus 99 Yrs-1958 (5L7, ex-libr, shake) 6.50
LEOPOLD, RICHARD WM-Robert Dale Owen-Cambr-1940-port-
470p (5q0) 12.50
LEOPOLD, W A, ed-Full hist of eventful life, crimes, repentance &
death on gallows of JnMWilson-(Norristown, Pa, 1887)-wrps
    (5g4, sp tn) 7.50
LE PAGE DU PRATZ, ANTOINE S-History of Louisiana-Lond-1763-
calf-2 vols-12mo-2 fldg maps (5s9, rbnd, maps in facs, tn) 175.00
--same-Lond-1774-Becket-2 fldg maps-mor-12mo-2nd Engl ed
    (5n1) 150.00
LE PAGE, W LAURENCE-The ABC of Flight-NY&Lond-1928-141p-
illus (5t7, libr labls) 6.00
LE PAULMIER, JULIEN-Traite du Vin & du Sidre-Rouen&Caen-
1896-2 vols in 1-ltd to 200c (5w6) 15.00
LE PRADE, RUTH, ed-Debs & the poets-Pasadena-(1920)-Upton Sinclair-
1st ed (5m2, sl fade) 7.50
LA PETITE RAPPORTEUSE-Lond-c1825-Darton-wrps (5v2, f) 12.50
LEPINE, AMBROISE D-Prelim investigation & Trial of....for murder
of Thos Scott-Montr-1874-Canadian Pr-127p-prntd wrps (5w8)45.00
L'EPINE, E-La legende de Croque mitaine-1863-4to-illus by
Gustave Dore- buck (5L7) 25.00
LE PLONGEON, ALICE D-Here & There in Yucatan-NY-(c1889)-
Lovell-8vo-buck-illus (4a3, sl chip) 15.00
LEPROHON, MME-Armand Durand-Montr-1869-16mo-hf calf
    (5w8, 2pg facs, wn) 10.00
LERNER, MAX-Amer as a Civilization-NY-1957-S&S-thk lg8vo-cl
    (5w0) 6.50 (5p9, 5x2) 7.50

LEROUX, GASTON-The Man Who Came Back from the Dead-Lond-
 1916-1st ed   (5ee3,vg) 7.50
--The Mystery of the Yellow Room-NY-1908-1st Amer ed-frontis
       (5ee3) 4.00
--The Perfume of the Lady in Black-NY-1909-1st Amer ed (5ee3) 5.00
LE ROW, CAROLINE B-English as She is Taught-NY-1901-Century
       (5m2, sl soil) 6.50
LEROY BEAULIEU, P-L'etat moderne et ses fonctions-1891-2nd ed
       (5L7) 10.00
LE SAGE, A R-Adventures of Gil Blas de Santillane-Lond-1819-
 T McLean-8vo-15 hand col plts-calf g.-3 vols (5i4) 50.00
--same-Oxford-1937-2 vols-sm folio-lin-ltd ed Club-autg-box
       (5b0) 35.00
--The devil upon two sticks-NY-1795-Swords, for Rivington-sheep-
 2 vols-12mo-in French & Engl (5i0, rub) 45.00
--The Hist of Gil Blas of Santillana-Phila-n.d.-3 vols-8vo-
 Jap vel papr-plts by Adolphe Lalauze-red buck (5t5) 15.00
LESCARBOT, MARC-History of New France-Tor-1907to14-
 Champlain Soc-3 vols-fldg maps (5zz8) 175.00
--Nova Francia-(Lond)&NY-1928-transl by Erondelle, 1609-
 lg8vo-cl-map   (5p5, dj) 10.00
L'ESCHOLE DE SALERNE-Paris-1650-(Louis Martin)-(19), 74p, (2)-
 8vo-bds-frontis-lea bk   (5c5, wn) 70.00
LESESNE, THOS P-Landmarks of Charleston-Richmond-1932-114p-
 illus   (5p0) 3.50
--same-Richmond-(1951)   (5h6) 3.50
LESKE, GOTTFRIED-I Was a Nazi Flier-NY-1941(5mm8) 4. (5p0) 7.50
LESLEY, J P-Iron Manufacturers Guide-NY-1859-cl (5ii8, rbnd) 50.00
LESLEY, LEWIS B, ed-Uncle Sam's Camels-Cambr-1929-1st ed-
 frontis-289p plus index
 (5k4, mint, dj) 25. (5zz5, bkplt, pres) 37.50 (5zz5, vg) 37.50
LESLEY, ROBT W-Hist of Portland Cement Industry in the US-Chig-
 c1924-330p-illus-imit lea (5w9, autg) 4.00
LESLIE, AMY-Some Players-Chig-1901-ports (5m1) 8.50
LESLIE, C E-The Sentinel-Chig-1885-Chig Music-160p-orig prntd bds-
 obl 8vo-cl sp   (5L8, sp wn) 10.00
LESLIE, ELIZA-Pencil Sketches-Phila-1833-label-orig cl
   (5m1, stnd, fade) 25. (5x1, labl rub) 37.50
--same-Phila-1835-2nd series-1st ed
  (5x1, wn, hng rprd) 27.50 (5ee3, wn) 15.00
LESLIE'S, FRANK-Illustrated Almanac-1877, 1878, 1879, 1880, 1881,
 1882, 1883, 1885, 1886, 1887, 1888, 1889, 1890, 1891, 1892-
 NY-1877 to 1892-pic wrps-col illus-4to (5t7) ea 4.00
--Illus Famous Leaders & Battle Scenes of Civil War-NY-(1896)-
 544p-cl (4g4, sl wn) 15.00 (5h1, wn) 12.50
--same-NY-(1896)-607p-illus-folio
 (4c1) 35. (5mm8) 17.50 (5L3, vg) 25. (5L3, f) 28.00
--Illus Historical Register of US Centennial Expos, 1876-NY-1877-
 folio-800 illus-foldout-scarce (5kk9, rbnd) 42.50
--Illus History of Civil War-NY-(1895)-Moat, ed-sm folio-512p
 (5s9, v wn) 17.50 (5t2, f) 18.50
--Pict & Descrpt Record of Cuban Rebellion-Wash-(1899)-folio-
 620p-cl   (5xx7, lacks bkstrp, wn) 17.50
LESLIE, JOHN-Short Account of Experiments & Instruments Depending
 on Relations of Air to Heat & Moisture-Edinburg-1813-1st ed-
 plt-179p-cl   (4d2, rbnd) 25.00
LESLIE, SIR JOHN-Discovery & Adventure in Polar Seas & Regions-
 Edinburg-1835-4th ed-rev&enlrgd-484p-illus-fldg map (5s0) 12.50
LESLIE, SIR JOHN R SHANE-Songs of Ariel-Dublin-1908-16mo-
 bds-cl bk-1st ed of auth's 1st book (5gg6) 15.00
LESLIE, COL K-Historical Records of the Family of Leslie-
 Edinburg-1869-3 vols   (5mm3) 15.00
LESLIE, MRS MADELINE-Governor's Pardon-NY-(1869)-286p-
 cl   (5h2) 12.50
--Little Robins in Trouble-Bost-(1860)-sq12mo-104p-illus (5v0) 5.00
--Worth & Wealth, or, Jessie Dorr-Bost, NY&Cinn-1865-12mo-
 263p-3 plts-Leslie Stories (5p1) 7.50
LESLIE, MISS-The Behaviour Book-Phila-1854-336p-4th ed
    (5w7, shake, poor) 7.50
--Directions for Cookery-Phila-1863-528p, 24p-59th ed
    (5c0, wn, lacks sp) 6.50
--The Gift for 1840-Phila-(1839)-328p-illus (5ee3, f) 25.00
--New Cookery Book-Phila-1857-662p, (58)-1st ed (5c0) 25.00
--same-Phila-n.d.-(1857)-662p, (24) (5c0, sp tn) 16.50
--75 Receipts for Pastry, Cakes & Sweetmeats-Bost-1832-16mo-
 104p-4th ed   (5xx7) 12.50
--same-Bost-by a Lady of Phila-2nd ed-100p (5c0, hng split) 25.00
LESLIE, PROF-Narra of Discov & Adven in Polar Seas & Regions...
 Whale Fishery-Edinb-1830-424p-map-plts-hf lea-16mo (5ss1) 17.50
LESLIE, SHANE-The Cantab-Lond-1926-1st ed (5r9, dj) 7.50
--Girlhood in the Pacific-Lond-1940-110p (5x9) 3.00
--The Irish Issue in its Amer Aspect-Lond-1918 (5q8) 6.50
--The skull of Swift-Indnpls-(1928)-BobbsMerrill-1st ed-illus (5m2)6.00

LESLIE, WARREN-Dallas Public & Private-NY-1964-o.p.(5a8, f,dj) 4.00
LESLY, PHILIP, ed-Public Relations Handbook-1962-PrenticeHall-
 901p-2nd ed   (5p0) 10.00
LE SOURD, PAUL, ed-Traite Pratique des Vins-Paris-n.d.-(ca1895)-
 illus-752p-hf calf   (5w1, rub) 25.00
LESPIAULT, MAURICE-Les Vignes Americaines dans le Sud Ouest
 de la France-Nerac-1881-77p(2)-wrps (5w1) 9.50
LESPINASSE, MLLE DE-Love Letters to & From Comte de Guibert-
 Lond-1929-553p-ports   (5a1) 5.00
LESQUEREUX, LEO-Atlas to Coal Flora of Penn &Carboniferous
 Formation thruout US-Harrisburg-1879-hf mor-18p text plus
 87 dblpg plts   (5w4) 10.00
LESSEPS, BARON DE-Journal Historique du Voyage de, employe
 dans l'Expedition-Paris-1790-(Imprimerie Royale)-2 vols in 1-
 2 fldg maps-calf-fldg plt (5s9, rbnd) 62.50
LESSER, ALEX-The Pawnee Ghost Dance Hand Game-NY-1933-
 Col U Contb to Anthrop Vol 16-338p-illus (5t3) 12.50
LESSING, GOTTHOLD EPHRAIM-Fables from the German of Mr
 Lessing-York-JRichardson, transl-12mo-calf
   (5xx6, lf tn wi loss of few wds) 85.00
LESSING, P-Only Hyenas Laugh-Lond-1964-263p-index
   (5x2) 3.50 (5c6, fine) 6.75
LESSLIE, JEREMIAH L-Doctrine of Modern Universalism Considered-
 Zanesvl-1836-252p-bds (5h1) 7.50
LESSON, RENE P-Voyage autour du Monde sur la Corvette la
 Coquille-Paris-1839-Pourrat Freres-2 vols-lg8vo-hf calf-
 42 plts-errat lvs   (5ss2, lt fox) 145.00
LESSONS FROM THE LOWLY-Old Eagle School, Tredyffin,
 Chester Co, Penna-Phila-c1902-illus-orig wrps-souvenir ed-
 ltd to 200c, nbrd   (5w5) 5.00
LESSONS OF VIRTUE-Balt-1814-Pomeroy, prntr-12mo-orig calf &
 bds-(Edw A Kendall)-1st Amer ed-rare (5i9, wn) 40.00
LESTER, C EDWARDS-The Life & voyages of Americus Vespucius-
 NY-1846-port-cl   (5g3, sp wn) 7.50
--The Life of Sam Houston-NY-1855-402p-port & 10 maps & plts
 (5ee3, lacks e.p.) 10. (5L3) 12.50
LESTER CO, FRANCIS E-Story of the Genuine Maztec Gem-
 Mesilla Park-n.d.-(ca1909)-16mo-wrps-20p (5g2) 7.50
LESTER, J C-Ku Klux Klan, its Origin, Growth & Disbandment-
 Nashville-1884-117p-12mo-orig prntd wrps (5m3) 150.00
--same-NY-1905-2nd ed-198p-cl-scarce (5h1, autg by ed) 22.50
LESTER, JAS W-History of the 2nd Regiment, NY Infantry, US V-
 Saratoga Sprngs-1899-75p-wrps (5j6) 6.00
LESTER, JOHN A, ed-A Century of Phila Cricket-Phila-1951-
 397p-illus   (5w4) 7.50
LESTER, JOHN ERASTUS-The Atlantic to the Pacific-Bost-map
       (5r7) 10.00
--same-Lond-1873-sm12mo-293p-illus-map (5w5, wn) 8.50
LESTER, MEMORY ALDRIDGE-Alldredge, Aldridge, Bracken, Nesmith
 Families and their kin-ChapelHill-1957-4to-priv prntd (5r7) 17.50
LESTER, WALTER F-Partners for 100 Yrs, New London Co Mutual
 Fire Ins Co-Norwich-1940-109p-illus (5h8) 6.75
L'ESTRANGE, A G-Hist of English Humour-Lond-n.d.-(ca1860)-
 thk12mo-grn cl-2 vols in 1 (5t0) 5.00
LE SUEUR, MERIDEL-North Star Country-NY-(1945)-336p, index-
 e.p.maps-1st ed   (5dd5) 7.50
--same-Book Find Club ed   (5dd5) 5.00
LET'S EAT-Boys'Shelter Club of Chig-n.p.-1931-170p
    (5c4, stns) 3. (4g9) 4.00
LETCHER, OWEN-Big Game Hunting in NE Rhodesia-Lond-1911-
 8vo-266p-photos-map-cl (4a6, sp fade) 8.50
LETCHWORTH, W P-Life of Sam'l F Pratt wi Account of Early Hist
 of the Pratt Family-1874-211p (5mm3) 10.00
LETHABY, W R-Medieval Art, 312 to 1350-Lond (1949)-rev by
 D Talbot Rice-illus (4a1) 12.50 (5m5) 22.00
LETTER FROM A GOLD MINER, A-Placerville, Calif Oct, 1850-
 SanMarino-1944-nar8vo-28p-bds-Friends of Huntington Libr-
 1st ed-ltd, nbrd   (5dd6) 12.50
LETTER FROM A MERCHANT AT JAMAICA-to Member of Parliament
 in Lond, touching the African trade-Lond-1709-12mo-31p-
 roan bk-1st ed-v scarce (5ss5, ex-libr, lacks 4 pgs) 15.00
LETTER FROM A WEST INDIA MERCHANT-To a Gentleman at
 Tunbridg-Lond-1712 - 18-lvs-priv prntd-v rare (5e2) 525.00
LETTER ON THE GENIUS & Dispositions of French gov by an Amer
 recently returned from Europe-Bost-1810-orig bds-2nd ed
    (5g4, libr disc) 6.00
LETTER TO THE FARMERS & Graziers of GrBritain to explain
 advantages of using salt in agriculture & in feeding farming
 stock-Phila-1819-stitchd (5g8, unopnd) 10.00
LETTER TO YOUNG LADIES ON MARRIAGE-from E B B Esk to His
 Ward Miss S L L-Bost-1837-8vo-orig wrps-14p (5m6) 12.50
LETTER WRITER, THE-Charlestwn(Mass)-1827-276p-calf
    (5w7, wn, fox) 9.50

LETTER WRITER, THE
--same-Bost-1835-12mo-144p-wdcut on t.   (5w7,wn)   8.50
LETTER WRITER'S OWN BOOK-Dayton,O-1842-192p-12mo-lea
             (5w7,wtrstnd)   9.50
LETTER WRITER'S OWN BOOK-Or,Art of Polite Correspondence-
   Phila-1844-180p,(12)-16mo-frontis   (5w7,sl wtrstn)   8.50
LETTERS FROM ABROAD TO KINDRED AT HOME-NY-1841-
   Harper-2 vols-12mo-orig cl-1st ed-(CMSedgwick) (5i0,vg) 17.50
LETTERS FROM AN AMER FARMER-Lond-1782-2 fldg maps-lea-
   12mo-1st ed-Howes 883-(MCrevecoeur) (5n9) 550. (5t7,rbkd) 400.00
LETTERS FROM A FARMER IN PENNA-to Inhabitants of British
   Colonies-Lond-1774-Almon-8vo-hf mor-2nd Engl ed (5n2)   75.00
LETTERS FROM THE NORTH OF ITALY-to HenHallam,Esq-Lond-
   1819-JnMurray-2 vols-8vo-orig bds-papr labls-1st ed-
   (WmSRose)   (5i8,f)   30.00
LETTERS OF AGRICOLA-on principles of vegetation &tillage,written
   for NovaScotia &publ 1st in Acadian Recorder by JnYoung-
   Halifax-1822-orig bds   (5g4,libr disc)   37.50
LETTERS OF DAME SHIRLEY,THE-SanFran-1933-Grabhorn Pr-
   2 vols-orig cl bkd bds-papr labls   (5m3,f,dj)   45.00
LETTERS OF SHAHCOOLEN,A HINDU PHILOSOPHER-Residing
   in Phila to his friend El Hassan-Bost-1802-calf-1st ed of
   Knapp's 1st book   (5gg6,sl wtrstn)   25.00
LETTERS TO MINISTRY-from Gov Bernard,Gen'l Gage & Com Howe-
   Bost-1769-Edes&Gill-sm4to-disbnd-1st ed (5n2,box) 175.00
LETTERS WRITTEN DURING LATE VOYAGE of Discovery in the
   Western Arctic Sea-by an Officer of Exped-Lond-1821-wrps-
   frontis-map-4 plts   (5w8)   30.00
LETTRES D'UN CULTIVATEUR AMERICAIN-Paris-1784-Cuchet-8vo-
   2 vols-calf bkd bds-1st French ed (5L1,pres) 95. (5n9) 150.00
LETTRES EDIFIANTES ET CURIEUSES-Paris-1780 to 83-Merigot-
   12mo-26 vols-calf-lea labls-56 fldg maps &plts-2nd ed
                        (5n9,vf)   850.00
LETTS,MALCOM-Sir John Mandeville,the Man & His Book-Lond-
   (1949)-illus   (5mm2,dj)   4.00
LEUBA,J H-Psychology of Religious Mysticism-1925 (5L7)   7.50
LEUENBERGER,HANS-Aethiopien-Zurich-1955-231p-44 plts
                      (5c6,f)   6.75
LEUPP,FRANCIS E-Geo Westinghouse-Bost-1918-304p-illus
      (4e4) 10.00 (5F0) 4.50   (5y2)   8.50
--In Red Man's Land-NY-(1914)-161p-9 photos (4b2)   4.00
--The Indian & His Problem-NY-1910-1st ed
   (5L7) 4.50 (5x5) 10. (5t3)   7.50
LEVASSEUR,A-Lafayette En Amerique-Paris-1829-Baudouin-2 vols-
   illus-fldg map-calf   (5qq8,rbkd)   37.50
LEVE & ALDEN'S-Tourist Tickets from Savannah etc-(NY,ca1881)-
   8vo-16p-illus-wrps-scarce   (5j5)   10.00
LEVEEN,JACOB-Hebrew Bible in Art-Lond-1944-140p-8vo (5ww3) 17.50
LEVENSON,J C-The mind &art of Henry Adams-Bost-1957-illus-
   Houghton-1st prntng   (5m2,dj)   6.00
LEVER,CHAS-The Bramleights of Bishops' Folly-Lond-1868-Smith,
   Elder-3 vols-orig cl-1st ed   (5ss3,sp def)   90.00
--Chas O'Malley,the Irish dragoon-Lond-1857-ChapmanHall-2 vols-
   8vo-orig cl-(not 1st)   (5xx6,fade)   5.00
--The Confessions of Harry Lorrequer-Dublin-1839-illus by Phiz-
   11 parts-8vo-orig pic pink wrps-1st ed of auth's 1st book-rare
             (5gg6,rprd,hf mor box)   150.00
--Davenport Dunn or the Man of our Day-Lond-1859-illus by Phiz-
   22/21 orig parts-lea-1st ed   (5hh1,vg)   60.00
--The fortunes of Glencore-Lond-ChapmanHall-3 vols-8vo-orig cl-
   1st ed -1857   (5x3,vf)   85.00
--Luttrell of Arran-Lond-n.d.-(1863 to 5)-16 parts in 15-8vo-
   orig pic wrps-ChapmanHall-1st ed (5x3,box,sl rprd) 75.00
--Our Mess-Dublin-1843-illus by Phiz-port-orig mor-tooling on bkstrp-
   3 vols   (5ss9,sig loose)   40.00
--Sir Brook Fossbrooke-Edinb-1866-3 vols-8vo-orig cl-Blackwood-
   1st ed-primary bndng-scarce   (5xx6,sl wn)   75.00
--Tom Burke of "Ours"-Dublin-1844-WmCurry,Jr-2 vols-t8vo-
   48 illus by Phiz-stmpd cl-1st ed   (5r9)   20.00
LEVER,DARCY-Arte de Aparajar y Maniobras de los Buques-Madrid-
   1842-2 vols-4to-orig pt calf-298p-125 plts-errat tip in
             (5ss2,sl wtrstn)   95.00
--The Young Sea Officer's Sheet Anchor-wi additions-NY-1858-
   Blunt-4to-orig calf-112 plts,2 fldg-lg margins
             (5ss2,hng broke)   125.00
--same-Bost-1938-illus-4to   (5t4)   27.50
LEVERHULME,WM H-6 Hour Day & other industrial questions-
   1919-SUnwin,ed   (5L7)   4.50
LEVERING,JULIA H-Historic Indiana-1909-Putnam's-538p-illus-
   1st ed   (5jj7,f)   15.00
--same-NY-1916-Centennial Ed-rev   (5x5)   7.50
LEVERMORE,CHAS H,ed-Forerunners & competitors of the Pilgrims
   & Puritans-Brooklyn-1912-2 vols-New Engl Soc (4c1) 15.00

LE VERT,MME OCTAVIA WALTON-Souvenirs of Travel-
   Mobile&NY-1857-SHGoetzel-2 vols-12mo-cl-1st ed-
   scarce   (5j5,ex-libr,wn)   25.00
LEVERTOV,DENISE-The Cold Spring & Other Poems-NY-1968-
   12mo-bds-papr labl-1st ed-ltd to 100c,nbrd,autg
   (5d8) 25. (5ss7,mint,dj,5b2,mint,dj)   35.00
--The Jacob's Ladder,Poems-NY-1961-New Directions-t8vo-
   orig dec wrps-1st ed   (5p5)   7.50
--Three Poems-1968-The Perishable Pr-12mo-wrps-1st ed-
   ltd to 250c   (5ss7,mint)   15.00
--With Eyes at the Back of Our Heads-NY-(1959)-lg12mo-cl-
   1st ed   (5ss7,vf,dj,autg)   18.50
LEBICK,M B-Tucson,Arizona-SanFran-(1911)-32p-photos-wrps-
   by Sunset Mag homeseekers bur   (5t3)   10.00
LEVINE,ESAR-Chastity Belts-NY-c1931-ltd to 2000c (5x7) 12.50
LEVINE,LOUIS-The Women's Garment Workers-NY-1924-8vo-
   illus-1st ed   (5ss5)   12.50
LEVINGER,ELMA EHRLICH-Playmates in Egypt & other stories-
   Phila-1920-Jewish Publ Soc of Amer-8vo-130p-pic cl-1st ed
                  (5p1,rub)   10.00
--They Fought for Freedom &other stories-NY-c1953-8vo-221p-illus-
   Riverdale Pr-Series No. 2   (5p1)   6.50
LEVINSON,RONALD B-In Defense of Plato-1953-Harvard Univ Pr-
   673p   (5p0)   12.50
LEVIS,H C-Baziliologia-NY-1913-Grolier Club-ltd to 300c on
   Jap vel-Chiswick Pr   (5i4,mint,unopened)   25.00
LEVY,ERNST-West Roman Vulgar Law,the Law of Property-Phila-
   1951-Philos Soc-Vol 29   (5w9,dj)   7.50
LEVY,HARRIET LANE-920 O'Farrell St-GarCty-(1947)-12mo-280p-
                 (5dd4)   6.50
LEVY,J de B-The Complete Herbal Book for the Dog-Lond-1955-
   272p-illus   (5w3)   4.00
LEVY,LUCIEN-Les Mouts & Les Vins en distillerie-Paris-1903-
   651p,(1)-limp cl   (5w1)   14.50
LEVY,RACHEL F-Life & Adven of John Levy-Lawrence-1871-
   Bower,prntr-83p-wrps   (4j4)   75.00
LEVY,ROGER-French Interests & Policies in Far East-NY-1941-
   209p-Inst of Pac Relations   (5x9)   5.00
LEWER,H W,ed-A Book of Simples-Lond-1908-Chiswick Pr-1st ed-
   222p(1)p-bds-center medalion   (5ii4,sl dmpstn) 35.00
LEWES,GEO HENRY-The Life of Goethe-Lond-1890-587p-port-
                  (5x0)   4.50
--On Actors & the Art of Acting-NY-1878-237p-Amateur Series
                  (5t4)   5.00
--Rug Weaving-Newton Centre,Mass-(1962)-160p-54 plts (5n7) 6.50
LEWIN,THOS-The Life & Epistles of St Paul-Lond-1878-2 vols-
   illus-pt lea-maps   (5ww4,sl dmpstn)   25.00
LEWIN,LT COL THOS H-A Fly on the Wheel-Lond-1912-
   Constable   (5p0)   6.00
LEWIN,W-Climbs -Lond-226p-cl   (5d7,lacks fly) 12.50
LEWIN,WM-Birds of Great Britain-Lond-1789 to 94-1st ed-323 plts-
   7 vols in 3-folio-mor-g.e.-3 index lvs-ltd to 60c
            (5z9,f,f bndg)   2,500.00
--same-Lond-1795 to 1801-2nd ed-336 hand col plts-8 vols in 4-
   orig bds-lg papr   (5z9,rbkd)   675.00
LEWINSKI CORWIN,EDW H-Political Hist of Poland-NY-1917-
   8vo-cl-628p-illus   (5t2)   5.00
LEWINSON,P-Race,Class & Party-NY-1932-1st ed (5x2) 10.00
LEWIS,A G,ed-Sport,Travel & Adventure-Lond-1915-352p-plts
                  (5a1)   5.00
LEWIS,A H-The Aaronsburg Story-NY-1955   (5x2,dj) 3.50
LEWIS,ALBERT ADDISON-Boxwood Gardens Old & New-Richmond-
   (1924)-191p-col illus   (5s7,hng loose)   10.00
LEWIS,ALFRED HENRY-American Patrician-NY-1908-Appleton-
   336p-cl-1st prntng indicated by (1) at end of pg 336
                  (5tt8,wn)   10.00
--The Apaches of New York-NY-(1912)-illus-1st ed (5ee3) 5.00
--Faro Nell & Her Friends-NY-(1913)-Dillingham-illus-348p-
   1st ed   (5g5) 12. (5ee3,f)   7.50
--Richard Croker-NY-1901-Life Publ Co-372p-cl (5tt8) 15.00
--same-NY-1901-illus-372p-2nd issue-1st ed (5ee3,f) 5.00
--The Sunset Trail-NY-1905-illus-1st ed   (5k4,f) 7.50
--same-1906-ALBurt-393p-cl-illus   (5g5)   5.00
--When men grew tall-NY-1907-Appleton-illus-pic cl-1st prntng
                  (5m2)   5.00
--Wolfville-NY-(1897)-12mo-FRemington,illus-orig pic cl-
   1st ed-auth's 1st book   (5tt6) 35. (5zz5,5gg6) 30.00
--same-NY-(1897)-Remington,illus-337p-2nd ed (5ee3,vg) 5.00
--same-NY-1897-Stokes-orig pic cl-3rd ed-Remington,illus
                (5m9,vg)   10.00
--Wolfville Days-NY-(1902)-frontis by Remington-1st ed
       (5ee3,f) 10. (5dd6)   10.50
--Wolfville Folks-NY-1908-1st ed-1st prntng-frontis
       (5m9,wn) 5. (5ee3,vg)   7.50

LEWIS, ALF HENRY-Wolfville Nights-NY-(1902)-326p-cl-
  1st ed-publ Sept 1902 (5ee3,pres) 35. (5dd5) 5.25 (5h2)   7.50
LEWIS, ALONZO-Hist of Lynn, Mass-1829-260p   (5mm3)   5.00
--Hist of Lynn including Nahant-1844-2nd ed-illus-lea-278p
       (5mm3)   6.00
--Hist of Lynn, including Lynnfield, Saugus, Swampscot & Nahant-
  1865-620p   (5mm3)   12.50
LEWIS & CO-Tea & Tea Blending-Lond-1886-117p,(9) (5w6)   4.50
LEWIS & DRYDEN'S-Marine Hist of Pac NW-NY-1961-illus-
  EWWright,ed-4to-ports-buck-reprnt-Antiquarian Pr-
  ltd to 750c   (5h5)   35.00
LEWIS, ANNA-Chief Pushmataha, Amer Patriot-NY-(1959)-204p-
  cl-1st ed   (5h7,f,dj) 4. (5t3,dj f)   7.50
--Diary of a Missionary to the Choctaws-1939-Chronicles of Okla-
  orig wrps   (5k2)   2.50
LEWIS, AUDREE S-Marriage Record for Steuben Co,Ind-1832 to 90-
  FtW-611p-cl-ltd to 50c   (5h2)   30.00
--Tombstone Inscriptions in Steuben Co,Ind-FtW-1967-cl-
  ltd to 50c   (5h2)   10.00
LEWIS, BERNARD-Behind the Type-Pittsb-1941-113p-Carnegie
  Instit of Tech   (5p7)   15.00
LEWIS, C B-Sawed Off Sketches-NY-1884-324p-cl (5h2)   15.00
LEWIS, C S-An Experiment in Criticism-Cambr-1961-1st ed
       (5r9,dj,f)   7.50
--The Last Battle-NY-(1956)-Macm-8vo-174p-1st Amer ed-
  Chronicles of Narnia ser   (5p1)   5.00
--Prince Caspian-NY-1951-Macm-8vo-186p-illus-1st Amer ed
       (5p1,scuff)   3.50
--Surprised by Joy-Lond-1955-1st ed (5r9,dj)   8.50
LEWIS, CHAS LEE-Adm Franklin Buchanan, Fearless Man of Action-
  Balt-1929-285p-illus col frontis-1st ed (5w4)   10.00
--Books of the Sea-Annap-1943-318p-cov (5s1,ex-libr)   5.00
--David Glasgow Farragut, our First Admiral-Annap-1942-
  36 illus   (5c1)   15.00
--Famous Old World Sea Fighters-Bost-(1929)-362p-illus (5t4)   12.00
LEWIS CO(WASH)-Inventory of the Archives of-1940-346p(5mm3) 7.50
LEWIS, D B WYNDHAM-At the Sign of the Blue Moon-Lond-(1924)-
       (5mm2)   4.00
--Francois Villon,a Documented Survey-NY-1928 (5t2)   3.00
LEWIS, DAVID-Recoll of a Superannuate-Cinn-1857-311p-cl-
  SMMerrill,ed-scarce   (5h1)   15.00
LEWIS, DIO-The New Gymnastics-Bost-1862-274p-300 illus-
  1st ed   (5t2,ex-libr) 4.50 (5w5)   8.50
--same-Bost-1864-274p-illus (5w7,wn)   8.50
--Oakland, (Calif), its climate etc,an address-SanFran-1877-
  Cubery-8vo-orig prntd wrps-1st ed-scarce (5i9,vg)   25.00
LEWIS, DORA S-Tomorrow's Homemaker-NY-(1960)-470p-illus
       (5w7)   3.50
LEWIS, EDW R-A Hist of Amer Political Thought from Civil War
  to World War-NY-1937   (5a8)   3.50
LEWIS, EDWIN H-White Lighting-Chig-1923-Covici Friede-354p
       (5x0)   6.00
LEWIS, ELISHA J-The Amer Sportsman-Phila-1855-lg8vo-orig cl-
  illus   (5t2,pres,fade)   35.00
--same-Phila-1857-510p-orig cl-illus-3rd ed of this title (5m3)   25.00
LEWIS, EUGENE W-Motor Memories-Detroit-1947-Alved-258p-
  illus   (5p0)   5.00
LEWIS, G C-Essay on Gov of Dependencies-Oxf-1891 (5r4)   15.00
LEWIS, G GRIFFIN-Practical Book of Oriental Rugs-Phila-1913-
  t.e.g.-maps-379p   (5qq7)   12.50
--same-Phila-(1920)-375p-illus-5th ed (5t7,dj)   8.50
LEWIS, G W-Reprt of Joint Comm on Treatment of Conscripts at
  Camp Lee-Richmond-1864-10p   (5j6)   12.50
LEWIS, SIR GEO CORNEWALL-An historical survey of astronomy
  of the ancients-Lond-1862-Parker, Son&Bourn-527p
       (5v6,bkstrp tn)   12.50
LEWIS, GEO E-The Indiana Company 1763 to 1798-Glendale-1941-
  358p-plts-map-g.t.   (5dd4)   18.50
LEWIS, GEO H-Nat'l Consolidation of RR's of the US-NY-1893-
  12mo-1st ed   (5m6)   7.50
LEWIS, H H,ed-A Gunner aboard the "Yankee"-NY-1898-312p-
  photos-4 col plts   (5s1,ex-libr)   6.00
LEWIS, HANNAH-Narr of Captivity & Suffering of Mrs-Bost-1817-
  Trumbull-12mo-hf mor-2nd ed-fldg frontis (5n1,wrps bnd in) 225.00
LEWIS, HAROLD MacL-Planning the Modern City-NY-c1949-2 vols-
  lg8vo-illus-charts-maps   (5w0,dj)   12.50
LEWIS, HARRIET NEWELL-Lady Kildare-NY-(1888)-RobtBonner-
  500p-frontis   (5x4)   9.00
LEWIS, HOWARD-Economic Resources of Pac NW-Seattle-(1923)-
  523p-illus-maps   (5s4,sl wn)   5.00
LEWIS, I N-Hist of Walpole, Mass-1905-217p (5mm3)   7.50

LEWIS, ISAAC-Divine Mission of Jesus Christ evident from his life,
  & from nature & tendency of his doctrines,a Sermon-NewHav-
  (1796)-T&S Green-30p-8vo-hf cl (5L1, lacks hf t.)   15.00
LEWIS, REV J W-Life, Labors & Travels of Elder Chas Bowles-
  Watertown-1852   (5x2)   35.00
LEWIS, JAS Francis Asbury, Bishop of Methodist Episcopal Church-
  Lond-1927-227p-plts-ports   (5a1)   5.00
LEWIS, JAS T-Cenadwri flynyddol...llywodraethwr talaeth
  Wisconsin-Milwkee-1865-WWColeman-8vo-orig prntd wrps-
  ltd to 5000c-(Welsh)   (5i9, vg)   27.50
LEWIS, JOHN-Complete Hist of Several Transl of Holy Bible &
  New Testament into Engl both in mss & in prnt-Lond-1739-
  2nd ed   (5t7,plt tn)   15.00
LEWIS, JOHN FREDK-The Hist of an Old Phila Land Title-Phila-
  1934-273p-illus (5mm3) 5. (5h9)   7.50
--Redemption of the Lower Schuylkill,the River as it was,as it is,
  as it should be-Phila-1924-City Parks Assn-t8vo-buck-photos-
  171p   (5j5,pres,soil)   7.50
LEWIS, JOS-Thos Paine, Author of Declaration of Independence-
  NY-1947-315p   (5h9)   5.00
--same-NY-1947-lea-ltd to 500c, nbrd (5w5,autg)   12.00
LEWIS, L-Hist of Bank of NoAmer-1882-4to-plts (5L7,ex-libr)   35.00
LEWIS, LLOYD-Capt Sam Grant-Bost-1950-Little, Brown-512p-
  frontis   (5mm8) 7.50 (5x0,5w9)   6.50
--Chig, the Hist of Its Reputation-NY-(1929)
       (5q8,sl fade) 6. (5w0)   7.50
--Granger Country,a pict Social Hist of the Burlington RR-Bost-
  1949-Little, Brown-4to   (5x5)   12.50
--John S. Wright, Prophet of Prairies-Chig-1941-215p-illus
       (5s4,dj)   10.00
--Myths after Lincoln-NY-HBr-1929 (5x0)   4.00
--same-wi intro by Sandburg-NY-1941-367p-Readers Club
       (5x0,5s9,dj)   3.50
--Sherman, Fighting Prophet-NY-(1932)-Harcourt, Brace-690p-
  illus-maps-cl-1st ed (5h7) 4. (4j4) 4.50 (5s9,5p0,5F9)   5.00
LEWIS MFG CO-Homes of Character-(BayCty, Mich, 1920)-sm4to-
  bds-159p of photos & plans   (5t0)   10.00
LEWIS, MARTHA L-The Harvest of Yrs-NY-1880-1st ed (5ee3,f) 12.50
LEWIS, MARY-The Marriage of Diamonds & Dollas-NY-1947-
  194p-photos   (5n7)   5.00
LEWIS, MATTHEW G-Journal of a West India Proprietor-Lond-1834-
  Murray-8vo-calf-t.g.   (4a3, rub,rbnd)   75.00
LEWIS, MERIWETHER-Die Reisen der Capitaine Lewis und Clarke-
  Lebanon,Pa-1811-Stoever-4 plts-12mo-1st Germ ed
       (4h0,wormhole,wn,Streeter copy,box)   1,000.00
--History of Expedition to Sources of Missouri River-NY-1893-
  Coues, ed-4 vols-1364p-orig cl-fldg map-ltd to 1000c
       (5m3,f)   125.00
--History of expeditions of,to sources of Missouri-NY-1902-3 vols-
  ports-maps-reprnt of 1814 ed-fldg pkt map-g.t. (5L3,vg)   22.50
--same-Chig-1924-2 vols-ports-maps(1 fldg)-g.t. (5dd5)   25.00
--Travels of, to Pacific Ocean-Lond-1809-Longman et al-8vo-
  hf calf-fldg map-1st Engl ed (5n9, cov dtchd) 150. (5nn8)   200.00
--Travels to Source of Missouri River-Lond-1814-lg4to-orig bds-
  lg fldg map-5 charts on 3 sheets-1st Engl ed
       (5n1,hf calf) 450. (5m4,rbkd)   275.00
LEWIS, MONTGOMERY S-Legends that libel Lincoln-NY&Tor-
  (1946)-239p   (5t4)   4.50
LEWIS, OSCAR-Bay Window Bohemia-1956-Dblday-12mo-cl-1st ed
       (5dd6,5h4,dj)   4.50
--Bonanza Inn-NY-1939-1st ed (4a5)   6.50
--same-NY-1940-346p (4a5) 4.50 (5c5)   5.00
--Calif in 1846,describd in Letters from Thos O Larkin-SanFran-
  1934-Grabhorn-ltd to 550c (5x5, fade dj) 30. (5x5,dj)   35.00
--Calif Heritage-NY-(1949)-4to-cl (5yy7) 8.50 (5h4) 12.50 (4n1) 9.00
--Here Lived the Californians-NY-(1957)-sm4to-cl-illus-1st ed
       (5jj7,f,dj) 10. (5h4,f,dj)   12.50
--High Sierra Country-(1955)-Duell, Sloan-(Amer Folkways Series)-
  8vo-cl-291p-1st ed   (5F5)   6.50
--I Remember Christine-1942-Knopf (5F1, mint,dj)   4.00
--The Lost Years-NY-1951-121p (5a8) 2.50 (5j6)   3.00
--Origin of the Celebrated Jumping Frog of Calaveros Co-SanFran-
  1931-4to-cl & bds-Grabhorn Pr-Book Club of Calif-
  ltd to 250c, nbrd   (5F5)   40.00
--Sagebrush Casinos-(1953)-Dbldy-illus-1st ed (5k4,f,dj)   3.50
--San Francisco Since 1872-SanFran-1946-US Ray Co-1946-101p-
  photos-folio   (4n1)   10.00
--Sea Routes to the Gold Fields-NY-1949-1st ed-12mo-cl
       (5s1,autg) 8. (5x5,5F5,vg,autg)   7.50
--Silver Kings-NY-1947-1st ed-286p plus index-illus
       (5jj1) 4.50 (5t3,dj)   7.50
--The town that died laughing-Bost-1955-235p (5m9) 10. (5s4)   7.50

LEWIS PUBL CO-Mem and Biogr History of counties of Fresno, Tulare and Kern,Calif-Chig-(ca1891)-ports-illus-4to-dec mor-beveled-822p   (5jj7,vf)   100.00
LEWIS,ROY-Shall I Emigrate?-Lond-1948-288p   (5a1)   5.00
LEWIS,SAM'L-Pipe Fitting & Marine Piping-Scranton-(1943)-49p-illus   (5s1)   3.50
LEWIS,SINCLAIR-Ann Vicers-GarCty-1933-1st ed-561p (5q0)   12.50
--same-1933-1st ed-ltd-on rag papr   (5mm2)   12.50
--Arrowsmith-NY-(1925)-1st ed-ltd to 500c,autg   (5ee9,box,4b1,f)   75.00
--Babbitt-(1922)-HB-1st ed-1st state   (5ww4)   12.50
--Bethel Meriday-NY-1940-1st ed   (5i3,dj,vf)   5.00
--Cass Timberlane,a novel of husbands & wives-NY-(1945)-Random-1st prntg   (5m2,dj,autg)   10.00
--Dodsworth,a novel-NY-(1929)-1st trade ed   (5m2)   5.00
--Elmer Gantry-NY-(1927)-Harcourt-cl-1st prntg,1st state (with G on sp like C)   (5z7,box) 25.   (5ee3,sl cov stn)   15.00
--same-NY-(1927)-Harcourt,Brace-1st ed-2nd issue   (5ss9,vg,tn dj)   15.00
--Free Air-NY-1919-pic cl-1st ed   (5mm1)   15.00
--The God Seeker-NY-(1949)-1st ed   (5ee3)   2.50
--It Can't Happen Here-NY-1935-1st ed   (5ss9,4p pres) 40. (5r9) 6.   (5m2)   6.50
--The Job-NY-(1917)-1st ed   (5ee3,vg)   27.50
--Kingsblood Royal-NY-(1947)-1st prntng (5r9,dj) 5. (5ee3,vg)   2.50
--Main Street-NY-1920-8vo-cl-1st prntng wi perfect type at bottom pg 387-1st ed   (5d3)   25.00
--same-NY-1920-cl-1st ed   (5b9,v wn) 5.   (5mm1)   6.00
--The Man who Knew Coolidge-NY-(1928)-1st ed (5ee3,mint)   15.00
--The prodigal parents,a novel-GarCty-1938-Dblday-1st prntng   (5m2)   6.00
--Selected Short Stories-NY-1937   (5p9)   3.50
--The Trail of the Hawk-NY-91915)-1st issue (5m4,bkstrp crease) 30.00
--same-NY-(1915)-2nd prntg-code K-P on copyrte pg   (5i3,mint)   10.00
LEWIS,THEODORE G-History of Waterbury-1763 to 1915-(1915)-286p-illus   (5e8) 9.75   (5mm3)   12.50
LEWIS,THOS M N-Tribes that Slumber-Knoxville-1958-192p plus index-illus-1st ed   (5t3,dj,f)   10.00
LEWIS,TRACY H-Along the Rio Grande-NY-1916-215p-illus-1st ed   (5ee3) 7.50 (5zz5,f)   15.00
LEWIS,VIRGIL A-Story of Louisiana Purchase-StL-1903-photos-300p-1st ed-cl   (4n9) 7.50   (5yy7)   8.50
LEWIS,W-The Wild Body,a Soldier of Humour etc-Lond-1927-cl bkd bds-ltd to 75c,autg-1st ed   (5a9,f)   75.00
LEWIS,W T-Lewis Family in Amer-1893-454p   (5t9)   40.00
LEWIS,WELLS-They Still Say No-(1939)-Farrar&Rinehart   (5F1,f,dj)   6.75
LEWIS,WM,ed-Ranald MacDonald-Spokane-1923-Estrn Wash State Hist Soc-1st ed-g.t.-ltd to 1000c-333p   (5s4,sl wn)   20.00
LEWIS,WM DRAPER-Life of Theo Roosevelt-n.p.-1919-544p-cl   (5h2)   7.50
LEWIS,WILLIE N-Between Sod & Sun-Clarendon-1938-244p-illus by Bugbee-1st issue-pic wrps-v rare   (4a5)   45.00
--same-Clarendon,Tex-1939-cl-244p-2nd prntg   (4h9,dj)   15.75
LEWIS,WYNDHAM-The Apes of God-NY-1932-8vo-625p-orig cl-1st ed   (5m2) 4.   (5t0)   5.00
--The Art of Being Ruled-NY-1926-8vo-cl-450p-1st ed (5t0)   5.00
--Blasting & Bombardiering-Lond-1937-1st ed-illus   (5r9,dj,5j2,dj)   20.00
--The Childermass,Section 1 (comes in 3 sections)-Lond-1928-Chatto-322p   (5p9)   5.00
--Collector's Progress-NY-1951-253p-bds-1st ed (5h7) 5. (5w9)   6.50
--Count Your Dead-Lond-(1937)-1st ed   (5r9)   15.00
--Francois Villon-NY-1928-pref by Hilaire Belloc-1st ed (5m1)   6.50
--Men Without Art-Lond-(1934)-Cassell-304p   (5p9)   5.00
--Rotting Hill-Chig-1952-1st Amer ed   (5r9)   5.00
--Tar-NY-1918-Knopf-379p   (5p9)   4.00
--Three Tours Through London in Yrs 1748,1776,1797-NewHav-(1941)-12p,135p-illus-12mo-cl-1st ed   (5t0,dj,f)   4.50
--Time and Western Man-Lond-1927-R8vo-cl-1st ed (5ss7,f,dj)   27.50
--Tutors'Lane-NY-1922-Knopf-8vo-cl   (5b2)   4.00
--The Writer & the Absolute-Lond-(1952)   -cl-1st ed   (5ss7,f,dj,review copy)   13.50
--The Yale Collections-NewHav-1946-54p-wrps   (5j4)   3.50
LEWISOHN,Ludwig-The Case of Mr Crump-Paris-1926-Titus-lg4to-prntd wrps-frontis-1st ed-ltd to 500c   (5ee9,unopnd)   25.00
--same-preface by Thos Mann-Paris-1931-8vo-wrps   (5ee9,unopnd)   25.00
--Expression in Amer-NY-1932-lg8vo-cl-32p,624p-1st ed(5t0,4L6) 5.00
--The Romantic,a Contemporary Legend-Paris-1931-Titus-8vo-bds & cl-g.t.-1st ed-ltd to 535c   (5ee9,box,autg)   25.00
--Trumpet of Jubilee-(1937)-Harper   (5F1,f,dj,pres)   10.00

LEWISOHN,LUDWIG (continued)
--Up Stream-NY-1922   (5x7)   4.00
LEWYS,GEORGES-Merry Go Round-(Lond)-1923-priv prntd-ltd to 999c   (5i4,dj)   15.00
--Temple of Pallas Athenae-n.p.-1924-priv prntd-ltd to 995c,autg-for Subscribers only (5nn2) 12.50 (5j3,dj) 10. (5i4,dj)   17.50
LEXBURN,J G-The Haitian People-1945-Yale Univ   (5x2)   6.00
LEXINGTON & DANVILLE RR-Third annual report-,Nicholasville, May 2,1854-Lexington(Ky)-1854-disbnd   (5g4)   20.00
--same-4th annual report-Lexington-1855   (5g4)   20.00
LEXINGTON,MASS-Record of Births,Marriages & Deaths to Jan 1,1898-Bost-1898-orig cl   (5x8,ex-libr)   6.00
LEY,J W T-The Dickens Circl-Lond-1919-2nd ed-ports-plts (4a8) 5.00
LEYBOURN,THOS-1806,9 & 14-New series of the mathematical repository-Lond-   WGlendenning-3 vols-8vo-calf-30 fldg plts   (5i8,lacks 2 labels)   30.00
LEYDA,JAY-Melville Log-NY-1951-2 vols-illus-8vo-cl-899p-1st ed   (5t0)   10.00
LEYDEN,JOHN-Scenes of infancy,descriptive of Teviotdale-Edinb--1803-Ballantyne-12mo-calf-frontis-1st ed   (5i8,rub)   20.00
LEYEL,MRS C F-Cinquefoil,Herbs to Quicken the 5 Senses-Lond-(1957)-368p-drwngs   (5w3)   9.50
--Compassionate Herbs-Lond-n.d.(1946)-224p-16 plts (5ii4)   8.00
--The Complete Jam Cupboard-Lond-n.d.-87p (5c5) 3.50 (5g9) 3.00
--Culpeper's Engl Physician-Lond-(1961)-illus   (5w3)   4.00
--Diet & Common Sense-Lond-1936-303p   (5c5)   3.50
--The Gentle Art of Cookery-Lond-(1935)-459p   (5c9)   5.00
--same-Lond-1925-461p   (5c5)   4.50
--Green Salads & Fruit Salads-Lond-n.d.-88p   (5w3)   3.50
--Hearts Ease-Lond-(1949)-333p-16 illus   (5s7)   7.50
--Herbal Delights-Bost-1938-8vo-cl-429p   (5t0,dj)   5.00
--same-Lond-(1937)-Faber&Faber-1st ed-429p (5ii4,dj,mint)   10.00
--Magic of Herbs-Lond-(1932)-320p-frontis   (5w3)   9.50
--Meals on a Tray-Lond-n.d.(c1925)-82p   (5c5)   3.00
--The Truth About Herbs-Lond-(1943)-106p   (5s7)   3.50
LEYMARIE,JEAN-Spirit of the Letter in Painting-(NY)-(1961)-90p-4to-lea-illus-Hallmark Cards,publ   (5t7,box)   17.50
LEYS,W A R-Ethics & Social Policy-1947   (5L7)   3.00
LEZARD,ADELE-The Great Gold Reef-Indnpls-1937-illus   (5h8) 5.50   (5x2)   5.00
L'HOMOND-Epitome Historiae Sacrae-Phila-1843-Thomas, Cowperthwait-24mo-156p-Long's Stereotype Ed-editio nova-editio viginti   (5p1,ink)   8.50
LHULLIER,C L-Dictionnaire des Termes Marines Francais Espagnol et Espagnol Francais-Paris-1810-2 parts in 1-8vo-bds   (5ss2,lacks hf t)   26.50
"LIAISON"-Biweekly Newsletter of Love-Vol 1,#1 to #16; Nov 17,1962 to June 15,1963-16 issues-wrps   (5ss9,vg)   15.00
LIBBEY GLASS MFG CO-Notes for An Epicure-(Toledo,O,1933)-43p pamph-illus   (5w1)   4.50
LIBBY,C T-Genealogical Dictionary of Maine & N.H.-1928-795p-6 parts   (5mm3)   50.00
LIBBY,C T-Libby Family in Amer-1882-628p   (5t9)   27.50
LIBBY,O G-The Arikara Narr of Campaign Agnst the Hostile Sioux, Jun 1876-Bismarck-1920-NoDak Hist Coll,Vol 6   (4k4,f,5yy7)   20.00
LIBER PSALMORUM HEBRAICE-Hilliard et Matcalf-1809-unbnd prntd sheets-495p-1st Amer prntg of Psalms in Hebrew&Latin-(for Harvard textbk)-12mo   (5cc6,sl stns,tn,box)   1,200.00
LIBER SCRIPTORUM-The Second Book of Author's Club-NY-1921-folio-lea-586p-Plimpton Pr-ltd to 251c-autg by all but six authors   (5d5)   35.00
LIBERATOR,THE-WLGarrison,ed-Bost-1833-Vol 3,#1 to #52,plus an extra-bnd(disbnd)   (5m3)   100.00
--Vol 26,#1 to #51-Bost-1856-lacking 3 issues-separate issues as publshd   (5m3)   60.00
LIBERTY AND ANTI SLAVERY SONG BOOK-Bost-1842-36p-wrps   (5x2)   27.50
LIBERTY BELL,THE-By Friends of Freedom-Bost-1839-Anti Slavery Fair-12mo-frontis-orig prntd bds-1st ed (5ss5,lacks bkstrp)   15.00
LIBERTY RECIPES-Lincoln,Neb-(1913)-HOBarber&Sons-52p-stiff papr wrps   (5c9)   3.00
LIBRARY-(Lond)-(1889,99)-10 vols-bd-Vol 1 thru 10   (5rr4,ex-libr)   150.00
LIBRARY BUREAU OF RWY ECONOMICS-List of Ref to Literature relating to Union Pac System-1922-299p-mimeo   (5d6)   25.00
LIBRARY CO OF PHILA-Charter,Laws & Catalogue of Books-Phila-1764-prntd by BFranklin & DHall-150p-hf lea   (5m4,blank lf cut)   275.00
--same-Phila-1789 to 1793-Poulson,Jr-lea-406p index plus 38p suppl,1793-lea   (5h9,cov wn)   35.00

LIBRARY OF FAMOUS FICTION-NY-1873-Ford&Co-lg8vo-
3/4 mor-1,065p-frontis　　　(5aa2)　10.00
LIBRARY SHAKESPEARE, THE-Lond-n.d.-(ca 1890)-4to-WMackenzie-
grn&g.cl-illus-g.e.　　　(5p6,f)　90.00
LICENSES TO TRADE WITH THE INDIANS-Wash-1826-(House Doc
118, War Dept)-4 fldg tabl-disbnd　(5g3)　10.00
LICHINE, ALEXIS-Wines of France-NY-1951-326p & index-scarce-
1st ed　　　　　　(5g9,dj)　6.00
--same-Lond-1951-illus-1st ed　(5w1)　5.00
LICHT, HANS-Sexual Life in Ancient Greece-NY-1932-Dawson,ed-
32p plts　　　　　(5j3)　12.00
LICHTEN, FRANCES-Decorative Art of Victoria's Era-NY-(1950)-
4to-cl-274p　　(5t7) 15.　(5w7,5p7)　12.50
--The Folk Art of Rural Pennsylvania-NY-1946-4to-276p-col plts-
1st ed　　　　　(5n7,5c3)　10.00
--Folk Art Motifs of Pennsylvania-NY-1954-96p-obl4to-spiral bnd-
col illus　　　　　(5n7)　7.50
LICHTENBERGER, HENRI-Germany & its Evolution in Modern Times-
Lond-1913-Constable-440p　(5p0)　7.50
LICK OBSERVATORY ON SUMMIT OF MT HAMILTON-n.p.-n.d.-
14p-fldg-pic wrps　　　(5r0)　7.50
LIDDELL HART, B H-Sherman, Soldier Realist American-NY-1920-
8vo-456p　　　　(4a7,fade)　15.00
--War in Outline, 1914 to 1918-1936-maps　(5L7)　5.00
LIDDELL, MARY S F-The Hon Geo Gray, 4th of Phila-n.p.-1940-
priv prntd-illus-226p-(100c prntd)　(5ii8)　30.00
LIDDELL, R SCOTLAND-50,000 Miles of Sun-Lond-1925-284p-
15 plts　　　　　　(5s6)　4.50
LIDDIARD, REV WM-A 3 months' tour in Switzerland & France-Lond-
Smith, Elder-1832-8vo-orig bds-prntd papr labl-frontis-3 plts-
fldg map-1st ed　　　(5i8,sp wn)　15.00
LIDDLE, R A-Geology & Mineral Resources of Medina County-
Austin-1918-177p-fldg map　(4a5)　6.00
--The geology of Venezuela & Trinidad-FtWorth-1927-JPMacGowan-
552p-pkt map　　　　(5v6)　12.50
LIDSTONE, RONALD A-The Art of Fencing-(1930)-224p-cl-
illus　　　　　　(5t2)　12.50
LIEBER, FRANCIS-Lecture on origins & Developments of 1st
constituents of civilisation(sic)-Columbia, SoCar-1845-stitchd
　　　　　　(5g4,fox)　7.50
--On Civil Liberty & Self Government-Phila-1859-lg8vo-cl-629p-
enlrgd ed　　　　(5t0,sp wn,fox)　8.50
--Popular Essay on Subj of Penal Law-Phila-1838-94p-disbnd-
mrbld bds　　　　　(5w5)　7.50
--The Stranger in Amer-Phila-1835-356p-hf lea (5ee3,hgn crk)　20.00
LIEBER, H-The Use of Coal Tar Colors in Food Products-NY-1904
　　　　　　(5w1,cov spot)　4.50
LIEBERMAN, MAX-Hollandisches Skizzenbuch-Berlin-1911-
JuliusBard-obl folio-cl-orig litho frontis-ltd to 500c (5d9)　100.00
--Sein Leben und Seine Werke-Berlin-1914-Cassirer-ErichHancke-
lg4to-548p-illus-orig 3/4 mor-orig self port frontis (5d5)　50.00
LIEBIG, JUSTUS-Familiar Letters on Chemistry & its Relation to
Commerce, Physiology & Agric-NY-1 43-54p, (2)-orig wrps
　　　　　　(5b8,soil,wn)　6.50
--Letters on modern agric-Lond-1859-Walton&Maberly-284p(5v6) 10.00
LIEBLING, A J-Telephone Booth Indian-GC, NY-Doubleday-1942-
1st ed-scarce　　　(5i1,g,wn dj)　35.00
--The Wayward Pressman-NY-1947-1st ed　(4a1)　10.00
LIEF, ALFRED-The Firestone Story-NY-(1951)-437p-illus
　　(5a9) 6.　(5t7) 5.　(5y2)　5.75
--Harvey Firestone, Free Man of Enterprise-NY-1951-324p-illus
　　　　　　(5y2)　4.50
LIFAR, SERGE-A Hist of the Russian Ballet-(Lond)&NY-1955-4to-
cl-illus　　　　　(5p5,dj)　15.00
LIFE & ADVENTURES OF ROBINSON CRUSOE-Lond-1790-WLane-
2 vols-sm8vo-hf calf-2 frontis-6 plts　(5aa2)　45.00
--same-Lond-1790-Logographic Pr-3 vols-t8vo-calf-plts
　　　　　　(5aa2,sl wn)　35.00
--same-Lond-(c1799)-C Cooke-3 vols-hf calf-6 plts
　　　　　　(5aa2,sl rub)　25.00
--same-Lond-1831-(Roscoe's Novelists Libr)-2 vols-sm8vo-pt mor-
port-16 plts　　　　(5aa2)　35.00
--same-Bristol, RI-1836-Gladding-sm8vo-orig prntd bds-134p-
4 hand col plts　　　(5aa2)　15.00
--same-Portland, Me-1841-Colesworthy-12mo-orig bds-134p-
hand col frontis-2 plts-(t.p. dated 1839)　(5aa2)　25.00
--same-Lond-1847-Bogue-sq8vo-620p-8 plts-dec cl (5aa2,rbkd)　15.00
--same-Lond-1858-reprnt of above-a.e.g.-WKent　(5aa2)　10.00
--same-Phila-1850-Journymn Pr Union-lg8vo-cl-7 plts-port
　　　　　　(5aa2)　20.00
--same-Lond-n.d.(ca 1855)-Read&Co-422p, (4) ads-24mo-18 col plts-
frontis-cl　　　　　(5p1)　18.50

LIFE & ADVENTURES OF ROBINSON CRUSOE (continued)
--same-Lond-1864-Routledge, Warne&Rutledge-lg sq8vo-dec cl-
a.e.g.-498p-100 illus by Watson　(5aa2)　25.00
--same-Lond-n.d.-Routledge&Sons-reprnt of above　(5aa2)　15.00
--same-Lond-n.d.-Routledge&Sons-reprnt-4to-pic glazed bds
　　　　　　(5aa2)　7.50
--same-Bost-(c1898)-DeWolfe, Fiske-Favorite Libr-12mo-192p-
pic grey cl-4 plts　　(5aa2)　4.50
--same-(c1901)-as above-yellow cl　(5aa2)　3.50
--same-NY-n.d.-McLoughlin-4to-dec cl-158p-frontis-
75 illus by Paget　　(5aa2)　4.50
LIFE & CONFESSION OF ANN WALTERS-female murderess,also
Dudley & Mary Runkle-n.p.-1850-illus-pic wrps (5g8,sl stn)　12.50
LIFE & DEATH OF JENNY WREN-NY-c1850's-JnMcLoughlin-
"Elton&Co" imprnt-9 col plts by Weir-sm8vo-12 lvs-The
Pleasure Bk Ser　　(5v2,fray)　40.00
LIFE & DEATH OF THE MERRY DEUILL OF EDMONTON-Lond-1819-
FrancisFaulkner-(T Brewer)-hf mor　(5ss3)　10.00
LIFE & MOST SURPRISING ADVENTURES OF ROBINSON CRUSOE-
Lond-1789-TMartin-sm8vo-calf & cl-314p-2 plts-16th ed
　　　　　　(5aa2,rbnd)　35.00
--same-Derby-1816-HenMozley-12mo-hf calf-286p-5 plts
　　　　　　(5aa2,sl rub)　15.00
--same-Dublin-1826-JohnJones-12mo-177p-6 plts-sheep-4th ed
　　　　　　(5aa2)　8.50
--same-Exeter&Lond-SHedgeland-Harvey&Darton(etc)-(1823)-
12mo-hf roan-246p-frontis　(5aa2)　35.00
LIFE & PUBLIC SERVICES OF HON ABRAHAM LINCOLN-of Illinois
& Hamlin-Bost-1860-Thayer&Eldridge-12mo-orig cl-320p-ports-
"Wide Awake Ed"　　(5t2,sl stn)　15.00
LIFE & STRANGE SURPRIZING ADVENTURES OF ROBINSON
CRUSOE-Lond-1719-prntd for WTaylor-8vo-calf-364p-frontis-
3rd ed-tailpiece pg 364 a lion　(5aa2)　250.00
--Lond-1766-JBuckland(&others)-2 vols-sm8vo-calf-frontis-10 plts-
fldg map-13th ed　　(5aa2,sl repr)　50.00
--same-Lond-1891-Cassell-Paget, illus-4to-416p-plts (5aa2)　7.50
--same as above-Phila-n.d.-Altemus-4to-dec blu cl-g.t.-445p-
plts　　　　　(5aa2,sl wn)　4.50
--same-NY-(189?)-McLoughlin-120 illus, Paget-4to-pic glazed
pink bds-cl back-416p-13 col plts　(5aa2)　6.50
--same-Bost-1908-HoughtonMif-4 vols-8vo-grn bds, buff bks-
16 plts-(lg papr ed, ltd to 180 nbrd sets)　(5aa2)　35.00
--same-Lond-1910-Frowde&Hodder&Stoughton-4to-dec tan cl-
labl-352p-24 mntd col plts　(5aa2)　10.00
--same-NY-1930-4to-limp cl-fldg map-bxd-(Grabhorn Pr, SanFran)-
Ltd Ed Club-ltd to 1500c, autg by artist　(5aa2)　65.00
--same-NY-1949-t8vo-dec cream cl-bxd-299p-Heritage Pr-illus
　　　　　　(5aa2)　7.50
LIFE BOAT, THE-Phila-(ca1870)-Protestant Episc Book Soc-16mo-
16p-prntd wrps　　(5c8)　3.00
LIFE, CAMPAIGNS, & PUBLIC SERVICES OF, GEN GEO B
McCLELLAN-Phila-(1864)-orig cl-g.　(5q8)　6.00
LIFE, CONDEMNATION-Dying Address & Trial of the 3 Thayers
who were executed for Murder of John Love of Buffalo, NY,
1825-Bost-n.d.(1825)-16p-orig plain wrps (5s2,wrps tn)　25.00
LIFE, EDITORS OF-America's Arts & Skills-NY-1957-folio-172p-
col illus　　　　(5xx7,dj)　15.00
--Life Book of Christmas-NY-c1963-3 vols-4to-illus (5w5,box)　15.00
--Memorable Life Photographs-NY-(1951)-Muse of Modern Art-
　　　　　　(5p7)　5.00
--Life's Picture Hist of Western Man-NY-1951-306p-illus-4to (5t4)8.00
--Life's Picture Hist of World War II-1950-folio-col plts (5L7)　20.00
--The World's Great Religions-NY-1957-illus-310p　9.50
--The World We Live In-NY-1955-304p　(5x7,5p7,box)　10.00
LIFE FOR A LIFE, A-Lond-1859-Hurst&Blackett-3 vols-8vo-
orig cl-1st ed　　(5xx6,shake)　35.00
LIFE IN AMERICA-NY-1939-(Met Mus of Art)-illus-orig wrps-
230p-Loan Exhibition World's Fair　(5ii3)　10.00
LIFE IN CALIFORNIA-by an Amer-to which is annexed Hist Account
of Origin, Customs & Traditions of Indians of Alta,Calif-NY-
1846-341p-mor-buck-t.g.e.-9 liths-1st ed　(5m3,f)　100.00
LIFE IN SING SING-by Number 1500-1904　(5L7)　3.50
LIFE IN THE WEST-or the Moreton Family-Phila-(1851)-258p-cl
　　　　　(5h2,wn,lacks fly)　5.00
LIFE IN WHITEHALL During the Ship Fever Times-Whitehall-1900-
8vo-cl-illus-76p-plts　　(5t2)　7.50
LIFE OF ABRAHAM LINCOLN-Chapter 1, Early Life-(NY-1860,
Greeley)-32p-self wrps-Tribune Tracts, No.6-(JLScripps)
　　　　　(5m3,wrps sl dmpstn)　52.50
LIFE OF JESUS OF NAZARETH, THE-Lond-n.d.(ca 1910)-4to-
80 col plts-dec cl-g.t.　(5p6,f)　10.00
LIFE ON DESOLATE ISLANDS-by Authr of "Tales of Northern Seas"-
Lond-(c1879)-RTS-12mo-dec red cl-128p-g.t.-plts (5aa2)　4.50

LIGHTFOOT, JOHN-Works of John Lightfoot & Mr of Katherine
Hall in Cambridge-Lond-1658-Crooke-2 vols-4to-calf-
lea labls-rare   (5h0) 600.00
LIGHTHALL, J L-The Great Indian Medicine Man & Dr W O Davis-
Peoria, Ill-1882-167p   (5s7)   7.50
LIGHTHALL, W D-Montreal After 250Yrs-Montr-1897-149p-index-
#8 of ltd, autg ed   (4b9)   10.00
--Outer Consciousness-Montr-1923-priv prntd   (5nn8) 20.00
LIGHTHALL, WM D, ed-Songs of the Great Dominion-Lond-1889-
465p-a.e.g.-1st ed   (5w5)   6.50
LIGHTON, WM BEEBEY-Memoirs of the Life of..written by Himself-
Wells River, VT-1835-White&Clark, prntr-illus-244p-24mo
                                                  (4L9)   12.50
LIGHTON, WM R-Sons of strength-NY-1899-Doubldy&McClure-
1st ed   (5m2)   8.50
LIGHTS OF EDUCATION-or, Mr Hope & His Family-by a Lady-
Balt-1825-frontis-179p-lea bk   (5w7, cov dtchd)   12.50
LIKINS, W M-The Trial of the Serpent-NY-1928-123p-12mo-illus-
scarce -wrps   (5x2) 20. (5jj9)   12.50
LILIENTHAL, OTTO-Birdflight as Basis of Aviation-Lond-1911-
Longm-139p-8 plts-illus   (5p0)   30.00
LILLARD, RICHARD G-Desert Challenge, Interpretation of Nevada-
NY-1942-illus-map-1st ed   (4a5, fox)   6.00
--The Great Forest-NY-1948-Knopf-399p-illus   (5p9)   6.00
LILLIE, ARTHUR-Modern Mystics & Modern Magic-NY-1894-172p-
                                                  (5w0)   8.50
LILLIE, LUCY C-Prudence, a story of aesthetic London-NY-1882-
Harper-illus-1st ed   (5m2)   6.50
LILLIPUT-Lond-1757-(D Garrick)-8vo-disbnd-1st ed (5x3)   95.00
L'ILLUSTRATION-Christmas Nbr, 1931-complete-16 col illus by
Clarence Gagnon   (5w8)   35.00
L'ILLUSTRATION-Paris-July to Dec 1861, July to Dec, 1863,
Jan to Dec 1864-Vols 38, 41, 43, 44-4 vols-illus-lea bkd bds
                     (5r7, Vol 44 ex-librr)   4 vols 75.00
LILLY-NY-1855-Harper-(Mrs S K Bowen)-330p-1st ed (5x4, fray) 12.50
LILLY, MRS CLYDE A-Woman's Club of Ft Worth Cook Book-
FtWorth-1928   (5a8)   6.00
LILLY, ELI-Hist of Little Church on the Circle-Indnpls-1957-
376p-cl   (5h7)   7.50
--Prehistoric Antiquities of Indiana-Indiana Hist Soc-1937-4to-
293p-illus   (5t3) 30. (5hh4, f)   35.00
LILLY, JOHN-Dramatic Works-Lond-1858-2 vols-(Lib of Old Authors)-
lg ppr ed   (5yy6, cov v poor)   15.00
LILLY, L-Hist of the Western States-Bost-1835-WmTicknor-156p-illus
                                      (5F9, rbnd, fox)   30.00
LILLY, LAMBERT-Early Hist of Southern States, Virg, N&S Car,
Ga-Bost-1834-WmTicknor-(cpyright 1833)-12mo-dec cl-
illus   (5c8, stnd)   17.50
--Story of Amer Revolution-Bost-1850-Ticknor, Reed&Fields-
204p-illus   (5mm8, sig loose)   5.00
LILLY, W E-Set my People Free-NY-1932   (5x2)   15.00
LILLY, WM S-On Right & Wrong-1892-3rd ed   (5L7)   6.00
LIMEBEER, ENA-To a Proud Phantom-Richmnd-1923-12mo-bds-
Leonard&Virginia Woolf-Hogarth Pr-1st ed   (5ee9)   7.50
LIMITED ED CLUB-See Author or Title
LIMPUS, LOWELL M-Hist of the NY Fire Dept-NY-1940-EPDutton-
380p-illus-cl   (5r0)   7.50
--Honest Cop, Lewis J Valentine-NY-1939   (5x7)   4.00
LIN, FRANK-What Dreams May Come-Chig-(Belford, Clarke)-
(1888)-12mo(G Atherton's 1st bk)   (5F6, bkplt remvd) 25.00
LIN, TSUIFENG-Cooking wi the Chinese Flavor-NJ-(1956)-
196p   (4g9)   3.50
LINCK, CHAS E-Edgar Rye-Commerce-1872-121p-illus-wrps (4a5) 5.00
LINCKLAEN, JOHN-Travels in Yrs 1791 & 1792 in Penn, NY & Vt-
NY-1897-illus-journals-1st ed-ltd to 500c (5q8) 19.50 (5jj3) 35.00
LINCOLN, ABRAHAM-Collected Works-NewBrunswick-1953 to
1955-9 vols-Bassler   (5j5) 42.50 (5j4, 5xx7)   75.00
--Illustrated Life, Serv, Martyrdom & Funeral of-Phila-1865-
299p-port-illus   (5j6) 6. (5h2)   12.50
--Life of Abraham Lincoln(caption title)-32p-sewed as issued-
(Chig, 1860)-(JohnJScripps)-1st issue of Chig ed(wi adv on
pg 32 in dbl colums)-rare   (4h2) 750.00
--Literary Works of-Menasha-1942-Ltd Ed Club-4to-illus-
ltd to 1500c, nbrd   (5w5, box)   22.50
--A Memorial of-Bost-1865-153p-cl   (5h7)   12.50
--Opinions of Abraham Lincoln upon Slavery & Its Issues-Wash-
1863-16p   (5j6)   17.50
--Political Debates Betwn Lincoln & Douglas-Columbus-1860-1st ed,
1st state-268p   (4j4) 125.00
--same-Columbus-1860-268p-cl-54th state of 3rd ed-preface letter
from Douglas   (5h1)   50.00
--Sketch of Life & Times of-Phila-(1865)-54p-wrps-rare pamphlet
                                          (5h1, sl wn)   60.00

LINCOLN, ABRAHAM (continued)
--Writings-1905-8 vols-plts-ABLapsley, ed-introd by Roosevelt-
Federal ed   (5L7)   50.00
--same-NY-1905, 6-Lapsley, ed-cl-8 vols-National ed (4h2) 20.00
--Writings of-NY-1923-Lapsley, ed-8 vols-8vo-cl-GPPutnam-
Constitutional Ed   (5t2)   25.00
LINCOLN, MRS ALMIRA H-Familiar Lectures on Botany-Hartfrd-
1829-H&FJHuntington-8vo-335p, (1), 4-13 plts-orig calf-
1st ed   (5L1)   55.00
--same-NY-1838-246p, 178p-illus-lea-7th ed, rev & enlrgd
                                          (5t0, sp wn)   7.50
LINCOLN, BENJ-Hints on present state of medical education &
influence of medical schools in New Engl-Burlington(Vt)-1833-
prntd wrps   (5g8, pres)   10.00
LINCOLN CENTENNIAL ASSOC PAPERS-Springfield-1927-112p
                                                  (5ww4)   5.00
LINCOLN, CHAS-A Calendar of John Paul Jones Manuscripts in
Libr of Congress-Wash-1903-316p   (5j4)   10.00
LINCOLN CITY GUIDE-Lincoln-1937-81p plus index-photos-
fldg map-wrps-Amer Guide Series-1st ed   (5L0)   12.50
LINCOLN ILLUS & LINCOLN'S GROWTH-Lincoln-1887-63p-
illus-wrps-1st ed   (5L0)   35.00
LINCOLN, MRS D A-Boston School Kitchen Text Book-Bost-1887-
1st ed-pic bds-237p, (5), 18p   (5ww2) 12.50
LINCOLN, JEANIE GOULD-Her Washington Season-Bost-1884-
1st ed   (5mm2)   7.50
--An Unwilling Maid-Bost-1897-HoughtonMif-263p-illus-1st ed
                                                  (5x4)   7.50
LINCOLN, JENNETTE E C-May Pole Possibilities-Bost-1907-
Amer Gymnasia-12mo-59p-frontis-4 plts   (5p1)   10.00
LINCOLN, JOS C-The Aristocratic Miss Brewster-NY-1927-
Appleton-1st ed   (5m2) 5. (4c6)   4.00
--The Big Mogul-NY-1926-Appleton-1st ed (5m2) 5. (4c6)   4.00
--Blair's attic-NY-1929-Coward, McCann-illus-1st ed
                                 (5m2, dj) 6. (4c6)   5.00
--Blowing Clear-NY-1930-Appleton-1st ed (5m2, dj) 6. (4c6) 4.00
--Cape Cod Ballads & Other Verse-Trenton-1902-12mo-cl-
Edw W Kemble drwngs-Brandt-1st ed of auth's 1st book
                         (5r9f, 5gg6) 15. (5p6) 20. (4c6) 25.00
--same-1924-Appleton Libr of Verse-12th ed   (4c6, dj) 15.00
--Cape Cod Yesterdays-Bost-1935-sm4to-two tone cl-slipcase-
ltd to 1075c, autgs   (5d8, box) 35. (4c6, fly cut, f) 35.00
--same-Bost-1935-286p-illus-1st ed
                (4c6, f, dj) 15. (5h9, f) 8.50 (4c6)   12.00
--Christmas Days-NY-1938-Coward, McCann-illus-pic cl-1st ed
                                 (4c6, autg) 15. (4c6)   10.00
--same-NY-1938-t8vo-orig vari col cl-mor labl-illus by Harold Brett-
ltd to 1000c, autgs   (5p5) 25. (4c6) 35.00
--Extricating Obadiah-NY-1917-Appleton-illus-1st ed
                                     (5m2) 5. (4c6)   4.00
--Mr Pratt-NY-1906-ASBarnes-frontis-1st ed   (4c6)   12.00
--Our Village-1909-green bndg, gilt-t.e.g.-1st ed (4c6, f) 45.00
--same-1909-2nd prntng-green bndg, gilt-t.e.g.   (4c6, f) 35.00
--same-1910-3rd prntng-green bndg, gilt-t.e.g.   (4c6, f) 35.00
--The Peel Trait-NY-1934-Appleton-1st ed
                             (5ee3, dj, autg) 8.50 (4c6) 8.00
--Queer Judson-NY&Lond-1925-DAppleton-1st ed-1st issue
                (5i4, autg, rub) 7.50 (5m2) 5. (4c6)   4.00
--Rhymes of the old Cape-1st ed   (4c6, f, dj) 50.00
--Rugged Water-NY-1924-Appleton-1st ed (5m2) 5. (4c6)   4.00
--Storm Signals-NY-1935-Appleton-1st prntg (5m2) 6.50 (4c6) 8.00
LINCOLN LIBRARY-1961-2 vols   (4e2)   10.00
LINCOLN, MARY J-A Book of Good Luncheons-NY-(1916)-244p-
14 plts-wrps   (5c0, 5g9)   5.00
--Home Science Cook Book-Bost-1904-vii, 281p (5c0, soil cov) 5.00
--The Peerless Cook Book-Bost-(1885, 1901)-(11)p, 140p-wrps-
new & enlrgd   (5c0, wn, tn)   3.50
--Pure Food Cook Book-Chig-1907-79p-frontis-port-wrps (5g9) 3.00
--The School Kitchen Textbook-Bost-1915-xi, 308p-illus
                                          (5c0, librr stmp) 5.00
LINCOLN MEMORIAL, THE-Record of Life, Assassination, &
Obsequies of the Martyred President-NY-1865-1st ed (5yy6) 15.00
LINCOLN, MRS-Boston Cook Book-Bost-1884(c1883)-brown cl &
mrbld bds of 1st ed- xiv, (1), 536p, 4p, (13 blanks)
                    (5c0, hng crack, lt wtrstn few pgs) 150.00
--same-1886-xiv, 536p, (8)   (5c0, shaken, hng broke) 12.50
--same-1890-xiv, (2), 536p, (8 & 12)p   (5c0, crack, chip) 10.00
--same-1909-rev ed-xviii, (1), 578p, (19)p   (5c0)   8.50
LINCOLN, MRS D A-Boston School Kitchen Textbook-Bost-1887-
illus-xxvii, 237p(16)-bds-1st ed   (5c0)   8.50
--Carving & Serving-Bost-1910, 1915-bds-52p, (4) (5c0)   5.00
--Frozen Dainties-Nashua-1902-White Mntn Freezer Co-32p-
wrps-illus   (5g9)   4.50

LINCOLN, MRS D A (continued)
--What to Have for Luncheon-NY-(1904)-244p-port-frontis-
illus-cl   (5g9,rub) 4.50 (5c0) 5. (5g9,f) 6.00
LINCOLN, ROBT W-Lives of the Presidents of the US-Battleboro-
1839-522p-illus-lea-8vo   (5ee3) 7.50
LINCOLN, SOLOMON-Annual Reprt,(1st),of the Bank Commissioners,
Dec,1851-Bost-1851-32p   (5h8,ex-libr) 12.50
LINCOLN, W E-Some Desc of Stephen Lincoln of Wymondham,
Engl-1930-322p   (5mm3) 12.50
LINCOLN, WM-History of Worcester, Mass etc-Worc-1862-illus-
448p   (5ii8) 17.50
LINCOLN, WM S-Alton Trials,of Winthrop S Gilman for Crime of
Riot-NY-1838-158p-frontis-orig cl-1st ed (5m3,rub) 22.50
LINCOLN'S DEVOTIONAL-Great Neck-(1957)-intro by Sandburg-
192p   (5t7,dj) 6.00
LINDBERGH, ANNE MORROW-Dearly Beloved-NY-(1962)-202p
(5t4) 4.00
--Listen, the Wind-NY-1938-1st ed (5ss1) 4. (5ee3,f,dj) 2.50(5yy6)5.00
--North to the Orient-NY-1935-frontis-maps-1st ed
(5ss,dj,vg) 4. (5ee3,f) 2.50
LINDBERGH, C A-Economic Pinch-Phila-(1923)-249p-scarce
(5ss1) 12.50
LINDBERGH, CHAS A-The Spirit of StLouis-NY-1953-562p-cl-
illus   (5t2,dj,f,4m9) 5.00
--We-NY-1927-318p-illus-1st ed (5ii3) 7.50 (5w5,5xx7) 6.00
--same-NY-1927-ltd to 1000c,autg by auth & publ
(5k2,mint) 75. (5p6) 38.00
LINDBERGH, CHAS A-(of Minn), Invisible Govt & Consequences of
It, Speech-Wash-1916-29p-orig wrps (5m2) 6.00
LINDEMANN, HANNES-Alone at Sea-NY-1958 (5c1) 6.50
LINDEN, ANNIE-"Gold" a Dutch Indian Story-NY-1896-258p-cl
(5h1) 8.50
LINDERMAN, FR ANK B-American, life story of a great Indian-NY-
(1930)-JnDay-cl-12mo-illus-313p-1st ed
(5h5, vg,fade dj) 15. (5k4,wn dj) 10. (5zz5,dj) 17.50
--same-NY-(1930)-324p-illus-12mo-cl (5h4) 10. (5i3) 7.50
--same-NY-1931-3rd prntg-illus (5m9) 8.50 (4k4,f,dj) 10.00
--Beyond Law-NY (1933)-254p   (5dd9) 10.00
--Blackfeet Indians-StPaul-Grt Nthn RR-1935-folio-col illus
(4k4,dj,sp jammed) 20. (5zz5,dj,vg) 25.00
--Bunch Grass & Blue Joint-NY-1921-Scribn-frontis-115p-scarce
(5g6) 12.00
--How it Came About Stories-NY-(1921)-234p-col frontis
(5dd4, lacks fly) 7.00
--Indian Old Man Stories-NY-1920-4to-8 col plts by Chas M Russell-
4to-pic cl-1st ed-v scarce
(5m9, lacks fly) 10. (5dd5, lacks fly) 21.50 (5p5,f) 25.00
--Indian Why Stories-NY-1915-illus, CMRussell-1st ed-236p
(5jj3,sig loose) 20. (5zz5) 17.50
--same-NY-1915-Scribner's-1st ed, later issue-cl-16p,236p-
8 illus & cov illus   (5r0) 15.00
--same-Burt Reprint ed-(c1915)-pic cl (5m9,sl wn) 6.50
--Kootenai Why Stories-NY-1926-166p-illus (4b9) 8. (4k4,vg) 12.50
--Old Man Coyote-NY-(1931)-Stoops,illus-254p-1st ed (5t3) 12.50
--same-NY-1932-Stoops,illus-Jr Lit Guild
(5m9,sl wn) 5. (4k4,dj) 6.00
--On a Passing Frontier-NY-1920-214p (5ss1,sl loose) 10.00
--Recoll of Charley Russell-Norman-(1963)-8vo-cl-illus-1st ed
(5F4,f,tn dj) 7.50 (5k4,dj,mint) 10.00
--Red Mother-John Day-(1932)-illus-1st ed (5k4,f) 25. (5zz5,f) 20.00
LINDESTROM, PETER-Geographia Americae, wi account of Delaware
Indians-Phila-1925-illus-t.e.g.-lg fldg map
(5ii8) 45. (5w9,dj,box) 25. (5kk9,mint,box) 23.50
LINDGREN, WALDEMAR-Copper Deposits of Clifton Morenci Dist,
Ariz-Wash-1905-GPO-USGS Prof Paper #43-375p-4to-maps-
illus -wrps   (5h5, lacks bk wrp) 15.00
LINDLAHR VEGETARIAN COOK BOOK & ABC of Natural
Dietetics-Chig-(1922)-Vol 3 of "Natural Therapeutics", 16th ed-
535p   (5c5,lng broke,rn) 3.50
LINDLEY, HARLOW, ed-Capt Cushing in War of 1812-Columbus-
1944-133p-wrps   (5h7) 5. (5jj7,f) 6.00
--Indiana As Seen by Early Travelers-Indnpls-1916-596p-cl(5ff7)12.50
--Indiana Centennial 1916-Indnpls-1919 (4a9) 9.50 (5jj7,f) 12.50
LINDLEY, JOHN-Medical & Oeconomical Botany-Lond-1849-
Bradbury&Evans-8vo-orig cl-1st ed-illus (4i8,vg) 35.00
--Paxton's Flower Garden-Lond-1882 to 1884-plts-3 vols-orig cl-
4to-T Baines, rev   (5z9) 50.00
--Theory of Horticulture-NY-1859-illus-12mo-cl-364p-
2nd Amer ed   (5t0, libr labl) 5.00
LINDLEY, WALTER-Calif of the South-NY-1888-illus-maps-1st ed
(4a5, sp loose) 8.50
LINDNER, JOHN S-Catalogue Succession Sale of Estate of-NOrl-
1848-42p-wrps   (5h1) 7.50

LINDON, MAURICE-Catalogue of Well Known Coll of French
Glass Paperweights-Lond-Feb&July, 1957-8vo-2 parts-
19 plts-wrps-Sotheby-priced (5m6) 15. (5t0) 12.50
LINDQUIST, G E E-The Red Man in the US-NY-(1923)-461p-
photos-maps-1st ed
(5yy7,rbnd) 6. (4k4,crk) 8.50 (4b2,rprd) 9.50 (5t3) 10.00
LINDQUIST, MAUDE L-Early Days & Ways in Old NorWest-(Minn)-
NY-(1937)-295p-col frontis-dec cov (5s4) 5.00
LINDSAY, JUDGE BEN B-The Beast-NY-1910-8vo-cl-frontis-
1st ed   (5p5) 7.50
LINDSAY, D C, ed-Drying & Processing of Materials by Means of
Conditioned Air-Newark-(1929)-Carrier Engr Corp-208p-
bds-illus   (5s8) 10.00
LINDSAY, DAVID MOORE-Camp Fire Reminis-Bost-(1912)-234p-
frontis-plts   (5dd5) 10.50
LINDSAY, F-Cuba & Her People of Today-1911-plts (5L7) 4.50
LINDSAY FAMILY ASSN OF AMER-Annual Reports, 1904 to 1913-
264p-(bnd)   (5mm3) 30.00
LINDSAY, HOWARD-State of the Union-Random Hse-(1946)
(5F1,f,dj) 5.50
LINDSAY, J SEYMOUR-Iron & Brass Implements of Engl & Amer Homes-
Bost-(c 1926)-Medici Soc-4to-211p-illus (5ii2) 12.50
--Iron & Brass Implements of Engl House-Lond1(1927)-11p, 212p-
illus-4to-cl-1st ed   (5t0) 37.50
LINDSAY, J SEYMOUR-also see same title under LINDSAY, SEYMOUR
LINDSAY, MARTIN-Three Tot Through-Lond-1946-262p-plts-maps-
port   (5yy9) 5.00
LINDSAY, NORMAN-Madam Life's Lovers-Lond-n.d.-Fanfrolico Pr-
t8vo-189p   (5x0) 7.50
--Norman Lindsay's Pen Drawings-Sydney, Australia-(1931)-
Kyle Hse,publ-64p plts-stiff pic wrps (5p6, soil) 7.50
LINDSAY, PHILIP-Great Buccaneer-NY-(1951)-305p (5s1,f,dj) 4.00
LINDSAY, SEYMOUR-Iron & Brass Implements of the Engl & Amer
Home-Bost&Lond-n.d.(ca1927)-illus-212p (5w7) 30.00
LINDSAY, THOS M-A History of the Reformation-NY-1910-2 vols
(5x7) 5.00
LINDSAY, VACHEL-Collected Poems of-NY-1923-Macm-bds-
cl bk-1st ed-ltd to 400c,nbrd,autg (5ss9, sl spots) 27.50
--Collected Poems-NY-1925-illus-cl-Spec ed, ltd to 350c, nbrd
(5z7,f) 65.00
--The Congo & Other Poems-NY-1922-12mo-pic cl (5x2) 12.50
--Gen'l Wm Booth Enters into Heaven & Other Poems-NY-1913-
Kennerley-8vo-cl-1st ed (5ee9,pres) 60.00
--Going to the Sun-NY-1923-8vo-101p-illus(5m2) 6.50 (5mm0) 12.50
--Golden Whales of Calif & Other Rhymes in Amer Language-NY-
1920-1st ed   (5r9) 12.50
--A Handy Guide for Beggars-NY-1916-cl-scarce-1st ed
(5j3,bkplt rmvd) 10. (5mm0) 17.50
--The Litany of Wash Street-1929-Macm (5F1,tn dj) 8.00
--Rigamarole, Rigamarole-NY-1929-Random Hse-8vo-wrps-
ltd to 475c   (5b2,f) 7.50
LINDSEY, JUDGE BEN B-Companioniate Marriage-NY-1927 (5x7) 4.00
--The Dangerous Life-NY-c1931-450p (5w4) 5.00
--The Revolt of Modern Youth-NY-1925-(8th prntng, Oct, 1926)-
364p-Boni&Liveright (5p1,fade) 5.00
LINDSEY, BESSIE M-Lore of our Land pictured in Glass-Forsyth-
1950-Vol 2-280p-illus (5xx7) 10.00
LINDSEY, C-An Investigation of Unsettled Boundaries of Ontario-
Tor-1873-250p   (4e6, lacks 3 maps) 15.00
LINDSEY, C-Life & Times of Wm Lyon Mackenzie etc-Tor-1862-
2 vols-illus-buck (4b9,fox,plt tn,rbnd) 20.00
--same-Tor-1862-cl-2 vols in 1-illus (5r6) 16.00
LINDSEY, G B-Story of 4th Canadian Div 1916 to 19-Aldershot-
n.d.-51p-dec wrps (5a1,sl wn) 6.50
LINDSEY, JACK-Byzantium into Europe-Lond-(1932)-illus-1st ed
(5yy6) 10.00
LINDSEY, T J-Ohio at Shiloh-Report of Comm-(Cinn-1903)-photos-
fldg pkt maps-226p (5zz5) 7.50
LINDSEY, D P-The Manual of Takigrafy-NY, Chig & Bost-1878-
12mo-121p,(7)p-grn cl-2nd ed (5p1,wn) 7.50
LINDSLEY, PHILIP-Address deliv in Nashville Jan 12,1825-Nashville-
1825-48p-disbnd-1st ed-v scarce (5h6) 50.00
LINDSTROM, CLAES-Sofartens Historia-Stockholm-1951-illus
(5c1) 27.50
LINDSTROM, RALPH G-Lincoln & Prevention of War-Harrogate, Tenn-
1953-25p   (5t7,dj) 3.00
LINEHAN, JOHN C-The Irish Scots & the "Scotch Irish"-Concord-
1902-8vo-1st ed (5ss5,f,pres) 10.00
LINES ON LEAVING THE BEDFORD ST SCHOOLHOUSE-
(Bost,1880)-4p leaflet-1st ed of Geo Santayana's 1st publ-
v rare   (5gg6) 600.00
LING, LOUIS-A Century of Service-n.p.-1922-77p-wrps
(5h7, sl soil) 5.00

LING, MEI MEI-Chop Suey-Honolulu-(1953)-recipes-34p-
   wrps   (5g9)   3.00
LINGARD, JOHN-History & Antiquities of the Anglo Saxon Church-
   Lond-1845-2 vols   (5j2, libr stmp)   15.00
LINGARD, WM H-On the Beach at Long Branch Song Book-NY-
   (c1868)-col pic wrps   (5g8)   15.00
LINK, ARTHUR S-American Epoch-NY-1955-724p plus index-
   illus   (5r7)   7.50
--same-NY-1958-rprnt   (5q8)   7.50
LINK BELT ENGR CO-Modern Methods-Phila-1902-319p-illus
                                                 (5b8)   9.50
LINK, HENRY-Travels in Portugal & thru France & Spain-Lond-
   1801-hf calf-8vo-504p-scarce   (4e1)   45.00
LINK, JOHN THOS-The Toponymy of Nebraska, a Thesis-Lincoln-
   May 1932-186p-wrps   (5r0, pres) 10.00
LINK, MARGARET SCHEVILL, ed-The Pollen Path-Stanford-1956
                                                 (5t1)   20.00
LINK, WM F-The Hudson by Daylight-NY-(1878)-1st ed-32p-
   illus-col 9 ft fldg map-scarce   (5L3)   28.50
LINKLATER, ERIC-The Campaign in Italy-Lond-1951-maps-illus
                                                 (4a1)   8.50
--The Crusader's Key-NY-1933-Knopf-42p   (5m2, 5p0)   5.00
LINN CO, IOWA-Biographical Record of-Chig-1901-illus-993p-
   th4to-mor   (4kk4, rprd) 45.00
LINN, JOHN BLAIR-The Powers of Genius, a Poem in 3 parts-Phila-
   1802-191p-illus-calf-2nd ed, enlrgd (5i0) 40. (5ee3, fox) 17.50
--Valerian-Phila-1805-port-orig bds-1st ed (5tt6, f, hng weak) 75.00
LINN, JOHN J-Remin of 50 Yrs in Texas-NY-1883-cl-369p-1st ed
   (4c7, sl loose, mottled) 55. (4a5, vg)   100.00
LINN, W ARMIN-False Prophets of Peace-Harrisbrg-c1939 (5w0) 6.50
LINN, WM-The Character of Simon the Sorcerer, A Sermon-NY-
   1793-TGreenleaf-30p-8vo-cl   (5L1)   10.00
LINN, WM-Life of Thos Jefferson-Ithaca-1834-Mack&Andrus-267p-
   calf-1st ed   (5qq8) 7.50 (5ee3) 12.50
LINNEAN SOC OF LONDON-Catalogue of Printed Books &
   Pamphlets in Library of-Lond-1925-860p-new ed
                                       (5w3, hng crack) 17.50
LINNAEUS, CARL-Families of Plants with their Natural
   Characters-Lichfield-1787-2 vols-8vo-calf-lea labl-errata
                                            (5z9, vf)   100.00
LINNAEUS, CARLOUS-Genera Plantarum-Stockholm-1754-mor back-
   5th ed-v scarce   (5m2) 125.00
LINSLEY, R K-Connecticut Linsleys, The Six Johns-(1948)-144p-
   mimeo   (5t9) 12.50
LINTON, RALPH-Arts of the South Seas-NY-(1946)-col illus-
   Mus of Modern Art   (5m5) 24. (5x5)   12.50
LINTON, W J-The Masters of Wood Engraving-NewHav/Lond-
   1899-229p-lg folio-ltd to 600c, autg (5m5, ex-libr, crack) 45.00
LINTON, WM-Ancient & Modern Colours-Lond-1852-80p
                                         (5w3, fade)   7.50
LINWOOD, MARY-Miss Linwood's gallery of pictures, in worsted,
   Leicester Sq-n.p.-(Lond)-1815-12mo-orig wrps (5i8) 10.00
LINWOODS, THE-NY-1835-Harper&Bro-2 vols-cl-(CMSedgwick)-
   1st ed   (5ss3, def sp stnd) 20. (5x1, sp tn) 45.00
LINZ, MIKE-The Lobster's Kettle of Fish-NY-(1958)-338p-
   1st ed-hardbound   (5c9) 4. (5c0)   4.50
LION'S MASQUERADE, THE-a sequel to Peacock at Home-
   Lond-1808-Harris&Tabart-6 handcol plts-front wrp preserved
                             (5c8, recased, cor def)   35.00
--same-Lond-1888-Griffith&Farran-sq4to-orig wrps-facs of 1807 ed-
                                                 (5c8)   5.00
LIONEL LINCOLN-or The Leaguer of Boston-NY-1825 (1824)-
   Wiley-half calf-2 vols-12mo-1st ed-(Cooper, J F) (4h0, fox) 40.00
--same-Phila-1828-lea&bds-2 vols-3rd ed   (5t2)   10.00
LIONBERGER, DAVIS J-Slow Boat, Reflections from the Sea-Bost-
   1937-8vo-orig wrps-1st ed-Merrymount Pr (5p5, pres) 10.00
LIPKE, ALICE C-Under the Aurora-LosAng-(1938)-286p-photos
                                                 (5ss1)   7.50
LIPMAN, JEAN-Amer Primitive Painting-NY-1942-158p-102 plts-
   4to   (5x0) 15. (5ww3) 35. (5m5, sl shake)   25.00
LIPOVETZKY, P-Jos Trumpeldor life & works-Jerusalem-1953-
   12mo-103p-pict bds-2 plts   (5p1)   7.50
LIPPARD, GEO-'Bel of Prairie Eden-Bost-1848-Hotchkiss&Co-
   1st ed-88p-wrps   (4b1, sp chip) 75.00
--Herbert Tracy, or Legend of the Black Rangers-Phila-1844-
   1st ed   (5m4, lacks bk wrps) 40.00
--Legends of the Amer Revolution-Phila-(1876)-527p-port
                               (5m6, bkstrp tn) 10. (5ee3, f) 12.50
--The Mysteries of Florence-Phila-(1864)-Peterson-258p
                               (5x4, lacks wrp cov)   12.50
--Paul Ardenheim-Phila-TBPeterson-1876-536p   (5i1)   6.00
--same-Phila-n.d.(1848)-Peterson-cl-1st ed(wi correct Peterson
   St ads)-pic t.p.   (5x1, rbnd) 60.00

LIPPARD, GEO (continued)
--Washington & His Generals-Phila-(1847)-Peterson-2 vols-
   wrps   (5x4, bk wrp tn)   20.00
--same-Phila-1847-half mor-raised bands-illus-1st ed (5m2) 15.00
LIPPERT, JULIUS-Evolution of Culture-NY-1931   (4a1)   10.00
LIPPINCOTT, HORACE MATHER-Early Philadelphia-Phila-1917-
   8vo-illus-1st ed   (5m6)   15.00
--same-Phila-1917-facs of "List of Errata" typed & autg laid in-
   340p-illus   (5h9)   20.00
--Narr of Chestnut Hill-Phila-1948   (5L7)   6.00
--A Portraiture of the People called Quakers-Phila-1915-116p-
   bds-illus   (5w4, sl wn)   8.50
LIPPINCOTT, MARY S-Life & Letters of-Phila-1893-284p (5w4) 5.00
LIPPINCOTT, R B-Short Hist of Lloyd & Catherine Canby Balderston
   of Colora, Md-1959-260p   (5mm3)   8.50
LIPPINCOTT, SARA J-Merrie England-Bost-1855-Ticknor&Fields-
   illus-1st ed   (5m2, sl shake)   4.00
--Stories & Sketches-NY-(1892)-Tait, Sons-imprnt on spine Amer
   Publ Corp-1st ed   (5m2)   10.00
LIPPMAN, WALTER-Amer Inquisitors-NY-1928-Macm-120p (5p7) 3.75
--The Method of Freedom-NY-1934-117p-1st ed   (5w4)   7.50
--A Preface to Morals-NY-1929-348p-1st ed   (5d3, 5w5)   5.00
--A Preface to Politics-NY-1913-12mo-cl-1st ed of auth's 1st bk
                                                (5gg6)   10.00
--The US in World Affairs-NY-1932   (5q8) 6. (5x7) 5.00
LIPPS, OSCAR H-The Navajos-CedarRapids-1909-col frontis-
   photo-map-1st ed-Little Hist of NA Indians   (5yy7) 20.00
LIPS, EVA-Savage Symphony-NY-c1938   (5x7)   5.00
LIPS, JULIUS E-The Savage Hits Back-NewHav-1937-sm4to-254p-
   photos   (4a6, dj)   17.50
--NY-1966-illus   (5x2, mint, dj)   9.50
LIPS, MICHAEL A-Statistik von Amerika-Frankfurt-1828-Wilmans-
   8vo-hf calf-handcol fldg map-1st ed   (4h0, f)   60.00
LIPSCOMB, J F-We Built a Country-Lond-1956   (5x2, dj)   3.75
LIPSEY, JOHN J-Alias Diamond Jack-ColoSprngs-1956-19p-
   wrps-port-ltd to 200c, autg   (5g0, f)   7.50
LIPTON, LAWRENCE-Holy Barbarians-1959   (5L7)   6.50
LISIANSKY, UREY-A Voyage Round the World-Lond-1814-port-
   8 col maps(3 fldg)-5 plts-R8vo
                    (5dd4, rbnd, 4 plts & prelim lvs in facs) 285.00
LISSONE, SEBASTIANO-La Fabricazione e Conservazione Del Vino-
   Rome-1891-Torino-wrps-6th ed-100p, (1)   (5w1)   9.50
LISTER, RAYMOND-The British Miniature-Lond-1951-114p-4to-
   69 plts   (5ww3)   12.50
--Decorative Wrought Ironwork in Gr Britain-Bost-1957-265p-
   28 plts   (5n7)   6.50
LISTON-GRISWOLL, comp-Tracy Genealogy Family of Thos Tracy
   of Lenox, Mass-Malamazoo-1900-230p (5mm3) 7.50 (5a9) 12.50
LITCH, SAM'L-A concise treatise of rhetoric, extracted from
   writings of Dr Blair, Usher, etc-Jaffrey(NH)-1813-Salmon
   Wilder-16mo-orig qtr calf & bds-1st ed-v scarce (5i0, box) 75.00
LITCHFIELD COOKERY-Torrngtn-1897-Ladies of Methodist
   Episcopal Church-89p plus ads-wrps   (5c4, wrps soil) 6.50
LITCHFIELD CO-Biographical Review, Leading Citizens of-Bost-
   1896-671p-photos-Conn   (5c8) 22.75 (5mm3)   17.50
LITCHFIELD CO (CONN) ATLAS-1874-FWBeers&Co-69p-
   lg atlas folio   (5mm3, edge wn)   40.00
LITCHFIELD, GRACE DENIO-In the Crucible-NY-1897-Putnam-
   1st ed   (5m2, rbnd)   10.00
--The moving finger writes-NY-1900-Putnam-1st ed (5m2, weak) 5.00
LITCHFIELD H W-Ancient Landmarks of Pembroke-1910-illus-
   188p   (5mm3)   10.00
LITCHFIELD, SAM-Marks & Monograms on Old China, The Dresden
   Gallary-Lond-(c1884)-obl 12mo-tripl fld tabl-56p-priced cat
                                                 (5w7)   9.50
LITCHFIELD, W J-Litchfield Family in Amer-Parts 1 thru 5-
   (Oct 1901 to Nov 1906)-384p   (5mm3)   22.50
LITERARY & HISTORICAL SOC OF QUEBEC-Catalogue of Books
   in Library of-Que-1864-GTCary-114p, 22p
                              (5aa1, Henry Morgan's copy) 75.00
--Catalogue of Library of-Que-1845-Augustin Cote-44p (5aa1) 85.00
LITERARY ANNUAL, THE-NY-1848-(1), 378p-9 col lithos of
   flowers-unbnd   (5w7, fox)   5.00
LITERARY TREASURES OF 1927-Chig-1927-Cuneo Pr-ltd ed,
   many autgs   (4b4)   45.00
LITTEL, JR, SQUIRE-A Manual of Diseases of the Eye-Phila-1837-
   255p-papr over bds-embossed cl sp-orig papr labl (5s2, f) 125.00
LITTELL, C G-The Distinguished Collection of Americana formed
   by-Chig, NY-1945-Parke Bernet-276p-wrps
                      (5g4, unpriced) 7.50 (5j4, priced) 12.50
LITTELL, WM-Digest of Statute Laws of Kentucky-Vol 1(of 2)-
   Frankfrt-1822   (5h6, sl wtrstnd) 27.50

LITTLE, A W-From Harlem to the Rhine-NY-1936-R8vo-illus (5x2,dj) 12.50

LITTLE ADDISON-Phila-1825-ASSU-pict wrps-16mo-32p-frontis- by a Clergyman-No 139,Ser V (5rr2,fox) 10.00

LITTLE ANNIE'S ABC-Phila-1851-12mo-32lvs-1st ed (5v2) 12.50

LITTLE,ARCHIBALD-The Far East-Oxford-1905-334p (5p0) 7.50

LITTLE BLUE BAG-or a Visit to the Bazaar-Lond-1825-HHolloway- 12mo-60p-2 plts-grey bds-1st ed (5c8) 27.50

LITTLE BO PEEP & other Mother Goose Rhymes-Racine-1934- Whitman-39p-pic wrps-48mo (5p1) 5.00

LITTLE,C M-Hist of the Clan Macfarlane,Macfarlan,Macfarland, Manfarlin-Charleston-1968-252p-illus-reprnt-ltd to 500c (5mm3) 10. (5mm3) 15.00

LITTLE CODFISH CABOT AT HARVARD-Cambr,Bost-(c1924)- 12mo-(60)p-JnWLuce-pic bds (5p1,dj) 6.50

LITTLE DR COMFORT-c1870-McLoughlin Bros-sewn-col illus (5v0,lacks bk wrp) 6.50

LITTLE,ELBERT L-Check List of Native & Naturalized Trees of US (incl Alaska)-Wash-1953-Agric Handbk #41-472p (5s7) 5.00

--Southwestern Trees,Guide to Native Species of New Mex & Ariz-Wash-1950-109p-wrps (5n4) 3.50

LITTLE FOLKS ABC,THE-McLoughlin-c1905-Wrps-folio-10p- col illus-glazed wrps (5v2) 6.50

LITTLE FOLK'S TRIP ABROAD-Bost-n.d.-(after 1883)-4to- col liths-8 panels accordion-DeWolfe Fiske(5p1,edge wn) 15.00

--same-Bost-c1895-lg Panorama-4to-col plts-6 panels-heavy bds- opens to 6' (5v2,vf) 20.00

LITTLE FORGET ME NOT-a Token of Love-NewHav-(ca1845)- SBabcock-wdcuts-12mo-24p-pic wrps (5c8,wn,fox) 6.00

LITTLE FROG & PRETTY MOUSE-McLoughlin Bros-sq16mo-8p- 4 col plts-Little Pleasewell Ser (5v0,f) 6.50

LITTLE,G-The Angler's Complete Guide etc-Lond-(ca1880)- 200p plus ads-illus-a.e.g. (5a9,f) 9.50

LITTLE,G T-Desc of Geo Little of Newbury,Mass-1882-620p- 2nd ed (5mm3) 40.00

--same-1877-82p (5mm3) 17.50

LITTLE GARDEN SERIES-Bost-1922 to 1928-8 vols-illus (5q0) 15.00

LITTLE GLEANER,THE-Lond-Jan 1885 to Dec 1886-Houlston&Sons- 24 issues bnd in 1 (5rr2) 12.50

LITTLE,GEO-The Amer Cruiser,a tale of the last war-Bost-1847- WmJReynolds-12p illus-12mo-orig cl-2nd ed (5x1) 20.00

--Life on the Ocean or 20 Yrs at Sea-Bost-1845-295p-cl- Waite,Peirce & Co-3rd ed (5d6,wn) 12.50

LITTLE,GEO-History of Lumsden's Brigade-Tuskaloosa-(1905)- wrps-70p (4h1) 20.00

LITTLE HARRY'S PRIMER-NY-(c1850)-Leavitt&Co-12mo-wrps- 12p wi 5p illus ABC's-45 wdcuts-sewn (5v2,f) 20.00

LITTLE HELPERS-Bost-1833 thru 1887-Woman's Baptist Foreign Mission Soc-Vol 1 thru 5-illus-part calf (5rr2) 17.50

LITTLE HELPS FOR HOME MAKERS-Bost-(1909)-(4),341p,10p (5w7) 6.50

LITTLE HISTORY OF THE US-NY-(c184?)- 191p-wdcuts- cl-"Tom Thumb Ser"-2-1/2" x 3-1/8" (5c8) 15.00

LITTLE,JAS A-What I Saw on the Old Santa Fe Trail-Plainfield,Ind- (1904)-ports-127p-cl case-lea labl-wrps (4b6,box) 100.00

LITTLE,JOE K-The Tinsmith's Pattern Manual-Chig-1901-Amer Artisan Pr-248p-illus (5hh7) 5.50

LITTLE,KATHARINE DAY-Francois de Fenelon-NY-(1951)-Harper- 8vo-273p-frontis-1st ed (5p1,dj) 6.50

LITTLE LAME PRICE,THE-& his Travelling Cloak-Chig,NY & Lond- (c1909)-HDunlap,illus-121p-8vo-pic labl (5p1) 7.50

LITTLE LEARNER'S ABC-McLoughlin Bros-(1899)-color (5v0,f) 7.50

LITTLE LIBRARY,THE-Lond-1850-Religious Tract Soc-32 miniature chapbooks-ea 8p wi woodcut on 1st pg-wrps-scarce set (5rr2,f) 90.00

LITTLE,LUCIUS P-Ben Hardin-Louisville-1887-1st ed-illus-640p (5i3) 25.00

LITTLE LUCY-or,the Birthday Presents-Lond-1819-JHarris-16mo- 72p-6 illus-wrps (5v0,rbnd,f) 30.00

LITTLE MISS GIANT-(c1870)-McLoughlin Bros-12mo-8p-4 plts- v scarce (5v0,sl stn) 15.00

LITTLE MATCH GIRL,THE-a poem by a lady of Charleston,SC- Charleston-n.d.-(c1870)-Fogartie's Book Depos-prntd in Phila- 12mo-orig glazd prntd wrps-1st ed (5i9) 25.00

LITTLE MOTHER GOOSE-NY-1918-col illus-176p-obl cl (5c8,lacks e.p.,sl stn) 15.00

LITTLE NATURE LIBRARY-NY-1922,1934-col illus-8vo-Vol 1 thru 5- (5qq7,vg) 15.00

LITTLE,NINA F-Abby Aldrich Rockefeller Folk Art Collection- Bost-(1957)-4to-col plts-1st ed (5yy6) 17.50

LITTLE OBJECT FINDERS ABC-NY-c1875-8vo-10p-col illus- McLoughlin,publ-4 games illus on bk wrp (5v2,vg) 27.50

LITTLE OLD WOMAN,THE-Susie Sunshine Ser-c1870-illus- 12mo-ip-McLoughlin Bros-scarce (5v0,f) 20.00

LITTLE PET'S PICTURE ALPHABET-c1875-12mo-14 lvs-col illus- sewn-McLoughlin Bros-scarce (5v0,wrps wn) 7.50

LITTLE PILGRIM,THE-Phila-Jan 1860 to Dec 1861-Vol 7,#1 to Vol 8,#12-bnd in 1 vol (5rr2) 7.50

LITTLE PILGRIM, THE-Phila-1865-Jan to Dec Vol 12,#1 thru #12- 12 issues (5p1,crude bnd) 20.00

LITTLE POEMS FOR LITTLE FOLKS-Phila-(c1845)-Peck&Bliss-192p- wdcut-dec cl-3" x 2-3/8" (5c8,lt soil,fade) 7.50

LITTLE PRIMER, THE-or First Lessons for Children-Newark-1844- BOlds-24p-wdcuts-sewn (5v0) 20.00

LITTLE RED RIDING HOOD-(Phila)-1834-WmW Weeks-16mo-8p- crude Amer chapbk-wdcuts (5c8,rbnd) 15.00

LITTLE RED RIDING HOOD-Lond-c1880-Tuck-sq12mo- 6 col embossed plts-plts perfect-moveable plt bk (5v2,vg,pencil) 35.00

LITTLE RED RIDING HOOD-NY-1890-Nelson-illus-pict glazed bds- a.e.g.-8 col plts (5v0,f) 4.50

LITTLE RED RIDING HOOD-NY-1933-HaroldLenz-lg,th8vo- 1 pop illus (5v2,vg) 7.50

LITTLE REVIEW, THE-Paris-Juan Gris Number,Autumn Winter, 1924,1925-sm4to-imprntd wrps-(Hemingway) (5ss7,vf) 45.00

LITTLE ROBINSON CRUSOE,THE-Bost-1856-JBuffum-32mo- 97p-frontis-g.t.-45 plts-dec brown cl (5aa2) 15.00

LITTLE ROCK-Selected Views of-Little Rock-c1945-24p-wrps (5j6) 6.00

LITTLE ROCK & FORT SMITH RWY-Homes in Arkansas for sale- StL-(1881)-folder wi info of RR,weather at LittlRock,distances, misc info on Ark,9 panels in German-lg map of RR & its lands in Ark on reverse-scarce (5t3) 15.00

LITTLE,SHELBY-Geo Washington-NY-1929-481p (5h9) 6.50

LITTLE SKETCHBOOK,THE-NY-n.d.(1835)-Kiggins&Kellogg-8p- prnt wrps-illus-toy book-Rosenbach 807 (5rr2,fox) 10.00

LITTLE STORIES FOR LITTLE CHILDREN-NY-(ca1825 to 1830)- Mahlon Day-16p-prnt wrps-3 & nine sixteenths by 2-1/4 (5rr2,f) 20.00

LITTLE TALES FOR LITTLE HEADS & LITTLE HEARTS-Lond-(ca1835)- Effingham Wilson-sq12mo-163p-g.pict cl-8 plts-2nd ed (5c8,marg dmpstn) 10.00

LITTLE TOM & JERRY WITH THEIR FRIEND LOGIC-or Juvenile Life in London-Lond-(ca1822)-Hodson & Co-12mo-orig wrps- 14p handcol-prntd on single lfs-scarce (5c8,lt soil,wrps sl wn) 65.00

LITTLE TRUTHS FOR INSTRUCTION OF CHILDREN-Vol 2-Phila- 1812-prntd bds-12mo-12 illus-Rosenback 456 (5rr2,f) 40.00

LITTLE VERSES FOR LITTLE GIRLS-Charlestwn-n.d.-chapbook- col wdcuts-ornamental borders-12p-orig pict yellow wrps (5c8,sl stns) 8.50

LITTLE,W-Hist of Warren,N Hamp,incl sketch of the Pemigewasset Indians-1854-170p-250c prntd (5t9) 15.00

LITTLE,WALTER-The First Nantucket Tea Party-NY-(1907)-4to- pic cl-illus,illuminated (5p6) 7.00

LITTLE,WM S-Descriptive Cat of Fruit Trees,etc-Rochester NY- 1882 (5w1) 6.50

LITTLE WILLY-A Story for Little Children-Northampton-n.d.- ETurner-16mo-16p-plts-wrps (5v0,f) 10.00

LITTLE'S-Encyclopedia of Classified Dates-1899 (4e2) 25.00

LITTLEHALES,EDW B-Journal Written by...of Explor Tour....From Navy Hall, Niagara to Detroit Feb & Mar, 1783 by Simcoe- Toronto-1889-wrps-23p (5dd7,f) 40.00

LITTLEHALES, G W-Development of Great Circle Sailing-Wash- 1899-US Hyrdr pub #90-63p-illus-maps-lea bkstrp (5s1,wn) 5.00

LITTLER,MRS PRINCE-For the Actors' Orphanage,Our Favorite Dish-Lond-1952-282p (5g9) 7.50

LITTLETON, H A-Digest of Fire Ins Decisions in Courts of Great Brit & No Amer-Dubuque,Iowa-1862-calf- 1st ed (5ss5,rub) 15.00

LITTLETON, MARTIN W-My Partner in Law-NY-1957-256p (5y2) 4.50

LITTLEWOOD, LETTY,ed-The Bower Book of Simple Poems for Boys & Girls-Lond&NY-n.d.-(pref 1922)-267p-8vo-frontis- 9 col plts-pic cl (5p1) 6.50

LITTLEWOOD, S R-Elizabeth Inchbald & Her Circle-Lond-1921- 136p-ports (5a1) 4.50

LITZ, FRANCIS A-Father Tabb,a Study of his Life & Works-Balt- 1923-JohnsHopkins Pr-12mo-cl-frontis-303p-1st ed (5j5) 20.00

LIU, C C-Amphibians of West China-Chig-1950-Fieldiana,Zool Mem V 2-400p-frontis-10 plts (8 col)-wrps-4to (4p6) 12.60

LIVE & LET LIVE-or, domestic service illus-NY-1837-Harper- 12mo-orig cl-(CMSedgwick) (5x1,sp fade) 30.00

LIVE BOYS-or Charley & Nasho in Texas-Bost-1879-12mo-cl- 1st ed of auth's 1st book (5gg6) 50.00

LIVE BOYS IN THE BLACK HILLS-Bost-(1880)-illus-12mo-cl (4c1) 25.00

LIVE STOCK LAWS OF ARIZONA-Phoenix-issued Sept 1,1901 by Live Stock Sanitary Board-36p-wrps (5t1) 85.00

LIVELY, W IRVEN-Camp & Trail - n.p.-n.d.-70p-cl (5ii9)   5.00
--The Mystic Mountains-Phoenix-1955-8vo-prnt wrps-1st ed (5g6) 5.00
LIVEMORE (MAINE) NOTES-Hist, Descriptive & Personal-1874-
    169p   (5t9)   10.00
LIVERMORE, A A-War wi Mexico Reviewed-Bost-1850-310p-
    1st ed   (5h1, cov wn) 12.50   (4a5)   17.50
--same-Bost-1850-Amer Peace Soc-12mo-cl-7th thousand
                                  (4a3, fray)   25.00
LIVERMORE, MARY A-My Story of the War-Hartf-1888-illus-
    3/4 mor-g.-g.t.   (5r7, f bndg)   15.00
--same-Hartf-1889-700p-plts (5mm8) 6. (5t0,crack) 4. (5ww4) 10.00
--same-Hartf-1890-illus   (5tt5)   6.50
--same-Hartf-1892-th8vo-cl-illus-700p   (5t2)   5.00
--The Story of my Life-Hartf-1897-120 illus-ports (5x5)   15.00
--same-Hartf-1898-730p-illus   (5w4)   12.50
--same-Hartf-1899-th8vo-illus   (5x2)   22.50
LIVERMORE, S T-Hist of Block Island from its Discov-1877-orig ed-
    371p   (5mm3)   17.50
--Block Island - a Map & Guide; a History(abridged)-Hartf-
    1882-map-plts-12mo-orig wrps-125p (5m6)   10.00
--Hist of Block Island 1514 to 1876-1877-371p,(15)p-reprntd 1961
                                  (5mm3)   6.00
LIVERMORE, S T-Condensed Hist of Cooperstown, NY-1862-276p-
    unbnd   (5mm3)   7.50
LIVERMORE, SAM'L Treatise on Law Relative to Principals, Agents,
    Factors, Auctioneers & Brokers-Bost-1811-8vo-orig bds-
    1st ed   (5ss5, ex-libr, rbkd)   25.00
LIVERMORE, SOLOMON KIDDER-On the practice of music-
    Amherst, NH-1809-wrps   (5g4, stnd, fox)   10.00
LIVERMORE, THOS L-Days & Events 1860 to 1866-Bost-1920-
    HoughtonMiff-485p-illus-t.e.g.-cl bk bds (5mm8)   12.50
--History of the 18th New Hamp Volunteers 1864,5-Bost-1904-
    illus   (5F0, dj)   5.00
--Numbers & losses in the Civil War 1861 to 65-Bost-1900-
    lf of errata laid in   (5g4)   10.00
LIVES AND SPEECHES-of Abraham Lincoln & Hannibal Hamlin-
    Columbus-1860-406p-port   (5t7)   7.50
LIVES OF DISTINGUISHED SHOEMAKERS-Portl-1849-sm8vo-
    340p-1st ed   (5v0, f)   10.00
LIVEZEY, HERMAN-Sleet-Camden, NJ-1927-1st ed (5m2)   5.00
LIVEZEY, WM E-Mahan on Sea Power-Norman-U Okla Pr-1947-
    334p-illus-1st ed   (5s1, dj)   5.00
LIVINGSTON CO, ILLINOIS-History of-Chig-1878-4to-part calf-
    896p-map-illus-ports   (5jj7, f)   55.00
LIVINGSTON, EDW-Introductory Reprt of Code of Prison Discipline,
    State of Louisiana-Phila-1827-78p-unbnd (5m2)   10.00
LIVINGSTON, GORDON-Livingston's Guide Book to St John, N B
    for 1870-StJohn-1870-fldg maps-16mo-prntd wrps-
    (2)p,138p,ii,(4) plus unnbrd lf of advs (5a3)   100.00
LIVINGSTON, JOHN-Livingston's Law Register for 1852-NY-
    1852-Office of US Law Magazine-8vo-cl-port-291p,56p(5j5) 35.00
LIVINGSTON, PETER-Poems & Songs-Dundee-1866-140p-10th ed
                                  (5a1)   15.00
LIVINGSTON, ROBT R-Essay on Sheep-NY-1810-Collins & Perkins-
    12mo-orig bds-fldg frontis-1 plt-164p-2nd ed, enlrgd (5j5) 45.00
--same-Trenton-1810-12mo-hf lea   (5m2, scuff)   25.00
--same-Concord, NH-1813-143p   (5t4) 20. (5s2, f)   17.50
LIVINGSTON, SAML-Remin of Plymouth, Luzerne Co, Pa-(NY)-
    (1915)-illus-94p   (5kk8)   10.00
LIVINGSTON, WM-Laws of NY, from 11th Nov 1752 to 22nd May,
    1762-NY-Weyman-2nd Vol-folio-calf-errata lf & 3 pg list
    of subscribers   (5r7, v dmpstnd)   50.00
LIVINGSTON, WM FARRAND-Israel Putnam-NY-1901-8vo-cl-
    419p-illus-Amer Men of Energy Ser (5t2, libr labl)   3.50
LIVINGSTONE, ALEX, ed-Complete Story SanFran's Terrible
    Calamity of Earthquake & Fire-n.p.-n.d.-272p-photos
                                  (5s4, cov sl stn)   6.50
LIVINGSTONE, BELLE-Belle out of Order-NY-1959-Holt-341p-
    illus   (5p0)   4.50
LIVINGSTONE, DAVID-Missionary Travels & Researches in SoAfrica-
    NY-1858-port-maps-illus   (5j2)   15.00
--Narr of Dr Livingston's Discoveries in Central Africa from 1849
    to 1856-Lond-1857-pref Jan 1857-(name misspelled thruout)-
    fldg wdct map-v rare-reprnted from "British Banner" newspaper
                                  (5gg6)   75.00
--Narr of Exped to the Zambesi & its Tributaries, etc-NY-1860-
    22p,638p-illus-map   (5t4)   10.00
--same-NY-1866-illus-r8vo   (5ii8) 15. (5x2)   20.00
--Travels & Researches in SoAfrica-Phila-n.d. (ca1860)-lg12mo-
    440p-illus-cl   (4a6, bkstrp dtched, wn)   7.50
LIVINGSTONE, R W-Defence of Classical Education-Lond-1916
                                  (4a1)   8.00

LIVIUS, TITUS-History of Rome-Phila-1836-GBarker, transl-
    2 vols-lea & bds-frontis-illus   (5kk9)   26.50
L'IVRESSE-Bibliotheque des Curiosities-Paris-1868-12mo-168p-
    prntd wrps   (5w6, sp split)   5.00
LIZARS, K M-Humours of 37-Tor-1897-map-369p (4e6, ex-libr)   12.00
LLOYD, A P-Family of Aaron & Sarah Bradley of Guilford, Conn-
    1879-46p   (5mm3)   12.50
LLOYD, B E-Lights & Shades in San Francisco-SanFran-1876-
    Bancroft-523p-illus-cl (5tt0,fade,4n1,rbnd) 20. (5F5,rub,soil) 35.00
LLOYD, E R-Rouse, Clasping Hands wi Generations Past-1932-
    228p   (5mm3)   7.50
LLOYD, EVERETT-Law West of the Pecos-SanAntonio-1936-
    124p-photos-3rd ed   (5s4, autg, sl warp)   5.00
--same-SanAntonio-(1936)-photos-88p-7th prntg (5yy7)   3.00
LLOYD, F C-The Art & Technique of Wine-Lond-(1936)-253p (5w1) 12.50
LLOYD, F E J-2 Years in Region of Icebergs & What I Saw There-
    Lond-n.d.-(ca 1890's)   (4e6)   25.00
LLOYD FAMILY-Papers of...of Manor of Queens Village, Lloyd's
    Neck, L I, NY-NY-1927-2 vols-th8vo-NYHist Soc (5r7)   30.00
LLOYD, FRANCES-Guayule-Wash-1911-213p-46 plts-May, 1942
    by Lippincott, Phila-4to-wrps-supplement laid in (5s7, f) 7.50
LLOYD, FRANK-Catalogue of Frank Lloyd collection of Worcester
    Porcelain of Wall Period-Lond-1923-British Mus-4to-bds-
    cl bk-84p plts-1st ed-scarce   (5p5)   35.00
LLOYD, GEO, ed-Narr of a journey from Caunpoor to Boorendo
    Pass in Himalaya mntns by Maj Sir Wm Lloyd-n.p.-(Lond)-
    1840-JMadden & Co-2 vols-8vo-orig cl-1st ed (5i8, fade) 25.00
LLOYD GEORGE, DAVID-War Memoirs-Bost-1933-3 vols-illus
                                  (4b7)   17.50
LLOYD, HANNIBAL EVANS-Alex I, Emperor of Russia; or, a
    sketch of his life-Lond-1826-Treuttel&Wurtz-8vo-orig bds-
    papr labl-frontis & 1 plt-1st ed (5i8, vg)   17.50
LLOYD, HOWARD WILLIAMS-Manuscripts from the collections of-
    Lancaster-1912-437p   (4b6, unopnd)   15.00
LLOYD, J A T-Fyodor Dostoevsky-NY-1947-8vo-cl-324p-1st ed
                                  (5t0)   4.00
LLOYD, JOHN URI-Etidorpha;or, End of the Earth-Cinn-1897-
    RobtClarke-386p   (5x4)   12.50
--Our Willie-Cinn-(c1934)-8vo-cl-illus-Kidd (5b2, f, dj)   7.50
--Red Head-NY-1903-illus-1st ed   (5b2) 6. (5mm2,autg)   15.00
--Scroggins-NY-1904-Dodd, Mead-8vo-dec cl-g.t.-illus (5b2)   4.50
--Stringtown on the Pike-NY-1900-414p-1st ed
              (5ee3,autg) 10. (5b2,5d3) 7.50 (5hh3)   5.00
--same-NY-1901   (5h6)   3.50
--Warwick of the Knobs-NY-1901-12mo-illus-1st ed (5x2)   5.00
LLOYD, LLEWELLYN-Game Birds & Wild Fowl of Sweden & Norway-
    Lond-1867-Warne-8vo-cl-t.e.g.-2nd ed-fldg pkt map-
    52 plts   (4h0, crack)   125.00
LLOYD MANUSCRIPTS-Welsh Records of Howard W Lloyd-
    Lancaster-1912-437p   (5m2) 15. (5h9)   13.50
LLOYD, NELSON-The Chronic Loafer-NY-1900-1st ed (5mm2)   10.00
--The Robberies Company, Ltd-NY-1906-frontis-1st ed (5ee3)   4.00
LLOYD, THOS-Trials of Wm Smith & Sam'l Ogden-NY-1807-
    I Riley & Co-287p-calf   (5tt8, rebkd)   30.00
LLOYD, MAJ SIR WM-Narr of Journey from Caunpoor to Boorendo
    Pass etc-Lond-1840-2 vols-maps (5xx7)   15.00
LLOYD'S-Register of Amer Yachts, inc Canada, West Indies, SoAmer-
    NY-1929-529p-13p ads-loose 22p suppl "Corr to 9/30/1929"
                                  (5s1, ex-libr)   12.00
LLOYD'S-Register Shipping-Rules, regulat for construction,
    classification wood vessels-Lond-1917-94p plus sections tabls-
    fldg diagr   (5s1)   15.00
--same-Steel vessels-1924-300p   (5s1, ex-libr)   20.00
LLOYD'S-Register Shipping-July, 1933 to June 1934-Vol 1 only,
    Register-Lond-1933-lea cov   (5s1, sl wn)   20.00
--same-Vol 1 & Vol 2, Jul 1936 thru Jun 1937-Lond-1936-
    2 vols   (5s1, sl wn)   45.00
LLOYD'S REGISTER-Annals of-(Lond)-1934-Centenary Ed-251p
    plus 23p-illus-photos-deluxe ed-g.e. (5s1)   12.50
LLYFR ATHRAWIAETH A CHYFAMM ODAU-Merthyr-Tydfil-1851-
    Book of Mormon in Welsh, John Davis, transl-304p-lea-rare
                                  (5t3, bndg wn)   100.00
LOBAGOLA, BATA K A-Ibn Lobagola-NY-1930 (5x2, dj)   12.50
LOBB, JOHN, ed-Uncle Tom's Story of his Life-Lond-1876-port
                                  (5x5)   25.00
LOBO DE BARBOZA-Tratado Theorico e Pratico da Agricultura
    das Vinhas-Lisboa-1822-239p-calf-fldg tabl & 2 fldg plts
                             (5w1, rbnd, marg stns)   65.00
LOBO, FATHER JEROME, A Portuguese Jesuit-A Voyage to
    Abyssinia-Lond-1735-Sam'l Johnson, transl (his 1st book)-
                                  (5gg6, rprd)   100.00
LOCHHEAD, MARION-The Scots Household in the 18th Century-
    Edinb-(1948)-410p-24 plts   (5w7)   8.50

LOCHHEAD, MARION (continued)
--Their First 10 Years-Lond-(1956)-Murray-8vo-247p-8p illus
(5p1)   7.50

LOCK, ROBT H-Recent Progress in the Study of Variation, Heredity
& Evolution-NY-(1916)-348p-illus
(5t4)   5.00

LOCKE, A-The Negro & His Music-Wash-1936-Assoc in Negro
Folk Educ-142p-wrps   (5x2)   22.50

LOCKE, A A-Seymour Family, History & Romance-Lond-1911-386p
(5mm3)   7.00

LOCKE, ALAIN, ed-Four Negro Poets (cover title)-NY-(c1927)-
8vo-wrps-Simon&Schuster   (5b2,cov tn)   7.50

LOCKE AMSDEN-or the schoolmaster, a tale-Bost-1847-12mo-
orig cl-Benj B Mussey-1st ed   (5x1,f)   45.00

LOCKE, DAVID ROSS-The Nasby lettrs, the orig Nasby lettrs-
Toledo-(1893)-Toledo Blade-1st ed   (5m2)   12.50

LOCKE, E W-Three Years in Camp & Hospital-Bost-(1870)-408p
(5q0) 10. (5j6) 5. (5w5)   7.50

LOCKE, EMMA P B-Colonial Amherst, the Early History, Customs,
Homes, etc-1916-122p-illus   (5mm3) 10. (5e8)   10.75

LOCKE, JOHN-Collection of Several Pieces-Lond-1720-Bettenham-
8vo-calf-plt-errata pg-3 pg ads-1st ed   (4h0, rbkd)   250.00

LOCKE, JOHN-An Essay concerning Human Understanding-Phila-
1852-8vo-lea-523p   (5t2)   4.00

--same-Oxford-1894-2 vols-Clarendon Pr-A C Fraser, ed-535p &
495p   (5p0)   14.00

--The Philosophical Works of-Lond-1902-2 vols   (5x7)   4.50

--Works-Lond-1727-Prntd for Arthur Bettesworth-3 vols-4to-
port-calf-blind & g.-3rd ed   (5b0, crack)   225.00

LOCKE, A H-Capt John Locke of Portsmouth & Rye, NH & Desc-
1916-720p   (5mm3)   17.50

LOCKE INSULATOR CORP-Locke Catalog #27-Balt-Sept 1, 1927-
308p-illus   (5b8, mint)   6.00

LOCKE, UNA-Festal & Floral Days in NewEngl & Old England-
NY-(1870)-126p-12mo-3 wdcuts (5w7, ex-libr, wn, pg tn)   8.50

LOCKE, WM C & CO-Hudson Rivr & Hudson Rivr RR-NY-(1851)-
50p-map & wdcut views-prntd wrps   (5t4, wrp loose)   20.00

LOCKE, WM H-Story of the Regiment, (11th Pa Inf)-Phila-1868-
401p-cl   (5h7, pres)   10.00

LOCKE, WM JOHN-At the Gate of Samaria-Lond-1895-12mo-
buck-1st ed of auth's 1st book   (5gg6)   10.00

LOCKER-LAMPSON, FREDERICK, ed-Lyra Elegantiarum-Lond-
1867-16mo-g.-dec cl-1st ed-rare orig ed   (5r9)   10.00

LOCKETT, H C-Along the Beale Trail-Lawrence-1940-56p-wrps-
obl 12mo-photos   (5g0)   4.00

--Woodchuck Cave-Mus of No Ariz-1953-Bull #26-8vo-wrps-33p-
plates-illus   (5g5)   5.00

LOCKHART, CAROLINE-The Dude Wrangler-GarCty-1921-frontis-
1st ed   (5ee3)   3.50

LOCKHART, JOHN G-Ancient Spanish ballads-Edinb-1823-
Blackwood-4to-half mor-1st ed   (5i8, scuff)   22.50

--same-NY-1842-8vo-orig pic cl-272p   (5t2)   5.00

--Life of Robt Burns-Edinb-Constable-1828-446p-hf calf-1st ed
(5a1, sl fox)   10.00

--same-Liverpl-1914-2 vol-cl-vel bk-ltd to 500 sets, nbrd, autg
(5ss9, vg)   45.00

--Life of Sir Walter Scott-(n.d.)-c1903-3/4 red lea-
g.tooling on sp-t.e.g.-10 vols-Millet Co   (5ss9)   80.00

LOCKHART, MARION-Standard Cook Book for all occasions-
NY-(1925)-12mo-115p   (5c0)   3.00

LOCKHART, SIR ROBT-Marines were there-Lond-(1950)-229p-
maps   (5s1, dj)   4.00

LOCKHART, SIR ROBT BRUCE-Scotch the whisky of Scotland in
fact & story-Lond-(1952)-(5), 184p   (5w1)   5.00

LOCKLEY, FRED-Capt Sol Tetherow-Portland-c1925-26p-wrps
(4a5)   7.50

--same-Portland-n.d.-8vo-wrps-27p-scarce (5h5) 5. (4c1)   6.00

--Hist of the Columbia Rivr Valley-Chig-1928-3 vols-illus-4to-
fab   (5F5, sl stn)   30.00

--Oregon Folks-NY-1927-220p   (5ss1, dj)   7.50

--Oregon Trail Blazers-NY-1929-369p   (5s4, dj, sl soil)   7.00

--Oregon's Yesterdays-NY-1928-350p   (5ss1)   7.50

--Recollections of B F Bonney-Eugene-1923-20p-reprnt
(5xx8, orig wrps)   3.00

--Vigilante Days at Virginia City-Portland-(1924)-8vo-wrps
(5k4, bnd) 5. (4c1, pres) 6. (5zz5)   4.00

LOCKMAN, JOHN-Travels of the Jesuits-Lond-1743-2 vols-
2 fldg maps & 3 fldg maps-fldg plt-orig bds wi vel (5x5, f)   350.00

--same-(Lond)-1762-Piety-2nd Engl ed-5 fldg maps-2 vols-calf
(4n5, lacks 1 map) 65. (5n1, 4h0)   150.00

LOCKRIDGE, NORMAN-Lese Majesty-NY-1952-190p-illus-
cl-1st ed   (5t0)   5.00

LOCKRIDGE, ROSS-Old Fountleroy Home-1939-1st ed (4a9, ex-lib) 7.00

--Raintree Country-Bost-1948-12mo-cl   (4c2)   15.00

LOCKSMITH OF PHILA-NY-1849-Meth Ep Church-4p ads at end
(5cc6)   12.50

LOCKWOOD, C A-Through Hell & Deep Water-NY-1956-23 photos
(5c1)   8.50

LOCKWOOD, FRANK C-The Apache Indians-NY-1938-348p-8vo-
1st ed   (5ii8) 27.50 (5xx5) 40. (5h5, f, dj, 5s4, dj)   30.00

--Apaches and Longhors, Remin of Will C Barnes-LosAng-1941-
Ward Ritchie Pr   (5x5)   30.00

--Arizona Characters-LosAng-1928-8vo-230p-1st ed-scarce
(5hh4, vg)   30.00

--Life in Old Tucson, 1854 to 1864-1943-Ward Ritchie Pr-8vo-
cl-illus-1st ed   (5s4) 10. (5F5, sl stn) 15. (5zz5, dj)   20.00

--More Ariz Characters-1943-U of Ariz Bull #6-79p-wrps
(5jj7, 5zz5)   10.00

--Life of Edw E Ayer-Chig-1929-plts-1st ed (4a4) 15. (5kk4, box) 25.00

--Pioneer Days in Ariz-NY-1932-387p-8vo-illus-1st ed
(5dd4, vg) 32.50 (5x5, sl stn) 30. (5F5 vg) 25. (5zz5)   27.50

--Thumbnail Sketches of Famous Desert Riders-1946-Bull #11 of
Univ of Ariz-8vo-30p-wrps-scarce (5g5) 10. (5jj7, f)   8.50

--Tucson, the Old Pueblo-Phoenix-n.d.-8vo-94p-illus-cl
(5zz5, autg) 30. (5hh4, vg) 12.50 (5zz5)   27.50

--With Padre Kino on the Trail-Tucson-1934-Univ of Ariz Soc
Sci Bull #5-illus-orig prntd wrps-fldg map-1st ed
(5g5) 10. (5jj7, f)   12.50

LOCKWOOD, GEO B-The New Harmony Communities-Marion, Ind-
1902-Chronicle Co-282p-illus-2nd ed-(reprint?) (5qq8)   8.50

--The New Harmony Movement-NY-1905-Appleton-404p-ads-
illus   (5qq8) 12.50 (4a9, 5t4)   10.00

LOCKWOOD, INGERSOLL-Travels & Adventures of Little Baron
Trump & his wonderful dog Bulger-NY-1890-287p-pic bndg-
8vo-illus   (5p1)   17.50

LOCKWOOD, ISABEL I-Oriental Brasses & Other Objects for
Temple & Household Use-Glendale-1935-340p-g.t.-illus-
ltd ed of 500c, nbrd   (5r8)   37.50

LOCKWOOD, J H-Westfield, Mass & Its Historic Influences-1922-
2 vols   (5mm3)   17.50

LOCKWOOD, JOHN H-Western Mass, a History-NY-1926-4to-
4 vols   (5mm3) 25. (5r7)   40.00

LOCKWOOD, LAURA E-Lexicon to the Engl Poetical Works of
John Milton-1907-Macm Co-th8vo   (5ss9, rprd)   15.00

LOCKWOOD, LUKE VINCENT-A Collection of Engl Furniture
of the 17th & 18th Centuries-NY-1907-Tiffany Studios-4to-
illus-ltd to 500c   (5m6, sl rub)   35.00

--Colonial Furniture in Amer-NY-(1901)-Scribner-371p-293 hftone
plts-lg4to-cl-t.e.g.   (5m5, sp crack)   25.00

--same-NY-1921-2 vols-4to-new & enlrgd ed-illus (5j3, vg)   25.00

--Colonial Furniture in Amer-NY-1957-2 vols in 1-   4to-cl-
354p-3rd ed   (5q0) 12. (5w4, dj, 5j3, dj, vg)   10.00

LOCKWOOD, MARY-Story of the Records, DAR-Wash-1906-
326p   (5t9) 4.50 (5j4)   8.50

LOCKWOOD, SARAH M-Antiques-NY-1926-(3), 161p-4to (5w7) 7.50

--New York-NY-1926-197p-illus   (5x0)   5.00

LOCKWOOD, T D-Practical Information for Telephonists-NY-
1882-12mo-1st ed   (5ss5)   7.50

LOCOMOBILE, THE CAR OF 1912-Locomobile Book, the 14th
annual catalog of Locomobile Motor Cars-Bridgeport, Conn-
(1911)-210p-illus   (5t7, hng weak)   55.00

LOCOMOBILE, BOOK OF THE-n.p.-1920-sm thn4to-bds-
21p text-photos-catalog   (5t0, bkstrp wn)   30.00

LODGE, EDMUND-Portraits of Illustrious Personages of Great Britain-
Lond-1849-(Bohn)-8 vols-ports (5m6, ex-libr) 17.50 (5tt5)   27.50

LODGE, EDWIN A-Art of Manufacturing Perfumery-Cinn-1849-
120p-12mo   (5w3, cov dtchd)   22.50

LODGE, HENRY CABOT-Alex Hamilton-Bost-c1898-t.e.g.-
illus-311p   (5w9)   4.00

--Andre's Journal-Bost-1903-Bibliophile Soc-2 vols-4to-vel-
ports-facs & maps-487 sets prntd   (5x5, orig box)   75.00

--Daniel Webster-Bost-1890-371p, (2)p-hf mor-raised bands
(5w0)   7.50

--same-Bost-c1899-375p-illus-t.e.g.   (5w9)   4.00

--Early Memories-NY-1913-362p-1st ed   (5t2) 3.75 (5w9)   7.50

--Frontier Town & Other Essays-NY-1906-274p-1st ed (5i3, f)   3.50

--Geo Washington-Bost-1889-2 vols   (5q8)   6.00

--same-Bost-c1898-2 vols-349p & 427p   (5w9)   7.00

--same-Bost-c1899-Amer Statesmen-341p & 399p   (5h9, f)   6.00

--History of Nations-NY-Collier-1913-25 vol-lea-t.e.g.-
Ghent Ed   (5i1, f)   27.50

--Life of Geo Wash-Bost-(1920)-2 vols-g.t.   (5a8, vg)   6.50

--Senate & League of Nations-NY-1925   (5w5) 6. (5q8)   6.50

--Short History of English Colonies in Amer-NY-1881-560p-
hf mor   (5i3, rbnd, fine bndg) 10. (5h9)   10.00

--Story of the Revolution-NY-1898-2 vols-illus-t.e.g.-
(5mm8, shake) 6. (5h2, sp fade) 7.50 (5t4, fade)   8.50

LODGE, HENRY CABOT (continued)
--War with Spain-NY-1899-12mo-cl-276p-illus-1st ed
          (5m6) 10. (5t0)   4.50
LODGE, JOHN C-I Remember Detroit-Detroit-1949-illus-1st ed
          (4b7)   7.50
LODGE, O R-The Recapture of Guam-Wash-GPO-1953-214p-
maps-(Marine Corps Monographs)   (5x9)   6.00
LODGE, SAML-Scrivelsby, Home of the Champions, Marmion &
Dymoke Families-1893-199p   (5mm3)   10.00
LODGE, TOM-Beyond Great Slave Lake-Lond-1957-198p-plts-
maps   (5dd0)   4.50
--same-NY-1959-illus-198p   (5ss1)   3.50
LODI WOMAN'S CLUB COOK BK-Lodi-1929-268p-ads-col t.p.-
photo-Glozer #201   (5c4)   7.50
LOEB, C H-The Future is Yours-Cleve-1947-illus   (5x2)   6.50
LOEB, JACQUES-Dynamics of Living Matter-Columbia U Pr-1906-
illus-1st ed   (4b6)   25.00
LOEB, L-Venom of Heloderma-Wash-1913-cl-244p-4to-
Carnegie Inst Wash Pub #177-v scarce   (4p6)   35.00
LOEB, ROBT H, JR-She Cooks to Conquer-NY-(1952)-121p-4to-
col illus   (5c0)   3.50
--Wolf in Chef's Clothing-Chig-(1950)-4to-illus-123p, (2) (5c5)   3.00
LOEDERER, R A-Voodoo Fire in Haiti-NY-1935-wd block illus-
1st ed   (5x2)   10.00
LOENING, GROVER C-Military Aeroplanes-1915   (5aa4)   40.00
--Military Aeroplanes Simplified, Enlarged-(Bost)-1918-photos-
8vo-5 fldg plts-cl   (5b0)   27.50
LOETSCHER, L A-Presbyterianism in Phila since 1870-1944-38p-
sewn   (5L7)   2.50
LOEWENBERG-Annals of Opera-1943   (4e2)   20.00
LOEWENFELD, CLAIRE-Britain's Wild Larder, Nuts-Lond-(1957)-
312p   (5c5)   5.00
LOEWENSTEIN, KARL-Brazil Under Vargas-NY-1942-Macmillan-
8vo-cl-map-2nd prntg   (4a3)   12.50
LOFBERG, LILA-Sierra Outpost-NY-(1941)-453p   (5t7, dj)   5.00
LOFLAND, CHAS-List of All Entries in Virginia Military District-
Columbus-1821-32p-sewed as issued   (5jj9)   175.00
LOFTHOUSE, JOS-1000 Miles from a Post Office-Lond-1922-184p-
11 plts-map   (4a8)   20.00
LOFTIE, W J-Orient Line Guide-Lond-1890-439p-cl-illus-maps-
h.t. by KGreenaway-4th ed   (5yy3)   25.00
--A Plea for Art in the House-Phila-n.d.-100p-14 wdcuts-
    (5w7, wn)   5.50
LOFTING, HUGH-Dr Dolittle & Green Canary-Phila-1950-1st ed-
8vo-dec cl-col frontis-plts   (5dd0)   6.50
--Dr Dolittle & Secret Lake-Phila-1948-Lippincott-1st ed-8vo-
pic cl-col frontis-plts-366p   (5b9) 5. (5dd0)   6.50
--Doctor Dolittle in the Moon-Phila-1928-Stokes-8vo-1st ed-
dec cl-frontis-plts-307p   (5dd0, sl wn)   7.50
--same-(NY, 1928)   (5v2, lt wn)   7.50
--Doctor Dolittle's Caravan-NY-(1926)-Fred A Stokes-1st ed
    (5ss3, stnd dj)   10.00
--Doctor Dolittle's Circus-NY-(1924)-1st ed   (5v0, lt soil)   7.50
--Doctor Dolittle's Garden-NY-(1927)-1st ed   (5v2, f)   12.50
--Doctor Dolittle's Post Office-NY-1923-Stokes-1st ed-8vo
pic cl-frontis-plts-359p   (5m2) 7.50 (5v2, 5dd0)   8.50
--Doctor Dolittle's Return-Cape-1933-1st Engl ed-8vo-dec cl-
288p-frontis-plts   (5s6)   7.50
--same-NY-1933-Stokes-273p   (4h8, f, autg) 22.50 (5v2, vf)   15.00
--Doctor Dolittle's Zoo-NY-1925-Stokes-1st ed-dec cl-8vo-
frontis-plts-338p   (5m2) 7.50 (5v0, 5s6)   8.50
--The Story of Doctor Dolittle-NY-1920-Stokes-12mo-frontis &
2 plts inserted-orange cl prntd in lt blue, duplicate of frontis
on upper cover-180p-pic e.p.-tissue over frontis (4h8, vg, 5p1) 50.00
LOFTON, RACHEL-The Rachel Plummer Narr-n.p.-1926-wrps-
118p-photos   (5t3)   17.50
LOFTS, NORAH-I Met a Gypsy-NY-1936-Knopf-1st Amer ed-
ltd to 250c, nbrd, autg by publ   (5ee3, f, box)   15.00
LOFTUS'S, WM R-New Mixing & Reducing Book-Lond-n.d.-
(?188-)-96p, (24)-frontis   (5w1, crack)   8.50
"LOFTY"-Adven & Misadventures or an Undergraduate's Exper in
Canada-Lond-1922-219p-port-13 plts   (5a1)   7.50
LOG CABIN-or, the World before you-Phila-1844-Appleton-12mo-
orig cl-1st ed   (5x1, f)   60.00
LOG OF US GUNBOAT GLOUSTER-Annap-1899-188p-illus-
dec cl   (5s1, sl warp)   6.50
LOGAN-The Master's House, a Tale of Southern Life-NY-illus-
1st ed   (5F0, crack)   8.00
LOGAN, ALGERNON S-Amy Warren, a Tale of the Bay Shore-
NY-1900-1st ed   (5mm2)   12.50
--Not on the Chart, a Novel of Today-NY-1899-1st ed (5mm2)   10.00
LOGAN, CLARENCE A-Mother Lode Gold Belt of Calif-Sacramento-
1935-maps-illus-240p   (4b3)   10.00

LOGAN CO DIRECTORY (ILL)- & Statistical Record-Dwight-
1880-Hyde, comp-8vo-map-381p   (5jj5, f)   50.00
LOGAN COUNTY, ILL-Biographical Record of-Chig-1901-
654p-cl   (5ff7, rbnd)   50.00
LOGAN, DEBORAH NORRIS-Memoir of Dr Geo Logan of Stenton-
Phila-1899-Hist Soc of Penna-207p-illus-4to-ltd to 250c
    (5mm8)   12.50
LOGAN, F A, ed-Memoir of Dr Geo Logan of Stenton-Phila-1899-
4to-ltd to 250c   (5ii8)   25.00
LOGAN, GEO-Letter to Citizens of Penna on necessity of
promoting agriculture, manufac & useful arts-1800-30p-buck-
2nd ed   (5L7, rbnd, sl tn)   15.00
LOGAN, HARRY B-Orchids are easy to Grow-Englewood Cliffs-
(1955)-312p-col plts   (5s7)   7.50
LOGAN, HERSCHEL C-Buckskin & Satin-Harrisburg-(1954)-illus-
1st ed   (5zz5, dj) 5.   (5kk4, f, dj)   3.50
LOGAN, JAMES-The Scottish Gael-Bost-1833-illus-1st Amer ed-
calf   (5yy6, rub, fox)   27.50
--same-Hartford-1845-520p-illus-buck   (5ii2, rbnd)   7.50
LOGAN, JOHN A-The Great Conspiracy, its Origin & History-
NY-1886-810p-ports & 3 maps   (5x2) 15. (5r7) 10. (4j4)   6.50
--Speech of Maj Gen-Cinn-1863-Caleb Clark-32p-pamph (5mm8) 17.50
--Volunteer Soldier of America-Chig-1887-706p
    (5h6, cov sl loose)   8.00
LOGAN, MRS JOHN A-The Home Manual-Bost-(1889)-vi, (1), 507p-
4to-illus-frontis   (5w7, pres)   10.00
--same-Chig, Phila & Oakland-(1889)-533p-illus-cl & lea (5t7)   7.50
--Remin of a Soldier's Wife-NY-1913-illus-1st ed   (4b7)   15.00
--30 Yrs in Washington-Hartford-(1901)-752p-cl
    (5j6, autg) 8.50 (5h1) 5. (5w9)   6.00
LOGAN, DR JOHN H-History of Upper Country of SoCarolina-
1960-reprnt-521p   (5h9)   15.00
LOGAN, OLIVE-Before the Footlights & Behind the Scenes-Phila-
1870-612p-cl   (5y0)   15.00
LOGAN, OLIVE-Chateau Frissac;or, Home Scenes in France-NY-
1865-Appleton-12mo-cl   (5b2, wn)   7.50
LOGAN, R W-The Negro & the Post War World-Wash-1945-
Minorities Pub   (5x2)   15.00
--What the Negro Wants-1944-Univ NoCar   (5x2)   12.50
LOGAN, SPENCER-Negro's Faith in America-NY-1946
    (5x2, dj) 6.   (5L7)   4.50
LOGAN, WALTER S-Irrigation on the Yaqui River(Sonora)-
(n.p., 1892)-map-wrp t.   (5g3)   6.00
--Arizona & Some of Her Friends-n.p.-1891-wrps-48p-scarce
    (4n8)   25.00
LOGGINS, V-The Negro Author, His Development in Amer to 1900-
Port Wash-1964-Kennikat Pr   (5x2, mint)   12.50
LOGIC-or Art of Thinking etc-Lond-1685-247p, 8p-TB, prntr-
12mo-lea & bds   (5t0, marg mss notes)   25.00
LOGUE, ROSCOE-Tumbleweeds & Barb Wire Fences-Amarillo-
1936-110p-photos-orig wrps-1st ed-v scarce
    (5k4, rbnd) 17.50 (5zz5, sl chip)   37.50
LOHER, FRANZ-Geschichte und Zustander der Deutschen in
Amerika-Cinn-1847-544p-cl bk bds   (5ff7)   40.00
LOHMANN, KARL B-Principles of City Planning-NY-1931-
McGrawHill-395p-illus-sm4to-cl-1st ed   (5m7)   30.00
LOHMEYER, FRANCES C-Recoll of Cleveland & Detroit-n.p.-
1948-77p-bds-priv prntd   (5h2)   7.50
LOI RELATIVE A LA PECHE DE LA BALEINE & du Cachalot dans les
Mers du Nord & du Sud-(Paris, l'Imp Royale 1792)-4to-33p-
unbnd   (5ss2, stnd)   42.50
LOISE, FERDINAND-Histoire de la poesie mise en rapport avec la
civilisation en Italie-Paris-1895-482p-cl-t8vo (5p6, rbnd)   16.00
LOKKEN, ROSCOE L-Iowa, Public Land Disposal-IowaCity-1942-
8vo-cl-318p   (5a9, 5m8)   10.00
LOLLI, GIAMBATISTA-Osservazioni teorico pratiche sopra Il
Giuoco degli Scacchi-Bologna-1763-4to-calf-1st ed
    (5b0, lt fox)   75.00
LOLME, J L de-Constitution de l'Angleterre-Geneve-1790-2 vols
    (5r4, rbnd)   15.00
--Constitution of England-1822-new ed-buck   (5L7, rbnd)   12.50
LOMAN, ALAN-Mister Jelly Roll-(1950)-Duell, Sloan (5F1, f, dj)   7.50
LOMAN, S-Lowmans in Chemung Co, NY-1939-237p (5mm3)   7.00
LOMAS, THOS J-Recoll of a Busy Life-(Cresco, Iowa, 1923)-
220p-lea-2 photos-ex rare-prntd for family   (5zz5, f)   225.00
LOMAX, A-The Rainbow Sign-NY-1959-1st ed   (5x2, dj)   7.50
LOMAX, JOHN-Cow Camps & Cattle Herds-Austin-1967-illus-
ltd to 750c, autg   (4c7)   27.50
LOMAX, JOHN A-Adventures of a Ballad Hunter-NY-1947-
302p   (5c3)   6.50
--Cowboy Folk Songs & Other Frontier Ballads wi Music-NY-
1910-8vo-cl-1st ed   (5p5)   12.50
--Cowboy Songs-NY-1930-8vo-cl-Barrett Wendell, intro (5p5)   8.50

LOMAX, JOHN A (continued)
--Folk Songs-NY-c1947-4to-407p-reprnt ed (5w5) 6.50
--Negro Folk Songs,as sung by Lead Belly-NY-1936-Macmillan-
242p-1st ed (5x5,lt dust) 27.50
LOMBARDO TOLEDANO, VICENTE-The US & Mexico-NY-1942-
Council for Pan Amer Dem-12mo-22p-port-wrps (4a3) 7.50
LOMBROSO, CAESAR-The Female Offender-NY-1912-313p-illus
(5t4) 4.25
LOMEN, CARL J-50 Yrs in Alaska-NY-(1954)-302p-endmaps-
scarce (5w9,dj pasted) 6.50 (5ss1,dj) 10.00
LOMEN, G J,comp-Genealogies of the Lomen(Ringstad), Brandt
& Joys Families-Northfield, Minn-1929-361p-separate supplement
charts-g.,maroon cov (5s4) 15.00
LONDON & COUNTRY BREWER, THE-2nd ed to which is added
...Strong October Beer-Lond-1736-(5),138p-disbnd (5w1) 45.00
--same-7th ed in 3 parts-Lond-1759-calf-(3)p,332p, (2) (5w1) 30.00
LONDON APHRODITE, THE-Lond-Aug 1928 to Jul 1929-6 numbers-
unbnd (5a9) 37.50
LONDON, CHARMIAN-The Book of Jack London-NY-1921-2 vols-
frontis (5ss9, rprd) 25.00
--Our Hawaii-NY-1922-rev ed-illus
(5hh1,fray dj,9 li pres) 25. (4a1) 7.50
LONDON GAZETTE, THE #9818-From Tues Aug 15 to Sat Aug 19,
1758-(Lond)-sm folio-4p (5zz7,vg) 45.00
LONDON GAZETTE, THE-Supl to...14th of Mar...Mar 15,1815-
Lond-1815-small folio-unbnd & untrmd-4p-(nbrd 501-504)
(5a3) 50.00
LONDON, HANNAH R-Portraits of Jews by Gilbert Stuart &
other early Amer artists-NY-(1927)-197p-37 plts-bd&cl-Rudge-
1st ed-ltd ed (5t0) 15.00
--Shades of My Forefathers-Springfield-1941-59 illus-199p, (1)-
4to-ltd to 500c,autg (4m2) 22.50 (5n7) 18.50
LONDON, JACK-The Abysmal Brute-NY-1913-12mo-cl-1st bdng
stmpd in yellow & drk grn wi "May 1913" on copyr pg-
1st ed (5d9,dj) 50.00
--Adventure-1911-1st ed-Variant red cl bdng wi white lettring-
WLT Bibl #85-scarce (4t6,lacks fly,ex-librr) 20. (5t6,f) 30.00
--same-NY-1911-1st ed (5mm1) 15.00
--The Apostate-Girard, Kans-n.d.-Blue Book #640 (5x4) 5.00
--Before Adam-NY-1907-Macmillan-1st ed
(5x4,soil,5nn2) 12.50 (4t6,bkstrp lt fade) 15. (4t6) 17.50
--same-1907-variant bdng-wi bkstrp lettrng not edged in white
(see WLT 52) (4t6,sl wn) 20.00
--Burning Daykight-NY-1910-Macmillan-361p
(5t6,vg) 12.50 (5x4,5t6,vf) 15.00
--The Call of the Wild-NY-1903-8vo-vertical ribbed cl-1st bdng-
PhilipRGoodwin&Chas L Bull,illus-1st ed
(5ee9) 30. (5v2,vg) 35. (5d3,ex f,dj,4a5,vf,box) 75.00
--same-Lond-1908-Heinemann-part mor (4b5,sl fade) 20.00
--A Daughter of the Snows-1902-1st ed (5t6,vf) 20.00
--Faith of Men & Other Stories-NY-1904-1st ed (5mm1) 15.00
--The Game-NY-1905-illus-1st ed (5mm1) 10.00
--same-Metro Mag Co-rubber stmp on cpyrt pg-1905-1st ed,
2nd issue (5t6,f) 12.50
--The House of Pride & Other Tales of Hawaii-NY-1912-1st ed-
Macmillan (5ee3,vg) 12.50 (5mm2) 10. (5ss9,vg) 20.00
--The Iron Heel-NY-1908-Macmillan-1st ed
(5b2,lt stn,rub) 6.50 (5mm2) 12.50
--Jerry of the Islands-NY-1917-1st ed (5mm1) 12.50
--John Barleycorn-NY-1913-Century-illus by Dunn-1st ed
(5mm2,5ee3) 10. (5x4) 7.50 (5j3,vg,5t2,f) 15.00
--Little Lady of the Big House-NY-1916-Macmillan-1st ed
(5ee3) 7.50 (5hh1,hng rprd,5mm2) 10.00
--Lost Face-1910-1st ed (5t6,vf) 15.00
--same (5t6,hng rpd,sl rub) 10.00
--Love of Life-NY-1907-1st ed
(5mm2) 12.50 (5ee3,f,5nn2,vg) 15. (5t6,vg) 17.50
--Martin Eden-1909-1st ed-scarce (5t6,f,rub stmp) 20.00
--Michael, Brother of Jerry-NY-1917-1st ed-344p-cl
(5zz9, rub) 7.50 (5hh1,f,4b5,name on fly) 12.50
--Moon Face-NY-1906-1st ed (4t6,sl wn) 22.50
--The Mutiny of the Elsinore-NY-1914-1st ed-frontis (5mm2) 10.00
--A Nose for the King-The Black Cat-Bost-1906-Shortstory Pub-
(wrps) (5x4) 12.50
--On Makaloa Mat-NY-1919-1st ed-229p-cl
(5zz9,sl dmpstn) 10. (5mm1) 15. (4t6,vg) 20.00
--The People of the Abyss-1903-Macmillan-lg8vo-cl-photos-
1st ed-scarce (5h4,sl wn,sl soil,5t6,f,lt rub) 25.00
--The Scab-Chig-(n.d.)-Chas H Kerr-2nd separate ed-25p-12mo-
orig wrps-WLT #1038 (4b5) 25.00
--The Scarlet Plague-NY-1915-Macmillan-1st ed
(5x4, fair) 7.50 (4t6,cov spots) 17.50
--The Sea Wolf-NY-1904-1st ed (5t2,4t6,soil,wn) 15.00

LONDON, JACK (continued)
--same-NY-1904-prntd Nov 1904,month following orig publ-
366p-cl (5zz9, crack) 5.00
--same-n.p.-(1916)-publ by The Daily Worker-8vo-cl-322p (5t2) 3.00
--Smoke Bellew-NY-1912-Century Co-1st ed
(4b5,f) 22.50 (5mm2) 12.50
--A Son of the Sun-1912-Dblday, Page&Co-1st ed
(5hh1,ex f) 27.50 (5mm2) 12.50
--Son of the Wolf Tales of the Far North-Bost & NY-1900-
1st ed of author's 1st book-orig gray cl stmpd in silver-
1st state of bndg (4b1) 90.00
--South Sea Tales-NY-1911-frontis-1st ed (5mm1) 12.50
--Stories for Boys-NY-(1936)-illus-1st ed (5mm1) 10.00
--The Strength of the Strong-NY-1914-1st ed-frontis
(5ee3,f) 15. (5mm2) 12.50
--The Sun Dog Trail & Other Stories-NY-(1951)-224p (5ss1) 4.50
--Tales of the Fish Patrol-NY, Lond-1905-1st ed-MacM Co
(5mm1) 17.50 (5hh1) 15. (5t6,f, corners sl wn) 20.00
--same-reprinted Dec 1905 (5t6,f) 12.50
--The Turtles of Tasman-NY-1916-MacM-1st ed
(4t6,f) 25. (5ss9) 15. (4t6,f) 25.00
--White Fang-NY-1906-MacM-illus-1st ed
(4t6,sl loose,sl wn,5hh1,5ee3,5v0) 10. (5mm1,5v2,vf) 15.00
LONDON, JOAN-Jack London & His Times-NY-1939-1st ed
(5mm1) 10.00
LONDON MAGAZINE, THE-or Gentlemen's Monthly Intelligencer-
Vol 30 for yr 1761-Lond-1761-bds-prntd at Rose in Pater Noster
Row (5t7,lacks Feb issue) 12.50
LONDON PRACTICE OF MIDWIFERY-NY-1820-16mo-303p-
calf-JasVSeaman (5xx7,lacks fly) 15.00
LONDON, R C,ed-Conrad to a Friend-150 Selected Letters-1928-
8vo-cl-1st ed (5ee9) 25.00
LONDON, UNIV, INST OF HISTORICAL RESEARCH(1923 to 40)-
Bulletin Vol 1 to 17-bd (5rr4,ex-librr) 125.00
LONDRES, ALBERT-Road to Buenos Ayres-NY-1928-8vo-251p (4a6) 3.00
LONE, E M-Check List 1st Editions of Works of John Ross Browne,
Calif Pioneer-NY-1930-Lathrop C Harper-16p-wrps in case
(4n1) 10.00
--Some Noteworthy Firsts in Europe during 15th Century-NY-1930-
8vo-illus-cl-Southworth Pr-425c prntd (4c1,box) 20.00
LONE STAR ANNUAL FOR 1885-El Paso-(1884)-S H Newman-
56p-wrps (5yy3) 25.00
LONG, A L-Memoirs of Robt E Lee-NY-1887-707p (5j6,fox,loose) 7.50
LONG, A W-Irish Sport of Yesterday-Bost-1923-illus-288p(5ee3) 9.00
LONG, ALICE M-My Lady Beautiful or the Perfection of Womanhood-
Chig-1908-206p-26 photos-rev ed (5n7,cov stnd) 5.00
LONG BEACH, CALIF, QUEEN OF THE PAC-LosAng-(1919)-
Julius J Hecht-18 lvs-illus-sm folio-wrps (4a5) 7.50
LONG, REV EDWIN M-Illus History of Hymns & their Authors-
Phila-c1875-560p-illus (5w5) 7.50
LONG, ELIAS A-Ornamental Gardening for Americans-NY-1885-
illus-8vo-pic cl-381p (5t2) 4.50
--same-NY-1915-390p-illus (5s7) 4.50
LONG, GENEVIEVE-The Blue Grass Cook Book-Chig-(1903)-
308p (5g9) 8.50
LONG, HANIEL-Interlinear to Cabeza de Vaca-SantaFe-1936-
Writers' eds-12mo-bds-v scarce (5b2,f) 20.00
--Pinon Country-1941-318p-1st ed-end map-Amer Folkways Ser
(5r1,vg) 17.50
--The Power Within Us-(Lond)-(1946)-Lindsay Drummond-
Transf Libr 3-12mo-cl (5b2,f,wn dj) 7.50
--Spring Returns-(NY)-(c 1958)-Pantheon-8vo-cl (5b2,dj,f) 5.00
LONG, HENRY C-Report....on Condition & Prospects of City of
Cairo-NY-1850-prntd wrps (5g4) 30.00
LONG, HUEY PIERCE-My First Days in White House-Harrisburg-
1935-1st ed-illus (5yy6,lacks fly) 6. (5tt5) 7.50 (5m6) 13.50
--Share Our Wealth-Wash-n.d.-32p-wrps (5q8) 5.00
LONG ISLAND HISTORICAL SOC-Proceedings and Annual Reports,
1864 thru 1883-(1870 to 76 not publ)-10 vols-wrps
(5dd4,lacks 1878) 23.50
LONG, J C-Kossuth & Capt Long Misunderstanding, Official Corres-
Wash-1852-unbnd (5c1) 15.00
LONG, JAMES L-First Boy, Land of Nakoda-Helena-1942-illus-
284p-1st ed-rare (5zz5,ex-librr) 75.00
LONG, JOHN-John Long's Voyages & Travels in the Yrs 1768 to
1788-Chig-1922-Lakeside Classic (4e9,f) 20. (5w8) 15.(5h9) 12.50
--Voyages & Travels of an Indian Interpreter & Trader-Lond-1791-
fldg map-hf mor-4to-1st ed (5n1) 285. (5e2) 400.00
LONG, JOHN D-New American Navy-NY-1903-1st ed-2 vols-
illus-287p & 238p-map (5i3) 12.50
LONG, HON JOHN D,ed-The Republican Party-Bost-1888-
Wm E Smythe-427p-plts (5qq8) 6.00

LONG, JOHN DAVIS-Oration, Boston, Jul 4, 1882-Bost-1882-
43p-wrps   (5t4)   5.00
--Papers of, 1897 to 1904-n.p.-1939   (5w5,unopnd)   12.50
LONG, JOHN LUTHER-Madame Butterfly, Purple Eyes-NY-1898-
Century-224p-bds-1st ed   (5x4,scuff)   5.00
--Naughty Nan-NY-1902-Century-8vo-dec cl-frontis   (5b2)   4.00
LONG, JOS W-Amer Wild Fowl Shooting-NY-1879-330p-cl
  (5h1,wn,rprd)   5.00
LONG, JULIA G-ed-Life & Corres 1664 to 1722, Lady Martha
Gifford-Lond-1911-370p-ports   (5a1)   6.50
LONG LANCE, CHIEF BUFFALO CHILD-Long Lance-NY-1928-
278p-ports-1st ed (5aa0) 7.50 (5t3,pres) 10.   (4k4,f)   8.50
--same-1929-Cosmopolitan-illus   (5k4,f)   5.00
--same-1932-reprint-smaller format   (4d1)   4.50
LONG, LAURA-Square Sails & Spice Islands-NY-1924-249p (5t4) 5.75
LONG, MARGARET-Shadow of the Arrow-Caldwell-1941-Caxton-
310p-photos & maps-1st ed   (4b3,rbnd) 10. (4n1,dj)   15.00
--same-1950-rev, enlgd-354p   (4n1,dj)   7.00
--Smokey Hill Trail-(Denver-1943)-fldg maps-errata slip-1st ed-
scarce   (5zz5,dj)   25.00
--same-(Denver,1953)-fldg maps-3rd ed   (5zz5,dj)   12.50
LONG, MASON-Life of...Converted Gambler-Chig-1878-212p-
cl-1st ed-scarce   (5h7)   15.00
--same-FtW-1882-280p-cl-2nd ed   (5h7,sl wn)   10.00
--same-FtW-1883-280p-cl-3rd ed   (5h7)   8.50
--same-FtW-1883-280p-cl-4th ed   (5h7)   7.50
--same-FtW-(1882)-280p-cl-5th ed   (5h7,rub)   7.50
--Converted Gambler-Cinn-1884-280p-cl   (5h2,soil)   7.50
LONG, LT GENL ROBT B-ed-Corres of-Lond-(1951)-304p-port-
frontis-sm8vo-cl-4 maps   (5t0,dj,f)   4.50
LONG, S H-Specification of certain improvements in locomotive
engine-Phila-1826- -4 plts-wrps   (5g3)   30.00
LONG, STEPHEN H-Voyage in a 6 Oared Skiff to Falls of St Anthony
in 1817-Phila-1860-Ashmead-8vo-half mor-map-1st ed (5n9)   75.00
--same-Phila-1860-1st ed-wrps-map-88p   (4k4,f)   15.00
LONG, W G-Long Family of Pennsylvania-1930-365p   (5t9)   20.00
LONG, WM J-Following the Deer-Bost-1903-illus-193p-1st ed
  (5ee3)   3.00
--Fowls of the Air-Bost-1902-Antheum Pr-illus-4th ed (4a0)   5.00
--How Animals Talk & other pleasant studies of Birds & Beasts-
NY-(1919)-Harper-302p-illus   (5x0)   5.00
--Northern Trails-Bost-1905-390p-frontis-illus   (5ss1)   4.50
--Wood Folk Comedies-   1920-307p-col illus   (4b9)   10.00
LONGAKER, MARK-Ernest Dowson-Phila-1945-illus (5mm2)   8.50
LONGFELLOW, ERNEST WADSWORTH-Random Memories-Bost-
1922-8vo-cl-263p-illus   (5t2)   5.00
LONGFELLOW, HENRY W-Aftermath-Bost-1874-Osgood-144p-
2nd ed   (5x4)   7.50
--Christus, a mystery-Bost-1873-in 3 parts-Osgood-BAL #12530-
1 vol ed   (5x4)   10.00
--Complete Poetical Works-Bost-1922-HEScudder, ed-Cambridge ed-
  (5p9)   4.75
--Courtship of Miles Standish & Other Poems-Bost-1858-1st Amer ed-
Ticknor & Fields-1st prntng wi publ's cat dated Oct 1858
(5p7,5w9,split,wn) 20. (5ss3,stn,crack,5rr2,fox)   30.00
--same-Bost-1858-orig cl-1st ed, 1st issue-gilt extra-BAL 12122
  (5yy4,vg)   30.00
--same-Bost-1858-Ticknor & Fields-sm8vo-1st Amer ed, 1st prntng-
gift binding   (5ss3)   75.00
--same-Bost-1859-Ticknor & Fields-1st ed-4th prntg (5x4,wn)   7.50
--same-1903-BobbsMerrill-Howard C Christie, illus   (5hh3)   8.50
--The Divine Comedy of Dante Alighieri-Bost-1867-transl by
Longfellow-3 vols-1st ed   (5mm2,vg)   25.00
--Divine Tragedy-Bost-1871-1st ed   (5r9,4b4)   12.50
--The Estray, a coll of poems-Bost-1847-Ticknor-BAL #12088-bds-
1st ed (5b2,stnd,crack,lacks bkstrp) 10.
  (5mm2,rbkd) 15. (5x4,lacks bkstrp)   25.00
--Evangeline-(1905)-Bobbs-Merrill Co-H C Christy, illus-132p
  (5p9)   6.00
--Final Memorials-Bost-1887-Ticknor   (4b4)   10.00
--The Golden Legend-Bost-1851-302p-Ticknor, Reed & Fields-
catalog dated Oct 1851   (5x4,fray,5jj0)   15.00
--Hyperion, a Romance-NY-1839-Sam'l Colman-1st ed-orig bds-
2 vols   (4b5,vg,box)   150.00
--same-Lond-1853-1st illus ed-mor-g.e.   (4b4)   25.00
--In the Harbor-Bost-1882-1st ed   (5mm2)   5.00
--Kavanagh, a Tale-Bost-1849-1st prntg, wi catalog dated May 1,
1849   (4b4)   22.50
--same-Lond-1849-Slater-16mo-cl   (5i9)   10.00
--Keramos, & Other Poems-Bost-1878-Houghton, Osgood-cl-148p-
1st ed-1st bind   (5ee2) 10. (5x4,stnd)   15.00
--Le ministre de Wakefield-Bost-1831-Gray&Bowen-12mo-orig cl
& bds-papr labl-Longfellow, ed-scarce   (5i0,labl rub)   50.00
--The Masque of Pandora & Other Poems-Bost-1875-1st issue (5jj0) 10.00

LONGFELLOW, HENRY W (continued)
--New England Tragedies-Bost-1868-179p-1st pub ed
(5e8) 7.50 (5ss9) 10. (5r9)   12.50
--Outre Mer-NY-1835-2 vols-cl   (5i3,rub)   20.00
--same-Bost-1846-2nd ed   (5mm2)   7.50
--Poems-Bost-1850-2 vols   (5mm2)   10.00
--The Poetical Works-Bost-1881, 82, (83)-HoughtonMiff-3 vols-
thk lg4to-orig g.lettr d-mor-g.e.-full pg wdcuts-Riverside Pr-
  (5j5)   60.00
--same-Bost-(1886)-6 vols-HoughtonMif-lg4to-g.t.-illus-dark
grn cl   (5p6,vg)   36.00
--The Poets & Poetry of Europe-Phila-1845-thk R8vo-3/4 mor-
800p-1st ed-scarce   (5p5)   17.50
--Prose Works-Bost-1886-2 vols-frontis-8vo-cl (5t2, lacks flys)   5.00
--Saggi de Novellieri Italiani d'Orni Secolo-Bost-1832-12mo-
1st ed   (5cc9,fade,chip)   20.00
--The Seaside & the Fireside-Bost-1850-1st ed, ads dated Oct 1,
1849   (5ee3,vg)   12.50
--The Song of Hiawatha-Bost-1855-1st issue-orig cl-12mo
(5tt6,f) 55. (5ee9,4b4)   75.00
--same-Bost-1855-Ticknor & Fields-2nd prntng   (5ss3)   10.00
--same-Cambr-1891-Riverside Pr-lea-lea corners-t.e.g.-
Remington illus   (4a9,chip,repr)   25.00
--same-Bost-1895-HoughtonMiff-t.e.g.-180p-brick cl-
Remington illus   (5F9)   9.00
--same-Bost&NY-1906-242p-Remington illus   (5m1)   10.00
--The Skeleton in Armor-Bost-1877-Osgood-8vo-orig stmpd mor-
g.e.-unpgd-18 plts   (5j5,f)   15.00
--Tales of a Wayside Inn-Bost-1863-g.t.-12mo-1st issue wi "nearly
ready"on pg 11 of adv (4b4,rprd) 35. (5ee9) 35. (5jj0) 30. (5x4) 37.50
--Three Books of Song-Bost-1872-1st ed   (5mm2)   12.50
--Ultima Thule-Bost-1880-1st ed   (5mm2)   5.00
--Voices of the Night-Cambr-1839-orig brown bds-1st ed
  (4b4,sp chip)   65.00
--The Work s of-NY-(1909)-10 vols-The Davis Pr-cl-lea labls-
illus-deluxe ed   (5p0)   25.00
LONGFELLOW, SAML-Life of Henry W Longfellow-Bost-1886-
2 vols-illus-uncut   (5mm2)   13.50
LONGINOS MARTINEZ, JOSE-Calif in 1792-San Marino-1938-
map-111p-8vo-orig cl-1st ed-Simpson, transl   (4c1)   25.00
LONGLEY, ELIAS-New Amer Manual of Phonography...Pitman's
Phonetic Shorthand-Cinn-1877-139p, (1)-illus   (5n7,wn)   5.00
--The Transition Reader-Cinn-1855-Amer Phonetic Publ Assoc-
24mo-96p-lea bkd bds-view "Hughes City High School, Cinn"
lower cov   (5p1,wn)   10.00
LONGMAN, E D-Pins & Pincushions-Lond-1911-43p-illus-186p-
1st ed   (5c3, lt fox) 7.50 (5q0)   12.00
LONGMAN, W-Tokens of the 18th Century Connected wi Booksellers
& Bookmakers-Lond-1916-Longmans, Green&Co-8vo-cl-illus
  (5b0, libr stmp)   17.50
LONGMEADOW, MASS-Centennial Celeb of-1884-321p-
97p of genealogy   (5e8)   19.75
LONGMORE, T-Treatise on Gunshot Wounds-Phila-1863-132p-cl
  (5h1, lacks sp)   7.50
LONGNON, HENRI-French Provincial Furniture-Phila-1927-
/1 illus-map-1st ed   (5w7) 12.50 (5yy6)   17.50
LONGSTAFF, MAJ F-Book of the Machine Gun-Lond-1917-plts-
fldg plans-v scarce   (5u7)   22.50
LONGSTAFF, TOM-This My Voyage-NY-(1950)-324p-illus-cl-
Scribners   (5d7)   10.00
LONGSTREET, AUGUSTUS B-Georgia Scenes-by a Native Georgian-
Augusta-1835-12mo-bds-label-anon-1st ed of auth's 1st book
  (5gg6,def pg,new label)   150.00
--same-NY-1840-2nd ed, wi orig illus-12mo-papr label-cl
  (5gg6,chip)   50.00
LONGSTREET, HELEN D-Lee & Street at High Tide-Gainesville-
1904-illus-346p   (5kk4,wn)   15.00
LONGSTREET, JAS-From Manassas to Appomattox-Phila-1896-
690p-dec cl-plts-col maps-1st ed
(5zz5,sl wn) 30. (5ee3,vf) 45. (5kk4,f)   32.50
--same-Phila-1912-Lippincott-698p-thk8vo-illus-col maps-
2nd ed, rev   (5s5,f)   25.00
LONGSTREET, R J-Bird Study in Florida-Daytona Beach-1930-illus
  (5r7)   10.00
LONGSTREET, STEPHEN-Century on Wheels-NY-(1952)-1st ed-
illus   (5ii3,pres)   12.50
LONGSTRETH, T MORRIS-The Adirondacks-NY-1917-370p-illus-
maps-cl   (5d7)   4.50
--same-NY-1920-370p-illus-maps   (5t4)   5.00
--The Catskills-NY-1918-photos-map   (5q8) 3.75 (5t0)   5.00
--same-NY-1921-321p-illus   (4t4)   10.50
--Lake Superior Country-NY-(1924)-cl-360p   (5zz9)   8.50

LONGSTRETH, T MORRIS (continued)
--The Laurentians, Hills of the Habitant-NY-(1922)-459p-illus-
 maps-cl-Century (5d7) 4.50
--To Nova Scotia-NY&Lond-1935-photos-maps (5w8) 7.50
--The Silent Force -1927-383p-illus-map (4b9) 10.00
--same-NY-(1928)-lg fldg maps-2nd prntng (5t3) 5.00
--Tad Lincoln, the President's Son-Phila (1944)-263p (5t4) 4.00
LONGUS-Daphnis & Chloe-1923-Golden Cockerel Pr-4to-cl-bds-
 ltd to 450c (5t5) 18.50 (5mm2) 17.50
LONGWORTH, ALICE ROOSEVELT-Crowded Hours, Remin of-
 NY-1933-355p-illus (5p9) 4.50 (5t7) 5.00
LONGYEAR, BURTON O-Trees & Shrubs of the Rocky Mntn Region-
 NY-1927-244p-9 col plts (5s7) 6.00
LONGYEAR, MARY BEECHER-History of a House-Brooklin-1925-
 thn8vo-cl-illus (5t2) 4.00
LONN, ELLA-Foreigners in Union Army & Navy-Baton Rouge-(1951)-
 frontis-1st ed (5yy7) 20.00
--Reconstruction in Louisiana after 1868-NY-1918-1st ed (5x2) 25.00
LOOFBOUROW, LEON L-In Search of God's Gold-Stockton-1950-
 314p-illus-1st ed (5dd6) 4.50
LOOK & COOK-Los Angeles Section Natl Council of Jewish Women-
 LosAng-n.d.-spiral bnd-152p (4g9) 4.00
LOOK, EDITORS OF-Look at America-Bost-(1948)-illus-maps(4a1) 7.50
LOOK MAGAZINE-The Story of the FBI-NY-1947-286p-illus-
 Dutton (5p9) 4.00
LOOKER, EARLE-The White House Gang-NY-1929-Revell (5p0) 4.00
LOOKING GLASS FOR THE MIND, THE-or the Intellectual Mirror-
 Lond-1792-E Newbery-(viii), 271p-6 1/2"x4"-74 cuts by Bewick-
 frontis-tooled calf-lea labl (5p1) 200.00
LOOMIS, REV A W, ed-Confucius & the Chinese Classics-SanFran-
 1867-432p-cl-A Roman & Co (5dd5) 15.00
--Oration deliverd at Centennial Celeb of Evacuation of Fort
 Duquesne, Pittsburgh, Nov 25, 1858-Pitts-1859-33p-8vo-cl
 (5L1) 20.00
LOOMIS, ALFRED F-Ranging the Maine Coast-NY-1939-sm4to-
 cl-274p-illus-1st trade ed (5t0) 7.50
--Yachts Under Sail-NY-1933-illus-4to (5q0) 7.50
LOOMIS, ANDREW-Figure Drawing for all it's Worth-NY-1946-
 204p-cl-4to-illus (5t7) 5.75
LOOMIS, CHAS BATTELL-Cheerful Americans-NY-1903-illus-
 1st ed (5ee3, pres) 7.50
--The 4 Masted Cat Boat & Other Truthful Tales-NY-1899-241p-
 dec bds-illus-1st ed (5ee3, f, pres) 20.00
--I've Been Thinking-NY-1905-Pott-8vo-bds-cl bk-frontis (5b2) 3.50
LOOMIS, E S-Some Account of Jacob Oberholtzer-1931-412p
 (5mm3) 10.00
LOOMIS, EBEN J-An Eclipse Party in Africa-Bost-1896-8vo-illus-
 1st ed (5m6) 10.00
LOOMIS, ELIAS-Descendants of Joseph Loomis in Amer & His
 Antecedents in the Old World-1909-859p (5mm3) 75.00
LOOMIS, GEO B-Progressive Music Lessons-NY, Chig-1875-
 1st bk-Ivison, Blakeman-cl bkd bds-54p-16mo (5p1, wn) 6.00
LOOMIS, NOEL M-Texan Santa Fe Pioneers-Norman-1958-1st ed
 (4a5) 10. (5a0, pres) 9.50
LOOMIS, ROGER SHERMAN-The Art of Writing Prose-NY-(1943)-
 646p-rev ed (5m3) 6.00
LOONEY, LOUISA PRESTON-Tennessee Sketches-Chig-1901(5h6)8.00
LOOS, ANITA-Gentlemen Prefer Blondes-NY-1925-1st ed-
 1st issue-Boni&Liveright-(incorr spell in Contents pg, Chapt 4)
 (5ss9, vg) 15.00
--same-NY-1925-1st ed-illus (5i3, f, pres) 12.50 (5tt2) 20.00
LOPES DA SILVA, BALTASAR-O Dialecto Criolo de Cabo Verde-
 Lisbon-1957-sm4to-391p-wrps (5c6, f) 12.50
LORANT, STEFAN-FDR, a pictorial Biog-NY-1950-4to-bds-cl sp-
 (5t8) 5. (5w5) 6.50
--Lincoln, his life in photographs-1941-4to-illus (5L7, 5s9, dj) 6.00
--Lincoln, picture story of his life-1952-folio-illus (5L7) 10.00
--The New World-NY-(1946)-1st ed-4to-plts
 (5ss5, f, box) 15. (5ff7, f, dj) 12.50 (5g6, f, 4a4, autg) 20. (5qq5) 18.50
--The Presidency-NY-1951-illus (5s9, dj) 15.00
LORD, AM ROGERS-1st Book Upon Birds of Ore & Wash-Portland-
 1902-304p-illus (5s4, fair) 3.50
LORD, ARTHUR-Plymouth & the Pilgrims-Bost-1920-Brown Univ,
 Colver Lectures (5q8, dj) 3.50 (5w4) 5.00
LORD, CLIFFORD L-Historical Atlas of the US-NY-1944-4to-cl-
 553p-1st ed (5g2) 10.00
LORD, E-Principles of Currency & Banking-NY-1829-G&C&H Carvill-
 sp labl-131p-cl (5a0, labl tn) 8.50
LORD, E W-Story of Templeton, Mass-1939-285p (5mm3) 6.00
LORD, EDW O, ed-History of 9th Reg NH Vol-Concord-1895-
 171p-illus (5mm8) 5.00
LORD, ELIOT-Comstock Mining & Miners-Wash-1883-(USGS, Vol 4)-
 4to-3 maps(2 fldg) (4a1, bndg brok) 32.50 (5x5, lea, vg) 40.00

LORD, ERNEST E-Shrubs & Trees for Australian Gardens-Melbourne-
 (1948)-col frontis-col plts-sq8vo-cl (5z9, dj) 25.00
LORD, ISABEL ELY-Everybody's Cook Book-NY-1924-Pratt Instit-
 916p-illus-4to (5c0) 3.50
--The Household Cookbook-NY-(1936)-486p (5c0) 3.50
--The Modern Woman's Cook Book-NY-1939-479p-photos (5c0) 2.50
LORD, J C-The Higher Law-NY-1851-Union Safety Committee-
 16p-wrps (5x2) 45.00
LORD, JOHN-Frontier Dust-Hartf-1926-Shipman, ed-illus-
 ltd to 1000c (5k4, f, dj) 10. (5zz5) 8.50
LORD, JOHN K-History of Hanover, NHamp-1928-wi appendx-
 339p-illus-maps (5mm3) 7.50
LORD, JOHN KEAST-The Naturalist in Vancouver Island & British
 Col-Lond-1866-2 vols in 1-cl-illus (5w8, rbnd) 50.00
LORD, K-Desc of Thos Lord, orig proprietor of Hartford, Conn-
 1946-482p (5t9) 12.50
LORD, KENNETH-Certain Members of Lord Family who settled in
 NY City in Early 1800's-1945-90p (5mm3) 15.00
LORD, MYRTLE SHAW-A Sacramento Saga-Sacramento-(1946)-
 428p-plts-1st ed (5dd5) 11.50
LORD, PERCEVAL BARTON-Algiers, wi notices of the neighbouring
 states of Barbary-Lond-1835-Whittaker&Co-2 vols-8vo-1st ed-
 frontis-fldg map (5i8, vg) 25.00
LORD, RUSSELL-Forever the Land-NY-(1950)-Harper-1st ed-394p-
 illus (4n8) 6.50
LORD, W G-Some of the Desc of Nathan Barker of Sandisfield,
 Mass-1931-101p (5mm3) 6.00
LORD, W W-The Complete Poetical works of-NY-1938-Random House-
 Mabbott, ed-narr R8vo-dec buck-port-ltd to 750c, nbrd
 (5b2, fray) 7.50
LORDS OF THE HOUSETOPS-13 cat tales-NY-1921-dec cl-
 1st ed (5r9) 10.00
LORD'S PRAYER-NY-(ca1830)-D Fanshaw for Religious Tract Soc-
 16mo-16p-wdcut designs (5c8, lt stns) 5.00
LORENZ, CARL-Tom L Johnson, Mayor of Cleveland-NY-1911-
 203p-cl (5h7) 5. (5q8) 6.00
LORENZ, LINCOLN-John Paul Jones, Fighter for Freedom & Glory-
 1943-US Naval Inst-846p-ltd to 500c (5p7) 8.50
--Life of Sidney Lanier-NY-1935-Coward, McCann-8vo-cl-
 frontis (5b2) 7.50
LORENZINI, CARLO-Pinocchio-Phila&Lond-(c1915)-234p-
 Lippincott-8vo-M L Kirk, illus-frontis-7 plts-5th impression-
 pic cl (5p1) 5.00
LORETTE-The History of Louise, daughter of a Canadian nun-NY-
 1833-WmAMercein-12mo-orig cl & bds-1st ed-rare
 (5x1, wn, cov loose) 100.00
LORGNETTE, THE-or Studies of the Town, by an Opera Goer-NY-
 1851-Vol 1-12mo-294p-cl-Stringer&Townsend-6 plts by Darley-
 5th ed (5j5, f) 15.00
LORGNETTE, THE 1886-NY-(1886)-obl 12mo-cl-1st ed of auth's
 1st book-cartoons by SW Van Schaick (5gg6) 50.00
LORIMER, DLR, transl-Persian Tales-Lond-1919-345p-16 col plts
 (5t0) 7.50
LORIMER, GEO HORACE-Jack Spurlock, Prodigal-NY-1908-8vo-
 illus-cl (5b2) 7.50
--Letters from a Self made Merchant to his son-1902 (5L7, rub) 3.50
--Old Gorgon-NY-1904-308p-illus (5ss1, pencil) 3.50
LORING, CALEB WM-Nullification, Secession etc-NY-1893-
 Putnam's-171p (5m2) 6. (5qq8) 7.50
LORING, GEO B-95th Anniv of Settlement of Ohio at Marietta-
 Marietta-1883-bnd (5jj3) 12.50
LORING, JAS SPEAR-Hundred Boston Orators-Bost-1852-694p-
 1st ed (5g1) 7.50
--same-Bost-1853-cl-2nd ed, enlrgd (5g4, fray) 7.50
LORINI, M C-How to Restore Antique Furniture-NY-(1949)-illus-
 214p (5w7) 5. (5t4) 4.50
LORNE, MARQUIS OF-Canadian Pictures Drawn with Pen & Pencil-
 Lond-1892-3rd ed-224p-illus-lg fldg map-pict cl (4b9, vf) 25.00
--same-Lond-1885 (4b9) 25.00
--same-Lond-n.d. (4b9) 25.00
LORRAINE, E-Central Water line from Ohio Riv to Virginia Capes, etc
 Richmond-1869-96p-fldg map-prntd wrps-2nd ed (5y0) 17.50
LORRAINE, M J-The Columbia Unveiled-LosAng-1924-Times Mirror
 Pr (5x5, lacks fly) 5.00
LORREQUER, HARRY-Charles O'Malley, the Irish Dragoon-
 Dublin&Lond-1841-Curry&Orr-2 vols-illus by Phiz-1st ed-
 6p ads front of Vol 1 (5i4) 15.00
LORSCH, A P, compl-The Mining Handbook of Canada-Tor-(c1924)-
 12mo-orig prntd wrps-6th ed-Investors' Mining Handbook Co
 (5w8) 5.00
LOS ANGELES-a Guide to City & Its Environs-NY-1941-1st ed-
 433p (5w0) 7.50 (5x5, dj) 10. (4n1, dj) 8.50

LOS ANGELES AQUEDUCT-Complete Report on Construction-LosAng-1916-4to-maps-photos　(5h4) 5.　(5xx5)　8.50
LOS ANGELES & VICINITY-Selected Views of-(LosAng)-1900-photos-sm folio-24 lvs-wrps　(4a5)　12.50
LOS ANGELES CORRAL-Brand B ook #1-LosAng-1947-(1948)-176p-ltd to 600c (5tt0) 50.　(5yy7,dj) 45. (5cc5,f,dj)　40.00
--same-Brand Bk #2-LosAng-1948-(1949)-176p-ltd to 400c-49 illus　(5tt0) 45.　(4n1,dj,5cc5,f,dj)　40.00
--same-Brand Bk #3-(LosAng-1950)-264p-58 illus-ltd to 400c-contains "West in Bronze"　(5cc5,f,dj),　125.00
--same-Brand Bk #4-(LosAng-1951)-232p-64 illus-ltd to 400c　(5cc5,f,dj)　40.00
--same-Brand Bk #5-(LosAng-1953)-180p-51 illus-ltd to 400c　(5L2) 35.　(5cc5,f,dj)　40.00
--same-Brand Bk #6-(LosAng-1956)-164p-58 illus-ltd to 400c　(5cc5,f,dj)　40.00
--same-Brand Bk #7-(LosAng-1957)-293p-86 illus-ltd to 475c　(5cc5,dj,mint)　40.00
--same-Brand Bk #8-(LosAng-1959)-232p-54 illus-ltd to 525c　(5cc5,dj,mint)　40.00
--same-Brand Bk #9-(LosAng-1961)-268p-53 illus-ltd to 550c　(5x5,dj) 35.　(5cc5,dj,mint)　40.00
--same-Brand Bk #10-(LosAng-1963)-242p-44 illus-ltd to 525c　(5cc5,dj,mint)　40.00
--same-Brand Bk #11-(LosAng-1964)-250p-36 illus-ltd to 525c　(5cc5,dj,mint)　40.00
--same-Brand Bk #12-(LosAng-1966)-211p-57 illus-ltd to 500c　(5cc5,plastic wrps,mint)　40.00
--same-complete set-Vols 1 thru 13-LosAng-1947 to 1969-13 vols-priv prntd　(5zz1)　800.00
LOS ANGELES CO, CALIF-Illustrated History of-Chig-1889-835p-mor　(5jj9)　50.00
LOS ANGELES CO PIONEERS-Annual Reports-LosAng, 1911, 12　(5x5)　10.00
--same-LosAng-1913, 14　(5x5)　10.00
--same-LosAng-1914, 15　(5x5)　10.00
LOS ANGELES CO REGIONAL PLANNING COMM-Comprehensive Report on Master Plan of Highways for Los Ang-1941-96p-maps in pocket-cl-Vol I (all?)　(5yy3)　10.00
--Report of Highway Traffic Survey in Co of Los Angeles-Los Ang-1937-62p-fldg map-cl　(5yy3)　10.00
LOS ANGELES TIMES-Prize Cook Book-LosAng-1923-bds-340p-A L Wyman, ed　(4g9,f)　7.50
LOSKIEL, GEORG HEINRICH-Geschichte der Mission der evangelischen Bruder unter den Indianern in Nordamerika-Barby-1789-784p-hf calf-1st issue wi 6 line errata (5d6)　80.00
--History of Mission of United Brethren Among Indians in NoAmer-Lond-1794-1st Engl ed-3 parts in 1-v scarce　(4L3,mor,f) 125. (5n1) 250.　(5e2,fldg map)　350.00
LOSSING, BENSON J-Harper's Popular Cyclopedia of US History-NY-1892-2 vols-rev, enlrgd-buck　(5w0,hand rbnd)　12.50
--History of the Civil War-NY-(1912)-16 parts as issued-512p-16 col plts by Ogden-Brady photos-wrps　(5p9,5mm8)　20.00
--History of Civil War 1861 to 65 & Causes etc-NY-1912-512p-illus-4to-cl-Brady photos (5w9) 30. (5s9,nick) 25. (5mm8)　17.50
--History of the US of Amer-NY-(1913)-lg8vo-illus-cl-papr labls-8 vols　(5t2)　22.50
--Home of Washington-Hartford-1870-1st ed-a.e.(4n9)8.50 (5q8) 6.00
--The Hudson from Wilderness to Sea-Troy, NY-(ca1866)-306 illus-464p　(5t4)　10.50
--same-Lond-1868-306 engrvs-pic cl　(5c1,vf)　35.00
--Life & Times of Philip Schuyler-1860-2 vols-504 & 499p-index　(5ff2,cov dmgd)　12.50
--Mary & Martha-NY-1886-348p-illus-facs-drawngs-g.e.　(5h9,sl rub)　7.50
--Mount Vernon & its Associations-NY-1859-engrvngs-lea-g.e.　(5L3,sl chip)　5.00
--Our Country-(1879)-illus-3 vols-hf lea-1846p (5ff2,scuff)　18.00
--same-NY-1878-Vol 3 (only)-4to-illus　(4b3)　12.50
--same-NY-1878-2 vols-thk4to-3/4 mor-illus-1st ed　(5p5)　25.00
--same-NY-1895-3 vols-illus-dec bds　(5b1,f)　22.50
--Pictorial Field Book of the Revolution-NY-1851-2 illus-2 vols-1st ed-frail cl (5x5,1 pg ALS) 35. (4L3,rbnd,f) 50. (5ee3,f)　35.00
--same-NY-1859-2 vols-col frontis-illus-bds-blind stmpd & g.　(5j3,crack)　20.00
--same-1860-index-2 vols　(5ff2,rprd)　27.50
--Pictorial Field Book of the War of 1812-NY-1868-1084p-illus-buck-1st ed　(5ee3,vf)　30.00
--same-NY-1869-1084p-illus-part mor　(5t7)　15.00
--Pictorial History of the Civil War-Phila-1866-2 vols (5j6,loose)10.00
--same-Phila-(1866)-illus-lea-2 vols　(5t4)　10.00
--Seventeen Hundred & Seventy Six-NY-1847-510p-illus (5mm8)　6.00

LOSSING, BENSON J (continued)
--same-NY-1852-510p-illus　(5mm8)　6.00
--Two Spies, Nathan Hale & John Andre-NY-1899-illus-169p　(5i3)　6.00
--Washington & the Amer Republic-NY-ca1870-3 vols-illus-4to-g.e.-raised sp bnds　(5h9,sl rub)　32.50
LOSSOW, FREDERIK-The Light Headed Puss-NY-(c1875)-tall 8vo-pict bds-Stroefer & Kirchner-16p,ea a plt　(4a8)　6.50
LOST CHILDREN-or Example of Efficacy of Prayer of Faith-Cleve-n.d.-(ca 1850)-208p-cl-scarce　(5h7)　15.00
LOST HUNTER, THE-A Tale of Early Times-NY-1856-1st ed(5ee3) 7.50
LOT, FERDINAND-L'Art Militaire et les Armees au Moyen Age etc-Paris-1946-2 vols　(5xx7,mint)　20.50
LOTH, D-Royal Charles, Ruler & Rake-1930-illus　(5L7)　6.00
LOTH, DAVID-Swope of G.E.-NY-1958-309p(5x0,4m9) 5. (5y2) 4.50
LOTHE, ADA B-Best from Midwest Kitchens-NY-(1946)-284p (5g9)5.00
LOTHIAN, MARQUESS OF-Auction Catalogue-NY-1932-folio-Amer Art Assoc, Anderson Galleries-col illus-wrps (5d5)　15.00
LOTHROP, AMY-Dollars and Cents-NY-1852-2 vols-sm8vo-1st ed　(5v0,f)　15.00
LOTHROP, CHAS H-History of 1st Reg Iowa Cavalry Veteran Volunteers;also a roster of regiment-Lyons, Iowa-1890-ports　(5k4)　125.00
LOTHROP, D & CO-The Patient Blind Boy-Bost-n.d.-16mo-plts-col cl covs of snowball fight　(5v0,vf)　12.50
LOTHROP, HARRIET MULFORD-The Pettibone Name-Bost-(1882)-1st ed　(5ee3)　5.00
LOTHROP, MARGARET M-The Wayside, Home of Authors-(1940)-Amer Book Co-illus-202p　(5p9)　4.25
LOTHROP, S K-Archaeology of the Diquis Delta, Costa Rica-4to-wrps-142p　(5g5)　8.00
--The Indians of Tierra Del Fuego-NY-1928-Heye Foundation-plts-244p　(4k4,f)　12.50
--Metals from the Cenote of Sacrifice, Chichen, Yucatan-Cambr-1952-folio-wrps-139p-illus　(5F5,vg)　17.50
LOTHROP, THORNTON KIRKLAND-Wm Henry Seward-Bost-1899-423p　(5j6)　3.00
LOTI, PIERRE-An Iceland Fisherman-Stockholm-1931-sm folio-liths-cl & bds-ltd to 1500c,nbrd,box,autg-Ltd Ed Club (5b0) 25.00
--Madame Chrysantheme-Lond-(ca 1900)-crushed levant mor-sp g.　(5d2,fine bndg)　10.00
--A Sphai's Love Story-Paris-1907-8vo-dec bds-cl sp-col frontis-6 etchngs by Trilleau-ChasCarrington-ltd to 1000c　(5b0,sl rub)　12.50
LOTT, ABRAHAM, ed-Journal of Votes & Proceedings of the Colony of NY-NY-1764 to 66-Gaine-folio-2 vols-calf-1st ed-wi lf (found only in some copies) containing Act of Parliament for reversing Attainder　(5n2,hng weak)　150.00
LOTT, ELSIE MOORE-Wagons Rolled West, & other poems-SaltLkCty-1955-72p-illus　(5r8)　7.50
LOTT, MILTON-Dance Back the Buffalo-Bost-1959-406p-e.p.maps-1st ed　(5s4)　6.50
LOTZ, P H, ed-Rising Above Color-NY-1943　(5x2)　8.50
LOU, WILLY-Willy Lou's House Book-Indpls-(1913)-175p　(4g9,sl stn)　7.50
LOUBAT, ALPHONSE-The Amer Vine Dresser's Guide-NY-1872-123p-frontis-French & Engl ed　(5w1,autg)　25.00
LOUCHHEIM, ALINE B-5000 Yrs of Art, in Western Civilization-NY-(1946)-Art News Book-199p-4to-illus-cl (5m5,sl tn)　15.00
LOUD, JEREMY-Gabriel Vane, His Fortune & His Friends-NY-1856-orig cl-1st ed-scarce　(4m8,hng crack,rub) 10.(5mm2)　15.00
LOUD, LLEWELLYN L-Lovelock Cave-Berk-1929-wrps-67 plts-U Cal Pr-maps　(4k4,f)　12.50
LOUDON, A-Selection of Some of Most Interesting Narr of Outrages Committeed by Indians in Their Wars With the White People-Carlysle-1811-Vol 2(only)-orig calf-369p-pgd erratically　(5r5, few pgs wn affect text)　350.00
LOUDON, J C-The Villa Gardener-Lond-1850-516p-illus-orig cl-2nd ed-Mrs. Loudon, ed　(4g0, rprd)　25.00
LOUDON, JOHN C-Arboretum et Fruticetum Britannicum, or Trees & Shrubs in Britain-Lond-1854-mor-412 col plts(some fldg)-8vo-g.t.-8 vols　(5z9, fine bndg)　200.00
LOUDON'S ENCYCLOPEDIA OF PLANTS-Lond-1855-illus-1574p　(5q0)　20.00
LOUDON, JANE MRS-Gardening for Ladies, & Companion to The Flower Garden-NY-1859-430p-illus-orig cl-2nd Amer　(4g0) 12.50
--Ladies Country Companian-Lond-1845-12mo-396p-illus (4g0) 25.00
LOUDON, W J-The Small Mouthed Bass-Tor-1910-8vo-cl-illus-103p　(5t0)　4.00
LOUGHEED, VICTOR-Vehicles of the Air-Chig-1909-lg8vo-cl-479p-254 photos-1st ed　(5t2)　22.50
LOUGHRIDE, R M-English & Muskokee Dictionary-Creek Mission-Indian Terr-Phila-1914　(4k4,f)　35.00

LOUHI, E A-The Delaware Finns-NY-(1925)-331p   (5ii8) 22.50

LOUISBOURG JOURNALS, 1745-NY-1932-Soc of Colonial
Wars in State of NY-illus   (5w8) 22.50

LOUISE, HELEN SISTER-Sister Louise, Amer Foundress of Notre
Dame de Namur-NY-1931-Benziger Bros-336p-illus (5r0,dj) 7.50

LOUISIANA, A GUIDE TO THE STATE-NY-1945-e.p. map-photos-
maps-3rd prntg-734p plus index   (4L5) 8.50

LOUISIANA-Resources, Possibilities, Offerings & Advantages
of Queen of Southern States-Baton Rouge-1899-illus-fldg map-
wrps-208p   (4h9,f) 15.00

LOUISIANA HISTORICAL SOCIETY-Publications-NewOrleans-
1895 to 1918-Vols 1 thru 10-wrps-lacks Vol 2, Pt 1&2 (5yy3) 30.00

LOUISIANA PURCHASE EXPOS-Glimpses of the.....& City of
StLouis-Classic Gems-32 views-text-obl 24mo-g.cl.
   (5ii4,crack) 10.00

LOUISIANA PURCHASE EXPOS-Greatest of Expositions...Official
Views of-StL-1904-obl 4to-286p-index-photos (5xx7,hng wk) 10.00

LOUISIANE-Code Civil De L'Etat De La Louisiane-1825-publ by
a Citizen-791p-orig calf   (5j6,5m4) 25.00

LOUISVILLE & FRANKFORT RR-7th annual report July 16, 1855-
Louisville-1855-disbnd   (5g4,writing on t.p.) 20.00

LOUISVILLE COOK BOOK-Young Ladies Miss Soc of 1st Christian
Church-Louisvl-n.d.-(?1890)-133p-ads-limp cl (5c4) 6.50 (5h1) 10.00

LOUISVILLE, A GUIDE TO FALLS CITY-NY-1940-WPA-Amer
Guide Ser-112p-cl   (5h1,f,dj) 8.50

LOUNSBERRY, ALICE-Gardens near the Sea-NY-1910-274p-
8p col plts-pic cl   (5t0) 5.00

--A Guide to the Trees-NY-(1900)-313p-64 col plts-2nd ed
   (5p7) 5. (5s7) 6.50

--A Guide to the Wild Flowers-NY-(1899)-347p-64 col plts-
4th ed,rev   (5p7) 5. (5s7) 6.00

LOUNSBERRY, CLEMENT A-NoDakota, history & people-Chig-
1917-3 vols-thk4to-3/4 mor-maps-ports   (5k4) 50.00

--Early History of NoDakota-Wash-1919-645p-4to-illus (5k4,f) 25.00

LOUYS, PIERRE-The Adventures of King Pausole-n.p.-n.d.-
Soc of Sophisticates-8vo-ltd ed-tip in plts   (5b0,sl rub) 5.00

--Satyrs & Women-NY-1930-4to-Mojeska,illus   (5j3) 10.00

--The Songs of Bilitis-Lond&NY-1904-HMBrown, transl-8vo-
bds-linen sp-Aldus Soc   (5t5) 15.00

--same-NY-1926-Engl by AlvahC Bessie-Willy Pogany, illus-8vo-cl-
Macy Masius-ltd to 2000c,autg   (5b0) 12.50

--same-n.p.-1928-Franz Felix, illus-cl-4to-t.e.g.-Pierre Louys
Soc-ltd   (5b0,sl chip) 10. (5p9) 15.00

--The Twilight of the Nymphs-n.p.-1927-Clara Tice, illus-
Pierre Louys Soc-ltd to 1250c,nbrd   (5j3,vg) 10.00

--Woman & Puppet-1930-priv prntd-illus by Siegal-ltd
   (5i4,box) 15. (5w9,sl chip) 10.00

LOUX, DUBOIS H-Maitland Varne-NY-1911-DeThaumaturge Co-
8vo-cl   (5b2) 6.00

--Ongon-NY-1902-182p-orig wrps   (5xx8) 15.00

LOVAT, ALICE LADY-The Life of St Teresa-StL-n.d.(ca 1925)-
8vo-cl-frontis-31p,629p   (5t0) 5.00

LOVE BALLADS OF THE 16th CENTURY-EastAurora-(1897)-
The Roycrofters-8vo-crimson cl & bds-deckled e.-illum lettrs-
prntd in red & black   (5p6,f) 15.00

LOVE, J F-Papal Invasion or Roman Catholic Methods to Date-
Nashvl-(1912)-67p-wrps   (5h2) 4.00

LOVE, NAT-The Life & Adven of..better known in Cattle Country
as "Deadwood Dick"-LosAng-1907-162p-illus
   (5k4,stain) 50. (5zz5,cov spots) 65. (5t1) 95.00

LOVE, PHILIP H-Andrew W Mellon-NY-1929-319p-1st ed (5k1) 4.00

LOVE, ROBERTUS-The Rise & Fall of Jesse James-1926-Putnam's-illus-
1st ed (5jj7,ink name,5yy2,sl wn) 15. (5jj7,dj,vf,5yy2,f,5yy8) 25.00

--same-2nd prntng   (5yy7) 12.50

LOVE TOKEN FOR CHILDREN, A-for Sunday School libraries-NY-
1839-Harper-24mo-142p, 16p ads-cl   (5p1,fox,wn) 7.50

LOVE, W DeL-Colonial History of Hartford, Conn-1914-ltd to 350c
   (5t9) 17.50

LOVECHILD, MISS-The Ladder to Learning-NY-c1850-NY-
Edw Dunigan-12mo-8p-illus-wrps-sewn-hand col illus-rare ABC
   (5v2) 17.50

LOVECHILD, MRS-Easy Readings-Lond-Jun, 1814-WDarton-12mo-
wdcuts-lea & bds-scarce   (5c8,lacks 16 lvs) 35.00

--Poetical Alphabet, The-Concord-1855-JAMerriam-12mo-24p-
wdcuts-wrps   (5v2,f) 17.50

LOVECRAFT, H P-Marginalia-SaukCty-1944-Arkham House-8vo-
cl-illus-1st ed   (5d9,dj) 20.00

--Something About Cats & Other Pieces-SaukCty-1949-Arkham House-
8vo-cl-1st ed   (5d9,dj) 20.00

LOVEJOY, E MW-Hist of Royalton, Vermont with Family Genealogies-
1911-1146p-2 vols in 1-plts & maps   (5t9,rbnd) 45.00

LOVEJOY, ESTHER POHL-Certain Samaritans-NY-1927-MacM Co-
302p-illus   (5r0,dj) 7.50

LOVEJOY, J C-Memoir of Elijah P. Lovejoy-1838 (5L7,rbnd) 15.00

--Memoirs of Rev Charles T Torrey-Bost-1847-frontis-364p (5i3) 12.50

LOVEJOY, OWEN-Speech of Owen Lovejoy from Illinois-1861-
House of Rep-8p-orig wrps   (5x5) 10.00

LOVELACE, RALPH MILBANKE-A Fragment of Truth concerning Geo
Gordon Byron-Lond-1905-6 ports-8 facs-sm4to- linen bkd bds-
1st ed-v scarce   (5r9,sl rub) 35.00

LOVELAND, SAM'L C-Correspondence by letters between Sam'l C
Loveland & Rev Jos Labree-Windsor, Vt-12mo-67p-Spooner
   (5t4,lacks bkstrp) 10.00

LOVELESS, RICH WM-200 Amer Ancestors, Progenitors of-1968-
48p   (5mm3) 8.50

LOVELL, A A-Worcester Mass in the War of the Revolution-1876-
128p   (5mm3) 5.00

LOVELL, CAROLINE-Golden Isles of Georgia-Bost-1932-300p-
1st ed   (5yy8) 12.50

LOVELL, F W-Ancestry of Thos Lovell & His Wife Mary Ellen Ricker-
1940-172p   (5mm3) 15.00

LOVELL, JAS-Oration Delivered April 2d, 1771...to Commemorate
the bloody Tragedy-Bost-1771-Edes&Gill-4to-mor
   (5n2,lacks hf t.,wn) 125. (5n2) 225.00

LOVELL, JAS-Sketches of Man "As He Is" Connected with Past &
Present Modes of Education-Bost-1808-cov title-sewn
   (5ii4,chip,autg) 20.00

LOVELL, M S-Edible Mollusks of Great Britain & Ireland wi Recipies
for Cooking Them-Lond-1867-12p illus-pic cl-207p,24p
   (5ww2) 18.50

LOVELL, MRS F S-Hist of the Town Rockingham-1958-553p & map-
   (5mm3) 17.50

LOVEMAN, ROBT-A Book of Verses-Phila-1900-Lippincott-sm8vo-
buck-scarce   (5b2,rub) 10.00

LOVEMAN, SAM'L,ed-21 Letters of Ambrose Bierce-Cleve-1922-
Geo Kirk-12mo-bds-ltd to 950c,nbrd   (5ss9,vg) 15.00

LOVERIDGE, A-I Drank the Zambezi-NY-1953-14p plus 296p-
16 plts-index-map e.p.   (5c6,vg) 6.75 (5x2) 5.00

LOVERIDGE, A-Reptiles of the Pacific World-NY-1945-259p-
7 plts-cl-8vo   (4p6) 8.00

LOVERING, REV MARTIN-Hist of Holland, Mass-1915-749p-
illus   (5mm3) 15.00

LOVET, H T-Treatise on the human hair, with particular reference
to greyness & baldness-NY-1851-27p, (1)-wrp t.   (5g8) 10.00

LOVETT, W J-Applied Naval Architecture-Lond-1920-654p (5s1) 8.00

LOVETTE, LELAND P-Naval Customs, Traditions & Usage-Annap-
1939-404p-illus-1st ed   (5s1,dj) 6.00

LOVEWELL, CAROLINE B-The Fireless Cooker-Topeka, Kans-1908-
211p-illus   (5c0,cov wn) 8.50

LOVIBOND, THOS W-Brewing wi Raw Grain-Lond-1883-(1),75p
   (5w1) 7.50

LOVING BALLAD OF LORD BATEMAN, THE-Lond-1839-32mo-
illus-wrps   (5t7) 10.00

LOW, PROF A M-Mine & Countermine-NY-(1940)-224p-photos
   (5s1,ex-libr) 4.50

LOW, A P-Rept of Dominion Govt Exped to Hudson Bay & Arctic
Islands-Ott-1906-355p-plts-fldg map   (5a1) 12.50

LOW, A MAURICE-Woodrow Wilson-Bost-1918-port   (5q8) 3.50

LOW, ALBERT H-Technical Methods of Ore Analysis-Wiley-1927
   (5a6) 3.50

LOW, BENJ R C-The sailor who has sailed & other poems-NY-1911-
John Lane-1st ed of auth's 1st book   (5m2,autg) 6.00

LOW, CAPT CHAS P-Some Recollections...1847 to 1873-Bost-1906-
GHEllis-12mo-cl-port   (5j5) 17.50

LOW, DAVID-Breeds of Domestic Animals of British Islands-Lond-
1842-57 col plts-2 vols in 1-folio-mor-g.e.-1st ed (5z9,vg) 500.00

LOW, GORHAM P-Sea Made Men, story of a Gloucester Lad-
1937-illus-presented by R W Babson   (5L7) 4.00

LOW, LYMAN HAYNES-Hard Times Tokens-NY-1900-2 vols(1 of
text & 1 of plts)-4to-cl-65p-15 plts-2nd ed, rev & enlrgd (5t4) 35.00

LOW, NATHANIEL-An astronomical diary, or almanack for...1768-
Bost-(1767)-12 lvs-stitchd   (5g4) 12.50

--same-for year of Christian Aera 1783-Bost-20p-v hard papr
   (5a0,rprd) 15.00

LOW, WILL H-A Painter's Progress-NY-1910-Scribner's Sons-
301p-illus-g.-demy 8vo   (4a0) 17.50

LOW'S ALMANACK, & AGRICULTURAL REGISTER, FOR 1816-Bost-
(1815)-18 lvs-sewed   (5ff7,sl wn) 6.50

LOWDERMILK, WM H-History of Cumberland, Maryland-Wash-1878-
hf calf-extra illus   (5tt8,author's copy wi clippings) 50.00

--same-Wash-1878-cl-illus   (5ii8,f) 75.00

LOWE, BRUCE-Breeding Racehorses by the Figure System-Lond-
(1913)-illus-263p   (5yy8) 20.00

LOWE, CLEMENT B-A Syllabus of Botanical Natural Orders (1888)-
(Pa)-1893-obl 12mo-66p   (5w3) 4.50

LOWE, E A-A 6th Century Fragment of Letters of Pliny the
Younger-Wash-1922-Carnegie Inst-20 plts-orig wrps-67p text-
4to   (5tt9, unopnd)   20.00
LOWE, E J-Natural History of New & Rare Ferns-Lond-1862-8vo-
72 col plts-orig cl-1st ed   (5z9)   5.00
--Ferns, British & Exotic-Lond-1872-479 col plts-8 vols-orig cl-
2nd ed   (5z9)   50.00
LOWE, JUDGE J M-National Old Trails Road-KansCty-1925-
rev ed-284p-illus-maps-scarce   (5ii1)   15.00
LOWE, JOHN-Ancestors of John Lowe Family Circle & Desc-
1901-189p   (5mm3)   10.00
LOWE, MARTHA PERRY-Story of Chief Joseph-Bost-(1881)-40p-
1 photo-illus-1st ed   (5L0)   8.50
LOWE, PAUL E-20th Century Book of Toasts-Phila-(1910)-180p
                                             (4g9)   4.00
LOWE, PERCIVAL G-Five Years a Dragoon ('49 to '54) & Other
Adventures on Great Plains-KansCty-1906-photos-1st ed (5yy7) 30.00
LOWE, ROBT W-Bibliographical Account of English Theatrical
Literature-NY-1888-384p-ltd ed   (4b4)   27.50
LOWE, W B-Heart of Northern Wales, as it was & as it is-1912, 27-
illus-2 vols   (5L7, sl wn)   15.00
LOWELL, A LAWRENCE-Government of England-NY-1912-Macm-
2 vols-New ed   (5ii4, ex-libr)   10.00
LOWELL, AMY-John Keats-Bost-1925-2 vols-illus (5p0,5mm1)   15.00
--Sword, Blades & Poppy Seeds-NY-1914-12mo-orig bds-papr labls-
cl-1st ed   (4m8) 8.50 (5t5)   12.50
--What's O'Clock-1925-HoughtonMiff-12mo-cl bk bds-1st ed
                                             (5ss9)   12.50
LOWELL, CHAS R-Memoirs of the War of '61-Bost-1920-ports(5g3) 5.00
LOWELL, D O S-Ancestors of Andrew Chauncey Munsey & Mary
Jane Merritt Hopkins-1920-216p   (5mm3)   5.00
LOWELL, GUY-More small Italian villas & farmhouses-NY-1920-
Archi Book Pub Co-folio-cl-plts   (5m5, ex-libr)   18.00
LOWELL, JAS R-Among My Books-Bost-1870-1st ed-Fields, Osgood
& Co   (5ss3) 7.50 (5mm1)   10.00
--Bigelow Papers-Cambridge-1848-163p-1st ed (5e8)   25.00
--same-Bost-1867-2nd ser-1st issue of 1st US ed (5mm2)   12.50
--The Cathedral-Bost-1870-title in red & black-1st ed (4b4)   12.50
--Complete Works-NY-(1899)-cl-Scully & Kleinteich-Univ ed
                                             (4F3, f)   22.50
--Conversations On Some of the Old Poets-Cambr-1845-1st ed
                       (4m8, orig wrps, fox) 15.00 (5mm2)   12.50
--The Courtin'-Bost-1874-Winslow Homer, illus-4to-t.p.-1st ed in
book form-silhouette illus-scarce   (5mm2)   27.50
--My Study Windows-Bost-1871-1st ed-1st issue, wi publishers'
monogram on sp   (5ss9, vg, 5r9, f)   15.00
--Poems-Cambr-1844-279p-bds-papr labl-uncut-1st ed & ser-
scarce   (5hh3, hf calf, hng loose) 25. (5mm1, sl case, bkplt) 40.00
--A Year's Life-Bost-1841-12mo-bds-papr labl-errata slip-
1st ed of auth's 1st book   (5gg6, f)   100.00
LOWELL, JOAN-Cradle of the Deep-NY-1929-261p-illus
                                             (5s1, fade)   5.00
--same-1929-port-2nd prntng   (5s1, dj)   4.00
LOWELL (MASS)-As it Was & As It Is-1845-234p (5mm3)   5.00
LOWELL (MASS)-Director for 1859-1858-271p   (5t9)   3.00
LOWELL, PERCIVAL-The Evolution of Worlds-NY-1909-Illus(5m2) 8.50
--Mars & Its Canals-1906-illus-buck   (5L7, ex-libr)   7.50
--Mars as the Abode of Life-NY-1908-illus-1st ed (5m2)   8.50
LOWELL, ROBT- Fall 1961-Milford-1965-Broadside-1st ed-
115c prntd   (5ss7, autg, mint) 75.00
--For the Union Dead-NY-(1964)-Farrar, Straus & Giroux-1st ed
                             (5dd8, f, dj, 5ss9, f, dj)   7.50
--Life Studies-NY-(1959)-8vo-cl-1st ed   (5dd8, f, dj)   15.00
--The Mills of the Kavanaughs-NY-(1951)-12mo-cl-1st ed
                                             (5ss7, vf, dj)   25.00
--Near the Ocean-NY-(1967)-Farrar, Straus & Giroux-1st ed
                                             (5ss9, f, dj)   10.00
LOWELL, ROBT-A Story or two from an old Dutch town-Bost-1878-
Roberts-1st ed   (5m2)   7.50
LOWELL TRI WEEKLY AMERICAN-Vol 1, Nos. 1 to 153-Lowell,
May 28, 1849 to May 27, 1850-folio-calf bk bds
                                             (5ss5, cov loose) 32.50
LOWENSTEIN, A K-Brutal Mandate-NY-1962   (5x2, dj)   7.50
LOWER, A R M-Canadians in Making-Tor-1958-plts-476p (5dd0)   7.50
--Unconventional Voyages-Tor-1953-156p   (4b9)   6.00
LOWER, J L-Lower Family in Amer-n.d.-144p   (5mm3)   15.00
LOWER, M A-Contributions to Literature Histroical, Antiquarian &
Metrical-Lond-1854-illus   (5mm2)   7.50
LOWERY, MARGARET R-Windows of Morning-NewHav-1940-8vo-
249p-wrps-illus   (5t0)   5.00
LOWES, JOHN LIVINGSTON-Convention & revolt in poetry-
Bost-1919-Houghton-1st ed   (5m2)   6.50

LOWES, MRS-Chats on Old Lace & Needlework-Lond-(1919)-
386p-76 photos   (5n7)   8.50
LOWIE, ROBT H-Vol 21, Parts 1 to 5, Anthropological Papers of
Amer Mus of Natural Hist-NY-1917 to 1924-365p plus index-
photos-bnd in 1 vol-cl wi orig wrps bnd in   (5t3)   25.00
--Crow Indians-NY-(1935)-350p-illus (4k4, f, dj) 30. (5s4)   22.50
--Indians of the Plains-(1954)-McGrawHill-illus-maps-222p
                       (5yy8) 8.50   (5k4, mint, dj)   10.00
--Primitive Religion-1924   (5L7)   3.50
--same-NY-1948   (5qq5)   5.00
--Primitive Society-NY-1920   (5qq5)   7.00
--Societies of the Crow, Hidatsa & Mandan Indians-NY-1913-
Amer Mus of Nat Hist-wrps-illus   (4k4, f)   13.50
LOWINSKY, RUTH-More Lovely Food-Lond-1935-Nonesuch Pr-
169p-illus   (5c5) 5. (5g9, fade)   4.50
LOWNDES, R-Law of General Average (Engl & Foreign)-Lond-
1874-2nd ed   (5r4, rbnd)   10.50
LOWREY, GROSVENOR-English neutrality, is the Alabama a
British pirate?-NY-1863-glazed orang wrps-2nd ed, rev
                                             (5g8, wrp tn)   7.50
LOWRIE, DRUCELLA-The Standard Book of Sewing-GarCty-(1947)-
237p   (5n7)   2.00
LOWRIE, J K, comp-County Pioneer History of Ohio-Niles-1888-
64p-wrps-Part 1, #1   (5ff7)   8.50
LOWRIE, SARAH DICKSON-Strawberry Mansion-n.p.-c1941-
224p-illus-g.t.   (5h9)   6.00
LOWRIE, WALTER-Short Life of Keirkegaard-Princeton-1946-8vo-
cl-271p   (5t0)   5.00
LOWRY, DELVALLE-Conversations on Mineralogy-Phila-1822-
Uriah Hunt-fldg plts-12mo-1st Amer ed   (4b6, wrp)   20.00
LOWRY, JAS H, comp-History of the Texas Press & Tesas Press
Assoc-Dallas-1929-folio   (5n4)   45.00
LOWRY, MALCOLM-Under the Volcano-NY-(1947)-1st ed
                       (5j3, sl soil) 12. (5d8, dj)   25.00
LOWRY, R-History of Mississippi-Jackson-1891-errata pg-648p
                                             (5yy8, pres)   50.00
LOWRY, ROBT-Filthy Poems-Italy-1945-48mo-16p-orig wrps-
autg-1st ed-ltd to 125c   (5ss9, vf)   25.00
LOWTHER, CHAS C-Dodge City, Kansas-(Phila, 1940)-illus-
1st ed-scarce   (5k4, f, dj, pres) 50. (5yy2)   25.00
--Panhandle Parson-Nashville-1942 (4a5, dj) 10. (5dd6)   9.50
--A Tale of the Kansas Border-NY-1949-190p   (5t1)   45.00
LOWTHER, M K-Hist of Ritchie Co, W Virg & Remin of Rev etc-
Wheeling-(1911)-illus-681p-v scarce   (4m2)   40.00
LOWTHER, MINNIE K-Mount Vernon, Its Children, Its Romances,
Its Allied Families & Mansions-(1930)-Winston Co-illus-282p
                                             (5yy8)   10.00
LOWTHER, MINNIE KENDALL-Blennerhassett Islands Romance and
Tragedy-(1939)-187p-wrps   (5t9)   7.50
LOYAL LEGION OF US-War Papers Read before Indiana
Commandery Military Order of-Indnpls-1898-521p-cl (5h1)   12.50
LOYAL PUBLICATION SOC #61-Sherman vs Hood-(NY-1864)-4p-
unbnd as issued   (5h1)   4.00
LOYALISTS' AMMUNITION, THE-Phila-1863-16p-wrps (5j6)   2.50
LOYD, SAM-Cyclopedia of Puzzles-NY-(1914)-Franklin Bigelow
Corp-lg 4to-384p-illus-scarce   (5rr2)   17.50
LUBBOCK, BASIL-Adventures by Sea from Art of Old Time-Lond-
1925-4to-ltd ed-1st ed-115 plts & maps(22 mounted)
                                             (5ii3, bndg fade) 45.00
--The Arctic Whalers-Glasgow-1937-1st ed-483p-illus-scarce
                                             (4e9)   35.00
--The Blackwall Frigates-Glasgow-1922-1st ed-illus-332p
                                             (5ee3) 5. (5s1) 8.00
--The China Clippers-Bost-(1914)-Laurian-illus & plans-8vo
                       (5s1) 12.50 (5ss5)   15.00
--same-Glasgow-(1946)-plts-4to   (4b6)   25.00
--Colonial Clippers-Bost-1921-Lauriat-1st ed-illus-432p (4e3,vg)15.00
--same-Bost-(1925)-3rd ed-433p-illus   (5s1, dj)   10.00
--same-1921-plts-2nd ed   (5L7)   7.50
--same-Glasgow-(1948)-384p-illus-plans (5s1, dj, ex-libr)   7.50
--Jack Derringer, tale of deep water-1906   (5L7)   3.50
--The Last of Windjammers-Bost-1927-(29)-photos-2 vols-thick
sm4to   (4b6)   50.00
--The Log of the "Cutty Sark"-Glasgow-1924-illus-plans-8vo-
1st ed   (5ss5)   12.50
--same-Bost-(1924)-422p-illus   (5s1, ex-libr)   8.00
--The Opium Clippers-Glasgow-1933-63 illus-7 plans (5c1)   22.50
--same-Glasgow-(1946)-392p-port-illus   (5s1, ex-libr, f) 9.50
--The Romance of the Clipper Ships-Lond-(1927)-Blue Peter Publ Co-
4to-30 col plts-lg fldg map-blue cl-g.-1st impress of 1000c-
scarce   (5b0, lt spot)   95.00
--same-NY-1949-sm4to-col illus   (5113)   10.00

LUBBOCK, BASIL (continued)
--The Western Ocean Packets-Bost-1925-8vo-illus
    (5s1) 12.50   (5m6)   10.00
LUBBOCK, F R-Six Decades in Texas-Austin-1900-685p-1st ed
    (4j4)   55.00
LUBBOCK, SIR JOHN-On Origin & Metamorphoses of Insects-
  Lond-1874-illus-12mo-1st ed   (5jj3, lacks flys)   15.00
--Origin of Civilisation & Primitive Condition of Man-NY-1870-
  380p-illus   (5s4, rprd, ex-libr)   6.00
LUBBOCK, PERCY, ed-Letters of Henry James-NY-1920-2 vols-
  Scribner's Sons-2nd prntng   (5ss9)   15.00
--same-NY-1920-2 vols   (5mm2)   20.00
LUBKE, WILHELM-Outlines of the History of Art-NY-1881-
  2 vols-571p-illus-ed by Cook   (5t4)   8.50
--same-1885-2 vols-ed by Cook-illus, Dodd-lea sp & tips
    (5ww4, rub, libr nbrs)   12.50
--same-NY-1911-2 vols-illus-index-ed & rev by Russell Sturgis
    (5m2, sl stnd)   17.50
LUBSCHEZ, BEN JUDAH-Manhattan, the Magical Island-NY-1927-
  4to-photos-1st ed   (5m6, dj)   8.50
LUCAS COUNTY, IA, 1881-History of-DesMoines-1881-8vo-743p-
  hf lea-illus-scarce   (5m8, hng weak)   45.00
LUCAS, DAN'L R-Paul Darst-Oskaloosa, Iowa-Central Book Concern-
  1877-206p   (5m1)   25.00
LUCAS, E V-Edwin Austin Abbey-NY-1921-Scribner's Sons-2 vols-
  illus-crown 4to   (4a0)   60.00
--Four & Twenty Toilers-NY-n.d.-(ca1900)-folio-35p-24p col illus-
  pic cov labl-FDBedford, illus-McDevitt, Wilson's   (5p1)   25.00
--Letters of Chas Lamb to which are Added Those of his Sister
  Mary Lamb-(Lond)-(1935)-Dent & Methuen-3 vols, dj   (4p1, dj)   45.00
--The Life of Chas Lamb-NY-1905-2 vols-illus   (5mm2)   10.00
--A Wanderer in Holland-NY-(1924)-illus-hf green mor-330p (5t4)6.50
LUCAS, EDW, ed-Book of Verses for Children-Grant Richards-1904-
  8vo-dec cl-col pict-350p   (5s0)   8.50
LUCAS, EDW V, ed-Forgotten Tales of Long Ago-Lond-Wells, Gardner-
  1906-425p-col frontis-plts-1st ed   (5a1, sl fox)   10.00
--Runaways & Castaways-Lond-1908-Wells, Gardner-sq8vo-dec cl-
  t.e.g.-310p-col frontis-FDBedford, illus   (5aa2)   10.00
--300 Games & Pastimes, or What Shall We Do Now?-Lond-
  Chatto&Windus-1925-354p-illus-9th ed   (5a1)   7.50
LUCAS, ELIZ-Mrs Lucas's French Cookery Book-Lond-(1929)-231p
    (5g9)   4.50
LUCAS, FRED W-Appendiculae Historicae, or Shreds of History Hung
  On A Horn-Lond-1891-216p-4to-frontis-orig dec bds-
  errata slip-scarce   (5j2, cov wn, 4e6, f)   50.00
LUCAS, HENRY STEPHEN-The Low Countries & 100 Yrs' War-
  Ann Arbor-1929-Univ of Mich-fldg map-696p   (5q0)   10.00
LUCAS, MATTIE DAVIS-A History of Grayson Co, Texas-Sherman-
  1936-209p   (5yy7, 5n4, fox, stnd, autg)   15.00
LUCE, EDW S-Keogh, Comanche & Custer-n.p.-(1939)-127p-
  photos-ltd ed, pres-v scarce   (5t3, vg, 5k4, f)   125.00
--same-bnd in brown padded Dupong fab-ltd to 25c thus
    (5k4, vf)   150.00
LUCK, MRS BRIAN-The Belgian Cook Book-NY-(1915)-151p(5g9) 5.00
LUCKENBACH, A-46 Select Scripture Narr from the Old Testament-
  NY-1838-transl into Delaware Indian-for use of Indian Youth-
  engrvngs-304p-calf-Dan'lFanshaw   (5d6)   45.00
LUCKIESH, M-Color & Its Applications-Vol 1-NY-1915-& Light &
  Shade & Their Applications-Vol 2-NY-1916-8vo (5ww3)   22.50
--Science of Seeing-NY-(1938)-charts   (5tt5, autg)   10.00
LUCKNER, COUNT-Sea Devil-GarCty-1927-illus-1st ed
    (4m3, pres, broke)   15.00
LUDLOW, FITZ HUGH-Heart of Continent-NY-1870-568p-8 plts-
  1st ed   (5yy7) 20.   (5i4, wtrstnd)   17.50
LUDLOW, HELEN, ed-10 Yrs' Work for Indians at Hampton Normal
  & Agric Inst at Hampton, 1878 to 1888-(Hampton, 1888)-8vo-
  78p-wrps   (5j5, wrps tn)   12.50
LUDLOW, JAS MEEKER-The Captain of the Zanizaries-NY-1886-
  1st ed   (5ee3)   5.00
--A King of Tyre-NY-1891-1st ed   (5mm2)   5.00
--That Angelic Woman-NY-1892-Harper-149p-1st ed (5x4)   6.00
LUDLOW, LOUIS-In Heart of Hoosierland-Wash-(1925)-329p-cl
    (5h2)   7.50
LUDLOW MFG ASSOCIATES-Jute, an Account of Its Growth &
  Manufacture-(Bost)-1928-t8vo-orig bds-priv prntd-1st ed(5m6) 7.50
LUDLOW, WM-Report of a Reconn from Carroll, Montana Terr on
  Upper Missouri to Yellowstone Natl Park & return made in
  summer of 1875-GPO-1875-40-cl-plats-2 fldg maps
    (5zz5) 27.50 (5k4, f) 20. (5t0)   25.00
--Report of a Reconn of the Black Hills of Dakota made in summer
  of 1874-Wash-1875-124p-plts-wrps-fldg map   (5n4)   9.50
--same-GPO-1875-4to-cl-maps-plts   (5k4, f)   25.00

LUGRIN, N de B-Pioneer Women of Vancouver Island, 1843 to 1866-
  Victoria-1928-312p-ports-e.p.maps-Vol 1(all publ)
    (4a8) 15.   (5dd7)   14.00
LUHAN, MABEL DODGE-Edge of Taos Desert-NY-(1937)-photos-
  1st ed   (5zz5)   20.00
--Lorenzo in Taos-Knopf-1932-illus-3rd prntg   (5kk4)   8.50
--Movers & Shakers-NY-(1936)-illus-542p-Vol 3 of Intimate
  Memories   (5t0, f, dj) 6.   (4b3)   15.00
--Winter in Taos-NY-(1935)-246p-plts-1st ed(5x5)12.50(5dd6) 17.50
LUI, GARDING-Inside Los Angeles Chinatown-(LosAng, 1948)-
  207p-maps-plts   (5dd4)   10.00
LUKAS, JAN-Shrine of Baroque Sculpture-Prague-1953-4to-plts
    (5yy6)   10.00
LUKE, MRS S-A Sequel to the Female Jesuit-NY-1853-Dodd-
  12mo-197p-cl   (5j5, sp def)   22.50
LULL, DeLOS-Father Solon, or, the Helper Helped-NY-(1888)-
  2nd ed   (5mm2)   12.50
LULL, R S-A Remarkable Ground Sloth-NewHav-1929-Mem Peabody
  Museum(Yale)-20p-9 plts-stiff wrps-4to   (4p6)   15.00
LUM, E H-Genealogy of Lum Family-(1927)-270p   (5t9)   10.00
LUMBERMAN'S HOUSE PLAN BOOK-Chig-(1907)-Radford Archit Co-
  illus-8vo-bds-215p   (5q0)   8.50
LUMHOLTZ, CARL-New Trails in Mexico-1912-397p-1st ed-illus
    (5d2, mor, f bndg) 50.(5zz5, ex-libr, 5r1, chip)   25.00
--Unknown Mexico-NY-1902-Scribner-2 vols-lg8vo-dec cl-g.t.-
  2 col fldg maps-15 col plts-v scarce (4a3) 50. (5x5)   95.00
LUMIERE ELECTRIQUE JOURNAL-Universel d'Electricite, 3rd yr-
  #27, 2 Jul 1881 to #52, 28 Sept 1881-lg4to-hf lea-427p
    (5hh7, lacks pt sp)   17.50
LUMMIS, CHAS F-The Awakening of a Nation, Mexico of Today-
  NY-1898-179p-fldg mpa-illus-1st ed (5w0, lt dmpstn, 5g6)   7.50
--same-NY-1898-(later prntng)   5m9)   4.50
--same-NY-1899-photos-179p   (5L7, spot) 5. (5zz5)   6.50
--A Bronco Pegasus-Bost-1928- ports-plts   (5r8)   8.50
--Flowers of Our Lost Romance-Bost&NY-1929-illus-pict cl (5m9) 6.50
--Gen'l Crook & the Apache Wars-Fiske, ed-Flagstaff-1966-
  special ed-ltd to 250c, autg, box   (5g2, mint)   15.00
--The Land of Poco Tiempo-1893-Scribner's-8vo-3/4 lea-illus-
  1st ed   (5h4)   12.50
--same-NY-1902-310p-illus   (5s4)   8.00
--same-1913   (5s4)   7.00
--same-NY-1925-310p-illus   (5t2)   5.00
--The Man Who Married the Moon & Other Pueblo Indian folk
  stories-NY-1894-Century-12mo-239p-illus-pic cl (5p1, soil)   7.50
--Mesa, Canon & Pueblo-Century-(1925)-517p-1st ed-photos
    (5r1, ex-libr) 12.50 (5a0, ink)   13.50
--A New Mexico David-NY-1891-12mo-cl-1st ed   (5h5)   6.00
--Some Strange Corners of Our Country-NY-1892-1st ed-illus-
  270p-37 plts   (5r8) 9.50   (4n8, 5x5)   7.50
--The Spanish Pioneers-1893-292p-illus-1st ed (5r1, vg)   25.00
--same-Chig-1918-photos-7th ed-292p   (5yy7)   4.00
--A Tramp Across the Continent-NY-1913-12mo   (5r8)   9.50
--The Works of Chas F Lummis-LosAng-1928-Lummis Foundation
    (5d6)   3.00
LUMNER, G LYNN-Abraham Lincoln-NY&Lond-(1922)-31p-port
    (5t7)   3.50
LUMPKIN, K D-The Making of a Southerner-NY-(1946)-Knopf-
  248p   (5p7)   3.75
--The South in Progress-NY-1940   (5x2)   5.00
LUMSDEN, JAS-Through Canada in Harvest Time-Lond-1903-
  map & illus   (5w8)   7.50
LUNAN, JOHN-Hortus Jamaicensis-Jamaica-1814-orig cl-4to-
  2 vols-poor papr   (4d2, fox, fade)   100.00
LUNCEFORD, A M, JR-Early Records of Taliaferro Co, Georgia-
  1956-127p   (5t9)   7.50
LUNCHEON RECIPES-Lutheran Women's Welfare League-Minn-
  1940-73p-mimeo-wrps-tied   (5c4)   3.00
LUNDBERG, FERDINAND-America's 60 Families-NY-(1937)-
  544p   (5p9) 5.   (4b3)   10.00
--same-NY-(1946)-Citadel-578p-8vo   (5j5)   7.50
--Imperial Hearts, a social biography-NY-(1936)-406p (5dd6) 10.50
LUNDBORG, EINAR-The Arctic Rescue, How the Nobile was Saved-
  NY-1929-illus-221p   (4e6)   12.00
LUNDY, BENJ-Life, Travels & Opinions of-Phila-1847-Thos Earle, ed-
  lea sp   (5a8, lacks map)   50.00
L'UNIVERS EN MINIATURE-ou les Voyages du Petit Andre sans
  Sortir de sa Chambre, Amerique-Paris-1839-16mo-8 hand col plts-
  illus bds   (5v0)   20.00
LUNKENHEIMER CO-Illus Catalog & Price List-Cinn-1908-565p-
  cl   (5h1)   10.00
LUNN, A-Saint in the Slave Trade, Peter Claver-Lond-1947-
  12mo   (5x2)   10.00
LUNN, ARNOLD-John Wesley-NY-1929-371p-port   (5t7)   5.00

LUOMALA, KATHARINE Maui of a Thousand Tricks-Honolulu-1949-
(Bishop Mus Bull 198)-sm4to-300p-wrps   (5F5,underline)   8.00
--Navaho Life of Yesterday & Today-Berkeley-1938-Western Mus-
115p-plts-maps-wrps   (4k4,f,5g5)   15.00
LUQUIENS, F B-Spanish Amer Literature in Yale Univ Library-
NewHav-1939-335p   (5yy1)   17.50
LURCAT, JEAN-Designing Tapestry-Lond-1950-61p-53 plts
(5a9,5F9)   5.00
LUSKA, SIDNEY-As It Was Written-NY-(1885)-12mo-cl-
1st ed of auth's 1st book-1st issue, without adv on pg (255)
(5gg6,f)   20.00
--Grandison Mather-NY-(1889)-1st ed   (5r9)   12.50
LUSTGARTEN, EDGAR-Verdict in Dispute-NY-1950-253p-bds
(5t2)   4.00
LUSTIG, LILLIE S-Southern Cook Book-n.p.-Culinary Arts Pr-48p-
wrps-(c1938)   (5g9)   2.00
LUTES, DELLA T-The Country Kitchen-Bost-1936-264p   (4g9)   5.00
--same-1955   (4g9)   4.50
--Country Schoolma'am-LB-1941-328p-1st ed   (5e8)   5.00
--Home Grown-Bost-1937-272p-1st ed   (4g9)   7.50
--Millbrook-LB-1938-330p   (5e8)   4.50
--Table Setting & Service for Mistress & Maid   (5c9)   3.50
LUTHER, FRANK-Americans & Their Songs-NY-1942-Harper-
323p   (5p7)   4.50
LUTHER, MARTIN, ed-Book of Vagabonds & Beggars wi Vocabulary
of their Language-Lond-1860-Chiswick Pr-64p-Hotten, tr-
sm4to-lea bk   (5ff6, lea dmgd)   45.00
LUTHER STANDING BEAR-My People the Sioux-(1928)-
HoughtonMiff   (5x5,pres)   20.00
LUTHER, TAL-High Spots of Custer & Battle of Little Big Horn
Literature-KansCty,Mo-1967-36p-frontis-1st ed-ltd to 250c,
autg   (5t3)   10.00
LUTHER'S-Smaller & Larger Catechisms wi Hist Intro to which are
added Hymns & Prayers-Newmarket,(Va)-1852-transl from
German   (5h6, fox)   4.00
LUTHERANER, DER-Sept, 1847 to Aug, 1850, Vol 4,#1 to Vol 6,
#26-72 issues bnd in 1 vol-StL-tall German text-8p ea issue-
rare   (5t3, lacks 1 nbr)   50.00
LUTHERISCHE KALENDER 1881-Allentn-(1880)-47(1)p-self wrps
(5h7)   2.50
LUTHIN, REINHARD H-The Real Abraham Lincoln-Englewood Cliffs-
(1960)-778p   (5t7,dj)   8.50
LUTTIG, JOHN C-Journal of a Fur Trading Exped on Upper Missouri,
1812,1813-StL-1920-SMDrumm,ed-8vo-cl & Bds-map-illus-
g.t.-ltd to 365c   (5a3)   50.00
LUTZ, FRANK E-Field Book of Insects-NY-1918-Putnam-509p-
illus   (5p7)   3.50
--A Lot of Insects-NY-(1941)-Putnam-304p-illus   (5p7)   6.00
LUTZ, H-Lord Grey & the World War-1928   (5L7)   6.50
LYALL, SIR A-Life of Marquis of Dufferin & Ava-Lond-1905-Nelson-
579p-frontis   (5dd7)   4.00
LYALL, A C-The Relation of Witchcraft to Religion-NY-1873-
sm12mo-32p plus ads   (5x7, lacks wrps)   3.00
LYALL, DAVID C-Catalogue of Pictures-NY-1903-(Amer Art Assn)-
105 plts-ltd to 500c-vel   (5ii3)   20.00
LYALL, EDNA-Knight errant-Lond-1887-3 vols-Hurst&Blackett-
8vo-orig scarlet cl-1st ed   (5xx6, lf tn, lend libr lbl)   27.50
LYBECK, OTTO, ed-Nordens Batar-Stockholm-1939 to 1941-3 vols-
small folio-dec canvas cov-339p-illus   (5ss2, mint)   27.50
LYCOMING RUBBER CO-Catalogue & Price List 1899 to 1900,
Rubber Boots & Shoes—Williamsport-1899-sm8vo-fldg bds-55p
(5hh7)   5.75
LYDEKKER, JOHN W-The Faithful Mohawks-1938-Cambr Univ Pr
(5x5)   12.50
LYDEKKER, R-The Game Animals of Africa-Lond-1926-483p-illus-
2nd ed-scarce   (4a6) 20. (5ss8)   13.50
LYDEKKER, RICHARD, ed-Library of Natural History-Akron, Ohio-
1904-Saalfield-6 vols-72 col plts   (5x0) post extra   20.00
LYDEKKER, R-Reptiles, Amphibia, Fishes & Lower Chordata-Lond-
1912-510p-8vo-36 plts(4 col)-fldg map-cl-scarce   (4p5)   20.00
LYDENBERG, HARRY M-Crossing the Line-NY-1957-illus (5ii3)   7.50
LYELL, CHAS-Geological Evidences of Antiquity of Man-Phila-
1863-2nd Amer Ed-wdcuts   (5h6) 12.   (4b7)   12.50
--Guide to Niagara Falls-1868-62p-illus-cl   (5ff2)   8.50
--Principles of Geology-Lond-1830,32,33-Murray-3 vols-8vo-
calf-7 plts-4 maps-labls-1st ed   (4h0,f,rprd)   550.00
--same-1837-illus-1st Amer ed-2 vols   (5L7,ex-libr,wn)   25.00
--Second Visit to the US of NoAmer-1849-2 vols-hf mor
(5L7, ex lend libr)   25.00
--same-NY-1868-Harper-2 vols   (5u3)   7.00
--Travels in NoAmer-NY-1845-2 vols in 1-7 plts (incl fldg frontis)-
(4m3,vg)   32.50
--same-Lond-1855-2nd ed-7 illus & maps   (4e9)   40.00

LYELL, D D-Nyasaland for the Hunter & Settler-Lond-1912-8vo-
103p-advs-photos-maps   (4a6)   7.50
LYFORD, C P-Mormon Problem-NY-1886-323p-cl   (5y0)   15.00
LYFORD, CARRIE A-The Crafts of the Objiwa-Phoenix Indian School-
1943-Ind Handcraft Ser #5-145plts-illus wrps (5m9) 6. (4k4,f)   7.50
--Iroquois Crafts-(Lawrence, Kans, 1945)-wrps   (4k4,f)   6.50
--Ojibwa Crafts (Chippewa)-(Lawrence,Kans)-n.d.-216p-photos-
cl   (5t3,rbnd)   6.50
--Quill & Beadwork of the Western Sioux-Lawrence,Kans-1940-
116p-photos-map-orig cl-scarce   (5t3)   10.00
--same-Ofc of Indian Affairs-n.d.-cl-illus   (4k4,f)   12.50
LYFORD, J O, ed-History of Concord, N Hamp from 1725-(1903)-
illus-2 vols   (5t9)   12.50
LYLE, EUGENE P, JR-Don Swashbuckler-Lond&NY-(1898)-Neely-
1st ed   (5m2)   8.50
LYLE, W W-Lights & Shadows of Army Life-Cinn-1865-2nd ed-
403p-cl   (5ff7)   20.00
LYMAN, ALBERT-Journal of Voyage to California etc-Hartford-
1852-ET Pease-192p-orig wrps   (5tt0)   175.00
LYMAN, CHESTER S-Around the Horn to the Sandwich Islands &
Calif, 1845 to 1850-NewHav-1924-328p
(5h5) 17.50   (5p9) 15.   (5s2,f,dj)   20.00
LYMAN, GEO D-John Marsh, Pioneer-NY-1930-1st ed-illus
(5jj1) 12.   (4m2,5i3)   12.50
--same-NY-1931-illus-394p   (4b3)   10.00
--same-NY-1934-394p   (4a5) 4.50   (5L3) 8.50   (5yy6)   7.50
--Ralston's Ring-NY-1937-368p-1st ed-illus
(4n1,dj) 8.50   (5x5,dj) 12.50   (5k4,f,dj,4m2)   7.50
--same-Scribner-1944-photos-8vo   (5F5,dj)   10.00
--same-NY-1945-illus-368p   (4b3)   10.00
--Saga of Comstock Lode-NY-1934-frontis-illus-407p
(5s4,autg) 15.   (5ee3,f,dj,5L3) 12.50 (5a9,5i3,f,dj,5x5)   10.00
--same-NY-1941-illus   (4m2,dj)   6.00
--The Sponge-NY-1928-4to-illus-wrps-reprntd   (5m9)   7.50
LYMAN GUNSIGHT CORP-Ammunition Reloading Handbook-
41st ed-8vo-172p plus-wrps-spiral bnd   (4a6)   6.00
LYMAN GUN SIGHT CORP-Catalogue #25-Middlefield,Conn-
1937-64p plus inserts-illus   (5b9,vf)   5.00
LYMAN, HENRY M-Hawaiian Yesterdays-Chig-1906-281p-illus
(5q0, libr labls)   10.00
LYMAN, JOS-A Sermon, Preached Before His Excellency James
Bowdoin, May 30, 1787-Bost-n.d.-(1787)-61p-disbnd (4h2)   15.00
LYMAN, OLIN L-Commodore Oliver Hazard Perry & War of the
Lakes-NY-1905-246p-1st ed   (5ee3)   6.00
LYMAN, P W-History of Easthampton, Mass-1866-194p (5mm3)   10.00
LYMAN, THEODORE-Meade's Headquarters 1863 to 1865-Bost-
1922-Atlantic Mo Pr-371p-illus-bds & cl   (5mm8)   7.50
--Papers Relating to the Garrison Mob-Cambr-1870-73p-wrps-
"College duplicate" stmpd on front wrp
(5x5, libr dupl) 12.50   (5ss5)   7.50
LYMAN, WM D-Columbia River-NY-1909-plts-fldg maps-409p
(5tt9)   15.00
--same-NY-1917-3rd ed-rev & enlrgd-plts-maps-418p   (5s0)   15.00
LYMINGTON, LORD-Spring Song of Iscariot-Paris-1929-8vo-wrps-
125c on Van Gelder papr of an ed of 175c-Black Sun Press
(5d1)   25.00
LYNAM, C C-Log of Blue Dragon-Lond-1907-299p-illus
(5s1, rprd)   4.50
LYNCH, MRS A T-Remin of Adams, Jay & Randolph Counties,(Ind)-
n.p.-n.d.-(FtWayne, ca 1896)-352p-cl   (5y0, rub)   22.50
LYNCH, ANNE C-The Rhode Island Book-Prov-1841-352p-illus
(5t7)   15.00
LYNCH, ALICE CLARE-The Kennedy Clan & Tierra Redonda-
(SanFran, 1935)-12mo-cl-264p-illus   (5h5,autg)   12.50
LYNCH, BOHUN-The Prize Ring-Lond-1925-4to-plts-vel bk-
ltd to 750c-scarce   (4j3,sl rub)   57.50
LYNCH, D T-"Boss Tweed"-NY-1927-illus   (5yy6)   5.00
LYNCH, JAS-With Stevenson to California-Oakland-(1954)-
62p-col fldg map-Calif Rel #36-500c prntd   (5dd6)   10.00
LYNCH, KATHLEEN M-Social Mode of Restoration Comedy-NY-
1926-242p-8vo-cl   (5t0)   5.00
LYNCH, L G-The Formation of the Negro-NY-1963 (5x2,dj)   10.00
LYNCH, LAWRENCE-Mountain Mystery, Outlaws of Rockies-
Chig-1887-600p-illus   (5s4,wn)   7.50
LYNCH, PATRICK-Guinness's Brewery in The Irish Economy 1759 to
1876-Cambr-1960-278p-10 plts-fldg tabl   (5w1)   12.50
LYNCH, R IRWIN-The Book of the Iris-Lond-1904-214p-photos
(5s7)   6.00
LYNCH, V E-Thrilling Adven, Guiding, Trapping, Big Game Hunting-
(Portl-1928)-174p-cl-priv prntd   (5h2)   10.00
LYNCH, COM W F-Narr of US Exped to River Jordan & Dead Sea-
Phila-1849-2 maps-28 illus-R8vo-dec cl-1st ed   (5p5)   15.00
--same-Phila-1858-332p-12mo-dbl pg map-condensed ed (5t0)   3.75

LYNCH, WM O-50 Yrs of Party Warfare, 1789 to 1837-1931-
 BobbsMerrill-1st ed   (5x5,dj)   10.00
LYNCHINGS & WHAT THEY MEAN-Atlanta-1931-Southern
 Comm on study of Lynching-76p-wrps-bds   (5x2)   25.00
LYND, ROBT-Rambles in Ireland-Lond-1912-Mills&Boon-25 photos-
 5 col illus-cl-1st ed   (5ss3,fade)   35.00
LYND, ROBT S-Middletown, a Study in Contemp Amer Culture-
 NY-1929-HBrace-550p   (5p7) 6.   (5w0)   7.50
--Middletown in transition-NY-1937-Harcourt, Brace-604p (5u3) 5.00
LYNDE, BENJ-Diaries of...& Benj Lynde, Jr, wi appendix-Bost-
 1880-8vo-priv prntd   (5m6)   17.50
LYNDE, FRANCIS-The Donovan Chance-NY-1921-1st ed (5ee3,f) 5.00
--A romance in transit-NY-1897-Scribner-1st ed-Ivory Ser
                            (5m2,sl stn)   10.00
--The Wreckers-NY-1920-1st ed-frontis   (5ee3,f)   5.00
LYNDOE, EDW-Everybody's Book of Fate & Fortune-NY-1938-
 576p-imit lea   (5w0)   6.50
LYNE, MONCURE-From Alamo to San Jacinto-NY-1904-320p-
 illus   (4a5)   10.00
LYNES, RUSSELL-The Domesticated Americans-NY-(1957)-4to-
 308p-illus   (5w7)   6.50
--The Tastemakers-NY-(1954)-362p,(1)-illus (5p0) 5. (5w7)   6.95
LYNN, ERNEST-The Blazing Horison-Chig-(1929)   (5k4)   5.00
LYNN, ETHEL-Gen'l Frankie, A Story for Little Folks-NY-1863-
 1st ed   (5mm2)   7.50
LYNN, FRANK-Blue Coats & Grey, a Tale of the Rebellion-
 Binghamton-1877-RE Ely, Publ-24mo-wrps
               (5b2, lf misbnd, sp sl wn)   40.00
LYNN, J & CO-Latest Catalogue & New Guide to Rapid Wealth-
 NY-1895-240 engrvs   (5t4)   7.50
LYNN, WM-Serious Consideration on Election of President-NY-
 1800-36p-disbnd   (5tt8)   15.00
LYNNHURST CONGREG CHURCH-Cook Book of Tested Recipes-
 Minn-1913-179p-(17 ads)- & ads   (4g9,soil)   7.50
--same-Minn-1920-215p-ads   (5c4)   4.00
LYNWOOD-Lynwood on Long Beach Blvd-LosAng-(before 1920)-
 22p-wrps-HTCoffin, JFBailliet, Owners   (5d6)   15.00
LYON, G F-Brief Narr of Unsuccessful Attempt to Reach Repulse Bay-
 Lond-1825-part lea-198,(1)-plts-fldg map (5aa9)   25.00
LYON, GEO F-Narr of Travels in Northern Africa in Years 1818,
 1819 & 20-Lond-1821-lg4to-383p-fldg map-15(of 17)-col plts-
 bds-cl sp   (5q1,rbkd,box)   100.00
LYON, HARRIS MERTON-Sardonics-NY-(1908) (5r9,pres)   15.00
LYON, I W-Colonial Furniture of New England-1924-113 plts-
 new ed   (5L7)   30.00
LYON, L B, comp-Glimpse of a Marvelous City-Watertown, SoDak-
 (Watertown-1889)-illus-maps-obl 8vo-(75p) (5q0)   12.50
LYON MFG CO-Lightning Rods, Otis' Patent-NY-1854-12mo-33p-
 orig wrps   (5ss5)   6.50
LYON, MARGUERITE-Hurrah for Arkansas-Indnpls-(1947)-1st ed-
 illus   (4a1)   7.50
LYON, WM H-The People's Problem & Its Solution-SiouxFalls-
 (1886)-1st ed-166p-v scarce   (5L5)   35.00
LYON CAEN, C-Traite de Droit Commercial-Paris-1906 to 7-
 4 vols in 5   (5r4)   22.50
LYONS, A B-Lyon Memorial, Massachusetts Families-1905-491p-
 Vol 1 only   (5t9)   10.00
LYONS, B J-Thrills & Spills of a Cowboy Rancher-(1959)-Vantage Pr-
 1st ed   (5k4,dj,mint)   6.00
LYONS, DIANE-How to Cook for a Wolf-n.p.-(1951)-28p-wrps
                                     (5c0)   3.00
LYONS, EUGENE-Our Unknown Ex President, port of Herbert Hoover-
 GarCty-1948-337p   (5ss1)   5.00
LYONS, LORENZO-Na Haawina Kamalii-Honolulu-1838-12mo-
 152p-43 wdcuts-cl bk bds   (4h0)   400.00
LYRE, P INCHBECK-Poems-Lond-1931-Duckworth-bds-1st ed(5ss3) 15.00
LYRIC WORKS OF HORACE, THE-Original Poems-Phila-1786-
 Oswald-8vo-frontis-orig wrps-1st ed-18 pgs of subscribers'
 names & 6p of addenda   (5n2,vg,sl chip)   1,500.00
LYSANDER, JAS C-Annals of the Corporation, relative to late
 contested elections-NY-1802-stitchd-88p
            (5g4,unopnd,lacks postscript)   15.00
LYTERIA-a Dramatic Poem-Bost-1854-12mo-cl-(Josiah P Quincy)-
 1st ed of Quincy's 1st book   (5gg6)   10.00
LYTLE, HORACE-How to Train your Bird Dog-Dayton-1944-224p-
 illus   (5t7)   5.50
LYTTON, EDW GEO BULWER-The New Timon, a Romance of London-
 Lond-1846-200p-part mor-1st ed   (4b4,scuf,ex-libr)   22.50
LYTTON, EDW BULWER-Novels of-Bost-1891-32 vols-illus-col frontis-
 Estes&Lauriat-3/4 mor-raised bands-inlay work-ed deluxe-
 ltd to 1000sets, nbrd   (5p6,mint, f bndg)   400.00
LYTTON, EDW BULWER-The Works of-Lond-n.d.-26 vols-cl-
 GeoRoutledge   (5p9)   40.00

MAASS, JOHN-The Gingerbread Age-NY-(1957)-4to-illus-cl-
 212p   (5j5,dj)   5.00
MABBOTT, THOS O-A Childs Reminiscence, collected by-1930-
 Univ of Wash-4to-orig cl bk bds-1st ed-ltd to 430c, nbrd
                                  (5ss9,vg)   25.00
MABEL LEA-A novel-NY-1872-Appleton-8vo-orig cl-frontis-
 1st ed-3 plts   (5i9,rub)   12.50
MABERLY, J-The Print Collector-NY-1880-illus-336p   (5q0)   15.00
MABIE, HAMILTON WRIGHT-A Child of Nature-NY-1901-illus-
 127p   (5t7)   6.00
--Norse Stories Retold from the Eddas-Bost-1882-12mo-cl-1st ed
 of auth's 1st book   (5gg6,pres)   15.00
--Old English Love Songs-NY-n.d.-8vo-illus by Edwards (5p5)   7.50
--William Shakespeare Poet, Dramatist & Man-NY-1900-8vo-
 421p-illus-suede(g.t.)   (5t7,dj)   10.00
MABON, MARY FROST-ABC of America's Wines-NY-1942-233p-
 fldg map-1st ed   (4g9)   5.00
--A Meal in Itself, Book of Soups-NY-(1944)-168p (5c0,5c9)   3.50
MABY, J CECIL-The Physics of the Divining Rod-Lond-1939-plts-
 468p-1st ed   (5dd4)   19.50
McADAM, DAVID, ed, & Others-History of the Bench & Bar of NY-
 NY-1897, 1899-2 vols-8vo-ports-mor   (5ss5,sl rub)   25.00
McADAM, ROGER W-"COMMONWEALTH", Giantess of the Sound-
 NY-1959-120 illus   (5c1)   7.50
--The Old Fall River Line-Brattleboro-Stephen Daye Pr-1937-
 190p-illus   (5p7)   4.50
McADOO, ELEANOR WILSON-The Woodrow Wilsons-NY-1937-
 Macm-301p   (5ee3) 3.   (5p0)   5.00
McAFEE, ROBT B-History of Late War in Western Country-Lexington-
 1816-Worsley&Smith-8vo-calf-wi final leaf of apology to
 Winchester   (5i4, fox)   135.00
--same-BowlingGrn-(1919)-591p-cl-reprnt of 1816 ed
                      (5y0) 12.50 (5jj7,f)   17.50
McALEER, GEO-Origin & Significance of Surname McAleer-1909-
 103p   (5mm3)   8.50
McALLISTER, ANNA-Ellen Ewing Wife of Gen Sherman-NY-1936-
 379p-cl   (5h1)   7.50
McALLISTER & BROS-Catalogue-prices & illus-scientific & math
 instruments, etc-Phila-1855-84p-3rd ed   (5yy0)   24.50
McALLISTER, WARD-Society As I Have Found It-NY-(1890)-12mo-
 frontis-orig prntd wrps   (5t2,5p0)   5.00
--same-NY-(1890)-4to-Deluxe ed-469p-ltd to 400c, autg (5w7) 18.50
McALMON, ROBT-A Companion Volume-(Paris, 1923, Contact Publ
 Co)-8vo-orig gray wrps-266p-1st ed (5d9,unopnd)   95.00
--Portrait of a Generation-Paris-(1926)   -covrd wrps-1st ed-
 Contact Editions   (5ss7,unopnd,sl soil)   55.00
--Post-Adolescence-n.p.-(Dijon)-n.d.   -covrd wrps-1st ed-
 Contact Publ Co-orig tissue sleeve as issued
                        (5ss7,unopnd, mint)   85.00
McANDREW, M J-History of Hawley, Pa-n.p.-1927-illus-orig wrps-
 187p   (4m2)   10.00
MACARIA-or, altars of sacrifice-by author of "Beulah"-Richmond-
 1865-orig prntd wrps-2nd ed   (5g3)   50.00
McARTHUR, ALEX-Our Winter Birds-Winnipeg-1887-No. 28 of
 Hist & Sci Soc of Manitoba-12p-prntd wrps (5w8)   12.50
MacARTHUR, BURKE-Rivers into Wilderness-NY-1935-295p-1st ed
                                 (5s4,dj,vg)   6.00
--United Littles-NY-1955-127p   (5n7)   4.50
MacARTHUR, JOHN R-Ancient Greece in Modern America-Caldwell-
 1943-illus   (4a1, lt underscoring)   15.00
MacARTHUR, LEWIS-Oregon Geographic Names-Portland, O-1928-
 -illus-maps-charts   (5s4,autg)   15.00
--Oregon Place Names-Portland-1944-R8vo-120p-1st ed (5dd9) 10.50
McARTHUR, PETER-In Pastures Green-(Tor, 1948)-   (5w8)   6.00
--The Last Law Brotherhood-Tor-(c1921)-Allen (5nn8)   10.00
MacARTHUR, WILSON-Traders North-NY-1952-240p-illus-
 1st Amer ed   (5ss1)   4.00
MACARTNEY, CLARENCE E-Highways & Byways of the Civil War-
 Phila-(1926)-1st ed-illus   (5yy6) 6. (5j6,autg)   8.50
--Mr. Lincoln's Admirals-NY-1956-illus (5dd6) 7.50 (5c1)   8.50
MACASKILL, JOS R-Indians Around Lake Superior-Albany-1804-
 316p-map-cl-v rare   (5kk3,v wn, tn)   120.00
MACASKILL, W R-Out of Halifax-NY-1937-Derrydale Pr-photos-
 ltd to 450c   (4b9,sl wn)   35.00
MACAULAY'S DIALOGUES FOR LITTLE FOLKS-NY-1876-DeWitt-
 192p,(6) (ads)-16mo-cl bkd pict bds (5p1,edges wn)   6.00
MACAULAY, LORD-Miscellaneous Works-NY-(ca 1900)-
 Lady Trevelyan, ed-5 vols   (5q0)   20.00
MACAULAY, LORD-Miscellanies-Bost-2 vols-HM-(1900) (5x0)   10.00
MACAULAY, R H H-Trading Into Hudson's Bay-Winnipeg-1934-
 folio-108p   (5dd7, cov stn)   11.00
MACAULAY, T B-Essays, Critical & Misc-NY-1873-744p-orig calf-
 New & Rev ed   (4b4)   12.50

MACAULAY, T B-Works-Longman's Trevelyan Edition-8 vols-
Lond-1879-3/4 calf-calf onlays   (5d2, f bndg)   100.00

MACAULAY, THOS B-Lays of Ancient Rome-Lond-1842-1st ed
(5ss9, box, autg)   85.00

MACAULAY, THOS BARINGTON-Critical, Historical & Miscel
Essays & Poems-Bost-n.d.-3 vols-hf mor   (5w9)   10.00

--History of England from Accession of James II-Bost-n.d.-5 vols-
hf mor-illus   (5w9)   20.00

--Pompeii, a Poem-(Cambr, 1819)-8vo-mor-g.-g.e.-1st ed of
auth's 1st book   (5gg6, f bndg)   75.00

McAULEY, JEREMIAH-Transformed, or, the History of a River Theif-
n.p.-1876-cl   (5j6, vf)   20.00

McAULEY, THOS-Narr of revival of religion within bounds of
Presbytery of Albany in year 1820-Schenectady(NY)-1821-
Isaac Riggs, prntr-8vo-disbnd-1st ed-v scarce   (5i0)   22.50

McBETH, KATE C-Nez Perces since Lewis & Clark-NY-1908-
photos-272p   (5jj1) 15. (5yy7)   17.50

MacBETH, R G-Making of Canadian West, Being Remin of an Eye
Witness-Tor-1905-2nd ed-279p-illus   (4b9)   15.00

--Policing the Plains-Lond-1921-1st ed-illus-Russell-frontis-320p
(5i3, vg, 5L2, wn) 12.50 (5L2, vg)   17.50

--same-NY-n.d.-illus-320p   (5ss1)   6.50

--Romance of Canadian Pacific Rail Way-Tor-1924-263p-illus
(4b9, f) 8. (5dd7, autg, 5w8)   6.00

--The Romance of Western Canada-Tor-1918-illus   (5r7)   12.50

--same-Tor-1920-2nd ed   (4b9, cov spot) 5. (5t2, pres)   7.50

McBIRNEY, NETTIE-Aunt Chick's Pies-Tulsa-1941-39p-wrps-
illus   (5g9)   3.00

McBRIDE, HERBERT W-A Rifleman Went to War-Marines, NoCar-
(1935)-8vo-398p-port   (4a6)   12.50

McBRIDE, MARY MARGARET-Harvest of Amer Cooking-NY-(1957)-
453p-illus   (5c0, 4g9, mint)   7.50

M'BRIDE, R E-In the Ranks-Cincinn-1881-16mo-246p-buck
(4a7, rbnd)   12.00

McBRIDE, ROBT M-A Treasury of Antiques-NY-(1946)-4to-160p-
illus   (5t4)   10.00

MacBRIDE, THOS H-In Cabins and Sodhouses-IowaCty-1928-8vo-
368p-cl   (5m8) 10. (5a9)   16.50

McBRYDE, FELIX-Cultural & Hist Geogr of SW Guatemala-GPO-
(1945)-Smithsonian-47 plts-25 maps-wrps   (4k4, f)   15.00

McCABE, CHAS R-Damned Old Crank-1951-Harper-1st ed (5ww4) 5.00

McCABE, JAS D-Centennial History of the US-Phila-ca1875-
pt lea-925p-raised bands-illus   (5h9)   7.50

--Great Fortunes-Phila-1871-g.e.-illus-633p-deluxe ed-lea (5s4)10.00

--Illus History of the Centennial Exhibition-Phila-(1876)-illus-
874p   (5q0, 5jj9) 10. (5kk8, lea, rub)   15.00

--New York by Sunlight & Gaslight-Phila-1882-672p-cl-illus(5jj9) 10.00

MacCAFFREY, J-History of the Catholic Church from Renaissance to
French Revolution-1915-2 vols   (5L7, rbnd)   25.00

McCALEB, WALTER FLAVIUS-Aaron Burr Conspiracy-NY-1936
318p-cl   (5tt8) 25. (4a9, dj) 17.50 (5dd4)   22.50

--Brotherhood of Railroad Trainmen-NY-(1936)-Boni-12mo-
cl   (5h4, dj, f)   7.50

--Conquest of the West-NY-1947-336p-1st ed (5s4) 6. (4a5)   9.50

--Spanish Missions of Texas-SanAntonio-(1954)-1st ed-photos-
scarce   (5zz5)   12.50

McCALL, GEO A-Colonel McCall's Reports in Relation to NewMex-
Wash-1851-SED 26-23p   (5n4)   15.00

McCALL, JAS-French & Engl Systems of Cutting, Fitting & Basting
Ladies Garments-Wash-1882-1st ser-96p-4to   (5n7, fox)   12.50

McCALL, PEARL D-Holland Jackson Record wi related Hoyle
Swofford Hist-1959-333p   (5mm3)   20.00

McCALL, SAM'L W-Thaddeus Stevens-Bost-1899-hf mor-369p-
t.e.g.-raised bands-1st ed   (5w0)   7.50

--Thos B. Reed-Bost-1914-303p-illus-t.e.g. (5p7) 3.50 (5w9)   4.00

McCALLIE, S W-Prelim Report on the Roads and Road Building
Materials of Georgia-1901-lg8vo-259p   (5h6)   6.00

McCALLUM, JOHN-6 Roads from Abilene-Seattle-1960-132p
(5s4, 2 autgs, f)   8.00

McCALLUM, THOMSON MURRAY-Adrift in the South Seas-LosAng-
1934-Wetzel Pub-324p   (5x9, pres)   6.00

McCAMPBELL, COLEMAN-Saga of a Frontier Seaport-Dallas-1934-
(4a5, f, pres) 30. (5a8)   20.00

McCANDLESS, B-Flags of the World-Wash-1917-1197 col flags-
Natl Geog   (5c1)   20.00

McCANN, E A, ed-The Shipmodeler-Official Journal of Ship
Model Makers Club-Brooklyn-1929 to 1933-5 vols-8vo-illus-
3/4 calf-Vols 1 thru 5   (5ss2, 2 ads tn out)   35.00

McCANN, E ARMITAGE-Ship Model Making-NY-1926-8vo-cl-
129p-illus & plans in pkt in rear   (5t0)   5.00

McCANN, FRANKLIN T-English Discovery of Amer to 1585-NY-
1952-246p-indexed   (5t1)   25.00

McCANN, CAPT IRVING GOFF-With the Nat'l Guard on the
Border-StL-1917-12mo-cl-271p-scarce   (5h5, vg)   17.50

McCARTER, MARGARET HILL-Winning the Wilderness-Chig-
1914-McClurg-1st ed-illus   (5ee3, f)   5.00

McCARTHY, CARLTON-Detailed Minutiae of Soldier Life in Army
of Northern Virg-Richmond-1882-224p-illus   (5mm8)   12.50

McCARTHY, CHAS H-Lincoln's Plan of Reconstruction-NY-1901-
531p-hf lea-1st ed   (5ee3)   47.50

McCARTHY, E T-Incidents in Life of a Mining Engineer & Further
Incidents-Lond-(1918)-2 vols-port   (5dd0)   12.50

McCARTHY, FREDK D-Australian Aboriginal Decorative Art-
Sydney-1938-Australian Mus-48p-4to-wrps-33 illus (5m5)   15.00

McCARTHY, J R, ed-California Series-SanFran-1929-Powell Pub-
9 vols   (4n1)   75.00

McCARTHY, JAS REMINGTON-The New Pioneers-Indnpls-(1934)-
1st ed   (4a1, pres, hng split)   12.50

--Rings Through the Ages-NY-1945-202p-illus   (5t7)   8.00

McCARTHY, SEN JOS-Treason in Wash-(StL, Christian Nat'l
Crusade, 1950)-12mo-128p-orig wrps   (5m6)   10.00

McCARTHY, JUSTIN-Story of Gladstone's Life-NY-1898-illus-
516p-2nd ed-rev & enlgd   (5q0)   10.00

--Violets-Lond-1881-16mo-vel-g.e.-1st ed of auth's first book
(5gg6, pres)   25.00

McCARTHY, MARGUERITE G-Aunt Ella's Cook Book-Bost-1949-
205p-1st ed   (5c9)   3.00

--The Cook is in the Parlor-Bost-(1947) (5c0, 5c9)   3.50

--The Queen is in the Kitchen-NY-(1954)-231p (5c9)   4.00

McCARTY, DWIGHT G-History of Palo Alto Co, Iowa-Cedar Rapids-
1910-photos-map-168p-cl   (5zz5, autg, sl fleck)   17.50

McCARTY, DWIGHT G-The Territorial Governors of the Old
Northwest-IowaCty-1910-210p   (5t7)   8.50

McCARTY, JOHN L-Adobe Walls Bride-SanAnt-1956-281p-illus-
8vo-cl   (5g5, dj) 5.75 (5dd5)   7.25

--Maverick Town-Norman-1946 (5dd6) 10.50 (5h0, dj)   12.50

McCARTY, RICHARD J-Work & Play-(1925)-priv prntd-253p-
photos-v scarce   (5zz5)   15.00

McCARTY'S AMER PRIMER-Phila-McCarty & Davis-(1828)-16mo-
36p-illus wrps-10p of A, B, C's-wdcuts by Gilbert (5v0, f)   25.00

MacCAZMROIL, SEASAN-Calendar of the Saints-Dublin-1907-
Maunsel & Co-12 engrvs-obl bds-1st ed   (5ss3, stn)   25.00

McCLANE, A J-The Wise Fishermen's Encyclopedia-NY-1953-
1336p-illus   (5t7)   8.00

MacCLAY, EDGAR S-Hist US Navy-NY-1897-2 vols-illus-g.t.-
maps-lea cor-bkstrp   (5s1)   12.50

--Reminiscences of Old Navy from Journals etc-NY&Lond-1898-
362p-cl-ltd to 750c   (5jj9)   10.00

MACLAY, WM-Journal of-NY-1927-429p   (4m2)   12.50

McCLELLAN, ELISABETH-Historic Dress 1607 to 1800-Lond-1906-
lg4to-cl-385 illus-407p-1st ed   (5t0)   25.00

--Historic Dress in Amer, 1607 to 1800-Phila-(1904)-lg4to-
illus-407p-hf lea-raised bands   (4m2)   35.00

--History of Amer Costume-NY-1937-4to-661p-illus (5xx7)   17.50

--History of Amer Costume, 1607 to 1870-NY-1942-Tudor-cl-
lg thk4to-661p-col plts & photos   (5t2, dj, f)   12.50

McCLELLAN, GENERAL, (GEO B)-Life, Campaigns & Public
Serices of-Phila-(1864)-194p-cl-advs (5s2) 10. (5h1)   8.50

McCLELLAN, GEO-Army of the Potomac-NY-1864-Putnam-
frontis-maps   (5mm8)   5.00

--McClellan's Own Story-NY-1887-8vo-678p
(5x0, 5s9, crack, 5b1, 5yy7, sl wn)   7.50

--Manual of Bayonet Exercise, prepared for Use of Army of US-
Phila-1862-Lippincott-illus-118p-cl
(5x5, 5j5) 15. (5mm8) 8.50 (5g4)   10.00

--Mexican War Diary-Princeton-1917-map-illus (4b6) 20.(5xx5) 17.50

--Report of-Chig-1864-147p   (4b3)   10.00

--Report of Sec of War-Wash-1857-A O P Nicholson-360p-illus
(5mm8)   15.00

--Report on Organiz & Campains of Army of Potomac-NY-480p-
Sheldon&Co-maps(some fldg) (5r7, wn) 7.50 (5mm8) 6.(5zz9) 12.50

--same-Wash-1864-GPO-242p (5j6) 4. (5i1) 8.

McCLELLAN, H B-I Rode with Jeb Stuart-Bloomington-(1958)-ports-
maps   (5tt5)   7.50

--The Life & Campaigns of Maj Gen J.E.B. Stuart-Bost-1885-
1st ed-frontis-   -7 maps (3 pkt)
(5s9, nick, fade) 35. (5ee3, cov wn)   32.50

M'CLELLAN, JOHN-State of Account of Collector of Excise,
York County, from 1st Nov 1786 till 1st Aug 1787-Phila-1788-
7p-8vo-unbnd   (5g4, unopnd)   25.00

McCLELLAN, R GUY-Golden State-Phila-(1872)-Wm Flint-685p-
illus-maps-mor   (5ff7, rbnd cl) 12.50 (5yy8)   15.00

McCLELLAN, M G-Mammy Mystic-NY-1895-16mo (5x2)   10.00

McCLELLAND, NANCY-Duncan Phyfe & the English Regency,
1795 to 1830-NY-(1939)-sm folio-illus-ltd to 1350c (5ii8)   55.00

McCLELLAND, NANCY-Furnishing the Colonial & Federal House-Phila-1936-Lipp-164p-204 illus   (5p0) 10.00
--same-Phila-1947-173p-202 photos-rev ed   (5w7) 5.00
--Historic Wallpapers from their inception to intro of machinery-1924-4to-plts   (5L7) 75.00
--Practial Book of Decorative Wall Treatments-Phila-1926-273p-t.e.g.-plts   (5w7,chip) 9.50 (5w5,unopnd,dj) 17.50
--The Young Decorators(juvenile)-NY-1928-117p-col plts   (5w7,wn) 3.50
McCLENACHEN, C T-History of Most Ancient & Honorable Fraternity of Free & Accepted Masons in NY-NY-1888 to 1894-4 vols-illus   (5r7) 40.00
M'CLEOD, MALCOM-Macleod's History of Witches,etc-Newark-1811-18mo-orig bds-lea bk-106p-Wm Tuttle   (5j5,fox) 15.00
McCLINTOCK, CAPT-In the Arctic Seas-Phila-n.d.-375p-maps-illus   (4b9,5ss0) 10.00
--A Narr of discovery of fate of Sir John Franklin & his companions-Lond-1859-402p-maps-illus-hf lea   (5ss1,cov loose) 12.50
--same-NY-1860-JTLloyd-maps-illus   (5w8) 12.00
--same-Bost-1860-375p-cl   (5h2,sp wn) 7.50
McCLINTOCK, F L-Voyage of the "Fox" in Arctic Seas-Lond-1859-illus-403p-fldg pkt map-1st ed   (5dd7) 27.50
McCLINTOCK, GILBERT S-Valley Views of NoEastrn Pennsylvania-Wilkes-Barre-1948-4to-illus-scarce   (5ii8) 25.00
McCLINTOCK, JAS H-Mormon Settlement in Arizona-Phoenix-1921-illus-map-307p   (5yy7,f,4b3,f) 35.00
McCLINTOCK, JOHN S-Pioneer days in the Black Hills-Deadwood-(1939)-photos-336p-1st ed   (4n8,last lf wn,5yy7,sl wn) 50. (5cc5,orig wrps) 60.00
McCLINTOCK, WALTER-Old Indian Trails-Bost-1923-336p-cl-illus-1st ed (5jj9,rub,lacks fly) 12.50 (5zz5,vg) 20. (4k4,vf,dj) 25. (5ee3,vg,5ii8) 17.50
--Old North Trail,or,Life,legends & religion of Blackfeet Indians-Lond-1910-col plts (5L7) 12.50 (5yy7,5ii8,4k4) 25.00
M'CLINTOCK, WM L-John Beedle's sleigh ride,courtship & marriage-NY-1841-CWallis-12mo-bds-rebkd in calf-1st ed-3 plts   (5x1,plts stnd,wtrstnd) 60.00
McCLUNE, H H-Miscellanea-n.p.-1907-port-214p-scarce (4m2) 12.50
McCLUNG, JOHN A-Sketches of Western Adventure-Louisvl,Ky-1879-illus-reprnt   (5jj7) 20.00
McCLUNG, NELLIE L-Clearing in the West-NY-(1936)-wrps-378p   (5yy7) 4.50
McCLURE, A K-Abraham Lincoln & Men of War Times-Phila-1892-496p-illus-4th ed (5t7) 10. (5s9) 6.00
--Old Time Notes of Penna-Phila-1905-2 vols-illus-g.t.e.-pic cl-ltd to 1,000c-auth's auto ed (5w5,dj) 45. (5qq8,4m2) 35.00
--3,000 Miles thru the Rocky Mnts-Phila-1869-cl-456p (5zz9) 20.00
McCLURE, ABBOT-Making Built In Furniture-NY-1914-12mo-(8)p,52p-illus   (5n7,autg) 4.50
McCLURE, ALEX K-The Annals of the War-Phila-1879-800p-illus- (5w9,crack) 25.00
--Recoll of Half a Century-Salem-1902-502p-illus-t.e.g. (5w4) 8.50
McCLURE, C BOONE-History of the Manufacture of Barbed Wire-Canyon-1958-125p-cl-barbed wire set in cov   (5n4) 9.50
McCLURE, C P-Pioneer McClure Families of Mononogahela Valley-(1924)-171p   (5mm3,wn) 25.00
McCLURE, DAVID-Diary 1748 to 1820-NY-1899-frontis-priv prntd-ltd to 250c   (5t7) 15.00
McCLURE, J B-Abraham Lincoln's Stories & Speeches-Chig-1904-illus-4to-cl   (5p5,f) 20.00
--Anecdotes of Abraham Lincoln & Lincoln's Stories-Chig-1879-frontis-8vo-illus (5ww4,wn) 15. (5m6,frontis tn) 10.00
--Edison & His Inventions Including etc-Chig-1879-171p(36)p-cl   (5h1) 12.50
--same-Chig-1879-wrps   (5w5,rprd,fade) 6.50
--Lincoln's Stories-Chig-1879-1st ed-frontis-illus-188p (5i3,rub) 10.00
McCLURE, J D-Calif Landmarks,photographic Guide to State's Historic Spots-Stanford U-(1948)-illus-149p   (4n1) 8.50
McCLURE, W K-Italy in NoAfrica-Lond-1913-Constable-328p-maps(1 fldg)-photos   (4t5,cov stnd) 15.00
McCOLLUM, E V-The Amer Home Diet-Detroit-1920-237p-illus   (5c5) 4.00
M'COLLUM, WM-Calif As I Saw It-Talisman Pr-1960-8vo-cl bk bds-ltd to 750c (5dd5) 25. (5F5,f,dj) 17.50
McCOMAS, E S-Journal of-1954-ltd to 500c   (5k0) 10.00
MACOMB, CAPT J N-Report of Exploring Exped from Santa Fe-Wash-1876-152p-col lithos-fldg map-cl   (5tt0,wn) 25.00
MACOMBER, FRANK GAIR-Collection of Arms & Armor-NY-1936-sm4to-illus-orig wrps   (5ii3) 10.00
MACON COUNTY, ILL-History of-Phila-1880-folio-hf mor-242p-map-ports-litho views   (5jj7,f) 65.00
McCONNELL, H H-Five Yrs a Cavalryman-Jacksboro -1889-319p (5t3,fleck) 25. (4a5,f) 65.00

McCONNELL, J P-Negroes & Their Treatment in Virginia from 1865 to 1867-Pulaski-1910-126p   (5r5) 35.00
McCONNELL, JOS CARROLL-West Texas Frontier-(Jacksboro)-(1933)-photos-334p-1st ed   (5yy7,sl wn) 45.00
McCONNELL, S D-History of the Amer Episcopal Church-NY-1890- (5q8) 4. (5t2) 3.50
McCONNELL, W J-Early History of Idaho-Caldwell-1913-420p-Caxton-8vo-cl (5m9,wn) 12.50 (5F5,crack) 15.00
M'CONOCHIE, JAS R-Leisure Hours-Louisville-1846-frontis-276p   (5yy8) 20.00
McCOOK, GOV E-Biennial message to Legislature of Colo Jan 4,1870-CentralCty-1870-disbnd   (5g3,lacks wrps) 37.50
McCOOK, HENRY C-The Honey Ants of Garden of the Gods & Occident Ants of Amer Plains-Phila-1882-13 plts-8vo   (5m6,libr stmp) 7.50
--Martial Graves of Our Fallen Heroes in Santiago de Cuba-Phila-1899-448p-illus-maps-plts   (5w0,crack) 7.50
MacCORD, CHAS WM-Kinematics-NY-1883-8vo-illus-1st ed   (5m6) 10.00
McCORD, DAVID-Oddly Enough-Cambr-1926-12mo-bds-cl bk-1st ed of auth's first book   (5gg6,pres) 50.00
McCORD, JAS B-My Patients Were Zulus-NY-1951-Rinehart-308p (4t5,autg) 6. (4t5,dj) 5.00
McCORD, M H-Report of Gov of Ariz-Wash-1897-illus-142p-scarce   (4a5) 15.00
McCORMACK, EUGENE I-Colonial Oppostion to Imperial Authority During the French & Indian War-Berkeley-1911-98p (5t1) 15.00
McCORMICK, A P-Scotch Irish in Ireland & Amer-1897-247p-v scarce   (5t9) 35.00
McCORMICK, CYRUS-Century of the Reaper-Bost-1931-302p-illus   (4e4) 10.00
McCORMICK, E D-McCormick,Hamilton,Lord,Day Ancestral Lines-1957-1136p   (5mm3) 27.50
McCORMICK, EDITH ROCKEFELLER-Collection...Laces,Jewelry, Furs Fr&Engl Silver,etc-NY-1934-(Amer Art Assn)-catalog-plts-ltd to 700c-bnd   (4j3,f,box) 37.50
McCORMICK, HARRIET HAMMOND-Landscape Art, Past & Present-1923-Scrib-56 plts-3/4 lea-ltd to 1200c   (5ww4) 30.00
McCORMICK, L HAMILTON-Characterology,etc-Chig-1920-646p-illus-t.e.g.   (5w5) 6.50
McCORMICK, RICHARD C-Visit to Camp before Sevastopal-NY-1855-3 fldg liths-1st ed   (5i3) 17.50
McCORMICK'S ALMANAC FOR YEAR 1872-Portland,Ore-(1871)-70p   (5yy3) 25.00
McCORNACK, ELLEN CONDON-Thos Condon,Pioneer Geologist of Oregon-Eugene-1928-355p-illus-map   (5s4,f) 10.00
McCOSKER, M J-The Historical Collection of the Insurance Co of NoAmer-Phila-1945-4to-cl-176p-plts   (4b3,vg) 10. (5t4) 6. (4m9,f) 15.00
McCOWAN, DAN-Animals of the Canadian Rockies-NY-1936-301p-illus   (5w4,autg) 6.00
--same-Tor-1950-302p-18 plts   (5aa0) 5.00
--Hill Top Tales-Tor-1948-266p-plts (5s6,autg) 5. (5dd7) 3.50
--A Naturalist in Canada-Tor-1948-plts-294p   (4a8) 5.00
--Outdoors wi Camera in Canada-Tor-1945-102p-plts (5s6,autg) 4.50
--Tidewater to Timberline-Tor-1951-plts-205p   (5s6) 5.00
McCOWN, MARY H-Soldiers of War of 1812 Buried in Tenn-JohnsonCty-1959-156p-wrps   (5ff7) 10.00
McCOY, F-Prodromus of Zoology of Victoria-Lond-1885 to 1890-hf lea-200 plts-sm4to-2 vols-ex rare   (4p5,vf) 375.00
McCOY, HORACE-Kiss Tomorrow Goodbye-(1948)-Random House- (5F1,vf) 10.00
--They Shoot Horses, Don't They-1935-Simon&Schuster-auth's 1st novel   (5F1,dj,mint) 17.50
McCOY, ISAAC-Country for Indians West of the Mississippi-Wash-1832-HD172-15p   (4n4) 17.50
--History of the Baptist Indian Missions-Wash-1840-611p-bds-mor sp,labls-1st ed (5yy8,wn) 85. (5m3,fox,t.p.rprd) 100. (5z7,rbnd) 150.00
McCOY, J MIKE-History of Cedar Co, Nebraska-n.p.-n.d.-(ca1937)-189p-photos-bds   (5t3,ex libr,wn) 30.00
McCOY, JOS G-Historic Sketches of Cattle Trade of West & SW-KansasCty-1874-427p-illus   (4a5) 300.00
--same-Wash-1932   (5x5) 30. (5yy6) 17.50
--same-Glendale-1940-illus-Bieber,ed (4a5,f) 32.50 (5yy7,unopnd) 20.00
--same-facs reprnt by Long's of 1874 ed-1951 (5k1,dj) 15.00
McCOY, RAYMOND-The Massacre of Old Ft Mackinac-BayCty-(1946)-169p-illus-maps-papr cov   (5h6) 3.50
McCOY, SAM'L DUFF-Nor Death Dismay-NY-1944-248p(5s1,dj) 4.50
McCRACKEN, DUANE-Strike Injunctions in the New South-1931-Univ of NoCar Pr-1st ed   (5x5) 10.00
MacCRACKEN, H N-Old Dutchess Forever-(1956)-503p (5t9) 10.00

McCRACKEN, HAROLD-Alaska Bear Trails-GarCty-1931-260p-
photos   (5ss1,pres) 12.50
--The Chas M Russell Book-GarCty-1957-35 col plts-1st trade ed
   (5L2) 23.50 (5cc5,mint, 5m9,dj) 20. (5x5,5k2) 25.00
--Frederic Remington, Artist of the Old West-(1947)-Lippincott-
   1st ed (5jj7,f,dj) 30. (5x5,dj,5zz5,fray dj) 25.
                                      (5k0,dj,5cc5,f,dj) 35.00
--The Fred'k Remington Book-GarCty-1966-lea-box wi lea labl-
   ltd to 500c,nbrd,autg   (5cc5,mint) 100.00
--same-NY-1966-Dblday-285p-illus-R4to   (4a0) 22.00
--Geo Catlin & the Old Frontier-NY-1959-Dial Pr-folio-36 col illus-
   1st trade ed (5m9,dj) 18.50 (5zz5) 17.50 (4k4,f,dj) 22.50
--same-NY-c1959-Bonanza-216p-plts   (5F9,mint,dj) 7.50
--Portrait of the Old West-NY-1952-McGrawHill-232p-illus-
   demy 4to (5r8) 30. (5cc5,f,dj,5d6) 25.   (4a0) 37.50
--Remington's Own West-Dial Pr-1960
   (5zz5,mint,dj) 10. (5xx8,5m9) 7.50
MacCREAGH, G-The Last of Free Africa-NY-1935-12p plus
   361p plus 63 plts   (5x2) 10. (5c6) 6.75
--same-NY-1928-Century-361p-photos   (4t5) 5.00
McCREARY, GEO W-The Ancient & Honorable Mechanical Company
   of Baltimore-Balto-1902-illus-157p   (4h8) 17.50
McCREATH, ANDREW S-The New River Cripple Creek mineral region
   of Virginia-Harrisburg-1887-pkt map-stiff prntd wrps (5g8) 6.00
McCREIGHT, M I-Buffalo Bone Days-(Sykesville,Pa-1939)-illus-40p-
   1st ed-bound   (5jj7,f,pres) 25.00
--Chief Flying Hawk's Tales-NY-(1936)-56p plus photos-1st ed
   (5yy7,pres,4k4,dj,f) 15.00
--Firewater & Forked Tongues-Trail's End Pub Co-1947-illus by
   C M Russell-delux ed-ltd to 250c-180p-demy 8vo-autg
   (5zz5,v sl wtrstn) 30. (4a0) 35.00
--same-Pasadena-1947-1st ed (5zz5,dj) 8.50 (5k4,f) 12.50
--Young Man Go West-(Sykesville,Pa-1941)-wrps-48p
   (5jj7,f,pres) 20.00
MacCUAIG, W W-Songs of a Shanty Man & Other "Dialect" Poems
   of Fr Can Life-Tor-n.d. (pref 1913)-illus-scarce (4e9) 10.00
McCUDDEN, JAS B-Flying Fury-Lond-1930-illus (5u7,fade) 6.50
McCUE, LILLIAN-The 60 Minute Chef-NY-1947-222p (5c0) 3.00
McCUE, J N-McCues of the Old Dominion-1912-287p (5mm3) 20.00
--same-1912-170p   (5mm3) 12.50
McCULLAGH, CAPT FRANCIS-Red Mexico-NY-1928-Carrier-8vo-
   cl-illus   (4a3) 12.50
McCULLERS, CARSON-Le Coeur est un Chasseur Solitaire-Paris-
   1947-   wrps-nbrd ed   (5ss7,vf) 12.50
--Reflections in a Golden Eye-Cambr-1941-HoughtonMiff-1st ed
   (5ss9,vg,dj) 15.00
McCULLEY, J-The Flaming Stallion-NY-1932-1st ed
   (5yy6,dj,pres) 10.00
McCULLEY, JOHNSTON-Range Land Justice-NY-(1934)-1st ed-
   authr sgd pres   (5yy6,vg,dj,pres) 10.00
McCULLOCH, HUGH-Men & Measures of Half a Century-NY-1889
   (4a9) 6. (5ii8) 6.50
M'CULLOCH, J R-Universal Gazetteer, a Dictionary Geogr,
   Statistical & Hist of Various Countries,etc-NY-1843-2 vols-
   44 fldg maps   (5yy0) 15.00
McCULLOCH, J R-A Dictionary, Geogr, Statistical & Historical-
   Lond-1841-2 vols-6 lg fldg maps   (5c1) 125.00
McCULLOCH, M C-Integration, Promise, Process, Problems-
   Fisk UnIv-1952-77p-wrps   (5x2) 10.00
McCULLY, ANDERSON-Amer Alpines in the Graden-NY-1931-
   251p-photos   (5s7,sl soil) 4.00
McCUNE, ALICE P-History of Juab County-Springville,Utah-1947-
   301p-photos-1st ed   (5L2) 15.00
McCUNE, ELIZ CLARIDGE-Memorial to, by Susa Young Gates-
   SaltLkCtv-1924-117p-wrps-illus   (5t4) 5.00
McCURDY, EDW-Leonardo Da Vinci's Note Book-NY-1923-8vo-
   cl-plts   (5p5) 7.50
--Roses of Paestum-Portland,Me-1912-ThosB Mosher-bds-papr labl-
   ltd to 700c-8vo   (5b0) 5.00
McCURDY, F ALLEN-Two Rough Riders-NY-c1902-53p plus plts-
   tissue guards   (5w4,sl soil) 8.50
MacCURDY, GEO G-Early Man-Phila-1937   (5qq5) 10.00
MacCURDY, GEO G-Human Origins-NY-1924-illus-2 vols-
   1st ed   (5zz5) 20.00
McCURDY, JAS G-By Juan da Fuca's Strait-Portland-1937-312p-
   ports-plts   (5s0,pres) 15.00
McCURDY, ROBT M-Garden Flowers-NY-(1927)-Nature Library-
   311p-48 col illus-lg8vo   (5s7,f) 5.00
--Book of Garden Flowers-NY-1931-illus   (5qq7) 2.50
McCUSKEY, DOROTHY-Bronson Alcott, Teacher-NY-1940-1st prntg
   (5jj1,dj,f) 7.50
McCUTCHEON, GEO B-Beverly of Graustark-NY-1904-1st ed-
   illus by H Fisher (5i3,f) 5. (5ss9,f) 7.50

--Books Once Were Men-NY-1931-cl bkd bds-12mo-1st ed-ltd ed
   (5b2,f,wn box) 8.50 (5r9,f) 7.50
--Castle Craneycrow-Chig-1902-Herbert S Stone-1st ed
   (5ss3) 10. (5i3,vg,5b2,vg) 7.50
--Graustark, the Story of a Love Behind a Throne-Chig-1901-12mo-
   cl-1st ed of auth's first book-1st issue wi textual error on pg 150
   (5gg6,f,als) 50.00
McCUTCHEON, JOHN-In Africa, Hunting Adven in the Big Game
   Country-Indnpls-1910-illus-402p   (4t5) 20.00
McCUTCHEON, JOHN T-Bird Center Cartoons-Chig-1904-pict bds-
   (ca200p) (5ff7,sl wn) 15. (5b9,scuff) 17.50
--Drawn from Memory-(1950)-Bobbs   (5ww4,dj) 7.50
McDANIEL, BRUCE W-The Desert, God's Crucible-Bost-(1926)-
   illus-118p (5dd9) 9. (5p5) 10.00
McDANIEL, RUEL-Vinegarroon, Saga of Judge Roy Bean-Kingspt-
   (1936)-cl (5h7) 4. (5yy7) 3. (5g5,f) 5.00
McDERMOTT, JOHN F-George Caleb Bingham, River Portraitist-
   U of Okla Pr-1959-454p-   (4a0,dj) 25.00
--Old Cahokia-StL-1949-355p-illus-maps   (5h9,rub) 8.50
--The Russian Journal & Other Selections from Works of Lewis
   Carroll-NY-(1935)-Dutton-1st ed   (5hh1,dj) 10.00
--Tixier's Travels on Osage Prairies-Norman-1940-illus-maps-
   309p   (4b3,f,dj) 17.50 (4k4,dj,f) 17.50
--Western Journals of Washington Irving-Norman-1944-illus-
   1st ed   (4k4,dj,f) 10.00
McDERMOTT, WM A-Mr. Billy Buttons,a novel-NY-1896-
   Benziger Bros-2nd ed(same yr as 1st)-pict cl-scarce (5m2) 10.00
McDEVITT, BROTHER V EDMUND-The First California's Chaplain-
   Fresno-1956-259p-illus-8vo   (5h5) 12.50
McDEVITT, WM-Jack London as Poet & as Platform Man, Did Jack
   London Commit Suicide?-SanFran-1947-orig wrps-ltd to 500c
   (4t6,mint) 25.00
--Jack London's First-SanFran-1946-orig wrps-ltd to 500c
   (4t6,vg) 25.00
MacDONAGH, THOS-Songs of Myself-Dublin-1910-Hodges,
   Figgis&Co-12mo-cl-1st ed   (5ss3,als) 35.00
MacDONALD, A B-Hands Up as told by Fred E. Sutton-Indnpls-
   (1927)-photos-303p-1st ed (5yy7,sl wn) 7.50 (5yy7,wn dj) 12.50
MacDONALD, ADRIAN-Canadian Portraits-Tor-1923-230p(5yy9) 5.00
MacDONALD, BETTY-The Egg & I-1945-1st ed   (5s4,dj) 9.50
MacDONALD, CHAS B-Scotlands Gift,Golf-NY-1928-illus-
   ltd to 260c,autg   (5xx7) 10.00
McDONALD, DANL-20th Century History of Marshall Co,Ind-Chig-
   1908-2 vol-648p-cl   (5h7,rbnd) 50.00
McDONALD, EDW D-Drexel Institute of Technology 1891 to 1941-
   336p-illus   (5b8) 6.75
--McDONALD, EDW D-Phoenix, the Posthumous Papers of
   DHLawrence-NY-1936-Viking Pr-1st ed   (5ss9,dj,vg) 15.00
McDONALD, F V-Inquiries Relating to Ancestors & Descendants of
   Job of Cumberland, RI & Greenwich,NY-1881-46p-ports (5mm3) 35.00
MacDONALD, GEO-At Back of North Wind-NY-(1890)-Routledge-
   8vo-dec cl-g.t.-378p-76 illus   (5s0) 5.00
--same-Phila-1919-McKay-8 col plts by Jessie Wilcox Smith-lg8vo-
   cl-342p-pic cl labl   (5j5) 12.50
--Letters from Hell-NY-1885-12mo-1st Amer ed-by LWJS (5yy6) 6.00
--Within & Without, A Dramatic Poem-Lond-1855-12mo-cl-1st ed
   of auth's first book-inserted adv dated March, 1855
   (5gg6,wn,pres) 50.00
MacDONALD, LT GRANT-Sailors-Tor-1945-153p-drawings
   (5s1,stn,warp) 7.50
MacDONALD, HUGH-Thos Hobbes,a bibliography-Lond-1952-
   frontis-illus-101p-4to-bds-linen bk   (4c1) 15.00
MacDONALD, J A-Troublesome Times in Canada-Tor-1910-255p-
   illus   (4b9) 10.00
McDONALD, MRS J R-Baptist Missions in Western Canada, 1873 to
   1948-Edmonton-1948-prntd wrps-61p-fldg map   (5yy9) 6.50
MacDONALD, JAS-Food from the Far West-Lond-1878-313p plus
   index-1st ed-scarce   (5t3,rub) 10.00
McDONALD, JAS J-Life in Old Virginia-Norfolk-1907-374p-illus-
   1st ed (5h6) 8. (5w9,fade) 10.00
McDONALD, JOHN-Biogr Sketches of Gen Nathaniel Massie,
   McArthur, Wells & Kenton etc-Cinn-1838-1st ed-rare (5zz9) 65.00
McDONALD, GEN JOHN-Secrets of the Great Whiskey Ring-StL-
   1880-346p,62p-rev & enlrgd ed   (5w4,sl crack) 10.00
MacDONALD, LADY-Fortunes of a Family through 9 Centuries-1928-
   264p-2nd ed   (5mm3) 12.50
MacDONALD, MALCOLM-Down North-Lond-1943-274p-plts-map
   (4a8) 4.50 (5ss1) 4.00
MacDONALD, RANALD-Narrative of His Early Life on Columbia
   Under Hudson's Bay Co-Spokane-1923-plts-maps-333p-g.t.
   (5zz1) 22.50
McDONALD, VEN ARCHDEACON-Grammar of the Tukudh
   Language-Lond-1911-201p-scarce   (5t1) 75.00

McDONALD, WM N-A History of the Laurel Brigade-(Balt, Sun
Job Prntng Office)-1907-499p-cl-illus
(5r0, pres, lacks 1 photo)   30.00

MacDONELL, ARTHURA-History of Sanskrit Literature-NY-1900-
orig ed   (5tt5, sp wn)   6.00

MacDONELL, SIR JOHN-Great Jurists of the World, Vol 2 of
Continental Legal Hist Ser-Bost-1914-Little-607p-port (5p9)   12.50

MacDOUGAL, D T-Course of Vegetative Seasons in Southern Arizona-
n.p.-1908-52p-illus-wrps   (4a5)   5.00

McDOUGAL, HENRY CLAY-Recollections, 1844 to 1909-KansCty-
1910-466p   (5k0)   10.00

MacDOUGALL'S, A F-Cook Book-Bost-1935-292p-8 photos (5c0)   5.00

MacDOUGALL, ALICE FOOTE-The Autobiogr of a Business Woman-
Bost-1928-205p-frontis   (5c5)   3.00
--Coffee & Waffles-NY-1927-131p   (5c0, fade)   3.50

MacDOUGALL, C D-Hoaxes-1940-buck-plts   (5L7, ex-libr)   7.50

MacDOUGALL, DONALD, REV-The Conversion of the Maoris-Phila-
1899-216p-illus   (5r0)   10.00

McDOUGALL, FRANCES H W-The mechanic-Providence-1842-12mo-
Burnett&King-orig violet cl-1st ed-scarce   (5x1, fade, pres)   65.00

MacDOUGALL, J-Forest, Lake & Prairie-Tor-n.d.-267p   (4e9)   10.00

MacDOUGALL, J B-Two Thousand Miles of Gold from Val D'Or to
Yellowknife-Tor-1946-234p-illus   (4b9)   12.00

McDOUGALL, JOHN-Pathfinding on Plain & Prairie-Tor-1898-
illus-1st ed   (4k4)   15.00
--Saddle, Sled & Snowshoe-Cinn-(1896)-282p-cl (5h1, bkplt)   10.00
--same-Tor-n.d.-282p-illus   (4b9, f)   10.00

McDOWELL, CATHERINE W, ed-Now You Hear My Horn-Austin-
1967-deluxe ed-autg-ltd to 250c (4c7, box, lacks mini knife)   75.00

MacDOWELL, LLOYD W-Alaska Glaciers & Ice Fields-Seattle-1906-
(4p), photos(some col)-pict wrps-Alaska Steamship Co-scarce
(5t3)   7.50
--Alaskan Indian Basketry-Seattle-1906-3rd ed-(13p)-photos-
some col-wrps-Alaska Steamship Co-   (5t3)   7.50
--The Totem Poles of Alaska & Indian Mythology-Seattle-1906-
2nd ed-(13p)-photos-wrps-Alaska Steamship Co   (5t3)   7.50

McDOWELL, WM-Shape of Ships-Lond-1950-232p-illus, 16 col
plts   (5s1, dj)   4.00

McDUFF, MARIHELEN-Taste of Texas-NY-(1949)-x, 303, (6)p-
J Traney, ed   (5c4)   3.50

McDUFFEE, FRANKLIN-History of Rochester, NHamp from 1722 to
1890-2 vols in 1-688p-buck   (5mm3, rbnd)   20.00

MACE, AURELIA G-The Aletheia, Spirit of Truth-Farmington-1907
plts-2nd ed   (5r7)   15.00

MACE, GUSTAVE-My first crime-Lond-1886-Vizetelly-12mo-
orig prntd bds-1st ed in Engl-frontis-2 plts (5xx6, chip)   20.00

MACE, JEAN-Mace's Fairy Book, Home Fairy Tales-NY-1868-8vo-
304p   (5v0)   6.50

MACE, RICHARD-The First Families-NY-1897-Munsey-12mo-cl
(5b2)   6.00

MacEIRE, FERGUS-The sons of Eire-Lond-1872-T Cautley Newby-
3 vols in 1-12mo-orig cl-1st ed   (5xx6, crack)   22.50

McELDOWNEY, JOHN C-History of Wetzel Co, West Virginia-n.p.-
1901-1st ed-183p, (84)p-photos-scarce   (5L2, wn)   50.00

MacELREE, WILMER W-Down the Eastern & Up the Black Brandywine-
n.p.-(West Chester)-1906-lg8vo-176p-illus-scarce
(5w0, rbnd, rprd)   37.50

McELROY, JOHN-Andersonville-Toledo-1879-illus-pt lea-654p
(4h1, rbnd) 8.50 (5t7) 12.50 (5L5) 15. (5q0, rprd, chip)   17.50
--same-Wash-1899-2 vols-wrps   (5j6)   10.00
--This Was Andersonville-NY-1957-4to-illus-cl&bds
(5r7) 15. (4a7)   16.50
--Struggle for Missouri-Wash-1913-illus-maps-293p-orig wrps
(5h2) 7.50 (4a1, 4p2, sl tn) 10. (5w0)   12.50

McELROY, JOS C-Chickamagua, Record of Ohio Chickamagua &
Chatanooga Nat'l Pk Comm-Cinn-1896-199p-illus (5w5, lt wn) 6.50

McELROY, LUCY CLEAVER-Juletty a Story of Old Kentucky-NY-
(1901)-280p-cl   (5jj9)   17.50

McELROY, ROBT-Grover Cleveland, the Man & the Statesman-NY-
1923-2 vols-frontis-g.t. (5h9) 7.50 (5yy8, 5w5, 5p9)   10.00
--Jefferson Davis; the Real & the Unreal-Harper-1937-illus-2 vols-
1st ed   (5yy8)   17.50

McELROY, ROBT McN-Kentucky in the Nation's History-NY-1909-
illus-map-590p   (4m2)   17.50

McELWAINE, EUGENE-Truth about Alaska The Golden Land of
Midnight Sun-(Chig)-1901-Regan Prntg Hse-cl-445p-illus-
maps-v scarce   (4L9)   25.00

MacELWEE, ROY S-Economic Aspects of the Great Lakes, St. Lawrence
Ship Channel-NY-1921-Ronald-8vo-cl-fldg charts-291p (5j5) 7.50
--Ports & Terminal Facilities-NY-1918-315p-illus   (5s1)   3.50

McENTEE, GIRARD-Italy's Part in Winning the World War-
Princeton-1934-114p-photos-1st ed   (5w4)   6.50

McEVORY, J P-Bam Bam Clock-Chig-(1920)-Volland Co-sm8vo-
illus by Johnny Gruelle-pic bds   (5c8)   5.00

McEVOY, B ERNARD-History of 72nd Canadian Inf Battalion-
Vancouver-1920-plts-maps-311p   (5dd0, cv sl wn)   8.50

McEVOY, HENRY N-Galesburg, Monmouth, Knoxville & Abingdon
Directories 1857-Chig-1857-168p(incl ads)-ex rare
(5zz5, sl wn)   75.00

MacEWAN, GRANT-Between the Red & the Rockies-Tor-1952-300p-
maps   (5aa0)   5.00
--The Sodbusters-Tor-n.d.-240p-col frontis-illus   (5s0)   6.50

McEWEN, INEZ PUCKETT-So This is Ranching-Caldwell, Id-1948-
270p-photos-1st ed-ltd to 1000c, autg, nbrd   (5s4, f, dj)   10.00

MACFADDEN, BERNARD-The Miracle of Milk-NY-1924-204p-
port   (5c5)   3.50
--Physical Culture Cook Book-NY-1926-372p-illus   (5c5)   2.50
--Strength from Eating-NY-1901-194p-12mo   (5c5, fade)   2.50
--The Truth about Tobacco, How to Break the Habit-NY-1921-8vo-
cl-port-1st ed   (5p5, dj)   7.50

MACFADDEN, HARRY A-Rambles in the Far West-Holidaysburg-
c1906-278p-illus   (5s4, sl wtrstnd) 12.50   (5w5)   18.50

MacFALL, H-The Wooings of Jezebel Pettyfer-NY-1925 (5x2, dj) 10.00

MacFALL, HALDANE-Art of Hesketh Hubbard-Lond-1924-87p-8vo
(5ww3)   15.00
--Aubrey Beardsley.....the Clown, etc-NY-1927-illus-4to-1st ed
(5j3, vg) 15.   (5yy6)   17.50
--Aubrey Beardsiey, the Man & His Work-Lond-1928-John Lane,
The Bodley Head-110p-12 plts-4to-cl   (5m7)   35.00
--Beautiful Children-NY-1909-mounted col plts-tissue guards-
g.t.-col labl-318p   (5kk8)   17.50
--The Book of Lovat Claud Fraser-Lond-1923-col plts-1st ed
(5v2, vg)   25.00
--Whistler-Lond-1905-Spirit of Age Series, #1-T N Foulis-70p-
illus   wrps   (5p5) 7.50 (4a0)   10.00

McFARLAND, J HORACE-Garden Bulbs in Color-NY-1938-296p-
lg8vo-illus(col & b&w)   (5s7)   7.50
--How to Grow Roses-NY-1937-192p-col & b&w plts-18th ed (5s7) 3.00
--same-14th, 16th & 17th editions   (5s7) each 3.00

McFARLAND, C-Judicial Control of Fed Trade Comm & Interstate
Commerce Comm, 1920 to 1930-Cambr-1933   (4c1)   10.00

McFARLAND, CARA LEE-U S Nat'l Bank of Portland, Ore-Portland-
(1940)-147p-roster, index-fldg chart tip in-lea bkstrp bds(5s4) 7.50

MacFARLANE, ANNIE ROBERTSON-Children of the Earth-NY-
1886-Holt-12mo-limp cl-Series #4   (5b2)   6.00

MacFARLANE, CHAS-Japan, Early, Geogr & Hist from Earliest Period
Lond-1852-435p-8vo-cl-illus-1st ed-scarce (5p5, chip)   25.00
--Extraordinary Tales & Lives of Robbers & Bandits in all Parts of
the world-Lond-n.d.-270p-5th ed   (5t4, spotted)   4.00
--Lives & exploits of banditti & robbers in all parts of the world-
Lond-1833-2 vols-EdwBull& JAndrews-12mo-orig bds-papr labls-
1st ed-frontis each vol & 12 plts   (5i8, f)   30.00

MacFARLANE, JAS J-History of Early Chestnut Hill-Phila-1927-rev-
illus-map-ltd to 500c   (5ii8)   17.50

MacFARLANE, JAS-Coal Regions of America-NY-1873-illus-maps-
3 fldg maps-679p-1st ed-v scarce   (5ii8, rebnd)   40.00

MacFARLANE, JOHN-Antoine Verard-Lond-1900-176p-4to-illus-
bds-linen bk-g.t.   (4c1)   75.00

MacFARLANE, JOHN J-Manufacturing in Phila, 1683 to 1912-
(phila)-1912-priv prntd-illus(some fldg)   (4b6)   15.00

MacFARLANE, R-Notes on Mammals Collected & Observed in
N Mackenzie Riv Dist-Wash-1905-5 plts   (5dd0)   7.50

MacFARLANE, ROBT-History Propellers & Steam Navigation-NY-
1851-illus   (5s1, soil)   8.50

McFARLAND, DANIEL-The trial of...for the shooting of Albert D.
Richardson....by a practical law reporter-NY-(1870)-
(WEHilton imprint)   (5g4, lacks wrps)   10.00

MacFARLAND, WM H-Report of Board of Visitors of Virginia
Military Institute, July 1863-Richmond-1863-111p   (5j6)   12.50

McFARLING, LLOYD, ed-Exploring the Northern Plains, 1804 to
1876-Caldwell-1955-maps-1st ed   (5yy7, dj)   12.50

McFEE, INEZ N-Young People's Cook Book-NY-(1925)-290p (5x5) 3.00

McFEE, WM-Casuals of the Sea-Lond-1916-MartinSecker-12mo-cl-
cl case-1st ed-adv dated 1916   (5ss3, sp def, stn)   35.00
--same-Lond-(1920)-MartinSecker-cl-2nd Engl ed (5ss3, crack, box) 5.00
--Harbours of Memory-NY-1921-1st ed   (5yy6, vg, dj)   6.00
--Law of Sea-NY-1950-12mo-cl-318p-1st ed   (5t0, dj, f)   3.50
--Life of Sir Martin Frobisher-NY-1928-276p-fldg maps-illus
(4b9) 15.   (5hh1)   12.50
--More Harbours of Memory-NY-1934-1st ed   (5ii3)   7.50
--North of Suez-NY-1930-1st ed   (5ii3)   5.00
--same-NY-1930-Dblday, Doran-1st ed-ltd to 350c, nbrd-autg, boxed
(5hh1, bkplt) 15. (5ss3, pres) 25. (4b4)   22.50
--Pilgrims of Adversity-NY-1928-1st ed   (5ii3)   5.00
--Race-NY-1924-1st ed   (5yy6, dj, f) 6.   (5ii3)   7.50

McFEE, WM (continued)
--The Reflections of Marsyas-Gaylordsville-1933-t8vo-dec bds-
Slide Mntn Pr-1st ed-ltd to 300c-autg   (5r9)   15.00
--Sailors of Fortune-NY-1929-1st ed   (5ii3)   5.00
--Sir Martin Frobisher-Lond-1928-Gold Hind Series-288p-maps-
illus-1st ed   (5hh3)   10.00
MACFIE, D T-Lilies for the Garden & Greenhouse-Lond-(1947)-
151p-photos   (5s7)   5.00
MACFIE, H-Wasa Wasa-Lond-1951-244p   (4b9, dj)   6.00
MACFIE, M-Vancouver Island & Brit Col-Lond-1865-illus-2 maps-
574p-calf   (4e9, lacks hf t., f bndg) 110.00
McGAFFEY, G W-Gen Hist of McGaffey Family-1904-145p
                                              (5mm3)   22.50
McGARVEY, LOIS-Along Alaska Trails-NY-(1960)-200p-o.p.
                                           (5ss0, dj, f) 6.00
M'GAW, JAS F-Philip Seymour, or Pioneer Life in Richland Co-
Mansfield-1858-279p-cl-scarce-fiction   (5jj9)   15.00
McGEE, A-Black America Abroad-Bost-1941-illus (5x2)   25.00
McGEE, T D-Popular History of Ireland-NY-1863-823p-hf lea
                                           (4b9, rub)   15.00
McGEE, THOS D'ARCY-The Irish Position in British & Republican
No Amer-Montreal-1866-Longmoore-2nd ed   (5nn8)   65.00
McGEHEE, RAMIEL, ed-"Fit For a King", The Merle Armitage Book
of Food-NY-1939-photo plts-258p-1st ed   (4g9, dedicat cpy) 12.50
MacGIBBON, DUNCAN-Canadian Grain Trade-Tor-1932-503p
                                              (4d0)   12.50
MacGIBBON, ELMA-Leaves of Knowledge-Spokane-1904-237p-
frontis-g.dec white cov   (5s4)   8.00
McGIFFERT, ARTHUR CUSHMAN-Luther, the Man & His Work-NY-
1914-Century-397p   (5p0)   5.00
McGIFFERT, J N-Hist of the Presbyterian Church of Ashtabula, Ohio-
Ashtabula-1876-18p-orig wrps   (5m2)   5.00
McGILL, V J-August Strindberg-NY-8vo-cl-459p-illus (5t0) 4.00
McGILL, WM M-Caverns of Virginia-n.p.-1933-sm4to-187p-illus-
maps-cl&bds-1st ed   (5w4, pres) 12.50
MacGILLIVRAY, C HOLMES-The Shadow of Tradition-Ottawa-(1927)-
Graphic Publ-prntd wrps   (5w8, rprd)   9.00
MacGILLIVRAY, W-Travels & Researches of Alexander von Humboldt-
NY-1833-J&J Harper-12mo-367p-calf &bds-1st Amer ed(5i4) 25.00
McGILLYCUDDY, JULIA B-McGillycuddy Agent-Stanford-(1941)-
291p-photos-1st ed-scarce   (4k4, f, dj, 5xx5, 5yy7, wn dj) 30.00
McGINNIS, E L'H-Yarn of the "Yampa"-NY-1898-160p-photos-
dec cov   (5s1)   3.00
McGINNIS, EDITH B-The Promised Land-(Boerne, Tex, 1947)-
1st ed   (5cc5, f) 12.50
McGIRR, N F-Bio Bibliography of Peter Force, 1790 to 1868-
Hattiesburg, Miss-1941-30p-wrps-246 entries-ltd to 150c(5n4) 12.50
McGIVERN, ED-Ed McGibern's Book on Fast & Fancy Revolver
Shooting & Police Training-Springfld-1938-1st ed (5cc5, f) 22.50
--same-Springfld-1945-reprint   (5yy7, dj)   7.50
McGLASHAN, CHAS F-History of the Donner Party, a Tragedy of
the Sierras-Truckee, Calif-(1879)-cl-v rare (5s9, sl rub) 175.00
--same-SanFran-1880-illus-2nd ed   (5x5, fray) 50.00
--same-Stanf U-(1940)-illus-316p   (4n1)   8.00
McGLOIN, JOHN BERNARD, S J-Eloquent Indian, the life of
Bouchard, Calif Jesuit-Stanford-(1950)-illus-ports (5r8) 9.50
MAGOFFIN, SUSAN SHELBY-Down the Santa Fe Trail & into
Mexico, Diary of...1846 to 47-NewHaven-1926-1hotos, fldg map-
276p-1st ed-Stella M Drumm, ed   (5yy7, dj) 30.00
McGONNIGLE, ROBT D-When I Went West-Pittsburg-1901-illus-
pict cl-1st ed   (4b6, pres) 50. (4n1, autg) 35.00
McGOVERN, JAS J, ed-Life & Letters of Eliza Allen Starr-Chig-
1905-452p-cl   (5h1)   10.00
McGOVERN, PATRICK A-History of the Diocese of Cheyenne-n.p.-
1941-12mo-cl-249p-illus   (5h5)   6.00
McGOVERN, WM MONTGOMERY-Jungle Paths &Inca Ruins, the
Record of an Expedition-Lond-Hutchinson-381p-illus-map-cl
                                              (5d6)   10.00
--To Lhasa in Disguise-NY-1924-Cent   (5p0)   6.00
McGOWAN, EDW-McGowan vs. Calif Vigilantes-Oakland-1946-
4to-214p-facs-Calif Relations, Vol 7-ltd to 675c, nbrd, autg
                                             (5dd5)   21.00
MacGOWAN, KENNETH-Footlights Across America-NY-(1929)-
8vo-398p-illus-1st ed   (5t0)   5.00
--The Living Stage-NY-1955-4to-illus-g.dec cl (5p5)   17.50
--Masks and Demons-n.p.-1923-Harcourt, Brace&Co-8vo-cl-
papr labls-illus   (5b0)   10.00
--The Theatre of Tomorrow-NY-1921-B&L-302p-illus (5p0, fade) 10.00
McGRANE, REGINALD C-Wm Allen, Study in Western Democracy-
(Colum-1925)-279p-cl   (5h7)   5.00
McGRATH, F SIMS-Pillars of Maryland-Richmond-1950-thk8vo-illus-
maps   (5yy6, pres) 17.50   (5h9, f, autg)   10.00

McGRATH, HAROLD-Arms & the Woman, a Romance-NY-1899-
12mo-cl-1st ed of auth's first book   (5gg6, vf) 10.00
McGRATH, J J, ed-Church & State in Amer Law-1962
                                         (5L7, ex-libr) 7.50
MAGRATH, THOS W-Authentic Letters From Upper Canada-Tor-
1953-Pioneer Books-plts-207p   (5dd0)   4.50
McGRAW, MYRTLE B-The Child in Painting-NY-(c1941)-Greystone-
4to-16p-frontis-48 plts-bds   (5p1)   5.00
McGREGOR, CHAS-History of the 15th Reg, NH Vol-(Concord, NH)-
1900-624p-illus   (5mm8, ex-libr) 6.00
MacGREGOR, FRANCES C-20th Century Indians-NY-1941-4to-
buck-photos-1st ed   (4k4, f) 10.00
MacGREGOR, G-Thundering Scott; portrait of John Knox-1958
                                              (5L7)   4.50
MacGREGOR, GORDON-Warriors without Weapons-Chig-(1946)-
2nd impr   (4k4, f, dj) 8.50
McGREGOR, J C-Winona Village, a 12th Century Settlement-
Flagstaff-1937-Mus of NoAriz Bull #12-53p-8vo-stiff wrps-
plts   (5g5)   4.50
MacGREGOR, J C-Disruption of Virginia-1922-map (5L7)   5.00
MacGREGOR, JAS G-Blankets & Beads-Edmonton-1949-278p-
illus-maps   (5a1)   5.00
--Land of Twelve Foot Davis-Edmonton-n.d.-395p-plts-illus-
maps   (5s0)   5.00
McGREGOR, JAS H-The Wounded Knee Massacre from the Viewpoint
of Sioux-Mnpls-(1950)-illus-140p-2nd prntg-scarce
                                   (4k4, f) 10. (5yy7) 12.50
McGREGOR, JEREMIAH S-Life & Deeds of Dr John McGregor-
Foster(RI)-1886-196p-12mo-cl-port   (5r7)   15.00
MACGREGOR, JESSIE-Gardens of Celebrities & Celebrated
Gardens in & around Lond-Lond-(1918)-326p-illus (5t7) 10.00
McGREGOR, JOHN C-Southwestern Archaeology-NY-1941-
1st ed   (5t3) 25. (5x5) 15. (4k4, f, dj) 20.00
MacGREGOR, MARSHALL-Studies & Diversions in Greek Literature-
Lond-(1937)   (4a1)   7.50
MACGREGOR-MORRIS, PAMELA-Clipperfields' Circus-Lond-1957-
8vo-cl-18 plts-1st ed   (5p5, dj) 10.00
McGREW, C B-Italian Doorways-Cleve-1929-folio-cl-195 drwngs
& photos   (5m2)   20.00
McGREW, CLARENCE A-City of San Diego & San Diego Co, the
Birthplace of Calif-Chig-1922-Amer Hist Soc-cl-4to-2 vol (4t1) 32.50
McGROARTY, JOHN S-California, Its History & Romance-LosAng-
1911-1st ed-illus (4a5, fox) 10. (5w9, autg, 5ee3)   7.50
                                  (4n1) 8.   (5h9)   8.50
--Calif of the South, a history-Chig-1933 to 35-5 vols-ports-plts-
R8vo   (5dd6, vg)   55.00
--History of Los Angeles County-Chig-1923-3 vols-Amer Hist Soc-
cl   (5d6) 30.   (4t1)   25.00
--Los Angeles, from the Mountains to the Sea-Chig-n.d.-Amer Hist Soc-
part lea-4to-2 vol-spec ltd ed (4t1) 25. (5h4, vf) 20.00
--Pioneer, Story of Stage Coach-LosAng-1925-Hellman Comm Trust
& Savings Bank-20p-wrps   (5tt0)   5.00
--Southern California-SanDiego-1915-Pan Expo Comm-4to-263p-
plts-wrps   (5g0)   5.00
McGUFFEY   -McGuffey's Fourth Eclectic Reader-NY, Cinn&Chig-
(1879)-256p-prntd bds-rev ed   (5t7)   6.50
--McGuffey's New Eclectic Speaker-Cinn-(1858)-504p-cl
                                        (5jj9, sl wn)   8.50
--McGuffey's New Eclectic Spelling Book-Cinn-(1865)-144p-
pict bds   (5h7, vg)   7.50
--same-Cinn&NY-(1865)-Wilson, Hinkle-illus ABC (4F6, vg) 15.00
--New Fifth Eclectic Reader, Selected & Orig Exercises for Schools-
Cinn&NY-(1857)-338p-electrotype ed   (5t7)   6.50
--McGuffey's Newly Revised Eclectic Spelling Book-Cinn-(1846)-
prntd bds-144p-Winthrop B Smith, pub   (5kk2)   15.00
--same-Cinn, Sargent, Wilson & Hinkle, NY, Clark&Maynard-(c1846)-
144p-imprvd stereotyped ed-wdcuts-cl bkd pic bds (5p1, wn) 8.50
--McGuffey's Newly Rev Eclectic Third Reader-Cinn-(1853)-
WBSmith-12 mo-roan bk-228p-illus-12p of ads for Pinneo's
Engl grammars-prntd bds   (5j5, bkstrp v wn, fox) 15.00
--McGuffey's New Sixth Eclectic Reader-Cinn-(1857)-Wilson, Hinkle-
(4F6, sp tn, stnd) 17.50 (4c3, cov v stnd, spn tn) 25.00
--McGuffey's Rhetorical Guide; or Fifth Reader of the Eclectic Series-
Cinn-(c1849)-WBSmith-orig sheep black lea labl-by publishers
of 1st ed of 1844   (5v2, f)   27.50
McGUIER, HENRY-A concise history of High Rock Spring-Albany-
1868-16mo-illus-pict wrps   (5g8, wrps creased) 5.00
McGUINNESS, CHAS J-Sailor-Phila-1935-313p, photos
                                       (5ss1, shaken)   4.00
McGUIRE, C E, ed-Catholic Builders of the Nation-Bost-1923-5 vols-
illus-fab-Continental Pr   (5p0)   20.00
McGUIRE, E C-Religious Opinions & Character of Washington-NY-
1836-Harper-12mo-414p-sprigged cl   (5j5)   15.00

McGUIRE, HARRY-Tales of Rod & Gun-NY-1931-illus-218p
(5ss8)   5.00

McGUIRE, HUNTER-Geo L Christian-Richmond-1907-229p-cl-
illus-1st ed   (5t2, pres)   12.50

McGUIRE, J A-In the Alaska Yukon Gamelands-Cinn-(1921)-215p-
photos   (5ss8)   10.00

McGUIRE, JOS D-Pipes & Smoking Customs of the Amer Aborigines-
Wash-1899-from Rpt of US Nat'l Mus for 1897-p351 to 645(295p)-
maps-wrps-an unusual association cpy, as this was from the
libr of noted Frederic Hodge
(5t3, cl, Fredk Hodge copy) 20. (5r7)   10.00

McGUIRE, LELIA-Old World Foods for New World Families-Detroit-
1946-112p-illus-sprial bnd bds   (5c0)   5.00

MACHADO, JOSE BETTENCOURT-Machado of Brazil-NY-1953-
Bramerica-8vo-cl-port   (4a3)   7.50

MACHARD, HENRI-Traite Pratique sur Les Vins-Besancon-1860-
12mo-hf calf-344p-3rd ed   (5w1)   9.50

MACHEN, A W-Treatise on Modern Law of Corp with Ref to
Formation & Operation under General Laws-Bost-1908-2 vols-
(5r4)   12.50

MACHEN, ARTHUR-The Anatomy of Tobacco-NY-1926-cl-papr labl-
12mo   (4i1) 8. (4b5)   10.00

--The Angels of Mons-Lond-1915-Simpkin, Marshall, Hamilton, Kent-
bds-1st ed   (5ss3, chip)   10.00

--Bowmen & Other Legends of the War-Lond-1915-heavy wrps-
16mo   (5i4, f, cl fldg case) 12.50   (4b5)   15.00

--The Canning Wonder-Lond-1925-Chatto&Windus-1st ed
(4b5, mint)   10.00

--The chronicle of Clemendy-Carbonnek-1888-8vo-orig qtr vel-
bds-frontis-priv prntd for Soc of Pantagruelists-1939-orig-
ltd to 250c   (4m8, rub, dust soil) 17.50 (5xx6, sl wn)   40.00

--same-Carbonnek-1923-priv prntd-ltd ed, nbr, autg-331p-
hf parch   (5dd0, 5jj0)   15.00

--Dog & Duck-Lond-(1924)-JCape-bds-ltd to 900c (4b5, mint, dj) 15.00

--same-NY-1924-Knopf   (4b5, mint, dj)   15.00

--Dreads & Drolls-Lond-1926-t8vo-bds-1st ed-ltd to 100c, autg, nbrd-
(5r9, dj)   30.00

--Fantastic Tales or The Way to Attain-Carbonnek-1923-bds-
ltd to 1050c, autg-priv prntd
(5ss3, fade, dj fade) 20. (4b5, mint, dj, unopnd)   40.00

--The Glorious Mystery-Chig-1924-CoviciMcGee-1st ed
(4b5, vg, dj)   10.00

--The Grande Trouvaille-Lond-n.d.-4to-8p wi 2-1/2p text-3 wdcuts-
priv prntd-1st ed Bookshop-ltd to 250c, autg, nbrd (5ee9)   25.00

--The Great God Pan & The Inmost Light-Lond-1894-cl-JnLane-
1st ed   (5ss3, chip)   35.00

--The Green Round-Lond-(1938)-Ernest Benn-1st ed (4b5, mint, dj) 12.50

--Hieroglyphics-NY-1923-Knopf-1st ed   (4b5, mint, dj)   10.00

--Hill of Dreams-Lond-1907-frontis-1st ed   (5mm1)   30.00

--same-Bost-1907-1st Amer ed   (5r9)   10.00

--The London Adventure or the Art of Wandering-Lond-(1924)-
MartinSecker-8vo-bds-ltd to 200c, autg-lg papr (5ss3, fade)   25.00

--same-Lond-(1924)-M Secker   (4b5, f, dj)   15.00

--Ornaments in Jade-NY-1924-Knopf-ltd to 1000c, autg
(4b5, mint, box)   22.50

--Precious Balms-Lond-1924-sq8vo-buck-g.t.-1st ed-
ltd to 265c, autg, lg papr   (5r9)   15.00

--The Shining Pyramid-Chig-1923-8vo-cl-g.t.-242p-illus by
Wallace Smith-ltd to 875c-1st ed   (5ee9)   20.00

--same-Lond-1925-Secker-1st Engl ed   (4b5, f)   7.50

--Strange Roads & With the Gods in Spring-Lond-1923-Classic Pr-
sketches by Simpson&Millar-1st ed   (5ss3, sp fade)   7.50

--Strange Roads-Lond-1923-Class Pr-ltd ed-16mo-limp cl
(4b5, vg)   15.00

--The Terror-Lond-(1917)-Duckworth&Co-bds-1st ed
(5ss3, dj, hng crack)   15.00

--Things Near & Far-Lond-(1923)-MSecker-cl-1st ed
(5mm2) 5. (5ss3, fade, dj)   10.00

McHENRY, D E-Third Force in Canada-1950-351p   (4b9)   10.00

MACHETANZ, FREDK-Panuck, Eskimo Sled Dog-NY-(1939)-94p-
illus-Juvenile   (5ss1, pres)   7.50

--On Arctic Ice-NY-(1940)-105p-illus-1st ed   (5ss0, pres)   5.00

MACHETANZ, SARA-The Howl of the Malemute-NY-1961-204p-
photos   (5ss1, dj)   6.00

--Where Else But Alaska?-NY-(1954)-214p-illus
(5ss0, f) 5. (5ss1, pres)   6.00

MACHIAS COOKERY-"Like Mother Used to Make"-Machias-1926-
210(18)p-bds-rev ed   (5c4)   4.00

MACHIAVEL, NICHOLAS-The Art of War, in Seven Books-Albany-
1815-Southwick, prntr-8vo-349p-unbnd   (5t4)   15.00

MACHIAVELLI, NICCOLO-Opere-Gaetano Cambiagi-Firenze-
1782, 1783-6 vols-4to-frontis-calf   (5b0, lt rub)   225.00

McILHANY, EDW W-Recollections of a '49er-KansasCty-1908-
212p-12mo-illus-orig pict cl-1st ed (4c1, sl fade) 25. (5yy7)   20.00

McILHENNY, E A-Autobiography of an Egret-NY-(1939)-illus
(4a1, pres)   15.00

McILHENY, E A, ed-Befo' De War Spirituals-Bost-1933-illus(5x2)17.50

McILRAITH, J-Life of Sir John Richardson-Lond-1868-280p-calf-
2 plts-1st ed   (4e9, rub)   40.00

McILVAINE, CHAS-1000 Amer Fungi...giving Full Botanic
Descriptions-Indnpls-(1900)-78 plts-1 vol in 2-4to-part mor
(5z9, f bndg)   50.00

McILVAINE, CHAS P-Present Condition & Chief Want of the Church-
Gambier-1836-28p-disbnd   (5w5, bkstrp taped)   6.50

McILWAIN, CHAS HOWARD-The Growth of Political Thought in
the West-NY-(1932)-Macm-417p   (5p0)   7.50

McILWAINE, H R, ed-Legislative Journals of Council of Colonial
Virginia, 1918 to 1919-3 vols-4to-bds-hf cl-ltd to 500 sets
(5h9, mint) 38.50 (5g3)   22.50

McILWAINE, SHIELDS-Memphis...Down in Dixie-NY-c1948-400p
(5h6) 7. (5w5)   6.50

--The Southern Poor White, from Lubberland to Tobacco Road-
Univ of Okla Pr-1939-1st ed   (5x5)   10.00

McILWRATH, T F-The Bella Coola Indians-Tor-1948-Vols 1 & 2
(5qq5)   30.00

McILWRAITH, THOS-Birds of Ontario-Tor-1894-2nd ed, rev-426p-
illus   (5dd0)   6.50

MacINNES, C M-In the Shadow of the Rockies-Lond-1930-347p-
photos-2 fldg maps   (5ss1, pgs dmgd)   5.00

MACINNES, C M-England & Slavery-Lond-1934-12mo (5x2, dj)   15.00

McINNES, G-Canadian Art-Tor-1950-140p-illus (4b9, mint, dj)   20.00

MACINNES, TOM-Chinook Days-n.d.-206p-11 illus (4b2, sl soil)   6.00

--High Low Along-Vancouver-1934-69p   (4b9)   12.00

--Oriental Occupation of BC-Vancouver-1927-Van Sun-170p-wrps
(5dd7)   12.00

--Rhymes of a Rounder-NoVancouver-n.d.-(1931?)-stiff wrps
(4b9, sl loose)   10.00

McINTOSH & TWYMAN-The Archko Volume-Phila-1896-
Antiquarian Book Co   (5b9, vf)   25.00

McINTOSH, BURR-The Little I Saw of Cuba-Lond&NY-(1899)-
173p-illus   (5t4, hng crack)   5.00

McINTOSH, C F-Brief Abstract of Lower Norfolk Co & Norfolk Co
Wills, 1637 to 1710-Norfolk-1914-223p   (5j4, fox)   7.50

--Brief Abstracts of Norfolk Co Wills 1710 to 1753-Norfolk-1922-
343p   (5j4, fox)   7.50

M'INTOSH, CHAS-The Greenhouse, Hot House & Stove-Lond-1840-
415p-a.e.g.-cl-18 hand col liths-new ed (5hh7, sl wn)   30.00

MacINTOSH, J-Discovery of Amer by Christopher Columbus & Origin
of North Amer Indians-Tor-1836-bds-152p incl 2p subscr (4b2) 22.50

McINTOSH, MARIA J-Alice Montrose; or, the lofty & the lowly-
Lond-1853-Bentley-3 vols in 1-12mo-hf calf-1st Engl ed
(5i9, rub)   22.50

--Charms & counter charms-NY-1848-Appleton-12mo-orig black cl-
1st ed   (5x1, cov wn)   40.00

--Evenings at Donaldson Manor-NY&Phila-1851-Appleton-illus-
dec cl-1st ed, 1st state, wi advts dated '51   (5m2)   7.50

--The Lofty & Lowly-NY-1853-Appleton-2 vols-1st ed
(5x4, e.p. cut)   17.50

--Minnie; or, the Little Woman, a Fairy Story-Bost-1857-12mo-165p-
illus-1st ed-scarce   (5v0, f)   8.50

-- Two lives; or, to seem & to be-NY-1846-Appleton-12mo-
orig purple cl-1st ed   (5x1, fade)   30.00

--Woman in America, Her Work & Her Reward-NY-1850-155p-
orig prntd wrps-1st ed   (5m3, sl dmpstnd)   22.50

MACINTYRE, CAPT DONALD-The Thunder of the Guns, a Century of
Battleships-NY-1960-352p-maps   (5s1) 5. (5w5)   4.50

--U-Boat Killer-NY-1957-7 photos   (5c1)   7.00

MACINTYRE, NEIL-Attack on Everest-Lond-(1936)-Methuen-172p-
cl   (5d7)   6.00

McINTYRE, W I-Colored Soldiers-Macon, Ga-1923
(5x2, stdn) 12.50 (5x2)   17.50

MacINTYRE, W IRWIN-An Amer Princess-Bost-(1926)-illus-maps-
177p   (4b2)   3.00

MacIVER, H IAN-Amateurs Afloat-Lond-1927-222p-photos-maps
(5s1)   4.50

McIVOR, A-The Overlord-NY-1904-423p   (4b9)   10.00

MACK, ARTHUR C-Palisades of Hudson-Edgewater-(1909)-illus
(5tt5, bdng spotted)   6.00

MACK, C E-Two Black Crows in the A E F-NY-1928   (5x2)   7.50

MACK, EBENEZER-The Life of Gilbert Motier de Lafayette-Ithaca-
1841-8vo-calf-lea labl-illus-1st ed   (5m6, rub, fox)   10.00

MACK, EDWIN F-Old Monroe Street-Chig-1914-bds-83p-illus
(4i2)   17.50

MACK, EFFIE MONA-Mark Twain in Nevada-1947-Scribner's-
illus-t8vo-1st ed   (5dd6) 14.50 (5h5, f, dj)   15.00

MACK, GERSTLE-Gustave Courbet-NY-1951-Knopf-4to-429p-cl-plts-1st ed (5m7) 15.00
--The Land Divided-1944-Knopf-4to-cl-illus-maps-1st ed (5h4,f,dj,pres) 20.00
--Toulouse Lautrec-NY-1938-Knopf-370p-illus (5x0) 7.50
MACKAIL, J W-The Life of Wm Morris-Lond&NY-1899-2 vols-lg8vo-illus (5p6) 15.00
--same-Lond-1901-illus-2 vols (5mm2) 12.50
--The Odyssey-Lond-1903-JnMurray-3 vols-orig cl (5ss3,fade) 25.00
MACKAIL, WM W-Leonard L Mackall,a Character Sketch-Savannah-1938-illus-12mo-cl-100c prntd (4c1) 6.00
MACKALL, LAWTON-Knife & Fork in NY-NY-(1948)-249p (5g9) 3.50
MACKANESS, GEO-The Life of Vice Admiral Wm Bligh, R N-NY-n.d.-8vo-cl-2 vols in 1-illus (5t2) 7.50
MACKAY, ALASTAIR I-Farming & Gardening in the Bible-Penn-(1950)-Rodale Pr-280p-frontis-1st ed (5s7) 7.50
MACKAY, ALEX-Die Westliche Welt, Reise durch die Vereinstaaten von Amerika-transl by Marie Heine-Leipzig-n.d.-(ca 1861)-4 vols in 1-8vo-cl-4 plts (5ss5) 10.00
--The Western World-Lond-1849-Bentley-2nd ed-3 vols-illus-2 fldg maps-orig cl (5L1) 60. (5n9,hf mor) 65. (5tt6) 80.00
--same-Phila-1849-Lea&Blanchard-2 vols-cl (5tt0,ex-libr,wn) 10. (4m2,ex-libr,vg) 25.00
MACKAY, ANDREW-The Complete Navigator, to which is added a concise system of calculations by P Delamar-Phila-1807-8vo-calf-7 plts-1st Amer ed (5m3) 75. (5L1) 25.00
--Descrip & Use of the Sliding Gunter-1812-2 plts-buck-2nd ed,imprvd (5L7,rbnd) 12.50
McKAY, C-Banjo-NY-1929-1st ed (5x2) 15.00
--same-not 1st ed (5x2) 10.00
--Harlem, Negro Metropolis-NY-1940-illus (5x2) 35.00
--Home to Harlem-NY-1929-1st ed (5x2) 12.50
--Selected Poems-NY-1953-1st ed (5x2,dj,mint) 15.00
MACKAY, CHAS-Life & Liberty in America-NY-1859-illus-1st Amer ed (5yy6) 17.50 (5ee3) 22.50
--Memoirs of Extraordinary Popular Delusions-Lond-1841-3 vols-ports-part calf-a.e.g.-1st ed (5nn2,f bndg) 35.00
--The Mormons-Lond-(1951)-illus-326p-adv (5i3) 15. (4n4) 27.50
McKAY, CLAUDE-Banana Bottom-1933-Harper (5F1,dj sl wn) 27.50
--Harlem, Negro Metropolis-NY-(1940)-illus-1st ed (4b6) 15.00
--A Long Way from Home-(1937)-Lee Furman-v scarce (5F1,dj) 25.00
--Quartier Noir-(Home to Harlem)-Paris-1932-286p-wrps (5r7) 7.50
McKAY, D-A Gentleman in a Black Skin-NY-1932 (5x2) 7.50
McKAY, DONALD-Some Famous Sailing Ships & Their Builder-NY-1928-10p col plts (5c1) 50.00
MacKAY, DOUGLAS-The Honourable Company-Tor-1949-illus-maps-2nd (rev) ed (5aa0) 10. (4e9) 15.00
--same-Indnpls-(1936)-1st ed, Toronto impr-maps-plts-396p (5dd9,autg) 22.50
--same-Tor-1938-photos-maps-396p (5ss4,fade) 12.50
--same-NY-1938-maps-396p (4m2) 15.00
MACKAY, E-Monroes in France, Hist of a Branch of the Family Desc from Chief of the Clans-1908-(text in French & Engl)-20p (5mm3) 10.00
McKAY, G L-A Bibliog of Robert Bridges-NY-1933-215p-g.t.-only 550c prntd (5p6,f) 16.00
McKAY, G L-Principles & Practice of Butter Making-NY-1908-350p, 19p-illus-2nd ed, rev & enlgd (5c5,fade) 3.50
McKAY, GEO L-Amer Book Auction Catalogues, 1713 to 1934-NY-1937-540p-8vo-wrps (4c1) 25.00
McKAY, HUGH-Geneaology of, & His Desc, 1788 to 1895-n.d.-76p (5mm3) 8.00
MACKAY, J A-Psalms & Hymns in the Language of the Cree Indians-Lond-(1935)-cl (4k4,f) 10.00
MACKAY, JOHN RUSSELL-Sea Weavers & Other Poems-Antwerp-n.d.-114p-1st ed-ltd to 500c,autg (5s1,pres) 6.00
MACKAY, JOHN W-Mark!-NY-(1956)-121p-illus (5t7,dj) 10.00
MACKAY, MALCOLM S-Cow Range & Hunting Trail-1925-243p-illus(3 by Russell)-1st ed-scarce (5r1,vg,dj) 50. (5zz5,autg) 45. (5zz5) 40.00
McKAY, MARTHA N-When the Tide Turned In the Civil War-Indnpls-1929-Hollenbeck Pr (5x2,5s4,dj,f) 15.00
MACKAY, PIONEER MISSIONARY-of the Church Missionary Soc to Uganda, by his sister-NY-1890 (5x2) 5.00
McKAY, R H-Little Pills-Pittsburg, Kans-1918-127p-cl-Pittsburg Headlight (5d6) 20. (5zz5) 25. (4m2,f) 22.50
McKAY, RICHARD C-Some Famous Sailing Ships & Their Builder-NY-Putnam-1928-395p-illus (5p9) 15.00
McKAY, RICHARD C-South Street-NY-(1934)-460p-illus (5q0) 25. (5p7) 16. (5t7) 15.00
MACKAY, ROBT-Letters to His Wife-Athens-(1949)-illus (5yy6) 10.00
MACKAY, ROBT W S-The stranger's guide to...Montreal-Montreal-1848-32mo-prntd wrps-fldg map-plts (5g3) 12.50

McKAY, SETH S-Debates in Texas Constit Convention of 1875-Austin-1930-471p (4j4,f) 18.50 (4c7,dj) 12.50
--Texas Politics, 1906 to 1944-Lubbock-1952-486p (5n4) 12.50
MacKAY, W A-Pioneer Life in Zorra-Tor-1899-400p (4e6) 20.00
McKAY, W J STEWART-Evolution of the Endurance, Speed & Staying Power of the Racehorse-Lond-1937-320p-illus (5w4) 7.50
MACKAY, WM R-Skein of Life-Phila-1897-260p-cl (5h1) 12.50
McKAY, J-The Mastership & Its Fruits-NY-1864-38p-wrps-Loyal Pub Soc (5x2) 27.50
MacKAYE, PERCY-Jeanne d'Arc-NY-1918-Macmillan-12mo-166p-ads-8th ed-frontis-pic cl (5p1,soil) 5.00
--Johnny Crimson,a Legend of Hollis Hall-Bost-1895-8vo-wrps-illus-cov by Eric Pape-1st ed of auth's 1st book (5gg6,pres) 100.00
--Ode on the Centenary of Abraham Lincoln-NY-1909-sm4to-orig cl-1st ed (5p5) 7.50
M'KEAN CO, PA-Map of, 1856-Phila-(1856)-ca 27x25-fld in 12mo cl covs (5g3) 20.00
McKEAN, F G-History, Notes, being quotations from History & Other Records-1906-250p (5mm3) 20.00
McKEARIN, GEO S-Amer Glass-NY-(1941)-4to-cl-622p-illus (5t7) 12.50
--same-NY-1942-illus-622p-4to (5h9) 10.00
--200 Yrs of Amer Blown Glass-NY-1950-382p-4to-col-ltd ed (5w1) 20.00
McKECHNIE, HECTOR-Lamont Clan, 1235 to 1935-1938-602p-36 plts (5t9) 30.00
McKEE, HARLEY, J,ed-Architecture Worth Saving in Onondaga Co-Syracuse U-(1964)-sq8vo-202p-illus-pict wrps (5j5,autg) 7.50
McKEE, IRVING-The Trail of Death, Letters of Benj M Pettit-1941-Vol 14,#1-wrps (4a9) 5.00
McKEE, JAS C-Narr of Surrender of a Command of U S Forces at Ft Fillmore, July, 1861-1960-reprnt-ltd to 550c (5hh3) 7.50
McKEE, OLIVER-U S "Snap Shots"-Bost-(ca1892)-col plts (5yy6) 10.00
McKEE, RUTH KARR-Mary Richardson Walker, Her Book-Caldwell-1945-357p-illus (5s4,dj,f) 10.00
McKEE, THOS H-Gun Book For Boys & Men-NY-1918-illus-362p (5ss8,pres) 12.50
McKEEN, SILAS-History of Bradford-1875-459p & errata (5e8,hngs broken) 8.75 (5mm3) 10.00
McKEEVER, HARRIET B-Edith's Ministry-Phila-1864-Lindsay & Blakiston-431p-not 1st ed (5x4,sl wn) 7.50
McKEEVER, WM A-The Pioneer, Verse-Topeka-1911-101p-wrps-illus-punched wi cord (5s4,autg) 4.00
McKELLAR, HUGH-Presbyterian Pioneer Missionaries in Man, Sask, Alb & BC-Tor-1924-249p-ports (5a1) 6.50
McKELLAR, K D-Tennessee Senators-Kingsport-1942-625p-1st ed (5yy8,pres) 12.00
MacKELLAR, SMITHS & JORDAN CO-Specimens of Printing Types-Phila-June, 1890-512p-(19th issue)-cl (5yy3,few small cut outs) 65.00
--same-Phila-1890-illus-510p (5yy0) 24.50
McKELVEY, BLAKE-Rochester, Water power City, 1812 to 1854-Cambr-1945-illus (5yy6) 6.00
McKELVEY, SUSAN DELANO-The Lilac,a Monograph-NY-1928-Macm-581p-4to-4 pkt charts (5x0) 60.00
--Yuccas of the Southwestern US-Jamaica Plain-1938, 1947-2 vols-145 plts-sm4to-prntd wrps (5z9) 27.50
--same-in1 vol-buck (5z9) 27.50
McKELVIE, B A-Early History of Province of Brit Columbia-Tor-1926-118p-illus (5dd7) 8. (4b9) 10.00
--Fort Langley, Outpost of Empire-Vancouver-1947-4to-bds-98p-col frontis-2 maps (4a8) 10.00
--Maquinna the Magnificent-Vancouver-1946-illus-4to-bds-cl bk-col plts-65p (4a8) 15.00
--Pageant of B C-Tor-1955-263p-plts (5dd0) 5.00
--same-Tor-1957-Centenial ed-illus (5dd7) 6.50
McKENNA, CHAS F-Under the Maltese Cross-Pittsburg-1910-sm4to-817p (4a7,rub,new e.p.) 32.50
McKENNA, J A J-Hudson Bay Route-Ottawa-(1907?)-illus-53p-fldg maps-stiff wrps (4e6) 20.00
McKENNA, JAS A-Black Range Tales-NY-1936-300p-illus (5m9,5s4,warp,stns) 15. (5zz5) 25. (5g0,f,dj) 35.00
McKENNEY, THOS-History of the Indian Tribes of NoAmer-Phila-1855-Rice-3 vols-120 ports (5t1) 350.00
--The Indian Tribes of NoAmer-Edinb-1933-thk8vo-123 col plts-3 vols-orig cl-new ed, ed by Hodge-John Grant (5x5,f,dj) 125. (4d2) 250.00
--Memoirs, Official & Personal, wi sketches of Travels Among the Northern & Southern Indians-NY-1846-2 vols in 1 (5zz5) 35. (5L3) 32.50
MACKENSIE, DR R S,ed-Memoirs of Houdin, written by himself-Phila-1859 (5t4) 7.50

MACKENZIE, A–History of the Frasers of Lovat, with genealogies–
1896–buck   (5L7, rbnd)   25.00
MACKENZIE, A DeB–Gazzam History–1894–72p   (5mm3)   10.00
MACKENZIE, A L–Clarence Milton, the Heroic Fireman–Cleve–
1900–cl–296p–illus   (4h1, rub)   15.00
MacKENZIE, ADELHEID Z–His sweetheart–Phila–1877–Moore–pic cl–
1st ed   (5m2)   10.00
McKENZIE, AIMEE L, transl–The George Sand, Gustave Flaubert
Letters–Lond–(1922)–8vo–cl–33, 382p   (5t0)   7.50
MACKENZIE, ALEX–Alexander Mackenzie's Voyage to Pacific Ocean
in 1793–Chig–1931–Lakeside Classic–frontis–fldg map
                         (5p7) 6.   (5L0)   7.50
--Reisen Von Montreal Durch NordwestAmerika Nach Dem Eismeer
Und Der Sud See in Den Jahren 1789 Und 1793–Hamburg–1802–
part mor–585p–1st German ed–errata   (4n4)   110.00
--Voyages dans l'Interieur de l'Amerique Septentrionale, Faits en
1789, 1792 et 1793–Paris–1802–3 vols–plts–map
                         (5e2) 250.   (4n4)   125.00
--Voyages from Montreal on River St. Laurence through Continent
of NoAmer to Frozen & Pac Oceans–Lond–1801–lea–maps–
1st ed   (4L3) 225.   (4n4, sp crack) 450. (5x5)   400.00
--same–NY–1802–map–lea–296p–1st Amer ed   (5t2)   85.00
--Voyages from Montreal Thru Continent of NoAmer to Frozen &
Pac Oceans in 1789 & 1793–NY–1922–fldg map–2 vols
                         (4e9) 25.   (5nn2)   12.50
--Voyage to Pacific Ocean in 1793–Chig–1931–Lakeside Classics–
port–fldg map   (5s6) 10.   (5w8)   17.50
MACKENZIE, ALEX–Hist of the Camerons–Inverness, Scotland–
1884–478p   (5t9)   25.00
MACKENZIE, ALEX–Life of Paul Jones–NY–1848–2 vols–port–
16mo   (4L3) 15.   (4m2)   17.50
--Oliver Hazard Perry–NY–1916–436p–illus–g. (5s1)   3.00
MACKENZIE, COLIN, ed–Chas Lillie, the British Perfumer–Lond–
1822–372p–orig cl–2nd ed   (5s7, cov soil, lacks e.p.)   23.50
---5000 Receipts–Phila–1825–670p, (2), (9)–cl bk–bds–1st US ed
                                             (5c0, ex-libr, rbnd)   25.00
--same–Phila–1829–546p–calf   (5w1, stnd, wn) 20.00
--same–Phila&Pittsb–1830–456p–8vo–orig sheep–from latest Lond ed–
                                             (5L1)   15.00
MACKENZIE, COMPTON–Extraordinary Women–Lond–1929–
st trade ed   (5yy6, sp wn, Dorothy Gish bkplt)   10.00
--The Savoy of London–Lond–1953–141p–illus–bds (5y2)   4.50
MACKENZIE, D R–Sprit Ridden Konde–Phila–1925–8vo–318p–map–
photos   (4a6)   10.00
MACKENZIE, F A–Landru–Lond–1928–cl–illus–Famous Trials Series–
244p   (5t2, fray)   4.00
--20th Century Crimes–Bost–1927–Little–273p–illus (5p9)   6.00
MACKENZIE, SIR G S–Treatise on Diseases & Management of
Sheep–NY–1810–bds   (5L7, rbkd, ex-libr)   27.50
--Travels in Island of Iceland During Summer of Year 1810–Edinb–
1811–lg4to–calf–(2)491p(1)–15 plts–2 maps(1 fldg) (4e1, rbkd) 175.00
MACKENZIE, GERTRUDE–My Love Affair with the State of Maine–
(1955)–311p   (5e8)   3.85
MACKENZIE, H H–Mackenzies of Ballone–Enverness–1941–198p–
                                             (5t9)   12.50
MACKENZIE, HENRY–Report of Committee of Highland Soc of
Scotland...Ossian–Edinb–1805–8vo–343p–col frontis–plts–bds
                                             (5i4, f)   100.00
MACKENZIE, J ROSS–Brewing & Malting–Lond–(1921)–143p, (9)–
illus   (5w1, fox)   6.50
MACKENZIE, SIR JAS–The Castles of England–Lond–1897–imp 8vo–
orig cl–40 plts–plans–2 Vols   (4e1)   45.00
MACKENZIE, JEAN K–African Clearings–NY–1924–HoughtonMiff–
270p–pic cov   (4t5)   10.00
--African Trail–W Medford, Mass–1917–United Study of Foreign
Missions–222p–photos   (4t4)   7.50
--Black Sheep–NY–1916–HoughtonMiff–314p   (4t5)   10.00
--Friends of Africa–Cambr–1928–photos–250p   (4t5)   5.00
MACKENZIE, JOHN–Day Dawn in Dark Places–Lond–n.d.–(c1883)–
Cassell–278p–illus–pict cov   (4t5, pres)   35.00
MACKENZIE, KENNETH–Living Rough–Lond–1936–288p (4d1)   6.50
MACKENZIE, R SHELTON–Life of Chas Dickens, with Letters by
'Boz'–Phila–1870–port–484p, 6p–1st ed   (4a8)   7.50
MACKENZIE, ROBT–America, a History–Lond–1892–571p (5h9)   7.50
MACKENZIE, W DOUGLAS–John Mackenzie: So African Missionary
& Statesman–NY–1902–12&564p   (5c6)   13.25
--South Africa, Its Hist, Heros & Wars–Vancouver–1899–MacGregor–
4 vols in 1–photos–682p   (4t5)   15.00
MACKENZIE, W L–Mackenzies Own Narr of the Rebellion....Siege
of Toronto....Dec 1837–Tor–1937–30p   (4e9)   25.00
MACKENZIE, WM–A practical treatise on diseases of the eye...from
last London ed–Bost–1833–bds–cl bk–papr labl–Mass Med Soc,
Vol 3   (5g4)   12.50

MACKENZIE, WM L–Lives & Opinion of Benj Franklin Butler...
& Jesse Hoyt–Bost–1845–152p–wrps   (4h2) 10.   (5r7)   12.50
MACKENZIE'S–10,000 Receipts–Phila–1866–cl–487p–2nd ed
                                             (5hh7, wn)   8.50
McKEOWN, MARTHA F–Alaska Silver–NY–1951
            (5ss0) 5.   (5m9) 3.50   (5zz8)   4.50
--Them Was the Days–NY–1950–282p   (5ss1, autg)   6.00
--The Trail Led North–NY–1948–222p–map
            (4b9) 8.   (5zz8, autg, 5ss0, 5t3)   5.00
McKERN, W C–Prelim Report on Upper Mississippi Phase in Wisc–
Milwaukee–1945–(Bull of Pub Mus of Milwa#3)–109p to 285p–
plts 20 to 71   (5h4)   5.00
McKERROW, RONALD–Intro to Bibliography for Literary Students–
Oxford–(1928)–8vo–cl–360p–2nd impress wi corr (5ee9)   15.00
McKESSON & ROBBINS–Prices Current of Drugs, Chemical &
Pharmaceutical Preparations–NY–1881–flexible cl–130p(5hh6) 8.50
--The Road to Market–n.p.–1958–62p–illus   (5y2)   4.00
MACKEURTAN, GRAHAM–Cradle Days of Natal–Lond–1930–
Longmans, Green–348p–photos   (4t5)   15.00
MACKEY, A G–History of Freemasonry–NY–(1898)–7 vols–illus–
4to   (5ii2)   47.50
--same–NY–(1906)–Masonic Hist Co–4to–hf lea (5p0, chip)   25.00
--Encyclopedia of Freemasonry & Its Kindred Sciences–Chig–1925–
2 vols–rev–illus–913p   (4b3)   12.50
MACKEY, MARGARET–Los Angeles, Proper & Improper–LosAng–1938–
Goodwin–181p–photos–sm folio   (4n1)   7.00
MACKIE, PAULINE BRADFORD–Mademoiselle de Berny–Bost–1897–
8vo–cl–illus–Lamson, Wolffe–g.t.   (5b2, f)   6.00
--Pauline Bradford Hopkins, a Georgian Actress–Bost–1900–296p–
illus   (5m1)   8.50
MACKIE, T C CAMPBELL–Pattern–Lond–1928–53p–illus–frontis(5n7) 2.00
McKIM, RANDOLPH H–A Soldier's Recoll...Young Confederate–
NY–1911–Longm–362p   (4p7, sp sl tn)   15.00
--same–NY–1910   (5h6)   20.00
MACKINAC UNDER 3 FLAGS–MackinacIsle–(1928)–46p–wrps (5h7) 5.00
McKINLEY, SILAS BENT–Woodrow Wilson, a biography–NY–(1957)–
284p–illus   (5t4)   4.50
McKINLEY, WM–Life of, 1843 to 1901–NY–PFCollier–lg4to–photos–
dec bds–cl bk   (5r0)   15.00
McKINNEN, DAN'L–Tour thru British West Indies in yrs 1802 &
1803–Lond–1804–8vo–hf calf–1st ed–rare   (5i0)   100.00
McKINNEY, EMMA–Aunt Caroline's Dixieland Recipes–Chig–(1922)–
(7), 147p–4th ed   (5c4)   3.50
McKINNEY, ROLAND–Thos Eakins–NY–1942–Crown Publ–111p–
illus–4to   (4a0)   20.00
--Thos Eakins–NY–1942–Crown Publ–29p–illus–crown 4to (4a0,dj) 17.50
McKINNIE, P L–From Tide to Timber Line–Chig–1895–151p–illus–
1st ed   (5ee3)   7.50
MacKINNON, J G–Old Sydney, Sketches of Town & Its People in
Days Gone By–Sidney–1918–DonMacKinnon, prntr–cl–16mo–
143p   (4t1)   12.50
MacKINNON, CAPT R N–Atlantic & Transatlantic–NY–1852–
324p   (5s1, ex-libr) 9.00
MACKINNON, W H–Journal of CIV in So Africa–Lond–1901–
12&252p–16 plts–2 maps   (5c6)   9.50
MACKINSTRY, E–The Fairy Alphabet–NY–1933–plts–1st ed (5v2) 10.00
McKITTRICK, MYRTLE M–Vallejo, Son of Calif–Port–(1944)–photos–
365p–1st ed–scarce   (5zz5, dj wn) 17.50
McKNIGHT, CHAS–Captain Jack, the Scout–Phila–(1873)
                         (5mm1) 12.50   (4a9)   15.00
--Old Fort Duquesne, or, Capt Jack, the scout–Pittsb–1873–People's
Monthly Publ–8vo–orig brick dec cl–frontis–1st ed (5i0)   15.00
--same–Phila–1874–Peoples Monthly Publ   (5x4)   9.00
--Our Western Border–Phila–1875–756p–1st ed–hf lea
                         (5yy0) 12.50   (5ii9, rbnd)   30.00
--same–Phila–1876–8vo–illus–2nd ed   (4k5) 15.   (5ss5)   12.50
--same–n.p.–n.d.–(ca1880?)–442p–cl   (5ff7)   12.50
McKNIGHT FAMILY CIRCLE–1889–98p   (5mm3)   20.00
McKNIGHT, GEO–Modern English in the making–NY–1928–590p–
illus–1st ed   (5p6, f)   10.00
--English Words & Their Background–NY–1925–Appleton–449p(5p7) 4.50
MacKNIGHT, JAS–A New Literal Translation from Orig Greek of
all the Apostolical Epistles–Edinb–1795–3 vols–4to–calf–
2nd ed–1st of subscribers   (5i3)   50.00
MACKNIGHT, THOS Life of Henry St John–Lond–1863–pt mor–
728p   (5aa0, sl rub) 25.00
McKNIGHT, W J–Pioneer Outline History of NW Penna, 1780 to
1850–Phila–1905–illus–maps–4to–749p–scarce   (4m2)   35.00
MACKOY, R S–Cabin in the Sunshine–Cinn–1936 (5x2, dj)   5.00
McKUNE, ROBT H, comp–Memorial of Erection of Lackawanna Co,
Pa–Scranton–1882–frontis–115p   (4m2)   8.50
McLACHLAN, R W–First Mohawk Primer–Mont–1908–13p–stiff wrps
                                             (4e9, autg)   20.00

MacLAGAN, E R D-Prophetic Books of Wm Blake, Jerusalem-
Lond-1904-Bullen-127p-4to-bds   (5m7, shaken)   20.00
McLAIN, J S-Alaska & the Klondike-NY-1905-330p-illus
(5ss1,4e6)   15.00
McLANATHAN, RICH B K-Ship Models-Bost-1957-photos-
stiff wrps   (5c1)   4.50
McLANE, LUCY NEELY-A Piney Paradise by Monterey Bay-SanFran-
1952-Lawton Kennedy-sm4to-cl-231p (5h4,bkplt) 10. (4t1) 20.00
MacLANE, MARY-Story of Mary MacLane by Herself-Chig-1902-
Herbert S Stone-12mo-322p-frontis-t.e.g.-1st ed (5p1,fade) 10.00
MacLAREN, HALE-Be Your Own Guest-Bost-1952-178p (5c0) 3.00
McLAREN, J-Law of Wills & Succession as Admin in Scotland-Edinb-
1894-2 vols-3rd ed   (5r4)   13.50
McLAREN, JACK-My Odyssey-Lond-(1928)-8vo-187p-photos(4a6)4.00
McLAREN, JOHN-Gardening in Calif Landscape & Flower-SanFran-
1914-illus   (5m9)   7.50
--same-SanFran-1924-lg8vo-cl   (5h5, vg)   5.00
McLAREN, L L-High Living Recipes from Southern Climes-SanFran-
(1904)-58, (3)p-Paul Elder   (5c0,fade)   14.50
--same-SanFran&NY-(1907)-Paul Elder-58, (3)p (5c4,wtrstn) 12.50
--Pan Pacific Cook Bk-SanFran-1915-170p-illus-dec cl (4g9) 7.50
McLAREN, M-Lord Lovat of the '45-1957-plts (5L7) 5.00
McLAREN, WALTER S BRIGHT-Spinning Woollen & Worsted-Lond-
1893-Cassell-sm12mo-cl-256p   (5j5)   6.00
McLAREN, WM-Unity of the Human Race-Belleville, Ont-1860-
Chronicle-lecture....Belleville YMCA   (5nn8)   20.00
McLAUGHLIN, A C-Cyclopaedia of Amer Government-1914-3 vols-
(5L7,ex-libr)   25.00
McLAUGHLIN, ANDREW C-The Confederation & the Constitution-
NY-1905-port-maps   (5r7)   7.50
McLAUGHLIN, DAN'L-Sketch of a Trip from Omaha to Salmon River-
Chig-1954-18p-bds   (5d6)   25.00
McLAUGHLIN, GERALD, L S J-Counsellor's Guide to the Social
Services of Mass-(1959)-266p   (5e8, dj)   3.50
McLAUGHLIN, J FAIRFAX-Matthew Lyon-NY-1900-531p-cl
(5tt8)   30.00
McLAUGHLIN, JAS-My Friend the Indian-Bost-1910-8vo-cl-
1st ed   (5hh4,vg) 20. (5zz5, f)   25.00
--same-Bost-1910-illus-404p plus index-1st ed, 3rd prntg
(4k4,5yy7)   15.00
McLAUGHLIN, M-China-Painting-Cinn-1880-69p-bds
(5ii2, lacks sp)   7.50
--same-Cinn-1894-103p   (5n7, wn)   6.50
--Pottery Decoration Under the Glaze-Cinn-1880-95, (7)p-12mo-
wrps   (5n7)   5.00
McLAUGHLIN, MRS MARIE L-Myths & Legends of the Sioux-
Bismarck, ND-1916-1st ed   (4k4, dj, f)   17.50
McLAUGHLIN, N MONROE-The Last Man-Wash-1900-221p-cl
(5h7)   10.00
McLAUGHLIN, ROBT W-Caleb Matthews-NY-(1913)-Eaton-83p
(5x0)   4.00
--Wash & Lincoln-NY-1912-illus-calf by Riviere-extra illus wi
37 ports   (5g4, f bndg)   15.00
McLAURIN, COLIN C-My Old Home Church in Rural Ontario-
Edmonton-1937-134p-plts   (4a8)   6.50
McLAURIN, JOHN J-Sketches in Crude Oil-Harrisburg-1896-illus-
8vo-cl-406p-1st ed   (5L7) 12.50 (5g5)   20.00
--same-Harrisburg-1898-frontis-2nd ed-452p-illus (5yyU) 9.50
MACLAY, EDGAR S-A History of Amer Privateers-NY-1924-
Appleton-519p-illus   (5p0)   12.50
--History of the US Navy from 1775 to 1893-NY-1894-2 vols-
Appleton-cl   (5q8) 12. (5ss5) 12.50 (5d6)   20.00
--same-NY-1897-illus-2 vols   (5ee3)   15.00
--Reminiscences of Old Navy -NY-1898-362p-index (5ii2) 7.00
--same-NY-1898-362p-cl-ltd to 750c (5h2) 10. (5ee3) 12.50
MacLEAN, ANNIE MARION-Some Problems of Reconstruction-
Chig-1921   (5t4)   5.00
McLEAN, BETH B-Good Manners-Peoria-(1934)-128p (5w7) 2.50
MacLEAN, CATHERINE M-Born Under Saturn-NY-1944-8vo-cl-
631p-illus   (5t0, dj)   5.00
McLEAN COUNTY, ILLINOIS-History of...-Chig-1879-1078p-cl
(5zz9, rebnd)   52.50
MACLEAN, EVA-Unser Kamerun von Heute-Munich-1940-159p-
56 plts-sm4to   (5c6, vg)   13.75
MACLEAN, GRACE E-"Uncle Tom's Cabin" in Germany-NY-1910
(5jj3)   10.00
McLEAN, J H-By command, all nations to keep the peace-1880-
4to-buck   (5L7, rbnd)   12.50
McLEAN, J H-Family Almanac & Recipe Book for Year of Our Lord,
1859-StL-1859-Wiebusch&Son-3rd ed   (4b3)   17.50
MacLEAN, J KENNEDY-Heroes of the Polar Seas-Lond-n.d.-
(ca1910)-8 illus-2 fldg maps   (5c1)   12.50

MacLEAN, J P-Biblio of Shaker Literature-Columbus-1905-frontis-
71p   (4h8, lacks front wrp)   12.50
--History of MacLean Clan from its First Settlement at Duard Castle
in Isle of Mull-1889-480p   (5t9)   25.00
--Hist Account of Settlements of Scotch Highlanders in Amer-
Cleve-1900-459p-cl   (5h7, libr stmp)   25.00
--Journal of Michael Walter-n.p.-1899-(177)-188p-wrps-
Wstn Resv Hist Soc #89   (5h7, sl chip)   3.00
--Mound Builders-Cinn-1879-233p-fldg map-cl-1st ed-scarce
(5y0)   17.50
--same-Cinn-1887-233p-fldg map-illus-maps (5ii8) 22.50
--Renaissance of the Clan MacLean-1913-208p (5mm3) 17.50
M'LEAN, JOHN-Notes of a 25 Yrs' Service in Hudson's Bay
Territory-Lond-1849-2 vols-1st ed   (4n4)   185.00
MacLEAN, JOHN-History of the College of New Jersey-Phila-
1877-Lippincott-2 vols-hf calf-g.dec (5qq8) 12.50 (5ii8) 20.00
MacLEAN, JOHN-Vanguards of Canada-Tor-1918-262p-plts-
fldg map   (5s0, autg)   8.50
McLEAN, N B-Report of Hudson Strait Expedition-Ottawa-1929-
wrps-221p-fldg maps-plts   (4d0)   12.50
MACLEAN, NORMAN-Africa in Transformation-Lond-1913-Nisbet-
263p-map(fldg)-photos   (4t5)   10.00
McLEAN, OLIVE GALE, illus-Flowers of Hawaii-text by Frear-
NY-1938-4to-cl   (5h4)   5.00
MACLEAN, ROBINSON-John Hoy of Ethiopia-Tor-1936-Oxf Un Pr-
264p-photos   (4t5)   7.50
McLEAN, ROBT N-That Mexican-NY-(1928)-184p-plts-1st ed
(5dd6,pres)   13.50
MACLEAR, ANNE BUSH-Early New England Towns-NY-1908-181p-
orig wrps-1st ed   (5yy6)   10.00
MacLEISH, ARCHIBALD-Conquistador-Bost-1932-t8vo-cl-1st ed
(5ee9,vg)   20.00
--Nobodaddy-Cambr-1926-Dunster House-1st ed-ltd to 750c
(5ss9, f,5ss3)   20.00
--Streets in the Moon-Bost-1926-1st ed-ltd to 550c (4b1) 27.50
McLELLAN, GEO - McLellan's Own Story-NY-1887-8vo-678p-
hf lea-illus-maps   (5m8, f)   7.50
McLEMORE, JEFF-Indianola & Other Poems-SanAntonio-1904-
165p   (4b4)   10.00
MacLENNAN, EWEN-Songs of the Neukluk-Council, Alaska-
May 15, 1912-30p-illus-cl-verse, priv prntd (5r0) 10.00
McLENNAN, J C-Industrial Research in Canada-Tor-1916-43p-
wrps-Roy Can Inst   (5a1)   4.50
McLENNAN, WM-In Old France & New-Tor-1900-Copp, Clark
(5nn8)   10.00
McLEOD, A J-The Notary of Grand Pre-Bost-1901 (5w8) 17.50
McLEOD, ALEX-Pigtails & Gold Dust-Caldwell-1947-8vo-
illus-1st ed   (5t3,dj) 10. (5h5,vg)   12.50
--same-1948-2nd prntg   (5t3, f,dj)   6.50
M'LEOD, D-Brief Review of Settlement of Upper Canada by U E
Loyalists & Scotch Highlanders in 1783,etc, wi Brief Sketch of
Campaigns-Cleve-1841-292p   (5w8)   350.00
McLEOD, DONALD-History of Wiskonsan from its 1st Discovery-
Buffalo-1846-1st ed-16mo-310p-4 plts-lg fldg map-part mor
(4L3, f)   285.00
MacLEOD, FIONA -At the Turn of the Year-Lond-(1913)-illus-
1st ed   (5r9)   10.00
--From the Hills of Dream-Portland, Me-1901-148p-16mo-prntd papr-
ltd to 925c   (5t7)   7.50
--The House of Usna, a drama-Portland, Me-1903-orig wrps over bds-
ltd to 450c-Mosher Pr   (5j2)   10.00
--The Immortal Hour, a play-1907-Mosher-sq8vo-bds-ltd to 500c
(5t5)   7.50
McLEOD, JOHN-Voyage of H M S "ALCESTE"along Coast of Corea
to Island of Lewchew-Lond-1818-3 qtr calf-5 aquatint plts
(5c1)   40.00
McLEOD, MALCOLM-The Pacific Railway-(1875)-Woodburn-
Brittanicus' letters   (5nn8)   50.00
--The Problem of Canada-Ottawa-1880-Citizen Prntg & Pub-wrps-
errata slip-72p   (5aa1, sl fray)   75.00
MACLEOD, WM-Catalogue of the Paintings, Statuary, Casts,
Bronzes, etc of Corcoran Gallery of Art-Wash-1884-67p-wrps
(5j4, wrp loose)   4.50
MACLEOD, WM-Harper's NY & Erie RR Guide Book-NY-1855, 6-
188p-fldg map-136 illus-8th ed   (5ee3)   20.00
MACLEOD, WM C-Amer Indian Frontier-1928-Knopf-maps-1st ed
(4k4, vg) 22.50 (5cc5, f,dj)   25.00
MacLOC, J-New Complete & Universal Nat'l History of quadrupeds
birds, fishes, reptiles etc-Phila-1821-57 engrs-lea-348p
(4L3, sl fox)   50.00
McLOUGHLIN, JOHN-Letters from Ft Vancouver-Tor-1941 to 44-
Champlain Soc-3 vols-port-plts-maps   (5zz8)   85.00

McMAHAN, VALRIE-Bumps, the Golf Ball Kid & Little Caddie-
EastAurora-(1929)-col illus-Roycroft   (5c8, f)   12.50

MacMAHON'S, ALBERT C-Latest Recipes & Amer Soda Water
Dispensers Guide-Chig-1893   (5w1, rprd, lacks frontis) 10.00

McMAHON, JOHN R-The Wright Brothers-Bost-1930-Little-308p-
illus   (5p0)   5.00

McMAHON, WM E, ed-Two strikes & out-GarCty-1939-156p(5v6)   4.00

McMANIS, J A-Flesh of My Brother-Hollywd-1946-illus (5x2, dj) 4.50

McMANUS, BLANCHE-Cathedrals of Northern France-Bost-1904-
Page-400p-illus-sm8vo-bds-t.e.g.   (5m5, wn)   9.00

McMANUS, GOE-Bringing Up Father-NY-c1929-Cupples&Leon-
lg8vo-(136p)-stapled-cl bkd pict bds-Big Book #2
                (5p1, wn, 1952 McManus Xmas card laid in) 35.00

MacMANUS, SEUMAS-Story of the Irish Race-NY-(1949)
                                               (4a1, pres) 10.00

McMANUS, THEO F-Men, Money & Motors-NY-1929-284p (5w5)   5.00

MacMARTIN, D F-Thirty Yrs in Hell-Topeka-(1921)-1st ed
                                               (5cc5, pres) 30.00

McMASTER, A C H-Holbrook & Allied Families-1942-177p(5mm3) 10.00

McMASTER, G-Apology for Book of Psalms-1818-buck (5L7, rbnd) 10.00

McMASTER, JOHN B-Penna & the Federal Constit-n.p.-1888-illus-
4to-scarce   (4m2)   30.00

McMASTER, JOHN BACH-Dan'l Webster-1902-plts (5L7, rub)   4.00
--same-NY-1939-illus   (5q8, fade)   3.00
--A History of People of the US from Rev to Civil War-NY-
Vols 1 to 6-1886, 1895, 1900   (5r7)   50.00
--same-NY-1893 to 1913-8 vols (5w5, Vol 5 ex-libr, crack) 50.00
--Lewis & Clark Expedition-NY-1922-3 vols-12mo-maps-ports-g.t.
                                               (5dd5)   15.00

MacMILLIAN, MIRIAM-Green Seas & White Ice-NY-1948-287p-
plts-map   (4a8)   5.00

McMICHEN, GILBERT-Abortive Fenian Raid of Manitoba-Winnipeg-
1888-11p-prntd wrps-No. 32 of Hist & Sci Soc of Manitoba
                                               (5w8)   15.00

MACMILLAN, DONALD B-Etah & Beyond-Bost-1927-287p-illus-
maps   (4b9, ex-libr) 8. (4c6, pres) 15. (5r0) 7.50 (5ss0, 5zz8) 8.50
--Four Years in White North-Bost-1925-428p-new ed-plts-maps
                                               (5dd0)   7.50
--same-NY-(1918)-photos-426p (5ss1, wn) 6.50 (5zz5)
                                               (5ss0)   5.00
--Kah Da-NY-(1930)-237p-illus   (5ss0)   4.00

MacMILLAN, SIR ERNEST, ed-Music in Canada-Tor-1955-232p(5s0) 5.00

McMILLAN, G-Racial Violence & Law Enforcement-Atlanta-1960-
31p-wrps-So Regional Council   (5x2)   6.00

MACMILLAN, HUGH-The Poetry of Plants-Lond-1902-386p (5s7)   5.00

MACMILLAN, J W-Limits of Social Legislation-Tor-1933-priv prntd-
34p   (4b9)   6.00

MACMILLAN, JOHN C-History of Catholic Church in Prince Edward
Island, 1885 to 1891-Quebec-1913-ports-plts-486p
                (5s6)   17.50   (5r0)   12.50

MacMILLAN, MIRIAM-Etuk, the Eskimo Hunter-NY-c1950-8vo-177p-
Dodd Mead-illus by Kurt Wiese-3rd prntng (5p1, dj, autg) 5.00
--Green Sea & White Ice-NY-1948-287p-illus (5ss0) 6. (4b9) 8.00

MacMILLAN, CAPT NORMAN-Art of Flying-Hartford-ca1930-illus
                                               (5xx7)   6.00

MACMILLAN, R H-Automation, Friend or Foe-Cambr-1956 (5x7)   3.50

McMINN, EDWIN-The Eaglesmere Trio-Phila-(1883)-illus-orig cl-
1st ed   (5mm2)   10.00
--A German Hero of Colonial Times of Penna-Moorestown-1886-
305p-illus   (5w5)   17.50
--On the Frontier with Col Antes-Camden, NJ-1900-photos-496p-
1st ed, ltd to 1000c-scarce   (5s5)   30.00

MacMINN, GEO R-The Theater of the Golden Era in Calif-Caldwell-
1941-Caxton-8vo-illus-cl-1st ed   (5F5, f)   12.50

McMINN, HOWARD E-Illustrated Manual of Pacific Coast Trees-
Berkeley-1935-409p-col frontis-1st ed   (5s7)   5.00
--same-Berkeley-1937-col frontis-limp cl-12mo (5z9)   3.00

McMORRIES, EDW YOUNG-History of 1st Reg Alabama Vol Infantry-
Montgomery-1904-142p-pamph-orig wrps
                (5L5, chip) 20. (5mm8, 4a7, rbnd)   25.00

MacMULLEN, JERRY-Paddle Wheel Days in Calif-Stanford-1944-
21 photos-24 drwngs   (5c1)   12.50

McMULLEN, THOS-Hand Book of Wine-NY-1852-327p, 3p
                                               (5w1, chip) 18.50

McMULLIN, MAUD L-A Child's Story of Oklahoma-OklaCty-
(1941)-map   (5zz5, pres) 4.00

MacMURCHY, M-The Canadian Girl at Work-Tor-1919-152p(4b9) 6.00

McMURPHY, MRS HARRIET S-The Ideal Receipt Book-Southington-
(1898)-64p-illus-wrps   (5c9, lacks cov) 3.50

McMURRY, CHAS A-Pioneers of Mississippi Valley-NY-1905-12mo-
illus-281p   (5s4, ex-libr)   4.00
--Pioneers of Rocky Mntns in West-NY-1905-12mo-248p-cl (5g2) 5.00

McMURRY, DONALD-Coxey's Army, a study in industrial unrest,
1893 to 1898-Bost-1929-331p-illus   (5t1)   35.00

McMURTRIE, DOUGLAS-Amer Imprints Inventory, No 5, Check List
of Ky Imprints-Louisville-1939-1st ed-wrps-203p(102)p plus
index-mimeo   (5yy7)   7.50
--Amer Imprints Inventory, No 32-Chig-1942-285p-orig stiff wrps
                                               (5ii1)   7.50
--Amer Imprints Inventory, No 36-Check List of Utica NY Imprints,
1799 to 1830   (5k0)   6.00
--Amer Imprints Inventory, No 39-Little Rock-1942-139p-wrps
                                               (5ii1)   7.50
--Amer Imprints Inventory, No 52-Detroit-1942-224p-wrps (5ii1) 7.50
--Amer Type Design in the 20th Century-Chig-1924-cl bkd bds-
64p   (4i2, dj)   15.00
--Bibliography of Chicago Imprints 1835 to 1850-Chig-1944-
112p-cl   (5jj9)   12.50
--Biblio of Mississippi Imprints 1789 to 1830-Beauvoir-1945-168p
                                               (5ii8)   22.50
--Book Decoration-Pelham-1928-63p   (5j4)   10.00
--Checklist of 18th Century Albany Imprints-Albany-1939-83p-wrps
                                               (5yy1)   4.00
--The Disabled Soldier-NY-1919-Macmillan-illus (5mm8)   15.00
--Early Printing in N M-NM Historical Review, Vol 8, #2, 1933
                                               (5g5)   7.50
--El Payo de Nuevo Mejico-Albuquerque-1933-11p-illus-facs-
priv prntd-200c prntd   (5g5)   7.50
--First 12 Years of Printing in North Car-Raleigh-1933-8vo-wrps
                                               (4c1)   7.50
--First Printing in Province of Quebec-Chig-1928-wrps-12p-
ltd to 350c   (5r6)   7.50
--The Golden Book-NY-1934   (5jj0) 6.   (5p7)   8.50
--Gutenberg Documents-NY-1941-239p-1st ed-ltd to 900c (5jj0) 20.00
--History of Printing in the US-NY-1936-Bowker-cl-462p-
Vol 2(all publ)   (5tt9)   25.00
--Indiana Imprints 1804 to 1849-Indnpls-1937-87p-wrps (5h2) 5.00
--Initial Letters-Pelham-1928- bds-wi 40p of plts (5j4) 10. (5d5) 5.00
--Jotham Meeker, Pioneer Printer of Kansas-Chig-1930-169p-
ltd ed of 650c, autg   (5t3) 10.   (5k1)   15.00
--Montana Imprints, 1864 to 1880-Chig-1937-fldg frontis-1st ed-
82p-scarce   (5yy7, vg)   35.00
--McMurtrie Imprints-Biloxi, Miss-1946-16p-wrps-supplement
                                               (5j4)   12.50
--A Note on P Jos Forster, Pioneer Alabama Printer-Hattiesburg,
Miss-1943-12p   (5j6)   6.00
--Oregon Imprints, 1847 to 1870-Eugene-1950-206p-cl (4a5)   12.50
--Pacific Typographical Soc & Calif Gold Rush of 1849-Chig-1928-
8vo-bds   (4c1, pres)   10.00
--Pamphlets & Books Printed in Buffalo Prior to 1850, a Supplement to
List by Severance...(Vol 16, #4 of Grosvenor Libr Bull)-Buffalo-
1934-107p-8vo-orig wrps   (5m6)   7.50
--Pioneer Printer of NewOrleans-Chig-1930-Eyncourt Pr-17p-wrps-
ltd to 250c   (5yy1)   7.50
--Pioneer Printing in Ohio-Cinn-1943-10p-wrps (5ii1)   3.00
--Preliminary Short Title Check List of Books, Pamphlets & Broadsides
Printed in Florida, 1784 to 1860-Jacksonville-1937-mimeo on
15 lvs-scarce   (5j4)   12.50
--Some Facts Concerning the Invention of Printing-Chig-1939-42p-
wrps   (5j4)   8.50
--Typographical Style Governing Use of Marks of Quotation in
Italian Composition-Greenwich-1922-4p-offprnt (4c1)   6.00

MACNAMARA, M H-Irish Ninth in Bivouac & Battle-Bost-1867-
12mo-306p-buck   (4a7, rbnd, text fade)   30.00

McNAMEE, MARY-Dominica Sister, Willamette Interlude-Palo Alto-
(1959)-Pacific Bks-302p-illus   (5r0, dj)   7.50

McNEAL, T A-When Kansas Was Young-NY-1922-cl
                (5m9) 12.50   (5jj7)   8.50

McNEER, MAY-The Mexican Story-NY-(1953)-Ariel Books-
sm4to-96p-liths-cl bkd bds-1st ed   (5p1, fade, dj) 10.00
--Prince Bantam-NY-1929-229p-illus   (5c3, wn)   4.50
--Story of the Great Plains-NY-(1943)-(32p)-col liths (5yy7) 4.00

MacNEICE, LOUIS-Poems 1925 to 1940-NY-(1940)-Random-
1st prntng   (5m2, dj)   6.50
--Zoo-Lond-(1938)-Michael Joseph-8vo-cl-255p-illus by Nancy
Sharp   (5j5, dj)   15.00

MacNEIL, ALAN-Garden Lilies-NY-1946-226p-plts (5s7)   4.00

McNEIL, E-Shores of Adventure-NY-1929-371p   (4b9)   8.00

McNEIL, EDNA V-First Foods of Amer-LosAng-(1936)-150p-
frontis-illus   (5c9)   5.00

McNEIL, SAMUEL-Mc'Neils Travels In 1849-(NewHaven-1958-
Yale UP)-8vo-40p-facs of 1850 ed-wrps-ltd to 300c
                (4a3) 12.50 (5hh3) 25.   (5yy7, f)   20.00

McNEILE, CYRIL-Bull Dog Drummond's Third Round-NY-(1924)-
1st Amer ed   (5ee3)   3.50

McNEILL, F MARIAN-The Book of Breakfasts-Lond-1932-170p
                                               (5c5)   3.00

McNEILL,GEO-The Labor Movement-NY-1888-illus-628p-1st ed
(5L3) 17.50

MacNEILL,HECTOR-The poetical works-Lond-1801-Bensley,prntr-
2 vols-8vo-calf-plts-1st ed (5i8,vg) 25.00

McNEILL,JOHN C-Lyrics from Cotton Land-Charlotte-1907-illus-
pict cl (5x2) 17.50

--same-Charlotte-1922-port-ABFrost&Kemble,illus
(5p5) 12.50

McNEILL,WARREN A-Cabellian Harmonics-NY-1928-1st (ltd) ed
(5mm2) 10. (5b2,f) 12.50

McNEILLY,J H-Religion & Slavery-Nashville-1911-12mo
(5x2,rbnd) 35.00

McNICKLE,D'ARCY-They Came Here First-Phila-(Peoples of Amer
Ser)-(1949)-8vo-cl-1st ed (5h9) 7.50 (5h4,5m2) 6.00

McNICHOLAS CHAS L-Crazy Weather-NY-1944-Macmillan-
195p (5v2,vf,dj) 6. (5g0,5p1) 4.00

--Old Fort Duquesne-Pittsb-1873-illus-1st ed
(5mm2) 10.00

MacNUTT,FRANCIS A-Fernando Cortes,His 5 Letters-Cleve-1908-
illus-maps-2 vols-1st ed-ltd (5zz5) 50.00

MACOMB,J N-Report of Exploring Exped from Santa Fe,NMex to
Junc of Grand & Green Riv....in 1859-Wash-1876-map-plts-
152p-folio-orig cl (4n4) 80.00

MACOMBER,BEN-The Jewel City-(Pan Pac Intl Expo in SanFran)-
SanFran-1915-204p-bds-75 illus (5xx5) 7.50

MACON COUNTY,MO-General History of-Chig-1910-(Henry
Taylor &Co)-945p-photos-1st ed (5zz5,rebnd) 60.00

MACOUN,JOHN-Manitoba & the Great NW-Guelph-1882-
World Publ-687p-maps-illus (4e3,lacks front cov) 10.00

McPHARLIN,PAUL-Life & Fashion in Amer,1650 to 1900-NY-
1946-40p-bds-16 col illus (5n7) 2.50

McPHERREN,IDA-Trail's End-(Caspar,Wyo-1938)-scarce (5r8,f) 25.00

McQUEEN,A S-History of Okefenokee Swamp-Clinton,SC-n.d.-
2nd ed (4a9,f) 9.00

McQUEEN,ANDREW-Clyde River Steamers of Last 50 Yrs-Glasgow-
1923-135p-photos (5s1,f) 6.00

MacQUEEN,PETER-In Wildest Africa-Bost-1909-8vo-402p-photos
(4a6) 7.50

M'QUIN,A D-Description of Picture Christ Rejected by the Jews,
Painted by Benj West-Phila-1830-8vo-orig wrps-16p (5m6,fox) 12.50

MacQUOID,KATHERINE S-At the red glove-Lond-1885-Ward &
Downey-3 vols-8vo-orig pict cl-1st ed (5xx6,rprd) 30.00

MacQUOID,PERCY-History of English Furniture-Lond-(1938)-illus-
folio-cl-260p-col plts (5q0) 25.00

--same-Lond-1925-Medici Soc-col plts-271p (5p0,f) 30.00

--Plate Collector's Guide Arranged-Lond-1904-199p-68 illus
(5w7) 8.50

MACRAE,DAVID-Americans at Home-NY-1952-606p-cl-reprint
(5h1) 5. (5q8) 7.50

--Amongst the Darkies & Other Papers-Glasgow-1880-Marr&Sons-
128p (5L3) 3.00

--same-Glasgow-1876-dec cl-12mo-1st ed (4n5) 5.00

MACRATE,ARTHUR N JR-History of the Tuna Club,Avalon,Santa
Catalina Isl-SantaCatalina Is-1948-lea-197p-8vo (5d6,4t1) 30.00

McRAVEN,WM HENRY-Life & Times of Edw Swanson-Nashville-
1937 (5h6) 10.00

McRILL,ALBERT-And Satan Came Also-OklaCty-(1955)-photos-
259p-1st ed in book form (5yy7) 15.00

MacRITCHIE,WM-Diary of Tour Thru Britain in 1795-Lond-1897-
169p (5a1) 4.50

McROSKEY,RACINE-The Missions of Calif-SanFran-1914-4to-
photos-cl&bds (5h4) 10.00

McSHANE,CHAS-The Locomotive Up to Date-Chig-1922-893p-
illus (5w5,crack) 17.50

--same-Chig-(1925)-Griffin&Winters-893p-illus-cl (5t0) 12.50

--1,000 Pointers for Machinists & Engineers-Chig-1896-scarce-
1st ed of 1st RR bk by auth (5b9,f) 50.00

McSHANE,HENRY,MFG CO-Plumber's Supplies,1904 Catalogue-
Baltimore-1904-4to-orig wrps-illus (5ss5,f) 9.00

McSPADDEN,J WALKER-Famous Painters of America-NY-1907-
Crowell-g.-362p-illus-demy 8vo (4a0) 25.00

McSWEENEY,E F-Judge Wm Gaston of N C,Gov Wm Gaston of
Mass,Col Wm A Gaston of Mass-(1926)-235p (5mm3) 15.00

M'TAGGART,MRS ANN-Constantia,a tragedy,in 5 acts & Valville-
Lond-1824-MANattali-12mo-orig bds-papr labl-1st ed (5i8,f) 25.00

McTAGGART,JOHN-Three Years in Canada-Lond-1829-2 vols-
scarce (5e2) 225.00 (4e9,rub) 175.00

McVAUGH,ROGERS-Edw Palmer,Plant Explorer of the Amer West-
Norman-c1956-403p-illus-maps-1st ed (5w5,dj) 6.00

--Farwelliana-Bloomfield Hills-1953-Cranbrook Inst Bull #34-
101p-illus (5w3) 4.00

McVEY,E E-The Crow Scout Who Killed Custer-Billings-1952-32p-
photos-wrps-1st ed (5t3,f) 3.00

McVICKAR,H W-Our Amateur Circus-NY-1892-obl 8vo-col plts-
text on tissue guards-cl (5v0,mint,box) 20.00

McVICKAR,H W (continued)
--Reptiles-(NY)-1905-Appleton-8vo-cl-illus (5b2,sl soil) 4.00

McWATTERS,GEO S-Knots Untied-Hartford-1871-illus (5L3) 5.00

--same-Hartf-1873-665p (5p7,rprd) 6.00

MacWETHEY,LOU D-Book of Names,Especially Relating to Early
Palatines & First Settlers in Mohawk Valley-1933-209p (5t9) 10.00

MacWHORTER,ALEX-Series of Sermons,upon Most Important
Principles of Our Holy Religion-Newark-1803-Pennington&Gould-
2 vols-thk8vo-cont calf-1st ed (5r7,lacks 1 cov) 35.00

McWHORTER,LUCULLUS VIRGIL-Tragedy of the Wahkshum-Yakima-
(Feb,1937)-44p plus 1p&map-photos-wrps-priv prntd-ltd to 750c-
scarce (5t3,pres) 15.00

McWILLIAMS,CAREY-Ambrose Bierce,a biogr-NY-1929-Boni-
1st ed (5m2,dj) 7.50

--Brothers Under the Skin-Bost-1943-325p-12mo-cl
(5x7) 5.50 (5x2) 4. (5t0) 4.50

--California,the Great Exception-NY-1949-1st ed
(5q8) 7.50 (5x5,dj) 10.00

--Factories in the Field-Bost-1939-334p (5x5,dj,5g2,dj,f,5t7,dj) 10.00

--Ill Fares the Land-Lond-1945-1st Engl ed (5q8) 5.00

--Louis Adamic & shadow Amer-LosAng-(1935)-Whipple-1st ed
(5b2,pres) 7.50 (5m2,dj) 6.50

--A Mask for Privilege-Bost-1948-299p
(5p5,dj) 10. (5m2,dj) 5. (5q8,dj) 7.00

--Prejudice,Japanese Americans-Bost-1944 (5q8,dj) 7.00

--North from Mexico,Spanish Speaking People of the US-Phila-
1949-Lippincott- -cl (5d6) 10.00

--Southern Calif Country,an Island in the Land-NY-(1946)-387p-
1st ed (4n1,dj) 7.00

--same-NY-1946-2nd prntg (5jj1,f) 8.50

McWILLIAMS,JOHN-Recollections-(Princeton)-n.d.-port
(5r7,cov stnd,pres,son's letter tip in) 100.00

McWILLIAMS,VERA-Lafcadio Hearn-Bost-1946
(5mm1,dj) 6. (5a9,f) 7.50 (5mm1,5ss9,5F1) 6.00

MACY & CO-Tea,Album,silk bound,of 42 tinted photos of tea-
n.p.-n.d.-(c1915) (5w1) 10.00

MACY,JESSE-Anti Slavery Crusade-NHav-1919-245p-cl-
Chron 8 Amer Ser (5h1,f,dj) 5.00

MACY,JOHN,ed-Amer Writers on Amer Literature-NY-1931-
539p (5m2) 6. (5p9) 7.50

--Between Dawn & Sunrise-NY-1930 (5p0) 4.00

MACY,OBED-History of Natucket-1880-313p-2nd ed (5e8) 28.75

MACY,WM F-The Natucket Scrap Basket-Nantucket-1916-183p
(5p9) 3.75

MADAME MERRI-Art of Entertaining for all occasions-Chig-1913-
355p-bds (5g9) 2.50

MADAN,FALCONER-Books in Manuscript-Lond-1893-Kegan Paul,
Trench,Trubner-188p (5F9,sp wn) 15.00

MADARIAGA,SALVADOR DE-Fall of the Spanish Amer Empire-Lond-
1947-8vo-cl-443p (5h5,f,dj) 10.00

--The Heart of Jade-NY-(c1944)-Creative Age-8vo-cl(4a3,fade) 4.00

--Vida Del Muy Magnifico Senor Don Cristobal Colon-BuenosAires-
(1940)-657p-port-fldg map (5r7) 10.00

MADAWASKA CLUB GO HOME BAY,1898 to 1923-n.p.-n.d.-
(1923)-illus-56p-stiff wrps-maps (4e6,f) 20.00

MADDEN,HENRY M-Xantus,Hungarian Naturalist in the Pioneer
West-PaloAlto-1949 (5x5,dj) 10.00

MADDE,JAS W-Chas Allen Culberson-Austin-1929-special ltd,
nbrds & autg ed (4c7) 15.00

--same-Austin-1929-trade ed (5a8) 6.00

MADDEN,RICH R-The United Irishmen,Their Lives & Times-Dublin-
1858-lg8vo-illus-cl-619p-2nd ser-2nd ed (5t2,libr bkplt) 5.00

MADDISON,IVY-Riding Astride for Girls-NY-1923-HenryHolt-
8vo-263p-frontis-22 plts-cl (5p1,fade) 7.50

MADDOCK,JAS-The Florist's Directory-Lond-1792-1st ed-orig bds-
6 col plts (5j3,crude rebk) 15.00

--same-Lond-1810-new ed-8 hand col plts-sm8vo-calf-new ed,
improved (4c2,rub,hng crack) 25.00

MADDOCKS,MILDRED,ed-The Pure Food Cook Book-NY-1914-
417p-illus (5c0) 5.00

MADDOCK,THOS SONS CO-Pottery A History of the Pottery
Industry..as applied to Sanitation-n.p.-n.d.-(c1910)-224p-
illus (5w7) 16.50

MADDUX,PERCY-City on the Willamette-Portl-(1952)-216p plus
index-photos-1st ed (5t3,dj) 5.00

MADEIRA,PERCY C-Hunting in Brit East Africa-Phila-1909-8vo-
304p-photos (4a6,shaken) 3.50 (5m6) 12.50

MADELEINE,AN AUTOBIOGRAPHY-NY&Lond-1919-329p-
cl bkd bds (4i2,rprd) 12.50

MADELEVA,SISTER M-Collected Poems-NY-1947-8vo-cl
(5b2,f,dj) 6.00

--Four Girls & Other Poems-Paterson-1941-St Anthony Guild Pr-
8vo-cl (5b2,f) 6.00

MADISON, JAS-Letters & Other Writings-1865-4 vols-buck
(5L7,rbnd) 40.00
--Papers of-Mobile-1842-orig sheep-3 vols (4L3,vg) 75.00
--The Writings of-NY-1900-cl-hf mor-port-Letterpress ed,ltd to
750 sets-9 vols-v scarce (5ii8,sl chip) 100.00
MADISON, L F-Lincoln-Phila-1928-368p-illus-1st ed (5a9) 5.00
MADISON, VIRG-Big Bend Country of Texas-Albuq-1955-263p-
1st ed (4a5) 12.50
MADISSES CLUB COOK BOOK-Brunswick,Maine-1926-83p-wrps-
1st Parish Church (5c4) 3.00
MAERCKER, M-Das Flussaurever,fahren In Der Spiritusfabrikation-
Berlin-1891-150p (5w1) 8.50
--Handbuch Der Spiritusfabrikation-Berlin-1898-783p,(48)-illus
(5w1,cov spots) 10.00
MAESER, KARL G-School & Fireside-(Provo?)-Skelton,Maeser & Co-
1898-8vo-358p-frontis-19 plts-hf lea (5p1,soil,sp tn) 35.00
MAETERLINCK, MAURICE-Aglavaine & Selysette-NY-1915-Dodd,
Mead-8vo-top g.-deluxe bndg (5i4) 15.00
--Children's Life of the Bee-NY-Dodd,Mead-1919-illus by Detmold-
8vo-192p-frontis-4 col plts-pict labl (5p1) 7.50
--The Life of the Bee-NY-1904-transl by Sutro-427p-8vo-cl (5t2) 4.00
--News of Spring-NY-1913-illus-18 col plts(of 20)-t.e.g.(5qq7) 20.00
--The Treasure of the Humble-Lond-1905-Humphreys-hf mor (5p7) 6.00
MAFFETT, R L-The Kingdom Within-NY-1955-1st ed (5x2,dj) 12.50
MAFFITT, CAPT JOHN N-Nautilus,or cruising under canvas-NY-
US Pub Co-SanFran-1871-Bancroft-pict cl-1st ed (5m2,lt spot)10.00
MAGARET, HELENE-Father De Smet,Pioneer Priest of the Rockies-NY-
1940-port-371p-e.p.maps (5nn2) 12.50
MAGAW, SAM'L-Address delivered in Young Ladies Academy at
Phila on Feb 8-Phila-1787-15p-wrps-1st ed
(5i9,disbnd) 35. (5m3,new wrps) 75.00
MAGDALENO, MAURICIO-Sunburst-(Lond)-(1945)-Lindsay Drummond-
8vo-cl (4a3) 7.50
MAGEE, DAVID-Catalogue of Some   Examples of Printing of
Edwin & Robert Grabhorn, 1917 to 1960-SanFran-1961-
Grabhorn Pr-63p-wrps-lg4to (5j4) 25.00
MAGEE, JAS D-Bordentown, NJ, 1682 to 1932-Bordentown-1932-
illus-145p (5ii8) 15.00
MAGEE, JAS F-Amer Student Abroad,from the letters of-Phila-
1932-illus-bds-1st ed-ltd to 517c,nbrd (5w5) 7.50
MAGENDIE, FRANCOIS-Phenomenes Physiques de la Vie-Paris-
1842-8vo-2 vols in 1-bds-calf bk (4n5,joints split) 15.00
MAGGIE'S COOK BOOK-LosAng-(1949)-St Alban's Episc Church,
Westwood Hills-252p-illus-spiral bnd (4g9) 5.00
MAGICIAN'S OWN BOOK-or, Whole Art of Conjuring-NY-(1857)-
362p,(10)-wdcuts (5w7) 7.50
MAGILL, FRANK N,ed-Masterplots-NY-1949-2 vols-Salem Pr
(5p7) 15.00
MAGINN, WM-The Odoherty Papers,annotated by Mackenzie-NY-
1855-2 vols-8vo-cl-frontis (5t2) 5.00
MAGNANIMOUS AMAZON, THE-or, adventures of Theresia,
Baroness van Hoog-Lond-1796-for Vernor&Hood-12mo-hf calf
(5xx6,lacks hf t.) 125.00
MAGNE, LUCIEN-Decor du Metal, Le Fer-Paris-1914-illus
(4j3,rbnd) 16.50
MAGNER, D-Art of Taming & Educating a Horse,etc-BattleCreek
1884-1088p-illus-lea (5t7) 15.00
--same-BattleCreek-1877-illus-calf (4m3,rub,sp tn) 10.00
MAGNER, JAS A-Men of Mexico-Milwaukee-(c1942)-Bruce-8vo-
cl-illus (4a3) 12.50
MAGNOLIA, THE-Or, Gift Book of Friendship-Clara Arnold,ed-
Bost-(1854)-6th in series-287p,(1)-plts-lea-g.t. (5w7,sl stnd) 3.50
MAGOFFIN, R V D-The Romance of Archaeology-NY-(1929)-lg8vo-
cl-348p (5t2) 4.50
MAGOFFIN, SUSAN S-Down the Santa Fe Trail & Into Mexico-
NewH-1926-294p-illus-1st ed (5t2) 25. (4L3,f) 32.50
MAGOON, REV E L-Eloquence of Colonial & Revolutionary Times-
Cinn-1847-91p-cl (5h2) 10.00
MAGOUN, F ALEXANDER-Frigate Constitution & other Historic Ships-
Ships-Salem-1928-Marine Res Soc,#16-Southworth Pr-folio-
charts-plts-scarce (5t4) 45. (5qq8) 62.50
MAGRIEL, PAUL-Chronicles of the Amer Dance-NY-1948-Henry
Holt-sq8vo-plts (5t8) 7.50
--Nijinsky-NY-(1947)-illus (5ii3) 7.50
MAGRUDER, ALLAN-John Marshall-Bost-1890-hf mor-t.e.g.-
raised bands (5w0) 7.50
MAGRUDER, GENEVIEVE K-The Upper San Joaquin Valley, 1772 to
1870-(Bakersfield)-1950-dbl pg & other maps-84p (4t1) 12.50
MAGRUDER, GEN J BANKHEAD-General Orders #16-Houston-
Dec 11, 1862-Hdq, Dist of Texas-broadside-lp-sm4to-rare(4a5)27.50
MAGRUDER, JULIA-At Anchor, & Honored in the Breach-Phila-1891-
stiff wrps-   1st ed (5ee3) 12.50
--A beautiful alien-Bost-1900-Badger-frontis-pict cl-1st ed (5m2) 8.50

MAGUIRE, JOHN FRANCIS-The Irish in America-Lond-1868-
lea (5j2,scuff) 10. (5ii8) 32.50
--Rome, its Ruler & Institutions-Lond-1857-Longmans-472p,(4)-
8vo-orig cl (4e1) 25.00
MAGUIRE, JOHN MacARTHUR-The Lance of Justice-1928-
Harvard Univ Pr-305p (5p9) 6.00
MAHAFFY, JOHN P-What Have the Greeks done for Modern
Civilization?-NY-1909-1st ed (4a1,stained) 8.50
MAHAN, A T-From Sail to Steam-NY-1907-326p-t.e.g.-1st ed
(5w5) 8.75
--Influence of Sea Power Upon History, 1660 to 1783-Bost-1894-
557p-maps-7th ed (5s1,f) 7.50
--same-Bost-1914-maps-557p (5ii8) 10.00
--Interest of Amer in Sea Power, Present & Future-1898 (5L7) 5.00
--Sea Power in its relations to War of 1812-Bost-1905-Little,Brown-
2 vols-cl (5d6) 15.00
--Types of Naval Officers Drawn from History of British Navy-Bost-
1901-illus-1st ed (5s1,rprd) 10. (5m2) 8.50
--The War in South Africa-NY-1902-oblong folio-illus (4b7) 20.00
--same-NY-1901-oblong folio-illus-208p (5t4) 15.00
MAHAN, BRUCE E-Old Ft Crawford & the Frontier-IowaCty-1926-
349p-illus-8vo-cl (5m8) 12.50 (5a9) 17.50
MAHAN, D H-An Elementary Treatise on Advanced Guard, Out Post
& Detachment Service of Troops,etc-NY-1847-168p (5t7) 10.00
--Treatise on Field Fortification...with Gen'l outlines Also of
Arrangement, Attack & Defence of Permanent Fortifications-
Richmond-1862-West&Johnson-16mo-orig calf bkd cl bds-
168p-4th ed,rev & enlrgd-12 fld plts & inserted lvs (5m3) 65.00
MAHAN, JOHN B, REV-Trial of, for felony-Cinn-1838-8vo-
Sam'l A Alley-orig pink prntd wrps-1st ed-scarce (5i0) 30.00
MAHIN, JOHN-Muscatine City Directory & Advertiser, 1856-
Muscatine-1856-12mo-orig prntd papr over bds-80p
(4c1,rbkd) 100.00
MAHONEY, ELLA V-Sketches of Tudor Hall & the Booth Family-
1928-61p (5t9) 5.00
MAHONEY, M J-Calif Sunshine,a book of verse-SanJose-1929-
12mo-114p-wrps-priv prntd (5dd4) 3.00
MAHONEY, TOM-The Great Merchants-NY-1955-Harper-340p
(5x0) 5. (5dd9) 5.25
MAHONING CO, OHIO-Atlas of-Phila-1874-95p-cl-map
(5h7,rbkd) 40.00
MAHONY, BERTA E-Contemporary Illustrators of Children's Books-
Bost-1930-Bookshop for Boys & Girls-4to-136p-illus-dec cl
(5p1,dj) 25.00
--Realms of Gold in Children's Books-GarCty-1937-Dblday Doran-
8vo-796p-frontis-2 col plts-5th ed Books for Boys & Girls
(5p1,dj) 12.50
--5 Years of Children's Books-GarCty-1936-Dblday Doran-8vo-599p-
suppl to Realms of Gold-1st ed (5pi,dj) 15.00
MAHONY, D A-The Prisoner of State-NY-1863-414p-cl
(4L9,fade,wn,fox) 15. (5w5,rbnd,sl stnd) 12.50
MAHOOD, RUTH I-Photographer of the Southwest, Adam C. Vroman-
1961-Ward Ritchie Pr-4to-1st ed (5x5,dj) 7.50 (5g0,f,dj) 12.50
MAHR, AUGUST C-The Visit of the "Rurik" to SanFran in 1816-
1932-Stanford Univ Pr-194p-cl (5d6) 20.00
MAIDEN, CECIL-Lighted Journey, The Story of the BC Electric-
Vancouver-1947-plts-170p-wrps (5dd7) 10.00
MAIDEN, RACHEL BELL-The Canape Book-NY-1934-95p (5c0) 3.00
MAIGNE, P-Nouveau Manuel Complet du Sommelier-Paris-1921-
499p-wrps (5w1,sp broke) 6.50
MAILE, JOHN L-Prison Life in Andersonville-LosAng-(1912)-
Grafton Pub Co-ltd to 500c,autg (5x5) 12.50
MAILER, NORMAN-Advertisements for Myself-NY-(1959)-Putnam's
Sons-1st ed (5ss9,vg,dj) 6.00
--Barbary Shore-NY-1951-Rinehart&Co-1st ed
(5F1,f,dj rub) 10. (5ss9,vg,dj) 12.50
--The Naked & the Dead-NY-1948-721p-1st ed of auth's first book
(4b4) 17.50 (5r9,fray dj) 20.00
MAILLARD, E-Old French Furniture & Its Surroundings-n.p.-1925-
4to-illus-128p (4a2,dj) 6.00
MAILLARD, LOUIS-La Cuisine des Familles-Geneva-1946-601p-
4p illus (5g9) 6.00
MAILLARD, N DORAN-History of Republic of Texas-Lond-1842-
512p-no map-1st ed-mor-v rare (4a5,lacks map) 150.00
MAILLIARD, JOS-Birds of the Bohemian Grove, Monte Rio, Calif-
n.p.-1931-16mo-cl-illus (5h4) 2.00
MAIN, ELIZ-High Life & Towers of Silence-Lond-1886-195p-
cl (5d7) 7.50
MAINE-Atlas of the State of, Geo N Colby & Co, Houlton, Me, 1884-
Phila-(1884)-folio-cl (5g4,v wn,lacks lea bk) 15.00
MAINE BUSINESS DIRECTORY-1888-692p (5t9) 5.00

MAINE COASTAL COOKING & the Accomplished Cook-
Rockland, Me-1963-86p, (4), (26)p-spiral bnd wrps   (4g9)   4.50
MAINE-Diocese of-100th Anniv of 1820 to 1920-1920-159p-illus
    (5e8)   7.50
MAINE, 1885-Fish & Game Laws of State of-Bangor-1885-16mo-
orig wrps-59p   (5ss5)   8.50
MAINE-A Guide "Down East"-Bost-1937-H M-Amer Guide Ser-
illus-1st ed-pkt map-WPA   (4L5, vg, dj)   10.00
MAINE REGISTER-State Year Book & Leg. Manual from May 1, 1893
to May 1, 1894-Portland, Me-1893   (5x0)   7.50
MAINE, FLOYD SHUSTER-Lone Eagle, the White Sioux-Albuq-1956-
208p-illus-1st ed   (5yy7, mint, dj)   8.50
MAINS, LURA A-Mizpah-GrndRap-1892-107, (1)p-cl   (5y0)   12.50
MAIR, CHAS-Tecumseh a Drama & Canadian Poems-Tor-1926-470p-
illus   (4b9) 15. (4b2, dj)   11.50
--Through Mackenzie Basin..also Notes on Mammals & Birds of
No Canada by Roderick Macfarlane-Tor-1908-ports-plts-fldg map-
part mor-494p   (5nn2, pres, f bndg)   25.00
MAIR, G H-Modern English Literature from Chaucer to the Present
Day-NY-1914-illus   (5mm2)   4.00
MAIR, JOHN-The Fourth Forger-NY-1939-8vo-cl-6 illus (5d5, dj)   3.00
MAIRE, F-Graining & Marbling-Chig-(1910)-161p-illus-12mo
    (5n7, spots)   6.50
MAIRS, THOS I-Some Penna Pioneers in Agriculture Science-
State College, Pa-(1928)-185p-photos   (5s7)   6.50
MAIS, S P B-A Modern Columbus-Phila-1934-photos-1st ed (5x5, dj) 7.50
MAISSIN, EUGENE-French in Mexico & Texas, 1838, 1839-Salado-
1961-254p-fldg map-ltd ed   (4a5) 25. (5h5)   27.50
MAITLAND, CHAS-The Church in the Catacombs-Lond-1847-
illus-calf   (5j2, vg)   12.00
MAITLAND, JAS-Historical sketch of Burlington-Burlington-1881-
wrps   (5g4)   22.50
MAITLAND, Lt LESTER J-Knights of the Air-GarCty-1929-338p-
illus-1st ed(so stated)   (5w4)   7.50
--same-1929-D Doran-338p-illus   (5v6, fade) 5.50 (5c1)   6.50
MAJDALANY, FRED-The Eddystone Light-Bost-1960-24 illus(5c1) 6.00
MAJORS, ALEXANDER-70 Years on the Frontier-Denver-n.d.-
12mo-col wrps   (4c1)   15.00
MAJOR, CHAS-Bears of Blue River-NY-1926-sq8vo-dec cl-g.-
277p-illus-Children's Classics ed   (5s4)   4.50
--Dorothy Vernon of Haddon Hall-NY-1902-1st ed-Christy, illus
  (5ii3) 10. (4F6, f)   6.50
MAJOR, GERTRUDE KEENE-Revelation in Mountain-NY-n.d.-
160p-photos   (5s4, pres 1909, rprd, shake)   6.00
MAJOR, HENRY-Portraits & Caricatures-NY-1927-4to-illus-
ltd ed 250c   (5ii3, autg)   12.50
MAJOR, MABEL-SoWest Heritage, a Literary History with
Bibliography-Albuq-1948-199p-8vo-cl-rev ed   (5g2)   5.00
--Southwest in Literature-NY-1929-367p plus index-photos-
1st ed   (5L0)   4.00
MAJOR, N L-C W Post, the Hour & the Man, a Biography-1963-
318p   (5mm3)   15.00
MAJORS, ALEXANDER-70 Years on the Frontier-Chig&NY-1893-
325p-illus   (5xx8, spot, rprd) 35. (5zz5, vg)   30.00
--same-Columbus-1950-325p-reprnt of 1893   (5k2, 5zz5, dj)   7.50
MAKARONY FABLES-Lond-1897-dec cl-uncut-258p-ltd to 300c
    (5aa0)   15.00
MAKATAIMESHEKIAKIAK, LIFE OF-or Black Hawk-Cinn-1833-
155p-bds-1st ed-v rare-Howes 120   (5y0, fox)   150.00
--same-Bost-1834-frontis-155p   (5s4, wn, ex-libr)   20.00
MAKEMSON, MAUD WORCESTER-The Book of Jaguar Priest-NY-
(c1951)-Henry Schuman-8vo   (4a3) 15. (5x5, 4a1)   10.00
--The Morning Star Rises-Yale U-1941-301p-8vo-cl
    (5F5, clip marks)   7.50
MAKEPEACE, LEROY McKIM-Sherman Thacher & His School-
NewHav-1941-Yale Univ Pr-205p-illus-cl   (5r0)   7.50
MAKERS OF CANADA-Tor-1906 to 11 - 21 vols-3/4 mor-
Parkman ed   (5yy9, sl fade)   65.00
--same-Tor-1909 to 11-Parkman ed-23 vols-qtr mor   (5dd0)   60.00
--same-Tor-1910-Morang-11 vols-University ed-cl-lea bks
    (5w8, def bkstrps)   30.00
MAKERS OF MILLIONS-n.p.-1951   (5h6)   5.00
MAKIGUCHI, TSUNESABURO-Philosophy of Value-Tokyo-1964-
trans by Overseas Bureau-199p-cl-8vo   (5t2)   5.00
MAKI, M-Monograph of the Snakes of Japan-Tokyo-1931-4 parts
85 col plts-folio-wrps-rare (4p6, box wi bone handled locks)   650.00
MAKINS, F K-British Trees in Winter-Lond-1946-64p-illus (5s7)   3.00
MAKIN, W J-South of Suez-NY-c1920-illus   (5x2)   7.50
--War Over Ethiopia-Lond-1935-287p-16 plts (5c6, spine nick)   10.75
MAKOWER, STANLEY V-Richard Savage-Lond-1909-343p-plts
    (5a1)   4.50
MALAMUD, BERNARD-The Magic Barrel-(NY, 1958)-1st ed
    (5r9, dj, f)   15.00

MALAN, CESAR-The Friend of Youth, or Stories for Children-
Edinb-1826-Wm Oliphant-12mo-228p-hf lea-plt
    (5c8, rub, lacks fly)   15.00
--Hymns....transl into English verse-Lond-1825-Jas Nisbet-16mo-
orig bds-papr labl   (5i8)   8.00
MALASPINA, ALESSANDRO-Viaje Politico Cientifico Alrdededor
del Mundo etc-Madrid-1885-folio-2nd ed-pt mor-681, (4)p-
6 plts-fldg map   (5aa0, f bndg, orig wrps bd in)   150.00
MALCOM, HOWARD-Travels in South Eastern Asia, embracing
Hindustan, Malaya, Siam, & China-Bost-1839-Gould, Kendall,
& Lincoln-2 vols-12mo-orig violet cl-fldg map-frontis ea vol-
1st ed   (5i8, f)   20.00
MALCOLM, SIR JOHN-Political History of India from 1784 to 1823-
Lond-1826-JnMurray-2 vols-8vo-hf calf-1st ed   (5i8, vg)   25.00
MALDEN, (MASS)-Bi Centennial Book of Malden-1850-251p
    (5mm3, wn)   4.50
--Memorial of the Celebration of the 250th Anniv-1900-340p-
illus   (5mm3)   6.00
--Past & Present-1899-112p   (5mm3, wtrstnd)   3.00
MALDEN & WORCESTER-Memoir of Mrs Mary H Adams, by her
husband-1865-144p   (5mm3)   4.50
MALET, LUCAS-History of Rich Calmady-Lond-1901-1st ed, 1st
issue wi Methuen's 48p catalog dated July 1901 (5k2, rub)   25.00
MALHAM, JOHN-Naval Gazetteer; or Seaman's Complete Guide-
Bost-1797-2 vols-17 fldg maps-orig calf (5c1, rbkd, brown)   100.00
MALIN, JAS C-US after the World War -(Bost, 1930)-590p-1st ed
    (5xx5)   11.50
MALINOWSKI, B-Sexual Life of Savages in No Westrn Melanasia-
NY-1929-603p-plts   (5qq5, 4L3)   15.00
--same-NY-(1929)-photos-2 vols-ltd to 2200c   (5j3)   15.00
--A Scientific Theory of Culture & Other Essays-Chapel Hill-1924-
12mo-cl-228p-1st ed   (5i2)   4.00
--same-Univ of NoCar-1944-228p   (5p0)   4.00
MALKIN, BENJ-Essays on subjects connected with civilization-
Lond-1795-8vo-hf calf-1st ed of auth's 1st book   (5x3)   40.00
MALL, THOS-History of the Martyrs Epitomised-Bost-1747-2 vols in 1-
8vo-calf-1st Amer ed   (5ss5, lacks label, sl wn)   22.50
MALLARME, STEPHANE-Throw of the Dice Never Will Abolish
Chance-Tiber Press-n.d.-transl by Aldan-lg8vo-orig cl-
1st ed-priv prntd   (5p5)   15.00
MALLARY, R DeWITT-Lenox & the Berkshire Highlands-NY-1902-
363p-8vo-illus-1st ed   (5mm3, 5m6)   5.00
MALLAS, A A -40 Years in Politics-Wayne State Univ-1947-
illus   (5x2, dj)   10.00
MALLERY, ARLINGTON H-Lost America-Wash-(1951)-illus-238p
    (5q0, dj, f)   7.50
MALLERY, REV C P-Ancient Families of Bohemia Manner, Their
Homes & Graves-1888-74p   (5t9)   7.50
MALLERY, GARRICK-Intro to study of sign language among NoAmer
Indians as illustrating the gesture speech of mankind-Wash-1880-
4to-prntd wrps-illus   (5g4)   12.50
MALLES DE BEAULIEU, MME-Le Robinson de Douze Ans-Paris-
1838-Lehuby-sm8vo-288p-calf-marbled sides-plts-14me ed
    (5aa2)   25.00
--same-Engl transl(The Modern Crusoe...)-NY-1857-Higgins &
Kellogg-12mo-g. t.-240p-plts   (5aa2)   8.50
MALLET, J W-Chemistry Applied to the Arts-Lynchburg-1868-38p
    (5hh7)   6.50
MALLET, PAUL-Northern Antiquities-Lond-1770-2 vols-8vo-
Percy, transl-calf   (5ss5, cov loose)   25.00
MALLET, CAPT THIERRY-Glimpses of the Barren Lands-NY-1930-
142p-illus-priv prntd (5dd7, 5h2, 4c1) 7.50 (5xx7, 5j5, 4b9)   10.00
--Plain Tales of the North-NY-1926-136p-illus   (4a8)   6.50
--same-NY-1925-illus-136p   (5ss0)   8.50
MALLETT, MARGUERITE-A White Woman Among the Masai-NY-1923-
8vo-288p-photos   (4a6, cov spots)   5.00
MALLETTE, GERTRUDE E-Chee Chako-NY-1938-299p-col frontis-
Juvenile   (5aa1)   3.50
MALLING, OVE-Great & Good Deeds of Danes, Norwegians &
Holsteinians-Lond-1807-Baldwin-4to-hf calf-328(4)p-port
    (5nn2, sl rub)   15.00
MALLISON, G-Color at Home & Abroad-Bost-1929 (5x2, dj)   35.00
MALLORY, DAN'L, ed-Life & Speeches of the Hon Henry Clay-
NY-1843-2 vols-orig cl-port-2nd ed   (5m2)   13.50
MALLORY, WALTER H-China, Land of Famine-NY-1926 (5x7)   8.50
MALONE, ANDREW E-The Irish Drama-NY-1929-8vo-351p-cl
    (5t0)   5.00
MALONE COOK BOOK-Woman's Aid Soc of 1st Congreg Church-
Rutland-1908-photo-ads   (5c4, crack, soil)   4.50
--same-NY-n.d.-(ca1917)-6th ed   (5g9, cov soil)   4.00
MALONE, DUMAS-Jefferson, the Virginian-Bost-1948-484p-illus
    (5h9)   6.00
--Story of Declaration of Independence-NY-Oxf Univ Pr-1954-
282p-illus   (5L7, 5p9)   7.50

USED BOOK PRICE GUIDE

MALONE, HENRY THOMPSON-Cherokees of the Old South-
Athen,Ga-(1956)-219p plus index-illus-1st ed (5t3,dj) 7.50
MALONE, JAS H-The Chickasaw Nation-Louisvl,Ky-1922-photos-
521p-2nd ed (5zz5) 45.00
MALONE, JOS S-Sons of Vengeance-NY-(1903)-299p-cl (5h7) 5.00
MALORY, THOS-Byrth,Lyf,Actes of Kyng Arthur & in the end,Le
Morte darthur-Lond-1817-2 vols-Robt Southey,ed-g.-lea
from Caxton 1485 ed (5P5,f bndg) 75. (5d2,f) 75.00
--La Mort d'Arthur-Lond-Geo Routledge-1893-Thos Wright,ed-
540p (5p7) 6.00
--same-Lond-1920-2 vols-Medici Soc-t thk8vo-orig grn dec cl,
g. lettring (5t8) 35.00
--Story of King Arthur-Lond-1936-Golden Cockerel Pr-3 vols-
sm folio-Ltd Ed Club-1500c,nbrd,boxed,autg (5b0) 45.00
--Romance of King Arthur & His Knights-NY-1917-Macmillan-
Rackham,illus-8vo-dec cl-g.t.-517p-23 plts(16col)-1st Amer ed
(5nn2) 25.00
MALOY, DR B S-A Negro Nation-Bost-1947 (5x2,dj) 20.00
MALOY, WALTER C-Madera Co,Calif-Madera-n.d.(ca1912)-
Chamber of Commerce,Tribune Print-24p plus 1p-illus-map
(5r0) 7.50
MALRAUX, ANDRE-Days of Wrath-NY-1936-1st Amer prnt
(4b4,mint,dj) 10.00
MALTBY, ISAAC-Treatise on Courts Martial & Military Law,etc-Bost-
1813-272p-lea-1st ed (5ee3) 25.00
MALTBY, LUCY MARY-It's Fun to Cook-Phila-(1938)-399p-4to-
illus-teenage (5c0) 4.50 (5c9) 5.00
MALTBY, WM J-Captain Jeff-Colorado-1906-161p (4a5) 37.50
MALTE-BRUN, CONRAD-Coup d'Oeil d'Ensemble sur es differentes
Expeditions Arctiques-Paris-1855-8vo-wrps-fldg map(5L1) 15.00
MALTE-BRUN, M-A System of Universal Geography & Atlas-Bost-
1836-Saml Walker-4to-illus-3 vols-calf (5t7) 27.50
MALTHUS, THOS R-1st Essay on Population,1798-Lond-1926-396p-
facs (5aa0) 15.00
MALVEZIN, FRANTZ-Le Vieillissement Artificiel des vins &
spiritueux-Paris-1906-94p,(12),-illus-wrps (5w1) 6.50
MALVEZIN, PHILIPPE-Etudes Sur La Viti Viniculture-Paris-1905-
4to-115p(6)p-col plt-wrps (5w1) 9.50
MALVEZIN, THEOPHILE-Les Grands Vins de Bordeaux-n.d.-
(ca1900)-Revue Mensuelle de Viticulture-64p-4to-map-
col wrps (5w1) 10.00
MAMA'S PRESENT-Derby-1835-Richardson-wdcuts-pt lea-bnd wi
"Select Poetry for Children" & "Select Fables" (5c8,chip) 20.00
MAMMALS OF AMERICA-(Nature Lovers Libr Vol 4)-NY-(1917)-
4to-cl-illus (5t7) 10.00
MAMMY TITTLEBACK & HER FAMILY-A True Story of Seventeen
Cats-by H H (Jackson)-Bost-1888-8vo-101p-illus (5v0) 7.50
MAN, THOS-A picture of Woonsocket-n.p.(Providence)-1835-
12mo-orig cl & bds-1st ed-for author (5i9,wtrstnd) 22.50
MAN TRAP-RedwoodCty,Ca-1951-St Peter's Epis Church-226p-
spiral bnd-illus (4g9) 4.50
MAN WORKING 1919 to 1962-Catalogue of Wm Faulkner Coll
at Univ of Virg-Charlottesville-(1968)-4to-cl-250p-18 plts
(5d5) 25.00
MANAGEMENT OF THE TONGUE-Bost-June,1814-Isaiah Thomas-
12mo-250p-orig bds-2nd ed (5j5) 20.00
MANAHAN, J E-Coppage,Coppedge Family-1955-113p-wrps
(5mm3) 5.00
MANAKEE, HAROLD R-Maryland in the Civil War-Balti-(1961)-
Hist Soc-8vo-cl-illus-173p (5j5,dj) 7.50
MANAOLANA, HUI-Japanese Foods-Honolulu-(1956)-118p-col plts
(5g9) 4.00
MANBY, G W-The History &Beauties of Clifton Hot Wells-Lond-
1806-84p-18 plts-12mo (5v0,wn) 10.00
MANBY, GEO WM-Lecture on Preservation of Persons in Hour of
Shipwreck-Lond-1814-72p-8vo-bds (5ss5,pres,rbnd) 15.00
MANCHESTER & LIVERPOOL RR-Descrip Catalogue of Padorama,or
the-Lond-1834-16p-illus (5k2) 27.50
MANCHESTER MANUFACTURER, A-England,Ireland & Amer by a-
Lond-1835-Jas Ridgway-160p-8vo-calf-1st ed(2nd ed same yr)
(5L1) 75.00
MANCHESTER, MASS-Vital Records of to end of year 1848-Salem-
1903-296p (5w0) 8.50
--same-to end of year 1849-Salem-1903 (5w9) 7.50
MANCHESTER DIRECTORY(N.HAMP)-with fldg map-1881,1883,
1888 each vol (5t9) 10.00
MANCHESTER, VT-Record of Soldiers of Civil,Spanish Amer &
1st World Wars from town of Manchester-1925-139p (5mm3) 5.00
MANCHESTER, H H-Story of Silk & Cheney Silks-S Manchester-
(1916)-63p-illus (4e4) 8.50
MANCHESTER, HERBERT-Wm Armstrong Fairburn-NY-1940-162p-
fldg bds (5y2) 5.75

MANCHURIA LAND OF OPPORTUNITIES-NY-SoManchuria
Rwy-1922-8vo-bds-113p-illus (5t0) 4.50
MANCHURIA YEAR BOOK 1932,33-Tokyo-1932-530p-plts-
fldg map (5s6) 4.50
MANDARIN CHOP SUEY COOK BOOK-Chig-1928-Pacific Trading
Co-96p-8vo-wrps-2nd ed (5g9) 3.50
MANDEL, B-Labor,Free & Slave-NY-1955-1st ed (5x2) 10.00
MANDEL, LEON-Robt Herrick,the Last Elizabethan-Chig-1927-
71p-hf lea-ltd to 490c (5k0) 7.50
MANDELBAUM, DAVID G-Soldier Groups & Negro Soldiers-
Univ Calif Pr-1952-142p-hard cover (5x2) 3. (5mm8,dj,vf) 5.00
MANDERSON, CHAS F-The Twin Seven shooters-NY-(1902)-
54p-photos-1st ed (5zz5) 12.50
MANDEVILLE, ERNEST W-Story of Middletown-Middletown,(NJ)-
n.d.-(c1927)-priv print-illus (4a9,g) 17.50
MANDRILLON, JOS,transl-Le voyageur americain...traduit de
l'Anglois-Amsterdam-1783-264p -fldg map-lea-2nd ed
(5m4) 100.00
MANELPHUS, J-Tradatus de Fletu et Lacrymis-Rome-1618-16mo-
calf (5j3,rprd) 55.00
MANFORD, ERASMUS-25 Years in the West-Chig-1873-priv prnt-
rev ed-cl (4a9) 17.50
--same-Chig-1885-rev ed-413p-ports (5m9,poor) 7.50 (4n8,cov wn) 15.00
MANEY, HENRY-Memories over the water,or stray thoughts on a
long stroll-Nashvl-1854-Toon,Nelson-8vo-orig cl-1st ed
(5mm2) 8.50 (5i9) 10.00
MANGIN, CHAS-Lettres du Soudan-Paris-1930-252p-1 plt-
2 maps(1 dbl pg) (5c6,defect wrp) 12.50
MANGIN, EWD-Stories for Short Students-1829-1st ed-JHarris,ed-
sm8vo-hf roan-188p plus 20p cat-plts (4d1) 20.00
MANGUM, A W-Myrtle Leaves,or Tokens of the Tomb-Raleigh-
1864 (5yy8,chip,lacks fly) 12.50
MANGUM, C S-Legal Status of Tenant Farmer in the Southeast-
1952 (5L7,ex-libr) 4.50
MANHATTAN, AVRO-Vatican in World Politics-NY-1949-444p-
12mo-cl (5t0) 4.00
MANHATTAN ELEC SUPPLY CO-Manual of Wireless Telegraphy
& Catalogue of Radio Telegraph Apparatus-NY-(1920)-#12-
fldg bds-198p-wi price list-illus (5b8) 12.50
-- Wireless Manual & Catalog of Radio Telegraph & Telephone
Apparatus· -NY-(1921?)-fldg bds-207p(1)-illus (5e4) 8.50
MANIAC BEAUTY, THE-n.p.-(Boston)-n.d.-(Gleason,1844)-8vo-
disbnd-1st ed-rare (5x1,rprd) 60.00
MANING, FREDK E-Old New Zealand-Auckland-(1906)-illus-
327p (5q0,dj) 12.50
MANITOBA-great agricultural Province of Manitoba-Winnipeg-
(ca1893)-photos-obl 4to-fldg map-wrps (5g3) 10.00
MANITOBE EN HET NOORDEWESTERN VAN AMERIKA-(Lond,
1882)-16p-illus (5r6) 60.00
MANITOU, COLO (COVER TITLE)-(Denv,1882)-(W H Lawrence &Co)-
folder of 20 views and 8 p text-small obl-cl (5L5) 10.00
MANITOU SPRINGS-Glimpse of...& Surroundings-CliffHouse,
ManitouSprngs-(ca1885to90)-illus-24mo-prntd wrps(5g8,sl stn) 7.50
MANJE, CAPT JUAN MATEO,UNKNOWN ARIZ & SONORA,
1693-1721-From Luz de Tierra Incognita-Tucson-1954-Engl
transl by Karns-photos-maps-col pkt map-ltd ed
(5g6,f,dj) 20. (5dd5,f) 23.50
MANKOWITZ, W-Concise Encyclopedia of English Pottery &
Porcelain-NY-1957-Chamberlin&Lucas-illus-312p-8vo (5ww3) 20.00
MANLEY, ATWOOD-Fredk Remington,in the Land of His Youth-
Ogdensburg(NY)-1961-4to-illus-wrps-priv prntd-1st ed-
scarce (5p5,autg) 15.00
MANLY, H-The Modern Motor Car-Chig-1918-illus (5b9,scuff) 20.00
MANLY, A STEWART-Hit &Miss-Chig-1889-428p-cl-Rhodes &
McClue Publ (5h2,dmpstn,wn) 7.50
MANLY, HOWARD P-Automobile Upkeep & Care-Chig-1920-cl-
308p-illus (5y2) 4.75
MANLY, JOHN MATTEWS-Specimens of the Pre Shaksperean
Drama-Bost-1903-2 vols-Ginn&Co (5x0) 10.00
MANLY, L-Southern Literature from 1579 to 1895-Richmond-1900
(5x2) 25.00
MANLY, WM L-Death Valley in '49-SanJose-1894-Pacific Tree &
Vine Co-orig cl-1st ed (5L7,5hh4,f,5zz5) 45. (5x5) 50.00
--same-Chig-1927-Lakeside Pr-frontis-map-307p (5ee3)10. (5p1) 12.50
--same-NY-(1929)-524p-illus-repnt (5zz5) 7.50 (5i3) 10.00
--same-SantaBarbara-(1929)-AlsonClark,ill -524p (4n1) 15.00
MANN, ALEX-Yachting on the Pacific-Lond-1909 (5c1) 15.00
MANN, B PICKINAN-Bibliogr of some of the Literature Concerning
Destructive Locusts-Wash-1880-24p-wrps (5j4) 3.00
MANN, BONITA H-History of Missouri School of Mines &Metallurgy-
Rolla,Mo-1941-1020p-photos-spec priv ed(very ltd) (5t3) 20.00
--same-1st ed-regular trade ed (5t3) 15.00

MANN,CHAS EDW-The Sargent Family & the Old Sargent
　Homes-Lynn-1919-64p-wrps　　　(5w5) 3.50　(5t9)　4.50
MANN,F W-Bullets Flight from Powder to Target-Huntington-1942-
　lg8vo-384p-illus-rprnt　　　　　　　(4a6)　22.50
MANN,GERTRUDE-Berry Cooking-(Lond 1954)-72p　(5c9)　3.00
MANN,HENRY-Features of Society in Old & In New England-
　Prov-1885-Rider-103p-ads-sq12mo　　(5qq8)　6.00
MANN,HORACE-Lectures on Education-Bost-1845-12mo-g.e.-
　orig roan-1st ed　　　　　　　　　(5gg6)　50.00
--Speech of Mr Horace Mann of Mass.on Subject of Slavery in
　Territories etc-Wash-1850-16p-orig wrps　(5x5)　25.00
MANN,MRS HORACE-Christianity in the Kitchen-Bost-1861-
　(1860)-189p　　　　　　　　　　(5c0)　14.50
MANN,MARY TYLER· Juanita,a Romance of Real Life in Cuba 50
　Years Ago-Bost-(1887)-1st ed　　(5ee3)　5.00
MANN,ROBT JAS,ed-The Colony of Natal-Lond-n.d.-(c1859)-
　maps(1 fldg)-229p　　　　　　　(4t5)　75.00
MANN,THOS-The Beloved Returns-1940-Knopf-1st Amer ed
　　　　　　　　　　　(5F1,f,dj,autg)　6.00
--Buddenbrooks-Lond-1924-M Secker-2 vols-8vo-cl-1st ed in Engl
　　　　　　　　　　　(5d9,dj)　25.00
--An Exchange of Letters-NY-1937-Knopf-12p-orig blue wrps-
　frontis-　　　　　　　　　　　(5ss9)　8.50
--Joseph & His Brothers-1934-Knopf-1st Amer ed (5F1,f,dj,autg) 6.75
--Nocturnes-NY-1934-liths by Lynd Ward-ltd to 1000c-
　autg,nbrd　　　　　　　　(5ss9,f,box,4b4)　35.00
--This Peace-NY-1938-Knopf-12mo-cl-38p-1st ed　(5j5)　7.50
--The Transposed Heads-1941-Knopf-1st Amer ed
　　　　　　　　　　　(5F1,mint,dj,pres)　17.50
--Young Joseph-1935-Knopf-1st Amer ed　(5F1,f,dj,autg)　7.50
MANNERS AND CUSTOMS-Newport(NH)-1837,Wilcox on upper
　wrapper-t.pg Merrifield,Windsor,Vt-ABC's-24mo-10p-wdcuts
　　　　　　　　　　　(5v0)　15.00
MANNERS,LADY VICTORIA-Angelica Kaufmann,R A-Lond-(1924)-
　illus-lg4to-bds-vel bk-268p-ltd ed　(5q0)　12.50
MANNERS-SUTTON,P-Black God-NY-1934-1st ed (5x2,dj)　3.50
--same-Lond-1934-299p　　　　　　　(4t5)　4.00
MANNHEIM,KARL-Ideology & Utopia-NY-1949-H Brace-1949-
　318p　　　　　　　　　　　　(5p0)　5.00
MANNING,CLARENCE A-The Siberian Fiasco-NY-(1952)-210p-
　　　　　　　　　　　　(5ss1)　3.75
MANNING,G C-Manual Naval Architecture..for Masters,Mates-
　NY-1930-183p-illus　　　　　　(5s1)　4.00
--Principles Warship Construction & Damage Control-Annap-1939-
　396p-plts　　　　　　　　　　(5s1)　6.50
MANNING,HELEN T-British Colonial Govt after Amer Revolution,
　1782 to 1820-1933　　　　　　　(5L7)　8.50
MANNING,J F-Federal Protection to Amer Commerce-NY-1882-
　8vo-48p-orig wrps-1st ed　　　(5ss5,loose)　5.00
MANNING,OLIVIA-Reluctant Rescue-GardenCty-1947-304p-map
　　　　　　　　　　　　(5c6)　6.75
MANNING,REG-Manning's Cartoon Guide of Ariz-NY-1944-
　121p-pkt maps-7th ed　　　　　(5s4,rprd)　3.00
MANNING,ROBT-History of the Massachusetts Horticultural Soc-
　Bost-1880-illus-545p　　　　　　(5w3)　6.50
MANNING,MRS TOM-Igloo for the Night-Lond-(1943)-232p-
　photos　　　　　　　　　　(5ss1)　3.00
MANNING,WM-Archaeologia Americana-Worcester-1820-Vol 1-
　maps-plts-cl　　　　　　　　(5x5)　40.00
MANNING,WM R-Nootka Sound Controversy-Wash-1905
　　　　　　　(5dd0,cov sl wn)　20.00
MANNIX,D P-Black Cargoes-NY-1962-illus　(5x2)　5.00
MANOLA,ADELAIDE-Poems of-Memorial by Rupert Hughes-NY-
　(1924)-Harper-12mo-1st ed　　(5ss9)　5.00
MANRIQUE,SEBASTIEN-Travels,1629 to 1643-Oxford-1927-2 vols-
　Hakluyt Soc-plts-maps　　　　(5s6)　15.00
MANROSS,WM-History of Amer Episcopal Church-NY-1935-404p-
　8vo-cl-illus　　　　　　　　(5t0)　5.00
MAN'S RANSOM,A-Pamphlet by "The Armstrong Assoc" for "Hampton
　Institute"-10p-illus-16mo-scarce　(5x2)　15.00
MANSBRIDGE,ALBERT-The Older Universities of England,Oxford
　& Cambridge-Bost-1923-cl-24p,308p　(5t2)　4.00
MANSFIELD AND HIGBEE'S-Memphis Family Almanac for use of
　Farmers,Planters,Mechanics & all Others,1873-Memphis-1873-
　48p-wrps-scarce　　　　　　　(5h6)　9.00
MANSFIELD (Conn)-A Passing Sketch of the Village,1685 to 1879
　by a Way Side Traveler-1880-(94p)-200c prntd-v scarce
　　　　　　　　(5t9,2p pres)　20.00
MANSFIELD,DAVID L-Hist of Capt John Kathan,1st Settler of
　Dummerston,Vt-1902-147p　　(5t9)　20.00
MANSFIELD,EDW D-Life of General Winfield Scott-NY-1846-
　366p-1st ed　　　(4L3,5mm8) 7.50　(4a5)　15.00

MANSFIELD,EDW D (continued)
--Life & Services of Gen'l Winfield Scott-NY-1852-Barnes-
　ads-illus-g.-cl　　　　(5mm8,rub) 8.50　(4h2)　12.50
--The Mexican War-NY-1848-323p　　(5s2)　12.50
--same-NY-1849-Barnes&Co-365p-illus-map　(5p7)　7.50
--Personal Memories...1803 to 1843-Cinn-1879-1st ed-348p (4L3) 20.00
--A Popular & Authentic Life of Ulysses S Grant-Cinn-1868-377p
　　　　　　　　　　　　(5j6)　6.00
MANSIFLED,H-Descendants of Richard Mansfield & Gillian of New
　Haven,1639-1885-193p　　　　(5mm3)　32.50
MANSFIELD,HOWARD-Descrip Catalogue of Etchings & Dry Points
　of...Whistler-Chig-1909-8vo-bds-cl bk-g.t.ltd to 303c
　　　　　　　　　　(4c1,box,f)　30.00
--same-Chig-1909-large type-4to-g.t.-linen sp　(5t8)　35.00
MANSFIELD,IRA F-Hist Collections Little Beaver River Valleys
　Penna Ohio-BeaverF-1911-224p-scarce　(5h1)　15.00
MANSFIELD,KATHERINE-The Aloe-Lond-1930-Constable&Co-
　ltd to 750c-1st ed　　　(5ss3,4b9,f,dj)　20.00
--same-NY-1930-Knopf-1st Amer ed-ltd to 950c
　　　　　　(5ss9,f,dj,box,unopnd)　15.00
--The Dove's Nest & Other Stories-Lond-(1923)-2nd ed
　　　　　　　　　　(5j3,vg,dj)　15.00
--The Garden Party & Other Stories-Lond-(1922)-12mo-cl-
　yellow letters on cov　　　　(4c2)　17.50
--same-Lond-(1922)-2nd issue　(5j3,vg,dj)　30.00
--same-NY-1923-255p-cl　　　(5t2)　3.00
--Je ne parle pas Francais-Hampstead-1919-Heron Pr-4to-
　orig green wrps wi prntd labl-1st ed　(5dd8)　350.00
--Letters-NY-1930-Murray,ed-2 vols　(5jj0)　7.50
--Poems-Lond-(1923)-t8vo-bds-cl bk-lea labl-t.e.g.-1st Engl ed
　　　　(4b5,vg,wn dj) 30.　(5ee9)　50.00
--Something Childish & Other Stories-Lond-(1924)-8vo-cl-1st ed
　　　　(5d9) 25.　(5j5)　20.00
MANSFIELD,LOUISE-An Artist's Herbal-NY-1937-4to-76p-
　38 plts　　　　(5x0) 5.　(5w3)　7.50
MANSFIELD,NORMA B-Keeper of the Wolves-NY-(1934)-308p-
　gloss　　　　　　　　　(5ss1)　2.50
MANSFIELD PARK-a novel-Lond-1814-TEgerton-3 vols-12mo-
　hf calf-mor labls-lf of ads at end of 3rd vol-1st ed
　　　　　　(5x3,new labels,f,fldg box)　825.00
MANSFIELD,RICH-Blown Away-Bost-1897-Page-12mo-180p-
　illus-t.e.g.-1st ed　　　(5p1,pres)　25.00
MANSIFLED,WM-Histology of Medicinal Plants-NY-(1916)-
　305p-127 illus　　　　　　(5w3)　5.50
MANSHIP,REV ANDREW-National Jewels,Washington,Lincoln
　& Fathers of the Revolution-Phila-1866-123p-2 ports-cl (5a0,f) 5.00
MANT,ALICIA CATHERINE-The Young Naturalist,a Tale-Bost-
　1827-Munroe&Francis-NY-CSFrancis-12mo-226p-frontis-
　cl-2nd ed　　　　　　　(5v0)　20.00
MANTAUK GUIDE & COOK BOOK-Montauk,NY-n.d.-maps-photos-
　spiral bnd-stiff wrps-212p-2nd ed　(4g9)　4.50
MANTEGAZZA,PROF PAOLO-Anthropological Studies of Sexual
　Relations of Mankind-NY-c1932-ltd to 1500c　(5x7)　15.00
--same-NY-c1937-500 illus　　　　(5x7)　8.75
--Physiology of Love-NY-1939　　(5x7)　7.50
MANTEGNA,ANDREA-von Fritz Knapp-Berlin-n.d.-193p-8vo
　　　　　　　　　　(5ww3)　15.00
MANTELLINI,G-Memoirs & Artistic Studies of Adelaide Ristori-
　NY-1907-263p-illus　　　　(5t4)　7.50
MANTER,ETHEL-Rocket of the Comstock-Caldwell-1950-256p-
　23p of illus,notes-port　　　(5dd6)　12.00
MANTLE,BURNS,ed-Best Plays of 1941,42-NY-1942-illus (4a1) 7.50
MANTLE FIELDING 'S-Dictionary of Amer Painters Sculptors &
　Engrav-NY-1865-JFCarr,comp-529p　(5t7)　10.00
MANTZIUS,KARL-Hist of Theatrical Art,Vol 6-Lond-(1921)-cl-
　361p-illus-1st ed　　　　　(5t0)　6.50
MANUAL ALPHABET-Used by the Deaf & Dumb-NY-c1840-32mo-
　16p-illus wrps-scarce　　　　(5v0)　15.00
MANUAL DEL COCINERO Y COCINERA-Puebla-1849-9 plts-
　397p(18)-lea bk-bds　　　(5c5,pg tn)　85.00
MANUAL DEL COCINERO-Mexico-1856-188p-lea-g.t.-
　MMurguia ed　　　　　(5c5,rbnd)　50.00
MANUAL FOR ARMY COOKS-Wash-1896-306p-lea (5c0,shake) 3.50
MANUAL FOR ARMY HORSESHOERS-Cavalry School,Wash-1920-
　8vo-114p-illus-wrps　　　　(4a6)　10.00
MANUAL FOR THE BATTERY COMMANDER-Heavy Artillery,
　Confidential-Wash-1918-12mo-orig limp cl-131p (5m6)　7.50
MANUAL FOR COURTS MARTIAL-Wash-1910-GPO　(5b9)　7.50
MANUAL FOR GAUGERS OF SPIRITS-prepared for US Treas Dept-
　Wash-(?1866)-185p-calf　　(5w1,chip)　7.50
MANUAL OF AMER COTTON INDUSTRY-Illus Descriptions of
　Various Machines-Bost-(ca1895)-138p　(5hh7)　12.50

MANUAL OF THE ARTS-for Young People-Bost-1857-450p(1)-calf   (5n7,wn)   8.50

MANUAL OF GUNNERY-For Her Majesty's Fleet-Lond-1873-22 plts-orig brass clasp-pkt size   (5c1)   40.00

MANUAL OF HERALDRY-Lond-n.d.-ca1862-16mo-cl&bds-132p col frontis   (5t9,rbnd)   5.00

MANUAL OF MATRIMONY-& Connubial Companion,by a Bachelor-NY-(1845)-127p-32mo   (5w7,chip)   6.50

MANUAL OF MESS MANAGEMENT-Military Service Pub Co-Harrisburg-(1941)-340p-illus   (5c9)   5.00

--Army Food & Messing-1942-418p-2nd ed-rev ed   (5c9)   5.00

MANUAL OF PRACTICAL NATURALIST-Bost-1831-frontis-12mo-1st ed   (5m6)   10.00

MANUAL OF SEAMANSHIP 1937-Vol 1-Lond-1942-446p-illus   (5s1)   4.00

MANUEL ABREGE DE CONTROVERSE-Quebec-1806-169p(2)-orig calf-nouvelle imprimerie   (5w8,libr stmp)   125.00

MANUEL GUIDE DES VOYAGEURS-aux Etats Unis de l'Amerique du Nord...par M F D G-Paris-1818-12mo-orig prntd wrps-196p   (5a3)   50.00

MANVILLE, MARION-Over the Divide & Other Verses-1888-Lipp-2nd ed   (5ww4)   5.00

MANWARING, CHAS W-Digest of Early Conn Probate Records, Hartford Dist 1635 to 1750-Vol 1 thru 3-1902 to 1906-3 vols   (5q0)   40.00

MANYPENNY, GEO-Claims for Indian Depredations in NewMex-Wash-1858-HED123-62p   (5n4)   25.00

MANZONI, ALESSANDRO-I Promessi Sposi-Verona-1931-illus-Ltd Ed Club Publ-ltd to 1500c-nbrd-autogs-box   (5F1,vf)   25.00

MAPES, DAVID P-History of the City of Ripon-Milw-1873 (5jj7)   20.00

MAPLET, JOHN-A Greene Forest, Or, a Naturall Historie-Lond-1930-4to-184p-ltd to 500c   (5w3)   12.50

MARACHE-Manual of Chess-NY-1866-1st ed   (5b9)   20.00

MARAINI, FOSCO-Meeting wi Japan-NY-c1959   (5x7)   5.00

--Secret Tibet-Lond-1954-251p-illus-cl-Readers Union (5d7)   8.50

MARAIS, BEN J-Colour, unsolved problem of the West-1952 (5L7) 5.00

MARAIS, JOSEF-Koos, the Hottentot-NY-1945-col illus-1st ed   (5v2,dj,mint)   10.00

MARAN, R-Batouala-NY-1932-lea tooled-Ltd Ed Club-ltd to 1500c-4to   (5x2)   65.00

--same-Lond-1922-1st Engl ed-ltd to 1000c   (5x2)   22.50

--same-NY-1922-1st Trade ed   (5x2)   10.00

MARAT, JEAN PAUL-Polish Letters-Bost-1904-R8vo-2 vols-orig bds-ltd to 445c-1st ed-illus   (5t5,boxes)   15.00

MARBAKER, THOS D-Hist of 11th NJ Volunteers From Its Organiz to Appomattox-Trenton-1898-illus   (4m2)   22.50

MARBEN, ROLF-Zeppelin Adventures-Lond-n.d.-illus   (5j2)   10.00

MARBLE, ANNIE-Pen Names & Personalities-Appleton-1930-255p   (5j4)   7.50

MARBLE, ANNIE R-From 'prentice to patron-NY-1935-8vo-cl(4c1) 7.50

MARBURG, THEO F-Small Business in Brass Fabricating-NY-1956-116p-illus   (5y2)   6.75

MARBURY, ELIZ-Manners, a Hand Book of Social Customs-NY-(1888)-12mo-114p,(6)   (5w7,stn)   3.50

MARBURY, MARY ORVIS-Favorite Flies & Their Histories-Bost-(1955)-4to-522p-illus   (5xx7,dj)   15.00

MARCEL, GABRIEL-Metaphysical Journal-1952   (5L7)   6.50

MARCELIN, P-Canape Vert-NY-1944-ELTinker, transl (5x2,dj)   10.00

--The Beast of the Haitian Hills-NY-1946   (5x2,dj)   10.00

--The Pencil of God, Novel of Haiti-NY-1951-1st Amer ed   (5x2,dj)   10.00

"MARCELINA"-Ireland's true daughter-Lond-1881-Remington&Co-3 vols-8vo-orig cl-1st ed   (5xx6,f)   35.00

MARCH, BENJ-China & Japan in Our Museums-NY-1929-illus-122p   (5ww3)   15.00

MARCH, DANIEL-Story of Massachusetts-(1938)-4 vols-Amer Hist Soc-illus   (5e8)   25.00

MARCH, FRANCIS A, JR-Athletics at Lafayette College-Easton-1926-Lafayette College-8vo-272p   (5p1,ex-libr)   6.50

MARCH, HAROLD-The 2 Worlds of Marcel Proust-1948-Univ of Pa-1st ed   (5ss9,dj)   7.50

MARCH, J-The jolly angler, or water side companion-Lond-n.d.-(1831)-12mo-orig qtr cl-frontis-1st ed   (5i8,rprd)   12.00

MARCH, JOS MONCURE-15 Lyrics-NY-1929-Fountain Pr-8vo-cl-Harbor Pr-ltd to 417c,autg   (5ee9)   10.00

--The Set Up-NY-1828-t8vo-1st ed   (5x2) 8.50   (5r9,dj)   10.00

--The Wild Party-1929-priv prntd-100p-ltd to 1000c (5x0) 7.50

MARCH, OTHNIEL C-Dinocerata-Wash-1886-4to-56p plts-buck-1 lin bkd fld out   (5w0,rbnd)   20.00

MARCH, WM-Some Like Them Short-1939-LittleBrown (5F1,dj,vf) 4.50

MARCHAND, E-Voyage autour du monde pendant 1790 to 1792-3 vols & atlas 1798 to 1800-folio-maps-buck   (5L7,rbnd)   300.00

MARCHAND, HENRY L-Sex Life in France-NY-c1935 (5x7)   22.50

MARCHANT, B-The Youngest Sister-1913   (4b9,rub)   6.00

MARCHANT, BESSIE-Queen of Shindy Flat-Wells Gardner-1905-8vo-216p-cel cl-g.-19 plts   (5aa3)   4.50

MARCHANT, W T-In Praise of Ale-Lond-1888-632p   (5w1)   20.00

MARCOSSON, ISAAC F-An African Adventure-NY-1921-Lane-288p-photos   (4t5)   10.00

--Anaconda-NY-1957-370p-illus   (5y2,5s4,5x0)   4.00

--The Black Golconda-NY-369p- 1924   -1st ed (5F6)5.50(5m6) 8.50

--Colonel Deeds-NY-1947-374p-illus   (5y2)   4.00

--Copper Heritage-NY-1955-254p-illus   (5p7) 5.   (5y2)   5.50

--Industrial Main Street-NY-1953-220p-illus   (5h8)   4.75

--Wherever Men Trade-NY-1945-263p-illus   (5y2)   4.50

MARCOY, PAUL-Travels in SoAmer from Pac Ocean to Atlantic Ocean-NY-1875-Scribner-Elihu Rich, transl-4to-illus-2 vols   (5p7)   30.00

--same-Lond-1875-illus-10 maps-2 vols-lg4to-cl g.e.   (4e1)   65.00

MARCU, VALERIU-Lenin-NY-1929-412p-photos   (5ss6)   5.00

MARCUS AURELIUS ANTONIUS-Meditations-NY-1900-Dutton-ed by WHDRouse   (5m2)   5.00

--Thoughts-Lond-1909-transl by Geo Long-illus-Medici Soc-ltd to 500c-Riccardi Pr-4to-   g. wi ties-t.e.g. (5b0,lt soil)   75.00

--same-Lond-1912-Medici Soc-8vo-cl-g.t.e.g.-illus (5b0,dj) 30.00

MARCUS, RICH-Korean Studies Guide-Berkeley-1954   (5x7)   6.50

MARCUS, STEVEN-The Other Victorians-NY-(1966)-Basic Books-8vo-cl-292p   (5j5,dj)   6.00

MARCY, MARY E-Rhymes of Early Jungle Folk-Chig-(c1922)-8vo-124p-wdcuts-1st ed   (5p1,dj)   7.50

MARCY, RANDOLPH B-Exploration of Red River of Louisiana-Wash-1853-plts-fldg map-1st issue-320p   (4n4)   25.00

--same-Wash-1853-Armstrong-65 plts-2 fldg maps in separate vol-Sen Ex #54   (4b6,ex-libr,maps wn)   25.00

--same-Wash-1854-AOPNicholson-plts-map folder-cl (5tt8)   25.00

--same-Wash-1854-286p-65 plts-2 lg fldg maps(in separate vol)   (5t3,wn, lacks map vol) 7.50 (4L3,vg)   55.00

--same-Wash-1854-310p-plts   (5xx7)   15.00

--Explor of Big Witchita & Head Waters of Brazos Rivers-Wash-1856-48p-lacks map(as usual)-SED60   (4n4)   20.00

--The Prairie Traveler, Hand Book for Overland Exped-NY-1859-16mo-cl-maps & illus-340p-fldg map (5zz5,5m9) 50. (5g5)   85.00

--same-West Virg-1961-maps-illus-ltd   (5x5,box,4n1)   15.00

--30 Yrs of Army life on the Border-NY-1866-442p-1st ed   (5zz5,wn)   15.00

--same-NY-1874-Harper-illus-442p   (5u3)   20.00

MARCY, W L-Strength of Army at Close of Mexican War-Wash-1848-HED 74   (4a5)   3.00

MARDIKIAN, GEO-Dinner at Omar Khayyam's-NY-1944-150p-1st ed   (5g9)   5.00

--same-1949 ed   (5g9)   4.50

MARDRUS, DR J C-The Queen of Sheba-Lond-n.d.-Casanova Soc-1st ed   (5x0)   4.00

MARECHAL, J-Le Point de depart de la metaphysique-1927-5 vols   (5L7,bndgs mixed)   15.00

MAREK, GEO R-Giacomo Puccini, a Biography-NY-1951-412p-illus   (5p0)   7.50

MARESCALCHI, A, ed-Storia Della Vite E Del Vino In Italia-Milan-1931-3 vols-4to-fldg map-29 plts(some col)-illus-ltd to 600 sets   (5w1)   750.00

MARETT, R R-Faith, Hope & Charity in Primitive Religion-1932   (5L7)   4.00

MARETZEK, MAX-Crotchets & Quavers-NY-1855-8vo-1st ed   (5m1,5m6)   10.00

MARGARET-A tale of the real & ideal, blight & bloom-Bost-1845-Jordan&Wiley-12mo-orig cl-1st ed   (5x1,sp wn)   20.00

MARGARET PERCIVAL IN AMERICA-Bost-1850-12mo-cl-1st ed of auth's 1st book   (5gg6,vf,autg)   10.00

MARGARITA, SAC CAMILLO-Del Modo Di Migliorare I Vini Di Lombardia-Milan-1851-78p-wrps   (5w1)   12.50

MARGE-Oh, Little Lulu!-n.p.-(c1945)-8vo-(62)p-pict bds   (5p1, fray dj)   12.50

MARGOLIOUTH, D S-Cairo, Jerusalem & Damascus-NY-1907-g.t.-58 pg col plts-thk4to-mor-1st ed   (5p5,rprd)   15.00

MARGRY, PIERRE-Decouvertes et Etablissments Des Francais dans L'ouest et dans Le Sud De L'Amerique Septentrionale (1614 to 1754)-Paris-1876,77,78,80,83,86-D Jouaust-6 vols-part mor   (5jj7,vf)   175.00

MARGUERITE KIRMSE'S DOGS-NY-1930-Derrydale Pr-plts-4to   (5q0, rub)   17.50

MARIA, MRS L-The Girl's Own Book-NY-(1833)-288p-12mo   (5w7,shake)   17.50

MARIANI, ANGELO-Coca & Its Therapeutic Application-NY-1892 & 1896-78p-frontis-illus   (5w3)   6.50

MARIANI'S COCA LEAF-NY-9 issues from Dec 1903 to Sept 1905   (5w3)   4.50

MARICE, A B-New York, Magical City, Notes by-NY-1925-
sq R8vo-70 illus   (5t8)   7.50
MARICOPA CO, ARIZ-Salt River Valley-(Phoenix)-n.d.-(1919)-
(14 dbl col pgs)-wrps-photos-map   (5t3)   8.50
MARIE, PETER-A tribute to the fair-NY-1864-Appleton-Sanitary
Commission-1st ed   (5m2)   6.00
MARIE, TANTE-La Veritable Cuisine de Famille-Paris-n.d.-480p-
illus-bds   (5g9)   4.50
--same-n.d.-new ed, rev & augmented   (5g9, browning) 3.50
--Tante Marie's French Kitchen-NY-1949-323p   (5g9)   5.00
MARIETTA & CINCINNATI RR-5th Annual Report...also Hillsboro'
& Cinn RR Co-Cinn-1855-disbnd   (5g4)   20.00
MARIETTA COOKBOOK-Minn-1947-48-typescript repro-ring bndg-
                                              (5c4)   3.00
MARIL, LEE-Savor & Flavor-NY-(1944)-63p-col illus (5s7)   3.00
MARILLIER, H C-"Christie's", 1766 to 1925-Lond-1926-4to-illus
                                              (5m2)   30.00
MARIN, JOHN-Drawings & Watercolors-NY-1950-ltd to 300c
                                              (5ww3)   115.00
--Watercolors, Oil Paintings, & Etchings-MOMA-1936-illus-100p-
8vo-ltd   (5ww3)   32.50
MARINE COPPERSMITHING-Mobile-1942-168p typescript-4to-
wrps-ring bndg   (5s1)   6.50
MARINE EINGINEERS' BENEFICIAL ASSN ANNUAL-Local 38, 1902
Seattle-n.d.-180p-photos-rosters   (5s1, sl shake) 10.00
--same-Seattle-1903-216p-photos-roster   (5s1, sl soil) 10.00
MARINE, F E-Sketch of Rev John Hersey, Minister of Gospel of
M E Church-1879   (5L7)   5.00
MARINE RESEARCH SOC-The Pirates Own Book-Salem-1924-8vo-
469p-cl-illus   (4a6)   12.50
MARINE SOCIETY OF CITY OF NY-Instituted 1769-NY-(1925)-
8vo   (5m6, sl stnd) 10.00
MARINE, WM M-The British Invasion of Maryland, 1812 to 1815-
Balt-1913-519p   (5ii8)   20.00
MARING, NORMAN H-Baptists in New Jersey-ValleyForge-1964-
379p-illus   (5w0)   3.50
MARIO, THOS-The Face in the Aspic-NY-1944-194p (4g9)   4.50
MARION CO, INDIANA-Directory for 1861 to 1862-Indnpls-1861-
Cullum&Sutherland-ads-illus-8vo-160p-cl   (4a9)   25.00
MARION CO, IOWA-History of-DesMoines-1881-8vo-hf lea-
807p-fldg map   (5m8, map split, cov spot)   42.50
MARION, F-Wonderful Ballon Ascents-Lond-n.d.-illus-224p
                                              (5rr9)   10.00
--same-NY-1870-218p-illus-1st ed   (5ee3)   7.50
MARION, GEN FRANCIS-The Life of-Phila-1829-by Horry&Weems-
252p-frontis   (5t7, sp rprd) 12.50
MARION, GEN'L-Life of-Bost&NY-1875-12mo-208p-7 plts-frontis-
dec cl-Young Amer's Libr of Famous Generals   (5p1)   6.50
MARION, LUCIE-The Home Chef-Lond-(1952)-255p (5g9)   3.50
MARIOTT, L-The blackgown papers-Lond-1841-Wiley&Putnam-
2 vols-12mo-orig cl-1st ed   (5xx6, f)   70.00
MARITAIN, JACQUES-Art & Scholasticism-NY-1930-232p (5v6)   3.50
--same-1947   (5L7)   3.50
--Bergsonian Philosophy & Thomism-1955   (5L7)   6.50
MARITIME COOK BOOK-Maritime Women's Club of Montreal-
n.p.-1939-127p   (5g9)   5.00
MARITIME DISCOVERY & ADVENTURE-Lond&Edinb-(c1898)-
Chambers-sm8vo-224p-plts-dec cl-g.t.   (5aa2)   5.00
MARJORAM, J-New Poems-Lond-1909-Duckworth&Co-cl-1st ed
                                              (5ss3, sp fade) 15.00
MARJORIBANKS, EDW-For the Defense-NY-1929-Macm-471p-
illus   (5p9)   6.00
MARKEVITCH, MARIE A-The Epicure in Imperial Russia-SanFran-
1941-Colt Pr-bds-500c publ   (5x5, rub)   15.00
MARKHAM, ALBERT H-Life of Sir Clements R Markham-Lond-1917-
plts-384p   (5zz8)   7.50
--A Polar Reconnaissance Being Voyage of the "Isbforn" to Novaya
Zemlya in 1879-Lond-1881-maps-illus   (5w8)   10.00
MARKHAM, C R-Threshold of the Unknown Region-Lond-1873-
357p-2nd ed-maps   (4e9, sp fade) 25.00
--same-1875-maps-3rd ed   (5L7, shaken) 7.50
MARKHAM, CLEMENTS-The Incas of Peru-NY-1910-Dutton-8vo-
cl-lg fldg map-16 illus   (4a3, map tn) 10.00
--Lands of Silence-Cambridge-1921-1st ed-plts-port-maps-539p
                                              (5s0)   25.00
--Travels in Peru & India-Lond-1862-572p, 12p-illus-maps
                                              (5w3, scuff, libr stmp) 18.50
--Voyages of Pedro Fernandez De Quiros 1595 to 1606-Lond-1904-
maps-2 vols   (5ii8)   20.00
MARKHAM, EDWIN-Calif the Wonderful-NY-1914-400p
                                              (4a5) 6.50   (4n1) 7.50
--Lincoln the Man of the People-NY-1922-Bernhardt Wall-
ltd to 300c, nbrd   (5ss9, autgs) 35.00

MARKHAM, EDWIN (continued)
--The Man with the Hoe & Other Poems-NY-1899-1st ed-
(1st issue, "fruitless" on pg 35, line 5)
(5k1, autg) 25. (5r9, 2p ALS) 25. (5m1, pres) 17.50
--same-NY-(1902)-McClure, Phillips-illus by Howard (5t4) 7.50
--New Poems, 80 Songs at 80-5th Book of Verse-NY-1932-Dblday,
Doran-ltd to 100c, nbrd, autg-lea bk   (5ss9, box) 25.00
--Real America in Romance-NY-1914-13 vols-hf mor-illus-t.e.g.-
"Art Edition"   (5w5)   42.50
--Shoes of Happiness & other poems-GardenCty-1924-Dblday, Page-
192p-pict cl-12mo-3rd book of verse   (5p1, pres, dj tn) 35.00
MARKHAM, FRANCIS-The Booke of Honour-Lond-1625-
Matthewes & Norton-(6), 200p-folio-calf-1st ed (4L1, f) 200.00
MARKHAM, GOV H H-Resources of Calif-Sacramento-1893-
lg fldg map-illus-pict wrps   (5g8)   6.00
MARKHAM, RICH-Colonial Days, being Stories & Ballads for Young
Patriots-NY-(1881)-Dodd, Mead-thk lg8vo-pict cl-698p-illus
                                              (5j5)   12.50
MARKLEY, WALT-Builders of Topeka-Topeka-1934-365p plus index-
photos   (5L0)   25.00
MARKS, DAVID-Life of-Limerick-1831-396p-calf-scarce   (5y0) 45.00
MARKS, E J-Genealogical Abstract of Pierrepont Descent from Sir
Hugh de Pierrepont of Picardy-1881-41p   (5t9)   12.50
MARKS, EDW B-They All Had Glamour, From the Swedish Nightingale
to the Naked Lady-NY-1944   (5p7)   6.00
--They All Sang, From Tony Pastor to Rudy Vallee-NY-1935-
Viking Pr-321p-illus   (5p7)   6.00
MARKS, HENRY K-Peter Middleton-Bost-(1919)-370p (5ss1)   3.00
MARKS, J J-Peninsular Campaign in Virginia-Phila-1864-Lippincott-
12mo-cl-444p-plts   (5j5)   10.00
MARKS, JEANNETTE-Genius & Disaster-NY-1925-Adelphi Co-
185p   (5p9)   5.00
--Thirteen Days-NY-1929-12mo-1st ed-scarce   (5ss5, dj) 15.00
MARKS, LIONEL S-Gas & Oil Engines & Gas Producers-Chig-1902-
75p, 61p-cl-illus   (5hh7)   8.50
MARKS, ROBT -Wines, How, When, & What to Serve-NY-1934-
Schenley Import Corp-63p-col illus-pict bds   (5c9)   5.00
MARKSMAN-The Dear Shot, or Sportsman's Complete Guide-NY-
1864-illus-282p   (5r5, f)   10.00
MARLE, RAIMOND VAN-Development of the Italian Schools of
Painting-Vol 2-Sienese School of 14th Cent-The Hague-1924-
Nijhoff-627p-4to-cl-10 col plts   (5m5)   75.00
MARLES, M DE-Amerique-Paris-1830-illus-2 vols-calf-12mo(4e1) 60.00
MARLETTE, GEO W-Schenectady Directory 1882-195p-ads-5th annual
                                              (5zz0)   7.50
MARLOWE, GEO FRANCIS-Churches of Old New England-NY-
1947-222p-illus-photos   (5h9)   7.50
--Coaching Roads of Old New England, Their Inns & Taverns-NY-
1945-Macm-197p   (5p9)   4.00
MARMADUKE MULTIPLY-NY-c1850-sq12mo-71p-illus-all
editions of this title are scarce   (5v0, lacks 1 lf) 10.00
--same-Bost-1839-sm sq12mo-71p(prntd 1 side)-70 hand col plts
                                              (5v0, wn)   17.50
MARMER, H A-US Coast Geo Surv-NY-1930-312p-45 illus(5s1, dj) 6.00
MARMETTE, JOS-Francois de Bienville, Scenes de la vie Canadienne
au 17th siecle-Montreal-1883-hf mor-2nd ed   (5w8)   10.00
MARMONT, MARSHAL-Spirit of Military Institutions-Columbia, SC-
1864-lea&bds-wi new version by Frank Shaller (5h6, lt scuff) 75.00
MARMONTEL, J F-Les Incas, ou la Destruction de l'Empire du Perou-
Berne&Lausanne-1777-calf-8vo-2 vols-10 plts   (4b6)   50.00
--same-Tours-1840-calf-4 plts   (5r7)   20.00
MARMONTEL, JEAN FRANCOIS-Belisarius-Lond-1767-12mo-
mor labl-calf-1st ed in Engl   (5xx6, vg) 35.00
MARMOR NORFOLCIENSE-by Probus Britanicus-Lond-1739-
for J Brett-8vo-hf mor-1st ed-rare-(Sam'l Johnson)
                                              (5x3, lacks hf t.) 600.00
MARMUR, JACLAND-Sea Duty-NY-(1944)-168p-1st ed (5s1)   2.50
MARO, PUBLIUS VIRGILIUS-The Georgics-Verona-1952-ltd to
1500c, nbrd-2 autgs-Limited Ed Club Publ   (5F1, f, dj) 25.00
MAROGER, E-La Goutte D'Eau-Paris-1924-428p-photos-fldg tabl-
2nd ed   (5w1)   15.00
MAROGER, JACQUES-Secret Formulas & Techniques of the Masters-
NY-1943-Studio Publ-lg8vo-plts-cl-1st ed   (5p5)   17.50
MARQUAND, J P-H M Pulham, Esq-NY-1941-cl-431p(1)p-
1st trade ed   (5mm0)   5.00
--Lord Timothy Dexter of Newburyport, Mass-NY-1925-8vo-cl
                                              (4c1)   7.50
--same-Lond-1926   (5mm2)   6.50
--Ming yellow-Bost-1935-Little, Brown-1st ed (5gg6)   35.00
--Prince & Boatswain-Greenfield, Mass-(1915)-12mo-cl (5gg6) 35.00
--Sincerely, Willis Wayde-Bost-1955-12mo-cl-1st ed (5t0, pres) 10.00
--Thirty Years-Bost-n.d.-466p-cl   (5t2)   4.00

MARQUAND, J P (continued)
--The Unspeakable Gentleman-NY-1922-12mo-cl-
1st ed of auth's 1st book   (5gg6,f,dj)   25.00
MARQUART, JOHN-600 Miscellaneous Valuable Receipts-
Lebanon, Pa-1860-311p   (5t7)   10.00
--600 Receipts, worth their weight in gold-Phila-(1867)-311p
                                 (5ee3,edges wn)   5.00
MARQUES, OSWALDINO, ed-Videntes e Sonambulos-(Rio de Janeiro)-
(1955)-lg8vo-wrps-Mini da Educ e Cultura, Serv de Docu(5b2)10.00
MARQUETTE, DAVID-History of Nebraska Methodism, 1st Half
Century-Cinn-1904-photos-1st ed (5t3,ex-libr) 7.50 (5w9) 12.50
MARQUETTE, LE PERE JACQUES-Au Mississippi, La Premiere
Exploration(1673)-Paris-1903-by Alfred Hamy-329p-maps-illus
                           (5s4, lacks part front cov)   17.50
MARQUIS, A N-The Book of Detroiters-1914-2nd ed (5t9,cov stnd) 7.50
MARQUIS, DON-The Almost Perfect State-NY-1927-hf cl-papr labl-
1st ed   (5r9,f)   8.50
--Archy & Mehitabel-NY-1927-1st prntg (5mm1)   10.00
--Archy Does His Part-NY-1935-1st ed
               (5F1,mint,dj) 7.50   (5r9,mint)   8.50
--Archy's Life of Mehitabel-NY-1933-Dblday-1st ed
               (5F1,fade dj) 8.50   (5tt2,f,dj)   15.00
--Carter & Other People-NY-1921-Appleton-1st ed
                            (5tt2,pres,good)   10.00
--Chapters for the Orthodox-NY-1934-12mo-cl   (5r9,dj)   7.50
--Cruise of the Jasper B-NY&Lond-1916-1st ed   (5jj0)   6.50
--Danny's Own Story-NY-1912-illus by Kemble-12mo-cl-
paste on illus front cov-1st ed of auth's 1st book(4m8)15.(5gg6) 25.00
--Her Foot is on the Brass Rail-(NY)-1935-8vo-bds-Marchbanks Pr-
dbl pg illus by Jas Thurber-scarce-ltd to 500c, nbrd (5b2) 12.50
--Noah An Johan An' Cap'n John Smith-NY-1921-157p-illus-
ads   (5t4,pres)   7.50
--Off the Arm-1930-Dblday   (5F1,f,tn dj)   4.75
--The Old Soak & Hail & Farewell-NY-1921-illus-1st ed
                        (5tt2,pres,rub) 10.   (5jj0)   6.00
--Prefaces-NY-1919-12mo-1st printing (5m2,pres) 10.(5jj0)   7.50
--same-NY-1919-Appleton-1st ed,2nd issue
               (5tt2,pres Aug 1921,fade,stnd)   10.00
--Sonnets to a Red Haired Lady & Famous Love Affairs-NY-1922-
D Page-138p   (5p7)   3.00
--Sons of the Puritans-1939-Dblday   (5F1,f,dj)   5.00
--When the turtles sing & other unusual tales-GardenCty-1928-
Dblday-1st prnting   (5m2,dj)   6.50
MARQUIS, T G-Canada's Sons on Kopje & Veldt-n.p.-n.d.(c1900)-
photos-488p-pic cov   (4t5)   15.00
--Giants of the Dominion from Carties to Laurier-n.p.-(1905)-
578p-illus   (4b9)   8.00
--Great Canadians From Cartier to Laurier-Phila-(1905)-illus-
578p   (5dd7)   9.00
MARQUIS, THOS B-Memoirs of a White Crow Indian-NY-(1928)-
12mo-cl-1st printing-illus (5zz5,4b2) 22.50   (5h5,f)   25.00
--Rain in the Face & Curly the Crow-1934-8p-orig wrps   4.00
--War Chief of Ottawas-Tor-1915-145p-lea-Chronicles of
Canada Series   (5h7,sp wn)   7.50
--A Warrior Who Fought Custer-Mnpls-1931-1st ed
               (4k4,dj,f) 50.   (5zz5,vg)   40.00
--Which Indian Killed Custer?Custer Soldiers Not Buried-
Hardin, Mont-1933-10p-wrps (5cc5) 3.   (5hh3)   4.00
MARR, G SIMPSON-Sex in Religion..Hist Survey-Lond-1936(5x7)7.50
MARRARO, HOWARD R-Philip Mazzei, Virginia's Agent in Europe-
NY-1935-106p-wrps   (4j4)   6.00
--Pioneer Italian Teachers of Italian in the US-n.p.-1944-wrps
                                 (5j4,pres)   4.00
MARRIED ABOVE HER-By a Lady of NY-Phila-(1884)-Peterson-
566p-1st ed   (5x4)   10.00
MARRET, J R DE LA-Race Sex & Environment-Lond-1936 (5qq5) 12.50
MARRIAGE, A NOVEL-Edinb-1818-3 vols-12mo-calf-hf titles-
1st ed of auth's 1st book-(Susan Ferrier)
               (5xx6, lacks hf t.) 65.   (5gg6,vf)   125.00
MARRIOTT, ALICE-Greener Fields-NY-(1953)-1st ed (4k5,f,dj) 10.00
--Hell on Horses & Women-Norman-(1953)-290p-illus-1st ed
               (5t3,dj) 7.50   (5cc5,mint,dj)   10.00
--Maria, The Potter of San Ildefonso-Norman-1948-294p-
1st ed-scarce-1st prntg (5zz5,dj) 20.   (4k5,autg,f,dj)   17.50
--same-later printing   (5zz5,no dj)   4.50
--The Ten Grandmothers-Norman-1945-320p-map-illus-1st ed
                                    (5dd6)   15.00
--The Valley Below-Norman-1949-254p-illus-1st ed (5xx5)   6.75
--Winter Telling Stories-NY-(1947)-col illus-84p (5yy7)   2.50
MARRIOTT, CHAS Masterpeices of Modern Art-Lond-n.d.-19p text-
40 col plts   (5w0,fade)   17.50
MARRIOTT, ELSIE Bainbridge Through Bifocals-Seattle-1941-
Gateway Prntg-292p-8vo-cl-scarce   (4t1)   20.00

MARRIOTT, HARVEY-Homilies for Young-Taylor&Hessey-1819-
sm8vo-hf calf-299p   (5s6)   5.00
MARRIOTT, J W-The Theatre-Lond-(1931)-272p-12mo-illus-cl
1st ed   (5t0,dj,f)   4.50
MARRIOTT, JOHN-A short account of John Marriott-Doncaster-
1803-12mo-calf-1st ed-lf of errata   (5i8,wn)   12.50
MARRIOTT, REV W-Vestiarium Christianum-Lond-1868-68 plts-
frontis-lg8vo-cl   (4a2,bkstrp tn)   15.00
MARROW, A J-Living without Hate-NY-1951-1st ed   (5x2)   6.50
MARRYAT, F-Codigo de Signaes Telegraphicos-Porto-(1839)-t8vo-
prntd wrps-5 plts of flags-6 parts   (5ss2)   25.00
MARRYAT, FRANK-Mountains & Molehills-Lond-1855-1st ed-
8 col plts-scarce   (4j3,bndg wn)87.50(5hh4,rbkd)   100.00
--same-NY-1855-illus-hf lea-1st Amer ed   (5s9)   47.50
--same-Stanford Univ Pr-(1952)-reprnt   (5x5,dj)   10.00
MARRYAT, FRANK S-Borneo & the Indian Archipelago-Lond-1848-
232p-roy 8vo-mor-illus-g.e.-1st ed (4e1,autg) 95. (4b6) 150.00
MARRYAT, CAPT FREDK-Complete Writings-Bost-(ca1900)-
Dana Estes&Co-auth's ltd ed-21 vols(of 24)-frontis-3 qtr mor
                                    (5c8,f)   100.00
--A Diary in America-Paris-1839,40-Galignani-2 vols-orig hf roan-
g.bkstrp-2 fldg maps   (5n9)   65.00
--same-NY-1839-orig bds
       (5L3) 13.50 (5tt6) 25. (5qq8,v frayed) 7.50 (5r6,stnd) 22.50
--same-Phila-1939-bds-263p   (5h2,wn)   10.00
--The Dog Fiend-Lond-1840-3 vols-2nd ed-hf lea   (5i3)   7.50
--Jacob Faithful-Lond-Constable-1928-8vo-2 vols-12 col plts-
dec cl-g.-ltd to 750 sets   (4d1)   25.00
--The Little Savage-NY-1850-Harper-8vo-250p-dec cl-g.t.
                                 (5aa2,wn)   3.50
--Masterman Ready-Lond-(c1890)-Warne-8vo-dec cl-334p-
frontis-g.t.   (5aa2)   5.00
--The Naval Officer, or, Scenes & Adventures in Life of Frank
Mildmay-Lond-1829-3 vols-sm8vo-hf calf-1st ed of auth's
1st novel   (5gg6,autg, lacks hf t. & adv)   25.00
--Novels of-Lond, Dent-NY, Groscup-Bost, L B-1895, 96-illus-
22 vols-750c-handmade papr-blu cov (5i1, lacks few pgs Vol 1) 30.00
--Percival Keene-Lond-1842-HenryColburn-3 vols-12mo-orig cl &
bds-papr labls-1st ed, primary bndg   (5xx6)   75.00
--same-R Bentley-1849-(Standard Novels)-sm8vo-dec cl-g.t.-
port   (4a8)   5.00
--Peter Simple-Lond-R Bentley-1839-1 vol-frontis &hf t (dated 1838)-
462p-hf calf   (5c8, rub)   8.00
--Poor Jack-Lond-1840-illus by Clarkson Stanfield-1st ed
               (5r9,hf mor) 35.   (5mm2)   15.00
--same-Lond-1846-illus by Stanfield-Imp 8vo-384p-hf calf
                                 (5c8, rub)   7.50
--same-Macmillan-1899-F Pegram, illus-8vo-dec cl-plts (4a8)   4.50
--Regimento de Signaes para os Telegraphos da Marinha-Lisbon-
1804-67p-8vo-prntd wrps- 1 plt of col flags   (5ss2)   45.00
--same-Lisbon-1824-12mo-stitchd wrps-35p-1 plt of col flags
                                    (5ss2)   27.50
--Second Series of Diary in America-Phila-1840-Collins-300p-
bds-cl sp   (5qq8, libr labl)   7.50
--Settlers In Canada-NY-1845-Appleton-2 vols-frontis ea-
ads-1st Amer ed   (5cc6)   25.00
MARRYAT, KAPITAN-Tagebuch In Amerika-Stuttgart-1845-2 vols-
2 fldg maps-16mo   (4n8)   15.00
MARS, AMAURY-Remin of Santa Clara Valley & San Jose, etc-
(SanFran-1901)-cl-276p-8vo   (4t1)   37.50
MARS, G C, ed-Brickwork in Italy-Chig-1925-Amer Face Brick Assoc-
298p-maps-illus   (5m5,crack)   18.00
MARSDEN, R G-Treatise Law of Collisions at Sea-Lond-1910-
607p plus 23p (Maritime Conv Act, 1911)-6th ed (5s1,ex-libr) 6.00
MARSDEN, WM-History of Sumatra-Lond-1811-fldg map-lg4to-
hf calf-enlrg 3rd ed   (4b6, rbkd, lakcs Vol of plts)   40.00
--Memoirs of a Malayan family, written by themselves-Lond-
1830-prntd for Oriental Transl Fund-8vo-orig bds-papr labl-
1st ed   (5i8)   15.00
MARSH, B-Personal Memoir of Dan'l Drayton, for 4 Yrs & 4 Months
a Prisoner in a Wash Jail-Bost-1853   (5x2)   35.00
MARSH, BARTON W-The Uncompahgre Valley & the Gunnison
Tunnel-Montrose, Colo-1905-152p-photos-1st ed (5zz5)   8.50
MARSH, C O-Odontornithes, a Monograph on Extinct Toothed Birds
of No Amer-Wash-1880-201p-plts-orig cl-4to-ltd to 3000c-
v scarce-(Vol 7)   (4p6)   75.00
MARSH, C W-Recollections, 1837 to 1910-Chig-1910-illus-299p-
1st ed   (5zz5)   10.00
MARSH, CHAS L-Opening the Oyster-Chig-1889-361p-illus
                                    (5mm2)   8.50
MARSH, DAN'L L-Charm of the Chapel(of Bost Univ)-Bost-Univ Pr-
1950-t8vo-plts-1st ed   (5p5,dj)   10.00

MARSH, D'ARCY-Tragedy of Henry Thornton-Tor-1935-293p-
illus (4b9) 8.00
MARSH, EDITH L-Birds of Peasemarsh-Tor-1919-233p-8 plts (4a8) 5.00
MARSH, ELSIE A G, comp-Economic Library of Jacob H Hollander-
Balt-1937-priv prnt-4to-324p-ltd to 500c (4b8) 15.00
MARSH, G P -Speech on the Mexican War-Wash-1848-16p (4a5) 6.00
MARSH, GEO-Toilers of the Trails-Phila-1921 245p (5ss1) 5.(4b9)8.00
MARSH, GEO P-Lectures on the English Language-NY-1860-cl-
lg8vo-697p (5t2) 7.50
--Man & Nature-NY-1865-560p-lg8vo-orig cl-1st ed (5t2, wn) 7.50
MARSH, J B T-The Story of the Jubilee Singers, With Their Songs-
NY-1883 (5x2) 10.00
--same-Bost-n.d. (5h6) 7.00
MARSH, JAS B-Four Years in the Rockies-NewCastle, Pa-1884-262p-
port-orig pic cl-1st ed-rare (5zz5, vg) 160.00
--same-NewCastle-1884-262p-ltd ed 1000c reprnt Columbus, 1950
 (5ii1, f, dj) 20.00
--same-Columbus, O-n.d.-262p (5t7, dj) 8.00
MARSH, L B-Bronsdom & Box-1902-311p (5mm3) 9.00
MARSH, L R, ed-Writings & Speeches of Alvan Stewart on Slavery-
NY-1860 (5x2) 32.50
MARSH, MARGARET ALEXANDER-The Bankers in Bolivia-NY-
(1928)-Vanguard-8vo-cl (4a3) 8.50
MARSH, O C-Statement of Affairs at Red Cloud Agency-(1875)-
38p-wrps (5t3, chip) 10. (5yy3) 15.00
MARSH, RICHARD-Datchet Diamonds-Lond-n.d.-illus-pict cl-
1st ed (4b7) 20.00
--Death Whistle-Lond-1903-1st ed (4b7) 17.50
MARSH, RICHARD OGLESBY-White Indians of Darien-NY-(1934)-
photos-maps-276p (5yy8) 6. (4b2, dj) 7.50
MARSH, W LOCKWOOD-Aeronautical Prints & Drawings-Lond-
1924-Halton&Truscott Smith-ltd to 100c, nbrd, 80 tipped in
col plts (5b0) 112.00
MARSH, WM J-Our President Herbert Hoover-New Milford-1930-
bds-44p (4h2, rub) 7.50
MARSHALL'S, MRS A B-Larger Cookery Book of Extra Recipes-
Lond-n.d.-(ca1902)-656p, 40p-ads (5c5) 10.00
MARSHALL, A J-Principles of Economics-1898-4th ed-Vol 1 (all pub)
 (5L7) 5.00
MARSHALL, ALAN-Speak for Yourself-NY-1937-8vo-ltd to 101c
 (5ss5, autg) 10.00
MARSHALL, ALBERT M-Brule Country-StPaul-1954-illus-1st ed
 (4b7) 10.00
MARSHALL, ARCHIBALD-Peter Binney, Undergraduate-Lond-1899-
12mo-pict cl-g.t.-1st ed of auth's 1st book (5gg6) 15.00
--same-NY-1921-279p (5t7, als tip in) 6.00
--Simple Stories-NY-1927-Harper-illus (5p7) 3.25
MARSHALL, ARTHUR-Short Account of Explosives-Phila-1917-
illus-1st Amer ed (4a1) 15.00
MARSHALL, B T-Modern Hist of New London County, (Conn)-1922-
3 vols-illus (5t9) 22.50
MARSHALL, C F D-History of the So Railway(British)-Lond-1936-
illus-708p (4p7) 12.50
MARSHALL, CATHERINE-A Man Called Peter-NY-c1951-342p
 (5w4, dj) 3.00
MARSHALL, CHAS-An Aide de camp of Lee, Being the Papers of...
Bost-1927-illus-maps (5yy7, dj) 15. (4b6) 12.50
MARSHALL, CHAS C JR-Hambletonian Winners 1926 to 1950-
1950-99p (5FF2) 10.00
MARSHALL, CHRISTOPHER-Extracts from Diary of...Kept in Phila
& Lancaster 1774 to 1781-NY-1877-Wm Duane (5m2, rbnd) 10.00
--Passages from His Diary, Vol 1, 1774 to 77-1839, 49-
Wm Duane, ed (5L7, sp tn) 6.00
MARSHALL, DAVID-Grand Central-NY-(1946)-294p-photos(5dd9)5.75
MARSHALL, DONALD-Ra'ivavae-NY-1961-Doubl-301p (5p7) 5.00
MARSHALL, E N-Gordons of the Deep South-1961-302p (5mm3) 15.00
MARSHALL, EDISON-Heart of the Hunter-NY-(1956)-illus (5F0) 4.00
--The Missionary-NY-1930-288p-illus (5ss1) 4.00
--Shikar & Safari-NY-1947-8vo-263p (4a6) 3.00
--The Voice of the Pack-Bost-1920-frontis-1st ed (5ee3, f) 3.50
MARSHALL, EDW-Broadway Jones-NY-(1913)-illus-1st ed (5yy6) 8.50
MARSHALL, F-Old English Embroidery-Lond-1894-4to-138p-
17 plts (5n7) 15.00
MARSHALL, F R-Breeding Farm Animals-Chig-1911-Breeders Gazette-
1st ed (5b1, sl scuff) 10.00
MARSHALL, G N, ed-Church of the Pilgrim Fathers-1950 (5L7) 3.50
MARSHALL, H R-Pain, Pleasure & Aesthetics-Lond-1894-369p (4a2) 4.00
MARSHALL, H-The Negro Tragedian-Lond-1958-illus (5x2, f, dj) 6.00
MARSHALL, HERBERT-Cathedral Cities of France-Lond&NY-1907-
281p-col illus (5t7) 10.00
MARSHALL HIGH SCHOOL STUDENTS-Sketches Drawn from Marshall
& Vicinity Past & Present-Marshall-1919-82p-illus (4c7, loose)62.50

MARSHALL, HOWARD-Men Against Everest-Lond-(1954)-
64p-cl-Country Life (5d7) 4.00
MARSHALL, HUMPHREY-History of Kentucky-Frankfort-1824-calf-
Vol 1 (5tt8) 50.00
MARSHALL, JAS-Elbridge A. Stuart, Founder, Carnation Co-LosAng-
1949-238p-photos-sm4to-1st trade ed (5y2) 8.50 (5yy7, 5s4) 6.00
MARSHALL, JAS-Santa Fe-NY-(1945)-illus-465p (5t3) 6. (5t7) 7.50
--same-NY-(1945)-8vo-orig cl-ltd ed-autg-32p photos
 (4c1, box) 20. (5x5) 22.50
MARSHALL, JAS S-Adventure in Two Hemispheres-Vancouver-1955-
15p charts (5s4, f, dj) 10. (5c1) 12.50
MARSHALL, J H-Report of Celebration of Centennial Anniv of
Buxton, Maine-1874-288p (5t9) 12.50
MARSHALL, JOHN-The Life of Geo Washington-Phila-1804 to 1807-
5 vols plus Atlas-port-calf-lea labls-1st ed-(Atlas is the 8vo issue)
 (5q8, rub, lacks atlas) 17.50 (5m3, f) 75.00
--same-Phila-1804 to 1807-5 vols & 1 vol maps-lea-(edition not
stated) (5xx7) 30.00
--same-Phila-1835-2 vols-12mo-port (5t7) 15.00
--same-Phila-1840-2 vols-orig lea-frontis-rev & cor by auth
 (5h9, rub) 15.00
--same-NY-1925-5 vols-WmHWise-illus-sm8vo-buck & lea-labls-
Fredericksburg ed (5t2, f) 20.00
--Speech, in House of Repr...on Edw Livingston, relative to Nash,
alias Jonathan Robbins-Phila-1800-16mo-stitchd (5g3, f) 12.50
--Writing of John Marshall-Bost-1839-Jas Munroe-728p (5qq8) 12.50
MARSHALL, JOHN A-American Bastile-Phila-1869-frontis-1st ed
1 plt-728p (5w5) 14.50
--same-Phila-1876-TWHartley-thk8vo-sheep-plts-768p-22nd ed
 (5j5) 10.00
MARSHALL, JOHN ALBERT-Manufacture & Testing of Military
Explosives-NY-1919-261p-cl-illus (5hh6) 5.50
MARSHALL, JOHN & CO, publ-The Popular Readers-Lond-(1880)-
sm8vo-dec cl-112p-40 illus (5s0) 7.50
MARSHALL, KATHERINE TUPPER-Together-NY&Atlanta-1946-292p-
illus (5t7, dj) 6.00
MARSHALL, LOGAN-Story of Panama Canal-n.p.-(1913)-illus-
maps-dec cov (5s1, sl wn) 4.50
MARSHALL, NINA L-Mosses & Lichens-NY-(1919)-345p-illus-
18 col plts (5t4) 7.50
--The Mushroom Book-NY-1903-illus-4to-cl-167p-t.e.g. (5q0) 10.00
MARSHALL, ORSAMUS H-Expedition of the Sieur de Champlain
Against the Onondagas in 1615-Albany-1885-26p-wrps-
ltd to 100c (5r6) 20.00
MARSHALL, P-Brown Girl, Brownstones-NY-1959-1st ed (5x2, dj) 20.00
MARSHALL, PERCIVAL-Wonderful Models-Lond-1928-2 vols-8vo-
red textured cl-g.-18 fldg plts (5b0) 45.00
MARSHALL, R-Arctic Village-NY-1933-399p-illus
 (4b9) 15. (5ss1, pres) 12.50
MARSHALL, SAM'L-Treatise on the law of insurance...First Amer-
Bost-1805-2 vols in 1-sheep (5g8, rub, libr labl) 10.00
MARSHALL, THOS C-Into the Streets & Lanes-Claremont, Ca-1948-
Saunders Pr-1,000c publ (5x5) 5. (4t1) 12.50
MARSHALL, THOS M, ed-Early Records of Gilpin County, Colo
1859 to 1861-Boulder-1920-301p plus index-fldg map-wrps-
Univ of Colo Hist Coll Vol 2-1st ed (5t3) 12.50
MARSHALL, THOS R-Recoll of...Vice President & Hoosier
Philosopher-Indnpls-c1925-397p-illus (5k0) 4. (5w9) 6.50
MARSHALL & CO, W E-Consider the Lilies-1927-92p-illus (5x0) 3.50
MARSHALL, W G-Through America; or, 9 months in the US-Lond-
1881-424p-photos-publ 32p cat bnd in (5u3, lacks wn) 3.00
MARSHALL, WM I-History vs The Whitman Saved Oregon Story-
Chig-1904-114p (5k1, autg) 8.50 (4a5) 10.00
MARSHALL, WM K-The Entering Wedge-Cinn, NY-(1904)-274p
 (5m1) 7.50
MARSILLAC J-La Vie de Guillaume Penn, Fondateur de la
Pensylvanie-Paris-1791-Cercle Social-2 vols(in 1)-1st ed
 (5m4, sl wn) 50.00
MARSON, CYRIL DARBY-Fishing for Salmon-Lond-1929-198p-illus
 (5t7) 8.00
MARSTON, ANNA LEE-Records of California Family-SanDiego-
1928-283p-map-15 illus-orig hf mor (5tt0) 100.00
MARSTON, LAURA-The Wonderfull, astounding, mysterious & strange
history of Laura A. Marston of Balti, Md-Balt-1850-46p-wrps-
1st ed (5p6) 8.00
MARSTON, MARY GILMAN-Geo White Marston-LosAng-1956-
Ward Ritchie Pr-2 vols-ltd to 550c (5jj1, mint, box) 20.00
MARSTON, R B-Walton & Some Earlier Writers on Fish & Fishing-
Lond-1894-264p (5a9) 6.50
MARTELL-Les Grandes Usine de Turgan, Les Establissements Martell
a Cognac(Charente)-Paris-1892-63p-4p of labls-2 dbl pg illus-
limp cl (5w1, stnd, shake) 9.50

MARTIAL, MARCUS-Martial's Epigrams-priv prntd-ltd to 990c-
v scarce   (5a6)   50.00
MARTIGNONI, MARGARET E, ed-Illustrated Treasury of Children's
Literature-NY-1955-G&D-512p-deluxe ed, boxed   (5p0)   6.00
MARTIN, ARCHER-Hudson's Bay Company's Land Tenures &
Occupation of Assiniboia by Lord Selkirk's Settlers-Lond-
1898-port-maps-238p   (5nn2, ex-libr)   20.00
MARTIN, C-Lord Selkirk's Work in Canada-Oxf-1916-maps-240p-
Vol 7 of Oxf Hist & Lit Studies   (4e6)   30.00
MARTIN, BENJ E-In the Foot Prints of Chas Lamb-NY-1890-
sq t8vo-illus-plts-g.t.-1st ed   (5t5)   15.00
MARTIN, BERNARD-Jn Newton:Biography-Lond-1950-372p-plts-
facs   (5a1)   4.50
MARTIN, CHAS-Civil Costume of England from the Conquest to the
Present Time etc-Lond-1842-etched by Leopold Martin-mor-
61p col plts   (5m4, chip)   75.00
MARTIN, CHAS-Pacific Area-Seattle-1929-U W Pr-405p-
wrps   (5s4, sl wn)   5.00
MARTIN, CHAS E-Proceedings of Nat'l Stock Growers'Convention
& Organiz of Nat'l Live Stock Assoc of US-Denv-1898-
359(360)p-photos-maps-1st ed-rare   (5L5)   45.00
MARTIN, CHAS L-A Sketch of Sam Bass, the Bandit-Univ of Okla Pr-
1956-illus-2nd ed   (5h6, dj, vg)   15.00
MARTIN, CLARA BARNES-Mount Desert, on the coast of Maine-
Portl-1885-(mounted photos)-6th ed   (5g3)   10.00
MARTIN, DAVID R-A Boy Scout with the "Sea Devil"-NY-1930-
33 photos   (5c1)   6.50
MARTIN, DOUGLAS-The Earps of Tombstone-Tombstone-1959-
65p-orig wrps-1st ed   (5zz5) 3. (5jj7, bound) 6. (5hh3)   4.00
--Tombstone's Epitaph-Univ of New Mex Pr-1951-1st ed
                     (5jj7, f, dj, 5zz5, dj, mint) 7.50 (5x5, dj)   10.00
--Yuma Crossing-Univ of NMex-1954-8vo-cl-243p
          (5zz5) 7.50 (5jj7, f, dj) 6.50 (5F5, dj, vg)   8.50
MARTIN, EDW A-Bibliography of Gilbert White-Lond-n.d.-orig cl-
frontis & map   (5j2, vg)   10.00
MARTIN, EDW SANDFORD-In a New Century-NY-1908-Scribner-
8vo-cl-g.t.   (5b2, f)   4.00
--A Little Brother of the Rich & Other Verses-NY-1890-91p-
t.e.g.-1st ed   (5w9)   5.00
--The Luxury of Children & some other luxuries-NY&Lond-1904-
Harper-8vo-frontis-214p-7 plts-pict labl-t.e.g.   (5p1)   17.50
MARTIN, EDW WINSLOW-Behind the Scenes in Wash-(Wash, 1873)-
518p-illus   (5r7)   12.50
--History of the Grange Movement-Chig-1874-544p plus ads-illus
                                        (5L0, pgs tn)   17.50
--History of the Great Riots-Phila-(c1877)-516p-orig cl-illus
                                     (5L7, 5m3)   25.00
MARTIN FABER-The story of a criminal-NY-1833-Harper-12mo-
orig light grn cl-papr labl-rare-(W G Simms)-1st ed of auth's
1st book   (5x1, lacks fly)   400.00
MARTIN FABER-The story of a criminal & other tales-NY-1837-
Harper-2 vols-12mo-orig brown cl-labls-(W G Simms)
                        (5x1, lacks e.p., libr bkplt)   75.00
MARTIN, FELIX-Life of Father Isaac Jogues, Missionary Priest of Soc
of Jesus, Slain by the Mohawk Iroquois-NY-1885-263p-maps-
port   (5t4)   8.00
MARTIN, JACK-Border Boss, Capt John R Hughes, Texas Ranger-
SanAnt-1942-236p-1st ed
                (5yy7, name on some pgs) 12.50 (5t1, dj)   45.00
MARTIN, J B-The Deep South Says Never-NY-1957-12mo (5x2,dj)6.50
MARTIN, J L-It Happened Here, In West Texas-Dallas-(1945)-
illus   (5s4, dj)   4.00
MARTIN, JOHN-Butcher's Dozen & Other Murders-NY-1950-cl-
275p-1st ed   (5t2, dj, f)   3.50
MARTIN, JOHN-The Children's Munchausen-Bost&NY-1921-
illus by Gordon Ross-185p-12 plts-frontis-pict labl-1st ed(5p1) 7.50
--Chubby Book for Chubby Children-NY-(1922)-illus-4to-pict bds-
1st ed   (5c8, lt rub)   12.50
--John Martin's Book-Magazine for Little Children-Jun, 1913 to
May, 1920-35 copies-col wrps   (5v2)   95.00
--same-1917 to 1924-orig col wrps-47 copies-incomplete years
                                          (4F6, f)   150.00
MARTIN, JOHN BARTLOW-My Life in Crime-NY-1952-Harper-
279p   (5p9)   4.00
--Indiana, an interpretation-NY-1947-Knopf-300p   (5u3)   4.00
MARTIN, JOHN HILL-Martin's Bench & Bar of Phila-Phila-1883
                                           (5kk8)   8.50
MARTIN, JOHN PAUL-The triumph of truth-Bost-1791-Isaiah Thomas
& Ebenezer Andrews-8vo-cl-1st ed   (5i0, rbnd)   22.50
MARTIN, JOS P-Narrative of....Adventures, Dangers & Sufferings
of a Revolutionary Soldier-Hallowell, Me-1830-213p-
prntd wrps over bds   (5s2, pres)   250.00

MARTIN, SADIE E-The Life & Professional Career of Emma Abbott-
Minneap-1891-8vo-illus-1st ed   (5m6)   10.00
MARTIN, T-Life of His Royal Highness the Prince Consort-NY-1875
to 1880-illus-ads-5 vols   (5yy0)   9.50
MARTIN, T COMMERFORD-40 Yrs of Edison Service-NY-1922-
181p-illus   (4e4)   8.50
MARTIN, THOS RICAUD-Great Parliamentary Battle & Farewell
Addresses etc-NY-1905-Neale-255p   (5qq8)   15.00
MARTIN, THOS W-Dr Wm Crawford Gorgas of Alabama & the
Panama Canal-1947-Newcomen Soc   (5hh3)   4.00
MARTIN, W A P-The Lore of Cathay-Edinb&Lond-1901-472p(5x9)6.50
MARTIN, W C L-A General History of Hummingbirds-Lond-1852-
orig cl-t.e.g.-232p-16 col plts-24mo-scarce (4p5, sp split)   42.00
MARTIN, W S-Martin Family Record from 1760 to 1963-n.p.-
ca1963-311p-port-wrps   (5r7)   10.00
MARTIN, WM-Parlour Book-Wm Darton & Son-(c1840)-sq8vo-
xv, 274p-hf roan-col frontis-15 plts   (5aa0, rub)   10.00
MARTINDALE, C C-African Angelus, Episodes & Impressions-Lond-
1933-Sheed & Ward-436p   (4t5)   12.00
MARTINDALE, J B-Martindale's Unclaimed Money, Lands, Estates
Manual-Chig-(1884)-208p   (5s4, sl wn)   8.50
MARTINDALE, JOS C-History of Townships of Byberry & Moreland
in Phila-Phila-n.d.(ca1900)-illus-A W Dudley, revsd (4m2)   20.00
MARTINDALE, THOS-Hunting in Upper Yukon-Phila-(1913)-320p-
8 plts-cl   (5L7) 5. (5r0, 5dd0)   7.50
--With Gun & Guide-Lond-(1907)-337p-illus   (5t7)   10.00
--same-Phila-(1910)-Jacob-337p-illus   (5r0)   7.50
MARTINDELL, E W-Bibliography of Works of Rudyard Kipling-Lond-
1922-111p-ltd to 450c   (5j4, box)   15.00
MARTINE'S, ARTHUR-Hand Book of Etiquette-NY-(1866)-
Dick&Fitzgerald-167p-bds   (5w7)   6.50
MARTINE'S SENSIBLE LETTER WRITER-NY-(1866)-206p, (4), (6)-
dec bds-cl-ads inside covs   (5w7, stns, sp split)   6.50
MARTINEAU, HARRIET-British rule in India, a historical sketch-
Lond-1857-Smith, Elder&Co-8vo-orig glazed lin-1st ed (5i8)   65.00
--The Charmed Sea-Hartf-1845-Andrus-1st Amer ed   (5i3, f)   10.00
--Deerbrook, a Novel-NY-1839-2 vols-1st Amer ed-orig bds-
cl bks   (5tt7, sl wn)   25.00
--Feats on the Fjord, a Tale-Lond-1899-sm12mo-237p-col frontis-
limp lea-12 Rackham illus-rare 1st ed   (5v0, wn)   15.00
--same-Lond-(1938)-12mo-128p-8 col plts by Rackham, dated
1899   (5v0, wn)   7.50
--Harriet Martineau's autobiography-Lond-1877-Smith, Elder&Co-
3 vols-8vo-orig lilac cl-6 plts-1st ed   (5x3, vf)   45.00
--History of 30 Years' Peace-(Bohn)-1877-4 vols (5tt5, wn)   10.00
--The hour & the man-Lond-1841-Edw Moxon-3 vols-12mo-hf calf-
fldg map-1st ed-v scarce   (5xx6, rub)   85.00
--Letters on the laws of man's nature & developement-Lond-1851-
JnChapman-8vo-orig yellow cl-1st ed-v scarce (5x3, vg)   60.00
--Miscellanies-Bost-1836-Hilliard, Gray-2 vols-12mo-orig cl-
1st ed   (5i8, mismatchd)   25.00
--Retrospect of Western Travel-Lond&NY-(1942)-2 vols-facs ed-
box   (5q0) 25. (4m2, f, dj)   22.50
--Society in Amer-Lond-1837-3 vols-12mo-1st ed-hf lea-scarce
                       (5mm0, rub) 50. (4m2)   35.00
--30 Years Peace-Lond-1850, 51-2 vols-illus-3 qtr lea
                                 (5t4, mismatchd)   20.00
MARTINEAU, JAS-Types of Ethical Theory-1891-2 vols in 1-
3rd ed, rev   (5L7)   7.50
MARTINEAU, MRS PHILIP-Cantaloup to Cabbage-Lond-(1929)-
130p-bds   (5m1)   3.50
MARTINET, DR-The Catechism of Nature for the Use of Children-
Bost-1793-Young&Etheridge-12mo-108p-rare (5v2, re-wrps)   110.00
MARTINEZ, EMILIO-Memoria Sobre El Cafe-NOrl-1887-
61p(1)p-wrps-2nd ed   (5w1, chip)   9.50
MARTINEZ, MAXIMINO-Las Plantas Medicinales de Mexico-
Ediciones Botas-1944-8vo-buck-630p-illus-(Tercera Edicion)
                                     (5h4, f, dj)   9.50
MARTINGALE, HAWSER-Tales of the Ocean & Essays for the
Forecastle-Bost-1845-WJReynolds-432p-cl-12mo-wdcuts
                                 (5j5, rbnd, sl tn)   15.00
MARTINI, FERDINANDO-Nell'Affrica Italiana-Milan-1891-1 plt-
2 fldg maps-qtr lea   (5c6, fox, rub)   13.50
MARTYN, CARLOS, ed-Wndell Phillips, the Agitator-NY-1890-
thk12mo   (5q8, 5x2)   5.00
MARTYN, CHAS-Life of Artemas Ward-NY-1921-Artemas Ward-
illus-g.t.   (5qq8, f) 12.50 (5ii8)   15.00
MARTYN, WYNDHAM-Anthony Trent, Master Criminal-NY-1918-
1st ed   (5ee3, vf)   5.00
MARTYR, PETER-De Orbe Novo Decades-Alcala-AGuillelmi-
1516-sm folio-84 unnbrd leaves-red crushed levant-1st ed
              (5hh0, fox, repair, Streeter cpy) 8,500.00

MARTYR, PETER (continued)
--de rebus Oceanicis & Orbe novo etc-Basle,Bebelius-1533-
folio-calf   (5n9,rprd)   375.00
--De Rebus Oceanicis et Novo Orbe,Decades Tres...Libri 3,
Lusitanicis & Hispanicis...Coloniae-1574-mor-sm8vo
                                    (5s9,rbnd,wormholes)   195.00
MARTYR'S MONUMENT NY-(1865)-297p-cl
                              (5h2,fade) 10.   (5a9)   7.50
MARTZOLFF,CLEMENT L-History of Perry County,Ohio-Columbus-
1902-195p-cl   (5ff7)   20.00
--Poems on Ohio-Colum-1911-221p-cl   (5h1)   5.00
MARVEL,ELINORE J-Cook It Ahead-Bost-(1951)-243p
                              (5c0) 3.   (5c9)   4.00
MARVEL,IK-Dream Life,a Fable of the Seasons-NY-1851-
Scribner-12mo-cl-frontis-286p-1st ed (5x4,ex-libr) 15. (5j5) 10.00
--Fresh Gleanings-NY-1847-1st ed of auth's 1st book-cl
                              (5yy6) 15.   (5gg6)   17.50
--same-NY-1847-orig prntd wrps-2 vols-1st ed (5gg6,rprd)   37.50
--Fudge Doings-NY-1855-Scribners-2 vols-1st ed-scarce (5k0) 10.00
--Reveries of Bachelor-NY-1884-Scribner's Sons-ltd to 250c-
deckel edges-bds   (5i4,cl chip)   17.50
--Seven Stories wi Basement & Attic-1864-Scribners-314p-1st ed
                                                (5k0)   5.00
MARVEL,TOM-New Congo-NY-1948-e.p.maps
                                 (5c6,ex-libr,bndg wn)   7.50
MARVELL,ANDREW-Works of...Poetical,Controversial & Political-
Lond-1776-3 vols-4to-calf-frontis-port & list of subscribers
                                        (5j2,rbkd)   80.00
MARVELOUS MUSICAL PRODGY,BLIND TOM-the Negro Boy
Pianist-Balt-(ca1867)-31p-orig pict wrps   (5m2)   10.00
MARVIN,C F-Barometers & Measurement of Atmospheric Pressure-
Wash-1894-GPO-Weather Bur Circ F-74p-illus-wrps(5hh7)   5.00
MARVIN,EDWIN E-5th Regiment,Connecticut Volunteers-Hartf-
1889-394p   (5j6,f)   12.50
MARVIN,HENRY-Complete History of Lake George-NY-1853-
16mo-102p   (5a0) 12 50   (5t4)   17.50
MARVIN,ISABEL-Bon Appetit:StLouis Cook Bk-Bost-1947-269p
                              (4g9) 5.   (5c0)   4.50
MARVIN,WINTHROP L-The Amer Merchant Marine-NY-1902-
444p   (5s1,ex-libr,stn) 5.   (5w0)   10.00
MARX,ENID-English Popular & Traditional Art-Lond-1946-illus
                                                (4a1)   5.00
MARX,GROUCHO-Groucho & Me-NY-(1959)-photos-344p-
1st ed   (4n1,dj)   4.00
MARX,KARL-Capital,a critical analysis of capitalistic production-
Lond-1887-2 vols-orang cl & marbled bd-1st Engl ed (5d2) 75.00
--Capital-NY-1889-Appleton&Co-816p-orig yellow cl-1st Amer
ed of 1st vol   (5d2)   75.00
--Das Kapital-Hamburg-1872-Meissner-8vo-hf cl-2nd ed-revised
                                        (4h0,rprd)   215.00
--A Discourse on Free Trade-Bost-1888-48p-orig prntd wrps-
1st Amer ed-very rare   (4b4,f)   125.00
MARX,MILTON-Enjoyment of Drama-NY-1940-242p-cl-1st ed
                                        (5t0,f,dj)   4.50
MARY,ANDRE-Le Chambre des Dames-Paris-Boivin-lg type-hf calf-
raised bands-g. -ltd ed   (5t5)   10.00
MARY ELIZABETH'S WAR TIME RECIPES-NY-(1918)-163p-port
                                                (5g9)   5.00
MARY HOLLIS,AN ORIGINAL TALE-NY-1822-Unitarian Book Soc-
22p-12mo-24ps-rare   (4b6)   40.00
MARY JANE'S BOOK OF HOUSEHOLD HINTS-Bost-(1915)-12mo-
illus-no pagination   (5w7)   4.00
MARY MILDRED,(SISTER)-Apostle of Alaska-Paterson-1943-292p-
plts   (5aa0)   8.50
MARY RICHMOND-A Day in the life of a Spoiled Child-NewHav-
c1835-SBabcock-16mo-24p-16 illus-wrps   (5v2,f)   12.50
MARY THEODORE,SISTER-Pioneer Nuns of Brit Col,Sisters of
StAnn-Victoria-1913-146p-ports   (5dd0,pres)   15.00
MARYLAND CASUALTY CO-Our First 50 Years-Balt-1948-4to-
illus-wrps   (4b8)   4.00
MARYLAND COOK BOOK-Oakland Civic Club-Oakland-1914-96p-
ads   (5g9)   5.00
MARYLAND COOKERY-Maryland Home Econ Assoc-n.p.-(1948)-
309p-spiral bnd wrps   (5g9)   3.50
MARYLAND GENERAL ASSEMBLY-Laws Made & Passed,Dec 30,
1839 to Mar 21,1840-Annap-1840-thk8vo-sewed (5r7,t pg tn) 20.00
MARYLAND,A GUIDE-to the Old Line State-NY-(1941)-
Oxf Univ Pr-561p-illus-Amer Guide Ser   (5x0)   5.00
MARYLAND NATL GUARD-5th Regiment Infantry US Vol,a History-
Balt-1899-illus-rev ed   (5m6)   10.00
MARYLAND RESOLUTIONS-& objections to them considered. By a
citizen of Maryland-Balt-1822-EJCoale&Co-8vo-disbnd-1st ed
                                        (5i0)   27.50

MARYLAND STATE COLONIZATION SOC-Maryland Colonization
Journal-Vol 4,#1 to 24,New Series-Balt-1847-394p-qtr lea
                                    (5c6,fox,rub)   45.00
MARYSVILLE-Colville's Marysville Directory Nov 1,1855-SanFran-
1855-Monson&Valentine-orig prnt bds-lea (5tt0,bkstrp wn) 250.00
MARYSVILLE,CA-Marysville City Directory,Aug 1853-
Marysville Herald Ofc-1853-8vo-orig calf bk mrbld bds-
1st ed-ads on vari col lvs-Hale & Emory
                          (4h0,bkstrp tn,Streeter cpy)   1,000.00
MARZIALS,FRANK T-Life of Victor Hugo-Lond-1888-Walter Scott-
224p-12mo   (5p9)   4.00
MASAOKA,NAOICHI,Ed-Japan to America-NY-1914-Putnams-
235p   (5x9)   4.50
--same-NY-1915-235p   (5p7)   4.00
MASEFIELD,JOHN-The battle of the Somme-Lond-n.d.(1919)-
Heinemann-8vo-orig qtr vel-papr bds-1st ed-ltd to 250c (5i8) 15.00
--The coming of Christ-NY-1928-Macm   (5mm2)   5.00
--same-NY-192-Macm-1st ed-ltd to 350c,autg
                     (5ss9,sl wn,fade) 10.   (4b5,vg,box)   12.50
--The Dream-Lond-(n.d.)-Heinemann-cl bkd bds-illus-1st ed
                     (5ss3,illus & auth autgs,sp stnd)   10.00
--same-NY-1922-cl&bds-ltd to 750c,autg   (5p5,5mm2,dj)   15.00
--Martin Hyde,the Duke's Messenger-Lond-(1910)-Wells Gardner,
Darton-illus by Dugdale-1st ed   (5ss3,dj,sp tn)   5.00
--Easter,a Play-NY-1919   -orig bds-cl bk-1st ed-ltd to 100c,
nbrd   (5p5)   12.50
--Enslaved-Lond-1920-8vo-bds-vel-g.t.-ltd to 250c,autg (5t8) 15.00
--Essays Moral & Polite,1660 to 1714-NY-n.d.-24mo-Chapbooks 2-
vel-lea ties-t.e.g.   (5j3)   8.00
--Gallipoli-Lond-1916-WmHeinemann-1st ed (5ss3,cov dtchd) 10.00
--Gautama the Enlightened & Other Verse-NY-1941-58p (5t7,dj) 5.00
--Good Friday-Lond-(1917)   (5mm2)   4.00
--King Cole-Lond-1921-8vo-bds-vel bk-t.e.g.-1st ed-
ltd to 750c,autg   (5dd8)   15.00
--same-NY-1921-MacMillan-cl bk bds-1st Amer ed (4b5,mint,dj) 8.50
--same-Lond-(1923)-Heinemann   (4b5,mint,dj)   7.50
--The Locked Chest & The Sweeps of 98-NY-1916-1st ed-
ltd to 850c   (5mm2)   8.50
--Lollington Downs & Other Poems-NY-1917-1st ed
                                        (5mm2,4b5,vf)   10.00
--Melloney Holtspur-Lond-1922-ltd to 535c,autg
                     (5t8,4b4) 15.   (4b5,vg)   20.00
--same-NY-1922-Macmillan-ltd to 1000c,autg
        (5p0) 7.50   (4b5,vg) 15.   (5ss9,sl stn,dj)   12.50
--The Midnight Folk-NY-1927-8vo-250c,autog-cl bk bds
                              (4c2,box,sp mended)   20.00
--same-Lond-1927-Heinemann-327p-1st ed (5F9,f,dj)   10.00
--Midsummer Night-Lond-(n.d.)-Heinemann-ltd to 275c,nbrd,autg
                                    (4b5,dj,mint)   30.00
--same-Lond-(1928)-Heinemann-1st ed   (4b5,vf,fade dj)   10.00
--Odtaa-Lond-(1926)-Heinemann-1st ed(4m8)5.(4b5,mint,dj) 15.00
--The Old Front Line-NY-1917-Macmillan-1st Amer ed (5ss9,f) 7.50
--Poetry-Lond-(1931)-Heinemann-1st ed   (4b5,mint,dj)   7.50
--Rosas-NY-1918-12mo-vel bk bds-1st ed-ltd to 750c,autg
                                        (5dd8,dj)   10.00
--Salt Water Poems & Ballads-NY-1916-plts   (5c1)   15.00
--Sard Harker-Lond-(1924)-Heinemann-1st ed
        (4m8) 5.00   (5ss3,stn,chip,dj) 5.   (4b5,mint,dj)   12.50
--Selected Poems-Lond-1922-8vo-bds wi vel bk-t.e.g.-frontis-
1st ed-ltd to 530c,nbrd,autg   (5dd8)   15.00
--same-(NY)-1923-Macmillan-ltd to 400c,nbrd,autg,box
                                    (4b5,unopnd,mint)   30.00
--Sonnets-NY-1916-8vo-bds-vel bk-t.e.g.-frontis-1st ed-
ltd to 500c,autg   (5dd8)   15.00
--South & East-Lond-1929-Medici Soc-1st ed-tip in plts-
ltd to 2750c   (4b5,f,dj)   7.50
--The Taking of Helen-NY-1923-8vo-bds & cl-papr labl-1st ed-
ltd to 750c,autg   (5dd8)   15.00
--same-Lond-1923-1st ed-ltd to 780c,nbrd,autg-cl&bds (5mm2) 15.00
--Trial of Jesus-Lond-1925-Heinemann-ltd to 530c,autg,nbrd
                                    (4b5,mint,dj)   15.00
--same-Lond-(1925)-Heinemann-1st ed (4b5,mint,sl fade dj) 5.00
--Tristan & Isolt,a Play in Verse-NY-1927-Macmillan-1st ed-
ltd to 350c,autg   (5tt2,vg)   15.00
--Wanderer of Liverpool-NY-1930-Macmillan-ltd to 350c,autg-
illus   (5i4,fray,rub)   20.00
MASK,THE-Vol 8,1918,1919-#1 thru 12-Monthly Leaflet of Art
of the Theatre-Florence-(Gordon Craig)-8vo-bds-cl bk-labl
                                                (5d1)   100.00
--same-Vol 9-illus-1923   (5d1)   100.00
MASKELL,HENRY P-Old Country Inns-Lond-1912-294p,31p-
photos   (5w1)   12.50

MASKELL, HENRY P (continued)
--Taverns of Old England-Lond-(1927)-235p-illus
        (5g9, lt fox) 6.50   (5w1)   7.50
MASON & WAAS-Miniature Flower Arrangement-Florida-n.d.-
   illus   (5qq7)   4.00
MASON, A E W-The Four Feathers-Lond-1902-Smith, Elder-8vo-
   orig light blu cl-1st ed   (5ee9) 50.00
--Life of Francis Drake-GardenCty-1942-349p-1st ed (5h9) 6.50
--A Romance of Wastedale-Lond-(1895)-12mo-cl-1st ed of
   auth's 1st novel-1st state, plus copy of later prntg
        (5gg6, 2 pg als) 2 books 50.00
MASON, A T-Bureaucracy Convicts Itself-NY-1941-illus (4a1) 10.00
MASON, ALPHEUS THOS-A Free Man's Life-NY-1946-713p-
   illus   (5p0)   6.50
MASON, AUGUSTUS-Our Pioneers...Struggle white Race wi Red
   Men for Possession of New World-n.p.-(1904)   -photos
              (5s4, wn, cov tn)   7.50
MASON, BENJ-Light Rising Out of Obscurity-Phila-Crukshauk-
   1790-46p-wrps   (5i1) 15.00
MASON, BERNARD S-Roping-NY-(1940)-140p-illus (5dd5) 4.00
MASON, CAROLINE A-A Titled Maiden-NY-(1889)-447p-illus-
   Pilgrim Prize Ser   (5r7)   7.50
--A Woman of Yesterday-NY-1900-367p-1st ed
        (5m2, vf) 10. (5ee3, f)   7.50
MASON, CHAS-Hist of Dublin (N Hamp)-1855-433p (5mm3) 10.00
MASON, DAN'L GREGORY-A Child's Guide to Music-NY-1909-
   Baker&Taylor-12mo-243p-frontis-11 plts-pict labl (5p1) 10.00
--Music in my Time-NY-1938-illus-1st ed (5jj3) 12.50
MASON, DEXTER-Tipple & Snack-NY-(1931)-83p-12mo (5w1,wn) 2.50
MASON, MRS E M-Faces that Follow-Tor-1898-illus (4b9) 8.00
MASON, E T, ed-Sam'l Johnson, His Works & His Ways-NY-1879-
   Harper-310p   (5x0)   4.00
MASON, E W-Robert Isbell Desc in Amer-1944-286p (5t9) 17.50
MASON, EDW G-Chapters from Illinois History-Chig-1901-322p-
   1st ed   (5jj7, f) 15.00
--Early Chicago & Ill-Chig-1890-illus-Chig Hist Soc
   (5t9, 5jj7, crack) 7.50   (5ii2, broke) 12.50
MASON, EDW S, ed-The Corp in Modern Society-Harvard Univ Pr-
   1959-335p   (5p0)   5.00
MASON, EMILY V-Southern Poems of the War-Balt-1867-456p-cl
       (5m2, wn) 6.50 (5jj9) 17.50
--same-Balt-1874   (5h6, loose)   5.00
MASON, F C-Borton & Mason, History of the Families in Europe &
   Amer-1908-264p & index   (5t9) 22.50
MASON, F VAN WYCK-Cutlas Empire-GardenCty-1949-illus(5r7) 5.00
--Fighting Americans-NY-(1943)-   (5h6)   4.00
MASON, FRANCES, ed-Creation by Evolution-NY-1928-392p-illus-
   1st ed   (5w4)   7.50
--John Norton & Sons, Merchants of London & Virg-Richmond-1937-
   Diez Pr   (5x5) 15.00
MASON, G W-Anc & Desc of Elisha Mason, Litchfield, Conn & wife-
   1911-120p   (5mm3)
MASON, GEO C-Application of Art to Manufactures-NY-1858-
   cl-344p-plts   (4e4, sl shaken) 15.00
--Life & Works of Gilbert Stuart-NY-1879-Scribner's Sons-1st ed-
   286p-illus   (4m2, f, unopnd) 35. (4a0) 40.00
--same-NY-1894-Scribners-286p-illus (5m5, crack, sl wn) 40.00
MASON, GREGORY-Remember the Maine-NY-(1939)-1st ed-illus
            (5tt5, dj)   6.00
--Silver Cities of Yucatan-NY-1927-illus-map-8vo-cl-340p
          (5t2, f, dj)   4.50
MASON, J D-History of Amador Co, Calif-Oakland-1881-
   Thompson&West-344p-orig cl&lea (5tt0) 200.00
MASON, J M-Our Town, the Story of Mesa, Ariz-Mesa-1948-181p-
   illus-wrps   (5d6) 10.00
MASON, JEREMIAH-Memoir & Correspondence-Cambr-1873-
   8vo-priv prntd-1st ed (5q8, sl soil) 30. (5ss5, sl rub) 15.00
--Memoir, Autobiogr & Corres of-KansasCty-1926-illus (5m2) 6.00
MASON, JERRY, ed-Family of Man-NY-(1955)-1st ed-illus-4to
          (4a1)   7.50
MASON, JOHN-A Brief History of the Pequot War-Bost-1736-
   Kneeland & Green-sm4to-g.t.mor-1st ed-v rare
       (5n2, repaired) 3,500.00
--same-NY-1869-8vo-20p-2nd ed   (5L3) 18.50
MASON, JN-Self Knowledge-Bost-Thomas-1793-211p-16mo-lea
       (5i1, fox, cov wn) 15.00
--same-Lond-1804-15th ed-orig bds-224p (5c8) 10.00
MASON, MAJ JOHN-History of Statue Erected to Commemorate
   Historic Achievement of Maj John Mason & His Comrades-Hartf-
   1889-8vo-58p-wrps   (5g5) 10.00
MASON, JOHN MONCK-Essay on antiquity & consti of parliament
   in Ireland-Dublin-1820-W Folds, prntr-8vo-hf crushed lev-t.e.g.-
   1st ed   (5i8, vf, wrps bnd in) 25.00

MASON, KENNETH-Abode of Snow-Lond-(1955)-372p-illus
          (5d7)   5.00
MASON, L R-To Win These Rights-NY-1952 (5x2)   7.50
MASON, LOUIS B-The Life & Times of Maj Jn Mason of Conn,
   1600 to 1672-NY-1935-8vo-illus-1st ed (5m6, dj, vg) 10.00
MASON, LOWELL-The New Carmina Sacra...Psalm & Hymn Tunes,
   wi music manual-Bost-(1869)-OliverDitson-380, 4p-lg obl 8vo-
   orig prntd bds   (5L8, wn)   7.50
--Primary School Song Book-Bost-1846-2 parts-96p-prntd bds(5h7) 12.50
MASON, MARY M-Mae Madden-Chig-1876-1st ed (5mm2) 20.00
MASON, MICHAEL H-The Arctic Forests-Lond-1934-299p-photos-
   fldg mapreprnt   (5ss1)   5.00
--Paradise of Fools-Lond-1936-photos-282p-map(fldg) (4t5) 8.50
MASON, OTIS TUFTON-Aboriginal Amer Basketry, Studies in a
   Textile Art without Machinery-Wash-1904-Govt Pr-248 plts-
   hf lea-Rpt US Natl Mus 1902, #128-v scarce (4b2, rprd, autg) 100.00
--NoAmer Bows, Arrows & Quivers from Annual Report of Smith Inst,
   1893-(Wash, 1893)-pp631 to 679 plus 57 plts bnd separately
   in 3 qtr lea   (5t3, pres to F Hodge) 15.00
--Papers Relating to Anthropology-(From Smith Report, 1886, Part 1)-
   pp205 to 239-26 plts-bds (5r0)   7.50
--Primitive Travel & Transportation-GPO-1896-wrps-illus-593p-
   US Natl Report for 1894 (4k4)   8.50
--Woman's Share in Primitive Culture-NY-1897-Appleton-illus-
   295p   (5p7, rbnd)   7.50
MASON, P F H-Desc of Richard Hull of New Haven-1894-82p
          (5t9) 15.00
MASON, PAUL-Constitution of State of Calif Annotated, 1946-
   (Sacramento)-1946-R8vo-1728p-buck (5xx5)   5.00
MASON, REDFERN-Song Lore of Ireland-NY-1910-8vo-cl-329p-
   illus   (5t2, lacks e.p.)   4.00
MASON, ROBT C-George Mason of Virginia, Citizen, Statesman,
   Philosopher-NY-1919-ltd to 1000c (4j4)   7.50
MASON, ROBT LINDSAY-The Lure of the Great Smokies-Bost-
   1927-plts   (5h6, rprd) 15.00
MASON, STUART-Bibliogr of Oscar Wilde-Lond-1914-TWerner Laurie-
   8vo-orig white cl-t.e.g.-plts-2 vols-deluxe ed-orig ed-
   ltd to 100c, autg   (5d3) 37.50
MASON, W A-History of the Art of Writing-NY-1920-502p-illus-
   1st ed-scarce   (5p6) 20.00
MASON, WM-Elfrida-Lond-1752-4to-1st ed-80p-sewn(5aa0) 12.50
MASON, WM-Pious Parent's Gilt...To Which is Added the Closet
   Companion & Swearer's Prayer-Hartf-1815-ODCooke-12mo-
   71p-frontis-orig prntd wrps dated 1814 (5rr2, f, fox) 20.00
MASON, WM-Works of Thos Gray wi Memoirs of His Life & Writings-
   Extracts Philological Poetical by Mathias-Lond-1814-2 vols-
   folio-buck-lea labls-port (5m4, rbnd) 50.00
MASON, WINFIELD-Frozen Northland Country-Cinn-1910-illus
         (5jj1, fray)   8.50
MASONICK MINSTREL-Dedham-1816-463p music-calf
        (5c3, cov dtchd) 18.50
MASONRY IN CALIF-50 Years of-SanFran-1897-Edwin A Sherman, ed-
   20 parts-orig wrps-v scarce (5h5) 30.00
MASONS-Bylaws of Warren Lodge #10 of Masons of State of Oregon-
   Jacksonville(Or)-1870-P D Hull-16mo-orig wrps (5i9, f) 17.50
MASONS, HISTORY OF-Bost&NY-1896-8vo-illus-3 qtr lea(5t7) 10.00
MASONS, PROCEEDINGS OF-Grand Lodge...of Montana, at its 9th
   annual...Oct 7, 1873-Helena-Rcky Mntn Publ Co-1874-8vo-
   orig blu prntd wrps (5i9, f) 40.00
MASPERO, G-History of Egypt, Chaldea, Syria, Babylonia, & Assyria-
   Lond-n.d.-(1920)-12 vols-Grolier Soc-AHSayce, ed-lg8vo-
   col plts-lg print (5p6, f) 72.00
--Life in Ancient Egypt & Assyria-NY-(1892)-390p-illus (5t4) 4.50
--Popular Stories of Ancient Egypt-NY-1915-316p-cl (5t2) 7.50
MASQUE OF POETS, A-Bost-1878-12mo-cl-1st ed (5gg6, hng tn) 15.00
MASSACHUSETTS, ACTS & LAWS-of His Majesty's Prov of Mass Bay
   in NEngl, wi Charter etc-Bost-1759(1761)-folio-calf-
   (2)p, 14, 24, 414p (5L1, rbkd) 125.00
--same-Bost-1789-Adams & Nourse-folio-pg 724 to 746 (5t4,rbnd) 25.00
--same-Bost-1795-Adams & Larkin-folio-pg 493 to 521 (5t4,rbnd) 25.00
--same-Bost-1796 to 1838-orig wrps-56 vols-broken run (5m6) 100.00
MASS, ANNUAL REPORT OF ADJ GEN-Bost-1863-470p, 38p
         (5j6)   6.00
--same-Bost-1864-1032p, 36p (5j6)   6.50
--same-Bost-1865-1099p, 80p (5j6)   7.50
--same-Bost-1866-767p, 36p (5j6, pres by APHooker) 9.00
MASSACHUSETTS-Houghton Mifflin-1937-WPA-Amer Guide Ser-
   1st ed   (5b5) 12.50
--same-Bost-(1937)-675p-illus-pkt map-WPA
     (5a9, f) 6. (4L5, vg, dj)   7.50
MASSACHUSETTS ANTI SLAVERY SOC-5th Annual Report of Board
   of Managers of-Bost-1837 (5x2, f, rbnd) 40.00

MASSACHUSETTS BAY-Journ of House of Rep of Prov of...in
New Engl-Bost-1764-Green & Russell,prntr-sml folio-
unbnd as issued-91p   (5L8,spot,libr release stmp) 38.50

MASSACHUSETTS BAY-Short View of History of Colony of wi....
Orig Charter & Constit-Lond-1769-Wilkie-hf mor-(4)p,71p-
8vo-1st ed-anon   (5L1,broke) 95.00

MASSACHUSETTS LAWS-Charter Granted by Their Majesties
King Wm & Queen Mary to Inhabitants of Prov of Mass Bay
in NEngl-Bost-1699-Green & Allen-folio-wi Acts & Laws-
(Bost-1700,1)   (5n2,rprd) 2,500.00

MASSACHUSETTS,CIVIL GOV OF-for year 1809,1810-n.p.-
(ca1810)-sm4to-orig wrps   (5m2) 15.00

MASSACHUSETTS-Collection of Portraits of Representative Men in
Business & Prof Life-1903-386p   (5t9) 5.00

MASSACHUSETTS,CONSTITUTION OF STATE OF-& that of US,
Declar of Independence wi Wash Farewell Address-Portl-
(1803)-Adams-orig calf bk bds-12mo-rare   (5n2) 85.00
--same-Bost-1805-Manning & Loring-12mo-orig calf bk bds (5n2) 55.00

MASSACHUSETTS CONSTITUTION OR FRAME OF GOV-Bost-1780-
stitched-53p   (5a3,f) 50.00
--same-Bost-1781-folio-Edes & Sons-stitched-24p-1st folio ed
   (5L1) 95.00

MASSACHUSETTS EMIGRANT AID SOC-Article of Agreement & Assoc
of Emigrant Aid Co-Bost-1854-8p-self wrps
   (5m3,f,leaflet laid in) 32.50

MASSACHUSETTS,ESSEX CO-Records & Files of Qurtly Courts of-
Vols 1 to 8,1636 to 1683-Salem-1911 to 1921-8 vols-
publ by Essex Insti   (5h9,f) 60.00

MASSACHUSETTS GENERAL HOSPITAL-Report of..Jan,1848-
Bost-1848-72p-frontis-8vo-qtr calf   (5L1) 150.00

MASSACHUSETTS HISTORICAL SOC PROCEEDINGS-Vols 65
thru 68,1932 to 1947-4 vols   (5h9,f) 50.00

MASSACHUSETTS HORTICULTURAL SOC-Transactions,Vol 1 #3-
Bost-1852-4 col plts-wrps   (5w3) 7.50

MASSACHUSETTS-Laws & Liberties of..-Cambridge-1929-t4to-
rprnt of 1648 ed   (5dd9) 10. (5p9) 12.50

MASSACHUSETTS LAW QUARTERLY-1915 to 1968-Vol 1 to 53-
bound   (5rr4,ex-libr) 850.00

MASSACHUSETTS MEDICAL SOC COMMUNICATIONS-Bost-
1790 to 1860-9 vols-8vo-hf calf   (4c1) 250.00

MASSACHUSETTS MEDICAL SOC-Pharmacopoeia-Bost-1808-
buck   (5L7,ex-libr) 100.00

MASSACHUSETTS,PRIV & SPEC STATUES OF-Commonwealth of
from 1780 to 1805..(to 1814)..(to 1822)-Bost-1805-(Vol 1 to 3)
& 1823 (Vols 4,5)-uniform cl,labls- v scarce   (5m3) 75.00

MASSACHUSETTS-Records of Mass Vol Militia Called Out by Gov
to Support Threatened Invasion During War of 1812 to 1814-
Bost-1913-448p   (5e8) 18.75

MASSACHUSETTS REGISTER-& Business Directory,1874-Bost-
1874-Sampson,Davenport-thk lg8vo-cl-828p plus ads,etc-
fldg col map   (5j5,wn,stnd) 20.00

MASSACHUSETTS REGISTER & US CALENDAR-for 1812-Bost-1811-
1st ed-orig hf calf   (5m2,rprd) 10.00
--same-Bost-1816-1st ed-bds   (5m2,hng loose) 10.00
--same-for 1819-Bost-(1818)-JasLoring-sm12mo-orig mrbld wrps-
252p   (5L8,sp wn) 17.50

MASS SENATE NO 5-Railway from Boston to Albany-Report-
Bost-1828-56p   (5q0) 45.00

MASSACHUSETTS SOC FOR PROMOTING AGRICULTURE-
Papers-Bost,1793 thru 1803-7 pieces,2 plts bnd in 1 vol-calf
   (5m3) 75.00

MASS SOLDIERS,SAILORS-& Marines in the Civil War-Norwood-
1931 to 1937-Norwood Pr-9 vols (8 text,1 index)
   (5mm8,vf,unopnd) 45.00

MASS VITAL RECORDS-
--Brewster-1904-281p   (5mm3) 10.00
--Bridgewater-1916-2 vols   (5mm3) 15.00
--Cohasset-1916-237p   (5mm3) 10.00
--Dartmouth-1929,30-3 vols   (5mm3) 22.50
--Leominster-1911-369p   (5mm3) 10.00
--Lowell-1930-4 vols   (5mm3) 35.00
--Lynn-1905,6-2 vols   (5mm3) 20.00
--Mansfield-1933-230p   (5mm3) 15.00
--Marblehead-1908-3 vols   (5mm3) 25.00
--Nantucket-1925 to 9- 5 vols   (5mm3) 50.00
--New Bedford-1932 to 41-3 vols   (5mm3) 25.00
--Newbury-1911-2 vols   (5mm3) 25.00
--Newburyport-1911-2 vols   (5mm3) 20.00
--Rowley-1928,31-537p,30p   (5mm3) 15.00

MASSACHUSETTS WCTU CUISINE-Bost-1878-128p & ads
   (5c4,ink,cov wn) 9.50 (5yy0) 12.50

MASSE,H J L J-Chats on old Pewter-Lond-1928-cl-12mo (4n5) 12.50
--The Pewter Collector-NY-1921-illus-8vo-cl-314p (5t2) 7.50

MASSECK,MAJ C J-Official Brief History 89th Div USA,
1917,18,19-n.p.-n.d.-48p-orig wrps   (5k1) 3.50

MASSETT,STEPHEN C-"Drifting About"-NY-1863-Carleton-
8vo-cl-illus   (5b2,sl tn) 12.50

MASSEY,JOHN E-Autobiog of-NY-1909-312p-cl-Eliz H Hancock ed
   (5r7) 8.50 (5h1) 12.50

MASSEY,V-On Being Canadian-1948-198p   (4b9) 8.00

MASSEY,WM C-The Castaldi Collection from Central and Southern
Baja Calif-Berkeley-Mar,1966-76p-illus-wrps (5d6) 6.00

MASSICOTE,E Z-Armorial Du Canada Francais,Deuxieme Series-
Mont-1918-151p-illus   (4b9) 10.00

MASSIE,DAVID M-Nathaniel Massie,a pioneer of Ohio-Cinn-
1896-port-cl   (5g4,loose,writing) 10.00

MASSIE,J W-Slavery,the Crime & Curse of America-Lond-1852-
g.e.-2x3"-bds-64p   (4j4) 7.50

MASSIE,S W,ed-Homes & Gardens in Old Virginia-Richmond-
1932-plts   (5tt5) 10.00
--same-Richmond-1930-illus   (5j6) 5. (5t7) 7.50

MASSIE,MRS WM R-Descriptive Guide Book of Virginia's Old
Gardens-Richmond-n.d.-Garden Club of Virg-88p (5p0) 5.00

MASSINGER,PHILIP-Plays of-Balt-1856-WmGifford,ed-529p
   (5p9) 10.00

MASSINGHAM,H W-A Selection from the Writings of...-Lond-
(1925)-J Cape-368p   (5p9) 6.50

MASSON,SIR IRVINE-Mainz Psalters & Canon Missae-Lond-1954-
folio-illus-tables-bds-cl bk   (4c1) 15.00

MASSON,L R-Les Bourgeois de la Compagnie du Nord Ouest,etc-
NY-1960-Antiquarian Pr-2 vols-8vo-cl-reprint(5h5,mint) 17.50
--Orig Journals,Narr Letters etc Relating to NW Co-NY-1960-
Antiquarian Pr-2 vols-700c for sale   (5x5) 20.00

MASSON,PHILIPPE-Le Canada Francais et la Providence-Quebec-
1875-Brousseau-57p-prntd wrps-pamph (5qq8,chip) 20.00

MASTER BAKER'S MANUAL-for Bakeries,Hotels,Restaurants,
Hospitals & other insti-Chig-(1930)-Calumet Baking Powder
Co-127p-18 pg col plts   (5g9) 4.50

MASTA,H L-Abenaki Indian Legends,Grammar & Place Names-
Victoriaville-1932-illus-stiff wrps-110p-scarce (4e9) 30.00

MASTER HENRY'S RABBIT-The Bees;& the Faithful Dog-Troy-
c1840-Meriam&Moore-16mo-24p-wdcuts-wrps (5v0,f) 12.50

MASTER J. SPRAGGLES-his Version of Robinson Crusoe as Narr-
NY-McLoughlin-(c1875)-sm4to-pict wrps-27p-11 plts(5aa2) 15.00

MASTERS,D C-Winnipeg General Strike-Tor-1950-plts-159p
   (5s0) 12.50

MASTERS,EDGAR LEE-Children of the Market Place-NY-1922-
469p-1st ed   (5a9) 5.00
--Domesday Book-NY-1920-1st ed (5b2) 5. (5F0) 4.50
--The fate of the jury-NY-1929-172p-1st ed (5p6) 8.00
--Gettysburg,Manila,Acoma-NY-1930-ltd to 375c,autg
   (5hh1,vg) 25.00
--Golden Fleece of Calif-Weston,VT-(1936)-Countryman Pr-
79p-illus-ltd to 550c,autg (5n1,writing on hf t) 20.00
--Great Valley-NY-1916-1st ed   (5mm1) 6.00
--Kit O'Brien-(NY)-1927-Boni&Liveright-1st ed (5ss3,dj,sp fade) 5.00
--Mitch Miller-NY-1920-illus-1st ed (5mm1,autg) 12.50
--same-1921-Sloan,Mac   (5ww4,vg,dj) 7.50
--Poems of People-NY 1936-Appleton-1st ed (5p7,dj) 5.00
--Skeeters Kirby-NY-1923-1st ed (5mm1,dj) 7.50
--Songs & Satires-NY-1916-1st ed (5m8) 6.50 (5ss3,sp stn) 5.00
--same-Lond-1916-Laurie-12mo-cl-172p-1st Engl ed (5j5) 7.50
--Spoon River Anthology-NY-1915-12mo-orig cl-1st issue(7/8-inch
across top of covers)-1st ed   (5i8,vg) 50.00
--same-Lond-n.d.-(1916?)-T Werner Laurie-8vo-orig qtr vel-
lin bds-papr labl-frontis-5 plts (5i8,dj,vf) 15.00
--same-NY-1942-lg8vo-buck-ltd to 1500c,nbrd,autgs-
Ltd Ed Club   (5b0) 50.00
--Starved Rock-NY-1919-1st ed   (5mm1) 6.00
--Toward the Gulf-NY-1918-1st ed (4b4,mint) 12.50

MASTERS IN ART-Series of Illus Monographs-Bost-1900 to 1908-
Vol 1 to 9-Bates&Guild-3 qtr lea-illus (5t7) 30.00

MASTERS,JOS-Stories of Far West-Bost-(1935)-297p-illus-
dec cov   (5s4,ex-libr) 9.00

MASTERS OF THE SCIENCE-Chig-(1900)-24ps (5ww4) 5.00

MASTERS,R D-Int'l Law in Nat'l Courts-NY-1932 (5r4) 15.00

MASTERS,THOS-The Ice Book-Lond-1844-8vo-dec cl-6 plts (4b6)35.00

MASTERSON,V V-The Katy Railroad & Last Frontier-Norman-
1952-maps-illus-312p-1st ed   (5yy7) 8.50
--same-Norman-1953-illus-321p-2nd prntg (5h0) 8.00

MASTERSON,W E-Jurisdiction in Marginal Seas-NY-1929 (5r4) 15.00

MASTON,T B-Segregation & Desegregation-NY-1959 (5x2,dj) 5.00

MASUCCIO-The Novellino-Lond-1895-2 vols-transl,W G Waters-
illus-sm4to-silk cl-Lawrence&Bullen (5t5) 20.00

MASUR,GERHARD-Simon Bolivar-Univ of NewMex-1948-737p-
8vo-cl-illus-scarce   (5h4,dj) 17.50

MASUROVSKY, B I-Sherbets, Water Ices & Modern Soda Fountain
Operation-Milw-(1933)-188p-illus   (5g9)   4.00
MASURY, J W-Hints on House Painting-NY-1868-84p-illus-wrps
                                          (5t4)   10.00
--How shall we paint our houses-NY-1868   (5g4,stnd) 15.00
--same-NY-1869-216p,(6)   (5n7,sp tn) 7.50
MATAMORPHOSES, THE-or, Effects of Education-WmDarton-
Jun,1818-12mo-frontis-hf roan-1st ed-164p (5s0)   12.50
MATEJCEK, ANTONIN-Modern & Contemporary Czech Art-
Lond-1924-4to-91p-illus   (5t0)   7.50
MATERNAL PHYSICIAN, THE-By an Amer Matron-NY-1811-291p-
hf lea   (5w7,wn,stnd) 35.00
MATHER, COTTON-Magnalia Christi Americana,or,the Ecclesiastical
History of New England-Lond-1702-Parkhurst-folio-calf-
fldg map   (5z7) 600.   (5n2,rbkd,rub) 385.00
--same-Hartford-1820-2 vols-calf-2nd ed   (5ee3,vg) 37.50
--same-Hartford-1853-R8vo-mor-2 vols   (5p5)   65.00
--Diary-1957-2 vols   (5L7)   12.00
--Essays to do Good-1822-sheep-new ed,imprvd by G Burder
                                       (5L7,crack) 12.50
--Johannes in Eremo-(Bost)-1695-24mo-calf-scarce
                                     (5g3,wn,lvs def) 150.00
--Ratio Disciplinae Fratrum Nov Anglorum-Bost-1726-S Gerrish-
12mo-orig sheep-207p(3)   (5L1)   150.00
--Wonders of the Invisible World-Lond-1693-for John Dunston-
4to-mor   (5n2,lacks hf t.) 1,250.00
MATHER, FRANK JR-Pageant of Amer, American Spirit in Art-
Yale Univ Pr-1927-Wash ed,Vol 12-g.t.-mor-354p-illus
crown 4to   (4a0)   27.50
--History of Italian Painting-NY-1923-Holt-495o-16mo-soft cl
                                        (5m5,crack) 11.00
--Western European Painting of the Renaissace-NY-1939-illus
                                            (5ww3)   15.00
MATHER, FRED-Modern Fishculture in Fresh & Salt Water-NY-
1900-332p-illus   (5t7)   6.00
MATHER, HELEN-One Summer in Hawaii-NY-(1891)-298p-illus
                                            (5xx7)   10.00
MATHER, INCREASE-A Discourse Concerning Earthquakes..also
2 sermons-Bost-1706-T Green-nar 12mo-131p-lea sp-1st ed
                                         (5L1,rbnd) 300.00
--Early History of New England-Bost-1864-309p-sm4to-orig grn cl-
facs rprnt   (5m3,f,lacks port) 25.00
--The First Principles of New England concerning The Subject
of Baptism & Communion of Churches-Cambr-1675-Sam'l Green-
40p,(8) 7-sm4to-hf lea (5L1,poor) 900.   (5z7,pgs reprd) 375.00
--Further Acc't Of Tryals Of The New England Witches..-Lond-
1693-part mor-1st Engl ed-(2),10,(4),40,(4)p-ex rare
                                  (5z7,lacks ad lf at end,few lvs tn) 750.00
--History of King Philip's War-Bost-1862-ports-fldg map-
orig cl-g.t.-250c prntd-scarce   (4c1,uncut) 30.00
--Remarkable Providences-Lond-1890   (5m2)   7.50
--Mystery of Israel's Salvation, Explained & Applyed-(Lond)-
1669-sm8vo-calf-period style   (5gg6) 600.00
MATHER, SAM'L-Abridgment of the Life of Cotton Mather-Lond-
1744-Oswald&Blackstone-12mo-hf roan-1st Engl ed (5n2) 75.00
--Apology for Liberties of Churches in New England-Bost-1738-
Fleet-8vo-calf-1st ed (5i0,vf) 80.   (5n2)   75.00
--The Fall of the Mighty Lamented-Bost-1738-J Draper-33p-
8vo-hf mor   (5L1,poor)   10.00
--The Figures of Types Of The Old Testament etc-Lond-1705-
2nd ed   calf-errata   (5z7,fox)   85.00
MATHER, WM W-Geology of New York-1843-639p-plts (5zz0) 20.00
--same-Albany-1842,3-fldg plts-4 vols-4to   (5yy0)   37.50
MATHERS, C W-The Far North-Edmonton-1902-4to-wrps-
27p mounted photos-scarce   (5dd7)   25.00
--Souvenir from the North-Edmonton-1901-Mathers-obl 8vo-
photos   (5nn8)   25.00
MATHERS, E P-Zambesia, England's El Dorado in Africa-Lond-
n.d.-(1891)-King, Sell & Railton-476p-maps-photos
                                 (4t5,lacks 1 map,ex-libr) 35.00
MATHERS, JAS-From Gun to Gavel-NY-1954-256p-1st ed (5xx5) 7.00
MATHES, J HARVEY-The Old Guard in Gray-Memphis-1897-
sketches   (5h6,sl stn) 30.00
MATHES, JAS M,ed-The Christian Record(magazine)-Bloomington-
1845-(1 yr),Vol 3-bound   (4a9)   50.00
MATHESON, E K,ed-Chapters in NW History Prior to 1890
Battleford-1927-(Can NW Hist Soc Pub,Vol 1,#3)-86p-ports-
wrps-86p   (4a8)   5.00
MATHESON, RODERICK O-Congressional Visit to Hawaii,1915-
Honolulu-(1915)-Advertiser Pr-72p-illus-wrps (5yy3) 10.00
MATHEW, D-Age of Charles I-1951   (5L7)   6.00

MATHEW, LT GEN EDW-Manuscript account of pay for him &
staff officers under his command 25th Aug to 24th Dec,1788,
Hdqrtrs-Granada-(1788)   (5t4)   10.50
MATHEWS, ALFRED-History of the Counties of Lehigh & Carbon, in
Penna-Phila-1884- 4to-hf mor-800p-col maps (5w5)   50.00
MATHEWS, B-Booker T. Washington-Lond-1949-SCM Pr Ltd-illus
                                            (5x2)   10.00
--The Clash of Color-NY-1924-12mo   (5x2)   6.00
MATHEWS, BASIL-Consider Africa-NY-1936-Friendship Pr-181p-
fldg map   (4t5)   5.00
--Livingstone the Pathfinder-NY-1912-Missionary Educ Mvmt-
213p-photos   (4t5,lacks fly) 5.00
--Wilfred Grenfell, Master Mariner-NY-(1924)-cl-178p-illus
                                         (5t2,f,dj)   4.00
--World Tides in the Far East-NY-c1934-184p (5w9)   3.50
MATHEWS, CHAS EDW-Annals of Mont Blanc, A Monograph-Lond-
1898-368p-illus-fldg map-Unwin (5p5,cl) 17.50 (5d7,hf mor) 20.00
MATHEWS, CHAS JOS-Life, Chiefly Autobiog,with Selections from
Corres & Speeches-Lond-1879-Chas Dickens (younger),ed-
2 vols extended to 4 vols-158 ex illus,etc -calf
                                      (5nn2,vf,f bndg) 175.00
MATHEWS, CORNELIUS-Pen & Ink Panorama of NYC-NY-1853-
16mo   (5xx7)   12.00
--Poems on Man-NY-1843-16mo-papr labl-1st Amer ed-bds
                                      (4c2,f,labl chip) 50.00
MATHEWS, F SCHUYLER-Field Book of Amer Trees & Shrubs-NY-
(1915)-Putnam-465p   (5p7)   3.50
--Field Book of Amer Wild Flowers-NY-1908-Putnam-552p (5p7) 4.50
--Field Book of Wild Birds & Their Music-NY-(1921)-Putnam-
325p-rev & enlgd   (5p7)   5.00
MATHEWS, G M-The Birds of Australia-Lond-1910 to 36-1st ed-
ltd to 225c-plts-18 vols in 14   (5z9,f,spec f bndg) 4,750.00
--Manual of Birds of Australia-Vol 1 (all pub)-Orders Casuarii to
Columbae-Lond-1921-c.-t.e.g.-lg8vo-279p-46 plts (10 col)-
v scarce   (4p5,dj)   47.00
MATHEWS, J M-Recoll of Persons & Events, Chiefly in City of NY-
NY-1865   (4b6)   12.50
MATHEWS, JOHN JOS-Life & Death of an Oil Man-Norman-1951-
259p-1st ed   (5h0,pres)   12.00
--The Osages-Norman-1961-maps-cl-1st ed   (4t3,dj,f) 15.00
--Sundown-NY-1934-312p-1st ed   (5t3,rbnd) 4.00
--Talking to the Moon-Univ Chig Pr-1945-244p-cl (5h0) 12.00
--Wah'Kon Tah-Norman-1932-illus-359p
(4b3,vg,5k2) 7.50 (4b2,dj,f) 8. (5m9) 4.50 (4t3,dj)   5.00
MATHEWS, JULIA A-Golden Latter Series, #1, 2, 3, 4, 6-NY-
1875-5 vols-16mo-green cl-plts   (5j5)   15.00
MATHEWS, LOIS K-Expansion of New England-Bost-1909-8vo-
cl-303p-1st ed   (5t2)   7.50
MATHEWS, MRS-What has been-Alexandria(Va)-1803-Cotton &
Stewart-2 vols in 1 (as issued)-12mo-hf calf-1st Amer ed
                                        (5i9,sl tn) 22.50
MATHEWS, MRS MARY McNAIR- 10 Years in Nevada-Buffalo-
1880-343p-illus-orig cl-1st ed   (5F0)   75.00
MATHEWS, SHAILER-The French Revolution-NY-1912-frontis-8vo-
cl-297p   (5t2)   4.00
MATHEWS, WM-Hours with Men & Books-Chig-1877-384p (5x0) 4.50
MATHEWSON, ANNA-Song of the Evening Stars-Bost-(1911)-
Caruso,illus-12mo-cl   (5t0)   6.00
MATHIEWS, FRANKLIN K-Boy Scouts Year Book-NY-(1927)-cl-
4to-240p-illus   (5t0)   4.00
--same-NY-(1928)-240p-illus   (5t0)   5.00
--same-NY-1929-cl-4to   (5m9)   7.50
MATINEAU, HARRIET-Society in America-NY-1837-2 vols-2nd ed
                                        (5w7,sl wn) 18.50
MATHIOT,GEO-On Electrotyping Operations of US Coast Survey-
NewHav-1853-15p,(1)-wrps-fldg plt (5hh7,libr stmp)   7.50
MATISSE, HENRI-Jazz-NY-n.d.-(Mus Mod Art)-obl 8vo-col illus-
1st Amer ed-prntd in Germany   (5ii3)   7.50
--Les Fleurs du Mal-(Paris, 1947)-Chas Baudelaire-4to-orig wrps-
loose in sheets as issued-slipcase-orig lith frontis-orig photo liths-
ltd to 320c,autg   (5d9)   375.00
--The Last Works of Matisse 1950 to 1954-(NY,1958)-folio-
41 col plts   (5d9)   65.00
--Pierre a Feu-Paris-(1947)-Maeght-4to-orig frontis-ltd to 950c
                                            (5ee9) 100.00
--Portraits-Monte Carlo-1954-Andre Sauret-4to-ltd ed (5ee9,box)75.00
MATOS, WM-Official Historical Souvenir, Phila, Its Founding &
Development 1683 to 1908-Phila-1908-4to-508p-illus
                             (5L7) 10.   (5w4)   8.50
MATSCHAT, CECILE HULSE-Mexican Plants for Amer Gardens-
Bost-1935-269p-photos   8.50
--Seven Grass Huts-NY-1939   (5w4,5x7)   4.00
--Suwannee River,Strange Green Land-NY-1938-The Rivers of Amer-
                                        (5k1,5p0)   4.00

MATSELL, GEO W-Vocabulum; or, the rogue's lexicon-compiled-
NY-1859-Matsell-12mo-orig cl-1st ed   (5i9)   20.00
MATSON, ANNA, ed-The City That a Cow Kicked Over-Chig-
(1881)-A H Andrews-21p-map-illus-pic wrps   (5r0)   10.00
MATSON, CLARENCE-Building a World Gateway-LosAng-1945
(5jj1, f)   8.50
MATSON, N-French & Indians of Illinois River-Princeton, Ill-1874-
260p-2nd ed   (5jj7, f)   20.00
--Memories of Shaubena-Chig-1878-drwngs-269p-1st ed (4t3, wn) 17.50
--same-Chig-1882-illus-252p-3rd ed   (5jj7)   15.00
--Remin of Bureau Co-Princton-1872-406p-cl-1st ed
(5h2, faded, wn)   25.00
MATSON, RUTH-Cooking by the Garden Calendar-GardenCty-
1955-258p-illus   (5c9, 5s7)   4.50
--Gardening for Gourmets-NY-(1959)-262p   (5c9, 5s7)   4.50
MATSON, WM A-The Adversary, His Person, Power & Purpose-NY-
1891-8vo-cl-1st ed   (5p5)   15.00
MATTAPOISETT & OLD ROCHESTER-& part of Marion & Wareham-
(1907)-424p-illus   (5t9)   10.00
MATTENKLODT, WILHELM-A Fugitive in SW Africa, 1908 to 1920-
Lond-1931-Butterworth-287p-map-O Williams, ed (4t5)   20.00
MATTERN, J-Principles of Constitutional Jurisprudence of German
Nat'l Republic-Balt-1928   (5r4)   12.50
MATTERN, J R-Handloading Ammunition-Small Arms Tech Publ Co-
(c1926)-8vo-380p-illus-handbook   (4a6)   12.50
MATTESON, DAVID-Analytic Index-NY-c1918   (5w5)   3.50
MATTESON, H M-The Trap-NY-(1921)-293p (5ss1, artist autg) 6.00
MATTHES, FRANCOIS-The Incomparable Valley, a Geologic Interpr
of Yosemite-U Calif-1950-160p-photos   (4n1, dj) 15.00
--Sequoia National Park, Geolog Album-U Calif-1950-sm4to-cl-
illus   (5p9, 5h5, f, dj)   5.00
MATTHEWS, BRANDER-Americanisms & Briticisms wi Other Essays
on Other Isms-NY-1892-190p-1st ed (5p7) 4.50 (5mm2) 6.00
--Ballads of Books-NY-1887-1st ed-174p   (5ee3)   4.50
--Check & Counter Check-Phila-(1887)-80p   (5x4)   6.00
--A Confident Tomorrow-NY-1900-Harper-300p-illus (5x4, dmgd) 5.00
--Introduction to Amer Literature-NY-(1896)-illus (5mm2) 5.00
--Moliere: His Life & His Works-NY-1916-385p-8vo-cl-frontis
(5t0)   4.50
--The Theatres of Paris-NY-1880-Scribner's-208p-orig cl-1st ed
of auth's first book   (5d6)   35.00
--These Many Years-NY-1917-8vo-463p-cl(5t2) 4. (5m2)   6.50
MATTHEWS, EDWARDS A-Horse and Buggy Days-1950-381p
(5e8, dj, autg)   10.75
MATTHEWS, FRANKLIN-With Atlantic Fleet-NY-1908-321p-
illus   (5s1)   8.00
MATTHEWS, J H-Hist Remin of Ohio Penitentiary-Col-1884-192p-
wrps   (5h1, wrps wn)   8.50
MATTHEWS, J M-Textile Fibres-NY-1924-4th ed-1053p
(5n7, ex-libr, shake)   3.50
MATTHEWS, JAS M-Statutes at Large of Confederate States of Amer,
1st session of 1st Congress, 1862-Richmond-1862- R M Smith-
sewn   (5j6)   25.00
--same-2nd Session of 1st Congress, 1862-Richmond-1862-R M Smith-
yellow wrps   (5j6)   25.00
--same-3rd session of 1st Congress, 1863-Richmond-1863-R M Smith-
yellow wrps   (5x5, lacks bk wrp) 30. (5j6) 22.50
--same-4th session of 1st Congress, 1863, 4-Richmond-1864-R M Smith-
wrps   (5j6)   22.50
MATTHEWS, JOHN-Matthews' Amer Armoury & Blue Book-Lond-
(1901)-8vo-illus   (5m6, fade)   15.00
MATTHEWS, KENNETH D, JR-Cities in the Sand-Univ of Penna Pr-
(1957)-4to-97 photos   (5c3)   5.75
MATTHEWS, LYMAN-History of Cornwall-1862-356p-illus (5e8) 29.75
MATTHEWS, SALLIE REYNOLDS-Interwoven-Houston-1936-suede-
rare   (5g6, cl) 150.   (4c7, crack, pres) 137.50
MATTHEWS, WASHINGTON-Ethnography & Philology of the
Hidatsa Indians-GPO-1877-cl   (4k4)   7.50
--Navaho Legends-Bost-1897-299p-49 illus(7 col)-music examps-
Amer Folklore Soc   (5c3)   8.00
--Navajo Weavers-GPO-1885-wrps-4to-plts-extract from 3rd
B A E annual Rept   (4k4, chip, pres loose)   6.00
MATTHEWS, WM-American Diaries-Berkeley-1945-Univ of Calif Publ-
Vol 16-8vo-orig wrps-1st ed   (5m6)   7.50
--British Diaries-Berkeley-1950-8vo-1st ed   (5m6, dj, mint) 7.50
--Canadian Diaries & Autobiographies-U of Calif-1950-130p
(4b9, dj)   15.00
MATTHIAS, BENJ-Politician's Register-Phila-1835-Key&Biddle-
12mo-104p-bds-roan bk   (5j5)   20.00
MATTHIES, KATH-Trees of Note in Conn-Conn DAR-1934-34p-
illus-rev   (5p9)   3.00
MATTHIESSEN, F O-The Achievement of T S Eliot-Lond-1939
(5mm2)   5.00

MATTHIESSEN, F O (continued)
--American Renaissance-NY-(1941)-678p-lg8vo-cl-1st ed (5p5) 15.00
--Henry James, The Major Phase-NY-1914-190p-frontis (5t2,pres) 7.50
--The James Family-NY-1947-illus-706p   (5q0, dj) 10.00
--Notebooks of Henry James-NY-1955   (5mm2)   7.50
--Sarah Orne Jewett-Bost-1929-illus   (5mm2)   7.50
MATTICE, HAROLD A-Perry & Japan-NY-1942-20p-pamplet-
orig wrps   (5jj3)   10.00
MATTIELLO, JOS J-Protective & Decorative Coatings, Paints,
Varnishes, Lacquers & Inks-NY-1946, 47-Vol 1 & 4-lg8vo-1237p-
illus-cl   (5p5)   15.00
MATTIMORE, JEAN-Cooking by the Clock-NY-1948-230p-illus
(5c0)   3.00
MATTINGLY, GARRETT-Catherine of Aragon-Bost-1941 (5x7) 5.00
MATTOCKS, JOHN-Address Delivered Before Vt Assn of Chicago
Jan 17, 1877-Chig-1877-23p-wrps   (5h2, wn, pres) 5.00
MATTOON, REV C H-Baptist Annals of Oregon, 1844 to 1900-
McMinnville, Ore-Vol 1 only(of 2)-(1905)-464p-illus
(5s4, ex-libr)   20.00
MATTSON, CHESTER-Wanderings from Line of Duty-Honolulu-(1944)-
64p-illus   (5s1, pres)   6.00
MATTSON, MORRIS-The Amer Vegetable Practice, wi Vol 2 "A
Guide for Women"-Bost-1841-24 col lithos
(5w3, stnd, lacks title & prelim pgs)   10.00
MATURIN, EDW-Montezuma: the last of the Aztecs-NY-1845-
Paine & Burgess-2 vols in 1-12mo-hf mor-1st ed (5x1,rbnd,wn) 27.50
MATY, M-Misc Wks of Late Philip Dormer Stanhope-Lond-1777-
2 vols-4to-plts-calf   (5xx7)   35.00
MATZ, B W-Dickensian Inns & Taverns-Lond-1922-1st ed-plts-illus
(4a8, pres to A Waugh) 7.50   (5w1)   12.50
MAU, AUGUST-Pompeii, Its Life & Art-NY-1899-8vo-cl & lea-
22p, 509p   (5t2)   10.00
MAUCH CHUNK, PA-Souvenir of...Switzerland of Amer-Portland,
Me-n.d.-(before 1893)-13 photos in album   (5b9, vf)   7.50
MAUCK, F F-Modern Tailoring for Women-NY-1947-178p (5n7) 4.00
MAUCH, J M-The Greek & Roman Orders-Wash-1910-4to-cl-plts-
W B Olmsted, ed   (5t2)   7.50
MAUDE CAMERON & HER GUARDIAN-Lond-1903-2 vols-16mo-
pt mor-Golden Birch Hse   (5xx7)   25.00
MAUDSLAY, ROBT-Texas Sheepman-Austin-1951   (5a8, dj)   5.00
MAUDSLEY, HENRY-Body & Mind-NY-1871-Royal College of
Physicians-16 mo-wi appendix   (5t4)   7.50
MAUGE, GILBERT-The Unknown Quantity-Lond-n.d.-(c1930)-
lea-1st ed-ltd to 45c, autg   (5ss9)   15.00
MAUGHAN, ILA FISHER-Pioneer Theatre in the Desert-SaltLkCty-
1961-8vo-172p-cl-illus   (5h5, vf, dj)   8.00
MAUGHAM, W SOMERSET-Ashenden, or, The British Agent-Lond-
1928-1st ed   (5r9, f, dj)   15.00
--Books & You-NY-1940-107p (5d9, pres) 25. (5j4, dj)   5.00
--The Book Bag-Florence(Italy)-1932-port-orig bds-cl bk-1st ed-
ltd to 725c, autg (5m1, lacks fly) 15. (4b5, f, dj, unopnd) 45.00
--Cakes & Ale-Lond-(1930)-Heinemann-1st ed
(5yy6, f, dj, 5ss3, dj, sp stnd) 15. (5d8)   20.00
--same-Lond-(1954)-8vo-bds-calf sp-port-nbrd, autgs, box-
18th Birthday edition   (5ss7, mint)   85.00
--The Casuarina Tree, Six Stories-Lond-1926-8vo-cl-1st ed (5d8) 15.00
--Christmas Holiday-Lond-(1939)-8vo-cl-1st ed (5d8, dj rprd) 10.00
--same-NY-(1939)-314p-(1st ed)   (5t7)   7.50
--Creatures of Circumstance-Lond-(1947)-1st ed
(5d8, pres) 50.   (4a1)   7.50
--Don Fernando-Lond-1935-Wm Heinemann-1st ed, spec ed,
ltd to 175c, autg   (5hh1, vg)   60.00
--same-GardenCty-1935-8vo-cl-1st Amer ed   (5d8, pres)   37.50
--East of Suez-NY-1922-Doran-1st Amer ed   (5ss9)   10.00
--The Explorer-1922-(Heinemann)-4 Acts   (5qq7)   7.50
--France at War-Lond-(1940)-8vo-orig prntd wrps-1st ed
(5ee9, pres)   60.00
--The Gentleman in the Parlour-Lond-(1930)-8vo-cl-1st ed
(5d8, pres, dj)   50.00
--The Judgement Seat-Lond-1934-Centaur Pr-8vo-cl-1st ed-
ltd to 150c   (5d9, pres)   75.00
--Land of Promise-Lond-1922-cl-159p-1st ed (5mm0, sl spot) 10.00
--The Letter-Lond-(1927)-8vo-cl-1st ed
(5d9, pres) 75.   (5ss7, pres, sl fade)   75.00
--Liza of Lambeth-Lond-1897-Cr8vo-dec cl-1st ed
(5d3, vf) 150.   (5ss7, ex f) 225.00
--The Making of a Saint-Bost-(1922)-St. Botolph Soc-8vo-cl-
new ed (1st publ was 1898)   (5ee9, pres)   40.00
--Maughamiana-Lond-(1950)-8vo-cl   (5d5)   5.00
--The Moon & Sixpence-Lond-1919-12mo-cl-1st issue wi 2 lvs of ads-
1st ed-on wartime paper   (5dd8)   75.00
--same-Lond-1919- Heinemann-4th issue(wi 4p of ads)-orig green cl
(5tt2, wn)   20.00

MAUGHAM, W SOMERSET (continued)
--same-NY-(1919)-314p-tan cl   (5m1)   6.00
--The Narrow Corner-Lond-(1932)-8vo-cl-1st ed   (5d8)   7.50
--Of Human Bondage-Lond-(1915)-12mo-cl-1st Engl ed
                                        (4c2,shaken)   37.50
--same-Lond-(1915)-Cr8vo-cl-1st ed
   (5d9,pres,broke,sp tn) 175. (5v5,hng crack,box)125.
                                        (5ss7,mor box,vf) 285.00
--same-NY-(1915)-Geo H Doran-8vo-green cl blocked in g.-
   1st issue wi misprint li 4,pg 257 & on heavier papr than later
   issue-2 lbs,1-3/4 ozs-1st ed   (5d3,rub,spot)   100.00
--same-GardenCty-1936-buck-4to-684p-ltd   wi 2 autgs,
   box   (5p6,f)   60.00
--On a Chinese Screen-Lond-1922-sq8vo-cl-1st Engl ed (5d8) 10.00
--same-Lond-(1927)-Cr8vo-cl-Travellers' Libr ed
                        (5ss7,pres to Princess Louise)   60.00
--Orientations-Lond-1899-Unwin-8vo-smooth olive green cl,
   blocked in black & lack publisher's imprnt foot of sp,3rd bndg-
   1st ed   (5d3,ex-libr)   15.00
--same-Lond-1899-Unwin-1st ed,2nd issue (4b5,lacks fly,1p TLS) 50.00
--The Painted Veil-NY-(1925)   (5j3)   15 00
--Princess September & the Nightingale-NY-(1939)-R C Jones, illus
   1st ed   (4f6,vf,dj)   20.00
--Purely for My Pleasure-NY-1963-4to-1st Amer ed (5r9,box) 15.00
--The Sacred Flame,a Play-NY-1928-12mo-cl-papr labls-1st ed
                                        (5ss7,vf,rprd dj) 22.50
--Six Stories Written in the First Person Singular-Lond-(1931)-
   8vo-cl-1st Engl ed   (5d8)   10.00
--Strictly Personal-GardenCty-1941-DbldayDoran
   ltd to 575c,nbrd,autg   (4b5,mint,box)   50.00
--The Summing Up-NY-1938-8vo-cl-1st ed
                                        (5ee9,pres,shake,poor) 50.00
--Theatre,a Novel-Lond-(1937)-8vo-cl-1st Engl ed (5d8)   5.00
--Then & Now-Lond-(1946)-Heinemann-1st ed (4b5,vg,dj)   7.50
--A Writer's Notebook-Lond-(1949)-8vo-cl-vel bk-1st ed-
   nbrd,autg,box   (5ss7,mint)   80.00
--same-GardenCty-1949-Dblday-ltd to 1000c,nbrd,autg
                                        (4b5,f,wn box)   40.00
--same-Lond-(1949)-1st trade ed   (4b5)   8.50
MAULSBY, F R-Douglas,Ariz-(Douglas)-n.d.-(ca1913,14)-15p-
   photos-map-wrps-Douglas chamber of com-scarce (5t3)   12.50
--Tucson,Ariz-SanFran-n.d.-(1913)-15p-photos-wrps-Chamber of
   Comm   (5t3)   10.00
--The San Simon Valley,Ariz-San Simon-1912-San Simon Comm'l
   Club-illus   (5g5)   17.50
MAUMENE, E J-Traite Theorique & Pratique du Travail Des Vins-
   Paris-1890-2 vols-4to-hf calf-3rd ed,rev
                                        (5w1,hng broke,brown) 12.50
--same-Paris-1874-680p-illus-2nd ed,rev (5w1)   15.00
MAUND, BENJ-Botanic Garden....of Hardy Ornamental Flowering
   Plants,cultivated in Gr Britain-Lond- 1825(-1851)-19 vols-
   8vo-hf calf-hand col plts   (5z9)   950.00
MAUNDE, COL FRANCIS-5 Yrs in Madagascar wi Notes on
   Military Situation-Lond-(1895)-8vo-port-map (5ss5)   10.00
MAUNDEVILE, SIR JOHN-The Voiage & Travaile of-Lond-1883-
   8vo-cl-illus-326p   (5t2,chip)   7.00
--same-Lond-1887-Ashton,ed-8vo   (5m6)   10.00
MAUPASSANT, GUY DE-Contes Choisis-Paris-1905-Societe d'Editions
   Litteraires et Artistiques-24mo-375p-a.e.g.-ed pour la Jeunesse-
   mor   (5p1)   22.50
--Oeuvres Completes-Paris-1908 to 10-29 vols-part mor
                                        (5yy6,sl rub)   87.50
--A Woman's Life-Lond-1942-illus-Nonesuch Pr (5ii3)   15.00
--The Works of-NY-(1923)-10 vols-Thompson Barlow-Flaubert,ed-
   cl   (5p7)   15.00
MAURELLO, S RALPH-How to Do Pasteups & Mechanicals-NY-
   c1960-sm4to   (5w5,dj)   5.00
MAURER, CHAS L-Early Lutheran Education in Penna-Phila-(1932)-
   294p   (5m2)   10.00
MAURER, DAVID W-The Big Con,Story of Confidence Man &
   Confidence Game-(1940)-Bobbs-1st ed (5jj7,f)   12.50
MAURER, HERRYMON-The End is Not Yet,China at War-NY-
   c1941   (5x7)   5.00
MAURICE, ARTHUR BARTLETT-History of the 19th Century in
   Caricature-NY-1904-363p-illus   (5t7)   15.00
MAURICE, FREDK,ed-Aide de Camp of Lee-Bost-1927-Little,Brown-
   287p-illus-maps (5mm8,ex-libr) 10.   (4a7,wtrstnd)   12.50
--Robt E Lee the Soldier-Bost-(1925)-313p-maps(1 fldg)-frontis-
   port   (5mm8) 4. (5p9)   5.00
--Soldier,Artist,Sportsman-Bost-1928-illus (4a1)   7.50
--Statesmen & Soldiers of the Civil War-Bost-1926-Little,Brown-
   173p-plts -   (5mm8) 6.00 (5q8)   6.75

MAURICE, J F,ed-The Franco German War 1870,71 by Generals
   & Other Officers-Lond-(1899)-687p-maps-crushed lev mor-g.t.-
   illus-7-1/2 by 11 inches   (5d2)   25.00
MAURICEAU, DR A M-Married Woman's Private Medical Companion-
   NY-1854-228p-cl   (5y0)   7.50
MAURICEAU, FRANCOIS-Diseases of Women with Child-Lond-1727-
   8vo-calf-8 plts-H Chamberlen,transl (4b6)   200.00
MAUROIS, ANDRE-Byron-NY-1930-596p-illus (5m1) 5. (5p7)   4.75
--Eisenhower-Paris-(1946)-Artheme Fayard-8vo-80 pict bds-illus
                                        (5p1)   5.00
--The French Boy-NY-n.d.-photos-4to-(48p) (5p1,dj)   4.50
--Prophets & Poets-NY-1935-Harper   (5p9)   6.00
MAUROIS, GERALD-Cooking with a French Touch-Lond-(1952)-
   208p-text illus   (5g9)   5.00
MAURY, A F,ed-Intimate Virginiana-Richmond-1941-R8vo-illus-
   1st ed   (5x2,dj)   10.00
MAURY, DABNEY H-Recoll of a Virginian in the Mexican,Indian,
   & Civil Wars-NY-1894-279p (5zz9,rbnd) 15. (4j4)   27.50
MAURY, M F-Physical Geography of the Sea-NY-1857-8vo-cl-illus-
   13 fld plts-360p   (5t2,fray)   6.00
--Physical Survey of Virginia-Richmond-1868-90p-hf lea-labls-
   3 fldg maps-1st ed   (5m3)   25.00
--same-NY-1869-2nd ed-100p-orig prntd wrps-3 fldg maps-revised
                                        (5m3,wrp loose) 20.00
MAURY, M F, JR-Resources of coal field of Upper Kanawha with
   sketch of iron belt of Virginia...fldg section-Balti-1873-wrps
                                        (5g8)   7.50
MAURY, R-The Wars of the Godly-NY-1928-illus-1st ed (5x2) 15.00
MAURY, SARAH MYTTON-An Englishwoman in Amer-Lond-1848
                                        (5j2,libr stmp) 25.00
--Statesmen of American in 1846-Phila-1847-Carey&Hart-261p-
   bds   (5qq8,v chip)   6.00
MAUS, C P-Puerto Rico in Pictures & Poetry-Caldwell-1947-
   illus   (5m2)   3.50
MAUS, CYNTHIA P-Christ & the Fine Arts-NY-(1938)-illus (5ii3)10.00
MAUZY, J H-Historical Sketch of the 68 Regiment-Rushville,Ind-
   1887-ltd to 100c-rare   (4a9,pres,hng rprd) 75.00
MAVERICK, MARY A-Memoirs of Mary A Maverick-SanAnt-1921-
   136p-stiff wrps   (4a5,f) 30. (5g0,f,autg)   20.00
--same-SanAnt-1921-wrps-8vo-136p-illus-1st ed,1st issue
   (see Howes 443)   (5h5)   15.00
MAVERICK, MAURY-A Maverick American-NY-1937-362p (5n4)   5.00
--Old Villita-SanAnt-1939-Amer Guide Ser-folio-1st ed-wrps-
   scarce   (4a5)   25.00
MAVOR, WM-The British Nepos,Lives of Illustrious Britons-Lond-
   1816-12mo-458p-frontis-24 port-3 qtr calf-12th ed (5v0,rub) 22.50
--Catechism of Botany-Bost-1814-24mo-prntd wrps-67p (5a3,fox) 20.00
--Catechism of History of England-Lackington-1816-12mo-wrps-
   72p-new & enlgd ed   (5s0) 5. (5a1)   4.50
--English Spelling Book,accompanied by Progressive Series of Easy
   & familiar Lessons-Lond-1806-R Phillips-T Bewick,illus-
   (pref "Woodstock,Feb 12,1806")-lg12mo-162p wi ads-roan
                                        (5c8,sp def)   45.00
--English Spelling Bk-Lond-Routledge-1885-108p-16mo-
   Greenaway,illus (5i1,loose,cov wn) 12.50 (5v0,rub,vg) 27.50
--History of Discovery & Settlement,to present time of No & SoAmer,
   & of West Indies-1810-buck-new ed   (5L7,rbnd,fox)   12.50
--History of Greece-Lond-1811,1812-2 vols-calf-frontis ea vol
                                        (4F6,hng crack)   10.00
MAWE, JOHN-The Linnaean System of Conchology-Lond-1823-
   col frontis-36 hand col plts-8vo-bds-1st ed (5z9,rebnd,f) 67.50
--Travels in Interior of Brazil wi notices on its Climate,Agriculture
   ...& Particular Account of Gold & Diamond Districts etc-Lond-
   1823-lg8vo-orig lea&bds-25 col plts-map-493p (5t2,wn) 85.00
MAWSON, SIR DOUGLAS-The Home of the Blizzard-Lond-(1938)-
   348p-maps-16mo-abridgd ed   (5ss1)   4.00
MAWSON, THOS A-Art & Craft of Garden Making-Lond-(1912)-
   illus-4to-cl-4th ed   (5z9)   35.00
--Life & Work of an English Landscape Artist-Lond-(1927)-4to-
   368p-28 plts-port frontis   (5w3)   12.50
MAXEY, CHESTER C-County Administration-NY-1919-illus
                                        (5r7,sp wn)   10.00
--Outline of Municipal Govt-NY-1925-Dblday Page-388p (5p7) 3.50
MAXFIELD, ALBERT-Roster & Statistical Record of Company D of
   11th Reg Maine Inf Vol-NY-1890-wrps-83p (4j4,vf)   9.50
MAXIM, SIR HIRAM S-Artificial & Natural Flight-Lond-1909-
   Whittaker-176p-95 illus-2nd ed   (5p0)   12.50
MAXIM, HUDSON-Chronology of Aviation-NY-1912-23p-reprnt-
   orig wrps   (4j3)   10.00
--Defenseless America-NY-(1915)-318p-port (5t7)   10.00
--same-NY-(1915)-Hearst's Intl-Amer Library ed (5r0,pres) 7.50
--Leading Opinions both for & Against Nat'l Defense-Hudson Maxim-
   (1916)-wrps   (5q0,sl fox)   5.00

USED BOOK PRICE GUIDE

MAXIM, HUDSON (continued)
--Remin & Comments as Reported by Clifton Johnson-NY-1924-
Dblday, Page-350p-map-illus (5r0,pres) 10.00
MAXIMILLAN, PRINZ ZU WIED-Reise in Das innere Nord America-
in Jahren 1832 biz 1834-Coblenz-1839, 1841-J Hoelscher-
4 vols-hf calf-48 plts (5tt0) 4,000.00
MAXIMILIAN ZU WIED NEUWIED, PRINCE-Reise in das Innere
Nord America-Coblenz(plts also Paris & Lond)-J Hoelscher-
1839, 41-2 vols-woodcuts-plan-table-map-2 atlases of 81
hand col plts by Bodmer-lg th4to-hf calf-1st German ed-
lg paper ed-Howes M443a (5hh0, lacks key plt,rbkd) 17,500.00
MAXIMOFF, G P-The Guillotine At Work-Chig-1940-illus-scarce
(5yy6) 10.00
MAXSE, F I-Seymour Vandeleur-Lond-1906-Heinemann-288p-
maps(7 fldg)-photos-pict cov (4t5, cov soil) 20.00
MAXWELL BRISCOE MOTOR CO-How to Judge an Automobile-
Tarrytown-190-?-fldg bds-28p (5hh6, sl stn) 8.75
MAXWELL, DONALD-Log of the Griffin-Lond-1905-16 col illus
(5c1) 15.00
MAXWELL, ELSA-How to Do It or The Lively Art of Entertaining-
Bost-(1957)-275p-photos-1st ed (5c9) 5.00
MAXWELL, HELEN B-The Way of Fire-NY-1897-Dodd, Mead-
244p-1st ed (5x4) 5.00
MAXWELL, HERBERT-Scottish Gardens-Lond-1908-32 col plts-
sm4to-part mor-ltd to 250c (5z9, rub, f bndg) 20.00
MAXWELL HISTORY & GENEALOGY-1916-642p-by F Houston et al-
v scarce (5mm3) 65.00
MAXWELL HOUSE COFFEE COOKBOOK-Lond-(1965)-274p
(5g9) 4.00
MAXWELL, HU-History of Tucker Co, W Virg-Kingwood-1884-575p-
cl (5jj9) 50.00
--Wood Using Industries of Maryland-Balt-1910-58p-fldg bds(5b8) 4.50
MAXWELL, HUGH-Trial of Jacob Barker etc-NY-1827-Coke Law Pr-
332p-hf calf (5tt8) 15.00
MAXWELL, SISTER MARY URSULA-Leadership of Mother Agatha
Reynolds, Ursuline of Roman Union-(SanFran,1941)-cl-
276p plus 12p (5r0) 7.50
MAXWELL, N-The Power of Negro Action-Lond-1965-59p-wrps
(5x2) 7.50
MAXWELL, W H-History of the Irish Rebellion in 1798-Lond-1886-
illus by Geo Cruikshank (5j2) 15.00
MAXWELL, WILL J-Greek Letter Men of the Pacific Coast &
Rocky Mntn States-NY-1903-696p-photos (5s4, wn, rprd) 7.50
MAXWELL, WM-The Dun Emer Press 1903 to 1907, Cuala Pr,
1908 to (1932)-priv prntd 1932-8vo-68p-cream bds
(5d3, sp broke) 100.00
MAXWELL, WM AUDLEY-Crossing the Plains, Days of '57-n.p.-
n.d.-(SanFran, 1915)-179p-illus-wrps (5g2) 10. (5t3) 7.50
MAXWELL, WRIGHT & CO-Commercial Formalities of Rio de
Janeiro-Balt-1830-Benj Edes-79p-wrps (5d6) 20.00
MAY, ARTHUR S-Marriage a la Mode-Lond-(1925)-Castle-320p
(5p9) 7.50
MAY, CAROLINE-Amer Female Poets-Phila-1848-1st ed (5mm1) 15.00
MAY, CLIFF-Western Ranch Houses-Sunset Lane-1947-plans-160p-
drawings-4to (5ww3) 10.00
MAY, EARL C-Canning Clan-NY-1937-487p-illus (5a9) 4.50
--Principio to Wheeling 1715 to 1945-NY, (1945)-illus-335p (4h8) 12.50
--The Prudential-GardenCty-372p-illus (5w4) 4.50 (5y2) 4.75
--2000 Miles Through Chile-NY-(c1924)-Century-fldg map-illus-
pic cl (4a3, insect dmgd) 5.00
MAY, EMILY J-Louis' School Days-Bath, Binns & Goodwin-(c1851)-
sm8vo-345p-dec cl-g.-illus-3rd ed (5aa0,bkstrp rprd) 6.50
MAY, F E-Yachting in Hong Kong-Hong Kon-n.d.-(preface 1905)-
134p-photos-maps (5s1, sl wn) 5.00
MAY, FLORENCE L-Hispanic Lace & Lace Making-NY-1939-4to-
map in cov-illus-417p (5n7) 14.50
MAY, GEO W-History of Massac Co, Illinois-Galesburg-(1955)-
232p-cl (5jj9) 7.50
MAY HOSIERY MILLS-The Story of Hosiery-Burlington-(193-?)-
fldg bds-101p, (3)-illus (5hh6) 10.00
MAY, J J-Nicholas Danforth of Framlingham, Eng & Cambridge, N.E.-
1902-476p (5mm3) 55.00
MAY, J LEWIS-Geo Eliot-(1930)-The Bobbs Mer (5p9) 5.00
MAY, JAS LEWIS-Anatole France-NY-(1924)-273p-illus (5t4) 5.00
MAY, JOHN B-Hawks of North Amer-NY-1935-orig ed-172p-
41 plts(37 col)-33 maps-cl (5cc1, vg) 22.50
MAY, JOHN RICHARD-Edw Howe Forbush, Friend of the Birds-
Bost-1929-32p-frontis-wrps (5w0, autg) 3.50
MAY, LIOY-Misplaced Glory-Phila-(1944)-353p-illus-
maps(incl fldg) (5w0, pres) 25.00
MAY, S-The Fugitive Slave Law & Its Victims-NY-1861-Amer
Anti Slavery Soc-168p-wrps-Anti-Slavery Tract #15 (5x2) 35.00

MAY, S J-Some Recoll of our Anti Slavery Conflict-Bost-1869
(5x2) 27.50
MAY, SAM'L J-The rights & condition of women-Syracuse-
(ca1846)-wrps (5g8, pres) 10.00
MAY, SOPHIE-Little Grandmother, Little Grandfather, Miss
Thistledown-Bost-1875-3 vols-16mo-green cl-frontis-
Lee&Shepard-#4, 5, & 6 of "Little Prudy's Flyaway Series."
(5j5) 10.00
MAY, STELLA BURKE-The Conqueror's Lady, Ines Suarez-NY-(1930)-
8vo-cl-1st ed (5h4) 4.00
MAY, THOS P-A Prince of Breffny-Phila-(1881)-1st ed (5mm2) 10.00
MAY, WM S-Never again-NY-1873-Putnam-advts dated Sept '72-
wdcuts (5m2) 6.50
MAYALL & MAYALL-Sundials-Bost-1938-illus-8vo-197p-1st ed
(5bb0) 9.50
MAYDON, MAJ H C-Big Game of Agrica-NY-1935-12mo-254p
(4a6) 6.00
--Big Game Shooting in Africa-Lond-1932-Vol 14 of Lansdale Library-
8vo-445p-photos (4a6, frontis loose) 15.00
MAYER, AUGUST L-Alt Spanien-Munich-1921-4to-176p-310 plts-
German text (5xx7) 15.00
MAYER, BRANTZ-Adventures of African Slaver-NY-(1928)-376p-
illus (5s1, pres) 5.00
--Capt Canot;or 20 Yrs of an African Slaver-NY-1854-Appleton-
448p plus ads-sm8vo-orig cl-1st ed (5x5, wn) 20. (5x2) 40.00
--same-NY-1855-448p-illus-plts (5L3, sp ragged) 8.50
--Mexico As It Was & As It Is-NY, Lond&Paris-1844-illus-8vo-cl
(5x5, wn, loose) 20. (4m2, shelf nbr, 4a3, stnd, ex-librr) 15.00
--Mexico;Aztec, Spanish & Republican-Hartford-1851-2 vols in 1-
illus-tooled lea (5t4, hng weak) 10.50
--same-Hartford-1852-2 vol-433, 398p-illus (5g1, sp torn) 12.50
--Tah Gah Jute-Albany-1867-mor & bds-820p, 204p-errata slip
tip in-Joel Munsell (5t4) 50.00
MAYER, E H-Our Negro Brother-NY-1945-juvenile (5x2, dj, mint) 2.00
MAYER, FRANK-The Buffalo Harvest-(Denver, 1958)-96p-illus-
ports-1st ed (5dd4) 5.00
MAYER, FRANK BLACKWELL-With Pen & Pencil on the Frontier
in 1851-StPaul-1932-illus-214p (4b3) 15.00
MAYER, GRACE M-Once Upon a City-NY-1958-Macm-4to-
511p-photos (5x0) 15. (5p5) 13.50
MAYER, J-Never To Die-NY-1938-illus-224p-8vo (5ww3) 12.50
MAYER, LOUIS-Vues en Egypte-Lond-1802-Bensley-lg folio-calf-
48 col plts-1st French ed-109p plus 1 lf (4e1, f) 480.00
MAYER OAKES, WM J-Prehistory of Upper Ohio Valley-Pitts-
1955-Carnegie Mus Annals, Anthro, Ser #2-290p-120 plts-
30 maps-1st ed (4t3, autg, dj) 20.00
MAYES, EDW-Gen of La mar Family-1935-74p-wrps (5t9) 7.00
MAYET, CHAS-Le Vin De France-Paris-n.d.-302p-3 maps-wrps
(5w1, pres, sp broke) 10.50
MAYET, VALERY-Les Insectes de la Vigne-Montpelier-1890-
5 plts(4 col)-470p(2)-wrps (5w1) 8.50
MAYFIELD, EUGENE O-Fairy Tales of the Western Range & Other
Tales-Lincoln-(1902) (5s4, ex-librr) 4.50
MAYFIELD, FRANK M-The Department Store Story-NY-(1949)-
260p-illus (5y2) 6.00
MAYFIELD, JOHN S-Mark Twain vs the Street Railway Co-1926-
priv prntd-25p-24ps-photo (5yy7) 3.00
--Sam Houston, Fugitive From Justice-(Austin)-1927-prntd by
Edwin W Numbers-ltd to 50c (5z7, vf) 75.00
--Sidney Lanier in Texas-Dallas-1932-Boyd Pr-limp bds-ltd to 119c
(5z7, vf) 65.00
MAYHEW BROS-Acting Charades, or Deeds Not Words-Lond-
D Bogue-(c1850)-smsq8vo-135p-hand col frontis-dec cl-a.e.g.-
1st ed (5a1) 12.50
MAYHEW, EDW-The Illustrated Horse Doctor-Phila-1868-522p-
illus-cl (5t0, fray) 7.50
MAYHEW, HENRY-Image of his Father-Bohn-1851-illus-1st ed
(5tt5, shaken) 15.00
--London Labour & the London Poor-Lond-1861&62-Griffin, Bohn-
4 vols-8vo-illus-hf mor-1st ed (5zz7, rub) 125.00
--The Mormons, or Latter Day Saints-Lond-1852-illus-320p-3rd ed
(4t3) 12.50
--The Wonders of Science-NY-1856-Harper-24mo-452p-cl-
frontis-7p illus-1st Amer ed (5p1, marg wtrstnd) 35.00
MAYHEW, IRA-Statutes of the State of Michigan, relating to
primary schools-Detroit-1847-wrps (5g3) 15.00
MAYHEW, RALPH-The Bubble Book-n.p.-(1919)-Harper-16mo-
14p-envelopes for 3 records-#1 of Harper Columbia Book That
Sings-pict bds (5p1) 15.00
MAYHILL, R THOS-Index & Abstract of Deeds of Lancaster Co, Pa,
Deed Books "A Through "K""(1729 to 1766)-159p (5m2) 10.00
MAYLARD, C G-A Glossary of Terms Used in Grecian, Roman &
Italian & Gothic Architecture-Oxf-1845-3 vols-mor &bds-illus-
4th ed (5j3, sl wn) 15.00

MAYNARD, ALICE-What to Knit & Crochet & How To Do It-NY-
n.d.-Lion Yarns-107p-photos-   (5n7)   2.00
MAYNARD, CHAS J-Manual of NoAmer Butterflies-Bost-1891-226p-
illus-10 hand col plts   (5w4)   17.50
MAYNARD, HORACE-Speech of Hon..of Tennessee On Negro
Enlistment Bill, Jan 31, 1863-ca1863-16p-wrps   (5x2)   65.00
MAYNARD, MILA T-Walt Whitman, the poet of wider selfhood-
Chig-1903-145p-cl & bds-1st ed-scarce   (5p6)   12.00
MAYNARD, MRS NETTIE COLBURN-Was Abraham Lincoln A
Spiritualist?-Phila-1891-264p-illus-1st ed (5a0, f) 10. (5w5)   9.00
MAYNARD, SAM'L T-Landscape Gardening as Applied to Home
Decoration-NY-1899-338p-illus-1st ed   (5s7, libr stmp)   4.50
MAYNARD, T-Story of Amer Catholicism-1943   (5L7)   6.00
MAYNARD, THEODORE-Orestes Brownson, Yankee, Radical,
Catholic-NY-(1943)-frontis-459p   (5t4)   7.50
--A Tankard Of Ale-NY-(1920)-205p   (5w1)   12.50
MAYNE, ETHEL-Life & Letters of Anne Isabella, Lady Noel Byron-
NY-1929-518p-illus   (5m1)   7.50
MAYNIAL, EDOUARD-Casanova & His Time-Lond-1911-illus-
E C Mayne, tr   (5mm1)   7.50
MAYO, A D-Symbols of Capital-1859-368p   (5FF2)   25.00
MAYO, BERNARD-Henry Clay-Bost-1937-HMifflin-570p-illus
(5p9) 7.50   (5yy0)   10.00
MAYO, REV E D-Southern Women in Recent Educational Movement
in South-Wash-1892-wrps   (5q8, sl fray) 7.50
MAYO, HERBERT-On Truths contained in Popular Superstitions wi
an acct of Mesmerism-Edinb-1851-248p plus 32p bk catalog
(5w0, sl wn)   7.50
MAYO, KATHERINE-Justice to All-1917-plts-2nd ed (5L7)   4.00
--The Standard Bearers-Bost-1918-324p-illus   (5w4)   6.50
MAYO, ROBT-Army & Navy Pension Laws & Bounty Land Laws of US-
Wash-1852-754p-calf-12p index   (5i3, hng cracked) 15.00
MAYO, DR ROBT-Political Sketches of Eight Years in Washington-
Balt-1839-216p-papr labl-Part 1(all publ)-1st ed
(5L3, 5m6, fade) 25.   (4h8)   22.50
MAYO, WM S-Never Again-NY-1873-1st ed   (5ee3)   5.00
--Romance dust from historic placer-NY-1851-Putnam-1st ed
(5m2, sl wn)   6.50
MAYORGA, MARGARET, ed-Short Plays of Tennessee Williams
1955 to 1956-Bost-(1956)-cl-12mo-1st ed   (5ss7, f, dj) 15.00
MAYS, GEO-The Jewish Colonists at Tower Hill, Schaefferstown,
Lebanon Co, Pa-Phila-1905-20p-orig wrps   (5m2)   4.00
MAZAMORRERO, UN LIMENO-Manual De Cocina Criolla-Lima-
n.d.-32p-pamphlet-12mo-Almuerzo   (5c5, brown)   10.00
MAZE, COLEMAN L, ed-Office Management, a Handbook-NY-
1947-Ronald Pr-870p   6.00
MAZO, EARL-Richard Nixon-NY-(1959)-309p   (4b3, f, dj)   5.00
MAZRO, MRS SOPHIA-Turkish Barbarity-   Prov-(1828)-12mo-
orig wrps-38p-fldg frontis-1st Amer ed (5m6, lacks bkstrp) 15.00
MAZUR, PAUL M-Amer Prosperity, its Causes & Consequences-NY-
1928-268p   (5w5)   5.00
MAZZA, IRMA G-Accent on Seasoning-Bost-(1957)-305p-1st ed
(5c9) 4.   (5c5)   4.50
--Herbs for the Kitchen-Bost-(1939)-orig ed-312p (5w3)   3.00
MAZZANOVICH, ANTON-Trailing Geronimo-Hollywd-1931-
12mo-cl-322p-3rd ed   (5h4) 8. (5yy7,5a9)   10.00
MBOYA, T-Freedom & After-Bost-1963-illus   (5x2, dj) 5.00
MEACHAM, A B-Wi ne ma(The Woman Chief) & her People-Hartf-
1876-illus-168p-1st ed (4t3, wn) 15. (5t4, pres) 10. (5L0, vf) 17.50
--Wigwam & Warpath-Bost-1875-700p-illus-calf   (5t4)   15.00
--same-Bost-1875-John P Dale-701p-illus-cl-2nd & rev ed
(5t0) 20. (5yy7, pt lea, rub) 15.00
MEACHAM, WALTER-Bonneville the Bold-Portland, Ore-1934-
47p-frontis-fldg map-wrps-1st ed   (5t3)   3.00
MEAD, DANIEL M-History of Greenwich, Fairfield Co, Conn-NY-
1857-318p   (5w4, fade) 22.50 (5e8, 5ii8)   27.50
MEAD, EDW C-Historic Homes of the SoWest Mtns Virg-Phila-
1899-illus-275p-1st ed-ltd to 750c   (4m2)   35.00
MEAD, ELWOOD-Report of Irrigations in Calif-Wash-1901-GPO-
4to-maps-photos   (5x5)   20.00
--Report of irrigation investigations in Utah-Wash-1903-GPO-
Bull #124-US Dept of Agri-330p-map-illus   (5u3)   9.00
MEAD, FRANKLIN B-Heroic Statues in Bronze of Abraham Lincoln-
FtWayne-1932-qtr cl-col frontis-4to-illus   (5r7)   10.00
MEAD, FREDK S, ed-Harvard's Military Record in the World War-
Bost-1921-Harvard Alumni Assoc-1142p-cl (5mm8) 4. (5w0)   8.50
MEAD, CMDR HILARY P-Sea Flags: Their Gen'l Use-Glasgow-(1938)-
12mo-cl-112p-col frontis-illus   (5t0, dj, f)   4.00
MEAD, HOMER-8th Iowa Cavalry in Civil War-Carthaga-(1927)-
118(20)p-wrps   (4t3)   25.00
MEAD, LEON-The bow legged ghost & other stories-NY-Werner-
(1899)-pict cl-port-1st ed   (5m2)   10.00

MEAD, MARGARET-An Anthropologist at Work-Bost-(1959)-583p-
illus   (5c3)   4.00
--Changing Culture of an Indian Tribe-NY-1932-304p plus index-
1st ed   (5L0)   12.50
--Coming of Age in Samoa-NY-1928-8vo-297p-photos-1st ed
(4a6, fade)   10.00
MEAD, PETER B-An Elementary Treatise on Amer Grape Culture &
wine making-NY-1867-483p-illus (5w1) 15.   (4g9, rprd) 18.50
MEAD, RICHARD-A Mechanical Account of Poisons, in Several Essays-
Lond-1747-320p-calf-4th ed corr   (5w3, plt tn, wn) 35.00
MEAD, WM E-Grand Tour in 18th Century-Bost-1913-480p-plts
(5aa0)   12.50
MEADE, BISHOP-Old Churches, Ministers & Families of Virginia-
Phila-1857-orig cl-illus-2 vols   (5ii8)   40.00
--same-1872-2 vols   (5mm3)   40.00
MEADE, C F-Approach to the Hills-NY-(1940)-Dutton-265p-cl-
illus   (5d7)   10.00
MEADE, GEO-The Life & Letters of Geo Gordon Meade, Maj Gen
US Army-NY-1913-2 vols-frontis-31 fldg maps-1st ed
(5ee3, f, autg of editor) 17.50
MEADE, GEO G-With Meade at Gettysburg-Phila-1930-illus-maps
(5m2)   6.50
MEADE'S, MAJ GEN (GEO GORDON)-Report of Military operations
& admin of civil affairs in 3rd Military District & Dept of South
for...1868 with doc-Atlanta-1868-prntd wrps   (5g3)   10.00
MEADE, MARTHA-Foreign Foods & Flavors-n.p.-n.d.-(ca193?)-
32p-wrps   (5g9)   2.00
MEADE, REBECCA PAULDING-Life of Hiram Paulding Rear Adm,
USN-NY-1910-Baker & Taylor-321p-plts   (5mm8)   7.50
MEADE, ROBT DOUTHAT-Judah P Benjamin, Conf Statesman-NY-
1943-8vo-432p   (4a7, lacks fly) 10.00
MEADER, J W-The Merrimack River-Bost-1869-fldg map-1st ed-
cr 8vo-307p-cl (5L3) 20. (5u9, map tn) 22.50 (5ii8)   25.00
MEADER, S W-Traplines North-n.d.-285p-illus   (4b9)   10.00
MEADOWS, CECIL A-Trade signs & their origin-Lond-(1957)-
Routledge-illus-1st prntng   (5m2)   7.50
MEADOWS, MRS F L S-Desc of Reade of Reed-1937-225p, 59p
(5t9)   15.00
MEADOWS, KENNY-Heads of People-Lond-n.d.-(19th cent)-plts-
2 vols-3/4 calf   (5j2)   15.00
MEADOWS, LINDON-Dame Perkins & Her Grey Mare-Lond-
1866-Sampson Low & Marston-col illus by Phiz-frontis & 7 plts-
pict cl-a.e.g.-(48p)-1st ed   (5p1)   25.00
MEADOWS, ROBT, comp-Private Anthropological Cabinet of 500
Authentic Racial Esoteric Photos & Illus-NY-c1934-priv issued-
ltd to 1500c, nbrd   (5w5)   25.00
MEADS, FRANK-They Meet at Eleven-Lond-(1956)-photos-folio-
illus   (5t7)   7.50
MEAGHER, GEO A-Guide to Artistic Skating-Lond-1919-167p-
plts   (5a1)   5.00
MEAKIN, JOHN PHILLIPS-Leaves of Truth, Utah & the Mormons-
SaltLkCty-1909-12mo-282p-plts   (5dd4)   7.25
MEANS, DAVID C-The Lincoln Papers-GardenCty-1948-2 vols
(5w0, dj, box) 14.50
MEANS, E K-Black Fortune-NY-1931   (5x2)   10.00
--E K Means(Negro Stories)-NY-1918-illus-1st ed (5x2)   15.00
--Further E K Means (Negro Stories)-NY-1921-illus-1st ed (5x2) 15.00
--More E K Means (Negro stories)-NY-1919-1st ed-illus (5x2) 15.00
MEANS, GASTON B-Strange Death of President Harding-NY-1930
(5x7)   3.75
MEANS, J H-Dorchester Past & Present, Sermon-1870-28p-wrps
(5t9)   2.50
MEANS, JAS-The James Means Control For Flying Machines-Bost-
1913-sm12mo-10p-illus-wrps-1st ed   (4F7, mint) 20.00
--Manflight-Bost-1891-wrps-29p-2 diagrams-8vo-1st ed
(4F7, mint) 50.   (5a3, f) 65.00
--The Problem of Manflight-Bost-1894-wrps-8vo-20p (5a3, f) 65.00
MEANS, P A-Racial Factors in Democracy-Bost-1919 (5x2, dj) 15.00
MEANS, PHILIP A-Fall of Inca Empire & Spanish Rule in Peru,
1530 to 1780-1932-Scribner's Sons-1st ed   (5x5)   15.00
--History of Spanish Conquest of Yucatan & of Itzas-Cambr-1917-
206p-plts-maps-errata slip   (5t3, 4k4) 12.50
--Newport Tower-NY-c1942-344p-illus-scarce (5r7) 7.50 (5h9) 15.00
--Peruvian Textiles-NY-1930-4to-cl-27p-24 photos
(5t7) 10.   (5F5, f) 12.50
--The Spanish Main-NY-1935-8vo-cl   (4c1)   7.50
MEANS, WM GORDON-My Guns-Dedham-1941-178p-illus (5t7) 10.00
MEANY, EDMOND S-Lincoln Esteemed Washington-Seattle-1933-
12mo-bds-57p-port-Dogwood Pr, Seattle-wide margin (5t7)   5.00
--History of State of Wash-NY-1924-412p-maps-ports
(5s4, ex-libr)   7.50
--Mt Rainier-NY-1916-plts-325p (5s6, autg) 15. (5d7, 5u6) 10.00

MEANY, EDMOND S (continued)
--Vancouver's Discovery of Puget Sound-NY-1907-ports-plts-
344p-maps-1st ed   (4b6,sl wn) 12.50   (5zz8,5s6,4e6)   20.00
--same-NY-1915-MacM-cl-17p&344p-reprnt   (5r0,autg)   10.00
--same-Portland-1942-344p-cl-ports   (5h2,f,5jj9,f)   7.50
MEARES, JOHN-Voyages Made In Years 1788 & 1789 From China
To NW Coast of Amer-Lond-1790-plts-maps-plans-4to
(4b1,rbnd,rprd) 450. (5ss2) 600. (4e1,f) 750. (5e2)   675.00
--Voyages de la Chine a la cote Nord Ouest d'Amer dans les
annees 1788 et 1789-Paris-1794-plts-maps-3 vols plus sml
folio atlas-Sabin 47262
(5t4, lacks vol of maps) 65. (4e1,vf) 350. (5e2)   225.00
MEARNS, DAVID C-The Lincoln Papers-GardenCty-1948-
2 vols-ports-slip case   (5w4,5yy8,5t4,4h2)   10.00
MEARNS, E A-Mammals of the Mexican Boundary of the US-
Wash-1907-wrps-530p-13 plts(incl 2 fldg maps)-Part 1(all publ)
(4p5)   12.75
MEARNS, HUGH, ed-Nathalia Crane-NY-c1926-Simon&Schuster-
8vo-(32)p incl wrps-stapld   (5p1, wrp tn)   3.50
MEARS, ANNE DE B-Old York Road & its Early Assoc of History
& Biography-Phila-1890-illus-map-4to-ex scarce   (4m2)   30.00
MEARS, ELIOT GRINNEL-Maritime Trade of Western US-Stanford U-
(1935)-538p   (5h4,dj) 8. (5s1,dj,f)   9.00
--Resident Orientals on the Amer Pacific Coast-Chig-(1928)-
12mo-cl-1st ed   (5t0)   4.50
MEARS, NEAL F-Hist of Heverly Family-1945-340p-illus (5t9)   17.50
MEASE, JAS, ed-Archives of Useful Knowledge-Phila-
July 1810 to April 1813-3 vols-12 numbers (all publ)-calf
& bds-8 plts (of 9?)   (5m3, lacks t.p. Vol 2, wn, ex-libr)   60.00
--The Picture of Philadelphia-Phila-1811-Kite-8vo-sheep-
fldg frontis-1st ed-376p
(5m3,crack) 25. (5n2,box) 75. (5kk8,hng weak)   35.00
MEAT & MEAT COOKERY-Chig-1942-Nat'l Live Stock & Meat
Board Comm-254p-wrps   (5c5)   2.50
MECHANICS FOR YOUNG AMERICA-Chig-c1905-8vo-96p-
wrps-reprntd from Popular Mechanics   (5p1)   7.50
MECHANICS' INSTITUTE OF CITY OF SAN FRAN-Report of 15th
Industrial Exhibition of-SanFran-1880-148p-orig wrps (5b8)   12.50
MECHANICS OF THE SEWING MACHINES-Monograph 5, Pratt
Inst-NY-1914-illus   (5e4)   8.50
MECHEM, KIRKE, ed-Annals of Kansas, 1886 to 1925-Topeka-
1954 & 1956-2 vols   (4i2)   20.00
--John Brown, a Play-Manhattan, Kans-1939-113p-1st ed
(5k2,autg)   4.00
--Mythical Jayhawk-16p-orig dec wrps   (5kk7)   3.00
MECKLIN, J M-Democracy & Race Friction-NY-1921 (5x2)   8.50
--The Ku Klux Klan:A Study of the Amer Mind-NY-1924-1st ed
(5x2,dj)   35.00
MECKLENBURG, GEO-Last of the Old West-Wash-(1927)-1st ed-
illus-149p   (5s4) 7. (5i3,dj,f)   8.50
MECQUIER, MARY JANE-Apron Full of Gold, letters of, from
SanFran, 1849 to 56-San Marino-1949-Huntington Lib -
Cleland, ed-99p-illus-1st ed   (4n1,dj)   12.50
MED ORNEN MOT POLEN-Stockholm-(1930)-488p-illus-maps-
hf calf   (5ss1)   12.50
MEDALL, THE-A Satyre against Sedition-By author of Absalom
& Achitophel-Lond-1682-20p   (5m4)   30.00
MEDALLION PAPERS,#38-Excavations at Snaketown 4-Reviews-
priv prntd for Gila Pueblo-Globe-1948   (5g5)   15.00
MEDBERRY, JAS K-Men & Mysteries of Wall Street-Bost-1870-
344p-cl   (5jj9,fade,5ss5,ex-libr)   10.00
MEDFORD, ROGUE RIVER VALLEY, SOUTHERN OREG-(Portland,
1912)-So Pac & Medford Comm Club-47p-photos-maps-wrps (5L0) 5.00
MEDICAL & AGRICULTURAL REGISTER-for Years 1806&1807(all pub)-
Bost-378p(2)-24 issues-calf bk   (5w3,scuff)   42.50
MEDICAL & SURGICAL HIST OF WAR OF REBELLION-Wash-1879-
Vol 1, Part 2, Medical History-2nd issue-folio-col plts
(5b1,shake)   35.00
MEDICAL CLINICS OF NO AMER-Jan 1957 thru Nov 1962-
6 vols-36 issues-illus-bl bnd   (5m2)   54.00
MEDICAL REPOSITORY-for Feb to April, 1805-(NY,1805)-8vo-
wrps   (5r7)   8.50
MEDICAL TRIAL TECHNIQUE QUARTERLY-(1954 to 69)-Vol 1 to
15-with index 1955 to 59-unbnd   (5rr4)   135.00
MEDICI SOCIETY BOOK-Forty Nine Poems-Lond-1928-Medici Soc-
8vo-cl-58p-1st ed   (5p6)   8.00
MEDICINE & ITS DEVELOPMENT IN KY-Louisville-1940-WPA-
illus-373p   (4p8)   15.00
MEDICUS-Twelve Days in the Saddle-Bost-1884-12mo-73p-
orig wrps-1st ed   (5m6)   10.00
MEDIEVAL FRENCH ROMAN D'ALEXANDRE-Princeton-1937-
2 vols-lg8vo-cl   (5t0)   25.00

MEDINA, JOSE TORIBIO-Discovery of the Amazon-NY-1934-
illus-Amer Geog Soc,#17-cl-4to   (5yy6) 7.50 (5h4)   17.50
--Ensayo Bio Bibliografico Sobre Hernan Cortes-Obra Postuma-
Santiago de Chile-1952-243p-4to-wrps-frontis (5r7,unopnd)   17.50
--Historia del Tribunal de la Inquisicion de Lima-Santiago-1956-
2 vols-4to-wrps   (5r7,unopnd)   30.00
MEDWIN, THOS-Conversations of Lord Byron: Noted during Residence
at Pisa...1821 & 1822-Lond-1824   (5mm1,rbnd)   20.00
--same-Lond-1824-Colburn-hf calf-new edition-fldg fac
(5i8, lacks hf t.)   10.00
MEECH, W W-Quince Culture-NY-1908-180p-illus   (5s7)   3.00
MEEHAN, THOS-Native Flowers & Ferns of US etc-Bost-
(1878 to 80)-192 plts-4 vols-orig cl-g.e.-1st & 2nd Series-
1st ed   (5z9, sp fade)   45.00
--same-Bost-1879-illus-2 vols-4to-col plts-a.e.g.   (5i8)   30.00
MEEHAN'S MONTHLY-Magazine of Horticulture etc-Vols 1 to 12
(all publ)-Germantown, Pa-1891 to 1902-138 col plts-lg8vo-cl-
g.e.-12 vols in 11-scarce   (5z9, vf)   40.00
MEEK, ALEX-The Red Eagle-NY-1855-108p-1st ed   (5m1)   13.50
MEEK, STEPHEN HALL-Autobiography of a Mountain Man, 1805 to
1889-Pasadena-1948-Dawson-23p   (4n1, fade)   7.00
MEEKER, EZRA-The Busy Life of 85 Years-Seattle-(1916)
(5w9, pres) 12.50 (5x5)   8.50
--Kate Mulhall, a Romance of the Oregon Trail-NY-1926-12mo-
287p-cl-map-illus   (5m8, dj, autg, 5s4, autg)   6.00
--Pioneer Reminiscences of Puget Sound-Seattle-1905-554p-photos-
(5s4, pres, rprd)   37.50
--70 Years of Progress in Washington-Seattle-1921-cl-383p plus
bnd in "Washington Terr West of Cascade Mtns etc" (brittle &
brown)   (5s4, hng rprd)   17.50
--Uncle Ezra's Short Stories for Children-Tacoma-n.d.-24mo-
100p-cl-prntd by D W Cooper   (5p1)   10.00
--Wash Territory West of the Cascade Mtns, Containing Descrip of
Puget Sound & Rivers Emptying into It-Olympia-1870-8vo-
orig prntd wrps-52p, 13, (1)-prntd at Transcript Ofc
(5a3, libr release stmp)   150.00
MEEKER, J EDW-Life & Poetry of Jas Thomson-NewHav-1917-
8vo-cl-148p-frontis   (5t2)   5.00
--Work of the Stock Exchange-NY-1922-631p-illus   (4b8)   10.00
MEEKER, O-Report on Africa-Lond-1955-illus   (5x2)   5.00
MEEKS FAMILY-Murder of..or Crimes of the Taylor Bros-KansCty-
(1896)-wrps-map-illus-58p-v rare-(A B McDonald)
(5zz5, wrp rprd)   150.00
MEEN, V B-Crown Jewels of Iran-Tor-1968-sm folio-81 col plts-
ed ltd to 75c-box-v scarce-fine bndg   (4n5)   250.00
MEERMAN, GERARD-Origines Typographicae-The Hague, Paris,
Lond-1765-calf-g.bk-2 vols in 1-4to-1st ed (4n5, libr stmp, vg)140.00
MEESE, WM A-Early Rock Island-Moline, Ill-1905-illus-97p-1st ed
(5zz5)   40.00
MEGGENDORFER, LOTHAR-From Far & Near, a movable toybook-
Lond-(ca1890)-lith bds, 13 by 9 & 1 hf inches (5d9, sl loose)   150.00
MEGGERS, BETTY-Archeological Investigations at Mouth of Amazon-
1947   (5qq5)   20.00
MEGROZ, R L-The Real Robinson Crusoe-Lond-n.d.-244p-8vo-
grey cl-Cresset Pr   (5aa2)   7.50
MEIER, FRANK-Fathoms Below-NY-1943-320p
(5s1, fair) 3. (5dd9, ex-libr)   6.25
--Hurricane Warning-NY-1947-254p-illus-1st ed (5t7) 5. (5dd9) 5.25
MEIER GRAEFE, JULIUS-Vincent Van Gogh-HB 1933-illus-240p-
8vo   (5ww3)   20.00
--same-Literary Guild-1933   (5ww3)   7.50
--same-NY-(c1933-Blue Ribbon-240p   (5x0)   5.00
MEIGHAN, CLEMENT W-Indian Art & History-Baja Cal Trav Ser,
Vol 13-12 col plts-map-fldg chart-79p-cl-Castle Pr (5d2)   10.00
MEIGHN, MOIRA-A Little Book of Conceited Secrets & Delights
for Ladies-Lond-1928-79p   (5w3)   5.00
MEIGS, CHAS D-Philadelphia Practice of Midwifery-Phila-1838-
370p-illus-calf   (5xx7)   15.00
MEIGS, CORNELIA-Critical History of Children's Literature-NY-
(1953)-1st ed   (5v2, 5p1)   12.50
--The Violent Men-NY-1957-278p   (5w4)   4.00
--Wind in the Chimney-NY-1934-Macm-8vo-144p-frontis-illus-
1st ed   (5p1)   5.00
MEIGS, J FORSYTH-Hist Of 1st Quarter Of 2nd Century of
Pennsylvania Hosp-Phila-1877-orig cl-illus   (5kk8, rub)   10.00
MEIGS, JOHN-Peter Hurd, the Lithographs-Lubbock-1968-folio-
ltd to 300c, autog-orig 10x14"-Hurd autg lith-spec bndg-box
(4a5, f)   200.00
MEIGS, PEVERIL, 3rd-The Kiliwa Indians of Lower Calif-Berkeley-
1939-wrps   (5gg1)   4.00
MEIKLE, WM, comp-Canadian Newspaper Directory or Advertisers'
Guide-Tor-1858-Blackburn's City Steam Pr-60p   (5aa1)   25.00

MEINERTZHAGEN, RICHARD-Birds of Arabia-Edinb-(1954)-cl-
4to-pkt map-plts   (5z9,dj)   20.00
MEINHARD, CARRIE-Across My Path-NY-1950-priv prntd (5r7)   7.50
MEINHOLD, WM-Sidonia the Sorceress-Lond-1926-the Julian
Editions-illus-4to-vel-t.e.g.-ltd to 225c   (5b0,box) 87.50
MEIRE-GRAEFE, JULIUS-Cezanne-Lond-1927-lg4to-plts-
ltd to 650c   (5ii8)   25.00
MEISSEN &OTHER CONTINENTAL PORCELAIN-in Irwin Untermeyer
Collection-Cambr-1956-text by Yvonne Hackenbroch-240 photos-
4to-cl-264p text   (5t0,dj,f) 25.00
MEITNER, LISE-Disintegration of Uranium by Neutrons-(Lond)-1939-
8vo-offprint from Nature, Vol 143-(4p)-last pg blank
                                                (5zz7,vf) 750.00
MELANCHOLY EXAMPLES & FRIENDLY ADVICE-(NY, (?)ca 1826)-
12p-stitchd   (5g8)   10.00
MELBO, IRVING R-Our Country's National Parks-Indnpls-(1941)-
2 vols-R8vo-photos-maps-1st ed   (5dd6)   5.00
MELBOURNE HOUSE-NY-1864-2 vols-frontis-1st ed-(S B Warner)
                                                (5F0)   10.00
MELCHER, EDW-Sketch of Destruction of Willey Family by White Mt
Slide on Aug 28, 1826-Lancaster-1879-Coos Repub Pr-16mo-
6p-wrps   (5u9,cov tn) 12.50
MELDEN, C M-From Slave to Citizen-NY-1921   (5x2)   22.50
MELENDY, MARY R-Ladies' Home Companion-Detroit-(1903)-
448p-illus-4to   (5w7,hng broke) 5.00
MELINE, JAS F-2000 Miles on Horseback-NY-1867-fldg map-317p-
1st ed-scarce   (4t3) 17.50   (5t2)   25.00
--same-1868-2nd prnting   (5yy7,fade) 10.   (4t3)   12.50
MELISH, JOHN-Geographical Description of US-Phila-1816-
T H Palmer,prntr-182p-fldg col map-maps..deckl papr-
lea sp-2nd ed   (5a0)   24.50
--same-Phila-1818-8vo-bds-4 maps-lea bk-3 rd ed (5m6,ex-librr) 17.50
MELL, DR & P H-Gen of Mell Family in the Southern States-1897-
89p   (5t9)   10.00
MELLEN, GRENVILLE-The martyr's triumph,buried valley,&other
poems-Bost-1833-Lilly, Wait, Colman & Holden-12mo-orig cl-
papr labl-1st ed   (5i0)   20.00
MELLICHAMPE-NY-1836-Harper-2 vols-12mo-orig blue cl-
papr labls-(W G Simms)-1st ed   (5x1,vg)   125.00
MELLICK, ANDREW D-Story of an Old Farm-Somerville, NJ-1889-
illus-scarce (5ii8, incl 24p prospectus) 90. (4m2,f)   75.00
--Lesser Crossroads-Schmidt, ed-n.p.-(New Brunswick)-1948-
                                                (5w0,dj)   8.50
MELLINGER, BONNIE E-Children's Interests in Pictures-NY-1932-
Col Univ-8vo-52p-#516   (5p1,dj)   7.50
MELLIS, J C-St Helena-Lond-1875-4to-cl-426p-col plts (5p6) 30.00
MELLON, ANDREW-Taxation, the People's Business-NY-1924
                                                (5x7)   5.00
MELLOR, J E M-Notes on Falconry-Cambr-1949-orig cl-16mo-
83p-frontis-scarce   (4p5)   17.50
MELMOTH, THE WANDERER-a tale-Edinb-1820-Constable-4 vols-
12mo-hf calf-1st ed-v scarce (5xx6,sp wn, lacks hf t.)   250.00
MELMOTH, WM-The Letters of Pliny the Consul, wi Occasional
Remarks-Lond-1748-2 vols-12mo-calf-Vol 1, 3rd ed-Vol 2,
9th ed - 1796   (5t4,mismtchd) 12.50
MELONE, HARRY R-Finger Lakes Region, Sesqui Centennial Souvenir-
1929-400p   (5t9)   12.50
--History of Central New York-1932-3 vols   (5ff2)   40.00
MELONEY, WM BROWN-Rush to the Sun-(1937)-Farrar&Rinehart-
ltd to 1000c,nbrd,autg   (5F1,mint,dj)   6.00
MELSEN, A G VAN-From Atomos to Atom-1952   (5L7)   6.00
MELTON, A B-70 Yrs in the Saddle & Then Some-KansCty-1950-
illus-117p-wrps-2nd ed   (5zz5)   15.00
MELTON, ELSTON J-Towboat Pilot-Caldwell-1948-279p-1st ed,
ltd to 1000c,autg (5dd4) 10. (5xx8,dj,5k0,dj)   12.50
--same-Caldwell-1948-photos-3rd prntg   (5s1,f)   10.00
MELVILL, ANDREW-Memoirs of Sir-Lond-1918-J Lane-297p-maps
                                                (5p7)   7.50
MELVILLE, GEO W-In the Lena Delta-Bost-1885-illus-maps
                (5t2) 6.50   (5ss5, hng crack)   7.50
MELVILLE, HERMAN-Apple Tree Table & Other Sketches-Princeton
Univ Pr-1922-1st ed-ltd to 175c   (5i4)   35.00
--same-Princeton&Lond-1922-cl&bds-8vo-(edition of 1675c)
                                                (5b2,sl wtrstns) 10.00
--Benito Cerene-Nonsuch Pr-Lond-1926-ltd to 1650c-illus
                                                (5ss9,5e8) 15.00
--The Encantadas or Enchanted Isles-Burlingame(Calif)-1940-113p-
cl&bds-illus   (5t2)   20.00
--John Marr & Other Poems-Lond&Princeton-1922-8vo-cl-
(edition of 1675c)   (5b2)   12.50
--Journal of a Visit to London & Continent-1948-Harvard Univ-
E M Metcalf,ed (5mm2,dj) 10. (5F1,f,dj)   15.00

MELVILLE, HERMAN (continued)
--Journal up the Straits October 11,1856 to May 5,1857-NY-1935-
Raymond Weaver,ed-labl-cl-1st ed-ltd to 650c (5m4)   40.00
--same-NY-1935-Colophon-cl-1st ed   (5d1)   25.00
-- Mardi, & A Voyage Thither-NY-1849-Harper-2 vols-1st ed-
8p ads Vol 2   (5x1,fox,vg) 200. (4b1,fox)   100.00
--same-NY-1925-Boni-546p   (5m2)   5.00
--Moby Dick or the Whale-NY,Harper-Lond,Bentley-1851-
orig cl-1st ed-1st state (wi publr name blindstmpd at center
of sides & orange yel e.p.)-(1),634p(8)   (5z7)   950.00
--same-NY-1851-Harper-12mo-orig blue cl-1st Amer ed-
orange e.p.--6p ads at back   (4h0,vg,sl dmpstnd)   1,500.00
--same-NY-1851-Harper-8vo-orig brown cl-yellow e.p.-
1st ed-(wi 2 prelim & 3 terminal blank lvs & 3 lvs of ads at
end-hf title   (5u5, sp wn, fox, mor case)   1,150.00
--same-Bost-(1921)-545p-illus-cl   (5t0)   4.00
--same-NY-1925-Boni-ed by Ramond M Weaver   (5m2)   5.00
--same-NY-1930-illus Rockwell Kent-sq8vo-Lakeside Pr
                (5ee3) 7.50   (5mm1,5v2,mint)   10.00
--same-NY-1930-Rockwell Kent,illus-1st Kent ed
                         (4a1,orig illus, Kent pres)   100.00
--same-Chig-1930-Riverside Pr-4to-buck-280 illus by Rockwell Kent-
3 vols-ltd to 1000c,alum box as issu   (5cc9,fade) 375.00
--same-NY-(1943)-Heritage Pr-illus by R Robinson-615p (5x0) 6.00
--Narr of a 4 Months' Residence among Natives of a Valley of
Marquesas Islands-Lond-1846-12mo-cl-1st ed of auth's 1st
book wi incorrect numeral XV for XX on the backstrip
                                                (5gg6)   375.00
--Omoo-Lond-1847-8vo-calf-g.-(publ a month before the Amer ed)
                                                (4c2,f)   75.00
--same-NY-1847-hf red lea-1st ed   (5ee3,vg) 50.00
--same-NY-1847-Harper-12mo-orig violet cl-3rd ed (5x1,fox) 25.00
--same-Bost-(1921)-365p   (5t0)   4.00
--The Piazza tales-NY-1856-Dix&Edwards-12mo-orig dark brwn cl-
1st ed   (5i0,sp rprd) 125.00
--Redburn, His First Voyage-NY-1849-1st ed
                (4b4,sl wn,fox) 47.50 (5x1,vg)   135.00
--same-NY-1924-Boni   (5m2,fade) 5.00
--Typee-NY-1846-12mo-cl-1st Amer ed of auth's 1st book
(5dd8,fox,wtrstn,box) 85. (5x1,vg) 225. (5gg6,vg,box)   250.00
--same-NY-1860-307p-rev ed wi sequel-map   (5mm2)   10.00
--same-NY-1876-Harper-307p   (5x4)   10.00
--same-Bost-(1921)-389p-frontis-port-cl   (5t0)   4.00
--The Whale-Lond-1851-Richard Bentley-1851-1st ed-
(precedes Amer ed)-3 vols-orig cl - v rare
                         (5tt2,new e.p.,sp sl wn)   4,000.00
--White Jacket, the World in Man Of War-NY-1850-465p-
1st ed (5ee9,box,sp rprd) 150. (5x1,rub) 70. (4b4,sp rprd) 85.00
--same-Bost-(1923)-374p-cl-illus   (5t0)   4.00
--The Works of-Lond-1922-Constable&Co-16 vols-Standard ed-
ltd to 750 sets,nbrd
        (5ss9,f mor bndg,orig cl bnd in) 400. (4h0,orig cl) 750.00
MELVILLE, JOHN-Guide to Calif Wines-NY-1955-270p (5w1)   4.00
MELVILLE, LEWIS-Life of Wm Makepeace Thackeray-Chig-1899-
ports & illus-2 vols   (4b4,f)   15.00
--The South Sea Bubble-Bost-1923-8vo-illus   (5m6)   10.00
MELVIN, A GORDON-Education, a history-NY-c1946-JnDay-
(374p)   (5p1,dj)   5.00
--Thinking for Every Man-NY-1942   (5p0)   4.00
MEMORIAL DES ALLIES-n.p.-1926-col illus-pub by Dan'l Jacomat
& Co-lg thk folio-folio size sheets in string tie,g.binder
                (5w9, lacks one sheet,sl soil)   30.00
MEMORIAL OF SIOUX INDIAN OUTBREAK 1862-Fairfax, Minn-
n.d.-(ca1927)-20p-photos-2 maps-stiff wrps (5t3, librr stmp) 8.50
MEMOIRES DE LA SOCIETE ROYALE DES ANTIQUAIRES DU NORD-
1840 to 1901-Copenhague-n.d.-(ca1841 to 1902)-t8vo-hf calf-
9 vols-illus   (5t2, lacks 1 vol)   30.00
MEMOIRES D'UNE POUPEE-Paris-(ca1845)-A Bedelet-qtr lea-
12 hand col lithos-6th ed   (5c8)   45.00
MEMOIRS OF AN AMERICAN LADY-Lond-1809-2nd ed-2 vols-
(Anne Grant)   (5ii3,bndgs wn) 20.   (5m3,f)   40.00
--same-Lond-1817-hf lea-2 vols in 1-3rd ed   (5t2)   30.00
MEMOIRS OF AN INFANTRY OFFICER (Sassoon)-Lond-1930-Faber-
ltd ed   (5ss3,autg) 25.   (5r9,f)   12.50
MEMOIRS OF A MONTICELLO SLAVE-Univ Virg Pr-1951-illus
                                                (5x2)   17.50
MEMOIRS OF A PROTESTANT, CONDEMNED TO GALLEYS OF
FRANCE FOR HIS RELIGION-Lond-1758-lg12mo-calf-2 vols-
1st ed of Goldsmith's 1st book (5i4,rbkd) 125. (5gg6,rbkd) 150.00
MEMORY OF ROSWELL SMITH-(NY, 1892)-8vo-orig bds-
priv prntd-(Geo W Cable)-1st ed   (5m6,pres) 12.50
MEMPHIS-Memphis-1913-photos-12 lvs-wrps   (4j4)   8.50

MEMPHIS COOK BOOK-Jr League-Memphis-nd.-(?195-s)-
259p-spiral bnd wrps   (5c4)   4.00
MEMPHIS RIOTS & MASSACRES-(Wash)-1866-House of Reps
Rept #101,39th Congr, 1st Sess-394p   (5w4)   15.00
MEN & MANNERS IN AMERICA-Edinb:Blackwd,& Cadell(Lond)-
1833-12mo- 2 vols-calf-g.-mor labls-1st ed   (5i8,pres)   70.00
--same-Phila-1833-sm8vo-410p-cl-1st Amer ed   (5t2,wn)   12.50
MEN BEHIND SEATTLE SPIRIT-Seattle-(1906)-Argus Cartoons,
ed by H A Chadwick-365p-lea cov-10x8"   (5s4)   10.00
MEN OF CALIFORNIA-SanFran-(1901)-ports-g.e.-440p-
(W C Wolfe)   (5xx5)   13.50
MEN OF CALIFORNIA-SanFran-(1925)-4to-buck-illus-206p(5h4)   6.00
MEN OF INDIANA IN 1901-Indnpls-1901-g.e.-scarce   (4a9)   10.00
MEN OF THE PAC COAST-SanFran-(1903)-Pac Art Co-mor-
634p-ports   (5r0)   17.50
MEN OF TIMBER-Peoria,III-1954-67p-photos   (5s4,ex-libr)   5.00
MEN OF TIMBER-Peoria,III-1955-Vol 2-88p-photos   (5s4)   5.00
MEN WHO MADE SAN FRANCISCO-SanFran-n.d.-Brown & Power
Sta Co-8vo-lea-274p   (4t1)   17.50
MENABONI, ATHOS-Manaboni's Birds-NY-(1950)-31 col plts
in text & same loose in portfolio-2 vols-4to-cl bkd bds-
ltd ed,autgs   (5z9,vf,box)   50.00
MENCHACA, ANTONIO-Memoirs-SanAnt-1937-Yanaglana Soc-
ltd to 500c,nbrd   (5g2) 5.   (4a5)   7.50
MENCKEN, AUGUST-By the Neck,a Book of Hangings-NY-1942-
cl-illus   (4a5) 5.   (5t2)   4.00
MENCKEN, H L-The Amer Language-NY-1919-Alfred A Knopf-
1st ed-ltd to 1500c (5r9) 15.   (5ss9,vg) 30.   (5mm2)   22.50
--same-NY-1930   (5mm2)   5.00
--same-NY-1937-769p-4th ed,enlgd   (5c3)   4.00
--Americana 1925-NY-1925-1st ed   (5mm2,wn dj)   10.00
--Americana 1926-NY-1926-1st ed   (5mm2)   7.50
--The Artist,a Drama without Words-Bost-1912-Luce & Co-33p-
bds-1st ed,2nd issue   (5ss9,vf)   10.00
--Bathtub Hoax & Other Blasts & Bravos From the Chicago Tribune-
NY-1958-1st ed   (5nn6,dj,f)   12.50
--Book of Burlesques-NY-1916-1st ed   (5mm1)   12.50
--Christmas Story-NY-1946-Knopf-12mo-1st ed
(4F6,mint,dj) 8.50 (5ss9,f,dj) 6.   (5mm0,dj)   5.00
--Geo Bernard Shaw,his plays-Bost-1905-107p   (5p6)   30.00
--The Gist of Nietzsche-Bost-1910-12mo-1st ed-orig cl-labls
   (4n5,vf)   35.00
--Happy Days, 1880 to 1892-NY-1940-Knopf
(4b4,mint,dj) 15.   (5p1) 7.50   (5mm0,dj)   10.00
--Heathern Days, 1890 to 1936-NY-1943-Knopf-1st ed
(4b4,mint, dj) 15.   (5hh1,dj)   10.00
--Heliogabalus,a Buffoonery in 3 Acts-NY-1920-Knopf-1st ed-
ltd to 2000c,nbrd   (5dd8) 30.   (5hh1)   25.00
--same-NY-1920-ltd to 60c,autgs   (5dd8)   75.00
--In Defense of Women-NY-1925-Knopf   (5p9)   3.50
--Men vs the man-NY-1910-252p-1st ed   (5p6)   16.50
--Menckeniana, A Schimpflexikon-NY-1928-8vo-bds & cl-labl-
1st ed-ltd to 230c,lg papr,autg   (5d8)   25.00
--Minority Report, H L Mencken's Notebooks-NY-1956-Knopf-
pst ed   (5p7) 3.50   (5ss9,f,dj)   6.00
--Newspaper Days, 1899 to 1906-NY-1941-port-1st ed
(4b4,mint,dj) 15.   (5mm1,dj)   12.50
--Notes on Democracy-NY-(1926)-1st ed   (5mm1,dj)   10.00
--Prejudices, First Series-NY-(1919)-12mo-cl-1st ed (5d8,fade) 15.00
--Prejudices, Second Series-NY-(1920)-Knopf-1st ed
(5xs9,sl fade) 7.50   (5mm2,autg)   15.00
--Prejudices, Third Series-NY-(1922)-8vo-cl-1st ed   (5ee9)   15.00
--Prejudices, Fourth Series-NY-(1924)-Knopf-1st ed (5ss3,dj) 20.00
--same-NY-(1924)-8vo-dec bds-cl bk-1st ed-ltd to 110c,autg
   (5d9,box)   37.50
--Prejudices, Fifth Series-NY-(1926)-Knopf-1st ed
(5ee9,dj,vf) 15.   (5ss3,dj,sl stn)   20.00
--Prejudices, Sixth Series-NY-(1927)-1st ed-errata slip
   (5mm1) 15. (5d8)   7.50
--same-NY-1927-1st ed-ltd to 140c,nbrd,autg   (5ss9)   30.00
--Treatise on the Gods-NY-1930-Knopf-364p-1st ed
(5j2,4b4) 10.   (5ss9)   7.50
--same-NY-1930-8vo-blue stained vel-t.e.g.-1st ed-
ltd to 375c,nbrd,autg   (5d8) 50.   (5mm0)   45.00
--Treatise on Right & Wrong-NY-1934-1st ed-331p-index
(5mm1,dj) 15.   (5m8,5mm0)   12.50
MENDE, ELSIE PORTER-An Amer Soldier & Diplomat Horace Porter-
NY-1927-379p-cl   (5g4,5h7)   7.50
MENDELSOHN, HENRIETTE-Das Werk der Dossi-Munich-1914-
Muller & Rentsch-225p-plts   (5m5)   60.00
MENDELSOHN, O A-The Earnest Drinker-Lond-(1950)-241p
   (5w1)   5.50

MENDELSSOHN CLUB COOK BOOK-Rockford-1909-
xxxii,339,(3)p   (5c4,cov wn)   5.50
MENDELSSOHN FAMILY-(1729 to 1847)from letters & journals
ed by Sebastian Hensel-NY-(1881)-2 vols-sm8vo-hf calf-
8 ports-2nd rev ed   (5t0)   10.00
MENDELSSOHN, FELIX-Letters of Felix Mendelssohn Bartholdy
from 1833 to 1847-Bost-1863-421p   (5p0)   5.00
MENEFEE, C A-Historical & Descrp Sketch Book of Napa, Sonoma Lake
& Mendocino-NapaCty-1873-illus-356p-1st ed-scarce
   (4t3,bkstrp sl wn) 50.   (4t1)   45.00
MENEFEE, E L-Hist of Tulare & King Co, Calif, Illus-LosAng-1913-
Historic Rec Co-in 1 vol-890p-a.e.g.-4to-hf lea
   (4t1,new hng)   65.00
MENEFEE, SELDEN C-The Pecan Shellers of San Antonio-Wash-
1940-GPO-8vo-82p-illus-wrps-WPA-scarce   (4a3)   15.00
MENENDEZ PIDAL, RAMON-Spaniards in their History-NY-
(1950)-Starkie,trans   (4a1)   7.50
MENKE, FRANK G-Encyclopedia of Sports-NY-c1960-2nd ed, rev
   (5w5)   7.50
MENN, ALFRED E-Texas As It Is Today-Austin-1925 (1926)-
photos-239p   (5yy7)   20.00
MENNONITE HISTORY-Scottsdale-1942-2 vols-illus   (5xx7)   20.00
MENNONITE QUARTERLY REVIEW-Goshen-Apr 1927 to Oct 1950-
vols 1 to 24-bnd in 12 vols   (5xx7)   40.00
MENOCAL, A G-Report of US Nicaragua Surv Party-Wash-1886-
GPO-4to-154p-fldg plts-plts   (5yy0)   27.50
MENOMINEE CO, MICH-Atlas-1912   (5mm7,chip)   50.00
MENOTTI, GIAN CARLOW-Amahl & the Night Visitors-
NY,Tor,Lond-(1952)-McGraw Hill-8vo-89p-pict cl-1st ed
   (5p1,dj)   15.00
MENPES, M-Rembrandt-Lond-1905-50p-16 col plts-lg4to-cl(5m5) 9.50
MENPES, MORTIMER-Whistler As I Knew Him-NY-Macmillan-1904-
153p-134 illus   (5i1,rprd)   15.00
--same-Lond-1904   (5t4)   6.00
MENUS FOR MINORS-n.p.-1948-illus-cl-Golden Gate
Kindergarten Aux-(ca 150p)   (4g9)   5.00
MENZEL, GOTTFRIED-Die Vereinigten Staaten von Nordamerika-
Berlin-1853-364p-8vo-sheets,unbnd,cl case-scarce (5L1) 35.00
MENZIES, H STUART-Let's Forget Business-Lond-1930-col illus-
unpgd   (5c7)   4.50
MENZIES, W J M-Salmon Fishing-Lond-(1950)-184p-illus-
Sportsman's Library   (5t7)   7.00
MENZIES, WM-Forest Trees & Woodland Scenery-Lond-1875-folio-
20 plts-151p   (5w3,bndg loose)   20.00
MERA, H P-Alfred I Barton Collection of SoWstrn Textiles-
SantaFe-(1949)-12mo-bds-illus-100p-ltd ed (5t0,pres,autg) 10.00
--Navajo Blankets of the "Classic" Period-SantaFe-1938-12mo-
wrps-4p plus 7 plts-Gen Ser Bull #3   (5g6)   3.00
--Style Trends of Pueblo Pottery in Rio Grande & Little Colo
Cultural Areas-SantaFe-1939-R8vo-172p-67 plts-fldg map
   (5dd6,ex-libr)   17.50
MERCANTILE DIRECTORY CO'S-Classified & Business Direc &
Mercantile Reg of Cleveland-n.p.-1901-168p-bds   (5ff7)   12.50
MERCANTILE LIBRARY ASSN-Report of..Erection of Edifice for-
SanFran-1859-orig prntd wrps-8vo   (5i9,f)   20.00
MERCANTILE PROTECTIVE AGENCY-Register, Brooklyn & vicinity,
1883 to 84-Brooklyn-1883-350p   (5u3,ex-libr)   10.00
MERCED CO-History of Merced Co-SanFran-1881-Wallace W
Elliott & Co-maps-lithos-232p-4to-orig cl & lea   (5tt0)   350.00
MERCED CO-Memorial & Biogr History of Co of Merced, Stanislaus,
Calaveras, Tuolumne & Mariposa-Chig-1892-Lewis Pub Co-
illus-408p-lea   (5tt0)   45.00
MERCEDES OF CASTILE-or, voyage to Cathay-Phila-1840-
Lea&Blanchard-2 vols in 1-12mo-roan & bds-1st ed (5x1) 40.00
MERCER, A S-The Banditti of the Plains-n.d.-c1930-facs ed (5x5) 25.00
--same-Sheridan-(1930)-orig wrps-166p-McPherren Edition
   (5xx5)   35.00
--same-SanFran-1935-Grabhorn Pr-illus-136p
(4t3,f) 30. (5x5) 35.   (5xx5)   32.50
--same-Okla-1944-8vo-bds   (5p5,dj)   12.50
--same-Norman-(1954)-195p   (5i3,f)   7.50
--Washington Territory-Utica, NY-1865-8vo-orig prntd wrps-
1st ed-rare   (5a3,f)   375.00
--same-Seattle-1939-8vo-cl-#2 of the Dogwood Pr-ltd to 350c
   (5h5,f)   17.50
MERCER, H C-The Lenape Stone or The Indian & the Mammoth-
NY-1885-illus-95p-1st ed-scarce   (5ii8,f)   25.00
MERCER, HENRY C-Ancient Carpenters' Tools-Doylestown-1951-
illus-(5)p,339p   (5n7)   5.00
--Bible in Iron-Doylestown-1941-sm4to-cl-313 illus-216p-
2nd ed,rev & enlrgd   (5t0) 25.   (5ii8)   32.50
--Guide Book to the Tiled Pavement in Capitol of Penna-ca1913-
95p-index-illus-   wrps   (5m2)   4.00

MERCER, SAML A B-The Pyramid Texts-NY-1952-4 vols-
out of print (5a8) 38.50
MERCER, WM, ed-Great Britain, Colonial Office List for 1925-
Lond-1925-88p ads-72&832p-38 col maps(31 fldg) (5c6,stn) 25.00
MERCERSBURG OLD MERCERSBURG, (PA)-by Woman's Club-
1912-215p-orig wrps (5t9) 17.50
MERCEY, ARCH A-Sea, Surf & Hell-NY-1945-352p-illus (5w5) 5.00
MERCHAN, R M-Free Cuba-1897-J Guiteras, ed-plts-buck
(5L7, rbnd) 15.00
MERCHANT & SEAMAN'S EXPEDITIOUS MEASURER, THE-
NY-1856-tall, nar 8vo-sheep-196p (5b8, bndg wn) 7.50
MERCHANT MARINE COMM-Report & Testimony at Hearings-
Vol 3 only(of 3 vols)-Southern Coast-Wash-1905-pgs 1483 to
1985-lea corners (5s1, ex-libr) 6.50
MERCHANT SHIPPING ACT-Act to Facilitate Erection &
Maintenance of Colonial Lighthouses...Amend Merchant Shipping
Act 1854-Que-1862-Trinity Hse, Montreal-46p English,
46p French (5w8) 25.00
MERCHANT SHIPS-World Built, Vessels 1,000 tons gross, over,
completed in year-Southampton, Eng-9 vols, 1954 to 1962-
pub by Adlard Coles-album style, 6x9"-photos-plans
(5s1, ex-libr) 75.00
MERCHANT VESSELS, USA, ANNUAL-Wash
--1890-460p-obl 4to (5s1) 17.50
--1915-481p-obl 4to (5s1) 15.00
--1941-775p-obl 4to (5s1) 10.00
--1944-752p-obl 4to (5s1) 10.00
--1945-773p-obl 4to (5s1) 10.00
--1946-813p-obl 4to (4a1) 10. (5s1) 9.00
--1947-831p-obl 4to (5s1) 8.00
--1957-991p-obl 4to (5s1) 7.50
MERCHANTS & BANKERS'ALMANAC FOR 1871-NY-(1871)-165p-
ads (4b8, lacks 2 pgs ads) 17.50
MERCHANT'S BANK OF BALTIMORE-Charter of the-Balt-1835-
21p, (3)p (5h8, lt fox) 10.00
MERCHANTS MAGAZINE & COMMERCIAL REVIEW-NY-1847-
Vol 16, Jan to Jun, 1847-8vo-lea (5t0) 7.50
--same-Vol 17, July to Dec, 1847-NY-1847-8vo-bds (5t0) 7.50
--same-Vol 23, July to Dec, 1850-NY-1850-8vo-bds-port (5t0) 7.50
--same-Vol 27, July to Dec, 1852-NY-1852-8vo-bds (5t0) 7.50
--same-Vols 1 to 63 (lacks title, index & last 2 nbrs of Vol 63)-
63 vols in 62-NY-1839 to 70-8vo (5g3, needs rebnd, ex-libr) 150.00
MERCIER, CARDINAL D F F-Manual of Modern Scholastic Philosophy-
3rd ed-Vol 1 only-1953-plts (5L7) 6.50
MERCIER, H-L'Avenir Du Canada-Montreal-1893-91p-wrps (4b9) 20.00
MERCIER, MRS JEROME-Father Pat, Hero of Far West-Gloucester-
1909-109p-plts-scarce (5dd0) 10.00
MEREDITH-or, mystery of the Meschianza-Phila-1831-12mo-
orig cl & bds-papr labl-1st ed (5x1, soil) 50.00
MEREDITH, DE WITT-Voyages of the Velero 3-LosAng-1939-4to-
ltd ed (5x5) 25.00
MEREDITH, G E-Desc of Hugh Amory, 1605 to 1805-Lond-1901-
373p-fldg chart-wrps (5t9) 7.00
MEREDITH, GEO-Amazing Marriage-Westminster-1895-2 vols-
1st ed (5mm1) 35.00
--Beauchamp's career-Lond-1876-Chapman&Hall-8vo-orig grn cl-
1st ed- 3 vols (5xx6, wn) 30.00
--Diana of the crossways-Lond-1885-Chapman&Hall-3 vols-8vo-
orig cl-1st ed (5xx6, rprd) 20.00
--The Egoist, for stage-Lond-1920-4to-orig wrps-cl case-
priv prntd by Clement Shorter-ltd to 30c-autg by Shorter
(5ss3) 75.00
--Emilia in England-Lond-1864-Chapman&Hall-3 vols-8vo-orig cl-
1st ed (5x3, vg) 75. (4h0, calf, f bndg) 75.00
--Evan Harrington-NY-1860-orig cl-1st ed-v scarce (5mm2, sl wn) 30.00
--Letters, collected & edited by his son-NY-1912-2 vols-illus
(5m1) 6.50 (5p0) 7.50
--Modern love & poems of English roadside-Lond-1862-Chapman &
Hall-12mo-orig cl-1st ed (5x3, vf) 70.00
--The Pilgrim's Scrip-Bost-1888-258p (5x0) 3.50
--Shaving of Shagpat-Lond-1856-12mo-cl (4c2, shabby) 15.00
--Tale of Chloe, etc-Lond-1894-1st ed-ltd to 250c, nbrd (5ss9) 17.50
--same-Lond-1894-1st ed (4m8) 5.00 (5mm1) 15.00
--The Tragic Comedians-Lond-1880-2 vols-12mo-crushed lev-g.t.-
orig cov bnd in (4c2, f bndg, rbnd) 25.00
MEREDITH, GRACE, ed-Girl Captives of Cheyennes-LosAng-1927-
123p-photos-map (5s4) 10.00
MEREDITH, LEWIS B-Rock Gardens-NY-(1923)-390p-col frontis-
3rd ed (5s7) 6.00
MEREDITH, LOUISE ANNE-Some of My Bush Friends in Tasmania-
Lond-1860 (to 1891)-plts-2 vols-folio-cl-g.e.-1st ed
(5z9, cov wn, pres) 50.00

MEREDITH, OWEN-Clytemnestra, the Earl's Return, the Artist &
Other Poems-Lond-1855-12mo-cl-1st ed of auth's 1st book
(5gg6, pres) 75.00
--Lucile-Lond-1860-8vo-orig green cl, 1st ed (4b6, box) 85.00
MEREDITH, ROY-The Face of Robt E Lee in Life & in Legend-
NY&Lond-1947-4to-illus (5x0,5s9,dj) 7.50
--Mr Lincoln's Camera Man, Mathew B Brady-NY-1946-4to-
1st ed (5s9, dj) 15. (5m2) 10. (5x5, dj) 20.00
--Mr Lincoln's Contemporaries-NY-1951-4to-ports
(5ii3) 10. (5s9,5m2,5t4) 7.50
MEREDITH, SCOTT, ed-Bar 3-NY-1954-1st ed
(5yy6, vg, dj) 5. (5nn6, dj) 7.50
MEREDITH, WM-Ships & Other Figures-Princeton-1948-12mo-
dec bds-cl bk-1st ed (5ss7, mint, dj, autg) 17.50
MERENESS, NEWTON D, ed-Travels in the Amer Colonies-NY-
1916-Col Dames of Amer-1st ed (5q8, shake) 15.00
MEREZHKOVSKY, DMITRI-Michael Angelo & other sketches-
NY-(1930)-mor-1st ed (5d2) 20.00
MERFIELD, FRED G-Gorilla Hunter-NY-1956-photos-238p
(4t5, dj) 4.00
MERGENTHALER-The Linotype Bulletin-Jan, 1920 to Oct, 1923,
in binder-22 numbers (5p7) 15.00
MERGENTHALER-Manual of Linotype Typography-Brooklyn-(1923)-
Wm Dana Orcutt, ed-256p-4to (5p7) 12.50
MERIAN, MARIA SIBYLLA-Over der Voortteeling en Wonderbearlyke
Veranderingen-Amsterdam-J Oosterwyk-1719-lg folio-72p-
72 plts-parch bds-2nd Dutch ed (5hh0, vf) 6,500.00
MERIDA, CARLOS, ed-Modern Mexican Artists-Mexico-1937-
(Frances Toor Studios)-12mo-illus (5h2, dj) 5.00
MERIDEN, CONN-Centennial of-1906-400p-illus (5t9) 7.50
MERILLAT, HERBERT L-The Island-Bost-1944-H M-283p-illus (5x0) 4.00
MERIMEE, M J F L-Art of Painting in Oil & Fresco-Lond-1839-
frontis (4b7, hng split) 12.50
MERING, A W-Mering Family-1929-50p-scarce (5mm3) 17.50
MERINGTON, MARGUERITE-The Custer Story-NY-1950-1st ed
(5yy7, dj, f) 7.50
MERIWETHER, LEE-Tramp at Home-NY-1889-Harper & Bros-296p-
illus-cl (5tt0) 15.00
MERIWETHER, NELSON HEATH-The Meriwethers & Their Connections-
Columbia-1964-690p plus index-illus (5r7) 17.50
MERKLEY, CHRISTOPHER-Biog of Christopher Merkley-SaltLkCty-
1887-wrps-46p-scarce (5dd6) 20. (5zz5) 12.50
MERLANT, JOACHIM-Soldiers & Sailors of France in Amer War
for Independence-NY-1820-illus (5ii8) 10.00
MERLE, MRS E I-Hist of Jericho, Vermont-Vol 2(only)-1963-
301p (5t9) 17.50
MERLIN, SIDNEY D-Theory of Fluctuations in Contemporary Economic
Thought-NY-1949 (5p0) 8.50
MERRIAM, ALAN P-Congo-Evanston-1961 (5tt5) 6.00
MERRIAM, C H-Dawn of the World-Cleveland-1910-A H Clark, publ-
illus (5h5) 20. (5r5,5s4,4k4, f) 15. (5x5) 17.50
--An nik a del-Bost-1928-160p plus index-photos-1st ed
(5t3, lt wtrstn) 7.50
--Results of a Biolog Surv of Mt Shasta Calif, No Amer Fauna #16-
Wash-1899-8vo-179p-5 plts-scarce-wrps (4p5) 5.00
--Studies of Calif Indians-Univ of Calif-1962 (5x5, dj) 5.00
MERRIAM, CHAS EDW-The Amer Party System-NY-1946-fldg map-
3rd ed (5q8) 7.50
MERRIAM, GEO ERNEST-More Precious than Gold, Wash
Commonplace Book-NY-1931-428p-illus-Collectors Edn (5h9) 6.00
MERRIAM, GEO S-The Life & Times of Samuel Bowles-NY-1885-
cl-2 vols (4h2) 15.00
MERRIAM, J C-The Felidae of Rancho La Brea-Wash-1932-
Carnegie Inst #422-231p-42 plts-cl-4to-v scarce (4p6,pres) 75.00
MERRIAM, RALPH-Claims Between Shippers & Carriers-Chig-1916-
1815p-LaSalle Ext U (5s1, ex-libr) 10.00
MERRICK, CAROLINE E-Old Times in Dixie Land-NY-1901-241p-
cl (5h2, sl dmpstn, pres) 7.50
MERRICK, ELLIOTT-From This Hill Look Down-1934-183p (5e8) 4.00
MERRICK, GEO B-Genealogy of Merrick, Mirick, Myrick of Mass-
1902-v scarce-494p (5mm3) 125.00
--Genesis of Steamboating on Western Rivers-Madison-1912-(52)p-
wrps (5y0) 7.50
--Old Times on the Upper Mississippi-Cleve-1909-8vo-cl-323p-
illus-map (5m8) 35.00
MERRICK, HENRIETTA SANDS-In the World's Attic-NY-1931-
259p-illus-fldg map-cl-Putnam's (5d7) 6.50
MERRICK, HUGH-The Perpetual Hills-Lond-Newnes-247p-cl-illus
(5d7) 5.00
MERRICK, LEONARD-Cynthia, a daughter of the Philistines-Lond-
1896-Chatto&Windus-2 vols-8vo-orig cl-1st ed (5xx6, f) 25.00
MERRICK, REBECCA-Rain Harbor-NY-(1947)-275p-1st ed (5s4) 3.50

MERRIFIELD, EDW-Story of Captivity & Rescue from the Indians
  of Luke Swetland etc-Scranton-1915-68p-orig wrps-v scarce
        (5w5, orig wrps) 25.   (4m2)   27.50
MERRILL, ARCH-River Ramble-Roch-(1943)-108p-cl (5h2, dj) 3.50
--The Towpath-Rochester-(1945)-illus   (5tt5, pres, 5r0) 7.50
--Upstate Echoes-NY-n.d.-illus   (5yy6)   4.50
MERRILL, D D-The Northern Route to Idaho & Pac Ocean-StPaul-
  (1864)-16mo-orig cl-lg fldg map-1st ed- ex rare-orig issue
  (without later changes)   (5n9) 1,800.00
MERRILL, ELIPHALET-Gazetteer of State of New Hampshire-Exeter-
  1817-8vo-calf-1st ed   (5ee3, crack) 17.50 (5ss5) 22.50
MERRILL, FREDK J H-Mineral Resources of NY State-Albany-1895-
  Bull NY State Mus, Vol 3, #15-fldg bds-maps (5b8, libr stmp) 5.00
MERRILL, G D-Hist of Androscoggin Co, Maine-1891-879p-illus-
  scarce   (5t9, f) 45.00
MERRILL, GEO P-Stones for Building & Decoration-NY-1897-lg8vo-
  cl-506p-2nd ed, rev & enlrgd   (5t2) 4.50
MERRILL, J M-Kilpatrick's Famous Ride-NY-Feb 1, 1890-24p-
  self wrps-War Library Ser #386   (5jj9) 7.50
MERRILL, J W, comp-Records of the 24th Independent Battery, NY
  Light Artillery, USA-Perry-1870-illus-map-280p plus 22p-
  1st ed   (5zz5) 15.00
MERRILL, JAS-First Poems-NY-(1950)-12mo-cl-1st ed of auth's
  1st book-issued in a nbrd ed   (5ss7, vf, dj) 17.50
MERRILL, JAS M-Rebel Shore-Bost-1957-plts (5dd6) 5. (5s9) 7.00
MERRILL, JOHN-Cosmogony:or thoughts on philosophy-EastCanaan-
  1860-prntd wrps   (5g4) 17.50
--Cosmogony...to which is added, a key to astronomy, & moon
  & tide influences-Flume House-1877-prntd wrps (5g4) 17.50
MERRILL, SAM'L-The Moose Book-NY-1916-366p-illus-fldg map
      (5aa0, sl wn, 5ss8) 12.50
MERRILL, SAM H-Campaigns of 1st Maine & 1st Dist of Columbia
  Cavalry-Portland-1866-Bailey&Noyes-436p-labl-lea-t.e.g.-
  1st ed   (5F9, rbkd) 30.00
MERRIMAN, HENRY SETON-Prisoners & captives-Lond-1891-
  Bentley-3 vols-8vo-orig cl-1st ed   (5xx6, wn) 20.00
MERRIMAN, MANSFIELD-Text Book on Roofs & Bridges, Part 2,
  Graphic Statics-NY&Lond-1900-234p &ads-illus (5t4) 7.50
MERRITT, ABRAHAM-The Moon Pool-NY-1919-12mo-cl(4c2) 27.50
--same-NY-1919-pic wrps-12mo-1st ed   (5gg6) 35.00
--Thru the Dragon Glass-Jamaica, NY-(1917)-16mo-wrps-stapled-
  ARRA Prntrs-1st separate ed   (5gg6) 20.00
MERRITT, EDWIN A-Civil War Recollections, 1828 to 1911-Albany-
  1911-188p-J B Lyon Co, Prntrs-lea   (5a0) 22.50
MERRITT, FRANK C-History of Alameda Co, Ca-Chig-1928-
  (S J Clarke)-illus-2 vols (4t3, rebnd, wtrstn, 5a0) 30. (5h4, f) 22.50
MERRITT, PERCIVAL, ed-Piozzi Marginalia, some extract: from-
  Cambr-1925-Harv Univ Pr-cl bkd bds-1st ed-ltd
      (5ss3, sp stn) 30.00
MERRITT, SR, W W-Iowa, History of Co of Montgomery from Earliest
  Days-Red Oak, Iowa-1906-344p-ports-illus-t.e.g. (5a9) 30.00
MERROW, O E-Henry Merrow of Reading, Mass & His Desc-1954-
  699p   (5t9) 15.00
MERRY FROLICS-& Comical Cheats of Swalpo-also, Merry Pranks
  of Roger the Clown-n.p.-ca1800-wdcuts-16mo-self wrps(5p5) 42.50
MERRY, THOS B-The American Thoroughbred-LosAng-1905-illus-
  244p-cl-scarce   (5yy8, spotted) 12.50 (4p2) 25.00
MERRY MOUNT-A Romance of the Massachusetts Colony-Bost-
  1849-JasMunroe-2 vols in 1-12mo-cl-1st ed (5x1) 25. (5ss3) 35.00
--same-Bost-1849-JasMunroe-2 vols-12mo-orig cl-1st ed-
  scarce 2 vol issue (5x1) 50. (5ss3, f) 85.00
MERRYMAN, WM N-Yankee Caballero-NY-(1940)-328p-plts-
  1st ed   (5dd4, spot) 5.00
MERRYWEATHER, F SOMMER-Bibliomania in The Middle Ages-
  NY-1900-ltd to 500, nbrd   (4m5) 15.00
--same-Lond-1933-ltd to 750c   (4m5) 12.50
MERSFELDER, L C-Cowboy, Fisherman, Hunter-KansCty-1941-271p-
  illus   (5h0, soil, dj) 8.00
MERSHON, W B-The passenger pigeon-NY-1907-225p-Outing Pub
  Co.   (5u3) 15.00
MERTINS, LOUIS-Intervals of Robert Frost-Berkley-1947-1st ed
      (5mm1, dj) 17.50
MERTON, THOS-Tears of Blind Lions-NY-New Dir-1949-32p
      (5i1, dj) 6.00
MERTZ, HENRIETTE-Pale Ink-Chig-(1953)-158p-maps-1st ed,
  signed by auth   (5t3, dj, mint) 10.00
--The Nephtali, One Lost Tribe-Chig-(1957)-107p-ltd to 1000c
      (5t3, autg, dj, mint) 10.00
MERVIN, SAM'L-My Favorite Club-NY-1933-illus-wrps
      (5qq7, autg, enclosures) 10.00
MERVINE, WM M, ed-Genealogical Register, Vol 1-Phila-1913-
  part lea-raised bands-332p-illus-g.e. (5kk8) 35.00

MERWIN, GEO H-Ye Church & Parish of Greenfield(wi Suppl
  1913 to 1931)-n.p.-n.d.-Tuttle, Morehouse & Taylor Pr-cl-
  12mo-107p, 125p   (4t1) 12.50
MERWIN, HENRY CHILDS-Aaron Burr-Bost-1909-Small, Maynard-
  150p-cl   (5tt8) 4.00
--Life of Bret Harte-Bost-1911-1st trade ed-illus (5i3, rub) 10.00
MERWIN, SAM'L-Old Concord, seen through Western Spectacles-
  Bost-1926-32p-hf cl-illus   (5w4, dj, autg) 3.50
--Rise and Fight Againe-NY-1935-257p-frontis (5y2) 4.00
MERWIN-WEBSTER-Calumet "K"-NY-1904-345p-cl (5h7) 5.00
MERY, JOS-La Floride-Paris-1859-288p-1st ed (4b4) 25.00
MERYON, CHAS-Masters of Etching-#14-Lond-1927-illus-21p-
  obl 4to-cl   (5t7) 7.50
MERZ, JOHN T-History of European Thought in 19th Century-
  Edinb-1912 to 23-4 vols-orig ed (5L7) 40. (5nn6) 35.00
MERZEL, W-History of Germany-(Bohn)-1852-3 vols
      (5tt5, bndg wn) 10.00
MESA VERDE NAT'L PARK, COLO-Wash-1928-62p-wrps-illus
      (4a5) 7.50
MESERVE, FREDK-Photographs of Abraham Lincoln-NY-(1944)-30p
      (5t7, dj) 10.00
MESSENGER, J R B-Niphrata Has Spoken-Maspeth-(1938)-8vo-328p-
  Tipharet Publ   (5j5, dj) 12.50
MESSENT, C J W-Weather Vanes of Norfolk & Norwich-Norwich-
  1937-127p-illus   (5n7) 6.50
MESSER, ASA-An Address, Delivered to Graduates of Rhode Island
  College Sept 7, 1803-Prov-1803-Nathaniel Heaton-12p-wrps
      (5r7) 15.00
--An Oration Delivered before Prov Assoc of Mechanics &
  Manufacturers Apr 11, 1803-Prov-(1803)-15p-sewed-wrps-
  John Carter   (5g4, f) 15. (5r7, unopnd) 25.00
MESSERVY, GEO P-The Quick Step of an Emperor, Maximilian of
  Mexico-Lond-1921   (5r7) 8.50
MESSITER, CHAS A-Sport & Adventures Among No Amer Indians-
  Lond-1890-orig illus, Chas Whymper-368p (5L0, 4b3) 25.00
MESSLER, A-First Things in Old Somerset-Somerville-1899-167p-
  scarce   (5ii8) 17.50
METCALF, FRNK J-History of the High School, Ashland, Mass-
  South Framingham-1890-Lakeview Pr-117p-12 photos
      (5p1, spots) 7.50
METCALF, FREDK-The Englishman & the Scandinavian-Bost-n.d.-
  (ca1880)-8vo-cl-25, 514p   (5t2) 7.50
METCALF, HENRY HARRISON-New Hampshire in History-Concord-
  1922-illus   (5q8) 3.00
METCALF, ISAAC STEVENS-Metcalf Genealogy-1898-62p (5t9) 10.00
METCALF, J G-Annals of the Town of Mendon, Mass, 1659 to 1880-
  1880-723p   (5t9) 7.50
METCALF, JOHN C-DeQuincey, a Portrait-1940-Harvard Univ Pr-
  1st ed   (5ss9, dj) 7.50
METCALF, SAM'L L-New Theory of Terrestrial Magnetism read before
  NY Lyceum of Natural History-NY-1833-Carvill-158p & errata 1f-
  8vo-cl   (5L1) 7.50
METCALF, W H-A summer in Oldport Harbor-Phila-1887-Lippincott-
  1st ed   (5m2) 7.50
METCALFE, J H-Tread of Pioneers-Tor-(1932)-305p-illus-ports
      (5aa0) 15.00
METCALFE-SHAW, GERTRUDE E-English Caravanners in the Wild
  West-Edinb-1926-400p-illus-fldg map-1st ed (5w4, autg) 10.00
METEOROLOGICAL REGISTER (1826 to 1830)-Phila-1840-fldg map-
  roan bk & corners-bds   (5g4, wn, ex-libr) 12.50
METFORD, J C J-San Martin the Liberator-NY-(1950)-Philos Libr-
  8vo-cl-port-fldg map   (4a3, sp faded) 7.50
METHLEY, NOEL T-Life Boat & Its Story-Lond-1912-67 illus (5c1) 12.50
METHODE ABREGEE-et facile pour apprendre la Geographie-Lyon-
  1780-Bernuset-515p-frontis-8vo-new ed, enlrgd (5L1) 55.00
METHODIST ALMANAC FOR 1834-NY-1833-Waugh & Mason
      (4a9, lacks hf pg 2) 3.00
METHODIST BOOK CONCERN-Centennial of the, 1789 to 1889-
  NY, Hunt & Eaton-SanFran-D J Hammond-8vo-15p-illus-stiff wrps
      (5r0) 7.50
METHODIST MAGAZINE, THE-for 1824, Volume 7-NY-1824-frontis-
  480p-lea-Bangs&Mason for Meth Episc Church (5a0) 10.00
--same-NY-1826-Vol 10-8vo-lea-frontis-for1827 (5t2) 8.50
MET LIFE INS CO-"A Friend in Need is a Friend Indeed"-NY-
  1898-91p-illus-fldg cl   (5hh6) 7.50
METROPOLITAN MUSEUM OF ART-Catalogue of Paintings in-NY-
  1912-227p-wrps   (5j4) 6.00
--Life in America-NY-1939-NY World's Fair-230p-illus-wrps-
  scarce   (5r0) 10.00
--Metropolitan Museum Studies-1931-Vol 3, pt 2-4to-orig wrps-
  pg135 to 255   (5t2) 5.00
METTEZ, T, prntr-Epistles & Gospels for All Sundays & Holidays etc-
  Detroit-1812-396p-new ed-lea-rare (5y0, sm libr stmp) 150.00

METZ, JACOB-Metz Family;genealogy of Jacob Metz-Altadena-
1932-Longyear,ed-64p-port-deckle edges-200c priv prntd
(5dd4)   15.00

METZELTHIN, PEARL V-World Wide Cook Book-NY-(1939)-681p
(5g9)   5.00

METZGER, ALFRED,ed-Musical Blue Book of Calif Season 1924,1925-
SanFran-1924-Musical Review Co-400p-cl-ports   (5r0)   7.50

METZLER, MAY SOWLES-Date Cook Book-Coachella Valley-(1919)-
73p-wrps   (5g9)   5.00

MEW, EGAN-Old Bow China-Lond-n.d.-plts-111p-8vo-
Vol 1 of 1st Series   (5x0) 10.   (5ww3,cor bent,5w7)   9.50

--Royal Sevres China-Lond-n.d.-sq8vo-15 col plts-orig blue buck
(5t5)   10.00

MEXIA, PEDRO-Historie of All the Romane Emperors-Lond-1664-
for Matthew Lownes-4to   (5j3,wn,rprd,pgs tn)   15.00

MEXICAN FOLKWAYS-n.p.-1927-Vol 3-#1 to 4-illus-orig wrps
bnd in-in Span & Engl-scarce   (5j3)   10.00

MEXICAN WAR, THE-By An English Soldier-NY-1853-frontis-288p-
1st Amer ed   (5ii8)   27.50

MEXICO, ANCIENT & MODERN-Works in Bancroft Library-
(Berkley)-1962-Univ of Calif Friends of Bancroft Libr-95p-illus-
pic bds-(Lawton Kennedy)   (5r0)   12.50

MEXICO & CENTRAL AMER PILOT-(West Coast)-Wash-1920-
423p-fldg map-6th ed   (5s1)   4.50

MEXICO IN 1842-Description of Country-NY-1842-illus-fldg map-
16mo-orig cl-Howes F226   (5x5,wn,fox)   75.00

MEXICO-New Railroad Law of, issued May 13,1899-MexicoCty-
n.d.-48p-stpld-wrps-Engl lang   (5s4,bndg wn)   7.50

MEYE, HEINRICH-Stone Sculptures of Copan & Quiriqua-NY-1883-
Dodd, Mead-23p-20 plts-eleph folio-cl-J Schmidt, text
(5m5, needs rbndg)   40.00

MEYER, A C-Travel Search for Bells-Chig-(1944)-sm8vo-cl-197p-
92 illus   (5t0, dj, f)   5.00

MEYER, A H-Soil Survey of Wash Co, Texas-Wash-1915-lg fldg map
(5kk6)   5.00

MEYER, CARL-Bound for Sacramento-Claremont-1938-298p-buck-
deckl edgd-ltd to 450c, nbrd   (5r8, t.pg in facs)   27.50

--Prospectus to Form a Society for Emigration to Calif-Claremont-
1936-Saunders-ltd to 440c-Ruth Frey Axe, ed   (4n1)   15.00

MEYER, CORD, JR-Peace or Anarchy-Bost-1948   (5x7)   4.00

MEYER, FRANZ SALES-Handbook of Ornament-Leipzig-(1892)-
548p-illus-8th ed   (5t7)   10.00

--Handbook of Ornament Systematically Arranged-Lond-1893-
580p-300 plts   (5n7,stnd)   5.00

MEYER, GEO HOMER-Outlawed-SanFran-1891-60p & ads-wrps-
Bear Flag Publ   (5d6)   30.00

MEYER, H-Meyer Family Genealogy-1890-131p   (5mm3)   8.00

MEYER, HAZEL-Gold in Tin Pan Alley-Phila-1958-Lipp-258p (5p0)5.00

MEYER, HENRY LEONARD-Illust of British Birds-Lond-n.d.(c1837
to 44)-4 vols in 2-folio-mor-318 hand col plts-1st ed-
probable 2nd issue   (5z9, lt fox,rprd)   850.00

MEYER, HERMANN-List of Works Relating to the Supreme Court of
the US-Wash-1909-124p-wrps   (4j6,f)   7.50

MEYER, HUGO-Public Ownership & Telephone in Gr Britain-NY-
1907-8vo   (5ss5)   7.50

MEYER, J-Meyer's Universum-NY-1852-2 vols-96 plts-oblong
(5yy0)   24.50

MEYER, JOHANN JAKOB-Sexual Life in Ancient India-NY-1930-
2 vols   (5j3, djs)   15.00

MEYER, MARTIN A-Western Jewry-SanFran-Emanu el June 1916-
245p plus 1p-illus-ports-purple suede-v scarce   (5r0)   35.00

MEYER, S A-50 Golden Years-Newport Beach-1957-Newport Harbor
Pub-cl-8vo-292p   (4t1)   12.50
--same-n.p.-n.d.   (5x5, dj)   7.50

MEYER'S UNIVERSUM-or View of Most Remarkable Places & Objects
of All Countries-NY-1852-HJMeyer-obl 4to-Vol 1 - 48 views-
extra engrv t.-pt roan-CADana, ed-295p (5j5, broke, fox)   95.00

MEYERS, LT CMNDR G J-Steam Turbines-Annap-1917-246p-illus
(5s1,stnd, rprd)   7.50

MEYERS LEXIKON-Leipzig-1924-16 Vols-illus-fldg maps & plts-
mor sp-sm4to   (5t5, rprd)   40.00

MEYERS, ROBT CORNELIUS V-The Colonel's Christmas Morning
& Other Stories-Phila-1900-340p-illus-1st ed   (5m1)   20.00
--Life & Adv of Lewis Wetzel-Phila-(1883)-414p-scarce
(5y0, rbnd)   20.00

MEYERS, WM H-Journal of Cruise to Calif & Sandwich Islands-
SanFran-1955-Book Club of Calif-hf mor-plts-map-ltd to 400c
(5d6, 5s6)   85.00
--Naval Sketches of War in Calif-NY-1939-Grabhorn Pr-Random Hse-
illus-bds & white sheepskin   (5d6)   125.00

MEYERSTEIN, E H W-Verse Letters to 5 Friends-Lond-Heinemann-
33p-illus   (5i1, dj,autg by Watson)   5.00

MEYLER, WM-Poetical amusement on journey of life-Bath-1806-
8vo-hf mor-1st ed   (5i8, rub, lacks hf t.)   22.50

MEYNELL, ALICE,ed-The Flower of the Mind-Lond-1897-1st ed
(5yy6)   10.00

--Poems-Lond-1893-Elkin Mathews & Jn Lane-t8vo-cl-lg papr-
1st ed-ltd to 50c, autg   (5dd8)   50.00

--The Poems of...complete edit-NY-1924-Scr-144p   (5p9)   3.50

MEYNELL, EVERARD-Giovanni Bellini-Lond-n.d.-Newnes-8vo-
64 plts-cl & bds   (5m5)   9.00

MEYNELL, VIOLA-Alice Meynell, a Memoir-Lond-(1929)-illus-
352p   (5t4)   5.00

MEYRICK, SAM'L RUSH-A Critical Inquiry into Ancient Armour-
Lond-1824-folio-3 Vols-mor-t.e.g.-80 plts-1st ed-
illum initials   (5b0, ALS, fade)   475.00

MEYROWITZ BROS OPTICIANS-Illus Catalogue of Optical Goods-
NY-1880-134p-orig wrps   (5m2)   12.50

MEZERIK, A G-Revolt of the South & West-NY-1946-1st ed
(5x2, dj)   5.00

MIAMI THE BEAUTIFUL-(Souvenir Brochure)-Miami-n.d.-(ca1915)-
horiz 8vo-pict wrps-30 col plts   (5x7)   3.00

MIARS, MARGUERITE S-Johannes Schenk of Bushwick, Long Isl &
His Desc-1948-87p-100c prntd   (5mm3)   20.00

MICHAEL, C D-The Slave & His Champions-Lond-1900-12mo-illus-
pict cl   (5x2)   32.50

MICHAEL, CHAS D-'Mid Snow & Ice-Tor-n.d.-318p-illus
(5ss1, fox)   3.50

MICHAEL, GEO-Handout-NY-1935-242p   (5w4)   3.75

MICHAEL, P-Ices & Soda Fountain Drinks-Lond-(ca1925)-184p
(5w1)   6.50

MICHAELIS, A-Ancient Marbles in Great Britain-Cambridge UP-
1882-833p-illus   (5ii2, lacks bkstrp)   9.50

MICHAUX, FRANCOIS-The North American Sylva-Phila-1857-
iw Nuttall's continuation-hand col plts-6 vols in 5-8vo-
hf mor-g.e.-reprnt   (5z9, vg)   265.00

--Travels to the Westward of the Allegany Mntns-Lond-1805-
Phillips-8vo-hf calf-fldg map(silked)-1st Engl ed   (5n9)   125.00

--Voyage a L'Ouest des Monts Alleghanys-Paris-1804-
Levrault&Schoell-8vo-hf mor-lg fldg map-1st ed   (5n9)   250.00

MICHEAUX, O-Case of Mrs Wingate-NY-1945   (5x2, dj)   6.00
--Story of Dorothy Stanfield-NY-1946   (5x2, dj)   6.00
--The Masquerade-NY-1947   (5x2, dj)   6.00
--The Wind from Nowhere-NY-1944   (5x2, dj)   6.00

MICHEL, EMILE-Rembrandt, His Life, His Work, & His Time-NY-1894-
by Stikeman-2 vols-4to-plts-3/4 mor   (5m6)   25.00
--Rembrandt-NY-1906-folio-70 plts   (5ww3, sp tn)   15.00

MICHEL, FERNAND-Le Repertoire de la Charcuterie-Paris-(1933)-
illus-280p   (4g9)   7.50

MICHEL, T-A Will & a Way-NY-1867-P O'Shea-orig dec cl-
6 col engrvngs-1st ed   (5c8, f)   15.00

MICHELER, NATH'L H-Routes From Western Boundary of Ark to
Santa Fe & Valley of the Rio Grande-Wash-1850-1st ed-HED 67
(4n4)   17.50

MICHELET, JULES-The Bird-Lond-1869-lg8vo-210 illus-340p-
crushed blue lev-a.e.g.   (5t2)   7.50
--Satanism & Witchcraft-NY-1939-illus   (5m2, dj)   4.50

MICHELL, E B-The Art & Practice of Hawking-Lond-1900-illus-
cl-g.t.-8vo-orig ed   (5b0, f)   55.00

MICHELSON, CHAS-The Ghost Talks-NY-1944   (5x7)   4.00

MICHELSON, MIRIAM-The Wonderlode of Silver & Gold-Bost-
1934-illus   (5x5, stn)   5.00

MICHELSON, TRUMAN-Contributions to Fox Ethnology-Wash-1927-
8vo-cl-168p-BAE bull 85   (4b2) 8.50   (5t7, libr stmp)   10.00

--Contributions to Fox Ethnology-II-Wash-1930-BAE bull 95-8vo-
plts-papr-183p   (5t7, libr stmp)   10.00

--Notes on the Fox Wapanowiweni-Wash-1932-BAE bull 105-
papr cov   (4b2) 7.50   (5h6)   4.00

--Notes on Buffalo head Dance of Thunder Gens of Fox Indians-
1928   (5L7)   3.50

--Observations of Thunder Dance   of Fox Indians-Wash-
1929-bull 89-hard cov   (4b2)   7.50

--Preliminary Report on Linguistic Classification of Algonquin
Tribes-1913-4to-pp221 to 290B of 28th Annual Reprt, BAE (5L7) 3.50

MICHENER, A O-History of the NoEast High School, Phila-n.p.-
1938-241 illus   (5w5)   5.00

MICHENER, CARRO K-Heirs of the Incas-NY-1924-8vo-cl-287p-
illus   (5t2) 5.   (4b2)   4.50

MICHENER, JAS A-The Fires of Spring-NY-(1949)-8vo-cl-1st ed
(5d9,autg)   10.00
--Return to Paradise-NY-(1951)-437p   (5t4)   6.00

MICHIE, ALLAN A-Dixie Demagogues-NY-(1939)   (5yy6)   6.00

MICHIGAN, BIOG HIST OF NORTHERN, Containing Biog of
Prominent Citizens-n.p.-1905-855p-mor-Streeter 367 (5h1)   45.00

MICHIGAN, Guide to Wolverine State-NY-(1949)-696p-cl-WPA-
5th printing   (5ff7)   5.00
MICHIGAN-The Iron Resources of & Gen'l Statistics of Iron-
Detroit-1856-24p-wrps-scarce   (5r7)   15.00
MICHIGAN, LAWS OF TERR OF-Detroit-1820-517p-lea
         (5h1, sl scuf, crack)   75.00
MICHIGAN LAW REVIEW-(1902 to 70)-Vol 1 to 68
        (5rr4, rbnd recently)   1,560.00
MICHIGAN-Memorial Record of the Northern Peninsula of Chig-
1895-4to-mor-illus-642p   (5jj7, f)   42.50
MICHIGAN NEWS CO-The Doomed City-Detroit-1871-8vo-54p-
orig wrps-fldg map-1st ed   (5ss5)   20.00
MICHIGAN STATE GAZETTEER-& Business Directory for 1863,4-
Detroit-1863-illus-8vo-cl&lea-2nd ed (5t0, cov chewed)   20.00
MICHIGAN, UNIV OF-Catalogue of officers & students in Dept of
Arts & Sci, 1846-Detroit-1846-16p-prntd wrps   (5g4)   10.00
MICHLER, GEN N-Military Maps...Armies of Potomac & James,
May 4, 1864 to Apr 9, 1865-NY-1867-15 maps mntd on lin
in lg folio   (5g8, lacks front cov)   40.00
MICHLER, N H-Letter from Secretary of War, rel to Routes from
Western Boundary of Ark to Santa Fe & valley of Rio Grande-
Wash-1850-HR67-12p-wrps   (5n4)   17.50
MICHNER, FANNIE L-Poetical Works-Phila-(1884) (5mm2)   4.50
MICKLEY, MINNIE F-Genealogy Of The Mickley Family of Amer-
Mickleys, Pa-1893-182p   (5m2) 10.   (5w5, ms laid in)   18.50
MICKWITZ, HAROLD VON-Memoirs of Harold Von Mickwitz-Dallas-
1936-Dealey&Lowe-116p   (4a5)   12.50
MIDDLE AMER RESEARCH INST-Inventory of Manuscript Collections
of-NewOrl-1939-MARI, Tulane Univ-WPA-No 2-Calendar of
Yucatecan Letters-4to-240p-wrps-scarce   (4a3, sl chip)   25.00
MIDDLEBROOK, LOUIS F-History of Maritime Connecticut During
Amer Revolu 1775 to 83-Salem-1925-illus-2 vols
  (4m2, f, dj, 5ii8, f, dj, 5w5)   25.   (5qq8, dj)   12.50   (5ss2)   17.50
MIDDLEBROOK'S NEW ENGL ALMANAC FOR 1861-Bridgeport-
1861   (4a9)   7.50
--same-for 1864-Bridgeport-1864   (4a9)   12.50
--same for 1885-Bridgeport-1885   (4a9)   10.00
MIDDLEBURY COLLEGE-The Undergraduate-Middlebury, Oct 28,
1830 to Oct 20, 1831-Vol 1-8vo-bds   (5t4, librr stmp)   20.00
MIDDLESEX CO(MASS) DIRECTORY-for 1873-Bost-1873-1st ed-
400p, 230p-illus-advs   (5m2)   10.00
--same-Bost-1884-470p-illus-adv-1st ed-for 1884 to 5 (5m2)   8.50
MIDDLETON-Historical Sketch of Parish Church of Holy Trinity-
(Formerly Christ Ch)-1887-52p-illus   (5e8)   7.75
MIDDLETON, A-Tropic Shadows-NY-n.d.-Barse-302p-illus(5p7) 5.00
MIDDLETON, C H-From Garden to Kitchen-Lond-(1937)-224p
        (5c9)   3.50
MIDDLETON, CONYERS-Hist of Life of Marcus Tullius Cicero-Lond-
authr-1741-4to-2 vol-564&591p-vignts-calf-1st ed (5a1)   25.00
MIDDLETON, G A T-Evolution of architectural ornament-Lond-
1913-Griffiths-117p-lg4to-cl-plts   (5s5)   25.00
MIDDLETON, HOWARD-The Conquest of Quebec, a Poem-Oxford-
1768-prntd at Theatre for J Fletcher-12p-4to-wrps (5e2)   600.00
MIDDLETON, JOHN W-History of Regulators & Moderators &
Shelby Co War in 1841 and 1842 in Rep of Texas-Austin-1930-
Gammel-wrps-40p   (5g6)   12.00
--same-Grand Prairie-1953-wrps-49p   (5n4)   12.50
MIDDLETON, L-Revolt U S A-NY-1938-illus   (5x2)   10.00
MIDDLETON, THOS-Some Notes on Bibliography of Philippines-
Phila-1900-58p   (5j4)   12.50
MIDDLETON, THOS C-Hist Sketch of Augustinian Monastery, Coll
& Miss of St Thomas of Villanova, Delaware Co, Pa-n.p.-
1893-illus-95p   (4m2)   6.50
MIDDLETOWN-Souvenir of, Orange Co, NY-Newburgh-1922-
illus-fldg map-wrps   (5r7)   7.50
MIDSUMMER EVE-NY-1928-Gaige-bds-ltd to 450c
      (5ss3, sp def, autg)   15.00
MIDWAY CITY COOK BOOK-Kearney-1899-1st Baptist Church-
136p, (1)   (5c7, stn, wn)   7.50
MIEROW, CHAS C-The Gothic History of Jordanes-Princeton-1915-
188p-errata   (5w9)   8.50
MIERS, E S-Big Ben-Phila-1942-1st ed   (5x2)   7.50
--General Who Marched to Hell-NY-1951-Knopf-349p
     (5x0) 6.   (5s9)   7.50
--Gettysburg-1948-Rutgers Univ Pr-308p-maps (5h6, 5s9)   6.00
--Lincoln Day by Day-Wash-1960-3 vols-buck-Lincoln Sesqui Com
     (5g4)   25.00
MIGEON, G-Collection Paul Garnier-Paris-1917-illus-112p-8vo-
wrps   (5bb0)   10.00
MIGHELS, ELLA STERLING-Wawona-SanFran-(1921)-illus-map-
117p   (4b2)   4.00
MIGHELS, HENRY R-Sage Brush Leaves-SanFran-1879-Edw Bosqui-
12p plus 335p-frontis-cl   (5r0)   10.00

MIGHELS, PHILIP V-Boy's Book of Indians-NY-243p-illus (4b2)   2.50
MIGNET, A F-History of French Revolution from 1789 to 1814-
Lond-1826-2 vols-calf   (5yy6, rub)   15.00
MIGOT, ANDRE-Tibetan Marches-Lond-1955-288p-illus-cl (5d7) 6.00
MIKHELSON, ANDRE-Kings & Knaves in the Cameroons-NY-1938-
Putnam's Sons-280p   (4t5)   8.00
MIKKELSEN, EJNAR-Conquering Arctic Ice-Lond-1909-470p-plts-
illus-maps   (5s6)   12.50
--same-Phila-n.d.-illus, maps-8vo   (5ss5, ex-libr)   10.00
--Frozen Justic-NY-(1922)-230p-motion pic illus (5ss1)   7.50
--Lost in the Arctic-Lond-1913-4to-395p-plts-fldg map
    (5a1) 8.50   (5ss1)   15.00
MILADY'S OWN BOOK-Ladies Aid Soc of Grace Methodist Church-
(Gallipolis-n.d.-ca1900)-54p-wrps   (5h7)   3.50
MILAM, TEXAS-Sketches of Character; Moral & Political Condition
of Republic; the Judiciary, etc-Phila-1839-16mo-cl
     (5a3, sp wn, libr stmps)   100.00
MILAM COUNTY-Inventory of the County Archives of Texas-
SanAnt-1941-131p-wrps   (5n4)   5.00
MILBURN, GEO-Flannigan's Folly-NY-1947-cl-240p (5h0)   5.00
MILBURN, WM H-Pioneer Preacher-NY-1859 (5yy8, bkstrp wn)   7.50
--Rifle, Axe, & Saddle Bags, & Other Lectures-NY-1857-frontis-
sm8vo-cl-309p   (5s4, fair) 6.50   (5t2)   6.00
MILES, ALFRED H, ed-52 Holiday Stories for Boys-Lond-(c1898)-
Hutchinson-8vo-dec cl-a.e.g.   (5aa2)   6.50
--52 More Stories for Boys-Lond-(c1890)-8vo-dec cl-a.e.g.-
448p-plts   (4a8)   6.50
MILES, ALLIE LOWE-Old San Fran, based on motion picture-NY-
(1927)-278p-photos   (5s4, sl soil)   3.50
MILES, EMMA BELL-Our Southern Birds-Morristown-(1922)-174p-
illus   (5h6)   3.50
MILES, GEO H-The governess-Bost-1883-Noonan-304p-reprint
     (5m2)   12.50
MILES, H H-Childs History of Canada for Use of Elementary Schools-
Montreal-1870-141p-illus-maps   (4b9, vf)   10.00
--History of Canada Under French Regime, 1535 to 1763-Montreal-
1872-Dawson Bros-maps-illus   (5w8, rprd)   6.00
MILES, MANLY-Silos, Ensilage & Silage-NY-1901-12mo-illus-
hf mor-100p   (5t4)   5.00
MILES, NELSON A-Personal Recoll & Observ...of Civil War etc-
Chig-1896-4to-mor-g.-1st issue(frontis "General")-
Remington, illus   (4t3, wn) 25.   (5yy7) 35.   (4c1, f)   37.50
--same-Chig-1896-Remington, illus-1st ed, 2nd issue
(frontis "Maj General")   (5m9, sp tn, ink) 25.   (5ee3, vg)   32.50
--same-Chig-1897-591p-Remington, illus & others-591p
    (5h6, hng broke, 4j4)   15.00
--Serving the Republic-NY-1911   (5a8)   20.00
MILES, WM-Journal of Sufferings & Hardships of Capt Park H French's
Overland Exped to Calif-Chambersburg-1851-26p-wrps-reprntd-
(NY, 1916)-ltd ed of 250c   (5r7)   20.00
MILESTONES MARKING-3 Qtrs of a Century of Achievement-NY-
1928-Home Ins Co-64p-illus   (5y2)   7.50
MILET, PIERRE-Relation de su Captivite parmi les Onneiouts en
1690, 1-NY-1864-Shea-8vo-orig cl-1st ed-(100c prntd)
     (5u9, box)   75.00
--Captivity among the Oneidas-Chig-1897-16mo-orig bds-hf mor-
ltd to 75c   (5n9, box)   50.00
MILFORD-Chronological List of Events for 50 Years-1930-248p-
illus   (5e8)   9.75
MILFORD, JOHN-Norway & her Laplanders in 1841-Lond-1842-
JnMurray-8vo-orig cl-1st ed   (5i8, vf)   25.00
MILFORT, GEN'L-Memoirs-Kennesaw-1959   (5r7, ex-libr)   7.50
MILHAM, WILLIS-Time & Timekeepers-NY-1915-617p-illus(5w5)10.00
MILHOLLAND, RAY-Splinter Fleet of Otranto Barrage-NY-(1936)-
307p-photos-maps-1st ed   (5s1, ALS)   7.00
MILHOLLEN, HIRST D-Presidents on Parade-NY-1948-425p-lg4to
    (5k0, 5x0, 5s9, dj)   7.50
MILITARY AERONAUTICS-Air Serv Medical, War Dept-Wash-
1919-illus-cl-446p   (5rr0, pres)   25.00
MILITARY COSTUME OF TURKEY-Lond-(1818)-Thos M'Lean-illus-
folio-mor-hand tooled-a.e.g.-29 col plts(of 30)   (5i4)   225.00
MILITARY HISTORY OF KENTUCKY-Frankfort-1939-illus-493p-
1st ed-Amer Guide Ser-scarce   (5u1)   15.00
MILITARY LAW REVIEW-1958 to 70, #1 thru 47-unbound
     (5rr4, lacks #8&18)   97.50
MILITARY MENTOR, THE-Series of Letters Recently Written by a
General Officer to His Son-Salem-1808-2 vols-329p, 310p-
orig papr bds, orange papr labls   (5m3, f)   30.00
MILITARY NOTES ON THE PHILIPPINES-Wash-1898-GPO-314p-
fldg maps-soft bnd   (5F9, chip)   15.00
MILITARY ORDER OF THE CARABAO-Constitu & Bylaws, etc-Wash-
ca1912-8vo-plts-bds-cl bk-1st ed   (5p5)   12.50

MILITARY POLICE HANDBOOK-Hawaiian Dept July 1938
Fort Shafter, Terr of Hawaii-51p plus fldg map-brown wrps
(5F9)   3.00

MILITARY ROAD, WESTERN FRONTIER, ETC-25th Congr-2nd sess-
Doc #278-n.p.-(c1838-Thos Allen-pamph-21p, (2) (5mm8) 17.50

MILITARY SERV PUBL-Map & Aerial Photograph Reading-1954-
lg8vo-174p-wrps-4th ed (5a6) 2.50

MILK FOR BABES-Northampton-1840-John Metcalf-prnt wrps-22p-
illus-16mo (5rr2, fox) 7.50 (5v0, f, 24 pgs) 7.50

MILL, JAS-Analysis of phenomena of human mind-Lond-1829-2 vols-
8vo-orig bds-papr labls-1st ed (5x3, labl rub) 85.00

MILL, JOHN STUART-Autobiography-Lond-1873-Longmans, etc-
8vo-cl-1st ed (5x3) 35. (5ss3, sp stn) 25.00

--Early Essays-Lond-1897-Bohn Libr (5p0) 3.50

--Principles of Political Economy-Lond-1848-John W Parker-2 vols-
orig cl-papr labls-1st ed,1st issue (5z7, vf) 125.00

--same-NY-1864-2 vols (4m3, rub, fade) 10.00

--The Subjection of Women-Lond-1869-Longmans, etc-cl-1st ed
(5ss3, hng crack, sp stn) 15.00

--Suffrage for Women, May 20, 1867-NY-(1867)-20p (5t7) 3.50

--Woman Suffrage Tracts, #3, Suffrage for women, 1867-Bost-1869-
stitchd (5g8) 5.00

--A System of Logic-NY-1881-65op-later ed (4b4) 12.50 (5p7) 7.50

--same-1925 (5L7) 5.00

MILLAIS, J G-Life & Letters of Sir John Everett Millais, Pres of
Royal Academy-1899-2 vols-4to-plts (5L7) 15.00

--Life of Fredk Courtenay Selous-Lond-1918-Longmans, Green-
illus-387p (4a6, fox) 12.50 (4t5) 18.50

MILLAIS, JOHN GUILLE-Rhododendrons-Lond-1917 to 24-
1st & 2nd series-34col plts-2 vols-folio-crushed lev-1st ed-
ltd to 550c-scarce (5z9, f, f bndg) 650.00

MILLAR, GEO R-A White Boat from England-NY-1951-16 illus-
7 maps (5c1) 6.00

MILLAR, J Y, CAPT-Brief Account of Voyage Around the World of
"Maulesden" in 1883-Oakland-1927-22p-stiff wrps-
5x7-1/2 (5r0, pres) 7.50

MILLARD, BAILEY-History of San Francisco Bay Region-Chig&SanFran-
1924-sml4to-ports-3 vols-Amer Hist Soc
(4t1, wi suppl) 65. (5F5) 30.00

MILLARD, F S-A Cowpuncher of the Pecos-1929-47p-orig prntd wrps-
one of 300c-scarce (5g2) 15.00

MILLARDET, M A-Etudes Sur Les Vignes D'Origine Americaine Qui
Resistent Au Phylloxera-Extrait, Academie Des Sci-Paris-1876-
48p-wrps-4to (5w1) 12.50

MILLAY, EDNA StVINCENT-Aria Da Capo-NY-1921-orig cl-1st ed
(5mm2) 12.50

--same-in The Chapbook, Aug 1920-(#14)-orig pic wrps (4b5, vg) 25.00

--Bibliography of works of...Karl Yost-1937-Harper-(1500c only)
(5F1, vg) 30.00

--Bright the Arrows, 1940 Notebook-NY-1940-Harper&Bros-
limp lea-orig box-1st ed (5hh1, f) 10.00

--Buck in the Snow-NY-1928-Harper-1st ed (5mm0) 7.50

--Collected Poems of-NY-1956-Haper (5p0) 7.50

--Collected Sonnets-NY-1941-full limp lea-t.e.g.-hand set at
Golden Hind Pr-1st ed-box (5ee9) 20. (5j2, cl) 15.00

--Conversation at Midnight-NY-1937-1st ed-Harper
(4b7, dj, bkplt) 7.50 (5m1, 5mm0, lacks e.p.) 5. (5p9, dj) 6.50

--same-Harper&Bros-1937-1st ed-ltd, autg (5ss9, f, unopnd, box) 30.00

--Fatal Interview-NY-1931-8vo-cl-"First Edition"
(5mm0, labl wn) 4. (5d3, 4b5, mint, dj) 15. (5mm0, dj) 10.00

--From a Very Little Sphinx, Poems set to music-NY-(1926)-
GSchirmer-4to-wrps-16p plus lf of ads-1st ed (5dd8) 20.00

--Harp Weaver & Other Poems-NY-1923-1st ed
(4b7, name on fly) 10. (5p6) 6.50 (5mm2, 5ss9) 7.50

--Huntsman, What Quarry-NY-1939-1st ed-Harper-94p
(4b4) 10. (5p9) 6.50 (5mm0, dj) 7.50

--The King's Henchman, Lyric Drama-NY-(1927)-Music by Deems
Taylor-JFischer&Bro-pict stiff wrps-1st ed-4to (5dd8) 25.00

--same-Play in 3 Acts-NY-1927-Harper&Bros-8vo-bds & cl-
(does not include score)-1st ed-ltd to 158c, autg (5dd8) 30.00

--The Lamp & the Bell-NY-1921-Frank Shay-bds-1st ed, 3rd bndg
(5ss3) 20.00

--Letters of-NY-1952-A R Macdougall, ed (5p9) 5.00

--The Lyric Year-NY-1912-Mitchell Kennerley-1st ed, 3rd issue-
Earle, ed (5ss3, sp chip) 10.00

--Make Bright the Arrows-1940 Notebook-NY-1940-sm8vo-cl&bds-
8,65p-1st ed-"Printed from type" (5t0) 7.50

--Murder of Lidice-NY-1942-12mo-wrps-32p-1st ed
(5j2, f) 10. (4c2, f) 17.50 (5mm0, f) 15.00

--Poems selected for young people-NY-Harper-1929-illus-1st prntng-
(5m2, dj, sl soil) 6.00

--same-NY-1929-1st ed-ltd to 1050c (5ee3, vg) 15.00

MILLAY, EDNA StVINCENT (continued)
--The Princess Marries the Page-NY-1932-illus-1st ed
(5ee3, lea, g.t.) 10. (5mm2, dj) 7.50

--Renascence & Other Poems-NY-1917-12mo-cl-1st issue-
Glaslan handmade papr-1st ed
(4c2, bkplt, dj) 250. (5m1) 100. (5ee9, vf) 125.00

--same-NY-1917-1st ed-2nd issue-handmade papr
(4b5) 40. (5tt6) 30. (5ss7, autg) 25. (5m4) 35.00

--Second April-NY-1921-M Kennerley-1st ed (5p0) 20.00

--Sunday after the War-New Directions-(1944)-1st ed
(5hh1, lt dust soil) 5.00

--There Are No Islands, Any More-1940-Harper&Bros-1st ed
(5mm2) 6. (5ss9) 4.00

--Wine From These Grapes-NY-1934-Harper-1st ed
(5mm0, 5x0, 5m1) 7.50

MILBOURNE MILLS CO-Its Antecedents & Present Operations &
Its Exhibit at Phila, Sept 15, 1887-n.p.-1888-8vo-17p-col illus
(5m6) 12.50

MILLBURY, MASS-Centennial History of town of...Millbury-1915-
illus-814p (4m2) 37.50 (5e8) 28.75

MILLBURY, MASS DIRECTORY-1871-83p (5t9) 4.00

MILLEN, G-Sweet Man-NY-1930 (5x2) 6.50

MILLENIUM HALL-& Country Adjacen, a Description of-Lond-
1762-Newbery-1st ed-12mo-calf-frontis-adv lf-by a
gentleman on his travels (5x3) 90.00

MILLENNIAL HARBINGER, THE-Bethany, W Va-5th Series-Vol 7,
#1 to 12, Jan to Dec 1864-3 qtrs roan (5m3) 32.50

MILLENNIAL PRAISES-Gospel Hymns, in 4 parts-Hancock-1813-
J Tallcott, Jr-288p plus index-12mo-orig sheep (5r7) 35.00

MILLER-Origin & Hist of Name, with Biographies-Crescent Family
Record-1902-112p (5mm3) 10.00

MILLER, A S-Racial Discrimination & Private Education-Univ No Car-
1947 (5x2, dj, mint) 3.25

MILLER, ADAM-Origin & Progress of German Mission in Methodist
Episcopal Church-Cinn-1843-16mo (5jj3) 12.50

MILLER, ALEC-Tradition in Sculpture-Lond-(1949)-illus-176p-8vo
(4a1) 10. (5ww3) 20.00

MILLER, ALEX-An Essay on Church Govt-Albany-1801-30p-8vo-cl-
Whiting&Leavenworth-slip of errata (5L1) 15.00

MILLER, MRS ALEX MC VEIGH-Senator's Bride-NY&Lond-(1887)-
Street & Smith-211p-cl (5h2) 15.00

MILLER, ALICE DUER-Cinderella-NY-Coward McCann-1943-illus-
unpaged (5i1, vg) 4.00

--White Cliffs-NY-Coward McCann-1940-70p-10th impress
(5i1, vg, pres cpy) 8.00

--same-NY-(1941)-Coward McCann-ltd ed (5i4, f) 15.00

MILLER, ANN-Matadors of Mexico-Globe, Ariz-1961-8vo-cl-307p-
1st ed (5g0, f) 7.50

MILLER, ANNA I-Independent Theatre in Europe-NY-1931-8vo-
cl-435p (5t0, f) 7.50

MILLER, ANNIE J-Physical Beauty How to Obtain & Preserve it-
NY-1892-246p, (7)-illus (5n7) 5.00

MILLER, ARTHUR-Death of a Salesman-NY-1949-Viking Pr-1st ed
(4b5, dj, vg) 22.50

--Focus-NY-(1945)-12mo-cl-1st ed (5j5, autg) 20. (5ss7, vf, dj) 13.50

--A View From the Bridge-NY-1955-1st ed (4a1) 5.00

MILLER, BASIL-Geo Washington Carver-Grand Rapids-1943
(5ww4) 5. (5x2) 4.00

MILLER, C C-Black Borneo-NY-1942-illus (5x2) 6.00

MILLER, C D-Fruits of Hawaii-Honolulu-1955-197p-photos (5c0) 4.00

MILLER, CHAS-"Cannibal," Cannibal Caravan-NY-1939-8vo-cl-
33 photos-1st ed (5p5) 7.50

MILLER, CHAS M-Kitecraft & Kite Tournaments-Peoria-(1914)-8vo-
illus (5ss5, ex-libr) 10.00

MILLER, CHAS T-Settlement of Rhode Island-Prov-1874-oblong 4to-
illus-1st ed (5c8, stnd, sp def) 10. (4b7) 17.50

MILLER, DAN'L-History of the Reformed Church in Reading, Pa-
Reading-1905-illus (5m2) 5.00

MILLER, DAVID H-Custer's Fall-NY-1957-map-illus-1st ed
(5dd9) 13.50 (5yy7) 10.00

MILLER, D HENRY-Bridal Days-NY-1883-154p-4to-illus
(5w7, cov soil) 5.00

MILLER, MRS D L-Letters to Young from Old World-MtMorris-1896-
258p-cl (5h7, sl rub) 5.00

MILLER, D R-Criminal Classes, Causes & Cures-Dayton-1903-227p-
cl (5h1, pres) 5.00

MILLER, DOROTHY C-Sculpture of John B Flannagan-NY-1942-
Mus of Modern Art-papr-40p-28 plts-5000c prntd-crown 4to
(4a0) 12.50

MILLER, DOUGLAS-You Can't Do Business With Hitler-Bost-1941
(5x7) 3.50

MILLER, E W-The Negro in America-Harvard Univ-1966-R8vo
(5x2, mint, dj) 6.50

MILLER, EDGAR G, JR-Amer Antique Furniture-NY-1937-
M Barrows-2 vols-sm4to-illus-orig ed (4p7) 30. (5w0) 25.00
--same-Vol 2 only (5t7) 16.00
--The Standard Book of Amer Antique Furniture-NY-(1950)-
illus (5j3) 10.00
MILLER, EDMUND E-The Hundred Year History of the German
Correspondent-Balt-1941-24p-fldg bds (5hh6) 4.00
MILLER, EDWIN L-Explorations in Literature-Phila-(1933)-Lipp-
802p-Amer Writers (5p0) 6.00
MILLER, ELEANOR-When Memory Calls-Gardena, Calif-1936-300p-
autg, ltd-priv prntd (5dd6) 12.50
MILLER, ELIZ CLEVELAND-Children of the Mountain Eagle-
GardenCty-1927-12mo-328p-pict cl-6 plts-1st ed (5p1, dj) 10.00
MILLER, ERNEST C-Oil Mania-Phila-(1940)-140p-cl-1st ed
(5h2, dj) 7.50
MILLER, FRANCIS T-Photographic History of the Civil War-NY-
1911-10 vols- (5yy7, 5s9) 65. (4j4, rprd) 80. (5m2) 75.00
--same-NY-1912-10 vols (5a9, 5p9, 5w5) 100.00
--Portrait Life of Lincoln-Springfield-1910-164p-cl
(5ff7, 5h2, 4b3) 7.50
--Lindbergh, His Story in Pictures-NY-1929-sm8vo-cl-320p-1st ed
(5p0) 5. (5t0, dj, f) 6.50
--Thos A Edison, Benefactor of Mankind-Chig-1931-320p-illus
(5p7) 4. (5v0) 5.00
MILLER, FRANK B, JR-A Diary Comes to Life-n.d.-n.p.(5x9) 5.00
MILLER, FREEMAN E-Oklahoma & Other Poems- 1895-24mo-
126p-blue cl (5h0, cov spot) 5.00
--Oklahoma Sunshine-Stillwater, Okla-1905-312p-red cl
(5h0, rbnd) 5.00
MILLER, G S-The Families & Genera of Bats-Wash-1907-Smi Inst,
US Natl Muse Bull 57-282p-14 plts-wrps-8vo-v scarce (4p5, wn) 20.00
MILLER, GEO-Missouri's Memorable Decade 1860 to 70-Columbia-
1898-frontis-175p-1st ed-scarce (4t3) 20.00
MILLER, GEO A-Interesting Manila-Manila-1906-8vo-illus-2nd ed
(5m6) 10.00
MILLER, GEO J-Trial of Frank James for Murder-(Columbia, Mo-1898)-
1st ed (5jj7) 20.00
MILLER, GEO J-Ye Olde Middlesex Courts-Perth Amboy-1932-
ltd to 232c (4m2, autg) 25.00
MILLER, GEN'L GUILLERMO-Memorias del...al Servicio de la
Republica del Peru-Madrid-1910-2 vols-port-wrps-reprint of
1829 ed (5r7, unopened) 25.00
MILLER, H-My Schools & Schoolmasters-Bost-1857-frontis-537p
(5yy0) 4.00
MILLER, HENRY-Account of a Tour of the Calif Missions-1952-
Grabhorn Pr-folio-ltd to 375c-boxed (5hh4, vf) 45.00
--The Air Conditioned Nightmare-(NY, 1945)-8vo-tan cl-
wi inserted repro of photos (as distinct from reprint in which
photos are prntd on text pgs)-New Directions-1st ed
(5tt2, vg, fray dj, 5d3, dj) 15.00
--Aller Retour NY-1945-priv prnt-8vo-cl-1st prntg-500c prntd
(4c2, soil, fade, bkplt removed) 15.00
--Black Spring-Paris-(June, 1936)-Obelisk Pr-orig pict wrps(5d2)75.00
--same-Paris-(1958)-Obelisk Pr-12mo-wrps (5tt2, wrps rprd) 7.50
--Colussus of Maroussi-SanFran-(1941)-Colt Pr-1st ed-papr labl-
cl-8vo (5tt5, M Milne, autg) 15. (5u5, fade) 20.
(5tt2, dj, autg) 27.50 (5tt2) 25.00
--Cosmological Eye-New Directions-(1929)
(5tt2, ink) 10. (5tt2, review cpy) 20.00
--same-Lond-1945-351p (5dd0, vg, sl wn dj) 15.00
--Max & The White Phagocytes-Paris-(1938)-Obelisk Pr-orig wrps-
1st ed (4b5, cl, orig wrps bnd in, autg) 100. (5hh1, pres) 125.
(5d2, Sept 1938) 75.00
--Plexus-Paris-n.d.-Olympia Pr-2 vols-orig wrps-ltd to 2000c
(4b5, vg) 45.00
--Remember to Remember-(NY, 1947)-cl-8vo-1st ed (5u5, dj) 15.00
--Sexus-Paris-1949-Obelisk Pr-orig cl-2 vols-1st ed-ltd to 3000c,
nbrd (4b5, lt stn) 50.00
--The Smile at Foot of the Ladder-NY-(1948)-illus-1st ed
(4b7, ink on fly) 15.00
--Sunday after the War-Norfolk-(1944)-New Directions-8vo-cl-
1st ed (5tt2, dj, vg) 20. (5j5, 5d9, dj) 15.00
--same-Lond-1945 (5tt2, scuff) 5.00
--Tropic of Cancer-Paris-1934-Obelisk Pr-1st ed of auth's
1st book-cl(wrps not bnd in) (4b5, later pres) 400.00
--same-NY-1940-Medusa-1st Amer ed-orig purple wrps
(4b5, advance copy, wrps tn) 75.00
--Tropic of Capricorn-Paris-(1939)- dec wrps-Obelisk Pr-
1st ed-errata slip-"First Publ Feb 1y39"
(5d8, vf) 150. (5ss7, mint, unopnd) 225.00

MILLER, HENRY (continued)
--Wisdom of Heart-Lond-1947-255p-autg (5dd0, autg, sl faded) 15.00
--same-Norfolk, Conn-(1941)-New Dir-cl-1st ed
(5F0) 7.50 (4b5) 6.00
MILLER, HON HENRY G-Chapters on Silver as Published in
Chicago Times-Chig-n.d.(1895?)-110p-wrps (5h1) 5.00
MILLER, HENRY WISE-All our Lives-NY-(1945)-229p (5t7) 7.50
MILLER, HUGH-My Schools & Schoolmasters-Edinb-c1856-sm8vo-
562p (5v0) 7.50
MILLER, HUGH GORDON-The Isthmian Highway-NY-1929-illus
(5r7, pres) 12.50
MILLER, HUNTER, ed & trans-Northwest Water Boundary, Report of
Experts Summoned by German Emperor-Seattle-1942-U Wash-
75p-map-wrps-7x10 (5dd7, mint) 12.00
MILLER, J C-Origins of the Amer Revolution-1943 (5L7) 5.00
MILLER, J MARTIN-Hunting Big Game in the Wilds of Africa-
n.p.(USA)-1909-map-photos-pic cov-384p (4t5) 10.00
MILLER, JAS-Alcohol: Its Place & Power-Phila-1866-Lindsay &
Blackiston-179p plus LIZARS, John, Use & Abuse of Tobacco-
137p-8th ed (5r0) 7.50
--same-NY-1875-138p (5w6, wn) 4.50
MILLER, JANET-Jungles Preferred-NY-1931-HoughtonMifflin-
photos-321p (4t5) 6.50
--same-Bost-(1931)-8vo-321p-photos (4a6) 4.00
MILLER, JOAQUIN-As It Was in the Beginning-(SanFran)-(1903)-
orig prntd wrps-99p (5F1) 7.50 (5zz7) 15.00
--Building of the City Beautiful-Trenton-1905-12mo-244p-sewed-
unbnd (5dd9, unopnd) 8.50
--Complete Poetical Works of-SanFran-1902-8vo-pict cl-illus-
rev ed (5h4) 6.00
--Danites & Other Choice Selections-NY-1878-160p-1st ed (5s4)10.00
--First Fam'lies of the Sierras-Chig-1876-12mo-cl-1st Amer ed
(5r9) 15. (5h4) 5. (5mm2) 12.50
--'49 Gold Seeker of the Sierras-NY&Lond-1884-Funk&Wagnalls-
orig wrps(usually bound)-1st ed (5tt6, f) 30.00
--In Classic Shades & Other Poems-Chig-1890-12mo-cl-1st ed
(5h4, shaken) 4.75 (5x5) 7.50
--Life Among the Modocs-Lond-1873-lea&bds-400p-1st ed (4n1) 85.00
--same-Hartf-1874-445p-illus (5L3, sl tn) 10.00
--Little Gold Miners of Sierras & Other Stories-Bost-(1886)-254p-
illus-dec cov (5s4, rprd) 6.50
--My Own Story-Chig-1890-12mo-cl (5h4, vg) 8.00
--The One Fair Woman-NY-1876-3 vols in 1-1st ed (5mm2) 10.00
--Paquita, the Indian Heroine-Hartf-n.d.-Amer Pub (5x4) 10.00
--A Royal Highway of the World-Portland-1932-4to-cl-
ltd to 245c, nbrd (5h4, f) 15.00
--Selections from Joaquin Miller's Poems-Oakland-1962-
Juanita Miller, ed-8vo-bds&cl (5h4, pres) 3.50
--Seven Songs-n.p.-1935-4to-wrps-words by Joaquin Miller,
music by Juanita Miller (5h4) 4.00
--Shadows of Shasta-Chig-1881-Jansen, McClurg-sm8vo-cl-
beveled edges (5b2) 10. (5mm2, f) 15.00
--Songs of Italy-Bost-1878-Roberts Bros-186p-1st ed (5q0) 10.00
--Songs of Sierras-Bost-1871-299(24)p-1st ed
(5xx8, sp fray) 5. (5s4, 4n1, rub) 4.00
--same-Lond-1871-Longmans-green cl-1st ed (5n8) 15.00
--same-lor-1871-Canadian News & Publ-8vo-cl (5b2, hng rprd) 15.00
--Songs of the Sun Lands-Bost-1873-1st ed (5mm2) 12.50
--True Bear Stories-Chig-(1900)-12mo-260p (5dd5) 5.00
MILLER, JOHN-New York Considered & Improved, 1695-Cleve-
1903-facs illus-8vo-bds (4c1) 10.00
--same-Cleve-1903-fldg plans & facs-ltd to 400c-bds (4a1) 15.00
MILLER, JOHN, JR-Guadalcanal, the First Offensive-Wash-1949-
GPO-413p (5x9, rbnd) 6.50
MILLER, JOHN A-At the Touch of a Button-Schenectady-1962-
209p-illus (5y2) 4.75
--Fares Please-NY-1941-204p-illus-1st ed (5y2) 5. (5m2) 7.50
--Workshop of Engineers-Schenectady-1953-4to-173p-illus (5y2) 6.50
MILLER, JOHN C-Origins of the Amer Revolution-Bost-1943-Little-
519p (5h9) 4.50 (5w4) 4. (5p0, 4a9) 5.00
--Triumph of Freedom, 1775 to 1783-Bost-1948-maps-718p (5ii8) 10.00
MILLER, JONATHAN W-History of Diocese of Central Penna,
1871 to 1909 & Diocese of Harrisburg, 1904 ro 1909-Frackville, Pa-
2 vols-1909-illus (5w0, lacks part bkstrps) 10. (5m2, rbkd) 20.00
MILLER, JOS-Arizona Indians-NY-(1941)-12mo-cl-ports (5h5) 5.00
--Arizona, the Last Frontier-NY-1956-8vo-cl-350p-1st ed
(5g2, dj) 8. (5yy7, dj) 6.50
--The Arizona Story-NY-1952-345p-8vo-cl (5g2) 10.00
--Monument Valley & Navajo Country-NY-(1951)-sq8vo-cl-96p-
photo (5h5, f) 5.00
MILLER, JUANITA J-Starward & Other Poems-Oakland-1948-8vo-
bds wi cl bkstrp (5h4, ALS, pres) 4.00

MILLER, KELLY-Kelly Miller's History of World War for Human
Rights-n.p.-n.d.-(c1919)-illus-pict cl-712o(28) (5mm8) 15.00
--same-Wash-1919-map-photos   (5x2) 22.50
--Progress & Achievements of Colored People-Wash-1917-illus
          (5x2,rbnd) 25.   (5x2) 27.50
--Race Adjustment-1908-Neale Pub   (5x2,ex-libr) 27.50
MILLER, KEMPSTER B-Amer Telephone Practice-NY-1899-458p-
illus   (5a9,vf) 15.00
--same-NY-1905-illus-lg8vo-888p-enlrgd (5ss5,rng crack) 10.00
MILLER, LEE G-Ernie Pyle Album-NY-(1946)-sm4to-157p-illus-
1st ed   (5xx7) 10.   (5w5) 6.50
MILLER, LEO E-In Wilds of South America-NY-1918-illus
          (5jj3) 10.   (5s6) 6.50
MILLER, M-Bliss Carman a Portrait-Tor-1935-136p (4b9,autg) 10.00
MILLER, MARGERY-Joe Louis, American-1945 (5L7,ex-libr) 4.50
MILLER, MARION MILLS-Amer Debate, Part 2, Land & Slavery
Question-NY-1916 -417p   (5t4) 8.50
--Great Debates in Amer History-(Vol #5(of 14)-States Rights
1798 to 1861, Slavery-NY-1913-illus   (5x2) 10.00
--Greek & Latin Classics-NY-(1909)-15 vols-Univ Edition-
Vincent Parke   (5p0) 60.00
--Practical Suggestions for Mother & Housewife-NY-1910-211p-
16mo   (5w7) 3.50
--Songs of Sappho-NY-1925-lg8vo-bds&vel-10 plts-13,435p
          (5t0) 12.50
MILLER, MAX-The Cruise of the Cow-NY-1951-256p-cl-map-
47 photos   (5r0) 10.00
--Fog & Men on the Bering Sea-NY-1936-272p-illus-map
          (4b9) 8.   (5ss1,4a8) 8.50
--same-NY-1938   (5c1) 9.50
--The Great Trek-NY-1935-illus-224p   (4h3,dj) 12.00
--I Cover the Waterfront-1932-Dutton-auth's 1st book
          (4m8,dj) 7.50 (5F1,dj,mint) 6.50
--Land Where Time Stands Still-NY-1943-photos (5x5,dj) 10.00
--Mexico Around Me-NY-(1937)-Reynal & Hitchcock-305p-plts
          (5qq8) 4.00
--Reno-NY-1941-267p-scarce   (5dd4) 12.50
--Town with the Funny Name-NY-1948-12mo-cl (5h4,pres,f,dj) 4.50
MILLER, MINNIE C-Tracht Family Tree-(1935)-33p-wrps (5mm3) 5.00
MILLER, NYLE H-Why The West Was Wild-Topeka-1963-illus-
1st ed   (5yy7,dj,f) 20.00
MILLER, OLIVE BEAUPRE-Heroes, Outlaws & Funny Fellows of
Amer Popular Tales-NY-1939-8vo-illus-1st ed (5ss5,stns) 7.50
--Little Pictures of Japan-Chig-Book Hse-1925-191p-
Sturges col illus   (5i1,vf) 9.00
--Tales Told of Holland-Chig-Book Hse-1926-190p-
Petersham col illus   (5i1,f) 9.00
MILLER, P E, ed-Esquire's Jazz Book-NY-1944-illus   (5x2) 6.50
MILLER, PERRY-Orthodoxy in Massachusetts-Cambr-(1933)-8vo-
cl-16p, 353p-1st ed   (5t0,dj,f) 4.50
MILLER, RAUP-Silhouettes on Blue-SanFran-1937-JohnHenry Nash-
8vo bds-cl bk   (5h4) 4.00
MILLER, RAYMOND C-Kilowatts at Work-Detroit-1957-lg8vo-
467p   (4i2,dj) 7.50
MILLER, ROBT C-Historic Views of Gettysburg-Gettysburg-1920-
80p-obl folio   (5j6) 4.50
MILLER, SAM'L-A Brief Retrospect of the 18th Century-Part First-
NY-1803-2 vols(all publ)-orig calf-1st ed
          (5h9,rub,hng weak) 100.00
MILLER, STEWART-Florida Fishing-NY-1931-8vo-illus-1st ed
          (5m6,ex-libr) 7.50
MILLER, T L-History of Hereford Cattle-Chillicothe-1902-illus-
592p-illus-v scarce   (5n4) 40. (4t3,bkstrp wn) 27.50
MILLER, THOS-Lady Jane Grey;an historical romance-Phila-1840-
Lea & Blanchard-2 vols-12mo-orig cl&bds-papr labls-1st Amer ed
          (5i0) 17.50
MILLER, THOS-Little Blue Hood-NY-1864-Gregory-sm sq8vo-dec cl-
95p-hand col frontis   (5s6) 8.50
MILLER, W-Centenary Bibliogr of Pickwick Papers-Lond-1936-223p-
ports   (4a8) 12.50
MILLER, W-The Costume of the Russian Empire-Lond-1811-
T Bensley-folio-mor-g.e.-72 col plts   (4n5,f) 350.00
MILLER, WARREN H-Camp Craft, Modern Practice & Equipment-NY-
1915-Scribners-292p-illus-cl   (5d7) 7.50
--The Lone Woodsman-Phila&Tor-(c1943)-Winston-sq8vo-230p-
dec orange cl-col frontis-plts   (5aa2) 5.00
MILLER, WILHELM-What England Can Teach Us About Gardening-
NY-1917-359p-illus   (5p7) 7.50
MILLER, WILLET G-Nickel Deposits of the World-Tor-1917-8vo-
maps-illus   (5m6) 12.50
MILLER, WM-Evidence from scripture(sic) & history of 2nd coming
of Christ, about year 1843-Troy(NY)-1836-8vo-orig qtr cl-
papr labl-2nd ed   (5i0,rprd) 100.00

MILLER, WM J-Geology of the Broadalbin Quadrangle,
Fulton, Saratoga Counties, NY-Albany-1911-65p-wrps (5p0) 3.50
MILLESON, ROYAL HILL-The Artist's Point of View-Chig-1912-
159p-cl-1st ed   (5g5) 6.00
MILLET, FRANK D, intro-Early English & Barbizon Paintings
Belonging to Wm H Fuller-NY-1898-(Amer Art Assn)-4to-bds-
plts-deluxe illus catalog-ltd to 250c (5ii3,sp frayed) 35.00
MILLET, J F-20 Etchings & Woodcuts-1881-folio-plts-India proof ed-
          (5L7,sl stn) 25.00
MILLET, SAM'L-A Whaling Voyage in the Bark "WILLIs"-Bost-
1924-46p-illus-priv prntd   (5c1) 35. (5p9) 12.50
MILLETT, FRED B-Art of the Drama-NY-(1935)-8vo-cl-253p-illus
          (5t0) 4.00
--Contemporary British Literature-NY-1935-8vo-cl-556p-
3rd rev ed   (5d3) 6.00
MILLETT, MARCUS W-Jungle Sport in Ceylon, from Elephant to
Snipe-Lond-(1914)-8vo-cl-illus   (5t0,ex-libr) 5.00
MILLHOLLAND, CAPT GEO H-Cavalry Examiner's Guide-
Harrisburg-(1929)-Telegraph Pr-8vo-133p-wrps   (4a6) 5.00
MILLIAN, JOHN-Life & Confession of-Virginia(Nevada)-Lammon,
Gregory & Palmer-sm8vo-wrps-16p-1868   (5t7) 10.00
MILLIGAN, R-Fetish Folk of West Africa-Lond-1912-Revell-photos-
pic cov-328p   (4t5,fox,lacks fly) 10.00
--The Jungle Folk of Africa-NY-1908-illus   (5x2,ex-libr) 8.50
MILLIKEN, CHAS F-History of Ontario County NY & Its People-
1911-2 vols-illus   (5ff2) 35.00
MILLIKEN, RALPH LEROY-The Plains Over, Remin of Wm Jasper
Stockton-Los Banos, CA-1939-Los Banos Enterprise-55p-frontis-
wrps-12mo   (4L9) 25.00
MILLIN, SARAH G-Cecil Rhodes-NY-1933-Harper-449p (4t5) 7.50
--General Smuts-Lond-1936-Faber & Faber-photos-2 vols (4t5,dj) 20.00
--God's Stepchildren-NY-1927   (5x2) 5.00
--The Coming of the Lord-NY-1928   (5x2) 7.50
--Rhodes-Lond-1933-Chatto Windus-e.p.-maps-389p (4t5) 8.50
--The South Africans-Lond-1926-280p-1st ed (5c6) 5.00
--The South Africans-Lond-1927-Constable-280p-5th reprnt (4t5) 7.00
--same-NY-1927-Boni Liveright-photos-287p (4t5) 6.00
MILLING, CHAPMAN-Exile Without An End-Columbia, S Car-1943-
Bostick&Thornley-88p-1st ed   (5F9,f,dj) 10.00
MILLINGEN, J G-History of Duelling-Lond-1841-R Bentley-8vo-
g.t.-2 vols-qrtr lev   (5i4,rbnd) 75.00
MILLIS, WALTER-James Forrestal, The Forrestal Diaries-NY-
1951-Viking Pr-581p   (5p9) 6.00
MILLOT, ABBE-Elements of General History, 2 vols-Worcester-1789-
Isaiah Thomas-calf-scarce-1st Amer ed (5v2,bndg v wn) 15.00
MILLS, ANSON-My story-Wash-1918-C HClaudy, ed-8vo-
maps & plans-1st ed-errata slip   (5h4,5yy7,5g2) 25.00
MILLS, CHAS-A History of Muhammedanism-Lond-1818-8vo-
3 qtr mor-2nd ed, rev   (5m6,fray) 10.00
MILLS, EDW LAIRD-Plains, Peaks & Pioneers-Portland-(1947)-234p-
plus index-photos-maps-1st ed   (5L2) 12.00
MILLS, ENOS A-The Grizzly-Bost&NY-1919-288p-illus (5t7) 5.00
--The Rocky Mntn Wonderland-Bost-(1915)-HoughtonMiff-363p-
illus-cl   (5d7) 6.00
--Spell of the Rockies-Bost-(1911)-336p-photos (5s4,lacks e.p.) 5.00
-- Waiting in the Wilderness-GardenCty-1921-Dblday-241p-
illus-cl   (5d7) 4.   (4,5w5) 4.50
--Wild Life in the Rockies-Bost-(1909)-illus (4a1,autg) 8.50
--same-Bost-1910   (5u3) 5.00
MILLS, FREDK C-The Wine Guide-Lond-1860-16mo-64p-limp cl
          (5w1) 10.00
MILLS, FREDK J-Life of John Carter-NY-1868-122p-illus-cl (5t2) 4.50
MILLS, GEO S-The Little Man with the Long Shadow-DesMoines-
1955-8vo-cl-254p-1st ed   (5m8,autg) 10.00
MILLS, DR H W-Mormon Bishop & His Son-(LosAng-1917)-91p-
illus-wrps   (5yy3) 20.00
MILLS, J HARRISON-Chronicles of 21st Regiment NY State Volun-
Buffalo-1887-348p, (40)p-cl   (5y0) 15.00
MILLS, J S-Mission Work in Sierra Leone, West Africa-Dayton, OH-
1898-United Breth Pub Hse-map(fldg)-pic cov-plts
          (4t5,plts crayon) 12.00
MILLS, JAS C-Our Inland Seas-Chig-1910-380p-cl-maps-illus
          (5ff7) 10.00
MILLS, JAS COOKE-Oliver Hazard Perry & Battle of LkErie-
Detroit-1913-278p, (6)p-frontis-author's autog ed, nbrd,
autg   (5w0,unopnd) 8.75
MILLS, JOHN-Christmas in the Olden Time-Lond-(1846)-
handcol frontis-5 plts-141p-1st ed (5nn2) 15.00
MILLS, JOHN-A Treatise on Cattle-Bost-1795-16mo-215p plus index-
calf   (5w9,rub,joints wn) 20. (4m6,rub) 50.00
MILLS, JOHN-The Sportsman's Library-Edinb-n.d.-(ca1845)-
431p-hf calf-illus   (5t2) 7.50

MILLS,JOHN S-San Diego,Calif,County Rich in Resources etc-
    SanDiego-n.d.-(ca1909)-Bd of Super-wrps-12mo-64p (4t1)   10.00
MILLS, LOIS-Three Together-NY,Chig,Tor-c1955-Follett-
    160p-8vo-illus   (5p1,dj,pres)   6.50
MILLS, RANDALL V-Stern Wheelers Up Columbia-PaloAlto-1947-
    212p-plts-maps   (5yy9) 12.50   (5dd9,5s1)   10.00
MILLS, ROGER Q-The Funding Bill-Wash-1881-14p (4a5)   4.00
MILLS, SAM'L J-Report of a missionary tour thru that part of US
    which lies west of Allegany Mntns-Andover-1815-64p-
    orig prntd wrps   (5i0,disbnd) 80. (5g3,vf,unopnd) 40.00
MILLS, W JAY,ed-Glimpses of Colonial Society & Life at Princeton
    College,1766 to 1773-Phila-1903-illus-1st ed (5tt5) 7.50 (5m6)8.50
--Historic Houses of New Jersey-Phila-1903-348p-illus-g.t.-
    Com Tr Issue(1902 edn)   (5h9)   15.00
--same-Phila-1912-illus   (5ii8)   32.50
MILLS, W S-History of Van Zandt County-n.p.-1950
         (5t9) 4.50   (5a8,f)   8.50
MILLS, W W-40 Years at El Paso-n.p.-1901   (4c7) 100.00
--same-El Paso-1962-Mesquite Ed-Tom Lea,illus-ltd to 100c,
    autg by editor   (4c7,box)   125.00
--same-El Paso-1962 (5k0,dj,autg) 15. (5x5,dj,3 autg) 22.50
MILLS, WEYMER J-The Girl I Left Behind Me-NY-1910-4to-bds-
    cl bk-90p,(5)p   (5w7,holes)   7.50
MILLS,WM-Life Experiences of The Mills Bros,Written by Themselves-
    Toledo-n.d.-(ca1900?)-40p-wrps   (5zz9)   12.50
MILLS, CAPT WM-Reports of,on Mullan wagon road,Montana Terr-
    Wash-1879-18p-unbnd-Ex Doc #3 (5dd6)   18.50
MILLS, WM C-Certain Mounds & Village Sites in Ohio,Vol 2-
    Columbus-1917-buck-plts   (4k4,f)   20.00
--same-Vol 2-Columbus-1917-illus-284p-ltd to 500 bnd copies
         (4t3)   25.00
--same-Vol 3-Columbus-1922-buck-illus   (4k4,f)   20.00
--same-Vol 4-Columbus-1926-buck-illus   (4k4,f)   20.00
--Excavations of the Adena Mound-Columbus-1902-buck-plts-4to
         (4k4,f)   6.00
--Explorations of the Edwin Harness Mound-Columbus-1907-plts-
    stiff wrps-4to   (4k4,f)   6.00
--Ohio Archaeological Exhibit at Jamestown Expos-Colum-n.d.-
    (1909?)-49p-cl   (5h7,autog)   5.00
MILMAN, HENRY H-The History of Christianity-NY-1881-2 vols-
         (5x7)   10.00
--History of Latin Christianity-NY-1881-8 vols in 4
         (5x7,hng crack)   20.00
--History of the Jews from Earliest-NY-1861-3 vols-8vo-cl
         (5t5,rbnd)   13.50
MILMINE, GEORGINE-The Life of Mary Baker G. Eddy & the
    History of Christian Science-NY-1909-8vo-cl-illus-1st ed
         (5d9)   55.00
MILNE, A A-Autobiography-NY-1939-315p-frontis-cl-1st Amer ed
         (5t2,5c8)   5.00
--Behind the Lines-Lond-(1940)-cl   (5d2,dj)   5.00
--Birthday Party & other stories-NY-1948 (5p7)   3.25
--By Way of Introduction-Lond-(1929)-1st Engl ed
    (5v0,autg) 25.   (5r9,f,5ss9,dj,vg)   8.50
--Chloe Marr-Lond-(1946)-1st Engl ed (5ss9,dj)   6.00
--The Christopher Robin Birthday Book-Lond-(1930)-Methuen-
    1st ed-215p-16mo   (5p1)   7.50
--For Luncheon Interval,Cricket & Other Verses-Lond-(1925)-
    12mo-1st ed-orig wrps (5yy6,autg) 22.50 (5r9)   5.00
--House at Pooh Corner-Lond-(1928)-1st ed-12mo-orig dj &
    linen wrps-dec by Shepard   (5ii3,f)   32.50
--same-Lond-(1928)-12mo-cl-g.t.-1st ed (5dd8,f)   25.00
--Michael & Mary,A Play-Lond-1930-Chatto&Windus-1st ed-
    ltd to 250c,autg   (5ss9,vg)   7.50
--same-Lond-1930-t.e.g.-buck-ltd to 260c,autg-1st ed (5u5) 45.00
--same-1st trade ed   (5u5,dj)   7.50
--Now We Are Six-Lond-(1927)-Methuen-dec by Shepard-cl
    (5ii3,dj) 35. (4d1,f,4F6,vg) 17.50 (4p2,lea) 25.
        (5dd2,vf,dj,5v2,vf,dj) 30. (5c8,f)   22.50
--same-NY-(1927)-large paper ed-ltd to 200c,autg by Milne &
    Shepard,orig box   (5v2,mint,dj)   165.00
--Once on A Time-NY-c1924-51 plts-col frontis-v scarce
         (4c3,wn dj,f)   17.50
--Peace With Honour-NY-c1934-1st Amer ed (5x7)   5.00
--Second Plays-NY-1922-Knopf-266p   (5p9)   3.00
--The Secret & Other Stories-NY-1929-12mo-cl-Fountain Pr-
    autg,ltd to 742c   (4c2) 20. (5a9)   25.00
--A Table Near the Band-NY-1950-1st Amer ed (5nn6,dj)   5.00
--Teddy Bear & Other Songs from When We Were Very Young-
    Lond-(1926)-brown bds & lin-dec by Shephard-1st ed (5d2) 25.00
--same-NY-(1926)-folio-1st Amer ed   (4F6,f)   17.50
--Those Were the Days-Lond-(1929)-12mo-cl-7p ads-1st trade ed
    (5u5,autg,mint) 35. (5v2,autg,mint,dj)   22.50

MILNE, A A (continued)
--same-Lond-(1929)-Methuen-ltd to 250c-1st ed
        (5u5,dj,5hh1,vg,dj)   50.00
--Toad of Toad Hall,a Play-Lond-(1929)-Methuen-1st ed
        (5hh1,vg)   7.50
--same-NY-1929-Scribners-168p-12mo (4F6,vg) 10. (5p1,wn) 3.50
--Two People-Lond-(1931)-cl-1st ed   (5d2,dj)   10.00
--same-NY-1931   (5b9,f) 3.   (5F0,vg)   4.00
--Very Young Verses-Methuen-1929-Shepard,illus-8vo-dec cl-
    88p-1st ed   (4a8)   7.50
--When We Were Very Young-Lond-(1924)-12mo-orig blue cl-
    g.t.-dec Shepard-1st ed (4c3,vg) 55. (5dd8,mint,box) 65.00
--same-NY-(1924)-Dutton-3 qrts mor-ltd to 100c,autg (4F6,vg) 90.00
--same-NY-(1924)-1st Amer ed   (5v2,f)   20.00
--Winnie the Pooh-Lond-(1926)-lg t8vo-bds-cl bk-dec Shepard-
    1st ed-ltd to 350c,lg papr,2 autgs
    (4F6,f,dj) 135. (5ee9,Rosenbach copy,dj) 175.00
--same-NY-(1926)-Dutton-dec cl-1st Amer ed (5c8,stn)   7.50
--Complete Set of the Pooh Books-When We Were Very Young,
    1924-Winnie the Pooh, 1926-Now We Are Six, 1927-The
    House at Pooh Corner, 1928-Lond-1st eds
        (5v2,f) 165. (4d2,vf,dj) 185.00
MILNE, ALAN A-When I Was Very Young-NY-1930-Fountain Pr-
    Shephard,illus-dec bds-28 illus-1st ed-ltd to 842c,nbrd
        (5nn2,autg)   35.00
MILNE, GORDON GEO-Wm Curtis & The Genteel Tradition-1956-
    Ind Univ Pr-illus-1st ed   (5m2,dj)   6.00
MILN, J-Excavations at Carnac(Brittany)-Edinb-1877-orig cl-4to-
    56 plts   (4e1)   35.00
MILNE, JAS-Epistles of Atkins-Lond-1902-12 plts (5c6,vg)   7.50
MILNER, DUNCAN C-Lincoln & Liquor-NY-1920-155p-port (5t7) 5.00
MILNER, JOE E-California Joe-Caldwell-1935-396p-photos-
    1st ed   (5yy7,pres) 30. (5dd5) 35. (4n8) 25.00
MILNER, VISCOUNT-Speeches Delivered in Canada, 1908-Tor-
    1909-93p   (5dd7)   10.00
MILNS,WM-Well Bred Scholar-Lond-1794-thk8vo-559p-orig bds
        (5tt6,unopnd)   40.00
--same-NY-1797-Literary Ptg Ofc-calf-284p (5w7,hng broke) 14.50
MILON, C-Denkwurdigkeiten zur Geschichte Benjamin Franklins-
    StPetersburg-1793-sm8vo-bds-g.labl (5L1)   65.00
MILORADOVICH, MILO-Art of Cooking wi Herbs & Spices-
    GardenCty-(1950)-304p   (5c9)   3.50
--Art of Fish Cookery-NY-1949-457p-1st ed (5c9)   3.00
--The Home Garden Book of Herbs & Spices-GardenCty-1952-
    236p   (5s7) 4. (5w3)   5.00
MILTON, CHAS J-Landmarks of Old Wheeling & Surrounding
    Country-Wheeling-1943-(99)p-cl-priv prntd-scarce (5h7) 10.00
MILTON, JOHN-Hymn on the morning of Christ's Nativity-
    Christmas, 1928-Ashendene Pr-8vo-blue wrps-16p-
    about 220c prntd   (5d1)   75.00
--L'Allegro & Il Penseroso-Art Union of Lond-1848-30p illus plus
    30p text-qtr mor-bds   (5ee3,vg)   4.00
--same-Lond-1855-illus-4to-26 lvs of cards-emboss cl-a.e.g.
        (5dd0,v sl fox)   15.00
--same-NY-1954-Limited Editions Club-Thistle Pr-4to-cl
    ltd to 1780c,box   (5ee9)   15.00
--The Mask of Comus-1937-Nonesuch Pr-sm folio-vel bds-
    col plts & music-ltd to 950c (5p6,sl soil,box fade) 35.00
--Paradise Lost & Paradise Regain'd-SanFran-1936-John Henry Nash-
    folio-ltd to 1500c,nbrd,autg-box (5b0)   25.00
--same-(Lond)-1937-sm folio-3 qtrs black pigskin-t.e.g.-
    Golden Cockerel-ltd to 196c,box (5d9) 225.00
--Paradise Lost A Poem in 12 Books-Lond-1725-350p plus index-
    prntd for Jacob Tonson-Vertue port of Milton-orig lea (5f9) 100.00
--same-Wash-1801-Mathew Carey-   (4m8)   0.00
--Poems in English-Lond-1926-Nonesuch Pr-illus by W Blake-
    2 vols-8vo-vel-g.t.-1450c (4c2,f) 75. (5b0) 125.00
--Poems,English,Latin,Greek & Italian-Lond-1925-Chatto&Windus-
    Florence Pr-2 vols-8vo-cl (5b0,edges slt brown) 17.50
--Poetical Works-Edinburgh & Lond-n.d.-Gall&Ingliss-cl (5i4) 7.00
--same-Sir E B Bart,ed-Lond-1835-John Macrone-lg12mo-illus-
    two tone cl-6 vols-g.t.   (5t5,rbnd)   37.50
--same-Lond-1906-Beeching,ed-lg16mo-hf calf-Oxford Complete ed-
        (5b0)   15.00
--The Poetical Works of...with a life of the author & illus-Bost-
    n.d.-4 vols-hand made papr edit-pigskin-ltd to 555 sets (5x0) 50.00
MILTON,JOHN M-A View of SoAmer & Mexico-NY-1826-
    2 vols in 1-orig calf   (5m2)   5.00
MILTON,WM-The North West Passage By Land-Lond-(1865)-
    Cassell,et al-8vo-hf mor-2 fldg maps-22 plts-1st ed (5n9) 125.00
--same-Lond-(1866)-400p plus illus-2 fldg maps-3 qtrs lea-
    raised bands-5th ed   (5t3)   27.50

MILTON, WM (continued)
--same-Lond-n.d.-3rd ed-397p-2 fldg maps(1 pkt)-cl-22 plts
(5i3, rbnd)   17.50
--same-Lond-(1867)-7th ed-calf-g.-plts-fldg map   (4a8)   15.00
MILTOUN, FRANCIS-Dickens' London-Lond-1904-300p-ports-plts
(4a8)   5.00
MILWAUKEE-Annual report of...for 1855-Milwkee-1855-8p-
Board of Trade   (5g8)   12.50
MILWAUKEE COUNTY-Memoirs of-Madison 1909-2 vols-4to-
part mor-illus by Watrous   (5jj7, f)   50.00
MILWAUKEE-Hist of, from Pre Historic Times to Present Date-1881-
1663p-illus-v scarce   (5t9, wn)   40.00
MILWAUKEE-100 Photogravures-Milwkee-1892-obl 8vo-orig limp cl-
32p text plus 100 illus-Pabst Brewing Co   (5ss5)   10.00
MILWAUKEE, WIS-Souvenir Presented by Phillip Best Brewing Co-
(NY, ca 1881)-obl 12mo-orig cl-24 lvs-fld out plus 8p text
(5m6)   17.50
--same-NY-1883-Wittemann Bros-58p-fld out   (5n4, f)   15.00
MIMS, E-The Advancing South-NY-1927   (5x2)   8.50
MINA, CURTISS, ed-Letters of Marcel Proust-NY-1949-Random Hse-
1st ed   (5ss9, dj)   10.00
MINARD, M E-Hist of Westminster, Vermont-1941-174p (5mm3)   7.50
MINCHIN, B-Worship in the Body of Christ-1961   (5L7)   7.50
MINCHIN, NYDIA E-The Jester's Purse-NY-(c1926)-Harcourt Brace-
12mo-203p-illus-Bookshop Play Series #1   (5p1)   6.50
MINCOFF, ELIZ-Pillow Lace, a Practical Hand book-NY-1907-
cl-50 illus   (5t2, libr mks)   7.50
MINELLE, JEAN-L'Agriculture a Madagascar-Paris-1959-378p-
22 plts-maps-wrps   (5c6, f)   12.50
MINER, CHAS-History of Wyoming-Phila-1845-plts-maps
(5t9, wn) 27.50   (5h9, lea) 25.   (5yy0, shake)   22.50
MINER'S, HARRY-Amer Dramatic Directory for 1885, 86-NY-1885-
336p-illus   (5m1sl wn)   10.00
MINER, LOUIE M-Our Rude Forefathers-CedrRapids-1937-1st ed
(5v0, pres, vf, dj)   10.00
MINER, MAUDE E-Slavery of Prostitution-NY-(1919)-319p (5t4)   7.50
MINER, T B-Amer Bee Keeper's Manual-NY-1849-349p-sm8vo-cl-
illus   (5t2, fray)   7.50
MINER, W H-Iowa-Cedar Riv-1911-Torch Pr   (4k4, f, 5L7)   7.50
MINERALS YEARBOOK 1936-Wash-1936-HR doc #42, 75th Cong,
1st sess-1136p   (5ss1)   4.00
MINERVA-Literary Entertaining & Scientific Journal-NY-1824-
Vol 1-New Series-416p-hf lea   (4b6, scuff)   35.00
MINES, JOHN FLAVEL-Tour Around NY & My Summer Place-NY-
1893-illus-1st ed   (4b7)   12.50
MINET, PIERRE-Circoncision du Coeur-Paris-1928-Edw W Titus-
8vo-wrps-1st ed-port-ltd to 300c   (5ee9, unopnd)   20.00
MINGOS, HOWARD-Flying for 1938-NY-(1937)-5th annual ed-
illus   (5jj3)   7.50
MINIFIE, WM-Text Book of Geometrical Drawing-Balt-1849-8vo-
166p-calf-plts   (5L1)   15.00
MINNESOTA ARROWHEAD COUNTRY-Chig-1941-(Am Guide Ser)-
216p-illus-map-1st ed-WPA   (4L5)   7.50
MINNESOTA-As a Home for Immigrants, being 1st & 2nd Prize Essay-
StPaul-1865-80p-disbound   (5yy0)   22.50
MINNESOTA FARMERS' DIARIES-StPaul-1939-247p-
Minn Hist Soc   (5t7)   7.50
MINNESOTA GAZETTEER & BUSINESS DIRECTORY FOR 1865-
StPaul-1865-8vo-prntd bds-lea bk   (5a3, ex-libr)   75.00
MINNESOTA HIST SOC-Collections of-Vol 1 to 17-StPaul-
v.d. (reprntd 1872)-8vo-cl-mor   (5g4, lacks Vol 2)   100.00
MINNESOTA-Illus Historical Atlas of State of-Chig-1874-Andreas-
39rp-maps-views&ports-orig lea & cl (5yy3, wn) 50.   (5t9)   40.00
MINNESOTA IN CIVIL & INDIAN WARS 1861 to 1865-StPaul-
1890-844p-bds-lea-Board of Commrs   (5t7)   20.00
--same-StP-1891-844p-2nd ed   (5a9, 5F9)   15.00
MINNESOTA, ITS ADVANTAGES TO SETTLERS-StP-1867-36p-
orig wrps-Pub by State   (5w4)   12.50
MINNESOTA-Its Progress & Capabilities-2nd annual report of
Comm of Statistics for 1860 & 1861-StP-1862-wrps-disbnd-
errata slip   (5g3, lacks bkstrp, ex-libr)   25.00
MINNESOTA-Its Resources & Progress etc-StP-1870-wrps-72p
(5q0)   10.00
MINNESOTA LAW REVIEW-1917 to 68-Vol 1 thru 53
(5rr4, recent rbnd)   1,100.00
MINNESOTA MASSACRE & SIOUX WAR-Thrilling Narrative of-
Chig-(1896)-illus   (5k4, f)   35.00
MINNESOTA-Men of Minnesota-StP-1915-520p-mor-ports-g.e.
(5xx5)   8.00
MINNESOTA-Sketch of Organiz, Objects & Membership of Old
Settlers'Assoc of Minn wi excursion to Red River, Oct 25 & 26,
1971-StP-1872-29p-wrps-v scarce   (5L0)   35.00

MINNESOTA-A State Guide-NY-1938-(Am Guide Ser)-511p-
photos-maps-1st ed-pkt map   (5x5, 4L5)   10.00
MINNESOTA TERRITORY-Rules for Gov of Council of etc,
Sept 3, 1849-StP-1849-16mo-15p-stitchd   (5a3, f)   85.00
MINNICH, HARVEY C, ed-Old Favorites from McGuffey Readers-
NY-(1936)-Amer Book Co-orig lea bkd bds-illus (5m2, sp wn)   4.00
MINNIE'S PET MONKEY-Bost&NY-1871-24mo-152p-frontis-
Vol 6 of "Minnie & her Pets" series   (5p1)   6.50
MINNIGERODE, MEADE-Certain Rich Men-NY-1926-210p-illus-
1st ed   (5w5)   6.50
--Jefferson, Friend of France-NY-1928-Putnam (5r0) 7.50 (5x5)   8.50
--Lives & Times-NY-1925-215p-illus-t.e.g.-1st ed   (5w5)   5.00
MINNIGH, LUTHER W-Gettysburg, "What They Did Here"-1892-
148p-wrps-map   (5j6)   4.50
MINNS, EDW W-Art of Restoring & Refinishing Antique Furniture-
n.p.-(1947)-8vo-illus-cl-165p-2nd ed   (5t0, dj, f)   5.00
MINOR, CHAS L C-The Real Lincoln-Gastonia-1928-273p-4th ed
(5t7)   5.00
MINOR, HENRY-Story of the Democratic Party-NY-1928-Macm-
8vo-cl-frontis-501p-Souvenir Ed   (5j5)   12.50
MINOR, RALEIGH C-A Republic of Nations-NY-1918 (5x7)   6.50
MINOR, THOS C-Athothis-Cinn-1887-194p-cl-Robt Clarke
(5ff7, pres)   12.50
MINOT, GEO RICHARDS-History of Insurrections in Mass in 1786
& Rebellion-Worcester-1788-part lea-192p-1st ed-rare
(5n2, disbnd) 85.   (4t3, hgn crack)   65.00
--same-Bost-1810-2nd ed-192p-orig bds-papr labl (5m3, sl soil)   22.50
MINOT, J G-Minot Family in Amer & England-1897-55p (5mm3) 32.50
MINSTRELSY OF THE WOODS-Harvey & Darton-1832-sm8vo-
hf calf-227p-16 col plts   (5s0)   25.00
MINUTE MAN, THE-Vol 1, #1, Feb 22, 1922 to Vol 1, #12,
Jan 22, 1923-Newark-120p-cl-lea bk-NJ Div Assn Agnst
Prohibition Amendment   (5r0, sl wn)   12.50
MINUTES OF DEBATES IN COUNCIL-on Banks of Ottawa(Maumee)
River, (Miamia of the Lake)-Phila-1792-8vo-22p, (2)p-
stitchd   (5a3, box)   750.00
MIRAGLIA, L-Comparative Legal Philosophy applied to legal
institutions-1912   (5L7)   7.50
MIRANDY-As Told To-Hollywood-(1938)-251p-pict cl-Oxford Pr
(5r0, autg)   10.00
MIRIAM COFFIN-NY-1834-Carvill-12mo-orig cl-2 vols-1st ed
(4h0, rbkd, fade, wtrstn) 100.   (5x1)   125.00
--same-NY-1835-Harper-cl-12mo-2 vols-paper labls
(5x1, fox, stnd)   50.00
MIRIAM COOK BOOK-Albion, MI-n.d.-(ca 1909)-Ladies Aid
Soc, M E Church-161p-illus ads-oilcloth (4g9, chip, rprd)   6.50
MIRROR, THE-Periodical Paper, publ at Edinburgh in 1779 & 1780-
2 vols-Bost-1792-1st Amer ed
(5v2, cov loose) 20.   (5ss5, sig loose)   12.50
MIRRORS OF WASHINGTON-NY-1921-Putnam-8vo-cl-illus-
256p   (5p7) 4.   (5j5)   7.50
MIRSKY, JEANNETTE-Elisha Kent Kane & The Seafaring Frontier-
Bost-(1954)-301p-1st ed   (5ss1, autg) 5.   (5s1, dj)   4.00
--To the North-NY-1934-386p-illus-fldg col map (5ss1, pres)   10.00
--The Westward Crossings-NY-1946-8vo-cl-1st ed
(5h4, f) 5.   (5m9)   7.50
--World of Eli Whitney-NY-1952-346p-illus   (5t4)   7.50
MIRVAL, C H De-Le Robinson des Sables du Desert-Paris-1837-
Lehuby-sm8vo-3 qrtrs calf-320p-3 plts   (5aa2)   25.00
MIRZA, YOUEL B-Myself When Young-GardenCty-1929-Dblday-
12mo-260p-illus-1st ed   (5p1)   12.50
MISCELLANIES IN PROSE & VERSE-Lond-1713-8vo-2nd ed
(5x3, rbkd)   45.00
MISCELLANIES, MORAL & INSTRUCTIVE-in Prose & Verse-
Phila prntd-Dublin reprntd-1789-198p-12mo-lea
(5c8, lea crack)   35.00
MISCHIEVOUS BOY, THE-A Tale of Tricks & Troubles-NewHav-
c1845-S Babcock-12mo-64p-wrps-8 plts   (5v0, sp wn)   12.50
MISHRA, RAMMURTI S-Fundamentals of Yoga, A Handbook-NY-
1959-Julian Pr-255p   (5p7)   4.25
MISISQUOI COPPER MINE-Canada East; Reports by Thos Petherick,
et al-Bost-1864-16p-fldg map & plt-wrps   (5x7)   10.00
MISS BROWNE-the Story of a Superior Mouse-Lond, NY-c1900-
4tp-bd lvs-col plts   (5v0)   12.50
MISS LESLIE'S MAGAZINE-Phila-(1843)-Vol 1-illus-part lea
(4b6)   25.00
MISS MARY'S VALENTINE-& Other Stories-Bost-1895-4to-col illus-
col pict bds-cl bk-1st ed   (5p5)   7.50
MISS SALAD & HER TROUSSEAU-1st Meth Episcopal Church-
Topeka-n.d.-(ca 192?)-38p-wrps-ads   (5g9)   3.00
MISSION FURNITURE HOW TO MAKE IT-Chig-(1909)-2 vols-
illus-cl   (5t4)   6.00

MISSION LA PURISIMA-La Purisima Concepcion Missions at Lompoc, Calif-(Lompoc, 1912)-56p inc ads-wrps   (5d6)   25.00

MISSIONARIES OF SOC OF JESUS-Dictionary of Kalispel or Flat Head Indian Language-Montana-1877,8,9-St Ignatius Pr-3 vols in 2-orig wrps(scrap)-1st ed-ex rare   (4F7)   300.00

MISSIONARY RECORDS-Northern Countries-Phila-1841-Presbyterian Board of Publ-279p-hf calf   (5s6)   10.00

MISSIONS BELGES DE LA COMPAGNIE DE JESUS-Congo:Bengale:Ceylon-Brussels-1899-sm4to-484p-illus-34p photos   (5c6, vg, re-wrp)   15.00

MISSISSIPPI-Commerce & Navigation of Valley of the-StL-(1847)-wrps-32p-rare pamphlet   (5L5)   250.00

MISSISSIPPI-A Guide to Magnolia State-NY-1938-545p-illus-fldg pkt map-WPA-1st ed   (5h9)   6.00
--same-NY-(1949)-4th prntg-Amer Guide Ser-maps   (4L5, dj)   6.50

MISSISSIPPI PANORAMA-City Art Museum of StL-1949-wrps-227p-illus-8vo-5 col plts   (4a0)   35.00

MISSISSIPPI-Revised Statutes of State of Mississippi-1836-buck   (5L7, rbnd)   25.00

MISSOURI BUR OF LABOR STATISTICS-1912,13,14-"Missouri Booster Pamphlet" Part 1, "1913 Red Book"-JeffersonCty-(1914)-609p plus index-photos-fldg maps-wrps-v scarce   (5t3)   20.00

MISSOURI-A Guide to the "Show Me" State-NY-(1941)-627p plus index-photos-maps-Amer Guide Ser-1st ed-WPA   (4L5)   10.00

MISSOURI HISTORICAL REVIEW-Columbia-Oct, 1906 to July, 1971-Vol 1 to 65-orig wrps-plus index Vols to 45   (5yy3)   275.00

MISSOURI HISTORICAL SOC -Bulletin of-Vols 1 to 21, #3, incl Vols 1 to 8 bnd in 5 vols, remainder in parts as issued-StL-1944 to 1964-illus-complete run   (5g4)   100.00

MISSOURI IRON CO-Prospectus of.., With Acts of Inc-n.p.-n.d.-(1837)-fldg frontis-wrps-map-36p-rare   (4t3, bkstrp chip)   75.00

MISSOURI, KANSAS & TEXAS RWY CO-(In Texas) & Its Auxiliary Lines-Charters, Acts of Incorp etc comp by Warner, Dean & Hagerman-Houston-1889-596p   (5s4, ex-libr)   40.00
--Report to Stockholders-(NY)-n.d.-(1910)-52p-wrps   (5L0)   5.00

MISSOURI-Organization & Status of Missouri Troops(Union & Confederate) in Service during Civil War-Wash, DC-1902-336p-scarce   (5yy7, rebnd)   15.00

MISSOURI PACIFIC RY-Statistics & Info concerning Indian Territory, Okla & Cherokee Strip-(StL)-n.d.-(1897)-wrps-85p plus ads-illus-fldg map-3rd ed-rare   (5L0,sl chip)   45.00
--Statistics & info concerning State of Texas...for Farmer & Stock Raiser-(StL, 1893)-93p-drawngs-8th ed   (5L0)   8.50
--Statistics & info concerning State of Nebraska-(StL, 1892)-illus-wrps   (5g3)   6.00

MISSOURI RY GUIDE-Official-Carthage, Mo, 1893, April ed-68p-photos-time tables-drawngs-ads-wrps-scarce   (5t3)   15.00

MISSOURI STATE GAZETTEER-& Business Directory, 1881-StL-(1881)-1215p plus ads-fldg map-papr on bds   (5zz5)   30.00
--same-1893,94-StL-1893-1915p plus ads-bds&cl (5zz5,ex-libr)   20.00

MISTAKES & FAILURES-of the Temperance Reformation-NY-1864-48p-wrps-Mason Bros   (5r7, ex-libr)   10.00

MR CROSWELL'S REPLY TO BOOK LATELY PUBLISHED-Bost-1742-Rogers & Fowle, prntr-23p-sewd, pamph   (5h2)   20.00

MR DOOLEY AT HIS BEST-NY-1938-Scribner's-291p-1st ed   10.00

MR DOOLEY IN PEACE & WAR-Bost-1898-12mo-cl-1st ed of auth's 1st book   (5gg6, dj, Merle Johnson Bkplt)   35.00
--same-Bost-1899-260p   (5t7, libr labl)   7.50

MR H OR BEWARE A BAD NAME-Phila-1813-12mo-36p-sewn-1st ed-orig state-ex rare   (5hh0, uncut)   1,150.00

MITCHELL, C AINSWORTH-Mineral & Aerated Waters-Lond-1913-227p   (5w1, shake)   3.50
--Oils, animal, vegetable, essential & mineral-Lond-(1916)-138p-illus-12mo   (5w1)   4.50
--Vinegar, Its Manufr & Examin -Lond-1916-5 plts-201p(32)p   (5w6, shake)   5.00

MITCHELL CITY-& Davison Co, SoDak Directory, 1928-Norfolk, Neb-n.d.-(1928)-459p-Keiter Directory Co   (5L2, wn)   7.50
--same, 1930, 31-Norfolk, Neb-n.d.-(1930)-493p   (5L2, wn)   7.50

MITCHELL, CLARA G-The "Original Book"-Denver-(1916)-242p-oilcloth-4th ed   (5c9)   5.00

MITCHELL, D G-Int'l Library of Famous Literature-NY-(1898)-20 vols-illus-hf mor-mrbld bds   (5yy0)   50.00

MITCHELL, DONALD G-About Old Story Tellers-NY-1878-Scribner, Armstrong-8vo-dec cl-237p-1st ed   (5rr2, bkstrp wn) 8.00   (5v0, f)   15.00
--Amer Lands & Letters, Mayflower to Rip Van Winkle-NY-1897-402p-illus-fldg chart-g.t.-1st ed   (5t2) 3.   (5h9)   5.00
--Amer Lands & Letters, Leather Stocking to Poe's Raven-NY-1899-412p-illus-g.t.-1st ed (5h9, pres, 5mm2) 5.   (5e8)   6.75
--The Dignity of Learning, Valedictory Oration..July 7, 1841-NHav-1841-8vo-orig prntd wrps-1st ed of auth's 1st publ (5gg6)   45.00

MITCHELL, DONALD G (continued)
--Doctor Johns-NY-1866-2 vols-1st ed   (5m1)   6.00
--The Lorgnette-NY-1850-2 vols-8vo-orig cl-plts   (5p5)   15.00
--Reveries of a Bachelor-NY-1850-hf mor & bds-a.e.g.-orig covs bnd in-1st ed   (5j3, f)   15.00
--same-NY-1931-R8vo-orig cl-1st ed-ltd, nbrd   (5t5)   12.50

MITCHELL, EDW P-Memoirs of an Editor-NY-1924-illus   (5mm2)   5.00

MITCHELL, EDWIN V-Maine Summer-NY-(1939)-210p-illus (5t4)   3.75
--Morocco Bound, Adrift Among Books-NY-1929-232p   (5t2, f, dj, 5j4, dj)   4.00
--It's An Old Penna Custom-NY-1947-262p-illus   (5h9)   4.00
--Yankee Folk-NY-1948-Vanguard-278p   (5p9)   3.50

MITCHELL, EWING-Kicked In & Kicked Out of the President's Little Cabinet-Wash-1936-8vo-illus-1st ed   (5ss5)   10.00

MITCHELL, G P, ed-A century of Iowa Baptist History, 1834 to 1934-Pella, IA-1934-Baptist Record-Vol 1(of 2)-601p   (5u3, lacks Vol 2)   6.50

MITCHELL, H E-Mitchell Group-1963-177p   (5t9)   10.00

MITCHELL, HELEN-Ships that Made History-NY-(1950)-96p-illus   (5s1, sl shake)   5.00

MITCHELL, HORACE-Game Farming-Portsmouth-8vo-162p-cl-illus   (5g6)   6.00

MITCHELL, ISAAC-The Asylum; or, Alonzo & Melissa-Poughkeepsie-1811-2 vols-12mo-sheep-1st ed of auth's only book   (5gg6, bk cov replaced)   175.00

MITCHELL, JAS T-Unequalled Collection of Engraved Portraits-Phila-(1907)-Davis&Harvey-illus-134p-8vp-pict labl-wrps   (4c1)   6.00

MITCHELL, JOHN-Map of British & Fremch Dominions in No Amer-Amsterdam-for Covens & Mortier-(1756)-8 sheets, ea ca 72x61 cm-col   (4e1)   1,750.00
--same-Lond-publ by authr-c1773-engr map in 2 sheets of 8 sections each 76x53"-linen bkd-3rd ed-Jefferys & Faden, prntr-Howes M678   (5hh0, f)   1,000.00

MITCHELL, JOHN-Jail Journal-Dublin-1913-illus-mor-a.e.g.-g.with shamrocks   (5j3, pres labl)   80.00

MITCHELL, JOHN AMES-The Last American-NY-(1902)-78p-Stokes-deluxe ed   (5x4)   7.50
--Life's fairy tales-NY-1892-Stokes-illus-pi c cl-1st ed (5m2)   6.50

MITCHELL, JOHN FOWLER, JR-The Rooster, Its Origin as Democratic Emblem (1840s)-Greenfield, Ind-1913-12mo-ports-32p-1st ed   (5m6)   10.00

MITCHELL, JOS-The Missionary Pioneer or Brief Memoir of Life, Labors & Death of John Stewart (Man of Color)-NY-1827-16mo-96p-bds-cl bk-(reprint Episc Church South NY, 1918) (5r0)   15.00

MITCHELL, JOS-McSorley's Wonderful Saloon-NY-(1943)-264p   (5dd6, spots)   5.00

MITCHELL, LT COL JOS B-Decisive Battles of Civil War-NY-(1955)-35 maps   (5s9, dj)   5.00

MITCHELL, LEONARD JAN-Luchow's German Cookbook-NY-1952-224p-illus   (5g9)   3.00

MITCHELL, MAIRIN-The Red Fleet & the Royal Navy-Lond-1942-8 photos   (5c1)   6.00

MITCHELL, MARGARET-Gone with the Wind-NY-1936-Macmillan-orig cl-1st ed, 1st issue (wi May copyrite)-1037p-auth's 1st&only book (5gg6, f, printed pres slip) 50. (4b4)   45.00
--same-NY-1936-1st ed-June prnt   (5i3, sl rub)   12.50
--same-NY-1939-Motion Picture Ed-illus   (5i3)   5.00
--same-NY-1940-wrps-391p-illus motion picture ed   (4b4)   7.50

MITCHELL, MARGARET J-The Fireless Cook Book-NY-1909-illus   (5g9, f)   5.00

MITCHELL, MISS-Tales of Instruction & Amusement Written for Use of Young Persons-Lond-E Newbery-1795-2 vol-sm8vo-frontis-calf-1st ed   (5a1, bkstr rprd)   85.00

MITCHELL, NAHUM-Mitchell's History of Bridgewater, Mass-Bridgewater-1897-(orig pub 1840)-facs reprint-424p-3 qrtrs lea   (5h9)   35.00

MITCHELL, P CHALMERS-Childhood of Animals-NY-n.d.(1912)-orig cl-12 col plts-269p-8vo-v scarce   (4p5, sl fade, scuff) 20.   (5yy6)   10.00

MITCHELL, R J-A History of the English People-Lond-1950-612p-illus   (5p0)   6.50

MITCHELL, RUTH COMFORT-Old San Fran, Blue for True Love etc-NY-1933-4 bks in 1 slcase-1st ed   (4a5)   10.50

MITCHELL, S A-Eclipses of the Sun-NY-1932-490p-8vo-cl-illus-col frontis   (5t2)   5.00

MITCHELL, S AUGUSTUS-Accompaniment to Mitchell's New Map of Texas, Oregon & Calif with Regions Adjoining-Phila-1846-46p-fldg col map inside bk cov- lea   (5t3, rub)   65.00
--Accompaniment to Mitchell's Reference & Distance Map of US-Phila-1834-324p-bds & lea   (5t4)   15.50
--Illinois in 1837-Phila-1837-map-143p-2nd issue   (5yy0)   22.50

MITCHELL, S AUGUSTUS (continued)
--Map of the State of NY-Phila-1839-col-21x18" fld to 16mo
cl case   (5t4)   20.00
--Map of the States of Ohio, Indiana & Illinois with settled part of
Mich-Phila-1835-fldg col map in bds-1st ed   (5L3)   40.00
--Mitchell's Modern Atlas-Phila-1871-folio-44 maps
(4F6, index incomplete)   35.00
--Mitchell's Nat'l Map with 32 cities & towns in Union-Phila-
1847-50x38" cl & rollers   (5t4)   75.00
--Mitchell's New General Atlas-Phila-1865-55 quarto maps-
orig cl & lea   (5yy3, wn)   50.00
--same-Phila-1867-maps-folio-92 col maps & plans-hf mor
(4c1, wn, cov loose)   50.00
--same-Phila-1870-96 maps in col   (5v2, vf)   50.00
--same-Census of 1860 & 1870-Phila-1872-63 maps-folio-orig bds-
(5L8, cov shabby)   32.00
--same-Phila-1886-series of 147 maps & plans-Wm M Bradley &
Bros   (5t4, cov stnd) 45.00
--same-Phila-1890-147 maps & plans-folio   (5w9, sl rub) 27.50
--Mitchell's School Geography-Phila-1847-Cowperthwait-
2nd rev ed-16 mo-lea & bds-336p-no atlas   (5ii4)   10.00
--Mitchell's Traveller's Guide thru the US-Phila-1836-18mo-lea-
fld map-78p   (5t4)   20.00
--same-Phila-1833-fldg col map-fldg index-cl folder (4t3,crack)35.00
--same-Phila-1837-mor-16mo-78p   (5yy8)   25.00
--same-Phila-n.d.-(map dated 1843)-fldg col map-32mo-roan
(5g8)   15.00
--Mitchell's Universal Atlas-New Universal Atlas-Phila-1850-
Cowperthwait-folio-72p(1 side)-col maps-3/4 lea-rare
(4t3, sl wn)   150.00
--same(cov title)-Phila-1854-Cowperthwait-129col maps-
atlas folio   (5n4)   145.00
--Mitchell's Universal Atlas-Phila-1855-Chas Desilver-folio-
hf calf-labl-129 col maps etc   (4c1)   85.00
MITCHELL, S L-Medical Repository & Review of Amer Publ on
Medicine-NY-1806-lea-454p-2nd Hexade, Vol 3   (4p8)   85.00
MITCHELL, S WEIR-Adventures of Francois-NY-1898-321p-illus-
Century-1st ed   (5x4)   7.50
--same-NY-1899-8vo-frontis-wrps-Int'l Paper Novels #4-
"Special Limited Ed"   (5b2)   4.00
--Dr North & His Friends-NY-1900-8vo-cl-g.t.-Century-
1st ed   (4m8) 5.00   (5b2, f, dj)   10.00
--Far in the Forest-Phila-1889-1st ed (4m8) 7.50 (5ee3) 5.00
--The Guillotine Club & Other Stories-NY-1910-285p-Century-
1st ed   (5x4)   10.00
--Hephzibah Guiness, Thee & You & Draft on the Bank of Spain-
Phila-1880-1st ed   (5jj0)   17.50
--Hugh Wynne, Free Quaker-NY-1897-Century-2 vols-12mo-
(trial or advance bndg tan, cl stmpd in brown)-last wd "in"
pg 54, Vol 1-"before us" li. 16, pg 260, Vol 2-1st ed, 1st issue
(4h0,f)   65.00
--same-NY-1897-2 vols-1st ed   (4m8) 20.   (5v2,f)   22.50
--same-NY-1899-Howard Pyle, illus-2 vols-Continental Ed
(5t4) 7.50   (5r9, f) 15.   (5h9)   10.00
--John Sherwood, Ironmaster-NY-1911-Century-8vo-cl-g.
(5b2, f, dj)   7.50
--Little Stories-NY-1903-Century-1st ed (4m8, 5m2, bkplt) 5.00
--A Madeira Party-NY-1910-165p-16mo-frontis (5w1, stain) 8.50
--Memory of Franklin-(NY)-1906-4p-1st prntg   (4c2, f)   25.00
--New Samaria & the Summer of St Martin-Phila-1904 (5x4) 7.50
--Philip Vernon, a tale in prose & verse-NY-1895-Century-
1st ed of one of his scarcer titles   (5m2)   6.00
--The Red City-NY-1908-Century-8vo-cl-illus-inset on upper cov
(4m8) 5.   (5x4, sl fray) 15.   (5b2, f, dj wn)   8.50
--A Venture in 1777-Phila-(1908)-Jacobs-120p-illus-1st ed (5x4) 7.50
--Westways, A Village Chronicle-NY-1913-8vo-cl-510p-1st ed
(4m8) 4.50   (5t2)   5.00
--When All the Woods are Green-NY-1894-Century-419p-1st ed
(5x4, name scratched)   10.00
--Works-NY-1905-12 vols-t.e.g.-Author's Definitive Ed (5w9) 17.50
--The Youth of Washington-NY-1904-290p-1st ed
(5xx5) 5.25   (5ee3, vg)   4.00
--same-Lond-1904   (5xx5)   5.25
MITCHELL, SIDNEY B-Iris for every Garden-NY-(1960)-216p-
col plts-rev ed   (5s7, pencil) 3.00
MITCHELL, STEWART-Horatio Seymour of NY-Cambr-1938-623p-
illus   (5t4)   8.50
--New Letters of Abigail Adams 1788 to 1801-Bost-1947-illus-281p
(4b3, f, dj)   7.50
MITCHELL, THOS-Rudimentary Manual of Architecture-Lond-1870-
Longmans&Green-304p-8vo   (5m5, bkstrp tn) 14.00

MITCHELL, THOS-Short Hand Phonography for the Million-
Lansingburgh, NY-1858-64p-12mo-orig prntd bds-1st ed (5L1) 20.00
MITCHELL, W H-Geographi & statistical history of Co of Olmsted,
togeth wi general view of State of Minn-Rochester-1866-
Shaver & Eaton-8vo-orig orange prntd wrps-1st ed (5i0) 120.00
--Geographi & statistical history of Steele Co(Minn) from its
earliest settlement to present time-Minnpls-1868-Tribune Prntg-
12mo-orig grey prntd wrps-1st ed   (5i0)   120.00
MITCHELL, WESLEY C-History of Greenbacks, with Spec Ref to
Economic Consequences of Their Issue, 1862 to 65-Chig-1903-
577p-v scarce   (5ii8)   35.00
MITCHELL, WM-New & Complete System of Bookkeeping, by Improved
Method of Double Entry-Phila-1796-orig calf (5m2)   12.50
MITCHELL, WM-Winged Defense-1926-illus-261p (5F2)   12.50
MITCHELL, WM A-Linn Co, Kans, a History-LaCygne, Ka & KansCty-
1928-404p-maps   (5t9) 15.   (5t3)   12.50
MITCHELL, WM M-Rise of Revolutionary Party in Engl House of
Commons, 1603 to 29-1947   (5L7)   6.00
MITCHELL-HEDGES, F A-Battles with Monsters of the Sea-NY-
1937-illus-3 maps   (5c1, cov wn) 10.00
MITCHENER, C H-Ohio Annals, Historic Events in Tuscarawas &
Muskingum Valleys-Dayton-1876-358p-1st ed (5jj7, sl wn) 25.00
MITCHELL, SAM'L L-Lecture on some parts of natural history
of NJ-NY-1828-orig wrps   (5g4)   25.00
MITFORD, BERTRAM-Aletta, Tale of Boer Invasion-Lond-1900-
8&302p-1 plt   (5c6)   7.50
--Expiation of Wynne Palliser-Lond-1896-8&342p-2 plts (5c6) 8.75
MITFORD, MARY RUSSELL-Atherton & Other Tales-Lond-1854-
3 vols-12mo-cl   (4c2, shabby) 15.00
--same-Bost-1854-port   (5mm2)   5.00
--Our Village-Lond-1893-illus (5p9, mor) 25. (5yy6)   22.50
--Poems-Lond-1810-12mo-mottled calf-g.bk-1st ed of auth's
1st book-lf of "Alterations" at end   (5gg6, vg) 50.00
MITFORD, WM-History of Greece-Lond-1838-8 vols-3/4 mor-
rev by Wm King   (5d2)   50.00
MITGANG, HERBERT-Lincoln, As They Saw Him-NY-(1956)-
536p-ports   (5dd6)   6.00
MITTELBERGER, GOTTLIEB-Journey to Penna in Year 1750-Phila-
1898-1st ed in English-8vo   (5jj3) 25.   (5m6)   17.50
MITTELHOLZER, WALTER-By Airplane Towards North Pole-Lond-
1925-176p-48 plts-maps   (5a1)   8.50
--same-Bost-1925-HoughtonMif-4 maps-illus-scarce (5s5) 12.50
MITTINEAGUE PAPER CO-Strathmore Quality Deckle Edge
Bookpapers-Mittineague, Mass-(1906)-illus-catalog-cl (5t4) 6.50
MITTON, G E, ed-Swiss Family Robinson-Phila-n.d.-Lippincott-
sq8vo-dec red cl-307p-illus-8 col plates-(Stories All
Children Love)   (5aa2)   4.50
MIVART, ST GEORGE-Dogs, Jackals, Wolves & Foxes-Lond-1890-
cl-4to-45 hand col plts-1st ed   (5z9, vg)   75.00
--Monograph of the Lories, or Brush Tongued Parrots-Lond-1896-
Quaritch-cl-g.t.-4to-65 col plts-4 maps   (4n5, vf) 1,250.00
MIX, DAVID E E-Catalogue of Maps & Surveys-Albany-1859-sheep
(4b6, wn)   20.00
MIXER, A-The Bartender's Friend-NY-1933-170p, (11)-4p of
glasses illus   (5w1)   6.50
MIXER, KNOWLTON-Porto Rico-NY-1926-Macm-329p (5p7)   5.00
--Old Houses of New England-NY-1927-346p-photos (5h9)   6.50
MIXER, M E-History of Trinity Church, Buffalo, NY-1897-130p
(5mm3)   3.00
MIYAKAWA, MASUJI-Life of Japan-NY-(1907)-Baker & Taylor-
301p   (5p7)   5.00
MIZER, L E-Genealogy of the Meisser Family-1966-631p (5mm3) 17.50
MIZNER, ADDISON-Florida Architecture of-NY-c1928-folio-
hf lin-184p, (1)p-185 plts-t.e.g.   (5w4)   25.00
MLIER, PIETER-Batiks, How to Make Them-NY-1919-lg8vo-cl-
plts-lg papr cpy-1st ed-scarce   (5p5)   12.50
MNEMONIKA-Balt-1812-346p-fldg plt-lea   (5y0)   12.50
MOAK, SIM-Last of the MillCreeks& Early Life in Northern Calif-
Chig-1923-wrps-8vo-48p   (4n1)   25.00
MOATS, LEONE-Off to Mexico-NY-1935-Scribner-186p-maps
(5x0)   5.00
--Thunder in Their Veins-NY-c1932-279p-illus (5x7, 5w4) 5.00
MOBERLY, H J-When Fur Was King-Lond-1929-illus-fldg map-
237p   (5dd7, f)   11.50
MOBILE, ALABAMA-Mobile-(1903)-24p-wrps   (5j6)   5.00
MOBILIZED WOMENS ORGANIZ OF BERKELEY-Conservation
Recipes-Berkeley-1918-ads-wrps-179(27)p-3rd ed (4g9, scuff) 7.50
MOCCASIN, THE-(Flagstaff, Ariz)-1924-Vol 1, #2-May 1924-illus-
18p-wrps   (4b3)   10.00
MOCK, ELIZ B-Architecture of Bridges-NY-1949-(Mus of Mod Art)-
illus-4to-127p   (5jj3) 12.50   (5ww3)   22.50
MOCKFORD, JULIAN-Golden Land, Background to So Africa-Lond-
1949-51&270p-31 plts   (5c6, vg)   6.75

MOCKING BIRD & OTHER STORIES-Also,Child's Book of True
  Stories-NY-1955-2 vols in 1,sm4to-wdcuts-scarce (5p5)   15.00
MOCQUET, JEAN-Voyages en Afrique,Asie,Indes Orientales, &
  Occidentales-Rouen-1665-Besongne-8vo-hf calf-5 plts (5n9) 150.00
MODDER, MONTAGU F-The Jew in Literature of England to end
  of 19th Cent-Phila-1939-435p   (5m1,dj)   8.50
MODERN BILLIARDS-Complete Text Book-NY-1891-thk8vo-plts-
  enlrgd ed-scarce -700p   (5p5)   25.00
MODERN BOOK PRODUCTION-Lond-1928-The Studio-4to-bds-
  parch bk-186p-facs inserts-col illus (5d5)   37.50
MODERN BRIT DOMESTIC ARCHITECTURE & DEC-Lond-1901-
  illus-212p-4to-hf mor-Studio   (4a2,rub)   10.00
MODERN CHARACTERS FOR 1778-By Shakespear-Lond-1778-
  12mo-hf calf-prntd by D Brown   (5x3,rbnd)   80.00
MODERN EXTRACTOR,THE-Pittsb-(1923)-179p-illus (5w1)   5.50
MODERN LANGUAGE INSTRUCTION-in Canada-Tor-1928-2 vols-
  Amer & Canadian Comm on Modern Languages-Vols 6 &7(5r7) 10.00
MODERN LETTER WRITER-On Love, Courtships,Marriage & Business-
  Bost-n.d.-(ca1846)-54p-12mo-dec wrps-wdcut (5w7,chip) 6.50
MODERN TRAVELLER-Mexico & Gautimala(sic)-Bost-1830-fldg map-
  6 plts-2 vols-orig cl-Wells&Lilly-1st Amer ed
                    (5xx5,fade,wn,hng loose)   16.50
MODERNE CAFES-Reataurants under Vergngungs-statten aussen-
  Berlin-n.d.-ca1930-4to-176p-plts   (5w1)   17.50
MODERWELL, HIRAM KELLY-The Theatre of Today-NY-1914-illus-
  J Lane   (5p0)   6.50
MODESTO CHAMBER OF COMMERCE-Modesto, Automobile Gateway
  to Yosemite-SanFran-n.d.(ca 1913)-Bolts&Braden-12mo-wrps-
  (32p)   (4t1)   12.50
MODISANE, B-Blame Me On History-NY-1963-1st ed
                    (5x2,mint,dj)   5.00
MODUPE, PRINCE-I Was A Savage-NY-1957-1st ed (5x2,dj)   4.50
--same-Lond-1958-illus-168p   (5c6,f)   7.50
MOE, ALFRED K-Honduras-Wash-1904-illus-fldg maps-#145,Pt 4,
  House Doc   (4b6)   25.00
MOERLEIN, GEO-A Trip Around the World-Cinn-1886-thk hf lea-
  extra col t.-map-prntd in oil colors (5c1,f,rbnd)   37.50
MOFFAT, R B-Moffat Genealogy, Descent from Rev John of Ulster
  Co, NY-1909   (5mm3)   12.50
MOFFAT, R BURNHAM-The Barclays of New York, Who They Are etc-
  NY-1904-474p   (5w5)   40.00
MOFFATT, JAS-George Meredith-NY-n.d.   (4a1,pencil)   10.00
MOFFETT, G-Moffett,Ballybay,Ireland Branch-1908-105p (5mm3)10.00
MOFFIT, ELLA B-The Cocker Spaniel-NY-1938-photos (5ww4) 5.00
--same-NY-1941-256p-illus   (5t7)   6.00
--Elias Vail Trains Gun Dogs-NY-1937-219p-illus (5t7,dj)   5.00
MOFIT, CAMBELL-The Arts of Tanning, Currying & Leather Dressing-
  Phila-1852-illus-557p, 16p   (5n7,sl wn)   17.50
MOFOLO, THOS-Chaka:Historical Romance-Lond-1931-15&198p -
  Dutton, trans   (5c6,vg)   13.75
MOHAWK VALLEY COOK BOOK-Ladies Soc of St Mark's
  Lutheran Church-Amsterdam-1906-53p-wrps (5c4,stn,wn)   4.50
MOHR, W H-Federal Indian Relations, 1774 to 78-1933-sewn (5L7) 4.00
MOIR, A L-Moir Genealogy & Collateral Lines-1913-429p
                    (5mm3)   10.00
MOISE, HAROLD-Moise Family of SoCarolina & Their Desc-1961-
  304p   (5mm3)   10.00
MOIVRE, ABRAHAM DE-Annuities on lives-Lond-1750-8vo-calf-
  mor labl-for A Millar-3rd ed   (5x3,f)   25.00
MOKLER, ALFRED-Ft Caspar(Platte Bridge Station)-Casper, Wyo-1939-
  75p-maps-illus-pict wrps-6x9-Prairie Pub -v scarce (5r0)   25.00
--Hist of Natrona Co,Wyo-Chig-1923-priv prnt-477p-t.e.g.-
  8vo-cl   (5bb4,4t1)   85.00
MOKVELD, L-The German Fury in Belgium-NY-n.d.-249p (5w4)   4.00
MOLDENHAWER, J V-The Voice of Books-NY-1940-174p (5j4)   5.00
MOLER, A B-The Manual of Beauty Culture-NY-(1928)-252p-
  plts   (5n7,scuff,plts rprd)   4.50
--Manual on Barbering, Hairdressing, Manicuring, Facial Massage,
  Electrolysis & Chiropody-Chig-1906-162p (5h0)   5.00
MOLES, H S-Observ on Range Sheep Management in New Mex-
  N M Col of Agri #80, Sep, 1924-27p-photos-wrps (5L5)   5.00
MOLESWORTH, MRS-"Us", An Old Fashioned Story-Lond-1886-12mo-
  240p-7 plts by Crane-1st ed-v scarce (5v0,vf)   30.00
MOLEY, R-Politics & Criminal Prosecution-NY-1929   (5r4)   10.00
MOLINA, J IGNATIUS-Geographical, Natural &Civil History of
  Chili-Middletwon,Conn-1808-2 vols-orig calf-map (4b1)   75.00
MOLLETT, J W-Illustrated Dictionary of Words Used in Art &
  Archaeology-Lond-1883-Sampson Low-350p-illus-lg8vo-cl
                    (5m5,sp crack)   14.00
MOLLHAUSEN, BALDWIN-Diary of a Journey from Missouri to Coast
  of Pacific-Lond-1858-2 vols-ads-col liths-buck-1st Engl ed
                    (4n1,rbnd)   175.00

MOLLIEN, G-Voyage dans la Republique de Colombia en 1823-
  Paris-1824-orig pap cov bds-calf sp-g.-8vo-plts-fldg map-
  2 vols-2 errata lvs-1st ed   (4e1)   155.00
MOLLINEUX, H-Popery Exposed by Its Own Authors & two Romish
  champions checked-1718-buck   (5L7,rebnd)   15.00
MOLLOY, FITZGERALD-Sir Joshua & His Circle-Lond-1906-t8vo-
  16p illus-2 vols   (5t8)   12.50
MOLLOY, ROBT-Charleston, A Gracious Heritage-NY-1947-illus
  by Suydam-311p-1st ed   (5h9)   8.50
MOLOHON, BERNARD-Sons of Marcus Whitman-Seattle-(1957)-
  151p-illus-1st ed-ltd   (5s4,pres)   3.50
MOLONY, EILEEN-Portraits of Mountains-Lond-(1950)-117p-
  cl-Dennis Dobson   (5d7)   3.00
MOLTER, BENNETT A-Knights of the Air-NY-1918-8vo-cl-plts-
  1st ed   (5p5)   12.50
MOLYNEAUS, P-The South's Political Plight-Dallas-1948-16mo
                    (5x2)   6.50
MOLYNEAUX, N Z R-History of Eaton Families-1911-782p (5mm3) 32.50
MOLYNEUX FAMILIES-History, Genealogical & Biographical of
  the-1904-370p   (5t9)   15.00
MOLYNEUX, PETER-Romantic Story of Texas-Dallas-1936-
  autograph Ed-ltd to 465c,autg-mor   (4c7)   47.50
--same-NY-1936-463p-1st ed   (5a8) 6.   (5w4)   8.50
MOMBERT, J I-Authentic History of Lancaster Co in State of Penna-
  Lancaster-1869-1st ed-illus-maps   (5yy6)   30.00
MON LIVRE DE CUISINE-Fribourg-1951-224p-bds-6th ed, rev
                    (5h9)   5.00
MONAGHAN, F-This Was New York-NY-1943-illus-1st ed (5yy6) 6.00
MONAGHAN, FRANK-French Travellers in the US 1754 to 1923-
  NY-1933-illus   (5v0,autg)   12.50
--Heritage of Freedom-Princeton-1947-4to-150p(5h9) 3.50 (5dd9) 5.50
MONAGHAN, JAS-The Great Deception-NY-c1913-213p
                    (5w9,dj)   3.00
MONAGHAN, JAY,ed-Book of the Amer West-NY-1963-608p-
  illus-separate portfolio of 6 Westrn prnts by Remington
         (5s4,f,dj) 22.50   (5m9,dj,mint,5hh3,dj)   25.00
--Civil War on the Western Border-Bost&Tor-(1955) (5s9,dj)   6.00
--Custer-Bost-(1959)-photos-map e.p.-1st ed-scarce (4t3,dj) 15.00
--Diplomat in Carpet Slippers-Indnpls&NY-(1945) (5s9,5t7,5w5) 5.00
--Last of the Bad Men-Indnpls-1946   (5jj1,sl fade)   7.50
--same-NY-(1946)-photos-1st ed   (5s4)   10.00
--Legend of Tom Hoen-Indnpls-(1946)-1st ed-illus (4t3)   8.50
--Lincoln Bibliography 1835 to 1939-Sprngfld-1943,1945-2 vols-
  cl   (4h2) 15.   (5j6)   12.50
--Overland Trail-Indnpls-(1947)-photos-423p plus index-1st ed
                    (4t3,dj,f)   12.50
MONAHAN, MICHAEL-Youth,a Poem of Soul & Sense, &other Poems-
  Albany-1895-12mo-buck-1st ed of auth's 1st book (5gg6,pres)10.00
MONAHAN, ROBT S-Mt Washington Reoccupied-Brattleboro-1933-
  1st ed-illus-270p   (5t2)   5.00
MONALDI, A TALE-Bost-1841-Little&Brown-12mo-orig cl-1st ed
                    (5x1)   45.00
MONARDES, NICHOLAS-Joyfull Newes Out of the Newe Founde
  Worlde-Lond-1925-2 vols-ltd ed   (5w3)   45.00
MONASTERE DE NOTRE DAME DES ANGES-HIstoire Du-Quebec-
  1882-lea sp-743p-bc de St Vallier   (4e9)   25.00
MONASTERY, THE, A ROMANCE-by author of "Waverley"-Edinb-
  1820-8vo-orig bds-cl bk-papr labls-3 vols-1st ed (5dd8,box) 50.00
MOMBERT, J I-Authentic History of Lancaster Co,Pa-Lancaster-
  1869-illus-maps-1st ed   (5nn6)   42.50
MONCEL, COUNT DU-The Telephone, the Microphone & the
  Phonograph-NY-1879-8vo-illus   (5ss5)   7.50
MONCKTON-or, the Fate of Eleanor-Lond-1802-3 vols-12mo-
  qtr calf-1st ed-rare   (5xx6,lacks hf t., rub)   125.00
MONCKTON, CAPT C A W-Taming New Guinea-NY-1921-8vo-
  337p-photos-fldg map   (4a6) 8.50   (5p0)   6.50
MONCKTON, H A-A History of English Ale & Beer-Lond-(1966)-
  238p-illus   (5w1)   6.00
MONCREIFFE, IAIN-Simple Heraldry-Lond-1953-63p (5t9)   5.00
MONCRIEFF, A R HOPE-Scotland Painted by Sutton Palmer-Lond-
  (1922)-8vo-cl-259p & index-32 col plts (5t2)   3.00
MONCURE BLANCHE E-Emma Jane's Souvenier Cook Book-
  Williamsburg-1937-87p-wrps   (5c7)   4.00
MONDOT, ARMAND-Histoire Des Indians Des Etats Unis-Paris-
  1858-hf lea-352p-illus   (5r6)   32.50
MONESSEN, PENN-Hist of Our City & Selections by the People
  of Our City & Their Friends-(1903)-101p (5t9)   5.00
MONETTE, JOHN W-History of Discovery & Settlement of Valley
  of the Mississippi by 3 Great European Powers, Spain etc-NY-
  1846-2 vols-hf mor   (5dd6,sl dmgd) 45.   (5x5,rbnd)   75.00
MONEY, A W-Guns, Ammunition & Tackle-NY-1904-illus-439p-
  g.t.-dec cov   (5ss8)   7.50

MONEY BY STEAM-John Law, His Body Moulders in the Ground-
(NY)-1864-8vo-orig wrps   (5ss5,wrp loose) 12.50
MONEY,EDW-The Cultivation & Manufacture of Tea-Lond-1878-
189p,(10)p,31p-3rd ed,enlrgd   (5w1,few loose pgs) 5.00
MONEY-MAKERS-NY-1885-Appleton-337p   (5x4) 12.50
MONGAN,AGNES-100 Master Drawings-Cambridge-1949-plts
208p, -cl   (5t2) 10.00
MONGER,MIRIAM-Tales from Toussaint-1945   (5L7) 3.50
MONHOLLAND,MARY-Life of-Chig-1894-183p-cl-Hyland Co
(5r0) 10.   (5h1,sl wn) 12.50
MONIER-WILLIAMS,MONTAGU-Figure Skating-Lond-1898-
316p-illus-1st ed   (5t2) 6.00
MONK,J A-Arizona Sketches-NY-(1905)-Grafton Pr-illus (5x5) 25.00
MONK'S-Standard Amer Map,US & Terr Mexico,Central Amer,
West India Islands,Canadas,New Brunswick & Nova Scotia-
Balt-1859-65x70"-cl & rollers-Jacob Monk   (5t0) 37.50
MONKHOUSE,COSMO-British Contemporary Artists-NY-1899-
illus-267p   (5p7) 10.   (5ww3) 17.50
--Corn & Poppies-Lond-1890-Elkin Mathews-4to-orig cl-frontis-
ltd to 50c,autgs-lg papr   (5ss3) 50.00
MONKMAN,NOEL-From Queensland to Great Barrier Reef-NY-
1958-182p-photos   (5s1,f,dj) 4.50
MONKS,NOEL-Squadrons Up-NY-(1941) -260p-illus (5mm8) 4.00
MONKSHOOD,G F-Less Familiar Kipling & Kiplingana-Lond-1917
168p   (5k1) 7.50
MONMARSON,RAOUL-L'Afrique Noire et Son Destin-Paris-1950-
365p-wrps   (5c6) 9.50
MONNER SANS,R-Liberia-Barcelona-1884-32p-wrps (5c6,pres) 8.75
MONNETTE,ORRA-First Settlers of Ye Plantations of Piscataway
& Woodbridge, Olde East NJ, 1644 to 1714,Part4-LosAng-
1932-illus-193p-orig wrps-ltd to 350c,autog (5kk8) 13.50
MONNIER,ADRIENNE-Dernieres Gazettes-Paris-1961-Cr8vo-
covrd wrps-1st ed-ltd to 20c on velin,nbrd (5ss7,unopnd) 15.00
MONOGRAFIA ILLUSTRADA-De La Provincia De Pichincha(Peru)-
n.p.-n.d.-(ca1940)-4to-cl-illus   (5h4,hng weak) 15.00
MONOGRAMS & ALPHABET ALBUM-NY-1871-sm4to-cl & Lea-
J Sabin 1871-78 plts   (5t0,scuff) 35.00
MONOGRAPHS ON COLOR-NY-(1935)-4to-bds-papr labl-
3 vols-fldg plts   (5d5,box,rub) 30.00
MONOHAN,FLORENCE-Women in Crime-NY-(1941)-306p
(5ss1,pres) 6.00
MONOTYPE COMPOSING MACHINE & TYPE CASTER-Phila-
(1914)-4to-thumb index-cl binder   (5ii2) 12.50
MONRO,HAROLD-Real Property-Lond-1922-Cr8vo-wrps-1st ed
(5ss7,pres) 10.00
--same-Lond-1922-Poetry Bookshop-sm4to-bds-ltd to 100c,nbrd
(5ss3,dj) 25.00
MONROE,ANNE S-Feelin'Fine!Bill Hanley's Book-GardenCty-
1931-320p-photos   (5dd6) 10.00
MONROE COUNTY,WIS-History of-Chig-1912-4to-part mor-
illus-946p   (5jj7,f) 50.00
MONROE,HARRIET-Poets & Their Art-NY-1926-301p-12mo-cl
(5m8,sl stn) 6.50
--A Poet's Life-1938-Macmillan   (5F1,f,dj) 6.00
--Valeria & Other Poems-Chig-1891-12mo-cl-vel bk-prntd for
author-1st ed of auth's first book-ltd to 300c-DeVinne Pr
(5gg6,ALS) 50.00
MONROE,HORACE-Elmley Lovett & the Moules of Sneads Green-
Lond-1927-26p   (5mm3) 10.00
MONROE,J-Science & Art of Chess-NY-1859-sm8vo-cl-281p
(5t2) 8.50
MONROE,JAS-Memoir of Jas Monroe,Esq-Charlottsville-1828-
sewed-60p   (4h2) 27.50
--Message from Pres of US to Both Houses of Congr-Wash-1823-
Gales & Seaton-1st ed-8vo-15p-disbnd-(Monroe Doctrine)-
Streeter #1735   (4h5,box) 400.00
--Narrative of a Tour of Observation-Phila-1818-1st ed-orig calf-
228p,(36) (5L8,rbnd,5tt6) 35.
(5ss5,hng weak,lacks labl) 17.50 (5m4,weak) 32.50
--Transmitting Report in relation to Dartmoor Prison in April last-
1816-sewn   (5L7) 7.50
--A View of the Conduct of Executive-Phila-1797-Benj Franklin
Bache-407p-1st ed   (4b6,wn) 25.   (5m2) 12.50
MONROE,JOEL H-Century & A Quarter of History of Geneva-
1912-324p   (4m2,stn) 12.   (4m2,rbnd) 16.00
--Schenectady Ancient & Modern-1914-285p-illus-maps
(5zz0) 15.   (5h9) 12.50
--Watertown-(from 1800 to 1912)-1912-261p   (4m2) 15.00
MONROE,N ELIZ-The Novel & Society-ChapelHill-1941 (5t4) 4.50
MONROE,PAUL-China,a Nation in Evolution-NY-1928-illus-
447p   (5t4) 4.50
MONS,BARBARA-High Road to Hunza-Lond-(1958)-157p-illus-cl
(5d7) 3.00

MONSARRAT,NICHOLAS-H M Corvette-Phila-1943-169p-
dec cov   (5s1,ex-libr) 5.00
--Cruel Sea-NY-1952-510p-plt   (5s1,pres) 3.50
MONSEIGNEUR LE VIN-Paris-1924 to 27-5 vols,complete-illus-
cl wrps as issued   (5w1) 60.00
MONSELET,CHAS-Les Vignes du Seigneur-Paris-1854-127p,(2)-
16mo-prntd in red-wrps   (5w6,pres) 12.50
MONSON-FITZJOHN,G J-Drinking Vessels of Bygone Days from
Neolithic age to Georgian-Lond-(1927)-144p-illus
(5g9) 15.   (5w1,fade) 9.50
--Quaint Signs of Old Inns-Lond-1926-157p,(1)-sq8vo-frontis-
70 sketches   (5w1) 11.50
MONTAGNE,PROSPER-Larousse Gastronomique-NY-(1961)-illus-
1101p-thk4to-1st Amer ed   (5g9) 16.50
MONTAGU,B-Summary of Law of Set off-NY-1806 (5r4,rbnd) 15.00
MONTAGUE,C E-Action & other stories-Lond-1928-1st ed-
Chatto&Windus   (5ss3,dj) 10.00
--Fiery Particles-Lond-1923-Chatto&Windus-12mo-cl-1st ed
(5ss3,dj,stn) 25.00
--A Hind Let Loose-Lond-(1910)-Methuen-cl-1st ed of auth's
1st book   (5ss3,crack) 15.   (5gg6) 25.00
--Right Off the Map-Lond-1927-Chatto&Windus-cl-1st ed
(5ss3,fade) 10.00
--The Right Place-Lond-1924-Chatto&Windus-1st ed
(5ss3,dj,sp fade) 10.00
--A Writer's Notes on His Trade-Lond-1930-8vo-bds&cl-t.e.g.-
ltd to 700c,autg by Tomlinson-1st ed   (5d5,dj) 15.00
MONTAGUE,GILBERT HOLLAND-Rise & Prog of Standard Oil Co-
NY-1904   (5xx8) 3.50   (5x7) 5.00
MONTAGUE,JOS-Wild Bill-NY-1926-Chelsea Hse-scarce
(5jj1,f) 8.50
MONTAGUE,SYDNEY R-I Lived with the Eskimos-NY-(1939)-
photos   (5ss1) 5.00
--North to Adventure-NY-(1939)-illus   (4b6) 5.00
MONTAGUE,WM P-Ways of Knowing-1928   (5L7) 8.50
MONTAIGNE,MICHEL DE-The Essays-Harvard Univ Pr-1925-
4 vols-R8vo-lg type-spec papr-orig brown cl-g.t.-uncut
(5t5) 35.00
--same-NY-1946-The Her Pr-3 vols-boxed   (5p7) 12.50
MONTALEMBERT,COUNT DE-The Monks of the West from
St Benedict to St Bernard-Bost-(1860)-2 vols-699p
(5t7,libr labl) 12.50
MONTANA CENTENNIAL TRAIN HISTORY,1964-(1965)-48p-cl-
photos-ltd to 500c   (5L2) 10.00
MONTANA-Constitution of State of,July 4,1889-Helena-(1889)-
76p-orig prntd wrps   (5x5,libr dupl,rprd,5m3,f) 25.00
MONTANA COOK BOOK-Ladies of Butte City-Lincoln,Neb-1881-
169p-cl-scarce   (5h5,cov wn) 27.50
MONTANA-8th Report of Bur of Agric,Labor & Ind of State of-
Helena-(1902)-772p plus index-photos-1 Russell illus-1st ed-
scarce   (5L2) 40.00
--same-9th Report-(1904)-564p-photos   (5L2) 15.00
MONTANA-Exhibit at World's Fair & Description of various resources
of State-Butte-1893-64p-16mo-wrps-scarce
(5g3,wn,tn) 8.50   (5t3) 12.50
MONTANA HISTORICAL SOC-Transactions,Act of Inc,Constit etc-
Helena-1876 to 1910-7 vols,Vol 1 thru 7-photos-maps
(5s4,ex-libr,sl stns) 225.00
--Contributions to-Helena-1900-Vol 3-361p plus index-photos-
1st ed-rare   (5t3,cov tn) 40.00
--same-Helena-1896-Vol 2-398p plus index-photos-rare (5t3) 45.00
MONTANA-Laws,memorials & resolutions of terr of,passed 1873-
Helena-1874-Daily & Weekly Herald-Fisk,public prntr-8vo-
orig blue prntd wrps   (5i9,vf) 45.00
MONTANA LAW REVIEW-1948 to 69-Vol 9 thru 30-bnd
(5rr4,ex-libr) 160.00
MONTANA-Profile in Pictures-NY-(1941)-WPA-illus-12mo-1st ed
(5ii3) 12.50
MONTANA-Progressive Men of State of Montana-Chig-n.d.-
(ca1905)-(A W Bowen & Co)-1886dbl pgs plus index-
illus(1 Russell)-4to-lea-rare (4t1,rbnd) 95. (5L2,hng weak) 125.00
MONTANA-Resources Opportunities Ed,Pub Dept Aggie,Labor-
Helena-June,1926-288p-#1,Vol 1,qrtrly (5s4,ex-libr,wn) 10.00
MONTANA-State Guide Book-NY-1939-WPA-Amer Guide Series-
illus-429p-fldg pkt map-1st ed-scarce
(4b3,wn,ex-libr) 15. (4L5) 17.50
MONTCLAIR'S TREASURE OF PERSONAL RECIPES-Montclair-
(1959)-124p-illus-sprial bnd wrps   (5g9) 3.50
MONTEFIORE,ARTHUR David Livingstone-NY-n.d.-
Fleming H Revell-map-6th ed   (4t5) 6.00
MONTEMERLI,COUNTESS MARIE-The Florentines-Lond-1870-
Tinsley-3 vols-8vo-orig cl-1st ed   (5xx6,shake) 22.50

MONTEREY (CALIF) & VICINITY-Handbook to...-Monterey-
 1875-sq12mo-orig prntd wrps-1st ed   (5i9) 100.00
MONTEREY (CALIF)-Historic Monterey & Surroundings-Monterey-
 1899-Spec Souvenir ed-photos-map-47p-rope bnd wi papr
 covers   (4p2,cov wn)   25.00
MONTEREY-History of Joint Anniv Celebration at Monterey,
 Calif,of 110th Anniv of Amer Ind & 40th Anniv-Monterey-
 1886-29 nbrd pgs-orig pict wrps-illus-in folder (5x5)   30.00
MONTEREY, CALIF-The Most Charming Winter Resort in the World-
 n.p.-(1880)-illus-16p-8vo-orig prntd wrps-map of Monterey
 & vicinity on bk cov   (4c1)   50.00
MONTEREY PENINSULA-Stanford-(1941)-207p-1st ed-WPA-
 Amer Guide Ser   (5h4) 10. (5n1)   7.50
--same-Stanford Univ-(1946)-200p-cl-Amer Centennial ed
                                  (5h2,sl soil dj)   5.00
MONTESQUIEU, BARON DE-Persian Letters-Lond-Tonson-1726-
 2 vols-calf-3rd ed   (5a1,bkstr wn)   8.50
MONTESQUIEU, C L de S-Spirit of Laws-Lond-1909-rev ed-
 T Nugent,tr-2 vols   (5r4) 10.00
--same-NY-1899-Colonial Pr-2 vols   (5p0)   8.00
MONTEZ, Lola-The Arts of Beauty-Lond-n.d.-123p-port-12mo-
 hf lea   (5n7) 16.50
--Lectures of Lola Montez including her Autobiography-NY-1858-
 292p-1st ed   (5F0) 4. (5p6)   8.00
MONTEZUMA CO,COLO-History of,land of promise & fulfillment-
 Mancos,Colo-1958-324p-photos-1st ed-priv prntd (5dd4) 10.00
MONTGOMERIE, NORAH, ed-Sandy Candy & Other Scottish
 Nursery Rhymes-Hogarth Pr-1948-sm8vo-191p-illus (5s0)   4.50
MONTGOMERY-or, West Indian adventurer-Jamaica-1812-by a
 gentleman resident in West Indies-Kingston Chronicle-3 vols-
 8vo-orig bds-1st ed   (5xx6,unmtchd bndgs) 600.00
MONTGOMERY, CORA-Eagle Pass-NY-1853-(403p)-bnd wi Life
 on the Isthmus by J Fabens   (4a5) 20.00
MONTGOMERY, DOUGLASS W-Collected Writings of-SanFran-
 1943-8vo-cl-2 vols   (5h4) 20.00
MONTGOMERY, FLORENCE-Behind the Scenes in the Schoolroom-
 Lond-1913-Macmillan-12mo-312p,(8) ads-cl-t.e.g. (5p1,rub) 12.50
MONTGOMERY, FRANCES T-Billy Whiskers Kidnapped-Chig-
 (1910)-sm4to-illus-1st ed-blk & w col illus by De Bebian
                                        (4j3,f) 15.00
--Billy Whiskers, Jr-Akron-1905-sm4to-col & blk & w illus-1st ed
                                        (4j3,f) 10.00
--Billy Whiskers' Vacation-Chig-1908-Brewer B-6 col plts-papr bds-
 1st ed   (4c3,vg) 17.50
--Frances & the Irrepressibles at Buena Vista FarmpNY,Akron,
 Chig-Saalfield-(c1905)-8vo-257p,(1) ads-photos-oval photo
 mounted upper cov   (5p1)   7.50
--On a Lark to Planets-Akron-1904-illus-1st ed-rare
                          (4j3,cov stn,pres,hng sprung) 37.50
MONTGOMERY, MRS FRANK C-Ft Wallace & Its Relation to the
 Frontier-(Topeka, 1928)-95p-stapld-self cov-separate prntng
                                        (5L0)   3.00
MONTGOMERY, H-The Life of Maj Gen Zachary Taylor-Phila-
 n.d.-(ca1847)   (5w5)   7.50
--same-Auburn-1850-462p-cl-illus   (5t2)   5.00
--Life of Maj Gen Wm H Harrison-Cleve-1853-Tooker & Gatchell-
 465p-frontis-2nd ed   (5qq8) 10.00
MONTGOMERY, HARRY E-Vital Amer Problems-Putnam's Sons-
 1908-384p-12mo-orig cl-1st ed   (5x5) 15.00
MONTGOMERY, HUGH-The Way Out-NY-(1895)-320p-cl (5h7) 7.50
MONTGOMERY, J S-The Shaping of a Battle:Gettysburg-Phila-
 1959-maps-1st ed   (5a9,dj,vf)   4.50
MONTGOMERY, JAS-Journal of Voyages & Travels by Rev Daniels
 Tyerman & Geo Bennett-Lond-1831-2 vols-2 ports-12 views-
 t8vo-calf &bds   (5c1,rbnd) 70.00
--same-Lond-1832-3 vols orig cl-2nd ed   (5c1) 35.00
--same-Bost-1832-Crocker & Brewster-3 vols-rev by Amer ed-
 12mo-labls   (5x5,sp tn,labls tn) 30.00
MONTGOMERY, JAS-Poetical Works...with Memoir of Author by
 Griswold-Phila-1846-Sorin & Ball-2 vols-12mo (5i4,sp fade) 10.00
MONTGOMERY, JAS-West Indies, & Other Poems-Lond-1810-
 16mo-g.-marbld bds-hf mor   (4b6) 20.00
MONTGOMERY, JAS E-Cruise of Admiral D G Farragut in
 Flag Ship Franklin-NY-1869-port-464p-illus-g. stmpd cov-
 scarce   (5s1,wn)   9.00
--Our Admiral's Flag Abroad,Cruise of Adm D G Farragut...in
 Flag Ship Franklin-NY-1869-8vo-illus-1st ed (5ss5,rub) 12.50
MONTGOMERY, LIZZIE W-Sketches of Old Warrenton,N C-
 1924-plts   (5L7,sl spot) 17.50
MONTGOMERY, REV M W-The Mormon Delusion-Bost-(1890)-
 354p   (5L7,ex-libr,5dd4)   7.50

MONTGOMERY, MORTON L-Historical & Biogr Annals of
 Berks Co,Pa-Chig-1909-hf lea-4to-ports-illus-2 vols (5ii8) 75.00
--History of Berks Co,PA in Revolution from 1774 to 1783-
 Reading-1894-illus-295p   (5ii8) 35.00
--History of Lodge No. 62 F & A.M.-Reading-1894-250p-illus
                                       (5w4)   6.00
--School History of Berks Co in Penna-Phila-1889-1st ed-illus-map
                                       (5jj3) 22.50
MONTGOMERY, RICH G-"Pechuck", Lorne Knight's Adventures
 in the Arctic-NY-1932-291p-photos   (5ss1)   4.00
--Young Northwest-NY-Random-1941-309p-illus (5s4) 6. (5p7) 4.50
--same-Portland-1948-318p-plts-2nd ed,rev   (5s6)   4.50
MONTGOMERY, RUTHERFORD-Timberline Tales-Phila-1939-illus-
 1st ed   (5jj1,vf)   8.00
MONTGOMERY WARD & CO-Catalogue No 18-Chig-Spring 1877-
 Ottaway & Colbert-120p-illus-3 3/4 x 6 7/8"-orig wrps
                                       (5yy3) 200.00
MONTHLY LAW REPORTER-Bost-1838 to 1860-Vol 1 thru 21
                                  (5rr4,rbnd) 200.00
MONTHLY REPOSITORY-& Library of Entertaining Knowledge-NY-
 1831-1st 12 issues (Jun 1830 to May 1831)-12mo-400p-bds
                                  (5v2,vg) 25.00
MONTHLY TRAVELLER, THE-or Spirit of the Periodical Press-Bost-
 Jan 1830 to Jan 1838-Vols 1 thru 8 & Vol 9,#1-8 vols-8vo-
 calf-v scarce   (5m6,sl rub) 75.00
MONTICELLO COOK BOOK-Monticello-1922-Presbyterian Church-
 165p   (5c7)   4.00
MONTORGUEIL, G-Henri IV-Paris-1907-Boivin-4to-72p-
 4 dbl pg illus-pict cl-a.e.g.-4 ports tip in (5p1,scuff) 25.00
MONTPELIER (VERMONT) DIRECTORY-1890,1891-108p-(1889)
                                     (5mm3)   4.00
MONTREAL(Mont-1877)-18 lfs,fldg style-cl-view bk (5h2)   5.00
MONTREAL ALMANACK, THE-Or Lower Canada Register, for 1830-
 Montr-1829-Robt Armour-168p,64p-orig prntd wrps
                                     (5w8) 75.00
MONTREAL ALMANAC-for Yr 1839-Montr-1832 & 1839-12mo-
 t.p. cov-bnd with same for 1833   (5w8,1 vol lacks cov) 75.00
MONTREAL GAZETTE-Vol 37, Feb 26,1829-4p & Vol 37,
 Mar 2,1829   (5w8) ea 25.00
MONTREAL GAZETTE,supplement-People's Almanac, 1891-Montr-
 1890-pict wrps-(78p)-cartoons   (5u6) 15.00
MONTREAL-Natural History Soc of, Constit & Bylaws of Montr,
 Directions for Preserving & Forwarding Objects of Natural
 History-Montr-1828-25p-wrps   (5r6) 42.00
MONTREAL IN PHOTOGRAVURE-Montr-n.d.-(?ca1898)-illus
                                   (5b9,vg) 10.00
MONTREAL OFFICIAL VOTER'S LISTS-(Printed)-Montr Centre-1867-
 8vo   (5w8) 65.00
MONTREAL OLD & NEW-Montr-n.d.-(ca1920)-4to-illus-
 edited by Prince,Gordon Smith,Deacon,Marcy (5w8) 25.00
MONTREAL-Traveller's guide to Montreal & its vicinity-Montr-
 1857-24mo   (5g3) 10.00
MONTROSE, DONALD-Story of a Parish, Its Priests, & its People,
 1860 to 1960-Anaheim-1961-St Boniface Parish-bds-8vo-504p
                                     (4t1) 15.00
MONTROSS, LYNN-The Reluctant Rebels-NY-1950-Harper
                                  (5m2,5p0)   6.00
--Rag,Tag and Bobtail-Harper-(1952)-519p   (5e8) 10.75
MONTROSS, MR N E-Notable Collection of Amer Paintings Offered
 for Sale at Amer Art Galleries, Feb 1919-NY-illus-8vo-wrps
                                    (5ww3) 15.00
MONTULE, E A-Voyage to No Amer & West Indies, in 1817-Lond-
 1821-liths (2 fldg)-   (4t3,lacks covs) 25.00
MONUMENTS OF WASHINGTON'S PATRIOTISM-Wash-1844-
 4to-lea(g.tooled)-108p-4th ed   (5t7) 10.00
MOOAR, G-Cummings Memorial-1903-532p   (5mm3) 20.00
MOODIE, MRS-Life in the Clearings Versus the Bush-NY-n.d.-
 12mo-cl   (4c1)   7.50
MOODIE, SUSANNA-Roughing It In the Bush-Lond-1854-3rd ed,
 wi additions-2 vols in 1-293p,336p   (4d1) 25.00
--same-Lond-1913-569p-17 plts   (5u6)   8.50
--same-Tor-1923-506p col illus   (4b9) 15.00
MOODY, C C P-Sketches of the Moody Family-1847-168p (5t9) 10.00
MOODY, DAN W-Life of a Rover-Chig-1926-116p (4h9) 15.00
MOODY, E C-Handbook Hist of the Town of York,Maine-1914-
 249p   (5mm3)   5.00
MOODY, REV GRANVILLE-Life's Retrospect, Autobiog of-Cinn-
 1890-486p-cl-Rev Sylvester Weeks,ed-1st ed (5h1) 12.50
MOODY, DR J P-Arctic Doctor-NY-1955-241p-illus
                             (4b9) 6. (5dd0)   5.00
MOODY, W L-Galveston Harbor, Argument for Improvement of-
 Austin-1884-10p-wrps-scarce   (5n4) 20.00

MOODY,WM R-The Life of Dwight L. Moody-Revell-1900-
   illus-g.e.-red lea-official authorized ed (5ww4,cov wn) 5.00
MOODY,WM VAUGHN-The Faith Healer-Bost-1909-HoughtonMiff-
   1st ed   (5ss3,sp stn) 10.00
--The Masque of Judgment-Bost-1900-Small,Maynard &Co-bds-
   1st ed-ltd to 150c-papr labl   (5gg6,unopnd) 25.00
--Poems-Bost-1902-HoughtonMiff   (5ss3,sp chip) 5.00
--Some Letters of-Bost-1913-HoughtonMiff-Mason,ed-1st ed(5ss3)5.00
MOODY'S,MRS WM VAUGHN-Cook Book-NY-1931-475p-1st ed
                      (5c9)   5.00
MOODY'S MANUAL-of RRs & Corp Securities-21st Annual Publ
   Utilities Section-NY-1920-2344p   (5h8) 10.00
MOON,BUCKLIN-The Darker Brother-NY-1943 (5xx2) 5.00
--The High Cost of Prejudice-NY-c1947-168p (5w4) 5.50
--Primer for White Folks-NY-1945 (5L7) 6. (5x2) 10.00
--Without Magnolias-NY-1949-1st ed   (5x2) 3.50
MOON,GRACE-Chi Wee & Loki of the Desert-NY-illus-col frontis-
                     (4b2) 4.00
--Lost Indian Magic-NY-(1918)-col frontis-col plts-318p (5dd5) 6.25
--The Runaway Papoose-GardenCty-Dblday Doran-1928-264p-
   Carl Moon,illus-frontis-1st ed (5p1) 10.00
--Singing Sands-NY-1946-245p   (4b2) 3.50
--Tita of Mexico-NY-1934-Stokes-12mo-213p-frontis-1st ed
                 (5p1,dj) 12.50
--Wongo Wise Old Crow-Chig-(1923)-188p-illus (5s4) 4.50
MOON,R C-Morris Family of Philadelphia-1898 to 1909-
   3 vols & 2 vols of supp (5t9,5L7,rbnd,ex-libr) 50.00
MOONEY,BOOTH-More Than Armies-Dallas-1948
         (5a8,autg by Cary) 6.50
MOONEY,H J-Fiction & Criticism of Katherine Anne Porter-
   Pitts-1962-66p-wrps   (5j4) 4.00
MOONEY,JAS-The Cheyenne Indians & Sketch of the Cheyenne
   Grammar-Lancaster,PA-1907-Amer Anthro Assoc-wrps-plts
                 (4k4,f) 12.50
MOONEY,ROBT S-Financial Interests of Baltimore-Balt-1913-
   lg4to-106p-illus   (4b8) 15.00
MOONLIGHT JACK-NY-(1867)-100p-col pict wrps-
   Robt DeWitt,publ-Claude Duval Ser #24 (5h2,sl wn) 10.00
MOORE,A-Annals of Gallantry,or Conjugal Monitor-Lond-
   1814 to 15-M Jones-3 vols-8vo-hf calf-mrbld bds-lea labls-
   a.e.g.-1st ed-2 ports-18 col plts
                 (4h0,f) 350.00
MOORE,A A-Moore Genealogy & Recollections-1915-170p(5t9) 17.50
MOORE,A W-The Alps in 1864,A Private Journal-Oxford-1939-
   2 vols-E H Stevens,ed-Basil Blackwell-cl (5d7) 10.00
MOORE,SIR ALAN-Sailing Ships of War,1800 to 1860-Lond-1926-
   14p,78p-(90 pg plts)-4to-cl-illus-ltd to 1500c (5t0,f) 37.50
MOORE,ALBERT B-Conscription & Conflict in the Confederacy-NY-
   1924-Macm-367p (4d9,crack) 10. (5s9,dj) 12.50
--History of Alabama-Nashville-1934-834p (5j6) 6.50
MOORE,ANNE CARROLL-A Century of Kate Greenaway-Lond-
   (1946)-Warne-15p-4to-col pict wrps-2 col plts-1st ed
               (5v2,ex-libr,vg) 15.00
--Children's Books of Yesterday-NY-1933-NY Publ Library-21p-
   wrps-stapled   (5p1) 3.50
--My Roads to Childhood-NY-1939-1st ed (5v2,ex-libr) 12.50
--New Roads to Childhood-NY-(1923)-Doran-12mo-209p-
   cl bkd bds-1st ed   (5p1,fade) 5.00
--Writing & Criticism-Bost-1951-(95)p-8vo-1st ed (5p1,dj) 12.50
MOORE,ANNIE E-Literature Old & New for Children-Bost,NY-
   HoughtonMiff-c1934-12mo-446p (5p1) 10.00
MOORE,ANON-John Harvey-Chig-1897-Kerr&Co-8vo-
   orig buck cl-1st ed   (5i0) 30.00
MOORE,BEN-Butterfield,7 Yrs with Wild Indians-
   (O'Donnell,Tx,1945)-photos-130p-1st ed (4t3) 12.50
MOORE,BRENT-A study of past,present & possibilities of hemp
   industry in Kentucky-Lexington-1905-wrps-thesis
               (5g4,libr stmps) 10.00
MOORE,C,ed-Leaflets of Masonic Biography-Cinn-1863-2nd ed
               (5jj7,sp sl wn) 10.00
MOORE,C-Life & Times of Chas Follen McKim-1929 (5L7,scuff) 17.50
MOORE,C C-Treatise on Facts-Northport-1908-2 vols (5r4) 12.50
MOORE,C T-Abstract of Wills of State of SoCarolina 1670 to 1740-
   Vol 1-(1960)-346p   (5mm3) 25.00
MOORE,CHAS,ed-Improvement of park system of Dist of Col-
   Wash-1902-Sen Report #166-GPO-179p-fldg maps (5u3) 10.00
MOORE,CHAS-Manuscripts in Public & Private Collections in
   US-Wash-1924-98p   (5j4) 12.50
MOORE,CHAS-The NW Under Three Flags,1635 to 1790-NY-1900-
   Harper-dec cl-illus F.Remington & others-1st ed
         (5jj7,f,als) 25. (5n4,pres) 8.50
MOORE,CHAS,ed-St Marys Falls Canal-Detroit-1907-286p-illus-
   red cl-sm4to   (5mm7) 20.00

MOORE,CHAS H-Development & Character of Gothic Architecture-
   NY-1899-454p-illus-8vo-2nd ed (5ww3) 15.00
--same-MacMil-1899 & 1905-plts-tall orig cl-2 vols (5t5) 12.50
MOORE,CHAS W-Timing a Century-Cambr-1945-Harvard Studies
   in Bus Hist,XI   (4F4,dj,f) 12.50
MOORE,CLARENCE-Antiquities of the St Francis,White & Black
   Rivers,Ark-Phila-1910-folio-wrps-plts (4k4) 20.00
--Certain Mounds of Ark & of Mississippi-Phila-1908-121p-4to-
   plts-Aca of Natural Sci   (5g5) 7.50
--Some Aboriginal Sites in Louisiana & in Ark-Phila-1913-folio-
   plts-cl   (4k4,f) 25.00
--Some Aboriginal Sites on Red River-Phila-1912-cl-folio-plts-
   reprnt from Jrnl of Academy of Nat'l Sci (4k4,f) 25.00
MOORE,CLEMENT C-The Night Before Christmas-Phila-c1883-
   Porter&Coates-12mo-a.e.g.-pict bevelled bds-(23 lvs)-
   The "Bells" Series   (5p1) 7.50
--same-Lond-(1931)-Harrap-illus by A Rackham-flex bds (5rr2) 10.00
--same-NY-1934-Dodd,Mead-24mo-(8p,16p)36p-T C Boyd,wdcuts
                 (5p1) 7.50
--same-NY-1942-col illus by Everett Shinn-4to-pict bds-cl bk-
   1st ed   (5p5,dj) 7.50
--same-Phila-n.d.-8vo-pict cl-36p-4 col plts-illus by A Rackham
             (5t2,dj,f) 7.50
--same-NY-n.d.-Bischoff,illus-tiny edition (4F6,f) 7.50
--A Visit From St. Nicholas-Mt Vernon-n.d.-Peter Pauper Pr-
   v t12mo-col illus   (5v0,mint,box) 5.00
--same-Cliffdale,NJ-1930-frontis-facs of autog cpy by author-
   thn8vo-mrbld bds-papr labl-12p-ltd to 550c,issued for Xmas
   by G A Zabriskie   (5j5) 6.00
MOORE,E FRANKFORT-Oliver Goldsmith,a Biography-(Lond)&NY-
   1911-lg thk8vo-cl-g.t.-orig ed (5p5) 15.00
MOORE,EDW-The Foundling-Lond-J Bell-1792-12mo-90p-
   2 engr hand col plts-wrps (5a1,rebnd) 4.50
MOORE,EDW A-Story of Cannoneer Under Stonewall Jackson-
   Neale,NY & Wash-1907-8vo-315p-buck (4a7,rbnd) 40.00
--same-Lynchburg-1910-8vo-331p (4j4) 15. (4a7) 40.00
MOORE,ELIZ C-Picture Book of Robinson Crusoe-NY-1931-
   (Macmillan Picture Bks)-4to-dec yellow cl-52p-28 col plts &
   illus (some dbl)   (5aa2) 4.50
MOORE,ELWOOD S-Mineral Resources of Canada-Tor-1933-
   maps-301p   (4a8) 5.00
MOORE,EMILY H-A Lost Life,a novel-NY-1871-297p-1st ed
                 (5p6) 7.50
MOORE,F A-Gems for You from New Hamp Authors-Manchester,NH-
   1850-312p-g.e.-cl   (5i0,vg) 300. (5s2,mint) 35.00
MOORE,FRANCIS,JR-Description of Texas-NY-1844-sm12mo-
   143p-orig cl-2nd ed(issued without map or plts) (5s9,sp tn) 95.00
MOORE,FRANCIS C-How to Build a Home-NY-1897-illus-
   12mo   (5w7,ex-libr,sp tn) 6.50
MOORE,FRANK-Amer Eloquence-NY-1857-2 vols-ports (5t7) 15.00
--Anecdotes,Poetry & Incidents of the War,North & South-NY-
   1866-560p   (5p9) 7.50
--same-NY-1882-frontis-g. (5s9,hng crack) 7.50
--Civil War in Song & Story,1860 to 1865-NY-1889-illus-560p
         (4b3) 6. (5t2,5c3) 5.00
--Diary of the Amer Revolution-NY-1860-2 vols-illus-maps(sm fldg)-
   Scribner   (5mm8) 20. (5ii8) 35.00
--same-Hartf-1875-1054p plus index (5yy7,rub) 10.00
--same-Hartf-1876-1084p-illus (5ee3,f) 15.00
--Heroes & Martyrs-1861-4to-illus-buck (5L7,rbnd) 12.50
--Lyrics of Loyalty-NY-1864-Putnam-336p 4"x6"-cl-lea sp(5a0) 5.00
--Rebellion Record-NY-1861-illus-3 vols-fldg maps (5yy0) 12.50
--same-NY-1862-illus-4 vols (5L3,f) 15.00
--same-NY-1867 to 71-illus-12 vols (5s9,Vol 1 cov shaken) 75.00
--Record of the Year,A Reference Scrap Book-NY-1876-2 vols-
   Vols 1 & 2,Jan thru Dec,1876-hf mor-t8vo (5m6) 15.00
--Women of the War-Hartf-1866-596p-illus (5w7,5m6) 7.50
        (5q8,5p7) 4. (5g4,5L3,f) 5.00
--same-Hartf-1867-illus   (5s9) 6.00
MOORE,FRANK F-Georgian Pageant-Lond-1908-346p-plts 5a1) 5.00
MOORE,FRED-With Japan's Leaders-NY-1942-Scribner-365p
                 (5p7) 5.00
MOORE,FREDK-America's Naval Challenge-NY-1929-166p
                 (5s1,dj) 3.00
MOORE,GEO-Anthology of Pure Poetry-NY-1925-Boni & Liv-
   182p   (5p9) 3.50 (5t0) 4.50
--Aphrodite in Aulis-Lond-(1930)-Heinemann-1st ed-
   ltd to 1825c,nbrd,autg-box (5ss3,soil) 15. (5ss9,vg) 25.00
--The Apostle-Lond-1923-Heinemann-ltd ed,autg
         (5ss3,hng crack) 10. (5t8) 15.00
--Avowals-NY-1926   (5mm2,wn dj) 3.50
--The Brook Kerlith-NY-1929-Macmillan-12 engr by Stephen Gooden-
   hf vel-ltd to 500c,autg-box (5ss9) 30.00

MOORE, GEO (continued)
--Celibates-Lond-1895-Walter Scott-1st ed-cl (5ss3, hng crack) 10.00
--Celebate Lives-NY-1927-Boni & Liveright (5ss9) 5.00
--Collected Works-NY-1922-22 vols-Boni&Liveright-Carra ed,autg
(5r9, f) 175.00
--The Coming of Gabrielle-Lond-1920-priv prntd for subscribers-
1st ed-ltd to 1000c,autg
(5ss3, stnd dj) 10. (5m4) 32.50 (5t2, f, dj) 20.00
--Conversations in Ebury Street-Lond-1924-t8vo-bds-ltd ed,autg
(5r9, dj) 20.00
--Esther Waters-Lond-1894-Walter Scott-cl-1st ed
(5ss3, hng crack) 15.00
--Esther Waters, A Play in 5 Acts-Lond-1913-Heinemann (5ss9) 5.00
--Esther Waters-Lond-1920-for subscribers-8vo-orig hf parch-
papr label-ltd to 750c,autg,nbrd
(5i8) 15.00
--Hail & Farewell-Lond-1911 to 1914-3 vols-1st eds-Ave is
1st issue-Salve is 1st issue wi errata slip-Vale is 2nd issue
with hf t. on a stub
(5r9, 2 1st issues & 3rd issue of Vale) 15. (5j3) 35.00
--same-NY-1925-2 vols-port (5mm2, dj) 7.50
--Heloise & Abelard-Lond-1921-2 vols-bds-for subscribers-1st ed-
ltd to 1500c,autg (5ss3) 20.00
--In Single Strictness-Lond-1922-thk lg8vo-bds-1st ed-
ltd to 1030c,autg (5r9, dj, unopnd) 15.00
--same-NY-1922-Boni & Liveright-1st ed-ltd to 1050c,nbrd,autg
(5ss9, f, dj) 20.00
--The Lake-Lond-1921-Heinemann (5ss3) 5.00
--Letters from Geo Moore to Ed Dujardin, 1886 to 1922-NY-1929-
Crosby Gaige-1st ed (5ss3, autg) 15.00
--same-NY-1929-bds-cl bk-ltd to 626c,nbrd (5ss9) 15.00
--Making of an Immortal-NY-1927-Bowling Green Pr-
ltd to 1240c,autg (5ss3) 10.00
--Memoirs of my Dead Life-Lond-1906-Heinemann-1st ed
(5ss9) 5. (5F1, pres, soil) 20. (5ss3, autg tip in,crack) 10.00
--same-NY-1920-Boni&Liveright-bds-ltd ed (5ss3, sp stn) 7.50
--A Mere Accident-Lond-1887-12mo-cl (4c2, hng cracked) 35.00
--A mummer's wife-Lond-1885-Vizetelly-8vo-orig cl-1st ed
(5xx6, soil, cir libr) 12.50
--same-Lond-(n.d.)-Walter Scott-20th ed (5ss3, pres) 15.00
--Pagan Poems-Lond-1881-8vo-orig cl-complete with t.pg-1st ed
(5d9) 250.00
--The Pastoral Loves of Daphnis & Chloe-Lond-1924-Heinemann-
1st ed-ltd to 1280c,autg (5ss3, dj, soil) 10.00
--Sister Teresa-Lond-1901-Unwin-cl-1st ed
(5ss9, dj) 12.50 (5ss3, hng crack) 7.50
--Spring Days-Lond-1888-Visetelli ed (4a4, f) 22.50
--A Story Teller's Holiday-Lond-1918-for Subscribers only-
1st ed-ltd to 1000c,autg (5ss3, chip dj) 15.00
--same-NY-1918-for Subscribers only-1st Amer ed-ltd to 1250c
(5ss3) 7.50
--same-1928-Wm Heinemann-2 vols-lg papr 1st ed-ltd format-
Lond (5i4) 20.00
--same-NY-1928-Liveright-2 vols-ltd to 1250 sets,autg,nbrd
(4L4, dj) 25.00
--Ulick & Soracha-Lond-1926-Nonesuch Pr-1250c, ltd,autg
(5dd0) 20. (5ss3, sp stn, dj chip) 15.00
--same-NY-1926-orig bds-ltd ed,autg (5ss3) 10. (5mm2) 12.50
--The Untilled Field-Lond-1903-1st issue in scarlet cl & wi 4p ads
at bk (5j3) 25.00
--Vain Fortune-Lond-(n.d.)-1st ed (5ss9, vg) 10.00
MOORE, GEO H-Notes on History of Slavery in Massachusetts-
NY-1866 (5x2, rbnd) 60.00
--Supplementary Notes on Witchcraft in Mass-Cambr-1884-
illus-25p-wrps (4b3) 10.00
--Treason of Chas Lee, Maj Genl-NY-1860-orig cl-port-fldg facs-
1st ed (4m2) 30. (5L1) 15. (5mm8, chip) 12.50
--Washington as an Angler-NY-1887-14p-sm4to-limp cl (5L1) 10.00
MOORE, GUY W-The Case of Mrs. Surratt-Norman-(1954)-illus-
142p (5t4, dj) 5.00
MOORE, H N-Life & Services of Gen Anthony Wayne-Phila-1845-
wdcuts-frontis-210p (5yy0) 12.50
MOORE, H P-Ensign John Moor of Canterbury, NH, Desc-1918-
370p (5m3) 15.00
MOORE, HARRY THORNTON-The Novels of John Steinbeck-Chig-
1939-Normandie Hse-8vo-cl-map-1000c prntd (5b2, sp fade) 17.50
MOORE, HORACE E-All Year Round Guide to Yukon-Whitehorse-
(c1947)-80p-plts-map-wrps (4a8) 5.00
MOORE, HUGH-Memoir of Col Ethan Allen-Plattsburgh-1834-252p-
orig cl-papr labl-1st ed (5m3) 20.00
MOORE, J B-Hist of Candia, N Hamp-1893-528p (5mm3) 15.00
MOORE, J HAMILTON-Young Gentleman & Lady's Monitor-Lond-
Prntd-NewLond-Reprntd-1794-396, (6)p-lea-Evans 27345
(5h7, lacks fly) 15.00

MOORE, J HAMILTON (continued)
--same-NY-1795-G Forman-12mo-403p-calf-4 plts on gestures
(5v0) 17.50
--same-Albany-1803-4 plts-orig calf (5mm2, lacks flys) 17.50
MOORE, J HAMPTON-History of 5 o'clock Club of Phila-n.p.-
(Phila)-1891-301p-illus (5w9, bkstrp wn) 7.50
--With Speaker Canon Through the Tropics-Phila-1907-410p-illus
(5p7) 4.50
MOORE, JACOB B-Laws of Trade in the US-NY-1840-12mo-lea-
360p (5t2) 7.50
--Lives of Governors of New Plymouth & Massachusetts Bay-Bost-
1851-lg8vo-cl-port-1st ed (5p5) 17.50
MOORE, JAS-Hist of Copper Shop Vol Refreshment Saloon-Phila-
1866-frontis-pict cl-1st ed (4b6, bk cov stn) 20.00
MOORE, DR JAS-Complete History of Great Rebellion-Phila-
1867-scarce (5h6, bkstrp wn) 10.00
MOORE, JAS CARRICK-Life of Lt Gen Sir John Moore, by his
brother-Lond-1834-JnMurray-2 vols-8vo-orig cl & bds-papr labls-
1st ed (5i8, rprd) 15.00
MOORE, COL JAS H-Roll of Honor-Wash-1866-35p-gray prntd wrps-
rare (5j6) 35.00
MOORE, JOHN BASSETT-Amer Diplomacy-NY-1905-1st ed-illus
(5tt5) 7.50
--History & Digest of Int'l Arbitrations to Which US has Been Party,
wi appendices-Wash-1898-6 vols-8vo-calf (5t0) 25.00
--Principles of Amer Diplomacy-NY-n.d.-476p-1m2o-cl (5t0) 3.75
MOORE, JOHN HAMILTON-New Practical Navigator-1796-
buck-12th ed (5L7, rbnd) 25.00
--same-Newburyport-1800-Edmund Blunt-570p, (2)-cl-7 plts(of 8)-
2nd ed, rev & corr (5m3, rbnd) 30.00
MOORE, JOHN R-Defoe in the Pillory & Other Studies-Bloomington-
(1939) (5mm2) 6.00
MOORE, JOHN TROTWOOD-Hearts of Hickory-Nashville-1926-
450p-frontis-1st ed (5mm8) 4.50 (5h6, autg) 6.00
--Ole Mistis-Phila-1909 (5x2) 12.50
--Songs & Stories from Tennessee-Chig-1897-pict cl-1st ed (5m2) 8.50
--A Summer Hymnal-Phila-1901-Coates-8vo-dec cl-illus
(5h6, shake) 3.50 (5b2, fade) 4.50
--Tom's Last Forage-Nashville-1926-16mo-36p-wrps (5x2) 12.50
--Uncle Wash, His Stories-Phila-1910 (5h6, shake) 3.50
MOORE, JOS W-Picturesque Washington, Pen & Pencil Sketches-
Prov-1884-308p-cl-map (5h7, rub) 5. (5w5) 6.00
MOORE, JULIA A-The Sweet Singer of Michigan-GrndRapids-
(1878)-Eaton, Lyon&Co-16mo-port-wrps-90p (5j5) 25.00
MOORE, REV L B-What the Negro Has Done for Himself-Wash-
16p-bds - (ca 1910) (5x2, ex-libr) 17.50
MOORE, LUCIA W-The Story of Eugene-NY-1949 (5x5) 10.00
MOORE, M B-The Dixie Speller, to Follow the First Dixie Reader-
Raleigh-1864-Branson&Farrar-8vo-orig prntd bds (5zz7, rub) 15.00
MOORE, M C-Report of Gov of Wash Territory-Wash-1889-60p-
col fldg map-prntd wrps (4a5, chip) 15.00
MOORE, MARIANNE-The Arctic Ox-Lond-(1964)-8vo-cl-
1st Lond ed (5dd8, autg, dj) 25.00
--Collected Poems-NY-1951-12mo-cl-1st ed (5ss7, dj, pres, vf) 45.00
--Le Mariage-NY-1965-sm12mo-dec wrps-ltd to 50c, nbrd
(5ss7, vf) 35.00
--Letters from & to Ford Motor Co-NY-1958-(Pierpont Morgan Liby)-
illus-ltd to 550c-scarce (4b7, f) 50.00
--Like a Bulwark-NY-1957-Viking-8vo-patternd bds (5b2, f, dj) 10.00
--Nevertheless-NY-(1944)-12mo-cl-1st ed (5ss7, pres, vf, dj) 45.00
--Observations-NY-1925-Dial Pr-bds-2nd prntng (5ss9, sl fray) 10.00
--The Pangolin & Other Verse-Lond-(1936)-lg8vo-dec bds-illus-
papr labl-1st ed-ltd to 120c-Curwen Pr (5ss7, pres, vf) 250.00
--Poems-Lond-1921-Cr8vo-dec papr wrps-labl-1st ed of auth's
1st book (5ss7, mint, pres) 250.00
--Poetry & Criticism-Cambr-(1965)-12mo-wrps-1st ed-
issued in ed of 200c (5ss7, mint) 25.00
MOORE, MARTIN-Memoir of (John) Eliot, Apostle to No Amer
Indians-Bost-1842-16mo-frontis-2nd ed, rev & corr (5h6, rub) 6.50
MOORE, MERRILL-The Noise that Time Makes-NY-1929-12mo-
bds-113p (5m8, autg port) 6.50
MOORE, MRS-Short History of France-Lond-1819-2 vols-sq16mo-
calf-(30 plts (of 32)-1st ed (5c8, chip, sl loose) 17.50
MOORE, N-Physician in Engl History-1913 (5L7) 4.00
MOORE, N HUDSON-The Collector's Manual-NY-(1906)-329p-
336 illus-lg4to (5w7, shake) 7.50
--same-NY-1935-329p-illus (5F9, underline, 5t4) 6.50
--same-NY-1939-329p (5h9) 6.50
--Delftware Dutch & English-Lond-n.d.-58 photo illus-(8),78p
(5w7) 7.50
--Flower Fables & Fancies-NY-1904-192p-48 photos (5w3) 5.00
--The Lace Book-Lond-1905-4to-206p-engrs (5xx7) 15.00
--same-NY-1937-Tudor-206p-plts-8vo-cl (5m5) 16.00

MOORE, N HUDSON-The Old China Book-NY-(1903)-300p-
   illus   (5t4)   8.00
--same-NY-1935-300p-illus-new ed-illus   (5h9)   6.50
--Old Clock Book-NY-(1911)-339p-illus   (5xx7)   10.00
--The Old Furniture Book with sketch of Past Days & Ways-NY-
   (1903)-254p-illus   (5t4) 6.50   (5h9,5w9)   8.50
--same-NY-1935-Tudor-254p-illus   (5p0) 6.   (5h9)   6.50
--Old Glass, European & Amer-NY-1935-394p-photos-lg8vo
                            (5w1) 10.   (5h9,5p0)   7.50
--same-NY-1938-thk4to-cl-lg papr-enlrgd ed   (5p5)   15.00
--Old Pewter, Brass, Copper & Sheffield Plate-GardenCty-(1933)-
   229p-illus   (5w7) 6.50   (5t7)   7.95
MOORE, PHIL H-The Castle Buck-Lond-1945-Longmans (5nn8) 4.50
MOORE, R-The Artizans' Guide & Everybody's Assistant-Montr-
   1873-284p, 57, 22(tables)   (5n7, sp tn)   5.50
MOORE, S S-Traveller's Directory, or, A Pocket Companion-Phila-
   1804-8vo-4p, 37p, 19p text-38 maps on 22 lvs-2nd ed (5t0) 25.00
MOORE, SALLY FALK-Power & Property in Inca Peru-NY-1958-
   Columbia Univ Pr-190p   (5p9)   4.25
MOORE, SAM'L-Historical outlines of Engl phonology & morphology-
   Ann Arbor-1925-4to-cl-153p   (5p6)   6.00
MOORE, SAM'L TAYLOR-America & the World War-NY-(1937)-
   Greenberg-309p-cl   (5mm8)   4.50
MOORE, T STURGE-Albert Durer-Lond-1905-343p-illus
                                      (5t7, libr stmp) 5.00
--Roderigo of Bivar-NY-1925-Rudge-51p-ltd to 500c (5p7) 7.50
--The Vinedresser & Other Poems-Lond-1899-12mo-80p (5w1) 6.50
MOORE, TEX-The West-Wichita Falls-(1935) (4c7,autg) 25. (5yy7)20.00
MOORE, THOS-British Ferns & Their Allies-Lond-1881-187p-
   11 illus   (5s7, rub)   7.50
MOORE, THOS-Irish Melodies-Jersey-1828-12mo-12 illus (5yy6) 10.00
MOORE, THOS-Lalla Rookh, an Oriental Romance-Lond-1817-
   Longman, Hurst-4to-3/4 mor-1st ed (5ss9, 1 pg ALS, fox) 75.00
--same-Lond-1817-lea-g.tooled-e.g.-Fore Edge Painting of Lond
                                              (5d2)   250.00
--same-Lond-1820-for Longman, Hurst-8vo-hf calf-g.-10th ed
                                      (5b0, lt rub)   5.00
--same-Lond-1860-Routledge, Warne & Routledge-illus-4to-
   g.back-a.e.g.   (5i4)   15.00
--same-Bost-1885-4to-wrps-273p-illus-silk portfolio-satin ties
                                            (5ii2)   12.50
--same-NY-n.d.-Leavitt & Allen-illus-heavy lea (5k1,sl scuff) 7.50
MOORE, THOS-Life of Lord Byron etc-Lond-1838 to 1844-2 vols-
   R8vo-calf-tooled-g.e.-ports by Finden-mor labls-JnMurray-
   scarce   (5p5, f, f bndg) 35.00
MOORE, THOS-Melodies, Songs, Sacred Songs & National Airs-NY-
   1825-orig bds   (4a4)   10.00
MOORE, THOS-Memoirs of Life of Rt Hon Richard Brinsley Sheridan-
   Lond-Longman-1825-lg4to-719p-port-calf-g.-1st ed (5a1) 25.00
MOORE, THOS-Odes of Anacreon-Phila-1804-301p-port-calf-
   1st Amer ed   (5m4)   20.00
MOORE, THOS-Poetical works of-Lond-Longmans-1869-10 vols-
   dec cl-lg prnt   (5p6, f)   20.00
MOORE, U S-Chonological History of Wm & Harriet Moore & Their
   Relatives & Desc-1904, 13-140p   (5mm3)   7.50
MOORE, WM E-US Official Pictures of World War-Wash-1920-
   576p-illus-olb-576p   (5x5)   12.50
MOORE, WM H-The Clash-Lond&Tor-1918-Dent   (5nn8)   5.00
MOORE, WM V-Indian Wars of the US from Discovery to Present Time-
   Phila-1840-1st ed-illus-321p   (5i3, wn)   10.00
--same-Phila-1860-illus-328p   (5ii7, f)   10.00
MOORE'S-Wholesale Price List of Newspapers & Magazines
   Winter 1901, 1902-Brockport-36p-illus-fldg bds (5e4,sl stns) 5.00
MOORE-WILSON, MINNIE-The Seminoles of Florida-Phila-1896-
   illus-cl-1st ed   (4k4, f)   10.00
MOOREHEAD, ALAN-No Room In The Ark-NY-c1959 (5x7,5x2)   3.00
--Russian Revolution-NY-1958-Harper-301p-illus (5p0)   4.50
MOOREHEAD, WARREN K-The Amer Indian in the US, 1850 to 1914-
   Andover-1914-434p plus index-illus-2 fldg maps-1st ed (5bb4)25.00
--Archaeology of Arkansas River Valley-Yake Univ Pr-1931-
   plts-4to-cl-1st ed   (4k4, f) 20.   (5bb4) 12.50
--Cahokia Mounds, a preliminary paper-Urbana-(1922)-16 plts-
   1st ed   (4k4, f)   7.50
--Cahokia Mounds-Urbana-(1929)-wrps-plts-map (4k4, f)   15.00
--Fort Ancient, The Great Prehistoric Earthwork of Warren Co, Ohio-
   Cinn-(1890)-photos-map   (5m2)   13.50
--Narr of Explorations in New Mex, Ariz, Ind, etc-Andover-1906-
   Bull #3-wrps-200p-photos   (5bb4, chip)   8.50
--Prehistoric Implements-Cinn-(1900)-illus-423p plus index-
   v scarce   (5j1)   35.00
--Prehistoric Relics, An Illus Catalogue-Andover-(1905)-162p plus
   bibli-1st ed   (5jj7, wrps) 7.50 (5t3, cl rbnd) 10.00

MOOREHEAD, WARREN K (continued)
--Report on the Archaeology of Maine-Andover-1922-plts-cl-
   4to-1st ed   (4k4, f)   20.00
--Report of Susquehanna River Exped-Heye Foundation-1916-
   142p-index-37 plts   (5zz0)   12.50
--Stone Age in No America-Bost-1910-photos-drawings-
   2 vols-1st ed   (4t3, 4p in facs) 75.   (4k4) 100.00
--Stone Ornaments etc-Andover-1917-illus-cl-4to-1st ed(4k4, f) 45.00
MOORES, CHAS W-Abraham Lincoln, lawyer-Greenfield, Ind-
   1922-(i e 1929)-wrps-Ind Hist Soc Publ   (5g3, unopnd) 5.00
MOORHEAD BOARD OF TRADE-Valley of Red River of North &
   City of Moorhead, Minn-Cleve-1883-44p,(20p ads)-illus-
   prntd wrps   (5g8)   25.00
MOORHEAD, ELIZ-Whirling Spindle-Pitts-1942-317p-illus (5m2) 6.00
MOORHOUSE, EDW-The Romance of the Derby-Lond-1908-
   Biographical Pr-2 vols-lg8vo-hf mor-a.e.g. (5b0)   75.00
MOORMAN, J J, MD-White Sulphur Springs, with analysis of its
   waters etc-Balt-1876-dbl pg map-wrps   (5g8)   10.00
MOORMAN, MADISON BERRYMAN-The Journal of....1850 to
   1851-SanFran-1948-t8vo-150p-Calif Hist Soc (4n1,5h5,fade) 8.00
MOORS, H J-With Stevenson in Samoa-Bost-(1910)-Small, Maynard-
   photos-1st ed   (5x5)   10.00
MOORS, J F-History of 52nd Regiment, Mass Vol-Bost-1893-
   Geo H Ellis-illus   (5mm8)   5.00
MOOSDORF, J-Flight to Africa-NY-1954-1st ed (5x2, dj)   3.50
MOOSE FORT JOURNALS 1783 to 85-Lond-1954-Hudsons Bay
   Rec Soc-392p-3 fldg maps-ltd ed   (5a1)   15.00
MOOSO, JOSIAH-Life & Travels of...Winfield, KS-1888-frontis-
   400p-1st ed-v scarce   (4t3)   85.00
MOOTZ, HERMAN EDWIN-"Pawnee Bill"-LosAng-(1928)-photos-
   285p-1st ed-scarce   (4t3) 12.50   (5xx5,autg) 20.00
MORA JO-Californios-GardenCty-1949-175p-cl-illus
                           (5d6) 10.   (5yy7, f, dj)   12.50
--Horsemen of the West-1952-Valley Nat'l Bank-portfolio of
   8 prnts   (5g5, f)   10.00
--Log of the Spanish Main-SanFran-1933-8vo-cl-illus (5h5) 3.00
--Trail Dust & Saddle Leather-NY-1946-illus
                      (5h5) 6.50   (4n1) 15.   (5xx5)   10.00
MORAIN, ALFRED-Underworld of Paris-NY-1931-320p-illus
                                            (5xx7)   6.50
MORAIS, HENRY S-Eminent Israelites of 19th Century-Phila-1880-
   371p-8vo-cl-1st ed   (5p5)   12.50
--The Jews of Phila-Phila-1894-(16)576p-v scarce (5ii8) 45.00
MORAN, CHAS-Money-NY-1863-228p-cl-labl
                            (4b8) 7.50   (5m6, f)   12.50
MORAN, E PERCY-Facsimiles of Water Colors-NY-(1894)-
   12 col plts   (5t4)   12.50
MORAN, EDW-13 Chapters of Amer History-n.p.-1905-illus (5j3)12.00
MORAN, FRANK F-Battles of the Confederacy-Balt-n.d.-(ca1890)-
   201p-illus-priv prntd   (5w5, lacks fly) 12.50
MORAN, HUGH ANDERSON-Makers of America-Ithaca-1936-wrps
                                           (5q8, tn)   4.50
MORAN, J BELL-Moran Family-Detroit-1949-152p
               (5jj9,pres) 12.50   (5t3,pres) 10. (5mm3) 22.50
MORAN, JOHN J, MD-A Defense of Edgar Allan Poe-Wash-
   1885-orig front wrp bnd in-port-1st ed   (5mm2)   20.00
MORAN, THOS-Explorer in Search of Beauty-NY-1958-
   East Hampton Free Libr   (5x5, d j)   7.50
MORAND, P-Black Magic-Lond-1929-illus-1st ed (5x2)   5.00
MORAND, P-Le Voyage-NY-1930-79p-red cl-illus tip in (5a9,f)10.00
MORAND, PAUL-Indian Air-Bost-1933-HoughtonMiff-12mo-cl
                                             (4a3)   5.00
MORANT, GEO SOUILE de-Chinese Love Tales-NY-
   Valenti Angelo, illus-Illust Edit Co -1935 (5p7)   3.25
MORAVIAN INDIAN BOY, THE-Phila-c1870-16mo-206p-frontis-
   2 plts-cl-Presby Board of Publ   (5p1, wn stns)   5.00
MORDAUNT, HARRY-Modest defence of publick stews;or,an essay
   upon whoring-Lond-1740-for T Read-8vo-mor-rare (5x3) 150.00
MORDECAI, MAJ ALFRED-Military Commission to Europe, 1855
   & 1856-Wash-1860-Bowman-232p-illus(sm fldg)
                           (5mm8) 10.   (5xx7)   15.00
--same-Wash-1861-4to   (5m6, lt stns)   17.50
--Report of Experiments on Gunpowder made at Wash Arsenal,
   1843, 44-1845-buck   (5L7, rbnd)   17.50
MORE, SIR THOS-Utopia-Lond-prntd for R Chiswell-1684-8vo-
   206p-calf-g.sp-1st ed of 2nd Engl transl-Wing M2691
                                           (5hh0, f)   750.00
--same-NY-1934-Limited Ed Club-ltd to 1500c
               (5i4,bkstrp wn,box) 20.   (5b0,box)   35.00
--same-Lond-n.d.-W Scott-268p   (5p0)   3.00
MOREARTY, ED F-Omaha Memories, Recoll-(cov t.is "36 Years
   in Omaha 1879 to 1917. Omaha Memories)-Omaha-1917-248p-
   frontis-scarce -1st ed   (5L2, sl wn, pres)   25.00

MOREAU DE ST MERY, M-Voyage aux Etats Unis de l'Amerique-
NewHav-1913-bds   (5cc6,shaken)   40.00
MOREAU, GEO-Theorie des Moteurs A Gaz Conferences faite a
L'Automobile Club de France-Paris-1902-224p   (5h8)   17.50
MOREAU, JACOB N,comp-Memorial,containing Summary View of
Facts-Phila-1757-Chattin-338p-buck-v rare
                              (4b1,rbnd,1 lf facs)   225.00
MOREAU, P-Les Sports Modernes Illustres-Paris-n.d.-4to-
Encyclopedie Sportive Illustree-813 Gravures (4j3,bndg wn) 15.00
MOREAU, VICTOR-Life & Campaigns of,by "an officer of the staff"-
NY-(1806)-288p-frontis-lea   (5t4)   15.00
MOREAU-BERILLON, C-Au Pays Du Champagne-Reims-(1924)-4to-
wrps-470p-illus   (5w1,shake,tape)   50.00
MORECAMP, ARTHUR-Live Boys,or Charley & Nasho in Texas-Bost-
1879-illus-308p-6p ads at end-"1879" on t.p.-(true 1st ed?)
                                       (4t3)   30.00
--same-Bost-(1878)-illus-12mo-cl (4c1) 25. (5jj7,vf) 40.00
MOREL DE VINDE, CH G-La Morale de l'Enfance-Geneve-1818-
Sestie et fils-sq12mo-112p-orig blue wrps-9th ed   (5c8) 20.00
MOREL, J J-Progressive Catering-Lond-(1953)-illus-4 vols
                                       (4g9,f)   25.00
MORGAN, CHAS L-The Gunroom-Lond-1919-12mo-cl-
1st ed of auth's 1st book   (5gg6)   35.00
MORGAN, DALE L-Calif as I Saw it-Los Gatos-1960-209p plus index-
1st ed,ltd to 750c-See Howes #M-55,Reprint of scarce 1850 ed
                                    (5t3,mint)   12.50
--The Great Salt Lake-Indnpls-(1947)-1st ed
               (5jj1,fade) 7.50   (4t3,dj)   10.00
--The Humboldt, Highroad of the West-(1943)-Farrar & Rinehart-
12mo-cl-1st ed   (5F5,dj,4t3,f,dj)   10.00
--Jedediah Smith & Opening of the West-Indnpls-(1953)-
BobbsMerrill-8vo-cl-scarce-1st ed
          (4t3,dj) 20. (5hh4,dj) 15. (5jj1,f)   23.75
--Overland Diary of Jas Pritchard from Kentucky to Calif in 1849-
Denver-1959-frontis-2 maps-1st ed(ltd)-200p plus index
                              (5yy7,dj,unopnd)   20.00
--Overland in 1846-Georgetwn,Calif-1963-2 vols-ltd 1st ed,
autg,box   (5t1,mint) 85.   (5h5,vf)   50.00
--Rocky Mntn Journals of Wm Marshall Anderson-San Marino-
1967-Huntingdon Libr-430p-ltd to 1500c   (5a0,f,dj)   15.00
MORGAN, EDMUND S-The Puritan Dilemna-Bost-1948-224p-
1st ed   (5h9)   4.50
MORGAN, EDW E P-God's Loaded Dice Alaska 1897 to 1930-
Caldwell-1948-Caxton Prntrs-298p-illus-cl-ltd to 1000c,autg
                                       (5r0)   10.00
MORGAN, F, ed-Connecticut as a Colony & as a State-1904-4 vols
                                   (5L7,rprd)   25.00
MORGAN, GENE-"Westward the Course of Empire"-Chig-1945-57p-
1st ed-illus   (4t3)   3.50
MORGAN, J McDOWELL-Military Medals & Insignia of the US-
Glendale-1941-GriffinPatterson-8vo-cl-141p-illus (5j5) 10.00
MORGAN, JAS-Abraham Lincoln, The Boy & the Man-NY-1908-
435p-illus   (5t7)   6.50
--The Birth of the Amer People-NY-1930-Macm-335p (5p7) 4.00
--Our Presidents-NY-1952-438p   (5t4)   5.00
MORGAN, JAS M-Recollections of a Rebel Reefer-Bost-1917-491p
          (4j4,sl wn) 20.   (5a9) 15.   (4m2)   22.50
MORGAN, JOHN HILL-John Singleton Copley, 1737 to 1815-Conn-
1939-Walpole Soc-25p-illus-175c prntd-wrps-rare
                               (4a0,autg)   23.50
--Paintings by John Trumbull at Yale Univ-Yale U Pr-1926-90p-
4to-wrps   (4a0)   12.50
--Two Early Portraits of Geo Washington painted by C W Peale-
Princeton-1927-29p-8vo   (4a0)   9.50
MORGAN, JOHN T-Navigation of Tennessee River-Wash-1906-
prntd wrps-fldg maps-72p   (4j4)   6.50
MORGAN, JOS-Sin its own Punishment-Bost-1728-Gamaliel Rogers-
12mo-stitchd limp bds   (5L1,chip,wn)   15.00
MORGAN, LEWIS H-The Amer Beaver & His Works-Phila-1868-
330p-orig cl-23 plts-fldg map-1st ed   (5m3)   50.00
--Ancient Society-NY-1877-1st ed   (5bb4)   17.50
--Diffusion against centralization-Rochester-1852-16mo (5g4) 6.00
--Houses & House Life of Amer Aborigines-Wash-1881-GPO-4to-
281p-orig cl-1st ed (4k3) 25.   (5m3,ex-libr)   35.00
--The Indian Journals, 1859 to 62-AnnArbor-(1959)-4to-16 col plts-
229p   (4b3,f,dj)   17.50
--League of Ho De No Sau Nee or Iroquois-Rochester-1851-
1st ed-hf lea-477p-col plts-scarce-lg linen map
            (5t3,lacks map) 30.   (5zz0)   85.00
--Systems of Consanguinity & Affinity of the Human Family-
(GPO, 1870)-Smi Contr to Knowledge-folio-cl bkd bds-590p
                                    (4k5,f)   75.00

MORGAN LIBRARY-Treasures from Pierpont Morgan Library-
NY-1957-illus-48p text-8vo-wrps-50th Anniv Exhib (5ww3) 8.50
MORGAN, M J-Catalogue of Art Collection of-NY-1886-4to-
hf mor-illus-ltd to 500c   (5ii2)   49.50
MORGAN, MANIE-The New Stars-n.p.-1951-301p (5w0,dj) 5.00
MORGAN, MINNIE B-Historical Souvenir of Central City Colo-
CentralCty-1941-40p-photos-map-wrps   (5t3)   5.00
MORGAN, MURRAY-Bridge to Russia-NY-1947-222p (5ss1) 4.00
--The Columbia-Seattle-1949   (5jj1,f)   7.00
--The Dam-NY-1954-illus-1st ed   (5jj1,f)   5.00
MORGAN, N H-Hist of Jas Morgan of New Lond, Conn & Desc-
1869-280p   (5mm3)   17.50
MORGAN, NATALIE-How to Make Paper Flowers & Party
Decorations-NY-(1947)-illus   (4a1)   8.50
MORGAN, OWEN-The Light of Britannia-Cardiff-n.d.-(1895)-
frontis   (5j2,crack,lacks e.p.)   25.00
MORGAN, R B,ed-Readings in English Social History-Cambr, Engl-
Univ Pr-1923-585p   (5x0)   12.50
MORGAN, R HAROLD-Beverage Manufacture(Non Alcoholic)-
London-1938-240p   (5w1)   12.50
MORGAN, RICHARD-Bibliography of Ohio Archaeology-Columbus-
1947-189p-wrps   (5jj9) 5.   (5jj7,f,bnd)   7.50
MORGAN, LADY SYDNEY-France in 1829, 30-Lond-1830-hf lea-
2 vols   (5t4)   10.50
--Italy-Lond-1824-3 vols-hf lea   (5t4)   15.00
--The novice of St Dominick-Lond-1806-for Rich Phillips-4 vols-
12mo-1st ed   (5xx6,lacks hf t.)   100.00
--Poems,dedicated by permission,to Countess of Moira-Dublin-
1801-prntd by Stewart&Philips(Lond)-8vo-hf calf-slim-
1st ed of auth's 1st book   (5i8,rprd,lacks hf t.) 75.00
--The wild Irish girl,a national tale-Lond-1806-Rich Phillips-3 vols-
12mo-hf calf-1st ed   (5xx6,wn)   35.00
MORGAN, THOS-Romano British Mosaic Pavements-Lond-1886-
8vo-323p-1st ed   (4m7)   30.00
MORGAN, THOS-My Story of the Last Indian War in the NW-
(Forest Grove, 1954)-8vo-29p-prntd wrps (5F5, autg) 3.50
MORGAN, THOS HUNT-Experimental Embryology-NY-1927-illus-
1st ed   (5jj3)   22.50
MORGAN, W H-Personal Remin of War of 1861 to 65-Lynchburg-
1911-sm8vo-286p   (4a7)   17.50
MORGAN, W SCOTT-History of Wheel & Alliance & Impending
Revolution-Ft Scott,Ka-1889-774p-illus-1st ed-v scarce
                               (5L0, lt wn)   20.00
MORGENTHAU, HANS J-Politics among Nations-NY-1949 (5x7) 5.00
MORGENTHAU, HENRY-Ambassador Morgenthau's Story-GardenCty-
1918-407p-illus-map   (5x7,5w4)   5.00
MORI, A-Life & Resources in Amer for circulation in Japan-Wash-
1871-illus-404p plus errata   (5ii8,pres)   25.00
MORICE, ADRIAN G-Catholic Church in Canadian NW-Winn-1936-
83p-ports-plts-wrps   (5a1)   6.50
--Histoire de L'Eglise Catholique Dans L'Ouest Canadien-1912-
illus-3 vols-buck   (4e9,rbnd)   40.00
--History of Northern interior of Brit Col, formerly New Caledonia-
Tor-1904-map-illus   (5g4)   7.50
--Thawing Out the Eskimo-Bost-1943-241p-port (5dd0,cov sl wn) 6.50
MORIER, JAS-Journey through Persia, Armenia & Asia Minor etc-
Lond-1812-1st ed-3 fldg maps-26 aquatints-440p-lg4to-
3/4 mor-g.bk   (4b6, f bndg)   150.00
MORIER, JAS-Adventures of Haji Baba of Ispahan-NY-1937-
sm4to-pict col cl-403p-illus-col plts   (5w9)   10.00
MORIN, E-Le Premier Livre Nouvel Alphabet-Paris-n.d.-(ca1880)-
pict bds-cl-4to-48p-col plts   (5p6,f)   16.00
MORIN, VICTOR-Old Montreal with Pen & Pencil-n.p.-1929-40p-
col illus   (4b9) 8.   (5w8)   7.50
--Traite d'Art Heraldique-1919-407p   (5t9)   7.50
MORISON, E E,ed-Letters of Theo Roosevelt-Cambr-1951-8 vols
                                    (5n4,f)   80.00
MORISON, ELTING E-Admiral Sims & Modern Amer Navy-Bost-1942-
illus-548p   (5s1,dj,sl soil)   7.50
MORISON, J L-The 8th Earl of Elgin-Lond-1928-plts
            (5dd7,f,dj) 12.   (4d2)   12.50
MORISON-Life of Hon Jeremiah Smith-Bost-1845-1st ed-port-516p
       (5ss5, lacks bkstrp) 6.   (5i3,f)   10.00
MORISON, SAML ELIOT-Admiral of the Ocean Sea-Bost-1942-8vo-
cl-2 vols-map-illus-ltd ed (5ss2,f,ex-libr) 42.50 (5t0,f,dj) 27.50
--Builders of the Bay Colony-Bost-1930-illus-8vo-cl-1st ed
          (5qq8) 15.   (4c1) 12.50 (5h9)   17.50
--Founding of Harvard College-Cambr-1935-illus-472p (5xx7) 15.00
--Growth of the Amer Republic-1946-2 vols-3rd ed (5L7,mismtchd) 7.50
--History of the US Naval Operations in WW II-Bost-1947 to 1963-
15 vols-photos-maps-diagrams   (5c1)   112.50
--Maritime History of Mass-Bost-1921-illus-1st ed
            (4m2) 15.   (4F4,crack)   17.50

MORISON, SAML ELIOT (continued)
--Maritime History of Mass-Bost-1921-1st ed-401p-lg papr-
ltd to 385c   (4c1) 30. (5w0, box) 32.50 (5ii8)   37.50
--The Ropemakers of Plymouth-Bost-1950-177p-col frontis-
illus   6.50   (5y2)
--Sources & Documents Illus Amer Revolution-Oxf-1929-2nd ed
(5yy6)   6.00
MORISON, STANLEY-Brief Survey of Printing History & Practice-
NY-1923-12mo-bds-cl bkstrp   (4c1)   6.00
--Talbot Barnes Reed, Author, Bibliographer, Typefounder-Cambr-
1960-t8vo-cl-plts-facs-ltd to 500c   (5ee9)   25.00
--Typographic Design in Relation to Photographic Composition-
1959-Black Vine Pr-8vo-Book Club of Calif-ltd to 400c (5h5) 15.00
MORISSET, GERARD-Coup d'Oeil sur les Arts en Nouvelle France-
Quebec-1941-8vo-32 engrs-prntd wrps   (5w8)   9.00
MORLAND, HAROLD-4 Plays for Boys-Lond&NY-n.d.-Nelson-
12mo-125p   (5p1)   4.00
MORLEY, CHRISTOPHER-Apologia Pro Sua Preoccupatione-NY-
1930-1st ed-ltd to 225c, autg, box   (5mm2)   17.50
--Christopher Morley's Briefcase-Phila-1936-12mo-64p-prnt papr
(5i8, f) 4.   (5t7)   3.00
--Born in a Beer Garden-NY-1930-118p, (1)-illus-ltd to 999c-
uncut   (5w7, unopnd)   8.50
--Don't Open Until Christmas-NY-1931-12mo-cl-dec bds-1st ed
(5cc9, bkplt) 5.   (5m2)   4.50
--Essays-NY-1928-DblDoran-1106p   (5p9)   5.00
--Ex Libris-NY-1936-12mo-cl-1st Nat'l Book Fair-1st ed
(5d5) 5.   (5t7)   7.50
--Ex Libria Carissimis-Phila-1932-8vo-bds-cl bk
(5b2) 10.   (5m2)   6.00
--Friends of the Library-NY-(1937)-(Marchbanks Pr)-12mo-10p-
papr-reprntd   (5t7)   4.00
--Footnotes for a Centennial-NY-1936-1st ed (5mm2)   7.50
--Forty four Essays-NY-(1925)-1st ed   (5mm2)   7.50
--The Goldfish Under the Ice-Lond-1929-ltd to 530c, autg
(5a9, dj) 10.   (5p1, dj)   12.50
--same-NY-1932-DbldayDoran-69p-pict cl-1st Amer ed (5p1,autg) 5.00
--Goodbye to Spring-Phila-1937-15p-dec bds-1st ed   (5t7)   7.50
--The Haunted Bookshop-NY-1919-┐ st ed   (5mm1)   10.00
--Inward Ho-NY-1923-1st ed   (5mm1)   6.00
--Kitty Foyle-Phila-(1939)-┐ st ed   (5r9, dj)   7.50
--Mince Pie-NY-(1919)-1st ed-bds   (5i3) 5.   (5mm1)   8.50
--Pipefuls-GardenCty, NY-1920-1st ed   (5r9) 15.   (5t7)   10.50
--Plum Pudding-NY-1921-1st issue   (5mm1)   15.00
--Powder of Sympathy-NY-1923-1st ed-illus (5i3) 5. (5mm1)   6.50
--The Rocking Horse-NY-1919-┐ st ed   (4b4)   10.00
--Thorofare-NY-(1942)-1st ed   (5mm1, dj)   6.00
MORLEY, F V-Whaling North & South-NY-(1926)-235p-photos-
maps-dec cov   (5s1, pres)   6.00
--same-Lond-1927-8vo-229p-cl-2 maps-47 illus (5t0)   7.50
--Wreck of the Active-Cambr-n.d.-347p-illus   (5w9)   4.00
MORLEY, HENRY-Palissy the potter-Lond-1852-Chapman&Hall-
2 vols-8vo-orig cl-1st ed   (5i8, fade)   22.50
MORLEY, IRIS-Soviet Ballet-Lond-1946-illus-71p-8vo (5ww3)   12.50
MORLEY, JOHN-Diderot & Encyclopaedists-Lond-1923-2 vols-
sm8vo-cl &bds   (5t0)   7.50
--Early Life & Letters of-Lond-1927-Macmillan-2 vols-1st ed-
by F W Hirst   (4p1, 1p auth's als) 22.50
--Edmund Burke-NY-1924-255p-ltd to 780c   (4b3)   12.50
--English Men of Letters-Lond-1904-Macm-38 vols in 19-hf mor
(5x0, sp fade)   85.00
--Life of Richard Cobden-(1881)-2 vols   (5L7)   7.50
--Literary Essays-Lond-1908-Arthur L Humphreys-sq8vo-3/4 lef-
g.bands-g.t.   (5t5)   20.00
--Recollections-NY-1917-2 vols   (5w9)   6.50
MORLEY, M W-Down North & Up Along-NY-1900-304p-illus-
maps   (4b9, lacks fly) 4.00
MORLEY, SYLVANUS G-The Ancient Maya-Stanford-(1946)-
32p, 520p-95 plts-lg8vo   (5t3, 5t2)   12.50
--Covered Bridges of Calif-1938-Univ of Calif-4to-92p-cl-illus-
1st ed   (5h5, f, dj)   10.00
--Introduction to Study of Maya Hieroglyphs-Wash-1915-BAE Bul #57-
284p-plts   (5t7, libr stmp) 10.   (4k4)   12.50
MORLEY, MRS WALTER S-History of Calif State Soc DAR-Berkeley-
1938-619p plus 2p index-ports   (5r0)   10.00
MORMON EXPOSITOR-Vol 1, #1(all publ)-SltLkCty-n.d. (c 1875)-
8vo-2 lvs   (5i0)   30.00
"MORMON" METROPOLIS, THE-Illus Guide to Salt Lake City &
its Environs-SaltLkCty-1888-(J H Parry&Co)-64p-1 fldg view
(5t3, lacks wrps)   15.00
MORMON READER-(phonetic alphabet throughout)-woodcuts-
Deseret 2nd Book, 1868 -12mo-pic cl-roan back (5i3)   15.00

MORMON READERS - 3 Readers-
Deseret First Book, 1868, prntd for the Univ-
Deseret Second Book, 1868, prntd for the Univ-
Book of Mormon, Pt 1, 1869, Russell Bros, prntrs-NY-pict bds
& roan bks   (5rr2)   100.00
MORMON TROUBLES IN MICH-Harrisb-1853-4p-unbnd as issued-
Democratic Union   (5h2)   8.50
MORMONISM UNVEILED-StL-1891-413p   (5t4, rprd)   17.50
MORMONS OR LATTER DAY SAINTS-Lond-(1851)-
National Illustrated Libr-illus-326p-cl   (5tt0)   20.00
--same-Lond-1852-illus-320p-orig cl-12mo-2nd ed (5t2)   8.50
MORNEWECK, EVELYN FOSTER-Chronicles of Stephen Foster's
Family-Pitts-1944-2 vols-illus   (5xx8)   25.00
MORNING HERALD-1st issue-NY-Wed Morning May 6, 1835,
(Vol 1,#1)-4p, fld   (5w4, sl tn) 10.00
MORNING RAMBLE, THE-NewLond-c1850-12mo-8 lvs-
pict wrps in col-hand col illus-verse   (4F6)   8.50
MOROSCO, HELEN M-The Oracle of Broadway-Caldwell-1944
(5p0)   6.00
MORPHY, COUNTESS-Recipes of all Nations-NY-1936-821p-
thk8vo-thumb index   (5g9)   10.00
--Lightning Cookery-Lond-(1931)-97p-illus-bds (5c5) 3.50 (5g9) 2.50
MORPURGO, E-Dictionary of Italian Clockmakers-Rome-1950-
239p-8vo-Italian text   (5bb0)   6.00
MORRAH, DAVE-Alice in Wunderbarland etc-Tor-(1957)-Rinehart-
77p-12mo-pict bds-1st ed   (5p1, rub, fade) 3.50
MORRAYE, CLEMENT-Les Lettres de Monsieur de Grandcru-
Bruxelles-(1946)-331p, (1)-18 plts-ltd ed-wrps (5w6)   16.50
MORRELL, BENJ-Narr of Four Voyages-NY-1832-J & J Harper-492p-
port-cl-1st ed   (4b1, rbnd) 125.   (5c1)   90.00
MORRELL, ED -The 25th Man-Montclair-1924-illus-1st ed
(5dd6) 10.   (4t6)   12.50
MORRELL, F V-Anc of Daniel Morrell of Hartford with Desc-1916-
126p   (5mm3)   6.00
MORRICE, ALEX-A Treatise on Brewing-Lond-1810-164p, (12), 16p-
bds   (5w1, v wn)   16.50
MORRICE, CAPT BEZALEEL-A voyage from the East Indies-Lond-
1716-J Roberts-8vo-hf calf-poem-hf calf-frontis-lf of ads-
1st ed- v scarce-hf t.   (5x3)   60.00
MORRILL, CHAS HENRY-The Morrills & Reminiscences-Chig-(1918)-
157p plus index-illus-extra photos tip in   (4t3, ex-libr) 5.00
MORRILL, MADGE HAINES-Fighting Africa's Black Magic-
Mountain View, CA-1938-Pac Pr-pic cov-155p (4t5) 8. (5x2)   5.00
MORRILL, MR-Report, The Chartering of Transport Vessels for the
Banks Exped-Wash-1863-SC75-128p   (5j6)   3.00
MORRIS, A-Nova Brittania-Tor-1884-187p (4b9,f,5nn8) 10. (5x6) 8.50
MORRIS, A M-Dusky Memories-Columbia-1932-12mo-bds (5h2)   10.00
MORRIS, ALEX-Treaties of Canada with Indians of Manitoba & the
NW Territories-Tor-(1880)-375p   (5dd7, vf)   24.00
MORRIS, ANN A-Digging in the SoWest-NY-1933-photos
(4k4, lt soil) 6.50   (5a6) 7.50   (5x5)   10.00
MORRIS, ANNE C, ed-Diary & Letters of Gouverneur Morris-NY-
1888-Scribner's-2 vols   (4d9)   8.50
MORRIS, B F-Life of Thos Morris-Cinn-1856-408p-cl
(5h2, ex-libr) 10.   (5zz9)   15.00
MORRIS, BARBARA-Victorian Embroidery-Lond-(1962)-238p-71 plts
(5n7)   8.25
MORRIS CANAL INVESTIGATION COMMITTEE-Report of the-
173p-maps-orig wrps-photos   (5m2)   10.00
MORRIS, CHAS-Aryan Race Origin Achievements-Chig-1888-347p
(4b2)   6.00
--Broken Fetters-NY-(1888)-602p-illus   (5w6, shake)   6.50
--Great Issues & Nat'l Leaders-Phila-1900-527p-illus(5w4,crack) 6.50
--The Great Republic-NY-1902-4 vols-illus (5ee3) 7.50 (5h9) 12.50
--New Century History of US-Chig-(1900)-JHMoore-lg8vo-illus-
pict cl-591p   (5j5)   15.00
--The SanFran Calamity by Earthquake & Fire, told by Eyewitnesses-
Phila-(1906)-446p-illus   (5t4)   10.00
--same-n.p.-(1906)-446p-illus (5b9) 4.   (5s4, soil)   6.00
MORRIS, CHARLOTTE S-Favorite Recipes of Famous Musicians-NY-
1941-photo-301p-scarce   (4g9)   7.50
MORRIS, CLARA-Stage Confidences-Bost-(1902)-Lothrop-316p-
illus   (5x0)   4.00
MORRIS, CONSTANCE L-Maria Theresa, the Last Conservative-
NY-1937-375p-illus-8vo-cl-1st ed   (5t0, dj)   4.00
MORRIS, DENNIS-The French Vineyard-Lond-1958-illus-223p
(5w1)   7.50
MORRIS, E P-The Fore & Aft Rig in Amer-NewHav-1927-8vo-215p-
illus-ltd to 1000c   (5p9) 10.   (5ss2, f)   20.00
MORRIS, EARL H-Anasazi Basketry-Wash-1941-(Carn inst of Wash,
Pub 533)-4to-66p-43p plts-wrps   (5h4)   17.50
--Marriage Records Harrison Co Va, 1784 to 1850-FtW-1966-262p-
cl-100c prntd   (5h1)   15.00

MORRIS, EARL   (continued)
--Temple of the Warriors, restoring, in Ruined Maya City of
  Chichen Itza, Yucatan-NY-1931-251p-photos
                            (5t3, 4b2, lacks fly)   8.50
MORRIS, EDW E-The Age of Anne-NY-n.d.-12mo-cl-251p-maps-
  plans   (5t2)   3.50
MORRIS, F O-A History of British Birds-Lond-1870-6 vols-hf lea-
  hand col plts-2nd ed   (5m4, sl rub)   135.00
--Natural History of British Moths-Lond-1872-132 col plts-4 vols-
  8vo-orig cl-2nd ed   (5z9, vf)   12.50
--Series of picturesque views of seats of noblemen & gentlemen of
  Great Brit & Ireland-Lond-(1866)-Mackenzie-6 vols-4to-
  g.stmpd lea-a.e.g.-col plts   (5m5, sl crack)   115.00
MORRIS, FRANCES-Antique Laces of Amer Collectors-NY-1926-143p-
  Part 5-illus-cl bk-bds-folio-Needle & Bobbin Club
                                 (5n7, sl wtrstn)   30.00
--Notes on Laces of the Amer Colonists-NY-1925-folio-14p-wrps-
  31 plts   (5n7)   10.00
MORRIS, FRANK-Our Wild Orchids, Trails & Portraits-NY-1929-
  454p-130 plts   (5s7) 15.   (5x0)   25.00
MOR RIS, GEO P-The Deserted Bride & other poems-NY-1838-
  Adlard&Sauders-8vo-orig cl-1st ed
               (5ss3, autg, sp def, stn) 75.   (5d6)   15.00
--The Deserted Bride & other productions-NY-1853-Scribner-lg8vo-
  g.orn red cl-port-12 plts-365p-gift ed   (5j5)   25.00
--The Gift Book of Amer Melodies-Phila-1854-286p-illus-pict cl-
  g.e.   (5m1)   6.50
--Woodman Spare That Tree-NY-(1837)-Firth&Hall-folio-8p with
  litho on pg 1-has corr "thee" for "the" but does not have
  notice, "New York Mirror Office"-1st ed of sheet music (5dd8)   50.00
--same-NY-(1837)-Firth&Hall-later prntg-Russell is correctly
  spelled-misspellings in stanza 4 corrected   (5r9)   7.50
MORRIS, GEO S-The Bottlers' Formulary-Kansas-(1910)-88p (5w1) 5.50
MORRIS, GOUVERNEUR-Aladdin O'Brien-NY-1902-Century-
  8vo-dec cl-g.   (5b2, rprd)   4.00
--Ellen & Mr Man-NY-1904-Century-8vo-dec cl-illus (5b2, sl rub)4.00
MORRIS, HARRIETT-Western Food-n.p.-150p-illus   (5g9)   4.00
MORRIS, HELEN-Portrait of a Chef-NY-1938-221p-7 photos (5g9) 6.50
MORRIS, HENRY C-History of Colonization-NY-1900-2 vols-
  scarce   (5tt5)   15.00
MORRIS, HENRY O-Waiting for the Signal-Chig-(c1897)-Schulte-
  8vo-cl-illus   (5b2, chip)   7.50
MORRIS, IVAN, ed-Modern Japanese Stories-Lond-(1961)-528p-
  Eyre&Spot   (5p7)   5.00
MORRIS, J B-Extracts from Correspondence & Minutes of Trustees
  of Bank of Maryland-Balt-1835-65p, (1)   (5h8)   8.50
MORRIS, J E-Stephen Lincoln of Oakham, Mass, His Anc & Desc-
  1895-109p   (5mm3)   7.00
MORRIS, JAS-As I Saw The USA-NY-c1956-245p   (5w4, dj)   4.00
MORRIS, JAS-Coronation Everest-NY-(1958)-Dutton-146p-illus-
  cl   (5d7)   3.00
--Islam Inflamed-n.p.-c1957   (5x7)   4.00
--Road to Huddersfield-NY-1963-11&235p-maps-8 plts (5c6, mint) 6.75
MORRIS, MRS JAS EDWIN-Travels of a Barnacle-NY-(c1901)-
  Abbey Pr-8vo-dec cl-frontis-g.   (5b2)   4.00
MORRIS, JAS O-Conflict Within the AFL-Ithaca-1958-Cornell Univ-
  319p   (5p7)   6.50
MORRIS, JOHN-Wanderlings of a Vagabond-NY-(1873)-8vo-1st ed
                                 (4m7)   15.00
MORRIS, JOS-Reminiscences of-Colum-1881-192p-cl (5h7, pres) 12.50
MORRIS, K-Story of the Can Pac Rwy-Lond-1916-illus-154p (4e9)10.00
MORRIS, LERONA ROSAMOND-Okla, Land of Opportunity-Guthrie-
  1934-9x18-106p-illus-wrps   (5h0)   7.50
--same-Guthrie-(1937)-4to-106p-heavy wrps   (5xx5)   15.00
--Okla Yesterday, Today, Tomorrow-Guth -1930-R8vo-944p-
  photos   (5xx5)   30.00
MORRIS, LEWIS-Papers of...Gov of Province of NJ, 1738 to 1746-
  NY-1852-orig cl-port-336p   (5ii8)   30.00
MORRIS, LLOYD-Incredible NY-NY-(1951)-illus (5p0) 5. (4a1) 6.50
--Not So Long Ago-NY-1949-Random-504p-illus   (5p0)   6.00
--Postscript to Yesterday-NY-1947-Random-475p
                                 (5p0, 5m0) 5.   (5yy6)   4.50
MORRIS, LUCILE-Bald Knobbers-Caldwell-1939-illus-250p plus index-
  1st ed-v scarce   (5yy7, dj, f)   20.00
MORRIS, LUCY, ed-Old Rail Fence Corners-(Austin, Minn)-1914-
  2nd illus-fldg map-324p   (4b3, 5ff7)   10.00
MORRIS MACHINE WORKS-Baldwinsville-1910-96p-obl 8vo-
  fldg bds-illus -catalog   (5b8)   7.50
MORRIS, MAURICE-Rambles in The Rocky Mntns With Visit to Gold
  Fields of Colo-Lond-1864-cl-264p-1st ed   (4n4, vf)   65.00
MORRIS, NEPHI L-Prophecies of Jos Smith & Their Fulfillment-
  SltLkCty-1920   (5x5, cov wn)   10.00

MORRIS, NEPHI L (continued)
--same-SaltLkCty-1931-illus-12mo-382p   (5dd5)   8.00
MORRIS, R A-Brief History of Greene Co-n.p.-n.d.-(1940)-
  44 dbl col pg plus questionnaire-photos-fldg map-wrps-
  spiral bnd   (5L0)   8.50
MORRIS, R B-Studies in History of Amer Law-NY-1930 (5r4)   10.00
MORRIS, R O-Contrapuntal Technique in 16th Century-Oxford-
  1922-Clarendon Pr   (5p0)   5.00
MORRIS, RICH B, ed-Encyclopedia of Amer History-NY-1953 et seq-
  maps   (5h9)   5.00
MORRIS, RICH B, ed-Select Cases of the Mayor's Court , 1674 to
  1784-Wash-1935-Amer Hist Assoc-Vol 2   (5p9)   12.50
MORRIS, ROBT-Courtship & Matrimony-Phila-(1858)-508p, (22)-
  frontis   (5w7, ex-libr)   5.00
MORRIS, ROBT-Freemasonry in the Holy Land-NY-1873-608p-
  8vo-cl-illus-4th ed   (5t0)   5.00
--Masonic Martyr, the Biography of Eli Bruce-Louisville-1861-
  Morris&Monsarrat-12mo-buck-map-2 views-316p-scarce
                                 (5j5, rbnd)   35.00
--Wm Morgan, or, Political anti masonry-1883-sewn   (5L7)   5.00
MORRIS, ROBT T-Nut Growing-NY-1931-236p-rev-frontis (5s7)   6.50
MORRIS, S-A Spirit Filled Life-KansasCty-(ca1900)-12mo-28p-
  wrps-Nazarene Publ Co   (5x2)   17.50
MORRIS, SAM-Wine, Women & Song-(Denton-1939)-119p-wrps
                                 (5h7)   3.00
--Worms Under the Bark-SanAnt-n.d.-(1941)-45p-wrps (5h7)   3.00
MORRIS, T S-Ephraim Morris & Pamela(Converse) Morris, their Anc
  & Desc-1894-207p   (5mm3)   12.50
--Records of Gilbert Ruggles & Evalina Christina (Snyder) Tucker-
  1901-305p-hf mor   (5t9)   15.00
MORRIS, THOS-Miscellanies in Prose & Verse-Lond-1791-prntd for
  Jas Ridgeway-port-rare   (5e2)   5,000.00
MORRIS, W-Out & Home Again by Way of Canada & US-n.d.-
  2nd ed-477p-buck-(pref 1875)   (4b9, rbnd)   15.00
MORRIS, W S-History 31st Reg Illinois Volunteers-Evansville-
  (1902)-8vo-237p   (4a7, sp chew)   35.00
MORRIS, WM-Art & Beauty of the Earth-Chiswick Pr-1899-'Golden'
  type   (5i4)   15.00
--Child Christopher & Goldilind the Fair-Hammersmith-1895-
  2 vols-24mo-bds-cl bks-ltd to 600c   (5j3, rprd)   50.00
--The Earthly Paradise-(Hammersmith 1896, 1897)-Kelmscott Pr-
  sq8vo-limp vel wi ties-ea vol in cl slip case-ltd to 225c -
  8 vols   (5d8)   450.00
--The Earthly Paradise, a Poem-Bost-1871-Roberts Bros-4 parts in
  3 vols   (5ss9)   15.00
--Poems by the Way-Lond-1891-port-sq12mo-cl-1st ed-publ 7 months
  before Kelmscott ed   (5r9)   12.50
--Well at World's End-Lond, NY&Bombay-1896-2 vols-bds-
  Chiswick Pr (5ss3,stn,crack) 25. (5i4, labels chip, bkplt removed)30.00
--same-Lond-1910-2 vols-bds-cl bks   (5mm2)   15.00
--The Water of the Wondrous Isles-Hammersmith-1897-Kelmscott Pr-
  lg4to-vel-ties-ltd to 250c   (4h5, vg)   400.00
MORRIS, WM G-Report Upon Customs District, Publ Serv & Resources
  of Alaska Terr-Wash-1879-GPO-SED #59-8vo-163p-fldg map
                                 (5q8, map tn)   12.50
MORRIS, WM H-Infantry Tactics, Comprising Schools of Soldier,
  Company, Instruction etc-NY-1865-2 vols-16mo-orig cl (5p5) 25.00
MORRIS, WRIGHT-The Home Place-1948-Scribner's Sons-1st ed,
  2nd issue   (5hh1, pres, f, dj)   35.00
--The inhabitants-NY-1946-Scribner's Sons-4to-1st ed (5ss9,dj)   35.00
--The Works of Love-NY-1952-Knopf-1st ed   (5ss9, f, dj)   10.00
MORRISEY, LOUISE L-An Odd Volume of Cookery-Bost-1949-215p
                                 (5g9)   5.00

MORRISON & FOURMY'S GENERAL DIRECTORY OF CITY OF
  DALLAS, 1886, 1887-Dallas-1886   (5a8, cov stnd)   47.50
MORRISON, ARTHUR-Chronicles of Martin Hewitt-2nd Series-
  Lond-1895-illus-1st ed   (4b7, bkplt)   35.00
--Martin Hewitt, Investigator-Lond-1895-illus-2nd ed-pict bndg
                                 (4b7, rub)   15.00
--Painters of Japan-Lond-1911-T C & E C Black-sm folio-cl-2 vols-
  122 plts(21 col)-   1st ed   (5t0)   125.00
MORRISON, C C-Unfinished Reformation-1953   (5L7)   5.00
MORRISON, DUNCAN-The Glorious Future of Canada, a Sermon-
  Owen Sound, Ont-1872-Rutherford   (5nn8)   15.00
MORRISON, EDITH L-Wm Tyrrell of Weston-Tor-1937-illus (5w8)10.00
MORRISON, ELSIE C & P N R-Calgary, 1875 to 1950-Calgary-1950-
  folio-pic wrps-250p-col plts   (5dd0)   5.00
MORRISON, G A-Clement King of Marshfield, Mass, 1668 & Desc-
  1898-65p   (5t9)   7.50
--Laurent Decamp of New Utrecht, NY & Desc-1900-77p (5t9)   10.00
--Desc of John Morrison & Prudence Gwyn-1907-31p-folio (5t9) 7.50
MORRISON, G R-Mixed Farming in East Africa-Lond-1935-
  East Africa(Newspap)-159p   (4t5, fox, dj)   7.50

MORRISON, HUGH-List of Books & Articles...Suez Canal-Wash-
1900-174p-wrps   (5j4)   12.50
--Preliminary Check List of Amer Almanacs, 1739 to 1800-Wash-
1907-160p   (5j4)   15.00
MORRISON, JOHN H-History of Amer Steam Navigation-NY-1903-
630p-frontis-1st ed-scarce   (5r7, ex-libr)   35.00
--same-NY-1958-illus-plts-630p   (5s6) 6.50   (5c1)   12.50
--History of NY Ship Yards-NY-(1909)-Sametz-illus-165p, (2)
       (5qq8)   10.00
MORRISON, L A-Hist of Morison or Morrison Settlers of
Londonderry, NH & Desc-1880-468p   (5t9)   15.00
--Kimball Family in Amer-1897-2 vols-1278p   (5t9)   75.00
--Norris Family in Amer from 1640 to 1892-1892-207p (5mm3)   15.00
--Hist of Windham, N Hamp-1883-862p   (5t9)   45.00
--Supplement to Hist of Windham-1892-169p (5mm3)   5.00
MORRISON, LACEY H-Amer Diesel Engines-NY-1939-489p-illus-
2nd ed, 5th impression   (5hh7)   5.75
MORRISON, N F-Garden Gateway to Canada-Tor-1954-344p
       (4e9)   20.00
MORRISON, W M-Texas Book Prices-Waco-1963-cl
   (5h5, f) 15.   (5kk6)   17.50
MORRISON, WM BROWN-Military Posts & Camps in Okla-OklaCty-
1936-180p-cl   (5h0, cov spot)   60.00
MORRISON, WM H-Stranger's Guide to City of Wash & Its Vicinity-
Wash-1852-12mo-   steel & wood engrs   (5m6)   10.00
--same-Wash-1860-rewritten-62, 2p-sm16mo-wood & steel engrs-
3 fldg plts-orig prntd glazed bds   (5L8, v wn, lacks sp)   6.00
--same-Wash-1864-illus-71p-orig brown cl-16mo   (4b3, vg)   15.00
--same-Wash-1873-12mo-74p-fldg plts-fldg plans-9th ed (5w7)   5.00
MORRISON, WM J-Charley Circus-M E Church, South-(1914)-
135p-frontis-pict cl   (5p1)   5.00
MORRISS, MARGARET S-Colonial Trade of Maryland, 1698 to 1715-
Balt-1914-157p-cl   (5y2, sl spot)   10.00
MORRISSEY, SISTER HELEN-Ethan Allen's Daughter-Que-(1940)-
157p-illus-1st ed   (5t7)   10.00
MORROW COUNTY & OHIO, HIST OF-Chig-1880-838p-mor
       (5h1)   50.00
MORROW, D F-Then & Now-Macon-1926   (5h6)   3.50
MORROW, ELIZ-The Painted Pig-NY-1930-Knopf-4to-(34)p-
prntd bds-1st ed   (5p1, fade)   10.00
MORROW, G-Colored Stories-1951-12mo   (5x2)   5.00
MORROW, H-Argonaut-NY-1933-316p (5ss1, wn) 4.   (4b9)   10.00
MORROW, HONORE WILLSIE-The Lost Speech of Abraham Lincoln-
NY-1925-56p-cl & bds   (5t7)   3.00
--Mary Todd Lincoln-NY-1928-248p-illus   (5t4)   4.50
MORROW, J D A-Family & Desc of Wm Barnes Adams & Martha
Larimore Adams of Laurel, Indiana-(1958)-180p   (5t9)   22.50
MORROW, KAY-New England Cook Book of fine Old Recipes-
Reading-1936-wrps-48p-illus   (4g9)   2.50
MORSE, A-Memorials of the Morses, comprising Hist of 7 Persons of
the Name-1850-171, (130)p   (5mm3)   30.00
MORSE, A-Desc of Several Ancient Puritans-1857-233p-
add mat'l to 1855 ed   (5t9)   30.00
--Memorials of the, Comprising History of 7 Persons of the Name-
1850-171, (130)p   (5mm3)   30.00
MORSE, A REYNOLDS-Works of M P Shiel-LosAng-1948-8vo-cl-
170p-illus-ltd to 1000c   (5m8, cov sl dmgd)   10.00
MORSE, BRICK-California Football History-Berkeley-1937(5jj1,f) 5.00
MORSE, CHAS W-Diamond Atlas, with Descriptions of all Countries...
Eastern Hemisphere-NY-1857-Gaston-sq12mo-mor-239p-
maps in col   (5t0, warp)   12.50
--Diamond Atlas, Amer...Western Hemisphere-NY-(1857)-sq8vo-
orig calf-a.e.g.-col maps   (5a8)   25.00
MORSE, EDW S-Japan Day By Day, 1877, 1878, 1882, 83-Bost-1917-
sm4to-2 vols-441p   (5t2, libr marks)   6.50
MORSE, FRANCES C-Furniture of the Olden Time-NY-1910-371p-
295 illus   (5L7, fray) 6.   (5w7)   5.00
--same-NY-1936-illus-New ed   (4b7)   12.50
--same-NY-1937-467p-illus-New ed   (5t7)   7.50
--same-NY-1943-sq8vo-cl-428 illus-20p, 470p-rev & enlrgd ed
       (5t0)   5.00
MORSE, H B-In the Days of the Taipings-Salem-1927-434p-illus
       (5t4)   4.75
MORSE, H G-Robt Louis Stevenson as I Found Him in His Island Home-
(n.p.)-(1902)-20p-orig pale blue wrps   (5ss9, cov sl tn)   10.00
MORSE, H H-Historic Old Rhinebeck, Echoes of 2 Centuries-1908-
448p   (5mm3)   17.50
MORSE, H S-Hist of Harvard, Mass 1732 to 1893-1894-605p (5t9) 30.00
MORSE, I H-Yankee in Africa-Bost-1936-297p-photos
   (4t5, autg) 5.   (4a6)   4.00
MORSE, JEDIDIAH-The Amer Gazetteer-Bost-1797-8vo-calf-1st ed-
7 fldg maps-lea labl
(5r7, rbkd) 20.   (5t4, hng weak) 18.50 (4c1, maps rprd, fox)   30.00

MORSE, JEDIDIAH   (continued)
--The Amer Universal Geography -Bost-1793-Thomas & Andrews-
2 vols-thk8vo-orig calf-g.t.-10 fldg maps-plate-1st ed
   (5tt0, map tn, Part 1 only) 40. (5n2, map rprd)   225.00
--same-Bost-Jun 1796-Thomas & Andrews-calf-lea labl-2nd ed-
692p-10 maps   (5ii4, wn, lacks hf map)   75.00
--Annals of the Amer Revolution-Harford-1824-400p, (50)-
6 plts(1 fldg)   (5mm8, fox) 17.50   (5L3, fox)   37.50
--An Appeal to the Public, on controversy respecting revolution in
Harvard College-Charlestown-1814-8vo-(192)p-hf lea (5p1)   85.00
--A Compendious History of New Engl-Amherst-1809-336p plus index-
fldg map-lea-2nd ed   (5t7)   15.00
--same-Charlestown-1820-324p-lea (5L3, lacks fly) 7.50 (5ee3)   10.00
--Elijah-Charlestown-1820-12mo-324p-1st ed   (5g1)   12.50
--Elements of Geography-Bost-May 1801-Thos & Andrews-24mo-
2 maps-143(1)p-dec papr cov, wd bds-lea bk   (5ii4, wn)   22.50
--Geography Made Easy-Bost-1806-Buckingham-432p-fldg maps-
calf   (5qq8)   7.50
--same-Bost-1812-360p-lea-fldg maps   (5L3, f)   18.50
--New Gazeteer of Eastern Continent-Bost-Thos & Andrews-1808-
thk 8vo-maps-2nd ed   (5v2, cov v wn)   8.50
--A Prayer & Sermon, Charlestown Dec 31, 1799, on death of
Washington-Lond-1800-J Bateson-8vo-cl-(9), 36p   (5L1)   20.00
--Report of Sec of War...on Indian Affairs-NewHav-1822-
96p, 400p-lea-labl   (5s2, vg)   65.00
MORSE, JOHN T, JR-Abraham Lincoln-Bost-1899-2 vols-hf mor-
t.e.g.-raised bands-Amer Statesmen ser   (5w0, f bndg)   12.50
--Amer Statesmen-Bost-1899, 0-HoughtonMifflin-32 vols-plts-cl-
       (5qq8, f)   75.00
--same-Bost-HoughtonMiff-(1898)-40 vols-cl-Standard Libr ed
       (5p9)   80.00
--Amer Statesmen-Bost-(1899 to 1917)-HoughtonMiff-41 vols-plts-
engr titles-gilt dec mor-(2 index vols)   (5qq8, f, f bndg)   275.00
--Benj Franklin-Bost-c1898-440p-illus-t.e.g.   (5w9)   4.00
--John Adams-Bost-1891-337p plus ads-hf mor-raised bands-t.e.g.
       (5w0)   7.50
--John Quincy Adams-Bost-1890-315 p-hf mor-raised bands-t.e.g.
       (5w0)   7.50
--Life & Letters of Oliver Wendell Holmes-Cambridge-1896-2 vols-
illus-1st ed   (5mm1) 10.   (5ee3, f)   7.50
--same-Cambr-1896-Riverside Pr-2 vols-ltd to 175c   (5ss3)   25.00
--Thos Jefferson-Bost-1898-326p-illus-t.e.g.   (5w9)   4.00
MORSE, SAM'L F B-Foreign Conspiracy Against the Liberties of US-
NY-1841-Chaplin-191p-5th ed   (5qq8)   7.50
--same-NY-1836-4th ed-cl   (5g4)   7.50
MORSE, SIDNEY-Household Discoveries-Petersburg, NY-(1913)-
thk 8vo-illus-rev ed-1173p   (4g9)   12.50
MORSE, WILLARD S-Howard Pyle, a record of his illustrations &
writings-Wilmington-1921-242p-frontis-orig bds-papr labl-
ltd to 500c, nbrd   (5c8, f)   25.00
MORSE, WM INGLIS-The Land of the New Adventure-Lond-1932-
illus-fldg pkt map-8vo-cl-ltd to 350c   (4c1)   12.50
--same-Lond-1932-158p-plts-2 fldg maps-ltd to 350c   (4a8)   35.00
MORSMAN, E M-E M Morsman-n.p.-(1942)-for family only-15p-
1st ed rare   (4t3)   17.50
MORSMAN, E M-Mary Morsman, Edgar & Truman & Their Anc in Amer-
1932-50p   (5mm3)   20.00
MORTENSEN, WM-Flash in Modern Photography-SanFran-(1941)-
illus   (4b7)   7.50
--Pictorial Lighting-SanFran-(1935)-illus   (4b7)   7.50
--Projection Control-SanFran-(1938)-illus-2nd ed   (4b7)   6.00
MORTIMER, W GOLDEN-Peru, History of Coca-NY-1901-576p
   (5p0, 5j1, sl spot) 15.   (5w3)   17.50
MORTON, EDW P-Mohawk Valley & Lake Ontario-Chig-(1913)-
99p-wrps-Grt Lk Ser   (5h1)   4.00
MORTON, ELEANOR-Josiah White, Prince of Pioneers-NY-(1946)-
8vo   (5jj1, f) 6.   (5w9, dj) 6.50 (5ss5, dj)   8.50
MORTON, ELSIE K-Crusoes of Sunday Island-NY-1958-Norton-
222p-illus   (5p7)   4.00
MORTON, GEO A-Law & Laughter-Lond-1913   (5r4)   10.00
--same-Lond-1914-259p   (5p9)   6.00
MORTON, GRACE M-Arts of Costume & Personal Appearance-NY-
(1943)-400p-4to-illus   (5n7)   4.50
MORTON, H V-Ghosts of London-NY-1940-illus-197p (5q0)   7.50
--In Search of So Africa-Lond-1948-Methuen-photos-maps-e.p. map-
359p   (4t5)   5.00
MORTON, HAWLEY-Details of Mill Construction-Bost-1907-4to-cl-
25 plts   (5t0)   4.50
MORTON HOUSE-NY-1872-(F Tiernan)   (5r7)   10.00
MORTON, J N-Morton Family Tree-1947-125p   (5mm3)   10.00
MORTON, J STERLING-Illus History of Nebraska-Lincoln-1907-
2 vols-R8vo-mor-illus-maps   (5dd6, sp wn)   50.00

MORTON, JAS-History of the Development of Fast Dyeing &
Dyes, a Lecture-Scotland-(1929)-61p   (5w3)   3.50
MORTON, JAS-Honest John Oliver-Tor-1933-illus-272p-1st ed
                                    (5dd7,autog)   12.00
MORTON, JOS W, JR, ed-Sparks from the Campfire-Phila-1890-illus-
580p-new & rev ed   (5s9,v shake,wn) 5. (5L3,f)   12.50
--same-Phila-1892-8vo-623p-col plts   (4a6,bnd rub) 15.00
--same-Phila-1893-new & rev ed-illus   (5tt5)   7.50
--same-Phila-1895-illus-688p   (5L3,f)   12.50
--same-Phila-1895-illus-676p   (5L3,vf)   11.50
MORTON, LOUIS-Robt Carter of Nomini Hall-Williamsburg-1941
                                    (5a8)   8.50
MORTON, NATHANIEL-New Engl Memoriall...with special
Reference to first Colony-Cambr-1669-for John Usher of Boston-
sm4to-mor   1st ed   (5n2,f)   6,500.00
--same-Newport-1772-Southwick-8vo-orig calf bkd bds-
mor pull case-3rd ed-8p list of subscribers
                            (5n2,sl chip,mor box)   185.00
--same-Bost-1826-Crocker&Brewster-map-481p-appendix-
orig calf-5th ed-errata   (5h9,rub,chip)   32.50
MORTON, OHLAND-Teran & Texas-Austin-1948-191p
            (4a5) 35.   (5x5,dj,autg)   25.00
MORTON, OLIVER T-Southern Empire & Other Papers-Bost-1892-
207p-cl   (5h7)   5.00
MORTON, OREN F-History of Pendleton Co, West Virg-Franklin-
1910-illus-fldg map-493p-v scarce   (4m2)   50.00
--Hist of Rockbridge Co, Virg-1920-574p   (5t9)   25.00
MORTON, ROSALIE SLAUGHTER-A Woman Surgeon-NY-1937-
399p-port   (5t7)   8.50
MORTON, S S-At the Dawning-Phila-1890-1st ed   (5mm2)   10.00
MORTON, SAM'L GEO-Inquiry into Distinctive Characteristics of
Aboriginal Race of Amer-Bost-1842-Tuttle&Dennett-37p-disbnd
                                    (5yy3)   10.00
--Types of mankind-Phila-1854-Lippincott-690p-4to-maps-cl
                            (5m5,cov v wn)   25.00
MORTON, SARAH WENTWORTH-Beacon Hill-Bost-1797-Book 1,
(all publ)-4to-56p-hf mor   (5L1,rbnd)   20.00
MORTON, T G-History of Penna Hospital, 1751 to 1895-4to (5L7) 12.50
MORTON, THOS-New Engl Canaan-Amsterdam-1637-Stam-
sm4to-g.tooled mor-1st ed
            (5L1,disbnd,t.pg in facs) 750. (5n2,bkplts) 2,500.00
MORTON, THOS-Speed the plough, a comedy-Phila-1822-T H Palmer-
12mo-76p-disbnd-scarce   (5m2)   10.00
MORTON, W L-Progressive Party in Canada-Tor-1950-331p (4e9) 20.00
MORTON'S HOPE-or Memoirs of a Provincial-NY-1839-2 vols-
12mo-cl-papr labls-1st ed of Motley's 1st book
                            (5gg6,hng rprd)   50.00
MOSBY, JOHN S-Mosby's War Remin & Stuart's Calvary Campaigns-
Bost-1887-frontis-256p-12mo (4t3,corners wn) 30. (4a7,sl rub) 35.00
MOSCHELES, FELIX-Fragments of an Autobiography-Lond-1899-
frontis-1st ed   (5jj3,pres)   15.00
MOSCOW, WARREN-Politics in the Empire State-NY-1948-Knopf-
8vo-cl-238p-1st ed   (5j5,dj)   6.00
MOSELEY, MARY-The Bahamas Handbook-Nassau-1926 (5x7)   4.50
MOSEMAN, C M-Moseman's Illus Guide for Horse Furnishings-
NY-1879-folio-303p-indexed-col plts   (5t1)   300.00
MOSENTHAL, PHILIP J-The City College-NY-1907-illus-565p-
t.e.g.   (4b6,unopnd)   17.50
MOSES, BELLE-Lewis Carroll, In Wonderland & at Home-1910-
D Appleton-296p-ads-cl-1st ed   (5hh1) 8.50   (5p1)   12.50
MOSES, BERNARD-So Amer on Eve of Emancipation-NY-1908-
Putnam-8vo-cl   (4a3)   10.00
--Spanish Dependencies in So Amer-Lond-1914-2 vols-8vo-cl
                                    (5h4,f)   15.00
MOSES, FREDK T-Firemen of Industry-Prov-1954-111p-illus (4b8) 5.50
MOSES, G H-New Hampshire Men, Collection of Biog Sketches-
1893-408p   (5mm3)   12.50
MOSES, HENRY-Collection of Antique Vases, Altars, Paterae,
Tripods, etc-Lond-(1814)-61p-170 engrs-dec bds-lea (5t4) 10.00
MOSES, JN-First Settlements in Illinois-FtW-1956-46p-wrps (5h1) 2.50
MOSES, JOHN-History of Chicago, Ill-Chig-1895-2 vols-cl
                                    (5zz9,rbnd)   35.00
MOSES, MONTROSE J-The Amer Dramatist-Bost-1911-Little-338p-
illus   (5p0)   6.50
--Children's Books & Reading-NY-c1907-Mitchell Kennerley-12mo-
272p   (5p1,sl wtrstn)   10.00
--Clyde Fitch & His Letters-Bost-1924-8vo-cl-406p-illus
            (4k3,2 pres) 12.50   (4p1)   17.50
-- Maurice Maeterlinck, a Study-NY-1911-12mo-cl-315p, 21p-
1st ed   (5t0)   4.00
MOSES, MYER-Full Annals of Revolution in France, 1830 &
Celebration of...in City of NY on 25th Nov, 1830-NY-1830-
12mo-225p, 151p-1st ed   (5ss5,ex-libr,crude rbk)   15.00

MOSES, ROBT-Yale Verse-NewHav-1909-1st ed-(Sinclair Lewis)
                                    (5d3)   37.50
MOSES, Z-Hist Sketches of John Moses of Plymouth, John of
Windsor & Simsbury etc-1890, 1907-2 vols in 1-298p (5mm3) 22.50
MOSGROVE, GLENNA J-Desc of Johann Georg Rinehart & Eliza
M. Reinhard-1954-9p, 286p-stiff wrps-illus   (5mm3)   25.00
MOSHEIM'S CHURCH HISTORY-of 1st 2 centuries-Milton-1847-
publ by Hoshour-prntd by C B Bentley-12mo-orig cl-papr labl
                            (5i0,labl rub)   25.00
MOSHER, LEROY E-"The Stranded Bugle" & other poems & prose-
LosAng-1905-396p-port   (5xx5)   5.00
MOSHER PRESS-The Mosher Books-Portland-1926-44p-wrps (5j4) 12.50
--The Bibelot, 1895 to 1914-NY-1925-12mo-21 vols(incl index)-
blue cl-papr labls   (5t4) 30. (5d5)   40.00
MOSHER, ROBT BRENT-Executive Register of the US, 1789 to 1902-
Wash-1905-GPO-8vo-cl-351p   (5j5)   5.00
MOSKOWITZ, HENRY-Alfred E Smith, an Amer career-NY-1924-
Seltzer-312p-8vo-cl-illus   (5j5)   7.50
MOSLEY, L-Haile Selassie, The Conquering Lion-1964-R8vo-illus
                                    (5x2,dj)   4.50
MOSORIAK, ROY-The Curious History of Music Boxes-Chig-1943-
4to-illus-1st ed   (5m6)   15.00
MOSS, ARTHUR-Legend of the Latin Quarter-NY-1946-Beechhurst Pr-
lg8vo-cl-1st ed   (5p5)   7.50
MOSS, EDW L-Shores of the Polar Sea-Lond-1878-83p-folio-a.e.g.-
16 chromoliths   (5w8) 75. (5t4)   65.00
MOSS, F-Pilgrimages to Old Homes, mostly on the Welsh border-
1903-illus   (5L7,sl shake)   7.50
MOSS, FRANK-American Metropolis-NY-1897-(Collier)-3 vols-
illus   (5q0)   12.50
MOSS, GEO H, JR-Nauvoo To The Hook-Locust-1964-sm4to-illus-
128p   (5w0)   10.00
--Steamboat To The Shore-Locust-1966-illus   (5w5)   8.95
MOSS, HOWARD-A Swimmer in the Air, Poems-NY-(1957)-12mo-
cl-1st ed   (5ss7,vf,dj)   7.50
MOSES, REV THOS-Poems upon several occasions-Lond-1827-
Phillips, ed-Bentley-8vo-orig bds-papr labl-priv prntd-1st ed-
errata slip   (5i8,vf)   22.50
MOSSE, A H E-My Somali Book-Lond-1913-314p-16 plts (5c6)   6.75
MOSSE, G L-Struggle for Sovereignty in Engl from reign of Queen
Eliz to Petition of Right-1950   (5L7)   5.00
MOSSER, MARJORIE-Foods of Old New England-GardenCty-1957-
428p   (4g9)   6.50
--Good Maine Food-NY-1939-Roberts-381p   (5t4)   6.00
--same-GardenCty-1946-381p   (4g9)   7.50
MOSSMAN, ISAAC-Pony Expressman's Recoll-1955-Champoeg Pr-
fldg map-photos-1st ed-ltd to 500c
            (5b0,5r0) 12.50   (5h4,mint) 15.   (4t3,f)   17.50
MOSSMAN, SAM'L-The Great Taiping Rebellion-Lond-n.d.-
(ca1899)-352p-illus   (5p0)   5.00
MOTELAY, P P-The Soldier in Our Civil War-NY-1890-folio-
illus-2 vols   (5yy0,poor)   17.50
MOTELS, HOTELS, RESTAURANTS & BARS-NY-1953-216p-illus-
4to-Arch Record Book   (5ww3)   15.00
MOTHER GOOSE-Chig-C1930-Volland Pop Ed-Eulalie Grover, ed-
Fredk Richardson, illus-108 col plts-pic cl   (4c3)   25.00
MOTHER GOOSE & SIMPLE SIMON-History of Mother Goose &
Her Son Jack & The Simple Story of Simple Simon in 6p-NY-
ca1865-Hurd&Houghton-wrps sewn-col illus   (5v0)   65.00
MOTHER GOOSE BOOK-MtVernon-1946-Peter Pauper Pr-oblong 8vo-
dec bds-78p-col illus   (5s0) 4.50   (4c3,mint,box)   8.50
MOTHER GOOSE FOR GROWN FOLKS-A Christmas Reading-NY-
1860-Billings, illus-12mo-111p-(By Mrs Whitney)-"Pop Art" bndg
                                    (5v0,vf)   15.00
MOTHER GOOSE IN HIEROGLYPHICS-Bost-c1849-60p, (4)-
Taggard&Thompson-pict red & blue wrps   (5p1,fox)   15.00
--same-Phila-(1849)-Appleton-illus-ob 16mo-60p   (5t4,wn)   10.00
MOTHER GOOSE JINGLES NY-(1907)-McLoughlin Bros-4to-lin-
3 plts-scarce   (4c3,3" sp tn)   15.00
MOTHER GOOSE MELODIES-set to music-NY-1873-Carleton&Co-
110p-12mo-illus-pict cl   (5p6,wn)   12.00
MOTHER GOOSE MELODIES-The Original-Bost-1878-sm, obl 8vo-
cov illus-by J F Goodridge-silhouette plts-1st ed-scarce (5v0) 17.50
MOTHER GOOSE MELODIES-3rd Ser with Magical Changes-NY-
(1879)-G W Carleton-sq8vo-pict wrps-8 changing plts
                                    (5c8,rbkd)   17.50
MOTHER   GOOSE MELODIES-Set to Music-NY-(ca1880)-
McLoughlin Bros-illus by Griset & others-Imp 8vo-111p-
pict bds-cl sp   (5c8,sl mend)   8.00
MOTHER GOOSE MELODIES-Bost-ca1890-4to-14p-col plts-bds
                                    (5v2,vg)   6.00

MOTHER GOOSE MELODIES-The Only True-Bost-(1905)-
repro of Munroe & Francis ed-(of 1833)-illus-bds (4c3, f) 12.50

MOTHER GOOSE MELODIES -Springfield-n.d.-McLoughlin Bros-
bds-col (4F6, f) 17.50

MOTHER GOOSE-Newly Feathered-Phila, Chig-(1903)-Natl Publ-
4to-pic bds-col illus (4F6, vg) 15.00

MOTHER GOOSE-The Old Nursery Rhymes-Lond-(1913)-
Heinemann-A Rackham, illus-13 col plts(tissues)-col pic cl-
159p (1) (5ii4, lt chip, sl spot) 45.00

MOTHER GOOSE-The Real-Chig-1916-illus by Blanche F Wright-
col plts (5v2, f) 17.50

MOTHER GOOSE RHYMES & MELODIES-Magical Picture Book of-
NY-(1908)-Geo W Dillingham-designed by Porteous-4to-dec cl-
18 "transformation" pictures (5c8, sl tn) 25.00

MOTHER GOOSE'S MELODIES-(Bost, ca1840)-Munroe & Francis-
(collation 9, 114p)-early grey bds (5c8, def, lvs dmgd) 22.50

MOTHER GOOSE'S NURSERY RHYMES-Tales & Jingles-F Warne-
(c1875)-sq8vo-dec cl-568p-frontis-illus (5s0) 10.00

MOTHER GOOSE'S NURSERY RHYMES-NY-(1886)-McLoughlin Bros-
320p-350 illus-8vo-pict bds- cl bk (5j5) 25.00

MOTHER GOOSE'S NURSERY RHYMES-NY-ca1900-McLoughlin
Bros-cl (4c3, vg) 10.00

MOTHER GOOSE'S NURSERY RHYMES-NY-n.d.-(ca1907)-8vo-
160p plus 2p ads-col frontis-pict col cl (5p1) 7.50

MOTHER GOOSE'S PICTURE PUZZLES-Phila-(1906)-Altemus-
60 plts ea containing hidden pict (4c3, vf) 25.00

MOTHER HUBBARD & HER DOG-Lond-(ca1830)-Dean & Mundy-
32p-frontis-hand col-wdcut-12mo-prntd wrps (5c8, soil, rprd) 13.50

MOTHER HUBBARD'S CUPBOARD-Young Ladies Soc 1st Baptist
Church-Roch-1887-87p-4th ed-wrps (5c4) 5.00

MOTHER LEE'S EXPER IN 15 YRS RESCUE WORK-Omaha-1906-
frontis-illus-219p (4b3) 7.50

MOTHER'S FABLES IN VERSE-Lond-1812-Darton, Harvey & Darton-
12mo-96p with 4p ads-grey bds-frontis-1st ed (5c8) 45.00

MOTHER'S GIFT, THE-A Present for All Little Boys Who Wish to be
Good-Hallowell(Maine)-1809-Cheever-24mo-62p-sewn-illus
rare (5v2, lacks bk wrp, sl holes) 27.50

MOTHER'S GIFT, A-Phila-c1852-Amer Sunday School Union-8vo-
64mo-192p-blind stmpd cl (5p1, fox, sl wn) 15.00

MOTHER'S GUIDE TO PHYSICAL EDUCATION-Greenfield(Mass)-
1846-Merriam&Mirick-84p-24mo (5p1, wrp tn, sl def) 5.00

MOTHER'S PRIMER-Palmer, Mass-(ca1855)-16mo-pict wrps-24p-
Woods&Allen (5t0) 4.00

MOTHERLESS MARY-A Tale-Lond-1816-16mo-67p-J Harris-6 illus-
wrps (5v2, f, rebnd) 30.00

MOTLEY, JOHN LOTHROP-Correspondence of-NY-1889-2 vols-
port (5q8) 8. (5t4) 10.00

--Historic Progress & Amer Democracy-NY-1869-8vo-orig wrps-74p-
1st ed (5ss5) 7.50

--History of the United Netherlands-NY-1861-Harper & Bros-
2 vols-cl-1st ed (5ss3, sp fade) 25.00

--same-NY-c1888-Harper-4 vols-ports-labls-g.t. (5h9) 17.50

--same-NY-c1888-Harper-2 vols-fldg map-ports (5h9) 10.00

--Hoe er Gestreden Werd en Waarom-Van Stockum-(ca1860)-
orig g. cl- 4 tinted liths (5c8, wn) 8.50

--Rise of the Dutch Republic-NY-1856-3 vols-1st ed(4m8)10.(5t4) 20.00

--same-NY-1874-Harper-t8vo-frontis-3/4 calf (5t2) 15.00

--same-NY-c1883-Harper-3 Vols-labls-frontis-g.t. (5h9) 12.50

--same-NY-n.d.-complete in 2 vols-illus (5h9) 7.50

--The Works of-NY-1900-17 vols-Library Ed (4m8) 45. (5m2) 65.00

--same-NY-1900-Netherlands Ed-orange cl-linen djs-
ltd to 500 sets -17 vols (4j3) 37.50

--same-NY-Harper-1900-17 vols-8vo-3/4 lea-Library Ed (5ss5) 60.00

MOTLEY, WILLARD-Knock On Any Door-NY-1947-8vo-cl
(5x2) 6.50 (5b2) 10.00

--Let No Man Write My Epitaph-NY-(c1958)-Random Hse-8vo-cl
(5b2) 5.00

--We fished All Night-NY-(1951)-560p-1st ed
(5m1, dj) 7.50 (5x2) 6.50

MOTOLINIA'S-History of Indians of New Spain-1950-Cortes Soc-
sm4to-cl-ltd to 500c (5F5, f) 17.50

MOTON, ROBT R-Finding A Way Out, an Autobiogr-NY-1920-
Dblday Page-9p plus 296p-cl (5r0, fray dj) 7.50

--What the Negro Thinks-NY-1936-267p
(5L7, bkplt rmvd) 5. (5ii8) 10.00

--same-NY-1942 (5x2) 8.00

MOTOR SHIP REFERENCE BOOK FOR 1938-Lond-n.d.-289p plus
32p ads-photos (5s1, dj, ex-libr) 3.50

MOTT, A, ed-Biogr Sketches & Interesting Anecdotes of Persons of
Color to Which is Added Selection of Pieces In Poetry-NY-
1837-2nd enlrgd ed (5x2, fox) 37.50

--Narratives of Colored Americans-NY-1882 (5x2, ex-libr) 37.50

MOTT, MRS D W-Legends & Lore of Long Ago, (Ventura Co) -
LosAng-1929-illus (4k5, dj, f) 12.50

MOTT, E-The Black Homer of Jimtown-NY-1900 (5x2) 10.00

MOTT, EDW HAROLD-Pike County Folks-NY-(1883)-12mo-cl-
1st ed of Mott's 1st book-Opper, illus (5gg6, Opper ALS) 25.00

MOTT, FRANK LUTHER-Amer Journalism-NY-1949-Macm-772p-
illus (5p7) 6.00

--Golden Multitudes-NY-1947-Macm-357p (5p0) 5.00

MOTT, HOPPER STRIKER-The NY of Yesterday-NY-1908-Putnam-
thk lg8vo-cl-78 maps & illus-g.t.-597p-ltd to 500c (5j5) 35.00

MOTT, JAS-Observations on Education of Children & Hints to Young
People-Lond-1822-NY prntd-York, reprntd-72p-orig bds (5c8) 8.50

MOTT, JAS-Life & Letters-Anna Davis Hallowell, ed-Bost-(1884)-
566p-cl (5h7) 10.00

MOTT, R L-Due Process of Law-Indnpls-(1926) (5r4) 10.00

MOTT, SMITH B-Campaigns of 52nd Reg, Penna Volunteers-Phila-
1911-sm8vo-266p-"Luzerne Reg" (4a7) 25.00

MOTT, T BENTLEY-Myron T Herrick, Friend of France-GardenCty-
1930 (5w9) 4.00

MOTTE, ELLEN N-The Opium Monopoly-NY-1920-8vo-illus-cl-
1st ed (5p5) 20.00

MOTTELAY, PAUL F-Bibliog History of Electricity & Magnetism-
Lond-1922-illus-1st ed (5nn6) 32.50 (5yy6) 22.50

--Frank Leslie's The Soldier in Our Civil War, Columbia Memorial
Ed-NY-1890-2 vols-folio-cl-illus (5t0) 20.00

--The Soldier in our Civil War, a Pict Hist of the Conflict-NY-
1884, 5-2 vols-illus-ports-maps-folio
(5m6, hng crack, bkstrp tn) 25. (5mm8, sp wn) 32.50

MOTTEN, CLEMENT G-Mexican Silver & the Enlightenment-
Univ of Penna-1950 (5a8) 5.00

MOTTLEY, JOHN-History of Life of Peter I, Emperor of Russia-Lond-
1739-for J Read-3 vols-8vo-calf-2 frontis-3 fldg maps-7 plts-
1st ed (5x3, lt wtrstn) 50.00

--Joe Miller's Jests-Lond-ca1788-Sabine&Son-12mo-61p-frontis-
g.lea-8th ed (4F6, hng crack) 45.00

MOULEN, FRED Orchids in Australia-Sidney-1958-prntd in
Switzerland-lg4to-148p-100 col illus (5s7) 15.00

MOULINIER, MARGARET ELEANOR BLACK-Genealogy Memoirs-
Cinn-1955-illus-ltd ed (5yy6) 7.50

MOULT, THOS-Barrie-NY-1928-Scribner's Sons-1st ed
(5t0) 4. (5hh1, vg) 6.00

MOULTON, AUGUSTUS F-Grandfather Tales of Scarborough-1925-
207p-illus (5mm3) 10. (5e8) 9.75

--Maine Historical Sketches-1929-293p-state publ (5e8) 6.00

MOULTON, E L-New Mexico's Future-Albuq-1945-lg fldg map
(4a5) 5. (5s4, dj) 4.50

MOULTON, H FLETCHER-Trial of Wm Henry Podmore-Lond-
1931-286p-illus-cl-Famous Trials Ser (5t2, fade) 4.00

MOULTON, HENRY W-Moulton Annals-1906-Claribel Moulton, ed-
454p-v scarce (5mm3) 75.00

MOULTON, LOUISE CHANDLER-Lazy Tours in Spain & Elsewhere-
Bost-1896-Roberts-8vo-cl (5b2, f) 5.00

--Poems-Bost-1878-sq16mo-pict cl-1st ed (5r9) 5.00

MOULTON, RICHARD G-Shakespeare as a Dramatic Artist-Oxford-
1897-8vo-cl-440p3rd ed, rev & enlrgd (5t2) 4.50

MOULTON, SHERMAN ROBERTS-The Boorn Mystery-Montpelier-
1937-104p-illus (5t4) 5.75

MOULTON, WM-A Concise Extract from the Sea Journal of-Utica-
1804-158p-calf-1p errata-v scarce (5w5, t.p. & intro in facs) 38.50

MT AUBURN-Catalogue of Lot Owners in Cemetery of-Bost-1891-
Mudge-16mo-299p-cl-fldg map (5j5) 7.50

MOUNT, CH MERRILL-John Singer Sargent-Lond-1957-illus-1st ed
(5jj3) 15.00

--same-NY-1935-illus (5p0, pres) 7.50

MOUNT HOOD, A GUIDE-(NY)-1940-photos-maps-125p plus index-
1st ed-Amer Guide Ser-WPA (4L5, dj, f) 6.00

MOUNT ROYAL, CITY OF-Montr-1898-48p-covs-illus-history-
ads (5b9, vf) 10.00

MOUNT VERNON, IOWA-Centennial Hist of, 1847 to 1947-n.p.-
1948-236p-cl (5h1) 10.00

MOUNT WASHINGTON IN WINTER-Bost-1871-frontis-map-illus-
363p-12mo-red cl-g. design of Cog RR-1st ed (5u9) 27.50

MOUNT WASH RWY CO-Bill to amend charter of-Concord-1891-
50p-col wrps (5s2, fade) 12.50

MOUNTAIN CAMPAIGNS IN GEORGIA-or war scenes on Western
& Atlantic-(c1887 by Jos M Brown)-4to-pict wrps-illus
(5g4, vg) 10.00

MOUNTAIN, HARCOURT-Old Tidewater Country(Poems)-Holland-
n.d.-1st ed (5tt5) 7.50

MOUNTAIN MEADOWS MASSACRE-with life, confessions &
execution of John D Lee, the Mormon-Phila-(1882)-(cov t.)-
64p-prntd wrps-4p plts (5t1) 45.00

MUCKENSTURM, LOUIS -Louis's Mixed Drinks-
-NY-(1906)-narr 4to-113p,(1)   (5w1,pres)   8.50
MUDD, JOS A-With Porter in No Missouri-Wash-1909-photos-
452p-1st ed-scarce   (4t3)   35.00
MUDDY RIVER &-Brookline Records, 1634 to 38-by Brookline Twn
Meeting-1875   (5L7,rbnd)   10.00
MUDD, DR SAM'L A-The Life of-NY&Wash&Marietta-1955-363p-
illus   (5t7)   10.00
MUDGE, ISADORE G-A Thackeray Dictionary-Lond-1910 (5ss9) 10.00
MUDGE, Z A-The Forest Boy-NY-(1867)-cl-321p
                                      (4h2,fade,sl spot)   10.00
MUDGE, ZACHARIAH-The Missionary Teacher-NY-1851-2nd ed-
220p-16mo-frontis-cl   (4a9,ex-librr,fair) 40.00
MUDIE, ROBT-Feathered Tribes of the British Isles-Lond-1888-2 vols-
35 col plts   (4d2)   20.00
MUEHLBACH, LOUISA-Jos II & his Court-Mobile-1864-SHGoetzel-
4 vols-orig prntd wrps-Rare Confederate Imprint:wrps prntd on
verso of wallpaper   (5r7,fray)   50.00
MUELLER, BERTHA-Goethe's Botanical Writings-Honolulu-(1952)-
258p-port frontis-4 plts   (5w3)   7.50
MUELLER, GERHARD F-Voyages et Decouvertes Faites par les Russes..
ver l'Amerique-Amsterdam-1766-Rey-2 vols-12mo-sheep-
lg fldg map-1st French ed   (5n9, rub)   185.00
MUENCH, JOYCE R-West Coast Portrait-NY-1946-sm4to-168p-cl-
1st ed   (5g5)   5.00
MUGGLEBEE, RUTH-Father Coughlin-NY-(1933)-illus (5q8)   5.00
MUHLBACH, L-The Historical Romances of-NY-1898-Brandenburg ed-
Mrs Coleman, trans-20 vols-ltd   (5yy0)   20.00
MUHLBACH, L-The Works of....transl from the German by
P Langley-NY-1912-Caldwell Co-18 vols-cl   (5p7)   32.50
--same-NY-1905-red&green cl-18 vols   (5kk8,vg)   20.00
MUHLENBERT, HENRY MELCHIOR-Journals of...-Phila-1942-
3 vols   (5nn6)   35.00
MUHS, HELEN K-Sunset's Host & Hostess Book-SanFran-1940-179p-
text illus-1st ed   (5g9)   4.00
MUIR, ALAN-Harold Saxon-Lond-1880-Smith, Elder-3 vols in 1-
8vo-orig cl-1st ed   (5xx6, soil)   22.50
MUIR, AUGUSTUS-How to Choose & Enjoy Wine-Lond-(1953)-160p
                                      (5w1) 3.50   (5g9) 4.50
MUIR, JOHN-Cruise of Corwin-Bost-1917-1st ed-plts-279p
                                      (5x5) 10. (5m8,4a8)   7.50
--same-Bost-1917-lg papr-ltd ed, nbrd (5x5,f,unopnd) 40. (5ss1) 15.00
--The Mountains of Calif-NY-1894-12mo-cl-1st ed of auth's
1st book   (4n1,rprd) 17.   (5gg6,f,dj)   35.00
--same-NY-1901   (5x5)   7.50
--same-NY-1911-389p-illus-cl-Century-9th ed, enlrgd (5d7)   15.00
--My First Summer in the Sierra-Bost-1911-HoughtonMiff-354p-cl-
illus-1st ed   (5m8) 10. (5d7) 20. (5s7)   17.50
--same-1911(but not on title pg)   (5s7)   12.50
--same-Bost-(1916)-plts-frontis   (5xx5)   10.50
--Our National Parks-Bost-1901-illus-t.e.g.-1st ed
                   (5x5,f,dj) 15. (5q8,hng weak) 6. (5t3,pres) 8.50
--same-Bost-1909-HoughtonMiff-382p-illus-cl-new & enlrgd ed
                                      (5d7,autg)   40.00
--same-Bost-(1916)-400p-illus   (5s7)   7.50
--Picturesque Calif & Region West of Rocky Mntns from Alaska to
Mexico-NY&SanFran-(1887)-2 vols-12 by 16 inches-many illus-
mor&cl   (5d2)   85.00
--Picturesque Calif, Rocky Mtns & Pac Slope -DewingCo, NY &
SanFran-(1894)-folio-hf lea (5x5,hng crack,bkstrp wn)   30.00
--Steep Trails-Bost-1918-1st ed-illus-391p (5i3) 12.50 (4n1) 10.00
--Stickeen, the Story of a Dog-Bost-1910 (4f9) 5. (5x5,dj) 5.00
--Story of My Boyhood & Youth-Bost-1913-1st ed-illus-294p-cl-
HoughtonMif-publ Mar 1913   (5i3,5a0,f)   12.50
--same-Bost-(1925)-293p-illus   (5w3)   7.50
--A Thousand Mile Walk to the Gulf-Bost-1916-illus
                                      (5b2,f,5jj1,f) 10.00
--Travels in Alaska-Bost-1915-8vo-cl-327p-illus-1st ed
          (5yy9) 6.50   (5m8, sl spot) 7.50 (5d7,5ii8) 12.50
--Two Essays on Mntn Meadows of Sierra Nevada-PaloAlto-1969-
R8vo-64p-e.p. map-1st ed-out of print (5r8)   17.50
--Works of John Muir-(1916)-HoughtonMif-Sierra Ed-10 vols-
sm8vo-orig green cl   (4f9) 60.   (5x5)   60.00
--Writings of John Muir-Bost-1916 to 1924-illus-hf purpl mor-
g.tooled-Manuscript ed(wi pg of mss) (5d7)   300.00
--The Yosemite-NY-1912-8vo-cl-1st ed (5h4,vg) 8. (5jj1,f)   10.00
--same-NY-1914-Century-284p-illus-cl (5d7)   10.00
--same-NY-1920-Century   (5x5)   8.50
--Yosemite & the Sierra Nevada-Bost-1948-65 full pg plts by
Ansel Adams-4to-cl-1st ed   (5p5,dj)   25.00
MUIR, LEO J-A Century of Mormon Activities in Calif-(1952)-
Deseret News Pr-2 vols   (5x5,4t1)   25.00

MUIR, P H-Book Collecting as a Hobby-NY-1947-181   pp-cl-
1st Amer ed   (5h6,sl wn dj) 5.00
--Talks on Book Collecting-Lond-(1952)-8vo-cl-15 illus (5d5,dj) 10.00
MUIR, PERCY H-Children's Books of Yesterday-A Catalogue-
Nat'l Bk League May, 1946-12mo-192p-pink wrps (5v2,vf,dj) 17.50
MUIR, RAMSAY-The Expansion of Europe-Bost-1919   (5x7)   5.00
MUIRHEAD, JAS-Historical Intro to Private Law of Rome-Lond-1899-
3rd ed-rev by Goudy   (5r4,rbnd)   15.00
MUIRHEAD, JAS F-The Land of Contrasts-Bost-1898-orig cl-g.-
1st ed   (5q8)   5.00
--same-Leipzig-1900-16mo-buck-Engl text-"Copyright Ed"
                                      (5w5,rbnd)   6.50
MUKERJI, DHAN GOPAL-Chief of the Herd-NY-1929-8vo-168p-
illus-1st ed-dec cl   (5aa0) 5.   (5p1)   7.50
MULDOON, SYLVAN-Alex Hamilton's Pioneer Son-Harrisburg-1930-
246p-map-e.p.-fldg facs-illus-ltd to 1000c (5w4,dj) 14.50
MULFORD, AMI FRANK-Fighting Indians in the 7th US Cavalry-
Corning, NY-(1879)-(probably ca 1930)-2nd ed (5yy7) 17.50
MULFORD, CLARENCE EDW-Bar 20-NY-1907-12mo-pict cl-
illus by Wyeth&Schoonover-1st ed of auth's 1st bk-1st issue
(on thicker papr, & reading "Blazing Star" in list of illus)
                                      (5gg6,f,autg, ALS) 35.00
--The Coming of Cassidy-NY-(1913)-AL Burt-col illus (5ee3) 2.50
--Cottonwood Gulch-GardenCty-1925-1st ed (5ee3)   3.50
--Hopalong Cassidy's Protege-GardenCty-1926-1st ed (5ee3)   5.00
--The Orphan-Chig-1924-ACMcClurg-frontis-1st ed
                                      (5ee3, fray dj) 7.50
MULFORD, PRENTICE-Story-Oakland-(1953)-R8vo-146p-lin-
gold papr labl-illus by Remington-Calif Rel,#35-ltd to 500c
                                      (5dd5)   20.00
--White Cross Library-NY-1901-Needham-6 vols-cl (5p7)   20.00
MULGRAVE, HELEN-Or Jesuit Executorship-(ca1850)
                                      (5t4, lacks fly) 10.00
MULHALL, MRS M G-From Europe to Paraguay & Matto Grosso-
Lond-1877-116p-fldg map-plts-Edw Stanford (5d6,plts sl worm)25.00
MULHALL, MARION McMURROUGH-Explorers in New World Before
& After Columbus-Lond-1909-maps(some fldg)   (5r7)   7.50
MULHOLLAND, JOHN-Quicker than the Eye-Indnpls-(1932)-cl-
illus-259p   (5t7)   6.00
MULKEARN, LOIS, ed-Geo Mercer Papers Relating to Ohio Co of
Virg-Pittsb-1954-731p-illus-fldg maps-ltd to 1,000c
                                      (5h9,mint)   11.50
MULLALY, J-A Trip to Newfoundland, Its Scenery & Fisheries,
With Acct of Laying of Submarine Telegraph Cable-NY-1855-
108p-v scarce-30 illus   (4e9, cov wn) 100.00
MULLAN, JOHN-Military Road From Ft Benton to Fort Walla Walla-
Wash-1861-HED 44-168p-1st ed-scarce   (4n4)   35.00
--Miners & Travelers' Guide to Oreg, Wash, Idaho, Mont, Wyo &
Colo-NY-1865-12mo-fldg map-1st ed   (4j3)   75.00
--Report of Sec of War...topogr mem & map of Col Wright's late
campaign against Indians in Oreg & Wash terr Feb 15, 1859,
(Senate 32) (Wash, 1859)-2 fldg maps-disbnd (5g3)   35.00
--Report & maps....Military Road from Ft Walla Walla-Wash-1863-
SED43-363p-plus errata 1f-4 fldg maps- 10 plts-hf mor (4n4) 45.00
MULLANEY, THOS W-Four Score Yrs-Rochester-1916-207p-illus
                                      (5w4, fade)   7.50
MULLENS, W H-Geographical Bibliog of Brit Ornithology from
Earliest Times-Lond-(1919-)1920-thk8vo-part mor-g.t.-1st ed
                                      (5z9, vg, spec f bndg) 60.00
MULLER, D L-Atlas of City of Schenectady 1905-1905-plts
                                      (5ff2, rbkd)   47.50
MULLER, DAN-Chico of the Cross Up Ranch-Chig-(1938)-illus-
249p-1st ed   (4m8) 5.00 (5yy7,dj,f)   8.50
--My Life with Buffalo Bill-Chig-(1948)-illus
                   (5yy6) 6.   (5g0,f,dj)   7.50
MULLER, F MAX-Auld Lang Syne-NY-1901, 1899-2 vols-Scribner-
port   (5x0)   9.00
MULLER, G F-Voyages from Asia to Amer, for completing Discov of
NW Coast of Amer....trans by Thos Jefferys-Lond-1764-
calf-4to-maps(2 fldg, 2 hf p.)-120p   (4e1)   450.00
MULLER, GERHARD-Voyages et Decouvertes faites par les Russes
le Long Des Cotes de la Mer Glaciale & sur L'Ocean Oriental-
Amsterdam-1766-sm8vo-hf mor-fldg map-2 vols in 1
                                      (4e1,rbnd)   275.00
MULLER, H J-Uses of the Past-1962   (5L7)   5.00
MULLER, J-Principles of Physics & Meteorology-Phila-1848-cl-635p-
2 col plts   (5hh7, sp wn) 10.00
MULLER, J W-"Ever Thine"....from the travel letters of-NY-
1928-Bartlett Orr Pr-123p   (5p7)   4.00
MULLER, MAX-The 6 Systems of Indian Philosophy-Lond-1903
                                      (5F0)   3.50
MULLIKIN, JAS C-Story of the Star Democrat, Easton, Md-
(Easton, 1948?)-88p-2 plts-fldg bds   (5hh6)   5.00

MULLIN,CORA PHEBE-Songs of the Indian Dances-(Omaha,1929)-
142p-1st ed　　　　　　　　(5dd6)　　6.00

MULLINS, EDGAR YOUNG-Freedom & Authority in Religion-
Phila-1913　　　　　　　　(5x7)　　3.75

MULLINS, J-Divining Rod, Its History,Truthfulness & Practical Utility-
War Office Auth-1905-Colerne, Box,Wilts-16mo-illus (5j2)　10.00

MULLINS,ROSCOE-Primer of Sculpture-Lond-1889-illus-108p-12mo
　　　　　　　　　　　　　(5ww3)　　5.50

MULVANEY,CHAS P-History of the NW Rebellion of 1885...Indian
Tribes of NW Canada-Tor-1885-424p　(5i3) 15.　(5r6)　17.00

MUMBY,FRANK A-George III & Amer Rev -Lond-1924-432p-ports
　　　　　　　　　　　　　(5a1)　　6.50

--Romance of Book Selling-Lond-1910-8vo-cl-490p-illus (5d5) 10.00

MUMEY,NOLIE-Alex T Rankin, His Diary & Letters-Denver-1966-
188p-illus-ltd to 400c,autg (5t1,mint) 45.　(4t3,mint)　17.50

--Alfred Edw Mathews-Boulder-1961-frontis-fldg map-78p-hf cl-
ltd to 350c　　　　　(5r7,f,unopnd)　10.00

--Anselm Holcomb Barker-1959-Golden Bell Pr-ltd to 500c, autg
(5x5) 25.　(4t3,mint)　20.00

--Barker Diary-Denv-1959-ltd to 500c,nbrd & autg (5hh3)　35.00

--Beckwourth 1856 to 1866;an enigmatic figure of the west-Denv-
1957-illus-lg fldg map-tip in frontis-232p-ltd to 500c,nbrd &
autg-scarce-out of print　(5xx5,f)　40.00

--Bloody Trails Along the Rio Grande-Denv-1958-Old West Publ-
cl-123p-fldg map-port-ltd to 500c,nbrd & autg
(5r0,4t3,dj,unopnd)　25.00

--Calamity Jane,1852 to 1903-Denv-1950-illus-fldg map-142p plus
index-2 pamph in pkt-ltd to 200c,autg-scarce (5yy7)　75.00

--Clark, Gruber & Co-Denv-1915-1st ed-88p plus index-illus-
ltd to 800c,autg　　　(4t3,unopnd)　30.00

--Colorado Territorial Scrip-Boulder-1966-R8vo-140p-plts-1st ed-
ltd to 350c,nbrd,autg-out of print (4t3,unopnd,mint)　20.00

--Creede-Denv-1949-illus-fldg map-177p plus index-1st ed-
ltd to 500c,autg　　(5yy7,unopnd,dj)　40.00

--Easter Island As It Is Today-Boulder-1963-xol-54p plus index-
ltd to 300c,autg　　(4t3,mint,unopnd)　12.50

--History of Early Settlements of Denver etc-Glendale-1942-200p
plus index-1st ed-scarce-ltd to 500c,nbrd,autg (4t3,f)　65.00

--History of Tin Cup, Colo-Boulder-1963-208p plus index-1st ed-
ltd to 300c,autg　　　(4t3,unopnd,f)　40.00

--Hoofs to Wings-Boulder-1960-116p-illus-fldg map-v scarce-
ltd to 200c,autg (5bb4) 50. (5k0)　60.00

--John Williams Gunnison-Denv-1955-Artcraft Pr-4to-189p-plts-
fldg map-ltd to 500c,nbrd,autg (5r8) 50. (5bb4) 30. (5F5,vf) 40.00

--Leaves of Yesterday & Other Poems-Denv-1944-151p-bds-cl bk-
1st ed-scarce　　　　　(5k1,autg)　15.00

--Life of Jim Baker-Denv-1931-1st ed-ltd to 250c,autg-rare
(4t3,lt wn) 125. (5bb4)　165.00

--Old Forts & Trading Posts of the West-Denv-1956-ltd to 500c,autg-
(5bb4, mint) 45. (5k2)　60.00

--Poker Alice,Alice Ivers-Denv-1951-orig stiff wrps-ltd to 500c,
autg　　　(4t3,vg,unopnd) 20. (5hh3)　35.00

--The Pot Shop & Other Poems-1942-Range Pr (5x5,autg)　15.00

--Prof Goldrick & His Denver-1959-ltd to 250c,autg
(5k1,4t3,dj,mint)　10.00

--Rocky Mntn Dick-Denv-1953-8vo-cl-ltd to 500c,autg
(5bb4,f,dj) 10. (5b0)　15.00

--Saga of Auntie Stone & Her Cabin-Boulder-1964-182p-illus-
ltd to 500c,nbrd,autg (5k1) 25. (4t3,mint,dj)　17.50

--The Teton Mntns-Denv-1947-447p plus index-photos-map-
fldg frontis-1st ed-ltd to 700c-v scarce (5t3)　75.00

--The Ute War-Denv-1964-192p-illus-map-orig wrps-fldg case-
reprnt -ltd to 300c　　　(4t3)　17.50

MUMFORD, JOHN K-Oriental Rugs-Scrib-1909-3rd ed-32 plts-
2 maps-2 fldg tables-278p-4to　(5ww3)　45.00

MUMFORD, LEWIS-The Golden Day-NY-1926 (5m2)　5.00

--Herman Melville-NY-1929-377p (5s1) 4.50 (5mm2)　6.00

MUMFORD, MILDRED-This is Waverly-(n.p.)-1954-8vo-cl-203p-
illus　　　(5j5,autg) 10. (5m2)　6.50

MUMM, A L-The Alpine Club Register 1857 to 1890-Lond-1923,1925,1
1928-3 vols-cl-Edwin Arnold　(5d7)　30.00

--5 Months in the Himalaya-NY-1909-LongmansGreen-263p-cl-
fldg maps-fldg views　　(5d7)　17.50

--My Climbs in the Alps & Caucasus-Lond-1895-TUnwin-360p-illus-
cl　　　　　　(5d7)　25.00

MUNBY, A N L-Catalogues of Manuscripts & Prntd Books of Sir Thos
Phillipps-Cambr,Engl-1954 to 60-8vo-cl-illus-5 vols
(5d3,djs)　45.00

MUNCHAUSEN,BARON-Adventur of...(ca1880)-F Warne-folio-
cl bk-104p-6 col plts-Rudolph E Raspe (5nn2)　12.50

MUNDAY,L-Mountys Wife-1930-217p-illus
London-　　(4b9) 12. (4f9)　12.50

MUNDY,TALBOT-The 9 Unknown-(1924)-1st Amer ed (5ee3)　3.50

--Rung Ho-NY-1914-12mo-cl-1st ed of auth's 1st bk (5gg6,dj,f) 25.00

MUNFORD,BEVERLY B-Virginia's Attitude Toward Slavery &
Secession-Richmond-(1915)-330p　(4m2) 15. (5x2)　12.50

MUNK,JOS A-Activities of a Lifetime-LosAng-1924-221p-photos
(5m9) 10. (5j1,sl wn)　8.50

--Arizona Sketches-NY-(1905)-230p-cl-1st ed
(5g6,pres) 20. (5dd4) 30. (5y0) 12.50 (5r1,f)　35.00

--History of Ariz Literature,an address-Flagstaff-Apr 1, 1925-12mo-
prntd wrps-scarce　　(5g6)　17.50

MUNKITTRICK, RICH K-Farming-NY-1891-102p-illus-orig pict bds-
ABFrost,illus　　(5mm2,pres)　12.50

--The Moon Prince & Other Nabobs-NY-1893-340p (5ee3)　4.50

MUNKS, BERTHA-Florida's Favorite Foods-Tallahassee-n.d.-
(ca1960)-Dept of Agric-202p-col plts-pict cov-wrps (5c9)　4.50

MUNN,C A-Three Types of Washington Portraits-NY-1908-illus-
8vo-cl-g.t.-priv prntd-ltd to 225c　(4c1,pres)　20.00

MUNN,CHAS CLARK-Uncle Terry, a story of the Maine Coast-
Bost-1900-Lee&Shepard-pict cl-1st ed (5m2) 5. (5b2)　4.00

MUNN,H T-Prairie Trails & Arctic Byways-Lond-1932-illus-288p
(4e9)　20.00

--Tales of the Eskimo-Lond-n.d.-196p-photos (5ss1,pres)　10.00

MUNNINGS,A J-Pictures of Horses & English Life-Lond-1939-4to-
20 col plts-2nd ed,rev　(5yy6)　28.50

MUNNS,E N-A Selected Bibliog of NoAmer Forestry-Wash-1940-
636p-wrps　　(5n4)　7.50

MUNRO,D J-The Roaring Forties & After,(1914)-Lond-1929-
31 photos　　(5c1)　15.00

MUNRO,DANA C-Treatment of Conquered Territory-Wash-
Mar,1918-64p-orig wrps-Part 2 of German War Prac,#8
(5w8,sl tn)　3.50

MUNRO,DAN'L C-You Can Live Longer Than You Think-NY-1948-
211p　　(5c5)　3.00

MUNRO FRASER, J P-History of Alameda County,CA-Oakland-
1883-MWWood,Pub-illus-1001p (5tt0) 45. (4L5,rebnd)　65.00

--Hist of Contra Costa Co,CA,illustrated-SanFran-1881-Slocum-
710p-lea-8vo　　(4t1)　150.00

--Hist of Santa Clara Co,CA-SanFran-1881-Alley,Bowen&Co-
ports-798p-sheep　　(5tt0)　75.00

--Hist of Solano Co-SanFran-1879-Wood,Alley & Co-503p-ports-cl-
lea bkstrp　　(5tt0)　50.00

MUNRO,H H-The Chronicles of Clovis-Lond-1912-JnLane-cl-1st ed
(5ss3,sp fade)　20.00

--The Square Egg & other sketches-Lond-(1924)-JnLane-cl-1st ed
(5ss3,fade)　20.00

--The Short Stories of Saki-(Lond)-(1930)-Lane-12mo-cl-718p
(5j5)　7.50

--The Unbearable Bassington-Lond-1912-JnHead-1st ed
(5ss3,sp fade)　15.00

MUNRO,J E C-Constitution of Canada-Cambridge U Pr-1889-356p
(4b9)　12.00

MUNRO,ROSS-Gauntlet to Overlord-Tor-1946-illus-477p (5dd7) 5.00

MUNRO,W B-Amer Influences on Canadian Gov-Tor-1929-
153p　　(4b9)　10.00

--Documents Relating to Seigniorial Tenure in Canada-Tor-1908-
Champlain Soc-380p　(5zz8)　35.00

MUNRO,W H-Hist of Bristol,RI,Story of Mt Hope Lands-1880-
396p　　(5t9)　20.00

MUNRO,WILFRED HAROLD-Tales of an Old Sea Port-1917-
Princeton Univ Pr-1st ed　(5F0)　4.50

MUNRO,WM BENNETT-Govt of the US-NY-1930-rev ed (5q8)　5.00

MUNRO'S TEN CENT NOVELS,#1-The Hunters,or, Life on the
Mountain & Prairie,by Latham C. Carleton-NY-(1864)-
IPBeadle & Co-96p-wrps　(5ee3)　25.00

--#2,The Trapper's Retreat-NY-(1863)-by LC Carleton-103p-wrps-
IPBeadle&Co　　(5ee3)　10.00

MUNROE,DAVID HOADLEY-The Grant National 1839 to 1930-NY-
(1930)-4to-map-illus-col frontis-ltd to 501c (5j2,f,box)　20.00

--same-NY-(1931)-4to-Huntington Pr-1st trade ed (5yy8)　20.00

MUNROE, F L-Practical Home Farmer-Chig-(1888)-illus-1115p-
Interstate Pub Hse　　(5t4)　10.00

MUNROE,HELEN-Classified List of Smithsonian Publ Available for
Distribution,Oct 1,1943-Wash-GPO-1943-47p-wrps (5j4)　3.00

MUNROE,KIRK-At War with Pontiac-NY-1895-illus-pict cl-
1st ed　　(5m1)　6.50

--Dorymates-NY-1890-illus　(5m1)　6.00

--The Fur Seal's Tooth-NY-1894-frontis-plts-map-1st ed
(5ee3) 10. (5dd5)　8.00

--The Golden Days of 49-NY-(1889)-351p-illus-1st ed
(4n1) 8.50 (5ee3,rub)　7.50

MUNROE, KIRK (continued)
--Raftmates-NY-1893-illus-1st ed   (5i3) 7.50
--With Crockett & Bowie-NY-1897-illus-1st ed (5i3) 7.50
--Through Swamp & Glade-NY-1899-col pict cl-illus (5r7) 7.50
--Wakulla, a Story of Adventure in Florida-NY-1886-illus-1st ed
    (5ee3,f) 7.50
MUNROE, RALPH-The Commodore's Story-n.p.-1930-384p-illus-
  pict cl   (5w0,pres) 7.50
MUNSELL, C G-Desc of Gerrit Fredericke Lansing Who Came to
  Amer from Hasselt, Holland 1640-1916-113p (5mm3) 22.50
MUNSELL, FRANK-Chips for the Chimney Corner, Gathered by-
  Albany-1871   (5g8) 10.00
MUNSELL, JOEL-Annals of Albany-1850 to 59, 1869-10 vols-illus-
  maps   (4b7, bndgs v poor) 150.00
--Catalogue of rare & extensive collection of books relating to
  Amer...library of Joel Munsell, of Albany-(NY-1865)-wrps
    (5g4) 10.00
--Webster's Calendar or the Albany Almanac-Albany-1860 to 1870-
  wrps-11 vols   (4j4) 22.50
MUNSELL, M E-Flying Sparks as Told by a Pullman Conductor-
  KansCty-1914-photos-159p-1st ed-rare (4t3,f) 35.00
MUNSELL, W W & Co-History of Queens County-1883-576p
    (4n2, rebnd) 47.50
MUNSELL'S-Guide to the Hudson River by RR & steamboat....from
  Staten Isl to Troy-Albany-1859-24mo-wrps-8 col maps(1 fldg)
    (5g8) 6.00
MUNSEY'S MAGAZINE-Vol 6, Oct 1891 to Mar, 1892-cl-
  (Horatio Alger, Jr)   (5p1, wn) 30.00
MUNSON, A J-Making a Country Newspaper-Chig-1899-12mo-
  1st ed   (5ss5) 7.50
MUNSON, GORHAM-The Dilemma Of the Liberated-NY-1930
    (5x7) 5.00
--Penobscott, Down East Paradise-Phila-(1959)-412p-illus (5t4) 4.50
MUNSON, JOHN W-Reminis of a Mosby Guerrilla-NY-1906-
  Moffatt-277p-illus-1st ed   (5x0) 17.50
MUNSON, LOVELAND-Early Hist of Manchester, Vermont-1876-
  63p   (5t9) 12.50
MUNSON, MYRON A-God's Doing & Man's Doing for Minisota-
  Chig-1871-24p-wrps   (5ff7) 20.00
MUNSTERBERG, HUGO-The Americans-NY-1904-619p-1st ed
    (5w9, autgs) 7.50
--On the Witness Stand-NY-1908-269p-1st ed (5w4) 6.50
--A Short History of Chinese Art-NY-E Lansing-Philos Library-
  (1949)-227p-plts-lg8vo-cl   (5m5) 12.00
--The War & Amer-NY-1914-210p-1st ed (5w5) 4.00
MUNTHE, AXEL-The Story of San Michele-Lond-(1929)-8vo-cl-
  JohnMurray-1st ed-wi slip   (5d9, box) 35.00
MUNTZ, E E-Race Contact-NY-1927   (5x2) 15.00
MUNTZ, EUGENE-Raphael, His Life, Works & Times-Lond-1888-
  R8vo-cl-43p plts-g.t.-enlrgd ed   (5p5) 15.00
MURAL PAINTINGS OF LIBRARY OF CONGR-Wash-n.d.-col-
  12 x 9½-wrps   (5ww4) 5.00
MURAT, PRINCESS LUCIEN-Private Life of Catherine the Great of
  Russia-NY-1928-212p-frontis   (5ss6) 4.00
MURCHIE, G-Saint Croix the Sentinel River-NY-1947-281p-illus
    (4b9) 10.00
MURCHIE, GUY-Song of the Sky-Bost-1954-438p-illus (5t7) 7.50
MURCHIE, R W-Agricultural Progress On The Prairie Frontier-Tor-
  1936-illus-maps-344p   (4e9) 20.00
MURCHISON, CARL, ed-The Case For & Against Psychical Belief-
  Worcester-1927-Clark Univ-lg8vo-cl-1st ed-scarce (5p5) 12.50
MURCHISON, CLAUDIUS T-King Cotton is Sick-Univ of NoCar-
  1930   (5x5, dj) 7.50
MURCHISON, RODERICK IMPEY-The Silurian System, Founded on
  Geological Researches...in two Parts-Lond-1839-John Murray-
  2 vols-4to-part calf-plts (some fldg)-1st ed
  (4h0, pres, lacks separate map) 450.00
MURDER BY A DEPUTY US MARSHAL-E M Dalton Waylaid &
  Assassinated in Cold Blood-SaltLkCty-1886-16 dbl col pg-
  map-no wrps-scarce pamphlet   (5t3) 50.00
MURDER OF CHRISTIAN INDIANS IN NO AMER-Dublin-1821-12mo-
  prntd by M Goodwin-disbnd-v rare   (5i0) 100.00
MURDOCK, CHAS A-Backward Glance at 80-SanFran-1921-275p-
  bds-ltd ed-autog (5h1, sp rprd) 7.50 (5h5) 6.00
MURDOCK, HAROLD-Bunker Hill-Bost-R8vo-Riverside Pr-lg type-
  ltd to 535c   (5t5) 17.50
--Earl Percy Dines Abroad-1924-spcl papr-H & M Co-R8vo-red cl-
  illus   (5t5) 15.00
--Earl Percy's Dinner Table-Bost-1907-HoughtonMif-Riverside Pr-
  8vo-cl-papr labl-frontis-ltd to 550c, nbrd (5ii8) 12.50 (5b0) 20.00
--19th of Apr 1775-Bost-1925-134p-illus-fldg map-hf cl
    (5mm8) 12.50

MURDOCK, JOHN R-Arizona Characters in Silhouette-Tempe-
  1933-wrps-100p-wrps   (4t3, chip) 25.00
--same-n.p.-1939-wrps-151p   (4t3) 25. (5g0) 20.00
MURDOCK, VICTOR-China, The Mysterious & Marvellous-NY-1920-
  8vo-cl-plts-1st ed   (5p5) 10.00
MURDOCH, W G BURN-Modern Whaling & Bear Hunting-Phila&Lond-
  1917-320p-illus   (5t4) 10.50
MURET, M-Traite des Festins-Paris-1682-(18), 230p, (24)-12mo-calf
    (5c5, sp rprd) 67.50
MURET, MAURICE-The Twilight of the White Races-NY-1926
    (5x7) 6.50
MURFIN, JAS V-Gleam of Bayonets-NY-(1868)-illus-maps (5tt5) 6.50
MURFREE, MARY N-Down the ravine-Bost-1885-Houghton-cl-illus-
  juvenile-1st ed   (5m2) 6.50
--Mystery of Witch Face Mntn & other stories-Bost-1895-Houghton-
  1st ed   (5m2) 6.50
--Where the Battle was fought-Bost-1884-Osgood-1st ed (5m2) 8.50
MURGER, HENRI-Bohemian Life-Phila-1899-Barrie-463p-illus
    (5p9) 4.00
MURILLO VELARDE, PEDRO-Historia de la Provincia de Philipinas-
  Manila-1749-folio-fldg map-frontis-limp vel-ric ppr-1st ed-
  rare-Sabin 51449   (5hh0, f, rprd) 1,350.00
MURNANE, LEONARD F-101 Adventures of Panamint Pete-
  Randsburg, Ca-(1947)-102p-1st ed   (5yy7) 3.00
MURPHY, ARTHUR-Life of David Garrick, Esq-Lond-1801-Foot-
  2 vols-8vo-hf calf-hf titles-1st ed   (5i8, f) 80.00
--The Works of Sam'l Johnson-1842-2 vols-1st Amer ed (5ee3, f) 3.50
MURPHY, BILL-Pictorial Hist of Calif-SanFran-(1958)-R8vo-212p-
  1st ed   (5dd6) 10.00
MURPHY, BLANCH, transl-Just Girard, Advent of a French Capt-
  NY-1878-dec cl-scarce   (5m9, lt wr) 20.00
MURPHY, CELESTE G-The People of the Pueblo-Sonoma, CA-1935-
  266p-illus   (5t1) 50.00
--same-(1948)-Binfords&Mort   (5x5, dj) 10.00
MURPHY, CHAS J-Amer Indian Corn-NY-1917-128p-rev ed (5c5) 3.50
MURPHY, CLAUDIA QUIGLEY-A Collation of Cakes-NY-1923-
  bds-29p(1)   (5c5, chip) 5.00
MURPHY, E G-Problems of the Present South-Lond-1910 (5x2) 17.50
MURPHY, EMILY-Janey Canuck in West-Lond-1910-306p-illus-
  col frontis-1st ed   (5aa0) 7.50
MURPHY, HENRY C-Catalogue of Library, unpriced-NY-1884-
  Geo A Leavitt, Auct-434p-sm4to-mor   (5L8, rprd) 25.00
MURPHY, J N-Terra Incognita-1873   (5L7, fray, ex-libr) 7.50
MURPHY, JOHN M-Sporting Adventures in Far West-NY-1880-
  469p-cl   (5jj9) 20.00
MURPHY, PAT   C-Behind Gray Walls-Caldwell-(1920)-83p-
  photos-autog   (5s4, soil, autg) 4.50
MURPHY, RICHARD C-History of Soc of Friendly Sons of St Patrick
  in City of NY-NY-1962-illus-566p   (5r7) 10.00
MURPHY, RICHARD J-Authentic Visitors' Guide to World's
  Columbian Expos & Chig-Chig-(1893)-67p-wrps (5h1) 3.00
MURPHY, ROBT CUSHMAN-Logbook for Grace-NY-1947-illus-
  1st ed   (5yy6, dj) 6.00
--Oceanic Birds of SoAmer-NY-(1936)-16 col plts-photos-2 vols-
  4to-cl-1st ed   (4p5, 5z9, vf box) 45.00
MURPHY, THOS D-On Sunset Highways-Bost-1915-380p-illus-
  map   (5a9, pres) 6.50
--same-Bost-1921-4to-g.t.- col plts-fldg map-rev ed
    (5p5, f) 15. (5L7) 7.50
--Oregon the Picturesque-Bost-1917-t8vo-40 plts-map-pict cl-
  1st impress   (5h4) 5. (5jj1) 7.50
--Wonderlands of the Amer West-Bost-(1925)-illus (4b7) 10.00
MURPHY VARNISH CO-Waterproof Polishing-Newark-1905-
  32p-illus-bds   (5hh7) 6.50
MURPHY, VIRGINIA REED-Across the Plains in the Donner Party
  (1846)-Century Mag-buck-18p-Remington illus-
  (Abstr Century Magazine)   (4n1, rbnd) 15.00
MURPHY, WM D-Biographical Sketches of State Officers etc-NY-
  1860-320p-frontis   (5qq8) 4.00
--same-in 1862 & 1863- 2 vols in 1-1863-437p (4n2) 10.00
MURRAY, ALAN E-Shoes & Feet to Boot-Chapel Hill-1950-illus-
  139p-orig wrps   (4a1, pres) 10.00
MURRAY, ALEX, M D-The Domestic Oracle-Lond-(1826)-(4), 568p-
  9 plts-lea   (5g9, lt fox) 65.00
MURRAY, ALEX S-Manual of Mythology-Phila-(1895)-sm8vo-cl-
  408p-12p plts   (5t2) 5.00
MURRAY, HON AMELIA M-Letters from the US, Cuba & Canada-
  NY-1856- 2 vols in 1-orig cl-1st Amer ed
  (5 6) 16. (5q8, chip, 5L7, rbnd) 12.50
MURRAY, ARTHUR-Down Memory Lane-NY-1954-4to-cl-photos-
  1st ed-scarce   (5p5) 10.00
--How to Become a Good Dancer-1947-Simon&Schuster-illus(5a6)3.50

USED BOOK PRICE GUIDE

MURRAY,CHAS A-The Prairie Bird-Lond-1844-3 vols
(4n4,Streeter & notes copy) 110. (5xx6,rub) 40.00
--same-NY-1844-cl-207p   (4n4,rbnd) 25.00
--same-NY-1845-cl-Libr of Select Novels #34-207p
(4n4,wrp bnd in) 30.00
--Travels in No America-Lond-1839-Bentley-2 vols-frontis
(5L1,calf,hng weak) 75. (5Z7,orig cl) 65. (5j3,hng crack) 80.00
--same-NY-1839-2 vols-12mo-lea (5yy6,hng weak,ex-libr) 52.50
MURRAY,CHAS H-Practice of Osteopathy-Elgin(Ill)-1918-8vo-432p-
illus-cl   (5p5) 17.50
MURRAY,FLORENCE-The Negro Handbook,1942-NY-1942 (5x2)25.00
--same,1944-NY-1944   (5x2) 17.50
--same,1946,7-NY-1947   (5x2) 17.50 (5x5) 12.50
--same,1949-NY-1949   (5x2,ex-libr) 10.00
MURRAY,GEO W-Race Ideals-n.p.-1910-66p-wrps (5j6) 10.00
MURRAY,GILBERT-4 Stages of Greek Religion-NY-1912-224p
(5w9) 7.50
MURRAY,GORDON-Nuts on the White House Table-SanFran-
(1936)-Hobart Bldg-76p-wros   (5r0) 7.50
MURRAY,H C-The Sight of Dawn-Poetry-NY-1959-1st ed
(5x2,dj) 10.00
MURRAY,H J R-A History of Chess-Oxford-lg thk8vo-g.t.
(5ww4,sl wn) 35. (5b0) 45.00
MURRAY,HUGH-Historical & Descriptive Account of British Amer-
NY-1840-2 vols-Harper   (5rr6) 27.50
--same-Edinb-1839-sm8vo-cl-3 vols-6 maps(2 fldg) (4e1) 60.00
MURRAY,J-Elements of Materia Medica & Pharmacy-Phila-1808-
2 vols in 1-447p-calf   (5w0,rub) 16.50
--Supplement to 1st ed of A System of Chemistry-Phila-1811
(5g4,ex-libr) 20.00
MURRAY,J CLARK-Handbook of Psychology-Bost-1890-435p
(5dd7) 4.50
MURRAY,J F-Picturesque Tour of River Thames in its western course-
1849-100 illus   (5L7,sl fray) 12.50
MURRAY,JAS-Impartial History of Present War in Amer-
Newcastle upon Tyne-(1778)-3 vols-8vo-27 ports-3 maps-
orig calf   (5L1,f,1 map tn) 450.00
MURRAY,JOHN-Jerubbaal-Newbury Port-1784-John Mycall-
12mo-75p-hf mor   (5L1,lacks hf t.) 15.00
MURRAY,REV JOHN-Life Of-Bost-1833-324p (5t7,chip) 5.00
MURRAY,JOHN-A System of Materia Medica & Pharmacy-NY-
1828-282p,278p-calf   (5w3) 18.50
MURRAY,JOHN F-Picturesque Tour of River Thames in its Western
Course-Lond-1845-1st ed-woodcuts-356p-dec cl-maps
(5i3,rub) 7.50
MURRAY,JN MIDDLETON-Keats & Shakespeare-Oxford-1925-
Univ Pr-cl-1st ed   (5ss3,spots) 10.00
--Wrap me up in my Aubusson Carpet-NY-1924-Greenberg 7.50
MURRAY,LT-Fanny Campbell,the female pirate captain-Bost-1845-
F Gleason-   disbnd-100p-1st ed   (5x1) 100.00
--The naval officer,or,the pirate's cave-Bost-1845-F Gleason-
8vo-illus-disbnd-1st ed   (5x1) 100.00
MURRAY,LINDLEY-English Reader-Rutland-1819-12mo-266p
(5xx7,lacks pt t.p.) 15.00
--same-Bost 1819-263p-calf   (5w5,sl wn) 12.50
--English Reader-Pitts-1834-204p-bds (5h7,wn,chip) 7.50
MURRAY,MARGARET A-The Splendour That Was Egypt-NY-(1957)-
335p plus index-photos-col plts-2nd impress (5t3,dj,f) 7.50
MURRAY,REV O E-The Black Pope;or, the Jesuits' Conspiracy
Against Amer Institutions-Chig-(1892)-Patriot Co-8vo-illus-
2nd ed   (5m6) 12.50
MURRAY,PAUL-Whig Party in Georgia,1825 to 1853-Chapel Hill-
1948-wrps-219p   (4j4) 8.50
MURRAY,ROBT H,ed-Maximilian, Emperor of Mexico-1934-
Yale Univ Pr-1st ed (5ss1,ex-libr) 6.50 (5x5) 15.00
MURRAY,STUART-The Complete Handbook of the Virgin Islands-
NY-1951-Duell-illus-maps-178p   (5p9) 2.50
MURRAY,THOS BOYLES-Pitcairn,The Island,People & Pastor etc
Lond-1853-12mo-illus-1st ed (5yy6,sl rub) 22.50
--same-Lond-(1860)-12th ed   (5nn6) 10.00
MURRAY,T H-Rhode Islanders, Irish, in the Amer Revolution-
1903-90p   (5t9) 4.00
MURRAY,THOS H-History of the 9th Regiment,Conn Vol Infantry-
NewHav-1903-446p   (5j6) 8.50
MURRAY,W H-The Negro's Place in Call of Race-Tishomingo-1945-
priv pub   (5x2) 30.00
MURRAY,WM H-Pocahontas & Pushmataha-OklaCty-1931-106p-cl-
2nd ed   (5h0,pres,cov dmgd) 6.50
MURRAY,WM H H-Adirondack Tales-Bost-1877-Golden Rule-459p-
1st ed   (5mm2) 10. (5x4) 17.50
--Adventures in the Wilderness-Bost-1869-illus-1st ed
(5j3,hng crack,wn) 10. (5t7,wn) 15.00
--same-Bost-1870-illus-ads   (5t4) 10.00

MURRAY,WM H H (continued)
--Daylight Land-Bost-1888-illus-1st ed (4b7,hng split,5s0) 12.50
--Deacons-Bost-1875-illus-82p   (5r7) 10.00
--The Doom of Mamelons-Phila-1888-136p-orig wrps-1st ed
(5m1,wn) 12.50
--Lake Champlain & Its Shores-Bost-(1890)-8vo-port
(5t4) 6.50 (5m6) 7.50
--The Mystery of the Woods & The Man Who Missed it-Bost-(1891)-
460p   (5t7) 10.00
--Phantom Falls, A Tale of the Adirondacks-n.d.-22p (4n2) 6.50
--Ungava-Bost-1889-Murray-1st ed-priv prntd-hf mor-rare (5i4) 20.00
MURRELL, JOHN A-Life & Adventures of...the great western land
pirate-NY-1848-HLong&Bro-8vo-22 illus-orig yellow prntd wrps-
2nd ed   (5x1,vg) 150.00
MURRELL,WM-Hist of Amer Graphic Humor-Vol 1,1747 to 1865-NY-
1933-Macmillan-245p-illus-demy 4to (4a0,dj) 35.00
--Hist of Amer Graphic Humor,Vol 2, 1865 to 1938-NY-1938-
Macmillan-271p-illus-demy 4to (4a0,dj) 35.00
MURREY,THOS J-Cookery for Invalids-NY-1887-16 mo-32p-
orig pict bds   (5t2) 4.50
--Fifty Salads-NY-1889-32p-6th ed-bds (5g9) 4.00
MURRIN,JAS A-With (Fighting) 112th Regiment in France-Phila-
1919-thk4to-cl-455p-32 plts-1st ed (5p5,pres) 10.00
MURRY,ANN-Mentoria-Lond-1787-Dilly-sm8vo-276p-plt-map-
calf-5th ed   (5a1) 15.00
--same-Lond-Dilly-1794-sm8vo-282p-plt-map-calf-7th ed (5a1) 10.00
MURRY,JOHN MIDDLETON-Countries of the Mind-NY-(1922)-
1st Amer ed   (5nn6,dj) 15.00
--Journal of Katherine Mansfield-NY-1927-8vo-illus-256p-cl
(5t0,dj) 5.00
--Son of Woman-NY-(1931)-Jonathan Cape-1st Amer ed
(5ss9,vg,fray dj) 12.50
MURY,PAUL-Les Jesuites a Cayenne-Paris-1895-283p-wrps-
fldg map   (5r7) 15.00
MUSCALUS, JOHN A-Bibliogr of Histories of Specific Banks-
Norristown-1942-16p-fldg bds-priv pub (5y2) 3.50
MUSCATINE,CHAS-Book of Geoffrey Chaucer-Book Club of Calif-
orig lf from undated (ca1561) Chaucer-folio-cl (5h5,mint) 40.00
MUSCATINE CO,IA-History of-Chig-1879-8vo-hf lea-692p-map
(5m8) 50.00
MEMPHIS-Special Report of Southern Regional Council-Atlanta-
1964-49p-wrps   (5x2) 6.50
MUSE,C-Way Down South-Hollywd-1932-R8vo-pict bds-loose lf
tied wi ribbon-1st ed-ltd to 1,000c,autgs (5x2) 22.50
MUSEUM OF ENTERTAINMENT-Lond-Gainsborough,H Mozley-
1802-12mo-156p-frontis-wrps (5a1) 12.50
MUSEUM OF MODERN ART-20 Centuries of Mexican Art-NY-
(1940)-illus-in Spanish & Engl-stiff wrps (5j3,vg) 8.00
MUSEUM OF MOSCOW ART-Western Art in-Moscow-1938-
series of 4to plts loose in orig cl portfolio-text in English-
orig issue   (5p5) 45.00
MUSGRAVE,GEO M-A ramble through Normandy-Lond-1855-
David Bogue-8vo-orig cl-frontis-plt-1st ed (5i8) 12.00
MUSGRAVE,MRS H-Illusions-Lond-1887-Bentley-3 vols-8vo-orig cl-
1st ed   (5xx6,dj) 27.50
MUSGROVE,J W-Waterfowl in Iowa-Des Moines-1943-orig cl-8vo-
122p-12 plts(8 col)   (4p5) 10.00
MUSGROVE,MARY D-Autobiogr of Capt Richard W Musgrove-n.p.-
1921   (5s2,f) 25.00
MUSICK, JOHN R-Hawaii, Our New Possession-NY-1898-
Funk&Wagnalls-56p plts (5p5) 15. (5x5,ex-libr) 20.00
MUSICK,L W-The Hermit of Siskiyou,or Twice old Man-CrescentCty-
1896-81p-6½ x 4   (5r0) 10.00
MUSKEGON & OTTAWA CO,MICH-History of-Chig-1882-151,
133p-lea bkd cl   (5jj9) 57.50
MUSKEGON CO,Mich-Inventory of the County Archives-1941-
318p-WPA Hist Records Surv (5t9) 7.00
MUSKOKA LAKES & GEORGIAN BAY GUIDEBOOK-n.p.-n.d.-
(ca 1888)-illus-127p-12mo-ads (5aa1,v fray,lacks bk wrp) 25.00
MUSPRATT,ERIC-Greek Seas-Lond-1933 (5c1) 6.00
MUSSELMAN,M M-Get a Horse-Phila-(1950)-8vo-304p-photos-
1st ed   (4a6) 7.50
MUSSER,A MILTON-Fruits of "Mormonism" by Non "Mormon"
Witnesses...-SaltLkCty-1878-35p-wrps-1st ed-scarce (4t3,f) 45.00
MUSSER,J-Establishment of Maximilian's Empire in Mexico-1918-
hf calf   (5L7,wn) 4.50
MUSSET,PAUL DE-Monsieur le Vent et Madame la Pluie-Paris-1846-
Hetzel-illus-1st ed   (5c8) 15.00
MUSSEY,ABIGAIL-Life Sketches & Experiences-Cambr-1866-227p
(5s2) 35.00
MUSSEY,BARROWS-Old New England-NY-(1946)-119p-engrs-
wdcuts   (5e8) 9.75

MUSSEY,BARROWS (continued)
--Yankee Life by Those Who Lived It-NY-1947-8vo-cl-543p-
illus   (5t2,dj,f)   5.00
--Young Father Time-NY-1950-illus-44p-8vo   (5bb0)   12.50
MUSSEY,HENRY RAYMOND-Combination in the mining industry-
NY-1905-wrps   (5g3,unopnd)   12.50
MUSSEY,J B,ed-The Cream of the Jesters-Boni-(1931)
                                              (5ww4,soil)   6.00
MUST,REV ISAAC-The Gun, Rod & Saddle,or 9 months in Calif-
Phila-1875-illus-278p-16mo   (5ss8)   15.00
MUTHER,RICHARD-History of Modern Painting-Lond-1907-
Chamberlin&Lucas-rev ed-4 vols-illus-8vo   (5ww3)   35.00
MUZUMDAR,HARDINAS T-Gandhi versus The Empire-NY-c1932
                                              (5x7)   5.00
MUZZEY,A B-Remin & Memorials of Men of Revolution & Their
Families-Bost-1882-424p-illus   (5x8) 7.50   (5ii8)   15.00
MUZZEY,DAVID SAVILLE-The Amer Adventure-NY-1927-2 vols-
illus-maps   (5h9,f) 12.   (5p9)   12.50
MY ABC BOOK-Saalfield-(c1904)-lg sq8vo-16p-prntd on muslin-
2 letters per pg   (5s6)   5.00
MY CANDY SECRETS-NY-(1919)-146p-sm4to-53 photo illus
                                              (5g9,vf)   6.50
MY CHINESE MARRIAGE-NY-1921-8vo-papr labl-g.t.-cl bk bds-
by MTF-auth's 1st bk   (4c2,sl soiled)   100.00
MY DESIRE-NY-Carter-1879-629p-1st ed   (5x4)   9.00
MY FLOWER POT-Concord-ca1835-R Merrill-orig pict wrps-16p-
13 wdcuts-4¼ x 2-3/4"   (5ii4)   10.00
MY INTIMATE ENEMY-A Story-Phila-1878-Claxton, Remsen &
Haffelinger-176p-1st ed   (5mm2)   40.00
MY LADY'S CASKET OF JEWELS-& Flowers for Her Adorning-Bost-
1885-obl 8vo-16 plts illum-impressd bndng-1st ed
                                              (5v2,mint,box) 50.00
MY LADY'S SCRAPBOOK-Vol 1,#2 Feb 1910 thru Vol 2,#1 Jan 1911-
12 issues-Richmond-96p ea-narr 12mo-wrps   (5w7)   7.50
MY LADY'S TOILETTE-Phila-(1911)-sq12mo-19 mechanical plts-
ribbon bndng   (5c8)   12.50
MY MOTHER-A poem for a good little girl-NewHav-1835-S Babcock-
16p-32mo   (5p1,stn)   10.00
MY MOTHER'S COOK BOOK-Revised-n.p.-n.d.-(ca 1880)-
2 prefaces-(10),226p (14)p-StL,Mo ads-Ladies of Church of
Messiah   (5c9)   12.50
MY PARTY BOOK-of Tested Chocolate Recipes-n.p.-1938-
Gen'l Foods-26p-illus   (5g9)   2.50
MY SISTER-Balt-1836-16mo-8p-hand col illus ea pg-illus wrps,
sewn   (5v0,wn)   15.00
MYCALL,JOHN-A Funereal Address on death of late Geo Washington
...Baptist Meeting House Feb 22,1800-Bost-(1800)-
Manning&Loring-27p   (5L1,lacks hf t.)   20.00
MY VINEYARD AT LAKEVIEW-By a Western Grape Grower(A N
Prentiss,Ohio)-NY-1866-143p-illus   (5w1)   7.50
MYER,RICHARD-Chats On Old Engl Tobacco Jars-Lond-n.d.-sm4to-
111,(14)p plus 55 plts   (5w9,fade)   14.50
MYERS,A C,ed-Hannah Logan's Courtship-1904   (5L7)   8.50
MYERS,ALBERT C-The Boy Geo Washington Aged 16-Phila-1932-
79p-illus-ltd ed,nbrd,autg   (5h9)   8.50
--Sally Wister's Journal-Phila-(1902)-illus-1st ed (4m2) 17.50
--Wm Penn's Early Life in Brief-Moylan,Pa-1937-83p plus plts
                                              (5w5,pres)   8.50
MYERS,ALLEN O-Bosses & Boodle in Ohio Politics-Cinn-1895-
293p-cl   (5h2)   10.00
MYERS,BERNARD S,ed-Encyclopedia of Painting-NY-1955-511p-
4to-cl-illus   (5t7)   12.00
MYERS,D P-Manual of Collections of Treaties & of Collections
relating to Treaties-1922   (5L7)   15.00
MYERS,ELIZ-Century of Moravian Sisters-NY-n.d.-col frontis-
illus   (4a9,underline) 10.00
MYERS,ELIZ-The Social Letter-NY-1918-147p   (5w7,chip)   4.50
MYERS,FRANK-The Comanches-1956-400p-facs of 1871 ed
                                (5a0) 12.50   (5hh3)   10.00
--Soldiering in Dakota Among the Indians-Pierre,S D-1936-wrps
                                              (5dd6,4k4,f)   7.50
MYERS,FREDK W H-Human Personality & Its Survival of Bodily
Death-NY-1903-2 vols-1st ed   (5t2,lt spot) 7.50
--same-Lond-1913-L Myers,ed-470p   (5w0)   6.50
MYERS,GUSTAVUS-Ending of Hereditary Amer Fortunes-NY-1939-
395p   (4b8)   10.00
--History of Bigotry in the US-NY-1943   (5x2)   10.00
--History of Great Amer Fortunes-Chig-1907 to 09-3 vols-cl
                                              (4b8,sl spot) 10.00
--same-Chig-1911-Kerr-3 vols-illus-hf titles (5qq8)   22.50
--History of the Supreme Court of the US-Chig-1912-823p-1st ed
                                              (5w5)   12.50
--Ye Olden Blue Laws-NY-1921-274p-illus-cl (5L7) 4. (5t2)   5.00

MYERS,J C-Sketches on a Tour through Northern & Eastern States,
the Canadas & Nova Scotia-Harrisonburg(Va)-1849-Wartmann-
16mo-sheep-1st ed   (5n9,mor box)   90.00
MYERS,J D,ed-Household Helps-Springfld-1932-294p (5w7,fade) 3.50
MYERS,JOHN M-Doc Holliday-Bost-1955-   1st ed
                                (5m9) 6.   (5a9,dj,mint)   4.50
--I, Jack Swilling, Founder of Phoenix,Ariz-NY-1961-320p-index-
1st ed   (5g2,dj)   6.00
--The Last Chance-NY-1950-260p-illus-1st ed   (5dd4)   12.00
MYERS,L H-The Orissers-Lond-(1922)-Putnam's Sons-8vo-
orig prntd bds-ltd to 250c,autg (5ss3,fade,dj fade)   35.00
MYERS,HON LEONARD-Abraham Lincoln-A Memorial Address
Delivered By-Phila-1865-15p-prntd wrps-Monaghan
                                              (5h1,pres)   15.00
MYERS,LOUIS G-Some Notes on Amer Pewterers-NY-1926-
Country Life Pr-96p   (4p7)   20.00
MYERS,PETER HAMILTON-The first of the Knickerbockers,a tale of
1673-NY-1849-Putnam-12mo-orig cl-2nd ed   (5x1)   15.00
MYERS,S D,ed-O W Williams,Pioneer Surveyor Frontier Lawyer-
El Paso-1966-Hertzog-8vo-cl-350p-maps-photos
                                (5g2,3 autg)   20.00
--same-Ft Stockton ed-Hertzog-8vo-hf lea-350p-one of 150c
spec prntd,boxed,autg-illus-v scarce   (5g2,f)   75.00
MYERS,WM E-Republican Nat'l Convention Cleveland,Ohio
June 10,1924-(Cinn,1924)-4to-illus-188p-cl   (5t7)   10.00
MYERS,REV WM H-The 19th Century Young Man-Phila-1890-164p-
port-lectures   (5w7,soil)   4.50
MYERS,WM STARR-The Hoover Administration-NY&Lond-1936-
port-553p   (5q8) 6.   (5ss1,5t7,dj)   6.50
MYLIN,A-State Prisons,Hospitals,Soldiers' Homes & Orphan Schools-
(Harrisburg)-1897-2 vols-photo-illus   (5ii2,shaken) 7.50
MYLONAS,GEO-Ancient Mycenae-Princeton-1957-illus (4a1)   15.00
MYRA'S COOKERY BOOK-Lond-n.d.-(ca1900)-416p
                                              (5g9,cov stn)   4.50
MYRDAL,GUNNAR-An Amer Dilemma-NY-1944-483p
                                (4j4) 12.50 (5p9,5x2)   10.00
--same-NY-1944-2 vols   (5ii8,5x2)   12.50
MYRES,S D,ed-Pioneer Surveyor,Frontier Lawyer-El Paso-1966
                                (4c7,dj,autg)   20.00
--same-Tex Westrn Coll Pr-1966-ltd to 150c,3 autg (5x5)   60.00
MYRES,SANDRA L-The Ranch in Spanish Texas-El Paso-1969-
spec cl bnd ed-autg by Hertzog & Cisneros-ltd to 50c (4c7) 87.50
--S D Myres,Saddlemaker-Kerrville-1961-4to-priv prntd-illus-
offset typed pgs-wrps   (4c7)   10.00
MYRICK,HERBERT-Cache la Poudre-NY&Chig-1905-illus-maps-
photos-202p-1sttrade ed (4t3,fleck,5x5,5s2,f,5yy7)   25.00
--same-NY-1905-illus-202p-4to-orig tan buckskin-ltd ed to 500c
                                (5dd9) 95. (4c1,f,5yy7)   65.00
MYRTLE,FREDK-Gold-SanFran-1916-Bohemia Club-bds
                                (4b5,London autg,vg)   35.00
MYRTLE,MINNIE-The Iroquois,or Bright Side of Indian Character-
NY-1855-plts-1st ed   (4k4)   15.00
MYSTERIES OF MANCHESTER,A TALE-No author-Manchester,NH-
1844-40p-orig blue dec wrps   (5s2,fray)   125.00
MYSTERIES OF MORMONISM-By an Apostle's Wife-(1882)-
69p+ads-papr covers-publ by Rich K Fox of Police Gazetre
                                (5h6)   15.00
MYSTERYCHEF'S,THE-Own Cook Book-GardenCty-(1943)-366p
                                (5c9)   3.50
MYSTIC BELL,THE-NY-1869-Putnam-12mo-176p- 3 plts-
purple beveled cl   (5p1,fade)   20.00
MYTHS & LEGENDS-Bost-n.d.-(after 1911)-David D Nickerson-
8vo-cl-t.e.g.-8 vols-Folklore ed-ltd to 1,000 c,nbrd (5p1) 100.00
MYTINGER,CAROLINE-Headhunting In the Solomon Island-NY-
1942-5 plts-425p-cl   (5x2) 2.50 (5t7) 4.50 (5cc1,f)   3.50
--New Guinea Headhunt-NY-1947-8vo-441p-illus-ports
                                (4a6,wn dj)   3.00
NABOKOV,VLADIMIR-Lolita-Paris-(1955)-Olympia Pr-orig wrps-
2 vols-1st ed-rare (5u5,rbnd 2 vols in 1) 75. (4b5,vg)   75.00
--9 Stories-NY-(1947)-8vo-1st ed-blu prntd wrps (5cc9)   27.50
--The Real Life of Sebastian Knight-NY-(1941)-12mo-rough cl-
papr labls-1st ed-correct 1st bndng   (5ss7,f)   25.00
NADAILLAC,MARQUIS DE-Pre Historic Amer-NY-1893-219 illus-
hf calf   (5r7)   20.00
--same-NY-1899-566p-illus   (4b2)   7.50
NADEAU,REMI A-City Makers,the Men Who Transformed LosAng
from Village to Metropolis During 1st Great Boom-NY-1938-
1st ed   (5x5,pres,lt stn,lacks dj) 15. (5x5,dj)   17.50
--LosAng,from Mission to Modern City-NY-1960-302p-illus-1st ed
                                (5t1)   20.00
--The Water Seekers-GardenCty-1950-pict wrps-scarce
                                (5m9,sl stn)   25.00

NAGEL,CHAS-A Boy's Civil War Story-StL-1934(1935)-420p-
  1st ed-scarce   (4t3)   20.00
--same-Phila-(1937)-340p   (4b3,f)   20.00
NAGEL,OSKAR-Mechanical Appliances of Chemical &
  Metallurgical Industries-NY-1908-307p-illus (5hh7) 6.50
NAGEL,W G,ELECTRIC CO-Radio Equipment & Supplies-Toledo-
  n.d.-(ca1922)-120p-wrps   (5h2)   4.00
NAGRA WALMENTA RAD-och Upplysningar for Swenska Utwandrare
  till Amerikanska staterna-Falun-1869-F L Schmidt-60p-fldg map-
  12mo-orig prntd wrps-rare   (5L1,vf) 200.00
NAGY,IMRE-On Communism-Lond-n.d.   (5x7)   4.50
NAHUM,DR PINHAS BEN-The Turkish Art of Love-NY-c1933-
  priv prntd   (5x7)   15.00
NAINS CELEBRES-depuis l'antiquite jusques et y compris Tom Pouce,
  par A d'Albanes et Georges Fath-Paris-(1845)-illus by Beaumont-
  part calf   (5c8,f)   20.00
NAKAMURA,GONGORO,ed-Japanese in So Calif,"A Hist of 70
  Yrs"-LosAng-1960-Japanese Chamber of Comm of SoCalif-8vo-
  cl-67p,(804)   (4t1)   25.00
NAKAMURA,ICHISABURO-Catalogue of Natl Treasures of Paintings
  & Sculptures in Japan-Kyoto,Japan-1915-169p (5j4) 15.00
NAKAMURA,KAJU-Prince Ito-NY-1910-Anraku Publ-114p (5p7)3.75
NAKAYA,U-Snow Crystals-NY-1954-Harv Pr-illus-510p-8vo
                (5ww3)   15.00
NAM-ECONOMIC PRINCIPLES COMMISSION-of NAM-NY-1946-
  2 vols   (5y2)   9.50
NAMIER,L B-1848,revolution of the intellectuals-1950 (5L7) 4.00
NANCE,R MORTON-Sailing Ship Models-Lond-1924-lg4to-cl-80p-
  124 plts   (5ss2,sp wn) 22.50
NANCREDE,P J G DE-L'Abeille Francoise,ou Nouveau Receuil
  de Morceaux Brillans-Bost-1792-Belknap-12mo-sheep
        (5n2,cov wn) 75.00
NANITA,ABELARDO-Trujillo-MexicoCty-1934-sm4to-bds-
  enlrgd ed   (5p5)   15.00
NANSEN,FRIDTJOT-Farthest North-Lond-(1897)-wrps as issued-
  plts-8vo-20 parts-(pre dates 1st ed)
     (4n5,chart tn,cov Vol 1 dtchd) 150.00
--Farthest North Voyage of the Fram-NY-1897-2 vols-ports-col plts-
  illus-map-1st ed   (5r6) 12.50 (5a1) 17.50
--same-Lond-1898-2 vols-illus-lg fldg map
  (4b9) 15. (5dd7,f bndg) 26.50 (5ss1) 12.50
--First Crossing of Greenland-1890-2 vols-buck-maps (5L7,rbnd)15.00
--same-NY-1897-453p-map-illus-cl   (5t0)   4.00
--Hunting & Adv in the Arctic-NY-1924-462p-1st ed-scarce
       (5dd7,f)   25.00
--In Nach und Eis,die Norwegische Polarexpedition 1893 to 96-
  Leipzig-1897-illus-maps-2 vols   (4d2) 10.00
--In Northern Mists-NY-1911-col frontis-384p-Vol 1 (of 2) (5ss1) 7.50
NAOMI-or Boston,200 yrs ago-Bost-1848-Crosby&Nichols-8vo-
  orig cl-1st ed   (5x1,fade) 12.50
NAPA CLASSIC,THE-New Series,Vol 14 #3-Napa,Calif-Sept 1888-
  12p   (5d6)   15.00
NAPA CO-Oakland-1878-Smith & Elliott-litho title-2 maps-
  15½x12¼"-orig cl-lea bkstrp-66p lithos & 4 dbl pg liths
        (5tt0) 250.00
NAPHEYS,G H-The Physical Life of Woman-Phila-1871-8vo-cl
        (5p5)   12.50
NAPIER,HENRY EDW-New Engl Blockaded in 1814-Salem-1939-
  illus-fldg map-88p-8vo-cl   (4c1) 12.50
NAPOLEON MINING CO,THE-Quartz Mining Dis,Gunnison Co,
  Col-(StL)-n.p.-n.d.-(ca1890)-wrps-7p-prospectus (5L5) 4.00
NAPP,R-Argentine Republic Centenary Exhibition-Phila-1876-
  maps-buck   (5L7,rbnd) 9.50
NAPTON,WM B-Over the Santa Fe Trail,1857-SantaFe-1964-73p
        (5n4)   6.00
NARES,GEO-The Naval Cadet's Guide-Lond-1860-141p-frontis-
  illus-8vo-cl-1st ed   (5ss2,cov wn) 17.50
NARODNY,IVAN-Amer Artists-NY-1929-Roerich Mus Pr-110p-
  illus-crown 8vo   (4a0)   8.50
NARR OF ARTHUR GORDON PYM OF NANTUCKET,NO AMER-
  Lond-1838-Wiley&Putnam,etc-8vo-orig cl-1st Engl ed-
  (E A Poe)   (5i9,cov wn) 125.00
NARR OF MASSACRE AT CHIG,AUG 15,1812 & OF SOME
  PRECEDING EVENTS-Chig-1844 -34p-map-mor-(Kinzie)-
  1st ed   (5m3,Newberry copy) 1,600.00
NARR OF MILITARY EXCURSION OF MONTREAL VOL MILITA
  RIFLES TO PORTLAND-Montr-1858-8vo-orig limp cl-(T Wily)-
  1st ed   (5m6,fade) 17.50
NARR OF OCCURRENCES IN INDIAN COUNTRIES OF NA-since
  Connexion of Selkirk with-Lond-1817-8vo-1st ed
  (5e2) 450. (5a3) 250.00

NARR OF PRIVATIONS & SUFFERINGS OF US OFFICERS &
  SOLDIERS-while Prisoners of War in Hands of Rebel Authorities-
  Phila-1864-283p-plts
  (5dd6,rbnd stiff wrps) 19.50 (5L1,cov wn) 35.00
NARR OF RESIDENCE IN BELGIUM-during campaign of 1815,by
  an Englishwoman-Lond-1817-Murray-8vo-hf calf-1st ed
       (5i8,sl crack) 12.50
NARR OF SUFFERINGS & ADVEN OF JOHN R JEWITT-NY-
  (ca1815)-12mo-orig prntd papr covered,cedar bds-frontis-illus
  -(John R Jewitt)   (5n9,chip) 125.00
--same-Middletown-1815-Richards-calf-12mo-frontis
      (5n9,frontis rprd,box) 185.00
NARR OF SPOILED CHILD-David Baldwin & the General's Widow-
  NY-n.d.-16mo-42p,26p,(50)-frontis-plt (5p1) 4.50
NASATIR,A P,ed-Before Lewis & Clark-StL-1952-5 fldg maps-
  2 vols-1st ed   (5yy7,dj,mint) 30.00
--French Activities in Calif-(1945)-Stanford Univ Pr-559p-cl
    (5tt0) 20. (5h5) 22.50
--A French Journalist in Calif Gold Rush-1964-Talisman Pr
      (5x5,dj) 12.50
NASBY,PETROLEUM V-"Swingin Round the Cirkle"-Bost-1867-
  Lee&Shepard-299p-Nast illus
  (5i1,sl shaken) 7.50 (5mm2) 10. (5q8) 8.50
NASH,C W-Vertebrates of Ontario-Tor-1908-122,18,107p-plts
      (5aa0,pres) 7.50
NASH,CHAS EDGAR-The Lure of Long Beach-Long Beach-1926-
  170p-illus   (5m2)   6.00
--The Magic of Miami Beach-Phila-1938-David McKay-143p-illus
      (5x0)   6.50
NASH,E-Farmer's Practical Horse Farriery-Auburn-1858-197p-cl
      (5h1)   12.50
--same-NY-1858-197p,(3)-flex cl (5w5,soil) 10.00
NASH,E T-50 Puritan Ancestors-1902-182p (5t9) 25.00
NASH,JOHN B-Trials & Travels of Bro John Israel,ex John B Nash-
  Emoryville,W Va-1922-74p-4½x6½ (5r0) 10.00
NASH,JOHN HENRY-Catalogue of Books Printed by-compiled by
  Nell O'Day-SanFran-1937-4to-bds lea labl-500c prntd by Nash
      (4h4) 17.50
--Fascinating San Francisco-SanFran-1924-12mo-52p-illus-
  orig wrps-for Chamber of Comm-1st ed (5dd6) 9.50
--Legend and Fact in Development of a Fine Press-Oakland-1948-
  sq8vo-ltd to 235c,nbrd-prntd by Alfred&Lawton Kennedy
      (5h4,rub) 12.00
--Monastery of Visitation of Blessed Virgin Mary...Piedmont Hills,
  Calif-SanFran-1929-3to-wrps-tied-ltd to 500c,nbrd (5h4,f) 10.00
NASH,JOS-Mansions of England in the olden time-Lond-1906-
  The Studio-8p text & 105 plts-4to-cl (5m5) 18.00
NASH,MAUDE-Children's Occupations-Vol 2 of "Kindergarten
  Children's Hour"-Bost-1920-illus-339p (5n7) 2.50
NASH,OGDEN-The Christmas That Almost Wasn't-Bost-(1957)-
  Little,Brown-Imp 8vo-63p-col illus-blue cl-1st ed (5c8) 6.00
--Free Wheeling-NY-1931-illus-12mo-cl (4c2) 10.00
--Hard Lines-NY-1931-Simon&Schuster-12mo-99p,(3)-cl-illus by
  Soglow-1st ed of auth's 1st book (5gg6,fade) 25. (5j5) 15.00
NASH,RAY-Amer Writing Masters & Copybooks-Bost-1959-79p,36p-
  illus   (5t4)   10.00
--Printing as an Art-Cambr-1955-Harvard Univ Pr-designed by
  Bruce Rogers-ltd to 1500c   (5p7) 5.00
NASH,RICHARD-Life of, of Bath,Esq-Lond-1762-calf sides-
  prntd for Newbery-(Oliver Goldsmith)-1st ed (5d2,f,rbkd) 100.00
NASH,ROY-Survey of the Seminole Indians of Florida-8vo-88p-
  prntd wrps-map   (5g6) 7.50
NASH,WALLIS-Oregon,There & Back in 1877-Lond-1878-285p plus
  ads-illus-col map-1st ed   (5t3) 12.50
--Two Years in Oregon-NY-1882-frontis-illus-311p
     (5i3) 12.50 (4t3,f) 8.50
NASHVILLE & KNOXVILLE RR-Charter....passed Dec 22, 1853-
  Nashville-1854-disbnd   (5g4) 27.50
  NASHVL & NW RR -Nashville-1854 (5g4,lacks wrps) 27.50
--Reports of president &engineers-Nashville-1854-disbnd (5g4) 25.00
NASON,E-Gazetteer of Massachusetts-1874-576p (5mm3) 7.50
--same-1890-724p   (5t9) 7.50
NASON, E H-Old Hallowell,Maine,on the Kennebec-1909-359p-
  illus   (5t9)   15.00
NASON,ELIAS-History of Dunstable,Mass to 1873-1877-316p
      (5mm3)   8.50
--Life & Times of Chas Sumner-Bost-1874-Russell-356p-frontis
     (5qq8) 4.50 (5L3) 4.75
--Memoir of Mrs Susanna Rowson-Albany-1870-Joel Munsell-8vo-
  cl-scarce   (5b2) 22.50

NASON, ELIAS (continued)
--A Monogram on Our National Song-Albany-1869-8vo-Munsell
     (5ss5)   7.50

--Sir Chas Henry Frankland, Baronet-Albany-1865-4to-crimson
   lev g.t. designs-g.t.-by Jas Forbes-129p-lg papr copy,
   extra illus   (5j5, f bndg)   87.50
NASON, G W-History & Complete Roster of Mass Regiments,
   Minute Men of '61, etc-Bost-1910-orig gl-g.-413p
     (4j4, f, mint)   12.50
NASSAU, DR H H-Fetichism in West Africa-NY-1904-illus-1st ed
     (5x2)   15.00
NASSE, HERMANN-Jacques Callot-Leipzig-n.d.-In series, Vol 1-
   100p text-98 plts-lg4to-bds-cl sp-Klinkhardt & Biermann-
   scarce   (5m5, wn)   40.00
NASSOUR, SARAH-Skin of Gods-NY-(1938)-225p (4b2, dj tn)   3.00
NAST, THOS-Christmas Drawings for the Human Race-NY-1890-
   4to-pict cl-64 designs (5c8, wn, pres, lacks 1 plt, stns)   45.00
--The Fight at Dame Europa's School-NY-(1871)-33 illus
     (5x4) 20.   (5m1, autg)   12.50
NATE, JOS COOKMAN-The History of Sigma Chi Fraternity 1855
   to 1925-n.p.-n.d.-2 vols-illus-t.e.g. (5w9)   7.50
NATHAN, ANNE-The Man Who Stayed in Texas-NY-1941 (5a8) 6.50
NATHAN, ISAAC-Fugitive pieces & remin of Lord Byron-Lond-
   1829-8vo-orig bds-papr labl-prntd for Whittaker, Treacher-
   1st ed   (5i8, pres, sp wn)   80.00
NATHAN, GEO J-The Amer Credo-NY-1921-12mo-266p-cl-
   rev & enlrgd ed   (5m8)   8.00
--Art of the Night-NY-1928-1st ed   (5r9)   8.50
--A Book Without a Title-NY-1918-Philip Goodman-1st ed-scarce
     (5r9)   12.50
--The Intimate Notebooks-NY-1932-Knopf-326p (5p9)   4.50
--The Theatre Book of the Year, 1946, 47-NY-1947-1st ed
     (5t4) 4.50   (5r9, dj)   7.50
--same-1948, 49-NY-1949-Knopf-363p   (5p0)   5.00
NATHAN, SIR NATHANIEL-Economic Heresies-Bost-1909-
   HoughtonMiff-423p   (5p7)   6.00
NATHAN, MANFRED-Voortrekkers of So Africa-Lond-1937-
   Gordon & Gotch-photos-illus-maps-427p (4t5)   12.00
NATHAN, ROBT-A Cedar Box & Other Poems-1929-Bobbs, Merrill-
   cl bkstrp-ltd to 1500c, nbrd-1st ed (5ss9, sp fray)   10.00
--The Concert-NY-1940-House of Books-ltd to 250c, nbrd, autg
     (5F1, f)   12.50
--The Enchanted Voyage-NY-1936-Knopf-8vo-cl (5b2, fj)   6.50
--One More Spring-NY-1933-Knopf-8vo-dec cl (5b2, dj)   6.00
--The Orchid-Indnpls-(c 1931)-8vo-cl-Bobbs, Merrill (5b2, dj) 6.00
--Portrait of Jennie-NY-1940-Knopf-8vo-cl-1st prntng wi various
   typogr errors   (5b2, f, dj)   7.50
NATION, CARRY A-Use & Need of Life of-Top-1905-201, (1)p-cl
     (5h7)   10.00

NATION'S HERITAGE-Vol 1, #I-NY-1949-folio-illus-cl-
   Heritage Magazine Inc publ   (5t7)   30.00
NATION'S HERITAGE, THE-A Bi-Monthly-1949-(all publ in 6 nos.)
   Vol 1, #3, 4, 5, 6-4tos   (5p9)   80.00
NATIONAL ADVISORY COMM FOR AERONAUTICS-Reports of...
   Yrs 1916, 1919, 1922, 1924, 1925-Wash-orig wrps (5p0) 125.00
NATL AERONAUTICS COUNCIL-Wurplane Spotters Manual, Part A-
   NY-1943-62p-illus-orig wrps   (5mm8)   4.00
NATL ASSOC OF HOSIERY-& Underwear Manufacturers, Convention
   & exhibition, May 1916-1916-4to-illus (5L7, sp wn)   10.00
NATL ASSOC OF TEACHERS IN COLORED SCHOOLS-Proceedings
   of 4th Annual Session at Hampton Insti Aug 1, 2, 1907-160p-
   wrps-illus   (5x2)   35.00
NATL BAPTISTS CONVENTION-Official program Annual Session
   Sept 1960-Phila-172p-wrps-4to-illus (5x2)   10.00
NATL CATHOLIC WELFARE CONFERENCE-Spanish Speaking of
   the SW-Wash-n.d.-Social Action Dept-8vo-44p-Report of
   Jul 20 to 23, 1943   (4a3, wrps)   12.50
NATL CITY CO-Over a Century of Railroading-NY-1929-36p-
   illus-fldg bds   (5hh6)   4.50
NATL CIVIC FEDERATION-Comm Regu of Public Utilities,
   Compilation & analysis of laws of 43 states & Fed gov-1913
     (5L7)   25.00
NATL CIVIL SERVICE REFORM LEAGUE-Proceedings at Annual
   Meeting-NY-1909-180p-wrps   (5q8)   6.00
NATL CLOAK & SUIT CO-Summer Styles for 1910, "National" Style
   Book for Sept 1911-NY-1910-52, 224p-8vo-pict wrps-illus
     (5r7)   35.00
NATL COOK BOOK-by a Lady of Phila-Phila-1855-301, 9p-
   5th ed   (5c0, cov dtchd)   25.00
NATL COMMERCIAL CONVENTION-Proceedings of the, Feb 1868-
   Bost-1868-251p-black cl-JHEastburn's Pr (5a9, chip)   8.50
NATL CONVENTION OF BUSINESS MEN-Proceedings of, at
   Phila Aug 1st-Phila-1837-wrps   (5g4)   10.00

NATL COUNCIL OF STATE GARDEN CLUBS-Cook Book-n.p.-1935-
   143p-8vo-1st prntng-fabr, ring bnd (5g9)   5.00
NATL DISTILLERS PRODUCTS CORP-Mine Host's Handbook-NY-1934-
   27p, (1)-12mo-wrps-illus   (5w1, soil)   2.00
NATL ECONOMIC LEAGUE-The Initiative & Referendum-Bost-
   (1912)-71p   (5q8)   3.50
NATL GALLERY LONDON-Art Treasures-NY-(1955)-folio-196p-
   100 col illus   (5xx7, dj)   17.50
NATL GEOGRAPHIC MAGAZINE-Wash-Jan to Dec 1908-illus-
   Vol 19-hf lea   (5q0, lacks top sp)   10.00
--same-1909-bnd vol(12 issues)-qtr lea (5u9, cov loose)   13.50
--same-May 1905 thru 1953-8 issues unbnd-89 vol bnd in black g.
   tooled lea-8 bnd special issues-cumulative cl bnd index from
   1899-1936, 1937 supp-Physiographic Regions of US, May 1895,
   orig brn wrps (5u9, f) post $75 extra   1,250.00
--same-run of 60 vols-Vol 35, 1919 thru Vol 94, 1948 plus 2 cumul
   index cols-buck & bds   (5cc1) post extra   350.00
--same-Jan 1948 thru Sept 1967(lacking 7 issues)-together 237 issues-
   wrps-shipment in USA   (5w4)   135.00
--same-Cumulative Index 1899 to 1936-Wash-1948-illus-tall 8vo
     (4b6)   35.00
NATL GEOGRAPHIC SOC-America's Wonderlands, Nat'l Parks-
   Wash-1959-509p-illus   (5p9)   7.50
--Book of Birds-Wash-19 7-2 vols-R8vo-cl-col illus (5t5)   15.00
--Book of Birds-Wash-(1939)-2 vols-740p-950 col plts
     (5t2, vf, 5ss8)   17.50
--Book of Dogs-Wash-1927-illus-109p (5ss8, shaken)   7.50
--Book of Fishes-Wash-1924-243p-illus   (5t7)   5.00
--Book of Fishes-1939-4to-367p-443 col photos-rev & enlrgd ed
     (5bb8) 6.50   (5t2)   7.50
--Book of Wild Flowers-Wash-1924-243p-col plts (5p7)   7.50
--same-Wash-1933-243p-col plts   (5ss1)   8.50
--Indian of the Americas-Wash-(1957)-424p plus index-illus-
   3rd prntng   (5t3)   6.50
--Our Insect Friends & Foes & Spiders-Wash-1935-258p-photos-cl
     (5cc1, vg)   8.50
--World in Your Garden-1959-col i!lus   (5qq7)   3.50
NATL GUARDSMAN-NY-Sat, Sept 11, 1869-Vol 1, #1, newspaper-
   8p   (5a0, mint)   10.00
NATL GUARDSMAN, THE-Vol 1 to Vol 2, #4, Aug 1, 1877 to
   Nov 1, 1878-NY-284p-orig 3 qrtrs roan-cl sides-4to-
   rare periodical   (5m3)   75.00
NATL HIST CO-History of Howard & Cooper Counties, Mo-StL-
   1883-illus-lea-1166p-1st ed-v scarce (4t3)   75.00
NATL HORSE SHOW-1946, Official Magazine-NY-1946-4to-146p-
   papr   (5t7)   5.00
NATL INSTI FOR PROMOTING INDUSTRY IN THE US-Circular
   & Address of-NY-1820-JSeymour-28p-orig plain wrps-
   1st ed-resolutions   (5m3, f)   27.50
NATL LIFE MAGAZINE-Al Smith's Life Story-NY-1928-
   Vol 1, #1-illus   (5b9, vf)   10.00
NATL LIVE STOCK ASSOC-of the US, Constitution & Bylaws-
   n.p.-n.d.-(1890s?)-(2p)-self cov (5L5, ex-libr)   12.50
NATL LOAN FUND LIFE ASSURANCE SOC-Premium tables,
   instructions etc-NY-Oct, 1849-36p-prntd wrps
     (5h8, lacks bk wrp)   12.50
NATL MANPOWER COUNCIL-Womanpower...statement by-NY-
   1957-371p-charts   (5w4, dj)   4.00
NATL NEGRO HEALTH WEEK-14th Annual Observance, Annual
   Tuskegee Negro Conference-Wash-1928-24p-wrps (5x2) 7.50
NATL ORANGE SHOW-Official Program-SanBernardino-Feb 20 to
   28, 1917-24p-wrps   (5yy3)   10.00
NATL ORANGE SHOW-Souvenir Magazine Edition of Evening Index-
   SanBernardino-1911-64p-illus-wrps (5yy3)   50.00
NATL PARKS PORTFOLIO-n.p.-n.d.-240p-photos-no t. pg-
   lea bkstrp-cors   (5s4, ex-libr)   7.50
NATL PARK SERVICE-Glacier Nat'l Park, Montana-Wash-1935-42p-
   wrps-fldg map rear   (5ss1)   2.50
--Mt McKinley Nat'l Park, Alaska-Wash-1934-28p (5ss1)   2.50
NATL PRIMER-Adapted to Capacities of Young Beginners-Balt-
   1823-MBRoberts-12mo-36p-t. pg reads "The New England Primer"-
   Phila-Griggs&Dickinson-n.d. (4F6, cov wn, crude reprd) 20.00
NATL PUBLISHING CO-RR, Post Office, Township & Co Map of
   Mass, R I & Conn-Bost-1900-36x38" lin bkd fld to 8vo-cl cov
     (5r7)   20.00
NATL REPUBLICAN CONVENTION-Journal of...Worcester,
   Oct 11, 1832-Bost-1832-Stimpson&Clapp-8vo-75p-sewed
     (5j5)   15.00
NATL SPORTSMAN-Sporting Goods Encyclopedia-Bost-(ca 1908)-
   12mo-384p-orig wrps   (5m6)   10.00
NATL SPORTSMAN-Vols 18, 19-Jan, 1907 to Dec, 1907-Bost-1907-
   lg8vo-cl-illus   (5t2)   4.00
NATL SUPPLY CO-Catalog D 1918-Tol-1918-1071p-cl
     (5h7, sl soil)   5.00

NATL WAR LABOR BD-Industry Statements Presented to Steel Panel
of-1944-2 vols   (5r4)   17.50
NATL WOMAN SUFFRAGE ASSN-Report of Council of Women ...
Wash, Mar 25 to Apr 1, 1888-Wash-1888-471p-frontis
(5w4, fade, edge wn)   7.50
NATURAL HISTORY OF BEASTS-Northampton-n.d.-Metcalf-
16mo-24p-orig prntd wrps-wdcuts   (5rr2, fox)   9.00
NATURAL HISTORY OF FISHES, A-40 wdcuts-Alnwick-c1815-
W Davison-12mo-36p-wrps-hand col illus-1st ed-scarce
(5v2, vg)   65.00
NATURAL HISTORY-Of Globe, Man, Beasts, Birds, Fishes, Reptiles,
Insects & Plants from writing of Buffon, Cuvier, Lacepede-Phila-
1831-illus-5 vols-New ed   (5yy0)   24.00
NATURAL HISTORY OF REMARKABLE BIRDS-Dublin-1821-16mo-
171p-20 plts(9 are duplicate)   (5v0, reprd)   22.50
NATURAL HISTORY OF REMARKABLE TREES, SHRUBS & PLANTS-
Dublin-1821-G Bull-12mo-sheep-178p-plts   (4a8, wn)   5.00
NATURALIST'S LIBRARY-Natural History of Ordinary Cetacea or
Whales-Edinb-1837-sm12mo-264p-calf-port-32 col plts
(5t0)   20.00
NATURE-Bost-1836-12mo-cl-1st ed of Emerson's 1st book-
1st issue, wi pg 94 misnbrd-copy of 2nd issue included
(5gg6, wn, lacks e.p.)   50.00
NATURE LOVERS LIBRARY-NY-(1917)1923-Vols 1 thru 6-4to-cl-
6 vols   (5z9, vf)   30.00
NATURE'S REMEDIES-Early Hist & Uses of Botanic Drugs-
Hammond-(1934)-200p-col plts-cl-(Jos Meyer)   (5h1)   4.00
NAUDEUS, GABRIEL-Instructions Concerning Erecting of a Library-
Camb-1903-12mo-bds&lea-designed by Bruce Rogers-ltd to
419c   (5d5, unopnd)   15.00
NAUMAN, MARY D-Eva's adventures in shadow land-Phila-1872-
Lippincott-illus-1st ed   (5m2)   7.50
NAUS, ALFRED R-West of the Mississippi-n.d.-73p-illus (5k2)   4.00
NAUTICAL REMINISCENCES-Providence-1832-216p-orig bds-
papr labl-(N Ames)-cl shelfbk-1st ed   (5m3)   27.50
NAUVOO GUIDE-Chig-1939-wrps-WPA-49p(2)p-scarce (5ff7)   12.50
NAVAJO SCHOOL OF INDIAN BASKETRY-Indian Basket Weaving-
LosAng-1903-103p-illus-woven cl   (5n7)   6.50
NAVAL & MILITARY TROPHIES & PERSONAL RELICS OF
BRITISH HEROES-Lond-1896-Nimmo-folio-orig cl-g.-36 col plts-
(5i4, sp wn)   85.00
NAVAL AVIATION-Textbk-Annap-(1933)-88p-illus-4to
(5s1, sl soil, ex-libr)   3.50
NAVAL COURTS & BOARDS-Navy Dept, Wash-1937-582p
lea   (5s1)   4.00
NAVAL ENCYCLOPEDIA-Phila-1884-L R Hammersly-cl-4to-872p-
15p ads   (4L9, hng rprd)   25.00
NAVAL LEADERSHIP-for Instruction of Midshipmen-Annap-(1952)-
324p-illus   (5s1)   3.00
NAVAL MACHINERY-Annap-(1914)-illus-about 576p-plans
(5s1, f)   6.00
NAVAL MONUMENT, THE-Accounts of All Battles Fought Betw
Navies of US & Great Britain...Annexed Naval Register-Bost-
1816-320p-sheep-1st ed-26 plts-errata slip   (5m3, sl tn)   30.00
NAVAL ORIENTATION-Bur Naval Personnel-n.p.-1948-621p-
wrps-illus-stitchd-10x8"   (5s1, hng rprd)   6.00
NAVAL REGISTER OF US-Bost-1815-34p-wrps-stitchd-rare
(5s1, pres, fox, ex-libr)   30.00
NAVAL TEMPLE, THE-Bost-1816-plts-calf (5g4, cracking, sl stns)   25.00
NAVIGATION-or Art of Sailing upon the Sea-Lond-1755-12mo-
calf-7 plts-208p, (1), (112), (2)   (5ss2)   65.00
NAVIGATION LAWS OF USA-Wash-1915-Dept Commer, Bur
Marine Insp, Navy-585p   (5s1)   4.00
NAVARETTE, MARTIN FERNANDEZ DE-Coleccion de los Viages
y descubrimientos, que hicieron por mar los Espanoles desde
fines del Siglo 15...Espanoles en Indias-Madrid-1825 to 1837-
5 vols-8vo-hf calf-3 fldg maps-28 ports   (5dd4)   190.00
NAVIN, THOS R-Whitin Machine Works Since 1831-Cambr-1950-
654p-illus   (5y2)   13.50
NAVY AT WAR, THE-Paintings & Drawings by Combat Artists-
NY-(1943)-Baldwin, text- 159p   (5t7, dj)   10.00
NAVY DEPT BULLETIN-Cum Ed-1948-Wash-645p-4to-illus (5s1)   6.00
NAYLOR, ROBT A-Across the Atlantic-Lond-1893-sm4to-305p
(5a1)   6.00
NAYLOR, WILSON S-Daybreak in the Dark Continent-NY-1905-
maps-photos-315p-2nd ed-Young Peoples Mis Movmt (4t5)   5.00
NEAD, PETER-Primitive Christianity -Staunton-1834-223p-
Harper prntr-lea   (4a4, fox)   5.00
NEAL, BIGELOW-Last of the Thundering Herd-NY-1933-287p-
illus   (5s4, dj)   4.00
NEAL, DAN'L-History of New England etc-Lond-1720-2 vols-
712p-fldg map-orig bds   (5L3, rbkd)   175.00

NEAL, DAN'L   (continued)
--same-Lond-1747-2 vols-8vo-hf mor-fldg map-for Ward,
Longman et al-2nd ed wi additions   (5n9)   150.00
--History of the Puritans-Lond-1732 to 1738-4 vols (5w5, rbnd)   50.00
--same-wi additional notes by Choules-NY-1843-2 vols-illus-
3 qrtrs lea   (5m3)   20.00
NEAL, JOHN-The down Easters etc-NY-1822-Harper-2 vols-12mo-
orig cl-papr labls-1st ed   (5x1, labl chip, box)   175.00
--Portland, Illustrated-Portl-1874-W S Jones, Pub-12mo-cl-160p
(4t1)   12.50
--True Womanhood, a Tale-Bost-1859-8vo-cl-1st ed
(5t2, libr labl)   8.75
--Wandering Recollections of a somewhat busy life-Bost-1869-
Robts Bros-8vo-orig cl-1st ed   (5i0, sl wn sp)   22.50
NEAL, JOS C-Charcoal sketches-Phila-1838-Carey & Hart-12mo-
orig figured cl-papr labl-4 etchings on buff papr-1st ed
(5i9, sl fox)   40.00
NEAL, MARIE C-In Honolulu Gardens-Honolulu-1929-12mo-illus-
336p-papr-Bishop Museum Publ 13 (5t7) 6.   (5h5, f)   7.50
NEAL, T A-Neal Record, Desc of John Neale, Early Settler of
Salem, Mass-1856-30p   (5mm3)   7.50
NEAL, W A-Illus History of Missouri Engineer & 25th Inf-Chig-
1889-305p-cl   (5jj9)   45.00
NEALE, JOHN MASON-Good King Wenceslas-Birmingham-1895-
Cornish Brs-illus-bds-1st ed   (5ss3, sp stn, rub)   10.00
NEALE, WALTER-The Betrayal, a Novel-NY & Wash-1910-8vo-cl
(5b2, cov spots)   4.50
NEAME, J ARMSTRONG-Among the Meadow & Alpine Flowers of
Northern Italy-Lond-(1937)-192p-16 col plts   (5s7)   4.50
NEANDER, AUGUSTUS-Gen'l History of Christian Religion & Church-
(Bohn)-1853 to 58-9 vols bnd in 10   (5tt5, bds wn)   17.50
NEAR HOME-Countries of Europe Described-NY-1854-16mo-
cl-wdcuts-orig ed   (5p5)   15.00
NEARING, HELEN-The Maple Sugar Book-NY-(1950)-illus-271p
(5g9)   4.50
NEARING, S-Black America-NY-1929-illus-1st ed   (5x2)   25.00
--Free Born-NY-1932-237p-wrps-Urquhart Pr   (5x2)   8.50
NEARING, SCOTT-Glimpses of the Soviet Republic-NY-(1926)-
32p-wrps-Social Science Publ   (5r0)   7.50
--War-NY-c1931   (5x7)   3.00
NEBRASKA-Check List of Nebraska Non Documentary Imprints,
1847 to 1876-Lincoln-1942-WPA-132p-stiff wrps (5yy1)   25.00
NEBRASKA, GUIDE TO CORNHUSKER STATE-NY-1939-illus-
fldg pkt map-412p plus index-1st ed-scarce-Amer Guide Ser-
WPA   (4L5)   10.00
NEBRASKA HIST SOC-Proceedings & collections-Vol 1, #3, ser 2,
Jan 1895-orig wrps-frontis   (5m2)   7.50
NEBRASKA-History of State of-Chig-1882-1506p-Andreas, publ-
fldg map-4to-illus-dbl column
(5dd9, rbnd, t. & 4p of index in facs)   40.00
NEBRASKA-Illustrated Review showing Commercial, Indus, Agric
& Hist Development of State of-Chig-(ca1917)-192 triple col pgs-
photos-col maps-1st 48p only on Nebraska-remainder an atlas-
rare   (5L0)   35.00
NEBRASKA-Inventory of County Archives of-Gosper Co, #37-
(Elwood)-Lincoln-1940-152p plus index-stiff wrps-1st ed (5L0)15.00
--same-Lincoln-1931- #47-Howard Co-(St Paul)-stiff wrps (5L0)   15.00
--same-Lincoln-1941- #58-Loup Co(Taylor)-stiff wrps (5L0)   15.00
--same-Lincoln-1941-#61-Merrick Co(Central Cty)-stiff wrps
(5L0)   15.00
NEBRASKA LAW REVIEW-1922 to 69-Vol 1 thru 48
(5rr4, recent rbnd)   850.00
NEBRASKA LAWS-Joint Resolu & Mem passed at 14th Session of
Legislative Assembly of State, Lincoln, Jan 2, 1877-StJos, Mo-
1877-8vo-orig sheep-lea labl-296p-Steam Prntng
(5j5, labl scuff)   17.50
NEBRASKA, NORTHEASTRN-Illus Biographical Album of-Phila-
1893-599p plus 123p illus-(Nat'l Publ Co)-1st ed-rare (5t3)   100.00
NEBRASKA-A Poem, Personal & Political-Cleve-1854-12mo-
mrbld bds-lea bk   (5b2, fade)   12.50
NEBRASKA STATE HISTORICAL SOC-Proceedings & Collections of-
Vol 15-Lincoln-1907-422p-black cl   (5a0) 10. (5F9, sl wn)   7.50
NEBRASKA STATE HISTORICAL SOC-Transactions & Reports-Vol 1
& 2-Lincoln-1885, 1887   (5dd6, f)   20.00
NEBRASKA TERRITORY-1st Annual Report of Comm of Common
Schools of...to 6th Legisl Assembly-1860 (5L7, ex-libr, sl fray)35.00
NEBRASKA TERR-Laws, Joint Resolutions & Memorials passed at
3rd Session of Legis Assembly of...at Omaha Cty, N T, Jan 5-
Brownville-310p   (5k0, lacks index pg)   25.00
--same-4th Session-OmahaCty-1858-72p-wrps   (4t3)   10.00
--same-9th Session-OmahaCty-1864-315p-prntd wrps (5j6, fox)   16.00
NECESSITY OF REPEALING AMER STAMP ACT-Lond-1766-Almon-
sm4to-disbnd-wrps-1st ed   (5n2)   125.00

NECK,JACOB VAN-Zwo underscheidliche newe Schiffarten(sic)-
Frankfurt-1605-Richtern-4to-calf-10 fldg plts-1st German ed
(5n9) 1,800.00

NECKER,ALBERTINE-Study of the Life of Woman-1833-buck
(5L7,rbnd) 7.50

NEEDHAM,J G-Life of Inland Waters-Ithaca-1916-illus-cl-8vo-
438p (4p5,stn,hng crack) 5.00

NEEDLEWORK GUILD COOK BOOK-Jamestn-1907-pp(12),314p,
(14 blanks)-photo (5c4,stn,hng crack) 6.50
--same-NY-1925-412p-3rd ed-1st Presby Church (5c4) 4.00

NEEL,F P W-Wilford,Williford Family Treks Into Amer-1959-
Vol 2(on sp)-437p,735p (5t9) 25.00

NEELY,FLORA-Handbook for the Kitchen & Housekeeper's Guide-
NewRochelle-(1878,1910)-364p-3rd ed,rev (5c0) 5.00

NEESER,ROBT W,ed-Dispatches of Molyneux Shuldham,Vice Admiral-
NY-1913-330p-ltd to 300c (4m2) 27.50
--Landsman's Log-NewHav-1913-199p-photos (5s1) 6.00
--Letters & Papers Relating to Cruises of Gustavus Conyngham-NY-
1915-Naval Hist Soc-241p-bds-vel bk-illus-g.t.-ltd to 600c
(5qq8,mint) 7.50
--Our Many Sided Navy-NewHav-1914-41 photos (5c1) 10.00
--Our Navy & Next War-NY-1915-205p (5s1,ex-libr) 2.50

NEFF,ANDREW L-History of Utah,1847 to 1869-SaltLkCty-c1940-
Deseret News Pr-cl-8vo-955p (4t1) 15. (5jj1,f) 25.00

NEFF,EMERY-Carlyle & Mill,Mystic & Utilitarian-NY-1924-
8vo-cl-334p (5t0,pres) 7.50

NEFF,JACOB K-Army & Navy of America-Phila-1845-Gable-624p-
illus-fldg plts-cl fldg frontis (5mm8,rbnd) 17.50 (5h9,sl rub) 22.50

NEFF,MARY K-Personal Memoirs of H P Blavatsky-NY-1937-
12 illus (5F0) 5.00

NEFF,PAT-Battles of Peace-FtWorth-1925-324p (4a5,autg) 10.00

NEFZAOUI-Le Jardin Perfume du Cheikh Nefzaoui-Paris-1886-
lea & bds-ltd to 220c,nbrd (5tt2,vg) 35.00

NEGRO AMERICANS-Report of Committee on Negro Amer-
Home Missions Council-1921-16p-wrps (5x2) 10.00

NEGRO COMMUNITY-Works in Behalf of Its Families-Wash-
1942-Office of Price Admin-8p-wrps (5x2) 8.50

NEGRO EDUCATION-Study of priv & higher schools for colored
people in the US-Wash-1917-sm4to (5x2) 40.00

NEGRO HANDBOOK-Compiled by Editors of Ebony-Chig-1966
(5x2,mint) 12.50

NEGRO HERITAGE LIBRARY-NY-1965-5 vols-4to-illus-1st ed
(5x2) 37.50

NEGRO IN CHICAGO-Chig-1922-thk R8vo-illus-fldouts-1st ed
(5x2) 50.00

NEGRO IN RICHMOND,VIRG-1929-Richmond Counc of Soc
Agencies-136p-wrps (5x2) 35.00

NEGRO IN VIRGINIA-NY-1940-380p-cl-WPA (5h1,dj) 10.00

NEGRO QUESTION-NY-ca1915-15p-wrps (5x2) 25.00

NEGRO RURAL FAMILY-Learns to Use Consumer Services of Its
Gov-Wash-1942-Office of Price Admin-13p-wrps (5x2) 10.00

NEGRO TYPES-Seen by the Camera-Lond-ca1920-64 photos-bds
(5x2) 8.00

NEGRO WHO'S WHO IN CALIFORNIA-1948-4to-illus (5x2) 27.50

NEGROES IN THE US,1920 to 1932-Wash-1935-4to (5x2) 45.00

NEHRLING,ARNO-Peonies,Outdoors & In-NY-(1960)-288p-
illus (5s7) 4.50

NEHRLING,DR HENRY-The Plant World in Florida-NY-1933-
Macm-A&E Kay,ed-304p-illus (5x0) 12.50

NEHRU,JAWAHARLAL- he Discovery of India-Calcutta-1946
(5x7) 6.50

NEIBARGER,WALT,ed-Sunflower Petals-Tonganoxie-1938-photos-
no pagination(30p) photos-stapled-self cov (5t3,f) 25.00

NEIDE,CHAS A-The Canoe Aurora-NY-1885-cl-215p
(4i2,ex-libr) 8.50

NEIDER,CHAS,ed-The Great West-NY-(1958)-illus-maps-4to-
457p (5t4) 7.50 (4b3) 12.50

NEIDHARD,C-Crotalus Horridus-NY-1868-cl-90p-8vo-2nd enlgd ed-
scarce (4p6,fox) 47.50

NEIDLINGER,W H-Small Songs for Small Singers-NY-c1896-4to-
57p-Schirmer-pict bds-col illus & music
(5p1,cor wn) 17.50

NEIGHBORHOOD COOK BK-Council of Jewish Women-Portl-
(1912)-334p (5c4,hng crack) 5.00

NEIHARDT,JOHN G-Black Elk Speaks-Morrow-1932-Standing Bear,
illus-1st ed (4k5,dj,f) 22.50

NEIHARDT,JOHN G-A Bundle of Myrrh-NY-1907-12mo-76p-
hf cl bds-illus-e.p. (5dd9) 15.00
--Collected Poems of-NY-1926-2 vols-8vo-cl-Macmillan-
ltd to 250 sets,autg (5ss3) 45.00
--The Divine Enchantment,a Mystical Poem-NY-1900-12mo-cl-
1st ed of auth's 1st book (5gg6) 250.00
--Indian Tales & Others-NY-1926-1st ed-306p (5t3) 6.50

NEIHARDT,JOHN G (continued)
--Poetic Values,their reality & our need of them-NY-1925-
12mo-154p (5m2) 5. (5dd9) 10.00
--The River & I-NY-1910-illus-325p-1st ed
(5u3) 7.50 (5t3,autg,4b3,autg) 15.00
--same-NY-1927-199p-photos (5dd4) 10. (5s4) 6. (5nn1) 7.00
--The Song of the Indian Wars-NY-1925-232p-illus-1st ed (5dd6)15.00
--same-NY-1925-8vo-bds&buck-illus by Allen True-Macmillan-
ltd to 500c,autg (5ss3) 35.00
--The Song of 3 Friends & The Song of Hugh Glass-NY-1924-12mo-
360p (5dd5) 15.00
--Splendid Wayfaring-1920 (5L7) 12.50
--Two Mothers-NY-1921-82p-1st ed (5L0) 7.50
--When the Tree Flowered-1951 (5L7) 6.00

NEIL,J E S-From Generation to Generation,Gen of Dwight Stone
& Olive Evans-1907-169p (5mm3) 25.00

NEIL,MARION H-Candies & Bonbons & How to Make Them-Phila-
(1913)-286p-illus (5g9) 5.00
--Canning,Preserving & Pickling-Phila-(1914)-284p-illus
(5g9,crack,rub) 2.50 (5g9) 5.00
--How to Cook in Casserole Dishes-Phila-(1912)-252p-illus
(5c0) 4. (5g9) 5.00
--Salads,Sandwiches & Chafing Dish Recipes-Phila-(1916)-262p-
illus (5g9) 4.50
--65 Delicious Dishes Made with Bread-n.p.-1919-32p-illus
(5g9) 3.00

NEILL,MISS E-The Every Day Cook Book & Encyclopedia-1888-
"Lord&Taylor's Family Cook Book"-315p-prntd wrps-
rear cov ad (5c0,chip) 7.50

NEILL,EDW D-Address at annual meeting of Old Settlers Assn-
Minneap-(1872)-(wrpr title) (5g3,f) 15.00
--The Founders of Maryland as Portrayed in Manuscripts,Provincial
Records & Early Doc-Albany-1876-Munsell-8vo-orig wrps-
1st ed (5m2,sl stn) 10. (5m6,sl tn) 22.50
--Glimpses of Nation's Struggle-StPaul-1890-pt calf-443p-
2nd series (5q0) 17.50
--History of Minnesota etc-Phila-1858-628p-illus-fldg map-
hf lea-1st ed (5i3,cracked) 20.00
--same-Mnpls-1882-Hist Soc-8vo-3 qtr lea-928p,10p,16p,4p
(4t1) 15.00

NEILL,JOHN-of Lewes,Del,1739 & His Desc-1875-127p (5mm3) 20.00

NEILL,PATRICK-The Practical Fruit, Flower & Vegetable Gardener's
Companion,with a Calendar-Adapted to US-NY-1859-408p-
illus (5s7,rprd) 6.50

NEILSON,CHAS-Burgoyne's Campaign & Memorable Battles of
Bemis's Heights-Bemis Heights-1926-12mo-cl-247p (5t2) 5.00
--Original,Compiled & Corr Account of Burgoyne's Campaign, &
Memorable Battles of Bemis's Heights-Albany-1844-Munsell-292p-
12mo-cl-fldg map-1st ed (5t4) 15. (5j5,wn,map tn) 12.50

NEILSON,HARRY B-The Fox's Frolic or A Day With Topsy Turvy
Hunt-obl 4to (5v2,shake) 12.50

NEILSON,DR J L HUBERT-Remin of War of 1812 to 14-Kingston-
1895-19p-orig prntd wrps-priv prntd-ltd to 30c (5w8) 45.00

NEILSON,WM A-The Facts About Shakespeare-NY-1918-273p-
frontis-sm12mo (5w9) 5.00

NEISON,ADRIAN-Practical Boat Building for Amateurs-NY-
1901-108p-illus (5s1) 2.50

NEITZEL,WILMERE JORDAN,ed-Flora & Fauna of Solano Co,
Calif-Fairfield-(1965)-8vo-cl-col illus-o.p. (5F5) 5.00

NEKLER,I-Die Bereitung Pflege und Unterfuchung Des Weines-
Stuttgart-(1930)-535p,(2)-illus (5w1) 16.50

NELLES,ANNIE-Or, the Life of a Book Agent-Cinn-1868-385p-
frontis-priv pub (5w7,pgs wtrstn) 9.50

NELMS,HENNING-A Primer of Stagecraft-NY-1941-158p-illus-
Dramatists Play Serv (5p0) 4.50

NELSON,B H-The 14th Amendment & the Negro Since 1920-
NY-1966 (5x2,mint) 7.50

NELSON,BRUCE-Land of the Dacotahs-(1946)-Univ of Minn Pr
(5x5,dj) 12.50
--same-Mnpls-(1947)-2nd prntd-photos (4t3,dj) 6.00

NELSON,DENYS-Fort Langley,1827 to 1927-Vancouver-1927-
wrps-ports-31p (4d1) 7.50 (5dd7) 8.00

NELSON,DICK-Only a Cow Country at one Time-n.p.-1951-
illus-105p-wrps-1st ed (4t3,autg) 12.50
--Wyo Has a Distinguished Heritage & Its Big Horn Basin-
(SanDiego-1957)-76p-map-wrps-1st ed (4t3,f) 7.50

NELSON,EDNA DEU PREE-O'Higgins & Don Bernardo-NY-1954-
Dutton-384p (5v6) 3.00

NELSON,EDW W-Report on Natural Hist Collections Made in
Alaska-Wash-1887-4to-Arctic Ser Sig Serv Publ #111-336p-
21 plts(12 col) (5ss1,pres) 30.00
--same-Wash-1887-Henshaw,ed-337p-21 plts(12 col) (4p5) 47.50

NELSON, GEO E, ed-Cavalcade of the North-NY-1958-8vo-
cl-640p-1st ed   (5g0)   5.00

NELSON, H L-Uniforms of the US Army-NY-(1959)-51p plus
44 col plts-folio-Yoseloff-paintings by H A Ogden (5c3) 15.00

NELSON, HARRIET S-Fruits & Their Cookery-NY-(1921)-209p-
(5c0)   4.50

NELSON, HORACE-Nelson's Amer Lancet, a Monthly Journal of
Practical Medicine-Vols 9 to 11-Plattsburgh-Apr 1854 to
Sept 1855   (5t4)   20.00

NELSON, J RALEIGH-Lady Unafraid-Caldwell-1951-cl-278p
(4i2, dj, autg)   7.50

NELSON, JAS P-Balla & Other Va Stories-Richm-1914-225p-cl
(5h7, pres)   5.00

NELSON, JOHN-Rhythm for Rain-Houghton-1937 (5F1, f, dj) 10.00

NELSON, LOWRY-Mormon Village, a Pattern & Technique of
Land Settlement-SaltLkCty-1952-plts-maps-296p (5dd0) 7.50

--Rural Cuba-Minnpls-(1951)-U of Minn Pr-8vo-cl-2nd prntg
(4a3)   8.50

NELSON, M E E -Desc of James Ensign & Wife Sarah Elson-(1960)-
809p, 68p   (5mm3)   15.00

NELSON, MARGARET-Yearbook of Contemporary Poetry, 1937-
NY-(1937)-Avon Hse   (5ss9, vg)   5.00

NELSON, O N-Hist of Scandinavians & Sucessful Scandinavians-
Mpls-1904-Vols 1 & 2 in 1 vol-illus-518p & 280p (5a9, f) 15.00

NELSON, RAPHAEL-Cries & Criers of Old London-Lond-(Oct 1941)-
Collins-4to-dec cl-30p wdblocks   (5c8)   12.50

NELSON, ROBT-Address to Persons of Quality & Estate-Lond-
for R S -1715-267p, 55p, (7)-calf-1st ed (5a1, sl wn) 35.00

NELSON, T-The Sin of the Prophet-Bost-1952-1st ed (5x2, dj) 4.00

NELSON, T O, comp-Plat Book of Polk County, Minn-FergusFalls-
(1946)-folio-wrps-62p   (4t1)   10.00

NELSON, THOS S-A full report of trial of Wm P Darnes...for
death of Andrew J Davis in StLouis, 1840-Bost-1841-wrps-
2nd ed   (5g8, lacks bk wrp)   7.50

NELSON, W R-Hist of Goshen, N Hamp-1957-471p (5mm3) 10.00

NELSON, WM-Calendar of New Jersey Wills, Vol 1, 1670 to 1730-
Paterson-1901-662p-indexes   (5h9)   17.50

--Josiah Hornblower & the first steam engine in Amer with Gen-
1883-80p-unbnd   (5mm3)   10.00

--The N J Coast in 3 Centuries-NY-1902-3 vols-4to-illus-
v scarce   (5m2)   45.00

--Edw Antill, NY Merchant of 17th Cent & Desc-1899-36p
(5mm3)   12.50

--Personal Names of Indians of NJ-Paterson-1904-ltd to 250c
(4m2, unopened)   17.50

NELSON, WM H· Alluring Arizona-SanFran-1927-plts-12mo-146p-
1st ed   (5dd4)   7.50

--same-SanFran-1929-illus   (4a5) 4.   (5n4)   4.50

--Fields of Glory-NY-c1960-316p-illus (5k0, dj) 10. (5w4, dj) 8.50

NELSON, WM ROCKHILL-Members of the Staff of Kansas City
Star-Cambr-1915-274p-1st ed   (5k0)   10.00

NELSON, WM STUART, ed-The Christian Way in Race Relations-
NY-1948-8vo-cl-1st ed   (5p5, dj)   12.50

NELSON'S GUIDE-To Lake George & Lake Champlain-Lond-1866-
48p-plts-col views   (5t4)   15.00

--same-Lond-1868-24mo-col plts   (5g4, ex-libr)   7.50

--same-Lond-1869-48p-col views   (5t4, hng weak)   10.00

--same-Lond-1896-16mo-48p-illus   (5xx7)   10.00

NELSON'S NORTHERN LANCET-and Amer Journal of Medical
Jurisprudence, Vol 5 to 8-Plattsburgh-Jan 1852 to Feb 1854
(5t4)   20.00

NELSON'S PICTORIAL GUIDE BOOKS-Central Pacific RR, a Trip
Across North Amer Continent from Ogden to SanFran-NY-
n.d.-(ca 1870)-32 double col pgs plus 12 tinted views-map
(5L2)   10.00

--same-SaltLkCty with Sketch of Route of Central Pacific RR from
Omaha to SaltLkCty, thence to SanFran-Lond, Edinb, NY &
SaltLkCty-n.d.-31p-col photos   (5L2)   3.50

--same-Union Pacific RR trip across North Amer Continent from
Omaha to Ogden-NY-n.d.(ca 1871)-46 dbl col pgs plus 12
tinted views-map   (5L2)   10.00

NEMCOVA, BOZENA-The Disobedient Kids & other CzechoSlovak
Fairy Tales-Prague-1921-B Koci-(48p)-4to-pict bds-illus
(5p1, lacks)   8.50

NEMEROV, HOWARD-Federigo or the Power of Love-Bost-(1954)-
bds-cl bk-1st ed   (5ss7, mint, dj)   7.50

--Storm Windows-n.p.-1965-(Perishable Pr)-4to broadside-
1st ed-ltd to 77c   (5ss7, mint)   20.00

NENNO, FAUSTINA-Placentia Round Table Club, 1st 35 Yrs-
Placentia-Placentia Courier Pub-c1938-cl-215p-8vo-ltd to 150c
(4t1)   25.00

NEON-The Great Delusion-NY-1927-lg thk8vo-cl (5p5) 10.00

NEOSHO VALLEY LANDS, KANS-KansCty Mo-n.d.-(1878)-
folder wi map of Kansas lands on reverse-publ Mo, Kan &
Texas RR-rare   (5t3, sl rprd)   75.00

NEQUATEWA, EDMUND-Truth of a Hopi & Other Clan Stories of
Shung opovi-Flagstaff-1936-Bul #8 Mus of NoAriz-114p-wrps-
frontis-1st ed-ltd to 600c-scarce (5g0) 7.50 (5L0) 10.00

NERVAL, GASTON-Autopsy of Monroe Doctrine-NY-1934
(5yy6, pres)   8.50

NESBIT, E-Children's Shakespeare-Lond-(1897)-Tuck-4to-98p-
1st ed-8 col plts by Brundage   (4c3, plt loose)   25.00

--Five of Us, & Madeline-Lond-(1926)-Unwin-2nd prntg (4c3) 8.50

--House House With No Address-NY-1909-1st Amer ed (4c3) 10.00

--Incomplete Amorist-NY-1906-illus- 1st Amer ed (4c3) 8.50

--The Railway Children-NY-(1913)-Macmillan-12mo-309p, 14p(ads)-
frontis-19 plts-dec cl   (5p1, cov wn)   4.00

--Story of the Treasure Seekers-NY-(1909)-Stokes-illus (4F6) 10.00

NESBIT, EVELYN-Prodigal Days-NY-(1934)-J Messner-315p (5p9) 5.00

NESBIT, WILBUR D-A Friend for Two-Volland-(1915)-16mo-col illus-
cov inset wi metallic plt-paprd bds & sp-1st ed (5v0, mint, box) 17.50

NESBITT, E-Algeria & Tunis-Lond-1906-8vo-col illus-pict cl
(5x2)   10.00

NESBITT, FLORENCE-Household Management-NY-1918-12mo-
170p, (1)-Social Work Series   (5w7)   3.50

NESBITT, HENRIETTA-The Presidential Cookbook, Feeding the
Roosevelts & Their Guests-NY-1951-246p (5c0) 3. (5c9) 3.50

NESBITT, L M-Desert & Forest, Explor of Abyssinian Danakil-Lond-
1935-Cape-photos-maps(1 fldg)-450p-3rd imp (4t5) 10.00

NESOR, ALBERT-The Mad Dog of Europe-NY-1939-307p-illus-
1st ed   (5w0, dj)   3.50

NESS, ZENOBIA B-Iowa Artist of the 1st 100 Years-1939-Wallace
Homestead Co-8vo-8 illus-253p   (4a0)   22.50

NESSMUK-Woodcraft-NY-(1884)-frontis-149p-illus-12mo
(5n7, scuff, fly loose)   4.50

--same-NY-1891-Forest & Stream Pub-149p-frontis-illus-red cl
(5g9, f)   7.50

NETHERCLIFT, J-Autograph Letters...from Corres of Illustrious &
Distinguished Women of Great Britain-Lond-1838-4to-36 plts
(4m6, crack)   15.00

NETTL, BRUNO-No Amer Indian Music Styles-Phila-1954-
Amer Folklore Soc, Vol 45-51p-wrps-1st ed-o.p. (5t3) 3.50

NETTLE, RICHARD-Salmon Fisheries of St Lawrence & its Tributaries-
Montr-1857-144p-cl-12mo
(5a3, autg of F Parkman, libr release) 200. (5nn8) 125.00

NETTLETON, L L-Geophysical Prospecting for Oil-NY-1940-illus
(5nn6)   12.50

NEUBERGER, RICHARD L-Integrity, Life of Geo W Norris-NY-1937-
Vanguard-401p-illus   (5qq8)   4.00

NEUBURG, VICTOR E-Chapbooks, bibliogr of references to Engl &
Amer Chapbook Literature of 18th & 19th cent-Lond-1964-
Vine Pr-lg8vo-88p-illus   (5c8)   7.50

NEUENBURG, EVELYN-California Lure-Pasadena-1946-1st ed
(4a1)   6.00

NEUESTE EISENBAHN-Post und Kanal Karte fur Reisende in den
Vereinigten Staaten von Nord Amerika-Bamberg-1855-Buchner-
42p text-fldg map-12mo-orig board case wi linen ties (5L1) 75.00

NEUHAUS, EUGEN-The Art of the Exposition-SanFran-(1915)-8vo-
91p-illus-linen   (5h5)   4.00

--The Art of Treasure Island, Golden Gate Int'l Expo 1939-Berkley-
1939-UC Pr   (4m9, dj, f)   8.50

--The Galleries of the Expo-SanFran-(1915)-98p-illus-8vo-lin
(5h5)   3.00

--Wm Keith, the Man & the Artist-1938-UC Pr-4to-cl-95p-illus
(5h4)   7.50

--World of Art-NY-1936-illus-292p-8vo   (5ww3)   12.50

NEUMAN, FRED G-Story of Paducah-Paducah-1920-104p-Young
Prntg Co   (5u3)   3.50

NEUMANN, ALFRED-Another Caesar-NY-1935-Knopf-1st Amer ed-
ltd to 750c-boxed   (5ee3, f)   12.50

NEUMANN, J B-Max Beckmann-NY & Munich-n.d.-47p-4to-
stiff wrps-(Artlover Libr Vol 5)-plts   (5m7)   12.50

NEUMANN, ROBT-23 Women-NY-1940-Dial Pr-316p (5p9) 4.50

NEUMANN, RUTH V-Cooking With Spirits-Chig-1961-249p
(5w1)   5.00

"NEUROTICA"-a quarterly-1949 to 51-#5 thru #9-orig wrps-
5 issues   (5ss9, vg)   30.00

NEUVAINE A-l'Honneur de St Francois Xavier-Montr-1811-
Montr-JasBrown-24mo-114p-orig old calf (5w8) 35.00

NEUVECELLE, JEAN-The Vatican-NY-c1955   (5x7)   3.50

NEVADA AT WORLD'S FAIR-CarsonCty-1893-J A Yerington-12mo-
pic wrps-12 lvs   (4a5)   12.50

NEVADA CONSOLIDATED COPPER CO-22nd Annual Report of-
for the Yr Ended Dec 31, 1928-4to-prntd wrps   (5g2)   3.00
NEVADA CONSTIT CONVENTION-Official Report of-CarsonCty,
July 4, 1864-SanFran-1866-8vo-orig sheep-Marsh, Official
Reporter   (5hh4, vf)   40.00
NEVADA, GUIDE TO SILVER STATE-Portl-(1940)-illus-fldg pkt map-
304p plus index-Amer Guide Ser-WPA-1st ed
      (4L5) 10.   (5x5, dj)   12.50
NEVADA HISTORICAL SOC-1st, 2nd, 3rd Biennial Rpts-CarsonCty-
1909 to 1913   (5t4) ea   5.00
--same-CarsonCty-1909-1st only   (5s4, sl stn)   7.50
NEVADA HISTORICAL SOC-Papers, 1917 to 20-Reno-1920
      (5x5, hng broke, scuff)   6.00
--same-1921, 1922-Reno-1922-State Prntng Off, CarsonCty, 1922-
237p incl index-illus-blue papr wrps   (5a0, f)   7.00
NEVADA-History of-Oakland-1881-680p-4to-cl-incl index by
Helen J Poulton-148p-wrps   (5dd6, 4p in facs, sl tn)   170.00
--same-Berkeley-1958-reprint   (5dd6)   20.00
NEVADA-Rand McNally Pocket Map & Shippers Guide of-Chig-
1906-12p-fldg map   (5k2)   8.50
NEVADA STATE HISTORICAL SOC PAPERS-Vol 2, 3, 4 & 5-Reno-
1920 to 26-(Vol 3 papr)-illus   (5t4) ea   5.00
NEVADA-Report of State Mineralogist of, for...1867 & 1868-
CarsonCty-1869-(F White)-disbnd   (5g3)   12.50
NEVADA-Report of Surveyor Gen'l & State Land Register of State
of for Yrs 1869 & 1870-(wrpr title)-CarsonCty-1871-8vo-24p &
2 fldg tables-orig wrps-(John Day)   (5a3)   30.00
NEVADA-Report of Surveyor Gen'l & State Land Register of State
of for 1875 & 1876-CarsonCty-1877-(John Day)-prntd wrps
      (5g3)   12.50
NEVADA-2nd Inaugural address of H G Blasdel, also 1st biennial
message-CarsonCty-1867   (5g3, lacks wrps)   25.00
NEVADA-Statutes of the State, 13th Session of Legislature, 1887-
CarsonCty-1887-State Prntg Off-8vo-orig sheep-lea labl-
170p, 18p   (5j5, cov loose)   15.00
NEVILE, SIR SYDNEY O-70 Rolling Years-Lond-(1958)-288p-
photos   (5w1)   6.50
NEVILL, RALPH-Old English Sporting Books-Lond-1924-lg4to-illus-
ltd to 1250c   (5m4)   35.00
--Old French Line Engravings-Lond-1924-4to-illus-plts-
Halton & T Smith   (5x0) 25.   (5m5, wn)   18.00
NEVILL, SAM'L-Acts of Gen'l Assembly of Province of New Jersey...
wi Proper Tables and index-(Phila)-1752-Wm Bradford-folio-
sheep-1st ed   (5n2, hng broke)   125.00
NEVILLE, A W-History of Lamar County-Paris-1937 (4c7, sl fade) 30.00
--The Red River Valley-Paris, Tex-1948-No Texas Publ Co-278p-
illus-scarce   (4n8, dj) 25.   (5yy7, dj, f)   20.00
NEVILLE, AMELIA R-The Fantastic City-Bost-(1932)-1st ed (4t3) 6.00
NEVILLE, R-Old Cottage & Domestic Architecture in SW Surrey-
1892-2nd ed-illus-maps-142p-4to-cl   (4a2, libr stmps)   4.00
NEVILS, COLEMAN-Miniatures of Georgetown-Wash-1934-
R8vo-cl-illus-ltd to 501c, nbrd   (5p5)   15.00
NEVIN, ADELAIDE MELLIER-The Social Mirror, Women of Pittsburg
(Penna)-Pittsburg-1888-199p   (5p7)   5.00
NEV, ALFRED-Centennial Biography, Men ot Mark of Cumberland
Valley, Pa, 1776 to 1876-Phila-1876-Fulton Pub-cl-4to-450p
      (4t1)   25.00
--Churches of Valley-Phila-1852-12mo- 1st ed   (5yy6)   15.00
--Encyclopaedia of Presbyterian Church in USA, 1884-4to-illus-
hf mor   (5r0) 15.   (5L7, wn)   25.00
NEVIN, FRANKLIN TAYLOR-The Village of Sewickley-Sewickley-
1929-cl&bds-227p-illus   (5w4, lt rub)   8.50
NEVIN, J W-History & Genius of Heidelberg Catechism-
Chambersburg-1847-12mo-1st ed   (5jj3, rub)   25.00
NEVINS, ALLAN-Amer thru British Eyes-NY-1948-530p (5r7)   10.00
--Amer Social History as recorded by British travellers-NY-(1934)-
frontis   (5g4)   15.00
--Diary of John Quincy Adams, 1794 to 1845-NY-1929-Longm-585p
      (5p9)   8.50
--The Emergence of Lincoln-NY-1950-2 vols, boxed
      (5s9) 10.   (5x5, 5t7)   12.50
--Fremont, Pathmarker of the West-NY-1939-8vo-cl-illus-1st ed
      (5h4, f, dj)   12.50
--Fremont, West's Greatest Adventurer-NY-1928-2 vols-cl-1st ed-
errata slip   (5jj9) 15.   (5r7) 30.   (5s9, 4t3)   20.00
--Hamilton Fish-NY-(1937)-lg8vo-cl-illus-932p   (5q8, 5t0)   10.00
--History of the Bank of NY & Trust Co-NY-1934-priv prntd-156p-
plts   (5p7) 6.   (5y2)   12.50
--Illinois-NY-1917-Oxford Univ Pr-378p   (5u3)   12.50
--John D Rockefeller-NY-1941-Scribner's-illus-2 vols (5qq8)   12.50
--Letters & Journals of Brand Whitlock-NY-1936-2 vols-illus-
1st ed   (4b7)   15.00

NEVINS, ALLAN (continued)
--Letters of Grover Cleveland 1850 to 1908-Bost-1933-640p-cl-
frontis-1st ed   (5t2) 6.   (5p9)   7.50
--Ordeal of the Union-2 vols-NY&Lond-1947-illus-box (5s9, 4t3)12.50
--Sail On-NY-(1946)-pub by US Linces Co-illus-103p-wrps-dec cov
      (5s1, ex-libr)   4.00
--The Statesmanship of the Civil War-1962-wrps-issued at 95¢
      (5h6)   2.00
NEVINS, F J-70 Years of Service-1922-48p-wrps   (5h0)   5.00
NEVINS, GROVER CLEVELAND-A Study in Courage-NY-1944-
8vo-cl-832p-illus   (5t0, dj)   8.00
NEVINS, WINFIELD S-The Intervale-1887-58p   (5mm3)   10.00
NEVINSON, H W-A Modern Slavery-NY-1906-illus-1st ed(5x2) 20.00
NEVINSON, HENRY W-Changes & Chances-NY-1923 (5p9)   4.50
--Goethe, Man & Poet-NY-1932-8vo-cl-256p-illus   (5t0, dj)   4.50
NEVIUS, REV JOHN L-China & the Chinese-NY-1872-Harper-
456p   (5x9)   7.50
NEW AGE(San Fran)-Weekly journal-Vol 1 complete 52 issues,
Jan to Dec 1865 bnd in 1 vol-sm folio-hf lea-scarce
      (5dd6, sl wtrstn)   25.00
NEW AMERICAN CLERK'S MAGAZINE & COMPLETE
CONVEYANCER-Hagerstown, 1806-calf-527(67)p
      (4h8, lacks fly, hng loose)   22.50
NEW AMERICAN COOK BOOK-(wrp title)-Springfield, O-(1897)-
383p-wrps-Brown 3704   (5ff7)   7.50
NEW AMERICAN PRIMER, THE-Cinn-n.d.-E Morgan & Co-22p
ABC's-illus text & wrps   (5v0, vf)   30.00
NEW BARTENDER'S GUIDE-..bnd wi The Up to Date Bartender's
Guide-US-1914, 1913-62p, 64p-32mo-wrps   (5w6)   3.00
NEW BATH GUIDE-or, Memoirs of the B-R-D Family, in series of
Epistles-Lond-1766-4to-hf calf-1st ed of Anstey's 1st book-
without the Epilogue   (5gg6)   25.00
NEW BRUNSWICK-An act to consolidate & amend laws-Fredericton-
1850-stitchd   (5g4, rprd)   15.00
NEW BRUNSWICK-An Almanack for 1825...calculated for Meridian
of St John, N B, by Uranophilus-St John-(1825)-Henry Chubb,
Market Sq-12mo-orig bds-mor bk   (5w8, rub)   75.00
NEW BRUNSWICK-Consolidated Statutes of-Fredericton-1877-
thk8vo-orig ½ calf-1187p   (5r7, cov wn)   25.00
NEW BRUNSWICK-Map of Province of-by Geo Hayward Perley-
StJohn-1853-lith by J H Bufford-fldg lin bkd map-21½ x 25 inches
      (5ss5)   22.50
NEW CAMPUS WRITING NO.2-NY-(1957)-12mo-cl-1st ed
      (5ss7, vf)   12.50
NEW CANAAN, CONN-History Readings in-1949-290p-illus-
1st ed   (5t9)   7.50
--Landmarks of-1951-505p   (5mm3)   15.00
NEW CHAIR, THE-& other stories-Phila-c1870-Prekenpine & Higgins-
24mo-116p, (2) ads-frontis-4 plts-dec cl-Snow Drop Libr
      (5p1)   7.50
NEW, CHESTER W-Lord Durham-Oxf-1929-port-612p   (4d1)   35.00
NEW CHURCHES ILLUSTRATED-Lond-1936-photos, plans & info
52 churches erected during yrs 1926 to 1936-Inc Church Bldg
Soc-152p-illus-lg4to-wrps   (5m7, wn)   12.00
NEW COBWEBS TO CATCH LITTLE FLIES-NY-(ca1860)-sm8vo-
250p-15 illus-orig cl-Carter&Bros   (5c8, rub)   12.50
NEW COLLECTION OF GENUINE RECEIPTS-or preparation &
execution of curious arts, etc-Bost-1831-12mo-102p, 6p-bds-
stereotype ed   (5c0, lacks sp, hng broke)   23.50
NEW COMICAL NURSERY RHYMES & FUNNY STORIES-(1870)-
Ward, Lock & Tyler-sm8vo-cl-192p-44 plts-g.t.
      (5yy9, lacks plt pg 164)   15.00
NEW COMPLETE LETTER WRITER-or Art of Correspondence, etc-
Albany-1802-12mo-(9), 240p-calf   (5w7, hng tn, fox)   15.00
NEW CONN COOK BOOK-NY-1947-338p   (5c4)   4.50
NEW CRIES OF LONDON-NewHav-1850-S Babcock-16mo-16p-
sewn-wrps-wdcuts   (5v2)   35.00
NEW DAILY FOOD-Ladies of StPaul's Church Morrisania-NY-
1885-128p-ads   (5c4, hng crack)   6.50
NEW DEALERS, THE-By Unofficial Observer-NY-(1934)-8vo-cl-
414p-Literary Guild   (5j5)   7.50
NEW DIRECTIONS-ed by Jas Laughlin-Norfolk, Conn-(1946)-
1st ed   (5r9, dj)   15.00
NEW DIRECTIONS-Spearhead, 10 Yrs Experimental Writing in Amer-
(1947)   (5ss9, vg, dj)   8.50
NEW EMPIRES IN THE NW-(wrpr title)-NY-(1889)-Vol 1, #8-
Library of Tribune Extras   (5g3)   7.50
NEW ENGLAND AID SOC-Florida, Advantages & Inducements
Which it Offers to Immigrants-Bost-(1868)-2nd ed-20p-stitched
      (5g3)   17.50
NEW ENGLAND ALMANACK-or Ladies & Gentleman's Diary
-Prov-(1776)-John Carter-16mo-sewn-B West, ed (5q0)   35.00

NEW ENGL ALMANAC & FARMER'S FRIEND FOR 1858-
NewLond-1858   (4a9,bent)   12.50
--same-for 1863-NewLond   (4a9,g)   12.50
NEW ENGLAND ANTI SLAVERY SOC-1st Annual Report of,
Jan 9,1833(bnd in slipcase)-Bost-1833   37.50
NEW ENGLAND ASSOC OF RR SUPTS-Reports & Other Papers of-
Bost-1850-8vo-orig wrps-48p-1st report   (5m6)   12.50
NEW ENGLAND AVIATORS 1914 to 1918-Bost&NY-1919-2 vols-
illus-C Ticknor,ed   (5q0,libr labl) 45.00
NEW ENGLAND-Brief Relation of State of-Lond-1689-Baldwine-
sm4to-g.tooled mor-1st ed,wi rare adv lf-Sabin 46642
                                          (5n2)   1,250.00
NEW ENGLAND COAL MINING CO-Report of,for Encouragement
from State & on Petitions in Aid of Same Before Select Spec
Committee of...Rhode Isl wi Report of Committee...Geolog &
Agric Survey of State,in 1838-NewEngl-1838-8vo-bds-hf-
calf bk-orig wrps bnd in-1st ed   (5ss5)   22.50
NEW ENGLAND CO-14 miles from Chattanooga,coal & iron
properties in Dade Co,GA-NY-ca1890-2 fldg maps-illus-
pict wrps   (5g8)   7.50
NEW ENGLAND COOK BOOK-Bost-(1905)-by Marion Harland,
Miss Parloa,Mrs Lincoln-illus-286p   (4g9)   10.00
NEW ENGLAND FAMILY HISTORY QUARTERLY-Me & Mass-
Vol 1 complete Jul 1907 to Apr 1908   (5t9)   3.50
NEW ENGLAND FARMER-Vol 2 (complete),Vol 3 (complete) &
Vol 4, #2-Bost-1823 to 5-lea bkd orig bds (5r7,bds wn) 40.00
NEW ENGLAND GAZETTEER-by John Hayward-Concord(NH)-
1839-thk8vo-calf-1st ed-scarce-illus   (5p5,rbnd) 25.00
--same-Bost-1902-approx 230p-fldg map of New Engl (5ee3) 4.00
NEW ENGLAND-A Handbook for Travellers-Bost-1873-maps & plans-
                                           (5g4)   6.00
NEW ENGLAND HISTORICAL & GENEALOGICAL SOC REGISTER-
--Vol 1, 1847 thru Vol 10, 1856-complete run-orig wrps as
issued   (5t9)   150.00
--same-Jul 1933,#348 to Oct 1958,plus suppl indexes-orig wrps-
102 nbrs plus indexes   (5mm3,lacks #405) 200.00
--same-Index of Persons-Vols 1 thru 50-A to G-493p-buck-Bost-
1906   (5r7,ex-libr) 20.00
--same-Memorial Biographies, 1845 to 55-Bost-1880-2 vols
                                           (5r7,chip)   15.00
--same-Memorial Biog, 1853 to 55-Vol 2-1881-533p (5t9) 7.50
--same-Proceedings-1868 to 1898-odd nbrs   (5mm3) ea   1.50
--same-Records of StPaul's Evang Lutheran Church-in Schohaire-
1915-84p   (5mm3,crude rbndg) 45.00
NEW ENGLAND HURRICANE-A Factual Pictorial Record-Bost-
(1938)-4to-illus   (5q8,dj)   4.50
NEW ENGLAND KITCHEN MAGAZINE-Vol 2 Oct 1894 to Mar
1895-Bost-308p,(2)-illus   (5c0,soil)   7.50
NEW ENGLAND MINING CO-Articles of assoc of-Bost-1846-
16mo-prntd wrps-betw Lake Superior & Keweenaw Bay,Mich
                                           (5g3,vg)   20.00
NEW ENGLAND NUN-& Other Stories-NY-1891-Harper-12mo-
dec cl   (5b2,lt stn) 12.50
NEW ENGLAND PALLADIUM-Bost-June 15,1804-Young & Minns
4p-Lewis & Clark Exped   (4n4,fox)   17.50
NEW ENGLAND PATRIOT,THE-Bost-1810-Russell&Cutler-8vo-
orig wrps-1st ed   (4h0,lacks bk wrp,fray) 50.00
NEW ENGLAND PRIMER ENLARGED-or Easy & Pleasant Guide to
the Art of Reading-T & T Fleet,prntr-n.d.-(inscr reads 1781)-
marbld papr over oak bds-wdcuts-Bost   (4F6,f,yellowd) 375.00
--same-Exeter-1816-32 lvs-plain wrps   (5v2,vg)   47.50
--same-Improved for more easy attaining true reading of Englis-
added Assembly of Divines,& Mr Cotton's Catechism-Bost-
1777-(reprint ca 1830)-32mo-bds & lea-Edw Draper,prntr (5t7) 12.50
--same-Improved-Bost-n.d.-Jas Loring-48mo-29 lvs-wooden cov-
(1797 to 1800?)   (5u9,lacks pt cov,fair) 25.00
--same-Bost-1777(reprinted in facs by Ira Webster,Hartf 1844)-
16mo-orig cl-Edw Draper   (5c8)   10.00
--same-Worcester,Wm Allen(ca 1840)-Assembly's Catechism,account
of burning of John Rogers,etc-intro by H Humphrey-frontis of
Isaac Watts-orig pict bds   (5c8,vg,sl tn) 15.00
--same-or, an easy & pleasant guide to Art of Reading-Bost-
(ca 1850)-Mass Sabbath School Soc-pict bds (5c8,wn)   10.00
NEW ENGLAND PSALTER-or Psalms of David with Proverbs of
Solomon & Christ's Sermon-Bost-1784-Edes&Sons-text dbl col-
12mo-171p-calf   (5c8,lacks 2 lvs,brownd,scuff) 30.00
NEW ENGLAND QUARTERLY-Vol 24,#1 thru #4-March to Dec,
1951-orig prntd wrps as issued   (5t4)   5.00
--same-Vol 25, #1 thru #4-March to Dec, 1952-8vo-orig prntd wrps
as issued   (5t4)   5.00
NEW ENGLAND TELEGRAPH CO-Dist #3 of western Div,official
Directory for Fitchburg,Mass,Keene NH,Bellows Falls,Vt &
that area-Portland-1887-narr 8vo-orig wrps-37p (5ss5) 15.00

NEW ENGLAND TELEPHONE & TELEGRAPH CO-Off Directory,
Jul 1,1896-(also)-Supplement,Oct 1,1896-2 vols-Bost-1896-
8vo-426p,222p-orig wrps   (5ss5)   17.50
--same-Jul 1899-Bost-1899-8vo-1027p-orig wrps (5ss5,cov loose)13.50
--same-Phone Directo for Western Section of Mass Jan 15,1905-
Bost-1905-8vo-170p-wrps   (5t7)   15.00
NEW ENGLANDER-Scenes in Rocky Mntns,Oreg,Calif,N Mex,
Tex & Grand Prairies-Phila-1846-303p-fldg map-cl-1st ed
                                            (5jj9,vg)   425.00
NEW ERA-Presenting Plans for New Era Union-Denver-(n.d.)-
(1897)-192p-cl-port-   (5r0,plan & sketch laid in) 10.00
NEW ESSAY-on Constitutional Power of Great Brit over colonies in
Amer-Lond-1774-Almon-8vo-disbnd-wrps-1st Engl ed
                                            (5n2,new wrps) 100.00
NEW FAMILY RECEIPT BOOK-NewHav-1819-(37),429p,(3)-
calf-12mo   (5c0,wn,fox) 35.00
NEW FINANCIAL PROJECT-togeth wi Some Remarks upon Currency
& Credit System of US-NY-1837-19p,(3)   (5e4)   7.50
NEW FOREST,THE-a Novel-Lond-1829-3 vols-hf calf-1st ed
                                            (5r9)   15.00
NEW FRANCE & NEW ENGLAND-Lond-1902-illus-maps (5q8)   4.00
NEW GOSPEL OF PEACE-according to St Benj(& same,Book 2nd,
Book 3rd & Book 4th)-NY-(1863 to 66)-4 vols-wrps
                                            (5g8,marg tn) 25.00
NEW HAMPSHIRE-Articles in addi to & amendment of Constitution
of State of agreed to...& submitted to people-Dover-1792-
12mo-stitched   (5g3,f)   50.00
NEW HAMPSHIRE BOOK,THE-Nashua-1842-391p-1st ed (5ee3,f) 10.00
NEW HAMPSHIRE,CONSTITUTION OF-as Altered & Amended by
Convention of Delegates,Held at Concord,in said State,by
Adjournment, on 2nd Wed of Feb,1792-Geo Hough-1792-
59p-wrps   (5t7,re-wrps,part of t. pg in facs,box) 35.00
--same-1st Wed of Sept 1792-Concord-1792-Geo Hough-sm8vo-
70p,(1)-stitched   (5L1,box)   150.00
NEW HAMPSHIRE-Constitution & Laws of State of,togeth wi
Constitution of US-Dover-1805-8vo-calf-lea
(5t2,lacks e.p., wn) 10. (5m6,hng sl crack,2 lvs dmpstnd) 15.00
NEW HAMPSHIRE-Guide to Granite State-Bost-1938-HoughtonMif-
Amer Guide Ser-WPA-559p-map   (5p0)   5.00
NEW HAMPSHIRE-Heads of Families First Census of US-1790-
146p   (5t9)   25.00
NEW HAMPSHIRE HISTORICAL SOC-Collections of,Vol 2-1827-
302p   (5t9,ex-libr) 15.00
--Collections of-Vol 5-1837-307p   (5t9)   15.00
--Proceedings of-Vol 2-Concord-1915-272p   (5s2,f)   12.50
NEW HAMPSHIRE-Journal of Proceedings of House of Rep of State of-
commencing Jun 1784,Oct 1784 & Feb 1785-3 pieces (5s2) 100.00
NEW HAMPSHIRE-Journal of proceedings of,21st Nov,1793-
Portsmouth-   67p-stitched   (5g8,unopnd) 17.50
NEW HAMPSHIRE LAWS-Acts & laws,passed-Bost-1716-(1726)-
sm folio-calf   (5a3,title lf in facs,wn) 250.00
NEW HAMPSHIRE-The laws of...Prntd at Portsmouth
--Nov, 1792-Evans 25876   (5g4,tn)   25.00
--Jun, 1793-Evans 25877   (5g4)   25.00
--Dec, 1793-Evans 27375   (5g4)   25.00
--Jun, 1794-Evans 27376   (5g4)   25.00
--Dec, 1794-Evans 29168   (5g4)   25.00
--Jun, 1797-Evans 32537   (5g4)   25.00
--Nov, 1797-scarce   (5g4)   30.00
--June, 1800-Evans 38053   (5g4)   20.00
--Nov, 1800   (5g4)   20.00
--Jun, 1801   (5g4)   20.00
NEW HAMPSHIRE LEGISLATORS-Souvenir of-1901-234p-Vol 3-
illus   (5e8)   3.75
NEW HAMPSHIRE,MERRIMACK & SULLIVAN CO,-Biographical
Review,Vol 22-Bost-1897-ports-4to-594p   (5yy0)   32.50
NEW HAMPSHIRE PROVINCIAL,TOWN & STATE PAPERS-1867 to
1939-(30 in all)-odd lot   (5t9)   160.00
NEW HAMPSHIRE REGIMENTAL HISTORIES-1st NH thru 18th N H
plus Register of N H Soldiers & Sailors in War of Rebell,N H
Surgeons in Rebell-20 vol-(10th N H never publ) (5s2,mint) 235.00
NEW HAMPSHIRE-Revised Statutes of the State wi Constitutions of
US & of State-Concord-1843-555p-sheep-lea labl (5r7) 12.50
NEW HAMPSHIRE-Sketches of Successful N H Men-1882-315p
                                            (5mm3)   6.00
NEW HAMPSHIRE-Tourists' Guide Book to State of-Concord-1902-
12mo-fldg maps-orig limp cl-publ by Rollins-1st ed
                                            (5ss5,map loose) 10.00
NEW HAMPSHIRE-Town & City Atlas of State of from Gov Survey,
Co Records & Personal Investig-Bost 1892-D H Hurd & Co-folio-
cl-maps-illus   (5t2,cov loose) 40. (5y7,f,part lea) 150.00

NEW HAMPSHIRE-Report of Adj General of State of for yr ending
  May 20, 1865-2 vols-Concord-1865-747p,856p-cl bkstrp-
  hvy wrps   (5w4,sl soil) 10. (5j4)   12.50

NEW HAVEN,CONN-Commemorative Biogr Record Containing
  Sketches of Prominent & Rep Citizens-1902-1,563p (5t9) 35.00

NEW HISTORY OF LIFE & ADVEN OF TOM THUMB-NewHav-1849-
  Babcock-16mo-wdcuts   (5c8,lacks last lf,wn) 9.00

NEW HISTORY OF TROJAN WARS-& Troy's destruction-in 4 books
  & siege of Troy-Lond-n.d.-(1728)-prntd for C Bates-12mo-
  3 wdcuts-frontis mounted-vel   (5xx6) 125.00
--same-Lond-1735-12mo-hf calf-frontis mounted-Bates&Hodges
    (5xx6,sl wn) 75.00

NEW JERSEY ALMANAC-for 1785-by Timothy Truman,Philom-
  Trenton-(1784)-16mo-disbnd   (5g3,libr stmp) 20.00
--same,for 1789-Trenton-(1788)-calculations by Wm Waring-
  16mo-disbnd   (5g3) 20.00

NEW JERSEY BOARD OF AGRICULTURE-9th Annual Report of NJ
  Board of Agric,1882-Orange-1882-444p-wrps (5e4,sl soil) 5.00

NEW JERSEY BELL TELEPHONE-Tales of New Jersey-(1963)-n.p.-
  43p-illus-bds   (5t7,box) 5.00

NEW JERSEY-Board of Gen'l Proprietors of Eastern Div-Bill in
  Chancery of NJ at suit of John Earl & otherproprietors against
  Benj Bond of Elizabethtown-1747-folio-3 fldg maps-hf mor
    (5L7) 650.00

NEW JERSEY CIVIL WAR CENTENNIAL COMM-Proceedings,4th
  Annual Amer History Workshop-NewBrunswick-1964-8vo-100p-
  wrps   (5j5) 4.50

NEW JERSEY-Guide to its present & past-1939-Amer Guide Ser-
  WPA-735p-pkt map   (5w4) 6.50 (5L7) 7.50

NEW JERSEY HISTORICAL SOC-Proceedings of-2nd Series,Vols 1
  to 13-1867 to 1895-index-bnd in 3 vols (5m2) 18.00
--Semi Centennial of,at Newark-1895-223p-port (5m2) 7.50

NEW JERSEY-A History,Biogr & Gen Records-Vol 5 only,Biogr-
  442p-ports-1930   (5t9) 7.50

NEW JERSEY-Inventory of Church Archives of Evangelical Church-
  Newark-1941-40p-stiff wrps   (5m2) 6.00

NEW JERSEY-Register of Commissioned Officers & Privates of
  N J Volunteers in Service of US-JerseyCty-1863-560p-wrps
    (5j6,v fox) 7.50

NEW JERSEY ZINC CO-First 100 Yrs of-NY-1948-69p-illus (5y2)7.50

NEW LETTER WRITER,A-For Use of Gentlemen-wi a New Letter
  Writer for Use of Ladies-Phila-n.d.-139p,139p (5w7,fox,wn) 5.50

NEW MEXICO-Brand Book of Territory of New Mex-Cattle Sanitary
  Board of New Mex-1907-536p-index,109p-orig cl (5yy3) 50.00

NEW MEXICO-Calendar of Annual Events in-Federal Writers'
  Project-SantaFe-1937-col illus-wrps   (5t1) 15.00

NEW MEXICO-Constitution of-Wash-1911-Sen Doc #835-8vo-47p-
  orig wrps   (5g6) 15.00

NEW MEXICO-Constitution of State of,1850-Intro by Jack D
  Rittenhouse-SantaFe-1965-Stagecoach Pr-frontis-map-
  ltd ed of 350c-autg by Rittenhouse (5g6,mint,dj) 9.00

NEW MEXICO-General Orders-SantaFe-Aug 24,1863-HQ Dept
  of NM,GO #21-Reg of Vol Officers-8vo-8 lvs-disbnd-rare
    (4n5) 100.00

NEW MEXICO-General Orders-Santa-Feb 18,1865-HQ Dept of
  NM-Synopsis of Indian Scouts & their Results...1864-#4 GO-
  8vo-8 lvs-fldg chart-stitched as issued-disbnd (4n5) 250.00

NEW MEXICO-Geological Soc-Guidebook of SWstrn NM by
  Frank E Kottlowski,et al,4th Field Conf-Socorro-Oct,1953-
  153p-plts-maps-fldg map in back   (5g5) 5.50

NEW MEXICO-Guide to Colorful State-NY-1940-WPA-Amer
  Guide Ser-1st ed-illus-458p-pkt map
  (4b3,dj,f) 10. (5b9,f) 10. (5t3) 8.50 (5x5,dj) 15.00
--same-NY-1945-illus-e.p. map-pkt map-439p-2nd ed-Amer Guide
  Ser-WPA   (5a0,f) 6. (4L5,dj) 7.50

NEW MEXICO HISTORICAL REVIEW-SantaFe-1926 to 1969-
  NewMex Hist Soc-Vol 1 to 45-ports (5yy3,lacks 6 nbrs) 125.00

NEW MEXICO HISTORICAL SOC-Charter,Constitution & Bylaws of
  with Inaugural Address by Hon W G Ritch-SantaFe-1881-27p
  plus ads-wrps-scarce form wi Ritch's address (5L0) 25.00

NEW MEXICO-Homesteaders' Guide Goodk to-SantaFe-1919-
  27p-prntd wrps   (5g2,f) 15.00

NEW MEXICO-Manual of Common School Course of Study for Public
  Schools of-SantaFe-1909-8vo-206p-orig wrps-index-ltd ed
    (5g2) 10.00

NEW MEXICO-The Mines of-SantaFe-1896-80p-fldg map-prntd wrps-
  issued by N M Bur of Immigration,May,1896-N M Prntg Co
    (5g5,mint) 35.00

NEW MEXICO-Private Land Claims in-Wash-1861-HED 28-
  72p   (5n4) 4.00

NEW MEXICO-Report of Gov of N M to Sec of Int-Wash-1885-
  11p-prntd wrp   (5n4,f) 13.50
--same-1889-25p   (5n4) 12.50
--same-1893-33p   (5n4) 12.50
--same-1896-75p   (5n4) 15.00
--same-1906-108p-fldg map   (5n4,fox) 15.00

NEW MEXICO-Rand McNally Pocket Map & Shippers Guide of-
  Chig-1910-19p-fldg map   (5k0) 12.50

NEW MEXICO TERRITORY-Sketch Map of oil lease holdings-
  Denver-1911-Clason Map Co-8½ x 11 (5g5) 15.00

NEW MEXICO TERRITORY-Acts,Resolutions,etc of-Wash-1852-
  74p-scarce   (5g5) 65.00

NEW MEXICO-Revised Statutes & Laws of Territory of-StL-1865-
  856p-calf-Spanish t.p.-Engl & Span text (5j6) 27.50

NEW MILWAUKEE COOK BK-Vol Comm of Visiting Nurse Assn-
  Milw-(1946)-320p-spiral bnd wrps (5c4) 3.00

NEW NATIONAL SECOND READER-NY&Chig-c1883-A S Barnes-
  12mo-176p-illus-dec cl   (5p1) 5.00

NEW NORTHWEST & TACOMA ITS METROPOLIS-Terminus of
  transcontinental RR etc-(Tacoma)-1890-Chamber of Comm-
  plts(prntd in blue)-orig prntd wrps (5g3) 30.00

NEW ORLEANS & ENVIRONS-NY-1885-W H Cole-prntd wrps-
  fldg map & illus-1st ed,1st issue (wiout Hearn's name on pg 299)-
  E H Holmes ad on wrps   (5q0,rbkd) 35.00

NEW ORLEANS CARNIVAL COOK BOOK-Women's Republican
  Club of La-NewOrl-1951-127p-wrps (4q9) 4.50

NEW ORLEANS CITY GUIDE-Bost-1938-Federal Writers' Proj-
  illus-pkt map-Am Guide Series (4j4) 8. (4m2) 7.50 (4L5) 8.50
--same-Bost-1952-HoughtonMif-416p-illus (5p9) 5.00

NEW ORLEANS IMPROVEMENT CO-Act to Inc-NOrl-1836-19p-
  sewed as issued   (5h1) 10.00

NEW ORLEANS-Souvenir of-(Columbus,1885)-12mo-18 plts-
  orig cl-fold out   (5m6,text loose) 10.00

NEW ORLEANS-Souvenir of..NOrl-(ca 1898)-Thos F Gessner-bds-
  33 lvs-photos   (4j4) 17.50

NEW PARLOR LETTER WRITER-Auburn-1854-144p-bds-calf sp
    (5w7,fox) 6.50

NEW PLATOON EXERCISE,THE-as Practised in 1756-Edinb-1756-
  8vo-16p-hf mor   (4a6) 65.00

NEW PROCESS CATALOGUE-& Cook Book-Cleve-1894-249p,(6)-
  ads   (5c0,lacks title,shake) 6.50

NEW REIGN OF TERROR-in Slaveholding States for 1859 to 1860-
  1860-Amer Anti Slavery Soc   (5x2) 35.00

NEW REPUBLIC,THE-Bost-1851-2nd ed (4a9,crude rpr) 12.50

NEW ROAD TO RUIN-or Intended RR from Bost,Portland &
  Portsmouth .....to Quebec-Quebec-1835(poetry)-11p (5e2) 250.00

NEW ROBINSON CRUSOE-an Instructive Entertaining History for
  Use of Children of Both Sexes-Lond-1788-Stockdale-sm8vo-
  calf-32 illus by Bewick-4 vols in 2-rare
  (5aa2,f,bkstrp sl rub,Lord StJohn's bkplt) 500.00
--same-Lond-Stockdale-1789-sm8vo-266p-32 plts-2nd ed (5aa2) 50.00
--same-Lond-1811-Stockdale-New ed-2 vols
  (5aa2,rbnd hf mor,tn frontis,libr labl) 35.00

NEW ROCHELLE,N Y-Charter,By Laws & Ordinances of Village
  of-MIVernon-1873-70p-orig wrps-"Chronicle" (5p7) 6.50

NEW ROCHELLE-Old Wills of,NY,1784 to 1850-DAR-1951-238p
    (5mm3) 7.50

NEW SOUTH WALES LAW REPORTS-1880 to 1900-bound-21 vols
  (all publ)   (5rr4,ex-libr) 500.00

NEW SOUTH WALES STATE REPORTS-1901 to 66-Vols 1 thru 66-
  bnd   (5rr4,ex-libr,mixed bndgs) 1,600.00

NEW SOUTH WALES,SUPREME COURT-Cases 1862 to 76-bound-
  14 vols(all publ)   (5rr4,ex-libr) 325.00

NEW SYDNEHAM SOC-Selected Monographs-Lond-1861-8vo-cl-
  329p-Society   (5j5) 20.00

NEW SYSTEM OF DOMESTIC COOKERY-Bost-1807-296p,(2)-
  red calf & bds-1st Amer ed   (5c0,cov dtchd) 45.00
--same-by a Lady-Lond-1807-thk16mo-hf black lea-blind t.sp-
  frontis-9 plts-2nd ed,enlrgd & imprvd (5b0) 75.00
--same-Phila-1808-24mo-263p-2nd Phila ed (5c0,rbkd,wn) 35.00
--same-NY-1814-316p-frontis-8 plts-calf (5c0,scuff) 35.00

NEW SYSTEM OF INFANTRY TACTICS-NY-1869-Appleton-392p-
  illus   (5mm8) 8.50

NEW SYSTEM OF PAPER MONEY-by a Citizen of Bost-Bost-1837-
  20p   (5e4) 7.50

NEW TESTAMENT-Ka Tite Tebeniminang Je Jezos,Ondaje Aking-
  Kanactageng,Lake of 2 Mtns-1861-hf mor-396p (5w8) 45.00

NEW TESTAMENT-of Our Lord & Savior,Jesus Christ,transl out of
  Orig Greek-Nashville-1861-orig bds-303p-scarce (5r5,wn) 100.00

NEW TESTAMENT-of Our Lord & Savior,Jesus Christ-Atlanta-1862-
  Augusta Confederate States Bible Soc-303p-(18mo)-prntd by
  Wood,Hanleiter Rice & Co   (5h6) 225.00

NEW TESTAMENT-Greek,Engl-authorized version of 1611,wi
rev version of 1881-1887 (5L7) 12.50
NEW TRANSLATION WITH NOTES-of 3rd Satire of Juvenal,misc
poems-NY-1806-12mo-orig mrbld bds-1st ed-addt'l errata lf
(5gg6,bkstrp def) 87.50
NEW UNIVERSAL LETTER WRITER-Phila-1830-228p-lea sp
(5w7,stns,sp wn) 9.50
NEW UNIVERSAL PARISH OFFICER-by a Gentleman of Middle
Temple-Lond-1771-16mo-2p,401p-calf-errata lf-prntd by
Strahan&Woodfall-3rd ed,enlrgd & corr
(5p1,sl stn,calf wn) 25.00
NEW VADE MECUM-or,Young Clerk's Magazine-Lansingburgh,NY-
1794-12mo-calf-346p-1st ed (5m6) 30.00
NEW VOYAGE TO GEORGIA-by a Young Gentleman-Lond-1735-
12mo-lea-61p-prntd for JWilford (5t7) 700.00
NEW VOYAGE TO THE NORTH-Lond-1706-hf calf-fldg frontis-
8vo-238p (4e1,rebnd) 75.00
NEW WORLD HEROES-Lincoln & Garfield-(Eva Hope)-Lond-
n.d.-(ca 1884)-Walter Scott,Ltd-363p-cl (5h2,bkplt) 12.50
NEW YORK-Abstracts of Wills on file,City of NY,1665 to 1880-
NY Hist Soc Coll-1893 to 1909-15 vls & 2 vols of corrections
(5mm3) 75.00
NEW YORK & HARLEM RR CO-Act to Incorporate-NY-1838-
16mo-52p-wrps (5t4) 75.00
--Proposals for Loan to-NY-1857-12p-wrps (5h1) 5.00
NEW YORK CENTRAL & HUDSON RR-The Hudson River Map,
What the Traveller Wishes to See & Know,etc-NY-(ca1870)-
16mo-(30p)-wrps (5t4) 15.00
NEW YORK & TEXAS LAND & EMIGRATION ASSN-Engr
Certificate for 5000 Acres,purchased by Jas Lawson-NY-
Mar 1,1848-sm4to in width (5r7) 25.00
NEW YORK AT GETTYSBURG-Final rept on battlefields of
Gettysburg-Albany-1902-3 vols-4to-1,462p (5w4,crack) 17.50
NEW YORK-Case of Officers & Independent Companies-n.p.-
n.d.-(ca1700)-1 lf folio wi docket lf.prntd on verso (5L1,box) 75.00
NEW YORK CENTRAL RR CO-Report of Committee,Oct 24,1855-
Bost-1855-Eastburn's Pr-8vo-47p-wrps (5j5) 25.00
NEW YORK AND ITS ENVIRONS-Views in City of-NY-1831-
Peabody&Co-illus by Dakin,egrvd by Barnard&Dick-8½x11-
parts 1 thru 5-fldg map of NY in col (5F9) 20.00
NEW YORK CITY AND VICINITY-Large 3 by 4 ft col map pub by
USGS,fld-1899 (5w0,vf) 12.50
NEW YORK CITY-Charter of with Acts of Legislature on additional
Powers in Mayor,Aldermen & Commonalty-NY-1805-8vo-240p,
1 vi-Jas Cheetham-sheep-reprints the Montgomerie Charter with
suppl Acts & Amend (5L1,broke) 25.00
NEW YORK DIRECTORY FOR 1786-NY-n.d.-fldg map-215p-
3/4 lea-facs reprint (4b3) 12.50
NEW YORK (CITY)DIRECTORY,The-& Register for Year 1790-
NY-1790-Hodge,Allen&Campbell-144p(pg123,4 in facs)-
fldg map-12mo-unbnd (5L1,box) 250.00
NEW YORK-Directory of Directors in City of-1940 ed-NY-(1940)-
thk8vo-cl-823p,407p-Directory of Directors Co (5j5) 7.50
NEW YORK CITY GUIDE-Federal Writers Proj-1939-pkt map-WPA-
648p (4n2) 9.50
--same-NY-1939-Random-680p-map-illus (5p0) 6.00
NEW YORK CITY-Laws & Ordinances,Ordained & Established by
Mayor etc-NY-1793-Hugh Gaine-8vo-calf-81p & 53p & (2)-
Parts 1 & 2 (only)-lacking Montgomerie Charter (5L1,vg) 45.00
NEW YORK CITY-Map of City & County of NY with...Brooklyn
& JerseyCty,&...Williamsburg wi directory of NY-1854-
(Thayer,Bridgman&Fanning)-fldg map-(2)p,28p(last pg unnbrd)
(4,versos blank)-col (5g4,f) 20.00
NEW YORK CITY-Public Parks-1st Annual Report of Bd of Comm of
Dept of,Year ending May 1,1871-NY-1871-427p-photos (5t4)20.00
NEW YORK CITY-The Wharves,Piers & Slips belonging to the
Corp of City of NY,East River-1868-NY Prntg Co-obl lg4to-
orig cl-lea sp & corners- 66p in col wi text (5t2) 35.00
--same-North River-1868-NY Prntg Co-obl 4to-orig cl-lea sp
& corners-65p plans in col-text (5t2) 35.00
NEW YORK CONFERENCE SEMINARY-Catalogue of Officers
& Students in,Charlotteville,Schoharie Co,NY-Albany-1852-
24p-prntd wrps (5p1) 10.00
NEW YORK CO-OP SOC-250th anniv of settlement of Jews in
US,addresses at Carnegie Hall-NY-1906-262p-bds (5u3) 4.50
NEW YORK-A Complete list...of individuals..who have filed
bankruptcy petitions for So Dist of NY-NY-1842-8vo-orig
prntd wrps (5t7) 20.00
NEW YORK-Glamour & Beauty-Baden,Baden-(1955)-4to-col
photos wi text (5r7) 7.50
NEW YORK GRAPHIC SOC-Mexico,Pre historic Paintings-(1958)-
folio-32 plts-Unesco (5p0) 17.50

NEW YORK-A Guide to the Empire State-NY-1940-
WPA Writer's Proj-739p-Oxford Univ Pr-fldg pkt map
(5p0) 5. (4n2,5t4) 6.50 (5x5,dj) 8.50
--same-NY-(1946)-photos-pkt map-739p-plus index-2nd prntg-
Am Guide Ser-WPA (4L5,dj) 8.50
NEW YORK HERALD-Separate issues betw Feb 1,1864 &
Sept 7,1865-folio-(fld)-ca215 issues(incomplete run) (5m3) 75.00
NEW YORK HERALD TRIBUNE HOME INSTIT-America's Housekeeping
Book-NY-1941-607p-illus (5w7) 5.00
NEW YORK HIST ASSN-Proceedings for 1906-1906-234p (5zz0) 12.00
--Proceedings of,Vol 13,1914-480p-illus (5h9) 8.50
NEW YORK HISTORICAL SOC-Arts & Crafts in NY 1777 to 1799-
NY-1954-484p-illus (5n7) 10.00
--Collections of,Vol 3,Part 1,1857-2nd Series-358p-bds-
cl sp (5h9) 12.00
--Collections...for Year 1868-NY-1868-Vol 1-bnd (5yy6) 15.00
--Collections...for Year 1885-NY-1886-678p (5p0) 7.50
--Diary of Wm Dunlap,1766 to 1839-NY-1931-964p-illus-8vo-
3 vols-ltd to 100c (4a0) 75.00
--Dictionary of Artists in Amer,1564 to 1860-NewHav&Lond-(1957)-
759p (5t7) 15.00
NEW YORK,A HISTORY OF-NY-1809-Inskeep&Bradford-2 vols-
12mo-orig sheep-1st ed-(W Irving) (5n2,vf,box) 375.00
--same-NY-1886-Grolier Club-8vo-2 vols-orig bds-l1 plts-
ltd to 175c (5n2,mint) 150.00
NEW YORK IMPROVEMENT-& Tunnel Extension of Penn RR-
Phila-Aug,1910-34p-illus-3 fld photo (5e4) 5.00
NEW YORK IN SPANISH AMER WAR,1898-3 vols-Albany-1900-
port-buck-report of Adj General (5t7) 20.00
NEW YORK-Laws of,from 1691 to 1741,incl-NY-1752-JasParker-
t4to-lea-488p-errata p & list of orig subscr
(5t7,bkstrp wn,chip) 50.00
NEW YORK-Laws of Her Maj Colony of NY,Apr 9,1691...to
12th of Nov,1709-(NY,1710,Wm Bradford)-3 vols-folio-
hf mor (5L1,def,broke) 2,000.00
--same-NY-1713-Bradford-folio-88p-disbnd-3rd revision
(5L1) 1,500.00
NEW YORK LEDGER-NY-1857 to 62-folio-3 vols-qtr lea-
Vols 12 to 17 (4b6) 150.00
NEW YORK LIFE INS CO-Record of a Single Year,NY,May,1892-
fldg bds-48p (5e4,sl stn) 6.75
NEW YORK-Manual of Board of Education of City & Co of NY-
NY-1847-Childs Prntr-136p plus 5p-cl-4x6 (5r0,fox) 12.50
NEW YORK MIRROR-Weekly Journal,Vol 10 #2 to 52,Jul 14,
1832 to Apr 20,1833-NY-4to-illus-bds (5t7,lacks 2 pgs) 25.00
NEW YORK-Natural History of-Albany-1842-24 vols-lg4to
(5t2) post extra 200.00
NEW YORK PANORAMA-A comprehensive view of metropolis-
NY-1938-Random Hse-526p-Amer Guide Ser (5u3) 5.00
--same-Lond-1939-illus (5q8) 5.00
NEW YORK,RR COMMISSIONERS-Annual Report of-Albany-
1881-Vol 1 only (5t2) 5.00
--same-Albany-1884-2 vols (5t2) 10.00
--same-Albany-1886-2 vols in 1 (5t2) 7.50
NEW YORK,REGIONAL PLAN OF-NY-1929-2 vols-atlas & descrip-
illus (5yy6) 17.50
NEW YORK SAFETY STEAM POWER CO-Builders of Steam Engines
& Boilers-NY-July,1876-sml 8vo-16p-illus-wrps (5b8) 12.50
NEW YORK SOCIETY LIBRARY-Alphabetical & Analytical Catalogue
of-NY-1838 (5g4,ex-libr) 7.50
NEW YORK SPELLING BOOK-or, Fourth Book-NY-1816-S Wood &
Sons-160p-title vignt-221 wdcuts-orig bds-v scarce (5u6) 85.00
NEW YORK STATE-Agricultural Soc-Transactions-Vol 14,1854-
Albany-1855-VanBenthuysen-thk8vo-cl-illus-951p (5j5) 20.00
NEW YORK STATE-Annual Report of Adj General of State of-
Albany-1863-1181p (5j6) 12.50
NEW YORK STATE ATLAS SHEETS-USGS,with State...approx
250 folio maps wi atlas index sheet; all maps present plus
duplicates & some subsequent-ca1895 to 1900-cl covered
holder (5w0,case wn) post extra 125.00
NEW YORK STATE,CANAL COMM-Annual Report of-Albany-
1855-fldg charts & maps-300p & index-wrps (5t2) 6.00
--same-Albany-1857-charts & maps-wrps-304p & index (5t2) 6.00
NEW YORK (STATE) CRIME COMM-Report 1st thru 4th-Jan to
May 1953-bnd in 1 vol (5rr4,rbnd) 15.00
NEW YORK STATE-Fisheries,Game & Forests of-5th Annual Reprt-
(Albany-1900,JBLyon)-thk4to-466p-pitct cl-col plts (5j5) 20.00
NEW YORK STATE-Forest Comm-1st Annual Report of for Year
1885-Albany-1886-8vo-fldg map (5m6) 8.50
NEW YORK STATE-General Regulations for Military Forces of,
1863-Albany-(1864)-plts & bds (5t4) 10.50

NEW YORK STATE-Journal of Convention of,at Poughkeepsie,
17th of June, 1788-Poughkeepsie-(1788)-Nicholas Power-
84(of 86)p-lg4to-unbnd(loose in sigs)-ex rare
(5L1,dmpstnd,lacks last lf) 200.00

NEW YORK STATE-Laws of,from 1st to 12th Session,incl-NY-
1789-Hugh Gaine-2 vols-folio-orig old calf
(5L1,hng weak,vg) 75.00

NEW YORK STATE-Laws of-1802-2 vols-buck (5L7,ex-libr) 25.00

NEW YORK (STATE) LEGISLATURE-Join Comm Investigating
Seditious Activities-Albany-1920-2 pts in 4 vols-filed April 24,
1920 (5r4) 55.00

NEW YORK STATE LIBRARY-Catalogue of Books on Bibliography,
Typography & Engraving-Albany-1858-3 qtr mor-143p (5p6) 17.00

NEW YORK STATE-Manual for Use of Legislature of,1866-
1866 (5L7,bndg v wn) 5.00

NEW YORK STATE-Map of-Rensselaer Co-by Lake & Beers-
Phila-1862-61x61"-mntd on cl & rollers-Smith,Mason & Co
(5t0) 40.00

NEW YORK STATE MEDICAL ASSOC-Transactions for 1884 to
1899-Vols 1 to 16 incl-NY-1885 to 1899 (5t7) 75.00

NEW YORK STATE PRISONS-Inspectors of State Prisons of-
21st Annual Report-Albany-1869-Van Benthuysen-8vo-
hf mor-dbl pg lith-(Sing Sing)-288p (5j5) 25.00

NEW YORK STATE -State Engineer & Surv on RRs-of-Annual Report-
Jan,1854-Albany-1854-fld out map showing water & rr lines-
cl-424p (5t4) 10.00

NEW YORK TABLE BOOK-NY-1822-v sm8vo-orig prntd wrps-24p
(4h8,resewn) 27.50

NEW YORK TIMES-The Times' Recipes-NY-(1876)-111p-illus-
rev & index (5c0,ex-libr,chip) 5.00

NEW YORK TIMES CO-Pictorial Portfolio of the World-NY-1922-
WW 1-t folio-480p-cl-photos (5j5) 17.50

NEW YORK TIMES-War of the Nations...Portfolio in photogravure-
NY-c1919-folio-528p (5w0) 15.00

NEW YORK TO WASHINGTON-A Complete Guide Book of Route-
NY-1876-Taintor Bros-12mo-96p plus ads-maps & wdcuts-
orig wrps (5ss5) 9.00

NY UNIVERSITY LAW REVIEW-1924 to 69-Vol 1 thru 44-bnd
(5rr4,rbnd) 795.00

--same-single bound volumes (5rr4) ea 22.00

NY WEEKLY MUSEUM-or Polite Repository-Vol #28 to 48-
NY-Nov 12,1814 to April 1,1815-8vo-sewed-1st Octavo
(5r7) 20.00

NY, VIEWS OF EARLY-wi illus sketches-prepared for NY Chap
of Colonial Order of Acorn-NY-1904-142p-illus-priv prntd-
ltd to 213c (5t4) 10.00

NEW YORKER,A-Historical Sketch of Rise & Progress of Metropolitan
City of Amer-by a New Yorker-NY-1853-illus-orig cl-a.e.g.
(5r7,stnd,fox) 25.00

NEWAYGO CO,MICH-Portrait & Biogr Album of-Chig-1884-
572p-mor-Streeter 5844-rare (5h1) 50.00

NEWBEGIN,MARION I-Canada-NY-c1926-308p-illus-
(Edinburgh) (5h9) 5.00

NEWBERRY,J S - Geological Report-Exped from Santa Fe,New Mex
to Junction of Grand & Green Rivers...in 1859, under Macomb-
Wash-1876-4to-cl-148p-8 plts-illus-map (5t2) 10.00

NEWBERRY,J S-The Later Extinct Floras of NoAmer-edited by
Hollick-(Monogr of USGS,Vol 35)-Wash-1898-4to-hf mor-
68 plts (5m6,rub) 15.00

NEWBERRY LIBRARY-Check List of 15th Century Books in the-
Chig-1933-388p-8vo-cl-Lakeside Pr-850c prntd (4c1) 35.00

NEWBERY,DIEGO-Pampa Grass-(Buenos Aires-c1953-Ed Guarania)-
8vo-bds (4a3) 12.50

NEWBOLT,HENRY-Drakes Drum & Other Songs of the Sea-Lond-
n.d.-(ca 1912)-12 mntd col plts-vel-t.e.g.-ltd to 250c-
autg by artist (5c1,als) 45.00

--Submarine & Anti Submarine-NY-1918-12mo-cl-312p
(5t0,libr labl) 4.00

NEWBURGH BASE BALL CLUB-By Laws & Rules & Regulations-
Newburgh-1858-16mo-lea (5r7) 15.00

NEWCOMB,B M-Andrew Newcomb & Desc,Rev ed of Newcomb
Family-1923-1021p (5t9) 30.00

NEWCOMB,HARVEY-How to be a Lady-Bost-1859-224p,(28)-
12mo (5w7,sl wtrstn) 5.50

NEWCOMB,M A-4 Years of Personal Reminis of the War-Chig-
1893-pict cl-7p plus 131p-port (5r0) 10.00

NEWCOMB,PEARSON-The Alamo City-SanAnt-(1926)-154p-cl-
illus-Standard Prntg (5r0,pres) 10.00

NEWCOMB,REXFORD-Franciscan Mission Architecture of Alta
Calif-NY-1916-tall folio-3 qtrs mor-41 plts-1st ed (5r7) 40.00

--Old Kentucky Architecture-NY-1940-130 plts (5qq7,dj) 20.00

NEWCOMB,REXFORD (continued)

--Old Mission Churches & Historic Houses of Calif-Phila-1925-
Lippincott-379p-illus-cl (5x5) 30. (5tt0) 32.50
(5y0, libr stmp,5h1,5h4) 20. (5F5,dj,vf) 25.00

--Spanish House for America-Phila-1927-illus
(5d2,5qq7) 10. (5hh4,dj,mint) 17.50 (5h5,f,dj) 12.50

NEWCOMB,WM W-The Culture & Acculturation of Delaware Indians-
1956-Univ of Mich-(Mus of Anth #10)-8vo-wrps-141p (5h5,f) 4.00

NEWCOMBE,W A-British Columbia Totem Poles-Victoria-1931-
R8vo-22p-wrps-10 plts (5dd5) 5.00

NEWDIGATE,BERNARD H-Art of the Book-Lond-(1938)-Studio-
illus-folio-cl-spec Autumn nbr-Shakespeare Head Pr (4c1) 17.50

NEWE ZEITUNG VON DEM LANDE-n.p.-1522-sm4to-sewn-
1st prntg of 1st Newsletter-ex rare-Sabin 54946
(5hh0,rprd,lacks 2nd & 3rd Newsltr) 5,000.00

NEWELL,CHAS M-The Isle of Palms-Bost-1888-DeWolfe,Fiske-
1st ed (5m2) 12.00

--Kalani of Oahu-Bost-1881-frontis-pict cl-1st ed (5m2) 8.50

NEWELL,CHESTER-History of Revolution in Texas-NY-1838
(4c7,sl fox,5n4) 150.00

--same-Austin-(1935)-facs of 1838 ed (5a8,f) 15.00

NEWELL,CICERO-Indian Stories-Bost-(1912)-illus-191p (5yy7) 4.00

NEWELL,D E-A Treatise on Fine Arts-NY-1930-87p (5p7) 3.50

NEWELL,F H-Report on agric by irrigation in Western part of US at
11th Census, 1890-Wash-1894-GPO-336p-illus-col maps (5u3) 8.50

NEWELL,GORDON-Paddlewheel Pirate-NY-1959-248p-1st ed
(5s4,dj,f) 5.00

NEWELL,H M-History of Fayette Co,Ariz-1960-461p (5t9) 18.00

NEWELL,MRS HARRIET-Life & Writings of-Phila-Amer Sunday
Sch Union-1832-24mo-267p-illus (5i1,cov wn) 6.00

NEWELL,PETER-The Hole Book-NY-(1908)-Harper&Bros-24 lvs ea
wi hole-1st ed-publ Oct,1908
(4F6,f) 40. (5c8,sl rub) 25. (5rr2,5d3) 35.00

--Peter Newell's Pictures & Rhymes-NY-(1899)-obl 8vo-illus
(5t7) 10.00

--The Rocket Book-NY-1912-Harper&Bros-48p-pict cl-plts-
1st ed-hole (5aa0,sl wn,lacks fly) 10. (5rr2) 30. (5d3) 37.50

--The Slant Book-NY-1910-Harper&Bros-slanted-pic glazed bds-
cl bk-22 col plts-46p-1st ed
(4d2,sl wn) 17.50 (4F6,f) 30. (5d3) 37.50 (5rr2,cov bent)32.50

--Through the Looking Glass-NY-1902-40 illus by Peter Newell-
wide pg borders-white bds-g.-orig box (5d2,dj) 12.50

NEWELL,"DOC" ROBT-The Mountain Journal-1959-Lawton
Kennedy-ltd to 1000c (5k2) 12.50

NEWELL,WM W-Games & Songs of Amer Children-NY-1883-
Harper-8vo-242p-frontis-pict cl (5p1) 25.00

--same-NY-1884-illus-242p-orig pict cl (5m1) 10.00

NEWGATE CALENDAR,THE-Hartf-1926-265p (5p9) 6.00

NEWGATE PRISON-Copper Hill,Conn-Souvenir of-Copper Hill-
1893-obl 16mo-illus-papr (5t7) 6.00

NEWHALL,CHAS L-Record of My Ancestry-1899-222p & Chart
(5mm3) 10.00

NEWHALL,CHAS S-Trees of NoEastrn Amer-NY-1894-250p-4to-
illus (5s7) 7.50

--Trees of NoEastrn Amer & Shrubs of NoEastrn Amer-Knickerbocker-
1911-2 vols in 1 (5qq7) 4.00

--Vines of NoEastrn Amer-NY-1897-207p-4to-illus-1st ed (5s7) 8.50

NEWHALL,J B-Sketches of Iowa,or the Emigrant's Guide-NY-
1841-JHColton-252p-green cl-scarce (5F9,lacks map,chip) 25.00

NEWHALL,J R-Lynn,Mass,or, Jewels of the 3rd Plantation-1880-
2nd ed (5mm3) 10.00

--History of Lynn,Essex Co,Mass-Lynn-1883-priv prnt-illus
(4b6,pres,reprd) 25.00

--Essex Memorial,for 1836-1836-283p (5mm3) 4.00

NEWHALL,NANCY-Paul Strand,Photographs 1915 to 1945-
MOMA-1945-23 photos-32p-8vo (5ww3) 22.50

--Time in New England-NY-1950-4to-248p-photos-1st ed (5w0) 12.50

NEWHALL,RUTH WALDO-The Newhall Ranch-1958-Huntington
Libr-120p-8vo-o.p. (5hh4,dj,mint) 10.00

NEWHALL,WALTER S-A Memoir-Phila-1864-140p-frontis-
cl bk bds (5mm8) 6.50

NEWHAUS,EUGENE-San Diego Garden Fair-SanFran-(1916)-
80p-photos-bds (5s4) 5.00

NEWHOUSE,S-Trapper's Guide-NY-1874-Oneida Comm-215p-
illus-ads-g.- (5dd7,vf) 30.00

--same-NY-1893-illus-127p (4e9) 10.00

NEWHOUSE,W H,ed-Ore Deposits as Related to Structural Features-
Princeton-1942-4to-maps-280p (5u6) 15.00

NEWILL,PHYLLIS K-Good Food & How to Cook it-NY-1939-
555p-illus (5c0) 3.50

NEWLAND,D H- N Y S Mus Handbook #19-Guide to Geology of
Lake Geo Region-Albany-1942-234p-wrps (5p0) 3.50

NEWLAND,D H (continued)
--NYS Museum Bull #123-Iron Ores of Clinton Formation in
  NYS-Albany-1908-76p-wrps   (5p0)   3.50
NEWMAN,BERNARD-Balkan Background-NY-1945-Macm (5p0) 5.00
NEWMAN,BERTRAM-Cardinal Newman-Lond-1925-8vo-cl-223p
                           (5t0,lacks fly,fade)   3.75
--Edmund Burke-Lond-1927-348p   (5a1)   5.00
NEWMAN,BURKITT J-Eagle of Washington-Louisvl-1859-   cl
                           (5h7,stn,wn)
NEWMAN,CLARE-A Cookbook of Leftovers-Bost-1941-421p (5c0) 2.50
NEWMAN,REV DR-Sermon...on Plural Marriage,to which is
  added An Answer by Elder Orson Pratt-SaltLkCty-1870-
  21 dbl col pg,removed-scarce pamph   (5t3)   25.00
NEWMAN,ERNEST-A Musical Critic's Holiday-NY-1925-Knopf-
  330p   (5p0)   6.00
NEWMAN,EVELYN-International Note in Contemporary Drama-
  NY-1931-12mo-208p-cl-1st ed   (5t0)   5.00
NEWMAN,H W-His Desc,Judge Thos Dent,who settled in Md-
  1963-176p   (5mm3)   10.00
NEWMAN,HENRY-Marine Pocket Dictionary of Italian,Spanish,
  Portuguese & German Languages,English French-Lond-1800-
  12mo-350p-orig bds-2nd ed   (5ss2,hng crack) 27.50
NEWMAN,JOHN HENRY-Apologia Pro Vita Sua-Lond-1864-
  127p-3 qrtrs mor-t.e.g.-1st ed   (4b4,f)   90.00
--A letter addressed to Duke of Norfolk on occasion of
  Mr Gladstone's recent expostulation-Lond-1875-B M Pickering-
  8vo-orig prntd wrps-1st ed   (5x3)   15.00
--Via Media of Anglican Church,illus in lectures,etc,1830 to 41-
  2 vols-1908 to 11   (5L7)   12.50
NEWMAN,JOS-Goodbye Japan-NY-1942   (5x7)   4.50
NEWMAN,MRS-Too late-Lond-1873-Henry S King & Co-8vo-
  2 vols in 1-orig cl-1st ed   (5xx6,soil)   15.00
NEWMAN,RICHARD B-The Belle Islers,a Novel-Bost-(1908)-
  Lothrop,Lee & Shepard-8vo-illus-pict cl (5b2)   4.00
NEWMAN,T-Southern Calif of Today,illustrating its Prominent
  Points of interest,beautiful Homes & Public Buildings-
  (ca 1897)-about 100p-open end 8vo pictorial (5h6)   12.50
NEWMAN,W THOS-Hidden Mines & How to Find Them-Tor-1895-
  148p   (5s6)   6.50
NEWMARK,HARRIS-60 Yrs in So Calif 1853 to 1913-Bost-1930-
  illus-photos-684p plus index-3rd ed,rev (4t3)   30.00
NEWMARK,MARCO R-Jottings in So Calif History-LosAng-
  (1955)-Ward Ritchie Pr   (5x5)   15.00
NEWMARK,MARUICE H-Census of the City & Co of LosAng,for
  the year 1850,with analysis & appendix-LosAng-1929-
  Times Mirror Pr   (5x5)   7.50
--60 Yrs in So Calif 1853 to 1913-NY-1916-688p-illus-1st ed-
  illus   (5a9,sl rub) 30.00
--same-1930-HoughtonMiff-182 illus-3rd & best ed (5x5,vg) 50.00
NEWNHAM-DAVIS,LT COL-Dinners & Diners-Lond-1901-376p-
  new ed   (5w1)   5.00
NEWNHAM,W-Essays on Superstition-Lond-1830-430p,(2)-
  bds-cl-1st ed   (5w0,wn)   20.00
NEWPORT ILLUSTRATED-in series of Pen & Pencil Sketches by
  Editor of Newport Mercury-NY-1854-Appleton-110p (5p9) 10.00
NEWS FROM NEW ENGLAND-...Lond,1676-20p-ads-reprinted
  by Drake,1850 (5s2,f,Drake bkpl) 12.50 (5ss5,unbnd) 8.50
NEWSHOLME,SIR ARTHUR-Medicine & the State-Lond-1932
                                           (5x7)   5.00
NEWSOM,J A-Life & Practice of Wild & Modern Indian-OklaCty-
  1923-212p-illus-orig wrps   (5ii1,reprd) 25.00
NEWSOM,T M-Thrilling Scenes Among the Indians-Chig-1884-
  drawings-Chig-1884-drawings-241p-1st ed (4t3)   20.00
--same-Belford,Clarke-1888-illus-cl   (4k5,vg)   12.50
NEWTON,A EDW-The Amenities of Book Collecting & Kindred
  Affections-Bost-1918-8vo-bds-cl bk-t.e.g.-1st ed-1st issue
  wi error on pg 268 & errat-col frontis-facs illus
           (5r9) 20. (5ee9) 25. (5tt7,f)   30.00
--same-Bost-(1918)-373p-bds-Atlantic Monthly Pr-1st trade ed
    (5h7,edges wn) 7.50 (5ss3,hng crack) 10. (5w9,fade) 8.50
--same-Bost-(1922)-Little-373p-illus (5p9) 5. (5n4,f) 8.00
--same-Bost-(1924)-382p-illus-cl & bds-5th prntg (5t4) 6.50
--same-Bost-1931-illus   (4a1,pres)   20.00
--Ascot...prntd,not published,for Friends of A Edw Newton,
  Christmas,1933-"Oak Knoll"-1933-orig blue wrps-
  unpaginated-frontis-orig envelope-inscribed,signed "A E N"
  (5dd8) 5. (5w9)   6.50
--Bibliography & Pseudo bibliography-Phila-1936-116p
            (5w9,dj,5mm2,dj) 10. (5j4,dj)   7.50
--Blake's Act of Creation-"Oak Knoll"-1925-lg8vo-frontis-
  mor&bds   (5w9,pres)   17.50
--Christmas Spirit-priv prntd-1930-blu wrps,tied (5i1) 6. (5w9) 5.00

NEWTON,A EDW (continued)
--Derby Day & Other Adventures-Bost-1934-illus-frontis-
  1st ed   (5yy6,f,dj) 10. (5ss3,sp fade) 7.50
--same-Bost-1934-389p-bds-cl-col frontis-tissue dj-
  ltd to l,129c,nbrd,autg,slipcase-wi C Bronte Novelette
                              (5j3,f) 25. (5w9)   20.00
--Edwin Forrest & His Noble Creation-Phila-1928-11p-illus-
  blue wrps-cord ties-orig envelope   (5w9)   6.00
--End Papers-Bost-1933-cl-1st ed (5h7) 7.50 (5yy6,f,dj) 12.50
--same-Bost-1933-235p-illus-bds-cl-unopnd-ltd to l,35lc,nbrd,
  autg   (5d3,5w9)   15.00
--The Greatest Book in the World,& Other Papers-Bost-c1925-
  451p-illus-bds&cl-1st ed   (5w9,autg,wn dj)   25.00
--same-LB-1925-451p-4th imprint-illus   (5e8)   4.00
--same-Bost-(1925)-8vo-bds & cl-g.t.-col frontis-illus-1st ed-
  ltd to 470c,autg   (5ee9)   25.00
--A Magnificent Farce-Bost-(1921)-12mo-illus-bds-cl bk-g.t.
                              (4c1) 7.50 (5m1)   6.50
--Thos Hardy,Novelist or Poet-1929-priv prntd-thn4to-cl bds-
  port-ltd to 950c   (5r9,f) 15. (5mm2)   17.50
--Oscar Wilde-"Oak Knoll" -c1912-27p-frontis-orig blue wrps-
  errat tip in   (5w9,autg)   12.50
--Pope,Poetry & Portrait-"Oak Knoll"-1928-illus-orig blue wrps
                                          (5w9)   5.00
--Reflections on the Character of Mme Thrale Piozzi-"Oak Knoll"-
  1921-7p-orig blue wrps   (5w9,pres)   10.00
--This Book Collecting Game-Bost-1928-1st trade ed-bds-cl bk-
  410p-plts-ports   (5w9,autg,5u6) 12.50 (5w9) 6.50
--same-Bost-1928-illus-ltd to 990c,autg,box
            (5d3,f) 20. (5mm1)   25.00
--A Tourist in Spite of Himself-Bost-1930-252p-illus
  (5w9,inscr by Mrs N) 7.50 (5m1,dj,5b2,f,dj)   5.00
NEWTON,A P,ed-Thos Gage the English American-(1946)-9 illus-
  3 maps-spec ed for El Patio,Guatemala Cty-407p (5yy8) 7.50
NEWTON,B C-Uncle Tom's Cadillac-Jacksonvl-1956-75p-
  wrps-priv publ-ltd to 1000c   (5x2)   8.50
NEWTON,BENIANS-So Fraica,Rhodesia & the Protectorates-
  Vol 8 of "Cambridge History of Brit Empire"-NY-1936-
  thk8vo   (5x2)   15.00
NEWTON CENTRE WOMAN'S CLUB,publ-Our Village Cook
  Book-Bost-1889-104p-ads   (5c4,brok hngs)   6.50
NEWTON,CLAIR A HEMENWAY-Capt John Whipple,1617 to
  1685 & his Descendants-Naperville-1946 (5jj3,pencil) 15.00
NEWTON,EARLE-Vermont Story,1749 to 1949-Montpelier-1949-
  4to-282p-cl-illus (5u9,f,dj) 14.50 (5z3,f,pres)   22.50
NEWTON,EPHRAIM H-History of Marlboro-1930-330p-
  500c prntd   (5e8)   12.75
NEWTON,FORSTER-or,the marchant service-Lond-1832-
  Jas Cochrane-3 vols-8vo-orig cl&bds-papr labls-1st ed
                          (5xx6,lacks flys,sl stns) 35.00
--same-Bentley-1838-(Standard Novels)-sm8vo-dec cl-g.t.-
  383p-frontis   (4a8)   4.50
NEWTON,H A-Metric System of Weights & Measures,Eaton's
  Common School Arith-Bost-1867-Taggard&Thompson-12mo-
  prntd wrps-pg 313 to 324   (5p1)   5.00
LORD,H W L-Lord Lyons-Lond-1913-2 vols-ports-1st ed (5q8) 22.55
NEWTON,ISAAC-The Method of Fluxions & Infinite Series-
  Lond-1736-H Woodfall,prntr-calf-4to-1st ed-frontis &
  errata lf (both misbnd)   (4h0,rebkd,f)   550.00
--Philosophiae Naturalis Principia Mathematica-Lond-1687-
  Jussu Soc Reg-4to-fldg plt-calf-g.bk-1st ed-Grolier 100
                          (5hh0)   8,500.00
--same-Lond-1726-calf,mor labl,raised bands-530p-lg papr ed
  (200c)   (5ee1,rbnd,f bndg,lacks port) 275.00
--same-Glasguae-1822-4 vols-editio nova   (5t7)   30.00
--Treatise of the System of the World-Lond-1728-calf bkd vel-
  8vo-154p-2 plts-errata lf-1st ed   (5ii0,f)   225.00
--Universal Arithmetick-Lond-1769-8vo-calf-lea labl-8 fldg tables-
  3rd ed in Engl   (4h0,sl worming) 120.00
NEWTON,J-Newton's Guide to Bd of Trade Exam of Master,
  Mates of Sailing Ships & Steam-Lond-1910-310p-illus-
  16th ed,rev   (5s1,rprd,ex-libr) 6.50
NEWTON,JAS-A Compleat Herbal-Lond-1802-(16)p-175 plts-
  frontis-bds-papr bk-6th ed   (5w3,crack)   47.50
NEWTON,JOHN-Capt John Brown of Harper's Ferry-NY-1902-
  288p   (5j6)   4.00
NEWTON,JOHN-Trigonometria Britanica,in Two Books-Lond-
  1658-R & W Leybourn-folio-calf-1st ed of 1st bk-1st Engl ed
  of 2nd bk   (4h0,rebkd)   400.00
NEWTON,JOS FORT-The Builders-CedrRapids-1921-Torch Pr-
  cl   (5p5)   7.50
--David Swing Poet Preacher-Chig-1909-273p-cl (5h7,f,uncut) 7.50
--Lincoln & Herndon-CedRap-1910-376p-cl   (5h2)   10.00

NEWTON, LADY-Lyme Letters 1660 to 1760-Lond-1925-342p-
plts-ports   (5a1)   4.50
NEWTON, RICHARD-Rills from Fountain of Life-NY-1870-220p-
cl   (5h1)   4.00
NEWTON, STANLEY-Story of Sault Ste Marie & Chippewa Co-
SaultSteM-1923-199p-wrps-priv pub-scarce   (5h2)   20.00
NEWTON, VIRGINIUS-Confederate States Ram Merrimac or Virginia-
Richmond-1892-W E Jones-28p   (5F9,f,unopnd) 10.00
NEWTON, W D-Westward with Prince of Wales-Tor-1920-351p-
port   (4f9,lacks fly) 4.50 (5dd0) 3.50
NEWTON, W M-Hist of Barnard, Vt-2 vols-(1928)-maps & illus
                                              (5t9)   15.00
NEWTON, WM-Twenty Years on the Saskatchewan, NW Canada-
Lond-1897-184p-port-illus (4f9) 25.   (4a8,pres,fly cut) 17.50
NEWTON-WHITE, E-Hurt Not the Earth-Tor-1958-188p-illus (5a1) 5.00
NEYHART, LOUISE A-Giant of the Yards-Bost-1952-illus
                               (5s4,f) 5. (5dd9) 8.25
NIAGARA-1883-R Lespinasse, copyrite-183p-hf lea (4m2) 15.00
NIAGARA ALBUM-n.p.-(ca1870)-12 fldg Ambertype views-
obl 16mo   (5t4)   4.00
NIAGARA FALLS-Great manuf village of West-Bost-1853-
Niagara Falls Hydraulic Co-fldg maps-wrps   (5g4)   7.50
NIAGARA, FALLS OF-Lond-1860-64p-cl-Dow p.1226 (5h1)   7.50
NIAGARA IN SUMMER & WINTER-(Phila,ca1904)-obl 8vo-
32p of illus   (5b9, 5w8)   5.00
NIAGARA HISTORICAL SOC-Bul #4-Niagara on the Lake-1898-
frontis-prntd wrps-plt   (5w8)   10.00
NIAGARA, THE WONDERS OF-Souvenir Pamph-1914-Shredded
Wheat Co-24p-col covs-illus   (5a6,f)   5.00
NIBLACK, ALBERT P-Coast Indians of So Alaska & No Brit Col-
Wash-1890-70 photos-maps-part lea-pg 225 to 386
                                        (4t3,ex-libr) 20.00
NIBLEY, PRESTON-Brigham Young, the Man & His Work-SaltLkCty-
1937   (5x5,crack)   10.00
--same-Independence-(1944)   (5a8)   3.00
--Jos Smith, the Prophet-SaltLkCty-1944-Deseret News Pr (5x5) 10.00
--Pioneer Stories-SaltLkCty-1944-4th prntg (5jj1,f)   8.00
--The Witnesses of the Book of Mormon-SaltLkCty-1946-
200p   (5r8)   15.00
NICKERSON, ANSEL D-A Raw Recruit's War Experience-Prov-
1888-16mo-63p   (4a7)   7.50
NICHOL, J P-Phenomena & Order of the Solar System-1842-
buck   (5L7,rbnd,stn) 15.00
--The planet Neptune, an exposition & history-Edinb-1848-
John Johnstone-8vo-orig cl-frontis-6 plts   (5i8,wn)   17.50
NICHOLAS, ANNA-An idyl of the Wabash & other stories-
Indpls-1899-Bowen Merrill-1st ed   (5m2)   12.50
NICHOLAS, EDW J-Toward Gettysburg-n.p.-(Univ Pk,Pa)-
1958-276p-illus   (5w4,dj)   5.00
NICHOLAS, GRIFFITH A-The Biddy Club-Chig-1888-308p
                                         (5w7,wn)   6.50
NICHOLL, EDITH M-Observations of a Ranchwoman in New Mex-
Lond-1898-Macm&Co-12mo-cl-   illus-1st ed-scarce
                                         (5hh4,f)   75.00
NICHOLL, JOHN-Desc of John Nicholl of Islip, England who
died 1467-(1894)-62p   (5mm3)   25.00
NICHOLLS, W-Sgt Francis Nicholls of Stratford, Conn 1639 &
Desc of his son, Caleb-1909-101p   (5t9)   10.00
NICHOLS, ALICE-Bleeding Kansas-NY-1954-1st ed (5jj3,f,dj) 10.00
NICHOLS, CHAS L-Issaiah Thomas, Printer, Writer & Collector-
Bost-1912-Merrymount Pr-8vo-bds&cl-110c prntd-Club of
Odd Volumes   (4c1)   35.00
NICHOLS, CLAUDE H-History of 1st Christian Church, Baxter
Springs, Kansas(cov title)-(Baxter Sprngs, 1961)-40p-photos-
wrps   (5t3)   4.00
NICHOLS, ED-Ed Nichols Rode a Horse-Dallas-1943(5a8,autg) 35.00
NICHOLS, EDW J-Toward Gettysburg-n.p.-(Univ Park)-1958-
276p-illus   (5w5,dj)   5.00
NICHOLS, EFFINGHAM H-Argument before Cox, in Support of
right of Central Branch Union Pac RR Co..-Wash-1869-44p-
disbnd-rare   (5L2)   20.00
NICHOLS, F M-Britton, an Engl Translation & Notes by-Wash-
1901   (5r4)   17.50
NICHOLS, FRANCIS H-Through Hidden Shensi-NY-1902-333p-
illus-cl   (5t2, libr labl) 5.00
NICHOLS, GEO WARD-The sanctuary, a story of the Civil War-
NY-1866-Harper-12mo-orig cl-frontis-5 plts-1st ed
                          (5i0, lend libr labl) 20. (5m2,ex-libr) 9.50
--Story of the Great March-NY-1865-cl-408p-map-illus
      (4h1,sl wn) 10. (5q8) 7.50 (5yy7,wn) 6. (5j6,5xx7) 8.50
--same-Lond-1865-288p-ads-fldg map-illus   (5mm8)   5.00
NICHOLS, MRS H S P-Phila New Century Club Book of Recipes-
1915-255p-blue cl   (5g9,f)   6.00

NICHOLS, HERBERT B-Historic New Rochelle-New Rochelle-
1938-illus-fldg map   (5yy6) 6. (5mm3)   7.50
NICHOLS, J L-Progress of a Race or Remarkable Advancement of
Amer Negro-Naperville-1920-illus   (5x2,rbnd)   25.00
NICHOLS, J P-Jas Styles of Kingston, NY & Geo Stuart of
Schoolcraft-1936-214p   (5mm3)   7.50
NICHOLS, JAS M-Perry's Saints or Fighting Parson's Regiment in
War of Rebellion-Bost-(1886)-299p-illus (5t4,hng weak) 10.50
NICHOLS, JAS T-New South & Old Mexico-DesMoines-(1927)-
12mo-128p-illus   (5dd6,lt fox)   4.75
NICHOLS, JEANNETTE-Alaska-Cleve-1924-fldg col map-photos-
map frontis-scarce-431p plus index (4t3) 40. (5ss1) 30.00
--Growth of Amer Democracy-NY-1939 et seq-819p-illus (5h9) 5.00
NICHOLS, L-Breakthrough on the Color Front-NY-1954-1st ed
                                              (5x2)   10.00
NICHOLS, MARIE LEONA-Ranald MacDonald, Adventurer-
Caldwell-1940-176p   (5dd9)   12.50
NICHOLS, NELL B-Good Home Cooking Across USA-Ames-(1952)-
560p-illus   (5c4)   7.50
NICHOLS, ROBT-Aurelia & other poems-Lond-1920-Chatto&Windus-
cl bkd bds-ltd to 110c,autg   (5ss3)   25.00
--The Budded Branch-1918-12mo-bds&cl-Beaumont Pr-ltd to 50c
                                            (5ee9)   10.00
--The Smile of the Sphinx-1920-8vo-dec bds-Beaumont Pr-
ltd to 35c,autg   (5ee9)   25.00
NICHOLS, THOS L-40 Years of Amer Life-Lond-1864-2 vols-
labls-cl   (5y0,rbnd,ex-libr) 37.50 (5L1,vg) 65.00
--Woman in All Ages & Nations-NY-(1849)-240p-cl (5h7)   5.00
NICHOLSON, BYRON-In Old Quebec & Other Sketches-Que-
1909-162p-col frontis-plts-2nd ed   (5a1)   4.50
NICHOLSON, ELIZ-What I Know-Phila-1856-12mo-156p
                                    (5c0,sp tn,stns)   20.00
NICHOLSON, ISAAC F-Baltimore Stock Exchange Historical Sketch-
Balt-1898-78p-illus   (4b8)   10.00
NICHOLSON, J D-On the Side of the Law-Edmonton, Alberta-
1944-288p-illus-map   (5xx5)   6.00
NICHOLSON, JAS R-History of the Order of Elks-NY-1953-
432p   (5u3)   4.00
NICHOLSON, JOHN-Martyrdom of Jos Standing-SaltLkCty-
1886-160p-1st ed   (4t3,sl wn)   35.00
NICHOLSON, M-The Cavalier of Tennessee-Indnpls-1928 (5x2,dj)5.00
NICHOLSON, M A-Carpenter & Joiner's Companion-Lond-n.d.-
(1837)-264p-plts-cl   (5jj9,rbnd)   25.00
NICHOLSON, MARGARET-Dictionary of American English Usage-
NY-1957-Oxford Univ Pr   (5p7)   4.75
NICHOLSON, MEREDITH-Broken Barriers-NY-1922-
8vo-cl   (5b2,dj,f)   5.00
--The Cavalier of Tennessee-NY-1928-Bobbs, Merrill
                          (5h6,lacks fly) 3. (5b2,f)   4.00
--same-Indnpls-(1928)-1st ed-ltd to 249c,autg-cl-box
                                  (5mm2,dj,mint)   15.00
--Hoosier Chronicle-Bost&NY-1912-606p-1st ed
                          (5xx8) 7.50 (5k0,f)   12.50
--The Hoosiers-NY-1915-1915 Centennial ed   (4a9)   6.00
--The House of a Thousand Candles-Indnpls-(1905)-col illus by
H C Christy-1st ed   (5ee3,f)   3.50
--Short Flights-Indnpls-1891-16mo-cl-1st ed of auth's 1st book
                                            (5gg6)   15.00
--Valley of Democracy-NY-1918-284p-illus   (5s4)   5.00
NICHOLSON, P-Encyclopedia of Architecture-1850-2 vols-4to-
illus   (5L7)   45.00
--The Carpenter's New Guide-Lond-1801-J Taylor-4to-10p,
73p text-78 plts-3rd ed   (5t0)   35.00
--New Carpenter's Guide-Lond&NY-n.d.-4to-cl-122p, 121 plts-
& 240p, 25 plts-incl Carpenter & Builder's Complete Measurer
                                            (5q0)   25.00
NICHOLSON, WM-An introduction to natural philosophy-Phila-
1788-calf-plts-1st Amer ed   (5g4,rub)   75.00
NICHOLSON, WM-An Almanac of 12 Sports-Lond-1898-by
Rudyard Kipling-folio-12 col plts-1st ed (5v2,rprd)   10.00
--Characters of Romance-Lond-n.d.-WmHeinemann-16 folio plts
in col-rare   (5v2,vg)   85.00
--The Pirate Twins-Great Britain-n.d.-obl 8vo-28 plts
                                      (5v2,ex-libr)   12.50
NICK OF THE WOODS-or Jibbenainosay-Phila-1837-Carey,
Lea&Blanchard-2 vols-12mo-orig cl-papr labls
                                  (5x1,hng rprd)   150.00
NICKEL, FRANK F-Direct Acting Steam Pumps-NY-1923-258p-
illus   (5t4)   6.00
NICKEL, OTTO-Destiny-NY-Farrar&Rinehart-1930-unpaged-
wdcuts   (5i1)   5.00
NICKELL, J M-Botanical Ready Reference-Chig-1881-268p-narr 8vo-
limp lea   (5w3,scuff)   9.50

NICKERSON,HOFFMAN-The Amer Rich-NY-1930-DblDay (5p9) 5.00
NICKERSON,M H-Carols of the Coast-Halifax-1892
(5w8,lacks fly)   15.00
NICKERSON,W SEARS-Land Ho!-Bost-1931-illus-fldg map-
buck & bds-illus   (5q8)   15.00
NICKERSON,WM-How I Turned $1,000 into a Million in Real
Estate in My Spare Time-NY-1959-S&S-497p (5t4) 4. (5p0)   4.75
NICKLIN,PHILIP H-Letters Descriptive of Virginia Springs,Roads
Leading Thereto & Doings there At-Phila-1837-248p-2nd ed
(5j6)   6.50
--Pleasant Peregrination thru Prettiest Parts of Penna Performed by
Peregine Prolix-Phila-1836-16mo-148p-orig bds-papr labl
(5m4)   30.00
NICOL,JOHN-Life & adventures of John Nicol,mariner-Edinb-
1822-Blackwood-12mo-215p-part calf-1st ed-half t. port-
rare   (5l9,rbnd cl) 200.   (5ss2,sp wn)   135.00
--same-NY-1936-4to-port-Gordon Grant,illus
(5s6) 15.   (5p5,dj)   12.50
NICOLAS,FRANCOIS-Proces Politique,La Reine vs Nicolas et
al-Montr-1838-12mo-43p-hf calf   (5w8,libr stmp)   160.00
NICOLAS,J H-A Rose Odyssey-NY-1937-238p-photos (5s7)   5.00
NICOLAY,HELEN-Lincoln's Secretary-NY-(1949)-illus-363p
(5t7,dj)   7.50
--MacArthur of Bataan-NY-1942-188p-illus (5w9,dj)   3.00
--Personal Traits of Abraham Lincoln-NY-1912-1st ed (5q8)   4.00
--same-NY-1939-386,(1)p   (5h7,f,dj)   4.00
NICOLAY,JOHN G-Abraham Lincoln,a History-NY-1890-
Century Co-10 vols-illus & maps-a.e.g.-3 qrtrs mor
(5w0,sl rub) 62.50   (5r7)   125.00
--same-NY-1909-10 vols-illus-t.e.g.   (5s9)   45.00
--Abraham Lincoln,A Short Life-NY-1919-12mo-cl-577p-port
(5t0)   4.50
--Complete Works of Abraham Lincoln-NY-(1894)-Tandy,Thomas Co-
12 vols-frontis-cl-lg margins   (5t0,unopnd)   35.00
--same-n.p.-(1894)-12 vols-hf lea-sponsors' ed (5ee3,sl wn)   27.50
--same-NY-(1905)-Lamb Pub Co-12 vols-8vo-ports-cl-ltd to
1000 nbrd sets-new & enlrgd ed   (5t0)   35.00
--The Outbreak of Rebellion-NY-1881-maps (5q8)   3.50
--Short Life of Abraham Lincoln-NY-1902-port-578p (4b3)   4.50
NICOLEANO,G N-Introduction a L'Ampelographie Roumaine-
Bucarest-1900-152p,(1)-wrps-4to (5w1,chip,top pgs tn)   18.50
NICOLL,ALLARDYCE-British Drama-NY-(1925)-549p-illus(5t4) 7.50
--History of English Drama,1660 to 1900-Cambr-1952-3 vols-
4th ed   (4j3,perf stmp on t.p)   15.00
--Stuart Masques & Renaissance Stage-NY-1938-224p-illus-cl
(5t2)   7.50
NICOLL,BRUCE H-Sam McKelvie,Son of the Soil-Lincoln-1954-
174p-photos   (5s4,f)   6.50
NICOLL,LUCIE G-The English Cookery Book-Lond-(1936)-402p
(5c5)   4.50
NICOLL,M J-Nicoll's Birds of Egypt-Lond-1930-Hugh Rees Ltd-
2 vols-col plts-maps-orig cl-folio-v scarce (5z9) 115. (4p5) 185.00
NICOLL,MICHAEL JOHN-3 Voyages of a Naturalist-Lond-1908-
cl-8vo-56 photos-1st ed   (5z9,f)   7.50
NICOLLET,J N-Report intended to illus a map of hydrographical
Basin of Upper Mississippi River-Wash-1843-calf-237p-fldg map-
1st ed-scarce   (4n4)   85.00
NICOLLS,WM J-Story of Amer Coals-1897   (5L7)   8.50
NICOLS,A-Snakes,Marsupials & Birds-Lond-n.d.-(early 1900)-
370p-4 plts-cl-12mo-v scarce   (4p5,crack,sp tn)   15.00
NICOLSON,H-Sir Arthur Nicolson,Bart,1st Lord Carnock-1930-
plt   (5L7)   6.50
NICOLSON,HAROLD-Aspects of his Life,Character & Poetry-
Bost-1925-HoughtonMiff-308p   (5p0)   6.00
--Dwight Morrow-NY-(1935)-illus-1st ed (5q8,autg)   4.00
NICOLSON,J U-The Sainted Courtezan-Pascal Covici-1924-
R8vo-illus-2 tone bndg-g.t.   (5t5,dj)   15.00
NICOLSON,MARJORIE HOPE-Conway Letters-NewHav-1930-
516p-cl-illus   (5t2)   7.50
NIDA,E A-Customs & Cultures-NY-1954   (5x2,dj)   3.00
NIDA,WM LEWIS-A Child's Robinson Crusoe-Chig-(copyrite 1916)-
8vo-160p-pict cl-160p-frontis-illus-Beckley Cardy (5aa2)   3.50
NIDEVER,GEO-Life & Adventures of,(1802 to 1883)-1937-
Univ of Calif-8vo-cl   (5h4,f,dj)   13.50
NIEBUHR,H R-Ministry in Historical Perspectives-1956 (5L7)   7.50
NIEBUHR,REINHOLD-Christian Realism & Political Problems (5L7)4.50
--Faith & History-NY-1949-sm8vo-cl-8,257p-1st ed (5t0,f,dj)   4.50
NIEDRACH,ROBT J-Birds of Denver & Mtn Parks-(Denv)-1939-
196p-cl   (5h7)   5.00
NIELSEN,B F-H C Andersen Bibliografi,digterens Danske vaerker
1822 to 1875-Kobenhavn-1942-462p-orig blue cardboard
(5c8,f,unopnd)   25.00

NIELSEN,KAY-East of the Sun & West of the Moon-Lond-n.d.-
orig cl-4to-frontis-24 col plts-illus   (4n5,rbkd)   75.00
--Hans Andersen Fairy Tales-Lond-n.d.-mtd col plts by Kay
Nielsen & others   (5jj3)   32.50
NIEMEYER,HARRY H-Yarns of Battery A-n.p.-n.d.-Souvenir ed-
ads-photos-wrps   (4b3)   10.00
NIEMOELLER,ADOLPH F-Amer Encyclopedia of Sex-NY-1935
(5x7)   12.50
--Sexual Slavery in Amer-NY-c1935-255p   (5w5)   12.50
NIERITZ,GUSTAV-Little Drummer,or,Filial Affection-Lond-
1852-Addey&Co-illus-orig dec cl   (5c8,sl wn)   8.50
NIESZ,JOHN-The Family Guide to Health & Husbandry-Canton,O-
1851-12mo-hf calf-5 illus-376p-some foxing (5w3,wn)   16.50
NIETLISPACH,MADAME F-Cold Dishes & Hors D'Oeuvres-
Lond-n.d.-63p-68 col plts   (5c9)   3.00
NIETZCHIE,FRIEDRICH-Thus Spake Zarathustra-NY-1914-
36, 458p-cl-ltd ed   (5t0)   5.00
--same-NY-1924-479p   (5p7)   3.50
NIGGLI,JOSEPHINA-Mexican Village-Chapel Hill-(c1945)-
UNC Pr-8vo-cl-illus-4th prntg   (4a3)   3.50
NIGHTINGALE,FLORENCE-Notes on Nursing-NY-1860-140p-
(5w0,5v0) 7.50   (5kk5,chip) 8.   (5ee3)   8.50
NIGHTS OF STRAPAROLA,THE-Lond-1894-2 vols-sm4to-plts-
silk buck-ltd ed   (5t5)   22.50
NIGNON,EDOUARD-Les Plaisirs de la Table-A Paris Chez
L'Auteur-n.d.-(ca1926)-333p-cl-frontis (5c9,1 pg loose)   10.00
NIKITINA-By Herself-Lond-1959-8vo-cl-frontis by Jean Cocteau-
23 plts-1st ed   (5p5,dj)   12.50
NIKKANOCHEE,OCEOLA-Narr of Early Days & Remin of-Lond-
1841-1st ed-illus-(A Welch)   (5tt6,f)   75.00
NILES,BLAIR-The James-n.d.-(c1939)   (4a9)   4.50
--same-Rivers of Amer-NY-1939-F&R-359p   (5x0)   5.00
NILES CENTER WOMAN'S CLUB COOK BOOK-(Niles Center,Ill)-
1942-62p-spiral bndg   (5g9,spiral broke)   2.50
NILES,EMORY-Amer Maritime Cases-Balt-1924-2 vols-1,743p
(5s1,sl soil)   8.00
NILES,GRACE G-Bog Trotting for Orchids-NY-1904-frontis-
24p col illus-310p   (5i3,f,5q0) 15.   (5ee3,f)   17.50
--Hoosac Valley-1912-549p-illus   (5zz0)   15.00
NILES,HEZEKIAH-Centennial offering-NY-1876-cl(5g4ex-libr) 10.00
--Journal of Proceedings of Friends of Domestic Industry-Balt-
1831-3 qrtrs lea-16, 44, 198p   (5m3,ex-libr)   32.50
--Principles & Acts of Revolution in Amer-Balt-1822-495p-hf calf
(5m3)   22.50
--Things as They are, or, Federalism turned inside out-1809-75p-
buck   (5L7,rbnd,sl rprd)   12.50
NILES,JOHN J-Singing Soldiers-NY-1927-171p-cl-illus-
1st ed   (5g5)   10.00
--Songs My Mother Never Taught Me-NY-(1929)-Gold Label Books-
227p   (5p0)   5.00
NILES,JOHN M-History of So Amer & Mexico-Hartford-1837-
2 vols in 1- 2 col maps-illus-lea-2nd ed (5i3) 65.   (4a5)   80.00
--same-Hartford-1839-2 vols in 1-orig calf
(4c7,chip,rprd,S Houston on autg)   50.00
--A View of So Amer & Mexico-NY-1825-2 vols-port-calf-
1st ed   (5L3)   35.00
--same-NY-1826-H Huntington-12mo-orig calf-2 vols in 1
(5x5,wn,v fox) 12.50   (5x5) 25.   (5L3,f)   27.50
NILES REGISTER, 1843-Vol 64-folio-416p-26 complete issues-
v scarce   (4n4)   115.00
NILES,SAML-Brief & Plain Essay on God's Wonderworking Providence
for N England-NLond-1747-16mo-(6),34p-sewn-1st ed-
T Green,ptr   (5hh0)   750.00
NILES WEEKLY REGISTER-1811 to 1848-1712 issues in 67 vols-
includes supplements   (4a5,lacks 2 vols)   850.00
--same-Vols 1 thru 50-Balt-1811 to 1836-49 vols-8vo-calf-
lea labels   (5m6,lacks 1 vol,rub)   450.00
NILES,WM OGDEN-The Tippecanoe text book-Balt-1840-
stitchd-port   (5g3,f)   10.00
NILES,WILLYS-500 majority-NY-1872-Putnam-8vo-orig cl-1st ed
(5i9)   12.50
NILSSON,SVEN-The Primitive Inhabitants of Scandinavia-
Lond-1868-16 plts-79p, 272p-cl   (5t2,rbnd)   8.50
NIMMO,JOS-Report in Relation to Proposed Imrpov of Harbor of
Galveston-Wash-SMD 111-1884-31p   (5n4)   15.00
NIMPORT-Wayside Series-Bost-1875-12mo-cl-1st ed of Bynner's
1st book   (5gg6)   7.50
NIMROD-The Chace,the Turf & the Road-Lond-1837-301p-8vo-
illus by Alken-3 qtrs calf-raised bands   (5p6)   45.00
--same-NY-1931-Georgian Pr-illus-lin sp   (5t5)   3.50
--Memoirs of Life of Late John Mytton of Halston Shropshire-NY-
1925-Longmans-8vo-col illus   (5ee3,sp fade)   5.00

NIMROD (continued
--Sporting,embellished by large engrs,etc-Lond-1838-folio-
144p-hf bnd-engrs   (5q1)   22.50
NIMUENDAJU,CURT-The Apinaye-Wash-1939-(Catholic U of
Amer Anth Series #8)-8vo-wrps-189p-illus   (5h5,f)   9.00
NIN,ANAIS-Children of the Albatross-NY-1947-E P Dutton-
1st ed   (5ss9,dj full pg pres)   15.00
--The Four Chambered Heart-NY-(1950)-1st ed   (5yy6)   12.50
--The House of Incest-Paris-(1936)-orig wrps-1st ed-ltd to 249c,
autg-Siana Editions   (5d2,unopnd,mint)   75.00
--Winter of Artifice-n.p.-n.d.-1st ed-ltd-(500c handsent by
author)   (5d9,pres)   75.00
1914 YEAR BOOK & CATALOGUE-Assoc of Amer Artists-NY-
1914-John Lane-98 illus-9p-8vo-wrps   (4e0)   25.00
1903 COOK BOOK-"Lend A Hand",comp-Berlin-26p-wrps (5c4) 5.00
90 YEARS,THE STORY OF WM PARMER FULLER-1939-Grabhorn Pr-
port-illus-sm folio-bds wi cl bk-5000c priv prntd
            (4p2) 15. (5jj1,f)   8.50
99 RECIPES-Portl,Maine-1917-24p-12mo-wrps-Ninety&Nine Club
            (5c4)   3.00
99 SALADS-& How to Make Them-NY-1897-57p-illus-wrps-
Gorham Silver Co   (5c5)   5.00
NIPHER,FRANCIS E-Thoughts on Our Conceptions of Physical Law-
KansCty-1878-8vo-orig wrps-9p   (5c5)   10.00
NIPS,JACK-The Yankee Spy-Bost-(1794)-20p-sewn-plain wrps-
prntd for John Asplund   (5m3)   67.50
NIRVANA-Commercial Cake Decoration-Lond-n.d.-95p-74 illus-
sm4to   (5g9)   4.50
NISHIMURA,SHINJI-A Study of Ancient Ships of Japan,Part 4,
Skin Boats-Tokyo-1931-25 plts-60 drawings-map (5c1)   50.00
--Reed Canoe-Tokyo-1925-10 plts-Engl text   (5c1)   25.00
NISTER,E-Nister's Panorama-Lond-(c1890)-folio-pict glazed bds-
cl bk-5 dbl col plts wi cut outs attached by tapes (4d1)   45.00
NITCHIE,EDW B-Lip Reading,Principles & practise-NY-(1919)-
illus-324p   (5t4)   6.00
NITCHIE,ELIZ-The Rev Colonel Finch-NY-1940-8vo-cl-109p-
illus   (5t0)   5.00
NITOBE,INAZO-Bushido,the Soul of Japan-NY-(1905)-
Putnam-203p   (5p7)   3.75
NITT,F-Decadence of Europe-1923   (5L7)   4.00
--Escape-NY-1930-267p-illus   (5t4)   5.00
NIVEN,FREDK-Hands Up-Lond-(1913)-316p plus ads (5dd5)   5.00
NIVEN,JOHN-Dynamic Amer-NY-(1958)-thk folio-illus
            (5yy6,box)   12.50
NIVOVA PAVHOSTO-The Four Gospels,transl for Cheyenne
Indians by Rodolphe Petter-Lame Deer,Mont-1928-273p
            (4b2,autg,mint)   22.50
NIX,EVETT DUMAS-Oklahombres,Particularly the Wilder Ones-
StL-1929-280p (4p2,5k2) 25. (4a5) 28.50 (5yy7,dj)20.
            (5h0)   22.50
NIX,JOHN W-A Tale of 2 Schools & Springtown Parker Co-Ft Worth-
1945-347p plus index-photos-1st ed-v scarce (5L0)   30.00
NIXON,HOWARD M-Styles & Designs of Bookbindings from
12th to 20th Century-Lond-1956-Broxbourne Libr-119 plts-
folio-t.e.g.   (5d5)   200.00
NIXON,LARRY-Vagabond Voyaging-Bost-1938-314p-photos-
dec cov   (5s1)   4.00
NIXON,LILLY LEE-James Burd,Frontier Defender-Phila-1941-
198p-frontis-port-map-1st ed   (5h9)   8.50
NIXON,OLIVER W-How Marcus Whitman saved Oregon-Chig-
1895-2nd ed-illus-339p   (4b3) 6. (5s4)   5.00
--same-Chig-1896-8vo-cl-339p-illus-5th ed (4f9) 5. (5m8)   3.00
--Whitman's Ride Thru Savage Lands wi Sketches of Indian Life-
1905-Winona Publ Co-illus   (5h6,4n8)   5.00
NIXON,PAT IRELAND-A Century of Medicine in San Antonio-
SanAnt-1936-405p-spec ed,ltd to 100c,nbrd-rare (5n4,mint) 45.00
--same-trade ed   (5n4,mint)   15.00
--History of Texas Medical Assn,1853 to 1953-Austin-1953-476p
            (4a5,dj)   15.00
--Medical Story of Early Texas,1528 to 1853-Lancaster-1946-
507p-v scarce   (5kk6,mint)   35.00
--same-Lancaster-1946-spec ed ltd to 100c,nbrd-rare (5n4,mint) 85.00
NIXON,RICHARD-Six Crises-NY-1962-DblDay&Co-460p-cl
            (5r0,dj,autg) 15. (5m8)   6.00
NOAKES,AUBREY-Sportsmen in a Landscape-Phila&NY-(1954)-
illus-224p   (5t7)   8.50
NOALL,CLAIRE-Intimate Disciple,Portrait of Willard Richards-
Univ of Utah Pr-1957   (5x5,dj)   8.50
NOBLE,ANNETTE L-Uncle Jack's Executors-NY-1880-1st ed
            (5mm2)   7.50
NOBLE,EDWIN-Old Anti Slavery Days,etc-Danvers,Mass-1893-
illus-151p   (4m2)   20.00

NOBLE,F A-The Mormon Iniquity-Chig-1884-1st ed-20p-wrps
            (5t3)   20.00
NOBLE,LAZ-Report of Adj General of State of Indiana-Indnpls-
1863-343p-wrps   (5j5)   10.00
NOBLE LIVES OF A NOBLE RACE-Odanah-1909-8vo-illus-cl
            (5mm7)   25.00
NOBLE,LOUIS L-After Icebergs with a Painter-NY-1861-336p-
col plts-bds   (5ss1,crack)   4.00
NOBLE,LUCRETIA-A reverend idol, a novel-Bost-1882-Osgood-
1st ed   (5m2)   5.00
NOBLE,OLIVER-Some Strictures...shewing the Power & Oppression
of State Ministers-Newburyport-1775-Lunt&Tinges-sm4to-cl-
1st ed   (5m2)   85.00
NOBLE,PETER-The Negro in Films-Lond-(1937)-illus (5x5,5x2)   20.00
NOBLE,RUTH CROSBY-The Nature of the Beast-NY-1945-Dblday,
Doran-224p   (5p7)   4.00
NOBLE,SAM-Sam Noble, Able Seaman...'Tween Decks in the 70's-
NY-1926-305p-map   (5w0) 5. (5c1)   8.50
NOBLE,SAML H-Life & Adventures of Buckskin Sam-RunfordFalls-
1900-frontis-185p-1st ed   (4t3,sl wn)   20.00
NOBLE SLAVES,THE-NY-1806-Evert Duyckinck-12mo-orig papr
covrd bds   (5i0,sl wn)   17.50
NOBLE-IVES,SARAH-Story of Teddy the Bear-NY-(1907)-
McLoughlin Bros-sm folio-col-1st ed   (4F6,vg)   27.50
NOCK,ALBERT JAY-Henry George   -1939   (5L7)   4.00
--Thos Jefferson,a Biography-NY-1926-340p-8vo-cl-plts (5p5)   10.00
--The Works of Francis Rabelais-NY-H Brace-1931-2 vols-t8vo-
illus   (5p7)   25.00
NODDER,F-Trials of Fredk Nodder, Mon a Tinsley Case -Winifred
Duke,ed-Lond-1950-Notable British Trials Ser (5ff4)   7.50
NOEL,CAPT JOHN-The Story of Everest-Bost-1927-Little,Brown-
258p-illus-cl   (5d7,als)   10.00
NOEL,JOS-Footloose in Arcadia-NY-(1940)-1st ed (5mm2,dj)   7.50
NOEL,LUCIE-Jas Joyce & Paul L Leon-NY-(1950)-Gotham Book
Mart-wrps   (5ss3)   12.50
NOEL,THEOPHILUS-Autobiography & Reminiscences of-Chig-1904-
illus-349p-1st ed-scarce   (5yy7,f) 25. (4j7)   50.00
NO FICTION or Test of Friendship-Balt-1821-2 vol in 1-360p-
lea-2nd ed   (5h7)   10.00
NOGARA,B-Art Treasures of Vatican-Bergamo,Italy-(1950)-4to-
plts   (5tt5)   10.00
--same-NY-1950-Tudor-308p-in Engl & Italian   (5x0)   7.50
NOICE,HAROLD-With Stefansson in Arctic-Lond-1924-270p-plts
            (5a1)   4.50
--same-NY-n.d.-photos-270p-fldg map   (5ss1,pres)   10.00
NOLAN,ALAN T-The Iron Brigade-NY-1961-Macm-412p-maps
            (5p0)   6.50
NOLAN,J. BENNETT-Annals of the Penn Square,Reading-Phila-
1933-106p-illus   (5w9,dj)   5.00
--Benj Franklin in Scotland & Ireland,1759 & 1771-Phila-1956-
229p-illus-bds-cl sp   (5h9)   6.00
--Early Narratives of Berks Co-Reading-(1927)-1st ed-illus (5jj3) 35.00
--The First Decade of Printing in Reading,Pa-Reading-1930-illus-
orig wrps-64p   (5m2)   3.00
--Israfel in Berkshire-Reading-1948   (5mm2)   3.00
--The Schuylkill-NewBrunswick-cl951-307p-illus (5w0,f,dj)   6.00
--Southeastern Pennsylvania-Phila-c1943-2 vols-4to-illus (5w4) 25.00
NOLAN,JEANNETTE-Hoosier City-NY-c1943-317p-illus
            (5w0, dj)   5.00
NOLAN,THOS-Publications of Geological Survey, 1879 to 1961-
Wash-1961-457p-wrps   (5j4)   8.50
NOLAN,W A-Communism Versus the Negro-Chig-1951 (5x2)   12.50
NOLEN,ORAN WARDER-Galloping Down the Texas Trail-
(Odem,TX,1947)-818p-1st ed   (4t3) 17.50 (5kk4,f)   12.50
NOLLE,ALFRED H-German Drama on St Louis Stage-Phila-1917
            (5jj3)   10.00
--Short History of Mexico-Chig-1890-294p   (4a5)   17.50
NOLLEN,J S-Grinnell College, 1953-283p-cl   (5a9)   5.00
NOLTE,VINCENT-50 Yrs in Both Hemispheres-NY-1854-484p-
1st ed   (5r7,rprd)   25.00
--The Memoirs of   -NY-1934-reprint-484p (5w5,5q8) 5.00
NONESUCH PRESS-The Temple-by Geo Herbert-Lond-1927-ltd to
1500c,nbrd-red embroidery   (4d4)   25.00
--The Iliad, the Odyssey-(Lond)-1931-4to-red mor-t.e.g.-
ltd to 1450c-2 vols-boxes   (5ee9)   150.00
--History of Herodotus of Halicarnassus-1935-lg4to-ltd to 675c
            (5ee9)   125.00
NONOTUCK SILK CO-How to Use Florence Knitting Silk-Bost-
1886-96p-illus   (5n7)   2.00
NOON,A-Ludlow,(Mass) a Century & a Centennial, with a Hist
of the Town-1875-208p   (5mm3)   7.50
--Hist of Ludlow, with Genealogies,Farm Histories, etc.-1912-
592p   (5t9)   15.00

NOONAN, D A-Alaska, the Land of Now-Seattle-1921-134p-
frontis-verse   (5ss1,pres)   6.00
NOORT, OLIVIER VAN-Neuwe Schiffart (sic) Warhafftige und
eygentliche-Frankfurt-1602-Becker-4to-calf-fldg plts-
1 fldg map-1st German ed   (5n9)   1,250.00
NORBECK, MILDRED E-Lure of the Hills-n.p.-(1931)-376p-cl
(5h7)   5.00
NORBERG, INGA-Good Food From Sweden-NY-(1939)-186p (5c5)3.50
NORCROSS, C A-Agricultural Nevada-SanFran-(1911)-64p-photos-
map-4 col illus-wrps   (5t3)   6.00
NORCROSS, CARL-The Aviation Mechanic-NY-(1941)-8vo-illus-
cl-563p,(9)-1st ed   (5t0)   5.00
NORCROSS, FREDERIC F-John H Wrenn & His Library, Notes &
Memories-Chig-1933-priv prnt-cl   (4a5)   25.00
NORD, SVERRE-Logger's Odyssey-Caldwell-1943-255p-photos
(5s4,dj)   7.50
NORDAU, MAX-Interpretation of History-1910 (5L7)   5.00
--Malady of the Century-1898   (5L7)   3.00
NORDELL, ESKEL-Water Treatment for Industrial & Other Uses-NY-
1951-illus   (5yy6,scuff)   12.50
NORDEN, CHAS-Panic Spring-Covici Friede-(1937)-scarce-
1st Amer ed   (5F1,mint,dj)   60.00
NORDENSKIOLD, A E-Voyage of the Vega Round Asia & Europe-
Lond-1881-Vol 1 (of 2)-524p-illus-maps-port (5ss1,rprd) 10.00
NORDENSKIOLD, ERIK-History of Biology, a Survey-NY-1928-
Tudor-629p   (5p7)   10.00
NORDHOFF, CHAS-California, A Book for Health, Pleasure &
Residence for Travellers & Settlers-NY-1872-illus-wrps-255p
& ads   (4n1,chip) 12.   (5s4,rprd,ex-libr)   15.00
--same-NY-1873-255p-illus   (5xx7)   7.50
--same-NY-1875   (4n1)   7.50
--same-NY-1882-206p-illus-map   (5ee3,f)   8.50
--Communistic Societies of the US-Lond-1875-illus-1st Engl ed
(4j3,rprd)   12.50
--same-NY-1875-439p-illus-8vo-cl (5t2,fray) 15. (5bb4)   17.50
--Crossing the Line-Lond-1893   (5c1)   15.00
--Man of War Life-NY-(1895)-286p-illus-dec cov (5s1,shake) 5.00
--Northern Calif, Oreg & Sandwich Islands-NY-1874-frontis-
illus-256p   (5rr9) 20.   (5t3)   10.00
--same-Lond-1874-256p-illus   (5r8,rbkd)   9.50
--Peninsular Calif-NY-1888-cl-130p-illus-8vo (5q8) 12.50 (5h5)10.00
--Politics for Young Americans-NY-1875-12mo-cl-259p-ads
(5m8,pres)   17.50
--Sailor Life on Man of War & Merchant Vessel-NY-1884-sm4to-
cl-473p   (5t2)   17.50
NORDHOFF, CHAS-Botany Bay-Bost-1941-374p-dec cov-e.p.maps
(5s1)   4.50
--Falcons of France-Bost-1936-Little-332p-illus (5p0)   4.50
--same-Bost-1940-332p-col frontis   (5t2)   4.00
--The Fledgling-Bost-1919-12mo-bds-papr labls-1st ed of auth's
1st book   (5gg6,f)   15.00
--Men Against the Sea-Bost-1934-1st ed (5yy6,f,dj)   8.50
--Mutiny on the Bounty-Bost-1932-1st ed
(5s1,sl shake) 6.   (5yy6,f,dj)   10.00
--Pitcairn's Island-Bost-1934-333(4)p (5F1) 4.   (5w9)   7.50
NORDYKE, LEWIS T-Angels Sing-Clarendon-1964-32p-Bugbee, illus-
ltd, nbrd-1 of the 50c in cl   (5g0)   20.00
--Cattle Empire-NY-1949-illus-map-scarce-1st ed
(5xx5,ex-libr,pres) 11.50   (5g5,f)   15.00
NORELIUS, E-Swedish Lutheran Family History-1890-871p-illus-
(Swedish trans)   (5t9)   22.50
NORFLEET, J FRANK-Norfleet-FtWorth-1924-340p (5yy8,rub)   7.50
NORFLEET, M B-Forced School Integration in the USA-NY-1961
(5x2,dj)   5.50
NORFOLK & BRISTOL HORSE THIEF DETECTING SOC-Constitution
of-Dedham, Mass-1842-8vo-16p-(unbnd) (5ss5)   10.00
NORFOLK, HORATIO EDW-Gleanings in Graveyards-Lond-1866-
208p   (5t4)   6.50
NORIE, J W-Complete Epitome of Practical Navigation-1844-illus-
buck-13th ed   (5L7,rbnd)   7.50
--same-Lond-1852-illus-2 vols-maps-calf (5s1,ex-libr,stn) 20.50
--same-1877-21st ed-complete in 1 vol (5s1,ex-libr,fair)   7.50
--New Piloting Directions for Mediterranean Sea, The Adriatic, of
Gulf of Venice-Lond-1831-364p-orig bds-papr labl
(5m3,chip)   22.50
NORMAN, B M-Rambles in Yucatan-NY-1843-304p-plts (5dd5) 30.00
NORMAN, C B-Corsairs of France-NY-(1929)-314p-illus
(5s1,ex-libr,dj)   5.00
NORMAN, CHAS-The Case of Ezra Pound-NY-1948-Bodley Pr-
12mo-orig stiff wrps-1st ed (5mm2) 7.50 (5ss9,vg)   12.50
--The Magic Maker, E E Cummings-NY-1958-Macm-1st ed
(5hh1,dj,vg)   7.50
--Northwest-Yukon-1945-illus-1st ed   (5yy6,pres)   7.50

NORMAN, CHAS (continued)
--So Worthy a Friend:Wm Shakespeare-NY-c1947-316p-illus
(5w9)   6.50
NORMAN, SIR HENRY-The Peoples & Politics of the Far East-
Lond-1907-Unwin-608p   (5x9)   7.00
NORMAN HORSES-Nat'l Register-Quincy-1883-Vol 2-frontis-
cl-8vo-401p   (5t0)   15.00
--same-Quincy-1884-Vol 3-index to Vols 1 thru 3-8vo-cl-642p
(5t0)   15.00
NORMAN, J R-Giant Fishes, Whales & Dolphins-Lond-1948-cl-
8 col plts-376p-16mo-2 parts   (4g5)   32.50
NORMAN LESLIE-NY-1835-Harper-2 vols-12mo-orig purple cl-
papr labls-1st ed   (5x1,lt stns,fade)   75.00
NORMAN, LUCIA-Popular History of Calif-SanFran-1883 (4a5)   5.00
NORMAN, PHILIP-London Signs & Inscriptions-Lond-1893-
Elliot Stock-illus-237p-cl-12mo   (5tt9,sl soil,hng weak)   7.50
NORMAN-NERUDA, L-The Climbs of Norman Neruda-Lond-1899-
Unwin-335p-illus   (5d7)   15.00
NORRIS & CURTIS-Costume & Fashion, 19th Century-Vol 6 (only)-
n.d.-illus   (5ww4,dj)   10.00
NORRIS, CHAS C-Eastern Upland Shooting-Phila-1946-lg8vo-plts-
408p-1st ed   (5p5)   10.00
NORRIS, EDWIN M-Story of Princeton-Bost-1917-illus-1st ed
(5tt5,f,dj) 6.   (5m2,5w9)   4.50
NORRIS, FRANK-Blix-NY-Dblday, McClure-1899-cl-338p-1st ed
(5x4,soil) 10.   (5ss3,box,5hh1)   15.00
--Collected Works of...-GardenCty-1928-Doubleday-10 vols-8vo-
simulated vel-g.stmpd sp & front cov-t.e.g.-Argonaut ed,
ltd to 245 sets-frontis   (4h0,dj)   400.00
--A Deal in Wheat & other stories of New & Old West-NY-1906-
12mo-280p   (5dd4)   8.50
--Frank Norris of "The Wave"-SanFran-1931-(Grabhorn Pr)-
8vo-bds wi cl bkstrp-ltd to 500c, nbrd-foreword by Chas G Norris
(5d8) 20.   (5hh4,unnbrd,f) 20.   (5hh4)   30.00
--McTeague-NY-1899-Doubleday&McClure-1st ed-1st issue-
orig cl-pg 106 ends wi "moment"
(4n5,vg,box) 110.   (5dd8,hng broke) 75. (5tt6,4g2)   70.00
--same-SanFran-1941-Colt Pr-ltd to 500c (4n5,cor sl wn)   27.50
--Moran of the Lady Letty-NY-1898-Doubleday&McClure-12mo-
cl-1st ed (5hh1,5i0) 20. (5ss3,sp stn,crack,box) 20. (5d9) 45.00
--The Octopus-NY-1901-Doubleday, Page-652p-cl-1st ed (5ff7) 10.00
--same-NY-1901-Doubleday, Page-cl-1st ed-1st issue (5ss3)   20.00
--same-NY-1906-652p-12mo   (5dd6)   10.00
--The Pit-NY-1903-1st trade ed-red cl-g.dec
(5u9) 9.50   (5mm2) 5.   (5ee3,5xx8)   10.00
--Vandover & the Brute-GardenCty-1914-Doubleday, Page-8vo-cl-
g.-1st trade ed   (5b2)   8.50
NORRIS, GEO W-Fighting Liberal-NY-1945-illus-1st prntg (5q8) 4.50
NORRIS, J PARKER-Portraits of Shakespeare-Phila-1885-266p-sm
folio-ltd to 500c, nbrd-33 plts   (4b4,wn)   30.00
NORRIS, J W-Gen'l Directory & Business Advertiser for Chig for
1844-1844, reprntd 1903   (5t9)   5.00
--same-reprint-1902   (4t1)   7.50
NORRIS, MARY H-The Gray House of the Quarries-Bost-1898-
frontis-1st ed   (5mm2)   12.50
NORRIS, P W-Calumet of Coteau & Other Poetical Legends of Border-
Phila-1884-275p-cl   (5h1,pres) 8.50 (4k5,f)   12.50
--same-Phila-1883-illus-275p   (4b2,wn,sl warp)   7.50
NORRIS, THADDEUS-Amer Angler's Book-Phila-(1864)-illus
(5s9,wn) 17.50 (5w0,rprd) 22.50 (5t7)   25.00
--Amer Fish Culture-Phila-1868-8vo-cl-illus-304p (5t2,lacks e.p.) 4.00
NORRIS, THOS WAYNE-Descrip & Priced Catalog of Books,
Pamphlets & Maps...Calif & Far West-Oakland-1948-
Grabhorn Pr-tall 4to-217p-illus-ltd to 500c (4g2)   40.00
NORRIS, ZOE A-Way of the Wind-NY-1911-orig bds-narr 8vo-
1st ed   (4m8)   7.50
NORRIS-NEWMAN, CHAS L-With the Boers in Transvaal & Orange
Free State 1880 to 81-Lond-n.d.-(c1885)-Abbott, Jones-
maps(3 fldg)-395p-2nd ed   (4t5)   15.00
NORTH & SOUTH HEMPSTEAD, LI, NY-Records of Towns of-
1896 to 1904-8 vols-scarce   (5zz0,rbnd)   150.00
NORTH-AMERICAN & WEST INDIAN GAZETTEER-Lond-1776-
2 fldg maps-lea   (5s9,cov loose,wn)   125.00
NORTH AMERICAN FISH & GAME PROTECTIVE ASSN-Minutes of
Proceedings of 1st Convention, Montreal, Feb 1900-Quebec-
1900-Darveau-12mo-cl-200p   (5j5)   25.00
NORTH AMERICA-History of...comprising Geograph & Statist View
of US & Brit Canadian Possessions-Leeds-1820-illus-2 vols
(5yy0)   17.50
NORTH AMERICAN SCENERY-from C J Way's Studies, 1863, 64-
Montr-(1864)-folio-orig mor-photos   (5w8,rub)   85.00

NORTH AMER WILDLIFE CONF-Transactions-1st-1936-77 plts-
Gov cl ed   (5cc1,vg)   7.50
NORTH ANNA,VA-Map,by Maj J E Weyss & others-(Wash)-1867-
Off Gov Map-col-16½ x 19 inches   (5r7)   20.00
NORTH,ARTHUR TAPPAN,FORE-Ralph Adams Cram,Cram &
Ferguson,NY-Lond-1931-Whittlesey-Contemporary Amer
Architects-11p & 104p & plans-4to-bds   (5m7,crack) 22.50
NORTH,ARTHUR WALBRIDGE-Camp & Camino in Lower Calif-
NY-1910-341p plus index-illus-maps(1 lg fldg)-1st ed
                   (5bb4,libr marks) 17.50 (5dd5) 37.50 (5x5) 30.00
--Mother of California-SanFran-(1908)-Paul Elder-photos-
maps(1 fldg)-169p-1st ed-scarce
     (4t3) 25. (5x5) 35.   (5d6) 20. (5r8) 30.00
NORTH BRITON XLVI-Notes & Collection of Proceedings in Hse
of Commons & Courts of Westminster Against Mr Wilkes-Lond-
1772-4 vol-4 ports-calf   (5a1)   85.00
NORTH BROOKFIELD,MASS HIST-Record of Soldiers & Sailors &
Others in War, 1861 to 65-1886-71p   (5mm3)   4.00
NORTH CAROLINA & ITS RESOURCES-State Board of Agric-Winston-
1896-413p-8vo-illus   (5ss5)   20.00
NORTH CAROLINA BAR ASSN-Reports-Vol 1 thru 45-bound-
(1899 to 1943)   (5ii7,ex-libr) 265.00
NORTH CAROLINA CONSTITUTIONAL CONVENTION,1868-
Constit,wi Ordinances & Resolutions-bnd wi Journal (5ii7) 25.00
NORTH CAROLINA-Guide to Old North State-Univ of No Car Pr-
1939-Amer Guide Series-illus-WPA   (5ss5) 9. (5p0) 5.00
NORTH CAROLINA-Hand Book of NC-Raleigh-1893-State Board
of Agric-sm8vo-orig pict wrps-333p-illus & map (5t2,bkstrp tn) 4.00
NORTH CAROLINA-Heads of Families at 1st census of US taken in
year 1790-Wash-1908-4to-orig wrps-292p-fldg map-orig ed
                                         (5w0)   10.00
NORTH CAROLINA-Journal of Senate,State of...(Caption)-
Edenton-(1789)-prntd by Hodge&Wills-41p-disbnd   (5g4) 50.00
NORTH CAROLINA LAW REVIEW-Vol 1 thru 48-1922 to 1970
                                         (5ii7,rbnd) 720.00
NORTH CAROLINA-Private Laws of State of passed by Gen'l
Assembly,1864,65-Raleigh-1865-50p   (5j6)   12.50
NORTH CAROLINA STATE BAR-Journal & Proceedings-Vol 1 thru
10-(1934 to 1943)   (5ii7,rbnd) 50.00
--same-single vols-wrps   (5ii7) ea   5.00
NORTH CAROLINA YEAR BOOK-& Business Directory for 1903-
Raleigh-1903-over 600p   (5h6)   15.00
NORTH,CHARLES C-Sketches of the War-NY-1863-174p
                                         (5j6,fox)   4.00
NORTH CLIFF MINING CO,(MICH)-Report of-Pittsburgh-1864-
wrps-fldg diagram   (5g8)   10.00
NORTH DAKOTA,DELUXE SUPPLEMENT-Chig-1917-ports-4to-
part mor   (5jj7,f)   20.00
NORTH DAKOTA-The Golden Wheat State-(Chig,1893)-map &
illus-prntd wrps in orig prntd envelope-World's Fair brochure
                                         (5g4)   5.00
NORTH DAKOTA-Guide to Northern Prairie State-Fargo-1938-
photos-fldg pkt map-360p plus index-1st ed-Amer Guide Ser-WPA
scarce-(only 300c printed)(5jj7) 35. (4L5) 25. (5kk4,f) 50.00
--same-NY-1950-2nd ed-map   (4k5,f,dj) 25.00
NORTH DAKOTA-Homes for All to be had along the Lines of NPacRR
in Garden of the Territory-StPaul,Minn-n.d.-(ca1883)-lg fldg
map-homesteader info   (5L0,f)   10.00
NORTH DAKOTA LAW REVIEW-1924 to 70-Vols 1 thru 46-bnd
                                         (5rr4,recent rbnd) 695.00
NORTH DAKOTA STATE HIST SOC-Collections of-Vol 1-1906-
500p   (5t9)   10.00
NORTH DEVON-Views of-Ilframcombe-n.d.-24 plts-obl 12mo-
no pagination   (5w7,cov wn) 5.00
NORTH EASTERN BOUNDARY DISPUTE-Report on-Wash-1838-
Sen Doc 287-8vo-16p-bds-2 fldg maps   (5L1)   45.00
NORTH GEORGIA GAZETTE-And Winter Chronicle-Lond-1821-
ed by Sabine-4to-hf lea-labl   (5j3,rprd) 40.00
NORTH GRANVILLE QUARTERLY-Wash Co,NY-NoGranville Ladies
Seminary,April 1864-Vol 1,#1-54p-prntd wrps-8vo-prntd by
Tuttle & Gay   (5p1)   10.00
NORTH HAVEN,CONN IN 19TH CENTURY-1901-207p-illus
                                         (5t9)   7.50
NORTH,J W-History of Augusta-Augusta-1870-illus-990p (4m2) 45.00
NORTH,MARY REMSEN-Down the Colorado-NY-1930-178p-31 illus-
1st ed   (5dd5)   12.00
NORTH MISSOURI AGRIC & MECHANICAL ASSOC-1st Fair of-
Hannibal-Sept,1869-23p-prntd wrps   (5n7)   10.00
NORTH MISSOURI RR-Annual report of-StL-1855-fldg map
                                         (5g4,lacks wrps) 25.00
NORTH ORANGE,MASS-Hist of, 1781 to 1924-1924-60p (5mm3) 12.50
NORTH PACIFIC COAST-Summer Trips to the-n.p.-(1912,NoPac)-
31p-photos-map-wrps   (5L0)   3.00

NORTH PACIFIC COAST-(Wash Territory)-a journal-New Tacoma
(W T)-North Pac Coast Publ Co-1880,1-folio-6 issues- 2 in
orig wrps-rest disbnd-Vol 1 #11 & Vol 2,#1 to 5(all prntd)-
rare   (5i9)   100.00
NORTH PACIFIC PORTS-Pacific Shipping Yearbook-Seattle-1915-
421p-2nd issue-rare   (5s1,ex-libr,rprd) 10.00
NORTH,S N D-Simeon North-Concord-1913-port-illus-207p
                                         (5q0)   25.00
NORTH SHORE RAILWAY-Rapports de l'Ingenieur en chef-Quebec-
1854-52p-lg fldg map-prntd wrps-Cote   (5w8)   45.00
NORTH,STERLING-So Red the Nose-NY-(1935)-35p-illus-bds
                                         (5w1)   4.50
--Speak of the Devil,An Anthology of Demonology-NY-1949-
1st ed   (5F0,dj)   3.00
NORTH YAKIMA,WASH-The Capital of the Apple Empire(cov titl)-
NoYakima-1911-Comm Club-8p-photos(2 in col)-wrps (5L0) 5.00
NORTHAMPTON & NORTHAMPTON INSTIT FOR SAVINGS-
Northampton-1931-128p-illus   (5y2)   5.75
NORTHAMPTON COUNTY-The Scotch Irish of...-(Easton,Pa)-
1926-illus-594p   (4m2)   25.00
NORTHAMPTON,MASS-Early-1914-339p   (5mm3)   5.00
NORTHAMPTON-Historical Localities in Northampton-(Northampton,
1904)-250th Anniv-40p-illus-wrps (5mm3) 4. (5r7) 7.50
NORTHAMPTON,MEADOW CITY-(1894)-108p-250 illus (5e8) 9.75
NORTHAMPTON,MASS-Representative Families of-Vol 1(all publ)-
1917-412p   (5mm3)   10.00
NORTHCOTE,JAS-Memoirs of Sir Joshua Reynolds-Lond-1813-
Colburn-4to-calf-g.dec-418p-ports-plt-facs (4d1,rprd) 75.00
--100 Fables,Original &selected-Lond-1833-GeoLawford-12mo-
272p-frontis-fldg facs-a.e.g.-3rd ed   (5p1,f bndg) 32.50
NORTHCOTE,ROSALIND-The Book of Herbs-Lond-1903-12mo-
18 illus   (5w3)   10.00
--same-Lond-1912-212p-illus   (5s7)   6.50
NORTHCOTT,W H-Lathes & Turning-Lond-1868-8vo-298p-illus
                                         (5bb0)   8.00
NORTHE,JAS NEILL,ed-Land of Gold (Tierra de Oro)-Ontario
(Calif)-(1934)-illus by Don Blanding-8vo-cl (5h4)   4.00
NORTHEN,REBECCA TYSON-Home Orchid Growing-NY-1950-
286p-col plts   (5s7)   8.50
NORTHEND,MARY HARROD-Amer Glass-NY-1926-209p-illus
                                         (5t4)   5.00
--Colonial Homes & their Furnishings-Bost-1912-252p-illus (5t4) 6.00
--same-Bost-1917-252p-117 plts   (5w7,sl brown) 5.00
--Historic Homes of New England-Bost-1914-274p-illus
                                  (5L7) 12.50 (5t7) 10.00
--Memories of Old Salem-NY-1917-341p-illus-t.e.g.-1st ed
                                         (5w4,cov stns) 10.00
--We Visit Old Inns-Bost-1925-176p-illus (5w5)   8.50
NORTHERN BANKING CO-Portland,Me-Portland-(1887)-12mo-
orig wrps-39p   (5m6)   7.50
NORTHERN GRIEVANCES-set forth in letter to Jas Madison by a
NoAmerican-NY-1814-stitchd-uncut   (5g4,scuff) 15.00
NORTHERN ONTARIO CANADA-A new land nearby-Tor-1916-
32p-wrps-photos-map-wrps   (5t1)   10.00
NORTHERN PACIFIC,THE-Philu-Jan,1872-#1-folio-4p-
issued by Jay Cooke & Co-map   (5g3)   10.00
NORTHERN PAC RR-Across the Continent Via the...to the
Pacific,Columbia River,Puget Sound & Alaska-StPaul-n.d.-
(ca 1890)-obl folder- 30 panels-wrps   (5L0,wn)   5.00
--Along the Scenic Highway-n.p.-(1914)-84p-photos-map-wrps
                                         (5L0)   4.00
--Boston Board of Trade-Report on the NoPac RR,Nov 27,1865-
Bost-1865-wrps   (5g8,f)   17.50
--Descriptive Map Folder,Facts for Homeseeker & Tourist-
(St Paul,1910)-17 panel fldr-map on reverse-wrps (5L0) 4.00
--Eastern Wash & Northern Idaho-n.p.-(1915)-NoPacRR-55p-
photos-maps   (5L0)   4.00
--Gallatin Valley,Mont-n.p.-n.d.-(1911)-(NoPac)-21p-photos-
map-wrps   (5t3)   5.00
--Guide to,& its Allied Lines-StPaul-1888-390p-sq8vo-cl-illus-
scarce   (5p5)   17.50
--La Cie de Chemin de Fer No Pac, La Route au Parc Natl
Yellowstone-Chig-(1893)-Rand,McNally-folder-map on verso
                                         (5nn8)   35.00
--North Pacific Coast Resorts-(StPaul)-1909-NoPac-79p-photos-
wrps-fldg map   (5L0)   3.00
--Official Guide-StPaul-1899-plts-442p   (5nn2,sl wn) 15.00
--Report in Re to Agreement made betw McCammon & Confed
Tribes of Flathead,Kootenay & Upper Pend d'Oreilles Indians
for Sale of a Reserv in Mont for Use of-Wash-1883-SD44-
28p-fldg maps   (5n4)   25.00

NORTHERN PAC RR (continued)
--Settlers' Guide to Oregon & Wash Territory & to lands of...
on Pacific Slope-Land Dept, NPRR-n.p.-(1872)-(wrpr titl)-
maps on versos of wrprs-Smith 7425   (5g3)   15.00
--Shields River Basin in Montana-StPaul-1913-24p-photos-wrps-
fldg map   (5t3)   5.00
--Through the Fertile NoWest-(StPaul,n.d.NoPac)-19p-photos-
map-wrps   (5L0)   3.00
--What Montana Has to Offer-(StPaul,1913)-13 panel fldr-
lg map on reverse   (5t3)   4.00
NORTHERN REGIONS-or Uncle Richard's Relation of Capt Parry's
Voyages for Discov of a NW Passage-NY-1827-256p-plts-
16mo   (5ss1,crack)   12.50
NORTHERN TRAVELLER & NORTHERN TOUR-wi Routes to
Springs, Niagara & Que etc-NY-1830-maps-32 engrs-12mo-
444p-bds-hf calf   (5i3,cracked)   17.50
--same-NY-1830-4th ed, rev   (5g4,v wn)   10.00
--same-NY-1844-24mo-cl-maps-illus   (5g8,libr labl)   15.00
NORTHEY, NEIL WAYNE-Wild Animals of Africa-MtnView,Ca-
1948-pic cov-illus-205p-juvenile   (4t5)   5.00
NORTHROP,ALICE RICH-Through Field & Woodland-NY-1925-
532p-illus   (5t2)   4.00
NORTHROP,BIRDSEY GRANT-Lessons from European Schools &
Amer Centennial-NY&Chig-1877-8vo-108p-A S Barnes-
stabbed-wrps   (5p1,2 lvs def)   15.00
NORTHROP,F S C,ed-Ideological Differences & World Order-
NewHav-1949   (5x7)   7.50
NORTHROP,H D-The College of Life,or Practical self-Educator,
a Manual of self-improv for colored race-Wash-1890-illus-
thk R8vo-pic cl   (5x2)   100.00
--Earth, Sea & Sky, or Marvels of the Universe-StPaul-(1887)-
864p-illus-lea   (5ww4,sl wn)   5.00
NORTHROP,HENRY-Indian Horrors or Massacres by the Red Men-
n.p.-n.d.-(ca 1891)-illus-600p (5w9,4t3) 8.50   (5jj9)   10.00
--Life & Public Services of Hon Jas G Blaine-Cleve-(1893)-cl-
604p   (4h2)   8.50
--Thrilling Adventures of Amer Pioneers & Heroes-(Wash,n.d.)-
col frontis-illus-256p   (5dd6,sl wn)   7.50
NORTHROP,N B-Pioneer Hist of Medina Co-Medina-1861-224p-
cl-Thomson 875   (5h7,rbnd)   45.00
NORTHRUP,A J-Desc of Jos Northrup,Settler of Milford,Conn
1639-1908-461p   (5t9)   45.00
NORTHRUP,A JUDD-Camps & Tramps in the Adirondacks-
Syracuse-1882-302p-2nd ed   (5p9)   7.50
--Slavery in New York-May,1900-NY State Bull Hist #4-67p-
wrps   (4n2,sl chip)   2.50
NORTHRUP,CLARK S-Bibliography of Thos Gray-Lond-1917-296p
        (4g2)   22.50
NORTHUP,GEO T-Intro to Spanish Literature-Univ of Chig-1929-
3rd impress   (5ss9,vg)   8.50
NORTHUP,S-12 Years a Slave-Auburn,NY-1853-illus-1st ed
        (5x2)   20.00
NORTHWEST BOUNDARY,THE-Discussion of water boundary
question-Wash-1868-GPO-270p-wrps-fldg map-Sen Exec
Doc #29   (5dd4)   25.00
NORTHWEST TERRITORIES-Consolidated Ordinances in Force
March 15,1899-Regina-1899-1102p-hf calf   (5a1)   25.00
--same-in Force Sept 1, 1905-Regina-1907-1351p   (5a1)   25.00
NORTHWESTERN LINE-Homesteads in Pine Ridge & Rosebud Indian
Reservations-Omaha-1911-16p-fldr-photos-map-wrps (5t3) 8.50
NORTHWESTERN MANUAL & TRAVELER'S DIRECTORY-Mar 1858-
pic wrps-16mo-ABElliott,ed-56p   (5ff9,f)   85.00
NORTHWESTERN PAC NEWS CO-California's Wonderland-
SanFran-(1912)-illus-sm folio-12 lvs   (5kk6)   9.50
NORTHWESTERN SCHOOL OF TAXIDERMY-Taxidermists Supplies-
Omaha-n.d.-(ca 1932)-40p-cov-illus   (5b9,vf)   6.00
NORTHWESTERN UNIV LAW REVIEW-1906 to 70-Vol 1 thru 64-bnd
        (5ii7,rbnd)   1,090.00
--same-single bound vols   (5ii7) ea   22.50
NORTHWESTERN YEAST CO-The Art of Making Bread-Chig-n.d.-
(ca 1920)-20p-col illus   (5g9)   2.00
NORTHWOOD, J D'ARCY-Familiar Hawaiian Birds-Honolulu-1940-
lg8vo-mor-12 col plts-ltd to 330c,autg (5z9,sl warped) 30.00
NORTON,A B-Great Revolution of 1840-Mt Vernon, OH & Dallas,TX-
1888-cl   (4h2)   15.00
NORTON,A BANNING-History of Knox County,Ohio-Columbus-
1862-424p-cl   (5y0)   50.00
NORTON,C-Opportunity in SoAfrica-Lond-1948-illus (5x2,dj) 5.00
NORTON,C-Historical Studies of Church Building in Middle Ages-
NY-1880-331p   (5ii2)   6.50
NORTON,C L-Canoeing in Kanuckia-NY-1878-illus-stiff prntd
wrps   (5w8,lacks bkstrp)   12.00

NORTON,CAROLINE-A Plain Letter to Lord Chancellor on the
Infant Custody Bill-NY-1922-8vo-bds-cl sp-papr labls-
ltd to 150c-Bruce Rogers,prntr   (5b0,chip)   15.00
NORTON,CAROLINE T-The Rocky Mntn Cook Book-Denver-(1903)-
346p   (4g9,soil,rprd) 5.   (4g9,rub,5c0,hng weak)   6.50
NORTON,CHAS B-Amer Breech Loading Small Arms-NY-1872-4to-
308p-illus   (5xx7)   35.00
NORTON,CHAS D-The Old Ferry at Black Rock(NY)-n.p.-n.d.-
19p-orig wrps-Hist Soc Club, Dec 14, 1863   (5k1)   3.00
NORTON,CHAS E-Correspondence of Thos Carlyle & Ralph Waldo
Emerson 1834 to 1872-Bost-1883-2 vols-illus   (5mm2)   15.00
--Historical Studies of Church Building in Middle Ages-NY-1880-
Harper-333p-sm4to-cl-t.e.g.   (5m5,shake)   20.00
--Letters of Jas R Lowell-NY-1894-2 vols   (5mm1)   12.50
--The New Life of Dante Alighieri-Bost-1867-4to   (5mm2)   10.00
NORTON,E F-The Fight for Everest, 1924-NY-1925-372p-illus-
fldg map-blue cl-Longmans, Green   (5d7)   20.00
NORTON,F L-Spain in America-NY-1877-mor-83p
        (5dd7,f bndg)   28.00
NORTON,FRANK H-The days of Dan'l Boone-NY-(1883)-Amer
News Co-pic cl-illus-1st ed-"Excelsior Ed"   (5m2)   10.00
--Illus Historical Register of Centennial Exhib,Phila,1876 & Expos
Universelle,Paris,1878-NY-(1879)-folio-hf mor-25 col art plts-
800 engrs-396p   (5m2)   35.00
--Life & Public Services of Winfield Scott Hancock-NY-n.d.-
(1880)-31p-pict wrps   (5h1,soil)   4.00
NORTON,HARRY J-Wonder land illus,or horseback rides thru
Yellowstone Nat'l Park-VirginiaCty-n.d.-(1873)-12mo-
orig cl-18 plts-scarce-Howes 205 (5i9,rub) 75.   (5g6,f) 85.00
NORTON,HENRY K-The Story of California-Chig-1913-390p-illus-
maps-1st ed   (5k0)   5.00
NORTON,J F,REV-Hist of Fitzwilliam, N Hamp-1888-827p (5t9) 30.00
NORTON,REV JOHN N-Allerton Parish-1863-366p (5zz0,wn) 12.00
NORTON,JOHN P-Elements of Scientific Agriculture-Albany-
1850-Pease-208p plus 4p ads-illus-bds-lea bk   (5r0)   7.50
NORTON,COL L A-Life & Adventures of-Oakland-1887-Pacific
Pr Pub Hse-8vo-cl-port-scarce (5r0,lg cov stn) 20. (4a3) 40.00
NORTON,MARY-The Magic Bed Knob-NY-1943-Hyperion-illus-
4to-bds & cl-46p-col plts-1st ed   (4a8)   5.00
NORTON,MARY AQUINAS-Catholic Missionary Activities in the
NW 1818 to 1864-Wash-1930-150p plus index-wrps-1st ed-
scarce   (5t3,ex-libr)   8.50
NORTON,OLIVER W-Strong Vincent & His Brigade at Gettysburg,
July 2,1863-Chig-1909-photo-57p-1st ed   (5yy7)   15.00
NORTON,PETER-The End of the Voyage-Lond-1959-19 plts-
35 plans-39 photos   (5c1)   6.50
NORTON,SARA-Letters of Chas Eliot Norton wi biographical
Comment-NY&Lond-1913-2 vols-illus   (5mm2)   10.00
NORWAY,ARTHUR H-Naples Past & Present-NY-1901-2 vols-
56 plts   (5s6)   5.00
NORWAY YEAR BOOK 1924-Christiana-(1923)-542p-fldg map rear
        (5ss1)   5.00
NOWELL,ELIZ,ed-Letters of Thos Wolfe-NY-(1956)-Scribner's-
cl-1st ed   (4p1,fade,dj fray)   8.50
NORWICH,CONN-Old Houses of 1660 to 1800-1895-621p-
maps-illus-port & Genealogies   (5t9)   30.00
NORWICH,CONN-Vital Records 1848-Parts 1 & 2   (5t9) ea   15.00
NORWOOD,GILBERT-Greek Tragedy-Bost-1920-8vo-cl-394p
        (5t0)   5.00
NORWOOD,JOS W-The Tammany Legend-Bost-1938-Meador Pub Co-
col frontis   (5x5,dj)   12.50
NORWOOD,THOS MANSON-True Vindication of South-Savannah-
(1917)-8vo-451p-tall 8vo-scarce   (4a7)   15.00
NORWORTH,HOWARD-Pathway of the Padres-LosAng-(1951)-maps-
illus-156p   (5xx5)   3.75
NOT LOST, BUT LAID ASIDE-NY-1861-Gen'l Protestant Epis S.
School Union-24mo-68p-frontis   (5p1)   5.00
NOTABLE LAWYERS OF THE WEST-Chig-(1902)-R8vo-186p-ports
        (5r8)   25.00
NOTED CALIFORNIANS-LosAng-1929-Noted Calif Co-139p-12mo-
cl   (4t1)   8.50
NOTES OF HOSPITAL LIFE-from Nov, 1861 to Aug, 1863-Phila-
1864-210p-1st ed   (5m1)   10.00
NOTES ON CAPT MEDWIN'S -Conversations of Lord Byron-n.p.-
(Lond)-n.d.-(priv prntd, 1824)-8vo-hf calf- v rare-1st ed
        (5x3)   200.00
NOTES ON EXHIBITION OF EARLY AMER LITHOGRAPHS-Bost-
1924-8vo-wrps-Club of Odd Volumes   (5gg6)   15.00
NOTHING TO DO-by a lady-NY-1857-57p-illus   (5t7)   7.50
NOTHING TO EAT-NY-1857-12mo-cl-117p   (5t2,stns)   5.00
NOTHING TO WEAR-NY-1857-68p-illus by Hoppin
(5v2,fox) 7.50   (5t7)   10.00

NOTICIAS DE CALIFORNIA-SanFran-1958-sm folio-cl bkd bds-
Book Club of Calif-ltd to 400c-orig mailing carton (5h5,mint) 25.00
NOTRE DAME LAWYER-Vol 1 thru 44-(1925 to 1969)
(5ii7,rbnd)   875.00
NOTT,CHAS C-Sketches of the War-NY-1865-184p (5j6,fox)   3.50
--same-NY-1911-Abbatt-201p   (5mm8)   7.50
NOTT,JOHN-Cook & Confectioners Dictionary-Lond-1724-
H P for C Rivington-8vo-calf-frontis-2nd ed   (5i4,wn)   45.00
NOTT,SAML,JUN-Appeal to Temperate on Vice of Intemperance-
Hartf-1828-120p-3 parts-bds-Sabin 56050   (5h7,fox)   15.00
--The freedom of the mind,demanded of Amer freeman-Bost-1830-
12mo-orig cl & bds-papr labl-1st ed   (5i0)   10.00
--The Telescope-Bost-1832-12mo-1st ed   (5m6)   6.00
NOTT,STANLEY CHAS-Voices from the Flowery Kingdom-1948-
Chinese Culture Study Group-4to-20 col plts-red cl (5t5)   15.00
NOURJSHAD,HIST OF-Lond-1927-120p-4 col plts-dec bds (5a1) 5.00
NOURSE,EDWIN G-America's Capacity to Produce-Wash-1934-
Brookings Inst-608p-charts   (5y2)   6.50
NOURSE,EVA M-Millar DuBois Family,its Hist & Genealogy-1928
(5mm3,wn)   17.50
NOURSE,HENRY S-Military Annals of Lancaster,Mass-1889-402p
(5t9)   15.00
NOURSE,J E-Amer Explorations in the Ice Zones-Bost-(1884)-608p-
map-illus-hf lea   (5ss1,sp tn,rprd)   7.50
--The maritime canal of Suez-Wash-1869-illus-wrps-fldg maps
(5g4,f)   15.00
NOURSE,MARY A-Ferment in the Far East-Indnpls-c1949 (5x7)   5.00
NOUVELLE MANIERE DE NEGOCIER LES PAIX ETC-(Brunswick)-
1798-48p-12mo-orig blue bds-(XYZ affair)   (5L1)   95.00
NOVA FRANCIA-Or Description of That Part of New France,which
is 1 continent wi Virginia-Lond-1609-Bishop-sm4to-tall copy-
g.tooled calf-1st Engl ed-1st issue-v rare-Sabin 40175
(5n9,f)   5,500.00
NOVA SCOTIA-Fair Representation of His Majesty's Right to-Lond-
1756-8vo-calf-64p   (5L1,broke)   60.00
NOVA SCOTIA LAWS,STATUTES ETC-1924 thru 1965-bound
(5ii7,ex-libr)   145.00
NOVA SCOTIAN-Descriptive Sketches of Nova Scotia,in Prose &
Verse-Halifax-1864-8vo-1st ed-scarce   (5ss5,sl dmpstn)   37.50
NOVI TRACTATUS DE POTU CAPHE:DE CHINENSIUM,& DE
CHOCOLATA-Geneva-1699-16mo-frontis-vel on bds-188p
(5w1)   150.00
NOVISIMO ARTE DE COCINA-Mexico-1831-245p-2 plts-calf bk
(5c5,stnd,wn,rbkd)   87.50
NOVUS ORBIS,ID EST-Navigationes primae in Americam-Rotterdam-
1616-Berewout-8vo-old vel-5th ed   (5n9)   125.00
NOWAK,CARL A-New Fields for Brewers-StL-(1917)-317p (5w1) 8.50
--Non Intoxicants-StL-(1922)-195p,(6)   (5w1)   6.50
NOWARRA,HEINZ-The Messerschmidt 109-LosAng-1963-4to-cl-
illus-1st ed   (5p5,dj)   12.50
NOWELL,ELIZ-Thos Wolfe,a Biography-NY-1960-port
(5k0,dj) 6.   (5F0)   5.00
NOWELL-SMITH,SIMON-The Legend of the Master-NY-1948-
Scribner-illus-1st prntng   (5m2,dj)   6.00
NOWLAND,JN H B-Sketches of Prominent Citizens of 1876-Indnpls-
1877-572p-cl   (5h2,cov soil)   12.50
NOWLIN,CLIFFORD H-My First 90 Years-KansasCty,Mo-1955-
8vo-145p-cl   (5m8,autg)   6.50
NOWLIN,WM-The Bark Covered House-Chig-1937-342p-cl-
Lakeside Classic   (5ff7) 10.   (5a9,f)   7.00
NOWOSIELSKI,LIEUT MRS SOPHIE-In the Hurricane of War,
Memoirs of a Woman Soldier-(Louisvl,1929)-124p-illus
(5r0,autg)   10.00
NOY,WM-Principal Grounds & Maxims wi Analysis of Laws of
England-Burlington,Vt-1845-8vo-219p-lea&bds-3rd Amer(5t2) 5.00
NOYCE,WILFRID-Mountains & Men-Lond-1947-160p-illus,Geoffrey
Bles   (5d7)   6.00
--Scholar Mountaineers,Pioneers of Parnassus-Lond-(1950)-164p-
illus-cl-Dennis Dobson   (5d7)   4.50
NOYER,LEON-Le Privilege Des Bouilleurs De Cru-Paris-1936-
346p,(1)-fldg tables-wrps   (5w1,chip)   5.00
NOYES,AL J-In the Land of the Chinook-Helena-(1917)-illus-8vo-
cl-scarce   (4c1,5dd4) 35. (5bb4) 25.(5w5) 28.50   (4m4)   40.00
--The Story of Ajax-Helena-1914-152p plus index-photos-1st ed
(5bb4)   125.00
NOYES,ALFRED-Book of the Earth-NY-1925-Stokes-1st ed
(5i4,pres,dj)   15.00
--Collected Poems-NY-(1913)-Stokes Co-2 vols
(5i4,pres,dj) 15. (5p9) 6. (5b0)   10.00
--Forty Singing Seamen & Other Poems-Edinb-1907-1st ed
(5r9,pres wi 4 li quote)   17.50
--If judgment comes,a poem-NY-1941-Stokes-1st US ed(5m2,dj)   4.00

NOYES,ALFRED (continued)
--Open Boats-NY-1916   (5c1)   7.50
--The Return of the Scare Crow-Lond-(1929)-210p-1st ed (5t7)   12.50
--Shadows on the Down & other poems-NY&Tor-(1941)-Stokes-
1st US ed   (5m2,pres)   6.00
--A Tale of Old Japan-Edinb-1914-12mo-1st separate prntg-
pic wrps   (4c2,pres)   15.00
--Watchers of Sky-NY-(1922)-Stokes-1st ed   (5i4,pres,dj)   15.00
NOYES BROS & CUTLER-Drugs,Chemicals,Patent Medicines,Paint
& Oils,etc-StPaul-1886-949p-cl-Vol 9-illus catalog (5yy3)   75.00
NOYES,C R-Institution of Property-NY-1936   (5ff4)   12.50
NOYES,CARLETON-The Enjoyment of Art-Bost-1903-8vo-orig bds-
1st ed   (5m6)   7.50
NOYES,G E-Bibliography of Courtesy & Conduct Books of 17th Cent
England-NewHav-1937   (5mm1)   15.00
NOYES,GEO F-Bivouac & Battle Field-NY-1863-1st ed (5tt5)   17.50
NOYES,H E- Desc of Jas,Nicholas & Peter Noyes-1904-2 vols-
575,437p   (5mm3)   40.00
NOYES,HARRIETTE-Memorial of Town of Hampstead,NH-Bost-
1899 to 1903-2 vols-8vo-illus-1st ed
(5mm3) 22.50   (5m6,crack)   30.00
NOYES,JOHN HUMPHREY-History of Amer Socialisms-NY-1961-
687p-ltd to 500c   (5w5,dj)   8.50
NOYES,PIERREPONT-My Father's House-1937-312p (5zz0)   10.00
NUERMBERGER,RUTH K-Free Produce Movement-1942-sewn(5L7) 4.00
NUEVO COCINERO AMERICANO-Paris-1858-1008p,(2)-plts-
col frontis-embossed lea   (5c5,rbkd,stns)   57.50
NUEVA COCINERA MEXICANA-Mexico-1841-12mo-256p-2 plts
(5c5,sl wn)   47.50
NUEVO COCINERO MEJICANO-Paris-1868-966p,(7),(5)-frontis-
5 plts(of 6?)-lea bk   (5c5,hng broke)   45.00
NUGENT,NELL MARION-Cavaliers & Pioneers-Richmond-1934-
ltd to 1000c,nbrd-1st ed   (5h9,f)   27.50
NULLI,NOTUS-Microcosmus Philadelphicus;In 2 Epistles to My
Cousin Tom in NY-Phila-1825-60p-scarce   (5m1)   42.50
NUMA-To the People,Particularly Farmers of New Hampshire-n.p.-
(Feb 28,1816)-8vo-8p-(unbnd,text loose)   (5ss5)   10.00
NUMISMATIC & ANTIQUARIAN SOC OF PHILA-Proceedings of..
29 year unbroken run 1880 thru 1909-Phila-illus-wrps as issued
(5w5,vg)   14.50
--same-Vols 20 to 33-Phila-1892 to 1946   (5L7)   50.00
NUMISMATIST(WICHITA)-Official publ,Amer Numismatic Assoc,
1957,Mar (Vol 70,#3) to 1967,Dec (Vol 80)-orig wrps-
9 vols in special Jones box holders   (5dd6,f)   75.00
NUNAN,THOS-Diary of an old bohemian-SanFran-(1927)- 176p-
Harr Wagner-pict cl-   (5r0,pres)   7.50
NUNEZ CABEZA DE VACA-Comentarios de,Adelantado y
Governador del Rio de la Plata-(Madrid,1736)-72p-sm folio-
qtr cl   (5r7)   25.00
NUNN,G E-Geographical Conceptions of Columbus-1924-maps
(5L7)   5.00
NUNN,LOTTIE-Ada Greenwood or Rescue the Perishing-Cinn-1882-
200p-cl-reprnt   (5h7) 7.50   (5m2,lt spots)   5.00
NUNN,W C,ed-Ten Texans in Gray-Hillsboro-1968-deluxe ed-
lea-ltd to 50c,autg   (4c7)   50.00
NUNN,WILFRED-Tigris Gunboats-Lond-1932-30 photos-2 maps
(5c1)   15.00
NUOVA PROVISIONE-Sopra la custodia delle vigne,&altri-
(Cesena)-19th of Aug,1581-4 lvs-wrps   (5w1,rprd)   125.00
NURSE LOVECHILD-Tommy Book for all Little Masters & Misses-
facs,c1950,of 1787-59 illus-wrps   (5v2,vf)   7.50
NURSERY,THE-Monthly magazine for youngest readers-Bost-1876-
JnLShorey-188p,Vol 19,#1 thru 6,Vol 20,#1 thru 6 in 1 vol-
lea&bds-12mo   (5p1)   22.50
NURSERY GIFT-or A Book of Books for Little Ones-NY-Francis-
(c1850)-smsq8vo-96p-46 handcol illus-wrps   (5a1)   10.00
NURSERY SONGS & BALLADS-Frank Leslie's Toy Books-lg4to-
10 lvs-6 col plts-col wrps-rare   (4F6,vf)   20.00
NURSEY,WALTER R-Isaac Brock...Saviour of Upper Canada-Tor-
1923-237p-plts-4th ed   (4a8)   5.00
NUSBAUM,AILEEN-Seven Cities of Ciboli,Zuni Folk-NY-1926-
dec e.p.-6 dbl pg col plts-1st ed   (4n3,dj,f)   15.00
NUSBAUM,DERIC-Deric in Mesa Verde-NY-1926-8vo-cl-166p
(5g5)   4.00
NUTCHUK,SIMEON OLIVER-Son of Smoky Sea-NY-1945-245p-
illus-ports   (5aa0,autg wi sketch)   7.50
--same-NY-(1941)-245p-illus   (5ss1)   5.00
NUTE,GRACE L,ed-Documents relating to NW Missions,1815 to
1827-StPaul-1942-469p   (5u6)   12.50
--Lake Superior-Indnpls-(1944)-illus-376p-Amer Lake Ser
(4f9) 8.50   (4b3,f,wn dj) 10. (5hh3) 5.   (5h9)   6.00
--The Voyageur-NY-1931-Appleton-288p-illus
(5t7,ex-libr) 6.50   (5jj7,f)   20.00

NUTE, GRACE L, ed (continued)
--same-StPaul-1955-reprnt (5jj7, mint, dj) 6.00
--The Voyageurs Highway-StPaul-1944-113p-illus-card cov (4b9)10.00
NUTT, C-Worcester & Its People-1919-4 vols (5mm3) 15.00
NUTT, FREDK-The Complete Confectioner-Lond-prntd-NY-reprntd-1807-frontis-91p-ads-12mo-calf-4th ed (5c0, wn, cov dtchd) 67.50
NUTTALL, THOS-The Genera of NoAmer Plants & a Catalogue of the Species, to Year 1817-Phila-1818-hf calf-2 vols in 1-12mo-1st ed (4h0, fox) 150.00
--An Intro to Systematic & Physiological Botany-Cambr-1827-Hilliard & Brown-12 plts-8vo-orig bds-orig papr sp labl-1st ed (4h0, fox, labl chip) 125.00
--Journal of Travels into Arkansa Terr...1819, etc-Phila-1821-fldg map-lea-lithos-296p-1st ed (4t3, ex-libr, marks) 100. (4n4, autg, name cut off) 350.00
NUTTALL, ZELIA-Fundamental Principles of Old & New World Civilizations-Cambr-1901-drwgs-Vol 2 of Papers of Peabody Mus-575 p plus index -1st ed (5bb4, rbnd) 15.00
NUTTING, HELEN C-Monadnock-Priv prntd-(1925)-273p (5e8) 6.50
NUTTING, J K-Desc of John Nutting of Groton, Mass-1908-277p-map (5t9) 22.50
--Desc of John Nutting of South Amherst, Mass-1929-334p (5t9) 15.00
NUTTING, WALLACE-Biography-Framingham-1936-Old Amer Co-illus (5e8, dj) 7.50 (5jj1, f) 7.50 4.50
--The Clock Book-NY-1935-312p-illus-8vo (5ww3) 20.00
--Connecticut Beautiful-Framingham-1923-illus-1st ed (5tt5) 6.00
--same-NY-(1935)-256p-illus (5h9) 6. (5p0) 4. (5jj3, 5j5) 7.50
--Correct Windsor Furniture-SaugusCenter, Mass-(ca 1918)-4to-illus-wrps-catalog-Wallace Nutting-48p (5t2) 7.50
--England Beautiful-NY-(1936)-illus (5yy6) 6.00
--Furniture Catalog, Final Edition-Framingham-1937-4to-photos-136p-wrps (5w7, chlp) 12.50
--Furniture Treasury-Framingham-1928 to 33-4to-orig cl-3 vols-photo illus-1st eds (5t2, libr labls, vg) 67.50
--same-NY-1948-2 vol-illus (5qq7, mint, 5w7) 25.00
--same-NY-1948, 1949-3 vols(Vols 1 & 2 in slipcase as issued)-sm4to-illus (5w0) 16.00
--Ireland Beautiful-NY-(1925)-illus (5yy6) 6.00
--Maine Beautiful-Framingham-(1924)-illus-302p (5t7) 5.00
--Massachusetts Beautiful-Framingham-1923-illus (5p9) 3.50
--same-NY-(1935)-illus (5jj3) 7.50 (5t2, f, dj) 5.00
--NH Beautiful-c1923-lg8vo-cl (4c5) 4.00
--Penna Beautiful(Eastern)-Framingham-(1924)-302p-illus (5p9) 4. (5ee3, f) 3.50
--Photographic Art Secrets-NY-1927-illus-133p-8vo (5ww3) 12.50
--Vermont Beautiful-GardenCty-c1936-254p-illus-deluxe ed (5h9, vg) 6.00
--Windsor Handbook-Framingham&Bost-(1917)-192p-illus (5t4) 15.00
NUTTING, WM W-Cinderellas of the Fleet-JerseyCty-c1920-bds-178p-illus (5s1, ex-libr) 8. (5w5, bkstrp tn) 5.00
--Track of the "Typhoon"-1925-plts (5L7) 3.00
NYABONGO, AKIKI K-The Story of an African Chief-NY-1935-illus (5j2) 7.00
NYBERG, DOROTHY HUSE-History of Wayne Co, Nebraska-Wayne-1938-wrps-304p-1st ed-photos-scarce (5L0) 30.00
NYE, ALVAN CROCKER-Furniture Designing & Draughting-NY-1907-2nd ed-illus (5q0) 6.00
NYE, BILL-Bill Nye & Boomerang-Chig-1881-illus-cl-12mo-1st ed of auth's 1st book (5gg6) 45.00
--Bill Nye, his own life story-NY-(1926)-Century-illus-1st ed (5m2) 6.50
--Bill Nye's History of US-Phila-(1894)-illus-1st ed (5mm1) 8.50 (4m8) 10.00
--Bill Nye's Sparks-NY-(1901)-181p-cl (5h1) 4.00
--Chestnuts, Old & New-Chig-1888-illus (4b6) 8.50
NYE, EDGAR W-See NYE, BILL-
NYE, ELWOOD L-Marching with Custer-Glendale, CA-1964-cl-53p-illus-ex illus laid in-ltd to 300c (4p2, vf) 30. (5kk4) 35.00
NYE, NELSON-Western Roundup-NY-1961-Macmillan-By Members of Western Writers of Amer-222p (5p0) 5.00
NYE, G H- Genealogy of Nye Family-1907-704p (5mm3) 25.00
NYE, G S-Biographical Sketches & Records of Ezra Olin Family-1892-441p & fldg chart (5mm3) 20.00
NYE, W S-Carbine & Lance, Story of Old Ft Sill-Norman-1937-photos-maps-419p-1st ed-scarce (5yy7, f, dj sl wn) 17.50
NYGARD, N E-Lew Reese & His Scio Pottery-NY-1948-176p-photos (5y2) 4. (5w7) 4.50
NYSTEL, O P-Lost & Found-Dallas-1888-26p-wrps-certification lf tipped in-rare (4j6) 200.00
NYSTEL, OLE T-From Bondage to Freedom or 3 Months wi Wild Indians-Keene, TX-1930-wrps-52p-2nd ed (4t3) 17.50
NYSTROM, ANTON-Before, During & After 1914-Lond-1915-368p (5w4) 5.00

NYSTROM-HAMILTON, LOUISE-Ellen Key...Her Life & Her Work-NY-1913-intro, Havelock Ellis-illus-187p (5w9) 4.50
O HENRY-The Voice of the City, Further Stories of 4 Million-NY-1908-McClure Co-8vo-cl-1st bndg wi "McClure" at bottom of sp-1st ed (5ee9) 15.00
"O-HI-O"-Cook Book & Instructions-For O-HI-O Steam Cooker wi Doors-Toledo, Ohio-(1903)-64p-recipes & ads-illus-wrps (5g9) 5.00
OAK LEAVES-Golden Jubilee of Sisters of Order of Pres of Blessed Virgin, 1854 to 1904-SanFran-1904-wrps-4to-illus (5F5) 5.00
OAK, H L-Nathaniel Oak of Marlborough, Mass & 3 Generations of His Desc-1906-90p (5mm3) 7.50
OAK, V O-The Negro's Adventure in Gen'l Business-YellowSprngs, Ohio-1949-Antioch Pr (5x2, dj) 17.50
OAK, V V-Institutions of Higher Learning Among Negroes in USA-Negro College Quarterly-Spec Issue-Wilberforce Univ-1947 (5x2) 35.00
OATES, JOYCE CAROL-By the North Gate-NY-(1963)-12mo-cl-1st ed of auth's 1st book (5ss7, dj, mint) 17.50
OAKES, MAUD-Beyond Windy Place-NY-(1946) (4a1) 6.00
OATES, WHITNEY J, ed-Stoic & Epircurean Philosophers-NY-1940-Random (5p7) 6.00
OAKEY, A F-Building a Home-NY-1881-Appleton-115p plus 19p ads-pic cl-illus (5r0) 7.50
OAKLAND, CALIF-Album of, Bird's Eye View of City-Descrip by Pres of Board of Trade-Oakland-1893-obl 8vo-scarce (5h4, vf)10.00
--same-special ed-Oakland-1894-Official Souvenir of 27th Annual Encampment, GAR (5h4) 10.00
OAKLAND-A Calif Wonder-(Tribune Publ Co, 1908)-obl folio-lea-about 100p-illus (5h4) 8.50
OAKLAND, CALIF-The City of Opportunity-(Oakland, Calif, Harrington & McInnis)-n.d.-(ca1904)-9p-illus-pic wrps (5r0) 7.50
OAKLAND-Greater Oakland, 1911-Oakland-1911-4to-buck-455p-illus (5h4, soil) 10.00
OAKLAND, CALIF-Illustrated Directory of-Oakland-Aug, 1896-Directory Co-obl folio-buck-104p & index-illus (5h4, vg) 17.50
OAKLAND, CALIF-Park System of-(Oakland)-n.d.-(ca1910)-8vo-cl-156p (5h4, vg) 5.00
OAKLAND, CALIF-Souvenir of-SanFran-c1898-Edw H Mitchell-photos-15 lvs-wrps (4a5) 15.00
OAKLEY, AMY-Kaleidoscopic Quebec-NY-1947-278p-illus (5h9, autgs, 5m2) 5.00
OAKLEY, IMOGEN B-6 Historic Homesteads-Phila-1962-4to-191p-illus-photos (5h9) 6.50
OAKLEY, VIOLET-The Holy Experiment-Phila-1950-4to-illus-ltd ed (5m2, autg) 8.50
--Sam'l F B Morse-Phila-c1939-97p-illus-ltd to 500c, nbrd, autg (5w4, box) 10.00
OAKMAN, JOHN-Moral Songs for Instruction & Amusement of Children-Darton & Harvey-1802-mrbld wrps-12mo-60p-illus-1st ed (4d1) 25.00
OATS, SERGEANT-Prison Life in Dixie-Chig-1880-209p plus ads-frontis-1st ed (5L0) 25.00
OAKUM, JOHN-Oakum Pickings-NY-1876-188p-1st ed (5m1) 8.50
OBATA, SHIGEYOSHI-The Works of Li Po-NY-(1928)-frontis (5F0) 3.50
OBER, CAROLYN F-Manhattan, Historic & Artistic-NY-c1892-Lovell, Coryell & Co-cl-12mo-232p (4t1) 7.50
OBER, FREDK A-Amerigo Vespucci-1907-Harpers-258p-cl (5g5) 5.00
--Camps in the Caribees-Bost-1880-Lee&Shepard-366p (5v6) 8.50
--Crusoe's Island-NY-1898-1st ed (5b9, shake) 8.50
--Mexican Resources, a Guide to & Thru Mexico-Bost-1884-57p, 37p-wrps (5n4, fox) 7.50
--Our West Indian Neighbors-NY-1904-illus-433p-fldg map-g.t.-pic cov (5kk9) 8.50
--The Silver City-Bost-c1883-Lothrop-8vo-(96)p-illus-pic bds (5p1, wn) 17.50
--Travels in Mexico-StL, MO-(1883)-illus-maps(1 fldg, col)-658p (4t3, wn) 12.50
--same-SanFran-1884-thk8vo-illus-1st ed (5yy6) 17.50
--same-Bost-1884-Estes&Lauriat-cl-illus-672p-8vo-col fldg map (5qq8, ex-libr, tn) 4.50 (4d9, rbnd) 8.50
--same-Bost-1887-lg8vo-cl-190 illus-rev ed (5h4, hng crack) 6.50
OBERBECK, GRACE J-Hist of La Crescenta La Canada Valleys-Montrose-1938-The Ledger-93p-12mo-cl (4t1) 12.50
OBERHOLSER, H C-The Bird Life of Louisiana-NOrl-1938-LA Dept of Cons Bull #28-834p-45 plts-cl (4p5) 20.00
--NoAmer Eagles & Their Economic Relations-Wash-1906-31p-wrps (5n4) 6.00
OBERHOLTZER, ELLIS P-Jay Cooke, Financier of the Civil War-Phila-(1907)-Jacobs&Co-thk8vo-2 vols-cl-1st ed (5ee3) 32.50 (5x5) 27.50
--History of the US since the Civil War-Vols 1 thru 5-1937 (5L7)30.00
--Referendum in Amer-NY-1911-new ed wi supplement (5m2) 5.00

OBERHOLTZER,ELLIS P (continued)
--Robt Morris,Patriot & Financier-NY-1903-illus   (4b6)   10.00
OBERHOLTZER,SARA L-Hope's Heart Bells-Phila-1884-Lippincott-
282p-1st ed   (5x4,pres card)   15.00
--Violet Lee & Other Poems-Phila-1873-1st ed   (4b4,f,pres)   25.00
OBERLIN EVANGELIST,Vol 2,Jan 1,1840 to Dec 16,1840-Oberlin-
1840-208p-lea bkd bds   (5h2,jts crack,sp wn)   15.00
--same-Vols 6 & 7 Jan 3,1844 to Dec 17,1845-Oberlin-1844,45-
lea bkd bds-2 yr run   (5h1,rub)   20.00
OBJECTIONS TO TAXATION OF OUR AMER COLONIES-Lond-
1765-Wilkie-8vo-20p-cl-1st ed   (5L1)   100.00
--same-Lond-1765-Wilkie-2nd ed-sm4to-calf-port inserted(5n2)100.00
OBOLENSKY,SERGE-One Man in His Time-NY-c1958-433p
  (5w4)   5.00
OBOOKIAH,HENRY-Memoirs of Henry Obookiah,a Native of
Owhyhee-Phila-1830-orig bds-126p   (5z7)   25.00
OBREGON,LUIS G-Mexico Viego y Anecdotico-Paris&Mexico-
1909-294p,(4)   (5n4)   15.00
--The Streets of Mexico-SanFran-transl by Wagner-sm4to-cl
1937   (5h4,f,dj)   5.00
OBREGON'S-History of 16th Cent Explorations-in Western Amer-
LosAng-1928-8vo-transl by Hammond&Rey-351p-fldg map-
errata slip   (5F5)   20.00
OBREITER,JOHN-History of 77th Penna Volunteers-Harrisburg-1905-
8vo-406p-fldg map   (4a7,sp fade) 25.   (5j6)   12.50
O'BRIEN,EDW J-Advance of the Amer Short Story-NY-Mead-1931-
314p-rev ed   (5x0)   4.50
--The Best Short Stories of 1927-NY-1927-Dodd,Mead-thk8vo-cl-
460p-1st ed   (5j5)   10.00
--Best Short Stories 1935 & yearbook of Amer short story-Bost-1935-
Houghton-1st ed   (5m2,fade)   6.00
O'BRIEN,FRANK G-Minnesota Pioneer Sketches-Minneapolis-1904-
8vo-cl-372p-illus   (5t9) 22.50   (4t1) 25.   (5m8)   35.00
O'BRIEN,FRANK M-Story of the Sun-NY-1928-8vo-cl-illus-
305p-new ed   (5t2)   5.00
O'BRIEN,FREDK-Mystic Isles of South Seas-NY-1921-8vo-534p-
photos   (4a6)   3.00
--White Shadows in the South Seas-NY-1919-Century-Marquesan
Islands-450p-illus   (5x2) 4.50   (5p7)   6.00
O'BRIEN,JOHN A-The Vanishing Irish-NY-c1953   (5x7)   4.50
O'BRIEN,JOHN EMMET-Telegraphing in Battle,Remin of the
Civil War-Scranton-1910-Raeder Pr-312p-maps-illus-cl (5r0) 10.00
O'BRIEN,JOHN S-By Dog Sled-Chig-1931-illus-2nd prntg
  (4m9,dj)   7.50
O'BRIEN,HOWARD V-Notes for a Book about Mexico-Chig-1937-
173p-cl   (5h7,wn dj)   3.50
O'BRIEN,MAURICE N-Maritime History of NY-320p-WPA(5ff2) 10.00
O'BRIEN,MICHAEL J-Hercules Mulligan-NY-(1937)-190p-frontis
  (5t4,autg)   7.50
--Hidden Phase of Amer History-Devin-1919-533p-illus (5e8) 15.00
--same-NY-1920-DoddMead-533p-cl-ports-8vo   (5j5)   22.50
--In Old New York,the Irish Dead in Trinity & St Paul's Churchyards-
NY-1928   (5t9)   6.50
--McCarthys in Early Amer History-NY-1921 (5jj1,libr nbr)   9.50
--Pioneer Irish in NewEngl-NY-(1937)-PJKenedy-325p (5p9)   5.00
O'BRIEN,P J-The Lindberghs-n.p.-1935-352p-illus-map (5w4)   5.00
--Will Rogers-n.p.-(1935)-photos-288p   (5yy7,fleck)   4.00
O'BRIEN,LIEUT PAT-Outwitting the Hun-NY-1918-8vo-cl-illus-
284p   (5t0,stn) 4.50   (5t2,dj,f)   5.00
O'BRIEN,ROBT-California Called Them-NY-1951-2nd prntg
  (5jj1,f,dj)   7.00
OBSERVATIONS BY MR DOOLEY-NY-1902-Russell-1st ed (5x4) 7.50
OBSERVATIONS ON INSLAVING-Importing & Purchasing of
Negroes-Germantown-1760-prntd by Christopher Sower-2nd ed-
wrps-16p   (5j6)   60.00
OBSERVATIONS ON PAPERS-Relative to rupture with Spain-Lond-
1762-for Nicoll-1st ed   (5x3,cov loose)   45.00
OBSERVATIONS ON PRESENT CONVENTION WITH SPAIN-(Lond)-
prntd in 1739-sm8vo-blue wrps   (5L1)   60.00
OBSERVATIONS ON WISCONSIN TERRITORY-Phila-1838-12mo-
cl-fldg map-Carey&Hart-1st ed   (5n9,ex-libr)   125.00
OBSERVATIONS UPON CERTAIN PASSAGES IN MR JEFFERSON'S
NOTES ON VIRGINIA-NY-1804-8vo-32p-wrps-1st ed
  (5gg6,5m6)   25.00
O'BYRNE,MRS ROSCOE C-Roster of Soldiers & Patriots of the Amer
Revolution Buried in Indiana-1938-DAR-407p-cl   (5a0)   15.00
O CAFE-No Segundo Centenario de sua introducao no Brasil-1934-
Rio de Janeiro-2 vols-961p-illus   (5w1,poor)   10.00
O'CALLAGHAN,E B-Calendar of Hist Manuscripts-Albany-1865 to
1868-4 vols   (5ii2,lacks bkstrp)   35.00
--Documentary History of State of NY-Albany-1850, 51-4 vols-
4to-maps-plts   (5t4) 40.   (5jj3,rub) 50   (4n2,mends)   45.00

O'CALLAGHAN,E B (continued)
--History of New Netherland-NY-1846-maps   (5jj3,sp wn)   20.00
--same-1848-Vol 1-396p-appendix-fldg map   (5zz0,v wn)   9.50
--Laws & Ordnances of New Netherlands,1638 to 74-1868-buck
  (5L7,ex-libr,fray)   17.50
--Remonstrance of New Netherland,& Occurrences There-Albany-
1856-4to   (4b7,pres)   27.50
O'CALLAGHAN,S-The Slave Trade Today-NY-1961   (5x2)   5.00
O'CALLAHAN,JOS T-I Was Chaplain on the Franklin-NY-1956-
Macm-153p   (5p7)   3.00
O'CASEY,SEAN-I Knock at the Door,Swift Glances Back at Things
That Made Me-NY-1956-2 vols-boxed   (5hh1)   12.50
--Inishfallen Fare Thee Well-NY-1949-396p (5ss9,dj) 4.95 (5t7)   5.00
--The Plough & the Stars-NY-1926-Macm-1st Amer ed
  (5ss9,pencil)   10.00
--Rose & Crown-Lond-1952-Macm-1st ed   (5ss3,dj,sp fade)   10.00
--The Silver Tassie-Lond-1928-Macm-cl bkd bds-1st ed
  (5ss3,sp stn,dj)   15.00
--Story of the Irish Citizen Army-Dublin-1919-Maunsel&Co-12mo-
orig prntd wrps-1st ed of auth's 1st book-pamph (5u5) 50. (5i8) 40.00
OCEAN-description of Wonders & Important Products of the Sea-Lond-
JohnHarris-illus-Little Library-1st ed -1833   (5c8)   12.50
--same-Lond-1835-Harris-2nd ed-enlrgd-12mo (5c8,cov dtchd)   12.50
OCEAN HIGHWAY-NY-(1938)-244p-cl-WPA (5h6) 4.   (5t4)   6.50
OCEAN PLAGUE-Or Voyage to Quebec in an Irish Emigrant Vessel...
by a Cabin Passenger-Bost-1848-orig painted wrps-1st ed-
scarce   (5m2)   15.00
OCHSE,J J-Fruits & Fruitculture in the Dutch East Indies-Batavia-
1931-cl-8vo-57 col plts   (5z9)   12.50
OCHSENFORD,S E-Muhlenberg College Quarter Centennial Mem
Vol-Allentown-1892-illus   (5m2)   5.00
OCHSENREITER,L G-History of Day Country from 1873 to 1926-
Mitchell,SD-(1926)-photos-258p-1st ed-scarce   (5yy7)   35.00
O'CONNELL,DAN'L-Upon Amer Slavery,wi Other Irish Testimonies-
NY-1860-wrps-48p-Amer Anti Slavery Soc Tract #5 (5x2)   25.00
O'CONNOR,BARRY-Turf Fire Stories & Fairy Tales of Ireland-
NY-1890-illus   (4a1,hng split)   10.00
O'CONNOR,EDWIN-The Last Hurrah-Bost-(1956)-LittleBrown-
8vo-cl-427p-1st ed   (5j5)   7.50
O'CONNOR,FLANNERY-A Good Man is Hard to Find & Other
Stories-NY-(1955)-1st ed   (5r9)   15.00
O'CONNOR,JACK-Big Game Rifle-NY-1952-Knopf-1st ed-lg8vo-
371p-illus   (4a6,f)   15.00
--Hunting in the Rockies-NY-1947-314p-photos-maps-4 col plts
  (5dd9)   9.00
O'CONNER,L P-O'Conner,Conner,Simmons Families-1941-81p
  (5mm3)   17.50
O'CONNOR,LESLIE M-Official Baseball including Official Rules
1945-NY-1945-illus-orig wrps   (5w4)   3.00
O'CONNOR,PAUL-Eskimo Parish-Milw-1946-x,134p-plts(5aa0) 5.00
O'CONNOR,RICHARD-Bat Masterson-GardenCty-1957-1st ed-263p
  (5k1) 4.   (5jj1,dj,f)   7.00
--High Jinks on the Klondike-Indnpls-(1954)
  (4a1) 7.50   (5w0,ltd,autg) 7.50   (5l0)   5.00
--Wild Bill Hickok-NY-1959   (5a8,dj)   5.00
O'CONNOR,T P-Memoirs of an Old Parliamentarian-NY-1929-
Appleton-2 vols   (5p0)   10.00
O'CONNOR,MRS T P-My Beloved South-NY-1914-427p plus ads-
frontis   (5w5)   5.00
O'CONNOR,WM DOUGLAS-Netty Renton,or the ghost-NY-1869-
Putnam   (5m2)   12.50
O'CONOR,NORREYS JEPHSON-A Servant of the Crown-NY-1938-
Soc of Colonial Wars-256p-illus   (5h9,mint)   6.50
O'COTTER,PAT-Rhymes of a Roughneck-Seward-1918-92p
  (5ss1,pres)   7.50
OCTAVE,ARIZONA-The Octave Mine & Mill-1902-4to-prospectus
& brochure,text & illus-photos-dbl pg illus   (5g6)   17.50
O'DALY,EDMUND E-History of the O'Daly's,Ancient Irish Sept
of Corca Adaimh-NewHav-1937-Tuttle,Morehouse & Taylor-cl-
8vo-546p   (4t1,pres,lacks t.p.)   15.00
O'DANIEL,V F-Snatches of O'Daniel,Hamilton & Allied Ancestry &
History in Maryland & Kentucky-Somerset,OH-1933-illus-101p
  (4p8)   15.00
O'DANIEL,GOV W LEE-Possibilities for Industrial Development of
Texas-Austin-c1941-62p-folio   (4a5)   10.00
ODART LE COMTE-Manuel Du Vigneron-Paris-1861-358p-3rd ed-
calf bk   (5w1,fox)   17.50
O'DAY,EDW F-Bel Air Bay,A Country Place by the Sea-LosAng-1927-
Young&McCallister-30p-4to-lea   (4t1,chip)   20.00
ODD FELLOWS-Constit,Bylaws & Rules of Order of Pacific Lodge
#155,IOOF of State of Calif-SanFran-1869-91p plus 1p-cl-
Winterburn Prntrs-4x6   (5r0)   7.50

ODD FELLOWS-Proceedings of R W Grand Lodge of Independent
Order of State of Nevada, 1st Annual Communication 1867 to
7th Annual, 1873-Sacramento&San Fran-1867 to 1873-sheep-
764p plus index 6p   (5r0, lacks bkstrp)   15.00
ODELL, GEO C D-Annals of the NY State-NY-1927-Vol 1 (to 1798),
Vol 2 (1798 to 1821)- 2vols-illus   (4j3)   50.00
--same-NY-1942-illus-Vol 12 (1882 to 1885)-4to   (5xx7) 15.00
--same-NY-1945-illus-cl-Vol 14 (1888 to 1891)   (5xx7) 15.00
ODELL, REV JOS H-Henry Martyn Boies-NY-1904-197p-illus-t.e.g.
(5w5)   5.00
ODELL, SAML W-Samson:an Historical Romance-Cinn-1891-284p-
cl-1891 on t.p.-(Earlier than Wright 4025)   (5h7)   17.50
O'DELL, SCOTT-Country of the Sun, Southern Calif-NY-1957-
310p   (4n1, dj)   6.00
ODELL, THOS E-Mato Paha-Spearfish, SD-184p-illus-maps-
stiff wrprs-priv prntd, 1942-1st ed   (5kk4, f)   12.50
ODEM, BILL-Early Days of Texas New Mexico Plains-Canyon-
1965-Haley publ-designed by Hertzog-ltd to 750c (4c7) 25.00
ODETS, CLIFFORD-The Country Girl, a play in 3 acts-NY-1951-
8vo-cl-1st ed   (5dd8, dj)   5.00
--Paradise Lost, a play in 3 acts-NY-(1936)-Random-frontis-
1st prntng   (5m2)   6.50
ODLUM, MRS CATHERINE-Life & Adv of Prof Robt Emmet Odlum-
Wash-1885-207p-cl   (5y0, rub)   12.50
O'DONNELL, BERNARD-The Old Bailey & Its Trials-NY-1951-
Macm-226p   (5p9)   3.50
O'DONNELL, EUGENE-Manual for Guidance of Apprentices on
Training Ships-Bost-(1918)-261p plus 26p   (5s1, f)   3.50
O'DONNELL, REV JOHN HUGH-Catholic Hierarchy of the US-
Wash-1922-Catholic Univ-223p-wrps   (5u3)   6.50
O'DONNELL, PEADAR-Adrigoole-Lond-(1929)-Jonathan Cape-
cl-1st ed   (5ss3, dj, fade)   10.00
--Islanders-Lond-(1928)-Jonathan Cape-1st ed-cl (5ss3, dj, fade) 10.00
--The Knife-Lond-(1930)-Jonathan Cape-1st ed (5ss3, dj, fade) 10.00
O'DONOGHUE, FREEMAN-Catalogue of Engraved British Portraits
preserved in Dept of Prints & Drawings in British Museum-Lond-
Brit Mus-1908 to 1914-4 vols-4to   (5m5, ex-librr) 50.00
O'DONOVAN, JEREMIAH-Brief Account of Auth's Interview with
his Countrymen-Pittsburgh-1864-382p-lea back bds-1st ed
(5jj9, sl wn)   50.00
O'DUFFY, EIMAR-King Goshawk & the Birds-Lond-1926-Macm-
cl-1st ed   (5ss3, dj, sp fade) 10.00
ODUM, HOWARD W-Cold Blue Moon-Indnpls-(1931)-BobbsMerrill-
(5x2) 10. (5F1, f, dj, autg) 12.50
--The Negro & His Songs-Univ NoCar-1925   (5x2)   25.00
--Race & Rumors of Race-Univ NoCar-1943   (5x2)   12.50
--Rainbow Round My Shoulder-Indnpls-1928-1st ed
(5x2, dj, autg)   15.00
--Social & Mental Traits of the Negro-NY-1910-Columbia Univ Pr-
R8vo   (5x2)   45.00
--Southern Regions of the US-Chapel Hill-(1943)-illus-maps-664p
(4p8)   15.00
OEHLER, ANDREW-The Life, Adventures...of-(Trenton)-1811
(5tt6, rbnd) 75. (5i0, stnd)   90.00
OEHLER, C M-The Great Sioux Uprising-NY-1959-illus(5L0,5r7) 7.50
OEHLER, GOTTLIEB F-Journey & Visit to Pawnee Indians on Platte
River, 1851-NY-1914-32p-wrps-scarce   (5dd4, chip)   21.00
OEHSER, PAUL H-Sons of Science-NY-1949-220p-illus (5y2)   4.50
OELSNER, G H-Handbook of Weaves-NY-1915-lg8vo-cl-402p-
v scarce   (5p5)   10.00
OEMLER, MARIE CONWAY-Johnny Reb, Story of SoCarolina-NY-
(1929)-433p   (4b3,5ee3)   3.50
O'FERRALL, CHAS T-40 Yrs of Active Service-NY-1904-Neale-
367p-frontis-8vo   (5mm8,4a7,rub)   20.00
L'OFFICE DE LA SEMAINE SAINTE-et de celle de Paque;Quebec-
1816-sm8vo-hf calf-new ed-in Latin & French-Nouvelle
Imprimerie   (5w8)   150.00
OFFICE OF THE HOLY WEEK-According to Roman Missal & Breviary
Containing Morning & Evening Serv in Latin & Engl-Balt-1810-
480p-dec lea-Dobbin&Murphy, prntrs-1st Amer ed (5r0) 100.00
OFFICER'S GUIDE, THE-Harrisburg, PA-(1942)-499p-illus (5t7) 6.00
OFFICERS OF OUR UNION ARMY & NAVY-Their Lives, Their
Portraits-Bost-(1862)-Vol 1-LPrang, Publ-148p plus ads-illus-
cl-scarce   (5t3, hng crack)   25.00
OFFICIAL ARMY REGISTER FOR 1847-Wash-1847-CAlexander-
54p-prntd wrps-officers of the Mexican War   (5n4)   35.00
--same, for 1848   (5n4)   35.00
OFFICIAL ARMY REGISTER-Volunteer Force of US Army for 1861 to
1865-Wash-1865-Pt 5-Ohio, Michigan   (5q0)   7.50
--same-for years 1861 thru 1865 for New Engl States-Wash-1865-
303p plus 102p   (5L3)   12.50
OFFICIAL AUTOMOBILE BLUE BOOK-For 1908, NewJersey, Penna
South & West, Vol 3-NY-1908-cl-610p   (4h1, cov rprd)   8.50

OFFICIAL AUTOMOBILE BLUE BOOK (continued)
--same-1919-Vol 7 covering Midwest-1144p-photos-maps-
lg fldg map   (5s4, soil, sl shake) 15.00
--same-1919-Vol 9 covering Wash, Ore, Id & BC-544p-illus-maps-
fldg map   (5s4, soil)   12.50
--same-1920-Vol 8-Calif, Nev, Utah & Ariz with routes into Ore,
Colo, Idaho, Wyo, NewMex-794p-illus-maps-ads-fab (5r0) 10.00
--same-Vol 1-NewEngl, NY, Lower Ontario, NorPa, QuebecCty,
Nova Scotia & NewBrunswick-Chig-1922-1,302p-imit mor-
fldg map   (5w5)   4.00
--same-Chig-1922-Vol2-Pa, WVa, Ky, Tenn, NC, SC, Ala, Miss,
Fla, La-1,066p-map   (5w5)   4.00
--same-Chig-1923-Vol 1-NE, NY, Lower Ontario, NorPa, QuebecCty,
Nova Scotia, New Brunswick-802p-immt lea   (5w9)   4.00
--same-Chig-1924-same as preceding except wi map holder & map
(5w9)   4.00
--same-Chig-1925-same as preceding-772p   (5w9)   4.00
OFFICIAL GUIDE OF THE RWYS & STEAM NAVIG LINES OF US-
June, 1945-1440p   (4d9, pgs bent)   30.00
OFFICIAL GUIDE-Shippers, Travellers, Osaka Shosen Kaisha SS Co-
Osaka, Japan-1926, 27-799p-g.e.-col maps-thumb indxd-
13th ann ed   (5s1, stns)   12.50
--same-1932, 33-657p-19th ann ed   (5s1)   12.50
OFFICIAL GUIDE TO THE KLONDYKE COUNTRY & GOLD FIELDS
OF ALASKA WITH OFFICIAL MAPS-Chig-1897-maps-296p
(4e9, fade)   20.00
OFFORD, C R-The White Face-NY-1943-1st ed   (5x2)   25.00
OFFORD, R M, ed-Jerry McAuley, Apostle to the Lost-NY-(1907)-
304p-cl   (5h7)   4.00
O'FLAHERTY, DAN'L-Gen'l Jo Shelby...Undefeated Rebel-
ChapelHill-(1954)-frontis   (5yy7, f, dj)   8.50
O'FLAHERTY, LIAM-The Assassin-Lond-(1928)-8vo-cl-1st ed-
ltd to 150c, nbrd, autg (5d3) 20. (5F9, mint dj) 30. (5a9, dj) 25.00
--The Black Soul-Lond-(1924)-8vo-cl-1st ed (5ee9, autg, 5ss3) 10.00
--The Child of God-Lond-1926-ltd to 100c, autg   (5a9)   25.00
--The Fairy Goose-NY&Lond-1927-sm12mo-dec papr bds-lin bk-
1st ed, autg, nbrd-Crosby Gaige, publ (5ss7, dj, unopnd) 8.50
--The House of Gold-Lond-(1929)-Cr8vo-cl-1st ed
(5ss7, f, autg) 6.50   (5ss3, dj)   7.50
--The Informer-Lond-(1925)-Jonathan Cape-1st ed (5ss3, dj) 20.00
--Red Barbara-NY-1929-ltd to 600c, autg   (5a9)   20.00
--A Tourist's Guide to Ireland-Lond-(n.d.)-Madrake Pr-1st ed
(5ss9) 7.50 (5ss3, dj)   10.00
--Two Years-Lond-1930-Jonathan Cape-1st ed
(5ss3, sp fade, chip dj) 7.50 (5ss9, vg, tn dj) 17.70
OGAN, LEW-Hist of Vinton Co, Ohio-(1953)-314p (5t9)   7.50
OGDEN, ADELE-The Calif Sea Otter Trade, 1784 to 1848-(1941)-
Univ of Calif (UC Pubs in Hist, Vol 26)-8vo-251p-wrps-scarce
(5h4)   40.00
OGDEN, C K-Bentham's Theory of Fictions-NY-1932 (5ff4)   12.50
OGDEN, HENRY A-8 Great Union Commanders in 8 Great Battles
of Civil War-n.p.-n.d.-4to-col illus-loose in fldr (5p9)   8.00
OGDEN, JAS-The British lion rous'd-or acts of the Brit worthies,
a poem in 9 books-Manchester-1762-RWhitworth-8vo-hf calf-
1st ed-v rare   (5x3, marg stns)   175.00
OGDEN, PETER SKENE-Snake Country Journals, 1824,5 & 1825,6-
Lond-1950-Hudson's Bay Rec Soc-13 fldg maps (5s6)   25.00
OGDEN, RUTH-Loyal Little Red Coat-NY-1890-60 illus-1st ed-
v scarce   (4F6)   40.00
OGDEN, SAM'L R-How to Grow Food For Your Family-NY-(1943)-
illus   (5s7)   4.00
OGG, D-England in the Reign of Charles II-1955- 2 vols (5L7) 12.00
OGG, F A-Reign of Andrew Jackson A Chronicle of Frontier in
Politics-NewHav-1920-Yale Univ Pr-249p-illus-t.e.g.(5F9) 6.00
OGG, GEO P-Graphic Account of Capture & Burning of Col Wm
Crawford by Indians-n.p.(Carey, OH)-n.d.(ca1902)-prntd wrps-
16p   (4h1)   12.50
OGG, OSCAR-The 26 Letters-NY-(1948)-Crowell-254p-illus (5p7) 4.50
OGILVIE, WM-Information Respecting the Yukon District-Ottawa-
1897-illus-65p-5 maps-scarce   (4n7, tn)   15.00
OGILVIES, THE-A Novel-Lond-1849-3 vols-12mo-cl-1st ed of
auth's 1st novel   (5gg6, short a.l.s.) 125.00
OGLESBY, CATHERINE-French Provincial Decorative Art-NY-
(1951)-4to-214p-plts   (5xx7)   10.00
--Modern Primitive Arts of Mexico, Guatemala & SW-NY-(1939)-
8vo-cl-226p   (5h4, f, dj)   10.00
OGLETHORPE, GEN'L-An Impartial Account of the Late Exped
Against StAugustine Under-Lond-1742-for Huggonson-
fldg map-lea-a.e.g.-68p   (5t7, rbnd, map def) 1,200.00
O'GORMAN, EDITH-Convent Life Unveiled-Aurora-n.d.(ca1913)-
264p-wrps-32nd ed   (4h7)   4.00
--Trials & Persecutions of Miss Edith O'Gorman, HudsonCty, NJ,
written by herself-Hartf-c1871-264p,(5) (5w5, edge wn, fade) 7.75

O'GRADY,ALICE-The Teachers' Story Teller's Book-Chig&NY-
(c1913)-RandMcNally-12mo-352p   (5p1)   5.00
O'GRADY,STANDISH-History of Ireland,the Heroic Period-Lond-
1878-2 vols-cl-Sampson Low,Searle,etc-1st ed
(5ss3,crack,fade)   35.00
OGRIZER,DORE,ed-North Africa-Lond-1955-4to-col illus-cl-
1st ed   (5p5)   12.50
O'HANLON,JOHN C-Irish Amer History of US-NY-1907-2 vols-
677p-mor-4to   (5q8) 15.   (5jj9,4m4)   17.50
--Life & Scenery in Missouri-Dublin-1890-292p-1st ed-rare(5L0)35.00
O'HARA,ELIOT-Watercolor Fares Forth-NY-(1938)-illus (5yy6)   5.00
O'HARA FAMILY-The Bit o' Writin & Other Tales-Lond-1838-
3 vols-1st ed-12mo-cl &bds-papr labls   (5xx6)   175.00
--Father Connell-Lond-1842-Newby&Boone-3 vols-12mo-hf calf-
papr labls-1st ed   (5x3,lend libr)   90.00
O'HARA,JOHN-And Other Stories-NY-1968-Random-ltd to 300c,
autg,nbrd   (4L4,box,mint)   30.00
--Appointment in Samarra-NY-(1934)-8vo-cl-1st ed of auth's
1st book   (5ee9,tn dj)   100.00
--A Family Party-NY-(1956)-Rand omHse-1st ed   (5tt2,dj)   10.00
--From the Terrace-NY-(1958)-RandomHse-1st ed (4b5,5r9,dj)   6.00
--Hellbox-NY-(1947)-RandomHse-1st ed   (5ss3,dj)   10.00
--Pal Joey-NY-(1940)-Duell,Sloan&Pearce-1st ed
(5v2,lend libr,dj,vf) 15.   (5ee3,f)   17.50
--Ten North Frederick-NY-(1955)-RandomHse-1st ed (5ss3,dj)   10.00
--Waiting for Winter-NY-1966-Random-ltd ed-300c autg,nbrd
(4L4,box, mint)   30.00
O'HARA,MARY-Green Grass of Wyoming-(1946)-Lippincott
(5F1,mint,dj)   3.50
--Thunderhead-(1943)-Lippincott   (5F1,vf,dj)   5.00
O'HARA,JOHN-From the Terrace-NY-(1958)-1st ed (5r9,dj,f)   6.00
O'HARA,MELITA L-Coast to Coast in a Puddle Jumper & Other
Stories-n.p.-(1930)-109p   (5s4,pres,fade)   3.00
O'HARRA,CLEOPHAS C-Black Hills Engineer,Custer Exped Numbers-
RapidCty-1929-illus-wrps   (4k5,f)   10.00
O'HART,JOHN-Irish Pedigree-Dublin-1892-Duffy-thk8vo-orig cl-
t.e.g.-5th ed in 2 vols   (4m9,hng crack)   65.00
--same-1923-Ltd Amer ed-2 vols   (5mm3)   75.00
OHIO-Acts Passed at 1st Session of 14th Gen Assembly of State of-
Chill-1816-484p-Imprints Invent #322   (5h1)   50.00
OHIO ARCHAEOLOGICAL & HISTORICAL PUBLICATIONS-Columbus
(1887 to 1921)-Vol 1 thru 30-illus-cl   (5w0)   150.00
--same-Vols 1 to 16(odd vols)-1887 to 1912   (5t9)ea   3.00
OHIO BAR-Vol 1 thru 43-(1928 to 1970)-bnd in 53 vols
(5ii7,rbnd) 1,020.00
OHIO-Biogr Encyclopaedia of Ohio of 19th Century-Cinn-1876-
illus-lea-667p plus index   (4t3) 20.   (5a9,vf)   30.00
OHIO COUNTY FAIR-Premiums & regulations for 4th Annual Fair
of Montgomery Co Agric Soc-Dayton-1855-stitchd (5g4)   6.00
OHIO GUIDE,THE-NY-(1940)-634p-cl-fldg pkt map-Amer Guide
Series-WPA   (5h2,wn)   5.00
OHIO LIFE INSURANCE & TRUST CO-Charter & bylaws of-Cinn-
1834   (5g8)   7.50
OHIO JOURNAL OF EDUCATION-Vol 4,Jan 1857 to Dec 1857-
Col-1857-392p-lea bkd bds   (5h2)   10.00
OHIO LAND GRANTS,Short Hist of-n.p.-n.d.-(Columbus 1939?)-
36p-wrps   (5h7)   2.00
OHIO-Map in Colors-by H Anderson-StClairsville-1853-43x34 inches-
mntd on cl & rollers   (5t0)   50.00
OHIO RR GUIDE,THE-illus,Cinn to Erie,via Columbus & Cleveland-
Columbus-1854-Ohio State Journal-12mo-orig blue sl-2nd ed
(5i9,fox)   45.00
OHIO RAILWAY MAP-Columbus-1901-shows all lines (5b9,vf)   5.00
OHIO UNIVERSITY 1875-Annual Catalog of-Athens-1876-96p-
wrps   (5h1)   8.50
OHLER,C P-Anc & Desc of Capt John Jas & Esther Denison of
Preston,Conn-1912-216p   (5mm3)   20.00
OHLER,CLARA P-Anc & Desc of David Paine & Abigail Shepard of
Ludlow,Mass-1913-252p-100c wre prntd   (5mm3,f)   60.00
OINOPHILUS,BONIFACE DE MONTE,FIASCONE-Ebrietatis
Encomium or The Praise of Drunkenness-NY-1922-2 frontis-
sm4to-177p-"Sallengre" on sp   (5w6,box)   18.50
OJIBWAY DICTIONARY-Cheap & Concise Dictionary of Ojibway
& Engl Languages-1907-card cov-177p   (4e9)   15.00
OJIBWAY-Gospel According to St Matthew-Engl & Ojibway-1897-
Colportage Mission-wrps-128p   (4e9)   20.00
OJIBWAY SCRIPTURE ABC BOOK-Tor,Sault Ste Marie-n.d.-
Algoma & NW Colportage Mission-wrps-15p (4e9)   15.00
OJIKE,M-I have 2 Countries-NY-1947)   (5x2,dj)   7.50
--My Africa-NY-1946-illus   (5x2,dj)   8.50
OKADA,Y-Catalogue of Vertebrates of Japan-Tokyo-1938-412p-
stiff wrps-8vo-v scarce   (4p6)   10.00

OKAKURA,KAKASU-The Ideals of the East,with Special Reference
to Art of Japan-NY-1904-8vo-cl   (5p5)   7.50
OKAKURA KAKUZO-The Book of Tea-NY-1906   (5F0)   3.00
--same-NY-1926-12mo-160p   (5w1)   2.50
--Ideals of the East-Lond-1905   (5F0,f)   3.50
OKAKURA YOSHISABURO-The Life & Thought of Japan-Lond-
1913-Dent-150p   (5x9)   3.50
OKANAGAN MANUEL-Engl Manual or Prayers & Catechism in
Engl Typography,1897-Kamloops-183p bnd wi Okanagan
Manual-50p-orig cl   (5d6)   40.00
O'KANE,WALTER-The Hopis,portrait of a Desert People-
(1953)-Univ of Okla-267p-cl-col photos-sm4to
(5F5,f,wn dj) 15.   (5x5,dj)   20.00
--Injurious Insects-NY-1914-414p-ads-illus-600 photos (5t4)   6.50
--Sun in the Sky-Norman-1950-maps-plts-1st ed (4k5,f,dj,4t3) 12.50
--Trails & Summits of the Green Mountains-Bost-1926-372p-illus
(5e8)   3.75
--Trails & Summits of the White Mountains-Bost-1925-illus-maps-
307p   (5t7)   6.00
O'KEEFE,JOHN-The castle of Andalusia,a comic opera in 3 acts,
wi additional songs-Dublin-1783-12mo-disbnd-1st (5x3)   40.00
--Fontainbleau;or,our way in France-A comic opera in 3 acts-
Dublin-1785-for W Wilson-12mo-disbnd-1st ed-rare
(5x3,t.pg tn)   35.00
--The highland reel,a comic opera-in 3 acts-Dublin-1789-12mo-
disbnd-prntd by TM'Donnel-1st ed-rare   (5x3)   40.00
OKESON,WALTER R-Spalding's Official Football Guide 1939-
NY-c1939-16mo-322p plus ads   (5w4,lacks wrps)   3.50
OKIE,HOWARD P-Old Silver & Old Sheffield Plate-NY-1936-
illus-420p-index   (5qq7,dj)   12.50
--same-GardenCty-1945-illus-420p   (5w5)   15.00
--same-NY-1946   (5F9,f)   6.00
OKLAHOMA-Norman-1941-1st ed-illus-pkt map (5kk4,f,dj)   20.00
--same-Norman-1945-photos,maps-pkt map-427p plus index-
2nd ed-Amer Guide Ser-WPA   (4L5,dj)   6.50
OKLAHOMA,THE BEAUTIFUL LAND-(By the 89ers)-OklaCty-
(1943)-photos-map-352p-1st ed-scarce (4t3,dj,f)   15.00
OKLAHOMA,CHRONICLES OF-(1921 to 1964)-Vols 1 to 42
(4a5,lacks 10 issues)   450.00
OKLAHOMA CITY-RL Polk&Co's OklaCty Directory for 1925-
1042p   (5h0)   5.00
--same-1919,1930,1931   (5h0) ea   5.00
OKLAHOMA HISTORICAL SOCIETY-Chronicles of Oklahoma-
OklahomaCty-1923 to 1968-Vol 1 to 46-orig wrps-plus index
1 to 37-   (5yy3,lacks part of 4 vols)   175.00
OKLAHOMA IMPRINTS 1835 to 1907-Norman-1936-illus-499p-
CTForeman,ed   (4g2)   20.00
OKLA LAW JOURNAL-Vol 1 thru 14(all publ)-1902 to 1916-bnd
(5ii7,rbnd)   210.00
OKLA MUTUAL TOWNSITE CO-A Cheap Trip to Oklahoma-
OklaCty-1904-wrps-illus-map   (5r5)   15.00
OKLA STATE BAR ASSN-Proceedings-Vol 1thru 26-(1907 to 1932)-
bnd   (5ii7,lacks Vol 1,3,ex-libr)   165.00
OKLAHOMA TERR-Report of Gov of-Wash-1893-wrps   (4a5)   12.50
OKUBO,MINE Citizen 13660-NY-1946-Col U Pr-8vo-cl-209p-
illus   (5j5)   10.00
OKUMA,THOS-Angola in Ferment-Bost-1962-137p (5c6,f)   6.50
OLAFSEN & POVELSEN-Travels in Iceland-Lond-1805-162p-
plts-wrps-fldg map   (5r7)   25.00
OLCOTT,CHAS-Wm McKinley-Bost-c1916-2 vols-illus-t.e.g.
(5w9)   7.00
OLCOTT,HENRY S-People From the Other World-Hartf-1875-
492p-illus   (5xx7,cov spot)   30.00
--Sorgho & Impee,the Chinese & African Sugar Canes-NY-1858-
352p-frontis-6th ed   (5s7)   20.00
OLCOTT,WMY TYLER-Star Lore of All Ages-NY-1911-Putnam-
illus-453p   (5p9)   7.00
--same-NY-(1929)-453p-64 plts   (5c3)   10.00
OLD ABE,THE 8th WISC WAR EAGLE-Madsn-1885-173p-cl-
by F.A.F.   (5h2,hngs rprd)   7.50
OLD AMERICAN COMIC ALMANAC,THE-Bost-1841-Dickinson-
(1840)-8vo-36p-sewed   (5j5)   25.00
OLD BREWERY,THE-The New Mission House at the 5 Points-NY-
1854-304p-frontis   (5j5,fox) 10.   (5w1)   7.50
OLD BUILDINGS OF NEW YORK CITY-NY-1907-Brentano-8vo-
cl-illus-179p   (5j5,sl dmpstnd)   10.00
OLD CALIFORNIA MISSIONS-SanFran-1889-H SCrooker-46p-
photos-wrps   (4a5,sp loose)   12.50
OLD CHINESE PORCELAIN-Lond-n.d.-7 col plts-wrps,tied-
(20p)   (5w7)   7.50
OLD COACHING DAYS-& the White Horse Cellar Piccadilly-
Lond-n.d.-obl 12mo-59p-wrps-8 col illus (5w1)   4.50

OLD COLONY,THE-or Pilgrim Land,Past & Present;Fall River
    Line & Old Colony RR-(Bost)-1889-8vo-orig wrps-illus-
    6 fldg maps   (5m6,dmpstnd)   7.50
OLD FLAG,THE-NY-1864-1st published by Union Prisoners at
    Camp Ford Tyler,Texas-17p-sm folio-rare   (5j6)   85.00
OLD FRANKLIN ALMANAC-Phila-1860 to 1872-John Haslett-bnd-
    12 issues   (5yy3,bndg broke)   15.00
OLD FRIENDS & NEW FACES-Cassell-1870-4to-dec cl-26p-
    24 col plts   (5s0)   21.00
OLD GAMEKEEPER,AN-Plain Directions for...Shooting on the Wing-
    NY-1873-frontis-88p-(8p) ads-8vo-orig   cl-g.-1st ed
                    (5zz7)   15.00
OLD HAUN,THE PAWNBROKER-Or, The Orphan's Legacy-NY-
    1857-(Rudd&Carleton)-463p-frontis   (5t7,wn)   6.00
OLD HELMET,THE-NY-1864-RobtCarter-2 vols-1st ed (5x4)   27.50
OLD HOUSE BY THE RIVER,THE-By Author of Owl Creek Letters-
    NY-1853-Harper-12mo-cl   (5b2,fade)   8.50
"OLD JACK"-& his Foot Cavalry-NY-1864-300p-cl-frontis-scarce
                  (5y0)   20.00
OLD LIBRARIAN'S ALMANACK,THE-Woodstock-1909-8vo-bds-
    cl bk-papr labls-1st ed of Pearson's 1st book (5gg6)   15.00
OLD MANORS,OLD HOUSES-1st Series-Quebec-1927-sm4to-
    prntd wrps-376p of photos-publ by Historic Monuments Comm
    of Prov of Quebec   (5t2)   10.00
OLD MASTERPIECES IN SURGERY-Omaha-1928-4to-cl&bds-263p-
    illus-priv prntd   (5p6)   15.00
OLD MEN'S TEARS FOR THEIR OWN DECLENSIONS-NewLond-
    1769-Green-12mo-motld calf   (5n2)   150.00
OLD MOTHER BANTRY-NY-c1870-McLoughlin Bros-col wrps-
    4 col plts-12mo-10p-scarce   (4F6,f)   17.50
OLD MOTHER HUBBARD & HER DOG-NY-c1870-McLoughlin Bros-
    12mo-8p-hand col illus   (4c3,sp taped)   15.00
OLD MR BOSTON DELUXE OFFICIAL BARTENDER'S GUIDE-
    Bost-1926-12mo-157p   (5w1)   2.50
OLD NICK'S POCKET BOOK-by himself-Lond-1808-prntd by JMoyes-
    8vo-orig prntd bds-fldg frontis-1st ed   (5i8,rbkd)   17.50
OLD NORTHWEST HISTORICAL SERIES-Vol 1 thru 4-Cleve,
    Glendale-1926 to 1941-Arthur H Clark Co   (5d6)   80.00
OLD NURSERY STORIES-NY-(1892)-McLoughlin Bros-sm8vo-
    pict bds-bnd vol of 6 toybooks ea wi 4 col plts (5c8,rub)   20.00
OLD PRINT SHOP PORTFOLIO-NY-1940 to 1962-181 issues-
    Vol 1,#1 to Vol 21,#10   (5j4,lacks some nbrs)   125.00
OLD RAIL FENCE CORNERS-the ABC's of Minnesota history-
    (Austin,Minn)-1914-324p-fldg map   (5dd6)   8.50
OLD,R O-Colorado,US America-its History,Geography & Mining
    incl cat of nearly 600 samples of ores-Lond-(1869)-orig wrps-
    map-1st ed   (5m4,slipcase)   150.00
OLD SAILING SHIPS OF NEW ENGLAND-Bost-(1927)-Chas E Lauriat-
    obl 4to-151p-cl-illus   (5t0)   10.00
OLD SANTA FE-SantaFe-c1910-24p-stif wrps-hand col-
    Fred Harvey Co   (5n4)   9.50
OLD SANTA FE-Twelve Hand Colored Views-KansasCty-c1900-
    Fred Harvey-oblong folio   (4a5,mint)   15.00
OLD SERJEANTS INN-Chancery Lane-(Lond)-1912-priv prntd for
    Law Union & Rock Ins Co-54p-frontis-illus   (5g9)   7.50
OLD SOUTH CHURCH LEAFLETS-(Bost)-Vol 1, #1 to 25-Vol 2,
    #26 to 50-2 vols   (5e8)   8.50
--same-(Bost, 1883 to 1909)-Vols 1 to 6-together 6 vols
              (5m6,sl dmpstn)   35.00
OLD TIME CONCORD RECIPES-Trinity Church,Concord-n.d.-
    iii,28,(3)p-spiral bnd wrps   (5c4)   3.50
OLD VANITY FAIR TEA ROOM-Recipes Gathered From Far & Near-
    (LosAng-1927)-purple ink-159p   (4g9,f)   7.50
OLD WEST,THE-Pioneer Tales of San Bernardino Co-SanBernardino-
    (1940)-Sun Co-Writers' Program-53p-8vo-wrps   (4t1)   15.00
OLD WOMAN WHO LIVED IN A SHOE,THE-NY-n.d.-12mo-
    wrps-(11)p-Little Folks Series   (5p1,wrps tn)   3.50
OLDBOY,OLIVER-Geo Bailey-NY-1880-288p-1st ed (5m1)   8.50
OLDE ULSTER-Jan 1908 thru Dec 1909-24 issues-orig wrps-
    magazine   (5ff2)   48.00
OLDEN,SARAH E-People of Tipi Sapa-Milw-(1918)-dec cov-
    illus   (5kk4,f)   12.50
OLDER,FREMONT-Calif Missions & Their Romances-NY-1945
        (4a5) 5.50   (5dd6)   7.50
--My Own Story-SanFran-1919-bds (5dd6) 15. (5n4) 9.50
              (5r7,pres)   10.00
OLDER,MRS FREMONT-The Socialist & the Prince-NY-1903-
    Funk&Wagnalls-8vo-dec cl-frontis by HFisher-g.t. (5b2,f)   4.50
OLDFIELD,DR JOS-Fruitarian Diet & Cookery-Lond-n.d.-56p-
    wrps-9th ed   (5c5)   9.00
OLDHAM,J H-Christianity & The Race Problem-NY-1926 (5x2) 10.00
OLDHAM,H P-How to Fly a Plane-Bost-1940-221p-illus-cl
              (5t2,libr labl)   3.50

OLDHAM,WILLIAMSON S-Digest of General Statute Laws of
    State of Texas-Austin-1859-836p   (4j7)   45.00
OLDMIXON,JOHN-British Empire in America-Lond-1741-calf-
    8vo-2 vols-2nd ed-corr-maps   (4j6)   285.00
OLDROYD,OSBORN H-Assassination of A Lincoln-Wash-1917-
    305p-fldg map-cl   (5h1)   7.50
--The Lincoln Memorial-NY-1883-Carleton-571p   (5p9)   10.00
--Lincoln's Campaign or the Political Revolution of 1860-Chig-
    (1896)-cl-14 ports-241p   (4h2)   10.00
--Soldier's Story of Siege of Vicksburg-Springfield-1885-8vo-200p
        (4a7,wn,lacks facs reprnt)   15.00
--Words of Lincoln-Wash-c1895-221p-illus   (5w5,pencil)   6.50
OLDS,GEO,ed-Brothers-(Muskogee)-n.d.-(1941?)-182p-photos
              (5t3)   17.50
OLDSMOBILE MODEL S FOR 1906-Detroit-1906-illus-catalog-
    16mo-wrps-16p   (5q0)   12.50
OLGIN,MOISSAYE J-A Guide to Russian Literature-NY-1920
        (5t0) 4.75   (5mm2)   6.00
OLIN,C C-Record of John Olin Family who came to Amer in 1678-
    1893-323p   (5t9)   15.00
OLIPHANT,LAURENCE-The Land of Gilead wi excurions in Lebanon-
    Edinb-1880-illus-fldg map-calf-g.t.   (5d2)   15.00
--Minnesota & Far West-Edinb-1855-1st ed-frontis-illus-fldg map-
    lea   (5i3,f)   35.00
--Narrative of the Earl of Elgin's Mission to China & Japan-NY-
    1860-lg8vo-cl-645p-frontis   (5t2,cov chewed)   5.00
--Russian Shores of Black Sea in Autumn of 1852-Redfield (NY)-
    1854-266p-map-illus-cl-ads   (5ee3) 4.   (5t0)   5.00
OLIPHANT,MARGARET-Memoir of Life of Laurence Oliphant &
    Alice etc-NY-1891-2 vols-port   (5q0)   10.00
OLIPHANT,MRS MARGARET-The ladies Lindores-Edinb-1883-
    Blackwood-3 vols-8vo-orig cl-1st ed-scarce (5x3,lend libr)   35.00
--The minister's wife-Lond-1869-Hurst&Blackett-3 vols-8vo-
    orig bevelled cl-1st ed   (5xx6,f)   75.00
OLIVE WREATH,THE-Monthly Magazine, Odd Fellowship-Chig-
    1867-Vol 1(complete)-386p   (5a8,rub)   10.00
OLIVE-BRANCH,REV SIMON-The Looker On: a Periodical Paper-
    Lond-J Evans-1794-2 vols-479&477p-calf   (5a1)   15.00
OLIVER CHILLED PLOW WORKS-The Oliver Alphabet with illus-
    SoBend-1889-24p-wrps-catalog-illus   (5hh6,sl soil)   9.50
OLIVER,ALFRED C,JR-This New America-Lond-1937-1st ed (5q8) 5.00
OLIVER,BENJ-Forms of Practice-Hallowell-1840-2nd ed-664p-
    calf   (5i3,lacks labls)   10.00
OLIVER,DANL-Flora of Tropical Africa-Lond-1868 to 1917-orig cl-
    8 Vols in 10-1st ed   (5z9)   140.00
OLIVER EVANS THE YOUNG MILL WRIGHT-Phila-1840-Lea &
    Blanchard-(Thos Jones)-28 plts-calf-10th ed,wi corr-scarce
              (4m9)   32.50
OLIVER,F L-Anc & Desc of Henry Oliver-Miner & Ann Turner
    of Mechanicville-1956-126p   (5mm3)   15.00
OLIVER,FREDK SCOTT-Alexander Hamilton-NY-1916-Putnam's-
    502p-frontis-fldg map   (5qq8)   4.00
--same-NY-Putnam-1923-502p-map-new ed   (5p9)   6.00
--Ordeal by Battle-Lond-1915-437p-3rd prntng   (5w5)   6.50
OLIVER,GRACE A-A Study of Maria Edgeworth...with Notices of
    Her Father & Friends-Bost-1882-571p   (5p9)   4.50
OLIVER,J A-Relationships & Zoogeography of Genus Thalerophis
    Oliver-NY-1948-Am Mus Nat Hist Bull V92,Art 4-cl-
    orig wrps-4to-plts   (4p6)   17.50
OLIVER,J K-Monterey & Its Environs,with Brief History,Legends,
    Views etc-Monterey-c1913-Mission Art & Curio Store-(44p)-
    obl 16mo-wrps   (4t1)   12.50
OLIVER,JAS H-The Ruling Power-Phila-1953-4to-(32p)-heavy wrps
              (5w9)   3.00
OLIVER,JENNIE HARRIS-Red Earth-KansasCty-1937-105p-cl-
    2nd ed   (5h0)   10.00
OLIVER,JOHN RATHBONE-Spontaneous Combustion-Chig-1937-
    Bds-Argus Book Shop-1st ed   (5ss3,review copy)   10.00
OLIVER,NOLA N-Natchez, Symbol of Old South-NY-(1940)-101p-
    cl   (5h7,4p8,dj)   4.00
OLIVER OPTIC-See OPTIC,OLIVER
OLIVER,PASFIELD,ed-Madagascar,or Robt Drury's Journal-Lond-
    1890-Unwin-pic cov-map(fldg)-illus-398p   (4t5)   25.00
OLIVER,PETER-A New Chronicle of the Compleat Angler-NY-
    1936-illus-301p-1st ed   (4g2)   25.00
OLIVER,RAYMOND-A Man's Cookbook-NY-1961-218p (5c0)   4.75
OLIVER,ROBT T-Syngman Rhee-NY-1955   (5x7)   4.00
OLIVER,STEPHEN-Scenes & Recollections of Fly Fishing in
    Northumberland etc-Lond-1834-12mo-part mor-g.t.-auth's 1st
    book   (4c2)   25.00
OLIVER,STUART-Wine Journeys-NY-(1949)-213p   (5g9)   4.00
OLIVER,SYDNEY-White Capital & Coloured Labour-Lond-1906-
    Socialist Libr Vol 4   (5z5,jnt splt)   25.00

OLIVER,WM-8 Months in Illinois-Chig-1924-reprint (5jj7,f)   15.00

OLIVERIAN CANAL ROUTE-Letter from Sec of War-Wash-1845-
House Doc 113-8vo-35p   (5ss5,text loose)   8.50

OLIVIA-Ellen Parry or trials of the heart-NY-1850-12mo-orig cl-
1st ed-Appleton   (5x1,sp def)   20.00

OLIVIER,STUART-Wine Journeys-NY-(1949)-312p   (5w1)   4.00

OLLIVANT,ALFRED-Bob, Son of Battle-NY-1898-1st ed wi gilt
dog's head within urn on cov-scarce 1st issue   (5v2)   25.00

OLMSTEAD,FRANK H- Gila River Flood Control-Wash-1919-
Sen Doc #436-91p plus 32 photo plts-maps(some fldg) (5L5)   10.00

OLMSTED,FREDK LAW-The Cotton Kingdom-NY-1953-Knopf-626p
           (5qq8,ex-libr,wn)   5.00

--A Journey in the Back Country-NY-1860-492p-orig cl-1st ed
(5m3) 20.   (5yy8,sl wn)   17.50

--A Journey in the Seaboard Slave States-NY-1856-4to-723p-
1st ed   (5m8,ex-libr) 15.   (5x2)   47.50

--Journey Thru Texas-NY-1857-516p-cl-fldg map-1st ed
(5n4,ex-libr,rbnd) 22.50 (5m8) 32.50 (5yy8,map tn) 25.
(5ee3,vg) 37.50 (5h2,sl rub)   35.00

--Walks & Talks of an Amer Farmer in England-NY-1852-2 vols-
stiff prntd wrps   (5g4,lt wn, ex-libr)   10.00
--same-Columbus-1859-12mo-cl-364p   (5t0,libr labl)   7.50

OLSEN,CHAS-In Cold Hell,in Thicket-Poems-SanFran-1967-
8vo-wrps-65p-Four Seasons   (5j5)   6.00

OLSEN,NIELS-American Yacht List for 1886-NY-1886-col plts-
ads-224p-narr obl 4to   (4m7)   10.00

OLSON,B G-Blood on the Arctic Snow-Seattle-(1956)-279p-
photos   (5ss1,mint,dj)   6.00

OLSON,CHAS-Call Me Ishmael-NY-(1947)-12mo-cl-1st ed
of auth's 1st book   (5ss7,pres,vf,dj)   150.00

--Mayan Letters-Mallorca-(1953)-sq8vo-prntd wrps-1st ed-
Divers Pr   (5ss7,f)   30.00

--O'Ryan 12345678910-(SanFran,1965)-12mo-dec wrps-
White Rabbit Pr-1st ed   (5ss7,pres,sl cov spot)   40.00

OLSON,EDMUND T-Utah-SaltLkCty-1931-illus-photos-col plts-
345p-1st ed-scarce   (4t3)   12.50

OLSON,ELDER-The Cock of Heaven-NY-1940-Macmillan-8vo-cl-
           (5b2)   6.00

--The Scarecrow Christ & other poems-NY-1954-Noonday Pr-
8vo-cl   (5b2,f,dj)   8.50

--Thing of Sorrow-NY-1934-Macmillan-8vo-cl   (5b2,fade)   8.50

OLSON,J E-The Northmen Columbus & Cabot-NY-1953-fldg map-
           (5c1)   6.50

OLSON,JAS C-History of Nebraska-Lincoln-1955-359p plus index-
photos   (5L0,dj) 8.50   (5dd4)   12.50

--J Sterling Morton-Lincoln-(1942)-illus-1st ed   (4a1)   17.50

OLSON,PHILIP-America as a Mass Society-Lond&NY-(1963)-576p
           (5u3) 4.   (5t7)   5.00

OLSON,RONALD L-Adze, Canoe & House Types of the NW Coast-
Seattle-1927-U of Wash Pubs in Anth-8vo-wrps-38p-plts (5h4) 2.75

--The Quinault Indians-Seattle-1936-U of Wash Pubs in Anth-
8vo-190p-wrps   (5h4)   5.00

OLSON,SIGURD F-Listening Point-NY-1958-243p-illus (5a1)   5.00

OLSSON,JAN-Welcome to Tombstone-Lond-1956-Elek Books-
164p   (5u3)   3.00

OLSZEWSKI,GEO-Covoare Vechi Romanesti-Rome-1926-folio-bds-
10 col plts tip in   (5n7,scuff)   18.50

"OLYMPIA"-Monthly Review from Paris-Vols 1 thru 4-Olympia Pr-
1962,63-4 issues   (5hh1,vg)   10.00

OLYMPIAD,10TH-LosAng-1932-Official pictorial souvenir of games-
(LosAng,1932)-R8vo-64p-wrps   (5dd6)   10.00

--same-Program-LosAng-1932-lg8vo-24p-illus-Coca Cola insert
           (5a8)   5.00

OMAHA & ENVIRONS-Pen & Sunlight Sketches of-Chig-(1892)-
4to-192p-illus   (4t1) 25.   (5t1)   50.00

OMAHA, GATE CITY OF THE WEST-Brooklyn-1917-Albertype-
48p-stiff wrps   (5n4)   8.50

OMAHA MANUFACTURERS ASSOC-Directory of Omaha
Manufacturers & Their Products-Omaha,(ca1920,1921)-48p-
photos-wrps   (5t3)   3.00

O'MALLEY,C D-Leonardo da Vinci, On the Human Body-drwngs-
transl,etc-1952-folio   (5L7)   25.00

O'MALLEY,M F-A Very woman-Lond-1876-Smith,Elder-3 vols-
8vo-orig green cl-1st ed   (5xx6,rub)   27.50

OMAN,CHAS-7 Roman Statesmen of the Later Republic-Lond-1902-
8vo-plts-cl-1st ed   (5p5)   10.00

OMAR KHAYYAM-Ruyaiyat of, the astronomer poet of Persia-Lond-
1872-Quaritch-sm4to-orig qtr roan-1st prntng of 3rd version
           (5i8,rub)   40.00

--same-Lond-1879-Quaritch-4th rev ed-112p-frontis-orig hf mor
(5i8,rub) 27.50   (5r9) 25.   (5z7,vg)   45.00

--same-NY-(1905)-Dodge-illus by Hanscom   (5m2)   6.50

--same-NY-1940-Heritage Club-illus by Szyk   (5p9)   5.00

OMAR KHAYYAM (continued)
--same-NY-n.d.-1st & 4th renderings-col plts-4to-dec cl-
illum dec by Willy Pogany   (5p5,pres by Pogany)   25.00

--same-NY-n.d.-ThosCrowellCo-illus by Pogany   (5p0)   6.00

--The Omar Sonnets-A New Sonnet Form & Lefra Lyrics-NY-1909-
Oliver OppDyke,ed-sm4to-bds-g.t.-1st ed-ltd to 250c-
priv prntd in red & black-rare   (5c5)   10.00

--Quatrains-Lond-1898-Villon Soc-ltd nbrd ed-bkplts-pic parch-
t.e.g.   (5i4,cov soil)   17.50

O'MEAGHERS OF IKERRIN-1890-216p-(unbnd)   (5mm3)   7.50

O'MEARA,JAS-Broderick & Gwin-SanFran-1881-Bacon&Co-16mo-
orig cl-1st ed   (5i9,sl chip)   20.00

O'MELIA,MRS J R-Roush Family (Rausch) in Amer-1942-579p
           (5mm3,few loose pgs)   20.00

OMMANNEY,F D-Isle of Cloves-Lond-1957-230p-8 plts-map
           (5c6,vg)   6.75

OMOHUNDRO,M H-Omohundros & Allied Families in Amer-1951-
1287p   (5mm3) 20.   (5t9)   20.00

OMWAKE,JOHN-Conestoga Six horse Bell Teams of Eastern Penna-
Cinn-1930-illus-sm4to   (5L7) 25.   (5yy6)   57.50

ON THE FRONTIER-Lond-(1938)-Cr8vo-cl-1st ed
           (5ss7,vf,dj,review slip)   30.00

ON GEN'L MANAGEMENT OF A FARM IN LOWER CANADA-
By a farmer in district of Montreal-StJohn-1851-New Brunswick
Soc-stitchd   (5g3)   7.50

ON THE PLAINS-Bost-1897-#13 in Companion Library-64p-illus-
stiff wrps   (5L0)   7.50

ON THE WAY-By A.L.O.E.-NY-1870-wood engrs   (5p5)   10.00

ONABAMIRO,SANYA DOJO-Why Our Children Die-Lond-1949-
Methuen-196p   (4t5)   10.00

ONDERDONK TRIAL-Proceedings of the Court..Rev Benj T
Onderdonk-NY-1845-orig wrps-333p (5r7,ex-libr) 10.
           (4j3,fox,fray)   25.00

ONE-The Homosexual Magazine-LosAng-Jan 1953 to Oct 1958-
Vols 1 thru 6-bnd in 4 vols-12mo-buck-orig wrps bnd in
           (4b6,ex-libr)   150.00

100 DAINTY DESSERTS WITH CREAM CHOCOLATE-Original-
Danvers,Mass-(1902)-64p-Roberts&Co-wrps   (5g9,chip)   3.50

150 RECIPES FOR APPLE DISHES-Omaha-n.d.(ca 1924)-Agric Dept
Union Pac System-36p-ads-wrps   (5g9)   2.50

150 SELECTED VIEWS OF CHATTANOOGA-Lookout Mtn-n.d.-
72p-fldg plt-wrps   (5ff7)   7.50

150 YEARS OF MERIDEN-Sesquicentennial, June 17 to 23,1956-
Meriden-1956-illus   (5q8)   6.00

100 INFLUENTIAL AMER BOOKS,PRINTED BEFORE 1900-NY-1947-
Grolier Club-illus-8vo-cl-cat & addresses   (4c1)   85.00

125 GLIMPSES OF BOSTON-Bost-1902-72p plus cov-photos
           (5b9,vf)   7.50

125 PHOTOGRAPHIC VIEWS OF CHICAGO-Chig&NY-c1910-
Rand,McNally-126p-red cl-5"x8"   (5F9,f)   4.50

125 YEARS OF PUBLISHING-Bost-1962-Little,Brown&Co (5j4,dj) 5.00

100 YEARS PROGRESS OF US-Hartf-1871-556p-280 engr-lea
           (5L3)   12.00

100 YEARS OF PUBLISHING-1837 to 1937-Bost-1937-History of
Little,Brown&Co-83p-illus-fldg bds   (5y2)   7.50

ONE SUMMER-Bost-1875-16mo-cl-1st ed of Blanche Howard's
1st book   (5gg6)   10.00

O'NEAL,CORA M-Gardens & Homes of Mexico-Dallas-(1947)-
illus-rev ed   (5a8)   4.50

ONEAL,JAS-The Workers in Amer History-NY-(1921)-Rand School-
208p-rev&enlrgd   (5p0)   5.00

O'NEAL,L R-A Peculiar Piece of Desert-LosAng-1957-Westernlore Pr-
illus-208p-ltd to 450c   (4n1,dj,autg)   12.00

O'NEALE,LILA M-Archaeological Explor in Peru, Part 3,Textiles
of Early Nazca Period-Chig-1937-Field Mus-folio-wrps-plts
           (4k5)   15.00

--Yurok Karok Basket Weavers-Berkeley-1932-U of Cal-57 plts-
wrps   (4k5,f)   12.50

ONEIDA & GANASTOTA,NY DIRECTORY-Incl Oneida Castle
& Durhamville, 1887,88-1887-160p   (5mm3)   15.00

O'NEIL,GEO-Tomorrow's House-NY-Dutton-1930-Rose O'Neil,illus-
159p-1st ed   (5c8)   12.50

O'NEIL,JAS B-They Die But Once-NY-1935-228p
           (4t4,dj,5h5,dj) 10.   (5s4)   12.50

O'NEIL,OWEN ROWE-Adventures in Swaziland-NY-1921-8vo-
381p-photos   (4a6)   7.50

O'NEILL,CHAS-A Dictionary of Calico Printing & Dyeing-Lond-
1862-215p   (5w3,chip)   12.50

O'NEILL,CHAS-Wild Train-NY-(1956)-illus-1st ed
           (5tt5,f,dj,autg) 7.50   (5u3)   4.50

O'NEILL,EUGENE-Ah, Wilderness-NY-(1933)-1st ed(so stated)-
Randome (5yy6,bkplt) 7.50   (5p7) 5.   (4b5,5ee3,f)   10.00

O'NEILL,EUGENE (continued)
--All God's Chillun Got Wings & Welded-NY-1924-1st ed
              (5r9) 7.50   (5x2)   15.00
--Anna Christie-NY-1930-4to-batik bds&cl-12 illus-ltd to 775c,
    autg   (5dd8,dj)   50.00
--Before Breakfast,a Play in 1 Act-NY-1916-orig wrps-1st ed
                   (5m4)   35.00
--The Complete Works of-NY-1924-Boni&Liveright-2 vols-1st ed-
    ltd to 1200 sets,autg   (5hh1,rub)   50.00
--Days Without End-NY-(1934)-1st ed-cl-Random Hse
             (5mm1,5ss3,4j2)   10.00
--same-NY-(1934)-Random Hse-8vo-blue calf-t.e.g.-1st ed-
    ltd to 325c,autg   (5d9)   50.00
--Dyanmo-NY-1929-HoraceLiveright-1st ed (5ss3,dj,sp fade)   8.50
--same-NY-1929-HoraceLiveright-blue vel-1st ed-ltd to 775c,
    autg   (5hh1,box,vg,unopnd)   40.00
--Emperor Jones, Diff'rent, The Straw-NY-(1921)-1st ed-cl&bds
                 (5mm1)   15.00
--GOLD,a play in 4 acts-NY-(1920)-1st ed-hardcover(5a6,f,dj) 17.50
--Hairy Ape,Anna Christie,First Man-NY-(1922)-1st ed-cl&bds
       (4b4) 25.   (5mm1,4j2,4n3)   15.00
--same-NY-1929-sq4to-batik bds-cl bk-ltd to 775c,autg
       (5ee9,dj) 75.   (4b5,rub)   50.00
--The Iceman Cometh-NY-(1946)-1st ed
       (5ee3,f) 7.50   (4b5,dj,4j2,dj)   10.00
--Lazarus Laughed-1927-1st ed (5k0,dj,5xx8,dj,4b5,dj)   10.00
--Long Day's Journey Into Night-NewHav-1956-Yale Univ Pr-
    1st ed   (4b5,dj)   15.00
--Lost Plays of-NY-1950-1st prntg   (5mm1)   12.50
--Marco Millions-NY-1927-1st ed-Boni (5k0,dj)   8.50
--same-NY-1927-t8vo-bds-lin sp-papr labl-ltd to 440c,autg
                 (5t8,mint)   25.00
--Moon for Misbegotten-NY-(1952)-12mo-cl bk bds
       (5ss9,vg) 5.   (4c2,f,dj)   15.00
--Mourning becomes Electra-NY-1931-1st ed
       (5m1,dj) 8.50   (4j2,dj)   10.00
--Plays of-NY-(1934,5)-Wilderness Ed-12 vols-ltd to 770 sets,
    autg-box   (4m5,mint) 350. (4F7) 275. (4h0,vf) 300.00

--The Provincetown Plays,First Series-NY-1916-67p-Frank Shay-
    orig wrps-scarce   (5ss9,wrps wn,spotted,fair)   25.00
--Strange Interlude-NY-1928-Boni&Liveright-1st ed
          (4j2,dj,5m1,dj,5ss9,f,dj)   12.50
--same-NY-1928-4to-vel over bds-prntd in 2 cols-1st ed-
    ltd to 775c,autg   (5ee9)   75.00
--A Touch of the Poet-NewHav-1957-1st ed
       (5r9,dj) 10. (4b5,f,dj)   6.00
O'NEILL,J M-Catholicism & Amer Freedom-1952 (5L7)   4.50
O'NEILL,OWEN H,ed-History of Santa Barbara Co...its People
    & Its Resources-SantaBarbara-1939-Harold M Meier-415p,496p-
    4to-lea   (4t1)   100.00
O'NEILL,ROSE CECIL-The Loves of Edwy-Bost-(1904)-Lothrop-
    illus-1st ed   (5x4)   35.00
ONLY TRUE MOTHER GOOSE MELODIES-Bost-(1905)-
    Lee&Shepard-sq8vo-100p-pict bds-cl sp (5c8)   17.50
ONLY WILLIAM,THE-The Flowing Bowl,When & What to Drink-
    NY-1892-294p-frontis-port   (5g9,rub)   7.50
ONONDAGA INDIANS-Report of Legislature on the-1883-48p
                 (5zz0)   10.00
ONONDAGA POTTERY CO-Little Romances of China-Syracuse-
    1919-56p-photos   (5w7,fade)   4.50
ONRAET,TONY-60 Below-Tor-(1944)-192p-v scarce (5ss1)   4.75
ONSTOTT,KYLE-Mandingo-Richmond-n.d.-Denlinger's-lg thk8vo
             (5m2,lt soil)   6.50
ONTARIO HISTORICAL SOC PAPERS & RECORDS-Tor-1915-
    Vol 13-orig prntd wrps   (5w8)   7.50
ONTARIO,PROVINCE-Bureau of Labour-Annual Reports for 1914
    & 1915-Prov of Ontario-260p (5dd0) ea   5.00
OPEN SESAME-NY-(1890)-sm4to-illuminated pict bds-90p-
    14 plts-illus   (5dd0)   12.50
OPERATION VITTLES COOK BOOK-(Germany)-Jan,1949-Amer
    Women in Blockaded Berlin-96p-illus (5c7,5g9)   5.00
OPIE, AMELIA-A Cure for Scandal-Bost-1839-208p-12mo
       (5w7,ex-libr,fox)   12.50
OPIE,IONA-The Oxford Dictionary of Nursery Rhymes-1951-
    Oxford U Pr-467p-illus   (5c3,pencil)   6.00
--Oxford Nursery Rhyme Book-Oxford-1955-1st ed-J Hassall,illus-
    224p   (5yy9) 7.50   (5c3)   4.75
OPIE,MRS-The Warrior's Return & Other Poems-Phila-1808-
    sm8vo-191p   (5v0)   7.50

OPLER,MORRIS-Character & Derivation of the Jicarilla Holiness
    Rites-Albuqu-1943-98p-wrps-1st ed-UNM Bull #390 (5g0)   6.00
--Dirty Boy-1938-8vo-wrps-80p-#52 of Amer Anthro Assn-1st ed-
    scarce   (5g5)   10.00
--Myths & Legends of Lipan Apache Indians-Soc Amer Folklore-
    1940   (5qq5)   8.50
--Myths & Tales of Chiricahua Apache Indians-Soc Amer Folklore-
    1942   (5qq5)   8.00
--Myths & Tales of the Jicarilla Apache Indians-Soc Amer Folklore-
    1938   (5qq5)   12.00
OPPENHEIM,EDW PHILLIPS-The battle of Basinghall Street-Bost-
    1935-Little-1st US ed   (5m2)   5.00
OPPENHEIMER, JANE M-New Aspects of John & Wm Hunter-1946
                 (5L7)   12.50
OPPER,F-Our Antediluvian Ancestors-Lond-1903-4to-49 plts-
    1st Engl ed   (4F6,f)   17.50
OPPORTUNITY-Bost-1867-Ticknor&Fields-1st ed (5x4)   12.50
OPTIC,OLIVER-All Aboard,or Life on the Lake-Bost-1856-1st ed
         (4F6,lacks fly)   20.00
--The Boat Club-Bost-1855-illus-1st ed (4c3,f,a.l.s.) 135.00
--In Doors & Out-Bost-(1854)-Brown,Bazin-1st prntg-pic cl-illus-
    extra t.p.   (5m2,sp wn)   8.50
--In School & Out-Bost-18640Lee&Shepard-16mo-286p-(2) (ads)-
    frontis-2 plts   (5p1)   12.50
--Oliver Optic's Magazine-Bost-1867-Lee&Shepard-Vol 1,#1 to
    Vol 2,#52-bnd in 1 vol   (5rr2)   20.00
--same-Bost-Oct 3 1868 to Sept 24 1869-#92 to 195-illus-102 copies
    (lacks 2 nbrs)-wrps   (4F6,vg)   175.00
--Our Standard Bearer-Bost-1868-illus-1st ed (5F0)   5.50
--Robinson Crusoe, Jr-Bost-1863-Lee&Shepard-Riverdale Bks-sq12mo-
    dec cl-g.t.-96p-4 plts   (5aa2)   10.00
--Taken by the Enemy-Bost-(1888)-illus-Blue & Gray Series (5m1) 6.50
--Try Again-Bost-1863-Lee&Shepard-12mo-dec cl-g.-281p-frontis-
    added engr title   (5yy9)   4.50
--A Victorious Union-Bost-(1893)-illus-Blue & Gray series (5m1) 6.50
ORAL DEBATE ON COMING OF SON OF MAN-bet Erasmus-
    Manford&Benj Franklin-Indnpls-1848-368p-cl
             (5h1,cov wn,lt fox)   12.50
ORANGE-City of...& its Adjacent Territory-Orange-n.d.(1914)-
    Press of Daily News-16p-wrps-narr 8vo (4t1)   15.00
ORANGE COUNTY-Directory 1939-Long Beach-1939-Western
    Directory Co-468p,258p,76p-8vo-cl (4t1)   10.00
ORANGE COUNTY HISTORY SERIES-Vol #3-SantaAna-1939-
    Orange Co History Soc-ports-plts-154p-scarce (5dd9)   25.00
ORANGE CO,IND-Hist of-Vol 1 (all publ)-Paoli-1950-320p-
    cl-rprnt of 1884   (5h1)   12.50
ORANGE GROVE-a tale of Connecticut-Worcester-1866-BG Howes-
    orig cl-1st ed   (5i0,sl rub)   15.00
ORANGE,TEXAS-The City of Your Future-Orange-1949-22p-wrps-
    illus   (5n4)   7.50
ORBELIANI,SULKHAN SABA-The Book of Wisdom & Lies-
    Hammersmith-1894-Kelmscott Pr-Wm Morris,prntr-vel
             (4h5,lacks 1 tie)   175.00
ORBIS PICTUS-Leipzig-(1852)-A H Payne-4to-lea- engravings
             (5c8,rub)   25.00
ORCHARD,WM C-Beads & Beadwork of the Amer Indian-NY-1929-
    140p plus 31 plts-Mus of Amer Indian, Vol 11-cl-scarce (5L0) 15.00
ORCUTT,REV JOHN-African Colonization,An Address Delivered
    before Amer Colonization Soc in Wash, Jan 19, 1875-NY-22p-
    orig wrps   (5x5)   15.00
ORCUTT,REGINALD-Merchant of Alphabets-GardenCty-1945-
    300p   (5ss1,autg)   4.00
ORCUTT,SAM'L-History of New Milford & Bridgewater-1882-
    909p-2 maps at back-additions & corr laid in (5t9)   27.50
--Hist of Torrington-1878-817p   (5t9)   27.50
ORCUTT,W B-Narrative Hist of Dorchester,Mass-1908-496p
             (5mm3)   15.00
ORCUTT,W P-Good Old Dorchester,a Narr of the Town-1893-
    496p   (5t9)   7.50
ORCUTT,WM DANA-The Book of Italy,During 15th & 16th Centuries-
    Lond-(1928)-folio-128 facs-cl&bds (5cc9)   37.50
--same-NY-1928-sml folio-illus-ltd to 750c (5m4)   35.00
--Celebrities off Parade-Chig-1935-8vo-1st ed (4m8,dj)   7.50
--From My Library Walls-NY-1945-246p-cl-1st ed
       (5h7,vg,sl wn dj) 5.   (5p7)   4.25
--In Quest of the Perfect Book-Bost-1926-frontis-illus-g.t.-1st ed
       (5r9) 15. (4m5,dj)   17.50
--same-Bost-illus-2nd ed-1926-317p   (4d8)   7.50
--same-Bost-1926-ltd to 365c,autg   (5d3)   20.00
--Kingdom of Books-Bost-1927-illus-1st trade ed-290p
       (5yy6) 5. (4d8) 8.50 (5p7)   7.50
--The Magic of the Book-Bost-1930-8vo-illus-cl-g.t.-1st trade ed
       (4c1,faded) 5. (5r9,dj,f)   15.00

ORCUTT,WM DANA (continued)
--Manual of Linotype Typography-Brooklyn-1923-folio-256p
(5j4) 12.50
--Mary Baker Eddy & Her Books-Bost-(1950)-198p-The Christian
Science (5p7) 2.50
--Miracle of Mutual Savings-NY-1934-127p-illus (4b8) 5.00
--The Princess Kallisto & Other Tales of the Fairies-Bost-1902-
Little Brown-4to-dec cl-139p-col illus-col plts-1st ed (4d2) 15.00
--Wallace Clement Sabine-Norwood-1933-Plimpton Pr-376p
(5v6) 6.50
ORD,ANGUSTIAS DE LA GUERRA-Occurrences in Hispanic Calif-
Wash-1956-Academy of Amer Franciscan Hist-sm4to-cl-98p
(5h5) 10.00
ORDEAL,THE-A Critical Journal of Politicks & Literature-Vol 1,
#1 to 26(all publ)-Bost-Jan 7 to Jul 1, 1809-8vo-old bds-calf bk
(5m6,ex-libr) 25.00
ORDISH,GEO-Wine Growing in England-Lond-1953-128p-17 photos
(5w1) 3.50
ORDISH,T FAIRMAN-Early London Theatres-NY-1894-298p-illus
(5t4) 7.50
ORDMOND,CLYDE-Hunting in the NW-NY-1948-col frontis-plts-
274p (4d8) 6.50
ORDNANCE & WAR SHIPS-Report of-Wash-1886-GPO-512p-
fldg plts (5mm8) 12.50
ORDNANCE,CHIEF OF-Annual Report to Sec of War 1872-Wash-1872-
180p-pt lea-illus (5xx7) 10.00
--Annual Report to Sec of War for...1876-Wash-1876-270p-plts-lea
(5xx7) 15.00
--Report to Sec of War for 1882-Wash-1882-541p-plts (5xx7) 15.00
ORDNANCE MANUAL-For Use of Officers of the Confederate States
Army-Richmond-1863-plts-546p-orig cl-(Mary Johnston,auth)
(5r5,auth's bkplt) 250.00
ORDONEZ,DR EZEQUIEL-El Volcan de Paricutin-Mexico-1947-
illus-181p-4to-text in Spanish & Engl-Spec ed (5x0) 10.00
ORDONNANCE DU ROY-Au Sujet des Deserteurs des troupes des
isles,francoises de l'Amerique-Du 11-Fevrier 1737-Paris-1737-
de l'Imprimerie Royale-sm4to-4p (5w8) 150.00
ORDWAY,ALBERT-Gen'l Index of Journals of Congr from 11th to
16th Congr incl-Wash-1883-118p (5j4) 15.00
ORDWAY,FREDK-Int'l Missile & Spacecraft Guide-NY-1960-illus-
4to-cl-1st ed (5p5) 25.00
ORDWAY,SAM'L H,JR-A Conservation Handbook-NY-1949-76p
(5t7) 6.50
--Little Codfish Cabot at Harvard-Cambr-1924-orig bds-illus-12mo-
1st ed (4m8) 10.00
--Resources and the Amer Dream-NY-c1953-55p (5w4,dj) 3.50
OREGON ALMANAC-Official Pamphlet-Portland-1915-296p-
maps-(Ore St Imm Comm) (5L0) 5.00
OREGON & CALIF-Description of,embracing an Account of the
Gold Regions-Phila-1849-Thos,Copperthwait&Co-18mo-
orig g.stamped pict cl-col fldg map-1st ed (5n9,vf) 375.00
OREGON-Biennial Report of the Sec of State Kincaid,20th Reg
Sess-Salem,Ore-1899 (5dd4) 5.00
OREGON CITY WOOLEN MILLS-Catalog-OregonCty-1915,16-
48p-wrps-col illus (5h7) 7.50
OREGON-Constitution,together wi session laws of Oregon,enacted
during 1st session-Salem-1860-Asahel Bush-8vo-orig light blue
wrps (5i0,f) 75.00
OREGON,END OF THE TRAIL-Portl,Or-(1940)-photos-maps-
fldg pkt map-e.p.map-535p-1st ed-Amer Guide Ser-WPA
(4L5,dj) 10.00
OREGON HIST SOCIETY QUARTERLY-Vol 4,#3,4-Sept&Dec,1903-
(5t9) 6.00
--same-Vol 21,#1-Mar,1920 (5t9) 3.00
--same-2 issues-Vol 15,#3-1914-Vol 20,#2,1919 (5g2) 3.50
--Same-Vol 30-(1929)-buck-bnd (5dd5) 5.50
OREGON IMMIGRATION BD-The New Empire,Oregon,Wash,Idaho,
its resources etc-Portland-(1889)-fldg map laid in-view bk wrpr-
pict wrps (5g8) 6.00
OREGON-The Land of Opportunity-(Portland,1909,Comm Club)-
62p,(64)-wrps (5L0) 4.00
OREGON LAW REVIEW-Vol 1 thru 48-(1921 to 1969)
(5ii7,lacks Vol 3 #4,rbnd) 625.00
OREGON PIONEER ASSN-Transactions of 3rd annual reunion of-
Salem(Oreg)-1876-EMWaite-8vo-orig mauve prntd wrps (5i9) 15.00
OREGON PRIMER-(Portland,1911,Cham of Comm)-92p-photos-
map-wrps (5L0) 4.00
OREGON-Rand McNally Vest Pocket Map of Oregon-Chig-1909
(5kk7) 7.50
OREGON RR & NAV CO-Map & Short Story of Pacific NW embracing
Ore,Wash-Portland-1904-18 panel fldr-map on reverse-photos-
wrps (5L0) 4.00

OREGON RR & NAV CO (continued)
--Oregon,Facts regarding its climate,soil,mineral & agric resources
(etc) for gen'l info-NY-1880-pict wrps-fldg map (5g3,wrp tn) 7.50
OREGON-Resources of Eastern Ore-Co of Baker,Malheur,Grant,
Union,& Wallowa-Salem-1892-Frank C Baker-12mo-orig
yellow prntd wrps-1st ed (5i9,vg) 22.50
OREGON-Resources of the state of Ore-rev-Salem-1892-wrps-
fldg map-State Board of Agric (5g3) 6.00
OREGON SHORT LINE RR-How to Get to American Falls,Idaho-
Portl-n.d.-Sunset Homeseekers' Bur-(8p)-12mo-wrps (4t1) 10.00
--How to Get to Blackfoot,Idaho-Portl-n.d.(ca 1909)-Sunset
Homeseekers' Bur-(8p)-12mo-wrps (4t1) 10.00
--How to Get to Boise,Idaho,1849 to 1909-Portl-(1909)-Sunset
Homeseekers' Bur-(8p)-12mo-wrps (4t1) 10.00
OREGON SPECTATOR INDEX, 1846 to 1854-Portl-1941-2 vols-
Hist Soc-R8vo-stif wrps-WPA (5dd4) 6.50
OREGON STATESMAN,THE-Vol 5,#10-Corvallis,Ore Terr-
Sat,May 19, 1855-4p of 6 cols ea (5L0) 10.00
OREGON,STATUES OF..2nd session-OregonCty-1851-280p plus
index-calf-1st ed (5L0,wn) 35.00
OREGON,STATUTES OF-5th & 6th Regular Sessions Thereof-Oregon-
1855-Asahel Bush,Public Prntr-654p-orig calf-rare
(5dd4,rub) 55.00
OREGON TERRITORY-Corres Relative to Negotiation of Question
of Disputed Right to Oregon Terr on NW Coast of Amer-Lond-
1846-prntd wrps-folio-71p (5e2) 375.00
OREGON TRAIL-Missouri Riv to Pac Ocean-NY-(1939)-illus-
230p plus index-fldg map-1st ed-Amer Guide Series (5dd1) 15.00
OREGON WASH RR & NAVIG CO-Land That Lures,Summer in the
Pac NW-Seattle-1911-12mo-wrps-46p (4t1) 7.50
O'REILLY,BERNARD-Greenland,Adjacent Seas & NW Passages to
Pacific Ocean-Lond-1818-3 maps-18 plts-lg4to-lea labl
(5tt6) 90. (5L1,broke) 50. (5n9) 85.00
O'REILLY,EDW-An Irish Engl Dictionary-Dublin-1864-sm thk4to-
lea bkd bds (5t7,scuff,wn) 20.00
O'REILLY,HARRINGTON-50 Yrs on the Trail-NY-1889-illus-
381p-1st Amer ed (4t3) 17.50
--Life Among the Amer Indians-Lond-1891-illus-381p
(4n7,shake) 7.50
O'REILLY,HENRY,ed-Origin & Objects of the Slaveholders'
Conspiracy Against Democratic Principles-NY-1862-16p,8p-
orig prntd wrps-1st ed-dbl cols (5m3) 22.50
O'REILLY,HENRY-Proposal on Mail & Telegraph Routes between
Atlantic & Pacific States,etc-1852-Sen Misc Doc #67-cl bds
(5x5,box) 20.00
O'REILLY,JOHN BOYLE-Songs from the Southern Seas & Other
Poems-Bost-1873-12mo-cl-1st ed of auth's 1st book
(5gg6,pres,f) 25.00
--Moondyne,a Story from the Under World-Bost-1879-12mo-cl-
1st ed (5m2,hng weak,fade) 10. (5gg6,f,pres) 25.00
O'REILLY,MILES-Irish Martyrs,Their Lives & Confessors-NY-1880-
751p-illus-thk R8vo-dec cl-g.e.-scarce (5p5) 15.00
ORFORD-Centennial Celebration of the Town of-(1865)-145p
(5mm3) 15.00
ORGA,IRFAN-Turkish Cooking-NY-(1958)-159p-1st Amer ed
(5g9) 3.00
ORIENTAL CARPETS-Runners & Rugs-Lond-1930-4to-22 col illus-
white buck-lg type (5t5) 37.50
ORIENTAL CERAMIC SOC-Transactions of, 1951, 1952 & 1952,1953-
1956-4to-illus (5j3,vg) 20.00
ORIENTAL NAVIGATOR,THE-or, New Directions for Sailing to &
from East Indies-Phila-1801-JasHumphreys-8vo-566p-orig calf-
leaf of errat (5ss2) 75.00
ORIENTAL RUGS-NY-1921-Scribners-32 plts-cl-4to-278p indexed
(5p6,sl wn) 17.00
ORIENTAL RUGS & CARPETS-NY-(1904)-illus-8vo-limp cl-116p
(5t0) 3.75
ORIENTALIST,THE-a volume of tales after the eastern taste-Dublin-
1764-JasHoby,Jr,prntr-12mo-calf-1st ed (5x3) 250.00
ORIGINAL HYMNS FOR SABBATH SCHOOLS-by the authors of
"Hymns for Infant Minds"-Hartf-1820-SG Goodrich-Hartf Sunday
School Repo-24p-plain brick wrps-5-1/8 x 3 (5p1,cor wn) 25.00
--same-Hartford-publ by Oliver D Cooke-1820-24p-tan prntd wrps
(5p1,sl worm hole,fox) 25.00
ORIGINAL PICAYUNE CREOLE COOK BOOK,THE-NOrl-(1938)-
438p-col frontis-9th ed-reprntd from 5th ed (5c9) 4.50
--same-NOrl-(1947)-446p-frontis-11th ed (5g9) 3.00
ORIOLI,G-Moving Along, Just a Diary-Lond-1934-Chatto&Windus-
illus (5x0) 6.50
ORION & OTHER POEMS-Phila-1880-12mo-cl-1st ed of Roberts
1st book (Sir Chas Geo Douglas Roberts) (5gg6) 25.00
ORIZU,A A NWAFOR-Without Bitterness-NY-1944-Creative Age Pr-
395p (4t5) 15.00

ORLEBAR,F-Orlebar Chronicles in Bedfordshire & Northamptonshire,
1553 to 1733-Lond-1930-337p   (5t9)   17.50
ORME,ALEXANDRA-Comes the Comrade-NY-1950   (5x7)   3.00
ORME,J B -Poems-Lond-1805-12mo-calf-1st ed   (5i8)   20.00
ORMEROD,LEONARD-The Curving Shore-NY-1957-331p-1st ed
              (5dd6) 5.   (5n4)   6.00
ORMES,MANLY DAYTON-The Book of Colorado Springs-
ColoradoSprngs-1933-366p plus 10p-illus-map-Dentan Prntg Co-
scarce   (5r0)   20.00
ORMOND,A T-Concepts of Philosophy-1906   (5L7)   6.50
ORMOND,CLYDE-Hunting in the NW-NY-1948-photos-274p
              (5s0) 6.50   (5xx5,5ss8)   8.50
ORMOND,J J-The Code of Alabama-Montgomery-1852-thk8vo
              (5x2,wn)   35.00
ORMSBEE,AGNES BAILEY-The House Comfortable-NY-1892-
232p-12mo   (5w7)   5.50
ORMSBEE,THOS H-Collecting Antiques in America-NY-(1940)-
319p-illus-1st ed   (5t4,dj)   6.00
--Early Amer Furniture Makers-NY-(1930)-illus-183p (5q0) 10.00
--same-NY-(1957)-illus-185p-new ed-rev   (5w7)   7.50
--English China & Its Marks-NY-(1959)-200p   (5w7)   8.50
--Field Guide to Amer Victorian Furniture-NY-(n.d.)-428p-illus
              (5t4,dj,f)   3.00
--Prime Antiques & Their Current Prices-NY-(1947)-illus-4to-
frontis-1st ed   (4j3,sl creased)   17.50
--Story of Amer Furniture-NY-1934-276p-117 photo illus-8vo-cl
              (5t0)   6.50
--same-NY-1946-276p-117 illus-4to   (5w7)   4.50
ORMSBY,M-B C,A History-Vancouver-1958-illus-558p-1st ed
              (5dd7)   10.00
ORMSBY,R McKINLEY-History of the Whig Party-Bost-1860-
Crosby,Nichols-377p-2nd ed   (5qq8)   6.00
--same-Bost-1859-cl-377p   (4h2)   15.00
ORMSBY,W L-Butterfield Overland Mail-SanMarino-1942-
Huntington Libr-179p   (4n1,dj)   12.00
ORPEN,ADELA E-Memories of the Old Emigrant Days in Kansas,
1862 to 1865-Edinb-1926-illus-324p-1st ed (5yy7,rebnd)   7.50
ORPHAN,THE-Phila-1831-Amer Sunday School Union-16mo-
16p wi orig dated wrps   (5c8)   7.00
ORPHAN RACHEL-or Fruits of Perseverance-Prov-1843- 16 mo-
orig prnt wrps-24p-illus-Geo P Daniels-frontis (5rr2)   17.50
ORPHEUS-A Symposium of the Arts-Lond-1948,49-John Lehmann,ed-
2 vols-1st eds   (5r9,dj)   12.50
ORPHEUS C KERR PAPERS,THE-NY-1862-12mo-cl-1st ed of
Newell's 1st book   (5b2,f) 12.50   (5gg6)   10.00
ORR,LIFE HISTORY OF THOS,JR-n.p.-1930-8vo-wrps-52p-
priv prntd   (5h4)   10.00
ORR,MRS N-DeWitt's Connecticut Cook Book & Housekeeper's Asst-
NY-1871-192p-pict bds   (5c4,wn,bkplt)   18.50
ORR,PHIL C-Customs of the Canalino-SantaBarbara-1956-26p-
illus-wrps-Mus of Natural Hist (5d6)   2.00
ORR,MRS SUTHERLAND-A Handbook to Works of Robt Browning-
Lond-1902-420p-Geo Bell   (5p7)   6.00
ORR'S GUIDE TO NIAGARA FALLS-1842-1st ed-lea (5kk5,f)   12.50
ORRED,META-Poems-Lond-1874-12mo-cl-1st ed of 1st book
              (5gg6,pres)   35.00
ORTEGA,JOSE-Apostolicos Afanes de la Compania de Jesus-
Barcelona-1754-Nadal-sm4to-vel-452p(7)-lf of errat (5L1) 500.00
ORTENBURGER,A I-Whip Snakes & Racers,Genera Masticophis &
Coluber-AnnArbor-1928-Mem U Mich Museums,Vol 1-247p-
36 plts-maps-graphs-cl-4to-scarce (4p6)   42.50
ORTH,SAML P-5 Amer Politicians-Cleve-1906-Burrows Bros-cl-447p
              (5tt8)   10.00
ORTIZ,FERNANDO-Cuban Counterpoint,Tobacco & Sugar-NY-1947-
Knopf-8vo-cl-illus-scarce   (4a3,dj)   15.00
ORTLOFF,HENRY STUART-A Garden Bluebook of Annuals &
Biennials-GardenCty-1924-245p-illus (5s7)   3.50
--Garden Planning & Building-GardenCty-1945-282p-illus-rev ed
              (5s7)   4.50
ORTON,ELLEN-Cooking with Whole grains-NY-(1951)-64p (5c9) 1.75
ORTON,JAS-The Andes &the Amazon-NY-1870-348p plus index-
fldg map   (5L0,fade)   5.00
ORTON,PROF JAS-4 Years in Vassar College-Worcester-1874-11p-
8vo-orig wrps   (5ss5)   6.00
ORTON,RICHARD H-Records of Calif Men in War of Rebellion
1861 to 1867-Sacramento-1890-State Office-887p-cl (5tt0) 30.00
ORTON,VREST-Dreiserana, A Book about His Books-NY-1929-
errata lf-1st ed-scarce   (4g2)   20.00
ORTON,WM-Argument...on the Postal Telegraph Bill-NY-1874-
wrps   (5g4)   15.00
ORVILLE,J-Incidents & Anecdotes of the War-NY-(1862)-400p-
1st ed   (5yy8,rub,wn)   7.50

ORVIS,CHAS F-Fishing with the Fly-Bost-1889-325p-cl-12mo
              (5t0)   7.50
ORWELL,GEO-Animal Farm,a Fairy Story-Lond-1945-12mo-green cl-
1st ed   (5d9,fade)   50.00
--same-NY-1946-1st Amer ed   (4b4)   12.50
--Down & Out in Paris & London-Lond-1933-12mo-cl-
1st ed of auth's 1st book-v scarce (5gg6)   50.00
--Inside the Whale-Lond-1940-12mo-cl (4c2,sp faded)   17.50
--1984-Lond-1949-Secker&Warburg-12mo-cl-1st ed (5d9,vf,dj) 50.00
OSAGE INDIAN TREATY-Wash-1868-HR63-23p-text of treaty
              (5n4)   5.00
OSARAGI,JIRO-Homecoming-NY-1954-8vo-cl-303p (5t0,dj,f)   4.50
OSBECK,PETER-A Voyage to China & East Indies-Lond-1771-illus-
2 vols-orig calf -plts-raised bands (5tt6)   75.00
OSBORN,ALBERT-Flower,Allen,Osborn...the Lineal Ancestors &
Descendants of Ransom & Amanda Allen Osborn-n.p.-1930-
24p-wrps   (5t9) 5.   (5w0)   4.50
OSBORN,CAMPBELL-Let Freedom Ring-Tokyo-(1954)-211p plus ads-
1st ed   (5yy7,dj)   7.50
OSBORN,CHASE S-The Andean Land-Chig-1909-McClurg-2 vols-
illus-maps   (5d6)   10.00
--Conquest of a Continent-Michigan-1939-190p (5s4,f,pres) 8.00
--The Iron Hunter-NY-1919-illus-1st ed   (5jj1)   5.50
OSBORN,FAIRFIELD-Our Plundered Planet-Bost-1948-217p (5s7) 3.00
--The Pacific World-NY-(1944)-illus-218-maps,some in col (5w3) 7.50
--same-NY-c1944-218p-illus   (5x7) 4.   (5w3)   4.00
OSBORN,FRANCIS-The Works of...in 4 several tracts-Lond-1682-
16mo-calf & bds-6281p-8th ed-prntd for RD (5p1,rbnd)   47.50
OSBORN,H-Palestine,Past &Present-Phila-1859-595p-maps-
col litho   (5ii2,ex-libr,rub)   12.50
OSBORN,HENRY F-The Age of Mammals in Europe,Asia & NoAmer-
NY-1910-illus-1st ed   (4k5,f)   15.00
--Cope,Master Naturalist-Princeton-1931-740p-illus (5w3) 7.50
--The Earth Speaks to Bryan-NY-1925   (5q8,fox)   3.50
--The Extinct Rhinoceroses-Vol 1,Pt 3-NY-1898-Amer Mus of
Nat'l Hist-plts-wrps-folio-v scarce (4p6,lacks bk wrp)   35.00
--From the Greeks to Darwin-NY-1908-Macm-259p (5p7)   5.00
--Men of the Old Stone Age-NY-1915-545p-illus-maps incl fldg-
1st ed   (4k5,5w9)   8.50
--same-NY-1916-lg8vo-cl-543p-illus-2nd ed   (5t2)   7.50
--same-NY-1923-Scribner-illus-559p-map   (5x0)   6.50
--The Origin & Evolution of Life-NY-1918-Scribner-322p-illus
              (5x0)   6.50
--same-NY-1923-136 illus   (4k5,f)   8.00
OSBORN,R-How to Shoot Quail-n.p.-(1941)-illus-dec bds (5t7,dj) 4.00
OSBORN,CAPT ROBT-A Narr or Journal of the Duke of Cumberland,
India man-Lond-1750-58p   (5t4)   10.00
OSGOOD,REV SAML-NY in the 19th Century-NY-1867-NY Hist Soc-
127p-pamph-orig prntd wrps   (5qq8,box,mint)   10.00
OSBORN,SHERARD-The Discovery of a NW Pasage by...Capt
R M'Clure-Lond-1865-358p-map-16mo-bds-4th ed (5ss1)   6.50
--Japanese fragments-Lond-1861-Bradbury&Evans-8vo-orig violet cl-
1st ed-6 hand col plts   (5x3,fade)   25.00
--On Explor of the North Polar Region-Lond-1865-orig prntd wrps-
22p-priv prntd   (5e2)   75.00
--Stray Leaves from an Arctic Journal-Lond-1852-320p-col illus-
fld map at bk-calf   (5ss1,sl scuff)   16.00
--same-NY-1852-216p   (5L0)   7.50
OSBORNE,D M &CO-Annual Catalog of Harvesting Machinery-
Auburn-1890-31,(1)p-col plts-wrps (5h7)   7.50
OSBORNE,MRS DAVID-The World of Waters-NY-1857-16mo-cl-
RobtCarter&Bros-363p-frontis-6 plts-Cater's Fireside Library 1
              (5p1,chip)   25.00
OSBORNE,DOD-Adventures in Chains-Lond-1957-16 photos(5c1) 6.00
OSBORNE,DUFFIELD-Engraved Gems-NY-1912-32 plts-lg8vo-cl-
424p,13   (5t2,libr marks)   8.50
OSBORNE,ED B-Letters from the woods-Poughkeepsie-1893 (5t4) 10.50
OSBORNE,H-Indians of the Andes,Aymaras &Quechuas-1952-illus
              (5L7,ex-libr)   5.00
OSBORNE,J A-Williamsburg in Colonial Times-Richmond-1936-
166p-illus   (5h9)   8.50
OSBORNE,LILLY DE JONGH-4 Keys to El Salvador-1956-illus
              (5L7)   4.50
OSBORNE,LUCY E-Notes on Errata from Books in Chapin Library-
Lond-1932-15p-4to-wrps-reprnt (4c1)   6.00
OSBORNE,MARGHERITA O-Favorite Fairy Tales-Phila-c1930-8vo-
365p-frontis-19 col plts-labl (5p1)   5.00
OSBORNE,MARJ N-Jolly Times Cook Book-Chig-(1934)-obl 12mo-
64p-col illus-bds   (5c5)   2.50
OSBORNE,THOS MOTT-Society & Prisons-1916-Yale Univ Pr-
246p   (5L7) 3.50   (5p9)   4.50
OSBORNE,WM H-History of the 29th Regiment of Mass Vol Infantry-
Bost-1877-393p   (4b3)   10.00

OSBOURNE,KATHARINE D-Robt Louis Stevenson in Calif-Chig-
1911-McClura-1st ed   (5x5.lacks fly)   7.50
OSGOOD,ERNEST STAPLES-Day of the Cattleman-Mnpls-1929-
illus-maps-268p plus index-1st ed
(5n4,Streeter copy,pencil) 65. (4t3,dj,f) 40. (4t3,vg) 35.00
OSGOOD,IRENE DE BELOT-The shadow of desire-NY-1893-
Cleveland Pub Co-1st ed   (5m2)   10.00
OSGOOD,SAML-Thos Crawford & Art in America-NY-1875-8vo-
orig prntd glazed wrps-40p   (5wn)   7.50
OSGOOD,W H-The Fur Seals & Other Life of the Pribilof Islands
Alaska in 1914-Wash-1915-plts-fldg maps-172p-cl-4to-Doc #820
(4p5)   17.50
O'SHAUGHNESSY,EDITH-Diplomatic Days-NY-(1917)-Harper-8vo-
cl-illus   (4a3)   8.50
OSTRANDER,A B-After 60 Years-(Seattle,1925)-8vo-cl-120p-illus-
1st ed   (5h5) 10. (5jj7,f)   12.50
--An Army Boy of the Sixties-Yonkers on Hudson-1924-illus-map-
272p-1st ed (4t3,autg) 12.50 (5jj7,5m9) 7.50 (5L0)   10.00
OSWALD,JOHN CLYDE-Benj Franklin in Oil & Bronze-NY-
1926-4to-58p-illus-dec cl   (5t4)   12.50
--Printing in the Americas-NY-(1937)-illus-565p-index-lg8vo-cl
(4b6,dj) 25. (4g2)   27.50
--same-Gregg Publ-1937-illus-545p& XLip-8vo-cl (5tt9)   12.50
OTA,AKIRA-Sei Shi Kakei Daijuten(Ota's Dictionary of Family Names
& Genealogy)-Tokyo-1934 to 36-3 vols (5t9)   35.00
OTERO,MIGUEL A-My Life on the Frontier, 1864 to 1882-NY-1935-
293p-illus-ltd,autg ed   (4a5,f) 30. (4c1)   40.00
--same-NY-1935-Press of the Pioneers-ltd to 750c,autg (5x5) 37.50
--My Life on the Frontier, 1882 to 1897-Vol 2-Albuqu-1939-1st ed-
rare   (5h5,f) 20. (5g0)   40.00
--My 9 Years ad Governor of Terr of New Mexico-Albuqu-1940-
8vo-cl-404p-1st regular ed (5yy7,dj,f) 10. (5h5,dj,f)   15.00
--same-Univ of NM-1940-spec ed of 400c,autg (5x5,dj)   37.50
--The Real Billy the Kid-NY-1936-illus-200p-1st ed
(5yy7,stained) 15. (4m2) 37.50 (5y0,5m3)   30.00
OTERO,NINA-Old Spain in Our SoWest-NY-(1936)-HarcBrace-
192p-illus   (4n8,dj wn)   15.00
OTHER END OF THE COUCH,THE-Cambr-1964-8vo-wrps-
priv prntd-about 151 nbrd copies"by many Hands" (5ss7,vf) 80.00
OTHER SIDE OF THE CHINESE QUESTION-SanFran-1886-
Woodward-8vo-orig prntd wrps-1st ed   (5i9,f)   22.50
OTHER SIDE OF THE QUESTION,THE-or a Defence of the Liberties
of NoAmer-NY-1774-Rivington-8vo-stitchd-(P Livingstone)-
1st ed-1st issue   (5n2)   125.00
OTIS,CHAS H-Mich Trees a Handbook-AnnArbor-1931-362p-cl
(5h2)   4.00
OTIS,ELWELL S-The Indian Question-NY-1878-283p-1st ed (5L0)12.50
OTISFIELD,MAINE TO 1892-Births,Marriages & Deaths-1948-348p
(5t9)   7.00
OTIS,H G-Letter from Hon Harrison G Otis to Hon Wm Heath...
for petitioning Congr against permitting merchant vessels to
arm-Bost-1798-orig mrbld wrps (5g4,title pg tn)   20.00
OTIS,HARRISON GRAY-A Letter from Harrison Gray Otis-
(LosAng,1917)-15p-wrps   (5d6)   10.00
OTIS,JAS-Rights of the British Colonies Asserted & Proved-Lond-
1766-Williams&Almon-sm4to calf-frontis port inserted-
Almon's 3rd ed,corr   (5n2)   100.00
OTIS,JAS-The Boys' Revolt-Bost-c1894-Estes&Lauriat-12mo-
illus-dec cl   (5p1)   7.50
--Capt Tom,Privateersman of Armed Brig Chasseur-Bost-1899-164p-
illus   (5s1,ex-libr,rprd)   3.00
--The Cruise of the Comet-Bost-1898-illus by AB Shute-1st ed
(4c3,f)   10.00
--Jack the Hunchback-Bost-(1892)-286p-illus-1st ed (5ee3,f)   4.50
--Life of John Paul Jones-NY-(1900)-407p-col frontis (5s1,spots) 2.00
--Lobster Catches,a Story of Coast of Maine-NY-(1900)-illus-
1st ed   (5ee3)   3.50
--The Minute Boys of Long Isl-Bost-c1908-DanaEstes-Bridgman illus-
342p-frontis-7 plts-pict cl-12mo   (5p1)   7.50
--The princess & Joe Potter-Bost-(1898)-Violet Oakley,illus-
Estes&Lauriat-pict cl-1st ed (5m2,joints weak)   4.00
--Toby Tyler or 10 Weeks wi a Circus-NY-1881-Harper&Bros-16mo-
pict cl-1st ed of Kaler's 1st book   (5gg6)   75.00
--same-NY-(1881)-Harper-dec cl-reprnt of 1st ed wi date dropped
from t.p.   (5rr2)   9.00
OTTAWA CO,OKLA-Story of Wm Turner & Ottawa Co-(Afton,Okla,
ca 1920)-26p-fldg map-wrps   (5t9)   15.00
OTTAWA VALLEY-Lumber Trade of the...Ottawa-1871-cl-64p-
2nd ed-scarce   (4e9)   40.00
--same-Ottawa-1872-Times Prntg&Pub-   wrps-53p-3rd ed
(5aa1,soil)   20.00

OTTLEY,WM YOUNG-A Descritive(sic) catalogue of pictures in
Nat'l Gallery-Lond-1832-Poulter-12mo-disbnd-guide book
(5i8)   7.50
--Inquiry Concerning Invention of Printing-Lond-1863-illus-377p-
4to-g.t.   (5m4) 40. (4g2,rebnd,stain)   47.50
OTTO,A F-Mythological Japan-Phila-1902-sq8vo-col plts-silk cl-
lin sp   (5t5)   17.50
OTTOLENGUI,R-Table Talks on Dentistry-NY-1935-4to-cl
(5p5)   25.00
OTWAY,THOS-Works of,in 2 vols-Lond-1712-lea-16mo
(4c5,lacks front cov Vol 1,lacks port)   22.50
--Writings-Lond-1768-3 vols-calf-calf labls   (5d2)   40.00
OUGHTON,CHAS E-Crazes,Credulities & Christian Science-
Chig-1901-priv prntd-8vo-cl-g.t.-scarce-1st ed (5p5)   10.00
OUIDA-Dog of Flanders-NY-n.d.-slim press bk in suede cov(5k1) 7.50
--Moths,a novel-Lond-1880-Chatto&Windus-8vo-orig cl-1st ed
(5xx6,lend libr)   35.00
OUR CHOICE RECIPES-Compiled by Florence Group of Lutheran
Ladies Aid-(Stanwood,Wa)-1946-194p-wrps-2nd ed (4g9)   4.50
OUR COOK BOOK-Molly Varnum Chapter DAR-Lowell-1910-
131p   (5c4,wn,soil,lack t.p.)   4.00
OUR COUNTRY-or the Amer Parlor Keepsake-Bost-(1854)-JMUsher-
12mo-orig roan-252p-4 plts-g.e.   (5j5,wn)   25.00
OUR COUNTRY COUSIN-The Handy Housekeeper...the "Farm
Journal"-Phila-1886-96p-prntd wrps   (5w7)   5.00
OUR COUNTRY,WEST-Companion Series-Bost-1902-illus
(5s4,wn,soil)   4.00
OUR FAMOUS WOMEN-Hartf-1884-1st ed-715p-illus-by 20 authors
(5g1,f)   5.00
OUR FIRST FAMILIES-by a Decendant of the "Pens"-Phila-1855-
408p-1st ed   (5m1)   12.50
OUR FIRST MEN-a calendar of wealth,fashion & gentility-Bost-
1846-wrps   (5g3) 17.50 (5m3,f)   32.50
OUR FOUR FOOTED FRIENDS-Familiar Series-c1880-sq8vo-
6 col plts-4p text   (5v0,f)   8.50
OUR GREAT INDIAN WAR-(1876)-Phill,Barclay Co-78p plus 1p-
illus-pict wrps-rare   (5r0,wrp rprd)   150.00
OUR HOMES-How to Beautify Them-NY-1883-198p-150 engrvs
(5w7,sl fox)   7.50
OUR LADY'S TUMBLER-Portl-1900-Mosher Pr-ltd to 450c-30p-
12mo-bds   (5p6,f)   7.00
OUR NORTHERN DOMAIN,ALASKA-Picturesque,Historic &
Commercial-Bost-(1910)-237p-photos-bds   (5ss1)   7.50
OUR OWN BOOK OF EVERY DAY WANTS-The Home Cook Book-
n.p.-n.d.-319p,(1)-12mo-ports-Weekly Gazette & Free Pr
(5c0,brown)   6.50
OUR PET COOK BOOK-Springfield Aux to Mass Soc for Prev of
Cruelty to Animals-Springfld-(1937)-274p,(27)-photos (5c7)   4.50
OUR PETS-Groombridge-(c1880)-sq8vo-dec cl-a.e.g.-12 col plts
(4a8)   6.50
OUR SOCIETY DIRECTORY-for SanFran,Oakland & Alameda-SanFran-
1888-8vo-lea   (5h5,cov fade,rub)   35.00
OUR TOWN,1749 TO 1865-Cat of exhibition at Gadsby's Tavern-
Alexandria-1956-114p-32 port,plts-1st ed   (5h9)   5.00
OUR VILLAGE COOK BOOK-Newton Centre Woman's Club,publ-
Bost-1889-104p-ads   (5c4,ads dtchd,hngs broke)   6.50
OUR WORLD-or The Slaveholder's Daughter-NY-1855-illus (5x2)20.00
OUR YOUNG FOLKS-Bost-Jan to Dec 1871-JasROsgood-Vol 7-cl
(5rr2,sl shake)   22.50
--same-complete run-(1865 to 1873)-9 annual vols-lg thk8vo-
luxury bndng-mor tips & sp-raised bands (5v2,f bndg)   250.00
OUR YOUNG FOLKS-Illus Magazine for Boys & Girls-#1 to
Vol 1,#12-Bost-1865-808p-cl   (5h1)   12.50
--same-Vol 5(complete)-Jan thru Dec 1869-thk8vo-cl-1st ed of
Aldrich,Story of a Bad Boy-wi 1870 date   (5d3)   37.50
OUSELEY,WM G-Remarks on statistics & political institutions of
US-Lond-1832-bds-labl   (5g4,ex-libr,wn)   15.00
--same-Phila-1832-8vo-orig bds-labl-1st ed   (5m6,rub)   25.00
OUSLEY,CLARENCE,ed-Galveston in 1900-Atlanta-1900-illus
(5jj1,f) 8.50 (5h2) 5. (4t1)   7.50
OUSPENSKY,P D-Tertium Organum-NY-1923-336p-8vo-cl (5t0) 5.00
--same-NY-1949-Knopf   (5p7)   5.00
OUTCAULT,R F-Buster Brown,His Dog Tige & There Jolly Times-
NY-(1906)-Cupples&Leon-obl folio-wrps-24 6 panel col plts-
1st ed   (4c3,wrps tn)   22.50
--Buster Brown,My Resolutions-NY-(1906)-FAStokes&Co-sm8vo-
red dec cl   (5c8,f)   15.00
--Buster Brown on Uncle Jack's Farm & Other Stories-NY-(1907)-
Cupples&Leon Co-sq12mo-illus-bds   (5c8)   6.00
--Tige,His Story-NY-(1905)-lg8vo-pict cl   (5c8,f)   17.50
OUT OF ALASKA'S KITCHENS-Anchorage-1947-illus-232p-
spiral bnd   (4g9,sl stn)   5.00
--same-1948-248p-2nd ed   (4g9)   5.00

OUT OF TOWN-Chig-1869-map-wrps   (5g8,wrps wn)   20.00
OUT OF TOWN-NY-1896-235p-illus-1st ed   (5m1)   8.50
OUT OF VT KITCHENS-Rutland-1949-400p-ads-spiral bnd wrps-
   Trinity Church   (4g9)   5.00
OUTDOOR LIFE'S GALLERY OF NOAMER GAMES-NY-(1946)-
   FLJaques paintings-folio-cl-142p-31 col repro-(loose lf bndg)
             (5t7)   15.00
OUTHWAITE, LEONARD-Unrolling the Map-NY-1935-56 maps-
   Gordon Grant,illus   (5c1)   12.50
OUTLAND,CHAS F-Man Made Disaster-1963-ArthurHClark-
             (5x5,dj)   9.50
OUTRAM, JAS-In Heart of Canadian Rockies-NY-1905-plts-maps-
   466p   (5d7) 10.   (5s0)   12.50
OUTRE MER-a Pilgrimage Beyond the Sea-Bost-1833,34-2 vols-
   8vo-hf calf-1st ed of auth's 1st book   (5gg6,box)   150.00
OVAL CLUB,UNIV OF WASH-Seattle-1926-64p-bds-6x9-
   frontis-(Seattle,Acme Pr)-ltd to 500c,nbrd
            (5r0,addenda laid in)   10.00
OVER,W H-Report on Investigation of Brandon Village Site & Split
   Rock Mounds-Vermillion-1941-WPA-mimeo-illus-stiff wrps
            (4k5,f)   5.00
OVER THE OCEAN-of Glimpses of Travel in Many Lands,by a lady
   of NY-NY-1846-12mo-a.e.g.-1st ed   (5ss5,pres)   9.50
OVER THE SIERRAS-Oakland Pier-1904-Denison News-32p-
   photogravures-bds   (4a5,sp weak)   13.00
OVERLAND MONTHLY-1st series-Vol 1,#1 to Vol 15, #6-Jul 1868
   to Dec 1875 (all publ)-orig wrps   (5n5,sm fray)   350.00
--same-Vol 1,2,3,4-SanFran-1868 to 1870-lg8vo-buck (5h4,vg)   50.00
--same-Vol 12,2nd Series-July to Dec 1888-SanFran-1888 (5r7)   17.50
--same-Vol 13,2nd Series-Jan to Jun 1889   (5r7)   17.50
--same-Vol 14,2nd Series-Jul to Dec 1889   (5r7)   17.50
--same-Bret Harte Memorial Nbr, Sept 1902-illus-rbnd in cl-
   scarce   (5m1)   12.50
OVERMAN, FRED-Moulder's & Founder's Pocket Guide-Phila-1878-
   252p-illus   (4e4,cl sl spot)   12.50
--Practical Mineralogy,Assaying & Mining-Phila-1851-sm8vo-cl-
   Lindsay&Blakiston-230p-2 lvs ads-1st ed   (5L1)   45.00
OVERS, JOHN-Evenings of a working man-Lond-1844-TCNewby-
   8vo-orig cl-1st ed   (5xx6,fade)   35.00
OVERSEAS MILITARY FORCES-Report of Ministry-Lond-1918-plts-
   fldg maps-533p   (4a8)   15.00
OVERTON, G L-Clocks & Watches-Lond-1922-127p-illus (5bb0)   3.50
OVERTON, G L-Water Transport-Lond-1923 to 1949-3 vols-catalog
   of model collection at Sci Museum-46plts-wrps   (5c1)   25.00
OVERTON, G S-How to Make Jewelry-Prov-1920-illus-8vo-274p
            (5bb0)   5.00
OVERTON, GRANT-Amer Nights Entertainment-NY-1923-1st ed
       (5ee3) 5.   (5ww4)   7.50
--Cargoes for Crusoes-NY-1924-416p-1st ed   (5k1)   4.00
--Portrait of a Publisher-NY-1925-96p-bds-illus   (5y2)   4.75
OVERTON, RICHARD C-Burlington West-Harvard U-1941-t8vo-
   cl-583p-(Railway ed)   (5h4,f,5j0,f,dj)   15.00
--Gulf to Rockies-Austin-1953-Univ of Texas Pr-illus-410p
   (5jj1,dj,autg,4m2) 10.   (5i3,dj,f,5ee3,dj,f) 12.50 (5h5,vg) 15.00
OVINGTON, MARY WHITE-The Walls Came Tumbling Down-NY-
   1947-307p-1st ed   (5w5)   8.50
OVITT, MABLE-Golden Treasure-Dillon,Montana-1952-8vo-cl-
   254p-illus   (5F5,sl stn)   6.00
OVID PUBLIUS-Ovid's Metamorphoses in 15 books-Lond-1717-
   calf-12 by 16 inches-frontis-Shakespeare Head (5d2,rbkd)   200.00
OWEN,CATHERINE-Choice Cookery-NY-1889-316p-12mo(5c0)   7.50
--Culture & Cooking-NY-1881-121p   (5c0,chip,ex-libr)   5.00
OWEN,CHAS-An Essay Towards a Natural History of Serpents,in
   Two Parts-Lond-1742-hf calf-4to-7 plts-1st ed   (4h0,f)   100.00
OWEN,DAVID DALE-1st Rpt of Geological Reconn of Northern
   Counties of Ark-LitRock-1858-256p-hf lea (5i9) 30. (4h1)   20.00
--Report of a Geolog Surv of Wisc,Iowa &Minn-Phila-1852-
   orig cl-folio-676p-illus (5cc1,lacks map,poor) 17.50 (4n4,f)   25.00
--same-Phila-1852-fldg plts-4to-638p   (5yy0) 24.50 (4n4,f) 25.00
--same-Phila-1852-2 vols-4to-illus
       (5yy8,bkstrp wn) 22.50   (5w4,bkstrp wn)   17.50
OWEN,MRS DE WITT C-Ripley's Sweet 16-Dixon-1898-12p-
   creped papr wrps   (5g9)   4.00
OWEN,DORA,ed-Book of Fairy Poetry-Longmans-1920-1st ed-4to-
   dec cl-16 mntd col plts   (5dd0)   25.00
OWEN,DOUGLAS-Ocean Trade & Shipping-Cambr-1914-277p-illus-
   2 sample documents in pkt   (5s1,ex-libr)   4.50
OWEN,H-Aids to Stability-Southampton-1901-70p-illus (5s1)   2.50
OWEN'S, JEANNE-Book of Sauces-NY-(1941)-156p   (5c9)   3.50
--Lunching & Dining at Home-NY-1942-284p   (5c0)   5.00
--A Wine Lover's Cook Book-NY-(1940)-197p   (4g9)   4.50

OWEN,JOHN-Journals & Letters of Maj..Pioneer of NW 1850 to
   1871-NY-1927-2 fldg maps-photos-2 vols-1st ed,ltd to 550c-
   scarce   (4t3,unopened,f)   50.00
--same-NY-1927-Eberstadt-367p-illus-maps-g.t.-boxed-
   ltd to 550c-Dunbar,ed   (5qq8)   35.00
OWEN,JOHN PICKARD-The Fair Haven-Lond-1873-orig cl-
   Trubner&Co   (5ss3,scuff)   25.00
OWNE,MERLE BANKHEAD-DeSoto & the Indians,a Play for
   Children-Montgomery-1919-Ala Cent Comm-pamph-18p
           (5h6,ex-libr)   3.50
OWEN,MARY A-Voodoo Tales, As Told Among the Negroes of the
   SW-1893-Putnams' Sons-310p-orig cl-1st ed
   (4b3) 15.   (5x2,5x5,f)   25.00
OWEN,MARY B,ed-Old Salem,North Carolina-(WinstonSalem)-
   c1941-Garden Club of NC-cl-4to-173p   (4t1)   12.50
OWEN,R-Lond-Odontography -text & atlas-hf mor-169 plts-1st ed
   Lond-1840   (4e5,f)   225.00
OWEN,ROBT DALE-Footfalls on the Boundary of Another World-
   Phila-1860-528p-cl-Lippincott   (5d6,wn,pres)   10.00
--Future of the NW in connection with Scheme of Reconstruction
   without NewEngl-Phila-1863-8vo-15p,(1)-orig wrps
      (5b2) 15.   (5L1) 20.   (5g3)   17.50
--Moral Physiology,or,a Brief & Plain Treatise on Population
   Question-NY-1831-Wright&Owen-12mo-bds-orig papr labl-
   frontis-2nd ed-v rare   (5gg6,rbnd)   250.00
--A New View of Society-Lond-1813-4 parts in 1 vol-8vo-bds-
   1st ed of auth's 1st book   (5gg6,rbkd,pres)   250.00
--The Wrong of Slavery-Phila-1864-246p-orig cl-1st ed (5m3,f)   22.50
OWEN,ROBT L-The Russian Imperial Conspiracy 1892 to 1914-n.p.-
   n.d.-154p-wrps   (5ss1,autg)   7.50
OWEN,RUSSELL-South of the Sun-NY-(1934)-288p   (5ss1)   4.00
OWEN,THOS-Dictionary of Alabama History & Biography-Chig-
   1921-4 vols   (5t1)   135.00
OWEN,THOS M,ed-Minutes of 11th Annual Reunion of United
   Sons of Confederate Veterans,New Orleans-Nashville-1907
           (5r7,ex-libr)   10.00
OWEN,THOS M-Checlist of Newspaper & Periodical Files in
   Dept of Archives & His of State of Ala-Montgomery-1904-
   65p-wrps   (5j6,fox)   5.00
OWEN,TOM-The Taylor Anecdote Book-NY-1848-150p plus ads-
   illus-hf mor   (5n4)   35.00
OWEN,CAPT W F W-Narr of Voyages to Explore Africa,Arabia,
   Madagascar-NY-1833-2 vols-260p & 240p (5s1,wn,ex-libr) 10.00
OWEN,WILFRED-Poems by Wilfred Owen-Lond-1920 -sq8vo-frontis-
   orig red cl-Chatto&Windus-1st ed-auth's only book (5u5)   125.00
OWENS,FERN R-Sky Pilot of Alaska-MntnView,Cal-(1949)-illus-
   175p   (5ss1)   4.00
OWENS',MRS FRANCES-Cook Book & Useful Household Hints-
   Chig-1883-372p-frontis   (5c0,brown)   5.00
OWENS,JOHN ALGERNON-Sword & Pen-Phila-1880-436p
      (5p7) 5.   (5j6,f)   4.00
--same-Phila-1883-516p   (5w4)   6.00
OWENS,WM A-A Slave Mutiny-NY-(1953)-illus
      (4p4) 5.   (5ii3,5x2)   7.50
--Texas Folk Songs-Austin-1950-Folklore #28-302p (5n4)   15.00
OWL CREEK LETTERS & OTHER CORRESPONDENCE-by W-NY-
   1848-12mo-cl   (5ss3,5gg6,autg)   20.00
OWSLEY,F L-Plain Folk of the Old South-Louisiana State U-1949
           (5x2,dj)   7.50
--States Rights in the Confederacy-Univ Chig Pr-1925-1st ed
           (5x2)   15.00
OXENDEN,REV A-My First Year in Canada-Lond-1871-128p-
   frontis-erratum sl   (4b9)   15.00
OXFORD,A W-English Cookery Books to the Year 1850-Lond-1913-
   192p,(4)   (5c7)   15.00
OXFORD & THE GROUPS-Oxford-1934-Cr 8vo-cl-1st ed (5ss7,f)12.50
OXFORD BOOK OF AMERICAN VERSE,THE-NY-680p-
   Bliss Carman,ed   (5t4) 5.   (5m2)   6.00
OXFORD BOOK OF CAROLS,THE-by Percy Dearmer et al-(1931)-
   Oxf Univ Pr-491p   (5p9)   4.00
OXFORD BOOK OF CHRISTIAN VERSE,THE-Oxf-(1951)-560p-
   Clarendon Pr-Lord David Cecil,ed   (5p7)   4.00
OXFORD DICTIONARY ON HISTORICAL PRINCIPLES-Shorter
   Version-1937-Oxf Univ Pr & Dblday,Doran-sq sm4to-black buck-
   labls-10 vols-rev ed by CT Onions   (5t5)   22.50
OXLEY,J MacDONALD-In the Wilds of the West Coast-NY-1905-
   398p-illus   (5s4,shake)   7.50
OZARK REGION-Reminis Hist of-1894-787p-illus-reprntd 1956
           (5t9)   15.00

PAAR,JACK-My Saber is Bent-NY-1961-S&S-236p (5p0)   4.00
PABOR,WM E-Colorado as an Agricultural State,Its Farms,Fields &
   Garden Lands-NY-1883-illus   (5x5)   10.00

PABST,A C S-Hist Atlas of Delaware Co,Ohio-1963-131p (5mm3) 37.50

--Nashes of Ireland,Richard & Alexander of Eastern Shore & Allied Families,1200 to 1956-1963-441p,71p,44p (5mm3) 50.00

--Some Records of Pioneers of Delaware Co,Ohio-1966-261p, indexed (5mm3) 25.00

PABST,ADOLF-Minerals of Calif-Sacramento-1938-Calif State Prntng Ofc-Bull #113 (5x5) 7.50

PABST BREWING CO-Milwaukee-(ca1885?)-24p fldng panoramas of Phillip Best Brewing Co-obl 16mo (5w1) 8.50

--Lond-n.d.-obl 12mo-46p pictures of brewery,6 col plts-56p,48p-hf red mor (5w1,pres,scuff) 27.50

PACH,ALFRED-Portraits of our Presidents-NY-(1943)-illus-12mo (4a1) 5.00

PACH,WALTER-Vincent Van Gogh,1853 to 1890-NY-1936-4to-cl-parch bk-30p plts-1st ed (5p5) 7.50

PACIFIC COAST ALBUM-SanFran-1888-41 views in cl fldr (5k0) 6.00

PACIFIC COAST AVIFAUNA,#1 to 23-Santa Clara,Hollywood, Berkeley-1900 to 1936-maps-plts-5 vols-8vo-cl-orig wrps bnd in-1st prntng (5z9,f) 160.00

PACIFIC COAST BORAX CO-Borax from Desert,Through Press,into the Home-Chig-(1896)-48p-wrps-WBConkey Co (5d6) 15.00

PACIFIC COAST FOURTH READER,THE-SanFran-1878-frontis-illus bds-ALBancroft&Co-rev ed (5dd6) 5.50

PACIFIC COAST LAND BUREAU-California Guide Book-SanFran-(1882)-74p-9p liths-fldg map-wrps-Central Pac & So Pac RR Co (5yy3) 50.00

PACIFIC ELEC RY CO,publ-Trolley Trail thru Heart of So Calif-n.p.-n.d.-(LosAng 1910)-32p-wrps (5h2) 4.00

PACIFIC GUANO CO-Its History,Its products & Trade-Cambr-1876-Riverside Pr-63p-wrps (5yy3) 7.50

PACIFIC NEWS-Weekly Pacific News for Steamer Oregon-SanFran-Mar 1,1850-Vol 1,#16-4p-prntd on brown wrapping paper (5tt0) 40.00

PACIFIC NORTHWEST-Information for Settlers & Others,Ore & Wash Territory-NY-1883-map-32p plus map-wrps-rare (5t3,sl cov spots) 35.00

PACIFIC NORTHWEST-Its Wealth &Resources-Portl-n.d.-(1896?)-128p-wrps (5h1,sl chip) 5.00

PACIFIC NORTHWEST TOURIST ASSN-Fishing in the Pacific NW-n.d.-photos-(22p)-wrps (5L0) 3.00

PACIFIC PALISADES WOMEN'S CLUB-Symphony in Foods-n.p.-ca 1950-spiral bnd-231p (4g9) 5.00

PACIFIC PORTS ANNUAL-Sup to monthly Pacific Ports-Seattle-Vol 4,Apr to Sept,1918-Frank Waterhouse pub (5s1) 6.00

--same-Vol 5-1919-553p (5s1) 6.00

--same-Vol 6-1920-626p (5s1) 6.00

PACIFIC RAILROAD DEBTS-Anti funding & Foreclosure Memorial of Calif State Convention-(SanFran,1896)-29p-wrps-v scarce(5L0)17.50

PACIFIC RAILROAD,THE-Open,How to go,what to see-Bost-1869-16mo (5g8) 15.00

PACIFIC RR EXPLORATIONS-Wash-1855 to 1859-13 vols-plts-charts-col liths-fldg maps-thk4to (4n4) 550.00

PACIFIC RR SURVEYS-Reports of Explor & Surveys...from Miss R to Pacific Ocean 1853,4-Wash-1856 to 1860-orig cl-12 vols in 13 (5tt0,wn) 350.00

PACIFIC SPECTATOR,THE-Quarterly-Stanford Univ Pr-Vol 1,#1 thru 4 & Vol 2,#1 thru 4-1947,8 (5h6) ea nbr 3.00

PACIFIC TRACT SOC-First Annual Report of-SanFran-1851-Alta Calif Steam Pr-8vo-wrps (4c1) 35.00

PACINI,SIGNOR GIOVANNI-Saffo...as performed at Howard Athenaeum,May 4,1847-Bost-1847-Eastburn's Pr-12mo-self wrapprd,sewn as issued (5b2) 15.00

PACK,CHAS L-Forests & Mankind-NY-1929-250p-illus (4b9) 6. (5s7,autg) 5.00

PACK,FRED L-Geology of Pioche,Nevada & Vicinity-Lancaster-1906-346p (5s4,ex-libr) 6.00

PACK,GRETA-Jewelry & Enameling-NY-(1945)-377p-illus (5n7) 3.50

PACKARD,A L-Thomaston,Maine,a Town that Went to Sea-1950-416p (5mm3) 7.50

PACKARD,A S-American Naturalist-Salem-(Mar 1867 thru Feb 1868)-Vol 1-14 plts-illus-bnd (4d9,hng crack) 7.50

PACKARD,MRS CLARISSA-Recollections of a Housekeeper-NY-1834-Harper-155p,(27)-12mo-orig cl-1st ed of auth's 1st book (5x1) 45.00

PACKARD,MRS E P W-Marital Power Exemplified in Mrs Packard's Trial etc-Hartf-1866-137,(1)p-wrps (5y0,wrps wn) 10.00

--The Prisoners' Hidden Life-Chig-1868-ABCase,Prntr-144p-cl (5d6,wn) 12.50

PACKARD,F A-Inquiry into Alleged Tendency of Separation of Conflicts,one from the other,to produce disease & derangement-1849-buck (5L7,rbnd) 15.00

PACKARD,FRANCIS R-The History of Medicine in the US-Phila-1901-lg8vo-cl-542p-illus (5t2) 10.00

--Some Account of Penna Hospital from its rise-Phila-1938-133p-illus (5h9,f) 10.00

PACKARD,FRANK L-The Miracle Man-NY-1914 (5ee3,f) 3.50

PACKARD,J F-Grant's Tour Around the World-Cinn-1880-802p-cl (5h1,hng crack) 4.00

PACKARD PIANOS-FtWayne-1926-trade catalog-sm obl 8vo-48p-illus-fldg bds (5e4) 4.00

PACKARD,REYNOLDS-Balcony Empire-NY-1942-cl-8vo (5p5) 7.50

PACKARD,REV THEOPHILUS,JR-Hist of the Churches & Ministers Franklin County Assoc,Mass-1854-456p (5mm3) 7.50

PACKARD,VANCE-The Pyramid Climbers-NY-1962 (5m2,dj) 5.00

PACKARD,WINTHROP-Old Plymouth Trails-Bost-c1920-351p-illus (5w0) 6.50

--White Mt Trails-Bost-1917-photos-8vo-312p-cl (5u9) 11.50

PACKER,THE-War Dept Training Manual-Pack Animals etc-1931-8vo-45p-self wrps (4a6) 10.00

PACKMAN,ANA BEGUE DE-Early Calif Hospitality-Fresno-1952-182p-illus (5c9) 10.00

--Leather Dollars-LosAng-c1932-(Times Mirror)-79p-illus-pict bds (4d6) 10.00

PACOTTET,P-Vins De Champagne & Vins Mousseux-Paris-1918-420p-wrps-illus (5w1) 7.50

PADDOCK,MRS A G-Fate of Madame La Tour-NY-1881-361p-cl (5h1) 7.50

--same-NY-1881-352p (5mm2) 8.50

--In the Toils-Chig-1879-cl-301p (5ff7) 12.50 (5mm2) 7.50

--Saved at last from among the Mormons-Springfield,Ohio-1881-Farm&Fireside Co-12mo-orig prntd wrps-scarce (5i9,wn) 7.50

PADDOCK,CAPT B B-History of Central & Western Texas-Chig-1911-Lewis Pub-897p-Vol 2 (only) (4j7) 45.00

PADDOCK,JUDAH-Narrative of Shipwreck of Ship Oswego on Coast of SoBarbary-NY-1818-t8vo-cl-329p-errat (5m8,rbnd,sl tn) 25.00

PADELFORD,FREDK M-Geo Dana Boardman Pepper-Bost-1914-60p-frontis (5s4,pres,autg) 7.50

PADEN,IRENE-The Big Oak Flat Road-SanFran-1955-1st ed-ltd to 1000c-Lawton Kennedy (5hh4,autg,f) 20.00

--Prairie Schooner Detours-NY-1949-illus-295p (4n1,dj,autg) 15. (5x5,dj,pres) 10.00

--Wake of the Prairie Schooner-NY-1943-illus-514p-1st ed (4n1,dj) 14. (4p2) 12.75 (5x5) 12.50

--same-1943-4th ed (4n1,dj) 10.00

PADLOCKS & GIRDLES OF CHASTITY-NY-1928-NY-1928-78p-bds-cl-illus-ltd to 545c,nbrd (5x7) 7.50

--same-n.p.-n.d.-115p-illus (5t4) 6.00

PADOVER,SAUL K-The Complete Jefferson-NY-(1943)-1322p-illus (5t7) 10.00

--A Jefferson Profile, as Revealed in His letters-NY-1956-8vo-cl-377p-1st ed (5p5) 7.50

PADRE ISLAND-By Writer's Round Table-SanAntonio-1950 (4c7,e.p.cut) 42.50

PADWICK,C E-Mackary of the Great Lake-Lond-1917-11&144p-12 plts(6 col) (5c6) 4.50

PAEZ,DON RAMON-Travels & Adventures in South & Central Amer-1st ser:Life in the Llamos of Venezuela-NY-1868-Scribner-473p-illus-map (5p7) 7.50

PAFF,WM J-The Geographical & Ethnic Names in the Pidriks Saga-Harvard U Pr-1959-238p (5c 3) 5.50

PAGAN,Y VEGA ERNESTO-Military Biogr of Genl Rafael Leonidas Trujillo Molina-Ciudad Trojillo DR-1956-199p plus 6p illus-cl-editorial atenas (5r0,dj) 7.50

PAGANI,CARLO-Italy's Architecture Today-Hoepli-1955-293p-illus-4to (5ww3) 22.50

PAGANINO,P A-Il Burato-Bergamo-1909 (5n7) 15.00

PAGANO,D A-Bluejackets-Bost-1933-Meador-138p-plts-cl (5mm8) 12.50

PAGANO,GRACE-Contemporary Amer Painting-NY-1945-Duell,Sloan,&Pearce-Encyclopedia Brit Coll-232p-illus-4to (4a0) 25.00

PAGE,ARTHUR W-The Bell Telephone System-NY-(1941)-illus (5F0) 3.50 (5y2) 4.50

--Our 110 Days' Fighting-GardenCty-1920-283p-maps-t.e.g. (5w4) 6.50

PAGE BELTING CO-Catalogue of Leather & Rubber Belting-Concord-1894-96p-cl-illus (5hh7) 10.00

PAGE,CHAS D-History of 14th Regiment,Conn Vol Infantry-Meriden-1906-509p-cl (5a0,f) 62.50

--Letters of a War Correspondent-Bost-1899-Page-397p-plts-maps(1 fldg) (5mm8) 6.00

PAGE,CHARLOTTE A-Under Sail & In Port in the Glorious 1850's-Salem-1950-8 plts (5c1) 7.50

PAGE,ELIZ-In Camp & Tepee-NY-(1915)-245p-photos-wrps-
  stitchd   (5s4)   7.50
--same-NY-1915-illus-245p-1st ed   (5bb4)   12.50
--Wagons West-NY-(1930)-illus-1st ed   (5yy7,fade) 8.50
--Wild Horses & Gold-NY-1932-362p-fldg maps (5r1) 15. (5u6) 12.50
PAGE,H S-Over the Open-1925-ltd ed,nbrd-col plts-155p (4a2) 3.00
PAGE,HENRY MARKHAM-Pasadena,Its Early Years-LosAng-1964-
  sm4to-o.p.-wrps-226p-illus   (5F5)   7.50
PAGE,MARY R-Memoir of-Cambr-1873-183p-photos (5t4)   7.00
PAGE,MOSES B-Speech of...of Berick,Maine in House of Rep,
  Feb 27,1863-Augusta-1863-8vo-unbnd   (5g5) 37.50
PAGE,ROSEWELL-Thos Nelson Page,a Memoir-NY-1923-port-
  ltd to 100c,lg papr   (5mm1,box) 12.50
--same-NY-1923-cl&bds   (5t2) 4.   (5mm2) 5.00
PAGE,THOS NELSON-Befo' De War Echoes in Negro Dialect-NY-
  1888-1st ed-dec cl   (5mm1)   20.00
--Bred in the Bone-NY-1904-illus-1st ed-1st issue
             (4n3) 5.   (5ee3)   3.50
--The Burial of the Guns-NY-1894-258p-1st ed (5x4) 7.50
--A Captured Santa Claus-NY-1902-illus-frontis-3 plts-81p-
  1st ed   (5x4) 5.   (5p1)   6.50
--Elsket & other stories-NY-1891-Scribner-1st ed (5m2) 5.00
--Gordon Keith-NY-1903-1st ed   (5h6,g) 3.50 (5x4,vg) 5.00
--In Ole Virginia-NY-1887-pic cl-1st ed,1st state-auth's 1st book-
            (4j2) 25.   (5gg6)   15.00
--same-NY-1903-12mo   (5x2)   5.00
--John Marvel,Assistant-NY-1909-1st ed   (4n3,f)   5.00
--Marse Chan-NY-1892-illus   (5ee3)   3.00
--Meh Lady,a Story of the War-NY-1893-Scribners-70p (5x4) 5.00
--Mount Vernon & its Preservation-n.p.-(1910)-84p-illus-1st ed
            (5ee3)   3.00
--same-(NY)-1932-84p-illus-rev ed   (5x0)   4.50
--The Negro,The Southerner's Problem-NY-1904-1st ed
            (4m2) 25.   (5x2)   17.50
--Old Gentlemen of Blackstock-NY-1900-illus by Christy-(not 1st)
          (5i4) 5. (5r7)   7.50
--same-NY-1909   (5x2)   5.50
--On New Found River-NY-1891-Scribners-240p-1st ed (5x4,4n3)5.00
--The Old South-NY-1919-(Chatauqua)-344p   (5h9)   4.00
--Red Riders-NY-1924-scarce   (5mm1,f,dj) 12.50
--Red Rock,a Chronicle of Reconstruction-NY-1898-Scribners-
  584p-illus-1st ed   (5x4)   5.00
--Robt E Lee..Man& Soldier-NY-1911-734p-t.e.g.-cl
           (5w5,sl soil) 7.50
--Robt E Lee the Southerner-NY-1908-312p   (4j4)   5.00
--Social Life in Old Virginia Before the War-NY-1897-1st ed-
  1st issue   (4j4)   8.50
--Two Little Confederates-NY-1888-1st ed-scarce
        (5v2,vf) 70. (4F6,f) 65.00
--Unc' Edinburg,a plantation echo-NY-1895-Scribner-illus
        (5m2,5x2)   5.00
--Under the Crust-NY-1907-8vo-cl-illus-1st ed (5dd8,5x4) 5.00
--Washington & Its Romance-NY-1923-196p-illus-col-g.t.-1st ed
          (5h9)   7.50
PAGE,VICTOR W-The ABC of Aviation-1918   (5zz4) 7.50
--Automobile Repairing Made Easy-NY-1918-1060p-illus-pic cl-
  fldg tbls-3rd ed   (5xx7,fray) 7.50
--Automobile Starting,Lighting & Ignition-NY-1917-12mo-cl-illus-
  519p   (5t2,shaken) 7.50
--Aviation Engines...Design,Construction,Operation & Repair-NY-
  1918-(589,(34)p-illus-"Censored" notice (WWI) (5w0) 20.00
--Automobile Starting,Lighting& Ignition-NY-1918-519p-illus-
  4th ed,rev   (5y2,ex-libr) 6.50
--Chevorlet Six Car & Truck-NY-1942-illus-photos-896p (4d9,f) 10.00
--Gasoline & Kerosene Carburetors-NY-1919-Henley-12mo-cl-illus-
  213p & 40p catalogue   (5j5)   6.00
--Henley's ABC of Gliding & Sailflying-NY-1930-294p-illus-cl
        (5t2,ex-libr)   4.00
--How to Run an Automobile-NY-1917-8vo-cl-fldg plts-1st ed(5p5) 12.50
--Modern Aircraft-NY-1928-855p-8vo-cl-illus   (5t2) 10.00
--Modern Aviation Engines-NY-1929-illus-976p (5q0,wn) 20.00
PAGE,WALTER H-Life & Letters of-NY-1922-2 vols-ports
        (5q8,sl soil) 4.00
PAGE,WM-The Victoria Hist of County of Norfolk-1906-Vol 2(only)-
  563p   (5t9)   15.00
PAGEANT,THE-Lond-1896,97-Vol 1 & 2 (all publ)-ed by Hazelwood
  & Gleeson White-4to-orig dec cl-1st ed-2 vols (5d3) 37.50
PAGEANT OF AMERICA-Ralph H Gabriel,ed-1925 to 29-Yale U Pr-
  part lev-t.e.g.-15 vols-Independence ed (4m9) 100. (5h9) 82.50
PAGES,P M DE-Voyages Autour Du Monde-Paris-1782-Moutard-
  2 vols-hf mor-1st ed-rare
       (4a5) 115. (5n2,stiff wrps) 150. (4j7) 100.00
PAGET,A M-People of the Plains-Tor-1909-199p-illus (4b9,f) 10.00

PAHK,INDUK-September Monday-NY-(1954)-283p (5t7,autg) 3.00
PAIGE,LT CHAS C-Story of Experiences of in Civil War of 1861 to
  65 as told by himself-Franklin,NH-1911-illus-8vo-orig bds-
  1st ed   (5ss5,lacks fly) 18.50
PAIGE,L R-Hist of Cambridge,Mass-1877-731p-illus (5mm3) 15.00
--Hist of Hardwick,Mass wi Gen Register-1883-555p (5t9,wn) 30.00
PAIGE,SID   -Reconn of Point Barrow Region,Alaska-Wash-1925-
  USGS Bul 772-32p plus index-photos-map in bk pkt-wrps (5L0) 5.00
PAILLERON,M L-Les Buveurs D'Eaux-Grenoble-(1935)-194p,(1)-
  80 illus-wrps   (5w1)   4.50
PAIN,BARRY-Eliza-Bost-(1904)-Dana Estes & Co-199p-illus-1st ed
        (5x4)   5.00
PAIN,S A-3 Miles of Gold...Kirkland Lake-Tor-1960-109p-maps-
  frontis   (5aa0)   4.50
PAIN,W B-Amer Notes...Being 15 months Impressions...&
  Observations in Kansas-Horsham(Engl)-1896-24p-wrps (5t1) 125.00
PAINE,A P-Saml Paine,Jr & wife Pamela Paine, of Randolph,Vt
  & their Anc& Desc-(1923)-218p   (5mm3) 10.00
PAINE,A W-Paine Genealogy,Ipswich Branch-1881-184p
        (5mm3) 8.50 (5m2) 12.50
PAINE,ALBERT BIGELOW-Arkansaw Bear-Lond-1919-pict bds-
  Geo D Harrap Ltd   (5c8,lacks e.p.) 10.00
--Definitive Edition of Complete Works of Mark Twain-NY-
  1922 to 1925-37 vols-8vo-bds-ltd to 1024 sets,nbrd
        (5h5,vg,autgs) 400.00
--Letters of Mark Twain-NY-1917-Harper-2 vols-illus (5p0) 7.50
--Mark Twain,A Biography-NY-1912-3 vols-illus-1st ed
        (5t4,5mm2) 15.00
--Sailor of Fortune-NY-1906-8vo-1st ed
        (5m6,autgs) 8.50 (5w4,sl wn) 7.50
--Thos Nast,his period & his pictures-NY-1904-4to-583p plus index-
  cl-1st ed-illus   (5p6)   20.00
PAINE,ALBERT TERHUNE-Lure of Mediterranean-NY-1921-394p-
  photos-dec cov   (5s1,rprd)   5.00
PAINE,BAYARD H-Pioneers,Indians & Buffaloes-Curtis-1935-illus-
  184p-1st ed   (4k5) 7.50 (5yy7) 15.00
PAINE,CHAS-The Elements of Railroading-NY-1885-154p
        (5e4,autg) 5.75
PAINE,HARRIET-Old People-Bost-1910-HoughtonMiff-8vo-cl
        (5b2,f)   5.00
PAINE,LAURAN-Northwest Conquest-Lond-n.d.-195p (5dd7,dj) 4.00
--Tom Horn, Man of the West-Barre-1963-8vo-cl-186p-1st ed
        (5g5,dj)   5.00
PAINE,NATHANIEL-Early Amer Imprints,1640 to 1700...Libr of
  Amer Antiquarian Soc-Worcester,1896-80p-wrps (4b4) 27.50
PAINE,R F W-Anc of Wm Alfred Paine-1936-80p (5mm3) 7.50
PAINE,RALPH-Fighting Fleets-Bost-1918-1st ed -o.p. (5s1) 6.50
--Greater America-NY-1907-327p-photos   (5m9,5s4) 6.00
--Joshua Barney a Forgotten Hero of Blue Water-NY-(1924)-illus-
  410p   (5q0) 10. (5s1,5L7) 5.00
--Lost Ships & Lonely Seas-NY-1921-8vo-412p-illus
        (4a6,sp fade) 4. (5L7) 3.50
--Old Merchant Marine-NewHav-1919-214p-deluxe ed
        (5s1,ex-libr)   3.50
--Roads of Adventure-Bost-1922-illus-452p-1st ed (5w9) 4.00
--Ships & Sailors of Old Salem-Chig-1912-McClurg-New Ed-
  515p-illus   (5qq8)   10.00
--same-Bost-1923-471p-illus-revised   (5e8,bkplt) 10.75
--same-Bost-1927-471p-illus-g.t.   (5s1)   8.00
PAINE,ROBT-Life & Times of Wm McKendree-Nashville-1885
        (5h6)   5.00
PAINE,ROBT TREAT-Pauperism in Great Cities Its 4 Chief Causes-
  Chig-1893-42p-cl   (5F0)   3.50
PAINE,S C-Family of Robt Treat Paine-1912-334p (5mm3) 25.00
PAINE,THOS-Age of Reason,Part the 1st,Part the 2nd-Lond-1796-
  Daniel Isaac Eation-50p,84p-orig front wrp-sewn (4c4,rprd) 42.50
--Complete Political Works,2 vols-NY-n.d.-Peter Eckler-illus-
  523p,509p   (5p0)   7.50
--Complete Works-NY-1954-Freethought Pr-2 vols (5tt5) 8.50
--same-NY-c1954-2 vols-simulated lea   (5w5) 7.50
--La Crise Americaine....trad de l'Anglois-Paris-(1794)-Buisson-
  124p,(4)-8vo-orig wrps   (5L1)   10.00
--The Crisis,in 16 numbers-Middletown,NJ-1839-8vo-orig bds-
  cl bk-papr labl   (5m6,ex-libr) 20.00
--The decline & fall of the Engl system of finance-NY-1796-
  stitchd   (5g4,wtrstnd) 25.00
--same-Phila-1796-33pg pamph-1st ed (5h6,wtrstnd,f) 20.00
--same-Lond-1796-8vo-removed   (4c1)   15.00
--Letter to the Earl of Shelburne,acknowledgement of Amer
  Independence etc-Lond-1792-D Jordan-sm4to-9th ed-wrps
        (5L8,re-wrps) 10.00
--Letter to Geo Washington-Phila-1796-disbnd-76p & 1p ads-
  1st issue   (5m2)   17.50

PAINE,THOS (continued)
--Letter to Mr Secretary Dundas,also 2 Letters to Lord Onslow-
Lond-1792-D Jordan-t8vo-16p,9p,2p blanks-removed-ex rare
(5L8,f)   27.50
--Life & Works-Patriots Edition-NewRochelle-1925-illus-8vo-
10 vols   (5p9) 25.   (4m7,1 vol sl shake)   27.50
--Life of-(Edinburgh? 1792?)-t8vo-18p-hf titl-3 qrtrs calf-
ps g.lettered   (5L8,f bndg)   12.50
--Political Writings of..-Charlestown,Mass-1824-2 vols-cl
(4m2,rbnd)   17.50
--Remarques sur les Erreurs de l'Histoire philosophique et Politique
de M Guillaume Thos Raynal-Bruxelles-1783-le Franc-8vo-
127p,(1)-orig wrps   (5L1)   10.00
--Rights of Man-Lond-1791,2-2 vols-buck-Vol 1,7th ed-
Vol 2,4th ed   (4b6,rbnd)   35.00
--same-Lond-1791-prntd for JS Jordan-sm4to-orig bds-5th ed
(5L8,crude rbkd,reprd)   10.00
--same-(Parts 1 & 2 in 1 vol)-Dublin-1791-mrbld bds-sheep bk &
cor   (5g8,wn)   15.00
--same-Lond-prntd 1792-Bost-1792,reprntd-Part the 2nd,combining
principle & practice-stitchd   (5g3)   10.00
--same-Dublin-1792-8vo-75p-(unbnd)-3rd ed   (5ss5)   10.00
--same-Lond-1792-HDSymonds-Pt 1,79p,pt 2,94p(5d6,t.pg tn)   25.00
--Writings of-Albany-n.d.-(1791,2)-7 sections-xii,60,186,41,70,
24,124p-lea-Howes P34   (5h1)   35.00
--Writings of-NY-1893 to 1896-6 vols-8vo-cl-g.t.-Conway,ed
(4c1,f)   75.00
PAINE,"THOS"-(i.e Robt Treat Paine,Jr)-The Ruling Passion,
An Occasional Poem-Bost-1797-Manning&Loring-32p-4to-hf mor-
(5L1,rbnd)   45.00
PAINESVILLE BOOK BK-Alumnae Assn of Lk Erie Seminary-
Painesvl-1896-172,(1)p-ads-bds-1st ed   (5c4)   6.50
PAINTER,C C-Condition of affairs in Indian Terr & Calif-Phila-1888-
wrps   (5g4)   10.00
--Visit to Mission Indians of Southern Calif & other Western
tribes-Phila-1886-wrps-Indian Rights Assoc   (5g4)   10.00
PAINTER,F V N-Poets of Virginia-Richmond-(1907)-ports (5r7)   15.00
PAINTER,GILDER & VARNISHER'S COMPANION-Phila-(1860-
216p,24p   (5n7,wn)   10.00
PAINTER'S,GILDER'S & VARNISHER'S MANUAL-Lond-1836-
207p   (5t7,cov loose)   16.00
PAINTER,O C-Family of Saml Painter, Gen & Biog Sketches of,
who settled in Chester Co,Pa in 1699-1903-lg folio-55p (5mm3) 10.00
--Wm Painter & His Father, Dr Edwin Painter, Sketches & Reminis-
1914-152p   (5mm3)   10.00
PAINTER,ORRIN C-Poems-Balt-1899-1st ed   (5b9,vf)   5.00
--Wm Painter & his Father, Dr Edw Painter-Balt-1914-folio-cl-
152p-t.e.g.-illus   (5hh7)   17.50
PAINTER,THOS-Autobiography-n.p.-1910-priv prntd-8vo-cl
(4c1)   20.00
PAIRPOINT,ALFRED J-Rambles in America,Past & Present-Bost-1891-
(5q8,autg)   6.00
PAIRS,FRANCKLYN-Personalities in Amer Art-NY-1930-Arch Forum-
112p-sm8vo   (4a0)   17.50
PAJEKEN,FRIEDRICH J-Im Wilden Westen und drei andere
Erzahlungen aus Nord und Sudamerika-Stuttgart&Leipzig-n.d.-
Wilhelm Effenberger-8vo-152p,(2)(ads)-frontis-3 plts-pict cl in
col-wire stitchd   (5p1)   20.00
PALACHE,JOHN G-Gautier & the Romantics-NY-1926-illus
(5mm2)   7.50
PALATISTS BOOK OF COOKERY-Hollywood-1933-Assistance League
of SoCalif-230p   (4g9)   6.00
PALEN,LEWIS STATON-The White Devil of the Black Sea-NY-1924-
8vo-cl-298p-1st ed   (5t2)   3.75
PALETTE PAINTING BOOK-NY-(c1892)-McLoughlin Bros-plts-
pic papr over bds   (5rr2)   12.50
PALEY,W-Treatise on Law of Principal & Agent-Phila-1822-2nd ed
(5r4,bndg poor)   12.50
PALEY,WM-Principles of moral & political philosophy-Lond-1785-
for R Faulder-4to-calf-1st ed   (5x3,hng wn)   75.00
--Works-Lond-1822-3 vols-16mo-lea   (5m1)   27.50
--The Works of-NY-1824-SKing-5 vols-sm thk12mo-orig prntd bds-
frontis   (5L8,rust spots)   12.50
PALFI,MARION-Suffer Little Children-NY-(1952)-4to-pict wrps-96p-
photos   (5t4)   7.50
PALFREY,DR-Remarks concerning Late Dr Bowditch wi Replies-
Bost-1840-26p-prntd wrps   (5r7)   8.50
PALFREY,JOHN G-Oration...Bost, July 4,1831-Bost-1831-
42p-wrps   (5t4)   5.00
PALGRAVE,FRANCIS T-The Golden Treasury of Best Songs &
Lyrical Poems in Engl Language-Cambr-1861-12mo-1st issue
(5ss5)   15.00

--Golden Treasury of Songs & Lyrics-NY-1911-Duffield&Co-
imp8vo-pict labl-col illus   (5p9) 10.   (5c8)   8.50
--same-NY-1911-Duffield&Co-sq4to-8p col illus-1st ed
(5v2,vf) 27.50   (5dd8)   20.00
--The Golden Treasury-NY-1945-maroon crushed lev mor by Maurin
(5d2,f bndg)   25.00
PALGRAVE,MARY E-Mary Rich,Countess of Warwick,
1625 to 78-1901-plts   (5L7)   3.50
PALGRAVE,R H INGLIS,ed-Dictionary of Political Economy-
Lond-1901-3 vols   (5w4,hng crack)   16.50
PALIMPSEST-Paris-1926-Cr8vo-cov wrps-1st ed-Contact Pr-HD
(5ss7,HD autg)   100.00
PALLADINO,L B-Indian & White in the NoWest-Lancaster,Pa-
1922-2nd ed,rev-scarce   (5s4,sl wn) 22.50   (5g4)   20.00
PALLAS,P S-Travels Through the Southern Provinces of the Russian
Empire-Lond-1802,03-2 vols-illus-col plts-maps-orig bds-
labls   (5j3,rbkd)   125.00
--same-Lond-1812-Stockdale-lg4to-mor-g.e.-2 vols-51 col plts-
4 fldg maps-2nd ed   (4e1,f bndg)   450.00
PALLEN,CONDE B-Crucible Island-NY-(1919)-Manhattanville Pr-
1st ed   (5m2)   6.00
PALLIS,MARCO-Peaks & Lamas-NY-1949-Knopf-illus (5p0)   7.50
PALLISER,JOHN-Exploration, British NoAmer-Lond-1859-folio-
orig prntd wrps-64p-9 maps-3 profiles-1st issue-v rare
(4n4,chip)   225.00
--The Solitary Hunter-Lond-1856-234p-illus-hf mor   (5d6)   20.00
--Solitary Rambles & Adventures of a Hunter in Prairies-Lond-
1853-JnMurray-326p-hf calf   (4n4) 85.   (5d2)   45.00
PALLISER'S NEW COTTAGE HOMES & DETAILS-NY-n.d.-
(ca1880)-4to-cl-drawings   (5t0,rbnd)   27.50
PALLUCCHINI,RODOLFO-Guardis Zeichnungen im Museum
Correr zu Venedig-Florenz-(1942)-G C Sansoni-4to-bds-
cl sp-illus-ltd to 5,000c,nbrd   (5b0,dj)   45.00
PALM BEACH,FLORIDA-Photogravures-KansasCty-1910-40p-
wrps   (5j6)   7.00
PALM BEACHES,FLORIDA-Souvenir Booklet-ca 1915-16p in col
(5a6,mint)   7.50
PALMA,RAFAEL-Our Campaign for Independence from Taft to
Harrison(1901 to 1921)-Manila-1923-Bur of Prntng-47p-wrps-
6 x 9   (5r0)   7.50
PALM & FECHTELER-Catalog of Transfer Carriage Ornaments-
NY-ca 1875-4to-66p plus ads-orig prntd wrps-v scarce (5t2)   50.00
PALMBORG,ROSA W-China Letters-Plainfield-1943   (5x7)   3.50
PALMDALE COLONY-Palmdale,LosAng Co-LosAng-1894-24p-
map-wrps-BRBaumgardt&Co,prntrs   (5d6)   50.00
PALMER,A,ed-Recording Britain-1946-Vols 1 thru 3 only (5L7)   30.00
PALMER,ABRAHAM,JR-History of 48th Regiment,NY State
Volunteers in War for Union-Brooklyn-1885-314p-cl-illus
(5j6)   8.50
PALMER,ALBERT W-Human Side of Hawaii-Bost-(1924)-Pilgrim Pr
(5x5,crease)   5.00
PALMER,ARNOLD-Movable Feasts-Lond-1952-153p-13p illus-bds
(5c9)   7.50
PALMER,B M-Life & Letters of Jas Henley Thornwell-Richmond-
1875-1st cd frontis-614p   (5L3)   7.50
PALMER,BENJ F-Diary of Benj F Palmer,privateersman-(NewHav)-
1914-illus-stiff prntd wrps-1 of 102c prntd for Acorn Club
(5g8,f,unopnd)   35.00
PALMER,BERTHA RACHAEL-Beauty Sports in NoDakota-Bost-
(1928)-266p-col frontis-autg ed-ltd to advance subscrip (5L0) 8.50
--same-1939-2nd ed   (5L0,dj)   5.00
PALMER,BROOKS-The Book of Amer Clocks-NY-(1950)-illus-
cl-4to-318p   (5t4)   12.50
PALMER,C H-The Salmon Rivers of Newfoundland-Bost-1928-
8vo-orig wrps-illus-271p-1st ed   (5m6)   10.00
PALMER,C J-Memorials of Family of Hurry of Great Yarmouth,
Norfolk & NY-Norwich,Eng-1873-104p   (5t9)   10.00
PALMER,CLARA S-Annals of Chicopee Street-Chicopee-1898-
Springfield Prntng-91p-12mo-cl   (4t1)   10.00
PALMER,E H-The Desert of the Exodus-Cambr-1871-2 vols-
illus-maps-3 qrtr lea   (5ww4,libr nbrs)   15.00
PALMER,E LAURENCE-Fieldbook of Mammals-NY-1957-
Dutton-321p-illus   (5p7)   3.50
PALMER,EDWIN O-History of Hollywood-1937-Vol 1 only-
Arthur H Cawston,pub   (5x5)   35.00
--same-Hollywood-1938-rev & extended ed   (5x5,dj)   30.00
--Third Galapagos Trip-(Hollywood-1934)-43p-wrps (5yy3,autg) 10.00
PALMER,ELIHU-Posthumous Pieces-Lond-1824-R Carlile-8vo-
disbnd-30p & leaf   (5L1)   30.00
PALMER,ELIZ-My Memories of Old New York-NY-1923 (4b7)   7.50

PALMER,FREDK-Clark of the Ohio-NY-1929-482p-illus-
1st ed   (5x5,dj) 20.   (5h9)   12.00
--In the Klondyke-NY-1899-218p-illus-1st ed
        (5r7,ex-libr) 10.   (5L0)   15.00
--Newton D Baker,Amer at War-NY-1931-2 vols-illus-lea-
1st ed-ltd ed   (5q8,unopnd,autgs)   17.50
--same-NY-1931-illus-2 vols   (5w4)   8.50
--This Man Landon-NY-1936-332p-frontis (5w9) 3.50
--With My Own Eyes-Indnpls-(1933)-396p-photos (5ss1) 5.00
PALMER G H-Altruism,its nature & varieties-1919 (5L7) 2.50
PALMER,GEO HERBERT-The Autobiography of a Philosopher-
Bost&NY-1930-12mo-cl-port-137p   (5t4)   5.00
--Life of Alice Freeman Palmer-Bost&NY-HoughtonMiff-1908-
354p-frontis-9 plts-cl-2nd impress-12mo (5p1,scuff) 5.00
PALMER,HENRIETTA LEE-Stratford Gallery-NY-Appleton-1865-
302p-8x11"-illus-dec lea   (5i1,scuf)   9.00
PALMER,HENRY R-Stonington by the Sea-Stonington-1913-8vo-
orig bds-illus-labl-1st ed (5m6,labl tn) 13.50
PALMER HOUSE COOK BOOK-Indnpls-(1933)-
by Amiet-1st ed   (5g9)   4.50
PALMER, J FREDK-Kodiak Bear Hunt-NY-(1958)-79p (5ss1,dj) 4.50
PALMER,J W-The New & the Old,or, Calif & India in Romantic
Aspects-NY-1859-13 illus-433p-frontis-1st ed
    (4p2) 12.50   (5r7)   15.00
PALMER,JAS CROXALL-Thulia:Tale of Antarctic-NY-1843-
Samuel Colman,publ-72p-cl-poems (5yy3) 35.00
PALMER,JAS W-Farmer's Almanac for the Year of Our Lord 1832-
Louisville-24p-unbnd   (5yy8)   6.50
PALMER,JOE-Amer Race Horses,1946-Annual Review-Sagamore Pr-
(1947)-4to-cl-illus-168p   (5j5)   12.50
--This Was Racing-NY-c1953-Red Smith,ed-imit lea-illus-
ltd to 1,000c,nbrd,autgs   (5w9,box) 10.00
PALMER,JOEL-Journal of Travels Over the Rocky Mntns to Mouth
of Columbia River...1845 & 1846-Cinn-1847-JA&UP James-
sm8vo-orig prntd wrps-stitchd-errat slip-1st ed-1st issue
    (4h0,box) 1,250.00
--same-Cinn-1847-James-12mo-roan bkd bds-1st ed with
date 1847 on title pg changed in ink to 1848 (5n9) 1,000.00
--same-Cleve-1906-Thwaites,ed-311p plus ads-facs of
title pg of orig   (5L0)   25.00
PALMER,JOHN-Journal of Travels in the US-Lond-1818-
Sherwood,et al-8vo-hf mor-fldg map-col map-1st ed
    (5n9,rprd) 85.00
PALMER,JOHN-Comedy of Manners-Lond-1913-8vo-cl-308p-
illus   (5t0)   7.50
PALMER,JOHN-Ben Johnson-NY-1934-illus (5mm2) 5.00
PALMER,JOHN McAULEY-Gen'l Von Steuben-Yale Univ Pr-
1937-frontis-maps-484p   (5mm8,dj) 10.00
PALMER,JULIUS A,JR-One voyage & its consequences-Bost-
(1889)-Lothrop-pic cl-1st ed (5m2,lt spots) 10.00
PALMER,L-Desc of John & Mary Palmer of Concord,Pa-1875-
474p   (5mm3)   20.00
PALMER,LOOMIS T-Standard Atlas & Gazetteer of the World
spec adapted for Commercial & Library Reference-Chig-
(1892)-Standard Columbian Co-illus-folio-World's Fair ed
    (5L3)   20.00
PALMER,LYMAN L-History of Mendocino Co,Calif-SanFran-1880-
Alley,Bowen&Co-676p-port-orig sheep-8vo (5tt0) 200. (4t1) 150.00
--History of Napa & Lake Counties,Calif...&Biogr Sketches-
SanFran-1881-Slocum,Bowen&Co-600p, 291p-8vo-lea-illus
    (4t1,rebkd) 100.00
PALMER,LYNDE-Helps Over the Hard Places-NY-1862-
(Am Tract Soc)-illus-frontis-12mo (4m3) 3.50
PALMER,M D-Lessons on Massage-NY-1912-8vo-illus-cl-1st ed
    (5p5)   12.50
PALMER,MARY E-Guide to Hotel Housekeeping-Charleston-
1908-108p   (5w7,soil)   5.00
PALMER, MRS MINNIE-The Woman's Exchange Cook Book-NY-
1902-527p-lg thk4to-frontis-illus-oilcloth cov (5g9,rprd) 10.00
PALMER,PETER S-History of Lake Champlain-Plattsburg-1853-
Tuttle-223p-part lea   (5qq8,lea wn) 12.50
--same-3rd ed-255p   (4m2)   20.00
PALMER,R R-History of the Modern World-1955-Knopf-900p
plus index-lg8vo   (5a6,f)   5.00
PALMER,RALPH S-The Mammal Guide-NY-1934-Dblday-384p-
illus   (5p7)   4.25
PALMER ROSE A-The No American Indians-(Wash-1934)-illus,
some col-309p-Vol 4 of Smi Sci Ser (4n7) 15.00
PALMER T H,ed-Historical Register of the US-Phila-1814-
Vols 1 & 2-orig bds-2nd ed   (5m2) 10.00
--same-Phila-1815, 16-4 vols-bds-roan bks (5g3,unmatchd bnds) 50.00

PALMER,T S-The Jack Rabbits of the US-Wash-1896-84p-wrps
    (4a5)   8.50
--same-Wash-1897-88p-wrps   (5n4)   4.50
--Places Names of Death Valley Region in Calif & Nev-(Wash)-
1948-80p-wrps   (5tt0)   12.50
PALMER,THOS W-Guide to Law & Legal Literature of Spain-
Wash-1915-(lib of Congr)-cl   (5yy6) 8.50
PALMER,V B-V B Palmer's Business Men's Almanac,1849-
(1848)-64p-wrps   (5yy3)   15.00
PALMER,GEN WM J-Report of Surveys Across the Continent in
1867,68-Phila-1869-WBSelheimer-250p-fldg profile-hf mor-
some copies issued w 1 map,others wi 3
    (5d6,lacks maps) 25. (5t3,wrps chip,1 map)100.00
PALMER,WM R-Pahute Indian Legends-SaltLkCty-(1946)-8vo-
134p-cl-illus-Deseret Book Co (5p1,dj) 5. (5h4) 6.00
PALMER'S POCKET SCALE-Warren,Ohio-1845-Tait&Walling,publ-
48p-cl   (5jj9)   10.00
PALMERSTON,LORD-on Treaty of Washington(1842)-(n.p.-ca 1842)-
wrps   (5g4)   10.00
PALO ALTO WOMEN'S CLUB COOKERY-PaloAlto-1903-oilcl cov-
95p-ads   (4g9,rub)   12.50
PALOCZI-HORVATH,GEO-Mao Tse Tung-NY-1963-Dblday-
393p   (5p0)   6.00
PALOU,FRAY FRANCISCO-Exped into Calif of Venerable Padre
Fray Junipero Sera &his Companions in Yr 1769-SanFran-1934-
Nueva Calif Pr-vel sp-ltd to 400c (5jj1,dj,f) 37.50
--Founding of the 1st Calif Missions Under Spiritual Guidance of
Junipero Serra-SanFran-1934-Nueva Calif Pr-4to-124p-bds-
ltd to 1000c   (5F5,f,dj fade) 25.00
--Historical Memoirs of New Calif-Univ of Calif-1926-cl-4 vols
  (5s4,ex-libr) 125. (5hh4,libr performances) 75. (5x5) 150.00
--Noticias de la Nueva California-SanFran-1874-Bosqui-4 vols-
8vo-part calf-18 plts-photos-ltd to 100c (4h0,rub) 385.00
--Relacion Historica de la Vida Apostolica Tareas del Venerable
Padre Fray Junipero Serra,y de las Misiones que fundo en la
Calif Septentrional etc-Mexico-1787-344p-port-4to-calf-
title & 13 prel lvs-fldg map of Calif
  (5s9,lacks map,v wormholed) 250. (5L1,f,rbkd) 600.00
PALSITS,VICTOR H-Minutes of Exec Council of Prov Adminis of
Francis Lovelace 1668 to 1673-Albany-1910-2 vols-buck (5t7) 10.00
PALTOCK,ROBT-Life & Adventures of Peter Wilkins-Dent-1928-
illus-4to-dec cl-17 col plts   (5s0) 8.50
PALTSITS,VICTOR HUGO,ed-Inventory of Rensselaerswyck
Manuscripts-NY-1924-54p-wrps (5j4) 7.50
--Narr of Amer Voyages &Travels of Capt Wm Owen & Settlement...
Fundy-NY-1942-illus-maps-169p-wrps (5yy6) 5.00
PAMBOUR,F M G DE-Practical Treatise on Locomotive Engines
Upon Railways-NY-1836-8vo-plts-orig bds &cl-122p,16p
    (5t2)   50.00
--same-Phila-1836-old roan-fldg plts (5g4,wn,fox) 25.00
PAMMEL,L H-Comparative Study of Vegetation of Swamp,Clay &
Sandstone areas in WWisc,SE Minn & part of Iowa-Davenport-
1905-92p-offprint   (4a5,wrp) 4.00
--Maj John F Lacey,memorial vol-(Torch Pr,CedarRapds)-1915-
Iowa Park & Forestry Assoc-454p-frontis (5u3,sl dmpstns) 7.50
PAN AMER PETROLEUM & TRANSPORT CO-Mexican Petroleum-
NY-1922-cl-12mo-pkt map-300p (4t1) 9.50
PANABAKER,FRANK-Reflected Lights-Tor-1957-159p-plts (5aa0) 6.50
PANAMA COOKERY BOOK-Favorite Recipes of Canal Zone
Fed of Women's Clubs-Mount Hope,CZ-1910-94p (5c5) 6.50
PANAMA PACIFIC EXPOS-Architecture & Landscape Gardening of
Exposition-SanFran-(1915)-illus (5xx7) 7.50
PANAMA PAC INT'L EXPO-San Fran,Calif, Invites the World-
SanFran-1915-Cardinell Vincent Co-12 lvs-photos-folio-wrps
    (4a5)   7.50
PANCHARD,EDOUARD-Meats,Poultry & Game-NY-(1919)-134p-
29 plts-frontis   (5c0)   4.00
PANCOAST,CHAS EDW-A Quaker Forty Niner-Phila-1930-
Univ of PA-Hannum,ed-8vo-cl-402p-2nd prntng (5h5) 10.00
PANCOAST,H-Covered Bridges to Yesterdays-Newark,Ohio-1959-
illus   (5m2)   6.00
PANCOAST,HENRY S-Impressions of Sioux tribes in 1882,with some
1st principles in the Indian question-Phila-1883-wrps (5g4) 10.00
PANDOSY,REV MIE CLES-Grammar & Dictionary of Yakama
Language-NY-1862-Cramoisy Pr-59p-wrps (5yy3) 10.00
PANHANDLE & SOUTH PLAINS OF TEXAS-1928-8x9-28p-illus-
wrps   (5h0)   2.50
PANHANDLE PLAINS HISTORICAL REVIEW-Canyon,Tex-1929 to
1970-38 vols   (4a5,lacks 5 vols) 200.00
PANIKKAR,K M-In Two Chinas-Lond-1955 (5x7) 5.00
PANNEKOEK,A-History of Astronomy-1961-illus (5L7) 7.50
PANNELL,WATLER-Civil War on the Range-LosAng-(1943)-48p-
16mo-orig pic wrps (4c1,f) 7.50 (5d6) 3. (5g5) 5.00

PANNELL,WALTER (continued)
----Redmen's Horizons-LosAng-1945-16mo-56p-wrps (5dd6)   2.00
PANOPLIST & MISSIONARY MAGAZINE-for Yr 1817-Vol 13 #1
to 12-Bost-1817-576p-lea   (5h1)   15.00
PANORAMA OF THE BUTTERFLY'S BALL-Otley,W Walker-ca 1845-
sq12mo-opens to 18 lvs 5"x67"-hand col wdcut-rare (5v2,f) 35.00
PANORAMA OF THE HUDSON..both sides of Rivr from NY to
Albany-NY-c1903-horiz 4to-orig heavy g. wrps-800 photos
(5w4)   8.50
PANORAMA OF WIT-Lond-JnSharpe-1809-357p-3 qrtrs lea-t.e.g.-
24mo   (5i1,fox,rub)   12.00
PANORAMIC VIEW FROM BUNKER HILL MONUMENT-(Bost,1848)-
8vo-accordion fashion to 47"   (5ss5,text loose,sl tn)   10.00
PANTHER JACK-NY-(1867)-100p-pict wrps-Munro's 10¢Novels#98
(5h7,dmpstn)   7.50
PANTOMIME BOOKS-Complete set of all 5 titles-NY-c1880-publ
by McLoughlin Bros-ea opens to dbl pg col view of theater-
overlays attached to center fold-col   (4c3,vg)   125.00
PANTON,CAPT EDW-Speculum juventutis,or,a true mirror-Lond-
1671-8vo-calf-1st ed   (5xx6,rbkd)   200.00
PANTRY PALAVERS-n.p.-1955-Covina Jr Women's Club-spiral bnd
(4g9)   4.50
PAPANIN,IVAN-Life on an Ice Floe-NY-(1939)-300p-photos-
frontis   (5ss1,mint)   7.50
--same-Lond-n.d.   (5ss1,dj)   7.50
PAPASHVILY,GEO-Yes & No Stories-NY&Lond-(1946)-Harper-
12mo-228p-1st ed   (5p1,dj)   5.00
PAPE,A G-The Alternative to Communism-Lond-c1932 (5x7)   3.00
--Is There A New Race Type-Edinb-1922-12mo-illus (5x2)   12.50
PAPINEAU,LOUIS J-Speech on the Hustings,at Opening of Election
for West Ward of City of Montreal-Montr-1827-wrps-48p-
sewn   (5w8)   45.00
PAPWORTH,JOHN B-Rural Residences-Lond-1818-for R Ackermann-
27 hand col aquatints-8vo-mor   (4c2)   125.00
PAQUET,L A-Etudes et Appreciations Nouveaux Melanges Canadiens-
Que-1919-Franciscan Missionary Pr-390p-wrps (5r7,unopnd) 15.00
PARADISE OF DAINTIE DEVICES-NY-1882-101p-(for Chas Pratt &
Co for Xmas token)-wrps   (5t4)   5.00
PARAGREENS,THE-on a Visit to Paris Universal Exhibition-NY-
1857-Edwards&Co-sm8vo-230p-cl   (5c8,rub)   4.00
PARAPHRASE ON PART OF "OECONOMY OF HUMAN LIFE-
Bost-1759-Green&Russell-8vo-disbnd-1st ed   (519)   150.00
PARCHMENT,S R-Astrology,Mundane & Spiritual-SanFran-(1933)-
charts-906p-1st ed   (5t7)   10.00
PAROD,ALEJANDRO-El Verdadero Practico con recetas
enteramente nuevas y ensayadas por su autor-Madrid-1914-287p-
frontis-illus-2nd ed   (5g9)   7.50
--Recetas practicas y escojidas del Prof de Cocina,Pasteleria Y
Reposteria-n.p.-n.d.-(ca 1890?)-251p-illus-cl&bds-
Mexican ads-1st ed   (5g9,hng crack)   17.50
PARDOE,G M-Gen of Wm Molyneaux & Desc-1894-24p (5mm3) 10.00
PARDOE,J-Louis Fourteenth & Court of France in 17th Century-
Lond-1886-3 vols-illus-calf   (5ii2,rub)   12.50
PARDOE,JULIA-The city of the Magyar,or Hungary & her
institutions-Lond-1840-Geo Virtue-3 vols-12mo-orig cl-
1st ed-8 plts   (5i8)   27.50
PAREDES,AMERICO-With His Pistol in His Hand-Austin-1958-262p
(5hh3,dj)   5.00
PAREDES,IGNACIO DE-Prompturio Manual Mexicano-Mexico-
1759-hf mor-rare   (4a5)   75.00
PAREDES Y ARRILLAGA,MARIANO-Manifiesto del Exmo-Mexico-
Aguila-26 July 1846-19p-4to-orig prntd papr wrps (5L1)   50.00
PARES,BERNARD-A History of Russia-NY-1944-8vo-cl-575p-
maps-4th ed   (5t0)   4.50
PARES,RICHARD-King George III & Politicians-Oxf-1954-214p
(5a1)   4.50
PARETO,VILFREDO-The Mind & Society-NY-(1935)-HBrace-4 vols-
A Livingston,ed   (5p9)   15.00
PARIKANINE,MAURICE-The Krassin-NY-(1929)   (5ss1)   4.00
PARIS,COMTE DE-History of Civil War in Amer-Phila-1875,1876,
(1888)-4 vols-maps   (5s9,v wn)   22.50
PARIS COOK BOOK-First Baptist Church-Paris,Missouri-n.d.-
(ca 191?)-141p-ads-wrps   (5g9,soil)   5.00
PARIS,J A-Pharmacologia-3rd Amer from 6th Lond-NY-1828-
corr & extended-544p-col wheel in front cov-calf
(5w3,cov dtchd)   15.00
--A Treatise on Diet-NY-1828-210p-lea sp-bds (5c7,soil,pencil) 18.00
PARIS,MATTHEW-English History from 1235 to 1273-(Bohn)-1852-
3 vols-Giles,tr   (5tt5,bndgs wn)   10.00
PARIS UNIVERSAL EXPOSITION,1867-General Surv of-Wash-1868
GPO-8vo-325p-wrps   (5j5,lack rear wrps)   10.00
PARIS,WM FRANCKLYN-Decorative Elements in Architecture-
NY-1917-illus-152p   (5q0,libr labl)   10.00

PARIS,WM FRANCKLYN (continued)
--Hall of American Artists-NY-1944-NYU-168p-8vo (4a0)   15.50
PARISET,CAMILLO-Della Trattazione Dei Vini Da Pasta E Communi-
Parma-1884-4to-39p-1 fldg plt-wrps   (5w1)   9.50
PARISH,JOHN CARL-John Chambers-IowaCty-1909-State Hist
Soc of Iowa-279p   (5u3)   6.00
--Persistence of the Westward Movement & Other Essays-U of Calif
Pr-1943   (5m9)   3.50
PARISH,R-Parish Families of New Engl-(1938)-502p (5t9)   12.00
PARISH SIDE,THE-NY-1854-258p-illus   (5t4)   5.00
PARISH WATSON & CO-Chinese Pottery of Han,T'Ang & Sung
Dynasties-NY-1917-109p-folio-17 tip in col plts (5ww3)   50.00
PARISOT,P F-Reminis of a Texas Missionary-SanAnt-1899-227p
plus index & ads-frontis-1st ed   (5L0)   15.00
PARK & TILFORD-Winter Quarterly 1915,16-catalog-141p-orig col
pic wrps-wine grocery price list,etc-illus (5m2)   5.00
PARK,BERTRAM-Roses-Lond-(1949)-col plts-141p (5s7)   3.00
PARK,JAS ALLAN-A System of the law of marine insurance-Bost-
1799-cont calf-2nd Amer ed   (5g8,wn hng broke)   10.00
PARK,LAWRENCE-Gilbert Stuart,illus descrip list of his works-
NY-1926-Rudge-4 vols-4to   (4a0,box)   325.00
PARK,MARY I-Dreams & Visions=(Tiffin-1925)-70p-wrps(5h1) 4.00
PARK,MUNGO-Travels in the Interior Districts of Africa-Phila-
1800-484p-illus   (5t7)   12.50
PARK,R E-Race & Culture-Free Pr-1950   (5x2,dj)   5.00
PARK,ROBT-History of the Okla State Penitentiary-McAlester-1914-
148p-wrps   (5h0,t.pg & 2 pgs in facs)   18.00
PARK,ROSWELL-An Eptiome of the History of Medicine-Phila-
1897-348p-8vo-cl-illus   (5t2,lacks fly)   7.50
--Pantology; or, a Systematic Survey of Human Knowledge-Phila-
1844-illus-580p   (5t4)   8.50
--Selections of Juvenile & Misc Poems-Phila-1836-Desilver,Thos
& Co-12mo-cl-labl-1st ed (5b2,pres) 25. (5ss3,stn,fox)   30.00
PARKE,ADELIA-Memoirs of an Old Timer-Weiser,Ida-(1955)-illus-
65p-wrps-1st ed   (5yy7)   8.50
PARKE,JOHN E-Recollections of 70 Yrs & Historical Gleanings of
Allegheny,Pa-Bost-1886-385p-port   (5m2)   12.50
PARKE,LT JOHN G-Report of Explor for portion of Railway Rt...
Dona Ana,on Rio Grande & Pimas Villages-(Wash-1855)-53p-
fldg map-disbnd   (5tt0)   25.00
PARKE,N G-Anc of Lorenzo Ackley & Wife Emma Arabella
Bosworth-1960-325p-wrps   (5mm3)   25.00
--Ancestry of Rev Nathan Grier Parke & Wife Anne Elizabeth
Gildersleeve-1959-146p-wrps   (5mm3)   15.00
--1st Presbyterian Church of Pittston,Pa-Pittston-1879-43p with
supplement   (5w0)   6.50
PARKE,THOS HEAZLE-My Personal Exper in Equatorial Africa-
NY-Scribner-1891-526p-illus   (5i1,lacks pocket map)   6.00
PARKER,A A -Trip to the West & Texas-Concord-1836-380p-orig cl
(5n4,sp rprd)   110.00
PARKER,AMASA J-Landmarks of Albany Co,NY-Syracuse-1891-
ports-g.t.-thk4to-cl-1st ed   (5p5,rebkd)   50.00
--same-NY-1897-557p,418p   (5t9)   25.00
PARKER,ARLITA D A-History of Pemaquid,with Sketches of Monhegan,
Popham & Castine-Bost-1925-8vo-orig wrps-226p-illus
(5ss5,pres)   10.00
PARKER,ARTHUR-Excavations in Erie Indian Village & Burial Site
at Ripley,Chautauqua Co,NY-Albany-1907-38 plts-wrps-
pg 459 to 554   (4b3)   12.50
--Iroquois Uses of Maize & Other Food Plants-Albany-1910-119p-
31 plts-wrps   (4b3)   10.00
PARKER,ARTHUR C-An Analytical History of the Seneca Indians-
Rochester,NY-1926-plts-wrps (4k5,f) 8.50 (5L0,rbnd in cl) 12.50
--Archaeological History of NY-NYS Museum Bul-1920-2 vols-
index   (5zz0) 15.   (5yy7,vg)   20.00
--Code of Handsome Lake,the Seneca Prophet-NY-1912-144p plus
index-photos-cl-NYS Museum Bul 163-scarce   (5L0)   15.00
--The Indian How Book-NY-1927-illus   (5m9)   4.50
--Iroquois Uses of Maize & Other Plant Foods-NYS Museum Bul #144
1910-114p   (5zz0,rbnd)   10.00
--Red Jacket,Last of the Seneca-NY-(1952)-219p-illus-map
e.p.   (4n2)   12.00
--Rumbling Wings & Other Indian Tales-Dbldy-1928-illus-1st ed
(4k5,f,dj)   6.00
--Seneca Myths & Folk Tales-Buffalo-1923-BuffHistSoc-cl-465p-
illus   (4k5,f)   12.50
PARKER,B F-Hist of Wolfeborough,NHamp-1901-557p (5t9) 12.50
PARKER,BENJ S-Cabin in the Clearing & Other Poems-Chig-1888-
303p-g.e.-mor-2nd ed   (5ee3)   12.50
PARKER,C E-Orange County,Indians to Industry-SantaAna-c1963-
O.C.Title Co-96p-4to-cl   (4t1)   7.50
PARKER,C S-Arlington,Mass,Past & Present-1907-331p (5mm3) 5.00

PARKER,CLEMENT C-Compendium of Works on Archery-Phila-
 1950-74p-ltd to 300c   (5w5)   5.00
PARKER,DOROTHY-Enough Rope-NY-1926-1st ed (5ee3)   5.00
--Here Lies-NY-1939-Literary Guild-1st ed (5hh1,dj) 7.50
--The Ladies of the Corridor-NY-1954-1st ed   7.50
--Not So Deep as a Well-NY-1936-Viking Pr-210p (5p9) 3.75
--Sunset gun-NY-1928-Boni&Liveright-cl-bds-1st ed (5m2,fade) 6.00
PARKER,E E-Hist of Brookline,NHamp-n.d.-664p-illus (5mm3) 12.50
PARKER,ELINOR-Cooking for One-NY-(1949)-122p (5c9)   3.00
PARKER,ERIC,ed-The Lonsdale Keeper's Book-Lond-(1952)-illus-
 256p   (5t7)   7.00
--Shooting by Moor,Field & Shore-Lond-1929-(Lonsdale Libr,Vol 3)-
 illus-375p   (5t7)   6.50
PARKER,F S-Ainsworth Family in Amer-1894-212p (5t9) 15.00
PARKER,FOXHALL-Fleets of World,Galley Period-NY-1876-235p-
 illus   (5s1,wn,ex-libr,fair) 12.50
--Squadron Tactics Under Steam-NY-1864-79 plts(2 fldg)
                                  (5c1,edges wn)   32.50
PARKER,FRANCES-Hope Hathaway-Bost-1904-408p-col frontis-illus
 by CMRussell-1st state(white spine stamping)-scarce (5L2) 17.50
--same-2nd state (with brown stamping)   (5L2)   15.00
--same as above but with new list of illus,with fewer illus-
 black&white frontis   (5L2,sl wn) 12.50
PARKER,FRANCIS J-Col Wm Prescott,the Commander in the Battle
 of Bunker's Hill...a Monograph-Bost-1875-8vo-orig wrps-21p-
 1st ed   (5ss5)   5.00
PARKER,GEO-Royal Double Ephemeris for Year of Our Lord 1704-
 Lond-1704-An Almanac-illus-g.dec (5F9,written records) 15.00
PARKER,DR GEO-Guaracha Trail-NY-1951-250p-1st ed (5dd6) 7.50
PARKER,SIR GILBERT-An Adventurer of the North-NY-1896-218p
                                            (5a1)   4.50
--Canada After 20 Years,an Address at Caxton Hall-(Lond)-(1905)
                                   (5nn8,pres)   25.00
--In Old Quebec-NY-1903-486p-plts-maps (5ee3,f)   2.50
--Judgment House-NY-1913-469p-frontis (5a1)   3.50
--Ladder of Swords-NY-1904-291p   (5a1)   3.50
--same-Tor-1904-cl   (5b2)   5.00
--The Lane that had no Turning-NY-1902-illus by Schoonover-
 1st ed   (5ee3)   3.50
--Old Quebec,The Fortress of New France-NY-1904-Macm-
 illus-g.t.   (5p7,5h9)   6.50
--When Valmond Came to Pontiac-NY-1898-222p (5a1)   3.50
--same-Tor-1898-312p   (5a1)   3.50
--Works-NY-1912 to 23-24 vols-lg8vo-3 qtr crushed mor-
 bks g.by Stikeman-"Imperial Ed"-ltd to 256 nbrd sets
                                     (5t2,f bndg)   150.00
PARKER,H W-The Snakes of Somaliland & the Sokotra Islands-
 Leiden-1949-115p-fldg map-wrps-8vo (4p6,sl scuff) 12.50
PARKER,H-Mail & Passenger Steamships of the 19th Century,
 MacPherson Collection-Lond-1928-Sampson Low,Marston&Co-
 16 col plts   (5t0,lacks frontis) 25. (5b0) 75.00
--same-Phila-n.d.-4to-illus-324p   (5t4)   35.00
PARKER,J M-An Aged Wanderer-SanAngelo,Texas(Bryan,Texas)-
 n.d.-32p-facs ed-hvy wrps-ltd to 500c,nbrd (5dd5)   5.00
PARKER,JAS-Conductor Generalis-Albany-1794-8vo-sheep(4c1) 30.00
PARKER,JAS-The Old Army Memories,1872 to 1918-Phila-(1929)-
 454p-illus-1st ed   (5L0)   20.00
PARKER,JOHN L-Unmasking Wall Street-Bost-1952-223p (5y2) 4.50
PARKER,JOHN R-The New Semaphoric Signal Book,in 3 Parts-
 Bost-1836-Light&Steans-40p,132p,19p-8vo-orig bds-pict labl-
 cl bk-col plts   (5j5,ex-libr) 27.50
PARKER,K T-North Italian Drawings of Quatrocento-NY-1927-
 Chamberlin&Lucas-illus-8vo   (5ww3)   25.00
PARKER,MARY M-This Was Alaska-Seattle-(1950)-237p (5ss1) 4.00
PARKER,DR M-The Arcana of Arts & Sciences Or,Farmers' &
 Mechanics' Manual-Wash,Pa-1824-calf-348p (5n7,fox) 150.00
PARKER,NH-Iowa As It is in 1855-Chig-1855-12mo-cl-264p-
 illus   (5t2) 15. (5m8,5n4)   17.50
--Iowa As It Is in 1856-Chig-1856-cl-plts
                         (5m8,lacks map) 15. (5s9) 25.00
--Minnesota Handbook for 1856,7-Bost-1857-col map-148p
                         (4p8) 15. (5n4)   22.50
--The Missouri Handbook-StL-1865-162p plus ads-2 fldg maps-
 1st ed   (5w5)   35.00
PARKER,R A-The Incredible Messiah-Bost-1937-1st ed (5x2) 17.50
PARKER,R D-Hist Recollections of Robertson Co,Texas-1955-254p
                                     (5mm3)   12.50
PARKER,R H- Hist & Gen of the Family of Deacon Lovel Parker of
 Barkhamsted Conn-1898-80p   (5mm3)   25.00
PARKER,RICHARD GREEN-School Compendium of Natural &
 Experimental Phylosophy-NY-1851-404p-illus-lea (5L3) 4.50
PARKER,ROBT ALLERTON-A Yankee Saint,John Humphrey Noyes
 & the Oneida Community-NY-1935-322p-illus-1st ed (5t4) 15.00

PARKER,ROBT J,ed-Chapters in Early Life of Thos Oliver Larkin,
 1939-Calif Histo Soc-Spec Publ #16-200c publ (5x5) 20.00
PARKER,SAML-Sylva-Lond-1701-for JP-8vo-calf-1st ed-scarce
                                     (5x3,wn)   40.00
PARKER,SAML-Journal of An Exploring Tour Beyond the Rocky Mntns-
 Ithaca-1838-orig cl-371p-map-1st ed
           (4n4,lacks map) 25. (4n4,mor)   85.00
--same-Ithaca-1840-12mo-cl-2nd ed (5t0,wn,facs of Oreg map) 30.00
--same-Ithaca-1842-408p-3rd ed
           (5t4,fray,lacks fldg map) 12.50 (5s9,facs map) 25.00
--same-Ithaca-1844-416p-4th ed-fldg map
           (5r1,map mend,chip) 15. (4n4,rprd)   25.00
--same-Auburn-1846-422p   (5yy8,lacks map) 12.50
--Rocky Mntn Indians-Bost-1836-Missionary Herald,Vol 1 32-
 1st ed -rare   (4n4)   125.00
PARKER,STUART C-Book of StAndrews-Tor-1930-142p-ports-plts
                                     (5a1)   4.50
PARKER,T-John Parker of Lexington-1893-528p (5t9)   7.50
PARKER,THEO-A Discourse Occasioned by Death of Dan'l Webster,
 1852-Bost-1852-cl-g.   (5q8)   8.50
--The Nebraska Question-Bost-1854-72p-wrps (5q8,lacks wrps) 7.50
--Proceedings of Penna Yearly Meeting of Progressive Friends-
 NY-1858-116p-8vo-orig wrps   (5m6)   10.00
--Sermon on Dangers Which Threaten Rights of Man in Amer-Bost-
 1854-56p-wrps   (5h7,dust soil) 5.00
--Slave Power-Bost-n.d.-centennial ed (5k1,fade)   5.00
--West Roxbury Sermons,1837 to 1848-Bost-1892-12mo-1st ed
                                     (5ss5)   15.00
PARKER,W B-Notes Taken During Exped Commanded by Capt
 R B Marcy Through Unexplored Texas-Phila-1856-242p-orig cl-
 1st ed   (4n4)   150.00
PARKER,WM B-Edw Rowland Sill,His Life & Work-Bost-1915-
 HoughtonMiff-307p-illus-1st ed   (4n8)   10.00
--Life & Public Services of Justin Smith Morrill-Bost&NY-1924-
 378p-illus   (5t7)   10.00
PARKER,THOS V-The Cherokee Indians with special reference to
 their relations with US Govt-NY-(1907)-Grafton Hist Series-
 116p plus bibl-illus-map   (5L3,f)   8.50
PARKER,CAPT WALTER H-Leaves From an Unwritten Log Book-(1929)
 Lond-n.d.-(ca 1930)-11 photos   (5c1)   10.50
PARKER,CAPT WM HARWAR-Recollections of Naval Officer,
 1841 to 1865-NY-1883-372p-plts   (5s1,ex-libr,wn) 17.50
PARKER,WYMAN W-Henry Stevens of Vermont-Amsterdam-1963-
 1st ed   (5q8,mint,dj)   7.50
PARKES,MRS WM-Domestic Duties-NY-1828-408p,(9)-cl bk-
 bds-3rd Amer ed   (5w7,scuff,sl stnd) 42.50
PARKHILL,FORBES-The Last of the Indian Wars-(1962)-Crowell
 Collier-12mo-cl-127p   (5F5,f,dj)   4.00
--The Law Goes West-Denver-(1956)-1st ed-photos (5bb4,dj) 6.50
--The Wildest of the West-NY-(1951)-illus-1st ed
                         (5yy6,f) 6. (5bb4,dj)   5.00
PARKHURST,CHAS H-Our Fight With Tammany-NY-1895-296p
                                     (5t4)   7.50
PARKHURST,D B-Painter in Oil-1898   (5L7)   5.00
PARKHURST,H E-Trees,Shrubs & Vines of the NE US-NY-1903-
 451p-illus   (5s7)   6.00
PARKHURST,JOHN H-Latin Lessons,For Children-Lahainaluna-
 1839-orig cartridge wrps-32p-16mo   (4h0,cov soil,wn) 350.00
PARKHURST,WINTHROP-The Encyclopedia of Music & Musicians-
 NY-1937-Crown-662p   (5p0)   7.50
PARKIN,SIR GEO R-Rhodes Scholarships-Bost-1912-250p-4 plts
                                     (5aa0)   4.50
PARKINS,ALMON E-Historical Geography of Detroit-Lansing-
 1918-356p   (4k5) 7.50   (4i2)   10.00
PARKINSON,C N,ed-The Trade Winds-Lond-1948-336p-illus-
 maps   (4b9)   12.00
PARKINSON,JOHN-Paradisi in Sole-1904-612p,(8)-folio-
 cl bk-bds-reprnt of 1629 ed   (5w3,crack)   50.00
--Theatrum Botanicum,The Theater of Plants-Lond-1640-wdcuts-
 sm thk folio-calf-errata lf   (5b0,repaired) 350.00
PARKINSON,THOS-Flower Painting Made Eash-Lond-n.d.(c 1770)-
 Robt Sayer-12p text-72 nbrd plts (hand col)-4to-3/4 calf-
 ex rare   (4L7,sl stns) 1,850.00
PARKMAN,REV EBENEZER-The Diary of...ed by H M Forbes-
 1899-Westborough Hist Soc-327p-illus (5p9)   15.00
PARKMAN,FRANCIS-Battle for NoAmer-NY-1948-John Tebbel,ed-
 746p   (5h9)   6.50
--The Book of Roses-Bost-1866-illus-1st ed (5mm2)   17.50
--The Calif & Oregon Trail,Being Sketches of Prairie & Rocky
 Mountain Life-NY-1849-orig wrps-1st ed-1st issue-1st state-
 2 vols-(only known copy in orig wrps)
                         (4n4,lacks bk wrp to Vol 1) 3,750.00

USED BOOK PRICE GUIDE

PARKMAN,FRANCIS (continued)
--The Calif & Oregon Trail-NY-1849-frontis-12mo-cl-
 (2nd prntg?)   (5gg6)   200.00
--Complete Works-Bost-1899-LittleBrown-lg type-8vo-green buck-
 g. lettering on sp-g.t.-12 vols   (5t5)   47.50
--Complete Works-Bost-1910-13 vol-port-maps-3/4 mor-mrbld sides-
 g.dec   (5a1,f)   60.00
--Complete Works-Bost-LittleBrown-16 vols-t8vo-illus,incl
 T Remington-buck-lg type-g.t.-Frontenac ed (5t5,rbnd) 85.00
--Complete Works-Tor-1899-Frontenac ed,nbrd-3/4 green mor-
 plts-16 vols   (4d8,f,f bndg) 85.00
--The Conspiracy of Pontiac-Bost-1899 et seq   -illus-fldg maps-
 g.t.   -Frontenac ed   (5h9)   17.50
--same-Bost-1903-2 vols-frontis-map-Works, New Liby edn,
 10,11   (5r7)   10.00
--same-Bost-1910-2 vols-381p, 484p-illus-maps-maroon cl-g.t.
                                      (5h9)   10.00
--Count Frontenac & New France Under Louis XIV-Bost-1910-
 523p-frontis-maroon cl-g.t.   (5h9)   6.00
--A Half Century of Conflict-Bost-1892-2 vols-12mo-cl-1st ed
                                      (5t0)   5.00
--same-Bost-1892-2 vols-one of 75 lg papr copies (5j3) 50.00
--same-Bost-1910-2 vols-368p, 417p-illus-maps-maroon cl-g.t.
                                      (5h9)   10.00
--same-Bost-1922-2 vols-368p, 416p-frontis-blue buck-labls-
 Centenary ed   (5h9)   8.50
--Historic Handbook of Northern Tour-Bost-1885-180, 12p-12mo-
 illus-pt lea-g.t.-1st ed   (5xx7)   25.00
--same-Bost-1899-illus-180p   (5t4)   10.00
--History of the Conspiracy of Pontiac-Bost-1851-maps-1st ed
                                      (5j3)   65.00
--same-Bost-1863   (5h6,hng crack) 10.00
--Jesuits in NoAmer in the 17th Century-Bost-1902-2 vols-
 280p,309p-illus-maps-g.t.-Frontenac ed (5h9)   15.00
--The Journals of-NY-1947-Wade, ed-2 vols-cl-8vo-illus-maps-
 1st ed   (5w0,5s4) 25.   (5r7,5L7,5h5,f) 17.50
--LaSalle & the Discovery of the Great West-Bost-1910-522p-
 frontis-maps-maroon cl-g.t.   (5h9)   6.00
--Montcalm & Wolfe-Bost-1899-2 vols-t.e.g.-45 plts-Holiday ed
                                      (5r7,f,cl djs) 25.00
--same-Bost-1902-3 vols-illus-maps-g.t.-Frontenac ed (5h9) 23.50
--same-Bost-1910-2 vols-maroon cl-g.t.-illus-maps (5h9) 10.00
--The Old Regime in Canada-Bost-1874-LittleBrown-cl-1st ed
                                      (5ss3,review copy,sp fade) 35.00
--same-Bost-1874-1 of 75 lg papr nbrd copies (5j3) 45.00
--same-Bost-1922-559p-frontis-map-maroon cl-g.t. (5h9) 6.00
--The Oregon Trail-Bost-1872-LittleBrown&Co-381p-orig cl-
 1st issue of revised ed   (5z7,vg) 55.00
--The Oregon Trail-See Calif & Oreg Trail for 1st ed
--same-Bost-1892-411p-illus by Remington (5g1,spot) 28.50
--same-Bost-1902-479p-illus-g.t.-Frontenac ed-deluxe ed (5h9) 7.50
--same-Bost-1906-plts by Remington   (5v0)   5.00
--same-Bost-1925-col plts-ltd ed   (5tt5) 57.50 (5kk5) 18.00
--same-NY-(1931)-illus, Jas Daugherty (5yy6)   5.00
--same-NY-1943-(Ltd Editions Club)-col plts-illus-calf-autg
                                      (4a1,lt rub) 27.50
--same-Heritage Illus Bookshelf (1943)-col illus (4d9,vf,box) 6.00
--same-NY-1945-Heritage Pr-lg8vo-dec cl-illus in tint by Dixton
                                      (5p5)   7.50
--same-NY-1946-col plts by Benton-328p (4b3,vg,dj) 7.50
--same-Literary Guild-illus-ltd ed of 1000c (5xx8) 5.00
--Pioneers of France in the New World-Bost-1902-2 vols-181p,
 311p-illus-maps-Frontenac ed   (5h9)   15.00
--same-Bost-1910-493p-frontis-maps-maroon cl-g.t. (5h9) 6.00
--Prairie & Rocky Mntn Life-NY-1853-8vo-orig cl-448p-2 frontis-
 3rd ed   (5t2,fray) 10.00
--Some of the Reasons Against Woman Suffrage-n.p.-n.d.-16p-
 wrps   (5g8) 5.   (5t7)   2.50
--Vassall Morton-Bost-1856-Phillips, Sampson-414p-1st ed
                                      (5x4,wn) 12.50
--Works of-Bost-1897-20 vols-deluxe ed-3/4 mor-t.e.g.-
 ltd to 300 sets, hand nbrd   (4n4)   250.00
--Works of-Bost-1898-Little Brown-12 vols-New Library ed-
 illus-maps-green cl-g.t.   (5h9)   48.50
--Works-Bost-1899-Frontenac Edition-blue cl-ports-illus-labls-
 maps-16 vols   (5s0)   65.00
--Works-Bost-1916 to 18-illus-maps-cl-12 vols (5nn2) 40.00
PARKS AIR NEWS-(E StL, Ill)-folio illus monthly publ of Parks Air
 College-complete Aug 1933 to Dec 1947-(Vol 1,#6 to Vol 14,#9)-
 (lacks Dec 1933 & July 1934)-also 2 issues not publ-153 issues
                                      (5dd6)   25.00
PARKS,GEO BRUNER-Richard Hakluyt...& Engl Voyages-NY-1930-
 (Amer Geog Soc)-illus-maps   (5yy6,5ss1) 10.00

PARKS,H B-Fauna & Flora of Big Thicket Area-n.p.-1936-
 51p-wrps   (5h2)   4.00
PARKS,MAL, ed-First Annual Soda Fountain Handbook-NY-1942-
 illus-184p-wrps-management ed   (5w1)   6.50
PARKS,SAML C-Great Trial of the 19th Century-KansasCty,MO-
 1900   (5k2,pres,ex-libr)   5.00
PARKYN,ERNEST A-Intro to study of prehistoric art-Lond-1915-
 Longmans-349p-16 plts-8vo-cl   (5m5)   12.50
PARLEY,PETER-Also See GOODRICH,S G
PARLEY,PETER-Parley's Ancient History & Customs-NY-1836-
 MahlonDay-12mo-31p-wrps-illus-scarce (5v2,vg) 30.00
--Peter Parley's Annual-Xmas & NewYear's Present for Young People-
 Lond-1851-Darton&Co-col frontis-tinted plts-sq4vo-376p-
 dec cl   (5c8,f)   17.50
--Peter Parley's Annual-Lond-1854-Darton&Co-chrom frontis-
 296p   (5c8,shake,crack) 10.00
--Peter Parley's Annual-1880-BenGeorge-sq8vo-dec cl-g.t.-
 312p-col plts   (4d8)   7.50
--Peter Parley's Annual-1886-296p-col plts (4d8) 7.50
--The Balloon Travels, or Robt Merry & His Young Friends-NY-
 1855-illus-scarce 1st ed   (5v0,vg) 20.00
--same-NY-1860-illus   (5v2,f)   15.00
--same-JasBlackwood-(c 1870)-sm8vo-dec cl-plts-242p (4a8) 5.00
--Book of Gymnastics-Lond-SLingham-(ca 1840)-4 plts-16mo-136p-
 orig dec cl-scarce   (5c8,wn) 20.00
--Book of Orinthology for Youth-Bost-1832-322p-lea sp-illus-
 1st ed   (5ee3,vg) 7.50
--Book of Travels & Adventures-NY-1857-thk8vo-plts (4c3,vg) 20.00
--Cabinet Library-Bost-1849-illus-20 vols-dec sp-(not 1st ed)
                                      (4c3,vg) 75.00
--Faggots for the Fireside-NY-1855-1st ed-12 tinted plts-gilt
 & enamel cov design   (4F6,fox,f,f bndg) 50.00
--same-NY-1868-Appleton-8vo-320p-dec cl-plts (5aa0) 7.50
--Heroism of Boyhood-Edinb-(c 1890)-Gall&Inglis-8vo-dec cl-
 g.t.-plts-282p   (4a8)   4.50
--Life of Benj Franklin-Phila-1838-lea&bds-illus-180p (5p6) 9.00
--Life of Siberian Sable Hunter-NY-(c 1870)-Williams-sm8vo-
 dec cl-g.t.-176p-illus-map   (5u6)   5.00
--Parley's Magazine-Bost-1833-Vol 1,#1 to Vol 1 #7-112p
                                      (5ff7,soiled) 12.50
--same-NY&Bost-Jan to Dec 1838-bnd in 1 vol (5rr2,shabby) 6.50
--same-for 1841-NY&Bost-3/4 lea-12 issues (4c3,rub,fox) 7.50
--Method of telling about Geography to Children-NY-n.d.-
 9 maps-75 engrs-sm8vo-120p-full pg maps-sm8vo-prntd yellow
 orig bds-cl bk-Collins&Hannay-cov imprint Hartford, F J
 Huntington   (5L1)   10.00
--Peter Parley's Own Story-NY-1864-illus (5m1)   6.50
--Tales of Peter Parley About Africa-Phila-1842-ThosCowperthwait-
 rev ed-12mo-144p-map   (4F6)   35.00
--Tales of Peter Parley About Europe-Bost-1828-SGGoodrich-
 1st ed-12mo-136p-illus-frontis-cl-v scarce (4F6,rbnd,vg) 150.00
--Peter Parley's Tales About Rome & Modern Italy-Thos Tegg-
 1839-lg sq1mo-dec cl-356p-illus-map-1st ed (4d1) 12.50
--Peter Parley's Tales About Sun, Moon & Stars-Phila-1833-116p-
 prntd bds-engrs   (5y0,chip) 12.50
--Peter Parley's Tales about the US of Amer-Lond-1839-Tegg-
 sq12mo-364p-cl-frontis-illus-4th ed-Chiswick Pr
              (4F6,f) 32.50 (5rr2,f) 12.50 (4b7) 17.50
--Peter Parley's Tales About the Widow's Family-R T Bowyer-
 (c1844)-sq12mo-dec cl-g.t.-188p-frontis (4d1) 7.50
--Travels, Voyages & Adventures of Gilbert Go Ahead in Foreign
 Parts-NY-1856-295p-illus-a.e.g.
              (5ee3,vg) 10. (5w9,wn,rprd) 6.50
--Peter Parley's Winter Tales-Bost-1830-Carter&Hendee-1st ed-
 8 col plts-orig black bds-(contains 1st Amer printing of
 Spider & the Fly   (4F6,f) 100.00
PARLIN,F E-Desc of Nicholas Parlin of Cambridge,Mass-1913-
 289p   (5mm3)   22.50
PARLOA,MARIA-The Aplledore Cook Book-Bost-1878(1872)-234p-
 new ed   (5c0)   7.50
--same-Bost-1884(1881)-new ed-240p & blanks (5c0) 6.50
--Choice Receipts-Dorchester-1893-32p-sm12mo-pict wrps of
 Walter Baker&Co   (5c0)   3.50
--Chocolate & Cocoa Recipes-Mass-1910-Walter Baker&Co-64p-
 col illus-wrps   (5g9)   4.50
--same-1914-64p   (5c0,5g9) 3.50
--Home Economics-NY-1898-378p-illus   (5w7)   6.50
--same-(1906)-416p-new&enlrgd ed   (5w7)   4.50
--Miss Parloa's Kitchen Companion-Bost-(1887)-966p-illus (5c0) 8.50
--Mrs Parloa's New Cook Book-Troy-1883-430p (5w0,wn) 7.50
--Miss Parloa's Young Housekeeper-Bost-1894-405p-illus (5c0) 6.50
--100 Ways to use Liebig Company's Extract of Beef-Lond-(1893)-
 95p-illus-pict wrps-rare   (5g9)   6.50

PARLOUR MAGIC-Lond-1838-Whitehead&Co-g. cl-sm8vo (5c8) 25.00
PARMELEE,M-Principles of Anthropology & Sociology in Their
Relation to Criminal Procedure-NY-1911 (5ff4,rub) 9.75
PARMELEE,MAURICE-Criminology-NY-(1918)-535p (5t4) 4.00
--Nudism in Modern Life-NY-1931-303p-illus (5w4,5x7) 6.00
--Povery & Social Progress-NY-1920-477p (5x7) 6. (5w4) 6.50
PARMENTIER,A A-Nouvel Apercu des resultats obtenus de la
fabrication des sirops & conserves de raisins..l'annee 1812-
Paris-1813-458p-calf bk-4 fldg plts (5w1,split) 22.50
PARMER,CHAS B-For Gold & Glory-NY-(1939)-Carrick&Evans-8vo-
cl-illus-352p (5j5) 7.50
PARMLY,L S-Practical Guide to Management of Teeth-Phila-
1819-16mo-lea-frontis-198p,9p (5t0) 25.00
PARNEL,JAS-Collection of Several Writings-n.p.-1675-
476p (5mm2,rbnd) 35.00
PARODY ON HOUSE THAT JACK BUILT,A-(Nonotuck Silk Co,
Florence&Leeds,Mass,c 1882)-(20)p incl wrps-illus-7th ed,rev-
24mo (5p1) 6.50
PARR,CHAS McKEW-So Noble a Captain-NY-(1953)-Crowell-
8vo-cl-illus-426p (5j5,dj) 7.50
PARR,V V-Ranch Organization & Methods of Livestock Production
in the SW-Wash-1928-Dept of Agri Tech Bul #68-104p-photos-
maps-wrps (5L0) 10.00
PARRAN,ALICE N-Register of Maryland's Heraldic Families 1634 to
1935-Balt-(1935)-404p (5m2) 5.00
--same-1634 to 1935-2 vols-1935 to 38-408p,352p (5t9) 12.50
PARRILLI,GUISEPPE-Vocabulario Militare di Marineria Francese
Italiano-Naples-1846,7-2 vols in 1-4to-qtr calf-8p,526p,(1)-
568p,(2)p (5ss2) 47.50
PARRINGTON,VERNON LOUIS-Main Currents in Amer Thought-
NY-1927 to 30-3 vols (5j2) 25.00
PARRISH,EDW-The Phantom Bouquet-Phila-1863-47p-5 plts (5s7) 10.00
PARRISH,LYDIA-Slave Songs of the Georgia Sea Islands-NY-
1942-Creative Age Pr-dec cl-4to (5ww4) 15.(5x2) 30. (5p5) 25.00
PARRISH,MAXFIELD-Knave of Hearts-NY-1925-Scribners-folio-
col plts-spiral bk-rare (4F6,f) 165.00
PARRISH,PHILIP H-Before the Covered Wagon-Portl-1931-1st ed
(5yy7) 7.50
PARRISH,RANDALL-The Air Pilot-Chig-1913-ACMcClurg&Co-
1st ed-illus in col by C Underwood (5ee3) 7.50
--Beth Norvell-Chig-1907-col frontis,NCWyeth-1st ed (4b4) 10.00
--Bob Hampton of Placer-Chig-1906-McClurg-384p-col illus &
frontis-1st ed (5dd6,ex-libr) 5. (5dd7) 5.00
--The Devil's Own-Chig-1917-McClurg-illus-1st ed (5ee3,vf) 7.50
--Gordon Craig,Soldier of Fortune-Chig-1912-McClurg-col illus-
1st ed (5ee3) 5.00
--The Great Plains-Chig-1907-399p-illus-2nd ed (5t2) 10.00
--same-Chig-1907-1st ed (5dd7) 10.00
--Historic Illinois-Chig-1907-480p-ports-plts-fldg map-3rd ed
(5s6) 6.50
--same-Chig-1905-1st ed-fldg map (5yy7,map tn) 8.50
--The Strange Case of Cavendish-NY-(1918)-1st ed (5ee3,f) 5.00
--When Wilderness Was King-Chig-1904-McClurg-387p-col illus-
1st ed (5b2) 5. (5x4) 7.50
PARRISH,WM E-Turbulent Partnership-Columbia-1963-242p (5j6) 4.50
PARROT,ANDRE-Sumer,the Dawn of Art-NY-1961-Golden Pr-
396p-illus (5x0) 25.00
PARROTT,THOS M-A Companion to Victorian Literature-NY-
(1955)-308p (5m1) 5.00
--Shakesperian Comedy-NY-1949-417p (5w9) 5.00
--Short View of Elizabethan Drama-NY-(1943)-sm8vo-cl-311p-
3 illus (5t0) 4.50
PARRY,ALBERT-Russian Cavalcade-NY-(1944)-334p-illus (5ss6) 6.00
--Whistler's Father-Indnpls-(1939) (5t2) 3.00
PARRY,ANN-Parry of the Arctic-Lond-1963-240p-plts (5a1) 4.50
PARRY,CALEB HILLIER-Cases of Tetanus, & Rabies Contagiosa-
Bath&Lond-1814-orig bds-lg8vo-14 plts-1st ed-218p
(5jj8,sl wn) 195.00
PARRY,E J-The Chemistry of Essential Oils & Artificial Perfumes-
Lond-1899-411p,(16)-illus (5n7) 6.50
--Parry's Cyclopedia of Perfumery-Phila-1925-2 vols-839p (5w3) 20.00
--Raw Materials of Perfumery-Lond-n.d.-12mo-112p,16p-illus
(5w3) 4.50
PARRY,EDW-Memoirs of Rear Adm Sir W Edw Parry-1857
(5ss1,lacks fly) 3.50 (5L7) 6.00
PARRY,EDW A-Scarlet Herring & Other Stories-Smith,Elder-1899-
8vo-253p-dec cl-a.e.g.-plts-1st ed (5aa0,lacks fly) 5.00
PARRY,SIR EDW ABBOTT-The Gospel & the Law-Lond-(1928)-
Heinemann-323p (5p9) 5.00
PARRY,EDWIN S-Betsy Ross-Chig-(1932)-252p-illus (5t4) 5.75
PARRY,ELLWOOD C-Friedrich Schiller in Amer-Phila-1905 (5jj3) 10.00
PARRY,FRANCIS-The Sacred Maya Stone of Mexico &its Symbolism-
Lond-1893-sm folio-8 plts-orig prntd wrps-1st ed (5t2,wrp tn) 8.50

PARRY,J W-The Spice Handbook-Brooklyn-1945-254p-photos-
illus (5w3,5s7) 7.50
PARRY,JOHN,ed-The London collection of glees, duetts &catches-
Lond-n.d.-(c 1820?)-Goulding&Dalmaine-obl 8vo-hf calf-
music wi words-in 4 parts (5i8,calf wn) 40.00
PARRY,JOS HYRUM,publ-The Mormon Metropolis,Guide to Salt
Lake Cty & its Environs-SaltLkCty-1883-44p-photos-removed
from bnd pamphlets-no wrps (5t3) 30.00
PARRY,LEONARD A-Some Famous Medical Trials-NY-1928-
Scribner-326p (5p9) 6.50
PARRY,WM E-Journal for Discovery of NoWest Passage-Lond-
1821-1st ed-3/4 calf-310p-plts-maps (5yy9,sl wn,bkstrp rprd) 100.00
--same-Lond-1821-lg4to-hf calf-310p-20 maps,plans & illus-
2nd ed (5L1,wn) 40.00
--Journal of a Second Voyage for Discovery of a NoWest Passage..
performed in Years 1821,22,23-Lond-1824-maps - plts
(5x2,cov loose,maps rprd) 50.00
--Journal of a Third Voyage of Discovery of a NoWest Passage
1824,5-Phila-1826-map-orig qrtr cl (5r7,map rprd,ex-libr) 35.00
--Parry's Third Voyage for Discovery of NW Passage in Years 1824
& 1825,with account of Esquimaux-Lond-n.d.-232p-16mo-
edited from Parry's 1st ed (5ss1,fly tn) 3.00
PARRY'S CYCLOPEDIA OF PERFUMERY-Phila-1925-2 vols-
839p (5w3) 20.00
PARSONS,ARTHUR-Catalog of the Gardiner Greene Hubbard
Collection of Engravings-Wash-1905-517p (5j4,rub) 20.00
PARSONS,BEATRICE-Gardens of England-Lond-1908-199p-20 col
illus (5s7) 8.50
PARSONS,C E-The Great Adventure,Story of Lafayette Escadrille-
1937-335p-1st ed (5F2) 15.00
PARSONS,C G-Inside View of Slavery,or a Tour Among the
Planters-Bost-1855 (5x2,fox) 28.50
PARSONS,C S M-China Mending & Restoration-Lond-(1963)-
4to-435p-photos (5n7) 15.00
PARSONS,CAROLINE-A Girl's Confessional & other Stories-
Bost-(1899)-1st ed (5ee3) 5.00
PARSONS,CHAS W-1788 to 1868,Memoir of Usher Parsons-Prov-
1870-72p-frontis (5qq8,pres) 7.50
PARSONS,MRS CLEMENT-Garrick & His Circle-Lond-(1906)-
illus (5mm2) 4.50
PARSONS,EDW ALEX-The Wonder & the Glory-NY-1962-4to-cl-
386p (5d3,dj) 12.50
PARSONS,J A-Eli Parsons of Enfield, Conn -1924-128p (5mm3) 10.00
PARSONS,ELSIE CLEWS-The Family-NY-(1912)-414p (5t4) 10.00
--Isleta Paintings, with commentary-ESGoldfrank,ed-1962-4to-
plt (5L7) 10.00
PARSONS,FLOYD W-New Jersey,Life,Industries & Resources of
a Great State-Newark-1928-4to-404p-illus (5m2) 6.00
PARSONS,EUGENE-A guidebook to Colorado-Bost-(1911)-390p-
map-illus-cl-Little,Brown (5d6) 6. (5s4) 7.50
PARSONS,FLORENCE CROSBY-Every Woman's Home Cook Book-
LosAng-(1911)-224p-Chig copyr (5g9) 4.00
PARSONS,FLOYD W-Everybody's Business-GardenCty-1923-503p
(5e4) 4.50
PARSONS,FRANCES THEODORA-According to Season-NY-1902-
197p-32 col plts-new & enlrgd ed (5s7) 6.00
--How to Know the Ferns-NY-1899-frontis-illus-215p (5ee3) 2.50
PARSONS,FRANCIS-The Friendly Club & Other Portraits-Hartf-
1922-EVMitchell-orig bds-illus-1st ed (5m2) 5.00
PARSONS,FRANK-Legal Doctrine & Social Progress-NY-1911-
(5x7,hng crack) 5.00
PARSONS,FRANK A-Interior Decoration,Its Principles & Practice-
NY-1915-284p-many illus (5w7) 3.50
--The Psychology of Dress-NY-1923-lg8vo-cl-358p-illus (5t2) 4.50
PARSONS,GEOFFREY-The Stream of History-NY-(1930)-4 vols-
illus (5t4) 10.00
PARSONS,HENRY S-Check List of Amer 18th Century Newspapers in
Libr of Congr-Wash-1936-401p (5n4) 12.50
PARSONS,HERBERT COLLINS-A Puritan Outpost-NY-1937-8vo-
illus-1st ed (5ss5) 7.50
PARSONS,HORATIO A-Book of Niagara Falls-Buffalo(Steele)-1836-
24mo-fldg map-fldg map (5g8) 7.50
--same-Buffalo-1838-Steele&Peck-12mo-orig cl-pattrnd-112p-
fldg map-5 plts-5th ed (5cc6,f) 12.50
PARSONS,JAS-Philosophical observations on analogy between
propogation of animals & that of vegetables-Lond-1752-for
CDavis-8vo-calf-fldg plt-1st ed (5x3,f) 40.00
PARSONS,JOHN E-The First Winchester-NY-1955-photos-200p-
Remington illus-1st ed (5yy7,dj) 10. (5jj7,mint,dj) 7.50
--Peacemaker & Its Rivals-NY-(1953)-illus-(not 1st) (5jj7) 6.00
PARSONS,KANSAS-The Wonder of the Great SoWest-Parsons
(prntd at Chig)-1887-12 panel fldr-illus-map of Kansas on
reverse-Parsons Board of Trade-v scarce (5t3) 20.00

PARSONS,KATHERINE B-History of 50 Yrs Ladies Literary Club, 1877 to 1927-SaltLkCty-1927-Arrow Pr Inc-cl-12mo-168p
(4t1,pres) 12.50

PARSONS,LEWIS B-Genealogy of the Family of...Parsons Hoar-StL-(1900)-Perrin&Smith Print-109p-8vo-wrps
(4t1) 12.50 (5mm3) 6.00

PARSONS,M A D-Anc of Nathan Dane Dodge & wife Sarah (Shepherd)-1896-76p (5t9) 5.00

PARSONS,MARION RANDALL-Old Calif Houses-Univ of Calif-1952-8vo-cl-143p-ports (5h5) 5. (5h5,pres,f) 6.50

PARSONS,MARY ELIZ-The Wild Flowers of Calif-SanFran-1907-417p-Cunningham,Curtiss&Welch-drawings (5s7,f) 6.00

PARSONS,R H-Early Days of the Power Station Industry-Cambr(Engl)-1939-prntd for Babcock&Wilcox Ltd-217p-plts
(5hh7) 13.50

PARSONS,S-Art of Landscape Architecture-1915-48 illus-347p-8vo
(4a2) 3.50

--Landscape Gardening-NY-(1891)-329p-frontis-illus (5s7) 10.00

--Landscape Gardening Studies-NY-1910-107p-illus-bds
(5s7,chip) 6.00

PARSONS,S B-The Rose,Its History,Poetry,Culture & Classification-NY-1847-4to-illus-hf lea-raised bands-280p (5m4) 30.00

PARSONS,S J,WILFRID-Mexican Martyrdom-NY-1936-Macmillan-304p (5x0) 4.50

PARSONS,SAML-Epistle of the Yearly Meeting of NY 1822-NY-1822-MahlonDay-4to-4p (5t4) 10.50

PARSONS,T-Memoir of Theophilus Parson-Bost-1859 (5r4) 10.00

PARSONS,THEOPHILUS-The Political,Personal & Property Rights of a Citizen of the US-Cinn-1876-744p-calf (5a8) 6.50

--Treatise on Law of Shipping & Law Practice Admiralty-Bost-1869-2 vols-law libr bndg (5s1) 10.00

PARSONS,THOS WM-The First 10 Cantos of Inferno of Dante Alighieri-Bost-1843-newly trans into Engl verse-8vo-orig bds-newly transl into Engl verse-1st ed of auth's 1st book
(5gg6,pres) 50.00

PARSONS,USHER-Address Delivered before Providence Assn for Promotion of Temperance-Prov-1831-16p-wrps (5h7,pres) 10.00

--Life of Sir Wm Pepperrell-Bost-1855-Little,Brown-352p (5qq8) 10.00

--same-Bost-1856-3rd ed-356p-illus-map (5i3,edge wn) 15.00

PARSONS,W D-Decatur Genealogy-1921-55p-only 50c prntd
(5mm3) 17.50

PARSONS,WM BARCLAY-Robert Fulton & The Submarine-NY-1922-Columbia Univ Pr-154p-illus (5s1,sl stns) 11.50 (5qq8,5t0) 12.50

PART,ALEX FRANCIS-Art & Practice of Innkeeping-Lond-1922-308p-frontis (5w1) 8.50 (5g9) 7.50

PARTICULAR ACCOUNT OF BATTLE OF BUNKER,OR BREED'S HILL-by a Citizen of Boston-Bost-1825-8vo-27p-sewn-2nd ed (5ss5) 10.00

PARTIES AND THE MEN,THE-or, Political Issues of 1896-n.p.-(1896)-544p-illus (5t7) 10.00

PARTINGTON,FRED E-The Story of Mohonk-Fulton-(1932)-85p
(5p7) 2.75

PARTISAN,THE-a tale of the Revolution-NY-1835-Harper-12mo-orig purple cl-prntd papr labls-1st ed-(WGSimms)
(5x1,cl v wn) 80.00

PARTNERS ALL-NY-1938-99p-sm folio (5y2) 6.50

PARTON,JAS-Carricature..&Other Comic Art-NY-1877-340(7)p-t.e.g.-203 illus (5w0,cov wn) 20.00

--Eminent Women of the Age-Hartf-1869-8vo-cl-plts-628p(5t0) 20.00

--Famous Americans of Recent Times-Bost-1867-Ticknor&Fields-cl-473p (5tt8) 15.00

--same-Bost-1890-cl-473p-8vo (5t2,ex-libr) 5.00

--Fanny Fern,a Memorial volume-NY-1873-Carleton-8vo-illus-cl
(5b2,lt fray) 7.50

--General Butler in New Orleans-NY-1864-649p-frontis
(5s9,wn) 5. (5mm8,shake) 4. (4j4,fox) 9.50

--same-NY-1864-661p-10th ed (4h1,rbnd) 7.50

--Great Commander, General Jackson-NY-1893-332p-frontis-illus (5g1,vg) 5.00

--History of the Sewing Machine-(Lancaster-1868?)-wrps-22(10)p of Howe Machines-reprnt Atl Monthly (May 1867)
(4h8,wn,lacks bk wrp) 12.50

--Le Parnasse Francais-Bost-1877-HoughtonMiff-8vo-hf calf(5b0) 7.50

--Life & Times of Aaron Burr-NY-1858-706p-orig cl
(5tt8) 15. (5L3,4a5) 10.00

--same-Bost-1880-Houghton,Osgood-2 vols-cl-enlrgd ed (5tt8) 10.00

--same-Bost-1882-HoughtonMiff-2 vols-frontis (5qq8,vf) 10.00

--Life & Times of Benj Franklin-Bost-(1864)-2 vols-3/4 lea (5h7) 10.00

--Life of Andrew Jackson-NY-1861-3 vol (5x5) 20.00

--Life of Horace Greeley-NY-1855-Mason Bros-442p-plts-cl-1st ed of auth's 1st book (5gg6) 10. (4h2) 8.50

--same-NY-1868-cl-598p (4h2) 7.50

--Smoking & Drinking-Bost-1868-Ticknor&Fields-12mo-cl-151p-1st ed (5k0) 5. (5w1,fade) 4.50 (5j5) 10.00

PARTON,SARA PAYSON-Ruth Hall, Domestic Tale-NY-1855-Mason Bros-cl-1st ed (4b4) 10.00

PARTRIDGE,THE-(Fur & Feather Series)-Lond-1893-276p plus ads-illus (5t7) 8.50

PARTRIDGE,BELLAMY-Amundsen,the Splendid Norseman-NY-1929-276p-photos-map e.p. (5ss1,wn) 4.00

PARTRIDGE,BURGO-A History of Orgies-NY-c1960 (5x7) 3.00

PARTRIDGE,C H-Progress of Man,the Spirit of Man Versus Machine-Lindsay,Ont-1943-Wilson&Wilson (5nn8) 5.00

PARTRIDGE,CHAS A-History of 96th Reg Illinois Volunteer Infantry-Chig-1887-8vo-938p (4a7,fray) 35.00

PARTRIDGE,EDW BELLAMY-Sube Cane-Phila-1917-8vo-cl-pic inset in cov (5b2,pres) 7.50

PARTRIDGE,ERIC-A Dictionary of Slang & Unconventional English-NY-1937-Macmillan-lg8vo-cl (5b0) 10.00

--Dictionary of the Underworld British & Amer-Lond-(1950)-sm4to-mor-g.-ltd deluxe ed-1 of 6 pres copies (5j2) 50.00

PARTRIDGE,G E-Studies in the Psychology of Intemperance-NY-1912 (5w1) 8.50

PARTRIDGE,G F-History of Bellingham, Mass-1919-221p (5t9) 10.00

PARTRIDGE,G H-Desc of Geo Partridge of Duxbury,Mass-1915-41p (5t9) 15.00

PARTRIDGE,PAULINE D-Wheatless & Meatless Days-NY-1918-225p (5g9) 5.00

PATRIOTS OF THE REVOLUTION OF '76-Bost-1864-8vo-20p-orig wrps-1st ed (5ss5) 5.00

PASADENA-Beautiful Pasadena Calif-LosAng-c1910-Julius J Hecht-photos-wrps-folio-18 leaves (5kk6) 6.50

PASADENA-Beautiful Pasadena Calif-Pasadena-c1910-Western Publ & Novelty Co-illus-wrps-folio (5kk6) 10.00

PASADENA BOARD OF TRADE-Pasadena,LosAng Co,Calif in 1900-n.p.-(1900)-Jackson Prntg Co-40p-16mo-wrps (4t1,libr stmp) 10.00

PASADENA CHILDREN'S TRAINING SOC-Tried Receipts of Pasadena-Pasadena-(1914)-ads-112p (4g9,dedic c) 8.50

PASADENA,LAND OF FLOWERS-Midwinter Photos by Hill-NY-1894-A Wittemann-18 lvs-photogravures-wrps (4a5,wrps) 19.50

PASADENA PREFERS RECIPES-Pasadena-1964-Jr League-illus-bds-spiral bnd-240p (4g9) 4.50

PASCAL-Thoughts on Religion & Other Subjects-Lond-1704-392p-lea (5p0) 7.50

PASCALIS-OUVIERE,TELIX-An Account of the Contagious Epidemic Yellow Fiver which Prevailed in Phila in Summer & Autumn of 1797-Phila-1798-8vo-180p (5r5) 45.00

PASCHALL,EDWIN-Old Times,or Tennessee History for Boys & Girls-Nashville-1869-sm12mo-scarce (5h6,cov stnd) 27.50

PASCOE,JOHN-Unclimbed New Zealand-Lond-(1939)-328p-illus-maps-cl-GeoAllen&Unwin (5d7) 7.50

PASHA,HOBART-Sketches from my Life-Lond-1886-cl (5q8) 5.00

PASKMAN,D-Gentlemen Be Seated-NY-1928-4to-illus-1st ed
(5x2,f,dj) 32.50

PASLEY,C W-Observations on Limes,Calcareous Cements,Mortars, Stuccos & Concrete-Lond-1838-288p, 124p-illus (5b8) 10.00

PASLEY,ADM SIR THOS-Private Sea Journals 1778 to 1782-Lond-1931-Dent (5p9) 12.50

PASLEY,VIRGINIA-The Christmas Cookie Book-Bost-1949-146p-illus-1st ed (5c5,5g9) 3.50

PASO ROBLES HOT SPRINGS-Paso Robles,Calif-(n.p.-n.d.)-(ca 1905?)-pict wrps-illus (5r0) 7.50

PASS,CRISPIN VAN DER-Hortus Floridus, 1st & 2nd Books-Lond-1928 to 29-Cresset Pr-plts-2 vols-obl 4to-mor bkd mrbld bds-500c prntd (5z9,f,dj) 40.00

PASSAGE OF THE ISTHMUS-or practical hints to persons about to cross the Isthmus of Panama-NY-1849-(Carrington)-14p, (2)-fldg map-disbnd (5g3) 175.00

PASSAGES FROM DIARY OF A LATE PHYSICIAN-Lond-1832-2 vols-16mo-calf-1st Engl ed-(Sam'l Warren) (5gg6) 37.50

PASSANO,E P-Index of Source Records of Maryland-1940-478p-scarce (5t9) 25.00

PASSION FLOWERS-Bost-1854-12mo-orig red cl-g.bk-1st ed of Mrs Howe's 1st book (5gg6) 15.00

PASSFIELD,SIDNEY-English Poor Law History by Sidney & Beatrice Webb-Lond-1929-2 vols (5ff4) 15.00

PASTERNAK,BORIS-Doctor Zhizago-NY-(1959)-illus-1st Amer ed
(5yy6,f,box) 8.50

--The Last Summer-Lond-(1959)-1st ed (5r9,dj) 10.00

PASTIME OF LEARNING,THE-with sketches of rural scenes-Bost-1831-Cottons&Barnard-260p-4 hand col plts-cl bk bds-John Cotton,prntr (5p1) 100.00

PASTON,GEO-"To Lord Byron" Feminine profiles based upon unpublished letters 1807 to 1824-Lond-(1939)-275p-illus-1st ed (5p6) 12.00

PATCH,JOS D-Reminis of Fort Huachuca,Ariz-n.p.n.d.-21p-maps-photos-8vo-prntd wrps-priv prntd-(200c prntd) (5g0,f,autg) 10.00

PATCHEN,KENNETH-Patchen's 1st Will & Testament-Padell,NY-
1948   (5ss9,f,dj)   10.00
--Memoirs of a Shy Pornographer-New Directions-(1945)-1st ed
    (5ss9,dj,autg)   20.00
--Pictures of Life & of Death-(NY Padell)-(1946)-8vo-wrps(5b2) 12.50
--Red Wine & Yellow Hair-New Directions-(1949)-1st ed
        (5ss9,vg) 7.50   (5ss9,f,dj)   12.50
--The Teeth of the Lion-New Directions-(1942)-orig wrps-1st ed
      (5ss9,dj,vg)   12.50
PATE,McCALL,ed-Naval Artificer's Manual-Annap-1918-797p-
illus-g.stmpd cov   (5s1)   6.00
PATENT FOR PLYMOUTH IN NEW ENGLAND,A-To which is
annexd extracts from records of that colony etc-Bost-1751-
JnDraper-sm4to-disbnd-1st ed-v scarce (5i0,mor box) 300.00
PATENT OFFICE SOCIETY-Journal,Vol 16 thru 51-1934 to 1969-
bound   (5ii7,lack Vol 21,#2,5) 495.00
PATENTS FOR INVENTIONS-Abridgements of Spec Relating to
Unfermented Beverages-Lond-1877-134p,26p-wrps(5w1,chip) 5.00
PATER ERRA-Book of Knowledge,Treating of the Wisdom of the
Ancients in 4 Parts-Glasgow-1786-16mo-wdcuts-bds-calf bk
    (5ss5)   12.50
PATER,WALTER-Appreciations with an essay on style-Lond-1889-
Macmillan-cl-1st ed   (5ss3,cov soil)   10.00
--Essays from the Guardian-Lond-1896-12mo-bds-for priv circulation-
Chiswick Pr-1 of 100c   (5ss3,cov soil)   35.00
--Gaston De Latour-Lond-1896-Macmillan-cl-1st ed
    (5ss3,sp def)   15.00
--Marius the Epicurean His Sensations & Ideas-Lond-1885-Macmillan-
8vo-orig cl-2 vols-1st ed   (5ss3,sp def) 50.   (5d3) 37.50
--Marriage of Cupid & Psyche-retold-NY-(1951)-Heritage Pr-
64p-illus   (5t4,box)   4.50
--Plato & Platoism-Series of Lectures-Lond-8vo-cl-283p(5t0) 5.00
--same-NY-1893-Macmillan-cl-1st Amer ed-ltd to 100c (5ss3) 25.00
--The Renaissance-1902-Mesher Pr-248p-ltd to 450c
    1(5m5,5k0,soil,5kk7)   10.00
--Studies in the History of the Renaissance-Lond-1873-12mo-cl-
1st ed of auth's 1st book (5ss3) 50. (5r9) 20. (5gg6,f) 25.00
PATERSON,A MELVILLE-Duval's Artistic Anatomy-Lond-1907-
348p-illus   (5w4)   5.00
PATERSON,GILBERT-Story of Our People-Tor-1936-illus-180p
    (5dd7,ex-libr)   3.00
PATERSON,M-Mountaineering below the snow line-Lond-1886-
GeoRedway-307p-cl   (5d7)   7.50
PATHFINDER,THE-or the Inland Sea-by auth of The Pioneers-Phila-
1840-Lea&Blanchard-2 vols-orig purple cl-labls-1st ed, 1st state-
(Vol 1 has no copyright notice & page (2) of Vol 1 is unpgd,
imprnt of Fagan & Collins near bottom outer edge copyright pg)-
(JFCooper) (5x1,labls wn) 150. (5z7,lt rub,box) 250.00
--same-Phila-1843-2 vols in 1-bds&lea   (5t2)   5.00
PATHFINDERS OF THE WEST-NY-1923-(c1904)-dec cl-many illus-
(Remington & others)   (5m9)   7.00
PATHWAY OF PROGRESS-Prov-1957-81p-illus (4b8)   5.00
PATMAN,WRIGHT-Complete Guide to the Robinson Patman Act-
PrenticeHall-1963-401p   (5p0)   11.00
PATMORE,COVENTRY,ed-Children's Garland from Best Poets-1862-
Macm-12mo-dec cl-1st ed   (4d4,f)   12.50
PATMORE,DEREK-Life & Times of Coventry Patmore-NY-(1949)-
8vo-cl-col frontis-8 illus-250p-1st ed   (5t0,f,dj)   4.75
PATNA LAW JOURNAL-Vol 1 thru 6-1916 to 1921(all publ)-bound
    (5ii7,rebnd)   97.50
PATON,HENRY-Gen of Symington Family-Edinb-1908-55p (5t9) 10.00
PATON,REV JAS-The Story of John G Paton-NY-1892-397p-illus-
Armstrong   (5p7)   4.00
PATON,JOHN G-John G Paton,Missionary to the New Hebrides-
Lond-1890-2nd Part-382p-Hodder&Stoughton (5x9)   4.50
PATON,WM A-Down the Islands,voyage to the Caribbees-1887
    (5L7)   9.50
PATRICK,DAVID-Chambers's Biographical Dictionary-Lond-c1900-
1,006p   (5yy1)   8.50
PATRICK,H R-The Ancient Canal Systems & Pueblos of the Salt River
Valley,Ariz-Phoenix-1903-(Bul #1 Phoenix Free Mus)-12p-
photos-fldg map-wrps-scarce   (5t3)   17.50
PATRICK,SIMON-The parable of the pilgrim,written to a friend-
Lond-RobtWhite-1678-sm thk4to-calf-5th ed (5xx6,hng wn) 40.00
PATRIGEON,DR GABRIEL-Le Mildiou(Peronosporta Viticola)-Paris-
1887-215p-4 col plts-hf cl   (5w1,brown)   9.50
PATRIOT'S MANUAL,THE-Utica,NY-1828-by Hopkins-220p-
lea-WmWilliams-1st ed   (5h9,crack)   8.50
PATRIOTIC FOOD SHOW-Official Recipe Book-StL-Feb 2 to 10,
1918-48p-wrps-8vo   (5g9)   4.00
PATRONIO,COUNT LUCANOR-or the 50 Pleasant Stories-Lond-
1899-246p-Gibbings-transl by JasYork (5p7)   10.00

PATTANGALL,WM R-The Meddybemps Letters-(Lewiston)-1924-
illus   (5r7)   7.50
PATTEE,FRED L-Development of the Amer short story-NY&Lond-
1923-388p   (5t7)   4.50
--A History of Amer Literature since 1870-NY-(1915)-449p (5t4) 5.00
--The New Amer Literature 1890 to 1930-NY-Century-1930-507p
    (5p0) 5.   (5p6,pres)   7.00
PATTEE,W S-Hist of Old Braintree & Quincy with Sketch of
Randolph & Holbrook-1878-660p   (5t9)   20.00
PATTEN,MRS FRANCIS J-Our New England Family Recipes-
(NY-1910)-134p-ltd to 500c-bds-nbrd   (5c4,wn)   5.00
PATTEN,GEO-Patten's Infantry Tactics & Bayonet Exercise-NY-
1861-JWFortune-149p-orig blue prntd wrps-illus-3rd ed
    (5m3,f)   20.00
--same-NY-1865-illus-16mo-stiff wrps-156p,(4) (5g8,libr labl) 15.00
PATTEN,MATTHEW-Diary of,of Bedford 1754 to 1788-1903-545p
    (5t9)   15.00
PATTEN,SIMON N-Consumption of Wealth-1889-79p-sewn(5L7) 2.50
--The Development of Engl Thought-NY-1899-8vo-cl-415p
    (5t2,lacks flys)   5.00
PATTEN,WM,ed-Book of Sport-NY-1901-lg4to-orig bds&cl-
12p,411p-1st ed   (5t0)   20.00
PATTERSON,A W-History of the Backwoods,or,Region of the Ohio-
Pittsburgh-1843-by the author-8vo-orig blind stmpd cl-
fldg map-1st ed   (5n9,rbkd,box) 285.00
PATTERSON,C L-Wilson County,Diversified Farming Center of SW
Texas-SanAnt-1939-32p-wrps   (5n4)   7.50
PATTERSON,CHAS-Address at Opening of 12th Exhibition of Amer
Academy of Fine Arts-NY-1826-46p   (5t2)   7.50
PATTERSON,CHAS H-Moral Standards-NY-Ronald Pr-1949-
514p   (5p0)   5.00
PATTERSON,GILES J-Journal of a Southern Student 1846 to 48 with
Letters of a Later Period-Nashville-1944-VU Pr (5h6)   8.00
PATTERSON,HAYWOOD-Scottsboro Boy-Lond-1950-1st Engl ed
    (5q8)   5.00
PATTERSON,J B-Autobiogr of Makataime,etc,or Black Hawk-
Oquawka,III-1882-208p-illus   (5L0,wn)   8.50
--same-n.p.(StL0-n.d. (1882)-Continental Prntg Co-orig cl-
3 plts   (5i0)   15.00
--Black Hawk's Autobiog Thru Interpretation of Antoine LeClaire-
RockIsl-1912-164p-cl   (5h7)   10.00
--Life of Ma Ka Tai Me She Kia Kiak or Black Hawk...dictated
by Himself-Bost-1834-port-orig bds-lin sp-labl-155p-
(orig ed was 1833)   (4m2)   45.00
--same-Bost-1834-155p-orig cl-papr labl-port of Black Hawk-
Russell imprnt   (5m3,sp split)   27.50
--Life of Black Hawk-Chig-1916-Lakeside Pr-illus-196p (5ee3,f) 10.00
PATTERSON,J H-In the Grip of Nyika-NY-1909-8vo-389p-photos-
1st ed   (4a6,sl wn)   10.00
--Man Eaters of Tsavo & Other East African Adventures-Lond-1911-
Macmillan-346p-photos   (4t5)   6.00
--same-Lond-1921-12mo-cl-350p-illus   (5t0)   5.00
--same-Lond-1926-8vo-351p-photos   (4a6)   6.50
PATTERSON,J T-The Drosophilidae of the SoWest-Austin-1943-
(Univ of Texas Pub #4313)-4to-cl-327p-illus (5h4,pres) 8.50
PATTERSON,J T-What Next?or The Honest Thief-(Lexington,Ky-
1899)-8vo-1st ed   (4m8,lacks fly,soil)   17.50
PATTERSON,JEAN RUSHMORE-Letter to Anne Lindbergh-NY-
1940-Lenox Hill Pr-17p   (5p7)   4.00
PATTERSON,MARJORIE-Fortunata-NY-1911-Harper-8vo-pic cl-
    (5b2,f)   4.00
PATTERSON,R M-The Buffalo Head-NY-1961-illus-1st ed
    (5tt5,f,dj)   5.00
--Dangerous River-NY-1954-314p-plts (5aa0) 5. (5t4) 4.50
PATTERSON,ROBT-Sage Grouse in Wyoming-Denv-1952-illus-
341p-o.p.   (5ss8,dj)   7.50
PATTERSON,SAML-Narr of Adventures & Sufferings of-Palmer(Mass)-
1817-8vo-orig sheep-1st ed   (5n9,rub) 185.00
--same-Fairfield,1967-144p-priv Pr-reprnt-ltd to 481c,nbrd(5w0) 5.00
PATTERSON,THOS L-Report of...in Relation to Bituminous Coal
Field near Oakland-Balt-(1857)-orig wrps-14p,(2)
    (5y2,ex-libr)   7.75
PATTIANI,EVELYN C-Queen of the Hills,Story of Piedmont,A Calif
City-Fresno-1954-Academy Libr Guild-179p-12mo-cl (4t1) 17.50
PATTIE,JAS O-Personal Narr of....during an Exped From St Louis,
Through Vast Regions Betw That Place & Pac Ocean-Cinn-1833
orig sheep-1st ed-1st state of text-p251 misnumbered 151-
2nd state of t.p.-300p-5 plts   (4n4,wn) 850.00
--same-Early Western Travels,Vol 18-Thwaites,ed-Cleve-1905-
illus-scarce   (5jj1,chip)   20.00
--same-Chig-1930-(Lakeside Classic)-428p-illus-g.t.-12mo(5h9)13.50
PATTISON,MARY-Principles of Domestic Engineering-Colonia,NJ-
(1915)-310p,(6)-frontis   (5w7,scuff)   3.50

PATTON,CORNELIUS H-The Lure of Africa-NY-1917-205p-
2 fldg maps-Missionary Edu Movmnt of US (4t5) 6.50
PATTON,FRANCES-Home & School Sewing-NY-(1901)-234p-
illus-Teacher ed (5n7) 2.50
PATTON,FRANCES GRAY-Good Morning,Miss Dove-NY-c1945-
Dodd Mead-218p-illus-Book club ed (5p1,fray,dj) 2.50
PATTON,GEO S,JR-War As I Knew It-Bost-1947-frontis-425p-
maps-1st ed (5w5,dj) 4.00
PATTON,JACOB H-Political Parties in the US,Their History &
Influence-NY-1902 (5m2) 6.50
PATTON,JOHN S-Monticello & Its Master-Charlottesville-1925-
78p-illus (5p0) 4.00
PATTON,JULIA-The English Village,a Literary Study-NY-1919-
12mo-bds-236p-1st ed (5t0) 5.00
PATTON,LEROY T-Geology of Potter County-Austin-1923-180p-
lg fldg map-wrps (4a5) 6.00
PATTULLO,GEO-Tight Lines-NY-(1938)-4to-cl-illus in tint-
1st ed-ltd to 300c,nbrd (5p5,pres) 25.00
--The Untamed, Range Life in the SW-NY-(1911)-illus (4b6) 7.50
PATTY PARSONS & THE PLUM CAKE-Phila-Amer Sunday School
Union-24mo-16p-wrps (5p1,wn) 4.00
PATTY'S PERVERSITIES-Bost-1881-12mo-wrps-Round Robin Series-
Arlo Bates's 1st book-later binding (of 1st ed?) (5gg6) 15.00
PAUL,ARTHUR G,ed-Riverside Community Book-Riverside-1954-
ArthurHCawston-496p-4to-cl (4t1) 35.00
PAUL,E J-Anc of Katharine Choate Paul,now Mrs Wm J Young,Jr-
1914-386p (5mm3) 8.50
PAUL,ELLIOT-Concert Pitch-(1938)-Random Hse (5F1,fray,dj) 4.00
--Ghost Town on Yellowstone-NY-(1948)-341p
(5yy7,f,dj) 5. (4b6) 6.00
--A Horse in Arizona-1936-Dblday (5F1,f,dj) 3.50
--Indelible,a Story of Life,Love & Music in 5 Movements-Bost-1922-
12mo-cl-1st ed of auth's 1st book (5gg6,editor pres) 10.00
--Intoxication Made Easy-NY-(1941)-145p,(3)-drawngs (5w1) 6.50
--The Life & Death of a Spanish Town-NY-c1937-427p (5w9,dj) 3.50
--The Pumpkin Coach-1935-Dblday-auth's 1st novel (5F1,mint) 5.00
PAUL,J H-Forest Groves & Canyon Streams-SaltLk-1913-228p-
photos (5s4,fair) 4.00
PAUL,J HARLAND-The Last Cruise of the Carnegie-Balt-1932-
198 photos (5c1) 10.50
PAUL,RODMAN W-California Gold-Cambr-1947-Harvard-illus-
380p-1st ed-cl (4n1,dj,5F5,f,dj wn) 15. (5dd6) 14. (5jj3) 12.50
--The Calif Gold Discovery-Georgetown,Calif-1965-250p-illus-
maps & index-ltd to 50c,in slipcase as issued (5t1) 75.00
PAUL,MRS SARA T-Cookery from Experience-Phila-(1875)-338p
(5c0) 7.50
--The Economical Cook Book-n.p.-(1905)-338p-illus-oilcloth cov
(5g9,hng loose) 3.50
PAULDING,DECATUR-The Brigantine-NY-(1864)-100p-wrps-
Beadle's New Dime Novels #484 (5h2) 10.00
PAULDING,JAS KIRKE-The backwoodsman,a poem-Phila-1818-
JMaxwell-12mo-orig bds-1st ed-rare 1st issue with Q4 & Q5
still present (5i9,box,cov loose) 100.00
--The Bulls & the Jonathans-NY-1867-WmlPaulding,ed-1st ed
(5r9,f,pres) 20.00
--Life of Washington-1848 (5L7,sl stn) 6.50
--Puritan & His Daughter-NY-1849-Baker&Scribner imp on sp-
hf lea-2 vols in 1-1st ed
(5ee3,cor ragged) 12.50 (5x4,rbnd) 25. (4g2) 35.00
--Reports Made by Board of Navy Officers on Colt's Improved
Repeating Fire Arms-Wash-1841-SD196-18p (5n4) 8.50
PAULDING,WM I-Literary Life of Jas K Paulding-NY-1867-port-
1st ed (5mm1) 12.50
PAULL,E M-Paull Irwin,Family Sketch-1936-268p (5t9) 15.00
PAULL,H B-The Cat Picture Book-Routledge-(c1872)-illus-lg sq8vo-
dec cl-96p-illus-plts (4d1) 10.00
PAULL,MRS H B,transl-Swiss Family Robinson-Phila-n.d.-
MacraeSmithCo-(Wash Sq Classics)-sq8vo-pict blue cl-569p-
7 col plts-g.t. (5aa2) 5.00
PAULL,M A-Vermont Hall,or Light Through the Darkness-NY-
Amer Tract Soc Fund-n.d.-402p-illus (5e8) 8.57
PAULL,MARY ANNA-Thistledown Lodge-Lond-1882-Hurst&Blackett-
3 vols-8vo-orig dec cl-1st ed (5xx6,wn,lend libr,crack) 17.50
PAULLIN,CHAS O-Atlas of Historical Geography of US-1932-
Carnegie Inst & Amer Geogr Soc-cl-166 plts-sm folio-cl
(5tt8) 75.00
--Commodore John Rogers-Cleve-1910-ArthurHClarkCo-434p-illus-
t.e.g.-cl (5mm8) 15.00
--Out Letters of Continental Marine Committee etc-NY-1914-
Naval Hist Soc-bds-vel bk-2 vols-illus-g.t.-ltd to 500c
(5qq8,mint) 12.50 (5L7,ex-libr,soil,4c1,boxes) 15.00
PAULMIER,HILAH,comp-Abe Lincoln-NY-1953-illus-1st ed
(5yy6,dj) 4.50 (5t7) 5.50

PAULSEN,FRIEDRICH-Introduction to Philosophy-NY-1898-
Holt-437p (5p7) 6.50
--A System of Ethics-NY-(1899)-Scribner-723p (5L7) 4.50 (5p0) 7.50
PAVLENKO,PIOTR-Red Planes Fly East-NY-(1938)-523p (5ss6) 6.00
PAVILLONS DES PUISSANCES MARITIMES EN 1819-n.p.-n.d.-
(1819)-obl 4to-bds-title-tabl of cont-50 lithog hand col plts-
(extra plts added) (5ss2) 165.00
PAXON,HENRY D-Sketch & Map of a Trip from Phila to Tinicum
Island, Delaware Co,Pa-Phila-1926-maps-many illus (5m2) 7.50
PAXSON,E S,illus-Henry Alfred,By Order of the Prophet,a Tale
of Utah-NY-1902-8vo-pict cl-402p-plts-1st ed-scarce (5g0) 8.50
PAXSON,F L-Independence of SoAmer Republics-1903 (5L7) 6.50
PAXSON,FREDERIC L-Amer Democracy & World War Postwar Years
Normalcy-Berkeley-1948-Univ of Calif Pr-401p (5qq8) 5.00
PAXSON,FREDERIC L-History of the Amer Frontier,1763 to 1893-
1924-HoughtonMiff-1st ed (5yy8) 14.50 (5x5) 15. (4m2) 17.50
--same-Bost-(1924)-Student's ed-598p-maps (5s4) 12.50
--Last Amer Frontier-NY-1924-402p (4a5) 3.00
--The New Nation-Bost-(1915)-HoughtonMiff (5p9) 4.00
PAXTON,A G-Vicksburg Campaign-n.p.-n.d.-17p-wrps (5ff7) 5.00
PAXTON,ALEX S-Memory Days-NY&Wash-1908-cl-287p
(4p2,dj) 10.00
PAXTON,ANNABEL-Washington Doorways-Richmond-1949-
illus-1st ed (5F0) 3.00
PAXTON,JOHN A-Phila Directory & Register for 1813-Phila-(1813)-
hf lea (5m4,f bndg) 40.00
PAXTON,SIR JOS-The Works of,1803 to 1865-by Chadwick-Lond-
(1961)-275p-phots-plans (5w3) 7.00
PAXTON,PHILIP -A Stray Yankee in Texas-NY-1853-Redfield-
frontis-1st ed-violet cl (5i9,fade) 25.00
--same-NY-1854-416p (4a5,rprd) 17.50
PAXTON,W M-Poems-KansasCty,MO-1887-1st ed-454p (5L0) 7.50
PAYEN & CHAPPELET-Art de Fabriquer Toute Espece de Bieres-
Paris-1844-119p,70p-prntd wrps-12mo (5w6,lacks illus) 7.00
PAYERAS,MARIANO,comp-Informe de la Confessiones,y
Communiones en Complimiento de la Iglesia-1818-1p (5d6) 100.00
PAYETTE,B C-The Northwest-Montr-1964-732p-photos-maps, 1 fldg-
priv prntd (5L0) 7.50
--The Oregon Country under the Union Jack-Montr-1962-682p-
priv prntd-postscript ed (5u3) 6.50
PAYNE,BRIGHAM-The Story of Bacchus,& Centennial Souvenir-
Hartf-1876-8vo-illus-1st ed (5ss5) 5.00
PAYNE,C HARMAN-The Florist's Bibliography-Lond-1908-80p-wrps
(5w3) 4.50
PAYNE,EDW B-The Soul of Jack London-Kingsport-1933-8vo-cl-
136p-illus (5t2,dj,f) 4.50
PAYNE,EDW F-Dickens Days in Boston-Bost-1927-1st ed-plts-ports-
275p (4a8) 15.00
--same-Bost-1927-8vo-orig bds-illus-cl bk-box-ltd to 150c,autg
(5m6,mint,box tn) 15.00
PAYNE,EDW J-History of New World Called America-Oxf-1892-
2 vols (5x5) 20.00
--Voyages of Elizabethan Seamen-Oxf-1936-12mo-415p (5h9,f) 6.50
PAYNE,EDW W-The Immortal Stone Age-Chig-(1938)-95p-photos
(5L0) 8.50
--Photographs of Interesting & Outstanding Specimens of Indian
Relics from the...Stone Age Collection-(Springfield,1937)-
obl 4to-156p (5hh4) 20.00
PAYNE'S,F M-Business Letter Writer-NY-(1894)-212p,(4)-bds-
cl sp (5w7,brown) 3.50
PAYNE,GEO HENRY-England, Her Treatment of Amer-NY-(1931)-
illus (5q8) 5.00
PAYNE,HENRY M-The Undeveloped Resources of the South-Wash-
1928 (5h6,sl stnd) 8. (5x2) 10.00
PAYNE,J W H-The unfortunate lovers,or,the affecting history of
Selim & Almena-NY-1823-Borradaile-8vo-orig prntd wrps
(5i0,soil) 65.00
PAYNE,JOHN HOWARD-Chas the Second,or,the merry monarch-A
comedy in 3 acts-Lond-1824-Longman,etc-8vo-disbnd-1st ed
(5i0) 75.00
--Clari,or,the maid of Milan,an opera,in 3 acts-Lond-1823-
JnMiller-8vo-disbnd-1st ed (5i0) 250.00
--Home Sweet Home-Bost-1882-plts by Miss L B Humphrey
(4F6,vf) 12.50
PAYNE,LEONIDAS W-When the Woods Were Burnt-Austin-1946-
Hertzog-11p-pamphlet (4a5) 15.00
PAYNE,PETER LESTER-The Savings Bank of Baltimore,1818 to 1866-
Balt-1956-188p-fldg bds (5hh6) 4.50
PAYNE,ROBT-The Canal Builders-NY-1949-278p-illus (5h8) 5.00
--The Chieftain-NY-(1953)-312p-scarce (4b2,dj,mint) 6.50
--Forever China-NY-c1945 (5x7) 5.00
PAYNE,THEODORE-Life on the Modjeska Ranch in the Gay Nineties-
(LosAng,Kruckeberg Pr)-1962-101p-illus (5r0,dj,pres) 7.50

PAYNE,W H-Afro Americans & the Race Problem-KansasCty-
1920-12mo-Burton Publ Co   (5x2)   30.00
PAYNE,WILL-On Fortune's Road-Chig-1902-McClurg-8vo-pic cl-
Fogarty drawings   (5b2)   4.00
PAYNE GALLWAY,SIR RALPH F-High Pheasants in Theory &
Practice-NY,Bombay&Calcutta-1913-4to-bds-79p (5q0)   10.00
PAYNTER,J H-50 Years After-NY-1940-illus   (5x2)   15.00
--Horse & Buggy Days with Uncle Sam-NY-1943-illus (5x2,dj) 10.00
--Joining the Navy-Hartf-1895-illus   (5x2)   35.00
PAYOT,J-Education of the Will-1914-5th Amer ed   (5L7)   4.50
PAYSON,J W-The Payson,Dunton & Scribner Manual of Penmanship-
NY-c1873-Ainsworth-106p plus 13p of litho alphabets & 5 plts
                                                 (5p1)   8.50
PAYSON,WM FARQUHAR-Mahogany,Antique & Modern-NY-
(1926)-illus-4to   (5m5) 30. (4m7)   15.00
PAYSON,WM FARQUHAR-The Title Mongers-NY-1898-Dodd,Mead-
333p-1st ed   (5x4)   7.50
PAZ,M-Hermano Negro-test in Spanish-Madrid-1931-12mo-211p-
wrps-1st ed   (5x2)   12.50
PAZOS,VICENTE-Letters on United Provinces of SoAmer-NY&Lond-
Seymour Miller-8vo-bds&calf-fldg col map(4a3,cov spot,rub)90.00
P E O COOK BOOK-Chapter "M",Knoxville,Iowa-Knoxville-1908-
175p-25 views-Souvenir ed   (4g9,soil) 10.00
PEABODY,ANDREW P-Harvard Reminiscences-Bost-1888-216p
                              (5e8) 4. (5u3)   3.00
PEABODY,C-Exploration of Mounds-Coahoma Co,Miss-1904-sewn
                                                 (5L7)   3.00
PEABODY,CECIL-Naval Architecture-NY-1907-616p-illus
                                          (5s1,fair)   6.00
--Propellers-NY-1912-132p-diagrams-1st ed   (5s1)   6.00
PEABODY,EPHRAIM-Wilton,NHamp,Address at Centennial
Celebration-1839-103p   (5t9)   4.00
PEABODY,FRANCIS G-Education for Life-NY-1919-R8vo-illus
                                                 (5x2)   37.50
--same-1922 edition   (5x2)   27.50
--same-NY-1926-Dblday,Page-orig cl (5x5,bkstrp stnd) 15.00
PEABODY,FRED W-Complete Expose of Eddyism or Christian Science-
Bost-1901-68p   (5xx8,lacks bk wrp)   10.00
--The Religio medical Masquerade-NY-(1915)-Revell-12mo-cl-
197p   (5j5)   6.00
PEABODY,GEO-Family Gatherings Relating to Smith & Blanchard
Families-1929-170p   (5t9)   10.00
PEABODY,GEO AUGUSTUS-South Amer Journals 1858,1859-Salem-
1937-Peabody Muse-R8vo-bds&cl-g.t.-fldg map-4 ports-
ltd to 581c   (4a3,box)   25.00
PEABODY,HENRIETTA C-Homemakers' Questions & Answers-Bost-
(1918)-133p-12mo-illus   (5w7)   4.50
PEABODY,HENRY G-Glimpses of the Grand Canyon of Arizona-
KansasCty-1902   (5x5)   15.00
PEABODY INSTITUTE LIBRARY-Second Catalogue of-Balt-1896-
1186p-2 vols(A thru D)   (5x2)   20.00
PEABODY,JOSEPHINE P-The Piper,A Play in 4 Acts-Bost&NY-1911-
cl bds   (5m1)   6.00
--Wolf of Gubbie-NY-1913-3 act comedy   (5qq7)   3.50
PEABODY LAW REVIEW(MAINE)-Vol 1 thru 5-1936 to 41(all publ)-
bound   (5ii7,rbnd)   87.50
PEABODY,MRS MARK-Miss Slimen's Window-1859-Derby&Jackson-
illus-1st ed   (5x4)   17.50
PEABODY MUSEUM OF SALEM-The Marine Room-Salem-1921-
188p-illus-catalog   (5t4)   10.00
PEACE DE RESISTANCE-by Women Strike for Peace-LosAng-n.d.-
illus-pict wrps-sprial bnd-152p   (4g9,wrps soil) 5.00
PEACE,M E-Darky Days in Dixie-SanAnt-1941   (5x2)   10.00
PEACE RIVER-A Canoe Voyage from Hudson's Bay to the Pacific-
Ottawa-1872-Durie-8vo-roig prntd wrps-fldg map-errat slip-
M McLeod,ed-1st ed   (5n9,box) 225.00
PEACE,WALTER-Our Colony of Natal-Lond-n.d.(c1883)-
Edw Stanford-174p-pkt map   (4t5)   25.00
PEACE WITHOUT DISHONOR-WAR WITHOUT HOPE-Bost-1807-
by a Yankee farmer-8vo-cl-43p   (5L1)   30.00
PEACOCK,THE "AT HOME"-A sequel to the Butterfly's Ball-
written by a Lady-Lond-1807-JHarris-sq16mo-prntd blue wrps-
6 plts-rare   (5v2,vf) 125.00
--same-Lond-1888-Griffith-   sq4to-wrps-facs of 1807 ed-
intro by ChasWelsh   (5c8)   5.00
PEACOCK,LADY-The Story of H R H Princess Elizabeth-n.p.-1949-
Told Mainly for Children   (5x7)   3.50
PEACOCK,THOS B-The Rhyme of the Border War-NY-1880-cl-162p
                                                (4p2)   10.00
PEACOCK,THOS LOVE-The genius of the Thames,a lyrical poem in
2 parts-Lond-1810-8vo-hf calf-mor labl-1st ed (5x3,rprd) 75.00
--Letters to Edw Hookham & Percy B Shelley-Bost-1910-Bibliophile
Soc-sm4to-hf vel-port-ltd to 483c   (5m2)   6.50

PEACOCK,THOS LOVE (continued)
--The philosophy of melancholy-Lond-1812-Shakespear Pr-lg4to-
cl-1st ed   (5x3,v fox)   70.00
PEACOCK,VIRGINIA TATNALL-Famous Amer Belles of the 19th
Century-Phila-1901-illus-296p   (5t4)   10.50
PEACOCKS PLEASAUNCE,THE-Lond-1908-257p,(22)-8 plts-by E V B
                                        (5w3,fade)   4.50
PEACH,ARTHUR WALLACE-The Country Rod & Gun Book-
Weston,Vt&NY-(1938)-224p-12mo-illus-cl   (5t0)   3.75
PEAK,HOWARD W-A Ranger of Commerce or 52 Years on the Road-
SanAnt-1929   (4a5)   10.00
PEAKE,ELMORE ELLIOTT-The Darlingtons-NY-1900-McClure,
Phillips-1st ed   (5m2,soil,sl wn) 7.50
PEAKE,HAROLD-Peasants & Potters-NewHav-1927-illus
                             (5t4) 4.50   (5jj3)   7.50
PEAKE,ORA BROOKS-The Colorado Range Cattle Industry-Clark,
Glendale-1937-8vo-cl-357p-illus-fldg map-1st ed (5h5) 25.00
PEALE,CHAS WILLSON-Catalogue of Exhibition of Portraits by...
Jas Peale & Rembrandt Peale-Penna Academy of Fine Arts-1923-
238p-illus-crown 4to   (4a0,lacks cov) 35.00
PEALE,REMBRANDT-An Historical Disquisition on the Mammoth,or
Great Amer Incognitum-Lond-1803-Peale plt   (5m2) 125.00
PEAPLES,F W-History of Great&Little Bolton Cooperative Society,
Ltd-1909   (5L7,sl stn)   6.00
PEARCE,CHAS E-"Polly Peachum"...the story of Lavinia Fenton &
"The Beggar's Opera"-Lond-(1913)-8vo-47 illus-cl-14p,382p-
1st ed   (5t0)   7.50
--Unsolved Murder Mysteries-Lond-1924-Stanley Paul-319p (5p9) 7.50
--same-NY-n.d.-(c 1925)-319p-frontis-cl   (5t2)   4.00
PEARCE,F B-Zanizibar-NY-1920-maps-illus   (5tt5)   10.00
PEARCE,HUGH NIGEL-Capt Nigel's Galaxy of Ships-Lond-
n.d.-(after 1945)-sm4to-col illus-207p   (5s1)   4.00
PEARCE,J E-Tales that Dead Men Tell-Austin-1935-118p-wrps
                                                (4j6)   6.00
PEARSON,JOS,ed-Memoirs of Colombo Museum-1914-illus-folio-
wrps-Ser A, #1, Bronzes from Ceylon (5ww3,cov detached) 30.00
PEARCE,THOS-Laws and customs of the stannaries in counties of
Cornwall & Devon-Lond-1725-for D Browne-folio-hf mor-
1st ed   (5x3,vg)   45.00
PEARCE,T M-The Beloved House-Caldwell-Caxton-8vo-cl-239p-
photos   (5F5,f,wn dj)   10.00
--The Engl Language in the SoWest-n.p.-1932-23p (5j4)   7.50
--Lane of the Llano-Bost-1936-8vo-cl-illus-1st ed (5p5) 17.50
--New Mexico Place Names-8vo-cl   (5g0,mint,dj) 15.00
--Southwesterners Write-Albuqu-1946-8vo-cl-365p (5g2) 12.00
PEARE,CATHERINE OWENS-John Woolman,Child of Light-NY-
c1957-254p-frontis   (5h9)   3.75
PEARL,RICH M-America's Mountain-ColoSprngs-(1954)-31p-map-
photos-(wrps)   (5L5)   2.50
--How to Know the Minerals & Rocks-NY-(1955)-McGrawHill-
192p   (5p7)   4.25
PEARLEY,S-Hist of Salem,Mass 1626 to 1716-1924,6,8-3 vols
                                                (5t9)   30.00
PEARSALL'S-Illus Handbook for Knitting in Silks-Lond-1902-illus
                                        (5n7,cov wn)   2.50
PEARSE,A S-The Emigrations of Animals From the Sea-NY-1950-
210p-cl-8vo-scarce-23 photos   (4p5)   12.50
--Fauna Of The Caves of Yucatan-Wash-1938-Carnegie Inst of
Wash Pub #491-plts-304p-stiff wrps-4to   (4p5)   27.50
PEARSE,A W-The World's Meat Future-NY-(1918)-335p-2nd ed
                                                (5c5)   3.00
PEARSON,REV C H-Cabin on the Prairie-Bost-1870-299p-1st ed
                                     (5s4,ex-librr,v poor) 3.00
--On the Frontier,or Scenes in the West-Bost-1864-320p-illus
                                     (5s4,ex-librr,fair) 12.50
PEARSON,C   -Emily Carr As I Knew Her-Tor-1954-162p-
col frontis   (5dd0)   5.00
PEARSON,DR-Special Report on Diseases of the Horse-Wash-1907-
Bur of Animal Indus-608p-illus-rev ed   (5t7)   15.00
PEARSON,E GILBERT-Birds of America-Univ Soc-1923-3 vols-
lg type-orig buck-4to-illus   (5t8,mint)   30.00
PEARSON,EDMUND L-Books in Black or Red-NY-1923-1st ed
                                      (5yy6,vg,dj)   7.50
--Five Murders-GardenCty-1928-299p-illus-cl (5p9) 4.50 (5t2) 3.50
--Instigation of the Devil-NY-1930-illus-8vo-1st ed (4m7) 7.50
--Queer Books-NY-1928-298p-cl-illus   (5t2)   5.00
--The Secret Book-NY-1914-12mo-cl-1st ed   (5d3)   7.50
--Studies in Murder-NY-1924-295p   (5p9) 6. (5x7) 5.50
--Voyages of the Hoppergrass-NY-1913-1st ed-scarce (4F6,vf) 40.00
PEARSON,EMILY C-Gutenberg,& Art of Printing-Bost-1871-illus-
292p   (5q0)   10.00
--Madonna Hall,the story of our country's peril-Bost-1891-Earle-
pic cl-reprnt   (5m2)   7.50

PEARSON,EMILY C (continued)
--Our Parish,a Temperance Tale-NY-1879-252p-cl
(5h7,priv bkplt) 7.50
PEARSON,FRANK A-Food-NY-1944
(5x7) 3.00
PEARSON,G M-Benjamin Pearson & Esther (Furnas)-Their Anc &
Desc-1941-538p (5mm3) 8.00
PEARSON,GARDNER W-Records of the Mass Volunteer Militia-
Bost-1913-Wright&Potter-448p-4to (5mm8) 12.50
PEARSON,GEO-Escape of Princess Pat-Tor-(1918)-227p-13 plts
(4d8,lacks fly) 6.50
PEARSON,HAYDN S-Country Flavor-(1945)-112p-illus-1st ed
(5e8,autg) 5.75
--The Countryman's Cook Book-NY-(1946)-311p-photos(5c0,autg) 5.00
PEARSON,HELEN-Vignettes of Portsmouth-Portsmouth-(1913)-54p-
illus (5p7,5mm3) 3.50
PEARSON,HENRY CLEMENS-Her opportunity-Bost-1888-
JasHEarle-1st ed (5m2,sl shake) 12.50
--same-Bost-1889 (5ee3) 5.00
--His opportunity-Bost-Earle-1887 (5m2) 5.00
PEARSON,HENRY GREENLEAF-Business Man in Uniform-1923-illus-
251p-1st ed (5F2) 15.00
--Jas S Wadsworth of Geneseo-NY-1913-Scribern's-321p-untrmd-
g.t.e.-port-maps (5mm8) 11. (5q8,soil) 10. (5xx7) 20.00
--Life of John A Andrew, Gov of Mass-Bost-1904-HoughtonMiff-
2 vols-illus-g.t. (5ss5,ex-libr) 12.50 (5qq8) 15.00
--Richard Cockburn Maclaurin-NY-1937-302p-illus (5w4,dj,autg)6.00
--Son of New England-Bost-1932 (5w5) 5. (5p0) 6.00
PEARSON,HENRY J-"Beyond Petsora Eastward"-Lond-1899-4to-
col frontis-88 plts-8 maps&plans-335p (5nn2) 17.50
PEARSON,HESKETH-Dickens, His Character,Comedy & Career-NY-
1949-361p-ports (4a8) 4.50
--Dr Darwin-Lond-1930-242p-ports (5a1) 4.50
--Gilbert & Sullivan, A Biography-NY-1935-Harper-317p (5p7) 4.50
--Oscar Wilde, His Life & Wit-NY-(1946)-Harper-345p-illus(5p7)5.00
--The Smith of Smiths-NY-1934 (5m1) 5.00
PEARSON,J-First Editions of 100 Books Famous in World's
Literature-Lond-c1880-Chiswick Pr-73p-wrps (5j4) 10.00
PEARSON,JIM BERRY-The Maxwell Land Grant-Univ of Okla-
(1961)-8vo-cl-305p-illus-scarce 1st ed
(5yy7,dj,mint) 10. (5h5,f,dj) 12.50
PEARSON,JOHN-An Exposition of the Creed-Lond-1659-
Roger Daniel-sm4to-calf-1st ed (4n5,rebkd) 125.00
PEARSON,JONATHAN-History of Schenectady Patent-Albany-
1883- index-28 illus-scarce (5zz0) 65.00
PEARSON,LEONARD-Diseases & Enemies of Poultry-Harrisburg-
1897-col plts-116p,750p-3/4 lea (5w4,in wrps,soiled,tape) 8.75
(5v6,bkstrp ragged) 11.50 (5m6) 30.00
PEARSON,R A-Notes Upon Dairying in Calif & Export of Calif
Butter to Orient-Wash-1900-29p-illus (4a5) 5.00
PEARSON,RALPH M-Experiencing Amer Pictures-NY-1943-Harper-
234p-illus-4to (4a0) 27.50
PEARSON,T GILBERT,ed-Birds of America-NY-1936-GardenCty
Publ-4to-106 col plts,Fuertes (5p7) 7.00
--same-NY-(1940)-4to-illus-cl-106 col plts by Fuertes (5t7) 15.00
--Portraits & Habits of our Birds-NY-1920-illus-50 col plts-1 vols
(5tt5) 8.50
--same-NY-1928-2 vols-illus-photos-50 col pltd (5w0) 10.00
PEARSON,W H-Recoll & Records of Toronto of Old-Tor-1914-illus-
orig bndg-272p (4e9) 20.00
PEARY,JOSEPHINE D-My Arctic Journal-NY-1893-240p-photos-
map-col plts (5t0) 5. (5ss1) 3.50
--Snow Baby-Lond-1902-4to-illus-1st Engl ed (4F6,f) 25.00
PEARY,MARIE AHNIGHITO-The Red Caboose with Peary in the
Arctic-NY-1932-12mo-128p-illus-pic cl-1st ed (5p1,dj) 8.50
PEARY,ROBT E-Nearest the Pole-NY-1907 -maps-illus-1st ed
(5ss1,ex-libr) 9. (5m6) 10. (5ss1) 16.50
--Northward Over the "Great Ice"-NY-1898-2 vols-maps-1st ed-
800 illus (5x0,5ss1,5ee3) 12.50
--The North Pole-NY-1910-373p-map-illus
(5x0) 7.50 (5ss1,fade) 9. (5t4) 10.00
PEASE,A-Desc of John Pease,Sr of Enfield,Conn-402p-Also Early
Hist of Pease Families in Amer-97p-1869 (5t9) 47.50
PEASE,JOHN C-Gazetteer of States of Conn & Rhode Island-
Hartf-1819-2 maps-2 ports-sheep (4b6,hng broken) 40.00
PEASE,JOSEPHINE-Nimbo-Chig-c1934-8vo-64p-Albert Whitman
(5p1) 7.50
PEASE,M B J-Mahlon Johnson Family of Littleton,NJ-1931-133p
(5t9) 12.50
PEASE,Z W-The Catalpa Expedition-NewBedford-1897-215p-illus-
1st ed (5ee3) 7.50
--Centenary of Merchants National Bank-NewBedford-1925-
91p-plts (4b8) 8.50

PEASE,Z W (continued)
--Visit to Museum of Old Dartmouth Hist Soc Bourne Whaling
Museum-NewBedford-1951-64p photos-dec cov-wrps (5s1) 2.50
PEAT,HAROLD-Private Peat-Indnpls-1917-ports-235p-plts (4d8) 5.00
PEAT,WILBUR D-Portraits & Painters of Governors of Indiana 1800 to
1943-1944-Ind Hist Soc-8vo-45p-wrps (4e0) 7.50
PEATTIE,DONALD CULROSS,ed-Audubon's Amer-Bost-(1940)-
HoughtonMiff-329p-col plts-4to (5w3) 9.50 (5p7) 10.00
--same-Bost-1940-4to-cl-illus-ltd to 3025c,autg
(5h4,sl sp soil) 15. (5h4,f,box) 20.00
--Green Laurels-NY-(1936)-368p-illus (5w3) 6.50
--same-NY-(1938)-368p-illus-deluxe ed (5s7) 7.50
--The Road of a Naturalist-Bost-1941-HoughtonMiff-315p
(5p7) 4.50 (5w3) 6.50
--Singing in the Wilderness-NY-1935-245p-illus
(5p7) 3.75 (5w3) 6.50
--Up country, a story of the Vanguard-NY-1928-Appleton-1st prntg
(5m2) 6.50
PEATTIE,RODERICK,ed-The Berkshires-NY-c1948-illus-414p
(5yy6) 6. (5h9,5p9) 5.00
--The Black Hills-Vanguard-(1952)-illus-1st ed (5kk4,f,dj) 10.00
--The Friendly Mountains,Green White & Adirondacks-NY-
(1942)-341p-cl-illus (5d7) 6.00
--Great Smokies & Blue Ridge-NY-c1943-illus-372p (5yy6,5w4) 7.50
--The Inverted Mountains,Canyons of the West-NY-(1948)-376p
plus index-illus-1st ed (5m9) 6. (5L0,dj) 6.50
--Pacific Coast Ranges-NY-1946-402p-29 plts-4 maps
(4f9) 8.50 (5u6) 10. (5t7) 8.00
--The Sierra Nevada, The Range of Light-NY-(1947)-398p-illus-
cl-Vanguard Pr (5d7) 10. (5w5,dj) 7.50
--Struggle On the Veld-NY-1947-photos-maps-263p (4t5) 8.00
PEBBLEBROOK & THE HARDING FAMILY-Bost-1839-BenjHGreene-
12mo-orig cl-1st ed-scarce (5x1,sp fade) 50.00
PECK,ANNE MERRIMAN-Roundabout America-NY-1933-234p-
1st ed-illus (5r1,vg) 10. (5dd9) 6.50
PECK,ANNIE S-Flying Over South Amer-Bost-1932-HoughtonMiff-
8vo-illus (4a3,fade) 7.50
--A Search for the Apex of America-NY-1911-DoddMead-370p-
illus-cl (5t7) 10. (5d7) 17.50
--South American Tour-1913 (5L7,sl fray) 5.00
PECK,C L-Thos Hatch of Barnstable & Some Desc-1930-356p (5t9) 20.00
PECK,CHAS H-The Jacksonian Epoch-NY-1899-472p (4m2) 12.50
PECK,DAVID W-The Greer Case-NY-1955-209p-S&S (5p9) 3.75
PECK,ELIZ-Amer Frontier-NY-1937-195p-illus (5s4,dj) 4.50
PECK,GEO-Sketches & Incidents-NY-1847-2 vols in 1 as issued-
166,197p-lea (5y0) 15.00
PECK,GEO-Wyoming,Its History,Stirring Incidents,etc-NY-1858-
illus (4m4) 20.00
PECK,GEO W-Melbourne & the Chincha Islands-NY-1854-294p-
frontis (5t7) 10.50
PECK,GEO W-Adventures of One Terence McGrant-NY-1871-
illus by HLStephens-12mo-cl-1st ed of auth's 1st book (5gg6) 15.00
--Peck's Bad Boy & His Pa-Chig-1883-illus-cl-1st ed-1st issue
(5v2,vf) 100.00
--same-Chig-1883-12mo-cl-1st issue(only 196p of text)-14p of ads-
1st ed-plus a copy of the 2nd prntg(with added text pp 197 to
256)- 8vo-orig cl (5ee9) 75.00
--same-Chig-(1900)-illus by Williams (5ww4,fair) 5.00
--same-Chii-188?-later printing (4F6,rub) 10.00
--Peck's Bad Boy in an Airship-Chig-(1908)-illus-257p (5q0) 12.50
--Peck's Bad Boy in an Airship-Chig-(1908)-illus-298p-pict cl
(5p6) 10.00
--Peck's Irish Friend-Chig,NY-1888-Phelan Geoheagan-
Household Library Ser-pic wrps-scarce (5v2,vg) 10.00
--Peck's Sunshine-Chig-(1893)-296p-illus (5xx7) 10.00
--Peck's Uncle Ike & the Red Headed Boy-Chig-1899-AlexBelford-
12mo-217p-pict cl (5p1,brown,cor wn) 12.50
--Sunbeams-Chig-1900-4to-dec cl-50 illus-1st ed (5p5) 10.00
PECK,HARRY T-The personal equation-NY-1898-Harper (5m2) 6.50
--20 Yrs of the Republic 1885 to 1905-NY-1907-frontis-811p
(5r7,ex-libr) 10.00
PECK,IRA B-Desc of Jos Peck,emig 1638 & records of his father's
& grandfather's families in England-1868-442p-v scarce
(5mm3,rbnd,facs t.pg) 75.00
PECK,J H-Deft Report of Trial...Impeachment..for High
Misdemeanors in Office by Arthur J Stansbury-Bost-1833
(5r4,rbnd) 12.50
PECK,JESS T-History of the Great Republic Considered from a
Christian Standpoint-NY-1868-hf lea-710p-frontis-34 ports-
raised bands (5h9) 10.00
PECK,JOHN-Facts & Calculations Respecting the Population &
Territory of the US-Bost-(1799)-8vo leaflet-7(1)p-folded as issued
(4m6,bkstrp tn) 62.50

PECK,JOHN M-A Guide for Emigrants,Containing Sketches of
Illinois,Missouri & the Adjacent Parts-Bost-1831-16mo-336p-
orig cl-papr labl-fldg col map-1st ed (5m3,rub,lacks e.p.) 42.50
--A New Guide for Emigrants to the West-Bost-1836-374p-cl-
enlrgd ed   (5m4) 40.   (5n9,box) 75.(5s2,f) 55.00
--Pecks Tourist's Companion to Niagara Falls,Saratoga Springs,
the Lakes,Canada etc-Buffalo-1845-194p-illus-maps-charts
(5t4) 20.50
PECK,LEIGH-Pecos Bill & Lightning-Bost-1940-1st ed-rare-
Kurt Wiese,col illus   (4F6,dj,vf) 20.00
PECK,MARY GRAY-Carrie Chapman Catt,a Biography-NY-1944-
illus   (5j3,Miss Catt's copy,a.l.s.) 15.00
PECK,SAML M-Alabama Sketches-Chig-1902-299p-cl-1st ed
(4m8) 5.00   (5h1) 7.50   (5b9,vf,dj) 12.50
PECK,T B-Richard Clarke,of Rowley,Mass & His Desc-1905-93p
(5t9) 10.00
--Wm Slade of Windsor,Ct & Desc-1910-197p   (5mm3) 10.00
PECK,THEODORE S-Revised Roster of Vermont Volun & Lists of
Vermonters who served in Army & Navy of US during War of
Rebellion-Montpelier-1892-4to-hf lea   (5mm3) 25.00
PECK,W F-Semi Centennial Hist of City of Rochester,etc-NY-1884-
maps-illus-frontis-736p   (5yy0,needs rbndg) 24.50
PECK,WALTER E-Shelley,His Life&Work-Bost-1927-2 vols-illus
(5mm1) 22.50   (5ss9) 17.50
PECK,WM DANDRIDGE-Natural History of the Slug Worm-Bost-
1799-8vo-wrps-14p-frontis-illus   (4c1,disbnd) 25.   (5m6) 35.00
PECK,WM HENRY-The Stone Cutter of Lisbon-NY-(1889)-
Robt Bonner-436p-1st ed   (5x4) 5.00
PECKHAM,HARRY H-Josiah Gilbert Holland in Relation to His
Times-Phila-1940-220p-frontis-8vo-cl-1st ed (5t0) 6. (5mm2) 7.50
PECKHAM,HOWARD H-Captured by Indians-NewBrunswick-1954-
235p plus index-illus-1st ed   (5dd6) 5.   (5L0) 6.50
--Pontiac & the Indian Uprising-Princeton-1947-332p plus index-
illus-maps-1st ed   (5L0,dj) 7.50
PECKHAM,JAS-Gen Nathl Lyon & Missouri in 1861-NY-1886-
447p-cl-12mo   (5j6,f) 6.50   (5m8) 6.00
PECORA,FERDINAND-Wall St Under Oath-NY-1939-8vo-cl-
1st ed   (5p5) 15.00
PEEBLES,J M-Seers of the Ages-Bost-1870-376p-3rd ed (5p7) 7.50
PEEBLES,L A,comp-Robt Peebles from Ulster 1718-1964-242p
(5t9) 15.00
PEEL,B B-Bibliography of Prairie Provinces to 1953-(1956)-680p
(4g2) 18.50
PEEL,MRS C S-The "Daily Mail" Cookery Book-Lond-1919-200p-
ads-dec bds-2nd ed   (5g9) 4.00
--The Labour Saving House-NY&Lond-1917-190p-46 illus
(5w7,soil) 4.50
PEEL,ROY V-Political Clubs of New York City-NY-1935-illus-
1st ed   (5tt5) 10.00
PEELE,GEO-Plays & Poems-Lond-1887   (5mm2) 4.00
PEEP AT BUFFALO BILL'S WILD WEST,A-c1890-lg4to-col plts-
8 lvs on thk bd-rare   (5v0,lacks cov) 15.00
PEEP AT OLD ASIA,A-Concord,NH-1847-RufusMerrill-24p-12mo-
24 engrs-pic wrps-Merrill's Pictorial Gallery(5p1,wtrstnd) 10.00
PEEPLES,E A-Swing Low-Bost-1945-12mo-1st ed   (5x2,dj) 4.50
PEET,REV L B-Preparation for Death,a Sermon-Bangkok-1845-
21p-ABCFM Pr   (5b6) 15.00
PEET,LOUIS HARMAN-Trees & Shrubs of Prospect Park-NY-(1902)-
237p-maps-diagrams-2nd ed   (5s7,pencil) 6.00
--Trees & Shrubs of Central Park-NY-(1903)-363p-illus-16 maps
(5s7) 7.50
PEET,LOUISE J-Household Equipment-NY-1934-315p-illus (5w7) 5.00
PEET,STEPHEN-History of the Presby & Congregational Churches &
Ministers in Wisc-Milwaukee-1851-SilasChapman-208p-cl
(5d6) 35.00
PEET,STEPHEN D-The Ashtabula Disaster-Chig-1877-cl-208p
(4h1) 12.50
PEFFER,NATHL-America's Place in the World-NY-1946 (5q8) 3.75
--China,the Collapse of a Civilization-Lond-1931-Routledge-
306p   (5x9) 6.50
PEGUES,A W-Our Baptist Ministers & Schools-Springfld-1892-
illus   (5x2) 60.00
PEGUY,CHAS-Prose & Poetry-(1943)-2 vols-8vo-cl   (5t2) 5.00
--same-NY-(1944)-A&JGreen,tr   (5mm2) 5.00
PENNSYLVANIA,WESTERN-Early History of-Pittsburg-1846-
Kauffman-1st ed-calf-8vo-2 fldg maps-(Rupp)   (5n9) 125.00
PEIRCE,A B-Knocking About-Yale Univ Pr-1924-176p-8vo-illus-
Leatherbee,ed   (5ww3) 15.00
PEIRCE,DR A C-A Man from Corpus Christi-NY-1894-252p-
10 illus-g.cl   (5ee3) 17.50
PEIRCE,B K-Audubon's Adventures,or Life in the woods-NY&Cinn-
1889-8vo-16mo-dec cl-7 plts-252p-frontis-8 illus   (5p1) 12.50

PEIRCE,CHAS-The Portsmouth Miscellany,or Lady's Library
Improved-Portsmouth,NH-1804-344p-calf-
(5d6,ink) 20.   (5i0) 40.00
PEIRCE,E W-Experiences & Incidents of Rev Gardner Dean with
Gen of Gardner,Dean & Hinds Families-1883-307p (5t9) 10.00
PEIRCE,EBENEZER W-Indian History, Biography & Genealogy-
NoAbington-1878-12mo-illus-1st ed   (5ss5,sl cov stns) 17.50
PEIRCE,F C-Posterity of John Pers of Watertown in N E-1880-278p
(5mm3) 18.50
PEIRCE,JOSEPHINE-Fire on the Hearth-Springfield-(1951)-254p
(5y2) 6.50   (5w7) 7.50
PEIRCE,MELUSINA FAY-Cooperative Housekeeping-Bost-1884-
12mo-189p   (5w7,bkstrp tn) 7.50
PEIRCE,PARKER I-Adventures of Antelope Bill in Indian War of 1862-
(Marshall,Minn)-(1898)-illus-244p-pic wrps-cov title
"Antelope Bill" a Minnesota Boy (5kk4,sl chip,sp tape) 200.00
PEIRCE,PAUL SKEELS-The Freedmen's Bureau,a chapter in history
of reconstruction-IowaCty-1904-Univ of Iowa-200p
(5u3,ex-libr) 4.00
PEITHMANN,IRVIN M-Echoes of Red Man-NY-(1955)-134p-cl-
1st ed   (5h1) 5.00
PEIXOTO,A-Clima e saude,introducao bio geografiga a civilizacao
brasileira-1938-sewn   (5L7) 3.00
PEIXOTTO,ERNEST-A Bacchic Pilgrimage-NY-1932-201p-illus-
1st ed   (5w1) 7.50   (5c9) 6.50
--Our Hispanic Southwest-NY-1916-illus   (5r7) 8.50   (4p8) 10.00
--Pacific Shores from Panama-NY-1913-illus   (4b6,5s4) 10.00
--A Revolutionary Pilgrimage-NY-1917-369p-illus   (5t7) 8.50
--Romantic Calif-NY-1910-1st ed
(4a5) 4.50   (5h9) 5.   (5s4,delux ed) 7.50
--Ten Drawings in Chinatown-SanFran-1898-Robertson-18p-
10 illus on cardboard-ltd to 750c   (4a0) 27.50
PEKING GAZETTE,THE-Shanghai-1876-fldg table-linen bndg
(5ii3,rub) 15.00
PELAYO,A STORY OF THE GOTH-NY-1838-Harper-2 vols-12mo-
orig cl-papr labls-(WGSimms)-1st ed   (5x1,lt wtrstns) 80.00
PELHAM,CAMDEN-The Chronicles of Crime,Or,the New Newgate
Calendar-Lond-1887-2 vols-illus   (5j2) 25.00
PELL,EDW L,ed-100 Years of Richmond Methodism-Richmond-1899-
8vo-illus   (5m6) 5.00
PELL,EDW LEIGH-McKinley & Men of Our Times-n.p.-1901-
544p-Hist Soc of Amer   (5w5) 5.   (5b1) 7.50
PELL,JOHN-Ethan Allen-Bost&NY-1929-331p-illus
(5t4) 7.50   (5t7,pres) 10.00
PELLA'S CHOICEST COOKING RECIPES-Ladies' Aux of Central
College-Pella,Iowa-1934-253p-wrps-3rd ed,rev (5g9) 4.00
PELLATI,FRANCESCO-Latest Archaeological Discoveries in Italy-
Treves-1932-Ente Nazionale Industrie Turistiche-8vo-111p
(5m5,sp crack) 10.00
PELLEGRINI,ANGELO-The Unprejudiced Palate-NY-1948-235p-
bds   (5g9) 4.50
PELLETIER,E&A-Le The & Le Chocolat dans l'alimentation publique-
Paris-1861-150p-mor   (5w1,stns) 28.50
PELLETREAU,WM S,ed-Silas Wood's Sketch of Town of Huntington,
L I-NY-1898-63p-ltd ed   (5ff2) 25.   (4t1) 17.50
PELLEW,CHAS E-Dyes & Dyeing-NY-1913-264p-3 col plts(5n7) 8.50
PELLEW,GEO-John Jay-Bost-c1898-354p-illus.t.e.g.   (5w9) 4.00
PELLICER y TOVAR,JOSE-Genealogia de la Noble,y antigua casa,
de Cabeza de Vaca-Madrid-Garcia y Morras-sm folio- 1652-
(6)100 leaves --sm folio-qtr calf-1st ed   (5L1) 150.00
PELLICO,SILVIO-My Imprisonments,Memoirs-NY-1833-Harper Bros-
8vo-cl-papr labl-1st Amer ed-scarce   (5p5) 20.00
PELLISSIER,GEO-Literary Movement in France During 19th Cent-
NY-1897   (5mm1) 10.00
PELLOW,R-Philosophy versus Corruption-1953   (5L7) 3.50
PELLOW,THOS-History & Long Captivity & Adventures of
Thos Pellow in South Barbary-Dublin-1753-1 fldg map-calf
(5c1) 45.00
PELTON,J M-Pelton Family in Amer,Desc of John-1892-722p
(5mm3) 20.00
PELTON,MABELL-A Tar Heel Baron-Phila-1903-Lippincott-8vo-
dec buck -illus   (5b2,sl rub) 5.00
PELTZ,MARY ELLIS-The Magic of the Opera-(NY)-(1960)-4to-
cl&bds-172p   (5t7) 10.00
PELTZ,W L L-Top Flight at #1 LaFayette St-Albany-1939-4to-buck-
ports-188p-priv prntd Yale U Pr-ltd to 300c   (5j5) 17.50
PELZER,LOUIS-Cattlemen's Frontier-Glendale-1936-351p-1st ed
(4j6,4d5) 35.00
--Marches of the Dragoons in Mississippi Valley-IowaCty-1917-
St Hist Soc of Iowa-263p-1st ed   (5yy7) 20.00

PEMBERTON,EBENEZER-Sermon preached at Presbyterian Church
  in City of NY on Death of John Nicoll,MD -NY-1743-
  JParker-sm8vo-32p-mor   (5L1)   85.00
PEMBERTON,HENRY-A View of Sir Isaac Newton's Philosophy-
  Lond-1728-4to-fldg plts-calf-labl   (5j3,rprd)   50.00
PEMBERTON,JOHN C-Pemberton,Defender of Vicksburg-
  ChapelHill-1942-8vo-cl-350p-illus-2nd prntg (5m8,dj) 10.00
--same-Univ of NC Pr-1945   (5x5) 10.00
PEMBERTON,MAX-Jewel Mysteries I Have Known-Lond-1894-
  illus-1st ed   (4b7,bkplt) 30.00
PEMBERTON,T E-Dickens & the Stage-Lond-1888-260p-plts
                                          (4a8,lacks t.p.) 3.50
--John Hare Comedian 1865 to 1895-Lond&NY-1895-1st ed (5m1) 7.50
--The Life of Bret Harte-Lond-1903-8vo-cl-357p-illus
                                          (5F5,fox,hng broke) 6.00
PENA,M T DE LA-Problemas Sociales y Economicos de las Mixtecas-
  Mexico-1950-4to-(Vol 2,#1)-182p-wrps-illus
                                          (5h4,sml libr stmp) 8.75
PENCE,M L-The Ghost Towns of Wyoming-NY-(1956)-242p-
  8 Russell illus   (5yy7,dj) 15.00
PENCIL,MARK-The White Sulphur papers-NY-1839-12mo-orig cl-
  papr labl-Sam'l Colman-1st ed   (5x1,t.pg tn)   45.00
PENDENNIS,ARTHUR,ed-The Newcomes-Lond-1854,5-2 vols in 1-
  thk8vo-hf calf-plts-1st ed   (5r9,fox)   25.00
PENDERGAST,A W-Cigar Store Figures in Amer Folk Art-Chig-
  (1953)-76p-illus   (5L0)   5.00
PENDEXTER,HUGH-The Gate Through the Mountain-Indnpls-(1929)-
  1st ed   (5ee3,dj,f)   3.50
PENDLETON,E H-Early N E Pendletons-(1956)-354p   (5j9) 10.00
PENDLETON,E R-Brian Pendleton & His Desc-1910-860p (5j9) 60.00
PENDLETON,GEO H-Copperhead Candidate for V Pres-Wash-1864-
  8p-unbnd as issued   (5h1)   5.00
PENDLETON,L-King Tom & the Runaways-NY-ca 1890   (5x2) 8.50
PENDLETON,LOUIS-Carita A Cuban Romance-Bost-1898-247p-
  Lamson,Wolfe-1st ed   (5x4)   7.50
PENDLETON,NATHL G-Military Posts,Council Bluffs to the
  Pac Ocean-1843-27th Congr,H Rep #31-map-78p-cl bds-
  scarce   (5s9,sewed) 75. (5x5,box) 65.00
PENDLETON,WM C-History of Tazewell Co & SW Virg-Richmond-
  1920-illus-700p   (4m4,4h1)   20.00
PENFIELD,THOS-Western Sheriffs & Marshals-Penfield-1955-G D-
  145p-4to-cl-illus-1st ed   (5g6,dj)   10.00
PENFOLD,JANE WALLAS-Madiera Flowers,Fruits & Ferns-Lond-
  1845-20 col plts-4to-orig calf bkd cl-lea labl-1st ed-v scarce
                                          (5z9,hng crack) 75.00
PENHALLOW,PEARCE W-Penhallow Family-Bost-1885-ports-
  thin8vo-47p   (4m6)   8.50
PENHALLOW,SAML-The History of the Wars of New Engl-Bost-
  1726-TFleet-sm4to-1st ed-134p plus errata lf
                            (5z7,sml holes in 2 pgs) 700. (5n2,f,box) 2,000.00
--History of Wars of New Engl with Eastern Indians-Cinn-1859-
  36p-cl-rubricated t.p.   (5h7) 40.   (5r6) 65.00
--Penhallow's Indian Wars-1925-facsim reprnt of 1st ed-buck-
  ltd to 250c   (5L7,rbnd)   10.00
PENINGTON,ISAAC-Few Experiences Concerning Some of the
  Weighty Things-Lond-(ca 1775)-8vo-disbnd-96p (4p3)   25.00
PENN,W A-The Soverane Herbe,a Hist of Tobacco-NY-1901-cl-
  326p-illus   (4i2,unopnd)   12.50
PENN,W E-Life & Labors of Maj W E Penn-StL-1869   (4c7) 25.00
PENN,WM-Charter of Liberties from Wm Penn to the Freed Men of
  Penna-Phila-1909   (5m2)   6.00
--Collected Works-Lond-1726-2 vols-lg4to-orig calf-J Sowle,prntr
                              (5m2) 45.   (4m4,rbnd)   40.00
--England's Present Interest Discovered-(Lond)-1675-sm4to-
  stitchd-1st ed-2nd issue-author's name on t. pg (5n2) 75.00
--Fruits of Solitude-Phila-1792-Benj Johnson-calf   (4b4) 17.50
--same-Phila-1794-Benj Johnson-orig calf-11th ed-2 t.pgs(5m2) 40.00
--Histoire abregee de l'origine et de la formation de la societe dite
  Quakers-Lond-1790-Bridel,transl-12mo-hf calf (5L1)   15.00
--A Memoir of-Phila-1858-172p-orig cl-pub by Assn of Friends-
  16mo   (5h9)   6.50
--Primitive Christianity Revided in Faith & Practice of People
  Called Quakers-Lond-1779-8vo-disbnd-83p-5th ed (4p3) 35.00
--Select Works....to which is prefixed a Journal of his Life-
  Lond-1771-lg folio-calf-mor labl   (5L8,2 pgs in facs) 38.50
--A Sketch of the Life & Character of-Phila-1885-36p-orig wrps-
  Soc of Friends   (5w4)   3.00
--Three Treatises, in Which Fundamental Principle...etc-Phila-
  1770   (5yy6)   37.50
PENNANT,THOS-The Antiquities of Lond-Lond-1825-8vo-104p-
  24 plts   (5v0,wn)   15.00
--Arctic Zoology-Lond-1792-24 hand col illus-2 fldg maps-3 vols-
  4to-lea labls-calf-2nd ed-v rare   (5z9,rebkd,vf) 975.00

PENNANT,THOS (continued)
--British Zoology-Warrington&Lond-1776,77-mor-4to-278 col plts-
  4 vols   (5jj8)   650.00
--Literary Life-Lond-B&JWhite-1793-lg4to-144p-ports-plt-
  lg ppr-1st ed   (5a1)   15.00
--Tours in Wales, with Notes-Lond-1810-44 plts(some fldg)-
  3 vols-8vo-hf calf   (4e1,rbkd)   75.00
PENNELL,ELIZ ROBINS-Art of Whistler-NY-1928-ModernLibr-
  201p-32 repro in aquatone-16mo-wrps   (4a0)   10.00
--Chas Godfrey Leland, a Biography-Bost-1906-2 vols-illus-
  1st ed   (5mm1)   10.00
--Delights of Delicate Eating-NY-1901-264p   (4g9,sp split) 17.60
--The Feasts of Autolycus-Lond-1896-12mo-264p (5c5,libr labl) 6.50
--A Guide for the Greedy by a Greedy Woman-Phila-(1923)-
  179p-bds-new&rev ed   (5c7) 10.   (5c9)   9.50
--Life of Jas McNeill Whistler-Phila-1908-Lippincott-2 vols-
  illus-1st ed-orig cl bk bds   (4a0)   60.00
--same-Lond-1908-Heinemann-2 vols-3/4 mor-sm folio-t.e.g.-
  ltd to 150c   (5d5,box)   75.00
--Life & Letters of Joseph Pennell-Bost-1929-2 vols-illus-
  1st Trade ed   (5yy6,als laid in) 25.00
--Nights-Phila-1916-Lippincott-8vo-buck-16 illus-g.t.(5b2,f) 6.00
--Whistler,the Friend-1930-Lippincott-illus-1st ed (5t0) 5. (5k1) 10.00
--The Whistler Journal-Phila-1921-Lippincott-1st ed illus-339p-
  4to   (5t2)   10.00
--same-Phila-1921-330p-illus-t.e.g.-ltd to 500c
                                      (5w9,autg,unopnd) 27.50
PENNELL,JOS-Adventures of Illustrator-Bost-1925-1st trade ed-
  folio-ports-plts-372p-(1st impr) (4d8) 15. (5w0,5k0) 20.00
--Etchers & Etching-NY-1925-Macmillan-illus   (5x0)   12.50
--same-NY-1926-343p,35p-plts-4th ed   (5t4)   10.00
--The Graphic Arts-Chig-1920-1st ed-illus
                          (4m5,5jj3,rub,hng split) 15. (4a1) 17.50
--A London Reverie-NY-1937-Macmillan-sm4to-56 drwngs (5p7) 5.00
--Pen Drawing & Pen Draughtsmen-Lond-1897-Macmillan-4to-
  3/4 crushd mor-g.-illus   (5b0,f bndg,sp fade) 55.00
--Jos Pennell's Pictures of Panama Canal-Phila-1912-28 plts
                                              (5w9)   7.50
--Play in Provence-NY-1892-202p-1st ed   (5m1)   6.50
--Quaint Corners in Phila-1922-174 illus-rev ed (5L7)   5.00
PENNELL MEMORIAL EXHIBITION-Catalog-1926-Phila Print
  Club & Penna Mus-18 plts-36 illus   (4e0)   20.00
PENNEY,CLARA L-List of books prntd before 1601 in library of
  Hispanic Soc of Amer-NY-1929-frontis   (5g4)   15.00
PENNEY,J C-50 Years with the Golden Rule-NY-1950-245p-
  frontis   (5y2)   4.75
PENNIMANS,THE-or,the triumph of genius-Bost-n.d.-c1862-
  GardnerAFuller-12mo-orig cl-frontis-1st ed (5i0)   17.50
PENNINGTON,HENRY-New Harlem Register-1903-lg folio-
  671p   (4n2)   125.00
PENNINGTON,PATIENCE-A Woman Rice Planter-NY-1913-
  450p-illus   (5t7,libr labl) 10.00
--same-NY-1914-illus   (5x2)   15.00
PENNSYLVANIA-Act of Assembly of Prov of-Phila-1775-21p,
  536p   (5h2,stn,rehnd) 35.00
PENNSYLVANIA & ADJOINING STATES-New County Map of,
  Showing Routes of Railroad-Phila-1863-col map-26x37"-
  fld into cl cov 6x4"-R L Barnes publ   (5h2)   10.00
PENNSYLVANIA ARCHIVES-8th Series,Vol 1 to Vol 8-cl
                                            (5m2,f)   45.00
--same-9th Series,Vol 1 to Vol 10-cl   (5m2,f)   50.00
--4th Series-Papers of the Governors-12 vols(complete)-Harrisburg-
  1900 to 1902-hf mor-a.e.g.   (5w5)   150.00
--6th Series-15 vols in 16-1906,07-buck   (5L7,rbnd)   85.00
PENNSYLVANIA AT COTTON STATES INTL EXPOS-Atlanta,1895-
  n.p.-(Harrisburg)-1897-155p-illus-hf mor   (5w5)   6.50
PENNSYLVANIA AT GETTYSBURG-(Harrisburg)-1904-2 vols-
  1154p plus index-illus-fldg map-1st prntng of rev ed (5L5) 10.00
PENNSYLVANIA AT JAMESTOWN EXPOS-Hampton Roads,Va-
  1907-Phila-1908-316p-illus-fldg map-g.t.   (5h9)   15.00
PENNA AUDITOR,GEN'L-Annual Report of & of Tabulations &
  Deductions from Reports of RR & Canal Co for 1866-Harrisburg-
  (1867)-8vo-cl-530p   (5t0)   12.50
PENNSYLVANIA BAR ASSOC QUARTERLY-Vol 1 thru 41-1929 to
  1970-bound   (5ii7,rbnd) 750.00
PENNSYLVANIA-Brief State of Prov of...Tru Cause of Encroachments
  of French....Riv Ohio-Lond-1755-Griffiths-sm4to-hf mor-
  (WmSmith)-2nd ed-Howes S686   (5n2)   125.00
PENNSYLVANIA-Brief View of Conduct of..1755..Gen'l Braddock-
  Lond-1756-Griffiths-1st ed-Howes S687 (5L1) 250. (5n2) 275.00
PENNSYLVANIA CAVALCADE-Phila-1942-illus-Amer Guide Series-
                                              (5m2   6.50

PENNA CAVALRY-3rd,60th Regt Penna Volunteers-Hist in Amer
Civil War-1905-4to-plt   (5L7)   10.00

PENNA CHURCH MUSIC & MUSICAL LIFE IN-In 18th
Cent-Phila-1926-Pa Soc Col Dames of Amer-Vol 1(only)-
261p-illus-g.t.-scarce   (5h9)   18.50

--same-Phila-1926 to 47-4 vols-Vol 3 in 2 parts as separate vols-
Pa Soc of Col Dames of Amer-illus-g.t.-scarce (5h9,unopnd) 60.00

PENNA CIVIL CODE-Report of Comm to Revise-Harrisburg-
1835,36-8vo-108p-(unbnd)   (5ss5)   9.00

PENNA,COLONIAL & FEDERAL-Jenkins,ed-Phila-1903-4 vol ed-
4to-illus-maps-g.t.-orig cl-deluxe ed-ltd to 300c (5h9) 42.50

PENNSYLVANIA,CONSTITUTIONAL CONVENTION 1873-
Debates-9 vols-bound   (5ii7,rebnd) 75.00

PENNSYLVANIA CONSTITUTION-Commemoration Committee(Pub)-
Federal Constitution Celebration 1937,38-n.p.-1938 (5x7) 3.00

PENNSYLVANIA-Constitution of Commonwelath of-Phila-1790-
Zachariah Poulson-29p-8vo-stitchd   (5L1,box,unopnd) 30.00

PENNA SOCY FOR PROMOTING ABOLITION OF SLAVERY-
& Relief of Free Negroes-Constitution of-Phila-1787 (5m4) 32.50

PENNA-Descriptive Review Showing Development of State of-
Chig-c1916-GeoFCram-folio-338p-illus-col maps (5w4)   10.00

PENNSYLVANIA DUTCH-Phila-1872-1st ed-12mo(P Gibbons)
                                                    (5jj3) 12.50

PENNA DUTCH COOK BOOK OF FINE OLD RECIPES-Reading-
1936-48p-wrps   (4g9)   2.50

PENNA FARMERS'CLUB-Minutes of Farmers' Club of Penna,1849 to
1919-1920   (5L7)   15.00

PENNA FISH COMM-Report of,for year 1903-(Harrisburg)-1903-
illus-3/4 lea-124p-col plts   (5t4)   10.50

PENNSYLVANIA FORGES & FURNACES IN THE PROVINCE OF-
Phila-1914-Pa Soc Col Dames-204p-illus-g.t.-scarce (5h9) 32.50

PENNSYLVANIA,FRONTIER FORTS OF-Report of Commis to
Locate Site of-2 vols-Harrisburg-1896-col plts & maps-
buck-1st ed   (5h9,rbnd) 36.00

PENNA GEOLOGICAL SURVEY-Annual Report,2d thru 4th,6th-
by HDRogers,1838 to 42(2d report also in German)-Contains
also Report on Swatara Mining District-1839-buck(5L7,rbnd) 25.00

PENNSYLVANIA,GENEALOGICAL SOC OF-Publ of...Vols 1
thru 7,1895 to 1920-orig wrps (5h9,lacks 3rd issue of Vol 1)125.00

--same-Vols 13 thru 24,1938 to 1968-orig wrps (5h9,f)   150.00

--same-Vol 4,#3,March 1911-Phila-1911-185p-includes index
Vol 4   (5h9)   6.50

PENNSYLVANIA GERMAN FOLKLORE SOC-n.p.-1936-Vol 1-
137p-illus   (5w4,hng crack)   8.50

--same-(Allentown,Pa,1943)-Vol 7-illus-170p   (5t4)   7.50

PENNSYLVANIA GERMAN SOC-Proceedings-Vol 39-Easton,
Oct 12,1928-The Society,1930-t8vo-illus-wrps-ltd to 750c
                                                    (5j5) 10.00

PENNSYLVANIA,A GUIDE BOOK-of Art, Architecture & Hispuric
Interests in-Phila-1924-Archambault,ed-509p-illus-maps
                                                    (5h9)   7.50

PENNSYLVANIA,GUIDE TO KEYSTONE STATE-NY-(1940)-660p-
photos,maps-pkt map-Amer Guide Ser-WPA-1st ed
                                        (4L5,dj,5w0,dj)   10.00

PENNSYLVANIA HERMIT,THE-Narr of Life of Amos Wilson-Phila-
1839-24p plus port-soft blu papr tied wi string (5a0)   20.00

PENNA,HISTORICAL SOC OF-Memoirs of-Phila-1864-Vol 1-
ltd ed of 1st Vol of Memoirs pub in 1826-495p (5h9)   10.00

--same-Phila-1858-Vol 6-429p-index   (5h9,unopnd) 12.50

--Charlemagne Tower Coll of Amer Colonial Laws-1890 (5L7) 15.00

PENNSYLVANIA HISTORICAL SURVEY-WPA Inventory of County
Archives of Penna,#7,Blair Co-Hollidaysburg-1941-293p(5u3) 3.00

PENNSYLVANIA HOUSE OF REPRESENTATIVES-Votes & Proceedings.
...14th day of Oct,1758-Phila-1775-HenryMiller-Vol 5-
560p-folio-calf   (5r7,hng broke)   35.00

PENNSYLVANIA IN WORLD WAR-illus hist of 28th Div-Pittsburgh-
1921-States Publ Soc-2 vols-cl   (5r0)   15.00

PENNSYLVANIA JOURNAL OF PRISON DISCIPLINE-&
Philanthropy-Vol 1,1845-Vol 2,1846-Vols 6,7,8(bnd in 1 Vol),
1851 to 1853-Phila   (5w5,needs rbndg) 20.00

PENNSYLVANIA-Journal of Senate of-2 vols-Harrisburg-1853-
971,632p-orig wrps   (5w4)   10.00

PENNSYLVANIA LAND CO-Act for vesting certain estates in Penna,
NJ & Maryland,belonging to...-(Lond,1760)-folio-buck-31p
                          (5g4,wtrstnd,pg 25 to 31 in facs) 100.00

PENNSYLVANIA PACKET-&Daily Advertiser-Phila-Sat,Sept 24,
1785-4p-ca19 x 12"   (5p1)   10.00

PENNA,PROVINCE OF-Forges & Furnaces in-Phila-1914-204p-
cl-t.e.g.-plts   (5hh6)   35.00

PENNA RR CO-Summer Excursion Book,Season of 1913-144p-illus-
fldg map-orig pict wrps   (5m2)   7.50

PENNA SOC FOR PROMOTING ABOLITION OF SLAVERY-
Constitution of-Phila-1787-wrps   (5g4)   15.00

PENNSYLVANIA SOC OF COLONIAL DAMES OF AMER-
Register of Phila-1907-304p-col frontis   (5h9,fade)   7.50

--same-1911-368p   (5h9,f)   8.50

--same-1928-499p   (5h9,f)   8.50

--same-1951-436p   (5h9,f)   6.50

PENNSYLVANIA STATE GRANGE COOK BK-1926,n.p.-168p-
4th ed   (5c4)   4.00

--same-1929-168p-7th ed   (5c4)   4.00

PENNA SUPT OF COMMON SCHOOLS-Report for year ending
June 4,1863-1863   (5L7)   6.00

PENNSYLVANIA,UNIVERSITY OF-History of US Army Base
Hospital #20 organized at...-Phila-1920-sm4to-257p-illus
                                                    (5w4)   7.50

PENNSYLVANISCHE VOLKS SCHULEN-Bericht des Superintendenten
(CRCoburn)...endende Schuljahr(1864)-Harrisburg-1864-
Eingerly u Myers-223p,99p-lg8vo-orig bds (5L8,fray,stns) 18.50

PENNY,ARTHUR-Great Undertakings, an Impression of British War
Effort-Quebec-1918-Chronicle Print   (5nn8)   5.00

PENNY,P   -A curious landlord-Tor,Lond,NY,Phila&SanFran-
1900-Drexel Biddle-1st ed   (5m2)   7.50

PENNY POST,THE-Weekly by Saml S Wilson-Vol 1,#1 thru 18-
Jan 25 to May 24,1834-Prov-1834-4to-bds-roan bk (5m6)   17.50

PENNY,PRUDENCE-Cookbook-NY-1939-385p   (4g9)   5.50

--Coupon Cookery-Hollywood-1943-128p   (4g9)   3.50

PENNY,VIRGINIA-Employment of Women-1863-bds
                                        (5L7,sp fray,stn)   4.50

PENNYBACKER,A J H-New History of Texas-Austin-1900
                                            (4a5,fox)   8.50

PENNYPACKER,ISAAC R-General Meade-NY-1901-12mo-402p-
Great Commanders Series   (4a7)   12.00

PENNYPACKER,MORTON-The Two Spies-Bost-1930-118p-illus-
labls-1st ed-ltd to 780c,nbrd   (5h9)   18.50

PENNYPACKER,SAM'L W-Annals of Phoenixville & its vicinity-
Phila-1872-Bavis&Pennypacker-8vo-orig cl-map-4 plts-
1st ed-scarce   (5i9,vf,a.l.s.)   27.50

--Autobiography of a Pennsylvania-1918   (5L7,rbnd)   8.50

--The Desecration & Profanation of the Penna Capitol-Phila-(1911)-
104p-illus   (5w5)   4.50

--Penna in Amer History-Phila-1910-494p-t.e.g. (5w4)   10.00

--Settlement of Germantown,Pa & Beginning of German Emigration
to NoAmer-Phila-1899-310p-illus-t.e.g.-ltd to 300c
                          (5m2,libr stmp) 27.50   (5w4)   45.00

--Valuable Library of-Phila-1906-123p-wrps   (5j4)   7.00

--same-Part 7-Phila-1908-181p-orig prntd wrps   (5c8)   8.50

PENROSE,CHAS B-Address....on subject of insurrection at
Harrisburg-Harrisburg-1839-207p-stitchd   (5g8)   25.00

PENROSE,CHAS B-The Rustler Business-Douglas-n.d.-8vo-56p-
pict wrps-publ by Douglas Budget-rare   (5g6,f)   17.50

PENROSE,CHAS W-"Mormon" Doctrine,Plain & Simple-SaltLkCty-
1888-69p   (5L0)   7.50

--same-1897-87p-(labeled 2nd ed)   (5L0)   6.00

PENROSE,MATT R-Pots 'O Gold-Reno-c1935-ACarlisle&Co-cl-
12mo-233p   (4t1) 15. (5jj7,cov letters fade) 20.00

PENROSE,STEPHEN B L-Whitman, an Unfinished Story-WallaWalla,
Wash-(1935)-256p-illus   (5s4,autg) 7.50 (5s4)   6.50

PENROSE'S PICTORIAL ANNUAL-Lond-(1908)-Vol 14,1908,9-
col plts-206p   (4d8)   10.00

PENSION LAWS-Now in Force in State of Main,1838-War Dept-
161p-3/4 lea   (5L3)   20.00

PENTAMERON & PENTALOGIA,THE-Lond-1837-by Mansell-
calf-g.-lea labls-hf title-errata slip-1st ed (5r9,f bndg,f) 45.00

PENTUCKET HOUSEWIFE-Haverhill-1882-136p-ads-1st Baptist
                                                    (5c4)   8.50

--same-Haverhill-1888-iv,(7),144p-ads   (5c4,fox,scuf) 7.50

PENZER,N M-The Book of the Wine Label-Lond-(1947)-4to-
143p-27 photo plts ea wi many examples   (5w6)   10.00

PENZER,N M-Book of the Wine Label-Lond-1947-144p-27 plts
                                                    (5g9) 10.00

PEOPLES'-Illus & Descriptive Family Atlas of World-Chig-(1889)-
466p-maps-col illus-folio-15th ed   (5i1,cov sl wn)   12.50

PEOPLE'S MAP & GUIDE OF SAN FRANCISCO-SanFran-1883-fldg
map-64p & 2p ads-3rd ed   (4L5)   17.50

PEORIA CO-Inventory of o Archives-WPA-1942-III Hist Records
Survey-423p-(mimeo)   (5mm3)   8.00

PEPE,WM-Narr of Political & Military Events which took place at
Naples-NY-(1822)-frontis-fldg map-130p-bds (5t0,map tn)   6.50

PEPLE,EDW-The Littlest Rebel-NY-Random-c1939-illus from
Shirley Temple motion picture-214p-glazed bds-12mo (5p1,dj) 10.00

--The Spitfire-NY-1908-Moffat, Yard-8vo-cl-illus by HCChristy
                                                (5b2,f)   4.00

PEPLER,DOUGLAS-The Devil's Devices or Control Versus Service-
Lond-1915-wdcuts by EricGill-Hampshire House Workshops-
12mo-pict bds   (5ss9,vg)   20.00

PEPLOW,BONNIE-Round Up Recipes-NY-(1951)-278p-1st ed
(5c9)   4.50

PEPOON,H S-Annotated Flora of Chig Area-Chig-1927-illus-maps-
554p-wrps   (4b6)   15.00

PEPPER,BEVERLY-The Glamour Magazine After Five Cookbook-
GardenCty-1952-narr 12mo-258p   (5c9) 2.50   (5c0)   3.50

--Potluck Cookery-GardenCty-(1955)-284p   (5c9)   4.00

PEPPER,GEO-Pueblo Bonito-NY-1920-AmMuseum of Natural Hist-
plts-wrps   (4k5,f)   13.50

PEPPER,GEO W-Under 3 Flags-Cinn-1899-photos-542p-errata p-
1st ed   (5yy7,wn)   15.00

PEPPER,GEO W-Philadelphia Lawyer-Phila-(1944)-Lippincott-
407p-illus   (5p9,5m2)   4.50

PEPPER,J W-#1,J W Pepper's Amer "Minstrel" Songster-formerly
Carncross' Songster(wrpr title)-Phila-1881   (5g8)   10.00

PEPPER,MARY-Maids & Matrons of New France-Bost-1901-8vo-
port-1st ed   (5m6)   10.00

--same-Tor-1902-286p-illus-ports   (5aa0)   5.00

PEPPERMAN,W L-Who Built the Panama Canal?-Lond-(1915)-
illus   (5t2)   4.50

PEPUSCH,JOHANN CHRISTOPH-Additional songs in operas of
Thomyris&Camilla as they are perform'd at New Theatre-Lond-
n.d.-folio-stitchd-1st ed-engraved music-v rare   (5x3)   130.00

PEPY'S,SAM'L-Diary & Correspondence-Lond-1875-5 vols-
t8vo-lg type-spcl papr-illus-Bickers&Son   (5t5,rbnd)   37.50

--same-Lond-1893 to 1899-GeoBell Sons-10 vols-8vo-g.-t.e.g.-
dark blue cl-illus-1st Wheatley ed   (5b0)   125.00

--same-Bost -(1892 to 1899)-CTBrainard-8vo-3/4 brown mor-g.-
t.e.g.-ltd to 1000 sets,nbrd-deluxe ed-text identical to
1st Wheatley ed -9 vols   (5b0)   95.00

PERCEVAL,DON-A Navajo Sketch Book-text by Clay Lockett-
Flagstaff-1962-Northland Pr-98p-cl-1st ed   (5d6)   20.00

PERCEVAL,JOHN-Things As They Are-Lond-1758-prntd for
S Hooper-wrps-112,(4)p-3rd ed,corrected   (5L8,f)   12.00

PERCHERON STUD BOOK OF AMERICA-Bloomington,Ill-
1905 to07,1915-Vols 6,7,8,17-8vo-hf lea   (5t0) ea 12.00

PERCIVAL,A B-Game Ranger's Note Book-NY-(1924)-illus
(5tt5,pencil)   6.00

--same-Lond-(1927)-8vo-369p-photos-map   (4a6,sp faded)   6.50

PERCIVAL,ALICIA C-The English Miss Today & Yesterday-Lond-
(1935)-(2)p,335p,(1)-15 plts   (5w7,crack)   9.50

PERCIVAL,C S-Hours of Musing-Utica-1841-12mo-cl-107p (5t2) 7.50

PERCIVAL,DEAN-A Thousand Miles in a Canoe-Bushnell,IL-1880-
orig prntd wrps-8vo-1st ed   (4h0,f,Streeter copy)   750.00

PERCIVAL,J G-Report of Geology of State of Conn-NewHaven-
1842-fldg map-495p   (5yy0)   12.50

PERCIVAL,MACIVER-The Glass Collector-NY-1919-331p-illus
(5w1)   6.50

--same-Lond-n.d.-12mo-cl-331p-illus-2nd ed   (5t2)   5.00

PERCIVAL,OLIVE-Our Old fashioned Flowers-Pasadena-1947-
245p-col frontis-bds-Ward Ritchie Pr-ltd ed of 1000c
(5F9) 4.   (5s7)   6.50

PERCIVAL,WALTER,ed-Friendship's Gift-Bost-1848-312p-plts
(5t4)   5.00

PERCIVAL,WALTER P-Across The Years,etc-Mont-1946-195p-illus-
ports   (5aa0)   5.00

--Lure of Montreal-Tor-1947-240p-illus (5dd7,f) 5.   (5aa0) 4.50

PERCY,ADRIAN-Twice Outlawed-Chig-n.d.-194p-cl(4p2,sp wn)20.00

PERCY ANECDOTES,THE-NY-1832-2 vols in 1-thk lg8vo-bds-
400p,240p-Harper-crude vel bk-scarce (5j5,lacks ports) 17.50

PERCY,EARL-Highlands of Asiatic Turkey-Lond-1901-EdwArnold-
338p-illus-fldg maps-hf mor-g.t.-g.e.   (5d7)   25.00

PERCY,THOS,ed-Northern antiquities-Lond-1770-TCarnan-2 vols-
8vo-calf-g.-mor labls-a.e.g.   (5x3)   50.00

--Reliques of ancient Engl poetry-Lond-1794-Nichols,prntr-
3 vols-8vo-mor labls-frontis-lf of music-4th ed (5x3,lt wtrstn)75.00

--same-Edinb-1858-JasNichol-3 vols-8vo-qtr lea (5c3,wn) 12.00

--same-Lond-1891-3 vols-Wheatley,ed   (5a1)   15.00

PERCY,BISHOP THOS-Folio MS Ballads & Romances together wi
Loose & Humorous Songs-Lond-1867,68-4 vols-orig hf mor-
orig wrps   (5j2,box)   60.00

PERCY,WM ALEXANDER-The Collected Poems of-1943-Knopf
(5F1,f,dj)   5.50

PEREIRA,JONATHAN-The Elements of Materia Medica &
Therapeutics-Phila-1852,1854-2 vols-JosCarson,ed -
3rd American edition, enlarged   (5w3,scuff)   18.50

--A Treatise on Food & Diet-NY-(1843)-ed by ChasALee-321p
(5c0)   9.50

PEREIRA SALAS,EUGENIO-Historia de la Musica en Chile-Santiago-
1957-illus-wrps   (5r7)   17.50

PERELMAN,S J-The Dream Department-(1943)-RandomHse
(5F1,mint,dj)   5.50

--The Swiss Family Perelman-NY-1950-Simon&Schuster-8vo-
213p-dec yello cl-tinted plts   (5aa2)   3.50

PERENNIAL CALENDAR & COMPANION TO THE ALMANACK-
Lond-1824-8vo-bds&lea-27p &803p-edited by TForster (5t2) 10.00

PEREYRA,CARLOS-Tejas,la Primera Desmembracion de Mejico-
Madrid-ca 1928-1st ed-252p-cl-mor labl-v scarce
(4j7,orig wrps bnd in)   75.00

PEREZ DE RIBAS,ANDRES-Historia de los Triumphos de nuestra
Santa fee entre Gentes las mas barbaras-Madrid-1645- de Paredes-
folio-20 lvs-764p-blind t.calf-1st ed-lg copy   (5L1,f)   825.00

PERFECT ADONIS,A-NY-1875-Carleton-8vo-cl-g.   (5b2)   12.50

PERFECT GENTLEMAN,THE-Or Etiquette & Eloquence-NY-1860-
335p   (5w7,fade)   4.50

PERFESSER TOM-Phila-1893-42p-illus   (5w5)   3.00

PERIAM & BAKER-Pictorial Cyclopedia of Live Stock & Complete
Stock Doctor-NY&StL-1884-1252p-illus-1st ed
(5b9,hng crack)   25.00

PERIAM,JONATHAN-The Groundswell-StL-1874-576p-illus-
1st ed   (5L0,pres)   20.00

PERILS OF PEARL STREET,THE-by a late merchant-NY-1834-
Betts&Anstice&Peter Hill-12mo-orig cl-1st ed   (5x1,rbkd) 37.50

PERKERSON,MEDORA F-White Columns in Georgia-NY-(1952)-
Rinehart-illus-4to-367p   (4d9,f)   6.50

PERKINS,CHAS-The Pinto Horse-SantaBarbara-1927-Hebbard-
frontis col-illus-76p-1st ed   (4n1,fade)   20.00

PERKINS,CHARLTON B-Travels From Grandeurs of West to
Mysteries of East-SanFran-(1909)-595p-photos-11x8
(5s1,ex-libr,rprd)   8.50

PERKINS,DEXTER-The US & the Caribbean-1947-Harvard Univ Pr-
253p   (5p9)   3.00

PERKINS,EDITH FORBES-Letters & journals-(Cambridge,Mass)-1931-
4 vols-8vo-cl-g.t.   (5g3)   20.00

PERKINS,ELDER ABRAHAM-Autobiography of-Concord,NH-1901-
22p-orig wrps   (5s2,f)   15.00

PERKINS,ELIZA-Memoirs & Moral Productions & Selections of,
who died in NY,June 20,1823,aged 18 yrs-NY-1823-96p-
sm8vo-orig bds-calf sp-GHillson   (5L1)   20.00

PERKINS,EVORA B-The Laurel Health Cookery-Melrose-(1911)-
525p-photos   (5c7)   5.00

PERKINS,FRANCES-The Roosevelt I Knew-NY-1946-illus-1st ed
(5yy6) 4.50   (5w9)   3.50

PERKINS,FRED B,comp-The Picture & the Men-NY-1867-cl-190p
(4h2,sl soil)   8.50

PERKINS,MRS GEO A-Early Times on the Susquehanna-Binghamton-
1870-8vo-1st ed   (5w4,fade) 25.   (5m6,sl fade)   20.00

PERKINS,GEO E-Pioneers of the Western Desert-LosAng-(1947)-
104p-illus-1st ed   (5dd4)   5.00

PERKINS,GEO R-Farmer's Alamanc for..1844..Calculated for the
Meridian of Detroit-Detroit-(1843)-16mo-36p-disbound(loose)
(5a3)   50.00

PERKINS,HENRY-The Perkins Library-Catalogue-Lond-1873
99p-half morroco   - priced   (5j4)   12.50

PERKINS,J R-Trails,rails & war-Indnpls-1929-BobbsMerrill-
371p   (5jj7,f) 12.50 (5u3) 15.   (4k5)   10.00

PERKINS,JAS H-Annals of the West-Cinn-1847-8vo-calf
(4c1,crack)   7.50

--same-StL-1850-2nd ed   (5L0,rbnd)   10.00

PERKINS,MARY E-Old Houses of Ancient Town of Norwich-1895-
621p-genealogies,photos   (5e8)   29.75

PERKINS,SAM'L-Historical Sketches of US-NY-1830-Converse-
444p-frontis-bds   (5qq8)   12.50

PERKINS,SIMEON-Diary-Vol1,1766 to 1780,Innis,ed-Tor-1948-
Champlain Soc-298p   (5nn2)   30.00

--same-vol 2,1780 to 1789-Harvey,ed-1958-531p-map-plts
(4d2) 25. (5nn2)   35.00

--same-Vol 4,1797 to 1803-Fergusson,ed-1967-facs-550p(5nn2) 35.00

PERKINS,T A-Jacob Perkins of Wells,Me & His Desc-1947-239p
(5mm3)   10.00

PERKIOMEN REGION,THE-(periodical)-Pennsburg-Oct,1934-
(184p)-orig wrps   (5w4)   4.50

PERLEY,M B V-Perley,Hist & Gen-1906-748p   (5mm3)   20.00

PERLOFF,HARVEY S-Puerto Rico's Economic Future-Chig-(1950)-
Univ of Chicago Pr-lg8vo-cl-maps-illus   (4a3)   12.50

PERLS,KLAUS G-Vlaminck-Hyperion-1941-76p-folio-16 col plts
(5ww3,fox)   15.00

PERNOLET,M A-L'Air Comprime et Ses Applications-Paris-1876-
8vo-illus- fldg tabls-cl   (5t0,fade)   6.00

PERNOUD,REGINE-The Retrial of Joan of Arc-NY-(1955)-
Harcourt Brace-264p-1st Amer ed   (5p1,dj)   12.50

PERRAUD,J-Etude Comparee De La Taille dans les differents
vignobles-Montpellier-1892-   prntd wrps (5w1,chip)   4.50

PERRAULT,CHAS-Contes de Fees-Paris-1812-Ancelle-frontis-
titl lf-14 plts-12mo-268p wi ads-calf
(5c8,f) 325.00
--same-Paris-(ca 1840)-thn8vo-illus-new ed-ACourcier-8 lithos
(5c8,bk cov dtchd) 35.00
--same-Lyon-1865-8vo-300p-dec calf-4 plts (5v0,hng split) 20.00
--Contes de ma mere l'Oye-(Paris,ca 1930s)-sq8vo-134p-orig col
wrps-illus de Renee Ringel-ltd prntg (5c8) 15.00
--Histoires or Tales of Past Times, told by Mother Goose with
Morals-Lond-n.d.-(ca 1930)-Fortune Pr-wdcuts-ltd to 1025c
(5c8) 20. (5p1) 17.50
PERRAULT,CLAUDE-Treatise of Five Orders of Columns in
Architecture-Lond-1708-Benj Motte-folio-calf-1st ed in Engl-
plts (4h0,rebkd) 300.00
PERRAULT,J F-Extraits ou Precedents,Tires des Registres de la
Prevoste de Quebec-Quebec-1824-8vo-orig bds-88p (5w8) 75.00
PERRAULT'S POPULAR TA LES-Oxf-1888-Clarendon Pr-
2 toned bds (5c8,rub) 15.00
PERRET,F A-The Vesuvius Eruption of 1906-Wash-1924-sm folio-
25 plts-151p-wrps (5cc1) 3.75
PERRIER,LOUIS-Memoire Sur Le Vin De Champagne-Paris-1865-
114p,(2),(1)-wrps (5w1) 17.50
PERRIN,M-Fables Amusantes-NY-1821-Duyckinck-12mo-180p-
calf (5c2,hng crack) 12.50
PERRIN,W H-Pioneer Press of Kentucky-Louisville-1888-4to-wrps-
illus-93p-Filson Club Pub #3 (4p8) 20. (5yy8) 15.00
PERRIN DU LAC,F M-Reise in Die Beyden Louisianen-Vienna-1807-
hf mor-364p-fldg map (4n4) 125.00
--Travels through the Two Louisianas & among savage nations of the
Missouri-Lond-1807-Phillips-8vo-bds-1st Engl ed
(5n9,rbnd) 80. (4j7,hf calf) 75.00
--Voyage dans les deux Louisianes, et chez les Nations Sauvages
du Missouri-Paris-1805-fldg map-fldg plt-calf-Howes P244
(5s9,rbnd) 475.00
PERRINE,FRED S-Military Escorts on the SantaFe Trail-N M Hist Soc,
Jul,1927-8vo-wrps-54p (5a9) 4. (5g2) 7.50
PERRINE'S NEW MILITARY MAP-Illustrating Seat of War-Indnpls-
1861-23x29"-folded into bds case (5h2,sl breaks at folds) 10.00
PERROT,GEO-History of Art in Persia-Lond-1892-Chapman&Hall-
R8vo-orig cl-12 plts (5t5) 8.50
PERRUCHOT,HENRI-Toulouse Lautrec-NY&Cleve-(1960)-317p-
illus-1st ed (5t7) 6.00
PERRY,B F-Reminis of Public Men-Phila-1883-ports-8vo-1st ed
(5h6,sl stns,5m6) 10.00
PERRY,BLISS-Life & Letters of Henry Lee Higginson-Bost-c1921-
557p-illus (5j6) 4.50 (5p0,5g4) 6.00
--The praise of folly & other papers-Bost-1923-Houghton-1st ed
(5p9) 4.75 (5m2) 6.50
PERRY,C B-Perry's of Rhode Island & Tales of Silver Creek-NY-
1913-illus-orig cl-t.e.g.-scarce (4m9) 20. (5mm3) 22.50
PERRY,CLAY-& John L.E.Pell-Hell's Acres-NY-(1938)-400p
(5t4) 7.50
PERRY,E G-Trip Around Cape Cod-Priv prntd-1898-267p-illus
(5e8) 12.75
PERRY,FRANCES-The Herbaceous Border-Lond-(1951)-120p-
illus-bds (5s7) 3.50
PERRY,FREDK-Fair Winds & Foul-Bost-1925-204p-illus (5t7) 7.50
PERRY,GARDNER B-History of Bradford to 1821-Priv prntd-1872-
69p-bds (5e8,hng weak) 6.00
PERRY,GEO SESSIONS-Hackberry Cavalier-NY-1944 (5a8,pres)20.00
--Hold Autumn in Your Hand-NY-1941 (5a8,f,dj,pres) 20.00
--My Granny Van-NY-1949-1st ed
(5a8,f,wn dj) 6. (5n4,pres,dj) 15.00
--Roundup Time-NY-1943-cl-1st ed (5a9,dj) 7.50 (5r1,dj,5g0) 10.00
--Texas, a World in Itself-NY-(1942)-illus,Fuller-293p
(4b3,5L3) 4. (5L3,pres) 7.75 (5s4,dj) 5.00
PERRY,HENRY FALES-History of 38th Regiment Indiana Vol Inf-
Palo Alto-1906-Stuart-385p-illus
(5mm8) 17.50 (5y0,autg) 32.50 (5r0) 15. (4p2,stnd) 20.00
PERRY,J ROY-Public Debts in Canada-Tor-1898-U of Tor Studies,
Econ Ser #1-wrps-88p (5aa1,fray) 12.50
PERRY,J T-Desc of John Odlin of Boston-reprntd 1887-8p (5t9) 4.00
PERRY,JOHN-Specific Inductive Capacity of Gases-Yokohama-
(1877?)-1p,15p,(1)-wrps-4 plts(3 fldg) (5hh7,stnd) 6.50
PERRY,JOSEPHINE-Around the World Making Cookies-NY-(1940)-
157p (5c7,ink) 3.00
PERRY,KATE E-Old Burying Ground of Fairfield,Conn-1882-241p
(5t9,wtrstnd) 15.00
PERRY,L-Perry Family Tree-1931-125p (5mm3) 5.00
PERRY,L DAY-Seat Weaving-Peoria,Ill-(1917)-84p-70 illus (5n7) 4.50
PERRY,MARSHALL S,MD-First Book of Fine & Useful Arts-Bost-
1832-sm8vo-orig bds-126p,(6)-Carter&Hendee-schoolbook
(5L1,sp dmgd) 15.00

PERRY,MATTHEW C-Narr of Exped of Amer Squadron to China
Seas & Japan...1852 to 54 under command of...-Wash-1856-
col illus-fldg charts-4to-3 vols (5yy0) 50.00
--same-Wash-1856-col plts-4to-cl-Exec Doc #97,Hse of Rep-
extract (5z9,rebnd) 15.00
PERRY, NORA-A book of love stories-Bost-1881-Osgood-1st ed
(5m2) 6.00
PERRY, ROBT E-The Secrets of Polar Travel-NY-1917-Century Co-
313p-pict cl-photos (5r0) 7.50
PERRY, THOS S-English Literature in 18th Cent-NY-1883-450p
(5m1) 6.00
PERRY,WM-Only Sure Guide to English Tongue-Greenwich-
Nov 1806-JohnHowe-1st improved ed-16mo-oak bds (5q0) 10.00
--Royal Standard English Dictionary-Bost-1802-Isaiah Thomas &
T Andrews-596p-6th Amer ed-lea (5ff7,wn) 15.00
PERRYMAN, L C-Message of Chief of Muskogees & Reply of Natl
Council in Extraordinary Session,April 4,1894, to Dawes
Commission-Eufaula, IT-(1894)-11p-wrps-rare
(5yy7,lacks bk wrp) 35.00
PERSECUTION OF CATHOLIC CHURCH IN THIRD REICH-NY-
1940-8vo-cl-565p-illus (5t0, dj) 4.50
PERSHING, JOHN J-Final Report of...-Wash-1920-GPO-96p-
maps (5ss1) 10. (5p7) 3.50
--My Experiences in the World War-NY-1931-cl-2 vols-1st ed
(5p0) 8.50 (5t4) 15. (5jj9,5w0,5h2) 10.00
--same-NY-1931-2 vols-photos-khaki col buck-ltd ed-
auth's autograph ed (5d2,autg,dj,f) 20.00
--Report of First Army, Amer Exped Forces-FtLeavenworth-1923-
Gen'l Serv Schools Pr-135p (5m8) 7.50
--Reports & Maps-In Letter to Sec of War,FROM GHQ, AEF,
Nov 20,1918-n.p.-1918-12mo-25p-limp mor-2 fldg maps in
back flap-scarce (5m6) 10.00
PERSINGER,JOS-The Life of Jacob Persinger-Mo-1861-8vo-
orig wrps-24p-"reprinted" (5g5) 7.50
PERSIUS,CHAS-he Academicians of 1823-Lond-1823-12mo-
col frontis-orig bds-cl sp-papr labl-1st ed-rare-(Chapter 8,
pg310 to 438 removed by publ because of libel) (5b0) 22.50
PERSON, HARLOW S-Mexican Oil-NY-1942-Harper-8vo-cl
(4a3) 10.00
PERSON,WM-Life & Letters, together with poetical & miscellaneous
pieces-Cambr-1820-Hilliard&Metcalf-12mo-hf calf-1st ed
(5l0,rub) 30.00
PERSONAL INJURY COMMENTATOR-Vol 1 thru 13-1958 to
1970-unbnd (5ii7,lacks index) 120.00
PERSONAL NARRATIVE-of First Voyage of Columbus to Amer-Bost-
1827-trans from Spanish-303p-bds-(ThosBWait&Son) (5t4) 15.00
PERSONAL RECOLLECTIONS OF JOAN OF ARC-NY&Lond-
1906-Harper-46p-frontis-35 plts (5p1) 5.00
PERSPECTIVES,USA-Vols 1 thru 16,Fall 1952 to Sept 1956,
complete-orig wrps (5ss9,vg) 40.00
--same-#15-NY-Spring, 1956-t8vo-prntd wrps-1st ed (5r9) 6.00
--same-#16-NY-Summer, 1956-t8vo-prntd wrps-1st ed (5r9) 6.00
PERTCHIK,BERNARD-Flowering Trees of the Caribbean-NY-1951-
4to-col plts (5j5,dj) 10. (5a8,f,dj) 5.00
PERU-Arbitration Between Peru & Chile-Wash-1923 to 24-
4 vols-bound (5ff4,ex-libr) 22.50
PERUCHO,JUAN-Joan Miro & Catalonia-NY-n.d.-plts-
text in Span,Fr.,Ger., & Engl-273p-8vo (5ww3) 30.00
PETALUMA-Her advantages & resources-Petaluma-1903-8vo-wrps-
16p-illus (5t1) 25.00
PETALUMA-The Lowell of the West-Petaluma,Calif-1906-24p-
map-illus-wrps-Chamber of Commerce (5r0) 7.50
PETER PIPER'S-Practical Principles of Plain & Perfect Pronunciation-
Brooklyn-c1936-Mergenthaler Linotype Co-8vo-99p-wrps
(5p1) 15.00
PETER 'POSSOM'S PORTFOLIO-Sydney,Aust-1858-8vo(R Rowe)-
1st ed (4m8) 25.00
PETER SCHLEMIHL-Lond-1824-3/4 calf-8 plts by Geo Cruikshank
(5v2,f) 85.00
PETER SCHLEMIHL IN AMERICA-Phila-1848-Carey&Hart-8vo-
orig violet cl-(Geo Wood) (5x0,fade,wn) 10.00
PETER SIMPLE-R Bentley-1852-(Standard Novels)-sm8vo-dec cl-
g.t.-462p-frontis (4a8) 4.50
PETERKIN,GEO W-Hist & Record of Protestant Church in Diocese
of W Va-(Charleston)-1902-856p-cl (5h7, cov fleck) 15.00
PETERKIN, JULIA-Black April, a novel-Indnpls-(1927)-1st ed-
BobbsMerrill (5x2) 5. (5m2) 10.00
--Bright Skin-(1932)-BobbsMerrill-prntd box on title pg-
1st ed (5F1,f,dj) 6.00
--same-lg papr-ltd to 250c,nbrd,autg-autograph ed
(5F1,vf,box dmgd) 12.50
--Green Thursday-NY-1924-1st ed-ltd to 2,000c (5x2) 15.00
--same-NY-1924-1st trade ed (5x2) 10.00

PETERKIN, JULIA (continued)
--A Plantation Christmas-Bost-1934-12mo (5x2) 7.50 (5x2,f,dj) 10.00
--Roll,Jordan,Roll-(1933)-BobbsMerrill-photos (5x2,5x5) 10.00
--same-NY-(1934)-RobtOBallou 7.50
--Scarlet Sister Mary-Indnpls-1928-1st ed (5x2) 5. (5b9) 8.50
PETERMANN-Vereinigte Staaten von Nord Amerika-Gotha-1874-
parts 1 thru 3-approx 48x14½ inches-lin mntd & fldng under cl
(5w0, cov stns) 16.50
PETERS,CHAS-Autobiography of...-Sacramento-(ca1915)-illus-
12mo-231p-orig wrps (4g6) 7.50 (4n1,5F9) 15.00
PETERS,DEWITT C-Kit Carson's Life & Adventures-Wash-1857-604p
(4a5) 20.00
--same-Hartf-1874-lg8vo-604p-35plts-enlrgd ed
(5yy7,wn) 8. (5v0,vg) 15. (5w9,wn) 12.50
--Life & Adventures of Kit Carson,Nestor of the Rocky Mntns-NY-
1858-534p-illus-WRC Clark (5p7,rbkd) 25.00
--same-NY-1859-534p plus adv-13 additional plts-orig plts
(4n4) 35.00
PETERS,E B-Bradley of Essex Co,Mass-1915-213p (5mm3) 7.50
PETERS,E F-Peters of New England-1903-444p (5mm3) 25.00
PETERS,FRED J-Railroad,Indian & Pioneer Prints-by N Currier &
Currier & Ives-NY-1930-illus-4to-cl-pict Check List-
ltd to 500c,nbrd (5t2,dj,mint) 7.50
PETERS,G S-ABC und Namen Buchlein for Kinder-Harrisburg-c1830-
12mo-36p-illus bds-wi 10p of stunning ABC's-50 wdcuts
(5v2, lt soil) 45.00
--same-Harrisburg-c1855-12mo-36p-illus-bds (5v2) 37.50
PETERS,H S-Birds of Newfoundland-StJohns-1951-col illus-431p
(5yy8,dj) 12.50
PETERS,HARRY T-California on Stone-GardenCty-1935-
Dblday Doran-112 plts-227p text-cl-4to-ltd to 501c
(5h2) 100. (5tt9,tn dj) 200.00
--same-Dblday, Doran-(1931)-415p-18 col plts-4to-cl-ltd to 751c
(5tt9,dj,box) 275.00
--Currier & Ives-GardenCty-1942-4to-192 plts(32 col)
(4b3,f,4m6,dj) 20. (4p2,5t7,4m9) 15.00
--Just Hunting-NY-1935-illus-tall8vo-buck-lea labls-1st ed
(4b6) 20.00
PETERS,HERMANN-Pictorial History of Ancient Pharmacy,with
Sketches of Early Medical Practice-Chig-1889-tall 8vo-180p-
illus (5v0) 22.50
PETERS,J P-Nippur or Explor & Adven on the Euphrates-U of Penn
Exped to Babylonia...1888 to 1890-NY-1897-plts-fldg maps-
2 vols-orig cl-8vo (4e1) 25.00
PETERS,MADISON C-Haym Salomon-NY-1911-47p(5ss1,cov stnd) 3.50
PETERS,P-Stevedore-NY-1934 (5x2,dj) 8.00
PETERS,R-Full & Arranged Digest of Decisions in Common Law,
Equity & Admiralty of Courts of US...1789 to 1847-NY-1854-
2 vols (5ff4,rebnd) 18.50
PETER,ROBT-Hist of Medical Dept of Transylvania Univ-Louisville-
1905-Filson Club Pub #20-ports-wrps-4to (5yy8) 15.00
PETERS,SAM'L-General History of Connecticut,from its First
Settlement-Lond-1781-JBew-8vo-436p-crushed lev mor-g.t.-
1st ed (5L1,f bndg,vg) 200.00
PETERS,T McCLURE-A picture of town government in Mass Bay
Colony at middle of 17th cent as illus by town of Boston-NY-
(1890)-wrps (5g4,libr stmps) 7.50
PETERS,WM E-Legal Hist of Ohio U,Athens,Ohio-Cinn-19190-
336p-fldg maps-cl-scarce (5h1,fleck) 17.50
PETERS,WM THEO-Children of the Week-NY-1886-88 illus-cl
(4F6) 8.50
PETERSBURG P T A-Cook Book-Petersburg,Alaska-1932-133p-wrps
(4g9) 5.00
--same-1947 ed-168p-spiral bnd wrps-illus (4g9) 5.00
PETERSEN,MARCUS-Fur Traders & Fur Bearing Animals-Buffalo-
1914-372p-cl (5h7,cov spots) 10. (5s4,5ss5) 15.00
PETERSEN,W J-Iowa Hist Reference Guide-1952-192p with index
(5bb4) 5. (5a9) 6.00
--Iowa,the Rivers of Her Valleys-1941-381p with index-red cl
(5a9) 12.50
--Steamboating on the Upper Mississippi-1937-575p with index-
g.cov (5a9) 45.00
--The Story of Iowa,the Progress of an Amer State-NY-1952-4 vols-
4to-cl-illus (5m8) 35.00
PETERSON,ANNA J-Delectable Dinners-NY-1939-459p (5c0) 4.50
PETERSON,ARTHUR EVERETT-NY as 18th Century Municipality
Prior to 1731-1917-199p-Vol 75,#1 (5ff2) 12.00
PETERSON,CHAS J-History of The Wars of the US-NY-1859-illus-
cl (4p2,wn) 10.00
--Military Heroes of War of 1812 with a narr of the War-Phila-
1848-illus-282p (5t4) 12.50
--Military Heroes of the War of 1812...wi War with Mexico-Phila-
1849-lea-illus (4m2,sl loose) 12.50

PETERSON,CHAS J (continued)
--same-Phila-1859-part mor-10th ed (5jj7,f) 12.50
PETERSON,CHRISTINE E-The Doctor in French Drama,1700 to 1755-
NY-1938-Columbia Univ Pr-8vo-cl-1st ed (5p5) 12.50
PETERSON,EDWIN L-Penn's Woods West-Pittsburg-c1958-4to-
249p-col illus (5w5,dj) 10.00
PETERSON,ELLEN W-A Kansan's Enterprise-Enterprise-c1957-
Enterprise Baptist Church-260p-12mo-cl (4t1,autog) 12.50
PETERSON,EMIL R-A Century of Coos & Curry-Portland,Ore-1951-
584p plus index-illus-1st ed (5m9,5bb4,mint) 6.00
PETERSON,ELLEN Z-The Spell of the Tabeguache-Denver-(1957)-
60p-photo-1st ed-scarce (5L0,dj,f) 7.50
PETERSON,FRED W-Desert Pioneer Doctor,& Experiences in
Obstetrics, in Two Parts wi Illus-Calexico-1947-130p,85p-
12mo-cl (4t1) 10.00
PETERSON,HAROLD L-The American Sword 1775 to 1945-New Hope-
1954-illus-274p (5q0) 10.00
PETERSON,HENRY-Pemberton or 100 Yrs Ago-Phila-1898-393p-
cl-reprint (5h7) 4.00
PETERSON,HOUSTON-Huxley-Lond-1932 (5x7) 5.00
--The Lonely Debate-NY-1938-Reynal-310p (5p9) 5.00
PETERSON,ORVAL D-Washington Northern Idaho Disciples-StL-
c1945-(Christ.Bd)-223p-illus (4d6) 6.50
PETERSON,RACHEL WILD-Long Lost Rachel Wild-Denver-1905
(5jj1) 6.00
PETERSON,ROGER TORY-Birds Over America-NY-DMead-1948-
105 illus -342p (5p7) 5.00
--Birds of Amer(ca1950)-Macmillan-50 selections Audubon Prints
(5t4,box) 15.00
--Bird Watcher's Anthology-NY-(1957)-illus-401p (5t7) 7.50
--Wild America-Bost-(1955)-434p-illus (5t7) 4.50
PETERSON,SCHAILER-How Well Are Indian Children Educated?-
1938-US Indian Service-182p (5ss1) 6.00
PETERSON,W H-Gen Records & Sketches of Desc of Lawrens
Peterson & Nancy Jones-1926-305p (5mm3) 27.50
PETERSON'S LADIES'NAT'L MAGAZINE-for 1854-hf lea-11 col
fashion plts,other plts (5ee3) 12.50
PETERSON'S MAGAZINE 1858-Phila-Jan to Dec 1858-pt lea-
11 col fashion plts (5q0) 8.00
--same-1859-hf mor-12 col fashion plts (5i3) 10.00
--same-Vols 35&36-1859-1 plain,11 col fashion plts-452p-
hf mor (5w7,wtrstnd) 7.50
--same-1862-full year-col fashion plts (5ee3) 12.50
--same-bnd vol for 1869-12 col fashion plts(dbl pgd)-hf mor
(5ee3,f) 15.00
--same-1870-12 dbl pg col plts (5jj3,3 plts incomplete) 15.00
--same-1871-bnd-hf mor-12 fldg col fashion plts (5i3,f) 10. (5q0) 7.50
--same-1872-hf lea-bound-12 fldg col fashion plts
(5q0,11 plts) 7.50 (5i3,f) 10.00
--same-1873-bnd-hf lea-12 fldg col plts (5i3) 10.00
--same-1881-12 dbl pg col costume plts (5jj3) 20.00
--same-1883-12 fldg col plts (5jj3) 20.00
PETIN,HECTOR-Les Etats Unis et la Doctrine de Monroe-Paris-1900-
8vo-hf mor-452p (5L1) 10.00
PETIT-DUTAILLIS,C-Studies & Notes Supplementary to Stubbs'
Constitutional History 1 & 2-Manchester-1923-2 vols in 1
(5ff4) 12.50
PETIT LAFITTE,AUG-La Vigne Dans Le Bordelais-Paris-1868-692p-
wdcuts-calf bk (5w6) 16.50
PETIT THOUARS,ABEL DU-Voyage Autour du Monde sur Fregate
Venus-Paris-1840 to 1843-fldg map-charts-4 vols-hf calf
(5tt0,lacks atlas) 200.00
PETITION OF CATO WEST & OTHERS-in Behalf of Themselves &
Other Inhabitants of Mississippi Terr-(Wash,1800)-27p-wrps-
uncut-rare pamphlet (5L2,unopnd) 50.00
PETO,FLORENCE-Historic Quilts-NY-1939-210p-illus (5h9) 12.50
PETO,SIR S MORTON-Resources & Prospects of America-Lond-1866-
Strahan-428p-2 col illus-1st ed (5qq8,ex-libr) 10.(5m6,pres) 12.50
--same-NY-1866-col illus-428p (5s4,ex-libr,shake) 12.50
PETOSKEY,BAY VIEW & HARBOR SPRINGS-StIgnace-1889-
E J Macadam-12mo-bds-12 lvs (4a5) 12.50
PETRARCA,FRANCESCO-Concordanaya Dalle Rime di Francesco
Petrarca-comp by KMcKenzie-Oxf&NewHav-1912-Italian text
(5j2) 50.00
PETRARCH,FRANCIS-Petrarch's Secret-Lond-transl by Draper-1911-
Chatto&Windus -192p (5p0) 4.50
PETRARCH'S SONNETS-Verona-1965-tall 8vo-lea sp-illus-Officina
Bodoni-Italian & Engl text-Lt Ed Club (5t8) 40.00
PETRE,F LORAINE-Napoleon's Last Campaign in Germany 1813-Lond-
1912-17 maps & plans-crushed Persian lev (5d2,f bndg) 15.00
PETRIFIED FORESTS OF ARIZ-Southern Pac RR-n.d.-brochure
(5g0) 5.00

PETROFF, IVAN-Prelim Report upon Population, Industry & Resources of Alaska-Wash-1881-86p-lg fldg map-HED 40 (4a5, fox) 37.50
--Report on Population, Industries & Resources of Alaska-(Wash, 1884)-189p-8 col plts-sm folio-hf mor-2 fldg pkt maps (5L1) 50.00
PETROFF, PETER-The Secret of Hitler's Victory-Lond-1934-128p-Hogarth Pr (5p0) 4.00
PETRONIUS ARBITER-The Satyricon of-Chig-1927-Pascal Covici-2 vols-illus (5x0) 8.50
PETRUCCI, RAPHAEL-Chinese Painters-NY-1920-Brentano's-lg8vo-155p-plts-cl&bds (5m5, cov stnd) 15.00
PETRULLO, VINCENZO-Puerto Rican Paradox-1947-Univ of Penna Pr-181p (5p0) 5.00
PETRY, A-Harriet Tubman, Conductor on the Underground RR-NY-1955 (5x2, f, dj) 3.50
--The Street-Cleve-1947 (5x2) 6.50
PETT, SAUL-The Torch is Passed...Assoc Pr Story of Death of a President-n.p.-n.d.-(ca 1964)-4to-cl-100p of photos & text (5t0) 6.00
PETTENGILL, SAM'L B-Smoke Screen-NY-(1940)-12mo-cl-126p-Southern Publs (5j5) 5.00
PETTERSSON, HANS-Westward Ho with the Albatross-NY-1953-55 illus (5c1) 6.50
PETTIGREW, R F-Triumphant Plutocracy-NY-1922 (5w5) 4. (5q8) 7.50
PETTIJOHN, JONAS-Autobiography, Family History & Various Reminis...among Sioux or Dakota Indians-ClayCenter, Kans-1890-12mo-orig cl (5a3) 50.00
PETTINGELL, JOHN M-Gen Desc of Richard Pettingell of Salem & Newbury-1906-582p (5t9) 40.00
PETTIS CO, MO-History of..Incl Authentic History of Sedalia-n.p.-1882-illus-1108p-v scarce (4t3, rebnd) 75.00
PETTIS, GEO H-Frontier Service During the Rebellion or Hist of Co K, 1st Inf Calif Volunteers-Prov-1885-wrps-54p-ltd to 250c-Ser 3, #14 (5mm8) 45.00
PETTIT, CHAS T-Ancestry of-of New Engl & Long Island-n.d.-40p-mimeo (5mm3) 12.50
PETTIT, E M-Sketches in the History of the Underground RR-Fredonia, NY-1879-McKinstry&Son (5x2, rbnd) 60.00
PETTOELLO, DECIO-Outline of Italian Civilization-Lond-(1932) (4a1) 12.50
PETTUS, DAISY CADEN-Rosalie Evans Letters from Mexico-Indnpls-1926-illus-1st ed (4n3, f) 9.00
PETTY, JENNIE M-"Nora" & Mercy's Angels-Phila-1880-1st ed (5mm2) 10.00
PETTY, WM-The Political Anatomy of Ireland-Lond-1691-for D Brown & W Rogers-8vo-part mor-1st ed (4h0, lt fox, f bndg) 215.00
PETULENGRO, GIPSY-A Romany Life-Lond-1935-1st ed (5b9, vf) 5.00
PETZOLDT, PATRICIA-On Top of the World-Lond-1954-Collins-254p-illus-cl (5d7) 6.00
PEVERIL OF THE PEAK-Phila-1823-Carey&Lea-3 vols-12mo-orig prntd bds-(Sir W Scott)-1st Amer ed (5i0, ex-libr, wn) 27.50
PEYOTE RITUAL, THE-Visions & Descript of Monroe Tsa Toke-SanFran-(1957)-Grabhorn Pr-66p, (67)-13 col plts-ltd to 325c-1st ed-ex scarce (5L5, f) 100.00
PEYRE, DR P-Les Vins & Cepages Du Roussillon & Du Languedoc-Strasbourg-1950-100p-wrps (5w1) 3.50
--Les Vins & Vignobles De La Seine-Paris-1950-115p-wrps (5w1) 4.50
PEYRE FERRY, FRANCOIS-The Art of Epistolary Composition-Middletown-1826-calf (5q8, wn) 17.50
PEYSER, ETHEL-The Book of Culture-NY-(1934)-780p (5t7) 8.50
PEYTON, GREENE-Amer's Heartland, the SoWest-Norman-1948-304p-photos-maps-1st ed (5dd6) 15.00
--For God & Texas-NY-(1947)-201p-photos-1st ed (5s4, dj) 4. (5L0, dj) 3.00
--San Antonio, City in the Sun-NY-1946 (5kk4) 4. (5w0) 6.50
PEYTON, J L-Hist of Augusta Co, Virg-1953-428p-2nd ed (5mm3) 15.00
PEYTON, JOHN L-Over the Alleghanies & Across the Prairies-Lond-1870-2nd ed (5jj7, f, pres) 35.00
PEZET, A W-Greatest Crimes of the Century-NY-1954-Stravon-127p (5p9) 3.50
PFAHLER, MURIEL B-Love of a Physician, Geo E Pfahler-1958 (5L7) 3.00
PFANN, HASN-Fuhrerlose Gipfelfahrten in den Hochalpen, dem Kaukasus, dem Tian Schan und den Anden-Berlin-(1941)-255p-illus-bds-Roth&Co (5d7) 6.00
PFATTEICHER, HELEN E-The Ministerium of Penna-Phila-1938-176p (5m2) 4.00
PFEFFERKORN, IGNAZ-Sonora, a Descrip of the Province-1949-Univ of NewMex-4to-329p-cl-illus-Coronado Hist Ser (5F5, f, frayd dj) 25.00
PFEIFFER, IDA-Journey to Iceland & Travels in Sweden & Norway-NY-1852-273p-16mo (5ee3, f) 5. (5ss1, fox) 3.00
--Visit to Iceland & Scandinavian north-Lond-1852-8vo-orig cl-g.sp-Ingram, Cooke&Co-7 tinted plts (5i8) 7.00
--A Woman's Journey Round the World-Lond-n.d.-(1852)-338p-illus (5ee3, f) 5.00

PFLEIDERER, O-Early Christian Conception of Christ-1905 (5L7) 4.00
PFLUEGER, DONALD H-Covina, Sunflowers, Citrus, Subdivisions-Covina-1964-372p-8vo-cl-ltd to 1000c (4t1) 25.00
--Glendora, the Annals of a Southern Calif Community-Claremont-1951-Saunders Pr-262p-8vo-cl-ltd to 1000c (4t1) 15.00
PHAEDRI FABULAE-or Phaedrus's Fables...by John Sterling-Lond-1750-ThosAstley-Imp 8vo-170p-roan (5c8, wn, sl tn) 12.50
PHANTOM FALLS-a Tale of the Adirondacks-(Alpine, ca 1936)-frontis-22p-cl bkd bds (5r7) 7.50
PHANTOMS OF THE FOOT BRIDGE-& Other Stories-NY-1895-Harper-353p-1st ed (5x4) 10.00
PHARES, ROSS-Reverend Devil-NOrl-(1941)-illus-map e.p.-unbnd-259p plus index-1st ed-scarce (5yy7) 10.00
--same-NOrl-(1941)-lea-ltd to 10c, lg papr (5kk4, f) 20.00
--Texas Tradition-NY-(1954)-239p-illus (5L3, dj, mint) 5.75 (5g5, dj) 6.50
PHARMACOPOEA BORUSSICA-Tertia Emendata Editio-Berolini-1813-208p-mrbld bds (5w3, wn, fox) 18.50
PHARMACOPOEIA OF THE US OF AMER-NY-1830- 2nd ed (from 1st ed pub in 1820) wi add & corr by Convention held in 1830-176p-calf (5w3, stnd) 27.50
--same-Phila-1831-By Auth of Nat'l Medical Conv, Wash, 1830-268p, (3)-calf (5w3, wn, stnd) 25.00
PHARMACOPOEIA OFFICINALIS & EXTEMPORANEA-Lond-1742-in 4 parts-700p-calf-12th ed, enlrgd & corr(5w3,wn,cov dtchd) 20.00
PHARR, HENRY NEWTON-Pharrs & Farrs with Other Desc from 5 Scotch Irish Pioneers in Amer-NOrl-1955-604p-illus (5r7,f) 17.50
PHELAN, GEO F, ed-Gleanings, From Our Own Fields-NY-1881 (5mm2) 12.50
PHELAN, J-The Ardent Exile-Tor-1951-317p (4b9) 5.00
PHELAN, JAS-History of Tennessee, the Making of a State-Bost-1888-478p-cl-fldg map (5h0) 22.50
PHELAN, M-Billiards without a master-NY-1850-127p-buck-illus-127p (5ii2, rbnd) 12.50
--The Game of Billiards-NY-1859-267p-rev&illus-4th ed (5w7, libr stmp) 6.50
PHELAN, RAYMOND-The Financial History of Wisconsin-Madison-1908-8vo-475p-wrps-Phd Thesis (5t0) 5.00
PHELPS, ALMIRA-Address on Subject of Female Education in Greece-Troy-1833-8vo-30p-(unbnd)-1st ed (5ss5) 12.50
--Lectures to Young Ladies-Troy Female Seminary-Bost-1833-308p, (3)-frontis (5w7, wtrstnd) 15.00
PHELPS & ENSIGN-Traveller's Guide Through US-NY-1844-16mo-illus-fldg map-cl-53p (5yy6) 37.50
--same-NY-1845-col fldg map-53p-mor (4h1, sl rub) 37.50
PHELPS, CLYDE W-The Foreign Expansion of Amer Banks-NY-1927-222p (5y2) 5.75
PHELPS, DUDLEY MAYNARD-Migration of industry to SoAmer-NY-1936-McGrawHill-335p (5v6) 6.50
PHELPS, ELIZ STUART-The Gates Ajar-Bost-1869-Fields, Osgood-cl-1st ed (5ss3, sp chip) 15.00
PHELPS, H-The Great West-NY-(ca 1850)-chart-23x30 inches mntd on cl & rollers-Ensign&Thayer (5t2) 35.00
PHELPS, HENRY P-World's Fair via Baltimore & Ohio RR-Balt-1893-orig wrps-94p-8vo-1st ed (4m6) 12.50
PHELPS'-Hundred Cities & Towns, etc-NY-1854-80p-14 maps-orig wrps as issued, all bnd in cl (5h6) 25.00
PHELPS, J A-Heroic Willards of '76-1917-113p (5mm3) 5.00
PHELPS, MRS LINCOLN-Ida Norman; or, Trials & Their Uses-NY-1854-2 vols in 1 (5F0) 4.50
PHELPS, MARTHA BENNETT-Frances Slocum, the Lost Sister of Wyoming-NY-1905-167p-col plts-t.e.g.-1st ed (5w5) 16.50
PHELPS, NETTA SHELDON-The Valiant Seven-Caldwell-1942-Caston-8vo-22p-illus-2nd prntng (5p1) 5.00
PHELPS, NOAH A-History of copper mines & Newgate Prison at Granby, Conn, etc-Hartf-1845-Case, Tiffany&Burnham-8vo-orig brown wrps-1st ed (5i0, f) 75.00
PHELPS, OLIVER S-Phelps Family of Amer & Their Engl Ancestors-Pittsfld-1899-2 vols-1865p-cl (5h7) 75.00
PHELPS, RICHARD H-Newgate of Conn Simsbury Mines etc-(1876)-117p (5e8) 6.75
PHELPS, RUTH S-Earlier & Later Forms of Petrarch's Canzoniere-Chig-(1925) (5mm2) 5.00
PHELPS STRANGERS & CITIZENS GUIDE-to NY City-NY-1857-maps & engrs-Humphrey Phelps (5t7) 18.00
PHELPS, LIEUT THOS STOWELL-The Indian Attack on Seattle-reprntd from Remini of Seattle, Wash Terr, United Serv Mag-with orig notes etc-Seattle-1932-collected by Mrs Carl F Gould-8vo-57p-wrps-ltd to 250c, nbrd-very scarce (5F5, Gould pres) 17.50
PHELPS TRAVELLERS' GUIDE-Through the US-NY-1847-24mo-col fldg map-orig mor (4c1, f) 40.00
--same-NY-1850-Ensign&Thayer-70p-fldg map-orig g stampd cov (5tt0) 45.00

PHELPS,WM LYON-Archibald Marshall-NY-1918   (5yy1)   7.50
--As I Like It-NY-1926-3rd Series-cl-309p-1st ed
       (5p7) 3.50   (5t2,dj,f)   3.75
--Autobiography with Letters-NY,Lond&Tor-1939-982p-illus
       (4j2) 5.   (5t7)   8.00
--Essays on Books-NY-1914-Macmillan-1st ed   (5m2)   5.00
PHI BETA KAPPA-Catalogue of Member,1806-Cambr-1806-12mo-
   15p-orig wrps   (5ss5,ex-libr)   12.50
PHI BETA COOK BOOK-n.p.-1942-LosAng Alumnae Club-
   pict wrps-spiral bnd-128p   (4g9)   4.00
PHILADELPHIA ALBUM-Ladies Literary Gazette-Phila-1827-
   Vol 2,#1 to #52-bnd in 1 vol   (5m2)   22.50
PHILADELPHIA AND POPULAR PHILADELPHIANS-1891-4to-illus
       (5L7)   15.00
PHILADELPHIA,ATLAS OF-Vol 1(22nd ward)-1876-folio (5mm3) 6.00
PHILADELPHIA-Atlas of Buroughs & Towns in Bucks & Montgomery
   Co on Line of No Penna RR & Branches(title)-Phila-1886-
   folio-col maps   (5w4,wn,rbkd,lacks map)   18.75
PHILADELPHIA,CENTENNIAL SOUVENIR 1876-Phila-1876-
   16 ambertype views,accordion fld to 18mo-cl case-
   Ostheimer Bros   (5t7)   5.00
PHILADELPHIA CHAMBER OF COMMERCE-Essay on Warehousing
   System & Government Credits of US-1828-57p-buck(5L7,rbnd)15.00
PHILADELPHIA COLORED DIRECTORY,1910-comp by RRWright-
   1910-wrps-sewn   (5L7,soil)   25.00
PHILADELPHIA DIRECTORY FOR 1805-AShoemaker,ed-1805-12mo-
   hf calf-unnbrd pg   (5w7,wn,sl stn)   37.50
PHILADELPHIA DIRECTORY FOR 1809-cl-lea labl-JasRobinson,ed
       (5tt6)   40.00
PHILADELPHIA DIRECTORY FOR 1816-hf lea-JasRobinson,ed
       (5tt6,hng weak)   45.00
PHILADELPHIA-Guide Book to the Principal Places of Interest in
   Phila-Phila-1896-obl 12mo-79p   (5w7)   6.50
PHILADELPHIA-Historical Sketches of Catholic Churches &
   Institutions of-Phila-1895-illus-orig wrps   (5m2)   6.00
PHILADELPHIA-Illus Phila...its Wealth & Industries...NY-c1889-
   sm4to-orig pict wrps-illus-288p-(Amer Pub & Engraving Co,pub)
       (5w0,bkstrp taped)   10.00
PHILADELPHIA IN 1824-Complete guide for strangers-Phila-
   24mo-fldg map-plts(1 fldg)-orig roan&bds-(Carey&Lea)
       (5g8,ex-libr,sl wn)   30.00
PHILADELPHIA-The Independence Square Neighborhood-Phila-1927-
   155p-illus-Penn Mutual Life Ins Co,pub   (5w9)   4.00
PHILADELPHIA JOURNAL-of the Medical & Physical Sciences-
   Phila-1820 to 27-hf lea-8vo-14 vols-complete run (5jj8,wn) 450.00
PHILADELPHIA MEDICAL MUSEUM-Vols 1 to 6(all publ)-Phila-
   1805 to 09-calf-8vo-6 vols   (5jj8)   180.00
PHILADELPHIA NATIONAL BANK-Century's Record,1803 to 1903-
   by a stockholder-Phila-1903-4to-illus(5ss5) 10. (5L7)   9.50
PHILADELPHIA-Official Directory of Bell Telephone of...
   Jan 1,1890-orig wrps   (4m2)   17.50
--same-April 1,1891-orig wrps   (4m2)   17.50
PHILA,POTTSVILLE & READING RR-Off Hand Sketches,a Companion
   for the Tourist & Traveller Over the,etc-Phila-1854-12mo-cl-
   illus-1st ed   (5ss5,rbnd)   20.00
PHILA SOCIETY FOR PROMOTING AGRICULTURE-Memoirs-
   Vols 1 thru 4-1808-buck   (5L7,rbnd)   45.00
--Sketch of the History of-Phila-1939-228p-illus   (5e4)   10.00
PHILADELPHIA SOUTHERN STEAMSHIP MANUFAC & MERCANTILE
   REGISTER-Phila-1866-illus-fldg map-ads-184p-scarce (4m2,f)25.00
PHILADELPHIA-Strangers Guide in Phila to all Public Buildings,
   Places of Amusement,etc-Phila-(1862)-
   272p-cl-illus-fldg map   (5t0)   7.50
PHILADELPHIANS IN CARTOON-As seen by Phila newspaper
   cartoonists-1906-illus   (5L7)   25.00
PHILANGUS & ASTRAEA-or,the loyal poem-Stamford-1712-
   prntd for author-sm folio-sewn-1st ed (5x3,lt dmpstnd) 100.00
PHILATELIC SOCIETY,THE-London,Compiler & Publisher-postage
   stmps,envelopes & postcards of NoAmer Colonies of Great Brit-
   Lond-1889,1887-6p plts-4to-hf crushed lev-t.e.g.-bnd with
   same of Australia & British Colonies of Oceania-(30p plts)-
   67p & 148p   (5w8,f bndg)   75.00
PHILBRICK,FRED A-Language & the Law-NY-1949-Macmillan-
   254p   (5p9)   4.50
PHILBROOK,H B-Astronomy Corrected-NY-JnPolhemus-1882-
   8vo-55p-orig cl   (5L1)   25.00
PHILBY,H ST. J B-Arabian Highlands-Ithaca-(1952)-771p-cl-
   Middle East Insti   (5d7)   7.50
PHILENIA-Ouabi,or the virtues of nature-Bost-1790-Thos&Andrews-
   8vo-stiff wrps-frontis-1st ed of auth's 1st book (5i9,sl stn) 75.00
PHILIDOR-Analysis of the Game of Chess-Lond-1790-8vo-
   2 vols in 1-calf-new ed   (5b0,rbkd,lacks frontis)   27.50
PHILIP,ALEX J-A Dickens Dictionary-Lond-1909-408p (4a8) 7.50

PHILLIP,ARTHUR-Voyage of Gov Phillip to Botany Bay-Lond-
   1789-fldg maps-thk lg4to-orig marbld bds-1st ed-errata lf
       (4b6,crude cl bk,broken)   375.00
PHILIP DRU:ADMINISTRATOR-a story of tomorrow-NY-1912-
   Huebsch-312p-1st ed   (5t1)   100.00
--same-NY-1919-Huebsch   (5ss9,hng rprd)   20.00
PHILIP 5th-Treaty of Peace & Friendship Between...Princess(Queen)
   Anne....&....Concluded at Utrecht-Lond-1714-sm4to-115p-
   sewn-1st ed   (5aa0)   65.00
PHILIPPE,CHAS LOUIS-Bubu of Montparnasse-Paris-1932-12mo-
   coverd wrps-1st ed-Crosby Continental Ed   (5ss7,sl soil) 17.50
PHILIPPI,FERDINAND-Geschichte der vereinigten Freistaaten
   von Nordamerika-Dresden-1826-12mo-bds-3 vols in 1 (5L1) 25.00
PHILIPPINE ISLANDS-Annual Reports of Sec of Int on...for
   1912,1913-Manila-1914-Bur of Printing-R8vo-cl-orig wrps
   bnd in-1st ed-rare-illus   (5p5)   32.50
PHILIPPINE ISLANDS-Census of-Year 1903-Wash-1905-GPO-
   4 vols-8vo-maps-illus   (4m7)   27.50
PHILIPPINE ISLANDS-Souvenir of-SanFran-n.d.-(ca 1900)-
   photogravures-obl-approx 100p photos   (5t4,hng crack)   7.50
PHILIPPINE LAW JOURNAL-Vol 1 thru 10-1914 to 31-bound
       (5ii7,rbnd)   165.00
PHILIPS,AMBROSE-Pastorals-Lond-1710-H Hills-8vo-disbnd-
   pirated 1st ed   (5x3)   35.00
PHILIPS,EDITH-The Good Quaker in French Legend-Phila-1932-
   cl bds-illus   (5mm2)   7.50
PHILIPS,FRANCIS CHAS-As in a looking glass-Lond-1889-
   Ward&Downey-4to-orig cl-13 plts by Geo DuMaurier
       (5xx6,rub)   17.50
--The dean & his daughter-Lond-1887-Ward&Downey-3 vols-
   8vo-orig cl-1st ed   (5xx6,vg)   35.00
PHILIPS,JOHN F-Speeches of....& Wm H Wallace...in the trial
   of Frank James-n.p.-n.d.(ca 1901)-wrps-pg 151 to 282-
   v scarce   (5yy7,lacks pt wrp)   25.00
PHILIPS,PAUL C,ed-40 Yrs on the Frontier as Seen in Journals &
   Remini of Granville Stuart-Cleve-1925-2 vols
       (5n4,Streeter set)   90.00
PHILIPS,SHINE-Big Spring-NY-1942-231p-1st ed-advance rev copy-
   Macmillan (5s4,cov tn,soil) 7.50 (5n4,review copy) 12.50
PHILISTINE,THE-Periodical of Protest-East Aurora,1895,1896-
   Vol 2,#1 to 6 complete-Dec,1895 to May 1896-16mo-
   orig wrps-bds&cl   (5dd8)   50.00
PHILLIMORE,J G-Principles & Maxims of Jurisprudence-Lond-
   1856   (5ff4,rebnd)   10.00
PHILLIP BEST BREWING CO,MILWAUKEE-Souvenir Presented by
   NY-1883-Witteman Bros-foldout-bds-16mo-24 leaves (4a5) 12.50
PHILLIPPE,A-Les Montres San Clef-Paris-1863-8vo-308p-
   3 fldg plts-cl   (5bb0)   30.00
PHILLIPPS,E MARCH-Gardens of Italy-Lond-1919-col frontis-
   illus-4to-cl-1st ed   (5z9,f)   25.00
PHILLIPS,S M-Famous Cases of Circumstantial Evidence-NY-
   1875   (5ff4,rebnd)   12.50
--Notes to Phillipps' Treatise on Law of Evidence by Esek Cowen-
   NY-1843-2nd ed-2 vols   (5ff4,rebnd)   17.50
PHILLIPPS,A & CO-Annual Guide to Calif-SanFran-(1883)-illus-
   narr 8vo-pict wrps   (5g3,sp wn)   15.00
PHILLIPS,A B,ed-The Inspired Version Compared with Other Bible
   Versions-Indep,Mo-n.d.-62 dbl col pgs-wrps   (5t3)   8.50
PHILLIPS,A V-Lott Family in Amer-1942-179p   (5mm3)   15.00
PHILLIPS,ALAN-Living Legend:Story of RCMP-Bost-1957-328p
       (5a1)   4.50
PHILLIPS,ALICE MARY-Los Angeles a Guide Book-LosAng-1907-
   151p-illus-cl-Neuner Co   (5d6)   10.00
PHILLIPS & HILL,eds-Classics of the Amer Shooting Field-Bost-
   1930-col frontis-illus-1st ed   (5kk7,dj,unopnd)   12.50
PHILLIPS,ANNA M L-Hooked Rugs & How to Make Them-NY-
   1925-154p-illus-12mo   (5n7)   3.00
PHILLIPS,ARTHUR B-Restoration Movement & Latter Day Saints-
   Indep-1929-rev ed-334p plus index   (5yy7)   7.50
PHILLIPS,ARTHUR S-My Wilderness Friends-FallRiv-1910-81p-
   plts   (5aa0)   5.00
PHILLIPS,C E L-The Vision Splendid-Lond-1960-illus (5x2,dj) 6.50
PHILLIPS,C J-Glass,the Miracle Maker-NY-(1941)-illus (5ii3) 15.00
PHILLIPS,CATHERINE C-Cornelius Cole,Calif Pioneer & Senator-
   SanFran-1929-Nash-illus-379p-mrbld cl-errata slip
       (4n1,box) 25.   (4L9)   20.00
--same-SanFran-1929-John Henry Nash-lg4to-errata slip-
   ltd to 250c,box   (4a5)   45.00
--Through the Golden Gate-LosAng-(1938)-1st ed (5h4,dj) 6.00
PHILLIPS,CHAS L-Fredk Young-Bost-(c1901)-8vo-dec cl-g.t.-
   illus   (5b2)   5.00
PHILLIPS,CLAUDE-Emotion in Art-NY-n.d.-illus-283p-8vo
       (5ww3)   15.00

PHILLIPS,D L-History of Griswold,Conn from the Earliest Times
to 1917-1929-456p   (5t9)   25.00

PHILLIPS,DAVID GRAHAM-The Fashionable Adventures of
Joshua Craig-NY-1909-Appleton-illus-1st ed   (5m2)   5.00

--The Plum Tree-Indnpls-BobbsMerrill-(1905)-pict cl-1st ed,
1st state(with advt for The Filligree Ball,etc) (5m2,v sl wn) 6.50

PHILLIPS,DUNCAN-The Enchantment of Art-Lond-1914-illus-
322p-8vo   (5ww3)   15.00

PHILLIPS,E P-The Genera of So African Flowering Plants-CapeTown-
1926-cl-8vo   (5z9)   12.50

PHILLIPS,EMMETT-Sacramento Valley & Foothill Counties of Calif-
Sacramento-1915-illus-orig dec wrps   (5jj1)   8.50

PHILLIPS,ETHEL CALVERT-A Name for Obed-Bost-1941-illus-8vo-
117p-cl-HoughtonMiff-1st ed   (5p1)   5.00

PHILLIPS,EVERETT FRANKLIN-Beekeeping-NY-1916-8vo-cl-illus-
457p   (5t2)   3.75

PHILLIPS,F C-A Question of Color-NY-1895-12mo-1st ed (5x2) 15.00

PHILLIPS,FREDERIC NELSON-Phillips' Old Fashioned Type Book-
NY-1945-252p-folio-cl   (4c1) 7.50   (4a1)   10.00

PHILLIPS,G JENKIN-System of Mining Coal & Metalliferous
Veins,etc-Phila-1858-86p-4 fldg plts   (5ee3)   6.50

PHILLIPS,GEO-Travels in NoAmer-Rivington-1831-plts-16mo-
qtr roan-168p   (4d2)   35.00

PHILLIPS,HENRY-Flora Historica-Lond-1829-2 vols (5w3,hgn wk)16.50

PHILLIPS,HENRY W-Red Saunders,His Adventures East & West-
1902-McClure&Phillips-210p-cl-2nd impress (5g5)   3.50

PHILLIPS,HUGH-The Thames About 1750-Lond-1951 (5c1) 22.50

PHILLIPS,ISAAC N-Lincoln-Chig-1910-117p-bds-Monaghan 1947
(5h7,stn)   5.00

PHILLIPS,JAS DUNCAN-Pepper & Pirates-Bost-1949-1st ed-illus
(4t0,5tt5)   4.50

--Salem & the Indies-Bost-1947-468p-illus-1st ed (5h9) 8.50

--Salem in 18th Century-Bost-1937-illus-533p-fldg maps
(5i3,dj,f) 12.50   (5c1)   20.00

PHILLIPS,JOHN C-Amer Game Mammals & Birds-Bost-1930-8vo-
639p-1st ed   (5ss5,dj)   25.00

--Classics of the Amer Shooting Field-Bost-1930-illus
(5p0) 6.50   (5ss8)   12.50

--A Natural History of the Ducks-Bost&NY-1922 to 1926-col plts-
118 maps-4 vols-4to-orig lin bkd bds-prntd labls-1st ed
(5z9,vf)   950.00

--Sportsman's Second Scrapbook-Bost&NY-1933-illus-197p(5q0) 7.50

PHILLIPS,JONATHAN-Messages of the Presidents of the US...
to inaugural address of Pres Harrison-Columbus-1841-lea-
Jonthan Phillips,pub   (5q8,wn)   10.00

PHILLIPS,LEROY-Bibliography of Writings of Henry James-Bost-
1906-1st ed-ltd to 250c,nbrd   (5g2)   27.50

PHILLIPS,LIONEL-Some Reminiscences-Lond-ca1925-lg8vo-
40&296p-16 plts   (5c6)   9.50

PHILLIPS,MARY E-Reminiscences of Wm Wetmore Story-Chig-1897-
illus-1st ed   (5mm1)   10.00

PHILLIPS,MICHAEL J-History of Santa Barbara Co,Calif-Chig-
1927-4to-2 vols-cl-illus   (5h4,vg)   35.00

PHILLIPS,MOWRY & CO-Union Steam & Water Heating Apparatus-
Sprngfld-1872-sm8vo-fldg plt-illus-88p-limp cl (5t7) 5.00

PHILLIPS,N F-US Taxation of Nonresident Aliens & Foreign Corps-
Tor-1952   (5ff4)   9.75

PHILLIPS,NORMAN-Tragedy of Apartheid-Lond-1961-217p-8 plts
(5c6,f)   6.75

PHILLIPS,P LEE-Alaska & NW Part of NoAmer,1588 to 1898,
Maps in Libr of Cong-Wash-1898-119p-wrps   (4a5,fox)   17.50

--Author List of Geographical Atlases in Libr of Cong-Wash-
1914-137p   (5j4)   12.50

--Check List of Large Scale Maps Published by Foreign Govts
(Great Brit excepted)-Wash-1904-58p-cl   (4j6)   13.50

--Descriptive List of Maps & Views of Phila,1683 to 1865-n.p.-
1926-frontis   (5L7,rbnd) 7.50   (4m2)   12.50

--Descriptive Lists of Maps of Spanish Possessions Within Present
Limits of the US, 1502 to 1820-Wash-1912-Lowery Collection-
567p   (5n4,f,pres)   30.00

--List of Atlases & Maps Applicable to the World War-Wash-
1918-202p   (5j4,lone pres)   22.50

--A List of Books,Magazine Articles & Maps Relating to Brazil,
1800 to 1900-Wash-1901-145p-wrps   (5n4)   8.50

--List of Geographical Atlases in Libr of Congress-Wash-1909-
tall thk8vo-4 vols   (4b6)   150.00

--List of Maps of Amer in Libr of Congress-Wash-1901-1137p-cl-
8vo-1st ed-rare (5tt0,ex-libr,shaken) 20. (4a1,hng cracked) 97.50

--List of Works Relating to Cartography-Wash-1901-90p-cl (5j4) 9.00

PHILLIPS,P LEE-Virginia Cartography,a Bibliographical Description-
Wash-1896-85p-wrps   (5j4)   12.50

PHILLIPS,P W-WW Brown,Host-NY-1941   (5x2,dj)   15.00

PHILLIPS,PAUL CHRISLER-The Fur Trade-Univ of Okla-(1961)-
2 vols-illus-1st ed-boxed   (5g6) 25.   (5h5,f)   20.00

PHILLIPS,S-The New Inferno-Lond-1911-4to-illus by Vernon Hill-
1st ed-ltd to 320c   (5yy6)   10.00

PHILLIPS,REV S-The Christian Home-Sprngfld,Mass-1868-plts-
376p,(6)   (5w7,fade)   4.00

PHILLIPS,S M-Famous Cases of Circumstantial Evidence-NY-
1874-JCockcroft-294p   (5p9)   6.50

PHILLIPS,S M A-Treatise on the Law of Evidence-NY-1820-23
lea labl-8vo-2 vols-calf-2nd Amer ed,enlgd (4m6)   15.00

PHILLIPS,SAM'L-Orthodox Christian;or Child Well Instructed-
Bost-1738-Kneeland&Green-calf-v rare
(5cc6,stnd,lacks 1st sig & last lf) 55. (4F6,last lf & hf t.in facs)125.00

--Political Rulers Authoriz'd & Influenc'd by God our Saviour to
decree & execute Justice,A Sermon...May 30,1750-Bost-1750-
59p,(4)-JnDraper   (5L1,dmpstnd)   15.00

--A Word in Season-Bost-1727-Kneeland&Green-213p,errata,4p-
ads-bds   (4b4)   27.50

PHILLIPS,SEMIRA A-Proud Mahaska,1843 to 1900-Oskaloosa-1900-
Herald Print-cl-8vo-383p   (5m8) 12.50 (4t1)   20.00

PHILLIPS,STEPHEN-Ulysses,a Drama in a Prologue & 3 Acts -NY-
1902-ltd ed-ltd to 100c on Jap vel   (5r9)   15.00

PHILLIPS,T E R-Splendor of the Heavens-NY-1931-cl-4to-992p-
25 col plts   (5cc1,cg)   7.50

PHILLIPS,TOM-Sketches of...-KansCty-1971-188p drawings plus
18p-2 col illus-col print laid in-orig drawing on cov-cowhide-
brand on cov-1st ed-ltd to 250c   (4L5)   75.00

PHILLIPS,ULRICH B-Amer Negro Slavery-NY-1929 (5x2) 35.00

--Life & Labor in the Old South-Bost-1929-375p-illus-lg fldg map-
2 nd prntng   (5w5)   10.00

--same-Bost-1931-cl-fldg map-375p   (4h7)   7.50

PHILLIPS,W S-Two Young Crusoes-Chig-c1905,6-Donohue-8vo-
pict buff cl-frontis-illus   (5aa2)   5.00

PHILLIPS,WALTER -Colour in Canadian Rockies-Tor-1937-125p-
25 col plts-e.p.maps   (5s4,dj,cov soil)   10.00

PHILLIPS,WALTER J-The Technique of the Color Wood Cut-n.p.-
1926-63p-cl-illus   (5t2,dj,f)   4.00

PHILLIPS,WENDELL-Constitution a Pro Slavery Compact-NY-
1856-208p   (4m4)   25.00

--Freedom for women,Speech at Worcester,Oct 15&16,1851-
wrpr title-NY-1867-wrps   (5g8,scuff,stns)   5.00

--No Slave Hunting in the Old Bay State-Bost-1859-16mo-
31p-wrps   (5x2)   35.00

--Philosophy of the Abolition Movement-Anti Slavery Tract #8-
NY-1860-47p-Amer Anti Slavery Soc   (5x2)   22.50

--Review of Lysander Spooner's Essay on unconstitutionality of
slavery-Bost-1847-95p-wrps   (5x2,loose)   50.00

--Review of Webster's Speech on Slavery-Bost-1850-44p-disbnd
(5x2) 40.   (5x5)   20.00

--Speeches,Lectures & Letters(Abolition Movement)-Bost-1863-
12mo   (5x2)   27.50

--same-2nd series-1894   (5x2)   22.50

PHILLIPS,WM-Conquest of Kans by Missouri & Her Allies-Bost-
1856-414p-cl-1st ed-Howes P 330   (5s4,wn,5s2,5h7)   15.00

PHILLIPS,WM BATTLE-Mineral Resources of Texas-Austin-1910-
45p-wrps   (4a5)   4.50

PHILLIPSON,WM M-Life & Voyages of-Sonora-(1924)-Banner-
114p-wrps   (5tt0)   25.00

PHILLPOTTS,EDEN-Children of the Mist-Lond-1898-ADInnes&Co-
cl-1st ed-1st issue   (5ss3,hgn crack,chip)   20.00

--A Comedy Royal in Four Acts-Lond-1925-priv prntd-ltd ed-
ltd to 275c, autg   (5r9,f)   15.00

--A Dish of Apples-Lond-(1921)-Hodder&Stoughton-3 col plts-
drawings by Rackham   (5c8,f)   17.50

--same-Lond-n.d.-sq8vo-4 col,7 b&w by Arthur Rackham-pict cl
(5t2)   15.00

--same-Lond-(1921)-illus by Arthur Rackham-white cl-g.t.-
3 mounted col plts-ltd to 500c,autgs   (4b7)   60.00

--The Girl & the Faun-Phila-1907-4to-col plts-dec in tint by
Brangwyn-dec cl   (5t5)   4.50

--A Hundred Lyrics-Lond-1930   (5mm2,dj)   4.00

--A Hundred Sonnets-Lond-1st ed-1929   (5r9,f,dj)   6.00

--My Adventure in the Flying Scotsman-Lond-1888-12mo-stiff wrps-
1st ed of auth's 1st book   (5gg6,rbkd)   50.00

PHILOPENA-or,Cousin Lill's Stories for her Pets-NY-(ca 1860)-
16mo-96p-red g. cl-JQPreble-2"x3"   (5c8,sml stn)   4.50

PHILOSOPHICAL INQUIRY CONCERNING HUMAN LIBERTY-
Lond-1735-99p-calf-3rd ed   (5m1,hng loose)   12.50

PHILOSOPHICAL RECREATIONS-or Winter Amusements-Lond-
(ca 1824)-ThosHughes-12mo-200p-orig prntd bds-col fldng
frontis   (5ss5,cov sl loose)   22.50

PHILOSOPHICAL VISIONS-Lond-1757-calf-12mo-rare (5xx6) 225.00

USED BOOK PRICE GUIDE

PHILOSOPHY IN SPORT MADE SCIENCE IN EARNEST-Lond-
1827-Longman,Rees,Orme,Brown&Green-3 vols-cl-papr labls-
wdcuts by GCruikshank-(JAParis)-1st ed
    (5rr2,bndg wn) 32.50   (5c8,rbnd,vg) 40.00
--same-Phila-1828-Carey,Lea&Carey-2 vols-24mo-lea sp & cor-
321p,351p   (5p1,cor wn) 30.00
--same-Lond-1833-1 vol complete-24 wdcuts by GCruikshank-
orig cl-papr labl-480p-new ed   (5c8,vg) 27.50
PHILPOT,H S-Prov of Nova Scotia,Resources & Development-
Ottawa-1930-Dept of Int-157p-illus-fldg col map-wrps-
4th ed   (4a8) 5.00
PHILPOT,HARVEY J-Guide Book to the Canadian Dominion-
Lond-1871   (5w8,pres) 15.00
PHILPOTT,WM B-Sponsor Souvenir Album & History of United
Confederate Veterans' Reunion 1895-Houston-1895-photos-
375p   (4j7,rare) 45.00
PHIN,JOHN-Open Air Grape Culture-NY-1862-375p (5w1) 7.50
--same-NY-1876-266p-rev ed   (5w1,chip) 5.00
--Trade Secrets & Private Recipes-NY-1887-96p (5n7) 3.50
PHINNEY,ELIAS-History of the Battle of Lexington-Bost-1825-
frontis-1st ed   (4m2) 25.00
PHINNEY,M A-Brief History of Jirah Isham(of New London,Conn)
& Desc-(1941)-179p   (5mm3) 22.50
PHINNEY,MARY A-Brief Hist of Ebenezer Phinney (of Cape Cod)
& His Desc-(1948)-146p   (5t9) 15.00
PHINNEY'S CALENDER-or Western Almanac for 1846-Cooperstown-
1846   (4a9) 12.50
PHIPPS,CONSTANTINE J-Voyage Towards North Pole undertaken
by His Majesty's Command,1773-Lond-1774-calf-4to-3 charts-
11 plts-1st ed   (4e1,rebkd) 100.00
--same-Dublin-1775-Sleater,Williams,Wilson-275p-fldg map-
2 plts-8vo-hf calf-plus 49p   (4e1) 20.00
PHIPPS,I N-The Forelopers-NY-1912-Neale-8vo-cl (5b2) 4.00
PHIPPS,JOS-Original & Present State of Man...by People called
Quakers-Phila-1783-reprntd by Crukshank-8vo-calf-209p,(4)-
    (5L1,ex-libr,rprd,5g3,rub) 15.00
--same-NY-1788-8vo-calf-2nd Amer ed
    (5g8,libr labl) 7.50   (5ss5,lacks fly) 13.50
PHISTERER,FREDK-NY in War of Rebellion 1861 to 1865-Albany-
1890-4to-532p   (4a7,sl wn,5t4) 17.50
PHOENIX CITY DIRECTORY-for 1916,5th Annual Directory-
Phoenix-1916   (5x5) 20.00
PHOENIX,JOHN-Phoenixiana-NY-1856-Appleton-pict cl-
1st ed   (5ee3,sl loose) 15. (5mm1) 25.00
--same-NY-1903-Appleton-8vo-pic cl-g.t.-illus by EWKemble-
intro by Bangs-new ed   (5b2,rprd) 7.50
--same-SanFran-1937-Farquhar,ed-Grabhorn Pr-illus-cl bds-
ltd to 500c (5mm2) 35. (5r0) 20. (5r8) 25.00
PHOENIX OF STORY BOOKS-Phila-(1844)-JasKSimon-sq12mo-
96p-orig cl-5 hand col wdcuts   (5c8,soil) 8.00
PHOENIX,S W-Whitney Family of Conn & Its Affiliations-1878-
3 vols   (5mm3) 37.50
PHOTO STORY GREATEST FLOOD OF CENTURY OHIO VALLEY-
n.p.-n.d.-(Cinn 1937)-(64)p-wrps   (5h7) 4.00
PHOTOMOBILE TOURIST-Oreg,Wash,Ida-Seattle-(1919)-416p-
photos   (5s4,cov wn & soil) 10.00
PHRENOLOGICAL ANNUAL-& Register Illustrated-Lond-1896-
Fowler&Wells-86p-7"x10"   (5F9) 4.00
PHYLLIDA-or, the Milkmaid-#1-SanFran-Jan 1,1897-4p (5d6) 7.50
PHYLON-Atlanta Univ Review of Race & Culture-1947-2nd qtr
    (5x2) 3.50
--same-1948-1st quarter   (5x2) 3.50
PHYSIOLOGIE DU GOUT-Paris-1847-474p-bds-half lea(5g9) 15.00
--same-Paris-1873-339p-lea & bds-new ed (5g9) 12.50
PIAGET,JEAN-Origins of Intelligence in Children-NY-c1952-
419p-8vo-Int'l Univ Pr   (5p1,dj) 4.50
PIATT,DONN-Lone Grave of Shenandoah,& Other Tales-Chig-1888
    (4b6) 20.00
PIATT,JOHN HAS-A dream of church windows,etc-Bost-1888-
129p-Houghton-rev ed   (5m2) 6.50
--The Hesperian Tree,Annual of Ohio Valley,1900-Cinn-(1900)-
Shaw-thk4to-cl-bds-1st ltd ed   (5m2,autg) 10.00
--Landmarks & other poems-NY-1872-Hurd&Houghton-Cambr,
Riverside Pr-1st ed   (5m2) 6.50
--Little New World Idyls & Other Poems-Lond-1893-port
    (5r7,unopnd) 7.50
PIATT,MRS S M-Voyage to Fortunate Isles,etc-Bost-1874-1st ed
    (5q0) 5.00
PICARD,GEO H-A Matter of Taste-NY-1885-illus(5ee3,cov soil) 5.00
PICARDI,GAETANO-Del Caffe Racconto Storico Medico-Napoli-
1845-126p-wrps   (5w1,fox,chip) 8.50

PICASSO,PABLO-Dans l'Atelier de Picasso-Paris-(1957)-Mourlot-
Jaime Sabartes-folio-orig Picass cov-bnd by Decauchelle-
calf-6 orig liths(incl 2 on cov) in col & 30 in b&w-extra
suite of 13 liths-ltd to 50c (5d1,box,autg) 2,500.00
--same-ltd to 200 copy edition-Paris-(1957) (5d8) 500.00
--Picasso,Seize Peintures 1939 to 1943-Paris-1943-intro by
Rbt Desnos-folio-in sheets-prntd wrps as issued (5d1) 37.50
--Lithographs 1945 to 1948-NY-1948-66p-illus-intro by Geiser
    (5t7) 3.50
PICAYUNE'S CREOLE COOK BOOK-NOrl-1922-390p-6th ed-
frontis   (4g9) 7.50
--same-1942-9th ed-438p   (4g9) 7.50
PICCARD,JACQUES-7 Miles Down-NY-1961-54 photos (5c1) 6.50
PICCIOCCHI,C-Manual Pratico de Vinificacao e Tratamento
de Vinhos-Lisboa-1927-160p-wrps (5w1,tn) 12.50
PICHON,LEON-The New Book Illustration in France-Lond-1924-
The Studio-168p-4to-plts   (5v2,f dj) 8.50
PICKARD,MRS KATE E R-The Kidnaped & The Ransomed-Syracuse-
1856-409p-buck   (5w5,crude rbnd,4m6,sl shake) 15.00
PICKARD,MADGE E-Midwest Pioneer,his ills,cures & doctors-
NY-1946 (5dd4) 10.50 (5L7) 8.50
PICKARD,SAM'L T-Life & Letters of John Greenleaf Whittier-Bost-
(1894)-2 vols-port   (5xx7) 15.00
--Whittier Land...A Handbook of N Essex-Bost-1904-160p-illus
    (5e8,5w5,dj) 5.00
PICKELL,JOHN-New Chapter in Early Life of Washington-NY-
1856-8vo-cl-159p & app   (5t2,pres) 5.00
PICKENS,W-Bursting Bonds-Bost-1929 (5x2) 22.50
PICKERING,ERNEST-The Homes of Amer-NY-(1951)-284p,(3)-
215 photos   (5w7) 6.50
PICKERING,ERNEST H-Japan's Place in the Modern World-Lond-
1936-Harrap-326p   (5x9) 4.50
PICKERING,H G-Dog Days on Trout Waters-NY-1933-78p-illus
Derrydale Pr-199c   (5i1,autg,soil) 5.00
PICKERING,JOHN-Eulogy on Nathl Bowditch-Bost-1838-101p-
disbnd-Sabin 62632   (5h7) 7.50
--Vocabulary-Bost-1816-Cummings&Hilliard-207p-hf mor (5yy3) 25.00
PICKERING,OCTAVIUS-Case of the Proprietors of Chas River Bridge
Against the Prop of Warren Bridge-Bost-1830-8vo-203p-sewn
    (5ss5,pgs loose) 10.00
PICKERING,TIMOTHY-Letter & reports of Sec of War to comm
naval equipment of US-(Phila,1796)-folio-orig wrps (5g8) 50.00
PICKETT,ALBERT JAS-History of Alabama-Sheffield,Ala-1896-
669p-cl-republ by Randolph   (5tt8,shaken) 10.00
PICKETT,DEETS,ed-Allied Reforms-Wash-n.d.-(ca 1920)-123p-
wrps-Bd of Temperance,etc   (5h7) 2.50
--Cyclopedia of Temperance,Prohibition & Public Morals-NY-
(1917)-406p-cl-(1917 Ed)   (5h7) 5.00
PICKETT,GEO E-Heart of Soldier as Revealed in Intimate Letters
of-NY-(1913)-215p-cl (5t4) 7.50 (5h2) 8.50 (4p2) 10.00
PICKETT,LA SALLE CORBELL-Literary Hearthstones of Dixie-
Phila-1912-Lippincott-8vo-illus-pic cl-g.t. (5b2,f) 7.50
--Pickett & His Men-Phila-1913-Lippincott-illus
    (5mm8) 7.50 (5w5) 15. (5kk5) 12.50
PICKETT,W P-The Negro Problem,Abraham Lincoln's Solution-NY-
1909-R8vo (5x2,rbnd) 37.50 (5x2) 40.00
PICKTHALL,MARMADUKE-Said the Fisherman-Lond-1903-Methuen-
12mo-orig cl-1st ed   (5ss3,pres,chip) 50.00
--same-NY-1925-Knopf-312p   (5p9) 5.00
PICKWELL,G-Amphibians & Reptiles of the Pacific States-PaloAlto-
1947-cl-236p-col frontis-64 plts-4to (4p6) 17.50
PICKWELL,GAYLE-Deserts-(1939)-Whittlesey Hse-4to-frontis in col-
2nd prntng   (5x5) 15.00
--same-NY-1939-cl-174p-63p plts-1 map-4to (4p5) 27.50
PICTORIAL HISTORY OF AMER REVOLUTION-NY-1846-Robt Sears-
432p-illus-fldg facs-cl   (5mm8) 6.00
PICTORIAL TRACT PRIMER-NY-c1860-12mo-108p-illus-
Amer Tract Soc   (5jj6) 6.50
PICTURE ALPHABET-or Child's A B C-Portland-c1845-24mo-16p-
illus wrps   (5v2,vf) 12.50
PICTURE BOOK FOR LITTLE BOYS & GIRLS-Phila-(c1832)-16p-
24mo-prntd wrps-12 wdcuts-Amer Sunday School Union (5p1) 15.00
PICTURE BOOK OF MERRY TALES-Lond-(ca 1855)-sq8vo-272p-
47p hand col illus-cl-Bosworth&Harrison (5c8,rbnd) 55.00
PICTURE STORY BOOK-Routledge-1850-sm8vo-illus-dec cl-a.e.g.-
3 handcol plts-1st ed-scarce   (4d1) 25.00
PICTURED A B C-NY&Phila-c1835-24mo-8p-pict wrps-illus-
Turner&Fisher   (5v0,f) 17.50
PICTURESQUE ALPHABET,THE-Providence-1843-16mo-(16p)-
wrps-stitchd-col engrs-GPDaniels (5p1) 25.00
PICTURESQUE AMERICA-NY-(1872)-illus-2 vols-4to-lea-sml folio
    (5q0) 35. (5tt7) 27.50

PICTURESQUE BOULDER & BOULDER CO-Hand Colored Views of
Nature's Playground-Boulder-(1915)-Fine&Coulson-12 lvs-
illus-folio-wrps   (4a5)   7.50

PICTURESQUE CHICAGO-Chig-1883-Chicago Engraving Co-
foldout-18 lvs-bds   (4a5)   27.50

PICTURESQUE MEXICO-The Country,the People & The Architecture-
Berlin-1925-4to-photos   (5x5)   15.00

PICTURESQUE NATURE AROUND COLORADO SPRINGS-
ColoradoSprngs-n.d.-(ca 1900)-16p plus covers-photos (5b9,f) 5.00

PICTURESQUE SAN ANTONIO-SanAnt-1907-32p-photos-wrps
          (4a5,mint)   20.00

PICTURESQUE SEATTLE-Seattle-1901-62p-wrps-album styled
cord & tie   (5s4)   5.00

PICTURESQUE SEATTLE & PUGET SOUND-Seattle-n.d.(ca 1915)-
64p-dec cov-stpld-Seattle Chamb Comm   (5s1)   3.00

PICTURESQUE SOUTHWEST-Vol 1,#1-1937-4to-200p (5g0) 3.00

PIDAL,RAMON M-El Romancero Espanol-1910-Hispanic Soc of Amer
          (5hh1)   15.00

PIDGEON,WM-Traditions of De coo dah,& antiquarian researches-
NY-1853-HoraceThayer-334p-cl-illus-fldg plt-fldg frontis
(5d6,lacks.map) 12.50   (5ee3,f)   30.00

PIDGIN,CHAS F-16 Blennerhassett,a Romance-Bost-1902-illus
          (4a9)   4.50

--Climax or What Might Have Been-Bost-1902-C M Clark-335p-cl
          (5tt8)   5.00

--Little Burr-Bost-1905-Luce Co-396p-cl   (5tt8)   5.00

--Quincy Adams Sawyer & Mason's Corner folks-Bost-1900-Clark-
frontis-pict cl-fldg map-auth's 1st book   (5m2)   8.50

PIER,ARTHUR STANWOOD-The Pedagogues,a Story of the Harvard
Summer School-Bost-1899-12mo-cl-1st ed of auth's 1st bk
          (5gg6)   5.00

PIERCE,ANNE-Home Canning for Victory-NY-(1942)-106p-
photo illus   (5c9)   3.00

--The Household Bookshelf-NY-(1950)-280p   (5c9)   3.50

PIERCE,CARL HORTON-New Harlem,Past & Present-NY-1903-
illus-338p-map   (5p0)   6.00

PIERCE CO PIONEER ASSOC-Commemorative Celebration at
Sequalitchew Lake,July 5,1906-(Tacoma,Vaughan&Morrill
Prntg Co)-101p-map-ports-illus-cl-2nd ed   (4L9)   10.00

PIERCE,EDW L-Index of Special RR Laws of Mass-Bost-1874-8vo-
calf-494p   (5m6)   15.00

--Treatise on the Law of RR-Bost-1881-575p-lea   (5t4)   7.50

PIERCE,E L-Lillie Family of Boston-1896-122p   (5mm3)   10.00

PIERCE,ELIZA-Letters,1751 to 75 With Letters from Her Son-Lond-
1927-124p-port-(Haslewood Bks)-ltd to 75c,nbrd   (5a1)   12.50

PIERCE,F C-Field Genealogy-1901-2 vols-1196p (5mm3,wn) 60.00

--Fiske & Fisk Family-1896-654p   (5t9)   40.00

--History of Grafton,Worcester Co,Mass-1879-623p (5mm3) 12.50

--Record of Posterity of Capt Michael Pierce-1889-441p (5mm3) 22.50

PIERCE,FRANKLIN-Message...in Regard to Slave & Coolie Trade-
Wash-1856-HED 5   (5j6)   12.50

--Indian Hostilities in Oregon & Wash Territories-Wash-1856-
HED 118-58p   (5n4)   4.50

PIERCE,FRANK R-Rugged Alaska Stories-Seattle-(1950)-432p-
col illus   (5ss1)   6.50

PIERCE,GERALD-Texas Under Arms-Austin-1969-Encino Pr-part mor-
ltd to 250c,nbrd-box   (4j7)   45.00

PIERCE,GILBERT A-The Dickens Dictionary....with Additions by
Wheeler-Bost-1900-ports-plts-573p   (4a8)   7.50

--Zachariah,The Congressman-Chig-1880-1st ed (5mm2) 10.00

PIERCE,HAYFORD-Byzantine Art-Lond-1926-Benn-4to-cl-plts-
56p text & 100 collotype   (5m5)   25.00

PIERCE,HENRY H-Report of exped from Ft Colville to Puget Sound,
Wash Terr by way of Lake Chelan & Skagit River,Aug & Sept,
1882-Wash-1883-GPO-8vo-orig blue prntd wrps-1st ed-
lg fldg map   (5i9,vf)   40.00

PIERCE,HIRAM DWIGHT-A Forty Niner Speak-Oakland-1930-
illus-74p-wrps-priv prntd   (5dd9)   17.50

PIERCE,JAS WILSON-Photographic History of World's Fair &
Sketch of City of Chicago-Balt-1893-8vo-illus-1st ed (5m6) 10.00

PIERCE,LORNE-Marjorie Pickthall,a Book of Remembrance-Tor-
1925-217p-plts   (5u6)   15.00

PIERCE,T M-White & Negro Schools in the South-Englewood Cliffs-
1955-cl&bds   (5dd5) 12.   (5x2,dj)   7.50

PIERCE,WM HENRY-From Potlatch to Pulpit-Vanc,BC-1933-
frontis-illus-176p-cl   (4L9,dj)   10.00

PIERCE,WM LEIGH-The Year:A Poem,in 3 Cantoes-NY-1813-1st ed-
David Longworth-191p,appendix,75p,(2)-18mo-cl   (5L1)   20.00

PIERCE, W M-Old Hancock County Families-Ellsworth-1933-
Hancock Co Pub-133p-8vo-wrps-(1st series,all pub) (4t1) 12.50

PIERCE,WINSLOW-Annual Report of Comptroller of State of
Calif,1854-n.p.-1854-52p-wrps   (4a5)   9.50

PIERCY,CAROLINE B-Shaker Cook Book-Not by Bread Alone-NY-
(1953)-283p   (5g9)   4.50

--Valley of God's Pleasure-NY-1951-illus-247p-1st ed
(5q0) 15.   (4a9) 7.   (5h2,f,dj)   7.50

PIERCY,FREDK-Route from Liverpool to Great Salt Lake Valley-
LosAng-n.d.-4to-fldg map-illus-JLinford,ed-facsimile reprnt-
1st ed   (5s4,dj,f)   50.00

PIERPONT,JOHN-The National Reader-Bost-1836-276p-lea (5s5) 7.50

--The Portrait,a Poem-Bost-1812-orig prntd wrps-8vo-
1st ed of auth's 1st publ   (5gg6)   25.00

PIERRE,BERNARD-A Mountain Called Nun Kun-Lond-(1955)-
189p-illus-cl-Hodder&Stoughton   (5d7)   5.00

PIERRE DAILY CAPITAL,THE-Special Edition-Pierre,S D-Apr,1890-
24p-wrps-10 x 13½   (5g5)   15.00

PIERRE,SAINT-Beauties of Studies of Nature, Selected from Works
of StPierre-NY-1799-332p-index-calf   (4b4,fox)   18.50

PIERS,HARRY-Rober Field-NY-1927-Sherman-197p-crown 4to
          (4a0)   45.00

PIERSON,A T-Forward Movements of Last Half Century-1900
          (5L7)   4.50

PIERSON,REV ABRAHAM-Some Helps for the Indians,a Catechism
in Quiripi language-Hartf-1873-67p-   intro by Trumbull-
reprntd-ltd to 100c   (5t4)   15.00

PIERSON,CHAS LAWRENCE-Ball's Bluff-Salem-1913-Salem Pr-
54p-frontis-t.e.g.   (5mm8)   12.50

PIERSON,DAVID L-Narratives of Newark (in NJ)-Newark-(1917)-
a.e.g.-illus   (4m2) 15.   (5w5) 6.50   (5m6)   10.00

PIERSON,D-Negroes in Brazil-So Ill Univ-1942-illus
          (5x2,mint,dj)   9.75

PIERSON,DR,ETC-Diseases of the Horse-Wash Dept of Agric-1903-
600p-illus-8vo-cl   (5t0,spots)   5.00

PIERSON,REV HAMILTON W-In the Brush-NY-1881-321p-cl-
12mo-illus,W L Sheppard   (4b3) 10.   (5m8)   12.50

PIERSON,HARRIET-Guide to Cataloguing of Serial Publ of Societies
& Instit-Wash-1919-105p-wrps   (5j4)   6.00

PIESSE,G W SEPTIMUS-The Art of Perfumery-Phila-1856-304p-
illus-1st Amer ed   (5n7,marg stnd)   15.00

PIFFARD,H G-Practical Treatise on Diseases of the Skin-NY-1891-
folio-50p plts-157p   (5yy0)   12.50

PIGAFETTA,ANTONIO-Magellan's Voyage around the World-Cleve-
1906-3 vols-maps-illus-350c prntd   (5m6)   90.00

PIGGOTT,N-Treatise of Common Recoveries,Their Nature & Use-
Lond-1770-2nd ed   (5ff4,rebnd)   22.50

PIGNATORRE,THEODORE-Ancient & Medieval architecture-Lond-
n.d.-Drane's-4to-cl-illus   (5m5)   11.50

PIGOT,BRIG GEN R-25 Years Big Game Hunting-Lond-n.d.-(1928)-
4to-307p-cl-photos-scarce   (4a6,spots)   22.50

PIKE,ALBERT-Prose Sketches & Poems,Written in the Western
Country-Bost-1834-200p-orig cl-1st ed (5t4,stn,fray) 200.00

PIKE & DUBOIS CO,IND-History of-Chig-1886-ports-illus-4to-
776p-part mor   (5kk4,vg)   60.00

PIKE,G D-The Jubilee Singers & Their Campaign for $20,000-
Bost-1873-orig cl-1st ed   (5x2) 20.   (5x5)   15.00

--same-Lond-1874-12mo   (5x2)   20.00

--Singing Campaign for 10,000 pounds,or Jubilee Singers in
Great Brit-NY-1875-appendix   (5x2)   22.50

PIKE,J -The Prostrate State-NY-1874   (5x2)   50.00

PIKE,JAS S-The Prostrate State,So Carolina Under Negro
Government-NY-1874-279p-1st ed   (4m4)   35.00

PIKE,JOSPH-An Epistle to the Nat'l Meeting of Friends, in Dublin,
Concerning Good Order etc-Phila-1757-B Franklin,prntr-23p-
pt mor   (5i9) 75.   (5z7)   95.00

PIKE,L O-History of Crime in England-Lond-1873,1876-2 vols
          (5r4) 27.50   (5tt7)   27.50

PIKE,NICHOLAS-A New and Complete System of Arithmetic-
Worcester-1797-Isaiah Thomas-516p-rev & corr
          (5t4) 10.   (5p5,f)   20.00

--same-Newburyport-1788-calf-lea labl-1st ed of auth's 1st book
          (4m7,2 lvs trim close)   25.00

--same-Bost-1802-352p-abridged for use of schools
          (5t4,wn,lacks e.p.)   7.50

PIKE,NICOLAS-Sub Tropical Rambles in Land of Aphanapteryx-
NY-1873-illus-map-509p   (5q0,5p7) 10.   (5ee3)   12.50

PIKE,WARBURTON-Barren Ground of Northern Canada-Lond&NY-
1892-300p-cl-2 fldg maps-1st ed   (5r6)   22.00

PIKE,Z M-Account of Exped to Sources of Mississ-Phila-1810-
Conrad-frontis-calf-8vo-6 maps(5 fldng)-3 fldg tabls
(4c7) 500. (5tt8,sl tn,stnd) 200.
(4c1,cov loose) 250. (5s9,rbnd,2 facs maps) 375. (4n5,mor) 385.00

--Expeds of...to Headwaters of Mississ Riv-NY-1895-3 vols-illus-
index by Elliot Coues-new map-new ed   (5s9)   145.00

--same-NY-1895-3 vols-hf cl-ltd to 150c   (5s9,mint)   195.00

PIKE, Z M   (continued)
--Exploratory Travels through Western Territories of NoAmer-
   Denver-1889-sm4to-orig blue cl   (5x5,f)   40.00
--Southwestern Exped of-Chig-1925-Quaife,ed-(Lakeside Classic)-
   239p-fldg map-frontis-12mo-g.t.   (5h9)   12.00
--Voyage Au Nouveau Mexique-Paris-1812-hf lea-2 vols-
   3 fldg maps-1st French ed   (4n4,sp chip)   185.00
PIKE'S PEAK & VICINITY-Denv-1885-H H Tammen-foldout-12 lvs-
   stamped bds   (4a5)   45.00
PIKE'S PEAK REGION,THE-Colorado-Denv-1893-from orig
   negatives & photos-34 views   (5L5)   7.50
PILAT,O-Sodom by the Sea-1941-plt   (5L7)   4.50
PILCHER,ELIJAH H-Protestantism in Mich-Detroit-1868-8vo-464p-
   cl   (5mm7)   12.00
PILCHER,RICHARD B-What Industry Owes to Chemical Science-
   Brklyn-1946-372p-illus-1st Amer ed   (5b8)   5.75
PILGRIM'S PROGRESS,THE-Life & Death of Mr. Badman-1928-
   Nonesuch Pr-wdcuts-ltd to 600c for US   (5a9)   25.00
PILGRIMAGE OVER THE PRAIRIES,A-Lond-1863-plts-cl-g.e.-
   2 vols in 1-1st ed-v scarce-(P Ruysdale) (4n4)   165.00
PILKINGTON,JAS-Artist's guide & mechanic's own book-Bost-
   c1841-illus   (5g8)   10.00
--same-NY-1841-cl-12mo-   (5t2,sp def,bkstrp tn) 7.50
--same-Portl-(1847)-frontis-490p   (5t4,fox)   7.50
--same-Portl-1853-490p-illus   (5n7,fade)   10.00
--same-Bost&Portl-(1856)-490p-frontis   (5t4)   10.00
--same-Bost-1857-12mo-cl-illus-490p (5b8,sl shake) 7.50 (5t4) 10.00
--same-Bost-1869-490p   (5t4,libr labl)   4.00
PILKINGTON,REV M-Dictionary of Painters-Lond-1810-4to-bds-
   cl bk-new ed with additions   (5j2,rprd)   18.00
PILINGTON,MARY-Historical Beauties for Young Ladies-Lond-
   1799-ENewberry-hf calf-2nd ed   (5c8,cov dtchd) 32.50
PILLEY,DOROTHY-Climbing Days-NY-(1935)-Harcourt,Brace-
   252p-illus-cl   (5d7)   7.50
PILLINGS,J C-Bibliography of Algonquian Languages-1891-
   Smithsonian BAE Bull #13-pt lea
              (5L7,rbnd) 25. (5y9) 17.50 (4k4,f)   20.00
--Bibliography of Athapascan Languages-Smithsonian-1892-
   BAE Bull #14-wrps   (5y9) 15.   (4b2)   12.50
--Bibliography of Chinookan Languages-Smithsn-1893-BAE Bull #15-
   wrps   (4k4) 15. (5y9) 15.   (5L7)   12.50
--Bibliography of Eskimo Language-Wash-1887-116p-wrps
              (5j4,wrps loose) 8.50   (4k4,f)   12.50
--Bibliography of the Iroquoian Languages-1888-BAE,B6-208p-
   hard cov   (4b2,rebnd) 15. (5L7,rbnd) 15. (4k4,wrps) 12.50
--Bibliog of the Muskhogean Languages-1889-BAE,B9-114p-wrps-
   scarce   (4b2,cl rebnd) 15. (4k4,f)   12.50
--Bibliography of Salishan Language-Smithsn,BAE,B16-1893-cl
              (5j4,cov dtchd) 8.50   (4k4,5y9)   12.50
--Bibliog of the Siouan Languages-1887-BAE,B5-87p-wrps
              (4b2,cl rebnd) 15. (5n4,4k4)   12.50
PILLSBURY,A J-Institutional Life-Sacramento-1906-12mo-cl-
   167p   (5h5)   3.00
PILLSBURY,DAVID B-The Pillsbury Family...of Newbury in
   NewEngl-Everett-1898-Mass Pub Co-part lea-12mo-307p(4t1)60.00
PILLSBURY,DOROTHY L-Adobe Doorways-Albuqu-(1953)-204p-
   hf cl   (5dd6,ex-librr) 3.50
--No High Adobe-1950-198p-1st ed   (5r1,dj)   13.50
--Roots in Adobe-UNM Pr-1954-8vo-cl-232p-1st ed (5g5,f,dj) 5.00
PILLSBURY,HOBART-New Hampshire,Resources, Attractions & Its
   People-1927-5 vols-Lewis Hist Publ Co-sm4to-cl
              (4t1) 40.   (5mm3)   17.50
PILLSBURY,LT J E-Gulf Stream Explorations-Wash-1890-GPO-
   USGS-4to-hf mor-maps-charts-369p-appendix #16,Rep for
   1889   (5p7)   12.50
PILLSBURY,PARKER-Acts of the Anti Slavery Apostles-Concord,NH-
   1883   (5x5)   25.00
--same-Bost-1884-503p   (4m2)   30.00
PILON,FREDK-The Fair American,a Comic Opera in 3 Acts-
   Dublin-1785-sm12mo-mor bkd bds-71p-prntd by JExshaw-
   1st ed   (5L8,rbnd)   35.00
PILOT,THE-a Tale of the Sea-NY-mor-2 vols-1st ed-(JFCooper)
   1823   (4j6,box)   75.00
--same-NY-1824-2 vols-2nd ed-(JasFCooper) (5mm1)   10.00
PILOT KNOB MEMORIAL ASSN-Meeting of-Sept 27,1904-33p-
   illus-wrps   (4b3)   35.00
PILOTE DE TERRE NEUVE,LE-(Paris,1763 to 92)- Depot Generale
   de la Marine, 1784 -lg folio-sheep-14 maps(13 fldng dbl sheets)-
   1st French ed-rare   (5n9) 1,250.00
PILSBURY,T-Report & Protest of Comm on Territories Against
   Dismemberment of Texas-Wash-1849-HR16-9p (5n4) 15.00
PINART,ALPHONSE-Journey to Ariz in 1876-LosAng-1962-sm4to-
   bds-Zamorano Club   (5h5,lt soil) 15.00

PINCHER,CHAPMAN-A Study of Fish-NY-(1948)-Duell-
   343p-illus   (5p7)   5.00
PINCHON,EDGCUMB-Dan Sickles-GardenCty-1945-8vo-280p
              (4j4) 4.   (4a7) 6.75   (5s9)   5.00
--Viva Villa-NY-c1933-383p-illus-1st ed (5w5,cov spots) 15.00
PINCHOT,GIFFORD-A Primer of Forestry-Part 1-The Forest-Wash-
   1900   (5b9)   10.00
--same-Wash-1903-Bull #24,US Dept of Agric-88p-47 plts-
   green cl   (5s7,f)   5.00
PINCHOT,GIFFORD-Giff & Stiff in South Seas-Phila-(1933)-
   241p-illus   (5s1)   4.00
--To the South Seas-Phila-(1930)-500p-maps-photos (5s1) 7.50
PINCKARD,GEO-Notes on the West Indies-Lond-1806-8vo-3 vols-
   orig calf-1st ed   (5L1,hng crack) 95.00
PINCKNEY,PAULINE A-Painting in Texas, 19th Century-Austin-
   1967-232p-illus-folio-col illus   (4j6)   15.00
PINCKNEY,S-National Guard Manual-1864-281p-illus-12mo
              (4a2,sp glued)   5.00
PINCOCK,JENNY-The Trails of Truth-LosAng-c1930 (5x7,stns) 3.00
PINDAR,PETER,JR-Parnassus in Philadelphia-Phila-1854-12mo-
   orig bds-1st ed   (5i0,sl wtrstnd) 17.50
PINE,GEO W-Beyond the West-Utica-1870-illus-pict cl-1st ed
              (5s4,ex-librr,fair) 35.   (5g3)   60.00
--same-Utica-1871-illus-483p-2nd ed   (4b6,rprd,ex-librr) 20.00
--same-NY-1873-illus-frontis-483p   (5yy0)   9.50
PINE,HESTER-Beer for the Kitten-(1939)-Farrar&Rinehart-
   auth's 1st novel   (5F1,f,dj)   8.00
PINE,JOHN-The Spanish Armada,1588-Bost-1878-4to-plts-
   orig bds   (5ss5,ex-librr,lacks bkstrp) 17.50
PINE,L G-The Story of the Peerage-1956-310p   (5t9) 5.00
PINERO,ARTHUR W-The Gay Lord Quex,a Comedy in 4 Acts-
   NY-1900-Russell-186p   (5p9)   3.50
PINGREE,HAZEN S-Facts & Opinions-Detr-1895-210p-wrps
              (5h2)   10.00
PINGRY,W M-Desc of Moses Pengry of Ipswich,Mass-1881-186p
              (5mm3)   25.00
PINK,L H-Candle in the Wilderness-NY-1957-Appleton-304p-
   illus   (5p7)   5.00
PINKERTON,ALLAN-Claude Melnotte as a detective-Chig-
   1875-Keen,Cooke&Co-8vo-orig dec cl-1st ed (5i0)   12.00
--The Detective & Somnambulist & Murderer & Fortune Teller-
   Chig-1875-illus-1st ed   (4m8,shake) 8.50 (5mm2) 10.00
--same-NY-1880-illus   (5r7,pres)   10.00
--The Expressman & the Detective-Chig-1875-Keen,Cooke&Co-
   278p-illus-(not 1st)   (5x4) 10.   (5m2,lacks e.p.) 6.00
--Mississippi Outlaws & the Detectives,Don Pedro & the
   Detectives,Poisoner & the Detectives-NY-1879-GWCarleton-
   377p-1st ed   (5x4,lacks e.p.) 20.00
--Molly Maguires & the Detectives-NY-1882-new&enlrgd ed-
   illus-12mo-cl   (4c1)   12.50
--Professional Thieves & the Detective-NY-1881-illus-1st ed (4j4) 10.00
--The Railroad Forger & the Detectives-NY-1881-364p,(8)-1st ed
              (5w9)   10.00
--The Spiritualists & the Detectives-NY-1877-illus-green cl-
   1st ed-1st issue,ads dated 1876 (5ee3,Ellery Queen's copy) 20.00
--Spy of the Rebellion-Chig-1882-688p-illus (5w5,stnd,crack) 5.00
--Tests on Passenger Conductors,made by the Nat'l Police Agency-
   Chig-1867-8vo-wrps-v rare-1st ed of auth's 1st publ (5gg6) 150.00
--30 Years a Detective-Phila-1884-1st ed   (5mm2)   10.00
PINKERTON,FRANK-Jim Cummings or the Great Adams Express
   Robbery-Chig-1887-162p-cl-Laird&Lee   (5h0)   15.00
PINKERTON,JOHN-Modern Geography-Lond-1802-2 vols-thk4to-
   calf-maps   (5r7,hng weak) 25.00
--Voyages & Travels-Lond-1809-Vols4,5,6 only-4to
              (5s1,rprd) ea vol   9.00
PINKERTON,KATHRENE-Adventure North-NY-(1940)-268p(5ss1)4.50
--Bright With Silver-NY-(1947)-347p-photos (5ss1)   5.00
--Three's A Crew-NY-(1940)-316p-photos   (5ss1)   6.00
--Two Ends to Our Shoestring-NY-1941-362p (5ss1,autg,5dd0) 5.00
PINKERTON,ROBT-Canoe,Its Selection,Care,Use-NY-(1914)-
   162p-photos   (5s4) 5. (5dd7) 4.00
PINKERTON,ROBT E-Hudson's Bay Company-NY-(1931)-366p-
   plts   (5r8)   30.00
PINKERTON,THOS A-A new saint's tragedy-Lond-1892-
   Swan Sonnenschein & Co-2 vols-8vo-orig cl-1st ed
              (5xx6,lend libr labl)   25.00
PINKERTON,WM A-Adam Worth....Theft & Recovery of
   Gainsborough's "Duchess of Devonshire"-NY-1902-23p-wrps-
   12 port   (5dd0)   15.00
--Bank..."Sneak"...Thieves-HotSprings-1906-53p-wrps-27 ports
              (5dd0)   15.00
--Train Robberies, Train Robbers & "Holdup" Men-Jamestown-1907-
   84p-prntd wrps-47 port   (5dd0)   25.00

PINKERTON'S NAT'L DETECTIVE AGENCY-Gen'l info issued
    to members of Amer Bankers' Assoc-(NY,1898 to 1909)-New
    Series-27 pamphlets-(odd nbrs)-photos-scarce periodical
        (5g4)   35.00

PINKERTON'S NAT'L DETECTIVE AGENCY-History & Evidence
    of Passage of Abraham Lincol from Harrisburg,Pa to Wash on
    22nd & 23rd of Feb,1861-(NY,1906)-42p-ports (5t4) 10.00

PINKHAM,LYDIA E-Guide to Health & Etiquette-Bost-n.d.-(1880's?)-
    wrps-95p   (5ff7) 4.00

PINKHAM,REBEKAH P-Narr of Life of Miss Lucy Cole of Sedgwick-
    Bost-1830-frontis-illus-108p   (5cc6,lacks pt frontis) 35.00

PINKLEY CALL,CORA-Pioneer Tales of Eureka Springs & Carroll
    Co-EurekaSprngs-1930-116p-photos-wrps-1st ed-scarce (5L5) 20.00

PINKNEY,EDW COOTE-Life & Works of-NY-1926-Macmillan-
    Mabbott&Pleadwell,ed-8vo-cl-6 plts (5b2,f,dj) 10.00

PINKNEY,NINIAN-Travels through the south of France-Lond-1809-
    TPurday-4to-hf calf-1st ed (5l8,hng wn) 15.00

PINKNEY,WM-Life of Wm Pinkney,by his Nephew...-NY-1853-
    port-scarce   (4m4,rebnd) 15.00

PINNEY,PETER-Legends of Liberia-n.p.-n.d.-(c1960?)-mimeo-
    249p-wrps   (4t5) 15.00

PINNOCK,WM-Catechism of Modern History-Lond-Whittaker-
    1821-12mo-72p-pr limp bds-9th ed (5a1) 4.50

--Catechisms-9 separate-Lond-n.d.-(ca 1844) (5p1) 35.00

--Catechisms-14 vols bnd in 3-Lond-1821 to 1831 (5c8) 50.00

PINO,PEDRO B-Noticias Historicas y Estadistican-Mexico-1849-
    Imprenta de Lara-102p-fldg map-wrps (5tt0) 125.00

PINSKI,DAVID-The Treasure,a Drama in 4 Acts-NY-1915-
    Huebsch-194p   (5p0) 4.00

PINSON,KOPPEL S-Modern Germany,Its History & Civilization-
    NY-1954-Macmillan-637p   (5p0) 6.00

PINTO,ORESTE-Friend or Foe-NY-1953-Putnam-243p (5p9) 5.00

PIOLANTI,AB GIUSEPPE-Il Bacco In Romagna-Roma-1839-308p,(1)-
    vel bk   (5w1) 16.50

PIOMINGO-The Savage-Phila-1810-12mo-calf-1st ed-v scarce
        (5ss5,cov loose) 25.00

PIONEER & GENERAL HIST OF GEAUGA CO-n.p.-1880-822p-
    cl-v scarce   (5h2) 55.00

PIONEER DENVER-Denv-1948-Dillingham Lithos-4to-
    ltd to 240c,autg   (5jj7,mint) 60.00

PIONEER RECORD,THE-Quarterly-Vol 1,#2 thru Vol 2,#4,
    Nov,1893 to May,1895,bnd together-plus Vol 3,#1,Aug,1895-
    stiff wrps-Verdon,Nebr-33p,36p & 16p (5L2) 45.00

PIONEER SETTLEMENT-Cooperative studies by 26 authors-
    NY-1932-Amer Geogr Soc Spec Publ 14-473p-hardbnd (5ss1) 8.50

PIONEER STORIES OF CUSTER CO,NEB-BrokenBow-1936-185p-
    stiff wrps-1st ed-scarce (4t3) 35.00

PIONEERING WITH FULLER IN 1849-100 Years,1949-SanFran-
    1949-Grabhorn   (5x5) 10.00

PIONEERS,THE-or Sources of the Susquehana-NY-1823-2 vols-
    12mo-orig calf & bds-(JasFenimoreCooper)-1st ed (issue?)
        (5t0) 25.00

PIONEERS OF THE SAN JUAN COUNTRY-Durango,Colo-(1946)-
    by DAR-Vol 2-photos-map-wrps-1st ed-scarce (5j1) 12.50

PIOUS PARENT'S PRESENT,THE-NY-1817-Sam'lWood&Son-
    24mo-67p-thin bds (5p1,chip) 22.50

PIPE OF TOBACCO,A-in imitation of 6 several authors-Lond-
    1736-LGilliver-8vo-disbnd-1st ed (5x3) 80.00

PIPER,CHAS V-Flora of State of Washington-Wash-1906-637p-wrps-
    scarce   (5s4,ex-libr,wn,4a5) 15.00

--same-Flora of the Northwest Coast-Lancaster,Pa-1915-8vo(5z9)3.00

--Forage Plants & their Culture-NY-1916-618p-illus (5s7) 6.00

PIPER,EDWIN FORD-Barbed Wire,& Other Poems-n.p.-1917-
    Midland Pr-cl bk bds (4b6) 10.00

PIPER,JOHN-Marine Electrical Installation-NY-1941-394p-
    plans-stmpd cov (5s1) 3.50

PIPER,JOHN J-Facts & figures concerning the Hoosac Tunnel-
    Fitchburg-1866-wrps (5g8) 5.00

PIPER,T W-Official Report of Trial of...for murder of Mabel HYoung-
    Bost-1887   (5ff4,rebnd) 15.00

PIPER,W S-Eagle of Thunder Cape-Tor-1926-301p-plts (5s6) 8.50

--same-NY-1924-plts-frontis-235p (4f9,lacks fly) 15.00

PIPER,WATTY-Little Folks of Other Lands-NY-c1929-Platt&Munk-
    (80)p-frontis-11 col plts-deluxe ed (5p1) 15.00

PIPES,J-Ziba-Univ Okla-1944   (5x2) 5.00

PIPES,JAS-The Fabulous 52-Natchez-1947-Carl Hertzog,prntr-
    wrps   (5g2,f) 5. (4a5) 7.50

PIPKIN,REV J J-The Story of a Rising Race-1920-Thompson Pub Co-
    R8vo-illus   (5x2) 65.00

PIQUE,RENE-Vinification & Alcoolisation Des Fruits Tropicaux
    & Produits Coloniaux-Paris-1928-296p-12mo-photos (5w6) 7.50

PIRATES OF PRAIRIES-or Fighting for Texas-n.p.-n.d.-
    (Chig-ca 1910)-57p-pict wrps (5h2) 3.50

PIRATES OWN BOOK-Portland-1837-illus (5ii3) 27.50

--same-NY,Edwards&Phila,Cowperthwait-1842-12mo-2nd ed
        (4c4) 42.50

--same-Salem-1924-469p-illus (5ee3) 8.50

PIRBRIGHT,PETER-Off the Beeton Track-Lond-(1946)-146p-
    col lithos-bds (5g9) 4.00

PIRENNE,HENRI-Mohammed & Charlemagne-NY-(1939) (5yy6) 5.00

PIRES,HOMERO-Anglo Amer Political Influences on Rui Barbosa-
    Casa de Rui Barbosa-1949-63p-illus-stiff wrps (5r0) 7.50

PIRKIS,MRS CATHERINE LOUISA-At the moment of victory-Lond-
    1889-Ward&Downey-3 vols-8vo-orig cl-1st ed
        (5xx6,lend libr) 22.50

--Saint & sibyl-Lond-1882-Hurst&Blackett-3 vols-8vo-orig cl-
    1st ed   (5xx6,lend libr) 20.00

PIRONE,P P-Maintenance of Shade & Ornamental Trees-NY-
    (1950)-Oxf Univ Pr-436p-illus (5x0) 7.50

PIROVANO,GAETANO-Trattato Di Vinificazione-Milano-1863-
    sm8vo-398p,(1)-illus (5w1) 30.00

PISANI,LAWRENCE FRANK-The Italian in America-NY-1957-
    Expo Pr-293p (5p9) 4.00

PISCATAQUIS CO,MAINE-Historical Collections of-Dover-
    1910-illus-bnd (5h6) 30.00

PISARRO,CAMILLE-Letters to His Son,Lucien-1943-JJRewald,ed
        (5L7,lf wrinkle) 12.50

PISTOL,THE-NY-1875-50p   (5ii2) 7.50

PITCAIRN'S ISLAND & ITS INHABITANTS-A Description of-NY-
    1838-16mo-303p (5q0) 6.00

PITEZEL,REV JOHN H-Lights & Shades of Missionary Life-Cinn-
    1883-12mo-468p-illus-cl-new ed-port (5mm7) 10.00

PITKIN,TIMOTHY-Mr. Pitkin's speech on the loan bill,Feb 10,
    Alexandria-1814-Snowden&Simms-8vo-stitchd as issued-
    1st ed   (5i9,unopnd) 15.00

--Political & Civil History of the US of Amer-NewHav-1828-
    Howe,Durrie&Peck-2 vols-8vo-calf-port-1st ed
        (5tt8) 25. (5q8,cov dtchd,wn) 15.(5n2) 55.00

--Statistical View of the Commerce of the US-Hartf-1816-8vo-
    cl-407p-labl-1st ed (5L1) 35.00

--same-NewHav-1835-Durrie&Peck-600p-lea
    (5qq8,ex-libr,crude rprd) 12.50

PITKIN,WALTER B-Capitalism Carries On-NY-c1935-282p
        (5w4,dj) 3.50

PITMAN,BENN-The Assassination of Pres Lincoln & Trial of the
    Conspirators-NY-(1954)-419p-illus-(Facsimile Ed)
        (5s9) 7.50 (5t7,dj) 10.00

--History of Short Hand-Cinn-1856-edited & engraved by
        (5t4,pgs stnd) 7.50

--The Little Violinist & other prose sketches-Amanuensis Style
    of Phonography-Cinn-1914-16mo-Phonographic Insti-47p,8(ads)-
    prntd wrps (5p1) 15.00

--Trials for Treason at Indianapolis-Cinn-1865-frontis-340p,16p
        (5yy8,wn,rbkd) 50.00

PITMAN,C R S-A Guide to the Snakes of Uganda-Kampala-1938-
    cl-362p-41 plts(23 col)-2 maps-8vo-ltd to 500c-ex rare
        (4p6) 850.00

PITMAN,F W-Development of the British West Indies,1700 to 63-
    1917   (5L7,lacks map) 7.50

PITMAN,H M-Ancestry of Richard W. Comstock-1964-452p
        (5mm3) 25.00

PITOU,AUGUSTUS-Masters of the Show-NY-1914-186p-illus-cl
        (5t4) 5.00

PITRAT,JOHN C-Paul & Julia,or,The Political Mysteries-Bost-
    1855-illus-1st ed (5mm2) 12.50

PITT,WM-Political debates-Paris(i.e.,Lond)-1766-orig wrps-
    reset from 1st prntng(same place & date) & distinguished
    by quotation "that the Stamp-Act be repealed absolutely,
    totally & immediately" (5g3,f) 35.00

PITT,WM,1st EARL OF CHATHAM-Correspondence,ed by executors
    of his son,John-1838 to 40-4 vols (5L7) 30.00

PITT,WM(THE YOUNGER)-War Speeches-Oxford-1940-3rd ed
        (4a1) 6.00

PITTARD,EUGENE-Race & History-NY-1926-maps
    (5yy6) 7.50 (5L7) 10.00

PITTENGER,WM-Capturing a Locomotive-Wash-1905-wrps-340p-
    Nat'l Tribune (5a0) 4.50 (4j4) 8.50

--Daring & Suffering-Phila-1863-288p-cl-frontis-1st ed
        (5L5,5jj9,fox) 20.00

--same-Phila-1870-Daughaday-288p-cl-port-12mo (5j5,rbnd) 17.50

--same-NY-1887-new ed-War Pub Co-enlrgd (5x5) 15.00

--The Great Locomotive Chase-NY-1891-illus-3rd ed
        (5s9,hng broke) 5.00

PITTMAN,PHILIP-Present State of the European Settlements on the
  Mississippi-Lond-1770-4to-calf-8 fldg maps & plans by
  Thos Kitchin-Nourse-1st ed   (5n9,f) 1,500.00
PITTSBURGH DIRECTORY FOR 1815-(facs Pitts-1940)-156p-cl
           (5h2) 5.00
PITTSBURGH,FORT WAYNE & CHICAGO RWY CO-History,
  Organization & Legal Proceedings Relative to-Pittsb-1863-
  8vo-168p-1st ed   (5m6,rub) 20.00
PITTSBURGH-History of Pittsburgh & Environs-by special
  contributors-1921-4to   (5L7) 10.00
PITTSBURGH PLATE GLASS CO-Glas,Paints,etc-Pittsb-1923-illus-
  208p,178p-4to-cl-a manual for users   (5hh6,f) 10.00
PITTSBURGH TESTED RECIPES-Ladies of Trinity M E Church-Pittsb-
  1885-178,(3)p   (5c4,bndg poor) 7.50
PIXLEY,FRANCIES W-A Hist of the Baronetage-1900-335p-
  ltd to 210c   (5t9) 10.00
PIXLEY,FRANK-King Dodo,Musical Comedy in 3 acts-NY-1901-
  4to-134p-pict wrps   (5t4) 6.50
PIXLEY,R B-Wisconsin in the World War-Milwkee-1919-photos
           (5ww4) 5.00
PIZARRO Y ORELLANA,FERNANDO-Varones Ilustres del Nuevo
  Mundo-Madrid-1639-Diaz de la Carrera-sm folio-limp vel-
  1st ed   (5n2) 350.00
PLACER MINING-Hand Book for Klondike & Other Miners &
  Prospectors-Scranton-1897-146p   (5n7,sl soil) 9.50
PLACERVILLE-Directory of City of-1862-Placerville Republican
  Print Office-128p   (5tt0,lacks pg55 to 60,wrp torn) 60.00
PLACID MAN,THE-or, memoirs of Sir Chas Beville-Lond-1770-
  for JWilkie-2 vols-12mo-calf-1st ed-v scarce (5xx6,rprd) 250.00
PLAGET,H F-The Watch,plus a short Essay on Clocks-NY-1860-59p-
  32mo   (5bb0) 20.00
PLAIDOYER de M O-Desmarais dans l'Affaire de Napoleon Demers-
  Montr-1896-76p-frontis-port-orig prntd wrps (5w8) 35.00
PLAIN & SEASONABLE ADDRESS,A-...on Present Posture of
  Affairs in Amer-Lond-1766-Richardson&Urquhart-8vo-disbnd-
  wrps-1st ed-(Stamp Act)   (5n2) 75.00
PLAIN TALK-& Friendly Advice to Domestics-Bost-1855
           (5w7,wtrstn) 7.50
PLAIN TRUTH-addressed to inhabitants of Amer-Lond-1776-
  Almon-8vo-bds-1st Engl ed   (5n2) 65.00
--same-Lond-1776-JAlmon-47p,(4),(1)-8vo-cl-2nd ed (5L1) 25.00
PLAN OFFERED BY EARL OF CHATHAM-...for settling troubles
  in Amer-Lond-1775-Almon-folio-bds-(Wm Pitt)-1st ed (5n2) 175.00
PLANCHE,J R-History of British Costume...to Close of 18th
  Century-Lond-1881-3rd ed-illus   (5yy6) 8.50
PLANCHON,G-Le Jardin des Apothicaires de Paris-Paris-1895-
  132p,(2)-wrps   (5w3,chip) 5.50
PLANIOL,M-Traite Elementaire de Droit Civil-Paris-1918-3 vols-
           (5r4,needs rbndg) 15.00
PLANTATION LULLABIES-Songs sung by Famous Canadian Jubilee
  Singers-Ontario-(ca1890)-53p-wrps-12mo-pic wrps (5x2) 17.50
PLASCHKE,P A-Club Men of Louisville in Caricature & Verse-
  East Aurora,NY-1912-illus   (5yy8) 8.50
PLAT,HUGH-The Garden of Eden-Lond-1653-for H R-sm8vo-calf-
  (16)175(40)p-1st ed-2nd issue(sheets of orig 1608 ed wi new
  t.lf)-v rare   (4h0,worming) 500.00
PLATNER,JOHN W-Religious History of New Engl...King's Chapel
  Lectures-Cambr-1917-356p-1st ed   (5w0) 17.50
PLATH,HENRY W-Plath Collection-NY-1959-Parke Bernet catalog
           (5m9) 15.00
PLATH,SYLVIA-The Colossus & Other Poems-Lond-(1960)-12mo-
  cl-1st ed-scarce   (5ss7,mint,dj) 45.00
PLATT & MUNK CO-8 titles-all copyrighted 1935-10 unnbrd pgs
  incl inner wrps,illus by Vernam in col & b&w-wrps stapled-
  #3300A to 3300H-8 x 6-3/4   (5p1) 8 items 22.50
PLATT,CHAS A-Italian Gardens-NY-1894-153p-52 illus-4to(5s7) 6.00
PLATT,E L-Geo Wood Platt & His Desc-1943-24p (5mm3) 7.50
PLATT,EDMUND-Eagle's Hist of Poughkeepsie-1905
           (5t9,needs rbndg) 12.50
PLATT,GEO W-A History of the Republican Party-Cinn-1904-
  8vo-cl-326p-illus   (5t0) 5.00
PLATT,JUNE-Best I Ever Ate-NY-(1953)-234p-scarce (4g9) 6.50
--June Platt's Party Cook Book-Bost-(1936)-277p-scarce (5c9) 5.00
--Serve It & Sing-NY-1945-70p-illus-scarce (5c9) 3.50
PLATT,RUTHERFORD-Our Flowering World-NY-1947-278p-4to
  168 photos   (5s7) 7.50
PLATT,WARD-Frontier-NY-(1908)-291p-photos-fldg map (4b2) 5.00
PLAUT,JAS S-Steuben Glass-NY-HBittner&Co-1951-4to-68p-
  2nd ed-rev&enlrgd   (5p0) 12.50
PLAYFAIR,JOHN-Euclid,Elements of Geometry-Edinb-1795-
  8vo-calf-lea labl   (5ss5,sl rub) 25.00
PLAYFAIR,NIGEL-Story of Lyric Theatre Hammersmith-Lond-
  1925-236p plus plts   (5c3) 5.00

PLEASANTS,HENRY-From Kilts to Pantaloons-WestChester-
  c1946-198p-illus-priv publ   (5w0,autg) 6.00
--NoMan's Land of Colonial Penna-Phila-1952-14p-map-wrps-
  pub by Soc Colonial Wars   (5h9) 3.50
--History of Old St David's Church...Radnor, Delaware Co-
  Phila-1915-394p-illus-g.e.-BiCentennial ed(Deluxe)-
  ltd to 150c-nbrd-raised bands-scarce (5h9,f bndg) 32.50
PLEASANTS,J HALL-Saint Memin Water Color Miniatures-
  Portl-1947-8vo-illus-orig wrps-29p   (5ss5) 7.50
PLEASANTS,W J-Twice Across the Plains, 1849....1856-SanFran-
  1906-orig pict cl-12mo-3 ports-10 plts-1st ed (4h0,box) 550.00
PLEASE TELL ME A TALE-Lond-1886-orig dec cl-6th ed (5c8) 5.00
PLEASING INSTRUCTOR,THE-1795-G G & J Robinson-sm8vo-
  calf-368p-6 plts   (4d2,cov wn) 35.00
PLEASING INSTRUCTOR-Northampton-1840-J Metcalf-8p-prnt wrps-
  3¼x1-7/8"   (5rr2) 9.00
PLEASING TOY FOR GIRL OR BOY, A-NY-c1830-MahlonDay-
  36mo-8p-wdcuts-orig Dutch paper wrps   (5v2) 35.00
PLEASURE BOAT,THE-Vol 1 thru 7, April 1, 1845 to Dec 23, 1852,
  weekly-JHacker,ed-2 vols-3/4 calf-lea labls-v scarce
        (5m3,lacks #3 of Vol 1) 225.00
PLEASURES OF HUMAN LIFE-Bost-1807-223p (5t4) 10.50
PLEASURES OF MEMORY,THE-Bost-1795-12mo-calf-lea labl-
  plts by Sam'l Hill-1st Amer ed   (5m6) 15.00
PLEASURES OF THE TABLE-NY-1902-illus-1st ed (4m2,cov soil) 20.00
PLEDGE,THE-or First Step to Fortune-NY-1850-84p-disbnd (5h7) 7.50
PLEDGE,H T-Science Since 1500-Lond-1939-illus-357p (5w9,dj) 5.00
PLEDGER,D J-Cotton Culture on Hardscrabble Plantation-Shelby,
  Miss-1951-234p-plts-1st ed   (5s7,f) 7.50
PLENN,J H-Saddle in the Sky-NY-(1940)-287p-1st ed (5s4) 7.50
--same-Indnpls-1940   (5a8) 6.00
PLESKE,F D-Birds of the Eurasian Tundra-Bost-1928-Memoirs of Soc
  of Natural Hist Vol 6,#3-lg4to-cl   (5jj8) 55.00
PLETSCH,OSCAR-Little Lasses & Lads-Bost-1869-cl-g.dec-8 col plts-
  4to-1st Amer ed   (4F6,lacks fly) 25.00
PLISCHKE,ELMER-Conduct of Amer Diplomacy-NY-1950-542p
           (5w0) 6.50
PLOMER,H R-Dictionary of Printers & Booksellers who were at work
  in England,Scotland & Ireland...1726 to 1775-Oxf-1932-cl bds-
  432p   (4g2,f,unopnd) 35.00
--English Printers' Ornaments-Lond-1924-4to-bds&cl-illus(5d5) 15.00
PLOMER,WM-Cecil Rhodes-Lond-1933-Davies-175p (4t5) 10.00
PLOOIJ,D-Leyden Documents Relating to Pilgrim Fathers-Leyden-
  1920-plts-ltd ed   (5jj3,f) 20.00
PLOT,ROBT-The natural history of Oxfordshire-Oxf-1705-
  LeonardLichfield-folio-calf-fldg map-16 plts-2nd ed,
  additions&corr   (5x3) 30.00
PLOUGH BOY,THE-104 weekly numbers from Jun 5, 1819 to May 26,
  1821-Albany, 1819 to 1821-2 vols-lg4to-qtr calf (5L1) 95.00
PLOUGHE,SHERIDAN-History of Reno County,Kans,Its People,
  Industries & Instit-Indnpls-1917-BF Bowen-404p-4to-cl-v scarce
  (4t1) 35.   (5t3) 55.00
PLOUGHED UNDER-Story of an Indian Chief-NY-1881-cl
      (5w9) 8.50   (5h2,fade,lacks flys) 10.00
PLUTARCH-Lives-Cambr-1676-John Hayes,prntr-thk folio-hf calf-
  1030p,90p-2 indexes   (4b4,edges wn) 150.00
--same-Dublin-T Ewing-1771-5 vol-ports-calf-Langhouse,ed
           (5a1) 50.00
--same-Worcester,Mass-Jun, 1804-6 vols-lg12mo-calf-red labls-
  Isaiah Thomas-1st Worcester ed(4m8) 15. (5L8,sl rust stns) 22.00
--same-Bost-1882-lg thk8vo-cl-787p-carmine e.-AHClough, transl-
  complete in 1 dbl col vol   (5t3) 10.00
--same-Lond-1895, 1896-6 vols-Englished by Sir Thos North-
  3/4 mor-bnd by Zaehnsdorf   (5j2,vg) 45.00
--same-Lond-1929, 1930-Thos North, transl-Nonesuch Pr-5 vols-
  lg4to-illus-papr labls-ltd to 1550c   (5m1) 50.00
--same-NY-1941-8 vols-Ltd Ed Club-8vo-lin in 2 slipcases-
  ltd to 1500c   (5b0) 65.00
--Dryden's, transl-NY-n.d.-rev by AHClough-Bigelow, Brown-
  5 vols-illus-cl   (5x0) 12.50
PLUTARCH-Plutarch's Lives for Boys & Girls....   Retold by
  W H Weston-Jack-n.d.-lg8vo-360p-dec cl-16 col plts (5aa0) 6.50
PLYMPTON,A G-The Mary Jane Papers-NY-1884-White, Stokes &
  Allen-16mo-127p-pict cl   (5p1) 8.50
POCKET ALMANACK-for Year of Our Lord 1785-Bost-1785-
  T&JFleet-84p-interlvd wi blank pgs-bnd wi string (5F9) 12.50
POCKET CHESTERFIELD,THE-Phila-(1920)-12mo-bds-illus(5w7) 4.50
POCKET LAWYER,THE-or Self Conveyancer-Pittsb-obl 16mo-
  bds-106p-4th ed   (5t7,lacks e.p.) 10.00
POCKET LETTER WRITER,THE-Providence-1836-frontis-256p,(25)-
  calf   (5w7,lt fox) 12.50
--same-1837-2nd ed   (5w7,hng broke,fox) 10.50
--same-Worcester-1852-plt-16mo-128p   (5w7,sp tn) 6.50

PODMORE,FRANK-Apparitions & Thought Transference-Lond-
1895-401p,(13)   (5w0)   6.50
--Mesmerism and Christian Science-Phila-1909-GeoW Jacobs&Co-
306p   (5v6)   17.50
PODMORE,HARRY,ed-Presbyterian Church of Lawrenceville,NJ-
n.p.-1948-250th Anniv   (5a8)   3.50
PODMORE,ST MICHAEL-Rambles & Adventures in Australia,
Canada & India etc-Lond-1909-288p-illus   (4b9)   10.00
POE,EDGAR A-The Bells-Phila-(1881)-separate poem-g.e.-illus-
1st ed   (5ee3,f) 5.00
--The Bells & other Poems-Lond-n.d.-4to-Hodder&S-E Dulac
                                            (5p9)   12.50
--A Chapter on Autobiography-NY-1926-DonCSeitz,ed-1st ed-
ltd to 750c (4m8,cor rub) 10.00 (5r9) 8.50 (5mm2) 12.50
--Complete Poems & Stories-NY-1946-intro by Quinn-bibliogra
notes by O'Neill-Kauffer,illus-2 vols   (5j3)   10.00
--Complete poetical works,with 3 essays on poetry-Oxf Univ Pr-
1919-RBJohnson,ed-3 qtr mor-port   (5m2,sl rub) 6.00
--Complete Works-Lond&Phila-1895-8 vols-24 illus-lg type-
8vo   (5t5,f,rbnd) 57.50
--Complete Works-NY-1902-Putnam-lg type-spcl papr-illus-10 vols-
t8vo-orig tan buck-labls-g.t.-Eldorado ed   (5t8)   115.00
--The Gift,a Christmas & New Year's Present for 1836-Phila-
ELCarey-embossed lea   (5p6,cov sl dmgd) 16.00
--Journal of Julius Rodman-Phila-Burton's Mag Jan to June 1840,
6 pts in 1 vol-part mor-1st ed   (4n4)   125.00
--same-SanFran-1947-Grabhorn-76p-ltd to 500c
(4n1,5F5,cor jam) 15. (4a5,mint) 27.50 (5ss9) 20. (5b0) 17.50
--La Chute de la Maison Usher-Paris-n.d.-Bibliophiles de la
Basoche-sm4to-wrps-8 etchings handcol-ltd to 1000c-
slipcase   (5b0,unopnd) 27.50
--Lenore-Bost-(1886)-illus-gift ed   (5p7)   3.50
--Letters & Documents in Enoch Pratt Free Library-NY-1941-
edited by Quinn&Hart-8vo-bds-cl bk-port & facs-Scholars'
Facs & Reprints-500c prntd   (5b2)   12.50
--Letters Till Now Unpublished-Phila&Lond-1925-Lippincott-facs-
15 illus-cl bkd bds-1st ed-ltd to 1500c   (4p1,box) 55.00
--The Murders in the Rue Morgue-Phila-n.d.-facs of ms (5a9) 15.00
--Pit & the Pendulum-Contained in "The Gift" for 1843-Phila-
Carey&Hart-1st of this tale-orig g.tooled lea (5ss9,stnd) 50.00
--Poems by-NY-1869-frontis-illus-278p-raised bands
                                            (5ee3,f,f bndg) 15.00
--Poems-with 3 essays on Poetry-Lond-1919-RBJohnson,ed(5mm2) 7.50
--Poems of-NY-1929-Spiral Pr-t4to-bds-lea bk-ltd to 585c,nbrd
                                            (5j2,vg) 15.00
--Poems-NY-1950-engrs by JGDarragnes-col illus-t.e.g.(5mm2)15.00
--Poems-NY-1950-4to-195p-mor-col engrs by JGDaragnes-t.e.g.-
ltd to 999c,nbrd   (5j5,f bndg) 35.00
--Poetical Works of...With Original Memoir-NY-1858-Redfield-
247p-orig mor-a.e.g.-1st ed   (4b4,f) 30.00
--Poetical works & essays on poetry,together with his Narr of
Arthur Gordon Pym-Lond-1888-Warne-Ingram,ed-illus-384p
Lansdowne Poets series   (5m2)   8.50
--The raven-Bost-Bibliophile Soc-for members only-sm4to-etchings-
ltd to 450c-1927   (5m2)   6.50
--Tales-NY-1845-Wiley&Putnam-1st ed-hf title adv lvs-1st issue
                                            (5z7)   800.00
--Tales-Chig-1930-(Lakeside Pr)-illus-ltd ed (5ii3,box) 15.00
--Tales and sketches,to which is added "The Raven,a Poem"-Lond-
1852-Routledge-8vo-hf calf-cheap format   (5i0)   17.50
--Tales of Mystery & Imagination-Halifax-1855-thk16mo-474p-
cl-frontis   (5v0)   15.00
--same-Baltimore-1941-4to-cl-Ltd Ed Club-ltd to 1td to 1500c,
nbrd,box,autg by illus   (5b0)   35.00
--same-NY-n.d.-4to-plts-illus-ltd ed-mounted col plts by
Harry Clarke   (5ii3)   20.00
--Tamerlane & Other Poems-SanFran-1923-John Henry Nash,prntr-
4to with 8vo facs of Bost 1827 ed-dec brown bds-labls with ties-
t.e.g.,box   (5b0)   45.00
--The Works of-Bost-(1884)-DanaEstes&Co-6 vols-illus-Cabinet Ed
half leather   (5p9)   22.50
--Works-Lond&Phila-1895-8 vols-illus-orig cl (5mm2) 22.50
--Works-of-NY-1913-5 vols-ABecher,illus   (5s5)   18.50
POE,ELISABETH E-Edgar Allan Poe,a High Priest of the Beautiful-
Wash-1930-orig wrps-112p   (5mm2,autg) 15.00
POE,JOHN W-Death of Billy the Kid-Bost-1933-cl-12mo-illus
(4a5,f,dj) 22.50 (5h5,f,5kk4,f)   15.00
--same-LosAng-1922-30p-wrps-priv prntd(55c printed)-
Brinstool,prntr   (5n4,autg of prntr) 35.00
--same-LosAng-n.d.-(ca 1923)-illus-orig wrps-priv prntd in ed
of 250c   (5kk4,pres) 35. (5g2,f) 20. (5i0,vf) 25.00
POE,SOPHIE -Buckboard Days-Caldwell-1936-292p-cl-1st ed
(5yy7,stnd,pres) 15. (5h1,dj,5jj1)   25.00

POEMS BY TWO BROTHERS-Lond-1827-16mo-orig bds(rebackd)-
orig papr labl-uncut-Simkin&Marshall-1st ed of Tennyson's
1st book-1st issue in bds without "Tennyson" on labl
(5i8,f bndg,grandson's autg) 350. (5gg6,lacks e.p.) 250.00
POEMS OF TWO FRIENDS-Columbus-1860-12mo-cl-g.t.-
1st ed of auth's 1st book-(WDHowells & JJPiatt) (5gg6,f) 50.00
POET AND THE PAINTER,THE-Or Gems of Art & Sond-NY-1869-
(DAppleton&Co)-a.e.g.-400p-4to-lea   (5t7)   10.50
POET AT THE BREAKFAST TABLE-Bost-1872-418p-1st ed,1st issue
(with "Talle" for "Table"p9)   (5w9,sl dmpstn) 16.50
POETRY,A MAGAZINE OF VERSE-Vol 21,#4, Jan 1923-
1st appearance of Hemingway's 5 poems-orig wrps (5hh1) 125.00
POGUE,J F-Ka Mooolelo Hawaii-Honolulu-1858-wrps bds-
86p-8vo-2nd ed   (4h0,rbkd,rprd) 200.00
POINCARE,H-Science & Hypothesis-Lond-1905   (5yy6) 12.50
POINDEXTER,CHARLOTTE M-Jane Hamilton's Recipes-Chig-
1909-191p,(32)   (5c0)   5.00
POINDEXTER,MILES-The Ayar Incas-NY-1930-2 vols-Liveright-
illus-1st ed   (5x5)   40.00
POINSETT,J R-Hostile Dispostion Upon Part of Indians on Western
Frontier-Wash-1838-10p-HD434   (4j7)   25.00
--Notes on Mexico,Made in Autumn of 1822,etc-Lond-1825-
298p & 138p of Documents-fldg map-rare   (4a5,sp chip) 110.00
--Report...in Relation to Cherokee Treaty of 1835-Wash-1838-
SD120-1090p plus 43p-fldg map   (5n4)   25.00
POINTER,JOHN-Rational Account of the Weather Shewing
Signs etc-Lond-1738-2nd ed   (5q0,rebnd) 20.00
POIRET,PAUL-King of Fashion-Phila-1931-15 plts
(5p5) 12.50   (5p0)   6.50
POKAGON,CHIEF-O Gi Maw Kwe Mit I Gwa Ki (Queen of the
Woods)-Hartf,Mich-1899-225p-CHEngle   (5k0)   20.00
POLAND,J S-Digest of Military Laws of US 1860 to 1867-Bost-
1868-calf-448p   (4j4,rprd) 12.50
POLAND,JN A-Then & Now-Chillicothe-1918-29p-cl-priv prntd
                                            (5h2)   5.00
POLDERVAART,ARIE W-Black Robed Justice-SantaFe-1948-8vo-
cl-222p-Hist Soc of NM-1st ed   (5g0)   5.00
POLE,WM-Handbook of Games-(Bohn)-1890-2 vols-enlrgd ed
                                            (5tt5,wn,shaken) 7.50
POLE,WM-On Whist-NY-1878-1st Amer ed   (5b9,scuff) 7.50
POLES OF CHICAGO 1837 to 1937-Chig-1937-256p-illus
                                            (5c3,sl tn) 4.50
PO LIN CAY SI-The Sun Girl-Berkeley-1941-47p-8vo-bds-
1st ed   (5g9,mint) 6.00
POLITICAL AFFAIRS (CHIG)-Vol 6 thru 48-1927 to 69-bound
(5ii7,rbnd,lacks Vol 47,#5)   1,565.00
POLITICAL MIRROR,THE-or Review of Jacksonism-NY-1835-12mo-
1st ed   (5m6,sl stnd) 20.00
POLITICAL SCIENCE QUARTERLY-Vol 1 thru 85-1886 to 1970
(5ii7,rbnd)   2,295.00
--same-single vols-bound   (5ii7) ea 28.00
POLITICUS-Impartial Enquiry into Certain Parts of Conduct of Gov
Lewis etc-NY-1806-141p-wrps   (5r7)   12.50
POLK,ANDERSON-Inert Pigments their Use & Abuse-Dayton-
1911-StL,Sept,1910-38p-fldg bds   (5b8)   4.50
POLK,J M-The Confederate Soldier & 10 Years in SoAmer-Austin-
1910-prntd wrps 57p   (4j7)   25.00
POLK,JAS K-Diary of,During his Presidency-4 vol-Chig-1910-
Quaife ed-bds (5ee3,mint) 50. (5h1,5g8,mint) 40.00
--Information in Relation to Calif & NewMex-Wash-1850-fldg maps-
976p-SED18   (4n 4) 80.00
--Message...Calling for Info Re to Mode of Raising Funds for
Carrying on War with Mexico-Wash-1846-18p   (4a5)   12.50
--Operation & Recent Engagements on Mexican Frontier-Wash-
1846-37p-SD388   (4a5)   18.50
POLLARD,ALFRED W-Early Illustrated Books-Lond-1893-Kegan Paul,
Trench,Trubner&Co-256p-illus   (5F9,sp wn) 15.00
--same-Lond-1917-254p-illus   (4j2)   12.50
--same-NY-1927-3rd ed-illus   (5yy6)   7.50
--English Miracle Plays-Oxf-1904-250p-illus-4th ed,rev (5x0) 5.00
--An Essay on Colophons-Chig-1915-Caxton Club-4to-bds-vel bk-
illus-DeVinne Pr-ltd to 252c,box   (5d5)   95.00
--Fine Books-NY-1912-thk4to-cl-332p-50 plts-orig Connoisseur's
Library format   (5d5)   25.00
--Last Words on History of Title Page with Notes on some Colophons
& 27 facs-Lond-1891-JohnCNimmo-buck-4to-ltd to 260c-
37p text   (5tt9,chip,labl wn) 27.50
--Romance of King Arthur & His Knights of the round table-NY-
1927-517p-illus by Rackham(b&w)   (5t4,5t8) 10.00
--Short Title Catalogue of Books Printed in Engl,Scotland & Ireland,
& English Books Printed Abroad,1475 to 1640-Lond-1926-
Biblio Soc-folio   (4b4) 65. (4c1,crack) 45.00

POLLARD, ALFRED W (continued)
--same-Lond-1950-bds-609p　　　　　(5yy1)　37.50
POLLARD,EDW A-Black Diamonds Gathered in the Darky Homes
　of the South-NY-1859-1st ed　　　(5x2)　45.00
--same-NY-1860-155p　　　　　　　(4m4)　27.50
--The Early Life, Campaigns & Public Services of Robt E Lee with
　Deeds of his Companions-NY-1871-30 ports　(5L3)　12.50
--1st Year of the War-Richmond-1862-map-illus　(5x2)　30.00
--same-NY-1863-illus-2nd ed　(4b3) 10.　(5ee3)　12.50
--The Last Year of the War-NY-1866-363p-orig cl-4 ports-
　1st ed-(small edition printed)　(5m3,ex-libr)　20.00
--Life of Jefferson Davis,with Secret History of Southern Confederacy-
　Phila-(1869)-536p-port　(4m6,rub) 12.50(5r7,sp rprd)　25.00
--The Lost Cause-NY-1867-752p-plts-hf cl-lea labl
　　　　　　(5w4) 15.　(5dd6,rbnd)　10.00
--same-NY-1866-ports-3 qtr lea-raised bands-752p (4p8,rub)　20.00
--Southern History of War-NY-1863-Richardson-plts-368p(2)
　　　　　　　　　　　　(5mm8)　12.50
--Southern History of the War-NY-1866-2 vols-676,644p plus ads-
　illus　　　　　　　　　(5L5,sp wn)　15.00
POLLARD,HUGH B C-Game Birds-Lond,Bost&NY-1924-4to-
　185p-col plts-cl　　　　　(5xx7)　35.00
--Gun Room Guide-Lond,Bost&NY-1930-4to-183p-col plts-
　ltd to 225c　　　　　(5xx7,autog)　40.00
--History of Firearms-Lond-(1926)-4to-320p-plts　(5xx7)　35.00
--The Sportsman's Cookery Book-Lond-(1926)-156p-8vo-bds&lin
　　　　　　　　　　(5c9)　6.00
POLLARD, JAS E-The Presidents &the Press-NY-1947-866p (5r7) 7.50
POLLARD,JNO GARLAND,comp-Virginia Born Presidents Addresses-
　NY-1932-Amer Book-232p-illus　(5qq8,dj)　5.00
POLLARD,JOS-The Land of the Monuments-Lond-1898-8vo-cl-
　illus-2nd ed　　　　　　(5t0)　4.50
POLLARD,JOSEPHINE-History of the US in One Syllable-NY-
　(c1880)-McLoughlin-lg sq8vo-108p-6 col plts　(4d8)　8.50
--Life of Washington,in Words of One Syllable-n.d.-120p-4to-
　6 col plts-cl　　　　　　(5v0,vf)　7.50
POLLARD,PERCIVAL-Dreams of Today-Chig-1897-264p-
　Way&Williams-1st ed-boxed　(5x4)　25.00
--Vagabond Journeys-NY-1911-8vo-orig cl-g.t.-1st ed
　　　　　　　　　(5p5,long pres)　10.00
POLLEN,JOHN H-A Description of the Trajan Column-Lond-1874-
　S Kensington Mus-188p-sm8vo-cl-wdcuts (5m5,ex-libr,wn)　20.00
POLLEN,MRS-True Stories about Dogs & Cats-Bost-1856-sm4to-
　cl-illus by Billings-1st ed　(5p5)　12.50
--The Old Garret,Part 2(complete in itself)-Bost-1856-sm4to-cl-
　illus by Billings-1st ed　(5p5)　15.00
POLLEYS,A D-Stories of Pioneer Days in Black River Valley-
　BlackRiver Falls-1948-Banner Journal-89p-illus-crepe wrps-
　9½ x 12-dbl columns　(5r0)　10.00
POLLITT,BASIL HUBBARD-A Lawyer's Story-Miami-(1958)-170p-cl
　　　　　　　　(5r0,autg)　7.50
POLLITT,MRS J MILTON-Dorothy Penrose-Lond-1893-3 vols-
　Eden,Remington&Co-8vo-orig cl-1st ed　(5xx6,lend libr)　12.50
POLLOCK,ADELAIDE L-Excursions about Birdland from the Rockies
　to the Pacific-Seattle-1925-191p　(5s4,f)　3.00
POLLOCK,CHANNING-Behold the Man-Wash-1901-16mo-cl-
　1st ed of auth's 1st book　(5gg6,f,pres)　15.00
--Harvest of My Years-Indnpls-1943-illus-1st ed(5qq7,8.50(5j5,dj) 10.00
POLLOCK,DAVID-Album of Eminent Ship builders & Notable Ships-
　(Lond)-1885-8vo-cl-frontis-ports　(5ss2)　10.00
--Modern Shipbuilding & the men engaged in it-Lond-1884-illus
　　　　　　　　　　(5c1)　15.00
POLLOCK,JOHN-Anatole France & Mrs. Grundy-Kensington-
　1926-(Cayme Pr)-32p-ltd to 750c -wrps　(5t7)　5.50
POLLOCK,FRED-Essays in Jurisprudence & Ethics-Lond-1882
　　　　　　　　(5ff4)　10.00
--Essays in the Law-NY-1922-Macmillan-303p　(5p9)　6.50
--Essay on Possession in the Common Law,Pts 1 & 2 by..,Pt 3 by
　R S Wright-Oxf-1888　(5ff4)　12.50
--The Etchingham Letters-NY-1899-DoddMead-343p (5p9)　5.00
--History of English Law Before the Time of Edw 1-Cambr-1895-
　Engl-Univ Pr　　　　　(5p9,pencil)　30.00
--Land Laws-Lond-1896-3rd ed　(5ff4)　9.00
--Law of Torts-NY-1892　　　(5r4)　10.00
POLLOCK,POLLY-Smelser Family in Amer-1961-278p-wrps-offset
　　　　　　　　　(5mm3)　10.00
POLLOCK,W-Fencing- Boxing by M Mitchell-Wrestling by
　W Armstrong-Lond-1897-8vo-42 illus-green mor-g.t. (5t5)　15.00
POLO,MARCO-Travels of-GardenCty-(1930)-8vo-cl-32p, 370p-
　Venetian ed,intro by Komroff　(5t0)　5.00
POLOWE,CAPT DAVID-Navigation for Mariners & Aviators-NY-
　1942-516p-illus　　　(5s1,ex-libr)　7.50

POLSZKY,A-Theory of Law & Civil Society-Lond-1888 (5ff4)　17.50
POMIANE,EDOUARD DE-Cooking in 10 Minutes-Oxf&LosAng-
　1948-wdcuts-145p-bds　(4g9)　4.50
POMEGRANATE SEED-Lond-1886-SampsonLow,etc-8vo-orig dec cl-
　3 vols-1st ed　　　　(5xx6)　25.00
POMEROY,A A-Hist of Genealogy of Pomeroy-1922-342p
　　　　　　　　(5mm3)　25.00
POMEROY,BRICK-Sense,or Saturday Night Musings-NY-1870-
　Carleton-illus　　　　(5x4)　7.50
POMEROY,EARL-In Search of the Golden West-NY-1957-photos-
　1st ed　　　　　　(5r8)　8.50
POMEROY,ELTWEED-Romance & Hist of Eltweed Pomeroy's Anc
　in Normandy & England-(1909)-81p　(5mm3)　12.50
POMEROY,JAS M-Constitution of State of Arkansas, Framed &
　Adopted at LittleRock Jul 14,1874-LittleRock-1876-70p plus
　index-wrps - 1st ed　(5t3,ex-libr)　12.50
POMEROY,JOHN NORTON-Treatise on Law Riparian Rights...
　Pacific States-StPaul-1887-307p-lea　(5s1,wn)　6.00
POMEROY,SETH-Journals & Papers of-(NY)-1926-8vo-cl
　(4c1) 15. (5t4) 12.50 (5h9) 13.50　(5w5)　14.50
POMET,PIERRE-A Compleat History of Druggs-Lond-1725-
　for Bonwicke&Wilkin-4to-orig calf-86 plts-419p-2nd ed
　　　　　　(4e5,rebkd,def lf)　275.00
POMFRET,JOHN E,ed-Calif Gold Rush Voyages, 1848 to 1849-
　San Marino-1954-Huntington Libr-246p-maps-pict bds-
　cl sp　　　　　　(5qq8,dj)　7.50
POMMERENKE,MILLICENT-Asian Women & Eros-NY-c1958(5x7)4.50
POMMEROL,JEAN-Among the Women of the Sahara-Lond-1900-
　photos-pic cov-343p　(4t5)　12.50
POMEY,NY-Reunion of Sons & Daughters of the Old etc-1875-
　431p-illus　　　　(5mm3)　12.50
PONCA CITY CHAPT,DAR-The Last Run, Kay Co, Okla 1893-
　PoncaCty-1939-photos-wrps-352p-1st ed-scarce　(4t3)　40.00
PONCA INDIANS-Removal of-Report of Select Comm on-US Sen-
　Report #670,46th Congr,2nd Ses-(Wash,1880,GPO)-502p
　　　　　　　　(5yy0)　12.50
PONCE DE LEON-the Rise of the Argentine Republic,by an
　Estanciero-BuenosAires-n.d.-　(5dd4)　7.50
PONCHON,RAOUL-La Muse Au Cabaret-Paris-(1937)-(4)p,
　312p,(1)p　　　　(5w1)　7.50
PONCINS,GONTRAN DE-Kabloona-NY-R&H-1941-illus (5x0)　3.75
POND,E LEROY-The Tories of Chippeny Hill,Conn-NY-1909-
　1st ed　　　　　　(5b1,vf)　15.00
POND,FRED E-Life & Adventures of "Ned Buntline"-NY-1919-
　R8vo-illus-orig bds-ltd to 250c　(5m1,wn,rbkd)　12.50
POND,J B-Eccentricities of Genius-NY-(1900)-illus-564p (4j2) 12.50
POND,MIRIAM BUCKNER-Heaven in a Wild Flower-NY-(1954)-
　101p　　　　　　(5w3)　4.00
POND,S A W-Family Records from Bartholomew,Botsford & Winston-
　1899-60p　　　　(5mm3)　5.00
PONFADINE,PIERRE-Life in the Moslem East-NY-1911 (5x7)　6.50
PONSONBY,SIR FREDK, ed-Letters of Empress Frederick-Lond-
　1929-492p-illus　(5t7) 6. (5m2)　6.50
PONTANI,IONNIS IOVANI-Carmina-Firenze-1902-2 vols-
　hf mor-bds-raised bands-269p,451p-Italian text (5w9)　8.50
PONTEY,WM-Forest Pruner, or Timber Owner's Assistant-Leeds-
　1826-plts-8vo-4th ed　(4m7)　15.00
PONTING,TOM CANDY-Life of-Evanston-1952-bds-cl sp-132p-
　illus-ltd to 500c　(5y2, mint)　14.50
PONTOPPIDAN,ERICH-Natural History of Norway...two parts-
　Lond-1755-ALinde-folio-28 plts-lg fldng map-calf-1st Engl transl
　(5b0,sl worming,rbkd) 95. (4h0,f,rbnd)　200.00
POOL,C W, Sec of State-Roster of Soldiers, Sailors & Marines who
　Served in War of Rebel,Spanish Amer & World Wars-Lincoln,
　1925-497p　　　　(5a9,cov soil)　5.00
POOL,DAVID DE SOLA-Portraits Etched in Stone-NY-(1953)-
　sm4to-cl-14p,543p-illus-maps　(5p5) 25. (5t2,f,dj)　12.50
POOL,MARIA LOUISE-Boss & other Dogs-NY-1896-Stone&Kimball-
　134p　　　　　(5x0)　4.00
--A golden sorrow-Chig-1898-Stone-1st ed　(5m2)　5.00
--In the first person-NY-1896-Harper-1st ed　(5m2)　8.50
--Out of Step-NY-1894-1st ed　(5ee3)　5.00
--Sand 'n bushes-Chig-1899-Stone-1st ed　(5m2)　4.00
--Tenting at Stony Beach-Bost-1888-1st ed　(5mm2)　7.50
--A widower & some spinsters-Chig-1899-Stone-illus-1st ed(5m2) 5.00
POOL,WM-Landmarks of Niagara County-1897-402p & 218p plus
　index　　　　　(4n2,rebnd)　27.50
POOLE,CAROLINE-Modern Prairie Schooner on Transcontinental
　Trail-SanFran-1919-4to-53p-mtd illus-fldg map-uncut-
　ltd to 250c-JHNash,prntr　(5xx7)　12.50
POOLE,D C-Among the Sioux of Dakota-NY-1881-1st ed-
　scarce　　　　　(5t3)　30.00

POOLE,E D-Annals of Yarmouth & Barrington,Nova Scotia in
   Revolu War-Yarmouth-1899-133p   (4b9,f,dj)   15.00
POOLE,ERNEST-Great White Hills of NH-GardenCty-1946-
   illus,GWilliams-1st ed-8vo-472p   (5u9,dj) 8. (4c5)   7.00
POOLE,ERNEST-The Village-NY-1918-Macmillan-8vo-cl
                      (5b2,review copy)   5.00
POOLE,JR,F A-Poole Family in Amer desc from John of Rockport,
   Mass-1927-hf mor   (5mm3,autg)   25.00
POOLE,HESTER M-Fruits & How to Use Them-NY-1890-242p
                      (5c0,chip)   4.50
POOLE,WM-Life of-NY-n.d.-(1855)-83p-ports-pict wrps
                  (5y0,wrps wn,fox)   15.00
POOLE,WM F-Catalogue of....Library of Late,Librarian of
   Newberry Library,Chicago-Bost-1900-76p-3/4 mor-priced
                  (5j4)   15.00
POOLE,WM FRED-Index to Periodical Literature-NY-1853-521p-
   buck-1st ed   (5w9,rbnd)   22.50
POOLEY,BEATRICE-"Millefleurs"(a Thousand Flowers) & how to
   use them-(Melbourne,1954)-obl 8vo-118p-photos (5s7)   5.00
POOLMAN,KENNETH-The Kelly,Lord Mountbatten's Destroyer-
   NY-(1955)-238p-photos-1st US ed   (5s1,ex-libr,dj)   5.00
POOR,CHAS LANE-Men Against the Rule-NY-(1937)-157p-photos-
   ltd ed   (5s1,f)   12.50
POORE,HENRY R-Conception of Art-NY-1913-2nd ed-illus-222p-
   8vo-rev ed   (5ww3)   12.50
POOR,HENRY V-Manual of the RR's of US for 1889-NY-c1889-
   maps-col fldg map   (5w0)   7.50
--same-NY-1885-8vo-illus-cl-1009p & advts   (5t4)   15.00
--same-NY-1890-8vo-cl-illus-1423p & advts   (5t0)   15.00
--same-1869, 1877 to 89, 1891, 1892, 1897 to 1903,1905 to 1907
   (26 vols in all)   (5t2) post extra   100.00
--Money & Its Laws-NY-1877-Poor-2nd ed-623p
       (5qq8,chip) 10.   (5L7)   17.50
POOR,HENRY VARNUM-An Artist Sees Alaska-NY-1945-illus-
   279p   (5yy7) 5.   (4d8)   4.50
POOR,HENRY W-Illus Cat of Valuable Artistic Furnishings &
   Interior Dec of-NY-1909-4to-plts-bnd   (5w7)   8.50
POOR,JOHN ALFRED-Intl Railway,etc-ed by Laura Poor-NY-
   1892-400p   (5w4)   12.50
POOR MAN'S HOUSE REPAIRED-Or,the Wretched Made Happy-
   NY-1834-16p-Amer Tract Soc   (5w6,wn)   3.50
POOR MAN'S ADVICE TO HIS POOR NEIGHBORS-A Ballad,to
   the Tune of Chevy Chace-NY-1774-sm4to-hf mor-1st ed-rare
                  (5n2)   185.00
POOR,M C-Denver South Park & Pacific-Denv-1949-4to-493p-
   illus-pkt map-ltd to 1000c,nbrd,autg
       (5h4,wi 1959 suppl) 225.   (5t1)   250.00
POOR RICH MAN AND THE RICH POOR MAN-NY-1836-Harper-
   12mo-orig cl-1st ed   (5x1,libr labl)   15.00
POOR RICHARD,IMPROVED-Phila-(1751)-BFranklin&Hall-12mo-
       (5cc6,rprd,trimmed close,disbnd)   125.00
POOR RICHARD'S ALMANACK-of 1733, 1749, 1757, 1758 First
   Written Under Saunders by Benj Franklin-NY-1928-facs-
   ltd to 350c,nbrd,box   (4g2)   37.50
POOR RICHARD'S ALMANACK FOR 1733-Appleton facs publ in
   1850-wrps-scarce   (5v2)   17.50
POOR WILL'S POCKET ALMANACK-For Year 1779-Phila-(1778)-
   JCrukshank-24p-interleaved-2½x4"-orig embossed wrps
              (5yy3,stained)   25.00
--same-for 1784-Phila-(1783)-16mo-stitchd   (5g3)   20.00
--same-for year 1797-Phila-JCrukshank-24mo-miniature almanac-
   orig Dutch papr wrps   (5v0)   20.00
POOR'S DIRECTORY-Railway Officials & Manual-NY-1892-illus
                  (5F0,f)   5.50
POORE,ALFRED-Memoir & Gen of John Poore-1881-332p-wrps
                  (5mm3)   10.00
POORE,B P,comp-Descrip Catalogue of Govt Publications,1774 to
   1881-1885-4to   (5L7,ex-libr,rprd)   35.00
--Federal & State Consti,Colonial Charters & Other Organic Laws
   of US-Wash-1878-4to-2 vols   (5r4,rbnd)   27.50
POORE,BENJ PERLEY-Life & Public Services of Ambrose E Burnside-
   Prov-1882-Reid-448p-illus-maps
    (5ee3,vg) 20.   (5mm8,chip) 12.50 (5w0,fade)   14.50
--Perley's Reminis of 60 yrs in Nat'l Metropolis-Phila-1886-2 vols-
   HubbardBros   (5w0)   17.50
POPE,ALEXANDER-An Essay on Critiscism-SanFran-1928-4to-
   blue bds-g.-t.e.g.-ltd to 250c,nbrd   (5b0,box)   45.00
--Essai sur l'homme-Lausanne&Geneva-1745-Marc Michel Bousquet-
   4to-hf calf-orig wrps bnd in-4 plts-port-in Engl & French
              (5x3,rbnd)   65.00
--Essay on Man-Phila-1778-JosCrukshank-43p-calf-bds-4th Amer ed
              (4b1,rbnd)   75.00

POPE,ALEXANDER (continued)
--same-Newbury-1780-J Mycall-55p-calf   (4b4,rub,fox)   15.00
--same-Phila-1821-72p-prntd bds   (5h1)   10.00
--On Characters of Men-Lond-1733-Gilliver-folio-bds-1st ed
              (5i4)   125.00
--Poetical Works-Lond-1831-3 vols-papr labls-orig cl-port (5m1)10.00
--Works-Edinb-1764-4 vols-calf-red labls-raised bands
           (5m1,f bndg,3 pg stns)   45.00
--Works of Mr-Lond-1717-WBowyer-priv prnt-calf-1st folio ed-
   port   (5i4,rbkd)   175.00
POPE& PAGAN-Or, Middleton's letter from Rome-Portl-1846-
   131p   (5t7)   5.00
POPE,ANTUINETTE-Antoinette Pope School Cookbook-NY-1948-
   366p-illus   (5c0)   2.50
POPE,BERTHA CLARK,ed-Letters of Ambrose Bierce-SanFran-1922-
   8vo-bds-port-Book Cluf of Calif-(ltd to 415c,nbrd) (5b2,f)   40.00
POPE,C H-Amphibians & Reptiles of the Chicago Area-Chig-1944-cl-
   275p-12 col plts-8vo-1st ed   (4p6,wrps bnd in)   12.50
--Notes from Amphibians From Fukien,Hainan & Other Parts of China-
   NY-1931-cl-plts-1 map-8vo-v scarce   (4p6)   27.50
--Reptiles of China,Turtles,Crocodilians,Snakes,Lizards-NY-1935-
   cl-604p-27 plts-fldg table-4to   (4p6)   45.00
POPE,C H-Hist of Dorchester Pope Family-1888-345p (5mm3)   17.50
--Hooper Genealogy-1908-313p-ltd to 150c   (5t9)   30.00
--Merriam Genealogy in England & Amer-1906-500p-v scarce
             (5mm3)   100.00
--Pioneers of Mass,a Descriptive List-Bost-1900-4to-hf lea-
   1st ed   (5ss5,rub)   17.50
--The Plymouth Scrap Book-Bost-1918-4to   (5q8)   10.00
--Prouty(Proute) Genealogy-1910-239p   (4t2)   17.50
POPE,ERNEST R-Munich Playground-NY-1941-Putnam (5p0)   4.50
POPE,F L-Practice of the Electric Telegraph-handbook-1869-buck
             (5L7,rbnd)   15.50
--Evolution of Electric Incandescent Lamp-NY-1894-91p-illus-
   2nd ed   (5xx7)   12.50
POPE,J-Corres of Sir John A MacDonald-Oxf U Pr-n.d.-502p-index
           (4b9,underlinings)   10.00
POPE JOAN-A Romantic Biography-Lond-(1954)-DerekVerschoyle-
   8vo-cl-1st ed   (5d8,dj)   35.00
POPE,JOHN-Tour Thru Southern & Western Territories of US etc-
   Richmond-1792-prntd by Dixon-8vo-105(1)p-orig calf-
   Sabin 64109   (5r5,f,hng loose)   10,000.00
POPE,JOHN-Report of Exploration of Terr of Minnesota-Wash-
   1850-SED42-56p-fldg map   (5g8) 12.50 (5n4)   15.00
--Report of Explor of Rt for Pacific RR...Red Riv to Rio Grande-
   (Wash-1855)-324p-disbnd-map   (5tt0,map tn)   20.00
--same-HED129-1855   (4n4)   35.00
--Report of-Wash-1863-8vo-256p
       (4a7,fade,pg chewed) 12. (5w4,sl stns)   10.00
--Report on Condition of Dept of Missouri-Wash-1866-15p-HED76
             (4j4)   15.00
POPE,KATHERINE-Hawaii The Rainbow Land-NY-(1924)-illus-
   fldg map   (5F0)   4.00
POPE,L-The Kingdom Beyond Caste-NY-1957-12mo (5x2,dj)   7.50
POPE MFG CO-Columbia Bicycles-Bost-1885-50p-illus-orig wrps
             (5m2)   10.00
--same-Bost-1885-illus-51p-orig wrps   (5m2)   10.00
POPE,SAXTON-Adventurous Bowmen,Field Notes on African Archery-
   NY-1926-photos-233p-Putnam's Sons   (4t5)   45.00
--Hunting with Bow & Arrow-SanFran-(1923)-illus-245p
            (5ss8,lacks 3 illus,fair)   10.00
--same-NY-1925-illus-257p   (5j5)   25.00
POPE,THOS-Treatise on Bridge Architecture in which the Superior
   Advantages of the Flying Pendent Lever Bridge are fully proved
   NY-1811-orig bds-18 plts-8vo-288p (5jj8,rebkd,fox,stn)   95.00
POPE,COL WM-Gen of Portion of Pope Family together wi Biog-
   1862-68p   (5mm3)   15.00
POPE HENNESSY,UNA-Canon Chas Kingsley-NY-(1949)-Macmillan-
   294p-frontis-8 plts   (5p1,dj)   4.50
--Chas Dickens,1812 to 1870-Lond-1945-ports-plts-476p (4a8)   3.50
POPENOE,PAUL B-Date Growing in the Old World & New-Altadena-
   1913-316p-illus   (4g0,hng loose)   20.00
POPENOE,WILSON-Economic Fruit Bearing Plants of Ecuador-Wash-
   1924-8vo-illus-134p-wrps-Smi Inst   (5t0)   3.00
POPEYE & THE PIRATES-NY-(1945)-4 moveable plts-obl 8vo
             (5v0,f)   15.00
POPHAM,A E-Drawings of Leonardo Da Vinci-NY-1945-320p-8vo-
   illus   (5ww3)   18.50
POPISH TREACHERY-Or, a Short & New Acct of Horrid Cruelties
   Exercised on Protestants of France-Lond-1689-10p,28p-disbnd
             (5h9,vg)   25.00
POPOFF,GEO-The Tcheka,The Red Inquisition-Lond-1925-308p-
   frontis-scarce   (5ss6,wn)   5.00

POPOL,VUH-Sacred Book of Ancient Quiche Maya-Norman-
(1950)-   (5jj3,5t2)   7.50
POPOWSKI,BERT-Crow Shooting-NY-(1946)-8vo-216p-illus
                                           (4a6,dj)   8.00
--Hunting Pronghorn Antelope-Harrisburg-(1959)-illus-225p-
pict cl   (5t7)   10.00
POPPENHEIM,MARY B-History of the United Daughters of the
Confederacy-Richmond-1938   (5j6)   3.50
POPPER,K R-Logic of Scientific Discovery-1959 (5L7)   6.50
POPPLE,LEONARD-Marline Spike Seamanship,The Art of Handling,
Splicing & Knotting Wire-Glasgow-1958-60 drwngs (5c1)   3.00
POPULAR ETHIOPIAN MELODIES-as sung at Sanford's Amer
Opera House-Phila-1856-pict wrps-3rd ed   (5g8)   15.00
POPULAR SCIENCE MONTHLY-Wood Carving & Whittling-
NY-(1936)-270p   (5t7,dj)   7.50
PORCUPINE,PETER-Bloody Buoy-Paradise(Pa)-1823-Henry Witner,
prntr-orig bds-calf back-ex scarce-2nd ed (4b1)   42.50
--A Kick for a Bite,or,Review upon Review-Phila-1795-32p-
orig wrps   (5w5,lacks front wrp) 25.00
--New Year's Gift to the Democrats-Phila-1796-TBradford-8vo-
wrps-1st ed-Howes 522   (5i0,sl fox) 35.00
--Political censor,or monthly review of most interesting political
occurrences,relative to the US-Phila-1796-orig prntd wrps
                                           (5g3)   20.00
--The Republican Judge,or,Amer Liberty of the Press-Lond-1798-
8vo-96p,(2)p-sewn   (5q8,sl dmpstn) 27.50
PORNAIN,E-Termes Nautiques(Sea Terms)-Toulon-8vo-prntd wrps-
2nd ed-Engl&French-159p -1880   (5ss2)   16.50
PORNY-The Elements of Heraldry-Lond-ThosCarnan-1787-calf-
4th ed-scarce   (5b9,wn)   25.00
PORT ARTHUR,TEXAS-by WPA Writers' Program-(1940)-164p(5t9) 4.00
PORT FOLIO,THE-Monthly Magazine-Bradford&Inskeep,Phila &
Inskeep & Bradford,NY-1809 to 1812-8 vols-(3rd Series)-
3/4 lea-illus-8vo   (5t7)   65.00
PORT FOLIO-New Series-July to Dec,1807-Phila-1807-416p-
qtr calf-Smith&Maxwell   (5r7)   35.00
PORTA,JOHN B-Natural Magick-Lond-1658-reprnt,Basic Books-
NY-1959-boxed   (5a9,f)   6.00
PORTAGE CO,OHIO,HISTORY OF-Chig-1885-927p-mor
                                           (5ff7,t.p.in facs) 45.00
PORTAGE CO,WISC-A Standard History of-Lewis Publ-1919-illus-
2 vols-part mor   (5jj7,f)   55.00
PORTAL,DEGRAFFIGNY-Les Merveilles De L'Horlogerie-Paris-
1888-295p-illus-cl   (5bb0)   30.00
PORTALIS,ROGER,ed-Researches Concerning Jean Grolier His Life
& His Library-NY-1907-sm folio-orig 3/4 mor-388p-14 col plts-
ltd to 300c   (5d5)   100.00
PORTER,A K-Lombard Architecture-Yale-1915-Vol 4,Atlas-folio-
244 plts   (5qq7,loose in box) 12.50
PORTER,ADMIRAL-Incidents & Anecdotes of the Civil War-NY-
1885-8vo-357p   (4a7,sl wn) 12.00
PORTER & HAFEN-Ruxton of the Rockies-1950-U Okla Pr-illus-
315p-1st ed   (5kk7)   10.00
PORTER,BERN,ed-The Happy Rock,A Book about Henry Miller-
Berkeley-1934-1st ed-750 nbrd cpy bnd for distri during 1945,
prntd on multicol papr   (5ss9,dj)   30.00
PORTER,CHAS T-Review of Mexican War,Embracing Causes of War,
etc-Auburn-1849-220p-calf (4a5,sp sl crack) 65. (5x5) 25.00
PORTER,CHAS T-Treatise on the Richards Steam Engine Indicator-
Lond-(1874)-illus-3rd ed,rev & enlrgd   (5t4)   7.50
PORTER,COLE-Song Book-NY-1959-S&S   (5p7)   7.50
PORTER,DAVID D-Adventures of Henry Marline,or,Notes from an
Amer Midshipman's Lucky Bag-NY-1885-illus-hf calf-1st ed
                                           (5mm2,wn,rprd) 7.50
--Memoir Comm David Porter,USN-Albany-1875-427p (5s1,wn) 12.50
--Naval History of the Civil War-NY-1886-R8vo-840p-frontis-
fldg plan   (5dd6,edge wn) 10.50
PORTER,DAVID-Giornale di una crociera fatta nell'Oceano Pacifico.
negli anni 1812 to 1814-Milan-1820-3 vols-12mo-wrps-port-
10 col plts-2 maps   (5ss2)   52.50
--Journal of a Cruise made to Pacific Ocean,in US Frigate Essex,
1812 to 1814-NY-1822-2 vols in 1-8vo-calf-242p,256p-port-
fldg map-fldg table-7 plts-2nd ed with additions
                                           (5ss2,1 lf replaced) 110.00
--Minutes of Proceedings of Courts of Inquiry & Court Martial,in
relation to Capt-Wash-1825-2 vols in 1-orig bds (5ss2,wn) 45.00
PORTER,DOROTHY B,ed-Catalog of African Collection in Moorland
Foundation-Wash-1958-lg8vo-398p-wrps   (5c6,vg)   10.75
PORTER,EDW C-Library of Mountaineering & Explor & Travel-Chig-
(1959)-74p-cl   (5d7)   10.00
PORTER,EDW G-Remarks concerning recent visit of Lieut Gen Geo
Digby Barker & diary of Lieut John Barker-Cambr-1898-9p-
wrps   (5g3)   4.00

PORTER,ELEANOR H-Pollyanna-Lond-1913-Pitman&Sons-
illus by StocktonMulford-frontis-7 plts-oval labl on cov-
310p,(24p ads)-12mo-1st Engl ed   (5p1)   20.00
--same-Bost-1913-illus-12th printing   (4F6,f)   5.00
--Pollyanna Grows Up-Bost-1915-illus-cl-308p-1st ed (5t2,pres) 10.00
PORTER,FAIRFIELD-Thomas Eakins-NY-1959-GeoBraziller-wrps-
127p-illus-crown 4to   (4a0)   15.00
PORTER,FLORENCE COLLINS-Collins,Our Folks & Your Folks-1919-
246p   (5mm3)   25.00
PORTER,GENE STRATTON-The Magic Garden-GardenCty-1927-
Dblday,Page-12mo-272p-decora by LeeThayer-e.p.prntd in
green-pict bndg-1st ed   (5p1,dj)   35.00
--Michael O'Hallorn-GardenCty-DbldayPage-1915-8vo-frontis-
560p-3 col plts-dec cl   (5p1)   7.50
--Moths of the Limberlost-NY-1912-8vo-1st ed-col illus-box
                                           (4m6,f)   12.50
--The Song of the Cardinal,a Love Story-Indnpls-(1903)-8vo-buck-
photos-1st ed of auth's 1st book   (5gg6,vf)   20.00
PORTER,H H-A Short Autobiography written for His Children &
Grandchildren-Chig-1915-8vo-illus-orig bds-1st ed-priv prntd
                                           (5ss5)   7.50
PORTER,GENL HORACE-Campaigning with Grant-NY-1897-illus-
546p   (5t7)   12.00
--same-NY-1906-plts   (5s9,sp wn) 6. (5h6)   8.00
PORTER,J T-In Spite of Handicaps-NY-1959-1st ed (5x2,dj) 7.50
PORTER,REV JAS-The Operative's Friend & Defence,or,Hints to
Young Laides-Bost-1850-229p   (5w7,chip)   7.50
PORTER,JAS A-Prince of Anahuac-Galion-(1894)-378p-cl-scarce
                                           (5h7)   15.00
PORTER,KATHERINE ANNE-A Christmas Story-NY-1967-Delacorte-
illus by Shahn-ltd to 500c,autgs,nbrd (5d8) 25. (5p1)   30.00
--The Flower of Flowers-(n.p.)-1950-(pub by Flair)-orig wrps
                                           (5ss9)   5.00
--Flowering Judas-NY-(1930)-12mo-bds-cl bk-1st ed-ltd to 600c-
orig glassine & prntd slip re the book   (5ss7)   95.00
--Leaning Tower & Other Stories-NY-(1944)-8vo-cl-1st ed
(5ss3,sp stnd,dj) 15. (4c2,sl stn,dj) 17.50 (5cc9,dj)   30.00
--Pale Horse,Pale Rider,3 Short Novels-NY-(1939)-8vo-cl-1st ed
                                           (5d3,pres)   50.00
PORTER,KENNETH WIGGINS-The Jacksons&the Lees-Cambr-1937-
illus-2 vols-8vo-cl   (4c1)   30.00
PORTER,L H-Cycling for Health & Pleasure-NY-1895-narr 12mo-
illus-195p   (5w7)   7.50
PORTER,NOAH-Books & Reading-NY-1887-434p   (5t7)   7.50
PORTER,PETER A-Guide to Niagara Falls River Frontier-Buffalo-
1901-311p-illus-maps   (5hh3)   4.00
PORTER,SIR ROBT KER-Travels in Georgia,Persia,Armenia,Ancient
Babylonia etc-Lond-1821-2 fldg maps-plts-2 vols-thk4to-
hf calf-1st ed   (4b6)   250.00
--Travelling Sketches in Russia & Sweden-Lond-1809-folio-
hf cl-2 vols(5 & 8)-303p,296p-2 fldg plts-plts wi orig
guard tissues   (4L7,f)   425.00
PORTER,T C-Impressions of Amer-Lond-1899-241p-ltd to 150c
                                           (5s4,fair,autg) 15.00
PORTER,THOS-Synopsis of Flora of Colorado-Wash-1874-180p-
wrps   (4a5)   4.50
PORTER,VICTOR W-Practical Candy Making-NY-1939-138p(5g9) 3.00
PORTER,WM S-Options-NY-1909-1st ed,1st issue (4b4)   13.50
PORTERFIELD,F B-The Porterfields of Scotland,Ireland & Amer-
(1947)-344p   (5t9)   12.50
PORTES,L-Traite de La Vigne & de ses produits-Paris-Vol 3-
891p,(1),(5)-wrps   (5w1)   10.00
PORTEOUS,ALEX-Forest Folklore,Mythology & Romance-NY-1928-
319p   (5w3,cov stnd) 12.50
PORTEOUS,S D-Psychology of Primitive People-NY-(1931)-illus-
maps   (5tt5)   12.50
PORTIGLIOTTI,GIUSEPPE-Some Fascinating Women of the
Renaissance-Lond-(1929)-16 illus-cl-285p-1st ed (5t2)   4.50
PORTINARI,HIS LIFE & ART-Univ Chig Pr-1940-intro by Rockwell
Kent-illus   (5x2)   25.00
PORTLAND,DUKE OF-Memoirs of Racing & Hunting-NY-1935-
4to-364p-illus   (5ii2)   9.50
PORTLAND,ORE-Album of Views-SanFran-n.d.-(ca 1900)-obl 12mo-
24 postcards bnd in pict wrps   (5w7)   4.50
PORTLOCK,NATHANIEL-Voyage Round World but more Particularly
to NW Coast of Amer,performed in 1785,1786 & 1788 in the
King George & Queen Charlotte-Lond-1789-John Stockdale-
4to-calf-1st ed-port-6 fldg charts-13 plts-2 lvs ads
(4h0,4 col plts,vf) 600. (5ss2,rbkd,cor rprd) 235.
                                           (5c1,rbkd) 250.00
PORTO,LUIGA DA-Rime et Prosa-Venice-F Marcolini-1539-
sm8vo-bds-3rd ed-Brunet 831 (5hh0,1 lf possible facs) 1,250.00

PORTO RICO-El Libro de Puerto Rico, The Book of Porto Rico-
Garcia,-ed-SanJuan-1923-4to-illus-cl-1188p-Span & Engl
texts-1st ed   (5t2,cov dmgd)   10.00

PORTOR,LAURA SPENCER-The Little Long Ago-NY-(1927)-
EPDutton-470p   (5p1,fray dj)   7.50

PORTSMOUTH,R I-Early Records of-1901-462p   (5t9)   15.00

PORTUGAL-A poem, in 2 parts-Lond-1812-Longman,etc-lg4to-
orig bds-1st ed of Nugent's 1st book   (5l8,rbkd)   20.00

POSADA,EDUARDO-Colombia,La Imprenta en Sante Fe De
Bogota en el Siglo 18-Madrid-1917-Libreria Gen'l De
Victoriano Suarez-t4to-calf bkd bds   (5L8,rbnd,vf)   18.50

POSEY,ALEXANDER-Poems of-Topeka-1st ed-red bndg (4k1,rub) 30.00

POSEY,WALTER B-The Development of Methodism in the Old SW,
1783 to 1824-Tuscaloosa-1933-151p   (4p8,rub)   12.50

POSNER,DAVID LOUIS-Love As Image-Lond-1952-Cr8vo-wrps-
1st ed   (5ss7,mint)   12.50

--S'un Casto Amor-Oxf-1953-Cr8vo-wrps-ltd to 30c for priv
circulation-Fantasy Pr   (5ss7,sl fade)   15.00

POSSELT,E A-Technology of Textile Design-Phila-1889-4to-illus
    (5m6)   20.00

POST,CHAS ASA-Doans Corners & the city 4 miles West-Cleve-
1930-CaxtonCo-210p-map-illus   (5u3)   3.00

POST,CHAS C-Driven From Sea to Sea-Chig-1884-Downey&Co-
335p-illus-scarce   (5mm2)   15.00

--same-Phila&Chig-1889-Elliott&Beezley-414p-enlrgd ed-
dec cov of covered wagons   (5ee3,f)   15.00

--Ten Yrs a Cowboy-Chig-1894-471p plus ads-(1st ed was prntd
in 1886)   (5a9,vg)   5.00

--same-Chig-1903-472p   (5r8,wn)   4.50

POST,EMILY-Cook Book-NY-1951-384p   (5c9)   5.00

--How to Behave,Though a Debutante-NY-1928-illus-227p,(7)-
cl sp   (5w7)   5.00

--Woven in Tapestry-NY-1908-12mo-orig stiff wrps-   1st ed
    (5ss5,long pres)   10.00

POST,J J-Abstract of Title of Kip's Bay Farm in City of NY ...
also early Hist etc-NY-1894-   (5r4,rbnd)   25.00

--Old Streets,Roads,Lanes,Piers & Wharves of NY-NY-1882-
RDCooke-76p-cl   (5tt8)   20.00

POST,LOUIS F-Henry George,the Prophet of San Francisco-
NY-1930-Vanguard-335p   (5p7)   5.00

POST,MARIE CAROLINE-Life & Memoirs of Comte Regis de
Trobriand-NY-1910-Dutton-539p-illus
    (5mm8,wn-ex-libr) 5.   (5m6,ex-libr,crack)   10.00

POST,MELVILLE D-Corrector of Destinies-NY-(1908)-1st ed
    (5tt5)   10.00

--Mystery at the Blue Villa-NY-1919-1st ed   (5yy6)   10.00

POST OFFICE CIRCULATION-for Mail Clerks on Grand Trunk
Rwy Betw Montreal & Tor-Tor-1866-Lovell&Gibson-fldg map
    (5w8)   25.00

POSTAGE STAMPS-Catalog of...Amer & Foreign-Cambr-1863-
Sever&Francis-78p-pict bds   (4c1,v chip)   50.00

POSTGATE,R W-That Devil Wilkes-NY-(1929)-8vo-cl-frontis-
port-275p-1st ed   (5t0)   4.00

POSTGATE,RAYMOND-The Plain Man's Guide to Wine-Lond-
(1952)-136p-frontis   (5c9)   3.50

POSTON,RICHARD WAVERLY-Small town renaissance-NY-1950-
Harper-231p-map   (5u3)   5.00

POT AU ROSES,LE-ou Correspondance Secrete et Familiere de
Hon Thos Boot-"Londres"-1782-12mo-96p-hf vel-pamphlet
    (5L1)   35.00

POTHIER,R J-Treatise on Obligations Considered in Moral & Legal
View-Newbern-1802-2 vols in 1   (5r4,rbnd)   25.00

--same-Phila-1826   (5r4,rbnd)   22.50

POTOMAC & ALLEGHANY COAL & IRON MFG CO-Documents
relating to-NY-(1841)-fldng profile & map-wrps   (5g8)   15.00

POTOUS,P L-My Enemy,the Crocodile-NY-1956-illus (5x2)   4.00

POTSDAM,NY-Historical Sketch of Trinity Church,1825 to 1898-
NY-n.d.-(ca 1898)-214p-illus-t.e.g.-ltd to 250c (5w0)   8.50

POTTER,A-Drinking Usages..lecture-Phila-1852-24p-wrps
    (5w1,chip)   4.50

POTTER,ALONZO-School & Schoolmaster-NY-1842-2 parts-
552p-lea bkd cl   (5h7,lt dampstn) 7.50   (5v0)   10.00

POTTER,BEATRIX-Art of-Lond-(1955)-130 col plts-1st ed
    (4F6,mint)   17.50

--Fairy Caravan by Beatrix Heelis-Lond-1929-225p-cl&bds-
col&blk&w illus-cpyrte by author-registered at Stationers Hall
    (5yy3,box,pres)   350.00

--Ginger & Pickles-Lond-1909-FredWarne&Co-sq8vo-pict bds-
1st ed   (5c8,chip)   35.00

--The Pie & Patty Pan-Warne-1905-sm sq8vo-maroon pict bds-52p-
col plts-1st ed-scarce-fragile   (4a8,sl rub)   35.00

--Tale of Benj Bunny-Lond-1904-Warne-tan bds-1st ed
    (4F6,lacks hf sp)   35.00

POTTER,BEATRIX (continued)
--Tale of the Flopsy Bunnies-Lond-FredWarne&Co-sq12mo-1909-
orig bds wi paste labl-prntd in col by EdmundEvans-1st ed
    (4F6,sl chip,5c8,recased,sp wn)   35.00

--The Tale of Little Pig Robinson-Lond-(cpyrte 1930)-Warne-
sq8vo-dec blue cl-g.t.-96p-6 col plts-b&w plts-1st ed
    (5aa2,pic dj)   12.50

--The Tale of Mr. Tod-Warne-1912-illus-col plts-94p-pict grey bds-
1st ed   (4d1,rebkd)   20.00

--Tale of Mrs Tiggy Winkle-Lond-1905-Warne-green bds-
1st ed   (4F6,sp reglued)   37.50

--same-Lond-(1918)-prntd bds-pic labl   (5c8,f,labl rub)   7.50

--Tale of Mrs Tittlemouse-Lond-1910-1st ed   (4F6,sl chip)   37.50

--Tale of Pigling Bland-Lond-1913-FredWarne&Co-sq12mo-
orig prntd bds wi paste labl-1st ed   (5c8,f)   40.00

--Tale of Samuel Whiskers,or the Roly Poly Pudding-Lond-(n.d.)-
FredWarne&Co-reprint ed wi e.p. designs of 4 sacks of meal,
oats,potatoes & bran-red bds   (5c8,f)   4.00

--Tale of Squirrel Nutkin-Lond-1903-Warne-1st ed
    (4F6,dark blu bds,sl crack) 50.   (4F6,grey bds,vg)   37.50

--The Tale of Timmy Tiptoes-Warne-1911-pict green bds-85p-
col plts-12mo-1st ed   (4d1,f)   35.00

--Tale of Tom Kitten-Lond-1907-Warne-1st ed
    (4F6,lacks hf t,sl crack)   32.50

--The Tale of Two Bad Mice-Lond-Warne-1904-sq12mo-85p-
col plts-labl-1st ed   (4d1,rebkd) 20.   (5c8,soil)   30.00

--Wag By Wall-The Horn Book-Bost-1944-(30p)-1st ed-t.e.red
    (5F1,f,dj) 10.   (5p1,dj)   15.00

POTTER,C E-Genealogies of Some Olf Families of Concord & Their
Desc-Vol 1 (all publ)-1887-143p   (5mm3)   22.50

POTTER,DAVID M-Trail to Calif-Yale-1945-fldg map-266p-1st ed
    (5x5,dj) 7.50   (4n1)   12.50

POTTER,ELISHA R-Early History of Narragansett-1835-315p-
Vol 3 of R I Hist Soc   (5t9)   18.50

POTTER,G-To the Golden Door-1960-plt   (5L7)   8.50

POTTER,H G-Album of Markesan,Wisc-Markeson,Wis,Aug 1897-
96 photos-11 x 8½   (5r0)   25.00

POTTER,HENRY-The Modern Man & His Fellow Man...Lectures
1902-Phila-1903   (5x7)   3.00

POTTER,JACK-Bibliography of John Dos Passos-Chig-1950-1st ed-
ltd to 365c,nbrd   (4g2)   25.00

POTTER,COL JACK M-Cattle Trails of the Old West-Clayton,NM-
1935-wrps-40 p-illus-ports-fldg map   (5t1,autg)   175.00

POTTER,JEAN-Alaska under Arms-NY-1942-200p(5ss1,5 aa0)   4.50

--Flying North-NY-1947-plts-ports-261p   (5s6)   5.00

POTTER,JOHN-Remin of the Civil War in US-Oskaloosa,Iowa-
Globe Pr-1897-196p   (5u3,pres)   6.50

POTTER,JOHN H-Under Cotton Canvas-Bost-(1892)-8vo-1st ed
    (5ss5)   6.50

POTTER,MARGARET H-Uncanonized-Chig-1900-McClurg-495p-
1st ed   (5x4)   7.50

POTTER,MARGARET Y-At Home on the Range-Phila-(1947)-
214p   (5c0)   3.00

POTTER,MARY KNIGHT-The Art of the Vatican-Bost-345p-illus
1903   (5t4)   3.50

POTTER,TRUMBULL H-Life & Remarkable Adventures of Israel R
Potter,native of Cranston RI-1824-16mo-bds   (5L7,wn)   15.00

POTTER,W W-History of Barry County-GrandRapids-(1912)-
Reed Tandler Co-cl-12mo-269p   (4t1)   25.00

POTTS,ABBIE F-Wordsworth's Prelude-Ithaca-1953-8vo-cl-1st ed
    (5t0,pres)   6.00

POTTS,CHAS S-Railroad Transportation in Texas-Austin-1909-
fldg maps-hf mor-214p-v scarce   (5z7)   65.00

POTTS,WM-From a New Engl Hillside-NY-1904-305p,(3)-12mo
    (5w7,sl soil)   4.50

POUCHER,W A-Perfumes & Cosmetics with Especial Reference to
Synthetics-NY-1923-1st ed-rare   (5n7) 7.50   (5kk5)   12.50

POUCHER,W A-The Magic of Skye-Lond-1949-Chapman&Hall-
223p-illus-cl   (5d7)   5.00

--Escape to the Hills-Lond-(1952)-Country Life-144p-illus-cl
    (5d7)   5.00

POUCHOT,PIERRE-Memoir Upon Late War in NoAmer, Betw French
& English,1755 to 60, followed by Observ Upon Manners &
Customs of Indians-Roxbury,Mass-1866-maps-hf lea-2 vols-
lg4to-ltd to 50c   (5r6)   60.00

POUGET,MARCEL-The Manual of the Professional Cook-n.p.-
1957-158p-illus   (5g9)   4.50

POUGH,R H-Audubon Bird Guide,Eastern Land Birds-NY-1946-
col illus-lea-1st ed   (5b1,f)   5.00

--Audubon Guides,All the Birds of Eastern & Central NoAmer-
NY-1953-Dblday-illus-352p   (5p7)   5.00

POUGHKEEPSIE CLOCK MFG CO-Report #88 in Sen of State of
NY of comm on manufactures for incorp of-Mar 7,1836-4p(5t7) 7.50

USED BOOK PRICE GUIDE

POULIOT,J CAMILLE-Quebec & Isle of Orleans-Que-1927-
224p-illus-extra title   (5a1,autog)   5.00
--same-French text   (5a1)   4.00
POULSEN,P-Canada,Som Det Moder Emigranten-Copenhagen-
1928-illus-fldg map-stiff prntd wrps   (5w8)   5.00
POULSON'S TOWN & COUNTY ALMANAC-Phila-1804-Jn bioren-
stitchd-48p   (5cc6)   4.00
POULSSON,EMILIE-Songs of a Little Child's Day-Music by
Eleanor Smith-Springfield-1915-MiltonBradley-lg8vo-117p-
frontis-illus   (5p1)   7.50
POULTER,G C B-Corbould Genealogy-Ipswich(Eng)-1935-168p
                                          (5mm3)   7.50
POULTNEY,EVAN-Report of Trial of,on Charge of Felony before
Harford Co Court,Mar Term,1836-Balt-1836-16p,(1) (5h8) 8.50
POULTNEY,VT-New History of Town of...to 1875-Poultney-1875-
369p-Joslin,ed   (4d9,sp crack) 22.50
POULTRY BOOK,THE-NY-1909-sm4to-cl-1299p &index-illus
                                          (5t0)   6.00
POUND,ARTHUR-Detroit,Dynamic City-NY-1940-illus by
EHSuydam   (5r7)   15.00
--Industrial America-Bost-1936-lg8vo-illus-cl-234p-1st ed
                                  (5t2) 5. (5y2)   6.50
--Johnson of the Mohawks-NY-1930-illus-556p-1st ed (5r7) 12.50
--Lake Ontario-Indpnls-1945-384p-illus
                   (5h9) 6.50 (5hh3,5p9) 5. (5t7)   6.00
--Native Stock-NY-1931-Macmillan-267p (5p7) 4. (5w9)   5.00
--Notes of Late Clarence W Barron-NY-1930-372p-illus-1st ed
                                          (5g5)   10.00
--The Penns of Penna & Engl-NY-1932-349p-1st ed (5w5)   7.50
--The Telephone Idea-NY-1926-ltd ed   (5yy6)   7.50
--The Turning Wheel-NY-1934-517p-1st ed (5ee3,wn dj) 3. (5h8) 4.50
POUND,EZRA-ABC of Reading-Lond-Routledge&Sons,Ltd-1934-
1st ed   (5ss9,vg,dj) 20. (5dd8,f,dj)   37.50
--Cantos LII-LXXI-Lond-(1940)-8vo-cl-1st ed (5d9,dj)   30.00
--Catholic Anthology,1914 to 1915-Lond-1915-illus bds-12mo-
1st ed-ltd to 500c   (5gg6)   250.00
--Certain Noble Plays of Japan-Churchtown,Dublin-1916-Cuala Pr-
orig cl bk bds-1st ed-ltd to 350c,nbrd   (5hh1,box,vg) 75.00
--A Draft of Cantos XXXI to XLI-Lond-(1935)-8vo-cl-1st Engl ed
                                          (5d9,dj)   20.00
--same-NY-n.d.-Farrar & Rinehart   (5hh1)   10.00
--Drafts & Fragments of Cantos CX to CXVII-(NY)-1968-
New Directions & Stone -errata sl-ltd to 310c,autg,nbrd
                                    (4L4,box,mint)   150.00
--The Exile-(Paris),Chig&NY-1927 & 1928-4 numbers(all publ)
                                          (5d8)   165.00
--same-#1,Spring 1927-(n.p.)-1927-orig orange wrps (5hh1) 50.00
--Exultations-Lond-1909-12mo-orig bds-1st ed (5yy6,sl rub) 47.50
--Gaudier Brzeska-Lond&NY-1916-4to-cl-illus-1st ed(correct
bndg wi embossed repro)   (5ss7,cov wn) 85.00
--Guide to Kulchur-New Directions-(n.d.)-1st ed (5hh1,vg) 7.50
--Homage to Sextus Propertius-Lond-(1934)-8vo-blue bds-
1st Separate ed   (5d9,dj)   30.00
--How to Read-Lond-(1931)-DesmondHarmsworth-1st ed
                                  (5ss9,vg,rprd dj)   20.00
--Imaginary Letters-Paris-1930-Black Sun Pr-sq8vo-prntd wrps-
in slipcase as issued-ltd to 300c-1st ed (5dd8)   50.00
--same-Paris-1930-Black Sun Pr-8vo-orig prntd wrps-in slipcase-
1 of 50c printd on Jap vel,autg   (5d3)   150.00
--Lustra-Lond-(1916)-Cr8vo-cl-frontis-1st ed-ltd to 200c,nbrd
priv prntd-auth's initials   (5ss7,vf)   310.00
--Make it New-Lond-1934-407p   (4b4,rub)   17.50
--Pavannes & Divisions-NY-1918-Knopf-1st ed,later state-
orig grey cl   (5ss9)   20.00
--Personae-Lond-1909-sm8vo-bds-1st ed-1st bndg in drab papr bds
                                  (5ss7,vf,erase)   90.00
--Personae:Collected Poems of-NY-1926-illus-1st ed
                   (5mm1,sl stn) 12.50 (5ss9)   17.50
--Poems 1918 to 1921-NY-(1921)-thn t8vo-vel bkd bds-1st ed
                                          (5r9)   12.50
--Polite Essays-Norfolk,Conn-(1940)-(700 c prntd)-1st US ed
                                  (5mm2,tn dj)   18.50
--Provenca-Bost-(1910)-16mo-bds   (5m1)   22.50
--Redondillas Or Something of That Sort-SanFran-1967-New
Directions-errata slip-ltd to 110c autg   (4L4,dj,f)   125.00
--The Spirit of Romance-Lond-(1910)-JMDent&Sons-8vo-cl-t.e.g.-
1st ed   (5ee9)   75.00
--same-Lond,Dent-NY,Dutton-n.d.-(1910)-Amer issue(wi Dutton
on sp & t.pg a cancel)-300c(from Engl sheets) were so issued
                                          (5b2,fox)   50.00
--Umbra,Early Poems-Lond-1920-128p-bds,cl bk-uncut (5dd0) 45.00
POUND,R-Criminal Justice in America-NY-1930 (5r4,rub)   10.00

POUND,R-Readings on History & System of Common Law-
Lincoln-1904   (5ff4,rebnd)   15.00
--same-Bost-1913-2nd ed   (5ff4)   9.75
POUPON,P-The Book of Burgundy-Lond-(1958)-78p-4to-plts
                                          (5w1,box)   15.00
POUSETTE-DART,NATHANIEL-Childe Hassam-NY-1922-Stokes-
4p text-64 illus-cr8vo   (4a0,dj)   20.00
--Jas McNeill Whistler-NY-1924-Stokes-65 plts-5p-"Distinguished
Amer Artists" ser   (4e0,dj)   12.50
--Robt Henri-NY-1922-Stokes-5p text-64 illus-cr8vo (4a0) 15.00
POUSSIN,GUILLAUME TELL-The US,its Power & Progress-Lond-
1851-488p-3/4 lea-raised bands-1st Engl ed (5L0,chip)   12.50
POWDERLY,T V-Labor Movement,The Problem of Today-NY-1891-
illus-frontis-639p   (5yy0,sp chip) 17.50
POWDERMAKER,HORTENSE-Copper Town,Changing Africa-NY-
1962-8 plts   (5c6,f)   8.75
--After Freedom-NY-1939-Viking-8vo-cl-408p (5j5)   15.00
POWELL,A C,SR-Palestine & Saints in Caesar's Household-NY-
1939-1st ed   (5x2)   22.50
--Picketing Hell-NY-1942-port-1st ed   (5ii3)   10.00
POWELL,A C,JR-Marching Blacks-NY-1945-1st ed (5x2)   15.00
POWELL,A G-I Can Go Home Again-Univ NoCar-1953 (5x2)   8.50
POWELL,AARON M-Personal Remin of Anti Salvery & Other Reforms
& Reformers-NY-1889-Caulon Pr-illus   (5x2)   50.00
POWELL,ADDISON M-Trailing & Camping in Alaska-NY-1909-
illus-8vo-1st ed   (4g6)   10.00
--same-NY-1910-379p-photos   (5ss1) 6. (5L7)   6.50
POWELL,ANTHONY-Afternoon Men-Lond-1931-12mo-cl-1st ed
of auth's 1st novel   (5ss7,f,dj)   50.00
POWELL,BADEN-A General & Elementary View of the Undulatory
Theory-Lond-1841-JWParker-8vo-orig bds-prntd sp labl-
errata lf-16p ads dated Oct 1841-1st ed   (4h0,sp chip) 25.00
POWELL,C L-Engl Domestic Relations 1487 to 1653-NY-1917
                                          (5ff4)   10.00
POWELL,C U-Description of Private & Family Cemeteries in
Borough of Queens-Jamaica-1932-illus-4to-orig wrps (5jj3) 12.50
POWELL,CUTHBERT-20 Years of Kansas City-(KansCty)-(1893)-
345p-illus-1st ed   (5L3,lacks fly) 28.50
POWELL,DONALD M-An Arizona Gathering-Tucson-1960-77p-
ltd to 400c   (5j4)   10.00
POWELL,E ALEXANDER-Asia at the Crossroads-NY-1922 (5x7) 5.00
--Beyond the Utmost Purple Rim-NY-1925-Century-photos-fldg map-
pic cov-431p   (4t5,wtrstn)   12.50
--By Camel and Car to the Peacock Throne-NY-1923-392p-cl-
illus   (5t2)   3.75
--End of Trail-NY-1914-fldg map-48 plts (5s4) 8. (5s6) 7.50
--same-NY-1919-463p-48 plts-fldg map   (5aa0)   7.50
--same-NY-1922-fldg map-48 illus-463p   (4n1,fade)   4.00
--Long Roll On The Rhine-NY-1934-231p-1st ed (5x7,5w4) 5.00
--The Map Is Half Unrolled-NY-1925   (5x2)   3.50
--Marches of the North-NY-1931-311p-illus (4b9) 8. (4d2,5r0) 5.00
--Some Forgotten Heroes-NY-(1922)-12mo-178p-illus (5dd9) 5.25
POWELL,FRANCES-The House on the Hudson-NY-1903-1st ed
                                          (5ee3,vf)   5.00
POWELL,FREDK-Bacchus Dethroned-NY-1882-268p-cl (5h7)   8.50
POWELL,FRED WILBUR,ed-Hall J Kelly On Oregon-Princeton U-
1932-8vo-411p-cl   (5t4) 12. (5h4,5j0)   15.00
POWELL,H-The Last Paradise-Lond-1930-illus (5x2)   3.00
POWELL,H M T-Santa Fe Trail to Calif-SanFran-1931-Grabhorn Pr-
2 fldg maps-4 fldg plts-272p-cl-300c-Book Club of Calif,
autgs   (5t1,5tt9)   400.00
POWELL,HARFORD,JR-Walter Camp,Father of Amer Football-Bost-
1926-8vo-cl-plts-1st ed   (5p1,sp wn) 7.50 (5p5)   10.00
POWELL,HICKMAN-90 Times Guilty-NY-1939   (5p9)   4.50
--What Citizens Should Know About Coast Guard-NY-(1941)-194p
                                          (5s1,dj,f)   3.00
POWELL,HORACE B-The Original Has This Signature,M W Kellogg-
Englewood Cliffs-1956-358p-illus (5t2,ex-libr) 3. (5y2) 4.50
POWELL,J H-Bring out Your Dead-1949   (5L7)   7.50
POWELL,J H-Books of a New Nation,US Gov Publ,1774 to 1814-
Phila-1957-170p   (5j4)   7.50
POWELL,J W-Exploration of Colorado River of West etc-Wash-1875-
Gov Print Off-291p-illus-profile in pocket-cl
                   (5tt0,wn) 25. (5ee3,edges wn)   22.50
--Intro to Study of Indian Languages-GPO-1890-cl-chars-2nd ed
                                          (4k5)   10.00
--9th Annual Report of Bur of Ethnology-1887-4to-6 col plts (5F0) 8.50
--9th Annual Report of USGS,1887,88-Wash-1889-4to-717p-illus-
maps   (5L3)   15.00
--Report of Explor in 1873 of Colorado of the West & Its Tributaries-
Wash-1874-Smi Insti-8vo-wrps   (5i9) 35. (5a3)   27.50
--Report on Lands of Arid Region of the US-Wash-1879-GPO-R8vo-
210p-3 lg fldng pkt maps-2nd ed   (5dd6,fade)   21.00

159

POWELL, J W (continued)
--7th Annual Report of Bur of Ethnology-1885-6 col plts (5F0)   8.50
--10th Annual Rpt of USGS to Sec of Int-Wash-1890-774p-cl
(5h2)   10.00
--21st Annual Report of Bur of Ethnology-1903-360p-Katchina doll-
col plts   (5r1,vg)   75.00
POWELL,COMM J W DAMER-Britol Privateers & Ships of War-Lond-
(1930)-Arrowsmith-412p-illus   (5p9)   15.00
POWELL, JOHN J-Essay upon the Law of Contracts & Agreements-
Walpole-1802-2 vols in 1-8vo-orig calf-DavidNewhall (5L1) 10.00
POWELL, JULIA MYGATT-Flashlights of A Lincoln-LosAng-(1921)-
92p-cl   (5h7)   5.00
POWELL,L W-Military Interference with Elections-Wash-1864-pamph-
orig wrps-38p,(1)   (5mm8)   22.50
POWELL,L P,ed-Historic Towns of Middle States, 1899...of
Southern States, 1900...Of Western States, 1901-NY &Lond-
Putnam's-illus-dec bndg-3 vols   (4d9,f)   12.50
POWELL, LAWRENCE CLARK-Books West Southwest-LosAng-1957
(5t1)   20.00
--Manuscripts of D H Lawrence,a Desc Catalog-LosAng-1937-
Ward Ritchie Pr-ltd to 750c-wrps   (4a5) 25.   (4c1)   17.50
--Philosopher Pickett, Life Story of Eccentric Pamphleteer-
Univ of Calif-1942   (5x5)   17.50
--Robinson Jeffers,The Man & His Work-LosAng-1934-Primavera Pr-
1st ed-ltd to 750c   (5hh1,lend libr)   15.00
--Southwestern Book Trails-Albuqu-1963-1st ed   (5g5,f,dj)   10.00
POWELL, LYMAN P-Historic Towns of the Middle States-Putnam-
1899-illus-439p   (4p8,spot)   6.50
--Historic Towns of New Engl-NY &Lond-1898-599p-illus
(5t4,bk cov dtchd)   10.00
--Historic Towns of the Southern States-NY-1900-604p-illus-g.t.
(5j6) 6.   (5h9)   10.00
--Historic Towns of the Western States-NY-1901-702p-illus-t.e.g.-
1st ed   (5L7,ex-libr) 4.50   (5w4)   10.00
--Mary Baker Eddy,A Life Size Portrait-NY-1930-lg8vo-cl-364p-
illus-1st ed   (5t2)   7.50
POWELL,SCOTT-History of Marshall Co from Forest to Field-
Moundsville-1925-334p-cl   (5jj9,rbnd)   35.00
POWELL, T-Attourneys Academy,or The Manner & Forme of
Proceeding Practically....-Lond-1630   (5ff4,rebnd)   47.50
POWELL, THOS-The Living Authors of Amer,First Series-NY-
1850   (5mm2,rbnd,sl stns)   12.50
POWELL,W B-How to Talk-Phila-c1882-Cowperthwait-208p-
lea bkd bds-illus-Powell's Langu Ser Part 1   (5p1)   7.50
POWELL, WALTER A-A History of Delaware-Bost-(1928)-1st ed-
455p plus index-photos-errata slip   (5L0,pres)   12.50
POWER,EILEEN-Medieval People-Bost-1925-12mo-map-216p-
8 illus-1st ed   (5t0)   5.00
POWER, J H-Review of Lectures of.Wm A Smith on Philosophy &
Practice of Slavery etc-Cinn-1859   (5x2,lt fox)   35.00
POWER,JOHN-Handy book about Books,for Book lovers, Book
buyers & Book sellers-Lond-1870-illus-scarce (4a1,bndg wn) 15.00
POWER, JOHN C-History of Early Settlers of Sangamon County,
Illinois-Springfld,IL-1876-illus-map-4to-797p-v scarce(4m4) 55.00
POWER, MABEL-Stories the Iroquois Tell Their Children-NY-(1917)-
216p-col plts-photos   (4b2,stns,warp)   3.50
POWER,SISTER MARY JAMES-In the Name of the Bee-NY-1944-
8vo-cl-frontis-Sheed&Ward   (5b2,f)   5.00
POWER,MRS S D-Anna Maria's Housekeeping-Bost-(1884)-348p-ads
(5w7)   8.50
POWER, TYRONE-Impression of America...1833,35-Phila-1836-
2 vols-orig cl   (5L7,ex-libr) 15.   (5tt6,bkstrp reprd)   35.00
POWERS, ALFRED-Early Printing in the Oregon Country-Portland-
1933-folio-16p-facs-Club of Prntng Hse Craftsmen-ltd to 500c,
nbrd   (5k0)   10.00
POWERS,GRANT-Address at Goshen Cent Celebration-1839-68p
(5e8,wrps)   7.50
--Historical Sketches of Discov,Settlement & Progress of Events
in Coos Country-Haverhill-1841-lea-16mo-238p-1st ed-lea labl
(4c5,fox)   35.00
POWERS, H H-The art of Florence,an interpretation-NY-1918-
Macmillan-461p-8vo-cl-plts   (5m5)   10.00
POWERS,KATE BALL-John Ball-Glendale,CA-1925-231p-photo-
illus   (5L5,dj)   12.50
POWERS, LAURA B-Historic Tales of Old Missions for Boys & Girls-
SanFran-(19 02)-155p-cl   (5jj9)   5.00
POWERS,MRS O A-The Maple Dell of '76-Phila-1889-24mo-16th ed
(4d9)   2.50
POWERS,ROBT B-Record of My Maternal Ancestors-1967-366p
(5mm3)   30.00
POWERS,STEPHEN-Afoot & Alone,a walk from sea to sea-Hartford-
1872-327p-illus-1st ed   (5ee3,lacks e.p.)   17.50
--In the Supreme Court of Texas,Bloomberg vs Andre & Schultz-
Galveston-1869-7p   (4j7)   20.00

POWERS,WM DUDLEY-Uncle Isaac;or,Old Days in the South-
Richmond-1899-245p-illus   (5x2)   15.00
POWICKE,F M-King Henry III & Lord Edward-Oxf-1947-2 vols-
maps   (5xx7)   12.50
POWLES, L D-Land of the Pink Pearl-1888-map   (5L7)   15.00
POWNALL,C A W-Thos Pownall,Gov of Mass Bay-Lond-1908-470p-
illus-errata slip   (4b9,spotted)   20.00
POWNALL, THOS-Memorial...on Present State of Affairs between
Old & New World-Lond-1780-Almon-8vo-orig bds-lf of adv-
2nd ed(same imprint as 1st ed)   (5n2)   75.00
--Topographical Description of Such Parts of NoAmer as Are
Contained in(Annexed) Map of Middle British Colonies etc
in NoAmer-Lond-1776-orig fldng map laid in-folio-
orig wrps-46p, 16p-1st ed-lg papr cpy   (5a3,box)   700.00
--Topographical Descr of Dominions of the US of Amer-Pittsbrg-
1949-lg4to-fldg map-235p-rev&enlrgd ed
(4m2) 25.   (5t2) 15.   (4m6)   20.00
POWYS, JOHN COWPER-Atlantis-Lond-(1954)-1st ed
(5ii3,f,dj)   15.00
--Autobiography-NY 1934-lg8vo-cl-595p-port-frontis (5t0)   5.00
--Confessions of Two Brothers-NY-1916-Manas Pr-12mo-cl-
papr labls-1st ed   (5r9,dj)   20.00
--100 Best Books-NY-1916-GArnold Shaw-73p   (5p0)   4.50
--Wolf Solent-NY-1929-2 vols-1st ed-3/4 mor   (4b7,rub)   20.00
POWYS, LLEWELYN-Black Laughter-NY-c1924   (5x7)   4.50
--same-NY-(1930)-8vo-216p   (4a6)   3.00
--Ebony & Ivory-NY-1923-1st ed   (5m1)   7.50
POWYS, T F-Christ in the Cupboard-Lond-1930-ELahr-orig wrps-
Blue Moon Booklets #5-ltd to 500c,nbrd,autg   (5ee9)   7.50
--The Dewpond-Lond-1928-prntd bds-ltd to 530c,nbrd (5a9,dj) 15.00
--Fables-Lond-1929-1st ed-4 drawings by GSpencer
(5ii3,bkplt remvd)   17.50
--The House with Echo-Lond-1928-uncut-1st ed-ltd to 200c,autg
(5mm1) 20.   (5F9,mint,dj)   25.00
--same-Lond-1928-1st trade ed   (5ss3) 10.   (5F9,f,dj)   12.50
--An Interpretation of Genesis-Lond-1929-Chatto&Windus-8vo-
cl bkd bds-1st ed   (5ss3,dj)   20.00
--The Key of the Field-Lond-1930-ltd to 550c-1st ed
(5ee9,autg) 10.   (5a9,vf)   17.50
--The Left Leg-Lond-1923-Chatto&Windus   (5ss3,dj)   10.00
--Mr Weston's Good Wine-Lond-1927-cl-ltd to 660c,autg
(5a9,f,dj)   25.00

--The Rival Pastors-Lond-1927-papr labl-stiff wrps-ltd to 100,autg
(5a9)   30.00
--The Soliloquy of a Hermit-NY-1916-12mo-cl-1st ed of auth's
1st book   (5ss3,pres) 45.   (5gg6)   15.00
--Soliloquies of a Hermit-Lond-1918-12mo-cl-1st Engl ed
(5ss3,dj) 20.   (5gg6,dj)   10.00
--The Two Thieves,In Good Earth, God & the Two Thieves-Lond-
1932-12mo-bds-cl bk-g.t.-1st ed-ltd to 85c,autg (5dd8)   15.00
--What Lack I Yet?-Lond-1927-orig wrps-1st ed-ltd to 100c,autg
(5a9)   17.50
--White Paternoster & Other Stories-Lond-1930-uncut-1st ed-
ltd to 200c,autg   (5mm1)   22.50
POYNTING,FRANK-Eggs of British Birds, with an Acct of Their
Breeding Habits-Lond-1895 to 96-pts 1 to 4(all pub)-54 plts-
thk4to-hf mor-g.t.-orig prntd wrps bnd in-1st ed (5z9,f)   50.00
PRACTICAL AMER COOK BOOK-By a Housekeeper-NY-1856-
267p   (5c0,wn)   8.50
PRACTICAL AMER GARDENER-By an Old Gardener-Balt-1822-424p-
calf   (5b8,lacks flys,crude rebkd)   20.00
PRACTICAL BOOK OF AMER ANTIQUES-GardenCty-(1927)-390p-
illus-rev with new suppl   (5t4)   10.00
PRACTICAL CHRISTIAN,THE-Vol 1,#1-Mendon,Mass,April 1,1840-
4p-Hopedale Community newspapr-ex rare (5m3,fray,sl loss) 15.00
PRACTICAL COOK BOOK-Phila-1857-Lippincott-303p-cl-
(Mrs Bliss)   (5p6,wn,sl loose)   12.50
PRACTICAL DRY FLY FISHING-NY-1912-lg 12mo-cl-216p
(5t2,lacks e.p.)   3.00
PRACTICAL ECONOMY-Lond-1822-12mo-379p,(4)-bds-2nd ed
(5w7,wn)   13.50
PRACTICAL ELECTRICS-Universal Handy Book-NY-1890-135p-
2nd ed   (5hh7)   5.75
PRACTICAL ETIQUETTE-Plain,Sensible Guide to Good Manners
for all people-Chig-(1881)-12mo-87p-N.C.   (5w7)   4.50
PRACTICAL GUIDE FOR EMIGRANTS TO NOAMER-Lond-1850-
Simpkin&Marshall-sm8vo-orig prntd wrps-fldg map-(Geo Nettle)-
1st ed-Howes N54   (5i0,f,5n9)   100.00
PRACTICAL HOUSEKEEPING-Minnpls-1881-670p-frontis
(5c0) 10.   (5c9)   12.50
PRACTICAL LAWYER-Vol 1 thu 16-1955 to 1970 (5ii7,rbnd) 215.00

PRACTICAL MAGICIAN & VENTRILOQUIST'S GUIDE-NY-(1876)-
92p-pict wrps   (5h1)   5.00
PRACTICAL MANUAL OF COMPASS-Annap-1921-173p
                                     (5ss1,ex-libr)   3.00
PRACTICAL TREATISE ON DYEING & CALICO PRINTING-NY-
1846-704p-10 plts   (5n7,rbnd,fox)   22.50
PRACTICAL USE OF METEOROLOGICAL REPORTS & WEATHER
MAPS-1871-GPO-80p-illus   (5a9)   7.50
PRADE, JEAN ROYER DE-Histoire du Tabac-Paris-1696-A Uvarin-
12mo-calf-172p-2 plts   (4e5,f) 175.00
PRADEAU, ALBERTO FRANCISCO-Numismatic History of Mexico-
Calif-1938-orig wrps-24 plts-rare   (5kk7,fray)   50.00
PRAED, MRS CAMPBELL-Affinities-Lond-1885-Bentley-2 vols in 1-
8vo-orig cl   (5xx6)   17.50
PRAED, WINTHROP MACKWORTH-Athens-n.p.-n.d.-(1824)-8vo-
disbnd-1st ed   (5i8)   25.00
--Poetical Works of-NY-1854-311p-12mo-cl   (5t0,v fade) 3.75
PRAEGER PICTURE ENCYCLOPEDIA OF ART-NY-Praeger-1958-
584p-plts   (5x0)   10.00
PRAEGER, S ROSAMUND-Further Doings of the Three Bold Babes-
Lond-(1898)-1st ed   (4F6,sl shake) 15.00
PRAGER, HANS G-Through Arctic Hurricanes-NY-n.d.-161p-
photos   (5ss1,dj)   4.00
PRAIRIE CRUSOE, THE-or, Adventures in the Far West-Bost-c1886-
Lee&Shepard-8vo-dec red cl-277p-Blue Jacket Series-g.t.
                                             (5aa2)   6.50
PRAIRIE GOLD-Chig-(c1917)-Reilly&Britton-illus-8vo-cl-g.-
By Iowa Authors & Artists   (5b2)   7.50
PRANG, LOUIS-Colour Instruction-Bost, NY&Chig-1893-Prang Educ
Co-12mo-12 plts-186p, 2-2 fldng diagr   (5p1)   17.50
--May Flower Memories of Old Plymouth, by L K Harlow-Bost-(1889)-
bds-10 col plts-obl 8vo-scarce   (4F6,vf)   22.50
PRASLOW, DR J-State of Calif, The-A Medico Geograph Acct-
SanFran-1939-transl by Cordes-12mo-cl-ltd to 250c, nbrd
                                          (5F5,pres)   10.00
PRATT & WHITNEY AIRCRAFT DIV-Pratt & Whitney Aircraft Story-
1950-illus-173p   (5F2)   7.50
PRATT, ANNE-Ferns of Gr Britain & Their Allies-Lond-n.d.-
orig cl-39col plts-g.e.-8vo-2nd ed   (5z9)   4.00
--Flowering Plants, Grasses, Sedges & Ferns of Gr Brit & Their
Allies-Lond-n.d.-Warne-317 col plts-6 vols-orig cl-g.e.-
reprnt   (5z9,f)   75.00
--same-5 vols & 2 vols-Lond-n.d.-(ca 1855)-8vo-cl-col illus
                                             (5t4)   50.00
PRATT, ALICE OLIVIA-Story of Grenell-1946-108p-photos(5ff2) 15.00
PRATT, ARTHUR-Pinciples of Combustion in Steam Boiler Furnace-
NY-(1920)-114p   (5s1,soil)   3.00
PRATT, DOROTHY-A Guide to Early Amer Homes North-NY-(1956)-
249p-illus   (5t7)   10.00
--same-NY-n.d.-2 vols in 1   (4h6,wtrstnd)   5.00
PRATT, E F-Phinehas Pratt & Desc-1897-164p   (5mm3)   8.50
PRATT, E J-The Titanic-Tor-1935-42p-hf lea   (4b9,rbnd) 15.00
PRATT, EDWIN A-Licensing & Temperance in Sweden, Norway
& Denmark-Lond-1907-117p   (5w1)   7.50
--same-1909-popular ed   (5w1)   6.50
PRATT, FLETCHER-Civil War in Pictures-NY=(1955)-illus-256p
                         (5yy7,dj) 8.50   (5s9,dj)   10.00
--Civil War on Western Waters-NY-(1956)-illus-maps
            (5L5,5tt5,vf,dj) 5. (5m2,dj) 4. (5s9,dj)   6.00
--Empire & the Sea-NY-(1946)-446p-illus-1st prntng
                                      (5s1,ex-libr,f)   6.00
--A Man & his Meals-(NY, 1947)-251p   (5c9)   3.50
--The Monitor & the Merrimac-NY-(1951)-illus (5s9)   4.00
--The Navy, Hist-NY-(1941)-496p-illus   (5s1,ex-libr) 6.00
--Navy Has Wings-NY-(1943)-224p-photos   (5s1,ex-libr) 5.00
--Ordeal by Fire-NY-1935-1st ed   (4k1)   10.00
--same-NY-(1948)-WmSloane-426p   (5p7)   6.00
--Stanton-NY-1953-Norton-520p   (5x0)   6.50
--War for the World-Yale Univ Pr-1951   (5x0)   4.50
PRATT, HARRY E-Lincoln 1840 to 1846-Sprngfld-(1939)-391p(5t7) 6.50
--The Personal Finances of A Lincoln-Sprngfld-1943-198p-port
                                          (5t4,5g4)   7.50
--The President's Words-Bost-1865-16mo-186p   (5t4)   5.00
PRATT, HARRY S, ed-Illinois as Lincoln Knew It-Sprngfld-1938-
8vo-illus-84p-wrps   (5j5)   7.50
PRATT INST-Mechanics of the Sewing Machines, Monograph 5-NY-
1914-80p-illus-fldg bds   (5b8)   8.50
PRATT, JOHN BARNES-Personal Recollections-NY-1942-67p-illus
                                             (5m1)   3.00
PRATT, L-Ezekiel Expands-Juvenile-Bost-1914-illus (5x2) 10.00
PRATT, MISS L J-The Unfortunate Mountain Girl-Bost-1860-160p-
illus   (5m1)   25.00

PRATT, LAURENCE-Saga of Paper Mill, Verse-Caldwell-1935-77p
                                          (5s4,dj,f)   4.00
PRATT, LEE S, ed-Galesburg Sketches-Galsbg-1897-76p-bds-250c
                                    (5h2,autog,sp wn)   8.50
PRATT, MARA L-Cortes & Montezuma-Bost-(1891)-99p plus ads-
illus-fldng frontis-juvenile   (5L0)   4.00
PRATT, ORSON-Absurdities of Immaterialism, or a Reply to TWP
Taylder's Pamphlet-(Liverpool, 1849)-32p-extract (5bb4) 12.50
--Divine Authenticity of the Book of Mormon-Parts 1 thru 6-
Liverpool-1851-96p-disbnd-pamphlets bnd together
                   (5k2, lacks port) 35. (5bb4)   25.00
--Divine Authority, or the Question, Was Jos Smith Sent of God-
(Liverpool, 1848)-16p, extract   (5bb4)   6.00
--Great First Cause or the Self Moving Forces of the Universe-
(Liverpool, 1851)-16p, extract   (5bb4)   6.00
--The Kingdom of God, Part 1 thru 4-(Liverpool, 1848, 1849)-
8p, 8p, 8p, 16p, extract   (5bb4)   15.00
--New Jerusalem;, or, the Fulfillment of Modern Prophesy-
(Liverpool)-1849-24p, extract   (5bb4)   6.00
--Remarkable Visions-(Liverpool, 1848)-16p, extract (5bb4) 6.00
--Was Jos Smith Sent of God?-Liverpool-n.d.-22p-wrps-
later prntg of 1848 issue   (5dd9)   8.00
--Publicist & Apostle of Church of Latter Day Saints, collection of 10
tracts, removed from bnd vol-Liverpool-1848 to 50 (5m3) 175.00
PRATT, P P-A Voice of Warning & Instruction to all People-NY-
1837-216p-16mo-hf mor-1st ed   (5tt6,f)   37.50
--same-NY-1839-216p-cl-2nd ed, rev   (5t4, lacks flys) 25.00
PRATT, RICHARD-Picture Garden Book & Gardener's Assistant-NY-
(1942)-143p-17 col plts-4to   (5s7,5qq7,dj)   6.50
--Second Treasury of Early Amer Homes-NY-(1954)-4to-cl-1st ed-
144p-1st ed   (5t7)   20.00
--Treasury of Early American Homes-NY-(1949)-4to-cl-1st ed-
(some illus not in 2nd ed)
        (5qq7,4p8,dj) 10. (5d2,5t7) 20. (5q0,f,dj,5x0) 15.00
PRATT, SARAH S-Old Crop in Indiana-Indnpls-1928-priv prnt
                                       (4a9,autg,vf)   15.00
PRATT, WALDO S, ed-St Nicholas Songs-juvenile-NY-(1885)-
Century-4to-cl-illus-190p   (5j5)   15.00
PRATT, WALTER M-Burning of Chelsea-Sampson-Bost-1908-149p-
illus   (5e8)   8.00
--Tin Soldiers-Bost-(1912)-Badger, The Gorham Pr-185p-illus
                                            (5mm8)   5.00
PRATT'S RIVER & RAILROAD GUIDE-NY-(1848)-24mo-prntd wrps-
illus maps-122p, (4)p   (5a3)   85.00
PRATT CHADWICK, MARY-The Alo Man, Stories from Congo-Yonkers-
1927-170p-illus   (5c6)   5.75
PRAY, R F-Dick Dowling's Battle-SanAnt-1936   (4j4)   17.50
PRAZ, MARIO-Studies in 17th Century Imagery-Lond-1939 to 47-
Warburg Inst-t4to-cl-233p, 209p-illus   (5m5)   50.00
PREBLE, EDW A-Biological Investig of Hudson Bay Region-
US Dept of Agric, Div of NoAmer Fauna #22-1902-140p-
plts-maps   (5ss1)   7.50
PREBLE, GEO HENRY-Diary of Ezra Green, MD-Bost-1875-
priv prntd-31p-wrps   (5p9)   5.00
--History of the Flag of the US of Amer-Bost-1880-Williams-cl-
col plts-815p(4)-2nd Rev Ed   (5qq8,fade) 12.50
--Our Flag-Albany-1872-col illus-1st ed   (4m2,rbkd) 27.50
--Gen Sketch of 1st 3 Gen of Prebles in Amer-1868-336p (5t9) 35.00
PREBLE, JACK-Land of Canaan-Parsons-1960-94p-wrps (5h7)   3.00
PRECAUTION, A NOVEL-NY-1820-2 vols-cl bk bds-12mo-
errata lf-1st ed of JFCooper's first book-BAL 3825-
togeth wi 1st Engl ed-Lond-1821-3 vols-orig bds-papr labl-
8vo-(anon)-v scarce   (5gg6)   300.00
PREECE, HAROLD-Living Pioneers-NY-(1952)-317p-1st ed
                         (5yy7,dj) 5.   (5s4,dj)   8.00
PREECE, W H A-NoAmer Rock Plants-(First Series)-NY-1937-illus-
204p   (5s7)   6.50
PREECE, WM-A Manual of Telephony-Lond-1893-8vo-illus-1st ed
                                            (5ss5)   6.00
--The Telephone-Lond-1889-8vo-illus-1st ed (5ss5)   6.00
PREGO, LOUIS G-Battles of San Juan & El Caney-Santiago de
Cuba-c1911-8vo-63p-wrps   (4a3)   10.00
PREHISPANIC ART OF MEXICO-Mexico-1946-12 p-263 plts-
Nat'l Inst of Antrop & Hist-stiff wrps   (5t3)   5.00
PREININGER, MARG-Japanese Flower Arrangement-Bost-1940-4to
                                          (5qq7,dj)   8.50
PREMIER BREWERS' CONCENTRATE-Its Uses & Economies in Modern
Brewing Practice-(Peoria, c1936)-33p, (2)p-4to-table (5w6,soil)3.50
PRENDERGAST, THOS F-Forgotten Pioneers-SanFran-1942-278p-
photos   (5s4,autg,f) 22.50

PRENTICE, ANDREW N-Renaissance architecture & ornament in
  Spain-Lond-n.d.-(ca 1924)-Batsford-4to-60 illus
      (5m5,wn,ex-libr) 20.   (5p5)   45.00
PRENTICE, ARCHIBALD-Tour in US-Halifax-1858-Milner&Sowerby-
  217p-orig cl   (5tt0)   20.00
PRENTICE, E PARMALEE-Amer Dairy Cattle, Their Past & Future-
  NY-1942-Harper-453p-illus   (5p7)   7.50
PRENTICE, GEO D-Biog of Henry Clay-Hartf-1831-304p-lea-
  1st ed   (4p8,wn) 12.50 (4h2)   20.00
PRENTICE, HARRY-Ben Burton, the slate picker-NY-(1888)-Burt-
  illus-pict cl-wdcut-1st ed   (5m2,fade)   7.50
PRENTICE MULFORD'S CALIF SKETCHES-1935-ed by FWalker-
  JnHenryNash-8vo-bds-cl bk-labl-ltd to 350c (5h4)   20.00
PRENTIS, NOBLE L-History of Kansas-Topeka-1909-403p (4a5)   3.00
--A Kansan Abroad-Topeka-1878-240p-1st ed   (5k2)   5.00
--Kansas Miscellanies-Topeka-1889-218p   (5k1)   5.00
PRENTISS, A-Hist of Utah Volunteers in Span Amer War & in
  Philippine Isls-(SaltLkCty)-(1900)-430p-illus (5yy8,rub) 20.00
PRENTISS, CHAS-Life of late Gen Chas Prentiss-Brookfield-1813-
  Merriam-448p-frontis-bds-label   (5mm8,chip) 22.50
--same-calf   (5mm8)   15.00
PRENTISS, DELIGHT-One Way Round SoAmer-Indnpls-(1905)-
  181p-cl   (5ff7)   7.50
PRENTISS, ELIZ-Henry & Bessie-NY-n.d.(after 1873)-Randolph&Co-
  16mo-198p-pic cl-frontis   (5p1,spots)   4.50
PRENTISS, MRS ELIZ-Aunt Jane's Hero-NY-(1871)-1st ed (5ee3) 5.00
--Fred, & Maria, Me-NY-1868-71p-illus   (5m1,sl wn) 10.00
--Life & Letters of-NY-1883-573p-illus-cl   (5t2)   5.00
PRENTISS, HENRY MELLEN-The Great Polar Current Polar Papers-
  NY-(1897)-12mo-1st ed   (5m6)   7.50
PRESBREY, F-History & Development of Advertising-1929-4to-
  350 illus   (4p4) 15. (5L7,ex-libr) 17.50
PRESBY, J W-Wm Presbey of Lond, Engl & Taunton, Mass & Desc-
  (1918)-151p   (5t9)   10.00
PRESBYTERIAN CHURCH IN USA-Digest Compiled from Records of
  Gen'l Assembly of-Phila-1820-391p-lea   (5t7)   12.50
PRESBYTERIAN CLERGYMAN LOOKING FOR THE CHURCH-
  By One of 300-NY-1855-8vo-cl-580p   (5t2,libr labl)   4.50
PRESBYTERIAN COOK BOOK-Dayton-1875-178p-8vo-Ladies of
  1st Presby   (5ww2,stnd) 12.50
--same-1886-illus-178p   (5ww2)   10.00
PRESCOTT, ABRAHAM-#1, Murder trials & executions in New Hamp-
  Report of trial of, for murder, Jun 23, 1833-Manchester, NH-1869-
  stitchd   (5g3)   12.50
PRESCOTT, ALBERT B-Chemical Examination of Alcoholic Liquors-
  NY-1875-108p, 48p   (5w1)   8.50
PRESCOTT, ALLEN-The Wifesaver's Candy Recipes-NY-(1934)-
  109p-reprint   (5g9)   2.50
PRESCOTT, ANNE M-Makapala by the Sea, Hawaii-Vol 1-Honolulu-
  1899-181p-cl-Hawaiian Gazette Co's Print (5yy3)   15.00
PREXCOTT, DANA G-Rough Passage-Caldwell-1958-1st ed
                (5yy6,f,dj,pres)   6.00
PRESCOTT, GEO B-Dynamo Electricity-NY-1884-867p-illus
                (5ii2)   6.50
--The Electric Telephone-NY-1890-illus-v scarce
               (5u7,hng crack) 12.50
--Electricity & Electric Telegraph-NY-1885-2 vols-1120p-6th ed
               (5h1,rub)   5.00
--History, Theory & Practice of the Electric Telegraph-Bost-1860-
  468p-lg12mo-orig cl-1st ed   (5L8,libr stmp) 35.00
--The Speaking Telephone, Talking Phonograph & Other Novelties-
  NY-1878-8vo-illus-1st ed   (5ss5)   15.00
PRESCOTT, HENRY B-Strong Drink & Tobacco Smoke-NY-1870
                (5w1)   8.50
PRESCOTT, LAWRENCE F-1896, Great Campaign or Political
  Struggles of Parties, Leaders etc-Cinn-(1896)-cl-512p (4k2) 7.50
--Living Issues of the Campaign of 1900 -Chig-(1900)-cl(4k2) 7.50
PRESCOTT, LUCY A-Emma Jane (Emmons) Brown, Descent-1965-
  41p(1 side only)   (5t9)   20.00
PRESCOTT, TH H-Amerikanisch Deutsche Encyclopedia-Columbus-
  1859-1,032p-orig mor-g.   (5yy1)   15.00
--The Volume of the World-Columbus-1853-J&HMiller-thk4to-
  100p wdcuts-orig stmpd roan (5j5,lacks world map,dmpstn) 10.00
--same-Balt-1860-1010p-lea   (5h0,rub)   9.50
PRESCOTT, W D-Amos Reed & Annie(Webb) Reed Gen & Biog Record-
  1956-265p   (5mm3)   30.00
--Gen & Biogr Record Concerning Mehitable(Reed) Lilly & Geo-
  1959-644p   (5mm3)   55.00
--Gen & Biog Record Concerning Phebe (Reed) Trott & John Trott
  & Desc-1954-235p   (5mm3)   30.00
PRESCOTT, W H-The Conquest of Mexico-NY-1922-2 vols-4to-
  intro by TAJoyce-480, 485p-illus-bev edges (5h9,vf) 28.50

PRESCOTT, W H (continued)
--History of the Conquest of Mexico-NY-1847-2 vols-frontis in ea-
  525, 519p plus index-1st ed   (5L0)   35.00
--same-NY-1848-3 vols-hf mor   (5w9,bkstrp wn) 15.00
--same-Phila-1873-ed by JnFosterKirk-3 vols-frontis (5t4) 10.00
--same-NY-1886-2 vols in 1-(467p, 490p)- (5L3,f) 10.00
--History of the Conquest of Peru-NY-1847-2 vols-8vo-cl-frontis-
  1st ed   (5t2)   15.00
--same-NY-1848-Harper&Bros-frontis-map-2 vols (4b3) 15.00
--same-Phila-(ca 1900)-2 vols-sm8vo-hf calf-t.e.g.-frontis (5j5)12.50
--same-MexicoCty-1957-4to-lea-Ltd Ed Club-ltd to 1500c, nbrd,
  autog, boxed   (5h5,vf)   50.00
--The Life of-Bost-1864-4to-mor-a.e.g.-illus-1st ed-spec wi arms
  of Prescotts on cov   (5j3, vg,pres from son) 80.00
--Works-Lond-1884-JnFosterKirk, ed-30 ports-15 vols-sm4to-cl-
  India papr-issued by Lippincott, Phila-ltd to 25 sets (5t2) 35.00
--same as above-ltd to 25 sets-bnd in red mor wi raised bands
                (5t0,f bndg) 100.00
--The Works of-(Montezuma Edition)-Phila-1904-Lippincott-22 vols-
  cl-papr labls-illus-ltd to 1000 sets   (5x0)   65.00
--Writings-ed by WHMunro-Phila-1904-illus-bnd in 3/4 purpl
  crushed levant mor-Ltd Montezuma Ed (5d2,f bndg) 250.00
PRESCOTT, WM HICKLING-Unpublished Letters to Gayangos in
  Library of Hispanic Soc of Amer-NY-1927-Hispanic Soc-12mo-
  cl-19 plts-Catalog Series   (4a3)   15.00
PRESENCE AFRICAINE-Deuxieme Congres des Ecrivains et Artistes
  Noirs, L'Unite des Cultures Negro Africaines-Paris-1959-428p-
  wrps   (5x2)   10.00
PRESENT, THE-Or A Gift for the Times-FAMoore, ed-Manchester-
  1850-12mo-192p-col frontis   (5w7,cov wn)   4.50
PRESENT DAY KU KLUX KLAN MOVEMENT-Report by Committee
  of Un American Activities-Wash-1967-371p-wrps (5x2) 10.00
PRESENT STATE OF GR BRITAIN & IRELAND, THE-Lond-1742-
  in 3 parts-cl   (5x7,rbnd) 35.00
PRESENT STATE OF NO AMERICA-Lond-1755-(John Huske)-4to-
  Part 1 (all publ)-1st ed   (5e2) 550.00
PRESENTATION OF FLAGS OF NY VOL REGIMENTS-& Other
  Organizations to Gov Fenton, July 4, 1865-Albany-1865-
  249p-illus   (5t7)   12.50
PRESIDENTIAL ELECTION, 1868-Proceedings of Nat'l Union
  Republ Conv at Chig May 20 & 21, 1868-Chig-Ely, Burnham &
  Bartlett-143p-Evening Journal Print   (5k0)   15.00
PRESIDENTS OF AMERICA, THE-Bost-1879-19 plts-4to-HWSmith, ed-
  1st ed   (4m6)   15.00
PRESS REFERENCE LIBRARY-Notables of the SoWest-LosAng-1912-
  500p-ports-4to-lea   (5w0,sl rub) 22.50
PRESSOIR, DR C-Elements de Geologie d'Haiti-Port au Prince-
  1943-135p-wrps-illus-French   (5x2)   7.50
PRESTON, E M, ed-Nevada County, The Famous Bartlett Pear Belt
  of Calif, Its Horticultural Resources, etc-NevadaCty-1886-
  94p plus ads-map-illus-prntd wrps   (5x5)   60.00
PRESTON, G H-Desc of Roger Preston of Ipswich & Salem Village-
  1931-355p   (5t9)   12.50
PRESTON, HOWARD WILLIS-Rhode Islands' Historic Background-
  1936- R I Tercentenary Comm-illus-wrps (5q8)   3.00
PRESTON, J C-Memoirs 1856 to 1926-(Sprngfld, 1927)-228p-
  wrps   (5s4,pres,soil) 10.00
PRESTON, JOHN HYDE-A Gentleman Rebel-NY-1930-370p
            (5p7) 6.   (5t4) 10.50
--Revolution 1776-NY-(1933)-440p-illus   (5t7)   6.50
PRESTON, KEITH-Pot Shots from Pegasus-NY-1929-243p (5p9) 6.00
PRESTON, L F-Uncle Bob, His Reflections-NY-1904-Grabhorn Pr
                (5x2)   12.00
PRESTON, MARGARET J-Beechenbrook, a Rhyme of the War-Balt-
  1866-94p   (5h1,rbnd)   5.00
--same-Balt-1867-106p   (5h6,scuff) 4. (5w5,wn) 6.50
PRESTON, RICHARD A, ed-Kingston Before The War of 1812-Tor-
  1959-Champlain Soc-ports-plts-428p (5L0) 10. (5s6) 12.50
--Royal Ft Frontenac-Tor-1958-Champlain Soc-ports-plts-503p
             (5dd0)   15.00
PRESTON, RICHARD J-Rocky Mntn Trees-Ames, Iowa-1940-maps-
  illus-hard bnd ed   (5s7)   4.50
PRESTON, T R-3 Years' Residence in Canada, from 1837 to 1839-
  Lond-1840-2 vols-errata slip in vol 1 (5w0) 75.00
PRESTON, THOS W-Historical Sketches of Holston Valleys-Kinsport-
  1926-186p-cl-scarce   (5j5,5y0) 15.00
PRESTON, W T R-My Generation of Politics & Politicians-Tor-
  1927-462p-port   (5aa0) 6.50 (4b9) 8. (5q8) 7.50
--Report Re NoAtlantic Steamship Combine by...Dec 31, 1924-
  (Ottawa, 1924)-sm folio-typescript cpy-orig wrps-56 lvs(5ss2) 25.00
PRESTON'S MANUAL OF BOOKKEEPING-NY-1829-2nd ed-
  8vo-calf & bds   (4c1)   15.00

PRETER,CARL JULIUS-Eine Kurze Beschreibung des Glaubens und
Praktischen Levens...Gewohnlich Genannt "Shakers"-
Union Village,Ohio-1888-8vo-orig wrps-32p-(only Shaker
tract prntd in German)-1st ed-scarce   (5ss5,v chip) 85.00
PRETLOW,MARY D-Old Southern Receipts-NY-1930-228p(5g9) 6.00
PRETTY PEGGY & OTHER BALLADS-NY-(1880)-Dodd,Mead-
prntd by Brett Lith-col illus-pict bds   (5c8,rub) 8.00
PRETTY PICTURE BOOK,A-Publ by NY Religious Tract Soc-n.d.-
DFanshaw,prntr-Series 1,#7-wdcuts-16p incl wrps
(5p1,wrp tn) 55.00
PRETTY PRIMER,THE-NY &Phila-ca1835-Turner&Fisher-24mo-
pict wrps-illus   (5v0,vg) 15.00
PRETTYMAN,W S-Indian Territory-Norman-(1957)-169p plus index-
illus-1st ed   (5dd5) 14.50   (5L0,dj) 10.00
PREVERT,JACQUES-Joan Miro-Maeght-1956-219p-8vo-orig dec wrps-
7 orig col liths   (5ww3) 65.00
PREVITE ORTON,C W-The Shorter Cambridge Medieval History-
Cambridge,Eng-1952-2 vols   (5q0) 15.00
PREVOST,ANTOINE F-Manon Lescaut-Lond-1928-folio-cl-
11 col plts-197p-ltd to 1850c,nbrd   (5nn2) 25.00
PREVOST,L'ABBE-Histoire de Manon Lescaut-Paris-1889-col plts by
Leloir-3/4 lea   (5yy6,rub) 12.50
PRIBRAM,DR ALFRED FRANZIS-Secret Treaties of Austria Hungary
1879 to 1914-Cambridge-1920-2 vols   (5q0) 20.00
PRICE,A G-White Settlers in the Tropics-Amer Geogr Soc-NY-
1939-illus   (5m2) 10.00
PRICE,ALFRED-Rail Life-Tor-1925-286p   (5aa0,pres) 8.50
PRICE,CON-Memories of Old Montana-Pasadena,Ca-(1945)-
154p-photos-paintng by CMRussell-1st ed   (5bb4,dj) 20.00
--same-deluxe ed-ltd to 125c   (5L2,autg) 50.00
--same-7th prntng   (5bb4,dj) 12.50
--Trails I Rode-Pasadena-(1947)-254p 1 col & 2 other illus by
ChasRussell-1st ed-photos   (5bb4) 15.00
--same-deluxe ed-ltd to 350c,autg   (5L2,dj) 35.00
PRICE,ELEANOR C-Miss Latimer of Bryans-Lond-1893-3 vols-
Bentley-8vo-orig blue cl-1st ed   (5xx6,lend libr) 30.00
PRICE,ELI K-Centennial Meeting of Desc of Philip & Rachel Price-
Phila-1864-disbnd-88p   (5w4) 8.50
PRICE,F A-Liberian Odyssey by Hammock & Surfboat-NY-1954-
Pageant Pr-photos-261p   (4t5) 12.   (5x2) 20.00
PRICE,F G H-Old Base Metal Spoons-Lond-1908-99p-16 plts
(5w7,cov stnd) 18.50
PRICE,F NEWLIN-Horatio Walker-NY-1928-Louis Carrier-7p-
38 illus-1st ed-ltd to 1024c-sm4to   (4a0) 25.00
PRICE,G A-Explorations of Capt Jas Cook-Heritage Pr-292p-illus
(4n1,box) 9.00
PRICE,G W-Giraud & the African Scene-NY-1944-1st ed (5x2) 5.00
PRICE,GEO F-Across the Continent with the 5th Cavalry-NY-
1959-705p-illus-t.e.g.-ltd to 750c   (5w0) 20.00
PRICE,GWYNNE-Clay Pigeon & Wing Shooting, & the Gun & How
to Use It-NY &StL-1884-58p-8vo-orig wrps-1st ed (5m6) 10.00
PRICE,HUGH D-The Negro & Southern Politics-NY-1957
(5x2,dj) 4.   (5w4,dj) 3.00
PRICE,JULIUS M-From Euston to Klondike-Lond-1898-map-illus
(5w8) 20.00
PRICE,LAWRENCE M-Inkle & Yarico Album-Univ of Calif Pr-
1937   (5ss9,dj) 12.50
PRICE,LITA-Maidcraft-(1937)-BobbsMerrill Co-216p-text illus
(5c9) 3.00
PRICE,M-The Negro & the Ballot in the South-Atlanta-1959-
Southern Regional Counc-83p-wrps   (5x2) 7.50
--The Negro Voter in the South-Atlanta-1957-Southern Regional
Counc-55p-wrps   (5x2) 10.00
PRICE,M PHILIPS-Amer After 60 Yrs-Lond-(1936)-235p-port
(5s4,f) 6.50
PRICE,RICHARD-Additional Observ on Nature & Value of Civil
Liberty-Lond-1777-Cadell-8vo-disbnd-1st ed (5n2) 85.00
--Observations on Importance of the Amer Revolution-Bost-1784-
8vo-hf mor-reprnted by Powars&Willis-1st Amer ed (5L1) 75.00
--same-NewHav-1785-Meigs Reprint-8vo-hf mor-Evans 19201
(5L1) 65.00
--same-Dublin-1785-1st Irish ed   (5q8,rbnd,libr bndg) 50.00
--Observations on the Nature of Civil Liberty-Lond-1776-T Cadell-
8vo-orig wrps-stitched-1st ed-scarce   (4h0,wrp dtchd) 100.00
--same-Lond-1776-T Cadell-128p,(8)-8vo-hf calf-2nd ed (5L1) 30.00
--Observations on the Nature of Civil Liberty, the Principles of
Government & the Justice & Policy of the War with Amer-
Lond-1776-8vo-disbnd-3rd ed   (5n2) 75.00
--same-5th ed-Lond-1776-8vo-cl-Adams 224e   (5L1) 30.00
--same-8th ed-Lond-1776   (5L1) 30.00
--Two Tracts on Civil Liberty,War with Amer & Debts & Finances
of the Kingdom-Lond-1778-TCadell-8vo-hf calf-fldg table-
112p,216p   (5g4,ex-libr,tn wi loss) 15. (5L1) 20.00

PRICE,ROSE LAMBART-Sport & Travel or the Two Americas-Phila-
n.d.-(ca after 1877)-illus-8vo-368p (5ee3) 12.50 (4m7,rub) 15.00
--The Two Americas, an Account of Sport & Travel-Phila-(1877)-
368p-illus-(1st Amer ed)   (5L0,wn,cov tn) 6.50
PRICE,S GOODALE-Black Hills the Land of Legend-LosAng-(1935)-
1st ed   (5kk4,f,pres) 12.50
--Saga of Hills-Calif-1940-245p-illus-1st ed
(5xx8) 7.50   (5m9,5yy7,5kk4,pres) 10.00
PRICE,WM T-Hist Sketches of Pocahontas Co,W Va-Marlinton-1901-
622p-cl-rare   (5h1,wn) 75.00
--same-Parsons-1962-facs rprnt   (5h1) 15.00
PRICHARD,H HESKETH-Hunting Camps in Wood & Wilderness-NY-
1910-274p-plts   (5dd0) 8.50
--Through Trackless Labrador-NY-Sturgis&WaltonCo,Lond-Heinemann
1911-244p-illus-cl-map   (5r0) 12.50
PRICHARD,HELEN M-Friends & Foes in the Transkei-Lond-1880-
Sampson,Low,Marston,etc-296p   (4t5,bndg broke) 20.00
PRICHARD,JAS C-Treatise on Diseases of Nervous System-Lond-
1822-12mo-hf calf   (4c2) 100.00
PRICHARD,SARAH J-The Only Woman in the Town & other Tales
of Amer Revolution-Waterbury-1898-1st ed   (5ee3,f) 10.00
PRIDE,W F-Hist of Ft Riley-n.p. 1926-339p-cl-fldg map
(5u3) 7.   (5h2,5g5,f) 7.50
PRIDEAUX,EDITH K-Figure Sculpture of the West Front of Exeter
Cathedral Church-Exeter,Commin-1912-35p-8vo-cl-33 plts
(5m5) 11.00
PRIDEAUX,MATHIAS-An Easy & Compendious Intro for Reading All
Sorts of Histories-Oxf-1672-Lichfield-sm4to-calf-2 vols in 1
(4n5,rebkd) 65.00
PRIDEAUX,TOM-World Theatre in Pictures from Ancient Times to
Modern Broadway-NY-(1953)-4to-illus   (4b7) 15.00
PRIDEAUX,W F-Bibliography of Works of Robt Louis Stevenson-Lond-
1918-401p   (4g2) 20.00
PRIDHAM,C H B-Superiority of Fire-Lond-1945-illus (5w0,dj) 7.50
PRIEST,ALAN-Aspects of Chinese Painting-NY-1954-4to-cl-134p-
illus   (5t7) 6.50
--Chinese Textiles-NY-1931-88p-(Metr Mus of Art) (5n7) 4.00
PRIEST,C D-Birds of So Rhodesia-Lond&Beccles-1936-Vol 4 only-
420p-10 col plts-cl-4to   (4p5,cov loose) 17.50
PRIEST,JOSIAH-Amer Antiquities & Discoveries in the West...-
1833-24mo-400p-map-2 plts-calf-Howes H592
(5L3,wn) 23.50   (5mm7) 32.50
--same-Albany-1833-2nd ed-400p-map-2 plts-calf-labl
(5i3,rub) 17.50 (5s9) 32.50   (5t7) 30.00
--same-Albany-1833-400p-illus-2 fldouts-orig lea-3rd ed
(5a9,sl fox,5q8,sl fox) 20.00
--same-Albany-1934-400p-4th ed   (5s4,wn) 20.00
--Indian Wars,Stories of Early Settlers in the Wilderness-Albany-
1837-JMunsell,prntr-fldg plt-papr wrps-orig ed of 1837 in 40p
(5a0,rprd) 25.00
PRIESTLY,HERBERT-The Mexican Nation,a History-NY-1926
(4a9,sl wtrstnd,dj) 12.00
PRIESTLEY,J B-Angel Pavement-Lond-1930-613p-1st ed (4b4) 12.50
--Brief Diversions-Cambr-1922-Bowes&Bowes   (5ss3,fade) 25.00
--Papers from Lilliput-Cambr-1922-Bowes&Bowes (5ss3,dj) 15.00
PRIESTLEY,JOS-Duty of Forgiveness of Injuries-Birmingham-1791-
42p-unbnd-stiff wrp-1st ed   (5yy6) 22.50
--Experiments & Observation on Different Kinds of Air-Lond-
1774 to 77-3 vols-orig hf calf-fldg plans   (5tt6) 300.00
--Experiments & Observ relating to various branches of Natural
Philosophy wi etc-Lond-1779 & Birmingham-1781-2 vols-
490 & 408p-fldg plans-orig hf calf   (5tt6,f) 200.00
--Familiar Letters,addressed to inhabitants of town of Birmingham-
Birmingham-JThompson,prntr-(Lond)-n.d.(1790)-(with) same-
Parts 2 to 5-5 parts in 1 vol-8vo-bds-1st ed (5x3,sp def) 60.00
--History & Present State of Electricity,with orig experiments-Lond-
1794-calf-8 fldg plts-4to-5th ed,corr
(5ee5,rebnd,plts sl dmpstn) 135.00
--Institutes of Natural & Revealed Religion-1782-2 vols-2nd ed
(5L7) 25.00
--Lectures on Hist & General Policy-Lond-1826-New ed-orig bds-
598p-fldg charts   (4d1,sl wn) 15.00
--Misc Observations Relating to Education-Bath-1778-8vo-calf-
1st ed   (4b6,f,reprd) 200.00
--Socrates & Jesus Compared-Phila-1803-8vo-disbnd-1st ed-scarce
(5i9) 35.00
PRIESTLY,H I,ed-The Luna Papers-Deland-1928-lg8vo-cl&bds-
maps&illus-2 vols-(Flor State Hist Soc)   (5g4,f) 35.00
PRIESTMAN,HOWARD-Principles of Worsted Spinning-Lond-1906-
8vo-cl-321p   (5t2) 5.00
PRIESTNALL HOLDEN,IVIE-750 Dishes from Overseas-NY-1945-
253p   (5g9) 3.50

PRIETO,GUILLERMO-San Francisco in the 70's-SanFran-1938-
Nash-plts-mrbld bds-91p-ltd to 650c
(4n1,dj) 20. (5h4,f,dj) 10. (5x5,dj) 25.00
PRIME,ALFRED COX-Arts & Crafts in Phila,Maryland & SoCar
1786 to 1800-Ser 2-(Phila)-1932-Walpole Soc-illus (5t7) 15.00
PRIME,MRS ALFRED COXE,ed-3 Centuries of Historic Silver-Phila-
1938-192p-illus-Pa Soc Col Dames of Amer-ltd to 1000c,nbrd
(5w0) 45. (5h9,f) 35. (5t2,mint) 40.00
PRIME,NATH'L S-History of Long Island...to 1845-NY-1845-1st ed
(4a1,chip) 42.50
PRIME,TEMPLE-Some Account of the Family of Prime of Rowley,
Mass-1897-79p-2nd ed (5mm3) 10.00
PRIME,W C-Along New England Roads-NY-1892-Harper-16mo-200p-
cl-t.e.g.-1st ed (4c5,f) 7.50
--Among the Northern Hills-NY-1895-Harper-16mo-209p-cl-t.e.g.-
1st ed (4c5,f) 7.50
--Boat Life in Egypt & Nubia-NY-1857-8vo-cl-illus-498p (5t2) 3.50
--Coins,Medals & Seals,Ancient & Modern-NY-1861-illus-292p-
frontis-1st ed (5j5,f bndg by Stikeman) 47.50 (5i3) 10.00
--I Go A Fishing-NY-1873-365p (5m1) 10.00
--Pottery & Porcelain of All Time & Nations-NY-1879-531p-illus
(5w7) 8.50
PRIMER,IMPROVED,THE-or The Child's Companion-Middlebury,Vt-
1817-48p-wdcuts-wrps-18mo-TCStrong (5t7) 10.00
PRIMULA-A Book of Lyrics-Lond-1858-16mo-hf mor-1st ed of auth's
1st book-(Richard Garnett) (5gg6,pres) 75.00
PRIN,ALICE-Education of a French Model-NY-1950-illus(5yy6) 7.50
PRINCE EDWARD IS-Memorial Volume,1772 to 1922-Summerside-
1922-127p-port (5u6) 15.00
PRINCE FREDK WINYAW PARISH-Register Book-SoCar-1713-246p
(5mm3,dmpstnd) 17.50
PRINCE,JANE-Letters to a Young Housekeeper-Bost-1917-167p-
bds (5w7,lacks fly) 5.00
PRINCE,L BRADFORD-Historical Sketches of New Mex from
Earliest Records to Amer Occupation-NY&KC-1883-327p-
1st ed (5g5) 15. (5yy7,lacks fly) 20.00
--New Mexico's Struggle for Statehood-SantaFe-1910-8vo-cl-
128p-1st ed (5h5,dmpstnd) 10. (5g2) 35.00
--Spanish Mission Churches of New Mexico-CedarRpds-1915-
373p-62 illus (5t1) 35. (5h5) 17.50
PRINCE LEE BOO-The Interesting & Affecting History of a Native
of Pelew Islands-Lond-1789-ENewbery-12mo-178p plus 6p ads-
frontis-vel sp-bds-1st ed (5v2,sp rprd) 175.00
PRINCE OF ABISSINIA,THE-a tale-Lond-1775-12mo-calf-
mor labl-for Strahan,Dodsley & Johnston-(Sam'l Johnson)-
5th ed (5xx6) 40.00
PRINCE OF KASHNA,THE-NY-1866-Carleton-450p-1st ed-
(Jos W Fabens) (5x4) 12.50
PRINCE,OLIVER H-Digest of Laws of State of Georgia-Athens-
1837-1046p-8vo-full calf- 2nd ed (5t0) 12.50
PRINCE,THOS-A Chronological History of New Engl in form of
Annals-Vol 1-Bost N E-prntd by Kneeland & Green for S Gerish-
1736 -lea (5t7,lacks t.p. & 2 pref lvs) 25.00
--same-Bost-1826-Kneeland&Green-4to-orig bds-1st complete ed
(5n2,rbkd,box) 85.00
--same-Bost-1852-(edited by Nathan Hale)-(18)p 3 to 12-5 to 439p-
lea&bds-Antiquarian Book Store-11 plts-3rd ed-v rare-
1 of only 30c (5m3,sl rub) 65.00
--Extraordinary Events...Occasion'd by Taking City of Louisbourg
on Isle of Cape Breton-Bost-1745-12mo-35p-(unbnd) (5ss5) 35.00
PRINCE WILLIAM OF SWEDEN-Among Pygmies & Gorillas with
Swedish Zoological Exped to Central Africa 1921-NY-n.d.-
8vo-296p-photos (4a6,shaken) 10.00
PRINCE WM REED-Memoir & Select Writings of-Portland,Me-1846-
300p-1st ed (5w5,wn) 7.50
PRINCE,WM R-The Pomological Manual,a Treatise on Fruits-NY-
1832-2 vols in 1-2nd ed (5yy8,rebnd,ex-libr) 12.50
PRINCESS DER LING-Old Buddha-NY-1928-347p-illus (5t7) 4.50
PRINCETON GUIDE-Princeton-1939-wrps-48p(7)p-WPA-Amer
Guide Series (5h1) 7.50
PRINCIPAL STAGE,STEAMBOAT & CANAL ROUTES,THE-in the
US..an accompaniment to Mitchell's Traveller's Guide-Phila-
1834-32mo-wrps-papr labl (5g3) 15.00
PRINCIPAL GAME BIRDS & MAMMALS OF TEXAS-Austin-1945-
Texas Game & Fish Comm-illus-maps (5a8) 6.50
PRINCIPLES OF MECHANICS-Explaining & Demonstrating,etc-
Lond-1758-4to-284p-orig calf-illus-43 plts-(Wm Emerson)
(5m4) 125.00
PRINCIPLES OF EQUITY-Edinb-1760-folio (5r4,rbnd) 27.50
PRINDLE,H G-Proceedings in Senate on Investig of Charges
Preferred Against-Albny-1874-2 vols (5r4,rbnd) 27.50

PRINDLE,L M-The Yukon Tanana Region,Alaska,descrip of
circle quadrant-Wash-1906-GPO-USGS Bull #295-27p-
fldg map (5ss1) 6.00
PRINDLE,P W-Van Derwerken,Van Derwerker Family-1966-370p
(5mm3) 15.00
PRING,DR-Particulars of Grand Suspension Bridge,Erected Over
Straits of Menai-Bangor-1829-40p-wrps-fldg frontis-10th ed
(5hh7) 8.50
PRINGLE,G C F-Adventures in Service-Tor-1929-282p-1st ed
(5dd7) 9. (4d2) 5.00
PRINGLE,HENRY F-Life & Times of Wm Howard Taft-Farrar-(1939)-
illus-2 vols (5yy8) 17.50
--Alfred E Smith,A Critical Study-NY-1927-402p (5x0) 4.50
PRINGLE,JAS R-History of Town & City of Gloucester,Cape Ann,
Mass-Gloucester-1892-illus-340p (5mm3,5h9) 8.00
--Mass Bay Colony at Cape Ann in 1623-Book of the 300th Ann
Observ of Foundation of-Gloucester-1924-280p-illus (5h9) 8.00
PRINGLE,SIR JOHN-Observ on Diseases of the Army, in Camp &
Garrison, In 3 Parts, etc-Lond-1753-Millar(etc)-8vo-calf-
g.back-2nd rev ed (5ee5,vf) 80.00
PRINT COLLECTOR'S BULLETIN-An Illus Catalog for Museums &
Collectors, Vol 1,#4-NY-1930-M Knoedler-wrps-71p-8vo-
50 liths by Whistler (4e0) 12.50
PRIOR, EDW S-Cathedral Builders in England-Lond-1905-Seeley-
112p-plts-4to-cl (5m5,ex-libr) 12.00
PRIOR,J-Voyage Along Eastern Coast of Africa to Mosambique,
Johanna & Quiloa to St Helena in Nisus Frigate-Lond-1819-
114p-map-disbnd (5x2) 32.50
PRIOR,JAS-Life of Oliver Goldsmith-Lond-1837-part mor-frontis-
facs-g. (4d1,f bndg) 35.00
PRIOR,MATHEW-Poems on Several Occasions-Aberdeen-1754-2 vols-
orig calf (5m4,joints weak) 20.00
PRIOR,CAPT SAM'L-All Voyages Round World from the 1st by
Magellan in 1520-Lond-1820-chart-12mo-sheep-72 illus
(4c1,rbkd) 75.00
PRINTING & THE MIND OF MAN-Catalogue of Display-Lond-
1963-wrps-pub FWBridges&Sons (5F9,f) 3.50
PRINTING INDUSTRY OF AMER-Composition Manual-n-c1953-
4to-311p-illus-Tools of Indus Series-Lakeside Pr (5w5) 6.50
PRINTING TRADES BLUE BOOK-Eastern Edition-NY-1948
(5b9,vf) 5.00
PRINTZ-"Printzess" Cloaks & Suits-Catalog Fall & Winter, 1903,04-
Cleve-1903-16mo-(32p)-illus-wrps-priced-Biderman&Co (5t4) 3.00
PRIOR,C M-Early Records of the Thoroughbred Horse-Lond-1924-
171p (5ii2) 7.50
PRISCILLA COOK BOOK-Priscilla Aid-Overton,Neb-1954-162p-
frontis-spiral bnd (5g9) 3.50
PRISON DISCIPLINE SOC-1st,2nd & 3rd Annual Report of,Bost,
Jun 2,1826-Bost-1827 to 1828-3 vols in 1-8vo-48p,100p,84p-
(unbnd)-5th ed (5ss5) 10.00
--same-1st,4th,5th,6th,8th,10th,11th & 12th Annual Reports-
in 1 vol-disbnd-Bost-n.d. (5w5,needs bndg) 10.00
PRITCHARD, JAS A-Overland Diary of-1959-Lawton Kennedy,prntr-
ltd (5b0,dj) 25. (4a4,5k1) 35.00
PRITCHARD, JAS B-Ancient Near Eastern Texts relating to Old
Testament-Princeton-1955-2nd ed-corr& enlgrd (5ii3) 17.50
PRITCHETT,C HERMAN-The Roosevelt Court-NY-1948 (5a8) 5.00
PRIVATE LAND CLAIMS-Florida-Letter fom Sec of Treas-Wash-
1830-8vo-sewn-159p-HD 51 (5ss5) 20.00
PRIVATE LIFE OF LEWIS XV-Lond-1781-Chas Dilly-4 vols-8vo-
port-calf (5L1,wn,broke) 75.00
PRIVATE PAPERS OF A BANKRUPT BOOKSELLER-NY-1932-306p
(5t7) 5.00
PROBLEMS OF COMMUNISM-(Wash)-Vol 1 thru 18-1952 to 69-
bound (5ii7,ex-libr) 245.00
PROBYN,J W,ed-Systems of Land Tenure in Various Countries-
1876 (5L7,ex-libr) 4.50
PROCEEDINGS OF GOV & ASSEMBLY OF JAMAICA-in regard
to Maroon Negroes-Lond-1796-frontis-4p,89p,1p,109p-calf-
lea labl-1st ed (5m3,rub,ex-libr) 125.00
PROCEEDINGS IN KU KLUX TRIALS-at Columbia,S C,Nov Term,
1871-Columbia-1872-836p,12p-sewn (5m3,box,lacks wrps) 45.00
PROCEEDINGS OF THE-2nd Nat'l Conference on Problems of Negro
& Negro Youth-Wash-1939-Dept of Labor-123p-wrps (5x2) 15.00
PROCES DE J BTE-Beauregard convaincu du meurtre d'Anselme
Charron-(Montreal,1859?) 52p (5w8) 35.00
PROCES DE PIERRE BARBINA DIT DUVAL-pour l'empoisonnement
de Julie Desilie,son epouse-Trois Rivieres-1863-21p-sewn
(5w8) 45.00

USED BOOK PRICE GUIDE

PROCES PROVENCHER BOISCLAIR-La Gazette de Sorel-1867-
prntd wrps   (5w8)   35.00
PROCOPIUS, CAESARIENSIS-The Secret History of Procopius-
Chig-1927-type by Douglas McMurtrie-ltd to 760c
                                        (5mm2,autgs)   22.50
PROCRASTINATION-or Maria Louisa Winslow-by a lady-Bost-1840-
DSKing-12mo-hf roan-1st ed   (5x1,scuff)   100.00
PROCTOR, EVERITT-Men Against the Ice-Phila-(1946)-148p-
Juvenile   (5ss1)   3.50
PROCTER, GIL-Tucson, Tubac, Tumacacori, Tohell-1956-108p-1st ed-
ltd-autg   (5r1,f,dj)   17.00
--same-Ariz Silhouettes-Tucson-(1957) (5x5,pres,cov nick)   7.50
PROCTOR, H G-The Iron Division, Nat'l Guard of Penna in World
War-Phila-c1919-297p-illus   (5w5)   5.00
PROCTOR, L B-Bench & Bar of NY-NY-1870-779 p
                                        (4b6, rub) 15. (5ff4,rebnd)   19.50
PROCTOR, R A-Expanse of Heave, series of essays on wonders of
the firmament-1911   (5L7)   4.00
--Our Place among Infinities-Lond-1886-288p-dec cl (5t0)   3.50
--Watched by the Dead-Lond-1887-166p-1st ed (4a8)   8.50
PROCTER, RICHARD W-The Barber's Shop-Manchester(Eng)-1882-
4to-plts-250p   (5n7,wn)   8.50
PRODGERS, C H-Adventures in Peru-Lond-(1924)-JnLane-250p-
illus   (5d6)   5.00
PRODUCTEUR, LE-Journal Des Interets Speciaux de la Propriete
Vignoble du Depart de la Gironde, 2nd Annee-Bordeaux-1839-
600p-12 fldg map s-lea bk-g.t.   (5w6)   22.50
PROFFATT, J-Curiosities & Law of Wills-SanFran-1876 (5ff4)   9.75
PROGRESS & STATE OF MISSION-at the Sandwich Islands-
(Bost, 1840?)-maps in text-wrpr title -24p   (5g8)   25.00
PROGRESS IN RACE RELATIONS 1924, 1925-Atlanta-1926-20p-
wrps-Comm On Interracial Co-Op   (5x2)   8.50
PROGRESS OF THE ART OF BUILDING-& a sure remedy for smoky
chimneys-Edinb-1864-WmPNimmo-8vo-orig cl-1st ed (5i8,f)   10.00
PROGRESS OF POPERY, THE-In British Dominions & Elsewhere-
Lond-1838-20p-prntd t.p.-cov-reprntd from "Blackwood's
Magazine" of Oct   (5w8)   7.50
PROGRESS OF THE RR-West from Omaha, Neb across the Continent...
820 miles completed Sept 20, 1868-NY-1868-40p-drawings-
map-wrps   (5L2)   20.00
PROGRESSIVE MEN OF STATE OF MONT-Chig-(1902)-lea-illus-
frontis-a.e.g.-1st ed   (4d5,cl dj,box,wn)   150.00
PROHIBITIONISTS' TEXT BOOK-NY-1882-(313)p-cl (5h7)   8.50
PROKOSCH, FREDERIC-Age of Thunder-NY-(1945)-8vo-cl-
sheet of the orig ms bnd in-g.t.-ltd to 45c, autg-1st ed
                                           (5d3,box)   37.50
--The Assassins-NY-1936-8vo-cl-1st ed   (5dd8,dj)   20.00
--The Carnival-NY-1938-Harper&Bros-1st ed-ltd 55c, nbrd &
autg-orig If of ms bnd in   (5ss9,box) 50. (5dd8)   37.50
--same-Lond-1938-8vo-cl-1st Engl ed   (5dd8,dj,autg)   7.50
--Death at Sea-NY-1940-8vo-cl-spec ed-1st ed-orig ms If bnd in-
ltd to 55c, autg, box   (5dd8,pres)   37.50
--same-NY-1940-8vo-cl-1st ed   (5dd8,dj)   15.00
--same-Lond-1940-8vo-cl-1st Engl ed (5dd8,pres,dj)   15.00
--Three Sorrows-NewHav-1932-wrps-8vo-& Three Images, NewHav-
1932-8vo-wrps-papr labl-ltd to 10c, lg papr ed-autg-12p ea
                                        (5d9,box,pres) 125.00
PROLETARIAN LITERATURE IN THE US-NY-(c1935)-Intl Publ-
8vo-cl-scarce   (5b2)   20.00
PROLIX, PERAGINE-Pleasant Perigrination thru the Prettiest Parts
of Pennsylvania Performed by....-Phila-1836-orig bds-lalb-16mo-
148p-scarce   (4m2,recased)   30.00
PROMINENT FEATURES OF A NORTHERN TOUR-from a brief diary-
Charleston-1822-for auth, by CCSebring-12mo-disbnd-1st ed-
rare   (5i9)   200.00
PRONOUNCING GAZETTEER-& Geographical Dictionary of
Philippine Islands-Wash-1902-GPO-thk8vo-cl-933p-maps-
charts   (5h5,shake,soil)   15.00
PROPER IDA SEDGWICK-Monhegan, the Cradle of New England-
Portland-1930-Southworth Pr-8vo-hf cl-illus-275p-ltd to 1000c,
autg   (5j5)   10.00
--same-Portland-1930-cl&bds-trade ed   (5t7)   6.50
PROPERTY-Its Duties & Rights Historically, Philos & Religiously
Regarded-Lond-1913   (5ff4,rebnd)   8.50
--same-NY-1922-new ed   (5ff4)   8.50
PROPHETICAL OBSERVATIONS OCCASION'D BY NEW COMET-
& by other signs in heavens-Lond-1723-prntd for Sam'l Harding-
8vo-disbnd-1st ed   (5x3)   22.50
PROPRIETORS OF ARCHITECTURAL LIBRARY OF BOSTON-Consti of,
15th Nov, 1809-Bost-1809-9p, blank, 5p-stitchd (5g3)   25.00
PROSCH, CHAS-Remin of Washington Territory-Seattle-1904-port-
plts-128p   (5cc4) 21. (5s4,pres,wn)   30.00

PROSCH, THOS W-Conkling Prosch Family-Seattle-1909-141p-
photos-ltd to 150c   (5s4,pres)   35.00
PROSE EPITOME-or, Elegant Extracts abridged-Lond-1791-CDilly-
sq12mo-456p-orig roan   (5c8,crack)   17.50
PROSE QUARTOS-NY-1930-stiff wrps-separate wks-boxed (4b1)   40.00
PROTESTANT COUNCIL OF CITY OF NY-Midcentury Pioneers &
Protestants, Surv...Puerto Rican Migration etc-(NY)-1954-
PCCNY-4to-mimeo-(28)p-wrps-2nd ed   (4a3)   12.50
PROTESTANT EPISCOPAL CHURCH-Documentary History in
Diocese of Vermont-NY-1870-418p   (5t4)   10.00
PROTESTANT JESUITISM-By a Protestant-NY-1836-8vo-(C Colton)-
1st ed   (5m6)   15.00
PROTHERO, ERNEST-All About Sailing Ships-Lond-n.d.-95p-illus
                                        (5s1,rprd,stnd)   4.00
PROUD, ROBT-History of Penna in NoAmer-Phila-1797, 8-Poulson-
2 vols-1st ed-port-fldg map-orig calf bds (4b1,f,rbkd) 200.00
PROUDFIT, ALEX-Practical Godliness in 13 Discourses-Salem-1813-
lea-399p   (5yy8)   10.00
PROUDHON, P J-What is Property, Inquiry into Principle of Right
& of Government-Lond-n.d.-Tucker, tr-2 vols in 1 (5r4)   12.50
PROUST, MARCEL-Cities of the Plain-NY-1927-2 vols-1st ed-
ltd to 2000c   (5ss9)   12.50
--Reviews and Estimates in English-Stanford Univ Pr-(1942)-
compiled by Gladys D Lindner-1st ed   (5ss9,dj)   10.00
--47 Lettres Inedites de Marcel Proust a Walter Berry-Paris-1930-
Black Sun Pr-4to-orig wrps-port-facs-1 of 200c-1st ed
                                        (5dd8,fade)   30.00
--Swann's Way-NY-1954-illus-ltd to 1500c, nbrd, autg-boxed-
Limited Edition Club publ   (5F1,f)   27.50
--The Works of..-7 vols-NY-1930-A&C-Boni   (5p9)   12.50
PROUT, EBENEZER-Counterpoint, Stric † & Free-Lond-(1890)-259p-
Augener   (5p0)   4.75
--Harmony, Its Theory & Practice-Lond-(1889)-266p-Augener-
13th ed   (5p0)   7.50
--The Orchestra-Lond-(1897, 1899)-2 vols-illus-8vo (5ss5,crack)   15.00
PROUT, SAM'L-Prout's Microcosm-1881-24 tinted liths-folio-
new ed   (5L7,spot)   25.00
PROUTY, F N-Hist of Holden, Mass-1941-370p (5mm3)   7.50
PROVIDENCE ANTI SLAVERY SOC-Tract indicating the philosophy,
principles & aims of-1833-12p-wrps   (5x2,stnd)   20.00
PROVIDENCE ASSOC OF MECHANICS & MANUFACTURERS-
Charter, By Laws, Rules & Regulations of-Providence-1860-wrps
                                             (5g4)   10.00
PROVIDENCE, R I-Early Records of-20 vols & index, 1892 to 1948-
                                            (5mm3)   35.00
PROVIDENCE, R I-Ship Registers & Enroll   of Providence,
1773 to 1939, (also) Ship Licences-Prov-1941-WPA-mimeo-
2 vols in 3   (4m7)   37.50
PROVIDENCE-250th Anniv of Settlement of, Jun 23, 24, 1886-Prov-
1887-City Council-lg4to-orig mor-frontis-a.e.g. (5L8)   20.00
PROVIDENT SAVINGS BANK, THE-A Unique Institution-Balt-1904-
illus-sm8vo-21p, (1)   (5e4)   5.75
PROVINCIAL AGRICULTURAL ASSOC OF LOWER CANADA-
Provincial Exhib, Sept, 1853-Montr-1853-16mo-52p-prntd t.p.-
cov   (5w8)   12.50
PROVISIONAL DRILL & SERV REGULATIONS FOR FIELD ARTILLERY-
NY-1917-Parts 1 thru 10, complete-8vo-cl   (4a6)   4.50
PROVISIONAL MACHINE GUN FIRING MANUAL, 1917-288p-
War Dept Doc #615-scarce   (5g5,f)   5.00
PROVO, PIONEER MORMON CITY-Portl-c1942-Binfords&Mort-
Amer Guide Ser-cl-12mo-223p-WPA-"First Publ in 1942" on
cpyrte pg   (5j1,4t1)   15.00
PROVOST, A J-Provost Family Biographical & Gen Notes-1895-
131p-300c prntd for priv distri   (5mm3)   20.00
PROVTER, GIL-Tucson, Tubac, Tumacacori Tohell-Tucson-1956-
8vo-110p-cl-illus-1st ed-ltd to 1000c, nbrd, autg
                                        (5hh4,f dj,pres)   10.00
PROWELL, GEO R-History of the 87th Regiment Penna Volunteers-
York-1901-305p, (25)-illus   (5w5)   12.50
PROWSE, G R F-Exploration of Gulf of St Lawrence, 1499 to 1525-
Winnipeg-1929-volio-23p & 14p-maps-orig wrps-2 vols(5jj3)   25.00
PRUDDEN, L E-Peter Prudden, Story of His Life at New Haven &
Milford-1901-   scarce   (5t9)   25.00
PRUDDEN, T M-On the Great Amer Plateau-NY-243p plus ads-
illus-fldg map-1st ed -1906   (5a9,underline)   5.00
PRUDDEN, T MITCHELL-Drinking Water & Ice Supplies & Their
Relations to Health & Disease-NY-1891-12mo-148p-illus
                                             (5w6)   5.00
PRUDENCE PENNY'S COOK BOOK-Popular dishes that men like
to cook-NY-1939-385p   (5c0)   3.50
PRUIETT, MOMAN-Criminal Lawyer-OklaCty-1945-580p-illus-
blue lea-2nd prntng   (5kk4) 35. (5k2)   45.00

165

PRUIETT, MOMAN (continued)
--same-OklaCty-1945-3rd printing(all printings are scarce)
(4k1,shake) 40.   (5kk5)   35.00
PRUNIER'S, MDME-Fish Cookery Book-Lond-(1947)-300p-illus-
reprint   (5c9)   4.50
PRUNTY, R E L-Brookfield Past & Present-Brookfld, Mo-n.d.-(ca 1905)-
276p-photos-wrps-scarce   (5t3)   15.00
PRUSSING, EUGENE E-Geo Washington, In Love & Otherwise-Chig-
1925-183p-illus-bds-cl sp-ltd to 1100c, nbrd, autg   (5h9)   7.50
PRUYN, J V L-Catalogue of Books Relating to Literature of Law-
Albany-1901   (5ff4)   32.50
--Report of Regents of Univ on Boundaries of State of NY-Albany-
1874   (5tt5)   25.00
PRYOR, MRS ROGER A-Remin of Peace & War-NY-1905-
rev & enlrgd ed-illus   (5r0,pres) 7.50   (5s9)   5.00
--same-NY-1924-418p-illus   (5ee3,vf,dj)   5.00
--The Mother of Washington & Her Times-NY-1903-367p-illus-
t.e.g.-1st ed   (5w9)   6.50
--My Day....Remin of a Long Life-NY-1909-454p-illus-t.e.g.-
1st ed   (5w5)   8.00
PSALM BOOK-The Whole Book of Psalms, in Metre, with Hymns
Suited to Feasts & Fasts of the Church-Phila-1790-calf-
lea bkstrp-Hall&Sellers,prntr   (5mm2,rprd)   25.00
PS ALMANAZAR, GEO-Memoirs of, a Reputed Native of Formosa-
By Himself-Lond-1764-364p-1st ed-lea   (5p6,bndg poor)   25.00
PSALMEN, DAVIDS-Das neue und verbesserte Gesang Buch,
worinnen die....vor die Evangelisch Reformirten Gemeinen in
den Vereinigten Staaten von America-Phila-1797-thk12mo-
calf-148p,(8),585p,(41)-g.e.-Steiner&Kammerer-rare
(5L1,crude bndg)   50.00
PSALMS-carefully suited to Christian Worship in US Allowed by the
Rev Synod of NY & Phila-NY-1797-Elizabethtown-
Shepard Kollock-314p & table-24mo-calf   (5r7)   35.00
PSALMS OF DAVID, THE-with Hymns & Spiritual Songs-also,
Catechism of Reformed Church in the Netherlands-NY-
1789-Hode, Allen&Campbell-thk12mo-calf-348p, 148p,(4)-
2nd ed without prntd music   (5L1,wn)   20.00
PSALTER-Das kleine Davidische Psalterspiel der Kinder Zions, etc-
Germantwun-1797-MichaelBillmeyer-572p,(24)-22p,(Suppl)-
(index)-12mo-orig calf   (5L1,v wn,rprd,lacks some text)   25.00
PSALTER, THE NEW ENGLAND-or, Psalms of David with Proverbs-
Bost-1761-prntd(ByBMecom)for Green&Russell-12mo-158p-rare
(5v2,vg,ex-libr)   300.00
PTOLEMY, CLAUDIUM-Liber Geographiae-Venice-1511-folio-
28 double pg woodcut maps-limp vel-Sabin 66477 (5hh0) 8,500.00
PUBLIC BUILDINGS OF CITY OF LONDON DESCRIBED-Lond-
1831-Little Library (Vol 7)-JnHarris-sq12mo-12 engr plts-
(C I Johnstone)   (5c8,sl spots)   25.00
PUBLIC LIBRARIES IN US OF A-Wash-1876-GPO-illus-1187p
(5yy0)   22.50
PUBLII TERENTII AFRI COMOEDIAE-Birmingham-1772-Baskerville Pr-
4to-g.bkstrp-a.e.g.   (5d1,f,f bndg)   200.00
PUBLOW, CHAS A-Fancy Cheese in Amer-C hig-1910-Amer Sheep
Breeder Co-96p-ads-illus 1   (5c5,4g9)   6.50
PUCK-Vol 1,#1-SanFran-Jan 7, 1865-4p   (5d6)   7.50
PUCKERTOWN'S WISDOM-Easthampton, Mass-n.d.-(ca 1905)-
Young Ladies' Missionary Soc-103p-cl   (5t4)   4.50
PUCKLER, MUSKAU, PRICE-Semilasso in Africa-Lond-1837-Bentley-
3 vols-12mo-hf calf-1st ed   (5i8,lacks 2 labls)   25.00
PUDDEFOOT, W G-Minute Man of Frontier-NY-(1895)-326p-
illus-g. dec cov   (5s4,fade,ex-libr)   6.50
PUDDEFOOT, WM G-Hewers of Wood-Bost-(c 1903)-Pilgrim Pr-
8vo-illus-dec cl   (5b2,f)   5.00
PUEBLO & DULUTH RR-Prospectus of the Pueblo Route-Neligh, Neb-
1891-43p-fldg frontis-illus-wrps-1st ed-rare   (5t3)   75.00
PUERTO RICO-A Guide to the Island of Boriquen-NY-1940-illus-
maps-pkt map-1st ed (5q8,lacks pkt map) 4.75 (5kk4,f)   7.50
PUFENDORF, BARON DE-Le Droit de la Nature et des Gens-
Amsterdam-deCoup-1712-2 vols-4to-port-calf (5a1,sl wn)   25.00
--same-1734-4to-calf-2 vols-5th ed   (5L7,sl stn)   25.00
--De jure naturae et gentium, libri octo, cum commentariis
J N Hertii atque J Barbeyraci-1744-2 vols-4to-vel (5L7)   25.00
PUGH, EDW-Forms of Procedure in Courts Admiralty USA-Phila-
1890-338p-lea   (5s1)   3.00
PUGH, EDWIN-Chas Dickens Originals-Lond-1912-1st ed-347p-
30 mtd ports   (4a8)   6.50
PUGH, JOHN-Remarkable Occurrences in Life of Jonas Hanway,
Esq, etc-Lond-1798-calf-fldg map-12mo-3rd ed
(5v7,fox,hng split)   12.50
PUGH, MARSHALL-Frogman, Cmndr Crabb's Own Story-NY-(1956)-
208p-photos   (5s1,dj,f)   5.00

PUGIN, A WELBY-Glossary of Ecclesiastical Ornament & Costume-
Lond-1844-HenryGBohn-222p text-73p illuminated plts-lg4to-
cl-g.t.-1st ed   (5s 5)   55.00
PUGIN, AUGUSTUS-Specimens of the Architecture of Normandy,
from the 11th to 16th century-Lond-1874-Blackie-lg4to-88p-
g.stmped cl-a.e.g.-illus-Richard Phene Spiers, ed (5m5)   42.00
PUGSLEY, CAPT R M-Navigator or Mariners' Guide-JerseyCty-1905-
202p-6 charts bk cov pkt-wrps-illus-10½x7"
(5s1,lacks some charts)   8.00
--same-1922-161p   (5s1)   6.50
PUHR, CONRAD-Modern Alaska & the Alcan-n.p.-n.d.-wrps-
ringbnd photos & descriptive text-wrps   (5ss1)   7.50
PUJOULX, J B-Livre du Second Age, ou Instructions Amusantes sur
l'Histoire Naturelle-Paris-An 11, 1803-Debray-frontis-18 plts-
3rd ed   (5c8,rub)   32.50
PULESTON, CAPT W D-Annapolis, Gangway to the Quarterdeck-NY-
1942-259p-illus   (5t7)   5.00
--Mahan, the Life & Work of Capt Alfred T Mahan, USN-Yale U Pr-
1939-illus   (5m2,als)   10.00
PULITZER, RALPH-Over the Front in an Aeroplane-NY-(1915)-sm8vo-
cl-illus-159p   (5t2,cov stns)   6.00
--NY Society on Parade-NY-1910-illus by Howard Chandler Christy-
141p,(5),(1)   (5w7)   8.50
PULITZER, WALTER-The Duel at the Chateau Barsanac-NY-1899-
Funk&Wagnals-120p-illus-1st ed   (5x4)   7.50
PULLEN, ELISABETH-Mr Whitman-Bost-(1902)-Lothrop-8vo-g.-
pict cl   (5b2,f)   4.50
PULLEN-BURRY, BESSIE-From Halifax to Vancouver-Lond-(1912)-
illus-8vo-1st ed   (4f9) 7.50   (5qq8) 6.   (4g6,chip)   12.50
PULLING, ALEX-Order of the Coif-Bost-1897-orig cl-g. pict bk-
(New ed)   (4m9)   15.00
PULP & PAPER INVESTIGATION HEARINGS-Wash-1908-3 vols-
hf lea   (4m5,sp tn)   35.00
PULSIFER, SUSAN N-Scenes from Life of Jesus in Woodcut-Bost-
1947-Beacon-sm folio-cl-168p   (5j5,dj)   15.00
PULSZKY, FRANCIS-White, Red, Black, Sketches of Amer Society-
NY-1853-2 vols   (5m6,ex-libr) 15.00   (4m2)   25.00
PULTE, MRS DR J H-Domestic Cook Book, A-Cinn-1888-370p,(1)
(5c0)   7.50
PULTENEY, WM-Considerations on Present State of Public Affairs &
means of raising Necessary Supplies-Lond-1779-Dodsley-
8vo-cl-52p,(4)-   (5L1,rbnd)   50.00
--Thoughts on the Present State of Affairs with Amer & the Means of
Conciliation-Lond-1778-JDodsley-t8vo-102p-wrps-4th ed
(5L8,re-wrps)   15.00
--same-Lond-1778-8vo-cl-111p-5th ed-2 appendices (5L1)   60.00
--same-1st ed-see under title
PULVER, JEFFREY-Biographical Dictionary of Old Engl Music-Lond-
1927-KeganPaul-537p   (5p7)   10.00
PUMPELLY, RAPHAEL-Across Amer & Asia-NY-1870-illus-maps-454p
(5yy0)   12.50
--same-NY-1871-cl-illus-maps-8vo
(5dd6,wn) 12.   (5v7,ex-libr)   12.50
--My Reminiscences-NY-1918-2 vols-illus-maps
(5g4) 12.50   (5dd9) 25.   (5t7,lib labl)   17.50
--Travels & Adventures of Raphael Pumpelly-NY-1920-illus-
ed by O S Rice   (5q8)   6.00
PUMPHREY, STANLEY-Indian Civilization-(Phila-1877)-intro John
Greenleaf Whittier-52p-fldg map   (5L7) 10.   (4i7)   20.00
PUMPHREY'S-Sectional Map of Western Washington-Seattle-
1891,92-2 col maps fldg into 4x6 cl cov   (5x5)   17.50
PUNCH-London Charivari-July to Dec-1915-452p-bnd (5i1)   6.00
PUNCHARD, GEO-History of Congregationalism from about AD 250
to 1616-Salem-1841-16mo-cl-388p   (5t4)   10.00
PUNCHINELLO-New Illus Humorous & Satirical Paper-Vols 1 & 2,
Apr , 1870 to Dec 24, 1870-NY-1870-4to-2 vols in 1
(5m6,wn)   25.00
PUNKIN, JONATHAN-Downfall of Free Masonry-(Harrisburg, PA)-
1838-Near Council Cham, Unction Room-illus-orig bds-linen sp-
1st ed-v scarce   (4g2,tn)   50.00
PUNSHON, E R-The Solitary House-NY-1918-AlfredAKnopf-bds-
1st ed   (5ee3,f)   10.00
PUPIN, MICHAEL-From Immigrant to Inventor-NY-1923-plts-396p
(4h8,photo mtd) 8.50 (5y2) 5. (5w5)   4.50
PUPPY DOG'S ABC-Father Tuck's Xmas Series 4570-Lond-(c1900)-
4to-16p in self wrps-illus shape book   (5c8)   7.50
PURCELL, M-The Great Captain-Lond-1962   (5c1)   5.00
PURCELL, MAE F-History of Contra Costa County-Berkeley-1940-
Gillick Pr-742p-8vo-cl   (4t1,pres)   40.00
PURCELL, POLLY JANE-Autobiography & remin of a pioneer-
(Freewater, Ore, n.d.)-unbnd 8vo-prntd on 1side of papr(5g3) 7.50

PURCELL,RICHARD J-Connecticut in Transition,1775 to 1818-Wash-
1918-fldg maps   (5q8)   10.00
PURDIE,SAM'L-Memories of Angela Aguilar De Mascorro & Sketches
of the Friends Mexican Mission-Chig-1885-Publ Assoc of Friends
(5x5)   20.00
PURDUE,A H-The Slates of Arkansas-LittleRock-1909-cl-170p-
2 fldg maps   (5h0)   3.50
PURDY,HELEN T-San Francisco As It Wash,As It Is & How To See It-
SanFran-(1912)-Tomary Pr-illus-221p-Paul Elder   (4n1)   6.50
PURDY,J-The New Sailing Directory for Strait of Gibraltar &
Western Div of Mediterranean Sea-Lond-1840 (5x2,rbkd)   25.00
PURDY,WM-London Banking Life-NY-(1876)-12mo-cl-243p(5t0)   4.00
PURITANS' FAREWELL TO ENGLAND,THE-April 7,1630-NY-1912-
reprntd for New Engl Soc 292nd anniv Forefathers Day-12mo-
10-10p-sp labl   (5h9)   5.00
PURMORT,B H-Purmort Genealogy-Philemon of Bost,1634,Anc &
Desc-1907-161p   (5mm3)   35.00
PURNEY,THOS-Works-Oxf-1922-111p-facs-Percy Rprnts #12 (5a1)4.50
PURPLE,E R-Contributions to Hist of Kip Family of NY & NJ-1877-
24p   (5t9)   6.00
PURRINGTON,WM A-Christian Science-NY-1900-8vo-1st ed
(5ss5,sl stns)   10.00
PURVIANCE,ROBT-Narrative of Events which Occurred in Baltimore
Town During the Revolution-Balt-1849-1st ed   (4m4)   35.00
PUSEY,E B-Marraige with a Deceased Wife's Sister,Prohibited by
Holy Scripture-Oxf-1849-lg8vo-cl-papr labl-1st ed-scarce
(5p5)   15.00
PUSEY,MERLO J-Eisenhower,The President-NY-1956-8vo-cl-
300p-1st ed   (5m8,dj)   4.50
--The Supreme Court Crisis-NY-1937   (5x7)   4.00
PUSS IN BOOTS-NY-(ca 1855)-Loomis&Co-12mo-col frontis-
10 illus-col printing-26p-pic wrps-Hewet's Illum Household
Stories for Little Folks,Vol 3   (5p1)   35.00
PUT'S GOLDEN SONGSTER-Calif songs-SanFran-(1858)-
DEAppletonCo-64p-pict wrps-4 x 5-3/4   (5r0)   12.50
PUTNAM,A E-Madami-NY-1954-illus   (5x2)   5.00
PUTNAM,ADA MacL-Selkirk Settlers etc-Tor-1939-57p-frontis-
ports   (5aa0,sl fade) 5.00
PUTNAM,ALFRED P-Sketch of Genl Israel Putnam-Salem-1893-
34p-wrps   (5t1)   10.00
PUTNAM,BRENDA-The Sculptor's Way-NY-(1939)-illus-4to
(5tt5,bndg rub) 10.00
PUTNAM,C-Race & Reason-Wash-1961   (5x2)   3.00
PUTNAM CO (OHIO) CENTENNIAL HIST-1834 to 1934-n.p.-n.d.-
(1934)-176p-wrps   (5h1)   7.50
PUTNAM,EBEN,ed-Lieut Joshua Hewes-(NY)-1913-656p-t.e.g.-
8vo-priv prntd-lea   (5t9) 27.50   (5hh4,f)   50.00
PUTNAM,ELLEN T H-Stories for the Strawberry Party-Bost-1857-
sm sq8vo-79p-wdcuts-1st ed   (5v0,f,pres)   12.50
PUTNAM,FREDK W-Reports upon Archaelogocial & Ethn Collections
from Vicinity of Santa Barbara, Calif & Ruined Pueblos of Ariz
& New Mex,etc-Wash-1879-485p plus index-plts-map
(5L0,rbnd)   20.00
PUTNAM,GEO-Salem Vessels & Their Voyages-Salem-1924 to 30-
illus-4 vols   (5q0)   20.00
--same-Salem-1924-Ser 2-illus   (5e8)   12.75
PUTNAM,GEO H-Amer Publisher's Biography,Life of Geo Palmer
Putnam-NY-1903-thk8vo-2 vols-848p-ports-bds-calf bks-g.t.-
1st ed-priv prntd-scarce   (5p5)   25.00
--Memories of a Publisher, 1865 to 1915-NY-1915-492p
(5ee3,5mm2)   5.00
--Memories of My Youth, 1844 to 1865-NY-1914-illus
(5q8,ex-libr)   5.00
--Prisoner of War in Virginia 1864 to 5-NY-1912-104p-cl
(5jj9) 8.50   (5w0)   10.00
--Some Memories of the Civil War-NY-1924-301p-frontis-1st ed
(5g4) 6.   (5L5,dj)   8.50
PUTNAM,GEO PALMER-Amer Facts-Lond-1845-8vo-ports-fldg map-
orig cl-1st ed   (5p5)   25.00
PUTNAM,GEO P-Andree-NY-1930-8vo-cl-illus-239p-1st ed
(5t2)   5.00
--Death Valley Handbook-NY-(1947)-e.p. maps   (5s4,dj)   4.50
--In the Oregon Country-NY-1915-52 illus   (5x5)   5.00
--Mariner of the North, Life of Capt Bob Bartlett-NY-1947-246p
(4e9)   6.00
--The Southland of NoAmer-NY-1913-425p-illus-map
(5d2,spec f bndg) 15.   (5p9)   5.00
--Wide Margins-NY-1942-351p   (5j4)   8.00
PUTNAM,GEO R-Sentinel of the Coasts-NY-(1937)-368p-frontis-
illus-1st ed   (5dd9)   6.25
PUTNAM,HERBERT-Library of Congr Exhibit of Books Printed During
15th Century & Known as Incunabula-Wash-1930-77p-wrps(5j4)10.00

PUTNAM,ISRAEL-General Orders Issued by Maj Gen, When in
Command of the Highlands in Summer & Fall of 1777-Brooklyn-
1893-8vo-map-orig wrps-WCFord,ed-ltd to 200c   (5ss5)   15.00
PUTNAM,J J-Line of Jos Converse of Bedford,Mass-1897-97p
(5t9)   10.00
PUTNAM,J PICKERING-The Open Fireplace, in all ages-Bost-
1881-202p-illus   (5w7) 8.50   (5t4)   10.00
PUTNAM,J W-Illinois & Michigan Canal-Chig-1918-312p-bds-
map-cl bk   (5t0,dj,mint)   7.50
PUTNAM,JEAN MARIE-Gardens for Victory-NY-(1942)-220p-
illus-1st ed   (5s7)   4.50
PUTNAM,MRS-A Primary Cook Book for new beginners in
housekeeping-Bost-1862-84p   (5c0,pencil)   7.50
--Receipt Book & Young Housekeeper's Assistant-Bost-1849-131p
(5c0,wn,tn) 10.00
--same-NY-1869-322p-enlrgd ed   (5c0)   6.50
PUTNAM,RUTH-California the Name-U Calif Pub in Hist-1917-
fldg map-wrps-64p   (4n1)   7.00
--William the Silent-NY&Lond-1898-illus-2 vols (5q0,libr labl) 10.00
PUTNAM'S HISTORICAL MAGAZINE-Vol 1-1892,93-bnd (5t9)   7.50
PUTNEY,EFFIE F-In So Dak Country-Mitchel-(1922)-176p-cl
(5h7) 4.   (5kk4,f)   10.00
PUTT,S GORLEY,ed-Cousins & Strangers-Harv U Pr-1956-1st ed
(5q8,dj)   5.00
PUTZEL,CHAS-Commercial Precedents Selected from Column of
Replies & Decisions of NY Journal of Commerce-Hartf-1892-
592p   (5t7)   8.50
PUVIS,M A-De La Culture De La Vigne-Bourg en Brese-1847-18p
(5wl)   8.50
PYATT,EDW C-British Crags & Climbers, An Anthology-Lond-
(1952)-DennisDobson-235p-illus-cl   (5d7)   4.50
PYE,ANNE BRISCOE-Navy Wife-NY-(1942)-335p   (5s1,dj)   2.50
PYE,DAVID-Geo Leigh Mallory,a Memoir-Lond-1927-Oxf Univ Pr-
183p-illus   (5d7)   25.00
PYLE,HOWARD-Book of Amer Spirit-NY-1923-4to-col plts-illus
(5t5,1 plt loose) 27.50
--same-NY-1923-20 col plts-1st ed   (4c3,col dj,mint)   65.00
--Book of Pirates-NY-1931-col plts-4to   (5tt 5)   22.50
--Gallantry-NY-1907-by Cabell-1st ed-4 col plts-silver bndg
(4c3)   17.50
--The Garden Behind the Moon-NY-1895-illus by Pyle-1st ed
(5v0) 6.50   (5ee3)   7.50
--History of NY-NY-1886-by W Irving-2 vols-ltd to 175c
(5jj6,chip) 17.50
--Howard Pyle's Book of Pirates-compiled by Merle Johnson-NY-
1921-sm folio-bds&cl-illus pasted to cov-col illus-246p,1p
(5dd8) 25.   (5s1,rprd,soil) 17.50   (5t0,rub)   20.00
--same-NY-(1949)-Harper&Bros-8vo-209p-col plts (4a6,soil)   5.00
--Men of Iron-NY-(1919)-illus-327p   (5q0)   6.00
--The Merry Adventures of Robin Hood-NY-1883-orig lea-
1st ed of Pyel's 1st book-rare (4c3,rbkd) 125. (4F6,f,sl chip)250.00
--same-Lond-1883-4to-cl-illus-1st Engl ed-(510c) (5gg6)   50.00
--same-NY-1905-illus   (5jj6)   8.50
--Merry Adventures of Robin Hood-NY-1915-296p(5t4,hng weak) 7.50
--A Modern Aladdin-NY-1892-illus by Pyle-1st ed
(5ee3,vg) 10.   (4j2)   15.00
--Otto of the Silver Hand-NY-1888-illus-cl sides-lea bk-
rare 1st ed   (5v2,lacks Pg & hf ads)   65.00
--Pepper & Salt,or Seasoning for Young Folk-NY-1886-Harper&Bros-
4to-1st ed   (5ss9)   50.00
--The Price of Blood-Bost-1899-Badger&Co-1st ed-col plts-98p
(4c3,rprd,rub) 10. (5rr2) 17.50 (5p7)   15.00
--Rejected of Men-NY-1903-1st ed-orig cl(4b7,4m8)10. (4j2) 25.00
--Rose of Paradise-NY-1888-231p-illus-1st ed   (4j2)   12.50
--The Ruby of Kishmoor-NY-1908-Harper-73p-1st ed
(5mm2) 11.50   (5p7)   17.50
--Saint Joan of Arc-NY-(1919)-by MTwain-5 col plts by Pyle
(4F6,f,tn dj) 17.50
--Stolen Treasure-Harper-(1907)-illus-254p   (5yy8)   6.50
--Story of the Champions of the Round Table-NY-1905-lg8vo-cl-
328p-1st ed   (5py,soil,crack) 7.50   (4c3,f)   20.00
--Story of the Grail & Passing of Arthur-NY-1910-39 illus-1st ed
(5jj6,f)   22.50
--Story of Jack Ballister's Fortunes-NY-1895-8vo-420p-14 illus-
1st ed   (5jj6,vg)   20.00
--Story of King Arthur & His Knights-NY-1903-8vo-dec cl-illus-
1st ed   (5r9)   20.00
--same-NY-1922-302p   (5t4)   7.50
--Twilight Land-NY&Lond-(1917)-Harper-12mo-438p-frontis-pic cl-
(5p1)   5.00
--Within the Capes-NY-1885-dec cl-1st ed
(4F6,pres,vg) 75.   (4j2) 15.   (5p6,f)   11.00

PYLE, HOWARD (continued)
--Yankee Doodle, an Old Friend in a New Dress-NY-1881-
   4to-illus-bds-1st ed of 1st book illus by Pyle(5gg6,cor rub)   50.00
PYLE, JOS G-The Life of Jas J Hill-GardenCty-1917-2 vols-ports-
   1st ed-scarce   (5dd6)   22.50
PRYNNE, WM-The Popish Royall Favourite-Lond-1643-
   Michael Spark, Sr-4to-hf calf-mrbld bds-1st ed   (4n5)   85.00
PYM, HORACE N, ed-Memories of Old Friends-Phila-1882-378p-
   cl   (5h1)   7.50
--same-Lond-1882-Smith Elder-2nd ed-2 vols   (4p1)   22.50
PYNE, HENRY R-History of the 1st NJ Cavalry (16th Reg, NJ Vols)-
   Trenton-1871-sm12mo-350p-dbl frontis (5w0,amateur rbnd)   22.50
PYNE, WM HENRY-History of Royal Residences of Windsor Castle,
   St James Palace, Carlton House etc-Lond-1819-mor-g.e.-
   3 vols-lg4to-plts-1st ed   (4h0,1p als,f bndg)   1,000.00
--On Rustic Figures, in Imitation of Chalk-Lond-1817-Ackermann-
   36p nbrd etchings on heavy drawing paper-lg4to-bds rare
                               (4L7,plts f)   225.00
PYNE, ZOE KENDRICK-Giovanni Pierluigi Palestrina-NY-1922-
   DoddMead-232p-illus   (5p0)   6.00
PYRNELLE, LOUISE CLARKE-Diddie, Dumps & Tot, or Plantation
   Child Life-NY-1882-Harper&Bros-pic cl-illus-1st ed (5c8,f)   50.00
Q P INDEX ANNUAL-for 1881,1882,1884,1885,1886-Bangor,Me-
   5 vols-thn8vo -cl- (Periodical Literature)   (5j5)   25.00
QUAD, M-Brother Gardner's Lime Kiln Club-Chig-1882-8vo-dec cl-
   Belford, Clarke-illus   (5b2) 12.50   (5x2)   20.00
--same-Chig-1888   (5x2)   17.00
--same-Chig-1894   (5x2)   15.00
QUAIFE, M M, ed-Absalom Grimes, Confederate Mail Runner-
   NewHav-1926-illus-216p-scarce (4b3,f,torn dj) 17.50 (5bb4)   12.50
--Adventures of the First Settlers on the Ore or Columbia River-Chig-
   1923-368p plus index-fldg map-Lakeside Classic   (5L0)   7.50
--The Bark Covered House-Chig-1937-16mo-cl-g.t.-2 ports-342p-
   Lakeside Pr   (5j5)   10.00
--Border & the Buffalo & Untold Story of SW Plains-1938 (5jj7,f)   8.50
--Capture of Old Vincennes-Indnpls-1927   (4j4)   7.50
--Captive of Old Vincennes-Indnpls-n.d.   (4a9,autg)   9.00
--Checagou, from Indian wigwam to modern city-Chig-(1933)
   map-index-224p   (5r8) 6.   (5u3)   6.50
--Chicago's Highways Old & New...-1923-8vo-278p-illus-maps
   (5mm7) 17.50   (5u3,5jj7)   12.50
--Chicago & the Old NW-Chig-(1913)-illus-1st ed (5jj7,f)   15.00
--The Convention of 1846-Madison-1919-Hist Soc of Wisc-
   Constit Ser Vol 2-illus   (5q8,sl shake)   7.50
--Detroit, 250 Yrs in pictures-Detroit-1951-4to-198p (5t4,dj)   6.00
--The Fur Hunters of the Far West-1924-317p-frontis
   (5jj7) 7.50   (5p1)   15.00
--The Indian Captivity of O M Spencer-188p-frontis-fldg map-
   #15 Lakeside Classics   (5p1)   15.00
--Kingdom of St James-NewHav-1930-275p plus index-illus-1st ed
                               (5L0)   10.00
--John Askin Papers-Detroit Libr Comm-1928,1931-plts-31 maps-
   part mor-2 vols   (5jj7,f)   65.00
--Kit Carson's Autobiography-Chig-1935-Lakeside Pr-170p plus
   index-1st prntng   (5a9)   8.00
--Lake Michigan-Indnpls-(1944)-1st ed-384p-Amer Lake Ser
   (4a9,autg) 10.   (5bb4,autg) 6.   (5dd9)   5.50
--Narr of Adventures of Zenas Leonard-Chig-1934(Christmas)-
   dec cl-g.t.-278p-fldg map-#32   (4d5)   10.00
--Narr of Texan, SantaFe Exped of Geo W Kendall-1929(5jj7,f)   12.50
--Personal Narr of Jas O Pattie of Kentucky-Chig-1930-415p plus
   index-illus-Lakeside Classic   (5jj7,f) 10.   (5L0)   8.50
--Pictures of Gold Rush California-Chig-1949-Lakeside Classics-
   1st ed   (5jj1,mint,5a9,f) 10.   (4d5,f)   12.50
--Pictures of Illinois 100 Years Ago-Chig-sm12mo-cl-g.t.-frontis-
   186p-Lakeside Classics Ser   (5j5)   10.00
--Pictures of 100 Years Ago-186p-frontis-Lakeside Classic #16
                               (5p1)   15.00
--The Siege of Detroit in 1763-Chig-1958-Lakeside Pr-274p plus
   index-maps-illus (5x5) 12.50   (5a9,mint,unopnd)   9.50
--3 Years Among the Indians & Mexicans-Xmas,1953-g.t.-
   Lakeside Classic #51   (4d5,f) 15.   (5jj7,f)   10.00
--A True Picture of Emigration-Chig-1936-Lakeside Pr-157p plus
   index-illus-fldg map   (5r8) 6.   (5a9,f)   7.50
--Uncle Dick Wootton-1957   (5jj7,f)   10.00
--War on the Detroit-Chig-Xmas,1940-Lakeside Pr-illus-fldg map
   (5a9,vf) 8.50   (5bb4)   7.50
--Western Country in the 17th Century-Chig-1947-Lakeside Classics
   (5a9,f) 10.   (5x5)   9.50
--Yellowstone Kelly, Memoirs of Luther S Kelly-Yale Univ Pr-
   1926-1st ed   (5x5,dj)   20.00

QUAIN, JONES-Series of Anatomical Plates with References &
   Physiological Comments-Phila-1842-Carey&Hart-thk lg4to-
                               (5t4,lacks bkstrp)   20.00
QUAINT OLD SAN ANTONIO-SanAnt-c1910-Alamo Chapel-
   12 lvs-illus-hand col   (4a5)   15.00
QUAKER NURSERY RHYMES-Bost-c1895-by Amer Cereal Co-
   sm shape book of Quaker Oats man-12 unnbrd lvs-wrps (5p1)   8.50
QUALEY, CARLTON C-Norwegian Settlement in the US-Norwegian
   Amer Hist Assoc-Northfield, Minn-1938   (5x5)   15.00
QUARLES, B-The Negro in the Civil War-Bost-1953   (5x2)   8.50
QUARLES, E C-History of the Penna Ave Subway & Tunnel-Phila-
   1894-sq8vo-unpaginated-pictorial   (5w5,ex-libr,crack)   7.50
QUARLES, FRANCIS-School of the Heart-Bristol-1808-47 plts
                               (4F6,cov loose)   20.00
QUARLES, J A-The Life of Prof F T Kemper-NY-n.d.-ca 1884-cl-
   492p plus 1p-illus-Burr Prntng Hse   (5r0,pres)   7.50
QUARTERLY CHRISTIAN SPECTATOR, THE-NewHav-1836-Vol 8-
   8vo-lea&bds-672p   (5t0)   10.00
QUARTERLY JOURNAL OF ECONOMICS-Vol 1 thru 78-Gen index
   Vols 1 thru 50-1886 to 1964-bnd (5ii7,rbnd) 2,083.50
QUATREFAGES, A DE-Rambles of a naturalist on coasts of France,
   Spain & Sicily-Lond-1857-Longman-2 vols-8vo-orig cl (5i8)   12.50
QUAYLE, WM A-The Prairie & the Sea-Cinn&NY-(1905)-illus-
   8vo-fabricoid-a.e.g.-342p-"Spec crepe papr ed"   (5t7)   7.50
QUEBEC & HALIFAX RWY-Final Report of Officers Employed on
   Survey of Line for...-Lond-1849-prntd by Wm Clowes-folio-
   col fldg map-73p-sewed as issued   (5aa1)   50.00
QUEBEC & LOWER ST LAWRENCE, THE-tourist's guide-Quebec-
   1875-24mo   (5g4)   10.00
QUEBEC BRIDGE, THE-New Liverpool-1907-32p plus cov (5b9,vf) 8.50
QUEBEC CITY-Illus Quebec Under French & English Occupancy-
   Montr-1891-McConniff-112p-illus-pict cov   (4b9,wn)   15.00
QUEBEC & ITS ENVIRONS-New Guide to-Quebec-1851-16mo-
   76p-fldg map 15x20 inches-P Sinclair-   (5w8)   35.00
QUEBEC PROVINCE-Dept of Colonization, Mines etc-Extracts
   Dist of Ungava-Que-1915-208p-plts-fldg map-wrps (5a1)   7.00
QUEBEC, PROVINCE OF-Municipal Code of the-Que-1870-
   prntd wrps   (5w8)   15.00
QUEBEC-Rapporte de l'Archiviste de la Province de Quebec,1921,
   1922,1924 to 1943,1947-23 yrs-sold as a run-orig prntd wrps
   as issued   (5w8)   87.50
QUEECHY-Phila-1888-Lippincott-2 vols(in 1)-8vo-dec cl (4a8)   5.00
QUEEN ALEXANDRA'S CHRISTMAS GIFT BOOK-Photos-Lond-
   1908-unpgd   (5w7)   10.00
QUEEN & CO'S-Manual of Engineers & Surveyors Instruments-
   Phila-ca 1898-plts-fldg bds-186p,2p   (5b8,sp wn)   10.00
QUEEN CITY COOK BOOK-Sioux Falls, SoDak-1891-1st Baptist
   Church-171p,(25)p with blanks-pic cov-v scarce
                               (5c9,soil,lacks e.p.)   12.50
QUEEN, ELLERY, ed-The Female of the Species-Bost-1943-Little
                               (5p9)   3.50
QUEEN ESTHER COOK BOOK-LosAng-1904-Boyle Hts Meth Epis-
   Church-ads-stiff fab cov-192p   (4g9,vf)   22.50
QUEEN OF HEARTS-or Stolen Tarts-Grandma Easy series-Albany-
   (ca 1860)-RHPearse-lg pict bk wi 8 lvs of hand col wdcuts &
   verse   (5c8,sl tn)   12.50
QUEEN, JAS-The Taylor's Instructor-Phila-1809-157p,1 lf of
   "Directions to Binder"-8 illus-8vo-orig bds-calf sp-ex rare
                               (5L1,facs plt & 2 lvs)   55.00
QUEEN MONEY-Bost-1888-Ticknor-400p-(E W Kirk)-1st ed (5x4) 9.00
QUEENS COUNTY, LI, NY, ATLAS OF-NY-1891-from Official
   Records-folio-maps   (4b7)   87.50
QUEENS COUNTY, HISTORY OF-NY-1882-(Munsell)-thk4to-
   illus-maps   (5yy6,sp tn)   27.50
QUEENSLAND LAW JOURNAL-Reports Vol 1 thru 11-1879 to
   1901(all publ)-bound   (5ii7,rebnd in 7 vols)   110.00
QUEENSLAND LAW REPORTS-Cases...ed by Beor-1876 to 78
   (all publ)-bound   (5ii7,rebnd)   20.00
QUEENSLAND, SUPREME COURT-Reports Vol 1 thru 5-1860 to 81,
   (all publ)-bound-Scott, Groom, Graham   (5ii7,rebnd)   95.00
QUEENY, EDGAR M-Prairie Wings, Pen & Camera Flight Studies-NY-
   1946-plts-4to   (5tt7,dj)   22.50
QUELCH, MARY T-Herbs & How to Know Them-Lond-(1946)-280p-
   drwngs by MEldridge   (5w3,stn)   4.50
--The Herb Garden-Lond-(1941)-234p   (5w3)   3.50
--Hers for Daily Use in Home Medicine & Cookery-Lond-(1945)-
   328p   (5s7)   4.00
QUELQUES REFLECTIONS-sur la derniere election du quartier ouest
   de la Cite de Montreal-(Montr,1832)-t.p.cov-15p-(M Bibaud)
                               (5w8)   35.00
QUENNELL, MARJORIE-The Anglo Sacon Viking & Norman Times-
   NY-(1927)-Putnam-216p-illus   (5p7)   5.00

QUENNELL,PETER-BYRON, The Years of Fame-NY-1935-320p-
Viking Pr   (5x0)   5.00
--Masques and Poems-1922-Golden Cockerel Pr-sq8vo-bds-lin sp-
papr labl-illus-ltd to 375c   (5t5)   12.50
QUENTIN DURWARD-By author of "Waverley"-Edinb-1823-8vo-
orig bds-cl bks-papr labels-3 vols-1st ed-(Sir W Scott)
                  (5x3,hng wn) 45.   (5dd8,box)   85.00
QUERVAIN,DR ALFRED D-Quer durchs Gronlandeis-Munchen-
1914-ErnstReinhardt-196p-map-illus   (5d7)   7.50
QUESADA,GONZALO DE-Cuba's Great Struggle for Freedom-n.p.-
c1898-758p-illus-map   (5w4,crack) 6.00
QUEVEDO VILLEGAS,FRANCISCO DE-The comical works-Lond-
1707-JnMorphew-8vo-calf-g.-JohnStevens,transl-port
                                             (5x3,rbnd) 200.00
--The visions-Lond-1668-for HHerringman-8vo-3rd ed,"corrected"-
sheep-license leaf   (5xx6,rbkd) 80.00
QUEZON,MANUAL LUIS-The Good Fight-NY-1946-336p(5x9) 5.00
QUICK,A C-Quick Family in Amer-(1942)-483p   (5mm3)   22.50
QUICK,HERBERT-American Inland Waterways-NY-1909-t8vo-map-
illus-1st ed   (5ss5)   10.00
--The Broken Lance-Indnpls-(c1907)-8vo-cl-Bobbs,Merrill (5b2) 3.50
--The Hawkeye-Indnpls-1923-12mo-cl-477p-illus-(adv) (5m8) 7.50
--The Invisible Woman-Indnpls-1924-12mo-cl-488p (5m8,dj) 5.00
--Mississippi Steamboatin'-NY-1926-342p-illus
                  (5w9,fade) 10.   (5r8)   17.50
--One Man's Life-Indnpls-(1925)-408p-illus-1st ed (5L0) 5.00
--Yellowstone Nights-Indnpls-(1911)-8vo-1st ed (4g6) 5. (5s4) 6.00
QUICK,J-Legislative Powers of Commonwealth & States of Australia
with proposed Amendments-Melbne-1919   (5ff4,rub) 9.50
QUICK,PROF M I-Complete Guide to Dancing, Ballroom Etiquette
& Quadrille Call Book-Chig-1903-8vo-dec cl-1st ed-scarce
                                             (5p5)   15.00
QUICK,O C-Doctrines of the Creed,their basis Scripture & their
meaning today-1949   (5L7)   4.00
QUICK,T-Original Life & Adventures of Tom Quick, the Indian
Slayer-Deposit,NY-1894-123p-poor papr   (5yy0,loose) 17.50
QUICKSILVER MINING CO-Apr 10,1866-Reports & exhibits,
annual meeting,NY,Feb 25,1874-NY-1874-8vo-orig prntd wrps-
DMurphy'sSon   (5i9)   17.50
QUIETT,GLENN-Pay Dirt,A Panorama of Amer Gold Rushes-NY-
1936-illus   (5kk4,f,dj) 15.   (5x5,dj)   20.00
--They Built the West-NY-1934-DAppletonCentury-1st ed
                                             (5x5,dj)   20.00
QUIGG,LEMEL E-New Empires in the NW-Libr of Tribune Extras-
Vol 1,#8 for Aug,1889-(NY)-84p-papr cov (5h6,cov tape) 17.50
QUIGLEY,DOROTHY-What Dress Makes of Us-NY-1897-133p-
illus   (5n7)   5.00
QUIGLEY,DR-The Irish Race in Calif & on PacCoast-SanFran-1878-
548p-cl-errata lf-8vo-scarce   (5h5,v rub,spots,5w4) 15.00
QUIGLEY,MARTIN-Decency in Motion Pictures-NY-1937-100p
                                             (4c9)   8.95
QUILL WHEEL-Aunt Emma's Story of the Harrises-Springfld-1880-
Atwood&Noyes,Pr-8vo-cl-(Mrs I N Mason)   (5b2)   6.00
QUILLER COUCH,SIR A T-Historical Tales from Shakespeare-
Arnold-1905-new illus ed-8vo-cl-16 plts-g.t.-368p (4a8) 5.00
--Notes on Shakespeare's Workmanship-NY-1917-8vo-cl-338p
                                             (5t0)   5.00
--On the Art of Reading-Cambr-1920-8vo-cl-237p-1st ed (5t0) 4.75
--On the Art of Writing-NY-1916-8vo-cl-302p (5p9)   5.00
--Oxford Book of English Prose-Oxf-1925-sm8vo-dec cl-1092p-
t.e.g.   (5aa2)   3.50
QUILLER COUCH,MABEL-The Treasure Book of Children's Verse-
Lond-(1911)-H&S-col illus   (5p0)   10.00
QUILLETUS,CLAUDIUS-Callipaedia,or,The Art of Getting Pretty
Children-Lond-1710-72p-lea   (5ee3,e.p.tn)   35.00
QUILTY,GLENN-Food for Men-NY-1954-352p   (5c5)   3.50
QUIMBY,GEO I-Indian Life in Upper Great Lakes 11,000 BC to
AD 1800-Chig-(1960)-182p-cl (5h1,dj) 5. (5L0,mint)   10.00
QUIMBY,M-Mysteries of Bee Keeping Explained-NY-1854-12mo-
cl-376p   (5t0,wn)   6.00
QUIMBY MANUSCRIPTS,THE-P P Quimby-NY-1961 (5x7)   6.50
QUIN,MICHAEL J-Steam Voyage down the Danube-Paris-1836-
Galignani-orig bds-fldg map-12mo-399p   (5v7)   22.50
QUIN,MIKE-More Dangerous Thoughts-SanFran-(1941)-158p-illus-
Peoples World   (5r0,autg) 10.00
QUINBY,H C-Gen Hist of Quinby, Quimby Family in Engl & Amer-
1915-602p   (5t9,wn)   40.00
--Quinby-Quimby Family of (Weare and) Sandwich, N H-
Vol 2(complete in itself)-1923-529p   (5mm3)   25.00
--Richard Harding Davis, a Bibliography-NY-1924-ltd ed (5yy1) 35.00
QUINCE,PETER-Parnassian shop, opened in Pindaric stile-Bost-
1801-prntd by Russell&Cutler-8vo-calf-mor labl-1st ed-
slip pasted on last lf   (5i0,rub,sl stns) 70.00

QUINCY & ADAMS COUNTY (ILL)-Hist & Representative Men-
Chig&NY-1919-2 vols-1502p-pt lea   (5y0)   50.00
QUINCY,EDMUND-Life of Josiah Quincy of Massachusetts-Bost-
1867-1st ed   (5q8,hng split) 5.00
--Bost-1868-560p-ports, index   (5h9)   7.50
QUINCY,JOHN,M D-Lexicon Physico Medicum-Lond-1730-
calf-8vo-4th ed with New Improvements   (4c8)   20.00
--Lexicon Physico Medicum Improved-NY-1802-orig calf (5d2) 35.00
QUINCY,JOSIAH-Considerations relative to library of Harvard
Univ-Cambr-1833-Chas Folsom-8vo-orig prntd wrps-1st ed
                                             (5i9,pres) 25.00
QUINCY,JOSIAH-Figures of the Past-Bost-1896-404p (5w4) 5.00
QUINCY,JOSIAH-History of Boston Athenaeum-Cambridge-1851-
1st ed   (5L3)   3.50
QUINCY,JOSIAH-Memoir of Life of John Quincy Adams-Bost-1858-
Phillips,Sampson-429p-frontis-1st ed (5L3) 5. (5qq8) 6.00
QUINCY,JOSIAH-Memoir of Life of Josiah Quincy Jun of Mass-
Bost-1825-Cummings,Hilliard-498p-cl-1st ed (5qq8,rbnd,vf) 20.00
--same-Bost-1875-431p-3rd ed (5w9,mounted autg) 32.50 (4m2)17.50
QUINCY,JOSIAH-Municipal History of Town & City of Boston
during 2 centuries-Bost-1852-frontis-map-orig tooled cl
                                             (5q8,wn)   8.50
QUINCY,JOSIAH,JR-Observations on Act of Parliament called the
Boston Port Bill-Bost-1774-hf lea-1st ed
          (5g3,rbnd,close trim, lacks some pg nbrs)   60.00
--same-Phila-1774-JnSparhawk-sm8vo-60p-hf mor-2nd ed (5L1) 85.00
QUINCY,JOSIAH P-The Peckster Professorship-Bost-1888-Houghton-
1st ed   (5m2,sl wn) 6.00
QUINCY,MASS-Atlas of City of-GeoWStadly&Co-1897-29p-
lg folio atlas   (4t2,wn)   47.50
QUINCY MINING COMPANY,(MICH)-Report of directors of,for
1862-NY-1863-wrps   (5g8)   7.50
--same-for 1863-NY-1864 -wrps   (5g8)   7.50
--same-for 1864-NY-1865 -wrps   (5g8)   7.50
QUINN,A H, ed-Edith Wharton Treasury-NY-(1950)-Appleton-
581p   (5p7)   6.00
QUINN,ALONZO H-100th Anniv of Nat'l Independence, July 4,
1876,Oration,Dover,NH-Dover-1876-51p-wrps   (5t4)   5.00
QUINN,ARTHUR H-Edgar Allen Poe, A Critical Biography-NY-
1941-illus   (5mm2,dj) 15.00
--History of the Amer Drama from the Beginning to Civil War-NY-
1923-8vo-cl-486p   (5t0)   7.50
--History of Amer Drama from Civil War to Present Day-NY-1927-
8vo-cl-2 vols-illus   (5t0)   10.00
--Literature of America-NY-1929-2 vols-1397p (5m1)   15.00
--Pennsylvania Stories-Phila-1899-illus   (5m2)   5.00
--Representative Amer Plays 1767-1923-NY-1925-1052p (5m1) 6.00
QUINN,CHAS R-Christmas Journey in the Desert-Downey-1960-
illus-pkt map -8vo-bds   (5g0,f)   7.50
QUINN,D A-Heroes & Heroines of Memphis,Remin of Yellow Fever
Epidemics-Prov,RI-1887   (5yy8,spot,libr stmp) 10.00
QUINN,DAVID B, ed-The Roanoke Voyages, 1584 to 1590-Lond-
1955-Hakluyt Soc-illus-maps-2 vols   (4m2)   35.00
QUINN,FRENCH-Short Short Story of Adams Co,Ind-Berne-n.d.-
(ca 1941)-142p-cl   (5h1)   8.50
QUINN,HENRY COLE-Bibliography of-NY-(1924)-294p-illus-
ltd to 1000c   (5mm2)   22.50
QUINN,JOHN-The Library of-NY-1923,24-Anderson Galleries-
5 vols-wrps-illus   (5n4)   27.50
QUINN,T C, ed-Massachusetts of Today-1892-619p-illus (5mm3) 5.00
QUINN,VERNON-Beautiful Canada-NY-1938-382p-plts
                                          (5s4,5dd0)   6.50
--Seeds,Their Place In Life & Legend-NY-1936-188p-drawings
                                             (5w3)   6.50
--Shrubs in the Garden & Their Legends-NY-1940-308p-
MLawson,illus   (5s7) 7.50   (5w3)   8.50
--War Paint & Powder Horn on the Old Santa Fe Trail-NY-1929-
illus-298p-map-1st ed   (5yy7)   12.50
QUINT,ALONZO H-Potomac & Rapidan-Bost-1864-407p-fldg map-
Crosby&Nichols   (5mm8)   10.00
QUINT,H H-Profile in Black & White-1958   (5L7)   6.00
QUINT,WILDER DWIGHT-The Story of Dartmouth-Bost-1914-
Little,Brown-8vo-285p   (5p1,ex-libr) 7.50
QUINTANAR,ANGEL-Manifiesto del Congreso General en el
presente ano-Mexico,Lara-29 July 1836-8vo-orig calf-20p
                                   (5L1,orig wrps bnd in) 85.00
QUINTANILLA,AN EXHIBITION OF DRAWINGS-NY-(1938)-
PierreMatisse Gallery-Hemingway pref-1st ed-leaflet (5ss9,f) 22.50
QUINTI HORATI FLACCI CARMINA SAPPHICA-Chelsea-1903-8vo-
orig white limp vel-Ashendene Pr-ltd to 125c (5ee9,box) 150.00
QUINTON,ROBT-Strange Adventure of Capt Quinton-NY-(1912)-
486p-port-dec cov   (5s1) 3.50   (5p7)   5.00

QUIROS,PEDRO FERNANDEZ DE-Relation...Von dem new
   erfundnem vierten theil der Welt...Terra Australis incognita-
   Augsburg-1611-Dabertzhofer-sm4to-bds-1st German ed
                       (5n9,stmp rmvd) 3,500.00
QUISENBERRY,A C-Life & Times of Hon Humphrey Marshall-
   Winchester-1892-Sun PubICo-142p-frontis (5h1,5qq8,sl dmpstnd)12.50
QUIVIRA SOCIETY PUBLICATIONS-#1 to 12 in 14 vols-LosAng-
   1929 to 51-cl bk bds   (5x5)   650.00
QUIVIRA SOCIETY PUBLICATIONS-
--II - Taraval,Father Sigismundo-The Indian Uprising in Lower Calif,
   1734 to 1737-LosAng-1931-1 of 35 nbrd cpys on Rives papr,
   autg by transl   (5F5)   40.00
--same-1 of 665c,not autg   (5F5)   25.00
--III-Gongora, Don Carlos de Siguenza y-The Mercurio Volante-
   LosAng-1932-1 of 35 nbrd cpys on Rives papr-autg by transl
                     (5F5)   32.50
--same-1 of 35c,nbrd & autg-sp soiled (5F5)   27.50
--same-1 of 665c,nbrd-not autg   (5F5,f)   20.00
--IV-Villagra, Gaspar Perez-History of NewMexico-Alcala-1610-
   Los Ang-1933-1 of 35c,nbrd on Rives papr,autg (5F5,pres) 45.00
--same-1 of 665c,nbrd-not autg (5F5,cor jammed,sl soil) 15.(5F5)22.50
--V-Celiz,Fray Francisco-Diary of Alarcon Exped into Texas,1718,
   1719-LosAng-1935-1 of 100c,nbrd,autg by transl (5F5,vf) 25.00
--same-1 of 600c,nbrd-not autg   (5F5)   15.00
--VI-Morfi,Fray Juan Agustin-History of Texas, 1673 to 1779-
   Albuqu-1935-2 vols-ltd to 500c,nbrd (5F5)   40.00
--VIII-New Mexico in 1602-Juan de Montoya's Relation of the
   Discovery of NewMex-Albuqu-1938-ltd to 550c,nbrd
         (5F5, sp sl soil) 15.   (5F5,f)   20.00
--IX-Spanish Approach to Pensacola, 1689 to 1693-Albuqu-1939-
   1 of 550c   (5F5)   25.00
--X-Bandelier, A F-A Scientist on the Trail, Travel letters of...
   1880, 1881-Berkeley-1949-ltd to 500c,nbrd (5F5)   15.00
--XI-3 New Mexico Chronicles-Albuqu-1942-ltd to 557c,nbrd
        (5F5,sp rub,soil) 20.   (5F5,f)   25.00
--XII-Galvez, Bernardo de-Instructions for Governing Interior
   Provinces of New Spain,1786-Berkeley-1951-ltd to 500c,
   nbrd   (5F5,f)   17.50
--XIII-The Frontiers of New Spain, Nicolas de LaFora's Description,
   1766 to 1768-Berkeley-1958-ltd to 400c (5F5)   20.00
RAB,FORDHAM-Guide to Law of Sea-NY-(1937)-2 vols-358p &
   270p   (5s1,libr labls)   12.50
RABB, KATE M,ed-A Tour Through Indiana in 1840-NY-1920-391p-
   illus-8vo-cl   (5jj7,f)   15.00
RABELAIS,FRANCOIS-5 Books of the Life, Heroic Deeds, & Sayings
   of Gargantua & His Son,Pantagruel-Lond-Matteus,transl-
   2 vols-4to-silk buck-ltd ed   (5t5)   20.00
-Gargantua & Pantagruel-Paris-1922-4to-French text-buck-
   vignettes by Hemard   (5t5,rbnd)   20.00
--same-NY-1936-Heritage Pr-lg thk8vo-illus by LyndWard-transl
                     (5p5)   12.50
-Works-NY-1931-2 vols-Nock&Wilson, ed-illus-maps (5mm2) 15.00
-Works of-Lond-1921-2 vols-illus by W HeathRobinson-8vo-cl-
   Navarre Soc   (5t2,cov dmgd)   8.00
--same-Lond-n.d.-2 vols-3/4 lev mor-Robinson,illus-Navarre Soc
                     (5d2)   40.00
--same-Lond-n.d.-frontis-cl-20p,640p-illus by Gustav Dore 7.50
--same-Lond-n.d.-Chatto&Windus-8vo-cl-640p-Dore,illus(5p6) 10.00
RABER, JESSIE B-Pioneering in Alberta-NY-(1951)-171p(4d2) 5.00
RABINOWICZ, OSHAR K-Winston Churchill on Jewish Problems-
   NY-1960   (5x7)   3.50
RABUTIN,ROGER DE COMTE DE BUSSY-The amorous history of the
   Gauls-Lond-1727-for S Illidge-12mo-hf calf (5x3)   40.00
RACE,NATION,PERSON-NY-1944   (5x2)   10.00
RACE RELATIONS LAW REPORTER-Vol 1 thru 12-1956 to 67
   (all publ)-bound   (5ii7)   308.00
RACHEL,S-De Jure Naturae et Gentium Dissertationes-Wash-1916-
   2 vols   (5r4)   17.50
RACIAL & CIVIL DISORDERS-in St Augustine,Report of Legislative
   Invest Comm-Tallahassee-1965-147p-wrps (5x2)   8.50
RACIAL DIGEST-Monthly-Feb, 1942 thru Aug, 1943-16 issues-
   (lacks some nbrs)-Detroit-Community Pub Co
             (5x2,16 nbrs) 65.   (5x2) ea 5.00
RACINE, LOUIS JOS Publ-Souvenirs historiques du Canada-Montr-
   1856-18mo-bds-calf bk-128p   (5w8)   20.00
RACINE & KENOSHA COUNTIES, (WISC)-History of-1879-illus-
   738p   (5t9)   22.50
RACINET, AUGUSTE-Le Costume Historique-Paris-1888-Didot-
   sq8vo-part vel-t.e.g.-1st ed-6 vols-Petit issue-errata lf
                (4h0,rbnd,lt fox)   375.00
RACK, JOHN-The French Wine & Liquor Manufacturer-NY-1863-
   268p   (5w0,cov tn,stnd)   10.00

RACK, JOHN (continued)
--same-NY-n.d.-273p-Fitzgerald PubCo-4th ed,rev&corr
            (5w1,crack) 7.50   (5g9)   10.00
RACKHAM,illus-also see author
RACKHAM, ARTHUR-Aesop's Fables-Lond-1912-white buck-t.e.g.-
   V Jones,transl-4to-13p col illus-ltd to 1450c,Rackham autg
                (5u5, sp fade)   200.00
--Alice's Adventures in Wonderland-Lond, Heinemann-NY,
   Dblday Page-(1907)-1st trade ed-13 col plts (4F6,vg) 42.50
--same-Lond-1947-sm4to-cl-13 plts   (5t5)   9.50
--The Allies'Fairy Book-Lond-(1916)-8vo-orig cl-12p illus in col-
   pict e.p. by Arthur Rackham-1st issue of 1st trade ed-(later
   issue does not have pict e.p.)   (5d1)   50.00
--same-Lond-Heinemann-(1916)-1st ed-12 col plts by Rackham-
   dec cl   (5c8, lt spots)   22.50
--same-Lond-(1916)-blue cl-ltd ed-autg-g.t.-12 mounted col plts
                  (4b7,f)   75.00
--Book of Pictures-Lond-Heinemann-(1913)-44 col plts-ltd to 1030c-
               (5il,f,autog)   135.00
--same-Lond-(1913)-4to-44p illus in col (5d1,dj)   37.50
--Arthur Rackham Fairy Book-Phila-n.d.-(ca 1930)-8 col illus
                (5ee3)   5.00
--same-Lond-(1933)-4to-vel-g.t.-8p col illus-60 b&w illus-
   ltd to 460c,Rackham autg   (5u5)   125.00
--Bracebridge Hall,or the Humorists-Washington Irving-NY &Lond-
   1896-thk8vo-blue cl-g. on cov & sp-g.t.-2 vols-657p-
   coated papr-illus   (5ee9,f)   60.00
--A Christmas Carol-Phila,Lond-(1915)-1st ed-12 col plts-dec cl-
                (5v2, mint, dj)   40.00
--same-Lond-1933-sq8vo-20 illus-8 plts in col-dec cl (5t5) 10.00
--same-Phila-(c 1930)-4 col plts   (4F6,cov v stnd) 7.50
--Cinderella-(1919)-Heinemann-4to-dec bds-col frontis-tinted plts-
   110p-1st ed   (5nn2, vf, dj)   35.00
--Dish of Apples-Lond-(1921)-sm4to-white cl-g.t.-3p col illus-
   pic e.p.-ltd to 500c,autgs   (5cc9)   125.00
--Evelina,or, History of a Young Lady's Entrance into the World-
   Lond-1898-8vo-cl-g.t.-16p illus   (5dd8)   20.00
--Goblin Market-Phila-(1933)-4 col plts-1st Amer ed
               (4F6, mint, dj)   25.00
--Gulliver's Travels-Lond-1909-Dent-12 col plts-(1st ed was 1899
   wi only 1 plt) (4F6,ex-libr,hng rprd) 27.50 (5v2,mint,dj) 40.00
--same-Lond-1909-cl-4to-13p col illus-ltd to 750c,autg (5d1) 200.00
--same-Lond-1939-lg8vo-cl-12 col plts   (5t5)   20.00
--The Haddon Hall Library-Lond-1899 to 1903-8vo-orig white vel-
   g.-cov illus by R-9 vols-ltd to 150 sets (5D1)   75.00
--Ingoldsby Legends-1898-Dent-8vo-dec cl-g.t.-plts(some col)-
   1st ed   (5nn2)   35.00
--The Ingoldsby Legends or Mirth & Marvels-Lond-1907-4to-white
   vel wi ties-24p col plts-12p tint plts-550p-ltd to 560c,autg
                (5d1)   150.00
--Irish Fairy Tales-Lond-1920-cl-1st trade ed-4to-16p col illus
                (5d1)   20.00
--same-Lond-1920-bds-g.t.-16p col illus-ltd to 520c,autg,box
          (5cc9,lttrng wn,fade)   150.00
--same-Lond-1920-ltd to 250c,autg,orig watercoll drwng
                (5dd8)   200.00
--King Albert's Book-NY-(1914)-1st Amer ed-tipped in col plts
                (4F6,f)   25.00
--Land of Enchantment-Lond-1907-Cassell&Co-1st ed-4to-dec cl
                (5c8, lt wn)   25.00
--Little White Bird-NY-1913-by Barrie-2 b/w plates by Rackham
                (4F6,vf)   30.00
--Legend of Sleepy Hollow-Lond-1928-illus-4to-ltd ed, autg-
   mounted plts   (4b7,f)   175.00
--A Midsummer Night's Dream-Lond-1908-lg4to-white vel-40 col plts-
   ltd ed,autg   (5v2,f) 185.   (5d9)   200.00
--Mother Goose,The Old Nursery Rhymes-Lond-(1913)-Heinemann-
   13 col plts-1st ed, 1st issue(wi pic e.p.)
         (4c3,lacks fr e.p.,fade)   35.00
--Peer Gynt,A Dramatic Poem-Lond-(1936)-4to-white vel-g.t.-
   12p col illus-e.p. by Rackham-ltd to 450c,autg (5d1) 150.00
--Peter Pan in Kensington Gardens-Long-1906-sq4to-orig brown cl-
   g.-50p illus in col-e.p. maps by Rackham-1st trade ed (5d1) 50.00
--same-Lond-1906-4to-vel-pic cov-t.e.g.-ties-50p col illus-
   e.p. maps by Rackham-ltd to 500c,autg (5d1) 250.00
--same-Lond-1907-2nd issue-50 col plts-tip in (4c3,pres,f) 135.00
--same-NY-1907(for Dec 1906)-Scribners-4to-dec cl-50 mtd col plts-
   126p-1st Amer ed   (5zz8, sl spots)   25.00
--same-NY-1914-16 col plts   (4c3,f)   17.50
--same-NY-1925-16 col plts   (4F7,f)   17.50
--Poor Cecco-NY-1925-Doran-sm4to-dec cl-g.t.-7 col plts-176p-
   1st ed-(1st issue wi pic e.p.)   (5nn2)   30.00
--Puck of Pook's Hill-NY-1906-4 col plts-1st Amer ed (4c3,f) 27.50

USED BOOK PRICE GUIDE

RACKHAM, ARTHUR (continued)
--Rip Van Winkle-Lond-1905-4to-vel-51p col illus-ltd to 250c,
autg-scarce   (5d9)   275.00
--same-NY&Lond-(1916)-24 col plts   (4F6,sl fox)   25.00
--River & Rainbow, 10 Miniatures for the Pianoforte-Lond-(1934)-
4to-wrps-12p & cov-lg col design 10 x8½ in col & t.pg (5d1) 40.00
--The Romance of King Arthur-NY-1920-16 plts in col-t8vo-
g. sp   (5t5)   20.00
--same-Lond-1917-lg4to-vel-t.e.g.-16p illus in col-ltd to 500c,
autg   (5dd8) 150.00
--Siegfried & The Twilight of the Gods-Lond-1911-4to-vel-g.t.-
ties-30p illus in col-ltd to 1150c,autg   (5cc9) 225.00
--Sleeping Beauty-Lond-(1920)-Heinemann-1st trade ed-1 col plt-
3 dbl pg silhouetts   (4F6,f)   25.00
--The Springtide of Life-Lond-1918-illus-1st ed   (5v0) 15.00
--same-Phila-1918-4to-8 col plts-1st Amer ed   (5t5) 17.50
--same-Lond-(1918)-4to-white bds-t.e.g.-9p col illus-
ltd to 765c,nbrd,autg   (5d9) 100.00
--Tales from Shakespeare-1905-Dent-(Temple Classics)-12mo-dec cl-
g.t.-col frontis-11 plts-362p-5th ed   (5nn2)   6.50
--same-Lond-1909-lg4to-white cl wi ties-13p col illus(including one
not in trade ed)-ltd to 750c,autg   (5d1) 150.00
--same-Dent-1909-(1st publ in 1899)-lg8vo-dec cl-12 col plts
(4d8,sl rub)   20.00
--same-Lond-(1957)-8 col plts   (4F6,mint,dj) 12.50
--Tales of Mystery & Imagination-4to-Lond-(1935)-vel-a.e.g.-
12p illus in col-ltd to 460c,autg (5d1,box) 175. (5v2,box) 200.00
--The Tempest-Lond-(1926)-4to-white pic bds-21p col illus-
ltd to 520c,autg   (5d9) 150.00
--Undine-Lond-1925-15 tip in col plts   (5v2,ex-libr) 12.50
--same-Lond-1909-4to-lev mor-5 bands-a.e.g.-15p col illus-
ltd to 1000c,autg   (5d1) 100.00
--Where the Blue Begins-Lond-1922-4to-4 col plts-dec cl (5t5) 15.00
--same-Lond-1925-4to-white bds-4p col illus-ltd to 175c,autg
(5d1) 150.00
--Wind in the Willows -NY-1940-folio-orig bds-cl bk-
designed by Bruce Rogers-ltd to 2020c,autg by Rogers(5nn7) 175.00
--same-NY-Heritage-12 col plts   (4c3,vg) 10. (5ee3,f,tn dj) 6.50
--same-Lond-(1951)-Methuen-4to-white lea-g.t.-12p col illus-
ltd to 500c,nbrd,box-(100th ed of)   (5cc9) 175.00
--A Wonder Book-NY-n.d.-8 col plts   (5ee3,f,dj)   6.00
--same-Lond-(1922)-lg4to-white cl-t.e.g.-24p col illus-
ltd to 600c,autg   (5dd8) 125.00
RACKHAM, BERNARD-A Book of Porcelain-Lond-1910-8vo-
28 col plts   (5ww3)   20.00
RADCLIFF, ELIZ W V-Capt Edw Richardson, a Memorial-1923-
81p-illus-priv print   (5p0)   15.00
RADCLIFFE, RICHARD-Letters 1755 to 83-Oxf-1888-306p-
fldg pedigree-(Oxford Univ Life)   (5a1)   7.50
RADCLIFFE, REV T, ed-Authentic Letters from Upper Canada-Tor-
1953-207p-illus   (4b9)   5.00
RADCLIFFE, WM-Fishing from the Earliest Times-Lond-1926 (5c1) 27.50
RADDON, SAM, JR-Portland Vignettes-Portl-n.d.-109p-illus
(5s4,sl wn)   8.00
RADEMAKER, JOHN A-These are Americans-PaloAlto-1951-278p-
Pacific Books   (5x9,ex-libr) 4.00
RADER, JESSE L-South of 40 from Mississippi to Rio Grande-Norman-
1947-336p-ltd to 1000c   (4a5) 45. (5g2,5yy7) 35.00
RADER, PERRY S-School History of State of Missouri-Brunswick, Mo-
(1891)-Rader, publ-illus-279p-orig cl   (4b3,faded) 10.00
RADFORD, HARRY V-Adirondack Murray-NY-1906-illus-84p (5t4) 10.00
RADFORD AMERICAN HOMES, THE-100 House Plans-Riverside, Ill-
(1903)-255p-illus-Radford Architectural Co   (5t4)   7.50
RADFORD'S ARTISTIC BUNGALOWS-Unique Coll of 208 Designs-
Chig-(1908)-Radford Architectural Co-4to-224p   (5t4)   5.00
RADFORD'S,(WM) BRICK HOUSES-& How to Build Them-Chig-
1912-219p,(3)   (5w7)   3.50
RADFORD'S COMBINED HOUSE-& Barn Plan Book-Chig-1908-287p
(5w7)   4.50
RADFORD IDEAL HOMES, THE-Chig-(1907)-sm4to-cl-111p-illus-
Radford Architectural Co   (5t2)   10.00
RADICALISM IN RELIGION, PHILOSOPHY & SOCIAL LIFE-4 papers
from Boston Courier for 1858-Bost-1858-12mo (5ss5,ex-libr) 8.50
RADIN, EDW-Crimes of Passion-NY-1953-247p-cl   (5v2)   4.00
RADIN, PAUL, ed-African Folk Tales & Sculpture-NY-(1952)-4to-
340p-cl-plts   (5xx7)   10.50
--Autobiography of a Winnebago Indian-Berkeley-1920-wrps
(4k5,f)   7.50
--Crashing Thunder-1926-203p-1st ed   (5r1,vg) 18.00
--Indians of SoAmer-GardenCty-1942-1st ed-scarce
(5h4,mint,dj,5L0,dj) 10.00
--Primitive religion-NY-1937-Viking-322p-1st ed   (5v6)   4.50

RADIN, PAUL, ed (continued)
--Story of the Amer Indian-NY-1927-6 col plts-44 photos-371p-
1st ed   (4b2,cov wn,hng rprd)   9.00
--same-NY-(1937)-377p plus index-photos-reprint
(4k5,f,dj) 5.   (5L2)   4.00
--same-GardenCty-(1937)-deluxe ed-illus-383p   (4b3,vg) 10.00
--same-1944-enlrgd ed-391p   (4f9) 7.50   (4b2,f)   7.00
--The Trickster-NY-(1956)-211p   (4b3,f,dj) 7.50
--same-Lond-1956-211p-1st ed (5s0) 5.   (5q8,dj,mint) 7.50
--Winnebago Hero Cycles-Balt-1948-(Indiana U Pubs)-4to-wrps-
168p   (5h5)   10.00
RADIO AMATEUR'S HANDBOOK-WestHartf-1932-214p-illus-
fldg bds   (5b8)   5.00
RADIO CORP OF AMER-Radiola 7, NY-1923-owner's manual-
fldg bds-14p-illus   (5b8)   7.50
--Radiola Super 8-RCA-NY-Feb 1925-owner's manual-fldg bds-
19p,5p-illus   (5b8)   8.50
--Radiola 30 Super Heterodyne-RCA-NY-(192?)-fldg bds-32p-
illus   (5b8)   7.50
--Radiola 3-A-RCA-NY-(192?)-owner's manual-fldg bds-16p-
illus   (5b8)   8.50
RADISSON, PIERRE E-Voyages of-Bost-1885-Prince Soc-buck
(orig wrps bnd in)-250c prntd   (5jj7) 125.00
RADZIWILL, PRINCES-They Knew The Washingtons-Indnpls-c1926-
256p   (5w0)   5.00
RAE, EDW-The White Sea Peninsula-Lond-1881-cl-plts-fldg map-
8vo-347p   (5v7)   12.50
RAE, JOHN-Correspondence with Hudson's Bay Co on Arctic Explor
1844 to 1855-Lond-1953-Hudson's Bay Rec Soc-plts-maps-401p
(5s6)   25.00
--Narr of Exped to Shores of Arctic Sea in 1846&1847-Lond-1850-
1st ed-maps-rare   (4a1,lacks bkstrp) 225.00
RAE, JULIA S E, ed-Old Stories Told Anew-Lond-1891-obl 8vo-
dec red cl-a.e.g.-67p-12 plts-Trischler&Co-(prntd in Bavaria)
(5aa2)   6.50
RAEBURN, HAROLD-Mountaineering Art-Lond-(1920)-illus-cl-274p-
TFisherUnwin   (5d7)   4.00
RAEMAKERS, LOUIS-Kultur In Cartoons-NY-1917-4to-219p-
pictorial in 2 col   (5w0,hng crack) 10.00
--Raemaker's Cartoon History of the War-Allison,comp-NY-1919-
3 vols   (5w4)   15.00
RAE, W FRASER-Facts about Manitoba from "Newfoundland to
Manitoba"-Lond-1882-TheTimes-131p-2 fldg maps-wrps-reprnt
(4d1,soil,rbkd) 15.00
RAE, WM FRASER-Columbia & Canada-NY-1879-316p-2nd ed-
Suppl to Wstward by Rail   (5aa0)   7.50
--Westward by Rail, new route to the East-NY-1871
(5L7,rprd,ex-libr) 6.   (5g2)   7.50
RAFF, EDSON D-We Jumped to Fight-NY-(1944)-illus-207p (5t7) 3.00
RAFF, GEO W-The War Claimant's Guide-Cinn-1866-477p
(5j6,fox)   6.00
RAFFALD, ELIZABETH-Experienced English Housekeeper-Lond-1780
7th ed-3 fldg plts-lea-352p, 363to379p, 398to412p(18)p
(5ww2,autg) 75.00
--same-Lond-1794-lea-3 fldg plts-port-11th ed   (4g9,autg) 75.00
RAFFLES, T S-History of Java-Lond-1817-for Black,Parbury&Allen-
4to-cl-lea labls-fldg col map-66 plts(9 col)-2 vols-1st ed
(4h0,vf,fade) 435.00
--same-Lond-1830-2nd ed-2 vols-cl   (4b6,recased) 60.00
RAFINESQUE, C S-Amer Manual of Grape Vines & Art of Making
Wine-Phila-1830-wrps-illus-2 plts-rare   (5ff9) 100.00
--Amer Manual of the Mulberry Trees-Phila-1839-prntd wrps-96p
(5ff9,f) 100.00
--Ancient History, or Annals of Kentucky-Frankfort-1824-for Author-
39p-8vo-disbnd   (5n2) 125.   (5L1)   85.00
--Genius & Spirit of Hebrew Bible-Phila-1838-12mo-wrps-264p-
1st series   (4c1,lacks front wrp) 75.00
--Western Minerva, or Amer Annals of Knowledge & Literature-
(1949)-Peter Smith-reprint(of 1821)   (5x5)   12.50
RAFN, CHAS CHRISTIAN-Memoire sur la decouverte de l'Amerique
au dixieme siecle-Copenhagen-1843-Societe Royale des
Antiquaires du Nord-2nd tirage-52p-plus Section Russe-12p-
9 plts-8vo-mor-bnd wi Memoires de Societe Royale des
Antiquaires du Nord, 1840 to 1844   (5L1)   50.00
RAFTERY, J H-A Miracle in Hotel Building-(Helena, ca1911)-illus-
8vo-orig wrps-15p   (4g6)   7.50
RAFTERY, JOHN H-The Story of the Yellowstone-(Butte)-1912-135p-
limp leatherette-scarce little book   (5L2)   7.50
RAGATZ, LOWELL JOS-Guide for Study of British Caribbean
History, 1763 to 1834-Wash-1932-8vo-1st ed   (4m7)   12.50
RAGG, LAURA M-The Women Artists of Bologna-Lond-1907-Methuen-
319p & 40p-lg8vo-Methuen cat bnd in-plts   (5m5,fade) 15.00

171

RAGGEDY ANN & ANDY-Animated by Julian Wehr-Akron-
(1944)-Saalfield Publ-6 moving plts-pict bds (5cs,f) 8.50
RAGLAND,J F-A Slice of Living-Richmond-1953-47p-wrps
  (5x2,autg) 20.00
RAGUET,C-Treatise on Currency & Banking-1840-hf calf-2nd ed
  (5L7,ex-libr,crack) 12.50
RAHT,CARLYLE G-Romance of Davis Mntns & Big Bend Country-
ElPaso-(1919)-381p-cl-1st ed-fldg map-plts
  (5h7) 35. (5L2,fleck,5jj7,f) 27.50
RAHV,PHILIP,ed-The Short Novels of Tolstoy-NY-(1960)-Dial Pr-
716p (5p7) 6.00
RAILEY,WM E-History of Woodford Co-Frankfort,Ky-1928-
394(395)p plus index-separate prntng of Ky Hist Soc,1920-1921-
illus-wrps-fldg map (5bb4) 17.50
RAILEY,W E-Raileys & Kindred Families-n.d.-113p (5mm3) 12.50
RAILROAD,THE-NY-1901-McClure,Phillips-fiction (5m2) 4.00
RAILROAD-An Act to Aid in Construction of a RR & Telegraph Line
from Mo Riv to Pac Ocean-Wash-1862-Doc #108-sewn-14p-
scarce (5bb4) 25.00
RAILWAY & CORP LAW JOURNAL-(NY)-Vol 1 thru 12-1887 to 1892-
bound-(lacks Vol 7) (5ii7,rbnd) ea 8.50
RR COMMISSIONERS-Report Board of-Calif,1st Biennial,1893,94-
Sacramento-1894-384p (5s4) 10.00
--same-Kansas-4th Annual,1886-Topeka-1886-322p (5s4,cov wn)10.00
--same-Michigan-15th An,1887-Lansing-1887-647p (5s4) 12.50
--same-Minnesota,yr end Nov 1893-Minnpls-1894-585p (5s4) 10.00
RAILROAD SYSTEM OF CALIF-Oakland & Vicinity-SanFran-1871-
Carmany&Co-48p-2 fldg maps-wrps-board folder (5tt0) 20.00
RAILWAY SIGNAL ASSOC-Digest of Proceedings of-Bethlehem,Pa-
1906 to 1911- Vols 1&2,rev ed-Vols 3 thru 6 plus index to
Signal Lit-Vol 1,Oct 1910-7 vols-8vo-illus-cl (5ss5) 27.50
RAINE,ALICE-Eagle of Guatemala-NY-(1947)-12mo-cl
  (5h4,review copy) 5.00
RAINE,JAS WATT-The Land of Saddle Bags-NY-(1924)-8vo-illus-
1st ed (5m6) 7.50
RAINE,WM MacLEOD-The Black Tolts-Houghton-1932 (5F1,f,dj)4.00
--Cattle-NY-1930-Dblday-plts-1st ed
  (5g6,pres to E M Rhodes) 50. (5jj7) 12.50
--Colorado-NY-1928-316p-cl-1st ed (5g5) 4.00
--Crooked Trails & Straight-NY-(1913)-339p-illus (5s4) 5.00
--A Daughter of Raasay-NY-(1902)-12mo-illus-1st ed of auth's
1st book (5gg6,dj) 15.00
--Famous Sheriffs & Western Outlaws-GardenCty-1929-294p-
1st ed (so stated) (5h6) 10. (5yy7) 8.50 (5yy7,wn) 6.50
--45 Caliber Law-(Evanston,1941)-8vo-64p-illus-pict cl
  (5bb4,5hh4) 4.00
--Guns of the Frontier-Bost-1940-1st ed-photos (5bb4,dj) 12.50
RAINES,C W-Analytical Index to Laws of Texas,1823 to 1905-
Austin-1906-559p-calf (4a5,chip) 135.00
--Bibliography of Texas-Austin-1896-268p-3/4 mor-ltd to 500c,nbrd
  (5j4) 110.00
--same-Houston-(1955)-(Frontier Pr)-268p-cl-boxed,ltd to 500c
  (5m9) 15. (5qq8) 10.(5j4) 12.50
--6 Decades in Texas-Austin-1900-685p-hf mor (5z7) 50.00
--Year Book of Texas-Austin-1903-483p (5n4) 18.50
RAINEY,GEO-The Cherokee Strip,It's (sic) History-Enid,Okla-
1925-wrps-30p-illus (5h0,sl spots) 40.00
--The Cherokee Strip-Guthrie-1933-illus-504p
  (4b3) 75. (5r8,5h0) 60.00
RAINEY,MRS GEO-Cherokee Strip Brands-Enid,Okla-1949-12mo-
68p (5h0) 5. (5g5) 6.00
RAINEY,T C-Along the Old Trail,Pioneer Sketches of Arrow Rock
& Vic-Marshall-1914-96p-cl-spec ed-ltd to 50c,autg,nbrd
  (4a5,5L0) 35.00
RAINIER,PETER W-My Vanished Africa-NewHav-1940-Yale U Pr-
maps-307p (4t5,ex-libr,4a6) 5.00
RAISIN-The Haskelah Movement in Russia-Phila-1913-1st ed
  (5b9,f) 8.50
RAIZISS,SONA-La Poesie Americaine "Moderniste"-Paris-1948-
Cr8vo-wrps-1st ed (5ss7,unopnd) 7.50
RAJBERTI,GIOVANNI-L'Arte di Convitare spiegata al popolo-
Milan-1850¡-1-2 parts bnd in 1-illus-bds (5w1,fox) 25.00
RAK,MARY KIDDER-A Cowman's Wife-Bost-1934
  (5bb4,pencil) 12.50 (5s4) 15. (5a8,f,dj) 22.50
RALEIGH & GASTON RR CO-Proceeding of 14th Annual Meeting-
Raleigh-1864-wrps-16p (5r5) 25.00
--same-15th Annual Meeting-Raleigh-1864-wrps-16p (5h6) 10.00
RALEIGH,LADY,ed-The Letters of Sir Walter Raleigh,(1879 to 1922)-
Lond-1926-Methuen-2 vols-illus (5p7) 12.50
RALEIGH,SIR WALTER-Discoverie of Large Rich & Bewtiful Empyre
of Guiana-Lond-Robt Robinson-1596-sm4to-(16),112p-mor g.-
g.e.-2nd ed-2nd issue-Sabin 67554 (5hh0,reprd) 2,500.00

RALEIGH,SIR WALTER (continued)
--same-Lond-1928-Argonaut Pr-frontis-2 maps-4to-cl-106p,182p-
ltd to 975c (5t0) 20.00
RALEIGH,SIR WALTER-Instructions for Youth, Gentlemen &
Noblemen-Lond-1722-Randal Minshull-12mo-328p-calf-1st ed-
rare (5v2) 75.00
RALEIGH,SIR WALTER-Instruction to His Son & to Posterity-Lond-
1927-PeterDavies-bds-64p-reprint-4-3/4 x 3 (5p1) 5.00
RALEIGH,SIR WALTER-The Last Fight of the REVENGE-Lond-n.d.-
SampsonLow-129p-illus (5p7) 10.00
RALEIGH,SIR WALTER-Prerogative of Parliament in England-
Midelburge-1628-sm4to-stitchd as issued-1st ed
  (5n2,f,box) 225.00
RALEIGH,SIR WALTER-Remains of Sir Walter Raleigh-Lond-1681-
396p-calf-12mo (4b4) 37.50
RALEIGH,WALTER-The History of the World-Lond-1614-Walter Burre-
790 lvs-8 dbl pg maps-calf over bds (4h5,rebkd,box) 850.00
RALEIGH,WALTER-The war in the air-Lond-1922-Oxf Univ Pr-
Vol 1 (only of 5 vols)-489p (5v6,autg) 12.50
RALEY,GEO H-Monograph on Totem Poles of Stanley Park,Vancouver-
Vanc-1937-dec wrps-24p-illus (5dd0) 4.50
RALLI,PAUL-Nevada Lawyer-Dallas-(1946)-12mo-162p-port
  (5dd4) 12.50
RALPH,JULIAN-Dixie,Southern Scenes & Sketches-NY-1896-illus-
412p-(some Remington illus) (4b3,5ee3) 7.50 (5w4) 12.50
--On Canada's Frontier-NY-1892-illus,Remington-325p-1st ed
  (5r6,4d4,cov sl wn) 25.00
--Our Great West-NY-1893-illus,Remington &others-1st ed
  (5m9) 20.00
--People We Pass-NY-1896-illus-12mo (5w4) 6.50 (4b7) 10.00
--A Prince of Georgia & Other Tales-NY-1899-Harper-162p-illus-
1st ed (5x4,wtrstnd) 5.00
RALSTON,LYCOMING CO PENN-Advantages of,for manufacture
of iron-NY-1843-wrps-fldg map (5g8,map tn) 10.00
RALSTON HEALTH CLUB-Book of Complete Membership in-Wash-
(1892)-Martyn Coll Pr Assn-8vo-cl-unpaged (5j5) 12.50
RALSTON,JACKSON,REPORT OF-Pious Fund of the Californias-
US vs Mexico-Wash-1903-GPO-8vo-891p-cl (5h5) 15.00
RALSTON,W R S-Russian Folk Tales-Lond-Smith,Elder&Co-1873-
thk8vo-382p-cl (5c8,wn) 20.00
RAM,J-Treatise on Facts as Subjects of Inquiry by a Jury-NY-
1870 (5ff4,rebnd) 7.50
RAMALEY,D-Most wonderful & valuable invention of 19th century,
the Abel combination loom-StPaul(Minn)-1871-DRamaley-8vo-
orig prntd wrps (5i8) 22.50
RAMBAUD,ALFRED-Russia-NY-1902- 2 vols-619p-illus-cl(5ss6) 5.00
RAMBLE,ROBT-A Portfolio for Youth-Phila-1835-1st ed-illus-12mo-
352p (5v0,rub) 8.50
"RAMBLER"-Guide to Florida-NY-1876-2 fldg maps-illus-24mo-
cl (5g8,spot) 22.50
RAMBLES-in the Mammoth Cave during 1844,by a visitor-Louisvlle-
1845-plts-16mo-errata slip-fldg map (5g3,map tn) 7.50
RAMBOSSON,(J)EAN-Histoire des Meteores et des Grands
Phenomenes de la Nature-Paris-1869-cl-408p-illus
  (4t7,rebnd) 42.50
RAMEL,L'ADJUTANT GEN JEAN PIERRE-Journal,l'un des Deportes
a la Guiane apres le 18 Fructidor-Lond-1799-orig wrps-159p-
copperplt port-3rd ed (5r7) 25.00
RAMEY,W SANFORD-Kings of the Battlefield-Phila-1887-illus-
525p (5yy7) 5.00
RAMON,THE ROVER OF CUBA-& other tales-NY-1843-8vo-orig cl-
frontis-9 plts-Nafis&Cornish (5x1,soil) 35.00
RAMOS,A-The Negro in Brazil-Wash-1951 (5x2) 4.25
RAMROD BROKEN-Bost-1859-300p-cl (5h7,lack fly) 12.50
RAMSAY,ALLAN-Gentle Shepherd-Lond-1790-1st ed-103,(7)p-
calf (5aa0,calf wn,t.p.cut) 12.50
RAMSAY,ANDREW MICHAEL-The travels of Cyrus-Lond-1730-
8vo-2 vols-calf-4th ed,enlrgd (5xx6,vg) 30.00
RAMSAY,DAVID-The History of the Amer Revolution-Phila-1789-
2 vols-calf-1st ed (5L3) 175.00
--same-Lond-1793-orig calf (5m4) 30.00
--History of Revolution of SoCar-Trenton-1785-Isaac Collins-2 vols-
5 fldg maps-plans-8vo-orig bds-1st ed (5L1,unopnd) 200.00
--Life of Geo Washington-port-calf-lea label-1st ed-port
NY-1807 (5j5,lacks port) 15. (5r7) 35.00
--same-Lond-1807-port-hf lea-1st Engl ed (5q8) 15.00
--Military Memoirs of Gr Britain....1755 to 63-Edinb-1779
  (5nn8) 175.00
RAMSAY,GEO M-Cosmology-Bost-1870-sm8vo-cl-illus-264p
  (5t2) 3.50
RAMSAY,SIR JAS H-Foundations of England-Lond-1898-3 vols-
maps-illus (5xx7) 12.50

RAMSAY, SIR JAMES H (continued)
--Genesis of Lancaster-Oxf-1913-2 vols-maps-illus (5xx7) 15.00
--Lancaster & York-Oxf-1892-2 vols-maps-illus (5xx7) 15.00
RAMSAY, ROBT-Rough & Tumble on Old Clipper Ships-NY-1930-
296p-illus (5s1) 8.50
RAMSAY, W M-The historical geography of Asia Minor-Lond-1890-
JnMurray-Vol 4, Royal Geogr Soc-495p-6 fldout maps (5v6) 7.00
RAMSAY, WM-A Book of Toasts-NY-(1906)-col frontis-dec bds
(5c9) 3.50
RAMSAY, WM-Gases of the Atmosphere-Lond-1896-Macm-8vo-
orig cl-8 ports-1st ed (4h0, vf, pres) 75.00
RAMSAYE, TERRY-A Million & 1 Nights-NY-1926-illus-868p-
ltd to 327 sets, nbrd, autg by Thos A Edison & author-2 vols
(4c9, cl) 350. (4c9, hf lea) 450.00
--same-NY-1926-1st ed-2 vols-t.e.g.-orig blu cl
(5b0, fade) 75. (4c9) 125.00
RAMSBOTTOM, F H-Pinrciples & Practices of Obstetric Medicine &
Surgery, in Ref to Process of Parturition-Phila-1842-R8vo-458p-
Lea&Blanchard-sheep-mor labl-1st ed-scarce (5p5, f) 35.00
RAMSDELL, CHAS W-Reconstruction in Texas-NY-1910-384p
(4j4) 75.00
RAMSDELL, G A-Hist of Milford, N Hamp-1901-1023p (5mm3, wn) 15.00
RAMSDELL, H J-Life & Public Services of Hon Jas G Blaine...
also Life of Gen John A Logan by Poore-Phila-(1884)-illus
(5q8, hng weak) 4.50
RAMSEY, A C, trans-The Other Side, or Notes for History of War
between Mexico & US-NY-1850-1st ed in Engl-458p-illus-
24 maps & plts(sm fldg) (5tt6) 65. (4a5, wn) 75.00
RAMSEY, A M-Gospel & the Catholic Church-1956 (5L7) 3.50
RAMSEY, ALEX-Address delivd....on 2nd Annual Territorial Fair,
held at Minnpls, MT, 1856-StPaul-1857-Minnesotian Office-
8vo-orig prntd wrps-1st ed (5i9, rprd) 45.00
RAMSEY, BRUCE-Ghost Towns of BC-Vanc-1963-226p-illus-map
(5a1) 5.00
RAMSEY, DAVID-History of SoCarolina-Charleston-1809-calf-
2 maps-Longworth, publ (5tt8, broken, maps tn) 35.00
RAMSEY, FRED-These Are My People-Detroit-1966-8vo-cl-87p-
1st ed-ltd to 600c (5g2) 15.00
RAMSEY, LT H C-Elementary Naval Ordnance, Gunnery-Bost-1918-
400p-illus-flex cov (5s1, libr labls) 5.00
RAMSEY, J C-Ramsey Family History-(1933)-216p-scarce (5t9) 22.50
RAMSEY, LEONIDAS-Garden Pools large & small-NY-1931-108p-
photos (5s7) 4.50
RAMSEY, S C-Small Houses of Late Georgian Period 1750 to 1820-
Lond-(1910)-folio-cl-100 photos (4a2, rub) 15.00
--same-Lond-1923, 4-Architectural Pr-lg4to-cl-2 vols (5m5) 30.00
RANALD, JOSEF-Hands of Destiny-NY-c1931 (5x7) 3.50
RANCK, GEO W-Hist of Lexington, Ky, its early Annals & Recent
Progress-1872-428p (5t9) 25.00
RAND, AUSTIN L-Amer Water & Game Birds-NY-1956-illus-4to-
239p-o.p. (5ss8, dj) 15. (5ww3) 20.00
RAND, AYN-Atlas Shrugged-NY-1957-1168p-1st prntng
(4b4, f) 18.50 (4k7, mint, dj) 25.00
--The Fountainhead-Indnpls-1943-754p-1st ed (4k7, f, pres) 30.00
RAND, B, comp-Classical Moralists-1909 (5L7) 6.00
RAND, CLAYTON-Men of Spine in Mississippi-Gulfpt-1940-
307p-cl (5h7) 5.00
RAND, EDW-After the Freshet-Bost-(1882)-Lothrop-423p-1st ed
(5x4) 7.50
RAND, EDW A-The Drummer Boy of the Rappahannock-NY&Cinn-
1889-12mo-386p-frontis-pict cl-1st ed (5p1) 10.00
RAND, F P-The Village of Amherst, Mass, a Landmark of Light-1958-
337p (5mm3) 5.00
RAND, HENRY A-Graphology, a Handbook-Cambr-(1947)-Sci Art-
200p (5p7) 3.00
RAND, J C-Massachusetts, 1 of a 1,000-1890-707p
(5mm3, lacks sp) 10.00
RAND McNALLY-Guide to Alaska & Yukon-NY, Chig-1922-175p-
photos-maps-fldg col map in bk (5r0) 7.50 (5L5) 4. (5x0) 5.00
--Indexed Co & Township Pocket Map & Shippers Guide of Ind-
Chig-(1910)-78p-fldg map (5ff7) 5.00
--Indexed Pocket Map & Shippers' Guide of W Va-Chig-(1917)-61p-
ads-lg fldg map-wrps (5h7) 5.00
--Pocket Map of Virginia, etc-(1908)-wrps-foldout map (5h6) 3.50
--Pocket Map of Western States(cov title)-New Township, Co &
RR Map of the NW-c1882-fld into 16mo cl cov-col (5g0, sp tn)15.00
--Township & Co & RR Map of Michigan, 1879- (4i2) 7.50
RAND, SILAS-Legends of the Micmacs-NY-1894-cl-452p
(4k5, hng crack) 15.00
RANDALL, DAVID A-Dukedom Large Enough-NY-(1960)-1st ed
(5v2, vf) 12.95
RANDALL, DEXTER-Democracy Vindicated & Dorrism Unveiled-
Prov-1846-Brown-100p-pamph-orig prnt wrps (5qq8) 12.50

RANDOLPH, E F-Inter Ocean Hunting Tales-NY-1904-illus-173p
(5ss8) 7.50
RANDALL, E O-Masterpieces of Ohio Mount Builders-Colum-1908-
126p-cl (5h7, fox) 7.50
--Centennial Anniversary Celebration at Chillicothe-Colum-1903-
730p-cl (5w5) 15. (5h2) 7.50
--The Serpent Mound, Adams Co, Ohio-Colum-n.d.-illus (5w5) 5.00
RANDALL, EMILIUS-History of Ohio-NY-1863-5 vols (5ji9, rbnd)40.00
RANDALL, F A-Randall & Allied Families-1943-582p (5mm3) 15.00
RANDALL, RT REV GEO M-Triennial Report of-(NY-1868)-map-
8vo-stitched as issued-25p(1) (4c1) 17.50
RANDALL, HENRY S-The Practical Shepherd-Rochester, NY-1863-
illus (5xx5) 20.00
RANDALL, J G-The Civil War & Reconstruction-Bost-(1937)-924p
plus index-illus-maps (5L5) 5.00
--same-Bost-1953-971p (4j4) 6.50
--Lincoln the Liberal Statesman-NY-1947-illus (5p9) 5. (5r7) 7.50
--Lincoln the President-NY-1945-2 vols (5w0) 17.50 (5t7, box) 12.50
--Lincoln the President, Midstream-NY-1952-DoddMead-467p-
illus (5p9) 7.50
RANDALL, JAS RYDER-Maryland, My Maryland & other Poems-
Balt&NY-(1908)-180p-port (5t7) 10.50
--The Poems of-NY-1910-TandyThomas-221p (5x4) 7.50
RANDALL, JOHN H-The Landscape & the Looking Glass-Bost-1960-
HoughtonMiff-1st ed (5m2, dj) 5. (5ss9) 7.50
RANDALL, L W-"Gay" Footprints along the Yellowstone-SanAnt-
(1961)-186p plus photos-1st ed (5L0, mint, dj) 5.00
RANDALL, M-Canadian Reader Designed for Use of Schools &
Families-Stanstead, L C-1834-Walton&Gaylord-sm8vo (5nn8)120.00
RANDALL, R H-The Key Letter-Marion, IA-1884-159, 1p with short
music manual-obl 8vo-orig prntd bds (5L8, wn) 28.50
RANDALL, RICHARD H-Amer Furniture in the Museum of Fine Arts,
Bost-Bost-(1965)-4to-18p, 276p-218 illus-boxed (5t4) 25.00
RANDALL, RUTH PAINTER-Mary Lincoln, Biography of a Marriage-
Bost-(1953)-illus-555p
(4b3, f, dj) 7.50 (5s9) 3.50 (5t4) 6.50 (5w9, 5x0) 4.00
RANDALL, THOS-The Farmer's Meditations, or Shepherd's Songs-
Limerick, ME-1833-265p (5t7, wn, lacks part 1 pg) 18.50
RANDALL, W M-Constitutional Guide or Pocket Companion-
Mansfield, OH-1865-32mo-cl-64p (5m8) 3.50
RANDELL, JACK-I'm Alone-Lond-1930-287p-ports-plts-maps
(5aa0) 6.00
--same-2nd impress-1931 (5aa0) 5.00
RANDOLPH, EDGAR F-Inter Ocean Hunting Tales-NY-1908-
173p-illus-1st ed (5ee3, pres, lacks e.p.) 6.00
RANDOLPH, EDMUND-Report of, Read in the House Dec 31, 1790-
(Phila, 1791)-folio-orig wrps (5g3) 35.00
--same-(Phila, 1791)-folio-32p-orig wrps-2nd ed (5g3) 30.00
--Vindication of Mr Randolph's Resignation-Phila-1795-8vo-cl-
103p-Sam'l H Smith-1st ed-2nd issue-errata corr (5L1) 35.00
RANDOLPH, EDMUND-Hell Among the Yearlings-NY-(1955)-
308p-illus (5s4, ex-libr, dj) 8.50
RANDOLPH, HELEN F-Mammoth Cave & the Cave Region of
Kentucky-Louisville-1924-illus-maps (5yy8) 12.50
RANDOLPH, HOWARD S F-La Jolla, Year by Year-LaJolla-1946-
142p plus index-photos-wrps-1st ed (5L5) 6.00
--Paramus, Bergen Co, NJ, Reformed Dutch Church Baptisms
1740 to 1850-Newark-1935-8vo-cl-224p (4t1) 12.50
RANDOLPH, JOHN-Texas Brags-Houston-1945-illus-orig stiff wrps
(5hh3) 3.50
RANDOLPH, MRS MARY-The Virginia Housewife or Methodical
Cook-Baltimore-1838-stereotype ed-lea (5ww2, rub) 80.00
RANDOLPH, P-From Slave Cabin to the Pulpit-Bost-1893 (5x2) 30.00
RANDOLPH, SARAH N-Domestic Life of Thos Jefferson-NY-1871-
432p-ports (5xx7) 15. (4m6) 8.50
--Life of Gen Thos J Jackson-1876 (5L7, sl wn) 6.00
RANDOLPH, THOS J-Memoir, Correspondence, & Miscellanies from
Papers of T Jefferson-Bost-1830-Gray&Bowen-4 vols-calf-2nd ed
(5yy3) 20.00
--same-Charlotteville-1829-1st ed-4 vols-8vo-port-calf-lea labl
(5ss5, cov sl loose) 30.00
RANDOLPH, VANCE-The Ozarks-NY-(1931)-Vanguard-illus-e.p.-
maps-310p (4d9, spot) 7.50
--Who Blowed Up the Church House?-NY-1952-232p-drawings-
1st ed (5bb4, dj) 5.00
RANDOLPH, WASSELL-Randolph Pedigree & Desc of Henry
Randolph-1957-277p-mimeo (5mm3) 17.50
RANGELEY LAKE VIEWS-Bost-n.d.-14 photos-"Albertype"-
Forbes Co-cl portfolio-(ca14x11) (5g4) 22.50
RANGERS, THE-Bost-1856(1851)-4th ed-12mo-orig cl-2 vols in 1
(4c5, fox) 19.50
RANHOFER, CHAS-The Epicurean-Evanston-(1920)-illus-thk4to-
1183p (4g9, mint) 25.00

RANKE, HERMANN-Art of Ancient Egypt-Vienna-1936-(Phaidon)-4to-illus-1st ed (4a1) 17.50
RANKE, LEOPOLD VON-History of the Popes-NY-1901-3 vols-Colonial Pr (5p0) 15.00
--History of Latin & Teutonic Nations-Lond-1909 (5tt5) 10.00
RANKIN, D J-History of the County of Antigonish, Nova Scotia-Tor-1929-Macmillan-390p (5x0) 20.00
--Our Ain Folk & Others-Tor-1930-208p (4b9) 6.00
RANKIN, DAN'L-The 1st Biography of Joan of Arc-(c1964)-Univ of Pittsburg Pr-156p-14p illus (5p1, pres) 12.50
RANKIN, HENRY B-Intimate Character Sketches of Abraham Lincoln-Phila-1924-ports (5q8) 5.00
--Personal Recoll of Abraham Lincoln-NY-(1916)-ports (5q8, autg) 5. (5t4) 6.00
RANKIN, JEAN S-Mechanics of Written English-Minnpls-1917-Augsburg-1st ed-illus-8vo-cl-plts (5u6) 8.50
RANKIN, MELINDA-20 Yrs Among the Mexicans-Cinn-1875-Chase&Hall-214p (4d9, ex-libr) 11.50(5dd5) 16.50
RANKIN, WM H-The Man Who Rode the Thunder-EnglewoodCliffs-c1960 (5x7, autg) 4.00
RANSLEBEN, GUIDO E-100 Yrs of Comfort in Texas-SanAnt-1954-239p (5n4) 25.00
RANSOM, J H-Who's Who in Horsedom-Lexington-1963-photos-419p (4p8) 10.00
RANSOM, JOHN CROWE-The New Criticism-NY-(1941)-12mo-cl-1st ed (5ss7, dj, pencil) 10.00
RANSOM, R C-The Pilgrimage of Harriet Ransom's Son-Nashville-ca 1930 (5x2) 27.50
RANSOM, STANLEY A, comp-History of Hartland-(1961)-189p-1st ed-ltd to 600c-illus (5e8, dj) 12.00
RANSOM, WILL-Private Presses & their Books-NY-1929-493p-illus-RRBowker-ltd to 1200c (5ee3, f, dj) 25.00
--same-NY-1929-Bowker-493p-cl (5tt9) 30.00
--Selective Check Lists of Press Books-NY-1963-Duschnes-420p-cl (5tt9) 25.00
RANSOM, WM L-Chas E Hughes...the Statesman as Shown in Opinions of Jurist-NY-c1916-353p (5w4) 7.50
RANSOME, ARTHUR-Great Northern?-NY-1948-350p-1st ed-illus (5s1) 4.00
RANSON, JOHN L-Andersonville Diary-Auburn-1881-304p-ports (5t4) 15.00
RANSON, NANCY RICHEY-Texas Wild Flower Legends-Dallas-(1933)-119p-illus-Kaleidograph Pr (5s7) 5.00
RANSON'S FAMILY RECEIPT BOOK-Buffalo-1894-82p-wrps (5g9) 3.50
RANTOUL, ROBT JR-Memoirs Speeches & Writings of-Bost-1854-Jewett-864p-frontis-L Hamilton, ed (5qq8) 10.00
RAOUL-Reminiscences of 20 Yrs' Pigsticking in Bengal-Calcutta-1893-12mo-160p&48p catalog-cl-photos (4a6) 27.50
RAPEE, ERNO-Encyclopedia of Music for Pictures-NY-1925-510p (4c9) 27.50
RAPER, CHAS LEE-NoCarolina-NY-1904-8vo-1st ed (5ss5) 12.50
RAPHAEL'S ALMANAC-or, the Prophetic Messenger & Weather Guide-1888, 1893, 1897, 1900, 1901-Lond-wrps (5t0) ea 3.00
RAPHAEL, JULIET-Madrigal & Minstrelsy-NY-1927-Boni-96p-4to-bds (5p7) 4.50
RAPHAEL, MAX-Prehistoric Cave Paintings-Pantheon-1945-Lucas-illus-100p-4to (5ww3) 17.50
RAPIN, H-La Sculpture Decorative Moderne-Series 1-Paris-(ca 1925)-photographic repros-30 plts loose in bds&cl portfolio tied-CHMoreau, ed-Rue de Prague (5t7, lacks 2 plts) 10.00
--same-Series 3-photographic repros-31 plts loose in bds&cl portfolio tied-(ca 1925) (5t7) 10.00
RAPIN, MONSIEUR (RENE)-Whole Critical Works of-Lond-Bonwicke&Wilkin-1716-2 vols-lea-2nd ed (5i1, hng crack) 35.00
RAPIN, RENE-Willa Cather-NY-1930-McBride-115p-port-(Modern Amer Writers series #8) (5p9) 4. (5m2, dj) 6.50
RAPPOPORT, A S-A Primer of Philosophy-NY-1905-Dutton-118p (5p0) 3.50
RASCOE, BURTON-Belle Starr, Bandit Queen-NY-1941-illus-340p-cl (5x5, lacks fly) 10. (4p2, 5x5) 15. (5L2, dj) 17.50
--Prometheans, Ancient & Modern-NY-1933-Putnam-296p (5p0) 6.00
--Theodore Dreiser-1925-1st ed (5ss9) 6.00
--Titans of Literature from Homer to the Present-NY-1932-Putnam's-lg8vo-dec cl-g.t.-496p-ports (5m2) 5. (5aa2) 4.50
RASKIN, XAVIER-The French Chef in Private Amer Families, a book of recipes-Chig-1922-700p (5c9) 6.00
RASMUSSEN, KNUD-Across Arctic America-NY-1927-388p-4 maps-64 illus (5ss1, autg card) 15.00
--Greenland-Lond-1921-4to-327p-fldg map-col plt-1st ed (5dd7) 20.00
--Min Rejsedagbog-Copenhagen-1927-183p-map (5ss1) 3.00
RASPAIL, JEAN-Terre de Feu Alaska-Paris-(1962)-233p-photos-col pict wrps (5r7) 7.50
RASPE, RUDOLPH-Singular Adven of Baron Munchausen-NY-1952-Ltd Ed Club-autg, box (4F6, mint) 15.00
--Singular Travels, Campaigns & Adventures of Baron Munchausen-Lond-1948-Cresset Pr-178p-illus-Cresset Library (5p1) 4.00
RAT TRAP, THE-or, cogitations of a convict in house of correction-Bost-1837-12mo-qtr mor-1st ed-v scarce (5i9) 40.00
RATCHFORD, FANNIE E, ed-Letters of Thos J Wise to John Henry Wrenn-NY-1944-Knopf-1st ed (4p1) 32.50
--Story of Champ D'Astile, as told by Two of the Colonists-Dallas-1937-Book Club of Tex-col illus-maps-ltd to 300c, box (4a5) 100.00
RATCLIFFE, DOROTHY UNA-Equatorial Dawn-Lond-1936-photos-304p-Eyre&Spottiswoode (4t5) 8.00
RATH, E J-Too Many Crooks-NY-(1918)-frontis-1st ed (5ee3, f) 5.00
RATH, IDA ELLEN-Early Ford County, (Kansas)-No Newton, KS-1964-267p-illus-1st ed-(100c, nbrd) (5k1) 10.00
--The Rath Trail-Wichita-(1961)-196p plus index-illus-1st ed (5L0, autg, mint, dj) 7.50
RATHBONE, A D-Shall We Scrap Our Merchant Marine?-NY-1945-397p (5s1) 3.00
RATHBONE, FREDK-Old Wedgewood-Lond-1898-Quaritch-royal folio-part mor-g.e.-col port-64 col plts-1st ed-ltd to 200c-v scarce (4h0, libr stmp, rub) 750.00
RATHBONE, PERRY T, ed-Mississippi Panorama-(StL-1950)-228p-188 illus-col illus-City Art Mus of StL, publ-cl (5h1) 12.50
--Westward the Way-StL-(1954)-City Art Mus-280p-col plts (4b3, f, dj) 25.00
RATHBORNE, ST GEO-Miss Fairfax of Virginia-NY-(1899)-289p-cl (5y0) 12.50
--Saved by the sword-NY-(c1898 by Neely)-370p-reprint (5m2) 5.00
RATHBUN, JOHN B-Aeroplane Construction-Chig-(1929)-John R Stanton-illus-392p (5q0) 15.00
--Motion Picture Making & Exhibiting-1914-236p (4c9) 22.95
RATHBUN, JONATHAN-Narrative-n.p.-(1840)-12mo-cl (4c1) 30.00
RATHBUN, RICHARD-National Gallery of Art-Wash-1909-illus-140p (4a0) 15.00
RATIGAN, WM-Adventures of Capt McCargo-NY-(1956)-245p-cl-1st prntg (5h7) 3.50
--Great Lakes Shipwrecks & Survivals-GrRap-(1960)-298p-cl-1st prntg (5h7, f, dj) 7.50
--Soo Canal!-GrRap-1954-186p-cl-2nd prntg (5h7, dj) 3.50
RATIONAL DAME, THE-Or, Hints toward supplying prattle for children-NY-1821-wdcuts-16mo-bds-105p (5t7) 12.50
RATNER, J-Spinoza on God-1930 (5L7) 4.00
RATTAN, VOLNEY-A Popular Calif Flora, or, Manual of Botany for Beginners-SanFran-1882-138p-illus-4th ed, rev-Bancroft (5s7) 7.50
--same-9th ed-SanFran-text illus (5s7, lacks e.p., Mss notes) 5.00
RATTAY, J E-East Hampton History & Genealogies-(1953)-619p (5mm3) 15. (5m2) 12.50
RATTI, ABATE ACHILLE-Climbs on Alpine Peaks-Bost-1923-HoughtonMiff-139p-illus-cl (5d7, wn) 4.50
RATTRAY, W J-Scot in British NoAmer-Tor-1880-4 vols (4b9, sp wn) 30.00
RAU, CHAS-Observations on a Gold Ornament from a Mound in Florida-Wash-1878-6p-1 drwng-wrps (5L0, f) 4.00
RAU, LOUISE-Three Physicians of Old Detroit-Detr-1929-(16)p-self wrps-Burton Hist Coll (5h7) 4.00
RAUCAZ, L M-In The Savage South Solomons-1928-Soc For Propagation of Faith-270p-maps-illus-scarce (5r0) 12.50
RAUCH, E H-Pennsylvania Dutch Hand Book-Mauch Chunk-1879-238p (5yy0) 17.50
RAUCH, JOHN H-Public Parks-Chig-1869-S G Griggs-8vo-84p-sewed (5j5, ex-libr) 17.50
RAUMER, FREDK von-American & the Amer People-NY-1846-1st Amer ed (4j3, needs rebndg) 20.00
--Die vereinigten Staaten von Nord Amerika-Leipzig-1845-2 vols-FABrockhaus-12mo-bds-lea labls-1st ed-map-4 fldg tabls (5i0) 60.00
--same-Phila-2 vols in 1-lea bkstrp-1846 (5m2, rprd crude) 13.50
RAUPERT, J GODFREY-The new black magic & the truth about the ouija board-NY-1920-Devin Adair-243p (5v6) 3.00
RAUSCHENBUSCH, WALTER-Christianity & the Social Crisis-NY-1907-sm8vo-cl-15p, 429p (5t2) 4.00
RAUSCHER, FRANK-Music on the March, 1862 to 1865 wi Army of the Potomac-114th Regt Penna Volun, Collis' Zouvas-Phila-1892-270p-illus (5w0) 15.00
RAUSSE, J H-Errors of Physicians & Others in Practice of the Water Cure etc-NY-1854-91p-wrps (5y0, wrps, soil) 5.00
RAVAZ, L-Le Pays Du Cognac-Angouleme-1900-(6)p, 307p, (2)-photos (5w1, wtrstns) 22.50
--Traite General De Viticulture 3me Parties, T 3, Le Mildious-Montpelier-1914-photos-(4)p, 198p, (4)-wrps (5w1, fox) 6.50

RAVAZ,L (continued)
--Les Vignes Americaines-Montpellier-1902-433 photos-4to-wrps-
376p   (5w1)   12.50
RAVENEL,HENRY WM-Private Journal of-Columbia-1947-8vo-
428p-ARChilds,ed   (4a7,mint) 12.50
RAVENEL,MRS ST JULIEN-Charleston,The Place &The People-NY-
1906-528p-illus-g.t.-1st ed   (5h9)   10.00
--same-NY-1912-illus-8vo-cl-528p   (5t2)   4.50
RAVENHILL,ALICE-Native Tribes of BC-Victoria-1938-142p-illus-
fldg map   (4a8,pres) 15.00
RAVENSCROFT,R T-Desc of John Blackman & Mary (Pond) of
Dorchester,Mass-1955-55p-mimeo   (5t9)   12.00
RAVERTY,MAJ H G-Dictionary of the Pukhto,Pushto Language of
the Afghans-Lond&Calcutta-1867-1166p-4to-orig cl-2nd ed,enlrgd-
ex rare   (5p5,rbkd) 35.00
RAVOUX,MONSIGNOR A-Reminiscences,Memoirs & Lectures-
StPaul-1890-ports-223p-1st ed   (4k5)   35.00
--Memoires,Reminiscences et Conferences-StPaul-1892-257p-
illus-2nd ed,enlrgd   (5L2)   15.00
RAWLE,WM-A view of the Constitution of the US-Phila-1829-
bds-cl bk-2nd ed   (5g4,ex-libr) 7.50
RAWLE,WM BROOKE-History of the 3rd Penna Cavalry-Phila-1905-
614p-photos-fldg maps-1st ed (5w4) 16.50 (5L5,f,unopnd) 25.00
RAWLINGS,MARJORIE-Cross Creek Cookery-NY-1942-illus-230p-
1st ed   (4g9)   7.50
--same-later printing   (5c4)   4.50
--The Yearling-NY-1938-Scribners-8vo-dec cl-illus-428p-
1st ed-1st issue   (5nn2)   15.00
RAWLINGS,MARY-The Albemarle(county)of Other Days-
Charlottesville-1925-8vo-orig bds-illus-1st ed (5m6)   5.00
RAWLINGS,THOS-Confederation of British NoAmer Provinces...
including British Col & Hudson's Bay Terr etc-Lond-1865-8vo-
orig limp cl-fldg map-4 plts-1st ed
(5L1) 85. (4k7,pres,Streeter copy)   65.00
RAWLINS,W D-Specific Performances of Contracts-Lond-1899
(5ff4)   6.50
RAWLINSON,ELEANOR-Intro to Literature for Children-NY-1931-
8vo-493p-Norton-1st ed   (5p1,lacks e.p.) 5.00
RAWLINSON,GEO-Seven Great Monarchies of Ancient Eastern
World-Phila&Chig-n.d.-part lea-illus-maps-3 vols-Edi
De Luxe-ltd to 1000 sets   (5kk7,sl rub) 12.50
RAWSON,JONATHAN-Compendium of Military Duty adapted
for Militia of the US-Dover,(NH)-1793-Eliphalet Ladd-
3 parts-12mo-lea-296p & index-1st ed (5t2,lacks back cov) 12.50
RAWSON,MARION NICHOLL-Candleday Art-NY-1938-383p-4to-
illus   (5n7,5m2) 7.50
--Country Auction-Dutton-(1929)-261p-illus-1st ed (5e8,faded) 12.00
--Little Old Mills-NY-(1935)-366p,(1)   (5n7,soil) 8.50
--New Hampshire Borns a Town-NY-1942-1st ed-illus (5tt5) 6.00
RAWSON,S S-Memoir of Edw Rawson,Sec of Colony of Mass Bay-
1849-146p   (5mm3)   17.50
RAWSON,T J-Statistical Survey of County of Kildare-1807-
plts-hf bds   (5L7,wn,plt tn) 5.00
RAWSTONE,L-Gamonia,or the Art of Preserving Game-Lond-1905-
cl-15 col plts-146p   (5cc1,f)   5.00
RAY,ANNA CHAPIN-The Brentons-Bost-1912-Little,Brown-8vo-
dec cl   (5b2)   4.00
--The Dominant Strain-Bost-1903-LittleBrown-illus-cl (5b2) 3.50
--Each Life Unfulfilled-Bost-1899-1st ed   (5ee3)   5.00
RAY,CLARENCE E-Rube Burrow,King of Outlaws & Train Robbers-
Chig-n.d.-191p-cl-Adams 1817   (5h7,rbnd) 10.00
RAY,CYRIL-The Compleat Imbiber-(Lond,1956)-256p-illus (5g9) 8.50
--same-NY-(1957)-256p-illus   (5w1)   7.50
RAY,G N,ed-Letters &Private Papers of Wm M Thackeray-Cambr-
1946-4 vols-illus   (5mm1)   45.00
RAY,GRACE ERNESTINE-Early Okla Newspapers-Norman-
Jun 15,1928-U of Okla-Studies #28-119p-photos-wrps (5L2) 7.50
RAY,GEO R-Kasba(White Partridge)-Tor-1915-259p (5a1)   4.50
RAY,GEORGES-Les Vins De France-Paris-1948-12mo-127p-wrps
(5w1)   4.50
RAY,ISAAC-Conversations on the Animal Economy-Portland-(1829)-
Shirley&Hyde-16mo-wdcuts-lea bk bds-lea corners-242p
(5p1,title tn,lacks e.p.) 125.00
RAY,JOHN-Collection of Curious Travels & Voyages,In 2 Tomes-
Lond-1693-8vo-calf-g.sp-1st ed   (4i0,sl brown) 125.00
RAY,JOS-Primary Lessons & Tables in Arithmetic-Cinn-(1857)-
96p-pict bds   (5h2)   7.50
--Ray's Eclectic Arithmetic-Cinn-1839-Truman&Smith-lea bkd bds-
239p-10th ed   (4k2,def final lf) 25.00
RAY,MR&MRS L P-Twice Sold,Twice Ransomed-Chig-1926-illus
(5x2)   35.00
RAY,P ORMAN-Convention that Nominated Lincoln-Chig-(1916)-
38p-wrps   (5h1)   3.00

RAY,P ORMAN (continued)
--Repeal of the Missouri Compromise,Its Origin & Authorship-
Cleve-1909-315p   (5m2,libr stmp) 15. (5x5,sl fox) 25.00
RAY,WM-Horrors of Slavery-Troy-1808-298p-orig calf
(5tt6,lacks fly) 60.00
--Poems,on various subjects-Auburn(NY)-Dblday-1821-8vo-orig bds-
prntd papr labl-1st ed   (5i0,t.p. tn) 60.00
--same-NY-1826-prntd for author-qtr calf-2nd ed-12mo
(5i0,lt wtrstnd) 20.00
RAY,WORTH S-Down in Cross Timbers-Austin-1947-ltd to 500c
(4c7)   15.00
--Genealogical & Hist Library of-Balt-1955-22p-wrps (5j4) 8.00
RAYBOLD,G A-Annals of Methodism-Phila-1847-12mo-orig cl
(5a8)   15.00
RAYMOND,DAN'L-Thoughts on Political Economy-In 2 parts-Balt-
1820-Fielding Lucas,Jr-8vo-orig pink cl-papr labl-1st ed
(5L1,fade,hng weak) 85.00
RAYMOND DE RIGNE-L'Abbaye du Bel Amour-Paris-1920-t8vo-
34 plts-buck-ltd to 500c   (5t5,rbnd) 20.00
RAYMOND,DORA NEILL-Capt Lee Hall of Texas-Norman-1940-
350p-illus by Lundean&Remington-map-1st ed
(5x5,dj) 25. (4b3,5bb4,dj) 20. (4c7,dj) 17.50
RAYMOND,E T-Disraeli,Alien Patriot-NY-(1925)-8vo-cl-illus-
346p   (5t2)   3.50
RAYMOND,ELEANOR-Early Domestic Architecture of Penna-
NY-1931-WmHelburn-4to-cl-photos   (5t0,lt fade) 25.00
RAYMOND,ETHEL T-Tecumseh,Chronicle of Last Great Leader of
His People-Tor-1915-159p-lea-Chronicles of Canada Ser
(5h7,sp wn) 7.50
RAYMOND,HENRY J-Life & Public Serv of A Lincoln-NY-1865-
8vo-808p-buck   (4a7,rbnd,5w0) 12.50
RAYMOND,HENRY W-Saranac,a Chapt in Adirondack History-
NY-1909-Grafton Pr-8vo-illus-dec cl-1st ed   (5p5)   10.00
RAYMOND,LOUISE-A Child's Book of Prayers-NY-1929-Random-
illus by Masha-4to-36p-cl bkd pict bds   (5p1,fray dj) 17.50
RAYMOND,M D-Desc of John Gray of Beverly,Mass-1887-316p-
scarce   (5m2) 55. (5mm3) 47.50
RAYMOND,M W-Architecture & Landscape Gardening of the
Exposition-SanFran-(1915)-202p-lin-2nd ed,rev (5h5)   4.00
RAYMOND,MARTHA GOULD-Ebell Club of Anaheim,Its Hist,
Nov,1907,July 1946-Placentia-n.d.-Placentia Courier-8vo-
part cl-110p   (4t1)   12.50
RAYMOND,ROSSITER W-Camp & Cabin-NY-1880-243p-frontis-
1st ed   (5L0,bkstrp wn) 7.50
--Mineral Resources of States & Territories west of Rocky Mntns-
Wash-1869-GPO-8vo-orig cl-256p   (5L1)   40.00
--Statistics of Mines & Mining in States & Territories West of
Rocky Mntns-1870-plts-buck
(5s4,ex-libr) 20. (5L7,rbnd,ex-libr) 25.00
--same-Wash-1872-fldg maps&charts-566p (4a5) 7.50 (4e4,cl wn)13.50
--same-Wash-1873-GPO-illus-maps-550p   (4n8,v wn) 10.00
RAYMOND,W-Excursion of 44 days thru Mexico...in Pullman
Palace cars-Bost-1885-80p-cl   (5n4)   10.00
RAYMOND,WALTER,ed-Standard Paper Money Catalogue-NY-
(1940)-8vo-cl-illus-106p   (5t4)   4.50
RAYMOND,WM O-River St John-StJohn-1910-1st ed-plts-illus-
maps   (5s6)   10.00
RAYNAL,ABBE-Revolution de l'Amerique-Lond-1781-Davis-12mo-
orig wrps-port-1st ed   (5n2)   55.00
RAYNAL,ABBE-Revolution of Amer-Edinb-1783-191p(5mm8,rbnd)10.00
RAYNAL,MAURICE-History of Modern Painting-Geneva-1949-
Chamberlin-col illus-folio-3 vols   (5ww3)   165.00
--History of Modern Painting from Picasso to Surrealism-Geneva-
c1950-4to-210p-tip in col plts   (5w5)   16.50
RAYNE,MRS M L-What A Woman Can Do-Petersburgh-(1893)-
528p,(24)-lea-cov   (5w7,cov dtchd)   5.00
RAYNE,MRS M LOUISE-Fallen among thieves & A Summer tour-
NY-1879-Carleton-1st ed-(advts dated '79) (5m2,sl wn) 10.00
RAYNER,B L-Life of Thos Jefferson-Bost-1834-Lilly,Wait,Colman
& Holden-431p,12p-frontis-1st ed   (5qq8)   15.00
RAYNER,CMDR D A-Escort,Battle of Atlantic-Lond-(1955)-250p-
photos-maps   (5s1,dj)   4.00
RAYNER,E-Handicapped Among the Free-NY-1903   (5x2)   15.00
RAYNOLDS,W F-Report of Explor of Yellowstone & Missouri Riv-
Wash-1869-174p-lg fldg map-prntd wrps   (4a5)   25.00
RAYNOR,TED-The Gold Lettered Egg & Other New Mexico Tales-
LasCruces-1962-8vo-wrps-54p-1st ed   (5g5,f)   5.00
--Old Timers Talk in SoWestern NewMexico-ElPaso-1960-86p-
photos-wrps-1st ed   (5L0)   4.00
--same-ElPaso-1960-100c bnd in cl-illus-Hertzog-3 autgs
(4c7,f,dj) 32.50 (5g0,2 autgs) 25.00

REA,GEO BRONSON-Facts & Fakes About Cuba-NY-(c1897)-
Munro's Sons-8vo-cl-illus-poor papr   (4a3,cov wtrstnd)   10.00
REA,LILIAN-The Life & Times of Marie Madeleine Countess of La
Fayette-Lond-(1908)-12mo-illus-3/4 lea-336p   (5t7)   10.00
REA,R R-Boone County (Ark) & Its People-1955-224p-Ark Hist Ser #4-
ltd to 1000c   (5mm3)   10.00
REACH,ANGUS B-A Romance of a Mince Pie-Lond-1848-illus by
Phiz-hf lea-104p-ads-frontis-illus   (5ww2)   25.00
READ,BENJ-History of Swanzey 1734 to 1890-(NH)-1892-585p-illus
(5e8) 24.75   (5mm3)   32.50
READ,BENJ M-Guerra Mexico Americana-SantaFe,NM-1910-illus-
photo   (5 x5,lacks e.p.)   25.00
--Illus History of NewMexico-n.p.-(SantaFe)-1912-4to-cl-
812p incl adv & plts-ltd to 500c,nbrd-errata slip
(5F5,pres,fade)   60.00
READ,COLLINSON-An Abridgement of Laws of Penna-Phila-1801-
Amer Biblio 1214-calf   (5m2)   6.00
READ,CONYERS-Social & Political Forces in the English Reformation-
1953   (5L7)   3.50
READ,D B-Lieut Governors of Upper Canada & Ontario-Tor-1900-
253p-illus   (4b9,f)   15.00
--Life & Times of Gen John Graves Simcoe,with some account of
Maj Andre & Capt Brant-Tor-1890-illus (5r6) 10.   (5w8)   15.00
READ,FLORENCE M-Story of Spelman College-Atlanta-1961-
399p-illus   (5p0)   5.00
READ,GEO H-Last Cruise of Saginaw-Bost-1912-128p-illus-photos
(5s1)   3.00
READ,GEORGIA W,ed-Gold Rush-NY-1949-Columbia Univ Pr-
frontis-illus-794p   (5x5,dj,5i3,dj,f)   17.50
--A Pioneer of 1850-Bost-1927-lg8vo-cl-184p (5t2) 7.50 (5h5)   12.00
READ,HERBERT-Art Now-NY-(1948)-illus-144p-photos (5t4)   4.50
--A Concise History of Modern Painting-NY-(1959)-illus (5m2)   5.00
--English Stained Glass-Lond-(1926)-4to-259p-69pg plts-ltd ed
(5xx7)   15.00
READ,HERBERT-Collected poems-Lond-1953-Faber&Faber-12mo-
orig cl   (5i8,autg,f,dj)   8.00
--The London Book of English Prose-Lond-1931-Eyre&Spottiswoode-
8vo-gl-g.t.-665p   (5aa2)   3.50
--The Sense of Glory-NY-(1930)-HBrace-228p   (5p9)   5.00
--A World Within a War,Poems-NY-(1945)-HarcourtBrace-
1st Amer ed   (5ss9,f,dj)   6.50
READ,J A-Journey to the Gold Diggins,by Jeremiah Saddlebags-
Facs of Orig Ed-Burlingame-1950-Grabhorn Pr-col illus-obl 8vo-
bds-ltd to 300c   (4g6,vf,f)   13.50
READ,J MARION-History of the Calif Academy of Medicine 1930 to
1960-1962-4to-cl-ltd to 1000c   (5h5,f)   10.00
READ,JESSIE-3 Meals a Day-Tor-1941-photos-480p-2nd rev ed
(5c5)   3.50
READ,JOHN MEREDITH,JR-Historical Inquiry Concerning Henry
Hudson,His Friends,Relatives & Early Life,etc-Albany-1866-
col frontis-8vo-part mor-1st ed   (4m6,sl rub)   12.50
READ,NATHAN S-An astronomical dictionary-NewHav-1817-
orig bds   (5g4,wn,ex-libr)   15.00
READ,THOS B-The Female Poets of Amer-Phila-1849-Butler&Co-
ports-lea-a.e.g.   (5ss9)   15.00
--Poetical Works of-Phila-1890-Lippincott-illus-346p-new rev ed
(5p7)   5.00
--A Summer Story,Sheridan's Ride & other poems-Phila-1865-
Lippincott&Co-12mo-cl-1st ed   (5ss3)   35.00
--Sylvia,or,the last shepherd-Phila-1857-Parry&McMillan-8vo-
orig cl-1st ed   (5i9,f)   10.00
--Paul Redding,A Tale of the Brandywine-Bost-1845-12mo-papr labl-
orig glazed bds-1st ed of auth's 1st book (5gg6,vf,box)   125.00
--Wagoner of Alleghanies-Phila-1865-276p-cl   (5h2,sp wn)   5.00
READ,THOS CARPENTER-Desc of Thos Lee of Charleston,SC-
(Columbia)-1964-465p-illus   (5r7,ex-libr)   15.00
READ,THOS THORNTON-Development of mineral industry
education in the US-NY-1941-Amer Insti of Mining & Met Engrs-
298p   (5v6)   4.00
READE,CHAS-The Cloister & The Hearth-Lond-1861-4 vols-
Trubner&Co-Vols 1,3 & 4 are 1st eds-Vol 2 is 3rd ed-orig cl-
djs have lea labls   (5hh1,box)   225.00
--same-NY-1861-8vo-1st Amer ed   (4m8)   15.00
--same-Lond-1902-illus by Hewerdine-655p-cl   (5t0)   4.00
--same-NY-1932-2 vols-illus by Lynd Ward-ltd to 1500c,nbrd,autg-
Limited Editions Club pub   (5F1,wn dj,soil box)   30.00
--Griffith Gaunt-Lond-1867-3rd ed-3 vols-12mo-cl   (4c2)   25.00
--"Love me Little,Love Me Long"-Lond-1859-2 vols-12mo-cl
(4c2)   75.00
--Terrible Temptation-Lond-1871-Chapman&Hall-3 vols-12mo-
orig cl-1st ed   (5xx6,rub,rprd)   50.00
--White Lies-Lond-1857-Trubner-3 vols-12mo-orig green cl-
1st Engl ed (4c2,sl shaken) 100.   (5xx6,sl rprd)   70.00

READE,CHAS (continued)
--A Woman Hater-Lond-1877-3 vols-12mo-orig cl   (4c2)   100.00
--The works of,complete in 16 vols-Bost-n.d.-(ca 1900)-DeWolfe,
Fiske-grn & crimson cl-g.t.-etched frontis   (5p6,f)   38.00
READE,COMPTON-Smith Family,Being a Popular Account-Lond-
1904-280p   (5i9)   12.50
READE,W WINWOOD-Savage Africa-NY-1864-Harper&Bros-452p-
illus-map-orig cl   (5x5)   25.00
READE,WINWOOD-The Martyrdom of Man-NY-1926-495p-reprint
(5w0)   8.50
READER,FRANK S-History of 5th West Virginia Cavalry-NewBrighton,
Pa-1890-304p-cl   (5ff7)   37.50
READER'S DIGEST FAMILY TREASURY-Of Great Painters & Great
Painting-col plts-illus-192p-cl   (4a2,dj,f)   6.50
READING,(MASS)-Hist Address & Poem at Bi Centennial Celebration-
1844-131p   (5mm3)   10.00
READING GUIDE-U of VA Law Library-Vol 1 thru 23-1946 to 68
(5ii7,rbnd)   150.00
READING,ROBT S-Arrows over Texas-SanAnt-(1960)-261p plus
index-illus-1st ed   (5L0)   7.50
REAGAN,ALBERT B-Don Diego of Pueblo Indian Uprising of 1680-
NY-(1914)-map-photos-music scores-352p   (4b2,stain)   6.00
--Notes on the Indians of Ft Apache Region-1930-Amer Mus of
Nat Hist-8vo-prntd wrps   (5g6,f)   3.50
REAGAN,JOHN H-Bridge over Rio Grande Betw City of Eagle Pass,
& Piedras Negras-Wash-1884-2p-HR 800   (4a5)   3.50
--Claims for Spoilations Committed by Indians & Mexicans-Wash-
1860-11p   (4a5)   12.50
--Memoirs-1906-Neale Pub Co-351p   (5yy8)   40.00
--Treaties of 1817 & 1819 with Cherokee Indians-Wash-1860-
HR534-13p   (5n4)   6.50
REAL,ANTONY-Ce Qu'il Ya Dans Une De Vin-Paris-1867-309p-
wrps   (5w1)   8.50
--The Story of the Stick in All Ages & Lands-NY-1891-illus-
254p   (5n7,wn)   7.50
REAL ESTATE ADVERTISER-Vol 1,#1-SanFran-Feb 1,1874-4p-
Berry&Capp   (5d6)   6.00
REAL HOME KEEPER,THE-A Perpetual Honeymoon for Vancouver
Bride-Vanc-n.d.-(ca 190?)-240p-4to-purpl papr bds wi
picture of bride   (5g9)   7.50
REAL PEN WORK PUBL CO-Real Pen Work,Self Instructor in
Penmanship-(By Successors to Knowles&Maxim)-Pittsfield,Mass-
1881-(1884)-obl 4to-frontis-48 lvs-orig glazed bds (5L8,wn) 26.50
REALITIES OF PARIS LIFE-Lond-1859-Hurst&Blackett-3 vols-8vo-
orig brick cl-frontis-1st ed   (5i8,wn,stn)   17.50
REAMY,MRS L B L-Tried Recipes-(Richmond,Ind)-1888-609p-cl
(5jj9,cov spot)   8.50
REARDON,JAS MICHAEL-Catholic Church in Diocese of StPaul-
StPaul-1952-cl-726p   (4i2)   10.00
REASON VERSUS PASSION-Lond-n.d.-(1809)-by W Lewis for
Wilson-8vo-disbnd-1st ed   (5i8)   75.00
REASON WHY-the Colored Amer is not in World's Columbian Expo-
(Chig(?),ca1893)-illus   (5g8)   15.00
REAU,LOUIS-French Painting in 14th,15th & 16th Centuries-
Lond-1939-Hyperion-41p text-12 col tip in plts-lg4to-cl-
disbnd   (5m5)   25.00
REAVIS,L-Commonwealth of Missouri-Lond-1880-disbnd-8vo-57p
(4p3)   20.00
REAVES,L U-The Great Empire of the West Beyond the Mississippi-
StL-1882-8vo-wrps-116p-illus-lg fldg map-NixonJones Prntg Co-
1st ed   (5g6,f)   35.00
--Saint Louis-StL-1871-3rd ed-214p-wrps (5mm3) 4.50 (4b3)   7.50
REBEC,MARY L-Poems-Eugene,Ore-1938-Nash,prntr-162p-
cl&bds-ltd to 350c,nbrd   (5p6)   10.00
REBECCA & ROWENA-Lond-1850-Chapman&Hall-hand col illus by
Doyle-orig pink bds-(Thackeray) -1st ed   (5c8,wn)   27.50
REBELS,THE-or,Boston before the Revolution-Bost-1850-Phillips,
Sampson-12mo-orig cl-2nd ed-rev ed-(Lydia M Child)
(5x1,sp wn)   12.50
REBER,L BENJ-History of StJoseph-StJos-1925-8vo-147p-illus-fab
(5mm7)   12.50
REBOUX,PAUL-Diet for Epicures-NY-1932-297p   (5c5)   3.50
REBUFFAT,GASTON-Mount Blanc to Everest-NY-(1956)-Studio-
158p-69 plts-cl   (5d7)   12.50
--Starlight & Storm-Lond-(1956)-Dent-122p-illus   (5d7)   7.50
RECEUIL DE VOYAGES AU NORD-Amsterdam-1725 to 38-Bernard-
10 vols-12mo-   orig calf-g.tooled-2 frontis-13 fldg maps-
26 fldg plts-   (5n9)   850.00
RECHERCHES HISTORIQUEST ET POLITIQUES-sur les Etats Unis-
Paris-1788-Froulle-8vo-4 vols-orig calf bkd bds-1st ed-
(F Mazzei)   (5L1) 95.   (5n2,5m4)   125.00
RECIPES FOR AMERICAN-& other Iced Drinks-Lond-n.d.-(ca 1900?)-
illus-ads-(ca 96p)   (5g9,soil)   5.00

RECIPES FROM OLD VIRGINIA-VA Fed of Home Demo Clubs-
Rich-1946-287p-spiral bnd wrps-illus
(5g9)   4.00

RECK, FRANKLIN M-On time-n.p.-1948-184p-illus-bds (5y2)   5.00

--One Man Against the North-NY-1940-244p-drwngs (5ss1,pres) 8.00

--Sand in Their Shoes-n.d.-(1952)-153p-illus   (5y2)   5.00

RECLUS, ELISEE-North America-Vol 1, British North America-NY-
1893-4to-496p-illus-maps-Earth & Its Inhabitants Series (5r7) 15.00

--Ocean, Atmosphere, Life-NY-1873-534p-illus-27 col maps
(5s1,ex-libr)   7.50

--South America-NY-1894-2 vols-4to-illus-8 maps-Earth & Its
Inhabitants Series   (5r7,f)   40.00

RECOLL OF AN EXCURSION TO MONASTERIES OF-Alcobaca &
Batalha-Lond-1835-1st ed   (5nn6,cov loose,lacks port) 15.00

RECOLL OF LIFE & DOINGS IN CHICAGO-from Haymarket Riot
to end of WW 1-Chig-1945-270p-cl-by an Old Timer (5h1)   7.50

RECONSTITUICAO DA VINHA EUROPEA-pela enxertia sobre cepas
Americanas-Quinta anno #12-Lisbon-1894-4to-wrps (5w1)   13.50

RECORD AMERICAN & FOREIGN SHIPPING - Amer Bureau Shipping-
NY-1918-g.cov-9½x9-1056p   (5s1,ex-libr)   40.00

--NY-1926-10 3/4x10-g.cov-1361p   (5s1,ex-libr)   30.00

RECORD AMERICAN BUREAU SHIPPING-Standard American
Classification of Vessels-1953-thumb index-1859p   (5ss1)   35.00

--1954-thumb index-1899p   (5ss1)   35.00

--1955-thumb index-1896p   (5ss1)   35.00

--1961-thumb index-1831p   (5ss1)   25.00

RECORD OF AN OBSCURE MAN-Bost-1861-Ticknor&Fields-8vo-
cl-(Mrs Putnam)   (5b2)   15.00

RECORD, SAMUEL J-Timbers of the New World-N H-(1947)-sm4to-
illus   (5yy6)   10.00

RECORD OF SERV OF CONN MEN-In War of Revolution, War of
1812, & Mexican War-Hartford-1889-3 parts in 1 vol-1st ed
(5L3)   28.50

RECORD OF SERV OF MICH VOLUNTEERS-in Civil War-Vol 23-
118p-cl-roster   (5a9)   8.50

RECORD, W-Race & Radicalism-Cornell Univ-1964-1st ed (5x2) 12.50

RECORDS OF BUBBLETON PARRISH-Bost-1854-1st ed-
(E W Reynolds)   (5mm2)   7.50

RECORDS OF SALEM WITCHCRAFT-copied from orig documents-
sm sq4to-bds-2 vols-prntd for Woodward-ltd to 215 sets
(5t0,cov loose)   15.00

RECREATION-Vol 8 #1 to Vol 10 #6-5 vols-(NY)-1898 to 1900-
hf lea-G O Shields,ed   (5h1)   45.00

RECREATION DES ENFANS-Illustree par Lassalle,texte de Mme
Salvage-Paris-(c 1820)-Eymery&Aubert-obl 8vo-orig bds-
20 hand col plts   (5c8,rub)   65.00

RECREATIONS OF CHRISTOPHER NORTH, THE-Edinb-1842-
Blackwood-3 vols-8vo-3/4 mor-(J Wilson)-1st ed (5i8,rub)   22.50

RECREATIONS OF A SOUTHERN BARRISTER-Phila-1859-Lippincott-
8vo-cl-(AHSands)   (5b2,sp labl)   17.50

RECTOR, GEO-Dine At Home with Rector-NY-(1938)-248p-port-
frontis   (5c9)   5.00

--Dining in New York with Rector-NY-1939-275p   (5g9)   4.50

--Wilson's Meat Cookery-Chig-1941-135p-illus-pict bds (5c9)   4.00

RECTOR, J L-Coachella, Riverside County-LosAng-(1904)-14p-
wrps-Baumgardt   (5d6)   7.50

RECUEIL D'ESTAMPES-representant les differents evenements de la
Guerre qui procure l'Independance aux Etats Unis de l'Amerique-
Paris-(1784?)-chez MPonce & chez M Godefroy-lg sq4to-
orig blue bds-16 views & maps incl t. plt   (5L1,vf)   150.00

RECUEIL DES LOIS CONSTITUTIVES-des Colonies Angloises,
Confederees sous la Denomination D'Etats Unis...Auquel on a
joint les Actes d'Independance, de Confed-Phila-(Paris)-
1778-Cellot&Hombert-12mo-sheep-1st ed (5n2,hng crack)   185.00

RECULET, C-Le Cuisinier Praticien our La Cuisine Simple et Pratique-
Paris-1859-510p   (4g9,rbnd,lacks 1st 3 lvs)   12.50

RED, WM STUART-History of Presbyterian Church in Texas-Austin-
1936   (4c7)   15.00

RED CROSS KNIGHTS OF SALVATION ARMY-By "Fidelis"-
1884-T Williamson&Co-16mo-reprnt   (5nn8)   10.00

RED IRON ORES OF E TENN-Nashville-1913-wrps-illus-173p-
fldg maps   (5z5,vf)   10.00

RED RIVER TRAILS-(StPaul)-1925-27p-map-drwngs-illus (5t3)   7.50

REDCAY, E E-County Training Schools & Public Secondary Educ for
Negroes in the South-Wash-1935-168p-wrps-John F Sluter Fund
(5x2)   20.00

REDDALL, HENRY FREDERIC-Columbus the Navigator-NY-(1892)-
285p-illus-maps   (5s1,wn,fair)   3.00

REDDAWAY, W F-Frederick the Great & Rise of Prussia-Lond-(1935)-
illus-368p   (5q0)   10.00

REDDICK, L D-Anti Semitism Among Negroes-1942-10p-wrps-
reprint   (5x2)   3.50

REDDICK, L D (continued)

--How Much Higher & Professional Education Does the Negro
Need-1948-reprntd-5p-wrps-bds   (5x2)   4.50

REDDING-Wakefield Souvenir of 250th Anniv of Ancient-1894-
116p-9x12-illus   (5e8,wrps detached)   4.75

REDDING, CYRUS-A History & Description of Modern Wines-Lond-
1833-407p   (5w1,stn,chip)   28.50

--History & Descr of Modern Wines-Lond-1851-(Bohn)-calf-illus-
3rd ed   (4j3) 13.50   (5w1)   15.00

--same-Lond-1860-440p-frontis-orig cl   (5c9,chip)   17.50

--History of Shipwrecks & Disasters at Sea-Lond-1843-2 vols-
2nd Series-orig g. dec cl   (5c8)   12.50

REDDING, MRS J H-Life & Times of Jonathan Bryan, 1708 to 1788-
Savannah-1901-sm4to   (4c1)   10.00

REDDING, J S-An Amer in India-Indnpls-1954-1st ed (5x2,dj)   12.50

--The Lonesome Road-NY-1958-1st ed   (5x2,dj)   12.50

--No Day of Triumph-NY-1942-1st ed   (5x2)   15.00

--On Being Negro in Amer-NY-1951-1st ed   (5x2)   15.00

REDDING, M W-Scarlet Book of Free Masonry-NY-1886-thk8vo-
cl-548p-illus   (5t2)   5.00

REDE, LUCY L-Flowers That Never Fade-(c1835)-Dean&Munday-
12mo-orig pict wrps-31p-handcol frontis-14 handcol illus
(4d1)   15.00

REDEDICATION OF OLD STATE HOUSE, BOSTON-July 11,1882-
Bost-1887-216p-illus   (5h9,rub)   6.00

REDFIELD, WM C-The New Industrial Day-NY-1912-213p (5t7)   7.50

REDFORD, A H-Western Cavaliers, Hist of Methodist Episcopal
Church in KY, 1832 to 44-Nashville-1876-548p   (4p8,wn)   8.50

REDINGER, DAVID H-The Story of Big Creek-LosAng-(1955)-
182p-illus-cl-Angelus Pr   (5d7)   5.00

REDLANDS, BOARD OF TRADE-Picturesque Redlands, Calif 1902-
Redlands-1902-Redlands Daily Facts-12mo-wrps-(16p) (4t1)   15.00

REDLANDS, CALIF-Souvenir of...n.p.-n.d.(ca 1901)-
F C Hoogstratt-12mo-suede-112p   (4t1)   27.50

REDLANDS DAILY FACTS-Illustrated Redlands-Redlands-Nov 26,
1 897-96p-illus-red lea-wrps bnd in   (5yy3)   50.00

REDLANDS-Golden Jubilee, Redlands, Calif, 1888 to 1938-Redlands-
(1938)-Citrograph Print Co-215p-illus-orig dec fab (5yy3)   25.00

REDMONDINO, C-History of Circumcision-Phila-1891-346p-
frontis   (5w5,libr labl)   7.50

REDOUTE & SON TEMPS-by Chas Leger-Paris-1945-lg4to-170p-
18 col plts-ltd to 980c   (5w3)   50.00

REDOUTE, PIERRE JOS-Roses, Parts 1 & 2-NY&Lond-(1954, 1956)-
folio-cl-wrps-43 col plts-2 vols   (5z9,dj)   20.00

REDPATH, J,ed-A Guide to Hayti-Bost-1861   (5x2)   25.00

REDPATH, JAS-Hand Book to Kansas Territory & Rocky Mntns' Gold
Region-NY-1859-Colton-1st ed-rare-2 fldg maps-177p plus ads
(4t8)   200.   (5n9)   325.00

--same-NY-(Denv-1954)-177p-cl-rprnt   (5h1)   10.00

REDPATH, JOHN-Public Life of Capt John Brown-Bost-1860-407p
(5r8) 8.50   (5s9,5t4) 5.   (4j4)   6.50

REDSKINS, THE-or, Indian & Injin-NY-1849-Stringer&Townsend-
2 vols in 1-12mo-orig brown cl-2nd ed bnd as Vol 29 in a
coll ed-(JFCooper)   (5x1,sp wn)   20.00

REDWING, MORRIS-Remarkable Captain-NY-April 21,1888-24p-
self wrps-War Libr Ser #293   (5jj9)   7.50

REDWOOD COUNTY-its advantages to settlers-StPaul-1879-map-
lg fldg map-2p frontis-15p (5p advts)-prntd wrps-issued Business
Men's Assoc of Redwood Falls   (5g3,sp wn)   60.00

REECE, BYRON HERBERT-Bow Down in Jericho-NY-1950-Dutton-
8vo-cl   (5b2,pres,dj)   5.00

REECE, J HOLROYD,ed-Keyserling, The Travel Diary of a
Philosopher-Lond-1925-2 vols-t8vo-cl   (5t5)   8.50

REED, ANDREW-Narr of Visit to Amer Churches by Deputation from
Congregtional Union of England & Wales-NY-1835-HarperBros-
dec cl-2 vols-scarce   (4L9)   25.00

REED, ANNA WETHERILL-Phila Cook Book of Town & Country-NY-
1940-346p-1st ed   (5c0) 5.   (5w5) 6.50   (5g9)   5.50

REED, CHAS B-First Great Canadian, Pierre Le Moyne-Chig-1910-
265p-plts-map   (5a1,sp fade)   5.00

--Masters of the Wilderness-Chig Hist Soc, Ft Dearborn Series-
Univ of Chig Pr-(1914)   (5x5)   10.00

REED, MAJ D W,ed-The Battle of Shiloh & Organizations Engaged-
Wash-1903-8vo-cl-122p-4 maps   (5m8)   12.50

REED, ELIZ A-Daniel Webster, a Character Sketch-Milwaukee-(1899)-
port-illus-12mo-112p   (5xx5,rprd)   4.00

REED, DAVID-Campaigns & Battles of 12th Reg Iowa Vet Vol Inf-
n.p.(Evanston)-n.d.(1903)-photos-319p-errata-pkt map-scarce
(4t8)   25.00

REED, DOUGLAS-Prisoner of Ottawa, Otto Strasser-Lond-1953-272p
(5dd0)   4.50

REED,EARL H-The Dune Country-NY-1916-287p-illus
(5xx7,pres,sketch) 30.00
--Silver Arrow & other Indian romances of Dune Country-Chig-
1926-illus-238p (5xx5) 4.00
REED,EDW O-Annual Report of Tech Director to Public Prntr-
Wash-GPO-1928-35p-wrps (5j4) 4.00
REED,E MILY H-Life of A P Dostie-NY-1868-Tom Linson-375p-
port-1st ed (5qq8,libr stmp,wn) 8.00
REED,ERIK K,ed-For the Dean-SantaFe-1950-illus-1st & only ed
(5g5,f) 10.00
REED,EVAN L-Ways & Means of Identifying Ancestors-Chig-1947-
(5yy6) 7.50
REED,G E-Catalogue of Law Books of Pa State Library-(Harrisburg)-
1899-4to-963p (5yy0) 27.50
REED,GEO E-Campaign of the 6th Army Corps, Summer of 1863-
Phila-1864-35p-orig wrps-scarce (5m1) 15.00
--Poetical Description of the 6th Army Corps during the year 1863-
Harrisburg-1887-48p (5j6) 3.00
REED,HENRY-Two Lectures on The History of the Amer Union-
Phila-1856 (4j4) 4.50
REED,HENRY E-Oregon, Story of Progress & Development-Portland-
1914-96p-photos-wrps (5L0,chip) 5.00
REED,ISAAC G-Erring, Yet Noble,a Tale of and for Women-Bost-
(1865)-Loring-(not 1st) (5ee3) 7.50
REED,J EUGENE,ed-Lives of the Roman Emperors & their
Associates-Phila-1883-Gebbie&Co-5 vols-illus (5p0) 30.00
REED,J S-Solomon Tuttle of Old Mt Comfort & His Desc-1961-
87p (5t9) 15.00
REED,J W-Map & Guide to the Kansas Gold Regions-(Denv-1959-
Mumey)-facs of 1859 ed-fldg map-12mo-orig wrps-24p-box
(4g6,mint) 10.00
REED,J W-Reed Family in Europe & Amer-1861-588p (5t9) 25.00
REED,W H-Johanna Philip Ried,Ried,Rieth,Riedt,Ritt,Rit,Rudt,etc
in Europe & Amer-1929-529p (5mm3) 20 00
REED,JOHN-Insurgent Mexico-NY-1914-Appleton-8vo-cl-scarce
(4a3,fray) 20.00
REED,JOHN-10 Days That Shook the World-NY-1919-
1st edition (5rr 6) 30.00
REED,JOHN A-History of 101st Reg Penna Veteran Vol Infantry
1861 to 1865-Chig-1910-4to-285p-fldg map
(5L5,fleck) 12.50 (4a7) 25.00
REED,JOHN C-The Brothers' War-Bost-1905-456p-1st ed (5yy8) 10.00
REED,JOHN D D-An Apology for Rite of Infant Baptism-Prov-
1806-Heaton&Williams,publ-1st ed-lea-errata slip (4a4,fox) 25.00
REED,JOHN ELMER-Gyantwachia 1732 to 1836-Erie-1926-27p-
wrps-illus (5w5,autg) 4.00
REED,JOHN SILAS-The Day in Bohemia,Or Life Among the Artists-
NY-1913-ltd to 500c-1st ed-stiff wrps-8vo (5gg6,box) 250.00
--Sangar, To Lincoln Steffans-Hillacre,Riverside,Conn-1913-
8vo-bds-1st ed of Reed's 1st (?) book (5gg6,als 2 poems) 100.00
REED,JOS-Tom Jones, a comic opera-Dublin-1769-for W&W Smith,
etc-12mo-disbnd-1st Dublin ed (5x3) 10.00
REED,JOS VERNER-The Curtain Falls-NY-(1935)-8vo-cl-illus-282p-
(5t2,pres) 5.00
REED,LANGFORD,ed-Nonsense Verses-Jarrolds-n.d.-sm4to-
143p-dec cl-illus (5aa0) 4.50
REED,MARJORIE-The Colorful Butterfield Overland Stage-(1966)-
Best West Publ-deluxe ed-col illus-ltd to 100c (5x5,dj) 20.00
REED,MYRTLE-The Book of Clever Beasts-NY-1904-8vo-cl-illus by
Peter Newell (5t5) 9.50
REED,NEWTON-Early History of Amenia,NY-Amenia,NY-1875-
151p (5x0) 20.00
REED,P FISHE-Beyond the Snow-Chig-1873-Lakeside Pr-12mo-cl-
326p (5p1) 25.00
REED,PARKER M-History of Bath and Environs, 1607 to 1894-1894-
526p-illus (5e8) 45.00
REED,R D-Structural Evolution of Southern Calif-Tulsa-1936-Amer
Asso of Petr Geolog-8vo-cl-157p-illus (5h5) 4.50
REED,RALPH D-Geology of Calif-Tulsa,Okla-1933-1st ed-355p-
(5x5,f) 17.50
REED,ROLAND-Indian Art-Ortonville-n.d.-16p-wrps-56 photos-
errata slip (5t3) 7.50
REED,S-Biographical Sketch of Thos Worcester-1880 (5L7) 4.00
REED,S B-House Plans for Everybody-NY-1884-8vo-cl-175 illus
(5p5) 15.00
REED,SAMPSON-Observations on the Growth of the Mind-Bost-
1829-16mo-orig bds-2nd ed (5ss5,cov loose) 15.00
REED,SARAH A-A Romance of Arlington House-n.p.-n.d.-116p
(5w5) 5.00
REED,TALBOT BAINES-The 5th Form at St Dominic's-Lond-n.d.-
Religious Tract Soc-pict cl-14 plts by Ray Potter (5p1) 7.50
--Kilgorman-Lond,Edinb&NY-1902-TNelson-420p-frontis-5 plts-
pict cl-Lone Star Series (5p1,rub) 7.50

REED,VERNER Z-Adobeland Stories-Bost-1899-16mo-
(5r7) 10.00
--Lo To Kah-NY-1897-illus-1st ed (4b2,sl wn) 7. (5mm1) 17.50
--Tales of the sunland-NY-Continental Pub Co-1897-1st ed-
pic cl (5m2,soil) 17.50
REED,WM-The Phantom of the Poles-NY-1906-283p-photos (5ss1) 4.50
REED,WM B-Among my books-NY-1871-Hale-1st ed-t. cov
"World Essays" (5m2,wn) 7.50
REED,WM H-Hospital Life in Army of Potomac-Bost-1866-199p-cl
(5jj9,fade) 10.00
REELING,VIOLA CROUCH-Evanston,Its Land & Its People-
Evanston-1928-468p-illus (5x0) 9.00
REEMELIN,CHAS-Vine Dresser's Manual-NY-1857-103p-illus-cl
(5h1,stns) 10.00
--same-NY-(1855)-frontis-103p (5w6,cov stn) 8.50
REES,JAS-The Life of Edwin Forrest-Phila-1874-524p
(5t4,wn) 8.50
REES,JOHN RAWLINGS-The Shaping of Psychiatry by War-NY-
c1945-158p-1st ed (5w0,dj) 5.00
REES,THOS-Egypt & the Holy Land Today-Springfld-1922-photos-
404p (4t5) 5.00
REESE,A M-The Alligator & Its Allies-NY&Lond-1915-cl-358p-
col frontis-28 plts-8vo-v scarce (4p6,libr stmp) 35.00
REESE,DAVID M-Humbugs of New York-NY-1838-cl-267p
(4h7,lack fly,sl dmpstn) 10.00
--Letters to Hon Wm Jay-NY-1835-120p-orig cl-1st ed
(5m3,fade) 27.50
REESE,GUSTAVE-Music in the Middle Ages-1940-lg8vo-cl-illus-
1st ed (5p5,dj) 15.00
REESE,JOHN J-Text Book of Medical Jurisprudence & Toxicology-
Phila-1889-646p,14p-2nd ed,rev&enlrgd (5t7) 10.00
REESE,LIZETTE W-A Branch of May-Balti-1887-12mo-cl-
auth's 1st book (4c2,sl cov stn) 100.00
--The Old House in the Country-NY-1936-1st ed-dec bds
(5b9,vf) 15.00
--A Victorian Village-(NY)-1929-285p,(6) (5w7,fade sp) 4.00
REEVE,CLARA-Destination:or,memoirs of a private family-Lond-
1799-for Longman&Rees -3 vols-12mo-qtr calf-1st ed-v scarce
(5xx6,lacks hf t.) 150.00
--The exiles,or,memoirs of the Count de Cronstadt-Lond-1788-
for THookham-3 vols-12mo-calf-1st ed (5xx6) 175.00
--The two mentors,a modern story-Lond-1783-for ChasDilly-
2 vols-12mo-calf-1st ed (5xx6) 175.00
REEVE,FRANK D,ed-Albert Franklin Banta,Ariz Pioneer-Albuqu-
1953-143p-wrps-Hist Soc of N M,Vol 14 (5g2) 8.00
REEVE,J STANLEY-Fox Hunting Formalities-Rumford Pr-(Suppl to
"Sportsman" Vol 6,#6 1924)-4to-24p-col plts-wrps-rare (4a6) 15.00
--Foxhunting Recollections-Phila-1928-320p (5ss8) 10.00
--same-Phila-1928-1st ed-320p-box -ltd to 250c,autg (4b1,f) 40.00
--Randor Reminiscences-Bost-1921-illus-204p (4m4) 17.50
REEVE,JAS KNAPP-Practical Authorship-NY-1905 (5p0) 3.50
REEVE,LLOYD ERIC-Gift of the Grape based on Paul Masson
Vineyards-SanFran-(1959)-314p-photos (5w1) 8.50
REEVES,A-Shooting at Sharpeville-Bost-1961-illus-1st ed (5x2,dj) 5.00
REEVES,CHAS EVERAND-School Boards-NY-1954-PrenticeHall-
368p (5p1) 5.00
REEVES,E M-Thos Reeves & Desc-1947-144p (5t9) 12.50
REEVES,FRANK,SR-A Century of Texas Cattle Brands-FtWorth-1936-
illus-stiff pict wrps-1st ed (5g2,mint) 15.00
REEVES,IRA L-Ol' Rum River-Chig-1931-383p-cl
(5h7,pres,wn dj) 5.00
REEVES,J STANLEY-Foxhunting Recollections-Phila-1928-illus-
320p (4m4) 25.00
--Radnor Reminiscences-Bost-1921-illus-204p (4m4) 17.50
REEVES,LE ROY-Ancestral Sketches-Lynchburg-1951 (5h6) 10.00
REFLECTIONS ON CONSERVATORY ELEMENTS OF AMER
REPUBLIC-Chillicothe-1842-55p-wrps-rare-by a lady
(5g4) 7.50 (5h2) 15.00
REFORMED PROTESTANT DUTCH CHURCH IN NO AMER-Vol 1,
from 1771 to 1812-NY-1859-8vo-cl-493p (5t2) 7.50
REFORMER'S YEAR BOOK, THE, 1903-Lond-1903-1st ed
(5b9,cov stn) 12.50
REGAN,J-First Things in Acadia-Halifax-1936-304p-illus (4b9) 12.00
REGAN,JOHN W-Sketches & Traditions of the NoWest Arm-Halifax-
1928-illus-181p plus ads (5w9) 6.50
REGICIDE,THE-or James the 1st of Scotland-Lond-1749-8vo-hf calf
(T Smollett)-1st ed (5x3,sl def) 135.00
REGIER,C C-West Liberty Yesterday & Today-n.p.-n.d.-(WLib-1939)-
221p-cl (5h7) 10.00
REGIONAL PLAN OF NY & ITS ENVIRONS-NY-1929-2 vols-
col maps (5x5) 40.00
REGISTER-of Commissioned & Warrant Officers of Navy of US, 1830-
Wash-1830-16mo-79p-orig wrps (5w0) 8.75

REGISTER-Commissioned,Warrant,Volunteer Officers,US Navy,
to July 1,1868-Wash-1868-74p-wrps   (5s1)   6.00
REGISTER-Commissioned,Warrant Officers US Navy,Marine Corps,
Jan,1932-Wash-1932-628p-wrps   (5s1)   4.50
REGISTER-of Confederate Dead,Interred in Hollywood Cemetary,
Richmond,VA-Richmond-1869-Gary,Clemmitt&Jones-116p
(5F9)   17.50
REGISTRAR'S BOOK,THE-of Gov Keith's Court of Chancery of
Prov of Penna,1720 to 1735-Harrisburg-1941-reprint(5m2)   6.00
REGLAMENTO E INSTRUCCION-para los presidios que se han de
formar en la linea de frontera de la Nueva Espana-Mexico-
1834-30p-sewn-31 x 21 cm   (5L1)   500.00
REGLAMENTO PARA EL GOBIERNO-de la Provincia de Californias
Aprobado,24 Oct 1781-Mexico-1784(prntd)-(reprntd SanFran,
1929)-(with same in Engl)-SanFran-1929-2 vols-8vo-bds-
300c prntd-Grabhorn Pr   (5a3)   75.00
REGULATIONS & INSTRUCTIONS-for General Government of
Several Commissioned & other Officers of Marine on Bombay
Estab-Bombay-1824-4to-qtr calf-130p,(3)-6 fldg tables
(5ss2,f)   67.50
REGULATIONS FOR ARMY OF US,1857-NY-(1857)-457p,21p
(5yy0)   9.50
REGULATIONS FOR EXERCISE-of Riflemen & Light Infantry,for
use of Penna Militia-1824   (5L7)   12.50
REGULATIONS FOR ORDER-& Discipline of Troops of US-Phila-
1809-Carey-72p-8 fldg plts-bds-lea sp   (5mm8)   17.50
REGULATIONS GOVERNING ADMISSION OF CANDIDATES-
into Naval Academy as Cadet Midshipmen,1878,79 (5g5)   7.50
REGULATIONS LATELY MADE,THE-concerning the Colonies & the
Taxes Imposed-Lond-1765-Wilkie-sm4to-disbnd-1st ed
(5L1) 50.   (5n2)   75.00
REHDER,ALFRED-Bibliog of Cultivated Trees & Shrubs Hardy in
Cooler Temperate Regions of No Hemisphere-JamaicaPlain-1949-
cl-4to   (5z9,autg)   35.00
--Manual of Cultivated Trees & Shrubs Hardy in NoAmer-NY-1940-
cl-8vo-map-2nd ed,rev   (5z9)   6.00
REICH,JEROME R-Leisler's Rebellion-Chig-1953-194p (5h9)   8.50
REICHARD,GLADYS A-Analysis of Coeur D'Alene Indian Myths-
Soc of Amer Folklore-Phila-1947-218p (5qq5) 10.   (4b2)   15.00
--Dezba,Woman of the Desert-NY-(1939)-161p-photos-1st ed-
scarce   (5yy7,dj)   15.00
--Navaho Grammar-NY-n.d.-(1951)-Amer Ethno Soc 21-
393p-v scarce   (5L2)   25.00
--Navajo Shepherd & Weaver-NY-(1936)-photos-1st ed,2nd prntg-
burlap-v scarce   (4t8,dj,mint)   20.00
REICHE,CARLOS-Flore de Chile,Vol 1 to Vol 6,pt 1-(all publ)-
Santiago-1896 to 1911-orig cl-8vo-6 vols-1st ed
(5z9,vg,rprd)   100.00
REICHE,CHAS CHRISTOPHER-15 Discourses on the Marvelous Works
in Nature-Phila-1791-calf-1st ed   (5v2,sp rprd)   35.00
REICHEL,LEVIN THEODORE-Early History of Church of the United
Brethren, Commonly Called Moravians, in NoAmer, AD 1734 to
1748-Nazareth,PA-1888-241p   (5h9)   18.50
REICHEL,WM C-The Crown Inn,Near Bethlehem,Penna,1745-
(Phila)-1872-8vo-illus-orig wrps-162p-ltd to 499c
(5m6,lacks bk wrp,stn)   10.00
--Historical Sketch of Nazareth Hall from 1755 to 1869-Phila-1869-
8vo-illus-1st ed   (5m6,rub)   7.50
REICHERS,LOU-The Flying Years-NY-(1956)-illus-1st ed-
auth sgd pres   (4b7,pres)   10.00
REICHERT,IRVING F-Judaism & the Amer Jew-SanFran-1953-
Grabhorn Pr-sm folio-cl-4to-ltd to 1500c
(5d1) 15.   (5r0) 10.50   (5h5)   12.50
REICHMANN,FELIX comp-Christopher Sower, Sr 1694 to 1758-
Phila-1943-wrps-79p   (4m4)   10.00
REID,A MAX-Mohawk Valley-1902-444p-photo   (5zz0)   15.00
REID,ALASTAIR-Ounce Dice Trice-Bost-(1958)-4to-drwngs by
Ben Shahn-1st ed   (5r9,dj)   15.00
REID,ARTHUR-Remin of the Revolution-Utica-1859-Roberts-8vo-
orig prntd wrps-1st ed   (5i0,f)   17.50
REID,B L-Art by Subtraction-Norman-(c1958)-Univ of Okla Pr-8vo-
dec cl-illus   (5b2,f,dj)   3.50
REID,C LESTOCK-An Amateur in Africa-NY-n.d.-(ca 1925)-8vo-
218p   (4a6)   5.00
REID,CHRISTIAN-After many days,a novel-NY-1877-t8vo-1st ed-
Appleton   (5m2,f)   11.50
REID,DAVID B-Ventilation in Amer Dwellings-NY-1858-120p-
27p plts-cl   (4e4,sp wn)   15.00
REID,ED-The Green Felt Jungle-NY-1963-4th prntg-o.p.(5m9)   4.50
REID,FORREST-Illustrators of the Sixties-Lond-(1928)-lg4to-cl-
g.t.-illus-1st ed   (5d3)   15.00

REID,HARVEY-Biographical Sketch of Enoch Long an Illinois
Pioneer-Chig-1884-port   (5ff7) 15. (4m4)   15.00
REID,HIRAM A-History of Pasadena-Pasadena-1895-675p-illus-
2 fldg maps-cl-Pasadena History Co   (5d6)   85.00
REID,HUGO-Acct of Indians of Los Angeles Co,Calif-Salem-1885-
Essex Inst-illus-wrps-33p   (4i7)   20.00
REID,IRA-Negro Membership in Amer Labor Unions-Nat'l Urban
League-1930-175p-wrps   (5x2)   22.50
REID,J H STEWART-Mountains, Men & Rivers, B C in Legend & Story-
Tor-1954-plts-229p   (4f9) 5. (4d2)   5.00
REID,J T-It Happened in Taos-Albuqu-1946-118p plus 63 photo plts-
1st ed   (5L2)   7.50
REID,JAS D-Telegraph in Amer-NY-1879-4to-846p   (4m2)   32.50
REID,JOHN C-Reid's Tramp-Selma-1858-Hardy-orig cl-237p-
1st ed-ex rare   (5tt0,box) 2,000. (4n4)   2,500.00
REID,JOS B-Trial of Rev John B Mahan, for felony-Cinn-1838-
88p-prntd wrps   (5g8,stn)   15.00
REID,MAYNE-Boy Hunters-Bost-1864-Ticknor&Fields-sm8vo-dec cl-
364p-plts   (5s0)   5.00
--Bruin, or Grand Bear Hunt-Routledge-(1875)-478p-plts (5s0)   5.00
--The Bush Boys-NY-1896-Putnam's-pic cov-388p   (4t5)   7.50
--Croquet-Bost-1864-12mo-frontis-orig limp wrps-48p (5m6)   6.00
--De Dochter van Den Squatter, uit het engelsch-Gouda-1877-
4 liths-cl-198p   (5c8)   10.00
--The Giraffe Hunters-NY-(1866)-298p-illus-dec cl   (5t4)   4.00
--Headless Horseman,a Strange Tale of Texas-Lond-(1866)orig cl-
2 frontis-18 plts-g. sp-2 vols-1st ed   (5z7,autg)   135.00
--same-Lond-(1865 to 1866)-orig 20 pts, 19 in orig prntd wrps-
v rare-as issued monthly   (5z7,hf mor box)   185.00
--same-NY-(1867)-408p   (5dd4)   15.00
--The Hunter's Feast-NY&Lond-(1879)-embossed cl (5m9,sp wn)   6.00
--Los Tiradores En Mexico-Mexico-1856-454p plus index-12mo-
hf calf   (5x5)   30.00
--Osceola the Seminole-NY-(1858)-illus-354p-1st Amer ed
(4b2,shake)   7.00
--The Plant Hunters-Lond-1858-1st ed-illus   (5i3)   7.50
--same-NY-(1884)-353p,(5)-illus-new ed   (5w3)   5.00
--Quadroon,or, A Lover's Adv in Louisiana-Lond-1856-8vo-
Geo W Hyde-orig orange cl-3 vols   (5zz7,lend libr lab)   125.00
--same-Lond-ca 1870-447p-illus   (5r7)   12.50
--The Scalp Hunters-1856-312p-1st ed   (5r1,sp reglued,rub)   10.00
--The War Trail-NY-(1857)-1st ed-489p-cl
(4b2,wn shake) 7.50   (5jj9)   10.00
--The White Chief-NY-(1860)-12mo-408p   (5dd4,edges wn)   12.00
--Wild Horse Hunters-NY-1877-16p-self wrps-Beadle's Half Dime
Libr   (5h1,fox)   10.00
--Wild Life-NY-1859-408p-orig cl-1st ed   (4j6)   22.50
--The Wood Rangers-NY-1883-illus-456p   (4b6)   10.00
--The Young Voyageurs-Lond-1854-1st ed-illus   (5i3,vg)   10.00
--same-Bost-1854-Ticknor&Fields-12 illus-360p-frontis-11 plts-cl
(5p1,sp wn)   12.50
REID,ROBT A-Puget Sound & West Washington-Sea-1912-192p-illus-
map   (5L2) 12.50 (5aa0,4g6,4t1)   8.50
--Sights & Scenes at Lewis & Clark Centennial Expos-Portland,Ore-
1905-pict stiff wrps-(94p) plts-6½ x 4 3/4   (5r0)   7.50
REID,ROBY L-Assay Office & Proposed Mint at New Westminster-
Victoria-1926-wrps-101p-13 plts-Arch of BC   (5yy9)   17.50
REID,S J-Sketch of Life & Times of Rev Sydney Smith-1885-plts
(5L7)   4.50
REID,S J-John & Sarah, Duke & Duchess of Marlborough-plts
(5L7,spots)   5.00
REID,SAMUEL C JR-Scouting Expeditions of McCulloch's Texas
Rangers-Phila-1860-reprnt-251p-illus   (5g5)   25.00
--same-Phila-1890-251p-cl   (5h7)   8.50
REID,T W-The Book of the Cheese-Lond-1901-200p-photos-4th ed
(5g9,lacks e.p.)   6.00
REID,THOS-Treatise on Clock & Watch Making-Phila-1832-476p-
orig cl-papr labl-20 fldg plts at back-1st Amer ed (5m3,rbkd) 85.00
--same-Glas-1839-hf lea-19 fldg plts-466p-8vo-7th ed (5bb0)   80.00
REID,THOS MAYNE SEE REID,MAYNE-
REID,W MAX-Lake George & Lake Champlain-NY-1910-illus-
381p-2 fldg maps   (5tt5) 12.50 (4t4) 20. (4n2)   16.50
--The Mohawk Valley,its Legends & its History-NY-1901-Putnam-
lg8vo-cl-455p-photos   (5t7) 17.50   (5j5,f)   20.00
--Old Fort Johnson-1906-illus-233p   (4n2)   20.00
--The Story of Old Fort Johnson-NY-1906-illus-240p
(5m6,ex-libr) 10.   (5t7,4m2)   12.50
REID,WHITELAW-After the War,a Southern Tour,May 1,1865 to
May 1,1866-Cinn&Lond-1866-8vo-7 plts-3 qtr calf-lea labls-
raised bands-1st ed   (5m6)   50.00
--Ohio in the War-Cinn-1868-cl-2 vols (5h2) 35. (4k2,wn)   25.00
REIDE,THOS-Treatise on Duty of Infantry Officers & Present System
of Brit Military Discipline-Lond-1798-12mo-238p-calf
(4a6, v wn)   35.00

USED BOOK PRICE GUIDE

REIGART,J F-Life of Robt Fulton-Phila-1856-plts-297p (5yy0) 42.50
REIK,HENRY OTTRIDGE-Tour of America's Nat'l Parks-NY-(1920)-
    209p-photos   (5s4,pres) 6.00
REILLY,C H-McKim,Mead & White-NY-1924-illus-24p-8vo-
    Masters of Arch Ser   (5ww3) 15.00
REILLY,JOS J-Of Books and Men-NY-1942-273p (5n4) 4.00
REILLY,O T-The Battlefield of Antietam-Hagerstown-c1915-34p-
    wrps-illus   (5j6) 3.00
REILLY,PAUL-Intro to Regency Architecture-Lond-1948-96p-
    8vo-cl-48 plts-Art/Technics   (5m5) 10.00
REIMANN,GEUNTHER-The Myth of the Total State-NY-1941
                                             (5x7) 4.00
REIMERS,A F-De Venditione Illicita Fructuum in Herbis-Halae
    Magdeburgicae-1738   (5r4,rbnd) 15.00
REIN,DAVID M-S Weir Mitchell As A Psychiatric Novelist-NY-
    (1952)   (5mm2,dj) 7.50
REINACH,SALOMON-Orpheus,Hist of Religions-NY-1930
                                (5x7) 6.50   (5j5) 7.50
REINER,IMRE-Modern & Historical Typography-NY-1946-illus-
    127p-8vo-bds-1000c printed   (4c1) 7.50
REINHARD,CHAS DE-Report at large of Trial of Chas de Reinhard
    for Murders-Montr-1819-JasLane-340p-orig gray bds
                                (5w8,4 lvs in facs) 350.00
REINHARD,JOHN R-The Old French Romance of Amadas Et
    Ydoine-Durham-1927   (5mm2) 6.00
REINSCH,PAUL S-Intellectural & Political Currents in the Far
    East-Bost-1911-HoughtonMiff-396p   (5x9,fade) 5.50
REINTHALER,FRANZ-Artificial Silk-Lond-1928-276p-illus-
    enlrgd&rev ed   (4e4) 7.50
REIS,A BATALHA-Vinho De Pasto -Lisboa-1900-355p-2nd ed,rev
                                             (5w1) 15.00
REIS,BERNARD J-False Security-NY-1937-Equimox Coop Pr-362p
                                             (5p0) 4.25
REISCHAUER,EDWIN O-The US & Japan-Cambr-1951-8vo-cl-357p
                                (5t2,f,dj) 4.00
REISNER,ED H-Evolution of the Common School-NY-1935-illus
                                             (5t4) 5.00
--Nationalism & Education Since 1789-NY-1925-575p (5w5) 5.00
REISNER,R G-Bird-NY-1962-R8vo-illus   (5x2,dj) 8.50
REITER,H W-The Merry Gentlemen of Japan-NY-1935-Bass-8vo-
    120p-frontis-11 plts   (5p1) 6.50
REITLINGER,HENRY SCIPIO-Old Master Drawings,a handbook-Lond-
    1922-Constable-188p-lg4to-hf cl-t.e.g.   (5m5,shake) 110.00
REITMAN,BEN L-The Second Oldest Profession-NY-1931-
    Vanguard Pr-266p   (5p9) 4.00
REITZ,DENEYS-Afrikander-NY-1933-Minton,Balch-320p (4t5) 10.00
--Commando-Lond-1929-Faber&Faber-331p-1st ed-3rd impression
                                (4t5,fox) 7.50
--same-2nd ed-rev 1935   (4t5,autg) 10.00
--No Outspan-Lond-1943-Faber&Faber-photos-maps(2 fldg)-288p
                                (5 tt5,sl fade,nick) 6.50
REITZ,ROSETTA-Mushroom Cookery-NY-(1945)-206p (5c9,mint) 4.00
REJECTED STONE,THE-or Insurrection vs Resurrection in Amer-
    by a Native of Virginia-Bost-1861-12mo-orig wrps-132p-1st ed
                                (5m6) 7.50
--same-Bost-1862-orig cl-2nd ed (5q8) 9.50
REJON,MANUEL CRESCENCIO-Observaciones del diputado...
    contra los Tratados de Paz-Queretaro,Lara-17 April,1848-
    62p,(2)-8vo-Spanish calf   (5L1) 200.00
RELACAM DO COMBATE-que entre si tiverao tres Naus du guerra
    Inglezas,com outras tres de Franca nos mares de America-
    Lisboa-1755-(Domingo Gonsalves)-sm4to-8p-limp bds-wdcut-
    ex rare   (5L1) 225.00
RELACION DEL VIAGE HECHO-por las Goletas Sutil y Mexicana
    en el ano de 1792 para reconocer el Estrecho de Fuca-Madrid-
    1802-Imprenta Real-8vo-186p-Atlas of 2 lvs,9 maps & 8 plts
    (mostly fldng)-lg4to-2 vols-calf-ex rare (5L1) 2,000.00
RELANDER,CLICK-Drummers & Dreamers-Caldwell-1956-332p plus
    index-illus-1st ed   (5L0,mint,dj) 10.00
RELATION HISTORIQUE DE L'EXPEDITION-contre Les Indiens de
    l'Ohio-Amsterdam-1769-Rey-8vo-hf roan-2 fldg maps-4 plts
    (2 fldg)-1st French ed   (5n9) 185.00
RELATION DE LA PRISE-des Forts de Choueguen ou Oswego & de
    ce qui s'est passe cette anne en Canada, 1756-(NY,1882)-8p-
    4to   (5w8) 100.00
RELATIONS DES JESUITES-contenant ce qui s'est passe de plus
    remarquable dans les Missions des Peres etc-Quebec-1858-3 vols-
    hf mor   (5s9) 195.00
RELATIONS DE LA LOUISIANE-et du Fleuve Mississippi-Amsterdam-
    1720-Bernard-12mo-calf-fldg map-14 plts-hf mor-2nd prntng
    in French   (5n9,box) 185.00
RELIGION AMONG AMER MEN-Committee on War & Religious
    Outlook-(Study in US Army)-NY-1920   (5x7) 4.50

RELIGION OF NATURE DELINEATED-Lond-1725-prntd by S Palmer-
    4to-calf-(B Franklin employed as a typesetter)
                                (5i0,stns) 75.00
--same-Lond-1726-prntd by Sam'l Palmer-4to-calf-index (5x3,f) 30.00
RELIGIOUS MONITOR & EVANGELICAL REPOSITORY-Vol 12
    Jun 1835 to May 1836-Albany-1835,36-384p-lea bkd bds
                                (5h2,crack) 7.50
RELIQUES OF ANCIENT ENGLISH POETRY-Phila-1823-3 vols-
    Jas E Moore-(T Percy)-1st Amer ed   (5v2,f) 125.00
RELYEA,PAULINE S-Diplomatic Relations Between the US & Mexico
    under Porfirio Diaz,1876 to 1910-Northampton,Mass-1924-
    91p-stiff wrps   (5n4) 10.00
REMARKABLE SHIPWRECKS-or Collection of interesting accounts of
    Naval Disasters,selected from Authentic Sources-Hartf-1813-
    Andrus&Starr-12mo-calf-419p   (5ss2,wn) 22.50
REMARKS ON ART OF MAKING WINE-Lond-1816-261p-hf calf-
    (JMcCulloch)   (5w1,rbnd,sl soil) 48.50
REMARKS ON AUCTION SYSTEM-wi an exam of report of exec
    committee on auction regulations-NY-1831-Elliott&Palmer-8vo-
    orig plain wrps-1st ed   (5i0) 20.00
REMARKS ON MR MASON'S TREATISE UPON TEA-Lond-1745-24p-
    disbnd-(J N,Surgeon)   (5w1) 28.50
REMARKS MADE ON A SHORT TOUR-betw Hartford & Quebec in
    Autumn of 1819-NewHav-1824-16mo-3 qtr lea-443p-2nd ed wi
    addi & corr-(B Silliman)   (5t4) 17.50
REMARKS UPON BANK OF THE US-Exam of Report of Comm of Ways
    & Means,Apr 1830-By a Merchant-Bost-Feb 1831-47p-
    orig prntd wrps-(D Henshaw)   (5m3,pres) 47.50
REMARKS UPON CONTROVERSY BETW MASS& SO CAR-by a
    friend to the union-Bost-1845-21p-wrps   (5x2) 27.50
REMARKS UPON GEN HOWE'S ACCOUNT-of his Proceedings on
    Long Island in Extra Gazette of Oct 10,1776-Lond-1778-
    for Fielding&Walker-8vo-54p-hf calf-Second Ed(so stated on
    t.pg)   (5L1) 75.00
REMARQUE,ERICH MARIA-Im Westen Nichts Neues-Berlin-1919-
    8vo-orig gray cl-1st ed   (5ee9) 30.00
--Three Comrades-Lond-n.d.-1st ed in English (5tt7,dj,f) 5.00
REMBAO,ALBERTO-Lupita,Story of Mexico in Revolution-NY-
    (c1935)-Friendship Pr-8vo-cl   (4a3) 6.00
REMBRANDT-Paintings of-Vienna-n.d.-(Phaidon Pr)-R8vo-plts-
    Bredius,ed   (5ii3) 22.50
REMEMBER WM PENN-Tercentenary Memorial-Harrisburg-1945-
    2 bks in 1-172p,78p-illus   (5h9,mint) 4.50
REMINGTON & SONS,E-The Type Writer,manufactured by-
    (1875?)-self wrps-front illus of machine-15p,(1)-illus on
    last pg   (5h8,vg) 27.50
REMINGTON,FREDERIC-Crooked Trails-NY-1898-Harper&Bros-
    pic cl-8vo-151p-illus by auth-1st ed (5x5,bkstrp stns) 35.
    (4a0,cov stns,ALS tip in) 200. (5h4,fox) 35. (5L2,f) 75.00
--same-NY-1899-illus-2nd ed-scarce   (5L3) 20.00
--same-NY-(1898)-150,(1)p-cl-Boy Scout Ed-(publ later)
    (5h7,cov soil) 7.50 (5s4) 8. (5kk6) 8.50
--Done in the Open-NY-1902-folio-bds-illus-intro by Wister
                                             (5ii2) 20.00
--same-NY-1903-Collier-folio-bds-illus   (5ii2) 12.50
--same-NY-1903-illus-pict bds-not paged-lg folio
    (5ee3,vg) 12.50 (5jj9,edge wear) 15. (5s4,bkstrp tn) 20.00
--same-NY-1904-folio-dbl pg col illus-hf cl-bds (5dd5,cov soil) 20.00
--Drawings by-NY-1897-Robt Howard Russell-61 plts-g.-obl folio-
    orig pict cov-scarce   (5hh4,cov soil,rub) 185.00
--Fredk Remington's Own West-NY-1960-Dial Pr-254p (5p9) 5.00
--John Ermine of the Yellowstone-NY-1902-illus-orig pict cl-1st ed
    (4j6,pres) 125. (5p5,f,5L2) 25. (5mm2) 22.50
--Men with Bark On-NY-1900-1st ed
    (5j6) 22.50 (5r9,f) 20. (5x5,fox) 25.00
--same-NY-1901-illus-209p-32 plts   (5L3,f) 17.50
--A Painter of American Life-Brooklyn-1943-8vo-spiral bndng-
    photos-port-ltd to 500c   (5q0,box) 12.50
--Pony Tracks-NY-1895-8vo-cl-1st ed of auth's 1st book
    (5L2,5t0) 75. (5j2,f) 135. (5d3,5m4,sl wn,5gg6) 100.00
--same-Columbus-1951-269p-(NY 1895) facs reprnt (5k2,dj) 5.00
--Song of Hiawatha-Bost-(1895)-wi 13 Remington illus-180p
                                (5s4,ex-libr,fair) 9.00
--Sundown Leflare-NY-1899-illus-1st ed   (4m2) 30.00
--Way of an Indian-NY-1906-251,(1)p-cl-1st ed,2nd issue(5y0) 22.50
REMINGTON,MARY MARGARET-Nature Fairy Stories-NY-(1902)-
    illus-12mo-1st ed   (4j3,f) 10.00
REMINISCENCES OF CHICAGO-Lakeside Classics-Chig-green cl-
    16mo
--During the Civil War-frontis-194p-#12   (5p1) 15.00
--During the 40s & 50s-frontis-137p-#11 (5p1,wtrstn) 5.00
--During the Great Fire-fldg frontis-140p-#13 (5p1) 15.00

180

REMINISCENCES OF–Chicago During Great Fire–Chig–1915–
140p–cl (5h2) 10.00

REMINISCENSE OF CIVIL WAR–Woman's Aux of Grant Co Vet
Assn–Blmngton–1902–46 lvs plus ads–ports–wrps–scarce
(5h1,soil) 10.00

REMINISCENCES OF A FIDDLE DEALER, THE–Bost–1925–t8vo–illus–
170p (5p6,f) 12.00

REMINISCENCES OF THE FRENCH WAR–wi New Engl Rangers–
Concord, NH–1831–illus–bds–273p–Luther Roby
(5t4,lacks port,broke) 100.00

REMLAP, L T, ed–The Life of Gen'l US Grant–Chig–1885–illus–
orig cl (5L3) 4.75 (5q8,chip) 4.50

REMSBURG, G W–The Pan American Diet Book–KansCty–1930–320p
(5c5) 3.50

REMUSAT, JEAN PIERRE ABEL–Iu Kiao Li: or, the two fair cousins,
A Chinese novel–Lond–1827–Hunt&Clarke–2 vols in 1–12mo–
hf calf–1st ed in Engl (5xx6) 60.00

REMY, JULES–Journey to Great Salt Lake City–Lond–1861–fldg map–
2 vols (5dd4,rbnd) 57.50 (5x5,fray) 80. (4t8) 95.00
––Voyage Au Pays Des Mormons Relations–Paris–1860–plts–map–
orig wrps–cl–2 vols–1st ed
(4n4,box) 115. (5n9,hf calf) 65. (5i0) 60.00

RENARD, G–Life & Work in Modern Europe–1926–plts (5L7) 5.00

RENAUD, HELENA–The Cook Book of the Stars–NY–(1941)–394p–
lg4to (5g9,f) 8.50

RENCHER, A–Indian Disturbances in Territory of New Mexico–Wash–
1861–17p–HED 24 (4j4) 22.50

RENDALL, VERNON–Wild Flowers in Literature–Lond–1934–
372p (5w3,pres) 12.50

RENDU, M LE CHANOINE–Theory of the Glaciers of Savoy–Lond–
1874–Macmillan–Forbes, ed–216p–cl (5d7) 6.00

RENDU, VICTOR–Ampelographie Francaise...(Premier et) Deuxieme
Partie–Paris–1854–col map–68(of 69) col plts–folio–calf&bds–
1st ed (5z9,vg,rbnd) 1,750.00
––same–Paris–1857–576p–map in facs–hand col–2nd ed (5w1) 25.00

RENEWAL OF YOUTH–Lond–1911–Cr8vo–wrps–(AE)–#7 of the
Orpheus Series–1st ed (5ss7,cov soil) 20.00

RENFROW, WM C–Report of Gov of Okla Territory–Wash–1893–
11p–prntd wrps (5n4) 12.50

RENGGER, J R–Reign of Dr Jos Gaspard Roderick de Francia, in
Paraguay–Lond–1827–bds–calf bk & cor–1st ed in Engl
(5ss5,ex-libr,wn) 45.00

RENIERS, PERCEVAL–The Springs of Virginia–ChapelHill–1941–
col illus–301p–1st ed (5p9) 7.50 (5w5,dj) 8.75

RENISON, ROBT J–One Day At A Time–Tor–1957–322p–ports–plts
(5dd0) 5.00

RENNER, F–A Selected Bibliography on Management of Western
Ranges, Livestock & Wildlife–Wash–1938–US Dept of Agri #281–
441p plus index–wrps–scarce (5L2) 15.00

RENOUIL, YVES–Dictionnaire Du Vin–Bordeaux–1962–1374p–
errata enclosure–6 col maps (5w1) 18.50

RENOWNED GUY, EARL OF WARWICK–(wrp title)–Lond–c1750–
wdcuts–chapbook–plt verso p23 (5rr7) 40.00

RENOWNED HISTORY & ADVENTURES OF ROBINSON CRUSOE–
Manchest–(c 1830)–ASwindells–chapbook–16p–11 illus–
3 3/4 x 6" (5aa2) 10.00

RENOWNED HISTORY–of Richard Whittington & his Cat–NewHav–
1825–Sidney's Pr–12mo–22p (5c8,lacks self wrps) 15.00

RENOWNED HISTORY OF THE 7 CHAMPIONS OF CHRISTENDOM–
and their sons–Lond–1824–450p–frontis–calf–32mo–red lea–
labels–g. (5p1,f bndg) 25.00

RENSCH, H E–Chronology for Tumacacori Natl Monument–Berkeley–
1934–4to–stiff wrps–84p–Civil Wks Program–scarce (5g5) 15.00
––Historic Spots In Calif–Southern Co, 1932–Valley & Sierra Co,
1933, Counties of Coast Range, 1937–Stanford U–(3 vols)(4n1) 40.00
––Historic Spots in California–Stanford U–1932–map–8vo–1st ed
(4g6) 6.00

RENVILLE & REDWOOD COUNTIES–Sketches of monuments &
tablets in, Indian outbreak of 1862–Morton–1902–illus–wrps
(5g4) 5.00

RENVILLE, J & SONS–Dakota Dowanpi Kin, Hymns in Dakota or
Sioux Language–Bost–1842–71p–1st ed–rare–wrps
(4L2,new wrps) 100.00

RENVILLE, MARY BUTLER–Thrilling Narrative of Indian Captivity–
Minnpls–1863–52p–1st ed–rare (4t8,re-wrp) 350.00

RENWICK, DR AM–Wanderings in the Peruvian Andes–Lond–(1939)–
228p–illus–cl–Blackie&Son (5d7) 10.00

RENWICK, JAS–Applications of the Science of Mechanics to
Practical Purposes–NY–1840–12mo–327p (5n7,fox) 8.50
––Outlines of Geology, for use of Junior Class of Columbia College–
NY–1838–Henry Ludwig–96p & slip of errata–12mo–orig cl
(5L1,soil) 25.00

REPEAL OF FUGITIVE SLAVE ACTS–Report of Select Comm
38th Congr Rep Com #24–Wash–1864–32p–wrps (5x2) 20.00

REPINGTON, LT COL C–The First World War 1914 to 1918–Bost–
1920–2 vols (5xx5) 7.50 (5w5) 8.75

REPLOGLE, C–Among Indians of Alaska–Lond–1904–182p–illus
(4b9) 25.00

REPLY OF MESSRS DE GASPARIN ETC TO LOYAL LEAGUE OF
NY WITH ADDRESS OF LEAGUE–NY–1864–30p–wrps–
Loyal Pub Soc (5x2) 25.00

REPORT OF BOARD OF NEGRO EDUCATION–& Evangelization
of Christian Church for 1893, 1894–Louisvl, KY–1895–40p–
wrps (5x2) 35.00

REPORT OF COMM OF INDIAN AFFAIRS–Fiscal Year Ended
Jun 30, 1909–Wash–1909–GPO (5x5) 7.50
––same–Fiscal Year Ended June 30, 1911–Wash–1912–GPO (5x5) 7.50

REPORT OF COMM OF PATENTS FOR YEAR 1860–Wash–1861–504p–
HED48–rare (4a5) 22.50

REPORT OF JOINT SELECT COMMITTEE–Appointed to Investigate
into Alleged Frauds & Corruption–Madison–1858–48p, 320p–wrps
(5h7,lack bk wrp) 15.00

REPORT OF SELECT COMM RELATIVE TO SOLDIERS' NAT'L
CEMETERY..PENNA–Mar 31, 1866–Harrisburg–1864–8vo–orig cl–
108p, 3p–2 fldg maps–Singerly&Myers, State Prntrs–rare printing
in book form of Lincoln's Gettysburg Address (5t2) 125.00

REPORT OF THE STATE TRIALS–Court Martial Held at Montreal in
1838,9: Late Rebellion in Lower Canada–Montr–1839–Vol 2 only–
565p–contem bds (5w8,rbkd) 185.00

REPORT ON ALLEGED OUTRAGES–In Southern States–by Select
Committee on Senate, Mar 10, 1871–Wash–1871–R8vo (5x2) 27.50

REPORT ON TRUSTEES OF AFRICAN CHURCH–in village of Rochester–
Rochester–1828–Marshall&Dean–12mo–disbnd–1st ed–frontis–rare
(5i9,stitch loose) 45.00

REPORTS OF AGENTS– & Others in Charge of Indians–(Carlisle, 1908)–
Indian Press–wrps (5r7,lacks t.pg) 15.00

REPORTS OF COMM ON CONDUCT OF WAR–Ft Pillow Massacre
& Returned Prisoners–Wash–1864–GPO (5x2) 40.00

REPORTS OF EXPLOR & SURVEYS–Route for a Railroad from
Mississippi River to Pac Ocean–Vol 2–1855 (5x5) 35.00
––same–Vol 3–1856 (5x5) 35.00
––same–Vol 4–1856 (5x5) 30.00
––same–Vol 5, Explorations in Calif 1853 (5x5) 45.00
––same–Vol 6–1857 (5x5) 35.00
––same–Vol 7–1857 (5x5) 35.00
––same–1855 thru 60 – 12 vols in 13 (5s2,f) 300.00

REPORTS OF MILITARY ENGINEERS–of Engagement of Enemy's Iron
Clad Fleet with Forts & Batteries...Harbor of Charleston, on 7th
of Apr, 1863–(Charleston, 1863)–10p (5m3,dmpstn) 55.00

REPP, THORL GUDM–Historical Treatise on Trial by Jury–Edinb–
(1832)–206p (5t4) 7.50

REPPLIER, AGNES–Books & Men–Bost–1888–12mo–bds–cl bk–papr labl–
1st ed of auth's 1st book (5mm1) 12.50 (5gg6) 15.00
––Compromises–Bost–(1904)–HoughtonMiff–277p (5p9) 4.00
––8 Decades, Episodes & Essays–1937–Houghton (5F1,dj) 5.00
––In Our Convent Days–Bost–(1905)–HoughtonMiff (5x0) 4.00
––Junipero Serra–GardenCty–1933–Dblday&Doran–312p–cl
(5r1,fade) 8. (5b2,f,dj,box) 15.00
––Pere Marquette, Priest, Pioneer & Adventurer–NY–(1929)–298p
(5h9) 6. (5L7) 3.50 (5s4,dj,rprd) 5. (5L2) 4.00
––Philadelphia, the Place & the People–NY–1898–392p–1st ed–
illus–g.t. (5h9) 7.50
––same–NY–1925–392p (5w0) 5.00
––To Think of Tea–Bost–1932 (4g9) 7.50
––same–Lond–(1933)–254p, (4) (5w1) 5.00

REPPY, A–Historical & Statutory Background of Law of Wills,
Descent & Distri, Porbate & Admin–Chig–1928 (5ff4) 7.50

REPRESENTATIVE NEW MEXICANS–Denver–1912–339p–illus–
hf mor–CSPeterson, pub (5a9,f) 7.50

REPTON, HUMPHREY–Art of Landscape Gardening–Bost–1907–plts–
col frontis–252p–8vo (4a2,ex-libr) 7.00

REPUBLIC OF RIO GRANDE–& Friend of the People–Republica de
Rio Grande y Amiga de los Pueblos–Vol 1, #2–Matamoros–
6 Jun, 1846–newspaper–2 lvs–folio–(32 x 22 cm)–text in
Engl & Span (5L1,dmpstns,sl loss of text) 125.00

REPUBLICAN ADDRESS–to the Free Men of Connecticut–n.p.–
(1803)–8vo–16p–(unbnd) (5m6) 15.00

REPUBLICAN CAMPAIGN TEXT BOOK, 1908–Phila–(1908)–548p–
narr 12mo–wrps–Dunlap Pr (5j5) 10.00

REPUBLICAN SCRAP BOOK–Bost–1856–8vo–stitchd–wrps–80p
(4c1) 10. (5r0) 15.00

REPUBLICAN VALLEY OF KANSAS–Homes for Thousands in Beautiful
ClayCenter, KS–(1878)–prntd in Topeka–wrps–29p plus 3p ads–
v rare (4L2) 50.00

REQUA,RICHARD S-Old World Inspiration for Amer Architecture-
Denver-1929-Monolith Portl Midwest Co,illus-144 plts-
sm thk folio   (4m9,dj)   35.00

RES GESTAE(INDIANA STATE BAR ASSN)-Vol 1 thru 14-1956 to
1970-bound   (5ii7,rbnd,lacks Vol 11#12)   175.00

RESCH,PETER-Shadows Cast Before-Kirkwood-1948   (5a8)   4.00

RESOLUTIONS,LAWS & ORDIN-Relating to Pay Commutation of
Half Pay....& Promises Made by Congress to Officers & Soldiers
of Revolution-Wash-ThosAllen,pub-1838-506p plus index-lea-
rare   (5L3)   37.50

RESOURCES OF CALIF-SanFran-Oct 1875-folio-8p
                                 (5g3,stn,unopnd)   5.00
--same-SanFran-Dec 1875   (5g3)   5.00
--same-SanFran-May,1881-sm folio   (5g3)   5.00

RESTARICK,REV HENRY B-Hawaii,1778 to 1920 from Viewpoint of
a Bishop-Honolulu-1924   (5x5)   17.50

RESTAURANT,RAYMOND-Hippocrate de l'Usage du Boire a la
Glace-A Pezenas-1677-(20)p,131p,(2)-wrps-2nd ed,rev
                                 (5c5,wrps)   50.00

RESUME POUR JOHN PRATT-n.p.-n.d.-capitaine du navire
Americain Le Federaliste de Charlestown-19p-4to-stitched-
(ca 1798)   (5L1)   50.00

RETAIL GROCERS COOK BOOK-Newark,NJ-n.d.-(ca 1925)-40p-
ads-wrps   (5g9)   2.50

RETANA,W E-Origenes de la Imprenta Filipina-Madrid-1911-
204p,2p-lg4to-calf bkd bds-ltd to 127c-Libreria Gen'l De
Victoriano Suarez   (5L8,mint)   25.00

RETI,RUDOLPH-Thematic Process in Music-NY-Macmillan-1951-
362p   (5p7)   4.50

RETURNS OF DESERTIONS,DISCHARGES,DEATHS,ETC-in Maine
regiments for months of Jun,Jul & Aug,1865-148p-wrps (5L3) 10.00

REUBEN,WM A-Hon Mr Nixon & Alger Hiss Case-(NY Action Books,
1956)-70p plus 72p appendix-illus-pict stiff wrps-5½ x 8½ (5r0) 10.00

REULEAUX,F-The Constructor,A Hand Book of Machine Design-NY-
1905-4to-illus-312p   (5t4)   15.00

REUSS,FRANCIS X-Biographical cyclopaedia of Catholic hierarchy
of the US-Milwkee-1898   (5g4,ex-libr)   6.00

REUSS,J D-Alphabetical Register of Authors in Great Britain,
Ireland & Amer wi Catalogue etc-Berlin-1791-459p-orig calf
          (5ii2,wi catalog) 50.   (4g2,f)   27.50

REUTER,E B-The Amer Race Problem-NY-1927   (5x2)   25.00
--Race & Culture Contacts-NY-1934-1st ed   (5x2)   20.00

REVEILLE,THOS-The Spoil of Europe-NY-c1941   (5x7)   5.00

REVERE,JOS W-Keel & Saddle-Bost-1872-Osgood-orig cl-360p
     (5L3,fox,hf lea) 16.50 (5m3,f) 25. (5cc6)   17.50
--same-Bost-1873-Osgood-360p (5c1) 20. (4d9,autg orig photo) 12.50
--Naval Duty in Calif-Oakland-1947-Biobooks-map-plts-
ltd to 1000c   (5x5)   25.00

REV DR WILLOUGHBY & HIS WINE-NY-1869-Nat Temp Soc-
458p-(Mrs M S Walker)-1st ed   (5x4)   17.50

REVERIE,THE-or,a flight to the paradise of fools-Lond-1763-
TBecket&P A DaHondt-2 vols-12mo-calf&bds-(Chas Johnstone)-
1st ed   (5xx6,f)   175.00

REVERIES OF A BACHELOR-or a Book of the Heart-NY-1850-
Baker&Scribner-cl-(D Mitchell)-1st bndng   (5ss3,chip)   25.00

REVERIES OF AN OLD MAID-NY-n.d.-188p-illus-reprnt (5x4)   20.00

REVES,EMERY A-Democratic Manifesto-NY-c1942   (5x7)   4.00

REVES,H F-The Reeves Family-1951-409p (5mm3) 8.50 (5m2)   10.00

REVIEW OF CONTEMPORARY LAW-   -Vol 1 thru 16-
1954 to 1969-unbnd -(Bruxelles)   (5ii7,lacks Vol 4#1)   100.00

REVIEW OF MILITARY OPERATIONS IN NO AMERICA-Lond-
1757-4to-(Wm Livingston)   (5e2)   950.00
--same-Lond-1757-New England(NewHaven)-reprntd 1758-This
Amer ed rare   (5e2)   875.00

REVIEWS OF JEFFERSON DAVIS-Constitutionalist(His letters,papers
& speeches)-Jackson-1924-Mississ Dept of Archives & History
                                 (5x2)   22.50

REVILLE,A-Les Religions du Mexique,de l'Amerique Centrale et du
Perou-Paris-1885-412p-buck   (5r7,rbnd)   20.00

REVISTA COLOMBIANA DE DERECHO INTERNACIONAL-Vol 1-
(1947(all publ)-bound   (5ii7)   20.00

REVISTA DE DERECHO PRIVADO-(Madrid)-Vol 1 thru 50 - 1913 to
1966-index 1913 to 56 in 3 vols-unbnd   (5ii7)   400.00

REVISTA JURIDICA-(Puerto Rico Univ)-Vol 1thru 39-1932 to 1970-
bound   (5ii7,rbnd)   585.00

REVOLUTION DE L'AMERIQUE-A Londres-(probably The Hague)-
1781-chez Lockier Davis-8vo-182p-orig wrps   (5L1)   50.00

REVOLUTION,THE-in New England Justified-& etc-Bost-1773-
sm8vo-59p-reprntd by Isaiah Thomas-v rare(5L1,rprd) 45.(5s9)150.00

REVUE CRITIQUE DE LEGISLATION ET DE JURISPRUDENCE DU
CANADA-Montreal-Vol 1 thru 3-1871 to 75(all publ)-bilingual-
bound   (5ii7,ex-librr,rub)   40.00

REVUE DE JURISPRUDENCE-Montreal-Vol 1 thru Vol 48 -
1894 to 1942(all publ)-bound   (5ii7,rebnd)   720.00

REVUE DE LEGISLATION ET DE JURISPRUDENCE-Montreal-
Vol 1 thru 3-1845 to 48(all publ)   (5ii7,rebnd)   45.00

REVUE DU BARREAU DE LA PROVINCE DE QUEBEC-Vol 1 thru 29-
1941 to 69   (5ii7,ex-librr,mixed bndg)   425.00

REVUE DU NOTARIAT-(Quebec)-Vol 1 thru 71-1898 to 1969
               (5ii7,ex-librr,mixed bndg)   700.00

REVUE LEGALE-(Montreal)-Vol 1 thru 21-1869 to 1892-n s,
Vol 1 thru 48-(1895 thru 1942) 1943 to 1969-96 vols
               (5ii7,mixed bnds) 1,200.00

REWALD,JOHN,ed-Degas,Works in Sculpture-Complete Catalogue-
NY-1944-Pantheon-144p-112 plts-lg4to-cl (5m7,shake)   50.00

REX,STELLA H-Choice Hooked Rugs-NY-1953-250p,(4)-illus
                                 (5n7)   6.50

REXFORD,EBEN E-Home Floriculture-Rochester-1890-226p-illus
                                 (5s7)   6.50

REXROTH,KENNETH-An autobiographical novel-GardenCty-1966-
Dblday-1st prntng   (5m2,dj)   6.00
--The Spark in the Tinder of Knowing-Cambr-(1968)-12mo-wrps-
1st ed-Pym Randall,publ-ltd to 200c,nbrd,autg (5ss7,mint)   12.50

REX,CAPT-Voyage from France to Cochin China-Lond-1821-
3/4 lea-dec bds   (5yy6)   25.00

REY,GUIDO-The Matterhorn-Lond-1907-TFisherUnwin-cl-mntd plts-
1st ed   (5d7)   17.50
--Peaks & Precipices-Lond-(1914)-TFisherUnwin-128p-illus-cl
                                 (5d7,fade)   15.00

REY,JAN-The World of Dance-Lond-n.d.-4to-photos-unpgd(5c3) 7.50

REYBAOUD,CHAS-Le Bresil-Paris-1856-244p-prntd wrps
                          (5r7,dmpstnd)   12.50

REYBURN,WALLACE-Some of it Was Fun-Tor-1949-199p-illus
                                 (5aa0)   5.00

REYES,GEN RAFAEL-Two Americas-Lond-n.d.-TWernerLaurie-
8vo-cl-g.t.-illus   (4a3,lt stn)   15.00

REYES,LIC RODOLFO-Mining Laws of Mexico-(c1910,-Amer Book
& Pr Co-12mo-buck   (4a3)   15.00

REYNARD,ELIZ-The Narrow Land-Bost-1934-326p-illus-map
1st ed   (5w0)   10.00

REYNARD THE FOX-renowned Apologue of Middle Ages,in rhyme
(by S Naylor)-Lond-1845-Longmans-251p-qtr lea rubbed-lettrs
in red,green & blue-1st ed   (5c8,rub)   20.00
--History of Reynard the Fox,wi some account of his friends &
enemies-verse by FSEllis-Lond-1897-illus devices by
Walter Crane-orig prntd cl-D Nutt   (5c8,unopnd,fade)   17.50
--Reynard the Fox-Bost-(1901)-pictured by JJMora-Dana Estes & C0-
24 tntd plts   (5c8)   7.50
--Story of-Lond-1861-TNelson-illus-6 plts from stuffed animals-
g.cl   (5c8,f)   17.50

REYNARDSON,C T S BIRCH-Down the Road-Lond-1875-col plts-
pic cl-1st ed   (5mm1,sl fray)   25.00

REYNIER,GUSTAVE-Le Roman Sentimental avant L'Astree-Paris-
1908-406p-cl   (5p6,librr stmp)   8.00

REYNOLDS,BUTCH-Broken Hearted Clown-(Lond)&NY-1955-8vo-
cl-21 illus   (5p5,dj)   10.00

REYNOLDS,C-Hudson Mohawk, Gen & Family Memorials-1911-
4 vols-illus   (5t9)   27.50

REYNOLDS,CHAS B-Old St Augustine-StAugustine-1891-12mo-cl
                                 (4c1)   7.50
--The Oldest House in the US-NY-1921-Foster&Reynolds-8vo-32p-
illus-wrps-2nd ed   (4a3)   7.50

REYNOLDS,CUYLER-Albany Chronicles-(1906)-817p-illus
               (5t9) 12.50   (4n2,rbnd)   17.50

REYNOLDS,E W-True Story of Barons of the South-Bost-1862-240p-
cl   (5h2) 10.   (5r0)   7.50

REYNOLDS,ELDER GEO-Are We of Israel?-SaltLkCty-1883-55p
                          (5t3,lacks wrps)   25.00
--The book of Abraham-SaltLkCty-1879-DeseretNews-8vo-
orange prntd wrps-1st ed   (5i9,cov tn)   17.50

REYNOLDS,ELON G,ed-Compendium of Hist & Biog of Hillsdale Co,
Mich-Chig-n.d.-(1930?)-460p-mor-not in Streeter
               (5h2,6p handwritten hist laid in)   50.00

REYNOLDS FAMILY ASSO-14th,15th,18th,23rd Annual Reunions-
1901 to 1929-wrps-v.p.   (5t9) ea   2.00
--same-1925 to 34-6 vols-wrps   (5v3) 6 vols   4.00

REYNOLDS,FRANCIS J-Story of Great War-NY-1916 to 20-
(Collier)-8 vols-illus-maps-cl   (4b7,rub)   37.50
--The US Navy from Revolution to Date-NY-1918-Collier-obl 4to-
144p-photos by Taylor-later cl   (5ss2,f)   12.50

REYNOLDS,FRANK W-Thru the Years to 70-n.p.-(1957)-map-
illus-284p plus 2 pt index-cl-8½x11-mimeo-100c priv prntd
                                 (5r0)   10.00

REYNOLDS,FREDK-The dramatist,a comedy in 5 acts-Dublin-1790-
PByrne-12mo-disbnd-hf t.-v scarce-1st ed   (5x3)   45.00
--Cheap living,a comedy in 5 acts-Dublin-1798-PByrne-disbnd-
1st Dublin ed   (5x3)   7.50
REYNOLDS,GEO-Complete Concordance to Book of Mormon-
SaltLkCty-1900-851p   (4t3)   45.00
REYNOLDS,H J-The world's oldest writing,man's earliest known
literary relics-Chig-(1938)-4to-dec cl-328p-index-illus
(5p6,f,dj)   16.00
REYNOLDS,HELEN W-Dutchess County Doorways-NY-1931-280p-
plts-204 photos   (5w7)   35.00
--Marriage & Deaths Dutchess County 1778 to 1825-1940-Vol 4-
140p-Dutchess Co Hist Soc   (5zz3)   15.00
--Poughkeepsie,The Origin & Meaning of the Name-1924-82p
(4n2)   9.50
REYNOLDS,J A-Heraldry & You-NY-c1961-184p-col illus
(5t9) 7.50   (5w5,dj)   6.50
REYNOLDS,J H-Case of Judge John C Watrous-Wash-1860-286p-
HR2   (4a5)   25.00
REYNOLDS,J J-The Allen Gang,Outlaws of the Blue Ridge Mntns-
Balt-1912-Ottenheimer-182p-ads-12mo-col pict wrps(5j5)   50.00
REYNOLDS,J N-Address on subject of Surveying & Exploring Exped
to Pac Ocean & South Seas-NY-1836-Harper&Bros-300p-
orig plain wrps   (5tt0,pres)   40.00
--Voyage of the US Frigate POTOMAC-NY-1835-cl(5c1,rbnd)   55.00
REYNOLDS,JAS-Ghosts in Amer Houses-NY-1955-Bonanza-229p-
illus   (5p7)   5.00
--Ghosts in Irish Houses-NY-1947-illus(some col)-4to-1st ed
(4j3,autg)   15.00
--same-NY-(1956)-276p-4to-col plts   (5c3)   5.00
REYNOLDS,JOHN-Pioneer history of Illinois-Belleville-1852-
N A Randall-12mo-orig cl-348p
(5i9,shake) 120.   (5m3,sl tn,fox)   150.00
REYNOLDS,JOHN-History of the 19th Regiment,Mass Volunteer
Infantry 1861 to 1865-Salem-1906-456p   (4j4)   12.50
REYNOLDS,JOHN E-In French Creek Valley-Meadville-1938-
illus-maps-352p   (4m4)   25.00
REYNOLDS,SIR JOSHUA-Discourses Delivered in the Royal Academy-
Bost-1821-2 vols in 1-12mo-calf-lea labl   (5m6)   15.00
REYNOLDS,SIR JOSHUA-Portraits-NY-1952-1st ed-181p-12 plts
(5aa0)   8.50
REYNOLDS,L B-Little Journeys Into Storyland-Negro Juvenile-
Nashvl-1947-illus-Southern Pub Co   (5x2)   12.50
REYNOLDS,M H-Desc of John & Sarah-1924-506p   (5mm3)   20.00
REYNOLDS,MATTHEW G-Spanish & Mexican Land Laws-New Spain
& Mexico-StL-1895-8vo-sheep-331p & index-errata slip
preceding preface-emendation tip in pg 29-scarce   (5h5)   40.00
REYNOLDS,MYRA-The Learned Lady in England-Bost-1920-8vo-
illus-cl-488p   (5t2)   6.00
REYNOLDS,QUENTIN-Courtroom-NY-1950 (5t0) 4.   (5x7)   3.50
--Fiction Factory or from Pulp Row to Quality St-NY-(1955)-illus-
col plts   (5v2,mint,dj) 12.50   (5y2,rubber stmps)   5.50
--I, Willie Sutton-NY-1953-Farrar   (5p9)   4.00
--They Fought for the Sky-NY-(1957)-illus-1st ed (5yy6,dj)   6.00
REYNOLDS,PHILIP KEEP-The Banana-Bost-1927-181p-map-photos
(5s7)   7.50
REYNOLDS,STEPHEN-Alongshore-NY-1910-320p-illus-dec cov
(5s1,libr labls)   4.00
REYNOLDSON,JOHN-Practical & Philosophical Principles of Making
Malt-Newark (Eng)-1808-293p,(1)-bds   (5w6,sp wn)   18.50
REZEK,ANTOINE I-History of Diocese of SaultSteMarie & Marquette-
Chig-1906, 07-4to-2 vols-deluxe ed-lea g.e.
(5mm7,autg,rub)   50.00
REZNIKOFF,CHAS-The Jews of Charleston-Phila-1950-illus
(5m2,dj)   6.00
--Louis Marshall,Champion of Liberty-Phila-1947-2 vols (4m4)   13.50
--Testimony-NY-(1934)-12mo-cl-papr labl-1st ed (5ss7,sl fade) 10.00
REZZORI,GREGOR VON-Tales of Maghrebinia-NY-1953 (5p7)   3.25
RHEAD,G W-Chats on costume-Lond-1906-Unwin-304p-8vo-cl-
117 illus   (5m5)   15.00
--same-Lond-(1926)-8vo-cl-304p-illus   (5t0)   6.00
RHEAD,LOUIS-Bait Angling for Common Fishes-NY-1907-152p-illus
(5t4)   7.50
--Bold Robin Hood & his Outlaw Band-NY&Lond-(1912)-285p
(5t4)   7.50
--Book of Fish & Fishing-NY-1908-306p-cl-illus (5t2,5a9)   4.00
RHEES,WM J-Account of the Smithsonian Institution-Catalogue of
the Indian Gallery-Wash-1858-58p-ads   (5s2)   17.50
--Catalogue of Publications of the Smithsonian Insti, 1846 to 1882 wi
index of Articles-Wash-1882-328p   (5j4)   25.00
--Manual of Public Libraries,Institutions & Soc in the US & British
Prov of NoAmer-NY-1859-667p   (5j4)   12.50

RHEES,WM J (continued)
--Smithsonian Institution:documents relative to its origin & history,
1835 to 99-1901-2 vols-map-buck   (5L7,rbnd)   17.50
RHETT,BLANCHE S-200 Years of Charleston Cooking-NY-(1934)-
L Gay,ed-rev ed-305p   (5g9)   8.50
RHEUMATISM:THE CAUSE & THE CURE-Jackson,Mich-n.d.-(ca1917)-
Magic Foot Draft Co   (5b9,vf)   3.50
RHIND,D W G-The High Priest of Israel-Lond-1868-folio-32p text-
2 hand col plts   (5x7,bkstrp dmgd)   20.00
RHINE,J B-New Frontiers of the Mind-(1937)-Farrar (5ww4)   8.50
RHOADS,THOS Y-Battle Fields of the Revolution-Bost-1856-
Crown&Co-336p-illus   (5mm8)   6.00
--same-Cinn-1879-illus-336p   (5L3)   8.25
RHODE,BILL-This Business of Carving-NY-1941-125p-drawings
(5c0)   3.50
RHODE ISLAND AMER & PROVIDENCE GAZETTE-Prov-Jan 2,1827
to Dec 26, 1828-206 issues-newspaper-thk lg folio-3/4 lea
(5m3,sp chip)   40.00
RHODE ISLAND & PROVIDENCE PLANTATIONS-Constitution of
State of-Prov-1842-24p-unbnd as issued   (5h2)   5.00
RHODE ISLAND & PROVIDENCE PLANTATIONS-in New England,
Records of the Colony of-Prov-1857-Vol 2, 1664 to 77-609p-
index-lea   (5h9,cov wn)   13.50
RHODE ISLAND BAR ASSOC-Report 1902, 1907, 1909, 1910,1912-
bound   (5ii7) ea   7.50
RHODE ISLAND,BOOK OF-(Prov)-1930-299p-cl   (5h2)   5.00
RHODE ISLAND,GENERAL LAWS OF-Prov-1909-rev of 1909-
sm thk4to-calf-16p,1408p   (5t2)   15.00
--Index to revision of 1909-Prov-1909-thk sm4to-calf-1622p
(5t2,lt stn)   15.00
RHODE ISLAND,GUIDE TO SMALLEST STATE-Bost-1937-photos-
maps-pkt map-e.p.map-479p-plus index-1st ed-Amer Guide Ser-
WPA   (4L5,dj)   10.00
RHODE ISLAND HISTORICAL SOC-Collection of...Vol 1 Containing
Roger Williams' Key to the Indian Language-Prov-1827-
John Miller-163p-orig wrps-1st ed   (4c4,sp dmgd)   150.00
RHODE ISLAND IMPRINTS, 1727 to 1800-NY-1949-8vo-cl-
J E Alden,ed   (4c1)   25.00
RHODE ISLAND IN WAR WITH SPAIN-Prov-1900 Freeman-417p-illus
(5mm8)   5.00
RHODE ISLAND,PICTURESQUE-Pen & Pencil Sketches of Scenery
& Hist of Its Cities & Towns-1881-304p   (5t9)   12.50
RHODE ISLAND-Public Laws of State of...& Providence Plantations
as revised Jan,1798-Prov-1798-Carter&Wilkinson-652p-8vo-
orig sheep-5th rev-300c prntd   (5L1)   55.00
RI SOLDIERS & SAILOR'S HIST SOC-Personal Narr of Battles of
the Rebellion-Prov-1878 to 1915-7 series-orig wrps-ltd
(5mm8,lacks 1 nbr)   475.00
RHODE,IRMA-The Viennese Cookbook-NY-1951-260p (4g9)   5.00
RHODE,JOHN-The Case of Constance Kent-NY-1928-cl-278p-
frontis-Famous Trials Ser   (5p9) 5.   (5t2)   4.00
RHODES,E C-Elementary Statistical Methoda-Lond-1933-8vo-cl-
243p-38 diagrams   (5t0,f,dj)   5.00
RHODES,EUGENE MANLOVE-Best Novels & Stories of-Dearing,ed-
Bost-1949-551p   (5g2,5L0,dj)   10.00
--Beyond the Desert-Bost-1934-cl-8vo-237p-1st ed (5g2,f,dj)   35.00
--Bransford in Arcadia-NY-1914-12mo-cl-236p-frontis-1st ed-
scarce   (5g2,f) 40.   (5L2)   35.00
--The Desire of the Moth-1916-149p-illus-1st ed   (5r1,f)   25.00
--Good Men & True-NY-1910-HTDunn,illus-12mo-cl-1st ed of
auth's 1st book   (5gg6,pres)   75.00
--The Little World Waddies-(1946)-illus-t8vo-cl-prntd by
Carl Hertzog-ltd to 1000c-scarce (5h4,vf,dj) 22.50 (5t3,f,dj)   50.00
--Say Now Shibboleth-Chig-1921-The Bookfellows-12mo-bds-
cl bk-papr labls-ltd to 400c   (5j3)   90.00
--Stepson's of Light-Bost-1921-1st ed (5x5,pres to Jim Tully)   35.00
--The Trusty Knaves-Bost-1933-1st ed   (5x5,dj)   20.00
--West is West-NY-1917-HKFly Co-illus by Harvey Dunn
(5x5, 10 li pres to Jim Tully)   60.00
RHODES,FREDK LELAND-Beginnings of Telephony-NY-1929-261p-
illus   (5w4) 7.50   (5y2)   12.50
--John J Carty,An Appreciation-NY-1932-8vo-orig bds-cl bk-
priv prntd-1st ed   (5ss5)   12.50
RHODES,HARRISON-Amer Towns & People-NY-1920-lg8vo-cl-
16 plts-1st ed   (5p5)   10.00
RHODES, H J-Desc of John & Hannah (Graves) of Gt Barrington-
1957   (5mm3)   25.00
RHODES,HARRISON-Guide to Florida for Tourists,Sportsmen &
Settlers-NY-1912   (4j4)   6.50
RHODES,LT HENRY-Uncle Sam's Blue Jackets Afloat...Foreign
Waters-Bost-(1897)-244p-illus-cov   (5s1,rprd)   3.00
RHODES,HENRY A-Memoirs of a Merchant-Seattle-1952-170p-
photos-ltd ed   (5s4,pres)   7.50

RHODES,JAS A-Short Hist of Ohio Land Grants-n.p.-n.d.-
(Col-1956)-36p-wrps   (5h1)   2.00
RHODES,JAS FORD-History of the US from Hayes to McKinley-
NY-1919-map   (5s8,wn)   3.00
--Lectures on the Amer Civil War...Univ of Oxford in Easter &
Trinity Terms 1912-NY-1913-206p-fldg col map-1st ed
(5s9) 5.   (5w9)   8.50
--McKinley & Roosevelt Administrations 1897 to 1909-NY-1922-
418p   (5L7)   7.50
RHODES,MAY D-Hired Man on Horseback-Bost-1938-illus-cl-
1st ed   (5L2,dj) 20.   (4p2)   22.50
RHODES,RUFUS R-Annual Report of Commissioner of Patents-
Richmond-1865-9p   (5j6)   15.00
RHODES,SUSIE R-Economy Administration Cook Book-NY-(1913)-
illus-frontis-322p-ports   (4g9)   8.50
RHODES,W H-Case of Summerfield-Tomoye Pr-1907-12mo-vel&bds-
Nash,prntr   (5ii2)   12.50
RHODIUS,APOLLONIUS-Argonautica-Athens-1957-transl by
E P Coleridge-illus-ltd to 1500c,nbrd,autg (5F1,f,box) 45.00
RHYMERS'CLUB-The Second Book-Lond-1894-sm4to-orig buck-
1st ed-ltd to 650c   (5p5,cov spots)   25.00
RHYMES FOR LITTLE READERS-Bost-1890-Lothrop-obl 4to-
col plates bds-25 lvs   (5v0)   8.50
RHYMES FOR THE NURSERY-NewHav-(ca1845)-Sidney Babcock-
wdcuts-16mo-16p-orig   wrps   (5c8)   8.50
RHYMING DICK & THE STROLLING PLAYER-Shewing Advantages
of Societies for Visiting the Sick-Notthingham-c1810-C Sutton-
rare 8p chap book   (5v2)   10.00
RHYNE,WILLEM TEN-Dissertatio de Arthritide,Mantissa Schematica,
de Acupunctura,et Orationes Tres-Lond-1683-R Chiswell-
22 lvs,334p-4 plts(3fldg)-sm8vo-vel   (4L7,rprd) 1,250.00
RHYS,ERNEST-A London Rose & Other Rhymes-Lond-1894-
Elkin Mathews & John Lane-8vo-cl-1st ed-ltd to 500c
(5b0,sl soil)   5.00
RHYS,J-The modern pedagogue,or,rustic reminiscences-Lond-1868-
Saunders&Otley-2 vols in 1-8vo-orig cl-1st ed   (5xx6)   17.50
RIBAUD,ROGER-Le Maitre de Maison De Sa Cave A Sa Table-
Paris-1945-illus-203p-prntd wrps-sq8vo-ltd ed   (5w6)   8.50
--same-Paris-1952-240p,(7)-photos-bds   (5w1)   5.50
RIBAUT,JEAN-The whole & true discoverye of Terra Florida-
Deland-1927-facs reprnt ed of 1563-illus-cl&bds-500c prntd
for Florida State Hist Soc   (5g8,unopnd)   10.00
RIBEIRO,L-Brazilian Medical Contributions-RiodeJaneiro-1938-
photos-181p-wrps-8vo   (4p6,sp tn)   25.00
RIBELLE,CHAS DE-Les Recits Amusants-Album de la jeunesse et
du foyer-Paris-1860-Amable Rigaud-sm4to-92p-frontis-pict cl-
7 hand cl liths   (5p1,t.lf rprd)   35.00
RICARD,ADOLPHE-Eloge de Jean Raisin-Paris-(1953)-281p-
sm12mo-lea bk   (5w6)   12.50
RICCARDI,SARO JOHN,comp-Penna Dutch Art & Architecture-
NY-1942-15p-orig wrps   (5jj3)   8.50
RICCI,MATTHEW-China in the 16th Century-NY-1953-Random
(5p0,stn)   7.50
RICCI,SEYMOUR DE-Louis XIV & Regency Furniture & Decoration-
NY-(1929)-illus-4to-cl-215p   (5q0)   20.00
--Louis XVI Furniture-Lond&NY-(1915)-illus-4to-cl-256p (5q0) 20.00
RICCIOTTI,G-Life of Christ-1948   (5L7)   7.50
RICCOUS-Le Bougainville de la Jeunesse,ou Nouvel Abrege des
voyages dans l'Amerique -Paris-(1834)-Martial Ardant-
12mo-328p-bds-3 plts-4th ed   (5c8,cov wn)   20.00
RICE,A H-The Shenandoah Pottery-Strasburg,Va-1929-279p-
photos-7 in col   (5w7)   8.50
RICE,ALICE HEGAN-The Buffer-NY-(c 1929)-Century-8vo-cl
(5b2)   3.50
--Calvary Alley-NY-1917-Century-8vo-cl-illus (5b2,f,dj)   4.50
--Lovey Mary-NY-1903-12mo-pic cl-1st ed   (5p1)   7.50
--Mrs Wiggs of the Cabbage Patch-NY-1901-16mo-cl-1st ed of
auth's 1st book-(2000c publ)   (5gg6,autg,ALS)   25.00
RICE,ALLEN T,ed-Remin of Abraham Lincoln by Distinguished
Men of his Time-NY-1886-656p   (5j2,pres) 15.   (5j6)   5.00
--same-NY-1888-cl-ports   (5q8)   5.00
RICE,BERTHA M-Popular Studies of Calif Wild Flowers-SanFran-
(1920)-127p-col photos-bds   (5x5) 5.   (5s7)   6.50
RICE,C S-Letters & Friendships of Sir Cecil Spring Rice, a Record-
Bost-1929-S Gwynn,ed-2 vols   (5r4)   10.00
RICE,CLATON S-Songs of "The Mormon Way"-n.p.-(1930)-71p-
8 x 4½-wrps   (5s4,cov soil)   3.00
RICE,CLAUDE T-Mines & Methods-Vol 1,#1 to Vol 1,#12-
SaltLkCty-1909-12 issues bnd in 1-wrps-1st year complete
(5x5)   45.00
RICE,CRAIG-45 Murderers-NY-282p   (5p9)   4.00
RICE,E A-A Text Book of Domestic Economy-Lond-n.d.-232p (5c9) 3.50

RICE,EDWIN W-Our 66 Sacred Books-Phila-1892-159p (5j4)   4.00
RICE,EDWIN WILBUR-After 90 Years-Phila-1924-167p-cl-illus-
Amer Sunday School Union   (5r0,autg)   7.50
RICE,ELMER-Imperial city, a novel-NY-1937-CowardMcCann-
1st ed   (5m2,sl wn)   5.00
RICE,ELMER A-Voyage to Purilia-Lond-1930-288p   (4c9)   7.59
RICE,ELMER L-The Adding Machine,a Play in 7 Scenes-GardenCty-
1923-143p-frontis   (5t7,pres)   6.00
RICE,H D-Reminiscences Read before Congreational Pioneer Soc-
Topeka-n.d.-8vo-wrps   (4c1)   20.00
RICE,HARRY E-Eva & the Evangelist-Bost-(c 1908)-Roxburgh-
8vo-illus-pict cl   (5b2,sp fade)   10.00
RICE,HENRY MOWER-Proceedings at unveiling of statue of-Wash-
1916   (5ss1)   5.00
RICE,HOWARD C-Barthe'lemi Tardiveau,a French Trader in the
West-Balt-1938-87p plus index-illus-fldg map-1st ed (5L0)   8.50
RICE,W G-Carillons of Belgium & Holland-NY-1914-illus-232p-
8vo   (5bb0)   9.50
RICE,WALLACE-Under the Stars & Other Songs of the Sea-Chig-
1898-Way&Williams-12mo-wrps-ltd to 1000c   (5b2,f)   8.50
RICE,WM-Indian Game-Lond-1884-illus-col liths-221p (5t7)   12.50
RICE,WM-Manual of the Geology of Connecticut-Hartf-1906-
273p-wrps   (5a8)   3.00
RICE,WM B-LosAngeles Star,Southern Calif's 1st Newspaper-
LosAng-1941-GlenDawson-ltd to 200c   (5x5)   15.00
RICH,ADRIENNE CECILE-A Change of World-NewHav-1951-
12mo-bds- 1st ed of auth's 1st book   (5ss7,vf,dj)   30.00
RICH,BEN E-Mr Durant of Salt Lake City-SaltLkCty-1893-1st ed
(4a9,lacks e.p.) 7.   (5L0,name)   6.00
--same-Chig-n.d.-16mo-220p-blue cl   (5m8)   4.50
RICH,DAN'L CATTON-Seurat &the Evolution of La Grande Jatte-
1935-Univ of Chig Pr-illus   (5x0)   7.50
RICH,E E-History of Hudson's Bay Co,1670 to 1870-Lond-1958 to 1959-
Hudson's Bay Rec Soc-ports-maps-2 vols   (5nn2,5w8)   45.00
--Hudson's Bay Co Minutes(1671 to 74,1679 to 84)-Champlain Soc-
1942 to 6-port-3 vols-3 Series(complete)   (5aa0)   50.00
RICH,EDWIN G-Hans the Eskimo-Bost-1934-Rockwell Kent,illus-
288p-juvenile   (5ss1,wn,ex-libr)   4.00
--Why So Stories-Bost01919-sq8vo-illus-dec cl-g.t.-col frontis-
plts-207p   (5nn2)   6.50
RICH,GEO-Desc of Jonathan Rich-1892-39p-stapled (5mm3)   12.50
RICH,JOHN L-Face of South America-NY-1942-sm4to-illus-
(Aer Geog Soc)   (5yy6)   10.00
RICH,LOUISE D-The Coast of Maine-NY-1956-CrowellCo-308p
(5b9)   4.50
--We Took to the Woods-Phila-1942-21 plts-1st ed (5b9,mint,dj) 4.50
RICH, M B-History of the First 100 Years in Woolrich,Pa-n.p.-
1930-236p-illus   (5m2)   8.50
RICH MEN OF MASSACHUSETTS-Bost-1852-Redding-224p,4to-cl-
mor bk-2nd ed   (5t2,crack) 18.50   (5L1,wn)   30.00
RICH,NORMAN-The Holstein Memoirs,Vols 1&2-Cambr-
1955 & 57-cl-216p,404p   (4t7,f dj)   17.50
RICH,WALTER H-Feathered Game of the Northeast-NY-(1907)-
432p-tall 8vo-illus   (4b6)   20.00
RICHARD EDNEY & THE GOVERNOR'S FAMILY-Bost-1850-
Phillips,Sampson&Co-12mo-illus-cl-1st ed   (5x1,rbnd)   25.00
RICHARD,EDOUARD-Acadia-NY-(c 1895)-2 vols-frontis-orig cl-
Home Book Co   (5m3)   35.00
RICHARD,LENA-New Orleans Cook Book-Bost-1940-145p (5c0)   5.00
RICHARD,O J-Rapport Sur Le Concours De Viticulture Americaine-
Poitiers-1889-39p-wrps   (5w1)   5.00
RICHARDS,A N-Methods & Results of Direct Investigations of
Function of the Kidney-Balt-1929-64p   (5m2)   5.00
RICHARDS, CAROLINE C-Village Life in Amer 1852 to 1872-NY-
1913-8vo-cl-plts-enlrgd ed   (5p5)   15.00
RICHARDS,ELLEN H-The Chemistry of Cooking & Cleaning-Bost-
1910-186p-3rd rev ed   (5w7,ex-libr)   7.50
--Food Materials & Their Adulterations-Bost-1886-183p-12mo
(5c0,pg tn)   7.50
RICHARDS,EVA ALVEY-Artic Mood-Caldwell-1949-282p-illus-
1st ed   (4g7) 2.00 (5ss1) 4.50   (5w5) 4. (5L0,dj)   5.00
RICHARDS, F DeB-Random Sketches-Phila-1857-344p-illus(5m1) 4.50
RICHARDS, FRANKLIN D-Compendium of Faith & Doctrines of
Church of Jesus Christ of Latter Day Saints-Liverpool-1857-
lea-243p-rare   (4t3,chip)   35.00
--The Pearl of Great Price-Liverpool-1851-56p-removed-fld plt
(5m3)   32.50
RICHARDS, GRANT-Author Hunting By An Old Literary Sports
Man-NY-1935   (5w5)   7.50
RICHARDS,I A-Nations & Peace-NY-1947-159p-cl-1st ed (5t2)   4.50
--Practical Criticism-NY-1929-8vo-cl-376p-1st ed   (5t0)   7.50
RICHARDS,J E,ed-Litchfield Co (Conn) Honor Roll of Revolutionary
Soldiers-1912-233p   (5mm3)   6.00

RICHARDS, J M-The Bombed Buildings of Britain-NY-Oxford-1943-4to-140p-illus (5t4) 10.00

RICHARDS, JOHN T-Abraham Lincoln,The Lawyer Statesman-1916-HoughtonMiff-illus (5ww4,dj) 10.00

RICHARDS, JOS W-Aluminium-Lond-1890-511p-cl-illus (5h8,wn) 5.00

RICHARDS, LAURA E-Captain January-Bost-1891-1st state-(ca1890)- (4a9,hng repr,cov soil) 16. (5jj6,sl chip) 75.00

--Julia Ward Howe, 1819 to 1910-Bost-1915-HoughtonMiff-Vol 1 (of 2 vols)-lg papr ed (5ss9) 20.00

--Melody-Bost-n.d.-12mo-90p-frontis-pict cl-Dana Estes (5p1) 4.50

--Mrs Tree-Bost-(1902)-12mo-illus-1st ed (5yy6) 6.00

--Sketches & Scraps-Bost-1881-Estes&Lauriat-sq8vo-pictures by Henry Richards-bright cols-pict bds-1st ed of auth's 1st book (5c8,f) 20. (4c3) 50.00

--Stepping Westward-NY-1935-illus-8vo-bds-405p (5t0) 4.00

--When I Was Your Age-Bost-1894-1st ed-illus (5r9,pres) 15.00

--The wooing of Calvin Parks-Bost-(1908)-Dana Estes-illus-pict cl-1st ed (5m2) 4.00

RICHARDS, PAUL-Book of Breads, Cakes,Pastries,Ices & Sweetmeats especially adapted for Hotel & Catering Trades-Chig-1907-2nd ed-168p-lea-port (5g9) 7.50

RICHARDS, RALPH-Headquarters House-FtScott,Kansas-1954-frontis-photo-76p-sprial bndng-wrps-sm ltd ed (5dd9) 10.00

RICHARDS STANDARD ATLAS-of City of Worcester-1922-31 dbl pg col maps-frontis-lg folio (4t2) 40.00

RICHARDS, T ADDISON-Amer Scenery Illustrated-NY-(1854)-Leavitt&Allen-4to-orig red wi green g. centerpeice-g.e.-310p-32 views (5j5) 50.00

--Appleton's Illustrated Hand Book of Amer Travel-NY-1857-illus-fldg maps (1 col)-orig cl-1st ed (4m4) 25.00

RICHARDS, T P-NY Commercial List-NY-Jn A Gray-1857-111p, plus (5i1) 10.00

RICHARDS, WM C-Henry Ford, Last Billionaire-NY-1948-Scribner-422p (5p7) 4.50

RICHARDSON, A E-Decorative details of the 18th century by Wm & Jas Pain-Lond-1948-Tiranti-8vo-cl-80p of measured drwngs (5m5) 6.00

--London Houses from 1660 to 1820-n.d.-(ca1911)-Lond-plans-illus-87p-8vo-plts (5m5) 18.50

--Regional Architecture of West of England-Lond-1924-illus-188p-lg4to (4a2) 10.00

--The Student's Letarouilly-Lond-1948-Tiranti-24p & 88 plts-lg4to-bds-cl sp-Scopas student's ed (5m5) 14.00

RICHARDSON, A W-The Old Inns of England-Lond-(1934)-photos-map-118p,32p (5w1,sp fade) 8.50

RICHARDSON, ALBERT D-Beyond the Mississippi-Hartford-1867-illus-1st ed-572p (5s4,rprd,5t0,5w5,crack) 10. (5jj3,wn) 12.50

--A Personal History of US Grant-Hartford-1869-560p-illus(5L3) 8.50

--same-Hartf-1885-630p-32 engr-facs-6 maps-cl (5h2) 7.50

RICHARDSON, BENJ W-On Alcohol-NY-1876-190p-cl (5h7) 7.50

--A Ministry of Health & other addresses-NY-1879-orig cl (5q8,wn) 5.50

--Temperance Lesson Book-NY-1883-220p-cl (5h7) 5.00

--same-NY-1888 (5h7,ex-libr) 3.00

RICHARDSON, C E-Chas Miner,a Penna Pioneer-Wilkes Barre-1916-195p-illus (5t7) 12.50

RICHARDSON, CHAS F-Amer Literature 1607 to1885-NY-(1888)-2 vols in 1-8vo-cl (5t2) 5.00

RICHARDSON, CAPT-Horsemanship-Lond-1853-illus-138p,24p (5yy8,hng rprd) 10.00

RICHARDSON, D A-Manual of Mexican Law-Denver-1910 (5ff4) 12.50

RICHARDSON, DOROTHY-Interim-Lond-(1919)-1st ed (5yy6,dj) 15.00

RICHARDSON, DOROTHY M-Deadlock-Lond-(1921)-1st ed (5r9,dj) 15.00

--Interim-Lond-(1919)-1st ed (5r9,dj) 17.50

--Revolving Lights-Lond-(1923)-1st ed (5yy6,dj) 15.00

RICHARDSON, E-History of Woonsocket-Woonskt-1876-264p-cl (5h2,5t9) 10.00

RICHARDSON, E P-Washington Allston,a Biog-NY-1948-Crowell-225p-plts-crown 8vo-wrps (4a0) 8.00

RICHARDSON, EVELYN N-We Bought an Island-Phila-1964-281p (5a1) 3.50

--We Keep a Light-Tor-1947-260p-illus-map (5dd0) 4.50

RICHARDSON, FRANK H-Motion Picture Handbook for Managers & Operators-NY-1910-186p-1st ed (4c9) 17.50

--same-432p-2nd ed (4c9) 14.95

--same-702p-3rd ed (4c9) 14.95

--same-942p-4th ed (4c9) 12.95

--Richardson's Handbook of Projection-NY-1929,30-illus-1247p-3 vols (4c9) 22.50

RICHARDSON, F H-Along the Iron Trail-Rutland-1938-illus (5m2) 6.50

RICHARDSON, G B-Report of Reconn in Trans Pecos Texas, N of Tex & Pac Rwy-Austin-1904-119p-wrps (4a5) 8.50

RICHARDSON, GEO-Book of Ceilings-n.p.-(1900s)-folio-48 plts-1774 reprnt-folder (4a2) 10.00

RICHARDSON, HARRY-Dark Glory-NY-1947-wrps-210p-1st ed (5z5,underline) 7.50

RICHARDSON, HENRY HANDEL-2 Studies-Lond-1931-Ulysses Pr-cl bkd bds-ltd to 500c,autg (5ss3) 20.00

RICHARDSON, HESTER D-Sidelights on Maryland History-Balt-1913-2 vols-1st ed-scarce (4m4) 40.00

RICHARDSON, JAS-Wonders of Yellowstone-NY-1873-256p-cl (5h7,rub) 8.50

--same-NY-1874-illus-fldg map (5s4,v wn) 10.00

--same-NY-1912-illus-256p-map (5s4) 4.50

RICHARDSON, JAS D-A Compilation of Papers & Messages & Papers of the Presidents, 1789 to 1897-Wash-1896-10 vols-orig cl-illus-ports-1st ed (4b6) 65. (5w9,sl dmpstn) 17.50 (5h9,vg) 32.50

--same-Wash-1896 to 99-GPO-10 vols (5yy0) 22.50 (5ww4,Vol 1 v wn) 25.00

--same-c1897-in 20 vols-mor-gilt (5w0,f bndg) 40.00

--same-1789 to 1905-part mor-8vo-gilt-11 vols (5g6,f) 45.00

RICHARDSON, JOHN-Fauna Boreali Americana-Lond-1829-orig bds-300p-28 plts(Landseer) (4n4) 385.00

RICHARDSON, MAJ JOHN-Movements of the British Legion, with Strictures on Course of Conduct Pursued by LtGen Evans-to close of Mar, 1837-Lond-1837-illus-hf calf (5w8) 100.00

--The Canadian Brothers, or A Prophecy Fulfilled-Montr-1840-2 vols-orig cl (5w8) 175.00

RICHARDSON, JOHN-Arctic Searching Expedition-NY-1852-516p-illus-hf lea (5ss1,scuff) 10.00

RICHARDSON, LEON BURK, ed-An Indian Preacher in England-Hanover, NH-1933-lg8vo-cl-376p-illus-1st ed (5t2,dj,f) 8.00

RICHARDSON, LYON N-History of Early American Magazines 1741 to 89-NY-1931-414p (4g2) 17.50

RICHARDSON, MARGARET STIMSON-A Handful of Nuggets-Austin,Texas-(1952)-illus-144p (5dd5) 5.00

RICHARDSON'S PAMELA-or Virtue Rewarded-Lond-1775-4 vols-vel wi red & Black sp labls-10th ed (5p6,vg) 30.00

RICHARDSON, R-Memoir of Josiah White,his connection with intro of coal & iron-1873-illus-buck (5L7,rbnd) 10.00

RICHARDSON, RICHARD-Genealogy of the Richardson Family of the State of Delaware-1878-60p (5m2) 17.50

RICHARDSON, ROBT-Memoirs of Alexander Campbell-Nashville-1956-2 vols in 1 (5p8,ink underline) 7.50

RICHARDSON, ROBT C, JR-West Point-NY-1917-8vo-354p-illus-1st ed (4a6) 5. (5ss5) 10.00

RICHARDSON, RUPERT N-Texas, Lone Star State-NY-1943-590p-illus-1st ed (4j6,ex-libr) 12.50

RICHARDSON, S C-In Desert Arizona-Indep,Mo-(1938)-184p-photos-1st ed (5L2) 10.00

RICHARDSON, SAML-Clarissa, or the History of a Young Lady-Lond-1748-calf-7 vols-1st ed (4k7) 475.00

RICHARDSON, SAML-The Novels of-Phila-1902-20 vols-12mo-illus-cl (5t0) 37.50

RICHARDSON, T C-East Texas, its History & Its Makers-NY-1940-4 vols-4to (5a8,sl fade) 60.00

RICHARDSON, T D-Modern Figure Skating-Lond-(1930)-sq8vo-cl-200p-1st ed (5t2) 7.50

RICHARDSON, U-Arctic Searching Expedition-Lond-1851-2 vols-10 col plts-fldg map-wdcuts (4b9,map rprd) 150.00

RICHARDSON, W-Texas Almanac for 1867-Galveston-1866-360p-g.-orig cl (4j6) 175.00

RICHARDSON, WM H-Journal of-NY-1848-the author-96p-removed-3 plts-"3rd Ed" (5m3) 45.00

RICHARDSON, WM H-Journal of....A Private Soldier in Col Donphan's Command-NY-1848-hf mor-84p-3rd ed-rare (4n4) 350.00

RICHARDSON, WM H-Picturesque Quality of Penna German-Lancaster-1904-illus-orig wrps (5jj3,pres) 10.00

--Washington & "Enterprise Against Powles Hook"-Jersey Cty-1929-illus-4to-69p-wrps (5yy6) 10.00

RICHARDSON, WILLIS-Plays & Pageants from the Life of the Negro-1930 (5L7) 6.50

RICHARDSON'S ALMANAC, COTTOM'S EDITION, 1862-Richmond-(1861)-36p-JW Randolph (5yy3) 75.00

RICHARDSON'S VIRGINIA & NORTH CAROLINA ALAMANC, 1863-Richmond-(1862)-Wynne,Prntr-West&Johnston, Publ-36p (5yy3) 100.00

RICHARDSON'S VIRGINIA & NO CAROLINA ALMANAC, 1862-Richmond-(1861)-Wynne, Prntr-A Morris, Publ-36p (5yy3,pgs tn,loss of sm text) 25.00

RICHARDSON'S VIRGINIA & NO CAROLINA ALMANAC, 1865-Richmond-(1864)-ChasHWynne, publ-36p (5yy3) 100.00

RICHBERG,D R–My Hero–NY–1954   (5ff4)   5.00

RICHELIEU & ONT NAV CO–From Niagara to the Sea–Official Guide–1908–Montr–(1908)–144p–illus–fldg map–orig prntd wrps   (5w8)   10.00

RICHERTER,EMMA C–History of Silver Lake,Kans–n.p.–(ca 1911)–Topeka Prntg–16mo–wrps–map–20p–errata   (4t1)   12.50

RICHFIELD,IDAHO–Richfield–n.d.–(1909)–Commercial Club–12mo–wrps–32p   (4t1)   10.00

RICHINGS,G F–Evidences of Progress Among Colored People–Phila–1902–illus   (5x2)   50.00

RICHMAN,IRVING B–Calif Under Spain & Mexico–1911–541p–HoughtonMiff–pkt maps–charts–plans–1st ed   (4g6,ex-libr) 17.50   (5dd5,ex-libr,5x5,f)   30.00

––Ioway to Iowa–IowaCty–1931–State Hist Soc–8vo–cl–479p   (4t1) 7.50   (5a9)   10.00

––Rhode Island–NY–1908–fldg map–2 vols in 1   (5tt5)   15.00

––San Francisco Bay & Calif in 1776–Providence–1911–maps–cl&bds–Merrymount Pr–ltd to 125c   (5tt0) 50.   (4c1)   35.00

––The Spanish Conquerors–NewHav–(c1919)–Yale UP–sm8vo–cl–g.t.–fldg map–illus–Chron of Amer, Vol 2 (4a3) 5.   (5h9)   4.50

RICHMAN,JACOB–Laughs from Jewish Lore–NY&Lond–(1926)–372p   (5w9,5t7)   5.00

RICHMOND,BERNICE–Our Island Lighthouse–(1947)–275p–1st ed   (5e8)   4.85

RICHMOND,REV CORA L V–My Experiences While Out of My Body & My Return after Many Days–Bost–(1923)–Part 2 & 2nd ed of Part 1–sm8vo–cl–111p   (5t2)   5.00

RICHMOND,DEAN–Design for Growth–Buffalo–1960–142p (5y2)   4.50

RICHMOND DURING THE WAR–4 Yrs of Personal Observ–By a Richmond Lady–NY–1867–buck–8vo–1st ed (4m7,rebnd)   17.50

RICHMOND,ILLUSTRATED–NY–1892–36p plus covs–photos   (5b9,vf)   7.50

RICHMOND,K F–John Hayes of Dover, NH, a Book of his family–1936–2 vols–911p   (5mm3)   18.00

RICHMOND,L–The Art of Painting in Pastel–Lond–1927–187p–40 col plts   (5w5,rbnd)   20.00

––Technique of Pastel Painting–Lond–1931–1Pitman–144p–illus   (5x0)   10.00

––same–n.d.–4to–col plts   (5L7)   5.00

RICHMOND,REV LEIGH–Dairyman's Daughter,an authentic narrative abridged–NY–(ca 1830)–Amer Tract Soc–32p–orig brown wrps   (5c8,sl soil)   4.50

––same–n.p.–(Bost?)–1835–8vo–prntd at New Engl Insti for Education of Blind–Amer Tract Soc–embossed roman lettrs–(1 of the earliest books made for the blind)   (5m6,rub)   32.50

RICHMOND,MARY E–Marriage & the State–NY–1929–395p–Russell Sage Found   (5p9)   3.00

RICHMOND,REBECCA–Chautauqua, An Amer Place–NY–c1943–illus–180p–1st ed   (5w0,dj)   4.50

––A Woman of Texas, Mrs. Percy V Pennybacker–SanAnt–1941   (5a8)   7.50

RICHMOND,(VIRG)–Shockoe Hill Cemetery Records–Vol 1, 1822 to 1850–100p   (5mm3)   12.50

––same–Vol 2, 1851 to 1950–276p   (5mm3)   17.50

RICHMOND STOVE CO–Catalogue of,–Norwich–(189-?)–76p–illus–fldg bds   (5hh7)   7.50

RICHMOND–The Strangers Guide,Official Directory for City of–(Richmond)–1863–Evans&Co–orig wrps–#1,Oct,Vol 1–rare   (5r5)   150.00

––same–(Richmond)–1863–(ca 1880)–reprint–16mo–wrps (5g8)   7.50

RICHMOND,VIRG–Photogravures–NY–1895–80p–bds–illus (5j6) 12.50

RICHMOND,W KENNETH–Climber's Testament–Lond–(1950)–246p–cl–illus   (5d7)   3.00

RICHMOND WHIG,THE–Richmond,Va–Apr 13,1865–folio–8p–Vol 1,#9   (5t7)   10.00

RICHMOND,SIR WM B–Assisi, Impressions of Half a Century–Lond–1919–Macmillan–Fine Arts Soc–col illus (5i4,unopened)   25.00

RICHMOND,WM E–9 Months on a Cruise & Experiences in Nicaragua–SanDiego–1912–Pub on USS Calif–illus–8vo–106(9)p   (4g6,crack)   15.00

RICHTER,CONRAD–The Light in the Forest–NY–1953–12mo–cl–1st ed   (5d3,dj)   5.00

––The Sea of Grass–NY–1937–1st ed–orig cl   (5m1)   8.50

RICHTER,GISELA M A–Catalogue of Engraved Gems of Classical Style–NY–1920–Metr Mus of Art–232p–illus–wrps–ltd to 1000c   (5x0)   20.00

RICHTER,JEAN PAUL FRIEDRICH–Flower,Fruit & Thorn Pieces–Lond–1877–565p–lg12mo–cl   (5t2)   5.00

––Levana,or doctrine of education–Lond–1891–GeoBell&Sons–12mo–413p(24)–Bohn's Standard Library   (5p1)   4.00

RICHTOFEN,WALTER BARON VON–Cattle raising on the Plains of NoAmer–NY–1885–16mo–102p plus ads–1st ed–v scarce   (5a3) 50.   (5L2)   40.00

RICKARD,F IGNACIO–Mineral & Other Resources of Argentine Republic in 1869–Lond–1870–Longmans,Green–8vo–cl–a.e.g.   (4a3,pres)   22.50

RICKARD,J H–Services With Colored Troops in Burnsides Corps–Prov–1894–43p–wrps–Soldiers & Sailors Hist Soc or RI–ltd to 250c   (5x2)   65.00

RICKARD,MICHAEL J–Across Continent with Soakems–NY–1906–illus   (4b7)   12.50

RICKARD,MRS "TEX"–Everything Happened to Him...Tex Rickard–NY–1936–368p–port   (4a8,sl wn)   4.50

RICKARD,R H–Prospectus of Hope Copper Mining Co–NY–1864–8vo–orig wrps–6p–fldg map–1st ed   (5ss5)   15.00

RICKARD,T A–A History of Amer Mining–NY–1932–414p plus index–1 photo–maps–1st ed   (5L0)   15.00

––same–NY–(1935)–414p plus index–1 photo–maps–3rd prntng(5L2)7.50

––Journeys of Observation–SanFran–1907–illus–cl (5x5,stn,5h5) 15.00

––Retrospect, An Autobiography–NY–(1937)–illus   (5q8,dj)   9.00

––Romance of Mining–Tor–1927–illus   (5dd7,dj,lacks fly) 10.   (5dd5)   17.50

––The Stamp Milling of Gold Ores–NY–1897–260p–cl–plts–fldg plt   (5a9) 9.   (5b8)   10.00

––Through the Yukon & Alaska–SanFran–1909–392p–maps–illus   (5ss1,5r0)   20.00

RICKARDS,COLIN–Buckskin Frank Leslie–El Paso–1964–illus–Hertzog–ltd to 450c   (4c7)   17.50

RICKARDS,CONSTANTINE GEO–The Ruins of Mexico–Lond–1910–4to–mntd photos–Vol 1(all publ)   (5h5) 15.   (5r7)   27.50

RICKENBACKER,CAPT EDW V–Fighting the Flying Circus–NY–(1919)–Fredk A Stokes Co–blu cl–pic papr over cl–1st ed–port frontis   (4a6,hng weak) 10.   (5u7,pres)   18.50

––Seven Came Through–GardenCty–1943 (5x9) 1.50   (5x7)   3.00

RICKET,E–The Gentleman's Table Guide–Lond–1871–53p,(45)–illus   (5w1)   10.00

RICKETT,H W–Wild Flowers of Amer–NY–(1953)–4to–400 col plts   (5x0) 9.   (5t9) 15.   (4p8,dj)   12.50

RICKETTS,CHAS–Bibliography of Books Prntd by Hacon & Ricketts–Lond–1904–sm4to–Vale Pr–bds&cl,as issued–in red&black–frontis   (5d1)   40.00

RICKERT,EDITH–Chaucer's World–Columbia Univ Pr–NY–1948–8vo–cl–illus   (5b0,dj)   6.75

––Babees Book, Medieval Manners for the Young–NY–Xmas 1913–priv prntd(Marchbanks Pr)–frontis–slim 8vo–bds–19p–ltd to 150c   (5c8)   6.50

RICKMAN,PHILIP–A Bird Painter's Sketch Book–Lond–1931–cl–plts–4to   (5z9,dj tn)   7.50

––same–Lond–1931–cl–vel bk–t.e.g.–4to–11 col plts–150p–ltd to 125c   (4p5,autg)   52.00

––Bird Sketches & Some Field Observations–Lond–1938–cl–papr labl–32 plts–frontis–4to   (5z9)   7.50

RICKMERS,W RICKMER–The Duab of Turkestan–Oxf–1913–cl–maps–illus–4to   (5v7)   35.00

RIX,G S–Am Hist & Gen of Ricks Family–1908–184p (5mm3) 17.50

RICORD,PHILIP–Venereal & Other Diseases Arising from Sexual Intercourse–Phila–1855–calf   (5j3)   12.00

RIDDELL,CHARLOTTE ELIZ–A mad tour–Lond–1891–Bentley–8vo–orig cl–1st ed   (5xx6,vg)   22.50

––The nun's curse–Lond–1888–Ward&Downey–3 vols–8vo–orig cl–1st ed   (5xx6,lend libr)   35.00

RIDDELL,ROBT–Carpenter & Joiner,Stair Builder & Hand Railer–Lond–(c 1860)–sm folio–cl–124p–fldg illus   (5t4)   17.50

RIDDELL,W–Diary of Voyage from Scotland to Canada in 1833–n.p.–n.d.–(1932?)–wrps–32p   (4b9)   10.00

RIDDELL,W R–Bar & The Courts of Province of Upper Canada,or Ontario–Tor–1928   (5ff4)   8.50

RIDDELL,W R–The Slave in Upper Canada–n.p.–n.d.–(reprint from Journal of Negro Hist, Vol 1 #4,Oct 1919)–372p,411p–orig prntd wrps   (5w8)   10.00

RIDDELL,WM R–Life of Wm Dummer Powell–Mich Hist Comm–1924–8vo–305p–illus–cl   (5mm7,ex-libr)   15.00

––Michigan Under British Rule–Lansing–1926–493p (5 ff 7,ex-libr) 7.50

RIDDELL,WM RENWICK–Some Epigrams of John Owen–(Tor)–(1922)–4to–rprnt from Amer Bar Assoc Journal   (5nn8)   25.00

RIDDLE,A G–Alice Brand–Cleve–1875–384p–cl–Cobb,Andrews&Co imprnt   (5h7)   10.00

––Ansel's Cave–Cleve–1893–249p–cl   (5h7,pres)   10.00

––The Life of Benjamin F Wade–Cleve–1886–310p   (5n4)   7.50

RIDDLE,ALBERT GALLATIN–Recollections of War Times–NY–1895–Putnam's–380p(4)   (5mm8)   9.00

RIDDLE BOOK–for the use of children–Concord–1843–Rufus Merrill–8p of rhymes–16mo–blue prntd wrps   (5ss5)   8.50

RIDDLE,DONALD W–Lincoln Runs for Congress–NewBrunswick–1948–port–illus–217p   (5t7)   5.00

RIDDLE,GEO W-History of Early Days in Oregon-Riddle,Ore-
1920-12mo-74p-port-wrps   (5dd4)   10.00
RIDDLE,JEFF C-Indian History of Modoc War etc-n.p.-(1914)-
295p-cl-8vo (5F5,soil,corners jam) 15. (5tt0) 20. (5hh4,f) 45.00
RIDDLE,WM-Nicholas Comenius-Lancaster-1898-8vo-469p-illus-
2nd ed   (5m1) 5.   (5v0,f)   8.50
RIDEING,WM H-The Captured Cunarder-Bost-1896-8vo-pict bds-
Copeland&Day   (5b2,f)   8.50
--A Saddle in the Wild West-NY-1879-orig wrps-12mo-165p-
1st ed   (4g6,ex-libr) 17.50
RIDENOUR,PETER D-Quantrill's Raid,Aug 21, 1863-Lawrence,Ka-
1963-32p-stiff wrps   (5hh3)   3.50
RIDEOUT,ERIC H-The American Film-Lond-1937-163p-illus
                                         (4c9)   125.00
RIDEOUT,HENRY MILNER-William Jones-NY-1912-Fredk A Stokes-
illus-212p-1st ed-v scarce   (4n8)   10.00
RIDEOUT,MRS J B-6 Years on the Border-Phila-(1883)-221p-illus-
Presby Bd   (5L2)   5.00
RIDER,FREMONT-Rider's California-NY-1925-28 maps &plts-
667p-48p ads   (4n1)   10.00
RIDER HAGGARD, H-Allan's Wife &Other Tales-Lond-1920-
Longmans Green-illus-331p   (4t5)   5.00
--Maiwa's Revenge-NY-1888-Longmans Green-pic cov-216p-
Author's ed   (4t5)   5.00
RIDER,SIDNEY S-Lands of Rhode Island as they were Known to
Caunounicus & Miantunnomu When Roger Williams Came-
Prov-1904-maps-illus-8vo-1st ed   (4m7)   17.50
RIDER'S CALIFORNIA-a Guide Book for Travelers-NY&Lond-1925-
28 maps & plans-thk16mo-cl-FTCooper (comp) (5m9)   4.00
RIDGE,JOHN R-The Life & Adventures of Joaquin Murieta-
Norman-1955-159p   (5k2,dj)   3.50
RIDGELY,DAVID-Annals of Annapolis....1649 to 1812-Balt-
1841-orig cl   (4m2,fox) 30.00
RIDGELY,JAS L-History of Amer Odd Fellowship,The 1st Decade,
6th Thousand-Balt-1878-528p-calf-illus   (5m6,crack) 10.00
RIDGELY,LAURENCE BUTLER-Santa Francesca,Our Lady of The
Golden Gate-SanFran-1935-Grabhorn Pr-49p-bds-vel bk-
250c prntd   (5r0)   5.00
RIDGER,A LOTON-A Wanderer's Trail-NY-1914-403p-60 photos
                                         (5s4,shake) 10.00
RIDGEWAY,GEO L-Merchants of Peace-NY-1938-419p-illus
                                         (5y2)   5.00
RIDGEWAY'S,JOHN-Statistical History of...Vertical Revolving
Battery-Bost-1865-prntd wrps-30p   (5g8)   15.00
RIDGWAY,ROBT-The birds of No & Middle Amer-Bull of US
Natl Mus-Wash-1901-GPO-Part 1,Family Fringillidae,The
Finches-Bull #50-715p-15 plts   (5u3,hng weak) 6.50
--same-Part 3-Wash-1904-GPO-801p-19 plts (5u3,scuff) 5.00
--Color Standards & Color Nomenclature-Wash-1912-53 col plts-
8vo-44p plus plts-2nd ed   (4c8)   85.00
--The Hummingbirds-Wash-1891?-hand bnd in hard cov-8vo-
46 plts   (4p5,lacks t.p.) 17.50
--Ornithology of Illinois-Springfld-1889-col frontis-32 plts-
orig cl-4to-520p   (4p5) 10. (5yy0)   12.50
--same-Vol 1,Pts 1&2,Vol 2,Pt 1(all publ)-Springfld-1889 to 95-
orig cl-col frontis-65 plts-lg 8vo-2 vols-1st ed
                             (5h0,soil,crack) 12. (5z9,vg) 35.00
RIDGEWAY'S PEERAGE-of United Kingdom for 1853-Lond
                                         (5r7,wn)   10.00
RIDING,LAURA-4 Unposted Letters to Catherine-Paris-(1930)-
Hours Pr-12mo-lea bk as issued-ltd to 200c,autg-1st ed (5ee9) 40.00
--Laura & Francisca-Majorca-1931-4to-dec bds-cl bk-1st ed-
ltd to 200c,nbrd,autg-orig glassine   (5ss7,vf) 35.00
--Progress of Stories-Majorca&Lond0(1935)-Cr 8vo-cl-1st ed
                                         (5ss7,cov soil) 15.00
--The Second Leaf-Majroca-1935-Broadside poem fld to make 4 lvs-
1st ed-(never for sale)   (5ss7,vf) 30.00
RIDINGS,SAM P-The Chisholm Trail-Guthrie-1936-fldg map-
photos (4a5) 40. (5x5,f,dj) 50.
    (4t8,dj,5k1,ex-libr,5L3,libr stmp) 45. (4c7,f,dj) 75.00
RIDLEY,BROMFIELD L-Battles & Sketches of Army of Tenn-
Mexico,Missouri-1906-scarce   (5h6,cov wtrstnd) 35.00
RIDPATH,JOHN CLARK-History of the US-NY-(1902)-McKinlay-
5 vols-illus-calf   (5qq8)   12.50
--Library of Amer History-Wash-c1900-6 vols
                                         (5w5,amateur rbndg) 30.00
--Life & Work of Jas A Garfield-Cinn-1882-illus-lg8vo-
orig pict cl-672p-Memorial Ed   (5t2,hng weak) 4.50
--Ridpath's Universal History-Cinn-Jones Bros-(1899)-17 vols-
4to-hf lea-g.bks   (5j5)   40.00
--Story of South Africa-n.p.-1899-Amer Hist Pr-col maps-photos-
illus-692p   (4t5)   10.00
--US,a History-Columbian Ed-(1891)-778p-illus(5ww4,pgs fade) 5.00

RIDPATH, JOHNSON-Official Portfolio of War & Nation-
(Gen Marcus Wright,ed)-(1907)-folio-cl-col plts-maps-
illus   (4d9)   37.50
RIEBEL,R C-Louisville Panorama-Louisvl-1954-illus-4to-231p
                                         (4p8)   7.50
RIEDESEL,FREIDRICH -Letters & Memoirs Relating to War of Amer
Ind & Capture of German Troops at Saratoga-NY-1827-8vo-
orig bds-papr labl-cl bk-1st ed in Engl (5ss5,cov loose) 25.00
RIEGEL,O W-Crown of Glory-NewHav-1935-1st ed-276p plus
index   (5L2,f,dj) 8.50
RIEGEL,ROBT E-American Moves West-NY-(1930)-maps-1st ed
                                         (5dd5)   8.75
--same-NY-(1931)-2nd ed   (5L2)   5.00
--Merchant Vessels-NY-1921-257p-illus   (5s1,ink notes) 4.50
--Story of Western Railroads-NY-1926-cl-1st ed-scarce
                             (5h2,sl fleck) 10. (5dd5) 35.00
RIEGO-or the Spanish Martyr,in 5 acts-Richmond(Va)-1850-
PDBernard-12mo-hf calf-1st ed-scarce   (5i9,rub) 30.00
RIEKER,HANS ULRICH-The Secret of Meditation-Lond-1955 (5x7) 3.00
RIEMAN,MARGO-12 Company Dinners-NY-(1957)-242p-
1st prntng   (5c0,5c9) 4.00
RIES,ESTELLE H-Amer Rugs-Cleve-(1950)-12mo-8 col plts-63p
                                         (5n7)   2.00
--Elias E Ries,Inventor-NY-1951-369p   (5b8,5x0) 5.00
RIES,HEINRICH-Clays of Texas-Austin-1908-316p-wrps (4a5) 8.50
RIESENBERG,EMILY-Easy Baking-NY-(1931)-287p (5c0) 3.50
RIESENBERG,FELIX-Cape Horn-NY-1939-photos-maps-4to-
452p   (4p8)   10.00
--East Side,West Side-NY-1927-HBrace   (5x0)   5.00
--Golden Gate-NY-c1940-347p-illus   (5h9)   6.00
--Pacific Ocean-NY-1940-322p-illus   (5s1)   7.50
--Portrait of New York-NY-1939-Macmillan-213p-illus (5x0) 5.00
--Standard Seamanship for Merchant Service-NY-(1936)-illus
                                         (5s1,f)   6.00
--Yankee Skippers to Rescue-NY-1943-283p-photos(5s1,5dd5) 5.00
RIESMAN,DAVID-The Lonely Crowd-(1952)-Yale Univ Pr-386p
                                         (5p7)   6.50
RIESS,CURT-Total Espionage-NY-1941   (5x7)   3.00
RIGAUD,MILO-Jesus Ou Legba-Vienne,France-1928-245p-wrps-
ltd to 100c   (5x2)   10.00
RIGBY,DOUGLAS-Lock, Stock & Barrell-Phila-(1944)-illus-570p-
1st trade ed   (5yy6) 6. (5h9)   5.00
RIGBY,ELIZ-Letters from the Shores of the Baltic-Lond-1844-
Murray-hf mor-160p-12mo   (5v7)   45.00
RIGDON,W T-Crossing the Plains, 1850-Salem,Ore-n.d.-4p
                                         (5t1)   25.00
RIGELE,FRITZ-50 Jahre Bergsteiger,Erlebnisse und Gedanken-
Berlin Wilmersdorf-1935-Verlags-373p-cl-"Sport und Spiel"
                                         (5d7)   6.00
RIGGS,ALFRED L-Wicoie Wowapi,Wowapi Pehanpi kin,World
Book Wall Roll-NY-n.d.-(ca late 1870s)-Amer Tract Soc for
Dakot Mission-25p-illus-31½ x 21½   (4k4,f)   100.00
--same-NY-1881   (4k4,f)   15.00
--same-NY-1887   (4k4,f)   15.00
RIGGS,MARY B-Early Days at Santee-Santee,Neb-1928-70p-
photos-wrps-1st ed-rare pamphlet   (5L0)   25.00
RIGGS,S R-Dakota ABC Wowapi-Santee,Neb-1929-20p-wrps-
rev ed   (5t3)   8.50
--Dakota English Dictionary-Wash-1890-665p-folio
                             (4a5) 15. (4t8,4b3,fade) 25.00
--Dakota Grammar,Texts & Ethnography-Wash-1893-Contb to
NoAmer Ethnology-Vol 9- 232p plus index-1st ed
                             (5m9,sl holes) 12.50 (4t8) 15.00
--Dakota Odowan,Hymns in Dakota Language-n.d.-Amer Tract
Soc-mor-brass clasp   (4k4,f)   10.00
--Dakota Tawoonspe (Dakota Lessons,Bk 1)-Louisville-n.d.-(1850)-
illus-cl over bds-48p-1st ed-rare   (4L2,ex-libr) 45.00
--Dakota Tawoonape,Wowapi 2,Dakota Lessons,Bk 2-Louisville-
n.d.(1850)-illus-wrps-48p-1st ed-rare   (4L2,ex-libr) 45.00
--Grammar & Dictionary of Dakota Language-1852-GPO-
Smithsonian Contr-cl-sm folio-1st ed   (4t8,4k5,f) 45.00
--Jeremiah,Ezekiel,Daniel,ga Wicasta Wokcan Toktokeca,
Dakota Lapi En,Tamakoce Okagn-NY-1877-267p,531p-
orig lea-1st ed-rare   (5t3)   150.00
--Mary & I-Chig-(Mar 1880)-Holmes-frontis-port-plts-388p
                                         (4d9,ex-libr) 47.50
--same-Bost-(1887)-ports   (4k5,f)   15.00
--Memorial Discourse on Rev Thos S Williamson,MD, Missionary
to Dakota Indians Oct 15,1880-NY-n.d.(1880?)-23p-frontis-
wrps-rare   (4t8,chip) 60.00
--Model First Reader,Wayawa Tokaheya prepared in English,
Dakota-Chig-(1873)-pic bds   (4k4,f)   25.00

RIGGS,S R (continued)
--same-Chig-(1885)-GeoSherwood&Co-112p   (5yy3)   15.00
--Pilgrim's Progress by John Bunyan in Dakota Language-n.d.-
   Amer Tract Soc-mor-brass clasp   (4k4,f)   25.00
--same-1892-Amer Tract Soc-cl   (4k4)   20.00
--Tah Koo Wah Kan -Bost-(1869)
   (4k5,libr stmp) 27.50   (5x5,pres) 25.   (4t8,4k5,f)   30.00
RIGGS,THEODORE F-Woyazanska Tuberculosis-Santee,Neb-
   1908-11p-wrps-1st ed-rare   (5t3)   20.00
RIGHT AND WRONG-exhibited in history of Rosa & Agnes-Lond-
   1815-JHarris-frontis-1st ed-12mo-192p   (5c8)   22.50
RIGHTS,DOUGLAS L-The Amer Indian in NoCarolina-Durham-
   1947-277p plus index-photos-maps(1 fldg)-1st ed (5L2) 10.00
RIGHT IS MIGHT-& other sketches-by the author of Peter Parley's
   Tales-Hartf,HHHawley;Utica,HawleyFuller-1850-frontis-
   144p-32mo-8 wdcuts   (5p1,wn)   7.50
RIGHT(THE) OF BRITISH LEGISLATURE-to Tax Amer Colonies
   vindicated-Lond-1774-TBecket-hf mor-8vo-58p (5L1)   150.00
RIGHTS OF COLONIES EXAMINED,THE-Providence-1765-
   Goddard-(SHopkins)-sm4to-hf mor- 1st issue,1st ed (5n2) 325.00
RIGHTS OF GREAT BRITAIN ASSERTED-against Claims of America-
   Lond-1776-Cadell-8vo-mor-frontis inserted-fldg tabl-hf title-
   (J MacPherson)-1st ed(of 20 editions publ in 1776) (5n2) 150.00
--same-London prntd:Phila reprntd-1776-sold by RBell-8vo-cl-
   1st Amer ed   (5i0,rbnd)   60.00
RIGHTS OF THE INDIANS-n.p.-n.d.-(dated at end Bost,Feb 22,
   1830)-8vo-16p-stitchd   (5L1)   35.00
RIGMAROLE,CRAYON-Bevil Faulcon,a Tradition of the Old
   Cheraw-Columbia(SC)-1842-ICMorgan,prntr-12mo-orig cl-
   papr labl-1st ed   (5x1)   350.00
RIGNAULT,HOMER-The Legend of Ermengarde-Paris-1929-
   Edw W Titus,At Sign of Black Manikin-8vo-prntd wrps-
   ltd to 250c   (5ee9,unopnd) 20.00
RIGNAULT DE GENOUILLY,(M L'AMIRAL)-Notice sue la
   Transportation a la Guyane Francaise at a la Nouvelle Caledonie-
   Paris-1867-lg8vo-qtr calf-95p-2 lg fldg maps (5ss2)   22.50
RIHBANY,ABRAHAM MITRIE-A Far Journey-Bost-(1914)-
   HoughtonMiff-352p-illus   (5p9)   5.00
RIIS,JACOB A-Battle with the Slum-1902   (5L7)   7.50
--How the Other Half Lives-NY-1892-illus-pict cl bds(5m2,als) 10.00
--The Making of an American-NY-1901-1st ed   (5q8)   4.00
--Theodore Roosevelt The Citizen-NY-1904-471p-illus-t.e.g.-
   1st ed   (5w9)   6.50
--same-NY-(1907)-Grosset&Dunlap rprnt-471p-cl (5h2)   4.00
RIKER,DOUGLAS H-The Wine Book of Knowledge-LosAng-1934-
   70p-illus-The Ascot Pr-8vo   (5g9,lacks wrps) 6.00
RIKER,JAS-Annals of Newtown in Queens County,NY-NY-1852-
   fldg map-427p plus index (4j3,rebnd) 35. (5zz0,ex-libr,rbkd) 45.50
RIKER,JAS-History of Harlem,Its Origins & early annals-NY-
   1904-thk8vo-illus-maps   (5x2)   37.50
--Revised History of Harlem-NY-1904-908p-illus (5p0)   17.50
RILEY,ARTHUR J-Catholicism in New England to 1788-(Wash,1936)-
   479p-8vo-orig prntd wrps   (4c1)   17.50
RILEY,B F-History of Baptists of Texas-Dallas-1907 (4c7,stnd) 25.00
--The White Man's Burden-Birmingham,AL-1910-priv pub (5x2) 32.50
RILEY,BENNETT-Gov Bennett Riley's Proclamation to People of
   Dist of SanFran,Jun 4,1849-LosAng-1956-priv prntd-15p-bds-
   ltd to 150c   (5x5)   7.50
RILEY,CHAS V-Notes on Aphididae of US...West of Mississippi-
   Wash-1879-32p-wrps   (4a5,autg)   4.00
--Report on the Cotton Worm-plus Boll Worm-Wash-1885-plts-
   maps-399p & 147p   (4j4)   12.50
RILEY,ELIHU-History of Anne Arundel Co in Maryland-Annap-
   1905-Feldmeyer-8vo-cl-169p   (4t1)   32.50
RILEY,FRANKLIN K-After Appomattox-NY-1922-illus-1st ed
                                             (5yy6,dj)   7.50
RILEY,H-The Mule,A Treatise-Phila-1869-Claxton,etc-107p-
   14p illus-orig cl-g.-16mo-v scarce   (4p5,ex-libr) 15.00
RILEY,H H-Puddleford & Its People-NY-1854-Samuel Hueston-
   illus-1st ed   (5q0) 7.50   (4b4)   12.50
RILEY,H T-Liber Albus:White Book of City of London-Lond-1861
                                             (5r4,rbnd)   12.50
RILEY,I WOODRIDGE-The Founder of Mormonism-NY-1902-
   1st ed-v scarce   (4t8)   30.00
--same-NY-1903-2nd ed-462p   (5L2,rbnd)   20.00
RILEY,J H-Birds from Siam & Malay Peninsula in US Natl Mus-
   Wash-1938-Smi Inst #172-wrps-581p   (4p5)   7.50
RILEY,J S-Science & Practice of Chiropractice, & Allied Sciences-
   NY-1919-lg8vo-cl-539p-illus-1st ed-v scarce (5p5)   15.00
RILEY,JAS-Authentic Narr of Loss of Amer Brig Commerce-Hartf-
   1817-8vo-calf-frontis-fldg map-illus   (5i4,sl wtrstn) 12.50
--same-NY-1817-illus   (4m4,rebnd)   15.00
--same-Hartford-1844-271p-cl   (5h2)   7.50

RILEY,JAS (continued)
--same-NY-1859-271p   (5e8,sl wn)   10.00
RILEY,JAS WHITCOMB-An Old Sweetheart of Mine-Indnpls-(1902)-
   BobbsMerrill-lea-g stmp on cov   (4h7,cl) 5.   (4h7)   7.50
--Armazindy-Indnpls-1894-BowenMerrillCo-12mo-1st ed
                                   (5m1) 5.   (5ss9,vg)   7.50
--same-Indnpls-1894-illus-169p-1st issue   15.00
--Book of Joyous Children-NY-1902-8vo-dec cl-g.t.-1st ed-
   illus by Vawter   (5p5)   10.00
--The Boys of the Old Glee Club-Indnpls-(1907)-BobbsMerrill-
   illus-dec cl-1st ed   (5x4)   6.00
--A Child World-Indnpls&KansasCty-1897-BowenMerrill-209p,
   (14)(ads)-frontis-g.-t.e.g.-smooth red cl-1st Amer ed-
   1st issue   (5p1,pres from Mrs Joe E Brown)   15.00
--same-Indnpls&KansasCty-1897-frontis-1st ed(not 1st prntng)
                                             (5ee3)   4.00
--Complete Works of...Memorial Ed-NY-1916-Harper-10 vols-
   cl   (5p0)   30.00
--Flying Islands of the Night -Indnpls-1892-1st ed
                              (5ee3,stn) 4.   (4b4)   4.50
--The Girl I Loved-Indnpls-1910-90p-HCChristie,illus (5xx8) 5.00
--Goodbye,Jim-(Indnpls,1913)-HCChristie,illus-boxed (5r9,f) 6.00
--His Pa's Romance-Indnpls-(1903)-BobbsMerrill-168p-1st ed
                                             (5x4)   6.00
--Home Folks-Indnpls-1900-g.t.-1st ed-1st issue(with error on
   pg 59)   (5k2,lacks fly)   25.00
--Love Letters...to Miss Elizabeth Kahle-Bost-1922-cl bkd bds-
   Bibliophile Soc-1st ed-ltd (5r9,f) 8.50 (5b2,f,wn box) 15.00
--Old Sweetheart of Mine,An-Indnpls-(1902)-illus by Christy
                                             (5i4)   5.00
--Out to Old Aunt Mary's-Indnpls-(1904)-1st ed-illus by Christy
                                             (5i3)   6.00
--Pipes O' Pan at Zekesbury-Indnpls-1889-pic cl-1st ed
   12mo   (4m8) 4.00   (5x4) 7.50   (5r9) 8.50   (5mm1)   10.00
--The Poems & Prose Sketches of-NY-1897,8-Scribner's-10 vols-
   frontis-g.t.-edges untrimmed   (5ee3)   22.50
--Poems Here at Home-NY-1893-illus-1st ed   (5kk7,5k2)   12.50
--Poems Here at Home-NY-1893-illus-1st ed, 1st state(pg 50,
   Girls spell correctly)   (4k1)   25.00
--Riley Farm Rhymes-(1921)-BobbsMerrill-191p (5p7)   2.50
--The Works of-NY-1913-Scribner-16 vols-cl   (5p7)   25.00
RILEY,MORGAN T-Dahlias,What is Known About Them-NY-
   1947-213p-illus   (5s7)   4.50
RILEY,PATRICK-Memories of a Blue Jacket,1872 to 1918-Lond-
   n.d.-Sampson Low(etc)-g.t.-308p-port- plts-lg8vo (5aa2) 5.00
RILEY,PHIL-Samuel McIntire, Woodcarver of Salem-Bost-1916-
   illus-167p-8vo-1st ed   (5ww3,hng crk)   25.00
RILEY,W-From Myth to Reason-1926   (5L7)   5.00
RILING,RAY-Powder Flask Book-NewHope-1953-4to-495p-plts
                                             (5xx7)   45.00
RILKE,RAINER M-Letters to a Young Poet-NY-(1934)-WWNorton-
   1st ed   (5hh1,dj)   6.00
RIMINGTON,CRISCHELL-Fighting Fleets, 1942, 1943, 1944-NY-
   1942 to 1944-3 vols-4to-cl-photos-1st eds (5p5)   20.00
RIMINGTON,CRITCHELL-Fighting Fleets-1943 Edition-NY-(1943)-
   8vo-illus   (5s1) 9.50   (5m6,dj)   7.50
--same-NY-1942-photos   (5s1)   10.00
RIMMER,ALFRED-Ancient Streets & Homesteads of England-Lond-
   1877-340p-illus   (5t4)   10.00
--same-Lond-1879-illus   (5yy6,hngs split)   7.50
--Rambles Round Eton & Harrow-Lond-1882-deluxe ed-4to-bds-
   plts&illus on China Paper-ltd to 250c-lg papr (4a2,soiled) 7.00
RIMMEL,EUGENE-The Book of Perfumes-Lond-1868-266p-
   g.e.-6th ed -over 250 illus   (4g0,hng loose)   25.00
RIMMER,DR WM-Art Anatomy-Bost-1877-Little,Brown-illus-
   3 edges glt-50 plts-22x14"-rare   (4a0)   225.00
RIMSKY KORSAKOFF,NIKOLAY A-My Musical Life-Joffe,transl-
   NY-390p-Tudor   (5p0)   7.50
RINDGE,FREDK HASTINGS-Happy Days in So Calif-Cambr&LosAng-
   (1898)-199p,(1)-pict cl-v scarce   (4L9)   35.00
RINEHART,E F-Wintering Range Stock-Boise-Sep 1931-8p-
   Col of Agri,Ext Cir #39-wrps   (5L5)   4.00
RINEHART,MARY ROBERTS-The Bat,novel from play by-(1926)-
   1st ed-scarce   (5p6,sl soil) 5.00
--Circular Staircase-Indnpls-(1908)-1st ed-frontis-illus (5i3,f) 12.50
--The Out Trail-NY-(1923)-246p-photos-1st ed
                          (5L2,dj) 6.   (5s4,tn dj)   6.50
--same-1931   (5s4)   4.00
--The Red Lamp-NY-(1925)-8vo-cl-publisher's device on cpyrte pg-
   1st ed   (5d3)   10.00
--Street of Seven Stars-Bost-1914-1st ed-1st prntng (5i3,vg) 5.00
--Through Glacier Park-Bost-1916-92p-photos-1st ed (5s4,5L2) 5.00
--same-GardenCty-1928   (5x7)   4.00

USED BOOK PRICE GUIDE

RINEHART'S INDIANS-(Omaha,Neb,1899)-1p text-49p plts(4 in
   col)-approx 9" x 7"-v scarce   (5L0) 45.00
RING,GEO C-Religions of The Far East-Milwkee-1950-350p-cl-
   illus-1st ed   (5t2,f,dj) 5.00
RINGBOLT,CAPT-Sailors' life & sailors' yarns-NY-1847-CSFrancis-
   orig cl-1st ed of auth's 1st book   (5x1) 27.50
RINGEL,FRED,ed-America as Americans See It-NY-1932-illus-
   1st ed   (5L3) 4.50
RINGWALT,J L-Diller Family,Desc Casper Diller of Pa-1877-56p-
   wrps   (5t9) 7.50
RIO,ANTONIO DEL-Descrip of Ruins of an ancient city discovered
   near Palenque in Kingdom of Guatemala-Lond-1822-128p-
   plts-calf-Henry Berthoud   (5d6,hng weak) 60.00
RIORDAN,JOS W-First Half Century of St Ignatius Church & College-
   SanFran-1905-cl-389p-illus-8vo   (5h5) 30.00
RIOTS IN NEW ORLEANS IN 1866-Report of Select Comm on
   NOrl Riots-Wash-1867   (5x2) 50.00
--same-original report #16 of 39th Congress-wrps (5x2) 35.00
RIP VAN WINKLE-ca1880s-lg4to-6 huge col plts-illuminated wrp
     (5v0,f) 10.00
RIPE CHERRIES-or history of Wm & Jane-NY-n.d.-
   Amer Tract Soc-16p incl wrps-9 wdcuts,7 in text & 1 on ea cov-
   Series 1,#13-3½ x 2½-(cira 1827 to 1833) (5p1) 27.50
RIPLEY,C S-Anc Lt Thos Tracy of Norwich,Conn-1895-100p(5t9)10.00
RIPLEY,C S-Ingersoll of Hampshire,in Line of John of Westfield,Mass-
   1893-107p   (5mm3) 12.50
RIPLEY,CLEMENTS-Clear for Action-NY-1942-310p (5s1) 3.50
RIPLEY,ELIZA-Social Life in Old New Orleans-NY-1912-Appl-
   scarce-332p   (4p7,sl cov stn) 25.00
RIPLEY,ELIZA M-From Flag to Flag-NY-1889-296p-cl
     (5h1,sl rub) 15.00
RIPLEY,H A-How Good A Detective Are You-NY-(1932-
   Blue Ribbon-177p   (5p9) 3.50
RIPLEY,H W-Genealogy of Part of Ripley Family-1867-48p
     (5mm3) 17.50
RIPLEY,M F-Oriental Rug Book-NY-1936-new ed-illus(5qq7) 7.50
RIPLEY,MARY C-The Chinese Rug Book-NY-1927-17 hftone illus-
   66p-   (5n7) 6.50
--Oriental Rug Book,The-NY-(1936)-310p-illus (5t7,dj) 10.00
RIPLEY(MISSISS)-Inventory of Tippah Co Archives,preliminary ed-
   1942-Hist Records Survey-WPA-157p-mimeo (5t9) 5.00
RIPLEY,O H-Barkhamsted Sesqui Centennial,Today & Yesterday in
   Hist of Town-1930-115p-ltd to 400c (5t9) 7.50
RIPLEY,R S-The War With Mexico-NY-1849-2 vols (5n4) 85.00
RIPLEY,THOS-They Died with Their Boots On-GardenCty-1935-
   photos-285p-1st ed-scarce   (5L0,f) 20.00
--same-Sidney,Aus-1936-Angus&Robertson-205p (4n8,fox) 15.00
RIPLEY,THOS E-A Vermont Boyhood-Appleton-1937-234p-1st ed
     (5e8) 6.25
RIPLEY,WM Z-Main Street & Wall Street-Bost-1927-2nd issue
     (4b8) 4.50   (5qq8) 5.00
--Railroads Finance & Organization-NY-1923-cl-638p (4i2) 10.00
RIPPERGER,HELMUT-Cheese Cookery-NY-(1941)-96p (5c0) 5.00
--Mushroom Cookery-NY-1941-95p (5c0) 5.50
--Spice Cookery-NY-1942-95p (5c9) 3. (5w3) 3.50
RIPPERGER,HENRIETTA-A Home of Your Own & How to Run it-
   NY-1940-443p-illus   (5w7) 4.50
RIPPEY,SARAH CORY-The Goody Naughty Book-Chig,NY-(1913)-
   col plts-(reversible book)   (5v2) 20.00
--The Sunny Sulky Book-Chig&NY-c1915-RandMcNally-pict bds-
   12mo-80p-reversible book (5p1,soil,cor wn) 7.50
RIS PAQUOT-Manuel du Collectionneur de Faiences Anciennes-
   Amiens-1877,8-343p,(2)-56 col illus-bds (5w7) 27.50
RISE & PROGRESS OF THE SERPENT-from Garden of Eden to
   Present Day,with Disclosure of Shakerism-Concord,NH-1847-
   c1847-port-frontis-268p-tan calf-orig labl-1st ed-scarce
     (5a0,cov wn) 27.50
RISHER,REV,ed-Right Hand Thunder,the Indian & the White Man-
   Indnpls-1880-515p-1st ed (5w5,fade) 10.00
RISLER,JEREMIAS-Leben August Gottlieb Spangenbergs Bischofs
   der evangelischen Bruederkirche-Barby-1794-516p,(20)p,(1)-
   sm8vo-orig bds-port   (5L1) 50.00
RISLEY,CHRISTINE-Machine Embroidery-NY-(1961)-4to-128p-
   34 plts   (5n7) 4.95
RISLEY,E H-Desc of Richard Risley of Newtown(Cambridge) Mass &
   Hartford,Conn-1909-306p (5t9) 15.00
RISLEY,RICH V-Men's tragedies-NY-1899-Macmillan-2nd prntng
     (5m2) 5.00
RISLEY,SARAH A-A Genealogy of the Lake Family of Great Egg
   Harbor,In Old Gloucester County-1915-376p (5m2) 27.50
RISTER,CARL COKE-Border Captives-Norman-1940-1st ed (5kk7) 7.50
--Border Command-Univ of Okla-1944-12mo-cl-fldg map
   (5yy7,f,dj) 12.50 (5h0,dj) 8.50 (5F5,f,dj) 10.00

RISTER,CARL COKE (continued)
--Comanche Bondage-Glendale-1955-203p plus index-photos-
   map-o.p.-1st ed   (5bb4,mint) 12.50
--Land Hunger-Norman-1942-illus-1st ed-scarce
   (5yy7,wtrstn) 10. (5yy7,dj,f) 20. (5xx5) 17.50
--Oil,Titan of the SW-Norman-1949-U of Okla Pr-467p-illus-1st ed
   (5yy6) 6. (5y2,5L2,wn) 6.50 (5yy7,f,dj,4n8) 10.00
--Robt E Lee in Texas-Norman-1946 (5kk6) 15.00
--The Southwestern Frontier,1865 to 1881-Cleve-1928-photos-
   maps-1st ed   (4t8,f) 35.00
--Southern Plainsmen-Norman-1938-279p plus index-photos-
   fldg map-1st ed-scarce (4g6) 27.50 (5bb4,dj) 32.50
RITCH,JOHNNY-Horsefeathers-Verse-Helena-(1940)-95p-
   Russel illus (5m9,wn) 5. (5s4) 10.00
--same-Helena-(1941)-95p-6 col illus & 7 engrs by Russell-
   2nd prntng(1st prntng there were no col illus)
   (5L2) 5. (5L2,f,autg) 7.50
--Shorty's Saloon-n.p.-n.d.-(Helena,ca 1940)-16p-wrps-illus
   (5L2) 1.50 (5g0) 2.50
RITCH,W G-Illustrated New Mexico-1883-140p-3rd ed-fldg map-
   illus-Bur of Emigr for terr of NM (5r1,pres,libr stmp) 45.00
--same-SantaFe-1885-illus-fldg views-wrps-5th ed-rev&enlrgd
     (5g4) 7.50
RITCHEY,CHAS J-Drake University thru 75 Years-DesMoines-1956-
   Drake Univ-288p   (5u3) 4.00
RITCHIE,A J-Sketches of Rabun County (Georgia) History-1948-
   503p   (5t9) 10.00
RITCHIE,ANDREW C-Abstract Painting & Sculpture in America-
   NY-1951-(Mus Mod Art)-plts (4a1) 10.00
--Catalogue of Contemporary Paintings & Sculpture-Buffalo-(1949)-
   sm4to-80p plts-Buffalo Fine Arts Acad (5jj3,dj) 12.50
--Catalogue of Paintings & Sculpture in the Permanent Collection-
   (1949)-(Buffalo Fine Arts Acad)-sm4to-87p plts (5jj3,dj) 12.50
RITCHIE,ANNA CORA-The Clergyman's Wife & Other Sketches-
   NY-1867-384p   (5F0) 3.50
--Mimic Life;or,Before & Behind the Curtain-Bost-1856-1st ed
   (5t2,fray,pres) 8. (5ee3) 7.50
--Twin Roses-Bost-1857-Ticknor&Fields-12mo-orig dark cl-1st ed
   (5i0,rub) 17.50
RITCHIE,ANNE THACKERAY-Chapters from some Unwritten
   Memoirs-NY-1895-Harper-8vo-106p,2 ads -dec cl-t.e.g.(5P1)7.50
RITCHIE,DAVID G-Natural Rights-Lond-1924 (5x7) 5.00
RITCHIE,GEO-List of Lincoliniana in Library of Congress-Wash-
   1903-75p   (4j6) 7.50
RITCHIE,JAS S-Wisconsin & Its Resources-Phila-1857-12mo-cl-
   illus-maps-312p   (5m8) 25.00
--same-Phila-1858-318p-3rd rev ed-fldg maps-plts (5y0,sl wn) 12.50
RITCHIE,LEITCH-Journey to St Petersburg & Moscow thru Courland
   & Livonia-Lond-1836-lea-plts-8vo-256p (5v7,fox) 38.50
RITCHIE,R L GRAEME-Normans in Scotland-Edinb-1954-illus-
   466p   (5q0) 10.00
RITCHIE,ROBT WELLES-Hell Roaring Forty Niners-NY-(1928)-
   illus-1st ed   (4b7,lacks fly) 8.50
RITCHIE,WM-Scripture Testimony Against Intoxicating Wine-
   NY-1874-213p-cl   (5h7) 7.50
RITCHIE'S ILLUSTRATED CATALOGUE-of Physical Instruments &
   School Apparatus-Bost-1878-111p,(5)-fldg bds (5hh7) 12.50
RITSON,JOS-Annals of the Caledonians,Picts & Scots;and of
   Strathclyde etc-Edinb-1828-2 vols-sm8vo-bds-1st ed
   (5t2,chip) 10.00
--The Caledonian Muse-Lond-prntd 1785 & now 1st publ by
   Triphook,1821-8vo-1st ed (5i8,crack) 30.00
--Robin Hood,a Collection-Lond-1820-12mo-240p-dec lea-
   Bewick cuts (5c8) 45. (5v2,rub) 75.00
--same-Lond-n.d.(ca 1850)-Cooke-8vo-122p-wrps-rare
   (4f6,wn) 12.50
--Select Collection of English Songs-Lond-1813-2nd ed-3 vols
   (5ii2,needs rbndg) 22.50
--same-Lond-1783-calf-3 vols-8vo-1st ed (5x3,wn) 175.00
RITTENHOUSE,JACK D-Horsedrawn Vehicles-LosAng-1948-illus-
   1st ed-ltd to 1000c (4p2,mint,dj) 15.00
--same-LosAng-1951-4to-218 illus-2nd deluxe ed (4p8) 10.00
--New Mexico Civil War Bibliography 1861 to 1865-Houston-1961-
   Stagecoach Pr-ltd to 400c (5g0,mint,dj) 10.00
RITTERSHAUS,CARL-Der Practische Konditor-Leipzig-1914-
   119p,98,47p-98 plts(83 in col) (5c5) 18.50
RITZ,MARIE LOUISE-Cesar Ritz Host to the World-Phila-(1938)-
   361p-plts   (5g9) 8.50
RIVARD,ADJUTOR-Chez Nous-Tor-(1929)-WHBlake,transl-cl-
   illus-201p   (5t0,f,dj) 4.00
RIVARD,M-La Gnomonique. Ou L'Art de Faire des Cadrans-Paris-
   1746-8vo-calf-fldg plts-raised g. bands (5p5,f bndg) 50.00

RIVAS VICUNA,MANUEL-Historia Politica y Parlamentaria de
Chile-Santiago-1964-3 vols-thk8vo-frontis-wrps   (5r7)   20.00

RIVERA,DIEGO-Portrait of Amer-NY-1934-illus-(1st ed) (4m9)   15.00

RIVERO,MARIANO EDW-Peruvian Antiquities-NY-1853-Putnam-
8vo-cl-illus-306p
(5m6,ex-libr) 15. (4a3,fray,darken papr) 40. (4p7)   30.00
--same-NY-1854-Putnam-306p   (5v6)   12.50

RIVERS,G R-The Governor's Garden-Bost-1898-259p,(5)-illus
(5w3)   4.50

RIVERS,GEO R R-Captain Shays,A Populist of 1786-Bost-1897-
358p-1st ed   (5m1)   6.00

RIVERS,JOHN-Greuze & His Models-Lond-1913-282p-plts-8vo
(5ww3)   15.00

RIVERS,THOS-The Miniature Fruit Garden-NY-(1866)-133p-illus
(5s7)   6.00

RIVERS,WM JAS-Sketch of the History of SoCar to Close of....1719-
Charleston-1856-McCarter-470p   (5qq8)   50.00

RIVERSIDE COOK BOOK-Collection of Tried & Approved Recipies-
All Saints Guild-Mrs Fessenden-1890-56p-ads-orig print
oilcloth cov   (5yy3,stain)   75.00

RIVERSIDE IN 1871-With a descrip of its improvements-Chig-(1871)-
illus-wrps   (5g8)   15.00

RIVERSIDE SOUVENIR,THE-Memorial Volume-NY-1886-Nations
Tribute to Gen Grant-4to   (5x0)   12.50

RIVERSIDE-Souvenir of-Photo Gravures-Riverside-1897-GeoCPoore-
40p-stiff wrps   (5n4)   12.50

RIVES,AMELIE-Hidden House-Phila-1912-Lippincott-8vo-cl-g.t.-
frontispiece   (5b2)   4.00
--The Quick of the Dead?A Study-Phila-1889-Lippincott-8vo-
cl-frontis   (5b2,f)   6.50

RIVES,HALLIE ERMINIE-A furnace of earth-NY-1900-Camelot-
1st ed   (5m2,autg)   6.00
--The Valiants of Virginia-Indnpls-(1912)   (5h6)   3.50

RIVETT,ROHAN D-Behind Bamboo-Sydney-1946-Angus&Rob
(5p7)   5.00

RIVIERE,F-La Vigne En Algerie Sa plantation & sa culture-Alger-
1873-52p-wrps   (5w1)   6.50

RIVLIN,JOS B-Harriet Martineau,Bibliography of Her Separately
Printed Books-NY-1947-NYPL-lg8vo-150p-wrps   (5v2,f)   15.00

RIVOIRA,G T-Lombardic Architecture,Its Origin,Development &
Derivatives-Lond-Heinemann-1910-2 vols-lg4to-plts-g.stmpd-
t.e.g.   (5m5,crack)   95.00

RIX,GUY S-Eastman Family of Amer-1901-2 vols-1000p (5t9)   50.00

RIXEY,R P-Rixey Genealogy-1933-427p   (5mm3)   15.00

RIXFORD,E H-The Wine Press & the Cellar-SanFran-1883-
240p-scarce   (5c9,fade)   28.50

RIXFORD,E M L-Rixford,Colonial Anc & War Service-1934-
367p   (5mm3)   17.50

RIZK,SALOM-Syrian Yankee-NY-1954-317p   (5w4,autg)   3.00

ROA,FERNANDO G-Lad Cuestiones Fundamentales de Actualidas
en Mexico-Mexico-1927-251p-wrps   (5n4)   9.00

ROACH,HATTIE JOPLIN-Hills of Cherokee-n.p.-1952
(4c7,autg)   32.50

ROAD REFERENCE-& Tourist's Guide of all States east of
Mississippi Riv,Eastern Ont,Quebec & Maritime Provinces-
Bost-1932-8vo-green cl-965p-maps   (5t0)   4.50

ROAD TO PEACE,COMMERCE,WEALTH & HAPPINESS-By an old
farmer-(Bost,1813)-stitchd   (5g4)   10.00

ROADS & RAILROADS-Vehicles & Modes of Travelling,of Ancient
& Modern Countries-Lond-1839-cl-340p-illus   (5hh7)   14.50

ROADS,SAML,JR-The History & Traditions of Marblehead-Bost-
1880-423p-1st ed-rare   (5L3) 40. (4t2)   60.00

ROANOKE,STORY OF CO & CITY-Roanoke-1942-WPA-1st(&only)
ed   (5z5,vf)   8.00

ROB OF THE BOWL,LEGEND OF ST INIGOE'S-Phila-1838-
Lea&Blanchard-1st ed-2 vols-lea&bds   (4b1)   85.00

ROB ROY-By author of "Waverley"-Edinb-1818-8vo-orig bds-
cl bk-labls-3 vols-1st ed   (5dd8,tn,wn,box)   50.00

ROBACK,C W-Mysteries of Astrology & Wonders of Magic-Bost-
1854-238p-illus   (5ii2) 12.50 (5d2) 10. (5t0)   13.50

ROBACKER,EARL F-Penna Dutch Stuff-Phila-1961-163p-illus
(5p0) 8.50 (5w4,dj)   7.50

ROBARTS,EDITH-Swiss Family Robinson,Retold for Little Folk-
Lond-n.d.-Blackie-4to-pict cl-80p-26plts(16 in col)(5aa2)   5.00
--Robinson Crusoe Retold for Little Folk-Lond-n.d.-Blackie-
4to-pict glazed bds-80p-7 col plts-illus   (5aa2)   5.00

ROBB,DAVID M-Art in the Western World-NY-1935-Harper-
708p-illus   (5x0)   8.50
--same-NY,Lond-1942-cl-2nd rev ed   (5m5)   6.00

ROBB,HARRY-Poddy,Story of a Rangeland Orphan-Trail's End,WY-
(1947)-illus-237p-1st ed   (5F5,autgs) 8.50 (4i7)   12.00

ROBB,J-Notable Angling Literature-Lond-   -illus-1st ed
(5a9,dj)   4.50

ROBB,MARSHALL J-Scotch Whisky-NY-1951-127p-32p of photos
(5w1)   5.50

ROBB,STEWART-Nostradamus on Napoleon,Hitler & the Present
Crisis-NY-1941-Scribner-8vo-cl-illus-218p-1st ed   (5j5)   7.50

ROBB,WINFRED E-The Price of Our Heritage-DesMoines-1919-
417p,(6)-4to-cl-photos   (5m8)   15.00

ROBBERSON,ELBERT-Small Boat Mechanics Handbook-NY-1956-
52 illus   (5c1)   6.50

ROBBINS,ARCHIBALD-Journal Comprising an Account of Loss of
Brig Commerce-Hartford-1818-7th ed-275p-fldg map(5i3,rub) 15.00
--same-Hartford-1821-fldg map-275p-lea   (5s1,stnd,wn) 12.50
--same-Hartford-1928-275p   (5L3)   20.00

ROBBINS,CAROLINE-Diary of John Milward,Esq-1938 (5L7)   7.50
--18th Century Commonwealthman-1959   (5L7)   7.50

ROBBINS,CHANDLER-History of the Second or Old North Church in
Boston-Bost-1852-illus   (5kk5)   17.50

ROBBINS,HAROLD-The Dream Merchants-NY-1949-Knopf-1st ed
(5x0)   5.00

ROBBINS,HELEN H-Our First Ambassador to China-Lond-1908-
JnMurray-479p   (5x9)   6.50

ROBBINS,J J-Report of Trial of Castner Hanway for treason,in
Resistance of Execution of Fugitive Slave Law of Sept,1850-
Phila-1852   (5x2,rbnd,f bndg) 50.00

ROBBINS,L H-Jersey Jingles-1907   (5L7)   3.00

ROBBINS,LEONARD H-Mountains & Men-NY-1931-324p-illus-
cl-Dodd,Mead   (5d7)   4.00

ROBBINS,LOUIS S-Robbins Process for Rendering Wood Imperishable
etc-Bost-1868-8vo-orig wrps-69p   (5m6,dmpstn)   7.50
--Treatise on the Robbins Process for Seasoning Wood & Preserving
It etc-Cinn-1869-8vo-orig wrps-91p   (5m6,ex-libr)   10.00

ROBBINS,PHYLLIS-Maude Adams,An Intimate Portrait-NY-1956-
8vo-cl-plts-1st ed   (5p5)   8.50
--same-(1956)-Putnam-illus-3rd ed   (5ww4,dj)   5.00

ROBBINS,ROLAND WELLS-Discovery at Walden(Stoneham,Mass)-
(1947)-illus-60p   (5t7,dj,pres) 10.50

ROBERSON,JOHN-The Chafing Dish Cook Book-NY-(1954)-
242p   (5c9)   3.50

ROBERT THE HERMIT-Life & Adventures of....of Mass who lived
14 years in a Cave-Prov-1829-HTrumbull-frontis-12mo-sewed-
36p-rare chapbook   (5j5,t pg tn)   35.00

ROBERT,FELIX-Scientific Bullfighting-(ElPaso)-(1910)-illus-30p-
pict tied wrps-v rare   (4p2,pres,tn cov) 25.00

ROBERT,H-D'Horlogerie-Paris-1852,4-plts-274p-8vo-French
text   (5bb0,rebnd)   35.00

ROBERT,MAURICE-Code for Collector of Beautiful Books-NY-
1936-Ltd Ed Club-55p-bds (4m8,sl rub) 7.50 (4i2,f)   15.00

ROBERT,NICOLAS-Variae ac Multiformes Florum species-Paris-
n.d.-(c1664)-F Poilly-31 nbrd plts-sm folio-1st & only ed
(4L7) 1,750.00

ROBERTS,A-Mammals of So Africa-Johannesburg-1954-orig
g.-4to-700p-77 plts(23 col)-map-2nd ed-scarce (4p5,sl wn) 87.75

ROBERTS,B H-The Missouri Persecutions-SaltLkCty-1900-333p-
frontis-ex rare   (5L0)   35.00
--The Mormon Battalion,Its History & Achievements-SaltLkCty-
1919-fldg map   (5bb4,wrps) 15. (5mm8) 15. (5x5)   20.00

ROBERTS,BRUCE-Springs from Parched Ground-1950-166p-priv prnt-
1st ed   (5r1,vg)   7.00

ROBERTS,C V-Early Friends of Upper Bucks(Co,Pa)-Phila-1925-
680p-illus   (5m2,bndg wn)   25.00

ROBERTS,CHAS-English Zulu Dictionary-Lond-1915-22&267p
(5c6,sl wn)   13.75

ROBERTS,CHAS G D-Discoveries & Explorations-Lond&Edinb-
also Phila&Tor-1905-part lea-illus-529p   (5dd7)   12.00
--The Raid from Beausejour & How the Carter Boys Lifted the
Mortgage-Montreal News Co-c1894-12mo-230p-map-frontis-
2 plts-dec cl   (5p1)   12.50
--Standard Dictionary of Canadian Biography-Vol 2,1875 to 1937-
478p   (5nn2)   20.00
--Watchers of the Trails-Bost-1904-361p-illus   (5t7)   8.00

ROBERTS,CHAS HUMPHREY-Down the O H I O-Chig-1891-c1891-
1st ed-blue cl   (5m2,sl wn) 8.50 (4a9,g) 12.00

ROBERTS,MRS D W-A Woman's Reminof 6 Years in Camp with
Texas Rangers-Austin-c1928-hf mor   (4a5,rbnd,stnd)   22.50
--same-Austin-n.d.-wrps   (4c7)   30.00

ROBERTS,CAPT DAN W-Rangers & Sovereignty-SanAntonio-1914-
port   (4c7, cov soil) 17.50 (4t8) 25.00

ROBERTS,DENNIS-I'll Climb Mount Everest Alone-Lond-(1957)-
158p-illus-cl-RbtHale   (5d7)   5.00

ROBERTS,DONALD R,ed-Tower & a Fortress-SanFran-1956-
priv prntd-12mo-cl-386p-ltd to 500c   (4t1)   12.50

ROBERTS,LT E M-A Flying Fighter-NY-1918-illus   (5u7,fade)   5.75

ROBERTS,E S-Preliminary Finding List of Southern Africa Pamphlets
in U of Cape Town Library-CapeTn-1959-203p-folio-wrps(5c6) 10.75

ROBERTS,EDWARDS-Santa Barbara & Around There-Bost-1886-
  illus-1st ed-scarce   (5yy7) 17.50
--same-Bost-1887-wrps-16mo   (5g3) 10.00
--Shoshone & Other Western Wonders-NY-1888-frontis-illus-275p-
  1st ed   (4a4,5i3,f) 10. (5L2) 7.50 (5k2) 15.00
--With the Invader:Glimpses of the SoWest-SanFran-1885-156p-
  drwngs-1st ed-rare   (5L2) 30.00
ROBERTS,ELIZ MADOX-A Buried Treasure-NY-1931-cl-
  1st ed-ltd to 200c,autg   (5a9,f) 12. (5d8,box) 20.00
--The Great Meadow-NY-1930-8vo-cl-g.t.-ltd to 925c,autg-
  1st ed   (5dd8,box) 25.00
--The Time of Man-NY-1945-Viking-pic cl-(not 1st)
    (5m2,sl wn box) 5.00
--Under the Tree-NY-1925-Viking&Heubsch-12mo-87p-bds-
  2nd prntng   (5p1,wn) 5.00
ROBERTS,FLORENCE-Dixie Meals-Nashville-(1934)-Parthenon Pr-
  310p   (5g9,rub) 4.50
ROBERTS,FRANK H H-Early Pueblo Ruins in the Piedra District-
  Wash-1930-BAE Bull #96-8vo-wrps-190p-55 plts (5g5) 5.00
--Ruins at Kiatuthlanna-Wash-1931-BAE #100-195p-wrps-maps-
  stpld   (5s4) 8.50
--Shabik'Eshchee Village, Late Basket Maker Site-1929-BAE # 92-
  plts-164p-fldg map-cl   (5g6) 5. (4b2) 10.00
ROBERTS,GEO-The 4 Years Voyages of-Lond-1726-Bettesworth-
  8vo-hf calf-fldg map-4 plts-1st ed   (5n9) 75.00
ROBERTS,H CHALMERS-Tales from Blackwood-DP-1903-12 vols-
  3/4 lea   (5e8) 12.75
ROBERTS,HAROLD D-Salt Creek,Wyoming-Denver-c1956-Midwest
  Oil Corp-8vo-cl-212p   (4t1) 9.50 (5h0) 5.50
ROBERTS,HELEN H-Report of Canadian Arctic Exped 1913 to 18-
  Ottawa-1925-wrps-506p   (5s6,rebkd) 15.00
--Songs of the Copper Eskimos-Ottawa-1925-(Vol 14)-wrps-506p
    (4d8) 15.00
ROBERTS,HELEN L-Putnam's Handbook of Etiquette-NY-(1913)-
  570p   (5w7) 2.50
ROBERTS,HENRY C-The Complete Prophecies of Nostradamus-NY-
  (1949)   (5p7) 4. (5F0,dj) 4.50
ROBERTS,JAS-Narrative of...AnnArbor-(ca 1938)-Heartman's
  Hist Series-wrps-32p-ltd to 136c   (4j4) 6.00
--same-Hattiesburg,Miss-1945-Heartman's Historical Series #71-
  8vo-orig wrps-32p-ltd to 136c   (5ss5) 12.50
ROBERTS,JAS A-NY in the Revolution as Colony & State-Albany-
  1898-4to-plts-534p-pict cl-2nd ed   (5t0) 15.00
--same-1904-534p & 336p-indexed-map (5ff2,cov stnd) 15.00
ROBERTS,JOS-Hand Book of Artillery for Service of the US...
  including new iron carriage-NY-1863-sm12mo-250p-cl-
  "5th ed"   (5t2) 10.00
ROBERTS,JOS K-Annotated Geological Bibliogr of Virg-Richmond-
  1942-726p-wrps   (4b6) 15.00
ROBERTS,KENNETH L,ed-Antiquamania-NY-1928-DDoran-260p
    (5x0) 6.00
--Arundel-NY-1930-1st ed(so stated)-1st issue (5ee3) 12.50
--The Battle of Cowpens-GardenCty-1958-illus-1st ed (5ee3,f,dj) 4.50
--Boon Island-GardenCty-1956-e.p. map-1st ed (5t4) 6.50
--Captain Caution,Chronicle of Arundel-NY-1934-1st ed
    (4b4,autg) 15.00
--Cowpens,the Great Morale Builder-Portland-1957-ltd to 400c,nbrd-
    (5t1) 25.00
--Europe's Morning After-NY-(1921)-8vo-cl-1st ed of auth's 1st book
    (5gg6,dj) 15.00
--Florida-1926-324p-cl-illus- DP Davis Properties Ed,by spec
  arrangement wi Harper   (5r0) 10.00
--Henry Gross & His Dowsing Rod-Double-1951-1st trade ed (5e8) 7.75
--I Wanted to Write-Dbl-1949-1st ed   (5e8) 9.75
--Lydia Bailey-NY-1947-g.t.-1st ed-ltd to 1050c,nbrd,autg,box-
  errata pg   (4g2) 65.00
--March to Quebec-Dblday-1938   (5F1,f,dj) 6.00
--same-NY-1938-frontis-map-657p-1st ed (5ee3,f) 15.00
--Moreau de St Mery's Amer Journey (1793 to 1798)-NY-1947-
  col frontis-1st ed   (4b7,dj) 15. (5t7) 8.50 (5x5) 10.00
--Northwest Passage-NY-1937-e.sheet maps (5h9) 5. (5dd6) 4.00
--same-GardenCty-1937-2 vols 1st ed-ltd to 1,050c,autg,box
    (5g1,mint,autog,dj) 90. (5t0,vf,dj) 45.00
--Oliver Wiswell-1st trade ed   (5k2) 5.00
--same-NY-1940-ltd to 1050c-2 vols-box,autg
    (5g1,mint,autog) 90. (4g2,f) 65.00
--Rabble in Arms-GardenCty-1933-870p-1st ed (5ee3,vg) 12.50
--Rabble in Arms-Dblday-1947-illus   (5k0,dj) 5.00
--The Seventh Sense-Double-1953-337p-illus (5e8) 5.00
--Sun Hunting-Indnpls-(1922)-BobbsMerrill-1st ed
  (5dd8,pres) 25. (4m8,dj) 8.50 (5ss9,fox) 10.00
--Trending into Maine-Bost-1938-NCWyeth,illus-394p (5t7) 10.50
--same-Bost-1938-Wyeth,illus-ltd to 1075c,autgs-394p (5m4) 65.00

ROBERTS,LESLIE-The Mackenzie-NY-(1949)-Rivers of Amer Ser-
  illus   (5ss1,dj,pres) 7.50
--These Be Your Gods-Tor-1929-illus-319p-ports (5s6) 5.00
ROBERTS,LLOYD-Book of Roberts-Tor-1923-147p (5a1,pres) 5.00
ROBERTS,LOUISA J-Biographical Sketch of-Phila-1895-Ferris-
  286p-illus-t.e.g.   (4n8,spot) 20.00
ROBERTS,M-Whig Party 1807 to 1812-1939 (5L7) 6.00
ROBERTS,MARTHA McM-Public Gardens & Arboretums of the US-
  NY-(1962)-4to-148p-10 col plts   (5w3) 5.00
ROBERTS,MARY FANTON-Inside 100 Homes-NY-McBride-1936-
  114p-illus-sm folio   (5p0) 7.50
ROBERTS,MILLARD F-Historical Gazetteer of Steuben County-
  1891-indexed-fldg map-2 vols in 1 (5ff2,newly rbnd) 24.00
ROBERTS,MORLEY-On the Old Trail, Through B C After 40 Years-
  Lond-1927-illus-242p-1st ed   (5dd7) 14.00
--The Private Life of Henry Maitland-Lond-1912-ENash-cl-
  1st ed-rev& ed by-1st ed (5ss3,dj, sp fade) 25.00
--W H Hudson, A Portrait-NY-(1924)-ltd ed (5mm2) 6.00
--The Western Avernus-Lond-1887-8vo-cl-1st ed of auth's 1st book-
    (5gg6,pres, 1 marg tn) 35.00
--same-Lond-n.d. (1924)-Dent-(Everyman)-238p (5dd7,f) 12.50
ROBERTS,OCTAVIA-Lincoln in Illinois-Bost-1918-lg papr ed-
  ltd to 1000c   (5p0,5q8,sl brown) 7.50
--With Lafayette in America-Bost-1919-HoughtonMiff-plts-
  293p,(1)   (5qq8) 6.00
ROBERTS,OSSEANNAH-Son of the North-Bost-1908-8vo-dec cl-
  illus   (5b2,f) 4.00
ROBERTS,PETER-Anthracite Coal Communities-NY-1904-illus
    (5q8,rprd) 10.00
ROBERTS,PHILETUS-Memoir of Mrs Abigail Roberts-Irvington,NJ-
  1858-port-plt-12mo-1st ed   (4m7,sl fox) 12.50
ROBERTS,RICHARD-The Unfinished Programme of Democracy-
  Lond-n.d.-sm12mo-bds   (5x7) 4.50
ROBERTS,ROBT-The House Servant's Directory-Bost-1843-180p
    (5w7,crack) 37.50
ROBERTS,S W-1st Annual Report of Little Schuylkill & Susquehanna
  RR Co, Jan 10, 1839-Phila-1839   (5m2) 6.00
ROBERTS,THOS S-Birds of Minnesota-Minnpls-1932-cl-92 col plts-
  5 maps-4to-2 vols-1st ed (5z9,autg,f) 55. (5cc1,pres,f) 75.00
--same-1936-revised ed-2 vols-cl   (5cc1,f) 67.50
ROBERTS,W A-Brave Mardi Gras-Indnpls-1946 (5x2) 10.(5x2,dj) 12.00
--Creole Dusk-Indnpls-1948-1st ed (5x2) 10. (5x2,dj) 12.50
--Lands of the Inner Sea-NY-1948-(pkt map in rear) (5x2) 15.00
--The French in the West Indies-Indnpls-1942-illus-1st ed (5x2) 17.50
--The Mind Reader-NY-1929-1st ed   (5x2) 25.00
ROBERTS,W ADOLPHE-The Book of the Navy-GardenCty-1944-
  302p   (5t4) 8.50
--Lake Ponchartrain-Indnpls-1946 et seq-376p-illus (5h9) 6.50
--Semmes of the Alabama-1938-BobbsMerrill (5g2) 10. (5x5) 12.50
ROBERTS,W F-Dixie Darkies-Bost-1942   (5x2,dj) 12.50
ROBERTS,W H-The British Winemaker & Domestic Brewer (with) A
  Suppl on Rhubarb Plant-Lond-1849-384p , 16p-5th ed
    (5w1,sl wn) 13.50
--The Scottish Ale Brewer & Practical Malster-Edinb-1847-251p,(1)-
  3rd ed   (5w6,cov spots) 18.50
ROBFRTS,WM-The Book Hunter in London-Chig-1895-McClurg-
  333p-illus-1st Amer ed   (5ee3,f) 12.50
ROBERTS,WM-Memoirs of the Life of Mrs Hannah More-Lond-1836-
  2 vols-thk8vo-orig dec cl   (5c8) 22.50
ROBERTS,WM-Poems-Lond-1774-for JWilkie,etc-8vo-calf-1st ed
    (5x3,f) 45.00
ROBERTSON,A-Regnum Dei-1901   (5L7) 4.50
ROBERTSON,ARCHIE-Slow Train to Yesterday-Bost-(1945)-8vo-cl-
  illus-1st ed   (5p5) 6.00
ROBERTSON,COLIN-Correspondence Book,1817 to 1822-Tor-1939-
  Champlain Soc-372p   (5s6) 25.00
--same-(Lond)-1939-EERich,ed-frontis-Hudson Bay Record Soc,II
    (5r7) 35.00
ROBERTSON,CONSTANCE-The Unterrified-NY-(1946) (5s9,dj) 3.50
ROBERTSON,DAVID-Reports of Trials of Colonel Aaron Burr-Phila-
  1808-Hopkins&Earle-2 vols-calf (5tt8,lacks hf t.,wn) 35.00
--Trial of Aaron Burr-NY-1875-2 vols-frontis (4a9,wn) 16.(5r7) 25.00
ROBERTSON,DOUGLAS S-To Arctic with Mounties-Tor-1934-plts-
  lg fldg map   (5a1,pres) 12.50
ROBERTSON,ELIZ W-Amer Quilts-NY-1948-167 illus-152p (5n7) 8.50
ROBERTSON,F A L-Keayne Keen(e), Keeney,Kinne(y) & Allied
  Families-1942-Vol 1(all pub)-183p   (5mm3) 20.00
ROBERTSON,F K-Book of Health, or Thomsonian Theory etc,also...
  Materia Medica by Silas Wilcox-Bennington,Vt-1843-calf-sm8vo-
  1st ed   (4c8,sl dmpstn) 17.50
ROBERTSON,F L K-Lovelace, Loveless & Allied Families-(1952)-
  203p   (5mm3) 22.50

ROBERTSON,FRANK C-A Ram in the Thicket-NY-1959-8vo-cl-
412p-illus-1st ed   (5g5,f,dj)   5.00

ROBERTSON,GEO-Discovery of Tahiti-Lond-1948-map-8vo-cl-
Hakluyt Soc   (4c1)   12.50

ROBERTSON,GEORGIA-Efficiency in Home Making & First Aid
to Good Cooking-Wash-(1915)-157p-qtr lea   (5g9)   4.50

ROBERTSON,HELEN-Merry Mixer Cook Book-NY-(1941)-628p-
rev&enlrgd ed   (5c0)   3.50

ROBERTSON,IGNATIUS L-Sketches of Public Characters Drawn From
the Living & Dead-NY-1830-hf calf-260p   (5tt8)   20.00

ROBERTSON,J G-The Life & Work of Goethe 1749 to 1832-NY-
1932-illus-350p   (5m1,dj)   7.50

ROBERTSON,J M-Mr. Shaw & The Maid-Lond-n.d.-115p (5p9)   4.50

ROBERTSON,J ROSS-Landmarks of Canada-Tor-Dec,1917(5w8)   7.50

--Old Toronto-Tor-1954   (5w8)   6.00

--Ornithological Collection-Tor-1919-Tor Pub Libr-88p-prntd wrps
(5w8)   5.00

ROBERTSON,JAS A-List of documents in Spanish archives relating
to history of US-Wash-1910-4to   (5g8)   7.50

ROBERTSON,JAS ALEX,ed-The relation of hardships suffered by
Gov Fernando de Soto & certain Portuguese gentlemen during
discovery of Florida-Deland-by a gentleman of Elvas-2 vols-
port-bds&buck-360c prntd-Publ #11 of the Florida Hist Soc-
1932-   (5g4)   40.00

ROBERTSON,JESSIE E-A Teacher's Life-Robt McQueen,ed-frontis-
Hamilton-1890   (5w8)   10.00

ROBERTSON,JOHN,ed-Michigan in the War-Lansing-1882-illus-
hf mor-1039p-illus-Part 3,Reg of Commissioner Officers
(5h7) 12.50   (5r7)   25.00

ROBERTSON,JOHN C-Reports of Comm on Publ Safety,People of
State of Texas-Austin-1861-JnMarshall-173p-rare(5n4,vf)   110.00

ROBERTSON,JOHN M-A Short History of Freethought,Ancient &
Modern-Lond-1899-8vo-1st ed   (5ss5)   15.00

ROBERTSON,JOHN R-Diary of Mrs. John Graves Simcoe w Notes
etc-Tor-1934-illus-440p   (4h3)   65.00

ROBERTSON,M L-Histoire De L'Amerique-Paris-1778-2 vols-lea-
(5x5,crack,rub)   25.00

ROBERTSON,M S-Rodeo Standard Guide to the Cowboy Sport-
Berkeley-1961-4to-cl   (5m9,vg,dj)   6.00

ROBERTSON,MARGARET M-Bairns or Janets Love & Service-Lond-
1883-10th ed   (4b9)   10.00

ROBERTSON,MAX-Mountain Panorama-Lond-(1955)-MaxParish-
128p-illus   (5d7)   2.00

ROBERTSON,NORMAN-History of County of Bruce-Tor-1906-
ports-plts-maps-560p (5s6) 15.   (4h3)   40.00

--same-Tor-1960-560p-ports-illus-maps-not 1st   (5a1)   8.50

ROBERTSON,R B-Of Whales & Men-Knoft-1954-illus
(5s1,5e8) 4.   (5hh6) 4.75 (5t2)   4.50

ROBERTSON,R S-Organization of Allen County-FtW-1954-49p-wrps
(5h1)   3.50

ROBERTSON,THOS A-A Southwestern Utopia-LosAng-1964-cl-
illus-206p   (5t2,dj,mint)   5.00

ROBERTSON,W GRAHAM-Gold,Frankincense & Myrrh & other
pageants for a baby girl-Lond&NY-1907-JnLane-4to-152p
(8)(ads)-frontis-11 col plts-pict cl   (5p1)   27.50

--Life was Worth Living,The Reminis of-NY-n.d.-illus-cl-344p
(5t2)   4.00

--A Masque of May Morning-Lond&NY-1904-JnLane-4to-
62p-4(ads)-frontis-11 col plts-pict cl   (5p1,rub,fox)   12.50

ROBERTSON,W M PARISH-A Visit to Mexico-Lond-1853-2 vols-
8vo-cl-fldg map,fldg frontis-subscribers ed-scarce (4a3,f)   65.00

ROBERTSON,WM-Historia de la America-Burdeos-1827-a vols-
16mo-calf-Spanish ed   (5r7)   20.00

--Historical & Other works of...-Edinb/Lond-1847-part mor-
8vo-2 vols   (4p3)   30.00

--History of America-Lond-1800-4 vols   (4k7,chip)   45.00

--same-Lond-1803-4 vols-lea-fldg map ea vol
(5L7,ex-libr) 15. (5i3,vg)   25.00

--same-Lond-1811-2 vols-lea-new ed   (5x5,rub,lt stns)   15.00

--same-Lond-1822-JRichardson-calf-4 vols(Vols 8 to 11)
(5qq8,cov loose)   15.00

--History of the Discovery & Settlement of Amer-NY-1828-
J&J Harper-orig papr bds-539p plus ad   (5a0,rbkd)   12.50

--History of the Reign of Emperor Charles V-Lond-1796-3 vols-
hf calf-8th ed   (5d6,cov wn)   100.00

--Works of-Lond-1829-2 vols-3 qtr mor   (5hh3)   20.00

ROBESON,ESLANDA GOODE-African Journey-NY-1945-John Day-
maps-photos-154p   (4t5) 6.   (5x2,dj)   5.50

--Paul Robeson,Negro-NY-1930-1st ed(so stated)-178p-tall 8vo-cl
(5w0,dmgd) 6.50   (5x2,4c5,wn dj,vg)   12.50

ROBESON,G F-Govt Special Charter Cities in Iowa-1923-
286p with index-t.e.g.   (5a9)   7.50

ROBESON,G M-Reports of Explor & Surveys for Location of
Ship Canal...thru Nicaragua-Wash-1874-GPO-20 fldg plts-
4to-143p   (5yy0)   22.50

ROBESON,GEO M-Instructions for exped toward North Pole from-
Wash-1871-wrps   (5g8)   10.00

ROBESON,GEO M-Method for Classifying Offences & Punishments
on Board Vessels of US Navy-(Wash,Navy Dept,Apr 4,1870)-
11p-pamph-soft cl   (5qq8)   10.00

ROBESON,P-Here I Stand-NY-1958   (5x2,dj)   10.00

ROBIDOUX,ORRAL M-Memorial to Robidoux Bros-KansCty,MO-
1924-illus-map   (5k1,f)   45.00

ROBIE,R E-Anc & Desc of Reuben Robie & Nancy Whiting-(1899)-
131p-2nd rev ed-200c prntd   (5mm2)   25.00

ROBIN HOOD-being a Complete History etc-Lond-Jun(1818)-
WDarton-sq8vo-32p-orig wrps -scarce chapbook-8 plts (5c8)   25.00

ROBIN L'ABBE-Nouveau Voyage dans L'Amerique Septentrionale-
Phila&Paris-Moutard-1783-8vo-2nd ed
(5L1,f,orig wrps) 35.   (5n9,sheep)   75.00

ROBIN,J-Vinification-Sucrage Des Vins-Montpellier-1888-79p-
wrps-3rd ed-rev&aug   (5w1)   8.50

ROBINET,EDOUARD,d'EPERNAY-Manual General Des Vins
2e Partie,Vins Mousseux Champagnes-Paris-(?1898)-364p,(14)-
5th ed,rev   (5w1,underline)   7.50

--Note sur la fabrication des Vins Mousseux-Paris-c1900-29p,(1)-
wrps   (5w1,wormholes)   6.50

ROBINS,BENJ-New Principles of Gunnery-Lond-1742-JNourse-
fldg plt & wd diagrams-wrps-1st ed-v scarce   (5jj8,f)   150.00

ROBINS,EDW-Chasing Iron Horse or Boy's Adven in Civil War-Phila-
(1902)-293p-cl   (5r7)   7.50

--Romances of Early America-Phila-1902-GeoWJacobs-illus-
268p   (5p7,5ee3)   6.00

ROBINS,ELIZABETH-The Florentine Frame-NY-1909-Moffat,Yard-
8vo-cl   (5b2,f)   4.00

--The Magnetic North-NY-(1904)-417p-fldg map   (5ss1)   4.50

ROBINS,ELIZ-Theatre & Friendship,some Henry James Letters-NY-
1932-Putnam's   (4p1)   10.00

ROBINS,RICHARD-Toasts & Responses at Banquests Given Lieut Gen
P H Sheridan-Chig-1882-8vo-ports   (5m6)   10.00

ROBINS,SALLY NELSON-Love Stories of Famous Virginians-
Richmond-1923-8vo-illus-1st ed   (5m6)   5.00

ROBINS,W P-Etching Craft-Lond-1922-8vo-orig bds-cl bk-illus
(5m6,warp)   7.50

ROBINSON,A-Life in Calif....Historical Acct of Origin,Customs &
Traditions of Indians-NY-1846-plts-lea&marbld bds-341p-
1st ed   (4n1)   125.00

ROBINSON,A H A-Mineral Industries of Canada-1934-Canada
Dept of Mines-   (5L7)   10.00

ROBINSON,ALBERT G-Old New England Doorways-NY-1919-illus
(5xx7) 10. (5ii2)   12.50

ROBINSON,B L-Fruit of Tropidocarpum-SanFran-1896-wrps(4a5) 3.50

ROBINSON,BEVERLY W-With Shotgun & Rifle in NoAmer-NY-1925-
illus   (5ss8) 7.50   (5t7)   8.50

ROBINSON,BOARDMAN-Boardman Robinson,93 Drawings-
ColoSprings Fine Arts Cntr-1937-16p-93 plts-sm4to   (4a0)   32.50

ROBINSON,C W-Canada & Canadian Defence-Tor-n.d.-186p-
3 fldg maps   (4b9,f)   15.00

ROBINSON,CHANDLER-J Evetts Haley, Cowman Historian-ElPaso-
1967-Hertzog-(600 copies printed)   (4c7) 27.50   (4j6)   17.50

ROBINSON,CHAS-Kansas Conflict-NY-1892
(5L0) 8.50   (5L0,autg,wn,5L7,rbnd)   7.50

--The Kansas Conflict-Lawrence-1898-487p (5t7,autg,libr stmp)   7.50

--Nebr & Kans,Rept of Comm of Massachusetts Emigrant Aid Co-
Bost-1854-sewn-32p-1st ed   (4k7)   30.00

ROBINSON,CHAS ALEX,JR-Alexander the Great-NY-1947-Dutton-
252p   (5p0)   5.00

ROBINSON,CHAS EDSON-Concise History of the United Soc
of Believers Called Shakers-East Canterbury-(1893)-134p-
illus-orig prntd bds   (5m3,sp def) 22.50   (5s2,f)   30.00

ROBINSON,CHAS MULFORD-Beautifying of Honolulu-Honolulu-
1907-39p-fldg map-wrps   (5yy3)   4.00

ROBINSON,CHAS N-Celebrities of the Army-Lond-(1900)-4to-
cl-col plts-144p   (5t4)   15.00

--Old Naval Prints-Lond-1924-4to-mtd col plts-ltd ed
(5tt5) 37.50   (5ss2,fade)   22.50

ROBINSON,CLEMENT-A Handful of Pleasant Delights-
Harvard Univ Pr-1924-Rollins,ed-145p   (5p9)   5.00

ROBINSON,CONWAY-Account of Discoveries in the West until
1519,etc-Richmond-1848-491p-scarce   (4m2,chip)   22.50

ROBINSON,CORINNE ROOSEVELT-My Brother Theodore Roosevelt-
NY-1921-365p-cl (5h1) 5. (5L7) 3.50 (5ss5,sl stn)   10.00

ROBINSON CRUSOE-Also See Defoe,Dan'l or title

ROBINSON CRUSOE-(Caption title)-Bost-(1859,Rock A Bye Libr)-
Taggard&Thompson-sm8vo-dec&pict yellow limp bds-16p-
hand col frontis-   hand col illus   (5aa2)   15.00
ROBINSON CRUSOE-Lond-1924-Milford-sm8vo-dec red cl-255p-
col frontis-(reprint,Herbert Strang's Library)   (5aa2)   3.50
ROBINSON CRUSOE-NY-(194-)-Books Inc-8vo-pict glazed wrps-
307p-(Giant Jr Classics)   2.50
ROBINSON CRUSOE-The Clever Cats,etc-A Picture Book for the
Nursery-Lond-(c1880)-Nelson-16 col illus-lg4to-dec cl-
16p text & 16 liths,mntd on lin   (5aa2)   25.00
ROBINSON CRUSOE-His Life & Adventures-Lond&NY-1887-Warne-
4to-dec col pict glazed bds-88p-12p col plts-wdcuts (5aa2)   6.50
ROBINSON CRUSOE-His Life & Strange Surprising Adventures
in Words of One Syllable(by Mary Godolphin)-Phila-(cpyrte 1897)-
12mo-pict cl-184p-frontis-plts-(Altemus'Young People's Libr)
                                            (5aa2)   4.50
ROBINSON CRUSOE-Rock A Bye Library-Bost-(1859)-16p-pict wrps-
hand col wdcuts-Taggard&Thompson   (5c8,tn)   7.50
ROBINSON CRUSOE-NY-(1897)-McLoughlin Bros-picture book
wi 6p col prnts-sq8vo-16p-self wrps   (5c8,rub)   7.50
ROBINSON CRUSOE-Toy Book-F Warne-(c1867)-sm4to-pict wrps-
19p-col plts   (5s0)   8.50
ROBINSON CRUSOE-Travels & Adventures-(Reading,PA)-(c1937)-
Spencer Pr-8vo-dec patent cl-311p-10 plts   (5aa2,sl wn)   4.50
ROBINSON,D S-Intro to Living Philosophy-NY-1932-381p (5p0)   5.00
ROBINSON,DOANE-Brief History of So Dakota-NY-c1905-
Amer Book Co-12mo-cl-224p   (4t1)   7.00
--History of SoDakota-Aberdeen-1904-2 vols-lea-1903p-illus
                                            (5t1)   100.00
--same-Vol 1(of 2)-n.p.-1904-BF Bowen Co-4to-part lea
                                    (4t1,lacks Vol 2)   25.00
--same-Minnpls-1956-reprint of 1904 orig-508p plus index-
illus-maps   (5L0)   10.00
--South Dakota-Chig-1930-3 vols   (5kk6)   35.00
ROBINSON,DUNCAN W-Judge Robt McAlpin Williamson-Austin-
1948-230p   (5n4)   8.50
ROBINSON,EDW-Memoir of Wm Robinson-1859-214p-3/4 lea
                                            (5e8)   7.50
ROBINSON,EDW A-The Gun Bearer-NY-1894-12mo-Ledger
Library #107-1st ed   (5ss5,pres)   7.50
ROBINSON,EDWIN ARLINGTON-Amaranth-NY-1934-12mo-105p-
cl-1st ed   (5m8,dj) 5.   (5b9,f)   8.50
--Avon's Harvest-NY-1921-Macmillan-1st trade ed,earliest bndng
                            (5ss3,dj) 15.   (4b7,dj)   20.00
--same-NY-1921-MacmillanCo-1st ed-2nd brdng (5ss3,dj)   7.50
--Capt Craig,a Book of Poems-Bost-1902-12mo-orig cl-t.e.g.-
(375c were issued)-1st trade ed   (5dd8)   50.00
--Cavender's House-NY-1929-ltd to 500c,autg
                            (5j2,unopnd) 20.   (5m4)   25.00
--Collected Poems-Cambr-(1927)-Dunster Hse-lg papr ed-5 vols-
ltd to 300 sets,autgs   (5d3)   75.00
--same-NY-1924-frontis-cl-591p   (5t2)   3.50
--Dionysus in Doubt-NY-1925-1st ed-ltd to 350c,autg,boxed
                            (5ss9,fade) 20.   (5m4)   25.00
--Glory of Nightingales-NY-Macmillan-1930-1st ed
            (5i1) 4.50   (5m8,soil) 3.50 (5ee3,f)   5.00
--same-NY-1930-cl-ltd to 500c,autg-Merrymount Pr-1st ed
                    (5mm1) 22.50   (5dd8,box)   20.00
--King Jasper-1935-Macmillan-1st trade ed,issued sub to ltd ed
                    (5F1,dj,f)   (5ee3,f,dj)   7.50
--same-NY-1935-8vo-bds-cl bk-1st ed-ltd to 250c,box (5ee9) 25.00
--Matthias at the door-NY-1931-Macmillan-1st trade ed
                    (5hh1,5m8,dj) 5.   (5m2)   6.50
--Nicodemus,a book of poems-NY-1932-Macmillan-1st trade ed
                    (5hh1,dj) 5.   (5m2)   6.50
--The Prodigal Son-NY-1929-Random Hse-8vo-wrps-poetry 4tos-
ltd to 475c   (5b2,v)   10.00
--Selections from the Letters of Thos S Perry   -NY-Macmillan-
1929-255p   (5p7)   4.50
--Sonnets 1889 to 1927-NY-Macmillan-1928-1st trade ed
                    (5m2) 6.50   (5b2,f,dj)   10.00
--The Three Taverns-NY-1920-Macmillan-cl-1st ed
                    (5ss3,sp stnd,crack,dj)   15.00
--Tristram-NY-1927-12mo-cl-1st ed-1st issue (wi "rocks" for
"rooks" pg 86)   (4a1,sl fray dj,5ee9)   15.00
--same-NY-1927-Macmillan-cl-1st ed-2nd state (5ss3,dj)   10.00
--Van Zorn,Comedy in 3 Acts-NY-1914-Macmillan-8vo-cl-
2nd bndng   (5b2,cov sl stn)   12.50
ROBINSON,ETHEL FAY-Houses in Amer-NY-(1936)-Viking Pr-
240p-illus-pict cl   (5p9) 6.   (5h9) 5.   (5r0)   7.50
ROBINSON,FAYETTE-Calif & Its Gold Regions-NY-1849-Stringer &
Townsend-137p-fldg map-cl&bds   (5tt0)   150.00

ROBINSON,FAYETTE   (continued)
--Acct of Organization of Army of the US etc-Phila-1848-2 vols-
1st ed-36 ports   (5ee3)   30.00
ROBINSON,FRANK T-Living New Engl Artists-Bost-1888-lg4to-
cl-plts   (5t2,hng weak)   7.50
ROBINSON,FRANKLIN W-Aural Harmony-NY-1918,1923-
2 vols-Schirmer   (5p7)   6.50
ROBINSON,FREDK-A Letter to Rufus Choate...Law Craft-n.p.-
1832-12mo-19p-stitchd-1st ed-prntd for Purchaser (5ss5,stnd) 8.50
ROBINSON,FREDK S-English Furniture-NY-1905-Putnam-4to-
orig buck-g.sp-plts   (5t5)   15.00
ROBINSON,G H-Handbook of Admiralty Law in the US-StPaul-
1939-Hornbrook Ser   (5ff4)   5.00
ROBINSON,GEO O,JR-The Oak Ridge Story-Kingsport-(1950)-
                            (5h6,dj,autg)   6.00
ROBINSON,GILMER GEO-Fly Casting-NY-(1942)-66p-illus(5t4) 4.00
ROBINSON,GREGORY-Ships...That Have Made History-NY-c1936-
4to-139p-col illus   (5w9,fade)   7.50
ROBINSON,H E-Wallace Fulham Robinson,His Anc etc-1917-
110p   (4t2)   4.00
ROBINSON,H L-Hist of Pittsfield,NH in the Great Rebellion-
Pittsfield-1893-sm8vo-illus-cl-2!7p   (4t2)   7.50
ROBINSON,H M-Great Fur Land-NY-1879-hf mor-348p-illus
                                            (5r6)   12.50
ROBINSON,MRS H M-The Practical Cook Book-NY-1864-225p
                            (5c0,brown)   12.50
ROBINSON,H W-Diary of Robt Hooke-Lond-1935-TaylorFrancis-
527p-11 plts   (5m5)   30.00
ROBINSON,HENRY-Science vs Crime-Indnpls-1935-303p-illus-
cl-1st ed   (5t0)   3.75
ROBINSON,HENRY CRABB-Diary,Remin & Corres of...Lond-
1869-port-lg8vo-hf mor-3 vols-1st ed   (5tt7)   20.00
--same-Bost-1870-cl-2 vols-1st Amer ed   (5p6)   15.00
ROBINSON,HENRY MORTON-Stout Cortez-NY=(1931)-344p plus
index-illus-map-1st ed   (5L2)   6.50
ROBINSON,IRWIN-Yankee Toolmaker-Bridgeport-1955-46p(5y2) 5.50
ROBINSON,J B-Pictures of Slavery & Anti Slavery-Phila-1863
                                            (5x2)   45.00
ROBINSON,J G,ed-A M E Church Review-Quarterly of African
Methodist Church-Jan 1938-44p-wrps-illus   (5x2)   10.00
ROBINSON,J H-A Brief Review of the 2 Systems of Medical Practice
...(wi) a Materia Medica-Bangor-1844-103p,(1) (5w3,stnd)   9.50
ROBINSON, DR J H-Silver Knife; Hunters of the Rocky Mntns-
Bost-1854-168p-scarce   (5s4,shake,poor)   37.50
ROBINSON, J H-German Bundesrath-1891-68p-sewn (5L7)   2.50
ROBINSON, J H-Guide to Nantucket-(1928)-98p-5th ed-illus
                                            (5e8)   3.50
ROBINSON,J H-Tomorrow is Today-Phila-1954   (5x2,dj)   7.50
ROBINSON, J M & CO-Catalogue of Cornice Breaks,Gutter Forms,
Bending Machines-Cinn-1892-wrps-84p-illus   (5hh7)   10.00
ROBINSON,JACOB S-Journal of Santa Fe Exped Under Col Doniphan-
Princeton U-1932-12mo-cl   (5F5)   12.50
ROBINSON,JAS,ed-Philadelphia Director for 1808-orig bds-
calf bk   (5m4,hng loose)   40.00
ROBINSON,JAS-Compend of Bookkeeping by Single Entry-Bost-
1833-2nd ed-8vn-prnt bds   (4c1)   10.00
ROBINSON,JAS-The Ordeal of Civilization-NY-1926-8vo-cl-
illus-769p-1st ed   (5t0)   4.00
ROBINSON,JAS H-Road without Turning,story of Rev Jas H
Robinson,an autobiogr-1950   (5L7)   4.00
ROBINSON,JOHN R-Marine Room of Peabody Museum of Salem-
Salem-1921-lg8vo-188p-plts   (5w9) 10.   (5h9)   25.00
ROBINSON,JOS S-The Story of Marblehead-(n.p.-)-1936-92p-
8vo-cl-illus   (5j5)   12.50
--Waymarks in Life of Mary Baker Eddy-Springfield-1942-108p-
illus   (5e8)   7.50
ROBINSON,JUDITH-Tom Cullen of Baltimore-Tor-1949-435p-plts
                                            (5s0)   5.00
ROBINSON,L B-Esquimalt,Place of Shoaling Waters-Vict-1947-
wrps   (4f9) 6.50   (5dd7)   6.50
ROBINSON,L L-Letter of to Joint Committee on RR's of Nev
Legislature-CarsonCty-1865-12mo-7p-prntd wrps
                            (5a3,wrps in facs)   125.00
ROBINSON,LENNOX-The White Headed Boy-Dublin-(1920?)-
12mo-bds   (4c2,faded)   20.00
ROBINSON,LURA-It's An Old New Orleans Custom-NY-1948-
322p-illus   (5x2) 3.   (5w5,dj)   6.00
ROBINSON,LUTHER E-Abraham Lincoln As A Man of Letters-Chig-
1918-illus-1st ed   (5m2,pres)   7.50
--same-NY-1923-8vo-cl-344p-illus   (5t2)   5.00
--Hist & Biog Record of Monmouth & Warren Co III-Chig-1927-
2 vols-565p-hf lea   (5h7)   47.50

ROBINSON,M S-A Pageant of the Sea,MacPherson Collection of-
Lond-1950-Halton&Co-4to-blue cl-col illus   (5b0)   55.00

ROBINSON,MABEL L-Runner of the Mountain Tops-NY-1939-
290p-cl-illus   (5t2) 4.50   (5w3)   5.00

ROBINSON,MARGARET-Arbitration & the Hague Peace Conference,
1899 &1907-1936-sewn   (5L7)   4.50

ROBINSON,MARION O-Give My Heart-GardenCty-1964-348p-
ports-plts   (5a1)   4.50

ROBINSON,MARY-Angelina,a novel-Lond-1813-3 vols-12mo-
hf calf-3rd ed-Minerva Pr   (5xx6,f,rbnd)   70.00

ROBINSON,NUGENT,comp-Collier's Cyclopedia of Commercial
& Social Info & Treas of Useful & Entertaining Knowledge-NY-
c1882-thk4to-g.dec cov-746p   (4g9)   17.50

ROBINSON,R E-Out of Bondage & Other Stories-Bost-1905-
12mo-1st ed   (5x2)   10.00

ROBINSON,ROWLAND E-A Danvis Pioneer-Bost-1900-HoughtonMiff-
8vo-dec cl   (5b2,f)   8.50

--In New Engl Fields & Woods-Bost-1896-sm12mo-1st ed
      (5w5,spots)   8.50

--Out of Bondage & Other Stories-Bost-1905-HoughtonMiff-12mo-
dec cl   (5b2,f)   8.50

--Sam Lovel's Boy-Bost-1901-HoughtonMiff-12mo-dec cl (5b2) 8.50

--Silver Fields & Other Sketches of a Farmer Sportsman-Bost-1921-
12mo-cl-261p-1st ed   (5t0,dj,f)   7.50

--Uncle Lisha's Shop-NY-1887-12mo-cl-1st ed (5b2) 8.50(5gg6)17.50

--Vermont,A Study of Independence-Bost-1892-HoughtonMiff-8vo-
cl-g.t.-map-Amer Commonwealths series-scarce   (5b2)   15.00

--same-Bost-1900-370p-fldg col map-g.t.-12mo-Amer
Commonwealths   (5b2,f)   7.50

ROBINSON,SARAH-Robinson,Saffords,Harwoods & Clarks,Hist of
families of-1837-96p   (4t2)   30.00

ROBINSON,SARA T L-Kansas,Its Interior & Exterior Life-Bost-
1856-366p-1st ed   (4n4,sp rprd)   20.00

--same-Lawrence,KS-1899-438p-illus-10th ed
      (5t7,libr stmps,pres)   10.00

ROBINSON,SAML-Catalogue of Amer Minerals with Their Localities-
Bost-1825-orig bds-1st ed-Sabin 72176   (5m2)   10.00

--A Course of 15 Lectures on Medical Botany-Columbus,O-1832-
16mo-206p,(2)-calf   (5w3,wn)   13.50

ROBINSON,SELMA-City child,poems-NY-1931-Colophon-
dec by Rockwell Kent-ltd to 300c,nbrd,autg by poet &
Kent's thumbprint-box   (5m2)   8.50

ROBINSON,SOLON-Guano-NY-1853-8vo-96p-wrps
      (4a3,lacks lower co)   12.50

--Hot Corn-NY-1854-408p-cl   (5h2,rub)   10.00

ROBINSON,T H-Robinson,Fragments of Family & Contempory
History-1867-141p   (4t2)   10.00

ROBINSON,T R-Modern Clocks & Their Repair & Maintenance-
Lond-1943-illus-193p-8vo-2nd ed   (5bb0)   5.00

--Modern Watch Repair & Adjusting-Chig-1933-illus-120p-8vo
      (5bb0)   6.25

ROBINSON,THOS H-Thos Robinson & His Descendants-Harrisburg-
1902-233p-illus   (5m2) 20. (5t9)   25.00

ROBINSON,VICTOR-Morals In Wartime-NY-1943-205p-1st ed
      (5w9,dj)   4.00

ROBINSON,W-The Garden Beautiful-Lond-1907-176p-bds (5s7) 7.50

--Mushroom Culture-Phila-n.d.-172p-frontis-illus (5s7) 4.00

--same-Lond-(ca 1890)-12mo-180p-illus   (5dd6)   7.50

ROBINSON,W HEATH-Illustrator of Works of Mr Francis Rabelais-
Lond-1924-Navarre Soc-2 vols-buck-ltd-t.e.g.-8vo (5ww3) 25.00

ROBINSON,W W-Bombs&Bribery-LosAng-Calif State College-
52p-2 col-7p illus-Famous Calif Trials,Vol 9   (5d2)   9.00

--Land in Calif-Univ of Calif-1948-(Chronicles of Calif)-cl-
291p-8vo   (5h5,vf,dj)   30.00

--Panorama-LosAng-1953-4to-wrps-78p-illus-1st ed (5s4) 4.(5g0) 5.50

--People vs Lugo-LosAng-1962-   -Famous Calif
Trials,2-ltd to 300c   (5F5,f)   15.00

--Ranchos Become Cities-Pasadena-1939-San Pasqual Pr-243p-
1st ed   (5F5) 17.50 (5x5,dj)   27.50

ROBINSON,WILL H-The Story of Ariz-Phoenix-(1919)-458p-illus-
scarce   (5dd4,wn) 23. (5r7) 35. (4t8)   25.00

--Under Turquoise Skies-NY-1928-photos-538p-1st ed
  (4b2,autg,5ee3,f) 12.50 (5ee3,5yy6) 10. (5x5) 15.00

--When the Red Gods Made Men-1935-priv prntd-8vo-wrps-34p-
illus-1st ed   (5g0,mint)   6.50

--The Witchery of Rita & Waiting for Tonti-Phoenix-1919-bds-
71p-cl bk-scarce   (5r0)   10.00

--Yarns of the SoWest-Chandler Arizonan Pr-(1921)-BerryhillCo-
pict stiff wrps   (5m2)   7.50

ROBINSON,WM ALBERT-10,000 Leagues Over the Sea-NY-(1932)-
379p-35 photos-maps   (5s1)   5.00

ROBINSON,WM DAVIS-Memoirs of Mexican Revol,Including Narr
of Exped of Gen Xavier Mina-Phila-1820-396p-3/4 mor-
1st ed   (4a5)   125.00

ROBINSON,WM MORRISON-The Confederate Privateers-NewHav-
1928-8vo-1st ed   (5ss5,dj)   16.00

ROBINSON,WM MORRISON,Jr-Confederate Privateers-Yale Univ
Pr-1928-372p-illus   (5mm8,dj) 10. (5x5) 15.00

ROBINSON,WIP,III-Early Amer Claims to Oregon Country-Norman-
1938-107p-hard cov-bndr-typescript,carbon-Master's thesis
      (5s4)   20.00

ROBINSONADE,MIRVAL,C H de-Le Robinson des Sables du Desert-
Paris-1837-PCLehurby-sm8vo-3/4 calf-3 plts (5dd0) 25.00

ROBISON,S S-History of Naval Tactics from 1530 to 1930-Annap-
(1942)-956p-illus-maps   (5s1,ex-libr)   10.00

ROBLES,M A-Perfiles Del Saltillo-Mexico-1933-141p-wrps (4a5) 8.50

ROBLES,VITO ALESSIO-Coahuila & Texas,Desde La Consumacion
De La Independencia-Mexico-1945-2 vols-wrps (5a8,mint) 42.50

--Coahuila Y Texas En La Epoca Colonial-1938-751p-maps-plts-
hf lea   (5r1,f)   30.00

--La Primera Imprenta En Las Provincias Internas De Orientes Texas-
Mexico-1939-79p-stiff wrps-illus-v scarce (5n4) 27.50

ROBLEY,T F-History of Bourbon County,Kansas,to close of 1865-
FtScott-1894-illus-210p-1st ed   (4L2)   37.50

ROBOTTI,FRANCES DIANE-Chronicles of Old Salem-Salem-1948-
illus-1st ed-o.p.   (5xx8) 7.50 (5h9) 6.00

ROBSON,CHAS-Biog Encyclopedia of Illinois of 19th Century-
Phila-1875-Galaxy Pub-4to-lea-a.e.g.-529p (4t1) 25.00

ROBSON,E I-A Wayfarer in French Vineyards-Lond-(1928)-212p-
illus   (5w1)   7.50

ROBSON,FRANCIS-The Life of Hyder Ally-Lond-1786-hf lea
      (5ee3,autg)   25.00

ROBSON,JOS-An Account of 6 Years Residence in Hudson's Bay-
Lond-1752-3 maps-calf-adv lf-rare (5m9,cov dtchd) 100.00

ROBY,H J-Intro to Study of Justinian's Digest-Cambr-1886
      (5ff4,rub)   15.00

ROCH,ANDRE-On Rock & Ice-Lond-1947-80p-cl (5d7) 5.00

ROCHE,JAS JEFFREY-The Story of the Filibusters-Lond-1891-8vo-
cl-373p-map-illus   (5r7) 10. (5m8) 15.00

ROCHE,JOHN-Inquiry,concerning author of Letters of Junius-
Lond-1813-12mo-294p-bds   (5xx7)   15.00

ROCHE,JOHN A-Life of John Price Durbin-NY-1889-369p-
1st ed   (5w5)   7.50

ROCHEBLAVE,S-French Painting of 19th Century-Paris-1936-
(Hyperion Pr)-thk4to-96 plts-1st ed   (5ii3)   35.00

ROCHEFORT,CHAS DE-Natuurlyke en Zedelyke Historie van
d'Eylanden de Voor Eylanden van Amerika-Rotterdam-1662-
Arnout Leers-475p-fldg plts-4to-vel-1st ed in Dutch (5j5,f) 475.00

ROCHEMONTEUX,LE P C DE,ed-Relation Par Lettres De L'Amerique
Septrent Ionelle-Paris-1904-215p-wrps   (4b9,f)   30.00

ROCHESTER & MONROE CO,NY-Rochester-1937-Federal Writers'
Proj-WPA-cl-460p-3 fldg maps   (4k2)   12.50

ROCHESTER (NY), DIRECDORY-for the Village of...(with) a
Sketch-Rochester-1827-141p,(1),(14)-16mo-fldg map-orig prntd
bds-calf bk   (5a3,title tn)   100.00

ROCHESTER-Great Republican meeting(caption)-(n.p.-1828)-8vo-
unbnd   (5g4)   40.00

ROCK COUNTY(WISC)-History of-1879-897p-illus (5t9) 30.00

ROCK ISLAND LINES-Calif,the Golden State-(Chig,1909)-48p-
wrps   (5dd4)   5.00

ROCK ISLAND PLOW CO-Cook Book-RockIsl-n.d.(ca 1910?)-
224p   (5t9)   3.50

ROCK,JAS L-Southern & Western Texas for 1878-StL-1878-282p-
illus-lg fldg map-rare   (4a5,wn)   42.50

ROCK OR THE RYE,THE-(Thos C DeLeon)-Mobile-1888-34p-wrps
      (5h1,wn)   8.50

ROCK PLANTS-Lond-1939-Hyperion Pr-1st ed-40 col liths
      (5qq7,dj)   40.00

ROCKEFELLER FOUNDATION INTERNES-Brooklyn Museum cat-
Exhibition of European Art 1450 to 1500-NY-1936-50p text-
304 plts-lg4to-wrps-cl sp   (5m5,soil)   14.00

ROCKEFELLER,H O-Rockefeller Genealogy-Vol 4-(1960)-401p
      (4t2)   17.50

--Transactions of the Rockefeller Family Assn for 1905 to 1909-1910-
383p   (5t9)   15.00

--same-for 1915 to 1925-1926-294p   (4t2)   12.50

ROCKEFELLER,JOHN D-The Colorado Industrial Plan-n.p.-1916-
orig wrps-12mo-95p-illus   (4g6)   5.00

--Random Reminiscences of Men & Events-NY-1909-1st ed-port
      (5jj3)   12.50

ROCKFELLOW,JOHN A-Log of Arizona Trail Blazier-1933-
1st ed-scarce   (5r1,vg,torn dj)   40.00

ROCKFORD (ILL)CITY DIRECTORY-& County Gazetteer for 1869-
Rockford-1869-Rockford Register Co-2 parts in 1-352p,72p-
fldg map-orig stmpd black cl   (5t1)   175.00

ROCKNE,KNUTE K-The Autobiography of-SoBend-c1931-296p-
illus-fldg chart-Notre Dame Ed-ltd to 2400c,nbrd,autgs(5w4) 10.00

ROCKWELL,A D-Rambling Recollections-NY-1920-332p-cl
    (5h2,rub)   8.50

ROCKWELL,F F-The Book of Bulbs-NY-1927-263p-illus (5s7) 5.00

--Flower Arrangement in Color-NY-(1940)-Wise&Co-238p-61 col
plts   (5s7)   6.00

--10,000 Garden Questions-2 vols   (5a6,f)   5.00

--Rock Gardens-NY-1928-Home Garden Handbooks-86p-illus
    (5s7)   2.50

--The Rockwells' Complete Book of Roses-NY-1958-332p-col plts
    (5s7)   4.50

--Save It For Winter-NY-(1918)-206p-illus   (5c5,shake)   3.50

ROCKWELL,G L-History of Ridgefield (Conn)-1927-583p
    (5m2,5t9,mor,pres)   25.00

ROCKWELL,JULIUS-Speech upon Question of Admission of Texas
as State-Wash-1845-16p   (4a5)   12.50

ROCKWELL,P G-Aiken as a winter resort-(n.p.-ca 1876)-16mo-
illus-pict wrps-BPChatfield,publ   (5g8)   7.50

ROCKWELL,WILSON-New Frontier, Saga of the North Fork-Denver-
1938-215p-photos-1st ed-v scarce   (4t8)   30.00

--Sunset Slope-Denv-(1956)-290p-photos-1st ed (5yy7,f) 7.50

--The Utes,a Forgotten People-Denv-(1956)-302p plus index-illus
    (5L0,mint,dj)   10.00

ROCKWOOD,HARRY-Neil Nelson,the veteran detective-Chig-
n.d.(c1885)-8vo-orig prntd wrps-Ogilvie-frontis-1st ed (5i9) 20.00

ROCKY MOUNT MILLS-Rocky Mount,NC-1943-51p (5p0) 3.00

ROCKY MOUNTAIN MAGAZINE-illus monthly-Helena,Mont-
Oct 1900,Vol 1,#2   (5p1)   5.00

ROCKY MOUNTAIN MINERAL LAW INSTITUTE-1st thru 15th-
1955 to 1969-index 1 to 10-bound   (5ii7,ex-libr)   325.00

ROCKY MOUNTAIN MINERAL LAW REVIEW-1963 to 68-Vols 1
thru 5-bound   (5rr4,recent rbnd)   60.00

ROCKY MNTN PARK WONDERLANDS-Denver-n.d.-Kendrick
Bellamy-illus-folio-12 lvs-wrps   (4a5)   6.00

ROD-For the Back of the Binder-Chig-1928-32p-lea labl-16 plts-
Donnelly&Sons-sm4to   (5j3) 8.   (5ee9)   15.00

RODBAUGH,JAS H-Robert Hamilton Bishop-Col-1935-216p-cl-
Ohio Hist Coll, Vol 4   (5h2,f)   5.00

RODAHL,KAARE-The Last of the Few-NY-(1963)-204p plus index-
1st ed-photos   (5L0,dj)   5.00

--North-NY-(1953)237p-photos   (5ss1)   4.50

--same-Lond-1954-224p-photos-reprint   (5ss1)   3.50

RODALE,J I-Encyclopedia of Organic Gardening-1145p-
thumb indexed   (5a6,mint,dj)   5.00

--Pay Dirt-NY-1949-244p   (5s7)   4.50

--Organic Merry Go Round-Emmaus,Pa-1954-64p-bds-Rodale Books-
    (5s7)   2.50

RODD,FRANCIS RENNELL-Gen Wm Eaton-Lond-1933-illus-maps
    (5g8)   10.00

RODD,RENNELL-Myrtle & Oak-Bost&Chig-1902-Forbes-sm4to-
calf-a.e.g.-port-1st Amer ed   (5i4,ex-libr)   17.50

--Songs in South-Lond-1881-sm4to-orig prntd wrps-auth's 1st book
    (4c2,sl chip)   15.00

RODDA,REV RICHARD-Youth's Manuel,or Guide to Happiness-NY-
1814-Hitt&Ware-366p-adv lf-16mo-2½x4"-1st Amer ed,rev
    (5c8)   9.00

RODDIE,STEWART-Peace Patrol-Lond-(1932)-illus (5x0,pres) 6.50

RODDIS,LOUIS H-Indian Wars of Minnesota-CedarRapids-(1956)-
1st ed-307p plus index-photos   (5bb4,dj)   25.00

RODEARMEL,WM-20th Century,Penna State Gov in Picture & Story-
1905-4to   (5L7)   25.00

RODEHEAVER,HERMAN-Song Stories of the Sawdust Trail-NY-
1917-1st ed   (5b9)   6.00

RODELL,MARIE F,ed-Denver Murders-NY-1946   (5t2,dj)   2.50

RODEN,H W-Wake for a Lady-NY-1946-Morrow (5x0,autg) 4.00

RODENBOUGH,THEO F-Afghanistan & the Anglo Russian Dispute-
NY-1885-3 maps-illus-cl-139p-1st ed   (5t0)   7.50

--Army of the US-NY-1893-740p-ports-v scarce   (5g5)   45.00

--Uncle Sam's Medal of Honor-NY-(1886)-8vo-424p-buck
    (4a7,rbnd)   17.50

RODGERS,CLEVELAND-NY,the World's capital city-NY-1948-
Harper-398p   (5u3)   5.00

RODGERS,DOROTHY-My Favorite Things-NY-1964-282p-illus-
1st ed   (5t4)   12.50

RODGERS,JOHN-Divine Goodness,displayed in the Amer Revolution,
a Sermon, Dec 11,1783-NY-1784-Loudon-42p-stitchd
    (5L1,hf mor box)   75.00

RODGERS,RICHARD-The King & I-NY-(1951)-8vo-cl-photos-
1st ed   (5dd8,dj)   5.00

RODGERS,ROBT L-Jeff Davis & the Pope-Aurora,Mo-(1925)-
91p plus ads-rare-wrps   (5bb4,f)   35.00

RODIER,CAMILLE-Le Vin De Burgoyne-Dijon-(1920)-fldg maps-
296p,(3)-(col illus)   (5w1,sl tn)   15.00

RODIER,PAUL-Romance of French Weaving-NY-1931-356p-t.e.g.-
2 col illus   (5w9,dj,box)   20.00

--same-NY-(1936)-illus-356p   (5t0) 7.50   (5p0)   10.00

RODIN,AUGUSTE-Short Notice on The Thinker..& Rodin Museum-
NY-1914-(Tiffany)-illus-12mo-vel   (5yy6)   10.00

RODING,JOHANN HINRICH-Allgemeines Worterbuch der
Marine in allen Europaeischen Seesprachen-Hamburg-(1793 to
1795)-4 vols-4to-orig bds-115p & fldg plts
    (5ss2,1 plt in facs)   400.00

RODMAN,HUGH-Yarns of Kentucky Admiral-Indnpls-(1928)-
320p-photos   (5s1,bkstrp tn)   7.50

RODMAN,M-Market Day for Ti Andre-NY-1952-R8vo-illus
    (5x2,dj)   6.00

RODMAN,O H P-The Saltwater Fisherman's Favorite Four-NY-
1948-illus-192p   (5t7)   5.00

RODMAN,SAML-The diary of-NewBedford-1927-t.e.g.-Reynolds Pr-
Pease,ed-349p   (5u3)   6.50

RODMAN,SELDEN-The Airmen-1941-RandomHse-
    (5b2) 3.50   (5m2) 5.   (5F1,f,dj)   4.75

--Lawrence,The Last Crusade-NY-1937-Viking-1st prntng
    (5b2,sl fade) 4.   (5m2,dj)   5.00

--Mexican Journal-1958-plts   (5L7)   6.50

--Renaissance in Haiti-NY-1948   (5x5,dj)   15.00

--The Revolutionists,A Tragedy in 3 Acts-NY-(c1942)-demy 8vo-
cl-illus   (5b2,dj)   5.00

RODNEY,GEO BRYDGES-In buff & blue-Bost-1897-Little,Brown-
1st ed   (5m2)   5.00

RODRIGO DE MORAES SOARES-Memoire Sur Les Vins Du Portugal-
Lisbonne-1878-42p,(1)-4to-wrps-3 fldg maps   (5w1)   14.50

RODRIGUEZ,JOS M-Como deben haverse los Vasallos con sus
Reyes-(Mexico)-1768-Jos Antonio de Hogal-sm4to-26p, 1p-
unbnd as issued-1st ed   (5L8)   38.50

RODRIGUEZ DE SAN MIGUEL,JUAN-Documentos relativos al
piadoso fondo de misiones...nueva Calif-Mexico-1845-
Luis Abadiano y Valdes-8vo-hf mor-1st ed   (5i9)   125.00

RODWAY,J-In the Guiana Forest-1912-plts-rev ed (5L7) 7.50

ROE,ALFRED S-History of the 1st Regiment of Heavy Artillery,Mass
Vol,1861 to 1865-(Bost)-1917-8vo-illus-1st ed   (5m6)   7.50

ROE,AZEL STEVENS-Jas Montjoy-NY-1850-Appleton-12mo-orig cl-
1st ed of auth's 1st book   (5x1)   27.50

--Looking Around-NY-1865-Carleton-312p-1st ed
    (5x4,lacks e.p.)   7.50

ROE,CHAS F-Custer's Last Battle-NY-1927-4to-40p-orig wrps-
illus   (5k4)   45.00

ROE,EDW-Barriers Burned Away-NY-1872-DoddMead-488p-1st ed
    (5x4,wn)   15.00

--A Day of Fate-NY-(1880)-DoddMead-450p-1st ed
    (5ee3,g) 5.   (5x4)   10.00

--Earth Trembled-NY-1887-1st ed   (5ee3,5mm1)   7.50

--Face Illuminated-NY-(1878)-1st ed (5ee3,5mm1) 5. (5x4) 7.50

--His Sombre Rivals-NY-(1883)-DoddMead-487p-1st ed
    (5mm2) 5.   (5x4)   10.00

--A knight of the 19th Century-NY-1877-DoddMead-582p-1st ed
    (5x4)   12.50

--An Unexpected Result & Other Stories-NY-(1883)-1st ed-scarce
    (5mm2)   10.00

--Young Girl's Wooing-NY-(1884)-1st ed   (5mm1)   5.00

ROE,F G-From Dogs to Horses Among Western Indian Tribes-
Ottawa-1929-prntd wrps-66p   (5u6)   5.00

--Indian & The Horse-(1955)-U Okla-434p-plts-fldg map-1st ed
    (4k5,di) 8.50   (4i7,dj)   10.00

ROE,F GORDON-Sporting Prints of 18th & Early 19th Centuries-
NY-1927-4to-50p text-col plts-Connoisseur Ser-1st ed
    (4a6,stnd,rprd)   17.50

ROE,FRANCES M-Army Letters from an Officer's Wife-NY-1909-
8vo-cl-illus-1st ed
    (4i7) 18. (4c1,5r0) 17.50 (5dd4) 31.50 (5bb4) 27.50

ROE,G M-ed-Our Police-Cinn-1890-413p plus index plus 68p-
photos-1st ed-rare   (5bb4,ex-libr,wn)   20.00

ROE,J R-Nehushtan-StL-1894-Christian Pub-8vo   (5b2)   7.50

ROE,JOHN MORIMTER-Poems-StL-1857-188p-2 illus-1st ed
    (5L0,wn)   6.50

ROEBLING,EMILY WARREN-Journal of Rev Silas Constant-Phila-
1903-plts-561p-4to-cl-1st ed-ltd to 300c,nbrd-for priv circ
ex **rare**   (5p5)   75.00

ROEBLING,JOHANN AUGUST-Diary of my Journey from
Muehlhausen etc-Trenton-1931-port-priv print   (5jj3)   22.50

ROEBUCK,LT THOS-English & Hindoostanee Naval Dictionary of
Technical Terms & Sea Phrases-Calcutta-1811-calf (5c1,rbnd) 48.50

ROEDER,RALPH-Juarez & His Mexico-NY-1947-Viking-2 vols-
8vo-cl-illus   (4b6) 20.   (4a3,box,f,5x5,box)   22.50

ROEDIGER,VIRGINIA MORE-Ceremonial Costumes of Pueblo
Indians-Berkeley-1941-40 col plts   (5r7)   12.50

ROELKER,WM G-Francis Wayland-Worcester-1944-8vo-54p-wrps-
rprnt   (5p1)   2.00

--150 Years of Providence Wash Ins Co-Prov-1949-priv pub-153p-
22 plts   (4b8)   7.50

ROEMER,J-Cavalry,Its History, Management & Uses in War-NY-
1863-8vo-cl-515p-illus   (5F5,fray,publ pres)   20.00

ROEMER,JACOB-Remin of War of Rebellion 1861 to 1865-Flushing-
1897-8vo-317p   (4a7)   35.00

ROENIGK,ADOLPH-Pioneer History of Kansas-(1933)-368p plus
index-photos-priv prntd-scarce   (5yy7,wn dj)   27.50

ROERICH,NICHOLAS-Heart of Asia-NY-1930-Roerich Mus Pr-cl
(5p5)   12.50

ROETHKE,THEODORE-Words for the Wind-Lond-1957-Cr8vo-cl-
1st ed   (5ss7,vf,dj)   25.00

ROFFEY,MABEL-Rush Work-Lond-1933-82p-45 illus   (5n7)   3.00

ROGER CAMERDEN,A STRANGE STORY-NY-1887-12mo-wrps-
1st ed of Bangs 1st book-rare   (5gg6,f)   50.00

ROGER,CHAS-Quebec As It Was & As It Is-Quebec-1867-5th ed-
wrps-138p   (5dd0)   6.50

ROGERS,AGNES-The Amer Procession-NY-1933-folio-photos
(5ee3,dj)   4.00

--I Remember Distinctly-NY-1947-500 picts-251p
(5L7) 7.50   (5xx5) 8.75   (4c9)   15.00

--Metropolis-NY-1934-photos-4to-1st ed (5c3,rub) 4.50 (5ii3)   7.50

--Vassar Women-Poughkeepsie-1940-223p-cl-1st ed   (5t0)   3.75

--Women Are Here to Stay-NY-(1949)-illus-bds-lg4to-220p
(4i2) 10.   (5p5,dj)   15.00

ROGERS,ANNA A-Sweethearts & Wives-NY-1899-Scribner's-
220p-1st ed   (5x4)   7.50

ROGERS,AURELIA SPENCER-Life Sketches of Orson Spencer &
Others & History of Primary Work-(SaltLkCty)-1898-333p-
photos-1st ed-scarce   (5t3)   15.00

ROGERS,BRUCE-The Psalms of David in metre-Cambridge(Mass)-
1928-8vo-blue cl-pgs ruled in red-ltd to 300c   (5d1)20.00

--The Rime of the Ancient Mariner-Oxford-1930-8vo-papr bds-
ltd to 750c ,dj   (5d1)   40.00

--Work of Bruce Rogers, Jack of all Trades, Master of One-NY-
1939-cl-8vo-plts-1st ed-Grolier Club Cat (4n5) 15. (4g2)   25.00

ROGERS,C-Sir Walter Scott,Genealogical Memoirs of the Family of-
Lond-1877-78p   (4t2)   6.00

ROGERS,CAMERON,ed-Full & By-NY-1925-4to-illus-1st ed
(5j3,5tt5)   10.00

--The Magnificent Idler-GardenCty-1926-312p-1st ed (5hh3)   5.00

--same-NY-1926-illus-1st ed-ltd to 250c   (5mm2)   10.00

ROGERS,REV CHAS-The Scottish Minstrel-Edinb-1872-lg8vo-cl-
507p   (5t2)   7.50

ROGERS,CHAS-Traits & Stories of the Scottish People-Lond-1867-
g. stmp cl-320p   (4t7,sl soil)   27.50

ROGERS,DAN'L-Report of trial of John Quay vs Eagle Fire Co of NY-
NY-1817-stitchd   (5g4,fox)   17.50

ROGERS,DAVID BANKS-Prehistoric Man of the Santa Barbara Coast-
SantaBarbara-1929-449p plus index & errata slip-photos-maps,
1 fldg-1st ed-ex scarce   (5x5)   35.00

ROGERS,ELDER SAML-Autobiography-Cinn-1880-8vo-1st ed
(5ss5)   7.50

ROGERS,ELLEN STANLEY-1800 Census of Kent Co,Delaware-
Bladensburg-1959-4to-104p-map-wrps   (5r7,ex-libr)   7.50

ROGERS,ERNEST E,ed-Sesquicentennial of Battle of Groton Heights,
etc-NewLond-1931-186p-illus-prntd wrps   (5mm8)   4.50

ROGERS,FRANCES-5000 Years of Glass-NY-1937-illus-303p
(5p0)   7.50

ROGERS,FRANK D-Confessions of an Undertaker-Chig-1900-87p-
cl   (5h2,spot)   10.00

ROGERS,FRED B-Bear Flag Lieutenant-SanFran-1951-reprint-4to-
cl-frontis   (5h5,pres,tls laid in)   22.50

--Montgomery & Portsmouth-(SanFran,1958)-145p-illus-
limited edition   (5s4,f,unopnd)   17.50

--A Navy Surgeon in Calif, 1846, 47-SanFran-1957-John Howell-
ltd to 600c   (5x5)   17.50

--Soldiers of the Overland-SanFran-1938-Grabhorn-ltd to 1000c
(5bb4) 25.   (5x5)   27.50

ROGERS,FREDK RAND-Dance,A Basic Educ Technique-NY-1941-
Macmillan   (5a6)   4.95

ROGERS,MRS G ALBERT-A winter in Algeria-Lond-1865-8vo-
SampsonLow-orig cl-frontis-5 plts-1st ed   (5i8,f)   10.00

ROGERS,GEO-Universalist Hymn Book-Cinn-1843-448p-2nd ed-
lea-Brooks,publ   (5y0)   8.50

ROGERS,GLENDON J-Kern County is Our Home-(Bakersfield)-
c1950-4to-cl-125p   (4t1)   12.50

ROGERS,H D-Geology of Pa,A Govt Survey-Phila-1858-illus-
fldg plts-col frontis-4to-2 vols-(wi scarce vol maps) (5yy0)   42.50

ROGERS,H J-Rogers Heritage,Family Memoirs-1937-360p (4t2)   30.00

ROGERS,HENRY C-History of Town of Paris,& Valley of the
Sauquoit-Utica-1881-White&Floyd-8vo-cl-398p   (4t1)   45.00

ROGERS,HESTER ANN-Acct of Experiences of-NY-1856-288p-
cl-sermon   (5h7,rub)   5.00

ROGERS,HOPEWELL L-Some Descendants of Giles Rogers,Immigrant
to Virginia in 1664-1940-priv prntd-4to   (5yy8)   15.00

ROGERS,HORATIO-Private Libraries of Providence,etc-Providence-
1878-hf lea-ltd to 250c   (4m5,wtrstn,hng crack)   20.00

ROGERS,HOWARD S-History of Cass Co from 1825 to 1875-
Cassopolis-1875-W H Mansfield, Vigilant-12mo-cl-406p (4t1)   35.00

ROGERS, J A-Nature Knows No Color Line-NY-1952
(5x2,mint,dj)   10.00

--Sex & Race-NY-(1940)-priv prnt-illus-3 vols   (4b6)   35.00

--World's Great Men of Color-NY-1947-Vol 2 only-illus (5x2)   10.00

ROGERS,JAS HARVEY-America Weighs Her Gold-Yale Univ Pr-1931-
245p-charts   (5qq8,dj)   7.50

ROGERS,JOHN-Sport in Vancouver & Newfoundland-Lond-1912-
maps-illus-8vo-cl-275p   (4m7) 13.50   (5j5,dj)   17.50

ROGERS, JOHN-Groups of Statuary 860Broadway,NY-n.p.-n.d.-
28p-prntd wrps-illus of 50 groups-obl 8vo-v scarce catalog
(5t0)   25.00

ROGERS,JOHN WM-Finding Literature on the Texas Plains-
Dallas- (1931)-Southwest Pr-57p-cl&bds   (5d6)   20.00

--Lusty Towns of Dallas-NY-1951-1st ed-port (5jj3,dj)10. (5yy7)   6.00

--Westward People-NY-1935-wrps-48p   (4j7)   25.00

ROGERS,JULIA E-Among Green Trees-Chig-1902-4to-202p-
25p illus   (5s7)   8.50

--A Key to the Nature Library-NY-1909-57p-illus   (5t7)   6.50

--The Shell Book-NY-1931-Dblday-R8vo-orig cl-8 col plts (5t5) 10.00

--The Tree Book-NY-1912-thk4to-16 col plts-cl   (5t5)   10.00

ROGERS,KENNETH-The Mermaid & Mitre Taverns in Old London-
Lond-(1928)-204p-plts   (5g9)   7.50

ROGERS,L W-The Ghosts in Shakespeare-(1925)   (5mm2)   4.00

ROGERS,LEBBEUS HARDING-The kite trust-NY-(1902)-illus-
pict cl-Kite Trust Pub-4th ed   (5m2,pres)   8.50

ROGERS,M R-Carl Milles,interpretation of his work-1940-folio-
163 plts   (5L7)   25.00

ROGERS,MARY COCHRANE-Glimpses of An Old Social Capital-
(Portsmouth, NH)-Bost-1923-4to-illus-buck&bds (5q8,rprd)   8.50

ROGERS,MEYRIC R-Amer Interior Design-NY-(1947)-Bonanza-4to-
cl-309p-illus   (5j5,dj)   7.50

--Italy at Work-Brooklyn Museum-Nov 1950 to Jan, 1951-illus-8vo-
catalogue-66p text-wrps   (5ww3)   9.50

ROGERS,NATHAN'L PEABODY-Collection of Newspaper Writings
of-Concord, NH-1847-8vo-port-frontis-1st ed (5m6,chip)   8.50

ROGERS,NORMAN McLEOD-Mackenzie King-Toronto-1935-
Morang,Nelson-212p-plts   (5qq8,dj)   5.00

ROGERS,PEET & CO-Jack's Funny Friend-NY-4to-24p-illus-
scarce   (5v2)   12.50

ROGERS,R V-Law of the Road;or, Wrongs & Rights of a Traveller-
SanFran-(1876)   (5r4)   12.50

ROGERS,ROBT-Journals of Maj Robt Rogers,etc-Lond-1765-236p-
adv lf-1st ed   (5e2) 500.   (5L1,vf)   325.00

ROGERS,ROBT CAMERON-Will o' the Wasp-NY-1896-Putnam-
frontis-1st ed-"Knickerbocker Series"   (5m2)   7.50

ROGERS,ROBT E-The Voice of Science...In 19th C Literature-Bost-
1924   (5x7) 4.50   (5m1)   6.50

ROGERS,SAML-Human Life,a Poem-Lond-1819-12mo-orig bds-
1st ed-v scarce   (5i8,lacks hf t.,calf) 8.   (5r9,als laid in)   50.00

--Italy,a Poem-Lond-1830-orig bds-papr labl-plts-1st ed-1st issue
(4b4,f)   27.50

--same-Lond-1830-for T Cadell,etc-8vo-red mor-g.-a.e.g.
(5x3,f bndg,sl rub,pres)   45.00

--same-Lond-1836-mor-g.sides-g.back-8vo-wi fore edge painting
(5tt7)   200.00

--Pleasures of Memory,Pains of Memory-NY-1820-12mo-142p-
frontis   (5v2)   8.50

--Poems-Lond-1834-orig bds-papr labl-plts-1st ed   (4b4,f)   25.00

--same-Lond-1838-Moxon-lg4to-mor-a.e.g.-60 plts-266p
(5dd0,sl fox)   15.00

ROGERS,STANLEY-The Atlantic-NY-(1930)-243p-illus (5s1)   5.00

ROGERS,THOS L-Mexico?Si, Senor-Bost-1893-maps-illus-8vo-
1st ed-priv prntd   (4g6)   12.50

ROGERS,VOLNEY-Partial Descrip of Mill Creek Pk,Youngstown-
(Youngstown, 1904-Vindicator Pr)-8vo-cl-120p   (4t1)   6.50

ROGERS,W B-Elements of Mechanical Philosophy-1852-buck
(5L7,ex-libr)   9.50

ROGERS,WALTER T-A Manual of Bibliography-Lond-1891-illus-
new ed   (4a1)   15.00

ROGERS,WM BARTON-Life & Letters-Bost-1896-2 vols-8vo-illus
        (5ss5,unopnd,f)   10.00
ROGERS,WILL-Acceptance of Statue of,State of Okla at US Capitol-
  Wash-GPO-1939-80p-frontis   (5dd5,lt stnd)   12.50
--His Wife's Story-1941-Bobbs Merrill Co-312p   (5p0)   4.50
--Rogersisms-NY-(1919)-16mo-bds-1st ed of auth's 1st book
        (5gg6,dj)   25.00
ROGERS,CAPT WOODES-A Cruising Voyage Round the World...
  begun in 1708 and finish'd in 1711-Lond-1712-A Bell & B Lintot-
  428p,56p-7 lvs index-5 fldg maps-8vo-calf-blind tooled-
  1st ed   (5L1)   275.00
ROGET,PETER MARK-Animal & Vegetable Physiology-(Bohn)-1867-
  illus-2 vols-4th ed   (5tt5,rub)   10.00
--Thesaurus of Engl Words & Phrases,etc-Lond-1852-8vo-g.t.-mor-
  1st ed   (5d3,rbnd)   50.00
--same-Bost-1854-8vo-1st Amer ed-revised   (4m8,f)   20.00
ROHAN,THOS-Confessions of a Dealer-Lond-(1924)-Mills&Boon-
  215p   (5x0)   6.00
ROHAULT,JACQUES-Physica-Lond-1718-for Knapton-8vo-calf-
  lea labl-27 fldg plts-4th Latin ed,wi lf of ads pre title
        (4h0,crack)   100.00
ROHDE,ELEANOUR SINCLAIR-Culinary & Salad Herbs-Lond-(1944)-
  106p   (5w3)   5.00
--Garden Craft in the Bible & Other Essays-Lond-1927-26 plts-
  242p   (5w3)   8.50
--A Garden of Herbs-Lond-1926-300p-9 illus-rev&enlrgd ed (5w3)9.50
--same-Lond-n.d.-224p   (5s7,fade)   6.50
--Herbs & Herb Gardening-Lond-(1936)-205p-illus (5w3,autg)   12.50
--The Old Engl Herbals-Lond-1922-4to-243p-col frontis-16 plts
        (5w3)   45.00
--The Scented Garden-Bost&Lond-n.d.-312p-frontis (5s7)   7.50
--same-Bost-1936-312p,(12)-16 photos-orig lg papr ed (5w3)   5.00
--The Story of the Garden-Bost-(1936)-326p-illus
        (5w3) 8.50   (5s7)   7.50
--Vegetable Cultivation & Cookery-Lond-(1938)-275p-illus
  (5c5) 5.   (5w3,hng weak)   4.50
ROHEIM,GEZA-Animism,Magic & the Divine King-NY-1930-
  Knopf-390p   (5x0)   8.50
ROHLFS,ANNA KATHERINE GREEN-Marked "Personal"-NY-1893-
  Putnam's-415p-1st ed   (5x4)   15.00
--The Sword of Damocles-NY-1881-Putnam's-540p-1st ed (5x4) 17.50
ROHMER,SAX-Moon of Madness-GardenCty-1927-1st ed (5ee3)   3.50
--Tales of Chinatown-NY-1922-1st ed   (5yy6)   7.50
--Tales of East & West-Lond-(1932)-Cassell-12mo-cl-288p-1st ed
        (5j5)   10.00
--The Trail of Fu Manchu-1934-Dblday-1st Amer ed (5F1,f,dj)   4.00
ROHN,MAHLON O-Mrs. Rohn's Lancaster County Tested Cook Book-
  Cleve-n.p.-1923-stiff wrps-2nd ed,rev (4g9,rprd,sl stnd) 6.00
ROJAS,LOLA,comp-Souvenir Book of Golden Anniv...Meth Epis
  Church in Mex 1873 to 1923-Mexico,DF-1924-Casa Unida de
  Pub-8vo-cl-210p   (4t1)   20.00
ROLAND,WALPOLE-Algoma West,Its Mines,Scenery & Industrial
  Resources-Tor-1887-map-2 plts-ads-8vo-217p-1st ed
        (5h6,stnd,lacks map) 15.   (4m7)   25.00
ROLDAN,SALVADOR CAMACHO-Abraham Lincoln-n.p.-n.d.-
  trans fr La Opinion,Bogota,Col, Jun 7, 1865-scarce (5y0)   35.00
ROLFE,MRS ANN-Choice & no choice-Lond-1825-Cook-2 vols-
  12mo-orig bds-prntd papr labls-1st ed   (5xx6,f)   150.00
ROLFE,FREDK-The Desire & Pursuit of the Whole-Lond-1934-
  Cassell-1st ed   (5hh1,dj)   30.00
ROLL,CHAS-Indiana, 150 Years of Amer Development-Chig-1931-
  5 vols-4to-illus-red cl   (4a9,mint)   50.00
ROLLAND,E-Faune Populaire de La France-Paris-1877 to 83-
  orig wrps bnd in-lea&mrbld bds-8vo-6 vols   (4p5)   27.50
ROLLESTON,MAUD-Yeoman Service-Lond-1901-Smith, Elder-310p
        (4t5,fox)   11.00
ROLLESTON,T W-Myths & Legends of the Celtic Race-NY-n.d.-
  457p plus 64 illus   (5c3)   5.00
ROLLINS,ALICE R-Antiques for the Home-NY-(1946)-232p-
  43 photos   (5w7)   4.00
ROLLINS,ALICE WELLINGTON-Story of a Ranch-(1885)-190p-
  1st ed-pic cl   (5r1,sp reglued) 8.50 (5m2)   7.50
--The three Tetons-NY-(1887)-Cassell-orig wrps-1st ed (5m2,wn) 8.50
--Uncle Tom's Tenement-Bost-1888-468p-cl-Wright 4670
        (5y0,faded)   10.00
ROLLINS,HYDER E,ed-A gorgeous gallery of gallant inventions-
  Harv Univ Pr-1926-4to   (5m2)   8.50
--A Pepysian Garland-Cambr Univ Pr-1922-491p-illus-hf cl(5c3) 5.00
ROLLINS,J R-Rawlins or Rollins Records-1874   (4t2)   12.50
ROLLINS,PHILIP A-The Cowboy-NY-1922-1st ed-353p-illus
        (5k0,pres,orig illus) 22.50 (5i3) 12.50
        (5xx7,dj,5L2,5dd6,5ww4)   15.00
--same-NY-1924-illus-353p   (5s4,pres,als)   20.00

ROLLINS,PHILIP A (continued)
--same-NY-1936-402p-illus-rev&enlrgd ed (5ee3,pres)   15.00
--Discovery of the Oregon Trail-NY-(1935) (5x5)   35.00
--Gone Haywire-NY-1939-illus-269p-cl-1st ed (4p2)   15.00
--same-NY-1941-cl-269p-illus   (5g2)   5.00
--Jinglebob-1928-3rd prntng   (5r1,cov soil)   11.00
ROLLINSON,JOHN K-Hoofprints of a Cowboy & US Ranger-
  Pony Trails in Wyoming-Caldwell-1945(1946)-411p-photos-
  map-3rd prntng   (5L2,f,dj)   8.50
--Pony Trails in Wyoming-Caldwell-1945-Caxton-8vo-425p-cl-
  photos-3rd prntng   (5F5)   6.00
--Wyoming Cattle Trails-Caxton-1948-366p-maps-ltd to 1000c,autg
        (5x5) 25. (5k2,5kk5)   20.00
--same-1948-1st trade ed (5dd4,5jj7) 15. (5x5,dj)   12.50
ROLLO AT SCHOOL-Bost-1839-sm8vo-cl-3rd ed(same yr as 1st)
        (4c2,fox,chip)   25.00
ROLO,CHAS J,ed-The World of Evelyn Waugh-Bost-1958-Little-
  411p   (5p0)   5.00
ROLLO,J H-Desc of Alex Rollo of East Haddam,Conn-1896-56p-
  wrps   (4t2)   10.00
ROLLO'S TRAVELS-Bost-1841-Gould,Kendall&Lincoln-Phila,
  Hogan&Thompson-frontis-2 plts-cl-189p-6½x4"
        (5p1,lacks e.p.)   12.50
ROLPH,GEO M-Something About Sugar-SanFran-1917-Newbegin,
  pub-19p plus 341p-illus-cl   (5r0)   7.50
ROLPH,WM K-Henry Wise Wood of Alberta-Tor-1950-235p-plat
        (5a1)   7.50
ROLT,L T C-Saml Williams & Sons Ltd 1855 to 1955-Lond-1955-
  26 photos-1 col plt   (5c1)   15.00
ROLT,RICHARD-History of the late war-Lond-1766-calf-sp labls
        (5g4,wn)   25.00
--Impartial history of conduct of...powers of Europe....in late
  general war (1739 to 1748)-Lond-1749,50-4 vols-calf
        (5g4,wn,cov loose)   35.00
--New & accurate history of SoAmer-Lond-1756-fldg map-calf
        (5g4,wn,lacks labls,cov loose)   37.50
ROLT WHEELER,FRANCIS-The Boy with the US Indians-Bost-(1913)-
  illus-410p-1st ed   (4n8) 5. (5L2)   4.00
ROLVAAG,O E-Giants in the Earth,Saga of the Prairie-NY-1927-
  465p-1st printing   (4j6,f) 25. (5i4,dj)   15.00
ROMAINE,LAWRENCE B-Guide to Amer Trade Catalogs, 1744 to
  1900-NY-1960-422p   (4j6)   12.50
ROMAINE,W-Discourses Upon Solomon's Song-Lond-1789-376p
        (5mm1,rbnd)   15.00
ROMAINE,WM-A Practical Comment on the 107thPsalm-Lond-
  1760-sm8vo-calf-268p-4th ed   (5t2)   7.50
ROMAN,ALFRED-Military Operations of Gen Beauregard in War
  Between States-NY-1884-2 vols-frontis   (5i2)   20.00
ROMAN,C V-Amer Civilization & the Negro-Phila-1916-R8vo-
  illus   (5x2,rbnd)   75.00
ROMANCE OF THE PYRENEES-Amherst(NH):prntd by JCushing-
  Newburyport(Mass)-1809-4 vols in 2(as issued)-12mo-sheep-
  1st Amer ed-(C Cuthbertson)   (5i0,rub)   27.50
ROMANCE OF TRAVEL-NY-1840-SColman-12mo-cl-1st ed-
  (NP Willis)   (5x1,rbnd,wtrstn)   25.00
ROMANOFF,A L-The Avian Egg-NY-1949-orig cl-8vo-918p
        (4p5)   25.00
ROMAUNT,CHRISTOPHER-The Island Home-Bost-Lothrop-n.d.-
  (c1861)-sm8vo-461p-g.t.-frontis   (5aa2)   5.00
ROMBAUER,IRMA S-The Joy of Cooking-Indnpls-(1953)-1013p
        (5c9)   4.50
ROMER,F-Makers of History-Hartf-1926-64p-illus-wrps-(by the
  Colt Co)-scarce-1st ed   (5bb4)   12.50
ROMER,J L-Romer,Van Tassel & Allied Families,Historical
  Sketches-(1917)-151p   (5t9)   12.50
ROMEYN,JOHN B-Catalogue of library of...Thos Bell&Co,NY-
  NY-Apr,1825-8vo-disbnd   (5i0)   90.00
ROMIG,EDGAR FRANKLIN-Tercentenary Year of Reformed (Dutch)
  Church in Amer-n.p.-1929-illus-sm4to   (5j3)   10.00
ROMIG,WALTER,comp-Book of Catholic Authors,2nd Series-Detroit-
  1943   (4b4)   10.00
ROMMEN,H A-Natural Law-1947   (5L7)   4.00
ROMULO,CARLOS P-I Saw Fall of Philippines-NY-1943-illus
        (5tt5,pres)   7.50
RONALD,J C-One Man's Philosophy-(Seattle,1939)-ltd to 100c
        (5s4)   7.50
RONALD,MARY-Century Cook Book-NY-1899-illus-photos-bds-
  588p   (4g9,rub)   7.50
--Luncheons-NY-1906-223p   (5g9)   4.00
RONALDS,ALFRED-Fly fisher's Entomology-Lond-1836-8vo-calf-
  19 col illus-g.t.-1st ed   (4c2,uncut)   125.00
--same-Lond-1921-152p-col illus   (5t7)   15.00

RONALDS,FRANCIS-Descriptions of an Electrical Telegraph & of
   Some Other Electrical Apparatus-Lond-1823-for Hunter-8vo-
   cl-mor cor &sp-frontis-7 plts(1 fldg)-1st ed (4F5,autg) 185.00
RONALDSHAY,EARL OF-Life of Lord Curzon-NY&Lond-(ca 1928)-
   3 vols-Ernest Benn Ltd-illus   (5t4) 12.50
RONAN,PETER-Historical Sketch of Flathead Indian Nation-
   Helena-(1890)-80p,(2)p-plts-v scarce   (4t8) 75.00
RONDELET,J-Memoire sur la Marines des Anciens et sur les Navires-
   Paris-1820-Chez l'Auteur-79p-10 fldg plts-lg4to-orig wrps
                (5ss2,sl fox) 65.00
RONSARD,PIERRE DE-Sonnets Pour Helene-Lond-1934-291p-
   ltd ed to 150c-boxed   (5k2,unopnd) 10.00
RONDTHALER,EDW-Life of John Heckewelder-Coates,ed-Phila-
   1847-149p-frontis-port-12mo   (5h9) 26.50
ROOD,HENRY E-The company doctor-NY-(1895)-Merriam-1st ed
                (5m2) 10.00
ROOF,KATHARINE M-The Life & Art of Wm Merritt Chase-NY-1917-
   352p-cl-51 illus   (5t2,libr mrks) 6.50
ROOKS,B-The Bottom Rail-NY-1960-1st ed (5x2,dj) 7.50
ROOKS MINING CO-Annual Report of,1884-(Bost)-1884-illus-
   47p-(Plymouth,Vt)   (5m6) 12.50
ROOME,WM-The Early Days & Early Surveys of East New Jersey-
   Butler,NY-1897-12mo-65p-wrps   (5t2) 3.00
ROOME,WM J W-Tramping Through Africa-NY-1930-8vo-photos-
   map   (5d7,fade) 5.   (4a6) 6.50
ROONEY,MIRIAM T-Lawlessness,Law & Sanction-1937-sewn
                (5L7) 3.50
ROORBACH,O A-Bibliotheca Americana...1820 to 52-NY-1852 to
   55-2 vols   (4g2) 52.50
ROOS,FRANK J,JR-Illus Handbook of Art History-NY-(1939)-
   Macmillan-304p-sprial bndng   (5x0) 4.00
ROOSE'S-Companion & Guide to Washington & Vicinity-(Wash)-
   1885-Gibson Bros-sq16mo-fldg map-144p-orig cl (5L8,wn) 5.00
ROOSEVELT,B-Life & Remin of Gustave Dore-NY-1885-lg8vo-illus-
   502p   (5p6) 14.00
ROOSEVELT,CLINTON-Mode of Protecting Domestic Industry-NY-
   1833-McElrath & Bangs-48p-pamph   (5qq 8) 7.50
ROOSEVELT,CORINNE-My Brother,Theodore Roosevelt-NY-1921-
   Scribner-365p-illus   (5p0) 4.00
ROOSEVELT,ELEANOR-Autobiography-NY-(1961)-illus-1st ed
                (5tt5,f,dj) 4.50
--Christmas-NY-1940-Knopf-Fritz Kredel,illus-32mo-42p-
   pict bds-1st ed   (5p1,dj) 15.00
--On My Own-NY-1958-8vo-cl-239p-illus (5t0,autg) 10.00
--This I Remember-NY-1949-387p-cl-1st ed (5x7) 4. (5j5) 7.50
ROOSEVELT,ELLIOTT-As He Saw It-NY-c1946 (5x7) 3.00
--F D R,His Personal Letters,Early Years-NY-(1947)-543p-illus-
   1st ed   (5ee3,dj,f) 3.50
ROOSEVELT,FRANKLIN D-The Democratic Book,1936-n.p.-
   1936-ports-illus-sm folio-lea-ltd,specially bnd ed,autog
                (5ss5) 47.50
--Looking Forward-NY-(1933)-8vo-cl-279p (5b9) 2. (5t2,dj,f) 4.00
--Official Inaugural Program...2nd Term..F D Roosevelt-Wash-
   1937-de luxe ed-illus-bnd   (4b7) 15.00
--On Our Way-NY-(1934)-8vo-cl-1st issue(with "party" for
   "property" last word line 13 on pg x)-1st ed (5dd8,dj) 25.00
--Public Papers & Addresses-NY-1938-Vols 1 to 5-1st ed
                (5jj3,f,dj) 45.00
--same-1938-RandomHse-5 vols-R thk8vo-blue cl (5t5) 30.00
--Public Papers & Addresses-NY-1938 to 41-9 vols-lg8vo-buck-
   Orig Random Hse Ed   (4b6) 125.00
--Wartime Corres between Pres Roosevelt & Pope Pius XII-NY-
   1947-8vo-cl   (4c1) 20.00
--Whither Bound?-Bost-1926-8vo-1st ed (4m6) 15.00
ROOSEVELT,MRS FRANKLIN D-A Trip to Washington with Bobby
   & Betty-n.p.-c1935-Dodge-91p-photos-4to-"2nd large printing"
   on dj   (5p1) 7.50
ROOSEVELT,HALL-Odyssey of an Amer Family-NY-1939-illus-
   1st ed   (5m6) 10. (4b7) 17.50
ROOSEVELT,KERMIT-The Happy Hunting Grounds-NY-1920-8vo-
   182p-photos   (4a6) 10.00
--The Long Trail-NY-1921-Review of Reviews-illus-autg ed
        (4L4,dj) 5. (5t7) 4.50 (5m6) 7.50
--War in the Garden of Eden-NY-1919-254p-illus (5t7) 5.00
ROOSEVELT,NICHOLAS-America & England-NY-(1930)-254p
            (5q8) 5. (5t7) 4.50
--The Philippines-NY-1926-Sears-315p (5p7) 5.00
--The Restless Pacific-NY-1928 (5x7) 6.00
ROOSEVELT,ROBT B-Florida & the Game Water Birds-NY-1884-
   illus-cl-443p-1st ed   (5t2) 7.50
--5 Acres Too Much-NY-1869-Harper-296p-1st ed (5x4) 15.00
--Superior Fishing-NY-1865-8p-304 illus (5t7) 12.50

ROOSEVELT,THEODORE-African Game Trails-NY-1910-illus-
   583p-1st ed   (4m8,rub,bkstrp tn) 6. (5t7) 20.00
--African Game Trails,An Acct of the African Wanderings of an
   Amer Hunter Naturalist-NY-1910-583p-illus (5dd6) 8. (5t7) 10.00
--same-NY-1910-Scribner-1 vols-illus-ltd to 500 sets,autg(5p0) 25.00
--same-NY-1910-Syndicate Pub-col plts (4t5,bk cov loose) 4.50
--An Autobiography-NY-1913-Macmillan-illus-647p
               (5p9) 6. (5r8) 8.50
--same-NY-1916-Macmillan-8vo-cl-illus-615p (5j5) 6.00
--same-NY-1920-597p-illus-cl   (5t2) 4.00
--Big Game Hunting in Rockies & on the Great Plains,Hunting Trips
   of a Ranchman,Wilderness Hunter-NY-1899-thk sm folio-
   cl-lea-illus by Remington etc-1st ed-ltd to 1000c,autg
               (5dd8) 85.00
--A Book Lover's Holidays in the Open-NY-1920-373p-illus(5t7) 5.75
--Diaries of Boyhood & Youth-NY-1928-illus-1st ed (5L3,dj) 4.00
--Fear God & Take Your Own Part-NY-(1916)-414p-cl
               (5h2,cov wn) 5.00
--The Foes Of Our Own Household-NY-c1917-347p (5w5) 5.00
--Hunting Trips of a Ranchman-NY-1886-Putnam's-cl-16p plus
   347p plus ads-illus-1st trade ed   (5r0) 10.00
--same-Lond-1886-1st Engl ed-24p illus-347p (5bb4) 10.00
--National Strength & International Duty-Princeton-1917-1st ed
               (5w9,sl stn) 6.00
--Naval War of 1812-NY-1882-orig cl-8vo-1st ed of auth's
   1st full length book (4m6,f) 50. (5gg6) 35.00
--same-NY-1898-Putnam-7th ed-enlgd to 549p-dec cl (5i3,f) 12.50
--same-NY-1927-new ed   (5q8) 5.00
--Outdoor Pastimes of an Amer Hunter-NY-1905-369p-
   1st ed   (5p0) 5. (5L3,5ee3) 8.50
--Ranch Life & the Hunting trail-NY-(1888)-186p-illus-1st prntng-
   Remington illus-rare 1st issue   (5bb4) 65.00
--same-NY-(1888)-186p-cl-1st ed   (5y0,wn) 22.50
--same-NY-1904-Century-186p-illus by Remington (5x0) 12.50
--Realizable Ideals-SanFran-1912-12mo-cl-frontis-1st ed
               (5dd8,autg) 15.00
--Revealing & Concealing Coloration in Birds & Mammals-NY-
   1911-wrps-8vo-Authors ed-extract-scarce (4p5,cov loose) 15.00
--The Rough Riders-NY-1899-298p-1st ed-illus
        (5bb4) 8.50 (5p9) 10. (5a9,5n4,f) 12.50
--same-NY-1899-8vo-cl-illus-298p-1st ed (5t2,autg) 40.00
--Stories from The Winning of the West-NY-1920-291p-illus-
   cl&bds   (5s4,5m9) 6.50
--Summer Birds of Adirondacks in Franklin Co,NY-n p.
   (Salem,Mass?)-n.d.(1877)-4p leaflet-1st ed-rare (Roosevelt's
   1st printed work)   (5gg6,5z9,sl soil) 100.00
--Theodore Roosevelt's To His Children-NY-1919-frontis
        (5q8) 3. (5L3,f) 4.00
--Through the Brazilian Wilderness-NY-1914-lg8vo-cl-photos-
   map-383p   (5j5,rub) 15. (5t2,rub) 10.00
--same-NY-1919-383p-illus   (5t7) 6.50
--The Wilderness Hunter-NY-(1893)-thk lg8vo-cl-plts by Remington,
   etc-1st ed   (5r9) 20.00
--Winning of the West-NY-1905-illus-6 vols
        (5jj9) 12.50 (4k1,rprd) 12.00
--Works-NY-1923-g.t.-illus-24 vols-Memorial ed-autg by
   Edith Kermit Roosevelt (5r0) 43. (5m4,f) 75.00
--Works of...NY-1927-Scribner-20 vols-National Ed-
   fabrikoid   (5x0) 40.00
ROOT,A I-The ABC & XYZ of Bee Culture-Medina,Ohio-1910-
   576p-illus   (5t7) 7.50
--same-Medina-1917-illus-806p plus dictionary (5t2) 5.00
--same-Medina-(1920)-A I Root Co-852p-illus (5t4) 6.00
ROOT,E MERRILL-Collectivism On The Campus-NY-1955 (5x7) 3.75
--Frank Harris-NY-1947-1st ed   (5mm2,dj) 5.00
ROOT,EDW W-Philip Hooker-NY-1929-4to-illus-ltd to 750c
               (5m6) 15.00
ROOT,ELIHU-Experiments in Gov & the Essentials of the Constitution-
   Princeton Univ Pr-1913-83p   (5p7) 4.00
--Missouri Troops in Service During the Civil War-Wash-1902-
   334p-wrps   (5j6) 7.00
ROOT,ERASTUS-Intro to Arithmetic for use of common schools-
   Bost-1806-106p-lea & shingle cov (5p6,chip,lacks fly) 12.50
ROOT,FRANK A-Overland Stage to Calif-Topeka-1901-fldg map-
   1st ed-630p (4t8,soil,wn) 40. (4n1) 85. (5r7) 75.00
--same-Columbus-1950-(reprint)-8vo-cl (5h4,f,dj) 20.00
ROOT,GEO F-The Bugle Call-Chig-(1863)-Root&Cady-62p-
   orig prntd orange wrps-songbook (5m3) 22.50
--Chapel Gems for Sunday Schools-(Chig,Root&Cady)-c1866-
   16mo-128p-cl bk bds-8 illus (5p1,sl tn) 25.00
--same-Chig-1868?-Root&Cady-sm sq12mo-orig prntd bds-
   enlrgd ed   (5L8) 18.50

ROOT, HARVEY W-The Unknown Barnum-NY & Lond-1927-376p-
illus   (5t4) 4.50   (5w5)   6.50
ROOT, HENRY-Personal History & Reminis-SanFran-1921-cl-
134p-8vo   (5h5, pres) 22.50
ROOT, J M-Speech of Mr...of Ohio-Wash-1846-Gideon-14p-
pamph-Dec 24, 1846   (5qq8)   12.50
ROOT, JONATHAN-One Night in July-NY-1961-Coward(5p0)   4.00
ROOT, M P-D A R Chapter Sketches, Conn Patriots' Daughters-
1904-390p   (4t2)   5.00
ROOT, RILEY-Journal of Travels from St Josephs to Ore-Galesburg(III)-
1850-Intelligencer Prnt-8vo-orig yellow prntd wrps-cl bk-
143p-1st ed   (5n9) 1,400.   (5x5, lt fox) 1,500.00
ROOT, W-Casablanca to Katyn-1946   (5L7)   6.00
ROOT, WAVERLEY-The Food of France-NY-1958-486p, (1)-4to-
illus   (5c5)   10.00
ROOT, WINFRED TREXLER-Relations of Penna with the British Gov,
1696 to 1765-NY-1912-U of Pa-422p   (5h9)   10.00
ROOTH, SIGNE ALICE-Seeress of the Northland-Phila-1955-
8vo-cl-illus-327p-Amer Swedish Hist Foundation (5j5, autg) 10.00
ROPER, WM W-Winning Football-NY-1921   (5x7, crack) 3.50
ROPES, JOHN CODMAN-The Campaign of Waterloo-NY-1906-
fldg map-crushed lev mor   (5d2)   15.00
--The Story of Civil War-NY-1894, 1898-Putnam's-2 vols-ads-
fldg maps   (5mm8)   10.00
ROPS, FELICIEN-A Study by Erastene Ramiro-Paris-1905-GPellet-
illus-R8vo-ed de luxe-ltd to 100c   (5t5)   35.00
RORER, D-Treatise on the Law of Judicial & Execution Sales-Chig-
1878-2nd ed   (5ff4, rebnd) 10.00
RORER, MRS S T-Home Cooking-NY-1905-wrps-63p (4g9)   3.50
--Hot Weather Dishes-Phila-(1888)-140p-ads   (4g9, f)   7.50
--Ice Creams, Water Ices, Frozen Puddings-Phila-(1913)-165p
(4g9, f)   5.00
--Mrs Rorer's Cakes, Icings & Fillings-Phila-(1905)-98p (4g9) 4.00
--Mrs Rorer's Every Day Menu Cook Book-Phila-(1905)-300p-
frontis   (5g9)   4.50
--Mrs Rorer's New Cook Book-Phila-(1902)-731p-plts (5g9, spot) 6.00
--Mrs Rorer's Philadelphia Cook Book-Phila-(1886)-581p
(5w0, 5c9)   8.50
--Mrs Rorer's Vegetable Cookery & Meat Substitutes-Phila-(1909)
Arnold & Co-328p   (4g0, crack)   5.00
ROSA, MATTHEW W-Silver Fork School-NY-1936-Columbia-223p-
cl-1st ed   (5t0)   6.00
ROSALIE-the Prarie Flower Melodist Songs & Ballads-Bost-(1859)-
72p-12mo-(unbnd)   (5m6)   6.00
ROSANNA-or, scenes in Boston-Cambr-1839-John Owen-12mo-
orig cl-1st ed-(HF Lee)   (5x1)   35.00
ROSCHER, WM-Principles of Political Economy-Chig-1882-2 vols-
lg8vo-cl   (5t2, sl tn) 7.50
ROSCOE, BURTON-Belle Starr the Bandit Queen-NY-1941 (4c7)20.00
ROSCOE, E S-Geo Selwyn, His Letters & His Life-NY-1900-8vo-
3/4 mor-1st Amer ed   (5m6)   10.00
--Growth of English Law-Lond-1911   (5ff4)   15.00
ROSCOE, HENRY-Life of Wm Roscoe-Lond-1833-2 vols-dec cl
(5c8, f)   17.50
ROSCOE, THEODORE-US Destroyer Operations in World War II-
Annap-1953-US Nav Insti-581p-4to-cl-illus   (5p5, dj) 17.50
--US Submarine Operations in World War II-Annap-US Naval Insti-
1950-577p-illus-maps   (5p5, dj) 15.00
ROSCOE, THOS-Tourist in Spain-Lond-1836-illus (5tt5, rub) 7.50
--Wanderings & Excursions in North Wales-Lond-n.d.-51 illus
(4a1, rub)   12.50
ROSCOE, W F-Icebound-NY-(1954)-132p-photos   (5ss1)   5.00
ROSE, A-America Divided-NY-1949   (5x2)   8.50
ROSE, A-So You Are Going to Be A Witness   (5ff4)   6.50
ROSE, ARNOLD-The Negro in America-NY-c1948
(5L7) 4.50   (5x7)   4.00
ROSE, AUGUSTUS-Copper Work-Worcester-1908-123p-illus (5n7) 2.50
ROSE CITY COOK BOOK-Portland, Ore-n.d.-(191?)-St Michael's
Epis Guild-8vo-ads-96p-wrps   (4g9)   5.00
ROSE CITY PARK COOK BOOK-Portl-1915-Domestic Sci Circle
of Rose City Park Club-8vo-61p-ads   (4g9, soil) 4.00
ROSE, DAN-The Ancient Mines of Ajo-Tucson-(1936)-67p-cl-
Mission Publ Co   (5L2, 5d6) 15.00
ROSE, GEO-The Great Country-Lond-1868-Tinsley Bros-416p
(5qq8)   12.50
ROSE, GEO MacL, ed-Cyclopedia of Canadian Biography-Tor-
1886-807p   (5dd0, hng rprd) 8.50
ROSE, HILDA-The Stump Farm-Bost-1928-plts-178p-ports
(4f9, loose, wn) 7.50   (5u6) 6.50   (5x5)   7.50
ROSE, ISAAC P-4 Years in the Rockies-Columbus-n.d.-12mo-262p-
(Reprint of 1884 ed)   (5dd4)   12.50
ROSE, J H-Wm Pitt & the National Revival-1923 (5L7)   14.50

ROSE, JOSHUA-Modern Machine Shop Practice-NY-1887, 88-
Scribner-illus-4to-2 vols   (4c8, rub, hngs broken) 20.00
--The Pattern Maker's Assistant-NY-1882-cl-324p-illus-3rd ed
(5b8, wn)   12.50
ROSE TREMAINE-Bost-1852-48p-cl   (5h2)   5.00
--same-Bost-n.d.-Crosby Nichols-24mo-48p, 16(ads)-8 wdcuts-
Young Peoples Libr(on sp)   (5p1)   7.50
ROSE, VICTOR-Ross' Texas Brigade-Louisville-1881-crushed lev-
raised bands-g.-g.t.   (5a8, rbnd) 200.00
ROSE, VICTOR M-Life & Services of Gen Ben McCulloch-Phila-
1888-cl-260p-ports-1st ed   (4d5, dj, sl wn) 175.00
--same-Austin-(1958)-Steck Co-cl   (5hh4, vf, box) 10.00
ROSE, WM-Men, Myths & Movements in German Literature-NY-
1931-8vo-cl-286p-1st ed   (5t0, dj, f) 8.00
ROSE, WM G-Cleveland the Making of a City-Cleve-(1950)-
-cl   (5L3) 6.   (5h2, autog)   10.00
ROSE-CHARMEUX, M-Culture Du Chasselas A Thomery-Paris-1863-
99p, 4-12mo-wrps   (5w1)   8.50
ROSEBERY, LORD-Miscellanies, Literary & Historical-Lond-(1921)-
8vo-cl-2 vols   (5t0)   8.50
ROSEBERRY, VIOLA M-Hist of Indian Baskets & Plates...Panama Pac
Inter Expo-1915-cards   (5m9)   7.50
ROSEBOOM, JANE-Poems on Various Subjects-Hillsdale-1869-
199p-cl   (5ff7)   10.00
ROSECRANS, GEN W S-Manifest Destiny, the Monroe Doctrine &
Our Relations With Mexico-n.p.-1870-23p-sewn (5n4)   15.00
ROSENBACH, A S W-A Book Hunter's Holiday...Adventures with
Books & Manuscripts-Bost-1936-illus-facs   (5w5)   16.50
--same-Bost-1936-1st ed-illus-ltd to 760c, autg-boxed
(5ee9) 25.   (5tt6, f, 5w9) 35.00
--Books & Bidders-Bost-1927-Little-311p-illus (5p9)   7.50
--same-Bost-1927-illus-1st ed-ltd to 785c, autg
(5tt6, box wn) 35.   (4g2, pres)   40.00
--Early Amer Children's Books-Portland, Me-1933-sm4to-illus-
ltd to 585c, autg-pict bds-mor back (5ii3, box) 100. (5v0, f) 125.00
--Libraries of Presidents of the US-Worcester-1935-wrps-illus
(4g2)   10.00
--The Unpublishable Memoirs-NY-1917-Mitchell Kennerley-8vo-cl-
frontis-1st ed   (5d8)   15.00
--same-Lond-(1924)-JohnCastle-8vo-cl-frontis-scarce (5b2, fade)10.00
ROSENBAUM, BEN-Green Nakedness-DesMoines-1929-8vo-bds-
67p-ltd to 50c   (5m8, pres, dj) 7.50
ROSENBERG BROS & CO-Years Mature-(SanFran, 1943, Lithogravure
by Crocker Union)-111p-map-illus-stif wrps-8½x11 (5r0)   6.00
ROSENBERG, J N-Columbia Verse, 1892 to 1897-NY-1897-12mo-
1st ed   (4b7)   17.50
ROSENBERG, LOUIS-Cottages, Farmhouses & other Minor Buildings
in England-NY-1930-cl-photos-9½x12½ (5d2, f, heavy djs) 10.00
--Davanzati Palace of Florence-NY-1922-sm folio (5qq7)   8.50
ROSENBERGER, FRANCIS, ed-Jefferson Reader-NY-1953-illus-
1st ed   (5q8, dj, 5h9) 5.00
ROSENBERGER, J L-Colver & Rosenberger, Lives & Times-(1922)-
407p   (5t9)   12.50
ROSENBERGER, JESSE L-In Pennsylvania German Land-Chig-(1929)-
1st ed-illus   (5jj3, t, dj) 7.50
ROSENBLOOM, MORRIS V-The Liquor Industry-Braddock, Pa-(1937)-
105p-frontis-wrps   (5w1)   7.50
ROSENFELD, DAVID-Porcelain Figures of the 18th Century in Europe-
NY-1949-Studio Publ-illus   (5p0)   10.00
ROSENGARTEN, A-A handbook of architectural styles-Lond-1876-
Chapman & Hall-509p-illus-8vo-cl   (5m5)   14.00
ROSENGARTEN, J G-French Colonists & Exiles in the US-Phila-
1907-234p   (4m4)   15.00
--German Soldier in Wars of US-Phila-1886-12mo-1st ed
(5yy6, ALS laid in) 22.50
ROSENLOF, GEO W-Masonry in Nebraska-Omaha-1962-180p-
photos   (5L0)   8.50
ROSENSTOCK-HUESSY, EUGEN-The Multiformity of Man-Norwich-
(1948)-70p   (5p0)   4.50
--Out of Revolution-NY-1938-Morrow-795p   (5p0)   7.60
ROSENTHAL, E-They Walk in the Night-Lond-(ca 1948)-illus
(5x2, dj)   7.50
ROSENTHAL, ERIC-Stars & Stripes in Africa-Lond-1938-Geo Routledge
photos-306p   (4t5, pres, 1 pg loose) 20.00
ROSENTHAL, JOE-Beaumont, Texas, A Statistical Review of City's
Progress for 1925-Beaumont-1925-96p-wrps-illus (5n4)   6.00
ROSENTHAL, MARIO-Guatemala-NY-c1962-327p-illus
(5L7, 5w4, dj) 4.00
ROSENTHAL, RUDOLPH-Story of Modern Applied Art-NY-(1948)-
lg8vo-cl-illus-208p-1st ed   (5t2)   4.50
ROSENWALD, LESSING J-5 Centuries of Print Making-Phila-1931-
catalog-illus-Print Club of Phila   (5m2)   7.50

ROSENZWEIG, A, ed-Guidebook of SoEastern Sangre De Cristo
  Mntns, N M-Socorro-Oct, 1956-151p-4to-plts-maps-illus
                    (5g5)   5.50

ROSEVEAR, ELIZ-Text Book of Needlework Knitting & Cutting Out-
  Lond-1893-460p-illus   (5n7, soil)   3.00

ROSEWATER, VICTOR-Back Stage in 1912-Phila-(1932)-8vo-
  illus-1st ed   (5m6)   10.00

ROSIN, JACOB-The Only Way Out-NY-c1955   (5x7)   3.00

ROSINGER, LAWRENCE K-China's Crisis-NY-1945 (5x7)   4.00

ROSKE, RALPH J-Lincoln's Commando-NY-(1957)-310p
         (5w4) 5.   (5t7, dj)   7.50

ROSNER, CHAS-Printer's Progress 1851 to 1951-Cambridge, Mass-
  1951-illus(some col)-4to-cl   (5p6, f) 7. (5yy8, dj) 8.50

ROSOK, INGWALD A-Retrospect, An Autobiography-Bisbee, Ariz-
  8vo-cl-323p-plts-priv prntd by Rosok-scarce (5g2, dj) 17.50

ROSS, ALEXANDER-Adventures of 1st Settlers on Oregon or Columbia
  River-Lond-1849-fldg map-orig cl-errata-352p-16p ads-
  1st ed   (4k7, rprd)   100.00
--same-Chig-1923-Lakeside Classics-388p-map
      (5h9, 5s6) 10. (5w8) 15. (5ss1) 13.50
--Fur Hunters of the Far West-Lond-1855-2 vols-calf-fldg map-
  1st ed   (4k7)   250.00
--same-Chig-1924-(Lakeside Classic)-Quaife, ed-317p-frontis-
  g.t.-12mo   (5L0) 7.50 (5w8) 10.00
--Red River Settlement-Lond-1856 (5w8) 125. (5nn8) 200.00
--same-Minnpls-1957-frontis-map on e.p.-416p-ltd to 1500c
        (5q0, dj) 10. (5h7) 7.50

ROSS & HIGHLAND CO, OHIO-History of-Cleve-1880-532p(1)-
  dbl columns-lea back cl-illus   (5jj9)   60.00

ROSS, CHRISTIAN K-The Father's Story of Charley Ross-Phila-
  c1876-431p-1st ed   (5w0, fade) 8.50
--same-Phila-1878-cl-431p   (4k2, 5h2) 10.00

ROSS, CLINTON-Improbable tales-NY-1892-Putnam-1st ed(5m2) 6.00
--The meddlings hussy-NY-1897-Stone&Kimball-1st ed (5m2) 7.50
--The Scarlet Coat-NY-1896-Stone&Kimball-16mo (5r7) 7.50

ROSS, CLYDE P-Geology & Ore Deposits of the Aravaipa & Stanley
  Mining Districts, Ariz-1925-USGS Bull #763-120p-illus-wrps-
  fldg map   (5g2)   6.50
--Routes to Desert Watering Places in Lower Gila Region, Ariz-
  1922-GPO-pkt maps   (5g2, f)   25.00

ROSS COUNTY, OHIO 1798 to 1848-Abstract of Wills-n.p.-
  n.d.-82p-cl   (5h2)   10.00

ROSS, DENMAN WALDO-On Drawing&Painting-Bost-1912 (5m2) 7.50

ROSS, EARLE D-Iowa agriculture-IowaCty-1951-State Hist Soc-
  226p   (5a9) 4. (5u3) 4.50

ROSS, EDW ALSWORTH-Changing America-NY-1912-236p (5w4) 5.00
--The Changing Chinese-NY-1911-Century-356p-illus (5p0) 6.00
--The Old World in the New-NY-1914-maps-t.e.g.-1st ed
        (5q8, rprd) 6.00
--South of Panama-NY-1921-8vo-cl-396p-illus (5t2) 4.00

ROSS, ELIZ W-A Road of Rememberance-Cinn-(1921) (5h6) 4.00

ROSS, ELLEN-Wreck of White Bear-Montr-1870-2 vols-1st ed
        (5s1, sl wn) 15.00

ROSS, G H-Beyond the River-Bost-1938-1st ed (5x2, autg) 22.50

ROSS, GEO-Tips On Tables-NY-(1934)-301p (5w1) 6.50

ROSS, HUGH R-35 Years in Limelight-Winnipeg-1936-205p-
  ports, plts   (5aa0, pres) 15.00

ROSS, I CLUNIES, ed-Australia & The Far East-Sydney-1935-310p-
        (5x9) 5.50

ROSS, ISHBEL-Proud Kate-NY-c1953-309p-1st ed (5w0, dj) 5.00
--Through the Lich Gate-NY-1931-4to-16illus, Boyer-ltd to 175c-
  3 autg   (4c8, f bndg, box) 35.00

ROSS, J K-Old Matt's View of It-Springfield-1936-wrps-33p-
  2 photos   (5L2) 5.00

ROSS, J K M-Boots & Saddles-NY-(1956)-4to-cl-plts-1st ed
        (5p5, dj) 8.50

ROSS, JAS-Voyage of Discovery & Research in Southern & Antarctic
  Regions during Years 1839 to 43-Lond-1847-2 vols-8vo-calf-
  8 plts-7 maps-plan   (5ss2, crack) 82.50

ROSS, REV JAS H-A Martyr of Today-Bost-1894-illus-180p (5t7) 12.50

ROSS, SIR JOHN-Narr of a Second Voyage in Search of NW
  Passage-Phila-1835-456p-fldg map-hf lea (5ss1, rprd) 25.00
--Relation du Second Voyage...1829 to 1833-Brussels-1835-3 vols-
  12mo-hf calf-fldg map   (5ss2) 15.00
--Voyage of Discovery...in HMS Isabella & Alexander-Lond-1819-
  40p, 252p & 144p-lg4to-7 maps & charts(fldg)-fldg plts-hf lea-
  raised bands-errata slip-1st ed (5L1) 100. (5tt6) 175.00

ROSS, JOHN, et al-Memorial of...Complaining of injuries done
  to Cherokees & Praying for Redress-Wash-1834-31p (4a5) 6.00

ROSS, JOHN-Book of the Red Deer & Empire Big Game-Lond-1925-
  lg8vo-illus-white cl-ltd to 500c (4g6, lt soil) 12.50

ROSS, LILLIAN BOS-The Stranger-1942-WmMorrow (5F1, dj, mint) 5.00

ROSS, MALCOLM-All Manner of Men-1948   (5L7)   6.00
--The Arts in Canada-Tor-1958-4to-176p-20 col plts (4d4) 15.00
--A Climber in New Zealand-NY-(1914)-LongmansGreen-
  316p-illus-cl   (5d7)   10.00
--Machine Age in the Hills-NY-1933-illus-8vo-1st ed (5m6) 12.50

ROSS, MARVIN C, ed-The West of Alfred Jacob Miller-Norman-
  (1951)-"first ed" on cpyrte pg-cl-200 plts-col frontis
      (5j0, f, dj, 4t8, wn dj) 25.00

ROSS, MARY-Writings & Cartography of Herbert Eugene Bolton-n.p.-
  1932-wrps   (5yy1)   8.50

ROSS, NANCY WILSON-Farthest Reach-NY-1941-illus-1st ed
      (4a1, pres) 8.50 (5dd6) 7.50
--Westward the Women-NY-1944-1st ed   (4a1) 6.00

ROSS, PATRICK H W-The Western Gate-NY-1911-maps-8vo-1st ed
        (4g6)   10.00

ROSS, T R-Jonathon Prentiss Dolliver-1958-366p with index-
  red cov   (5a9)   5.00

ROSS, W W-10,000 Miles by land & Sea-Tor-1876-cl
      (4g6, rub) 12.50 (5g4, pres) 20.00

ROSS, WALTER-The Present State of the Distillery of Scotland-
  Edinb-1786- 105p, (2)-disbnd   (5w1) 18.50

ROSS, WM ALEX-Pryology, or Fire Chemistry-Lond-1875-sm4to-
  346p-4 plts   (5hh7, lacks sp) 12.50

ROSS, WM D-Right & the Good-1930   (5L7)   5.00

ROSSEN, ROBT-Alexander the Great, Facts About the Film-
  (cc1956)-310p   (4c9)   22.50

ROSSER, CHAS M-Doctors & Doctors-Dallas-1941 (5a8, autg) 7.50

ROSSER, L-Experimental Religion-Richmond-1856-16mo-180p-cl-
  stereotyped in Phila   (5p1, chip) 5.00

ROSSETTI, CHRISTINA-Goblin Market & Other Poems-Bost-1866-
  256p-frontis-1st Amer ed-Auth's Ed (4d4) 12.50
--New Poems-NY-1896-ltd to 100c   (5v2, f) 45.00

ROSSITER, CLINTON-Bibliogr on the Communist Problem in the
  US-NY-1955-474p-folio   (5n4) 12.50

ROSSITER, E K-Modern House Painting-NY-1883-WmTComstock-
  4to-orig cl-20 col plts-2nd rev ed (5t2) 20.00

ROSSITER, HARRIET-Alaska Calling-NY-(1954)-200p-photos
      (5ss1, dj, pres) 8.00
--The Twins' Birthday Surprise-NY-(1954)-40p (5ss1, autg) 5.00

ROSSITER, WM-An Accidental Romance & Other Stories-NY-
  1895-Republic Pr-185p-1st ed   (5x4) 7.50
--Days & Ways in Old Boston-Bost-1915-144p-illus-bds
      (5j5) 6. (5t7) 7.50

ROSSKAM, EDWIN-Towboat River-NY-(1948)-1st ed-illus-4to
      (5ii3)   10.00

ROSTAND, EDMOND-Cyrano de Bergerac-NY-1936-Ltd Ed Club-
  4to-ltd to 1500c, nbrd   (5b0, box) 25.00
--same-MtVernon-(1941)-140p-bds(5d2, mor, fbndg) 20. (5ee3) 5.00

ROSTAND, J-Toads & Toad Life-Lond-1934-cl-192p-illus-12mo
      (4p6)   8.00

ROTH, D LUTHER-Acadie & the Acadians-Phila-1890-427p-
  frontis   (5w4)   7.50

ROTH, EDW-Christus Judex, Legend of the White Mntns-Bost-
  (c1892)-Cupples-8vo-cl-illus-olive&dark blue (5b2, f) 7.50

ROTH, H LING-Oriental Silverwork, Malay & Chinese-Lond-1910-
  illus-4to-cl-300p-1st ed   (5t2) 35.00

ROTH, HENRY-Call It Sleep-NY-(1934)-RobtOBallou-8vo-cl-
  1st ed   (5F1, libr stmp) 12.50 (5dd8) 50.00

ROTH, PHILIP-Goodbye Columbus-Paris-(1962)-Cr8vo-wrps-
  1st French transl-ltd to 31c, nbrd (5ss7, f, dj) 25.00

ROTH, SAML-Amer Aphrodite-NY-1955-Vol 4, #16-228p-illus
      (5x7)   7.50

ROTHA, PAUL-Movie Parade 1888 to 1949-Lond-1950-illus-160p
      (4c9)   22.50
--Portrait of a Flying Yorkshireman-Lond-1952-illus-231p (4c9) 12.95

ROTHBAUST, JOHN-The Franklin Harmony & Easy Instructor in
  Vocal Music-Chambersburg, Pa-(1830)-Henry Ruby-sm obl 4to-
  orig prntd bds-195p-2nd & imprvd ed (5L8, stnd) 12.00

ROTHENBERG, STANLEY-Copyright & Public Performance of Music-
  The Hague-1954-188p   (5p7)   5.00

ROTHENSTEIN, WM-Men & Memories-NY-n.d.-Tudor-2 vols in 1-
  illus   (5x0)   7.50
--24 Portraits-Lond-(1920)-GeoAllen&Unwin-8vo-t.e.g.-papr labls-
  1st ed-ltd to 2000c, prntd by Emery Walker (5b0) 12.50
--same-Lond-1923-Chatto&Windus-1st ed-ltd to 1500c (5ss3, dj) 25.00

ROTHENSTEINER, JOHN-Chronicles of an Old Missouri Parish-
  CapeGirardeau-1928-119p-photos-2nd ed-scarce (5bb4) 15.00
--History of Archdiocese of StLouis-StL-1928-(2 vols)-1st ed-
  illus-map   (4t2) 12.50 (5bb4) 25.00

ROTHERT, OTTO A-History of Muhlenberg Co-Louisville-1913-
  ports-1st ed-rare   (4d7) 65.00
--The Outlaws of Cave In Rock-Cleve-1924-345p-4to-cl-g.t.
      (4i7) 30. (5m8) 35. (5w5, 4d7) 40.00

ROTHERY,AGNES-Central Amer & the Spanish Main-1929-
HoughtonMiff-illus (5x5) 10.00
--New Roads in Old Virginia-Bost-1929-223p-illus (5h9) 5.00
--Virginia,The New Dominion-NY-1940-386p-illus-1st ed (5h9) 6.50
--Houses Virginians Have Loved-NY-c1954-319p-illus-4to-
1st ed (5h9) 8.50
ROTHMELL-Bost-1878-Lee&Shepard-(Mary A Denison)-371p-
1st ed (5x4) 12.50
ROTHSCHILD,ALONZO-Lincoln,Master Of Men-Bost-1906-531p-
ports-2nd impression (5w0) 7.50
--same-NY&Bost-1908-531p-port (5p0) 5. (5t4) 4.50
ROTHSCHILD,LIONEL-The Avifauna of Laysan & the Neighbouring
Island-Lond-1893 to 1900-folio-part lev-83 plts-1 vol in 2-
1st ed-ltd to 250c (5z9) 495.00
ROTHSCHILD,NATHAN-A Century Between,The Story of the
Desc of-1937-325p (4t2) 10.00
ROTHSCHILD,W-Monograph of the Genus Casuarius-Lond-1900-
Zoolog Soc of Lond,Vol 15,Pt 5-2 pts in 1 vol-cl-4to-plts-
v scarce-290p (4p5) 112.50
ROTHWELL,C F-Rothwell Family Register-(Ireland ca 1908)-
51p-typescript (4t2) 25.00
ROTHWELL,CLAIBORNE-Desc of,of Albemarle Co,Va thru 9
Generations-1964-434p (4t2) 15.00
ROTHWELL,M T-Geo Wash Carver,A Great Scientist-Chig-1944-
12mo-48p-wrps (5x2) 5.00
ROTONCHAMP,JEAN DE-Paul Gauguin 1848 to 1903-Paris-1925-
Cres-264p-8 plts-t8vo-wrps (5m7) 20.00
ROTTGER,H-Kurzes Lehrbuch Der Nahrungsmittel Chemie-Leipzig-
1903-illus-698p (5w1,tn) 7.50
ROUART,DENIS,ed-Corres of Berthe Morisot wi Her Family,Friends-
(Lond)&NY-1939-8vo-plts-cl (5p5) 15.00
ROUAULT,GEORGES-Reincarnations du Pere Ubu-Paris-1932-
Ambroise Vollard-folio-orig wrps bnd in-illus-ltd to 250c
(5d1,rbnd,f bndg,box) 1,750.00
ROUECHE,BERTON-The Delectable Mntns &-Bost-1953 (5p7) 3.25
ROUGEMONT,LOUIS DE-Adventures As Told By Himself-Lond-
1899-GNewnes-8vo-dec cl-g.t.-396p-port-plts-1st ed (5aa2) 8.50
--same-Lond-1899-Heinemann-8vo-cl-396p-port-plts-illus (5aa2) 8.50
ROUGERON,P N-Nouvelle Mythologie de la Jeunesse-Paris-
1811-12mo-368p-11 plts-calf (5v0) 30.00
ROUGH & READY ANNUAL-NY&Phila-1848-Appleton-20 ports &
plts-12mo-embossed sheep-a.e.g.-scarce (4a3,lacks bkstrp) 20.00
ROUGH & READY SONGSTER,THE-NY-n.d.-32mo-250p-lea-
by an Amer Officer-Mexican War-25 illus (5g1,chip) 5.00
ROUGHEAD,WM-Bad Companions-NY-Duffield-(1931) (5p9) 7.50
--Burke & Hare-Edinb-1921-lg papr-illus-412p-ltd to 250c-
1st edition (5i3,vg) 15.00
--same-NY-1927-JDay-280p-illus (5p9) 7.50
--Enjoyment of Murder-NY-1938-cl-310p-1st ed (5t2) 4. (5p9) 6.00
--The Fatal Countess & other Studies-Edinb-1924-WGreen&Sons-
298p-illus (5p9) 10.00
--Glengarry's Way & other Studies-Edinb-1922-WGreen&Sons-
307p-illus (5p9) 10.00
--Malice Domestic-Edinb-1928-Green (5p9) 7.50
--The Murderer's Companion-NY-n.d.-(ca 1935)-8vo-cl-365p-
Readers Club-foreword by Alex Wollcott (5t2) 4.00
--The Rebel Earl & other Studies-NY-1926-Dutton-310p (5p9) 10.00
--The Riddle of the Ruthvens & other Studies-Edinb-1919-544p-
WGreen&Son-illus (5p9) 10.00
--Trial of Dr Pritchard-Edinb-(1925)-343p-illus-WmHodge (5p9) 6.50
--Twelve Scots Trials-Edinb-WGreen&Sons-1913-302p-illus (5p9) 7.50
ROUGHLEY,T C-Fishes of Australia & Their Technology-Sydney-
1916-Tech Educ Ser #21-296p-70 plts-frontis-orig cl-1st ed-
v scarce (4g5) 97.75
ROULET,MARY F NIXON-Indian Folk Tales-NY-(1911)-192p-
Juv (5s4) 3.50
ROUNDY,R W-The Negro,An Asset of the Amer Nation-NY-
ca1920-wrps-15p (5x2) 15.00
ROUQUETTE,L F-Great White Silence-NY-1930 (4b9) 8.00
ROURKE,CONSTANCE-Audubon-NY-(1936)-cl-illus
(5m2,autg) 8.50 (5p1) 5. (5p0) 4.50
--Charles Sheeler,Artist in Amer Tradition-NY-1938-Harcourt,Brace-
203p-4to-illus (4a0) 35.00
--Roots of Amer Culture-NY-1942-305p-1st ed (5h9) 7.50
--Troupers of the Gold Coast or the Rise of Lotta Crabtree-NY-
(1928)-illus-262p (4n1,dj) 10.00
--Trumpets of Jubilee-NY-(1927)-lg8vo-cl-445p-illus-1st ed
(5t2) 7.50
ROURKE,L-Land of Frozen Tide-Lond-n.d.-illus-352p-1st ed
(5dd7,ex-libr) 12.00
ROURKE,THOS-Gomez,Tyrant of the Andes-NY-1941-12mo-cl
(5h4,dj) 5.00
--Man of Glory,Simon Bolivar-NY-1939-1st ed (5h4,f,dj) 6.50

ROUS,SAML HOLLAND-The Victrola Book of the Opera-
(camden,NJ,1917)-553p-illus-4th rev ed (5t7) 5.00
ROUSE,E S S-The Bugle Blast-Phila-1864-12mo-336p-buck
(4a7,fox,rbnd) 15.00
ROUSE,G H,ed-Intro to Bengali Language by late Dr Yates &
Dr Wenger-Calcutta-1891-8vo-cl-Vol 1 (5t0) 5.00
ROUSE,PARKE-The City That Turned Time Back-Williamsburg-1952-
wrps-photos (4j4) 4.00
ROUSE,W H D,ed-Marcus Aurelius Antoninus,Meditations-Lond-
1900-g.t.-white cl-spec papr (5t5) 9.50
ROUSE,W J-Life of Jas Wilson-n.d.-n.p.-(NY-ca 1887)-13p-
pict wrps (5h1,wn wrps) 5.00
ROUSE,WM-Doctrine of Chance,or the Theory of Gaming-Lond-
(1810)-fldg tables-8vo-orig bds-papr labl-1st ed
(4m7,rub,cov loose) 17.50
ROUSIERS,PAUL DE-La Vie Americaine-Paris-1892-4to-hf mor-illus-
orig wrps bnd in-698p-1st ed (5ss5,ex-libr) 12.50
ROUSSEAU,JEAN JACQUES-Confessions of-n.p.-n.d.-lg8vo-
cl-414p,19p (5t0,fade) 5.00
--same-NY-1955-illus-Ltd Editions Club-ltd to 1500c,nbrd,autg,box
(5F1,vf) 30.00
--Emilius & Sophia-Lond-1762,3-4 vols-12mo-calf-frontis ea vol &
plts in Vol 1-1st ed in Engl (5x3) 150.00
--Emile,ou de l'Education-Lond-1780-4 vols-12mo-calf-plts
(5c8,labl tn) 35.00
--La Nouvelle Heloise-Paris-1802-7 vols-16mo-orig pink wrps-
labls-deckled edges-new ed (5p6,lacks 1 bk wrp) 30.00
--Letters on Elements of Botany,Addressed to a Lady-Lond-White-
1791-503,(28p)-hf calf-3rd ed (5a1,sl wn) 17.50
ROUSSEVE,C B-The Negro in Louisiana-NewOr-1937-Xavier Univ-
(5x2,ex-libr)
ROUSSIN,B-Le Pilote du Bresil-Paris-1845-qtr calf-2nd ed
(5r7,wtrstnd) 20.00
ROUSTAN,M-The Pioneers of the French Revolution-Lond-1936-
EBenn-302p (5p7) 7.50
ROUTES FROM WSTRN BOUNDARY OF ARK-To Santa Fe & Valley
of Rio Grande-Wash-1850-12p-1st ed (4a5) 15.00
ROUTH,MARTHA-Memoir of Life Travels & Religious Exper of-
York-1824-307p-hf lea-2nd ed (5h1) 15.00
ROUTHIER,A B-Quebec-(Montreal,1904)-4to-illus
(4h3,cl) 10. (5w8) 12.00
ROUTLEDGE-NY-1860-Derby&Jackson-(Mrs M C Harris)-504p-
1st ed (5x4) 12.50
ROUTLEDGE'S BOOK OF ALPHABETS-Lond-c1877-4to-cl-
4 ABCs of 8 lvs ea-in col (5v2,vg) 35.00
ROUTLEDGE'S PICTURE GIFT BOOK-(c1866)-G Routledge-lg4to-
a.e.g.-cl-30p-24 col plts-lg type-thk papr (4d1) 35.00
ROUTLEY-The English Carol-NY-1959-1st ed-music (5b9) 10.00
ROUTT,JOHN L-Message of to Second Gen Assembly,Colorado...
Jan 3,1879(wrpr title)-Denver-1879 (5g8) 10.00
ROUX,ANTOINE-Ships & Shipping-Salem-1925-(Marine Res Soc)-
pict-sm4to-plts (5ii3,bndg stnd) 35.00
ROUX,POLYDORE-Ornithologie Provencale,etc-Marseille-
1825,1830-4to-441 col plts-2 vols-calf-rare
(5jj8,Vol 2 rbnd) 1,950.00
ROUX DE ROCHELLE,M-Etats Unis d'Amerique-Paris-1839-
scarce-map & 96 plts (4j3,rub) 27.50
ROUZIER,EDOUARD-Livre D'Or De La Gastronomie Francaise-
Paris-1931-illus-331p,(5)-ads-4to-wrps (5c7) 7.50
ROVASENDA,JOSEPH DE-Saggio Di Una Ampelografia Universale-
Torino-1877-206p-4to-wrps-fldg col plt (5w1) 15.00
--Essai D'Une Ampelographie Universelle-Traduit de l'Italien-
Montpellier-1881-4to-wrps-241p-fldg plt (5w1) 13.50
--same-Montpellier-1887-4to-wrps-247p,(2)-col plt-2nd ed
(5w1) 10.00
ROVERE,RICHARD H-The Gen'l & the President-(NY)-c1951-336p-
1st ed (5w4) 4.00
ROVINGS IN THE PACIFIC,FROM 1837 to 1849-With a Glance at
Calif,by a Merchant long resident at Tahiti-(Edw Lucatt)-Lond-
1851-Longman,et al-8vo-orig cl-4 tinted plts-2 vols in 1-
1st ed (4h0,f,sl rub) 250.00
--same-Lond-1851-Longman,etc-orig cl-2 vols-1st ed-4 tinted plts
(5i0) 160.00
ROWAN,A H-Report of Trial of Archibald Hamilton Rowan on
Info for Distribution of a Libel-NY-1794-Tiebout&O'Brien-
reprint-port-cl (5L1,rbnd) 50.00
ROWAN,CARL T-South of Freedom-NY-1952 (5x2,dj) 4. (5L7) 5.00
--Wait Till Next Year-NY-1960-illus-1st ed (5x2,dj) 8.50
ROWAN,MRS-A Flower Hunter in Queensland & New Zealand-
Lond-1898-272p-fldg map-dbl col plt (5w3) 16.50
ROWAN,RICHARD W-The Pinkertons,A Detective Dunasty-Bost-
1931-350p-illus (5y2,brochure laid in) 8.50
--same-Bost-1931-350p-illus (5t4) 5.00

ROWAN,RICHARD W (continued)
--Terror in Our Time-NY-1941-1st ed   (5F0)   3.00
ROWBOTHAM,THOS-Art of Landscape Painting in Water Colours-
Lond-n.d.(1880)-50p plus list-16mo-wrps   (5t2)   4.00
ROWCROFT,CHAS-The Australian Crusoes-Phila-1855-WP Hazard-
8vo-dec grn cl-512p-g.t.-plts   (5aa2)   12.50
--The Bush Ranger of Van Diemen's Land-NY-1846-8vo-bds-cl
146p-1st Amer ed   (5ss5,rbnd)   25.00
ROWE & SONS,AC-Underwriters Fire Extinguisher-NY-(1908)-
fldg bds-20p-illus   (5h8)   5.75
ROWE,E R-Highlights of Westbrook Hist-1952-242p   (4t2)   7.50
ROWE,FRANK H-Hist of Iron & Steel Industry in Scioto Co Ohio-
Col-1938-129p-cl   (5h1)   4.00
ROWE,G C-Our Heroes-Charleston,SoCar-1890-68p-wrps (5x2) 50.00
ROWE,H S-Anc of John Simmons,Founder of Simmons College-
1933-88p   (4t2)   5.00
ROWE,HENRY K-Tercentenary History of Newton,Mass-Newton-
1930-534p-illus   (5p7)   10.00
ROWE,J A-Calif's Pioneer Circus-A Dressler,ed-SanFran-1926-
ltd to 1250 c-illus-98p   (5a9,f) 13.50
ROWE,L S-The US & Puerto Rico-NY-1904-271p plus ads
(5w4,crack)   7.50
ROWE,N A-Samoa Under the Sailing Gods-Lond-1930-Putnam-
339p   (5x9)   5.00
ROWE,NICHOLAS,ed-Dramatic Works of Wm Shakespeare-NY-
1825-2 vols-calf-g.sp   (5yy1,chip) 15.00
ROWE,WM HUTCHINSON-Maritime History of Maine-NY-(1948)-
Norton-illus-1st ed   (5qq8,autg) 10.   (5h9)   7.50
ROWELL,GEO P-Amer Newspaper Directory-NY-1880-Rowell-
8vo-cl-1044p   (4n9) 15.   (5j5)   25.00
ROWELL,J C-The sonnet in Amer-Oakland(Calif)-1887-Pacific Pr
Pub Hse-8vo-orig prntd wrps-1st ed   (5i9,f) 15.00
ROWELL,R-Sam'l Rowell,Some of his Desc for 7 Generations-
1898-216p   (4t2)   10.00
ROWEN,RUTH HALLE-NY-1949-Columbia Univ Pr-sq8vo-
orig wrps-1st ed -Early Chamber Music   (5p5)   7.50
ROWLAND,BENJ-Jaume Huguet,A study-Cambr-1932-H U Pr-
236p & 62 plts-sm4to-cl   (5m5,crack) 30.00
ROWLAND,DUNBAR,ed-A Symposium on Place of Discovery of
Mississippi River by Hernado de Soto-Jackson-1927-103p-bds
(5w0)   7.50
ROWLAND,ERON-Varina Howell,Wife of Jefferson Davis-NY-
1927,1931-illus-2 vols-1st ed   (5bb5)   8.50
ROWLAND,HELEN-Reflections of A Bachelor Girl-NY-(ca1909)-
Dodge-8vo-pict cl   (5b2,f,dj)   4.00
--The Sayings of Mrs Solomon-NY-(c1913)-Dodge-8vo-pict cl-
labels-illus   (5b2)   4.50
ROWLAND,HENRY-The Countess Diane-NY-1908-Dodd,Mead-
8vo-cl-illus by John Rae-pict labl   (5b2)   3.50
ROWLAND,KATE MASON-The Life of Chas Carroll of Carrollton-
NY-1898-2 vols-illus-fldg chart-ltd to 750c (5r7,ex-libr) 20.00
--Life of Geo Mason 1725 to 1792-NY-1892-frontis-orig cl-g.t.-
2 vols   (5r7) 30.   (4m2)   47.50
ROWLAND,LEON-Annals of Santa Cruz-SantaCruz-(1947)-12mo-
wrps-155p & index-illus-ltd,nbrd ed   (5h5)   6.50
--Los Foundadores-Fresno-1951-12mo-56p   (5xx5)   11.50
ROWLAND,M-Bert Williams, Son of Laughter-NY-1923-illus
(5x2)   15.00
ROWLANDS,JOHN J-Cashe Lake Country-NY-1947-1st ed-272p-
plts-illus   (5yy9) 6.50   (5t4)   8.50
--same-Lond-1952-272p-plts   (5dd0)   5.00
ROWLANDSON,MRS MARY-Narrative of Captivity & Removes-
Lancaster-1828-16mo-cl bk bds-(not 1st)   (4b6)   35.00
--same-NY-1887-Libr of Univ Adventure-illus-23p (5g0) 3.50
ROWLANDSON,THOS-The Engl Dance of Death,From Designs of-
Lond-1903-Methuen-2 vols-red cl-papr labls-t.e.g.-illus
(5F9)   35.00
ROWLANDSON,THOS-The Watercolor Drawings of...Wiggin
Collection-NY-1947-4to-127p   (5t2,dj,f) 10.   (5w0) 16.50
ROWLEE,W W-Lieut Heman Rowlee & His Desc-1907-138p-illus
(4t2)   8.50
ROWLEY,D,ed-Arctic Research-n.p.-1955-261p-lg fldg map-illus-
cl-reprnt   (4b9)   10.00
ROWLEY,GORDON-Flowering Succulents-GrBritain-1959-80p-
col illus   (5s7)   2.50
ROWLEY,OWSLEY R-Anglican Episcopate of Canada & Newfdld-
Milw-1928-280p-ports   (5dd7,ink) 5.   (5aa0)   6.50
ROWNING,J-A Compendious System of Natural Philosophy-Lond-
1744,1742-4 pts-2 vols-fldg plts-8vo-calf (5m6,sl crack) 35.00
ROWNTREE,B S-Human Needs of Labour-1937 (5L7,fly cut) 3.50
ROWSON,SUSANNA-An Abridgement of Universal Geography
togeth wi Sketches of Hist-Bost-(1805)-David Carlisle,prntr-
1st ed-12mo-302p-errata sheet-calf   (5i4)   95.00

ROWSON,SUSANNA (continued)
--Charlotte Temple-Harrisburgh-1801-2 vols in 1
(5ff7,lacks bk cov)   15.00
--same-NewHav-1813   (5mm1)   15.00
--The history of Charlotte Temple-Hudson-1808-N Elliot,prntr-
12mo-orig papr cov bds-sheep sp   (5i0,v chip) 20.00
ROXBURGHE CLUB-Distribution of Books by Catalogue From
Invention of Printing to 1800-Cambr-1965-folio-428p-38 plts-
t.e.g.-ltd ed   (5d5)   325.00
ROXBURGHE CLUB OF SAN FRAN-Chronology of 25 Years-
(SanFran,1954)-lg4to-cl-Grabhorn Pr-200c prntd (5h4,mint) 40.00
ROY,JAS A-The Scot & Canada-Tor-1947-117p-frontis (4a8) 3.50
ROY,NANCY REBA-Descendants of Wm Duncan-
SanDiego-1959   (5r7,ex-libr) 15.00
ROY,P G-Les Monuments commemoratifs de la Province de Quebec-
Quebec-1923-4to-orig prntd wrps-illus-2 vols (5w8)   15.00
ROY,ULYSSE-Etude Chimique Des Vins etc-Poitiers-1856-47p-
wrps   (5w1,tn,libr stmp) 7.50
ROYAL ACADEMY OF ARTS-Catalog Intl Exhib of Chinese Art-
1953,6-3rd ed-263p & 288p of hftone plts & 32p adv-8vo-
hf lea   (5m5,rbnd) 18.00
ROYAL BAKING POWDER CO-My Favorite Receipt-NY-1895-
123p,4p-8vo-dec cl-7th ed   (5c9,hng loose) 6.50
--Royal Baker & Pastry Cook-NY-(1911)-43p-wrps (5g9,chip) 2.50
ROYAL BANK OF CANADA-Annual Report 1920-Montr-(1921)-
prntd wrps-60p-2 fldg graphs   (5w8)   10.00
ROYAL BOTANIC GARDENS KEW-Illus Guide-Lond-1951-134p-
fldg map-wrps   (5s7)   2.00
ROYAL CANADIAN MOUNTED POLICE-Act Respecting NoWest
Mounted Police-Ottawa-1886-9p-unbnd   (5dd7)   4.00
ROYAL CANADIAN QUADRILLES-Montr&Tor-(n.d. ca 1860?)-
4to-12p-publ by Nordheimer-beavers in wreath of maple
lvs on front cov   (5w8)   45.00
ROYAL HISTORICAL SOC-Lond-1928 to 1931 inc-Vols 11 thru 14-
4 vols   (5k2)   15.00
ROYAL,JOS-La Crise Actuelle-Montr-1894-Senecal-105p-orig
prntd wrps   (5qq8)   17.50
ROYAL NAVAL EXHIBITION-Chelsea-1891-570p handbk-358 ports-
wrps   (5c1)   42.50
ROYAL NW MOUNTED POLICE-Report, 1909-Ottawa-1909-wrps-
263p-30p photos   (5dd7,lacks bk wrp,tn) 15.00
ROYAL SOC OF LITERATURE-The 1880's-Cambr-1930-Univ Pr-
(De La Mare)   (5ss3,dj) 10.00
ROYCE,J-Race Questions,Provincialisms & other Amer Problems-
NY-1908-1st ed   (5x2)   25.00
ROYCE,JOSIAH-Calif From Conquest in 1846 to 2nd Vigilante
Comm in San Fran-NY-1948-319p (5h5) 6.   (4n1,dj) 10.00
--The Hope of the Great Community-NY-1916-Macmillan-136p
(5p0)   4.00
--Problem of Christianity-NY-1913-2 vols-1st ed (4a1) 12.50
--Spirit of Modern Philosophy-Bost-1892-519p (5w9) 4.50 (5L7) 6.00
ROYCE,S-Deterioration & Race Education-NY-1878(5x2,cov wn) 12.50
ROYCE,SARAH ELEANOR-A Frontier Lady-Yale-1932-map-158p-
1st ed   (4n1,dj) 15. (5h5) 10. (5dd6)   18.00
ROYCE,W H-A Balzac Bibliography-Chig-1929,30-2 vols (5n4) 25.00
ROYCROFT PRESS-Ali Baba of East Aurora-1899-ltd & autg-
Robarger, illum   (5ii2)   7.50
--Essays of Elbert Hubbard-1905-4to-312p-buck-illus (5ii2) 5.00
--Little Journeys....to Great Musicians-1901--ltd ed-suede-
illuminated   (5ii2,autg) 8.50
--Little Journeys to Homes of Artists-1902-165p-blue wrps-
ltd ed-Knight,illum   (5ii2)   7.50
--Little Journeys to Home of English Authors-1900-148p-suede-
ltd ed-illuminated   (5ii2)   6.50
--Little Journeys to Home of English Authors,Alfred Tennyson-
1901-suede-74p-t.p. & initials hand illuminated-ltd to 940c
(5ii2)   7.50
--Little Journeys to Homes of Famous Women-1896-4to-suede & bds-
193p-signed-ltd ed-rubr   (5ii2,autg) 9.50
--Shakespeare's Tragedy of Hamlet-E Aurora-1902-lea&bds-172p
(5ii2,bkstrp tn)   7.00
--So Here Then is Little Journey to Home of Joaquin Miller-1903-
106p-suede-illus   (5ii2)   6.00
--Ye Rime of Ye Ancient Mariner-1899-101p-suede-ltd ed-
illuminated   (5ii2,hng broke,autg) 7.50
ROYDE SMITH,NAOMI-Portrait of Mrs Siddons-NY-1933-illus-cl-
18,296p-1st ed   (5t0)   4.00
ROYER,JN S,ed & publ-School Visitor Devoted to Practical
Mathematics,etc-Gettysb & Versailles-1892,94-Vol 12 to 15-
(5h7,sl wn) 15.00
ROYS,AUREN-Brief Hist of the Town of Norfolk from 1738 to 1844-
1847-89p   (5mm3)   22.50

ROZET,GEORGES-La Bourgogne,Tastevin en main-Paris-1949-
    sq4to-12 plts-211p,(2)-wrps   (5w1)   9.50

ROZIER,L'ABBE-Memoire sur la meilleure maniere de faire & de
    gouverner Vins De Provence-Lausanne-1772-350p,(1)-wrps-
    3 fldg plts   (5w1,writing,bkstrp tn)   50.00

ROZWENC,EDWIN-Slavery as a Cause for the Civil War-Bost-
    1949-Heath&Co-104p-wrps   (5x5)   5.00

RUBAIYAT OF OMAR KHAYYAM-Ed N H Doe-Lond-1898-2 vols-
    Variorum Ed in Engl,French & German-8vo-illus-dec cl-
    g.tops-   (5t8)   10.00

RUBEL,R O,JR,& CO-Aeroplanes & Aeronautical Supplies Catalog
    #30-Louisvl-n.d.-(1910)-42p-wrps   (5h1)   100.00
--Catalog of Aeroplanes,Motor Supplies & Accessories-(Louisvl)-
    1911-40p-illus-wrps -#32   (5h1)   75.00

RUBICAM,HARRY C,JR-Pueblo Jones-NY-1939-illus-284p-
    1st ed   (5dd9)   12.00

RUBIN,DAN'L F-Mexico,Monumentos Historicos Y Arqueologicos-
    Mexico-1953-4to-487p-475 illus-ltd to 2000c-orig cl (5x5)   30.00

RUBIN,V-Tar & Feathers-Chig-1924   (5x2)   35.00

RUBINSTEIN,ANTON-Autobiography of-Bost-1890-Little (5p0)   6.00

RUBINSTEIN,HELENA-Collection,Modern Paintings & Sculpture,
    African & Oceanic Art etc-1966-4 vols-wrps   (5j4)   20.00

RUBLE,KENNETH D-Men to Remember-Chig-1947-1st ed-illus
       (5yy6) 6.   (5y2)   6.50

RUBLE,S & H-Agricultural Circular & Catalog Price List-1874-
    priced parts catalogue-illus-4 plts-23p-fldg bds (5hh6,wn)   12.50

RUCK,S K,ed-West Indian Comes to England-1960   (5L7)   5.00

RUCKER,MAUDE E-The Oregon Trail & Some of its Blazers-NY-
    1930-293p-photos-1st ed-scarce   (5L2,dj)   25.00

RUCKER,MRS JOS-A History of Colonial Dames of Amer,Nat'l Soc-
    Lamar-1934-illus-272p   (5h9)   6.50

RUDISILL,JAS JEFFERSON-The day of our Abraham,1811 to 1899-
    York,Pa-1936-illus   (5g3)   15.00

RUDKIN,CHAS-The First French Exped in Calif,Laperouse in 1876-
    LosAng-1959-148p-ltd to 350c   (5t1)   25.00

RUDOFSKY,BERNARD-Are Clothes Modern-Chig-1947-1st ed-4to-
    illus   (5jj3,dj)   15.00

RUDWICK,E M-The Unequal Badge-Atlanta -1962-14p-wrps-
    Southern Reg Counc   (5x2)   6.00

RUEDE,HOWARD-Sod house Days-NY-1937-Columbia U Studies-
    240p plus index-1st ed   (5L2)   15.00

RUEDEMANN,R-Cephalopoda of the Champlain Basin-Albany-
    1906-cl-plts-217p   (5t4) 5.   (5cc1)   7.50

RUFFIN,EDMUND-Report of Commencement & Progress of
    Agricultural Survey of SoCar for 1843-Columbia,(SC)-1843-
    56p-bds   (5m3,rbnd,wn)   22.50

RUFFNER,E H-Report on Lines of Communication Betw Southern Colo
    & No New Mex-Wash-1876-34p-prntd wrps-fldg map (5n4)   8.50

RUFFNER,W H-Report on Washington Territory-NY-1889-242p-
    fldg map-cl-illus-maps   (5x5) 20. (4a5,5s4)   15.00

RUFINUS,THE HERBAL OF-ed by Lynn Thorndike-Chig-(1949)-
    476p   (5w3)   9.50

RUGG,E R-Desc of John Rugg-1911-580p   (4t2)   27.50

RUGG,WINNIFRED KING-Unafraid,Life of Anne Hutchinson-Bost-
    (1930)-frontis   (4b6)   8.50

RUGGLES,ALICE McGUFFEY-Story of the McGuffeys-NY-(1950)-
    133p-cl   (5j4) 7.50   (5h7) 4.   (5t4)   4.50

RUGGLES,C L-The Great Amer Scout & Sp y,"Gen'l Bunker"-
    NY-1870-illus-3rd ed,rev   (5s9,wn,shake)   6.00

RUGGLES,ELEANOR-The West Going Heart-NY-(1959)-1st ed
       (5r9,dj,f)   6.00

RUGGLES,SAM'L B-Report of...in respect to the Enlargement of
    Canals for Nat'l Purposes-Albany-1863-8vo-105p-stitchd (5t0)   3.00

RUGGLES,THOS-Usefulness & Expedience of Souldiers as discovered
    by reason & experience-N Lond-1737-T Green-26p-hf calf-
    wn   (5d6)   85.00

RUKAVINA,KATHALEEN-Jungle Pathfinder-NY-1950-8vo-cl-
    299p-port   (5t0)   5.00
--same-NY-1951-Expos Pr-299p-2nd ed   (4t5)   3.50

RUKEYSER,WALTER ARNOLD-Working for the Soviets-NY-1932-
    12mo-cl-286p-1st ed   (5t0)   4.50

RUKEYSER,MURIEL-Beast in View-1944-Dblday- (5F1,pres)   13.50
--Willard Gibbs-GardenCty-1942-465p-illus-1st ed
       (5q8) 5.   (5w0)   8.50

RULE AND MISRULE OF THE ENGLISH IN AMER-by the Author of
    Sam Slick-Lond-1851-2 vols-lg12mo-orig cl-(Haliburton)
       (5r9)   35.00

RULE,EDITH-True Tales of Iowa-MasonCity-1932-12mo-cl-364p-
    1st ed-ltd to 1000c-scarce   (5m8)   17.50

RULE,J C-A Voice From the South-Bost-1930-poems in 7 parts
       (5x2)   8.50

RULE,W G-Means of wealth,peace & happiness-(StL,1947)-plts-
    frontis-ports-108p   (5dd9)   5.75

RULES & ARTICLES-for better Government of Troops,Raised or
    to be Raised & Kept in Pay etc-n.p.-n.d.-89p-pamph-
    rmvd-wi revisions dated Mar 3,1799   (5mm8)   87.50

RULES OF DISCIPLINE-of Yearly Meeting of Friends for Penna,NJ,
    Del & Eastern Part of Maryland,held in Phila (Apr 21 to 26,
    1834)-Phila-1834   (5x2,rbnd)   15.00

RUMBALL-PETRE,E A R-Rare Bibles-NY-1938-Philip C Duschnes-
    illus-12mo-bds-ltd to 500c   (4c1)   10.00

RUMBLE,JOSEPHINE R-History, Mill Creek Zanja-(SanBernardino-
    1937)-WPA-82p-mimeo-bds&fab-WPA Project #3428-(assembled
    in 1950)-18 illus-maps   (5yy3)   50.00
--History Old Government Road Across Mojave Desert-
    (San Bernardino-1937)-mimeo text-bds&fab-36 illus-WPA Project
    #3428   (5yy3)   50.00

RUMMELL,JOHN-Aims & Ideals of Representative Amer Painters-
    1901-E M Berlin-114p-8vo   (4a0)   15.00

RUMPLE,JETHRO-History of Rowan County,N Car-Salisbury-1881-
    428p-cl-(1929 reprint) (5ff7) 20.   (4k2)   22.50

RUNBECK,MARGARET LEE-Pink Magic-Bost-1949-HoughtonMiff-
    8vo-pict labl-231p-1st ed   (5p1,dj)   5.00

RUNCIMAN,STEVEN-A History of the Crusades-Cambr-1953-
    3 vols-illus   (5q0)   22.50

RUNDLE IN ALBERTA-1840 to 1848-n.p.-1940-32p-pict wrps-
    ports-illus   (5dd0)   3.50

RUNDLE,T-A Sermon preached at St George's Church...to recommend
    Charity for establishing New Colony of Georgia-Lond-1734-
    Woodward&Brindley-sm4to-sheep-1st ed
      (5x5,disbnd) 125. (5n2,f)   225.00

RUNES,D D -Dictionary of Philosophy-NY-1942-Philos Libr-
    343p   (5p0,spots)   6.00
--Encyclopedia of the Arts-NY-(1946)-8vo-1064p
      (4a1) 8.50   (5ww3)   12.50
--On the Nature of Man-1956   (5L7)   3.00

RUNKLE,P B-Bounties to Colored Soldiers-Wash-1870-254p-
    HED 241   (4j4)   5.00

RUNNELS,M T-Hist of Sanbornton,Annals & Genealogy-1881-
    569p-Vol 1 only   10.00

RUNNELS,M T-Runnels & Reynolds Genealogy-1873-355p (4t2) 25.00

RUNYAN,NICHILAS PATERSON-A Quaker Scout-NY-(1900)-
    Abbey Pr-277p-1st ed   (5x4)   7.50

RUNYON,DAMON-Guys & Dolls-NY-1931-intro by Heywood
    Broun-1st ed   (5j3)   25.00

RUPP,I DAN'L-A Collection of upwards of 30,000 Names of German,
    Swiss,Dutch,French & Other Immigrants in Penna from 1727 to
    1776-Phila-1876-8 plts   (5w5)   25.00
--same-Phila-1880-495p-2nd rev ed   (4m4)   20.00
--Geographical Catechism of Penna & Western States-Harrisburg-
    1836-1st ed-384p-orig calf & bds
   (4b1,sl wn,lacks maps,fox) 75. (5r5,wn,fox)   50.00
--same-Phila-1837-2nd ed-384p   (4m4,rbnd)   32.50
--He Pasa Ekklesia-Phila-1844-734p (5yy0) 17.50 (5h1,lea)   25.00
--History of Counties Berks & Lebanon-Lancaster-1844-illus-
    orig calf   (5tt6,lacks fly)   65.00
--History of Lancaster Co-Lancaster-1844-orig calf-litho-529p
      (5yy0) 37.50   (4b1)   75.00
--History of Northampton,Lihigh,Monroe,Carbon & Schuylkill Cos...-
    Harrisburg-1845-illus-568p
   (5yy0,rebnd) 24.50 (4m4) 37.50 (5ee3) 27.50
--History & Topogr of Northumberland,Huntingdon,Mifflin Centre,
    Union,Columbia,Juniata & Clinton Cos-1847-560p
      (5t9,wn,crack)   30.00
--Original History of Religious Denominations at Present Existing
    in US-Phila-1844-1st ed   (5yy6)   24.50
--30,000 Names of German,Swiss,Dutch,French & other Immigrants
    in Penna from 1727 to 1776-Phila-1876-2nd ed,rev&enlrgd-
    495p + 24p-8 plts-12mo-orig cl wi Centennial cov dec (5h9) 18.00

RUPPELT,EDW-The Report on Unidentified Flying Objects-
    GardenCty-c1956   (5x7)   4.00

RURAL GEM & FIRESIDE COMPANION-Worcester-1846-144p,
    144p-8 col plts-hf lea-2 parts   (5w7,sl wn)   7.50

RURAL HOURS-By a Lady(Susan Fenimore Cooper)-NY-1850-
    521p,(9)   (5w3,chip)   6.50

RURAL MAGAZINE,THE-& literary evening fire side Vol 1,
    #1 to 12(Jan thru Dec 1820)-all publ-bds-roan bk
      (5g4,ex-libr)   22.50

RURAL SCENES-Cooperstown-1841-Phinney-16mo-31p-orig wrps-
    wdcuts   (5rr2,wtrstn,rprd)   12.50

RUSCHENBERGER,W S W-Account of Insti & Progress of College of
    Physicians of Phila during 100 years-1887 (5L7)   5.00
--Voyage Round the World-Phila-1838-Cary,Lea & Blanchard-559p-
    calf-g.   (5tt0,spec bndg for Sultan)   100.00

RUSDAY,SOPHIE-Horsecars & cobblestones-NY-1948-Beechhurst Pr-
    240p   (5u3)   3.50

RUSH,C E,ed-Library Resources of Univ of NoCarolina-1945-
Univ NoCar Pr (5x2,dj) 15.00

RUSH,JOHN A-The City County Consolidated-LosAng-1941-
414p (5dd9) 10.00

RUSH,OSCAR-The Open Range & Bunk House Philosophy-Denver-
1930-110p-photos-1 Russell illus-wrps-1st ed
  (5dd4) 18. (5a8,5bb4) 10.00

RUSH,PHILIP S-Historical Sketches of the Californias,Spanish &
Mexican periods-(SanDiego,1953)-1st ed-maps-illus-102p
  (5dd6) 5.00

RUSH,RICHARD-Memoranda of a Residence at Court of London-
Phila-1833-orig bds-1st ed (5m2,cov wn) 10. (5p5,hf mor) 25.00
--same-Lond-1833-hf lea (5q8,sp loose) 12.50
--same-Phila-1845-640p-pt calf (4j6) 20.00
--same-Lond-1872-3rd ed-port-595p-hf lea (4b6,crudely rbkd) 20.00
--Washington in Domestic Life-Phila-1857-8vo-hf mor-85p,(15)-
ltd ed -Lippincott (5L1) 20.00

RUSH,THOS E-The Port of NY-GardenCty-1920-illus
  (5s1) 6. (5r7) 7.50

RUSH,WM MARSHALL-Wild Animals of Rockies-NY-(1942)-
296p-photos-1st ed (5s4,ex-libr,soil) 6.00
--same-NY-(1947)-296p-photos-2nd ed (5L2) 3.50
--Yellowstone Scout-NY-1945-184p (5s4) 4.50

RUSHTON,EDW-Poems-Lond-1806- McCreery-8vo-orig bds-
labl-1st ed (5i8,sp wn) 27.50

RUSK,FERN HELEN-Geo Caleb Bingham,the Missouri Artist-
JeffersonCty-1917-135p-illus-1st ed-ltd to 500c (5yy7) 35.00

RUSK,RALPH-The Life of Ralph Waldo Emerson-NY-c1949-592p-
frontis-1st ed (5w9,dj) 7.50
--same-NY-Columbia Univ Pr-1957-592p (5p7) 7.50

RUSKIN,JOHN-The Contemptible Horse-1962-8vo-bds&cl-
5 illus-280c prntd-Adagio Pr (5ee9) 15.00
--The crown of wild olives-Lond-1866-Smith,Elder-8vo-orig cl-
1st ed (5x3) 20.00
--The Elements of Perspective-NY-1887-Wiley-12mo-144p(5p1) 7.50
--The ethics of the dust-Lond-1866-Smith,Elder-8vo-orig cl-
1st ed (5x3) 20.00
--Letters to Chas Eliot Norton-Bost-1904-plts-ports-2 vols-1st ed
  (5nn2,sl wn) 12.50
--King of the Golden River-Lond-1859-illus by Richard Doyle-
g.-cl-4th ed (5c8) 15.00
--same-Lond&NY-1930-8vo-66p-6 plts-Noble,ed-ltd ed-
Rudge,prntr (5aa0) 7.50
--same-illus by A Rackham-Lond-(1939)-GeoHarrap-col frontis-
orig wrps-48p (5c8) 6.00
--same-NY-n.d.-Crowell-bds-cl back- 3 3/4 x 2 3/4"-
frontis-scarce (5rr2) 10.00
--Lectures on Art delivered before the University-Oxf-1870-
12mo-cl-1st ed (5d8) 25.00
--Modern Painters-NY-1873-5 vols-plts-by a Graduate of Oxford
  (5ii3) 40.00
--Mornings in Florence-Orpington-1875,7-GeoAllen-6 parts-8vo-
orig red leatherette-1st ed-scarce (5i8,mor box) 40.00
--The poems of John Ruskin, now 1st collected-Orpington-1891
GeoAllen-2 vols-lg4to-hf vel-Collingwood,ed-27 plts-
India papr-1st ed-ltd to 800 sets (5x3,f) 45.00
--Political economy of art-Lond-1857-Smith,Elder-orig cl bds-
1st ed (5x3) 30.00
--Precious Thoughts,Moral & Religious-NY-1866-8vo-orig dec cl-
g.t.-1st ed (5p5) 7.50
--The queen of the air-Lond-1869-Smith,Elder-8vo-orig cl-
1st ed (5x3,sl wn) 12.50
--Salsette & Elephanta,a Prize Poem,recited in the Theatre,
Oxford,Jun 12,1839-Oxf-1839-12mo-wrps-1st ed of auth's
1st publ (5gg6,lacks wrps) 35.00
--Sesame & Lilies-Lond-1906-Arthur L Humphreys-sm4to-g.t.-
ltd ed-prntd in black &red (5p5,f bndg) 12.50
--The Stones of Venice-Lond-1851-Smith,Elder-thk4to-illus-
embossed cl-g.t.-3 vols-1st ed (5d9) 60.00
--same-Lond-1886-calf-4to-illus-3 vols-4th ed (5tt7,rub,fade) 20.00
--The story of Ida-Orpington(Kent)-1883-GeoAllen-by Francesca-
8vo-orig papr bds-1st ed-1 of 250c on lg papr (5i8,f) 27.50
--same-NY-1886 (4j6) 6.00
--Two Letters Concerning "Notes on the Construction of Sheepfolds"-
Lond-1890-orig vel bds-priv distrib (5mm2) 25.00
--The Two paths-Lond-1859-Smith,Elder-8vo-orig cl-frontis-
1 plt (5x3) 22.50
--"Unto this last"-Lond-1862-Smith,Elder-8vo-orig cl-1st ed
  (5x3,vf) 35.00
--same-Lond-1902-ltd to 400c-Ballantyne Pr (5mm1) 12.50
--Works of-Lond-1903 to 12-lg8vo-39 vol-plts-red mor-g.t.-
Library ed-ltd to 2,062 sets (5hh0,fine bndg) 1,150.00

RUSKIN,JOHN (continued)
--The Writings-Bost-n.d.-26 vols-lev mor-100c only
  (5d2,f bndg) 175.00

RUSLING,J F-The Great West & Pacific Coast-NY-(1877)-515p-
col pkt map-illus-1st ed (5dd5) 20. (5L2,5t7) 25.00
--Men & Things I saw in Civil War Days-NY-1899-1st ed-frontis-
illus-411p (5ee3,5i3,5x5) 12.50
--The Railroads,The Stock Yards,The Eveners-Wash-1878-
Polkinhorn-23p-prntd wrps (5t1) 65.00
--Rusling Family-1907 -160p (5t9) 8.50

RUSO,J J-Discurso Sobre El Origen Y Fundamentos de la
Desigualdad Entre Los Hombres-Charleston-1803-192p-disbnd
  (5x5) 125.00

RUSS,CAROLYN HALE-Log of a Fortyniner-Bost-1923-8vo-cl bk bds-
illus-1st ed (4c1) 7.50 (5h5,sp sl tn) 10. (5yy8,fox,5r8) 12.50
--same-Bost-1923-183p-illus-1st ed-ltd to 155c,autg (5i3) 17.50

RUSSEL,FLORENCE-In West Point Gray-Bost-1908-Page-illus-
401p(4) ads-frontis-5 plts-pict cl (5p1) 7.50

RUSSEL,JOHN-Authentic History of Vermont State Prison-
Windsor,Vt-1812-sm12mo-orig bds-lea bk-91p-1st ed (5t0) 25.00

RUSSEL,ROBT R-Improvement of Communication with Pacific Coast
etc-CedarRapds-1948-Torch Pr-332p-cl (5tt0) 15. (5L2) 12.50

RUSSELL,A-Police Power of State & Decisions Thereon as Illust
Development & Value of Case Law-Chig-1900 (5r4) 15.00

RUSSELL,A G B-The Engravings of Wm Blake-Lond-1912-217p plus
index-ltd to 500c,autg (5a9) 25.00

RUSSELL,AUSTIN-Chas M Russell,Cowboy Artist-NY-(1957)-
247p-illus-2nd prntng (5L2,mint,dj) 5.00

RUSSELL,BERTRAND-The ABC of Atoms-Lond-1923-12mo-1st ed
  (5ss5,fade) 15.00
--The Amberley Papers-Lond-1937-2 vols-Hogarth Pr-1st ed-
boxed (5r9) 15.00
--Analysis of Matter-1927 (5L7) 6.00
--Freedom vs Organization, 1814 to 1914-1934 (5L7) 6.00
--A History of Western Philosophy-NY-S&S-1945-895p (5p0) 4.50
--Marriage & Morals-NY-1929 (4j6) 6.00
--New Hopes for Changing World-NY-(1951)-sm8vo-cl-213p(5t0)3.75
--Portraits From Memory-Lond-1956-1st ed (5x7,dj) 5.00
--The Practice & Theory of Bolshevism-Lond-(1920)-188p-12mo-
bds-1st ed (5t0) 4.50
--The Problem of China-NY-1922-Century-276p
  (5p6) 3.50 (5p0) 5.00
--Proposed Roads to Freedom-NY-n.d. (5x7) 4.00
--Why Men Fight-NY-1917-272p (5t7) 5.00

RUSSELL,C E-True Adventures of the Secret Service-NY-1925-
DPage-316p (5p9) 4.00
--Bare Hands & Stone Walls-NY-1933-1st ed-illus (5x2) 12.50

RUSSELL,CARL P-Guns on the Early Frontiers-Univ of Calif Pr-
395p-illus -1957 (5c3) 5.00
--100 Yrs in Yosemite-Stanford U-1931-illus-242p-1st ed
  (5d7) 10. (4n1,cov spot) 12.00

RUSSELL,CHAS E-Blaine of Maine-NY-1931-illus-446p
  (5yy6) 6. (5qq8) 4. (5p9) 5.00
--Haym Salomon & Revolution-NY-1930-port-8vo-cl (4c1) 7.50
--The Outlook for the Philippines-NY-1922-Century-411p-illus
  (5p7) 4.00
--A rafting on the Mississip-NY-(1928)-346p plus index-photos-
maps(1 fldg)-1st ed (5h6,5L2,f) 10.00
--The Story of the Nonpartisan League-NY-1920-1st ed (5q8,spot)7.50

RUSSELL,CHAS LORD-Diary of Visit to US of Amer in Year 1883-
1910-illus (5yy6,5g4) 6. (5w4) 10.00

RUSSELL,CHAS M-Back Trailing On the Old Frontier-GtFalls-
1922-wrps-56p-14p illus-1st ed-rare
  (4p8,sl fray) 85. (5h5,5x5) 75.00
--Cow Range & Hunting Trail-NY-1925-cl-8vo-21 plts-3 orig
drawings-scarce (4n5,dj) 60.00
--The Cowboy Artist-(1957)-Trail's End Publ-by Adams & Britzman-
lg8vo-350p-cl-3rd ed (5h5,vf,dj) 15.00
--Acceptance of Statue by State of Mont-Wash-1959-Sen Doc #133-
92p-photos-cl (5L2) 12.50
--Good Medicine-GardenCty-1929-col illus-sm folio
  (5L3,mint,dj) 20. (4j6) 15.00
--Good Medicine-GardenCty-1929-frontis-162p-col-1st ed-
ltd to 134c,dj rprd,orig box (4L5,dj rprd,orig box) 450.00
--Good Medicine-GardenCty-(1930)-illus-buck-col plts-1st trade ed-
sm4to (5L2) 45. (5q0) 20. (5r8) 40. (5L2,dj) 60.00
--Master Portfolio of Western Art-Helena-1965-14 col prnts in folio
24" x 30"-ltd to 500c (5L2) 50.00
--More Rawhides-GtFalls-1925- Russell drwngs-wrps-1st ed
59(60)p (5bb4,f) 50.00
--More Rawhides-Pasadena-1946-59p-illus-1st rev ed
  (5m9) 10. (5L2,dj,sl dmpstn) 7.50

RUSSELL,CHAS M (continued)
--same-1954-2nd prntng   (5L2,f,dj,5x5,dj)   12.50
--Rawhide Rawlins Stories-GtFalls-1921-illus-orig pic stiff wrps-
  60p-8vo-1st ed, 2nd prntng-("adios" inside bk cov)
                                          (5L2,4c1,f,cov fox) 35.00
--same-4th prntng before change-Mont-1921-scarce (5L2,mint)   35.00
--same-Pasadena-1946-60p-illus-Russell e.p.-lea-g. stmpd wi
  design of orig ed-1st rev ed-rare   (5bb4)   50.00
--Studies of Western Life-Cascade, Montana-(1890)-obl 8vo-orig cl-
  silk ties-1st ed of auth's 1st book-1st issue-later variant
                                          (5gg6)   500.00
--same-Spokane-n.d.(1919)-24p-12 Russell illus-obl,punched &
  tied-3rd ed-rare (5L2) 100. (5bb4,autg by Ben Roberts)   125.00
--Trails Plowed Under-GardenCty-1927-Dblday-illus-1st ed(so stated)
       (5L7) 25. (5kk7,5g0) 35. (4b6) 40. (5x5,5bb4)   30.00
--same-GardenCty-1928-lg8vo-cl-210p-5 col plts   (5t2)   12.50
--same-GardenCty-1936-Dblday, Doran-210p-brown cl (4b3,f)   20.00
--same-1938 edition   (5L2)   12.50
--same-NY-1944-illus   (4a5)   5.00
--Western Types-Compliments of GtFalls Evening Leader-(GtFalls)-
  n.d.-14 sketches loose in dark green envelope wi silhouette
  of cowboy in gold-cardboard-(lacks 1 print)-rare (5L2)   150.00
--Western Types-GtFalls-1927-16 loose prints,boxed,heavier
  stock than preceding   (5L2)   100.00
RUSSELL,CHAS THEO-Oration delivered before Municipal
  Authorities of City of Boston, July 4,1851-Bost-1851-33p-wrps
                                          (5t4)   5.00
RUSSELL,CHAS W-Memoirs of Col John L Mosby-Bost-1917-illus-
  1st ed   (5x5)   15.00
RUSSELL,FRANK-Explorations in the Far North-Univ of Iowa-1898-
  lg8vo-wrps-290p-plts   (5g2)   10.00
RUSSELL,G W-The Irish Home Rule Convention,Essays by-NY-
  1917-Macmillan-1st ed   (5ss3,dj)   10.00
RUSSELL,GEO WM-Collected Poems-Lond-1915-Macmillan-3rd ed-
  cl   (5ss3,sp faded)   7.50
RUSSELL,MRS HAL-Land of Enchantment-Evanston-1954-8vo-cl-
  158p-illus-ltd to 750c   (5F5,5g2)   17.50
RUSSELL,HENRY B-Lives of Wm McKinley & Garret A Hobart-
  Hartf-1896-546p-illus   (5w4)   5.00
--The Story of Two Wars-Hartf-1899-8vo-752p-illus (5m6)   8.50
RUSSELL,IRWIN-Christmas Night in the Quarters-NY-1917-
  1st ed-scarce-Kemble, illus   (4F6)   20.00
--Poems-NY-(1888)-12mo-orig figured cl-1st ed of auth's 1st book
       (5x2) 17.50   (5gg6)   25.00
RUSSELL,ISRAEL C-Exped to Mt St Elias, Alaska-Wash-(offprint
  Nat Geog Mag May 1891)-152p-20 plts-wrps (5aa0)   15.00
--Glaciers of NoAmer-Bost-1897-Ginn&Co-210p-illus (5p7)   6.50
--Lakes of NoAmer-Bost-1895-125p-illus-1st ed (5L3) 7.50 (5p7) 6.50
--Rivers of NoAmer-Bost-1898-Putnam-327p-illus   (5p7)   7.50
RUSSELL,J, JR-History of War Between US & GrtBritain-Hartf-1815-
  calf-1st ed   (5nn8,sl wn) 35. (5q8,wn) 27.50
--same-Hartf-1815-Russell-402p-ads-2nd ed-calf
       (5mm8,wn) 22.50 (5nn8,sl wn)   35.00
RUSSELL,J-Studies in Food Rationing-Wash-1947-wrps-404p-
  (OPA Ser Gen Pub # 31)   (5ff4)   9.50
RUSSELL,J H-The Free Negro in Virginia 1619 to 1865-
  Johns Hopkins Pr-1913   (5x2)   25.00
RUSSELL,J H-Cattle on the Conejo-1957-Ward Ritchie Pr
                                          (5h5,f,dj)   7.50
RUSSELL,JAS A-Report on Field Work wi the Rainbow Bridge
  Monument Valley Exped of 1934-(Fresno)-157p-mimeo-photos-
  wrps   (5d6)   35.00
RUSSELL,JESSE LEWIS-Behind These Ozark Hills-NY-1947-205p-
  photo-1st ed   (5L0,pres)   10.00
RUSSELL,JOHN-The Red Mark-NY-1919-12mo-cl (4c2,dj)   35.00
RUSSELL,JOHN H-The Free Negro in Virginia 1619 to 1865-Balt-
  1913-wrps-194p   (4m2)   15.00
RUSSELL,LINDSAY-America to Japan-NY-1915-318p (5p7)   4.00
RUSSELL,MORRIS C-Western sketches-LakeCty, Minn-1904-
  Home Printery-8vo-orig prntd wrps-1st ed (5i0,f,pres)   30.00
RUSSELL,OSBORNE-Journal of a Trapper-Portland-1955-maps-
  ltd to 750c-scarce   (5b0,5L2,mint)   25.00
RUSSELL,P-Acct of Indian Serpents, Collected on Coast of Coromandel
  (1796)-A Continuation of Acct (1801)-Lond-1796 & 1801-Imp folio-
  hand col plts-hf mor-port-g. on sp-cx rare (4p6,sl rprd) 1,750.00
RUSSELL,PHILLIPS-Benj Franklin-NY-1926-323p-illus (5h9)   4.00
--John Paul Jones-NY-1927-Brentano's-314p-illus
       (5j5) 8.50   (5p9) 5.   (4a9,f,dj)   6.50
--Red Tiger, Adventures in Yucatan & Mexico-NY-1929-illus
                                          (5tt5)   7.50
--The Woman Who Rang the Bell-ChapelHill-1949-lg8vo-plts-cl-
  1st ed   (5p5)   15.00
RUSSELL,HON R-Strength & Diet-Lond-1905-649p (5c7)   15.00

RUSSELL,ROBT R-Improvement of Communication with Pacific
  Coast as an Issue in Amer Politics, 1783 to 1864-CedarRpds-
  1948-maps-1st ed   (5L0,dj)   12.50
RUSSELL,SCOTT-Mountain Prospect-Lond-1946-Chatto&Windus-
  248p-illus-cl   (5d7)   3.50
RUSSELL,THOS H-The Girl's Fight for a Living-Chig-c1913-ports-
  frontis & 12p photos-pict labl-cl-200p-M A Donohue (5p1,soil) 10.00
--Great Titanic Disaster-Chig-(1912)-320p-photos-wrps (5s1)   3.50
--Life & Work of Theodore Roosevelt, Typical American-Wash-
  (1919)-512p-cl   (5h2)   5.00
--Sinking of the Titanic-(1912)-320p-official ed-illus
       (5e8) 10.   (5t7)   7.50
--Swept by Mightly Waters-Chic-(1913)-326p-1st ed-photos
                                          (5L0,f)   5.00
RUSSELL,VIRGIL Y-Indian Artifacts of the Rockies-Casper, Wy-(1945)-
  prntd at Douglas-112p-photos-1st ed-v scarce (5L0,pres)   10.00
RUSSELL,W CLARK-The Captain's Wife-Bost-1903-frontis-480p
                                          (5ee3,mint)   7.50
--The frozen pirate-Lond-1887-SampsonLow,etc-2 vols-8vo-
  orig cl-1st ed   (5xx6,f)   45.00
--Horatio Nelson & Naval Supremacy of Engl-NY-1890-557p-illus
                                          (5s1)   2.50
--The Hunchback's Charge-Lond-1867-3 vols-12mo-plain bds,
  untrimmed,wi ms titles on sp-1st ed of auth's 1st novel-
  ex rare   (5gg6,box)   500.00
--Representative Actors-Lond-n.d.-FredWarne&Co-496p (5p0)   5.00
--The tale of the ten-Lond-1896-Chatto&Windus-3 vols-8vo-
  orig cl-1st ed   (5x3,sl fade)   35.00
RUSSELL,WM H-Canada, Its Defences, Condtions & Resources...-
  Bost-1865-311p   (4d2) 12.50 (4b9,rbnd)   12.00
--Diary in the East, During Tour of Prince & Princess of Wales-
  Lond-1869-col plts-hf mor-1st ed   (4j3,rebnd)   12.50
--My Diary North & South-Bost-1863-Burnham-602p
       (5i3,5mm8) 15.   (5L3,f)   17.50
--same-1863-wrps-224p   (5yy0)   9.50
--Pictures of Southern Life-NY-1861-143p
       (4b3,ex-libr) 15.   (5a0,bnd in brown papr)   20.00
RUSSELL,WILLIS-Quebec, As It Was & Is-Quebec-1857-160p-
  prntd wrps   (5ff7,lacks bk wrp) 12.50 (5g3)   10.00
RUSSELL'S RAILWAY GUIDE-for Iowa,Minn, The Dakotas, Nebr-
  Northern Wisc & Missouri-Vol 12,#4(Sept 1901)-CedarRpds-
  1901-223p   (5t4)   10.50
RUSSIANS IN CALIF, THE-SanFran-1933-4to-wrps-(Calif Histor Soc)-
  scarce   (5h4)   10.00
RUSSO, ANTHONY J-Bibliography of Jas Whitcomb Riley-Indnpls-
  1944-illus-351p   (5h7) 15.   (4g2)   12.50
RUSSO, D R-Bibliography of Booth Tarkington, 1869 to 1946-Indnpls-
  1949-illus-303p   (4g2)   12.50
--Bibliography of Geo Ade 1866 to 1944-Indnpls-1947-cl-t.e.g.-
  314p-Lakeside Pr   (5hh3,ex-libr) 10.   (4i2,f)   20.00
--Bibliographical Studies of 7 Authors of Crawfordsville, Ind-Indnpls-
  1952-illus-486p   (4g2)   12.50
RUST,P R-First of the Puritans & Book of Common Prayer-1959 (5L7) 6.00
RUSTICUS-Hints for the people,wi some thoughts on the presidential
  election-(n.p., 1822,23)-prntd wrps   (5g4)   7.50
RUSTICUS, MERCURIUS-Bibliophobia-Lond-1832-8vo-orig bds-lg papr-
  papr labl-Henry Bohn-rare in bds-1st ed-ltd to 100c (5d5) 50.00
RUSTON, GEO FREDK-Wild Life in the Rocky Mntns-1926 reprnt-
  303p   (5r1,cov spots)   9.00
RUTGERS, J-The Sexual Life-n.p.-1934-448p (5w5)   7.50
RUTGERS LAW REVIEW-Vol 1 thru 24-1947 to 70 (5ii7,rbnd)   396.00
--same-Vol 1 thru 8-bnd   (5ii7)   ea 18.00
--same-Vol 9 thru 24-bnd   (5ii7)   ea 20.00
RUTHERFORD, ERNEST-Radio Activity-Cambr-1905-Univ Pr-8vo-
  orig cl-plt-2nd ed   (4h0,f)   75.00
--Radioactivity of Thorium Compounds-Lond-1902-Gurney&Jackson-
  8vo-orig prnt wrps-2 vols-1st prntg   (4h0,sp chip,box) 650.00
RUTHERFORD, LIVINGSTON-John Peter Zenger, His Press, His Trial
  & Bibliog of Zenger Imprints-NY-1904-illus-275p-ltd to 325c
       (5j2) 35.   (4g2)   37.50
--same-NY-1941-t8vo-illus   (5m6)   7.50
RUTHERFORD, MILDRED LEWIS-Measuring Rod to Test Text Books &
  Reference Books in Schools, Colleges & Libraries-Athens, Ga-
  (ca1919)-23p-wrps   7.50
--Truths of History-(Athens, Ga)-(n.d.)-(ca 1920)-cov title-
  11p plus 114p   7.50
RUTHERFORD, PEGGY,ed-Darkness & Light-Lond-1958-Faith Pr-208p
                                          (4t5,dj)   7.50
RUTHERFORD, SAM'L-The Due right of Presbyteries-Lond-1644-
  EGriffin-sm4to-hf mor-(24)p,768p   (5L1,f bndg)   95.00
RUTHERFORD, THOS-Ordo Institutionum Physicarum-Cambr-1756-
  4to-plts-calf-2nd ed   (5j3)   25.00

RUTHERFORD,W K-Gen Hist of the Halliburton Family-1959-
385p   (5t9)   20.00
RUTHVEN,A G-Variations & Genetic Relationships of the Garter
Snakes-Wash-1908-US Nat Mus Bull#61-201p-1 plt-cl-8vo
scarce   (4p6)   17.50
RUTLAND DIRECTORY 1905,6-City of Rutland,Towns of Rutland,
West Rutland & Proctor-Rutland-1905-360p-bds   (5t7)   12.00
--same-1909-340p   (4t2)   12.50
--same-1911,1916,1917 & 1919   (4t2) ea   5.00
RUTLEDGE,ARCHIBALD-An American Hunter-Phila-(c1937)-8vo-
later prntg-461p-frontis   (4a6,autg)   5.00
--God's Children-Indnpls-(1947)-1st ed-illus-ltd ed
                              (4a1,autg) 15.   (5x2)   10.00
--Home By the River-Indnpls-1941-R8vo-illus   (5x2)   10.00
--Peace in the Heart-NY-1931   (5x2)   6.00
--Wild Life of the South-NY-1935-Stokes (4d9,dj,pres)   7.50
RUTLEDGE,S A-Pen Pictures from the Trenches-Tor-1918-158p
                                        (4b9)   10.00
RUTT,CHRIS L-History of Buchanan Co & City of StJoseph & Rep
Citizens,1826 to 1904-Chig-1904-Biog Pub Co-photos-lea-
723p-scarce   (4t3)   75.00
RUTTENBER,E M-Catalogue of Manuscripts & Relics in Washington's
Headqrtrs,Newburgh-1879-75p-illus-wrps   (5r7)   10.00
--History of Indian Tribes of Hudson's River-Albany-1872-ports-
illus-8vo-cl-errata pg   (4c1,5a0) 50. (4t8,f)   100.00
RUTTER,FRANK R-SoAmerican Trade of Baltimore-Balt-1897-
fldg bds-87p   (4h8,unopened)   10.00
RUTTER,JOHN-Culture & Diseases of the Peach-Harrisb-1880-94p-
cl   (5h2)   4.00
RUTLEDGE,HUGH-Everest 1933-Lond-1934-Hodder&Stoughton-
390p-illus-fldg maps-cl   (5d7)   12.50
--Everest,The Unfinished Adventure-(1937)-Hodder&Stoughton-
295p-maps-portfolio of illus-cl   (5d7,wn)   15.00
RUTTY,JOHN-The Liberty of the Spirit & of the Flesh Distinguished-
Phila-1759-Franklin&H all-8vo-cl bkd bds-1st Amer ed
                                        (5n2)   125.00
RUTZEBECK,HJALMAR-Alaska Man's Luck-Lond-1925-304p(4d2) 4.50
--My Alaskan Idyll-Lond-1924-296p   (4d2)   4.50
RUUTZ REES,J E-Appleton's Home Books,Home Occupations-NY-
1883-155p,(12)-   (5n7)   4.50
--Home Decoration-NY-1881-120p plus ads-1st ed-Appleton's
Home Bks   (5w0,sl stns)   8.50
RUXTON,GEO F-Adventures in Mexico & the Rocky Mntns-Lond-
1847-12mo-1st ed (5tt0) 25. (4j3,rbnd,rub) 57.50 (4t8)   45.00
--same-NY-1848-312p-1st Amer ed
         (4n1) 22. (4n4) 45. (5y0,wn) 25. (4a3,rub)   35.00
--same-Lond-1849-new ed   (5x5,lacks fly,cov soil)   20.00
--same-NY-1860-2nd Amer ed-8vo (4g6,ex-libr,sig loose)   10.00
--In the Old West-NY-1915-345p plus ads-#1 Outing Adventure
Libr   (5w0)   6.50
--same-Cleve-(1915)-Kephart,ed   (5q8)   3.50
--Life in the Far West-Edinb-1849-cl-sm8vo-1st ed
                                   (4n5,joints wn)   45.00
--same-NY-1849-orig cl-235p &ads-1st Amer ed
              (4n4) 35. (4t8) 20. (5t4)   15.00
--same-Edinb-1869-new ed   (5t1)   25.00
--same-Univ of Okla-(1951)-Leroy R Hafen,ed-8vo-cl
           (4t8) 7.50 (5m8,dj) 5. (5h5,dj)   10.00
--Wild Life in the Rocky Mntns-NY-1916-303p-illus-map (5t4)   10.50
RUZICKA,RUDOLPH-Fairfield-Brklyn-1940-Mergenthaler Linotype-
illus-28p-8vo-200c issued in bds   (4c1)   10.00
--NY,A Series of Wood engravings in Color-NY-1915-4to-30 illus-
Grolier Club-ltd to 250c   (5d9)   35.00
RYALS,J V-Yankee Doodle Dixie-Rich-1890-532p-cl (5h7,rub)   8.50
RYAN,ABRAM J-Father Ryan's Poems-Mobile-1879-8vo-1st ed
                                        (4m8)   15.00
RYAN,C-Poems,Songs,Ballads-Montreal-1903 (4b9)   8.00
RYAN,DANL J-Civil War Literature of Ohio-Cleve-1911-518p-4to
                                        (5r7)   35.00
RYAN,DON-Angel's Flight-NY-1927-296p-1st ed (5dd6)   10.00
RYAN,GRACE L-Dances of Our Pioneers-NY-(1939)-8vo-cl-
illus-196p   (5j5,dj)   10.00
RYAN,KATE-Old Boston Museum Days-Bost-1915-illus
                                   (5mm2,pres)   7.50
RYAN,L R-Old St Peter's,the Mother Church of Catholic NY-
NY-1935-   (5t9)   7.50
RYAN,MARAH ELLIS-Flute of the Gods-NY-1909-part mor-g.-
338p-ltd to 500c   (4b2,autg,sl wn)   8.50
--same-NY-(1909)-338p-illus by ESCurtis (5h4) 4. (5a9,5L2)   3.00
--Indian Love Letters-Chig-1907-lea-g.-122p (4b2,cov wn)   3.00
--A pagan of the Alleghenies-Chig&NY-(1891)-RandMcNally-
1st ed   (5m2)   7.50
--Told in the Hills-Chig-(1914)-RandMcNally-col illus (5ee3)   4.00

RYAN,THOS FORTUNE-Collection of Gothic & Renaissance Art-
NY-1933-(Amer Art Ass'n)-folio-bnd-ltd to 600c-col & b&w plts
   (5t4,wtrstnd,dmgd) 8.   (5ii3,f,box)   40.00
RYAN,VICTOR A-Some Geographic & Economic Aspects of the
Cork Oak-Balt-1948-8vo-orig limp lea-116p-1st ed (5m6)   10.00
RYAN,VINCENT W-Mauritius & Madagascar-Lond-1864-
Seeley,Jackson & Halliday-340p tinted drawings (4t5,fox)   25.00
RYAN,W M-Shamrock & Cactus,Story of Catholic Heroes of
Texas Independence-SanAnt-1936-64p-wrps (4a5)   7.50
RYAN,WM R-Personal Adventures in Upper & Lower Calif-Lond-
1851-2 vols in 1-thk12mo-cl-23 drawngs (5h4,fade)   90.00
RYAN'S-Bottoms Up-NY-n.d.-46p-illus   (5w6)   2.50
RYBERG,OLOF-Studies on Bats & Bat Parasites-Stockholm-(1947)-
1st ed-4to-plts-orig wrps-330p   (5jj3,pres)   15.00
RYCAUT,SIR PAUL-History of the Turkish Empire,1623 to 77-Lond-
1687-J D-ports-tall folio-old calf-crude cl bk
                              (4b6,sl dampstns)   150.00
--Present State of the Ottoman Empire-Lond-1670-Starkey&Brome-
sm folio-hf calf-frontis-illus-3rd ed   (4n5,hng rprd)   45.00
RYDBERG,PER AXEL-Flora of the Prairies & Plains of Central
NoAmer-NY-1932-NY Bot Garden-lg8vo-cl-illus-969p (5j5)   10.00
RYDBERG,VIKTOR-Roman Legends about the Apostles Paul &
Peter-Lond-1898-lg12mo-cl-940p   (5t2)   3.50
--Singoalla-Lond-1904-227p-25 plts   (5c3)   5.00
RYDELL,CARL-Adventures,Autobiog of a Seafaring Man-Lond-
1924-308p-port-plts-map   (5a1,editor autog)   12.50
--On Pacific Frontiers-Yonkers-1926-267p-illus-map (5a1)   4.50
RYDER,DAVID W-A Century of Hardware & Steel-SanFran-1949-
illus-119p   (5x5,5y2)   8.50
--"Great Citizen"-SanFran-1962-8vo-cl-271p-illus (5h4,f)   8.50
--Memories of the Mendocino Coast-SanFran-1948-sm4to-
bds&cl   (5F5,f)   12.50
--Men of Rope-SanFran-1954-146p-illus (5x5) 10. (4e4)   12.50
RYDER,DON-Black Cotton Stockings-1954-photos-scarce (5zz0)   27.50
RYDER,JOHN-A Suite of Fleurons-Bost-(1957)-54p-illus-bds-
nar 12mo   (5n7)   3.00
RYDER-TAYLOR,HENRY-History of Alamo & of Local Franciscan
Missions-SanAnt-1935-95p-illus-wrps   (4a5)   6.00
RYDINGS,JOS-Country Walks in Many Fields-Paterson-1934-
338p-illus   (5w9)   6.50
RYDJORD,JOHN-Foreign Interest in the Independence of New
Spain-1935-Duke Univ Pr-347p-orig cl   (5x5,f)   20.00
RYE,JOHN-Kirby in the Dale-Lond-1884-3 vols in 1-8vo-
orig cl-1st ed-frontis   (5xx6,rub)   22.50
RYERSON,EGERTON-Annual Report of Normal,Model,Grammar
& Common Schools in Upper Canada for....1857-Tor-1858-
hf roan-392p   (5nn2,sl rub)   12.50
--My Dearest Sophie-Tor-1955-350p-ports-map (5aa0)   8.50
--Story of My Life-Tor-188 -614p-ads   (5dd7)   10.00
RYERSON,JOHN-Hudson's Bay-Tor-1855-1st ed-port-plts-190p
                                        (5yy9,sl fox)   45.00
RYERSON,STANLEY W-French Canada-Tor-1944-256p (5dd0)   4.50
RYHINER,P-The Wildest Game-Phila-1958-illus-1st ed (5x2,dj)   5.00
RYLE,J C-Only One Way...thoughts on Acts 4,12-Tor-1851
                                        (5nn8)   15.00
RYMER,T-Foedera-The Hague-1739 to 45-10 vols
                              (5r4,Vol 7 is reprnt)   950.00
RYNNING,THOS H-Gun Notches-NY-(1931)-332p
              (5x5,lacks fly,dj) 10. (5L2,dj)   17.50
--same-NY-(1931)-4th prntng   (5m9,ink)   7.50
RYUS,WM H-The 2nd Wm Penn-KansasCty-(1913)-pict wrps-
176p-illus   (5F5,f,4p8,5h2) 7.50 (5L2,5m9)   10.00
RYWELL,M-Tennessee Cookbook-Harriman-1951-64p-8vo-wrps
                                        (5g9)   3.00

SA,ZITKALA-Old Indian Legends-Bost-1901-illus-165p-juvenile
                                        (4b2,sl tn)   4.00
SAARINEN,ALINE-The Proud Possessors-NY-1958-lg8vo-cl (5p5)10.00
SABARTES,JAIME-Picasso,An Intimate Portrait-NY-(1948)-230p-
illus   (5t7)   4.50
SABATINI,RAFAEL-Scaramouche-Bost-1921-8vo-cl-1st ed (5d9)   25.00
--The Tavern Knight-Lond-1914-12mo-pict cl-1st ed of auth's
1st book   (5gg6,pres)   25.00
SABIN,EDWIN L-Building the Pacific Railway-Phila-1919-
Lippincott-22 illus-map-1st ed (5x5,lt stns) 10. (5bb4,vg)   17.50
--Gold-Phila-(1929)-336p-col plts-1st ed (5dd6)   9.50
--Kit Carson Days 1809 to 1868-Chig-1914-illus-maps-656p plus
index-1st ed   (5yy7)   35.00
--same-Chig-1919-656p plus index-illus-maps-2nd ed (5L0)   15.00
--same-NY-1935-2 vols-972p plus index-Press of the Pioneers-
illus-expanded&rev ed-
   (5h4,2 pgs wrnkld) 30. (5kk4,glassine wrps,5yy7)   40.00
--On the Plains with Custer-Phila-1913-308p-illus-1st ed
                                        (5bb4,cov tn)   4.00

SABIN,EDWIN L (continued)
--The Rose of Santa Fe-Burt-1923-8vo-cl-409p   (5g5)   4.00
--Wild Men of the Wild West-NY-(c1929)-Crowell-illus-cl-
    363p-scarce   (5jj7,vf,dj) 22.50   (5r1,5kk4,4p2)   20.00
--With Carson & Fremont-Phila-(1912)-302p-photos-9th prntng
                                            (5L2)   4.00
--With Geo Washington into the Wilderness-Phila-1924-298p plus ads-
    col frontis-plts-map-1st ed   (5dd6)   5.00
SABIN,ELIJAH R-Life & Reflections of Chas Observator-Bost-1816-
    Rowe&Hooper-12mo-sheep-1st ed   (5i0,scuff)   65.00
SABIN,JOS,comp-Catalog of Francis S Hoffman-NY-1877-hf calf-
    lg8vo-498p-priced-orig wrps bnd in   (5L8,rbnd)   18.50
SABIN,MARION S-Palmer Lake, A Historical Narrative-Denver-
    c1957-Sage-12mo-bds-116p   (5L2) 7.50   (4t1)   12.50
SABINE,SIR EDW-Acct of Experiments to Determine Acceleration
    of the Pendulum in Different Latitudes-Lond-1821-4to-disbnd-
    Bulmer&Nicol-28p-5 fldg tables-1st separate ed (5ee5,pres) 50.00
--On Length of the Seconds Pendulum in Observatory at Greenwich-
    Lond-1831-Bulmer&Nicol-4to-disbnd-459p to 488p-
    1st separate ed   (5ee5,pres)   32.00
SABINE,EDW-Journal of a Voyage for Discovery of a NW Passage...
    1819,20-Phila-1821-355p-chart-qtr lea   (5ss1,fox)   25.00
SABINE,GEO H-A History of Political Theory-NY-(1948)-Holt-
    797p   (5p0)   7.50
SABINE,LORENZO-Notes on Duels & Duelling-Bost-1855-394p-
    cl-1st ed   (5h2,lack fly) 12.50
--same-Bost-1856-Crosby Nichols-426p-2nd ed (5F9,poor)   7.50
--Report on Principal Fisheries of American Seas-Wash-1853-
    317p-8vo-orig cl (5g4,ex-libr) 10. (5ss2,phes,sl wn) 17.50
SABINE,W H W-Suppressed History of Gen'l Nathaniel Woodhull-
    NY-1954-maps-4to-typescript ed(bnd)   (5yy6)   12.00
SABONADIERE,G-O Fazendeiro De Cafe Dm Ceilao-Rio de Janeiro-
    1877-187p-2nd ed,rev   (5w1,lacks wrps)   8.50
SACCO VANZETTI CASE, THE-Transcript of Record of Trial...
    and sub proceedings,1920 to 7-Vols 1 thru 5,plus suppl Vol 6-
    NY-1928,29-orig cl   (5m3)   125.00
SACHS,EMANIE-"The Terrible Siren"...Victoria Woodhull-NY-
    1928-dec bds-1st ed   (4m7,pres) 12.50   (5w5,edge wn) 6.50
SACHS,H B-Heine in America-Phila-1916-   (5jj3)   10.00
SACHS,H-FREUD, Master & Friend-1944   (5L7)   3.50
SACHS,PAUL J-Modern Prints & Drawings-NY-(1954)-illus (5m2) 7.50
SACHS,WULF-Black Hamlet-Bost-1947-Little, Brown-324p
                                    (5x2,dj,4t5,dj)   5.00
SACHSE,JULIUS F,transl-Daniel Falckner's Curieuse Nachricht
    from Penna-Lancaster-1905-1st ed-German & Engl text
                                            (5jj3,rbnd)   20.00
--German Pietists of Provincial Penna-Phila-1895-illus-facs-4to-
    504p-scarce   (5L7) 35.   (4m4)   60.00
--Justus Falckner-Phila-(1903)-Ltd ed   (4m4)   25.00
--Wayside Inns of the Lancaster Roadside Between Phila & Lancaster-
    Lancaster-1912-illus-206p-scarce   (4m4)   32.50
SACK,A J-The Birth of the Russian Democracy-NY-1918-lg8vo-
    cl-illus-552p   (5t2,pres)   7.50
SACK,ALBERT-Fine Points of Furniture,Early Amer-NY-1955-
    Crown-303p-illus   (5p0)   8.50
SACK,ALBERT VON-Narr of Voyage to Surinam-Lond-1810-
    W Bulmer-4to-hf mor-frontis-2 plts   (4a3,fox)   60.00
SACK,JOHN-The Butcher,The Ascent of Yerupaja-NY-(1952)-
    213p-illus-cl-Rinehart   (5d7)   7.50
SACKETT,F-Brickwood's Sackett on Instructions to Juries-Chig-
    1908-3 vols-3rd ed   (5ff4)   16.50
SACKETT,WM E-Modern Battles of Trenton-Trenton-1895-illus
                (5m2) 7.50   (4b6) 10.   (5t0)   12.50
SACKVILLE,GEO GERMAIN-Proceedings of General Court martial
    held at Horse guards-1760-buck   (5L7,rbnd)   15.00
SACKVILLE WEST,VICTORIA-The dark island-Lond-1934-
    publ by Leonard&Virginia Woolf-Hogarth Pr-8vo-orig cl-
    1st ed   (5i8,pres)   10.00
--The Edwardians-(Lond)-1930-Hogarth Pr-hf vel-g.t.-lg ppr 1st ed-
    ltd to 125c,autg   (4b6)   30.00
--King's Daughter-Lond-1929-Cr 8vo-bds-1st ed-Hogarth Living
    Poets Ser   (5ss7,sl fade) 6.50
--Knole & the Sackvilles-Lond-(1926)-13 illus-230p,(1)-mor
                                            (5w3)   22.50
--same-"Cheap edition"-(1934)-smaller format (5w3,crack)   6.50
--Saint Joan of Arc-GardenCty-1936-Dblday Doran-395p-frontis-
    7 plts-cl-1st Amer ed   (5p1,fade)   6.00
--Seducers in Ecuador-Lond-1924-Leonard&Virginia Woolf-
    1st ed   (5ss3,dj)   15.00
--same-NY-1925-Doran   (5x0)   3.75
SACLEUX,C-Grammaire des Dialectes Swahilis-Paris-1909-27&335p-
    2 fldg tables   (5c6,vg)   22.50

SACRAE ROTAE ROMANAE-Decisiones Recentiores-Mediolani-
    1730-folio-5 vols   (5r4,rbnd)   87.50
SACRAMENTO,CALIF-Souvenir of-Brklyn-c1898-photogravures-
    19p-A Wittemann-bds   (5kk6,f)   22.50
SACRAMENTO,CALIF-Souvenir of-Brklyn-c1898-photogravures-
    Brklyn-1898-A Wittemann-40p   (5n4)   17.50
SACRAMENTO CO & ITS RESOURCES-A Souvenir of the 'Bee',
    1894-(Sacramento)-obl folio-bds-198p & index-illus-(2nd ed,
    1895)   (5h4)   12.50
SACRAMENTO CO IN HEART OF CALIF-Sacramento-(1915)-
    Bd Superv & Expos Comm-12mo-wrps-64p   (4t1)   12.50
SACRED DRAMAS-chiefly intended for Young Persons-Lond-1783-
    calf-(H More)-3rd ed   (5c8,t.pg cut) 35.00
SACRED HYMNS & SPIRITUAL SONGS-for Church of Jesus Christ
    of Latter Day Saints in Europe-Liverpool&Lond-1851-lea-
    words only-9th ed,rev-379p plus errata   (4t3,rub)   25.00
SADLEIR,MRS J-Elinor Preston-NY&Montr-12mo-cl-frontis
                                            (5w8,wn)   10.00
SADLEIR,MICHAEL-Excursions in Victorian Bibliography-Lond-
    1922-t8vo-g.t.-   (5r9,dj)   25.00
--Hyssop, A Novel-Lond-(1915)-12mo-cl-1st ed of 1st novel by
    Sadleir-   (5gg6)   25.00
--19th Century Fiction-Lond-(& Berkeley&LosAng)-1951-lg4to-
    buck-2 vols-48 plts-1025c prntd by Cambr Univ Pr (5dd8,djs)100.00
--Trollope, A Commentary-Lond-1927-Constable&Co-1st ed-
    ltd to 100c,nbrd,autg   (5ss9)   37.50
SADLER,SAM'L-Art,Science of Sailmaking-Lond-1892-137p(5s1) 8.00
SAEKI,P Y-Nestorian Documents & Relics in China-Tokyo-1951-
    Acad of Oriental Culture   (5p0)   7.50
SAELTZER,ALEXANDER-A Treatise on Acoustics in Connection with
    Ventilation etc-NY-1872-12mo-1st ed   (5ss5)   15.00
SAENZ,MOISES-Some Mexican Problems-Univ of Chig-(1926)-
    12mo-cl   (5h4,dj)   7.50
SAFFELL,W T R-Records of the Revolutionary War-Phila-1860
                                            (5m2)   17.50
SAFFIN,JOHN-John Saffin His Book-NY-1928-Harbor Pr-199p-
    ltd to 500c   (5qq8)   10.00
SAFFORD,JAS M-Geology of Tennessee-Nashville-1869-Mercer-
    8vo-cl-551p-7 plts-fldg view-scarce (5j5,lacks map,plt tn) 10.00
--Geological Reconnoissance of State of Tennessee,1st biennial
    report-Nashville-1856-col fldg map-buck
                (5L7,rbnd) 12.50   (5g8,libr labl)   20.00
SAFFORD,MARION FULLER-Story of Colonial Lancaster(Mass)-
    Rutland-1937-Tuttle-8vo-cl-illus-190p   (5j5)   15.00
SAFFORD,VIRGINIA-Food of my Friends-Minneap-(1944)-U of Minn
    Pr-300p-illus   (5c9)   4.50
SAFFORD,WM H-Life of Harman Blennerhassett-Chillicothe-1850-
    view-239p-cl   (5tt8,wn) 20. (4a9,cov wn) 30.(5i9) 25.00
SAFFLEY,JAS CLIFFORD-Mexican Vistas-SanDiego-1952-photos-
    225p-scarce   (5dd4)   12.50
SAGAN,FRANCOISE-Toxique-(NY,1964)-illus-4to-prntd wrps-
    1st Amer ed   (5r9)   10.00
SAGARD,GABRIEL-Le Grand Voyage du Pays des Hurons-Paris-
    1632-Moreau-frontis   (5e2)   4,000.00
--Histoire du Canada et Voyages les Freres Mineurs Recollects etc-
    Paris-1636-Chez Claud Sonnius-wi orig 3 leaves of music &
    1 blank lf-rare   (5e2)   10,000.00
--Long Journey to Country of the Hurons-Tor-1939-Champlain Soc-
    facs-maps-411p   (5zz8)   45.00
--Long Journey to Country of the Hurons-Tor-1939-Champlain Soc-
    facs-maps-illus-Limited Ed   (4c1)   60.00
SAGARIN,EDW-Science & Art of Perfumery-1945-1st ed (5kk5) 10.00
--same-NY-1955-220p-illus   (5w3)   7.50
SAGATOO,MRS M A-Wah sash kah moqua,or 33 Years Among
    the Indians-Bost-1897-12mo-illus-1st ed (5ss5)   17.50
SAGE,E J P-Sam'l Morrison & Some of His Desc-(1936)-98p (5t9)20.00
SAGE,E L-Gen Record of Desc of David Sage-1919-128p-scarce
                                            (5t9)   25.00
SAGE,EDMUND-Masters of the city-Phila-(1909)-Madoc Pub-
    127p   (5m2)   6.50
SAGE,ELIZ-A Study of Costume-NY-1926-Scribner-235p-illus
                                            (5x0)   6.00
--Occupations For Little Fingers-NY-1905-illus-cl-15p (5t2) 3.75
SAGE,LEE-The Last Rustler-Bost-1930-illus-8vo-cl-1st ed
        (5kk4) 12.50   (4g6,5L2) 8.50   (5h4)   10.00
SAGE,RUFUS B-Rocky Mountain Life-Bost-1857-363p-illus
                                    (5L0,stn,wn)   8.50
--same-1860   (5L0,wn)   8.50
--Scenes in the Rocky Mntns,& in Ore,Calif,NewMex,Tex &
    Grand Prairies-Phila-1846-mor-g.-303p-fldg map-1st ed-
    ex rare   (5s9,rprd,wn stnd) 575. (4n4,rprd,map wn) 375.00

SAGE,RUFUS B (continued)
--Wild Scenes in Kansas& Nebr,Rocky Mntns,Ore,Calif,
NewMex-Tex & Grand Prairies-Phila-1844-cl-303p-illus-
3rd ed-Miller   (5g6,vg)   15.00
--same-Phila-1855-Miller-303p-illus-3rd ed,rev   (5qq8)   12.50
SAGE,WALTER N-Sir Alexander Mackenzie & his influence on
history of the NW-Kingston(Ontario,1922)-wrpr title-18p-
(5g8)   7.50
SAGENDORPH,KENT-Michigan,story of the University-NY-
1948-EPDutton-8vo-384p-1st ed   (5p1)   10.00
--Stevens Thomson Mason,Misunderstood Patriot-NY-1947-447p-
cl-1st ed   (5h2)   5.00
SAGINAW CO,MICH-Atlas of-NY-1877-F W Beers-132p-lea bkd cl-
liths   (4h7,sp wn)   60.00
SAGINAW VALLEY,MICH-Resources & Prospects of-(East Saginaw,
1862?)-folded-self cov-15p   (4t3)   17.50
SAGLIO,ANDRE-French Furniture-Lond-1913-t8vo-60 plts-cl
(5t5)   7.50
SAILAND,ALBERT-The Viking Goes to Sea-LosAng-1924-
Times Mirror Pr   (5x5,pres)   12.50
SAILING DIRECTIONS FOR JAPAN-Korea,Adjacent Seas etc-
Lond-1904-872p-maps-1st ed   (5s1,soil,rprd)   15.00
SAILLET,ALEXANDRE DE-Les Enfants peints par eux memes;types,
caracteres et Portraits de Jeunes Filles-Paris-1842-frontis-
34 plts(index calls for 36 plts)-lea-lg8vo   (5c8,lt fox)   37.50
SAINER,A L-The Judge Chuckles-NY-1935   (5ff4)   7.50
SAINES,ALANSON A-History of the 15th Regiment NJ Volunteers-
NY-1883-illus   (5s9)   7.50
ST AUGUSTINE-Buffalo-c 1915-32p-wrps-illus   (5j6)   7.00
ST CHRISTOPHER & NEVIS-Laws,Statutes,etc-Lond-1922-bound
(5ii7,ex-libr)   12.50
ST CLEMENT,DOROTHY DE-White Gumbo-NY-1951   (5a8)   5.00
ST CROIX,JOHN W-Pictorial History of Hartford-1953-184p(5e8)9.75
ST CROIX VALLEY,THE-(Caption)-(Prescott,Peirce Co,1859)-
n.p.-n.d.-4p,(4)adv-8vo-unbound (5g4,stn) 15.   (5i9)   30.00
SAINT EXUPERY,ANTOINE de-Flight to Arris-NY-(1942)-
illus,Lamotte-8vo-hf calf-ltd to 500c,autg,box (5tt7,f)   27.50
--Night Flight-NY-1932-198p-1st ed in Engl   (4b4,f)   12.50
ST GAUDENS,AUGUSTUS-His Life & Art-Bost-1907-24 plts-
g.t.-R8vo-orig cl   (5t5)   10.00
SAINT GAUDENS,HOMER-American Artist & His Times-NY-1941-
Dodd,Mead-332p-illus-frontis-crown 4to   (4a0)   22.50
--same-NY-1941-illus-332p-1st ed-ltd to 155c   (4m4,box)   40.00
ST GEORGE,ELEANOR-The Dolls of Yesterday-NY-1948-illus-
204p-4to   (5w0) 16.50   (5n7) 10.   (5t4)   12.50
--Old Dolls-NY-1950-12mo-cl-134p   (5g0,f,dj)   7.50
ST GEORGE,MAXIMILIAN-A Trial on Trial-1945-Nat'l Civil
Rights Comm-503p-cl-illus   (5r0)   10.00
SAINT GERMAN,C-Doctor & Student-1886-rev by W Muchall
(5L7)   10.00
SAINT GERMAIN,COMTE C de-Study of Palmistry for Professional
Purposes-NY-(1949)-illus   (4b7)   12.50
ST JAMES'S MAGAZINE-& Heraldic & Hist Register-Lond-1850-
hf calf-15 plts   (5dd0,sl wtrstnd)   10.00
ST JOHN,CHRISTOPHER,ed-Ellen Terry & Bernard Shaw, A
Correspondence-NY-1931-1st ed-Merrymount Pr-ltd to 3,000c-
370p   (5i3,sl fade) 12.50   (5r9,box)   15.00
--same-NY-1932-Putnams- (5x7) 4.50   (5t4,5m1,5ww4)   5.00
ST JOHN,MRS EUGENA-Bella,or,the Cradle of Liberty-Bost-1874-
351p-3rd ed   (5m1)   6.50
ST JOHN,MOLYNEUX,comp-Prov of Brit Col,Canada...new field
opened up by Canadian Pac Rwy-n.p.-1886-wrps-2 fldg maps-
4 phototype-56p   (5aa1,soil)   65.00
ST JOHN,MRS HORACE-Audubon,Naturalist of the New World-Bost-
1866-Bost-1866-12mo-cl-311p-frontis   (5t2)   4.00
ST JOHN,J A-ed-John Locke,Philosophical Works-1894-2 vols-
(5L7)   10.00
ST JOHN,J HECTOR-Letters from an Amer Farmer-Lond-1782-
Davies&Davis-2 fldg maps-mrbld bds-calf sp-8vo-1st ed
(4c4,sp rprd)   525.00
ST JOHN,JAS AUGUSTUS-Isis,an Egyptian pilgrimage-Lond-1853-
Longman,etc-2 vols-8vo-orig cl-1st ed   (5i8,autg)   15.00
SAINT JOHN,NB-Plan of Saint John,NB for 1872-Gordon
Livingstone,publ-fldg map in card cov-folio (4b9,cov loose) 20.00
ST JOHN,PERCY B-The Arctic Crusoe-Lond-(1854?)-Clarke&Beeton-
3 qtr calf-197p-18 dbl pg plts   (5aa2)   17.50
--same-Bost-1870-Lee&Shepard-sm8vo-dec cl-g.t.-243p-plts
(5aa2)   5.00
--same-Bost-1874-illus   (5w8,wn,lacks flys)   7.50
--The Sea of Ice-Bost-1859-sm8vo dec cl-g.t.-243p-plts-
Mayhew&Baker   (5aa2)   8.50
--The Trapper's Bride,a Tale of the Rocky Mountains,etc-NY-
1845-cl-lea labl-48p-1st Amer ed   (4n4)   60.00

ST JOHN,ROBT-From the Land of Silent People-GardenCty-
c1942   (5x7)   4.00
--It's Always Tomorrow-GardenCty-1944-248p-1st ed (5i1,dj,pres)5.00
--The Silent People Speak-GardenCty-1948   (5x7)   4.00
--Through Malan's Africa-NY-1954-Dblday-e.p. maps-317p
(4t5,dj)   9.00
ST JOHN,SPENSER-Hayti or Black Republic-Lond-1884-map
(5L7) 10.   (5x2)   15.00
ST JOHN'S LAW REVIEW-Vol 1 thru 43-1926 to 69 (5ii7,rbnd) 650.00
ST JOHNS,ADELA ROGERS-Final Verdict-GardenCty-1962
(5t7) 5.   (5p9)   4.25
ST JOSEPH'S CONVENT-In the Early Days-StL-1925-B Herder Bk Co-
367p-illus-dec cl-2nd ed   (5r0)   7.50
SAINT JULIEN,CHAS-Voyage Pittoresque en Russie-Paris-
1853-Berlin Meprieur & Morizot-4to-hf lea-540p-g.e.-
plts(some col)   (5v7,lt fox)   65.00
SAINT LAMBERT,JEAN de-Poesies of Saint Lambert-(n.p. 1823)-
93p-frontis-8vo-bds&mor-illus   (5t2)   7.50
ST LAWRENCE COUNTY-Farm Directory & Reference Book of...
1918-fldg map-ads   (4m2,lacks map) 7.   (4m2)   12.00
ST LEGER,STRATFORD E-War Sketches in Colour-Lond-1903-4to-
dec cl-col plts-274p-ltd to 250c,nbrd   (5nn2,autg)   25.00
ST LEONARDS,LORD-Handy Book on Property Law in a Series of
Letters-Edinb-1869-8th ed   (5ff4,rebnd)   9.50
ST LOUIS ALBUM-View Book Containing 12 plts-StL-1887-
Jas Overton-obl 8vo   (4g6)   8.50
ST LOUIS,ART WORK OF-W H Parish Publ-1895-12 parts-folio-
photos   (4b3,vg,bndg wn)   50.00
ST LOUIS COUNTY,MO-Directory-StL-1922 (4b3,hng weak)   15.00
ST LOUIS,KANS CITY & NTHRN RY-Season of 1875-brief descrip-
of famous Rocky Mntn resorts in Colo etc-(StL,1875)-illus-
fldg map-pict wrps-(disbnd)   (5g3)   25.00
ST LOUIS LAW REVIEW-Vol 1 thru 21-1915 to 36-plus Vol 22
Wash Univ Law Qtrly   (5ii7,rbnd)   420.00
ST LOUIS PHOTOGRAVURES-StL-c1898-RAReid-66p   (5n4)   17.50
ST LOUISANS AS WE SEE 'EM-(StL)-n.d.-obl 8vo-261p-
(ca 1920?)-cartoons   (4b3)   15.00
ST LOUISANS,BOOK OF-StL-1912-StLouis Republic-2nd ed-rev-
4to-661p-orig cl   (4b3,f)   20.00
ST LUCIA,LAWS,STATUTES,ETC-Civil Code-Lond-1879-bound
(5ii7,ex-libr)   25.00
--Commercial Code of...-Lond-1916-Coller,ed-bound
(5ii7,ex-libr)   27.50
--Laws of...-Oxf-1889-new ed-bound   (5ii7,ex-libr)   17.50
--Laws of St Vincent-by authority-Lond-1864-bound
(5ii7,ex-libr)   17.50
ST NICHOLAS-NY-Nov 1877 to Oct 1878-Scribners-Vol 5-
bnd in 1 vol-calf&bds   (5rr2)   20.00
--same-NY-1878 to Oct 1879-Vol 6-cl   (5rr2)   22.50
--same-Vol 11,Pt 1,Nov 1883 to Apr 1884-4to-hf roan-plts-
504p   (4a8,sl rub)   6.00
--same-Vol 12,1884,5(complete)-2 vols-hf roan-plts   (4a8)   12.50
--same-Vol 14-Nov 1886 to Oct 1887-12 issues bnd in 1-hf lea
(5p1)   25.00
--same-Vol 34-Nov 1906 to Oct 1907-dec cl-2 vols (5p1)   20.00
ST NICHOLAS-Illus Magazine for Young Folks-Vols 9 thru 19
(22 bnd vols)-Nov 1881 to Oct 1892   (5t2) post extra   100.00
ST ONGE PRETRE,L N-Alphabet Yakama-Montreal-1872-1st ed-
104p-frontis-rare   (5y5)   200.00
SAINT PAUL-Stranger's Guide & Reference Book to City of-1878-
Kirby,publ-Smyth&Co,Pr-prntd bds-lea bkstrip
(5x5,bkstrp wn)   35.00
ST PAUL,JOHN-History of Nat'l Soc of Sons of Amer Revolution-
NOrl-(1962)-illus-256p   (5t7,dj)   7.50
ST PHILIP'S-NY-1855-Carleton-340p-1st ed-(Mrs M C Harris)
(5x4)   10.00
SAINT PIERRE,J H B-Beauties of the Studies of Nature selected
from Works of....-NY-1799-reprntd for H Caritat-sm8vo-orig
orig calf-332p,(3)   (5L1)   10.00
--Oeuvres Completes-Paris-1818-12 vols-plts-pt calf (5aa0)   85.00
--Paul & Virginia-Lond-1795-CG&J Robinson-1st Engl ed-lea-
12mo-212p   (5c8,rub)   85.00
--same-Wrentham(Mass)-1799-Hunter,transl-12mo-
180p-calf   (5c8,calf wn)   50.00
--same-Lond-(c1830)-JBailey-Williams,transl-12mo-88p-
hand col frontis-plain blue wrps   (5aa2)   10.00
ST ROMAIN,LILLIAN SCHILLER-Western Falls Co,Texas-Austin-
1951-136p plus index-port-maps (1 fldg)-1st ed   (5L0)   7.50
ST RONAN'S WELL-Edinb-1824-hf lea-3 vols-1st ed-
(Sir W Scott)   (5hh1,sl wn)   20.00
SAINTSBURY,GEO-Collected Essays & Papers of,1875 to 1920-
Lond-1923-3 vols-8vo-cl   (5t0,spot)   12.50
--The English Novel-Lond-1913-Dent   (5p9)   6.50

SAINTSBURY,GEO- (continued)
--History of 19th Century Literature,(1780 to 1895)-NY-1910-
Macmillan-477p   (5p0)   6.00
--Minor Poets of the Caroline Period-Oxf-1905-Clarendon Pr-
3 vols-blue cl-1st ed   (5ss9,f)   50.00
--Notes on a Cellar Book-Lond-1921-8vo-parchment papr bds-
cl bk-1st ed-ltd to 500c,autg   (5d1)   50.00
--same-NY-1933-174p   (5w1)   5.00
--A Scrap Book-Lond-1922-1st ed   (5r9)   7.50
SAKER,DORA G-Practical Cheddar Cheese Making-Eng-1917-
photos-(10p), 101p,(4)   (5c5)   4.00
SAKI,H H MUNRO-The Short Stories of...complete-NY-1943-
Viking Pr-718p   (5p9)   4.00
--Reginald-Lond-(1904)-12mo-cl-1st ed   (5ee9)   20.00
--The Square Egg & Other Sketches,wi 3 Plays-Lond-(1924)-8vo-
cl-illus-1st ed   (5ee9)   10.00
--The Westminster Alice-Lond-1902-Westminster Gazette-
sq4to-red cl-illus-1st ed-auth's 1st book   (5ee9)   25.00
SALA,G A-Quite Alone-Lond-1864-3 vols-12mo-cl
                                            (4c2,faded, hng crack) 15.00
SALA,GEO AUGUSTUS-Paris Herself Again-Lond-(1948)-illus-
orig liths-4to-cl-127p   (5t7)   10.00
--The Thorough Good Cook-NY-1896-492p,(2)-4to   (5c0,fade) 22.50
--A trip to Barbary by a roundabout route-Lond-1866-8vo-
orig red cl-1st ed   (5i8)   15.00
--Under the sun-Lond-1872-TinsleyBros-8vo-orig cl-1st ed
                                            (5i8, rprd)   12.00
SALAMAN,MALCOLM C-Etchings of Sir Francis Seymour Haden-
Lond-1923-34p text-97 plts-4to   (5xx7)   12.50
--The Etchings of Jas McBey-Lond&NY-1929-96 plts-4to-frontpiece
is an orig autg etching   (5k1)   35.00
--French Colour Prints of the 18th Century-Phila-1913-Lippincott-
sm folio-illus-50 col illus   (5x0)   35.00
--Old English Colour Prints-Lond-1909-4to-40 mounted col plts-
42p   (5nn2)   15.00
SALAME,ABRAHAM-Narrative of exped to Algiers in year 1816-
Lond-1819-JnMurray-8vo-hf calf-1st ed-port-fldg map-
2 fldg plts   (5i8)   17.50
SALAMONS,D L-Breguet 1745 to 1823-Lond-1921-plts-illus-
233p-8vo-wrps-1st ed-ltd to 1000c   (5bb0)   60.00
--same-Lond-1923-illus-330p-8vo-5th ed-(French)   (5bb0)   38.00
SALAZAR,ADOLFO-Music in Our Time-NY-1946   (5p0)   6.00
SALE,EDITH TUNIS,ed-Historic Gardens of Virginia-Richmond-
1923-Williams Byrd Pr-cl-col illus-355p -2nd ed   (5r0)   12.50
--same-Richmond-(1924)-thk8vo-cl-illus   (5yy6)   15.00
--same-Richmond-1930-374p-illus-col prints-rev ed (5h9)   15.00
--Interiors of Virginia Houses of Colonial Times-Richmond-1927-
Wm Byrd Pr-pict cl-503p-371 plts
                        (5w0) 25.   (5r0) 17.50   (5t4,4L9) 15.00
--Old Time Belles & Cavaliers-Phila-1912-Lipp-285p-
61 illus   (4p7)   25.00
SALE,FLORENTIA,LADY-A journal of the disasters in Afghanistan-
Lond-1843-JnMurray-8vo-orig cl-1st ed   (5i8,fade) 17.50
SALE,GEO-The Koran,New Ed with Memoir of-Lond-1825-
illus-4 fldg plts-2 vols in 1-orig bds-labl on sp
                                            (5F0, needs rebking) 6.50
SALE,J B-The Tree Named John-Univ NoCar-1929-illus (5x2)   12.50
SALE OF AUTHORS-a dialogue-Lond-1767-8vo-qtr calf-mor labl-
1st ed-(A Campbell)-lf of ads at end   (5x3)   125.00
SALEILLES,R-Individualization of Punishment-Bost-1911-Mod Criminal
Sci Ser #4   (5r4)   10.00
SALEM,ATLAS OF CITY OF-Phila-1874-G M Hopkins&Co-folio-
calf&cl   (4c1, lea wn)   25.00
--same-Bost-Walker Lith-1911   (4c1)   20.00
SALEM BOOK,THE-Prepared for Publ by Group of Salem's Sons
& Daughters-copyrite, Harriet M Williams, 1896-250p
                                            (4m2,sl tn,rebnd) 18.00
SALEM COLLECTION,THE-of classical sacred musick-Salem(Mass)-
1805-obl 8vo-bds-calf bk   (5g8, sp wn)   17.50
SALEM,OLD TIME SHIPS OF-Salem-1917-pub by Essex Insti-lea labl-
orig wrps-70p-col plts-4to   (5h9, wrps bnd in) 24.00
SALES,FATHER LUIS-Observations on Calif,1772 to 1790-LosAng-
1956-Rudkin, ed-218p-bds-12mo-Early Calif Travel Ser,#37-
ltd to 300c   (5dd6)   30.00
SALEY,MET L-Realm of the Retailer-Chig-1902-Amer Lumberman-
8vo-illus   (5ss5)   12.50
SALGADO,F DE SOMOZA-Tractatus De Regio Protectione vi
Oppressorum etc-Lugduni, Anisson-1647-670p-folio (5r4)   45.00
SALINGER,J D-The Catcher in the Rye-Bost-1951-12mo-cl-
1st ed of auth's 1st book (5gg6, writing on e.p.) 20.
              (4n5,dj) 75.   (4j6) 60.   (5hh1,marred dj)   30.00
--Franny & Zooey-Bost-1961-Little, Brown-1st ed
                        (5ss9,dj) 8.50   (5tt2,f,dj)   7.50

SALINGER, J D (continued)
--Nine Stories-Bost-(1953)-orig cl-8vo-1st ed   (4n5,dj,vf) 100.00
--Raise High the Roof Beam.etc-Bost-(1959)-12mo-cl-2nd issue
wi dedic before hf t.   (4c2,glue stns on sp) 30.00
SALISBURY,EDW E-Family Histories & Genealogies-n.p.-1892-
priv prntd-ltd to 250 sets-3 vols in 5-4to   (4b6)   75.00
--same-1892-5 vols   (4t2)   45.00
--Family Memorials-priv prntd 1885-2 vols   (5mm3)   30.00
SALISBURY,F S-Rambles in the Vaudese Alps-Lond-1916-154p-cl
                                                  (5d7)   5.00
SALLES,PROSPER-La Grande Cuisine Illustree-Monaco-1902-4to-
illus-lea&cl   (5g9,wn)   15.00
SALLEY,A S,JR-History of Orangeburg Co,SoCar from its First
Settlement to Close of Revolutionary War-Orangeburg-1898-
572p   (5h6)   35.00
SALM SALM,PRINCESS FELIX-Ten Years of my Life-Detroit-1877-
12mo-port   (4b7, hng split) 17.50
SALMAGUNDI-NY-1807,1808 -16mo-calf-(W Irving)-early issue
of Irving's 1st book-wdcut port present in 2 states
2 volumes   (5gg6, rbkd) 250.00
SALMON,D E-Proceedings of Interstate Convention of Cattlemen
held at FtWorth-97p-Wash-1890-hf mor-ex rare (5n4,box)   65.00
SALMON,THOS-A New Geographical & Historical Grammar-
Lond-1756-23 maps by Mr Jeffreys-640p-maps-calf
                                            (5m3, hng weak)   25.00
--Salmon's Geographical & Historical Grammar-Edinb-1771-
thk8vo-603p-calf- 23 dbl fld maps   (4F6)   35.00
SALMON,WM-Botanologia, the English Herbal Or, History of Plants-
Lond-1710-2 folio vols-calf-frontis-   (5w3, wn)   175.00
SALMONS,C H-Burlington Strike-Aurora-1889-480p-lea-scarce
                                                  (5y0, wn)   16.50
SALMOND,J-Principles of the Law of Contracts-Lond-1945(5ff4) 6.75
SALMONY,ALFRED-Antler & Tongue-Ascona-1954-illus-4to
                                                  (5tt5)   15.00
SALOMON,JULIAN H-Book of Indian Crafts & Indian Lore-NY-
(1928)-Harper&Bros-illus-1st ed   (5L2,wn) 3.50   (5x5)   12.50
SALOMON,MRS MIRA-Jewish Ritual Silver, the Renowned
Collection of-priced-NY-1949-catalog-Parke Bernet-illus-8vo-
orig wrps-66p   (5m6)   10.00
SALOMON'S-Carbonic Acid Gas Engine-Wash-1853-6p,(2)-
self wrps   (5b8, lt soil) 7.50
SALPOINTE,J B-Soldiers of the Cross-Banning-1898-St Boniface's
Industrial School-300p-cl-with Appendix #7 added in 1900
                                 (5p1) 75.   (5d6)   60.00
SALT,H S-Percy Bysshe Shelley, Poet & Pioneer-Lond-1896-12mo-
port   (4a1)   12.50
--Richard Jefferies, A Study-Lond-1894   (5mm2)   7.50
SALT LAKE CITY-A Sketch of Utah's Wonderful Resources-SaltLk-
1888-96p-photos-wrps-(SaltLk Chamb of Comm)-1st ed (5L2)   8.50
SALT LAKE HERALD ANNUAL 1882-Salt Lake City-(1881)-Salt Lake
Daily Herald-illus-wrps   (5yy3)   20.00
SALTEN,FELIX-Bambi-NY-1928-Simon&Schuster-1st Amer ed-
K Wiese,illus   (5aa0) 6.50   (5rr2,5w9,5p1)   15.00
--same-NY-1929-4th printing   (5v0, mint) 3.50
SALTER,ARTHUR-China & Silver-NY-1934-8vo-117p-prntd papr
                                                  (5t7)   6.50
SALTER,MARY J-The Lost Receipt, or Frustrated Designs-Bost-1881-
Wright&Potter-frontis-95p-wrps-12mo   (5j5)   7.00
SALTER,WM-Iowa, first free state in Louisiana Purchase-1905-plt
                                                  (5L7)   5.00
SALTER,WM-Memoirs of Jos W Pickett-Burlington&ColoSprings-1880-
cl-150p   (5r0, underline) 10.   (5m8)   12.50
SALTER,WM M-Nietzsche the Thinker, a study-1917   (5L7)   6.00
SALTONSTALL,WM G-Ports of Piscataqua-Cambr-1941-4to-244p-
illus-map   (5s1, pres, sl soil) 7.50   (5w9, dj)   10.00
SALTUS,EDGAR-Anatomy of Negation-NY-1886-scarce   (4j2)   15.00
--same-Chig-1889-Belford, Clarke-8vo-cl-rev ed   (5b2, rprd) 7.50
--Balzac-Bost-1884-port-1st ed of auth's 1st book
                                            (5ii3, fade, sl soil) 17.50
--Daughters of the Rich-NY-(1909)-1st ed   (4b7)   7.50
--Eden-Chig-(1888)-1st ed   (4j2)   10.00
--Enthralled-Lond-1894-12mo-wrps   (4b7, wrps rprd) 15.00
--Historia Amoris-Kennerley-1906-1st ed   (5ww4, autg) 25.00
--same-NY-1922   (5x7)   7.50
--Imperial Orgy-NY-1920-Boni&Liveright-237p-illus-1st ed
                                  (5d8, pg tn) 7.50   (5p6)   10.00
--Imperial Purple-Chig-1892-1st ed-MorrillHiggins-cl
              (4m8) 10.   (4b7, faded, hng split) 10.   (5d8) 22.50
--The Lords of the Ghostland-NY-1907-MitchellKennerley-12mo-
cl-g.t.-red lettering on t.pg-1st issue-1st ed   (5d8)   15.00
--The Lovers of the World-NY-(ca1890)-FCollier-3 vols-illus-
1st ed   (5r9)   25.00

SALTUS,EDGAR (continued)
--Madam Sapphira-NY-(1893)-12mo-wrps-1st ed-scarce (5r9) 15.00
--Mary Magdalen,A Chronicle-NY-(1891)-Belford-1st ed (5r9) 12.50
--The Monster-NY-1912-12mo-cl-1st ed
(4j2) 5.   (5d8,hng broke) 10.00
--Philosophy of Disenchantment-Bost-1885-HoughtonMiff-12mo-
orig cl-1st ed of auth's 2nd book   (5d8,vf) 25.00
--Transient Guest & Other Episodes-Chig-(1889)-1st ed
(4b7,bndg rub) 15. (4j2) 12.50
--The Truth About Tristrem Varick-Chig-(1888)-1st ed (5mm2) 12.50
SALTUS,FRANCIS S-Honey & Gall-Phila-1873-Lippincott-231p-
1st ed-auth's 1st book   (5x4) 25.00
SALTUS,MARIE-Edgar Saltus,the Man-Chig-1925-324p-illus-
1st ed   (5m1) 6.00
SALVATION ARMY OF AMERICA-Positive Facts etc-Atlanta-
(ca 1890)-8vo-64p-orig wrps-illus   (5m6) 6.00
SALVATION ARMY-21 Years-Lond-1891-254p-12mo-cl-illus(5t0)4.50
SALVATOR,LUDWIG L-Los Angeles in the Sunny Seventies-LosAng-
1929-lea labl   (5x5,rub) 20.00
SALWEY,CHARLOTTE M-Fans of Japan-Lond-1894-cl-bevelled bds-
4to-10 plts-39 illus-1st ed   (5m4) 75.00
SALZBACHER,JOS-Meine Reise nach Nord America im Jahre 1842-
Vienna-1845-cl-fldg map-8vo-479p   (5v7) 75.00
SALZMANN,C G-Gymnastics for Youth-Phila-1802-Duane,prntr-
432p-fldng frontis-9 plts-calf-1st Amer ed   (5p1,wn) 125.00
SAMMIS,J L-Cheese Making-Madison-1937-311p-illus-9th rev ed
(5c0,autg) 6.50
SAMPSON AGAINST THE PHILISTINES-or reformation of lawsuits-
Phila-1805-stitchd-2nd ed   (5g4,unopnd,f) 15.00
SAMPSON,A-Drum-Cambr-1957-illus   (5x2,dj) 8.50
SAMPSON,ARTHUR W-Important Range Plants-Wash-1917-63p-
wrps   (4a5) 4.50
SAMPSON,E S-Mammy's White Folks-NY-1920   (5x2) 6.00
SAMPSON,WM-Memoirs of-Leesburg-1817-2nd ed-rev-432p-calf-
label   (5i3,vg) 22.50
SAMS,C W-Conquest of Virginia,The Forest Primeval-NY-1916-
432p   (4j4) 3.00
SAMS,WM-A Tour Through Paris-Lond-(1825 to 28?)-folio-
mor&bds-21 handcol plts-a.e.g.-tissue guards (4h5,sl scuff) 350.00
SAMSON,HENRY T-War Story of C Battery-(Norwood,Mass)-1920-
Plimpton Pr-248p-illus   (5mm8) 8.50
SAMUEL,ARTHUR-Piranesi-Lond-1910-dbl pg plts (5j2,pres) 15.00
--G B Piranesei-Lond-(1912)-2nd ed-etching (5ii3,sp fade) 15.00
SAMUEL,ARTHUR MICHAEL-The Mancroft Essays-NY-n.d.-
287p-HarcourtBrace   (5p0) 5.00
SAMUEL,BUNFORD-Secession & Constitutional Liberty-NY-1920-
Neale-8vo-2 vols   (4a7,f) 12.50
SAMUEL,HORACE B-Shareholders' Money-Lond-1933-392p(5p0) 5.00
SAMUEL,M-The World of Sholom Aleichem-1943-Knopf-1st ed
(5ww4) 5.00
SAMUELS,E A-Ornithology & Oology of New England-Bost-1868-
col plts-587p-frontis   (5r5,hng wk) 85.00
SAMUELS,EDW A-With Fly Rod & Camera-NY-1890-sm4to-477p-
150 plts-1st ed   (5t0) 7.50
--With Rod & Gun in New Engl & the Maritime Provinces-Bost-
1897-540p-illus-a.e.g.-1st ed-tissue guards (5w4,5m6) 12.50
SAMUELS,LEE-A Hemingway Check List-NY-1951-Scribner-8vo-
750c prntd-erratum slip   (5b2) 15.00
SAMUELS,M-Memoirs of Moses Mendelsohn-Lond-1827-2nd ed
(4b7) 20.00
SAMUELS,MAURICE V-The Florentines,a Play-NY-1904-Brentano's-
1st ed   (5ss9,pres) 7.50
SAMUELS,CAPT SAMUEL-From the Forecastle to the Cabin-NY-
1887-Harper-12mo-cl-illus-308p   (5ee3) 5. (5j5) 6.00
SAMUELSON,JAS-The History of Drink-Lond-1878-288p(5w1) 16.50
SAMWELL,DAVID-Capt Cook & Hawaii-SanFran-1957-David Magee-
400c publ   (5x5) 12.50
--same-SanFran-1957-David Magee-sq8vo-cl-Lawton Kennedy,prnt-
ed of 750c   (5F5,f) 15.00
SAN ANSELMO COOK BOOK-San Anselmo-1908-cl-168p
(4g9,hng loose,cov wn) 12.50
SAN ANTONIO-A History & a Guide-(WPA)-SanAnt-1940-8vo-
111p-maps-illus-stiff wrps   (5m8) 4.50
SAN ANTONIO,SOUVENIR OF-n.p.-1900-12 fldg pgs
(4a5,mint) 15.00
SAN ANTONIO TELEPHONE DIRECTORY-Spring,1917 (5b9,f) 10.00
SAN DIEGO-San Diego-(1918)- I L Eno Co-18 lvs-photos-sm folio
(4a5,wrp) 6.00
SAN DIEGO,THE BEAUTIFUL-SanDiego-c1915-Christiance-18 lvs-
illus-hand col-folio-wrps   (4a5) 12.50
SAN DIEGO,CALIF-City & County-(SanD-1904)-(H P Wood)-(32p)-
wrps   (5h1) 4.00

SAN DIEGO-The Italy of Amer-C of C-SanD-(1907)-24mo-32p-
wrps-illus   (5m9) 3.50
SAN DIEGO CHAM OF COMM-The Southern Transcontinental
Rwy,Its Pacific Terminus-SanD-1870-wrps-8p-v rare pamph
(5t3) 85.00
SAN DIEGO-Souvenir of San Diego,Calif-with Brief Sketch of Its
History & Historic Photographs-Columbus-(1886)-16mo (5x5) 20.00
SAN DIEGO,SELECTED VIEWS OF-Brooklyn-1913-(Albertype Co)-
folio-24 lvs-wrps   (4a5) 6.00
SAN DIEGO LAW REVIEW-Vol 1 thru 7-1964 to 70 (5ii7,rbnd) 65.00
SAN FRANCISCO,CALIF-SanFran-c1916-Pac Novelty Co-24 lvs-
illus-folio-wrps   (4a5) 7.50
SAN FRANCISCO,THE BAY & ITS CITIES-NY-1940-photos-maps-
551p-1st ed-Amer Guide Ser-WPA   (4L5) 8.50   (5p5) 12.50
--same-1947-2nd ed-rev   (4L5,dj) 6.00
SAN FRANCISCO THE BEAUTIFUL-SanFran-1912-Pac Novelty Co-
12 lvs-illus-wrps-folio   (4a5) 7.50
SAN FRANCISCO BLUE BOOK-SanFran-1888-Bancroft Co-262p-
blue cl   (5yy3) 20.00
SAN FRANCISCO CHRONICLE & ITS HISTORY-SanFran-1879-60p-
frontis-t8vo-4 liths   (5F5,f) 75.00
SAN FRANCISCO DAILY GOSSIP-Vol 1,#1-SanFran-Jun 20,1878-
8p newspaper   (5d6) 20.00
SAN FRANCISCO DISASTER-Glimpses of-Chig-1906-obl 8vo-96p-
fldg map-illus-wrps   (5xx7) 7.50
SAN FRANCISCO HORROR-n.p.-(1906)-photos-408p   (5dd5) 7.00
SAN FRANCISCO,CALIF,INVITES THE WORLD-Panama Pac Intl
Expos-SanFran-1915-Cardinell Vincent Co-photos-wrps-folio-
12 lvs   (5kk6) 7.50
SAN FRANCISCO,MODERN-1907 to 08-SanFran-(n.d.)-c1908-
Western Pr Assoc-4to-illus-123p,nbrd-orig stiff wrps
(5x5,rprd) 15.00
SAN FRANCISCO,OAKLAND-Alameda & San Rafael,1889 to 90-
Calling & Address List of-SanFran-Crocker-suede-212p (5rr0) 15.00
SAN FRANCISCO,THE QUEEN CITY-SanFran-c1910 -Pac Novelty
Co-23 lvs-illus-folio-wrps   (4a5,sl stain) 11.00
SAN FRANCISCO-Panoramic San Francisco from Calif St Hill-1877-
Thos C Russell-fldg photo-bound   (4n1) 12.00
SAN FRANCISCO,SOUVENIR OF-SanFran-c1900-Cunningham,
Curtiss & Welch-33p-bds-photogravures   (4a5) 17.50
SAN FRANCISCO,SOUVENIR OF-SanFran-1902-Cunningham,
Curtiss & Welch-24p-photogravures   (4a5) 17.50
SAN FRANCISCO,CALIF-Souvenir of.."Queen City"-SanFran-
c1920-Pac Novelty Co-obl 8vo-wrps-62p   (4t1) 7.50
SAN FRANCISCO WOMEN'S LITERARY EXHIBIT-List of Books-
SanFran-1893-Raveley Prntng-52p-wrps   (5d6) 15.00
SAN JOAQUIN CO,CALIF-Illustrated History of-Chig-1890-
Lewis Publ Co-666p-lea   (5tt0,wn) 40.00
SAN JOAQUIN VALLEY,THE-(Fresno,1930)-16p-wrps (5dd4) 6.00
SAN JOAQUIN RIVER BASIN 1931-Sacramento-1934-State Prntng
Off-Bull #29-656p-plts-maps-illus-wrps   (5r0) 17.50
SAN JOSE & ENVIRONMENTS-Picturesque...Illus Statement...
Santa Clara Co,"Garden of the World"-SanJose-c1893-
Foote&Woolfolk-obl 12mo-wrps-(80p)   (4t1) 15.00
SAN JOSE,QUEEN OF THE MISSIONS-SanAntonio-1938-68p-
illus-wrps   (4a5) 8.50
SAN JOSE & VICINITY-Souvenir of-Albertype-NY-1894-
Crockwell&Williams(photo)-40p photos-2p text-7¼ x 5-
hard cov   (4n1) 10.00
SAN JUAN-Its Past & Present,Ways of Getting There etc-Denver-
1876-73p plus 20p ads-v scarce-C A Warner,publ-wrps(5L2) 65.00
SAN JUAN NATL FOREST,(COLO)-USDA-1942-22p-8vo-illus-
lg fldg map-prntd wrps   (5g5) 3.00
SAN LEANDRO,ALAMEDA CO,CALIF-(San Leandro Standard Pr)-
issued by Board of Trade,Sept 1906-pict wrps-24p-illus-
6½ x 5   (5r0) 7.50
SAN LUIS HOT SULPHUR SPRINGS-San Luis Obispo,Calif-(n.p.n.d.)
(ca 1909)-32p-illus-pict wrps-5 x 6½   (5r0) 7.50
SAN LUIS OBISPO CO,CALIF-History of-Oakland-1883-4to-illus-
Thompson&West-3/4 lea   (5F5) 185.00
SAN LUIS OBISPO,CALIF-Souvenir of-(Santa Clara,Nace,prntr)-
n.d.-(ca 1908)-50p-illus-wrps-9 x 4-(Chamber of Comm)(5r0) 7.50
SAN LUIS OBISPO FIRE DEPT-LosAng-1904-78p of illus-obl-
JHTigner-orig red cl   (5x5,f) 35.00
SAN LUIS OBISPO TRIBUNE-Souvenir RR ed,May 15,1894-
SanLuis Obispo-1894-Tribune-folio-wrps-104p   (4t1) 45.00
SANBORN,ALVAN F-Meg McIntyre's Raffle-Bost-1896-
Copeland&Day-1st ed-ltd to 1000c   (5ee3,f) 7.50
SANBORN COUNTY,(SD)-Pioneer Hist of-n.p.-1953-193p-cl
(5h1) 10.00
SANBORN,EDWIN D-History of New Hampshire-Dartmouth,
Manchester-1875-1st ed-tall 8vo-422p-cl-g.dec (4c5,fade) 17.50

SANBORN,EDWIN W-People at Pisgah-NY-1892-Appleton-
185p-orig bds-1st ed   (5m2,wn) 4.   (5x4,wn)   7.50
SANBORN,F B-Genius & Character of Emerson-Osgood-1885-447p
(5e8)   10.00
--Henry D Thoreau-HM-1882-324p   (5e8,covs sl wn)   10.75
--Life & Letters of John Brown-Bost-1885-Roberts-645p-illus
(5L2) 8.50   (5qq8)   12.50
--Personality of Emerson-Bost-1903-8vo-bds-cl bkstrp-ltd to 525c
(4c1)   25.00
--Personality of Thoreau-Bost-1901-Merrymount Pr-illus-8vo-cl bk-
515c printed   (4c2,darkened,unopnd)   25.00
--Recollections of 70 Years-Bost-1909-2 vols-illus-boxed-1st ed
(5p6,f)   14.00
SANBORN,JOHN B-Some Descriptions of Battles in which Commands
of,Participated in-n.p.-n.d.-(StP-1900)-56p-wrps (5h1)   12.50
SANBORN,KATE-Educated Dogs of Today-Bost-1916-priv distribu-
1st ed-4to-orig bds-77p(2)   (4m7)   12.50
--Hunting Indians in a Taxi cab-Bost-(1911)-74p-photos-scl-
v scarce   (5L0,tn) 7.50   (4g6)   15.00
--Memories & Anecdotes-NY-1915-219p-illus   (5t4,pres)   10.00
--Truthful Woman in SoCalif-NY-1893-192p-flex cov-7x4"(5s4)   4.00
--same-NY-1902-12mo-192p   (5dd6,lt soil)   3.00
SANBORN,V C-Amer & Engl Sambornes with a Notice of Rev
Stephen Bachiler-1895-25p-scarce   (5t9)   10.00
SANCEAU,ELAINE-Henry The Navigator-NY-(1947)-318p-illus
(5t7)   5.00
SANCHEY,NELLIE VAN DE GRIFT-Spanish & Indian Place Names
of Calif-SanFran-1922   (5x5,cov dtchd)   8.50
SANCHEZ,ANTUNANO,J A-Practical Education of the Pointing
Dog for Hunting & for Field Trials-Chig-1944-12mo-papr-illus-
164p   (5t7)   6.00
SANCHEZ,GEO I-Mexico,Revolution by Education-NY-1936-
Viking-8vo-dec cl-illus   (4a3,dj,f) 15.   (5h4)   5.00
SANCHEZ,INEZ,comp-Lola Montez' Secrets of the Toilet-NY-n.d.-
Popular Pub Co-wrps-col illus-64p   (4h8,sl stns)   10.00
SANCHEZ,MANUEL SEGUNDO-Bibliografia Venezolanista-
Caracas-1914-494p-wrps   (5p0)   35.00
SANCHEZ,N V-Spanish & Indian Place Names of Calif-SanFran-
1914-illus-446p   (4n1,5m2)   15.00
--same-SanFran-1922-472p-plts   (5dd9,lt spots)   10.00
--same-SanFran-1930-AMRobertson-343p-cl   (5d6)   5.00
--Spanish Arcadia-LosAng-(1929)-413p-illus   (5s4)   11.00
SANCHO,IGNATIUS-Letters of Late Ignatius Sancho,an African
with Memoirs,by Jos Jekyll-1783-2 vols in 1-2nd ed
(5L7,rbnd)   25.00
SAND,GEO-The Devil's Pool-Phila-1901-Barrie-209p-illus (5p9) 4.00
--Historic & Romantic Novels-Phila-1902-20 vols-GeoBarrie&Son-
illus-cl   (5x0)   50.00
SANDBURG,CARL-Abe Lincoln Grows Up-NY-(1930)-illus (5r7) 7.50
--Abraham Lincoln-NY-(1926 to 39)-illus-maps-6 vols
(5s9,5ii3,f) 40.   (5t4,mint) 30.   (5q8)   35.00
--same-NY-1940-6 vols-illus-Sangamon Ed   (5tt5)   22.50
--same-NY-(1944)-6 vols-The Sangamon Ed   (5a8)   32.50
--Abraham Lincoln, the Prairie Years-NY-(1926)-illus-lg8vo-
2 vols-1st ed   (5tt7,dj)   15.00
--Abraham Lincoln, the War Years-NY-(1939)-illus-lg8vo-
orig cl-4 vols-1st ed   (5tt7,box,mint)   40.00
--Abraham Lincoln, the War Years-NY-(1939)-illus-4 vols
(5ss5,box,sl dmpstn) 20.   (4b6)   25.00
--Abraham Lincoln,the War Years-NY-(1937)-4 vols-Morocco
buck-g.t.-boxed-1st ed-ltd to 525c,autg   (5g4,f)   112.50
--Abraham Lincoln,The Prairie Years and the War Years-NY-(1954)-
1 vol ed-762p-illus   (5t7,dj)   6.50
--American Song Bag-NY-(1927)-HarcourtBrace-1st ed-black cl
printed in orange   (5mm2) 12.50   (5q8,5t4)   10.00
--Bronze Wood-SanFran-1941-Grabhorn Pr-tall thn4to-title illus-
cl bds-ltd to 195c   (4b1,fly tn) 37.50   (5ss9,f)   30.00
--Chicago Poems-NY-1916-HenryHolt&Co-8vo-orig cl-1st ed-
adv not dated   (5d3) 30.   (4j2)   25.00
--Cornhuskers-NY-1918-Holt&Co-1st ed (4j2,5ss3,sp chip,dj)   10.00
--Early Moon-NY-HarcourtBrace-(1930)-Daugherty,illus-tall 8vo-
cl-137p-1st ed   (5j5,dj)   15.00
--Good Morning,America-NY-1928-1st ed (5mm1) 7.50 (5yy6)   10.00
--Lincoln & Whitman Miscellany-Chig-1938-Holiday Pr-8vo-
marb bds-cl bk-lea labl   (4c2,rub)   12.50
--Lincoln Collector-NY-1949-HarcourtBrace-1st ed-special ltd ed,
autg,box   (5d5) 37.50   (5ss9,f)   35.00
--same-NY-1950-344p-illus-1st trade ed (5s9) 6. (5ee3,f,dj)   5.00
--A Lincoln Preface-NY-(1953)-16p-1st ed-ltd ed (5yy6,bnd)   5.00
--Mary Lincoln,Wife & Widow-NY-(1932)-HarcourtBrace-1st ed-
ltd to 260c,autgs   (5hh1,f,box)   60.00
--same-NY-(1932)-illus-in 2 pts-357p   (5t7,dj)   6.50

SANDBURG, CARL (continued)
--M'Liss & Louis-LosAng-May 1929-Ward Ritchie,prntr-8p-
ltd to 150c-wrps   (5tt9,sl soil)   40.00
--The People, Yes-NY-(1936)-1st ed   (5mm1,dj,autog)   17.50
--Potato Face-NY-(1930)-1st ed   (5p6,f,dj,autg)   20.00
--Remembrance Rock-NY-(1948)-1067p-1st trade ed
(5d2,autg) 20.   (5k0,dj) 10.   (5t7)   6.50
--same-NY-1948-2 vols-1st ed,ltd,nbrd, & autg,box (4b4)   50.00
--same-NY-(1948)-2 vols-ltd 1st ed-ltd to 1000c,autg,box
(5F1,f) 40.   (5r9,f)   27.50
--Rootabaga Country-NY-(c1929)-Harcourt-4to dec cl-plts-
col frontis-258p   (4a8)   8.50
--Rootabaga Stories-NY-1922-HarcourtBrace-1st ed-8vo-dec cl-
col frontis-plts-230p   (5s0)   15.00
--same-1922-4th printing   (5s0)   5.00
--Slabs of Sunburnt West-NY-(1922)-1st ed   (4j2)   15.00
--Smoke & Steel-NY-1920-1st ed   (4j2)   12.50
--Storm over the Land-NY-(1942)-illus-1st ed   (5yy6,pres)   17.50
SANDEMAN,CHRISTOPHER-A Wanderer in Inca Land-NY-(1949)-
194p-photos-map   (5L0,dj)   12.50
SANDEMAN,F-By Hook & By Crook-Lond-1892-255p-illus-
col lithos-t.e.g.-1st trade ed   (5a9)   9.50
SANDER,CONSTANTIN-Geschichte des vierjahrigen Burgerkrieges
in der Vereinigten Staaten von Amerika-Frankfurt-1865-587p-
3 fldg maps-8vo-orig bds   (5L1)   25.00
SANDERS,ALVIN HOWARD-At the Sign of the Stockyard Inn-
Chig-1915-hf mor-322p (4i2) 25.   (5m2,autg,5g2,f,5FF7)   15.00
--The Cattle of the World-Wash-1926-cl   (4a9,vg)   25.00
--Short Horn Cattle-Chig-(1900)-illus-902p-2nd impr
(5g0,f) 10.   (4b3)   15.00
--same-Chig-1909-Sanders Pub-illus-902p-cl-lea sp-2nd ed
(4n8,hng split) 12.50   (5L2,rub)   10.00
--same-Chig-1916-illus-840p   (4b3)   12.50
--same-Chig-1918-8vo-calf-1021p-illus
(5bb4,pt lea,rub) 10.   (5m9,calf) 17.50 (5bb4,cl)   10.00
--The Story of the Herefords-Chig-1914-1087p-scarce
(5bb4) 15.   (5n4)   25.00
--The Story of the Int'l Live Stock Expos-Chig-1942 (5ww4)   10.00
SANDERS,CHAS W-Sanders Pictorial Primer, Sanders Bilder Fibel-
NY-(entered 1846)-illus-pic bds-in Engl & German (4h8)   12.50
--Sanders's Spelling Book-Cleve-1834-166p-pict bds (5h7,wn)   5.00
SANDERS,F C S-Calif as a Health Resort-SanFran-1916-illus
(5x5)   10.00
SANDERS,F W-Essay on Uses & Trusts & on Nature & Operation of
Conveyances at Common Law-Lond-1844-2 vols-5th ed (5ff4) 17.50
SANDERS, HELEN FITZGERALD-Trails Through Western Woods-NY-
1910-311p-photos-dec cov   (5s4,rprd)   6.00
--History of Montana-Chig-1913-3 vols-3/4 lea-1st ed
(4t8,sl rub)   125.00
SANDERS,J C-Gen of Cortland Co,NY Branch-(1908)-111p (4t2)17.50
SANDERS,J H-Breeds of Live Stock & Principles of Heredity-Chig-
1887-illus-3/4 lea-1st ed-scarce   (4t8)   30.00
--More Breeding-Chig-1885-249p   (5yy8,spot)   12.50
--Horse Breeding-Chig-(1893)-428p-illus   (5xx7)   10.00
SANDERS,JOHN-Early History of Schenectady-1879-336p-index
(5zz0)   35.00
SANDERS,LEON-Notable Democrats,Natl Democratic Convention,
StLouis Jun 14,1916-StL-1916-pict cl-ports-112p   (5r0)   10.00
SANDERS,SUE-Our Common Herd-NY-1939-lea-261p (5h0)   10.00
SANDERS,T W-Grapes,Peaches,Melons & how to grow them-Lond-
(1924)-150p-photos   (5w1)   6.50
SANDERS,WM PERRY-Days That Are Gone-LosAng-1918-134p-
orig pict wrps-scarce   (5x5,pres) 25.   (5dd4)   30.00
SANDERSON,ALFRED-Historical Sketch of Union Fire Co of
Lancaster,Penna-Lancaster-1879   -illus   (5w5)   8.50
SANDERSON,C MACKAY-Practical Breaking & Training of Gundogs-
Manchester(England)-n.d.-(ca 1910)-142p-illus   (5t7)   6.00
SANDERSON,E L-Waltham(Mass), As a Precinct of Watertown & as
a Town, 1630 to 1884-1936-168p   (4t2)   7.50
SANDERSON,EDGAR-Africa in the 19th Century-Lond-1898-Seeley-
photo-fldg map-335p   (4t5)   12.00
SANDERSON,IVAN T-Animal Treasure-NY-1937-Viking Pr-
pic cov-illus-325p (4a5,ex-libr) 7.50 (5kk7,fade) 8. (4t5)   10.00
--Living Mammals of the World-GardenCty-n.d.-190 col illus
(5tt7)   8.50
--Follow the Whale-Bost-1956-12mo-cl-423p-maps & charts
(5s1,dj) 5.   (5t0,dj)   4.00
SANDERSON,J E-First Century of Methodism in Canada-Tor-1908,
1910-2 vols-illus   (4b9)   25.00
--Messengers of the Churches-Tor-1901-illus-183p-2nd ser(5dd7) 6.50
SANDERSON,JAS GARDNER-Cornell Stories-NY-1898(5p7)   3.00

SANDERSON, JOHN-Biography of Signers of Declar of
Independence-Phila-1820-9 vols-illus-1st ed-3/4 mor
(5yy6, rub & weak)   50.00
--same-Phila-1828-8vo-5 vols-31 ports-4 plts of facs-old calf-
2nd ed, "Revised"   (5t2, wn)   17.50
--Republican Landmarks-Phila-1856 (5L7, rbnd) 12.50 (5yy6)   35.00
SANDERSON, JOHN-Travels in Levant-Hakluyt Soc-1931-
2nd Ser, #67-plts-ports-maps-322p   (5s6)   8.50
SANDFORD & MERTON, HIST OF-Lond-Stockdale-1787 to 9-
sm8vo-3 vols-calf-(Thos Day, ed)   (5a1, hng rprd)   45.00
--same-Lond-Routledge-(c1855)-sm8vo-462p-plts-dec cl-g.-
rev by Hartley   (5a1)   5.00
SANDERSON, MEREDITH-Introduction to Chinyanja-Glasgow-1953-
107p-39p-5th rprnt of 2nd ed   (5c6)   12.50
SANDHAM, ALFRED-Ville Marie-Montreal-1870-393p-plts
(5a1) 15. (5w8)   35.00
SANDHAM, ELIZ-History of Wm Selwyn-Lond-1815-Joan Harris-
frontis-295p-lea-1st ed-scarce   (5c8, sl crack)   25.00
SANDHURST, P T-Great Centennial Exhibition-1876-illus (5L7)   10.00
--Masterpieces of European Art-Phila-(c1890)-4to-hf mor-268p-
engrs   (5ii2)   9.50
SANDISON, G H-How to Behave & How to Amuse-NY-(1895)-
284p-16mo   (5w7, lacks fly, fox)   3.50
SANDOZ, MARI-Buffalo Hunters-NY-(1954)-1st ed-illus
(5s4, dj, ex-libr) 9.   (5jj3) 12.50   (5r7, 5bb4, dj)   10.00
--Capital City-Bost-1939-Little, Brown (5L2) 6.   (5F1, f, dj)   5.00
--The Cattlemen-NY-(1958)-plts-ports-527p-ltd deluxe, pre pub ed
(4p2, f, autg)   25.00
--same-NY-(1958)-527p-illus-1st trade ed
(5m9) 6.   (5L3, mint, dj, 5yy7, dj)   8.50
--Cheyenne Autumn-NY-(1953)-fldg map-276p plus index-
1st printing   (5yy7)   20.00
--Crazy Horse-NY-1942-1st ed (5a9, 5kk4, mint, dj) 25. (5yy7, dj)   30.00
--same-NY-n.d. (later ed)-8vo-fldg map-428p   (4i2, dj)   6.50
--Hostiles & Friendlies-Lincoln-1959-250p-photos-map-1st ed
(5bb4, f, dj) 8.50   (5kk4, mint, dj)   6.00
--Old Jules-Bost-1935-424p-1st ed
(5w9) 6.   (4j6) 5.   (5ee3, 5kk4, f, wn dj)   7.50
--Slocum House-Bost-1937-8vo-orig cl-1st ed   (5p5, autg)   15.00
--The Tom Walker-NY-1947-12mo-cl-1st ed   (5p5, f, dj)   5.00
SANDOZ, MAURICE-La Limite-Paris-1951-La Table Ronde-lg8vo-
illus de Dali-6 drwngs-wrps-ltd to 150c, autg-scarce (5m7)   37.50
--On the Verge-GardenCty-1950-Dali, illus-col frontis-plts-
127p-1st ed   (5nn2, f, dj)   35.00
SANDS, B A-Direct Forebears & All Desc of Richardson-1916-
99p   (4t2)   20.00
SANDS, FRANK-A Pastoral Prince, the History & Remin of
J W Cooper-SantaBarbara-1893-port-206p-priv prntd-
v scarce   (5cc4)   125.00
SANDS, LEDYARD-The Bird, the Gun & the Dog-NY-(1939)-
494p-illus-24 plts   (5t4)   10.00
SANDS, ROBT C-Life & Correspondence of John Paul Jones-NY-
1830-555p-frontis-1st ed   (5ee3, lacks errata)   15.00
--Writings of, in Prose & Verse-NY-1834-1st ed-2 vols (4j2)   37.50
SANDUSKY, OHIO-Views of...Portl-n.d.-L N Nelson-obl 8vo-
wrps-32p   (4t1)   10.00
SANDUSKY, MANSFIELD & NEWARK RR CO-20th Annual Report...
as reorganized for 1880-Sandusky-1881-Register Steam Pr-8vo-
56p-wrps   (5j5)   7.50
SANDWICH ISLANDS-History of-Phila-(ca 1840)-n.d.-Amer
SundaySchool Union-231p-label-map frontis   (5cc6)   20.00
SANDYS, EDWYN-Sporting Sketches-NY-1905-389p-illus
(5ee3, 5t7)   5.00
SANDYS, GEO-Relation of a Journey Begun An Dom 1610-Lond-
1637-Crooke-sm folio-Foure Bookes-calf-4th ed-fldg map
(5v7, cov loose, reprd)   75.00
SANDYS, WM, ed-Specimens of Macaronic Poetry-Lond-R Beckley-
1831-56p-facs   (5a1, rbkd)   8.50
SANFORD, E-History of the US before the Revolution with some
Account of the Aborigines-Phila-1819-341p-cl-lea labl
(5a9, rbnd, lacks part t.pg)   10.00
SANFORD, EDMUND C-On Certain Strange Phenomena Appearing
in Contents of Books-n.p.-(ca 1911)-ltd to 100c (5mm2)   6.50
SANFORD, FANCHON-Diamonds & Precious Stones-NY-1874-
292p-illus   (5n7, wn)   7.50
SANFORD, REV JOHN-Black Hills Souvenir-Denver-1902-222p-
photos   (5s4, fair)   15.00
SANFORD, MRS NETTIE-History of Marshall Co, Iowa-Clinton, IA-
1867-12mo-168p-orig cl   (5s9, cov tn)   42.50
SANGER, "LORD" GEO-70 Years a Showman-NY-(1926)-port-
249p   (5t4)   5.00
SANGER, MARGARET-An Autobiography-NY-(1938)-port-1st ed
(4j3, pres)   17.50

SANGER, WM W-The History of Prostitution-NY-1899
(5x7, crack)   10.00
--same-NY-1939-700p-Eugenics Pub Co   (5a6)   7.50
SANGREE, MIGONNETTE, An Ideal Love Story-NY-1885-324p
(5mm2)   10.00
SANGSTER, CHAS-Hesperus, & Other Poems & Lyrics-Montr&Kingston-
1860-embossed cl   (5w8)   25.00
SANGSTER, MARGARET E-Art of Being Agreeable-NY-(1897)-
320p   (5w7, fox)   4.50
--Art of Home Making-NY-1898-263p-4to-illus (5w7, lacks fly)   6.50
--Cross roads-NY-(1919)-Christian Herald-1st ed (5m2, autg)   6.00
--Good Manners for All Occasions-NY-(1910)-376p-illus
(5w7, wn, crack)   4.50
SANSOM, JOS-Sketches of Lower Canada-NY-1817-plain bds
(5w8, lacks frontis, cov loose)   35.00
SANSOM, KATHARINE-Living in Tokyo-Lond-1937-illus
(5tt5, pres)   10.00
SANSON, A J-Navigation dans l'air-Paris-1841-Ledoyen-8vo-
hf calf-t.e.g.-fldg plt   (5b0, sl rub)   95.00
SANSONE, ANTONIO-Printing of Cotton Fabrics etc-Manchester,
Eng-1887-385p-19 fldg plts-42 fabric samples-8vo-1st ed
(4m7, ex-libr)   15.00
SANSUM, OLIVER BARKER-Tables in Dollars & Cents, Showing the
Interest, at 6 & 7 Percent, on Any Sum from $1 to $10,000...
the decimal Value of Halifax Currency, from 1 Farthing to
One Thousand Pounds-Montr-1857-203p-orig mrbld bds-
hf calf   (5w8)   25.00
SANTA ANNA, ANTONIO LOPEX de-Discurso Pronunciado por...
Acto de Prestar El Juramento Al Tomar Posesion Del Gobierno
etc, 20 de Abril de 1853-Mexico-1853-7p-blue prntd wrps
(5n4)   30.00
--Gen Antonio Lopez de Santa Anna to the Mexican People-
Elizabethport, N J-1866-15p-prntd wrps-v rare   (5n4)   65.00
--Exposicion...Dirige a Los Exmos, Sres, Secretarios de la Camara
de Diputados-Mexico-1845-Imprenta de Lara-43p-blue pict wrps
(5n4, Streeter copy)   85.00
SANTA BARBARA-SantaBarbara-c1899-H A C McPhail-54p-
stiff wrps   (5n4)   15.00
SANTA BARBARA-Santa Barbara-c1900-H A C McPhail-photos-
27 lvs-wrps   (4a5, chip)   15.00
SANTA BARBARA-Santa Barbara-n.d.- W W Osborne-12 lvs-
hand col-illus-sm folio-wrps   (4a5)   11.50
SANTA BARBARA, CALIF-Santa Barbara-ca 1904-photos-52p-wrps-
map on back cov   (5dd6)   8.00
SANTA BARBARA, GUIDE TO CHANNEL CITY & ITS ENVIRONS-
NY-1941-206p-1st ed-Amer Guide Ser-WPA   (4n1, dj)   7.50
SANTA BARBARA JR LEAGUE COOK BOOK-(SantaBarbara)-1939-
News Press Pub-bds-spiral bnd   (4g9, rub)   5.00
SANTA BARBARA MUSEUM OF NATURAL HISTORY-Annual Reports
for Years 1933 thru 52 Consecutively-2 vols-bd   (5x5)   20.00
SANTA BARBARA RECIPES-by Ladies of 1st Congreg Church-
SantaBarbara-1888-Morning Pr Print Hse-106p-plus 4p ads-
1st SantaBarbara cook book-orig cl   (5yy3)   60.00
SANTA CLARA CO-Vol 1, #1-History, Climatology, Resources etc-
Sept, 1887-illus-Bd of Trade of San Jose-96p-map   (4t2)   45.00
SANTA CLARA CO & ITS RESOURCES-Historical Descrip, Statistical-
SanJose-1895-souvenir of SanJose Mercury-319p plus 6p-ports-
illus-pict bds-Smith&Eaton   (5r0, lacks map)   25.00
SANTA CLAUS BOOK OF GAMES & PUZZLES-NY-1865-8vo-
dec cl-illus-scarce   (5p5, rbkd)   17.50
SANTA CRUZ-The City of...& Vicinity-SantaCruz-1908-Bd of Trade-
2 maps-illus-68p-pict wrps-Sentinel Pr   (5r0)   7.50
SANTA CRUZ-Vistas de Santa Cruz-(LosAng, M Rieder, publ, press
Geo Rich Sons)-(n.d.)-illus-wrps   (5r0)   7.50
SANTA FE SYSTEM LINES-Wine of California-(1937)-35p-bds-
booklet   (5w1)   3.00
SANTA FE TRAIL, THE-NY-(1946)-editors of Look-272p-illus
(5dd9, cov soil)   8.50
SANTA GERTRUDIS BREEDERS INTL RECORDED HERDS-Kingsville-
1954-Vol 1-Hertzog-4to (5a8) 10.   (4c7, Kleberg, autg)   15.00
SANTANDER, CARLOS U-Diccionario de Medicacion Herbaria-
Santiago, Chile-1953-274p-wrps   (5w3, wrps tn)   4.50
SANTAYANA, GEO-Character & Opinion in the US with Reminis
of Wm James-NY-1920-Scribner-233p   (5p9)   4.00
--Dialogues in Limbo-NY-1925-Scribner-193p   (5p0, fade)   4.00
--Dominations & Powers-NY-1951-Scribner-481p   (5p0)   6.00
--The Last Puritan-1936-Scribner's (5a6) 6. (5F1, sl stn, dj, 4m8) 5.00
--Life of Reason or Phases of Human Progress-NY-1935 to 37-
5 vols   (5q0)   15.00
--The Middle Span-NY-1945   (5u6) 3.   (5t0, 5x7)   3.50
--Persons & Places-NY-1944-Scribner's (5k2) 3.50 (5p1, dj)   4.50
--Poems, selected by the author & revised-NY-1923-12mo-cl-
errata slip-1st Amer ed   (4c2, faded)   10.00

SANTAYANA,GEO (continued)
--Realm of Matter-NY-1930-Scribner-209p   (5p0) 5.00
--Scepticism & Animal Faith-Lond-(1923)-Constable (5x0) 6.00
--The Sense of Beauty-NY-Scribner's Sons-1896-1st ed (5ss9,fade)8.50
--Soliloquies in England-Lond-(1922)-8vo-cl (4c2) 10.00
--Soliloquies in England & Later Soliloquies-NY-1922-1st ed
                          (5yy6) 10.00
--Sonnets & Other Verses-Cambr&Chig-1894-1st ed of auth's 1st book-
   ltd to 450c   (5m4) 90.00
--Works of-NY-1936-Scribner-Triton ed-15 vols-ltd to 940 sets-
   autg-cl bks-papr labls-g.t.-8 boxes   (4b1) 225.00
SANTEE,ELLIS M-Genealogy of the Santee Family in America-
   Wilkes Barre-1927-illus-211p (5m2) 10. (4t2) 12.50
SANTEE,ROSS-Apache Land-1947-Scribner's Sons-1st ed-illus
           (5m8) 12.50 (5x5) 15.00
--Cowboy-NY-1928-Cosmopolitan Book Corp-illus by author-1st ed
      (5x5,5yy7,e.p.tn) 10. (5r7,5g0,f) 20.00
--same-NY-1928-pict cl-illus-reprint ed (5m9) 4.50
--Hardrock & Silver Sage-NY&Lond-1951-224p-illus (5t4) 5.00
--Lost Pony Tracks-NY-1953-303p-1st ed-illus-scarce
   (5dd4) 23.50   (5r1,vg) 20. (5yy7,dj) 12.50
SANTERRE,GEO H-White Cliffs of Dallas-Dallas-1955-tho not so
   stated,ltd to 450c   (5c8,pres) 22.50
SANTLEBEN,AUGUST-A Texas Pioneer-NY-1910-Neale-321p
                     (4j6,vg) 75.00
SANTLEY,MARY McDERMOTT-Indian Romances & Other Poems-
   Cleve-1911-115p-wrps   (5h2) 4.00
SANTMIER,ARTHUR-Glimpses of the Northland-Chig-(1905)-64p-
   photos-wrps-1st ed   (5L2,lacks wrps) 6.00
SANTOS-DUMONT,A-My Air ships-NY-1904-Century-356p-
   Century   (5h2) 12.50 (5p0) 20.00
SAPIR,EDW-Navaho Texts-IowaCity,Ia-1942-543p-H Hoijer,ed
                    (5L2) 25.00
SAPPER,DR CARLOS-Los Volcanes de la America Central-Halle-
   1925-116p-illus-wrps   (5d7) 7.50
SAPPHO IN BOSTON-NY-1908-Moffat,Yard-8vo-cl-g.-frontis by
   J M Flagg   (5b2,lt fade) 4.50
SAPPINGTON,DR JOHN-Theory & Treatment of Fevers-Arrow Rock-
   1844-(c1843)-priv prnt-1st ed-calf
        (5L0,hng broke,wn) 30. (4a9,fox) 40.00
--same-ArrowRock,Mo-1844-calf-12mo-revised by Stith,
   Franklin Tenn   (4c8,stn,crack) 25.00
SARDI,VINCENT,SR-Sardi's-NY-1953-244p-frontis (5e4) 4.50
SARETT,LEW-Slow Smoke-1925-104p-1st ed
     (5r1,vg) 5.50   (5ss1) 4.   (5dd5) 5.25
--Wings Against the Moon-NY-1931-8vo-cl-125p-1st ed (5m8,dj) 4.50
SARG,TONY-Tony Sarg's New York-NY-1926-col plts-thin 4to-
   buck-1st ed   (4b6) 25.00
--Tony Sarg's NY-NY-1927-col illus-4to-scarce (4j3) 25.00
--Tony Sarg's Magic Movie Book-NY-1943-1st ed-rotate disc
                    (5jj6) 15.00
--Tony Sarg's Savings Book-Cleve&NY-(1946)-9 col plts-1st ed
                    (5jj6) 12.50
SARGEANT,LEONARD-Trial,Confessions & Conviction of Jesse
   & Stephen Boorn-Manchester,Vt-1873-Journal Book & Job-
   48p-orig wrps   (5qq8) 15. (5m6) 12.50
SARGEANT,P W-Jerome Bonaparte,the burlesque Napoleon-NY-
   1906-illus-3/4 lev mor   (5d2,f bndg) 10.00
SARGENT,AARON-Sargeant Family,Desc of Wm of Malden,Mass-
   1858-108p   (5mm3) 6.00
SARGENT,ALICE APPLEGATE-Following the Flag-KansasCty-n.d.-
   291p-photo   (5L2) 5.00
SARGENT,C S-The Woods of the US-NY-1885
           (5m6,ex-libr) 7.50 (5m2) 6.00
SARGENT,CHAS S-Manual of the trees of NoAmer-Bost-1905-
   HoughtonMiff-644 illus-826p-t.e.g. (5u3) 6.00
--The Silva of NoAmer-Bost&NY-1891 to 1902-orig prntd bds-
   papr labl-740 plts-lg4to-14 vols-1st ed (5z9,vf) 500.00
--Trees & Shrubs,Vol 1,Pt 1 to Vol 2, Pt 4(all publ)-Bost&NY-
   (1902)1905 to 13-cl-orig prntd front wrps bnd in-1st ed
                    (5z9,f,rbnd) 140.00
SARGENT,D A-Athletic Sports-(NY)-1897-8vo-cl-318p-illus-The
   Out of Door Library Ser   (5t2) 3.75
SARGENT,EDWIN EVERETT-Sargent Record,Wm Sargent...wi his
   Desc & their Intermarriages-StJohnsbury,Vt-1899-Caledonian Co,
   8vo-331p-illus-frontis mounted (4t2) 25. (5j5,rbnd) 27.50
SARGENT,EMMA-Epes Sargent of Gloucester & His Desc-Bost-1923-
   sm4to-bds-cl bs-illus-ltd to 500c,nbrd (5w0,auth's bkplt) 60.00
--same-1923-416p   (4t2) 35.00
SARGENT,EPES,ed-Arctic Adventure by Sea & Land from Earliest
   Date to Last Explor in Search of Sir John Franklin-Bost-1857-
   illus   (5e8) 10.00

SARGENT,EPES (continued)
--Life & Public Services of Henry Clay-NY-1844-Greeley&
   McElrath-80p-pamph-rmvd (5t7,wrps) 6. (5qq8) 10.00
--same-NY-1848-8vo-new ed-rev&enlrgd (5m6) 7.50
--same-Auburn-1852-port-492p   (4p8) 7.50
--same-Phila-1852-423p   (5k2,ex-libr) 5.00
--School Primer,Part 2-Bost-1874-Billings,illus-12mo-pict bds
               (5c8,lf tn,lf def) 3.50
--Wonders of the Arctic World,including Polaris Exped-Phila-
   (1873)-dbl frontis-651p   (5ee3) 5. (5ss1) 7.50
SARGENT,GEO H-Amy Lowell,a Mosaic-NY-1926-(30p)-bds-
   ltd to 450c   (5w9) 10.00
--A Busted Bibliophile & his Books-Bost-1928-illus-box-ltd to 600c
         (5w9) 12.50 (5dd8,5j3,f) 15.00
--Writings of A Edw Newton-Phila-1927-lg8vo-52p-illus-t.e.g.-
   ltd to 110c,nbrd,autg   (5w9,dj,box) 17.50
SARGENT,GERTRUDE W-The Grand Master's Treasure-Brooklyn-
   (1911)-Gertreva Publ-8vo-cl-g.t.-uncut (5b2) 6.00
SARGENT,HARRY G-The Bradley massacre,address...before New
   Hamp Hist Soc-Concord-1891-wrps (5g4) 7.50
SARGENT,HELEN CHILD,ed-Engl & Scottish Popular Ballads-Bost-
   (1904)-HoughtonMiff-729p   (5t2) 6. (5p7) 5.00
SARGENT,J L MRS,ed-Amador Co History-Jackson-1927-
   Amador Co Fed of Women's Clubs-127p-wrps (5tt0) 10.00
SARGENT,JOHN-The mine,a dramatic poem-Lond-1785-for T Cadell-
   4to-disbnd-1st ed   (5x3) 35.00
SARGENT,JOHN SINGER-The Work of...-Lond-1903-Heinemann-
   plts-folio-1st ed   (5t2,libr,mrks) 17.50 (4c8) 30.00
SARGENT,JOHN W-Toasts for the Times-NY-1904-illus-(160p)
                    (5g9) 5.00
SARGENT,L M-Address Before Mass Soc for Suppression of
   Intemperance,May 27, 1833-Bost-1833-39p-stitchd as issued-
   2nd ed-uncut   (5w5) 5.00
SARGENT,LUCIUS M-The Temperance Tales-Bost-1853-2 vols in 1-
   332p-illus-"new illustrated ed"   (5t4) 6.50
SARGENT,M P-Pioneer Sketches,Scenes & Incidents of Former Days-
   Erie,Pa-1891-illus   (4p7,fade) 50.00
SARGENT,SHIRLEY-Pioneers in Petticoats-LosAng-(1960)-80p-
   illus-cl-Trans Anglo Books   (5d7) 3.95
SARGENT,WM M-Maine Wills,164o to 1760-Portland-1887-
   8vo-3/4 calf-953p plus inserted errata slip(5m6,hng split) 20.00
SARGENT,WINTHROP-Early Sargents of New England-n.p.-
   1922-51p-tip in illus-lt weight bds (5w0) 12.50
--History of Expedition Against Ft DuQuesne in 1775-Phila-1855-
   fldg maps-423p   (5yy0) 27.50
--same-Phila-1856-423p-illus-Lippincott for Hist Soc
           (5mm8) 15. (5h9) 22.50
--Life & Career of Maj John Andre-Bost-1861-Ticknor&Fields-
   471p-frontis-1st ed (5L1) 15. (5ee3) 20. (5mm8) 17.50
--same-Bost-1861-lg papr-ltd to 75c-471p (5w0,5h9) 45.00
--same-Bost-1871-2nd ed-478p-map-2 ports (5i3) 10.00
--same-NY-1902-543p-cl-illus-500c-Abbatt,ed (5h1) 15.00
--same-NY-1902-Wm Abbatt-new ed-illus-fldg map-ltd 75c-
   lg papr   (5tt8) 30.00
SARGENT'S BOOK OF DESIGNS-Sargent&Co-NY-191-?-hardware
   & locks-84p-plts   (5h8) 4.50
SARMIENTO,DOMINGO FAUSTINO-Vida de Abran Lincoln,
   decimo sesto Presidente de los Estados Unidos-NY-1866-Appleton-
   8vo-306p-port-orig cl-1st ed, 1st issue (5L1) 50.00
SARMIENTO,F L-Life of Pauline Cushman Union Spy & Scout-Phila-
   (1865)-illus   (5s9,shaken) 4. (5L3) 7.50
SARMIENTO,FERDINAND-The History of Our Flag-Phila-c1864-
   96p-orig wrps-1st ed   (5w4,wn) 8.50
SARON,GUSTAV,ed-Jews in So Africa-CapeTn-1955-17&422p-
   24 plts-fldg map   (5c6,f) 25.00
SAROYAN,WM-Daring Young Man on Flying Trapeze & Other
   Stories-NY-1934-1st ed(so stated)-auth's 1st book
        (5hh1) 20.   (5F1,libr nbrs) 17.50
        (5ss9,autg,dj) 35.   (5gg6,dj) 30.00
--Dear Baby-NY-(1944)-HarcourtBrace-1st ed (5ss9,dj) 7.50
--Don't Go Awa Mad & other plays-NY-(1949)-HarcourtBrace-
   cl-1st ed   (5ss3,dj) 15.00
--The Fiscal Hoboes-NY-1949-Press of Valenti Angelo-blue wrps-
   1st ed-ltd to 250c,autg   (5ss9,dj) 27.50
--Hairenik,1834 to 1939-Bost-1939-Hairenik Pr-8vo-orig cl-
   1st ed   (5p5) 20.00
--Hilltop Russians in San Francisco-1941-Grabhorn Pr-30 col illus-
   ltd to 500c   (5F5,f,tn dj) 25.00
--The Human Comedy-NY-(1943)-HarcourtBrace-illus-1st ed
         (5F1,f,dj) 10.   (5ss3,dj) 15.00
--Inhale & Exhale-NY-(1936)-Random Hse-8vo-cl-438p-1st ed-
   scarce   (5j5,fade) 22.50
--Little Children-(1937)-Harcourt   (5F1,mint,dj) 35.00

SAROYAN, WM (continued)
--My name is Aram-NY-(1940)-Harcourt-illus-1st prntng
                        (5m2,dj)   8.00
--same-NY-(1940)-HarcourtBrace-illus-Book of Month Issue
                        (5ss3,dj)   5.00
--A Native American-SanFran-1938-Geo Fields-lg8vo-orig cl-
   1st ed-ltd to 450c,autg (4h0,pres) 35. (5F1,hng weak) 25.00
--Razzle Dazzle-NY-1942-12mo-cl-frontis-1st ed
             (5hh1,pres) 25.   (5cc9,dj)   17.50
--Rock Wagram-GardenCty-1951-Dblday-1st prntng
               (5r9,f,dj,5ss3,dj)   10.00
--Saroyan's Fables-1941-Harcourt-illus-sm4to-cl-1st ed-
   ltd to 1000c,nbrd,autg   (5h5)   25.00
--The Trouble with Tigers-(1938)-Harcourt-scarce (5F1,mint,dj) 27.50
SARPI, FRA PAOLO-Histoire du Concile de Trente-Amsterdam-1751-
   3 vols-vel-engrvd prints   (5j3,labls chip) 30.00
SARRATT, J H-New Treatise on Game of Chess etc-Lond-1828-
   2 vols-2nd ed-bds   (5xx7,rebkd) 10.00
--Science & Art of Chess-NY 1859-281p-1st ed   (5xx7) 8.50
--Treatise on the Game of Chess-Lond-1808-2 vols-sm8vo-fabrikoid-
   1st ed   (5b0) 37.50
SARTAIN, J,ed-American Gallery of Art-Phila-1848-g.-111p-
   illus-Lindsay&Blakiston   (4a0,sp torn) 20.00
SARTAIN, JOHN-Reminof Very Old Man, 1808 to 1897-NY-1899-
   Appleton-1st ed-297p-illus-g.t.-8vo (5w0) 15. (4a0) 40.00
SARTOR RESARTUS-life & opinions of Herr Teufelsdrockh-in 3 books-
   Lond-1838-Saunders&Otley-12mo-hf mor-(T Carlyle)
                    (5x3,rbnd,scuff) 40.00
SARTORI, ANNA B-About My Pioneer Ancestors-1942-4to-115p &
   chart-(mimeo)   (4t2)   5.00
SARTORY, A-Visions Rouges-Paris-1935-wrps-350p-illus-ltd to 25c
                        (5v7) 17.50
SARTRE, JEAN PAUL-Portrait of the Anti Semite-(NY,1946)-27p-
   PR Series #1-prntd wrps   (5r9)   7.50
SARYCHEV, GARVRILLA A-Acct of a Voyage of Discovery to NE
   of Siberia-Lond-1806,1807-5 plts(2 col)-hf calf-8vo-2 vols in 1-
   70p,80p   (4g6,ex-librr) 135.00
SARZANO, FRANCES-Sir John Tenniel-Lond-1948-sm4to-cl-96p-
   illus   (5t0)   3.50
SASKETCHEWAN LAWS, STATUTES, ETC-Statutes of...1951,52 to
   1966,67-15 vols-bound   (5ii7) 70.00
SASS, HERBERT R-Hear Me, My Chiefs-NY-1940
      (5a9) 7.50   (5i1) 15.   (5yy7) 8.50
SASSE, FRED-Dan Patch Story-Harrisburg-1957-1st ed-wrps
                    (4a9,taped) 12.50
SASSOON, SIEGFRIED-Counter Attack & Other Poems-Lond-1918-
   64p-wrps-12mo   (4b4,wn) 15. (5j2) 20.00
--Collected Poems-Lond-(1947)-1st ed   (5j2,dj) 15.00
--Memoirs of Infantry Officer-Lond-(1930)-Faber&Faber-1st ed
                       (5i4) 22.50
--Satirical Poems-Lond-1926-1st ed   (4b4) 10.00
--Selected Poems-Lond-1925-1st ed   (5j2,dj,autg) 25.00
--To the Red Rose-Lond-(1931)-illus-16mo-wrps-4 lvs-1st trade ed
                     (5j2,f)   5.00
--To My Mother-Lond-1928-ltd to 500c,autg (5a9) 12.50
SASSURE, MONSIEUR CAESAR DE-A Foreign View of England in
   the Reigns of George I & Geo II-Lond-1902-map & illus-
   3/4 mor-g.   (5d2) 10.00
SATAN IN SOCIETY-By a Physician-Cinn-1880-412p-(C F Vent)
                   (5w5,sl wn) 6.50
SATCHELL, JOHN-Thornton Abbey,or,the persecuted daughter-
   Portsea-n.d.-(1814)-2 vols-8vo-hf mor-1st ed-for G A Stephens
                    (5xx6) 30.00
SATERLEE, HERBERT L-J Pierpont Morgan,An Intimate Portrait-NY-
   1939-Macmillan-595p-illus   (5m2) 6. (5p0) 6.50
SATTERLEE, L D-Amer Gun Makers-Buffalo-1940-Otto Ulbrich-
   186p   (5p9) 25.00
SATTERLEE ,MARION P-Detailed Acct of Massacre by Dakota
   Indians of Minnesota in 1862-Minpls-ca1923-wrps
         (5L0,wrps) 25.   (4k5,f) 35.00
SATTERTHWAIT, ELISABETH C-A Son of the Carolinas-Phila-1898-
   1st ed   (5mm2) 12.50
SATURDAY EVENING POST STORIES,1955-NY-(1955)-Random Hse-
   8vo-cl-345p-(1st printing,Faulkner's "Race at Morning")
                   (5j5,dj) 10.00
SAUCIER'S,TED-Bottoms Up-NY-(1952)-4to-270p-plts (5w1) 7.50
SAUDEK, ROB-The Psychology of Handwriting-NY-1926-Doran-
   illus suppl   (5p7)   7.50
SAUER, CHRISTOPH-Biblia, Das ist, Die Heilige Schrift, Altes und
   Neues Testaments-Germantown-1743-1st ed,2nd issue-scarce
                (5nn6,lacks fly) 300.00

SAUER,MARTIN-Acct of a Geographical & Astronomical Exped to
   Northern Parts of Russia...& of Islands in Eastern Ocean to
   Amer Coast...by Cmdr Jos Billings,1785 to 1794-Lond-
   1802-332p,58p,(1)-4to-hf calf-fldg map-14 plts-1st ed,
   complete with hf title & errata lf
        (5L1,hng crack) 135. (5x5,rbkd) 185.00
SAUER,MARTIN-Viaggio fatto..nel Mare Glacjale..e sulla costa
   Nord Ouest dell'America-Milan-1816-Sonzogno-2 vols-12mo-
   orig prntd wrps-8 col plts-1st Italian ed (5n9) 75.00
SAUER,MARTIN-Voyage Fait Par Ordre De L'Imperatrice De Russie...
   Asiatique,Dans La Mer Glaciale,Dans L'Amerique,Depuis
   1785,1794 etc-Paris-1802-2 vols-24p,385p &418p-cl
                (5r6,rbnd,lacks atlas) 95.00
SAULT STE MARIE CANAL & HAY LAKE CHANNEL-Duluth-
   1887-46p,(5)p-fldg table-fldg map-wrps-v scarce
       (5L0,chip) 15.   (5h7,sp sl wn) 27.50
SAUNDERS, AUDREY-Algonquin Story-n.p.-n.d.-photos-plts-
   196p   (4b2,dj,f)   3.50
SAUNDERS,CHAS FRANCIS-California Padres & Their Missions-
   HoughtonMiff-1915-418p-1st ed-illus (5r1,vg) 14. (5x5) 12.50
--Finding the Worth While in Calif-NY-1916-229p-illus-map
                      (5s4)   5.00
--Finding the Worth While in the SoWest-NY-1918-illus-1st ed
                      (5L2)   3.50
--same-NY-(1937)-4th ed-revised-semi flex cov (5s4) 3.50
--Indians of Terraced Houses-NY-1912-Putnam's-293p-photos(4g0)27.50
--Little Book of Calif Missions-NY-1925-McBride&Co-64p-cl
   23 sepia plates-12mo   (5h2,dj) 4.(4g0) 7.50(4a5) 4.50
--The Southern Sierras of Calif-Bost-1923-HoughtonMiff-367p-
   illus-cl   (5d7) 15.00
--The Story of Carmelita-Pasadena-(1928)-Vroman,Inc.-54p-
   illus-12mo   (4g0) 5.00 (5s7) 5.00
--Trees & Shrubs of Calif Gardens-NY-1926-cl-12mo-photos-323p
       (4g0) 10. (5s7) 7.50 (5h4,5z9) 4.00
--Under the Sky in Calif-NY-1926   (4a5) 5.00
--same-NY-1931-McBride-299p (5dd5,4go,fbd,5s4,tn,5p0) 5.00
--Western Flower Guide-GardenCty-1917-obl 16mo-286p-
   250 col drwngs-fabr   (5s7)   4.50
--same-1931 ed-236p-col illus   (5s7)   3.50
--Western Wild Flowers & Their Stories-GardenCty-1933-illus-
   320p-1st ed   (5g0) 10.00
--With the Flowers & Trees in Calif-NY-1919 (5x5) 7.50
--same-NY-1923-286p   (5s7)   5.00
SAUNDERS,GEO W-Trail Drivers of Texas-Nashville-1925-illus-
   2 vols in 1-2nd ed-revised-1044p (5yy7,dj) 30.00
SAUNDERS, HENRY S-Parodies on Walt Whitman-NY-1923-
   Amer Libr Serv-R8vo-cl   (5b2,fade) 7.50
SAUNDERS, JOHN-Israel Mort,overman-Lond-1876-Henry S King-
   3 vols-8vo-orig cl-1st ed   (5xx6) 30.00
SAUNDERS, KATHERINE-The high mills-Lond-1875-Henry S King-
   3 vols-8vo-orig cl-1st ed   (5xx6) 30.00
SAUNDERS, LYLE-Guide to Materials Bearing on Cultural Relations in
   NewMex-Albuqu-1944-470p plus indices-1st ed
       (5bb4,dj) 8.50   (5g0,mint,dj) 15.00
SAUNDERS,MARSHALL-Deficient Saints-Bost-1899-Page-431p-
   illus-cl   (5h0)   2.00
SAUNDERS,O E-English Illumination-Paris-1928-Pegasus Pr-
   hf mor-4to-cl-89 plts-2 vols (4n5,f bndg,brown) 225.00
SAUNDERS,WM-A Treatise on the structure, economy & diseases
   of the liver-Bost-1797-16mo-calf-1st Amer ed (5g4,librstmp) 25.00
SAUNDERS,WM-Scientific Farming...also Horse Breeding in
   Canada-Ottawa-1888-MacLean,Roger-64p (5aa1) 15.00
SAUNDERSON,M H-Economics of Range Sheep Production in
   Montana-Bozeman-1935-Mont St Col Agri Bul #302-55p-wrps
                    (5L5,dmgd) 5.00
SAUNIER,C-Prakischis Handbuch Fur Uhrmacher-Bautzen-1892-
   307p-8vo-illus   (5bb0) 22.00
SAUNIER,CLAUDIUS-Lehbuch Der Uhrmacherie-Bautzen-1902-
   8vo-3 vols(incl Atlas)-5 parts in 2 vols-1 vol plts (5bb0) 90.00
--Treatise on Modern Horology,Trans by Triplin & Rigg-part lea-
   844p-4to-illus   (5bb0) 50.00
SAUR,CHRISTOPH,prntr-Neu Eingerichtetes Gesang Buch in sich
   halten eine sammlung,etc-Germantown-1762-760,(40)p-lea
                (4h7,lacks clasps) 100.00
SAUR,MRS P B-Maternity,book for every Wife & Mother-Chig-
   1889-12mo-719p-lea   (5t0,fray) 3.75
SAURER, JULIA L-Fog Magic-NY-1943-Viking-107p-pict cl-
   1st ed   (5p1,dj) 7.50
SAUSE, M JUDSON-The Art of Dancing-NY-1880-cl-120p
                     (4h8,stns) 5.75
SAUSSURE, DR HENRI de-Synopsis of Amer Wasps-Wash-1875-
   Smi Misc Coll #254-4 col plts-8vo-orig wrps-392p
              (5ss5,lacks bk wrp) 7.50

SAUVIN,G-Un Royaume Polnesian Illes Hawaii-Paris-1893-
Librairie Plon-321p-wrps (5q8,rbnd hf lea) 12.50   (5x9)   8.50

SAVAGE,ALINE H-Dogsled Apostles-NY-1942-plts-231p
(4d4,autg)   8.50
--same-NY-1944-plts-231p   (5ss1)   5.00

SAVAGE,C R-Reflex of Salt Lake City & Vicinity-SaltLkCty-
(1893)-16mo-48p text-accordion folded album of 18p views
(5dd4,f)   16.50

SAVAGE,EDW H-Chronological History of Boston Watch & Police
1631 to 1865-Bost-1865-396p-1st ed   (5e8)   17.50
--same-Bost-1865-cl-408p-2nd ed   (5d6)   12.50

SAVAGE,F G-Shakespeare's Flora & Folklore-GB-1923-420p-
12 illus   (5w3)   10.00

SAVAGE,GEO-Ceramics for the Collector-NY-1949-illus
(5k1,dj)   7.50

SAVAGE,HENRY-A Long Spoon and the Devil-Lond-1922-
Cecil Palmer-1st ed   (5ss3)   7.50

SAVAGE,I O-History of Republic Co,Kans-Beloit-1901-
Jones&Chubbic-8vo-cl-enlrgd ed   (4t2,4t1)   45.00

SAVAGE,JAS-Genealogical Dictionary of 1st Settlers of New Engl-
Bost-1860,1862-4 vols-hf mor-1st eds
(4t2,bndgs wn,sp crude reprd) 125.   (5w9,f bndg)   250.00
--Letters to His Family-Bost-1906-8vo-port-(priv prntd)-1st ed
(5m6)   12.50

SAVAGE,JAS W-A Visit to Nebraska in 1662-Bost-1885-25p-
wrps   (5L2,wrps loose)   8.50

SAVAGE,JOHN-Compleat History of Germany-Lond-1702-2 vols-
port-calf   (5yy6,rub)   25.00

SAVAGE,JOHN,ed-Picturesque Ireland,etc-NY-(1884)-pict cl-
thk heavy 4to-640p-map-illus-a.e.g.   (4t7,recased)   37.50

SAVAGE,MINOT J-Life Beyond Death-NY-1905-Putnam (5p7)   4.00

SAVAGE,RICHARD-Progress of a Divine-Lond-1735-folio-qtr mor-
1st ed-rare   (514,sml libr stmp)   150.00

SAVAGE,RICHARD H-A Daughter of Judas-NY-1894-Neely-304p
(5x4)   10.00
--His Cuban sweetheart-NY-(1895)-Home Pub Co-1st ed (5m2)   12.50
--Landon,a story of modern Rome-Chig-(1899)-Rand,McNally-
pict cl-illus-1st ed   (5m2)   13.50
--Last Traitor of Long Island-NY-(1903)-341p-wrps-stpld
(5s1,stn)   3.00
--The little lady of the Lagunitas-NY-1892-Amer News Co-1st ed
(5m2)   8.50
--Lost Countess Falka,a story of the Orient-Chig-1896-Rand,
McNally-1st ed   (5m2,lacks frontis)   6.00
--The Passing Show-Chig-(1893)-326p plus 10p (5xx5,pres)   12.00

SAVAGE,SARAH-Scenes & characters illus Christian truth,#1,
Trial & self discipline-Bost-1835-Jas Munroe-12mo-calf-
1st ed-scarce   (5x1,wn)   50.00

SAVAGE,TIMOTHY,B C-The Amazonian Republic,recently
discovered in interior of Peru-NY-1842-Sam'l Colman-12mo-
orig bds-papr labl-1st ed-scarce   (5x1)   110.00

SAVAGE,W S-Controversy Over Distribution of Abolition
Literature 1830 to 1860-Wash-1938-1st ed   (5x2)   3.00

SAVAGE-LANDOR,A HENRY-Across Unknown SoAmer-Lond&NY-
1913-Hodder&Stoughton-12mo-2 maps-8 col plts-260 photos-
2 vols-1st ed   (4e4,dj,fox)   40.00
--Tibet & Nepal-Lond-1905-cl-4to-233p-frontis-75 plts(some col)-
fldg map   (5v7,pencil)   15.00

SAVANNAH-Savannah-1937-WPA-208p   (5j6)   7.50

SAVANNAH-Photogravures-Brklyn-1908-33p-folio-wrps   (5j6)   8.50

SAVANNAH,SOUVENIR OF-NY-1892-Wittemann-32p-illus
(5j6)   10.00

SAVARIN-Real French Cooking-GardenCty-(1956)-399p (5g9)   5.00

SAVARY,A W-Supplement to History of Annapolis Co (Nova Scotia)-
n.p.-1913-illus-142p   (5q0)   20.00

SAVARY,CHAS-Feuilles volantes-Ottawa-1890-hf mor (5w8)   10.00

SAVARY,JACQUES-Universal Dictionary & Commerce-Lond-1757-
2nd ed-frontis-fldg tables-2 vols-thk folio-calf
(4b6,lacks maps,rebk,crack)   75.00

SAVARY,NICHOLAS-Letters on Egypt-Lond-1787-fldg map&plans-
2 vols-calf   (4b6,hng reprd)   75.00

SAVIGEAR'S GUIDE-to Horsemanship & Horse Training-Lond-1904-
3/4 lev-g.tooled   (5d2,f bndg)   20.00

SAVIGNY,F K VON-Jural Relations...transl of 2nd Book...by
W H Rattigan-Lond-1884   (5ff4)   17.50

SAVILLE,FRANK-High Grass Trail-Lond-1924-Witherby-photos-
hf lea-255p   (4t5,fox)   15.00
--River of the Giraffe-Lond-1925-Witherby-photos-hf lea-217p
(4t5,fox)   15.00

SAVILLE,MARSHALL H-Earliest Notices Concerning Conquest of
Mexico by Cortes in 1519-NY-1920-Vol 9,#1-Heye Foundation-
wrps-54p   (5L2)   4.50

SAVILLE,MARSHALL H-The Goldsmith's Art in Ancient Mexico-
NY-1920-225p plus index-plts-v scarce-Mus of Amer Indian
Heye Foundation   (5L0,cov soil)   35.00

SAVOY,THE-An Illustrated Quarterly-Lond-1896-Leonard Smithers-
#1 to #8 complete in 3 vols as issued-cl-Symons,ed
(5ee9,Xmas card laid in)   250.00

SAVOY,W-Alien Land-NY-1949-1st ed   (5x2,dj)   10.00

SAWITZKY,WM-Matthew Pratt,1734 to 1805-NY-1942-NY Hist
Soc/Carnegie-103p-8vo-43 plts-ltd to 300c   (4a0)   40.00

SAWTELL,RUTH-Primitive Hearths in Pyrenees-NY-1927-illus-
307p   (4b2)   6.50

SAWTELLE,I B-Hist of Townshend,Mass-1878-455p   (4t2)   12.50

SAWTELLE,MRS MARY P-Heroine of '49-(SanFran)-1891-1st ed
(5mm1)   15.00
--same-n.p.-(SanFran copyr 1891)-248p-cl-2nd ed(so stated)
(5h1)   10.00

SAWTELLE,WM O-Mt Desert,Champlain to Berard-n.p.-n.d.-
(ca 1925)-58p-illus   (5w0,pres)   7.50

SAWVEL,FRANKLIN B-Lo gan the Mingo-Bost-(1921)-110p-photos-
1st ed   (5L0,dj)   7.50

SAWYER,ALBERT E-Prohibition,Confidential Reports-n.p.-1930-
Part 4,Sect 1(par 1 to 638)-4to-cl   (5p5)   12.50

SAWYER,CAROLINE M-The merchant's widow & other tales-NY-
1841-Price-cl-1st ed-scarce   (5m2,wn) 10.   (5x1,f)   50.00

SAWYER,CHAS J-English Books,1475 to 1900-Westminster-1927-
2 vols-illus-ltd to 2000 sets-scarce (5tt5) 37.50   (4b1)   42.50

SAWYER,CHAS W-Firearms in American History,1600 to 1800-
Bost-(1910)-1st ed-illus-237p-scarce (5tt5) 10.   (5t4)   15.00
--Our Rifles-Bost-1944-Williams Bookstore-412p-illus (5p9)   10.00
--same-Bost-1946-412p-illus   (5xx7)   10.00
--US Single Shot Martial Pistols-Bost-(1913)-100p-wrps-illus
(5ii2)   8.50

SAWYER,EDMUND OGDEN,JR-Our Sea Saga-SanFran-(1929)-
205p-illus-ports-maps   (5s1)   10.00

SAWYER,EUGENE-History of Santa Clara Co,Calif,Leading Men
& Women of the County-LosAng-1922-1692p-3/4 lea-4to
(5F5)   40.00

SAWYER,EUGENE T-Life & Career of Tiburcio Vasquez,Calif
Stage Robber-Oakland-1944-Grabhorn Pr-frontis-8vo-
ltd to 500c (5x5) 27.50 (5dd5) 38.50 (4g6,glassine dj)   35.00

SAWYER,GEO W-Fret Sawing & Wood Carving for Amateurs-
Bost&NY-1875-63p-cl-7 plts   (5hh7)   10.00

SAWYER,JOHN-History of Cherry Valley from 1740 to 1898-
CherryValley-1898-Gazette Print-12mo-cl-156p-rare (5j5,f)   45.00

SAWYER,JOS DILLAWAY-Romantic & Fascinating Story of the
Pilgrims & Puritans-NY-(1925)-HNichols-3 vols-t8vo-3/4 mor-
g.t.-illus   (5j5)   45.00
--Washington-NY-1927-illus-2 vols (5j3) 15.   (5r7,4b6)   20.00

SAWYER,LEMUEL-A Biography of John Randolph-NY-1844-295p-
3/4 lea-1st ed   (5L3)   10.00

SAWYER,LORENZO-Way Sketches-Cleve-Family Visitor,Vol 1,#30
to 44,Nov 14,1850 to Mar 13,1851,#40 in facs-mor bkd cl-
eleph folio-1st ed-(Holliday c)-ex rare   (4n4)   750.00
--same-NY-1926-8vo-125p-ltd to 385c
(5hh4) 40.   (5dd4) 45.   (5F9)   50.00

SAWYER,MOSES H-Lieut Colborn,or the disinherited-Portland-
1861-12mo-orig cl-1st ed   (5i9)   25.00

SAWYER,NEWELL W-Comedy of Manners from Sheridan to Maugham-
Phila-1931-8vo-bds&cl-275p-1st ed   (5t0)   5.00

SAWYER,ROBT V-Water Gardens & Goldfish-NY-1934-259p
(5s7)   5.50

SAWYER,ROBT W-Henry Larcom Abbot & Pacific RR Surveys in
Oregon,1855 Mar&June,1932-Oreg Hist Quarterly-48p-wrps-
reprnt   (5tt0)   10.00

SAWYER,TIMOTHY T-Old Charlestown-Bost-1902-West Co-527p
(5t9)   10.00

SAYLER,MILTON-Recent Election in SoCarolina-Wash-1877-
HR175-57p,242p   (4j4)   5.00

SAXBY,A-The Fiery Totem-Lond-n.d.   (4b9)   8.00

SAXE HOLME'S STORIES-NY-1874-1st ed-(H H Jackson)(5mm1)15.00
--same-2nd Series-NY-1878-Scribner-384p-1st ed   (5x4)   10.00

SAXE,JOHN G-Clever Stories of Many Nations-Bost-1865-illus
(5c8)   6.50
--Fables & Legends of Many Countries-Bost-1872-sm12mo-orig cl-
128p-1st ed   (5t0)   4.50
--Flying Dutchman-NY-1862-12mo-illus-1st ed (4b7,5b2)   10.00
--The Money King & Other Poems-Bost-1860-1st ed (5mm2)   6.50
--Poems-Complete 1 vol ed-Bost-1864   (5p9)   4.00
--Progress;a Satirical Poem-NY-1846-8vo-orig prntd bds-
1st ed of auth's 1st book-rare   (5gg6,rbkd,pres)   75.00

SAXIUS,CHRISTOPHORUS-Onomasticon Literarium sive
Nomenclator Historico Criticus-Utre cht-1775 to 90-8vo-
hf calf-8 vols-ex libr   (5t0,f)   80.00
SAXON,ISABELLE-5 Yrs within the Golden Gate-Lond-1868-
Chapman&Hall-315p-cl   (5d6)   25.00
SAXON,LYLE-Children of Strangers-Bost-1937   (5x2,dj)   8.50
--Fabulous New Orleans-NY-(1928)-Century-EHSuydam,illus-330p
(5x0) 7.   (5h9,5x2)   7.50
--same-NOrl-1954-Crager-plts-338p   (4d9,f)   3.50
--Father Mississippi-NY-(1927)-1st ed-illus-v scarce
(5ii3) 15.   (5L2)   25.00
--Friends of Joe Gilmore & some friends of Lyle Saxon-NY-1948-
illus   (5x2,dj)   6.50
--Gumbo Ya Ya-Bost-1945-581p plus photos-WPA   (5c3)   6.50
--Old Louisiana-NY-(1929)-2nd prntng-illus   (5ee3,pres)   7.50
--same-NY-1938-388p-illus-cl   (5t2)   5.00
SAXTON,A-Bright Web In the Darkness-NY-1958   (5x2,dj)   5.00
SAY AND SEAL-Phila-1860Lippincott-2 vols-12mo-orig cl-1st ed-
(Susan B Warner)   (5x4) 27.50   (5i9,fade,chip)   15.00
SAY,THOS-American Entomology-Phila-1824,25,28-Saml A Mitchell-
8vo-hf mor-54 col plts-3 vols-1st ed   (5jj8)   575.00
--Short Compilation of Extraordinary Life & Writings of Thos Say..
by His Son-Phila-1796-Budd&Bartram-36p,151p-calf
(5m3,wn)   37.50
--The Complete Writings...on the Entomology of NoAmer-NY-
1859-hf calf-g.t.-8vo-54 hand col plts-2 vols   (5z9,rub)   110.00
SAYBROOK PLATFORM-A Confession of Faith,Sept 9,1708-Lond-
1760-Timothy Green-t.lf & 118p-12mo-orig sheep-2nd ed
(5L1,t pg tn)   60.00
--same-Bridgeport-1810-Lockwood&Backus-144p-12mo-orig sheep-
3rd ed   (5L1)   35.00
SAYCE,R U-Primitive Arts & Crafts-Cambr-1933   (5qq5)   7.00
SAYER,ALEXIS-Soyer's Culinary Campaign-Lond-1857-frontis-
597p(2)   (5c5,crack)   28.50
SAYERS,E-Amer Fruit Garden Companion-Bost-1839-12mo-174p
(5w1,fade)   18.50
SAYERS,EDW-Amer Flower Garden Companion-Cinn-1846-207p ads-
rev&enlrgd-lea bkd cl   (5h2,wn corners)   7.50
SAYERS,J D-Can the White Race Survive-Wash-1929-illus (5x2) 20.00
SAYINGS & DOINGS-or Sketches from Life-Lond-1828-
HenryColburn-3 vols-hf lea-(T Hook)-1st ed   (5ss9)   35.00
SAYLE,R T D-Barges of the Merchant Tailor's Co-(Lond)-1933-
4to-7 plts-80p-(400c prntd)   (5s6)   12.50
SAYLER,H L-The Airship Boys Due North-Chig-(c1910)-
Reilly&Britton-335p-12mo-frontis & 3 plts-pict cl-
Airship Boys Series 3   (5p1)   7.50
SAYLER,J L-Sayler Family-1898-164p   (4t2)   20.00
SAYLER,OLIVER M-Our Amer Theatre-NY-1923-8vo-cl-illus-
399p   (5t0)   4.50
SAYLOR,HENRY H-Distinctive Homes of Moderate Cost-NY-
1910-folio-173p-illus   (5xx7)   12.50
SAYMORE,SARAH EMERY-Hearts Unveiled-NY-1856-12mo-cl-
300p-reprint   (5t0)   4.50
SAYRE,H M-Desc of Deacon Ephraim Sayre-1942-75p   (4t2)   15.00
SAYRE,J WILLIS-This City of Ours-n.p.-(Seattle)-c1936-191p-
cl-photos   (5mm3)   15.00
SAYRE,JOEL-Persian Gulf Command-NY-(1945)-12mo-illus-
140p   (5s1,ex-libr)   3.50
SAYRE,LUCIUS E-A Manual of Organic Materia Medica &
Pharmacognosy-Phila-1899-4to-684p,29p(4)-2nd ed rev
(5w3,broke)   6.50
SAYWARD,C A-Hist & Gen of Henry Sayward of York,Me-1890-
177p   (4t2)   10.00
SA ZITKALA-Old Indian Legends-Bost-1901-165p-illus (5s4,sl tn) 4.00
SBARBORO,CAV ANDREA-The Fight for True Temperance-
(SanFran)-n.d.(ca 1908)-HicksJudd Co-pict wrps-67p-illus-
v scarce   (5r0)   12.50
SCACHERI,MARIO-Indians Today-NY-(1936)-photos-182p-juvenile
(4b2,hng reprd,sl soil)   6.00
--Winnebago Boy-NY-(1937)-illus-182p   (4b2,cov sl wn)   4.00
SCADDING,HENRY-The 8th King's Regiment-Tor-1894-10p-
wire staples   (5w8)   12.00
SCAIFE,H LEWIS-History & Condition of Catawba Indians of
SoCar-Phila-1896-wrps-24p-1st ed-Indian Rights Assoc-
scarce   (5bb4)   8.50
SCAMMON,L N-Spanish Missions Calif,a portfolio of Etchings-
SanFran-1926-folio-ltd to 400c,autg-Grabhorn Pr
(5x5,fox,soil)   65.00
SCANLAN,CHAS M-Indian Massacre & Captivity of Hall Girls-
Milw-(1915)-photos-16mo-119p-wrps-scarce
(4b2) 7.50   (5bb4,cl,pres)   10.00

SCANLAND,JOHN MILTON-Life of Pat F. Garrett & the
Taming of the Border Outlaw..(ColoSprngs,1952)-42p-
illus-stiff wrps-reprint   (5L0,f)   3.00
SCARBOROUGH,A O-Following a Doctor's Satchel-GrandRapds-
1941   (5a8,dj)   3.50
SCARBOROUGH,D-On the Trail of Negro Folk Songs-Harvard U-
1925   (5x2)   22.50
SCARBOROUGH,KATHERINE-Homes of Cavaliers-NY-1930-
illus-1st ed   (5yy6)   10.00
SCARNE,JOHN-Scarne on Cards-NY-1949-illus-lg8vo-cl-
1st ed   (5p5,dj)   10.00
SCARRON,MON-The whole comical works of-Lond-1741-
2 vols-illus-5th ed   (5p6)   37.00
SCEARCE,STANLEY-Northern Lights to Fields of Gold-Caldwell-
1939-390p-col frontis-plts-scarce(5dd0,ex-libr) 12.50 (4t8) 17.50
SCENES & OCCURRENCES IN ALBANY & CAFFER LAND,
SO AFRICA-Lond-1827-Wm Marsh-12mo-214p-cl (4a6,rbnd) 45.00
SCENES IN THE ROCKY MNTNS-& in Oreg,Calif,NM,Texas
& Grand Prairies-Phila-1846-fldg map-cl-303p-1st ed
(5n9,box) 575.   (5jj9,vg)   425.00
SCENES OF ESTES PARK-& Rocky Mntn Natl Park,Playground of
the World-Estes Park-n.d.-J B Baird-hand col illus-folio-
12 lvs   (4a5)   12.50
SCENES THROUGHOUT FEATHER RIVER CANYON-SanFran-
c1913-Van Noy Interstate Novelty-hand col illus-sm folio-
13 lvs-wrps   (4a5)   7.50
SCHACHNER,NATHAN-By the Dim Lamps-1941-FredkStokes(5F1)4.50
--Thos Jefferson,a Biography-NY-1951-2 vols-frontis-notes
(5h9)   12.50
SCHADT,MABEL E-Cafeteria Recipes-NY-1927-12mo-112p(5c0) 3.50
SCHAEFER BREWING CO,F&M-Our 100th Year-Brklyn-1942-
44p-bds-illus-oblong   (5y2)   6.50
SCHAEFER-SIMMERN,HENRY-The Unfolding of Artistic Activity-
Univ of Calif Pr-1948-201p-illus   (5x0)   5.50
SCHAEFFER,REV C-Memoirs & Remini Together wi Sketches of
Early Hist of Sussex Co-1907-187p   (4t2)   27.50
SCHAEFFER,HEINZ-U-Boat 977-Lond-1953-11 photos (5c1) 6.50
--same-NY-(1952)-260p   (5ss1)   5.00
SCHAEFFER,L M-Sketches of Travels in SoAmer,Mex & Calif-
NY-1860-247p-scarce (4n1) 30.   (4j6) 12.50   (5L2)   15.00
SCHAF,PHILIP-Principle of Protestantism-1845 (5L7,broke) 3.00
SCHAFER,JOS-Calif Letters of Lucius Fairchild-Madison-1931-
Wisc Hist Publ Col-203p plus index   (5L2)   7.50
--History of Agriculture in Wisc-Madison-1922-212p-34 plts plus
frontis-16 maps plus 1 in pkt-ltd to 1600c   (5y2)   14.50
--History of the Pacific NoWest-NY-1918-1st of rev ed-307p plus
index-col map-photos   (5L2,cov stn)   5.00
--Social History of Amer Agriculture-NY-1936-maps-1st prntng
(5q8)   7.75
--The Winnebago Horicon Basin-Madison-1937-illus-Vol 6 (5q8) 7.00
SCHAFF,MORRIS-Etna & Kirkersville(Ohio)-Bost-1905-157p-cl
(4m2)   12.50
--The Spirit of Old West Point 1858 to 1862-Bost-1907-283p plus
index-photos-1st ed   (5L0)   7.50
--The Sunset of Confederacy-Bost-(1912)-8vo-302p
(5w5,crack) 8.50   (4a7,sl dmgd)   15.00
SCHAFF,PHILIP-History of the Christian Church-NY-1923-
2 vols   (5h9)   15.00
SCHAFFER,MARY T S-Old Indian Trails-NY-1911-360p plus index-
illus-fldg map-1st ed   (5L2)   6.50
SCHAICK,JN V-Characters in Tales of a Wayside Inn-Bost-(1939)-
199p   (5e8)   5.85
SCHALDACH,WM J-Coverts & Casts-NY-(1943)-Barnes-4to-
buck-4 col plts   (5j5,dj)   12.50
--Currents & Eddies-NY-c1944-4to-col illus-1st ed (5w5,dj) 10.00
--Fish by Schaldach-1937-4to-60 plts-illus-ltd ed (5L7) 25.00
SCHALIT,LEON-John Galsworthy,a Survey-NY-1929-8vo-cl-
333p-1st ed   (5t0)   4.00
SCHALK,EMIL-Summary of Art of War-Phila-1862-Lippincott-
maps(sm fldg)-182p,2p   (5j6) 6.   (5mm8)   7.50
SCHANTZ,F J F-Domestic Life & Characteristics of Penna German
Pioneer-Lancaster-1900-1st ed-illus   (5jj3)   17.50
SCHAPIRO,ELEANOR I-Wadsworth Heritage-Wadsworth-1964-
392p-cl   (5h1)   8.50
SCHAPIRO,MEYER-Vincent Van Gogh-NY-(1950)-Abrams-
130p-4to-50 col illus   (5x0)   10.00
SCHARF,J THOS-The Chronicles of Baltimore-Balt-1874-orig cl-
1st ed   (5h9,sl speck)   30.00
--History of Baltimore City & County-Phila-1881-2 vols-ports-
cl   (5m2,rbnd,facs t pgs)   30.00
--History of Confederate States Navy from its Organization to
Surrender of its Last Vessel-NY-1887-cl-824p
(5yy0,rbnd) 40.   (5a0,sl chip,4j6,rbnd)   65.00

SCHARF, J THOS (continued)
--History of Delaware-Phila-1888-2 vols-lg4tos-1358p-plts&facs
                (4b1,rebnd) 250.00
--History of Maryland from Earliest Period to Present Time-Balt-
  1879-3 vols-1st ed-illus-maps-v scarce   (4b1) 150.00
--History of Phila, 1609 to 1884-Phila-1884-illus-fldg plts-4to-
  3 vols   (5w5) 75.   (5h9,4m4) 85.00
--History of St Louis City & County-Phila-1883-L H Everts-a.e.g.-
  8vo-hf lea-1943p-illus-2 vols   (4t1,rebkd) 65.00
--History of Westchester Co-1886-2 vols-888p & 764p-index-
  scarce   (5ff2) 60.00
--Historyof Western Maryland-Phila-1882-illus-map-4to-2 vols
          (5yy0) 35.00
SCHAUB-KOCH, EMILE-L'Oeuvre d'Anna Hyatt Huntington-Paris-
  1949-Editions Messein-396p-illus-4to-wrps-ex scarce (4a0) 55.00
SCHAUFFLER, ROBT H-Beethoven, the Man Who Freed Music-
  GardenCty-1936-8vo-cl-693p-illus   (5t0) 4.50
--Romantic Amer-NY-1913-339p-illus-1st ed (5h9) 7.50 (5w5) 8.50
SCHAW, JANET-Journal of a Lady of Quality-Andrews, ed-1923
          (5L7) 5.00
SCHEER, ADM-Germany's High Sea Fleet in World War-NY-
  1934-376p-28 plans-1st ed   (5s1,sl wn) 10.00
SCHEIBERT, CAPT JUSTUS-7 Months in the Rebel States during
  NoAmer War, 1863-Tuscaloosa-1958-166p-frontis-orig hvy wrps-
  maps-Confed Cent Series-ltd to 450c   (5w9) 6.50
SCHEINER, DR J-Treatise on Astronomical Spectroscopy-Bost-
  1894-illus-8vo-cl-482p   (5t0,lacks bkstrp) 4.50
SCHEINFELD, A-Women & Men-1944   (5L7) 4.50
SCHELE DE VERE, M-Americanisms, The English of the New World-
  NY-1872-685p   (5yy0) 12.50
SCHELL, JAS PEERY-In the Ojibway Country-Walhalla-1911-
  photo-map-1st ed-v scarce (5dd6) 20. (5L2) 30.00
SCHELL, W G-Is the Negro a Beast-Moundsville, West Va-1901-
  12mo-illus   (5x2) 37.50
SCHELLEN, DR H-Spectrum Analysis in its application to
  Terrestrial Substances-NY-1872-illus &dec cl-455p (5t0) 7.50
SCHELLING, FELIX E-The English Chronicle Play-NY-1902-
  Macmillan-310p   (5p9) 5.50
--Engl Literature During the Lifetime of Shakespeare-NY-1910
        (5F0,sl wn) 3.50
SCHENCK, MRS E H-History of Fairfield, 1639 to 1818-NY-
  1889, 1905-2 vols   (4t2) 50.00
SCHENCK, EARL-Come unto These Yellow Sands-(1940)-
  BobbsMerrille-372p   (5p7) 6.00
SCHENECTADY, NY-Atlas of City of-Phila-1905-Miller&Mueller-
  folio-cl-maps   (5t2) 25.00
SCHENECTADY, (NY)-Hist of, during the Revolution-1916-304p
        (5t9) 17.50
SCHENKMAN, J-Prentenboek-Amsterdam-(ca 1880)-reprint-
  22 hf pg figures-12mo   (5c8) 8.50
SCHERER, JAS A B-First 49'r Story of Golden Tea Caddy-NY-1925-
  127p-bds-1st ed 7.50 (5dd4) 8.50 (4b3) 6. (5h1,5x5) 7.50
--Lion of the Vigilantes, Wm T Coleman etc-NY &Indnpls-(1939)-
  illus-335p (4n1,dj tn) 13. (5h5) 8. (5x5,dj) 10.00
--Romance of Japan thru the Ages-NY-1928-Dblday Doran-
  illus-Japan Soc   (5p7) 5.00
--31st Star-NY-1942-1st ed   (4a5) 7.00
SCHERER, WM C-Catalogue of Sash Doors, Moldings, etc-Balt-
  1902-185p-illus   (5b8) 12.50
SCHERMAN, DAVID L-Literary Amer, A Chronicle of Amer Writers
  from 1607 to 1932-NY-1932-4to-cl-photos-1st ed (5p5) 12.50
SCHERMAN, HARRY-The Promises Men Live By-NY-1938 (5x7) 5.00
SCHERMAN, KATHARINE-Spring on an Arctic Island-Bost-1956-
  plts-331p (4f9) 5. (5ss1) 5. (4d2) 5.00
SCHERMERHORN, FRANK EARLE-American & French Flags of the
  Revolution-Phila-1948-148p-col illus   (5w4) 8.50
SCHERMERHORN, H A-These Our People-Bost-1949 (5x2) 7.50
SCHERMERHORN, W E-Hist of Burlington from the early European
  arrivals in the Delaware to 1927-1927-388p (5t9) 10.00
SCHEVILL, FERDINAND-Siena, the Story of a Mediaeval Commune-
  NY-1909-8vo-cl-433p-illus-maps-1st ed (5t2) 7.50
SCHEVILL, MARGARET ERWIN-Beautiful on the Earth-SantaFe-
  (1947)-col plts-R8vo-172p   (5dd4) 35.00
--Desert Sheaf-Tucson-1942-Desert Pr-8vo-prntd wrps-1st ed
        (5g2) 2.50
SCHERZER, DR CARL-Travels in the Free States of Central Amer-
  Lond-1857-2 vols-12mo-cl-fldg map (5hh4,f) 32.50
SHIAVO, G-The Italians in Amer Before the Civil War-NY-1934-
  399p-illus   (5t1) 35.00
SCHIDER, FRITZ-An Atlas of Anatomy for Artists-NY-(1947)-116 plts
        (5t4) 5.00
SCHIDLOFF, B-Venus Oceanica-NY-1935-bds&dec cl-411p-
  ltd to 925c, nbrd   (5w5) 15.00

SCHIEL, J H-Journey Through Rocky Mntns & Humboldt Mntns
  to Pac Ocean-U Okla-1959-illus-maps-132p-1st ed (4n1,dj) 10.00
SCHIELDROP, E B-The Highway-Lond-(1939)-248p-illus
        (5xx7,libr stmp) 7.50
SCHIFF, MORTIMER L-Catalogue of Selected Portion of the
  Famous Library of-Lond-1938-Sotheby-illus-2 vols-8vo-
  cl-g.t.   (4c1) 25.00
SCHILLER, FREDK-The Robbers-Lond-1792-8vo-orig bds-
  1st ed in Engl (4m8, cov loose, chip) 15.00
SCHILLER, J-Wm Tell, a Drama-NY-1952-R8vo-illus-buck-1st ed
  Heritage Press   (5p5) 7.50
SCHILLING, BERNARD N-Human Dignity & the Great Victorians-
  NY-1946-8vo-cl-246p   (5t0,dj) 4.00
SCHILLINGER, JOS-The Schillinger System of Musical Composition-
  NY-(1946)-2 vols   (5t4) 20. (5p0) 40.00
SCHILLINGER, WM-Journal of-Columbus-1932-8vo-orig wrps-
  35p-reprintd   (5m6) 10.00
SCHILLINGS, C G-Flashlights in the Jungle-NY-n.d.-782p-
  302 photos   (5ss8) 10.00
--In Wildest Africa-NY &Lond-1907-lg8vo-716p-photos
        (5ss8) 10. (4a6,fox) 12.50
--With Flashlight & Rifle-Lond-1906-2 vols-lg8vo-782p-photos
        (4a6,wn) 20.00
--same-NY-1905-cl-18p, 421p-8vo   (5t0) 6.00
SCHLA GINTWEIT, ROBT VON -Pacific Eisenbahn in Nordamerika-
  Leipzig &NY-1870-frontis-fldg map-fldg table-203p-16mo-
  bds   (4b6,rbnd) 45.00
--Die Prairien des Amerikanischens Westens-Coln &Leipzig-1876-
  Mayer-sm8vo-frontis-orig hf cl -202p   (5L1) 45.00
SCHLARMAN, J H-From Quebec to NewOrl, Ft DeChartres-
  Belleville-1929-569p-illus-1st ed (5bb4,autg) 12.50 (5ee3,f) 17.50
SCHLARMAN, JOS H L-Mexico, Land of Volcanoes-Milwkee-
  (c1950)-Bruce-thk8vo-cl-maps-illus (4a3,5bb4) 12.50
SCHLEGEL, CARL W-German Amer Families in US-NY-1916-
  2 vols-4to-ports-ltd to 200 sets   (5yy6) 62.50
SCHLEGEL, J F W-Neutral Rights-Phila-1801-disbnd (5m2) 10.00
--Upon Visitation of Neutral Vessels under Convoy-Lond-1801-
  187p-disbnd   (5ii2) 9.00
SCHLESINGER, ARTHUR M, JR-The Age of Jackson-Bost-1945-
  577p   (5t7) 7.50
--same-NY-(1946)-Book Find Club-545p (5p7) 3.25
--A History of Amer Life-NY-(1927 to 1935)-5 vols-illus-
  Vol 6, 7, 8, 10, 11, 12   (5w5) 15.00
--A Thousand Days-Houghton-1965-lea-box-ltd to 1000c, nbrd,
  autg   (5F1) 25.00
--The Vital Center-Bost-c1949   (5x7) 4.50
SCHLESINGER, JULIA-Workers in the Vineyard-SanFran-1896-
  illus-288p   (4b3, chip) 10.00
SCHLESINGER, R-Soviet Legal Theory, its Social Background &
  Development-Lond-1945   (5ff4) 10.00
SCHLEY, FRANK-Frank Schley's Amer Partridge & Pheasant
  Shooting etc-Frederick-1877-illus-222p (5j3,5tt6) 25.00
SCHLEY, WINFIELD S-Report...Greely Relief Exped of 1884-
  Wash-1887-(Mis Doc #157)-4t0-75p-2 maps-3 ports-30 plts
        (4a8, sml libr stmps) 15.00
SCHLINK, F J-Meat 3 Times a Day-NY-1948-194p-illus (5c9) 3.50
SCHLOSS, HANNAH W-Short Cuts & Left Overs-NY-(1938)-130p
        (5c0,5c9) 2.50
SCHLUMPF, M W-The Gardeners Cook Book-Houston-1945-
  Tex Garden Clubs-361p   (5c7) 4.50
SCHLUNDT, HERMAN-Radio activity of Thermal Waters of
  Yellowstone Natl Park-Dept of Int-1909-35p-8vo-wrps-plts-
)5g6) 5.00
SCHMALENBACH, WERNER-African Art-NY-(1954)-175p-
  131 illus-16 col plts   (5t4) 10.00
SCHMALIX, ADOLF-Sind Die Roosevelts Juden?-Weimar-1939-
  46p-pamphlet-orig wrps   (5jj3) 25.00
SCHMALZ, JOHN BARNES-Nuggets from King Solomon's Mines-
  (Bost)-(1908)-suede bndg-g.t.-12mo (5tt5) 10. (5j5) 15.00
SCHMAUK, THEODORE E-Old Salem in Lebanon-Lebanon-1898-
  1st ed-frontis & dec   (5jj3) 25.00
SCHMECKEBIER, L F-Catalogue & Index of the Publications of
  the Hayden, King, Powell & Wheeler Surveys-Wash-1904-
  208p   (5j4) 25.00
SCHMEDDING, JOS-Cowboy & Indian Trader-1951-364p-illus-
  1st ed-scarce (5r1,f) 35. (5F5) 10.00
SCHMELTZER, KURT-The Long Arctic Night-NY-1952-illus
        (5ss1) 3.00
SCHMIDT, CARL F-Cobblestone Architecture-n.p.-1944-59p-
  illus   (5t4,autg) 10.50
SCHMIDT, ED-Gen Geo Crook His autobiography-U Okla Pr-
  1946-326p-1st ed   (5a9,dj) 12.50

USED BOOK PRICE GUIDE

SCHMIDT, EDMOND J P-Catalogue of Franciscan Missionaries in Texas, 1528 to 1859-Austin-1901-16p-nbrd, autg-wrps (4j6) 22.50

SCHMIDT, HUBERT G-Lesser Crossroads-NewBrunswick-1948-402p (5h9) 6.50

SCHMIDT, JULIUS-The Stone Sculptures of Copan & Quirigua-NY-1883-thin atlas folio-20 plts-qtr lea (5r7) 85.00

SCHMIDT, K P-Amphibians & Land Reptiles of Porto Rico, With a List from Virgin Islands, Vol 10, Part 1-NY-1928-wrps-160p-plts-8vo (4p6) 15.00

SCHMIDT, MINNA M-400 Outstanding Women of the World & Costumology of their time-Chig-1933-583p-illus (5t4) 10.00

SCHMIDT, ROBT-Das Porzellan Als Kunstwerk Und Kulturspiegel-Munich-1925-illus-261p-8vo (5ww3) 15.00

SCHMITHALS, HANS-Die Alpen, Das Gesampgebiet in Bildern-Berlin-(1930)-336p-illus-fldg map-cl (5d7) 10.00

SCHMITT, JO ANN-Fighting Editors-SanAnt-1948-8vo-cl-227p-illus-1st ed (5g2, dj) 6.00

SCHMITT, JARTIN, F-Cattle Drivers of David Shirk from Tex to the Idaho Mines, 1871 & 1873-Portl-1956-148p-ltd to 750c (5n4) 17.50

--Fighting Indians of the West-1948-Scribner's Sons-4to-270 illus-1st ed (5jj7) 20. (5yy7) 25. (5xx5,5x5) 30.00

--Gen'l Geo Crook, His Autobiog-Norman-1946-1st ed (5bb4) 17.50

--The Settler's West-NY-1955-Scribner's Sons-4to-1st ed (5m9,5dd5) 10. (5x5,dj) 12.50

SCHMOE, F W-Our Greatest Mountain, a Handbook for Mt Rainier Natl Park-NY-1925-Putnams-366p-illus-cl (5s4) 10.00

SCHMUCKER, SAM'L M-History of Civil War in US-Phila-(1865)-1021p-illus-lea (5xx7, cov loose) 20. (5h0, rbkd) 25.00

SCHNACK, FERDINAND J H-The Aloha Guide, Standard Handbook-(n.p.)-(1915)-206p plus index&ads-maps-16mo-orig stiff wrps-1st ed (5x5) 7.50

SCHNECK, B-The Burning of Chambersburg, Pa-1864-76p (5j6) 4.00

--Diezerstorung der Stadt Chambersburg-Phila-1865-41p, (7)-map (5w9, fox) 6.00

SCHNEIDER, CARL E-The German Church on Amer Frontier-StL-1939 (5x5) 35.00

SCHNEIDER, G-Book of Choice Ferns for Garden, Conservatory & Stove-Lond-1892 to 94-orig dec cl-g.e.-20 col plts-3 vols-1st ed (5z9, sl fox, vg) 45.00

SCHNEIDER, MANFRED-Goya, A Portrait of the Artist as a Man-NY-1936-Knight-337p-illus (5p7) 5.00

SCHNEUR & CANFIELD-Illustrated & Descriptive Guide Book of Mauch Chunk etc-Athens, Pa-1874-8vo-orig wrps-illus-72p-1st ed (5m6) 8.50

SCHNITZLER, A-Casanova's Homecoming-Lond-1922-175p-bds-Golden Cockerel Pr-ltd to 250c (5ii2) 9.50

--same-Lond-n.d.-Brent-175p (5x0) 3.50

--Couples-Paris-1927-Titus-8vo-limp white cl-10 illus-1st ed in Engl (so stated)-ltd to 500c (5ee9, sp tn) 37.50

--Fraulein Else-Lond-1928-Constable-sq8vo-bds-vel sp-col plts-Engl text (5t8) 10.00

--Hands Around-NY-1920-priv prntd-ltd to 1475c (5x0) 5.00

--same-NY-1929-223p-bds-cl-for Members of Schnitzler Soc-ltd to 1475c, nbrd (5w9, sl wn) 8.50

SCHOBERLIN, MELVIN-From Candles to Footlights-1941-Old West Pub-1st ed (5x5) 15.00

SCHOELLER, MAX-Mitteilungen Uber Meine Reise Nach Aquatorial Ost Afrika und Uganda, 1896 to 97-Berlin-1904-Dietrich Reimer-2 vols-photos-suede-g.e. (4t5) 75.00

SCHOELLKOPF, ANNA-Don Jose de San Martin-NY-1924-12mo-cl-illus (5h4) 6.00

SCHOEN, HAROLD, comp-Monuments Erected by State of Texas..-Austin-1938-illus-4to-214p (4n8, spot) 15.00

SCHOEN, JAS FREDK-Vocabulary of Haussa Language-Lond-1843-5&29&190p-hf lea (5c6, f) 50.00

SCHOENBERG, WILFRED P-Jesuit Mission Presses in Pacific NW-(Portland, Oreg)-1957-Champoeg Pr-ltd to 804c-orig imprint laid in (4t8, mint, 5F5) 15. (5x5, 4g2) 20.00

SCHOENMANN, L R- oil Survey of Bowie County, Tex-Wash-1921-lf gldg col map-wrps (4a5) 4.00

SCHOENRICH, OTTO-The Legacy of Christopher Columbus-Glendale-1949-2 vols-7 tabls(3 pkt)-ltd to 150 sets-30 plts & facs-scarce (5dd5, f) 45.00

SCHOETTLE, EDWIN, ed-Sailing Craft-NY-1937-786p-photos (5s1, fade) 11.00

--same-1942 (5s1, ex-libr) 9.50

--same-n.p.-1946-illus-sm4to-786p-cl (5t2) 6.00

SCHOFER, H M-Johan Georg Schofer Family History, 1832-1934-167p (5t9) 7.50

SCHOFF, W H-Atlantic Deeper Waterways Assn, 5th Annual Convention, New London, Sept 1912, Report of Proceedings-Phila-1912-8vo-407p (5ss5, ex-libr) 8.50

--Desc of Jacob Schoff-1910-163p (4t2) 6.00

--Ship "Tyre", symbol of fate of conquerors-1920 (5L7) 4.50

SCHOFIELD, J M-Freedmen's Affairs in Kentucky & Tennessee-Wash-1868-HED 329-51p (5j6) 5.00

SCHOFIELD, JOHN M-46 Years in Army-NY-1897-port-576p (5xx7) 17.50 (4t8, rprd) 20.00

SCHOFIELD, R J-Home Mechanic & Complete Self instructor in Carpentry, Painting, etc-1897-buck (5L7, ex-libr) 7.50

SCHOFIELD, W J-Prospector's Manual for discovery of quartz & placer indications of gold & silver mines-Bost-1875-16mo-wrps (5g8) 15.00

SCHOHARIE COUNTY DIRECTORY 1899-185p-fldg map (5ff2) 12.00

SCHOHARIE-Records of StPaul's Evangelical Lutheran Ch in Schoharie, Schoharie Co, NY-1915-84p-NY Gen & Biog Soc (5t9, amateur bndg) 45.00

SCHOLDERER, VICTOR-Greek Printing Types-Lond-1927-folio-cl&bds-ltd to 650c (5d5, dj) 37.50

SCHOLES, FRANCE V-Maya Chontal Indians of Acalan Tixchel-Carnegie Insti of Wash-1948-sm4to-565p-illus-1st ed-wrps (pub 560) (5F5) 15.00

SCHOLES, FRANCE V-Troublous Times in NewMex, 1659 to 1670-Univ of NM-1942-Vol 11-8vo-276p-wrps (5F5) 12.50

SCHOLL, JOHN W-Scholl Shull Genealogy, the Colonial Branches-NY-(1930)-Grafton-lg8vo-cl-plts-879p (5m2) 20. (5x5) 32.50

SCHOLTE, LEONORA R-A Stranger in a Strange Land-GrandRpds-1942-reprint-120p-frontis (5L2, autg) 5.00

SCHOMBERG, R C F-Between the Oxus & the Indus-Lond-1935-MartinHopkinson-275p-illus-cl (5d7) 7.50

SCHON, KARL-Biographical Dictionary, US Navy-NY-(1964)-280p-48 ports (5s1, dj) 9.00

SCHOOL DESEGREGATION-The 1st 6 Years-Atlanta-1960-Southern Regional Council-25p-wrps-fld out map (5x2) 6.00

SCHOOL FOR SCANDAL-Dublin-(1781)-J Ewling-8vo-rare-badly printed-(not 1st, which was 1780)-bnd wi 3 other plays-qtr calf (5i4, rprd) 125.00

SCHOOL FOR SCANDAL-by R B Sheridan-Oxf-1934-Limited Editions Club Publ-ltd to 1500c, nbrd (5F1, vf) 30.00

SCHOOL OF FASHION-A Novel-NY-1829-JJHarper-2 vols-orig bds-1st ed (5ss9, fox) 25.00

SCHOOL OF MINES AND OF SCI-Records of, Applied to Arts-Vol 1, Part 1-Lond-1852 (5j2) 20.00

SCHOOLCRAFT, HENRY R-A discourse delivered on anniv of Historical Soc of Mich, Jun 4, 1830-Detroit-1830-Whitney-8vo-disbnd-1st ed-v scarce (5i0) 110.00

--Incentives to the Study of Ancient Period of Amer History-NY-1847-orig wrps-38p (4F6, f) 8.50 (4c1) 15.00

--Indian in His Wigwam-Buffalo-1848 (5kk6) 35.00

--Info Respecting History, Condition&Prospects of Indian Tribes of the US-Phila-1853 to 57-massive folio-dec cl-maps-plts(some handcol)-6 vols-rare (4a5, autgs) 900. (4k5, bkstrp wn) 950. (4k5, f) 1,100.00

--Journal of a Tour into the Interior of Missouri & Ark-Lond-1821-102p-map-lea-1st ed-v rare (5s9, 5n9, box) 75.00

--same-VanBuren-1955-reprint edited by Hugh Park-cl-191p(5h0) 4.00

--Myth of Hiawatha, & other Oral Legends-Phila-1856-343p (4b4) 37.50 (4k5, f) 25.00

--Narr of Exped Thru Upper Mississippi to Itaska Lake-NY-1834-Harper-cl-papr labl-maps-1st ed (4j4, ex-libr) 55. (5n9, 4k5, vf) 125.00

--Narr Journal of Travels From Detroit NW Thru Great Chain of Amer Lakes...1820-Albany-1821-Hasford-8vo-fldg map-7 plts-1st ed (5s9, rbnd calf) 125. (4c4, map rprd, bndg wn) 110. (5m3, libr stmp) 100.00

--Notes on Iroquois-1846-285p-illus (5zz0, rprd) 45. (5r7) 40.00

--Notes on the Iroquois-Albany-1847-cl-2 col ports-enlrgd ed-498p plus pg (4k5, vf) 75.00

--Personal memoirs of a residence of 30 years wi Indian tribes of Amer frontiers-Phila-1851-cl (5g8, wn, lacks port) 30.00

--Scenes & Adventures in the semi Alpine region of Ozark Mntns of Missouri & Ark-Phila-1853-256+36p (5n4) 27.50

--A View of the Lead Mines of Missouri-NY-1819-294p plus index-3 plts (5t3, rbnd) 45. (5n9, sl stnd) 100.00

SCHOOLING, SIR W-Gov & Co of Adventurers of England Trading into Hudson's Bay during 250 Yrs-Lond-1920-plts-fldg map-folio-129p-heavy wrps (5dd7) 12. (5x5) 20. (5dd4) 16.50

SCHOOLMASTER IN COMEDY & SATIRE-for teachers-NY, Cinn, &Chig-(c1894)-Amer Book Co-592p-dec cl (5p1, wn) 7.50

SCHOOLMISTRESS, THE-Dublin-1824-12mo-roan-176p-frontis (5so) 6.50

SCHOONMAKER,EDWIN D-Our Genial Enemy France-NY-1932
(5x7)   4.50

SCHOONMAKER,FRANK-Amer Wines-NY-(1941)-illus-312p
(5w1) 8.50   (5g9)   7.50

--The Complete Wine Book-NY-1934-315p (5w1) 6.50 (5g9)   7.50

--Dictionary of Wines-NY-(1951)-120p-illus
(5w1)   3.00

SCHOONOVER,T J-Life & Times Gen John A Sutter-Sacramento-
1907-illus-315p-rev&enlrgd ed (4n1,cor rub) 8.50 (5bb4,sl wn)15.00

SCHOOR,G-Willie Mays-NY-1960   (5x2)   7.50

SCHOPF,JOH DAVID-Materia Medica Americana potissimum
regni vegetabilis-Erlangen-1787-Joh J Palm-170p-8vo-
white bds-1st ed-rare   (5L1,vg) 2,250.00

--Reise durch die mittlern und Sudlichen Vereinigten
nordamerikanischen Staaten nach Ost Florida und dem
Bahama Inseln...in den jahren 1783 und 1784-Erlangen-
1788-2 vols-fldg map-8vo-orig bds-1st ed (5L1,mismatchd) 385.00

SCHORER,MARK-Wm Blake,The Politics of Vision-NY-1946-
8vo-cl-524p-illus-1st ed   (5d5,dj)   15.00

SCHOTTER,H W-The Growth & Development of the Penna RR Co-
(Phila)-1927-518p-illus-map   (5w0)   10.00

SCHOTTMULLER,FRIDA-Furniture & Interior Decoration of the
Italian Renaissance-NY-1921-Brentano's-t4to-246p (5x0)   20.00

--same-NY-(1930)-4to-250p-590 illus-2nd ed rev   (5xx7)   12.50

SCHOULER,JAS-Americans of 1776-NY-1906-317p   (5t7)   10.00

--History of the USA,Vol 6,History of Civil War,1861 to 65-
1899   (5L7)   3.50

SCHOYER,WILL-Scaife Co & the Scaife Family-Pittsburgh-1952-
181p-illus   (5y2)   5.00

SCHRABISCH,MAX-Archaeology of Delaware Riv Valley Betw
Hancock & Dingman's Ferry-Harrisburg-1930-illus-181p-
volume 1   (5h9,5w0) 6.50   (4m4)   12.50

SCHRADER,F C-Economic Geology of the Independence
Quadrangle,Kans-Wash-1906-74p-plts-fldg map-unbnd-
USGS Bull 296   (5ss1)   4.50

--Geology & Mineral Resources of Portion of Copper Rivr Dist,
Alaska-1901-4to-sewn-94p-plt   (5L7,lacks bk cov)   10.00

--Prelim Report on Cape Nome Gold Region,Alaska-Wash-1900-
plts-fldg maps-56p   (4a5)   18.50

SCHRANTZ,WARD L-JasperCo,Missouri,in Civil War-Carthage,Mo-
1923-250p plus index-illus-map-1st ed-scarce
(5hh3) 32.50   (5bb4)   12.50

SCHREIBEIS,CHAS D-Pioneer Education in the Pac NW,1789 to
1847-Portl-n.d.-illus   (4m2)   6.50

SCHREIDER,HELEN-20,000 Miles South-NY-1957-287p-photos
(5s1,dj)   4.00

SCHREINER,GEO ABEL-From Berlin to Bagdad-NY-c1918(5x7)   4.50

SCHREINER,OLIVE -Dreams-(East Aurora,Roycroft,1901)-4to-
hf suede-85p-dec-g.t.   (5j5)   15.00

--same-Bost-1915-Little,Brown-lea-163p   (4t5,fox)   5.00

--From Man to Man-NY-1927-Harper-463p   (4t5)   5.00

--South African Question-Chig-1899-Sergel-123p   (4t5)   13.00

--Woman & Labor-NY-c1911-299p   (5w0)   5.00

SCHREPFER,LUKE-Pioneer Monks in Nova Scotia-NY-1947-ports-
288p   (4d8,autg)   8.50

SCHERER,JAS A-Thirty First Star-NY-(1942)-illus-8vo (4g6,dj) 10.00

SCHREYVOGEL,CHAS-My Bunkie & Others-NY-1909-obl folio-
36 plts   (5t1,vf) 350. (5d6,loose) 175. (5h5,sl crack,rub) 300.00

SCHRIBER,FRITZ-The Complete Carriage & Wagon Painter-NY-
1910-12mo-orig cl-177p   (5t2,vf)   12.50

SCHRIEKE,B,ed-The Effect of Western Influence on Native
Civlisations in Malay Archipelago-Batavia-1919-247p (5x9)   7.50

SCHRIFTGIESSER,KARL-Farmer from Merna-NY-1955-243p-
illus   (4b8,5y2) 5. (5tt5)   6.00

--Lobbyists,art & business of influencing lawmakers-1951
(5q8,dj) 6. (5L7,ex-libr)   6.50

--Oscar of the Waldorf-Phila-(1943)-248p-plts (5p5) 10. (5g9)   6.00

SCHROEDER,A T-Origin of Book of Mormon..Spaulding's-
SaltLkCty-1901-wrps-56p   (4t3)   17.50

SCHROEDER,EUG-Quer Durch Amerika-Leipzig-1906-Wanderer
Verlag-illus-fldg map-pict cl-226p   (4n8)   10.00

SCHROEDER,J F-Life & Times of Washington-NY-(1857)-illus-
4to-2 vols   (5yy0)   12.50

SCHROEDER,S-Half Century Naval Service-NY-1922-444p-
illus-g.stmpd cov   (5s1)   6.00

SCHROEDER,SEATON-Fall of Maximilian's Empire as Seen from
a US Gun Boat-NY-1887-port-12mo-1st ed (4g6,ex-libr)   10.00

SCHROEDER,THEODORE-Free Speech for Radicals-Riverside,Conn-
1916-bds-enlrgd ed   (5yy6,hng split)   12.50

--"Obscene" Literature & Constitutional Law-NY-1911
(4a1,bndg wn,crack)   12.50

SCHROEDER-LOSSING-Life & Times of Washington-Albany-
1903-2 vols-rev,enlrgd   (5t7)   20.00

SCHUBERT,PAUL-Sea Power in Conflict-NY-1942   (5c1)   8.50

SCHUCKERS,J W-The Life & Public Services of Salmon Portland
Chase-NY-(1874)-684p-port-lea&bds-1st ed
(5ss5,ex-libr) 12.50   (5t0)   7.50

SCHUETTE,MARIE-Perser Teppkhe-Leipzig-(1935)-62p-bds-
17 col illus   (5n7)   4.50

SCHULBERG,BUDD-The Harder They Fall-NY-1947-RandomHse-
1st ed   (5F1,f) 4.50   (5ss9,dj)   7.50

SCHULL,JOS-100 Yrs of Banking in Canada,Tor Dominion Bank-
Tor-(1958)-illus-222p   (4d2)   6.50

SCHULLIAN,D M-A Catalogue of Incunabula & Manuscripts in
the Army Medical Library-NY-n.d.-361p   (5j4)   12.50

SCHULMAN,HARRY MANUEL-Slums of NY-NY-1938-394p(5u3) 8.50

SCHULTE,PAUL-The Flying Priest Over the Arctic-NY-1940-
267p-illus   (5k2)   7.50

SCHULTEIS,HERMAN J-Report on European Immigration to the US-
Wash-1893-61p-wrps   (5q8)   7.50

SCHULTZ,A H-Studies on Growth of Gorilla & of other Higher
Primates-Pittsbgh-1927-wrps-86p-8 plts-folio-scarce(4p5)   10.00

SCHULTZ,CHRISTIAN-Travels on Inland Voyage thru NY,Penn,
Virg,O,etc-NY-1810-Isaac Riley-   port-2 plts-5 maps-
calf - 2 vol in 1   (5yy3,wn,libr discard)   100.00

--same-NY-1810-Riley-hf mor-2 vols-port-plate-5 fldg maps-
1st ed   (5n9)   200.00

SCHULTZ,GERARD-Early History of the Northern Ozarks-
JeffersonCty,Mo-(1937)-192p-1 illus-1st ed   (5L0)   12.50

SCHULTZ,JAS W-Bird Woman-Bost-1918-236p-plts-1st ed-scarce
(5dd4,spot)   25.00

--Blackfeet Tales of Glacier Natl Park-Bost-1916-242p-1st ed
(5r8,f)   15.00

--My Life as an Indian-HoughtonMiff-(1907)-photos
(5x5) 12.50   (4m9)   17.50

--same-Bost-1914-8vo-cl   (5h4,pres)   15.00

--On the Warpath-Bost-(1914)-245p-illus by Geo Varian-reprnt
(5L2)   4.00

--Plumed Snake Medicine-Bost-1924-245p-illus by Varian-
1st ed   (5L2,dj)   12.50

--Rising Wolf,the White Blackfoot-Bost-1919-253p-illus by
Schoonover-1 photo-1st ed (5m9) 10. (5L2,lt stn) 6. (5L2)   8.50

--Sahtaki & I-Bost-1924-col frontis-305p-1st ed   (5bb4)   15.00

--The Sun God's Children-Bost-1930-255p-frontis-ports-scarce-
1st ed   (5L2)   15.00

--Sun Woman,a novel-Bost-1926   (5yy7,dj) 15.   (5xx5)   21.00

--William Jackson,Indian Scout-Bost-1926-illus-201p-1st ed-
scarce   (5yy7)   25.00

--With the Indians in the Rockies-NY-(1912)(5L2,5x5,lacks fly) 6.00

--same-Bost-1925-cl-252,(1)p   (5h1)   8.50

SCHULTZ,JOHN S-New & Complete County Map of all RRs in
US & Canada in Operation & Progress-NY-1857-col fldg map
in folder   (4a5)   25.00

SCHULTZ,L P-Fishes of the Marshall & Marianas Islands-Wash-
1953 to 1966-3 vols-plts-(Vol 1 & 2 v scarce)   (4g5)   50.00

SCHULTZ,MR MAURICE-a German tale-Lond-1796-2 vols for
Vernor & Hood-12mo-qtr calf-v rare   (5xx6)   150.00

SCHULTZ,THEODORE W-Redirecting Farm Policy-NY-1943-bds
(5q8)   4.50

SCHULZ,ELLEN-Cactus Culture-NY-1947-rev ed   (5a8)   4.00

--500 Wild Flowers of San Antonio & Vicinity-SanAnt-1922-
priv prnt   (4a5) 25.   (4c7)   27.50

--Texas Cacti-SanAnt-1930-181p   (4a5,mint)   17.50

--Texas Wild Flowers-Chig-(1928)-505p-cl   (5h7)   10.00

SCHULZ,H C-French Illuminated Manuscripts-wi orig lf-
SanFran-1958-ltd to 200c-Grabhorn Pr   (5x5)   60.00

SCHULZE,J L-Reports of United German Evan Lutheran
Congregations in NoAmer,esp in Pa-Phila-1880-2 vols(5yy0) 17.50

SCHUMAN,FREDK L-Soviet Politics-NY-1948   (5x7)   5.00

SCHURE,EDOUARD-The Great Initiates-Phila-n.d.-port-756p-
2 vols-8vo-cl   (5p5,dj)   15.00

SCHURICHT,HERRMANN-History of German Element in Virginia-
Balt-1898,1900-2 vols in 1- port   (5jj3,rbnd)   35.00

SCHURZ,CARL-Abraham Lincoln,an Essay-Bost-(1899)-91p-
wrps   (5h1)   3.50

--Lebenserinnerungen-Berlin-1906 to 12-Reimer-3 vols-8vo-
orig cl   (5L1)   20.00

--Life of Henry Clay-1899-Houghton-2 vols
(4p8) 7.50   (5d2,mor,g.sp)   15.00

--Reminiscences-NY-1907-8vo-3 vols-1st ed   (5ss5)   22.50

--Reminiscences-NY-1908-3 vols-illus   (5jj3)   25.00

--Speeches of Carl Schurz-Phila-1865   (5x2)   40.00

SCHURZ,WM LYTLE-The Manila Galleon-NY-1939-maps-
1st ed-scarce   (5s1,ex-libr,wn) 25.   (5dd6)   50.00

SCHUSSLER,EDITH M-Doctors, Dynamite & Dogs-Caldwell-1956-189p-illus-1st ed (5L0,dj) 5.00

SCHUSSLER, HERMANN-Locality of the Broderick Terry duel on Sept 13,1859-SanFran-1916-JnHenry Nash-8vo-orig wrps-frontis-2 maps-1st ed (5i9) 7.50

SCHUSTER,CLAUD-Men, Women & Mountains, Days in the Alps & Pyrenees-Lond-1931-143p-illus-cl (5d7) 7.50

--Peaks & Pleasant Pastures-Oxf-1911-Clarendon Pr-227p (5d7) 6.00

SCHUSTER, LORD-Postscript to Adventure-Lond-(1950)-illus-cl-214p (5d7) 4.50

SCHUSTER,M LINCOLN-Eyes on the World-NY-1935-4to-1st ed (4a1) 10.00

--Treasury of the World's Great Letters-NY-1940-563p (5t7) 10.00

SCHUTZE'S JAHRBUCH FUR TEXAS UND VOLKS KALENDER FUR 1884-Austin-(1883)-Albert Schutze-200p-German text (5yy3, lacks back wrp) 15.00

SCHUTZENBERGER,P-Les Fermentations-Paris-1889-278p,(32)-illus (5w1) 8.50

SCHUYLER & BROWN CO, ILL-Combined Hist of-Phila-1882-412p-lea bkd bds-rare (5h1) 50.00

SCHUYLER,G S-Black & Conservative-NY-1966 (5x2) 4.50

--Black No More-NY-1931 (5x2,sl cov stns) 35.00

SCHUYLER,GEO W-Colonial NY-NY-1885-2 vols-8vo-1st ed (5ss5) 15.00

SCHUYLER,MONTGOMERY-Amer Architecture Studies-NY-1892-illus-8vo-suede-211p (5t2,libr mrks) 7.50

--Westward the Course of Empire-NY-1906-198p-illus-1st ed (5L2,dj) 3.00

SCHUYLER,PHILIPPA-Who Killed the Congo-NY-1962-illus (5x2) 3.50

SCHUYLKILL FISHING CO-of State in Schuylkill,a History of-Phila-1889-3/4 lea-raised bands-4to-446p-illus-g.t. (5h9) 36.00

SCHUYLKILL RIVER DESILTING PROJECT-Final Rept-n.p.-1951 (5x7) 6.50

SCHWAB,GEO-Tribes of Liberian Hinterland:Peabody Museum Exped-Cambr-1947-19&526p-44p glos-83 plts-pkt map (5c6,ex-libr,f) 42.50

SCHWACOFER,MARY A-Life & Surprising Adventures of Robinson Crusoe...words of One Syllable-NY-c1882-Cassell-sq8vo-dec cl-221p-8 plts-g.t. (5aa2) 7.50

SCHWAGERMAN,WM-Biography of an Inventor-Cranston-1941-photos-priv prntd-48p-wrps-ltd to 50c (5u0) 100.00

SCHWANTES,ROBT S-Japanese & Americans-NY-1955-380p (5t4) 5.00

SCHWARTZ,DELMORE-Vaudeville for a Princess & Other Poems-NY-(1950)-12mo-bds-1st ed (5ss7,vf,dj) 15.00

SCHWARTZ,H STANLEY-Alexandre Dumas,fils,Dramatist-NY-Univ Pr-1927-216p-8vo-cl-1st ed (5t0) 6.50

SCHWARZ,G FREDK-Forest Trees & Forest Scenery-NY-1901-183p-illus (5s7) 5.00

SCHWARZE,EDMUND-History of Moravian Missions Among Southern Indian Tribes of the US-Bethlehem,Pa-1923-Vol 1, Spec Series-324p-illus (5bb4) 15.00

SCHWATKA,FREDK-Alaska's Great River-NY-(1885)-360p-illus-maps-scarce (5ss1) 12.50

--Along Alaska's Great River-NY-(1885)-360p-illus-3 maps(2 fldg)-8vo-cl-g. (5i3,f) 12.50

--Nimrod in the North-NY-1885-198p-illus (5ss1,crack) 12.50

--Report of a Military Reconnaissance in Alaska,Made in 1883-Wash-1885-Sen Ex Doc #2-20 lg fldg maps-illus-3/4 mor (5r7,ex-libr,rprd) 25.00

--Summer in Alaska-StL,Mo-1894-418p (5r7) 15. (4m2) 12.50 (5ss1) 10.00

--Wonderland,or,Alaska & the Inland Passage-StPaul-1886-map&illus-pict wrps (5g3,sl tn) 7.00

SCHWEITZER,ALBERT-Animal World of...-Bost-1950-Beacon Pr-photos-207p (4t5) 7.50

--Forest Hospital at Lambarene-NY-1931-191p-plts (5c6,vg) 8.75

--More from Primeval Forest-Lond-1931-14&173p-16 plts-1st ed in Engl (5c6) 9.50

--On Edge of Primeval Forest-Lond-1922-180p-16 plts (5c6,underline) 5.75

--same-Lond-1953-Adam&Chas Black-128p (4t5,dj) 4.50

--Out of My Life & Thought-NY-1949-HenryHolt-274p-2nd prntg (4t5,dj) 4.00

--Paul & His Interpreters-Lond-1912-tall 8vo-1st Engl ed (5r9) 17.50

SCHWEITZER,S C-Preparation Manual for Accident Cases-NY-1935 (5ff4) 7.50

SCHWENDENER,NORMA-Legends & Dances of Old Mexico-NY-(1933)-8vo-cl-illus-111p (5F5) 6.00

SCHWENKFELDER-Genealogical Records of Desc of-1879-339p (4t2) 15.00

SCHWENFELDER FAMILY-Genealogical Record of,Saxony to Pa-2 vols in 1-1923-1752p (5t9) 25.00

SCIDMORE,ELIZ R-Appleton's Guide Book to Alaska & NW Coast-NY-1893-plts-fldg maps-156p-1st ed (5zz8) 20.00

--same-NY-1899-167p-plts-fldg map (5s6) 15.00

--Alaska,Its Southern Coast & The Sitkan Archipelago-Bost-(1885)-8vo-cl-333p-map-illus (5t2) 7.50

--Java,The Garden Of The East-NY-1899-Century-339p (5x9) 3.00

SCIENCE REVIVED-or Vision of Alfred-Lond-1802-2 plts-lg4to-3/4 lea (4a2,scuff) 9.50

SCIRMACHER,KAETHE-The Modern Woman's Rights Movement-NY-1912-8vo-cl-1st ed (5p5) 12.50

SCITUATE-Old Scituate-pub by D A R-1921-292p-illus (5e8) 14.75

SCLATER,P L-On The Curassows Now-wi supplement-Lond-1875, 1879-cl-4to-2 vols in 1-21 col plts-scarce (4n5,vf) 125.00

SCOBEE,BARRY-The Steer Branded Murder-(Houston,1952)-12mo-56p-illus-wrps-ltd to 350c (5g0,5dd4) 10.00

SCOBEY,F E-The Biographical Annals of Ohio,1902,1903-(n.p.-n.d.)-lg8vo-cl-illus-916p (5j5,ex-libr) 20.00

SCOFIELD,CHAS J-A Subtle Adversary, Tale of Callitso Co-Cinn-1891-640p-cl-Std Publ Co imprnt-prior printing of Wright (4823)?-(no mention of "First Thousand" in t.p.)-rare (5h7,pres) 20.00

--Hist Encyclo of Illinois & Hist of Hancock Co-Chig-1921-2 vols-hf lea (5h7,cov dmpstn) 45.00

SCOLLARD,CLINTON-Pictures in Song-NY-1884-12mo-cl-1st ed of auth's 1st book (5gg6) 10.00

SCORESBY,WM-Account of the Arctic Regions-Edinb-1820-plts-hf calf-2 vols (4d0) 85.00

SCOTT,A C-The Kabuki Theatre of Japan-Lond-(1956) (4t4) 4.50

SCOTT,ANGELO C-The Story of OklaCty-OklaCty-(1939) illus (5a8,5r7) 10.00

SCOTT,ALLEN M-Chronicles of Great Rebellion-Cinn-1864-344p-cl (5ff7) 10.00

SCOTT, MRS ANNA B-Mrs Scott's NoAmer Seasonal Cook Book-Phila-1921-252p-4to-oilcloth bndng (5c0) 6.50

SCOTT,C-Romance of Highways of Calif-Glendale-1946-Griffin Patterson-photos-320p (4n1,dj) 4.00

SCOTT,C A-Romanism & the Gospel-1946 (5L7) 3.50

SCOTT,CAPT C ROCHFORT-Excursions in the mountains of Ronda & Granada-Lond-1838-Colburn-2 vols-8vo-orig bds-papr labls-frontis-1st ed (5i8,vf) 25.00

SCOTT,C W A-Scott's Book-Lond-1934 (5x7) 10.00

SCOTT,CLEO M-Antique Porcelain Digest-Newport,Mon England-(1961)-4to-cl-illus(some col)-200p-1st ed (5t2,f) 17.50

SCOTT,CYRIL-Music,Its Secret Influence Throughout the Ages-Phila-n.d.-221p (5p0) 5.00

SCOTT,D C,ed-Poems of Archibald Lampman-Tor-1900-2nd ed-buck (4b9,rbnd) 12.00

SCOTT,DAN'L-History of Early Settlement of Highland Co,Ohio-Hillsborough-1890-192p-rare (5jj9,rbnd) 35.00

SCOTT,DAVID-70 Fathoms Deep-Lond-1931-42 photos (5c1) 9.50

SCOTT,DAVID C-Dictionary of Nyanja Language-Lond-1957-8&612p (5c6,f) 12.50

SCOTT,(DRED) vs. SANFORD(F.A.)-Report of Decision of Supreme Court in Case of,-Wash-1857-239p-Howes B-367 (5g1,vg) 22.50

SCOTT,DUNCAN CAMPBELL-The Magic House & other poems-Ottawa-1893-Durie-12mo-cl-1st ed (5ss3,pres) 35.00

SCOTT,E-Background in Tennessee-NY-1937-1st ed (5x2,dj) 7.50

SCOTT,EBEN G-Reconstruction During the Civil War-Bost-1895-1st ed-432p (5i3) 15.00

SCOTT,EDW B-The Saga of Lake Tahoe-(Crystal Bay,Lake Tahoe, 1957)-R8vo-634p-fldg map-photos (5xx5) 18.50

SCOTT,ELIZA JANE PULSE-Memorial Sketches-n.p.-n.d.-(ca 1900?)-294p-cl (5jj9) 12.50

SCOTT,EMMETT J-Amer Negro in the World War-n.p.(Wash)-(1919)-dec lg8vo-608p-illus (4t7) 15.00

--Booker T Washington,Builder of a Civilization-NY-1916-illus-331p-1st ed (5x2,4m2) 10.00

SCOTT,FLORENCE D-Montrose as It Was Recorded,Told about, & Lives-n.p.-1959-4to-illus (5r7,autg) 7.50

SCOTT,FLORENCE JOHNSON-Historical Heritage of Lower Rio Grande-SanAnt-1937 (4c7) 40.00

SCOTT,FRANK J-Art of Beautifying Suburban Home Grounds of Small Extent-NY-1881-illus-618p (5q0) 7.50

SCOTT,FREDK GEO-In the battle silences-Lond-1917-Constable-orig wrps-3rd impres (5m2,wn,als) 6.00

SCOTT,G G-Essay on History of English Church Architecture-Lond-1881-37 plts-cl (4a2,rub) 10.00

SCOTT,GEN-Life of-n.p.-n.d.-(Colum?-1852)-30p-sewed as issued-For sale by Scott & Bascom-rare (5h1,spot) 12.50

SCOTT,GENIO C-Fishing in Amer Waters-NY-1869-484p-illus (5ii2) 7.50 (5ee3) 10.00

SCOTT,GENIO C (continued)
--same-NY-1873-484p-illus   (5t7)   10.00

SCOTT,GEOFFREY-A Box of Paints-Lond-1923-Bookman's Journal-
1st ed-ltd to 1000c   (5ss3,dj)   15.00
--The Portrait of Zelide-Lond-1925-Constable-cl-1st ed
      (5ss3,fade)   10.00

SCOTT,GEO-Tamarack Farm-NY-(1903)-8vo-2 illus-1st ed
      (5ss5,pres)   10.00

SCOTT,GEO W-Black Hills Story-FtCollins,Colo-(1953)-wrps-
97p-1st ed   (5L2)   8.50

SCOTT,H L-Some Memories of a Soldier-NY-(1928)-illus-673p-
1st ed-scarce   (4i7)   18.00

SCOTT,H W-Courts of State of NY-NY-1909   (5r4)   12.50

SCOTT,HARVEY M-History of the Oregon Country-Cambr-1924-
6 vols-photos-maps-ltd to 500 sets   (5s4,autg)   135.00

SCOTT,HENRY T-Autograph Collecting-Lond-1894-415p (5x0)   7.50

SCOTT,HOWARD-Intro to Technocracy-NY-(1933)-JnDay-8vo-
prntd bds-61p   (5j5)   6.00

SCOTT,HUGH-Some Memories of a Soldier-NY-(1928)-Century Co-
illus-673p-1st prntg-scarce   (4n8) 15.   (5L2)   20.00

SCOTT,J D-Combination Atlas Map of Bucks Co,Pa-Phila-1876-
folio-109p-liths-buck   (5yy0,rebnd)   90.00

SCOTT,REV J L-Scenes Beyond the Grave,Trance of Marietta Davis-
Dayton-1859-225p-cl-16th ed   (5h2,wn)   5.00

SCOTT,J M-The Man Who Made Wine-NY-(1953)-12mo-124p,(1)-
illus   (5w1)   5.00

SCOTT, J W ROBERTSON-The Foundations of Japan-Lond-1922-
John Murray-446p   (5x9,pres)   5.00

SCOTT,JAS BROWN-De Grasse a Yorktown-Paris-1931-Ed Int'l-
363p-cl&bds   (5mm8,vf)   7.50
--The Hague Court Reports-NY-1916-Carn Endowment for Intl
Peace   (4j3)   15.00
--Survey of International Relations Between US & Germany-NY-
1917-390p   (5w4,underline)   8.50
--The US & France-NY-1926   (5q8,dj)   6.75

SCOTT,JAS K P-Story of Battles at Gettysburg-Harrisburg-1927-
301p   (4j4,f) 5.   (5r0)   7.50

SCOTT,JAS L-A Journal of a Missionary Tour...of the Great
Western Prairies-Providence-1843-12mo-orig cl-1st ed (5n9) 160.00

SCOTT,JOB-Journal of Life, Travels & Gospel Labours of-NY-
1797-Isaac Collins-360p-calf-labl-1st ed
  (5L3) 20.   (5m3,rbnd) 30.   (5m3,hng weak)   40.00
--same-Warrington,Eng-1798-orig calf-281p   (4m4)   17.50
--same-Mtpleasant-1820-303p-lea   (5y0,box)   25.00

SCOTT,JOCK-Greased Line Fishing for Salmon-Lond-n.d.-
thk8vo-orig buck-illus   (5t8)   7.50

SCOTT,MAJ JOHN-Barbarossa,The Lost Principle-Richmond-1860-
266p-1st ed   (5ee3,rbkd)   30.00

SCOTT,JOHN-Caves in Vermont,Location & Lore-1959-45p
    (5e8,wrps)   3.00

SCOTT,JOHN REED-The Imposter-Phila-1910-col illus-1st ed
    (5ee3,f,dj)   2.50

SCOTT,JONATHAN M-Blue Lights-NY-1817-Baldwin-12mo-
150p-prnt paper over bds-1st ed   (5i4,frayed)   30.00

SCOTT,KENNETH-Counterfeiting in Colonial America-NY-(1957)-
illus-cl-1st ed   (5h9,5t4,f,dj)   7.50

SCOTT,LENA B-Dawn Boy of the Pueblos-Phila-1935-Winston-
1st ed-8vo-dec cl-col frontis-plts   (4a8)   5.00
--same-NY-1935-illus-198p   (4b2,ex-libr,tn)   3.00

SCOTT,M-A Time to Speak-NY-1958-1st ed   (5x2,dj)   5.00

SCOTT,MAJOR GEN'L-Infantry Tactics-NY-1857-3 vols-16mo-
illus-lea&bds   (5xx7)   17.50
--same-NY-1861-3 vols-lea&bds-fldg charts (5p5,officer's autg) 37.50

SCOTT,MEL-Metropolitan Los Angeles,One Community-LosAng-
1949-maps-photos-R8vo-200p-1st ed   (5r8)   10.00

SCOTT,MILTON R-Supposed Diary of Pres Lincoln from Repeal of
Missouri Compromise-Newark-1913-140p-cl   (5h2)   8.50

SCOTT,NANCY E-Limits of Toleration within the Church of
England,1632 to 1642-1912   (5L7)   5.00

SCOTT,NATALIE-Gourmet's Guide to NewOrl-NOrl-1949-
116p-wrps   (5g9)   2.50
--200 Years of NewOrleans Cooking-NY-1931-238p-illus (5c0)   5.00

SCOTT,PETER-The Battle of the Narrow Seas-NY-1946-8 col illus
    (5c1)   10.00
--Morning Flight-Lond-(1936)-plts(some col)-4to-1st trade ed
    (5tt7,dj)   15.00
--Wild Geese & Eskimos-Lond-1951-illus-254p-1st ed (5dd7)   5.00

SCOTT,CAPT R F-Scott's Lost Expedition-NY-1913-2 vols-
1st Amer ed-illus-fldg map   (5i3) 15.   (5m6)   18.50
--same-Lond-1914-photos-maps-2 vols   (4p2)   17.50

SCOTT,REVA-Samuel Brannan & The Golden Fleece-NY-1944-
illus-462p-1st ed   (5x5,dj) 10.   (5L2) 6.50   (4n1)   8.50

SCOTT,RHEA C-Home Labor Saving Devices-Phila-(1917)-
illus-119p   (5w7)   6.50

SCOTT,S P,ed-Visigothic Code (Forum Judicum)-trans from orig
Latin-Bost-1910   (5r4)   17.50

SCOTT STAMP & COIN CO-Catalogue,1900-NY-1899 (5b9,f)   12.50

SCOTT,SYBIL,LADY,ed-A Book of the Sea-Oxf-1918-8vo-
dec cl-472p-g.t.   (5aa3)   3.50

SCOTT,TEMPLE,ed-Book Sales of 1895-Lond-1896-1st annual vol-
443p-Chiswick Pr   (5n4) 9.   (5yy6)   15.00
--Book Sales of 1897-Lond-1897-Chiswick Pr-priced   (4j6)   8.50
--Lord Chesterfield & His Letters to His Sons-Indnpla-1929-
Zinkin-ltd to 200c,autg   (5ss3)   7.50
--Oliver Goldsmith Bibliographically & Biographically Considered-
NY-1928-illus-4to-368p   (4g2)   25.00

SCOTT,THOS-Certaine Reasons & Arguments of Policie,why King
of England should ··· into warre with the Spaniard-(Lond)-
prntd 1624-sm4to-hf lea   (5L1)   100.00
--Experimentall Discoverie of Spanish Practices-(Lond)-prntd,Anno
1623---sm4to-hf lea   (5L1)   225.00
--Vox Populi,or Newes from Spayne-(Lond)-1620-sm4to-qtr calf-
14 unnbrd lvs   (5L1)   225.00

SCOTT,THOS-The Holy Bible Containing Old & New Testaments-
Bost-1832-6 vols-illus-8vo-calf   (5t7)   35.00

SCOTT, T H-Wild Flowers of the Wayside & Woodland-Lond-(1948)-
359p-col plts-Warne   (5x0)   5.00

SCOTT, W A-Trade & Letters-NY-1856-RobtCarter&Bros-168p-cl
    (5yy3)   10.00

SCOTT & SON,W & C-Sporting Breech Loaders-Lond-(1872)-47p-
illus   (5xx7)   15.00

SCOTT,SIR WALTER-The Abbot-Edinb-1820-3 vols-12mo-calf-
hf titles   (4k9) 50.00   (4c2)   50.00
--Anne of Geierstein-Edinb-1829-3 vols-12mo-calf
    (4c2,lacks hf t.)   25.00
--Complete Poetical Works-12 vols-12mo-frontis-3/4 mor-
g.t.   (5t8)   45.00
--The Doom of Devorgoil-Edinb-1830-8vo-mor-blind & g. stmpd-
g.e.   (4c2,fox)   35.00
--The field of Waterloo,a poem-Edinb-1815-Ballantyne-8vo-
orig wrps-1st ed -54p   (4m8,sp broke,box) 15.   (5x3,wn)   17.50
--Halidon Hill-Edinb-1822-Constable-8vo-orig cl-1st ed (5d8)   37.50
--Ivanhoe,a romance-NY-1940-2 vols-8vo-Ltd Ed Club-
ltd to 1500c,nbrd,autg,box   (5t8,sl chip) 12.50   (5b0)   25.00
--Journal of Sir Walter Scott-NY-(1890)-Harper&Bros-2 vols-
illus-cl   (5t4,hng crude rpr'd)   7.50
--Kenilworth-Burlington-1966-8vo-illus-Lane Pr-Lt Ed Club-
gold brocade cl   (5t8)   20.00
--The Lady of the Lake,a Poem-Bristol,RI-1836-Gladding-frontis-
32mo-orig bds-232p   (5j5,fray)   7.50
--same-Crowell-n.d.-limp lea cov   (5ww4)   5.00
--Letters on Demonology & Witchcraft-Lond-1885-intrc by Morley-
320p   (5w0)   6.50
--Memoirs of Capt Geo Carleton,an Engl officer-Edinb-1809-
Constable-8vo-calf-sp g.   (5xx6)   25.00
--Memoirs of the Life of-Phila-1838-7 vols-port-16mo-cl-
(Carey Lea & Blanchard)-by Lockhart   (5t7)   25.00
--Novels & Romances-Edinb-1833,(v.d.)-Constable-12mo-41 vols-
blue calf-g.t.-tooled sp-labls-Handy Edition
    (5t8,mint,f bndgs)   290.00
--Peveril of the Peak-Edinb-1822-4 vols-12mo-calf   (4c2)   25.00
--same-Edinb-1822-Constable-4 vols-8vo-orig bds-papr labls-
1st ed-errata slip   (4k9,rprd) 40.   (5xx6)   50.00
--The Pirate-Edinb-1822-3 vols-12mo-calf-1st ed
  (4k9) 75.   (5xx6,v wn) 10.   (4c2)   35.00
--The poetical works of-Balt-1813-JCushing-5 vols-24mo-calf
    (5p6,hng crack,scuff)   25.00
--Quentin Durward-Edinb-1823-Constable-3 vols-8vo-orig grey bds-
papr labls-1st ed   (4k9) 45.   (5xx6,hng sl wn)   45.00
--Redgauntlet-Edinb-1824-3 vols-12mo-calf-1st ed
  (4k9) 40.   (4c2,lacks hf titles)   25.00
--Rokeby,a Poem-Edinb-1813-330&116p-lg4to-hf calf-1st ed-
3p of ads at end   (5r9)   35.00
--St Ronan's Well-Edinb-1824-3 vols-12mo-calf (4c2,rebkd)   15.00
--Tales of a Grandfather-Edinb-1828-Cadell&Co-3 vols-5th ed-
1st series-roan & bds   (5rr2)   10.00
--same-Edinb-1829-2nd series-1st ed-3 vols   (5rr2)   15.00
--same-Bost-1829-orig bds-2 vols-2nd series (4k1,sp damgd)   15.00
--same-Edinb-1830-3rd series-1st ed-3 vols   (5rr2)   15.00
--same-Lond-1911-col illus   (4a1)   10.00
--Tales of My Landlord-Edinb-1832-4 vols-12mo-calf
    (4c2,lacks hf t.)   30.00
--Waverly Novels-Bost-1893-Estes&Lauriat-48 vols-8vo-3/4 red mor-
g.-#3 of "Conoisseur Edition" ltd to 70c,nbrd-xtra illus
    (5t2,f bndg post extra)   140.00

SCOTT, SIR WALTER (continued)
--same-Bost-1912-52 vols-3/4 black mor-plts-Caledonian Ed
(5d2) 250.00
--same-Phila-n.d.-Porter&Coates-48 vols in 24-red cl labls
(5p9) 45.00
--Woodstock-Edinb-1826-3 vols-12mo-calf (4c2,lacks hf t.) 25.00
--Works of-Bost-n.d.-Brainard Publ-48 vols in 24-cl-ed de luxe
(5p0) 50.00
SCOTT,WALTER-Specimen Days in America-Lond-1887-papr labl-
1st Engl ed (5ss9,labl fade) 10.00
SCOTT,WALTER DILL-The Psychology of Advertising-Bost-1908-
269p-illus (5t7) 10.00
SCOTT,WALTER S-White of Selborne-Lond-1950-260p-ports-plts
(5a1) 4.50
--White of Selborne & His Times-Lond-1946-4to-166p-ports-plts
(5a1) 4.50
SCOTT,WELLINGTON-17 Yrs in Underworld-NY-(1916)-119p-cl
(5h7,f) 5.00
SCOTT,WM -O Tempora, O Mores-Phila-1774-reprntd by Benj
Towne-8vo-cl-(12p),20p (5L1) 30.00
SCOTT,WM-Lessons in Elocution-Greenfield-Clark&Tyler-1821-
16mo-408p-lea (5i1) 6.00
--same-Bost-Ewer&Bedlington-1823-372p-4 plts-12mo-calf (5p1)15.00
SCOTT,WM B-History of Land Mammals in the Western Hemisphere-
NY-1913-Macmillan-693p-32 plts-lg8vo-cl-1st ed
(5j5,shake) 15.00
SCOTT,WM FORSE-Philander P Lane-n.p.-1920-port &maps-
296p (5q0) 10. (5u3) 12.50
--Roster of 4th Iowa Cavalry,Veteran Volunteers 1861 to 1865-
NY-1902-frontis-243p (4b3) 15.00
SCOTT,WM HENRY-British Field Sports-Lond-1818-8vo-plts-
bds-calf bk & cors (5ss5,cov loose) 20.00
SCOTT,WINFIELD-Infantry Tactics-NY-1861-3 vols-12mo-
lea&bds-fldg plts (5m2) 18.50
--Memoirs of Lt Gen Scott-NY-1864-cl-2 vols-1st ed
(5j6,chip) 9.50 (4k2) 17.50
SCOTT'S STANDARD COIN CATALOGUE #4-Silver & Gold-NY-
1893-208p-wrps-illus-index (5ii2) 6.60
SCOTT-GILES,C WILFRID-Civic Heraldry of England & Wales-
Lond-(1933)-336p-illus (5t9) 7.50
SCOTTISH CLANS & THEIR TARTANS-89 col plts-Edinb-n.d.(5t9)4.00
SCOUGAL,HENRY-Das Leben Gottes in der Seele des Menschen-
Phila-1756-Benj Franklin-(21)p,78p(1)-8vo-orig bds-lea bk-
1st ed (5L1,box) 475.00
SCOURGE OF THE OCEAN,THE-Complete in 1 vol-Phila-1851-
A Hart-R8vo-214p-(not 1st ed)-scarce (5mm2,rbnd) 35.00
SCOURING OF THE WHITE HORSE-or,Long Vacation Ramble of a
London Clerk-Cambr-1859-Macmillan-orig dec cl-228p-
adv dated 1858-illus (5c8,rub,soil) 17.50
SCRANTON LACE CO-Our First 50 Years-Scranton-1947-44p,(4)-
bds-illus (5hh6) 6.75
SCRIBLERIAD,THE-Heroic poem in 6 books-Lond-1751-for R Dodsley-
4to-hf calf-plts (5x3) 55.00
SCRIBNER,FRANK K-Honor of a Princess-NY-1897-1st ed-
v scarce (5mm1) 20.00
SCRIBNER,J M-Ready Reckoner for Ship Builders,Boat Builders etc-
Rochester-1871-16mo-bds (5q0) 7.50
SCRIBNER'S LUMBER & LOG BOOK-Rochester-1882-158p-bds-
illus (5h2,rub) 10.00
SCRIBNER'S MONTHLY ILLUS-May,Jun,1874 -orig wrps-2 parts
(5x4) 12.50
--same-May-1881-wrps-illus (5u9,worn,stnd) 4.50
SCRIBNER'S PRIVATE SCHOOL PRIMER-NY-1903-illus (5t7) 5.00
SCRIPPS,JOHN J-Life of Abraham Lincoln(caption title)-32p-
sewed as issued-(Chig,1860)-1st issue(wi adv pg 32 in dbl
column -rare (4h2) 750.00
SCRIPTURAL TALES-Lond-1854-Dean&Son-sq12mo-28 handcol plts-
dec cl (5v0,f) 12.50
SCROGGS,WM O-Century of Banking Progress-GardenCty-1924-
333p-frontis (4b8) 6.75
SCROPE,F POULETT-Memoir of Life of...Lord Sydenham-Lond-
1844-2nd ed-mor&cl-port-403p (5s6) 20.00
SCROPE,WM-Art of Deer Stalking-Lond-1839-New ed-plts-
440p-tall 8vo-g.pict cl (4b6) 25.00
SCRUGGS,ANDERSON M-Ritual for Myself-NY-1941-Macmillan-
1st ed (5ss9,dj) 4.50
SCRUGGS,MRS GROSS R-Gardening in the SoWest-Dallas-(1932)-
230p (5s7,fade) 7.50 (5r7,autg) 12.50
--Gardening in the South & West-GardenCty-1947-revised ed-
297p (5s7) 5.50
SCRYMSER,JAS A-Personal Reminis of-n.p.-(1915)-illus-lea
(5r7) 12.50

SCUDAMORE,T V-Lighter Episodes in Life of Prisoner of War-
Aldershot-(1933)-92p-port-illus (5dd0,pres) 6.50
SCUDDER,H E,ed-Men & Manners in Amer 100Years Ago-NY-
1887-illus-12mo (5jj3) 10.00
SCUDDER,HORACE E-Boston Town-Bost-1881-243p-illus
(5x0,ex-libr) 3.50 (5h9) 7.50
--Doings of the Bodley Family in Town & Country-Bost-1879-
later issue (5v0) 7.50
--James Russell Lowell-Bost-(1901)-2 vols-port
(5xx7) 12.50 (5mm2) 8.50
--Mr Bodley Abroad-Bost-1881-plt (5v0) 5.00
--Stories & romances-Bost-1880-Houghton-1st ed (5m2,sl wn) 7.50
SCUDDER,JANET-Modeling My Life-NY-1925-Harcourt Brace-
297p-illus (4a0) 20.00
SCUDDER,REV M L-Amer Methodism-Hartf-1868-thk8vo-illus-
cl-591p (5t2) 5.00
SCUDDER,SAM'L H-Everyday Butterflies-Bost&NY-1899-391p-
71 illus (5t4,libr stmp) 6.00
--Frail Children of the Air-Bost&NY-1897-279p,12p-illus
(5t4,libr labl) 4.00
--Insects of Unusual Interest from Tertiary Rocks of Colo & Wyom-
Wash-1878-25p-offprnt (4a5) 3.50
SCUDDER,TOWNSEND-Concord,American Town-LB-1947-1st
(5e8) 10.75 (5h9) 8.50
SCUDDER,VIDA-The Disciple of a Saint-NY-1907-1st ed(5b9,f) 5.00
--Life of the Spirit in Modern Engl Poets-Bost-1896-HoughtonMiff-
349p (5x0) 4.00
--Social ideals in Engl letters-Bost-1898-Houghton-1st (5m2) 6.00
SCUDERY,MADELEINE de-Almahide,or,the captive queen-Lond-
1677-folio-calf-mor labl-1st ed in Engl (5xx6) 250.00
SCULL,E MARSHALL-Hunting in Arctic & Alaska-Lond-1914-304p-
136 plts-11 maps (5dd0) 15.00
SCULL,GUY H-Lassoing Wild Animals in Africa-NY-1911-Stokes-
photos-135p-12mo (4t5,plt loose) 6. (4a6) 7.50
SCULL,JOHN-Ship Wiring-NY-1943-227p-illus (5s1,f,dj) 3.00
SCULL,PENROSE-Great Ships Around World-NY-1960-260p-
photos-4to (5s1,f,dj) 10.00
SCULL,WM ELLIS-Great Leaders & Nat'l Issues of 1896-Phila-
c1896-644p-illus (5w4) 6.50
SCHULLIAN,DOROTHY MAY-Catalogue of Incunabula &
Manuscripts in Army Medical Library-NY-1950-Schuman-
R8vo-orig buck-12 plts (5ee5,f) 28.00
SCULLY,MICHAEL-This Is Texas-Austin-1936-4to-illus
(5w5) 7.50 (5r7) 10.00
SCULLY,WM-Brazil,Its Provinces & Chief Cities,the Manners etc-
Lond-1866-398p-fldg map (5w4,rub) 10.00
SCURFIELD,GEO-Stickful of Nonpareil-Cambr-1956-illus-8vo-
cl-500c prntd,Xmas (4c1) 20.00
SCUTT,J F-Man Who Loved the Zulus-Pietermaritzburg-ca 1950-
12mo-illus (5x2) 5.00
--same-(ca 1951)-187p-10 plts (5c6,vg) 7.50
SEA,SOPHIE FOX-That Old Time Child, Roberta-Louisvl-1892-84p-
cl (5h7,dmpstn) 7.50
SEABROOK,KATIE-Gao of the Ivory Coast-NY-1931-col frontis-
illus-121p-juvenile (4t5) 4.00
SEABROOK,WM-These Foreigners-NY-1938 (5x7) 5.00
SEABROOK,WM B-Air Adventure-NY-1933-HarcourtBrace-
211p-illus (5p0) 6.00
--Jungle Ways-NY-1931-HarcourtBrace-308p-33p photos
(4t5,explibr) 3.50 (5c6,vg,4a6) 7.50
SEABURY,SAM'L-Amer Slavery,Distinguished from Slavery of
English Theorists,& Justified by Law of Nature-NY-1861-
319p (5L3,libr stmps) 22.50
--Free Thoughts,on Proceedings of Continental Congress-NY-
1774-24p-disbnd (5m2) 65.00
--Theory & Use of Church Calendar in Measurement & Distribution
of Time-NY-1872-224p (5t7) 10.00
SEACORD,M H-Historical Landmakrs of NewRochelle,NY-
NewRochelle-1938-Huguenot&Hist Assoc-135p-wrps (5p0) 5.00
SEAFORTH HIGHLANDERS OF CANADA-Souvenir,231st Overseas
Battalion CEF,3rd Battn-Vanc-1917-dec wrps-41p-ports-illus-
plus 30p ads (5u6) 12.50
SEAGO,EDW-With The Allied Armies in Italy-Lond-1945 (5x7) 5.00
SEAL,ETHEL D-Furnishing the Little House-NY-(1924)-200p,(1)-
illus-bds (5w7) 4.50
SEAMAN,HERVEY J-The Expert Cleaner-NY-(1899)-12mo-286p
(5w7) 5.00
SEAMAN,HOLLY S-Manitoba Landmarks & Red Letter Days-
Winnipeg-(c1920)-92p-illus-prntd wrps (5w8) 17.50
SEAMAN,N G-Indian Relics of the Pacific NoWest-Portland-
(1946)-153p plus index-illus-1st ed (5L2,dj) 5.00
SEAMAN,OWEN-War Time Verses-Lond-1915-Constable&Co-
8vo-hf crushed mor-t.e.g.-1st ed (4b0,f bndg,rbnd) 45.00

SEAMSTRESS,THE-NY-1848-400p   (5n7,wn)   9.50

SEANNELL,F-Christmas Visit-Lond-(ca 1890)-sq8vo-12p-bds-
picturebook-4 liths   (5c8)   6.00

SEARCHER,VICTOR-Lincoln's Journey to Greatness-Phila&Tor-
(1960)-279p-illus   (5t7,dj)   7.50

SEARIGHT,FRANK T-Amer Press Humorists' Book-LosAng-1907-
4to-illus   (5x5,crack)   25.00

SEARIGHT,THOS B-The Old Pike-Uniontown-1894-8vo-illus-cl
    (4c1)   20.00

SEARING,A E P-The Land of Rip Van Winkle-NY-1884-4to-
a.e.g.-illus-fldng panoramic view   (5r7)   17.50

SEARLE,TOWNLEY-Strange News From China-NY&Lond-n.d.-(1932)-
231p-illus   (5c5,fade)   4.00

SEARS,CLARA ENDICOTT-Bronson Alcott's Fruitlands-Best-1915-
185p-cl   (5h1) 5.   (5t2)   12.50

--Gleanings from Old Shaker Journals-Best-1916-illus-12mo-
cl-1st ed   (5t2)   12.50

--The Great Powwow-Best-1934-288p-illus   (5e8)   5.00

--same-Best-(1935)-8vo-illus   (5ss5)   9.00

--Highlights Among Hudson River Artists-Best-1947-HoughtonMiff-
216p-illus-4to   (4a0) 25.   (5t0)   10.00

--Somer Amer Primitives-NY-1941-Kennikat Pr-292p-illus-
demy 8vo   (4a0)   12.50

SEARS,CYRUS-11th Ohio Batt at Iuka-n.p.-n.d.-(Akron,1898)-
(10)p-prntd wrps-v scarce   (5y0)   12.50

SEARS,EDMUND H-Picturs of the Olden Time-Best-1857-1st ed
    (5mm2)   6.00

SEARS,ELINOR LATHROP-Pastel Painting Step By Step-NY-
1947-123p-illus   (5t7)   5.50

SEARS,FRED C-Productive Orcharding-Phila-(1914)-315p-
frontis-157 illus-Lippincott's Farm Manuals   (5s7)   6.00

SEARS,HAMBLEN-Fur & Feather Tales-NY-8vo-illus by ABFrost &
Others-1st ed -1899   (5ee3) 6.   (5m6)   10.00

SEARS,J H-Trust Estates as Business Companies-KansasCty,Mo-
1921-2nd ed   (5ff4)   7.50

SEARS,JOS HAMBLEN-The Career of Leonard Wood-NY-1919-
272p-1st ed   (5w4)   6.50

--Tennessee Printers 1791 to 1945-Kingsport-n.d.-(ca 1945)-
cl&bds   (5w0)   6.50

SEARS,LORENZO-Wendell Phillips-NY-1909-Dblday,Page-
379p-frontis   (5qq8)   6.00

SEARS,MINNIE EARL-Song Index-NY-1926-HWWilsonCo-650p-
tall 8vo   (5p7)   50.00

--Song Index Supplement-NY-HWWilsonCo-1934-367p (5p7)   25.00

SEARS,ROBT -New & PopularPictorial Descrip of England,Scotland,
Ireland,Wales & British Islands-NY-1855-554p-illus (5t7)   10.00

--Pictorial Description of US-NY-1860-648p-illus-cl-new edition
    (5tt0)   10.00

--Pictorial History of Amer Revolution-NY-1847-432p plus ads-
illus   (5w5,crude rbnd)   5.00

SEARS,R W-Survey of Cycle of Sod & Livestock Industries Here
& Abroad-LosAng-(1941)-1st ed-306p-illus   (5L2,dj)   5.00

SEARS ROEBUCK CATALOGS-#134,145,155 to 161,164,168 to
173,177,178-19 pieces-Chig,Phila or Best-1911 to 1939-
4to-illus-wrps   (5t0) ea 10.00

SEARS,ROEBUCK & CO-Agricultural Implements-Chig-1910-
illus catalog-52p   (5h8,soil)   5.75

SEARS,GEN W H-Notes from a Cowboy's Diary-Lawrence,Ka-n.d.-
wrps-(6p)-v scarce pamph   (5L2)   7.50

SEASONS-NY-1811-S Wood,16mo-44p   (5c8,s ln)   45.00

SEATON,A E-A Manual of Marine Engineering-Lond-1883-
70 illus-2nd ed   (5c1)   22.50

SEATON,C W-New York State Statistical Census-1877-465p
    (5t9)   10.00

SEATON,O A-Seaton Family with Gen & Biographies-1906-441p
    (5t9)   12.50

SEATON,WM C-Manual of Examination of Masters & Mates as
instituted by Dept of Marine & Fisheries of Canada-Quebec-
1875-Dawson&Co-8vo-cl-160,12p-2nd ed   (5t2,v wn)   4.50

SEATTLE-Seattle-(ca 1893)-Chas H Kittinger-obl 8vo-24p-
24 liths of public buildings,etc with text   (4g6)   17.50

SEATTLE BRIDES' COOK BOOK-Seattle-n.d.-(ca 1905)-pic bds-
122p-ads-lg8vo   (4g9,chip,rprd)   8.50

SEATTLE COOK BOOK-1st Christian Church-Seattle-1906-135p-
wrps-ads   (5g9,stnd)   5.00

SEATTLE CENTURY-Compiled by Seattle Hist Soc-Seattle-1952-
105p-illus   (5ss1)   4.00

SEATTLE MARINE SUPPLY CO-Marine Hardware,Fishing Supplies-
Seattle-n.d.-115p   (5s1,fade)   5.00

SEATTLE ON PUGET SOUND-Seattle-c1910-C P Johnston-24p-
stiff wrps   (5n4)   8.50

SEATTLE WRITERS CLUB-Tillicum Tales-Seattle-1907-illus (5z7)   7.50

SEAVER,GEO-Albert Schweitzer,The Man & His Mind-NY-
1947-Harper-photos-illus-346p   (4t5,dj)   9.00

--Edw Wilson of the Antarctic-Lond-1933-maps-26 Illus(7 col)
    (5c1)   8.50

--same-Lond-1936-236p-illus   (5ss1)   5.00

SEAVER,JAS E-Deh He Wa Mis-Batavia-1844-3rd ed-enlrgd ed-
calf-spine title "The White Woman"   (4a9,vf)   45.00

--Life of Mary Jemison,Deh he wa mis-NY-1856-312p-orig cl-
4 plts-4th ed   (5w5,rbnd) 15.   (5s9)   27.50

--Narr of Life of Mrs Mary Jemison-Canandaigua-1824-lea-
1st ed   (5m3,1 lf tn wi loss,4a9,vg)   225.00

--Narr of Life of Mary Jemison,white woman of the Genesee-
1918-plt-rev by CDVail-20th ed   (5L7)   7.50

--Narrative of Life of Mrs Mary Jemison-Canandaigua-1929-
16mo-calf&bds   (4c1)   7.50

SEAWANHAKA CORINTHIAN YACHT CLUB OF NY-Club Book of-
NY-1900-178p + 15p-col illus   (5s1,rprd)   4.50

SEAWELL,MOLLY ELLIOT-Papa Bouchard-NY-1901-Scribner-
12mo-cl-g.-illus   (5b2)   4.50

--Sprightly romance of Marsac-NY-1896-Scribner-illus-pict cl-
1st ed   (5m2)   8.50

SECCHI,P A-Le soleil,Expose des principales-1870-buck
    (5L7,ex-libr)   25.00

SECCOMBE,MAJOR-Army & Navy Drolleries-Lond-(188-)-Warne-
26p col lith-sq4to-cl-illus-3rd ed,imprvd   (5c8,wn)   37.50

SECCOMBE,T S-Comic Sketches from Engl History for Children of
All Ages-Lond-(1884)-WHAllen&Co-pict bds-col illus-1st ed
    (5c8)   20.00

--Good Old Story of Cinderella retold in Rhyme-Lond-(1882)-
Warne-dec cl-1st ed-scarce   (5c8)   20.00

--Military Misreadings of Shakespeare-Lond-GeoRoutledge&Sons-
(ca 1880)-orig pict bds-illus-1st ed-prntd in col by Edmund
Evans   (5c8)   32.50

SECHEVERALL,J HAMP-Journal Hist of 29th Ohio Vet Vol-
Cleve-1883-284p   (5h7,rbnd)   35.00

SECKER,THOS-Lectures on Catechism of Protestant Episcopal
Church-Col-1839-351p-cl   (5h2)   8.50

SECOMB,D F-Hist of Amherst,N Hamp-1883-978p-illus & map
    (5t9,wn)   25.00

SECOND BOOK OF READING LESSONS-Tor-(1869)-illus-232p
    (4a8)   5.00

SECOND TALE OF A TUB,A-or history of Robt Powel,the puppet
show man-Lond-1715-JRoberts-8vo-calf-frontis-1st ed
    (5xx6,hng wn)   175.00

SECOY,FRANK RAYMOND-Changing Military Patterns on the
Great Plains-LocustValley-(1953)-112p-maps-Amer Ethn Soc
#21-1st ed   (5L0)   7.50

SECRET & SCIENCE-of French Dry Cleaning-Minn-1912-120p-
illus-rev ed   (5b8)   5.00

SECRET DISPATCHES FROM ARABIA-Lond-(1939)-Golden Cockerel
Pr-4to-cl-mor bk-t.e.g.-1000c prntd   (5ee9,f bndg)   150.00

SECRET HISTORY-or Horrors of StDomingo-Phila-1808- R Carr,prntr-
by a lady at Cape Francois-calf-225p   (5tt8,wn)   30.00

SECRET HISTORY OF PERFIDIES-intrigues & corruptions of Tyler
dynasty etc-Wash&NY-1845-wrps   (5y4,fox)   20.00

SECRET HISTORY OF REIGNS OF CHAS II & JAS II-n.p.-
1690-18mo-bds&lea-214p   (5t4,close crop)   40.00

SECRET INTRIGUES-The Roman Empresses-Walpole Pr-1899-2 vols-
thk8vo-brown buck-ltd ed   (5t5)   15.00

SECRET MEMOIRS OF LATE MR DUNCAN CAMPBELL-Lond-
1732-8vo-calf-frontis-list of subscr-1st ed-(sp labld Defoe)-
(bogus ed)   (5xx6,rbkd)   150.00

SECRET MUSEUM OF MANKIND-NY-n.d.-lg8vo-5 vols in 1-illus-
photos   (5t2)   5.00

SECRET OUT,THE-or 1000 Tricks with Cards etc-NY-(ca 1870)-
Dick&Fitzgerald-398p & 10p-ads-12mo-pict cl   (5j5)   15.00

SECRET SPRINGS OF DUBLIN SONG-Dublin-1918-tall 8vo-
ltd to 500c,nbrd   (5r9,unopnd)   15.00

SECRETAN,J H E-Canada's Great Highway,From First Stake to
Last Spike-Lond,Ottawa-1924-plts-252p   (4f9)   12.50

--Out West-Ottawa-1910-206p-plts (5a1,wn) 6.50 (5dd0)   8.50

SECRETS OF MEAT CURING-& Sausage Making-Chig-(1911)-
303p-12mo-illus-pict bds   (5c0)   8.50

SEDDON,JAS A-Funds Required to Meet our Treaty Obligations
to Indian Nations-Richmond-1864-3p-Crandall #1312 (5j6)   10.00

--Officers Attached to & Employed in Different Depts & Bur in
City of Richmond-Richmond-1865-6p-Crandall #1313 (5j6)   8.50

SEDGLEY,G B-Burbank & Families of Bray,Wellcome etc-1928-
563p   (4t2)   17.50

SEDGWICK,CATHARINE MARIA-The Poor Rich Man & the Rich
Poor Man-NY-1837   (5ee3)   5.00

SEDGEWICK,ELLERY-Atlantic Harvest-Best-1947-679p (5k0,dj)   4.00

SEDGWICK,H D-Refutation of reasons assigned by arbitrators, for their award in case of 2 Greek frigates-NY-1826-JSeymour-8vo-disbnd-1st ed (5i0,facs t.pg) 25.00

SEDGWICK,HENRY DWIGHT-Cortes the Conqueror-Indnpls-(1926)-1st ed (4a3) 10. (5L2) 4. (5h4) 4.50

SEDGWICK,JOHN-Correspondence-n.p.-1902-2 vols-red cl-DeVinne Pr-ltd to 300c-v scarce (5ee3) 55. (5r7) 75.00

SEDGWICK,SARAH CABOT-Stockbridge 1739 to 1939-Great Barrington-1939-306p-blue cl-illus-Bicentennial Ltd ed (5a0) 10.00

SEDGWICK,THEODORE-Public & Private Economy-NY-1836-Part First-263p-orig cl-papr labl (5m3,fox) 25.00

SEDGWICK,THEO,JUN-Memoir of Life of Wm Livingston-NY-1833-port-449p (4b6,pres) 22.50

SEDGWICK,MRS WM T-Acoma,the Sky City-Harvard U-1926-bds-8vo-cl bkstrp-1st ed (5r8) 26. (5w0,wn) 16.50 (5h5,f) 17.50
--same-Cambr 1927-309p plus index-illus-2nd impres (5L2) 12.50

SEDLEY,CHAS-The infidel mother,or,3 winters in London-Lond-1807-3 vols-12mo-hf calf-2nd ed-rare (5xx6,rub) 50.00

SEDWICK,HENRY DWIGHT-Cortes the Conqueror-Indnpls-(c1926)-BobbsMerrill-8vo-cl-illus (4a3) 10.00

SEEBOHM,BENJ-Memoirs of Life & Gospel Labours of Stephen Grellet-Phila-1860-2 vols (5w4,wn) 10.00

SEEBOHM,FREDERIC-The Engl Village Community-Lond-1896-8vo-cl-464p-maps (5t2,lacks e.p.) 7.50
--same-NY-1915-reprnt from 4th ed(1905) (5r4) 10.00

SEEBOHM,HENRY-Siberia in Europe-Lond-1880-& Siberia in Asia-Lond-1882-Murray-2 vols-8vo-lea-g. illus-fldg maps (5v7) 35.00

SEEGER,ALAN-Poems-wi an intro by Wm Archer-NY-1916-12mo-cl-1st ed of auth's 1st book (5r9) 10. (5gg6) 20.00

SEEGER,EUGEN-Chicago the Wonder City-Chig-1893-451p (4h7) 10.00

SEEGMILLER,W-Primary Hand Work-(1906)-illus-12mo-136p(5n7)2.50

SEELEY,E L-Stories of the Italian Artists from Vasari-Lond-1914-Chatto&Windus-325p-8 col plts-4to-cl (5m5,crack) 10.00

SEELEY,H G-Dragons of the Air-Lond-1901-orig cl-12mo-80 illus-1st ed (4n5,sl soil) 15.00

SEELEY,L B-Horace Walpole & His World-NY-n.d.-296p,7p-illus-cl (5t2) 5.00

SEELINGSON,LELIA-A History of Indianola-Cuero-n.d.-16p-wrps-scarce (5n4,mint) 9.50

SEELY,HOWARD-Ranchman's Stories-NY-1886-12mo-cl-2nd ed (4c1) 7.50

SEELY'S,MRS -Cook Book-NY-1902-432p-illus (5c5) 8.50

SEEMANN,BERTHOLD-Botany of Voyage of HMS Herald,under ...Kellett....1845 to 51-Lond-1852 to 57-col frontis-97 plts-2 maps-4to-cl-1 vol in 2-1st ed-rare (5z9,rbnd,libr stmp) 750.00

SEEMULLER,ANNE M CRANE-Reginald Archer,a Novel-Bost-1871-8vo-cl-Osgood (5b2,f) 12.50

SEEWERKER,JOS-Nuestro Pueblo,Los Angeles,City of Romance-Bost-1940 (5x5,dj,pres) 15.00

SEGAERT,HENRI-Une Terme au Congo Belge-Brussels-1919-269p-15p ads-wrps (5c6,vg) 11.50

SEGALE,SISTER BLANDINA-At the End of Santa Fe Trail-(Columbus-1932-Columbian Pr)-illus-347p-scarce (5L2,rbnd,4n8) 20.00
--same-Milwkee-(1948) (5xx5) 12.50 (5x5) 10.00
--same-Milwkee-1949-298p-illus-3rd prntng (5w5) 7.50
--same-Milwkee-(1951)-illus-298p-4th prntg (4b3) 10. (5L2) 5.00

SEGAR,LT NATHAN'L-A Brief Narrative of Captivity & Sufferings-Paris(Maine)-1825-sm8vo-wrps-for Author-1st ed-rare (5n2,box) 850.00

SEGER,JOHN H-Early Days Among the Cheyenne & Arapahoe Indians-1934-U of Okla Pr-Stanley Vestal,ed-1st ed-155p (5x5,f,dj) 30.00
--Tradition of the Cheyenne Indians-n.d.(1906?)-orig wrps-11p in board folder -Arapaho Bee Print (5m3) 37.50

SEGOE,LADISLAS-Land Use & Community Facilities,Report to Richmond City Planning Comm-Cinn-1951-4to-84lvs plus tables-maps-wrps-pkt map (5j5) 7.50

SEGUR,COUNT PHILIP DE-History of Exped to Russia,undertaken by Emperor Napoleon-Lond-1825-2 vols-map-7 engrs-calf-tooled-rev&corr 2nd ed (5d2,f bndg) 20.00
--Memoirs & Anecdotes of the Count de Segur-NY-1928-286p-illus (5t7) 7.50

SEGUY,E A-Les Laques du Coromandel-Paris-n.d.-eleph folio 50 plts-tied (5n7) 38.50

SEGY,L-African Sculpture Speaks-NY-1952-4to-illus (5x2) 25.00

SEHNER,S M-Schner Anc-1896-6p-(75c printed) (4t2) 10.00

SEIDEL,A,ed-Geschichten und Lieder der Afrikaner-Berlin-1896-12&340p (5c6,bndg stn) 22.50

SEIDELL,ATHERTON-Solubilities of Inorganic & Organic Substances-NY-1907-8vo-1st ed (5ss5,ex-libr) 7.50

SEIDENADEL,CARL W-First Grammar of Language Spoken by the Bontoc Igorot,etc-(Philippines)-Chig-1909-lg4to-plts-592p (4k5) 65.00

SEIDENSTICKER,OSWALD-Geschichte der Deutschen Gesellschaft von Pennsylvanien etc-Phila-1876-336p-8vo-orig cl (5L1) 20.00

SEIDLITZ,W von-History of Japanese Colour Prints-Lond-1910-plts(some col)-4to-1st ed (4j3,hngs weak,scuff) 17.50

SEILHAMER,G O-The Bard Family-Chambersburg-1908-Kittochtinny Pr-8vo-cl-ltd to 300c (4t1) 25. (4t2) 23.50

SEISBERGER,D-Diary of..A Moravian Missionary Among the Indians of Ohio-Cinn-1885-2 vols (5yy0) 24.50

SEITZ,DON C-Artemus Ward-NY-(1919)-Harper-illus-1st prntng (5m2) 8.50
--The Dreadful Decade, 1869 to 1879-Indnpls-(1926)-illus (5t0) 4.50 (5m2) 7.50
--From Kaw Teepee to Capitol-NY-1928-photos-223p (5L2) 3.50 (4b2,soil) 6.00
--The Great Island-NY-1926-251p-illus-port (5aa0) 6.50
--Horace Greeley,Founder of NY Tribune-Indnpls-(1926)-433p-cl-plts (5h7,lacks fly) 5. (5p5) 12.50
--The Jas Gordon Bennetts Father & Son-Indnpls-1928-405p-illus-1st ed (5hh6) 6.75
--Joseph Pulitzer,His Life & Letters-NY-1924-Simon Schuster-cl-1st ed (5F0) 5. (4p1,fade) 8.50
--Lincoln,the Politician-NY-(1931)-487p-cl (5h1) 5.00
--Monogatari,Tales from Old & New Japan-NY-1924-Putnam-327p (5p7) 4.50
--Newfoundland-Lond-1927 (5aa0) 6.50
--Paul Jones, His Exploits in English Seas during 1778 to 1780-NY-1917-hf mor-col frontis-8vo-de luxe ed-ltd to 43c,autg (4n5) 25.00
--Under Black Flag-NY-1925-Dial Pr-8vo-341p-frontis-Rogues Libr (4a6,cov spot) 10.00

SEITZ,MARY A-History of the Hoffman Paper Mills in Maryland-Towson-1946-priv pub-63p-illus (5y2) 12.50

SELBIT,THE MAGICIAN'S HANDBOOK-Lond-1902-Marshall & Brookes-8vo-cl-illus-188p-2nd ed (5j5,crack) 15.00

SELBY,PAUL O-Bibliography of Missouri Co Histories & Atlases-Kirksville,Mo-1966-44p-wrps-o.p.-2nd ed (5t3) 5.00

SELDEN,DUDLEY-Conveyances on Record in Register's Office... from Jan 1825 to Jan 1838-NY-1838-fldg maps-1st ed. (5tt5) 35.00

SELDEN,JOHN-Historie of Tithes-(Lond)-1618-calf-4to-1st ed (4n5,rbnd) 100.00

SELDEN,JOHN-Table Talk of...ed by Pollock-Lond-1927-Quaritch-191p (5p9) 7.50

SELDES,GEO-The Catholic Crisis-NY-c1939 (5x7) 5.00
--Lords of the Press-NY-(1938)-408p-1st ed (5t4,pres) 5. (5j5) 10.00
--The Stammering Century-NY-JDay-1928-414p-illus (5p9) 6.00
--You Can't Print That-NY-1929-thk8vo-cl-465p (5j5) 7.50

SELDES,GILBERT-The Future of Drinking-Bost-1930-173p-illus (5w6) 4.50
--Hour with Movies & Talkies-Phila-1919-12mo-cl-156p-1st ed-One Hour Series (5t0,dj) 7.50

SELECT COMMITTEE OF SENATE-to Investigate Alleged Outrages in Southern States-Sen Report #1,49th Cong-48p-wrps-1871 (5x2) 17.00

SELECT TALES-Being a Compil of Singular Interesting Remarkable & Auth Narr,Ancient & Modern-Charlottesvl-1833-orig calf-424p (5r5) 65.00

SELECT TRACTS RELATING TO COLONIES-Lond-(1732)-Roberts-8vo-cl-1st ed (5n2) 175.00

SELECT VIEWS OF CATALINA ISLAND-Avalon-(1913)-Catalina Novelty-hand col illus-folio-12 lvs-wrps (4a5) 7.50

SELECTED RECIPES-Woman's Amer Baptist Foreign Mission Soc-Chig-(ca 1916)-55p-wrps (5g9) 4.50

SELER,EDWARDS-Mexican & Central Amer Antiquities-Wash-1904-BAE #28-Bowditch-8vo-cl-682p (5t0) 10.00

SELF INSTRUCTION IN REAL PEN WORK & PENMANSHIP-Pittsfield,Mass-(1881)-50p-illus-bds (5t4) 17.50

SELF,MARGARET C-The Horseman's Encyclopedia-(1946)-Barnes Co-illus-519p (4p8) 5.00

SELFRIDGE,T O-Reports of Explor & Surv to Ascertain Practicability of Ship Canal between Atlantic & Pacific Oceans....Isthmus of Darien-Wash-1874-GPO-illus-4to-16 fldg plts-268p (5yy0) 32.50

SELFRIDGE,THOS O-Trial of,for killing Chas Austin in Boston, Aug 4,1806-Bost-(1806)-8vo-169p-plt-2nd ed-(unbnd) (5ss5) 7.50

SELIGMAN,GERMAIN-Roger de La Fresnaye-NY-1945-Valentin-9 plus 52p-lg4to-bds-plts-1st ed-ltd to 775c (5m7,wn) 25.00

SELIGMANN,H J-Race Against Man-NY-1939 (5x2) 7.50
--The Negro Faces America-NY-1924-319p-wrps (5x2) 22.50

SELIGMANN, HERBERT-D H Lawrence,an Amer Interpretation-NY-1924-12mo-1st ed-wrps (4c1) 20.00
SELIGMAN, KURT-The History of Magic-NY-c1948 (5x7) 25.00
--same-NY-(1948)-Pantheon-504p-255 illus (5c3) 6.00
SELKIRK, THOS DOUGLAS-Diary, 1803 to 1804-Tor-1958-Champlain Soc-port-maps-359p (5zz8) 40.00
--Observ on Present State of Highlands of Scotlands-Lond-1805-R Taylor & Co,prntr (5nn8) 150.00
--same-Edinb-1806-8vo-orig bds-232p & 61p-2nd ed (5q8,ex-libr) 80. (5r7) 40.00
SELL, HENRY B-Buffalo Bill & the Wild West-NY-1955-278p-1st ed (5t7,dj) 10. (5s4,dj,5ee3,f) 5. (5hh3,5h5) 7.50
SELLERIER, CARLOS-Data Referring to Mexican Mining-Mexico-1901-Hoeck&Co-folio-140p-wrps-scarce (4a3,chip) 25.00
SELLERS, CHAS-Oporto Old & New-Lond-1899-314p-illus (5w1,stn) 30.00
--Tales from the lands of Nuts & Grapes-Lond-1888-178p&ads (5t4) 7.50
SELLERS, CHAS COLEMAN-Artist of Revolution,Early Life of Chas W Peale-Hebron,Conn,1939 & Phila,1947-2 vols-8vo-plts (4a0,dj) 90.00
SELLERS, E J-De Carpentier Family of Holland-1909-59p (4t2) 17.50
--Gen of Jacquett Family-1896 (4t2) 25.00
--Genealogy of the Kollock Family of Sussex Co,Delaware 1657 to 1897-1939-72p (4t2) 10. (5w4) 15.00
--Dr Francis Jos Pfeiffer of Phila,Gen of-1899-67p (5t9) 17.50
--Partial Gen of Sellers & Wample Families of Pa-1903-139p (4t2) 10.00
--Allied Anc of Van Culemborg Family-1915-161p (4t2) 10.00
SELLERS, ELIZ J-From 18 to 20,a novel-Phila-1888-Lippincott-pict cl-1st ed (5m2,fade) 10.00
SELLERS, SARAH P-David Sellers,Mary Pennock Sellers-Phila-1928-157p-illus (5h9,mint) 35.00
SELLIER, RICHARD-Twin Brother Hell-Lond-1960-208p (5c6,mint) 5.75
SELLIN, T-Pioneering in Penology-1944-illus (5L7) 3.50
SELLSTEDT, LARS GUSTAF-From Forecastle to Academy-Buffalo-1904-353p-illus-8vo (4a0) 30.00
SELOUS, FREDK C-Hunters Wanderings in Africa-Lond-1895-8vo-455p-illus-4th ed (4a6,cov stnd) 12.50
--Sunshine & Storm in Rhodesia-Lond-1896-29&290p-9 plts-fldg map (5c6,vg) 16.50
--Sport & Travel East & West-Lond-1901-311p-illus-plts (5a1) 6.50
--Travel & Adven in SE Africa-Lond-1893-8vo-503 plts-3rd ed-calf&bds (4a6,lacks map) 15.00
SELTMAN, CHAS-Wine in the Ancient World-Lond-(1957)-196p-illus (5w1) 6.00
SELVAGEM, CARLOS-Tropa d'Africa-Paris-1925-332p-wrps (5c6) 10.00
SELWYN, WM-Abridgment of Law of Nisi Prius-Albany-1811-2 vols-8vo-calf-labels (5i3,f) 17.50
SEMENOFF, VLADIMIR-The Price of Blood-Lond-1910-3/4 blue mor-tooled (5d2,f bndg) 10.00
SEMINAR-Annual extraordinary # of the Jurist-Vol 1 thru 13-1943 to 54(all publ)-bound (5ii7,ex-libr) 40.00
SEMMENDINGER & CO-FtLee-1876-Photographic apparatus-4p folder-4to (5e4) 10.00
SEMMES, J E-John H B Latrobe & His Times,1803 to 91-1917-col plts (5L7) 20.00
SEMMES, R-Cruise of Alabama & Sumter-NY-1864-port-328p-2 vols in 1 (4b3) 22.50 (5t7) 20.00
SEMMES, RAPHAEL-Campaigns of Gen Scott in Valley of Mexico-Cinn-1852-367p-fldg map (4a5) 35.00
--same-Cinn-1852-map-8vo-2nd ed (4g6,sl loose) 15.00
--Service Afloat & Ashore During Mexican War-Cinn-1851-480p (5g8,wn) 20. (4j4) 65.00
--same-Balt-1887-cl-833p (4j4,rebnd) 12.50
SEMPLE, ANNE-Ties That Bind-Durant,Okla-n.p.-n.d.-104p-papr (5h0,pres) 4.50
SEMPLE, ELLEN CHURCHILL-Amer History & Its Geographic Conditions-Bost-(1903)-8vo-cl-illus-maps (5t2,crack) 6. (5u3) 6.50
SEMPLE, ROBT H-Memoirs on Diphtheria-Lond-1859-New Sydeham Soc-8vo-cl-407p (5j5) 20.00
SEMPILL, ROBT-The Sempill Ballates-Edinb-1872-283p (5c3) 6.00
SENAN, JOSE-Letters of Jose Senan-SanFran-1962-Lawton Kennedy-frontis-fldg map-1st ed-1000c (5L0,mint) 15.00
SENDAK, MAURICE-Where the Wild Things Are-NY-1963-Harper & Row-1st ed-obl 4tl-pict bds-40p (5s0,mint) 7.50
SENDERS, ROBT,prntr-Genealogy of Lairds of Ednem & Duntreth from Year 1063 to Year 1699-(Glasgow,1699)-reprntd Thos G Stevenson-Edinb,1834-ltd (5b0,f bndg) 75.00
SENECA-Canoe & Camp Cookery-NY-1885-16mo-96p (5ss8,poor) 3.50
--same-NY-1893-96p (5c0) 5.00

SENECA CO,OHIO-Centennial Biographical History of-Chig 1902-757p-mor (5ff7) 55.00
SENECA COUNTY, OHIO-Rural Route Directory of-Tiffin-1904-32p-wrps (5h1) 5.00
SENECA INDIANS-Home Life & Culture-York,Pa-1944-125p-illus-map-1st ed (5L0) 8.50
SENEFELDER, ALOIS-Invention of Lithography-NY-1911-cl-illus 229p (4c1,crack) 25.00
SENEGAL, LE-Paris-430p-13 fldg plts-fldg maps-wrps-(for Expos Universelle of 1900) (5c6,wrps wn) 20.00
SENG, R A-Brink's the Money Movers-Chig-1959-128p-illus (5y2) 5.50
SENGSTACKEN, AGNES-Destination,West-Portland-(1942)-219p (5s4,dj,f) 5.00
SENIOR, F DOROTHY-Life & Times of Colley Cibber-NY-n.d. (ca 1925)-illus-cl-16p,268p (5t0) 5.00
SENN, C HERMAN-The Book of Sauces-Chig-1915-128p-vest pkt ed (5g9) 3.00
--Breakfast Dishes & Savouries-Lond-1923-126p-illus (5g9) 4.00
SENN, EDW L-Deadwood Dick & Calamity Jane-Deadwood,SD-(1939)-15p-wrps-1st ed-scarce (5L2) 15.00
SENN, NICHOLAS-In Heart of the Arctics-Chig-1907-336p-plts (5s6) 12.50 (4b9) 20.00
SENOUR, CARO-Master St Elmo-Chig-(c 1904)-Juvenile Book Co-153p-pict cl-illus (5p1,pres) 8.50
SENOUR, F-Morgan & His Captors-Cinn-1865-389p (5L3) 6. (5ee3,edge wn) 8.50
SENSENIG-The Sensineys of Amer-1943-159p (5t9) 10.00
SENTER, O S-The Health & Pleasure Seeker's Guide-Phila-1874-12mo-126p-1st ed (4c8) 12.50
SEQUIN, L G-Rural England-Lond-(1880)-illus-folio-ed de Luxe-ltd to 300c for England & 300c for Amer (5q0) 20.00
SEQUOYAN LANGUAGE-Laws of US Regul Trade & Intercourse with Indian Tribes etc-(Tahlequah I T)-1879-rare-66p (4L5) 400.00
SERANNE, ANN-The Complete Book of Home Preserving-GardenCty-(1955)-384p (5c9) 4.00
SERGEANT ATKINS-By an officer of the US Army-Phila-1871-Lippincott-12mo-orig cl-frontis-plts-1st ed (5i0,f) 17.50
SERGEANT BELL & HIS RAREE SHOW-Phila-1854-sq12mo-144p-17 plts (5v0,f) 12.50
SERGEANT, JOHN-Letter from Revd Mr Sergeant of Stockbridge to Dr Colman of Boston,re Indian Children-1929-16p-facs (5L7) 6.00
SERGEANT, T-Constitutional Law-Phila-1822-Abraham Small,Prntr (5ff4,rebnd) 19.50
SERIES OF LETTERS-written during Residence in SoAmer by an Engl Gentleman-Lond-1804-8vo-3/4 calf-64p-frontis-(J C Davie) (5ss2) 85.00
SERIOUS CONSIDERATIONS ON MEASURES-of the Present Admin-(Earl of Bute's)-Lond-1763-20p,1p-sq4to-wrps (5L8,new wrps) 18.50
SERMOLINO, MARIA-Papa's Table d'Hote-Phila-(1952)-253p (5g9) 3.00
SERMONS PREACHED IN BOSTON ON DEATH OF A LINCOLN-Bost-1865-379p-cl (5h2) 12.50
SERMONS TO CHILDREN-to which are added etc-Hartf-1808-Lincoln&Gleason-by a Lady-72p-wrps (5d6) 20.00
--same-Bost-1814-T B Wait & Sons-wrps-91p-by a Lady (5rr2,fox) 20.00
SERRA, JUNIPERO-Founding of the 1st Calif Missions-SanFran-1934-Nueva Calif Pr-sm4to-ltd to 1000c (5x5,vf,dj) 35.00
--Life & Times of-Wash-(1959)-R8vo-2 vols-frontis-maps-plts-by M J Geiger (5dd6) 12.00
SERVANTS' GUIDE & FAMILY MANUAL-Lond-1832-frontis-288p,24p-3rd ed (5w7,fox) 16.50
SERVEN, JAS E-Colt Firearms,1836 to 1954-SantaAna-1954-4to-384p-illus (5xx7dj) 15. (5x0) 17.50
SERVICE, ROBT W-Ballads of a Bohemian-NY-(1921)-Barse&Hopkins-port-1st ed (5m2,vg,wn dj) 5.00
--Ballads of a Cheechako-Tor-1909-illus-1st ed (5tt7,f) 20.00
--Bar Room Ballads-1940-Dodd,Mead (5F1,mint,dj) 4.00
--Harper of Heaven-NY-1948-452p-1st(4f9) 10. (5dd7,dj,f) 7.00
--Master of the Microbe-NY-1926-424p (5a1) 4.50
--Ploughman of the Moon-Lond-1946-port-396p (4d2) 5.00
--Poisoned Paradise-Lond-1924-412p (5dd7,f) 3.50
--The Pretender-(1914) (4h3,sl soil) 4.00
--Rhymes of a Red Cross Man-Tor-1916-Wm Briggs-cl-1st ed (5ss3,rub) 25.00
--same-NY-1916 (4b4) 4.50
--Rhymes of a Rolling Stone-Tor-1912-1st ed (5hh1,vg) 12.50
--Why Grow Old-Lond-1932-224p (4d8) 5.00
SERVIER, J-Memoires Du Sieur de Pontis-Paris-1898-4to-col plts (5jj3,rub) 35.00
SESSIONS, F C-Sessions Family in Amer-1890-252p (4t2) 10.00

SESSIONS,FRANCIS-From Yellowstone Park to Alaska-NY-1890-
12mo-cl-bds-186p-ads-Welch Fracker Co-1st ed   (5g2)   12.00
SET OF FLOWERS,A-Alphabetically Arranged,for Little Children-
NY-Sam'lWood&Sons-n.d.-16mo-24p-wrps-sewn-v rare
(5v2,wn)   25.00
SETH,RONALD- Spy Has No Friends-n.p.-(Lond)-n.d. (5x7)   3.50
SETON,ANYA-The Turquoise-Bost-(1946)-378p   (5L0)   3.00
SETON,ERNEST THOMPSON-Animal Heroes-NY-1905-362p-
drwngs -1st ed   (5L0,fade)   6.50
--Animal Tracks & Hunter Signs-GardenCty-1958-158p plus index-
drwngs -1st ed   (5L2,dj)   5.00
--The Arctic Prairies-(NY-1911)-308p-illus   (4h3,lacks fly)   18.00
--same-NY-1920-photos-2nd impr-308p   (5L0)   5.00
--Bannertail,Story of a Gray Squirrel-Lond-(c1922)-230p-plts-
1st Engl ed   (5a1)   5.00
--Biogr of a Grizzly-NY or Tor-1900-(140)p-plts-vignts-1st ed-
cl   (5a1) 5.   (5t0) 10. (5v0,vf) 6.   (4t8)   7.50
--The Biogr of an Arctic Fox-1937-Appleton,Century (5F1,f,dj) 5.50
--Birch Bark Roll of Woodcraft-NY-(c1925)-493p-illus-20th ed
(5aa0)   6.50
--The Book of Woodcraft & Indian Lore-GardenCty-1915-551p plus
index-drwngs   (5L2,f,dj)   6.50
--same-NY-1922-illus-590p   (5t7)   10.50
--Krag & Johnny Bear-NY-1902-12mo-148p   (5x5,sl stn)   9.50
--Library of Pioneering & Woodcraft-1925-5 vols-illus (4m2,f)   20.00
--same-NY-1927,8,9-illus-6 vols   (5L2)   20.00
--Lives of Game Animals,Cats,Wolves & Foxes-Bost-(1953)-plts-
12 maps-2 vols-o.p.-cl   (5cc1,mint)   19.00
--same-Skunks,Wolverine,Weasels & Otters-Bost-(1953)-382p-
plts-7 maps-cl   (5cc1,mint)   9.50
--same-Antelope,Wild Goats & Sheep,Muskox,Buffalo-Bost-
(1953)-372p-plts-5 maps-o.p.-cl   (5cc1,mint)   9.50
--same-Squirrels,Rabbits,Armadillo & Oppossum-Bost-(1953)-
2 vols-plts-20 maps-o.p.-cl   (5cc1,mint)   19.00
--Lives of the Hunted-NY-1901-Scribner's Sons-1st ed-illus-
DeVinne Pr   (5t7) 10. (5L2,fade,5cc1,f) 6. (5i4,5dd9)   8.50
--same-NY-1915-360p   (5t4)   7.00
--Lobo & Other Stories from Wild Animals I Have Known-Lond-
n.d.-125p-plts-illus   (5a1)   4.50
--Lobo,Rag & Vixen & pictures-NY-1914-154p-illus (5xx5)   4.50
--Monarch The Big Bear of Tallac-NY-1904-pict cl-100 drwngs-
1st ed   (5r9,f)   12.50
--same-NY-1922-12mo-100 drwngs   (5xx5)   5.00
--Natural History of the 10 Commandments-NY-1907-12mo-78p-
wrps   (5dd4)   9.00
--The Preacher of Cedar Mountain-GardenCty-1918-frontis-440p
(5xx5)   8.00
--Rolf in the Woods-NY-(1911)-456p-illus   (5xx5)   8.00
--Rolf in the Woods-NY-1922-plts-cl-452p   (5cc1,vg)   5.00
--Sign Talk,a Universal Signal ode..Cheyenne Indians-GardenCty-
1918-illus by author-1st ed-scarce   (4t8)   40.00
--The Trail of the Sandhill Stag-NY-1899-illus-1st ed (5m1,autg)8.50
--same-NY-1899-Japan vel-1st ed-ltd ed of 250c   (5v2)   20.00
--Two Little Savages-NY-1903-cl-illus-552p-1st ed
(5mm2) 8.50 (4h8,sl soil) 17.50   (5r9,5cc1,f)   12.50
--Wild Animals I Have Known-Scribner's Sons-1898-358p-
drwngs-8vo   (4a0)   10.00
--same-NY-1904-359p-30 plts-cl   (5cc1,vg)   5.00
--Woodland Tales-GardenCty-NY-1922-235p plus ads-drwngs
(5L2)   5.00
--Woodmyth & Fable-Lond-1905-Hodder&Stoughton-red dec cl-
1st Engl ed   (5c8,f)   7.50
--same-n.p.-1905-illus-1st ed   (5mm2)   7.50
--Works,uniform format-GardenCty-1923-DbldayPage-8vo-cl-
illus-6 vols   (5t2,f,dj)   15.00
SETON,GRACE THOMPSON-Poison Arrows-NY-(1940)-304p-
illus   (5t7)   5.75
--A Woman Tenderfoot-NY-1900-361p-illus-1st ed
(5s4) 6.   (5m9) 4.50   (5L2)   4.00
SETON,JULIA M-Pulse of Pueblo-1939-249p-1st ed (5r1,dj,f)   11.00
SETON-WATSON,H W-Bear hunting in the White Mntns or Alaska
& British Columbia-1901-illus   (5L7)   5.00
SETON-WATSON,HUGH-The East European Revolution-NY-1951-
8vo-cl-406p-2 maps   (5t0)   5.00
SETSER,V G-Commercial Reciprocity Policy of the US,1774 to
1829-1937-sewn   (5L7)   5.00
SETTLE,RAYMOND W-Empire on Wheels-Stanford Univ-(1949)-
4to-cl-illus   (5L0,5F5,vf,dj) 10.   (5xx5)   12.50
SEUSS,DR-500 Hats of Bartholomew Cobbins-NY-(1938)-1st ed-
black bds   (4F6,vf)   40.00
--Seven Lady Godivas-NY-(1939)-1st ed   (4F6,vf,dj)   65.00

SEVEN & NINE YEARS AMONG THE CAMANCHES & APACHES-
JerseyCty,N J-1873-Clark Johnson-8vo-orig cl-plts-
(E Eastman)-1st ed   (5n9,box)   75.00
--same-JerseyCty-1874-illus-309p-cl
(5r5,wn) 12.50   (5r7,rub,4i4)   20.00
--same-JerseyCty-1879-309p-cl-8vo   (5g0)   7.50
SEVEN CHAMPIONS OF CHRISTENDOM-The Surprising Adventures
of-Lond-ca 1830-16mo-wrps-fldg hand col frontis (5v0,f) 22.50
727TH RAILWAY OPERATING BATTALION IN WW2-NY-1948-
4to-102p   (4p7)   10.00
SEVEN LITTLE SISTERS WHO LIVE ON THE ROUND BALL THAT
FLOATS IN THE AIR-Bost-1861-12mo-1st ed of auth's 1st book
(5gg6) 15.   (4c3,f)   40.00
SEVEN WIVES & SEVEN PRISONS-NY-1870-frontis-205p-
(L A Abbott)   (5t7,stnd) 8.   (5x4,cov wn)   17.50
SEVEN WONDERS OF THE WORLD & OTHER MAGNIFICENT
BLDGS etc-NY-1816-S Wood&Sons-pic wrps-col illus-
cov impr of Amer Antiq dated 1816   (5jj6,fox)   35.00
--sane-NY-1822-SWood&Sons-chapbook-42p-&3p adv-slim 12mo-
pic self wrps   (5c8,cov tn)   27.50
17th VERMONT REGIMENT-Rosters of Survivors of 17th Vt
Reunion Assoc-St Johnsbury-1900-16mo-wrps-32p (5q0)   10.00
SEVENTH REGIMENT-Nat'l Guard,S NY,Manual of the-(NY)-
1868-Board of Trustees-8vo-cl-frontis-col plt-239p (5j5)   10.00
SEVENTY YEARS,THE FOLEY SAGA-(Los Ang,1945)-R8vo-204p-
hf cl-fldg maps-illus   (5dd4,autg)   15.00
75 YEARS OF PROGRESS-NY-1927-Hanover Fire Ins Co-48p-
bds-illus   (5y2)   6.50
77TH PENNA AT SHILOH-History of the Regiment-(Harrisburg)-
1905-(J Obreiter)-406p-photos-fldg maps-1st ed   (5L5)   12.50
SEVERAL HANDS-Collection of Poems in 6 Volumes-Lond-1763-
6 vols-calf-g.dec-engr-Dodsley   (5aa0)   65.00
SEVERAL HANDS-New Signatures,Poems By Several Hands-Lond-
1932-Cr 8vo-bds-1st ed   (5ss7)   10.00
SEVERAL PROCEEDINGS & RESOLUTIONS OF HOUSE OF PEERS-
in relation to Lords Impeached or Charged-Lond-1701-100p-
folio-hf mor   (5L1)   200.00
SEVERANCE,F B-Genealogy & Biog of Desc of Walter Stewart of
Scotland & John etc-1905-215p   (4t2)   25.00
SEVERANCE,FRANK H-Old Frontier of France-NY-1917-2 vols-
illus-maps-ports   (5aa0)   35.00
--Old Trails on the Niagara Frontier-Buffalo-1899-321p-frontis
(5aa0)   15.00
--same-1903-260p   (5zz0,fox)   8.00
SEVERANCE,HENRY ORMAL-Story of a Village Community
(Walled Lake,Mich)-NY-1931-maps   (5yy6)   6.00
SEVERANCE,J F-Genealogical Hist Severans-1893-78p (5t9)   17.50
SEVERANCE,JULIET H-A Discussion of the Social Question-Milwkee-
1891-46p-orig prntd wrps   (5w5)   5.00
SEVERANCE,L-Speech on the Mexican War-Wash-1847-16p(5n4) 6.00
--Speech On the War Against Mexico-Wash-1846-8p (5n4)   6.00
SEVERANCE,MARK-Hammersmith,His Harvard Days-Bost-1878-
524p-Houghton,Osgood-1st ed   (5x4,sl fray)   17.50
SEVERIN,ERNEST-Svenskarne I Texas I Ord Och Bild, 1838 to 1918-
(Austin-1919)-604p-photos   (4a5)   25.00
SEVERIN,KURT-To the South-NY-1944-Eagle Bks-8vo-cl-244p-
illus   (5v7)   7.50
SEVERSKY,ALEXANDER DE-Victory Through Air Power-NY-1942
(5q2) 3.   (5x7)   3.50
SEVILLE,WM P,ed-Narr of March of CoA,Engineers from
Ft Leavenworth to Ft Bridger & Return May 6 to Oct 3,1858-
Wash-1912-#48-US Army-46p-oilcloth cov-rare (5bb4)   45.00
SEWALL,HENRY D,ed-Collection of Psalms & Hymns for Social
& Private Worship-NY-1820-12mo-calf-1st ed-(1st of
W C Bryant's hymns)   (5gg6,crack,wn)   250.00
SEWALL,JOHN IVES-A History of Western Art-NY-(1953)-Holt-
957p-illus   (5p7)   9.00
--Ancient Dominions of Maine-Bath-1859-366p-cl-illus-1st ed
(5g8) 27.50   (5t2)   17.50
--Sketches of St Augustine-NY-1848-orig cl-6 engrs-1st ed
(5i0,pg 39,40 in mss) 35.   (5m4)   125.00
SEWALL,SAML-History of Woburn-Bost-1868
(5yy0,needs rbndg) 12.50   (5ii8)   17.50
SEWALL,SAML E-The Legal Condition of Women in Massachusetts-
Bost-1870-16mo-24p-rev ed-Woman's Suffrage Tracts #5
(5t7) 3.   (5g4)   5.00
SEWALL,WM WESLEY-Clocks & Early Timing Pieces of London-
Lond-1887-plts-368p-fldg plt-rare   (5e0,plt tn)   215.00

SEWARD,ANNA-Memoirs of Life of Dr Darwin-Phila-1804-313p-
bds-scarce   (5h7,sp wn,stns)   12.50

USED BOOK PRICE GUIDE

SEWARD, ANNA (continued)
--same-Lond-1804-hf mor-8vo-1st ed-errata lf   (5i8)   35.00
--Monody on Major Andre-Bost-1798-Spotswood&Wayne-sm8vo-
22p-orig grey wrps   (5L1,sl tn,box)   20.00
--Monody on Major Andre,To Which Are Added Letters-Litchfield
(Eng)-1781-4to-47p-2nd ed-removed   (5m3,autg)   65.00
SEWARD,FREDK W-Eilliam H Seward-NY-1891-822p (5j6)   5.00
SEWARD,GEO F-Chinese Immigration in its social & economical
aspects-NY-(1881)-435p   (5t4)   7.50
SEWARD,HERBERT-Marine Engineering-NY-1942,4-2 vols-4to
(5s1)   12.50
SEWARD,OLIVE RISLEY-Wm H Seward's Travels Around the
World-NY-1873-orig sheep-illus-raised bands-1st ed
(5s1,wn) 7.50   (5w5,f bndg)   12.50
SEWARD,WM H-An autobiography from 1801 to 1834-NY-1891-
lg8vo-3 vols-illus   (5g3)   20.00
--California,Union & Freedom-Wash-1850-leaflet-14p-8vo (4g6) 6.00
--Life & Public Services of John Quincy Adams-Auburn-1849-
404p-1st ed   (5L3,f) 7.50   (5t7)   10.00
--Travels Around the World-NY-Appleton-1873-dec cl
(5dd6,bkstrp tn)   5.00
SEWEL,WM-History of the Rise, Increase & Progress of the Christian
People Called Quakers-Lond-1795-2 vols-calf-3rd ed
(5r7,broke)   20.00
SEWEL,WM-History of the rise, increase & progress of Christian
people called Quakers-Burlington,NJ-1774-Isaac Collins-
folio-calf-2nd Amer ed   (5i0,rub)   65.00
SEWELL,A-Black Beauty-Bost-(1890)-orig bds-1st Amer ed(?)
(4F6,f)   25.00
SEWELL,E M-The Experience of Life-NY-1853-379p-1st ed
(5t4,sp wn)   6.50
SEWELL,ELIZ M-Katharine Ashton-Lond-(ca 1875)-522p-1st ed
(5t7)   6.00
SEWELL,HELEN-Broomsticks & Snowflake-NY-1933-1st ed-illus
(4F6,ex-libr)   6.00
SEWELL,S-Hist of Woburn,Mass-1868-657p   (4t2)   15.00
SEWELL,WM-History of the Rise,Increase & Progress of the Quakers-
Burlington,NJ-folio-calf-labl-Isaac Collins-3rd ed,corr-
812p,16p   (5L8,rust)   32.50
--same-Phila-1832-orig calf-new ed in 2 vols   (5m2)   12.00
SEXBY,J J-The Municipal Parks,Gardens & Open Spaces of
London-Lond-1905-646p-photos-"cheap ed"   (5w3)   12.50
SEXTON COOK BOOK-John Sexton & Co-(Chig,1950)-432p-
1st ed   (5c9)   5.00
SEXTON,GEO-A Portraiture of Mormenism,or Animadversions on
the Doctrines & Pretensions of the Latter day Saints-Lond-
1849-113p-errata-hf lea-1st ed-v rare   (5t3)   85.00
SEXTON,LYDIA-Autobiography-1882   (5L7)   10.00
SEXTON,R W-Amer Theatres of Today...plans,sections,details-
NY-1927-4to-175p   (4p7)   12.50
--Spanish Influence on Amer Architecture & Decoration-NY-
1927-Brentano's-sm folio-cl-illus(5w7,stn,scuff) 8.50 (4m9) 20.00
SEYBERT,A-Statistical Annals-1818-4to-buck (5L7,ex-libr)   17.50
SEYBERT COMMISSION ON SPIRITUALISM-Prelim Report of-
Univ of Pa-Phila-1887-159p   (5w0)   10.00
SEYBOLT,PAUL-Catalogue of 1st Editions Books in Collection of-
Bost-1946-8vo-bds-cl bk   (5gg6)   5.00
--First Editions of Ike Marvel,a Checklist-Bost-1930-12mo-8p-
priv prntd-ltd to 100c-nbrd   (5ss9,fade)   5.00
SEYD,ERNEST-Calif & Its Resources-Lond-1858-plts(8 col)-
2 fldg maps-168p-1st ed-wi reproduction of Calif-gold slug
on cov   (4n1,rub)   100.00
SEYMANN,J-Colonial Charters,Patents & Grants to Communities
Comprising City of NY-NY-1939   (5ff4)   15.00
SEYMOUR CASH REGISTER CO-New Peerless Detail Adding
Cash Register-Detroit-(191-?)-12p-illus   (5h8)   6.50
SEYMOUR,CHAS-Diplomatic Background of War,1870 to 1914-
NewHav-1916   (4b7,pencil)   10.00
--How The World Votes-Springfield-1918-2 vols   (5x7)   7.50
SEYMOUR,E L D-Favorite Flowers in Color-NY-1949-Wise&Co-
634p-300 col plts-pict cl   (5s7)   7.50
--The Garden Encyclopedia-NY-1939-Wise&Co-1300p-
illus   (4g0)   10.00
SEYMOUR,FLORA WARREN-Indian Agents of the Old Frontier-
NY-1941-8vo-cl-402p-illus-1st ed (5L0) 15. (5F5,f,dj)   12.50
--Lords of the Valley-1930-278p   (4m2)   17.50
--Pocahontas,Brave Girl-NY-(1946)-illus-192p-1st ed-juvenile
(4b2)   3.00
--Story of the Red Man-Lond,NY&Tor-1919-1st ed
(5kk7) 10.   (5bb4,dj)   12.50
--same-NY-1934-illus-maps   (4b2)   10.00

SEYMOUR,GEO D-Captain Nathan Hale,1775 to 76,Maj John
Palsgrave Wyllys 1754 to 90-NewHav-1933-illus-Ltd ed
(5p0) 12.50   (4m4)   27.50
--Documentary Life of Nathan Hale-NewHav-1941-priv prntd-
454p plus appendix   (5L 3,appndx pgs stuck)   7.50
--A History of the Seymour Family-NewHav-1939-662p-illus
(5p0)   27.50
SEYMOUR,H D-Russia on the Black Sea & Sea of Azoff-Lond-1835-
cl-8vo-361p-fldg maps   (5v7)   17.50
SEYMOUR,HORATIO-Lecture on Topography & History of NY-
Utica-1856-8vo-orig wrps-41p-1st ed   (5m6)   6.50
SEYMOUR,JOHN-One Man's Africa-Lond-1955-illus (5x2)   4.00
SEYMOUR,MAURICE-Ballet-NY-1949-Pellegrini-4to-101 photos
(5p0)   12.50
--Ballet Portraits-NY-1952-Pelegrini&Cudahy-4to-165p-photos
(5p0)   12.50
SEYMOUR,R-Squib Annual of Poetry,Politics & Personalities for
1836-Lond-1836-Chapman&Hall-16mo-hf mor-raised bands-
g.t.-1st ed   (4n5,sl soil)   75.00
SEYMOUR,ROBT-Humorous Sketches-Lond-1866-illus by Crowquill-
8vo-cl-g.e.-New ed   (4c2,sp wn,crack)   15.00
SEYMOUR,SILAS-Incidents of a Trip through the Great Platte
Valley....in Fall of 1866 etc-NY-1867-129p-1st ed-scarce
(5L2,bkstrp wn)   25.00
SEYMOUR,WM N-Madison Directory & Business Advertiser-
Madison-1855-Atwood&Rublee-orig bds-192p-roan-1st annual ed
(5m3,rub,lacks map)   25.00
SHABEENY,E H A S-Account of Timbuctoo & Housa,Territories
in Interior of Africa-Lond-1820-2 fldg maps-547p-buck
(5m4,ex-libr,rbnd)   55.00
SHACKELFORD,SHELBY-Electric Eeel Calling-(NY-(1941)-illus
(5jj3)   10.00
SHACKLEFORD,WM Y-Belle Starr,the Bandit Queen-Girard,Ka-
(1943)-24p-wrps-1st ed   (5bb4)   3.00
--same-1946-12mo-63p-Little Blue Book #1846   (5g6)   3.00
--Gun fighters of the Old West-Girard,Ka-(1943)-24p-wrps-1st ed
(5bb4)   3.00
SHACKLETON,E H-Heart of the Antartic-Lond-1909-Wm Heinemann-
thk8vo-g.t.-2 vols-1st ed (5L7) 15. (5j5) 35. (5n9)   45.00
SHACKLETON,EDW-Arctic Journeys-NY-n.d.-F&R-(ca 1936)-
illus-map-photos   (4m9)   10.00
SHACKLETON,SIR ERNEST-South,The Story of Shakleton's Last
Expedition 1914 to 1917-MM-1920-380p-illus   (5e8)   5.00
SHACKLETON,ROBT-Adventures in Home Making-Phila-1922-
350p-photos   (5w7)   3.50
--The Book of Antiques-Phila-(1938)-Penn Publ-284p-illus (5x0) 6.50
--The Book of Chicago-Phila-1920-illus   (5yy6)   5.00
--The Book of New York-Phila-1917-375p-illus-col frontis
(5L3,lacks fly) 3.50   (5h9)   5.00
--The Book of Philadelphia-Phila-1918-413p-illus-1st ed (5w4)   5.00
--The Great Adventurer-NY-1904-Dblday,Page-8vo-dec cl (5b2) 4.00
SHADDINGER,A E-Micheners in America 1686 to 1958-1958-627p
(4t2)   13.00
SHADOWS OF THE PEOPLE-Bost-(ca 1870)-A Williams&Co-sm8vo-
pict bds-12 plts   (5c8)   12.50
SHADWELL,CHAS-The fair Quaker of Deal-Dublin-1757-12mo-
disbnd   (5x3)   10.00
SHADWELL,THOS-Complete Works of-Lond-1927-Fortune Pr-
ed by Summers-4to-bds-lin bk-5 vols-ltd to 1200c-scarce
(5d1)   150.00
SHADY SIDE,THE-or,Life in a Country Parsonage,by a Pastor's
Wife-Bost-1853-Jewett-349p-2nd issue-(Mrs M Hubbell) (5x4)12.50
SHAEFER,P W-Historical Map of Pennsylvania-Phila-1875-
col fldg map-scarce   (4m4)   17.50
SHAFER,DON CAMERON-Smokefires of Schoharie-1938-357p-
1st ed   (5ff2)   16.00
SHAFER,T B-Sutton Beasley Family of Brown Co,Ohio-1946-97p
(4t2)   8.50
SHAFFER,E T H-Carolina Gardens-NC Pr-1939-illus (5qq7)   7.50
--same-1939-Uof NoCar Pr-illus-336p-Garden Club Ed (4d9,f)   4.50
SHAFFER,ELLEN-The Garden of Health,an Account of 2 Herbals-
SanFran-1957-Bk Club of Calif-sm folio-ltd to 300c (5d8)   55.00
SHAFFNER,TAL P-The War in Amer-Lond-(1862)-col fldg map-
418p   (4b6,pres,ex-libr)   35.00
SHAFFORD,JOHN CONRAD-Narr of Extraordinary Life of-NY-
1840-1st ed-24p-frontis-qtr mor   (5s6,orig cov bnd in)   65.00
SHAFTER,ALFRED M-Musical Copyright-Chig-1932   (5p7)   6.50
SHAFTER,O L-Life...Diary & Letters of-SanFran-1915-Blair
Murdock-illus-col frontis-323p-1st ed   (4n1,sp dark)   16.50
SHAFTESBURY,EDMUND-Life Building Method of the Ralston
Health Club-n.p.-1920-240p   (5c5,pencil)   5.00
--Transference of Thought-Wash-(1896)-272p-8vo-cl-2nd ed
(5t2,sl shake)   5.00

SHAFTSBURG,ANTHONY,EARL OF-Characteristicks of Men,
Manners,Opinions,Times-Birmnghm-Jn Baskerville-1773-
3 vols-calf-g.dec-5th ed   (5a1,f)   165.00

SHAHN,BEN-The Sorrows of Priapus-(NY,1957)-Edw Dahlberg-
8vo-g.t.-extra lith-Thistle Pr-ltd to 150c   (5d8,box)   85.00

SHAH,SAYED IDRIES-Oriental Magic-NY-(1957)-illus
(5F0,dj) 4.50   (5t4)   7.50

SHAHMAH IN PURSUIT OF FREEDOM-by an Amer citizen-NY-
1858-port   (5g8,libr labl)   7.50

SHAHN,BEN-Partridge in a Pear Tree-Curt Valentin-1949-
obl 8vo-wrps   (5ww3)   15.00

SHAKER CHURCH COVENENT-ShakerVillage,NH-1889-12p text-
wrps   (5t4)   15.00

SHAKER VILLAGE-Catalog of Fany Goods...made at Shaker
Village,Sabbathday Lake,Maine-n.p.-1907-obl 12mo-
orig prntd wrps-illus-v scarce   (5t0)   30.00

SHAKERS-Summary View of the Millennial Church-Albany-1823-
orig sheep-12mo-1st ed   (5i0,f)   45.00
--same-Albany-1848-sheep-384p-2nd ed,revised   (5t2,sm3)   25.00

SHAKESPEAR,CAPT HENRY-The Wild Sports of India etc-Bost-
1860-Ticknor&Fields-12mo-cl-283p-16p ads-1st Amer ed (5j5)15.00

SHAKESPEARE BIBLIOGRAPHY-Wm Jaggard,ed-1911-8vo-
729p   (4g2,f,unopened)   45.00

SHAKESPEARE,WM-As You Like It-n.d.(ca 1910)-8vo-col plts tip in-
col illus by Hugh Thompson   (5p6,sl wn)   7.00

--Comedies,Histories & Tragedies-Lond-1632-Tho Cotes-port-
folio-2nd ed,1st state,1st issue-vel   (4c0,rbnd,box)   12,500.00

--Comedies,Histories & Tragedies etc-Lond-1685-Herringman,
Brewster & Bentley-port-folio-272p-plus 1f of actors,328p,
303p-calf-4th edition   (5c0,sl repr)   9,000.00

--Comedies-NY-1896-Harper-8vo-drwngs by E A Abbey-bds-
lin sp-papr labls-g.t.-4 vols   (5s5)   17.50

--The Comedies,Histories & Tragedies-NY-1939,1940-Ltd Editions
Club-37 vols-illus-Bruce Rogers   (5d2)   175.00

--same-NY-Ltd Ed Club-1939,40,41-incl 2 vols poems-39 vols-
box   (5b0)   400.00

--The Complete Works-Phila-1889-896p-mor-"The Fine Avon Ed"
(5b9,f,f bndg)   15.00

--Complete Works-Gollancz,ed-1899-JMDent-Cr 8vo-green buck-
g.t.-illus-12 vols   (5t8,f)   47.50

--Complete Works-ChasKnight,ed-Lond-1890-Rutledge-6 vols-
3/4 red mor-8vo-illus-raised bands   (5t8,f bndg)   39.00

--Complete Works...intro by Sidney Lee-NY-(1906 to 08)-
Harper-8vo-papr labls-g.tops-20 vols   (4m8)   30.00

--Complete Works gathered into 1 vol-Oxford-1934-3/4 crimson mor-
g. seal on cov -Shakespeare Head Press   (5d2)   25.00

--Complete Works of-Lond-1952-WJCraig,ed,Dublin-India papr-
1166p-3/4 mor   (5k1,f bndg,box)   12.50

--Essays of-NY-c1947-GeoCoffinTaylor,ed-144p   (5w9,dj)   3.00

--Hamlet,Prince of Denmark-Barcelona-(1930)-4to-173 sheets of
cork-95 lvs in Engl & 78 lvs in Span-on goatskin-ltd to 100c
(5d1,sl def)   150.00

--Life & Complete Works-Bost&NY-1901-20 vols-8vo-illus-lg type-
buck   (5t5,rbnd)   95.00

--A Midsommer Nights Dreame-Lond-1632-from 2nd folio-
complete in 18p-(pg 153 is misnbrd 151)-cl bds-mor back
(5j2,f bndg,sl rprd)   150.00

--Midsummer Night's Dream-Lond-Heinemann-1908-4to-134p-
40 mntd col plts-Rackham illus-dec cl-g.   (5a1)   20.00

--same-Lond-1908-lg4to-vel-40p mounted col illus by Rackham-
ltd to 1000c,autg by artist   (5d1)   200.00

--same-NY-1911-illus Rackham-2nd imp-8vo-plts-dec cl (5i3,f)25.00

--same-Lond-1912-Heinemann-sm4to-col illus by Rackham-
pict bds-cl bk-134p   (5t2)   25.00

--same-Lond-1914-illus(W Heath Robinson)-R8vo-12 col plts-
pict cl   (4n5)   30.00

--same-NY-1914-illus by W H Robinson-4to-1st Amer ed-
mounted col plts   (5ii3)   17.50

--Mr Wm Shakespeares Comedies,Histories & Tragedies-Lond-1632-
publ according to true Originall Copies-2nd impre-for Tho Cotes
for Robt Allot-folio-a.e.g.-brown russia-2nd folio-
2nd ed of Shakespeare's works
(5ee9,3 facs lvs) 2,750.   (5d1,rprd)   5,000.00

--The Passionate Pilgrim-Oxf-1905-Clarendon Pr-sm4to-vel
(5b0,lacks ties)   7.50

--Plays of Wm Shakespeare, in Miniature-Lond-   9 vols-
calf-1st ed-Sharpe's Ed-rare -1803,4   (5v2,hng rprd)   50.00

--The Plays & Sonnets-Lond-1867-Clark&Wright,ed-fore edge
painting of Globe Theatre   (5d2)   60.00

--Poems....to which is added acct of his life-Bost-1807-
12mo-calf-1st Amer ed-Oliver&Munroe&Belcher&Strong
(5i0,wn)   40.00

SHAKESPEARE,WM   (continued)
--Poems & Sonnets-Cambr Univ Pr-1967-Ltd Ed Club-4to   (5t8)   25.00

--Romeo & Juliet-NY-1892-Duprat&Co-4to-170p-wrps-frontis-
15 plts-ltd to 300c   (5p1)   17.50

--Shakespeare-Phila-n.d.-Handy Stratford Shakespeare-12 vols-
5x3½-flex red lea bndgs-a.e.g.   (5u9)   13.00

--Songs & Sonnets-Lond&Cambr-1865-g.e.-red mor-fore edge
painting   (5h6)   50.00

--Sonnets of-Latin trans by Barton-Lond-1923-bds-papr labl
(5mm2)   12.50

--Venus & Adonis-Rochester-1931-R Kent,illus-Leo Hart-
ltd to 1250c   (5i4,box,Kent autg)   17.50

--Venus & Adonis-Oxf-1905-Clarendon Pr-sm4to-vel-ltd to 1000c,
autg by Lee   (5b0,lacks ties)   7.50

--Venus & Adonis-Lond-1948-designed by Peter Rudland-87p-
ltd to 986c   (5t7)   10.00

--Works of-Lond-1728-9 vols(of 10)-illus-sm8vo-orig sheep&bds-
Pope's 2nd ed   (5ii3,lacks Vol 1)   75.00

--Works-Lond-1842-Chas Knight,ed-tall 8vo-crimson buck-
10 vols-2nd ed   (5t8,f,rbnd)   60.00

--Works of-Bost-1878-illus-2 vols in 1-1120p-pict cl-g.dec-a.e.g.
(5u9)   9.50

--Works-Lond-1891-Rev Alex Dyce,ed-Swan Sonnenschein-
10 vols-8vo-3/4 wine mor-t.e.g.   (5b0)   200.00

--Works-Lond-1891-WmAldisWright,ed-Cambridge Shakespeare-
tall 8vo-9 vols   (5t3,rbnd)   95.00

--Works-NY-1929 to 1933-7 vols-8vo-sheep-g.t.-H Farjeon,ed
(4c2)   450.00

--Works-H Farjeon,ed-Cambridge Univ Pr-(1929 to 33)-mor-8vo-
7 vols-ltd to 1600 sets   (4h5,f)   425.00

--Works of Shakespere,Imperial Edition-Lond-1875-2 vols-
lg folio-3/4 mor-illus   (4j6)   45.00

SHAKESPEARE CLUB COOK BOOK-Pasadena,Calif-n.d.-153p
(5g9)   6.50

SHAKESPEARE'S ENGLAND-An Acct of the Life & Manners of
his Age-Oxf-1916-Clarendon Pr-in the Tercentenary Yr-
2 vols in 4-8vo-3/4 dark brown mor-g.t.e.g.-plts-illus
(5b0)   150.00

SHALER,N S-Kentucky,a Pioneer Commonwealth-Bost-1884-433p
(4j4)   5.00
--same-Bost-1895-fldg map-433p-g.t.   (5h9)   8.50

SHALER,WM-Sketches of Algiers-Bost-1826-Cummings,Hilliard-
310p-orig hf calf   (5d6,rprd)   25.00

SHALET,SIDNEY-Old Nameless-NY-1943-177p-port   (5s1)   5.00

SHALLCROSS,WM J-A Boy's Way of Life-LosAng-(1950)-208p-
cl   (5r0,dj)   7.50

SHAMBAUGH,B F-Constitutions of Iowa-382p with index-cl-
t.e.g.   (5a9)   5.00

SHAMBAUGH,BENJ F-The Old Stone Capitol Remembers-
IowaCty-1939-8vo-cl-435p   (5a9,5m8)   12.50

SHAMBAUGH,BERTHA M H-Amana That Was & Amana That Is-
1932-502p with index-t.e.g.   (5a9)   15.00

SHANACHIE,THE-A Irish Miscellany Illustrated-Dublin-1906,1907-
#1 to 6 complete-8vo-orig prntd wrps   (5dd8)   150.00

SHANAFELT,T M-Baptist History of SoDakota-SiouxFalls-(1899)-
photos-1st ed-v scarce   (4t8,mildew marks)   40.00

SHAND,ALEX-Soldiers of Fortune-Lond-1907-3/4 mor (5d2)   10.00

SHAND,P MORTON-A Book of Food-NY-1928-319p-bds (5g9)   5.00
--Book of French Wines-Lond-1928-247p   (4g9)   7.50
--A Book of Wine-Lond-Cloister Pr-1926-320p   (5g9)   10.00

SHANER,DOLPH-Story of Joplin-NY-c1948-Stratford House-12mo-
cl-144p   (4t1,autg) 12.50   (5dd6)   10.00

SHANKLE,GEO E-Amer Nicknames,Their Original & Significance-
NY-1937-lg8vo-cl-599p-1st ed   (5t0)   10.00

SHANKMAN,SAM-The Peres Family-Kingspt-n.d.-(1938)-
241p-cl   (5h2)   5.00

SHANKS,DAVID C-As They Passed Through the Port-Wash-(1927)-
351p-illus   (5t4)   6.50

SHANKS,HENRY T-The Secession Movement in Virginia-Richmond-
(1934)-Garrett&Massie-8vo-1st ed   (5m6,dj)   10.00

SHANNAHAN,JOHN H K-Steam Boat'n Days-Balt-1930-
18 illusts-ltd to 300c   (5c1)   12.50

SHANNON,A H-Racial Integrity of the Amer Negro-Wash-1953
(5x2)   15.00

SHANNON,HOWARD J-The Book of the Seashore-NY-1935-
281p-illus   (5p7)   12.50

SHANNON,JAS P-Catholic Colonization of the Western Frontier-
Yale Univ Pr-1957   (5x5)   7.50

SHANNON & CO,J JACOB-Catalogue of Builders' Hardware-
Phila-Jul,1888-292p-4to   (5ss5,f)   27.50

SHANNON,K-Integration Decision is Unconstitutional-
LittleRock-1958-60p-wrps   (5x2)   8.50

SHANNON,L W-Underdeveloped Areas-NY-1957   (5ff4)   7.00

SHANNON,MARTHA A S-Boston Days of Wm Morris Hunt-Bost-
1923-illus-165p-bds&cl-ltd ed (5t2,libr mrks) 7.50 (5m2) 12.50

SHANNON,P-State of Dakota,How it may be Formed-Yankton-
1883-wrps-58p   (4L5,underline) 100.00

SHANTY,FOREST & RIVER LIFE IN BACKWOODS of CANADA-
Montr-1883-361p-cl   (5h1) 15.00

SHANTZ,H L-Arizone & Its Heritage-Tucson-1936-Univ of Ariz-
291p-wrps   (4a5) 9.50

SHANTZ,J Y-Relation d'un Voyage a Manitoba-Ottawa-1873-
wrps-30p-1st ed   (5r7,f) 55.00

SHAPIRO,H L-Migration & Environment-Lond-1939-Oxf Univ Pr-
                                       (5x5,dj) 20.00

SHAPIRO,HARRY L-Descendants of Mutineers of Bounty-Honolulu-
1929-sm folio-wrps   (4c1) 15.00

SHAPLAND,H P-The Practical Decoration of Furniture-Lond-
1926,27-3 vols in 1-4to-cl-144 plts-1st ed (5m6) 25.00

SHAPLEY,HARLOW-A Treasury of Science-NY-c1958-776p-bds
                                       (5w4) 4.50

SHAPLEY,RUFUS E-Solid for Mulhooly-Phila-1889-Gebbie-210p-
ads-illus-pict cl   (5qq8) 6. (5m1) 12.50

SHARFMAN,I L-Interstate Commerce Comm;a Study in Admin Law
& Procedure-NY-1931 to 37-4 vols in 5 (5r4,rub) 85.00

SHARP,MRS ABBIE-History of the Spirit Lake Massacre-DesMoines-
1885-314p-illus   (5L2) 15.00
--same-DesMoines-1902-5th ed-rev-312p-illus (5i3) 10.00
--same-LakeOkoboji,la-(1910)-386p-6th ed (5L2,ex-libr) 6.00

SHARP,DALLAS LORE-Where Rolls the Oregon-Bost-(1914)-245p
plus index-(not 1st ed)   (5bb4) 3.00

SHARP,ELIZ A-Wm Sharp(Fiona Macleod) A Memoir-NY-1910-
illus-cl   (5t2) 4.50

SHARP,GRANVILLE-Declaration of People's Natural Right to a
Share in Legislature-Bost-1774-Edes&Gill-sm4to-hf mor (5n2)85.00
--Representation of Injustice & Dangerous Tendency of Tolerating
Slavery...in 4 Parts-Lond-1769-167p-orig bndg-with appendix,
Lond-1772-28p   (5tt6) 100.00

SHARP,MORRIE L-Camellias Illustrated-Portland,Ore-1949-
159p-col illus   (5s7) 5.00

SHARP,PAUL F-Whoop Up Country-Helena-(1955)-map-illus-
368p-1st ed   (5L0) 6.50 (5dd4) 8.50

SHARP,W C-Chatfield Family-1896-32p   (5t9) 22.50

SHARP,DR W H H-Prophetic History & Fulfillment of Prophecy
from 600 Years BC-SaltLkCty-1883-42p-orig wrps-illus-
Deseret Home Co-"Book First"   (5m3,f) 27.50

SHARP,WM,ed-The Essays of Sainte Beuve-Lond-1901-3 vols-
Gibbings&Co   (5p9) 15.00
--Life of Percy Bysshe Shelley-Lond-1887-cl-Walter Scott-
1st ed   (5ss3,chip,pres) 35.00

SHARPE,CHAS KIRKPATRICK-Historical Acct of Belief in
Witchcraft in Scotland-Lond-1884-orig cl-8vo-268p (5ee5) 18.00

SHARPE,D R-Walter Rauschenbusch-1942   (5L7) 5.00

SHARPE,EDMUND-Treatise on Rise & Progress of Decorated Window
Tracery in England-Lond-1849-103 illus-111p (5t7) 7.00

SHARPE,LANCELOT,ed-Poems,supposed to have been written at
Bristol by TRowley & others-Cambr-1794-8vo-hf calf (5gg6) 50.00

SHARPE,MAY CHURCHILL-Chicago May,Her Story-NY-1928-
336p-illus-Macaulay   (5w5,5p0) 5.00

SHARPE,PHILIP B-Complete Guide to Handloading-NY-1937-
4to-465p-illus   (4a6,autg) 35.00
--same-NY-(1952)-4to-232p-illus-3rd ed   (5xx7) 15.00
--The Rifle in America-NY-1938-4to-641p-plts-lea-1st ed
(5xx7,autog) 25. (4a6,box,autg) 40.00
--This Handloading Game-Chig-(c1936)-4to-48p-illus-wrps-rprnt
                                       (4a6) 10.00

SHARPE,R BOWDLER-Analytical Index to Works of Late John Gould-
Lond-1893-4to-375p   (5nn2) 65.00
--Lloyd's Natural History-Lond-1896 to 97-12mo-orig cl-
484 col plts-16 vols-scarce-complete   (4p5,sp fade) 85.00
--Monograph of the Hirundinidae or Family of Swallows-Lond-
1885,1894-cl-104 handcol plts-4to-2 vols
(4n5,recased,vf) 1,150.00
--Monograph of Paradiseidae-Lond-1891-mor-elephant folio-
g.e.-79 handcol plts-2 vols-1st ed-ltd to 350c
(5z9,f bndg,vf 3,500.00

SHARPE,S G-Tobe-Univ NoCar-1944-juvenile-4to-photos
                                       (5x2,dj) 2.50

SHARPE,W C-South Britain-Priv prntd-1898-167p (5e8) 27.75

SHARPLES,ADA WHITE-Alaska Wild Flowers-Stanford U Pr,Calif-
(1938)-156p   (5s7) 2.75

SHASTA,KEYSTONE OF CALIF SCENERY-SanMateo-1887-col illus-
4to-col pict lin wrps   (5g3,f) 25.00

SHASTA COUNTY-Resources of Shasta Co,Calif-(1892)-World's
Fair Comm-16mo-10p-prntd wrps-(accordion fold) (5g4,f) 7.50

SHATTERED IDOLS-Lond-1865-Hurst&Blackett-3 vols-8vo-
orig blue cl-2nd ed   (5xx6) 15.00

SHATTUCK,G B,ed-Bahama Islands-1905-4to-illus (5L7) 32.50

SHATTUCK,HARRIETTE R-The Woman's Manual of Parliamentary Law-
Bost-1896-12mo-285p-illus-6th ed,rev   (5w7,sp tn) 3.50

SHAW,ALBERT-Abraham Lincoln-NY-1929-2 vols-cartoons-4to-
orig cl-port   (5m3,pres) 30. (5w5) 15.00
--Cartoon History of Roosevelt's Career-NY-1910-4to-cl-253p
(5m8) 5. (5L7) 7.50

SHAW,ALONZO-Trails in Shadowland,Story of a Detective-
(Columbus-1910)-cl-298p-rare   (4k2,dmpstn) 8.50

SHAW,ANNA H-Story of a Pioneer-NY&Lond-(1915)-illus
(5kk3,5i3) 5. (5qq8,5s4) 7.50

SHAW,ARCHER H-The Lincoln Encyclopedia-NY-1950-395p
(5t4) 7. (5h6) 8.00
--The Plain Dealer,100 Yrs in Cleveland-NY-1942-illus-1st ed
(5yy8) 6.00

SHAW,CLIFFORD R-The Jack Roller,a Delinquent Boy's Own
Story-Jun,1930-U of Chig Pr   (4m9,dj) 12.50

SHAW,D A-Eldorado or Calif as seen by Pioneer 1850 to 1900-
LosAng-1900-Baumgardt-313p-cl (5tt0) 6. (5bb4,pres) 12.50

SHAW,EDW-Rural Architecture-Bost-1843-Jas B Dow-4to-108p text-
48p plts-orig calf   (5t0,wn,lt stns) 100.00

SHAW,ELTON R-The Curse of Drink Or,Stories of Hell's Commerce-
n.p.-(1910)-544p-photos   (5w6) 8.50
--Conquest of Southwest-Berwyn-(1924)-138p-cl (5jj9) 10.00
--Stories of Hell's Commerce of Liquor Traffic in Its True Light-
GrndRpds-(1909)-544p-cl   (5h7) 7.50

SHAW,FRANK H-Full Fathom Five-NY-1930-Macmillan-8vo-
301p   (5s1) 6. (5j5) 7.50

SHAW,FRED G-The Science of Fly Fishing for Trout-Lond-1925-
341p-illus   (5t7) 10.00

SHAW,GEO-General Zoology or Systematic Natural History,
Vol 3,Pt 1 & 2 Amphibia (incl Reptiles)-Lond-1802-2 vols(part
of 14 vol set but complete on reptiles & amphibians),plts-lea-
g.sp-8vo-v scarce   (4p6) 75.50
--Naturalist's Miscellany-Lond-(1789 to 1813)-calf-lea labls-
1,065 handcol plts-8vo-24 vols-1st ed-in Engl & Latin
(5z9,1 lf tn,2 plts rprd) 1,000.00

SHAW,GEO BERNARD-The admirable Bashville in 3 acts-Lond-
1909-Constable-12mo-orig prntd wrps-1st ed (5i8) 10.00
--The Adventures of the Black Girl in Search for God-Lond-(1932)-
Constable-bds-illus   (4b5,mint) 20.00
--same-NY-1933-illus   (5x2) 5.00
--same-Edinb-1932   (4b4) 10.00
--Androcles & Lion,Overruled,Pygmalion-Lond-1916-8vo-cl-
1st ed   (5cc9) 10.00
--The Apple Cart,Political Extravaganza-Lond-1930-1st ed
(4b4) 12.50 (5ss3,lacks front cov) 10.(4b5,mint,dj) 15.00
--Back to Methuselah-Lond-1921-12mo-cl-1st ed-267p
(5t0,5cc9,5dd0,5tt7,vf,dj) 15.00
--same-NY-1939-Ltd Ed Club-lg8vo-ltd to 1500c,nbrd,box(5b0)20.00
--Bernard Shaw & Mrs Patrick Campbell,Their Corres-NY-1952-
Knopf-1st Amer ed   (4p1) 10.00
--Bernard Shaw through the Camera-Lond-1948-8vo-cl-128p-
238 photos   (5t0) 3.50
--Cashel Byron's Profession-(Lond)-1886-The Modern Pr-8vo-
cl-9 3/4 x 6¼"-1st ed   (5ee9) 175.00
--same-9 x 5 5/8"-1st ed   (5dd8) 50.00
--Common Sense of Municipal Trading-Westminster-1904-16mo-
cl   (4c2,darkened) 15.00
--same-NY-1911-Lane   (4b5,mint) 7.50
--Doctor's Dilemma-Lond-1911-12mo-cl-1st ed
(5cc9,bkplt) 10. (4b5,sl dust) 12.50(4c2,vg) 25.00
--Doctor's Dilemma-Lond-1913   (5tt7,dj) 15.00
--Dramatic Opinions & Essays-NY-1906-2 vols-12mo-cl-
papr labls-1st ed-issued prior to Engl ed (5r9,f) 25.00
--same-Lond-1913-Constable-2 vols   (4b5,mint) 20.00
--Everybody's Political What's What?-Lond-(1944)-8vo-cl-
port-1st ed   (5cc9,dj) 7.50 (5j2) 8.00
--Fabian Essays in Socialism-Lond-1889-The Fabian Soc-dec cl-
1st issue   (5j2,sl wn) 65.00
--Fabianism & the Empire-Lond-1900-12mo-wrps (4c2,wrps tn) 27.50
--Geneva-Lond-(1939)-12mo-pict bds   (4c2,fox) 10.00
--Heartbreak House, Great Catherine &Playlets of War-Lond-
1910-Constable-12mo-cl-1st ed   (5ss3,5cc9,dj) 10.00
--How to Settle the Irish Question-Dublin&Lond-(1917)-orig wrps-
32p-8vo-1st ed   (4m8) 7.50
--Intelligent Woman's Guide to Socialism & Capitalism-Lond-1928-
8vo-cl-g.t.-1st ed   (5r9,dj) 10. (4c2,f) 20.00
--same-Lond-1928-1st issue with all the errors (5k1,pres) 100.00
--same-NY-1928-lg8vo-1st Amer ed (5w4,5x7) 5. (5tt7,f) 10.00

SHAW,GEO BERNARD (continued)
--John Bull's Other Island & Major Barbara-Lond-1907-12mo-cl-
　1st ed (5dd8,pres,box) 100. (4c2,crack) 17.50 (4tt7) 12.50
--Love Among the Artists-Chig-1900-Herbert S Stone (5v0,vg) 12.50
--Man & Superman-Westminster-1903-12mo-cl-g.t.-wiout catalog
　　　　　　　　　　　　(4c2,hng cracked) 22.50
--same-MtVernon-1962-Ltd Ed Club-2 vols (5t8) 32.50
--Misalliance-Lond-1914-12mo-cl-t.e.g. (4c2,dj,f) 20.00
--On Going to Church-East Aurora-1896-ElbertHubbard-12mo-
　cl bkd bds-1st ed (5ss3,sp stn,Hubbard pres) 45.00
--same-Bost-1905-12mo (4a1,4b5) 5.00
--Peace Conference Hints-Lond-1919-16mo-wrps-108p-1st ed
　　　　　　　　(4c2,browned) 10. (4m8) 7.50 (4c2) 10.00
--Perfect Wagnerite-Lond-1898-12mo-buck-cl bkstrp-t.e.g.-
　1st ed (5cc9) 25. (4c2,darkened) 20.00
--Plays,Pleasant & Unpleasant-Chig-1904-2 vols-12mo-(not 1st)
　　　　　　　　(4a1) 7.50 (5t0) 6.50
--Quintessence of Ibsenism-Lond-1891-12mo-blue cl
　　　　　　(4c2,sp faded,cracked) 25.00
--St Joan-Lond-1924-Constable-12mo-cl-1st ed
　(4b5,fade) 8.50 (5cc9) 7.50 (4c2,4b5,mint,dj)1 15.00
--The Sanity of Art-Lond-1908-16mo-prntd brown wrps-
　ex scarce-1st issue (4c2,sl chip,f) 65. (5j2,underline) 50.00
--The Sanity of Art-NY-1908-new Preface (4a1) 15.00
--Socialism,the Fabian Essays-Bost-(1894)-12mo-pict red cl-218p-
　ChasE Brown (5j5,sp tn) 12.50
--Three Plays for Puritans-Lond-1901 (4b6) 60.00
--Translations & Tomfooleries-Lond-1926-12mo-cl-1st ed
　(5cc9,dj) 10. (5t0,4b5,mint) 7.50
--Two Plays for Puritans-NY-tall 8vo-red dec cl-Ltd Ed Club(5t8)
　　　　　　(5t8) 30.00
--The Unprotected Child & the Law-n.d.-issued by the Six Point
　Group-8p-prntd wrps-8½x5½ (5p1) 25.00
--Widowers' Houses-Lond-1893-12mo-1st ed-olive green (5cc9) 37.50
SHAW,GEO C-Chinook Jargon & How to Use It-Seattle-1909-
　wrps-65p (4b2,cov sl tn) 7.50
SHAW,GEO RUSSELL-Knots-Bost-1933-2nd ed-illus (5tt5) 7.50
SHAW,HELEN LOUISE-The First 100 Years of St Mary's Hall on
　the Delaware-Burlington College-1936 (5p9) 5.00
SHAW,HENRY-Details of Elizabethan Architecture-Lond-1839-
　lg4to-orig bds-plts-(some col) (4m6,ex-libr,lacks bkstrp) 20.00
--Dresses & decorations of the Middle Ages-Lond-1843-
　WmPickering-2 vols-lg8vo-hf cl-1st ed-94 plts (5x3) 175.00
SHAW,IRWIN-Act of Faith & Other Stories-NY-(1946)-RandomHse-
　1st ed (5hh1,dj) 5.00
SHAW,JAS-Early Reminiscences of Pioneer Life in Kansas-n.p.-
　(Atchison,Ka)-(1886)-238p-1st ed (5s4,soil) 12.50 (5bb4) 15.00
SHAW,JAS C-North From Texas-Evanston-1952-Branding Iron Pr
　reprnt-ltd to 750c (4c7) 38.50
SHAW,JOHN-Poems by the late Dr John Shaw to which is prefixed
　a biogr sketch of the author-Phila&Balt-1810-252p-calf (5d6) 50.00
SHAW,JOHN R-Narrative of Life & Travels of...the Well digger-
　Lexington-1807(reprint Louisvl,1930,ltd to 300c)-qtr cloth
　　　　　　(5m2) 15.00
SHAW,LLOYD-Cowboy Dances-Caldwell-1940-illus-372p (5yy8) 5.00
SHAW,LUELLA-True History of Some of Pioneers of Colorado-
　Hotchkiss-1909-1st ed-frontis-illus-268p-wrps
　　　　(5i3,f) 17.50 (5bb4) 15. (5a0,f) 22.50
SHAW,MABEL-God's Candlelights-Lond-1933-197p (5c6,vg) 5.50
SHAW,OLIVER-The Providence selection of psalm & hymn tunes
　...for use of schools & churches-Dedham-1815-bds-calf bk
　　　　(5g4,wn,fox) 17.50
SHAW,OSBORN-History of Storms & Gales of Long Island &
　Hurricane of 1938,by Dorothy Quick-Bay Shore,LI Forum-
　(1939)-12mo-wrps-illus-27p-(ltd to 500c,nbrd) (5j5) 7.50
SHAW,PRINGLE-Ramblings in Calif-Toronto-(1856?)-JasBain-
　239p-cl (5tt0,worn) 30.00
SHAW,R C-Across Plains in Forty Nine-Farmland,Ind-1896-
　frontis-16mo-priv prnt (4b6,box) 100.00
--same-Chig-1948-Lakeside Pr-illus-map (5a9,f) 10.00
SHAW,MAJOR SAML-The Journals of-Bost-1847-360p-port-
　1st ed (5L3) 10.00
SHAW,THOS-Travels,or Observations,Relating to Several Parts
　of Barbary & the Levant-Edinb-1808-plts-calf&bds-2 vols-
　3rd ed (4j3) 17.50
SHAW,THOS-Management & Feeding of Cattle-NY-1914-frontis-
　494p plus ads-illus (5dd6,sl soil) 5.00
SHAW,THOS GEO-Wine,the Vine, & The Cellar-Lond-1864-
　fldg frontis-540p-fldg table-2nd ed (5w6,dmpstnd) 28.50
SHAW,THURSTAN-Excavation at Dawu-Edinb-1961-lg4to-
　8&129p-55 plts (5c6,mint) 15.00
SHAW,W J-Solomon's Story-Cinn-1880-illus-1sted (5mm1) 12.50

SHAW,WILFRED B,ed-From Vermont to Michigan-1936-301p-
　illus (5e8) 5.75
SHAW,WM H-History of Essex & Hudson Counties,NJ-Phila-
　1884-illus-4to-1332p-2 vols (4m4,rebnd) 75.00
SHAW,WM W-Reveries of a Drummer-LosAng-(1926)-200p-illus-
　imit lea (5h7) 4.00
SHAW-SPARROW,WALTER-Frank Brangwyn & his Work-Bost-
　(1911)-4to-cl-illus-258p (5t7) 12.50
SHAWNEE HIGH SCHOOL GIRLS-Flood Stories by-Louisville,KY-
　Louisvl-1937-92p-cl-scarce (5h1) 8.50
SHAY,FRANK-The Best Men are Cooks-NY-1941-281p (5c5) 5.00
--Drawn from the Wood-NY-(1929)-illus-186p (5w6,fade) 7.50
--Iron Men & Wooden Ships-GardenCty-1924-folio-154p-illus
　　　　(5t7) 10.00
--A Treasury Of Plays for Women-Bost-1922-443p (5w9) 5.00
--25 Short Plays-NY-1925-1st ed (4a1) 7.50
SHAYLOR,JOS-Some Favourite Books & Their Authors-Lond-
　1901-sm8vo-cl-282p-g.t.-Grant Richards (5aa2) 3.50
SHEA,JOHN GILMARY-Catholic Church in Colonial Days-NY-
　1886-663p-illus (5xx7) 15. (5w4,crack) 17.50
--Discov & Explor of Mississippi Valley-Redfield-1852-frontis-
　fldg map-1st ed (5x5,ex-libr) 50. (4t8,bkstrp wn) 35.00
--same-Albany-1903-268p-ltd to 500c (4j4) 25.00
--History of the Catholic Missions Among the Indian Tribes of
　the US-NY-(n.d.)-(ca 1882)-P J Kennedy Sons-514p-cl-illus-
　reprint (5r0,ex-libr) 12.50
SHEA,JOHN C-The Only True History of Quantrell's Raid Ever
　Published-KansCty-1879-1st ed-rare-wrps-27p (4t8,chip) 175.00
SHEAHAN,JAS W-Great Conflagration-Chig-1871-Union Publ-
　8vo-illus (5dd6,5yy8,stn) 10.00
--The Life of Stephen A. Douglas-NY-1860-528p-port (5t4) 4.50
SHEAR,G WILLARD,photographer-Panorama of the Hudson-
　NY-1888-Bryant Literary Union-4to-orig wrps-cl sp-96 plts-
　800 photos-1st ed (4c4) 35.00
SHEAR,JOHN K,ed-Religious Buildings for Today-NY-1957-Dodge-
　4to-cl-illus (4m9,dj tn) 7.50
SHEARMAN,M-Athletics-Lond-1898-8vo-mor-raised bands-
　g.t.-61 illus (5t5,f bndg) 15.00
SHEARWOOD,F P-By Water & The Word-Tor-1943-illus-1st ed-
　215p (5dd7) 8.50
SHEBA,S-Sheba's Practical English Japanese & Japanese English
　Conversations-Honolulu-1913-Hawaii Shinpo Sha-448p-ads-
　8x3 3/4"-wrps (5yy3) 15.00
SHEELAH-The Mother's Request,or Ballyshan Castle-1866-355p
　　　　(5x4) 10.00
SHEEN,FULTON J-Communism & the Conscience of the West-
　Indnpls-1948 (5x7) 3. (5L7) 3.50
SHEEN,JAS RICHMOND-Wines & Other Fermented Liquors-Lond-
　(?1864)-12mo-292p (5w1,hng broke) 10.00
SHEFFLY,L F-Life & Times of Timothy Dwight Hobart 1855 to 1935-
　Canyon,Tx-1950-Panhandle Plains Hist Soc-322p-illus-scarce
　　　(4i7) 20. (4t8) 25.00
SHEFFIELD,JOHN BAKER HOLROYD-Observations on Commerce
　of the Amer States-Lond-1784-Debrett-287p-12 fldg charts&
　tables-8vo-calf-new ed (5L1) 30.00
SHEIL,R L-Sketches of the Irish Bar-NY-1854-2 vols (5r4) 12.50
--same-1856-2 vols-hf lea (5r4) 17.50
SHELBY,CHARMION-Printed Work of Spanish Intellectuals in
　the Americas-Stanford Univ Pr-(1950)-Span&Engl text (5x5,dj)12.50
SHELBY CO,ILL-Historic Sketch & Biographical Album of-
　Shelbyville-1900-313,(5)p (5y0,rbnd) 50.00
SHELBY COUNTY,OHIO-Hist of-Phila-1883-406p-cl (5h2) 50.00
SHELBYVILLE,MO-Here & There in-Shelbyville-1915-76p-
　photos in fldr-untied (5L0) 12.50
SHELDEN,HAROLD P-Tranquillity,Tranquillity Revisited,
　Tranquillity Regained-1945-Countryman Pr-3 vols-ltd to 5000c
　　　(5kk7,dj,box) 25.00
SHELDON,ADDISON ERWIN-History & Stories of Nebraska-Chig-
　1913 (4a5) 3.50
--Land Systems & Land Policies in Nebraska-Lincoln-1936-
　illus-400p-Nebr Hist Soc (5dd6) 5.00
--Nebraska,The Land & the People-Chig-1931-Vol 1 & 3-photos-
　dec cov (5s4,lacks Vol 2) 22.50
SHELDON,CHAS-Wilderness of Denali-NY-1930-lg fldg map-
　illus-412p (4b6) 12.50
--Wilderness of the No Pacific Coast Islands-NY-1912-illus-8vo
　　　(5m9) 10. (4g6,5zz8) 12.50
--Wilderness of the Upper Yukon-NY-1911-illus-maps-364p-1st ed
　　　(4m2) 12.50 (5w8) 20.00
--same-Lond-1911-cl-8vo-354p-col plts-maps (5v7) 25.00
--same-NY-1919-364p-photos (5ss1,pres) 20.00
SHELDON,E M-Early Hist of Michigan-NY-1856-409p-cl-1st ed-
　Howes S 374 (5h7,stn) 17.50

SHELDON,FREDK M-Practical Colorist-Burlington-1900-
238p-illus   (5hh7, v wn) 6.50   (5xx7)   15.00
SHELDON,G W-Selections in Modern Art after works of recent
Contemporaneous Artists-NY-(1885, 86)-folio-illus-2 vols
(5yy0)   27.50
SHELDON,G W-Story of Volunteer Fire Dept..NY-NY-1882-
145 illus-575p   (5yy0,hng brok)   9.50
SHELDON,GEO WM-Recent Ideals of Amer Art-NY-1888-
Appleton-g.e.-184 illus-ltd to 500c   (4e0)   125.00
SHELDON,GEO-Heredity & Early Environment of John Williams-
Bost-1905-149p-cl   (5i3,f) 12.50   (5t4)   15.00
SHELDON,GEO-History of Deerfield-1895-2 vols-scarce-red cl
(5e8,vg)   75.00
SHELDON,COL HAROLD P-Tranquility-NY-(1936)-Derrydale Pr-
ltd to 950c   (5j3)   20.00
--Tranquility Revisited-NY-(1940)-4to-illus-ltd to 485c
(5j3,pres)   25.00
SHELDON,HENRY-Northwest Corner-NY-1948-photos (5q8)   5.00
SHELDON,HENRY DAVIDSON-History & Pedagogy of Amer
Student Societies-NY-1901-Appleton-12mo-orig wrps-366p-1st ed
(5m6,wrp loose)   10.00
SHELDON,J ARMS-John Sheldon & the Old Indian House
Homestead-Greenfield,Mass-1911-21p-wrps   (5L2)   3.00
SHELDON,J P-Dairy Farming-Lond-c1890-4to-570p-col plts
(5ii2,needs bndg)   9.50
SHELDON,MARK-An Autobiographical Sketch-SanFran-n.d.-
(1913)-8vo-wrps-120p-port   (5h5)   25.00
SHELDON,STEWART-Home Missions in Southern Dakota-n.p.-
(Yankton?)-(1884)-21p-fld-rare   (5L5)   50.00
SHELDON,WM H-Penny Whimsy-NY-(1958)-352p-illus (5t4)   7.50
SHELDON WILLIAMS,RALF-Canadian Front in France & Flanders-
Lond-1920-32 col plts-208p   (4d2)   8.50
SHELFORD,VICTOR-Naturalist's Guide to the Americas-Balt-
1926-illus-1st ed   (5kk7)   12.50
SHELL,DAVID L-The Shell Family-Dexter,Ma-1953-127p-
2 photos-1st ed-scarce   (5L2)   10.00
SHELLABARGER,SAML-Lord Chesterfield & His World-Bost-1951-
456p-port   (5a1) 5.   (5t0)   4.50
SHELLER,ROSCOE-Courage & Water-Portland-(1952)-263p-
photos   (5s4, dj)   7.50
SHELLEY,ER M-20th Century Bird Dog Training & Kennel
Management-(Jackson,Tenn)-1921-98p-illus   (5t7)   5.00
SHELLEY,GEO ERNST-Monograph of Nectariniidae or Family
of Sun Birds-Lond-1876 to 80-lg4to-mor-g.e.-121 hand col plts-
1st ed   (5z9,vf,f bndg,pres)   1,050.00
SHELLEY,GEO F-Early History of Amer Fork with Some History
of a Later Day-AmerForkCty-1945-152p-photos-scarce (5L2)   20.00
SHELLEY,GERARD-The Speckled Domes-NY-1925-256p-photos
(5ss6)   4.00
SHELLEY,HENRY C-Inns & Taverns of Old London-Bost-1909-
366p-col frontis-48 illus   (5w1)   12.50
--Literary By Paths in Old England-Bost-1906-Little-400p-illus
(5p9)   5.00
SHELLEY,MARY W-Frankenstein-Phila-1833-Lea&Blanchard-
3 qtr calf-2 vols in 1-1st Amer ed   (4b5)   150.00
SHELLEY,PERCY B-The Banquet of Plato-Bost-1908-12mo-bds-
(Bruce Rogers-1 of 440 nbrd copies   (5r9)   10.00
--The Cenci-Lond-1819-for C&J Ollier-mor-1st ed-ltd to 250c
(5tt2,f)   375.00
--Complete Poetical Works-Cambr-1892-Riverside Pr-tall 8vo-
port-bds-linen sp-labls-ltd to 250 sets-8 vols   (5t8)   100.00
--Complete Poetical Works of-Bost&NY-1901-651p-pt mor-g.-
Cambridge Ed-raised bands   (5xx8)   15.00
--Complete Works of-Lond-1927-E Benn-10 vols-Ingpen&Peck,ed-
parch&cl-Julian edition   (5p9)   125.00
--In Memoriam,Adonais-SanFran-1922-col frontis-4to-t.e.g.-
blue wrps-ltd to 150c,nbrd   (5b0,box)   45.00
--Prometheus Unbound-Lond-1829-Ollier-8vo-mor-raised bands-
1st ed,2nd issue   (4n5)   300.00
--Queen Mab,a Philosophical Poem-NY-1821-hf calf-16mo-
1st Amer ed   (5tt7)   50.00
--same-Lond-1821-W Clark-orig cl-1st trade ed (4b5,sl fox)   85.00
--The revolt of Islam,a poem,in 12 cantos-Lond-1818-for C&J Ollier-
8vo-orig bds-labl-1st ed,2nd issue (5i8,wn,lacks errata lf)   175.00
--The Works of...-Lond-1836-Chas Daly-thk16mo-hf calf-port
(5tt7)   10.00
SHELLEY ROLLS,JOHN C E-Yachts of the Royal Yacht Squadron,
1815 to 1932-Lond-1933-folio-col frontis-483 plts-265p (5nn2)25.00
SHELTON,A C-Newfoundland,Our North Door Neighbor-NY-
1943-cl-R8vo-78 plts-116p   (4p3)   15.00
SHELTON,JANE deF-The Salt Box House-NY-(1900)-302p (5w7) 7.50
SHELTON,L-Beautiful Gardens in Amer-NY-1915-4to
(5ii2) 7.   (5w4) 10.   (5qq7)   7.50

SHELTON,L (continued)
--same-NY-1924-4to-274p-illus   (5xx7) 6.   (5t5)   6.50
--Continuous Bloom in Amer-NY-1915-145p-plts   (5s7)   4.50
--The Seasons in a Flower Garden-NY-1909-117p-plts-2nd ed
(5s7,soil)   2.50
SHELTON,CHIEF WM-Story of the Totem Pole-Everett,Wa-1923-
photos-80p   (4b2,autg)   5.00
SHELTON,WM HENRY-The Jumel Mansion-Bost-1916-4to-illus-
pict cl-800c prntd   (5g3)   10.00
--Salmagundi Club-Bost-1918-illus-1st ed (5t0,4b7,pres,sp wn) 15.00
SHELVOCKE,GEO-Voyage Round World by Way of Great South Sea...
1719 to 22 in Speedwell-Lond-1726-for Senex-8vo-calf-
4 plts(2 fldg)-fldg map-1st ed   (4h0,rbkd)   400.00
--same-..in Yr 1718-Lond-1757-476p-fldg map-4 plts-imit mor-
2nd ed,rev&republ   (5ss2)   85.00
SHENK,HIRAM H-Encyclopedia of Penna-Harrisburg-1932-539p-
illus   (5w5,bkstrp tn)   25.00
SHENSTONE,WM-Works in verse & prose of...-Lond-1764-
for Dodsley-2 vols-disbnd   (5v6)   32.50
SHENTON,JAS P-Robt John Walker,a Politician from Jackson to
Lincoln-NY-1961-288p   (5q8) 5.   (5w5,dj)   4.50
SHEPARD,CHAS E-Found in Bagdad & Other Divagations Of A
Lawyer-NY-1928-233p-illus   (5w4)   4.50
SHEPARD,CHAS UPHAM-Report on Geological Survey of Conn-
NewHav-1837-8vo-orig wrps-188p   (5m6,ex-librr)   6.00
SHEPARD,MRS D ELLEN GOODMAN-Cut Flowers, a Collection
of Poems-Springfld-1854-1st ed of Holland's 1st book
(5gg6,lacks port)   7.50
SHEPARD,EDW-Martin Van Buren-Bost-1892-t.e.g.   (5q8)   3.50
SHEPARD,ELIHU H-The Autobiography of-StL-1869-275p-
2 photos   (5L2,ex-librr)   27.50
--History of StLouis & Missouri from its 1st Explor-etc-StL-1870-
170p   (5L0,wn)   35.00
SHEPARD,KATHARINE-First Steps in Cooking-NY-1946-174p (5c0)2.50
SHEPARD,O L-Story of Lakeside-Lkside-1923-99p-wrps-scarce
(5h1)   8.50
SHEPARD,ODELL-Connecticut,Past & Present-NY-1939-Knopf-
136p-illus   (5p7)   4.50
--Pedlar's Progress-Bost-1937-Little,Brown-1st ed-ltd to 450c
(5ss9)   22.50
--same-Bost-1937-bds-hf cl-ltd to 500c,autg   (5mm2)   15.00
--same-Bost-1937-Little,Brown-8vo-546p-2nd prntng (5p1,dj)   7.50
SHEPARD,THOS-New Englands Lamentations for Old Englands
present errours & divisions etc-Lond-1645-GeoMiller-sm4to-
title lf&6p-mor   (5L1)   450.00
SHEPERD,CHAS R-The Case Against Japan-NY-1938-242p(5x9)   3.00
SHEPHERD & HIS FLOCK,THE-Portland-1820-WmHyde-16mo-
35p-frontis-wrps-rare chapbook   (5v0,rbkd,wn)   40.00
SHEPHERD BOY,THE-Wendell,Mass-1832-JMetcalf-48mo-18p-
wdcuts on wrps   (5p1,rprd,sl dmpstn)   15.00
SHEPHERD,C W-Wines,Spirits&Liqueurs-NY-(1959)-160p-photos
(5w1)   4.50
SHEPHERD,CHAS R-Story of Chung Mei-Phila-1938-Judson Pr-
264p-illus   (5r0)   5.50
SHEPHERD,GRANT-Silver Magnet-1938-302p-1st ed-illus
(5r1,spots)   11.00
SHEPHERD,J C-Italian Gardens of the Renaissance-NY-1925-folio-
cl-91 plts   (5z9,sp rprd)   45.00
--same-1925-(England)-atlas folio-92p plts   (4a2,rub)   25.00
SHEPHERD,DR J S-Journal of Travel Across the Plains to Calif &
Guide to the Future Emigrant-Racine-1851-reprntd Jan,1945-
n.p.-(1945)-(orig wrps bnd in)-45p   (5t4)   10.00
SHEPHERD,MARGARET L-My Life in the Convent-n.p.-n.d.-
(Tol-1920's)-258p-wrps-Export ed publ for the trade   (5h7)   4.00
SHEPHERD,PETER-With Glowing Hearts-Tor-(c1946)-prntd wrps
(5w8)   3.50
SHEPHERD,R H-Bibliography of Carlyle-Lond-(1881)   (4g2)   17.50
SHEPHERD,R H-Bibliography of Coleridge-Lond-1900-ltd to 30c
(4g2)   22.50
SHEPHERD,RICHARD-Bibliography of Thackeray-Lond-(1880)-8vo-
qtr mor-61p   (4m8)   27.50
SHEPHERD,R H W-African Contrasts,story of a SoAfrican People-
Oxf Univ Pr-1947-R8vo-illus   (5x2,dj)   15.00
--same-Cape Town-1947-266p-90p illus   (5c6)   10.75
--Bantu Literature & Life-Lond-1955-198p-6 plts-wrps (5c6,vg) 8.75
--Lovedale,So Africa,Story of a Century,1841 to 1941-Lovedale-
n.d.(c1941)-Lovedale Pr-photos-fldg map-531p (4t5,autg)   15.00
SHEPHERD,MAJ W-Prairie experiences in handling cattle & sheep-
Lond-1884-Chapman&Hall-266p-map-illus   (5u3,v wn)   11.50
--same-NY-1885-illus-215p-1st Amer ed-scarce   (5bb4)   17.50
SHEPHERD,WM R-Historical Atlas-NY-1924-sm4to-cl-216p of maps-
94p index-4th ed,rev   (5t0)   8.50
--Historical Atlas-NY-Holt-1927-216 col maps-99p text (5x0)   10.00

USED BOOK PRICE GUIDE

SHEPPARD,C B-Desc of Richard Beckley of Wethersfield,Conn-
1948-406p   (4t2)   10.00
SHEPPARD,W-Law of Common Assurances,Touching Deeds in
General-Lond-1669-John Streater-folio   (5ff4,rebnd) 85.00
SHEPPERD,E-Plantation Songs for My Lady's Banjo & Other Negro
Lyrics & Monologues-NY-1901-illus   (5x2)   20.00
SHEPPERSON,AL B-Cotton Facts-NY-1884-cl-125p-limp cl (4j4) 4.50
SHEPPERSON,ARCHIBALD BOLLING-John Paradise & Lucy
Ludwell of London & Williamsburg-Richmond-1942-501p-illus
(5h9) 8.50   (5w0,dj)   14.50
SHERARD,ROBT H-Bernard Shaw,Frank Harris & Oscar Wilde-
NY-(1937)-Greystone Pr-299p   (5x0)   5.00
--Life of Oscar Wilde-NY-1928-8vo-cl &bds-470p-uncut-
1st ed   (5t0)   5.00
SHERBORN,CHAS DAVIES-A History of the Family of Sherborn-
Lond-1901-frontis-ltd to 250c   (5r7)   15.00
SHERBURNE,ANDREW-Memoirs of-Utica-1828-Wm Williams-
262p-1st ed-calf labl-errata pg
(5mm8,rub) 12.50 (5L3,f,5m4) 25. (5i9,fox) 22.50
--same-Prov-1831-HHBrown-sm8vo-312p-orig sheep-rebd,enlrgd
(5L1,lacks frontis) 15.00
SHERBURNE,JOHN HENRY-Life & Character of Chevalier John
Paul Jones-Wash-1825-Wilder&Campbell-364p-bds
(5mm8,chip,lacks frontis) 7.50 (5ee3,vg) 20.00
SHERCLIFF,JOSE-Jane Avril of the Moulin Rouge-Phila-(1954)-
illus-256p-cl &bds   (5t7)   6.00
SHERIDAN,C MACK-The Stag Cook Book-NY-(1922)-197p-scarce
(5c0) 6.50   (5c9)   7.50
SHERIDAN,CLARE-Arab Interlude-Lond-1936-photos-384p (4t5) 5.00
--My Amer Diary-NY-1922-lg8vo-cl-plts-1st ed (5p5) 10.00
--West & East-NY-c1923   (5x7)   4.00
SHERIDAN,F-History of Camden County in the Great War 1917,1918-
Camden-1919-234p-illus   (5a9)   7.50
SHERIDAN,P H-Personal Memoirs of-NY-1888-2 vols-cl
(5w0,mor,f bndg) 25. (5h1) 10. (5a9,f,4t8) 15.00
--Record of Engagements with Hostile Indians-Chig-1882-
Headquarters,Military Div of Mo-120p-wrps-v scarce
(5yy3,repaired) 50. (4t8,pres,1 lf in facs) 55.00
--Reports of Inspection Made in Summer of 1877 by...of Country
North of UPRR-Wash-1878-10 fldg maps-110p-1st ed
(5bb4,7 autgs) 60. (5L7,lacks sp) 15.00
--Report of an Explor of Parts of Wyo,Idaho&Mont in Aug&Sept,
1882-Wash-1882-GPO-80p-fldg map-orig prntd wrps (5dd4) 49.50
SHERIDAN,RICHARD B-Critic-Lond-1781-1st ed-96p
(5aa0,rub,lacks hf t.,5x3) 25.00
--The Duenna,A Comic Opera in 3 Acts-Bost-n.d.(ca 1925)-
4to-cl-27,105p-12 col illus   (5t0)   5.00
--The Plays of-Lond-1886-Routledge-320p-7th ed (5p7) 2.50
--Plays-Lond-1900-Macmillan-tall 8vo-lg type-buck
(5t8,sp sl tn) 6.50
--The School for Scandal,a Comedy-Phila-1802-John Conrad-
18mo-102p-disbnd   (5j5)   10.00
--same-Oxf-1934-tall 8vo-bds-Ltd Ed Club-ltd to 1500c,nbrd
(5b0) 30.00
--A trip to Scarborough,a comedy-Dublin-1781-Marchbank-
12mo-disbnd   (5x3,1 lf tn) 25.00
SHERIDAN,SOL N-History of Ventura Co,Calif-Chig-1926-
S J Clarke-2 vols-illus-cl   (5yy3)   75.00
--The Little Spotted Seal-NY&Lond-1929-8vo-frontis-4 plts-(193p)-
pict cl-2nd prntng   (5p1)   4.50
SHERIDAN,WILBUR F-Life of Isaac Wilson Joyce-Cinn-(1907)-
281p-cl   (5h7)   10.00
SHERINGHAM,HUGH-Book of the Fly Rod-Bost-1931-plts(3 col)-
4to   (5t0) 12.50   (5tt7,box) 27.50
SHERLOCK,CHESLA C-Homes of Famous Americans-DesMoines-
c1926-2 vols-illus-48 plts-g.t.-scarce-orig cl (5h9) 24.00
SHERMAN,ALLAN-A Gift of Laughter-NY-Atheneum-1965-
335p   (5p0)   6.00
SHERMAN,REV ANDREW-Life of Capt Jeremiah O'Brien-
(Morristown)-1902-247p-illus   (5s1)   10.00
SHERMAN,ANDREW M-Phil Carver,A Romance of the War of
1812-Morristown,NJ-(1902)-GSherman-1st ed (5m2,pres) 5.00
SHERMAN,CHAS P-Roman Law in the Modern World-NY-1937-
3rd ed-3 vols   (5r4)   30.00
SHERMAN CO(OREG),STANDARD ATLAS OF-Chig-1913-Ogle-
lg folio-87p & suppl   (4t2)   50.00
SHERMAN,REV D-Sketches of New England Divines-NY-1860-
443p-cl   (5jj9)   10.00
SHERMAN,EDGAR J-Recollections of a Long Life-Salem-1908-
priv prnt   (4a4,pres)   7.50
--Some Recollections of a Long Life-Bost-1908 (5ff4) 7.50

SHERMAN,F F-Sonnets Suggested by Paintings-Westport-1937-
illus-priv prntd-ltd to 75c   (5kk7)   12.50
SHERMAN,FRANK DEMPSTER-Madrigals & Catches-NY-1887-
16mo-cl-1st ed of auth's 1st book   (5gg6)   10.00
SHERMAN,FRANKLIN J-Modern Story of Mutual Savings Banks-
NY-1934-193p-illus   (4b8)   6.50
SHERMAN,FREDERIC FAIRCHILD-Amer Painters of Yesterday
& Today-NY-1919-priv prntd-illus-69p-4to-ltd to 500c (4e0) 27.50
--Early American Painting-NY-1932-Century-289p-illus-8vo-
scarce   (4a0)   35.00
--Early Amer Portraiture-NY-1930-illus-priv prntd-ltd to 250c
(5m2) 20.00
--Landscape & Figure Painters of Amer-NY-1917-priv prntd-
illus-71p-ltd to 500c   (4e0)   27.50
--Richard Jennys,New Engl Portrait Painter-Springfield-1941-
lg8vo-bds&cl-96p-1st ed   (5t0)   15.00
SHERMAN,G B-The Negro As A Soldier-Soldiers&Sailors Hist Soc
of RI-1913-34p-wrps-ltd to 250c   (5x2)   60.00
SHERMAN,HAROLD M-Tahara Among African Tribes-Chig-1933-
Goldsmith Pub-246p-juvenile   (4t5)   4.00
SHERMAN,HENRY C-Food Products -NY-1917 (5x7)   2.50
SHERMAN,HERBERT LEROY-The King of Cuba-NY-(1899)-
F Tennyson Neely-1st ed-scarce   (5ee3)   10.00
SHERMAN,JOHN-Recollections of 40 Years in the House,Senate
& Cabinet-Chig-1895-2 vols-illus-lea-1st ed
(5q8) 7.50   (5dd6,5k2) 10.00
--same-Chig-1895-2 vols-1st ed-ltd to 1000c,autog-pt lea-
t.e.g.-illus-lg8vo   (5i3) 15. (5x5,f) 35. (5t4,f) 25.00
--Speech by Hon John Sherman of Ohio on Emancipation Feb 2,
1864-Wash-1864-16p-disbnd   (5x5,sl stnd) 35.00
SHERMAN,LYDIA-The poison fiend,Life,crimes & conviction of-
Phila-1872-illus-pict wrps   (5g3,sp wn)   15.00
SHERMAN,S N-Eulogy upon Pres Lincoln....Apr 19,1865...-
Grafton-1865-wrps-14p-rare   (4t3,sl wn)   75.00
SHERMAN,TEXAS-Sherman,Richardson & Sanders-c1904-photos-
wrps-20 lvs   (4a5)   12.50
SHERMAN,GEN'L-Home Letters of-NY-1909-M A DeWolfe Howe,ed-
412p-port   (5t7)   10.50
SHERMAN,GEN WM T-Life & Remin   ...-Balt-1891-479p-cl
(5h7) 7.50
--Recollections of Calif 1846 to 1861-Oakland-1945-8vo-cl-
1 of 625c   (5b0)   17.50
--Personal Memoirs-NY-1891-4th ed-2 vols in 1-port
(5yy6,bndg wn) 6.00
--Memoirs of...-NY-1875-2 vols
(5L5,4j4) 8.50 (5dd5,fldg map) 15. (5w9,pkt map) 22.50
SHERRARD,ROBT A-Narr of the Wonderful Escape & Dreadful
Sufferings of Col Jas Paul-Cinn-1869-sewed
(5h6,lacks bk cov) 15. (5s9) 30.00
SHERRATT,HARRIOTT W-Mexican Vistas-Chig-1899-illus-8vo-
3/4 mor-1st ed   (4g6,sl rub)   7.50
SHERRIFF,R C-Journey's End-Lond-1929-12mo-prntd wrps-1st ed
(5r9) 10.00
SHERRILL,CHAS H-French Memories of 18th Century Amer-NY-
1915   (5t2) 5.   (5r7)   12.50
--Modernizing the Monroe Doctrine-Bost-1916-8vo-1st ed
(5a8) 2.   (5m6,pres)   8.50
--Stained Glass Tours in England-Lond-1910-lg8vo-plts-maps-
dec cl-g.t.-1st ed   (5p5)   10.00
SHERRILL,CAPT C O-Military Map Reading-n.p.-c1912-63p-
illus-maps-fldg charts   (5w4)   4.50
SHERROD,ROBT-History of Marine Corps Aviation in WW2-Wash-
(1952)-496p-cl-1st ed (5x9,dmpstnd,5ff7) 7.50 (4h4) 15.00
SHERRY,LAURA-Old Prairie du Chien-Paris-1931-EdwWTitus-
8vo-bds&cl-1st ed-ltd to 400c   (5ee9,dj)   20.00
SHERWELL,SAM'L-Old Recollections of an Old Boy-NY-1923-port-
271p-1st ed-v scarce   (5bb4,pres) 40.00
SHERWIN,MRS D S-Why,or tried in the crucible-By D D S-Bost-
(1884)-JasH Earle-1st ed   (5m2)   12.50
SHERWIN,OSCAR-Mr Gay-NY-1929-184p-frontis-bds-cl bk-
1st ed   (5t0)   4.50
--Prophet of Liberty-NY-1958-814p   (5x2) 8.   (5w0) 8.50
SHERWIN,REIDER T-The Viking & the Red Man-8 vols-NY(Vols 1&2)-
Bronxville(Vols 3 to 8)-1940 to 1956-1st eds (5L0)   30.00
SHERWIN WILLIAMS CO-Your Home & Its Decoration-n.p.-
1910-4to-12 col illus-204p-bds   (5w7,wn,soil) 7.50
SHERWOOD,A-Daniel L Sherwood & Paternal Anc in England &
Amer-1929-390p   (4t2)   12.50
SHERWOOD,MARY M-Shanty the Blacksmith-(c1840)-Darton&Clark-
t12mo-dec cl-g.t.-176p-3 plts   (4d4)   10.00
SHERWOOD,BOB-Hold Yer Hosses,the Elephants are Coming-NY-
1932-illus-1st ed   (5yy8,dj)   6.00

SHERWOOD,MRS E W-The Art of Entertaining-NY-1892-404p
 (5w7,soil)   6.50
SHERWOOD,MRS JOHN-Manners and Social Usages-NY-c1884-
 496p-t.e.g.   (5w0)   6.50
--same-NY-(1887)-487p-frontis   (5w7)   4.50
SHERWOOD,MRS-History of Emily & Her Brother-Bost-1821-
 24p-illus wrps-3rd ed   (5v0,sp tn)   15.00
--The Orphan Boy & Other Tales-(Phila)-1842-18mo-cl-152p-
 frontis   (5t0)   6.50
--The orphans of Normandy-Lond-1822-12mo-hf calf-frontis-2 plts-
 1st ed   (5xx6)   35.00
--The Recaptured Negro-Lond-1840-Houston&Stoneman-72p-
 24mo-11th ed   (5x5)   35.00
SHERWOOD,ROBT E-Petrified Forest-NY-1935-1st ed (5yy6)   6.00
--Roosevelt & Hopkins-NY-1948   (5F0,5h7) 3.   (5x7)   4.50
SHERWOOD,SAML-The Church's Flight into the Wilderness-
 NY-1776-SamlLoudon-sm8vo-54p-cl   (5L1,rbnd)   85.00
SHERWOOD,WARREN G-History of Town of Lloyd-1952-
 180p-illus-maps   (5ff2)   10.00
SHETRONE,HENRY CLYDE-The Mound Builders-NY-1930-
 lg8vo-508p-cl-illus-1st ed-scarce (5L0,5x5) 30.   (5hh4)   27.50
SHEW,JOEL-Hydropathy-NY-1844-304p-illus-cl (5t2,stn,crack) 4.00
SEYMOUR,F W-Indian Agents of the Old Frontier-NY-1941-
 photos-1st ed   (5yy7)   12.50
--Story of the Red Man-NY-1929-plts-maps-421p   (4i7)   10.00
SHEYS,B-The American Bookkeeper-NY-1818-8vo-calf (4c1)   20.00
SHIEL,M P-Dr Krasinski's Secret-NY-1929-8vo-wrps-260p-
 Book League of Amer   (5j5)   10.00
SHIELDS,C W-Final Philosophy-1879-2nd ed,rev   (5L7)   5.00
SHIELDS,E L-Knit One Purl One-NY-1938-illus-95p   (5n7)   3.50
SHIELDS,G O-The Big Game of NoAmer-Chig-1890-581p-illus-
 1st ed   (5L2) 10.   (5t0)   7.50
--The Blanket Indian of the NoWest-NY-1921-col frontis-illus-
 1st ed-ltd to 500c,autog   (5bb4)   30.00
--Cruising in Cascades-Chig-1889-339p-port-plts (5u6) 15. (5s4)17.50
--Hunting in the Great West-Chig-1884-frontis-illus-306p
 (5i3) 12.50   (5ee3)   15.00
SHIELDS,JOS H-Natchez,Its Early Hist-Louisville-1930-274p
 (4p8)   20.00
SHIELDS,JOS W,JR-From Flintlock to M1-NY-(1954)-4to-
 220p-illus   (5xx7)   17.50
SHIELDS,WALTER C-The Ancient Ground-Nome-1918-47p(5ss1) 5.00
SHIELS,ARCHIE W-San Juan Islands,The Cronstadt of the Pacific-
 Juneau-1938-Empire Prntng Co-275p-cl-(ltd to 500c)
 (5d6) 25.   (4d0,autg)   50.00
--Sewards Icebox-Bellingham-(1933)-ltd ed-419p
 (5u6,5ss0,wn,bkstrp loose)   35.00
SHIER,MORLEY-Fireside Mining-n.p.-n.d.-79p-port-illus (5s0) 10.00
SHILLABER,B P-Partingtonian Patchwork-Bost-1873-Lea&Shepard-
 12mo-cl-360p-plts   (5j5,shake)   7.50
--Rhymes with Reason & Without-Bost-1853-12mo-cl-1st ed of
 auth's 1st book   (5gg6,pres)   35.00
SHIMIZU,SEKIJO,ed-Book of gun's tools-Kyoto-1808-5 vols-
 Imp 8vo-wrps-bone clasps-rare-(Chinese text)   (5t4)   40.00
SHINDLER,HENRY-Ft Leavenworth,Its Churches & Schools-1912-
 Army Serv Sch Pr-photos-176p-wrps-rare (4t8,author's pres) 45.00
SHINE,MICHAEL A-Nebraska Aborigines As They Appeared in
 the 18th Century-Lincoln-(1913)-23p-wrps-Neb Acad Sci
 Vol 9,#1   (5L2) 3.   (4t7)   7.50
SHINN,CHAS H-Graphic Descrip Pacific Coast Outlaws,etc-
 LosAng-1958-Westernlore-illus-107p (4n1,dj) 10. (5r8,pres) 15.00
--Mining Camps-NY-1885-11,316p-orig cl-1st ed (5m3,stn) 50.00
--same-NY-1948   (5L2,dj)   6.00
--Story of a Mine-NY-1896-photos-272p-1st ed   (5bb4)   10.00
SHIP & GUN DRILLS-Correct to 1914...Navy Dept-NY-1918-
 16mo-289p-illus   (5s1)   4.00
SHIP REGISTERS & ENROLLMENTS-Bristol Warren,RI,1773 to 1939-
 Providence-1941-Survey of Fed Archives-WPA-4to-orig wrps-
 354p,72p,9p-mimeo   (5m6,f)   27.50
SHIP'S MEDICINE CHEST-& First Aid at Sea-Wash-1929-207p
 (5ss1)   2.50
SHIPLEY,JONATHAN-A speech,intended to be spoken on bill
 for altering charters of Colony of Massachusett's Bay-Lond-
 1774-stitchd-1st ed-(Adams 141a)   (5g4,blank cor tn)   27.50
--same-Lond-1774-(for TCadell)-crushed mor-(Sabin 80511)
 (5s9,rbnd)   22.50
--same-Lond-1774-TCadell-(Sabin 80513,Adams 141c)-36p-
 8vo-hf mor   (5L1)   35.00
--same-Lond-(1774)-sm8vo-disbnd-wrps-(Sabin 80515) (5n2) 55.00
SHIPLEY,JOS T-Encyclopedia of Literature-NY-(1946) (4a1)   8.00
SHIPMODELER,THE-Ship Model Makers' Club-Brklyn-1929,30-
 Vol 1-McCann,ed-illus   (5t4)   7.50

SHIPPEN,EDW-Naval Battles,Ancient,Modern-SanFran-1883-
 719p-calf-illus   (5 s1,wn,tn)   10.00
SHIPPEN,NANCY-Nancy Shippen Her Journal Book-Phila-1935-
 Armes,ed-fldg chart   (5h9) 8.50   (4m4)   10.00
SHIPPEY,L-It's An Old Calif Custom-NY-1948-292p (5a9,f,dj) 3.00
SHIPPEY,LEE-It's An Old Calif Custom-NY-1948 (4a5) 4.50 (5r8) 4.00
--The Los Angeles Book-Bost-1950-photos   (4a1)   5.00
SHIPS & SHIPMASTERS OF OLD PROVIDENCE-Prov-1919-illus-
 8vo-bds-51p   (5t0)   3.50
SHIPS OF ESSO FLEET WORLD WAR II-n.p.-1946-534p-illus
 (5s1,wtrstnd)   8.00
SHIPTON,CLIFFORD-Rogert Conant-Cambr-1945-170p-illus-
 fldg map   (5w0)   6.50
--Isaiah Thomas,Printer,Patriot & Philanthropist-Rochester-1948-
 LeoHart-8vo-cl-23 illus   (5d5)   7.50
SHIPTON,E E-Nanda Devi-Lond-(1936)-Hodder&Stoughton-310p-
 illus-cl-1st ed   (5d7)   25.00
--same-(1939)-3rd ed   (5d7)   8.50
SHIPTON,ERIC-Blank on the Map-Lond-(1938)-Hodder&Stoughton-
 299p-illus-fldg map-cl   (5d7)   40.00
--Men Against Everest-EnglewoodCliffs-(1955)-161p-illus-cl-
 Prentice,Hall   (5d7)   5.00
--The Mt Everest Reconnaissance Exped-NY-(1952)-Dutton-illus-
 cl-128p   (5d7)   10.00
--Mountains of Tartary-Lond-Hodder&Stoughton-224p-illus-cl
 (5d7)   7.50
SHIPWAY,W-The Campanalogia,or Universal Instruction in Art
 of Ringing-Lond-1816-185p-3 parts-4" x 7"   (5bb0)   24.00
SHIRAS,GEO-Hunting Wild Life with Camera & Flashlight-Wash-
 1935-Natl Geog Soc-2 vols   (5cc1,5kk7) 10. (5ss8)   12.50
--same-Wash-1936-2 vols-illus   (5t7)   15.75
SHIRCLIFFE,ARNOLD-The Edgewater Beach Hotel Salad Book-Chig-
 (1926)-265p-col plts-green fabr-lg4to-(2nd prntng of 1st ed?)
 (5c9)   10.00
--same-1944 ed   (5c9)   7.50
SHIRER,WM L-Berlin Diary-NY-1941
 (5w0) 4. (5m2,autg,dj) 5.   (4h4,dj)   6.50
SHIRK,DAVID-The Cattle Drives of,from Texas to the Idaho Mines,
 1871 and 1873-(Portland,Oreg)-1956-MFSchmitt,ed-176p-
 3 illus-1st ed-Lawton Kennedy-ltd to 750c   (5dd4)   25.00
SHIRK,GEO H-Oklahoma Place Names-Norman-1956-cl-233p-
 2nd prntg   (5h0)   4.95
SHIRLEY,DAME-The Shirley Letters from Calif Mines-SanFran-
 1922-8vo-cl bk-bds-hand col plts-1st ed-ltd to 200c,nbrd,
 Russell autg   (5h4,f) 50.   (5yy7,f)   75.00
SHIRLEY,GLENN-Buckskin & Spurs-NY-1958-224p-36 illus-
 1st ed   (5L0,pres,dj) 5. (5k2,autg,dj) 6.50 (4i7)   6.00
--Heck Thomas,Frontier Marshal-Phila-(1962)-12mo-cl-231p-
 1st ed-o.p.   (4i7,dj) 7.   (5F5,5m9)   5.00
--Law West of Ft Smith-NY-(1957)-photos-333p-1st ed
 (5h0) 10. (5yy7,f,dj)   7.50
--Pawnee Bill-Albuqu-1958-256p-illus-Adams Guns #2013
 (5h0,dj) 6.50 (4i7,dj) 7. (5bb4,dj,mint)   7.50
--Six Gun & Silver Star-Albuqu-1955-map-236p
 (5h0) 6.50   (4i7,dj,5bb4,dj)   7.50
--Toughest of Them All-U New Mex Pr-1953-145p
 (5bb4,dj,mint) 5. (5h0) 3.50 (5L3,dj,mint)   5.75
SHIRLEY LETTERS-From the Calif Mines,1851,52-NY-1949-
 intro by Carl I Wheat   (5x5,dj)   12.50
--Shirley Letters-Also See SHIRLEY,DAME
SHIRLEY,J C-Redwoods of Coast & Sierra-U Calif-1937-photos-
 plts-84p-2nd ed,rev   (4n1,dj)   7.50
SHIRLEY,JOHN M-The Dartmouth College Causes-StL-1879-
 cl   (5q8)   15.00
SHIRLEY,WM-Conduct of Maj Gen Shirley,late Gen'l & Commander
 in Chief of HM Forces in NoAmer-Lond-1758   (5e2)   525.00
SHIRLEY,WM-Letter fom...to...Duke of Newcastle, with a journal
 of siege of Louisbourg-Bost-(1746)-hf lea
 (5g3,rbnd) 100.   (5L1)   110.00
SHISHMAREF DAY SCHOOL-Eskimo Cook Book-(1952)-wrps-
 36p   (4g9)   1.50
SHIVELY,J M-Route & Distances to Oregon & Calif with Description-
 Wash-1846-12mo-orig prntd front wrp-15p
 (5a3,bk wrp replaced) 2,500.00
SHLAKMAN,VERA-Economic History of a Factory Town-
 Smith College-Northampton-1935-204p-heavy papr wrps
 (5e8)   27.50
SHOBERL,FREDERIC,Ed-The World in Miniature,Persia-Lond-
 (1822)-Ackermann-3 vols-30 col plts-12mo-orig varnished
 yellow paper bds-prntd labls   (4L7,sp chip)   125.00
SHOEMAKER,ALFRED I-A Check List of Imprints of the German
 Press of Lehigh Co,Penna,1807 to 1900-Allentown-1947-240p
 Vol 16-Lehigh Co Hist Soc   (5w5)   12.50

USED BOOK PRICE GUIDE

SHOEMAKER,B H,3rd-Guide to Shoemaker Pioneers in Colonial
Amer-1955-155p-mimeo   (4t2)   20.00
SHOEMAKER,BENJ H-Shoemaker Family of Cheltenham,Pa-
1903-524p   (4t2)   45.00
SHOEMAKER,D,ed-With All Deliberate Speed-NY-1957 (5x2,dj) 6.00
SHOEMAKER,FLOYD C,ed-Missouri Day By Day-(JeffersonCty)-
1942,43-State Hist Soc-2 vols-1st ed   (5dd9,f) 7.50
SHOEMAKER,H W-Black Forest Souvenirs-Reading-1914-1st ed-
illus-404p   (5w0,pres) 25.   (5yy6) 20.   (5m1) 17.50
--Byron Hinckley Tells a Tale-Harrisbrg-1952-mimeo-7p (5kk7) 8.00
--In Seven Mountains-Reading-1913-1st ed-illus (5jj3) 25.00
--Indian Folk Songs of Pennsylvania-Ardmore-1927-ltd to 300c
                                              (4m4)   10.00
--Juniata Memories-Phila-(1916)-illus   (5m1,sl cov stn) 15.00
--More Allegheny Episodes-Altoona,Pa-1924-2 vols-544p-illus-
orig pict wrps   (5m1)   17.50
--North Pennsylvania Minstrelsy....1840 to 1910-Altoona-1919-
orig wrps-176p-1st ed   (4m4)   15.00
--Origins & Language of Central Penna Witchcraft-Reading-1927-
bnd-23p-illus   (5jj3)   10.00
--Some Stories of Old Deserted Houses In Central Penna Mntns-
Altoona-1931-orig wrps-81p   (5jj3) 10. (5w5)   12.50
--South Mountain Sketches-Altoona-1920-illus-scarce (4m4) 25.00
--Tales of the Bald Eagle Mntns in Central Penna-Reading-1912-
illus-scarce   (5m2)   12.50
--Two Old Christmas Stories of the "Great North Road"-Altoona-
1930-31p-orig wrps   (5w0)   10.00
SHOEMAKER,MICHAEL M-Great Siberian Railway-NY&Lond-
1903-illus-243p   (5q0)   10.00
--Islands of the Southern Seas-NY-1898-Putnam's Sons-illus
                                              (5x5,rprd) 15.00
SHOEMAKER, MYRON E-Fresh Water Fishing-GardenCty-1942-
illus-18 col plts   (5t4,dj) 6.50
--same-GardenCty-1945-218p-col plts   (5w9)   6.50
SHOEMAKER,VAUGHAN-1940 A D Cartoons-Chig Daily News-
1941-pict bds-ltd ed of 500c   (5r0,pres) 10.00
SHOEMAKER,W D-Trade marks-Wash-1931-2 vols   (5r4)   12.50
SHOENFELD,A H-The joy peddlar-NY-1927-Penuel Pr-sm4to-
ltd to 1285c   (5m2,autg) 7.50
SHOLL,CLARENCE VREELAND-Sholl's Humanitone-NY-1936-
413p   (5p0)   5.00
SHONE,A B-Century &a Half of Amateur Driving-Lond-1955-
hf mor-4to-14 col plts-110p-2 parts in 1-ltd to 500 proof copies
                                              (5nn2)   25.00
SHOOK,CHAS A-Cumorah Revisited-Cinn-1910-577p plus index-
maps-1st ed-scarce   (5L2,f) 20.00
--The True Origin of Mormon Polygamy-Cinn-1914-213p-illus-
1st ed   (5L2,f) 15.00
SHOOK,CHESTER E-The Lincoln Story-Cinn-(1950)-140p-priv prntd-
wrps   (5h2,pres) 5.00
SHOOLMAN,REGINA-Six Centuries of French Master Drawings
in Amer-NY-1950-4to-cl-256p-illus   (5t7)   12.00
SHOPPELL,R W-Modern House Beautiful Homes-NY-c1887-4to-
366p-illus   (5w5,wn) 17.50
SHORE,W TEIGNMOUTH-Charles Dickens & His Friends-Lond-
1909-ports-323p   (4a8)   5.00
SHORT ADVICE TO THE COUNTIES OF NY-By a Country
Gentleman-NY-1774-Jas Rivington-sm8vo-15p-calf-g.e.
                                              (5L1)   150.00
SHORT CHRONOLOGICAL ABSTRACT-of Rise of Reformation,&
Protestant Succession-Lond-1774-Glove-36p-wrps (5p1) 50.00
SHORT HISTORY,A-of Conduct of Present Ministry with regard
to Amer Stamp Act-Lond-1766-JAlmon-8vo-21p-roan
                                              (5L1,lacks sp) 30.00
SHORT HISTORY OF THE SALEM VILLAGE WITCHCRAFT TRIALS-
Salem-1911-(M V B Perley)-illus   (5g4)   4.00
SHORT LINE BLUE BOOK,JUNE 1907-Guide to Colorado-Denver-
1907-Vol 7,#4-65(68)p incl ads-photos-wrps   (5L5)   5.00
SHORT NARRATIVE OF HORRID MASSACRE IN BOSTON-Bost-
1770-8vo-mor-(title lf & pp73 to 88 inlaid)-fldng frontis-
3 plts inserted-1st ed,4th issue(wi pagination corr from 3rd
issue & wi additions)   (5n2)   375.00
--same-Lond-1770-Dilly&Almon-8vo-hf mor-frontis-2nd Engl ed
                                              (5n2)   550.00
--same-NY-1849-facs of Revere engr-fldng Plan-122p-8vo-
orig cl   (5L1)   10.00
SHORT,PEARLE ROSE-Chosen Sweets-Chig-1923-63p (5c5)   4.00
SHORT STORIES IN RHYME-NY-(c1860)-sq12mo-64p-illus (5v0) 10.00
SHORT STORY OF RISE,REIGN & RUIN-of the Antimonians,
Familists & Libertines That Infected Churches of New England-
Lond-1692-Parkhurst-sm4to-hf mor-3rd ed   (5n2)   150.00
SHORT TREATISE ON GAME OF WHIST-n.p.-(ca1820)-16mo-
216p-lea-(Hoyle)   (5xx7)   10.00

SHORT VIEW OF HISTORY OF COLONY-of Massachusetts Bay,
wi respect to their Orig Charter & Constitu-Lond-1769-
Wilkie-sm4to-hf mor-1st ed   (5n2,rprd) 100.00
SHORTER CATECHISM,THE-Bost-1765-Thos&John Fleet-12 lvs-
wrps   (5v2,f) 95.00
--same-NY-1791-Prntd for Macgill-16mo-111p-wrps-scarce
                                   (5L1,lf tn wi loss,lack bk wrp) 35.00
SHORTER,CLEMENT K-Victorian literature-NY-1897-Dodd,Mead-
1st ed   (5m2,lacks e.p.) 6.00
SHORTHOUSE,J H-John Inglesant;a romance-Birmingham-1880-
Cornish Bros-8vo-vel-1st ed   (5ss3,stnd,pres) 45.00
SHORTT,ADAM,ed-Canada & Its Provinces-Tor-1914 to 1917-
23 vols-4to-mrbld bds-hf mor-t.e.g.-Archives Ed (5w8) 200.00
--Documents Relating to Constitutional History of Canada-
Ottawa-Parts 1&2-1918-2 vols-2nd &rev ed-prntd wrps (5w8) 30.00
SHOTWELL,JAS T-Heritage of Freedom-NY-1934-136p (5aa0) 4.50
--War As An Instrument of National Policy-NY-c1929-310p(5w5) 5.00
SHOUER,LOUELLA G-Quick & Easy Meals for Two-NY-(1952)-
274p-illus   (5c0)   2.50
SHOULER,JAS-History of the US...Under the Constitution-NY-
c1880-5 vols   (5w9)   15.00
SHOWALTER,MARY EMMA-Mennonite Community Cookbook-
Phila-1953-494p-col plts   (4g9)   5.00
SHOWERMAN, G -A Country Chronicle-NY-1917-Century-
illus   (5m2,pres) 6.00
SHREVE,ROYAL ORNAN-The Finished Scoundrel-Indnpls-c1933-
                                              (5w5,sl wn) 5.00
SHRIVER,H C-Justice Oliver Wendell Holmes-NY-1936-
Central Book Co-280p   (5p9)   5.00
SHRIVER,J ALEXIS-Lafayette in Harford County,1781-Bel Air-
1931-orig wrps-ltd to 100c   (5m2,box) 10.00
SHRIVER,WM P-Immigrant Forces-NY-1913-fldg table-1st ed
                                              (5q8)   4.50
SHRYOCK,R H-Georgia & the Union in 1850-1926- (5L7)   9.50
SHUB,DAVID-Lenin-A biog-GardenCty-1951   (5x7)   4.50
SHUCK,EDITH-The Chicago Daily News Cook Book-(Chig,1930)-
                                              (5c9,5g9) 4.00
SHUCK,OSCAR T-Bench & Bar in Calif-SanFran-1887-sm4to-
543p & index-hf mor   (5xx7)   12.50
--Bench & Bar in Calif-SanFran-1887 to 1889-Occident Printg House-
3 vols-cl   (5tt0)   15.00
--Bench & Bar in Calif-SanFran-1889-8vo   (4g6,stn) 16.50
--California Scrap Book-SanFran-1869-illus-hf lea (5x5,crack) 15.00
--History of Bench & Bar of Calif-LosAng-1901-Commercial Print
House-1152p-cl   (5tt0) 20. (5h5,crack)   15.00
--Representative & Leading Men of Pacific-SanFran-1870-
Bacon&Co-port-702p-cl   (5tt0)   20.00
SHUEY,A M-The Testing of Negro Intelligence-Lynchburg,-1955-
R8vo   (5x2)   15.00
SHUEY,LILLIAN HINMAN-Don Luis' wife-Bost-1897-Lamson,Wolffe-
1st ed   (5m2)   6.50
SHUFELDT,R W-Reports of Explor & Surv to ascertain Practicability
of Ship Canal...Isthmus of Tehuantepec-Wash-1872-GPO-
illus-4to-20 fldg plts-151p (5yy0) 22.50 (5g0,4g6,ex-libr) 15.00
SHUFELDT,R W-Studies of the Human Form-Phila-c1908-lg8vo-
642p-illus-gilt   (5w5,rprd) 65.00
SHULER,ELLIS W-Geology of Dallas County-Austin-1918-54p-
2 lg fldg maps   (4a5)   5.00
SHULIM,JOS I-The Old Dominion & Napoleon Bonaparte-NY-
1952-332p-cl-1st ed   (5t2)   7.50
SHULMAN,HARRY M-Slums of NY-NY-1938-8vo-cl-394p
                                   (5t0) 5.   (5w4)   6.00
SHULMAN,IRVING-The Amboy Dukes-1947-Dblday   (5F1)   8.00
SHUMAKER,E S-Descendants of Henry Keller of York Co,Penn
& Fairfield Co,Ohio-Indnpls-(1924)-594p-cl (5y0,f) 15. (5t9)17.50
SHUMWAY,A L-Oberliniana...1833 to 1883-Cleve-(1883?)-
pict bds-175p,(?)p   (4h7)   10.00
SHUNK,CAROLINE S-An Army Woman in the Philippines-KansCty-
1914-12mo-bds&cl-183p-illus   (5h5)   3.00
SHURBURNE,ANDREW-Memoirs of-Utica-1828-262p-calf-12mo-
errata lf-1st ed   (5m2)   32.50
SHURTLEFF,HAROLD R-The Log Cabin Myth-Cambr-1939-
SEMorrison,ed-243p-index-illus   (5t1)   50.00
SHURTLEFF,J B-The Governmental Instructor-NY-1857-Collins&Bro-
189p,(2)(ads)-lea bkd pict bds-rev ed   (5p1)   12.50
SHURTLEFF,NATHANL B,ed-Records of Colony of New Plymouth
in New England-Bost-1855 to 61-12 vols in 10-4to-cl
                                              (5g4,hng weak) 300.00
--Topographical & Historical Description of Boston-1890-illus-
3rd ed   (5L7)   10.00
--same-Bost-1891-719p-illus-fldg maps-bev edges-lg8vo (5h9) 13.50

SHUSHANNA,CHISANA-Gold Fields via Cordova & Copper Riv
& NW RR-Cordova-(1913)-fld-6 panels of text,4 panels of
photos-ca 16x21"-scarce   (5t3)   12.50
SHUTE,HENRYA-Adventures of Several Hard Characters-Exeter,NH-
1897-Newsletter Pr-t8vo-97p-photos-(50c prntd)-v rare
                                                    (4F6,vg)   250.00
--Sequil,or Things Whitch Aint Finished in the First-Bost-1904
                                                    (4F6,vg)   7.50
--Youth Plupy-Bost-1917-Houghton-8vo-253p-cl-6 plts-1st ed
                                                    (5aa0)   6.50
SHUTE,NEVIL-Requiem for a Wren-Lond-(1955)-1st ed (5r9,f,dj)   7.50
--A Town Like Alice-Lond-(1950)-1st ed   (5r9)   7.50
SHUTE,MISS T S-The American Housewife,Cook Book-Parts 1 & 2-
Phila-1880-Lewis&Menzies-356p-cl-ads   (5ww2)   20.00
SHUTE,W,transl-Triumphs of Nassau-Lond-1613-prntd by Adam Islip-
vel-394p   (5t4)   40.00
SI,"SHORTY" & BOYS ON MARCH TO SEA-Wash-1902-312p-wrps-
(J McElroy)   (5ff7)   5.00
SIA,M-Mary Sia's Chinese Cookbook-Honolulu-1961-U of Hawaii Pr-
148p-illus   (5g9)   3.50
SIBELL,MURIEL V-Cloud Cities of Colorado-Denver-(1934)-(82p)-
wrps-1st ed-rare pamph   (5L2)   25.00
SIBLEY,FREDK O-Zanee Kooran-NY-(c1901)-8vo-dec cl-port
                                                    (5b2,f)   4.00
SIBLEY,JOHN-Louisiana-Portsmouth Oracle,Feb 25,1804-
complete issue-4p-1 ad lf   (4n4,ad lf rprd) 45.00
SIBLEY,JOHN L-History of Union-1851-540p   (5e8)   39.75
SIBLEY,ROBT-The Golden Book of Calif-(Berkeley)-1937-4to-
cl-illus-1296p   (5dd5,5h5)   5.00
--Romance of the Univ of Calif-1928-Crocker Co-illus-orig stiff wrps-
                                                    (5x5)   5.00
SIBLEY,WM G-French Five Hundred-Gallipolis-1933-priv prnt
                                                    (4a9)   6.00
SIBLY,E-New & Complete Illustration of the Occult Sciences-
Lond-1807-4to-orig calf-1130p   (5w0,cov dtchd)   45.00
SIBREE,JAS-Madagascar & Its People-Lond-1870-576p-illus-
8 plts   (5c6,ex-libr)   16.50
--50 Years in Madagascar-NY-1924-HoughtonMiff-map-photos-
353p   (4t5)   7.50
SICHEL,ALLAN-A Guide to Good Wine-Lond-(1952)-200p-
photos-maps   (5g9)   7.50
SICHEL,WALTER-Emma Lady Hamilton from new & original sources
& documents-Lond-1905-551p-illus-2nd ed   (5t7)   6.50
SICHLER,ERNEST G-From Maumee to Thames & Tiber-NY-
Univ Pr-1930   (5ss9,f)   12.50
SICKEL,H S J-Thanksgiving...its source,philosophy & history-
Phila-1940-258p   (5w5)   6.50
SICKELS,D K-U S Mining Laws & Decisions of Comm of General
Land Office-SanFran-1881   (5r4,rbnd)   25.00
SICKERT,BERNHARD-Whistler-Lond-1909-Duckworth-26 plts-
175p-16mo   (4e0)   15.00
SIDENBLADH,E-Urmaker I Sverige Under Aldre Tider-Stockholm-
1947-129 plts-256p-4to-wrps   (5bb0)   30.00
SIDNEY,ALGERNON-Discourses concerning Government-Lond-
1698-folio-462p,5p-calf-1st ed   (5L8,wn)   65.00
--same-NY-1803 to 5-3 vols-John Toland,ed-buck
                                         (5g4,ex-libr,wn,crack) 10. (5L7) 35.00
SIDNEY,EDW WM-The Partisan Leader,a Tale of the Future-
n.p.(Wash,DC)-1856-JasCaxton,prntr-2 vols-12mo-qtr mor-
1st ed-ex rare-(suppressed)   (4i3,f)   650.00
SIDNEY,MARGARET-5 Little Peppers & How They Grew-Bost-
(1880)-1st ed,later issue ("phronsie" on pg 231)-scarce (4F6) 90.00
--same-Bost-(1881)-illus-scarce Lothrop ed in col bds (4F6)   10.00
--Golden West As Seen by Ridgway Club-Bost-(1886)-388p-
illus-dec cov   (5s4,wn,rprd)   10.00
SIDNEY,SIR PHILIP-Astrophel & Stella-Lond-1931-Nonesuch Pr-
1210c,ltd-dec bds   (5dd0,box)   20.00
--Sir Philip Sidney's Arcadia,modernized by Mrs Stanley-Lond-
1725-folio-calf-mor labl   (5x3,vg)   85.00
SIDON,ALICE-Continental Dessert Delicacies-NY-(1950)-186p
                                                    (5c9)   5.50
SIEDENTOPF,A R-Last Stronghold of Big Game-NY-1946-
Natl Travel Club-202p-maps-photos   (4t5)   5.00
SIEBERT,WILBUR H-The Mysteries of Ohio's Underground Railroads-
Columbus-1951-cl-330p   (4h7)   12.50
--Underground Railroad from Slavery to Freedom-NY-1898-cl-
478p-1st ed-scarce   (4h7)   35.00
SIEGFRIED,ANDRE-Afrique du Sud,Notes de Voyage-Paris-1949-
160p-wrps   (5c6)   7.25
--African Journey-Lond-1950-Cape-maps   (4t5,dj)   3.50
--America Comes of Age-NY-c1927   (5t0) 4. (5x7)   5.00
--Democracy in New Zealand-Lond-1914   (5tt5)   8.50

SIEGFRIED,ANDRE (continued)
--Suez,Panama et les Routes Maritimes Mondiales-Paris-1940
33 charts & maps-hf mor   (5r7,f)   12.50
SIEGMEISTER,ELIE-Music Lover's Handbook-1943 ed-
W Morrow,Publ-817p   (5a6,f)   3.50
SIEMENS,GEORG-History of House of Siemens-Munich-1957-
2 vols   (5jj3,f,dj)   18.50
SIERRA CLUB BULLETIN-VOL 9,#2-SanFran-1913-129p-illus-
stiff wrps   (4a5,unopened) 15.00
SIERRA CLUB BULLETIN-annual issues,91 vols-SanFran-1893 to 1963-
Sierra Club-orig wrps-incl index vol   (5d7)   400.00
SIERRA CLUB BULLETIN-Vol 1,1893 to Vol 38,1953-orig prntd wrps-
complete set in parts   (5n5)   500.00
SIERRA CLUB BULLETIN-1893 to 1905-SanFran-1950-5 vols-
reprinted   (5x5)   35.00
SIERRA CLUB,A HANDBOOK-edited by D R Brower-SanFran-1947-
124p-illus-1st ed   (5dd9)   7.50
SIERRA LEONE,LAWS,STATUTES,ETC-Laws of the Colony &
Protectorate....Jan 1,1946-Lond-1946-rev ed-4 vols-bound
                                              (5ii7,ex-libr)   45.00
SIERRA MADRE SOUVENIR & BOOK OF RECIPES-Sierra Madre-
1929-illus-ads-pict wrps-ring bnd-90p   (4g9)   7.50
SIERRA MINING CO OF LAKE VALLEY,NM-Letter Press Book...
Feb 12,1884 to Mar 15,1885..from F M Endlich....to Pres
of Mining Companies in Phila-rare-(ca 900p)   (4t3)   250.00
SIEVEKING,ALBERT FORBES-The Praise of Gardens-Lond-1899-
423p-34 plts   (5s7,rprd)   8.50
SIFTON,CLIFFORD-Speech on the Canadian Yukon Railway-
Ottawa-1898   (5nn8)   35.00
SIGAUD,LOUIS A-Belle Boyd,Confederate Spy-Richmond-(1944)-
illus-254p   (5b1,5h0,f) 7.50   (5t7,dj) 5.   (5r8)   8.75
SIGEL,F P-Lectures on Slavonic Law-Lond-1902   (5r4)   12.50
SIGERIST,HENRY E-Socialized Medicine-NY-c1937   (5x7)   5.00
SIGERSON,DORA-Love of Ireland-Dublin-1916-Maunsel&Co-
mor-1st ed-ltd to 25c   (5ss3)   45.00
SIGLER,PHARES O-Numismatic Bibliography-Dearborn-(1951)-
189p   (4h8)   10.00
SIGNOURNEY,MRS L H-The Girls Reading Book in Prose & Poetry
for schools-NY-1839-18mo-bds-243p   (5t7,stnd)   6.50
--Letters of Life-NY-1866-Appleton-8vo-cl-port   (5b2,f)   10.00
--Letters to Young Ladies-Hartf-1835-212p   (5w7,ex-libr) 9.50
--Lucy Howard's Journal-NY-1858-343p   (5w7)   10.00
--Olive Buds-Hartf-1836-WmWatson-24mo-136p-cl   (5p1,v wn)   7.50
--Past Meridian-NY-1854-1st ed   (5yy6)   10.00
--Pleasant Memories of Pleasant Lands-Bost&Cambr-1856-a.e.g.-
395p,4p-3rd ed   (5t7,pres) 10.00
--Poems for Children-Hartf-1836-Canfield&Robins-sq12mo-cl-
91p-frontis-g.t.   (5s0,sl wn) 15.00
--The Religious Souvenir for 1840-NY-1845   (5mm2)   10.00
--Scenes in My Native Land-Bost-1845-319p-16mo
                                              (5i0,sl loose) 10. (4b6) 17.50
--Sketches-Phila-1834-Key&Biddle-1st ed-cl
                               (5i4,hng split) 17.50 (5x1,sp wn) 25.00
--Water drops-NY-1838-RobtCarter-cl-1st ed   (5x1)   25.00
--The western home & other poems-Phila-1854-Parry U McMillan-
port-1st ed   (5m2)   6.50
--The Young Ladies' Offering-Bost-1848-8vo-264p-illus (5v0,f) 7.50
SIGSBEE,CHAS-Deep Sea Sounding,Dredging-Wash-1880-221p-4to-
illus   (5s1,ex-libr) 12.50
--The "MAINE"-NY-1889-270p-photos-port-scarce   (5s1)   7.50
SIHLER,K ELY-Against Odds-StL-1917   (4a9,vg)   7.00
SIKES,EARL R-State & Federal Corrupt Practices Legislation-
Durham-1928-321p   (5w4,dj)   3.00
SILHOUETTES D'AVIONS,ALLIES ET ENNEMIS-(Paris,1918)-
obl 12mo-illus-wrps-v scarce   (5t2)   12.50
SILHOUETTE HANDBOOK OF USAAF AIRPLANES-Dayton,
Wright Field-1942-48p plus wrps-restricted   (4n6,sl stn) 10.00
SILHOUETTES,1st SERIES-Bost-1878-orig wrps-sq8vo-(by Church)-
12 plts   (4m8)   10.00
SILK-Its Origin,Culture & Manufacture-Mass-1911-illus of
Corticelli Mills-47p-12 col plts   (5n7)   2.50
SILL,EDW ROWLAND-Around the Horn-Yale U-1944-79p-8vo-
cl&bds   (5h5)   5.00
--The Poems of-Cambr-1902-Riverside Pr-tall 8vo-cl bkd bds-
ltd to 500c,nbrd   (5b2,unopnd) 10. (5r9)   17.50
--The Poetical Works of-Bost-1906-423p-a.e.g.-8vo-illus-calf
                                                 (5t2)   12.50
SILL,FRED S-A Year Book of Colonial Times-NY-1899-Dutton
                                                 (5p9)   3.50
SILL,JOHN-Gen of Desc of,who settled in Cambridge, Mass in
1637-1859-108p   (5t9)   20.00
SILLIAMAN,SUE I-St Joseph in Homespun-3 Rivers-1931-213p-wrps
                                                 (5h2)   10.00

SILLIMAN, AUGUSTUS E-A Gallop among American Scenery-
  NY-1881-illus-not 1st   (4b6) 15. (5h2,5ss5,ex-libr) 10.00
SILLIMAN, BENJ-Amer Journal of Science & Arts-NewHav-1823-
  hand col fldng map-plts(some fldng)-hf lea-408p
                                (5r7,wn,map rprd) 35.00
--Description of the Recently Discovered Petroleum Region in Calif-
  NY-1864-Francis&Loutrel-orig prntd wrps-disbnd-1st ed
                        (4h0,Streeter bkplt) 750.00
SILLITOE, HELEN-A History of the Teaching of Domestic Subjects-
  Lond-1933-245p   (5w7) 8.50
SILLS, THEO B-How The West Was Won-Cinerama art ed-
  prntd in Switzerland-obl 8vo-pict bds   (5m9) 3.00
SILSBEE, M C D-A Half Century in Salem-Bost-1888-HoughtonMiff-
  136p-4th ed,enlrgd   (5p9) 4.00
SILTZER, FRANK-Story of British Sporting Prints-Lond-1929-4to-
  413p-new ed, rev&enlrgd   (5x0) 35.00
SILVA, A A-Baldaque da Estado Actual das Pescas em Portugal-
  Lisbon-1891-4to-519p,(1)-3/4 mor-col plts-fldg map (5ss2,f) 45.00
SILVA, VICENTE-New Mexico's Vice King of the Nineties-n.p.-
  n.d.-by DeBaca-12mo-40p-wrps-scarce   (5dd5) 18.50
SILVER, ARTHUR P-Farm Cottage, Camp & Canoe in Maritime Canada-
  Lond-n.d.-249p-illus   (4a8) 6.50
--same-Lond-(1908)-illus-8vo-1st ed (5m6,ex-libr) 10.00
SILVER JUBILEE MEM CONVENT-of Our Lady of The Sacred Heart,
  Oakland,Calif,1868 to 1893-SanFran Pr Co-1893-dec cl-
  172p-illus   (5r0) 7.50
SILVER,S W & CO-Handbook to Canada-Lond-1883-288p-
  col fldg map-wrps   (4a8) 6.50
--Publrs Handbook to Canada-Lond-1881-288p-col fldg map
                         (5dd0) 5.00
SILVERSMITH, JULIUS-The New Northwest-Cheyenne-1869-
  LBJoseph-8vo-orig yellow prntd wrps-32p(incl last 4p of ads)-
  1st ed-ex rare   (5i9,lacks map,Streeter copy) 350.00
SIMCOE, JOHN G-Simcoe's Military Journal-NY-1844-328p-
  10 maps-orig bds-rare
        (5L7,rbnd,hole in t. pg) 75 (5L3,rbkd,vg) 175.00
SIMCOE, MRS JOHN GRAVES-The diary of-Tor-1934-440p-maps-
  238 illus-revised   (5w4,underline) 27.50
SIMCOX, E J-Primitive Civilizations-Lond-1894-2 vols (5rr9) 25.00
SIMES, THOS-A Treatise on Military Science which Comprehends
  the Grand Operation of War-Lond-1780-frontis-4to-calf
                        (5b0,rprd) 60.00
SIMKIN, COLIN,ed-Currier & Ives' America-NY-1952-obl folio-
  cl-bds-col illus   (4m9) 15. (5t2,dj,mint) 12.50
--The Story of the Charter Oak-Hartf-1938-12mo-illus-28p-
  simulated wd sides-boxed-ltd to 1500c,autg-Charter Oak Fire Ins
                        (5j5) 6.00
SIMKINS, FRANCIS-Women of the Confederacy-NY-n.d.(c1936)-
                          (4a9,f) 17.50
SIMKINS, FRANCIS BUTLER-The South,Old & New-NY-1949-
  Knopf-527p   (4j4) 3.00
SIMMONDS, J H-Trees from Other Lands for Shelter & Timber in
  New Zealand-Auckland-1927-cl-4to-plts (5z9) 30.00
SIMMONDS, RALPH-All About Aircraft-Lond-1915-illus-pic cl-
  th8vo   (5j7) 9.50
SIMMONDS, W H-Boy's Book of the Sea-Lond-n.d.-Partridge-
  8vo-318p-col frontis-dec red cl-plts-g.t. (5aa2) 4.50
SIMMONITE, WM J-The Simmonite Culpeper Herbal Remedies-Lond-
  (1957)-123p   (5w3) 3.95
SIMMONS, AMELIA-Amer Cookery-facs of 1796 ed-NY-1958-
  47p-bds-ltd ed   (5c0) 15.00
--Amer Cookery-Conn-1937 reprint-69p-cl bk-prntd bds-
  ltd to 185c   (5c0) 15.00
SIMMONS, EDW-From Seven to Seventy-NY-1922-Harper-344p-
  illus-demy 8vo   (4a0,dj) 18.50 (4a0) 17.50
SIMMONS, ERNEST J-Leo Tolstoy-Bost-1946-8vo-cl-illus-790p
                       (5t0) 4.50
SIMMONS, FRANK E-History of Coryell County-Coryell Co News-
  1936-102p-1st ed-stiff wrps-scarce
          (4a5,stns,pres to Pres Roosevelt) 60.00
SIMMONS, GEO F-Birds of the Austin Region(Tex)-Austin-1925
  cl-illus-432p   (5cc1) 10.00
SIMMONS, JAS RAYMOND-The Historic Trees of Massachusetts-
  Bost-1919-139p-illus-bds-1st ed (5h9) 10.00
SIMMONS CO, JOHN-Steam, Water,Gas,Oil & Fire Protection
  Lines-NY-1916-604p-illus   (5b9) 7.50
SIMMONS, L A-History of 84th Reg't Ill Volunteers-Macomb-1866-
  1st ed-345p, lp-scarce   (5bb4) 40.00
SIMMONS, LEE-Assignment Huntsville-Univ of Texas Pr-1957-
  illus   (5h6) 5.00
SIMMONS, LEO W-The Role of the Aged in Primitive Society-
  NewHav-(1947)-308p plus index-2nd prntng (5L0,dj) 6.00

SIMMONS, LEO W (continued)
--Sunchief,The Autobiography of a Hopi Indian-NewHav-
  1947-illus-2nd printing   (4k5,f) 17.50
SIMMONS, VIRGIL-Air Piloting-NY-(1938)-8vo-cl-illus-284p
                      (5t2,dj,fine) 5.00
SIMMONS, WM JOS-The Klan Unmasked-Atlanta-(1923)-illus
                         (5x2) 60.00
--same-Atlanta-(1924)-illus-298p   (5rr3) 25.00
SIMMS, FLORENCE M-Etoffe du pays-Tor-n.d.-illus (5w8) 5.00
SIMMS, HENRY H-Emotion at High Tide-(Richmond)-1960-243p-cl
             (5w9,5h1) 4.   (5x2) 6.50
SIMMS, JEPTHA R-The Amer spy-Albany-1857-JMunsell-8vo-
  orig prntd wrps-2nd ed   (5i0) 25.00
--Trappers of NY-Albany-1850-illus-1st ed-12mo-280p-glt dec cl-
          (5u9,sl fox) 25. (4m2,cov wn) 40.00
--same-1871-289p   (5zz0,rbkd) 20.00
--same-1935-MacWethy edition-294p (5zz0,rbnd) 15.00
SIMMS, P MARION-The Bible in Amer-NY-1936-illus-1st ed
                       (5yy6) 7.50
SIMMS, WM GILMORE-Border Beagles,Tale of the Mississippi-
  (anon)-Phila-1840-Carey&Hart-12mo-orig qtr cl-labls-2 vols-
  1st ed-scarce   (4i5,vf) 350.00
--Border Novels & Romances of the South-n.d.-Vol 4,Charlemont,
  Pride of the Village   (5h6,wn) 5.00
--Carl Werner-(anon)-NY-1838-Geo Adlard-12mo-orig cl-labls-
  2 vols-1st ed   (5x1,Swann copy) 350.00
--Confession,or The Blind Heart-NY-1856-new & rev ed (4j2) 12.50
--The Damsel of Darien-(anon)-Phila-1839-Lea&Blanchard-12mo-
  orig cl-labls-2 vols-1st ed   (4i5,f) 200.00
--Eutaw-NY-n.d.-(1880's?)-582p-cl-new & rev ed (5h2,crack) 4.00
--The Forayers,or the raid of the Dog Days-NY-1855-Redfield-
  8vo-orig cl-frontis-1st ed   (4i3) 27.50
--Golden Christmas,a Chronicle of St John's,Berkeley-(anon)-
  Charleston-1852-WalkerRichards&Co-8vo-orig cl-1st ed
                      (4i5,chip) 27.50
--Life of Capt John Smith,founder of Virginia-Bost-1855-379p-
  illus   (5L3) 12.50
--same-Bost-n.d.(ca 1850)-375p-illus-cl-6th ed (5t2) 5.00
--Life of the Chevalier Bayard-NY-1847-Harper-401p-1st ed
                       (5x4) 37.50
--Life of Francis Marion-1844-1st ed (5L7,bndg marked) 25.00
--Life of Nathanl Green-NY-(1849)-Cooledge&Bros-393p-illus-
  Amer Lib Series-1st ed   (5x4) 17.50
--Martin Faber, Story of a Criminal-(anon)-NY-1833-Harper-
  12mo-orig cl-labl-rare   (5x1,sl wn,lacks fly) 400.00
--Martin Faber, Story of a Criminal & Other Tales-(anon)-NY-
  1837-Harper-12mo-orig cl-labls-2 vols-1st ed-scarce
               (4i5,sl wn,lack e.p.) 75.00
--Mellichampe-(anon)-NY-1836-Harper-12mo-orig cl-labls-
  2 vols-1st ed   (5x1,vg) 125.00
--same-Redfield-1854-frontis-revised ed (4j2) 12.50
--Norman Maurice,or the Man of the People-Richmond-1851-
  Jno R Thompson,pub-MacFarlane&Fergusson,prntrs-8vo-
  disbnd-1st ed-scarce   (5xx9) 45.00
--The Partisan-(anon)-NY-1835-Harper-12mo-orig cl-labls-
  2 vols-1st ed (5ee3,sl wn) 75. (4i5,sl wn) 80.00
--The Partisan,a Romance of the Revolution-NY-1870-12mo-cl-
  531p-frontis-new & rev ed   (5m8,cov spot) 5.00
--same-NY-n.d.-(1880's?)-cl   (5h2,5h6) 5.00
--Pelayo,Story of the Goth-(anon)-NY-1838-Harper-12mo-
  orig cl-labls-2 vols-1st ed   (4i5,sl wtrstn) 80.00
--Sack & Destruction of City of Columbia,etc-(anon)-Columbia-
  1865-Power Pr Daily Phoenix-8vo-hf mor-1st ed-scarce
                       (5xx9) 225.00
--The Scout,or,The Black Riders of Congaree-Chig-1887-8vo-
  cl-472p-new& rev ed   (5g5) 5.00
--Southward Ho!-NY-n.d.-(1880's?)-472p-cl (5h2) 5.00
--Supplement to Plays of Shakespeare-Phila-1855-JasB Smith-
  8vo-orig cl   (4i3) 17.50
--Woodcraft-NY-n.d.-(1880's?)-518p-cl (5h2,hng crack) 4.00
--The Works of-16 vols(of 17)-NY-1864-WJWiddleton-cl-
  new & rev ed   (5p7) 80.00
SIMON, ANDRE-The Art of Good Living-Lond-1929-201p (5w1) 6.00
--Bibliotheca Bacchica-Tome 1-Incunables-Lond-1927-facs-
  237p,(1)-4to-ltd ed   (5w1) 115.00
--The Blood of the Grape-Lond-(1920)-301p,(2) (5w1,rub) 15.00
--Bottlescrew Days-Lond-(1926)-273p-illus (5w1,wn) 10.00
--By Request-Lond-1957-180p-5 illus   (5w1) 10.00
--Champagne-Lond-(1934)-12mo-140p,(3) (5w1,fade) 10.00
--Dictionary of Wine-Lond-(1938)-266p-6 maps (5w1,wormhole) 6.50
--A Dictionary of Gastronomy-NY-1949-264p (5g9) 7.50
--French Cook Book-Bost-1948-342p-col illus-rev by Crosby Gaige
                       (5g9) 6.00

SIMON, ANDRE (continued)
--Madeira, Wine, cakes & Sauce-wi Eliz Craig-Lond-(1933)-
153p, (5)-12mo   (5w1, rub)   10.00
--Table of Contents-Leaves from my diary-Lond-(1933)-180p
                                              (5w1)   12.50
--In Vino Veritas-Lond-(1913)-202p, (1)   (5w1)   8.50
--Vintagewise-Lond-(1945)-174p   (5w1, 4g9)   5.00
--What About Wine-Lond-(1953)-12mo-56p-photos (5w1)   8.50
--Wine & Spirits, The Connoisseur's textbook-Lond-(1919)-
272p, (1)   (5w1)   6.50
--A Wine Primer-Lond-(1946)-148p-maps   (5g9)   5.00
--Wines of the World Pocket Library-7 vols-Lond-(1950)-bds-
ca 15p ea vol-maps-box   (5g9, box scuff)   6.50
SIMON, OLIVER-Printing of Today-Lond-1928-Peter Davies-
illus-4to-cl   (5t2) 12.50   (5p5) 17.50 (5t8) 15.00
SIMON, SANDOR, ed-R Vogeler, E Sanders & Their Accomplices
Before the Criminal Court-Budapest-1950-309p-illus-orig wrps
                                              (5x7)   6.50
SIMONDS, FRANK H-History of World War-NY-(1917 to 20)-
5 vols-8vo-photos-maps   (4a6, shaken &stn) 20. (5w0) 12.50
SIMONDS, J-The Amer Book of Recipes-Bost-1854-16mo-72p-
wrps   (5c0, wn, wtrstnd) 12.50
SIMONDS, J C-Story of Manual Labor in all Lands & Ages-Chig-
1886-illus-715p   (5yy0, hngs brok) 12.50
SIMONDS, WM A-Kamaaina, a Century in Hawaii-Hawaii-1949-
8vo-bds-105p-ltd-illus   (5h5)   4.00
SIMONIS, H-The Street of Ink-Lond-1917-ports (4b6)   15.00
SIMONS, A M-Class Struggles in Amer-Chig-1906-64p-wrps
                                              (5x2)   10.00
--Social forces in Amer history-NY-1911-325p (5u3)   6.50
SIMONSON, LEE-The Stage is Set-NY-(1932)-8vo-cl-585p-
illus-1st ed   (5t0, dj)   7.50
SIMOONS, FREDK J-NW Ethiopia, Peoples & Economy-Madison-
1960-17&250p-32 plts-3 sketches-10 maps   (5c6, f)   7.50
SIMPLE COBBLER OF AGGAWAM-in America-Lond-1647-
Bowtell-4to-mor -2nd ed   (5n2, f)   450.00
--same-Bost-1713-Henchman-sm8vo-mor-1st Amer ed
                                         (5n2, sl rprd) 300.00
SIMPLE POEMS FOR INFANT MINDS-NY-(ca 1840)-Kiggins &
Kellogg-2nd series, #11-wdcut-16mo-16p-orig yellow wrps-
stitchd   (5c8, sl soil)   6.00
SIMPSON, ALAN-Puritanism in Old & New England-1955 (5L7) 4.00
SIMPSON, ALEX-The Life & Travels of Thos Simpson-Lond-1845-
8vo-424p-frontis-fldg map-calf-1st ed (4e9) 110. (5s9, rbnd)100.00
SIMPSON, ALYSE-Red Dust of Kenya-NY-1952-Crowell-282p
                                          (4t5, dj)   3.50
SIMPSON, C-A Yankee's Adventures in SoAfrica-Chig-1902-illus
                                          (5b9, f)   5.00
--Life in Far West-1910-261p   (5r1, fade, sp loose) 8.00
--Wild Life in Far West-Chig-(1896)-264p-cl   (5h1)   7.50
SIMPSON, CHAS-Life in the Mines-Chig-1905-343p (5s4, wn) 4.00
SIMPSON, CHAS TORREY-In Lower Florida Wilds-NY-(1920)-
404p, (2)-col frontis-2 maps   (5w3, pres)   15.00
--same-NY-(1920)-2nd printing   (5m6, pres)   9.00
--Ornamental Gardening in Florida-LittleRiver, Fla-(1926)-243p-
plts   (5s7, rub)   7.50
--Out of Doors in Florida-Miami-1923-8vo-illus-1st ed
                                          (5m6, pres)   12.50
SIMPSON, DOROTHY-The Maine Islands-Lipp-(1960)-256p-1st ed
                                          (5e8, dj)   6.75
SIMPSON, LT EDW-Treatise on Ordnance & Naval Gunnery-NY-
1862-492p-plts   (5xx7, lacks flys) 15.00
SIMPSON, EDW J-Sedalia, Queen of the Prairies-50th Anniv
Souvenir-(Sedalia, 1909)-(48p)-photos-wrps-tied (5t3)   15.00
SIMPSON, ELIZABETH M-Bluegrass Houses & Their Traditions-
Lex-1932-scarce   (4d7)   30.00
SIMPSON, GEO-Overland Journey Round the World, During Years
1841 & 1842-Phila-1847-orig cl-1st Amer ed-2 pts in 1 vol
                                        (4n4, inscr)   110.00
SIMPSON, GEO-Part of Dispatch....(1828 Journey to the Columbia)-
Lond-1947-Hudson's Bay Rec Soc-277p   (5nn2)   3.50
SIMPSON, GEO GAYLORD-Attending Marvels, a Patagonian Journal-
NY-1934-Macmillan-295p-tall 8vo-cl-illus   (5j5)   7.50
SIMPSON, JR, GEO LEE-The Cokers of Carolina-Univ of NoCar Pr-
1956   (5x0)   4.50
SIMPSON, HENRY-Lives of Eminent Philadelphians, Now Deceased-
Phila-1859-44 illus-993p   (4m4, rebnd)   17.50
SIMPSON, J C-Horse Portraiture-NY-(1867)-462p (5ii2, chip) 9.50
SIMPSON, JAS H-Journal of Military Reconn from Santa Fe, New Mex
to Navajo Country-Phila-1852-maps-plts-140p-1st ed
                            (4n4) 90.   (5r1)   75.00
--Report & Map of Route from Ft Smith, Ark, to Santa Fe, New Mex-
Wash-1850-cl-lea labl-25p-4 fldg maps-SED 12 (4n4)   35.00

SIMPSON, JAS H (continued)
--Report & Map of Wagon Road Routes in Utah Territory-Wash-
1859-SED 40-84p-fldg map   (5n4) 15. (5g4)   25.00
--Route from Ft Smith to Santa Fe-Wash-1850-HED 45-89p-2 plts-
fldg map   (5n4)   25.00
--same-SD 12-25p wiout March's report, but wi map (5n4) 15.00
--Report on Union Pac RR & Branches etc-Wash-1866-disbnd-(136p)
                                          (4n4, 5tt0)   15.00
--Report & Map of Wagon Road Routes in Utah Territory-Wash-
1859-fldg map-84p-1st ed   (4n4)   30.00
SIMPSON, JOHN-A Complete System of Cookery-Lond-1816-16mo-
illus-cl-revised & enlrgd   (5b0)   55.00
SIMPSON, L E-The Weaver's Craft-Leicester, Eng-n.d. (ca 194-)-
136 illus-200p-4to   (5n7)   3.50
SIMPSON, LESLEY BYRD-California in 1792-SanMarino-1938-
8vo-cl   (4c1)   10.00
--The Encomienda in New Spain-Vol 19-Univ of Calif-1929-
t8vo-297p-1st ed   (5F5)   15.00
--Many Mexicos-NY-1946-Putnam   (5x0)   4.50
SIMPSON, M, ed-Cyclopaedia of Methodism-1881-4to-lea sp-
4th rev ed   (5L7, rub)   17.50
SIMPSO POFFENBARGER, LIVIA NYE-Battle of Pt Pleasant-
PtPleas-1909-141p-cl-scarce   (5h2)   12.50
SIMPSON, SAML L-Gold Gated West-Phila-1910-308p (5s4, soil) 6.00
SIMPSON, THOS-Narr of Discoveries on North Coast of Amer-
Lond-1843-1st ed-orig cl-2 fldg maps   (5s6)   125.00
SIMPSON, WM HASKELL-Along Old Trails-Bost-1929-89p (5s4,dj) 3.00
SIMPSON, WM R-Hockshop-NY-1954-311p-illus   (5hh6)   4.75
SIMS, J MARION-Story of My Life-NY-1888-471p-cl (5ff7)   12.50
SIMS, JOS P-Old Phila Colonial Details-NY-(1914)-Architectural
Book Publ-folio-cl&bds-55 plts   (5t0, cov soil) 25.00
--The Phila Assemblies-Phila-c1947-51p-illus-ltd to 2400c(5w9) 6.00
SIMS, ORLAND L-Gun Toters I Have Known-Austin-1967-
ltd to 750c, autg   (4c7) 30.   (4j6)   17.50
SIMS, RICHARD-A Manual for the Genealogist-1888-542p (5m2) 10.00
SIMS, WM-Kansas, Siene Hulfskvuellen etc-Topeka-1883-60p-
illus-fldg map-wrps-rare   (5t3)   65.00
--Kansas, Velstandstandskilder Produktionsevne, Beliggenhed etc-
Topeka-1883-59(60)p-illus-fldg map-wrps-rare (5t3)   65.00
--Kansas Information Concerning Its Agriculture, Horticulure &
Live Stock-Topeka-1884-59(60)p-illus-fldg map-wrps-rare
                                              (5t3)   60.00
--Kansas, Auskunst uber seinen ackerbau etc-Topeka-1884-59(60)p-
illus-fldg map-wrps-rare   (5t3, chip)   60.00
--Special Report of Kans State Board of Agriculture for Info-Topeka-
1886-31p-fldg map-wrps   (5t3)   50.00
SIMS, WM SOWDEN-Victory at Sea by Rear Adm Sims-GardenCty-
1920-Dblday, Page-410p-frontis   (5mm8)   6.50
SIMSAR, MUHAMMED AHMED-Oriental Manuscripts...of John
Fredk Lewis Collection in Libr of Phila-Phila-1937-lg8vo-
248p-illus   (5w9)   10.00
SIMSON, JAS-Contributions to Natural History & Papers on Other
Subjects-NY-1878-8vo   (5ss5)   10.00
SIMSON, ROBT-Elements of the Conic Sections-NY-1804-
W Falconer-8vo-calf-14 fldg plts   (5j5)   32.50
SINCLAIR, CATHERINE-Holiday House-Ward, Lock-(c1903)-8vo-
dec cl-320p-frontis   (5s0)   5.00
SINCLAIR, GORDON-Foot Loose in India-NY-1933-cl-8vo-
312p-plts   (5v7)   6.50
--Loose Among Devils-Tor-1935-Dblday-photos-276p (4t5)   5.00
SINCLAIR, HAROLD-Port of New Orleans-GardenCty-1942-
plts-frontis   (4j4) 8. (5dd9) 12.00
SINCLAIR, ISABELLA-Indigenous Flowers of the Hawaiian Islands-
Lond-1885-folio-orig g. cl-g.e.-44 col plts (5z9, rbkd) 300.00
SINCLAIR, JOHN L-In Time of Harvest-1943-Macmillan
                                          (5F1, mint, dj) 6.00
SINCLAIR, MARY D-Pioneer Days-Steubenvl-1962-172p-cl-
priv publ   (5h7)   8.50
SINCLAIR, MAY-Uncanny Stories-NY-1923-illus-1st ed (5ee3) 12.50
SINCLAIR, UPTON-The Brass Check-Pasadena-n.d.-publ by author-
1st ed   (4b5)   7.50
--same-Pasadena-1931-rev ed   (5p7)   3.50
--Capt of Industry-Girard-1906-142p-cl-1st ed-White lettring
                           (5h1) 7.50   (5b2, f)   15.00
--The Cry for Justice-Phila-c1915-891p-1st ed (5w5)   12.50
--The Epic Plan for Calif-n.p.-n.d. (1934)   (5w5, dj)   8.50
--Flivver King-Pasadena-1937-119p-orig wrps-1st ed-publ by author-
                    (5tt2, fade) 5. (5mm7, 5r9, 5ss5, pres) 10.00
--same-Detroit-(1937)-119p-wrps-United Auto Workers of Amer,
publ   (5h2)   5.00
--The Goose Step-Pasadena-(1923)-thk12mo-cl-488p-The Author
                                              (5j5)   10.00

SINCLAIR,UPTON (continued)
--The Goslings-Pasadena-(1924)-publ by author-1st ed
(4b5,mint) 7.50
--The Jungle-NY-(1906)-413p-cl-v.scarce 1st issue with Jungle
Publ Co imprnt-"Sustainer's Edition" slip pasted to fr e.p.
(4m8,lacks slip, flake) 7.50 (5h2) 20.00
--same-Dblday,Page&Co imprnt-NY-1906
(5p5,5ss9) 10. (5x0) 25. (5h2,5p6) 12.50
--Jungle-Girard,Kans-(1924)-Haldeman Julius Co-6 vols-16mo-
blue wrps-scarce (5i4,f) 20.00
--King Coal-NY-1917-Macmillan-1st ed (5hh1) 7.50
--King Midas-NY-1901-frontis-1st ed (5i3,sl rub) 7.50
--Love's Pilgrimage-NY-(1911)-663p-cl-1st ed (5h7) 7.50
--Prince Hagen A Phantasy-Bost-1903-L C Page-orig pict cl-1st ed-
scarce (4g2) 35.00
--A World to Win-NY-1946-Viking-1st ed (4g8,dj) 6.50
SINCLAIR,W-Dictionary of Naval Equivalents Covering Engl,French,
Italian,Span,Russian, Swedish, Danish,Dutch & German-incl
an index vol-Lond-1922,24-2 vols (5c1) 25.00
SINDING,PAUL C-Scandinavian Races-NY-(1880)-frontis-500p-
3rd ed (5t4) 6.50
SINGER,C-White Africans & Blacks-NY-1929-4to-col illus(5x2)17.50
SINGER,C-History of Technology-Vol 3,from Renaissance to
Industrial Revolution, 1500 to 1750-1957 (5L7) 20.00
SINGER,C G-SoCarolina in the Confederation-1941-sewn (5L7) 5.00
SINGER,CAROLINE-White Africans & Black-Cape Coast-1949-
Methodist Book Depot-2nd impres (4t5,dj) 10.00
SINGER,DANL-Big Game Fields of Amer,No & So-NY-(1914)-
368p (5ss8) 7.50
SINGER,H W-Etching,Engraving & Other Methods of printing
pictures-Lond-1897-plts-illus-ltd to 50c-scarce (5tt5) 42.50
SINGER,H W-Stories of the German artists-Lond-1911-314p-
9 col plts-4to-cl (5m5) 14.00
SINGER SEWING MACHINES-Catalogue of,for Family Use-
(NY,1893)-12mo-orig wrps-illus-32p (5ss5) 7.50
SINGER SOUVENIRS OF PORTLAND-11 views of Portl,7x4½"
in pict mailing envelope-n.p.-n.d.(ca 1905)-Lewis&Clark Fair
(5r0) 7.50
SINGLETON,ESTHER-The Collecting of Antiques-NY-1926-
4to-illus-338p (5w7) 7.50
--same-1941-4to-illus (5yy6) 6.00
--The Furniture of Our Forefathers-NY-1908-664p-photos (5w7) 7.50
--Historic Buildings in America-NY-1906-illus-1st ed (5qq7) 10.00
--Historic Landmarks of America-NY-1907-305p-illus (5xx7) 7.50
--The Shakespeare Garden-NY-1922-360p-pict cov (5s7) 8.50
--Social New York Under Georges-NY-1902-396p-illus
(5ff2) 8. (5h9) 12. (5w9) 12.50
SINGLETON,G A-The Romance of African Methodism-NY-
1952 (5x2) 3.00
SINGMASTER ELSIE-Ellen Levis,a novel-Bost-1921-Houghton-
1st ed (5m2,sl soil) 5.00
SINGSTAD,OLE-Queens Midtown Tunnel under the East River
betw Mid Manhattan & Queens-(NY)-1944-84p-illus
(5t7,pres) 7.50
SINIGAGLIA,LEONE-Climbing Remin of the Dolomites-Lond-
1896-T Fisher Unwin-224p-illus (5d7) 8.50
SINJOHN,JOHN-From the Four Winds-Lond-T Fisher Unwin-
1897-8vo-orig cl-t.e.g.-500c prntd-author's 1st book-1st ed
(5ee9) 200.00
SINNETT,CHAS N -Historic Lebanon-Haverhill-1903-
CC Morse&Son-12mo-wrps-16p (4t1) 5.00
SINNETT,MRS PERCY,ed-Lady's Voyage Around the World-
Harper-1852 (5e8,bkstrp torn) 4.00
--Manners & Customs of Various Nations-Lond-(ca 1840s)-
Chapman&Hall-sq8vo-2 vols in 1-orig dec cl-8 plts (5c8) 22.50
SIOUX CITY & PAC RR-Elkhorn Valley Route,Free Homes in
Northern Nebr on Line of-Chig-n.d-(ca 1882,3)-fldr-map on
back-rare (5L2) 35.00
SIOUX CITY,IOWA-NY-1890Albertype Co-12mo-illus-16 lvs-bds
(4a5,vf) 12.50
SIOUX CITY,IOWA-Three Quarters of a Century of Progress-
SiouxCty-1923-104p-col plts-stiff wrps-map (5m8) 7.50
SIOUX FALLS ILLUSTRATED-Omaha-1888-62p-wrps-1st ed-scarce
(5L2,chip) 50.00
SIOUX FALLS,SOUTH DAK-cover tiel Sioux Falls,Metropolis of
South Dakota,Leading City of New State-SiouxFalls-1889-
32p-illus-map-wrps-Commercial Club (5L2,sl tn) 65.00
SIPE,C HALE-Fort Ligonier & Its Times-Harrisburg-1932-illus-699p
(4m4,pres) 25.00
--The Indian Chiefs of Penna-Butler-1927-569p-frontis-scarce
(5h9,5L7) 20.00
--The Indian Wars of Penna-Butler-1929-761p plus index-
photos-pkt map-1st ed (5L2,pres) 30.00

SIPES,WM B-The Penna RR,its Origin etc-Phila-1875-illus-
4to-scarce-281p (4p7,rebkd,ex-libr) 35.00
SIRDAR IKBAL ALI SHAH-Westward to Mecca-Lond-1928-cl-
8vo-224p-plts (5v7) 12.50
SIREN,OSVALD-China & Gardens of Europe in 18th Century-
NY-(1950)-cl-4to-192 illus (5z9) 45.00
--Essentials in Art-Lond-1920-J Lane-157p-illus (5x0) 6.00
--Gardens of China-NY-(1949)-cl-4to-200 illus (5z9) 45.00
SIRINGO,CHAS A-Cowboy Detective-Chig-1912-1st ed-illus-
519p-v scarce-cl (5tt6) 65. (4a5,vg) 75.00
--Lone Star Cowboy-SantaFe-1919-illus-291p-scarce-1st ed
(5L2) 27.50 (4p8) 22.50 (5bb4,pres,spot) 27.50
--Riata & Spurs-Bost-1927-suppressed 1st issue-276p-scarce
(4c7,dj) 65. (5bb4,dj,f) 40. (5ee3,5yy8) 35. (5a0) 37.50
--same-Bost-1927-261p (4a5,stns) 25.00
--same-Bost-1931-261p-photos (5ww4) 20. (5s4) 15.00
--A Texas Cowboy or, 15 Yrs on the Hurricane Deck of a Spanish
Pony-Chig-1885-12mo-cl-illus-chrom lith frontis-1st ed of
auth's 1st book- v rare (5gg6,rprd) 750.00
--same-Chig-1893-(Eagle Publ Co)-347p plus ads-illus-
3rd Eagle Co ed-scarce (5L2) 12.50
--same-NY-1950-illus (5m2,5L2,dj) 10.00
SISTERS OF ST ANN-Chaplet of Years, 1858 to 1918-Victoria-(1918)-
dec wrps-110p-plts-port (5dd0) 15.00
SITES,I A-Reformed Robbers-Alliance-(1899)-139p-wrps-Not in
Wright (5h2) 15.00
SITGREAVES,CAPT LORENZO-Report of Expedition down Zuni &
Colorado Rivers-Wash-1853-198p-lithos-plts-map
(4n4,wrps,lacks map) 22.50 (5tt0,wn) 30. (5g6,f) 40.00
--Report of Exped down Zuni & Colorado Rivers-Wash-1854-
plts-maps (5L0,lacks map,rbnd) 15. (5yy6) 37.50
SITWELL,BUCHANAN-Fine Bird Books 1700 to 1900-Lond-1953-
lg folio-hf lev-16 col plts-1st ed-ltd to 295c,autg,box
(5z9,f) 200.00
--same-hf buck-1st trade ed (5z9,rprd dj) 75.00
SITWELL,EDITH-Alexander Pope-Lond-1930-illus-8vo-cl-g.t.-
1st trade ed (4c2,sp darkened) 10.00
--Five Poems-Lond-1928-Duckworth-sm4to-cl-1st ed-
ltd to 250c,autg (5ee9,dj,unopnd) 85.00
--Gold Coast Customs-Lond-(1929)-Duckworth-12mo-black cl-
frontis-1st ed (5c6,wn) 6. (5d9,pres) 50.00
--The Mother & Other Poems-Oxf-1915-Cr 8vo-wrps-1st ed of
author's 1st book (5ss7,vf) 125.00
--The Song of the Cold-NY-(1948)-Vanguard Pr-1st ed (5ss9,dj) 6.00
SITWELL,SIR GEO-On the Making of Gardens-NY-(1951)-76p-
16 plts (5w3) 4.50 (5s7) 4.00
SITWELL,GEO P-Tales of My Native Village-Lond-1933-illus-
8vo-cl (4c2,pres,crack) 20.00
SITWELL,OSBERT-Argonaut & Juggernaut-Lond-1919-12mo-cl
(4c2,vg) 22.50
--Escape With Me-Lond-1939 (4g8) 25.00
--Out of the Flame-Lond-1923-8vo-cl (4c2,faded) 12.50
--The Winstonburgh Line-Lond-(1919)-8vo-19p-pict wrps (5r9) 20.00
SITWELL,SACHEVERELL-British Architects & Craftsmen (1600 to 1830)-
Lond-(1945)-1st ed-illus (5tt5) 7.50
--same-NY-1946-illus-196p (5q0,torn dj) 8.50
--German Baroque Art-Lond-1927-Duckworth-109p-4to-cl
(5m5,bkstrp tn) 55.00
--The Gothick North-Bost-1929-8 plts-454p- (5q0) 10.00
--same-Lond-1929,1930-8vo-cl-illus-3 vols-1st ed (5ee9,dj) 20.00
--Great Flower Books, 1700 to 1900-Lond-1956-folio-hf cl-
36 plts(20 col)- (5w3,5z9,rprd dj) 60.00
--The 101 Harlequins-Lond-1922-Grant Richards Ltd-cl-1st ed
(5ss3,fade) 10.00
--The Hunters & the Hunted-NY-1948-1st Amer ed
(4g8) 10. (5b9vf) 8.50
--Old Fashioned Flowers-NY-1939-pt lea-11 prints (5qq7,scuff) 18.50
--Two Poems, 10 Songs-Lond-1929-4to-dec bds-ltd to 275c,autg-
1st ed (5ee9) 50.00
$600 A YEAR-Bost-1867-183p-cl (5w7) 9.50 (5m1) 15. (5h1) 12.50
SIX MONTHS IN KANSAS-Bost-1856-orig cl-231p-1st ed-
by a Lady (4n4) 15. (5g3,5L2,wn) 10.00
SIX TALKS-by the Jolly Fat Chauffeur with the Double Chin-
Detroit-1911-16mo-illus-40p-orig wrps (5m6) 12.50
16TH ANNUAL ARCHITECTURAL EXHIBITION-Phila-1910-The
T Square Club & AIA-(Phila,1910)-Penna Academy of Fine Arts-
Catalog-illus-4to-cl-292p (5t7) 12.00
16TH ANNUAL REPORT-of Amer Soc for Colonizing the Free
People of Color-Wash-1833-40p-wrps (5x2) 27.50
SIZER,THEODORE,ed-Autobiography of Col John Trumbull-NewHav-
1953-Yale U Pr-404p-8vo (4a0) 37.50
SKAGGS,W H-The Southern Oligarchy-NY-1924-thk8vo-1st ed
(5x2) 17.50

SKAL,GEO VON-History of German Immigration in US &
Successful German Americans & Their Descendants-(NY)-
1908-4to-ports-lea-277p-1st ed   (5m6,rub)   22.50

SKAVLEM,M L-Gen Record & Pioneer Hist of Skavlem &
Odegaarden Families from Norway-1915   (4t2)   20.00

SKEAT,WALTER,ed-Fables & Folk Tales from an Eastern Forest-
1901-Cambr U Pr-lg sq8vo-dec cl-g.t.-plts-92p-1st ed-
scarce   (5nn2)   12.50

SKEEL,E E F,comp-Bibliography of Writings of Noah Webster-NY-
1958-illus-655p-ltd to 500c,nbrd   (4g2)   35.00

SKELDING,SUSIE BARSTOW-Flowers from Dell & Bower-NY-
1890-128p-12p col plts   (5s7,soil)   6.50

SKELLEY,LELOISE D-Modern Fine Glass-GardenCty-(1942-4to-
144p-photos   (5s7)   7.50

SKELTON,C O-Gordons Under Arms-(Vol 3 of Gordon Hist)-
Aberdeen-1912-595p   (5mm3)   25.00

SKELTON,ISABEL-The Backwoodswoman-Tor-1924-illus-261p
                                          (5s0)   7.50

--Life of Thomas D'Arcy McGee-Gardenvale-1925-mor-g.-
plts-554p-Deluxe ed   (4d2)   27.50

SKELTON,OSCAR D-Canadian Dominion-NewHav-1919-296p-
plts-maps   (5a1)   5.00

--Railway Builders-Tor-1916-254p-lea-Chronicles of Canada Ser-
                                          (5h7,sp wl wn) 7.50

SKELTON,R A-Decorative Printed Maps of the 15th to 18th
Centuries-Lond-(1952)-Staples Pr-4to-cl-g. (5b0,dj)   45.00

SKETCHES BY A TRAVELLER-Bost-1830-Carter&Hendee-12mo-
buck-1st ed   (5x1,rbnd,libr stmp) 35.00

SKETCHES FROM CAMBRIDGE-By a Don-Lond-1865-12mo-cl-
1st ed-(L Stephen)   (5gg6)   25.00

SKETCHES OF BUNKER HILL-Battle & Monument -Charlestown-
1843-16mo-172p-1st ed   (5w4,stnd)   15.00

SKETCHES OF HISTORY, LIFE & MANNERS IN US-By a Traveller,
(Anne Royall)-NewHav-1826-bds-12mo-scarce-1st ed of
auth's 1st book (5gg6,broke) 100.   (4c4,crack,stn,box) 190.00

SKETCHES OF THE INTER MOUNTAIN STATES...1847 to 1909-
SaltLkCty-1909-(Tribune)-369p plus index-photos-limp lea
              (5dd9,wn) 17.50   (5L2,vg)   45.00

SKETCHES OF MISSION LIFE AMONG INDIANS OF ORE-NY-
1854-illus-5 plts-orig cl-scarce   (5m9)   50.00

SKETCHES OF A NEW ENGLAND VILLAGE-in the last century-
Bost-1838-JasMunroe-12mo-orig cl-1st ed   (5x1)   35.00

SKIDMORE,HUBERT-Heaven Came So Near-1938-Dblday
                                          (5F1,f,dj)   5.00

SKILLMAN'S-New York Police Reports-NY-1830-illus-orig bds-
scarce   (5g4,wn)   15.00

SKILTON,I D-Dr Henry Skilton & Desc-1921-412p (4t2)   18.50

SKINKER,T K-Saml Skinker & His Desc-1923-298p (4t2)   17.50

SKINNER,ADA M-Child's Book of Modern Stories-NY-1920-
Duffield-8vo-341p-1st ed   (5p1)   10.00

SKINNER,ALANSON-Mascoutens or Prairie Potawatomie Indians-
Mus of City of Milw-Nov,1924,June,1926 & Jan,1927-3 parts-
cl   (5L0,rbnd)   17.50

--Material Culture of the Menomini-NY-1921-393p plus index-
illus-Heye Foundation   (5L0,f)   12.50

--Medicine Ceremony of Menomini,Iowa & Wahpeton Dakota-NY-
1920-illus-cl   (5L0,mint) 15.   (4k5)   12.50

--The Menomini Indians-NY-1915-Amer Mus of Nat Hist-
Parts 1 to 3-546p-photos-cl-v scarce   (5L0,rbnd)   25.00

--Notes on Iroquois Archeology-NY-1921-Mus of Amer Indian-
16mo-cl-illus-216p   (5L0,f) 8.50   (5j5)   10.00

SKINNER, CARL H-Good Indians-NY-1958-8vo-cl-150p-1st ed
                                          (5g6,f,dj)   3.00

SKINNER,CHAS M-Amer Myths & Legends-Phila-1903-2 vols-
illus-12mo-cl-1st ed   (5t0)   10.00

--Flowers in the Pave-Phila-1900-12mo-216p-illus (5w0,crack) 4.50

--Myths & Legends Beyond Our Borders-Phila-1899-319p-photos-
g.t.   (5s4,rprd)   7.50

--Myths & Legends of Flowers, Trees, Fruits & Plants-Phila-1911-
302p-illus   (5w3)   10.00

--Myths & Legends of Our New Possessions & Portectorate-Phila-
1900-354p-illus   (4t8,lacks fly) 3.50

--Myths & Legends of Our Land-Phila-1896-illus-2 vols
              (5j5) 15. (4m2,5ss5,vf) 10. (5mm6)   12.50

SKINNER,CONSTANCE-Adventurers in the Wilderness-NewHav-
(1925)-350p plus index-photos-maps-frontis-Vol 1, "Pageant
of Amer Series"   (5L0)   5.00

--Beaver, Kings & Cabins-NY-1933-illus-273p-1st ed
              (4e9) 15. (4t8)   8.50

--The Search Relentless-Lond-(1925)-252p- (5s 5,pres)   5.00

SKINNER,ELEANOR L-Children's Plays-NY&Lond-1921-Appleton
illus-270p-frontis-pict cl-3rd ed   (5p1)   5.00

SKINNER,GEO,ed-Pennsylvania at Chikamauga & Chattanooga-
Harrisburg-1897-illus-499p   (4j4)   7.50

SKINNER,JOHN-Amusements of leisure hours-Edinb-1809-
John Moir-8vo-orig bds-1st ed   (5i8,rbkd)   25.00

SKINNER,JOHN R-History of 4th Illinois Vol in Relation to
Spanish American War-Longansport-(1899)-illus-461p (4b3,f) 15.00

SKINNER,JOS-Present State of Peru-Lond-1805-hf calf-4to-
20 col engr-487p,(1)   (4e1,rprd,t.soil) 175.00

SKINNER,M P-Bears in the Yellowstone-Chig-1925-12mo-cl-
158p-illus   (5p5) 8.50 (5h5)   4.00

--Yellowstone Nature Book-Chig-1926-221p-photos-fldg map
                                          (5s4,soil)   6.00

SKINNER,OTIS-Footlights & Spotlights-Indnpls-1924-
Bobbs,Merrill   (4c8,autg) 10. (5p0)   5.00

--same-Indnpls-(1924)-8vo-illus-ltd ed to 500c,autg (5m6,als) 10.00

SKINNER, ROBT P-Abyssinia Today-NY-1906-226p-32 plts (5c6)12.50

SKITT-Fisher's River Scenes & Characters-NY-1859-12mo-illus-
orig cl-269p-1st ed   (5t2,fray)   10.00

SKOGMAN,C-Fregatten Eugenie Resa omkring Jorden aren
1851 to 1853-Stockholm-(185-)-2 vols in 1-8vo-orig cl-
20 plts in col-3 fldg maps   (5ss2,map tn,hng crack) 52.50

SKOMOROVSKY,BORIS-The Siege of Leningrad-NY-1944-
196p-photos   (5ss6,dj)   5.00

SKOTTSBERG,CARL-The Wilds of Patagonia-Lond-1911-EdwArnold-
336p-map-illus-cl   (5d7)   10.00

SLACK,J H-Practical Trout Culture-NY-1872-lg12mo-cl-143p-
illus-1st ed   (5t2)   4.00

SLADE,DANL DENISON-The Evolution of Horticulture in
New England-NY-1895-180p-12mo   (5w3)   5.00

SLADE,WM F-Federation of Central Amer-1917-new buck
                                          (5L7,rbnd)   5.00

SLADEN,DOUGLAS-How to See the Vatican-Lond&NY-1914-
440p-8vo-cl-plts   (5m5,ex-libr) 14.00

SLANG DICTIONARY-Etymological, Historical & Anecdotal-
Lond-1874-382p, 48p-rev&corr   (5t7,wn)   10.00

SLARE,FRED-Experiments & Observations upon Oriental & Other
Bezoar Stones etc-Lond-1715-hf cal-8vo-1st ed (5jj8)   95.00

SLATER,ELSIE M-El Paso Birds-ElPaso-1945-Hertzog-illus
                                          (4a5, Hertzog autg) 15.00

SLATER,J H-Book Collecting,a Guide for Amateurs-Lond-1892-
130p   (5n4)   6.00

--The Library Manual-Lond-1892-3rd ed   (5yy6)   6.00

SLATIN,R-Fire & Sword in the Sudan-Lond-1935-19&416p-
16 plts   (5c6, vg, Gen Wingate autg)   20.00

SLATKIN,CHAS E-Treasury of Amer Drawings-NY-1947-
Oxf Univ Pr-163 plts-35p-4to   (4e0) 17. (5ii3)   15.00

SLATTERY,CHAS LEWIS-Felix Reville Brunot, 1820 to 1898-NY-1901-
illus-map-340p-1st ed   (5w4) 7.50 (5L2)   8.50

SLAUGHTER,P-Hist of Bristol Paris,Virg,with Gen of Families
connected therewith-1879-237p-2nd ed   (4t2)   17.50

SLAUSON,ALLAN-Check List of Amer Newspapers in Library
of Congress-Wash-1901-292p-cl   (5yy1)   12.50

SLAUSON,H W-Everyman's Guide to Motor Efficiency-NY-
1926-450p-illus   (5y2)   10.00

SLAVE,THE-or memoirs of Archy Moore-Bost-1836-John H Eastborn-
2 vols-12mo-orig cl&bds-papr labls-1st ed (5x1,sl dmpstnd) 125.00

--same-Bost-1840-Mass Anti Slavery Soc-2 vols in 1(as issued)-
12mo-orig cl&bds-papr labl-3rd ed   (5x1)   50.00

SLAVERY IN THE US-Its Evils, Alleviations & Remedies-Bost-
1857-36p-wrps   (5x2)   37.50

SLEE,RICHARD-Dr Berkley's Discovery-NY&Lond-1899-219p
                                          (5m1)   12.50

SLEEPER,JOHN-Waco & McLennan County, Texas-Waco-1876-
171p-rare   (5n4,rbnd)   60.00

SLEEPER,JOHN-History of the Sleeper Family of Waco &
McLennan Co,Texas-Waco-1930-55p-orig wrps-illus (5w5)   7.50

SLEEPING BEAUTY IN THE WOODS-c1870-illus in col-
Fairy Moonbeam Series   (5v0,f)   15.00

SLEFFEL,CHAS C-Working in Metals-NY-1916-419p (5n7,wn) 2.50

SLEIGHT,HARRY D-The Whale Fishery on Long Island-
Bridgehampton-1831-232p   (5t7,spots)   12.00

SLESSER,H-Trade Union Law-Lond-1927-3rd ed (5ff4)   5.50

SLEVIN,J R-The Amphibians of Western NoAmer-SanFran-1928-
Occ Pap Calif Acad Sci 16-cl-152p-23 plts-4to-v scarce
                                          (4p6)   30.00

SLICER,THOS R-From Poet to Premier-1909-Grolier Soc-
6 etchings-ltd to 1250c,autg (5ee3) 12.50 (5ss9,fade) 15.00

SLICK,SAML-The Clockmaker-Concord-1838-262p-2nd ed (4j6) 15.00

--same-NY-1840-1st Series   (5mm2)   25.00

--same-(&) The Bubbles of Canada-Paris-1839-A&W Galignani-
R8vo-hf calf   (5mm2)   17.50

SLICK,SAM,JR-Adventures of an Office Seeker-Richmond-
1904   (5r7)   7.50
SLIJPER,E J-Whales-NY-1962-cl-   -plt-v scarce (4p5,dj) 27.50
SLIM JACK-or,history of a circus boy-Phila,NY&Bost-(c1847)-
Amer Sunday School Union-frontis-32mo-107p-illus (5p1) 15.00
SLOAN,EDW L-Gazeteer of Utah & Salt Lake City Directory,1874-
SaltLkCty-1874-326p-fldg map-1st ed-v scarce (5dd1) 100.00
SLOAN,MAURICE M-The Concrete House &its Construction-
Phila-1912-Assn of Amer Portland Cement Mfrs-224p-illus
                              (5hh7)   5.75
SLOAN,RICHARD E,ed-History of Arizona-Phoenix-1930-Record Publ-
4 vols-illus-lea   (5gg5,f) 150.   (4t1)   100.00
--Memories of an Arizona Judge-Stanford-1932
          (4b3,stn) 17.50   (5r1,fade)   20.00
SLOAN,ROBT W-Gazetteer & Directory of Logan,Ogden,Provo
& Salt Lake Cities for 1884-SaltLkCty-1884-advs-634p-
lg fldng map in col   (5t1)   150.00
SLOAN,SAML-City & Suburban Architecture-Phila-1867-folio-
cl-131 illus-101p   (5t4,bkstrp loose)   35.00
SLOAN'S ALMANAC-& Traveler's Guide for 1851-Chig-(1850)-
WBSloan-32p-stitchd   (5L1,box)   50.00
SLOANE,ERIC-Eric Sloane's Americana-NY-1954-W Funk-
3 vols   (5p0)   10.00
SLOANE,JULIA M-Smiling Hill Top & Other Calif Sketches-NY-
1927   (4a5)   5.00
SLOANE-STANLEY,CAPT CECIL-Reminis of a Midshipman's Life
from 1850 to 1856-Lond-1893   (5c1)   15.00
SLOANE,T O'CONOR-Liquid Air & Liquefaction of Gases-NY-
1899-12mo-cl-illus-356p   (5t0)   3.50
--Standard Electrical Dictionary-NY-1901-682p-illus-rev&enlrgd
                            (5hh7)   7.50
SLOANE,WM MILLIGAN-Greater France in Africa-NY-1924-
16&293p-20 plts-2 fldg maps (5c6,bndg stn)   6.75
--The Life of Napoleon Bonaparte-NY-1916-4 vols-rev&enlrgd-
ports   (5yy6)   12.50
--same-NY-1939-2 vols-illus (4a1)   12.50
SLOCOMBE,GEO-Rebels of Art-NY-1939-plts-304p-8vo-1st ed
                            (5ww3)   15.00
SLOCUM,CHAS ELIHU-Life & Services of Maj Gen Henry Warner
Slocum-Toledo-1913-Slocum Publ-391p-illus
    (5mm8) 9.   (5w4) 8.75   (5L5,5s9)   7.50
SLOCUM,HEI RY WARNER-In Memoriam-Albany-1904-publ by
State of NY-lg4to-illus&maps (5t2,v wn) 6. (5s9,soil) 7.50
SLOCUM,JOSHUA-Sailing Alone Around the World-NY-1900-
illus-294p-1st ed   (5ss5) 15. (5tt5) 22.50 (5aa2,4b7) 20.00
--same-Lond-1900-plts-port-scarce 1st Engl ed (4d4) 35.00
--same-NY-1905-294p   (5s1,pres,stnd)   7.50
--Voyage of The Liberdade-Bost-1894-lg sq12mo-cl-161p-illus
                            (5t2)   8.00
SLOCUM,VICTOR-Capt Joshua Slocum-Lond-1952-illus-maps
                            (5c1)   7.50
SLOSS,ROBT-The Automobile-NY-1910-194p (5xx7)   8.50
SLOSSON,ANNIE T-Seven Dreamers-NY-1891-281p-cl-1st ed
                    (5h1,sl soil,5m2)   5.00
SLOSSON,ELVENIA,comp-Pioneer Amer Gardening-NY-1951-
306p-illus   (5w3)   4.00
SLY,JOHN F-Town Gov in Mass-Harv Univ Pr-1930-244p (5qq8) 7.50
SLY,WINFIELD SCOTT-Chronicles of a Farm House-Lansing-
1923-lg8vo-274p-cl   (5mm7,autg) 10. (5mm7)   8.50
SMALL(et al)-Studies on Drug Addiction-Public Health Reports
Supp#138-1938-143p   (5ii2)   6.50
SMALL,A R-Robertson,Small & Related Families-1907-258p (4t2) 17.50
SMALL,AUSTIN J-The Frozen Trail-Bost-1924-305p (5ss1) 3.00
SMALL,H B-The Canadian Handbook & Tourist's Guide-Montr-
1866-J Taylor,ed-photos-8vo-1st issue (5ss5,rub) 15.00
--same-Montreal-1867-8vo-photos   (5ss5)   12.50
SMALL,H BEAUMONT-Products & Manufactures of New Dominion-
Ottawa-1868-Desbarats-fldg map-156p-5 lf nds (5aa1) 15.00
SMALL,JOHN KUNKEL-Ferns of the vicinity of NY-Lancaster-
1935-Science Pr-285p-illus (5x0)   10.00
--Ferns of the Southeastern States-Lancaster-1938-517p (5x0) 10.00
SMALL,JOHN W-Scottish Woodwork of 16th & 17th Centuries-
Stirling&Lond-1878-100 plts-lg sq folio-dec cl (4a2,blister) 15.00
SMALL,KATHLEEN E-History of Tulare Co,Calif,Illus-Chig-
1926-S JClark-4to-cl-2 vols (4t1) 50. (5h4)   27.50
SMALL,MARIE-Four Fares to Juneau-NY-1947-237p-illus (5dd0) 4.50
SMALL,TUNSTALL-Architectural Turned Woodwork of 16th,17th,
& 18th Centuries-NY&Lond-n.d.-portfolio-20p plts-4to-
orig bds-loose as issued,ribbon ties (5m6,f) 12.50
SMALLEY,EUGENE V-History of Northern Pac RR-NY-1883-illus-
437p-5 maps   (4b6)   25.00
SMALLEY,GEO W-London Letters & Some Others-NY-1891-2 vols-
8vo-cl-uncut-1st ed   (5t2)   8.50

SMALLWOOD,JOS R,ed-Book of Newfoundland-St John's-1937
2 vols-ports-maps-plts   (5s6) 65.   (4t2)   50.00
SMALLWOOD,M B-Birch,Burch Family in Great Brit & Amer wi
Allied Fam-1957-2 vols-423p,491p   (4t2)   35.00
SMALLZRIED,KATHLEEN ANN-The Everlasting Pleasure-NY-
(1956)-344p-illus   (5c9)   8.50
SMAMMERDAM,JAN-The Book of Nature-Lond-1758-for Seyffert-
lg folio-orig bds-vel bk-53 plts-1st ed wi Engl text (5ee1,f) 425.00
SMART,ADAM-Words at Play-SanFran-1939-4to-illus-Grabhorn
                            (5x5)   10.00
SMART & CORNERED-How to Get a Mine without Finding,Opening
or Working One-By a Quartz Miner-SanFran-1860-8vo-hf mor-
orig wrps bnd in   (5a3)   100.00
SMART,BILL-Mexico to Montreal on a Cow Pony-FtWorth-1928-
208p   (5n4)   6.00
SMART,BORLASE-The Technique of Seascape Painting-NY-(1946)-
4to-cl-129p-illus   (5t7)   10.00
SMART,DR CHAS-Driven from Path-NY-1873-467p-cl
                   (5h7,rub,lacks fly)   8.50
SMART SET,THE-A Magazine of Cleverness,Vols 1&2,March,1900,
Dec 1900-2 vols-bound   (5p7)   12.50
SMART,STEPHEN F-Colo Tourist & Illustrated Guide via Golden
Belt Rte-KansCty-1879-KansPac RR-illus-72p-tooled calf-
v scarce   (4t8,rub,lacks map)   30.00
SMEAD& COWLES'-Gen'l Business Directory of City of Cleveland
for 1848,49-Cleve-1848-Stephenson,ed-map-plan-12mo-
orig cl-sheep sp   (5s9,crack)   97.50
SMEAD,W H-Land of the Flatheads-StPaul-1905-144p-illus-wrps
          (5L2,cl) 40.   (5L2) 30.   (5t1)   65.00
SMEATON,JOHN-Reports of the Late-Lond-1812 to 1814-4 vols-
4to-plts-calf&bds-1st ed   (5ss5,wn,cov loose) 75.00
SMEDLEY,AGNES-Battle Hymn of China-NY-1943 (5x7)   3.00
--same-NY-1945-illus   (4a1,pres)   10.00
SMEDLEY,FRANK E-Harry Coverdale's Courtship-Lond-n.d.-
8vo-bds-illus-col frontis   (5t5)   7.50
SMEDLEY,R C-History of the Underground RR in Chester &
Neighboring Co of Pa-Lancaster-1883-illus-407p-scarce
                            (4m2,5x2)   45.00
SMELLIE,REV C-Memoir of Rev John Bayne of Galt-Tor-1871-
139p   (4b9,wn)   10.00
SMELLIE,WM-Philosophy of Natural History-Dover,NH-1808-
8vo-orig calf-552p- nd ed   (5L1)   10.00
SMET,PIERRE JEAN DE-Oregon Missions &Travels Over Rocky Mntns
in 1845,46-NY-1847-fldg map-Edw Dunigan-412p-15 tinted plts-
hf calf   (5tt8,stnd) 100.00
--same-NY-1847-orig cl-480p-map-13 tinted plts-1st ed (4n4) 150.00
--Missions De L'Oregon et Voyages...1845,46-Gand-(1848)-
Vander Schelden-389p-orig prntd yell wrps-15 plts-
3 fld maps   (5m3,wrp loose,unopnd)   100.00
SMILES,SAML,ed-A Boy's Voyage Round the World-Lond-1871-
JnMurray-sm thk8vo-calf-304p-illus (5L8)   35.00
--Life of Geo Stephenson,Rwy Engineer-Lond-1857-3rd ed-rev-
546p-frontis   (4e4,sl wn)   20.00
--A Publisher & His Friends-(Lond-1891)-2 vols-2nd ed (5xx0) 32.50
--Round the World by a Boy-NY-1872-286p-illus
                   (5s4,pres,ex-libr)   10.00
SMILLIE,JAS-Mount Auburn,Illus-NY-1847-R Martin-plts-a.e.g.-
4to-cl-119p   (4t1)   10.00
SMITH,MRS A-An Autobiography-Chig-1893 (5x2)   15.00
SMITH,A D HOWDEN-John Jacob Astor,Landlord of NY-NY-1929-
296p-frontis   (5aa0)   6.50
SMITH,A DONALDSON-Through Unknown African Countries-Lond-
1897-illus-6 maps   (5m2)   13.50
SMITH,A H-Classified Catalog of Books,Pamph & Maps in Libr of
Sec for Promotion of Helenic & Roman Studies-Lond-1924-bds
                            (5yy6)   15.00
SMITH,MRS A MURRAY-Westminster Abbey-Lond-1904-illus-
3/4 mor   (4b7)   15.00
SMITH,AARON-The Atrocities of the Pirates-Lond-1824-8vo-
214p-hf cl-1st ed   (5L1,ex-libr)   45.00
SMITH,ADAM-Inquiry into Nature & Causes of Wealth of Nations-
Dublin-1776-calf-3 vols-lea labls-8vo (4c8) 250.00
--same-Lond-1789-prntd for A Strahan &T Cadell-calf-3 vols-
5th ed   (5z7,rebkd)   60.00
--same-Lond-1796-3 vols-8th ed-calf
          (5aa0,sl wn,lacks lettrng piece)   25.00
--same-Hartf-1818-calf-2 vols-lea labls-from 11th Lond ed
                            (5ss5)   20.00
--same-Lond-1921-2 vols-8vo-Bohn Library (5p5)   10.00
SMITH,ADAM-Theory of Moral Sentiments-1817- 2 vols in 1-
buck-new ed   (5L7,rbnd)   15.00
SMITH,ALBERT-The wassail bowl-Lond-1843-Bentley-2 vols-12mo-
orig red cl-frontis-1st ed (5xx6)   17.50

SMITH, ALBERT   (continued)
--Wild oats & dead leaves-Lond-1860Chapman&Hall-8vo-
orig dec cl-1st ed   (5xx6)   22.50
SMITH, ALBERT-History of Peterboro-1876-375p-illus
(5e8, hngs weak)   19.75
SMITH, ALBERT-The Story of Mt Blanc-NY-1853-Putnam-208p-cl
(5d7)   7.50
SMITH, ALBERT W-John Edson Sweet-NY-1925-ASME-220p-
illus   (5y2)   7.50
SMITH, ALEX H-The Mushroom Hunter's Field Guide-AnnArbor-
(1958)-197p-155 photos-narr 4to   (5s7, mint)   6.50
SMITH, ALEX-Dreamthorp-Portland-1913-sq8vo-buck-Mosher-
hand made papr   (5t5, rbnd)   7.50
--Poems-Lond-1853-12mo-cl-1st ed of auth's 1st book-inserted adv
dated Nov, 1852   (5gg6, sl fade)   25.00
--A summer in Skye-Lond-1865-AlexStrahan-2 vols-8vo-orig cl-
1st ed   (5x3)   22.50
SMITH, CAPT ALEX-Complete History of Lives & Robberies of most
notorious Highwaymen, Footpads, Shoplifts & Cheats of Both
Sexes-Lond-1933-pop ed   (5x7, dj)   12.50
SMITH, ALFRED E-Campaign Addresses-Wash-c1929-322p-illus-
1st ed   (5j5, 5w5)   7.50
--Up To Now-NY-1929-illus-bds-vel bk-1st ed-ltd ed
(4j3, f, autg)   17.50
SMITH, ALICE R HUGER-Chas Fraser-NY-1924-F Sherman-priv prnt-
58p-frontis-crown 4to-ltd to 325c   (4a0)   45.00
SMITH, ALSON JESSE-Brother Van-NY-(1948)-235p plus index-
photos-2 Russell illus-1st ed-scarce   (5L2, f, dj)   12.50
SMITH & CHILDS, ed-Mason Smith Family Letters 1860 to 1868-
Columbia-1950-8vo-292p   (4a7, mint)   8.50
SMITH, ANITA M-Woodstock, History & Hearsay-1959-190p plus index
(4m2, dj fade)   12.50
SMITH, ARTHUR D H-John Jacob Astor, Landlord of NY-Phila-
1929-1st ed   (5r8) 6.   (5s4, soil)   10.00
--Mr House of Texas-NY-1940-1st ed   (4a5)   7.50
--Narrative of Saml Hancock 1845 to 1860-NY-1927-217p-
map-1st ed   (5L2, f, dj)   8.50
--Old Fuss & Feathers-NY-1937-illus-386p-1st ed
(5yy8) 7.50   (5bb4) 5.   (5w9, dj)   6.50
--Porto Bello Gold-NY-(1924)-330p-col illus-de luxe pub (5s1, f)12.50
SMITH, ASA-Smith's Illustrated Astronomy-NY-1849-illus-4to-
bds-67p-4th ed   (5t7, hng loose)   6.50
SMITH, ASHBEL-Remin of the Texas Republic-Galveston-1876-orig
prntd wrps-1st ed-ltd to 100c-v rare   (5z7, f, mor box)   250.00
--Yellow Fever in Galveston, 1839-Austin-1951-C D Leake, ed
(5a8) 5.   (5dd4)   6.00
SMITH, B WEBSTER-To the South Pole-Lond&Glasgow-n.d.-8vo-
maps-plts   (5ss5, ex-libr)   6.00
SMITH, BENJ-A Fugitive from Hell-(Joplin-1935)-frontis-122p-
1st ed-v scarce   (4t8)   20.00
SMITH, BENJ G-War With the South-NY-(1862)-illus-4to-3 vols
(5yy0)   12.50
SMITH, BERNARD-European Vision & the South Pacific 1768 to 1850-
Oxf-1960-4to-287p-plts-171 illus   (5w3)   17.00
SMITH, BERTHA H-Yosemite Legends-SanFran-(1904)-sm4to-64p-
dec cl-col plts   (5s4) 10.   (5dd6) 7.50 (5w5)   8.50
SMITH, BESSIE WHITE-Romances of the Presidents-Bost-(1932)-
Lothrop-400p-illus   (5w5)   5.00
SMITH, BRADFORD-Bradford of Plymouth-Phila-1951-Lippincott-
338p   (5qq8) 4.   (5h9, 5p7)   5.00
SMITH, BUCKINGHAM-Inquiry into Authenticity of Documents
Concerning Discovery in NoAmer Claimed to Have Been Made
by Verrazzano-NY-1864-31p-fldg map (5L0, sl spot) 25. (5L1)30.00
--Rudo Ensayo, Tentativa de Una Prevencional Descripcion
Geographica de La Provincia de Sonora-San Augustin de la
Florida-1863-208p-160c total prntd-1 of few on laid papr
(5n4)   185.00
SMITH, C-Does the Bible Sanction Amer Slavery-1863-128p(4b9) 25.00
SMITH, C ALPHONSO-O Henry Biography-GardenCty-1916-
258p   (5x0) 5.   (5n4)   8.00
SMITH, C C-Life & Work of Jacob Kenoly-Cinn-(1912)-160p-cl
(5h1)   5.00
SMITH, C D-Peck Family Record, Male & Female Lines-Vol 1,
#1 to 8(all pub)-Rome-1916 to 18-32p   (4t2)   15.00
SMITH, C E-Pioneer Times in the Onondaga Country-Syracuse-1904-
illus-415p   (4m2)   32.50
SMITH, C FOX-Sailor Town Days-Bost-1923-182p-6 plts (4a8)   4.50
SMITH, C HENRY-Coming of the Russian Mennonites-Berne-1927-
Mennonite Book Concern-296p-illus   (5qq8)   7.50
--Mennonite Immigration to Penna in 18th Century-Norristown-
1929-1st ed-illus   (5jj3)   15.00

SMITH, C HENRY   (continued)
--Mennonites of America-Goshen, Ind-1909-1st ed-priv print-
scarce   (5jj3)   32.50
--Story of the Mennonites-Berne, Ind-(1941)-illus-1st ed (5jj3)   10.00
SMITH, C S-A Monograph, Life of Danl Alexander-Nashvl-1894-
57p-bds-scarce   (5j6)   10.00
SMITH, C W CO-Curtain poles, grilles-(Norwalk-1895)-36p-illus-
wrps-trade catalog   (5h2)   7.50
SMITH, C W-Journal of Trip to Calif...Summer of 1850-Manchester-
1920-79p   (4k1)   12.50
SMITH, CALVIN-The Western Tourist & Emigrant's Guide-NY-1839-
J H Colton-16mo-col fldng map in rear-1st ed (5x5, fox)   200.00
SMITH, CHARD POWERS-The Housatonic, Puritan River-(1946)-
Rinehart-illus-Rivers of Amer Series
(5h9) 6.   (5j5) 8.50   (5ww4, 5p9)   5.00
SMITH, CHAS-The Amer War from 1775 to 1783 with Plans-NY-1797-
183p-rare   (5a0, bnd wiout plans & ports)   150.00
--The Monthly Military Repository-NY-Davis, 1796 & Buel, 1797-
2 vols in 1-8vo-hf mor-9 plts-3 ports-& added map (5L1, f)   400.00
SMITH, CHAS-University of Virginia in Woodcuts-Richmond-
1937-t8vo-32 wdcuts-1st ed   (4n6, vf, dj wn)   12.50
SMITH, CHAS A-Comprehensive History of Minnehaha Co, SoDakota-
Mitchell-1949-504p-illus-1st ed   (5dd9, 5L2, mint)   15.00
SMITH, CHAS M-From Andersonville to Freedom-Providence-1894-
5th Series, #3-74p-wrps-ltd to 250c   (5L5, chip)   20.00
SMITH, CHAS P-Lineage of Lloyd & Carpenter Family-Camden-
1870-S Chew-4to-wrps-88p   (4t1)   15.00
SMITH, CHAS W-Pacific Northwest Americana-NY-1921-339p
(5yy1) 20.   (4g2)   30.00
--Portland-1950-3rd ed-rev by Mayhew   (5dd0)   25.00
SMITH, CHAS W-Old Virginia in Block Prints-Richmond-1929-4to-
flex mor-ltd to 1000c, nbrd   (5w5)   16.50
SMITH, CHARLOTTE-Elegaic sonnets-Lond-1792-prntd by R Noble-
8vo-calf-6th ed-5 plts   (5x3, rprd)   20.00
--The young philosopher, a novel-Lond-1798-for T Cadell-4 vols-
12mo-hf calf-1st ed-v scarce   (5xx6)   250.00
SMITH, CLARK ASHTON-The Double Shadow & Other Fantasies-
(Auburn-1933)-orig wrps   (5F1, f, pres)   20.00
--Nero & Other Poems-Lakeport-1937-Futile Pr-1st ed-orig wrps-
12mo-1st ed (corr on pg 21 by hand)   (4b5, f)   60.00
--Odes & Sonnets-SanFran-1918-8vo-bds with lin bkstrp-
ltd to 300c, nbrd   (5h4, lt soil)   15.00
SMITH, D-Biography of Rev David Smith of A M E Church-Xenia-
1881-12mo   (5x2)   50.00
SMITH, D MURRAY-Arctic Exped from British & Foreign Shores-
Edinb-1877-Thos C Jack-col illus-maps-sm folio-calf-g.
(4e1, g.broken)   65.00
SMITH, DAMA MARGARET-Hopi Girl-Stanford-1931-273p-
1st ed-scarce   (5t1) 15.   (5L0, dj, f)   10.00
--I married a ranger-Stanford-1930-Stanford Univ Pr-179p (5u3)   5.00
SMITH, DR DANL-The Reformed Botanic & Indian Physician-Utica-
1855-419p-frontis   (5w3, bndg poor, lacks 1 pg of index)   20.00
SMITH, DANL M-Robt Lansing & Amer Neutrality-Berkeley-1958-
241p-frontis-orig prntd wrps   (5mm8)   7.50
SMITH, DAVID-The Dyer's Instructor-Phila-1853-330p, 24p
(5w3, sl soil)   14.50
SMITH, DAVID MURRAY-Tales of Chivalry & Romance-Lond-1869-
12mo-illus-1st ed   (4a1)   7.50
SMITH, DECOST-Martyrs of the Oblong & Little Nine-1948-
Caxton Prntrs-illus-1st ed-ltd to 1000c
(4d9, dj, unopened) 17.50 (5h5, f) 8.50 (5x5, dj)   10.00
--same-Caldwell-1948-illus-310p
(5L2, dj, mint) 5. (4b2, dj, f) 10. (4b2, dj)   7.50
--Red Indian Experiences-Lond-(1949)-photos-illus-387p-scarce
(4b2)   10.00
SMITH, DELAZON-A history of Oberlin-Cleve-1837-12mo-
Underhill&Son-orig green prntd wrps-1st ed-v rare
(5i0, f, box)   350.00
SMITH, DONAL V-Chase & Civil War Politics-Col-1931-181p-cl
(5h2, f)   5.00
SMITH, E-The Compleate Housewife, or Accomplish'd Gentlewoman's
Companion-Lond-1739-9th ed-Pemberton-(16), 354p-frontis-
6 fldg plts-lea   (5ww2, f)   79.50
--same-Lond-1741-frontis-5 fldg plts-lea-354p (5ee0, crack)   25.00
SMITH, E-Inquiry Into Scriptural & Ancient Servitude, etc-
Mansfield, OH-1852-cl-244p-rare   (4h7, fox, sp tn)   22.50
SMITH, E BOYD-Chicken World-NY-(1910)-obl 4to-25 col plts-
1st ed-scarce   (5v2)   12.50
--Fun in the Radio World-NY-1923-Stokes-obl 8vo-col plts
(5rr2, mint) 7.50   (5jj6, vf)   15.00
--Story of Noah's Ark-Bost&NY-1905-obl 4to-col plts-1st ed
(5v2, sl soil)   15.00

USED BOOK PRICE GUIDE

SMITH,E C-Dictionary of Amer Family Names-(1956)-244p (4t2)   8.95
SMITH,E W-Aggrey of Africa-NY-1930-illus   (5x2,dj)   15.00
--The Golden Stool-NY-1928   (5x2,dj)   8.50
SMITH,E W-The Ila Speaking Peoples of Northern Rhodesia-Lond-
1920-illus-qtr calf-scarce-2 vols   (5tt5,f)   50.00
SMITH,EDMOND REUEL-The araucanians or,Notes of a Tour
Among the Indian Tribes of Southern Chili-NY-1855-8vo-
plts-1st ed-scarce   (5h4,vg) 10.   (5ss5,ex-libr)   25.00
SMITH,EDMUND-Phaedra & Hippolitus-Lond-n.d.-Bernard Lintott-
8vo-1st ed-calf   (5b0,rbkd)   15.00
SMITH,EDMUND WARE-Further Adventures of a One Eyed Poacher-
1947-Crown-illus-ltd to 750c   (5kk7,autg)   12.50
SMITH,EDW CONRAD-The Borderland in the Civil War-NY-1928-
8vo-412p   (4a7)   17.50
SMITH,EDW GARSTIN-The Real Roosevelt-HighlandPark-(1910)-
205p plus advts-illus-cl   (5r0)   7.50
SMITH,EDW M-Documentary History of Rhinebeck-1881-239p-
fldg map   (5ff2)   25.00
SMITH,EDW P-Incidents of Shot & Shell-Phila-1888-512p-illus
(5L3,f)   11.50
SMITH,EDWIN W-The Golden Stool-NY-1928-Dblday-327p
(4t5)   7.50
--Life & Times of Danl Lindley-Lond-1949-30&456p-23 plts
(5c6,vg)   15.75
SMITH,ELBERT H-Ma Ka Tai Me She Kia Kiak,or,Black Hawk &
Scenes in the West-NY-1848-illus-1st ed (5M1) 6.   (5L1)   10.00
SMITH,ELIAS-Hymns,Original & Selected for the use of Christians-
Bost-1805-Manning&Loring-16mo-144p-pine bds (5t7,wn)   10.00
SMITH,ELIZ OAKES-The salamander,a legend for Xmas-NY-1848-
Putnam-12mo-orig cl-illumin t.pg(dated 1849)-plts-1st ed
(5x1)   25.00
SMITH,ELIZABETH W-Model Housekeeper-Louisvl-(1911)-416p-
(5c0,scuff,fade)   4.50
SMITH,ELLEN GALUSHA-How to Shade Embroidered Flowers &
Leaves-Chig-1888-127p-illus   (5t4)   8.00
SMITH,ELVA S-The History of Children's Literature-Chig-1937-
1st ed-scarce   (5v2,ex-libr)   20.00
SMITH,EMORY EVANS-The Golden Poppy-PaloAlto,Calif-
1902-230p-col frontis-illus-pict cov   (5s7,f)   15.00
SMITH,ESTHER RUTH-History of Del Norte Co,Calif-Oakland-
1953-ports-1st ed   (5h4,5dd9)   17.50
SMITH,ETHAN-View of the Hebrews-Poultney,Vt-1823-
Smith&Shute-187p-12mo-orig sheep-1st ed (5L1,tn,sl loss)   30.00
SMITH,EUGENE W-Trans Atlantic Passenger Ships,Past & Present-
Bost-1947-1st ed-2nd prntg   (5hh3)   10.00
SMITH,F HOPKINSON-American Illustrators(in 5 parts,Part 1 to 5)-
NY-1892-Scribner's-folio-15 plts-67p-1st ed-ltd to 1000c
(4e0)   65.00
--same-NY-1893-folio-5 parts-loose as issued in orig wrps-
orig bd folio-2nd ed   (5ss5)   17.50
--Caleb West Master Diver-Bost-1898-HoughtonMiff-illus-cl-378p-
1st ed   (5t0) 4.50   (5x4)   5.00
--Col Carter of Cartersville-Bost-1891-illus-12mo-1st issue (4m8)15.00
--Col Carter's Xmas-NY-1903-bds wi fold over flaps-1st ed-
ltd to 500c,autg   (5v2)   12.50
--same-NY-1903-cl-g.t.   (5r9,f)   7.50
--In Dicken's London-NY-1914-4to-illus-ltd to 1000c (5mm2)   8.50
--The Other Fellow-Bost-1899-HoughtonMiff-218p-1st ed (5x4)   7.50
--Outdoor Sketching-NY-1915-Scammon Lectures-145p-illus-
demy 8vo   (4a0)   17.50
--White Umbrella in Mexico-Bost-1889-227p-illus-1st ed
(5xx7,bkstrp soil)   5.00
SMITH,FANNY MORRIS-A Noble Art-NY-(1892)-DeVinne Pr-
8vo-illus-orig wrps-160p-1st ed   (5m6)   12.50
SMITH,FITZ HENRY,JR-French at Boston During the Revolution-
Bost-1913-illus-wrps-ltd to 80c   (4m4)   10.00
SMITH,FRANCES R-Mission of San Antonio de Padua-1932-
Stanford Univ Pr   (5x5)   20.00
SMITH,FRANK-Thomas Paine,Liberator-NY-1938-port-1st ed
(4b7)   10.00
SMITH,FRANK KINGSTON-Week end Pilot-NY-1957-Random-
242p-illus   (5p)   4.00
SMITH,FRANK M-San Francisco Vigilance Committees of '56-
SanFran-1883-83p-wrps-v scarce   (4t8)   40.00
SMITH,FREDK-Stone Ages in NoBritain & Ireland-Glasgow-1909-
377p-illus   (5m4)   25.00
SMITH,FREDK M-The Higher Powers of Man-Lamoni,la-1918-
232p-1st ed   (5L0,pres)   20.00
SMITH,G ELLIOT-Elephants & Ethnologists-Lond-1924-illus-
lg8vo-1st ed-scarce   (4b2,cov bent)   10.00
SMITH,G ELLIOT-Elephants & Ethnologists-Lond-1924-Kegan Paul-
wdcuts-135p   (5x0)   15.00

SMITH,G F H-Gem stones & Their Distinctive Characters-Lond-
(1923)-4th ed-illus   (5tt5)   7.50
SMITH,G H-Elements of Right & of the Law,to Which is Added....
Essay Upon Several Theories of Jurisprudence-Chig-1887-2nd ed
(5ff4)   7.50
SMITH,G W-History of Illinois & Her People-Chig-1927-Amer Hist
Soc-lg8vo-cl-t.e.g.-6 vols-illus   (4t1)   60.00
SMITH,GEO-of Kendall,Westmorland-A Compleat Body of Distilling-
Lond-1738-150p-frontis-calf-3rd ed   (5w1,wn)   65.00
SMITH,GEO-Cabinet Maker & Upholsterer's Guide-Lond-1826-
4to-135 plts(2 col)-orig bds&lea   (5xx7,wn)   35.00
SMITH,GEO-The Hebrew People-NY-1856-8vo-lea-614p (5t2)   7.50
SMITH,GEO-Hist of Delaware Co,Pa-Phila-1862-fldg map frontis-
plts-fldg maps-buck (5yy0,rebnd) 37.50 (4m2) 40. (5h9)   32.50
SMITH,GEO-Assyrian Discoveries-NY-1875-orig cl-fldg map-
4 photos-illus-8vo   (4e1)   30.00
SMITH,GEO-The Oldest London Bookshop-Lond-1928-Ellis-illus-
8vo-cl   (4c1)   10.00
SMITH,PRES GEO A-Rise,progress & travels of the Church of Jesus
Christ of Latter Day Saints-SaltLkCty-1869-49p-wrps (5g8)   15.00
--same-SaltLkCty-1872-71p-8vo-disbnd-2nd ed   (5t7)   25.00
SMITH,GEO BARNETT,ed-Illus British Ballads,old & new-Lond,
Paris&NY-1881-4to-frontis-2 vols in 1-384p,384p   (5p1)   25.00
SMITH,GERRIT,ed-Lies & Libels of Frank Harris-NY-1929-
Antigone Pr-1st ed   (4p1,dj)   15.00
SMITH,GORDON-Monograms in 3 & 4 Letters-NY-(ca 1870)-4to-
lea-illus-70p-a.e.g.-(New Series)   (5t7,hng loose)   18.00
SMITH,GUSTAVUS W-Battle of 7 Pines-NY-1891-202p-buck-
v scarce   (5h6,rbnd)   40.00
SMITH,H ALLEN-Robt Gair,a Study-NY-1939-Dial-12mo-cl-port-
118p   (5j5)   10.00
SMITH,H CLIFFORD-Sulgrave Manor & Washingtons-Lond-(1933)-
illus-4to   (5tt5) 17.50   (4p7)   15.00
--same-NY-1933-cl   (5w9)   7.50
SMITH,H M-Annotated Checklist & Key to Snakes of Mexico-Wash-
1945-Smi Inst,US Nat Mus Bull #187-buck-239p-8vo-scarce
(4p6,libr stmp)   10.00
--Handbook of Lizards-Ithaca-1946-557p-135 plts-maps-cl-8vo
(4p6,ex-libr)   10.00
SMITH,H MAYNARD-Frank,Bishop of Zanzibar-Lond-1926-photos-
326p   (5c6) 8.25   (4t5)   8.50
SMITH,H P-Hist of Addison Co,Vt-1886-774,63p-g.e. (5t9,f)   45.00
SMITH,H P-Hist of Rutland Co,Vt-1886-959p   (5t9)   35.00
SMITH,H PERRY-History of the City of Buffalo & Erie Co-Syracuse-
1884-2 vols-ports-4to-orig cl-mor bks
(5t9,wn) 15.   (5ss5,wn)   32.50
SMITH,HARLAN I-Archaeology of Yakima Valley-NY-1910-
Amer Mus of Nat Hist-171p plus 16 photos-drwngs-fldg map-
wrps   (5L2,lack back wrp)   8.50
--Archaeological Coll from Southern Interior of BC-Ott-1913-
39p-16 plts-maps-pict wrps-Dpt of Mines   (5a1)   6.00
SMITH,HARRIET LUMMIS-Pollyanna of the Orange Blossoms-
Bost-1924-Page-illus-313p-wrps-frontis-5 plts-3rd Glad Book-
1st ed-   ads   (5p1)   7.50
SMITH,HARRY B-First Nights & First Editions-Bost-1931-325p
(5j4,dj)   8.50
--same-Bost-1931-8vo-cl-illus-325p-1st ed,boxed-ltd to 260c,
autg,box   (5t0)   25.00
--A Sentimental Library-(NY)-1914-lg4to-priv prntd-332p (5d5) 37.50
SMITH,HARRY WORCESTER-A Sporting Family of the Old South-
Albany-1936-477p-illus   (5L1) 10.   (5w0,dj)   17.50
SMITH,HARVEY H-Lincoln & the Lincolns-NY-1931-thk8vo-
illus-1st ed   (4b7)   15.00
SMITH,HELEN A-Historyof Russia in Words of One Syllable-
NY-(1887)-Routledge-sq8vo-dec bds-224p-plts   (5dd0)   7.50
SMITH,HENRY-The Master Book of Soups-Lond-n.d.-233p (5g9)   4.00
SMITH,HENRY H-Minor Surgery-Phila-(1850)-455p-illus
(5t4,lacks last index pg)   7.50
SMITH,HERBERT H-Brazil,The Amazons & the Coast-NY-1879-
644p-illus-cl-Scribners   (5d6)   15.00
SMITH,HERMAN-Kitchens Near & Far-NY-1944-277p-frontis
(5g9)   4.50
SMITH,HORATIO-Festivals,Games & Amusements,Ancient &
Modern-NY-1836-illus-1st Amer ed   (5v2)   12.50
SMITH,HUGH,M D-Letters to married women on nursing &
management of children-Phila-1792-Mathew Carey-16mo-
calf-167p-1st Amer ed-rare   (5p6,hng crack)   35.00
SMITH,HURON H-Ethnobotany of Menomini Indians-Milwk Mus-
1923-wrps-plts   (4k5)   15.00
--Ethnobotany of Meskwaki Indians-Milwkee-1928-plts-wrps
(4b3) 20.   (4k5,f)   12.50
--Ethnobotany of Ojibwe Indians-Milwkee-1932-plts-wrps
(4b3) 25.   (4k5,f)   15.00

SMITH, ISABEL C-The Blue Book of Cookery-NY-1940-566p-
photos   (5c0)   3.00
SMITH, J ALDEN-Biennial Report of State Geologist of State of
Colo ending Dec 31, 1880-(wi) Catalogue-Denver-1881-
Tribune Pub-8vo-75p-orig wrps   (5L1)   15.00
SMITH, J BURRITT-"High Joe" or the Logger's Story-Madsn-(1892)-
240p-wrps-v scarce   (5h7, dmpstn)   17.50
SMITH, J C-Remin of Early Methodism in Indiana-Indnpls-1879
     (4p8)   17.50
SMITH, J CALVIN-Illustrated Hand Book-NY-1849-Sherman&Smith-
234p-fldg map-cl   (5tt0)   40.00
--Western Tourist & Emigrants Guide-NY-1839-180p-map-orig cl
     (5s2, map tn)   65.00
--same-NY-1853-fldg map-89p   (4t8)   20.00
SMITH, J D-History of the Chisum War-(Electra, Tex-1927)-illus-
70p-stiff wrps-1st ed   (5kk4)   45.00
SMITH, J E A-History of Pittsfield(Berkshire Co), Mass-Bost&Sprngfld-
1869, 1876-Lee&Shephard & C W Bryan-8vo-cl-2 vols   (4t1)   35.00
SMITH, J FOSTER-Stage Point & Thereabout-c1929-21p-maps&plan-
stiff wrps   (5e8, pres)   9.75
SMITH, J FRAZER-White Pillars-NY-1941-1st ed-illus-4to
     (5jj3) 25.   (4j3) 15.   (5a8)   17.50
--same-NY-(1941)-252p-cl-rprnt Howes S604   (5m2, 5h1)   7.50
SMITH, MRS J GREGORY-Ann Eliza-Atla, a story of the lost island-
NY-1886-Harper-1st ed   (5m2, sl wn)   6.50
SMITH, J I-New Washington & Cranberry Tp-New Wash-Herald Job
Prnt-1889-104p-cl-rare   (5h1)   25.00
SMITH, J J-Rhode Island Civil & Military List, 1800 to 1850-
Vol 2 only-1901   (5t9)   7.50
SMITH, J L-History of the Corn Exchange Regiment, 118th Penna
Vol-Phila-1888-746p-illus-1st edition   (5w9, lt wn)   18.75
SMITH, J M-A Work on Revivals-StJos, Mo-1885-port-priv prntd-
enlrgd ed-304p   (5yy8, rub)   6.50
SMITH, J THORNE, JR-Out O'Luck-(1919)-Stokes   (5F1, f, soil dj)   6.00
--Topper, An Improbable Adventure-1926-RobtM McBride
     (5F1, f, soil dj)   10.00
SMITH, JAS-Acct of Remarkable Occurrences in Life & Travels of
Col Jas Smith-Lex-prntd by Jn Bradford-1799-8vo-88p-
hf calf-1st ed-ex rare   (5hh0, rprd, stns)   12,500.00
--same-Phila-1834-Grigg&Eliot-162p-orig bds-12mo
     (5L1, lacks 3 lvs of Intro)   50.00
SMITH, JAS, M D-The commonwealth's man-NY-1806-A Foreman-
8vo-stitchd as issued-1st ed   (5i0)   25.00
SMITH, JAS-History of Christian Church...Incl Cumberland
Presbyterian Church-Nashville, Tenn-1835-lea-687p-scarce
     (5yy8, stn, rprd)   30.00
SMITH, JAS-Voyage & Shipwreck of StPaul-Lond-1848-4 plts-
3 charts   (5c1)   50.00
SMITH, JAS C-Commission of Christ's Ambassadors-Ottawa-1868-
Times Steam Power Wks   (5nn8)   10.00
SMITH, JAS EDW-Intro to Physiological & Systematical Botany-
Bost-1814-bds-labl-15 plts-8vo-1st Amer ed   (4m6, rebnd)   25.00
SMITH, JAS H-History of Duchess County, NY-Syracuse-1882-
thk4to-il lus   (5yy6) 37.50   (4t2, rbkd)   60.00
SMITH, JAS H-Vital Facts Concerning the African Methodist
Episcopal Church-(n.p.)-(1941)-photos-rev ed   (5x5)   7.50
SMITH, JAS L-Autobiography of-Norwich-1881   (5x2)   45.00
SMITH, JAS THORNE-Biltmore Oswald, Diary of a Hapless Recruit-
NY-(1918)-12mo-pict bds-1st ed of auth's 1st book
     (5gg6, vf, dj)   25.00
SMITH, JEROME V C-Natural History of the Fishes of Massachusetts-
Bost-1833-orig cl-papr labl-1st ed   (5m3, fade, pres)   95.00
SMITH, JOHN-Sea mans Grammar & Dictionary-Lond-1692-
sm4to-2 parts-fldg plt-fold table-calf-reissue of 4th ed-
prntd for Dring&Griffin   (5hh0, sml worming)   875.00
SMITH, JOHN-Horological Disquisitions Concerning the Nature
of Time-Lond-1694-lea-2 fldg tables-92p-4x6½"   (5bb0)   385.00
SMITH, JOHN-Iconographia Scotica-Lond-1798-folio-bds-69p
     (4p3)   40.00
SMITH, CAPT JOHN-Adventures & Discourses of-Lond, Paris&NY-
n.d.-Cassell&Co-309p-illus   (5h9)   8.50
--Advertisements for the unexperienced Planters of New England-
Lond-1631-Haviland-sm4to-g.tooled mor-fldg map(silked)-
1st ed-v rare   (5n2)   6,500.00
--Description of New England-Bost-1865-Veazie-89p-map-
sm4to-ltd to 250c   (5qq8) 12.50   (5s2)   35.00
--Generall Historie of Virginia, New England & the Summer Isles-
Lond-1627-for M Sparkes-lg4to-mor-4 fldng maps(silked)-
facs port inserted (not called for)   (5n9, vf)   5,000.00
--same-Glasgow-1907-fldg maps-illus-8vo-hf vel-100c   (4c1)   40.00
--same-Together with True Travels, Adventures & Observations
& A Sea Grammar-Glasgow-1907-2 vols-MacLehose-8vo-cl-
vel backs-maps-facs ports-ltd to 100c on handmade papr(5ss2) 37.50

SMITH, CAPT JOHN   (continued)
--New England Trials-(Prov-1867)-4to-ltd to 60c-facs of 2nd ed-
wrps   (4c1)   20.00
--The True Travels-Richmond-1819-Franklin Pr-8vo-2 vols-
tooled mor-fldng map-4 plts(2 fldg)-1st Amer ed
     (5x5, wn) 60.   (5n2)   85.00
--same-NY-1930-Rimington&Hooper-folio-buck-facs-ltd to 375c-
Georgian Pr   (4a3, labl chip)   27.50
SMITH, JOHN B-Insects of New Jersey-Trenton-1910-8vo-cl-
illus-885p-fldg map   (5t2, pres)   7.50
SMITH, JOHN L-Indiana Methodism-Valparaiso-1892-482p-
cl-scarce   (5h7)   17.50
SMITH, JOHN M-Hist of Sunderland, Mass-1899-684p   (5t9)   45.00
SMITH, JONATHAN-History of Old Trinity Lodge of Lancaster, Mass-
Clinton-1896-g.embossed cov-1st ed   (5b9, mint)   20.00
SMITH, JOS-Bibliotheca Anti Quakeriana-Lond-1873-474p-scarce
     (4m4, sl wn)   30.00
SMITH, JOS, JR-The Book of Mormon-Palmyra-1830-8vo-orig calf
with final lf"Testimony of 3 Witnesses" & "And Also Testimony
of 8 Witnesses"-1st ed   (5ee9, box, sl rprd)   750.00
--same-Nauvoo, Ill-1840-3rd ed-rev by transl-571p(3p)-lea-
see Howes 623   (5jj9)   85.00
--same-In Mormon characters, or the Deseret alphabet-NY-1869-
Deseret Univ-8vo-cl-1st ed   (5g6, bkstrp dmgd)   85.00
--Llyfr Athrawiaeth a Chyfammodau-Merthyr Tydfil-1851-304p-
lea-Book of Mormon in Welsh, transl by John Davis-rare
     (5L2, chip)   100.00
SMITH, JOS JENCKS, comp-Civil & Military List of RI 1647 to 1800-
Prov-1900-Preston&Rounds-3 vols   (5mm8)   27.50
SMITH, JOS LINDON-Tombs, Temples & Ancient Art-Norman-
(1956)-335p plus index-photos   (5L0, dj, mint)   8.50
SMITH, JOSHUA HETT-Authentic Narrative of Causes Which Led
to Death of Maj Andre-Lond-1808-map-357p
     (5ff2, mend) 27.50   (5L1, f)   25.00
--same-NY-1809-sm8vo-calf-port   (5L1)   20.00
SMITH, JOSHUA TOULMIN-Journal in Amer 1837 to 1838-
Metuchen, NJ-1925-ltd to 99c-54p-3/4 mor-1st ed
     (4t8, cl) 17.50   (4t8, unopnd, lt rub)   20.00
SMITH, JULIE P-Kiss and be friends, a novel-NY-1879-Carleton-
1st ed-1st state with advts title as "new" (5m2, lacks e.p.)   10.00
SMITH, JUSTIN H-Struggle for the 14th Colony-Putnam-1907-
2 vols-315 illus-maps   (5e8)   27.50
--The War with Mexico-NY-1919-2 vols-maps-1st ed
     (5L2) 45.   (5h9)   57.50
SMITH, K D-The Story of Thos Duncan & His 6 Sons-1928-174p
     (5mm3)   17.50
SMITH, KATE-The Kate Smith Company's Coming Cookbook-NJ-
(1958)-312p   (5c9)   4.50
SMITH, L BERTRAND-Jesse Smith, His Ancestors & Descendants-
NY-1909-187p-12mo-g.t.   (5h9, 5t9)   7.50
SMITH, L WALDEN-Saddles Up-1937-276p-1st ed-illus(5r1, dj, f) 35.00
SMITH, LAURA A-The Music of the Waters-Lond-1888   (5c1)   35.00
SMITH, LAURA CHASE-Life of Philander Chase-NY-1903-8vo-
cl-341p-illus-1st ed   (5t2)   5.00
SMITH, LAWRENCE B-Amer Game Preserve Shooting-GardenCty-
(1937)-175p-illus   (5t7)   12.50
--Fur or Feather, Days with Dog & Gun-NY&Lond-1946-144p-
illus   (5t7)   10.00
--Dude Ranches & Ponies-NY-1936-1st ed (5s4) 12.50 (5x5)   15.00
--Shotgun Psychology-NY-1938-illus-295p   (5ss8, dj)   12.00
--Sunlight Kid & Other Western Verses-NY-(1935)-photos-1st ed-
121p   (4t8)   5.00
SMITH, LEWIS WORTHINGTON, ed-Women's Poetry Today-
NY-(1929)-237p   (5p7)   4.00
SMITH, LOGAN P-Afterthoughts-Lond-1931-orig bds-1st ed-
ltd to 100c, autg   (5hh1, fade)   20.00
--Prospects of Literature-Lond-1927-Hogarth Pr-16mo-1st ed-
dec wrps-Vol 8   (4c1)   6.00
--Trivia-Lond-1918-Constable-cl bkd bds-1st ed (5ss3, fade)   10.00
--More Trivia-Lond-1922-Constable-cl bkd bds-1st ed
     (5ss3, dj, fade)   15.00
--The Youth of Parnassus-Lond-1895-Macmillan-12mo-cl-
1st ed   (5ss3, pres, sp stnd)   50.00
--Unforgotten Years-Lond-(1938)-8vo-cl-1st ed (5r9, mint, dj)   10.00
SMITH, LUCIUS E-Heroes & Martyrs of Modern Missionary-
Enterprise-Hartf-1852-ports-frontis-508p   (5yy0)   7.00
SMITH, LUCY-History of Jos Smith-SaltLkCty-1958-355p (4t8)   7.50
SMITH, M-General View of European Legal History & Other
Papers-NY-1927   (5ff4)   15.00
SMITH, M-Development of European Law-NY-1928   (5ff4)   10.00
SMITH, M-Monograph of The Sea Snakes-Lond-1926-cl-130p-
2 plts-8vo-orig ed-rare   (4p6, libr stmp)   25.75

SMITH,M A-Fauna of British India,Ceylon & Burma;
Reptilia & Amphibia Vol 3,Serpents-Lond-1943-cl-
583p,6p-fldg map-8vo-orig ed-rare   (4p6,sp fade) 57.00

SMITH,M L-Officers & Soldiers of Artillery & of 3rd Brigade-
Vicksburg-July 12,1862-prnt leaflet-2p
   (5yy3,wi mss endorsement of Girault)200.00

SMITH,MARGARET V-Virginia,1492 to 1892-Wash-1893-
illus-459p   (4b6) 15. (5L7,ex-libr) 17.50

SMITH,MATTHEW HALE-Sunshine & Shadow in NY-Hartf-
1868-718p-lea-illus-1st ed   (5L3,sp crack) 6.50
--same-Hartf-1870-illus   (5jj3) 15.00
--20 Years Among Bulls & Bears of Wall St-Hartf-1870-
12 plts-1st ed-scarce   (5i3) 25.00

SMITH,MAXWELL-East Coast Marine Shells-AnnArbor,Mich-
1945-314p-77 plts-illus-3rd ed,rev&enlrgd   (5t4) 10.00

SMITH,MINNA-Red Top Ranch-NY-(1907)-illus-213p (5s4) 6.00

SMITH,MR-Rosine Laval,a novel-Phila-1833-Carey,Lea &
Blanchard-12mo-orig cl&bds-papr labl-1st ed (5x0,soil) 90.00

SMITH,MORTON-First 100 Years in Cooke County-SanAntonio-
1955   (4a5,vg) 25.00

SMITH,MOSES-History of the Adventures & Sufferings of...from
1806 to Jun 1811-Albany-1814-16mo-bds&lea-146p (5t0) 35.00

SMITH,NATHAN-Practical Essay on Typhous Fever-NY-1824-
Bliss & White-orig bds-1st ed   (4h0,rbkd) 225.00

SMITH,NICOL-Burma Road-NY-npls-c1940   (5p1) 3.50

SMITH,NILA BANTON-Amer Reading Instruction-NY-(c1934)-
Silver Burdett-287p-"Sample Copy"   (5p1) 12.50

SMITH,NORA ARCHIBALD-Boys & Girls of Bookland-Phila-
c1923-100p-4to-frontis-10 col plts-pict labl (5p1,dj) 15.00
--Kate Douglas Wiggin-Bost-1925-383p-1st ed
   (5ee3,autg,photo laid in) 5.00
--Under the Cactus Flag-Bost-1899-illus-photos-orig pict cl
   (5m9) 7.50

SMITH,O H-Early Indiana Trials & Sketches-Cinn-1858-640p-
1st ed   (4a9,wn) 10. (5y0,rub,pres) 20.00

SMITH,O W-Trout Lore-NY-(1917)-203p-illus-photos (5t4) 6.50

SMITH,P R-Geology & Mineral Resources of NoWestern Alaska-
USGS Bull 815-1930-351p-plts-2 pkt maps   (5ss1) 20.00

SMITH,PAUL J-A Key to the Ulysses of Jas Joyce-Chig-1927-
bds-cl bk-1st ed-ltd to 960c   (5hh1,cor wn) 15.00
--same-NY-(1934)-map   (5mm1,dj) 10.00

SMITH,PHILIP H-Acadia,A Lost Chapter in Amer History-Pawling-
1884-illus   (5w8) 50.00
--Green Mountain Boys, or Vermont & the NY Land Jobbers-
Pawling-1885-130p   (5e8) 9.75
--Legends of Shawangunk & Its Environs-illus (5ff2) 20.00

SMITH,PRESERVED-History of Modern Culture-1930,34-2 vols-
8vo-cl   (5t0) 12.50

SMITH,R,ed-SoCarolina Ballads-Harvard Univ-1928-R8vo (5x2) 35.00

SMITH,R A-Smith's Illus Guide to & through Laurel Hill Cemetery
etc-Phila-1852-WPHazard-8vo-col map-cl-147p,53p-illus-
1st ed
   (5j5,sl dmpstn) 40.00

SMITH,R D HILTON-Alice One Hundred-Victoria,BC-1966-
Adelphi Book Shop-8vo-77p-pict wrps-illus (5p1) 15.00

SMITH,R C-Concise & Practical System of Geography-NY-1847-
4to-8 Amer col maps   (5yy0,cov soil) 12.50

SMITH,R R-Ohil Valley Saffords-rev by S M Culbertson-1932-230p
   (4t2) 25.00

SMITH,RALPH D-History of Guilford,Conn-Albany-1877,J Munsell,
Prntr-8vo-cl-219p   (4t2) 10.00

SMITH,RAY B,ed-History of New York State, Political & Governmental
Governmental-1922-6 vols   (5zz0) 30.00

SMITH,RAY M-Story of Pope's Barrels-Harrisburg-(1960)-Stackpole-
4to-cl-illus-210p   (5j5,dj) 15.00

SMITH,RICHARD G-Ancient Tales & Folklore of Japan-Lond-
1908-361p plus 62 col plts   (5c3) 10.00

SMITH,ROBT-A Compleat System of Opticks-Cambr-1738-
83 plts-4 pts in 2 vols-4to-calf   (4c2) 150.00
--Compleat System of Opticks in 4 Books-Cambr-1738-for the author-
4to-calf&bds-63 plts,plus 20 plts-orig ed
   (5ee5,lacks 1 plt,rebnd,libr stmp) 185.00

SMITH,ROBT-Baseball,a Historical Narr of the Game-NY-1947-
Simon&Schuster-8vo-cl-362p   (5j5) 7.50

SMITH,ROBT H-Address to Citizens of Alabama on Constitution
& Laws of Confed States of Amer by the Hon-Mobile-1861-
Mobile Daily Register Pr-24p   (5d6,lacks bk cov) 40.00

SMITH,ROSWELL C-English Grammar-Phila-1861-EHButler-
192p,16p(catalogue)-lea bkd bds   (5p1,v wn) 3.00

SMITH,S F-History of Newton,1630 to 1880-1880-851p (5t9) 12.50

SMITH,S R-The Wyoming Valley in 1892-Wilkes Barre-1892-
ports & illus   (5r7) 25.00

SMITH,S R-Lectures to Youth-Phila-Thos Cowperthwait-1843-
Gihon,Fairchild&Co,prntrs-lea bkd bds-241p (5p1) 32.50

SMITH,S S-Essay on Causes of Variety of Complexion & Figure
in Human Species-1810-calf-2nd ed   (5L7,ex-libr) 15.00

SMITH,SAML-History of Colony of Nova Caesaria or NJ-
Burlington-1765-JasParker-1st ed-573p-hf calf-(10)573p,(1)p-
1st issue(wiout punctuated date)   (4b1,f,rbnd) 225.00
--same-Trenton-1877-573p-map   (5ii2) 12.50

SMITH,SAML-History of Province of Pennsylvania-Phila-1913-
231p-Mervine,ed   (4m4) 20.00

SMITH,SAML STANHOPE-Essay on Causes of Variety of
Complexion & Figure in the Human Species-NewBrunswick-
1810-410p-orig bds-enlrgd&improvd 2nd ed
   (5m3,unopnd,sl wtrstnd) 95.00

SMITH,MOTHER SARAH-Life Sketches of-Moundsvl-1902-
72p-wrps   (5h7) 7.50

SMITH,SEBA-'Way Down East,or,Portraitures of Yankee life-
NY,Bost,Cinn-1854-illus-1st ed   (5m2) 13.50

SMITH,SOL-Theatrical Management in the West & South for
30 Years-NY-1868-illus-275p-1st ed (5ee3,libr stmp,sp tn) 15.00

SMITH,SOUTHWOOD-Treatise on Fever-Phila-1835-8vo-lea-
326p-3rd ed   (5t0) 17.50

SMITH,SYDNEY-Works-1845-3 vols-3rd ed   (5L7,rub) 15.00

SMITH,MRS SYDNEY-Old Yorktown & Its History-Yorktown-
1920-wrps-illus-23p   (4j4) 7.00

SMITH,THEODORE CLARKE-Parties & Slavery 1850 to 1859-
NY-1906-illus   (5x2) 12.00

SMITH,T R,ed-Poetica Erotica-NY-1921-Vol 1 only-
hf vel-ltd to 1500 sets-for subscribers only (5k2,f,dj) 25.00
--same-1929-Boni Liveright-8vo-bds-vel sp-ltd ed-for
subscribers only   (5t5) 20.00
--same-NY-H Liveright-1931   (5x0) 5.00

SMITH,T V-Promise of Amer Politics-U of Chig-1936-1st ed (5q8) 7.50

SMITH,THOS-Extracts from the Diary of a Huntsman-Lond-
1838-8vo-cl-Whittaker-1st ed   (5ss3,chip) 35.00

SMITH,THOS L-History of Town of Windham-Portl-1873-
Hoyt&Fogg-8vo-cl-104p   (4t1) 12.50

SMITH,TIMOTHY-Gen of Timothy Smith Family, 1620 to 1910-
n.d.-48p   (5t9) 17.50

SMITH,TRUMAN-Speech of...of Conn...on Physical Character of
Northern States of Mexico...Also New Mex & Upper Calif-
(Wash-1848)-31p-self cov-rare pamph
   (5z7) 45. (5g4) 25. (5L2) 35.00

SMITH,TURNSTALL,ed-Richard Snowden Andrews-Balt-1910-
8vo-156p   (4a7) 20.00

SMITH,URIAH-Marvel of Nations-BattleCr&Okla-1886-289p-cl
   (5h7) 5.00
--The US in the Light of Prophecy-BattleCr-1874-Steam Pr of
Seventh Day Adventist Publ Assn-160p-orig cl-incl catalog(16p)-
1st ed   (5m3,f) 27.50

SMITH,VIDA E-Young People's History of Church of Jesus Christ
of Latter Day Saints,Vols 1 & 2-Lamoni,Iowa-1914&1918-
photos-map-2 vols-1st eds   (4t3) 15.00

SMITH,VINCENT A-Early History of India-Oxf-1914-512p-illus-
map-3rd ed,rev&enlrgd   (5w9) 12.50

SMITH,W-Newburyport (Mass) Directory-1849   (5t9) 5.00

SMITH,W ANDERSON-Temperate Chile,a Progressive Spain-
Lond-1899-399p-map-illus   (5p7) 6. (5L7) 10.00

SMITH,W B-The Color Line,A Brief in Behalf of the Unborn-NY-
1905   (5x2) 35.00

SMITH,W B-On Wheels & How I Came There-Cinn-1893-338p-cl
   (5h2) 8.50

SMITH,W C S-A Journey to Calif in 1849-n.p.-n.d.-(NapaCty-
ca1925)-8vo-orig wrps-36p   (5h5,f) 20.00

SMITH,W G-Building the Nation...Churches' Relation to
Immigrants-Tor-1922-wrps-plts-202p   (5dd0) 5.00

SMITH,W H,comp-Brooklyn Directory,Eastern Dist,for Year Ending
May 1,1857-Brklyn-1856   (4j3,rebnd) 17.50

SMITH,W H-A Political History of Slavery-NY-1903-2 vols(5x2)50.00

SMITH,W H B-Basic Manual of Military Small Arms-Harrisburg-
(1945)-4to-351p-illus   (5xx7) 17.50

SMITH,W L-The Marshall Tragedy,Its Cause-75p-4to-typescript-
in fldr   (5n4) 17.50

SMITH,W PRESCOTT-History & Description of the Balt&Ohio RR-
Balt-1853-200p-plts-map   (5hh7,ex-libr,wn) 50.00

SMITH,W S-Trails of Wm S Smith & Sam'l G Ogden-NY-1807-
287p-wrps   (5r4) 15.00

SMITH,W T-Complete Index to Names of Persons,Places & Subjects
in Littell's Laws of Ky-1931-213p   (4t2) 10.00

SMITH,W W-True Record of Marriages,Deaths,Accidents etc-
Owensville-1891-1st ed-111p   (4a9) 12.00

SMITH,WALLACE-Garden of the Sun-Fresno-c1960-Max Hardison-
8vo-cl-567p   (4t1) 17.50
--Oregon Sketches-NY-1925-247p-illus-"Oregon Journal" ed
   (5ss1,dj) 6.00

SMITH,WALLACE (continued)
--Prodigal Sons-Bost-(1951)-8vo-cl-434p   (5h4,autg,wn)   13.75
--On the Trail in Yellowstone-NY-1924-105p-illus   (5s4)   4.00
SMITH,WALTER-Examples of Household Taste-NY-(1875)-4to-
521p-illus   (5w7)   7.50
SMITH,WALTER H B-N R A Book of Small Arms-Harrisburg-(1946)-
2 vols-illus   (5xx7)   20.00
SMITH,WALTON H-Liquor The Servant of Man-Bost-1940-273p
(5w1)   5.00
SMITH,WARREN H-Originals Abroad-NewHav-1952-205p-plts
(5a1)   5.00
SMITH,MRS WHITE MOUNTAIN-Indian Tribes of the SoWest-
Stanford U-(1933)-illus-1st ed-scarce   (4t8)   12.50
SMITH,WILL-War Work of Skinner,Eddy Corp,Seattle-Seattle-
(1919)-4to-illus-ports-pgs unnbrd   (5s1,sl stnd)   10.00
SMITH,WM,ed-Dictionary of Greek & Roman Antiquities-Lond-
1878-engr-thk8vo   (5yy6,bndg wn)   17.50
SMITH,WM-(of Nevis)-A Natural History of Nevis & Rest of
English Charibee Islands in Amer-Cambr-1745-JBentham-8vo-
318p,(9)-calf-1st ed   (5L1)   125.00
SMITH,WM,(of SoCar)-Comparative view of constitutions of several
states wi each other & wi that of US-Phila-1796-4to-
6 fldg tabls-bds-calf bk   (5g8)   37.50
SMITH,WM-Eulogium of Benj Franklin...deliv Mar 1,1791-
Phila-1792-8vo-disbnd-1st ed   (5i9,lacks stitching)   40.00
SMITH,WM-Oration In Memory of Gen Montgomery & of Officers
& Soldiers Who Fell with Him Dec 31,1775,Before Quebec-
Phila-1776-Dunlap-8vo-port laid in-1st ed
(5n2,box re-wrps)   125.00
SMITH,WM-History of Canada-Quebec-1815-prntd for author-
2 vols-wi slip "Nbr of Souls"etc   (5e2)   450.00
--same-Quebec-1815(actually 1826)-2 vols in 1-calf&cl-
errata lf   (4d1,sl wn)   250.00
SMITH,WM-History of NY from First Discov....wi a Continuation
to Year 1814-Albany-1814-8vo-calf-lea labl (5ss5,crack)   37.50
--Histoire de la Nouvelle York-Lond-1767-12mo-calf-1st ed in
French-scarce   (4a1,rub) 37.50   (5t4)   45.00
--History of Province of NY,from 1st Discov to Year 1732-Lond-
1757-Thos Wilcox-fldg map-lg4to-mor-lg papr-g.sp-g.e.-
255p-1st ed-f bndg-box   (4e1,Rice Menzies copy) 1,500.00
--same-Phila-1792-2nd ed-calf-scarce   (5yy6,wn,fox)   22.50
SMITH,WM-History of the Post Office in British NoAmer 1639 to
1870-Cambr U Pr-1920   (5w8)   75.00
SMITH,WM A-Lectures on Philosophy & Practice of Slavery-
Nashvl-1856-328p-orig cl-1st ed (5x2,fox) 37.50 (5m3,rub)   42.50
SMITH,WM C-The Book of Vetch-n.p.-n.d.-(ca1913-Des Moines?)-
157p-plts   (5s7)   7.50
SMITH,WM C-Indiana Miscellany-Cinn-1867-1st ed-scarce
(5m2)   18.50
SMITH,WM D-The Bible,Confession of Faith & Common Sense-
Springfield-1844-251p-cl   (5h7,fox)   15.00
SMITH,WM ERNEST-The Francis Preston Blair Family in Politics-
NY-1933-2 vols-illus   (5t7,libr labls)   25.00
SMITH,WM F-Diamond Six-NY-1958-1st ed (5m9,dj) 5. (5tt5)   7.50
SMITH,WM GEO,ed-Oxford Dictionary of English Proverbs-Oxf-
(1936)-Clarendon Pr 644p   (5p7)   5.00
SMITH,WM HAWLEY-Evolution of "Dodd"-Chig-(1884)-153p-
wrps-RandMcNally imprnt   (5h1,sl wn)   10.00
--same-Chig&NY-1897-pic cl-245p   (5p1,Denslow autg)   10.00
SMITH,WM HENRY-The History of the State of Indiana-Indnpls-
1897-2 vols-1st ed-illus   (5L3,f)   27.50
--The St Clair Papers-Cinn-1882-2 frontis-fldg map-2 vols (4t8)   45.00
SMITH,WM J,ed-Corres of Richard Grenville,Earl Temple, & Rt Hon
Geo Grenville,their friends & contemporaries-1852,53-4 vols
(5L7)   40.00
SMITH,WM JAY-Typewriter Town-NY-Dutton-(c1960) (5b2)   5.00
SMITH,WM R-Africa Illustrated-NY-1889-A W Lovering-
pict cov-200p-g.e.   (4t5,sp loose)   20.00
SMITH,WM R-The History of Wisconsin-Madison-1854-
Beriah Brown-Vols 1&3(all publ)-cl (4t8,wn) 15. (5d6)   20.00
--Incidents of a Journey from Penna to Wisc Terr in 1837-
Chig-1927-ltd to 115c,nbrd-82p   (5L2)   15.00
SMITH,WM WHITE-The Prophets,or,Mormonism Unveiled-Phila-
1855-8vo-412p-illus-stmpd cl-1st ed   (5g5)   25.00
SMITH,Z F-History of Kentucky-Louisville-1895-illus-848p,31p
(5yy8,sl wn) 40.   (5m6)   17.50
SMITHE,GEO C-Glimpses,Places,People & Things-Ypsilanti-
1887-191p-cl   (5jj9,cov spot)   10.00
SMITHERS,WM W-The life of John Lofland-Phila-1894-Leonard-
illus-1st ed-ltd to 500c,nbrd   (5m2)   7.50
SMITHEY,ROYALL BASCOM-History of Virginia,a Brief Text
Book for Schools-NY,etc-(1898)   (5h6)   4.00

SMITHSONIAN INST-BAE Annual Reports-
--2nd-477p-col plts-calf   (4t8,chip,ex-libr)   20.00
--3rd-606p-col plts   (4t8)   20.00
--5th-564p-col plts-3/4 lea   (4t8,ex-libr)   15.00
--6th-675p-3/4 lea   (4t8)   15.00
--7th-409p-col plts-calf   (4t8)   15.00
--8th-298p-col plts   (4t8,rbnd)   17.50
--16th-326p-plts-3/4 lea   (4t8,ex-libr)   15.00
--19th-576p-calf   (4t8)   15.00
--23rd-634p-3/4 lea-col plts   (4t8,ex-libr)   30.00
SMITHSONIAN INST-also see US GOV, or AUTHOR or SUBJECT
SMITHSONIAN SCIENTIFIC SERIES-C G Abbott,ed-1929-12 vols-
illus   (5L7)   65.00
SMITHWICK,NOAH-Evolution of State-Austin-1900-cl-12mo-354p
(4c7) 35.   (5F5)   30.00
SMOKE RINGS & ROUNDELAYS-Lond-(1924)-cl-320p-
(Wilfred Partington)   (4i2)   20.00
SMOKE SIGNAL,THE-Tucson-1965-pub by The Westerners-
12 issues,May 1960 (reprnted 1964) to Fall 1965-bound in bds
(5x5)   20.00
SMOLKA,H P-40,000 Against the Arctic-Lond-1938-288p-illus-
2 fldg maps   (5ss1)   4.00
SMOLLETT,TOBIAS-Adventures of Ferdinand Count Fathom-Lond-
1753-2 vols-12mo-calf-1st ed   (5xx6,rub,box)   400.00
--The Adventures of Peregrine Pickle-Oxf-1936-2 vols-sm folio-
buck-Ltd Ed Club-ltd to 1500c,autg,nbrd,box   (5b0)   35.00
--Complete Works-Edinb-1820-6 vols-ports-extra illus wi
Cruikshank plts-crimson mor   (5tt2,f bndg,rbkd)   150.00
--Complete Works-Lond-12 vols-Geo Saintsbury,ed-g.t.-
lg12mo-3/4 red lev-Gibbings&Co-Frank Richards,illus-
raised bands   (5t5,f,bndg)   65.00
--Exped of Humphry Clinker-Lond-1671(sic,for 1771)-(Salisbury)-
3 vols-calf-1st ed   (5xx6,lacks hf t.)   250.00
--History & adventures of an atom-Lond-1769-2 vols-
Robinson&Roberts-12mo-calf-1st ed   (5xx6,box)   275.00
--same-Lond-1769-Robinson&Roberts-1st ed,2nd issue-12mo-lea-
2 vols   (5tt2,rbkd,split,chip)   65.00
--History of England-Lond-1825-t8vo-618p-calf-t.-raised bands
(5p5,f bndg)   15.00
--Memoirs of a Lady of Quality-1751-Lond-1925-Peter Davies-4to-
Willoughby,illus-orig g. bds-vel sp-ltd to 500c   (5t5)   15.00
--Travels through France & Italy-Lond-1766-R Baldwin-2 vols-
8vo-1st ed   (5x3,rbkd)   125.00
SMUCKER,SAM'L M-Arctic Explor & Discov During 19th Century-
NY-1857-517p-illus-hf lea   (4b9,rbnd)   12.00
--same-NY-1860-517p-illus-buck   (4b9,rbdn)   12.00
--same-NY-1886-640p-illus-bds   (5ss1)   5.00
--Life of Col John Chas Fremont,etc-NY&Auburn-1856-illus-
orig cl-493p   (4n4) 10. (5tt0,soil) 7.50 (5ee3,4t8)   8.50
--Life of Dr Elisha Kent Kane & other Distinguished Amer Explorers-
Phila-1858-406p-frontis   (5ss1) 4.   (5t4)   7.50
--Life,Speeches & Memorials of Daniel Webster-Bost-1859-
Crown-548p-frontis   (5qq8) 5. (5L3,vf)   7.50
--Religious,Social & Political History of the Mormons-NY-1856-
460p-illus-frontis   (5L2,ex-libr,wn)   5.00
SMUGGLER,THE-a Tale-Lond-1831-Colburn&Bentley-3 vols-
1st ed-hf mor   (5xx6)   75.00
SMULL,JOHN A-History of Harrisburg Cemetery Assoc-Harrisburg-
1876-Telegraph Prntg Hse-12mo-wrps-67p (4t1,lacks bk cov) 12.50
SMUTS,J C-Africa & Some World Problems-Oxf-1930-Clarendon Pr-
184p-map(1 fldg)-2nd impr   (4t5,dj)   10.00
--Jan Christian Smuts,by His Son-Lond-1952-Cassell-maps-photos-
568p   (4t5,dj) 9.   (5c6,f)   8.75
--Plans for a Better World: Speeches of-Lond-1942-288p-8 plts
(5c6)   10.75
SMYLIE,JAS-Brief History of Trial of Rev Wm Scott...in New
Orleans-NewOrl-1847-74p   (4j4)   12.50
SMYTH,ALBERT H-Philadelphia Magazines & Their Contributors,
1741 to 1850-Phila-1892-264p-scarce   (4g2)   20.00
--Writings of Benj Franklin-NY-1907-Macmillan-10 vols-red cl
(5ee3,sl wn)   17.50
SMYTH,ALEX-Regulations for Field Exercise,Manoeuvres, & Conduct
of Infantry of the US-Phila-1812-Finley-225p-calf-lea labl-
2nd ed(Smyth's name on t.pg)-lf of errata-34 fld plans at bk
(5m3)   45.00
SMYTH,MAJ G CARMICHAEL-History of the Reigning Family
of Lahore-Calcutta-1847-W Thacker-263p (5x9,ex-libr)   12.50
SMYTH,ROBT CARMICHAEL-Employment of the People & Capital
of Great Britain in her own Colonies,etc-Lond-1849-map
(5e2)   225.00
SMYTH,T-Unity of the Human Races Proved to be the Doctrine
of Scripture,Reason & Science-NY-1850   (5x2)   22.50

SMYTH,REV THOS-The Nature & Claims of Young Men's
Christian Associations-Phila-1857-1st ed-12mo   (5m6)   7.50

SMYTH,W -Narr of a Journey from Lima to Para-Lond-1836-Murray-
8vo-hf mor-3 maps(2 fldg)-10 plts-1st ed (4h9,rbnd)55 (5n9)   65.00

SMYTHE,F S-An Alpine Journey-Lond-1934-Gollancz-351p-cl
(5d7)   10.00

--Climbs in the Canadian Rockies-Lond-(1950)-Hodder&Stoughton-
260p-cl   (5d7)   12.50

--Camp Six-Lond-(1956)-219p-illus-cl   (5d7)   6.00

--Climbs & Ski Runs-Edinb-1929-illus-307p-cl-Blackwood (5d7) 12.50

--Edward Whymper-Lond-(1940)-Hodder&Stoughton-330p-illus-
cl-fldg maps   (5d7)   17.50

--The Kangchenjunga Adventure-Lond-1930-Gollancz-464p-
illus-cl-1st ed   (5d7,fade)   15.00

--Kamet Conquered-Lond-1932-Gollancz-420p-illus-fldg map-
cl-1st ed   (5d7)   20.00

--The Mountain Scene-Lond-1937-Black-153p-illus-cl (5d7)   7.40

--Rocky Mountains-Lond-1948-1st ed-4to-149p-16 col plts plus
48 plts   (4a8) 10.   (4b9,dj tn)   12.00

--The Valley of Flowers-Lond-1938-322p-2 maps-16 col photos
(5w3,fade) 6.50 (5d7)   10.00

SMYTHE,H-Historical Sketch of Parker Co & Weatherford,Texas-
StL-1877-cl-476p-ads-1st ed
(4d5,sl wn,box) 200.   (5z7,f bndg)   185.00

SMYTHE,R M-Obsolete Amer Securities & Corp-NY-1904-
illus-979p-lg8vo-cl-1st ed-scarce   (5p5)   22.50

--Valuable Extinct Securities-NY-1929-398p   (5h8)   10.00

SMYTHE S M-Ten Months in Fiji Islands-Oxf&Lond-1864-illus-
282p   (5q0,libr labls)   10.00

SMYTHE,W-Narr of Journey from Lima to Para-Lond-1836-Murray-
8vo-part mor-3 maps (2 fldg)-10 plts-1st ed
(4h0,rbnd,lacks 2p ads,vg)   55.00

SMYTHE,WM E-History of San Diego,1542 to 1908-SanDiego-
1908-History Co-2 vols in 1-buck   (5tt0)   30.00

SNAITH,STANLEY-At Grips with Everest-Lond-1937-240p-illus-
cl-Percy Pr   (5d7)   7.50

SNAPE,ANDREW-Anatomy of an Horse-Lond-1683-M Flesher-
2 parts in 1-(12)237p,45(6)p-49 plts-folio-part mor-illus-
1st ed   (4t9)   600.00

SNEAD,THOS L-Fight for Missouri from Election of Lincoln to
Death of Lyon-NY-1886-maps-1st ed   (5m2)   8.50

SNEDEKER,CAROLINE DALE-Theras & His Town-GardenCty-
1924-illus-252p-frontis-1st ed   (5p1,spot)   5.00

SNEDEKER,FLORENCE W-A Family Canoe Trip-NY-1892-illus
(5c1)   15.00

SNELGRAVE,WM-New Account of Some Parts of Guinea & The
Slave Trade-Lond-1734-Knapton-fldg map-8vo-calf-288p-
1st ed   (4e1,rbkd)   350.00

SNELL,DAN'L W-Manager's assistant:being a condensed treatise
on cotton manufacture-Hartf-1850   (5g4)   15.00

SNELL,GEO D-Root,Hog & Die-Caldwell-1936-8vo-418p-1st ed
(5g2)   8.00

SNELL,JAS-A practical guide to operations on the teeth-Phila-
1832-plts-orig bds-cl bk-papr labl   (5g3,libr labl)   27.50

SNELL,ROY J-Arctic Stowaways-Chig-1935-180p   (5ss1)   2.00

SNIDER,C H J-Glorious "Shannon's" Old Blue Duster etc-Tor-
1923-430p-plts   (4f9) 12.50   (5aa0) 8.50   (5p9)   10.00

--The Griffon-Tor-1956-24p-illus-bds-ltd ed (5w8) 15. (4h3) 20.00

--Story of the "Nancy" & Other 1812ers-Tor-1926-334p-7 col plts-
5 maps   (4f9,f) 12.50   (5aa0)   5.00

SNIDER,DENTON J-Writer of Books in His Genesis-StL-n.d.-
(1910)-668p-cl-scarce   (5h2)   10.00

SNIVELY,JOHN H-Treatise on Manufacture of Perfumes & Kindred
Toilet Articles-Nashvl-1877-illus-8vo   (4m6,rub,soil)   15.00

--same-Nashvl-1890-248p-illus   (5w3,crack)   6.50

SNIVELY,R D-Pottery-NY-(1946)-Old Deerfield Series of
Handicraft Manuals-86p   (5n7)   2.50

SNOHOMISH COUNTY,WASH-The Richest on Puget Sound-
Press of Everett Daily Herald-Jun 1905-59p-illus-pict wrps,
flds to 10x4½   (5r0)   12.50

SNOW,CALEB H-History of Boston-Bost-1825-maps-400p-illus
(4b3,needs rbndg)   25.00

--same-Bost-1828-Abel Bowen-8vo-orig bds-3 maps-14 plts-
2nd ed   (5L1,rprd)   20.00

SNOW,EDGAR-Christmas Escapade in Japan-(Phila-Ruttle,Shaw &
Wetherill)-n.d.-dbld sheets-ed of 300c,nbrd   (5b2)   5.00

SNOW,EDW ROWE-Famous New Engl Lighthouses-Bost-(1945)-
457p-plts   (5c3)   5.00

--Great Storms & Famous Shipwrecks of the New Engl Coast-
Bost-1943-338p-illus-col frontis-1st ed
(5h9,autg) 10.   (5m2,fade)   8.50

--New England Sea Tragedies-NY-1960-310p-illus (5h9,f) 6.50

SOCIETY FOR PROPAGATING THE GOSPEL AMONG INDIANS-
(Cambridge)-1887-sm4to-ltd to 225c   (5xx7)   17.50

SOCIETY OF COLONIAL WARS-Complete Set of Registers-
NY,BOST,etc-1894 to 1941-10 vols-ex scarce   (5h9)   185.00

SOCIETY OF 1st DIVISION-History of 1st Div During the WW,
1917 to 1919-Phila-1922-Winston-1st ed-450p-col illus (5mm8)10.00

SOCIETY OF FRIENDS,LONDON-Yearly Meeting,Meeting for
Sufferings,Facts Relative to Canadian Indians...-Lond-1839-
Harvey&Darton-8vo-unbnd   (5mn8)   55.00

SOCIETY OF ILLUSTRATORS-NY-1911-annual-Vol 1-illus-4to
(5ww3)   20.00

SOCIETY OF MAYFLOWER DESCENDANTS IN STATE OF NY-
NY-1912-illus-orig g.dec cl-4th rec bk,Oct 1912-ltd to 750c
(4m9)   20.00

SOCIETY OF NAVAL ARCHITECTS & MARINE ENGINEERS-
Transactions of-Vols 1 to 68-1893 to 1960 (5s1,f,lacks Vol 65) 600.00

SOCIETY OF PRIVATE BIBLIOPHILES-Memoirs of Dolly Morton-
Phila-1904-303p-illus-16mo-wrps   (5t4)   25.00

SODDY,FREDK-Interpretation of Radium & Structure of the Atom-
NY-1920-8vo-cl-260p-4th ed,rev   (5t0)   5.00

SODERHOLTZ,E E-Colonial Architecture & Furniture-Bost-(1895)-
58 plts,loose as issued-cl case wi ties   (5t2,sl fray)   18.50

SOHMER & CO-Catalogue,pianos-NY-1885-wrps-24p-14 illus
(4h8,wn)   12.50

SOIL & WATER-Albuqu-1936-USDA-4to-173p-mimeo-illus (5g6) 17.50

SOILAND,ALBERT-Saga of Newport Bay & Newport Harbor
Yacht Club-LosAng-(1936)-12mo-bds-66p   (4t1,pres)   12.50

--The Viking Goes to Sea-LosAng-1924-Times Mirror-126p-
illus-cl   (5d6)   10.00

SOKOLOFF,BORIS-Napoleon,A Doctor's Bibliography-NY-1937-
292p-illus   (5t4)   10.50

SOLA,A E IRONMONGER-Klondyke,Truth & Facts of New
El Dorado-Lond-1897-port-3 maps-4to-102p-24 plts (5zz8) 35.00

SOLANO & NAPA CO,CALIF-History of-LosAng-1912-lea-4to-
illus   (5F5,crack)   40.00

SOLBERG,THORVALD-Copyright in Congress,1789 to 1904-Wash-
1905-468p   (5j4)   15.00

--Copyright in England-Wash-1912-54p-wrps   (5j4)   6.00

SOLDIER TURNED FARMER-Northampion-1840-J Metcalf-wrps-
tiny 8p chapbook   (5v2)   8.50

SOLDIER'S ALBUM,A-Lond-1826-prntd by & for SWFores-12mo-
col frontis-bds-1st ed   (5t4,wn,pres)   15.00

SOLDIERS' & SAILORS' HALF DIME TALES-of the late Rebellion-
NY-1868-Soldiers'&Sailors' Pub Co-Vol 1,#1-pict wrps-
1st ed   (5m2,wn)   8.50

SOLDIER'S GUIDE,THE-By an officer in US Army-Phila-(c1861)-
prntd wrps   (5g4)   10.00

SOLDIERS HYMN BOOK WITH TUNES-NY-n.d.(ca 1864)-128p-
pict bds   (5h7,wn)   5.00

SOLEY,JAS RUSSELL-The Blockade & The Cruisers-NY-1888-
257p-maps-Navy In Civil War Series   (5w4)   6.50

--The Sailor Boys of '61-Bost-(c1888)-Estes&Lauriat-381p-
frontis-pict cl   (5p1)   7.50

SOLICITOR-Journal for Solicitors & Their Managing Clerks-
(Lond)-Vol 1 thru 28-1934 to 61-bound
(5ii7,ex-libr-lacks Vol 19,20,21)   195.00

SOLICITOR QUARTERLY-Lond-1962 to 65-Vol 1 thru 4,(all publ)-
bnd   (5ii7,ex-libr)   45.00

SOLIS,ANTONIO DE-Historia de la Conquista de Mexico-Barcelona-
1691-Llopis-lg4to-vel-titl in red & black-2nd ed (5n9) 185.00

--same-Paris-1827-calf-5 vols   (5qq8,v wn,lacks sps)   20.00

--History of Conquest of Mexico-Lond-1724-Woodward-port-
2 maps-6 plts-folio-hf mor-1st Engl ed   (4e1)   100.00

SOLLY,V N-Gardens for Town & Suburb-NY-(1926)-112p-plts-
bds   (5s7,rub)   5.00

SOLMS BRAUNFELS,CARL-Texas,1844,45-Houston-1936-1st Amer ed-
141p-port-map   (5i3,f)   17.50

SOLON,L M-The Art of the Old English Potter-Lond-1885-illus
(5j3)   25.00

SOLON,LEON V-Polychromy-NY-1924-8vo-orig bds-cl bk-illus-
1st ed   (5m6)   12.50

SOLORZANO PEREIRA,JUAN DE-Politica Indiana-Antwerp-1703-
Verdussen-sm folio-vel-port   (5n2)   225.00

SOME ACCOUNT OF CONDUCT OF RELIGIOUS SOCIETY
OF FRIENDS-towards Indian Tribes in Settlement of Colonies
of East & West Jersey and Pa-Lond-1844-Edw Marsh-frontis-
2 col maps-247p-scarce   (5t3,rbnd)   15.00

SOME LETTERS OF EDGAR ALLAN POE-To E H N Patterson of
Oquawka,III-Chig-1898-Caxton Club-32p-6 facs(5ww4,stnd) 25.00

SOME MERCHANTS & SEA CAPTAINS OF OLD BOSTON-Bost-
(1918)-53p-wrps-State St Trust Co   (5jj9)   4.00

SOME THOUGHTS CONCERNING DOMESTIC SLAVERY-Batl-
1838-(John L Carey)-1st ed (5ss5,ex-libr) 22.50 (5m4)   40.00

SOMERVELL,T HOWARD-After Everest-Lond-339p-illus-cl-
    Hodder&Stoughton -1936   (5d7)   10.00

SOMERVILLE,ELIZ-Flora,or The Deserted Child-1800-12mo-calf-
    Longman&Rees-g.borders-120p-frontis-1st ed   (4d1)   35.00

--History of Little Phoebe & the Reclaimed Child-Hartf-(1815)-
    Sheldon&Goodwin-illus wrps   (5v2,chewed)   32.50

SOMERVILLE,J A-Man of Color-LosAng-1949-1st ed   (5x2)   8.50

SOMERVILLE,MARY-Physical Geography-Lond-1858-8vo-port-
    4th ed,rev   (5m6)   7.50

SOMMERS,JANE R-Two Bequests-Phila-(1870)-1st ed-v scarce
    (5mm1)   50.00

SOMMERVILLE,MAXWELL-Siam on the Meinam from The Gulf
    to Ayuthia-Phila-1897-Lippincott-237p-map-illus   (5p0)   7.50

SOMERVILLE,THOS-Hist of Great Brit During Reign of Queen Anne-
    Lond-Strahan-1798-lg4to-674p-hf mor (5a1,sl hng damage)   20.00

SOMERVILLE,W-Hobbinol,Field Sports & the Bowling Green-
    Lond-1813-R Ackermann-4to-hf calf   (5b0)   45.00

SOMERVILE,WM-The Chase to which is annexed,Field Sports wi
    life of author-Lond-1809-Albion Pr-fore edge painting (5d2)100.00

SON OF A GENIUS-A Tale,for the use of Youth-Lond-1812-
    J Harris-(B H Hofland)-1st ed-frontis-advts at front & bk
    (5c8)   35.00

SONG,REV ELI S-Lyndon B Johnson-Seoul,Korea-1964-229p-illus
    (4c7,dj,sl case)   12.50

SONGS FOR GRAND ARMY-1898-Wait & Dana,Howard,publ
    (5yy3)   5.00

SONGS FOR MY CHILDREN-Bost-(1861)-sm12mo-192p-col frontis-
    (5v0,wn)   6.00

SONG OF SONGS,THE-Lond-1950-Collectors Book Club-folio-
    mor-Wigmore Bindery-ltd to 100c   (5d9)   75.00

SONGS FOR THE LITTLE ONES AT HOME-NY-(c1852)-Amer
    Tract Soc-288p-frontis-cl blind stmpd-a.e.g.-24mo
    (5p1,rub)   15.00

SONNECK,OSCAR-Catalogue of First Editions of Edward McDowell-
    Wash-1917-cl-89p (5yy1,autg) 9.50 (5p7) 12.50 (5j4)   7.50

--Dramatic Music,Catalogue of Full Scores-Wash-1908-170p-
    wrps   (5p7) 15. (5j4)   12.50

--Orchestral Music Catalogue-(Class M 1000 to 1268)-Scores-
    Wash-1912-GPO-663p   (5p7)   32.50

SONNENBERG,G J-Radar & Electric Navigation-Lond-1951-
    272p-illus   (5s1)   5.00

SONNERAT,PIERRE-Voyage uax Indes Orientales et a la China-
    Paris-1782-Chez l'Auteur,et al-8vo-calf-lea lables
    7 fldg plts-3 vols-2nd ed   (4h0,chip,crack)   125.00

--Voyage a la Nouvelle Guinee-Paris-1776-Ruault-4to-
    tooled calf-120 plts(some fldng)-1st ed   (5n9)   250.00

SONNICHSEN,ALBERT-Ten Months a Captive Among Filipinos-
    NY-1901-Scribners-388p   (5x9)   4.50

SONNICHSEN,C L-Alias Billy the Kid-Albuqu-1955-8vo-
    illus-photos-1st ed   (4t8,5m9) 6.50   (5g2,f)   7.00

--Billy King's Tombstone-Caldwell-1942-1st ed   (5kk4,f,dj)   17.50

--same-Caldwell-1946-cl-233p-2nd printing (5m9) 8. (4t8)   6.50

--Cowboys & Cattle Kings-Norman-1950-1st ed (5g2,f,dj,autg) 12.50

--I'll Die Before I'll Run-NY-(1951)-294p-   1st ed-scarce
    photos   (5yy7)   10.00

--Roy Bean:Law West of the Pecos-NY-1943-207p-1st ed-scarce
    (4t8) 8.50   (5a8)   10.00

--Ten Texas Feuds-1957-Univ of NewMex Pr-1st ed
    (4t8,dj,5x5,dj)   7.50

SONNINI,C S-Travels in Upper & Lower Egypt-Lond-1799-40 engr-
    8vo-calf-g.bks-3 vols   (4e1)   35.00

--same-Lond-1800-4to-illus-map   (5yy6,rbnd)   20.00

SONOMA CO,CALIF-Illustrated History of-Chig-1889-Lewis-
    ports-4to-lea-scarce   (5F5,crack)   65.00

SONS OF CONFED VET,THE-The Gray Book-(n.p.,n.d.)-
    (ca 1920)-dec wrps-53p plus 1p   (5r0,underline)   7.50

SONTIE,M-The Wolf Cub-Indnpls-1927-281p-illus   (5a9)   5.00

SONVESTRE-Popular Legends of Brittany-Bost-1856-sm8vo-
    16 hand col plts   (5v0)   10.00

SOPHOCLES-ANTIGONE-Chapman,transl-Bost-1930-Houghton,Miff-
    8vo-dec bds-ltd to 550c,nbrd(4m8,box)10.(5b0,box,unopnd)   12.50

SOPHOCLES-The Tragedies-(Thos Francklin,transl)-Lond-
    R Francklin-1758,9-4to-2 vol in 1-cl-1st ed (5a1,wtrstn) 17.50

SORCHO SUGAR-Experiments wi Chinese Cane-Cinn-(c1857)-
    wrps-illus-120p-catalog   (5yy0,lacks front wrps)   12.50

SOREL,E-La Grande Industrie Chimique Minerale-Paris-1902-
    809p-illus   (5w1,ex-libr)   5.00

SORENSEN,CHAS E-My 40 Years with Ford-NY-1956-Norton-
    345p-illus   (5p7)   5.00

SORENSEN,THEODORE C-Kennedy-(1965)-Harper-orig glassine
    wrpr,boxed-ltd to 1963c,nbrd,autg   (5F1,vf)   27.50

SORENSON,ALFRED-History of Omaha,from pioneer days to
    present time-Omaha-1889-342p-ports-illus (4t2) 12.50 (4t8)15.00

--Story of Omaha from Pioneer Days etc-Omaha-1923-651p plus
    index   (4t8,pres)   15.00

SORLEY,M E-Lewis of Warner Hall-1935-887p   (5t9)   37.50

SOROKIN,P A-Reconstruction of Humanity-1948   (5L7)   4.50

SOROKIN,PITIRIM A-Systematic Source Book in Rural Sociology-
    Minnpls-1930-2 vols-1st ed (5w5,sl underline)   25.00

SORREL,G MOXLEY-Recoll of a Confed Staff Officer-NY-1905-
    frontis-315p-1st ed   (4t8,ex-libr)   45.00

SOSEY,FRANK H-Robt Devoy-(Palmyra-1903)-172p-v scarce
    (5y0,stnd) 10.   (4t8,pres)   12.50

SOTELO,REGIL,LUIS F-Campeche En La Historia-Mexico-1963-
    2 vols-stiff wrps   (5n4)   15.00

SOTHEBY,S L-Principia Typographica-Lond-1858-3 vols-folio-illus
    (5ii2,wn)   150.00

SOTHEBY,WM,transl-The Georgies of Virgil-Middletown,Conn-
    1808-12mo-bds-45p,(1)   (5t2,crude rbnd)   5.00

SOTHERAN,CHAS-Horace Greeley...& Other Pioneers of Amer
    Socialism-NY-1892-343p plus ads-Soc Sci Libr   (5w4)   7.50

--same-NY-1915-Kennerley-349p   (5qq8)   6.00

SOUDER,MRS EDMUND A-Leaves From the Battle Field of
    Gettysburg-Phila-1864-144p-1st ed (5w0,pres) 12.50 (5r0) 7.50

SOUILLARD,F A-The Pharmaceutical Practical Recipe Book-NY-
    (?186-)-12mo-wrps-94p   (5w3,wn)   12.50

SOULE,CMDR C C-Intern'tl Law for Naval Officers-Annap-1928-
    245p   (5s1,wn)   3.50

SOULE,FRANK-Annals of San Francisco-NY-1855-illus-fldg maps-
    lea-824p-1st ed (5g4,rehngd) 32.50 (4n1,rbnd) 60.
    (5dd5,crack) 45.   (4n1,rbkd)   75.00

--same-Palo Alto-1966-reprint-ltd to 60c-lea,box (5t1,mint) 150.00

SOULE,S H-Rand McNally Guide to Great Northwest(incl BC &
    Alaska)-Chig-1903-366p-illus-68p adv-port-cl
    (5s0,ex-libr,soil) 10.   (5aa0)   15.00

SOULE,WINSOR-Spanish Farm Houses & Minor Public Bldgs-NY-
    1924-4to-98p of plts   (5xx7)   12.50

SOULES,FRANCOIS-Hoistoire des Troubles de l'Amerique Anglaise-
    Paris-1787-Chez Buisson-4 vols-3 fldng maps-bds-calf bks-g.
    (5L1)   50.00

SOURCES OF INFORMATION ON MILITARY PROFESSIONAL
    SUBJECTS-Wash-1898-501p-wrps   (5yy1)   25.00

SOUSA,JOHN PHILIP-The Fifth String-Indnpls-(1902)-blu cl-
    illus by H C Christy-1st ed   (5ee3)   3.50

SOUSA SARMENTO,PEDRO DE MARIZ DE-Preceitos de Construccao
    de Navios etc-Lisbon-1789-sm4to-wrps-185p,(2)-fldg table
    (5ss2)   57.50

SOUTH,THE-Letter from a Friend in the North-Phila-1856-8vo-
    46p-wrps-The Author-(S Colwell)   (5j5)   15.00

SOUTH AFRICA-Ofc Year Book of Union & of Basutoland,
    Bechuanaland Protectorate & Swaziland-Pretoria-1934-Gov Prntr-
    #15,1932,33-1119p-maps (4 fldg)   (4t5)   10.00

SOUTH AFRICA,UNION OF-Rpt on Natives of SW Africa & Their
    Treatment by Germany-Lond-1918-212p-13 plts-lg folio
    (5c6,wrp defects)   47.50

--State of the Union-Year Bk 1956 to 60-J'burg-1959-449p
    (5c6,f)   13.75

SOUTH AMERICA-View of SoAmer & Mexico,etc-by a citizen of
    the US-NY-1825-Huntington,Jr-12mo-frontis-calf-2 vols in 1
    (4c4,cor wn) 60.   (5y0)   25.00

SOUTH AMERICA PILOT-Wash-1916-2 vols-buck-fldg maps &
    charts-1st ed   (5dd5)   10.00

SOUTH & EAST AFRICA-Year Book & Guide,1937 ed-Lond-Sampson
    Low,Marston-1168p plus 64p maps-pict cov   (4t5)   10.00

SOUTH BEND & ST JOSEPH CO-In Northern Ind-Hist Background of-
    Schuyler Colfax Chapt DAR,comp-(SoBend)-1927-71p-bds(5h1)6.50

SOUTH BOSTON & DORCHESTER,MA -Atlas-Vol3-Phila-1874-
    GMHopkins&Co-folio-cl-73p&4p-maps in col   (5t2)   20.00

SO CAR & GA,HISTORICAL ACCOUNT OF-Lond-1779-
    Donaldson-2 vols-4to-calf-1st ed   (5n1,rprd,box)   275.00

SOUTH CAROLINA-Constitution of...adopted by Constitutional
    Conv-Charleston-1868-Reconstruction Constitution-stitchd
    (5g4,lf tn wi loss)   10.00

SOUTH CAROLINA-Constitution of State of With Ordinances
    Appended-Charleston-1868-Denny&Perry-46p-self wrps-
    Reconstruction Constitution   (5m3,t.pg sl tn)   45.00

SOUTH CAROLINA-Economic & Social Conditions in 1944-1945-
    Univ SoCar Pr   (5x2,wn)   20.00

SOUTH CAROLONA,GUIDE TO PALMETTO STATE-NY-(1941)-
    photos,map-pkt map-e.p. map-1st ed-Amer Guide Ser
    (4L5,dj,stns) 6.   (5p9) 5.   (5x5,dj)   10.00

SOUTH CAROLINA-Journal of provincial congress of SoCar-1776-
    Charleston prntd,Lond reprntd,1776-JnAlmon-8vo-disbnd-
    lf of ads-rare   (5i9)   175.00

SOUTH CAROLINA LAW REVIEW-1948 to 69-Vol 1 thru 21-
bound   (5rr4, recent rbnd) 350.00
SO CAROLINA LAW REVIEW-1948 to 70-Vol 1 thru 32-bnd
                         (5ii7) 380.00
SO CAROLINA-Public Laws of,(1694 to 1788)-n.p.-(ca 1790)-
4to-   (5r7, v poor, lacks 26 lvs) 40.00
SOUTH ILLUSTRATED, THE-NoCarolina, The South Illustrated-
Aiken, SoCar-Bost-(ca 1880)-illus-pic wrps (5g3) 15.00
SOUTH DAK HISTORICAL COLLECTIONS-State Hist Soc-
Vol 3, 1906-Aberdeen-1906   (5L2, ex-libr, stnd) 8.50
--same-Vol 10, 1920-Pierre-(1921)   (5L2) 8.50
--same-Vol 22, 1946-Madison-n.d.   (5L2) 5.00
SOUTH DAK HIST RECORDS SURVEY-Inven of Co Archives of So Dak-
Mitchell-1940 to 41-stiff wrps-4to-5 vols   (4i2) 35.00
SO DAK HISTORICAL REVIEW-Vols 1, #1, Oct, 1935 thru Vol 2, #4,
Jul, 1937(all publ)-orig wrps bnd in   (5L2, rbnd) 15.00
SOUTH DAKOTA-Memorial & Biographical Record-Chig-1898-
Geo A Ogle&Co-1st ed-1102p-photos-lea-scarce (4t8, chip) 85.00
SOUTH DAKOTA-More facts about-(Milwkee, 1893, 4)-illus-wrps
                         (5g4, sl tn) 15.00
SOUTH DAKOTA WRITERS' PROJECT-Legends of the Mighty
Sioux-Chig-1941-WPA   (4k5) 20.00
SOUTH DAKOTA'S-Beautiful Black Hills-Mitchell-(1926)-265p-
photos-ports   (5s4, wn) 12.50
SOUTH HANOVER COLLEGE & IND THEOLOGICAL SEMINARY-
Catalog of Officers & Students of SoHanover-1834-16p-disbnd
                         (5h1) 12.50
SOUTH IN THE BUILDING OF THE NATION, THE-A History-
Richmond-1909-12 vols-illus   (5m2, bkstrps v wn) 25.00
SOUTH KENSINGTON MUS-Catalog, Descrip of the Glass Vessels
in-Lond-1878-4to-22 plts(9 col)-218p-lea   (5w7, scuff) 14.50
SOUTH, ROBT-Sermons Preached Upon Several Occasions-Oxf-
1679-H Haall-12mo-300p   (5t7, rbnd) 20.00
SOUTH SEA BUBBLE, THE-& Numerous Fraudulent Projects to which
it gave rise in 1720-Lond-1825-ThosBoys-sm12mo-143p-
orig prntd bds   (5s9, wn, stnd) 20.00
SOUTHARD, C Z-Evolution of Trout & Trout Fishing in Amer-NY-
1928-4to-254p-col illus-maps   (5ii2) 7.50
SOUTHARD, CHAS Z-Trout Fly Fishing in Amer-NY-1914-4to-cl-
15p, 288p-20 col plts-Leonard   (5t0) 25.00
SOUTHBY, SUSAN-Costumes of the Holy Land-Beirut-1953-
ltd ed in folder-6p col drawings-folio   (5jj3) 17.50
SOUTHERDEN, SAM'L-The censor or gleanings in Sussex-Lond-
1807-M Allen-12mo-hf calf-1st ed   (5l8, rub, stns) 15.00
SOUTHERN BAPTIST REVIEW-Nashvl-1858-Vol 4, 4 nbrs-buck
                         (5h6, rbnd) 30.00
SOUTHERN CALIFORNIA-1892-98p-wrps-maps   (5r1) 10.00
SOUTHERN CALIF HISTORICAL SOC ANNALS-1890 to 1939-
wrps(most in folders)   (4n1, lacks 1892) 195.00
SOUTHERN CALIFORNIA ILLUSTRATED-Geo Rice, Publ, LosAng-
(LosAng, 1883)-4to-col pict wrps-map&illus   (5g3) 10.00
SOUTHERN CALIFORNIA-Illus History of-Chig-1890-Lewis-
plts-mor-898p   (4n1, hng crack) 35.00
SOUTHERN, KATE-Sad Case of Mrs Kate Southern-Phila-(1878)-
31p, (1)p-wrps   (4t7, chip) 12.50
SOUTHERN LADIES-The Living Female Writers of the South-
ed by Author of "Southland Writers"-Phila-1872-Claxton,
Remsen&Haffelfinger-sm sq4to-hf calf-568p   (5L8) 17.50
SOUTHERN LADY'S COMPANION, THE-A Monthly-Vols 6 & 7,
Apr, 1852 thru Mar, 1854   (5h6, cov wn) 60.00
SOUTHERN LAW REVIEW-Nashville, StLouis-1872 to 83- Vol 1
thru 11, (all pub)-bnd   (5ii7, ex-libr) 125.00
SOUTHERN N ENG TYPOGR SERV-Type Specimen Book, #6-
NewHav-n.d.-(ca 1945)-sm4to-pict bds-109p-spiral bnd(5t0) 7.50
SOUTHERN PACIFIC CO-Road of a Thousand Wonders, Coast Line
Shasta Route from Los Ang to Portland-SanFran-1907-4to-
pict cards-72p-col illus (5s4) 5.   (5m9) 7.50
SOUTHERN PACIFIC CO-Sunset Route & Scenic Wonders of Ariz
from ElPaso, Tex to LosAng, Calif via-n.p.-n.d.c1910-
25 col views-obl-orig pict wrps   (5x5) 7.50
SOUTHERN PRIMER, THE-or Child's 1st Lessons in Spelling & Reading-
Charleston(S C)-1860-WmR Babcock & M'Carter on wrp-
impr of Adolphus Morris(t.pg)-12mo-36p-scarce (5v2, f) 32.50
SOUTHERN RHODESIA-Standing Rules & Orders of Legis Assembly
Relating to Publ Business & Priv Bills-Rhodesia-1934-Gov Prntr-
302p   (4t5, dj) 10.00
SOUTHERN SCENES & SCENERY-Charleston-By a southern lady-
1856-Southern Baptist Publ Soc-12mo-cl-1st ed (5i9, fox) 80.00
SOUTHERN SENTINEL, THE-Vol 1, #18-Alexandria, La-Jul 14, 1863-
1p prntd on wallpapr   (5d6, wn) 60.00
SOUTHERN TABLE BOOK-Charlstn-1857-24p-pict wrps(5h2) 10.00

SOUTHERN TRANSCONTINENTAL RWY, THE-Its Pacific Terminus-
SanDiego-1870-SanDiego Chamber of Comm-8p-wrps-rare pamph
                         (5L2) 75.00
SOUTHERN WORKMAN, THE-May & Jun, 1903-Hampton-2 vols
                         (5z5, vg) 17.50
--same-Hampton-Feb, May, Jun, 1902   (5x2) ea 7.50
SOUTHERNER, THE-A Press Reference Book-NewOrl-1945-456p
                         (4p8) 12.50
SOUTHESK, EARL OF-Saskatchewan & Rocky Mountains-Edinb-
1875-1st ed-448p-illus-2 fldg maps   (5i3, hng sl weak) 25.00
SOUTHEY, ROBT-Metrical Tales & other poems-Lond-1805-Longman,
etc-12mo-cl-1st ed   (5l8) 40.00
--Poems, containing the Retrospect, Odes, Elegies, Sonnets etc-
By Robt Lovell & Robt Southey, of Baliol(sic)College, Oxf-Bath-
1795-12mo-cl-labl-auth's 1st book-1st ed   (5gg6) 37.50
--Poems-Bristol-1797-8vo-calf-mor labl-N Biggs, prntr-
2nd ed(so stated)-final lf of ads   (5x3, f) 60.00
--Thalaba the Destroyer-Lond-1801-2 vols-sm8vo-orig calf-1st ed-
scarce   (5p5, f) 35.00
SOUTHGATE-Thru my window at Southgate-LosAng-(1918)-
ChasB Hopper-31p-wrps   (5d6) 10.00
SOUTHOLD, L I-Yennycott Folks-NY-(1910)-illus-1st ed
                         (5jj3, dj) 15.00
SOUTHWARD, JOHN-Principles & Progress of Printing Machinery-
Lond-n.d.(ca1890)-Menken-4 fldg plts-156p-orig cl (5tt9) 10.00
SOUTHWEST HISTORICAL SERIES-Glendale-1931 to 42-12 vols-
4to-g.tops-maps-plts   (5dd9) 350.   (5m8) 195.00
SOUTHWEST REVIEW-Winter, complete issue-Dallas-1945 (4a5) 12.50
--New Mexico Special Number-Summer, 1946   (4a5) 8.50
SOUTHWEST TEXAS FROM SAN ANTONIO TO EL PASO-Houston-
1911-Passenger Dept, Sunset Rte-12mo-wrps-90p   (4t1) 10.00
SOUTHWESTERN LAW JOURNAL-SMU-1947 to 68-Vol 1 thru 22-
bnd   (5ii7) 495.00
SOUTHWESTERN LAW REVIEW-LosAng-1916 to 18-Vol 1 & 2-bnd
                         (5ii7) 28.50
SOUTHWORTH, A S-4,000 Miles of African Travel-NY-1875-
maps-illus   (5x2) 15.00
SOUTHWORTH, MRS EMMA-A noble lord-Phila-(1872)-Peterson-
1st ed (ads dated '72)   (5m2) 10. (5i0, vf) 12.50
SOUTHWORTH, J R-The Mines of Mexico-Mexico-(1905)-
Engl & Spanish text-folio   (5x5) 35.00
SOUTHWORTH, MAY-101 Beverages-SanFran-(1904)-87p, (3)-
narr8vo   (5w1) 5.00
--One Hundred & One Entrees-SanFran-(1904)-Paul Elder-
pict stiff wrps-88p   (4g9, scuff) 7.50
--101 Desserts-SanFran-(1907)-Paul Elder-pict cl-88p (4g9) 7.50
--101 Mexican Dishes-SanFran-(1914)-Paul Elder-pict stiff wrps-
88p-scarce   (4g9) 10.00
SOUVARINE, BORIS-Stalin:A Critical Survey of Bolshevism-NY-
(1939)-690p-2nd prntg   (5ss6) 5.00
SOUVENIR-Also see Place or Subject
SOUVENIR OF CALIF MID WINTER INT'L EXPO-SanFran-1894-
JosAHofmann-37p-photogravures   (4a5) 27.50
SOUVENIR OF CENTENNIAL EXHIBITION-or, Connecticut's
Representation at Phila, 1876-Hartf-1877-8vo-illus (5m6) 10.00
SOUVENIR GOLDEN JUBILEE-Nov 20, 21, 22, 1910-StFrancis
Solanus Parish & Franciscan Fathers-n.p.-n.d.-(Quincy-1910)-
212p-cl   (5h1) 10.00
SOUVENIR OF PORTLAND, ORE & VICINITY-Portl-1904-
J K Gill-31 plts-obl 12mo-orig wrps   (4g6, sl shaken) 9.00
SOUVENIR OF A RIDE ON THE FERRIS WHEEL-at World's Fair,
Chig-Chig-1893-obl 4to-orig wrps-16p-13p illus
                         (5m6, bk cov tn) 30.00
SOUVENIR OF SETTLEMENT OF THE NW TERRITORY AT MARIETTA,
O-View Book-Marietta-1888-Chamberlain&Strecker-12mo-
orig cl-12 lvs-fld out   (5m6) 10.00
SOUVESTRE, EMILE-Attic Philosopher in Paris-NY-1894-194p-
12mo   (5ww3) 12.50
SOVIET LITERATURE MONTHLY-for 1949-Moscow-1949-12 nos.-
wrps   (5r9) 12.50
SOWDEN, LEWIS-South African Union-Lond-1945-Robt Hale-
220p plus 26p photos   (4t5, dj) 5.00
--Union of SoAfrica-NY-1943-illus-1st ed (5x7) 5. (5x2, dj) 6.50
SOWELL, A J-Early Settlers & Indian Fighters of SoWest Texas-
Austin-1900-844p-photos   (5L2, rbnd) 125. (4t8, spots) 145.00
--Life of "Big Foot" Wallace-Austin-(1957)-facs of orig ed-123p-
photos   (5L2) 7.50
--Rangers & Pioneers of Texas-SanAnt-1884-411p-illus-cl-
1st ed-rare   (5t3, fade) 235.00
SOWER BIBLE-Biblia, Das Ist-Germantown-1743-1st ed, 2nd issue-
Christoph Sauer-calf bk, metal corners-scarce
                         (5nn6, lacks fly) 300.00
SOWERBY, A De C-Nature in Chinese Art-NY-1940-illus (5t5) 6.50

SOWERBY,A De C (continued)
--Naturalist in Manchuria-Tientsin-1923 to 30-Tientsin Pr-orig cl-
plts-fldg map-Vols 2 to 5(only) bnd in 2 vols-4to-v scarce
(4p5) 92.00

SOWERBY,MILLICENT-Rare People & Rare Books-Lond-(1967)-
Constable-t8vo-248p-orig buck (5L8,mint,dj) 7.50

SOWERBY,JAS-British Minerology-Lond-1804 to 1811-4 vols-mor-
g.-a.e.g.-400 hand col plts (5j2) 95.00

SOWERS,PAULINE B,transl-Joan the Maid of Orleans-SanFran-
1938-Grabhorn-wdcuts-folio-ltd to 525c (4n1,dj) 20.00

SOWLE,HENRIETTA-I Go A'Marketing-Bost-1900-237p
(5c0,broke) 7.50

SOYER,ALEXIS -Modern Housewife or Menagere-NY-1866-
364p,10p (5c0,shake) 10.00

--A Shilling Cookery for the People-Lond-1855-12mo-194p-port
(5c5,rbnd) 7.50

SOYER,NICOLAS-Soyer's Paper Bag Cookery-NY-1911-12mo-
130p (5c0) 3.50

--Soyer's Standard Cookery-NY-1912-436p-col illus (5c0,soil) 8.50

SPAETH,SIGMUND-A History of Popular Music in Amer-NY-(1948)-
RandomHse-8vo-cl-729p (5j5) 7.50

--Read 'Em & Weep-GardenCty-1927-267p-illus (5w9) 6.50

--same-NY-(1945)-Arco-248p (5p7) 5.00

SPAFFORD,HORATIO G-Gazetteer of State of NY-Albany-1813-
map-8vo-calf-fldg frontis (4c1) 15.00

--same-1824-620p-map (5ff2,rbnd) 20.00

SPAIGHT,A W-The Resources,Soil & Climate of Texas-Galveston-
1882-360p (5n4) 17.50

SPAIN & SPANISH AMERICA-In Libraries of Univ of Calif,A
Catalogue of Books-Berkeley-1928-4to-cl-2 vols (4j6) 125.00

SPAKES,EDWIN E,ed-Lincoln Douglas Debates of 1858-Sprngfld-
1908-627p-3/4 lea (5h2) 7.50

SPALDING,ALBERT G-America's National Game-NY-1911-illus-
8vo-orig bds-cl bk-542p-1st ed
(4c8,crack) 15. (5ss1,hng loose) 12.50 (5w5) 22.50

SPALDING,C C-Annals of City of Kansas-KansCty-1858-plts-
116p-ex rare-lea (5cc4,rbnd) 485.00

--same-(Columbia,Mo-1950)-1950 reprint (5k2) 8. (5h5) 10.00

SPALDING,CHAS W-Spalding Memorial-1897-2nd ed-1276p-cl
(4n9,4t2,stn) 35.00

SPALDING,HENRY H-Indians West of the Rocky Mountains-Bost-
Missionary Herald,Mar,Oct,Dec 1837-orig wrps-3 vols-
1st ed-v rare (4k7) 125.00

--Oregon Indians, Letter from Mr Spaulding-Bost,Missionary Herald,
Oct 1838, Dec 1839, June, 1840-orig wrps-rare (4n4) 85.00

SPALDING,HENRY S-Sheriff of Beech Fork-NY-(1903)-223p-cl
(5ff7,f,dj) 5.00

SPALDING,J A-Illustrated Popular Biography of Connecticut-
Hartf-1891-ports-4to (4b6) 10.00

SPALDING,JOHN L-Kentucky Pioneer-(Champaign-1932)-cl
(5ff7) 6.50

SPALDING,M J-Sketches of Early Catholic Missions of Kentucky-
Louisville&Baltimore-n.d.-308p (5jj9,rbnd lea) 55.00

--Sketches of Life,Times & Character of Rt Rev Benedict J Flaget-
1852-1st issue (5L7,rprd,wn) 50.00

SPALDING,PHINEAS-Spalding Memorial & Personal Reminis-
(Haverhill,NH)-1887-323p-port (5t9) 7.50 (5t4) 6.00

SPALDING,SUSAN M-Winter Roses-(1888)-EdwNewton&Co-
lea bk&bds (5mm2,7 li inscr by Newton) 30.00

SPALDING,WM-Italy & the Italian Islands-Edinb-(1841)-
Oliver&Boyd-fldg maps-thk8vo-calf-3 vols in 1 (4c1) 35.00

SPALDING,WM A-History & Remin,LosAngeles City & Co,Calif-
LosAng-(1931)-J R Finnell-4to-t.e.g.-cl-3 vols (4t1) 37.50

SPALTEHOLZ,WERNER-Hand Atlas of Human Anatomy-Phila-n.d.-
3 vols-4to-col illus-cl-2nd ed (5p5) 35.00

SPANISH AMERICAN DIRECTORY-Directorio Hispano Americano-
LosAng-1921-27&28p-wrps (5d6) 15.00

SPANISH AMERICAN WAR-Note on the Office of Naval
Intelligence-Wash-1900-maps-8 items in 1,as issued,ea wi
orig wrps in orig cl (5ss5) 17.50

SPANISH AMERICAN WAR-Pictorial Souvenir of..-NY&Phila-1899-
lg8vo-fldg bds-16 plts (4h8,f) 7.50

SPANISH & INDIAN NEW MEXICO-Denver-1895-cl folder with
long foldout of photos (4a5) 15.00

SPANISH INTERIOR-14th to 17th CENTURY-NY-n.d.-lg4to-cl-
illus-136 plts-Architectural Bk Publ (5xx7) 15.00

SPANUTH,JURGEN-Atlantis,The Mystery Unravelled-NY-1956
(5a8,f,dj) 5.00

SPARGO,JOHN-Return of Russell Colvin-Bennington-1945-8vo-
87p-wrps-illus (5q0,5xx7) 10.00

--Stars & Stripes in 1777-Bennington-1928-4to-col frontis-illus-
qtr mor-57p (5t0,pres) 7.50

SPARGO,JOHN (continued)
--Two Bennington Born Explorers & Makers of Modern Canada-
n.p.-1950-135p-plts-port (5dd0) 8.50 (5e8,autg) 7.50 (5w8)10.00

SPARHAWK,FRANCES C-A lazy man's work-NY-1881-Holt-
1st ed (5m2) 6.50

SPARKES,BOYDON-The Witch of Wall St-GardenCty-1935-338p-
illus (5w5,stn) 3.50

SPARKS,EDWIN ERIE-The Expansion of the Amer People-Chig-
1900-461p-illus-maps-g.t.-12mo (5h9) 8.50

SPARKS FROM A FLINT-Odd Rhymes for Odd Times-Lond-1890-
by E V L-16mo-cl-1st ed (5gg6) 25.00

SPARKS,JARED-Life & Treason of Benedict Arnold-Harper-1860-
Lib Amer Biog (5e8,sl wn) 8.00

--The Life of Geo Washington-Bost-1839-562p-lea (5s2,f) 22.50

--same-Bost-1855-Little,Brown-562p-frontis (5qq8) 4. (5xx5) 6.75

--Life of Gouverneur Morris-Bost-1832-Gray&Bowen-3 vols-
orig cl &bds (5tt8,shaken,lacks labels) 30.00

--Life of John Ledyard-Cambridge-1828-Hilliard&Brown-1st ed-
325p-orig bds,cl bkstrp (5w5) 110.00

--same-Cambr,Mass-1829-pict cl-310p (4p2,rub,fox) 14.75

--same-Bost-1847-12mo-orig cl-419p-illus-Lib Amer Biog (5h9) 8.50

SPARLING,H HALLIDAY-The Kelmscott Press & Wm Morris
Master Craftsman-Lond-1924-8vo-bds-cl bk-frontis-
16 plts (5ee9,dj) 37.50

SPARRMAN,ANDREW-Voyage to Cape of Good Hope etc...
1772 to 1776-Lond-1785-for Robinson-4to-mor-fldg map-
10 plts-2 vols-1st ed in Engl (4h0,f,sl rub) 250.00

SPARROW,WALTER SHAW-Geo Stubbs & Ben Marshall-NY-1929-
Scribner-80p-plts-t4to-ltd to 250c (5x0) 25.00

--Henry Akin-Lond-1927-1st vol of series-4to-55p-8 col plts
(4a6,fox,dj) 40.00

--Our Homes & How to Make the Best of Them-Lond-1909-280p-
4to-30 col plts(6 dbl pg) (5w7,chip) 12.50

--Prints & Drawings by Frank Brangwyn wi some other phases of
his art-Lond-1919-Lane-288p-lg4to-col plts
(5m7,hng broke,wn) 18.50

SPARROY,WILFRID-Persian Children of the Royal Family-
Lond&NY-1902-8vo-349p,(4)-42 plts-dec cl (5p1,ex-libr) 10.00

SPARRY,C-The Illustrated Christian Martyrology-Phila-1851-
Gihon-t8vo-cl-254p-woodcuts (5j5) 25.00

SPAULDING,CHAS S-Acct of Some of Early Settlers of West
Dunstable-Monson&Hollis-1915-251p (5e8) 10.75

SPAULDING,E WILDER-New York in Critical Period 1783 to 89-
1932-315p (5ff2) 10.00

SPAULDING,EDW S-Adobe Days Along the Channel-n.p.-
(SantaBarbara)-1957-illus(some col)-ltd to 1015c
(4t8,4n1,box,5x5) 25.00

--Ed Borein's West-SantaBarb-1952-lg4to (4a5) 25.00

--Santa Barbara Club,a History-SantaBarb-1954-Schauer Prntg-
8vo-cl-col frontis-131p-ltd to 250c (4t1) 17.50

SPAULDING,JOHN H-Historical Relics of White Mntns-Bost-1855-
frontis-1st ed-16mo-96p-cl-g.stmpd (5u9,f) 30. (5i3) 20.00

SPAULDING,THOS M-Early Military Books in Univ of Mich
Libraries-AnnArbor-1941-45p-37 plts-4to (5u1) 12.50

SPEAKMAN,HAROLD-Mostly Mississippi-NY-1927-illus-360p
(4j4) 5.00

SPEAKMAN,THOS H-Divisions In The Society of Friends-Phila-
1869-16mo-63p-1st ed (5w5) 6.50

SPEAR,ELSA-Ft Phil Kearny Dakota Territory 1866 to 1868-
Sheridan,Wyo-1939-(36p)-(9 photos)-wrps-1st ed-ltd to 500c
(5L2,f) 5.00

SPEAR,JOHN W-Grace Winslow-NY-1883-Tibbals-1st ed (5x4) 12.50

SPEARE,D E-American Watch Papers-Worcester-1952-wrps-3 plts-
76p-4to (5bb0) 6.00

SPEARE,EVA A-Colonial Meeting Houses of New Hampshire compared
with their contemporaries in New Engl-n.p.-(1938)-DAR-sm8vo-
cl-15p,238p (5t2) 5.00

SPEARE,JACK W-In Rochester 100 Years Ago & Now-Rochester-
1931-46p-illus-bds (5hh6) 5.75

SPEARING,HERBERT G-Childhood of Art-Lond-1930-Benn-
417 plts & illus-548p-thk8vo-2 vols-cl-2nd ed rev (5m5) 32.00

SPEARMAN,ARTHUR D-5 Franciscan Churches of Mission Santa
Clara-PaloAlto-(1963) (5x5,dj) 15.00

SPEARMAN,C-Abilities of Man,Their Nature & Measurement-
Lond-1927-Macm-8vo-orig cl-1st ed (5ee5) 25.00

--same-Abilities of Man-NY-1927-1st ed (5yy6) 10.00

SPEARMAN,FRANK H-Nan of Music Mountain-NY-1916-8vo-cl-
430p-Wyeth,illus-4 col plts (5t2) 8.50

--The Strategy of Great RR's-NY-1904-maps-287p
(5ee3) 4.50 (5t4) 6.00

--Whispering Smith-NY-1906-Scribner-NCWyeth,illus
(5F1,rub) 8.50 (5b2) 10.00

SPEARS, GEO M-Dear Old Kentucky-Cinn-1900-296p-cl
(5ff7,pres)   7.50
SPEARS, JOHN R-American Slave Trade-NY-1900-232p-illus
(5xx7)   25.00
--Capt Nathaniel Brown Palmer-NY-1922-252p-illus (5w0)   10.00
--David G Farragut-Phila-(1905)-407p-maps-frontis-1st ed
(5ee3,f,pres)   10.00
--The Fugitive, A Tale of Adventures of Clipper Ships-NY-1899-
Scribner's-325p-illus   (5x4)   10.00
--History of Mississippi Valley-NY-1903-1st ed-illus-maps-416p
(5i3)   12.50
--History of Our Navy-NY-1897-4 vols-illus-maps (5w5,spots)   15.00
--same-NY-1899-Scribners-5 vols-8vo-illus-orig buck
(5s1) 25.   (5t5)   15.00
--Illus Sketches of Death Valley & Other Borax Deserts of Pacific
Coast-Chig-1892-226p-wrps-   (5h7) 35.   (5L0,chip)   25.00
--Short History of Amer Navy-NY-1907-134p-pict bds (5h2)   5.00
--Story of the New Engl Whalers, 1640 to 1901-NY-1910-10 illusts
(5c1)   15.00
SPEARS, RAYMOND S-Trip on Great Lakes...Summer, 1912-Columbus-
1913-212p-plts-maps-by a skiff traveler   (5aa0)   7.50
SPECK, FRANK G-Beothuk & Micmac-1922-illus-map (4k5)   7.50
--Chapters on Ethnology of Powhatan Tribes of Virginia-NY-
1928-Mus of Amer Indian-455p-photos-wrps-fldg map (5L0,f)   7.50
--Montagnais Art in Birchbark-NY-1937-157p-illus-16mo-
card cov-Mus of Am Indian   (4b9)   15.00
--A Study of the Delaware Indian Big House Ceremony-Harrisburg-
1931-Pa Hist Comm-Vol 2-8vo-wrps-192p-illus
(5h5) 7.50   (5h9)   13.50
--The Tutelo Spirit Adoption Ceremony-Harrisburg-1942-8vo-cl-
125p-illus   (5h5)   8.00
SPECTATOR, THE-Lond-1712 to 1715-8 vols-8vo-dec mor-g.e.-
(Jos Addison,ed)   (5d9, Maj Abbey copies)   350.00
--same-Lond-n.d.-(ca 1788)-8 vols-12mo-frontis-g.-crushed mor
(5b0,f bndg)   55.00
--same-Lond-1803-mor-g.labls-engrs-16mo-8 vols   (5.bb1)   75.00
--same-Lond-1822-calf-6 vols   (5bb1)   60.00
--same-Phila-1830-2 vols in 1-lea   (5k1)   15.00
SPECTORSKY, AUGUST C,ed-The Book of the Sea-NY-1954-
64p of illus   (5c1)   12.00
SPECTRE MOTHER, THE-or the haunted tower-NY-1823-
W Borradaile-12mo-blue wrps-1st Amer ed-col frontis (5i0)   30.00
SPECULATION, OR MAKING HASTE TO BE RICH-Bost-1840-
80p-cl-Wright 2483-scarce   (5h7,wn,stn)   22.50
SPEDON, A L-Tales of the Canadian Forest-Mont-1861-221p
(5dd7)   12.00
SPEECHLY, WM-Treatise on Culture of the Pineapple & Management
of Hot House-NY-1796-orig bds-8vo-6 plts(some fldg)-2nd ed
(5z9,cov wn)   27.50
--Treatise on the Culture of the Vine-Lond-(1779)-6 plts-
300p,(12)-calf   (5w1,rbkd)   60.00
SPEED, JAS-Opinion on Constitutional Power of the Military to
Try & Execute Assassins of the President-Wash-1865-16p-
wrps   (5r7) 7.50   (5g3,f)   10.00
SPEED, JOHN GILMER-The Horse in Amer-NY-1905-8vo-illus-
1st ed   (5m6)   12.50
SPEER, JOHN-Life of Gen James H Lane-GardenCty, Kans-1896-
1st ed (5ii1,lacks fly) 22.50 (4t8) 20. (5k0) 35. (5yy8,pres)25.00
SPEER, O-Texas Jurists-1936   (5ff4,ex-libr)   10.00
SPEER, R E-Of One Blood-NY-1924-12mo   (5x2)   10.00
--Race & Race Relations-NY-1924   (5x2)   10.00
SPEER, WM S-The Encyclopedia of the New West-Marshall, Tex-
1881-US Biog Publ-1010p plus index-ports-t.lea-rare
(5L2,rub)   150.00
SPEIDEL, WM C, JR-You Can't Eat Mt Rainier-Portl-1955-134p-
illus   (5g9)   3.00
SPEILMAN, M H-Kate Greenaway-Lond-1905-A&CBlack-20p, 301p-
col illus-lg8vo-cl   (5t2,fade)   18.00
SPEISER, EPHRAIM A-Mesopotamia Origins-Phila-1930 (5x7)   7.50
SPEKE, JOHN HANNING-Journal of the Discovery of the Source
of the Nile-NY-1864-map-ports-illus-orig cl   (5j2)   15.00
SPELL, LESLIE D-Forgotten Men of Cripple Creek-Denv-1959-
Big Mountain Pr   (5x5)   7.50
SPELLER, FLORENCE C-Garden Clubs, Their Activities &
Organization-NY-1931-159p-plts-frontis   (5s7)   5.00
SPELTZ, A,ed-Coloured Ornament of All Historical Styles-n.d.-
folio-3 vols-plts in fldrs   (5L7)   45.00
SPENCE, CATHERINE ELLEN-The author's daughter-Lond-1868-
Richard Bentley-3 vols-8vo-orig cl-1st ed (5x3,lacks labls) 55.00
SPENCE, G-Equitable Jurisdiction of Court of Chancery-Phila-
1846 to 50-2 vols   (5ff4,rebnd)   17.50
SPENCE, JAS-The Amer Union-Lond-1862-4th ed-scarce
(5m2,autg)   18.50

SPENCE, JOS-Anecdotes, Observ & Characters of Books & Men-
Lond-WHCarpenter-1820-501p-illus (5a1) 25. (5mm2,rbnd) 22.50
SPENCE, LEWIS-The Magic & Mysteries of Mexico-Lond-n.d.-
illus   (5x5)   12.50
--Myths & Legends of NoAmer Indians-1922-393p-col plts
(4b9,sp wn)   12.00
--Myths of the NoAmer Indians-Lond-1930-col plts-map-393p
(4d2)   12.50
--same-NY-n.d.-374p plus index-illus-30 col plts   (5L2,f)   10.00
--Myths & Legends of Ancient Egypt-Lond-1949-lg8vo-cl-370p-
frontis   (5t2,f,dj)   5.00
SPENCE, ROBT J-John Markle, Representative American-NY-1929-
8vo-illus-crushed mor-raised bands-ltd to 300c
(5ss5,f bndg,pres)   30.00
SPENCE, T H-Martin Larwin-NY-1954-1st ed   (5x2,dj)   8.50
SPENCE, THOS-Manitoba et le Nord Ouest du Canada, etc-Ottawa-
1875-Seconde Ed rev   (5nn8)   55.00
--Prairie Lands of Canada....compared with...of US-Montr-
1879-Gazette Prntg House-56p-12p ads   (5aa1)   25.00
--Saskatchewan Country of NW of Dominion of Canada...latest
info-Montr-1877-Lovell-fldg map-60p   (5aa1)   100.00
--Settler's Guide in the US & British NoAmer Provinces-NY-1862-
frontis-col map-illus   (5w8)   50.00
SPENCER, AMBROSE-Narrative of Andersonville-NY-1866-272p-cl
(5jj9)   15.00
SPENCER, BELLA-Tried & True-Springfield-1866-394p (4b4,fox) 7.50
SPENCER, CHAS L-Knots, Splices & Fancy Work-Glasgow-1944-
193p,8p   (5n7)   3.50
SPENCER, DORCAS JAS-History of WCTU of No & Central Calif-
Oakland-(1913)-WestCoast Prnt-cl-illus-ports-169p-errata sheet
(4L9)   15.00
SPENCER, EDW-Cakes & Ale-England-1913-282p-4th ed (5g9)   5.00
--The Flowing Bowl-Lond-1903-Grant Richards Pr-243p-bds (5g9) 6.50
SPENCER, FRANK C-Education of the Pueblo Child-Columbia Univ-
Doctoral thesis-NY-1899-wrps   (5g4)   10.00
SPENCER, HERBERT-The Principles of Psychology-Lond-1855-8vo-
orig cl-1st ed   (5ee9)   75.00
--Social Statics-Lond-1851-8vo-cl-1st ed of auth's 1st book
(5gg6,hf t.rprd)   25.00
SPENCER, J A-Complete History of the US of Amer-n.p.-Phila-c1878-
4 vols in 2-sm4to-hf mor-illus-a.e.g.-raised bands (5w5)   15.00
--History of the US,...to the Adminis of J Buchanan-NY-(1858)-
3 vols-plts-hf lea-4to   (5ee3)   25.00
--History of the USA-NY-(1874)-4to-illus-4 vols   (5yy0)   17.50
SPENCER, J W-Reminis of Pioneer Life in the Mississippi Valley-
Davenport(Iowa)-1872-8vo-port-cl-73p-for complimentary
distribution-v scarce   (5a3)   75.00
SPENCER, J W-Early Day of Rock Isl & Davenport-Chig-1942-
302p plus index-frontis-Lakeside Classic (5a9) 7.50 (4t8)   6.50
SPENCER, LLOYD-History of the State of Wash-NY-1937-4 vols-
4to-buck-illus-Amer Hist Soc   (5F5)   37.50
SPENCER, O M-The Indian Captivity of-Chig-1917-12mo-g.t.-188p-
frontis-(Lakeside Classic)   (5h9)   10.00
SPENCER, OMAR C-Story of Sauvies Island-Portl-c1950-
Binsford&Mort-12mo-cl-134p   (4t1)   6.50
SPENCER, PLATT R-Spencerian Key to Practical Penmanship-
NY-1869-176p-illus   (5n7,wn)   4.50
SPENCER, R H-Thomas Family of Talbot Co, Md & Allied Families-
1914-180p-ltd to 150c   (4t2)   30.00
SPENCER, S R-Booker T Washington & the Negro's Place in
Amer Life-Bost-1955-1st ed   (5x2)   4.50
SPENCER, STANLEY-Scrapbook Drawings of Stanley Spencer-Lond-
1964-Lion&Unicorn Pr-Royal College of Art-sm folio-60p illus-
ltd to 400c   (5d9)   25.00
SPENCER, SYDNEY-Mountaineering-Lond-Lonsdale Libr Vol 18-
383p-illus-cl-Seeley, Service   (5d7)   10.00
SPENCER, SYLVIA-Up From the Earth, A Collection of Garden Poems-
Bost-1935-305p   (5w3,fade)   6.50
SPENCER, THEODORE, ed-A Garland for John Donne-1931-
Harvard Univ Pr   (5ss9,f,dj)   10.00
--The Paradox in the Circle-Norfolk-1941-New Directions-
1st ed-orig red wrps   (5tt2)   7.50
SPENCER, THOS E-A Missourian Worth Remembering-StL-1930-wrps-
44p-2 photos-1st ed-priv prntd-ltd to 100c   (5L2)   20.00
SPENCER, WM L-A plucky one-NY-(1886)-Cassell-pict cl-
1st ed   (5m2,sl shake)   13.50
SPENDER, STEPHEN-Forward from Liberalism-Lond-1937-8vo-cl-
1st ed   (5dd8,dj)   15.00
--Learning Laughter-Lond-(1952)-Weidenfeld&Nicolson-8vo-cl-
1st ed   (4g1,f,dj)   15.00
--The New Realism-Lond-1939-Hogarth Pr-12mo-orig wrps-24p-
1st ed   (4g1)   12.50

SPENDER,STEPHEN (continued)
--Poems of Dedication-Lond-(1947)-Faber&Faber-1st ed
    (4g1,sp fade) 7.50
--World Within World-(Lond,1951)-1st ed
    (5r9) 10.00
SPENDLOVE,F StGEO-The Face of Early Canada-Tor-1958-
   Royal Ontario Museum-4to-128 illus (5w8) 15.00
--Collector's Luck-Tor-(1960)-illus-20p,208p (5w8,5t4) 15.00
SPENGLER,OSWALD-Decline of the West-NY-1926-Knopf-
   2 vols (4b5) 30.00
--Der Untergan Des Abendlandes-Munich-1920,22-2 vols-1st ed
    (5j2,crack) 35.00
SPENSER,EDMUND-Daphnaida & Other Poems-WLRenwick,ed-
   Lond-1929-Scholartis Pr-243p-cl-ltd ed (5m1) 7.50
--The Faerie Queene,Disposed into Twelve Bookes,Fashioning 12
   Morall vertues,The 2nd Part...Containing 4th,5th &6th Bookes-
   Lond-1596-Wm Ponsonby-4to-mor-by Riviere-2 vols-
   1st complete ed (4L1,f bndg,neatly annotated) 4,000.00
--Faerie Queen-Lond-prntd by HL for Mathew Lownes-1611,13-
   sm folio-illus-calf-1st collected ed,2nd issue (5hh0) 400.00
--The Faerie Queene...new ed,wi notes by Ralph Church-Lond-
   1758,9-WmFaden,prntr-4 vols-8vo-hf mor-1st prntg,this ed
    (5x3) 50.00
--The Faerie Queene,Disposed into 12 Bookes Fashioning 12
   Morall Vertues-1923-Ashendene Pr-folio-180c prntd
    (4h5,spec bndg) 950.00
--The Faerie Queene-Lond-1897-Dent-2 vols-4to-g.t.-
   Muckley,illus-t.pgs in blk & red-orig g.dec cl-ltd to 1250 sets
    (5t5) 37.50
--Poetical Works-Bost-1839-Little,Brown-8vo-orig cl-5 vols
    (4h0,f) 45.00
--The Poetical Works of-Lond-1926-JCSmith,ed-Oxf Univ Pr-
   736p (5p9) 3.50
--The Works of-Oxf-1930-Shakespeare Head Pr-4to-mrbld papr bds-
   calf sp-8 vols-illus-ltd to 350 sets (4h5,sp dark) 275.00
SPENSER,MARY CLARE-Brinka,An Amer Countess-NY-1888-
   Spenser-8vo-dec cl (5b2) 6.00
SPERANSKY,A D-Basis for the Theory of Medicine-1935 (5L7) 10.00
SPERANZA,G-Race or Nation-Indnpls-1925 (5x2) 12.50
SPERLIN,OTTIS BEDNEY-Heart of the Skyloo-Portl,Or-1934-
   e.p. maps-344p (4b2,pres,sl soil) 6.00
SPERLING,H,transl-The Zohar-Lond-1931-Soncino Pr-g.t.-5 vols-
   t8vo-orig cl-ltd ed (5t5) 35.00
SPERRY,ALBERT L-Avalanche-Bost-(1938)-165p-photos (5s4,fade)12.50
SPERRY,ARMSTRONG-Wagons Westward-Chig-1936-276p-cl-
   illus-1st ed (5g5) 5.00
--same-Phila-1936-Winston-276p-illus (5p7) 4.00
SPETTIGUE,D-The Friendly Force-n.d.-(ca 1951)-134p-illus(4b9)6.00
SPICE ISLANDS COOK BOOK,THE-Menlo Pk,Calif-(1961)-
   4to-illus-hard bnd (5c0) 5.00
SPICER,DOROTHY G-From an English Oven-NY-1948-123p (5c5)4.50
SPICER-SIMSON,THEODORE-Men of Letters of the British Isles-
   NY-1924-Rudge-4to-cl bkd bds-Bruce Rogers-1st ed-ltd to 520c
    (5r9) 20.00
SPIELMANN,M H-Kate Greenaway-Lond-1905-frontis-cl-
   col plts-1st ed (5c8,lacks frontis) 15. (5v2,fade) 25.00
--same-Lond-1905-thk4to-orig cl-26 col illus-ltd to 500c,autg John
   Greenaway-orig pencil drawing bnd in (5tt7) 200.00
--History of "Punch"-NY-1895-592p-g.t.-1st ed-4to
   (5p5) 15. (4b4,4F6,f bndg) 20.00
--Hugh Thomson,His Art,his Letters,his Humour & his Charm-Lond-
   1931-269p-illus-cl-1st ed (5c8) 17.50
--The Rainbow Book,Tales of Fun & Fancy-Lond-1912-8vo-290p-
   col frontis-illus by Rackham&others-1st ed (5v0,f) 20.00
SPIELMANN,PERCY EDWIN-Catalogue of the Library of Miniature
   Books,collected by-Lond-(1961)-4 plts-ltd to 500c,nbrd
    (5c8,mint,dj) 25.00
SPIER,LESLIE-Analysis of Plains Indian Parfleche Decoration-Seattle-
   1925-(U of Wash Vol1,#3) (5h4) 2.00
--Ghost Dance of 1870 Among the Klamath of Oregon-Seattle-
   1927-(Uof Wash Vol 2,#2) (5h4) 2.75
--Growth of Japanese Children Born in Amer & in Japan-Seattle-
   1929-(U of Wash Vol3,#1) (5h4) 2.50
--Wishram Ethnography-Seattle-1930-(U of Wash Vol 3,#3)-8vo-
   wrps (5h4) 10.00
SPIETH,J-Die Religion der Eweer in Sued Togo-Gottingen-1911-
   316p-wrps (5c6,vg) 15.75
SPIKES,NELLIE W-Through the Years,History of Crosby Co,Texas-
   SanAnt-1952-493p-illus (4a5) 20. (5a8) 15.00
SPILLER,BURTON L-Grouse Feathers-NY-(1935)-4to-illus-
   Derrydale Pr-ltd to 950c (5j3) 18.00
--same-NY-1947-illus (5kk7,dj) 9. (4a1) 12.50
--More Grouse Feathers-NY-n.d.-(c1938)-Derrydale Pr-illus-
   ltd ed-ltd to 950c (4a9,ink on h.t.) 40.00

SPILLER,BURTON L (continued)
--Thoroughbred-NY-(1936)-sm4to-illus-ltd (5yy6,sl rub) 15.00
SPILLER,R E,ed-Literary History of US-NY-1948-3 vols (5mm1) 20.00
SPILLER,ROBT E-Descriptive Bibliography of Writings of Jas
   Fenimore Cooper-NY-1934-illus-260p-1st ed-ltd to 500c (4g2)45.00
--Fenimore Cooper,Critic of His Times-NY-1931-illus-1st ed
    (5mm2) 10.00
SPILSBURY,E G-Wire Rope Tramways-Trenton,NY-1890-Trenton
   Iron Co-8vo-flex cl-illus-35p (5j5) 7.50
SPINDEN,HERBERT J-Ancient civilizations of Mexico & Central
   Amer-NY-1917-227p-1st ed (5L2) 7.50
--same-NY-1922-242p-Amer Mus of Nat Hist-Handbook Ser #3,
   2nd&rev ed (5x0) 7.50
--same-NY-1948-8vo-cl-fldg map-47 plts-3rd &rev ed-4th prntg
    (4a3) 5.00
--same-NY-1949-photos-258p plus index (5L2) 5.00
SPINDLER,WILL H-Bad Lands Trails-Mitchell,SD-(1948)-
   12mo-96p-ports-stiff wrps (5L2) 7.50 (5dd6) 8.50
--same-Mitchell-(1952)-2nd prntg (5L2) 3.00
SPINGARN,J E-History of Literary Criticism in Renaissance-
   NY-1925 (5yy6) 6.00
SPINK,J G TAYLOR-Official Baseball Record Book 1942-StL-
   c1942-495p,17p-illus 1 (5w4,lacks front wrp) 3.50
--The Sporting News Dope Book 1948-StL-c1948-illus-157p,(3)-
   pict wrps (5w4) 4.00
SPINKS,WM WARD-Tales of the British Columbia Frontier-Tor-
   1933-134p-10 plts (4d2) 12.50
SPINNERS' BOOK OF FICTION-SanFran-(1907)-illus-8vo-
   1st ed-1st bndg(tweed cl) (5b2) 12.50 (4m8) 15.00
SPIRIT OF THE NATION,THE-Ballads & Songs-Dublin-(1882)-
   JasDuffy&Sons-frontis-4to-cl (5t7,libr labl) 20.00
SPIRIT OF THE ROANOKE,THE-A Pageant of Halifax Co History-
   Roanoke Rapids-1921 (5h6) 10.00
SPIRIT OF THE TIMES-NY-Aug 1884 to Jul 1886-Vols 108 thru 111-
   bnd in 2 vols-thk folio-hf roan (5r7,cov loose) 75.00
SPIVAK,JN L-Devil's Brigade-n.p.-(1930)-325p-cl-1st ed
    (5h1,dj,5x5) 17.50
SPLAINE,HENRY-Memorial History of 17th Regiment,Mass Vol Inf
   in Civil War-Salem-1911-illus-(14)402p(1) (5mm8,pres) 5.00
SPLAN,JOHN-Life With the Trotters-Chig-1889-8vo-1st ed
    (5m6) 9.00
SPLAWN,A J-Ka mi akin,Last Hero of Yakimas-(Portl,Or)-1917-
   photos-1st ed-v scarce (4t8,cov wn,hng weak) 35.00
SPLINT,SARAH F-The Art of Cooking & Serving-Cinn-(1926)-
   Proctor & Gamble-252p (5c9) 2.50
--The Rumford Modern Methods of Cooking-Prov,RI-n.d.-64p
    (5g9) 3.00
SPOFFORD,AINSWORTH-Amer Treasury of Facts,1886-Rochester-
   1886-HHWarner-12mo-312p-prntd wrps (5j5) 7.50
--Public Libraries of US-NY-1870-23p-wrps (5yy1) 6.50
--Rare books relating to the Amer Indians-NY-1901-15p-wrps(5j4)6.00
SPOFFORD,MRS HARRIET ELIZ-Azarian,An Episode-Bost-
   1864-Ticknor&Fields-251p-1st ed (5x4) 12.50
SPOFFORD,HARRIET PRESCOTT-The Elder's People-Bost-1920-
   Houghton-1st ed (5m2) 5.00
--The Servant Girl Question-Bost-1881-181p (5w7) 5.00
--The Thief in the Night-Bost-1872-1st ed (5mm2) 7.50
SPOFFORD,HORATIO GATES-Gazetteer of New York State-
   Albany-1813-Southwick-8vo-fldg frontis map-2 plts-1st ed
    (4c4,fox,scuff) 45.00
SPOFFORD,J-John Spofford,Desc who settled at Rowley,Mass in
   1638-1869-127p (4t2) 10.00
--Gen Record of Families Spelling their name Spofford,Spafford,
   Spafard-1888-502p (4t2) 30.00
SPOFFORD,THOS-Illinois Farmers' Almanac for...1843-
   Chig&Illinois-(1842)-S F Gale & Co-12mo-stitched-18 lvs-rare
    (4c1,lf tn wi sl loss) 125.00
SPOLANSKY,JACOB-The Communist Trail in Amer-NY-1951
    (5x7) 3.75
SPOONER,SHEARJASHUB-Anecdotes of Painters,Engravers,Sculptors
   & Architects & Curiosities of Art-NY-1853-Putnam-3 vols
    (4e0,fade) 30.00
SPOONER-Records of Wm Spooner of Plymouth,Mass-Cinn-1883-
   Vol 1(all publ)-694p (5a9) 20. (4t2) 22.50
SPOONER,WALTER W-Back Woodsmen-Cinn-1883-608p-cl-
   1st ed-v scarce (5jj9,sl rub) 35.00
SPORTING SCENES & SUNDRY SKETCHES-NY-1842-Gould,
   Banks&Co-2 vols-12mo-3/4 mor-t.e.g.-1st ed (5x1,f bndg) 45.00
SPORTSMAN'S ENCYCLOPEDIA-NY-(1947)-311p-illus (5t7,dj) 7.50
SPORTSMAN'S LIBRARY,THE-NY-1940-ltd to 600c-Ernest R Gee,ed
    (4g2) 22.50
SPOTSWOOD,ALEX-Official Letters of-Richmond,(Va)-1882-
   8vo-cl-frontis-2 vols (5t2,libr labl) 15.00

SPOTTISWOODE,WM-A Tarantasse Journey Through Eastern
Russia in Autumn of 1856-Lond-1857-hf lea-8vo-258p-col plts-
fldg map   (5v7,hng split,ex-libr)   10.00

SPOTTS,DAVID L-Campaigning with Custer & the 19th Kans
Vol Cavalry-LosAng-1928-Brininstool,ed-8vo-cl-215p-map-
13 plts-800c prntd-nbrd-(many were burned) (5h4,2 autg) 37.50
--same-LosAng-1928-rare lg papr ed(many were burned)
         (5kk4,f)   65.00

SPRAGUE,CHAS-The Prize Ode written...&Recited at
Representation of Shakespeare Jubilee,Boston,Feb 13,1824-
(Bost,1824)-8p-8vo-sewn as issued-1st ed of auth's 1st publ
         (5gg6)   25.00

SPRAGUE,ISAAC-Beautiful Wild Flowers of Amer-Troy-1887-
10p col plts-folio-1st ed   (5ee3,rub)   5.00

SPRAGUE,J T-The Treachery in Texas,etc-NY-1862-Pr of Rebellion
Record-64p-wrps   (5z7,vf)   25.00
--same-NY-1862-wrps-36p,dbl col   (4t8)   15.00

SPRAGUE,JESSE RAINSFORD-An Amer Banker-NY-1929(5F0,f) 5.50

SPRAGUE,JOHN FRANCIS-Sebastian Rale-Bost-1906-illus (5g4) 6.00

SPRAGUE,JOHN T-Annual Report of the Adj Genl of State of NY-
Albany-1864-2 vols-cl   (5j6)   12.50

SPRAGUE,MARSHALL-Massacre,the Tragedy at White River-Bost-
(1957)-8p-illus-photos-1st ed (4t8,f,dj) 6.   (5hh3,dj)   7.50
--Money Mountain-Bost-(1953)-330p plus index-photos-1st ed
         (4t8,dj)   7.50

SPRAGUE,WARREN V-Sprague Families in America-Rutland-1913-
Tuttle Co-8vo-cl-578p,8p   (4t1)   37.50

SPRATLIN,V B-Juan Latino,Slave & Humanist-NY-Spinner Pr-
1938-R8vo   (5x2)   35.00

SPRATLING,WM-Little Mexico-NY-(1932)-illus-1st ed
         (4t8,pres)   12.50

SPRENGEL,C M-Allgemeines historisches Taschenbuch...enthaltend
fuer 1784 die Geschichte der Revolution von Nord America-
Berlin-(1783)-Haude&Spener-24mo-orig dec bds-g.e.-
col fldng map-18 plts(3 col)   (5n2)   175.00

SPRENGER,J A-The Leave Areas of the Amer Exped Forces,
1918,19,Records-Phila-1928   (5p0)   4.00

SPRIGGE,ELIZ-Gertrude Stein,Her Life & Work-NY-Harper&Bros-
1957-1st ed   (5ss9,f,dj)   8.50

SPRIGLE,RAY-In the Land of Jim Crow-NY-1949-215p
        (4j4,ex-libr) 3.50 (5x2)   6.50

SPRING,AGNES WRIGHT-Caspar Collins,Life & Exploits of an
Indian Fighter of the 60s-NY-1927-Columbia U Pr-cl-187p-
illus-map   (4L9,dj) 10. (5bb4,wn dj)   12.50
--The Cheyenne & Black Hills Stage & Express Routes-Glendale-
1949-17 plts-1st ed   (4t8)   30.00
--The Cheyenne Club-KansCty-1961-wrps-1st ed-(118c printed)-
v scarce   (4k1) 25. (5hh3,publ autg) 20. (4t8) 40.00
--Pioneer Years in Black Hills by Rich B Hughes-Glendale-
1957-photos-1st ed   (4t8,unopened)   25.00
--Wm Chapin Deming of Wyoming,Pioneer Publisher etc-Glendale-
1944-531p-photos-g.t.,ltd (5dd5) 12.50 (5s4,autg,f) 15.00

SPRING,ARTHUR L-Beyond the Rio Grande-Bost-1886-orig wrps-
8vo-70p-1st ed   (4g6,lacks bkstrp)   5.00

SPRING BLOSSOMS-a Choice Collection of Hist & Literary
Essays & Orig Poems-Ogden,Utah-May, 1880-48p,removed-
no wrps   (5t3)   15.00

SPRING FLOWERS-NY-1948-Hyperion Pr-32 litho-sm folio
        (5qq7,dj)   25.00

SPRING,GARDINER,ed-Memoirs of Rev Sam'l J Mills,Late
Missionary to the SW Section of the US-NY-1820-247p-
orig bds-1st ed   (5m3,wn)   37.50

SPRING,JAS W-Boston & the Parker House-Bost-1927-cl-230p-
illus   (5t0)   4.00

SPRING,LEVERETT WILSON-Kansas-Bost-(1885)-(Commonwealth
Series)-327p plus index-fldg map   (4t8)   6.50

SPRING-RICE,SIR CECIL-Letters & Friendships of,A Record-
Bost-1929-2 vols-Gwyn,ed   (5q8)   10.00

SPRINGER,JOHN S-Forest Life & Forest Trees-NY-1851-illus-
259p-g.t.   (5w3,scuff)   12.50
--same-NY-1856-illus-2nd ed (5m6,ex-libr)   12.50

SPRINGER,T G-The Californian-NY-(1936)-1st ed (5yy6,pres) 7.50
--Dword Peddler-NY-1928-1st ed   (5yy6,pres)   6.00
--Sagebrush Buckaroo-NY-1932-1st ed (5yy6,vg,dj)   6.00

SPRINGETT,EVELYN CARTIER-For My Children's Children-Montr-
1937-illus   (5w8)   35.00

SPRINGFIELD,ATLAS OF CITY OF-Springfield-1899-L J Richards-
folio-calf&cl   (4c1,lea wn)   30.00

SPRINGFIELD,(MASS)-History of Dept of Police Services 1636 to
1900-1900-105p-illus   (5e8)   8.75

SPRINGFIELD FIRE & MARINE INS CO-1849 to 1949,a Century
of Achievement,History of the-Springfield-1949-4to-66p-illus
        (5y2)   6.00

SPRINGS,ELLIOTT WHITE-The Rise & Fall of Carol Banks-
GardenCty-Dblday,Doran-1931-8vo-cl-glazed lin-
ed of 200c   (5b2,vg)   25.00

SPRINGSTEED,ANNE FRANCES-The Expert Waitress-NY-1894-
131p   (5w7) 5. (5g9)   4.50

SPRINGWATER,DR-Cold Water Man or Pocket Companion for
Temperate-Albny-1832-216p-cl (5h7,lack fly)   15.00

SPROGLE,H O-Phila Police,Past & Present-Phila-1887-illus-
ads-671p   (5yy0)   9.50

SPROUT,HAROLD-Toward a New Order of Sea Power-Princeton-
1943-336p-illus-maps   (5s1,f,dj)   6.00

SPRUNT,A,Jr-SoCarolina Bird Life-Columbia-1949-col frontis-
orig cl-4to-34 col plts-585p-1st ed (4p5) 15. (5w0) 16.50

SPRY,CONSTANCE-Constance Spry's Garden Notebook-NY-1940-
217p-illus-photo plts   (5s7)   5.00
--Winter & Spring Flowers-Lond-1953-sm4to-140p-24 hand col
photos-12 plts   (5s7)   5.00

SPURLING,FANNIE S,ed-Postmarked Vermont & Calif 1862 to 1864-
Rutland-(1940)-illus-202p   (5t4)   7.50

SPURR,GEO-Land of Gold,Tale of '49-Bost-1883-dec cl-3rd ed-
9p,271p-rev-(novel)   (5r0,pres)   15.00

SPURR,JOSIAH E-Atlas to Accompany Monograph 31 on Geology
of the Aspen District,Colo-Wash-1898-lg folio-orig cl-
(27 col maps & sec views)   (5m3,f)   60.00
--Thru the Yukon Gold Diggings-Bost-1900-illus-8vo-1st ed
        (4g6)   25.00

SPURZHEIM,J G-Phrenology-Bost-1833-plts-359p
        (5yy0,needs rebndg)   12.50

SPYRI,JOHANNA-Heide,Her Years of Wandering & Learning-
Bost-1885-2 vols in 1-cl-1st ed in Engl-v rare (5v2) 175.00

SQUAW BOOK,THE-Syracuse-(1909)-short stories,poems-wrps
        (5h6)   5.00

SQUIER,E G-Ancient Monuments of Mississippi Valley-
Wash(Prntd NY)-1848-maps,drawings-1st ed-v scarce
        (4t8,ex-libr)   60.00
--Nicaragua,its people,Scenery,etc-NY-1852-D Appleton-2 vols-
views-maps   (4j6,rbkd)   30.00
--Notes on Central Amer-NY-1855-397p-fldg maps-tinted lithos
        (5n4,vf)   25.00
--Peru-NY-1877-HarperBros-illus-8vo-orig cl-599p-1st ed
        (4e1,sp chip)   25.00
--Serpent Symbol & Worship of Reciprocal Principles of Nature-
NY-1851-illus-1st ed (4b7,bndg wn) 40. (5m9,wn) 25.00

SQUIER,E S-Tricks & Magice Made Easy-NY-1912-12mo-cl-1st ed
        (5p5)   10.00

SQUIER,EMMA LINDSAY-Bride of the Sacred Well-NY-1928-
illus   (4b2,lacks e.p.)   5.00
--Children of the Twilight-NY-1926-257p (4b2)   5.00
--Gringa-Bost-1934-illus-8vo (4g6,5x0)   5.00

SQUIRE,ANNA-Social Washington-Wash-(1923)-81p (5w7) 2.50

SQUIRE,J C-Contemporary Amer Authors-NY-1928-Holt-236p-
illus   (5p9)   4.50
--The Gold Tree-Lond-1917-MartinSecker-cl-ltd to 500c,autg
        (5ss3,tn dj)   15.00

SQUIRE,JOHN,ed-Cheddar Gorge-NY-1938-181p-illus-4to(5g9)7.50
--same-Lond-(1937)   (5g9)   7.50

SQUIRE,LORENE-Wildfowling with a Camera-Phila-1938-4to-
plts   (4a1) 12.50 (5t7)   15.00

SQUIRE,W C-Report of Gov of Washington Territory-Wash-1885-
77p-wrps   (4a5,fox)   12.50
--Resources & Development of Washington Territory-Seattle-1886-
72p-fldg map   (4a5)   22.50

SQUIRES,FREDK-Architec tonics,Tales of Tom Thumtack Architect-
NY-1914-12mo-cl-R Kent,illus-1st ed (5d9,rprd dj,Kent autg) 65.00

SQUIRES,W H T-Through Centuries Three-Portsmouth-1929-illus-
605p-1st ed,nbrd   (4b6,autg)   25.00
--Unleashed At Long Last-1939-Printcraft Pr-R8vo-illus-1st ed
        (5x2)   30.00

SRYGLEY,F D-70 Years in Dixie-Nashvl-1914-8vo-cl-400p-
illus   (5m8,pencil)   8.50

STABLES,GORDON-'Twixt School & College-Lond,Glasgow &
Dublin-n.d.-Blackie-352p-(ads)-frontis & 7 plts(2 in sec)-
pict cl   (5p1)   6.50

STACEY,C P,ed-Records of Nile Voyageurs, 1884 to 1885-Tor-
1959-Champlain Soc-285p-ports-plts-maps (5zz8) 35.00

STACKPOLE,EDOUARD A-The Sea Hunters-Phila-(1953)-
Lippincott-8vo-cl-510p-illus (5h9) 8.50 (5j5,dj) 10.00

STACKPOLE,EVERETT S-History of New Hampshire-NY-(1916)-
8vo-4 vols-buck-t.e.g.   (4c5,f)   29.50

STACKPOLE,MARKHAM W-World War Memoirs of Milton Academy-
1940-449p   (5e8)   4.00

STACY,NATHAN'L-Memoirs of the Life of-Columbus,Pa-1850-
523p-frontis   (5w0,als)   40.00

STACY-JUDD,R B-Ancient Mayas-LosAng-(1934)-plts-map-
273p   (4i7,tn dj)   12.00
STADEN,HANS-True History of His Captivity,1557-NY-1929-
McBride-8vo-buck-wdcuts-Argonaut Ser   (4a3,f)   15.00
STAEHLIN,J von-An Acct of the Northern Archipelago-Lond-
1774-Heydinger-4to-bds-cl bk-118p-fldg map-2p advts at end
                                        (5ss2,rbnd)   250.00
--Original anecdotes of Peter the Great-Dublin-1789-calf-
prntd by J Rea   (5x3,f)   25.00
STAEL-HOLSTEIN,MME de-Delphine-Lond-1803-J Mawman-
6 vols-12mo-calf-1st ed in Engl-scarce   (5xx6,wn)   95.00
STAFF,WALTON-Falmouth on Cape Cod-Bost-1925-47p-illus-
1st ed-ltd to 300c   (5a9,f)   7.50
STAFFORD,CORA E-Paracas Embroideries-Augustin,NY-(1941)-
4to-107p-31p plts-col frontis   (5F5,f)   15.00
STAFFORD,DAVID W-In Defense of the Flag-Warren-1912-12mo-
95p-orig papr wrps   (4a7,rub)   12.00
STAFFORD,M H-Desc in the Male Line of Ensign Jas Kidder-
(1941)-749p   (4t2)   50.00
STAFFORD,M K-Stafford Lineage Book, Descent from Jarvis-
1932-(122p)   (5t9)   15.00
STAFFORD,MRS MALLIE-The March of Empire thru 3 Decades-
SanFran-1884-12mo-cl-port-189p-scarce
(5bb4) 50.   (5r0) 35.   (5F5)   27.50
STAFFORD,W P-Wendell Phillips, A Centennial Oration-
ca 1912-NAACP-39p-wrps   (5x2)   27.50
STAFFORDSHIRE,THE HERALDIC VISITATIONS OF-in 1614 &
1663, 64-Part 2,Vol 5-Lond-1885-436p-bev edges-scarce
                                          (5h9)   15.00
STAHL,JN M-Battle of Plattsburg-n.p.-(1916)-166p-cl
                                        (5h2,cov spot)   7.50
STAHL,P J-Mademoiselle Lili a la Campagne-Paris-(ca 1870)-
J Hetzel-4to-56p-24 illus-pict bds   (5c8,rub)   15.00
STAHLE,WM-Description of Borough of Reading,Pa-Reading-
1841-orig bds-68p   (4m4)   32.50
STAHL,WM-Grower of High Grade Fruit Trees-Quincy-n.d.-
(1890?)-48p-col wrps-trade cat   (5h2)   10.00
STAINBANK,H E-Coffee in Natal-Lond-1874-78p,(8) (5w1,stnd)   5.00
STAINER,C-A Dictionary of Violin Makers-Lond-n.d.-ca 1890-
102p-bds   (5t2)   7.50
STAIR,J L-The Lighting Book-Curtis Lighting,Inc.-Chig-1930-
4to-315p-illus   (5hh6)   8.50
STALEY,MILDRED E-A Tapestry of Memories-Hilo Tribune Herald-
(1944)-illus   (5x5)   7.50
STALLINGS,LAURENCE,ed-1st World War-NY-1933-photos-
1938-4to   (4h4)   8.00
STAMBAUGH,J LEE-History of Collin Co,Texas-Austin-1958-
303p   (4a5)   12.50
STAMP,C W-Dudley Stamp Lost in the Rocky Mntns-Chig-(1913)-
151p-illus-col frontis   (5s4,wn) 10.   (5L2)   4.00
STAN,ANISOARA-The Romanian Cook Book-NY-1951-229p(5g9)   5.00
STANARD,MARY N-The Dreamer-Phila-1925   (5mm2)   10.00
--Colonial Virginia,Its People & Customs-Phila-1917-Lippincott-
93 illus-1st ed   (5x0,5x5)   15.00
--Richmond,its People & its Story-Phila-1923-Lippincott-239p-
cl-03 illus-1st ed   (5m6) 7.50   (5x2) 15.   (5j5)   12.50
--Story of Virginia's 1st Century-Phila-1928-331p-illus-g.t.-
1st ed   (5h9)   10.00
STANDARD AMERICAN COOK BOOK-Springfield,O-(1897)-
illus-383p-pic wrps   (5ww2,cov loose)   9.50
STANDARD ELECTRIC TIME CO-catalog-NewHav-1891-26p-
illus-8vo-orig wrps   (5ss5)   6.50
STANDARD HANDBOOK ON WINES & LIQUORS,THE-NY-
1907-A M Hirschfeld-61p,(7)-   (5w1,rub)   10.00
STANDARD HOMES CO-Better Homes at Lower Prices-Wash-1923-
100 illus p   (5b9,fray)   5.00
STANDARD LIBRARY CYCLOPEDIA-n.p.-1853-4 vols (5tt5,wn)   15.00
STANDARD LIGHTING CO-New Process Catalogue & Cook Book-
Cleve-(1894)-illus-249p   (4g9,hng loose,writing)   12.50
--Catalog of New Process Ranges & Stoves-(1897)-bds-sq8vo-
52p-illus   (5hh7)   8.50
STANDARD OIL CO-Aladdin Security Oil Sold in Barrels & by
Tank Wagon-n.p.-n.d.-4 pg adv folder-5 col illus-
2 cotton wicks mounted inside   (5hh6)   25.00
STANDARD,PAUL-Calligraphy's Flowering, Decay & Restoration-
Chig-1947-Soc of Typogr Arts-32p-cl   (5tt9)   7.50
STANDARD,STELLA-Whole Grain Cookery-NY-(1951)-240p(5c9)   5.00
STANDING BEAR,LUTHER-My People the Sioux-Bost-(1928)-
288p-photos-1st ed   (5L2,stn) 10.   (4k5,f,dj)   12.50
--Stories of the Sioux-HoughtonMiff-(1935) (4k5,f,dj)   8.50
STANDING,PERCY C-Guerilla Leaders of the World-Bost-1913-
maps-illus   (4t8)   15.00

STANDISH,BURT L-Frank Merriwell's Book of Athletic
Development-NY-(1901)-Street&Smith-8vo-148p & 12p ads-
wrps-Diamond Hand Book Ser #6   (5rr2,sl chip)   15.00
--Frank Merriwell at Yale-Racine,Wisc-(c1935)-Whitman Publ-
sq12mo-bds-scarce-Big Little Book #1121
                                  (5rr2,bkstrp torn,scarce)   12.50
STANDISH,MYLES-Standishes of Amer-1895-145p   (5t9)   30.00
STANDISH,ROBT-The First of Trees-Lond-(1960)-108p-illus (5s7)   3.50
STANDLEY,PAUL-Contributions from the US Natl Herbarium-
Vol 13,Pt 6...Type Localities of Plants,1st Described from
New Mex-Wash-1910-(104)p-orig wrps   (5w4,unopnd)   6.00
STANDLEY,WM H-Admiral Ambassador to Russia-Chig-1955(5x7)   6.00
STANEK,V J-Introducing Dragons-Lond-n.d.-cl-79p-90 photo-
4to-scarce   (4p6)   8.00
STANFORD,ALFRED-Ground Swell-NY-1923-301p (5s1,sl soil)   3.00
--Navigator-NY-1927-Morrow-308p-1st ed (5e8) 5.   (5w0)   6.50
STANFORD,DON-New England Earth & Other Poems-SanFran-
1941-Colt Pr-8vo-300c-wrps   (4c2,sl stn)   10.00
STANFORD,LELAND-History of Life of-by H H Bancroft-Oakland-
1952-R8vo-hf lea-plts-Calif Relations,#34   (5dd5)   20.00
--Trotting Stock at Palo Alto,property of-SanFran-1882-8vo-
74p-wrps   (5F5,cov dtchd)   15.00
--same-San Mateo-1891-8vo-313p-wrps   (5F5)   13.50
--same-(Palo Alto)-1897-8vo-wrps-173p   (5F5)   12.00
--same-(Palo Alto)-1898-8vo-wrps-141p   (5F5)   10.00
STANFORD,MARTHA PRICHARD-of New Orleans,La-The Old &
New Cook Book-NOrl-1904-296p   (5c0,wn,stnd)   22.50
STANFORD UNIV-Memorial Library of Music at-Stanford-1950-
(LosAng,Ward Ritchie Pr)-310p-illus-cl-8½x11   (5F5)   15.00
STANHOPE,CHAS VINCENT MAHON-Principles of Electricity-
Lond-1779-Elmsley-4to-calf-263p-6 fldg plts-orig ed (5ee1)   200.00
STANHOPE,EARL-History of England 1701 to 13-Lond-1870-
584p   (5a1)   7.50
--same-Lond-1872-2 vol-port-4th ed   (5a1)   5.00
--Life of Wm Pitt-Lond-1861, 1862-ports-4 vols-1st ed (4d1)   17.50
STANLEY,ARTHUR,ed-Bedside Book for Children,an Anthology-
Lond-1950-Gollancz-sm8vo-cl-g.t.-333p   (5aa2)   3.50
STANLEY,ARTHUR PENRHYN-Dean Stanley's Historical Memorials-
3 vols-Phila-n.d.-sm4to-mor&bds-t.e.g.-tip in plts-tissue guards-
LP Edition-ltd to 250c,nbrd   (5w9,cov wn)   50.00
STANLEY,E J-Life of Rev L B Stateler-Nashville-1907-photos-
356p-scarce   (4t8)   25.00
STANLEY,EDWIN-Rambles in Wonderland,Up Yellowstone...&
Natl Park-NY-1878-179p-illus-map
                      (4t8) 15.   (5s4,lacks e.p.)   12.50
STANLEY,F-The Apaches of New Mexico,154 to 1940-(Pampa,Tex-
1962)-1st ed-438p plus index-autg-scarce (5bb4,mint,dj)   20.00
--Civil War in New Mexico-Denv-1960-508p-1st ed
              (5k0,autg,mint) 15.   (5bb4,autg,mint,dj)   20.00
--Ciudad Santa Fe,Mexican Rule,1821 to 1846-(Pampa,Tex-1962)-
285p plus index-ltd to 500c,autg-1st ed,rare 1st state(wi t.pg
& dj reading Cuidad)   (5bb4,mint,dj)   30.00
--same-wi dj correct Ciudad & corr title superimposed (5bb4)   12.50
--Clay Allison-(Denv-1956)-1st ed-236p-autg-scarce
                                      (5bb4,mint,dj)   30.00
--Despreadoes of New Mexico-(1953)-320p-1st ed-ltd to 800c,autg
              (5r1,f,dj) 40.   (5bb4)   25.00
--Fort Bascom,Comanche Kiowa Barrier-(Pampa,Tex-1961)-
224p-1st ed   (5bb4,mint,autg,dj)   15.00
--Fort Union(New Mex)-n.p.-(1953)-305p-illus-1st ed-scarce
                                      (5bb4,dj,autg)   25.00
--The Grant That Maxwell Bought-(Denv-1952)-1st ed-ltd to 250c,
autg-256p,dbld col-pkt map-photos-v rare (5bb4,vg)   100.00
--Jim Courtright,2 Gun Marshall of Ft Worth-(Denv,1957)-
234p-photos-1st ed-ltd to 500c,autg   (5bb4,dj,mint)   15.00
--same-2nd printing   (5bb4)   7.50
--Longhair Jim Courtright-Denv-1957-Ltd Ed,autg-500c
                      (5k2,dj) 12.50   (5g6)   15.00
--No Tears for Black Jack Ketchum-(Denv,1958)-148p-stiff wrps-
1st ed-ltd to 500c,autg   (5bb4,mint)   7.50
--One Half Mile from Heaven-(Denv-1949)-155p-illus-wrps-
1st ed-autg-rare   (5bb4)   60.00
--The Private War of Ike Stockton(cov title)-(Denv,1959)-169p-
1st ed-ltd,autg   (5bb4,dj,mint)   12.50
--Raton Chronicle-(Denv-1948)-1st ed-146p-(ltd to 500c)-illus-
wrps-v scarce   (5bb4)   60.00
--Rodeo Town(Canadian,Tex)-(Denv-1953)-418p-photos-1st ed,autg-
ltd to 500c   (5bb4,f,dj)   20.00
--Socorro,the Oasis-(Denv-1950)-1st ed-221p-photos-rare
                                      (5bb4,wn)   50.00
STANLEY,MRS H M-London Street Arabs-Lond,Paris&Melbourne-
1890-8vo-pict cl-5th thous-28 plts-12p   (5p1,soil)   5.00

STANLEY,HARVEY-Pilate & Herod-Phila-1853-2 vols-12mo-cl
                    (4c2,sl stn)   20.00
STANLEY,HENRY M-Autobiography of...-NY-1909-HoughtonMiff-
    551p-fldg map-photos-2nd impr   (4t5)   5.00
--The Congo & the Founding of its Free State-NY-(1885)-2 vols-
    maps & illus   (5j2)   18.00
--In Darkest Africa-NY-1890-illus-pkt maps-2 vols (5x2) 22.50
--In Darkest Africa-NY-1890-Scribner-2 vols-orig green mor & vel-
    t.e.g.-demi 4to-lg pap ed,ltd to 250c,autg-extra proof illus
    (some autg)-40 plts-3 maps(2 fldg bkd on lin) (5m3,f) 125.00
--same-NY-1891-Scribner's-illus-maps(2 fldg pkt)-pict cov-2 vols
                    (4t5)   20.00
--My Dark Companions & Their Strange Stories-Lond-1893-335p-
    18 plts-illus   (5c6)   16.50
--My Early Travels & Adventures in Amer & Asia-NY-1895-ports-
    2 vols   (5q0)   10.50
--Through the Dark Continent-Tor-1878-John B Magurn-maps-
    2 vols   (4t5)   25.00
--same-NY-1878-2 vols-8vo-illus-maps-pkt maps
               (4a6,wn,hng broken) 12.50
STANLEY,MARY-Measure for Measure-NY-1883-Carleton-
    1st ed   (5x4,wn)   7.50
STANLEY,MRS-Sir Philip Sidney's Arcadia, modernized by-Lond-
    1725-folio-calf-g.-mor labl-1st ed-lg papr
    (5t7,lacks fly,stnd) 25.   (5xx6,f,lg papr cpy) 85.00
STANLEY,RANDALL J-History of Jackson Co,Fla-1950-281p(5j6)7.50
STANLEY,REVA-The Archer of Paradise-1937-Caxton Prntrs-
    photos-1st ed   (5L0,dj) 10. (5x5,dj)   17.50
STANLEY STEAM CARS-Catalog of-Newton,Mass-1910-8vo-
    36p-orig wrps-illus   (5m6,lacks 1 lf)   22.50
STANNARD,HAROLD-Rome & Her Monuments-NY-1924 (5ii3) 10.00
STANSBURY,ARTHUR J-Elementary Catechism on Constitution of
    the US-Bost-1831-(Hilliard,Gray,Little&Wilkins)-78p-
    bds&lea   (5t7)   6.00
--Report of Trial of James H Peck-Bost-1833-Hilliard,Gray-592p-
    disbnd   (5tt8) 20.   (4g6,crack)   17.50
STANSBURY,CHAS F-The Lake of the Great Dismal-NY-1925-
    8 photos-238p-fldg map-1st ed   (5ee3) 8.50 (5L7) 15.00
STANSBURY,HOWARD-Exploration & Survey of Valley of the
    Great Salt Lake of Utah-Phila-1852-Lippincott,Grambo&Co-
    2 vols-487p-57 plts-2 fldg maps
            (4n4) 80. (5x5,maps tn) 60. (5n9) 85.00
--same-Phila-1852-487p-map&57 plts-orig cl-2 lg fldg maps in
    sep vol-1st ed-Sen Exec Doc 3   (5m3)   50.00
--same-Phila-1852-487p-plts-Sen Spec Sess,Exec #3 (5t4) 20.00
--same-Exploration & Survey of Valley of Great Salt Lake-Wash-
    1853-cl folder-views-2 fldg maps   (5tt0)   25.00
--Survey of Cumberland River, Letter from Sec War-House Doc 171-
    Wash-1835-fldg maps-8vo-sewn-24p (5ss5,text loose) 15.00
STANSFELD-HICKS,C-Yachts,Boats & Canoes,design & construction-
    Lond-1887-9 drwngs-16 fldg plts-3/4 calf-t.dec- (5c1) 35.00
--same-NY-1888-pict cl   (5c1)   25.00
STANSFIELD,HERBERT H-Sculpture & the sculptor's art-Lond-
    1918-Jack-164p-In series,Through the Eye-plts (5m5) 10.00
STANSBIE,J H-Iron & Steel-1907   (5L7)   7.50
STANTON,DAN'L-Journal of the Life,Travels...of,late of Phila,
    etc-Phila-1772-184p,4p-cl-bds   (5m4)   22.50
STANTON,EDWIN-Report on the War Claims at StLouis-Wash-
    1862-41p-HED 94   (4j4)   6.00
STANTON,EDWIN F-Brief Authority...Recollections of China-
    Thailand-NY-c1956   (5x7)   4.50
STANTON,EDWIN M-Condition of Affairs in Texas-Wash-1867-
    4p-HED 61   (4j4)   3.50
--Transportation of Troops Between Missouri Riv & Pac Coast-
    Wash-1862-2p   (4n4)   7.00
STANTON,MRS FLORENCE K-Practical Housekeepr & Cyclopedia
    of Domestic Economy-Phila-1901-621p-illus (5c0,fade) 8.50
STANTON,FRANK-Comes One with a Song-Indnpls-1899-200p-cl-
    port-1st ed   (5m1) 6.50 (5h2)   5.00
--Songs from Dixie Land-Indnpls-(1900)-illus (5r7)   10.00
--Up from Georgia-NY-1902-12mo-1st ed (5tt5) 10. (5m2) 6.00
STANTON,G S-When The Wildwood Was In Flower-NY-(1909)-
    Ogilvie Pub-illus-pict cl-230p-1st ed (5bb4,4n8) 20.00
STANTON,IRVING W-60 Yrs in Colorado-Denver-1922-port-
    320p-scarce   (4p7,fade)   50.00
STANTON,MARY OLDSTED-A System of Practical & Scientific
    Physiognomy-Phila-1890-2 vols-1222p plus 32p catalog-illus
                  (5w5,sl wn)   10.00
STANTON,THEODORE,ed-Manual of Amer Literature-NY-1909-
    493p   (5p0)   4.50
--The Woman Question in Europe,Series of Original Essays-NY-
    1884-Putnam's-478p-cl   (4L9,ex-libr)   12.50

STANTON,V H-Place of authority in matters of religious belief-
    1891   (5L7)   4.00
STANTON,W-The Leopard's Spots-Univ Chig-1960-R8vo (5x2,dj) 5.00
STANWELL FLETCHER,THEODORA C-Clear Lands & Icy Seas-
    NY-1958-264p-plts   (4f9) 5. (5aa0) 4.50 (5ss1) 4.00
--Tundra World-Bost-1952-266p-col frontis   (5dd0)   4.50
STANWOOD,EDW-History of the Presidency-Bost-1898-cl
               (5kk7,fray)   7.50
--same-from 1788 to 1897-Bost-c1898-2 vols-1st ed (5w9) 17.50
--Jas Gillespie Blaine-Bost-c1908-377p-illus-t.e.g. (5w9) 4.00
STANYAN,JOHN M-History of 8th Reg of NH Vol-Concord-1892-
    Ira C Evans-583p-illus   (5mm8) 5. (5bb4) 12.50
STAPEL,H F,pub-Biogr History,Atchison Co,(Rockport,Mo,1905)-
    photos-lea-obl-798p plus index-1st ed (4t3,rub,hngs wn) 60.00
STAPLES,C R-Hist of Pioneer, Lexington, 1779 to 1806-1939-361p
                (5t9)   30.00
STAPLES,W R-Annals of the Town of Providence,RI,from its 1st
    Settlement to 1832-1843-670p   (5t9)   12.50
STAPLES,WM R-Destruction of the Gaspee-Prov,RI-1845-
    56p-   original wrps-Documentary Hist of (5h9) 12.50
--Rhode Island in the Continental Congress-Prov-1870-Providence Pr-
    725p   (5qq8)   12.50
STAPLETON,BRIAN-Wealth of Nigeria-NY-1958-228p-13 tables-
    10 maps   (5c6,mint)   3.00
STAPLETON,ISAAC-Moonshiners in Arkansas-(Independence,Mo)-
    1948-wrps   (4j4)   7.50
STAPLETON,JAS W-Gate Hangs Well,A Kenya Diary-Lond-
    1957-234p   (5c4,mint)   5.00
STAPP,EMILIE B-Bread&'Lasses-DesMoines-1902-12mo-cl-illus
    94p   (5m8,f,autg)   7.50
--The Little Streets of Beacon Hill-Cambr-1928-15p-6 etchings
    by J A Stewart,ea autg-limp suede-ltd to 100c,autg (5k0) 10.00
STAPP,WM PRESTON-The Prisoners of Perote,etc-Phila-1845-
    G B Zieber & Co-orig cl   (5z7,fox,fade) 100.00
STAR IDENTIFICATION TABLES-Wash-1909-HO #127-364p-
    album style-g.cov   (5s1,sl wn)   3.00
STAR SPANGLED BANNER,THE-Lond-(not before 1776,not after
    1782)-folio-removed-4p, 1st blank-prntd by Longman&Broderip-
    1st ed, 1st issue   (5L8,vg) 875.00
STARBUCK,ALEX-History of Nantucket Co,Island & Town-Bost-
    1924-Goodspeed-3 fldg plts-8vo-3 fldg maps-871p-1st ed
            (4c4) 42. (5c1) 100.00
STARBUCK,EDWIN D-A Guide to Literature for Character
    Training-Vol 1,Fairy Tale,Myth&Legend-NY-1929-Macmillan-
    389p-8vo-2nd prntng   (5p1,ex-libr)   5.00
STARK,CALEB-History of Dunbarton 1751 to 1860-272p (5e8) 27.50
--Memoirs & official corres of Genl John Stark-Concord-1877-
    495p   (5s2)   20.00
STARK,GEO W The Best Policy-Detroit-1959-251p (4b8) 5.00
STARK,JAS H-History & Guide to Barbados & Caribee Islands-
    Bost-(1893)-illus-12mo   (4b7)   8.50
--same-Bost-1903-maps-illus   (5x2)   15.00
--Loyalists of Massachusetts&the other side of the Amer Revolution-
    1910-509p   (5t9)   15.00
--Stark's antique views of ye towne of Boston-Bost-(c1901)-4to-
    cl-maps-plts   (5g8)   17.50
--Stark's Illus Bermuda Guide-Bost-(1890)-12mo-illus-maps-
    pict cl-157p   (5t2)   4.50
STARKE,AUBREY H-Sidney Lanier-ChapelHill-1933-525p (4b4) 17.50
STARKE,DR J-Alcohol,The Sanction for Its Use-NY-1907-317p,(3)
                (5w1)   4.50
STARKEY,DAN B-Geo Rogers Clark & His Illinois Campaign-
    Milwkee-1897-Parkman Club #12-38p-wrps-scarce (5bb4) 7.50
STARKEY,MARION L-The Cherokee Nation-NY-1946-355p plus
    index-illus-map-1st ed   (5bb4)   10.00
--The Devil in Massachusetts-NY-1949-310p-1st ed
           (5t2,f) 5. (5w5,autg) 6.50
--same-NY-1950-Knopf   (5L7,5F9,f,dj,5qq8,dj) 3.50
STARLING,ERNEST H-The Action of Alcohol on Man-Lond&NY-
    1923-291p   (5w1)   5.00
STARNES,E-The Slaveholder Abroad,or Billy Buck's Visit with
    His Master to England-Phila-1860 (5x2,fox) 40.00
STARR,B P-History of the Starr Family of New England-1879,80-
    589p(incl suppl)-v rare   (4t2,rbkd) 250.00
STARR,ELIZA ALLEN-Patron Saints-Chig-1896-8vo-cl-2 vols-
    illus   (5t2)   7.50
STARR,F F-Goodwins of Hartford,Conn-1891-798p (5mm3) 25.00
STARR,FREDK-The Ainu Group at the St Louis Expos-Chig-1904-
    118p-photos-1st ed   (5L2)   7.50
--Indian Mexico-Chig-1908-Forbes&Co-thk8vo-425p-1st ed
           (5L2) 22.50 (5x5) 30.00
--Mexico & the US-Chig-(c1914)-Bible Hse-8vo-cl-maps-illus-
    scarce   (4a3,fade)   15.00

STARR,JIMMY-365 Nights in Hollywood-Hollywd-Fischer Corp-
1926-365p-1000c-1st ed   (5i1,cov wn)   7.50
STARR,JOHN W JR-Lincoln & the RRs-NY-1927-Dodd,Mead-
325p-illus-ltd to 287c,nbrd,autg (5qq8,crack)   10.00
--same-NY-1927-illus-1st trade ed   (5m2)   6.50
--Lincoln's Last Day-NY-(1922)-illus   (5s9)   3.00
STARR,LOUIS M-Bohemian Brigade-NY-1954 (5bb4,5s9,dj)   5.00
STARR,RALPH S-Physical Geography of Empire State-1902-383p-
index-illus   (5zz0)   12.00
STARR,SYLVIA-Pueblo Boy-Phila-1938-McKay-(44p)-pict bds
   (5p1,dj)   4.00
STARR,WALTER A-My Adventures in Klondike & Alaska,1898 to
1900-n.p.-n.d.-(1960)-fldg map-68p-Lawton Kennedy
   (5s6,pres)   15.00
STARR,WALTER A,JR-Guide to John Muir Trail & High Sierra
Region-SanFran-1934-145p-pkt map-cl-1st ed (5d7)   6.00
STARR,WM H-Discourses on Nature of Faith & Kindred Subjects-
Chig-1857-289p-cl   (5ff7)   17.50
STARRETT,VINCENT-All About Mother Goose-1930-Merrymount Pr-
8vo-bds&cl-ltd to 275c   (5ee9)   15.00
--Autolycus in limbo-NY-1943-Dutton-1st prntng-ltd to 1500c
   (5m2)   6.00
--Bookman's Holiday-NY-(1942)-312p-cl-1st prntg
   (5h7) 6.50   (5r9,f)   15.00
--Books Alive-NY-1940-1st ed
  (5dd8,dj,5m1,dj,autg) 10. (5r9,mint,dj) 17.50
--Ebony Flame-Chig-(1922)-76p-ltd to 350c (5t4,pres)   6.00
--Et Cetera-Chig-1924-Pascal Covici,pub-253p-ltd to 625c
   (5k1,pres)   6.50
--Oriental Encounters,Two Essays in Bad Taste-Chig-1938-
Normandie Hse-8vo-cl-ltd to 249c,autg (5d5,box) 20.00
--Snow for Christmas-n.p.-1935-Eileen Baskerville-32p-
orig parch wrps-1st ed-ltd to 125c,nbrd (5m2,wn)   6.50
--A Student of Catalogues-CedarRapds-1921-8vo-bds-parch bk-
ltd to 250c   (5b2,pres)   12.50
STARS & STRIPES,THE- A E F,France-Feb 8,1918 to Jun 13,1919-
pict Suppl-Victory Ed-folio-ea 8p-cl-71 nbrs(all publ)
   (4c1,box) 175.00
STASON,E B-Law of Administrative Tribunals-Chig-1947-2nd ed
   (5ff4)   10.00
STATE BAR JOURNAL-Calif-1926 to 70-Vol 1 thru 44-bnd
   (5ii7) 660.00
STATE OF BRITISH & FRENCH COLONIES IN NO AMER-with
respect to the Number of People,Forces,Forts,Indians,
Trade,etc-Lond-1755-(2p),190p-8vo-hf mor
  (5L1,broke) 110. (5e2) 400.00
STATE COINAGES OF NEW ENGLAND-NY-1920-4to-cl-76p-
plts & extra material-200c reprntd from Amer Journal of
Numismatics   (5t7,f) 100.00
STATE BANKS,THE-Condition of-Treas Dept Doc #79,Jan 8,1838-
Ho Reps-856p   (5e4)   25.00
STATE OF DESERET,THE-SaltLkCty,Apr,July,Oct,1940-Utah
State Hist Soc Vol 8,#2,3,4-WPA project,Utah Hist Rec Surv-
65p,239p plus index-map frontis-wrps (5L0) 12.50
STATE LAW INDEX-GPO-1925 to 48-Vol 1 thru 12,(all publ)-
   (5ii7)   65.00
STATE MINING JOURNAL(Calif)-Vol 1,#1 to 31-Jan 20 to
Nov 20,1896-hf calf   (5n5,f,sp weak) 17.50
STATE TRIUMVIRATE,THE-A Political Tale-NY-1819-12mo-
orig prntd bds-v scarce   (5b2,rub)   50.00
STATEN ISLAND-Gravestone Inscriptions in St Andrews Cemetary,
Richmond-1923-unbnd-109p-Davis,Long&Vosburgh 37.50
--Records of St Mary's Church at West New Brighton,Staten Island,
NY-NY-1923-72p-unbnd   (5t9)   30.00
STATES,JAS N-Genealogy of the States Family-NewHaven-1913-
8vo-wrps-187p   (4t1)   20.00
STATHAM,H HEATHCOTE-Short Critical History of Architecture-
Lond-Batsford-1912(?)-586p-4to-cl-illus (5m5) 16.00
STATISTICS OF WOOLLEN MANUFACTORIES IN THE US-By
Proprietor of Condensing Cards-NY-1845-190p (5n7) 37.50
STATLER,OLIVER-Japanese Inn-NY-1961-Random-365p
  (5p7) 6.   (5t4)   7.50
STAUFFER,FRANK H-The Queer,The Quaint & The Quizzical-
Phila-c1882-367p-t.e.g.   (5w0)   8.50
STAUNTON,GEO-Authentic Acct of an Embassy from King of Gr
Britain to Emperor of China...from-Lond-1797-W Bulmer-
frontis-illus-calf-4to-2 vols-folio vol of plts
  (4c4,lacks folio vol of plts)   80.00
STAUNTON,HOWARD-Chess Player's Hand Book-NY-1859-
518p-illus   (5xx7)   6.50
STAVEACRE,F W F-Tea & Tea Dealing-Lond-1929-136p,24p
  (5w1) 4.50 (5c9)   5.00

STEAD,J D-Doctrines & Dogmas of Brighamism Exposed-n.p.-
1911-281p-errata sl-scarce   (4t3,f)   12.50
STEAD,WM T-If Christ Came to Chicago-Chig-1894-470p-wrps
  (5ff7)   10.00
--same-Lond-1894-Review of Reviews-frontis-fldg plt-1st Lond ed
   (5m2)   10.00
STEADFAST,JONATHAN-Count the cost,address to people of
Conn-Hartf-1804-Hudson&Goodwin-8vo-disbnd-23p-1st ed-
scarce   (5j5) 20.   (5r9)   25.00
STEAMBOAT DISASTERS & RR ACCIDENTS IN THE US etc-
Worcester-1846-408p-illus   (5t4,wn)   7.00
STEARNS,AMANDA AKIN-The Lady Nurse of Ward E-NY-1909-
Baker&Taylor-312p-illus-pict cl (5r0)   10.00
STEARNS,CHAS-The Ladies'Philosophy of Love-A Poem in 4 Cantos
written in 1774-Leominster,Mass-1797-JohnPrentiss-sm4to-
orig papr cov woodn bds-76p (5t2,shake,poor) 12. (5L1) 75.00
STEARNS,CHAS-The Black Man of the South & the Rebels-NY-
1872-562p-8 plts-orig cl (5m3,rub) 20. (5x2) 40.00
STEARNS,E S-Genealogical & Family History of State of NHamp-
NY-1908-hf lea-4 vols-ports-4to (4c5,bndg g) 23.50 (4c5,f)42.50
--History of New Hampshire-NY-(1916)-4 vols-buck-8vo-t.e.g.
   (4c5,f)   29.50
--Hist of Ashburnham,Mass,1734 to 1886-1887-1022p-ports (4t2) 20.00
--Hist of Rindge,N Hamp,1736 to 1874-1875-788p (5t9) 25.00
STEARNS,FRANK PRESTON-Life & Genius of Nathanl Hawthorne-
Phila-1906-1st ed   (5r9)   15.00
--same-Bost-(1906)-Badger-463p   (5p0)   6.50
--The mid summer of Italian art-Bost-1914-338p-16mo-cl-32 plts
   (5m5)   9.50
STEARNS,G C-A Family Memorial Containing Hist & Gen Records
of Stearns,Chapin,Raynolds,Parsons & Pease Families-1891-
68p   (4t2)   35.00
STEARNS,GUSTAV-From Army Camps & Battlefields-Minneap-
1919-67 illus   (5ww4,soil)   5.00
STEARNS,HAROLD E,ed-America Now-NY-(1938)-Literary Guild-
lg8vo-606p   (5j5)   7.50
STEARNS,MARSHAL-Just Memories-n.p.-1932 (5ss8,autg)   6.00
STEARNS,SAM'L-The Amer Herbal or Materia Medica-Walpole-
1801-16mo-360p-lea-1st NoAmer herbal (5t4,sp tn,sl wtrstn) 75.00
STEARNS,WINFRID A-New Engl Bird Life-Bost-1883-328p-illus-
rev by Dr Coues,Part 1,Oscines (5t7)   7.50
STEBBINS,GILES B-Amer Protectionist's Manual-Detroit-1883-
192p-cl   (5h7)   7.50
STEBBINS,J E-50 Yrs History of Temperance Cause-Hartf-1876-
500p-cl   (5h7) 10. (5w1,chip)   7.50
STEBBINS,LUCY P-A Victorian Album-NY-1946-226p-12mo-cl-
1st ed   (5t0,dj,f)   4.00
STEBBINS,LUKE-Stebbins Gen,of Family of Sam'l & Hannah
Stebbins 1707 to 1771-1879-31p-reprint in ltd ed of 100c of
1771 ed   (4t2)   30.00
STEBBINS,SARAH B- The annals of a baby...by one of its slaves-
NY-1877-Carleton-1st ed (5m2)   5.00
STEBBINS,WM-Journal,Stratford (Conn) to Washington in 1810-
n.p.-1968-Publ #31 of Acorn Club-ltd to 750c (5g4)   7.50
STEDMAN,CHAS-History of Origin,Progress & Termination of Amer
War-Dublin-1794-2 vols-orig bds (5tt8,wn) 40.00
--Geschichte des Ursprungs,des Fortgangs under die Beendigung
des Amerikanischen Kriegs-Berlin-1795-2 vols-8vo-hf calf-
2 fldg plans   (5L1)   30.00
STEDMAN,EDMUND C-An American Anthology 1787 to 1900-
Cambr-1900-2 vols-ltd to 300c (5mm1) 27.50
--same-Bost-1900-Houghton,Miff-878p (5p9) 12.50
--Edgar Allan Poe-CedarRapds-1909-8vo-g.t.-ed of 200c
   (5b2,f)   15.00
--The Nature & Elements of Poetry-Bost-1892-1st ed (5m1,als)   8.50
--Poems-NY-1860-Scribner-1st ed-auth's 1st book
  (5gg6,auth's own book,photo tip-in) 100. (5x4,als) 27.50
--The Prince's Ball,a Brochure,from "Vanity Fair"-NY-1860-illus-
1st ed   (5m1)   7.50
STEDMAN,EDMUND,ed-Library of Amer Literature from Earliest
Settlement to Present Time-NY-1892-Webster-11 vols-g.t.-lea-
illus   (5x4)   75.00
STEDMAN,S O-Allen Bay,a story-Phila-1876-152p-1st ed
   (5mm2,mint)   30.00
STEED,VIRGIL-Kentucky Tobacco Patch-Indnpls-(1947)-illus-
1st ed   (5yy8,autg)   5.00
STEEDMAN,ANDREW-Wanderings & adventures in the interior of
Southern Africa-Lond-1835-Longman-2 vols-8vo-orig cl-
frontis-plts-fldg map-1st ed (5x3,vf) 100.00
STEEGMAN,MARY G-Bianca Cappello,Grand Duchess of Tuscany-
Lond-1913-Constable-293p-illus (5p7)   5.00
STEEL,F A-The Complete Indian Housekeepr & Cook-Lond-1898-
373p,(2)   (5c5)   5.00

STEEL,FLORA A-Adventures of Akbar-Heinemann-1913-
 sq8vo-204p-dec cl-8 col plts   (5aa0)   5.00
STEEL,JAS-Selection of Practical Points of Malting & Brewing
 etc-Lond&NY-1881-spon-10 fldg plts-130p-errata-cl (4n0) 15.00
STEEL,JOHN H-Analysis of the Congress Spring,with practical
 remarks on its medical properties-NY-1856-16mo-frontis-
 rev by John L Perry   (5g8,ex-libr)   8.50
--same-NY-1861-32p-frontis   (5t7)   6.50
STEEL,W G-Mountains of Oregon-Portland,O-1890-111p-illus
                            (5s4,stnd)   10.00
STEELE,ASHBEL-Chief of the Pilgrims-Phila-1857-Lippincott-
 416p-illus   (5qq8,rprd) 15.   (5h9) 18.50 (5i3,chip) 17.50
STEELE,ELIZA R-Summer Journey in the West-NY-1841-278p-
 1st ed   (5g1)   13.50
STEELE,G F-My New Cocktail Book-NY-1934-2nd ed-190p(5w1) 4.50
STEELE,HAMPTON-History of Limestone Co,Texas:1833 to 1860-
 Mexia-c1925-37p-wrps   (4a5)   25.00
STEELE,J E-Naval Architecture,Part 1-Lond-1917-141p-illus
                            (5s1,ex-libr)   3.00
STEELE,JAS-Old Calif Days-Chig-1889-BelfordClarke Co-227p-
 cl   (5tt0)   12.50
--The Klondike,New Gold Fields of Alaska & Far NW-Chig-
 1897-80p-map-wrps-1st ed-scarce   (5t3,fade) 50.00
STEELE,JAS W-Frontier Sketches-Chig-1883-Jansen,McClurg-
 329p-ads   (5mm8,stns,4i7,rbnd) 10.   (4L0) 25.00
--Guide to the Pacific Coast,Santa Fe Route-Chig&NY-1891-
 illus   (5m9,crack)   6.00
--same-Chig-1893-212p-illus-fldg map   (5i3)   8.50
--Rand,McNally & Co's Guide to Southern Calif Direct-Chig-
 1886-139p-drwngs-map-lg fldg map in front   (5L2) 12.50
--Sons of the Border-Topeka-1873-260p-1st ed-rare (4L0) 40.00
STEELE,MATTHEW FORNEY-American Campaigns-Wash-1935-
 2 vols   (4a1) 32.50   (4j3)   17.50
STEELE,RICHARD,ed-The Ladies Library,Written by a Lady-Lond-
 1714-for Jacob Tonson-12mo-calf-frontis-3 vols
                        (5i7,rebkd,scuff)   95.00
STEELE,SIR RICHARD-Political Writings of-Lond-1715-12mo-
 1st Collected ed-calf   (5yy6,sp wn)   27.50
STEELE,ROBT,transl-Renaud of Montauban-Lond-1897-284p-
 8vo-dec cl   (5p1)   15.00
STEELE,ROBT-The Russian Garland of Fairy Tales-NY-1916-243p-
 col illus   (5c3,rub)   4.50
STEELE,SILAS S,ed-Book of Drawing Room Plays & Evening
 Amusements-Phila-1870-352p-8vo-cl   (5p5)   15.00
STEELE,THOS SEDGWICK-Canoe & Camera-NY-1880-illus(5r7) 7.50
STEELE,WM O-The Buffalo Knife-NY-(1952)-juvenile (5h6,pres) 5.00
STEELL,WILLIS-Benj Franklin of Paris-NY-1928-227p-plts
          (5qq8) 5.   (5w0) 6.50   (5qq8,5t7)   5.00
STEELE,ZADOCK-The Indian Captive:or a Narr of the Captivity &
 Sufferings of-Montpelier,Vt-1818-142p,(2)-12mo-1st ed
 (4p2,v wn,lacks lf) 35.   (5ss5,3 lvs tn wi loss) 22.50
                            (5L1,broke)   50.00
--same-Springfield-1908-Huntting-12mo-frontis-bds&cl-166p-
 ltd ed,box   (5t2,f)   7.50
STEELE'S-Book of Niagara Falls-Buffalo-1847-24mo-prntd wrps-
 new series maps&plts-fldg map   (5w5)   6.00
STEEN,MARGUERITE-Oakfield Plays-Lond-1932-plts-R8vo-cl
                            (5ww3,rub)   12.00
--The Sun Is My Undoing-NY-1941-1176p   (5c6)   6.50
--Wm Nicholson-Lond-1943-illus-1st ed   (5v0,f)   8.50
STEEN,RALPH W-Texas Story-Austin-1948-illus-451p (4a5)   5.00
STEENDAM,JACOB-Memoir of the First Poet in New Netherland-
 NY-1908-port-map-12mo-cl   (5L1)   15.00
STEERE,THOS-History of Town of Smithfield,1730 to 1871-
 Providence-1881-230p   (5w5) 8.50   (5t9)   10.00
STEEVENS,G W-From Capetown to Ladysmith-Lond-1900-
 Blackwood&Sons-180p-maps(1 fldg)-2nd impr (4t5,lacks fly) 7.50
--same-NY-1900-illus   (5x2)   4.00
--The Land of the Dollar-Lond-1897-WmBlackwood-316p (5x0) 5.00
--With Kitchener to Khartum-Lond-n.d.   (5x7)   4.50
STEFAN,PAUL-Arturo Toscanini,His Life & Career-NY-1938-t8vo-
 cl-plts   (5p5)   10.00
STEFANSSON,EVELYN-Here is Alaska-NY-(1943)-154p-map-
 photos   (5ss1,dj,pres)   8.50
--Within the Circle-NY-(1945)-160p-photos   (5ss1,pres) 7.50
STEFANSSON,V-Adventure of Wrangel Island-Lond-1926-
 1st Engl ed-416p-plts-fldg map   (5ss1,5s6) 10.00
--same-NY-1925-52 illus   (5ss1,pres) 15.   (5c1)   10.00
--Fat of the Land-NY-1957-339p   (5a1)   6.50
--The Friendly Arctic-NY-1921-cl-thk8vo-784p-fldg maps-1st ed
                            (4b6,pres)   40.00
--same-NY-1922-784p-2 gldg pkt maps-illus   (4d1,5ee3) 8.50
--Greenland-GardenCty-1942-1st ed-338p-plts   (5s6)   6.50

STEFANSSON,V (continued)
--Hunters of the Great North-NY-1922-illus-301p-map-1st ed
          (5ss1,pres) 12.50   (5dd7,hng rprd)   6.00
--Kak,the Copper Eskimo-Lond-1925-208p-illus   (5a1)   5.00
--My Life with the Eskimo-NY-1913-1st ed-illus-538p-fldg map
          (4b6) 25.   (5i3)   12.50
--Northward Course of Empire-NY-1924-plts-map-274p (5s0) 5.00
--same-Lond-n.d.(1922)-frontis-plts-fldg map-274p (4f9) 12.50
--Northward Ho-NY-1929-plts-181p   (4d1)   5.00
--Not By Bread Alone-NY-1946-339p   (5ss1,pres) 9.00
--Unsolved Mysteries of Arctic-NY-1939-1st ed-maps (5aa0) 7.50
--same-NY-1938-maps-381p-spec ltd ed for Explorers Club-
 autg,box   (5ss1)   30.00
STEFFENS,LINCOLN-The Autobiography of-NY-1913-1st ed
                            (5w5)   8.50
--same-NY-1931-884p-illus   (5w0,dj)   5.00
--The Shame of the Cities-NY-1904-12mo-cl-1st ed of auth's
 1st book   (5gg6,vf)   25.00
STEFFERUD,ALF,ed-Wonderful World of Books-Bost-1953-319p-
 cl-1st prntg   (5h7,dj)   4.00
STEGNER,WALLACE-Mormon Country-NY-(1942)-362p(5s4,f,dj) 7.50
STEICHEN,EDW-US Navy War Photographs-NY-1945-wrps (5c1) 10.00
STEILL,BENJ-Pictorial Spelling Book-1842-Steill-sm8vo-dec cl-
 126p-frontis-illus   (4d4)   15.00
STEIN,A-Hurrah for the Holidays-Bost-1857-220p-col lithos-
 scarce-juvenile   (5yy0)   34.50
STEIN,EMANUEL-The Labor Boycott,a Bibliography-NY-1938-
 WPA-mimeo-112p   (4j6)   8.50
STEIN,GERTRUDE-The autobiography of Alice B Toklas-NY-1933-
 Harcourt,Brace-8vo-orig cl-1st ed
          (5i8,fade) 6.   (5F1,f,dj) 15.   (5ss9,vg)   10.00
--Brewsie & Willie-NY-(1946)-Random-1st ed
          (5b2,f,dj) 8.50   (4b5,dj)   10.00
--Dix Portraits-Paris-Ed de la Montagne-8vo-wrps-ltd to 500c-
 (1 of 400 on Alfa papr)   (4g1,sl chip,unopened) 45.00
--An Elucidation-(Lond)-April,1927-12mo-orig wrps
          (4c2) 37.50   (4g1)   35.00
--Everybody's Autobiography-NY-(1937)-RandomHse-318p (5p9) 5.00
--Four in America-1947-Yale Univ Pr-1st ed (5hh1,f,dj) 17.50
--Four Saints in Three Acts-NY-1934-1st ed-RandomHse-cl-57p
          (5yy6) 15.   (5j5)   22.50
--Geography & Plays-Bost-(1922)-1st ed
          (4g1,vg,tn dj) 40.   (4b7)   45.00
--How to Write-Paris-(n.d.)-Plain Ed-12mo-bds-ltd to 1000c-
 1st ed   (4g1,sl fade)   45.00
--Ida,a Novel-NY-(1941)-1st ed   (4a1)   15.00
--In Savoy, or 'Yes' is for a very young man-Lond-(1946)-
 Pushkin Pr-12mo-orig wrps-1st ed   (4b5,f,dj) 27.50
--In Savoy-Lond-(1947)-Pushkin Pr-12mo-wrps   (4c2,dj) 20.00
--Lucy Church Amiably-Paris-1930   (4g8,wn)   35.00
--Literally True, From To Do-Remembrance of Gertrude Stein-
 Tujunga,CA-1946-leaflet 3x5-1 sheet fldg in qtrs (4g1) 20.00
--Love Like Anything-(Bilignin-1939)-ltd to 50c-1 pg fldg twice
                            (4g1,f) 150.00
--The Making of Americans-(Contact Editions,Three Mtns Press,
 Paris,1925)-4to-orig wrps-1st ed-(500c prntd)
     (5ss7,rbnd) 275.   (4g2,sl chip) 350.   (5u5,vf,fldg box)425.00
--same-NY-(1934)-Harcourt,Brace-8vo-orig cl-1st ed
          (5b2,f,dj) 20.   (4g1,sp sl discol) 15.00
--same-NY-1966-Something Else Pr-lg8vo   (4b5,f,dj) 15.00
--Paris France-NY-1940-12mo-cl-1st Amer ed-Scribner's
          (4c2,pict dj,5b2) 10.   (5ss9,vg,dj) 12.50
--Picasso-NY-1946-illus-1st Amer ed   (4b7,bkplt) 12.50
--Portraits & Prayers-NY-RandomHse-(1934)-1st ed
          (4g1,pres) 150.   (5hh1)   17.50
--Transition,#10,Jan 1928-orig wrps   (4b5,sl soil) 25.00
--same,#14,Fall,1928,orig wrps   (4b5,rub)   25.00
--same,#16,17-Spring,Summer-orig wrps (4b5,unopend,sl soil)25.00
--Three Lives-NY-1909-Grafton Pr-orig cl-1st ed of auth's 1st book
                            (4i1,rub) 175.00
--Two,Gertrude Stein & Her Brother &other early portraits-NewHav-
 1951   (5mm1,dj) 15.   (5b2,wn dj)   7.50
--Wars I Have Seen-NY-1945-Random-1st Amer ed
          (5b2,dj) 7.50   (4b5,5m1)   6.00
STEIN,L-Racial Thinking of Richard Wagner-NY-1950 (5x2,f) 15.00
STEIN,MAX,comp-Francisco "Pancho" Villa Peon Chief Terror of
 Mex-Chig-1916-64p-pict wrps-illus   (5h1)   5.00
STEIN,THEODORE-Historical Sketch of German English Independent
 School of Indianapolis-n.p.-n.d.-(Indnpls, 1913) (4a9) 13.00
STEINBECK,JOHN-Bombs Away-NY-1942-Viking-1st ed
          (5t5,dj) 15.   (4b5,sl tn dj,5mm0)   10.00
--Burning Bright-NY-1950-Viking-1st ed
          (5F1,f dj) 8.   (4b5,vg,sl fray dj)   12.50

USED BOOK PRICE GUIDE

STEINBECK, JOHN (continued)
--Cannery Row-NY-1945-1st ed-thin 12mo-208p-canary cl-
  wartime book (5m1,5u9) 6.50   (5ss1,vg,5p6,f,dj) 5.00
--Cup of Gold-NY-1929-1st issue of auth's 1st book-Aug,1929
  on copyr pg (4g2) 95. (5d3) 100.00
--East of Eden-NY-1952-1st ed
  (5u5,dj) 20. (5hh1,dj) 6.50 (5r9,dj) 7.50 (5mm1,dj) 15.00
--East of Eden-NY-1952-1st ed-8vo-cl-ltd to 1500c,autg (5u5) 50.00
--First Watch-LosAng-1947-Ward Ritchie Pr-32mo-orig wrps-8p-
  1st ed-ltd to 60c-orig envelope (5p1) 400. (4b5,f) 300.00
--Forgotten Village-NY-1941-Viking-1st ed
  (4b5,sl soil) 4. (4g8,dj) 20. (4b5,sl fray dj) 15.00
--Grapes of Wrath-NY-(1939)-1st ed(wi top stained yellow &
  reads publ April) (5xx8,dj) 40. (4g2,dj,f) 75. (5u5,f) 37.50
--same-NY-(1939)-Viking-1st trade ed (4b5) 12.50
--same-NY-(1940)-Heritage Pr-litho Thos H Benton
  (4b5,fade) 15. (5ss1,box,sp fade) 20.00
--same-NY-1940-Ltd Ed Club-4to-cl & rawhide-2 vols-illus-
  ltd to 1146c,autg,box (4b5) 125.00
--In Dubious Battle-NY-(1936)-cl-1st ed (5u5,bkstrp sl tn) 25.00
--The Long Valley-NY-1938-Viking-1st ed
  (5ss1,dj) 22.50 (5i3,f,dj) 17.50 (4g2,dj,mint) 40.00
--Moon is Down-NY-1942-Viking-1st ed (5ss1,dj,4b4,4b5,dj) 5.00
--Of Mice & Men-NY-(1937)-orig cl-8vo-cl-2500c were prntd
  (4n5,f,chip dj) 50.00
--same-NY-(1937)-1st ed-later issue (5i3,5b9) 3.50
--same-NY-(1938)-sm8vo-limp cl-1st Modern Libr ed
  (4b5,mint,dj) 10.00
--Once There was War-NY-1958-1st ed (4b7,dj) 7.50
--The Red Pony-NY-1937-Covici,Friede-1st ed-ltd to 699c,nbrd,
  autg,box (4g2,f) 110. (5ee3,f,5hh1,f) 125. (5h5,sl fade) 75.00
--same-NY-1945-Viking-1st illus ed
  (5g6) 6. (5v0,mint,box) 6.50 (5ss1,box) 5.00
--Russian Journal-NY-1948-Viking-cl bkd bds-illus by Robt Capa
  (4b5,sl fray dj) 15.00
--Saint Katy the Virgin-(NY,1936)-orig bds-12mo-g.bk-
  glassine wrps-1st ed-199c,autg,issued wi prntd announcement
  slip (4n5,vf) 400. (5ss7,mint,box) 300.00
--Sea of Cortez-NY-1941-Viking-1st ed-cl
  (5z9,f,dj) 55. (4n3,mint,dj) 85. (4b5,vg dj) 75.00
--To a God Unknown-NY-(1933)-Robt O Ballou-orig green cl-
  g.t. on sp-1st issue of 1st ed (5zz7,fray dj,autg) 125.00
--same-NY-(1933)-12mo-cl-1st ed (5ss7,fade,dj) 35.00
--Tortilla Flat-NY-Cocici Friede-(1935)-1st prntg,rare
  (5ee3,vf,dj) 50.00
--Their Blood is Strong-SanFran-1938-1st ed-orig wrps (5hh1,vg) 60.00
--The Wayward Bus-NY-1947-312p-8vo-cl-1st ed
  (5mm2,dj) 12.50 (5t2) 5.00
STEINER,EDW A-Introducing the Amer Spirit-NY-c1915-274p
  (5w4,rub,pres) 6.50
--The Immigrant Tide, Its Ebb & Flow-NY-1909-illus (5m2) 5.00
--Uncle Joe's Lincoln-NY&Chig-(1898)-171p-illus (5t7) 5.00
STEINER,M S-John Coffman-SpringGrove-n.d. (4a9,wn,soil) 4.50
STEINITZ,W-Modern Chess Instructor-NY-1889-illus (4b6) 25.00
STEINMETZ,ANDREW-The Gaming Table,Its Votaries & Victims-
  Lond-1870-2 vols-sm thk8vo-cl-lea labls (5b0) 37.50
STEINMETZ,CHAS P-Theory & Calculation of Transient Electric
  Phenomena & Oscillations-NY-1909-8vo-1st ed (5m6) 10.00
STEINWAY & SONS'-Pianos,Illustrated Catalogue of..-NY-
  (1884)-fldg bds-24p-2 folio sheets laid in (4h8,pgs dmgd) 13.50
STEINWAY,THEODORE E-People & Pianos-NY-1953-122p-illus
  (5y2) 6.50
STEJNEGER,L-Check List of NoAmer Amphibians & Reptiles-
  Cambr-1933-cl-185p-8vo-3rd ed (4p6,libr stmp) 7.50
--Herpetology of Japan & Adjacent Territory-Wash-1907-
  Smith Inst,Nat Mus Bull #58-577p-35 plts-wrps-8vo-scarce
  (4p6) 47.50
--The Poisonous Snakes of NoAmer-Wash-1895-Smi Inst,Rep US
  Nat Mus 1893-plts-lea-   wrps (4p6,hng crack) 27.50
STEKEL,DR WM-Bi-Sexual Love-Brklyn-1933 (5x7) 4.00
--The Homosexual Neurosis-Bost-c1922-322p (5w5) 6.50
STELLE,ABEL C-1861 to 1865 Memoirs of Civil War-31st Rgmt
  Wisc Vol Inf-n.p.-n.d.-(New Albany-1904)-87p-wrps-scarce
  (5h7) 25.00
STELLE,J P-The Gunsmith's Manual-NY-(1883)-illus-376p
  (5ss8,poor) 12.50
STELLMAN,LOUIS J-Mother Lode-SanFran-(1934)-ports-318p-12mo
  (5dd9,autg spot) 12.50
--same-SanFran-(1939)-12mo-cl-2nd prntg (5h5,f) 5.00
--Sam Brannan,Builder of San Francisco-NY-(1953)-254p-
  1st ed (5dd4) 12.50
--The Vanished Ruin Era-SanFran-1910-(4a5,lacks sp) 5. (5h4) 10.00

STEMBRIDGE,J H-Canada Bound-1941-155p-illus (4b9,faded) 5.00
--A Portrait of Canada-Lond-1944-164p-illus (5w9,dj) 4.50
STEMONS,J S-The Key,a Tangible Solution of the Negro
  Problem-1916-Neale Pub-12mo (5x2) 25.00
STEMPFEL,THEO,Sr-Ghosts of the Past-Indnpls-1936-101p-
  ltd to 500c (4p8) 6.50
STENDHAL,BEYLE,HENRI-Journal,Publiees Sours La Direction De
  Paul Arbelet Et Edouard Champion-Paris-1923 to 34- 5 vols-
  plus 2 suppl-orig wrps-ltd to 1235 sets (5ss9) 50.00
STENHOUSE,T B H-Rocky Mntn Saints-1873-749p-1st ed-illus
  (5r1,vg) 52.50 (5L2,vg) 25.00
STENHOUSE,MRS T B-Tell It All-Hartford-1874-623p-illus-
  1st ed (5x5,crack) 10. (5L2) 12.50
--same-Hartf-1875-illus-623p
  (5g0,f) 15. (5i3,rub) 10. (5L2,wn) 8.50
STENNIS,MARY A-Florida Fruits & Vegetables in the Family
  Menu-Mar,1939-131p-col plts-wrps (5c9) 4.00
STENSRUD,E M-The Lutheran Church & Calif-SanFran-1916-4to-cl-
  282p-illus (5h5) 17.50
STENT,VERE-Personal Record of Some Incidents in Life of Cecil
  Rhodes-Capetown-1925-Maskew Miller-87p (4t5) 6.00
STENZEL,H B-Geology of Leon County,Texas-Austin-1938-
  295p-lg fldg map-wrps (4a5) 6.00
STEP,EDW-Wild Flowers month by month in their natural haunts-
  Lond-n.d.-407p-4 col plts-photos (5s7) 6.50
STEPHANINI,J-Personal Narrative of Sufferings etc-NY-1829-
  16mo-132p-cl (5xx7,rbnd,ex-libr) 20. (5d6) 20.00
STEPHEN,A M-Land of Singing Waters-Lond-1927-189p-1st ed
  (5dd7) 5.00
STEPHEN DANE-Bost-1867-Lee&Shepard-8vo-orig cl-1st ed
  (5i0,rub) 17.50
STEPHEN,H L-State Trials Political and Social-Lond-1899 to 1902-
  4 vols (5r4) 25.00
--same-Lond-1899-2 vols (5r4) 15.00
STEPHEN,HOMER-Frontier Postmasters-Stephenville-1952-
  102p-wrps (4a5) 7.50
STEPHEN,J F-Digest of the Ciminal Law(Crimes&Punishments)-
  StL-1878 (5ff4) 7.00
--General View of Crimnal Law of England-Lond-1863
  (5ff4,rebnd) 10.00
--History of the Criminal Law of England-Lond-1883-3 vols (5r4) 20.00
STEPHEN,LESLIE,ed-Henry Fielding,Works-Lond-1882-10 vols-
  illus-pt lea-nbrd,ltd (5q0,hng weak) 75.00
STEPHEN,LESLIE-Geo Eliot (Engl Men of Letters Series)-NY-
  1902-lg12mo-cl-213p (5t2) 4.00
STEPHEN,W L,comp-Penna German & Huguenot Antiques-
  Reading-1925-2nd ed-illus-32p-orig wrps (5jj3) 10.00
STEPHENS,ALEXANDER-History of the Wars which arose out of the
  French Revolution-Phila-1804-calf-2 vols (5x7,rub) 12.50
STEPHENS,ALEXANDER H-Comprehensive & Popular History of
  the US-Phila-c1882-calf-illus (5w5,crude rprd) 8.50
--Constitutional View of Late War Betw the States-(1868,70)-
  2 vols-map-illus (5i3,5m8) 20. (5L3) 25. (5m3,4c8,rub) 22.50
--Recollections of..His Diary-NY-1910-DblidayPage-472p-
  ed by M L Avary (5p9) 8.50
STEPHENS,MRS ANNS-Ladies Complete Guide to Crochet,Fancy
  Knitting & Needlework-NY-n.d.-117p-obl 12mo-6 fldg plts
  (5n 7,tn) 3.50
--Malaeska,Indian Wife of White Hunter-NY-(1929)-254p-
  reprnt (4b3,f) 10. (4b2,rprd) 8.00
--Phemie Frost's Experiences-NY-1874-Carleton-408p-1st ed
  (5x4) 15.00
STEPHENS,C A-Adventures of 6 Young Men in Wildes of Maine
  & Canada-Lond-(c1890)-239p-plts (4d2) 12.50
--Great Years of Our Lives-Bost-(1912)-313p (5e8) 4.00
--The Knockabout Club Alongshore-Bost-(1882)-Estes&Lauriat-
  240p-lg8vo-pict cl-illus (5j5) 7.50
--Left on Labrador or Cruise of Schooner Yacht "Curlew"-Phila-
  1873-illus (4b9,faded) 10.00
--Off to the Geysers,or the Young Yachters in Iceland-Bost-1872-
  dec cl-sm8vo-238p(24) (4t7,sl loose) 15.00
--same-Phila,Chig&Tor-(1873)-Winston-Vol 3 of Camping Out
  Series-238p-(19)(ads)-frontis-7 plts-pict cl (5p1) 5.00
STEPHENS,G W-St Lawrence Waterway Project-1930-460p-
  2 lg fldg maps-illus (4b9) 20.00
STEPHENS,GEO W-Report on British & Continental Ports with View
  to Development of Port of Montreal,etc-Lond-1908-hf mor-
  151p-11 col maps-2 fldg charts (4d4) 15.00
STEPHENS,HENRY L-Cinderella or the Glass Slipper-NY-1866-
  8vo-10p plus 6 inserted plts-cl (5i3) 7.50
--The Comic Natural History of the Human Race-Phila-(1851)-
  illus-v scarce (5m6,wn,tn,pres)15.(5w0,v poor,lacks pgs) 20.00

USED BOOK PRICE GUIDE

STEPHENS, HENRY L (continued)
--The Prince's Ball-NY-1860-Rudd&Carleton-cl-12mo
(5cc0,autg) 15.00
--Puss in Boots-NY-Hurd&Houghton-plts-1st ed (5cc0,wn) 15.00
STEPHENS, JAS-Incidents of Travel in Greece, Turkey, Russia &
Poland-NY-1838-Harper-sm8vo-cl-illus-fldg map-2 vols (5v7) 38.50
STEPHENS, JAS-Collected poems-NY-1926-Macmillan-268p
(5v6) 10.00
--same-Lond-1926-Macmillan-lg papr-1st ed-ltd to 500c
(5ss9,vg,autg) 30.00
--The Crock of Gold-Lond-1912-Macmillan-8vo-orig cl-1st ed
(5d3,f,dj) 85. (4g1,hng weak) 75.00
--same-Lond-1926-4to-orig hf cl-12 mount illus in col by
Mackenzie-ltd to 525c (5r9,scuff) 25. (5j2) 30.00
--same-NY-1942-illus by Robt Lawson-sm folio-cl-box,autg
Limited Editions Club (5b0) 30.00
--Etched in Moonlight-Lond-1928-Macmillan-1st ed (5ss9,dj) 10.00
--Green Branches-NY-1916-Macmillan-bds-vel bk-1st ed-
ltd to 500c (5ss9) 15.00
--Irish Fairy Tales-NY-1920-sm sq12mo-cl-16p illus in col by
Rackham (5t5,rbnd,f bndg) 49.50 (5t2,f,dj) 14.50
--Strict Joy-NY-1931-Macm-1st ed (4g1) 4.50
STEPHENS, JOHN L-Incidents of Travel in Central Amer, Chiapas,
& Yucatan-NY-Harper-1841-2 vols-8vo-dec cl-424p,474p-
fldg map-1st ed (5j5,wn,tn) 25. (5dd5,rbnd) 22. (5s9,rbnd) 75.00
--same-Lond-1841-Murray-2 vols-cl (5j5,shabby) 25.00
--same-1854-rev by F Catherwood-buck-plts (5L7) 17.50
--same-NewBrunswick-1949-Predmore,ed-2 vols-illus-cl&bds-
346p,401p-Rutgers Univ Pr (5t2) 7.50
--Incidents of Travel in Yucatan-NY-1843-Harper-2 vols-illus-
459p,478p-illus (5s9,rprd) 65. (5L0,f) 40.00
--same-NY-1848-orig lea-8vo-map-illus-2 vols
(4g6,cov loose,rprd) 15.00
--Viaje A Yucatan,1841,42-Mexico-1937-2 vols-wrps-illus-
orig wrps (5x5) 20.00
STEPHENS, L DOW-Life Sketches of a Jayhawker of '49-(San Jose)-
1916-wrps-68p-6 plts-1st ed-300c printed-scarce
(5F5,f) 45. (4L0) 65.00
STEPHENS, STEPHEN DEWITT-The Mavericks, Amer Engravers-
1950-Rutgers U Pr-219p-crown 4to (4a0,dj) 37.50
STEPHENS, W A-Hamilton & Other Poems & Lectures-Tor-1871-
2nd ed (4b9) 20.00
STEPHENS' PHILA DIRECTORY FOR 1796-Phila-1796-orig calf
(5m4,f) 150.00
STEPHENSON, MRS FREDK C-100 Years of Canadian Methodist
Missions-Tor-1925-265p-vol 1 (5dd0) 7.50
STEPHENSON, ISAAC-Recollections of Long Life-Chig-1915-264p-
cl (5mm7,autg) 22.50 (5y0) 15. (5m8,autg,underline) 12.50
STEPHENSON, J NEWELL-Pulp & Paper Manufacture-NY-1950-
3 vols (4m5,wn) 10.00
STEPHENSON, JOHN-Medical Botany-Lond-(1827 to)1831 -
mor-8vo-185 handcol plts-4 vols-1st ed (5z9,sl fox) 225.00
STEPHENSON, NATHANIEL WRIGHT-Autobiography of Abraham
Lincoln-Indnpls-(1926)-illus-501p (4b3,fade) 2.50 (5t7) 6.00
--Lincoln, An Account of His Personal Life-Indnpls-(1922)-
8vo-cl-illus-478p (5t2) 5.00
--Texas & Mexican War-NewHav-1921 (4a5) 6.00
STEPHENSON, O W-Ann Arbor, First Hundred Yrs-AnnArbor-
1927-478p-cl (5h7) 10.00
STEPHENSON, TERRY E-Caminos Viejos-SantaAna-1930-
SantaAna High School & Jr Coll-8vo-cl-111p-ltd to 500c(4t1) 50.00
--Shadows of Old Saddleback-SantaAna-1931-SantaAna High
School & Jr Coll Pr-8vo-part lea-209p-ltd to 500c (4t1) 50.00
STEPHENSON, WM B-Land of Tomorrow-NY-1919-plts-240p
(5s0,pres) 8.50 (5a1) 6.50
STERLING, ADA-A Belle of the Fifties-NY-1905-8vo-illus-386p-
cl (5m8) 6. (5L2) 10.00
STERLING, A M-Sterling Genealogy-1909-2 vols-1407p-
1 of 50c prntd-50 spec illus-scarce (5t9) 50.00
STERLING, F W-Internal Combustion Engine Manual-Annap-1911-
146p-illus-cl-1st ed (5y2,lt spots) 5.75
STERLING, FRANK, ed-Marine Engineers' Handbook-NY-1920-
illus-1486p-1st ed (5s1) 7.50
STERLING, GEO-Beyond the Breakers-SanFran-1914-A M Robertson-
8vo-cl (4g1,pres) 40.00
--The Caged Eagle & Other Poems-SanFran-1916-Robertson-
12mo-cl-1st issue(wi To for Too line 5,pg 34)
(5ee9,pres,auth's corrections) 75.00
--Lilith-SanFran-1920-Book Club of Calif-ltd to 350c (4a5) 27.50
--Ode on Opening of the Panama Pac Intl Expos-SanFran-1915-
8vo-bds-ltd to 525c (5F5,soil) 12.50
--Testimony of the Suns-Book Club of Calif-1927-thin folio-
bds-ltd to 300c (5ww3,sp weak) 40.00

STERLING, GEO (continued)
--Yosemite-SanFran-1916-sq8vo-wrps-1st ed (5F5) 6.00
STERLING, ROBT-Lighthouses of Maine Coast & Men Who Keep
Them-Brattleboro-1935-234p-illus (5s1,fade) 7.50
STERN, BERNHARD-The Family, Past & Present-NY-1938 (5qq5) 12.50
--The Lummi Indians of NoWest Washington, Cycle of Life,
Tribal Culture, Legend & Lore-Columbia Univ Pr-1934-
1st ed (5x5,dj) 20.00
STERN, G B-Bouquet-Lond-1927-13 illus-map-246p,(1)
(5g9) 6.50 (5w1) 7.50
--No Son of Mine-NY-1948-Macmillan-328p (5p0) 5.00
--Tents of Israel-Lond-1924 (4b6,pres,mor box) 25.00
STERN, PHILLIP VAN DOREN-The Confederate Navy-NY-1962-
Dblday-253p-4to (5p7) 10.00
--Life & Writings of Abraham Lincoln-NY-(1940)-Modern Library
Giant-863p (4b3) 2.50
--The Man Who Killed Lincoln-NY-1939-8vo-408p
(5L3) 3.50 (4a7) 6.50
STERNBECK, ALFRED-Filibusters & Buccaneers-1930-plts (5L7) 6.50
STERNBERG, MARTHA L-Geo Miller Sternberg, a Biography-
Chig-1920-326p plus index-illus-1st ed (5L2,f,unopnd) 25.00
STERNE, LAURENCE-Complete Works-NY-1904-FF Taylor-t8vo-
illus-buck-g.t.-labls-12 vols-Ltd York Ed (5t8,mint) 57.50
--Life & Opinions of Tristam Shandy & Sentimental Journey-
Lond-1900-2 vols-Macmillan (5t8) 12.50
--Life & Opinions of Tristam Shandy, Gentleman-2 vols-3/4 lea-
g.tooled -Lond-1911 (5t7) 15.00
--same-NY-1935-8vo-hf cl-Ltd Ed Club-ltd to 1500c,box,autg
(5b0) 30.00
--Original Letters of...-Lond-1788-Logographic Pr-calf-hf t.-
1st ed (5tt7,rebkd) 27.50
--Sentimental Journey Through France & Italy-NY-1884-illus by
Leloir-orig pic wrps (5yy6) 7.50
--same-NY-1930-3 Sirens Pr (5a6,vf) 7.50
--same-NY-1930-illus-Editions Co (5a6,f) 5.00
STERNER, R-The Negro's Share-NY-1943 (5x2,dj) 12.50
STERRETT, JOS-Fiscal & Economic Condition of Mexico-n.p.-n.d.-
(1928)-4to-256p-wrps (4a3) 25.00
STERRETT, LAURA C-The Erie Cook Book-Erie, Pa-1881-Atkinson's
Steam Pr House-272p-oilcloth (5g9) 20.00
STETSON, OSCAR F-Art of Ancestor Hunting-Brattleboro-1936-
1st ed (5yy6) 10.00
--Sketch of Cornet Robt Stetson of Plymouth Colony Troopers 1658-
(1929)-144p (5e8) 7.75
STETSON, W W-History & Civil Govt of Maine & Govt of US-
(1898)-340p (5e8) 4.75
STEUART, E H,comp-Gems from a Texas Quarry-NewOrl-1885-
300p (4j6) 27.50
STEUART, J-Bogota in 1836,7-NY-1838-Harper-12mo-cl
(4a3,ex-libr) 75.00
STEUART, J A-Robt Louis Stevenson, Man & Writer-Tor-1924-
2 vols-lg8vo-cl-port (5t0) 10.00
STEUBEN, BARON DE-Regulations for Order & Discipline of
Troops of US-NY-1809-16mo-engrs (5jj3,worn) 32.50
STEUBEN, F W A-The Military Companion, etc-Newburyport-1808-
bds-2 plts-12mo-47p-calf bk-2nd ed (4c8) 20.00
STEVENS, ABEL-History of the Methodist Episcopal Church in the
US-NY-1866,67-4 vols-sm8vo-cl-frontis (5t2) 8.50
--Memorials of the Early Progress of Methodism in the Eastern
States-Bost-1852 (5F0) 8.50
STEVENS, ALDEN G-Lion Boy-NY-1938-Lippincott-pict cov-233p
(4t5) 4.00
STEVENS, CAPT C A-Berdan's US Sharpshooters in Army of Potomac
1861 to 1865-StPaul-1892-8vo-555p (4a7,rub,fade) 75.00
STEVENS, C E-Anthony Burns, A History-Bost-1856-illus (5x2) 75.00
STEVENS, CLARA SHERWOOD-Passages from Philosophy of Herbert
Spencer-Portland-1910-Mosher Pr-ltd ed (4b4) 17.50
STEVENS, D L-Bibliog of Municipal Utility Regulation & Municipal
Ownership-Cambr-1918 (5r4) 10.00
STEVENS, DAN'L GORDON-First 100 Yrs of The Amer Baptist
Publication Soc-Phila-n.d.-(ca 1924)-illus-120p (5w9) 5.00
STEVENS, DORIS-Paintings & Drawings of Jeannette Scott,
1864 to 1937-1940-priv prnt-96p-ltd to 500c-R4to (4a0) 10.00
STEVENS DURYEA CO-Catalogue-ChipFalls-1907-lg4to-63p-
17p illus-g. cl sp (4h8,sl wn,5cc7) 42.50
STEVENS, EZRA A-Geographical Keys-Portsmouth, NH-1819-
52p-disbnd (5g3) 25.00
STEVENS, FRANCES-The Usages of the Best Society-NY-1884-
201p (5w7,fade) 4.50
STEVENS, FRANK WALKER-Beginnings of the NY Central RR-
NY-1926-408p-illus-t.e.g.-1st ed (5w0,dj) 12.50
STEVENS, G A-Garden Flowers in Color-NY-1939-320p-
col plts (5s7) 4.50

STEVENS, G A (continued)
--Roses in the Little Garden-Bost-1926-118p-photos (5s7) 3.50
STEVENS, GEO A-Songs, Comic & Satyrical-Oxf-1782-247p-
calf-2nd ed (5a1, needs rebnd) 15.00
STEVENS, GEO T-Three Years in the 6th Corps-Albany-1866-
1st ed-illus (5tt5, pres) 17.50
--NY-1870-2nd ed-rev & corrected-ports (5tt5) 10.00
STEVENS, GORHAM PHILLIPS-Italian Doorways-Cleve-1929-
Jansen-8p text-194 plts-lg4to-cl (5m5) 30.00
STEVENS, H N-Lewis Evans, His Map of Middle Brit Colonies in
Amer-Lond-1905-41p-Chiswick Pr-wrps (5yy6) 25.00
STEVENS, HAZARD-Life of Isaac Ingalls Stevens-Bost-1900-2 vols-
photos-maps (5L0) 20. (5L7) 12.50 (5s4, sl wn) 17.50
STEVENS, HELEN N-Memorial Biography of Adele M Fielde,
Humanitarian-Seattle-(1918)-377p-photos (5s4, soil) 9.00
STEVENS, HENRY, comp-Analytical Index to Colonial Documents
of NJ-NY-1858-504p (4m4, 5tt5) 17.50
--The Bibles in Caxton exhibition 1873-Lond-1873-12mo-cl-
rev & cor (4c1) 6.00
--Catalogue of My English library-Lond-1853-107p
(5p9, lacks bkstrp) 10.00
--Historical & Geographical Notes on Earliest Discoveries in
America, 1453 to 1530-NewHav&Lond-1869-6 pkt maps-
orig cl (5m3) 125.00
--Historical Nuggets-Lond-1862-2 vols (5n4, chip) 37.50
--Recoll of Mr Jas Lenox...NY & Formation of His Library-Lond-
1887-(Chiswick Pr)-12mo-ports-3/4 vel (5yy6, f) 17.50
STEVENS, HENRY N-New Light on Discovery of Australia-
Hakluyt Soc-1930-2nd Ser, #64-261p-maps (5s6) 10.00
--Ptolemy's Geography-Lond-1908-2nd ed-Chiswick Pr-orig wrps-
scarce (5yy6) 25.00
STEVENS, HORACE NATHAN'L-Nathan'l Stevens 1786 to 1865-
NoAndover-1946-Merrymount Pr-illus D B Updike (5r0) 6.50
STEVENS, ISAAC INGALLS-Report of Explor of Route for Pacific RR-
(Wash-1855)-599p-index-disbnd-2 maps(of 3) (5tt0) 25.00
--same-Wash-1855-599p-1st ed-HED 129 (4n4) 35.00
STEVENS CO, J & E-Export Catalog of Pistols for Harmless Paper
Caps, Toy Banks, etc, #51-Cromwell-(1924)-obl 8vo-illus-26p-
wrps (5t7) 17.50
STEVENS, JAS-Homer in the Sagebrush-NY-1928-313p (5s4) 6.00
STEVENS, JOHN AUSTIN-Colonial Records of the New York
Chamber of Commerce 1768 to 1784-NY-1867-172p-
plts(some fldg) (5t4) 15.00
--Expedition of Lafayette against Arnold-Balt-1878-36p-
orig prntd wrps (5mm8) 5.00
STEVENS, JOHN H-Personal Recoll of Minn & Its People, etc-
Minnpls-1890-illus-8vo-1st ed
(5t9) 25. (4g6, rub, sig loose) 15.00
STEVENS, JOHN L-Picturesque Hawaii...Her Unique History,
Strange People, etc-Phila-1894-obl 4to-illus-cl&lea-126p-
photos (5t0) 15.00
STEVENS, JOSEPH E-1798 to 1948 Amer Dyewood Co-n.p.-1948-
cl-120p-illus (5hh7) 10.00
STEVENS, MARY-The Easy Way in Cookery-(BayCty, Mich, 1922)-
280p-fabr-lg8vo (5c9, rub) 4.50
STEVENS, MONTAGUE-Meet Mr Grizzly-1943-Univ New Mex Pr-
2nd prntng-autogd check laid in-scarce (5g6, autg laid in) 15.00
STEVENS, O B-Georgia, Historical & Industrial-Atlanta-1901-
(Dept of Agric)-thk8vo-illus (4a1, hng sprung) 15.00
STEVENS, ROBT C-History of Chandler, Ariz-Tucson-1955-106p-
wrps (4a5) 9.50 (5g0) 4.00
STEVENS, SUSAN SHEPPARD-I am the King-Bost-1898-Little,
Brown-pict cl-1st ed (5rr6) 10.00
STEVENS, SYLVESTER, ed-Chronicles of Northwestern Penna
Wilderness-Harrisburg-1941-342p-illus-maps (5h9) 12.50
STEVENS, THOS-Around the World on Bicycle-NY-1894-illus-
Vol 2 (only) (5ii3) 15.00
--Through Russia on a Mustang-Lond-1892-cl-8vo-334p-plts(5v7)12.50
STEVENS, THOS WOOD-The Entrada, The Coronado Cuarto
Centennial Comm-Albuqu-1940-1st ed (5g0) 7.50
--Lettering-NY-(1916)-illus-4to-cl-113p (5t7) 7.50
STEVENS, W J-Chip On My Shoulder-Bost-1946 (5x2, dj) 12.50
STEVENS, WALLACE-The Auroras of Autumn-NY-1950-Knopf-
12mo-orig cl-1st ed (4h0, f, wn dj) 20.00
--The Collected Poems-NY-1955-Knopf (5p9) 5.00
--The Man With the Blue Guitar & Other Poems-NY-1937-1st ed
(5r9) 15.00
--Transport to Summer-NY-1947-cl bkd bds-1st ed (5r9, dj) 12.50
STEVENS, WALTER B-Centennial History of Missouri-StL, Chig-
1921-6 vols-3/4 lea (5ff7) 50.00
--Missouri, The Center State 1821 to 1915-Chig-1915-photos-
illus-part lea-4 vols-1st ed (4t3, sl reprd) 30.00

STEVENS, WALTER B-100 Yrs of the StLouis Republic-StL-1908-
28p-wrps-v scarce (5L2) 8.50
--St Louis, Fourth City 1764 to 1909-Chig&StL-1909-3 vols-
hf lea (5y0, jnts wn) 25. (5dd4, rub) 75.00
--same-1909-1132p (4t2) 40.00
--A Trip to Panama-StL-1907-obl 4to-illus-1st ed (5ss5) 7.50
--Through Texas-n.p.-(StLouis)-1892-8vo-orig prntd wrps-
1st ed-scarce (5i0, f) 75.00
STEVEN, WM-Memoir of Geo Heriot-1845-buck-map (5L7, rbnd) 12.50
STEVENS, WM B-History of the 50th Reg of Infantry Mass Vol
Militia-Bost-1907-395p-illus-map-1st ed (5mm8) 5. (5L5) 10.00
STEVENS, REV WM BACON-History of Georgia from its First
Discov by Europeans-NY-1847-Appleton-Vol 1(only)-503p-
illus-fldg plt-cl-1st ed (5F9, wn) 15.00
STEVENS, WM CHASE-Kansas Wild Flowers-Lawrence-1961-446p
plus index-photos-frontis (5L0, f, dj) 8.00
STEVENS, WM O-Annapolis, Anne Arundel's Town-NY-1937-illus-
cl-339p (4i2, dj) 10.00
--Boy's Book Famous Warships-NY-1916-236p-4 col plts (5s1) 3.50
--Charleston, Historic City of Gardens-NY-1937-331p-col frontis-
illus (5h9) 7.50
--same-NY-1940 (4j4) 4.50
--Discovering Long Island-NY-1939-illus-349p (5t7) 10.00
--History of Sea Power-NY-1932-458p-maps (5s1, ex-libr) 6.00
--Nantucket The Far Away Island-NY-1937-illus (5F0, autg) 4.50
--same-NY-1944-316p-illus (5t7, dj, autg) 7.50
--Old Williamsburg & Her Neighbors-NY-1938-337p-illus-
col frontis (5p7) 5. (5h9) 6.50
--The Shenandoah & its Byways-NY-1941-Dodd, Mead-illus-
281p (5p7) 5.00
--Story of Our Navy-NY-(1918)-maps-339p (5s1, rprd) 3.00
STEVENS-NELSON PAPER CATALOGUE-(NY, ca 1953)-lg4to-
patternd bds-mor bkstrp (5ee9) 100.00
STEVENSON, ADLAI E-Something of Men I Have Known-Chig-
1909-cl-442p-2nd ed (4h7) 10.00
STEVENSON, ALEX-Battle of Stone's River Near Murfreesboro, Tenn,
Dec 30, 1862 to Jan 3, 1863-Bost-1884-cl-197p-2 fldg maps
(4t7, wn) 15.00
STEVENSON, ANNA B-Beams from Lone Star-SanAntonio-1949
(4a5) 3.00
STEVENSON, B F-Cumberland Gap-Cinn-1885-8vo-orig wrps-22p
(5m6) 8.50
STEVENSON, BURTON, ed-The Home Book of Proverbs, Maxims
& Familiar Phrases-NY-1948-2957p (5c3) 15.00
--Home Book of Verse-NY-(1923)-Holt-4009p-India papr-5th ed, rev
American & English (5p7) 15.00
STEVENSON, E L-Maps Illustrating Early Discovery & Explor in
Amer-NewBrunswick-1906-folio-maps-orig wrps (5jj3, sp tn) 27.50
STEVENSON, ELDER EDW-Remin of Joseph, the prophet & the
coming forth of the book of Mormon-SaltLkCty-1893-8vo-
orig prntd wrps-frontis-4 plts-1st ed (5i9) 20.00
STEVENSON, ELIZ-The Crooked Corridor-NY-1949-172p (5mm2) 5.00
STEVENSON, G J-Wesley Family-1876-562p (5t9) 30.00
STEVENSON, J H-Songs & Poems of the Old West by an Old Cowboy-
n.p.-1937-t8vo-(98p)-priv prntd-1st ed-scarce (5g0) 12.00
STEVENSON, JOHN-British Fungi-Lond-1886-2 vols (5s7, fade) 10.00
STEVENSON, R SCOTT-In Search of Spanish Painting-Lond-(1955)-
illus (5ii3) 10.00
STEVENSON, ROBT L-Across the Plains-Lond-1892-4to-lg papr-
(100 prntd)-cream col cl-1st ed (5hh1, sl fray) 37.50
--same-Hillsborough, Calif-1950-LDAllen Pr-t8vo-dec cl-illus-
ltd to 200c (5ee9) 37.50
--Ballads-Lond-1890-sq t8vo-buck-Ltd Ed-ltd to 100c, nbrd
(5r9, sl fade) 15.00
--The Black Arrow-NY-1916-4to-14 col plts-328p-pict cl-
NCWyeth, illus (5t2) 7.50
--Catriona-Lond-1893-1st ed (5r9) 8.50
--A Child's Garden of Verses-Lond-1885-12mo-orig blue cl-g.t.-
earliest bndng wi apostrophe in normal state(later bndg it looks
like fig 7)-1st ed (5dd8, vg) 175.00
--same-NY-1895-Scribner's Sons-illus by Robinson-sm8vo-137p-
orig pict cl (5c8, sl rub) 25.00
--same-Lond-1896-illus (5i3, rub) 5.00
--same-Chig-(c1916)-Donohue-illus by Myrtle Sheldon-8vo-96p-
pict cl (5p1) 3.00
--same-NY-1923-Scribner-illus by Jessie Willcox Smith
(5hh3) 5. (5x0) 3.50
--same-Springfield-(c1946)-(cov title)-(12p) & 6 pop ups-ca 8x10"-
pict glazed bds-The Jolly Jump Ups-McLoughlinBros(5p1) 10.00
--Diogenes in London-SanFran-1920-Grabhorn-t8vo-papr cov bds-
labls-1st ed-ltd to 150c (5ee9) 75.00
--The Ebb Tide-Chig-1894-Stone&Kimball-1st ed (5i3, f) 7.50
--Fables-NY-1902-Scribner's-92p-24mo-cl-t.e.g. (5p1, spots) 3.50

STEVENSON,ROBT L (continued)
--Father Damien-SanFran-1930-bds-t.e.g.-ltd to 250c,nbrd,box
        (5b0)   45.00
--A Footnote to History-Lond-1892-1st ed (5mm2,als tip in)
        37.50
--same-NY-1892-Scribner's Sons-1st Amer ed   (5ss9) 10.00
--The History of Moses-"Oak Knoll"-1919-10p-col frontis-facs-
   blue wrps-orig mailing env   (5w9,AENewton autg) 15.00
--An Inland Voyage-Lond-1878-12mo-cl-1st ed of auth's 1st book
        (5gg6)   75.00
--Island Nights' Entertainment-Lond-1893-Cassell-1st ed-illus-
   orig pic cl (5tt7) 15. (5j2) 20. (5tt6,5mm2,4b5,5dd8) 25.00
--same-NY-1893-1st Amer ed-illus   (5i3)   5.00
--Kidnapped-n.d.-(Lond)-1886-Cassell&Co-1st ed-1st state(wi advts
   dated 4/86 etc)-fldg map frontis (5ss9,vg) 50. (5v2,vg) 45.00
--same-Lond-1876-fldg map-1st ed (4F6,rprd) 27.50 (5mm2) 25.00
--same-NY-1886-Scribner's-1st Amer ed (4b5,spot,rub) 25.00
--same-NY-1938-Ltd Ed Club-ltd to 1500c,box (5b0) 20.00
--Letters of...to His Family & Friends (Sidney Colvin,ed)-NY-
   1902-Scribner's - 2 vols   (4p1) 17.50
--same-NY-1911-Scribner-sm8vo-cl-4 vols-frontis-ports-"A new ed"
        (5t2)   12.50
--The Master of Ballantrae,a Winter's Tale-Lond-1889-Cassell-
   dec cl-"12th thousand"(same yr as orig prntng) (5c8) 5.00
--The Merry Men & Other Tales & Fables-Lond-Chatto&Windus-8vo-
   orig blue cl-1st ed -1887   (5dd8) 35.00
--Prayers Written at Vailima-NY-1904-Scribner's Sons-12mo-bds-
   Merrymount Pr-cl bk-1st ed   (5ss9,vg) 7.50
--Poems Hitherto Unpublished-Bost-1916-2 vols-4to-green cl-t.e.g.-
   frontis-Bibliophile Soc-ltd to 484c-for members (5b0) 75.00
--same-Bost-1916-R8vo-2 vols-g.t.-3/4 orig vel-ltd to 480c-
   for members of Bibliophile Soc   (5t8,mint) 32.50
--same-Bost-1921-port-hf vel-boxed-Bibliophile Soc-ltd to 450c
      (5d3) 15. (5m2)   8.50
--St Ives,Being Adventures of a French Prisoner in England-NY-
   1897-Scribner'sSons-1st ed(Amer preceded Engl) (5ss9,vg) 25.00
--San Fran-1890,Modern Cosmopolis-SanFran-1963-Book Club of Calif-
   ltd to 450c (4b4,f) 25. (5h5,vf) 20.00
--The Sea Frogs-SanFran-(1907)-Paul Elder-16mo-bds-parch sp-
   1000c prntd   (5ss9,f,dj) 20.00
--Silverado Journal-SanFran-1954-illus-4to-Book Club of Calif-
   Grabhorn Pr-ltd to 400c (4g6,mint) 50. (5ss9,f) 65.00
--The Silverado Squatters-Lond-1883-12mo-hf mor-1st ed (5r9) 17.50
--same-SanFran-1952-Grabhorn   (5ss9,f,5dd5,5x5) 20.00
--A Stevenson Medley-Lond-1899-Chatto&Windus-1st ed-
   ltd to 300c-hf lea,as issued   (4b5) 40.00
--Stevenson's Workshop-Chig-1921-29 Ms facs-priv prntd for
   Mrs Francis S Peabody-1st ed-orig white bds,boxed (5ss9,f) 22.50
--Story of Monterey,The Old Pacific Capital-SanFran-1944-
   Colt Pr-500c   (5x5) 20.00
--Strange Case of Dr Jekyll & Mr Hyde-Lond-1886-Longmans,Green-
   orig tan cl-1st Engl ed   (5hh1,vg) 95.00
--same-NY-1886-Scribner's Sons-1st Amer ed (5hh1,vg) 37.50
--Travels with a Donkey in the Cevennes-Lond-1879-16mo-cl-illus g.
        (4c2,crack,rub) 25.00
--Travels with a Donkey-NY-1957-ltd to 1500c,nbrd-Ltd Ed Club-
   boxed   (5F1,f) 25.00
--Treasure Island-Leipzig-1884-Tauchnitz-24mo-287p-lea&bds
        (5p1,edges wn) 5.00
--same-NY-1911-1st ed-N C Wyeth,illus   (5v2,f) 20.00
--same-Chig-(c1915)-Milo Winter,illus-258p-14 plts-pict labl-
   Rand,McNally-Windermere Series   (5p1) 5.00
--same-NY-1926-273p-N C Wyeth,illus   (5t4) 8.00
--same-NY-1931-273p-N C Wyeth,illus-4to-9 col plts-pict cl
        (5t2)   7.50
--same-NY-1941-8vo-illus-Ltd Ed Club-ltd to 1500c,box
        (5b0,fade) 20.00
--same-NY-(1941)-Heritage-illus-8vo-273p (5p1,box) 7.50
--Will O'The Mill-Bost-1895-JosKnight-illus-dec blu cl-16mo-
   (64p) (2)-Cosy Corner Series   (5p1,sl stn) 12.50
--Works,(28 vols)-Edinb&Lond-1894 to 1910-8vo-orig cl-labls-t.e.g.-
   (plus 5 vols)-Edinb ed-ltd to 1035c (4h0) 33 vols 150.00
--The Wrecker-Lond-1892-1st ed-illus (5i3) 22.50 (5ss9) 20.00
--The Wrong Box-Lond-1889-1st ed-ads   (4b7) 25.00
STEVENSON,ROBT L & LLOYD OSBOURNE-The Wrong Box-NY-
   1889-244p-(piece of newspapr clipping pasted on front) (5t4) 10.00
STEVENSON,MRS ROBT LOUIS-Cruise of "Janet Nichol"-NY-
   1914-illus-1st ed   (4b7) 10.00
STEVENSON,WM G-13 Months in Rebel Army-NY-1862-232p-
   cl-1st ed   (5h1) 12.50
STEVENSON-HAMILTON,J-The Low Veld-Lond-1929-Cassell-
   287p-photos   (4t5) 22.50
STEVERS,MARTIN D-Sea Lanes-NY-(1938)-illus-326p-de luxe ed
        (5q0)   10.00

STEWARD,AUSTIN-22 Years a Slave & 40 Yrs a Freeman,etc-
   Rochester-1857-bds-360p-12mo   (4t7,recased) 47.50
STEWARD,JULIAN H,ed-Handbook of SoAmerican Indians-Wash-
   1946 to 50-illus-fldg maps & others-6 vols (4m4) 90.00
--Handbook of SoAmer Indians,Vol 3,Tropical Forest Tribes-1948-
   8 maps-126 plts-986p-scarce-BAE,B143-hard cov (4b2) 30.00
STEWARD,WM-First Edition of Steward's Healing Art,Corrected &
   Improved by Orig Hand...To Which He Has Added a Concise
   Herbal-Saco,Me-1827-Putnam&Blake,prntrs-8vo-calf-calf labl
        (5zz7,rebnd) 75.00
STEWART,A C-The Beaver & Other Odds & Ends-Tor-1918 (5w8) 10.00
STEWART,A T-Catalogue of the Collection of Paintings,Sculptures
   & Other Objects of Art-Kirby,comp-Amer Art Assoc-NY-1887-
   ltd to 100c,lg papr   (5ss5,bkstrp tn) 30.00
STEWART,C S-Private Journal of the Rev...-Dublin-1830-12mo-
   orig cl-labl-1st Irish ed   (4h0,hng crack,libr labl on sp) 155.00
STEWART,C S-Visit to South Seas,in Ship Vincennes-NY-1831-
   John Haven- 2 vols-orig bds   (5tt8) 50.00
STEWART,C S-Brazil & La Plata-NY-1856-2 plts-1st ed
        (5s9,dmgd bndg) 15.00
STEWART,CECIL-Topiary-Golden Cockerel Pr-col plts-sq t8vo-
   dec cl-ltd to 500c   (5t5) 12.50
STEWART,CHAS EDW- A collection of trifles in verse-Sudbury-
   1797-4to-orig wrps-1st ed   (5x3,sp def) 35.00
STEWART,DAVID A-Glimpses at Manitoba History-Winn-1932-
   15p-wrps   (5a1,autog) 5.00
STEWART,E I-Custer's Luck-U of Okla Pr-1955-522p-illus-maps-
        (5a9)   10.00
STEWART,EDGAR I-Washington-NY-(1957)-4to-photos (5s4) 65.00
STEWART,ELIHU-Down the Mackenzie & Up the Yukon in 1906-
   Lond-1913-30 illus-map (5q8) 7.50 (5r7) 10.00
STEWART,ELINORE P-Letters of a woman homesteader-Bost-1914-
   Houghton,Miff-282p-illus (5u3) 7. (5m9) 8.00
--Letters on An Elk Hunt By A Woman Homesteader-Bost-1915-
   162p   (5ss8) 6.50
STEWART,F L-Sugar Made From Maize & Sorghum-Wash-1878-102p
        (5c5)   7.50
STEWART,F H-Indians of Southern New Jersey-1932-sewn-94p
        (5L7)   5.00
STEWART,FRANK H-Notes on Old Gloucester Co,NJ-n.p.-1917-
   Vol 1-342p-illus-Soc of Penna   (5w4) 22.50
--Our New Home & Old Times-Phila-(1913)-orig wrps-illus-48p
        (4m4)   10.00
STEWART,GEO B,ed-Centennial Memorial-Harrisburg-1894-435p-
   illus   (5r7,unopnd) 17.50
STEWART,GEO-Names on the Land-NY-(1945)-1st ed
      (5yy6) 5. (5h9)   4.50
--The Opening of the Calif Trail-Univ of Calif-1953-cl
        (5h5,f,dj) 10.00
--Ordeal by Hunger-1936-321p-1st ed-illus (5r1,vg) 17.50
--Take Your Bible in One Hand,Life of Wm Henry Thomes-SanFran-
   1939-Colt Pr-folio-bds-illus-ltd to 750c
   (4a3,lt soil) 12.50 (5h4,fade) 10. (5x5) 15.00
STEWART,GEO W-Big Trees of The Giant Forest,Sequoia Natl Park-
   SanFran-1930-104p-pict bds-(Bruce Brough Pr)-scarce (5r0) 10.00
STEWART,HOMER L-Celery Growing & Marketing-Tecumseh,Mich-
   1891-frontis-151p-13 plts   (5s7,rub) 6.50
STEWART,J A-Descendants of Valentine Hollingsworth-Louisville-
   1925-208p   (5a9) 15.00
STEWART,J A-Robt Louis Stevenson,Man & His Work-Lond-n.d.-
   c1924-Sampson,Low,Marston-1st ed-2 vols (5ss9,dj) 20.00
STEWART,JAS-Index or Abridgement of Acts of Parliament...1424
   to 1707-Edinb-1707-16mo-old calf   (4b7,wn) 25.00
STEWART,JAS-Steam Engineering of Sugar Plantations,Steamships
   & Locomotive Engines-NY-1867-Russell's Amer Steam Pr House-
   138p-cl-errata slip   (5a0,f) 7.50
STEWART,JAS M-Rudyard Kipling,a Bibliographical Catalog-Tor-
   1959-673p-ltd to 750c   (4g2) 27.50
STEWART,JOHN-Travels over Most Interesting Parts of the Globe-
   ca 1789-16mo-2 vols-buck   (5L7,rbnd) 15.00
STEWART,JOHN STRUTHERS-Hist of NW Ohio-Indpls-1935-cl-
   3 vols-1118p-scarce   (5h7) 50.00
STEWART,LAWRENCE O-Rainbow Bright-Phila-(1923)-illus-145p
        (4h4,dj)   7.50
STEWART,LUCY SHELTON-The Reward of Patriotism-NY-1930-
   Walter Neale-484p-illus   (5p0) 7.50
STEWART,MARCUS A-Rosita,A Calif Tale-SanJose-1882-72p-
   cl-Mercury Steam Print   (5r0,soil,wn) 20.00
STEWART,MARY-Way to Wonderland-NY-(1917)-col illus-1st ed
        (5yy6)   6.00
STEWART,MOTHER-Crusader in Great Brit-Sprngfld-1893-396p-cl
        (4h7)   7.50

STEWART,MOTHER (continued)
--Memories of Crusade-Columbus-1888-535p-cl (5h7) 10. (5w0) 8.50
--same-Columbus-1889-535p-cl-2nd ed (4h7) 7.50
STEWART,PHILEMON-A Holly,Sacred & Divine Roll & Book...In
Two Parts,Par 1(2)..Canterbury,NH-1843-prntd in the United
Soc-405p-calf-1st ed (5m3) 50.00
STEWART,R-Col Geo Steuart & His Wife Margaret Harris,Their Anc
& Desc-1907-522p (4n2) 12.50
STEWART,ROBT-American Farmer's Horse Book-Cinn-1867-600p-
lea-illus (5y0) 13.50
STEWART,ROBT L-History of the 140th Regiment Penna Vol-n.p.-
1912-cl-504p (4k2) 15.00
--Sheldon Jackson,Pathfinder & Prospector of Missionary Vanguard
in Rocky Mntns & Alaska-(1908)-Revell Co-1st ed
(5x5,wn) 12.50 (5x5) 17.50
STEWART,ROSS-Home Decorations Its Problems & Solutions-NY-
(1935)-68 plts-323p (5w7,fade) 3.50
STEWART,T D,ed-Basic Readings on Identification of Human
Skeletons-NY-1954-(Wenner Gren)-illus-4to-wrps (4b7) 15.00
STEWART,VIRGINIA-45 Contemporary Mexican Artists-Sanford Univ
Pr-(1951)-1st ed (5x5) 22.50
STEWART,W F-Geological Report upon "Golden Fleece" Gold
& Silver Mine,Peavine Mining Dist,Washoe Co,Nev,by-(wrpr t.)-
Reno-1879-8vo-orig wrps-12p (5a3,wrp sl tn) 125.00
STEWART,W K-Brown's Signalling-(1941,reprnt)-220p-illus-
bds (5s1) 3.00
STEWART,W M-Policy of Extending Government Aid to Additional
RR's to Pacific-Wash-1869-Sen Rep Com #219-31p-spec wrps-
scarce (5L2,f) 25.00
STEWART, COL WM H-Spirit of South-NY-1908-Neale Pub-238p
(4b3,cov fleck) 10.00
STEWART'S COOK BOOK-Louisville-(ca 1910)-Stewart's Dry
Goods Co-wrps-96p (5yy8) 5.00
STICKLE,ARTHUR W,ed-State of Texas Book, 100 Yrs of Progress-
Austin-1937-Bur Research & Publ-4to-cl-496p (4t1) 15.00
STICKLEY,GUSTAV-Craftsman Homes-NY-(1909)-4to-illus-cl-
205p (5t7) 12.50
STICKNEY,GARDNER P-Nicholas Perrot-Milwkee-1895-Parkman
Club Publ#1-15p-wrps (5L2) 6.50
--Use of Maize by Wisc Indians-Milwkee-1897-Parkman Club Publ
#13-(25p)-wrps (5L2) 7.50
STICKNEY,JOS L-Life & Glorious Deeds of Adm Dewey-Springfield-
(1899)-photos (5s1) 4.00
--Life of Adml Geo Dewey & Conquest of the Philippines-
Phila-(1899)-Ziegler-lg8vo-pict cl-photos-412p (5j5,f) 15.00
STICKNEY,L W-Dest of Robt Kinsman of Ipswich-1876-258p(5t9) 25.00
STICKNEY,MATTHEW ADAMS-The Stickney Family-Salem-1869-
526p-cl (5h2) 35.00
--Desc Philip & Mary Fowler of Ipswich-1883-247p (4t2) 12.50
STICKNEY,MARY E-Brown of Lost River-NY-1900-Appleton-
309p-fiction-1st ed (5s4,ex-libr) 4. (5x4) 10.00
STIEFEL,H C-Slices from a Long Loaf-Pittsb-(1905)-221p-cl
(5h1,sl rub) 8.50 (5jj9,pres) 12.50
STIEFF,FREDK P-Eat Drink & Be Merry in Maryland-NY-(1932)-
326p (4g9) 8.50
STIELER,K-The Rhine,From its Source to the Sea-Lond-1878-
Bickers&Son-folio-mor-a.e.g.-425 engrs-1st Engl ed
(4h0,f,fox) 60.00
STIFF,EDW-The Texan Emigrant,etc-Cinn-1840-Geo Conclin-
367(1)p-hf mor-1st ed-rare (5z7,f bndg) 275.00
STIFLER,JAS MADISON-"My Dear Girl"-NY-1927-279p-illus-
1st ed (5h9,pres) 13.50
STIGAND,C H-Game of British East Africa-Lond-1909-310p-
photos-4to (4p5) 48.75
--Land of Zinj-Lond-1913-8vo-351p-photos-pkt map
(4a6,lt fox) 12.50
STILES,BERT-Serenade to the Big Bird-NY-(1952)-216p-1st ed
(4h4,tn dj) 7.50
STILES,EDW H-Recollections & sketches of notable lawyers and
public men of early Iowa-DesMoines-1916-Homestead Publ-
988p (5L2,rprd) 15. (5u3) 12.50
STILES,EZRA-History of 3 of the Judges of King Charls I-Hartf-
1794-Elisha Babcock-357p-lf of adv-12mo-calf-pasted slip
of errata (5i9,frontis & 8 plts) 70. (5L1,frontis & 8plts,rbkd)35.00
--Literary Diary of Ezra Stiles-NY&NewHaven-1901 to 1916-
3 vols-cl (5tt8) 50. (4c1) 75.00
--Oratio Inauguralis habita in Sacello Collegii Yalensis-Hartf-
1778-Watson&Goodwin-sm4to-disbnd-wrps-1st ed (5n2) 75.00
STILES,H R-Civil,Political,Prof & Ecclesiastical Hist...of Co
of Kings & City of Brooklyn-NY-(1884)-illus-ports-4to-
1408p-buck (5yy0,rebnd) 75.00
--Gen of the Conn Family-1895-782p (5t9) 27.50

STILES,HELEN E-Pottery of the Amer Indians-NY-1939-165p
plus index -photos-1st ed (5L0) 15.00
STILES,HENRY REED,M D-Bundling,Its Origin,Progress & Decline
in Amer-Albany-1869-Munsell-12mo-1st ed-scarce (4c8) 37.50
--same-Albany-1871-1st ed (5jj3) 20.00
--same-NY-(1934)-cl-146p (5dd4) 8.50 (4t7) 8.50
--same-n.p.-n.d.-bds-cl bkstrp-t.e.g.-for subscribers only
(5h9) 5. (5w5) 7.50
--same-MtVernon-(n.d.)-sm8vo-patternd bds-88p-Peter Pauper Pr-
boxed (5j5) 6.00
STILES,J C-Modern Reform Examined,or the Union of North &
South on Subject of Slavery-Phila-1858 (5x2) 27.50
STILES,ROBT-Four Years under Marse Robert-NY-1904-Neale-368p-
frontis-3rd ed (5mm8) 15.00
STILL,ANDREW T-Autobiography of-Kirksville-1897-illus-460p
(4b3) 10. (4k8) 17.50
"STILL ANOTHER" COOK BOOK-by Ladies Aid Soc of 1st Congreg
Church-Oakland-1888-120p-red limp fabr-8vo-Pac Press Pub Hse
3rd edition (5c9,scuff) 20.00
STILL,BAYRD-Mirror for Gotham-NY-1956-illus-1st ed (5ii3,f) 10.00
STILL,JAS-Early Recollections & Life-1877 (5L7) 30.00
STILL,JAS-Hounds on the Mountain-1937-Viking Pr-ltd to 750c,nbrd
(5s4,soil) 3.50 (5F1,f,dj) 7.50
STILL,WM-Still's Underground Railroad Records-Phila-1886-cl-
780p,(5)p-ports-rev ed (4n7) 25.00
--same-Phila-1883-70 illus -revised edition (5s9,rub) 15.00
--The Underground Railroad,a Record of Facts-Phila-1872-illus-
buck-780p (5yy0,rebnd) 12.50 (5m2) 13,50
STILLE,ALFRED-Therapeutics & Materia Medica-Phila-1868-2 vols-
4to-3rd ed (5w3,broke,5t7) 15.00
STILLE,C J-Memorial of Great Central Fair for US Sanitary
Commission held at Phila,June 1864-4to-plt (5L7,ex-libr) 12.50
STILLE,CHAS J,ed-Life & Writings of John Dickinson-Phila-
1891,1895-port-2 vols-scarce (4m2) 27.50
--Maj Gen Anthony Wayne & The Penna Line in Continental Army-
Phila-1893-441p-illus-ltd to 150c,nbrd,autg (5w4) 32.50
STILLMAN,J D B-The Horse in Motion as shown by Instantaneous (5z9)
Photography...-Bost-1882-orig cl-4to-107 plts(12 col)-1st ed 65.00
--Seeking the Golden Fleece-SanFran-1877-1st ed-352p-plts
(5dd9,fade) 28.50
STILLWELL,JOHN E-Hist & Genealogical Misc Data Relating to
Settlement & Settlers of NY & NJ-NY-1903 to 16-4to-4 vols
(4m2) 100.00
STILWELL,GEN JOS-The Stilwell Papers-NY-1948
(5x7) 3. (5x0) 4. (5q8) 4.50
STILLWELL,L-John Cabell Breckinridge-Caldwell-1936-12mo-illus
(5x2,dj) 15.00
STILLWELL,LEANDER-Story of a Common Soldier of Army Life in
Civil War-1920-Franklin Hudson Pub-278p-illus (5t4,autg) 10.00
STILLWELL,MARGARET B-Noah's Ark in Early Woodcuts & Modern
Rhymes-NY-(1942)-Brick Row-8vo-ltd to 300c (4c1) 6.00
STILWELL,ARTHUR EDW-Cannibals of Finance-Chig-(c1912)-
Farnum Pub-3rd ed-8vo-cl-illus (4a3) 12.50
STILWELL,HART-Fishing in Mexico-NY-1948 (5kk6) 5. (5n4) 8.00
--Hunting & Fishing in Texas-NY-1946 (5t7) 8. (5a8) 6.00
STIMPSON,JAS-Exposition of Some of Natural Mechanical Actions,
Connected wi Running Gears of RR Carriages-Balt-1838-8vo-
illus-orig wrps-1st ed-scarce (5m6,stn) 20.00
STIMSON,A L-History of the Express Companies-NY-1858-illus-
8vo-2nd ed (4c8,tn) 15.00
--History of the Express Business-NY-1881-illus-Baker&Godwin-
388p plus subscribers sheet-"best edition" (5t1) 125.00
STIMSON,E R,ed-History of Separation of Church & State in
Canada-Tor-1887-201p (4b9) 12.00
STIMSON,F J-American Statute Law...in force Jan 1,1886 with 1888
suppl-Bost-1886 (5ff4) 12.50
--Law of Fed & State Constitutions of US-Bost-1908 (5r4) 12.50
STIMSON,F J-My Story-NY-1917-Scribner's-622p-port-map
(5mm8) 6.00
STIMSON,H K-From Stage Coach to Pulpit-StL-1874-8vo-427p-cl
(4g6,sl rub,fade) 7.50 (5ff7) 10.00
STIMSON,LEWIS A-Civil War Memories Of-NY-1918-76p-frontis
(5w9) 7.50
STINE,J H-History of the Army of the Potomac-Phila-1892
(5s9,crack) 12.50
STINE,THOS OSTENSON-Scandinavians on the Pacific,Puget
Sound-Seattle-1900-4to-208p-92 photos&ports
(5s4,ex-libr,wn) 12.50
STINETORF,LOUISE-White Witch Doctor-Phila-1950-276p
(5c6,vg) 6.75

STIPP, G W-John Bradford's Historical Notes on "Kentucky"-
SanFran-1932-Grabhorn Pr   (5m8,f) 45.   (5x5)   50.00
STIRLING, M W-3 Pictographic Autobiographies of Sitting Bull-
Wash-1938-Smi Misc Col #5-57p-46 plts-1st ed-scarce (5L0) 10.00
STIRLING, MATTHEW W-Indians of Americas-Wash-1963-col plts-
432p   (4b3,f)   7.50
STIRLING, WALTER-Early Impressions-(c1835)-E Lacey-hf calf-
140p-6 plts(4 handcol)-2 vols in 1   (4d4)   12.50
STIRLING, WM-Some Apostle of Physiology, being an Account of
Their Lives & Labours-Lond-1902-Waterlow-orig prntd bds-
32 plts-folio-129p-rare   (4e5)   90.00
STITH, WM-First Discovery & Settlement of Virginia, The History of..
Virginia-prntd Lond-reprntd for S Birt-1753- 1st Lond ed-rare
(5h9)   250.00
STIVERS, C E-Rare promotional item-WhiteOaks, NM-17 photos-
1900   (5g5)   35.00
STOCK, D-Jazz Street-NY-1960-4to-1st ed   (5x2,dj)   12.50
STOCK EXCHANGE IN CARICATURE, THE-NY-1904-2 vols-
sm folio-cl-illus-ltd to 177c, nbrd   (5t2)   35.00
STOCK, RALPH-Confessions Of A Tenderfoot-Lond-1913-
Grant Richards Ltd-illus-260p   (4n8)   15.00
STOCKARD, S W-The History of Alamance-Raleigh-1900-166p-
illus   (5a9,wn)   9.00
STOCKBRIDGE, BERTHA-What to Drink-NY-1920-177p (5w1)   6.50
STOCKBRIDGE, FRANK-Florida in the Making-NY-1926-351p-
illus   (5L7) 4.50   (5h9,5x7) 3.   (5hh3)   4.00
STOCKING, AMER MILLS-The Saukie Indians & Their Great Chiefs
Black Hawk and Keokuk-RockIsl-1926-299p-illus-maps
(5xx5) 7.50   (5w4,pres)   10.00
STOCKING, CHAS H W-The Tefft Ancestry-Chig-1904-Lakeside Pr-
lg8vo-cl-1st ed-scarce   (5p5)   22.50
STOCKING, GEO W-Monopoly & Free Enterprise-NY-1951
(5tt5)   10.00
STOCKLEY, V M-Big Game Shooting in India, Burma & Somaliland-
Lond-1913-illus-282p   (5ss8, hng wk)   15.00
STOCKTON ILLUSTRATED-in Photogravure-SanFran-1894-88p
(5n4)   25.00
STOCKTON, CALIF-Souvenir of-SanFran-Crockwell&Williams-
40p-photogravures   (5kk6,f)   32.50
STOCKTON, FRANK R-The Adventures of Capt Horn-NY-1895-
1st ed   (5ee3,f)   4.50
--Amos Kilbright-Scribner-1888-146p-1st ed   (5e8)   3.00
--Captin's Toll gate-NY-1903-illus-lg papr ed-ltd to 160c-
frontis
(5yy6, cov soil, autg tip in) 20. (5ee3, autg tip in, sl dmgd) 35.00
--same-NY-1903-Appleton-1st ed   (5x4)   6.00
--Casting Away of Mrs Lecks & Mrs Aleshine-NY-(1886)-130p-
1st ed-Century   (5q0)   15.00
--same-NY-(c1886)-Century-1st ed, 1st state (5b2, lt fade) 27.50
--A Chosen Few, Short Stories-NY-1895-Scribner-hf calf-g.t.-
240p   (5j5, joints wn)   7.50
--Clocks of Rondaine & Other Stories-NY-1892-12mo-pict cl
(5ee3, lacks fly, 4c2, sl shake)   10.00
--The Dusantes-NY-(1888)-1st ed-150p   (5q0)   15.00
--Fanciful Tales-NY-1894-Scribner's 8vo-135p-frontis-3 plts-
pict cl-Gullans & Espey 214   (5p1, publ pres)   8.50
--The Late Mrs Null-NY-1886-437p-1st ed, 1st issue
(5x4) 10.   (5ee3, rub) 5.   (5w9)   7.50
--same-NY-1891-Scribner's Yellow Cover Series (5b2,f)   5.00
--The Novels & Stories-NY-1899-Scribner-23 vols-cl-
Shenandoah Ed   (5x0)   75.00
--Pomona's Travels-NY-1894-plts-275p-1st ed-1st bndg-Frost, illus
(5nn2) 12.50   (5ee3)   7.50
--Rudder Grange -NY-1879-270p-illus-1st issue-18 chaptrs-
1879 on t.p.   (5ee3) 12.50   (5mm1)   13.50
--Ting a Ling-NY-1870-12mo-cl-1st ed of auth's 1st book
(5p6,wn) 17.   (5v0, sl rub) 55.   (5gg6)   50.00
STOCKTON, J ROY-Gashouse Gang-NY-(1947)-photos-283p
(4b3)   5.00
STOCKTON, THOS COATES-The Stockton Family of N J & Other
Stocktons-Wash-1911-350p-illus (5t9) 20. (5w9)   27.50
STOCKWELL, W P-Arizona Cacti-Univ of Ariz-1933-(Biol Sci Bull,
#1)-8vo-wrps-116p-illus   (5dd6) 7.50 (5h5)   3.50
STODDARD, AMOS-Sketches, Historical & Descriptive of Louisiana-
Phila-1812-publ by Mathew Carey-hf t.calf   (5s9)   150.00
STODDARD, CHAS AUGUSTUS-Beyond the Rockies, Spring Journey
in Calif-NY-1894-214p   (5s4, ex-libr) 6. (5r0)   7.50
STODDARD, CHAS WARREN-Apostrophe to the Skylark-LosAng-
(1909)-sq12mo-bds-(Calif Classics Series) (5F5,f) 3. (5m2)
--A Bit of Old China-(SanFran)-1925-orig bds-29p-4to
(4g6, sl soil)   6.00
--In the Footprints of the Padres-SanFran-1911 (4a5, lacks e.p.) 3.00

STODDARD, CHAS WARREN (continued)
--Island of Tranquil Delights-Bost-1904-12mo-cl-g.t.(4c2,pres) 17.50
--Poems-SanFran-1867-8vo-cl-1st ed of auth's 1st book-
750c prntd   (5gg6, autg tip in)   37.50
--South Sea Idyls-NY-1892-Scribner   (5m2,pres)   7.50
--A Trip to Hawaii-SanFran-1892-8vo-pic wrps   (4c1)   10.00
STODDARD, HENRY L-As I Knew Them-NY-1927-illus
(5jj3) 7.50   (5x0)   6.00
STODDARD, HERBERT L-The Bobwhite Quail-NY-1931-559p-
col illus-1st ed-scarce   (5ee3)   35.00
--same-1946-Scribners-illus-photos   (5kk7)   20.00
STODDARD, LOTHROP-Racial Realities in Europe-NY-1925-
fldout col maps   (5x2)   8.50
--Revolt Against Civilization -NY-1922-274p
(5w9,5L7) 5.   (5x2)   8.50
--The Rising Tide of Color Against White World Supremacy-
NY-1920-1st ed   (5m6,ex-libr, stn) 12.50 (5x2)   8.50
--Stakes of the War-1918-maps   (5L7)   4.50
STODDARD, RICHARD H-Foot Prints-NY-1849-8vo-orig prntd wrps-
1st ed of auth's 1st book-1 of great rarities of Amer lit
(5gg6)   750.00
--Town & Country & the voices in the shells-NY-1857-Dix, Edwards-
illus-1st ed   (5m2, sl soil)   4.00
STODDARD, S R-The Adirondacks-Albany-1875-16mo-pict wrps-
3rd ed   (5g3)   7.50
--The Adirondacks-NY-1884-illus & maps-232p-cl   (5t2)   7.50
--Lake George; A Book of To Day-Albany-1875-184p &ads-illus
(5t4)   7.50
--Lake George & Lake Champlain, A book of Today-Priv prntd-
(1906)-208p-maps-ads-wrps   (5e8)   5.75
--Midnight Sun-GlenFalls-1901-(ca 250p)-4to-photos
(5s1, pres, sl soil)   7.50
STODDARD, WM O-Chumley's Post, Story of Pawnee Trail-Phila-
1895-368p-illus   (5s4, soil)   6.50
--John Adams & Thos Jefferson-NY-1887-358p-illus-1st ed-
Lives of the Presidents Series   (5w9)   5.00
--Little Smoke-NY-1891-illus-295p
(4b2, ex-libr, rprd, tn) 15. (5i3, rprd) 12.50 (4c3) 17.50
--On the Old Frontier-NY-1893-illus-pict cl-1st ed (5m1)   7.50
STODDART, THOS TOD-The Angler's Companion to the Rivers &
Lochs of Scotland-Lond-1923-320p-illus   (5t7)   6.50
STOKER, BRAM-Famous Imposters-1910-illus   (5L7)   5.00
--Personal Reminiscences of Henry Irving-NY-1906-2 vols-illus
(5xx7, faded) 15.   (5mm1)   12.50
STOKER, H G-Straws in the Wind-Lond-1925-315p (4h4, sl cov stn) 7.00
STOKES(publ)-Indian Fairy Book from Orig Legends-NY-1916-
303p-col illus   (5L2, dj)   3.00
STOKES, ANSON PHELPS-Cruising in the West Indies-NY-1902-
Dodd, Mead-126p-cl   (5s1) 8.   (5d6)   6.00
STOKES, ANTHONY-View of Constitution of British Colonies-Lond-
1783-mor-555p   (5qq8, ex-libr)   20.00
STOKES, C S-Sanctuary-Capetown-1943-illus   (5tt5)   10.00
--same-(Capetown)-(1946)-8vo-474p-photos-5th ed (4a6)   5.00
STOKES, E-Life, Trial & Conviction of Edw Stokes..Life & Eventful
Career of Josephine Mansfield-Phila-(1873)-prntd wrps-illus-
111p   (5yy0)   12.50
STOKES, ETHEL W-The Main Line Cook Book-NY-(1950)-277p
(5g9)   5.00
STOKES, FREDK A-College Tramps-NY-1880-8vo-1st ed (5ss5)   7.50
STOKES, GEO STEWART-Agnes Repplier, Lady of Letters-Phila-
1949-274p-illus-1st ed   (5mm2) 4. (5w0)   5.00
STOKES, H G-English Place Names-Lond-1948-120p   (5t9)   4.00
STOKES, HUGH-Francisco Goya-NY&Lond-1914-Putnam's/Jenkins-
400p-48p plts-cl-4to-t.e.g.   (5m7, ex-libr, wn)   9.00
--French art in French life-Lond-1932-Allen-272p-plts-8vo-cl
(5m5)   10.00
STOKES, I N PHELPS-American Historical Prints-NY-1932-
N Y Public Library-327p-illus-cl   (5tt8)   50.00
STOKES, J-Cabinet Maker & Upholsterer's Companion-Phila-1901-
illus-cl-190p   (5q0)   12.00
STOKES, J-Thunder Cave-SaltLkCty-1945-illus   (5x2)   10.00
STOLL, WM T-Silver Strike-1932-273p-1st ed-illus   (5r1)   11.50
STONE, A H-Studies in the Amer Race Problem-NY-1908-1st ed
(5x2)   30.00
STONE, A L-Following Old Trails-Missoula-1913-illus-304p-
1st ed-scarce   (4i7)   45.00
STONE, ARTHUR F-Vermont Today-1929-4 vols   (4t2)   25.00
STONE, ARTHUR L-Following Old Trails-Missoula-1913-304p-illus-
1st ed-v scarce   (5t1) 100. (5L2)   65.00
STONE, CHAS F-The Story of Dixiesteel-Atlanta-1951-177p-
plts   (5y2)   5.75
STONE, EDWIN M-Our French Allies...of Amer Rev-Prov-1884-
maps-illus-51p-1st ed-scarce   (4i9)   35.00

STONE,ELIZ A-Unita County,Its Place in History-Laramie-
1924-Laramie Prntg-8vo-cl-176p-scarce (4t1) 50. (5dd6)   25.00

STONE,ERIC-Medicine among the Amer Indians-NY-1932-
125p plus map & index-photos-ex scarce   (5L0)   12.50

STONE,GEO CAMERON-Glossary of Construction, Decoration
& Use of Arms & Armor-Portland-1934-4to-694p-illus-
Southworth Pr   (5xx7)   20.00

STONE,HERBERT L-Millions for Defense-NY-(1934)-Derrydale Pr-
t4to-illus-ltd to 950c,nbrd   (4b6)   35.00

--The "America's" Cup Races-NY-1930-Macmillan-8vo-cl-illus-
photos-359p   (5j5)   6.50

STONE,HERBERT STUART-First Editions of Amer Authors-Cambr-
16mo-cl-1st ed-ltd to 450 sm papr copies (5gg6,f,autg)   35.00

STONE,HUGH E-A Flora of Chester Co,PA-Phila-1945-illus-
1470p-2 vols-scarce   (4m4)   42.50

STONE,IRVING-Men to Match My Mountains-NY-1956-459p
(4n1,dj,5L0,f) 6.   (5s0)   6.50

--same-NY-1956-Far West ed-ltd,nbrd,autg   (5hh1,f)   20.00

--The President's Lady-GardenCty-1951   (5h6)   3.50

--Sailor On Horseback-1938-Riverside Pr-facs letter included
(5a9,f,dj)   10.00

STONE,JAS S-Woods & Dales of Derbyshire-Phila-1894-
Jacobs&Co-ltd to 400c-illus   (5i4)   25.00

STONE,LEE ALEX-The Power of a Symbol-Chig-1925-Pascal Covici-
8vo-bds-lin sp   (5t5)   10.00

STONE,LIVINGSTON-Domesticated Trout-Charleston,NH-1896-
367p-illus   (5t4)   10.50

STONE,LLOYD-In this Hawaiian Net-Honolulu-1945-illus-8vo-
97p-novelty bds tied wi rafia   (5t7)   6.50

STONE,MILDRED F-Since 1845-Rutgers U Pr-1957-236p-illus
(4b8)   5.00

STONE,M T-Hist of Troy,NHamp-1897-576p   (5t9)   17.50

STONE,R C-Gen of the Stone Family Originating in Rhode Island-
1866-193p   (5t9)   40.00

STONE,REYNOLDS-A Book of Lettering-Lond-(1943)-
A&C Black-48p-bds   (5tt9)   5.00

STONE,RUFUS B-McKean,The Governor's County-NY-1926-
orig cl-illus-315p (5ss5) 12.50 (5h1) 10.   (4m4)   15.00

STONE,W L-Uncas & Miantonomoh-NY-1842-109p (5yy0)   12.50

STONE,W L,ed-Washington Co,NY,Its History to the Close of the
19th Century-1901-570p,318p   (5t9)   75.00

STONE,WILBUR F-History of Colorado,Illustrated-Chig-1918-
S J Clarke-4to-cl-3 vols   (4t1,5d6)   60.00

--same-Chig-1918,19-4 vols-cl   (5h7)   65.00

STONE,WILBUR MACEY-Book Plates of Today-NY-1902-Tonnele-
62p-illus-crown 4to   (4a0,dj)   32.50

--4 Centuries of Children's Books-Newark-1928-Public Library-
32p-wrps-stapld   (5p1)   5.00

--The Gigantick Histories of Thos Boreman-Portland-1933-
Southworth Pr-8vo bds&cl-ltd to 250c-illus   (5ee9)   10.00

--Women Designers of Book Plates-NY-1902-(57p)-36 bkplts-bds
(5n7,scuff)   4.50

STONE,WM-Pepe Was the Saddest Bird-NY-1944-Knopf-8vo-(64p)-
pict bds-1st ed   (5p1,tn dj)   15.00

STONE,WM-Tale of a Plain Man-Phila-1918-port-2nd ed (4a1)   5.00

STONE,WM L-Campaign of Lt Gen John Burgoyne & Exped of
Lt Col Barry St Ledger-NY-1877-illus-map-461p (5m2,5t4)   10.00

STONE,WM L-History of New York City-1872 to 85-illus-658p-
appendix-index   (5ss0,pres) 25.   (5u3)   12.50

STONE,WM L-Life & Times of Sa Go Ye Wat Ha, or Red Jacket-
Albany-1866-497p plus index (5ff2,f) 30.   (5p0)   17.50

STONE,WM L-Life of Jos Brant Thayendanegea-NY,1838-
Cooperstown,1845-2 vols-calf
(5ff2,crude mend,5m2,rbnd,lacks map) 22.50
(5ee3) 45.   (5t4,mismtchd)   35.00

STONE,WM L-The Poetry & History of Wyoming-Albany-1864-
Munsell-406p-3rd ed with index   (5p0)   12.50

STONE,WM L-Remin of Saratoga & Ballston-1875-451p (5ff2)   10.00

STONE,WM L-Starin Family in America-1892-233p (4t2,weak)   30.00

STONE,WM L-Tales & sketches,such as they are-NY-1834-Harper-
2 vols-12mo-orig cl-labls-1st ed   (5x1)   70.00

STONE,WM L-Visits to Saratoga Battle Grounds 1780 to 1880-
Albany-1895-Munsell-344p-illus (5mm8,cov badly spot)   5.00

STONE,WM S-Ship of Flame-NY-1945-illus-1st ed-4to-dec bds-
166p-frontis   (5s6) 6.50 (5s1)   7.50

STONE,WITMER-Annual Report of NJ State Museum,3rd Report-
Trenton-1907-orig cl-8vo-211p-69 plts-13 photos-v scarce
(4p5)   8.50

--Bird Studies at Old Cape May-Phila-1937-illus-4to-2 vols
(5z9) 45.   (4m4,f)   75.00

STONEBRAKER,J CLARENCE-Unwritten South,Cause,Progress &
Results of Civil War-Wash-c1903-lg16mo-bds-193p-1st ed
(5w5)   10.00

STONEHAM,C T-Hunting Wild Beasts with Rifle & Camera-
Lond-n.d.-(ca 1935)-8vo-219p-photos   (4a6)   12.50

STONEHENGE-British Rural Sports-Lond-1865-Fred'k Warne-
thk12mo-hf mor-6th ed   (5i4,dmpstn)   22.50

STONEHILL,CHAS A-Anonyma & Pseudonyma-Lond-1926-4 vols
(4b4)   45.00

STONEMAN,VERNON C-John & Thos Seymour,Cabinetmakers in
Boston-Bost-1959-4to-boxed   (5m2,vg,lt spot)   40.00

STONER,DAYTON-Ornithology of the Oneida Lake Region-NY-
1932-wrps-2 col plts-498p-118 photos   (5cc1)   4.00

STONEY,S G-Black Genesis-NY-1930   (5x2)   15.00

STRONG,PHIL-Gold in Them Hills-GardenCty-1957-209p (5s4,f) 6.50

--Horses & Americans-NY-1939-1st trade ed-328p plus index-illus-
frontis   (5L2,dj)   10.00

--same-NY-1939-special ed of 500c,autg   (5x5)   40.00

--same-reprint-GardenCty-(1946)   (5L2,dj)   4.50

--State Fair-NY-1932-12mo-cl-266p-1st ed   (5m8,wn)   7.50

--A Village Tale-NY-1934-12mo-cl-1st ed   (5m8,dj)   8.50

STOPES,H-Malts & Malting-Lond-1885
(4n0,dmpstn) 22.50   (5w6,chip)   42.50

STORER,J-Illus of University of Cambridge-Cambr-(before 1835)-
lg4to-bds-roan sp-32 illus   (4e1,sp broke)   50.00

STORER,J R-Criminal Abortion,its Nature,its Evidence & its Law-
Bost-1868   (5ff4)   8.50

STOREY,HARRY-A Ceylon Sportsman's Diary-Colombo,Ceylon-
1921-8vo-274p-photos   (4a6,fox)   7.00

STOREY,M-Negro Suffrage Is Not A Failure-Bost-1903-19p-wrps
(5x2)   17.50

STORIES BY AMER AUTHORS-NY-1900-Scribner's-10 vols (5x4) 17.50

STORIES FROM THE HARVARD ADVOCATE-Cambr-Harvard U-
1896-1st ed-ltd ed   (5m2)   15.00

STORIES OF THE RAILWAY-NY-1893-Scribners-1st ed-195p-
illus-12mo   (5i3,sl rub)   12.50

STORIES OF THE WAR OF 1812-& the Mexican War-Phila-1852-
illus-sq16mo-cl-juvenile   (5g4,fray)   10.00

STORKE,C A-The English Storkes in Amer-SantaBarbara-1935-
4to-cl-illus   (5t9) 15.   (5h4)   12.50

STORKE,E G-The Family Householder's Guide-Auburn-(1859)-
frontis-238p-illus   (5ww2,chip,fox)   27.50

STORKE,T M-California Editor-LosAng-1958-Westernlore-illus-
489p-1st ed   (4n1) 12.   (5dd5)   14.00

STORM,BARRY-Thunder Gods' Gold-Tortilla Flat,Ariz-1945-
1st ed   (5m9) 7.50 (5L2,f,dj)   12.50

STORM,COLTON-Invitation to Book Collecting-NY-1947-281p-
cl-maps-prnts-1st ed   (5h7,dj)   10.00

--A Pretty Fair View of the Eliphent-Chig-1960-prntd for Everett
D Graff-45p-bds   (5d6)   25.00

STORM,HANS OTTO-Count Ten-NY-1940-Longmans,Green-8vo-
cl   (5b2,f,dj)   7.50

--Full Measure-NY-1929-Macmillan-8vo-cl-auth's 1st book
(5b2,f,dj)   12.50

STORM,JOHN-An Invitation to Wines-NY-1955-201p-bibliog-
illus-cl   (5g9)   5.00

STORRS,AUGUSTUS-Collocation of the Indians-Balt-Feb 26,1825-
Niles Register   (4n4)   25.00

--Santa Fe Trail,first reports,1825-1960-69p-Ltd Ed-550c
(5g0,dj) 8.50   (5s2,dj)   10.00

STORRS,RICHARD S-The Early Amer Spirit & the Genesis of it-
NY-1878-t8vo-hf orig roan-ltd to 150c,lg papr   (5m6)   13.50

STORY,DR CHAS A-Alcohol Its Nature & Effects-NY-1868-
12mo-392p   (5w1,stns)   9.50

STORY,J-Commentaries on Equity Jurisprudence as Admin in
Engl & Amer-Bost-1836-2 vols   (5r4,rbnd)   17.50

--Commentaries on Law of Partnership, as Branch of Commercial &
Maritime Jurisprudence-Bost-1868-sheep-6th ed   (5ff4)   9.50

--Selection of Pleadings in Civil Actions,Subsequent to Declaration-
Salem,Mass-1805-1 vol extended to 2-8vo-calf-lea labls-1st ed-
scarce   (5ss5)   47.50

--Sketch of the Life of Sam'l Dexter-Bost-1816-8vo-20p(unbnd text
loose)-1st ed   (5m6)   8.50

STORY OF DAVID DOUBTFUL-or,the Reprobate Reformed-Lond-
1798-Vernor&Hood-12mo   (5c8,lacks prelim lf)   20.00

STORY OF MARY & HER LITTLE LAMB,THE-as told by Mary & her
neighbors & friends-Dearborn-1928-12mo-(6p,41p)-photos-
publ by Mr&Mrs Henry Ford   (5p1)   4.00

STORY OF A SLAVE,THE-n.p.-1894-orig pict wrps-illus-publ for
the trade   (5j2,fray)   40.00

STORY,WM W-Roba Di Roma-Lond-1864-2 vols-4th ed (5mm1)   10.00

STOTT,WM T-Indiana Baptist history-1908-Franklin-381p (5u3)   5.00

STOTZ,CHAS MORSE-Early Architecture of Western Penna-NY-
1936-illus-folio-cl-290p (5p9) 22.50 (5t7) 35.   (5m2)   42.50

--same-Pittsburgh-1936-lg4to-illus-290p   (4j9)   65.00

STOTZ,LOUIS-History of Gas Industry-NY-1938-534p-illus
(4e4,vg) 12.50

STOUDT,JOHN BAER-The Folklore of the Penna-German-
Lancaster-1915-153p-orig wrps (5w5) 12.50
--Liberty Bells of Penna-Phila-1930-illus-ltd to 1000c
(4b3,autg) 12.50 (4j9,f,unopened) 25.00
--Nicolas Martiau,The Adventurous Huguenot-Norristown,Pa-
1932-illus (4m4) 15.00

STOUDT,JOHN JOS-Pennsylvania Folk Art-Allentown-1948-col plts-
2nd ed (5jj3,f,dj) 15.00

STOUGHTON,J A-Windsor Farmes,Glimpse of an Old Parish-1883-
148p (5t9) 15.00

STOUT,ARTHUR B-An essary on public education in Calif-SanFran-
1866-Agnew&Deffebach-12mo-orig yellwrps-1st ed (5i9) 25.00

STOUT,GEO DUMAS-Edward Mallinckrodt-StL-1933-priv prnt-
frontis-illus-88p-orig cl (4b3) 17.50

STOUT,H -The Staudt,Stoudt,Stout Family of Ohio-1935 (5a9) 12.50

STOUT,P F-Nicaragua,past,present & future-1859
(5L7,lacks map) 4.50

STOUT,REX-Forest Fir-(1933)-Farrar&Rinehart- (5F1,f,dj) 6.00
--Golden Remedy-1931-Vanguard Pr (5F1,f,dj) 7.50
--How Like a God-1929-author's 1st book -Vangd (5F1,f,dj) 20.00
--The League of Frightened Men,A Nero Wolfe-(1935)-
Farrar & Rinehart (5F1,f,dj) 5.00
--Mr Cinderella-Farrar & Rinehart-(1938) (5F1,f,dj) 4.75
--O Careless Love-(1935)-Farrar&Rinehart (5F1,mint,dj) 6.50
--Seed on the Wind-1930-Vanguard Pr-auth's 2nd book (5F1,f,dj)10.00
--The Second Confession-NY-(1949)-8vo-cl-1st ed (5d3) 5.00

STOUT,TOM,ed-Montana,Its Story & Biography-Chig-1921-
3 vols-photos-1st ed-Adams #2149 (5L2,ex-libr) 50.00

STOUT,W W-DeWolf Hopper,Once A Clown,Always a Clown-
Bost-1927-Little-illus (5p7) 4.50

STOUT,WAYNE-Hosea Stout,Utah's Pioneer Statesman-SaltLkCty-
1953-279p plus index & 4p frontis-1st ed (5L2,cov spot) 15.00

STOUT,WESLEY W-The Great Detective-Detroit-1946-98p-illus
(5b8) 5.00

STOUT,WILBER-Geology of Southern Ohio-Columbus-1916-
723p-cl (5h1) 7.50

STOUTENBURGH,JOHN L JR-Dictionary of Amer Indian-(1955)-
459p-1st ed (5r1,dj,f) 11.00

STOVALL,ALLAN A-Nueces Headwater Country-SanAntonio-
(1959)-438p plus index-photos (5L0,dj) 12.50

STOVE PILOT-Women's Club,Maxwell AFB-Montgomery-1948-
2nd ed-spiral bnd wrps -334p (5g9) 3.50
--same-1951 ed (5g9) 3.50

STOW,BELL & HAYDEN-Furniture Designs of Chippendale,
Hepplewhite & Sheraton-NY-1938-illus-128p-4to
(5bb0,bndg tn) 5.00

STOWE & MANSFIELD-Lamoille Co,Vt-1940-Inventory of Town
Archives-130p-wrps-WPA Hist Records Surv (5t9) 4.00

STOWE,CALVIN E-Prussian System of Public Instruction-Cing-
1836-107p-16mo-1st ed-unbnd (5yy6) 10.00

STOWE,HARRIET B-Betty's Bright Idea-NY-1876-illus-1st ed
(5mm1) 15.00

--Dred-Bost-1856-2 vols-1st ed
(5k1,fray shake) 8. (5mm1,f) 17.50 (5x4,sp dmgd)15.(5x2) 25.00
--same-Bost-1856-2 vols-75th Thousand (5yy8) 20.00
--De Negerhut-Nijmegen-(ca 1900)-4to-pict cl-1st illus Dutch ed
of Uncle Tom's Cabin (5x2,rbkd) 25.00
--Earthly Care-Bost-1856-(wrp dated 1855)-orig wrps-24mo-16p-
scarce (4m8,cov tn,pencil) 17.50
--La Case De L'Oncle Tom-Paris-1853-563p-1st French ed-wrps
(4b4,chip) 75.00
--Key to Uncle Tom's Cabin-Bost-1853-262p-Jewett,etc-1st ed
(5m2,sl soil) 7.50 (5x2,wn) 17.50 (5ee3) 10.00
--same-Lond-1853-8vo-orig violet cl-(publ same year as 1st Bost ed)-
port -Thomas Bosworth (5i0,fade) 17.50
--Lady Byron Vindicated-Bost-1870-1st ed (5mm1) 10.00
--The May Flower & Misc Writings-Bost-1869-471p-later ed (5t4) 5.00
--Men of Our Times-Hartf-1868-Hartford Pub-illus-1st ed-
575p (5mm2) 7.50 (5x4) 12.50
--The Minister's Wooing-NY-1859-Derby&Jackson-578p-1st ed
(5mm2) 5.00
--Oldtown Fireside Stories-Bost-1872-illus-1st ed
(5mm1,lacks fly) 10.00
--Oldtown Folks-Bost-1869-Fields,Osgood-1st ed -608p
(5mm2) 6.50 (5ss9,sp wn) 12. (5x4,sp wn) 12.50
--Onkel Tomms Hutte-Stuttgart-n.d.-(ca1906)-pict bds-152p
(4h7,lacks fly) 5.00
--Pink & White Tyrrany-Bost-1871-Roberts-331p-1st ed
(5x4,lacks e.p.) 10. (5mm2) 7.50 (5b2) 8.50
--Religious Poems-Bost-1867-Ticknor&Fields-8vo-cl-bevelld edges-
(5b2,sl rub) 7.50

STOWE,HARRIET B (continued)
--Sunny Memories of Foreign Lands-Bost-1854-2 vols-1st ed-
Phillips,Sampson (5x4) 20. (5mm1) 22.50
--same-Lond-1854-1st Engl ed-2 vols-frontis-illus
(5s6,cov sl wn) 5.00
--same-Lond-1854-Low-Author's Edn-illus-1st authorized Lond ed-
advts dated Sept '54 (5m2) 6.50
--Uncle Tom's Cabin,or Life Among the Lowly-Bost-1852-
Hobart&Robbins on cpyrt pg-JP Jewett&Co foot of spines-2 vols-
12mo-6 plts-orig brown gilt cl-title vignts,repeated in g.
front covs & blind on bk covs-1st ed-1st issue-rare in fine cond
(5hh0,fine,sml wtr stn) 1,750.00
--same-Bost-1852-JohnP Jewett&Co-orig dec cl-2 vols-1st ed-
1st issue,Hobart&Robbins on cpyrt pg-with Jewett&Co at
foot of sp (4g2,f,lacks fly) 550.00
--same-Bost-1852-JohnP Jewett-2 vols-1st ed-1st issue
(4b4,some wear) 250.00
--same-Bost-1852-illus-12mo-part mor-raised bands-2 vols-
1st ed (4m8,rebnd,f bndg) 125.00
--same-Bost-1852-2 vols-40th thousand (5t4,wn) 15.00
--same-Bost-1852-2 vols-3/4 lea-120th thousand (5x5) 25.00
--same-Lond-1852-391p-27 illus by Cruikshank (4j6) 50.00
--same-Lond-1852-illus (5mm2) 10.00
--same-Uncle Tom's Cabin-Lond-1852-cl-329p-not 1st ed(4h7,f) 20.00
--same-Bost-1853-orig cl-1st illus ed
(5hh1,bndg wn) 25. (5mm2,mor) 40.00
--same-Bost-1883- illus-wi bibliog by Geo Bullen (5mm2) 12.50
--same-NY-1938-16 liths-sm folio-Ltd Ed Club-ltd to 1500c,box,
illus autg (5b0) 60.00
--We & Our Neighbors-NY-(1875)-illus-1st ed-Ford-480p
(5x4) 15. (5mm1) 8.50

STOEW,J M-History of the Town of Hubbardston...from 1686-
Hubbardston-1881 (5mm3) 17.50 (5a8,wn) 32.50

STOWE,LELAND-Crusoe of Lonesome Lake-NY-(1957)-Random-
234p-e.p. maps (4f9) 5.00 (5aa2) 5.00

STOWE,LYMAN BEECHER-Saints Sinners & Beechers-Indnple-
1934-450p-8vo-cl-illus-1st ed (5t0) 5.00

STOWELL,J S-Methodist Adventures in Negro Education-NY-
1922-12mo-illus (5x2) 15.00

STOWELL,JOHN-Don Coronado thru Kansas-(Seneca,Ka,1908)-
384p-illus-scarce -1st edition (5L2) 12.50

STOWELL,T-Statutes & Ordinances of Isle of Man-1792-C Briscoe,
Douglas-171p-calf (5yy3,rebkd) 85.00

STOWELL,W H H-Record of the Desc of Sam'l Stowell of Hingham,
Mass-1922-980p-ports-illus-cl (5t9) 50.00

STRACHAN,JOHN-Letter Book,1812 to 1834-Tor-1946-Ont Hist Soc-
port-279p (5s0) 15.00
--Remarks on Emigration from the United Kingdom-Lond-1827-cl-
96p-orig bndg (5r6,rbnd) 95.00

STRACHEY,JOHN-Nature of Capitalist Crisis-NY-1935
(4m9,pres) 10.00

STRACHEY,LYTTON-Books & Characters French & English-NY-
1922-324p-cl (5h7) 5.00
--Elizabeth & Essex-NY-1928-t8vo-hf cl-illus-ltd ed,autg(5tt7) 20.00
--same-Lond-1928-t8vo-cl-6 plts-1st ed (5d3) 7.50

STRADLING,JAS M-His talk with Lincoln-1922-Riverside Pr-16mo-
33p-cl&bds-boxd-535c prntd (5t7) 8. (5g4,unopnd) 6.00

STRAHAN,EDW,ed-A Century After,Picturesque Glimpses of Phila
& Penna-Phila-1875-lg4to-lea-360p-a.e.g. (4t7) 25.00
--Chefs D'Oeuvre d'Art of the Paris Universal Exhibition-Phila-
1878-hf lea-folio-t.e.g.-plts (4t7) 42.50

STRAHORN,CARRIE ADELL-15,000 Miles by Stage-NY-1911-Putnam-
illus by ChasMRussell&others-673p-cl
(5yy7) 55. (5d6,t pg spot) 60. (5m3) 75.00

STRAHORN,ROBT E-Handbook of Wyoming-Cheyenne-1877-8vo-
249p-orig prntd wrps-ads-1st ed-rare (5g6) 75.00
--same-Cheyenne-1877-(prntd in Chig)-272p-illus (5jj7,f) 125.00
--Resources of Mont Terr & Attractions of Yellowstone Natl Park-
Helena-1879-map-77p-9 plts-3p ads-wrps
(4b6,autg,lacks bkstrp) 100.00
--The Resources & Attractions of Idaho Terr-BoiseCty,Ida-1881-
88p plus ads-fldg map-illus-errata slip-wrps-1st ed-scarce
(5h6,brittle) 20. (5t3) 50.00
--To the Rockies & Beyond-Omaha-1878-141p-fldg map-limp cl-
1st ed-scarce -illus (5L2) 30.00

STRALEY,W-Archaic Gleanings-Nelson,Neb-1909-49p plus 9 plts-
fldg map-frontis-ltd ed-v scarce (5L2) 15.00
--Pioneer Sketches,Nebraska & Tesas-Hico,Tex-1915-58p-photos-
drawngs-wrps-1st ed (5L2) 17.50

STRALEY,WILSON-Comanches-KansasCty-1938-(12p)-poetry-
frontis-v scarce (5L2,autog,chipped) 6.50

STRANAHAN,C H-History of French Painting-Lond-1889-index-
496p-8vo-16 plts (5ww3,wrps) 12.50

USED BOOK PRICE GUIDE

STRAND MAGAZINE
--Lond-Feb 1893-blue wrps-illus-(Sherlock Holmes)   (5d2)   15.00
--Lond-Apr 1893-blue wrps-illus-(Sherlock Holmes)   (5d2)   15.00
--Lond-Jun 1893-blue wrps-illus-(Sherlock Holmes)   (5d2)   15.00
STRAND MAGAZINE,THE-An Illustrated Monthly-ed by Geo Newnes-
    4to-blue cl as issued-first 25 yrs-Jan 1891 to Dec 1915-50 vols
                                          (5d9)   350.00
STRANDES, JUSTUS-Portuguese Period in E Africa-Nairobi-1961-
    13&371p-5 plts-fldg map   (5c6,f)   10.75
STRANG, HERBERT-The Air Scout-Lond-1912-Henry Frowde,Hodder&
    Stoughton-12mo-432p-col illus-pict labl   (5p1,hng tn)   15.00
STRANG, JESSE-Confession of...Who Was Executed at Albany
    Aug 24 for Murder of John Whipple-Albany-1827-stitchd-8vo-
    1st ed-McDade 935   (519,soil)   25.00
STRANG, LEWIS C-Celebrated Comedians of Light Opera & Musical
    Comedy in Amer-Bost-1901-Page-illus   (5p0)   4.50
--Famous Actors of the Day...in Amer-2nd Series-Bost-1902-
    16mo-343p-illus-t.e.g.   (5w5)   5.00
--Prima Donnas & Soubrettes of Light Opera-Bost-270p-illus-
    L C Page -1900   (5p0)   4.50
STRANGE & SURPRISING ADVENTURES OF ROBINSON CRUSOE-
    rewritten for Children-Bost-n.d.-Lothrop-4to-48p-cl bk-
    pict glazed bds-plts   (5aa2)   5.00
STRANGE, E F-Stories from the Pentamerone of Basile-Lond-1911-
    sq R8vo-orig red cl-g.-spec papr-Macmillan   (5t8)   22.50
STRANGE, EDW F-Alphabets,a Handbook of Lettering wi Historical
    Critical & Practical Descriptions-Lond-1895-t8vo-prntd wrps-
    296p-196 plts-Jap vel-ltd to 75c   (5ee9)   45.00
--Alphabets,a Manual of Lettering for the Use of Students-Lond-
    1898-Chiswick Pr-200 illus-1st ed   (5p5)   12.50
STRANGE MANUSCRIPT FOUND IN COPPER CYLINDER-Lond-
    1888-291p-plts-2nd ed-(Jas DeMille)   (5a1)   7.50
STRANGE,WM-Canada,Pacific & War-Tor-1937-220p-map (5dd0)   4.50
STRANGER IN LOWELL-Bost-1845-156p-lea&bds-1st ed (5m4)   45.00
STRANGER'S GUIDE-Official Directory for City of Richmond-
    Geo P Evans&Co-1863-#1,Oct,Vol 1-orig wrps-rare   (5r5)   150.00
STRANSKY, JOSEF-Modern Paintings by German & Austrian
    Masters-NY-1916-plts   (5tt5,sp wn)   10.00
STRAPAROLA, GIOVAN-The Facetious Nights of Straparola-
    Lond-1898-8vo-t.e.g.-pict cl-4 vols-priv prntd for Soc of
    Bibliophiles-ltd to 1000c   (5p1)   50.00
STRASSBURGER,R B-Penna German Pioneers 1727 to 1808-
    Morristown-1934-3 vols-1st ed   (4m4)   65.00
--Strassburger & Allied Families of Penna-Gwynedd Valley-
    1922-illus-4to-520p   (4m2) 20.   (5w0,5mm3)   15.00
STRATEMEYER,EDW-On to Pekin or Old Glory in China-Bost-
    1900-Lee&Shepard-12mo-frontis-7 plts-pict cl-322p(4) (5p1)   7.50
STRATFORD, JESSIE PERRY-Butler County's 80 Years 1855 to 1935-
    n.p.-n.d.(1934)-photos-map-401p-1st ed-scarce   (4L2)   45.00
STRATTON, ARTHUR-The English Interior-Lond-1920-Batsford-
    folio-115 plts-cl   (5m5)   30.00
--The orders of architecture,Greek,Roman & Renaissance-Lond-
    1931-Batsford-lg4to-cl-80 plts   (5m5)   25.00
STRATTON, ELLA HINES-American Indian & His Daring Deeds-
    n.p.-(1902)-illus-photos-311p   (4b2,rebnd)   7.50
--Wild Life Among the Indians-n.p.-(1916)-illus-254p-New ed
                            (4b2,hng loose) 3.   (4b3)   3.50
--Wild Life Among the Redman-n.p.-(1902)-illus-254p
                            (4b2,wn,hng loose)   4.00
STRATTON, HELEN-A Book of Myths-NY-1920-Putnam-
    340p-20 orig col drwngs   (5x0)   6.50
STRATTON, H R-Book of the Strattons-1908,18-2 vols-894p (5t9)   40.00
STRATTON, R B-Captivity of Oatman Girls-SanFran-1857-
    Whitton,Towne-231p-map-cl-2nd ed
        (4h0,sp wn,5tt0) 200. (4n4,sl wn) 225.   (5n9)   250.00
--Captivity of the Oatman Girls-Chig-1857-Scott-12mo-hf mor-
    map-port-(pub same year as 1st ed)   (5n9,box)   250.00
--same-NY-1858-Carlton&Porter-20th thousand-12mo-290p-
    frontis-4 plts-map-cl-sp g.-3rd ed wi add material-12(ads)
    4(Notices of the Press) (4p2,v wn,loose) 10. (5p1)   30.00
--same-1909-119p-reprnt-soft cov-rev   (5r1)   10.00
--Life Among the Indians-SanFran-1935-illus-Grabhorn Pr-
    ltd to 550c   (5m9,cov wn)   20.00
STRATTON,W C-Catalogue of Calif State Library-Sacramento-
    1866-460p & 207p-3/4 mor   (4a5)   35.00
STRAUB, JACQUES-Drinks-Evanston-1914-106p-pkt book for chefs
                                        (5c9)   2.00
STRAUCH BROS-Manufacture of Pianoforte Action its Rise &
    Development-n.p.-1904-lea-68p-illus   (5b8,sp wn)   17.50
STRAUS,RALPH-Charles Dickens,Biography from New Sources-
    NY-1928-ports-340p   (4a8)   3.50

STRAUS,RALPH   (continued)
--Lloyd's, Gentlemen of Coffee House-NY-1938-ports-plts (5a1)   5.00
STRAUSS,M-White Lady-NY-1932-1st ed   (5x2)   6.00
STRAVINSKY,IGOR-An Autobiography-NY-1936-288p-illus(5p0)   4.00
STRAY, ERMINA C-The Golden Link-Almont,Mich-1891
    cl-rare   (5ff7)   15.00
STREAKS OR SQUATTER LIFE-& Far West Scenes-Phila-1847-
    Carey&H-12mo-9 plts-Howes R335 (5cc6,fox,plts crude col)   75.00
STREBOR, EIGGAM-Ambition,or,The Launch of a Skiff upon the
    Sea of Life-NY-1876-224p-illus   (5m1)   15.00
STRECKER, HERMAN-Lepidopter etc-Reading-1872 to 1877-
    col illus-15 orig pts-wrps-col plts-rare
                            (5cc6,lacks suppl,wrps tn)   375.00
STREDDER,E-Lost in Wilds-n.d.-scarce   (4b9)   8.00
STREDDER, ELEANOR-The price of silence-Lond-1873-T Cautley
    Newby-3 vols-12mo-orig cl-1st ed   (5xx6,rub)   20.00
STREET, ALFRED B-Frontenac,Atotarho of the Iroquois-NY-1849-
    324p-rare   (4b2,fox,shake)   12.50
--Frontenac, a Poem-Lond-1849-Bentley-8vo-cl-precedes NY ed
                            (5b2,pres,rprd,sl fray)   22.50
STREET, ALFRED B-Woods & Waters-NY-1860-345p-illus-map
                                        (5xx7)   10.00
STREET,C H & CO-California,Topography,Soil Climate etc-
    SanFran-ca 1888-illus-72p-wrps   (4b6)   10.00
STREET, CHAS R-Huntington,NY Town Records,including Babylon,
    1653 to 1873-3 vols-1887 to 9   (5mm3)   35.00
--Opinion Upon Powers & Duties of Trustees...Huntington...-NY-
    1872-John DeVries-8vo-wrps-51p   (4t1)   12.50
STREET,G S-Ghosts of Piccadilly-1907-illus   (5L7)   3.50
STREET, H A-Street Genealogy-1895-542p   (4t2)   20.00
STREET, JULIAN-Amer Adventures-NY-1917-681p-illus-1st ed
                (5h9) 6.   (5L2,hng weak)   3.00
--Where Paris Dines-GardenCty-1929-321p-illus   (5g9)   6.50
--Wines,their selection, care & service-NY-1948-rev by A Street-
    288p & index-map   (5g9)   4.00
STREETER, BERTHA-Home Making Simplified-NY-1922-243p (5w7)   4.00
STREETER, DANIEL W-Arctic Rodeo-NY-1929-356p-24 plts-map
                (5aa0) 4.50   (5L2)   4.00
--Camels-NY-1927-8vo-277p-photos   (4a6)   5.00
--Denatured Africa-GardenCty-1929-photos-338p-9th impr
                (5x2) 4.50   (4t5)   3.00
STREETER, EDW-Dere Mable-NY-(1918)-12mo-orig pict bds-
    1st ed of auth's 1st book   (5gg6,dj,vf)   25.00
STREETER,EDW-Skoal Scandinavia-NY-(1952)-238p-photos
                                        (5ss1,dj)   5.00
STREETER, EDWIN W-Great Diamonds of the World-Lond-(1882)-
                                        (5yy6)   10.00
--Precious Stones & Gems-Lond-1877-Chapman&Hall-photos-
    col plts-264p-hf mor   (5x0,plt tn)   20.00
STREETER,FLOYD B-Ben Thompson,Man with a Gun-NY-1957
                (4a5) 6.   (5hh3,dj)   5.00
--The Kaw-n.d.-c1941   (4a9,vf)   6.00
--Prairie Trails & Cow Towns-Bost-1936-illus-236p-12mo-orig cl
        (4c1,dj) 50.   (5x5,dj) 60. (5L2,f,dj)   65.00
STREETER, THOS-Bibliography of Texas 1795 to 1845-Cambr-
    1955 to 1960-Harvard Univ Pr-5 vols-cl
        (5tt0) 250.   (4j6,mint) 450. (4g2,vf,dj)   400.00
--Celebrated Collection of Americana Formed by-NY-1966 to 70-
    illus-8 vols   (4c1) 235.   (4g2,f)   250.00
STRENGTH OUT OF WEAKNESSE-(John Eliot)-Lond-1652-
    sm4to-(6th of Eliot's Indian Tracts)-1st ed (?)   (5zz7)   450.00
STRETCH, L M-Beauties of History-Lond-1808-Vol 1(only)-12mo-
    illus-288p-tree calf   (5c8)   12.50
'STRETTON, HESBA'-Jessica's First Prayer-n.d.-R T S-dec cl-
    95p-illus-sm8vo-g.t.   (4a8)   3.50
STRETZER, THOS-New description of Merryland-Lond-1742-
    for E Curll-8vo-calf-10th ed   (5xx6)   100.00
--Merryland-NY-1932-136p-ltd to 777c-priv issued   (5x0)   6.50
STREVELL,CHAS NETTLETON-As I Recall Them-n.p.-n.d.-
    (SaltLkCty? ca1944)-304p,(4)-illus-simulated lea
                (5jj7,f,pres) 20.   (5w9)   25.00
STRIBLING, THOS S-Clues of the Caribees-GardenCty-1929-
    Dblday-illus-1st prntg   (5m2)   6.50
--The Cruise of the Dry Dock-Chig-(1917)-12mo-cl-1st ed of
    auth's 1st book-250c prntd   (5gg6,vf,dj)   50.00
--The Store-NY-1932   (5h6)   3.00
STRICKLAND, AGNES-Lives of Queens of England-(Bohn)-1864,65-
    6 vols-ports   (5tt5,rbnd)   15.00
--same-1902-16 vols-col illus   (5L7)   30.00
--same-Phila-(1902)-sm8vo-brown mor-xtra panelled sp-a.e.g.-
    16 vols-GeoBarrie&Sons-Royal Edition-ltd to 39 sets
                                        (5t0,f)   300.00

STRICKLAND,AGNES   (continued)
--The Rival Crusoes-NY-1864-Blakeman&Mason-12mo-dec cl.-
   g.t.-160p-frontis   (5aa2)   6.50
STRICKLAND,JANE-Moral Lessons & Stories-NY-1839-JohnSTaylor-
   24mo-190p(2)ads-frontis-11 plts-cl   (5p1,wn,tn) 15.00
STRICKLAND,SAM'L-27 Years in Canada West-Lond-1853-
   RichardBentley-2 vols-calf-rare   (5s9,cov loose) 75.00
STRICKLAND,W P,ed-Autobiography of Rev Jas B Finley-Cinn-
   1855   (4a5)   10.00
--Peter Cartwright the Backwoods Preacher-Cinn&NY-(1856)-
   525p   (4p8,wn)   6.00
--The Pioneers of the West-NY&Bost-(1856)
                  (5s4,wn) 6. (5h6,fox)   5.00
STRICKLER,H M-Forerunners,a History or Genealogy of Strickler
   Families-(1925)-illus 425p   (4d9) 8.50   (4t2)   15.00
--Massanutten-n.p.-(1924)-stiff wrps-8vo-illus-fldg map-183p
                  (4d9) 4.50   (4t1,autg)   12.50
STRICKLER,THEODORE D-When & Where We Met Each Other on
   Shore & Afloat-Wash-(1899)-wrps-219p(1)p-Nat'l Tribune
                  (5ff7,5mm8)   7.50
STRINGER,ARTHUR-House of Intrigue-NY-(c1918)-363p (5a1)   4.50
STRINGFIELD,E E-Presbyterianism in the Ozarks-1909-Presbytery
   of Ozark-439 plus index-photos-fldg map-1st ed (5L2)   15.00
STROBEL,REV P A-The Salzburgers & Their Descents-Balt-1855-
   2 plts-1st ed   (4c3)   17.50
STROBRIDGE,IDAH M-In Miner's Mirage Land-LosAng-1904-
   col illuminations-3/4 mor-ltd ed   (4b6,2 autg) 35.00
STRODE,HUDSON-Jefferson Davis, Confederate President-NY-
   1959-Harcourt,Brace-556p   (5p0)   5.00
--Pageant of Cuba-1936   (5L7)   5.00
--South by Thunderbird-NY-(1937)-illus-388p   (5t7,dj)   6.50
--The Story of Bermuda-NY-1932-col frontis-374p-photos-
   1st ed   (5t4)   6.50
STROFFER,D H-Virginia Illustrated-NY-1857-300p-illus-lea-
   1st ed   (5a9)   35.00
STROM,S A E-And So To Dine-Lond-(1955)-12mo-99p-frontis-
   illus   (5w1)   5.00
STRONG,A B-Illustrated Natural History of the Three Kingdoms-
   NY-1848,49,50-3 vols-8vo-hf calf-142 plts(some col)-
                  (5ss5,cov loose)   30.00
STRONG,ANNA LOUISE-I Change Worlds-NY-1937-422p
                  (5p7,5ss6)   4.00
STRONG,BENT T-3 Years or During the War-Olathe,Ka-1913-
   (26p)-photo-wrps-1st ed-ltd to 300c-scarce   (5L5)   17.50
STRONG,CAPT-My Frontier Days & Indian Fights on Plains of
   Texas-n.p.-n.d.-(Dallas,ca 1926)   (4c7)   12.50
STRONG,GEO T-Diary of-NY-1952-illus-4 vols-Nevins,ed-
   scarce   (4j9)   50.00
STRONG,GRACE-Worst Foe,a Temperance Story-Wheeling-1891-
   385p-cl-"13th Ed" on t.p.   (5h7)   5.00
STRONG,HENRY W-My Frontier Days & Indian Fights on the Plains
   of Texas-n.p.-n.d.-(ca 1926)-122p-wrps   (5L2)   10.00
STRONG,JAS C-Wah kee nah & Her People-NY-1893-1st ed-
   275p   (5L0)   7.50
STRONG,L A G,ed-By Haunted Stream-NY-1924-Appleton&Co-
   bds   (5i4)   12.50
--A Defence of Ignorance-NY-1932-12mo-cl-ltd to 200c,nbrd,
   autg   (5dd8)   15.00
--The Sacred River-Lond-(1949)-Methuen-1st Engl ed (5ss9,f,dj) 7.50
STRONG,MARGARET M-Genealogy of Ragland Families-StL-
   1928-121p-cl   (5jj9) 10. 7.00
STRONG,MOSES M-Hist of Territory of Wisc from 1836 to 1848-
   Madison-1885-port-637p   (5n4) 17.50 (5t9) 20. (5m6) 22.50
STRONG,PHIL-Gold in Them Hills-NY-1957-209p-1st ed
                  (4n1,dj) 8.   (5L0,dj)   5.00
STRONG,RICHARD P,ed-African Republic of Liberia & Belgian
   Congo-Cambr-1930-2 vols-8 col plts
                  (5c6,ex-libr,vg) 40. (5t2,dmpstn) 20.00
STRONG,SYDNEY-South African Sermons to Boys & Girls-Oak Park-
   1904-Acorn Pr-24p   (5yy3)   4.00
STRONG,T G-Joseph H Choate-NY-1917   (5ff4)   8.50
STRONG,T M-History of the Town of Flatbush-NY-1842-188p
                  (5m2,5t9)   4.50
STRONG,W W-History of 121st Reg Penna Volunteers-Phila-1906-
   8vo-305p   (4a7)   22.50
STRONG,WM DUNCAN-Introduction to Nebraska Archeology-
   Wash-1935-Smi Misc Col Vol 93,#10-315p plus index-125 plts-
   wrps-1st ed   (5L2)   12.50
STROPE,JEREMY-Snowflake-(NY)-1030-ltd ed-14p-8vo-white bds-
   wrps-Yule greeting   (5ww3)   12.50
STROYER,J-My Life in the South-Salem-1885-83p-wrps-
   new&enlrgd ed   (5x2)   45.00
STRUNSKY,ROSE-Abraham Lincoln-NY-1914-331p   (4j4)   4.00

STRUTT,JACOB GEO-Sylva Britannica-Lond-1822(to 1826)-
   lg folio-hf mor-frontis-49 plts-1st ed   (5z9,plts fox) 100.00
STRUTT,JOS-Chronicle of England-Lond-1779-2 vols-4to-plts-
   calf-1st ed   (5yy6,rub) 37.50
--A Complete View of Dress & Habits of People of England-Lond-
   1796 to 99-prntd by J Nichols-lg4to-calf-151 handcol plts-
   2 vols-1st ed   (5i7,rebkd) 150.00
--Glig Gamena Angel Deod,or The Sports & Pastimes of the
   People of England-Lond-1810-4to-t.e.g.-calf-39 plts-
   2nd ed   large paper   (5b0,f bndg) 125.00
--Sports & Pastimes of the people of England-Lond-1838-new ed
   by Wm Hone-140 engrs-8vo-calf-420p   (5p6,scuff) 15.00
STRUVE,GUSTAV VON-Handbuch der Phrenologie-Leipzig-1845-
   Brockhaus-8vo-calf bkd bds-frontis-5 plts-illus-376p-1st ed
                  (4j5,sl fox)   35.00
STRYKER,LLOYD PAUL-Andrew Johnson,a Study in Courage-NY-
   1930-881p   (5h6)   17.50
STRYKER,WM S-Battle of Monmouth-Princeton-1927-illus-303p
                  (4m2)   30.00
--Forts on the Delaware in Revolutionary War-Trenton-1901-illus-
   map-51p-1st ed-scarce   (4m4)   17.50
--Official Register of Officers & Men of NJ in the Revolution-
   1872-878p   (5t9)   35.00
--Record of Officers & Men of NJ in the Civil War-Trenton-
   1876-2 vols-thk4to-   (5r7,ex-libr) 50.00
STUART,ANDREW-Letters to Rt Hon Lord Mansfield-Lond-1773-
   39,64,47,47p-calf   (5aa0,rbkd) 21.00
STUART,C-Emigrants Guide to Upper Canada-Lond-1820-335p-
   hf lea-wi 4p catalog   (4b9,rbnd) 150.00
STUART,CHAS B-Naval Dry Docks of the US-NY-1852-Norton-
   mor-g.e.-folio-23 plts(of 24)-11 by 13(11 lbs)-(4)p,126p,94p
                  (4L9,rprd,rub) 75.00
STUART,D-Canadian Desert-Tor-1938-88p-card cov   (4b9)   6.00
STUART,DAN'L-Peace & Reform against war & corruption-
   1794-buck-101p   (5L7,rbnd) 15.00
STUART,DOROTHY M-Daughters of George III-Lond-1939-plts
                  (5a1)   6.50
--The English Abigail-Lond-1946-220p,(1)-illus   (5g9,5w7) 7.50
STUART,FRANK S-City of the Bees-NY-1949-243p-12mo-cl (5t0) 4.00
STUART,GRANVILLE-40 Years on the Frontier-Cleve-1925-
   PCPhillips,ed-2 vols-illus   (5kk4)   60.00
--same-Glendale-1957-Paul C Phillips,ed-2 vols in 1 (4k1)   22.50
STUART,I L-History of Franklin Co,Iowa-Chig-1914-SJClarks-
   4to-hf lea-2 vols   (4t1)   40.00
STUART,I W-Life of Jonathan Trumbull-Bost-1859-Crocker&Brewster-
   700p-col illus   (5ee3,rub,5qq8,fade) 15.00
STUART,JAS-3 Years in NoAmer-Edinb-1833-8vo-2 vols-calf-
   fldg map-1st ed   (5n9)   65.00
STUART,JESSE-Foretaste of Glory-NY-1946-1st ed
                  (5ss9,pres,dj) 20.00
--Huey the Engineer-StHelena,Calif-1960-JasEBeard-patternd bds-
   ltd to 585c   (5b2,f)   15.00
--Men of the Mountains-NY-1941-2nd prntng-scarce   (5p6)   12.00
STUART,JOHN LEIGHTON-50 Years in China-NY-1954-
   RandomHse-346p   (5x9)   5.00
STUART,JOS ALONZO-My Roving Life-Auburn,Ca-1895- 12mo-
   orig cl bkd bds-labl-2 vols-ltd ed(50 copies?) (4h0,chew) 900.00
STUART,MOSES-Conscience & the Constitution-Bost-1850-8vo-
   orig wrps-119p-1st ed   (5x2) 25.   (5m6)   12.50
STUART,REGINALD R-Calvin B West of the Umpqua-1961-
   Calif Hist Soc-ltd to 250c   (5x5)   17.50
STUART,ROBT-Discovery of the Oregon Trail-NY-1935-1st ed-
   392p-10 maps&ports-Rollins,ed
        (5i3,autg by ed) 50.   (5s4,soil) 30. (5yy6,f,dj) 42.50
STUART,RUTH M-Golden Wedding & Other Tales-NY-1893-
   366p-cl   (5jj9,lacks fly,5x2) 10.00
--Gobolinks, or Shadow etc-NY-1896-Century-pict bds-73p-
   24mo   (5p1,wn) 17.50
--Plantation Songs-NY-1916-12mo-illus   (5x2)   12.50
--Solomon Crow's Christmas Pockets & Other Tales-NY-1897-
   illus-12mo   (5x2)   10.00
--In Simpkinsville-NY-1897-Harper-illus-1st ed   (5m2)   12.50
--Moriah's Mourning & Other Half Hour Sketches-NY-(1898)-
   illus-1st ed   (5r7,5x2) 7.50
--Sonny's Father-NY-1910-Century-24mo-240p-frontis-dec cl-
   10 plts   (5x2) 6.50   (5p1)   7.50
STUART'S ATLAS-of the State of Maine-Phila-(1903)-folio-cl-
   12th ed   (5g4,lacks bk cov) 10.00
STUBBS,ADDISON W-The Indian Princess & Other Poems-Bost-
   1912-illus-1st ed   (5hh3,pres) 5.00
STUBBS,BURNS-Paintings,Pastels,Drawings,Prints & Copper Plates
   Attributed to Amer & European Artists-Wash-1948-wrps-152p-
   20 illus-8vo   (4a0)   20.00

STUBBS,CHAS WM-Cambridge & Its Story-Lond-1903-Dent-
4to-291p-28 plts-24 tinted liths-t.e.g.-hf mor-Edition de luxe
(5p1,cov wn)   20.00
STUBBS,R ST G-Prairie Portraits-Tor-1954-176p-ports (5dd0)   5.00
STUBBS,STANLEY A-Bird's Eye View of the Pueblos-Univ of Okla-
(1950)-8vo-cl-1st ed   (5h4,f)   6.50
STUBBS,T McA-Account of Moods of Charleston,SC-(1943)-
246p   (4t2)   12.50
STUBBS,WM-Constitutional History of England-Oxford-1903-3 vols
(5q0)   12.50
--same-1883 to 96-4th,5th ed-3 vols-buck   (5L7,rbnd)   25.00
--The Early Plantagenets-NY-n.d.-(ca 1900)-12mo-cl-2 maps-
"Epochs of Modern Hist" series   (5t2)   3.50
STUBBS,DR WM-Descendants of Mordecai Cooke-NewOrl-1923-
286p plus index-illus   (5L2,fleck)   10.00
STUBBS,WM HENRY-Stubb's Manual,Practical Treatise on Linotype-
(Balt,1902)-16mo-39p-illus   (5m6)   7.50
STUCK,HUDSON-The Ascent of Denali(Mt McKinley)-NY-1914-
Scribner's-188p-illus-fldg map-cl   (5d7)   10.00
--Ten Thousand Miles with Dog Sled-NY-1914-Scribners-1st ed-
420p-plts-fldg map   (5i3,f) 25. (4g6,crack) 16. (5dd7)   20.00
--Voyages on Yukon & Its Tributaries-NY-1917-1st ed-397p-
plts-2 fldg maps   (5i3,dj,vf)   20.00
--Winter Circuit of Our Arctic Coast-NY-1920-1st ed-plts-
2 fldg maps-360p   (5i3)   12.50
STUDEBAKER,JOHN-An American Dream-NY-(1948)-1st ed-illus
(5tt5)   4.50
STUDENT & SCHOOLMATE-& Forrester's Boys & Girls Magazine-
Vol 6,#6(Oct 1858) & 5 other issues ending Vol 15,#6 (5aa0) 15.00
STUDENT LAWYER-1955 to 70-Vols 1 thru 15-bound
(5rr4,recent rbnd)   132.50
STUDER,JACOB H-Columbus,Ohio,Its History etc-Columbus-1873-
12mo-cl-584p   (4t1) 15. (5m6,ex-libr) 10. (4m4)   20.00
--Studer's Popular Ornithology,Birds of NoAmer-with Ornithology,
or Science of Birds-Columbus-(1874 to)1878-folio-orig mor-
g.e.-2 vols-1st ed-plts   (5z9,rub)   45.00
STUDLEY,J T-Journal of Sporting Nomad-1912-303p-illus
(4b9) 10. (5t7)   8.50
STUFF,HARRY S-The Siwash,His Book-Seattle-1908-shaped like
teepee-scarce-wrps   (4b2,f)   3.50
STUHLDREHER,HARRY A-Knute Rockne-Phila-1931-1st ed-
1st prntng of autog ed-335p-illus-rare   (5L3)   50.00
STUMP,A-Hist of the Evangelical Lutheran Synod of West Penna-
Chambersburg-1925-696p-illus-1st ed   (5m2)   10.00
STURGE,GORDON W-Hannibal's Historical Highlights-
(Hannibal,NY)-1949-illus-wrps & spec bndg   (4a1)   10.00
STURGEON-Genealogical Hist of Sturgeons of NoAmer-ca 1926-
293p   (5t9)   17.50
STURGES,A A,transl-Momin Pan Luk Ronamau-Honolulu,Oahu-
1866-51&48p-2 title pgs   (5yy3)   60.00
STURGES,EDW B-The Druggist's Legal Directory-Phila-1870-4to-
(16),366,(4)pgs   (5n7,5w3,hinges weak)   25.00
STURGIS,ROGER F-Edw Sturgis of Yarmouth,Mass-1914-88p(5t9)12.50
STURGIS,JULIAN-Dick's wandering-Edinb-1882-Blackwood-3 vols-
8vo-orig cl-1st ed   (5xx6,lt soil,pres)   27.50
STURGIS,RUSSELL-The appreciation of sculpture-NY 1905-235p-
plts-4to-cl   (5m5)   10.00
STURGIS,THOS-Prisoners of War 1861 to 65-NY-1912-illus
(5ee3)   10.00
STURGIS,WM-The Oregon Question-Bost-1845-32p-map-wrps
(4a5) 17.50 (5r6) 24. (5m3)   30.00
STURTEVANT,J M-3 Months in Great Britain-Chig-1864-43p-wrps
(5y0)   12.50
STURTEVANT,RALPH ORSON-Hist of 13th Regiment Vermont Vol,
War of 1861 to 1865-n.p.-1910-4to-cl-illus-896p (5t0)   20.00
STUTENROTH,STELLA MARIE-Daughters of Dacotah-Mitchell,SD-
(1942)-157p-photos-1st ed   (5dd9) 10. (5L2)   7.50
STUTFIELD,HUGH E M-Climbs & Exploration in the Canadian
Rockies-Lond-1903-Longmans,Green-343p-illus-fldg map-
cl   (5d7)   10.00
STUTTERHEIM,MAJ GEN-Battle of Austerlitz-Lond-1807-12mo-
mor   (5t4)   10.00
STYLES,JOHN-Life of David Brainerd,Missionary to the Indians-
Bost-1821-12mo-lea-280p   (5t0)   4.75
STYLES,S-Gentleman Johnny-NY-1963-243p 1st ed (5F9,f,dj)   2.50
STYLES,SHOWELL-Mountains of the Midnight Sun-Lond-(1954)-
Hurst&Blackett-208p-illus-cl   (5d7)   6.00
STYRON,WM-The Confessions of Nat Turner-NY-(1967)-8vo-
cl-1st ed-ltd to 500c,autg,box   (5ss9)   35.00
--Les Confessions de Nat Turner-Paris-(1969) Cr 8vo-covrd wrps-
1st French Transl-#2 of 46 nbrd copies   (5ss7,unopnd)   27.50
--Lie Down in Darkness-Indnpls-1951-1st ed of auth's 1st book
(4b4) 12.50 (5dd8) 20. (5r9,dj)   15.00

STYRON,WM   (continued)
--Set This House on Fire-NY-(1960)-8vo-cl-1st ed
(5ss9) 6. (5dd8,dj)   7.50
SUAREZ DE FIGUEROA,CHRISTOVAL-Hechos de Don Garcia
Hurtado de Mendoza-Madrid-1613-Imprenta Real-sm4to-vel-
1st ed   (5n9)   785.00
SUBARAYA,MOHEI-(Seaman's Manual)-Bunka era(1810)-8vo-
wrps-(102)p-3 illus   (5ss2)   37.50
SUBMARINE CABLES-1892-Govt pub,Navy Dept #103-67p-
map-illus   (5s1)   8.00
SUBMARINE CHASER MANUAL-Wash-1943-US Navy-316p-
illus-wrps-stitchd   (5s1,sl tn)   4.00
SUCCESSFUL HOUSEKEEPER,THE-Detroit-1882-608p-cl-col plts-
(5h1)   7.50
--same-Detroit-1885-Ellsworth-lg8vo-cl-608p-col frontis-illus
(5t2,stnd)   5.00
SUCKOW,RUTH-Country People-NY-1924-8vo-1st ed of auth's
1st book   (4m8,fj)   7.50
--same-NY-1924-12mo-bds-cl bk-1 of 600 issued for Amer
Booksellers' Assoc   (5gg6)   10.00
--The Folks-NY-1934-8vo-cl-727p-illus   (5m8)   6.50
SUDAN-Reports on the Finance & Condition of the Sudan,1908-
Khartoum-Govt of Sudan-229p,plus 717p   (4t5)   35.00
SUDDELL,RICH-Landscape Gardening-Lond-1939-illus-480p-
index   (5qq7)   10.00
SUDWORTH,GEO B-Forest Trees of Pacific Slope-Wash-1908-
441p-illus-wrps-Forest Service   (5tt0) 7.50 (5x5)   10.00
SUE,EUGENE-The Wandering Jew-Lond-1844-Chapman & Hall-
3/4 mor-3 vols-1st Engl ed-t.e.g.   (5z7) 85. (4b7,f)   75.00
--same-Lond-1844-cl-3 vols-1st ed in Engl-cheap ed wiout plts
(5xx6)   20.00
--same-NY-1845-EWinchester-668p-cl   (5r9,rbnd)   25.00
SUES,OTTO L-Grigsby's Cowboys-Salem,SD-1900-illus-8vo-
359,3p   (4g6,worn)   20.00
SUESS,EDUARD-Future of Silver-Wash-1893-8vo-hf mor (4c1)   5.00
SUFFERINGS OF JOHN TURNER-Lond-(ca 1805)-ThosTegg-
sm8vo-wrps-28p-fldg frontis   (5aa2)   17.50
SUGAR LANDS IN TEXAS-Houston-(1909)-Sunset Route-
18p-photos   (5L0)   5.00
SUGDEN,A V-A History of English Wallpaper 1509 to 1914-Lond-
(1925)-281p-folio-illus   (5w7)   85.00
SUGGESTIONS IN BRICKWORK-with Cat of Bricks-Hydraulic
Press Brick Cos-Wash-1895-photos-195p-4to   (5w7)   12.50
SUGGS,ROBT CARL-Archeologyof Nuku Hiva,Marquesas Islands,
French Polynesia-NY-1961-(Amer Mus Nat Hist,Vol 49,Part 1)-
4to-wrps-205p-plts   (5F5)   10.00
SUGRANES,EUGENE-The Old San Gabriel Mission-SanGabriel-
1909-104p-wrps   (5F5) 5. (5L 2)   7.50
SUIT OF ARMOR FOR YOUTH,A-Lond-1824-frontis-11 plts-
moveable flap-1st ed   (5c8,hng crack)   85.00
SULLIVAN,ALAN-Aviation in Canada,1917,1918-Tor-(1919)-
318p-plts   (4a8,sl wn)   12.50
--Brother Blackfoot-NY-(1927)-illus-dec cov-300p (4b2,wn)   4.00
SULLIVAN,EDMUND J-The Art of Illustration-NY-n.d.-257p-
illus-Scribner   (5x0)   7.50
SULLIVAN,EDW-The Book of Kells-Lond-1914-The Studio-4to-
orig white cl-24 col plts-1st ed   (4h0,sml libr stmp)   45.00
SULLIVAN,SIR EDW-Yachting-Bost-1894-Badminton Libr Sports
& Pastimes-   2 vols-894p   (5s1,rprd)   15.00
SULLIVAN,EDW D-Benedict Arnold Military Racketeer-NY-1932-
Vanguard-306p-frontis-1st ed   (5mm8)   6.00
--Chicago Surrenders-NY-(1930)-239p-cl 1   (5ff7)   5.00
--This Labor Union Racket-NY-1936 (5m2,dj) 4. (5x7)   5.00
SULLIVAN,EDW ROBT-Rambles & Scrambles in No & SoAmer-
Lond-1852-orig cl-424p-1st ed   (4n4)   60.00
SULLIVAN,GERALD E,ed-Story of Englewood 1835 to 1923-
Englewood-c1924-Foster&McDonnell-12mo-cl-224p (4t1)   15.00
SULLIVAN,J T-Report of Hist & Tech Info re...Interoceanic
Communication...Amer Isthmus-Wash-1883-GPO-maps-
5 fldg plts-4to-217p   (5yy0)   17.50
SULLIVAN,JAS-History of the District of Maine-Bost-1795-
I Thomas&ETAndrews-1st ed-421p-errara-fldg map-orig calf
(4b1,map rprd)   95.00
SULLIVAN,JAS-History of NY State 1523 to 1927-1927-6 vols-
illus   (5ff2)   25.00
--same-NY-(1927)-5 vols-4to-hf lea-illus (5t9) 15. (5m6)   17.50
SULLIVAN,JOHN-Of Berwick, New Eng & of the O'Sullivans of
Ardes,Ireland,by Thos Coffin Amory-Cambridge,Mass-1893-
170p   (4p7,cov spot)   15.00
SULLIVAN,MAJ GEN JOHN-Journals of Military Expedition
Against the 6 Nations of Indians in 1779-Auburn-1887-
fldg map-illus-579p   (5s4,wn) 15. (5m2)   10.00

SULLIVAN,MAJ GEN JOHN (continued)
--Letters & Papers of...,Continental Army-Concord-1930 to 39-
3 vols-frontis   (5q8,sl bndg spot)   22.50

SULLIVAN, JOHN L-Observations on Thomas's Naval Architecture...
(wrpr title)-NY-1825-wrps   (5g3,lacks bk wrp)   10.00

SULLIVAN, JOSEPHINE-History of C Brewer&Co-Bost-1926-8vo-
cl-193p-illus   (5t1) 25.   (5r0) 15. (5h5)   10.00

SULLIVAN, KATHRYN-Maryland & France, 1774 to 89-1936-sewn
(5L7)   7.50

SULLIVAN,M J,ed-Intl Blue Book Publication,a Deluxe Issue
on SE Texas-Memphis-1912-124p   (5n4)   35.00

SULLIVAN, MARK-Our Times-NY-1926 to 35-6 vols
(5w5,4k2) 35.   (4n6,vf,5j2) 40.   (5j5)   37.50

SULLIVAN, MAURICE S-Jedediah Smith, Trader & Trail Breaker-
NY-1936-illus-sm4to-1st ed
(5L2,dj,4g6) 22.50 (5x5,dj,5hh4,sp tn,dj)   27.50

--The Travels of Jedediah Smith-Santa Ana-1934-sm4to-cl-
fldg map   (5h4,cov soil) 75.(5a3) 100. (5b0,sl fade)   95.00

SULLIVAN, MAY K-Trail of a Sourdough-Bost-1920-frontis-258p
(4F9)   10.00
--Woman Who Went to Alaska-Bost-n.d.-(1903?)-   3rd ed-
392p-illus   (4b9)   12.00
--same-Bost-1910-plts-292p   (4F9)   10.00

SULLIVAN,SGNT W J L-12 Years in the Saddle for Law &
Order on the Frontiers of Texas-Austin-1909-284p-hf mor-
v scarce   (5yy7,wn rprd) 70.   (5n4)   85.00

SULLIVAN,WM-Public Men of the Revolution-Phila-1847-
Carey&Hart-463p-frontis   (5qq8) 10.00 (5ee3)   15.00

SULLIVANT'S ABC ZOO-NY-Old Wine Press-1946-4to-
pict bds   (5c8,rub)   6.00

SULLY, JAS-The Human Mind-NY-1892-2 vols   (5t4)   10.00
--Illusions-NY-1881-372p-1st ed-Intl Sci Series   (5w0)   7.50

SULTE, BENJ-Histoire des Canadiens Francais, 1608 to 1880-
Montr-1882 to 84-7 vols in 3   (5nn8)   125.00
--same-Montr-1882 to 84-lea bks & corners-4to-8 vols in 4
(4m6,sl loose,ex-libr)   100.00
--Les Coureurs de Bois au Lac Superieur-Ottawa-1912-18p-
prntd wrps   (5w8)   10.00
--Les Francais dans l'ouest en 1671-Ottawa-1918-prntd wrps (5w8) 12.00

SULZ,CHAS H-A Treatise on Beverages-NY-1888-818p,(1)
(5w1,broke,soil)   12.50

SULZER, ROBT FREDK-Planting the Outposts-Phila-1913-133p-
photos-1st ed   (5L2)   5.00

SUMERTON, WINTER-Will He Find Her?-NY-1860-491p-
Derby&Jackson-1st ed   (5x4)   15.00

SUMIDA, SHOJCHI-Japan & China Ship Encyclopedia-(Edo,1944)-
8vo-cl-429p-profusely illus   (5ss2)   17.50

SUMMARY OF EVIDENCE-Produced Before a Committee of House
of Commons, Relating to the Slave Trade-Lond-1792 (5x2)   32.50

SUMMARY VIEW OF THE MILLENIAL CHURCH-or United Soc
of Believers, commonly called Shakers-Albany-1848-12mo-
384p-orig sheep-lea labl-enlrgd 2nd ed (5t4,ex-libr) 10. (5r7) 20.00

SUMMER, G L-Newberry Co,SoCar, Historical & Genealogical-
n.p.-1950-480p   (4j4)   12.50

SUMMER RAMBLES-via Rome, Watertown & Ogdensburg RR-
(NY, 1886)-fldng brochure-orig wrps-8vo-illus-opening to
43 inches   (5m6)   10.00

SUMMERHAYES, MARTHA-Vanished Arizona-Salem, Mass-(1911)-
319p-illus-2nd ed   (5L0)   15.00
--same-Chig-1939-illus-337p-Quaife, ed   (4b3,5a9)   10.00

SUMMERING IN COLORADO-Denver-1874-158p-ads-cl-
15 mntd photos bnd in   (5h7)   30.00
--same-no illus(as issued)   (5h7,wn)   15.00

SUMMER LAND, THE-A Southern Story-By a Child of the Sun-
NY-1855-246p   (5i9) 15. (5w7,fade)   10.00

SUMMERLY, FELIX,ed-Pleasant History of Reynard the Fox-Lond-
1843-JosCundall-4p ads at end-40 liths-sm8vo-hf calf
(5c8,rub)   55.00

SUMMERS, LEWIS-History of SW Virginia 1746 to 86 & Wash Co
1777 to 1870-Richmond-1903-1st ed-maps-911p
(4m2) 45.   (4m6,mint)   35.00

SUMMERS, MONTAGUE,ed-Complete Works of Thos Otway-
Bloomsbury-1926-4to-batik bds-3 vols-ltd to 90 sets-
Nonesuch Pr   (5d9)   150.00
--The History of Witchcraft & Demonology-NY-1926-353p-
8 plts   (5c3)   8.00

SUMMERS, RICHARD-Dark Madonna-Caldwell-1937-294p-scarce
1st edition -(novel)   (5dd4)   15.00
--The Devil's Highway-NY-1937-8vo-cl-299p-1st ed (5g5,dj) 10.00

SUMMERS, T O,ed-Confederate States Almanac 1862-Nashville-
1862-Southern Methodist Publ House-32p   (5yy3)   125.00

SUMMERS, THOS O-The River-Nashville-1857-53p plus 2p ads-
hf lea-cpyrte date 1855   (5L2,lacks fly)   8.50

SUMMIT MAGAZINE-Vols 1 thru 9 bnd in 4 vols, vols 10 thru 14
in wrps as issued-Huntington Park & Big Bear, Nov 1955 to
Mar 1968-(May 1959 not issued)   (5d7)   165.00

SUMNER,CHAS-The Crime Against Kansas-Bost-1856-port-12mo-
orig cl wrps-95p-a.e.g.   (4g6)   8.50
--Orations & Speeches-Bost-1850Ticknor&Fields-2 vols-1st ed
(5kk5,fade,rub)   15.00
--Prophetic Voices Concerning America-Bost-1874-Lee&Shepard-
frontis   (5qq8) 5.   (5m2) 8.50 (5L2)   6.00

SUMNER, CHAS A-Odd Fellowship-Virginia-1964-24p-8vo-
prntd wrps   (4c1)   50.00
--Poem..delivered at Metro Theatre, SanFran, Calif, May 6,1863-
SanFran-1863-16mo-orig yellow prntd wrps-1st ed-scarce
(5i9,f)   27.50
--'Round the Horn, a Christmas yarn-n.d.-(ca 1870)-Bacon&Co-
8vo-orig prntd wrps-1st ed   (5i0,f)   60.00

SUMNER, E B-Anc & Desc of Amaziah Hall & Betsy Baldwin-
1954-255p   (4t2)   12.50
--Anc of Edw Wales Blake & Clarissa Matilda Glidden-1948-
322p   (4t2)   12.50

SUMNER, G LYNN-Abraham Lincoln As A Man Among Men-
NY-(1922)-31p   (5m2,pres)   3.50
--Meet Abraham Lincoln-NY&Chig-1946-port-1st ed
(5yy6,pres) 6.   (5t4) 3.50   (4a1)   5.00

SUMNER, HELEN L-Equal Suffrage, results of an investigation in
Colorado-NY-1909-318p   (5dd4)   4.50

SUMNER,WM GRAHAM-Science of Society-NewHav-1927-
(Yale Univ Pr)-4 vols   (5q0) 17.50   (4j3)   35.00
--same-Yale Univ Pr-1927-2 vols   (5p9)   15.00

SUMNER,WM H-History of East Boston-Bost-1858-J E Tilton-
8vo-bds-801p   (4t1,rebkd)   15.00

SUMPTION, LOIS L-Cookies & More Cookies-Peoria-(1938)-
182p-illus   (5g9)   3.00

SUNDAY AFTERNOONS WITH MAMA-Lond-(c1864)-sm sq8vo-
80p-plts-dec cl-a.e.g.   (5a1)   8.50

SUNDAY SCHOOL BOY-Phila-(ca 1835)-Amer Sunday School
Union-8p-yellow wrps-wdcuts   (5c8,rbkd)   12.50

SUNDBORG, GEO-Hail Columbia-NY-1954-467p
(5dd6) 5.   (5s4,dj,f)   7.50

SUNDERLAND, EDSON R-History of the Amer Bar Assoc & its
Work-1953-251p   (5p9)   5.00

SUNDERLAND, EDWIN S S-Abraham Lincoln & the Illinois
Central RR-NY-1955-illus-pict cl-priv prntd   (5r7)   10.00

SUNDERLAND, LA ROY-The Testimony of God against Slavery-
Bost-1836-12mo   ·labl-2nd ed   (5ss5,chip)   12.50

SUNKIST RECIPES FOR EVERY DAY-Calif Fruit Growers Exch-
LosAng-1929-illus-pict wrps-36p   (4g9)   3.50

SUNKIST RECIPES ORANGES, LEMONS-Calif Fruit Growers Exch-
LosAng-1916-illus-pict wrps-64p   (4g9)   5.00

SUN MAID RAISINS-Their Food Value & 92 Selected Recipes-
n.p.-n.d.-(ca 1915)-22p-col illus   (5g9)   5.00

SUNNY SIDE-or, the Country Minister's Wife-Phila-(1851)-
Amer Sunday School Union-198p   (5x4)   7.50

SUNNY SOUTH, THE-or, The Southerner at Home-Phila-1860-
526p & 18p advts-1st ed   (5m4)   45.00

SUNNYSIDE IRRIGATION PROJECT OF US RECLAMATION
SERVICE-Sunnyside, WA-(ca 1908)-illus-obl 8vo-orig wrps-
72p   (4g6)   7.50

SUNSET ALL WESTERN FOODS-What They Are etc-1947-
284p-illus-scarce   (4g9)   6.50

SUNSET CHEFS OF THE WEST-1952-224p-scarce   (4g9,f)   6.50

SUNSET FLOWER GARDEN BOOK-SanFran-(1950)-252p-illus-
Lane Pub-rev&enlrgd-stiff papr wrps-spiral bnd   (5s7)   3.50

SUNSET'S HOST & HOSTESS BOOK-1940-illus-Muhs, ed (4g9) 5.00

SUNSET KITCHEN CABINET COOK BOOK-1938-stiff wrps-
spiral bnd-illus-223p   (4g9)   5.00

SUNSET KITCHEN CABINET RECIPES-Vols 1,2 & 3,1944 to 45-
3 vols-illus-128p ea   (4g9)   7.50

SUPPRESSED BOOK ABOUT SLAVERY-NY-1864-illus-
GeoWCarleton Pub   (5x2)   37.50

SURFACE, FRANK M-The Grain Trade During the War-NY-1928-
tables in fold-679p   (4p7)   10.00

SURFACE, H A-The Serpents of Penna-Harrisburg-1906-Mo Bull
Div Zool, Vol 4 #4&5-plts-wrps-8vo   (4p6,lacks bk wrp)   12.50

SURFACE, HENRY-Bibliography of the Pulp & Paper Industries-
Wash-1913-48p-wrps   (5j4)   6.00

SURRATT, JOHN H-Trial of John H Surratt in Criminal Court-
Wash-1867-GPO-2 vols-1383p-bds-papr labls   (5r7)   50.00

SURRATT, MARY, TRIAL-Proofs of Falsity of Conover's Testimony
Before Military Court at Wash City-Montreal-1865-20p-rare
(5r5)   45.00

SURTEES,ROBT S-Handley Cross, or, Mr Jorrock's Hunt-Lond
1854-illus(some col)-1st ed in bk form-
       (4j3,needs rebndg) 17.50 (5p5,f)   25.00
--Jorrock's Jaunts & Jollities-Lond-Downey-1901-4to-2 vols-
62 plts-lg papr-90c   (5i1)   85.00
--"Plain or Ringlets?"-Lond-1860-illus-col engrs-1st ed in bk form-
lea&bds   (4j3,rebnd)   25.00
--Sporting Novels-Lond-n.d.-for Subscribers from plts of orig ed-
6 vols-sp g. tooled-hand col plts-part calf (4a6,f bndg) 65.00
SUSQUEHANNA CO-History of-1873-ECBlackman, ed-illus
      (5L7,rbnd)   25.00
SUSQUEHANNA SYNOD-of Evangelical Lutheran Church in
US-n.p.-1917-publ by the Synod-illus   (5m2) 8.50
SUSSEL COLLECTION-Arts & Crafts of Penna & other Notable
Americana-NY-1958,59-Parts 1 to 3-8vo-orig prntd wrps-
illus-priced-Parke Bernet   (5t2)   17.50
SUTCLIFFE,DENHAM,ed-Untriangulated Stars-Cambr-1947
Harvard U Pr   (4p1)   10.00
SUTERMEISTER,EDWIN-The Story of Papermaking-Bost-1954-
SDWarrenCo-209p-illus-cl   (5hh6,spot)   5.00
SUTHERLAND,A H-Victoria,Brit Columbia-Vict-1938-illus-
stiff wrps-32p   (5dd7,autg)   11.00
SUTHERLAND,ALEX-Summer in Prairie Land-Tor-1882-198p-
2nd ed   (4a8)   12.50
SUTHERLAND,DONALD-Gertrude Stein,a Biography of Her
Work-1951-Yale Univ Pr-1st ed   5m2,dj)   5.00
SUTHERLAND,EDWIN H-Principles of Criminology-1955-
Lippincott-lg8vo-(5th ed,rev by Cressy) (5a6,vf) 6.50
SUTHERLAND,HALLIDAY-Lapland Journey-Lond-1938-295p(5s6) 3.50
SUTHERLAND,J G-At Sea With Jos Conrad-Lond-1922-
Grant Richards Ltd-bds-1st ed-ltd to 1250c (5ss3,stnd) 5.00
SUTHERLAND,JAS-Defoe-Phila-1938-Lippincott-8vo-red cl-
300p-ports   (5aa2)   5.00
SUTHERLAND,MRS MARY A-Story of Corpus Christi-n.p.-
1916   (4a9,f) 17.50 (4c7)   27.50
SUTHERLAND,W A-Treatise on Code Pleading & Practice
Also Containing 1900 Forms-SanFran-1910-4 vols (5r4) 25.00
SUTLEY,ZACK T-The Last Frontier-NY-1930-Macmillan-map-
350p-1st ed-fldg map (4n8,5h1) 10. (5w9) 12.50 (5yy7) 10.65
SUTLIFFE,G H-Sutcliffe,Sutliffe Family in Amer,Desc of
Nathan'l-(1903)-242p   (5t9)   17.50
SUTPHEN,W-Golfer's Alphabet-NY&Lond-1898-Frost,illus-
orig pict cl bds   (5m1)   35.00
SUTRO,A-Mineral Resources of US...reference to Comstock
Lode & Sutro Tunnel-Balt-1868-frontis-4to-fldg maps-
232p   (5yy0)   27.50
SUTRO TUNNEL-Report of Commissioners in Regard to The
Sutro Tunnel-Wash-1872-8vo-a.e.g-988p (5F5) 17.50 (5x5) 30.00
SUTRO,THEODORE-13 Chapters of Amer History-(n.p.)-1905-
Edw Moran Series   (5x5)   15.00
SUTTER,JOHANN A-Diary of Johann A Sutter-SanFran-1932-
col fldg plt-Grabhorn   (5x5)   50.00
SUTTER,JOHN A-New Helvetia Diary-SanFran-1939-4to-
ltd to 950c -Grabhorn Press (5r8) 45. (5F5,f)   40.00
SUTTEY,ZACK T-The Last Frontier-NY-1930-350p-fldg map-
1st ed   (5ee3,f)   8.50
SUTTON,AMOS-Narrative of Mission to Orissa-Bost-1833-
frontis-calf-424p   (5q0)   10.00
SUTTON,DENYS-Discussions on Art,Amer Painting-Lond-1948-
Avalon Pr-31p-illus-crown 4to   (4a0,dj)   10.00
SUTTON,ERNEST V-A Life Worth Living-(1948)-Trail's End Pub Co-
1st ed-ltd to 2000c,autg
  (5jj7) 7.50   (5L2,f,dj,5m9,5F5) 10. (5x5,dj) 12.50
SUTTON,FRED E-Hands Up-NY-1927-303p-illus (5dd9,5kk6) 8.50
SUTTON,GEO MIKSCH-Eskimo Year-NY-1914-illus-1st ed
      (4a1,autg)   8.50
--Mexican Birds-Norman-(c1951)-Univ of Okla-lg8vo-cl-
16 col plts-o.p.   (4a3,f,dj)   22.50
SUTTON,HORACE-Footloose in Canada-1950-illus (5L7) 4.00
SUTTON,J J-Hist of 2nd Regiment West Virg Cavalry Vol-
Portsmouth-1892-262p-cl-rare   (5y0,spots)   50.00
SUTTON,R-Report of Debates & Proceedings of Convention for
Revision of Constit of Kentucky-1849-Frankfort-1849-1107p
plus index-lea   (5L2,rub)   25.00
SUTTON,RICHARD L-Tiger Trails in Southern Asia-StL-1926-
8vo-207p-115 photos   (4a6)   15.00
SUTTON,SAM'L-Historical Account of a New Method for extracting
foul air out of ships etc-Lond-1749-sm4to-disbnd-120p-fldg plt-
2nd ed   (5ss2)   15.00
SVERDRUP,OTTO-New Land -Vol 2 only (of 2)-504p-illus-
2 pkt maps-Lond-1904   (5ss1)   10.00
SVIVINE,PAUL-Picturesque US of Amer 1811,12,13-NY-1930-
lg4to-52 illus   (4p8)   17.50

SVIVINE, PAUL (continued)
--Life of Gen Moreau-NY-1814-hf lea-24mo-107p (5L3) 13.50
--Some Details Concerning Gen Moreau-Bost-1814-N Willis-
port-107p-cl   (5yy3,rbnd)   10.00
SWAIN,J E-Struggle for Control of the Mediterranean prior to 1848-
n.d.-sewn   (5L7)   3.50
SWAIN,JOHN-Pleasures of the Torture Chamber-Lond-1931-
Noel Douglas-t8vo-mor sp-labl-illus   (5t8)   20.00
SWALES,FRANK-Driving as I Found It-Lond-1891-illus-180p-
ads-g.pic cl-scarce   (4p2,hng crack)   10.00
SWALLOW BARN-or A Sojourn in the Old Dominion-Phila-1832-
2 vols-orig bds-(J P Kennedy)-1st ed (5m4,cov loose) 47.50
SWALLOW,G C-1st & 2nd Annual Reports of Geological Survey
of Missouri-JeffersonCty-1855-plts-maps(some fldg & col)-
207p,239p-errata p-1st ed   (4t3)   12.50
--Geological Report of Country along Line of SW Branch of
Pac RR,State of Missouri-StL-1859-91p-fldg col map-
2 illus-1st ed-scarce   (5L0)   15.00
SWAN,A M-Albuquerque Illustrated-1900-Democrat Pub-obl 8vo-
50p-plts-illus   (5g0)   10.00
SWAN,ANDREW-Remarkable Story of...-Lond-1933-254p (5yy8) 7.50
SWAN,JAS G-Haidah Indians of Queen Charlotte Islands,
Brit Col-Wash-(Aug 1874)-Smi Inst-4to-Orig wrps-
2 lvs,15p-7p plts   (5w8)   22.50
--Indians of Cape Flattery...Wash Terr-(Wash-1869-Smi Inst)-
wrps-4to-108p   (5w8)   25.00
--same-Wash-(1870)-Smi Contrib to Knowl #220-illus-108p-
3/4 lea-scarce   (5yy7)   30.00
--Northwest Coast-NY-1857-Harper&Bros-435p-illus-fldg map-cl
    (5tt8,pres) 35.   (4d0,rbkd,sl wn)   35.00
SWAN,JOHN A-A Trip to the Gold Mines of Calif in 1848-
SanFran-1960-orig bds-8vo-Book Club of Calif-ltd to 400c
    (5hh4,mint) 32.50   (4g5,mint)   27.50
SWAN,OLIVER G-Deep Water Days-Phila-(1929)-506p-illus(5t4) 8.00
SWANBERG,W A-Citizen Hearst-NY-(1961)-photos-555p
    (4n1,dj) 6.50   (5t7)   7.50
SWANDER,JOHN I-Evolution of a Farmer Boy-Tiffin-1919-270p-
cl   (5h2)   10.00
SWANK,JAS-Cambria County Pioneers-Phila-1910-scarce (4m4) 16.50
--Introduction to a history of Ironmaking & Coal Mining in Penna-
Phila-1878-125p   (5w4)   20.00
--Notes & Comments on Industrial,Economic,Political etc-Phila-
1897-Amer Iron & Steel Assoc   (5m2,pres)   7.50
--Progressive Penna-1908   (5L7)   7.50
SWANN,ARTHUR-Collection of 1st editions of Amer Authors
formed by-NY-1961-catalogue-8vo-bds   (5b2,f)   7.50
SWANN,H K-A Monograph of the Birds of Prey-Lond-1930 to
45-4to-hf mor-39 col plts plus 17 plts-2 vols (4h0) 150.00
SWANN,JOHN-Title Map of Coal Field of Great Kanawha Valley-
NY-1867-59 x 54"-fold to 8vo-rare-col   (5y0)   60.00
SWANNER,CHAS S-Santa Ana,A Narr of Yesterday,1870 to 1910-
Claremont-1953-Saunders Pr-8vo-cl-158p-ltd to 2000c
    (4t1) 20.   (5h5,f,dj)   7.50
SWANSON,E W-Public Education in the South Today & Tomorrow-
Univ NoCar-1955   (5x2,dj)   12.00
SWANSON,NEIL H-First Rebele being a lost Chapter of our
History etc-NY-(1937)-Farrar&Rinehart-393p-plts-maps-cl
    (5F1,5mm8) 6.   (5h9)   8.50
--same-(1937)-Farrar&Rinehart-ltd to 1000c,nbrd,autg (5F1,f,dj) 6.00
--Unconquered-GardenCty-1947-Dblday-1st prntng (5m2) 6.00
SWANSON,ROBT E-Rhymes of a Lumberjack-Tor-1943-illus-
58p-wrps-2nd ed   (4t7)   5.00
SWANSON,W E-Modern Shipfitters' Handbook-NY-1940-269p-
12mo-flex cov-fldg plans-   (5s1,dj)   3.50
SWANSON,W W-Rail,Road & River-Tor-1937-121p(4f9)6.(5aa0) 4.50
--Wheat-Tor-1930-320p-map-chart (5a1) 4.50 (5w8) 7.50
SWANTON,JOHN R-Early History of Creek Indians-BAE Bul#73
      (4k4,f)   15.00
--Haida Texts,Masset Dialect-Leiden,Holland&NY-1908-Part 2,
Vol 10,Memoir Amer Mus Nat Hist,Jesup No Pac Exped-
folio-Eng & Haida text   (4b2,unopened,4h3)   20.00
--Haida Texts & Myths(Skidegate Dialect)-Wash-1905-448p-
BAE #29 (4k4,cl,f) 6. (5ss1,hf mor)   13.50
--Indian Tribes of NoAmer-Smi Insti BAE Bul#145-Wash-1952-
cl-8vo-fldg maps-1st ed (4k4,f) 27.50 (5qq5) 15.(5ss5,mint)25.00
--Myths & Tales of SE Indians-cl-BAE Bull #88 (4k4,f) 10.00
--Source Material...Choctau Indians-BAE Bull #103-wrps (4k4,f) 10.00
--Tlingit Myths & Texts-Wash-1909-BAE Bull #39-451p
    (5qq5) 12.   (4h3)   20.00
SWARD,KEITH-The Legend of Henry Ford-NY-1948-550p
    (5p0) 6.50   (5h8,5hh6)   5.00
SWASEY,CHAS A G-Amer Caricatures,Pertaining to the Civil War...
79 cartoons-NewBedford,Mass-(ca 1880) (5t4)   15.00

SWAYNE, J S-The Story of Concord-1906-314p-illus
(5t9,5k0)   3.50

SWEDENBORG, EMANUEL-Doctrine of the New Jerusalem
Concerning the Sacred Scripture-Bost-1795-orig wrps-186p
(5ss5,sl dmgd)   17.50

SWEDENBORG, A HERMETIC PHILOSOPHER-NY-1858-Appleton-
12mo-cl-352p-6p ads-1st ed-scarce-(EAHitchcock) (5j5)   25.00

SWEDISH SMORGASBORD-Stockholm-(1934)-70p-illus-
Engl text   (5g9,chip)   3.00

SWEENEY, J J,ed-African Negro Art-NY-1935-R8vo-illus-
fldg maps   (5x2,f,dj)   30.00

SWEENEY, JAS JOHNSON-Joan Miro-NY-(1941)-Met Mus of Art-
t8vo-illus-1st ed   (5m6,dj)   7.50

--Plastic Redirections in 20th Century Painting-(1934)-Univ of
Chig Pr-104p   (5x0)   6.00

--Three Young Rats & other rhymes-NY-(1946)-Mus of Modern Art-
4to-134p-drawngs, Calder-2nd ed   (5p1,dj)   7.50

SWEENEY, LT THOS W-Journal of -Woodward,ed-LosAng-(1956)-
port-plts-278p   (5dd5)   15.00

SWEENEY, W A-History of the Amer Negro in the Great World
War-Chig-1919-illus   (5x2)   35.00

SWEET, ALEX E-On Mexican Mustang Through Texas-Hartf-1883-
672p   (4j6,f) 35.   (5ee3,f) 15.   (5L3,vg)   16.50

--Sketches from Texas Siftings-NY-1882-228p (5t7) 8.50 (5n4)   7.50

SWEET, FREDK A-Catalog, Sargent, Whistler & Cassatt-Chig Art
Inst-1954-101p-illus-8vo   (4a0)   17.50

SWEET, H C-Memorial to Gov & Legislature of State of Texas-
Mangum, Tex-1887-8p-wrps-rare   (5n4)   25.00

SWEET, ROBT-Flora Australasica-Lond-1827,28-hf calf-bd-
56 handcol plts-1st ed-v rare   (5z9,cov wn,sl wtrstnd)   550.00

--Geraniaeceae-Lond-1820 to 30-mor bkd bds-500 handcol plts-
5 vols-1st ed   (5z9,vf,errata lf)   1,300.00

SWEETMAN, LUKE D-Back Trailing on Open Range-Caldwell-
1951-248p-illus   (5g0,dj)   7.50

SWEETS FROM FAIRY LAND-Lond-(1895)-ErnestNister 630-
8 changeable slot picts-4to-pict bds-cl sp   (5c8,f)   65.00

SWEETSER, ALBERT R-Key & Flora-Bost-(1908)-157p-fabr (5s7)   5.00

SWEETSER, KATE-Book of Indian Braves-NY-(1913)-illus-184p-
juvenile   (4b2,lacks 2 illus,tn) 6.   (4b2,fair)   7.00

SWEETSER, M F-Osgood's White Mntns-Bost-1876-1st ed-16mo-
436p-cl g. stmpd-6 fldg maps(incl pkt)   (5u9)   22.50

--Views in the White Mntns-Portland-1879-1st ed-crown 8vo-
cl-g. dec   (5u9,wn) 4.50   (5ss5) 7.50   (5t7)   6.50

SWEETSER'S-The White Mntns,a Handbook for Travelers-Bost-
1893-12th ed-revised-5 maps   (4c5,lacks map)   15.00

SWEM, E G,ed-Brothers of the Spade-Barre-1957-196p-2 ports-
map   (5t4)   8.00

SWENSON, OLAF-Northwest of the World-NY-1944-270p-illus
(4b9) 8.   (5ss1)   6.50

SWETE, H B-Church Services & Service books before the
Reformation-1896   (5L7)   4.00

SWETNAM, GEO-Pittslvania country-NY-1951-Duell,Sloan&Pearce-
315p-Amer Folkways ser-1st ed   (5ss5,autg)   7.50

SWETT, LUCIA G-New England Breakfast Breads-Bost-1891-
obl 12mo-129p-illus   (5c4,faded)   6.50

SWEET, SAM'L-Who Was the Commander at Bunker Hill-Bost-
1850-8vo-orig wrps-39p-1st ed   (5ss5)   6.00

SWETT, SOPHIE-The Lollipops' Vacation & other stories-Bost-
c1896-Estes&Lauriat-12mo-260p-dec cl-illus   (5p1)   10.00

SWICHER, CARL BRENT-Roger B Taney-NY-1935-Macmillan-
608p-illus   (5qq8,vf)   12.50

SWIETEN VAN, BARON GERARD-Diseases Incident to Armies-Phila-
1776-164p-8vo-hf mor-1st Amer ed (4c1,rbnd,libr stmp)   300.00

--same-Bost-1777-reprntd by W Draper-sm8vo-orig hf calf-167p-
scarce   (4t9)   775.00

SWIFT, DEAN-Gulliver's Travels & The Adventures of Baron
Munchausen-NY-1883-JohnBAlden-12mo-334p,125p-
Cyclopedia of Choice Prose for Young People   (5p1)   5.00

SWIFT, H H-North Star Shining-NY-1947-illus   (5x2,dj)   12.50

SWIFT, HELEN-My Father & My Mother-Chig-1937-157p-illus-
Lakeside Pr   (5p7)   5.00

SWIFT, JOHN L-About Grant-Bost-1880-206p-cl
(5h1,cov spot,rprd)   4.00

SWIFT, JONATHAN-Gulliver's Travels-Lond-1839-Scott,Webster &
Geary-12mo-333p-frontis   (5c8)   6.00

--same-NY-1869-AllenBros-orig g.cl-1st illus ed by HKBrowne
("Phiz")   (5c8)   12.50

--same-Lond-1883-WmNimme-Ballantyne Pr-t8vo-etched port &
4 orig etchings by ADLeLoir-brown lev-raised g.bands-
g.top-ltd to 40c   (5t5)   85.00

--same-Lond-1894-100 illus by ChasEBrock-8vo-g.dec blue cl-
g.e.   (5t5)   10.00

SWIFT, JONATHAN   (continued)

--same-Lond-1900-JMDent-12 illus by Rackham-sm12mo-363p-
limp lea covers   (5v0,rub)   17.50

--same-NY-1940-illus-Heritage Pr (5p1) 7.50   (5t4,5p9)   6.00

--same-NY-c1947-Crown 8vo-358p-24 prints & 160 drwngs by
Quintanilla-labl   (5p1,dj)   12.50

--Miscellaneous Poems-REllis Roberts,ed-1928-Golden Cockerel Pr-
bds-ltd to 375c   (5ss9,f,dj)   30.00

--A Tale of a Tub-Lond-1704-8vo-calf-2nd ed, corrected
(4c2,rbkd)   100.00

--same-Lond-1733-prntd for Benj Motte-7p plts-12mo-8th ed-lea
(5ss9,rub)   30.00

--Travels Into Several Remote Nations of the World, in 4 Parts,
by Lemuel Gulliver-Lond-1724-for Benj Motte-port-mor-
6 maps & plans-a.e.g.-1st ed-2 vols   (5z7,f,f bndg)   275.00

--same-Lond-1747-Bathurst-5th ed-12mo-296p-6 maps (4F6,vg)   37.50

--same-Lond-1894-Macmillan-a.e.g.-100 illus by CEBrock
(5c8,f)   8.50

--The Travels of Lemuel Gulliver-(Balt)-1929-Ltd Ed Club-
lin wi pigskin sp-ltd to 1500c,autg by King,box
(5p1,box rub) 45.   (5b0)   60.00

--Voyages de Gulliver-Paris-1838-Ledentu-2 vols in 1-16mo-
qtr red lea   (5c8)   6.00

--Works-Edinb-1824-t8vo-19 vols-3/4 mor-lg type-g.tooled sp-
raised bands-2nd ed-ex scarce   (5t8,f bndg)   210.00

SWIFT, LINDSAY-Brook Farm-NY-1904-sm8vo-cl-303p
(5t2,lacks e.p.)   5.00

SWIFT, LOUIS W-The Yankee of the Yards-Chig&NY-1927-
218p-illus-1st ed   (5s4,autg) 7.50 (5k0,pres)   6.00

SWIFT, S-Food & Drugs Administration-Lond-1947   (5ff4)   8.75

SWIFT, SAMUEL-History of Middlebury-1859-444p-illus (5e8)   28.75

SWIFT, Z-Digest of the Law of Evidence, in Civil & Criminal
Cases-Hartf-1810   (5r4,rbnd)   15.00

SWIGART, WM R-Biography of Spring St in Los Angeles-LosAng-
(1945)   (5x5,pres,dj)   10.00

SWIGGETT, HOWARD-The Great Man...As A Human Being-NY-
1953-1st ed   (5yy6)   6.00

--The Extraordinary Mr Morris-NY-1952-illus-1st ed
(5yy6,5p0)   5.00

--Jas Oliver Curwood-NY-(1943)-Disciple of the Wilds-8vo-plts-
orig cl-1st ed   (5p5,dj)   7.50

--The Rebel Raider-Indnpls-(1934)-Bobbs Merrill-341p-plts-
1st ed   (5mm8,dj)   17.50

--same-GardenCty-(1937)-341p   (5yy8)   6.00

--War out of Niagara-NY-1933-309p-illus   (5t7)   10.00

SWIGGETT, CAPT S A-The Bright Side of Prison Life-Balt-(1897)-
254p plus photos-scarce   1st edition   (5L5,f)   35.00

SWINBORNE, J-Mechanism of the Watch-Lond-1950-88p-8vo-illus
(5bb0)   4.00

SWINBURNE, ALGERNON CHAS-Anactoria & Other Lyrical
(Erotic) Poems-NY-1906-sm4to-orig bds-cl bk-ltd to 1000c-
prntd for Mitchell Kennerley   (5p5)   10.00

--Atalanta in Calydon, A Tragedy-Hammersmith-1894-Kelmscott Pr-
lg4to-vel-ltd to 250c   (4h5,lacks ties)   200.00

--same-Portland,Me-1907-Mosher Pr-925c-wrps   (5x0)   4.00

--Bothwell,a Tragedy-Lond-1874-thk12mo-orig cl-8p ads
(5r9,wn)   10.00

--Grace Darling-Lond-1893-4to-orig vel bds-for priv circ-
1st ed-supposedly ltd to 33c   (5i8,sp def)   60.00

--Holy Spirit of Man-n.p.-1945-Hertzog-wrps-rare   (4a5)   35.00

--The Jubilee-Lond-1887-8vo-cf-hf t-(Thos Wise forgery)
(5cc9,bkplt)   125.00

--Letters of...(Gosse&Wise,eds)-Lond-1918-Heinemann-2 vols-
1st ed   (4p1)   22.50

--Notes on poems & reviews-Lond-1866-JohnCamdenHotten-
8vo-bnder's cl-1st ed-orig printing of this pamph(issued
wiout wrps) was 1000c-genuine 1st ed-(not the forged one
wi only the printers' names in the imprint)   (5i8)   100.00

--Pasiphae, A Poem-1950-Golden Cockerel Pr-cl-ltd (5ss9,f)   30.00

--A Pilgrimage of Pleasure-Bost-1913-Badger-181p-ltd to 500c
(5p0)   7.50

--Poems-NY-1904-6 vols-bds-cl backs   (5ii3,rub)   40.00

--The Poems,in 6 vols & the Tragedies in 5 vols-Lond-1904 to
1906-Chatto&Windus-1st collected ed-orig issue of all vols-
11 vols-8vo-cl-g.-t.e.g.   (5b0)   100.00

--The Queen Mother Rosamund,Two Plays-Lond-1860-12mo-
cl-papr labl-1st ed of auth's 1st book-1st issue wi Pickering
t.p.   (5gg6,f labl def)   100.00

--Songs Before Sunrise-Portland-1901 Moser Pr-ltd to 400c(4b4) 12.50

--Springtide of Life-Phila-1918-4to-mountd col plts, Rackham-
ltd ed-autg-3/4 mor   (5yy6,f,rbnd,autg by Rackham)   112.50

--same-Lond-(1918)-sm4to-cl-8 col plts by Rackham-133p
(5c8,f) 25.   (5t2)   22.50

SWINBURNE,ALGERNON CHAS   (continued)
--A Study of Shakespeare-Lond-1880-orig cl-sm8vo-32p ads-
   errata sl-1st ed-1000c printed   (4n5,f,pres)   175.00
--same-NY-1880-319p-1st Amer ed   (5p5)   12.50
--A Study of Victor Hugo's "Les Miserables"-Lond-1914-
   (for Thos J Wise)-8vo-orig blue prntd wrps bnd in-calf bndg by
   Riviere-for priv circ-ltd to 30c   (5dd8,f bndg)   60.00
SWINBURNE,H-Briefe Treatise of Testaments & Last Wills-Lond-
   1635-prntd by W S-orig bndg-corr & augm-wi tables
                                        (5ff4,poor)   75.00
SWINBURNE,HENRY-Travels in the Two Sicilies...in the Years
   1777 to 1780-Lond-1783,85-map-fldg table-2 plans-2 plts-
   lg4to-calf-g.-1st ed-2 vols   (4e1,hng weak)   150.00
SWINDLER,MARY H-Ancient Painting From Earliest Times to
   Period of Christian Art-NewHaven-1929-illus-4to-v scarce
          (5ii3) 72.50 (4m4,f) 40.   (4j3)   52.50
SWINEFORD,A P-Alaska,Its History,Climate & Natural Resources-
   Chig-(1898)-256p-photos-fldg map   (5ss1)   7.50
--History & Review of the Copper,Iron...of South Shore of Lake
   Superior-1876-plts-cov t.'Mineral Resources'-scarce
          (5mm7,lacks t.p.,ex-libr,wn) 15.   (5g8)   15.00
SWING,GILBERT S-Biographical Sketches of Eminent Men-
   Camden,NJ-1889-398p-cl   (5jj9) 25.   (5t2)   30.00
SWINGLE,CALVIN F-Automobile Catechism & Repair Manual-
   Chig-(1916)-16mo-153p&index-lea-illus   (5xx7)   6.50
--Art of Railroading-Chig-1906,7-hf mor-fldg plns-7 vols (5t0) 35.00
SWINNERTON,FRANK-Bookman's London-GardenCty-1952-
   161p-cl-1st ed   (5h7,dj)   7.50
--The Elder Sister-NY-1925-1st ed   (4b4)   10.00
--Georgian Literary Scene, 1910 to 1935-NY-(n.d.)Farrar,Straus-
   8vo-cl   (4g1,sl dustsoil)   10.00
--The Georgian Scene-NY-1934-522p-F&R   (5x0)   4.50
SWINTON,WM-Campaigns of Army of the Potomac-NY-1866-
   ports-maps-640p   (5xx7,hng weak,5mm8)   15.00
--same-NY-1882-revised-plts (5s9,tn) 9.50 (5L7) 6. (5L5,rub)   8.50
--History of 7th Reg,Nat'l Guard,State of NY during War of
   Rebellion-NY-1876-501p-illus   (5t4,libr stmp)   15.00
--McClellan's Military Career Reviewed & Exposed-Wash-1864-
   Towers-32p-pamph   (5x5) 10.   (5mm8)   12.50
--War For the Union-NY-1864-wrps-20p   (4j4)   3.00
--Word Primer,Beginner's Book-NY-1878-12mo-pict bds-cl bk-
   1st ed   (5p5)   7.50
SWIRE,J-Kind Zog's Albania-NY-(1937)-33 illus   (4b6)   15.00
SWISHER,CARL B-Stephen J Field,Craftsman of the Law-Wash-
   cl-473p -1930   (5h4,f,dj) 10.   (5x5)   15.00
--Growth of Constitutional Power in the US-Chig-c1946 (5x7)   6.50
--Motivation & Political Technique in Calif Constit Con 1878,79-
   Claremont-1930-Pomona College-132p-cl   (5tt0)   10.00
SWISHER,J A-Amer Legion in Iowa 1919 to 29-303p-t.e.g.-cl
                                        (5a9)   12.50
--Iowa Dept of Grand Army of Republic-1936-t.e.g.-194p(5a9)   5.00
--Iowa in Times of War-IowaCty-1943-395p-deckle edged
                                     (5m8,5a9)   10.00
--Iowa,Land of Many Mills-1940-317p-cl   (5a9)   12.50
--Leonard Fletcher Parker-1927-199p-t.e.g.   (5a9)   7.50
--Robt Gordon Cousins-1938-307p-cl   (5a9)   6.50
SWISHER,JAS-How I Know-Cinn-1881-cl-illus   (5jj7,wn)   15.00
SWISHER,COL JOHN M-Swisher Memoirs-SanAntonio-1932-63p-
   wrps   (4a5)   15.00
--Title of Greer County Investigated-Austin-1883-16p-wrps(5n4)30.00
SWISS AMER HIST SOC-Prominent Americans of Swiss Origin-
   NY-1932-266p-scarce   (5t9)   15.00
SWISS FAMILY ROBINSON,THE-Lond-1864-sm8vo-illus by John
   Gilbert-Routledge,Warne&Routledge-roan&cl-410p-16 plts-
   map-new ed   (5aa2)   8.50
same-(ca 1875)-GRoutledge&Sons-dec green cl-sl larger format-
   g.t.   (5aa2)   6.50
SWISS RECORD,THE-Brown Swiss Cattle Breeders' Assoc-Vol 1-
   Oswego,NY- 1908-Nixon,ed-8vo-840p-plts (5m6,sl shake)   12.50
SWISSHELM,JANE GREY-Crusader & Feminist...Letters of-StPaul-
   1934-327p-illus-fldg facs   (5w4)   6.50
--Half a Century-Chig-1880-cl-363p-2nd ed   (4h7,sp sl wn)   12.50
SWITZER,STEPHEN-The Practical Fruit Gardener-Lond-1724-
   Half Moon-3 fldg plts-calf-1st ed-rare-(28)323p, (16)-
                                     (4g0,f)   75.00
SWOLLEN HEADEN WILLIAM-Lond-1914-Methuen&Co-lg8vo-
   pict col bds-5th ed of "painful stories & funny pictures" (5c8)   6.00
SWYGERT,MRS LUTHERS,ed-Heirlooms from Old Looms-Chig-
   1955-8vo-cl-406p-nearly 400 plts-priv prntd-rev ed (5t0)   10.00
SYDNEY,ALGERNON-Works-Lond-1772-W Strahan Jun,etc-
   4to-calf-g.borders-New Ed   (4d1,sl wn)   35.00

SYDNEY,ALGERNON-Letters of,in Defence of Civil Liberty
   & against the Encroachments of Military Despotism...to
   which are added an Appendix,etc-Richmond-1830-8vo-
   65p-disbnd-TW White   (5L1)   75.00
SYDNEY,CLIFTON-or,vicissitudes in both hemispheres-NY-
   1839-Harper-2 vols-12mo-orig cl-papr labls-1st ed(5x1,f)   150.00
SYDNEY,WM CONNOR-England & the English in 18th Century-
   Lond-1892-2 vols-2nd ed   (4o1)   15.00
--Social Life in England from Restoration to Rev-1892 (5L7,spot)   5.00
SYKES,GODFREY-Colorado Delta-Wash-1937-193p-illus-map
                                     (5s4)   15.00
--Westerly Trend-1944-Ariz Pioneer Hist Soc-325p-1st ed-illus
     (5g2,dj,5L2,dj) 5.   (5h5,5x5,dj)   7.50
SYKES,JAS-Mary Anne Disraeli-NY-1928-8vo-cl-246p (5t0)   4.50
SYKES,McCREADY-Poe's Run & other Poems-Princeton-1904-
   84p   (5m2,sl wn) 6.   (5p7)   8.50
SYLIE,JAS HAMILTON-History of England under Henry Fourth-
   Lond-1884 to 1898-4 vols   (5q0)   15.00
SYLVESTER,CHAS H-Journeys through Bookland-Chig-1909-11 vols-
   illus-red cl   (5p7)   25.00
SYLVESTER,HERBERT M-IndianWars of New England-Bost-1910-
   1st ed-3 vols-thk4to-papr labls (4b1) 85. (5xx5,ex-libr)   55.00
--Maine Coast romance-Bost-1904-5 vols-illus-cl-papr labls-
   Author's Edition,autg   (5g4,sl wn)   35.00
SYLVESTER,NATHAN'L BARTLETT-Historical Sketches of Northern
   NY & Adirondack Wilderness-Troy-1877-316p-ports   (5t4)   20.00
SYMES,MAJ MICHAEL-Account of Embassy to Kingdom of Ava-
   Lond-1800-Bulmer-1st ed-2 fldg maps-24 plts(of 26)-lg sq4to-
                            (4b6,disbnd,fox)   100.00
SYMINGTON,JAS-Thos Moore, the Poet-NY-1880-Harper-255p
                                     (5p9)   4.00
SYMMES,FRANK R-History of the Old Tennent Church-Cranbury-
   1904-illus-2nd ed   (5m2)   13.50
SYMONDS,JOHN ADDINGTON-Autobiography of Benvenuto
   Cellini-NY-1946-Dblday-Dali,illus-4to-cl-ltd to 1000c
                                (5m7,wn box)   75.00
--The Escorial,a Prize Poem-recited in the Theatre-Oxford-
   Jun 20,1860-1st ed of auth's 1st publ   (5gg6)   25.00
--Life of Benevenuto Cellini-Lond-1899-464p-illus   (5t4)   8.00
--Wine,Women & Song-Lond-1884-12mo-orig vel-1st ed (5dd8)   20.00
--Walt Whitman,A Study-Lond-1893-Nimmo-sm4to-cl-bds-
   lg papr ed-port-4 illus-1st ed   (5mm2)   22.50
SYMONDS,R W-Book of English Cocks-Lond-1948-illus-80p-
   sm8vo   (5bb0)   3.50
--Masterpieces of English Furniture & Clocks-Lond-1940-folio-
   illus(some col)-172p   (5bb0)   35.00
--Present State of Old English Furniture-NY-n.d.(ca 1925)-
   4to-cl-12p,132p-116 illus   (5m5,sl soil) 20.   (5t0)   22.50
SYMONS,A J A-The Quest for Corvo-NY-1934-Macmillan-
   293p   (5p9)   4.00
--same-Lond-(1934)-8vo-cl-1st ed   (5ee9,dj)   50.00
SYMONS,ARTHUR-A Book of 20 Songs-Lond-1905-Dent-sq12mo-
   344p-1st ed -wrps   (5j5)   10.00
--The Cafe Royal & Other Essays-1923-8vo-dec bds-Jap vel-
   ltd to 80c,3 autgs-Beaumont Pr   (5ee9)   25.00
--An Intro to the Study of Browning-Lond-1886-12mo-cl-1st ed of
   auth's 1st book   (5gg6,f)   15.00
--Notes on Jos Conrad-Lond-1925-8vo-orig bds-port-1st ed
                                     (5ee9)   15.00
--Parisian Nights,a Book of Essays-1926-8vo-dec bds-Beaumont Pr-
   1 of 80c,3 autgs   (5ee9)   25.00
--Plays Acting & Music,a book of Theory-Lond-1909-Constable-
   8vo-cl-1st ed   (4g1,dustsoil)   10.00
--Studies on Modern Painters-NY-1925-Rudge-1st ed-88p-4to-
   no illus   (4a0) 42.50   (5r9)   20.00
--Studies in Two Literatures-Lond-1897-1st ed-3/4 mor
                            (5yy6,rbnd,rub)   10.00
--William Blake-NY-1907-433p   (5q0)   10.00
SYMONS,H E-Two Roads to Africa-Lond-1939-Travel Book Club-
   320p-fldg map   (4t5)   7.50
SYMONS , THOS W-Report of an Exam of Upper Columbia River,
   etc-Wash-1882-maps-8vo-fldg map
          (4g6) 12.50   (5L7,rbnd) 15.   (5s4)   30.00
SYNGE,J M-Playboy of the Western World;a Comeday in 3 Acts-
   Dublin-1907-8vo-1st ed   (5r9,fade)   17.50
--Riders to the Sea-Bost-1911-JohnWLuce&Co-cpyrite dated 1916
                                     (5l4)   7.50
SYNGE,M B-Book of Discovery-NY-n.d.-maps-illus-8vo-cl (4c1)7.50
--same-Jack-n.d.-sq8vo-554p-plts   (5aa0)   5.00
SYNON,MARY-McAdoo...the Man & His Times-Indnpls-c1924-
   355p   (5w1)   5.00
SYPHER,J R-History of Penna Reserve Corps-Lancaster-1865-8vo-
   723p-cl   (4a7,rebnd)   40.00

SYPHER, J R (continued)
--School History of Penna-Phila-1869-Lippincott-364p-12mo-cl-
    4p ads-1st ed   (5j5)   10.00
SYRACUSE LAW REVIEW-1949 to 69-Vol 1 thru 20-bnd (5ii7) 385.00
SYRETT, IRIS-Rum in the Kitchen-Lond-n.d.-illus-19p-wrps (5w1) 2.00
SYRETT, NETTA-Tinkelly Winkle-NY-1923-Dodd, Mead-8vo-157p-
    frontis-7 col plts-pict cl   (5p1)   5.00
SYSTEM OF INFANTRY DISCIPLINE-Phila-1814-4 parts plus
    appendix-   284p   (5t0)   25.00
SYSTEM OF TARGET PRACTICE, A-For use of troops when armed
    with musket, rifle, musket, rifle or carbine-prepared from the
    French-Wash-1862-illus-pict wrps   (5g3)   20.00
SZE, MAI MAI-Tao of Painting-NY-1956-Chamberlin-2 vols-
    illus-748p-4to   (5ww3)   50.00
SZYK, ARTHUR-Haggadah-ed by Cecil Roth-Lond-(1939)-
    Beaconsfield Pr-lg4to-mor-raised bands-ltd to 250c, autgs,
    box-49 miniature paintings by Szyk   (5d9, f bndg) 1,400.00
--Ink & Blood-NY-1946-small folio-lea-g.t.-74 plts-
    ltd to 1000c, autg-slipcase   (5d9)   150.00
--The New Order-NY-1941-illus-8vo
            (5ww3) 15. (5ij3, dj) 10. (5j3)   12.00
TABART, BENJ-Popular Fairy Tales, or a Liliputian Library-Lond-
    n.d.-(ca 1835)-353p-illus-bds   (5t7)   10.00
TABB, JOHN B-Later lyrics-Lond&NY-John Lane at the Bodley
    Head-1902-12mo   (5m2)   6.00
--Two Lyrices-Bost-1900-12mo-bds-cl bk-illumin by hand by
    Hapgood Jr-ltd to 375c, autg-Craftsman's Guild-1st ed (5ee9) 25.00
TABER, C W-The Business of the Household-Phila-1918-438p
                                          (5w7, crack)   4.00
TABER, GRAHAM-Hist of Logansport & Cass County-(Loganspt-1947)-
    142p-wrps   (5h1)   10.00
TABER, J H-Story 168th Infantry-2 vols-t.e.g. (5a9)   22.50
TABLER, EDW C-Far Interior-CapeTn-1955-443p-4p maps-8 plts-
    fldg map-lg8vo   (5c6, f)   17.50
TABOR, GRACE-The Landscape Gardening Book-NY-1911-180p-
    photo illus-4to   (5s7, rub)   6.50
--Old Fashioned Gardening-NY-1925-McBride-263p-illus (5x0) 6.50
TACHE, J C-De la tenure seigneuriale en Canada-Quebec-1854-
    hf calf   (5w8)   50.00
--Des provinces de l'Amerique du Nord et d'une Union Federale-
    Queben-1858-hf calf   (5w8)   55.00
--Forestiers et Voyageurs-Montr-1884-prntd wrps (5w8, pres) 25.00
--Les asiles d'alienes de la Province de Quebec et leurs
    detracteurs-Hull-1885-51p-orig prntd wrps   (5w8)   17.50
TACITUS, C CORNELIUS-The Works of-Dublin-1728-4 vols-
    12mo-calf-trans by T Gordon   (5j3)   15.00
TACOMA ILLUSTRATED-Chig-1889-illus-4to-orig wrps-98p-
    dbl col-Tacoma Chamb of Comm-1st ed   (4g6)   15.00
TACOMA, THE WESTERN TERMINUS-of the Northern Pac RR-
    Tacoma-Wash Territory-1887-43p-fldg lith-fldg map-illus -wrps-
    Ledger Steam Book & Job Pr House   (5g5)   10.00
TAFT, ALLEN-American Story-NY-1947-1st ed (4b7, pres)   8.50
TAFT, ALPHONSO-A lecture on Cincinnati & her RR's-Cinn-
    1850-Young Men's Merc Libr Assoc-52p-orig prntd wrps
                                          (5g8, wrp tn)   25.00
TAFT, EDNA-Puritan in Voodoo land-1938-illus   (5L7)   5.00
TAFT, H W-Century & a Half at the NY Bar-NY-1938
                                      (5p9) 7.50 (5ff4)   9.50
TAFT, ROBT-Artists & Illustrators of the Old West 1850 to 1900-
    NY-1953-Scribner's-90 illus-400p-8vo-1st ed
        (5F5) 22.50 (4e0) 30. (5dd1, 5s4)   25.00
--Photography & the Amer Scene-NY-1938-516p plus indices-
    photos-1st ed-scarce   (5L2) 30. (5jj7, f)   27.50
TAFT, ROBT A-A Foreign Policy for Americans-GardenCty-1951
            (5q8) 3.50   (5x7)   3.25
TAFT, RUSSELL W-John Godfrey's Saxe-Burlington, Vt-1900-
    75p-port-cl-100c prntd   (5t4, autg)   10.00
TAFT, S H-A discourse on the character & death of John Brown,
    deliv Dec 12, 1859-DesMoines-1872-prntd wrps-2nd ed (5g4) 17.50
TAFT, WM H-The United States & Peace-NY-1914-1st ed
                                          (5tt5, dj)   6.00
TAFUR, PERO-Travels & Adventures, 1435 to 1439-Lond-1926-
    8 plts-fldg map-mor&cl-g. ship on sp   (5c1)   40.00
TAGGARD, GENEVIEVE-Monologue for Mothers(Aside)-NY-
    1929-Random Hse-poetry quartos-8vo-wrps-ltd to 475c
                                      (5dd8) 10. (5b2, f) 6.00
--Travelling Standing Still-NY-1928-Knopf-1st ed-ltd to 110c,
    autg, box   (5ss9)   25.00
TAGGART, CYNTHIA-Poems-Prov-1834-Cranston&Hammond-
    8vo-bds-sheep bk-g.sp   (5b2)   12.50
TAGGART, DONALD G-History of the 3rd Infantry Div in World
    War II-Wash-c1947-4to-574p-col plts-maps-1st ed (5w9) 12.50

TAGORE, RAJAH SOURINDRO MOHUN-Orders of Knighthood,
    British & Foreign, Part 1 only-Calcutta-1883-Catholic Orphan
    Pr-plts-4to-mor-g.tooled borders-g.e.   (4b6)   25.00
TAINE, H-Lectures on Art-NY-1875-2 vols   (5ii3)   10.00
TAINE, H A-History of English Literature-Lond-1883-3 vols-
    cl-paper labls   (5i3)   10.00
TAINE, HIPPOLYTE A-History of English Literature-NY-n.d.-
    (Nottingham Soc)-4 vols-illus   (5jj3)   17.50
TAINTOR, CHAS M-Genealogy & History of Taintor Family-
    Greenfield-1847-Merriam&Mirick-16mo-wrps-82p
                                      (4t1) 15. (5t9)   12.00
TAINTOR GUIDE BOOKS-The Hudson River Route-NY-1883-
    16mo-maps-illus-pict wrps   (5g8)   7.50
TAIT, R H-Newfoundland-(n.p.-1939)   (5g8)   10.00
TAIT, WM-Cruise of HMS Cleopatra 1892 to 95-Plymouth-(c1896)-
    4to-136p-plts-ports   (4d4)   15.00
TAKAHASHI, S-Nippon Hebirui Taikwan (Terrestrial Snakes of
    Japan)-Tokyo-1930-cl-178p-66 col plts-4to-v rare (4p6) 87.50
TAKAYAMA, MR-Basic Knowledge of Wooden Ship Construction-
    Tokyo-1943-lg 12mo-stiff wrps-383p-illus-text foxed (5ss2) 12.50
TAKEN BY SIEGE-a Novel-Phila-1887-294p-1st ed (5m1)   12.50
TALABOT, MME EUGENIE-Alphabet Pittoresque des Enfants
    Sages et Bien Obeissants-Paris-(ca 1840)-Faye-sq8vo-132p-
    24 plts hand col-pict bds   (5c8, f)   75.00
TALBOT, C R-Historic California in Bookplates-LosAng-1936-
    hf lea-159 illus   (5zz3)   27.50
TALBOT, CATHERINE-Works-Lond-Rivington-1812-427p-port-
    hf calf-8th ed   (5a1, wn)   10.00
TALBOT, CONSTANCE-The Complete Book of Sewing-NY-(1943)-
    4to-319p-illus thruout   (5n7)   3.00
TALBOT, D AMAURY-Woman's Mysteries of a Primitive People-
    Lond-1915-8&252p-41 plts-cl   (5c6, sl bubbled) 22.50
TALBOT, DAN'L-A Treasury of Mountaineering Stories-NY-
    (1954)-337p-cl-Putnam's   (5c6)   4.00
TALBOT, E A-Sam'l Chapman Armstrong-NY-1904-1st ed (5x2) 15.00
TALBOT, BISHOP E-My People of the Plains-NY-1906-1st ed
                        (5L7) 5. (5s4) 8. (5m9)   7.50
TALBOT, EDW A-Five Years' Residence in the Canadas-Lond-
    1824-1st ed-2 vols-calf-plts (4h0, rbnd, rprd) 75. (5e2, 4d2) 150.00
TALBOT, ELEANOR-Wonder Eyes & What For-Lond-(1880)-sm4to-
    28 lvs(prntd 1 side)-col illus-col bds   (4c3, f)   20.00
TALBOT, ETHELBERT-My People of the Plains-NY-1906-illus-
    265p-1st ed   (4i7, cov wn)   5.00
TALBOT, F L-Souvenir StLouis Police Dept, 1902-(StL-1902)-
    (ca 250p)-photos-ads-stiff wrps-heavy slick papr-9x12-rare
                                                (5dd1)   40.00
TALBOT, FRANCIS-Jesuit Education in Philadelphia-Phila-1927-
    146p-illus   (5w5)   6.00
--Saint Among Savages-NY-n.d.-(c1935)
                        (4a9, f) 12. (5j4) 7.50 (5ii3)   10.00
TALBOT, FREDK-Aeroplanes & Dirigibles of War-Phila-1915-
    12mo-illus-scarce   (5jj3)   20.00
TALBOT, FREDK A-The Oil Conquest of the World-Phila-1914-
    8vo-cl-410p-1st ed   (5g0)   8.00
TALBOT-BOOTH, LT E C-Cruising Companion, Ships & the Sea-
    Lond-1937-752p-illus-maps-album style 4½x5½" (5s1, wn) 8.50
--His Majesty's Merchant Navy-Lond-n.d.(after 1942)-571p-
    album style 4½x5½"   (5s1, rprd)   8.00
--Merchant Ships, 1943-Lond-1944-pgs not nbrd-illus-thk4to-
    album style   (5s1, stn)   35.00
TALBOT, JOHN L-The Western Practical Arithmetic....Revised
    & Improved-Cinn-1844-240p, 7p, 5p-prntd bds (4h7, sp sl chip) 7.50
TALCOTT, A-Wm Chittenden of Guilford, Conn & Desc-(1882)-
    262p   (5t9, wn)   35.00
TALCOTT, S V-NY & New Engl Families, Genealogical Notes of-
    Albany-1883-747p plus 49p-bev edges   (5h9)   46.50
TALE OF A TUB, A-Lond-1704-for John Nutt-8vo-qtr mor-
    2nd ed, "corrected"   (5xx6)   125.00
--same-Lond-Jn Nutt-1705-sm8vo-322p-calf-4th ed
                                    (5a1, margin notes)   15.00
TALES & SKETCHES-Second series-NY-1844-Harper-12mo-orig cl-
    1st ed   (5x1)   20.00
TALES FROM AMERICAN HISTORY-NY-1830-Wm Burgess-12mo-
    bds-calf sp-plts-extra t.p.   (5rr2)   27.50
TALES FROM AUNT AMY'S PORTFOLIO-a Book for the Young-
    Lond-(ca 1865)-Dean&Son-6p list at end-3 plts, cl (5c8, soil) 7.50
TALES FROM McCLURE'S-The West-NY-1897-Dblday&McClure-
    12mo-illus-1st ed   (5m2)   8.50
TALES IN RHYME FOR GIRLS-by Old Humphrey-Lond-(1851)-
    Religious Tract Soc-108p-g. dec cl   (5c8)   6.00
TALES OF THE FIRESIDE-By A Lady of Boston-Bost-1827-
    Hillard, Gray, Little&Wilkins-rust marked-t12mo-labl-
    1st ed wi 13p list of subscribers   (5L8, rbnd, fair) 25.00

TALES OF GLAUBER SPA-By Several Amer Authors-NY-1832-
orig bds-8vo-2 vols-276p,263p (5zz7,sp sl fade) 75.00
TALES OF A GRANDFATHER-being Stories taken from Scottish
History-1st series in 3 vols-second series,in 3 vols-3rd series,
vols 2&3 only(of 3)-Edinb-1828,29,30-12mo-frontis-qtr lea-
(Sir W Scott) (5c8) 27.50
TALES OF THE GREAT & BRAVE-Lond-1838-Harvey&Darton-
sm8vo-322p-dec cl-1st ed with a Baxter print (5c8,1 lf def) 20.00
TALES OF MY LANDLORD-The second series-Edinb-1818-4 vols-
calf-1st eds-(Sir W Scott) (5d2) 35.00
TALES OF THE NORTHWEST-or,Sketches of Indian Life & Character-
Bost-1830-16mo-old calf-1st ed of Snelling's 1st book
(5x1,ex-libr,1 lf of pref in facs,rbkd) 85. 150.00
TALES OF OTHER DAYS-Lond-1830-Effingham Wilson-
250p-bds-6 plts by Geo Cruikshank-1st ed (5c8,lacks sp) 15.00
TALES OF THE PURITANS-NewHav-1831-AHMaltby-12mo-
orig bds-labl-1st ed of auth's 1st book-(D S Bacon) (5x1,rbkd) 30.00
TALES OF THE WHITE HILLS-Bost-n.d.-Riverside Pr-32mo-illus-
N Hawthorne-grn cl-c1879 (5u9) 5.50
TALES OF THE WOODS & FIELDS-second series-Lond-1836-
Saunders&Otley-3 vols-12mo-hf calf-mor labls (5xx6) 30.00
TALISMAN,THE-A Tale for Boys-Bost-1829-Wait,Greene&Co-frontis-
scarce (5v2,vf) 30.00
TALLACK,WM-The Calif Overland Express-LosAng-1935-
Ward Ritchie Pr-8vo-cl&bds-ltd to 1500c (5b0) 45.00
--Friendly Sketches in America-Lond-1861-1st ed
(5jj3,needs rebndg) 12.50
TALLAMY,B D-St Lawrence Seaway Project-Buffalo-1940-129p-
maps-cl-4to (5s1,f) 7.50
TALLANT,ROBT-The Romantic New Orleans-NY-1950-384p
(5x2,5x0) 5. (5c3) 4. (5h9) 6.00
--Voodoo in New Orleans-NY-1946 (5x2) 6.00
TALLEY,T W-Negro Folk Rhymes-NY-1922 (5x2) 27.50
TALLMADGE,SAML-Orderly Books of 4th NY Regiment,1778 to
80,2nd NY Regt 1780 to 83...etc-Albany-1932-lg4to-illus-
933p (5w5) 18.50 (4m4) 25.00
TALLMADGE,THOS E-Story of Architecture in America-NY-
(1927)-illus-313p (5q0) 10.00
TALLMAN,MARJORIE-Dictionary of American Folklore-NY-(1959)
(5yy6) 6.50
TALMADGE,MARGARET L-Talmadge Sisters-Phila-1924-
photos-245p (4c9) 17.95
TALMAGE,J E-The Theory of Evolution-Lecture,Provo City,
Mar 8,1890-n.p.-n.d.-(1890)-17p-no wrps-scarce (5t3) 20.00
TALMAGE,JAS E-The Vitality of Mormonism-Bost-(1919)-361p-
1st ed (5L2) 4.00
TALMAGE,T DE WITT-Crumbs Swept Up-Phila-1875-illus-445p
(4b6,5r7) 10.00
--Social Dynamite-Phila-1888-574p-illus (5r7) 10.00
TALMAN,JAS J,ed-Loyalist Narratives from Upper Canada-Tor-
1946-Champlain Soc-411p (5zz8) 50.00
TALMEY,A LLENE-Doug & Mary & Others-NY-1927-181p (4c9) 12.95
TAMBLYN,W F-These Sixty Years-Lond-1938-illus-135p (4b9) 8.00
TAMMEN,H H-Objects of Interest from the Plains & Rocky Mntns-
Denver-1886-orig wrps-8vo-32p-catalog (4g6) 15.00
TANEY,RODGER B-Report of Decision of Supreme Court of US
...in Case of Dred Scott-Wash-1857-BCHoward-hf lea-1st ed-
scarce (5m2) 13.50
TANGERMAN,E J-Design & Figure Carving-NY-(1940)-289p-
illus (5t7) 10.00
TANGUAY,CYPRIEN-Dictionaire Genealogique des Families
Canadiennes-Que-1871 to 80-cl&calf-8vo-7 vols
(5w8) 350. (4m6,rprd) 250.00
TANGYE,H LINCOLN-In New So Africa-Lond-1900-431p-
illus-13 plts-fldg map (5c6,pres) 12.50
TANGYE,SIR RICHARD-The Two Protectors-Lond-1899-302p-
illus-t.e.g. (5w9) 8.00
TANNEHILL,WILKINS,ed-Portfolio,or Journal of Freemasonry &
Gen'l Literature-Nashville-1848 to 50-Vols 1 to 3-bds,cl bk-
plts-complete run-scarce (5dd0,bndg sl wn) 50.00
--Sketches of History of Literature from Earliest Period to Revival
of Letters in 15th Century-Nasvhille-1827-hf cl (5h6,rub) 50.00
TANNENBAUM,F-Slave & Citizen-NY-1947 (5x2,dj) 7.50
TANNENBAUM,SAML A-A Concise Bibliography (Thos Middleton)-
NY-1940-ltd to 300c (4g2) 15.00
TANNER,E F-Desc of Thos Tanner Sr of Cornwall,Conn-1893-110p
(4t2) 35.00
TANN ER, G C-Desc of Wm Jr Tanner of So Kingstown,RI & Desc-
1910-516p (5t9) 27.50
TANNER,H S-Map of Calif NMex Texas etc-NY-1849-about
18¼x23 3/4"-col-folds out to 24mo-cl cov
(5a3,dtched at sp,folds wn) 200.00

TANNER,HENRY-Dominion of Canada,Successful Emigration to
Canada-Ottawa-1886-Dept Agri-fldg map-32p-rev ed(5aa1) 35.00
TANNER,J M-Biogr Sketch of Jas Jensen-SaltLkCty-1911-illus-
16mo-buck (4b6,rbnd) 25.00
TANNER,JOHN-The Hidden Treasures of the Art of Physick Fully
Discovered-Lond-1672-(7),324p,(11)-12mo-lev mor-3rd ed
(5w3,rbnd,wn) 87.50
TANNER,JOHN-Narrative of Captivity & Adventures of John
Tanner-NY-1830-Carvill-426p-uncut-calf-Howe 42
(5yy3,reprd) 200.00
TANNER,V-Outlines of Geography,Life & Customs of Newfoundland,
Labradore-Helsingfors-1944-2 vols-plts-illus-maps-wrps (5s6) 50.00
TANNER'S UNIVERSAL ATLAS-Accompaniment to-Phila-1843-
Carey&Hart for Justin Pierce (5r7) 15.00
TANSILL,CHAS C-Back Door to War-Chig-1952 (5yy6) 7.50
--Congressional Career of Thos Francis Bayard,1869 to 1885-
Wash-1946-frontis (5r7) 12.50
--Foreign Policy of Thos F Bayard,1885 to 1897-NY-1940-800p-
port (5r7) 12.50
TAPESTRIES OF IMPERIAL VIENNA COURT-Vienna-1922-4to-
bds&cl-44p plts-1st ed-text in Engl (5p5) 25.00
TAPLEY,CHAS S-Rebecca Nurse-Bost-1930-105p (5p9,5e8) 4.00
TAPLEY,HARRIET SYLVESTER-Chronicles of Danvers,(Old Salem
Village)-Danvers-1923-283p-Hist Soc (5p0) 25.00
--Salem Imprints 1768 to 1825-Salem,Mass-1927-Essex Inst-512p-
illus-g.t. (5qq8) 20.00
TAPLIN,WM-Gentleman's Stable Directory-(Vol 1),12th ed-port-
& Vol the 2nd-3rd ed-Lond-1793-504p, 417p-calf-lea labls
(5m3,f) 35.00
TAPPAN,EVA M-The Out of Door Book-Bost-(1907)-Houghton,Miff-
Children's Hour,Vol 7-sm8vo-517p-col frontis-plts-2 tone cl
(5aa2) 3.50
TAPPAN,MASON W-The Union As It Is-Wash-1861-Natl Rep Off-
7p rmvd (5qq8) 15.00
TAQUET,PAUL-La Distillerie Dans Le Monde Entier-Paris-(1900)-
folio-photos (5w1,broke) 20.00
TARAKANOFF,VASSILI P-Statement of My Captivity Among the
Californians-LosAng-1953-50p-wdcuts-Plantin Pr-Early Calif
Travel Series-ltd to 200c (5t1) 30.00
TARAVAL,SIGISMUNDO-Indian Uprising in Lower Calif,1734 to
1737-LosAng-1931-Quivira Soc-R8vo-parch bk bds-9 plts-
ltd to 35c,nbrd (4a3,f) 75.00
TARBELL,IDA M-All in The Day's Work,an autobiography-NY-
1939-Macmillan-illus-1st prntng (5m2) 4.00
--The Early Life of Abraham Lincoln-NY-1896-20 ports-1st ed
(5w4) 8.50 (5ee3) 5.00
--He Knew Lincoln & Other Billy Brown stories-NY-1931-179p
(5t7,dj) 3.50
--The History of the Standard Oil Co-NY-1937-2 vols in 1-illus
(5w5) 7.50
--In the Footsteps of the Lincolns-NY-1924-illus-418p-1st ed
(4b6,5r7) 12.50
--The Life of Elbert H Gray-1925-illus-cl-361p
(5s4,soil) 6. (5m2) 8.50 (5e4) 6.75
--The Life of Abraham Lincoln-NY-1902-2 vols (5j6) 7.50
--same--NY-1924-4 vols-illus-fabr-Lincoln Hist Soc-Sangamon ed
(5t7) 7.50
--same-NY-1924-illus-2 vols (5p7) 7.50
TARBOX,INCREASE N-Life of Israel Putnam-Bost-1876-Lockwood,
Brooks-389p-illus-map (5mm8) 12.50
TARG,WM,ed-Bibliophile in the Nursery-Clev-(1957)-illus-1st ed
(5v0) 15. (4a1) 22.50
--Carrousel for Bibliophiles-NY-1947-cl-8vo
(5u8,dj) 20. (4m5,sl soil,dj) 12.50
--Making of Bruce Rogers World Bible-Cleve-(1949)-8vo-cl
(4c1,e.p. fox, box) 10.00
--Rare Amer Books Valued from $50 to $25,000.00-Chig-1935-
wrps-1st eds (5j4) 5.00
--Targ's Amer First Editions & their Prices-Chig-1931-cl-122p
(5t2) 4. (5j4) 7.50
TARKINGTON,BOOTH-Beauty & the Jacobin-NY-1912-8vo-
cl-illus-1st ed (5dd8) 5.00
--The Conquest of Canaan-NY&Lond-1905-1st ed
(5b2) 4.50 (5hh3) 5.00
--The Fascinating Stranger & Other Stories-NY-1923-492p-
ltd to 377c,autg,boxed (5m1) 22.50
--Gentleman From Indiana-NY-1899-cl-12mo-1st ed-
1st issue-ear of corn on spine tipped up (priority unknown)-
author's 1st book (4c2,wtrstnd,crack) 17.50
--same-NY-1899-1st ed-ear of corn on sp upside down-
all points (5ee9) 15.00
--same-NY-1899-1st ed-1st issue (pg 245,li 12,last wd "eye"
& li 16 "so pretty")-ear of corn upside down (5ee3,rub) 10.00

TARKINGTON,BOOTH (continued)
--The Midlander-NY-1928-   1st ed,autg
    ltd to 377copies   (5mm2,dj,f,wn box)   25.00
--Monsieur Beaucaire-NY-1900-illus-1st ed,1st issue
                            (5tt7,sl spot)   15.00
--Mosieur Beaucaire-NY-1900-1st ed
                            (4b4)   4.00
--Penrod-GardenCty-1914-1st ed,1st issue-(Scence,pg 19)-
    meshed cl   (5c8) 10.   (5i3)   17.50
--Penrod-GardenCty-1914-Gordon Grant,illus-1st ed-8vo-
    dec cl-plts-345p-(1st bndg,blu mesh-2nd sheets,pg 19 corrected
                            (4a8)   12.50
--Penrod & Sam-GardenCty-1916-Dblday,Page-illus-1st ed,
    1st state(wiout type wear)   (5m2,fade)   6.50
--Penrod Jashber-GardenCty-1929-Gordon Grant,illus-1st ed-
    8vo-dec cl-frontis-321p   (4a8)   5.00
--Seventeen-NY-(1916)-illus-1st ed(B-Q foot of copyrite)
                            (5tt7,pres,sl fade)   27.50
--Some Old Portraits,A Book About Art & Human Beings-NY-1939-
    4to-cl-g.t.-12 ports-ltd to 247c,autg,box-1st ed (5ee9)   25.00
TARVER,M-The Western Journal & Civilian-StL-1851-Vol 7-
    435p(436p)-2 illus-frontis   (5dd1,rbnd,sl wtrstn)   17.50
TASHLIN,FRANK-The Bear That Wasn't-Lond-(1946)-(51p)-4to-
    pict bds-1st Engl ed   (5p1,autg)   10.00
--The Possum That Didn't-NY-Farrar Straus(c1950)-4to-(61p)-
    pict cl   (5p1,autg,dj)   7.50
TASKER,L H-The United Empire Loyalist Settlement at Long Point,
    Lake Erie-Tor-1900-frontis-map-illus-Being Ont Hist Soc
    Papers & Records,Vol 2   (5w8)   25.00
TASMAN,ABEL JANSCOON-& Discovery of New Zealand-
    Wellington-1942-4to-prntd wrps over bds   (4c1)   25.00
TASMANIA LAW REPORTS-1905 to 40-Vol 1 thru 35-bnd
                            (5ii7,ex-libr)   650.00
TASMANIA STATE REPORTS-1941 to 65-bound (5ii7,ex-libr)   500.00
TASMANIA,SUPREME COURT-Reports...Nicholls & Stops-1897
    to 1904-2 vols (all publ)   (5ii7,rebnd)   27.50
TASSE,ELIE-The North West,Prov of Manitoba & NW Territories-
    Ottawa-1880-48p-La Canada Ofc   (5aa1)   40.00
TASSE,JOS-Les Canadiens de l'ouest-Montr-1878-qtr calf-
    illus-2 vols   (5w8,ex-libr)   50.00
TASSIN,ALGERNON-The Magazine in America-NY-1916-frontis-
    374p-1st ed   (4g2)   22.50
TATE,ALLEN-The Fathers-1938-Putnam's (5F1,f,dj) 10. (5b2)   12.50
--The Forlorn Demon-Chig-1953-Regnery-8vo-cl-scarce (5b2,f)   15.00
--Jefferson Davis,His Rise & Fall-NY-1929-8vo-311p (4a7)   7.50
--Reason in Madness-NY-(1941)-Putnams-1st ed   (4g1)   15.00
--Stonewall Jackson,the Good Soldier-NY-(1928)-8vo-322p
                    (4a7,fray) 6.   (5x0)   5.00
--Two Conceits for the Eye to Sing,if Possible-Cummington-1950-
    sm12mo-wrps-papr labl-1st ed-300c prntd at Cummington Pr
                            (5ss7,mint)   27.50
--The Vigil of Venus,Per Vigilium Veneris-Cummington-(1943)-
    8vo-cl-1st ed-Latin & Engl-Cummington Pr-400c,nbrd for sale-
    orig glassine   (5ss7,mint)   15.00
--same-Cummington Pr-(1943)-cl-ltd to 430c-1st ed
                    (5cc9) 30.   (5b2,f)   20.00
TATE,CHAS SPENCER-Pickway,a True Narrative-Chig-1905-photos-
    159p plus ads-cl-1st ed (5ff7) 10.00 (5dd1,bkstrp wn)   15.00
TATLOW,A H,ed-Natal Province,Descriptive Guide & Official
    Hand Book-Durban-1911-SoAfrican Rwys Pr-photos-maps-574p-
    pict voer   (4t5,maps loose)   32.50
TATUM,FRANCES C-Old Westtown,a collection-1888-illus(5L7)   7.50
TATUM,GEO B-Penn's Great Town 250 Years of Philadelphia
    Architecture-Phila-(1961)-lg4to-352p-illus (5w4) 12.50(4m4)   30.00
TATUM,GEORGIA LEE-Disloyalty in Confederacy-ChapelHill-
    1934-8vo-176p   (4a7,mint)   12.50
TATUM,LAWRIE-Our Red Brothers & the Peace Policy of Pres
    U S Grant-Phila-1899-photos-366p-1st ed-v scarce
                            (5dd1,rbnd)   40.00
TAUBES,FREDERIC-The Quickest Way to Paint Well-NY-(1950)-
    illus   (5t7)   3.50
--Technique of Oil Painting-NY-1952-illus   (5t7)   5.00
TAUSEY,THOS G-Military History of Carlisle & Carlisle Barracks-
    Richmond-1939-Dietz Pr   (5x5,dj)   17.50
TAUSSIG,CHAS W-Rum,Romance & Rebellion-NY-1928-
    Philip Kappel,drwngs   (5q8,pres)   5.50
--Some Notes on Sugar & Molasses-NY-1940-233p-illus
                            (5y2,rub)   8.50
TAUSSIG, V ADM JOS-Our Navy,a Fighting Team-NY-(1943)-
    239p-photos   (5s1,dj,f)   4.50
TAVARES DE SA,HERNANE-The Brazilians,People of Tomorrow-
    NY-(1947)-12mo-cl   (5h4,f)   4.00
TAVERNER,ERICK-Salmon Fishing-Lond-1931-thk8vo-307 illus-cl
                            (5t8)   7.50

TAVERNER,ERICK (continued)
--Trout Fishing From All Angles-Lond-1933-thk8vo-250 plts(5t8)   7.50
TAVERNER,P A-The Birds of Canada-Ottawa-1934-illus-445p
                            (5nn2,5yy8)   12.50
--same-Tor-1945-revised-col plts-446p   (4d8)   12.50
--same-Tor-1953-446p-new & rev ed-173 col plts (4b9)   10.00
--Birds of Western Canada-Ottawa-1926-cl-84 col plts-380p
                            (5nn2,rebnd)   10.00
--Canadian Land Birds,a pkt Field Guide-Phila-1939-col illus-
    277p   (4d4)   6.50
TAVERNIER,JEAN BAPTISTE-6 Voyages...Through Turkey,into
    Persia & East Indies...a Voyage into the Indies-Lond-1677,78-
    sm folio-calf-25 plts-264p & 214p-Littlebury,Prntr
                            (5ff6,rbkd)   450.00
TAVISTOCK,MARQUESS OF-Parrots & Parrot like Birds in
    Aviculture-Lond-(1929)-orig cl-lg8vo-8 col plts-1st ed-
    v scarce   (5z9)   35.00
TAX INSTITUTE,UNIV OF SO CALIF-Proceedings 1948 to 68
    (lacks 1949,1950,1963,64)-17 vols-bnd (5ii7,ex-libr)   525.00
TAX LAW REVIEW-1945 to 71-Vol 1 thru 3-bnd (5ii7) ea   25.00
--same-Vol 4 thru 26-bnd   (5ii7) ea   22.00
TAX LAWYER-1947 to 69-ABA-Vol 1 thru 22 (5ii7,rbnd)   260.00
TAXES,THE TAX MAGAZINE-1923 to 67-Vol 1 thru 45
                        (5ii7,rbnd)   1,350.00
TAYLOR,A E-Elements of Metaphysics-NY-1912-8vo-cl-419p-
    2nd ed   (5t0)   5.00
TAYLOR,ALBERT D-The Complete Garden-GardenCty-(1921)-
    440p-50p photos-9 col plts-4to   (5s7)   7.50
TAYLOR,ALICE-Gold Rush of '49-NY-(1960)-illus-wrps-62p
                        (4n1,cov reprd)   7.50
TAYLOR,ALLAN-What Everybody Wants to Know About Wine-
    NY-1934-312p-illus   (5g9,5w0) 7.50 (5w1)   6.50
TAYLOR & TAYLOR-Types,Borders & Miscellany of Taylor&Taylor-
    SanFran-1939-Taylor Taylor-qtr calf-ltd to 330c,nbrd-8vo
                        (5b0,sp sl fade)   37.50
TAYLOR,ANN-also see Taylor,Jane
TAYLOR,ANN-City Scenes,or a Peep into London for Children-
    Lond-1814-Darton,Harvey&Darton-37 plts-72p text
                    (4F6,rbnd,f bnds,sl rprd)   250.00
--Corres Between a Mother & Her Daughter-Lond-1818-Taylor &
    Hessey-4th ed-frontis-lea labl-24mo-146p   (5p1)   37.50
--same-Lond-1821-frontis-6th ed-164p-lea labl   (5c8)   17.50
--Original Poems for Infant Minds-Vol 1,29th ed;Vol 2,26th ed-
    Lond-1832,33-12mo-frontis dated 1826-qtr lea-Harvey&Darton
                            (5c8)   35.00
--same-Phila-1835-LBClarke-12mo-144p-wdcuts-orig lea bkd bds
                            (5v0)   20.00
--The "Original Poems" & Others-Lond-Wells,Gardner-(1903)-
    sq4to-411p-col frontis-plts-dec cl-1st ed   (5a1)   8.50
--same-Lond-1905-2nd ed-(same format)   (5a1)   7.50
--Rural Scenes-Harvey&Darton-(c1818)-hf calf-60p-29 plts (5s0) 12.50
--same-c1826-qtr roan   (5s0)   12.50
TAYLOR,ARIEL-Numerology Made Plain-Chig&NY-(1930)-190p-
    illus-cl   (5t0,dj,f)   3.50
TAYLOR,B-A Journey to Central Africa-NY-1854-illus (5x2)   15.00
TAYLOR,BASIL-Impressionists & Their World-Lond-(1953)-4to-
    plts   (5yy6)   10.00
TAYLOR,BAYARD-Byways of Europe-NY-1869-8vo-orig cl-470p-
    frontis   (5p5,autg tip in)   17.50
--Colorado,A Summer Trip-NY-1867-12mo-1st ed
                (4g6,fade) 6.50 (5s4,wtrstnd)   6.50
--Egypt & Iceland in the year 1874-NY-1874-Putnam-1st ed
                        (5m2,rub)   5.00
--Eldorado-1850-8 tinted plts-2 vols-251p,247p-1st ed-1st state
                    (4n1,fox,libr bkplt)   50.00
--same-Lond-1850-2 vols-stiff bds   (4n1,sp wn)   30.00
--same-NY-1850-2 vols in 1-3rd ed   (5x5)   15.00
--same-NY-1854-2 vols in 1   (5s5,wn)   12.00
--same-NY-1855-illus-444p   (5ee3)   7.50
--same-NY-1860-444p-hf calf-18th ed   (5s4)   12.50
--same-NY-1864-444p-frontis   (4a5) 5. (5x5)   10.00
--same-NY-1949-375p-illus   (5L2,dj)   5.00
--Hannah Thurston-NY-1863-1st ed   (5mm1)   18.50
--Picturesque Europe-(1875)-Appleton-2 vols-a.e.g.-lea-g. trim
                            (5ww4)   50.00
--Poems of Home & Travel-Bost-1855-1st ed   (4b4)   12.50
--The Poems of..-Bost-1865-Ticknor&Fields-419p-1st ed (5x4,wn)5.00
--The Story of Kennett-NY-1866-3/4 calf-1st ed (5m2)   10.00
--Studies in German Literature-NY-1879-Putnam-1st ed (5m2)   5.00
--Views A Foot,or Europe seen wi Knapsack & Staff-NY-1865-
    506p   (5ss1,v wn)   4.50
--same-1889   (5L7)   5.00

USED BOOK PRICE GUIDE

TAYLOR,BENJ C-Annals of Classic of Bergen,of Reformed Dutch
Church-NY-1857-Hosford-12mo-cl-479p   (4t1)   20.00
TAYLOR,BENJ F-Between The Gates-Chig-1878   (4a5)   4.00
--Pictures of Life in Camp & Field-Chig-1884-270p-cl-3rd ed
                                            (5h7)   8.50
--World on Wheels & Other Sketches-Chig-(1874)-illus
                            (4b6) 8.50   (5m2)   7.50
TAYLOR,MRS BASIL-Japanese Gardens-NY-1912-Dodd,Mead-
sm4to-298p-28 col plts   (5p7)   15.00
TAYLOR,C W,comp-Masters & Masterpieces of the Screen-NY-
1927-folio-illus-112p   (4c9)   27.50
TAYLOR,C W,Jr,Pub-Eminent Californians 1953-(Angwin,CA,1953)-
cl-ports-592p-Pac Union   (4L9)   15.00
TAYLOR,CHAS J-History of Great Barrington-1882-1st ed-cl-
12mo-516p   (4c5,f,pres) 17.50
TAYLOR,CHAS M,JR-Touring Alaska & the Yellowstone-Phila-
c1901-388p-illus-t.e.g.-1st ed   (5m9,pres) 5. (5w4) 6.50
--Vacation Days in Hawaii & Japan-Phila-(1898)-361p-illus(5t4)10.00
TAYLOR,CHAS W-Biogr Sketches & Review of Bench & Bar of
Indiana-Indnpls-1895-lea-848p   (5t4)   17.50
TAYLOR,DEEMS-Pictorial History of the Movies-NY-(1943)-illus-
folio-350p   (4n1,dj) 10. (5yy8) 8.50
--Of Men & Music-NY-1937-Simon&Schuster-318p (5p0) 4.00
--Some Enchanted Evenings-NY-c1953-244p-illus-1st ed (5w0) 6.50
--A Treasury of Stephen Foster-NY-1946-4to-illus (5a8,cor bent) 3.50
--Walt Disney's Fantasia-NY-1940-Simon&Schuster-4to-illus-158p
                                            (5p7)   15.00
TAYLOR,D W-Resistance of Ships & Screw Propulsion-NY-1893-
234p   (5s1)   8.50
--Speed & Power of Ships-NY-1910-4to-2 vols-plts-album style-
1st ed-scarce   (5s1)   27.50
--same-in 1 vol-1933-rev-US Shipping Board-4to-367p
                                        (5s1,soil)   15.00
TAYLOR,EDW B-Primitive Culture,Researches into Develop etc-
NY-1889-2 vols-3rd Amer ed   (4k5,f) 18.50
TAYLOR,EDW LIVINGSTON-Ohio Indian & Other Writings-
Columbus-1909-347p-photos-maps-priv prntd-scarce
                                        (5L2,bkstrp wn) 10.00
TAYLOR,EMERSON-Practical Stage Directing for Amateurs-NY-
1916-Dutton-194p   (5p0)   4.00
TAYLOR,EMILY-The Ball I Live On-Lond-n.d.-illus (5jj6)   7.50
TAYLOR,F-A Sketch of the Military Bounty Tract of Illinois-Phila-
1839-12mo-12p-disbnd   (5a3) 125.00
TAYLOR,F SHERWOOD-A History of Industrial Chemistry-Lond-
1957-467p-illus   (5e4)   5.50
TAYLOR,F W-Grammar of Adamawa Dialect of Fulani Language-
Oxf-1953-14&124p-2nd ed   (5c6,f)   6.75
TAYLOR,FITCH W-Voyage Round World...Frigate Columbia-
NewHav-1848-2 vols in 1-frontis-illus   (5i3)   15.00
--same-NY-1854-illus-2 vols in 1   (5j2)   12.00
TAYLOR,FRANCIS HENRY-Fifty Centuries in Art-NY-1954-
(Met Mus of Art)-4to-illus-1st ed (4a1,pres) 22.50 (5w5) 8.50
--Taste of Angels-Bost-1948-1st ed-12 col plts-661p-8vo (5ww3) 15.00
TAYLOR,FRANCIS R-Life of Wm Savery of Phila-NY-1925-474p-
illus   (5m2) 7.50   (5t0) 5.   (5h9,mint,dj) 10.00
TAYLOR,FRANK H,ed-City of Philadelphia-(Phila,1900)-4to-
illus-ads   (5ss5)   10.00
--Phila in Civil War 1861 to 1865-Phila-1913-illus-8vo-360p
                            (5a8,stnd) 5.   (5h9)   7.50
TAYLOR,FRANK J-Black Bonanza-NY&Lond-1950-Whittlesey Hse
                    (4m9,dj) 7.50 (5m2,dj) 5. (5dd5) 6.50
--Calif,Land of Homes-SanFran-1929-1st ed   (4a5)   8.00
TAYLOR,G-Voyage to NoAmer,Perform'd...in the Yrs 1768 &
1769,etc-Nottingham-1771-for author-(8)248p (5e2) 1,500.00
TAYLOR,G-Memoir of Robt Surtees,Esq,author of History of County
Palatine of Durham-1852-J Raine,ed   (5L7)   7.50
TAYLOR,GEN'L-Life of,hero of Okee Chobee etc-Bost&NY-1875-
12mo-227p-frontis-7 plts-dec cl-Young American's Libr of
Famous Generals   (5p1)   6.50
TAYLOR,GEOFFREY-Some 19th Century Gardeners-Lond-(1951)-
175p-5 illus   (5w3,5s7)   5.00
TAYLOR,GRIFFITH-Canada,a Study-NY-(1950)-Dutton-8vo-cl-
illus-526p   (5j5,dj)   7.50
TAYLOR,H-Science of Jurisprudence-NY-1908   (5ff4)   7.50
TAYLOR,H C-An Amer Peeress-Chig-1894-1st ed (5ee3)   7.50
--Decline of Landowning Farmers in England-Madison-1904-
wrps-66p   (5ff4)   5.75
TAYLOR,H S-The Battle Cry-Cinn-1887-160p words & music(5w6)7.50
TAYLOR,HANNIS-Origin & Growth of Amer Constitution;an
Historical Treatise-Bost-1911-676p (5r7) 8.50 (5r4) 15.00
TAYLOR,HENRY HAMMOND-Knowing,Collecting & Restoring
Early Amer Furniture-Phila&Lond-(1930)-156p-illus (5t4) 3.50

TAYLOR,HENRY OSBORN-Ancient Ideals-NY-1909-2 vols (5q0) 12.50
--Medieval Mind-Lond-1911-2 vols   (5xx7,ex-libr) 15.00
--same-NY-1919-2 vols-3rd Amer ed   (5h9)   12.00
--same-Lond-1927-2 vols-4th ed   (5q0,libr stmp) 10.00
--Thought & Expression in 16th Century-NY-1920-2 vols (5q0) 12.50
TAYLOR,IDA S-Story of Christopher Columbus told in rhyme-Lond-
(ca 1895)-RaphaelTuck&Sons-col illus-pict bds(5c8,bds loose) 7.00
TAYLOR,ISAAC-The Alphabet,an Acct of Origin & Development of
Letters-Lond-1883-Kegan Paul,Trench&Co-cl-2 vols (5tt9) 40.00
--Ancient Christianity & Doctrines of the Oxford Tracts-Phila-
1840-cl-554p   (4t7) 17.50
--Beginnings of European Biography,The Early Ages-Lond-(1827)-
JnHarris-12mo-150p-bds-12 plts wi 24 engrs-1st ed-rare (5v2)65.00
--same-The Latter Ages-Lond-(1829)-J Harris-textually complete wi
only 11(of 24)engrs-260p-orig prntd bds (5c8,soil rub,def) 8.50
--Character Essential to Success in Life-Lond-1820-frontis-4p ads-
lea-2nd ed(same year as 1st)   (5c8,rub) 15.00
--History of the Alphabet-Lond-1899-2 vols-cl-8vo-illus(5p6,f)30.00
--History of Transmission of Ancient Books to Modern Times-Lond-
1827-256p-part calf-1st ed   (5u6) 35.00
--same-Liverpool-1879-12mo-rev&enlrgd ed   (4a1) 12.50
--The Mine-Lond-1831-JnHarris-16 engrs-sq16mo-215p-17 plts
3rd ed   (5v0,lacks fly,chip) 12.50
--same-Phila-1861-sm4to-cl-16 engrs   (5p5,rbkd) 17.50
--Scenes in America,for the...Little Tarry at Home Travellers-
Lond-1821-JHarris-12mo-illus bds-col fldg map of Americas-
28 plts-rare 1st ed   (5v0,vg) 55.00
--same-Lond-1822-J Harris-14 plts-orig bds-2nd ed
                                         (5c8,sl dmgd) 15.00
--same-Hartf-1825-Silas Andrus-12mo-illus (5rr2,plt tn) 20.00
--Scenes in Africa & America etc-Lond-(1829)-JHarris-intro verse-
continuous pgination-maps-32 plts-New Ed
                            (5c8,maps rprd,cov dtchd) 20.00
--Scenes in Asia-Lond-1822-Harris&Son-22(of 28) plts-orig prntd bds-
fldg frontis-3rd ed   (5c8,lacks 6 lvs)   6.50
--Scenes of Commerce By Land & Sea-Lond-1836-12mo-395p-
66 illus-lea bk-bds   (5n7,lea tn) 15.00
TAYLOR,REV ISAAC-Scenes of Wealth etc-Hartf-1826-68 plts-
12mo-orig prntd bds-roan bk
                    (5t0,wn,A Van Buren autg) 35. (5x2,sl wn) 32.50
TAYLOR,J-Pondoro,last of the Ivory Hunters-NY-1955-illus-1st ed
                                            (5x2)   6.00
TAYLOR,JAS W-History of the State of Ohio,First Period 1650 to
1787-Cinn-1854-557p-8vo-orig cl   (5L1)   50.00
TAYLOR,JANE also see TAYLOR,Ann
TAYLOR,JANE-Display,a Tale-Lond-1816   (5c8,cov dtchd) 20.00
--A Day's Pleasures,to which are added,Reflections on a Day's
Pleasure-NY-1833-MahlonDay-12mo-12 lvs-illus (5c8) 22.50
--Hymns for Infant Minds-Newburyport-1814-W&J Gilman-16mo-
71p-illus-wrps-sewn   (5v2,wrps fade) 125.00
--Little Ann & Other Poems-Lond-1882-Routledge&Sons-64p-
col illus by Greenaway-bds-1st ed(for sale 1883)(5F9,vg) 30.00
--same-Lond-(1883)-Routledge-illus by Kate Greenaway-4to-cl-
64p-1st ed   (5m7,soil,cov wn) 25.00
--The Snow Drop-NewHav-c1835-SBabcock-16mo-24p-6 plts-
wrps   (5v0,lacks wrps) 15.00
TAYLOR,JEFFERYS-A Month in London-Lond-1832-Harvey&Darton-
6 hand col plts-cl wi g.Tower of London-1st ed-deluxe issue
                                            (5c8)   50.00
--Parlour Commentaries on the Constitution & Laws of England-Lond-
1825-JnHarris-12mo-205p-dec bds-6 prints-engr-1st ed (5c8) 15.00
TAYLOR,JOHN-All the Workes-Lond-prntd by JB for Jas Boler-
1630-sm folio-mor-g.e.-1st collected ed-v rare
                                    (5hhc,rbnd,f bndg) 1,300.00
TAYLOR,JOHN-Inquiry into Principles & Policy of Gov of the US-
Fredericksburg-1814-8vo-556p(1,errata)-calf (5a3,crack) 55.00
--New Views of Constitution of the US-Wash-1823-316p-8vo-calf
                                    (5a3,ex-libr,crack) 40.00
TAYLOR,JOHN-African Rifles & Cartridges-Georgetown-(1948)-
lg8vo-431p-photos   (4a6)   12.50
TAYLOR,JOHN-Big Game & Big Game Rifles-Lond-(1953)-8vo-
215p   (4a6,wn dj)   5.00
TAYLOR,JOHN L-Memoir of His Honor Saml Phillips-Bost-1856-
Congrega Board of Publ-391p-frontis-3 plts-1 fldg facs-cl
                                    (5p1,pres,cov wn) 32.50
TAYLOR,JOHN M-Witchcraft Delusion in Colonial Connecticut-
NY-(1908)-frontis   (5g4) 7.50   (4m2) 10.00
TAYLOR,JOHN W-Iowa,the "Great Hunting Ground" of the Indian,
etc-Dubuque-1860-Pamph #1-16p-2 drwngs-1st ed-rare
                        (5a3) 50. (5dd1,lacks wrps) 35.00
TAYLOR,JOS-Tales of the Robin & other Small birds etc-Lond-1808-
W&TDarton-12mo-qtr lea-3 plts-rare (5c8,lacks pg E2 to E5) 35.00

TAYLOR, JOS H-Beavers, Their Ways & other Sketches-Washburn,
ND-1906-illus-dec cl-rev&enlrgd   (5m9)   25.00
--Frontier & Indian Life & Kaleidoscopic Lives-1932 anniversary ed-
327p-illus-scarce   (5r1,dj)   40.00
--Sketches of Frontier & Indian Life on Upper Mo etc-Pottstown,Pa-
1889-illus-200p-12mo-orig roan&bds-scarce
          (4c1,wn) 100.   (5m3)   125.00
--same-Bismark-1897-photos-306p   (5s4,v wn)   25.00
TAYLOR, JOS R-Story of the Drama-Bost-1930-8vo-cl-555p-
illus-1st ed   (5t0)   6.00
TAYLOR, KATHERINE AMES-Lights & Shadows of Yosemite-
SanFran-(1906)-86p-photos   (5L2)   2.50
TAYLOR, LANDON-The Battle Field Reviewed-Chig-1881-375p-2
2 illus-1st ed   (5L2)   8.50
TAYLOR, LILLIE JANE ORR-Life History of Thomas Orr Jr-
(Placerville)-1930-51p-wrps   (5tt0)   7.50
TAYLOR, M M-Heart of Black Papua-NY-1926-illus-1st ed (5x2) 8.50
TAYLOR, MARIE HANSEN-Letters to a Young Housekeeper-NY-
1892-219p   (5w7,soil)   6.50
TAYLOR, MARSHALL W-The Fastest Bicycle Rider in the World-
Worcester-1928-Wormley Pub   (5x5,dj,5x2,dj)   15.00
TAYLOR, MARY IMLAY-The house of the wizard-Chig-1899-
McClurg-frontis-1st ed   (5m2,lacks e.p.)   10.00
TAYLOR, MATTHEW-England's Bloody Tribunal or Popish cruelty
displayed-1773-4to-buck   (5L7,ex-libr)   25.00
TAYLOR, CAPT MEADOWS-Ralph Darnell-Edinb-1865-Blackwood-
3 vols-8vo-orig cl-1st ed   (5x3,unopnd)   50.00
TAYLOR, MRS, OR ONGAR-Practical Hints to Young Females-
Bost-1820-Wells&Lilly-12mo-189p-bds-2nd Amer ed (4c3,f)   35.00
TAYLOR, NORMAN-The Garden Dictionary-Bost-1936-4to-col plts-
mor-888p-thumb indexed-1st ed   (5w5)   15.00
--same-Bost-c1938-4to-888p   (5w0)   12.50
--A Guide to the Wild Flowers, East of the Mississippi & No of Va-
GardenCty Publ-(1928)-357p   (5s7,5x0)   5.00
TAYLOR, PAUL SCHUSTER-An Amer Mexican Frontier, Nueces Co,
Tex-ChapelHill-1934-Univ of NCar Pr-8vo-buck-v scarce
          (4a3)   15.00
TAYLOR, PETER-A Long 4th & Other Stories-NY-(1948)-12mo-cl-
1st ed of auth's 1st book   (5ss7,vf,dj)   35.00
TAYLOR, PHILIP MEADOWS-Confessions of a Thug-Lond-1839-
3 vols-12mo-orig bds-papr labls-1st ed of auth's1st book(Vol 1
does not contain publ catalog)   (5gg6)   185.00
TAYLOR, RACHEL ANNAND-Leonardo the Florentine-Lond-1927-
Richards-580p-4to-9 plts-cl   (5m5,wn)   12.00
--same-NY-(1928)-illus   (4a1)   7.50
TAYLOR, RICHARD-Destruction & Reconstruction-NY-1879-1st ed-
274p   (5a8,cov marks) 15.   (5i3,fox,5h1,pres)   20.00
--same-Lond-1879-calf-labl-1st Engl ed   (5a8,rub)   32.50
--same-NY-1893-274p   (5j6)   9.00
--same-NY-1955-Longman-380p   (5p0)   7.50
TAYLOR, RICHARD C-Statistics of Coal-Phila-1848-754p-charts-
fldg maps   (5h2,rbnd,libr stmps)   12.50
TAYLOR, ROBT LEWIS-W C Fields, His Follies-NY-1949-340p
          (4p7) 6.   (5p0,5m2)   5.00
TAYLOR, RUPERT-The political prophecy in England-NY-1911-
Columbia Univ-cl-165p   (5p6,pres)   10.50
TAYLOR, RUTH-The Kitchenette Cook Book-NY-1936-299p-
spiral bnd wrps   (5c0)   3.00
TAYLOR, S-Angling in All Its Branches-Lond-1800-298p-ads(5a9)12.50
TAYLOR, SARAH E L,ed-Fox Taylor Automatic Writing, Unabridged
Record-Bost-1936-Bruce Humphries-4to-cl-g.t.-6 plts-400p-
scarce   (5j5,f)   25.00
TAYLOR, STELLA WEILER-Rosemary-(Hamilton-1940)-illus-thk8vo-
2 vols   (4b6)   20.00
TAYLOR, T-Final Report to Sec of Army on Nuernberg War Crime
Trials-Wash-1949-wrps-345p   (5ff4)   9.50
TAYLOR, T U-The Austin Dam-Wash-1900-orig cl-plts-fldg maps
          (4a5)   30.00
--Irrigation Systems of Texas-Wash-1902-137p-illus   (4a5)   15.00
--Water Powers of Texas-Wash-1904-116p-illus-wrps   (4a5)   7.50
TAYLOR COLLECTION, TALBOT J-NY-1906-sm4to-cl-187 illus
          (5t2)   7.50
TAYLOR, THOS E-Running the Blockade-Lond-1896-illus (5h6) 12.50
--same-Lond-1912-Murray-frontis-180p(8)-maps(1 fldg) (5mm8) 10.00
TAYLOR, TOM,ed-Life of Benj Robt Haydon, historical painter-
Lond-1853-Longman, etc-3 vols-8vo-orig cl-1st ed
          (5x3,sp fade)   45.00
TAYLOR, W-Story of My Life-NY-1895-R8vo-illus (5x2)15.(4L9) 12.50
--The Flaming Torch In Darkest Africa-NY-1898-thk8vo-illus
          (5x2)   17.50
TAYLOR, W C-Biog of Elder Alfred Taylor-by his son-Louisville-
1878-123p   (4p8)   10.00

TAYLOR, W D-Jonathan Swift, A Critical Essay-Lond-1933-1st ed
          (5ss9)   6.50
TAYLOR, W G LANGWORTHY-The Saddle Horse, his Care,
Training & Riding-NY-1925-Holt-8vo-cl-illus-270p (5j5)   6.00
TAYLOR, WALTER H-Four Years with General Lee-NY-1878-
Appleton-199p   (5mm8)   22.50
TAYLOR, WALTER P-Mammals & Birds of Mt Rainier Nat'l Park-
Wash-1927-(US Dept Int)-wrps-plts-249p-fldg map (4d4)   6.50
TAYLOR, WM-Vines At Langleat-Lond-1882-84p-12mo-limpcl
          (5w1,shake)   6.50
TAYLOR, WM-Calif Life Illustrated-NY-1858-illus-8vo-1st ed
          (4g6,pres,sl stn on t.)   10.00
--same-NY-1858-348p plus ads-16 illus-1st ed-not 1st prntng
          (5L2,fox,sl wtrstns,cov wn)   5.00
--same-NY-1859-16 engr-348p-buck   (4n1,fox,rebnd)   7.50
--Christian Adventures in So Africa-NY-1880-Phillips&Hunt-
557p   (4t5)   12.00
--Seven Years Street Preaching in San Francisco-NY-1856-
394p-illus (5L2,wn) 3.50 (5hh3) 6.00   (5k1,fox,rub)   5.00
--same-NY-(1856)-354p-18th thous-illus   (5ee3,f)   7.50
--same-NY-1857-394p   (5s4,wn,fox,fair)   7.50
--Story of My Life-NY-1896-Eaton&Mains-photos-770p (4t5)   15.00
TAYLOR, WM H, MD-DeQuibus, Discourses & Essays-Richmond-
(1908)-8vo-cl-380p   (5j5)   12.50
TAYLOR, WM H-Yachting in NoAmerica-NY-(1948)-4to-750p-
photos-1st ed   (5s1,sl soil)   20.00
TAYLOR, WM H C-Garde of Happy Valley-KansasCty-1925-306p-
wrps   (5h0)   4.50
TAYLOR, WINNIE L-His Broken Sword-Chig-1888-354p-cl (5h1) 8.50
TAYLOR, ZACHARY-Info In Relation to Calif & New Mex-Wash-
1850-SR18-976p-fldg maps   (5n4)   40.00
--Letters of-Rochester-1908-4to-illus-ltd to 300c (4b3,v wn)   15.00
TAYS, GEO-Historical Sites & Landmarks of Alameda Co, Calif-
Oakland-1938-Alameda Co Library-WPA-4to-buck-349p-
offset typewriter copy-scarce   (5F5)   37.50
TCHITCHINOFF, ZAKAHAR-Adventures in Calif Of-LosAng-1956-
bds&cl-(Early Calif Travels Ser)-ltd to 225c-12mo (5h5,f)   15.00
TEA & TEA BLENDING-Lond-1886-117p, (9) (5w1,lacks fly)   4.50
TEA CUP READING-& Art of Fortune Telling by Tea Leaves-By a
Highland Seer-NY-n.d.-10 illus-94p   (5g9)   4.50
TEA DISTRICTS LABOUR ASSN-Handbook of Castes & Tribes
Employed on Tea Estates in NE India-Calcutta-1924-360p
          (5z5,scuf)   20.00
TEACHWELL, MRS-Fables in Monosyllables...to which are added
Morals etc-Phila-1898-Dodson-sm8vo-dec wrps-2 full pg wdcuts-
60p, 39p   (5u6)   75.00
TEAGUE, CHAS C-Fifty Years a Rancher-n.p.-1944-199p-2nd ed-
(Calif Fruit Growers Exch, prnt)   (5r1,vg) 10.   (5dd6)   7.50
TEAKLE, THOS-Spirit Lake Massacre-IowaCty-1918-Iowa State Hist
Soc-336p-1st ed   (4g6) 30.   (4i7)   18.00
TEAL, ANGELINE-John Thorn's Folks-Bost&NY-1884-187p (5m1) 10.00
TEALE, EDWIN W-Autumn Across Amer-NY-1956-8vo-cl-photo-
386p-Amer Seasons Series   (5t0)   3.75
--Days Without Time-NY-1948-283p-illus   (5p7) 6. (5t4)   7.50
--Near Horizons-NY-1942-1st ed-illus   (5tt5)   6.00
TEALE, THOS P-Brooklyn City Directory...1848, 49...Manual of
Kings Co-Brklyn-1848-E B Spooner-12mo-part cl-286p, 191p
          (4t1)   20.00
TEALL, GARDNER-The Pleasures of Collecting-NY-1920-328p-
illus   (5t4)   6.00
TEASDALE, SARA-Flame & shadow-NY-1920-Macmillan-1st ed
          (5m2)   6.50
--Strange Victory-NY-1933-Macmillan-1st ed (5F5) 5. (5j5)   7.50
TEBBEL, JOHN-Geo Horace Lorimer & The Saturday Evening Post-
GardenCty-1948-335p   (5y2,autg) 5.75   (5w5)   5.00
--Wm Randolph Hearst, His Life & Good Times-NY-1952-8vo-cl
          (5p5)   10.00
TEBIEN'KOV, MIKHAIL D-(Atlas of NW Shores of Amer)-
(StPtrsbrg)-1852-8vo-2 vol-39 maps-litho view-atlas folio-
blu wrps-1st ed-Wickersham   (5hh0, Assn copy) 2,500.00
TECHNO CHEMICAL RECEIPT BOOK, THE-from the German-
Phila-1902-78 engrs-495p   (5g9, hng loose)   6.50
TECHY, MARGARET-Filet Crochet Lace-NY-1943-80p-57 illus
          (5n7)   4.50
TEDLOCK, E W, JR-The Frieda Lawrence Collection of D H Lawrence
Manuscripts-1948-Univ of NewMex-1st ed   (5ss9,f,dj)   15.00
TEDROW, WM L-Our Church-AnnArbor-1894-illus   (5m2)   11.00
TEE-VAN, HELEN DAMROSCH-Red Howling Monkey-NY-1926-
Macmillan-142p-frontis-3 col plts-pict cl-1st ed   (5p1)   15.00
TEELE, A K-History of Milton, Mass, 1640 to 1887-(Bost)-1887-
illus-8vo-668p   (5t9) 15.   (4c8)   22.50
TEETERS, NEGLEY K-Penology From Panama to Cape Horn-Phila-
1946-for Temple U-8vo-cl-illus-scarce   (4a3)   15.00

TEETOR,HENRY B-Past & Present of Mill Creek Valley-Cinn-
1882-328p-cl   (5y0)   15.00

TEFFT,BENJ FRANKLIN-The shoulder knot-NY-1850-Harper-
12mo-orig cl-1st ed   (5x1,libr labl) 35.00

TEGETMEIER,W B-Horses,Asses,Zebras,Mules & Mule Breeding-
Lond-1895-frontis-orig cl-8vo-166p-v scarce   (4p5)   15.00

--Pigeons,Their Structure,Varieties,Habits & Management-Lond-
1868-orig cl-lg8vo-g.e.-16 col plts-1st ed (5z9,sp wn,fox) 47.50

TEGGART,F J-Idea of Progress-1949-rev ed   (5L7)   10.00

TEGNAEUS,H-Blood Brothers-NY-1952-4to-illus   (5x2)   15.00

TEGNER,ESAIAS-Fridtjof's Saga,a Norse Romance-Chig-1905-
12mo-cl   (5t0)   4.00

--same-Stockholm-1953-illus-ltd to 1500x,nbrd,box-Limited Edition
Club Publ   (5F1,f)   27.50

TEICHERT,MINERVA-A Romance of Old Fort Hall-Portland-1932-
165p-illus-1st ed-scarce   (5L2,dj) 8.50 (5s4)   12.50

TEICHMANN,EMIL-A Journey To Alaska In The Year 1868-
Kensington-1925-ed by his son Oskar-272p-ltd to 100c(5u3) 50.00

TEIGNMOUTH,LORD-Memoirs of the Life, Writings & Corres of
Sir Wm Jones-Phila-1805-8vo-lea-419p-frontis   (5t2)   6.50

TEIT,JAS H-The Middle Columbia Salish-Seattle-1928-U of Wash
Pubs in Anth,#4-8vo-wrps   (5h4)   4.00

TEIXEIRA DE OLIVEIRA,JOSE-Historia do Estado do Espirito Santo-
RiodeJaneiro-1951-fldg maps-500p-wrps (5r7,unopnd,ex-libr) 12.50

TEIXEIRA PINTO,JOAO-A Ocupacao Militar da Guine-Lisbon-
1936-219p-18 plts-fldg table-fldg map (5c6,lt fox,pres) 17.50

TEIXIDOR,FELIPE-Ex Libris y Bibliotecas de Mexico-Mexico-1925-
550p-wrps   (5j4)   25.00 ·

TELEGRAPH HERALD'S ABRIDGED HISTORY-of the State of Iowa &
Directory of Jackson Co-n.p.-1907-322p plus 71p-100 photos
                                           (5L0,lacks fly) 12.50

TELEKI,COUNT LADISLAS-The case of Hungary stated-Lond-1849-
Effingham Wilson-8vo-disbnd-1st ed   (5i8)   7.50

TELEMACHUS & MENTOR-A dialogue between,on rights of
conscience & military requisitions-Bost-1818-16mo-orig plain
wrps-16p   (5g4,wtrstnd) 25.00

TELFER,J BUCHAN-The Crimea & Transcaucasia,being a Journey
in Kouban in Gouria, Georgia, Armenia-Lond-1876-cl-8vo-
illus-fldg maps-2 vols   (5v7)   35.00

TELLER,D W-Hist of Ridgefield,Conn-1878-251p   (5t9)   10.00

TELLER,JUDD L-Scapegoat of Revolution-NY-1954-352p (5t4)   6.00

TELLER,WALTER,Ed-Five Great Sea Captains..under Sail-NY-1960-
431p-ports-1st ed   (5s1)   8.00

TELLMAN,JOHN-Practical Hotel Steward-Chig-1913-illus-248p-
4th ed   (4g9,rub)   6.00

TELLO,ANTONIO-Cronica Miscelanea De La Sancta Provincia De
Xalisco,Libro 3 & 4-Guadalajara-1942,45-8vo-wrps-2 vols-
reprnt of 1891 ed-ltd to 1000c   (4t1)   30.00

TEMPERANCE FAMILY ALMANAC-for Yr of Our Lord 1835-Bost-
(1834)-24 lvs-sewed as issued-Drake 4089 (5h7) 8.50 (5s9) 27.50

--same-Albany-(1835)-24p-sewed as issued   (5jj9)   7.50

--Temperance Almanac,1838-Albany-(1837)-Packard & Van
Benthuysen-48p-Drake 7598   (5yy3)   15.00

TEMPERANCE SERMONS-Delivered in Response to Invitation of
Natl Temp Soc & Publ House-NY-1874-400p-cl
                                           (5h7,lacks flys) 7.50

TEMPLE,THE-Lond-1927-8vo-red brocade bndg-Nonesuch Pr-
Ltd Ed,boxed   (5t7,f)   15.00

TEMPLE,CHARLOTTE-Lamentable History of the Beautiful &
Accomplished-Phila-(1865)-Barclay-8vo-pict wrps-58p,(13)-
wdcuts-only correct & authentic ed   (5j5,fray) 25.00

TEMPLE DE HIRSCH-Famous Cook Book-Seattle-1916-Ladies Aux-
349p-ads   (4g9,cov dtchd,writing) 10.00

TEMPLE LAW QUARTERLY-1927 to 70-Vol 1 thru 43-index 1 thru 25
                                          (5ii7,rbnd) 967.50

TEMPLE LAW QUARTERLY-1927 to 70-Vols 1 thru 43-bound wi
index 1 to 25   (5rr4)   967.50

TEMPLE,J H-History,Framingham,Mass,Early Known as Danforth's
Farms-1887-794p   (5t9)   20.00

--Hist of North Brookfield-1887-824p-illus   (4t2,wn) 17.50

--Hist of the Town of Palmer,Mass-1889-602p   (4t2)   25.00

TEMPLE,NEVILLE-Tannhauser-Mobile-1863-125p   (4b4)   35.00

TEMPLE,SIR RICHARD-The Story of My Life-Lond-1896-2 vols-
299p-cl   (5t2)   6.50

TEMPLETON,FAITH-Drafted In-NY-(1888)-1st ed   (5mm2)   13.50

TEMPLETON,WM C-Proposals for & advantages of a regular mail
communication by steam packets between NewOrl & Vera Cruz-
Wash-1851-RobtA Waters-8vo-orig wrps-1st ed   (5i0)   27.50

TEMPLIN,LUCINDA DE LEFTWICH-Remin of Lindenwood College-
StCharles-1920-166p-photos-wrps-scarce   (5L2)   15.00

--The Sibleys(cov t.)-StCharles,Mo-1926-32p plus photos-wrps
                                                 (5L2)   7.50

TEMPTED OF THE DEVIL-Lond-1882-Remington-3 vols-8vo-
orig cl-1st ed   (5xx6,rub)   27.50

TEMPTING KOSHER DISHES-Cinn-1930-158p-col illus-
in Engl & Hebraic-bds-3rd ed   (5c9)   4.00

TEN ACRES ENOUGH-NY-1864-12mo-cl   (5t0) 5. (5w9)   8.50

TEN LITTLE NIGGERS,THE-NY-c1880-4to-10 lvs-McLoughlin,publ
                                                 (5v2,wn) 12.50

TEN LITTLE NURSERY DOLLS-Lond-(1900)-RaphaelTuck&Sons-
obl 4to-bds-col illus-sections at top shift dolls (5c8)   15.00

TEN SINGERS,AN ANTHOLOGY-Lond-(1925)-Crown 8vo-
stiff wrps-1st ed   (5ss7,mint)   16.50

TEN THOUSAND A YEAR-Edinb-1841-Blackwood-3 vols-8vo-
hf calf-(Sam'l Warren)-1st Engl ed   (5xx6,scuff) 25.00

TEN THOUSAND MILES ON A BICYCLE-NY-1887-12mo-cl-
107p,800p-frontis   (5t0)   6.50

TEN YEARS A COWBOY-Chig-1888-Rhodes&McClure-471p-illus
                                                 (5m1)   22.50

--same-(C C Post)-Chig-1889-471lp-cl-an early edition (5h2) 12.50

TENCH,WATKINS-A Narr of the Exped to Botany Bay-NY-1789-
sm8vo-wrps-(5),(11),64p-Swords-rare 1st Amer ed(same year
as 1st)   (5n9)   225.00

TENENBAUM, DR JOS-Races,Nations & Jews-NY-1934-8vo-cl-
1st ed   (5p5)   10.00

TENENBAUM,S-Why Men Hate-Phila-1947-R8vo   (5x2)   6.50

TENESLES,NICOLE-Indian of New Engl & NEastern Provinces etc-
Middletown,Conn-1851-24p-lea&bds-pamph as issued (5r6)   27.00

TENISON,E M-Louise Imogen Guiney,Her Life & Works-Lond-1923
                                               (5mm1)   12.50

TENNAL,RALPH-History of Nemaha Co,Kans-Lawrence-1916-
816p-illus-3/4 lea   (5t3,cor wn)   50.00

TENNEH LANGUAGE-Catholic Prayers & Hymns-bnd wi Tenneh
Indian Catechism of Christian Doctrine-Kosoreffski,Indian Boys
Pr-1897-limp flowrd cl-39p,22p   (5a3)   85.00

TENNESSEE BAR JOURNAL-1965 to 69-Vol 1 thru 5 (5ii7,rbnd) 47.50

TENNESSEE-a guide to the state-NY-1939-Viking-558p-pkt map-
WPA-Amer Guide Series   (5u3)   6.50

TENNESSEE,MEN OF-n.d.-(ca in the teens)-(ca 175p)-ports
                                                 (5h6)   6.00

TENNESSEE,JOURNAL-Proceedings of Conven of Delegates to
Amend,Revise or Form & Make a New Constitution for State,
Nashville,Jan 10,1870-Nashvl-1870-wrps-32p
                 (5L1,M Filmore's copy) 200. (5h6,lea)   50.00

TENNESSEE LAW REVIEW-1922 to 69-Vols 1 thru 36-bound
                                        (5rr4,recent rbnd) 570.00

TENNESSEE VALLEY AUTHORITY-Telephone Directory for
Knoxville,Norris & Norris Dam-July 1,1942-wrps   (5rr6)   3.50

TENNEY,EDW P-Coronation,a story of forest & sea-Bost-1877-
Noyes,Snow-1st ed   (5m2)   10.00

TENNEY,M J-Desc of Thos Tenney of Rowley,Mass,1638 to 1890-
1891-369p   (4t2)   10.00

--Tenney Family-1904-691p-rev   (5t9)   45.00

TENNEY,W J-Military & Naval History of Rebellion in US-NY-
1865-843p-illus-mrbld bds-pt lea
(5xx7) 15. (5s1,wn) 17.50 (5x5,lea) 20. (5ee3,f,f bndg) 22.50

--same-NY-1867-ports-lea   (5x5)   20.00

TENNYSON,ALFRED-Becket,a Drama-Lond-1884-1st ed (5r9)   12.50

--Bibliography of Tennyson-Lond-1896-priv prnt-lg papr-ltd to 35c
                                                 (4b4)   35.00

--same-Exhibited at Grolier Club Nov 5,1897-12mo-3/4 grey lev-
labls-raised bands-g.t.   (5t5,f bndg) 17.50

--Bibliography of the First Editions-NY-1901-Dodd,Mead-
papr bds-Ltd Ed   (5t5)   15.00

--Death of Cenone Akbar's Dream & Other Poems-Lond-1892-
12mo-hf lea   (5hh1)   8.50

--Enoch Arden etc-Lond-1864-16mo-dec lea by Riviere-t.e.g.-
1st ed   (5ss9,f,f bndg)   40.00

--same-Bost-1864-Ticknor,Fields-cl-1st Amer ed (5i4,sm wtrstn) 3.50

--Idylls of the King-Lond-1859-16mo-dec lea-1st ed
                        (5r9) 20. (5hh1,f,f bndg)   40.00

--Life & Works-NY-1899-crown 8vo-green cl-g.sp-floral cov design-
g.t.-port   (5t5)   15.00

--Maud & Other Poems-Lond-1855-dec lea by Riviere-1st ed
                                        (5ss9,f,f bndg)   40.00

--same-orig cl   (5ss9,f)   30.00

--same-E Aurora-1900-Roycrofters-ltd to 100c (5ii2,2 autgs) 8.50

--Memoir by His Son-NY-1897-illus-2 vols
                 (5q0) 12.50 (5i1,fox) 7.50 (5mm2)   8.50

--Ode on the Death of the Duke of Wellington-Lond-1852-
Edw Moxon-16p-orig pale blu wrps-1st ed (5ss9,vg,box)   50.00

--Poems of Imagination & Fancy-Phila-1868-124p-illus-g.e.-
g.design-1st Amer ed   (5ee3,f,f bndg)   5.00

TENNYSON,ALFRED (continued)
--Poetical & dramatic works of-Bost-(1929)-7 vols-Houghton,Miff-
Riverside Pr-lg8vo-cl&bds-deckle edged-illus-Lg Paper Ed
(5p6,f,unopnd) 40.00
--Seven Poems & Two Translations-1902-8vo-limp vel-Doves Pr-
ltd to 325c (5d8) 75.00
--Works-NY-1903-6 vols-red cl (4a1,sl rub) 17.50
--The Works of-Lond-1911-Macmillan-12mo-901p-frontis-calf-
bnd by Bicker&Son (5p1) 12.50
TENNYSON,HALLAM-Jack & The Beanstalk-Lond-1886-Macmillan-
illus by Randolph Caldecott-pic cl (5c8) 20.00
TENT,DEXTER FELLOWS-Circus Saints & Sinners-NY-1957-illus-200p
(5p0) 5.00
10TH MICH CAVALRY RECORD-Civil War 1861 to 65-(Kalmz-1905)-
n.p.n.d.-155p-cl (5h2) 12.50
TERESAH-A Doll,2 Children & 3 Storks-NY-(1931)-Dutton-
Dorothy Emmrich,transl-8vo-178p-illus-1st Amer ed (5p1) 15.00
TERHUNE,ALBERT PAYSON-Caleb Conover,Railroader-NY-1907-
12mo-cl-1st ed (5gg6,f) 25.00
--A Dog Named Chips-NY-1931-1st ed (5ee3,dj) 17.50
--Lad,a Dog-NY-(1919)-1st ed-scarce (4c3,f,als & photo) 70.00
--The Life of Edw Fitzgerald-Yale Univ Pr-1947-1st ed
(5mm2,dj) 6. (5ss9,f,dj) 12.50
--My Friend the Dog-NY-Harper-1926-col illus-317p-1st ed
(5i1,autg tip in) 10. (4a6) 7.50
--Syria from the Saddle-Bost-1896-illus-8vo-1st ed of auth's 1st book-
(4m8) 20.00
--To the Best of My Memory-NY-1930-Harper-272p-illus (5p0) 4.50
TERMAN,LEWIS M-Children's Reading-NY&Lond-1926-Appleton-
(365)p-1st ed (5p1) 5.00
TERMINAL FACILITIES NORTH PACIFIC PORTS-Oregon,Calif,
Wash-1914-336p-12mo (5s1) 5.00
TERRELL,C V-The Terrells-Austin-1948 (4c7) 32.50
TERRELL,CAPT J C-Remin of Early Days of Ft Worth-FtWorth-1906
(4c7,resewn,box) 110.00
TERRINGTON,WM-Cooling Cups & Dainty Drinks-Lond-n.d.-
(c1869)-223p,(15) (5w1,crack) 12.50
TERROU,FERNAND-Legislation For Press,Film & Radio-Paris-1951-
420p-wrps (4c9) 17.50
TERRY,A H-Copies of Gen Terry's Reports on Georgia-Wash-1870-
207p-HED 288 (4j4) 12.50
TERRY,ELLEN-Memoirs-NY-1932-illus-1st ed (5k0,5tt5) 5.00
TERRY,FRANK TAYLOR-The Aborigines of the NoWest-Milwkee-
1896-wrps-Parkman Club Publ #4 (5L2,unopnd) 6.50
TERRY,HENRY-Amer Clock Making-Waterbury-1870-J Giles&Son-
frontis-8 illus-orig wrps-27p pamphlet-1st ed-rare (4c4) 37.50
--same-n.p.-n.d.-(c1871)-frontis-19p-orig prntd wrps (5m3,f) 20.00
TERRY,MARIAN D,ed-Old Inns of Connecticut-Hartf-1937-4to-cl
illus-mor bk-box-ltd ed (5m2) 35.00
TERRY,T B-Our Farming-Phila-1893-367p-illus (5w0,sl dmpstn) 7.50
TERRY,T PHILIP-Terry's Guide to the Japanese Empire-Bost-1928-
lg12mo-cl-maps-rev ed-8 maps-21 plans (5t2,f,dj) 3.00
--Terry's Guide to Mexico-Hingham-1947-thk12mo-932p plus ads-
rev ed-fldg & other maps (5dd6) 4.00
TERSTEEGEN,GERHARD-Geistliche Brosamen-Vol 1,in 2 parts,
bnd together-Reading-1807-JRiter-thk8vo-calf-lea labl (5r7) 35.00
TERWILLIGER,CHAS-The Horolover Collection-Bronxvle-1959-
illus-4to-143p-ltd prntg (5bb0) 12.00
TESSIER-Complete Treatise on Merinos & other sheep-1811-calf
(5L7,ex-libr,broke) 17.50
TESTED RECIPES-Prepared by W H M S-Algona Methodist Church-
n.p.-(Iowa,1938)-56p-ring bnd wrps (5g9) 3.00
TESTIMONIES OF CAPT JOHN BROWN-At Harper's Ferry,wi his
Address-NY-1860-Anti Slavery Tract #7-16p-wrps-Amer
Anti Slavery Soc (5x2) 25.00
TESTIMONY OF THE RELIGIOUS SOC OF FRIENDS AGAINST
SLAVERY-Bost-1847-12p-wrps (5x2) 20.00
TESTIMONY OF CHRIST'S SECOND APPEARING-Lebanon(Ohio)-
1808-press of JnM'Clean,Off of Western Star-thk12mo-calf-
mor labl-1st ed (5i0,f,Streeter copy) 200.00
--same-(Albany 1856)-24p,631p-4th ed-United Soc Called Shaker
(5t4) 35.00
TESTUT,L-Traite d'Anatomie Humaine-Paris-1899 to 1901-illus(some
col)-4th ed-4 vols (4j3,rub) 32.50
TEUFFEL,BLANCHE W-Aunt Serena-Bost-1881-1st ed (5ee3) 5.00
--A Fellow & His Wife-Bost-1892-1st ed (5ee3) 5.00
--Guenn A Wave on the Breton Coast-Bost-1884-Osgood-439p-
illus-1st ed,1st issue (5x4) 12.50
--Tony the Maid-NY-1887-Harper-166p-1st ed (5x4) 7.50
TEUFFEL'S HISTORY OF ROMAN LITERATURE-Lond-1900-
rev&enlrgd ed-2 vols (5q0) 17.50
TEVIS,REV A H-Beyond the Sierras,Observations on PacCoast-
Phila-1877-259p-illus (5s4,fade) 10.00

TEVIS,JAS H-Arizona in the '50's-Univ of NewMex Pr-1954
(5x5,dj) 10.00
TEVIS,MRS JULIA A-60 Years in a School Room-Cinn-1878-489p
(4p8) 25.00
TEXARKANA GATEWAY,THE-to Texas & the Southwest-StL-(1896)-
maps-illus-wrps (5g3) 10.00
TEXAS ALMANAC FOR 1860-(Galveston-1859)-228p,ads-prntd wrps-
(4b0,wn,lacks back wrp) 55.00
--same-for 1870-Galveston-1869-Richardson-cl (4j6,rbnd) 60.00
TEXAS & PACIFIC RY-Sketches of Principal Cities & Towns of the
Line of the-n.p.-Nov,1880-17 panel fldr,col map on reverse-
scarce (5L0) 15.00
--West Texas,the "Land of Opportunities" reached via-n.p.-(1907)-
23p-photos-map-wrps (5L0) 7.50
TEXAS BAPTISTS-Centennial Story of-Dallas-1936 (5x5) 15.00
TEXAS CENTENNIAL,AN EXHIBITION-Wash-1946-54p-illus-
catalogue-wrps (4a5) 10.00
TEXAS COAST COUNTRY-Houston-1912-Sunset Central Lines-
12mo-wrps-46p (4t1) 10.00
TEXAS CONSTITUTION-As Amended in 1861-wrps-12p (5ff4) 15.00
TEXAS,GUIDE TO LONE STAR STATE-NY-1940-illus-maps-e.p.map-
700p plus index-1st ed-Amer Guide Ser-WPA
(4L5,5a8) 10. (5t3) 7.50 (5k0,5hh3) 8.50
TEXAS,HISTORY OF-Lewis Pub Co-Chig-1895-730p-illus-folio-
orig mor (5n4,vf) 160.00
TEXAS LAW REVIEW-1922 to 71-Vol 1 thru 49 (5ii7,rbnd) 885.00
--same (5ii7) ea 22.00
TEXAS LAW REVIEW-1922 to 1970-Vols 1 thru 48-bound
(5rr4,recent rbnd) 865.00
TEXAS,LAWS OF-Alphabetical Index to-(Houston,1839)-12p
(5n4) 45.00
TEXAS,LAWS PASSED-by 6th Congr of Republic of Texas-Austin-
1842-S Whiting-128p (5n4) 40.00
TEXAS-RandMcNally Pocket Map & Shippers Guide-Chig-1910-
75p-fldg map (5k1) 12.50
TEXAS SAMPLER,A-1941-129p-1st ed (5r1,dj) 5.00
TEXAS STATE FAIR-Second Grand State Fair of Agric,Mech & Blood
Stock Assoc of Texas...(at) Houston-Galveston-1871-wrps
(5g4) 20.00
TEXAS TOURIST POINTS & RESORTS-Houston-1912-Sunset Central
Lines-12mo-wrps-30p (4t1) 10.00
TEXAS WESTERN RR CO-Charter of & Extracts from Reports of
Col A B Gray & Sec of War on Survey of Route-Cinn-1855-8vo-
fldg map-disbnd (5a3) 85.00
TEXIER,EDMOND-Lettres Sur L'Angleterre (Souvenirs de
l'Exposition Universelle)-Paris-1851-Gernier-qtr lea-8vo-
269p (4e1) 25.00
TEXTBOOK OF SMALL ARMS-Lond-1929-Her Majesty's Sta Ofc-
4to-427p-red cl-illus (4a6) 25.00
TEXTE,JOS-Jean Jacques Rousseau & the Cosmopolitan Spirit in
Literature-Lond-1899-Duckworth-8vo-cl-g.t.-393p (5aa2) 12.50
TEXTILE MANUFACTURES OF ALL AGES-of the World-By an
experienced manufacturer-illus (5L7,wn) 7.50
TEZUKA,KANEKO-Japanese Food-Tokyo-1936-84p-col plts-wrps
(5g9) 3.00
THACHER,JAS-American Medical Biography-Bost-1828-
Richardson,Lord,Cottons,Barnard-15 ports-2 vols-hf mor(5tt8) 75.00
--Amer modern..adapted to use of medical practitioners of US-
Bost-1826-hf calf-new ed,improved (5g4,ex-libr) 25.00
--The Amer orchardist-Plymouth,Mass-1825-16mo-bds-roan bk-
2nd ed (5L3,f ox) 10. (5g4,cov loose) 22.50
--History of town of Plymouth-Bost-1832-frontis-cl-fldg map-
1st ed (5m3,rbnd) 25.00
--History of the Town of Plymouth....wi Concise History of
Aborigines etc-Bost-1835-401p-orig cl-papr labl-frontis-map-
2nd ed,enlrgd (5m3) 25.00
--Military Journal During Amer Revolutionary War-Bost-1823-
Richardson&Lord-603p-orig calf
(5tt8,stns) 75. (5s9,rbnd pigskin) 145.00
--same-NY-1860-illus-486p-g.e. (5L3,f) 27.50
--same-Hartf-1862-618p (5L3,f) 30.00
--Observations on Hydrophobia-Plymouth,Mass-1812-8vo-calf-
orig lea labl-lettering in g.-1st ed (4c1,hng weak,fox) 60.00
--A Practical Treatise on the Management of Bees-Bost-1829-12mo-
cl&bds-162p (5g8) 15. (5t2) 12.50
THACHER,JOHN B-Cabotian Discovery-Ott-1897-port-7 facs-
Royal Soc of Can (5aa0,pres,orig cov bnd in) 12.50
THACHER,JOHN BOYD-Charlecote-NY-1895-hf calf-
ltd to 356c,nbrd (4b4) 10. (5b2) 8.50
THACKERAY,WM M-The Chronicle of the Drum-NY-1882-sm4to-
illus by H Pyle,ABFrost & others (5t4) 7.50
--A Collection of Letters of Thackeray,1847 to 1855-NY-1887-
illus (5m1) 10.00

THACKERAY,WM M (continued)
--Complete works-NY-1903-26 vols-t8vo-red buck-illus-
Anne Ritchie,intro-g.t.-spcl ed   (5t5)   57.50
--Denis Duval-Lond-1867-Smith,Elder&Co-8vo-orig cl-1st ed
(5xx6,rprd)   20.00
--English Humourists of the 18th Century-NY-1853-Harper-
1st Amer ed   (5x3) 15.   (4b5)   10.00
--The four Georges-Lond-1861-Smith,Elder-8vo-orig cl-
1st Engl ed(publ previous year in NY)   (5i8,hng wn)   8.00
--The History of Pendennis-Lond-1850-hf lea-2 vols-illus-1st ed
(5r9)   30.00
--Jeames's Diary-NY-1853-sm12mo-mor-bk&t.g.-16p of ads at end-
1st ed   (5r9,f bndg)   15.00
--Letters & Private Papers-Gordon N Ray,ed-Cambr-1945,46-
Harvard Univ Pr-4 vols-8vo-cl-g.   (5b0,dj,boxes)   55.00
--Loose Sketches-Lond-1894-Chiswick Pr-lg papr   -publ autg-
ltd to 100c   (5p6,sl rub) 22.50   (5ss9)   30.00
--Mr Brown's Letters to a Young Man About Town-NY-1853-
sm12mo-3/4 mor,g, t, -bndg by Stikeman-1st ed-rare early
issue wi last letter of "with" lacking on t.pg   (5r9)   20.00
--same-Cambr-1901-Riversde Pr-ltd to 500c-box-autg by Bruce
Rogers   (5i4)   25.00
--The Newcomes-Lond-1853 to 55-orig wrps-24 parts in 23(in 2
folders)-1st ed in orig parts-8vo
(5nn2,sl wn) 100.   (4m8,lacks 1 back wrp)   75.00
--same-Cambr-1954-2 vols-illus-Limited Edition Club publ-
ltd to 1500c,box,illus autg,nbrd   (5F1,vf)   32.50
--The Rose & the Ring-NY-Christmas, 1942-4to-frontis-
6 hand col plts-pict cl-Limited Editions Club   (5p1,box)   17.50
--same-NY-(1942)-Heritage Pr-4to-pict bds-illus by Fritz Kredel
(5c8,soil)   6.00
--same-abridged by Amy Steedman-Lond-(ca1907)-Jack-sm8vo-
8 col plts-cl labl   (5c8)   8.50
--Sultan Stork & Other Stories & Sketches-Lond-1887-8vo-1st ed
(5x3,f) 10.   (5r9) 15.   (4m8)   22.50
--The Thackeray Alphabet-NY-1930-Harper-illus-1st prntg
(5m2,dj)   6.00
--Thackeray's Letters to an Amer Family-NY-1904-Century-
cl bkd bds-1st ed-Merrymount Press   (4p1,labl scuff)   12.50
--Vanity Fair-NY-1848-Harper-illus-1st Amer ed
(5yy6,bndg poor,rbnd) 22.50   (5r9,rbnd)   17.50
--same-Lond-1868-illus-2 vols-hf calf   (5q0)   10.00
--same-Oxford-1931-4to-2 vols-Ltd Ed Club (5b0,box) 45. (5t8) 27.50
--same-NY-1940-Heritage Pr-759p-no box   (5p7)   7.50
--The Virginians-Lond-1857 to 59-8vo,in orig 24 parts-1st ed-
1st issue ("actresses" pg 207)   (4n5,vf)   275.00
--same-Lond-1858-Bradbury & Evans-illus-mor&bds-2 vols in 1-
1st ed   (5z7,f)   65.00
--The Works of...-NY-(1910)-Harper-Centenary Ed-illus-26 vols-
hf bds-papr labls   (5x0)   100.00
THANE,ELSWYTH-Ever After-NY-(1945)-1st ed (4b7,pres)   10.00
THANE,ERIC-High Border Country-(1942)-Duell,Sloan-cl-335p-
1st ed   (5F5,f,dj)   6.50
--The Majestic Land-Indnpls-(1950)-330p plus index-1st ed-photos
(5dd1,dj)   7.50
THANET,OCTAVE-The Missionary Sheriff-NY-1897-illus by
ABFrost& C Carleton-1st ed   (5ee3,f)   10.00
--Stories of a Western Town-NY-1893-Scribner-8vo-cl-illus by
ABFrost   (5b2)   7.50
THARIN,R S-Arbitrary Arrests in the South-NY-1863-12mo-245p(2)
(5mm8,chip) 12.50   (4c8,ex-libr)   25.00
THARP,B C-Vegetation of Texas-Houston-1939-Anson Jones Pr-
74p-wrps   (4a5)   6.50
THARP,LOUISE H-The Peabody Sisters of Salem-Bost-1950-8vo-cl-
illus-372p   (5p1,dj) 4.50   (5t2,f,dj)   3.50
THATCHER,B B-The Boston Book-Bost-1837-Light&Stearns-8vo
(5b2,chip)   15.00
--Indian Biography-NY-1832-2 vols-4 x 6-3/4 lea   (5e8)   15.75
--same-NY-1837-Harper&Bros-2 vols-12mo-calf&bds-frontis
(5i4,rub)   22.50
--same-NY-1900-16mo-2 vols   (4b2,sl wn)   7.50
--same-Akron-(1910)-350p   (4b2,sl soil)   5.00
THATCHER,CAPT MARSHALL P-A Hundred Battles in the West-
Detroit-1884-416p-1st ed-scarce   (5L5,wn)   30.00
THATCHER,OLIVER J-Source Book for Medieval History-NY-(1905)
(4a1,wn)   7.50
THATCHER'S WIFE-or,an account of Mary Camps-Lond-1818-
JNisbet-frontis-54p-12mo-cl bkd bds   (5c8)   15.00
THAXTER,CELIA-Among the Isles of Shoals-Bost-1873-sm12mo-
cl-184p-1st ed   (5t2)   5.00
--The Heavenly Guest,wi Other Unpublished Writings-(Andover,
Mass,1935)-12mo-cl-port-177p-ed by Oscar Laighton-
priv prntd   (5j5)   7.50

THAXTER,CELIA (continued)
--Letters of-Bost-1896-12mo-cl-230p-illus-port-frontis (5t2)   3.50
--Poems-NY-1872-12mo-orig brown cl-g.e.-1st ed of auth's
1st book   (5gg6,vf)   35.00
THAYER,E H-Wild Flowers of Rocky Mntns-NY-1889-54p-4to-
24p col illus   (4b9,sl fade)   12.00
THAYER,ELI-New England Emigrant Aid Company-Worcester-
1887-48p-wrps   (5w5,fray)   5.00
THAYER,EMMA HOMAN-Wild Flowers of Colorado-NY-(1885)-
col plts-4to-1st ed   (4g6,rub,soil)   10.00
--Wild Flowers of the Pac Coast-NY-(1887)-4to-pict cl-col illus
(5j2,sl tn)   15.00
THAYER,FRANK S-Gems of Colorado Scenery-Denver-1892-
Publisher's Pressroom-folio-cl-48p   (4t1)   10.00
THAYER,JOHN-Astir,a Publisher's Life Story-Bost-1910-302p
(5j4)   6.00
THAYER,TIFFANY-Mona Lisa-NY-1956-3 vols-1st ed (5hh3)   10.00
THAYER,WM M-Chas Jewett,Life & Recollections-Bost-1886-
464p-cl   (5h1)   7.50
--Marvels of the New West-Norwich-1887-714p-maps-illus-
1st ed-scarce   (5dd1) 10.   (5g0,f)   15.00
--The New West-Norwich-1888-715p-illus
(5n4) 4.50   (5s4,wn) 8.   (5w5,rub)   10.00
--same-Norwich-1889-lg8vo-calf-36p,715p-illus
(5s4,sl wn) 7.   (5t2,f)   7.50
--same-Norwich-1890-8vo-illus-maps-715p (4d9) 6. (5s4,sl wn) 7.00
--same-Norwich-1892-715p-maps-stmpd lea cov
(5dd1,cl,f) 7.50   (5s4)   10.00
--A Youth's History of the Rebellion-Bost-1864-Walker-16mo-
347p-frontis-3 plts-5th thousand   (5p1)   7.50
THAYER,WM ROSCOE-The Art of Biography-NY-1920-Scribner
(5p9)   4.00
--George Washington-Bost-c1922-274p-illus   (5h9)   5.00
--The Life & Times of Cavour-Bost-c1911-2 vols-illus-maps
(5p0) 10.   (5w9)   7.50
--Life & Letters of John Hay-(1915)-Houghton,Miff-2 vols
(5w9) 7.   (5w5,5t2)   7.50
--Theodore Roosevelt-Bost-1919-474p-illus (5h2) 4. (5t2)   4.50
THEAL,GEO McCALL-Progress of South Africa in the 19th Century-
Lond-1901-Linscott Publ-photos-522p-19th Cent Ser Vol 10
(4t5)   15.00
THEARLE,SAM'L-Modern Practice of Shipbuilding in Iron & Steel-
Vol 2 only-Lond-n.d.-plts-no pg nbrs-no text-4to
(5s1,ex-libr)   5.00
--Theoretical Naval Architecture-Lond-n.d.-2 vols-4to (5s1)   15.00
THEATRE GUILD ANTHOLOGY-NY-1936-1st ed-buck-961p
(5qq7)   10.00
THEBAUD,REV AUG J-Gentilism,Religion Previous to Christianity-
NY-1876-Sadlier-lg8vo-cl-15p,525p, 1st ed   (5t2)   7.50
--Louisa Kirkbride,a tale of NY-NY-1879-Collier-illus-lg8vo-
illus-1st ed   (5m2)   10.00
THEIRS,LOUIS ADOLPHE-History of the French Revolution-
Phila-1894-5 vols-illus-tissue guards-t.e.g.   (5w9)   22.50
THELLER,E A-Canada in 1837 to 38-Phila-1841-1st ed-2 vols
(4b1)   75.00
THEOBALD,WM H-Defrauding the Govt-NY-1908-508p-cl
(5x7) 5.   (5h2)   7.50
THEOPHILANTHROPIST,THE-By A Society-NY-1810-#1 thru 9(all)-
384p-calf-scarce   (5m3,rub)   85.00
THERE WAS AN OLD WOMAN-who lived in a Shoe & other
Nursery Jingles-Bost-(ca 1890)-DeWolfe,Fiske&Co-lg8vo-32p-
pict bds-liths   (5c8,chip)   4.50
THERESE,M-French Cooking for Amer Kitchens-NY-1929-295p-
photos-bds   (5g9,rub)   5.50
THESIGER,ERNEST-Adventures in Embroidery-(Lond)-1947-4to-
96p-4 col plts-rev ed   (5n7)   5.00
THICKNESSE,PHILIP-A Year's Journey Through France & part of
Spain-Bath-1777-R Cruttwell-fldg plt-5 plts-1 dlb p.music plt-
2 vols in 1-1st ed   (4e1,rebkd)   50.00
THIEL,ALBERT W-Chinese Pottery & Stoneware-Calif-1953-illus-
204p-8vo   (5ww3,water stns,rebnd)   12.50
THIEL,RUDOLF-And there was light-NY-1957-illus (5t4,5j5)   7.50
THIERS,ADOLPHE-Mississippi Bubble,a Memoir of John Law-NY-
1859-338p   (4j4)   7.50
THIESSING,FRANK C,ed-Erni,Elements of Future Painting-St Gall-
1948-Zollikofer-103p-13 col plts-4to-cl   (5m7,fade)   12.75
THIMBLE CLUB,THE-Choice Collection of Cherished Recipes-
Manchester,NH-1937-296p-spiral bnd bds   (5g9)   5.00
THINGS AS THEY ARE-or,Notes of a Traveller Through Some of the
Middle & Northern States-NY-1834-Harper-252p-plts
(5r0,fox)   15.00
THIRD BOOK OF LESSONS-for the Use of Schools-Montr-1850-
Armour&Ramsay-orig cl   (5w8)   12.50

THIRKELL, ANGELA-Coronation Summer-Lond-(1953)-1st ed
(5r9,f,dj)   10.00
--The Duke's Daughter-Lond-(1951)-1st ed   (5r9)   8.50
--Grateful Sparrow & Other Tales-H. Hamilton-n.d.-sm4to-87p-
pic bds-24 col plts-1st ed   (5aa0)   5.00
13 MONTHS IN REBEL ARMY-NY-1862-Barnes&Burr-232p-frontis
(5mm8) 5.   (5m6)   7.50
THIRTY FAVORITE PAINTINGS-(NY)-(1908)-Collier&Son-ob folio-
bds   (5t0,5q0,wn)   10.00
32nd DIVISION(WISC) IN WW-Madison-1920-deluxe lea ed-1st ed
(5b9,soil) 5.   (5z5,vf)   12.50
"THIS QUARTER"-Vol 1,#1-Paris-(1925)-orig prntd wrps-1st ed
(5dd8,unopnd)   100.00
"THIS QUARTER"-Vol 4,#2-Dec 1931-Paris   (5ss9,vg)   25.00
THISELL, A G-Junior Watchmaker-1925-91p-sm8vo   (5bb0)   6.50
--Science of Watch Repairing Simplified-1942-38 plts-208p-8vo
(5bb0)   5.00
THISSELL, G W-Crossing the Plains in '49-Oakland-1903-illus-
pict cl-16mo-1st ed-priv prntd-11 plts-176p
(5hh4, cov sl soil)   45.00
THOBURN, JOS B-Oklahoma-NY-1929-Lewis Pub-t.e.g.-4to-
part lea-4 vols   (4t1, lacks Vol 4)   35.00
THOINOT, L-Medicolegal Aspects of Moral Offenses-Phila-1913-
478p   (5w5)   8.50
THOM, ADAM-The Claims to the Oregon Territory Considered-Lond-
1844-44p   (5n4,f)   35.00
THOM, CHAS-The Electric Telegraph A Manual of Complete
Instruction-Chig-1912-lg8vo-illus   (5b8)   7.50
THOMAJAN, P K-Hades & Jades-NY-1949-ltd to 500c
(4b7, autg)   15.00
THOMANN, G-Amer Beer, Glimpses of its history..manufacture-NY-
1909-104p,(1)   (5w1,ex-libr)   12.50
THOMAS, ABEL-Strictures on religious tests-Phila-1838-disbnd
(5g4,fox)   10.00
THOMAS, ALFRED BARNABY-After Coronado-Norman-1935-map-
1st ed   (5dd1,cov dmgd)   20.00
--The Plains Indians & New Mex, 1751 to 1778-Univ of New Mex-
1940-232p-(Coronado Cuarto Cent Publ, Vol 11)-v scarce
(5h5) 35.   (5dd1,unopnd)   60.00
--Teodoro de Croix & the Northern Frontier of New Spain, 1776 to
1783-Norman-1941-273p-illus-fldg map-1st ed
(5F5,f,dj,pres) 15.   (5L2,dj)   15.00
THOMAS, A R-Records & Sketches of Wm Thomas of Hardwick,
Mass-1891-221p   (5t9)   17.50
THOMAS, ARAD-Pioneer History of Orleans County, NY-Albion-
1871-illus-463p   (4m2)   35.00
THOMAS, ARTHUR-In the Days of Brigham Young-NY-1914-8vo-
cl-109p-1st ed   (5g5)   3.50
THOMAS, BENJ P-Abraham Lincoln-NY-1952-illus-548p
(5t4) 6.   (5p0,5w4)   5.00
--Lincoln's New Salem-Springfld, Ill-1934-illus-128p   (5t7)   4.50
THOMAS, C-Frontier Schoolmaster, Autobiography of a Teacher-
Montr-(1880)-477p   (5t4) 6.50   (5w8)   10.00
THOMAS, C-History of Shefford-Montr-1877-wrps-152p-ports
(5r6, cov tn)   40.00
THOMAS, CHAS G-Johannesburg in Arms 1895 to 1896-Lond-1896-
Smith, Elder-photos-120p   (4t5, lack fly)   12.50
THOMAS, CYRUS-Contributions to History of the Eastern Townships-
Montr-1866   (5w8)   75.00
--Indian Languages of Mexico & Central America-1911-BAE Bul #44-
fldg map-108p-hard cov   (5t0) 5.   (4b2)   10.00
--Work in Mound Exploration of Bureau of Ethnology-1887-15p-
wrps-stpld-BAE, Bul #4   (4b2)   7.50
THOMAS, DAVID-Travels through Western Country, 1816-Auburn-
1819-16mo-hf mor-errata slip-1st ed-box
(5n9) 150.   (4b6,3 lvs tn, loss of words)   100.00
THOMAS, DYLAN-Adventures in the Skin Trade-(NY)-(1955)-
New Directions-1st ed   (4b5,f,dj)   15.00
--A Child's Christmas in Wales-NY-1954-1st ed-bds-New Directions
(4b4,dj) 27.50 (5hh1,vg)   8.50
--Deaths & Entrances-Lond-(1946)-12mo-cl-1st ed (5ss7,vf,dj)   60.00
--The Doctor & the Devils-Lond-(1953)-12mo-cl-1st ed
(5d9,dj) 25.   (5ss9,f,dj)   30.00
--Dylan Thomas Letters to Vernon Watkins-Lond-(1957)-Dent&Faber,
etc-1st ed   (4p1,dj)   17.50
--18 Poems-Lond-n.d.(1942)-4to-green cl-2nd ed
(5ss9) 35.   (5cc9,dj)   37.50
--In Country Sleep-NY-1952-New Directions-bds-1st ed
(4b4,dj) 30.   (4g1,vg)   20.00
--Letters to Vernon Watkins-NY-1957-1st Amer ed   (4b4)   10.00
--New Poems-Norfolk-1943-wrps   (4b4)   35.00

THOMAS, DYLAN   (continued)
--Quite Early One Morning-Lond-(1954)-12mo-cl-port-1st ed-
1st impress-(lacks comma after "sailors" p.3 & 11)
(5ss9,f,dj) 30.   (5cc9,dj)   35.00
--same-NY-1954-New Directions-1st Amer ed-cl
(4b4,dj) 22.50 (5hh1,vf,dj)   15.00
--Twenty six Peoms-Lond-(1949,1950)-JMDent&Sons-lg4to-dec bds-
cl bk-labl-Officina Bodoni in Verona-1st ed-ltd to 140c, box
(5d9)   200.00
--Twenty Years a Growing-Lond-1964-1st ed-bds   (4b4)   10.00
--Under Milk Wood-Lond-(1954)-12mo-cl   (4c2,dj)   67.50
--same-NY-(1954)-New Directions-1st Amer ed (4b5,vg,dj)   12.50
THOMAS, E-The Young Lady's Piece Book-Phila-1829-16mo-
180p-4 hand col plts-Dutch papr over bds-1st ed   (5v0)   12.50
THOMAS, E S-Remin of the last 65 Years-Hartf-1840-2 vols-1st ed
(5yy8,pres,rprd) 20.   (5ee3,f) 35.   (5i3)   25.00
THOMAS, EDITH L R-A Night in Sitka-NY-1948-84p
(4d4,sl wrinkled)   4.50
THOMAS, FRANK A-Wines, Cocktails & Other Drinks-NY-1936-
228p   (5w1)   4.50
THOMAS, G-Earl of Albemarle-Lond-1852-2 vols   (5ii2)   12.50
THOMAS, GABRIEL-Account of Pennsylvania & West New Jersey-
Cleve-1903-reprnt-map-bds-ltd to 250c,nbrd   (4a1)   15.00
--Historical & Geogr Acct of Prov & Country of Penna & of West
NJ, in Amer-Lond-1698-A Baldwin-fldg map-calf-v rare-
(8),55p,(11),34p   (5z7, last lf in facs)   600.00
--same-NY-1848 reprint og above   (5tt8)   10.00
THOMAS, GEO C, JR-Game Fish of the Pacific, Southern Calif
& Mexican-Phila-1930-Lippincott-293p-illus-cl   (5d6)   15.00
--Golf Architecture in Amer-LosAng-1927-4to-cl-illus-1st ed
(5p5)   15.00
--Practical Book of Outdoor Rose Growing-Phila-1917-4to-
90 plts-g.t.-dec cl-col plts-Edition Deluxe   (5p5)   15.00
--Roses for all Amer Climates-NY-(1924)-col frontis-plts (5s7)   5.00
THOMAS, H H-The Rose Book-NY-n.d.-(ca 1926)-287p-8 col plts
(5s7)   7.50
--Garden Flowers as They Grow-Lond-1913-197p-thk8vo-20p col
plts   (5s7)   6.50
THOMAS, HENRY-Life & Adventures of....Western Burglar &
Murderer & Thrilling Narr of Mrs Whipple & Jesse Strang-
Phila-(1848)-(T B Peterson)-illus-141 dbl col p-rare
(4L5,tn, lacks wrps)   25.00
THOMAS, HENRY-Early Spanish Bookbindings-Lond-1939-
100 collotype plts-111p-8vo-bds&lin bkstrp-g.t.   (4c1)   45.00
THOMAS, HENRY-Living Biographies of Famous Novelists-
GardenCty Publ-1943-lg8vo-dec cl-g.t.-305p-20 ports (5aa2) 5.00
THOMAS, HENRY W-History of the Doles Cook Brigade, Army of
Northern Virginia-Atlanta-1903-ports-632p-v scarce
(5h6,rbnd) 60.   (5r7,sp rprd)   40.00
THOMAS, HOWARD-Boys in Blue from the Adirondack Foothills-
Prospect, NY-1960-illus-maps-8vo-cl-297p-1st ed (5t2,f,dj)   5.00
THOMAS, HUGH KERR-Worm Gearing-NY-1916-96p-2nd ed,
rev&enlrgd   (5b8)   5.00
THOMAS IRON CO, THE-1854 to 1904(title)-n.p.-n.d.(1904)-
illus-maps-pkt bklet   (5w5)   10.00
THOMAS, ISAIAH-The Diary of, 1805 to 1828-Vol 2,only-Worcester-
1909-Benj Th Hill, ed   (5t2)   7.50
--History of Printing in America-NY-1874-2 vols-2nd ed
(4g2,sl wn)   75.00
--same-NY-n.d.-2 vols-R8vo-cl   (5p5)   25.00
THOMAS, J MEREDITH-The professor & his daughters-Lond-1883-
3 vols-8vo-orig cl-Remington&Co-1st ed   (5xx6,f)   35.00
THOMAS, JAS A-A Pioneer Tobacco Merchant in the Orient-
Durham, NC-1928-8vo-illus-1st ed-scarce   (5ss5)   17.50
THOMAS, JEAN-Devil's Ditties-Chig-1931-180p-cl-1st ed
(5y0,dj)   18.50
--Sun Shines Bright-NY-1940   (4j4)   4.00
THOMAS, JERRY-The Bar Tender's Guide-NY-1862-12mo-cl-
1st ed   (5gg6)   100.00
--same-NY-(1887)-137p   (5g9)   5.00
--The Bon Vivant's Companion-NY-1928-illus-169p,(5) (5w1)   5.00
THOMAS, JOHN J-Farm Implements & the Principles of Their
Construction & Use-NY-1860-267p-illus-cl   (5t2,stn)   5.00
--The Fruit Culturist-NY-1897-758p-20th ed   (5w1)   8.50
THOMAS, JOS B-Hounds & Hunting-NY-(1937)-4to-233p
(5yy8,dj)   10.00
THOMAS, JULIAN P-The Advantages of Raw Food-NY-1905-
63p-frontis   (5c5)   3.50
THOMAS, L.B.-Thomas Book-1896-627p   (5t9)   50.00
THOMAS, L O-Prov of New Brunswick, Natural Res & Develop-
Ottawa-(1930)-Dept of Int-166p-illus-maps-wrps   (4a8)   5.00
THOMAS, LATELY-Aimee Semple McPherson, the Vanishing Evangelist-
NY-1959-348p-photos-1st ed   (5xx5)   12.00

THOMAS,LEWIS F,ed-Valley of the Mississippi Illus-StLouis-
1948-Drawn & Litho by JC Wild,StLouis,1841,42-rprnt-
ltd to 300c   (5kk5)   45.00

THOMAS,LEWIS H-Struggle for Responsibl Gov in NW Territories
1870 to 97-Tor-1956-maps-276p   (4d2)   15.00

THOMAS,MARCIA A-Memorials of Marshfield & Guide Book-Bost-
1854-12mo-orig cl wrps-108p-1st ed-plts (5t9) 10. (5m6)   12.50

THOMAS,MARY-Dictionary of Embroidery Stitches-Lond-(1935)-
234p   (5n7)   4.50

--Embroidery Book-Lond-(1935)-304p-350 illus   (5n7)   5.00

--same-NY-1936-304p   (5x0)   4.50

THOMAS,NORMAN-The Conscientious Objector in America-NY-
1923-12mo-cl-papr-1st ed of auth's 1st book   (5gg6,f)   15.00

THOMAS,O-Catalogue of Marsupalia & Monotremata in Coll of
Brit Mus (Natural Hist)-Lond-1888-orig cl-401p-28 plts(4 col)-
8vo-scarce   (4p5)   47.50

THOMAS,P-Epics,Myths & Legends of India-Bombay-n.d.-
Taraporevala-134p-4to-illus   (5p0)   7.50

THOMAS,PAUL-Secret Messages,How to Read & Write Them-
NY-1929-8vo-cl-rare   (5p5)   12.50

THOMAS,R-Authentic Acct of Most Remarkable Events-NY-1836-
2 vols in 1-wdcuts-calf   (5m3)   25.00

THOMAS,R-Pictorial History of US of Amer-Hartford-1845-E Strong-
755p-wdcuts-calf   (5tt0,wtrstnd)   10.00

--same-Hartf-1847-755p-illus-lea   (5h9)   20.00

THOMAS,RICHARD H-Penelve or Among Quakers-Lond-1898-
366p-cl   (5h2,sl soil)   7.50

THOMAS,ROBT BAILEY-No 1,the Farmer's Almanac for Year of
Our Lord 1793-Bost-(1792)-12mo-illus-sewn as issued-1st of
the series   (5gg6,sl stn)   500.00

THOMAS,ROBT E-Salt & Water Power & People-Niagara Falls-
1955-109p-illus   (5y2)   4.75

THOMAS,SIDNEY J-Six & One Abroad-Austin-1914-281p (5n4)   6.00

THOMAS,T H-French Portrait Engraving of 17th & 18th Centuries-
Lond-1910-illus-8vo-cl   (4c1,pres)   15.00

THOMAS,THEO G,ed-Liste des Francois & Suisses-NY-1888-
Knickerbocker Pr-sm4to-wrps-map   (5cc6)   22.50

THOMAS,THEODORE MRS-Our Mountain Garden-NY-1904-
Macmillan-illus-1st ed-12mo-212p-cl-g.dec.t.e.g. (5u9,f)   7.50

THOMAS,VALENTINE-John Paul Jones,Father Amer Navy-Cleve-
(1942)-608p   (5s1,dj)   5.00

THOMAS,W-The Seeking-NY-1953-1st ed   (5x2,dj)   15.00

THOMAS,W G-Northern Italian Details-1916-4to-illus-bds in
portfolio   (5L7)   12.50

THOMAS,W H-The Amer Negro-NY-1901   (5x2,lacks fly)   27.50

THOMAS,W H-Running the Blockade-Chig-1883-474p-illus
     (5s1,rprd)   7.50

THOMAS,W R-Life Among the Hills & Mountains of Kentucky-
Louisvlle-(1926)-cl-414p-illus-(Ser #1)   (4L9)   10.00

THOMAS,WM S-Trails & Tramps in Alaska & Newfoundland-NY-
1913-8vo-147 illus-330p   (4g6) 12.50   (5ss1)   7.50

THOMAS'S MASS,CONN,RI NH & VT ALMANACK-withEphemeris
for Year of 1797-prntd at Worcester,Mass for Isaiah Thomas-
48p-tied with string   (5a0,sl stns)   22.50

THOMAS-STANFORD,CHAS-Leaves from a Madeira Garden-Lond-
1909-289p,(20)-illus   (5w3,fox)   6.50

THOMASON,GEO-Catalogue of Pamphlets,Books,Newspapers &
Mss Relating to Civil War,Commonwealth & Restoration...1640
to 61-Lond-1908-2 vols   (4g2)   60.00

THOMASON,JOHN W,JR-and a Few Marines-NY-1943 (5a8)   12.50

--Fix Bayonets-NY-(1926)-not 1st   (5a8)   10.00

--Gone to Texas-NY-1937-illus   (5p9) 6.50   (5a8)   12.50

--Jeb Stuart-NY-1930-8vo-illus-1st ed (5w5) 7.50   (5ss5)   10.00

--Lone Star Preacher-NY-1941-illus-8vo-296p
    (4a7,5p5) 15.   (5x5,dj)   12.50

THOMASSY,R-Geologie pratique de la Louisiane-NewOrl&Paris-
1860-264p-6 plts-4to-g. reliue bk-g.e.   (5L1)   95.00

THOME,J A-Anti Slavery Examiner #7,Emancipation in the West
Indies-NY-1838-fldg map-orig prntd bds-127p,32p
    (5ee3) 20.   (4m4)   25.00

--same-1839-fldg map   (5ee3)   17.50

THOME,JAS A-Emancipation in the West Indies-NY-1838-fldg map
    (5j2,sl dmpstn)   40.00

THOMES,WM H-The Belle of Australia-Bost-1883-illus-1st ed
     (5ee3)   7.50

--On Land & Sea-Bost-1884-351p-illus
   (5s4,ex-libr,wn) 13.50   (5xx5,cov wn)   21.00

--A Slaver's Adventures on Land & Sea-Chig-1885-illus (5x2)   6.00

--The Whalemen's Adventures in the Sandwich Islands & Calif-
Bost-1872-illus-444p-Ocean Life Series   (5t4)   5.00

--same-Chig-(1890)-illus   (4b7,faded)   12.50

THOMPSON,A-Gold Seeking on the Dalton Trail-Bost-1925-
327p-col illus   (4b9,f)   10.00

THOMPSON & WEST-History of Nevada-1958-1000p-280 illus-
reprint offset of 1881 ed   (5xx8)   20.00

THOMPSON,ALICE SMITH-The Drake Family of New Hampshire-
Concord-1962-illus   (5t9) 15.   (5r7,f,ex-libr)   17.50

THOMPSON,ANNIS G-The Greatest Airlift....315th Air Div-
Tokyo-(1954)-photos-cl-464p   (4p2)   18.50

THOMPSON,ARTHUR R-Gold Seeking on the Dalton Trail-Bost-
1925-Little-illus-327p   (5p9)   3.50

THOMPSON,BENJ F-History of Long Island-1839-690p-index-
1st ed   (5zz0)   37.50

--History of Long Island from its Discov & Settlement to Present
Time...wi additions-NY-1918-orig cl-8vo-papr labl-3 vols-
de Luxe ed-600c on hndmade papr-plts (4n5) 75.   (5t9)   50.00

THOMPSON BLUE BOOK ON ADVERTISING,THE-NY,Chig&Bost-
NY-(1904)-8vo-orig limp blu cl-288p-illus   (5m6)   8.50

THOMPSON,C H-Desc John Thomson of Plymouth-1890-272p
     (5t9)   12.50

THOMPSON,C J S-The Mystery & Lure of Perfume-Phila-(1927)-
247p-26 illus   (5n7)   8.50

--The Quacks of Old London-NY-(1928)-Brentano's-cl-illus
    (5b0,dj)   10.00

THOMPSON,CHAS MINER-Independent Vermont-Bost-1942-
illust-1st ed   (5yy6,dj)   6.00

THOMPSON,CHAS WILLIS-Presidents I've Known-Indnpls-1929-
386p   (5p0) 5.   (5t2)   4.50

THOMPSON,CRAIG-Gang Rule in NY-NY-1940-406p-illus (5t4)6.50

--Since Spindletop-Pittsb-1950-110p-illus-4to   (5y2)   4.00

THOMPSON,D G-Mojave DesertRegion Calif-Wash-1929-GPO-
35 plts-wrps-759p   (4n1,sp rub)   25.00

THOMPSON,D G BRINTON-Ruggles of NY-NY-1946-222p-
illus-fldg map   (5w4)   6.50

THOMPSON,D P-History of Town of Montpelier,Vt-Montpelier-
1860-port-312p   (4t2) 10.   (4m2)   15.00

THOMPSON,D P-May Martin,or the Money Diggers-Canandaigua,
NY-1849-16mo-cl&lea-171p   (5t0,bkstrp dmgd)   7.50

THOMPSON,DAVID-History of the Late War between Grt Britain
& US of Amer,etc-Niagara,U C-1832   (5e2,5w8)   125.00

THOMPSON,DAVID-Narrative,1784 to 1812-Tor-1962-Champlain
Soc-new ed-map-ltd ed-410p   (5s6,mint)   125.00

THOMPSON,DAVID G-The Mohave Desert Region,Calif-Wash-
1929-GPO-759p-orig wrps   (5x5)   25.00

THOMPSON,DOROTHY-Once on Christmas-Lond,NY&Tor-(1939)-
Oxford Univ Pr-8vo-bds-(48p)-8th printing   (5p1,dj)   2.50

THOMPSON,E B-American Daughter-1946-Univ Chicago-1st ed
    (5x2,dj)   10.00

THOMPSON,ED PORTER-A Young People's History of Kentucky-
StLouis-1897-A R Fleming-344p-frontis-12mo-1 plt-fldg map
    (5p1,cov wtrstnd)   5.00

THOMPSON,ERNEST SETON-Wild Animals I Have Known-NY-
1898-illus-1st ed,1st issue-ex rare-(last paragr pg 265 "Angel
whispered don't go" omitted)   (4c3,f,A Swann copy)   115.00

--same-NY-1899-358p,4p-illus   (5t7)   7.50

THOMPSON,F M-History of Greenfield Shiretown of Franklin Co,
Mass 1682 to 1900-2 vols-1904-with History of Greenfield 1900
to 29 by L C Kellogg-1931-3 vols   (4m4)   42.50

THOMPSON,FRANCIS-Poems-Lond-1893-81p-1st ed-500c,ltd-
dec bds-81p   (5dd0,cl sl wn) 12.50   (5r9)   15.00

--Sister Songs-Lond-1895-65p-1st ed-frontis
   (5dd0,sl stn) 10.   (5r9,f)   7.50

--Works-Lond-(1913)-Burns&Oates Ltd-3 vols-red lea-later issue
    (5ss9,vg)   40.00

THOMPSON,GEO-A Description of Royal Palace & Monastery of
St Laurence Called The Escurial & of Chapel Royal of Pantheon-
Lond-1760-Dryden Leach-lg4to-lea-359p-12 plts (5m5,v wn)150.00

THOMPSON,GEO (CHARLES)-View of Holy Land-Wheeling-1850-
495p-errata-lea   (5h7,scuf)   5.00

THOMPSON,GEO-Prison Life & Reflections-Oberlin-1847-orig cl-
417p-1st ed-scarce   (4m2,sl wn)   30.00

--same-Hartf-1849-3 pts in 1 vol-3rd ed   (5q8)   9.50

--same-Hartf-1851-frontis   (5yy8,sl wn)   7.50

--same-Hartf-1853-377p   (5xx8)   6.00

--Africa in a Nutshell-Oberlin-1886-3rd ed-priv prnt-port-fldg map-
12mo   (4a9,vg)   10.00

THOMPSON,GRACE E-Prince of Scandal-1931-illus (5L7)   4.50

THOMPSON,H-YATES,Illustrations of 100 Manuscripts-Lond-
1907 to 18-Chiswick Pr-folio-buck-g.t.-7 vols-deLuxe ed-
ltd to 100 sets   (4n5,pres)   350.00

THOMPSON,H T-Ousting the Carpetbagger from SoCarolina-
Columbia-1927-RLBryan Co-illus   (5x2)   45.00

THOMPSON,HAROLD W-Body,Boots & Britches-Phila-1940-
529p-illus   (5t7) 5.   (5g4) 6.   (5c3)   5.50

THOMPSON,MRS HARRY-Clayton,the Friendly Town in Union
Co,New Mex-(Denver,1950)-illus-170p-stiff wrps-ltd ed,
nbrd,autg   (5dd9)   10.00

THOMPSON,HENRY-Food & Feeding-Lond-1891-222p-7th ed
         (4g9,sl soil,hng crack)   7.50

THOMPSON,HOLLAND-New South-NewHav-1919-250p-cl-
Chron of Amer Ser   (5h1,f,dj)   5.00

THOMPSON,J ERIC-Civilization of the Mayas-Chig-1927-
Field Mus of Natl Hist-110p-map-14 plts-wrps-1st ed (5dd4)   6.50
--same-Chig-(1958)-6th ed   (5dd4)   4.00

THOMPSON,J M-Leaders of French Revolution-NY-1929-ports
         (4a1)   10.00

THOMPSON,J P-The Sergeant's Memorial by His Father-NY-
1863-242p   (5j6)   4.50

THOMPSON,J W-Authentic History of the Douglass Monument-
NY-1903-Rochester Herald Pr-illus   (5x2)   50.00

THOMPSON,JAMES-The City of Dreadful Night-Portland-1892-
Mosher Pr-ltd to 400c,nbrd   (4b4)   30.00

THOMPSON,JAS-Walt Whitman the Man & the Poet-Lond-1910-
105p-orig stiff wrps   (5m1,unopnd)   7.50

THOMPSON,JAS-Complete Treatise on the Mensuration of Timber-
Troy,(NY)-1805-(Wright,Wilbur&Stockwell)-16mo-lea-illus-
87p   (5t7,wn)   6.50

THOMPSON,JAS H-History of County of Highland in State of Ohio-
Hillsboro-1878-132p-wrps   (5jj9) 20.   (5i0)   27.50

THOMPSON,JAS WESTFALL-Economic & Social History of Middle
Ages-NY&Lond-(1928)-2 vols   (5q0)   12.50
--Feudal Germany-Chig-(1928)-fldg map-710p   (5q0)   10.00
--History of Historical Writing-NY-1942-2 vols-frontis (5q0)   17.50
--Middle Ages,300 to 1500-NY-1931-2 vols   (5xx7)   15.00

THOMPSON,JEAN-Over Indian & Animal Trails-NY-(1918)-
illus-263p   (4b2)   6.00

THOMPSON,JEANETTE R-Hist of Stratford 1772 to 1925-(New Hamp)-
Pub by town-1925-525p-illus   (5e8) 19.75   (4t2)   20.00

THOMPSON,JOHN-Life of,a Fugitive Slave-written by himself-
Worcester-1856-143p   (5s2)   12.50

THOMPSON,JOHN H-Jubilee History of Thorold Township & Town-
Thorold-1897-8p,212p,77p-plts-ports   (5aa0)   20.00

THOMPSON,JOS P-The Right & Necessity of Inflicting Punishment
of Death for Murder-NewHav-1842-8vo-orig wrps-54p-1st ed
        (5ss5)   8.50
--A Short History of Charlestown for Past 44 Years-Charlestown-1848-
8vo-orig wrps-71p-1st ed   (5ss5)   7.50

THOMPSON,KAY-Eloise-NY-1955-Simon&Schuster-4to-64p-
drwngs by Hilary Knight-1st ed   (5p1,dj)   25.00
--Eloise at Christmastime-NY-(1958)-4to-(47p)-pict bds-drwngs by
Hilary Knight-1st ed-Random   (5p1,dj)   7.50
--Eloise in Paris-NY-1957-Simon&Schuster-4to-(64p)-drwngs by
Hilary Knight-pict bds-1st ed   (5p1,dj)   7.50

THOMPSON,MAURICE-Alice of Old Vincennes-Indnpls-1900-
Bowen,Merrill-419p-illus-1st ed-pict cl-1st issue (5ee3,f)   17.50
--same-Indiana-(1900)-Bowen,Merrill-419p-1st ed,2nd issue
        (5ee3) 3.50   (5x4)   5.00
--Hoosier Mosaics-NY-1875-16mo-cl-1st ed of auth's 1st book
        (5gg6)   25.00
--Stories of the Cherokee Hills-Bost-1898-Houghton-1st ed
        (5m2,sl soil)   7.50

THOMPSON,R A-Conquest of Calif-SantaRosa-1896-Sonoma
Democrat Publ Co-33p-wrps-v scarce
   (5tt0,close trim) 12.50 (5dd1) 45. (5h4,f)   30.00
--The Russian Settlement in Calif,Fort Ross-Oakland-1951-R8vo-
60p-illus-Calif Relations Series,27   (5dd4)   15.00

THOMPSON,R W-Wild Animal Man-NY-1934-Morrow-illus(5p7) 4.50

THOMPSON,RALPH-American Literary Annuals & Gift Books 1825
to 65-NY-1936-183p   (5j4) 12.50   (4g2)   25.00

THOMPSON,RICHARD W-Recoll of 16 Presidents from Washington
to Lincoln-Indnpls-1894-illus-2 vols   (4j4)   12.50

THOMPSON,ROBT-The Gardener's Assistant,Practical & Scientific-
Lond-(ca 1859)-774p-col plts-thk4to   (4gQ,rbnd)   22.50

THOMPSON,ROBT A-Historical Atlas Map of Sonoma Co-Oakland-
1877-ThosH Thompson&Co-102p-maps-liths-cl lea bkstrp
        (5tt0)   150.00

THOMPSON,ROBT J-England & Germany in the War-Bost-c1915
        (5x7)   5.00

THOMPSON,ROBT LUTHER-Wiring a Continent-Princeton-1947-
544p-illus-maps-fldg chart   (5dd1,dj) 8.50 (5w4,dj)   10.00

THOMPSON,ROBT MEANS-Confidential Correspondence of Gustavus
Vasa Fox-1918-DeVinne Pr-2 vols-4to-bds-vel bk-ltd to 1200c,
nbrd   (5h4,f)   37.50
--same-NY-1920-vel-2 vols-ltd to 1200c   (5j6)   12.50

THOMPSON,RUTH-Eating Around San Francisco-SanFran-(1937)-
Sutton House-296p   (4g9,sp fade)   7.50

THOMPSON,S-Remin of a Canadian Pioneer for the Last 50 Years-
Tor-1884-cl   (5w8,rbnd)   25.00

THOMPSON,LIEUT S D-Recollections with the 3rd Iowa Reg-Cinn-
1864-12mo-396p-cl (5m8,rbkd) 15. (5u3,lacks bkstrp)   12.50

THOMPSON,S MILLETT-13th Reg of NH Vol Inf in War of Rebel-
Bost-1888-Houghton,Miff-717p-illus-maps   (5mm8)   5.00

THOMPSON,SILVANUS P-Dynamo Electric Machinery,a Manual-
Lond&NY-1886-527p-illus-2nd ed,enlrgd&rev-cl (5b8,rprd)   12.50

THOMPSON,SLASON-Cost Capitalization & Estimated Value of
Amer Railways-Chig-1908-175p-cl-3rd ed   (5h0)   3.50
--Eugene Field-NY-1901-2 vols-illus-g.t.-1st ed
        (5mm2,5ee3,vf)   10.00
--Short History of American Railways-Chig-1925-2nd ed-rev-
473p-illus   (4e4)   10.00

THOMPSON,STITH,ed-Round the Levee-Austin-1935-cl-
1st Dobie ed-Folklore Soc Vol 1   (4a5)   12.50
--Tales of the NoAmerican Indians-Cambr-1929-386p-fldg map-
1st ed-scarce   (5L2,f,dj)   22.50

THOMPSON,W H-Sicily & Its Inhabitants-Lond-1813-3 views-
fldg frontis-4to-hf calf   (4b6,reprd,ex-libr)   75.00

THOMPSON,WADDY-Recollections of Mexico-NY-1846-
Wiley&Putnam-304p-ads (5qq8,vf) 17.50 (5kk6,rbnd)   25.00

THOMPSON,WALLACE-The Mexican mind-Bost-1922-Little,Brown-
303p   (5v6)   5.00
--The People of Mexico-NY-(1921)-Harper-428p (5x0,pres)   4.00
--Rainbow Countries of Central Amer-NY-(1926)-8vo-cl-283p-illus
        (5t2)   5.00
--Trading with Mexico-NY-1921-Dodd,Mead-8vo-cl (4a3)   7.50

THOMPSON,WM-Remin of a Pioneer-SanFran-1912-187p-illus
   (5r0) 10. (5dd1) 15. (5x5)   17.50

THOMPSON,WINFIELD M-The Lawson History of the America's Cup-
Bost-1902-4to-402p-col plts-t.e.g.-ltd to 3,000c,nbrd
        (5w0,libr labl)   22.50

THOMPSON,ZADOCK-Geography & history of lower Canada-
Walton&Gaylord,publ-Stanstead&Sherbrooke,L C-1835-
116p-bds   (5t7,lacks hf of map,wn)   15.00
--The Green Mountain Repository for the Year 1832-Burlington,Vt-
1832-EdwSmith-12mo-cl-run of 12 issues-bnd (5i0,rbnd)   75.00
--Guide to Lake George,Lake Champlain,Montreal & Quebec-
Burlington-1845-24mo-fldg map-stiff prntd wrps (5g8,f)   25.00
--same-Burlington,(Vt)-1851-fldg map-24mo-stiff prntd wrps-
2nd ed,corr&enlrgd   (5g4) 15. (5t4)   17.50
--History of the State of Vermont from its Earliest Settlement thru
1832-Burlington-1833-252p-hf lea-bds-1st ed (5L3,fox)   20.00
--History of Vt,Natural,Civil,& Statistical-Burlington-1842-
3 pts-map   (5q0) 20. (5ee3)   15.00
--Natural History of Vt,An Address,Boston Soc of Natural Hist,
Jun 1850-Burlington-1850-CGoodrich-8vo-32p-qtr cl
        (5L1,rbnd)   10.00

THOMS,H-Chapters in Amer Obstetrics-1933   (5L7)   3.50

THOMS,WM J,ed-A Collection of Early Prose Romances-Lond-
1828-WmPickering-3/4 lea-3 vols   (5hh1)   25.00

THOMSON,ALEX,MD,ed-Letters of a Traveller,on the Various
Countries of Europe,Asia & Africa-Lond-1798-JasWallis-8vo-
calf-524p   (5j5)   27.50

THOMSON,ALLEN W-The Horses of Windsor County(Vt) & History
of Windsor Co Fair-Bost-1893-8vo-wrps-56p   (5t0)   7.50

THOMSON,BASIL-The Story of Scotland Yard-NY-1936-
Liter Gld-347p   (5p9)   5.00

THOMSON,SIR C WYVILLE-Report on Scientific Results of Voyage
of HMS Challenger,1873 to 76-Lond-1895,1882-thk lg4to-cl-
plus Narrative,Vol 2-3 vols   (4b6)   500.00

THOMSON,D CROAL,ed-50 Years of Art 1849 to 1899-Lond-1900-
folio-illus-cl-376p-a.e.g.   (5t7)   15.00

THOMSON,DAVID-Handy Book of Fruit Culture Under Glass-
Lond-1881-321p,(37)   (5w1)   8.50

THOMSON,G M-Wild Life in New Zealand,Pt 1,Mammalia-
Wellington,NZ-1921-NZ Bd Sci & Art,Man#2-cl-8vo-112p-
v scarce   (4p5)   12.00

THOMSON,GEO-Anatomy of Human Bones With Acct of Muscular
Motion & Circulation of Blood,also of Digestion & Nutrition-
Lond-1734-for R Ware-8vo-calf-15 fldg plts-1st ed
        (4j5,f,sl reprd)   145.00

THOMSON,GEO-Prison Life & Reflections-Dayton-1860-cl-
377p-3 pts in 1 vol (as issued)   (4h7,cor wn)   8.50

THOMSON,GLADYS SCOTT-Life in a Noble Household-Lond-
(1937)-406p-7 plts   (5w7)   8.50
--A Pioneer Family-Lond-1953-frontis-1st ed (5q8,dj)   6.00

THOMSON,H B,publ-As We See 'Em-KansCty,Mo-c1905-412p
        (5hh3)   12.50

THOMSON,H C-China & The Powers-Lond-1902-Longmans,Green-
30 illus-285p-2 maps   (5x9)   4.00

THOMSON,HUGH-Quality Street,a Comedy in 4 Acts-Lond-
Hodder&Stoughton-n.d.-198p-t4to-ltd to 1000c-illus,autg-
parch   (5x0)   25.00
THOMSON,IGNATIUS-Generaology of John Thomson-1841-24mo-
84p   (5L3) 20.   (5t9)   17.50
--The Patriot's Monitor for Vermont...Adapted For the Use of
Schools-Randolph(Vt)-1810-12mo-orig bds-Wright 1810
(5n2,back def)   45.00
THOMSON,J-Through Masai Land-Lond-1887-illus (5x2,rbnd) 15.00
--Straits of Malacca,Indo China & China-NY-1875-546p-illus
(5ii2)   8.50
THOMSON,J ARTHUR-Outline of Science-NY-1922-cl-4 vols-
illus-4to   (5cc1,f)   9.50
THOMSON,REV J B-Jos Thomson,African Explorer-Lond-1901-
12mo-358p-photos   (4a6)   10.00
THOMSON,JAS-The City of Dreadful Night & Other Poems-Lond-
1880-12mo-cl-auth's 1st book-1st ed (4c2,crack,lacks errata) 22.50
--Poetical Works,with Life & Notes-Edinb-1853-t8vo-3/4 pink mor-
g.top by Merrell-g.sp   (5t5,f,f bndg) 20.00
--The Seasons-Lond-1730-4to-calf-1st collected ed
(4c2,crack) 27.50   (5x3) 90.   (5ss9)   60.00
--same-Lond-1744-243p-illus-orig lea-tooled-a.e.g.
(5m4,sl loose)   20.00
--same-Lond-1805-JWallis-calf-286p,(6)p-9 engr by Bewick
(5aa0,sl rub)   40.00
--same-Chiswick-1820-211p-a.e.g.-raised bands (5w5) 12.50
--same-Lond-1927-Noneusch Pr-sm4to-5 col plts-198p-ltd to 1500c
(5nn2) 15.   (5c9,mint)   25.00
THOMSON,SAM'L-A Narr of the Life & Medical Discoveries of-
Columbus,O-1835-253p-16mo-calf   (5w3,wtrstnd) 13.50
--New Guide to Health-Bost-1835-12mo-228p,168p
(5w3,hng split)   35.00
THOMSON,SPENCER-Wild Flowers-Lond-n.d.(ca 1887)-322p-
col illus-dec cov   (5s7,2 lvs loose) 8.50
THOMSON,WM-Great Cats I Have Met-Bost-1896-12mo-174p-
illus   (4a6)   3.50
THOMSON,WM-A Practical Treatise on the Cultivation of the
Grape Vine-Lond-1890-105p,32p-illus   (5w1)   7.50
THOMSONIAN RECORDER-Columbus-416p-cl bkd bds-Oct 12,1833
to Sept 27,1834   (5jj9)   17.50
THOMSONIAN SCOUT-Burlington,Vt-(1842)-Vol 1-104p-
orig bds   (5t4)   20.00
THONNER,F-Flowering Plants of Africa-Lond-1915-cl-8vo-
fldg map-150 plts-1st ed   (5z9)   30.00
THORBURN,ARCHIBALD-Naturalist's Sketch Book-Lond-1919-
cl-lg4to-60 plts-1st ed   (5z9)   35.00
THORBURN,GRANT-40 Years' Residence in Amer-Bost-1834-
Russell,Odiorne&Metcalf-264p-1st ed
(5qq8,ex-libr) 20.   (5w3,sp broke,fox)   18.50
--Sketches from the Notebook of Laurie Todd-NY-1847-32p-
wrps-port-front wrps   (5w3,wrp tn,autg) 15.00
THOREAU,HENRY D-Cape Cod-Bost-1865-1st ed(4g2,reprd) 50.00
--same-Bost-1896-illus-2 vols   (5m8) 15.   (5tt5,f) 30.00
--same-Bost-1899-Houghton,Miff-2 vols   (5ss9,lacks flys) 20.00
--same-Bost-1914-Riverside Pr-illus (5ee3) 2.50 (5t2) 3.00
--same-NY-1951-300p-illus   (5h9,f,dj)   6.50
--Concord Saunterer-Middlebury-1940-12mo-dec bds (4c1) 7.50
--Early Spring in Mass-Bost-1881-Houghton,Miff-1st ed
(4b5,sl cov spots)   40.00
--Excursions-Bost-1863-Ticknor&Fields-1st ed
(4b1,sl wn) 37.50   (5dd3,f)   2.50
--same-Bost-1888-319p   (4g2)   75.00
--Letters to Various Persons-Bost-1865-Ticknor&Fields-1st ed
(4g2)   50.00
--The Maine Woods-Bost-1864-1st ed
(4b4,sl chip) 22.50   (4g2,box)   75.00
--same-Bost-1898-442p-cl-Vol 3 of "Riverside Edition" (5t0) 3.75
--Men of Concord & some others-Bost-1936-FrancisH Allen,ed-
8vo-cl-255p-10 col plts (4b5,mint,dj) 20. (5t2,f,dj) 8.50
--Night & Moonlight-NY-1921-HubertRBrown-16mo-bds-24p-
papr labl-Rudge,prntr-(Bruce Rogers)-ltd to 40c (5j5) 15.00
--Sir Walter Raleigh-Bost-1905-Bibliophile Soc-3/4 lea-boxed-
ltd to 489c,1st ed   (5hh1,vg)   20.00
--The Transmigration of the 7 Brahmans-NY-1932-Arthur Christy,ed-
Rudge-30p-ltd to 1200c   (5p7)   6.50
--Walden or Life in the Woods-Bost-1854-Ticknor&Fields-1st ed,
wi April Advts   (4g2,f,mor box) 275.00
--same-Bost-1854-Ticknor&Fields-1st ed,wi May Advts
(4g2,sl stn)   175.00
--same-Chig-1930-Lakeside Pr-intro by Raymond Adams-lg8vo-
pattrnd bds-cl bk-355p-ltd to 1000c   (5j5,box)   50.00
--same-NY-(1946)-391p-illus-Modern Library ed (5q0,dj) 5.00

THOREAU,HENRY D (continued)
--A Week On the Concord & Merrimack Rivers-Bost&Cambr-1849-
Ticknor&Fields-orig cl-12mo-1st ed-auth's 1st book
(4c4,wn,hng tn,box) 395.   (5gg6,f) 1,000.00
--The Writings of...Walden edit-Bost-1906-Houghton,Miff-cl-
20 vols   (5w0,wn)   100.00
--Writings-Bost-1906-Houghton,Miff-plts in col & tint-3 qtr green
crushed mor-g.over mrbld bds-Manuscript Edition-ltd to 600c,
nbrd,wi lf of a Thoreau ms bnd in Vol 1 (5b0,f bndg,f) 850.00
--A Yankee in Canada,with Anti Salvery & Reform Papers-Bost-
1866-lea bk-1st ed   (5m1,crack)   12.50
THOREK,MAX-A Surgeon's World-Phila&NY-(1943)-410p
(5t7,dj,libr stmp)   5.00
THORINGTON,J M-Glittering Mountains of Canada,Old Trails
of Rockies-Phila-1925-illus-maps-310p-ltd to 1500c (4p8) 12.50
--The Purcell Range of Brit Columbia-NY-1946-152p-cl-pkt map-
illus-Amer Alpine Club   (5d7)   15.00
--Survey of Early Amer Ascents in Alps in 19th Century-(NY)-1943-
83p-illus-cl-Amer Alpine Club   (5d7)   10.00
THORN,C JORDAN-Handbook of Old Pottery & Porcelain Marks-
NY-(1947)-Tudor-176p   (5x0) 4.   (5w7)   3.95
THORN,J C-3 Years a Prisoner in Germany-(Vanc)-1919-151p-plts
(5aa0)   4.00
THORNBER,JOHN JAS-The Fantastic Clan-NY-1932-194p-col plts-
1st ed   (5s7) 8.50   (5dd1)   10.00
THORNBOROUGH,LAURA-The Great Smoky Mountains-NY-
(1938)-photos   (5h6)   4.00
THORNBURY,D L-Calif's Redwood Wonderland,Humboldt Co-
(SanFran,1923)-R8vo-174p-buck-photos-maps-1st ed (5r8) 18.00
THORNBURY,WALTER-The Buccaneers,or Monarchs of the Main-
Lond-1858-GRoutledge-8 illus-8vo-orig cl-1st ed (4c4,sl tn,wn)
(4d4,sl tn,wn)   47.50
--Old & New London-Lond-n.d.-new ed-6 vols-illus (5ii3) 32.50
--The Fables of Jean de La Fontaine-Phila,Chig,StL&Atlanta-
(n.d.)-4to-733p-illus by Gus Dore-a.e.g.-(The Art Edition)
(5t7)   7.50
THORNDIKE,ASHLEY H-English Comedy-NY-1929-8vo-cl-635p
(5t0)   5.00
THORNDIKE,CHUCK-The Business of Cartooning-NY-1939-55p-
wrps-mimeo   (4t7)   15.00
THORNDIKE,LYNN-History of Magic & Experimental Science-NY-
1923-Vols 1&2-1st ed   (4b6)   17.50
--Science & Thought in the 15th Century-NY-1929-Columbia Univ
Pr-387p   (5p9)   6.50
THORNDIKE,R S,ed-Sherman Letters-NY-1894-398p-ports-t.e.g.
(4j4) 5.   (5s9) 7.50   (5L3)   5.00
THORNDIKE,RUSSELL-The Tragedy of Mr Punch-Lond-(1923)-
illus in col by Arthur Watts-4to   (5j2,vg)   15.00
THORNDIKE,THADDEUS-Life & Exploits of the Daring Frank &
Jesse James-Balt-c1909-185p-orig pict wrps-Oppenheimer
(5w5)   7.50
THORNE,ATWOOD-Pink Lustre Pottery-Lond-1926-38p-2 plts
(5xx7)   15.00
THORNE,EDW-Decorative Draperies & Upholstery-GrandRapds-
1929-4to-277p-74 col illus   (5w7)   10.00
THORNE,TERESA A-Kate Comerford or Sketches of Garrison Life-
Phila-1881-beveled bds (4a9,sl wn) 22.50 (5mm2)   25.00
THORNTHWAITE,C WARREN-Climate & Accelerated Erosion
in Arid & Semi Arid SW-Wash-1942-illus-maps-USDA Tech
Bull #808-wrps   (4a5)   7.50
THORNTON,COL-Sporting Tour thru Various Parts of France in
the Year 1802-Lond-1806-Longmans-4to-hf lea-2 vols (5x0) 25.00
THORNTON,J QUINN-The Calif Tragedy-(Oakland,1945)-161p-
pict cl-illus-errata slip-Gillick Pr-1500c prntd
(5r0,dj) 10.   (5dd1,publ autg)   20.00
--Oregon & Calif in 1848,with Appendix Incl...Gold Mines of
Calif,etc-NY-1849-col fldg map-orig cl-12 plts-2 vols-1st ed
(4n4,f)   150.00
THORNTON,JOHN WINGATE-Colonial Schemes of Popham &
Gorges-Bost-1863-Blanch-thn8vo-buck-20p (5j5,rbnd)   12.50
--Historical Relation of New Engl to the English Commonwealth-
(Bost)-1874-105p   (5t7,pres)   10.00
--Pulpit of the Amer Revolution-Bost-1860-8vo-illus-ports-
1st ed   (5m6,pres,fade) 17.50
THORNTON,JOS F-The Annals of A Family-(n.p.-n.d.)-(ca 1941)-
149p-illus   (5r0)   10.00
THORNTON,R J-Politician's Creed-1799-3 vols in 1-buck
(5L7,rbnd)   17.50
THORNTON,RICH,ed-Recognition of Robert Frost,25th anniv-
NY-(1937)-Holt&Co (5t7) 7.50 (5mm1,dj) 12.50 (5ss9) 15.00
THORNTON,RICH H-An American Glossary-Lond-1912-2 vols
(5mm2)   15.00
--same-Phila-1912-lg8vo-cl-2 vols   (5t2)   12.50

THORNTON,ROBT JOHN-New Illus of Sexual System of Carolus
  von Linnaeus...& Temple of Flora-Lond-(1799)-1807-atlas
  folio-hf mor-g.e.-1st ed   (5z9,f) 4,750.00
--Temple of Flora-Lond-1812-Lottery Edition-mor (5z9,f) 650.00
--Thornton's Temple of Flora with plates-Lond-1951-20p-eleph-
  12 col,24 blk&wh plts (5z9,ltd,autg) 50. (5w3) 35.00
THORNTON,THOS-Sporting Tour Through Northern Parts of
  England-Lond-1804-1st ed-4to-calf-16 plts-g. (5s6) 65.00
THORNTON,WILLIS-The Country Doctor-Dionne quintuplets-
  NY-(c1936)-Grosset&Dunlap-8vo-frontis-cl bkd pict bds-
  (131p)-20th Cent Fox-Jean Hersholt (5p1) 15.00
--The Nine Lives of Citizen Train-NY-c1948-327p-illus (5w4,dj) 6.50
THORNWELL,EMILY-The Lady's Guide to Perfect Gentility-NY-
  1856-226p-frontis   (5w7,fade,chip) 4.50
--same-NY-1858-226p   (5ii2) 6.50
THORNWELL,J H-The state of the country,an article republished
  from Southern Presby Review-Columbia-1861-32p-stitchd-
  3rd ed   (5g8) 25.00
THORNWELL,JAS H-Our Danger & Our Duty-Richmond-n.d.-
  16p-Soldiers' Tract Assoc   (5j6) 15.00
THOROWGOOD,THOS-Jews in America,or Probabilities etc-Lond-
  1660-Henry Brome-sm4to-72 lvs-qtr mor (5L1,f,rbnd) 500.00
THORP,JAS-Geography of the Soils of China-Nanking-1936-
  552p   (5x9,pres) 8.50
THORP,JOS-Early Days in the West,along the Missouri 100 Years
  Ago-(Liberty,1924)-95p-wrps-scarce (5dd1) 12.50
THORP,L ASHTON-Manchester of Yesterday-Manchester-c1939-
  Granite State Pr-8vo-cl-561p-illus (4t1) 20.00
THORP,N H-Story of the SoWestern Cowboy,Pardner of the Wind-
  Caldwell-1945-301p plus index-illus-2nd prntg (5L2,dj) 6.00
--same-1st ed-scarce in the 1st (5L2,fade) 17.50
--Tales of the Chuck Wagon-SantaFe-(1926)-123p-wrps
        (5dd1) 6.50 (5g2) 7.50
THORP,N HOWARD-Pardner of the Wind-Caldwell-1945-illus-
  cl-309p   (4p2,dj) 15.00
THORP,RAYMOND-Bowie Knife-(Albuqu)-1948-12mo-184p-
  illus-1st ed (5dd1,dj) 10. (5dd9) 12.50
--Spirit Gun of the West-Glendale-1957-Clark-cl-266p-1st ed
       (5dd1,mint,dj) 10.00
THORP,WILLARD-Lost Tradition of Amer Letters-Phila-1945-
  for Philobiblon Club-8vo-bds-cl bkstrp (4c1) 6.00
THORPE,CARLYLE-A Journey to the Walnut Sections of Europe
  & Asia-LosAng-1923-101p-photos-bds (5s7) 4.50
THORPE,CORA W-In the Path of the Trade Winds-NY-1924-
  198p   (5ss1) 6.00
THORPE,F N,ed-Benj Franklin & Univ of Penna-Wash-1893-illus-
  450p-scarce   (4m4,rebnd) 15.00
THORPE,FRANCIS NEWTON-Constitutional Hist of Amer People,
  1776 to 1850-NY-1898-2 vols-maps-1st ed (4b7) 15.00
--The Divining Rod-Bost-1905-Little,Brown-8vo-pic cl (5b2,f,dj) 5.00
--Federal & State Constitutions,Colonial Charters...-Wash-1909-
  7 vols   (5p0) 30. (5h1) 35. (5r4) 50.00
THORPE,JAS-Bibliography of the Writings of Geo Lyman Kittredge-
  1948-Harvard-125p   (5j4,ex-libr) 6.50
THORPE,LOUISA-Bonbons & Simple Sugar Sweets-Lond-1921-
  81p-bds   (5g9,ex-libr) 2.50
THORPE,ROSA HARTWICK-Curfew Must Not Ring Tonight-
  Bost&NY-1883-1st ed-1st issue di dated t.p. &ad at end
       (5xx8,sl rub) 15.00
THORPE,T B-Life & Public Services of Gen Z Taylor-NY-1846-
  H Long-56p-sewn   (5n4) 13.50
THORPE,W A-English & Irish Glass-Lond-(1927)-60 photos-35p-
  5 col plts   (5w1) 35.00
THORPE,WALTER-Hist of Wallingford,Vermont-1911-222p-illus
       (5t9) 10.00
THORSON,ALICE OTILLIA-Tribe of Pezhekee-Minnpls-1901-
  illus-232p   (4b2,sl wn) 4.00
THOUGHTS IN THE CLOISTER & THE CROWD-Lond-1835-12mo-
  orig bds-papr labl-1st ed of A Helps'1st book (5gg6) 15.00
THOUGHTS ON DESTINY OF MAN-(Harmony)-1824-96p-
  blu wrps-by Harmony Soc   (5h7) 225.00
THOULESS,ROBT H-Straight & Crooked Thinking-NY-(1932)-
  Simon&Schuster-261p   (5p7) 3.50
THOUSAND ISLANDS-Sunlight Pictures of the-NY-c1895-
  photos by McIntyre-horiz 8vo-67p plts-tip in col fldg map
       (5w5) 6.50
THOUSAND ISLANDS,RIVER ST LAWRENCE-Over 100 illus-
  GrandRapds,Mich-(ca 1899)-obl 8vo-stiff prntd wrps (5w8) 10.00

THRALL,HOMER S-People's Illus Almanac,Texas Handbook &
  Immigrants Guide-StLouis-1879-201p-wrps-v rare (4a5) 185.00
--Pictorial History of Texas-StLouis-1879-3rd ed-calf-fldg map
       (4c7,rbnd) 85.00
--same-StLouis-1883-888p-rev&enlrgd (4a5) 75.00
THREE ACRES ENOUGH-(1864)-255p (5e8) 3.75
THREE BEARS,THE-(ca 1870s)-McLoughlin,publ-12mo-col illus
  each pg   (5v2,f) 15.00
THREE CHILDREN SLIDING ON THE ICE-Lond&Sydney-(ca 1889)-
  24mo-8 lvs-cl bkd bds-7 illus incl centerfld (5p1,rub) 7.50
THREE EXPERIMENTS OF LIVING-Bost-1837-WmSDamrell-12mo-
  orig yellow wrps-1st ed   (5x1,f) 100.00
THREE LITTLE CROWS-c1870-McLoughlin Bros-lg8vo-6 lvs prntd
  one side   (5v0) 17.50
THREE LITTLE KITTENS-NY-(ca 1877)-narr4to-6 lvs & 8 hand col
  plts(incl inside wrps)-sewn-McLoughlin Bros (4c3) 20.00
THREE NEW MEXICO CHRONICLES-Albuqu-1942-facs-cl&bds-
  557c prntd for Quivira Soc   (5g2) 85.00
THREE YEARS BEHIND THE GUNS-NY-1908-293p-photos-dec cov-
  by L G T   (5s1) 4.00
THREE YEARS IN CHILE-NY-1863-Follett,Foster-12mo-cl (4a3) 20.00
THREE YEARS IN A MAN TRAP-Phila-1872-Stoddart-364p-
  illus-1st ed-(T S Arthur) (5x4,wn) 10.00
THREE YEARS IN THE PACIFIC-Phila-1834-441p-orig cl bk&bds-
  (WSWRuschenberger)   (5m4) 85.00
304th ENGINEER REGIMENT-The Official History of,79th Div,USA-
  Phila-1920-415p-illus-maps   (5m2) 12.50
347th MACHINE GUN BATTALION-History of-Oakland-n.d.-
  Horwenski Co-(1919?)-140p-cl-frontis-plts-Smith 1386 (5r0) 7.50
THRICE THROUGH THE FURNACE-A Tale of Times of the Iron
  Hoof-Pawtucket,RI-1852   (5x2) 27.50
THRILLING ADVENTURES IN THE FOREST & FRONTIER-NY-n.d.-
  295p-illus   (5s4,pres) 7.50
THRILLING NARRATIVE OF ADVENTURES,SUFFERINGS &
  STARVATION OF PIKE'S PEAK GOLD SEEKERS-Chig-1860-
  by one of the survivors-Evening Journal Steam Pr-12mo-
  hf mor-1st ed-ex rare-(D Blue)
     (5i0,t.pg restored,Streeter copy) 2,000.00
THRILLING NARR OF MINNESOTA MASSACRE & SIOUX WAR
  OF 1862,63-Chig-(1896)-273p-illus-(A P Connolly) (5t3) 40.00
THRILLING STORIES OF THE GREAT REBELLION-by a Disabled
  Officer-Phila-1865-thk12mo-cl-384p-JEPotter (5j5,wn) 22.50
THROOP,GEO H-Lynde Weiss,An Autobiography-Phila-1873
       (5m2) 8.50
THROOP,LUCY ABBOT-Furnishing the Home of Good Taste-NY-
  1920-illus-251p   (5q0) 15.00
THROSBY,JOHN-History & Antiquities of Town & Country of Town
  of Nottingham,etc-Notthingham-1795-Burbage&Stretton-
  frontis-23 plts-lg4to-calf   (5ff6,rbkd) 225.00
THROUGH THE SW ALONG SANTA FE-KansasCty-c1895-
  Fred Harvey-obl folio-col views (4a5) 15.00
THRUM,THOS G-Hawaiian Almanac & Annual for 1884-Honolulu-
  (1884)-82p plus ads-orig wrps (5x5) 35.00
--More Hawaiian Folk Tales-Chig-1923-McClurg-323p (5x9) 5.00
THRUSTON,GATES P-Antiquities of Tennessee & the Adjacent
  States-Cinn-1890-362p plus index-photos-1st ed
     (5h6,lacks fly,5t3,f) 35.00
THUDICHUM,J L W-A Treatise on Wines-Lond-1896-cl-379p
     (5b8,unopnd,fade) 6.75
--same-Lond&NY-1872-illus-760p-8vo (4j1,crack,ex-libr) 17.50
THUMB,SIR THOMAS-The History of Sir Thos Thumb-Edinb-
  1855-illus-a.e.g.-orig bndg-(CYonge)-1st ed (4j3,sl fade) 67.50
--History of England-Lond-1749-MCooper-ports-8vo-304p-
  hf calf   (5c8,box) 600.00
• THUNBERG,C P-Voyages au Japon-Paris-(1796)-port-fldg plts-
  4 vols-8vo-hf calf (4b6,reprd) 275.00
THUNDER,CHIEF RIGHT HAND-Indian & White Man-Indnpls-1880-
  515p-dec cov   (5s4,soil,wn) 7.50
THUNDERSTORM,THE-Assu-Phila-(1826)-#73,1 Ser-wrps-
  tiny 12mo-illus (4h8,age darkened) 14.50
THURBER,FRANCIS B-Coffee,from Plantation to Cup-NY-1881-
  illus-416p   (4g9,hng loose,rub) 15.00
--same-1884-8th ed   (4g9,crack) 12.50
--same-1884-9th ed   (4g9,vg) 17.50
--same-NY-1886-416p-frontis-illus-12th ed (5g9,f) 15.00
THURBER,GEO-Amer Weeds & Useful Plants-NY-1859-illus-cl-
  460p-2nd ed   (5t2) 5.00
THURBER,JAS-Fables for Our Time-NY-(1940)-8vo-illus bds
     (4c2,dj,fox) 22.50
--The Great Quillow-NY-(1944)-Harcourt,Brace-illus by Doris Lee-
  54p-labl-cl-1st ed (4g1) 10. (5p1,lt soil) 7.50

THURBER, JAS (continued)
--Is Sex Necessary-NY-1929-Harper-frontis-drwngs-8vo-hf cl-
1st ed   (5j5,fray dj)   15.00
--The Last Flower-NY-1939-Harper-obl 4to-pict bds
    (5b2,vf,dj,misbnd)   17.50
--Let Your Mind Alone-1937-Harper   (5F1,dj,fade)   5.75
--Many Moons-(1943)-Harcourt-illus by Slobodkin (5F1,f,wn dj)   6.00
--The Middle Aged Man on the Flying Trapeze-1935-Harper
    (5F1,f,dj)   7.50
--The Seal in the Bedroom & Other Predicaments-NY-1932-
Harper-4to-pict bds-illus-unpgd-1st ed   (5p5,5j5)   15.00
--The 13 Clocks-NY-(1950)-Simon&Schuster-illus by Simont-
124p,11p bkd bds-1st ed (5p1,pres,dj) 37.50   (5p1)   25.00
--Thurber's Dogs-NY-1955-12mo-cl bk bds (4c2,dj,bk stnd)   10.00
--The White Deer-NY-(1945)-4 plts-115p-1st ed
    (5p1) 6.   (5v0,mint,dj) 7.50   (5p1,rprd dj)   8.50
--The Wonderful O-NY-1957-12mo-bds-72p-illus-1st ed
    (5p1,dj) 7.50   (5t0,dj) 5.   (5p1)   6.00
THUREAU-DANGIN,P-English Catholic Revival in the 19th
Century-(1899)-2 vols-rev by WWilberforce
    (5L7,ex-libr,fade)   12.50
THURMAN,H-The Greatest of These-Mills College,Calif-1945
Eucalyptus Pr   (5x2,dj)   25.00
--Meditations for Apostles of Sensitiveness-Mills College,Calif-
1947   (5x2)   22.50
--The Negro Spiritual Speaks of Life & Death-NY-1947-16mo
    (5x2,dj)   10.00
THURN,EVERARD F IM-Among the Indians of Guiana-Lond-1883-
Kegan Paul-53 illus-lg8vo-orig buck-illus(3 in col)-map-
445p,32p-1st ed   (5L8,f)   28.50
THURNWALD,RICHARD-Banaro Society-Lancaster-1916-orig wrps
    (5jj3)   10.00
THURSDAY CLUB MEMBERS-Delicacies by...-SanDiego-1929-
wrps-160p-2nd ed   (4g9,stn)   5.00
THURSFIELD,H G,-ed-Brassey's Naval Annual,1943-NY-1944
282p-116 plts-cov embossed-illus   (5s1)   6.50
--same-1944-116 plts   (5s1,dj)   6.50
THURSTAN,VIOLETTA-Weaving Patterns of Yesterday & Today-
Leicester(Eng)-n.d.-42p-obl 12mo-limp cl   (5n7)   2.00
THURSTON,ADA,comp-Check List of 15th Century Printing in
Pierpoint Morgan Library-NY-1939-348p-8vo-cl (4c1,5yy6,f)37.50
THURSTON,BROWN-Thurston Genealogies-1880-598p (4t2)   27.50
THURSTON,FLORENCE-Three Centuries of Freeport-1940-
254p-illus-priv prntd   (5e8)   12.00
THURSTON,GEO H-Allegheny County's Hundred Years-Pittsb-
1888-8vo-orig stiff wrps-312p-map-plts-1st ed
    (5ss5,hng broke)   22.50
THURSTON,HOWARD-50 New Card Tricks-NY-1905-8vo-illus-
pict wrps-1st ed   (5p5)   10.00
--400 Tricks you can do-NY-(1940)-2 vols in 1-186p-illus
    (5t4)   4.50
THURSTON,J S-Laguna Beach of Early Days-(CulverCty,1947)-
8vo-cl-198p-illus   (5h5)   10.00
THURSTON,LORRIN A-Hand Book On Annexation of Hawaii-
StJos-1898-A B Morse-12mo-wrps-maps-83p   (4t1)   20.00
THURSTON,SAML R-Geographical Statistics,Oregon,its Climate,
Soil Production,etc-Strykers Amer Register,July 1850 (4n4)   60.00
THWAITE,L-Alberta,Account of Its Wealth & Progress-1912-
250p-illus   (4b9)   12.00
THWAITES,REUBEN GOLD,ed-Civil War Messages & Proclamations
of Wisc War Govs-Wisc Hist Conn Reprints #2-319p-wrps
    (5ww4) 10.   (5w0)   7.50
--Collections of State Hist Soc of Wisc-Madison-1895-515p-
Vol 13-cl   (5h7)   7.50
--The Colonies,1492 to 1750-NY-1893-Longmans-4 maps-301p
    (5p9)   4.00
--Daniel Boone-NY&Lond-1916-frontis-later ed   (5h6)   4.00
--Down Historic Waterways-Chig-1902-12mo-300p-1st ed-map-
plts   (5dd4)   8.50
--Early Western Travels-Cleve-1905-illus-Vol 2 (5jj3)   17.50
--same-Vol 10-Cleve-1904-illus-Hume   (5r7)   35.00
--same-Cleve-1904 to 07-32 vols incl atlas & 2 vol index
    (4k5,sl fade)   750.00
--France in America-NY-(1905)-8vo-cl-frontis-maps-320p-
Vol 7,The Amer Nation   (5t2)   4.50
--Frontier Defense of the Upper Ohio,1777,1778-1912-Wisc Hist
Soc   (5ww4)   15.00
--Historic Waterways-Chig-1888-12mo-cl-1st ed of auth's 1st book
    (5gg6)   25.00
--How Geo Rogers Clark Won the Northwest-Chig-1904-2nd ed
    (5jj7)   17.50
--same-Chig-1927-378p-cl-5th ed   (5h1)   5.00

THWAITES,REUBEN GOLD,ed (continued)
--The Indians of North Amer-NY-(1927)-maps-2 vols-8vo-cl
    (4c1)   22.50
--Original Journals of Lewis & Clark Expedition 1804 to 06-
NY-1904,05-maps-illus-7 vols plus atlas-8vo-cl-Centenary ed
    (4e1,vg)   450.00
--The Romance of Mississippi Valley History-CedarRapds-1907-
32p-orig prntd wrps   (5w5)   5.00
--Travels in the Far West,1836 to 41-1906-Arthur H Clark-
2 vols   (5x5,cov spots)   40.00
THWING,EUGENE-The Man from Red Keg-NY-1905-Dodd,Mead-
8vo-dec cl-   (5b2)   3.50
TIBBETS,J C-Hist of Coffee Creek Baptist Assn-Cinn-1883-224p-
cl-scarce   (5h2)   22.50
TIBBITS,ETHEL B-On to the Sunset-Tor-1953-155p   (5dd0)   3.50
TIBBLES,T H-Nebraska Redeemed-Lincoln-1897-119p plus index
& errata p-1st ed   (5L2)   15.00
TIBBLES,THOS H-Hidden power-NY-1881-Carleton-1st ed
advertisements dated '81   (5m2,wn)   8.50
TIBBLES,THOS HENRY-Buckin & Blanket Days-NY-(1957)
    (5F0,dj) 5.50   (5s4) 8.50   (5dd1,f,dj)   7.50
TICE,J H-Over the Plains & On the Mountains-StLouis-1872-
illus-262p plus index-1st ed   (4L0,sl wn)   17.50
TICE,JOHN H-Elements of Meteorology-Part 2 Cycles-StL-1875-
Met Research & Publ-208p-frontis-8vo-orig cl-g.   (5L1)   15.00
TICHY,HERBERT-Cho Oyu,By Favour of the Gods-Lond-(1957)-
Methuen-196p-illus   (5d7)   10.00
TICKELL,JERRARD-Gentlewomen Aim to Please-NY-1940-illus-
141p   (5w7)   3.00
TICKNOR,ALMON-The Columbian Calculator-Phila-1854-
Lippincott,Grambo-12mo-264p-lea bkd prntd bds   (5p1)   7.50
TICKNOR,CAROLINE,ed-Dr Holmes's Boston-Bost-1915-
Houghton,Miff-illus-ltd to 750c   (5p0)   7.50
--Glimpses of Authors-Bost-1922-illus   (5mm2)   7.50
TICKNOR,GEO-History of Spanish literature-NY-1849-Harper-
3 vols-8vo-orig cl-1st ed   (5i0,lt fox)   40.00
--Life,Letters & Journals of-Bost-1876-Jas R Osgood&Co-2 vols-
illus   (4b3)   15.00
--Life of Wm Hickling Prescott-Bost-1864-491p(5mm2) 7.50 (5t7)12.50
TICKNOR'S NEW ENGLAND-Handbook for Travellers-Bost-1887-
453p-6 maps-11 plans   (5ee3,vf)   7.50
TIDBURY,G E-Clove Tree-Lond-1949-212p-17 plts
    (5c6,f) 6.75   (5s7)   7.50
TIDY,GORDON-Surtees on Fishing-NY-1931-63p-7 hand col plts-
t.e.g.-1st Amer ed-ltd to 500c   (5w9)   15.00
TIEMANN,GEO & CO-American Armamentarium Chirurgicum-
NY-(1886)-sm4to-cl&lea-illus-846p   (5t0,broke)   27.50
TIERNAN,FRANCES C-A question of honor,a novel-NY-1875-
Appleton-1st ed   (5m2)   6.50
TIERNAN,MARY F-Homoselle-Bost-1881-Osgood-Round Robin
series-advts dated Aug '81-1st ed   (5m2,sl soil)   8.50
TIETZE,HANS-European Master Drawings in the US-NY-1947-
Augustin-326p-sm folio-cl-illus   (5m5)   60.00
--Genuine & False-NY-1948-Chanticleer-In series-Approach to Art-
80p-73 plts-4to-cl   (5m5)   10.00
--Masterpeices of European Painting in Amer-Lond-1939-45p-
Allen&Unwin-4to-cl-plts   (5m5,ex-libr)   15.00
--same-NY-(1939)-317 repro   (5tt5)   10.00
--Tintoretto,The Paintings & Drawings-NY-1948-Phaidon-4to-cl
107p text&cat-3 col plts-289 hftone(1 fld out) (5m5,ex-libr) 28.00
--Treasures of Great National Galleries-NY-1954-(Phaidon)-
4to-plts   (4a1)   10.00
TIFFANY,FRANCIS-Life of Dorothea Lynde Dix-Bost-1891-frontis-
cl-392p,13p   (5t0)   5.00
TIFFANY GLASS& DECORATING CO-Memorial Tablets,Ancient
& Modern,Honorary & Mortuary,in Bronze,Brass,Mosaic
& Marble-NY-(1896)-18mo-wrps-24p   (5t2)   7.50
TIFFANY,H T-Law of Real Property & Other Interests in Land-
Chig-1920-enlrgd ed-3 vols   (5r4)   16.50
TIFFANY,J K-History of the Postage Stamps of the US-StL-1887-
320p-port-cl-scarce   (5a9)   9.50
--Stamped Envelopes,Wrappers & Sheets of US-NY-1892-126p-
illus-plts   (5ii2)   6.50
TIFFANY,NINA MOORE-Harm Jan Huldekoper-Cambr-1904-
386p-illus-t.e.g.   (5w0)   10.00
--Samuel E Sewall a Memoir-Bost-1898-frontis   (5qq8)   5.00
TIFFANY TABLE SETTINGS-NY-(1960)-4to-cl-196p-illus-1st ed
    (5t2,dj,f)   10.00
TIFFIN,WM-A New Help & Improvement of the Art of Swift Writing-
Lond-(1751)-Hart-8vo-bds-52p-12 plts-1st ed (5ee5,rbnd)   32.00
TIFFT,M E-Partial Record of Desc of John Tefft-1896-159p (4t2)   40.00
TIGHT,W G-Songs of the University of NewMex-Albqu-1905-
4to-cl-96p-ads   (5g6,bndg dmgd)   10.00

TIJTGAT,EDGARD-Le Petit Chaperon Rouge-Lond-1917-16p of
text-col plts-bds-bnd Japanese style-ltd to 40c   (5v2,f) 40.00

TILBY,A WYATT-English People Overseas-Lond-1911-Vol 3,
Brit NoAmer-441p   (4d2) 6.50

TILDEN &CO-Catalogue of Pure Medicinal Extracts-NY-1852-
28p,(4)-prntd wrps-rear illus   (5hh6,sl stn) 14.50

TILDEN,EMILY ESTER IRISH-Genealogy of Johnson Tozer Family
& Hist Sketches-n.p.-(Lorain)-1917-262p-cl (5h1,discol) 17.50

TILDEN,JOE-Joe Tilden's Recipes for Epicures-SanFran-1907-
12mo-drwngs   (5c0,sl soil) 7.50

TILDEN,WM T-Match Play & the Spin of the Ball-NY-1925-355p-
illus-1st ed   (5w5) 5.00

TILGHMAN,ZOE A-Marshall of the Last Frontier-Glendale-1949-
1st ed-9 plts-fldg map
   (5jj7,f) 25. (5F0,f) 22.50 (5dd1) 30. (4i7) 35.00

--Outlaw Days-OklaCty-1926-138p-illus-wrps
   (5dd1) 12.50 (4a5) 17.50 (4i7) 12. (5h0) 15. (5L3,vf) 16.50

--Quanah, Eagle of the Comanches-OklaCty-1938-Harlow Pub-illus-
e.p. map-1st ed-scarce   (5kk5) 30.00

TILING,MORITZ-German Element in Texas-Houston-1913
   (4c7,sl rub) 50.00

TILKE,M-Orientalische Kostume in Schnitt und Fabre-Berlin-1923-
4to-128 col plts-32p text   (5xx7) 20.00

TILLEY,JOHN SHIPLEY-Lincoln Takes Command-ChapelHill-(1941)-
8vo-334p   (4a7) 7.50

TILLMAN,S F-Christopher Reynolds & His Desc-ChevyChas-1959-
sm4to-464p-illus   (5w5) 8.50 (4t2) 15.00

TILLOTSON,F H-How to be a Detective-KansCty-1909-illus-
limp leatherette   (5k1) 10. (4L0) 15.00

TILLOTSON,HARRY STANTON-The Beloved Spy-Caldwell-1948-
illus-195p-deckle edge-ltd to 1000c,autg   (5t7,dj) 10.00

TILLOTSON,LEE S-Ancient Craft Masonry in Vermont-Montpelier-
1920-193p   (5t4) 7.50

TILLOTSON,M R-Grand Canyon Country-Stanford-1929-116p-
plts-1st ed   (5xx5) 6.50

--same-Stanford-1935-photos-dec cov (5dd9) 5. (5s4,f) 6.00

TILLSON,BENJ-Complete Automobile Instructor-NY-1907-
1st ed-3 qtr lea-213p-illus-2nd thous-frontis (4e4) 12.50

TILLSON,CHRISTIANA HOLMES-A woman's story of pioneer
Illinois-Chig-1919-Lakeside Pr-12mo-orig cl- ports
   (5h9) 8.50 (5i9) 12.00

TILMAN,H W-China to Chitral-Cambr-1951-Univ Pr-
illus-cl   (5d7) 6.00

--Mischief in Patagonia-Cambr-1957-Univ Pr-185p-illus-cl
   (5c1) 5. (5d7) 4.50

--Mount Everest 1938-Cambr-1948-Univ Pr-160p-illus-cl (5d7) 6.00

--Nepal Himalaya-Cambr-1952-Univ Pr-272p-illus-cl (5d7) 10.00

--When Men & Mountains Meet-Cambr-1946-Univ Pr-232p-
illus-cl   (5d7) 7.50

TILLMANS,EMILE-Porcelaines de France-Editions Mondes-1953-
tip in col plts-320p-4to   (5ww3) 30.00

TILTON,CECIL G-Wm Chapman Ralston,Courageous Builder-Bost-
(1935)-8vo-cl-474p-illus   (5F5,f,dj) 12.50

TILTON,ELEANOR M-Amiable Autocrat-NY-(1947)-470p-illus-
1st ed   (5t4) 5. (5m2,dj) 6.50

TILTON,G H-Hist of Rehoboth,Mass-1918-417p (5t9) 22.50

TILTON,CAPT GEO F-"Cap'n Geo Fred" Himself-NY-1928-
295p-illus-photos-g.stmpd cov-1st ed   (5s1,rprd) 10.00

TILTON,THEODORE-Biography of Victoria C Woodhull-NY-1871-
16mo-35p(1)-orig prntd wrps-Golden Age Tracts #3 (4c1) 35.00

--Golden Haired Gertrude-NY-1865-6 tintd plts-cl-bevelled edge-
1st ed-scarce   (5v2) 20.00

--Henry Ward Beecher,Verbatim Report by-NY-1875-3 vols-
8vo-ports-calf-1st ed   (5m6,crack) 30.00

--Tempest Tossed-NY-1874-Sheldon-606p-1st ed (5x4) 10.00

TIMASHEFF,NICHOLAS S-The Great Retreat,The Growth and
Decline of Communism in Russia-NY-1946-470p-charts(5ss6,dj) 6.00

TIMBERLAKE,CRAIG-The Bishop of Broadway-NY-(1954)-8vo-
cl-491p-Library Publs   (5j5,dj) 10.00

TIMBERLAKE,HENRY-The Memoirs of Lieut Henry Timberlake-
Lond-1765-fld map-plt-calf-orig ed-rare
   (5s9,rbnd,facs map & plt) 200.00

TIMBS,J-Abbeys,castles & ancient halls of England & Wales-Vol 1,
The South-Lond-1862-578p-4to-cl-illus (5m5,x-libr) 9.50

TIMBS,JOHN-English Eccentrics & Eccentricities-Lond-1875-illus-
pict cl-578p & ads   (5t0) 4.00

--Nooks & Corners of Engl Life...Past & Present-Lond-1867-cl
   (5x7,cl blister) 8.50

--Wonderful Inventions-Lond-1868-300p-illus (5t7,wn) 6.00

TIMOVSKI,M G-Voyage A Peking a Travers la Mongolie,en 1820
et T821,etc-Paris-1827-8vo & 4to (atlas)-hf lea-fldg map-
plts-2 vols   (5v7) 65.00

TIMLIN,WM-South Africa,a Series of Pencil Sketches-Lond-
1927-A&C Black-16p text,24p sketches (4t5) 10.00

TIMMERMAN,JOHN-John Timmerman,Pioneer Citizen of Stella,
Richardson Co,Nebr-n.p.-n.d.-4p-self cov-slim,tall-scarce
   (5L2) 5.00

TIMMONS,WM-Twilight on the Range-Austin-(1962)-214p plus
index-illus-1st ed   (5dd1,f,dj) 8.50

TIMPERLEY,C H-Encyclopea of Lit & Typogr Anecdote-Lond-1842-
2nd ed-frontis-illus-plus Printers Manual-1838-115p-mor
bnd together   (5i3) 75.00

TINCKER,MARY AGNES-Aurora-Phila-1886-Lippincott-315p-
1st ed   (5x4) 7.50

--The jewel in the lotos,a novel-Phila-1884-Lippincott-illus
1st edition   (5m2) 6.00

TINDAL,N-A Guide to Classical Learning-Lond-1777-JDodsley-
calf-12 plts   (5v2,crack) 20.00

TINEE,MAE-Life Stories of the Movie Stars-Ohio-1916-64p(4c9)12.50

TINGLEY,R M-Desc of Sam'l Tingley of Malden,Mass,1666-
1910-894p   (4t2) 20.00

--Some Ancestral Lines-1935-465p   (4t2) 20.00

TINKCOM,H M-Historic Germantown from Founding to Early Part
of 19th Century-Phila-1955-photos-maps-154p-tall 4to
   (4m4,f,dj) 15.00

TINKCOM,HARRY MARLIN-John White Geary,Soldier Statesman-
Phila-1940-155p-1st ed   (5w9) 6.50

TINKER,CHAUNCEY BREWSTER-Dr Johnson & Fanny Burney-NY-
1911-8vo-cl-1st ed of auth's 1st book (5gg6) 10.00

TINKER,E-Toucoutou,Creole Stories-NY-1928 (5x2) 7.50

--Closed Shutters-NY-1931-12mo   (5x2) 6.00

TINKER,EDW LAROCQUE-Creole City,its Past & its People-NY-
1953-Longmans-8vo-cl-illus-359p-1st ed (5j5,autg) 10.00

TINKER,SPENCER WILKIE-Hawaiian Fishes-Honolulu-1944-illus-
pict bds-404p   (5t7) 8.00

TINKHAM,GEO H-Calif Men & Events,1769 to 1890-Stockton-
Dec,1915-336p-cl-rev 2nd ed (5tt0) 10. (5n1) 7.50

TINKLER,E D-The History of the Rocking Chair Ranche-Canyon,
Panhandle Plains-1942-96p-stiff wrps-maps (5n4) 6.00

TINSLEY,LAURA R-Practical & Artistic Basketry-NY-(1904)-
photos-143p   (4L0,f) 5.00

TINTINNABULUM-Sporting Intelligence,The Race for the Mitre-
Tor-1866   (5nn8) 15.00

TIPPECANOE,WHITE,JASPER,NEWTON,BENTON,WARREN &
PULASKI CO,IND-Biog Hist of-Chig-1899-2 vols-1075p-
3/4 lea   (5h1) 50.00

TIPPETT,EDWIN JAS,JR-Who Won the War?-(Tol-1920)-222p-
wrps   (5h2,sl soil) 7.50

TIPPETT,T-When Southern Labor Stirs-NY-1931-illus-1st ed(5x2)15.00

TIPPETTS,W H-Lake George,the Queen of Amer Lakes-Caldwell-
1901-67p-illus-pict wrps   (5t4) 6.50

TIPPING,H AVRAY-Grinling Gibbons & the Woodwork of his age,
1648 to 1720-Lond-1914-folio-bds-cl sp-illus (4m4) 37.50

--Old Engl furniture,its true value & function-Lond-1928-
Country Life-24p-50 plts-4to-bds   (5m5) 8.50

TIPPLE,EZRA S-Francis Asbury Prophet of Long Road-NY-(1916)-
333p-cl   (5h1) 5.00

TIPTON,EDNA S-Table Decorations for All Occasions-NY-1924-
photos-128p   (5w7) 5.00

TIPTON,EDNA S-Menus for every Occasion-NY-1927-217p
   (5c9,f) 4.50

TIPTON,THOS W-40 Yrs of Nebraska,at Home & in Congress-
Lincoln-1902-570p   (4j4,f) 15.00

TIPTON,W HORD-Tipton Family History-(1948)-325p (4t2) 25.00

TIRPITZ,VON-Grand Admiral,My Memoirs-NY-1919-2 vols-
Dodd,Mead   (5p7) 12.50

TISCHNER,RUDOLF-Telepathy & Clairvoyance-NY-1925 (4b7) 12.50

TISDALE,C W WALKER-Butter&Cheese-Lond-(1920)-140p-illus-ads
   (5g9) 4.50

TISSANDIER,GASTON-Application de l'Elictricitie a la
Navigation Aerienne-Paris-1884-fldg chart-8vo-16p (5xx4) 35.00

TICOMB,SARAH ELIZ-Early New England People-Bost-1882-
288p(5)   (4j1,5ii3) 17.50

TITCOMB'S,TIMOTHY-Letters to Young People,Single & Married-
NY-1859-251p   (5w7,fox) 7.50

TITFORD,WM JOWIT-Sketches Towards a Hortus Botanicus
Americanus-Lond-1812-calf bkd bds-4to-handcol frontis-
17 handcol plts-1st ed (5z9,sp wn,sl fox) 225.00

TITHERINGTON,R H-History of Spanish Amer War of 1898-
NY-1900   (5j5,5L7,ex-libr) 7.50

TITIAN-Paintings & Drawings-Phaidon-1937-illus-359p-8vo
   (5ww3) 20.00

TITMARSH,MR M A-The Irish Sketch book-Lond-1843-2 vols-
Chapman&Hall-12mo-cl-1st ed   (5x3) 60.00

TITMARSH,MR M A (continued)
--The Kickleberys on the Rhine-4to-plts by Thackeray-green lev-
  g.raised bands-g.sp-g.t.-bndg by Tout-rare 1st ed
                  (5t5,f bndg)   55.00
--The Paris sketch book-Lond-1840-JnMacrone-12mo-orig cl-
  2 vols-1st ed   (5x3,rub)   90.00
--Mrs Perkin's Ball-Lond-(1847)-sq8vo-mor-a.e.g.-20 handcol plts-
  frontis-46p-1st ed   (5nn2,f bndg)   75.00
--The Rose & the Ring-Lond-1855-illus-orig pink bds-1st ed-
  scarce   (4F6,rbkd,cov stnd)   45.00
TITTERWELL,ESQ-Yankee notions,a medley,by Timo-Bost-1838-
  Otis,Broaders&Co-8vo-orig cl-papr labl-1st ed (5x1)   30.00
TIXIER,VICTOR-Tixier's Travels on the Osage Prairies-Norman-
  1940-297p plus index-illus-2 fldg maps-1st ed (4L0,f,dj)   15.00
TIZZARD,SAM'L-The new Athenian oracle or ladies' companion-
  In 2 books-Carlisle(Pa)-1806-from press of A Loudon-8vo-
  1st ed-scarce   (5i9,rub)   75.00
TOBIN,JOHN-The curfew,a drama-NY-1807-Longworth-12mo-
  disbnd-prntd same year as Lond   (5i0)   7.50
TOBIN,RICHARD L-The Center of the World-NY-1951-Dutton-
  1951-1st ed   (5x0,dj)   5.00
TOCQUEVILLE,ALEXIS DE-Democrary in America-NY-1838,40-
  Vols 1&2-orig cl   (5m3,wn)   35.00
--Democracy in Amer,Part the Second,Social Influence of
  Democracy-NY-1840-355p-1st Amer ed   (5ee3,f)   22.50
--same-NY-1845-4th ed-2 vols   (5tt5)   22.50
--same-Cambr-1862-Sever&Francis-2 vols (5qq8)   12.50
--same-NY-1899-2 vols-Colonial Pr   (5p9)   10.00
--same-NY-(1900)-Colonial Pr-plts-2 vols (5qq8)   6.50
--De La Democratie en Amerque-Paris-1874-Levy-3 vols-mor
                   (5qq8,f)   17.50
--The Republic of the USA-NY-1849-cl-2 vols in 1,as issued-
  471p,404p   (4k2)   15.00
TODD,CHAS BURR-Burr Family in Amer-1878-457p   20.00
--General History of Burr Family-NY-1902-Knickerbocker Pr-
  600p-cl-4th ed   (5tt8,rub)   40.00
--In Olde Conn-Grafton-1906-244p-2nd prntg (5e8)
  (5e8) 10.75 (5w4)   7.50
--The Story of the City of NY-NY-1888-478p-illus-fldg maps-
  1st ed   (5h9)   6.50
--same-NY-1902-illus facs-fldg maps-Great Cities of Republic
  Series   (5w5)   5.00
--The True Aaron Burr-NY-1902-cl-77p (5tt8)   10.00
TODD,FRANK MORTON-Eradicating Plague from SanFrancisco-
  SanFran-1909-313p-illus   (4L0)   4.00
--Romance of Insurance-SanFran-1929-283p-illus (4b8)   12.50
--Story of the Exposition-(Intl Celebration..SanFran,1915...
  Discov of Pac Ocean etc)-NY-1921-5 vols-4to-illus-
  61 col plts-scarce   (5ii3)   125.00
TODD,H G-Armory & Lineages of Canada-NY-1919-7th annual issue-
  122p-plts-scarce   (5dd7,f)   18.00
TODD,HELEN-A Man Named Grant-Bost-1940-598p-8vo (4a7)   7.50
TODD,JOHN-The Young Man-Northptn-1845-Butler-2nd ed-
  calf   (5cc6)   8.50
TODD,JOHN-Practical Seamanship...in Merchant Marine-Lond-
  1890-345p-illus   (5s1,fair,ex-libr)   13.50
--same-1903-385p-5th ed,enlrgd-illus (5s1,ex-libr,rprd)   12.50
TODD,JOHN-Calif & Its Wonders-1880-plts-new ed,rev
         (5L7,lend libr labl)   7.50
--same-Lond-1884-illus   (4a5)   5.00
--Early Settlement & Growth of Western Iowa-DesMoines-1906-
  port-8vo-1st ed (5m8) 12.50 (4g6) 17.50 (5F9,f)   25.00
--same-DesMoines-1906-frontis-87p plus index-cl wi wrps
  bnd in (recent reprint?)   (4L0)   5.00
--John Todd,the Story of His Life Told Mainly by Himself
              (5t7,5x2)   7.50
--The Sunet Land-Bost-1869-1st ed (4a5)   12.50
--same-Bost-1870-322p-cl (4L0,fade) 5. (5h2)   7.50
TODD,MABEL L-Bolts of Melody,new Poems of Emily Dickinson-
  1945-Harper&Bros-1st ed   (5ss9)   5.00
--Corona & Coronet-Cambr-1898-383p-illus-1st ed (5s1)   7.00
--Footprints-n.p.-Amherst-1883-8vo-wrps-scarce (5b2)   35.00
--Letters of Emily Dickinson-Bost-1894-RobertsBros-orig green cl-
  2 vols-1st ed,1st issue   (5ss9,fade)   25.00
TODD,MATTIE P-Hand Loom Weaving-NY-1902-illus-160p(5n7) 2.50
TODD,W E C-Birds of Western Penna-Pittsburgh-1940-cl-
  22 col plts-725p-4to-maps   (5cc1,vg)   50.00
--Birds of Santa Marta Region of Colombia-Pittsburgh-1922-cl-
  8 plts-619p-fldg map   (5cc1,f)   15.00
TODD,WM-The 79th Highlanders, NY Vol in War of Rebel-Albany-
  1886-Brandow, Barton-513p-illus-maps-g.t. (5mm8)15. (4L0) 17.50

TODD,WM J
--Port...buying,serving,storing-Lond-1926-illus-95p-12mo (5w1)7.50
TODD,WM J-A Handbook of Wine-Lond-(1922)-103p (5g9)   4.00
TODHUNTER,JOHN-Ye Minutes of Ye CLXXVIIth Meeting of Ye
  Sette of Odd Volumes extracted from Ye Diary of Samuel Pepys,
  Esq-Ashendene-1896-orig wrps-8&32p-ltd to 154c-16mo-rare
               (4h5,box,f)   600.00
TOILET,THE-Rock Bros&Payne-(c1845)-12mo-mor-g.t.
               (5s6,sl wn)   85.00
TOILET OF FLORA,THE-for the use of ladies-Lond-1779-252p-
  frontis-calf bk-new ed,impr   (5w3)   25.00
TOKEN & ATLANTIC SOUVENIR,THE-Bost-1833-354p-1st ed
  Gray & Bowen   (5x4)   17.50
TOKSVIG,SIGNE-Emanuel Swedenborg,Scientist & Mystic-
  NewHav-1948-8vo-cl-illus-389p   (5t0)   5.00
--Life of Hans Christian Andersen-Lond-1933-Macmillan
              (5c8 f,pres)   15.00
--same-NY-1934-illus-8vo-cl-289p (5k2) 3.50 (5t0)   5.00
TOKUTOMI,Iichiro-Japanese Amer Relations-NY-1922-207p-cl
              (5t2)   4.00
TOKYO NAT'L MUSEUM-Pageant of Japanese Art,Textile &
  Lacquer-Tokyo-c1958-bds-illus in col (5x7)   3.50
TOLBERT,CAROLINE-History of Mt Rainier Nat'l Park-Seattle-
  1933-Lowman&Hanford-60p-illus-fldg map-cl (5r0,pres)   7.50
TOLBERT,FRANK X-Dick Dowling at Sabine Pass-NY-(1962)-
  1st ed (5L3,mint,dj) 5. (5a8,mint,dj)   7.50
--Neiman Marcus,Texas,the story of the proud Dallas store-
  NY-(1953)-190p-ports-illus-hf cl bds (5dd6)   5.00
TOLBLOOM,WANDA N-Arctic Bride-NY-1956-port-plts-256p
              (5s0)   4.50
TOLD BY THE PIONEERS-Remin of Pioneer Life in Washington-
  (Olympia)-1937,1938-3 vols-WPA,Fed Proj #5841 (5mm3)   25.00
--same-1938-(n.p.Olympia)-222p-stiff wrps-sm4to-frontis-
  WPA Proj #5841,Vol 2(only of 3)   (4L9)   10.00
TOLD UNDER THE GREEN UMBRELLA-NY-1930-8vo-frontis-
  2 col plts-Macmillan-189p-1st ed (5p1,fray dj)   12.50
TOLEDO DIRECTORY-Toledo-1858-prntd bds-294p-1st directory-
  Hosmer&Harris-rare   (5jj9,rebkd)   125.00
TOLEDO MUSEUM OF ART-Catalogue of Inaugural Exhibition
  Jan,Feb 1912-lg4to-bds-163p-ltd to 1000c (5m5)   15.00
TOLFREY,FREDK-Sportsman in Canada-Lond-1845-plts-2 vols
              (5e2)   100.00
TOLKIEN,J R R-Sir Gawain & the Green Knight-Oxf-1925-
  Clarendon Pr-1st ed   (4g1,ink,fly cut)   50.00
TOLL,ROGER W-Mountaineering in Rocky Mntn Nat'l Park-Wash-
  1919-illus-106p-wrps   (4b3,wrps wn)   7.50
TOLLAND & WINDHAM CO,CONN-Commemorative Biographical
  Record of-1903-JHBeers&Co-1358p (5t9)   30.00
TOLLES,FREDK B-Geo Logan of Philadelphia-NY-1953-8vo-cl-
  19p,362p-1st ed   (5t0,f,dj)   5.00
TOLLIVER,ARTHUR S-Wild Adventures of Davy Crockett-1944-
  HaldemanJulius-8vo-wrps-23p (5g5)   3.00
TOLMACHOFF,I P-Siberian Passage-NewBrunswick-1949-cl-
  8vo-238p   (5v7)   6.50
TOLMAN,BETH-Country Dance Book-NY-(1937)-192p-illus (5c3)4.50
TOLMAN,J E-Build It Yourself-25 Furniture Designs-NY-1951-
  obl 8vo-51p   (5n7)   2.50
TOLSON,F-Hermathenae-n.p.-(c1740)-Vol 1(all pub)-176p-
  engrvs   (5aa0,rbnd)   35.00
TOLSON,M B-Libretto for Republic of Liberia-NY-1953-1st ed
              (4b4)   12.50
TOLSON,R J-A History of Wm Cameron &Co-Waco-1926-folio-
  illus-ltd ed   (5n4)   30.00
TOLSTOY,COUNTESS ALEXANDRA-The Tragedy of Tolstoy-1933-
  Yale Univ Pr-1st ed-ltd to 1000c,autg (5hh1)   15.00
TOLSTOY,LEO-Anna Karenina-prntd in Moscow-1933-2 vols-
  col liths-boxed-Ltd Ed Club (5t8,ink on fly)   20.00
--Christ's Christianity-Lond-1885-Kegan Paul-384p-plus 44p ads-
  1st Engl ed   (4b4,fox)   37.50
--Kreutzer Sonata-Berlin-1890-117p-1st ed-rare (4b4)   75.00
--War & Peace-NY-1886-Gottsberger-orig cl-g.stmpd-6 vols-
  1st ed in Engl-Clara Bell,transl-v rare (5z7,mint)   300.00
--same-NY-1938-Heritage Pr-2 vols   (5p5)   10.00
TOM CRINGLE'S LOG-Lond-1833-2 vols-12mo-cl-(M Scott)-
  "A" bndg-1st ed   (5gg6,rprd)   50.00
TOM,FREDK C-Court Tennis-1909-Lippincott-illus-115p (5a6)   3.00
TOM THE PIPER'S SON-A Continuation of...Part the Second-
  Phila-1808-WmCharles-sm8vo-orig prntd wrps (4h8)   87.50
TOM THE THIEF-McLoughlin Bros-(ca 1870)-col illus-lin book-
  12mo-8p-v scarce   (5v0,crack,soil)   7.50
TOM THUMB-Adventures of-NY-(1897)-McLoughlin Bros-4to-
  6 col plts-pic wrps   (4c3,f)   12.50

TOM THUMB'S PLAY BOOK- Newcastle-1824-GAngus-sq12mo-
48p-frontis-orig blu wrps-wdcuts   (5c8,f)   45.00

TOMB,EVA S-Bowling Green Cook Bk-BowlGr-1929-132p-wrps
   (5h1,soil,wn)   3.00

TOMBLESON'S VIEWS OF THE RHINE-Lond-1852-illus-1st ed
   (5yy6,bndg tn)   20.00

TOMBES,ROBT-The Champagne Country-NY-1867-12mo-1st ed
   (4j1)   12.50

TOMILIN,A G-Kitoobraznie (Cetacea)-Moscow-1957-cl-4to-
756p-12 col plts-Vol 9 of Series-scarce   (4p5)   21.00

TOMKINS,H M-Bibliotheca Jeffersoniana-NY-1887-187p-
ltd to 350c,nbrd   (4q2,sp rub)   27.50

TOMKINS,WM-Universal Indian Sign Language-SanDiego-
77p-illus-cl-1st ed -(1926) (5L0) 5. (5L0,prs)   7.50
--same-SanDiego-(ca 1929)-wrps   (4k5,f,pres)   5.00
--same-(1959)-14th ed-wrps   (5L0)   1.50

TOMKINSON,G S-Select Bibliography of Principal Modern Presses
Public & Private in Great Britain & Ireland-Lond-1928-lg4to-
col illus-bds&cl-238p-First Ed Club   (5d1) 75. (4p7,f)   200.00

TOMLINS,W L-Children Songs-n.p.-1892(wrpr t.)-4to (5p1)   5.00

TOMLINSON,H M-All Our Yesterdays-Lond-1930-539p-1st ed
   (4b4,4g1)   7.50
--same-NY-1930-Harper-445p-ltd to 350c,autg-boxed (5p7)   12.50
--same-Lond-1930-R8vo-buck-g.t.-Ltd Ed,autg (5t8) 10. (5t5)   12.50
--Gallions Reach-1927-Harper&Bros-1st ed-ltd to 350c,autg
   (5hh1)   12.50
--Great Sea Stories of All Nations-Lond-(1930)-8vo-cl-1108p
   (5aa2) 4.50 (5t0)   4.00
--London River-Lond-1921-1st ed-268p-frontis   (5s6)   6.50
--Norman Douglas-Lond-1931-Chatto&Windus-63p-ltd to 260c
   (5p9)   10.00
--same-1931-Harper&Bros-1st ed   (5ss9,f,dj)   10.00
--Old Junk-Lond-1933-new&rev ed-224p   (5s6)   4.50
--Pipe All Hands-NY-1937-12mo-cl-326p-1st Amer ed (5t0)   4.50
--The Sea & the Jungle-Lond-(1912)-1st ed of auth's 1st book
   (5r9,f)   25.00
--same-Lond-1930-t8vo-orig green cl-wdcuts-ltd to 550c,autg
   (5t8,mint)   20.00
--Under the Red Ensign-Lond-1926-1st ed-195p (5t9,5s6)   7.50

TOMLINSON,IRVING C-12 Years with Mary Baker Eddy-Bost-
1945-277p-illus   (5k2)   3.50

TOMLINSON,WM P-Kansas in 1858-NY-1859-304p-ads-
1st ed   (5s4,ex-libr,wn,5L2,wn)   12.50

TOMLINSON,WM WEAVER,ed-Songs & Ballads of Sport & Pastime-
Lond-n.d.-12mo-red vel sp-g.t.   (5t8)   10.00

TOMMY THUMB'S SONG BOOK-(facs,NY 1946)-By Nurse
Lovechild-Worcester-1788-16mo-64p-wrps   (5c8)   10.00

TOMPKINS CO,NY-Gazetteer & Business Directory for 1868-
240p-map-HChild,ed   (4d9,map damaged)   12.50

TOMPKINS,ELIZ K-Her majesty,a romance of today-NY-1895-
Putnam-1st ed   (5m2)   4.00

TOMPKINS,M D,E P-The Natural Bridge & its Historical
Surroundings-Natural Bridge,Va-1939-147p-illus (5p0)   3.50

TOMPKINS,COL FRANK-Chasing Villa-(Harrisburg)-1934-
Military Ser Pub-8vo-270p-cl-illus (4a3) 25. (4b3,f,dj)   17.50

TOMPKINS,RAYMOND S-Brief History of a Bank-Balt-1938-
priv pub-illus-68p,11p   (4b8)   7.50

TOMPKINS,STUART R-Alaska-Norman-1945-350p-8 maps
   (5L7) 5. (5s6)   8.50

TOMPKINS,W A-Santa Barbara's Royal Rancho-Berkeley-(1961,
2nd prntg)-Howell North-illus-282p   (4n1,autg,dj)   10.00

TOMPSON,BENJ-New England's Crisis-Bost-1894-Club of Odd Vols-
sm4to-bds-roan bk-34p-ltd to 100c (5q0,chip,lacks e.p.)   10.00

TONER,J M-Address before the Rocky Mntn Medical Assoc Jun 6,
1877-Wash-1877-414p   (5w0)   12.50
--Contributions to Annals of Medical Progress & Medical Education
in US-Wash-1874-GPO-118p-interleaved   (5t2)   7.50
--Washington's Rules of Civility & Decent Behavior in Company
& Conversation-Wash-1888-34p-orig wrps-cl bkstrp (5x5)   6.00

TONEY,MARCUS B-The Privations of a Private-Nashville-1905-
133p-illus-priv publ   (5h6)   17.50
--same-Nashville-1907-enlarged ed-12mo-158p-buck (4a7,rbnd)   10.00

TONG,WM-A Defence of Mr M H's Brief Enquiry into the Nature
of Schism-Lond-1693-sm4to-papr bds   (5j2,rbnd)   25.00

TONGATABOO-Authentic Narr of 4 Yrs Residence at...One of
Friendly Islands in South Sea-(Geo Vason)-Lond-1810-map-
frontis-8vo-calf-234p-errata lf-1st ed-rare (4e1,rebkd)   200.00

TONKAWA TRIBE OF INDIANS OF OKLA-Constitution & By Laws
of-Wash-1938-prntd wrps   (4a5)   22.50

TONKIN,R DUDLEY-My Partner,The River-(1959)-U Pittsburgh Pr-
illus-276p   (4d9,dj,f)   6.50

TONTY,HENRI DE-Relation...concerning explorations of
LaSalle from 1678 to 1683-Chig-1898-transl by Anderson-
bds-vel bk-ltd to 197c-Caxton Club (5g3,unopnd)   35.00

TOOGOOD,GRANVILLE-Huntsman in the Sky-NY-1930-Brewer-
1st ed   (5x0,dj)   6.00

TOOKE,ANDREW-Pantheon representing fabulous histories of
Heathen Gods-Lond-1810 -28 plts   (5c8,cov dtchd)   7.50
--Tooke's Pantheon of the Heathen Gods & Illustrious Heroes-
Balt-1838-sm8vo-lea-illus-305p-revsd   (5t2)   4.00

TOOKE,C W-Cases on Law of Municipal Corporations-NY-1931-
3 vols   (5ff4)   12.50

TOOKE,JOHN HORNE-(Greek Title)or The Diversions of Purley-
Lond-1798 to 1815-part mor-2 vols-2nd ed-4to
   (4d1,wn,cov dtchd)   15.00

TOOKE,WM-Life of Catherine II-Lond-1798-Longman&Debrett-
3 vols-7 ports-map-8vo-orig bds-1st ed (5i4,hng weak)   45.00
--View of the Russian Empire-Lond-1800-fldg map-8vo-calf-
3 vols-2nd ed   (4e1,hng weak)   50.00

TOOKER,ELVA-Nathan Trotter...Philadelphia Merchant,1787 to
1853-Cambr-1955-1st ed-maps (4a1) 6. (5t4)   5.00

TOOKER,WM WALLACE-John Eliot's First Indian Teacher &
Interpreter-Lond-1896-Stevens'-60p-illus-ltd to 215c (5qq8)   15.00

TOOLE,K ROSS,ed-Probing the Amer West-SantaFe-(1962)-cl-
216p-8vo-o.p.   (5h5,f,dj)   5.00
--Montana,an Uncommon Land-Norman-(1959)-1st ed,
1st printing-photos-o.p.   (4L0,mint,dj)   8.50

TOOLEY,R V-Maps & Map Makers-Lond-(1949)-8vo-illus-
1st ed   (5m6,dj)   10.00

TOOMBS,SAM'L-NJ Troops in the Gettysburg Campaign-Orange-
1888-Evening Mail Publ Hse-406p-illus-maps
   (5mm8) 6.50 (5w4,cov soil)   8.50

TOOR,FRANCIS-Early Arts & Crafts of Mexico,Mexican Folk Ways
Spec Nbr,Popular Plastic Arts-MexicoCty-1935wrps (5g6)   7.50
--Mexican Popular Arts-Mexico-1939-sm4to-cl-illus (5h4)   5.50
--Motorist Guide to Mexico-MexicoCty-1938-1st ed-340p(5ww3)12.50
--A Treasury of Mexican Folkways-NY-(1947)   (5a8)   3.00

TOPLIS,GRACE,ed-Richard Jeffries,The Early Fiction-Lond-1896-
frontis   (5mm2)   8.50

TOPONCE,ALEXANDER-Reminiscences of,Pioneer 1839 to 1923-
SaltLkCty-(c1923)-248p-illus-scarce (5a0,f) 30. (5a9,f)   20.00

TOPPAN,ROBT NOXON-Edward Randolph-Bost-1898 to 1909-illus-
7 vols-sm4to-250c by Prince Soc-wrps   (4c1)   75.00

TOPSFIELD,IPSWICH,ESSEX,HAMILTON & WENHAM-Atlas of-
Bost-1910-folio-calf-cl (4c1,cov detached,lacks lea)   20.00

TOPSYS&TURVEYS-NY-1893-obl 8vo-orig pict bds-reversible-
1st ed of Peter Newell's 1st book-scarce (5gg6,wn)   45.00

TORBET,R G-Social History of Phila-1944-Baptist Assoc-sewn
   (5L7)   6.50

TORBETT,J W-The Doctor's Scrapbook-Marlin-1947(5a8,autg)   5.00

TORCHIANA,H A VAN COENEN-Story of the Mission Santa Cruz-
SanFran-1933-8vo-cl-460p-illus-scarce
   (4L0,dj) 25. (5dd1) 25. (5H5,f,dj)   22.50
--Tropical Holland-Chig-1921-Univ of Chig Pr   (5x9)   6.50

TORNEL,JOSE MARIA-Carta de Gen Jose Maria Tornel a Sus
Amigos-Mexico-1839-Impreso por Ignacio Cumplido-25p-
blue pict wrps-fldg chart   (5n4)   75.00
--Tejas y los Estados-Unidos de America,en sus relaciones con la
Republica Mexicana-Mexico-1837-Cumplido-8vo-98p-
Spanish calf   (5L1)   200.00

TORNQUIST,KARL G-Naval Campaigns of Count De Grasse During
the Amer Revolution-Phila-1942-illus-charts-203p (5m4)   12.50

TORONTO BOARD OF TRADE-Annual Report...with Statistics of
Trade of the City for year 1858-Tor-1859-40p-prntd wrps(5w8)25.00

TORONTO-Illustrated Guide Book & Souvenir-Tor-n.d.-(1897?)-
GMRose&Sons -oblong 8vo   (5w8)   10.00

TORONTO TYPEFOUNDRY CO-Descriptive Catalogue & Price List
of Wood Furniture,Cylinder Presses etc-Tor,etc-(1910)-t8vo-
illus   (5w8,few items clipped)   15.00

TORRANCE-Torrance,The Modern Industrial City-LosAng-(1913)-
ThosDCampbell&Co-32p-wrps   (5d6)   17.50

TORRANCE,JARED S-Descendants of Lewis Hart & Anne Elliott-
LosAng-1923-illus-361p-t.e.g. (4p8) 17.50 (5w5)   18.50

TORRE,LILLIAN DE LA,ed-Villainy Detected-NY-1947-Appleton-
243p   (5p9)   4.50

TORRENCE,CLAYTON-Old Somerset on the Eastern Shore of
Maryland-Richmond-1935-583p   (5m2)   12.50

TORRENCE,FREDERIC RIDGELY-The House of a Hundred Lights-
Bost-1900-narr 16mo-bds-g.-1st ed of auth's 1st book-750c
were printed at Heintzemann Pr   (5gg6,pres)   50.00

TORRENCE,RIDGELY-Granny Maumee,The Rider of Dreams,Simon
the Cyrenian-NY-1917-1st ed   (5x2)   22.50
--Hesperides(Poetry,1st ed)-NY-1925   (5x2)   15.00

USED BOOK PRICE GUIDE

TORRENCE,RIDGLEY   (continued)
--Poems-NY-1952   (5x2,dj)   8.50
--The Story of John Hope-NY-1948-1st ed
                                   (5x2,dj)   10.00
TORREY,BRADFORD-Birds in Bush-Bost-1885-1st ed-16mo-300p-
   pic cl-g.dec   (5u9,sl bubbled) 10.50
--Field Days in Calif-Bost-1913-Houghton,Miff-235p-illus (5x0) 6.50
--The Foot Path Way-Bost-1892-1st ed-16mo-245p-cl (5u9) 7.50
--Footing It In Franconia-Bost-(1901)-1st ed-251p-16mo-cl-g.dec
                                   (5u9)   11.50
TORREY,REV DAVID-Memoir of Maj Jason Torrey-1885-131p-
   wi 50p suppl interleaved   (4t2)   12.50
TORREY,EDWIN C-Early Days in Dakota-Minnpls-(1925)-1st ed
                                   (5jj7,f,autg) 25.00
TORREY,JESSE-The Moral Instructor & Guide to Virtue & Happiness-
   Ballston Spa(NY)-1819-frontis-228p-calf
                                (5w7,v wn,cov dtchd) 9.50
--same-1824-Kinber & Sharpless-calf-8vo-300p-4th ed,rev
                                (5rr2,hngs wn) 8.50
TORREY,RAYMOND H-New York Walk Book-NY-1923-illus-
   fldg maps-Amer Geogr Soc   (5p7) 4.50   (5zz0)   6.50
--same-NY-1951-3rd ed-illus-12mo (5yy6) 7.50 (5p0)   4.00
TORREY,RUFUS C-History of Fitchburg,with History of Lunenburg-
   1865-128p   (5e8)   8.75
TORRINGTON,O M,compl-Catalogue of Etchings of Levon West-
   NY-1930-(Rudge)-4to-125 plts-ltd ed (5ii3,f,box) 25.00
TORRUBIA,F GIUSEPPE-I Moscoviti nella Calif-Rome-G Salomoni-
   1759-sm12mo-1st ed-wrps   (5hh0,Streeter copy) 8,500.00
TORY,A-Frankie in Wonderland,With Apologies to Lewis Carroll-
   NY-1934-EPDutton Co-24p-16mo   (5r0)   7.50
TORRY,D-Torrys in America-1890-145p (5t9)   12.00
TOTHEROH,DAN-Wild Birds,A Play in 3 Acts-GardenCty-1925-
   Dblday,Page-8vo-cl-Totheroh's 1st book(5b2,autgs of cast) 12.50
--Wild Orchard-NY-(c1927)-Doran-8vo-cl (5b2,autg,dj) 6.00
TOUEY,JOHN P-Are Mediums Really Witches-Lancaster-1927
                                   (5x7,autg)   4.50
TOULMIN,HARRY-Western Country in 1793-SanMarino,Calif-
   1948-Huntington Libr   (5x5,dj)   10.00
TOURGEE,ALBION-An Appeal to Caesar-NY-1884-12mo (5x2) 12.00
--Bricks without straw-NY-Fords,etc-(1880)-1st ed-1st state-
   pic cl-erratum slip   (5m2)   6.50
--Figs & Thistles,A Romance of the Western Reserve-NY-(1879)-Fords,
   Howard&Hulbert-1st ed   (5x4)   10.00
--A Fool's Errand-NY-1879   (5x2)   7.50
--A Fool's Errand-NY-(1880)-521p-enlrgd-illus (5yy8) 10. (5x2)17.50
--Hot Plowshares-NY-1883-Fords,Howard&Hulbert-610p-1st ed
                                   (5x4)   10.00
TOURIST,THE-or pocket manual for travellers-Albany-1831-
   24mo-bds-cl bk-papr labl-fldg map-2nd ed,enlrgd (5g8,fox) 7.50
--same-NY-1841-Harper&Bros-fldg map-108p-cl-9th ed
                        (5tt0) 10. (5t4,lacks map)   12.50
TOURISTS'GEM,THE-ManitouSprngs-(ca 1887)-orig wrps-16mo-
   16p-illus   (4g6)   6.00
TOURIST'S GUIDE THROUGH THE EMPIRE STATE-Albany-1871-
   Mrs S S Colt,ed-illus-239p   (5q0)   10.50
TOURISTS' MANUAL-to health & pleasure resorts of golden
   Northwest(Wisc,Iowa & Minn)etc-(Milwkee)-1880-illus-
   pict wrps   (5g3,sp wn)   7.50
TOURTELLOT,ARTHUR B-Be Loved No More-Bost-1938-Houghton,
   Miff-8vo-cl-9 plts-381p   (5j5)   6.50
--The Charles(The Rivers of Amer)-NY-(1941)
                    (5F0,dj) 3. (5s1,pres)   4.50
TOURTOULON,P de-Philosophy in the Development of Law-1922
                                   (5L7)   12.50
TOUS,GABRIEL-Ramon Expedition,Espinosa's Diary of 1716-Austin-
   1930-24p-offprnt-wrps   (4a5)   8.50
TOUSEY,SINCLAIR-Indices of Public Opinion-NY-1871-128p-
   blu cloth over soft bds-priv cir (5a0)   12.50
TOUSLEY,ALB S-Where Goes the River-IowaCty-(1928)-296p-
   cl-illus-priv prntd   (5h7,f,dj) 10. (5hh3)   6.00
TOUSSAINT,PIERRE-Memoir of-Born A Slave in St Domingo-Bost-
   1854-Crosby,Nichols-124p-cl-port (5r0)   20.00
TOUT,O B-The First 30 Years in Imperial Valley,Calif,1901 to 1931-
   SanDiego-1931-427p-illus   (5a9)   30.00
TOUT,T F-Chapters in Admin History of Medieval England-
   Manchester-1920-5 vols   (5q0) 1   45.00
TOVEY,CHAS-Wine & Wine Countries-Lond-1877-frontis-20 plts-
   519p   (5w1,shake) 16.50 (4g9,hng loose,lacks e.p.) 25.00
TOVEY,DUNCAN C,ed-Gray & His Friends-Cambr-1890-312p
                                   (5a1)   5.00
TOWARD THE POLES-Wash-1950-224p-fldg maps-230p-card cov
                                   (4b9)   10.00

TOWER,CHARLEMAGNE-The Charlemagne Tower Collection of
   Amer Colonial Laws-n.p.(Phila)-1890-sm4to-298p-frontis-
   t.e.g.-1st ed   (5w0) 25. (4j1) 17.50
--The Marquis De La Fayette in the Amer Revolution-Phila-1895-
   2 vols-ports-maps   (5m2)   17.50
TOWER,PHILO-Slavery Unmasked-Rochester-1856-frontis-8vo-
   1st ed   (5ss5,wtrstnd,bkstrp tn)   12.50
TOWERS,JOHN-A Friendly Dialogue between Theophilus &
   Philadelphus-Lond-1776-12mo-24p-bds (5L1,rbnd)   65.00
TOWLE,E R-Reuben Towle of Ranklin,Vt-1892-79p (5t9) 12.50
TOWLE,N C-History & Analysis of Constitution of US-Bost-1873-
   3rd ed-rev&enlrgd   (5ff4,shake)   9.75
TOWLE,NANCY-Vicissitudes Illustrated-Charleston-1832-
   frontis-1st ed-294p-errata-sm12mo-orig calf (4b1,f) 100.00
TOWN,SALEM-Analysis of Derivative Words in the Engl Language-
   NY-1836-164p-3rd ed-revsd&enlrgd (5t7)   6.50
--The Progressive Speller,for common schools & academies-Bost-
   ChasHWhiting-(c1859)-16mo-168p-cl bkd bds (5p1,wn) 5.00
TOWNDROW,THOS-Trial & acquittal of Ezra Haskell-Bost-1833-
   stitchd   (5g8,lt stn) 6.00
TOWNE,ARTHUR W-Pioneer in Paper,Story of Blake,Moffitt & Towne-
   (SanFran)-1930-50p-ltd to 50c for Roxburghe Club Feb 1931
                                   (5tt0)   10.00
TOWNE,CHAS H-Ambling Thru Acadia-NY-1923-250p-illus-plts
                        (5a1) 4.50 (5t0)   4.00
--Jogging Around New England-NY-1939-illus by Gillette (5t4) 7.00
--The Rise & Fall of Prohibition-NY-1923-Macmillan-12mo-cl-
   frontis-220p-1st ed   (5j5)   7.50
--This New York of Mine-NY-1931-Cosmo Bk Corp-290p-illus
                                   (5x0)   4.50
TOWNE,CHAS W-Shepherd's Empire-Norman-1945-cl-364p-
   "First Edition" on copyrite pg-scarce (4L0) 8.50 (4k6) 12.50
--same-1946-2nd printing   (4L0,dj)   6.50
TOWNE,HENRY ROBINSON-A Treatise on Cranes-Stamford-1883-
   ESDodge-191p-8vo-cl-g.crane on front cov (5L1)   35.00
TOWNE,ROBT D-Teddy Bears at the Circus-Chig-(1907)-
   Reilly&Britton Co-sm8vo-16p-col illus (5c8,soil)   8.00
TOWNER,H M-Hist Sketches Relating to Spencer,Mass-1901,2,3,9-
   4 vols   (5t9)   30.00
TOWNES,WM T-With Hooks of Steel-NY-1913-Neale-8vo-
   embossed cl   (5b2,flake)   4.00
TOWNSEND,CHAS W-Along the Labrador Coast-Bost-1907-289p-
   plts   (5s6)   8.50
--Sand Dunes & Salt Marshes-Bost-(1913)-311p (5e8)   6.75
TOWNSEND,E D-Anecdotes of the Civil War in the US-NY-1884-
   287p & ads   (5t4)   7.50
TOWNSEND,E W-Chimie Fadden Explains-1895-US Book Co(5x2)7.50
TOWNSEND,EDW W-A Daughter of the Tenements-NY-(1895)-
   1st ed,2nd issue   (5m2) 6.50 (5ee3)   5.00
TOWNSEND,ELIZ W-The White Dove,& other poems for children-
   NY,Bost,Cinn-1855-16mo-128p-frontis-3 plts
                        (5p1,chip,lacks e.p.)   7.50
TOWNSEND,GEO A-The Entailed Hat,or Patty Cannon's Times-
   NY-1884-orig pict cl-1st ed   (5m2)   12.50
--Los Abroad-Hartford-1870-frontis-594p-1st ed-scarce (4g2,f) 32.50
--Rustics in Rebellion-ChapelHill-(1950)-8vo-292p
                        (4a7,5yy6) 6. (5x2,dj) 6.50
--Tales of the Chesapeake-NY-1880-1st ed-port (5tt6) 15.00
TOWNSEND,REV GEO F-Three Hundred Aesop's Fables-NY-
   n.d.(1875?)-McLoughlin Bros-16mo-114 illus-230p-pict cl
                                   (5p1,rub)   15.00
TOWNSEND,H-A Touchstone for Silver-NY-1917-Gorham Co-
   41p-illus-lea   (5w7)   6.50
TOWNSEND,J D-The Divine Art-(1931)-illus by King-pict suede-
   183p   (5p6,f,dj)   5.00
TOWNSEND,J W-Piano Jim & the Impotent Pumpkin Vine-1950-
   8vo-wrps-ltd to 200c   (5g6)   7.50
TOWNSEND,J W-The Old "Main Line"-n.p.-1922-114p (5w4) 5.00
TOWNSEND,JOHN-Extracts from a Priv Journal Kept...During
   a Journey Across the Rocky Mntns in 1834-Phila-Supl to
   Waldie's Select Circ Libr,Dec 29,1835-folio-rare (4n4) 85.00
TOWNSEND,JOHN KIRKE-Narr of a Journey Across Rocky Mntns
   to Columbia River,etc-Phila-1839-orig cl-8vo-1st ed
   (5s9) 125. (5z9,pres,chip,box) 200. (4n4) 90. (5tt6,rbnd) 100.00
--Sporting Excursions in the Rocky Mntns-Lond-1840-part calf-
   2 vols-1st Engl ed   (4n4)   90.00
TOWNSEND,JOHN W-Kentuckians in History & Literature-NY-
   1907-189p   (5t2)   4.00
TOWNSEND,JOHN WILSON-Ambrose Barbour & His Idelberg
   Papers-Lexington-1951-152p-ltd to 200c,autg,nbrd
                                   (5yy8,autg) 20.00
TOWNSEND,LUTHER TRACY-History of the 16th Reg,New Hamp
   Vol-Wash-1897-574p   (5j6,fox)   8.50

TOWNSEND,MALCOLM-The Townsends-(1895)-(110p) (5t9) 15.00
TOWNSEND,REGINALD T-Mother of Clubs-NY-1936-237p-
cl-t8vo-ports&views-ltd to 1500c,nbrd (5j5) 15.00
TOWNSEND,THOS S-Honors of Empire State in War of Rebellion-
NY-1889-sm8vo-416p-buck (4a7,rbnd) 15.00
TOWNSEND,VIRGINIA F-A Boston girl's ambitions-Bost, Lee&
Shepard-NY, Dillingham-1887-1st ed (5m2,broke) 7.50
--Lenox Dare-Bost-1881-Lee&Shepard-451p (5x4) 12.50
TOWNSEND,W C-Lives of 12 Eminent Judges of the Last & Present
Century-Lond-1846-2 vols (5r4,ex-libr,rub) 17.50
TOWNSEND,W G PAULSON-Embroidery or the Craft of the Needle-
Lond-1899-illus-115p (5t4) 7.50
--same-Lond-1907-illus-308p(4)-col frontis (5n7) 8.50
TOWNSEND,WM H-Lincoln & the Bluegrass-(Lexington,Ky,1955)-
392p-illus-CMClay Edition (5t7,dj,autg) 7.50
--Lincoln the Litigant-Bost&NY-1925-illus-bds-116p (5t7) 10.00
TOWNSENDWARNER,SYLVIA-Elinor Barley-1930-R8vo-g.t.-
dec bds-vel sp-g.t.-ltd to 350c,autg,box-CressetPr (5t7) 17.50
TOWNSHEND,C H-Townshend Family of Lynn in Old & New
England-(1882)-138p-3rd ed (4t2) 15.00
TOWNSHEND,CAPT CHAS-Capt Chas Hervey Townshend-Mystic-
1940-4to-illus-ltd to 100c (5q8) 12.50
TOWNSHEND,CHAUNCEY,HARE-Facts in Mesmerism with Reasons
for a Dispassionate Inquiry Into It-NY-1841-illus-388(8)p-
(5w0,wn) 10.00
TOWNSHEND,F TRENCH-10,000 Miles of Travel,Sport & Adventure-
Lond-1869-275p-frontis-3/4 lea-raised bands -1st edition
(5dd1,hng rprd) 17.50
TOWNSHEND,HENRY H-New Haven & the First Oil Well-NewHav-
1934-priv prnt-8vo-wrps (4c1) 6.00
TOWNSHEND,R B-Last Memories of a Tenderfoot-Lond-(1926)-
John Lane-illus-270p-1st ed (4n8,4L0,f) 15.00
--A Tenderfoot in Colorado-Lond-(1923)-282p plus ads-2 photos-
1st ed(1st publ in 1923 on copyrite pg) (4k6) 20. (4L0) 12.50
--A Tenderfoot in NewMexico-Lond-(1923)-illus-257p-1st ed
(5yy8,fox) 12.50 (5a8,5dd1) 17.50
TOWNSON,ROBT-Travels in Hungary with a Short Acct of Vienna
in Year 1793-Lond-1797-calf-4to-plts-fldg map-506p
(5v7,broke) 47.50
TOY BOOK-Country Visit-NY-1904-McLoughlin-lg8vo-
pict glazed wrps-10p test-illus (5s0) 4.50
TOY BOOK-Death & Burial of Cock Robin-NY-n.d.- McLoughlin-
lg8vo-pict wrps-10p-illus-Sunshine Ser (5s0) 4.50
TOY BOOK-Domestic Animals-NY-1900-McLoughlin-sq8vo-
pict glazed wrps-10p-illus (5s0) 4.50
TOY,EDDIE-The Technic on How to Become Scientific in Manly
Art of Self Defense-NY-n.d.(?191-)-119p-12mo-illus
(5w7,stn) 5.00
TOYE,WM-The St Lawrence-Tor-1959-296p-plts-map (4a8) 5.00
TOZZER,ALFRED M-Excavation of a Site at Santiago Ahuitzotla,
D F Mexico-1921-BAE,B74-l9 plts incl map-56p-hard cov(4b2) 7.50
--Value of Ancient Mexican Manuscripts in the Study of the
General Development of Writing-Wash-1912-(14p)-wrps-
sep prntg (5L0) 3.00
TRACT PRIMER,THE-NY-(ca 1850)-Amer Tract Soc-16mo-illus-
108p-g.pict cl (5j5) 8.50
TRACY,CYRUS MASON-Studies of the Essex Flora-Lynn,Mass-
1892-99p (5s7) 6.00
TRACY,E E-Ancestry & Desc of Lt Thos Tracy of Norwich,Conn-
1898-294p (4t2) 27.50
TRACY,GILBERT A-Uncollected Letters of Abraham Lincoln-NY&Bost-
1917-264p-illus-cl&bds (5t7) 10.00
--same-Bost-1917-port-illus-1st ed-ltd to 550c (5m2) 7.50
TRACY,J-Since Emancipation-ca 1870-3p tract-wrps (5x2) 15.00
TRACY,JOS-History of American Missions to the Heathen-Worcester-
1840-illus-maps-726p-1st ed-scarce (4L2,fade,5r0) 50.00
TRACY,LOUIS-Wings of the Morning-Chig-(1924)-319p (5t7) 5.00
TRACY,MARIAN-The Care & Feeding of Friends -NY-(1946)-
128p (5c0,5c9) 3.00
--Casserole Cookery-NY-1943-154p-spiral bnd-8vo-bds (5c9) 3.00
--Coast Cookery-Bloomington,Ind-1952-318p (5g9) 6.00
--Marian Tracy's Complete Chicken Cookery-Indnpls-(1953)-
234p-illus (5c9) 4.50
TRACY,MILTON-The Colonizer -El Paso-1941-8vo-cl-381p-
illus-1st ed (5g2,dj) 10.00
TRACY,S-Mother & Her Offspring-NY-1860-453p (5ii2) 5.00
TRACY,WM-Notices of Men & events connected with early history
of Oneida Co-Utica-1838-orig prntd wrps-45p-scarce
(5g3,pres) 50.00
TRADEMARK DESIGN-Chig-1952-1st ed-illus-171p-4to (5ww3) 10.00
TRADE MARKS OF JEWELRY & KINDRED TRADES-NY-1950-
388p-illus-6th ed (5y2) 10.00

TRADER VIC'S-Bartender's Guide-NY-1947-illus-437p (5w1) 3.50
--Book of Food & Drink-NY-1946-272p-12mo-illus (5w1) 5.00
--Kitchen Kibitzer-GardenCty-1952-223p-illus (5g9) 4.50
TRAFFIC & USE OF OPIUM,THE-in our own & other countries-
Providence-1882-wrps (5g8) 7.50
TRAFFORD,F G-Phemie Keller,a novel-Lond-1866-3 vols-
Tinsley Bros-8vo-orig cl-1st ed (5xx6,sl loose) 35.00
TRAGER,MARTELLE W-Nat'l Parks of the Northwest-NY-1939-
216p-photos-fldg maps-1st ed (5s4) 7.50 (5L0) 5.00
TRAGICAL DEATH OF A APPLE PIE-cut in pieces and eat by etc-
Chig-(ca 1900)-Geo MHill Co-illus-bds (5c8,crack) 10.00
TRAHEY,JANE,ed-A Taste of Texas-NY-(1949)-for Neiman Marcus-
303p (5g9) 3.00
TRAIL GUIDE-The Kansas City Posse of the Westerners-Vol 1,#1 to
Vol 6,#4 incl Sept 1955 to Dec 1961-24 nbrs (5k0) 42.00
TRAIL OF THE MAINE PIONEER-Lewiston,Maine-1916-ltd to 2000c
(5x5) 15.00
TRAILL,MRS-Afar in the Forest-Lond,Edinb&NY-1869-illus
(5w8,v wn) 12.50
TRAILL,CATHERINE PARR-Afar in the Forest-Lond,Edinb&NY-1873-
Nelson-16mo-107p-illus-col frontis-cl-Pict Libr of Travel &
Adven (5p1,sl wn) 15.00
--Backwood of Canada-Tor-1929-buck (4b9,rbnd,ex-libr) 12.00
--Canadian Crusoes-Lond-1859-Hall, Virtue&Co-agnes Strickland,
ed-sm8vo-illus-dec cl-362p-plts-g.t.-2nd ed (5aa2) 20.00
TRAILL,H D-Life of Sir John Franklin-Lond-1896-ports-facs-maps-
12p,454p (4a8) 12.50
--Social England-NY-1901 to 1904-GPPutnam's Sons-6 vols in 12-
8vo-crushed lev mor-g. over cl-a.e.g.-illus ed
(5b0,f bndg) 400.00
--same-Lond-1902 to 1904-6 vols-sm4to-col plts-fldg maps
(5x7,crack) 50.00
TRAILL,R T-The Illustrated Family Gymnasium-NY-(1857)-215p,(4)-
illus (5w7) 12.50
TRAILL,THOS W-Chain Cables & Chains,etc-Lond-1885-illus-
19 plts-sm folio-1st ed (4m6,autg) 17.50
TRAIN & BANK ROBBERS OF THE WEST-Chig-(1880)-313p & 287p-
2 frontis-illus-cl-(2nd pt is Appler's work)-rare (5zz5) 75.00
TRAIN,ARTHUR-From the District Attorney's Office-NY-1939-
Scribner's-illus-1st ed (4L4,autg) 7.50
--Mc Allister & his Double-NY-1905-12mo-buck-1st ed of auth's
1st book (5gg6,pres) 25.00
--On the Trail of Bad Men-NY-1925-427p-1st ed (4L0) 8.50
--Mr Tutt's Case Book-NY-1936-Scribner (5p9) 6.00
--Puritan's Progress-NY-1931-477p (5r7) 7.50
--Story of Everyday Things-NY-(1941)-1st ed-illus
(4b7) 12.50 (5t0) 7.50
--Tutt for Tutt-NY-1934-1st ed (5mm2,dj) 8.50
--Yankee Lawyer-NY-1943-464p-Scribner (5p7) 4.00
TRAIN,C R-Precedents of Indictments & Special Pleas-Bost-1855
(5r4,rbnd) 15.00
TRAIN,ELIZ P-Madam of The Ivies-Phila-1898-Lippincott-1st ed
(5m2) 6.00
--A Queen of Hearts-Phila-1898-1st ed (5ee3) 5.00
TRAIN,GEO F-An Amer Merchant in Europe, Asia & Australia-
NY-1857-512p (5ii2,rub) 5.50
--My Life in Many States & in Foreign Lands-NY-1902-photos-
348p (4h7) 10. (5dd1) 8.50
--Young America in Wall Street-NY-1857-12mo-cl-406p
(5m8,underline) 10.00
TRAIN,PERCY-Medicinal Use of Plants by Indian Tribes of Nevada-
Wash-1941-mimeo-WPA-3 vols-cl-151p plus (48p) (5dd1,rbnd) 60.00
TRAIN TO YESTERDAY-1955-RRs of Amer-4to-maps & illus (5g0) 7.50
TRAITE SUR LA CULTURE DU TABAC CANADIEN-n.p.-ca 1882-
wrps (4c1) 10.00
TRAITS & STORIES OF THE IRISH PEASANTRY-Dublin-1833-
Wakeman-2nd series-3 vols-12mo-orig cl&bds-paper labls-
1st ed (5xx6) 150.00
TRAITS OF ABORIGINES OF AMERICA-A Poem-(Lydia H Sigourney)-
Cambridge-1822-284p (5yy8,wn,rprd) 15.00
TRAITS OF AMER INDIAN LIFE-by a Fur Trader-SanFran-1933-
4to-Grabhorn Pr (5r8) 30. (5x5) 40.00
TRAITS OF THE TEA PARTY-NY-1835-By a Bostonian-265p-port
(5m4,ex-libr) 27.50
TRALL,R T-The Hydropathic Encyclopedia...in 8 Parts-NY-n.d.
(1851)-cl-504p-scarce (4t8,rbnd) 22.50
--Illustrated Family Gymnasium-NY-(1857)-illus-cl
(5v0) 8.50 (5t7) 10.00
--The New Hydropathic Cook Book-NY-1854-12mo (5m6) 10.00
--same-NY-1857-illus-226p-orig red cl-g.lttrng
(5ww2,lack e.p.) 11.50
TRANE AIR CONDITIONING MANUAL-May 1941-Trane Co-
lg4to (5a6) 7.50

USED BOOK PRICE GUIDE

TRANOWSKY,BENJ-Anthropological,Legal & Medical Studies
on Pederasty in Europe-NY-n.d.-bds-ltd to 1500c,nbrd(5x7) 12.50
TRANS AFRICAN HIGHWAYS-(Jo'burg?)-1949-Auto Assn of So
Africa-16&406p-150p maps-fldg pkt map   (5c6,vg)   12.50
TRANS CONTINENTAL-Published Daily on Pullman Hotel Express
betw Bost&SanFran-Vol 1,#1 thru 12(all publ)-WRSteele,ed-1870-
4to-cl   (5g8)   50.00
TRANSFORMED-or Hist of a River Thief-Jeremiah McAuley?-
n.p.-(1876)-78p-cl   (5h7)   10.00
TRANSITION-#1 to 27(all publ)-Paris-1927 to 1938-8vo & 12mo-
orig wrps-27 nbrs in 25-complete run,as issued (5d5) 475.00
TRANSITION-Aug 1927,#5-Paris-1927-Shakespeare&Co-orig wrps
                                            (5hh1)   35.00
TRANSITION FORTY EIGHT-#1-Paris-(1948)-12mo-pict wrps-
1st ed   (5r9)   10.00
TRANSITION STORIES-NY-1929-12mo-pict bds-cl bk-1st ed
                                          (5ss7,f,dj)   30.00
TRANSPLANTED ROSE,A-NY-1882-Harper-1st ed (5m2,sl stn) 5.00
TRANSPORTATION IN AMER-RR Comm for Study of Transportation-
Wash-1947-391p-4to   (4e4)   5.00
TRANSPORTATION ON GREAT LAKES-Wash-1937-Trans Ser #1-
wrps-fldg maps-illus-441p-rev ed-sewn   (5s1,f)   6.00
TRANTER,G J-Plowing the Arctic-Lond-1944-illus-256p-cheap ed
                                          (5dd7,dj)   4.50
TRANTHAM,HENRY-Diamond Jubilee-Waco-1921-4to-190p-
illus   (4c7)   20.00
TRAPHAGEN,ETHEL-Costume Design & Illustration-NY-1918-197p-
plts   (5n7,stn,shake)   3.50
TRAPPROCK,WALTER E-The Cruise of the Kawa-NY-(1921)-illus-
146p   (5ss1,pres)   5.00
--My Northern Exposure-NY-1922-245p-illus (5ss1,pres)   6.00
TRAQUAIR,R-Old Silver of Quebec-Tor-1940-16p of photos-
169p,(3)   (5w7)   18.50
TRASK,KATRINA-Lessons in love-NY-1900-Harper-frontis-1st ed
                                             (5m2)   13.50
--White Satin & Homespun-NY-(c 1896)-Anson DF Randolph-g.-
narr 12mo-buck   (5b2,libr stmp) 8.50
TRASK,SPENCER-Bowling Green-1898-84p   (5t9)   3.00
TRATTNER,ERNEST R-Architects of Ideas-NY-(1938)-8vo-ports-
1st ed   (5m6,dj)   7.50
TRAUBEL,HORACE-Chats Communal-Bost-1904-1st ed
                                        (5mm2,pres)   17.50
TRAVELER,THE-Directory Guide & Handbook of LosAngeles &
Southern Calif-(1909)-64p-wrps   (5d6)   6.00
TRAVELER'S GUIDE TO NEW GOLD MINES IN KANS & NEBR-
(Denver-1949-Mumey)-facs of 1859 ed-16mo-orig wrps-16p-
ltd to 400c   (4g6,box)   10.00
TRAVELLERS' GUIDE FOR MONTREAL & ITS VICINITY-Montreal-
1857-32p-wrps   (5ff7)   15.00
TRAVELER'S GUIDE-for Montreal,Quebec & Saratoga Springs-
Montreal-1859-24mo-illus-wrps   (5g4)   6.00
TRAVELLER'S GUIDE-for..Montreal,Quebec,Ottawa etc & rivers
St Laurence & Saguenay-(wrpr title)-Montreal-1871 (5g3) 5.00
TRAVELLING WITH TRAMPS-By A #1-Erie-1920-pict wrps-1st ed-
wdcuts   (5m2)   6.00
TRAVELS & ADVENTURES-of Wm Lithgow in Europe,Asia & Africa-
1825-Falkirk-16mo-24p-self wrps-rare   (5p5)   37.50
TRAVELS IN THE INTERIOR PARTS OF AMER-Lond-1807-part calf-
fldg table-116p-1st Engl ed-rare   (4j4)   275.00
TRAVELS OF BARON MUNCHAUSEN-NY-1929-4to-208p-
lea bkd cl-t.e.g-ltd to 1500c,nbrd-Ltd Edit Club (5p1) 25.00
TRAVELS OF SEVERAL LEARNED MISSIONERS OF SOC of JESUS-
Lond-1714-R Gosling-336p-index-plts-calf (5yy3)   85.00
TRAVELS ON WESTERN SLOPES OF MEX CORDILLERA-SanFran-
1857-438p-illus-(M T Wheat)   (4a5,cov wn)   35.00
TRAVEN,BRUNO-The Death Ship-NY-1934-12mo (5gg6,dj)   25.00
TRAVERS,BENJ-Further Inquiry Concerning Constit Irritation,
& Pathology of Nervous System-Lond-1826,1835-for Longman(etc)-
8vo-hf calf-bds-2 vols-errata lf   (4e5,rebkd)   75.00
TRAVERS,P L-Mary Poppins Comes Back-Lond-(1935)-1st ed-illus
        (5i3,autg,dj) 25.   (5v0,autg,mint,dj)   27.50
--Mary Poppins Opens the Door-NY-(1943)-Reynal&Hitchcock-
1st ed   (5rr2,autg,spot)   7.50
TRAVIS,DAN'L-MDCCXXI,An almanack...for...1721-Bost-1721-
16mo-stitchd   (5g3,1st lf tn wi loss) 30.00
TRAVIS,EDMUNDS-A Century of Usury in Texas-Dallas-1940-
wrps-73p   (5a8)   5.00
TRAVIS,ELMA-The Pang Yanger-NY-1905-McClure,Phillips-8vo-
dec cl   (5b2,fleck)   5.00
TRAVIS,LORENA L-Walter Scott Richards,Pioneer of the SW-
Muskogee-1956-123p-wrps   (5h0)   5.00
TRAVIS,REV WM-History of the Germantown Academy-Phila-1882
HWSmith,ed-64p plus illus-tip in frontis-250c prntd(5w4,lt soil)14.50

TRAYLOR,SAM'L W,SR-Out of the SoWest,A Texas Boy-n.p.-
(Allentown,Pa)-(1936)-255p-cl-illus   (5t2,4L0)   5.00
TREADWELL,EDW F-The Cattle King-NY-1931-Macmillan-
"Publ Apr 1931" on copyrite pg-367p-cl-1st ed
        (4k6) 25.   (4L0) 30.   (5x5,dj)   12.50
--same-Bost-(1950)   (5d6)   22.50
TREADWELL,JOHN H-Manual of Pottery & Porcelain for Amer
Collectors-NY-1872-161p-illus   (5w7)   4.50
TREANOR,THOS C-John Treanor-LosAng-1937-Zamorano Club-
8vo-green cl-85p-port-wrps   (5h5,f)   10.00
TREASHER,RAY C-Bibliography of Geology & Mineral Resources
of Oregon-Portland-1936-Conger Prntg Co-5p plus 224p-
stiff wrps-Oreg State Planning Board-WPA Project 498(3) A
                                           (5r0)   12.50
TREASURED RECIPES FROM SEATTLE-Women's Univ Club-Sea-
(?1944)-400p-illus-spiral bnd wrps   (5g9,5c4)   3.50
TREASURED RECIPES FROM SPOKANE-(Cover title)-(n.p.,1948)-
98p-plts-spir bnd-pict wrps   (5g9)   4.00
TREASURY OF PLEASURE BOOKS FOR YOUNG PEOPLE-Lond-
1856-Sampson,Low&Son-blu g.cl   (5c8,fray,shake) 37.50
TREASURY OF TRAVEL & ADVENTURE IN N & S AMER,EUROPE,
ASIA & AFRICA-NY-1865-456p-illus-1st ed (5s4) 6.50 (5L3) 7.50
TREATIES OF AMITY & COMMERCE-& of Alliance Eventual &
Defensive, betw His Most Christian Majesty & the 13 United
States of Amer-Hartf-1779-8vo-32p-stitchd (5a3,f)   100.00
TREATIES & CONVENTIONS-concluded betw the US of Amer &
Other Powers since Jul 4,1776...Wash-1871-thk8vo-cl-
912p-SED 36   (5j5,wn)   15.00
--same-Wash-1889-enlrgd ed-1434p   (5j5)   25.00
TREATISE ON CAKE MAKING-to Assist the Baker-NY-(1935)-
Fleischman Div-468p-4to-illus   (5c5,libr stmp) 4.50
TREATISE ON THE MANUFACTURE-Imitation,Adulteration &
Reduction of Foreign Wines,Brandies,Gins,Rums-Phila-1870-
(JnStephen)-208p   (5w1)   15.00
TREATISE ON PATRIARCHAL-or Coop System of Soc as it Exists in
Some Gov etc,Under the Name of Slavery-By an Inhabitant of
Florida-(n.p.-Tallahasee?)-1829-16p-orig plain wrps-2nd ed
        (5m3,f,unopnd) 50.   (5x5)   60.00
TREATISE ON POLICE OF LONDON-By a magistrate-Phila-1798-
1st Amer ed-calf   (5g3,ex-libr,wn,cov dtchd) 12.50
TREATT,STELLA COURT-Sudan Sand,Filming the Baggara Arabs-
Lond-1939-Geo G Harrap-photos-251p   (4t5)   12.50
TREATY BETWEEN THE US & MEXICO-Wash-1858-SED52-384p
                                           (5n4)   45.00
TREATY OF PEACE-betw Allied & Assoc Powers & German...
signed Versailles,Jun 28,1919-Lond-(1919)-453p-folio-fldg maps-
wrps   (5j5)   17.50
TREE,HERBERT BEERBOHM-Thoughts & After Thoughts-NY&Lond-
1913-315p-illus   (5t7)   10.00
TREGASKIS,RICHARD-Guadalcanal Diary-NY-c1943
        (5x7) 3.   (5m2,dj) 4.   (5s1)   4.50
TREGO,CHAS B-Geography of Penna....wi descrip of each county...
(&) a travellers' guide-Phila-1843-map-illus-orig roan
                                    (5g4,wn,sl dmpstn) 25.00
TREGO,FRANK H-Boulevarded Old Trails in the Great SuWest-
NY-(1929)-262p-photos-map   (5dd1) 7.50   (5x5)   15.00
TRELAWNEY-ANSELL,E C-I Followed Gold-NY-1939-312p(4b9)15.00
TRELOAR,WM P-Wilkes & the City-Lond-1917-300p-16 plts(5a1) 6.00
TREMAIN,HENRY EDWIN-Last Hours of Sheridan's Cavalry-NY-
1904-Bonnell,Silver&Bowers-563p-illus   (5mm8)   10.00
TREMAN,E M-Treman,Tremaine,Truman Family in Amer-1901-
2 vols-2129p   (5t9)   35.00
TREMAUDAN,A H de-Hudson Bay Road(1498 to 1915)-Lond-1915-
264p-30 plts-2 fldg maps   (4a8,pres)   15.00
TREMENHEERE,HUGH S-Notes on Public Subjects Made During
Tour in US & Canada-Lond-1852-fldg map-320p (5dd0)   25.00
TREMONT BAPTIST CHURCH-Collection of Choice, Well Tried
Recipes-Pasadena-ca 1915-ads-wrps-178p   (4g9)   8.50
TRENCK,BARON FREDERIC-Life of-Albany-1794-16mo-345p-lea
                                      (5xx7,lacks flys) 10.00
TREND,J B-Bolivar & the Independence of SoAmer-n.p.-1951-
242p-map   (5w5)   3.00
TRENHOLM,VIRGINIA C-Footprints on the Frontier-(Douglas,Wyo)-
(1945)-365p plus index-illus-ltd to 1000c,autg (4L0)   45.00
TRENT,LUCY-John Neely Bryan-Dallas-1936   (4c7)   20.00
TRENT,META CATHERINE-Incidents by the Way-(LosAng,1935,
GeoRice&Sons Pr)-cl-g.t.-6p plus 342p-illus-ltd to 150c,nbrd
                                       (5r0,sl tn)   15.00
TRENT,S M-My Cousin,Will Rogers-NY-1938-266p-illus (5s4) 7.50
TRENT,W P-Cambridge History of Amer Literature,The-NY-(1925)-
4 vols   (5t4)   10.00
--Defoe,How to Know Him-Indnpls-1916-Bobbs,Merrill-8vo-cl-
329p-port   (5aa2)   5.00

291

TRENT,W P (continued)
--Southern Writers-NY-1905   (5mm2)   7.50
TRENY,M-La Californie Devoilee-Paris-1850-8vo-orig prntd wrps-
    2nd ed   (4h0,lacks sp)   40.00
TRESCOT,WM H-The Diplomacy of the Revolution-NY-1852-
    Appleton-sm8vo-169p-orig cl   (5L1)   10.00
TREUSSART,GEN-Essays on Hydraulic & Common Mortars & on
    lime burning-Phila-1838-plts-buck   (5L7,rbnd)   15.00
TREVELYAN,GEO M-England Under Queen Anne-Lond-1932 to 4-
    3 vols-ports-maps   (5a1)   17.50
--English Revolution, 1688,89-1939   (5L7)   4.00
--English Social History-Lond-1943-628p   (5c3)   4.50
--Garibaldi & the Thousand-NY-1909-8vo-cl-illus-maps-395p
                                         (5t0)   5.00
--Garibaldi's Defence of the Roman Republic-Lond,NY,Bombay &
    Calcutta-1910-illus-maps-387p   (5t7)   8.50
--Illustrated English History-Lond-v.d.-4 vols-8vo-cl (5p5,dj,f) 20.00
TREVELYAN,GEO OTTO-The Amer Revolution-Lond-1899,1914-
    together,6 vols-8vo-cl   (5g3)   20.00
--same-1909,07-Vols 1 to 3 in 4 vols   (5L7)   17.50
TREVES,SIR FREDK-The Cradle of the Deep-Lond-1908-44 photos-
    4 maps   (5c1)   8.50
--same-NY-1908-maps-illus-t.e.g.   (5w4)   5.00
--Uganda for a Holiday-Lond-1913-JMurray-photos-230p
                                       (4t5,dj)   12.50
TREVOR,ROY-My Balkan Tour-Lond-1911-cl-8vo-465p-plts-map
                                         (5v7)   12.50
TREVOR-BATTYE,AUBYN-Ice Bound on Kilguev-Westminster-1895-
    cl-8vo-458p-illus-fldg maps   (5v7) 15. (5ss1)   12.50
TREZEVANT,DR D H-Burning of Columbia,S C-Columbia-1866-
    SCPower Pr-31p-wrps   (5yy3)   40.00
TRI-STATE COOK BOOK-Keokuk,Iowa-n.d.(ca 1890)-1st Unitarian
    Church-269p & ads   (5g9,rub)   7.50
TRIAL OF THE ASSASSINS-& Conspirators for Murder of...
    V P Johnson etc-Phila-(1865)-8vo-illus-pict wrps-102p (5t7) 25.00
TRIBUNE ALMANAC,THE-& Political Register for 1861-(wrpr title)-
    NY-(1860,61)   (5g4)   7.50
TRIBUNE BOOK OF OPEN AIR PORTS,THE-NY-1887-Henry Hall,ed-
    t8vo-orig cl-500p-illus-1st Linotype book (5d1)   85.00
TRICKS & KNACKS OF FISHING-Bristol,Conn-1911-115p-illus
                                         (5t7)   5.00
TRICKS OF THE TOWN-...Mr John Thomson(pseudonym?)-Lond-
    1732-for J Roberts-8vo-disbnd-1st ed-v rare (5i7)   200.00
TRIDENT SOC,Ed-Book of Navy Songs-NY-1945-4to-illus-194p-
    dec   (5s1,ex-libr)   7.50
TRIED & APPROVED-Buckeye Cookery-Minnpls-1883-536p-
    rev&enlrgd   (5c0,broke)   7.50
TRIED RECEIPTS OF PASADENA-Scripps Home for Aged People-
    (cpyrte by M Honberger,1914)-112p   (5g9,pres,soil)   6.50
TRIFLES FROM MY PORT FOLIO-By a Staff Surgeon-Quebec-
    1839-2 Vols(Vol 2 only)-orig bds-cl bk-252p (5w8)   50.00
TRIGGS,H INIGO-Formal Gardens in England & Scotland-Lond-
    1912-122 plts loose in 3 portfolios of cl bkd bds
                                     (5z9,cov soil & wn)   35.00
--Town Planning Past, Present &Possible-Lond-1911-334p-Methuen-
    334p-2nd ed-cl-t.e.g.-scarce   (5m5,broke)   45.00
TRIGGS,J H-Hist & Directory of Laramie City,Wyo Terr-Laramie-
    1955-facs of 1875 & 76-2 phamph,boxed-ltd to 500c (4L0,f) 15.00
TRIGGS,OSCAR L-Chapters in the History of the Arts & Crafts
    Movement-Chig-1902-photos-198p   -bds,4to (5n7)   12.50
--Selections from the Prose & Poetry of Walt Whitman-Bost-1898-
    8vo-cl-g.t.-port-Small,Maynard   (5b2)   6.00
TRIGONOMETRY-Together with Logarithmic & Other Tables-
    Cambr-1822-Univ Pr-orig bds-cl-plts   (5j3,rbnd, v fox)   30.00
TRIM-Le Calcul Amusant,La Table de Pythagore,servie aux petits
    enfants-Paris-(c 1860)-4to-22 lvs-orig pict bds (5c8,cov stnd) 17.50
TRIM-Plume le Distrait-Paris-(ca 1860)-Hachette-4to-25p-
    pict book   (5c8)   17.50
TRIMBLE,MRS JANE-Memoir of-Cinn-1861-177p-cl-(Jos M Trimble)
                                         (5h7)   7.50
TRIMBLE,WM J-Mining Advance Into the Inland Empire-Madison-
    1914-Univ of Wisc Hist Ser-pg 137 to 392-cl-scarce
                                     (4L0,rbnd,ex-libr)   17.50
TRIMEN,HENRY-HandBook to the Flora of Ceylong-Lond-1893 to
    1900-orig cl-8vo-2 col fldg plts-100 litho plts-5 pts in 5 vols-
    wi atlas of plts loose in portfolio,4to,cl-1st ed (5z9,f) 200.00
TRIMMER,F M-The Yukon Territory-Lond-1898-1st ed-wdcuts-
    illus-438p-fldg map-8vo   (5i3)   20.00
TRIMMER,MRS-A Series of Prints Taken from the New Testament-
    Lond-(1790)-JnMarshall-plts dated Feb 1,1790-1st ed-64 plts
                                     (5v2,rbnd,f)   35.00
--Some Account of the Life & Writings of Mrs Trimmer wi orig letters-
    Lond-1814-2 vols-Imp 8vo-frontis-calf (5c8,rub)   45.00

TRIMMER,SARAH-Descrip of Set of Prints of Ancient History,
    wi series of prints-1828-Baldwin&Cradock-12mo-roan-2 vols-
    32 plts   (4d1)   20.00
--New & Comprehensive Lessons Containing General Outline of
    Roman History wi series of prints-1816-J Harris-lg sq12mo-roan-
    2 vols-40 plts   (4d1)   25.00
--Scripture Lessons Designed to Accompany a Series of Prints from
    New Testament,wi series of prints-1825-Baldwin Cradock&Joy-
    12mo-roan-2 vols-64 plts   (4d1)   25.00
TRINITY COUNTY,CALIF-& Summary of Its History from May,1845
    to Sept 1926-Weaverville,Ca(1926)-(prntd at Sacr)-28p plus
    index-wrps-1st ed-scarce   (5t3,pres,als laid in)   30.00
TRINKA,ZENA IRMA-NoDakota of Today-Bismarck-1919-253p plus
    index-photos-1st ed   (5dd1,lt wn)   10.00
--same-StPaul-1920-illus-3rd ed   (5jj7,f)   8.00
--Out Where the West Begins-StPaul-1920-432p-photos-fldg map-
    scarce   (5jj7,f) 15. (5dd1) 20. (5s4,soil)   17.50
TRIPLER LIQUID AIR CO-Bost-1900-8vo-orig wrps-16p-several illus
                                         (5ss5)   15.00
TRIPLETT,F F C-Analytical Digest of Pension & Bounty Land Laws-
    Wash-1854-Sheep   (5r4,needs rebndg)   10.00
TRIPLETT,FRANK-Conquering the wilderness-NY-1883-illus-
    pict cl-1st ed   (4L0,wn) 8.50 (5g8)   15.00
--Conquering the Wilderness-NY-1890-742p-illus
                                     (5L2,tn,rprd)   6.50
--Conquering the Wilderness-Chig-1895-cl   (5h1)   7.50
--History, Romance & Philosophy of Great Amer Crimes &
    Criminals-Hartford-1885-calf-illus-659p-scarce (5dd1,wn)   15.00
--Life, Times & Treacherous Death of Jesse James,the Only
    Correct & Authorized Ed-Chig-1882-416p-illus-orig calf-
    1st ed-1st prntg-ex rare   (4L0)   275.00
TRIPLETT,JUNE-Salt Water Taffy-NY-1929-206p-illus (5s1)   4.00
TRIPP & FIFIELDS-Durohercules Water Wheel-Camden,NY-1868?-
    illus front & rear-4p-4to folder   (5b8,f)   14.50
TRIPP, C E-Ace High, The Frisco Detective-SanFran-1948-
    reprntd from Beadle's Half Dime Library-sm folio-cl&dec bds-
    10 illus-ltd to 500c-Grabhorn Pr   (5d1)   25.00
TRIPP,WM H-There Goes Flukes-Reynolds-1925-262p-illus-
    autg   (5e8)   37.50
--same-NewBedford-1938-262p-illus   (5t4,autg)   70.00
TRIPP'S WHITE MNTNS GUIDE BOOK-Bost-(1852)-4th ed-24mo-
    108p-illus-maps-cl-g.stmpd   (5u9)   17.50
TRIPPENSEE,REUBEN E-Wildlife Management,Upland Game &
    General Principles-NY-1948-cl-489p-illus (5cc1)   9.95
TROBRIAND, REGIS DE-4 Years with the Army of the Potomac-
    Bost-1889-port-maps   (5s9,libr labl)   22.50
TROLLEY TRIPS THROUGH SOUTHERN NEW ENGLAND-Hartford-
    (1907)-108p-16mo-prnt wrps-illus   (5q0)   10.00
TROLLOPE,ANTHONY-The Amer Senator-Detroit-1877 (5mm2)
--same-NY-(1940)-ltd to 310c-Trollope Soc (5mm2)   15.00
--An autobiography-Edinb-1883-Blackwood-2 vols-8vo-orig cl-
    1st ed-cl-port   (5x3,fade)   40.00
--same-NY-1883-Harper-port-1st US ed   (5m2,sl soil)   6.00
--Can You Forgive Her?-Lond-1864-Chapman&Hall-illus-2 vols-
    8vo-1st ed-calf-g.   (5b0,chip)   60.00
--Four Lectures-Lond-(1938)-NorrisLParrish,ed-1st ed-ltd to 150c
                                     (5m1,mint)   20.00
--Framley Parsonage-NY-(ca 1860)-Harper-12mo-cl-plts-
    530p-10p ads   (5j5,fray)   10.00
--The Golden Lion of Granpere-Tor-1872-Hunter, Rose&Co (5w8) 17.50
--Harry Heathcote of Gangoil-Lond-1874-Sampson Low, etc-
    orig cl   (5x3,lacks e.p.)   30.00
--He Knew He Was Right-Lond-1869-Strahan&Co-2 vols-
    lg12mo-g.sp-illus-1st ed
               (5xx6,lt dmpstn) 25.(5b0,lt fade) 55. (5r9)   35.00
--How the "Mastiffs" Went to Iceland-Lond-1878-Mrs Blackburn,
    illus-4to-orig cl-g.-a.e.g.   (5b0,lt soil)   95.00
--Hunting sketches-Lond-1865-Chapman&Hall-8vo-hf mor-
    t.e.g.,by Zaehnsdorf-1st ed-scarce   (5x3)   35.00
--same-NY-1933-Sign of Gosden Head-sq4to-calf sp-g.t.-
    ltd to 950c,nbrd   (4b6)   17.50
--same-Lond-1934-illus by Robt Ball-4to   (5j2)   10.00
--Last Chronicle of Barset-Lond-1867-1st ed-2 vols-orig cl-illus
               (5tt6,wn) 25. (5r9,hf mor)   25.00
--A Letter from...describing a visit to Calif in 1875-Colt Pr-
    bds-ltd to 500c-wdcuts -1946(JGrabhorn pres)(5ss9,pres,f)   20.00
--Linda Tressel-Edinb-n.d.-Wm Blackwood-2 vols in 1-8vo-
    orig cl   (5xx6,hng wn)   60.00
--Lotta Schmidt, & other stories-Lond-1867-Alexander Strahan-
    8vo-orig cl-1st ed   (5xx6,sp fade)   80.00
--The Macdermots of Ballycloran,a Historical Romance-Lond-1848-
    3 vols-8vo-hf calf-1st ed,2nd issue of Trollope's 1st book-
    ex rare   (5gg6,box)   350.00

TROLLOPE, ANTHONY (continued)
--same-Lond-1880-Chapman&Hall-1880-orig pic bds-12mo(5xx6) 6.00
--North America-NY-1862-623p-cl   (4m4)   15.00
--same-Phila-1862-cl-2 vols   (5q8,sl soil)   17.50
--same-NY-1951-lg8vo-bds wi cl-555p-8p index   (5t0)   5.00
--Orley Farm-Lond-1862-Chapman&Hall-JEMillais,illus-1st ed-
   20 pts with orig front wrps bnd in (5b0,lt rub) 75. (5tt2)   125.00
--same-Lond-1862-Chapman&Hall-illus-3/4 mor-2 vols-1st ed
    (5z7,sl fade)   65.00
--Phineas Redux-Lond-1874-1st ed-2 vols-illus (5tt6,rbnd)   30.00
--Ralph the Heir-Lond-1871-1st ed in 1 vol-illus-3/4 lev mor-
   a.e.g.-scarce-(publ same yr as 3 vol ed)   (5ii3,rub)   50.00
--The Small House at Allington-Lond-1864-18 illus by Millais-
   Smith, Elder&Co-2 vols-8vo-lea&bds-1st ed-g.   (5b0)   75.00
--Travelling Sketches-Lond-1866-112p-1st ed-(1st issue wiout
   pub cat)   (5nn2)   75.00
--Two Heroines of Plumpington-NY-1954-Oxford Univ Pr-8vo-
   cl-illus   (5b0,dj)   10.00
--The Vicar of Bullhampton-Lond-1870-Bradbury,Evans&Co-8vo-
   hf calf-t.e.g.by Riviere-30 illus by HWoods-1st ed
    (5b0,f bndg)   95.00
--The Way We Live Now-Lond-1875-Chapman&Hall-8vo-orig grn cl-
   Chapman&Hall-40 illus by Fildes-2 vols-1st ed-yell e.p.   100.00
TROLLOPE,MRS FRANCES-The Barnabys in Amer-Lond-1843-
   Henry Colburn- 3 vols-12mo-hf calf-1st ed-6 plts-frontis
    (5xx6,scuff,sl rprd)   25.00
--Domestic Manners of the Americans-Lond-1832-2 vols-336p,272p-
   24 plts-3/4 lea-hf lea-Whittaker,Treacher&Co-1st ed
    (5L3) 50.   (4b5)   75.00
--same-Lond-1832-cl-8vo-24 liths-2 vols-2nd ed (5v7)   35.00
--same-Lond-1832-325p-8 plts-4th ed (5ee3,sl wn)   15.00
--same-Lond-1839   (5ee3)   5.00
--same-NY-1949-illus-cl&bds-454p
   (5q0,dj) 10.50 (5m2,5q8,dj) 7.50 (4p8)   6.50
--The Life & Adventures of Michael Armstrong,the Factory Boy-
   Lond-1840-illus-hf lea-1st ed   (5mm2)   15.00
TROLLOPE,T ADOLPHUS-Artingale Castle-Lond-1867-3 vols-
   Chapman&Hall-8vo-orig cl-1st ed   (5xx6,rub)   40.00
--Summer in Brittany-Lond-1840-1st ed-2 vols-12 plts
   (5i3) 12.50 (5i8)   35.00
TROMHOLT,SOPHUS-Under the Rays of the Aurora Borealis-Bost-
   1885-Siewers,ed-orig ed in 2 vols-illus-fldg map (5ss1)   13.50
TROOST,G-4th Geological Rpt to 22nd Gen Assembly of State of
   Tenn-Nashvl-1937-37p-lg fldg map disbnd   (5h7)   15.00
--same-3rd Geological Rpt to 21st Gen Assembly-Nashvl-1835-
   32p-disbnd   (5h7,lacks map)   12.50
TROTSKY,LEON-History of the Russian Revolution-NY-1932-
   3 vols-illus   (5m2)   12.50
--Lenin-NY-(1925)-216p-frontis   (5ss6)   6.50
--Lessons of October, 1917-Lond-1925-wrps   (4b4)   20.00
--Our Revolution-NY-1918-220p   (5t7)   6.50
--The Real Situation in Russia-NY-(1928)-364p-6 supl-scarce
    (5ss6,dj)   6.00
--Stalin,An Appraisal of the Man & His Influence-NY-(1941)-
   516p-supl-photos-1st ed   (5ss6,dj)   7.50
TROTT,NICHOLAS-The Laws of the British Plantations in Amer in
   One Volume-Lond-1721-prntd for B Cowse-folio-1st ed
    (5s9,rprd)   345.00
TROTTA,VINCENT-Screen Personalities-NY-1933-illus-109p
    (4c9)   12.50
TROTTER,J M-Music & Some Highly Musical People-Bost-1882-
   illus   (5x2)   27.50
TROTTER,REGINALD G-Canadian History,A Syllabus & Guide to
   Reading-NY-1926-cl-162p   (5r6)   6.00
TROTTER,THOS-View of the Nervous Temperment-Troy-1808-
   Wright(etc)-sm8vo-orig sheep-338p,1 leaf (4e5,rub)   150.00
TROUBETZKOY,AMELIE RIVES-Phila-1898-Lippincott-illus-
   1st ed -A Damsel Errant-211p   (5m2)   4.00
TROUGHTEN,ELLIS-Furred Animals of Australia-NY-1947-25 col plts-
   1st ed   (5kk7,dj)   7.50
TROUP,MRS ALEX C-Once upon a time in Nebraska-Omaha-
   1916-91p-2nd ed   (4L0)   3.00
TROUP,LORIS-The Tasting Spoon-NY-(1955)-286p
   (5c9) 4.50 (5w3)   5.00
TROUP,ROBT-A letter to the Hon Brockholst Livingston...on the
   lake canal policy of State of NY-Albany-1822-disbnd
    (5g4,t.pg tn)   20.00
TROW,JAS-Manitoba & NW Terr,Letters-Ottawa-1878-8vo
    (5nn8)   60.00
TROWBRIDGE,F B-Desc of Henry Champion of Saybrook &
   Lynne,Conn-1891-560p   (4t2)   15.00

TROWBRIDGE,J M-The Cider Maker's Hand Book-NY-1890-119p
   (5e4) 7.50 (5w1)   6.50
TROWBRIDGE,JOHN T-A Chance for Himself-Bost-1872-
   Jas R Osgood&Co-8vo-cl-sp g.-illus-1st ed (5rr2,bkstrp wn)   7.50
--Cudjo's Cave-Bost-1864-Tilton-cl-1st ed,2nd state,wi 21 chapt
   listed in Contents but L'Envoy pg wrong (5rr2) 17.50 (5v0)   30.00
--same-Bost-1904-cl   (5p5,5x2)   7.50
--Darius Green & His Flying Machine-Bost-1910-Houghton,Miff-
   54p-1st ed-illus   (5x4)   10.00
--My Own Story-Bost-1903-illus-482p-g.t.-illus-1st ed (5ee3)   10.00
--Neighbor Jackwood-Bost-1895-459p-frontis-port-rev (5t4)   4.50
--Picture of Desolated States-Hartford-1868-690p,46p
   (5q0) 10.   (5L3,f)   13.50
--The South-Hartford-1866-590p-illus-maps
   (5hh3) 10. (5ee3) 17.50 (5r7)   15.00
--The Vagabonds-NY-1868-Hurd&Houghton-illus by Darley-8vo-
   orig stmpd mor   (5j5,wn)   7.50
TROWBRIDGE, M E D-Pioneer Days-Phila-(1895)-frontis-
   160p(7-10 detached)   (5t4)   18.50
TROWBRIDGE,W P-Report on Power & Machinery Employed in
   Manufactures-Vol 22 of 10th Census-Wash-GPO-lg4to-cl-
   12p,294p,64p,27p,66p,106p and 41p (5hh7,sl wn)   28.50
TROXELL,GILBERT McCOY-The Elizabethan Club of Yale University-
   n.p.-n.d.-8vo-8pg fold   (5p1)   5.00
TROY,N Y-Manual of the Common Council of City of...ending
   Mar,1867-By Hubbell-Troy-1866-173p   (5p7)   10.00
TROYAT,HENRY-Firebrand,Life of Dostoevsky-NY-1946-illus-
   8vo-cl-438p   (5t0)   4.50
TRUAX,CHAS & CO-Price List of Physicians' Supplies-Chig-1890-
   20p,1080p-illus-lg thk8vo-cl-illus-5th ed (5t0)   15.00
TRUDEAU,EDW L-An Autobiography-Phila-1916-illus-1st ed
    (5m2,5t4)   7.50
TRUDEL-Genealogie de Dosithee Trudel Pretre-L'Institut
   Genealogique Drouin-Montreal-1942-2 vols-lea-illus-
   delux lea -406p & 62p   (5t9)   150.00
TRUDELLE,JOS-Les Jubiles et les eglises et chapelles de la Ville
   et de la Banlieue de Quebec,1608 to 1901-(Vol 2 only)-
   Quebec-1904-ports-illus   (5w8)   25.00
TRUE,ALFRED C-A History of Agricultural Education in the US
   1785 to 1925-USDA Misc pub #36-1929-436p (5w3)   9.50
--History of Agricultural Experimentation & Research in US 1607 to
   1925-Wash-1937-321p   (5e4)   12.50
--History of Agriculture Extension Work in US 1785 to 1923-
   Dept of Agric-Wash-1928-220p   (5e8)   3.75
TRUE & IMPARTIAL STATE OF PROVINCE OF PENNA-Phila-
   1759-Dunlap-4to-hf mor-1st ed-rare
   (5m4,rbnd) 250. (5n2,ex-libr)   275.00
TRUE BLUE COOK BOOK-Oak Park alll-1895-1st Presbyterian Church-
   194p-blue ink-oilcloth cov   (5g9,hng loose)   7.50
TRUE,CHAS K-John Winthrop & the Great Colony-NY&Cinn-
   c1875-16mo-208p-frontis & 1 plt-cl   (5p1,pres)   17.50
TRUE NATURE & CAUSE OF THE TAILS OF COMETS-Byan Enquirer-
   Bost-1772-sm4to-disbnd   (5a3)   250.00
TRUE PICTURE OF EMIGRATION-Chig-1936-Lakeside Pr-12mo-
   cl-167p   (5t0)   7.50
TRUE POLITENESS-A Hand Book of Etiquette for Gentlemen-NY-
   (1848)-32mo-64p   (5w7,crack)   6.50
TRUE WEST-Vol 1,#4(whole #4),Vol 16,#6(whole #94)-89 numbers
   (5s4,lacks Oct '63)   90.00
TRUEBLOOD,SARAH E-Cats by the Way-Phila-1904-illus-1st ed
    (4a1)   15.00
TRUEMAN,TIMOTHY-Burlington Almanack for NJ for 1774-
   Burlington-(1773)-16mo-stitched-Drake 5110 (5g4,lacks 1 lf) 20.00
--same-for 1779-Trenton-(1778)-16mo-stitched-16 lvs-Drake 5116
   (5a3,lf tn wi loss)   40.00
TRUESDALE,CAPT JOHN-The Blue Coats-Phila-(1867)-illus-510p-
   orig cl   (5q8,sl shake) 3.50 (5L3)   6.50
TRUESDELL,AMELIA WOODWARD-A Calif Pilgrimage-by One of
   the Pilgrims-SanFran-1884-12mo-cl-2nd ed (5h4)   3.00
--Francisca Reina-Bost-1908-8vo-wrps-orig illus by Maynard Dixon
    (5F5)   5.00
TRUETT,RANDALE BOND-Lincoln in Philately-Wash-1959-8vo-
   illus-wrps-35p&supplement   (5t7)   5.00
--Trade & Travel Around the Southern Appalachians Before 1830-
   ChapelHill-1935-8vo-map-5 illus-1st ed (5ss5)   12.50
TRUMAN,MAJ BEN C-The Field of Honor-NY-1884-557p
   (5tt8,shake) 10. (5ss8) 12.50 (5xx7)   17.50
--Occidental Sketches-SanFran-1881-1st ed-scarce
   (5dd1) 20. (5r0,autg) 15. (5x5)   25.00
--Semi Tropical Calif-SanFran-1874-ALBancroft-pict cl-204p
    (4L9)   25.00

TRUMAN,HARRY S-The Man of Independence-Phila-(1950)-
1st ed   (5yy6,dj,f)   5.00
--Memoirs-NY-1955-Dblday-2 vols
              (5qq8) 4.50   (5k1,dj) 8.   (5m8,5r8,5t7)   10.00
TRUMBULL,ANNIE ELIOT-A Cape Cod Week-NY-1898-1st ed
                                     (5m2,5ee3)   5.00
--Mistress Content Cradock-NY-1899-pict cl-1st ed   (5m2)   5.00
TRUMBULL,BENJ-A Century Sermon or Sketches of The History of
    the 18th Century-NewHav-1801-Read&Morse-8vo-orig wrps-
    papr labl-stitchd-1st ed   (5n2)   45.00
--Compendium of Indian Wars in New England-Hartford-1926-4to-
    stiff wrps-62p-ltd   (5e8) 10.   (4c1,5q8)   12.50
--A Complete History of Connecticut - Vol 1(all publ)-NewHav-
    1797-567p-lea   (5t2,cov loose,ed)   18.50
--same-Hartf-1797-Hudson&Goodwin-587p-fldg map-3 ports-
    8vo-orig calf-1st ed   (5L1,re-hinged) 45.00
--A Plea, in vindication of Connecticut Title to Contested Lands
    Lying west of Province of NY-NewHav-1774-T&S Green-
    8vo-160p-lf of errata-hf vel-2nd ed(same year as 1st) (5L1) 100.00
TRUMBULL CO,OHIO-Combination Atlas Map of Chig-1874-cl-
    122p   (4h7,rebkd)   55.00
TRUMBULL,H CLAY-Captured Scout of Army of the James-Bost-
    1869-60p-cl   (5h1)   8.50
--The Knightly Soldier-Bost-1865-plts-331p-1st ed (5L3,vf)   6.50
TRUMBULL,HENRY-History of Discovery of Amer-Bost-1810-276p-
    lea   (5g1)   15.00
--same-Norwich-1812-Springer,prntr-calf
              (5i4,lacks 1 plt & part of frontis)   10.00
--History of the Indian Wars-Phila-1854-col plts-320p
                         (4k5) 5.   (4L0)   10.00
--Indian Wars-Norwich-1810-lea   (5kk5)   15.00
--Life & Remarkable Adven Of Israel R Potter-Prov-1824-frontis-
    12mo-scarce   (5s9) 25.   (5dd6,rbnd)   35.00
TRUMBULL,J R-Hist of Northampton,Mass-1898,1902 -illus&map-
    2 vols   (5t9)   35.00
TRUMBULL,JAS HAMMOND-Memorial Hist of Hartford Co,Conn-
    Bost-1886- 4 maps-67 plts-imit lea-2 vols (4i2) 42.50 (5t9) 27.50
--Natick Dictionary-1903-BAE Bul 25-4to-347p-hard cov
              (5p7) 8.50   (4b2)   15.00
TRUMBULL,JOHN-Autobiog, Remin & Letters of-NY-1841-
    Wiley&Putnam-439p-23 illus-8vo
              (4a0) 60.   (4c1) 25.   (5w0,wn)   35.00
--same-1953-illus-ed by T Sizer (5q8,dj) 8.50   (5L7)   12.50
--M'Fingal, A Modern Epic Poem-Hartf-1856-183p plus ads-
    a.e.g.-rev&corr   (5w0)   10.00
--same-NY-1881-Amer Book Exchange-322p   6.00
--The poetical works-Hartf-1820-Lincoln&Stone,prntrs-8vo-
    orig bds-papr labls-plts-1st ed   (5m2) 15.   (5l0)   27.50
TRUMBULL,LYMAN-Speech of Lyman Trumbull of Illinois on
    amending Constitution to prohibit slavery-Mar 28, 1864-8p-
    disbnd   (5x5,fox)   12.50
TRUMBULL,ROBT-The Raft-NY-(1942)-205p-photos
                                     (5s1,dj,ex-libr) 4.00
--Silversides-NY-(1945)-1st prntg-217p-photos (5s1,f,ex-libr) 5.00
TRUSLER,REV DR-The Progress of Man & Society-Bath,prntd by
    JBrowne,Lond-16mo-260p,(8)-wdcuts-lea bkd bds (5p1) 95.00
TRUSTA,H-The Last Leaf from Sunny Side-Bost-1853-1st ed (5ee3) 12.50
TRUSTS & ESTATES-NY-1949 to 69-Vol 88 thru 108
                                     (5ii7,rbnd) ea 20.00
TRUTH ABOUT WHISKY,THE-Lond-1879-103p,(6)-fldng tinted lithog-
    2nd rev ed   (5w1)   35.00
TRUTH & TRUST-Alfred in India,Moral Courage,Clever Boys-
    Chambers' Libr for Young People-Edinb-1848-4 vols in 1-
    1st ed-sm8vo-hf calf   (5c8,rub)   17.50
TRUTH,S-Narrative of Sojourner Truth-Bost-1850-bds-1st ed
                                     (5x2)   75.00
TRYAL OF CAPT WM KIDD,THE-for Murther & Piracy,upon 6
    several Indictments...London,May 1701-n.p.-n.d.(early 18th
    century)-folio-cl -pg 451 to 500 (5L1)   30.00
TRYALS FOR HIGH TREASON-& Other Crimes-Lond-1720 to 1731-
    calf-Vols 1 to 9   (5tt5)   100.00
TRYON,WARREN S,comp-Mirror for Americans-Chig-(1952)-
    3 vols-illus-4to   (4a1)   18.50
TSCHICHOLD,JAN-An Illustrated History of Writing & Lettering-
    NY-(1948)-Col Univ Pr-70p plts-18p text-bds (5tt9,dj) 5.00
--Designing Books-NY-n.d.-Wittenborn,Schultz,Inc-58 plts-
    21p text-bds   (5tt9,dj)   12.50
TSCHIRKY,OSCAR-The Cook Book by "Oscar" of the Waldorf-
    Chig-(1896)-907p-4to-1st ed-port (5c0,scuff)   12.50
TSCHUDI,DR J J VON-Travels in Peru, During Years 1838 to
    1842-Lond-1847-David Bogue-8vo-cl-frontis-scarce
                                     (4a3,fray)   50.00

TSCHUDI,DR J J VON   (continued)
--same-NY-1854-Barnes-12mo-cl-frontis-new ed (4a3,chip) 20.00
TSUDA,NORITAKE-Handbook of Japanese Art-Tokyo-1935-
    Chamberlin&Lucas-345 plts-527p-8vo (5ww3,top pgs wtrstnd) 15.00
TSUI CHI-A Short History of Chinese Civilization-Lond-1942-
    illus-8vo-cl-335p   (5t2)   4.50
TSURUMI,YUSUKE-Present Day Japan-NY-(1927)-Columbia Univ Pr-
    114p-Japan Soc   (5p7)   3.00
TUBI,GRAZIONO-Manuale Di Vinificazione-Milano-1868-96p-
    wrps-fldg table-2nd ed   (5w1)   12.50
TUCK,CLYDE E-The Bald Knobbers-Indnpls-1910-1st ed-illus
                                     (4a9)   10.00
TUCK,R-Robinson Crusoe-Lond-ca 1870-(Combined Expanding Toy
    & Painting Book Series)-sm sq8vo-pict blazed bds-cl bk-10p text
    & 6 col plts-3 dimensional pict   (5aa2)   35.00
TUCKER,A-A Maasai Grammar with Vocabulary-Lond-1955-317p-
    fldg map   (5c6,f)   9.50
--Non Bantu Languages of NE Africa-Lond-1956-228p-40p bibliog-
    2 fldg maps,(1 pkt)   (5c6,f)   8.50
TUCKER,ARTHUR H-Hope Atherton & His Times-Deerfield,Mass-
    1926-72p-8vo-orig bds   (5m6)   10.00
TUCKER,BENJ-An Epitome of Ancient & Modern History-Phila-
    D Hogan-JAnderson, Prntr-16mo-368p-calf-enlrgd-1822
                                     (5p1,crude rprd) 10.00
TUCKER,BEVERLY-Key to Disunion Conspiracy-NY-1861-392p-
    ads   (5qq8,vf)   17.50
--The Principles of Pleading-Bost-1846-Little, Brown-12mo-disbnd-
    220p-1st ed-scarce   (5j5)   32.50
TUCKER,ELIZ S-A Cup of Tea-NY-(1892)-obl 4to-1st ed-col plts
                                     (4F6)   15.00
--Leaves from Juliana Horatia Ewing's "Canada Home"-
    Bost-1896-8vo-8 col illus-1st ed (5m6,dj)   10.00
TUCKER,GEO-Life of Thos Jefferson...with parts of his
    Correspondence-Phila-1837-port-sm4to-2 vols-1st ed (4m4) 30.00
TUCKER,GEO F-The Boy Whaleman-Bost-1925-283p-illus (5t7) 4.50
--The Monroe Doctrine-Bost-1885-138p-orig cl (5m2)   7.50
TUCKER,GEO FOX-A Quaker Home-Bost-1891-426p (4b6) 7.50
TUCKER,G W-Lee & Gettysburg Campaign-n.p.-(1933)-61p-illus
                                     (5mm8)   7.00
TUCKER,GILBERT M-The Path to Prosperity-NY&Lond-1935-312p
                                     (5t7,pres)   6.00
TUCKER,GLENN-Poltroons & Patriots-Indnpls-(1954)-maps-2 vols
                                     (4m4,dj)   15.00
TUCKER,J R-Constitution of the US-Chig-1899-2 vols (5r4) 16.50
TUCKER,JOSIAH-Selection from His Economic & Political Writings-
    1931   (5L7)   6.50
TUCKER,L NORMAN-Western Canada-Lond-1908-plts-fldg map-
    164p   (4a8)   12.50
TUCKER,LEVI-Lectures on Nature & Tendency of Modern Infidelity-
    Cleve-1837-189p-cl   (5h1,sp chip,pres) 8.50
TUCKER,LOUISE E-Historical Plays of Colonial Days for 5th Year
    Pupils-Lond-1914-frontis-157p   (5t7, libr labls) 6.00
TUCKER,PATRICK T-Riding the High Country-Caldwell-1933-
    fab-210p-1st ed   (4k6,f)   20.00
TUCKER,POMEROY-Origin,Rise & Progress of Mormonism-NY-1867-
    302p-orig cl-frontis-1st ed (5L2,sl wn,wtrstnd) 12.50 (5m3) 27.50
TUCKER,S G-Dissertation on Slavery:with Proposal for Gradual
    Abolition of it in State of Virg-Phila-1795(NY,1861,rprnt)
                                     (5r4,rbnd)   22.50
TUCKER,SARA-The Rainbow in the North-Lond-1852-fldg map-
    illus   (5w8)   45.00
--same-Lond-1853-JasNesbit&Co-222p-plts-fldg map-12mo-
    orig cl-"4th thous"   (5L1)   35.00
TUCKER,SOPHIE-Some of These Days-NY-1945-Dblday-309p
              (5x7) 4.50   (5p7) 4.   (4c9,autg)   8.95
TUCKER,T W-Waifs from way bills of an old expressman-Bost-
    1872-port-16mo   (5g8)   6.00
TUCKER,WM-The Family Dyer & Scourer-Phila-n.d.(ca 1831)-
    cl bk-bds-180p   (5w3,stnd,wn)   47.50
TUCKERMAN,BAYARD-Wm Jay & the Constitutional Movement for
    the Abolition of Slavery-NY-1894-illus (4m4)   17.50
TUCKERMAN,HENRY T-America & Her Commentators
                                     (5q8,ex-libr)   20.00
--Book of Artists-NY-1867-Putnam-2nd ed-(wi tip in leaf so
    stating)-639p-8vo-orig cl   (4a0) 40.   (5m3)   25.00
--The Criterion-Bost-1866-Dutton,NY, Hurd&Houghton
                                     (5b2,sl fray)   12.50
--Isabel or, Sicily-Phila-1839-Lea&Blanchard-12mo-orig cl-
    1st ed   (5x1,fade)   35.00
--The Italian Sketch book-NY-1848-JCRiker-12mo-orig cl-
    3rd ed, "rev&enlrgd"   (5x1)   20.00
--The Optimist-NY-1850-273p-orig cl   (4b4)   15.00

TUCSON,ARIZONA-Tucson-(1917)-R Rasmessen-12 lvs photos-
   folio-wrps   (4a5)   6.50

TUCSON,ARIZ-Man Building in the Sunshine Climate-Tucson-
   n.d.(ca 192?)-Sunshine Club-8vo-prntd wrps-28p-
   photos   (5g0) 5.   (5t3)   4.00

TUDHOPE,JOHN-Voortrekkers of South Africa....2 Lectures...
   Aug 17th & Sept 14th, 1891-Durban-1891-P Davis & Sons-
   54p-wrps   (4t5,fox)   13.50

TUDOR,ALICE-A Little Book of Healing Herbs-Lond-(1927)-
   12mo-bds-73p   (5s7) 4.   (5w3)   5.00

TUDOR,EMMA-October Dawn-Cambr-1926-63p-bds (5w1) 6.50

TUDOR,WM-Life of Jas Otis-Bost-1823-Wells&Lilly-illus-508p-
   pt calf   (5mm8,cov loose,ex-libr)   12.50

TUER,ANDREW W-The Follies & Fashions of Our Grandfathers(1807)-
   Lond-1886,7-38 plts-366p,8p-bds   (5w7,hng crack) 14.50

--History of the Horn Book-Lond-1896-Leadenhall Pr-2 vols-
   vel-4to-illus-v rare -1st edition   (5u5,4c3,vf) 300.00

--same-Lond-1897-1 vol ed-3 hornbooks in pkt   (4F6,f) 125.00

--London Cries,with 6 Charming Children-Lond-(c 1884)-4to-
   hf cl-red&brown prntg-illus-labl   (5c8) 50.00

--Old London Street Cries & the Cries of Today-Lond-1885-
   Leadenhall Pr-illus chapbooks-NY imprint on cov-12mo-
   dec bds   (5c8) 12.50

--Pages & Pictures from Forgotten Children's Books-Lond-1898,9-
   Leadenhall Pr-orig pict cl-400 plts-510p
       (4g2,5tt9) 25.   (4F6,vg) 27.50

--same-Lond-1898,9-cl-g.t.-520p-400 illus-ltd to 112c,lg papr
       (5d3,mint) 50.00

--"Quads" for Authors, Editors & Devils-Lond-1884-sq16mo-
   94p-illus-orig vel jacket-enlrgd ed-scarce   (5v2) 15.00

--Stories from Old Fashioned Children's Books-Lond-1899,1900-
   Leadenhall Pr-1st ed wi 'Aug 99' adverts at end-250 cuts
       (4c3,f) 30.   (5c8,f) 20.00

TUFFNELL,F-The gentleman's pocket farrier-Bost-1832-24mo-
   plt-stiff prntd wrps-34p   (5g4,fox) 10.00

TUFFY,TIM-Thrilling Life Sketches of Peggy Tommy-(Delta,Colo)-
   1953-128p-photos-stiff wrps   (5L0) 5.00

TUFLONGBO & LITTLE CONTENT-Lond-(ca 1870)-Warne's
   Fairy Libr-pict cl-ads at end-8 illus by W Sharpe (5c8) 10.00

TUFTS,JAS W-Soda Water Apparatus, Book of Directions-Bost-
   n.d.(?1887)-4to-illus -190p (5m6) 15. (5w1) 27.50

TUGBYS ILLUS GUIDE TO NIAGARA FALLS-Niagara Falls-
   n.d.-(ca 1890s)-32 illus-stiff wrps-32p text-mounted illus
       (4b9,fade) 12.00

TUKER,M A R-Cambridge-Lond-1907-Adam&ChasBlack-8vo-
   396p-fldg plan-frontis-76 plts-dec cl   (5p1) 15.00

TULARE COUNTY-Business Directory & Hist Descriptive Hand Book
   of Tulare Co,Calif-TulareCty-1888-222p-prntd bds-Pillsbury&
   Ellsworth   (5d6) 100.00

TULEY,WM FLOYD-Tuley Family Memoirs-NewAlbny-1906-
   75p-cl-very scarce   (5h2) 18.50

TULIN,ADAM F-Practical Shell Developing for Steel Shipbuilders-
   NY-1941-158p-illus   (5s1) 5.00

TULLIDGE,EDW W-History of Salt Lake City & Its Founders-(1886)-
   3/4 lea-ports-over 1,000p-2nd impress   (5h6) 30.00

--Life of Jos (Smith) the Prophet-NY-1878-545p-ports-g.embossed cl-
   1st ed-rare   (5r7) 100.00

TULLOCH,JOHN-Theism,witness of reason & nature-1855-buck
       (5L7,rbnd) 7.50

TULLY,ANDREW-Berlin, The Story of a Battle-NY-1963 (5x7) 4.00

---CIA,the Inside Story-NY-1962-Morrow   (5p7) 3.50

TULSA CO IN THE WORLD WAR-Tulsa-1919-cl-294p-illus (5h0) 6.50

TUMIN,M M-Segregation & Desegregation-NY-1957-112p-wrps
       (5x2) 7.50

TUMULTY,JOS P-Woodrow Wilson As I Know Him-NY-1924-
   Dblday,Page-553p   (5p0) 7.50

--same-n.p.-(1921)-frontis-8vo-cl-553p-for Literary Digest
    (5L7,wn) 3.50 (5x7) 3. (5t0) 4.50

TUNA CLUB-History of the Tuna Club-(n.p.)-(1948)-1st ed (5x5)25.00

TUNNEY,GENE-Arms for Living-NY-1941-   (5yy6) 5.00

TUNSTALL,BRIAN-Adm Byng & Loss of Minorca-Lond-1928-293p-
   plts   (5a1) 5.00

TUNSTALL,NANNIE W-"No.40", A romance of Fortress Monroe
   & The Hygeia-Richmond-1884-McCarthy-orig wrps-1st ed
       (5m2,autg) 7.50

TUOMEY,HONORIA-History of Sonoma Co,Calif-SanFran,Chig-
   1926-2 vols-fabr-illus-ports-4to   (5h5) 42.50

TUPPER,SIR CHAS-Recollections of 60 years in Canada-Lond-1914-
   414p-illus-ports (5aa0) 15. (5a1,pres) 25. (5r7) 12.50

TURBERVILLE,A S-English Men & Manners in 18th Century-Oxf-
   1926-531p-plts   (5a1,5w7) 10.00

--same-Oxf-1929-539p-2nd ed-illus (5aa0) 10. (5t0) 7.50

TURCK,HERMAN-Man of Genius-Lond-1923   (4b7) 12.50

TURENNE D'AYNAC,GABRIEL L-Quatorze mois dans l'Amerique
   du Nord-Paris-1879-A Quantin-2 vols-12mo-orig prntd wrps-
   1st ed   (5i0,wn) 30.00

TURGENEV,IVAN-Fathers & Sons-NY-1951-Limited Edition Club
   Publ-ltd to 1500c,nbrd-boxed   (5F1,f) 15.00

TURGEON,CHARLOTTE-Cooking for Christmas-NY-1950-116p
       (5c0) 3.00

TURI,JOHAN-Turi's Book of Lappland-NY-n.d.(ca 1910)-292p-
   EGNash,transl   (5ss1,dj) 6.50

TURKISH FAIRY TALES-& Folk Tales, coll by Dr Ignatius Kunos-
   Lond-1896-Lawrence&Bullen-275p-illus-1st Engl ed (5c8) 10.00

TURLEY,CHAS-Nansen of Norway-Lond-1933-210p-plts-ports-
   maps   (5a1) 4.50

--The Voyages of Capt Scott-NY-1919-440p-8vo-cl-frontis-map
       (5t2) 4.00

TURNBULL,A B-Wm Turnbull, 1751 to 1822-(NY)-(1933)-priv prntd-
   illus-175p-fldg chart   (4m2) 22.50

TURNBULL,ARCHIBALD D-Commodore David Porter-NY-Century-
   (1929)-326p-8vo-cl-16 plts-1st ed   (5j5) 7.50

--John Stevens, An Amer Record-NY-1928-545p-1st prntg-illus
       (5h9,f) 13.50

TURNBULL,D-Travels in the West,Cuba-1840-buck (5L7,rbnd) 15.00

TURNBULL,FRANCESE HUBBARD-The Catholic Man, A Study-
   Bost-(c1890)-311p   (5m1) 8.50

TURNBULL,HENRY-History of the Indian Wars-Bost-1846-new ed
       (5jj7) 7.50

TURNBULL,JOHN-Reise um die Welt in den Jahren 1800 bis 1804-
   Vienna-1806-8vo-orig bds-436p-fldg map-2 plts (5ss2) 67.50

TURNBULL,ROBT-The Theatre,in its influence upon literature,
   morals, & religion-Bost-1839-16mo-2nd ed (5g4) 7.50

--World We Live In-Hartf-1852-illus-540p   (5L3) 7.50

TURNER&BRIDGERS-History of Edgecombe Co,NoCar-Raleigh-
   1920-1st ed   (5b9) 25.00

TURNER & NELSON-Contributions to the Natural History of Alaska
   betw May 1874 & Aug 1881-Wash-1886-4to-mor-337p-
   26 col plts-#2,Arctic series   (5ss1) 50.00

TURNER,B L-The Legumes of Texas-Austin-1959-284p-illus
       (5k0,dj) 5.00

TURNER,MRS C H-The Floral Kingdom-Chig-1877-4to-424p
       (4p3) 25.00

TURNER,DAWSON-Fuci, or Colored Figures & Descrip of Plants
   Referred by Botanists to Genus Fucus-Lond-1808 to 19-thk,lg4to-
   bds-lea bks-258 col plts-4 vols in 2-rare (4t9,lea bk rub) 695.00

TURNER,E S-What the Butler Saw-1963   (5L7) 6.00

TURNER,EDW-Elements of Chemistry-Phila-1840-6th Amer ed-
   666p-calf   (5w5,rub) 7.50

TURNER,EDW R-Negro in Pennsylvania...1639 to 1861-Wash-
   1911-(12)314p-scarce   (4m4) 25.00

TURNER,EDW RAYMOND-New Market Campaign,May 1864-
   Richmond-1912-Whittet & Shepperson-203p-illus
    (5mm8) 12.50 (5m6,bk cov sl dmpstn) 20.00

TURNER,ELIZ-The Blue Bell-1838-Derby,Mozley-sm8vo-dec cl-
   g.t.-6 plts-137p-scarce   (4d4) 17.50

--The Daisy-NY-(ca 1845)-12mo-96p-25 hand col wdcuts-cl
       (4c3,vg) 22.50

TURNER,ETHEL DUFFY-Murtlnez,Pablo,a History of Lower Calif-
   MexicoCty-1960-4to-545p-illus-maps   (5g6,f) 10.00

TURNER,GEO E-Victory Rode the Rails-(1953)-BobbsMerrill-1st ed
       (5x5,dj) 20.00

TURNER,J,ed-A Treasury of English Wild Life-NY-n.d.-324p-
   48 col plts-cl-8vo   (4p5,dj) 5.50

TURNER,J B-Mormonism in All Ages-NY-(1842)-304p plus ads-
   1st ed-v scarce   (5t3,rbnd) 100.00

TURNER,J K-History of Edgecombe County,NCar-Raleigh-1920-
   illus-maps-486p   (4m2) 35.00

TURNER, JOHN KENNETH-Barbarous Mexico-Chig-1911-
   ChasHKerr-8vo-cl-illus-1st prntg   (4a3,sl stn) 15.00

TURNER,JOHN PETER-The NW Mounted Police 1873 to 1893-
   Ottawa-1950-2 vols-photos-fldg map   (5L0) 25.00

TURNER,JOS ADDISON-Autobiography of "The Countryman",1866-
   Atlanta-1943-Emory U Libr-THEnglish,ed-8vo-20p-wrps (5j5) 6.00

TURNER,JOSIE-Elsie Dinsmore On the Loose-NY-(1930)-8vo-
   166p-JonathenCape&Harrison Smith-cl&pict bds-1st ed
       (5p1,rub) 5.00

TURNER,L D-Africanisms In the Gullah Dialect-Univ Chig Pr-
   1949   (5x2,dj) 25.00

TURNER,L M-Contributions to the Natural History of Alaska-Wash-
   1886-26 plts(10 col)-4to-1st ed (4p5) 20. (4g6) 22.50

TURNER,LINCOLN,UNION & CLAY CO,SO DAK-Memorial &
   Biographical Record of-Chig-1897-(GeoAOgle&Co)-
   560p-photos-rare   (5t3,rbnd) 75.00

TURNER,LUTHER W-The Basket Maker-NY,Chig-(1909)-illus-61p
       (5n7) 3.00

TURNER,NANCY BYRD-The Mother of Washington-Hartf&NY-
1930-284p-illus   (5h9)   8.00
TURNER,OWEN-Pioneer History of Holland Purchase of Western NY-
Buffalo-1849-666p-illus-cl   (5h9,5zz0,rbnd)   35.00
--History of Pioneer Settlement of Phelps & Gorham's Purchase-
1851-684p   (5zz0)   27.50
TURNER,R-Easy Intro to the Arts & Sciences-Lond-1791-SCrowder-
illus-12mo-248p-3rd ed   (5c8)   27.50
TURNER,R-The Parlour Letter Writer & Secretary's Assistant-Phila-
1845-288p   -mor   (5w7,scuff)   6.50
--same-NY-1854-16mo-cl   (5w7)   5.50
TURNER,R W-Equity of Redemption-Cambr-1931-Cambr Studies
in English Legal History   (5ff4)   17.50
TURNER,RALPH E-Relations of Jas Silk Buckingham with East India
Co 1818 to 36-Pittsb-1930-145p-wrps   (5h2)   4.00
TURNER,ROSS-On the Use of Water Colors for Beginners-Bost-1886-
LPrang&Co-sq4to-6 col plts-orig bds-29p-1st ed (5ss5,ex-libr) 15.00
TURNER, CAPT SAMUEL-Account of Embassy to Court of Teshoo
Lama in Tibet-Lond-1806-2nd ed-fldg map-lg4to-calf-
12(of 13) plts   (4b6,wn,loose)   50.00
TURNER,SAM'L-My Climbing Adventures in 4 Continents-Lond-
1911-Unwin-283p-cl   (5d7)   10.00
--same-NY-n.d.-283p-74 illus-cl   (5t2, libr labls) 3.50
--Siberia-Lond-1905-cl-plts-fldg maps-8vo-420p (5v7) 15.00
TURNER,T G-Turner's Guide,From the Lakes to the Rocky Mntns-
Chig-1868-cl-288p-8vo-adv-1st ed   (5g6,dmgd)   35.00
TURNER,THOS-An Epitome of Bookkeeping by Double Entry-Portland-
1804-16mo-148p,(2)   (4c1) 35.   (5p1,lacks sp) 25.00
TURNER,TIMOTHY G-Bullets,Bottles & Gardenias-Dallas-1935
(5a8,dj) 15.   (5x5,dj,pres)   20.00
TURNER,W J-British Craftsmanship-Lond-1948-48 col plts-327p-8vo
(5bb0)   4.25
TURNER,W W-Fundamentals in Arch Design-NY-1930-plts-folio
(5qq7,wn sp)   7.50
TURNER,WM-Turner on Birds-Cambr-1903-cl-8vo-Evans,ed (5z9) 5.00
TURNER,WM-Book of Wines-NY-1941-12mo   (5w1)   30.00
TURNER-TURNER, J-Three Years' Hunting & Trapping in Amer &
Great NW-Lond-1888-182p plus ads-illus-2 maps-1st ed
(5dd1,lt wn) 17.50   (5r7,ex-libr)   30.00
TURNEY-HIGH,HARRY H-Flathead Indians of Montana-Menasha-
1937-Amer Anthro Assn #48-wrps-161p   (4L0)   10.00
TURNLEY,PARMENAS T-Reminiscences of Chig-(priv prntd,1892)-
8vo-orig cl-7 plts-1st ed-(300c only for author's friends)-
inserted index& Comments dated 1893   (5n9) 125.00
TURNOR,REGINALD-19th Century Architecture in Britain-Lond,
NY,Tor&Sydney-(1950)-illus-118p   (5q0)   7.50
TURPIN,E A-Merchant Marine Officers' Handbook-NY-1942-
12mo-illus-740p   (5s1,dj,ex-libr) 4.00
TURQUOISE TRAIL,THE-Bost-1928-Alice Henderson,ed-1st ed-
(containes EMRhodes)-scarce   (5g2)   25.00
TURRELL,EBENEZER-Life & Character of Rev Benj Colman-Bost-
1749-calf-238p-list of subscr   (4k9,cov wn)   20.00
TURRILL,CHAS B-California Notes-SanFran-1876-Bosqui&Co-232p-
cl-Vol 1(all publ) (5tt0) 15. (5i0,pres) 30. (5r7,dmpstn) 20.00
--Catalogue of Products of Calif-NewOrleans-1886-W B Stansbury-
208p-wrps   (5tt0)   15.00
--Deuteronomy Brown,A Real Estate Transaction-(SanDiego)-n.p.-
1888-8vo-wrps-scarce   (5b2,f)   25.00
TURRILL,GARDNER STILSON-A Tale of the Yellowstone or in a
Wagon through Western Wyo & Wonderland-Jefferson,Ia-1901-
128p-photos-cl-1st ed   (4L0) 125.00
--same-Jefferson-1901-photos-128p-wrps   (5dd1) 150.00
TURRILL,W B-Jos Dalton Hooker, Botanist,Explorer & Administrator-
Lond-(1963)-228p-3 maps & 25 plts   (5s7)   5.00
--The Royal Botanic Gardens Kew Past & Present-Lond-(1959)-
256p-27 photos-fldg map   (5w3)   5.00
TUSHINGHAM,S-Etchings & Dry Points-Lond-n.d.-39 plts (5ii3) 10.00
TUSKOGEE INSTITUTE-NewOrleans-(1910)-APBeldon-48p-wrps-
illus   (5j6)   8.00
TUSSER,THOS-500 Points of Good Husbandry-Lond-1931-sm4to-
Hermitage-336p-calf bndg   (5w3)   35.00
TUTHILL,MRS L C-I Will Be A Sailor-Bost-1864-Crosby&Nichols-
195p-frontis-2 plts-16mo   (5p1,wn)   5.00
--The Juvenile Library-Bost-1862-Crosby&Nichols-8 vols-24mo-
yellow-e.p.-mulberry cl-sp g.   (5p1)   32.50
TUTHILL,W B-The Suburban Cottage-NY-1885-11p,101p,(3)-illus
(5w7,cov stnd)   7.50
TUTT,EPHRAIN-Yankee Lawyer-NY-1943-464p-cl   (5t0)   3.50
TUTTLE,A C-Keene Business Directory,1871,2-60p   (4t2)   7.50
TUTTLE,CHAS C-Our North Land-Tor-1885-illus-maps-hf calf
(5w8)   20.00
TUTTLE,CHAS R-Alaska,Its Meaning to the World-Seattle-1914-
318p-cl-fldg pkt map-Franklin Shuey (5d6) 10. (5w4) 12.50

TUTTLE,CHAS R   (continued)
--General History of Michigan,the Peninsular State-Detroit-1874-
illus-cl   (5hh3,sp tn)   12.00
--General History of State of Michigan-Detroit-1873-ports-illus-
735p-wrps   (4b6,re wrps)   35.00
--Illus History of State of Iowa-Chig-1876-RichardSPeale-
8vo-cl-fldg map-732p   (4t1)   17.50
--Illus History of the State of Wisc-Bost-1875-fldg map-ports-illus-
800p   (5xx5,fade)   12.00
TUTTLE,REV D S-Reminis of Missionary Bishop-NY-1906-498p-
illus   (5s4,ex-libr)   30.00
TUTTLE,EDMUND B-Boy's Book About Indians-Phila-1874-
illus-207p-2nd ed-scarce   (4L0,cov stn,wn)   15.00
TUTTLE,MRS GEO FULLER-3 Centuries in Champlain Valley-
Plattsburgh-1909-illus-8vo-Tercentenary ed-485p (5t7,4c8)   15.00
TUTTLE,HARLEY A-Palmyra My Old Home Town-Palmyra,OH-
1930-84p-prntd wrps   (4h7)   8.50
TUTTLE,HERBERT-History of Prussia,1134 to 1757-Bost-1883 to 96-
4 vols-8vo-cl-maps&illus   (5t2)   12.50
TUTTLE,JAS-The Field & the Fruit-Bost-1891-illus-8vo-1st ed
(4g6)   10.00
TUTTLE,JOS F-Assassinated Presidents, Lincoln & Garfield-
(Crawfordsvl-1881)-18p-wrps   (5h7)   12.50
TUTTLE,REV JOS F-The Life of Wm Tuttle-NY-(1852)-16mo-
192p-frontis   (5t4)   7.50
TUTTLE,STEPHEN-My Services & Losses in Aid to the King's Cause
during Amer Rev-Brooklyn-1890-16mo-wrps-24p-Hist Prntng
Club-ltd to 250c   (5t7,wn)   5.00
TWAIN,MARK-Adventures of Huckleberry Finn-NY-1885-port-
green cl-pg 155 lacks the second 5-frontis has table cloth
clearly visible-1st ed   (5v2,mint) 400.00
--same-NY-1885-illus-lg8vo-orig cl-1st ed,early issue
(4c3) 75.   (4b6,fray,5c8,vg,box) 200.00
--same-NY-1885-Webster&Co-cl-illus captioned Him & another
Man listed as at pg 88; pg 57,11th line from bottom reads:...
with the was; pg283,If is a cancel; pg 155,final 5 has been
replaced wi larger size & extends below line-1st ed,3rd state
(5m8) 150.   (5F1,sp sl wn) 185.00
--same-NY-1885-illus-8vo-cl-1st Amer ed
(4c2,rub) 100.   (5t8) 75.   (5p6,crack)   60.00
--same-NY-1885-1st ed,later issue   (4b5,wn)   20.00
--same-NY-1933-Limited Edtions Club-8vo-illus-cl-t.e.g.-
ltd to 1500c,box   (5p1)   40.00
--same-NY-1950-Chanticleer Pr-Cresset Library-12mo-292p
(5p1)   3.50
--The Adventures of Tom Sawyer-Hartf-1876-Amer Publ Co-4to-
orig blu cl-1st prntng on wove papr,triple flys-a.e.g.-1st ed
(5d3,box,sp sl wn) 800.00
--same-Hartford-1876-lg8vo-frontis-illus-orig blu cl-1st prntg of
1st Amer ed-4p ads-Engl ed preceded this   (5hh0,vg) 675.00
--same-Leipzig-1900-G Frentag-8vo-2 parts-orig cl,(pt 1)-
prntd wrps(pt 2)-Notes in German-rare
(4h0,pres,f) 175.   (5p1,pres)   85.00
--same-NY-1930-RandomHse-Donald McKay,illus-rag papr-
dec fab-4to-ltd ed-artist autg-box   (5c8)   10.00
--same-Phila,Chig&Tor-c1931-Winston-Peter Hurd,illus-8vo-
264p(1)-frontis-3 plts-pict labl   (5p1)   7.50
--The Amer Claimant-NY-1892-ChasLWebster-277p plus ads-
orig cl-1st ed (5ee3,crack,rub) 3. (4u5,4j6,4b5,f,lacks flys)15.00
--same-Lond-1892-Chatto&Windus-1892-1st Engl ed (4b5,stnd) 6.00
--Celebrated Jumping Frog of Calaveras Co-NY-1867-12mo-
brn cl g.-1st ed-1st prntg-ads-frog wi head point up on front
& back cover   (5hh0) 1,500.00
--same-NY-JohnPaul,ed-CHWebb-1867-8vo-orig cl wi frog in
lower left corner-1st ed,1st issue wi inserted leaf of advs,
unbroken "i" in folio pg 21,pg 66,last line the "e" in "life"
unbroken; last line pg 198 the "i" in this is unbroken
(5ee9,sl soil,hng rprd,box) 225.00
--same-NY-1867-12mo-cl-1st state-1st ed of 1st issue
(5gg6,cov crease,sp rprd) 200.00
--Christian Science-NY&Lond-1907-1st ed & 1st issue-orig cl
(5ee3,fade) 5.   (5m1) 10.   (5ee3)   12.50
--A Connecticut Yankee in King Arthur's Court-NY-1889-cl-
1st ed,1st issue (wi Sking plate pg 59)
(5jj6,sl wn) 32.50 (5d2)   50.00
--same-NY-1889-1st ed,2nd issue-lea   (5k2,rbnd)   35.00
--same-NY-1890-Webster   (5e8) 5.75   (5v0)   6.50
--same-NY-1949-orig wrps-box-Limited Editions Club (5a0,f) 30.00
--A Dog's Tale-n.p.(Lond)-Natl Antivivisection Soc-1903-illus-
9p-orig buff wrps   (5tt2,f,hf mor box) 125.00
--A Dog's Tale-NY-1904-HarperBros-1st ed   (5ss9)   12.50
--A Double Barrelled Detective Story-NY-1902-Harper&Bros-
8vo-cl-t.e.g.-illus-1st ed   (5d3,dj) 35.   (5ss9)   15.00

TWAIN, MARK (continued)
--Editorial Wild Oats-NY&Lond-1905-illus-1st ed (5m1) 8.50
--same-NY-1905-t8vo-plts-1st ed-dec cl (5p5,5t2,fade) 12.50
--English as She is Taught-Bost-(1900)-Mutual Book-29p-1st ed, 2nd state (5k0) 5. (5x4) 7.50
--Eve's Diary-NY-1906-Harper-109p-1st ed (5t7) 9. (5x4,fade) 7.50
--Extracts from Adam's Diary-NY-1904-Harper-89p-1st ed (5b2) 10. (5x4,5t7) 7.50
--Extract from Capt Stormfield's Visit to Heaven-1909-Harper&Bros-1st ed (5m1) 12.50 (5x4,5g1) 10. (5ss9) 8.50
--Following the Equator-Hartford-1897-Amer Publ Co-712p-1st ed, 1st issue-(wi only 1 publsher's imprint) (5e8) 22.50 (5tt2,5j5,4F6) 25.00
--same-Hartf, Amer Bk Co-NY, Dblday&McClure-1897-1st ed-not 1st state-blu cov-gilt (5i1) 12.50
--The Gilded Age-Hartf-1873-illus-574p-1st ed-illus (5p6,wn,lacks fly) 18.00
--A Horse's Tale-NY-1907-1st ed-Harper&Bros (5x4,fade) 7.50 (5mm2) 10. (5hh1,vg) 12.50
--The Innocents Abroad-Hartf-Amer Pub-1869-651p-1st ed,1st state (5x4,wn) 20.00
--same-Hartf-1869-Amer Pub Co-3/4 lea-1st ed,2nd state (5g1,rbnd,crack) 7.50 (5hh1,sl scuff) 15.00
--same-Amer-1871-illus (5e8) 4.75
--same-Leiptzig-1879-Tauchnitz-2 vols-1st Tauchnitz ed-orig wrps (5x4) 27.50
--same-Bost-1895-2 vols-8vo-red cl (5t0,mint,dj) 8.50
--Is Shakespeare Dead?-NY-1909-Harper&Bros-150p-t.e.g.-cl-dbl frontis-1st ed,1st issue (4b5,f) 20. (5g1) 11.50 (5x4,5w9) 10.00
--King Leopold's Soliloquy-Bost-1905-1st ed-illus-PRWarren Co (5x2,rbnd) 27.50
--same-Bost-1905-wrps-56p-illus-2nd ed-(wi publishers slip on hf title) (5m8) 10.00
--Life on the Mississippi-Bost-1883-JasROsgood&Co-thk8vo-orig brown cl-gilt-1st ed-1st issue wi Mark Twain portrayed in flames on pg 441 & legend StLouis Hotel on pg 443 (5ee9,box,4pg leaflet laid in) 150.00
--same-Bost-1883-Osgood&Co-1st ed,1st state(Mark Twain going up in flames on pg 441)-(pg 443 reads St Charles Hotel) (5L3) 28.50 (5dd8,f,5ss9,hng rprd) 50.00
--same-Lond-1883-Chatto&Windus-8vo-orig pict cl-32p ads dated Mar 1883-1st ed (5mm2,cov stn) 27.50 (5d3) 50. (4h0,f,bkplt) 60.00
--same-Bost-1883-1st ed,2nd issue (5w9) 10. (5L3,vf,5x4,f) 25.00
--The Man That Corrupted Hadleyburg-NY-1900-Harper-398p-1st ed,1st state (5x4,fade) 15.00
--same-NY-1900-1st ed,3rd state-orig cl (5hh1,vg) 30.00
--Mark Twain Birthday Book-Lond-1889-John MacQueen-12mo-cl (4b5) 12.50
--Mark Twain's Autobiography-NY-1924-Harper&Bros-g.t.-2 vols-2 ports- (5m1,5j5,shake) 10. (5j5,4b5,f,dj) 25. (5L3,vf,5dd4) 17.50
--Mark Twain's(Burlesque) Autobiog & First Romance-NY-(1871)-Sheldon-47p-grn cl (5i1,wn) 8. (5p6) 12.50 (5e8) 7.50
--same-NY-(1871)-Sheldon-12mo-orig wrps-47p-2nd state (5t4) 20. (5ss9,vg) 25.00
--Mark Twain in India-Karachi,India-n.d.-Prof. Vaswani-Vol #1-Abridged-(wrps)-78p-3rd ed (5x4) 7.50
--Mark Twain's Letters from the Sandwich Islands-Stanford Univ Pr-(1938)-Ezra Dane,ed-1st ed (4b5,mint,dj) 20. (5x5,dj) 22.50
--same-SanFran-1937-Grabhorn Pr-ltd to 550c (4b5,mint) 30.00
--Mark Twain's Letter to the Calif Pioneers-Oakland-1911-(reprnt of Elmira,1869,issue)-12mo-stiff wrps-13&p-ltd to 750c (5h5,vf) 5.00
--Mark Twain's Notebook-NY-1935-t8vo-cl-1st ed (5cc9) 25.00
--Mark Twain's Sketches,#1-NY-(1874)-Amer News Co-32p-authorized ed-pict prntd wrps-fragile pamph-1st issue wi back wrpr blank-rare (5j2,sl fray) 100.00
--same,New&Old,Now 1st Published in Complete Form-Hartf-1875-Amer Publ Co-4to-orig cl-g.-illus-1st issue wi footnote on pg 119 repeated on pg 120&erratum slip tipped in-1st ed (5ee9,hng broke,sl fray,box) 95. (4h0) 140.00
--same-Hartf-1875-Amer Publ Co-4to-cl-320p-illus-1st ed,2nd issue (5ss9,vg) 35. (5g1,vg) 22.50 (5p6,sl wn) 30. (4b5,fray,fly tn) 15.00
--same-Hartford-1889-Amer Publ-320p (5x4) 6.00
--Mark Twain's Speeches-NY-Harper-1910-port-1st ed (5m2,sl soil) 6.50
--Mark Twain's Travels with Mr. Brown,etc-NY-1940-port-1st ed (5mm2,mint,dj) 12.50
--The New Pilgrims Progress-Lond-n.d.-(1872)-GeoRoutledge&Sons-Auth's Engl ed-orig pic wrps (4b5,lacks most of sp) 35.00

TWAIN,MARK (continued)
--The Niagara Book-Buffalo-1893-Underhill&Nichols-orig green cl-1st ed-4th issue (5tt2,f,dj) 25.00
--same-1901-Dblday,Page&Co (5hh1,f) 7.50
--Notebook-Albert Bigelow Paine,ed-NY&Lond-1935-1st ed (5k1) 10.00
--Old Times on the Mississippi-Tor-1876-Belford Bros-unauthorized version-orig dec cl-g.-variant (5c8) 35.00
--The 1,000,000 Bank Note & Other Stories-NY-1893-1st-260p (5x4) 25. (5mm2) 17.50 (5g1) 12.50
--same-Lond-1893-Chatto&Windus-red dec cl-1st Engl ed with adverts correctly dated Apr 1893 (5c8,lt fade) 12.50
--Personal Recollection of Joan of Arc-NY-1896-Harper-1st ed-1st state adv("just ready")-illus-461p (5x4,fade) 12.50 (5g1,vg) 17.50
--same-Lond-1896-illus-435p-cl-1st Engl ed (5t2) 25.00
--The Prince & the Pauper-Bost-1882-441p-1st ed, 1st issue(with Franklin Pr imprint on cpyrite pg) (5w9) 27.50 (5g1,5p6,sl scuff) 25. (4F6,vg) 40.00
--same-Lond-1882-Chatto&Windus-1st Engl ed,secondary issue (5c8,f) 10.00
--Pudd'nhead Wilson,A Tale-Lond-1894-Chatto&Windus-8vo-orig red cl-pict design-port-advt dated "Sept 1894"-1st ed-precedes Amer ed (5d3) 50.00
--Roughing It-Hartford-1872-1st ed-1st issue-illus (5L3,rbnd) 35. (5L3,lt rub) 60. (5d2,rbnd,f) 65.00
--same-Hartf-1872-illus-1st ed,2nd issue wi loss of type on pg 242-thk R8vo-orig pict cl (5g1,vg) 20. (5m1) 30.00
--Saint Joan of Arc-NY&Lond-(1919)-Howard Pyle,illus-320p (5t7) 8.00
--same-NY-(1919)-Harper-32p-Pyle illus in col-2nd state (5x4,vg) 12.50
--SanFrancisco Virginia City Territorial Enterprise Correspondent-Smith&Anderson,ed-1957-Allen Pr-illus-sm4to-ltd to 400c (5hh4,mint) 45.00
--The $30,000 Bequest & Other Stories-NY-1906-Harper-523p-1st ed,2nd state (5x4,fade) 10.00
--1601,A Tudor Fireside Conversation-NY-priv prntd-ltd-frontis-80p-box-illum intro-FMeine,bibl (5jj6,mint) 12.50 (5g1,mint) 25.00
--same-Lond-1936-sml folio-illus-ltd ed (4j6) 12.50 (5tt2,box) 20.00
--Sketches now 1st published in complete form-n.p.(Tor)-1880-Slemin&Higgins (5m2,shake,sl wn) 5.00
--Sketches of the Sixties-SanFran-1926-cl bkd bds-1st ed-ltd ed (5m4,f,dj) 30. (5ss9,vg,dj) 27.50
--Speeches at the Lotos Club-NY-1911-488p-1st ed (5x4) 12.50
--The Stolen White Elephant,etc-Bost-1883-Osgood-16mo-306p-pict cl-1st ed(wi 10p of ads dated March 1883) (5m1,sl wn) 17.50 (5j5) 25. (5g1,vg) 27.50
--Tom Sawyer Abroad-Bost-1882-1st ed, 1st issue-green cl (4c3,lt rbu) 40.00
--same-Lond-1894-Chatto&Windus-orig pic cl-12mo-26 illus-1st Engl ed (5u5) 35.00
--The Tragedy of Pudd'nhead Wilson & the Comedy of Those Extraordinary Twins-Hartf-1894-t8vo-orig cl-g.-marginal dec-1st Amer ed-1st state(sheets 1-1/8 inches & title lf conjugate wlth lf (13) (5w9,edge wn,sp tn) 20. (5ee3,hf mor,g.e.,f) 45. (5d3,vf) 50.00
--same-Hartford-1894-1st ed,1st prntng (5m4) 40. (5w9,edge wn,sp tn) 20. (5ee3,hf mor,g.e.,f) 45.00
--same-Hartford-1894-lg8vo-illus-orig cl-1st ed (5L0) 15. (5jj6,vg) 20. (5t2,sp wn) 17.50
--A Tramp Abroad-Hartford-1880-Amer Publ Co-1st ed,2nd issue (4b5,lt wn) 25.00
--same-Lond-1880-Chatto&Windus-2 vols-8vo-orig brown cl-1st Engl ed(same year as Amer)-v scarce (5l0,sl wn) 65.00
--same-Tor-1880-Slemin&Higgins-410p-1st Canadian ed (5x4,lacks e.p.) 35.00
--same-Tor-n.d.(ca 1880)-Rose Belford Publ Co-illus-pict sl (5m1) 10.00
--The Washoe Giant in San Francisco-SanFran-1938-Franklin Walker, ed-8vo-bds&cl-Ward Ritchie Pr-1st ed (5dd8,rprd dj) 15.00
--What is man? (Issue for Rationalist Pr Assoc)-Lond-1910-Watts-1st Lond ed-also 1st trade ed - (5m2) 8.50
--same-NY-1906-The DeVinne Pr-8vo-orig bds-anon-250c prntd-(Feb 8,1917)-(S L Clemens)-1st ed (5d3) 150.00
--Works-1901-Amer Publ Co-plts-8vo-red buck-g.t.-22 vols (5t5,f bndg,rbnd) 100.00
--The Works of-NY-(1912)-Collier&Son-25 vols-cl (5p7) 37.50
--Works-Author's National Edition-25 vols (5e8,vg) 65.00
--Works-NY-1928-HarperBros-Authorized Ed-25 vols-lg type-frontis-illus-Cr8vo-greej buck-g.letterng (5t8,f) 37.50

TWAIN,MARK (continued)
--The Writings of-NY-1912-Harper-25 vols-Author's Nat'l Edit-
cl   (5p0,sp fade)   50.00
--A Yankee at the Court of King Arthur-Lond-1894-Chatto-A New
Ed-298p   -advts dated Nov 1896-orig pict bds (5m2,edge wn) 5.00
--Yankee in King Arthur's Court,(cov title)-NY-1889-illus-1st ed
                                       (5g1,vg)   37.50
TWEDDEL,COLIN E-Snoqualmie Duwamish Dialects of Puget
Coast Salish-Seattle-1950-Univ of Wash-78p-wrps (5dd1)   3.00
TWEEDIE,MRS ALEC-Mexico As I Saw It-NY-Macmillan Co-472p-
photos-col fldg map-thk8vo -1901   (5x5)   25.00
TWEEDSMUIR,LADY-Canada-Lond-1941-48p-plts (4b9,sp split)   5.00
TWEEDSMUIR,LORD-Hudson's Bay Trader-NY-1951-195p-plts
(4f9) 7.50   (5dd0)   4.50
TWELVE YEARS' MILITARY ADVENTURE-in Three Quarters of the
Globe-NY-1829-2 vols-8vo-orig bds-cl bks-labls-1st Amer ed
                                       (5m6,fox)   15.00
TWELVE YEARS A SLAVE-Auburn-1853-(Derby&Miller)-336p-
Narr of S Northup-illus   (5q0,hng loose)   15.00
TWENEY,GEO H-Jack London,A Bibliography-Georgetown-1966-
1st ed-(750c prntd)   (4t0,mint,dj)   35.00
TWENTIETH CENTURY COOK BOOK-Berkeley,Calif-(1914)
                                       (5x5)   10.00
TWENTY CENTURIES OF MEXICAN ART-NY-1940-(Mus Mod Art)-
4to-plts-1st ed-Engl&Spanish (5ii3) 12.50   (5x5)   15.00
TWENTY FOUR IVANS-NY-1946-4to-pict bds-32p-plts (4a8)   4.50
TWENTY ONE MISSIONS OF CALIF-Repro from Paintings by Edwin
Deakin-Berkeley-1902-illus   (4a5)   6.00
TWICE A YEAR-Book of Literature,Arts & Civil Liberties-Dbl #5 &
6-1940,41-566p-bds   (5b9)   10.00
TWINING,ELIZABETH-Illus of Natural Orders of Plants with Groups
& Descriptions-Lond-1868-orig cl-g.e.-160 col plts-2 vols-
2nd ed   (5z9,f)   45.00
TWINING,THOS-Science Made Easy-Lond-1880-6 vols-4to-orig
wrps-illus-2nd ed   (5ss5)   12.50
--Travels in America 100 years ago-NY-(cpyrite 1893)-32mo-port-
prntd bds   (5g3)   15.00
--same-NY-1894-16mo-port-(Harper's Black&White Ser) (5yy6)   7.50
TWISS,RICHARD-Chess-Lond-1787,1789-2 plts-2 vols in 1 (4L1) 50.00
--Travels Through Portugal & Spain in 1772&1773-Lond-1775-
fldg map-5 plts-lp.engr music-lg4to-hf mor-1st ed
                                       (4e1,rub,wn)   95.00
TWISS,TRAVERS-The Oregon Territory,Its History & Discovery-
NY-1846-264p-1st Amer Ed (4a5,rebnd) 30. (5s2,red lea)   75.00
TWITCHELL,R E-Desc of Benj Twitchell,Dorchester,Lancaster,
Medfield & Sherborn,Mass 1632 to 1927-1929-707p (4t2)   30.00
TWITCHELL,RALPH EMERSON-History of the Military Occupation
of Territory of NewMexico from 1846 to 1851-Denver-1909-
Smith,BrooksCo-394p-illus-maps-pict cl
(4L0) 20.   (5h5,sp tn) 15.   (5h5,pres)   22.50
--Leading Facts of New Mexican History-CedarRapids-1911 to 17-
Torch Pr-t.e.g.-R8vo-cl-5 vols-subscribers'ed-ltd to 1500c,
nbrd,autg
(5m9,crack) 250. (5h5,vg) 275. (4t1,fade) 300. (5g2,f) 475.00
--same-CedarRapids-1911-Torch Pr-illus-2 vols-buck (5tt0)   25.00
--Old Santa Fe-SantaFe-(1925)-488p-photos-maps-Subscrip Ed-
ltd to 1000c-scarce   (5n4,rbnd) 30.   (5dd1)   25.00
--The Spanish Archives of NewMexico-CedarRapids-1914-2 vols-
lg8vo-cl-illus   (5h5,pres) 75.   (5g2,dj,f)   85.00
--The Story of the Conquest of SantaFe-SantaFe-1921-NM Hist Soc
Paper #24-8vo-wrps-63p-illus   (5g6)   6.75
TWITCHELL,W I-Hartford in History-1899-268p   (4t2)   6.00
TWO ADMIRALS,THE-A tale-Phila-1842-Lea&Blanchard-2 vols-
12mo-orig violet cl-papr labls-1st Amer ed-(J F Cooper)
                                       (5x1,fade)   50.00
TWO AMERICAS,THE-NY-1881-833p-22p plts   (5ww4)   10.00
TWO CENTURIES OF NAZARETH-By Various Contributors-
Nazareth,Pa-1940-imit lea-illus-276p plus patron list (5w9)   8.50
TWO CENTURIES OF TYPEFOUNDING-Annals of Letter Foundry
Est by Wm Caslon-Lond-1920-93p-folio   (5j4)   10.00
TWO LEGACIES,THE-Cambr-1863-Riverside Pr-8vo-orig qtr roan-
1st ed-(G L Putnam)   (5i0,rub)   6.00
TWO PHILOSOPHERS,THE-a quaint sad Comedy-Bost-(1892)-8vo-
1st ed of Chapman's 1st publ-v rare   (5gg6)   100.00
TWO QUAKER SISTERS-from Orig Diaries of Eliz Buffun Chace &
Lucy Buffun Lovell-NY-1937-183p-illus (5t7)   10.00
TWO WEALTHY FARMERS-or History of Mr Bragwell-Dublin-
Wm Watson (ca 1815)-in 7 pts-12mo-(inscr dated 1816)-lin
                                       (5c8,f)   40.00
TWO WEEKS OF HAWAIIAN HISTORY-Brief Sketch of Revolution
of 1893-Honolulu-1893-illus   (5x5)   60.00
TWO WEST NEW JERSEY TRACTS WI APPENDIX-cov title-(Phila-
Collins,Jul 1880)-wrps   (5h9) 20.   (5j5)   17.50

TWO WORLDS-a Literary Quarterly,Vol 1,#1,2,3&4-NY-
1925,26-8vo-wrps(as issued)-(Contains first 4 instalments
of Jas Joyce's new unnamed work)   (5ss9,box)   85.00
TWO YEARS BEFORE THE MAST-NY-1840-16mo-orig prntd cl-
illus opp pg 33-State 1,wi 105 titles only listed in bk cov-
1st ed of Dana's 1st book-1st issue,wi perfect type in cpyrite
notice & running head on pg9-Harper's Family Library
No CVI   (5gg6,vf) 1,500.00
--same-NY-1840-Harper-12mo-orig cl-1st ed(probably 2nd printing,
wi undotted "i" in copyright)
                     (4h0,fox,sl wn) 250.   (5ee9,vg)   150.00
TWYFORD,H B-Storing,Its Economic Aspects,Proper Methods-NY-
1918-200p-illus   (5s1)   3.50
TYBOUT,E M-Poketown People-NY-1905-illus   (5x2)   10.00
TYLER,B E-Souvenir of the Copper Co of Upper Peninsula of Mich-
Houghton-1903-1p text,plus photos-cl   (5a8)   8.50
TYLER,C B-Autobiog of Wm Seymour Tyler & Related Papers-1912-
324p   (4t2)   10.00
TYLER,C W-The K K K -NY-(1902)-Abbey Pr-8vo-359p-cl-
scarce novel   (5i4)   20.00
TYLER,DANIEL-Concise History of Mormon Battalion in Mexican
War (SaltLkCty)-1881-376p-cl
(5tt0,rbnd,stnd) 40.   (5dd5,pres,mor,g.e.) 125. (5n9,box) 150.00
TYLER,DAVID BUDLONG-The Bay & River Delaware-Cambr,Md-
1955-244p-illus   (5h9)   10.00
--Steam Conquers the Atlantic-NY&Lond-1939-425p-illus (5t4)   6.50
TYLER,EDW L-Primitive Culture,etc-Bost-1874-cl-8vo-2 vols-
1st Amer ed-scarce   (4t7)   42.50
TYLER,GEO C-Whatever Goes Up-Indnpls-(1934)-illus-1st ed
                                       (4a1)   6.50
TYLER,GEO-History of Bell County-SanAntonio-1936 (5a8,lt stn) 35.00
TYLER,JOHN-Relations with Mexico-Wash-1842-42p (4a5)   25.00
TYLER,JOHN M-The New Stone Age in Northern Europe-NY-1921
                  (5L2) 3.   (5x7)   5.00
TYLER,JOHN W-Life of Wm McKinley,Soldier,Statesman&President-
Phila-c1901-520p-illus   (5w5,fade)   3.00
TYLER,JOSIAH-40 Yrs Among the Zulu-Bost-1891-300p-17 plts-
map   (5c6,ex-libr)   20.00
--Livingstone Lost & Found, or Africa & Its Explorers-Hartf-1873-
8vo-782p-lea-illus-maps   (5t2)   5.00
TYLER,LYON GARDINER-The Cradle of the Republic-Richmond-
1900-187p-illus-orig cl-bev edges-maps (5h9)   15.00
--England in Amer 1580 to 1652-NY-1904-8vo-cl-frontis-maps-
339p-Vol 4 of Amer Nation Series (5q8) 4.   (5t2)   4.50
--Original Narratives of Early Virginia, 1606 to 1625-NY-1907-8vo-
cl-500p-1st ed-map   (5p5)   15.00
--Propaganda in History-Richmond-1921-Richmond Pr-8vo-20p-
wrps-2nd ed,rev-cov title   (5r0)   7.50
TYLER,MASON WHITING-Recollections of the Civil War-NY-
1912-Putnam's-379p-plts   (5mm8,vf,dj)   6.00
TYLER,MOSES COIT-A History of Amer Literature during the
Colonial Period-NY-(1878)-8vo-cl-2 vols in 1-"Students' Ed"
                                       (5t2)   7.50
--same-NY-1879-g.t.-bev edges-2 vols   (5h9)   26.50
--Literary History of Amer Revolution 1763 to 1783-Lond-(1897)-
2 vols in 1-8vo-cl-527p   (5t2)   10.00
--same-NY-1898-cl-t.e.g.-2 vols-2nd ed (4i2,libr stmp)   12.50
--Patrick Henry-Bost-1889-t.e.g.-hf mor-raised bands-398p
                                       (5w0)   7.50
--same-Bost-1897 et seq-Amer Statesmen (5h9)   4.00
TYLER,ROBT-Memoir of Brevet Maj Gen...wi 2 Months Travel in
Brit & Farther India-Phila-1878-ltd   (5yy6)   35.00
TYLER,ROBT LEE-A Yale Man-NY-1896-Street&Smith-1st ed
                  (5m2) 13.50   (5ee3,f)   12.50
TYLER,S-Memoirs of Roger Brooke Taney-1872-buck (5L7,rbnd) 10.00
TYLER,SYDNEY-SanFrancisco Great Disaster...Earthquake-Phila-
1906-Ziegler-424p-illus   (4p7,stn)   5.00
TYLER,WM F-Pulling Strings in China-Lond-1929-Constable-
306p   (5x9)   4.00
TYLERTOWN,MISSISSIPPI-Inventory of Walthall Co,Archives-
1942-   Prelim ed by Hist Records Survey,WPA-125p(mimeo)
                                       (5y9)   4.50
TYLOR,EDW B-Anahuac or Mexico & the Mexicans,Ancient &
Modern-Lond-1861-maps-frontis-3 tinted plts-crushed mor-
gilt tooled   (5d2,f bndg)   30.00
--Primitive Culture-NY-1889-8vo-2 vols-cl-3rd Amer ed
                                       (5t2,sl crack)   8.75
TYMESEN,MILDRED McC-The Norton Story-Worcester-1953-
326p-illus   (5y2)   5.75
TYNAN,JAS J-Shooting of Dan McGrew-NY-1924-283p-plts
                                       (5a1)   5.00
TYNDALE-BISCOE,E D-50 Years Against the Stream-Mysore-1930-
Wesleyan Mission Pr-96p-48p illus-pict cl-errata slip (5p1)   12.50

TYNDALL, J-Hours of Exercise in Alps-NY-1875-437p-illus (5ii2) 7.50
TYNDALL, JOHN-Faraday as a Discoverer-Lond-1868-port-8vo-
1st ed (5ss5, pres) 13.50
TYNDALL, JOHN-The Glaciers of the Alps-Lond-1896-Longmans,
Green-445p-illus-cl (5d7) 10.00
--Mountaineering in 1861, a vacation tour-Lond-1862-105p-
cl (5d7, lacks bkstrp) 7.50
TYNG, STEPHEN H-The Captive Orphan, Esther, Queen of Persia-
NY-1860-1st ed (4m8, rub, dmpstnd) 15.00
--Memoir of Rev Gregory T Bedell-Phila-1836-402p-cl-1st ed
(5h1) 8.50
TYPICAL ELIZABETHAN PLAYS-NY-(1949)-thk lg8vo-cl-1065p-
3rd ed, rev by Felix Schelling (5t0) 5.00
TYPOGRAPHIA-an Ode On Printing-Roanoke-1926-photo facs-
8vo-bds-lea bkstrp (4c1, chip) 15.00
TYPOGRAPHY-1936, 7-Shenval Pr-8 issues, complete-stiff wrps-
spiral bndg (5tt9) 40.00
TYRE, ROBT-Saddlebag Surgeon-Tor-1954-261p-port (5a1, sp fade) 5.00
TYREE, MARION CABELL, ed-Housekeeping in Old Virginia-Louisvl-
1890-528p (5c0, wn, shake) 12.50
TYROLESE MINSTRELS-By a lady-Bost-1841-GeoWLight-16mo-
orig cl-1st ed-frontis (5x1) 20.00
TYROLESE ALPINE SINGERS-Collection of Tyrolese Songs sung by-
Balt-1837-stitchd (5g8) 15.00
TYRRELL, EDITH-I Was There-Tor-1938-131p-ports-plts (5a1) 10.00
TYRRELL, FRED-Lectures of Sir Astley Cooper on Principles &
Practice of Surgery-Phila-1826-2 vols in 1-4 plts-calf (5i3) 17.50
TYRRELL, J B, ed-Documents Relating to Early History of Hudson Bay-
Tor-1931-Champlain Soc-plts-facs-maps-419p (5zz8) 75.00
--Journals of Sam'l Hearne & Philip Turnor-Tor-1934-Champlain Soc-
ltd to 550c (5w8) 100.00
TYRRELL, JAS W-Across the Sub Arctics of Canada-Tor-1897-
W Briggs-map-illus-8vo-orig cl-230p (4e1) 30.00
--same-Tor-1908-3rd ed-rev-280p-plts-maps (4a8, sl wn) 17.50
TYRRELL-GREEN, E-Parish Church Architecture-1931-illus (5L7) 5.00
TYSON, CARROL B-The Poconos-Phila-1929-193p-illus-map
(5w0, 5m2) 6.50
TYSON, LT-Le Polaris le Radeau de Glace 1870 to 73-(Paris, 1875)-
48p-illus-sml folio-wrps (5r7) 15.00
TYSON, PHILIP T-First Report of Philip T Tyson-Annap-1860-wrps-
col liths-fldg map-145p, 20p (5hh7, sl stn) 12.50
--Geology & Industrial Resources of Calif-Balt-1851-maps-plts-
8vo-2nd ed (4g6, ex-libr) 57.50
--Info in Relation to Geology & Topography of Calif-Wash-1850-
127p & 37p-fldg maps&plts-scarce (4a5) 18.50
TYTLER, ALEX FRASER-Elements of General History-Concord-
ca1894-527p plus 44p-12mo-lea (5h9) 7.50
TYTLER, PATRICK F-Historical View of Progress of Discov on More
Northern Coasts of Amer-Edinb-1832-1st ed-444p-illus-fldg map
(5u6) 35.00
--same-Edinb-1833-2nd ed (5w8, fox) 25.00
TYTLER, SARAH-Landseer's Dogs & their Stories-Lond-1877-8vo-
149p-a.e.g.-cl-6 chrom liths (4a6) 7.50
UBBELOHDE-DOERING, HEINRICH-The Art of Ancient Peru-NY-
1952-sm4to-cl-240p-400 illus (5t2, dj, f) 20.00
UBIQUE-Gun, Rod & Saddle-Lond-1869-8vo-orig cl-295p (5g5) 7.50
UDALL, DAVID KING-Arizona Pioneer Mormon-1959-304p-1st ed
(5r1, f, dj) 20.00
UDDEN, J A-Geology of Muscatine County-DesM-1899-140p-
wrps-Iowa Geol Surv (5h2) 3.50
--Sketch of Geology of Chisos Country, Brewster Co, Tex-Austin-
1907-101p-wrps (4a5) 3.50
UDDERZOOK, WM E-The Goss Udderzook Tragedy-Balt-1873-
8vo-port-orig wrps-59p-1st ed (5m6) 7.50
UDELL, JOHN-Incidents of Travel to Calif, across the Great Plains-
Jefferson, Ohio-1856-for Author-8vo-orig cl-port-1st ed
(5n9) 125.00
--Journal Kept During a Trip Across the Plains...in 1859-LosAng-
1946-illus-reprnt (4m2) 12.50 (5hh3, dj, 4n1) 15.00
UEBER NORDAMERIKA UND DEMOKRATIE-"Koppenhagen"
(Konigsberg)-1782-sm8vo-212p-bds-1st ed-(Schmohl) (5L1) 50.00
UEBERWEG, FRIEDRICH-History of Philosophy, from Thales to Present
Time-NY-(1871 to 73)-thk lg8vo-cl-Scribner (5j5) 15.00
UGARTE, JOSE B-Compendio de Historia de Mexico-Mexico-1946-
286p-calf (5n4) 12.50
UGARTE, MANUEL-Destiny of a Continent-NY-1925-Knopf-8vo-
batik bds-cl bk (4a3) 7.50
UKERS, WM H-All About Coffee-NY-1935-sm4to-col frontis-plts-
818p-2nd ed (5nn2) 15. (5w1) 35.00
--All About Tea-NY-1935-2 vols-4to-1152p-illus(5w1, libr stmp) 42.50
--The Romance of Coffee-NY-1948-280p-55 plts (5w1) 10.00
--The Romance of Tea-NY-1936-276p-illus (5w1) 10.00
ULANOV, B-Duke Ellington-(Biorgraph)-NY-1946-illus (5x2) 8.00

ULLMANN, EGON V-Diet in Sinus Infections & Colds-NY-
1937-166p (5c7) 2.00
ULLMAN, JAS RAMSEY-High Conquest-NY-1941-illus (5t4) 4.50
--same-Phila-(1941)-Lippincott-334p-illus-cl (5d7) 5.00
--Kingdom of Adventure, Everest-NY-(1947)-411p-illus-cl-
Sloane (5d7) 4.00
ULLMAN, JOE-What's the Odds?-NY-1903-8vo-illus-dec cl-
1st ed (5p5) 7.50
ULLYET, K-British Clocks & Clockmakers-Lond-1947-32 plts(8 col)-
48p-lg8vo (5bb0) 3.50
ULMANN, ALBERT-A Landmark History of NY-1901-285p-illus
(5p0) 6. (5t4) 10.50
--New Yorkers-NY-1928-267p-illus-1st ed (5w5) 6.00
ULMER, GEO T-Adventures & Remin of a Volunteer-n.p.-1892-
wrps-77p (4j4, fox) 5.00
ULRICH, CAROLYN F-Books & Printing-Woodstock-1943-NY Publ
Libr-256p-8vo-wrps (4c1) 7.50
ULSTER CO-Medical Soc-Code of Medical Ethics & By Laws-
Rondout-Horatio Fowes-1866-8vo-23p-wrps (5r7) 10.00
UMFREVILLE, E-Present State of Hudsons Bay-Tor-1954-illus
(4b9, dj) 20. (5w8) 15.00
UMLAUFT, F-The Alps-Lond-1889-523p-illus-cl (5d7) 10.00
UN THE DANS LE MONDE DES CHATS-Paris-(ca 1880)-Hachette
et Cie-lg8vo-col illus (5c8, sp wn) 12.50
UNAUTHORIZED PRACTICE NEWS-1934 to 67-Vol 1 thru 32
(5ii7, rbnd) 375.00
UNCLE BARNEY-Carrollton, Ill-1877-Gazette Steam Pr House-
258p-port (5r0, names on flys) 15.00
UNCLE DANIEL'S STORY-of "Tom Anderson" & 20 Great Battles-
By an Officer of the Union Army-NY-1886-ARHart-435p-
12mo-cl-illus-1st ed (5j5) 20.00
UNCLE DICK'S SERIES-My Mother-ca 1860-8 lvs-4 col plts (5v2) 10.00
UNCLE EZEKIEL'S YOUTH'S CABINET-Concord-1844-Witherell-
Vol 1, #2, 3, 6, 9, 10-orig prntd wrps-illus-6x4¼" (5rr2, f) 12.50
UNCLE FRANK'S-Select Faboes for Good Boys & Girls-NY-ca 1840-
12mo-34p-5 vols-17 illus ea vol-illus wrps-(5 vols of 6)-
WHMurphy (5v0, vf) 40.00
UNCLE HUMPHREY'S-Tales of Wonder & Delight-Lond-(ca 1855)-
Thos Holmes-sm8vo-dec red cl-g.t.-284p-plts (5aa2) 6.50
UNCLE JOHN-Illus Songs & Hymns for the Little Ones-Lond-
ca1850-lg8vo-201p (5v0) 8.50
UNCLE MADISON-Little Things, or, One Step at a Time-Bost-
(ca 1845)-32mo-cl-96p-illus (5t7) 6.00
UNCLE NICK-Among Shoshones-SaltLkCty-(1910)-Skelton Publ-
222p-plts-cl (5yy3, wn) 25.00
UNCLE RUFUS & MA-n.p.-Aug 1882-16mo-cl (5g8, erasure) 15.00
UNCLE TOBY'S SERIES-Enraged Miller, 3 Tiny Pigs-NY-(ca 1880s)-
McLoughlin Bros-ea wi 4 col plts-12p in pict wrps-12mo-
2 vols (5c8, lt soil, sl tn) 3.50
UNCLE'S PRESENT, THE-A New Battledoor-Phila-n.d.-ca1810-
Jacob Johnson-4 lvs-Rosenbach 428-rare (5v2, f) 200.00
UNDERHILL, FRANCIS T-Driving for Pleasure, or the Harness Stable
etc-NY-1896-orig 3/4 lea-suede sides-4to-1st ed (4c8) 37.50
UNDERHILL, LAW-Edw Small of New England, Desc & Allied
Families-1910-3 vols (5mm3) 17.50
--Desc of Edw Small of New England & Allied Families-1934-
1868p-3 vols-rev ed (5t9) 30.00
UNDERHILL, REUBEN L-From Cowhides to Golden Fleece, a Narr of
Calif-Stanford Univ Pr-1939 (5h5) 12.50 (5kk3, autg, dj) 20.00
--same-(1946)-2nd, revised ed (5h5) 10.00
UNDERHILL, RUTH-Autobiography of a Papago Woman-1936-
8vo-stiff wrps-64p-Amer Anthr Assn #46
(5g6, autg) 5. (4k5, f) 6.00
--First Penthouse Dwellers of Amer-SantaFe-(1946)-plts-176p-
2nd ed, rev-scarce (5xx5) 17.50 (4L0) 8.50
--Here Come the Navaho-(Lawrence, 1953)-orig cl-285p-1st ed-
photos (4L0, rbnd) 10. (4k5, f) 7.50
--Indians of the Pac NW-Riverside-1945-illus-fab (4k5, f) 6.50
--Indians of Southern Calif-(Lawrence, Kans, n.d.)-74p-wrps-
photos (4k5, 5dd4) 3.50
--Northern Paiute Indians of Calif & Nevada-1941-US Off of
Indian Affairs, Sherman Pamph #1, 1st ed-4to-78p-photos (5g5) 4.50
--same-Lawrence-n.d.-wrps-illus (4k5) 4.50
--Papago Indians of Ariz & their Relatives the Pima-(Lawrence,
Kans, 1940)-68p-wrps-photos (5dd4, 4k5, f) 3.50
--People of the Crimson Evening-Riverside, Ca-1951-wrps-illus-
127p-1st ed (5L0) 5. (4k5, f) 6.50
--Pueblo Crafts-US Indian Serv-(1944)-illus-pic cl (4k5, f) 7.50
--same-(Lawrence, Kans, 1948)-R8vo-148p-illus wrps (5dd4) 3.50
--Red Man's America-Chig-(1953)-369p plus index-illus-1st ed
(5L0, f, dj) 10.00
--Singing for Power-Berkeley-1938-illus-158p-unbound, uncut
sheets (4L0) 12.50

USED BOOK PRICE GUIDE

UNDERHILL, VER A-Creating Hooked Rugs-NY-1951-110p-
  4 col plts-photos   (5p0)   7.50
UNDERSEA WARFARE-Wash,DC-1949-Natl Res Councl (4j3) 12.50
UNDERWOOD, ADIN B-Three Years' Service of 33rd Mass
  Infantry Reg 1862 to 1865-Bost-1881-8vo-299p-buck
                    (4a7,rbnd) 25.00
UNDERWOOD, FRANCIS H-Cloud pictures-Bost-1872-Lee&Shepard,
  etc-1st ed   (5m2,sl spots) 8.50
--Life of Henry Wadsworth Longfellow-Bost-1882-355p-cl (5h1) 7.50
UNDERWOOD, J C-Trail's End, Poems of NM-SantaFe-1921-
  79p-1st ed   (4i7,fray) 6.00
UNDERWOOD, JOHN C-Analytical Compilation of Regulations
  & Army Register I O O F-Cinn-1892-obl 8vo-illus-269p-
  col plts   (4b3,vg) 25.00
UNDERWOOD, JOHN J-Alaska, An Empire in the Making-NY-
  1913-map-illus-8vo-1st ed (4L0,lacks e.p.) 6.50 (4g6) 8.50
--same-NY-1915-440p-photos-map   (5ss1,pres) 8.50
UNDERWOOD, LORING-The Garden & Its Accessories-Bost-1907
  215p-photos   (5s7,rub) 5.00
UNDERWOOD, LUCIEN M-Moulds, Mildews & Mushrooms-NY-
  1899-236p-col-frontis-9 plts (5s7) 10.00
UNDERWOOD, M A-Spoor Family in Amer-1901-165p (4t2) 12.50
UNDERWOOD, OSCAR-Drifting Sands of Party Politics-NY-
  1928-422p   (5w4) 5.00
--same-NY-c1931-port   (5q8,5x7) 4.50
UNDSET, SIGRID-Sigurd & His Brave Companions-NY-1943-Knopf-
  illus-140p-10 col plts(1 dbl pg)-Borzoi Books for Young People-
  1st ed   (5p1) 10.00
UNGER, F W-With Bobs & Kruger-Phila-1901-illus (5x2) 10.00
UNIFORM REGULATIONS FOR OFFICERS OF THE FLEET-Lond-
  1893-folio-24 col plts   (4p3) 30.00
UNION BANK OF LOUISIANA-Charter of-n.p.-1832-16p(5h8) 25.00
UNION COAL CO-Charter of, Somerset Co, Pa-Balt-1853-
  JohnWWoods-8vo-orig prntd wrps-4 lg fold outs (5i9) 10.00
UNION HISTORY COMPANY-History of Jackson Co,MO-KansCty-
  1881-illus-fldg map-1006p-1st ed-v scarce
         (4t3,rebnd,wtrstn,chip) 85.00
UNION LEAGUE CLUB of NY-Report of Spec Comm, Amendment
  for Abolition of Slavery, Jan 31, 1865-NY-1865-8vo-24p-
  sewn   (5m6) 12.50
UNION OF SOUTH AFRICA-All South Africa Law Reports-1947
  to 67-83 vols-bnd (5ii7,ex-libr) 975.00
--South African Law Reports-Witwatersrand Local Div-1910 to 46-
  bnd   (5ii7,ex-libr) 700.00
--South African Tax Cases-1921 to 66-Vol 1 thru 28-bnd
         (5ii7,ex-libr) 495.00
UNION PACIFIC RR CO(listed by year)-Geological & Agricultural
  Survey of 100 Miles West of Omaha-NY-1886-44p-1st ed-
  v scarce-wrps-Amer Bur of Mines (5L0,cor front wrp clipped) 20.00
--Union Pac RR,the Great Natl Highway betw Mntns & East...
  Open from Omaha to Julesburg-Chig-1867-16p plus fldg map-
  wrps-1st ed-(Chig before fire imprint) (5L0) 65.00
--Progress of Their Road West from Omaha....500 Miles Completed
  Oct 25, 1867-NY-1867-24p-wrps-1st ed (5L2) 25.00
--Progress of their Road West from Omaha,Nebr across the Continent,
  540 Miles Completed-NY-1868)Apr 2, 1868)-32p-map-scarce
         (5L0) 20.00
--Progress of the...West from Omaha,Nebr across the Continent,
  828 miles completed Sept 20, 1868-NY-1868-40p-map-wrps
         (5L0) 20.00
--Eastern Div or (Kansas Pac Ry),Importance of its route to all
  sections of the country-Wash-1868-50p-fldg map-1st ed-
  scarce   (5h2) 20. (5L2,lt stn) 40.00
--Great Nat'l Highway Betw Missouri R & Calif-Chig-1868-
  map on bk cov-8vo-prntd wrps-end pg 13 "New York, Feb 1868"
         (4c1) 25.00
--The Great Nat'l Highway betw The Missouri River & Calif, open
  from Omaha to the Mntns-Chig-1868-13p,(15)-map on bk wrp-
  wrps-pre Chig fire imprint-scarce-prntng before May 1
         (5L2,chip) 60.00
--Report of G M Dodge, Chief Eng on a Branch RR Line from Union Pac
  RR to Idaho, Montana, Oreg & Puget's Sound, Wash-1868-13p-
  fldg map-wrps-rare (5L5) 85.00
--Union Pac RR Lines, 12 Million Acres-Omaha-1870-map-8vo-
  44p-wrps   (5q0,wrps) 10.00
--Pass of Central Branch Union Pac RR 1871-stiff cardboard,signed-
  scarce   (5L2) 10.00
--Affairs of the Union Pac RR Co,the Credit Mobilier of Amer &...
  Wash-1873-1st ed-H of R Rpt #78,26 & 768p plus index-
  scarce   (5L2,wn) 25.00
--Guide to Union Pac RR Lands-Omaha-1878-orig wrps-32p-
  8vo-2 fldg maps   (4g6) 17.50

UNION PACIFIC RR CO (continued)
--Oregon Short SE Line Country,a description of Oregon,Wash
  & Idaho,facts for settlers-Omaha-1885-illus-prntd wrps-
  map on bk   (5g3) 20.00
UNION PACIFIC TOURIST,THE-Illus Sketches of Principal Health
  & Pleasure Resorts of Great West & NW....publ by Passenger
  Dept-Buffalo-1884-map-illus-4to-pict wrps-61p plus ads &
  index-scarce   (5dd1) 25.00
UNION QUESTIONS-on select portions of scripture-Phila-
  Amer Sunday School Union-32mo-3 vols-1831,1834,1830-
  fldg map in ea-lea bkd bds (5p1) 15.00
UNION REPUBLICAN CAMPAIGN DOCUMENTS #2-Colum-1867-
  14p-sewed as issued-rare (5h2) 10.00
UNITED BRETHREN,THE-Historical Sketch of Church & Missions
  of,Commonly called Moravians-Bethlehem,Pa-1848-
  Held,prntr-93p plus list of Indian Missions-blue wrps(5h1) 25.00
UNITED BRETHREN IN CHRIST-Origin,constit,doctrine &
  discipline-Circleville,Ohio-1837-16mo-qtr roan-1st ed
         (5i9,f) 40.00
UNITED CONFEDERATE VETERANS-Battles of Atlanta-Atlanta-
  1895-31p pamph-foldout map (5h6) 10.00
UNITED DAUGHTERS OF CONFEDERACY-Remin of Women of
  Missouri during the Sixties-n.p.-n.d.(ca 1913)-311p-scarce
         (5L0) 15.00
UNITED FARM WOMEN,ALBERTA-Recipes...-Calgary-1928-
  220p   (5kk7,writing) 5.00
UNITED GERMAN EVANGELICAL LUTHERAN CONGREG IN
  NO AMER-Reports of-Reading-1882-illus-Vol 1(all?)-
  new ed-Pilger Book Store (5m2) 12.50
UNITED NATIONS DEPT OF ECON & SOCIAL AFFAIRS-Economic
  Survey of Africa since 1950-NY-1960-248p-wrps (5c6,f) 6.00
UNITED NATIONS DOCUMENTS INDEX-1950 to 62-Vol 1 thru 13
         (5ii7,rbnd) 390.00
UN MONTHLY CHRONICLE-NY-1964 to 69-Vol 1 thru 6
         (5ii7,rbnd) 65.00
UNIVERSAL BIOGRAPHICAL DICTIONARY-Hartford-1847-cl-
  444p-new ed   (4k2) 12.50
UNIVERSAL MAGAZINE-of Knowledge & Pleasure-Vol 65-monthly-
  6 issues-Jul thru Dec 1779-fldg plts-US mdps-lea-orig labl
  John Hinton,ed-379p plus index-London (5a0,chip) 20.00
UNIVERSAL SONGSTER,THE-& museum of mirth-Bost-1835-
  (words only)-frontis-24mo-prntd bds-sheep bk
         (5g3,wn,libr labl) 20.00
UNIVERSALIST COMPANION-with Almanac & Reg...for 1849-
  Bost-(1848)-60p-wrps (5h1) 4.00
UNIV COMMISSION ON SOUTHERN RACE QUESTION- R8vo-
  illus-Organiz Meeting-Nashville,May 24,1912)-Lexington-
  1914   (5x2) 25.00
UNIVERSITY LAW REVIEW-NY-1893 to 97-Vol 1 thru 3
         (5ii7,rbnd) 50.00
UNIVERSITY LIBRARY OF AUTOBIOGRAPHY-NY-1927-Nat'l
  Alumni-15 vols-ltd to 1007 sets (5p9) 60.00
UNIVERSITY OF ALABAMA-Tuskaloosa-(ca1900)-wrps-folio-
  12 lvs of photos   (4j4) 12.50
UNIV OF BRIT COL-Record of (War) Service-Vanc-1924-146p
         (5aa0) 5.00
UNIV OF CHICAGO LAW REVIEW-1933 to 71-Vol 1 thru 38-
  bnd   (5ii7,rbnd) 690.00
--same-single vols (5ii7,rbnd) ea 22.00
UNIV OF CINCINNATI LAW REVIEW-1927 to 1970-Vol 1to 25-
  bnd   (5ii7) ea 30.00
--same-Vol 16 thru 39-bnd (5ii7) ea 22.00
UNIV OF COLO LAW REVIEW-1928 to 70-Vol 1 thru 41(Vol 1 thru
  34 as Rocky Mountain Law Rev)-bnd (5ii7) 485.00
UNIV OF FLORIDA LAW REVIEW-1948 to 69-Vol 1 thru 22
         (5ii7,rbnd) 500.00
UNIV OF ILLINOIS LAW FORUM-1949 to 68-Vol 1 thru 20
         (5ii7,rbnd) 400.00
UNIV OF MICHIGAN-Catalogue of Graduates,Non graduates,Off
  & Members of Faculties,1837 to 1921-AnnArbor-1923-1379p
         (5j4) 10.00
UNIV OF NEWARK LAW REVIEW-1936 to 42-Vol 1 thru 7
         (5ii7,rbnd) 65.00
UNIV OF PENNA ILLUSTRATED-(Phila)-1906-1st ed (5m6) 7.50
UNIV OF PENNA LAW REVIEW-1852 to 1971-Vol 1 thru 119
         (5ii7,rbnd) 2,350.00
--same-Single Vols (5ii7) ea 25.00
UNIV OF TENNESSEE-Catalogue of Officers & Students of East Tenn
  Univ for 1858,59-Knoxville-1859-12p (5h6,lacks back wrp) 15.00
UNIV OF VIRGINIA-Photogravures-Charlottesville-1895-24p-
  wrps   (5j6) 8.50
UNIV OF WISC-12th Annual Rpt of Bd of Regents of-Madison-1860-
  83p-wrps   (5h2,stn) 8.50

300

UNONIUS,GUSTAF-Minnen fran en sjuttonarig vistelse i nordvestra
Amerika-Upsala-1861, 1862-WSchultz-8 plts-2 vols-hf calf
(5d6,wn) 75.00

UNTERMYER COLLECTION-Harvard Pr-1956-264p-159 plts-4to-
Y Hackenbroch,ed (5ww3) 35.00

UNTERMEYER, JEAN STARR-Steep ascent-NY-1927-Macmillan-
1st prntng (5m2) 6.50

UNTERMEYER,LOUIS-Adirondack Cycle-NY-1929-The Poetry
Quartos-8vo-wrps-1st ed-ltd to 475c (5b2,f) 4. (5dd8) 7.50

--A Century of Candymaking 1847 to 1947-Cambr-1947-New
England Confectionery Co-sml folio-84p-col plts (5b8) 8.50

--A Critical Anthology-NY-(1936)-Harcourt, Brace-Modern Amer
Poetry,Modern British Poetry-combined edit-654p,549p (5p7) 7.50

--First Words Before Spring-1933-AlfredAKnopf-8p-16mo-
orig wrps,in envelope-1st ed,#6 of the Chap Books (4b5,f) 5.00

--The Forms of Poetry-Pocket Dictionary of Verse-NY-1932-
12mo-cl-156p (5t0) 3.50

--Including Horace-NY-1919-159p-Harcourt, Brace &Howe-
12mo-bds-1st ed (5r9) 7.50

--Modern Amer Poetry,An Intro-NY-1919-Harcourt, Brace & Howe-
8vo-bds-cl bk (5b2,f) 12.50

--Moses-NY-1928-1st ed (5b9,vg) 7.00

--The New Adam-NY-1920-Harcourt, Brace & Howe-12mo-pict bds-
cl bk-120p-1st ed (5j5) 7.50

--New Songs for New Voices-NY-(1928)-Harcourt, Brace-4to-
buck-drwngs by Peggy Bacon-258p (5j5,dj) 10.00

--Poems of Heinrich Heine-(NY-(1923)-(rev ed)-port (5F0,f) 3.00

--Robert Frost,a Backward Look-Wash-1964-24p plus bibliog-
orig pict wrps (5ss9,vg) 3.50

--This Singing World-NY-(1924)-Harcourt, Brace-illus by Florence
Wyman Ivins-12mo-445p-frontis-pict cl-3rd prntng (5p1) 4.00

--A Treasury of Laughter-NY-1946-712p (5k2) 3.50

UP DE GRAFF,F W-Head Hunters of the Amazon-NY-(1923)-
337p-photos (5w3,fade) 5.00

UP TO THE CLOUDS ON MULEBACK-Worcester-1938-158p-bds-
illus-1st ed-(Chas W Kellogg) (5dd6,pres) 5.00

UPDIKE, D B-Amer Printer & His Merrymount Press-NY-1947- cl
Amer Inst of Graphic Arts (4p9,f,dj) 25.00 (5j4,5tt9) 10.00

--The Book of Common Prayer-Bost-1930-Merrymount Pr-folio-
ltd to 500c-pigskin-wi care of bndg slip (4n5,vf) 200.00

--In the Day's Work-Harvard Univ Pr-1924-70p (5p9) 5.00

--Notes on the Merrymount Press & its Work-Cambr-1934-orig cl-
8vo-13 views-ltd to 500c (4n5,unopened) 50.00

--Printed Types-Cambr-1951-2 vols-2nd ed (5r5,dj) 15.00

--Printed Types,Their History,Forms & Use-Harvard Univ Pr-
1927-2 vols (5p7) 11.00

--same-Cambr-1937-Harvard Univ Pr-2 vols-cl (5tt9,sp fade) 12.50

UPDIKE, JOHN-The Centaur-NY-1963-8vo-cl-1st ed (5d9,dj) 15.00

--Midpoint & Other Poems-NY-1969-Knopf-ltd to 350c,autg,nbrd-
(4L4,box,mint) 25.00

--The Music School,Short Stories-NY-1966-8vo-cl-1st ed,1st issue
(5d9,dj) 37.50

--same-NY-1966-Knopf-bds-8vo-1st ed (4g1,dj) 4.95

--Of the Farm-NY-1965-8vo-cl-1st ed (5d9,dj,4g1,f,dj) 10.00

--Poorhouse Fair-NY-1959-12mo-bds (4c2) 20.00

--Rabbit, Run-NY-1960-12mo-bds-cl bk-1st ed
(5hh1,vg,dj) 10. (5ss7,vf,dj) 25.00

UPDIKE,W-Episcopal Church in Narragansett,RI-1847-533p(5t9) 7.50

UPHAM, ALFRED H-Old Miami-Hamilton,Ohio-161p-illus (5p0) 5.00

UPHAM,C E-Salem Witchcraft in Outline,etc-Salem-1895-frontis-
12mo-161p (4m2) 7.50

UPHAM,CHAS W-Salem Witchcraft-Bost-1867-2 vols (4b6) 40.00

--same-Bost-1867-ltd to 100 sets-1st ed-2 vols bnd in 4-t.e.g.
(5m4) 100.00

UPHAM,CHAS WENTWORTH-Life Exploration & Public Services
of John C Fremont-Bost-1856-Ticknor&Fields-256p-illus-cl-
1st ed (5dd1,wn) 3. (5tt0) 10. (5s4,sl wn) 6. (5dd1) 7.50

UPHAM,N G-Rebellion,Slavery & Peace-NY-ca1861-Loyal Pub
Soc-24p-wrps (5x2) 25.00

UPHAM,THOS C-Elements of Mental Philosophy-NY-1861-2 vols-
lea (5t2) 5.00

UPHAM,WARREN-The Glacial Lake Agassiz-USGS Monogr 25-
Wash-1895-GPO-4to-hf mor-g.e.-658p-38 plts (5L1) 25.00

UPHAM,WM P-A memoir of Gen'l John Glover of Marblehead-
Salem-1863-4to-port-mor-orig wrps bnd in (5g3,rbnd) 7.50

UPS AND DOWN-A Book of Surprise Pictures-Lond-c1880-ENister-
tab operated slats (5v2,f) 67.50

UPS & DOWNS-in Life of a Distressed Gentleman-NY-1836-
Leavitt, Lord&Co-225p (5x1) 45. (5t4) 20.00

UPSHUR,GEO LYTTLETON-As I Recall Them,Memories of Crowded
Years-NY-1936-259p plus index-illus-1st ed-ltd to 750c (5L2) 15.00

UPSHUR,T T-Sir Geo Yeardley or Yardley,Gov of Va-(1896)-
36p (4t2) 17.50

UPSON,ARTHUR-The collected poems-Minnpls-1909-
Richard Burton,ed-EdmundDBrooks-2 vols-8vo-orig cl-1st ed
(5t5) 6.50 (5i8,photo laid in) 10.00

UPSON,WM HAZLETT-The Piano Movers-StCharles,Ill-1927-
16mo-bds- 1st ed of auth's 1st book (5gg6,dj) 10.00

UPTON,EMORY-Infantry Tactics Double & Single Rank,adapted to
Amer etc-NY-1884-16mo-lea-445p-rev ed (5t2) 5.00

--Military Policy of the US-Wash-1904-495p-2 fldg maps (5L2) 7.50

--same-Wash-1907-2nd impr-495p-2 fldg maps (5dd1) 5.00

--same-Wash-1916,1917-2 items bnd as 1-23p,495p (5w4) 8.50

--A New System of Infantry Tactics, Dbl & Single Rank-NY-1867-
24mo (5x5) 12.50

--same-NY-1868-illus-12mo (5s9,sp wn) 6.00

UPTON,FLORENCE K-Adventures of Borbee & the Wisp-Lond-
1908-1st ed-col illus-sq4to-pict bds (5c8) 15.00

UPTON,JOHN-Critical observations on Shakespeare-Lond-1746-
for GHawkins-8vo-1st ed-scarce (5x3,rbkd) 50.00

UPTON,LOUISE R-Castles in Air-NY-1878-1st ed-frontis-v scarce
(5tt6) 40.00

URBAIN-DUBOIS-Cuisine de Tous les Pays-Paris-1897-cl-thk4to-
illus-col frontis-7th ed-54p,799p (4g9,f) 35.00

--La Cuisine Artistique-Etudes de L'Ecole Moderne-Paris-n.d.-
576p-lg thk4to-red cl-plts -14th edition (5g9) 30.00

URBAN,JOHN W-In Defense of the Union-(n.p., Hubbard Bros,
1887)-thk8vo-pict cl-plts-633p (5j5) 10.00

URBAN,JOS-Theatres-NY-1929-4to-col frontis-plts-ltd (5tt5) 17.50

URBINO,MADAME L B-Art Recreations-Bost-1863-illus-336p
(5t4) 7.50

URE,D-History of Rutherglen & East Kilride-Glasgow-1793-
334&22p-subscr list-18 plts-8vo-ex scarce (4p6,lacks bndg) 97.50

URE,PERCY N-Black Glaze Pottery from Rhitsonia in Boeotia-
Lond-Oxf-1913-Studies in Hist & Arch-illus-8vo-orig bds-64p-
19 plts (4m6,ex-libr, lacks bkstrp) 15.00

URIBE,C,ANDRES-Brown Gold-NY-(1954)-255p-32 photos(8 col)
(5w1) 8.50

URMY,CLARENCE T-A Calif Troubadour-SanFran-1912
(5x5,cov soil) 5.00

URQUHART,FRANK J-Short History of Newark-Newark-1910-
Baker Prntg-12mo-cl-158p (4t1) 6.50 (5a8) 10.00

URQUHART,H M-History of the 16th Battalion(Can Scottish),
CEF in Great War 1914 to 1919-Tor-1932-ports-plts-15 fldg maps
(4d1,vf) 25.00

URQUHART, JOHN-Electric Shiplighting,Handbook-Lond-1900-
308p-illus (5s1) 5.00

URSULINES OF QUEBEC-Glimpses of the Monastery-Quebec-
Demers et Frere-1897-8vo-cl-418p-184p-8 illus-2nd ed,rev
(5L1) 15.00

URWICK,T A-Urswyk,Urswick,or Urwick,Records of the Family-
Lond-1893-224p-fldg chart (5t9) 30.00

US ARMY ENGINEERS-Report Upon Geog Explor & Surv West
of 100th Meridian-Wash-1875-Vol 5,Zoology-4to-1021p-
plts (5cc1,rbnd) 37.50

US ARMY REGULATIONS, OF 1861-Revised-Phila-1863-Geo Childs-
594p (5mm8) 15.00

US ATTORNEY GENERAL-Attorney General's Survey of Release
Procedures-Wash-1939-wrps-5 vols (5tt4) 29.50

US ATTORNEY GENERAL-Committee on Administrative Procedure-
Monographs-mimeo-27 vols in 34 (5ii7) 200.00

--1940 printed ed-76th Cong-13 pts in 1 vol (5ii7) 25.00

--1941 printed ed-77th Cong-14 pts in 1 vol (5ii7) 25.00

US CAMERA,1945-U S A At War-NY-(1944)-1st ed-illus-4to-
Tom Maloney,ed (5ii3) 10.00

U S CARTRIDGE CO-Illus Catalog of Collection of Firearms-
Lowell-n.d.-140p-illus-wrps (5xx7,wrps) 10.00

--Where to Hunt Amer Game-Lowell-1898-8vo-cl-illus-288p
(5t2) 3.75

US CATHOLIC HIST SOC-Historical Records & Studies-Thos F Meehan,
ed-Vol 22-1932-cl-286p (5r0) 7.50

--same-Vol 26-1936-cl-183p (5r0) 7.50

US CODE CONGR & ADMIN SERV-Internal Revenue Acts, Code
& Fed Tax Regulations-1954 to 63-14 vols-bnd (5ii7) 95.00

US COMPTROLLER OF THE TREAS-Decisions-1894 to 1940-
Vol 1 thru 27(all publ) (5ii7,rbnd) 225.00

US COURT OF CLAIMS-Reports-Vol 1 thru 192-bnd (5ii7) 2,000.00

US CUMULATIVE BOOK AUCTION RECORDS-
--1940,1 (4a4) 10.00

--same-1940,2 (4a4) 15.00

--same-1942,3 (4a4) 10.00

--same-1943,4 (4a4) 10.00

--same-NY-1946-index for 1940 to 45-thk8vo (5ii2,hng broke) 12.50

US DEPT OF AGRICULTURE-Climate & Man,Yrbk 1941-Wash-1941-
illus-1260p-cl (5cc1,f) 7.50

US DEPT OF AGRICULTURE (continued)
--NoAmer Faunn-#1 to 60-(#6&9 never issued)-Wash-1889 to
1950-Bur of Biol Survey-wrps-ex scarce   (4p5)   200.00
--Soils & Mne,Yrbk 1938-Wash-1938-col fldg map-illus-cl-
1246p   (5cc1,vg)   7.50
US DEPT OF STATE-Papers Relating to Foreign Relations 1861 to
1942-204 vols-bnd   (5ii7,ex-libr) 5,000.00
US FEDERAL TRADE COMMISSION-Annual Report 1916 to 66-
51 vols bnd in 19 books   (5ii7,rbnd)   450.00
US HORSE SHOE CO-ca 1908-12mo-16p-self wrps   (4a6)   10.00
US HYDROGRAPHIC OFFICE-Africa Pilot-Wash-1923,24-2 vol-
5&661&597p-3 fldg maps-West Coast,So&E Coasts (5c6,stn) 25.00
US INFANTRY TACTICS-Phila-1861-1st ed-12mo-drawings
                                         (5jj3)   25.00
--same-Wash-1863-Gov Print Office-370p-plts-cl (5yy3,stns) 25.00
US INTL BOUNDARY COMM-Joint Report...Boundary Between
US & Canada-Wash-1921-folio-linen-g.-plts-104p
                                     (5dd7,mint)   35.00
US LAWS,STATUTES,ETC-Statutes at Large-1968-Vol 1 thru 82,
bnd in 132 vols   (5ii7,ex-libr) 2,450.00
US LIBRARY OF CONGRESS-Annual Report 1900 to 40-bnd
                                     (5ii7,ex-libr)   125.00
US MAGAZINE & DEMOCRATIC REVIEW-Vol 8-Wash-1840-538p-
bds   (5h1,rub)   10.00
US MAGAZINE RIFLE,MODEL OF 1903-Wash-1906-illus-bds-
57p   (5q0)   5.00
US NAT'L LABOR RELATIONS BOARD-Annual Report-1936 to 65-
1st thru 30th-30 vols bnd in 15   (5ii7)   335.00
--Decisions-Vol 1 thru 161-bnd (5ii7,lacks 1 vol,ex-libr) 1,550.00
US NAVAL INST-Proceedings of the US Naval Instit-(Vol 39 #2
Mar,1913) to Vol 89,#10(Oct,1963)-599 numbers-wrps
                                 (5s1,f,incomplete)   400.00
US NAVAL TRAINING CAMP,CHARLESTON,SC-Charleston-
(ca 1915)-illus-wrps-24 lvs-Albertype   (4j4)   7.50
US NAVY-Ship & Gun Drills-NY-(1914)-32mo-289p (5q0)   5.00
US PATENT OFFICE-Decisions of Commissioner 1900 to 1957
                                     (5ii7,lacks 1905)   450.00
--Index of Patents 1877,1880,1882,1884,1899,1903,1913
                                         (5ii7) ea   5.00
--Index of Trade Marks-1929 to 1950   (5ii7) ea   5.00
US SECURITIES & EXCHANGE COMMISSION-Annual Report-
1st to 33rd-1935 to 67-33 vols bnd in 11   (5ii7)   280.50
US SERVICE MAGAZINE-NY-1864 to 65-4 vols (4j4,fox,stnd) 17.50
US SUPT OF DOC-Index to Reports & Documents-Vol 1 to 43-
54th to 72nd Cong-43 vols-2nd ed-1895
                                 (5ii7,incomplete run)   195.00
US SUPREME COURT-Reports-Vol 1 thru 388-cl-Official ed
                                 (5ii7,some ex-libr) 2,200.00
US TREATIES & OTHER INTL AGREEMENTS-1950 to 60-Vol 1
thru 11-28 vols-bnd   (5ii7) 1,400.00
US WAR DEPT-Gunnery & Explosives for Field Artillery Officers-
Wash-1911-16mo-1st ed-100p   (5z5)   10.00
--Small Arms Firing Manual-Wash-1918-rev to 3/15/18-12mo
                                         (5z5,vg)   3.50
--Technical Manual TM 9-1575,Ord nance,Time Pieces-Wash-
1945-illus-224p-8vo   (5bb0)   2.50
US WAR DEPT-BOARD OF CONTRACT ADJUSTMENT-Decisions
1919 to 21-Vol 1 thru 8(all publ)   (5ii7)   95.00
USE,DISPOSITION OF SHIPS-Shipyards end of WW II-Wash-
1945-Off Doc #48,wrps-illus-325p-stapled   (5s1)   6.00
USEFUL ARTS EMPLOYED-in Construction of Dwelling Houses-
Lond-1844-215p-illus-cl-g.   (5hh7)   12.50
USEFUL ARTS EMPLOYED-in the Production of Clothing-Lond-1851-
199p-12mo-2nd ed   (5n7)   7.50
USEFUL COLLECTION of Down to Date Recipes-1912-(LosAng)-
Wilshire Presbyt Church Guild-156p-ads (5g9,sl soil)   7.50
USSHER,PERCY A-The Midnight Court and Adventures of a
Luckless Fellow-Lond-1926-1st ed   (5ss9)   10.00
UTAH-Acts,Resolutions & Memorials,passed by First Annual,& Spec
Sessions,of Legis Assembly of Terr of,22nd Day of Sept,1851-
Great SaltLkCty,U T-1852-BrighamHYoung,prntr-258p-
removed   (5m3,lacks 14 lvs)   45.00
UTAH-Constitutional Convention 1895-Official Report- 2 vols
                                         (5ii7,rub)   22.50
UTAH-General report of auditor (A Calkin) for Terr of-Great
SaltLkCty-1854-Cain-8vo-unbnd as issued-(100c prntd)
                                         (5i0,f)   85.00
UTAH-A Guide to the State-NY-(1941)-WPA-Amer Guide Ser-1st ed-
illus-595p   (4b3,vg,dj,4a4,f,dj)   15.00
UTAH,THE INLAND EMPIRE,ILLUS-SaltLkCty-1902-R8vo-110p-
orig wrps   (5r8,lt chip)   8.75
UTAH-its history,people,resources,attractions & institutions-
SaltLkCty-1937-12mo-96p-wrps-photos   (5dd5)   5.00

UTAH-Its People,Resources,Attractions & Institutions-SaltLkCty-
n.d.-(ca 1907)-62p-wrps   (5h1) 4.   (5dd1)   3.50
--same-(ca 1909)-illus-wrps-94p   (5k2,cov sl stn)   3.00
--same-Bur of Info,SaltLake-1910-wrps-94p-12mo (5g5)   5.00
--same-(ca 1913)-photos-96p-wrps   (5dd3)   3.00
--same-SaltLkCty-n.d.(ca 1920)-wrps-95p,(1) (5h7)   3.00
UTAH LAW REVIEW-1949 to 65-Vol 1 thru 9 (5ii7,rbnd)   280.00
UTAH-Laws in Utah(To accompany bill HR#1089)-Wash-1870-
Hse Report 21,Pt 2-15p-sewed   (5r7)   15.00
UTAH-Report of Utah Commission to Secr of Interior-Wash-
1883 to 1896-9 vols-orig prntd wrps-v rare-9 separate reports
                                         (5n4,box)   80.00
UTAH-Report of Gov of Utah-Wash-1887-1896-8 vols-orig prntd wrps-
8 separate spec annual reports- v rare   (5n4,box)   80.00
UTAH-Resources & Attractions of Territory of Utah-Omaha-1879-
Utah Bd of Trade-wrps-74p-illus-rare   (5L2)   35.00
UTAH-resources & attractions of Utah-Chig-1889-prntd wrps-
-2nd ed,rev&enlrgd-(map on verso of front)-scarce-issued
by Union Pac RR   (5g3,f)   7.50
UTAH-The Tourist Guide,Its People,etc-c1920   (5k2)   3.00
UTAH'S GREATEST MANHUNT-By an Eye Witness-(SaltLkCty,1913)-
142p-illus-wrps-(B E Gallagher)   (5t3)   6.00
UTAH'S STORY-SaltLkCty-1942-90p-plts-WPA-maps-1st ed-
v scarce-Amer Guide Series   (5g5)   10.00
UTBERG,NEIL S-The Coins of Mexico, 1536 to 1962-4to-wrps-41p
                                         (5g5)   3.50
UTE INDIAN OUTBREAK-Testimony in relation to-Wash-1880-
Doc #38-204p plus index-disbnd-   (4L0)   35.00
UTICA CITY DIRECTORY FOR 1852 to 1853-(B S Merrell)-28p ads-
                                         (4m2)   10.00
UTINSKY,MARGARET-"Miss U"-SanAntonio,Texas-1948-
Naylor Co-172p   (5x9)   3.00
UTLEY,FREDA-The China Story-Chig-1951   (5x7)   4.00
--The High Cost of Vengeance-Chig-1949   (5x7)   3.50
UTLEY,H M-Michigan as a Province,Territory & State-1906-
4 vols-plts   (5L7)   25.00
UTLEY,ROBT M-Custer & the Great Controversy-LosAng-1962-
177p plus index-illus-1st ed   (4L0,mint,dj)   12.50
--The Last Days of the Sioux Nation-NewHav-1963-314p plus
20p photos   (5k0,dj) 10.   (4L0)   8.50
UTLEY,WM L-Annual Report of Adj Gen'l of State of Wisc for
Year 1861-Madison-1861-Smith&Cullaton-57p (5a0,vf)   35.00
UTTER,WM T-Granville-Granville-Granville Hist Soc-1956-
347p-illus   (5p7)   5.00
UTZ,W H-Biogr Sketches of Bartlett Marshall Duncan & Henry Utz
Family-StJos-1935-illus-137p-1st ed-v scarce (4L0,autg)   17.50
UZANNE,OCTAVE-The Sun shade, the Glove,the Muff-Lond-
1883-t8vo-illus   (5ss5,cov lt soil)   10.00
VACATION GUIDE TO CUSTER STATE PARK-in Black Hills of
SoDak-n.p.-1938-photos-wrps-32p-1st ed-Amer Guide Ser-
scarce-WPA   (4L5)   10.00
VACCINATION-History of Inoculation & Vaccination-Lond-(1913)-
Burroughs Wellcome-sm8vo-orig cl-310p-ports-maps-plts(some
col)   (5ee5)   15.00
VACHELL,HORACE A-Life & Sport on the Pacific Slope-NY-1901-
illus   (5x5)   5.00
--Sport & Life on the Pacific Clope-Lond-1908-340p-illus-1st ed
                                         (5ee3)   7.50
VACHON'S-Book of Economical Soups & Entrees-Evanston-1903-
85p-pkt book for chefs   (5c9)   2.50
VAERST,EUGEN-Gastrosophie oder die Lehre von den Freuden
der Tafel-Leipzig-1851-2 vols-8vo-prntd papr wrps-1st ed-
scarce   (5b0,wn)   57.50
VAHL,M AMDRUP,ed-Greenland-Copenhagen&Lond-1928,1929-
3 vols-maps-illus-4to-orig wrps   (4m6)   30.00
VAIHINGER,H,ed-Commentar zu Kants Kritik der reinen Vernunft-
1881 to 1892-2 vols   (5L7,sl brown)   25.00
VAIL,ALFRED-American Electro Magnetic Telegraph,etc-Phila-
1845-unbnd-8vo-208p-81 illus-1st ed   (4m6)   30.00
--same-Phila-1847-208p-illus-prntd wrps (5g4)   35.00
--Description of Amer Electro Magnetic Telegraph now in Operation
betw....Wash&Baltimore-Wash-1845-8vo-prntd wrps-24p-
illus   (5hh7,lacks wrps) 22.50 (5a3,f)   25.00
VAIL,GILBERT-A History of Cosmetics in America-NY-(1947)-
139p-bds   (5n7)   5.00
VAIL,H H-Pomfret,(Vt)-(1930)-2 vols-maps-illus
                                 (5m2) 20.   (5t9)   25.00
VAIL,J P A-Vail's Poughkeepsie City Directory 1873,74-
PoughkeepsieCity-c1873-Vail&Co-8vo-part lea-254p (4t1)   15.00
VAIL,MARY BEALS-Approved methods for Home Laundering-Cinn-
(1906)-illus-74p,(1)   (5w7)   4.50
VAIL,R W G-Frederic Remington,Chronicler of Vanished West-NY-
1929-NY Publ Libr-7p-illus-crown 4to-wrps (4a0)   15.00

VAIL, R W G (continued)
--Literature of Book Collecting-NY-1936-50p-wrps   (5j4)   7.50
--Revolutionary Diary of Lt Obadiah Gore Jr-NY-1929-34p-wrps
 (5h7)   3.00
--Voice of the Old Frontier-Phila-1949-492p-1st ed
 (5qq8,mint,4g2) 25.   (5s4)   22.50
--same-NY-n.d.-(prntd Phila,1949,reprntd
 (5ff7,5x5,dj,5g4,mint,dj)   10.00
VAILL,THEODORE F-History of 2nd Conn Heavy Artillery-Winsted,
 Conn-1868-366p   (5t2)   12.50
VAIL,THEODORE NEWTON-Views on Public Questions-n.p.-1917-
 mor-priv prntd-8vo-1st ed   (5ss5,rub)   10.00
VAIL,W P-Genealogy of Some of the Vail Family Desc from Thos etc-
 1937-592p   (4t2)   25.00
--Moses Vail of Huntington-1947-524p   (4t2)   20.00
VAILLANCOURT,EMILE-Broad Side-Montrl-1936-108p-dec wrps
 (5a1)   4.50
VAILLAND,AUGUSTE NICOLAS-Voyage Autour Du Monde execute
 pendant...1836 et 1837 sur La Corvette La Bonite-Paris-1840
 to 52-text,14(of 15) vols in 17-orig prntd bds-1st ed
 (5z9,wn,1 vol lacks t.&h.t.) 4,850.00
VAILLANT,GEO C-Artists & Craftsmen in Ancient Central America-
 NY-1949-102p-wrps-illus   (5dd4)   3.50
--Aztecs of Mexico-GardenCty-1944-325p plus index-illus-map
 (4L0)   6.00
--same-GardenCty-1950   (4L0,dj)   6.00
VAILLANT,LEON-Recherches sur les Poissons des Eaux Douces de
 l'Amerique Septentrionale-Paris-(ca 1875)-folio-wrps-plts-
 154p-offprint   (5j5)   20.00
VALCARCEL,LUIS E-Indians of Peru-NY-(1950)-photos
 (4a1) 15.   (5x5,dj)   10.00
VALDES,A PALACIO-Joy of Capt Ribot-NY-1900-276p-dec
 (5s1,ex-libr)   3.00
VALDES,ANTONIO-Derrotero de las Costas de Espana en el
 Oceano Atlantico-Madrid-1789-Por la Viuda de Ibarra-
 4to-calf-g.border cov   (5L8)   75.00
VALDES,MANUEL ANTONIO-Gazetas de Mexico,Compendio de
 Noticias de Nueva Espana-Ontiveros,Mexico-1788,1789-
 Tomo Tercero-448p-3 plts-vel-Zuniga (5d6,sml wormholes) 100.00
--same-Ontiveros,Mexico-Tomo Quarto-456p & index-Don Felipe
 de Zuniga-dbl plt -1790,1791   (5d6)   75.00
--same-Ontiveros,Mexico-1792,1793-Tomo Quinto-716p-vel-
 plt-de Felipe de Zuniga   (5d6,lacks 6 lvs)   100.00
--same-Ontiveros,Mexico-1794-Tomo Sexto-716p-calf-
 Herederos de Felipe de Zuniga   (5d6,wormed)   75.00
--same-Ontiveros,Mexico-1795-Tomo Septimo-562p-vel-de
 Don Mariano de Zuniga   (5d6,lacks bkstrp,wormed)   100.00
VALDIVIA,FRANCISCA-Recetas Para Cocina-Guadalajara-1898-
 214p-lea bk-12mo-2nd ed,corr&enlrgd (5c5,fade)   16.50
VALE,JOS G-Minty & The Cavalry-Harrisburg-1886-Meyers-
 550p-illus   (5mm8) 13.50   (5i3,rub) 20. (5L3)   22.50
VALE,GILBERT-Fanaticism;Its Source & Influence-NY-1835-
 2 parts in 1-12mo-orig bds-cl bk-1st ed (5ss5,rub)   10.00
VALENTE-PERFEITO-Let's Talk About Port-(Porto)-1948-100p,(1)-
 12 illus   (5w1)   13.50
VALENTIA,GEORGE-Voyages & Travels to India,etc-Lond-1809-
 illus-3 vols-4to-3/4 mor-g.e.   (4c2)   75.00
VALENTINE,ALAN-Vigilante Justice-NY-1956-173p
 (5dd9) 8.25   (5w9)   5.00
VALENTINE & ORSON-Goody Goodchild's Series-Lond-(ca 1860)-
 Dean&Son-hand col illus & text on 8 leaves-yell pict wrps
 (5c8)   15.00
VALENTINE,B B-Ole Marster & Other Verses-Richmond-1921-12mo-
 1st ed   (5x2,dj)   12.50
VALENTINE,D T-City of New York-NY-n.d.-coll of Notices,etc
 from Contempory Pr-2 illus   (4a1)   17.50
--History of City of New York-NY-1853-illus-maps
 (5yy6,f,sl map repair)   37.50
--Manual of Corp of City of NY,1861-(NY-1861)-fldg maps & illus-
 12mo-orig cl   (4c1,mended)   7.50
--Manual of Corp of City of NY,1866-(NY-1866)-fldg map & illus-
 12mo-820p   (4c1) 10.   (5a9)   12.00
VALENTINE,D W-The US Half Dimes-NY-1931-Amer Numismatic
 Soc-plts-79p   (5t7)   25.00
VALENTINE,DAVID T-Obsequies of Abraham Lincoln in the City
 of NY-NY-1866-illus-sm folio-254p
 (4j4,fox) 8.50 (5s9,v wn) 5. (5w5,5j2,sl wn)   10.00
VALENTINE,EDW PLEASANTS-Papers,Abstracts of Records in Local
 & General Archives of Va-(1929)-4 vols-2768p (4t2)   50.00
VALENTINE,LEWIS J-Night Stick,Autobiog-NY-1947 (5x7)   3.75
VALENTINE,MRS-Shakspearian Tales in Verse for Children-NY-
 c1882-McLoughlin Bros-4to-(64p)-col illus-pict bds-
 wire stitchd   (5p1,wn)   7.50

VALENTINE,T W-The Valentines in America-NY-1874-248p-
 illus-orig cl   (5h9,wn)   25.00
VALENTINE'S-Manual of Old NY-NY-1920-#4,New Series-
 illus-maps   (4b7,hngs split)   7.50
--same-NY-(1921)-#6-prnts-col liths-pt lea (5ii3,rub)   10.00
VALENTINER,W R-Jacques Louis David & French Revolution-NY-
 1929-illus-4to-orig box-ltd to 160c,priv prntd (5j2,mint,dj) 25.00
--Late Years of Michel Angelo-NY-1914-ltd to 300c-illus(5tt5) 12.50
--Tino di Camaino-Paris-1935-Pegasus-168p-illus-ltd to 450c
 (5m5)   50.00
VALENTINER,WILHELM R-The Art of the Low Countries-NY-1914-
 Dblday,Page-251p-illus   (5p7)   7.50
--Catalogue of Loan Exhibition of Paintings by Old Dutch Masters...
 Metr Mus of Art....Hudson Fulton-NY-1910-folio-mor-t.e.g.-
 149 illus-Deluxe ed-Box   (4h0-f bndg-sml libr stmp,f)   150.00
--Henry Goldman Collection-NY-1922-priv prntd-14p text,
 22 tip in full pg plts-on heavy stock,ea wi cover sheet & c 2pg
 of notes-elephant folio-t.e.g.-lea&bds-ltd to 200c
 (5m5,edges wn)   35.00
VALENTINI,PHILIPP J J-The Katunes of Maya History-Worcester-
 1880-60p-orig wrps-map   (5w4,ex-libr)   7.50
VALERIO,KATHERINE-Ina-Bost-1871-1st ed   (5F0)   5.50
VALERY,PAUL-Monsieur Teste-NY-1947-Knopf-8vo-dec cl
 (5b2,f,dj)   7.50
--Le Serpent-Lond-(1924)-8vo-black cl-1st ed-ltd to 525c(5ee9)25.00
VALLANCE,A-Old Crosses & Lychgates-Lond-1920-237 illus-
 198p-4to-cl-g.t.   (4a2,sp rprd)   5.00
VALLANCE,AYMER-Wm Morris,Hist Art,His Writings,& his Public
 Life,A Record-Lond-1897-Geo Bell & Sons-36 plts incl col
 frontis-462p-prntd cl   (5tt9)   45.00
VALLANDIGHAM,CLEMENT L-Trial of-Cinn-1863-cl-272p-v rare
 (4h7,rbnd)   40.00
VALLANDINGHAM,JAS L-Life of Clement L Vallandigham-Balt-
 1872-573p-cl   (5h2,rebnd)   12.50
VALLE,RAFAEL HELIODORO-Bibliografia Maya-Mexico-1937-
 404p-hf mor   (5r7,rbnd,wrps bnd in)   30.00
VALLENTIN,A-H G Wells,Prophet of Our Day-NY-(1930)-
 (5ww4,dj)   7.50
VALLENTIN,ANTONINA-Leonardo Da Vinci-NY-1938-1st ed-
 illus-561p   (5qq7,dj) 10.50   (5k2)   7.50
VALLETTE,ELIE-Deputy Commissary's Guide within Province of Md-
 Annapolis-1774-12mo-sheep   (4c1,wn)   25.00
VALLEY ROAD,THE-SanFran-1896-ports-part lea-224p-(A Wheeler)
 (5tt0) 25.   (4p2,spot,sl fray)   30.00
VALLEY SUNSET ROUTE,CALIF TO ARIZ-(Phoenix)-c1910-
 Denison News Co-24 lvs-view book-folio-wrps   (4a5)   7.50
VALLISNERI,ANTONIO-Dell'Uso E Dell'Abuso Delle Vevande E
 Bagnature Calde,O Fredde-Napoli-1727-4to-124p,   48p-
 3rd impress   (5w1,fox,worm,facs t.)   85.00
VALLOIS,G M-Antiques & Curios in Our Homes-Lond-1927-t8vo-
 62 illus-bds-vel sp   (5t5)   10.00
VALOIS,ALFRED DE-Mexique,Havane et Guatemala-Paris-(1861)-
 446p-qtr cl   (5r7)   20.00
VALTIN,JAN-Out of the Night-NY-1941-840p-1st ed
 (4j6,dj,vf)   15.00
--same-GardenCty-c1942   (5x7)   3.50
VALUABLE SECRETS-in Arts, Trades, Etc Adapted to...the US-NY-
 1809-380p-lea   (5n7,rbkd,lacks index)   42.50
--Concerning Arts & Trades,or,Approved Directions-Norwich-
 1795-ThosHubbard,prntr-240p-calf   (5n7,wn)   50.00
VAMBERY,ARMINIUS-Travels in Central Asia-Lond-1864-illus-
 hf lea   (5xx7)   10.00
VAMPYRE,THE,A TALE-Lond-1819-8vo-orig plain wrps-2nd issue
 of Sherwood,Neely&Jones ed   (5x3,box,f)   80.00
VAN ALSTYNE,L-BuryingGrounds of Sharon,Conn-NY-1903
 (5yy6)   17.50
--Diary of Enlisted Man-NewHav-1910-Tuttle,Morehouse&Taylor-
 348p-frontis   (5mm8) 12.50   (4a7,emboss libr stmp)   15.00
VAN AMBURGH,I A-brief biographical sketch of...& illus &
 descrip....mammoth menagerie-(NY,ca 1840 to 50)-pict wrps
 (5g4)   35.00
VANAMEE,LIDA OSTROM-An Adirondack Idyl-NY-(1893)-
 Dillingham-pict cl-1st ed   (5m2)   10.00
VAN ARSDALE,MAY B-Our Candy Recipes-NY-1922-202p-illus-
 1st ed   (5g9)   4.00
VAN BENSCHOTEN,W H-Van Bunschoten or Van Benschoten
 Family in Amer-1907-813p   (5mm3)   50.00
VAN BRUYSSEL,E-Population of an Old Pear Tree-1870-Macm-
 sm8vo-dec cl-a.e.g.-plts-221p-1st ed   (4d1)   15.00
VAN BUREN,MARTIN-Annexation of Texas to US-Wash-1837-
 18p-HED 40   (4a5)   22.50
--Boundary Between US & Republic of Mexico-Wash-1837-94p-
 HED 42   (4a5)   27.50

VAN BUREN, MARTIN (continued)
--Message-Wash-1838-HED 74-62p (4j7) 37.50
VAN BUREN, SARA-Good Living-NY-(1908)-643p-thk8vo-
oilcloth cov-3rd ed (5g9) 7.50
VANCE, C H, ed-Rev Sam'l Seabury, Letters of a Westchester
Farmer-White Plains, NY-1930-Hist Soc (5x0) 5.00
VANCE, J T-Background of Hispanic-American Law-NY-1943
(5r4) 15.00
VANCE, LOUIS JOS-Sheep's Clothing-Bost-1915-Little, Brown-
J M Flagg, illus-8vo-cl (5b2, f, dj) 5.00
VANCE, MARGUERITE-Lady Jane Grey, Reluctant Queen-NY-
1952-Dutton-illus-8vo-184p-frontis-1st ed (5p1, autg, fray dj) 6.50
VAN CLEVE, MRS CHARLOTTE OUISCONSIN-Three score years
& ten-n.p.(Minnpls)-1888-8vo-orig green cl-1st ed, 1st issue,
(with cpyrte slip pasted on bk of t.pg) (5i9) 22.50
--same-n.p.(Minnpls)-1888-1 photo-176p-1st ed
(5dd1, autg) 17.50 (5dd1) 15.00
VAN COURT, CAT HERINE-In Old Natchez-GardenCty-1937-
119p-illus-1st ed (5w0) 5.00
VANCOUVER-Civic Center-Report by Plans Committee, Apr 8, 1915-
Vanc-1915-folio-plts-18p-appendix-wrps (5dd7) 10.00
VANCOUVER-Fireman's Benefit Assn, pub-Souvenir of Vancouver
Fire Dept-Vanc-1911-folio-136p-photos-ads-col wrps (5dd7) 15.00
VANCOUVER-Greeter's Tourist-& Shopping Guide-Vanc-1924-
72p-plts-map-wrps-adv (4a8) 7.50
VANCOUVER(CANADA)-Phone Directory-1954-wrps-686p(5ss4) 4.00
VANCOUVER-Plan for City of-Vanc-(1930)-4to-388p-illus-maps-
plans (5a1) 6.50
VANCOUVER, GEO-Voyage de Decouvertes, les annees 1790 to
1795-Paris-(1801, 2)-Didot Jeune-atlas wi 17 plts-9 maps(8 fldg)-
calf-t.e.g.-6 vols (5L1) 125. (4b6, f) 350.00
--Voyage of Discovery to N Pacific Ocean-Lond-1798-4to-
3 vols-(plus folio atlas in facs)-1st ed-pt mor-t.e.g.-23 plts-
11 maps & chts-atlas ltd to 60c (5aa0, sl fox) 1,750.00
--same-Lond-1801-Stockdale-8vo-calf-mor labls-19 views &
charts-"New ed wi Corr"-6 vols
(5L1, hng weak, calf wn)200.(4h0, 2 Vols rbkd, covs sl wn) 375.00
VAN DEMAN, R-Aunt Sammy's Radio Recipes Revised-Wash-
1931-GPO-142p-wrps (5c9) 2.50
VAN DE MARK, MARTIN V B-Early Recollections of Cloud Co,
Kans-n.p.-n.d.-74p-wrps-o.p.-scarce (5t3) 15.00
VANDEN BERGH, DR LEONARD JOHN-On Trail of the Pigmies-
NY-(1921)-8vo-264p-photos-map (4a6) 12.50
VANENBURG, ARTHUR H-Greatest American Alexander Hamilton-
NY-1921-Putnam's-plts (5t2) 4.50 (5qq8, dj) 7.50
--If Hamilton Were Here Today-NY-1923-Putnam-illus-366p
(5x0) 6.00
--Private Papers of Senator Vandenberg-Bost-1952-illus
(5w5) 6. (5p0) 7.50
VAN DENBURGH, ELIZABETH-My Voyage in US Frigate "Congress"-
NY-(1913)-338p-illus-g.t. (5s1, unopnd) 5.00
VAN DENBURGH, J-Garter Snakes of Western NoAmer-SanFran-
1918-Proc Calif Acad Sci, 4th Ser, Vol 8#6-2 fldg maps-orig wrps-
4to (4p6, sl scuff) 20.00
--Reptiles of Western NoAmer-Vol 1, Lizards, Vol 2, Snakes &
Turtles-SanFran-1922-Calif Acad Sci, Vol 10-plts-orig wrps-
4to-2 vols (4p6, soil) 42.00
VAN DE PUT, ALBERT-Hispano Moresque Ware of 15th Century-Lond-
1904-illus-199p-2 vols (5ww3) 15.00
VANDERBILT, ARTHUR T-Men & Measures in the Law-NY-1949-
Knopf-156p (5p9) 4.00
VANDERBILT, CORNELIUS-Farewell to 5th Avenue-Lond-1935-
320p-illus (5p9, 5t7) 5.00
--The Living Past of America-NY-1955-Crown-234p-4to
(5p0, 5t4) 7.50
--Man of the World-NY-1959-Crown-342p (5p9) 5.00
--Reno-NY-(1929)-Macaulay-2nd prntng (5x0, dj, autg) 5.00
VANDER BILT, GERTRUDE L-Social History of Flatbush, & Manners
& Customs of Dutch Settlers in King's County-NY-1881-1st ed
(5tt5) 10.00
VANDERBILT, HAROLD-Enterprise-NY-1931-4to-cl-illus
(5ss2, sl stn) 22.50
VANDERBILT LAW REVIEW-1947 to 70-Vol 1 thru 23
(5ii7) ea 12.50 (5ii7, rbnd) 280.00
VANDERBILT, WM K-Taking One's Own Ship Around the World-
NY-1929-4to-col illus-orig mor bkd bds-priv prntd-
ltd to 200 spec bnd copies (5ss5, rub, pres) 15.00
VANDERCOOK, JOHN W-Black Majesty-NY-1928-8vo-(209p)-
drawings (4a6) 4.50 (5x2) 3.50
--Dark Islands-NY-1937-illus (5p7) 4.50
--same-Lond-1938-illus (5x2) 3.50
--Fool's Parade-NY-1930-1st ed (5L7) 4.50 (5x2, dj) 6.50
--King Cane-Harper-1939-8vo-cl-illus (5h4) 5.00

VANDERCOOK, JOHN W (continued)
--Tom Tom-NY-1926-1st ed (5x2) 3.50
VAN DER ELSKEN, ED-Bagara:Photographs of Equatorial Africa-
NY-1961-4to-174 plts(17 col)-29p text in pkt (5c6, mint) 12.00
VAN DER ELST, JOS-Last Flowering of Middle Ages-NY-1944-
4to-plts-1st ed (4a1, pres) 25.00
VAN DER HEYDEN, REV JOS-Life & Letters of Father Brabant,
a Flemish Missionery Hero-Louvain-ca1913-wrps-249p, (3)-
illus (5r6) 25.00
VANDERLIP, W B-In Search of a Siberian Klondike-Lond-1906-
FU-cl-8vo-315p (5v7) 27.50
VANDERPOEL, EMILY N-Amer Lace & Lacemakers-NewHav-
1924-14p-110 photos-plts-folio (5v0) 25.00
VANDERPOEL, EMILY NOYES-Chronicles of a Pioneer School from
1796 to 1833-Cambr-1903-lg8vo-465p-65 plts-1st ed (5v0) 27.50
--Color Problems-NY-1902-117 col plts-8vo-137p (4m6) 35.00
VANDERPOL, ALFRED-La Doctrine Scolastique du Droit de Guerre-
Paris-1919-534p (5t7, rbnd) 12.50
VANDERPOOL, EUGENE-Waste of Energy in Production of Water
Gas-Newark-(1879?)-wrps-23p, (1) (5hh7, libr stmp) 7.50
VAN DER POST, LAURENS-Dark Eye in Africa-NY-1955-224p
(5c6, vg) 6.25
--Lost World of Kalahari-NY-1958-279p (5c6, f) 5.00
--Venture to the Interior-NY-1951 (5x2) 2.50
--same-Lond-1952-241p (5c6, vg) 5.00
VAN DERSAL, WM R-The American Land, Its History & its Uses-
NY-1943-Oxf Univ Pr-215p-illus (5p7) 6.00
--Native Woody Plants of the US-Wash-1939-US Dept of Agri #303-
illus-362p-wrps (5dd1) 4.00
VAN DER SLEEN, DR W G N-4 Months' Camping in the Himalayas-
Lond-1929-Philip Allan-123p-illus-cl (5d7) 20.00
--same-Rotterdam-1927-orig Dutch ed (5d7) 12.50
VAN DER SLICE, HOWARD-Van Der Slice & Allied Families-
1931-index-287p (4t0) 25.00
VANDERSLICE, JOHN M-Gettysburg....A History of the Gettysburg
Battlefield Mem Assn-Phila-1897-320p-fldg col map (5w4) 15.00
VAN DER VEER, KATHERINE-Herbs for Urbans-NY-1939-95p-
spiral bnd wrps (5w3) 4.00
VAN DER VEER, LT NORMAN, ED-Blue Jacket's Manual US Navy-
NY-1918-821p plus index-16mo-illus (5s1, libr labl) 5.00
VANDERWALKER, F N-Interior Wall Decoration-Chig-(1924)-
sm8vo-451p, (2)-limp cl (5n7) 5. (5t4) 6.50
VANDERWATER, ROSALIE-Two Tea Parties-NY-(1882)-Cassell,
Peter, Galpin&Co-bds (5c8, rub) 12.50
VAN DER ZEE, JACOB-The British in Iowa-IowaCty-1922-State Hist
Soc-port-340p (5yy8, spot)8.50(5m8) 10. (5a9) 9.50
--Hollanders of Iowa-1912-453p wi index-t.e.g. (5a9) 12.50
VAN DEUSEN, J G-The Black Man in White America-Wash-1944
(5x2, mint, dj) 4.00
VAN DEVENTER, H R-Telephonology-NY-1910-586p-cl-illus
(5b8, sl wn) 10.00
VAN DEWATER, F-We're Still in the Country-NY-(1938)-frontis-
253p-2nd prntng (5ee3, f, dj) 3.50
VAN DE WATER, FREDK F-The Captain Called it Mutiny-NY-
1954-1st ed (5m2) 4.00
--Glory Hunter-Indnpls-1934-Bobbs, Merrill-1st ed-plts
(4i7, fade) 30. (5dd4) 37.50 (4L0, 5ii1) 25.00
--same-Indnpls&NY-1934-illus-Burt reprint (5m9, dj) 8.00
--Lake Champlain & Lake George-Indnpls-1946-1st ed-381p-
illus (5h9, autg) 6.50
--Reluctant Republic-NY-(1949)-John Day-344p-illus-pict cl
(5qq8, dj) 6.00
--Rudyard Kipling's Vermont Feud-NY-(1937)-8vo-cl-119p-illus
(5t0) 5.00
--same-Weston, Vt-(1937)-illus-ltd to 700c-1st ed, autgs (5m1) 8.50
VAN DE WATER, VIRGINIA-Present Day Etiquette-NY-(1924)-
381p, (5w7) 3.00
VAN DE WIELE, ANNIE-The West in My Eyes-NY-1956-illus
(5F0, dj) 4.00
VAN DEUSEN, GLYNDON-The Life of Henry Clay-Bost-1937-
illus-1st ed (5x5, dj) 15.00
--Thurlow Weed, Wizard of the Lobby-Bost-1947-illus
(5t0, f, dj) 4.50 (5s9, dj) 5.00
VAN DEVENTER, C I-Sketches of Methodism in NW Missouri etc
St Jos-1894-photo-156p plus ads-1st ed-scarce (5dd1) 10.00
VAN DINDERN, ADRIAN-County of Mountains of Moon-NY-
1951-149p-52 fullpg illus(23 col)-ltd to 600c (5c6, f) 10.75
VAN DINE, S S-The Green Murder Case-NY-1928-Scribner's-
black cl-8vo-1st ed (4g1, sl fade, cor bump) 6.00
VANDIVEER, C A-Fur Trade & Early Western Exploration-Cleveland-
1929-Clark-316p-6 plts-g.t.-1st ed (4i7) 25.00

VAN DOREN,CARL-The Amer Novel-NY-1921-295p-12mo-
cl-1st ed   (5t0)   4.00
--same-NY-1940-Macmillan-406p-rev&enlrgd ed (5p9)   6.00
--Benjamin Franklin-NY-1938-845p-illus-1st trade ed
              (5t0,5h9) 4.50   (5t7) 7.50   (5w5)   6.50
--same-NY-1938-3 vols-Viking Pr-1st ed-ltd to 625 sets,autg,
boxed   (5ss9,5x5)   50.00
--Benj Franklin's Autobiographical Writings-NY-1945-810p
              (5p7) 5.   (5t2) 3.50   (5t7)
--The Great Rehearsal-NY-1948-1st ed-illus-336p
              (5L3,mint,dj) 3.   (5L7) 5.   (5h9)   3.50
--same-NY-1948-cl-1st ed,ltd to 380c,nbrd,autg,box (5h5,vf) 25.00
--James B Cabell-NY-1925   (5mm2)   8.50
--Jane Mecom-NY-1950-255p   (5h9,5m2,dj,5p9)   5.00
--The Literary Works of Abraham Lincoln-NY-1942-302p
                                           (5j6,dj)   5.00
--Many minds-NY-1924-Knopf-1st ed   (5m2)   6.50
--Mutiny in January-NY-1943-288p-illus-fldg map-1st ed
                                          (5mm8,dj)   5.00
--Secret History of the Amer Revolution-NY-(1941)-Viking Pr-
534p   (5p9)   5.00
--Swift-Lond-1931-267p-ports   (5a1)   5.00
--Three Worlds-1936-Harper   (5F0,dj) 3.50 (5F1,vf,dj) 5.00
VAN DOREN,MARK,ed-An anthology of world poetry-NY-1928-
Literary Guild-1318p   (5v6,lt fade)   1.50
--An Autobiography of Amer-NY-1929-752p   (5dd5)   6.75
--Country Year-NY-Wm Sloan-1946-1st prntg
                                         (5i1,dj,autg) 6.00
--Edw Arlington Robinson-NY-1927-Literary Guild (5hh3) 4.00
--The Lost Days of Lincoln-NY-1959-152p   (5j6)   5.00
--The Mayfield Deer-(1941)-Henry Holt   (5F1,f,dj)   7.50
--Noble Voice-NY-1946-12mo-cl-328p   (5t0)   4.50
--Travels of Wm Bartram-NY-1940-Facsimile Library-12mo-cl-
414p   (5t0)   5.00
--The Travels of Wm Bartram-NY-(1928)   (5q8)   6.50
--Windless Cabins-(NY)-(1940)-Holt (5F1,vf,dj) 6. (5b2,dj) 5.00
VAN DRESSER,JASMINE STONE-How to Find Happyland-NY&Lond-
1907-Putnam's-8vo-frontis-123p-10 col plts   (5p1)   12.50
VAN DRUTEN,JOHN-And Then You Wish-1937-Little,Brown
                                        (5F1,vf,tn dj) 5.50
VAN DUKE,JOHN C-New New York-NY-1909-425p-illus
                                             (5xx7)   10.00
VAN DYK,HARRY STOE-Theatrical portraits,with other poems-
Lond-1822-for JnMiller,etc-hf calf-1st ed (5i8,wn)   15.00
VAN DYKE,HENRY-The Builders & Other Poems-NY-1897-
orig dec cl-1st ed   (5m1)   7.50
--Broken Soldier & Maid of France-Harper-1919-70p-1st ed (5e8) 2.50
--The Christ Child in Art-NY-1898-8vo-illus-cl-236p (5t0) 4.50
--Companionable Books-Scribner-1922-391p (5e8,fade)   2.75
--same-NY-1924-391p-cl   (5h7)   4.00
--A Creelful of Fishing Stories-NY-1932-419p-illus (5t7) 6.50
--Fighting for Peace-NY-1917-247p   (5t7)   4.00
--Fisherman's Luck etc-NY-1899-247p-illus
              (5xx7,ALS laid in) 12.50   (5t0)   4.00
--The First Christmas Tree-NY-1897-dec cl-g.o.t.-4 plts by Pyle-
1st ed   (5ee3,pres) 7.50   (5r9)   7.50
--Flirtation Camp-NY-1881-1st ed-299p   (5i3,f)   12.50
--Little Rivers-NY-1900-12mo-cl-illus-291p   (5t0)   3.75
--The Man behind the Book-NY-1929-357p (5m2) 5. (5j4)   4.50
--The story of the other wise man-NY-1896-Harper-illus-1st ed
                                              (5m2)   6.50
--Works-NY-1920-17 vols-frontis-8vo-hf cl-papr labls-504c on
Stratford papr-autg ed   (4c2,unopened)   75.00
VAN DYKE,JOHN C-Amer Painting & Its Tradition-NY-1919-
Scribner's-24 illus-270p-sm8vo   (4a0)   27.50
--The Desert-NY-1907-233p-frontis-2nd ed   (4L0)   5.00
--same-NY-1925-12mo-cl-photos   (5h5)   5.00
--The Grand Canyon of the Colorado-NY-1920-218p-photos-
1st ed   (5s4,rprd,soil) 5.   (4L0)   6.50
--same-NY-1924-218p-illus-Scribner's (5g0) 5. (5t7)   7.50
--The New New York-NY-1909-illus-425p   (5q0)   12.50
--The Open Spaces-NY-1922-frontis-272p-1st ed (4L0)   7.50
VAN DYKE,LOUISE-Tasty Tarts & Savory Sauces-n.p.-1915-
(23p)-hand painted cov   (5c0,soil)   3.00
VAN DYKE,MONA-Cooking With Wine Recipes-Lodi,CA-(1935)-
32p-wrps   (5w1)   2.50
VAN DYKE,T S-City & Co of San Diego,Illus,etc-SanDiego-
1888-Leberthron & Taylor-8vo-lin cov   (4t1,5hh4)   27.50
--Flirtation Camp-NY-1881-299p   (5t7) 6. (5m1)   6.50
--Southern Calif,Its Valleys,Hills & Streams-NY-1886-8vo-1st ed
        (5hh3) 5.   (4g6,ex-libr) 7.50   (4L0)   6.50
--The Still Hunter-NY-1921-illus-390p   (5t7)   12.50

VAN DYNE,EDITH-Aunt Jane's Nieces-Chig-(1906,reprinted
1912)-Reilly&Britton Co-illus-dec cl   (5c8)   5.00
VANE,SIR HENRY-Life & Death of..-(Lond)-1662-sm4to-hf mor-
2 ports inserted-1st ed-rare-(Geo Sikes) (5n2,sl rprd) 275.00
--Tryal of...wi what he intended-(Lond)-1662-1st ed-rare
                                         (5n2,rprd)   325.00
VAN EMDEN,F W-Sure Enough,How Come?-SanAntonio-1938-
122p-rev ed   (5xx5)   4.50
VAN EVERY,DALE-Chas Lindbergh,His Life-NY-1927-8vo-cl-
photos-1st ed   (5p5)   7.50
--Men of the Western Waters-Bost-1956-244p-illus
              (5L3,mint,dj) 3.   (5L7)   6.00
VAN EVERY,E-Joe Louis,Man & Super fighter-NY-1936-1st ed
                                              (5x2)   12.50
VAN EVERY,EDW-Sins of New York-NY-1930-illus-4to (5yy6) 6.00
--same-NY-1930-wdcuts-299p-3rd prntg   (5dd1)   12.50
--Sins of Amer-NY-Stokes-1931-orig cardinal cl-illus-297p-4to
                                             (5dd1)   15.00
VAN EVRIE,J H-Negroes & Negro "Slavery"-Balt-(1853)-32p-
wrps-scarce   (5h6)   20.00
--White Supremacy & Negro Subordination-NY-1868-illus-339p &
60p   (4m2)   30.00
--same-NY-1870-col illus   (5x2)   45.00
VAN FLEET,J A-Old & New Mackinac-GrandRapids-1880-illus-
map-173p-2p addenda   (4d9)   8.00
VAN GOGH-Letters to an Artist-NY-1936-illus-1st Engl ed
                                          (5ii3,dj)   12.50
VAN GUNDY,JOHN C-Remin of Frontier Life on Upper Neosho
in 1855 & 56-n.p.-(1925)-illus-wrps-41p-1st ed-scarce (4L2) 17.50
VAN HALEN,J-Narr of Don Juan Van Halen's Imprisonment in
Dungeons of Inquisition at Madrid,etc-Lond-1827-hf lea-port-
fldg view-8vo-2 vols   (5v7,fox,sl wtrstn)   42.50
VAN HEUBEL,J-El Dorado-NY-c1844-Winchester-166p-fldg map-
qtr roan-scarce   (5h9,rub)   28.50
VAN HISE,CHAS R-Conservation of Natural Resources-NY-
1912-12mo-cl-413p   (5t0)   4.50
VAN HISE,CHAS R-Prelim report on Marquette Iron Bearing Dist
of Mich-Wash-1895-sm4to-illus-maps (5mm7,wrp chip)   8.50
--Atlas to Accompany Monogr 28 on Marquette Iron Bearing Dist
of Mich-Wash-1896-lg folio-orig cl-36 maps with col geolog
sections(1 fld)   (5m3,f)   60.00
VAN HOOSEAR,D H-Desc of John Fillow,a Huguenot Refugee-
1888-274p   (4t2)   15.00
--Desc of Rinear Van Hoosear-1902-96p   (4t2)   15.00
VAN HORN,H T-Central Pacific Rwy Route-KansasCty,Mo-1858-
Western Journal of Commerce Print-16p-stapld prntd wrps-
wrpr in facs   (5t1,vf,fldg box)   650.00
VAN HORNE,THOS B-Life of Maj Gen Geo H Thomas-NY-1882-
Scribner's-502p-ads-port-maps   (5mm8,rub)   9.00
VAN HULLE,H J-Culture De La Vigne Sous-Gand-1884-51p-
wrps-1 plt-4th ed,rev   (5w1,chip)   8.50
VAN LAER,A F J-Corres of Maria Van Rensselaer,1669 to 1689-
Albany-1935-cl-206p   (4i2) 7.50   (5t7)   4.50
--same-Albany-1932   (5q8,ex-libr) 10.00
VAN LAER,ARNOLD J H,transl-Lutheran Church in NY,1649 to
177?-NY-1946-4to-frontis-orig wrps   (5jj3)   10.00
VAN LAER,J J F-Minutes of Court of Ft Orange & Beverwyck
1652 to 56 & 1657 to 60-Albany-1920,23-2 vols-index
                                             (5ff2)   10.00
VAN LAREN,A J-Cactus-LosAng-Abbey San Encino Pr-cl-4to-
col frontis-133 col plts   (5z9)   35.00
--Succulents other than Cacti-LosAng-1934-Abbey San Encino Pr-
v lg4to-bds-col illus tip in -ltd to 1000copies (5s7) 15.00
VAN LAUN,HENRI-History of French Literature-NY-1877-3 vols
                                              (5m1)   17.50
VAN LOON,HENDRICK-America-NY-1933 et seq-463p-illus
                                              (5h9)   3.50
--Ancient Man-NY-1920-Boni&Liveright-4to-pic cl-plts-maps-
1st ed-121p   (5nn2)   10.00
--The Arts-NY-1937-1st ed   (5L7) 5.   (5k0)   6.50
--Elephant Up a Tree-NY-1933-Simon&Schuster-lg8vo-206p-
illus-col plts-1st ed   (5aa0,vf,dj)   15.00
--Life & Times of Pieter Stuyvesant-NY-(1928)-1st ed-illus
                                             (5q8,dj)   6.00
--Life & Times of Simon Bolivar-NY-1943-Dodd,Mead-1st ed-
sq8vo-cl-plts-146p   (5s0)   5.00
--My School Books-1939-8vo-24p-DuPont advertising bk for
World's Fair-illus   (5p1) 4. (5v2,mint) 5.00
--Observations on Mystery of Print & Works of Johann Gutenberg-
NY-1937-illus-12mo-1st ed   (4a1,f,dj)   5.00
--R V R Life & Times of Rembrandt van Rijn-Tudor-1936-illus-
570p-8vo-dec e.p.   (5ww3) 10.   (5t7)   7.50

VAN LOON,HENDRICK   (continued)
--Re An Elephant up a Tree-NY-1933-Simon&Schuster-lg8vo-
  dec cl-g.t.-206p-col plts-1st ed   (5u6,vf,sl wn dj)   12.50
--Ships & How They Sailed the Seven Seas-NY-1934-311p (5s1)   4.50
--same-1935-6th prntng   (5s1,5j5)   7.50
--Sons of Sinbad-NY-1940-429p-photos-dec cov-1st ed (5s1)   9.00
--Songs We Sing-NY-1936-Simon&Schuster-1st ed-obl 8vo-dec bds-
  64p-col plts-music   (5yy9,vf)   12.50
--The Story of Mankind-NY-1921-illus-479p-1st ed
                                    (5ee3,f,wn dj)   5.00
--The Story of the Pacific-NY-(1940)-Harcourt,Brace-387p-illus
                                    (5p7)   5.00
--Story of Wilber the Hat-NY-1925-Liveright-4to-pict bds-cl bk-
  110p-col plts   (4a8)   3.00
--Van Loon's Geography-NY-1932-lg8vo-525p-illus   (4a6)   3.00
VAN LOOT,CORNELIUS O-The Collector's Whatnot-1923-
  147p-line drwngs   (5w7)   5.00
VAN MAANEN-HELMER-What to do About Wines-NY-1934-
  maps-184p   (5t2) 4.   (5w1)   4.50
VAN MAANEN-HELMER,ELIZ-The Mandates System In Relation
  To Africa & Pacific Islands-Lond-1929-PSKing&Son-331p (5x9) 7.00
VAN METRE,T W-Trains, Tracks & Travel-NY-1939   (5x5)   7.50
VAN MUYDEN EVERT-Catalogue of Etched Work of-NY-1894
  sm4to-port-ltd to 230c-A Curtis,ed   (5ii3,rub)   25.00
VAN NADA,L BELLE-Poems-Indnpls-1881-150p   (5t7,pres)   4.00
VAN NEST,A R-Memoir of Rev Geo W Bethune-NY-1867-446p-cl
                                    (5h1)   7.50
VAN NOSTRAND,JEANNE-Calif Pictorial-Univ of Calif-1948-
  4to-cl-(Chron of Calif) (5F5,vf,dj,autgs) 22.50 (5F5,f,dj)   20.00
VAN NOY INTERSTATE CO-Handcolored Views of Beautiful
  Mt Shasta,Calif-SanFran-1914-wrps-sm folio-12 lvs (5kk6)   7.50
VAN OOSTKERKE,PIETER-The Picture Frame-Lond-1947-12 col illus-
  4to   (4j3,pres)   30.00
VAN OSDEL,A L-Historic Landmarks-n.p.-n.d.(1915)-hf lea-
  400p-illus   (4L0,rbnd) 10.   (5dd1)   15.00
VAN PATTEN,NATHAN-The Medical Literature of Mexico &
  Central Amer-Chig-1931-wrps   (5d6,autg)   15.00
VAN PELT,GARRETT,JR-Old Architecture of Southern Mexico-
  Cleve-1926-JHJansen-125p-folio-1st ed   (5x5)   20.00
VAN PELT,JOHN-Selected Monuments of French Gothic
  Architecture-NY-1924-100 plts-4to-214p-Pencil Point Pr-
  Libr of Arch Doc Vol 3   (5t2)   7.50
VAN PUFFELEN,JOHN-Watch Repair Course-1946 to 50-
  Home Study Course,Units 100 to 600-600 illus-200p-mimeo-
  binder   (5bb0)   10.00
VAN RAUMER,FREDK-Amer & the Amer People-NY-1846-8vo-
  512p-cl-scarce   (5m8,rub)   15.00
VAN RENSSELAER,EDW,ed-Encyclopedia of Bird Pictures-NY-
  c1966-sm4to   (5w4)   7.50
VAN RENSSELAER,MRS JOHN KING-The Goede Vrouw of Mana
  Ha Ta,At Home & in Society, 1609 to 1760-NY-1898-418p-
  1st ed   (5h9)   10.00
--New Yorkers of the 19th Century-NY-c1897-F Tennyson Neely-
  folio-bds-56p   (4t1)   35.00
--Prophetical,Educational & Playing Cards-Phila-(1912)-392p-
  illus-1st ed   (5xx7)   15.00
VAN RENSSELAER,M-Annals of Van Rensselaer in US-1888-
  241p   (4t2)   17.50
VAN RENSSELAER,MARTHA-A Manual of Home Making-NY-
  1919-661p,(6)-illus-Rural Manual Ser   (5w7)   6.50
VAN RENSSELAER,MRS SCHUYLER-Many Children-Bost-1921-
  Atlantic Monthly Pr-12mo-cl-84p-g.t.-illus-Merrymount Pr
                                    (5j5)   5.00
VAN RENSSELAER,SOLOMON-Narr of the Affair of Queenstown in
  War of 1812-NY-1836-fldg map-95p plus ads-1st ed (5dd1)   15.00
VAN RIET LOWE,C,ed-The Monuments of SoAfrica-Pretoria-1941-
  Govt Prntr-maps(1 fldg)-photos-174p   (4t5)   12.50
VAN SALVERDA,J G W FIJNJE-Aerial Navigation-NY-1894-
  Appleton-Waring,transl   (5p0)   17.50
VAN SANTVOORD,C W,comp-History of County of Schenectady-
  Schentdy-1887-Barhyte&Birch-16mo-cl-54p   (4t1)   15.00
VAN SCHAACK,HENRY C-Life of Peter Van Schaack-NY-1842-
  Appleton-490p-cl-port-1st ed (5tt8) 25. (5ss5,bkstrp tn)   15.00
VAN SCHAICK,JOHN,JR-Characters in Tales of a Wayside Inn-
  Bost-(1939)-Universalist Pub House-illus-1st ed (5m2,autg)   6.50
VAN SICKLE,H-Utah Desperadoes-13p-photostat of orig in Bancroft
  Library   (5ii1)   12.50
VAN SIDEREN,ADRIAN-Blake the Mystic Genius-Syracuse-1949-
  4to-cl-12 col plts   (5d5,dj)   10.00
--Foundation Stones-NY-1952-4to-hf buck-priv prntd-ltd to 700c
                                    (5r7)   17.50
VANSITTART,R G V BARON-Lessons of My Life-1943 (5L7)   3.50

VAN SLYCK,J D-Representatives of New Engl Manufacturers-
  Bost-1879-1st vol(complete in itself)-ports-views-lg4to-
  orig mor-555p   (5ss5)   15.00
VAN STANTVOORD,C-Memoir of Eliphalet Nott-1876-390p
                                    (4m2,sl crack)   20.00
VAN STEEN,M-Pauline Johnson Her Life & Work-Tor-1905-279p
                                    (4b9,mint,dj)   5.00
VAN TASSEL,C S-Book of Ohio & Its "Centennial"-Bowling Green &
  Toledo-n.d.-3 vols-half lea-   photos   (5ff7)   40.00
--Grounds of Maumee Valley-BowlGr&Tol-n.d.(ca 1904?)-
  Rait-port vol-71p-prntd 1 side only   (5h1)   10.00
VAN TRAMP,JOHN C-Prairie & Rocky Mntn Adventures-Columbus-
  1858-640p-hf lea-1st ed-scarce (5ff7,wn) 75.   (4n4)   60.00
--same-StLouis-1859-plts-640p   (5L3)   17.50
--same-Columbus-1866-Gilmore&Segner-stmpd lea-649p
                 (5tt0) 10. (5qq8) 15. (5t4)   18.50
--same-Columbus-1868-775p-lea cov   (5s4,cov wn)   17.50
--same-Columbus-n.d.-670p   (5s4,hng rprd)   20.00
VAN TYNE,CLAUDE H-The Amer Revolution-NY-c1905-369p-
  frontis-maps-(The Amer Nation,Hist Series)
                 (5r7) 7.50 (5w5) 3. (5t2)   6.50
--Causes of War of Independence-NY-c1922-499p-1st vol-
  (Hist of Founding of Amer Repub) (5h9) 8. (5r7)   7.50
--England & Amer,rivals in the Amer Revolution-1927 (5L7)   5.00
--Guide to the Archives of the Gov of the US in Wash-Wash-1904-
  3/4 lea   (5r7,ex-libr,rprd)   20.00
--The War of Independence,Amer Phase-Bost-1929-Houghton,Miff-
  2nd vol-518p   (5p9)   6.00
VAN URK,J BLAN-Story of Amer Foxhunting From Challenge to Full
  Cry-NY-(1940,1)-Derrydale Pr-ltd to 950c-2 vols (5tt6,f)   100.00
VANUXEM,L ARDNER-Geology of NY-1842-306p   (5zz0)   12.50
VAN VALKENBURGH,R F-Dine Bikeyar-WindowRock,Ariz-1941-
  US Dept of Int,Off of Indian Affairs,Navajo Serv-180p plus
  bibl-maps-wrps-scarce   (5a9,wtrstnd)   25.00
VAN VALKENBURG,RICHARD-A Short History of the Navajo
  People-Window Rock-1938-4to-56p-wrps-mimeo-scarce
                                    (5g5,autg)   12.00
VAN VECHTEN,CARL-Bibliography of Writings,by Scott Cunningham-
  Phila-1924-8vo-port-ltd to 300c,nbrd   (5r9)   7.50
--Excavations,a Book of Advocacies-NY-1926-12mo-cl-285p-
  1st ed   (5m8)   6.50
--Firecrackers-NY-1925-Knopf-1st ed (5p0,dj)   5.00
--Music After the Great War-NY-1915-12mo-cl-papr labl-
  1st ed of auth's 1st book   (5gg6,fade)   25.00
--Nigger Heaven-NY-1926   (5x2)   5.00
--same-1926-AlfredAKnopf-orig cl-1st ed-ltd to 195c,autg
                 (5tt2,hgn crack) 15. (4g1,sl fade)   22.50
--Peter Whiffle,His Life & Works-NY-1922-Knopf-1st ed
                 (5F1,fade dj) 5. (5r9)   8.50
--Sacred & Profane Memories-NY-1932-12mo-cl-230p-illus-
  1st ed-ltd to 2000c   (5m8,wn dj)   15.00
--Selected Writings of Gertrude Stein-NY-(1946)-RandomHse-
  1st ed   (5ss9,vg,tn dj)   10.00
--Spider Boy,a scenario for a moving picture-NY-1928-297p-
  1st ed-ltd to 210c,autg   (5t7)   10.00
--same-1928-Knopf   (5F1,f,dj)   13.50
--The Tattooed Countess-NY-1924-8vo-dec bds&cl-1st ed-
  ltd to 150c,autg   (5d9,wn box)   20.00
VAN VOGT,A E-Out of the Unknown-LosAng-(1948)-Fantasy Pub Co-
  1st ed   (5ss9,pres)   15.00
VAN VOORHIS,JN S-Old & New Monongahela-Pittsb-1893-486p-
  cl-scarce   (5h7,spot) 25. (5t9)   20.00
VAN WELL,MARY STANISLAUS-Educational Aspects of Missions
  in the SW-Milwkee-1942-154p plus index-wrps-(for PHD degree)-
  v scarce   (4L0)   25.00
VAN WERT,CO,OHIO-Complete Directory of-Portl-1909,10-
  324p-fldg map-bds   (5h2)   10.00
VAN WINKLE,EDW-Manhattan,1624 to 1639-NY-1916-4to-fldg map
                                    (5jj3)   10.00
VAN WINKLE,EDW D-Hist of Municipalities of Hudson Co,1630 to
  1923-1924-3 vols   (5t9)   20.00
VAN WYCK,CAROLYN,ed-Photoplay's Cook Book-Chig-1929-
  pict wrps-64p   (4g9)   5.00
VAN WYCK,FREDK-Ancestry of Gov Dongan-Bost-1935-8vo-
  orig bds-cl bk-illus-ltd to 150c (4t2) 8.50 (5m6)   10.00
--Recollections of an Old New Yorker-NY-(1932)-4to-421p-illus
                 (5p5) 15. (5r7) 8.50 (5t7)   10.50
--Select Patents of NY Towns-1938-47p,180p   (4t2)   15.00
VAN WYCK,K L-Pettit Families in America-1936-80p-mimeo
                                    (5t9)   17.50
VAN WYCK,WM-On the Terrasse-Paris-1930-Titus-4to-bds-
  illus-ltd to 100c   (5ee9)   35.00

VAN WYCK,WM (continued)
--Robinson Jeffers-LosAng-1938-WardRitchie Pr-1st ed-ltd to 250c
(5ss9) 35.00
--Some Gentlemen of the Renaissance-Paris-1928-Titus-4to-
bds-prntd wrps-4 ports-ltd to 250c
(5ee9) 30.00
VAN ZILE,EDW S-Kings in adversity-NY-1897-Neely-sm8vo-
1st ed (5m2) 8.50
VAQUERO-Adventures in search of a living in Spanish America-
Lond-1911-JnBale,Sons&Danielsson-304p (5v6) 4.00
VARADY,RALPH-Many Lagoons-NY-(1958)-illus-192p-cl&bds
(5t7,dj) 5.00
VARE,WM S-My 40 Years in Politics-Phila-1933-RSwain Co-225p
(5p7) 3.75
VARENIUS,BERNHARD-Descriptio Regni Japonis et Siam,etc-
Cambr-1673-J Hayes for S Simpson-8vo-calf (4e1,f) 200.00
VARGA,MARGIT-Waldo Peirce-NY-1941-Hyperion Pr/Harper&Bros-
76p-illus-10 x 13½" (4a0) 20.00
VARIETY,POETRY & PROSE-by Bard of Niagara-Montr-1872-port-
1st ed (5w8) 7.50
VARILLE,MATHIEU-La Cuisine Lyonnaise-Lyon-1928-sq8vo-136p,(1)-
illus-ltd to 900c (5c5) 10.50
VARLEY,TELFORD-Winchester-Lond-1910-200p,(3)-24 col plts
(5w7) 5.00
VARLO,C-New System of Husbandry-Phila-1785-2 vols-calf-
fldg chart (5L7,ex-libr,wn) 25. (5m3,f) 75.00
VARNER,JOHN GRIER-The Florida of the Inca-Austin-1951-
Univ of Texas Pr-655p-illus (5ee3,f,dj) 12.50
VARNUM,JAS M-The Case,Trevett against Weeden....Paper Bills-
Prov-1787-John Carter-wrps-60p-4to-1st ed
(5L1,ex-libr,buck) 45. (5m3,rbnd cl,libr stmp,4c4,rbkd) 150.00
VARNUM PAPERS,JOS B,THE-NY-1928-Amer Art Assoc-8vo-illus-
wrps (5t4) 7.50
VASARI,GIORGIO-Lives of the Most Eminent Painters,Sculptors
& Architects-Lond-1878-cl-5 vols (5d2) 40.00
--same-NY-1896-4 vols-Lives of Seventy-ltd ed-r8vo (5ii3) 40.00
--same-NY-1917-Scribners-4 vols-8vo-cl (5t8) 15.00
VASEY,FITZGERALD,B-British Bats-Lond-1949-bds-4 col plts-
8vo-61p (4p5) 12.00
VASEY,G-Monograph on Genus Bos-Lond-1857-orig cl-8vo-
72 engr-v scarce (4p5) 37.00
VASON,GEO-Authentic Narr of 4 Yrs Residence at Tongataboo-
Lond-1810-map-frontis-8vo-calf-234p-errata 1f-1st ed-rare
(4e1,rbkd) 200.00
VASSA,G-Interesting Narr of Life of Olauda Equiano or Gustavus
Vassa,the African-Halifax-1812-3/4 lea (5x2,rbnd) 200.00
VASSAR-Life at Vassar,75 Years in Pictures-Poughkeepsie-(1940)-
4to-cl-125p-photos-1st ed (5t0) 5.00
VASSAR COLLEGE GROUP-At Sign of Rolling Pin-Middletn-1916-
12mo-225,(2)p-Brown #2266 (5c4) 5.00
VASSAR MISCELLANY MONTHLY-A Book of Vassar Verse-
(Poughkeepsie)-1916-8vo-bds-cl bk-g.t.-1st state (wi misprint
on pg 130) (5b2) 15.00
VASSILI,PAUL-Confessions of the Czarina-NY-c1918 (5x7) 5.00
VASSOS,JOHN-Contempo -tx by Ruth Vassos-NY-1929-thn4to-
1st ed (5r9) 8.50
VASSOS,RUTH-Ultimo-NY-1930-4to-dec cl-1st ed-illus-scarce
(5p5,autg) 12.50
VATTEL,E DE-Law of Nations-Phila-1844-6th Amer ed from a New
ed by Jos Chitty (5ff4) 9.50
VAUCAIRE,MICHEL-Histoire de la Peche a la Baleine-Paris-1941-
8vo-262p-illus-wrps (5ss2) 12.50
VAUGHAN,AGNES CARR-Within the Walls-NY-1935-Macmillan
(5x0,dj,autg) 4.00
VAUGHAN,BEATRICE-Yankee Hill Country Cooking-Brattleboro-
1963-202p-illus (5g9) 3.00
VAUGHAN,C J-Osage Co Directory & Statistical Compendium-
Linn,Mo-1915-fldg map-197p-1st ed (4t3) 30.00
VAUGHAN,C W-Illustrated Laconian-1899-248p (5t9) 10.00
VAUGHAN,H W-Types & Market Classes of Live Stock-Columbus-191
1915-448p-illus-index-1st ed (5dd6,rub) 7.50
--same-Columbus-1917-442p plus index-photos (4 L0,sl wn) 4.00
VAUGHAN,JOHN-Wild Flowers of Selborne & Other Papers-Lond-
1906-247p (5w3,hng weak) 6.50
VAUGHAN,ROBT A-Hours with the Mystics-Lond-1895-2 vols in 1-
cl (5t2,sp stn) 4.00
VAUGHAN,SAM'L-Appeal to the Public on Behalf of-Lond-1770-
(bnd wi) Refutation of False Aspersion-Lond,1769-8vo-cl
(5a3,rbnd,libr stmp) 45.00
VAUGHAN,THOS W-International Aspects of Oceanography-Wash-
1937-fldg maps (5tt5) 10.00
VAUGHAN,W-Life & Work of Sir Wm Van Horne-NY-1920-388p-
map-illus (4b9,hng weak) 12.00

VAUGHAN'S VEGETABLE COOK BOOK-NY-1898-Vaughan's
Seed Store-64p-cl-scarce (5g9,5c9) 6.00
VAUGHN,FLOYD L-The US Patent System-Norman-1956-355p
(5y2) 7.50
VAUGHN,HAMPTON-Ebba Borjeson-(Wilmington,Del,1894)-
1st ed (5mm2,pres) 12.50
VAUGHN,J W-With Crook at the Rosebud-Harrisburg,Pa-
1955-240p-index-illus (4L0,dj) 8.50
VAUGHN,ROBT-Then & Now-Minnpls-1900-461p-photos-
1st ed (5t4) 35. (5ii7,vf,4L0) 40.00
VAUGHT,ELSA,ed-The Diary of an Unknown Soldier,Sept 5 to
Dec 7,1862-VanBuren,Ark-1959-45p-2 maps-wrps-1st ed
(5h0,5t3) 5.00
VAUX,CALVERT-Villas & Cottages-NY-1857-318p(2)-plts
(5w7,wn,stnd) 18.50
VAY DE VAYA-The Inner Life of the US-Lond-1908 (5q8,wn) 5.00
VAYER,LAJOS-Master Drawings from Collection of the Budapest
Museum of Fine Arts,14th to 18th Centuries-NY-(1956)-Abrams-
folio-cl-109 color repro (5b0,dj) 40.00
VEALE,E-Brownies & Other Stories-Chig-n.d.(ca 1916)-illus by
Palmer Cox-MADonohue-320p-12mo-pict cl (5p1,rub,hng crack)5.00
VEATCH,A C-Quito to Bogota-NY-(1917)-Doran-338p-illus-cl
(5d6) 10.00
VEBLEN,THORSTEIN-The Laxdaela Saga-NY-1925-BW Huebsch-
8vo-302p-blind stmpd cl (5p1) 12.50
--Theory of the Leisure Class-NY-1899-400p-1st prntg (4b4) 75.00
VECELLIO,CESARE-Pizzi Antichi-Milano-1886-obl 8vo-116 plts-
ltd to 492c-reprint ed (5n7) 17.50
VEDDER,ELIHU-Digressions of-Bost-1910-Houghton,Miff-2 vols-
sm4to-nbrd (4a0,autg) 65.00
--same-Bost-1910-lg sq8vo-dec cl-illus-26p,521p-1st ed
(5t0) 10. (5m2) 8.50
--A Monk's Thoughts-Rome-1875-sm4to-vel-g.-by C L W-
1st book illus by Vedder (5gg6,vf,orig imit lea dj) 35.00
VEDDER,J V-History of Greene County 1651 to 1800-1866-207p-
wrps-reprint (5ff2) 12.00
VEECH,JAS-Monongahela of Old-Pittsb-1858 to 92-frontis-259p
(5yy0) 17.50
--same-Pittsb-(1910)-port-259p (5t4) 25.00
VEENSTRA,J-Een Blanke Vrouw Onder De Kannibalen-GrandRapids,
Mich-1928-illus-Swedish (5x2) 7.50
VEER,GERRIT DE-3 Voyages of Wm Barents to Arctic Regions-
buck-1876-illus-ed by Beke&Beynen (5L7,rbnd) 25.00
VEGA,GARCILASO DE LA-The Florida of the Inca-Austin-1951-
655p (5n4) 5.50
--Royal Commentaries of the Incas & General History of Peru-
Austin-1966-2 vols (5n4) 12.50
VEGETABLE GROWERS ASSOC OF AMER-Milwkee-1930-198p-
wrps (5s7) 1.50
VEHLING,JOS D-America's Table-Chig-1950-(5),882p,(13)
(5c5) 12.50
VELARDE,PABLITA-Old Father the Story Teller-Flagstaff-1960-
4to-bds-60p-col plts-1st ed (5g6,mint) 10.00
VELASCO IN TEXAS HISTORY-Angleton,Tex-1936-19p-stiff wrps
(5n4) 15.00
VELEZ,ILDFFONSO V-Historia de Coahuila-Coahuila-1870-192p-
stiff wrps (5n4) 5.00
VELTER,J M-Arctic S O S-NY-1935-278p (4b9) 8.00
VENABLE,VERNON-Human Nature,the Mexican View-NY-1945
(5x7) 4.00
VENABLE,W H-The School Stage-Cinn&NY-(c1873)-VanAntwerp
Bragg-12mo-234p-30 wdcuts-marbled edges (5p1,cov sl wtrstn) 20.00
VENABLE,WM HENRY-A dream of empire-NY-1901-Dodd,Mead-
1st ed (5m2,lacks fly) 5.00
VENABLES,REV R LISTER-Domestic scenes in Russia-Lond-1839-
Murray-8vo-orig bds-1st ed (5i8,sp wn) 25.00
VENABLES,ROBT-The Experienced Angler-Lond-1825-
Septinus Prowett&T Gosden-16mo-calf-g.e.-illus mounted
(4c2) 35.00
VENEGAS,MIGUEL-Histoire Naturelle Et Civile De La Californie-
Paris-1768-16mo-calf-3 vols-1st French ed (5x5,f) 150.00
--A Natural & Civil History of Calif-Lond-1759-Rivington&Fletcher-
2 vols-mor-fldg map-4 plts-8vo-1st Engl ed
(5a3,lacks 2 plts,f bndg) 325. (5n2,f,box) 450. (5x5,box) 500.00
--Noticia de la California,y de su conquista temporal y espiritual,
hasta el tiempo presente-Madrid-1757-3 vols-sm4to-orig vel-
4 fldg maps-1st ed (5L1,sl tear in 1 map) 600.00
VENEZUELA,LAWS,STATUTES,ETC-Recopilation de leyes y decretos
de Venezuela-1830 to 1942-Vol 1 thru 65-bnd in 69 vols
(5ii7,ex-libr) 750.00
VENNER,TO-A Briefe & Accurate Treatise of Tobacco-SanFran-1931-
mor&bds-Book Club of Calif-ltd to 200c-4to-Windsor Pr
(5b0,box) 27.50

VENNER,TO (continued)
--Treatise of Tobacco-SanFran-1931-ltd to 200c,boxed-Book
Club of Calif (5x5,rub) 30.00
VENNING,MARY A-Geographical Present, being Descr of Principal
Countries of the World etc-Lond-1820Harvey&Darton-tall 12mo-
hf roan-144p-60 handcol plts-3rd ed (4d1) 65. (5c8,rbkd) 85.00
VENNOR'S WEATHER BULLETIN-Vol 1,complete in 11 numbers-
plus Vol 2,#1 thru 4-Montr-Jan 1882 to Apr 1883-4to-stapled
(5r7,als laid in) 40.00
VENTRE,JULES-Instructions pratique Pour La Vinification-
Montpellier-1913-102p -wrps (5w1) 7.50
--Traite De Vinification pratique & rationelle-Montpellier-(1947)-
2 vols-illus-(not 1st ed) (5w1) 15.00
VENTURA,L D-Misfits & Remnants-Bost-1886-Ticknor-12mo-cl
(5b2,autg) 8.50
VENTURE,THE-An Annual of Art & Literature-Lond-1903-dec bds-
4to-15 plts-249p (5nn2) 15.00
--same-Vol 2-Lond(1905,publ Nov 1904)-4to-pic cl-(contains
Jas Joyce)-also Vol 1 (5d8) 85.00
VENTURI,LEONELLO-Pitture Italiane in America-Milan-1931-
Ulrico Hoepli-lg v thk folio-438 hftone plts ea wi pg of descrip-
ltd to 1425c (5m5,shake,cl wn) 95.00
--Painting & Painters-NY-1945-Scribner (5x0) 5.00
VERAX-Calumnies of Verus-Phila-1792-Johnston&Justice-58p-
sm8vo-ex rare (5L1) 175.00
VERBRUGGHE,LOUIS-Promenades et Chasses dans L'Amerique Du
Nord-Paris-1879-351p-wrps-1st ed (5h7) 12.50
VERCHERES de BOUCHERVILLE,THOS-Merchant's Clerk in Upper
Canada, Journal-Tor-1935-Rons&Mann-26p (5dd0,cov sl wn) 6.50
--War on the Detroit-Lakeside Classic-1940-347p-map
(5w8) 12.50 (5k2) 6.00
VERDOORN,FRANS,ed-Plants & Plant Science in Latin Amer-
Waltham-1945-84 illus (5r7,pres) 15.00
VERDUN DE LA CRENNE,DE BORDA-Voyage Fait....en Diverses
Parties de l'Europe,de l'Afrique et de l'Amerique-Paris-1778-
Imprimerie Royale-2 vols-4to-t.calf-4 fldg maps-27 plts(25 fldg)-
1st ed (5n9) 225.00
VEREINIGTEN NORDAMERIKANISCHEN PROVINZEN,DIE-
Leipzig-1798,99-PPWolf-thk12mo-2 vols-12 engrs-
(J Milbiller) -half calf (5L1) 95.00
VERGA,GIOVANNI-The house by the medlar tree-NY-1890 -
Harper (5m2) 5.00
--Little Novels of Sicily-NY-1925-8vo-cl-1st ed (5dd8,f,dj) 25.00
--Mastro Don Gesualdo-NY-1921-8vo-cl-1st ed-DHLawrence,transl
(5dd8,dj) 25.00
VERGNE,GEO DE LA-At Foot of the Rockies-NY-(1901)-209p
(5s 4,cov wn) 6.00
VERHOEFF,MARY-The Kentucky Mountains,Transportation &
Commerce from 1750 to 1911-Louisvl-1911-wrps-4to-208p-
illus-Filson Club Pub #26 (5yy8) 15.00
--The Kentucky River Navigation-Louisvl-1917-wrps-illus-257p-
Filson Club Pub #28 (5yy8) 15.00
VERLAINE,DEE-Nets Upon the Morning-LosAng-1930-bds-cl bk-
1st ed-ltd to 175c,nbrd (5ss9,pres) 7.50
VERLAINE,PAUL-Romances Sans Rarales-Paris-1921-col illus by
Leon Lebegue-orig wrps-ltd to 1500c,nbrd (5ss9,sp sl wn) 10.00
VERMONT LAWS-Acts & Laws,Passed by the Gen'l Assembly of
State of Vt(caption)-(Windsor,1783)-sm folio-12p-disbnd
(5a3) 350.00
--same-at Their Sessions at Bennington,in Feb & Mar,1784(caption)-
(Windsor,1784)-15p-disbnd-small folio (5a3) 300.00
--same-at Newbury,second Thurs of Oct,1787(caption)-(Windsor,
1787)-16p-disbnd -4to (5a3) 150.00
--same-at Manchester,second Thurs of Oct,1788(caption)-
(Windsor,1788)-28p-4to-disbnd (5a3) 150.00
--same-at Westminster,second Thurs of Oct,1789(caption)-(Windsor,
1790)-19p-4to-stitchd (5a3,fox) 100.00
VERMONT CLOCK CO-Fair Haven,Vt-Catalog of Clocks Manufacture
Manufactured 1900-Rutland-1900-illus-wrps-32p (5q0) 50.00
VERMONT-Guide to Green Mt State-Amer Guide Series-WPA-
1937-372p-illus-map in pkt
(4c5,lacks pkt map) 8.50 (5e8) 11.75 (5t9) 10.00
VERMONT HISTORICAL GAZETTEER-v.p.-v.d.-6 vols-lg thk8vo
(5u9,4 vols rbnd) 450.00
VERMONT HIST SOC COLLECTIONS-1871-Vol 2-530p (5t9) 4.00
VERMONT HIST SOC-Proceedings of...for Years 1919,1920-n.p.-
c1921-300p-orig heavy wrps (5w5) 7.50
VERMONT IN SPANISH AMER WAR-Montpelier-1929-illus-
163p (5q0) 12.50
VERMONT MERINO SHEEP BREEDERS' ASSOC-Register-Rutledge-
1879,1883-2 vols-illus-8vo-lea (5t4) 25.00
VERMONT-Natural & civil history of Vt-Burlington-1809-2 vols-
fldg map-calf-2nd ed,corr&enlrgd (5g4,sp wn,crack) 35.00

VERMONT-Statutes of State of,Rev & Estab in Year 1787-
Bennington-1791-Anthony Haswell-8vo-orig sheep-315p,(5)
(5L1) 40.00
VERNADSKY,GEO-A History of Russia-(1929)-Yale Univ Pr-
397p (5p0) 6.00
--Political & Diplomatic History of Russia-Bost-1936-maps (5tt5) 7.50
VERNE,J-Fur Country of 70 Degrees North Latitude-Lond-n.d.-
334p-illus-calf (4b9) 10.00
VERNE,JULES-Adventures in the Land of Behemoth-Bost-1874-
Henry LShepard-Ferrat,illus-12mo-190p-frontis-plts-pict cl-
10th thous (5p1,sp wn,fox) 12.50
--Around the World in 80 Days-Lond&NY-n.d.-Pitman-16mo-
184p-8(catalog)-cl-Pitman's shorthand-20th ed (5p1,wn) 5.00
--Dr Ox & other stories-Bost-1874-JasROsgood-GeoM Towle,transl-
Authorized ed-292p(1)(ads)-t.pg in red&black-a.e.red-
brick col cl-1st ed in Engl-24mo (5p1) 47.50
--From the Earth to the Moon-NY-1886-8vo-323p-78 plts-
illus-not 1st (5v0,vf) 6.00
--Godfrey Morgan,a Californian Mystery-NY-ca1870-illus (5r7) 7.50
--Martin Paz-Lond-1876-126p-illus-1st Engl ed (5ee3) 5.00
--Michael Strogoff,A Courier of the Czar-NY-(1927)-Wyeth,illus-
9 col plts-4to-pict cl-397p (5t2) 7.50
--The Moon Voyage-Lond-n.d.-frontis in col (5ee3) 5.00
--Mysterious Island-NY-1875-Scribner's Sons-48 illus (5hh1) 8.50
--same-NY-1926-Wyeth,illus-9 col plts-4to-pict cl-493p
(5t2,dj,f) 8.50
--North against South-Chig-n.d. (5h6) 10.00
--The Tour of World in 80 Days-Bost-1873-12mo-1st Amer ed-
Towle,transl-scarce (5ss9,sl cov wrinkle) 7.50
--Twenty Thousand Leagues Under the Sea-LosAng-1956-handcol illus-
ltd to 1500c,nbrd-Limited Edition Club-boxed,autg by illus
(5F1,f) 30.00
--Vingt Mille Lieues Sous Les Mers-Paris-(n.d.)-(ca 1875)-cl-
lea gk (5ss9) 25.00
--Voyages et Aventures du Captain Hatteras-Paris-(ca 1850)-R8vo-
dec orig cl-g.e.-wdcuts-dbl pg map-illus by Riou (5p5) 22.50
--Wreck of Chancellor & Martin Paz-Bost-1875-Towle,transl-
285p-stmpd cov-1st Amer ed (5s1,rprd,sl shake) 3.00
--Works of-NY-(1911)-Daniels-illus-t.e.g.-15 vols-ChasFHorne,ed-
blue mor-ribbed bands-flowers on sp (5tt2,f,f bndg) 200.00
VERNER,COOLIE-Carto Bibliographical Study of the English Pilot,
4th Book-Charlottesville-1960-8p-maps-12mo (5h9, mint) 8.50
VERNEY,MARGARET M LADY-Verney letters of 18th Cent from MSS
at Claydon House-Lond-(1930)-Benn-ports-2 vols-lg8vos-
1st ed (5m2) 7.50
VERNEY,MAJ F E-H R H,a Character Study of the Prince of Wales-
Lond-(ca 1940)-285p-illus (5t7) 10.00
VERNEY,MICHAEL P-Practical Conversions & Yacht Repairs-Lond-
1951-illus (5c1) 6.00
VERNON,ANNE-A Quaker Business Man-Lond-1958-207p-illus
(5y2) 4.50
VERNON,ARTHUR-Calif Tin Types-Los Ang ed-n.p.-n.d.-152p-
photos (5r0) 7.50
--History & Romance of the Horse-NY-(1941)-illus (5yy8) 7.50
VERNON,FRANK-20th Century Theatre-Bost-n.d.-12mo-cl-159p
(5t0) 3.75
VERNON,GRENVILLE-Yankee Doodle Doo,a collection of songs
of the Early Amer Stage-NY-(1927)-4to-cl&bds-165p(5p6) 12.00
VERNON,IDA S W-Pedreo de Valdivia-Austin-1946-1st ed-
illus-map (5ii3) 8.50
VERNON,JOS S-Along the Old Trail-Cimarron,Ka-(1910)-110p-
photos-8vo-wrps (5F5) 7.50 (4L0,f) 12.50
VERNON,PAUL E-Coast to Coast by Motor-NY-1930-12mo-128p-
8 col plts-fldg map (5r8) 3.50
VERPLANCK,JAS DE LANCEY-A Country of Shepherds-Bost-(1934)-
63p-photos-1st ed (5dd9) 5. (4L0,dj) 7.50
VERPLANCK,WM-The Sloops of the Hudson-NY-1908-13 illus
(5c1,ex-libr) 17.50
VERRAZZANO,GIOVANNI DA-The Voyage of,by Henry C Murphy-
NY-1875-206p-g.t.-fldg & other maps-priv prntd (5dd5) 30.00
VERRILL,A HYATT-An Amer Crusoe-NY-c1914-Martin Lewis,illus-
8vo-dec yell cl-251p-4 plts (5aa2) 5.00
--American Indian,No,So & Central America-NY-(1943)-reprnt-
485p (5dd4) 5. (4b2,f,4L0) 4.00
--Harper's Wireless Book-NY-c1913-185p-illus (5w5) 7.50
--Old Civilizations of New World-Indnpls-(1929)-1st ed-393p-
illus-8vo (4a2) 4.50
--Perfumes & Spices-Bost-(1940)-304p-illus (5w3) 7.50
--same-n.p.-(1940)-illus-304p (5hh6) 6.50
--same-Bost-1945-304p-illus (5n7) 7.50
--The Real Americans-NY-(1954)-illus-309p (5L0,dj) 4. (4i7,dj) 10.00
--The Real Story of the Pirate-NY-1923-illus-1st ed (5F0) 5.50
--Smugglers & Smuggling-NY-1924-illus-frontis-327p (5r8, 5rr9) 6.00

VERRILL,A HYATT (continued)
--Strange Customs,Manners & Beliefs-NY-(1946)-illus (4a1) 7.50
VERSES-By H H-Bost-1870-16mo-cl-1st ed of Mrs Jackson's 1st book-
948c prntd (5gg6,als) 50.00
VERSTEEG,DINGMAN-Manhattan in 1628-1904-203p-hand made
papr-ltd ed (5ff2) 30.00
VERTES,MARCEL-Art & Fashion-NY-(1944)-1st ed-4to-plts
(5yy6) 15.00
VERVE-An Artistic & Literary Quarterly,Vols 1 thru 3,#1 to 12-
Paris-1937 to 1945-4to-dec wrps-col illus-12 vols in 11-
scarce-Engl text (4h0,boxes,f) 225.00
--Vol 1,#1 for Dec,1932-Paris-1937-lg4to-dec wrps-illus
(5p5,vf) 45.00
--same-Vol 1,#3-dec wrps-4to (5p5) 35.00
--same-#5,6,July,Oct 1939-World's Fair Number-folio-220 illus
(5x0) 20.00
--same-Vol 7,dbl number 25,26-folio-wrps-Picasso's paintings-
Paris-1951 (5d9) 50.00
--same-Paris-1955-Vol 8-folio-dbl number 31,32-160p-bds-
col plts (5d9) 65.00
VERY LITTLE TALES FOR VERY LITTLE CHILDREN-in single
syllables-Phila-1851-Appleton-32mo-frontis-253p-2nd series-
11 wdcuts-1st Amer from 5th Lond ed (5p1,wn,stn) 12.50
VERY,LYDIA L A-Poems-Andover-1856-12mo-cl-1st ed of
auth's 1st book (5gg6,pres,bkstrp sl wn) 25.00
VESALIUS,ANDREAS-Illustrations from the works of, of Brussels-
Cleve-1950-4to-cl-252p-96 plts (5t2) 7.50
VESSEY,JOHN HENRY-Mr Vessey of England-NY-(1956)-port-
Waters,ed (5q8,dj) 4.50 (5yy6) 6.00
VEST POCKET PASTRY BOOK,THE-Chig-(1905)-90p-
(J E Meister) (5g9) 1.50
VESTAL,STANLEY-Bigfoot Wallace,a Biography-Bost-1942-291p
plus index-illus-map e.p.-scarce-1st ed (5cc5,f,dj) 20. (4L0) 17.50
--Dobe Walls a Story of Kit Carson's SW-1929-Houghton,Miff-
8vo-cl-313p-1st ed-scarce
(5g2,bndg dmgd) 15. (5cc5,sl cov spot) 20.00
--Fandango,Ballads of the Old West-Bost-1927-66p-1st ed of
auth's 1st book-scarce (4L0,dj,vg,5jj7,mint,dj) 25.00
--Jim Bridger,Mountain Man-NY-1946-8vo-cl-333p-1st ed
(5cc5,mint,dj) 15. (5h5,vg,wn dj) 12.50
--Joe Meek,the Merry Mountain Man,a Biography-Caldwell-1952-
Caxton-t8vo-336p-photos-cl
(5F5,vg) 12.50 (5cc5,mint,dj) 15. (5F5,f,dj,4L0,dj) 20.00
--same-Caldwell-1952-Caxton-pict cl-336p-illus
(4L9,dj,5L7) 10.00
--King of Fur Traders-1940-1st ed-326p
(5r1,dj) 35. (4L0,dj) 25. (5cc5,f,dj) 17.50
--Kit Carson,Happy Warrior of the Old West-Bost-1928-1st ed-
8vo-297p-map e.p.
(5ii1) 12. (5jj7,f,dj,5x5) 12.50 (5h0,f,dj) 15. (4L0,f,dj)17.50
--same-Bost-(1928)-reprint-297p-map e.p. (5dd1) 3.00
--same-Bost-1928-cl-297p-(not 1st ed)
(5m8) 7.50 (5p0) 4. (4k5,f,dj) 5.00
--same-Lond-n.d.-Hodder&Stoughton-297p (5u3) 4.00
--The Missouri-NY-(1945)-Rivers of Amer-354p plus index-
maps-illus-1st ed (5L0,dj) 7.50 (5cc5) 10.00
--Mountain Men-Bost-Houghton,Miff-1937-296p illus-1st ed
(5cc5,f,dj) 22.50 (5x5,f,dj) 20.
(5x5,fade,4L0,fade) 15. (4L0,dj) 30.00
--New Sources of Indian History 1850 to 1891-Norman-1934-
illus-351p-1st ed-v scarce
(5cc5,mint,dj) 40. (4L0,fade,autg) 50.00
--The Old Santa Fe Trail-Bost-1939-photos-1st ed
(4L0,f,dj,5cc5,f,dj,5ww4,fade) 15. (5x5,dj) 20.00
--Queen of the Cowtowns,Dodge City,etc-NY-(1952)-298p-
illus-1st ed (5cc5,f,dj) 12.50 (4L0,wn dj) 10.00
--same-2nd issue (5cc5,f,dj) 12.50
--same-Lond-(1955) (4L0,f,dj) 7.50
--Revolt on the Border-Bost-1938-1st ed
(5cc5,paste on sp) 6. (5jj7,ex-libr) 5. (5x5,dj) 20.00
--Short Grass Country-NY-(1941)-Duell,Sloan-297p plus index-
map e.p.-1st prntng (5F5,f) 7.50 (5jj7,f,dj,5L2) 10.00
--Sitting Bull,Champion of the Sioux-Bost-1932-illus-8vo-1st ed
(4L0) 12.50 (4k5,f,dj) 15. (4g6,sp wn) 13.50
--same-Norman-1956-350p-ports-facs-map (5a1) 6.00
--same-Norman-(1957)-1st ed of revised ed-illus-map
(5m9,tn dj) 6. (5cc5,mint,dj,4L0,dj) 10.00
--Wagons Southwest-NY-1946-map-50p-slick wrps-1st ed-Amer
Pioneer Trails Assn-scarce (5cc5,f,4L0) 5.00
--Warpath-NY-1934-photos-maps-291p-1st ed-scarce
(4b2,dj mend,sl soil) 30. (5dd1) 35.00

VESTAL,STANLEY (continued)
--Warpath & Council Fire-NY-(1948)-RandomHse-1st ed
(5x5,dj,sl holes) 12.50 (4k5,f,dj) 20. (4L0) 15.00
VETH,CORNELIS-Norwegian Work of W H Singer,Jr-Amsterdam-
1923-Frans Buffa & Zonen-36p-16mo-illus (4a0) 15.00
VETANCOURT,AGUSTIN DE-Arte de Lengua Mexicana-Mexico-
1673-F R Lupercio-sm4to-vel-1st ed (4i0,sl spot) 350.00
VETROMILE,EUGENE-The Abnakis & their History,or,Historical-
NY-1866-illus (5w8) 50.00
--Indian Good Book,...for benefit of Penobscot,Passamaquoddy,
St John's,Micmac & other tribes of Abenaki Indians-NY-1857-
12mo-stmpd mor-a.e.g.-tinted lithos (5w8,bkstrp wn) 50.00
VETTER,ERNEST G-Fabulous Frenchtown-Wash-1955-Coronet Pr-
320p-illus (5p0) 6.00
VEVERS,G M-Animals of the USSR-Lond-1948-cl-illus-4to-95p
(4p5) 7.25
VEXILLA REGIS QUOTIDIE,(by) L B S-Bost-1893-orig bds-12mo-
cl bk-ltd to 100c,prntd by Updike,his 1st book
(4m8,soil cor rub) 9.50
VEYSEY,ARTHUR HENRY-A Cheque for Three Thousand-NY-1897-
1st ed (5ee3) 7.50
VHAY,A L MURPHY-Architectural Byways in New Spain-NY-(1939)-
4to-photos-cl-182p (5h5) 12.50
VIAL,A E LOCKINGTON-Alpine Glaciers-Lond-(1952)-Barchworth-
126p-illus-cl (5d7) 3.00
VIAL DU CLAIRBOIS-Dictionnaire Encyclopedique de Marine-
Paris-1793-Panckouke-4 vols-4to-calf-g.-175 fldg plts-fldg
table (5ss2,scuff) 350.00
VIALA,PIERRE-Ampelographie-Paris-1901 to 10-7 volio vols-
500 col plts-cl-wrps bnd in (5w1,rbnd) 650.00
VIALX & RAUAZ,L-American Vines(Resistant Stock) etc-SanFran-
1903-(Press of Freygang Leary Co)-cl-299p-illus (5r0) 7.50
VICAIRE,G-Bibliographie Gastronomique-1890-4to-971p-
prntd wrps-orig ed (5c5) 50.00
--same-1954-reprint of 1890 ed-971p (5w1) 20.00
VICAR OF WAKEFIELD,A TALE-Salisbury-1766-B Collins,prntr-
2 vols-12mo-calf-1st ed
(5hh0,rub) 1500. (5xx6,vg,rbkd,box) 1,400.00
--same-Dublin-1767-for W&WSmith-2 volsin 1(as issued)-calf
(5x3,soil) 35.00
VICKERY,JAS B-History of Unity-(1954)-254p (5e8) 14.75
VICTIM OF CHANCERY,THE-or a debtor's experience-NY-1841-
12mo-orig cl-1st ed-(F Jackson) (5x1,dmpstn) 50.00
VICTOR,BENJ-History of theatres of Lond&Dublin from year 1730
to present time to which is added etc-Lond-1761-for TDavies,etc-
2 vols-12mo-hf cal-1st ed (5x3) 150.00
VICTOR,MRS FRANCES FULLER-All Over Oregon & Wash-
SanFran-1872-1st ed-368p
(4b6,lacks fly,rprd) 15. (5w4,rbnd) 22.50
--Atlantis Arisen,or,Talks of a Tourist about Oregon&Wash-
Phila-1891-412p-photos-map-1st ed
(5s4,soil,lacks fly) 15. (5dd9) 13.50 (5L0) 12.50
--The New Penelope & Other Stories & Poems-SanFran-1877-
Bancroft-8vo-cl-scarce (5b2,sl fray,pres) 25.00
--The River of the West-Hartford-1870-illus-lea-1st ed
(5t2) 45. (5ee3,sl crack) 45.00
--same-Hartf&Toledo-1870-reprint Columbus,1950
(5q0,dj) 15. (5dd1,dj) 10.00
VICTOR,METTA V-Maum Guinea & Her Plantation Children-Lond-
(1861)-Beadle&Co-1st Engl ed-orig purple cl-g.pic sp
(5qq0,f,publ pres) 75.00
VICTOR,ORVILLE J,ed-Incidents & Anecdotes of the War-NY-
(1862)-Torey-400p (5t0,5mm8) 5. (4j4,fox) 7.50 (5t7) 15.00
VICTOR,OSMUND-Salient of So Africa-Lond-1931-190p-maps-
illus (5c6,fly fox) 7.50
VICTOR,RALPH-The Boy Scouts in the Black Hills-NY-(1913)-
drawings-194p (4L0) 4.00
VICTOR TALKING MACHINE CO-Automatic Electrola Radiola
#954-Camden-1929-owner's manual-bds-18p,2p-illus-bds
(5e4,vf) 5.75
--same-#1069-Camden-1929-owner's manual-16p-illus (5e4) 5.75
--Catalogue of Victor Records-(ca 200 pgs)-photos-green soft
papr covs -Camden,NJ (5F9,sp tape) 7.50
--Music Appreciation wi the Victrola for Children-Camden-(1923)-
Educational Dept-12mo-288p,(2)(ads)-pict cl (5p1) 17.50
--Victrola Book of the Opera-Camden-c1917-553p-illus-heavy
green cl-t.e.g. (5F9) 5.00
VICTORIA(CANADA) DIRECTORY-
--1958-sm4to-868p (5ss4) 8.50
--same-1959-sm4to-868p (5ss4) 10.00
VICTORIA ILLUSTRATED-Vict-1891-Colonist-folio-linen-86p-
photos-scarce (5dd7,mint) 25.00

VICTORIA PRIMER-or First Book for Children-York-(c 1840)-
J Kendrew-12mo-pict wrps   (5c8,sl fade) 16.00

VICTORY,BEATRICE M-Benj Franklin & Germany-Phila-1915-
orig wrps   (5jj3) 10. (5h9) 8.50

VIDAL,GORE-Dark Green,Bright Red-NY-1950-Dutton-8vo-
cl   (5b2,f,dj) 8.50

--Messiah-NY-1954-1st ed   (5r9,dj) 10.00

--A Thirsty Evil,Seven Short Stories-NY-1956-1st ed (5r9) 8.50

VIDE,V V-Sketches of aboriginal life-NY-1846-Buckland&Sumner-
12mo-orig cl-1st ed   (5x1,fox) 30.00

VIE ET LES AVENTURES SURPRENANTES DE ROBINSON CRUSOE-
(Parts 1&2) Traduit de l'Anglais-Neuchatel-1776-Sam'l Fauche-
4 vols-t12mo-calf-9 plts-New ed   (5aa2,sl rub) 35.00

VIELE,EGBERT L-Hand Book for Active Service-NY-1861-Van
Nostrand-252p-illus   (5s9,fade,rub) 5. (5mm8) 12.00

--Report on civic cleanliness & economical dispostion of refuse
of cities-NY-1860-illus-wrps   (5g8) 10.00

VIELE,MRS EGBERT-Following Drum-NY-1858-256p-1st ed
(4c7,chip,fox) 60. (5xx5,rbnd) 32.50 (5L2) 35. (4j6) 45.00

VIELE,HERMAN K-The Last of the Knickerbockers-Chig-1901-
Herbert S Stone-12mo-pict cl-g.t.-354p-1st ed-Lakeside Pr
(5j5) 6.50

VIEN,JOS MARIE-Caravanne du Sultan a la Mecque-n.p.(Paris)-
n.d.(1749)-sm folio-bds-lea bk-engr t.-29(of 31)numbered plts-
1st ed-lg paper   (4e1,rub) 285.00

VIERECK,GEO SYLVESTER-As They Saw Us-NY-1929-illus-
1st ed   (5F0) 3.50

--The Candle & the Flame,Poems-NY-1912-mounted port+8vo-
bds-1st ed-ltd to 110c   (5r9,sp fray) 10.00

--Roosevelt A Study in Ambivalence-NY-1919-Jackson Pr-
8vo-cl-illus   (5b2,lt mark) 5.00

VIERTEL,PETER-The Canyon-NY-(1940)-288p-1st ed (5dd6) 7.50

--The Persimmon Tree-NY-(c 1956)-8vl-cl-Scribner (5b2,f) 4.00

VIETH,FREDK H D-Recollections of Crimean Campaign-Montreal-
1913-plts-309p   (5dd0) 12.50

VIETOR,JOHN A,JR-Time Out-NY-1951   (5x7) 3.00

VIETZEN,RAYMOND C-The Ancient Ohioans & Their Neighbors-
1946-photo-maps-439p-1st ed-priv prntd   (5L2) 10.00

VIEWS IN MASSACHUSETTS FOR THE YOUNG-Worcester-n.d.-
(ca 1855)-Enos Dorr&Co-64p-disbnd,but complete-views
(5rr2,fox) 10.00

VIEWS IN NORTH BRITAIN-illustrative of Works of Robt Burns-
Lond-1805-8vo-20 hand col plts-1st ed
(5j3,vg) 10. (5v0,rbnd,vf) 30.00

VIEW OF THE CONTROVERSY-betw Great Britain & her Colonies...
NY-1774-Rivington-12mo-37p-qtr mor-(Sam'l Seabury)
(5n2) 650. (5L1,close crop) 125.00

VIEW OF SOUTH AMERICA AND MEXICO-By a Citizen of the
US-NY-1825-calf-16mo-2 vols in 1
(5ss5,cov loose,stnd) 9. (5t0,lacks e.p.) 12.50

--same-NY-1826-cl-2 vols in 1-211p,254p (4p2,rbnd,fox) 20.00

VIEW OF VALLEY OF MISSISSIPPI-or Emigrants & Traveller's
Guide to the West-Phila-1834-HSTanner-12mo-orig cl-labl-
fldg maps-2nd ed   (5x5,fox) 50.00

VIEW OF THE WHITE MOUNTAINS-Portland-1908-48p plus covers-
photos   (5b9,fray) 5.00

VIGER,DENIS,ed-Siege de Quebec,en 1759-Quebec-1836-
Presses de Frechette et Cie-8vo-disbnd-1st ed (5i9) 40.00

VIGILANCE COMMITTEE OF 1856-(Jas O'Meara)-SanFran-1887
(cov t. date 1890)-wrps-57p-scarce   (4t3) 20.00

VIGNAUD,HENRY-Toscanelli & Columbus-Lond-1902-facs-map-
ltd 200c-hf vel   (5yy6) 42.50

VIGNETTI E VINI LARIANI-Como-1954-fldg col map-1 plt-
4to-wrps-27p,(1)   (5w1) 12.50

VIGO,GIOVANNI DA-The vvhole worke of that Famous Chirurgion
Maister John Vigo,Newly Corrected,by Men Skilfull in
that Arte...works compiled & Published by Thos Gale-Lond-
1586-for Thos East-sm4to-4th Engl ed-calf
(5ee1,rebkd,lacks wks by Gale)1,100.00

VIGUERS,RUTH HILL-Illustrators of Children's Books 1946 to
1956-Bost-1958-Horn Book-4to-299p (5p1,dj) 15.00

VIKING TALES OF NORTH-Chig-1889-12mo-cl-17,370p (5t0) 4.00

VIKINGS OF TODAY-or Life & Medical Work Among Fishermen
of Labrador-Lond-1895-12mo-cl-photos-1st ed-Grenfell's 1st
book   (5gg6) 15.00

VILAPLANA,HERMENEGILDO DE-Vida Portentosa del....Margil de
Jesus-Mexico-1763-Bibliotheca Mexicana-4to-port-1st ed
(5n9,lt stn) 475.00

--same-Madrid-1775-sm4to-8 lvs-335p-orig vel   100.00

VILAS,WM F-A View of the Vicksburg Campaign-(Madison,Wisc)-
1908-104p-fldg map-Wisc Hist Comm   (4L1) 5.00

VILLAFRANCA,RICHAR D-Costa Rica,Gem of Amer Republics-
1895   (5a6,autg,f) 5.00

VILLAGE ANNALS-Containing Austerus & Humenus,a Sympathetic
Tale-Phila-1814-24mo-35p(incl illus)-orig mar wrps
(5a3,frontis pasted to cov) 22.50

VILLAGE READER,THE-Springfield-1845-24mo-300p-hf lea-
frontis -G & Merriam   (5p1,v wn) 6.50

VILLAGRA,GASPAR PEREZ DE-History of New Mexico,1610-
LosAng-1933-Quivira Soc-308p-ltd ed   (4a5) 30.00

VILLANOVA LAW REVIEW-1956 to 70-Vol 1 thru 15
(5ii7,rbnd) 300.00

VILLANUEVA,JAIME-Viage Literario a las Iglesias de Espana-
Madrid&Valencia-1803 to 1852-8vo-calf-22 vols in 7-
1st ed-rare   (4e1) 350.00

VILLARD,HENRY-Lincoln on the Eve of '61-NY-1941-1st ed
(5q8) 6.50

--Memoirs of Henry Villard-Bost-1904-2 vols-maps-photos-1st ed-
(5L7,pres) 12.50 (5L0) 25.00

--The Past & Present of Pike's Peak Gold Regions-Princeton-
1932-fldg map-illus-reprint of 1860 ed   (4L0) 12.50

VILLARD,OSWALD G-Germany Embattled-NY-1915 (5x7) 3.75

--The German Phoenix-NY-1933-358p   (5t7) 5.00

--John Brown,1800 to 1859-Bost-1910-illus-8vo-cl (4c1) 7.50

--Prophets True & False-NY-1928-1st ed   (5yy6,dj) 6.00

--True Story of the Lusitania,reprinted from Amer Mercury
8vo-orig wrps-14p-n.p.-n.d.   (5ss5) 2.50

VILLARD,PAUL-Up To Light-Tor-1928-plts-237p (5s6) 5.00

VILLARS,MEG-Dining Out in Paris-Paris-n.d.(ca 1920)-12mo-
bds-91p,(1)   (5w1,chip) 4.50

VILLIERS,A J-Falmouth for Orders-NY-(1929)-301p-photos
(5s1,ex-libr) 4.50

--same-Holt-1931-301p   (5e8) 4.50

--Whaling in the Frozen South-NY-1931-12mo-cl-301p-
not 1st ed   (5t0) 7.50

VILLIERS,ALAN-Grain Race-NY-1933-Scribner's Sons-cl-
331p-illus   (5r0,dj,long pres) 10.00

--Men Ships & the Sea-Wash-(1962)-Natl Geogr Book Serv-
4to-illus-436p   (5t4) 12.50

--The Sea in Ships-NY-1933-8vo-cl-illus-11p-fldng sketch(5t4) 8.50

VILLIERS,MARJORIE- Grand Whiggery-Lond-1939-405p-ports
(5a1,sl faded) 5.00

VILLON,FRANCOIS-The Poems-Lond-1912-Stacpoole,transl-
4to-g.t.-frontis-calf-raised bands (5t5,rbnd,f bndg) 40.00

--The Lyrics of-Ltd Ed Club-Croton Falls-1933-sm folio-
1500c,nbrd,box,autg-Spiral Pr   (5b0) 25.00

VINAL,HAROLD-The Compass Eye-NY-(1944)-Comet Pr-1st ed
(5m2,pres) 5.00

--Hurricane,a Maine Coast Chronicle-Brattleboro-1936-1st ed
(5r7) 7.50

--Hymn to Chaos-Brattleboro-1931-Stephen Daye Pr-8vo-cl-85p-
1st ed   (5t2) 5.00

--White April-NewHav-1922-8vo-pict wrps over thin bds-
Yale Ser of Younger Poets -46p   (5b2) 4.00

VINAZA,EL CONDE DE LA-Bibliografia Espanola De Lenguas
Indigenas de America-Madrid-1891-427p-dec blue lea
(5j4,f bndg,pres) 35.00

VINCE,CHAS-Storm on the Waters-Lond-1948-18 photos (5c1) 4.00

VINCE,S-The elements of astronomy-Phila-1811-1st Amer ed
(5g4,ex-libr,wn) 15.00

VINCENT,FRANK-Around & About South Amer-NY-1890-illus-
maps-437p-g.e.-hf calf   (4b6,chip,ex-libr) 15.00

VINCENT,GEO E,ed-Theodore W Miller, Rough Rider-Akron-1899-
179p-cl   (5ff7) 12.50

VINCENT,H-History of the Camp meeting & Grounds at Wesleyan
Grove-Bost-1870-258p   (5e8) 4.75

--History of Wesleyan Grove,Martha's Vineyard,Camp Meeting,
...1835 to That of 1858,incl-Bost-1858-12mo-frontis-1st ed
(5ss5) 10.00

VINCENT,JOHN H-The Chautauqua Movement-Bost-1886 (5q8) 5.00

VINCENT,LEE-Earthly Footsteps of the Man of Galilee-(1894)-
Thompson Pub-500 orig photos-406p-map-hf lea (5ww4,rub) 10.00

VINCENT,LEON H-DeWitt Miller, Biographical Sketch-Cambr-
1912-148,(1)p-ltd to 100c,nbrd   (5h7,autg) 10.00

VINCENT,W D-Contributions to History of Pac NW-Pullman,Wa-
1928-Study Series Wash State Col-Astorians-28p-wrps (5s4) 2.50

--same-on Hudson's Bay Co-1927-34p-wrps   (5s4) 2.50

--same-on Lewis&Clark Exped-1929-wrps-40p   (5s4) 2.50

--same-on Northwest Company-1927-28p-wrps   (5s4) 2.50

--same on Northwest History-1930-23p -wrps   (5s4) 2.00

VINCENT,WM,Transl-Voyage of Nearchus from Indus to the
Euphrates-Lond-1797-6 maps & charts-calf   (5c1) 65.00

VINCENZ,STANISLAW-On the High Uplands-NY-n.d.-344p-
illus   (5c3) 4.00

VINE IN EARLY CALIF,THE-13 numbers-1955-Adrian Wilson,prntr-
ea wi a view-ltd to 950c   (5m9) 10.00

VINE MANUAL,THE-or Instructions for cultivation of-Lond-
n.d.(?188-)-illus-139p-12mo   (5w1,shake) 7.50

VINER,GEO H-Descrip Catalogue of Book Plates Designed and
Etched by Geo W Eve-KansasCty-1916-lg8vo-orig bds-1st ed-
ltd to 250c-for members of Amer Book Plate Soc-Torch Pr-
rare   (5p5) 15.00

VINES,ROBT A-Trees,Shrubs & Woody Vines of the SW,Guide
for Ark,LA,NM,OKL & TEX-Austin-1960-folio-illus-1104p
  (4j4) 30.00

VINEY,JOHNNY-"Hi Hattie,I'M In the Navy Now" Letters-
NY-(1941)-dec cartoons   (5s1,dj,ex-libr) 2.50

VINGUT,MRS GERTRUDE-Irene-Bost-1853-frontis-orig cl-1st ed
  (5mm2) 12.50

VINING,EDW P-Inglorious Columbus-NY-1885-23p,788p-map
  (5xx7) 15.00

VINING,ELIZ GRAY-Windows for the Crown Prince-Phila-(1952)-
Lippincott-320p   (5p7) 4.50

VINOGRADOV,A-The Black Consul-NY-1935-1st ed (5x2,dj) 10.00

VINOGRADOFF,P-Essays in Legal History Read Before Intl Congress
of Historical Studies-Lond-1913   (5ff4) 25.00

--Growth of the Manor-Lond-1911-2nd rev ed (5ff4) 17.50

--Intro to Historical Jurisprudence-Lond-1920 (5ff4) 12.50

VINTON,J A-Desc of John Vinton of Lynn-1858-unabridged ed-
538p   (5mm3) 30.00

--Gen Sketches of the Desc of John Vinton of Lynn-1858-236p
  (5t9) 6.00

--Richardson Memorial-1876-944p   (5t9) 60.00

VIOLLET LE DUC,EUGENE-Dictionnaire Raisonne du Mobilier
Francais-Paris-1874 to 76-Morel-8vo-hf mor-t.e.g.-col plts-
6 vols-2nd ed   (4h0,sl rub) 100.00

VIOLLIS,ANDREE-A Girl in Soviet Russia-NY-1929-8vo-cl-345p
  (5t2,stnd) 3.50

VIPER OF MILAN,THE-Lond-1906-12mo-pict cl-1st ed of auth's
1st book   (5gg6) 10.00

VIRGIL'S AENEID-NY-1944-Heritage Pr-R8vo-embossed cl-illus
  (5p5) 7.50

VIRGIL-Works,Translated into Engl Prose with Latin Text-Lond-
JFuller-1763-2 vols-illus-calf-4th ed   (5a1) 15.00

VIRGIL,WORKS OF-John Dryden,transl-NY-1880-425p-24mo
  (5ss1,wn) 3.00

VIRGINIA-The Address of the Minority in the Legislature.....
Alien & Sedition Laws-(Richmond,1799)-8vo-stitched-16p
  (5a3,lt stn) 50.00

VIRGINIA BAR NEWS-1953 to 68-Vol 1 thru 16 (5ii7,rbnd) 110.00

VIRGINIA COMEDIANS,THE-Old Days in the Old Dominion-
NY&Lond-1854-2 vols-orig cl-1st ed(Vol 2,pg 249 is earsed
for erased in 1st ed)   (5mm2,vg) 60.00

VIRGINIA-Constitution of Virginia...Passed Apr 17,1868-
Richmond-1868-New Nation-40p-self wrps (5g4) 7.50

VIRGINIA-Economic & Civic-Richmond-1933-Virg Polytech Insti-
ltd to 700c   (5h6) 8.00

VIRGINIA-Guide to the Old Dominion-NY-(1940)-699p-pkt map-
fldng illus-Amer Guide Ser-WPA-1st ed (5t3) 6.50 (5h9) 7.50

--same-NY-1941-710p-illus-fldg pkt map (5h9) 6.00

--same-NY-(1946)-photos-maps-pkt map-e.p.map-673p plus
index-3rd prntg-Amer Guide Ser-WPA (4L5,dj) 6.50

VIRGINIA-Historic Gardens-Richmond-1923-Edith T Sale,ed-
355p-illus-col prints-2nd ed-James River Garden Club (5h9) 15.00

VIRGINIA,A-Historical Library-formed by an Old Virginia
Collector-NY-1925-Anderson Galleries-75p-wrps (5j4) 3.50

VIRGINIA HISTORICAL SOC-Catalogue of Mss in Collec...& also-
Richmond-1901-WEJones-8vo-120p-prntd wrps-supplement
  (5j5) 10.00

VIRGINIA-History of-Lond-1722-Tooke-calf-8vo-14 plts-
frontis-2nd ed rev-Howes B410   (5n1) 225.00

VIRGINIA ILLUSTRATED-A Visit to the Virginian Canaan-NY-1857-
Harper-illus-300p (D H Strothers)-1st ed
(4p7,poor) 10. (5mm2,sl fox) 45.00

--same-NY-1871-Harper-300p-cl   (5t2) 12.50

VIRGINIA LAW REVIEW-1913 to 70-Vols 1 thru 56-bound
  (5ii7) 1,120.00

--same-single volumes-bound   (5ii7) ea 25.00

VIRGINIA MAGAZINE-of History & Biography-Vols 1 to 74-
Richmond-1893,4 to 1966-Vols 1 to 56 cl-Vols 57 to 74
orig wrps   (5r5,f) 1,000.00

--same-Vol 7-Richmond-1900-bnd (5h6,bndg loose) 10.00

VIRGINIA-Plantation of,Proclamation for Setling 1625-Charlottesville
1946-facs-4to-wrps-40p   (5t7) 8.00

VIRGINIA PREHISTORIC & ANTEBELLUM-Danville-1899-
119p   (5r5) 10.00

VIRGINIA REAL ESTATE JOURNAL-Vol 3,#3-Richmond-1882-
Chaffin&Co-8vo-orig wrps-48p   (5ss5) 12.50

VIRGINIA UNIV MAGAZINE-Vol 11 for year 1872,73-a monthly-
bound   (5h6,scuff) 15.00

VIRKUS,F A,ed-Compendium of American Genealogy-Vol 1-1925
  (4t2) 35.00

--same-Vol 2-Abridged Compendium of Amer Gen-1926-628p
  (4t2) 22.50

--same-Vol 3-Abridged Compendium of Amer Gen-1928-810p
  (4t2) 22.50

--same-Vol 4-1930-909p   (4t2) 25.00

--Handbook of Amer Genealogy-1932 to 43-Vols 1,2,3 (4t2)ea 10.00

--same-Vol 1-1932   (5ss1) 10.00

--same-Vol 3-1937   (5hh3) 12.50

VIRTUE,GEO,pub-Virtue's Picturesque Beauties of Grt Britain-
Lond-(c1834)-4to-orig bds-130 views-fldg map-132p
  (5nn2,rebkd) 35.00

VISCHER,EDW-Missions of Upper Calif,1872 etc-SanFran-1872-
4to-lg papr copy-(4p)44p,viii,iv-stiff wrps (4c1) 100.00

--same-SanFran-1872-Winterburn&Co-56p-wrps (5tt0) 20.00

--Vischer's Pictorial of Calif,wi Missions of Upper Calif,1872...
a supplement-SanFran-1870-Winterburn-Supl,8vo,orig wrps-
SanFran-1872-3 vols-169 plts   (4h0) 750.00

VISCOSE CO-Story of Rayon-1929-7 col plts-63p,1p-frontis-
2nd ed   (5b8) 5.00

--same-NY-1937-95p-illus-3rd ed   (5b8) 4.50

VISIT TO TEXAS-Austin-1952-facs of 1834 ed (5m9,f) 10.00

VISHITA,SWAMI BHAKTA-Genuine Mediumship or The invisible
Powers-Chig-(1919) 12mo-cl-277p   (5t0) 5.00

VISIAK,E H-Medusa,a Story of Mystery& Ecstasy & Strange Horror-
Lond-1929-1st ed   (5ee3,wn dj) 5.00

--The Mirror of Conrad-Lond-(1955)-illus (5mm2) 3.50

VISION OF RUBETA-Epic Story of the Island of Manhattan-
Bost-1838-Weeks,Jordan&Co-1st ed-illus-orig papr bds
  (4b1,wn) 40.00

VISIONS IN VERSE FOR ENTERTAINMENT & INSTRUCTION OF
YOUNGER MINDS-Lond-Dodsley-1767-(Nath'l Cotton)-sm8vo-
141p-frontis-calf-7th ed   (5a1) 15.00

--same-1794-prntd at Exeter by Henry Ranlet-18mo-orig calf
  (5g3) 25.00

--same-Lond-1798-6 plts by Ridley-orig bds-144p-new ed (5c8) 37.50

--same-Lond-1808-Darton&Harvey-12mo-144p-bds-frontis-
new ed   (5v2,f) 25.00

VISIT TO AUNT AGNES,A-(c1864)-sm sq8vo-80p-dec cl-g.-
4 col plts- RTS   (5aa0) 8.50

VISIT TO LONDON-(by S W)-Lond-(c1835)-WmDarton&Son-
sm8vo-232p-flowered cl-8 plts   (5c8) 17.50

VISIT TO TEXAS-NY-1834-Goodrich&Wiley-8vo-orig cl-fldg map
(silked)-4 plts-1st ed   (5n9) 225. (5j1) 175.00

--same-Austin-1952-fldg map-264p-facs repro of above (5n4) 10.00

VISSCHER,W L-Black Mammy-(Dialectical Poetry)-Cheyenne,Wyo-
1885-illus-1st ed   (5x2) 35.00

--same-2nd ed   (5x2,autg) 35.00

VISSCHER,WM-Blue grass ballads & other verse-NY-Caldwell-
(1900)-1st ed-frontis   (5m2) 5.00

--Poems of the South & other verse-Chig-1911-Clarkston-1st ed-
illus   (5m2) 6.00

--The Pony Express-Chig-1908-illus-1st ed (5hh3) 10.00

--Thrilling & Truthful Hist of Pony Express-Chig-(1908)-98p-cl-
illus
(5h6) 12. (5h7,cov soil) 7.50 (5x5,5yy8,wn,4L0,sl dmpstn)10.00

--same-Chig-1946-98p-ports-illus-reprnt (5s6) 8.50 (5g2,dj) 5.00

VISSER-HOOFT,JENNY-Among the Kara Korum Glaciers in 1925-
Lond-1926-303p-illus-cl   (5d7,fade) 10.00

VISTAS IN SOUTHERN CALIFORNIA-LosAng-1893-A C Bilicke-
48p-illus-wrps   (4a5) 15.00

VITRUVIUS-Ten Books on Architecture-Cambr-1914-M H Morgan,
transl-illus   (5yy6) 12.50

VITRY,PAUL-Paul Manship,Sculpteur Americain-Paris-1927-
Editions de la Gazette des Beaux Arts-46p-80 plts-crown 4to
  (4a0) 40.00

VITTORINI,ELIO-In Sicily-(1949)-Intro by Hemingway-New
Directions   (5ss9,dj,vg) 5.00

VIVANCO,AURELIO DE-Baja,Calif Al Dia-n.p.-c1924-fldg map-
4to-wrps-579p   (4t1) 40.00

VIVIAN,H HUSSEY-Notes of a tour in Amer from Aug 7 to Nov 17,
1877-Lond-1878-fldg map   (5q8,sp loose) 9.00

VIZCAINO,FR JUAN-The Sea Diary of,to Alta Calif,1769-LosAng-
1959-12mo-50p-hf cl-1st ed-Early Calif Travel Ser #49-
ltd to 225c   (5dd6) 25.00

VIZETELLY,ERNEST ALFRED-The True Story of the Chevalier
D'Eon-Lond-1895-Chiswick Pr-crushed lev mor-ltd ed (5d2) 10.00
VIZETELLY,H-4 Months Among the Goldfinders of Calif-Phila-
1849-buck-94p-1st Amer ed   (4n1,rebnd) 25.00
VIZETELLY,HENRY-Facts About Champaigne & Other Sparkling
Wines-Lond-1879-235p-112 illus-ads (5w1) 15.   (4g9) 18.50
--History of Champagne With Notes etc-Lond-1882 g.stmp cl-
4to-263p-a.e.g.-illus-fldg map   (4t7) 32.50
--The Wines of the World-Lond-1875-202p,(5)-wrps
(5w1,bndg loose) 12.50
VLEKKE,BERNARD H M-Hollanders Who Helped Build Amer-NY-
1942-ports-4to-323p   (4t2) 5.   (5h9) 10.   (4b6) 17.50
VLIEGER,J-Amsterdam-Amsterdam-ca 1910-29 photos-obl 12mo-
accordion fldg-cl hinges   (5ww3) 12.50
VOCINO,MICHELE-Ships through the Ages-Milan-(1951)-folio-
moire cl-g.-330p-8 col plts-Luigi Alfiere-3rd ed (5ss2,f) 20.00
VOGEL,E-Los Horrores De La Trata De Negroes En El Africa Por
Humanus-Madrid-1888-129p-wrps-map-in Spanish (5x2) 25.00
VOGEL,EDW-The Practical Brewer-StL,Mo-1946-Master Brewers
Assoc-226p-illus   (5t7) 6.50   (5g9) 7.50
VOGEL,KARL-Aloha Around the World-1923-Putnam's Sons
95 photos-2nd impress   (5x5) 12.50
VOGEL,PETER-Tale of a Pioneer Church-Cinn-1887-350p-illus-
fldg chart-1st ed   (5w9) 7.50
VOGEL,WM & CO-Catalogue of Tin Ware-Brooklyn-n.d.(ca1865,
'75)-8vo-orig prntd wrps-39p   (5t2) 7.50
VOGEL,Z-Reptile Life-Lond-n.d.(195-?)-cl-80p-150 plts (4 col)-
4to   (4p6) 15.00
VOGT,E Z-Navaho Means People-Cambr-1951-Photos (5t1) 25.00
VOGT,WM-Birds of America by Audubon-NY-1944-Macmillan-
sm4to-435 col plts   (5t4) 15.00
--same-NY-1946-Macmillan-4to-cl-435 col plts-frontis (5t4) 12.50
--Road to Survival-NY-(1948)-335p   (5w3,5s7) 5.00
VOGUE'S COOKERY BOOK-Lond-(1939)-HPowell,ed-Conde Nast-
248p-1st ed   (5c9) 5.00
--same-1947-263p-2nd ed   (5c9) 4.50
VOGUE'S MANUAL-of Smart Service & Table Setting-NY-1930-
90p-illus   (5w7,lacks fly) 3.00
VOICE FROM ABROAD-or Thoughts on Missions...Sheldon Dibble-
Lahainaluna-1844-Press of Mission Seminary-132p-emboss cl-
lea sp   (5s2,f) 75.00
VOICE FROM THE NEWSBOYS-1860-Benefit of Author-135p-
orig cl-port   (5m3,soil) 25.   (5j5,f) 22.50
VOICES OF THE STONES-Lond-1925-Macmillan&Co-1st ed-
(Geo W Russell)   (5ss3,dj,sp fade) 10.00
VOIGT,HARRY-Concordia,Missouri,a Centennial History-
Concordia-1960-wrps-137p plus 56p-plts-wrps (5t3) 10.00
VOLCANO UNDER THE CITY,THE-By A Volunteer Special-
NY-1887-350p-orig cl-fldg map   (5m3) 22.50
VOLLARD,AMBROISE-Degas,an Intimate Portrait-NY-1927-
149p-illus   (5ww3) 10.00
--Renoir,An Intimate Record-NY-1925-Knopf-248p-illus (5x0) 6.00
--La Vie et L'Oeuvre de Pierre Auguste Renoir-Paris-1919-
thk4to-dec wrps-370 illus&orig liths-lg papr-1st ed-ltd to
525c,nbrd-for subscribers   (5p5) 175.00
VOLLMER,WM-The US Cook Book-Phila-1865-165p-in German &
Engl   (5c0) 10.00
VOLLMER,WM A-A Book of Distinctive Interiors-NY-1912-
128p-4to   (5w7) 5.00
VOLNEY,C F-Tableau Du Climat et Sol des Etats Unis d'Amerique
etc-Paris-1826-Jas Lane   (5nn8) 65.00
--The ruins...(with)Volney's answer etc-NY-1890-illus (5m2) 6.00
--View of Climate & Soil of USA-Lond-1804-1st Engl ed-orig bds-
roan bk & corners-504p-fldg maps (5a0,rbkd) 40. (5yy9) 65.00
--same-Phila-1804-1st Amer ed-illus-fldg maps-446p-orig lea
(5cc6,bk cov dtchd) 35.   (5tt6,vf) 125.00
VOLTAIRE,F MARIE AROUET-Candide,or Optimism-Lond-1939-
Nonesuch Pr-col illus (4b4,box) 17.50 (5b0,cov sl browned) 10.00
--Henriade,An Epick Poem,in Ten Cantos-Lond-1732-311p-
frontis-sheep-1st ed in Engl   (4b4,crack) 125.00
--La Pucelle,The Maid of Orleans-Lond-1899-Lutetian Soc-2 vols-
8vo-cl-g.-500c   (5b0,lt fade) 15.00
--Philosophical Dictionary-NY-1952-10 vols in 2   (4a1) 10.00
--The Princess of Babylon-Lond-1927-Nonesuch Pr-ltd to 1500c,
boxed   (5F9,f,unopnd) 22.50   (5a9,mint) 12.50
--same-NY-1928-Art Studio Pr-frontis-mor sp-ltd to 750c-bds
(5ee3,f) 10.00
--Romances, Tales & Smaller Pieces of-Lond-1794-prntd for
P Dodsley-12mo-hf lea-2 vols   (5t2,rbnd) 7.50
--Works of-Lond-(1901)-Dumont-42 vols-Wm Fleming,transl-
ltd to 660 sets-3 qtr green mor,ea vol boxed (5p6,boxes wn) 160.00
--The Works of-Paris-Ferney ed-ltd to 190 nbrd sets-42 vols-
illus-3/4 mor   (4b4) 250.00

VOLTAIRE   (continued)
--The Works of-Paris-Ferney ed-ltd to 190 nbrd sets-42 vols-
illus-3/4 mor   (4b4) 250.00
--Works of-42 vols-NY-Dumont-Hulbert Guild-cl
(5x0,post extra) 50.00
VOLUME from life of Herbert Barclay-Balt-Wm&Jos Neal-1833-
12mo-orig cl-labl-1st ed of auth's 1st book-rare
(5x1,fox,labl chip,pres) 275.00
VOLWILER,A T-Geo Croghan & the Westward Movement 1741 to
1782-1926-sewn   (5L7) 10.00
VON ABELE,RUDOLPH-Alex H Stephens-NY-1946-8vo-illus-
1st ed   (5p9,5m6,f,dj) 6.00
VON FALKE,OTTO-The Guelph Treasure,the Sacred Relics of
Brunswick Cathedral-Frankfurt-1930-illus-mor-9½ x 13"
(5d2,mint) 125.00
VON HAGEN,VICTOR-Ancient Sun Kingdomes of the Americas-
Cleveland-(1960)-illus(some col)-617p-1st ed (4b2,dj) 12.50
--The Aztec & Maya Papermakers-NY-(1944)-Augustin-frontis-
29 plts-120p-cl   (4b6) 17.50   (5tt9,f,dj) 27.50
--Fredk Catherwood,Architect-NY-1950-Oxford Univ Pr-177p-
illus   (5p7) 6.50
--Green World of the Naturalists-NY-1948-Greenberg-392p
(5p7) 5.00
--Maya Explorer, John Lloyd Stephens & Lost Cities of Central
Amer & Yucatan-Norman-1948-illus-fldg map-324p
(4p8,dj) 6.   (5h4) 5.   (5t2,f,dj) 6.50
--South America Called Them-NY-1955-4 maps-28 illus-311p
(5w3) 7.50
VON HENNEBERG,FREIHERR A-The Art & Craft of Old Lace-
NY-1931-(prntd in Germany)-folio-181 plts(8 col)-49p text
(5n7) 27.50
VON HOFE & CO,EDW-Catalog,Fine Fishing Tackle-NY-1928-
12mo-orig prntd wrps-171p   (5t0) 5.00
VON HOFFMAN,CARL-Jungle Gods-NY-(c1929)-A L Burt-8vo-
286p   (4a6) 7.50
--same-NY-1929-ELohrke,ed-illus-pict cl   (5x2) 10.00
VON HORN,W O-The Rhine-Wiesbaden-n.d.-38 engrs (5yy6) 10.00
VON HUTTEN,BARONESS-What Became of Pam-Lond-1906-
Heinemann-8vo-cl   (5b2) 4.00
VON KLARWILL,VICTOR,ed-The Fugger News Letters-Lond-
(1924)-JLane-illus-284p   (5p9) 6.00
VON LIEBIG,JUSTUS-Natural Laws of Husbandry-NY-1863-
387p-cl-labl   (5hh7) 7.50
VON MISES,LUDWIG-Socialism-NY-n.d.-transl from 2nd German
ed(1932)   (4a1) 10.00
VON MUNCHHAUSEN,KARL-Travels of Baron Munchausen-Chig-
1929-sm folio-cl-Ltd Ed Club-ltd to 1500c,box,autg (5b0,dj) 27.50
VON REBER,FRANZ-History of Ancient Art-NY-1887-8vo-cl-
310 illus   (5t0) 4.50
VON SACHER MASOCH,LEOPOLD-Venus in Furs-NY-1928-
218p-illus   (5q0) 10.00
VON SCHMIDT PAULI,E-We Indians-NY-(1931)-248p plus index-
col frontis   (4L0) 8.50
VON SHON,H-Report on Hydro electric Power Development on
Pennington Creek,Ind Ter-1906-maps-ca 100p-cl (5h0) 50.00
VON SCHONBERG,ELIZ-Sonnets of San Fran in Swingtime &
Other Poems-(SanFran,1937)-8vo-114p-suede (5h4) 2.75
VON SCHRODER,JANET-The Quest-SanFran-1914-8vo-t.e.g.-
green crushed mor-1 of 8c prntd by RJOrozco (5b0,lt rub) 27.50
VON SKAL,GEO-History of German Immigration in US etc-NY-
n.d.-ports   (5jj3,lacks sp) 12.50
VON SUTTNER,BERTHA-Lay Down Your Arms-NY-1914-435p
(5ss1) 3.00
VON TIRPITZ,ADM-My Memoirs-NY-1919-2 vols-376p-scarce
(5s1,sl cov soil) 15.00
VOORHEES,D W-40 Yrs of Oratory-2 vols-Indnpls-1898-782p
(5a8,sl soil) 7.50   (5h1) 12.50
VOORHEES,H C-Law of the Public School System of the US-
Bost-1916   (5ff4) 7.50
VOORHEES,JAS PAXTON-Caverns of Dawn-Plainfield-1910-
519p-cl   (5jj9,sl cov dmpstn) 10.00
VOORHEES,LUKE-Personal Recollections of Pioneer Life on
Mountains & Plains of the Great West-(Cheyenne,1920)-sm8vo-
cl-76p   (5t2,pres) 15.00
VOORHIES,FELIX-Acadian reminiscences-Opelousas-1907-
Jacobs News Depot-107p   (5u3) 4.50
VOORHIS,ROBT-Life & Adventures of...The Hermit of Mass-
(Henry Trumbull)-Prov-1829-sm8vo-frontis-orig wrps-
ex rare issue wi "Voorhis" in title   (4n5) 275.00
VORCE,C M-Gen & Hist Record of Vorce Fam in Amer-1901-111p
(4t2) 25.00
VORS,FRED-Bibelots & Curios-NY-1879-12mo-116p,(12)(5w7) 4.50

USED BOOK PRICE GUIDE

VORSE, MARY H-The Breaking of a Yachtman's Wife-NY-1908-
276p-illus-orig pict cl-auth's 1st book   (5m1)   10.00
--Growing Up-NY-(1920)-1st ed   (5m1)   7.50
VOSBURGH, R W-Hist of St Paul's Evangelical Lutheran Church of
Berne, Albany Co, NY-1916-24p-wrps   (5t9)   15.00
--Hist of Zion's Evangelical Lutheran Church of Cobleskill-1916-
40p-wrps   (5t9)   25.00
--Records of 1st Congr Church of Stillwater & 1st Presbyterian Church
Saratoga Co, NY-1919-48p-wrps   (5t9)   25.00
--Records of German Reformed Church in New Rhinebeck, near
Dorlach(or Sharon)-1915-21p, 202p-unbnd-typescript (5t9)   55.00
--Records of the Reformed Dutch Church of Owasco, NY-1919-
33p-wrps   (5t9)   20.00
--Records of the Reformed Protestant Church of Caughnawaga, now
Reformed Church of Fonda, NY-1917-Vol 1-224p
    (5t9, home bndg)   85.00
--Records of the Reformed Prot Dutch Church of Herkimer-1920-
Vol 3-163p   (5t9, home bndg)   60.00
VOSE, C E-Caucasians Only-Univ Calif   (5x2, dj)   4.50
VOSE, JOHN-A System of Astronomy-Concord-1827-Jacob B Moore-
8vo-orig hf sheep-252p-1st ed   (5j5, lacks plts, fox)   10.00
VOSSLER, KARL-Mediaeval Culture-NY-(1929)-2 vols (5j3, dj)   25.00
VOTH, H R-Traditions of the Hopi-Chig-1905-wrps-319p
    (4p2, f, unopened) 25.   (4L0, lacks wrps)   15.00
VOX POPULI-Geneva-(press of Albert Kundig, 1932)-Vox Populi
Committee-dec bds-83p plus 3p-ltd to 500c, nbrd (5r0)   7.50
VOYAGE A LA MARTINIQUE-Paris-1763-fldg map-Bauche-
4to-1st edition   (5n9)   125.00
VOYAGE & VENTURE-Phila-1854-300p-illus w/line engrs(5ii2) 7.50
VOYAGE AUTOUR DU MONDE-Paris-1772-Saillant&Nyon-8vo-
2 vols-calf-21 fldg maps-3 fldg plts-2nd ed, enlrgd (5n9) 150.00
--same-1773-12mo-Neuchatel, Societe Thypographique-2 vols in 1
    (5n9)   85.00
VOYAGE EN CALIFORNIE 1850 et 1851-Paris-1851-Garnier Freres-
48p-wrps   (5tt0) 40.   (4h0)   35.00
VOYAGE PITTORESQUE DE PARIS-Ou Description de tout ce
qu'il ya a de plus beau etc-par M.D.-Paris-1770-illus-lea-
483p-5th ed   (5t7)   20.00
VOYAGES, LES-Paris-1706-Cellier-12mo-calf-2 fldg maps-
1st French ed-(L Wafer)   (5n9)   65.00
VOYAGES, ADVENTURES-& Miraculous Escape of Geo Andrew
Barton-Lond-(ca1800)-8vo-wrps-38p-hand col frontis-3rd ed-
J Ker   (5aa2, rewrps)   35.00
VOYAGES & ADVENTURES OF CAPT ROBT BOYLE-of Richard
Castelman-Lond-1726-Watts-8vo-frontis-1st ed-calf-
(Wm Chetwood)   (5n9, box, rbkd)   150.00
VOYAGES & ADVENTURES OF ROBINSON CRUSOE-Moveable
Book-Dean&Son(1873)-8vo-pict bds-cl back-8p text (5s0) 65.00
VOYAGES & CRUISES-of Commodore Walker, during late Spanish
& French Wars-Lond-1760-12mo-2 vols-calf-1st ed   650.00
VOYAGES & DISTRESSES-of Capt T James & Mr Henry Ellis for
Discovery of a NW Passage to South Seas-1820-J Arliss-12mo-
orig bds-frontis(1807)-60p   (4d1)   25.00
VOYAGES, DANGEROUS ADVENTURES-& Imminent Escapes of
Capt Rich Falconer-Lond-1724-Marshal et al-12mo-calf-
frontis-2nd ed, corr   (5n9)   85.00
VOYAGES ET AVANTURES-de Jacques Masse-Bordeaux(i e La Haye?)-
1710-chez Jaques l'Aveugle-12mo-calf-1st ed (5i8, rub) 70.00
VOYAGES ROUND THE WORLD-Edinb-1843-448p
    (5aa0, f, unopen)   17.50
VOYAGES, TRAVELS & ADVENTURES-of Wm Owen Gwin Vaughan,
etc-Lond-1736-prntd for JWatts-12mo-calf- (5xx6) 275.00
VOYAGEUR AMERICAIN-ou Observations sur l'Etat actuel-
Amsterdam-1783-Schuring-264p-map-8vo-3 fldg tables-calf
    (5L1, rub)   85.00
VOYNICH, E L-The Gadfly-NY-1897-1st ed   (5yy6)   15.00
VROOMAN, JOHN J-Forts & Firesides of Mohawk Country-1943-
266p-index   (5ff2)   20.00
VROOMAN, WALTER-Government Ownership in Production &
Distribution-Balt-1895-fldg maps-1st ed   (5m2)   10.00
VULLIAMY, C E-John Wesley-NY-1932-port-8vo-cl-370p-
1st ed   (5t0)   5.00
--Our Prehistoric Forerunners-NY-1925-209p plus index-illus
    (4L0)   4.00
--Royal George-Lond-1940-318p-ports   (5a1)   4.50
--Unknown Cornwall-1925-col plts   (5L7)   3.50
VYNNE, HAROLD RICHARD-The Woman That's Good-Chig&NY-
(c 1900)-Rand, McNally-8vo-dec cl   (5b2)   4.50
WA BO KIE SHIEK COOK BOOK-Prophetstown-n.d.-(ca 1905)-
162p-oilcloth(Indian illus)-ads-rare (4g9, scuff, sl stns) 25.00
WABASH CO, IND-Atlas of-Phila-1875-maps-65p-cl-illus-
scarce-LeGear. III3   (5h1)   55.00

WABASH VALLEY REMEMBERS-A Chronicle-n.p.-n.d.-
(TerreH-1938)-111p-cl   (5h1)   10.00
WACH, JOACHIM-Sociology of Religion-Chig-1944-412p
    (5L7, 5w9)   4.00
W A D-Mss by WAD....collection of writings of Dwiggins-NY-
1947-152p-illus-typophiles, publ(950c prntd) (5w5) 3.50
WADDEL, MOSES-Memoirs of Life of Miss Caroline Eliz Smelt-
NY-1818-Fanshaw-12mo-orig sheep-lea labl-175p
    (5j5, sheep wn)   17.50
WADDELL, JOS A-Annals of Augusta Co, Virg 1726 to 1871-
Staunton-1902-fldg map-4to-545p-2nd ed-rev (4m4, recased) 40.00
WADDINGTON, ALFRED-The Fraser Mines Vindicated-Vanc-1949-
Robt Reid, prntr-reprnt-ltd to 110c, nbrd-sq8vo-hf mor-93p-
port, plt   (5u6)   175.00
WADDINGTON, MARY KING-My War Diary-NY-1917-8vo-
1st ed   (5m6)   6.50
WADDINGTON, RICHARD-Salmon Fishing-Lond-(1959)-plts-8vo
    (5tt7, dj)   7.50
WADDY, FREDK-Cartoon Portraits & Biogr Sketches-Lond-1873-
4to-147p-illus-pt mor-a.e.g.-Tinsley Bros (5xx7) 25.00
WADE, ALLAN-Bibliography of Writings of W B Yeats-Lond-1951-
390p   (4b4)   18.50
WADE, B F-Report on the Attack on Petersburg-Wash-1865-272p-
SR114   (4j4)   8.50
--Report on Treatment by Rebels of Remains of Officers & Troops
at Manassas-Wash-1862-SR41   (4j4)   8.00
--Returned Prisoners-Wash-1864-6 illus-40p-HR67 (4j4) 6.50
WADE, F MASON-The French Canadians, 1760 to 1945-Lond-1955-
Macmillan-1136p-1st ed   (5u3)   9.00
WADE, H T, ed-With Boat & Gun in the Yangtze Valley-Shanghai-
1895-sm4to-maps-1st ed   (4c8)   20.00
WADE, HERBERT TREADWELL-Brief History of Colonial Wars in
Amer 1607 to 1775-NY-1948-illus-120p-Publ #51 (5t4) 7.50
WADE, HOUSTON-Dawson Men of Fayette County-Houston-1932-
86p-index   (4a5)   12.50
--Members of the Texas Veteran's Assoc, 1st&2nd Class-42p-
type script in stiff wrps   (5n4)   25.00
WADE, JOHN DONALD-Augustus Baldwin Longstreet-NY-1924-
Macmillan-392p   (5x0)   10.00
WADE, MARY HAZELTON-10 Big Indians-Bost&Chig-(1905)-256p-
illus   (5t4)   5.00
WADE, MASON-Francis Parkman, Heroic Historian-NY-1942-
456p plus index-photos-1st ed   (5L0, dj)   6.00
--French Canadian Outlook-NY-1947-192p (5a1, lack fly) 4.50
--Journals of Francis Parkman-NY-1947-718p-cl-1st ed-2 vols
    (5ff7, dj, box) 12.50   (4L0, dj, box)   15.00
--Margaret Fuller, Whetstone of Genius-NY-1940-illus-304p
    (5mm1, dj) 10.   (5p7)   6.00
WADE, W P-Treatise on Law of Notice as Affecting Civil Rights &
Remedies-Chig-1878-sheep   (5ff4, rub)   9.75
WADHAM, CAROLINE R-Simple Directions for the Chambermaid-
NY-1917-12mo-col frontis-82p   (5w7, buckled) 3.00
WADIA, A S-The Belle of Bali-Lond-1936-R8vo-illus-1st ed
    (5x2, dj)   4.00
WADLIN, HORACE G-Public Library of Boston-1911-236p-illus
    (5e8)   4.75
WADSWORTH, BENJ-The imitation of Christ, a Christian duty-Bost-
1722-BGreen-8vo-calf-1st ed   (5i0, lacks fly) 35.00
--The Way of Life opened in the Everlasting Covenant-Bost-1712-
BGreen-12mo-148p, (4)-orig sheep   (5L1, wn) 50.00
WADSWORTH, JOHN-Counter Defensive-Lond-(1946)-plts-tall 8vo-
hf mor-g.t.   (4b6)   17.50
WADSWORTH, SAML-Historical Notes with Keyed Map of Keene &
Roxbury, Cheshire Co, NH-Keene-1932-Sentinel Prntg-8vo-
cl-86p-ltd nbrd ed   (4t1)   15.00
WADSWORTH, WALLACE C-The Real Story Book-Chig&NY-(c1927)-
Rand McNally-136p-frontis-labl-4to-1st ed (5p1) 12.50
WADSWORTH, WM H-of Kentucky, on Enlistment of Negro Soldiers,
Jan 30, 1863-Wash-1863-8p-wrps   (5x2)   65.00
WAERN, CECILIA-John LaFarge-Lond-1896-illus-pt lea-104p
    (5q0, libr labl)   7.50
WAFER, LIONEL-Les Voyages de Lionnel Waffer-Paris-1706-398(4)p-
calf-2 fldg maps-1st French ed   (5ff7)   100.00
--New Voyage & Descrip of Isthmus of Amer-Cleve-1903-
GPWinship, ed-maps-plts(all fldg)-212p-g.t.-ltd to 500c-
scarce   (5dd6)   28.50
WAGENKNECHT, EDW-Abraham Lincoln, His Life, Work &
Character-NY-1947-661p-1st ed (4b7, autg) 10. (5t4) 5.00
--A Guide to Bernard Shaw-1929-Appleton-12mo-1st ed (5ss9, dj) 5.00
--Joan of Arc-NY-1948-Creative Age Pr-421p-1st ed (5p1, dj) 7.50
--Mark Twain, the Man & His Work-Yale Univ Pr-1935 (5ss9, dj) 15.00
--Utopia Americana-Seattle-1929-Univ of Wash Chapbooks #28-
port-40p-orig wrps   (5c8, f, unopnd)   25.00

WAGENSELLER,G W-Wagenseller Family in Amer-Middleburgh-
1898-225p   (4t2,cov stnd)   12.50

WAGGAMAN,M T-Little Missy-NY-1900-12mo-Juvenile (5x2) 4.50

WAGGAMAN,W H-Review of Phosphate Fields of Idaho,Utah,
& Wyo-Wash-1910-48p-wrps   (4a5)   3.50

WAGGONER,GEO A-Stories of Old Oregon-Salem-1905-12mo-
292p-plts   (5dd4)   10.00

WAGNER,ANTHONY RICHARD-Heralds & Heraldry in Middle Ages-
Lond-1939-157p   (5q0)   10.50

WAGNER,ARTHUR L-Service of Security & information-Wash-1893-
254p plus index-illus-2nd ed   (5dd1,bkstrp tn)   8.50

WAGNER,BLANCHE C-Tales of Mayaland-Pasadena-1938-
SanPasqual Pr-8vo-part cl-88p-ltd to 1000c
    (4t1) 10.   (5dd4) 8.50   (5F5,pres)   5.00

WAGNER,CHAS L H-Wagner's Blue Print Text Book of Sign & Show
Card Lettering-Bost-(1926)-4to-71 plts-buck
    (4m6,ex-libr,rebnd)   15.00

--Story of Signs,an Outline History-Bost-1954-122p-illus (5hh7) 6.50

WAGNER,GLENDOLIN DAMON-Blankets & Moccasins-Caldwell-
1933-photos-col dec e.p.-304p-1st ed
    (4b2,dj sl wn) 17.50   (4L0)   20.00

--Old Neutriment-Bost-(1934)-illus-256p-1st ed-v scarce
    (5L2,f) 40.   (4m2)   45.00

WAGNER,HENRY R-Antonio de Herrera,Historia General de las
Indias Occidentales-Berkeley-1924-4to-wrps-14p-reprint
from Span SW-v scarce   (5F5)   8.00

--(Biblio of Printed Works Relating to Those Portions of US Which
Formerly Belonged to Mexico)-Santiago,Chile-1917-wrps-
43p-rare   (5z7,pres)   125.00

--Calif Imprints-Berkeley-1922-8vo-wrps (4c1,pres) 20.00

--Calif Voyages,1539 to 1541-SanFran-1925-JnHowell-95p
    (5p9)   30.00

--Cartography of NW Coast of Amer to Year 1800-Berkeley-1937-
Univ of Calif Pr-maps-2 vols-4to
    (5tt0) 125.   (5ss2,tn dj) 75. (5h4,box) 100.00

--same-2 vols in 1-linen bndg   (5h4)   87.50

--Catalogue of Imprints in Collection of....LosAng-1938-Ritchie Pr-
bds-ltd to 250c   (4g2,sl wn)   15.00

--Creation of Rights of Sovereignty through Symbolic Acts-
1938-reprnt from Pac Hist Review-32p (5tt0,pres) 10.00

--Nueva Bibliografia Mexicana Del Siglo XVI-Mexico-1940-
lg folio-wrps-illus-548p-ltd ed   (4j7)   60.00

--Peter Martyr & His Works-Worc-1947-Amer Antiqu Soc-8vo-
52p-reprnt-wrps   (4a3,f,autg)   12.50

--Peter Pond,Fur Trader & Explorer-Yale Univ Library-1955-
103p-boxed wi 3 separate maps in folder-ltd to 500c
    (5r6) 25.   (5F5)   15.00

--Plains & the Rockies-SanFran-1920-174p-v rare (4j7) 90.00

--same-SanFran-1921-hf buck-193p   (4j7)   55.00

--The Plains & Rockies...1800 to 65-Columbus-1953-illus-601p-
3rd ed   (4j6,f) 45.   (4g2)   85.00

--same-Columbus-1953-deluxe ed-ltd to 75c,box-extra illus
    (5x5,f)   150.00

--Rise of Fernando Cortes-(LosAng)-1944-Cortes Soc-illus
    (4c1,pres)   50.00

--Sir Francis Drake's Voyage Around World-SanFran-1926-maps-
illus-4to-cl-Howell   (5a3) 60. (4c1,pres,5h4,f) 50.00

--Some Imaginary Calif Geography-Worcester-1926-Amer
Antiquarian Soc-49p-maps-wrps   (5F9,f)   20.00

--Spanish Voyages to NW Coast of Amer-SanFran-1929-maps-
illus-571p-4to-cl-Calif Hist Soc #4 (4L0,wn) 65. (4c1) 100.00

WAGNER,LAURA V-Through Historic Years with Eliza Ferry Leary-
Seattle-1934-Dogwood Pr-ports-plts-93p (4d8) 15. (4g6) 17.50

WAGNER,LEOPOLD-More London Inns & Taverns-Lond-(1925)-
256p   (5w1)   7.50

WAGNER,PHILIP M-Amer wines & how to make them-NY-1933-
295p   (4g0)   6.50

--Amer Wines & Wine Making-NY-1956-264p-13 photos (5w1) 5.00

--Wine Grapes-NY-(1937)-illus-297p   (4g0)   8.50

--A Wine Growers Guide-NY-1945 (4g0) 5. (5w1) 4.50

WAGNER,RAY-Amer Combat Planes-NY-1960-1st ed-illus-4to
    (5ii3,f,dj)   10.00

WAGNER,RICHARD-My Life-1936-Tudor-911p (5p0) 7.00

--Rinegold-4to-g.lettering-col plts by ArthurRackham-vel-
Ltd ed,autg by Rackham   (5t8,f)   185.00

--The Ring of the Niblung-Lond-1910,1911-thk8vo-orig cl-
64 col plts by Rackham-2 vols-1st trade ed (4n5,hng weak) 75.00

--The Valkyrie-col plts by Rackham-vell-Ltd Ed-autg by Arthur
Rackham   (5t8,f)   185.00

--The Rhinegold & The Valkyrie-GardenCty-1939-4to-cl-183p-
illus by Arthur Rackham   (5t2,f,dj)   17.50

WAGNER,ROB-Rob Wagner's Calif Almanack for 1924-1924-60p-
obl 8vo-illus-Times Mirror Pr-1st ed   (5g2,pres)   3.00

WAGONER,J J-History of Cattle Industry in Southern Ariz,1540 to
1940-Tucson-1952-illus-132p-wrps(4a5) 9.50 (5g6,4b3) 7.50

WAGSTAFF,A E-Life of David S Terry-SanFran-1892-8vo-cl-
526p-5 plts-1st ed   (5h5,cor bumped)   40.00

WAGSTAFF,DAVID-Upland Game Bird Shooting in Amer-NY-
1930-249p-col plts-Derrydale Pr   (5xx7)   25.00

WAGSTAFF,WM R-History of Soc of Friends-NY-1845-
Wiley&Putnam-400p plus errata slip-Part 1(all publ)
    (5F9,sp wn) 25.   (5a0)   37.50

WAHL,JEAN-Marc Chagall....Illustrations for Bible-NY-(1956)-
plts&liths-ltd ed-scarce   (5yy6)   225.00

WAHL,NATALIE RICE-200 & other Stories-Portland,Org-1932
    (5p7)   3.25

WAINWRIGHT,GEN JONATHAN M-Gen'l Wainwright's Story-
GardenCty-1946-314p   (5x9,5x7)   3.50

WAINWRIGHT NICHOLAS B-Colonial Grandeur in Phila-Phila-
1964-169p-illus-ltd to 2000c   (5h9)   10.00

--History of the Phila Electric Co-Phila-1961-416p-illus (5y2) 4.75

--History of the Phila Nat'l Bank-Phila-1953-illus (5w9) 5.00

WAINWRIGHT,LT COMM RICHARD-Log of US Gunboat Gloucester
& Official Reports etc-Annapolis-1899-illus (5yy6,pres) 12.50

WAIT,BENJ-Letters from Van Dieman's Land-Buffalo-1843-356p-
fldg map-frontis   (5r6,dmpstn,5a3,wtrstnd) 100.00

WAIT,L-Fairchild Tropical Garden-NY-(1948)-381p (4g0) 10.00

WAITE,ARTHUR EDW-Real History of the Rosicrucians-Lond-
1887-1st ed   (5x7,wn)   16.50

WAITE,MRS C V-The Mormon Prophet & His Harem-Cambr-1866-
280p-illus-ads-orig cl-1st ed-scarce   (5g5,f)   17.50

--same-Cambr-1866-frontis-280p-3rd ed (4L0,ex-libr) 5.00

WAITE,F D,ed-San Diego,the City & the County-SanDiego-1888-
dbl pg map-col pict wrps   (5g3,f)   25.00

WAITE,FREDK CLAYTON-The Story of a Country Medical College-
Montpelier-1945-213p-ports   (5t4)   10.00

WAITE,M W-Wheelock Family of Calais,Vt-1940-175p (4t2) 15.00

WAITE,MARJORIE P-Yaddo...Yesterday &Today-SaratogaSprngs-
1933-91(2)p-illus-bds-illus   (5w0)   4.00

WAITE,OTIS F-History of Claremont 1764 to 1894-Manchstr-
1895-illus-540p-fldg map   (5e8) 19.75 (5mm3) 17.50

--New Hampshire in the Great Rebellion-Claremont-1870-part mor-
608p   (4j4)   9.50

--Vermont in the Great Rebellion-NH-1869-288p-illus-cl (5t2) 5.00

WAITE,W H-Modern Dahlia Culture-NY-1928-132p-plts-2nd ed
    (5s7)   3.50

--same-1931-col plts-3rd ed,rev   (5s7)   4.00

WAITES,K A,ed-First 50 Years Vancouver High Schools-n.p.-n.d.-
160p-illus   (4b9)   10.00

WAITING AT TABLE-By a Member of the Aristocracy-Lond-1894-
115p,(4)   (5w7)   5.00

WAITT,GEO O-3 Years with Counterfeiters,Smuglers & Boodle
Carriers-Bost-1875-436p-cl   (5h1,rbnd)   7.50

WAKE,JOAN-Brudenells of Deene-Lond-1954-illus-(2nd ed)
    (5tt5)   6.00

WAKEFIELD,HOMER-Wakefield Memorial-1897-352p (4t2) 25.00

WAKEFIELD,JOHN A-History of the War betw the US & Sac &
Fox Nations of Indians in years 1827,1831&1832-Jocksonvl-
1834-Calvin Goudy-12mo-142p-orig cl(muslin)-label-
prntd on poor paper-1st ed   (5L1,fox)   225.00

WAKEFIELD,PRISCILLA-Domestic Recreation-Phila-1805-16mo-
Jacob Johnson-orig hf roan-frontis-5 plts (5r7) 35.00

--A Family Tour thru the British Empire-Lond-1826-Harvey&Darton-
fldg frontis-469p-roan   (5c8,soil,chip) 12.50

--Instinct Displayed-Lond-CFCock-(c1830)-12mo-180p-engr-
qtr roan   (5a1)   8.50

--same-Lond-Darton&Harvey-1836-sm8vo-303p-frontis-cl-g.
    (5a1)   6.50

--Intro to Botany-Bost-1811-Belcher&Burdett-216p-12 plts-
2 fldg tables-12mo-orig sheep   (5L1)   35.00

--same-Lond-Darton,Harvey-1812-8vo-180p-11 plts-calf-6th ed
    (5a1)   12.50

--same-1831-Harvey&Darton-8vo-orig bds-handcol plts-10th ed
    (5zz8)   15.00

--Juvenile Travellers-Lond-Darton&Harvey-1801-8vo-357p-(18p)-
fldg col map-hf calf-1st ed   (5a1)   15.00

--same-Lond-1818-fldg frontis-hf roan-12 th ed (5c8,v rub) 12.50

--Mental Improvement-NewBedford-1799-Abraham Shearman-
8vo-264p-calf-1st Amer ed-rare   (5rr2,lt fox)   45.00

WAKEFIELD,RUTH G-Toll House Cook Book-Bost-1937-212p-
orig ed   (5c0)   5.00

--Ruth Wakefield's Toll House Tried & True Recipes-NY-1945-
275p-plts   (5c9)   4.00

WAKEFIELD,SHERMAN DAY-How Lincoln Became President-NY-
1936-WilsonErickson-184p-illus-ltd to 650c (5x0,autg) 7.50

WAKELEY,ARTHUR C,ed-Omaha,Gate City &Douglas Co-
Chig-1917-SJClarke-photos-part lea-2 vols   (4t3,chip)   40.00
WAKELEY,J B-The Heroes of Methodism-NY-(1856)-Carlton&Porter-
thk12mo-cl-3 ports   (5j5,autg)   10.00
--Lost Chapters Recovered from Early History of Amer Methodism-
NY-1858-594p-illus-1st ed   (4L0)   12.50
WALAM OLUM-Migration Legend of Lenni Lenape or Delaware
Indians-Indnpls-1954-I H S-4to-linen buck-t.e.g.-Lakeside Pr-
                                          (4a9,vf)   20.00
WALBRIDGE,WM-Amer Bottles Old & New-Toledo-1920-Owens
Bottle Co-illus-112p,(1)   (5w7,ex-libr)   12.50
WALCOTT,J-Figures,Descrip,& Hist,of Exotic Animals,comprised
under Classes Amphibia & Pisces of Linnaeus-Lond-1788-lea-
marbld bds-(65p)-60 plts(1st 3 crudely col)-8vo-v rare
                                          (4p6,bds wn)   100.00
WALCOTT,MARY VAUX-Illus of NoAmer Pitcherplants-Wash-1935-
Maps&15 col plts loose in orig portfolio wi silk tie-1st ed-
ltd to 500c   (5z9,f,autg)   45.   (5m6,vf)   25.00
--No Amer Wild Flowers-Wash-1925-400 col plts & text loose in
5 portfolios-1st ed-deluxe issue-ltd to 500 sets,autg
                     (5a9,f)   500.   (5z9,mint)   250.00
--same-trade ed-in 5 portfolios   (5z9,mint)   150.00
--same-NY-(1953)-in 1 vol-4to-cl   (5z9,dj)   7.50
WALD,LILLIAN D-The House on Henry Street-NY-1915-photos
                                          (5q8)   7.50
--Windows on Henry Street-Bost-1934-illus (5q8) 6.50 (5u3)   10.00
WALDACK,CHAS-Treatise of Photography on Collodion-Cinn-
1858-bds-150p-2nd ed   (5e4,wn)   14.50
WALDECK,PHILLIPP-Diary of the Amer Revolution-1907 (5L7)   3.50
WALDEN,A V-List of Birds Known to Inhabit Island of Celebes-
Lond-1872-Zoolog Soc of Lond,Vol 8,Pt 2-10 col plts-4to-
orig wrps bnd in   (4p5,rebnd)   75.00
WALDEN,ARTHUR T-Dog Puncher on the Yukon-Bost-1928-289p-
plts   (5yy9)   8.50
--same-Bost-1931-illus-289p   (4L0)   4.00
WALDEN,MARY A-The Housekeeper's Directory-NY-1858-
48p-wrps   (5c0,stnd,chip)   7.50
WALDEYER-HARTZ,HUGO VON-Admiral Von Hipper-Lond-1933-
26 illus   (5c1)   22.50
WALDMAN,L-Labor Lawyer-NY-1944   (5ff4)   7.00
WALDO,EDNA LAMOORE-Dakota,an Informal Study of Territorial
Days-Bismark-(1932)-1st ed-(200c printed) (5kk4,pres)   45.00
--same-Caldwell-1936-459p-illus
                  (4L0,f,autg) 15.   (4a5,autg,5s4,pres)   20.00
--From Travois to Iron Trail-NY-(1944)-photos-189p
                  (4b2,cov broken)   6.50   (4L0)   5.00
WALDO,FULLERTON-Down the Mackenzie Through the Great
Lone Land-NY-1923-Macmillan-251p-illus-pict cl (5r0)   7.50
--With Grenfell On The Labrador-NY-c1920-189p-illus
                                          (5w0,2 autgs)   6.50
WALDO,MYRA-Beer & Good Food-NY-1958-264p-col plts (5g9) 5.00
WALDO,S PUTMAN-Life & Character of Stephan Decatur-
Middletown-1822-calf&bds-4 plts-2nd ed,revised (5c1,fox)   25.00
--Memoirs of Andre Jackson-Hartf-1819-J&W Russell-326p-
frontis-calf-5th ed   (5qq8)   15.00
--same-Hartf-1820-12mo-lea-336p-frontis-"5th ed,imprvd"(5t2) 7.50
--Tour of James Monroe in Yr 1817-Hartford-1818-lea-288p-
1st ed   (5L3)   20.00
--same in 1817...1818 -Hartf-1820-348p-port-calf-2nd ed
                  (5L8,ex-libr) 10.   (5mm7,stn,chip)   15.00
WALDORF ASTORIA,THE-A Souvenir of-(Long IslCty)-1929-
illus-sq8vo-orig wrps-16p-orig mailing envelope-mor bndg
                                          (5ss5,vf)   10.00
WALDRON,HOLMAN D-With Pen & Camera Thro the White Mntns-
Portland,Me-1896-lg obl 4to-orig wrps-46 plts (5m6)   10.00
--same-Portland-1901-ChisholmBros-(ca 50p)-stiff paper covs
                                          (5ee3)   5.00
WALDRON,MALCOLM-Snow Man-Bost-1931-plts-292p (5s6)   7.50
WALDRON,WEBB-We Explore Great Lakes-NY-(1928)-384p-
illus   (5s1,soil)   4.50
WALDRON,WM WATSON-Pocahontas,Princess of Virginia & other
Poems-NY-1841-Dean&Trevett-12mo-cl-108p-1st ed
                                          (5j5,lacks sp)   15.00
WALDSEEMULLER,MARTIN-Cosmographiae Introductio-NY-1907-
(US Catholic Hist Soc)-maps   (5yy6)   32.50
WALDSTEIN,CHAS-Herculaneum...Past,Present&Future-Lond-
1908-sm4to-324p-illus-col maps   (5w9)   16.50
WALES,B N-Memories of Old St Andrews & Historical Sketches of
Seigniory of Argenteuil-(Lachute,1934)-illus (5w8)   17.50
WALEY,ARTHUR-Translations from the Chinese-NY-1941-Knopf-
illus   (5ee0,box) 7.50   (4k0,f)   10.00

WALFORD,LIONEL A-Marine Game Fishes of Pac Coast from
Alaska to Equator-Berkeley-1937-cl-4to-col frontis-69 plts
(37 col)-1st ed   (5h4,f,dj) 35.   (5z9,dj,f)   65.00
WALGAMOTT,CHAS S-Six Decades Back-1936-Caxton Prntrs-
illus-1st ed   (5x5,dj)   25.00
--Reminiscences of Early Days of Snake River-Vol 2 only-1927
                                          (5L7)   12.50
WALKER,A-System of Familiar Philosophy-Lond-1802-12 lectures-
2 vols-new ed-4to-49 plts   (5jj3)   17.50
WALKER,A-Woman,physiologically considered as to mind,morals,
marraige,matrimonial slavery,etc-1842-16mo
                                          (5L7,fray,v stnd)   3.00
WALKER,A EARL,MD-Penicillin In Neurology-Sprgfld,Ill-(1946)-
cl-203p-1st ed   (4t7,pres)   15.00
WALKER,A K-Braxton Bragg Comer,His Family Tree from Virginia's
Colonial Days-1947-364p   (4t2)   20.00
WALKER,ADAM-Journal of 2 campaigns of 4th Reg of US Inf in
Mich & Ind Terr...during years 1811 & 12-Keene,(NH)-1816-
Sentinel Pr-12mo-hf mor-rare   (5i0)   475.00
WALKER,ALDACE F-Vermont Brigade in the Shenandoah Valley,
1864-Burlington-1869-191p(4j4) 9.50 (5t7) 6.50 (5m6)   8.50
WALKER,ALEXANDER-Beauty.. Analysis & Classification of
Beauty in Woman-Lond-1836-illus-395p-lev mor (5p7)   15.00
--same-Lond-1852-Bohn-cl-8vo-frontis-22p plts (5p5)   35.00
WALKER,ALEXANDER-Jackson & NewOrleans-NY-1856-411p,(7)-
frontis   (5w9)   16.50
--The Life of Andrew Jackson-1858-414p   (5L3)   7.50
WALKER,ALICE-Historic Hadley-NY-1906-Grafton-130p,(5)(ads)-
frontis-6 plts-cl   (5p1,cl def) 5.   (5t9)   7.50
WALKER,ALLAN S-Middle East & Far East,Medical Series-NY-
(1959)-maps-photos-718p-1st Amer ed   (5dd6)   6.00
WALKER,AMASA-Abstract Exhibiting Condition of Banks in Mass
on 1st Sat of May,1851-Bost-1851   (4b8,ex-libr)   12.50
WALKER,ARDIS M-Garces,Pioneer Padre of Kern-(Kernville,Calif,
1946)-108p-cl&bds-ltd to 500c,nbrd,autg-illus (5dd9,rbnd)   25.00
WALKER,BENJ,ed-Life of Rear Adm J P Jones-Phila-1845-illus
                                          (5m2,rbkd)   6.50
WALKER,BEN B-The Indian Practice of Medicine-Louisville-
1847-120p   (5yy8,sl shaken)   15.00
WALKER,C-Mississippi Valley & Prehistoric Events-Burlington-
1880-784p   (5r7,wn)   25.00
--same-Burlington-1881-illus-maps-784p   (4p8,wn)   17.50
WALKER,C IRVING-The Romance of Lower Carolina-Charleston-
(1915)   (5h6)   8.00
WALKER,C M-History of Athens Co,Ohio-1869-illus-map-600p
                                          (4m4)   37.50
WALKER,REV C T-Reply to Wm Hannibal Thomas,Author of
"The Amer Negro"-(ca 1902)-31p-wrps   (5x2)   45.00
WALKER,CHAS I-The NW during the Revolution-Madison-1871-
44p-wrps-1st ed   (5L2)   5.00
WALKER,CHAS M-Sketch of Life Character & Public Serv of Oliver
P Morton-Indnpls-1878-191p-cl   (5h7,sl soil)   8.50
WALKER,COMMODORE-The Voyages & Cruises of-Lond-1928-
Cassell-illus-plts-2 maps   (5p9)   7.50
WALKER,DAVID-Storms of our Journey & Other Stories-Tor-1963
                                          (5w8)   4.00
WALKER,DAVID H-Pioneers of Prosperity-SanFran-1895-12mo-cl-
191p plus ads   (5a0)   17.50
WALKER,DUGALD STEWART-Dream Boats & Other Stories-
GardenCty-1918-Dblday,Page-8vo-frontis-219p-19 plts-cl-
ports-1st ed   (5p1,rub)   10.00
--same-1924-cl   (5p1,lt soil)   4.50
WALKER,EDWIN FRANCIS-5 Prehistoric Archaeological Sites in
Los Angeles Co,Calif-LosAng-1951-R8vo-116p-illus-stiff wrps
                                          (5dd6)   3.50
WALKER,ELLA JACOBY-Fortress North-Montreal-1956-illus-
frontis-436p   (5dd5,lt spots)   8.00
WALKER,ERNEST GEO-48 Gridiron Years-Wash-1933 (5x0)   6.50
WALKER,F-A Literary History of Southern Calif-Berkeley&LosAng-
1950-271p-illus-1st ed   (5a9,f,dj)   7.50
WALKER,F-Statistics of Wealth & Industry of the US-1870-
folio-buck   (5L7,rbnd)   25.00
WALKER,F D,CAPT-Log of The Kaalokai-Hawaiian Gazette Co-
1909-64p plus map-illus-wrps-6 x 8 1/2"   (5r0)   7.50
WALKER,FRANCIS A-General Hancock-NY-1894-Appleton-
illus-t.e.g.-332p,8p   (5mm8,pres)   7.50
--History of 2nd Army Corps in Army of Potomac-NY-1886-
Scribner's-737p-port-maps   (5mm8,pres)   10.00
--Making of the Nation,1783 to 1817-Lond-1896-maps-314p
                                          (5dd4)   3.50
--Memorial of Philip Henry Sheridan from The City of Boston-
Bost-1889-mor-a.e.g.-121p-ltd ed   (4j4)   8.50
--Statistical Atlas of US-n.p.-1874-Julius Bien,lith-folio-
qtr mor   (4b6,ex-libr)   60.00

WALKER,FRANKLIN-A Literary History of Southern Calif-
Berkeley-1950-282p-8vo-1st ed-Chronicles of Calif Series
(5F9,f,dj) 7.50 (5g5,f,dj) 5.00
--San Francisco's Literary Frontier-NY-1943-AlfredKnopf-8vo-
cl-400p-illus (5x5,dj,orig Mss pg insert) 25. (5x5,dj) 17.50
(5h5,dj,5ss9,f,dj) 12.50
--Seacoast of Bohemia,Account of Early Carmel-SanFran-1966-
Book Club of Calif (4a5) 17.50
--same-SanFran-1966-sm4to-ltd to 500c-Book Club of Calif
(5h5,mint,wi prospectus) 35.00
--The Washoe Giant in San Francisco-SanFran-1938-GeoFields-
8vo-bds&cl (5h4,f) 12.50
WALKER,GEO-Cribbage Made Easy-NY-n.d.-143p,(28)-12mo-
pict bds (5w7,scuff) 3.50
WALKER,G F-Person(s) Lineage-(1951)-192p (4t2) 20.00
WALKER,G L-Hist of First Church,Hartford,Conn-1884-503p
(4t2) 12.50
WALKER,HAYES,ed-Where Herefords Are Produced to Supply
the Nation wi Beef-Marfa,Texas-1919-Breeders Prntng Co,
KansCty,Mo-(70p)-photos-wrps-Highland Hereford Breeders
Assoc-rare pamphlet -11" x 6" (5L5) 75.00
WALKER,HOVENDEN-A Journal,or Full Acct of Late Exped to
Canada-Lond-1720-Browne-1st ed
(5e2) 350. (5n9) 225. (4L8) 375.00
--Walker Exped to Quebec-Tor-1953-Champlain Soc-plts-maps-
441p (4d4) 35.00
WALKER,HUGH-The Greater Victorian Poets-Lond-1895-8vo-
cl-332p (5t0) 5.00
WALKER,ISAAC-Dress,As It Has Been,Is,& Will Be-NY-1885-
210p,(1)-illus (5n7) 8.50
WALKER,JAS B-Experiences of Pioneer Life in Early Settlements
& Cities of The West-Chig-1881 (4a5) 15.00
WALKER,JAS B-The Epic of Amer Industry-NY-1949-513p (5y2) 4.50
WALKER,COL JAS D,comp-Penna at Andersonville,Georgia-
n.p.-1905-94p-illus (5w5) 5.00
WALKER,JANET-Vegetarian Cookery Book-Lond-(1959)-220p
(4g0) 5.00
WALKER,JEANIE MORT-Life of Capt Jos Fry,The Cuban Martyr-
Hartf-1875-JBBurr-589p-a.e.g.
(5v6,marg dmpstn) 7.50 (5s1,bkstrp wn) 15.00
WALKER,JOHN-Great Amer Paintings from Smibert to Bellows-
Lond&NY-1943-Oxford Univ Pr-104 illus-31p
(4a0) 17.50 (5ww3) 22.50
WALKER,JOHN-Critical Pronouncing Dictionary & Expositor
of the English Language-Lond-1791-sml folio (4j6,rbkd) 45.00
--Elements of Elocution-Bost-1810-DMallory-8vo-orig calf-
port-2 plts-379p (5j5) 15.00
WALKER,JOHN-Treatise on Baptism-Mtpleasant-1824-274p-lea-
errata (5y0,fox) 22.50
WALKER,JUDSON E-Campaigns of Gen'l Custer in the NW &
Final Surrender of Sitting Bull-NY-1881-illus-135p plus ads-
cl-scarce (5kk4,f,5dd1) 100.00
WALKER,LYDIA LeB-Home Craft Rugs-NY-1929-421p-17 photos
(5n7,ex-libr) 5.00
WALKER,M-For My People-Poetry-Yale Univ-1942 (5x2) 12.50
WALKER,MARY E-HIT-NY-(1871)-177p,(6)-frontis
(5w7,libr labl,stnd,wn) 15.00
WALKER,MRS MARY S-Rev Dr Willoughby & His Wine-NY-1869-
458p-illus-1st ed (5i3,cl damage) 12.50
WALKER,ROBT S-Lookout, Story of a Mountain-Kingsport-1941-
(5h6) 4.50
--Torchlight to the Cherokees-NY-1931-1st ed-fldg map-v scarce
(5L2,dj,pres) 27.50 (5kk7,underline) 12.50
(5dd1,e.p.writing) 17.50
WALKER,SHIRLEY-Margaret Hall Walker-SanFran-1952-cl-75p-
fldg map-map-illus-priv prntd-ltd to 135c(for the family)
(5r0) 100.00
WALKER,STANLEY-City Editor-NY-1934 (5x7) 5.00
--Home to Texas-NY-c1956-307p-1st ed
(5n4,pres) 6.50 (5w9,dj) 3.50
--Mrs Astor's Horse-NY-1935-illus-errata slip-1st ed
(5u3) 2.50 (5b1) 3.00
--The Night Club Era-NY-1933-4to-327p-frontis (5w6,fade) 8.50
WALKER,T C-The Honey Pod Tree-NY-1958 (5x2) 8.50
WALKER,THOS-The Art of Dining & the Art of Attaining High
Health-Phila-1837-ELCarey&AHart-267p-orig cl-sml 16mo-
1st ed (5L8,ex-libr,rprd,chip) 18.50
WALKER,TACETTA B-Stories of Early Days in Wyo-Casper-(1936)-
maps-268p plus index-scarce (4L0) 40.00
WALKER,W H-Odd Fellowship in America & in Texas-Dallas-
1911-512p (4j7) 25.00
WALKER,GEN'L WM-The War in Nicaragua-Mobile&NY-1860-
col fldg map-port-431p (5r0,lacks map) 20. (5t7) 25. (5ss2) 27.50

WALKER,WM C-History of 18th Reg,Conn Vol in War for Union-
Noriwch-1885-444p (5j6,stns) 8.50
WALKER'S MANLY EXERCISES-Lond-1847-sm8vo-267p-cl-
44 plts-revised-8th ed (5c8,f) 15.00
WALKINSHAW,LEWIS C-Annals of SoWestern Penna-NY-(1939)-
4 vols-illus-4to (5m2) 35.00
WALKINSHAW,ROBT-On Puget Sound-NY-1929-294p-illus
(5L2,dj,lacks e.p.) 5. (4n9) 7.50
--same-NY-1930-illus-294p (5s4) 5.00
WALKLEY,A B-More Prejudice-NY-1923-Knopf-255p (5p9) 5.00
WALKUP,FAIRFAX P-Dressing the Part-NY-1938-lg8vo-cl-
illus-1st ed (5p5) 15.00
WALL,A J-Sketch of Life of Horatio Seymour,1810 to 1886-
NY-1929-111p-ltd to 300c,nbrd (4j4) 9.50
WALL,BERNHARDT-Following Abraham Lincoln 1809 to 1865-
LimeRock-1943-415p-illus-1st ed (5w5) 10.00
WALL,C A-Historic Boston Tea Party of Dec 16,1773-Worcester-
1896-88p-wrps (5t1) 5.00
WALL,F-How to Identify the Snakes of India-Karachi-1923-
cl&bds-56p-illus-folio (4p6,rebnd,sm worm holes) 25.00
--Snakes of Ceylon(Ophidia Taprobanica)-Colombo-1921-cl-
591p-map-8vo-scarce (4p6) 97.80
WALL,REV HENRY-Fashion,A Humorous & Satirical Poem,in 2 parts-
Richmond-1870-West&Johnston-8vo-wrps-errata slip
(5b2,cov stn) 10.00
WALL,M-Splinters from an African Log-Chig-1963-Moody Pr-
illus (5x2,dj) 3.50
WALL,O A-Sex & Sex Worship-StL-1920-608p-illus (5t4) 10.00
--same-StL-1922-R8vo-orig blu cl-illus (5t4) 9.50
WALL,OSCAR GARRETT-Recollections of the Sioux Massacre-
(LakeCty,Minn)-1909-ports-illus-288p-priv prntd-1st ed
(5dd9) 26.50
WALL,WM E-Graining Ancient & Modern-Somerville,Mass-1905-
137p-illus (5t4) 12.50
WALLA WALLA VALLEY,WASH-WallaWalla-(1910)-Comm Club-
64p-photos (5L0) 5.00
WALLACE,A E-Land Cruising & Prospecting-Columbus,Ohio-(1908)-
sm12mo-illus-175p (5t2) 3.75
WALLACE,ALFRED R-Darwinism-Lond&NY-(1897)-494p-map&illus
(5t4) 7.50
--Is Mars Habitable?-Lond-1907-110p-frontis (5t4) 10.00
--Island Life or the Phenomena & Causes of Insular Faunas
& Floras-Lond-1895-Macmillan-563p-map-2nd rev ed (5P1) 10.00
--The Malay Archipelago-NY-1869-638p-maps-illus
(5w3,fox,crack) 7.50
--Natural Selection & Tropical Nature-Lond-1895-8vo-new ed wi
corr (5m6) 10.00
WALLACE,ANTHONY F C-King of the Delawares,Teedyuscung-
1949-U of Pa Pr-291p plus index-1st ed (5L2,dj) 8.50
WALLACE,MRS CHANDOS-366 Menus-Lond-(ca 1885)-(8),166p,
(18)p-pict cl (5c9) 15.00
WALLACE,CHAS-Confession of the Awful & Bloody Transactions
in Life of-NewOrl-1851-wrps-32p-illus (5m6) 37.50
WALLACE,D D-Constitutional Hist of SoCar from 1725 to 1775-
Abbevl-1899-93p-wrps (5h7) 7.50
WALLACE,DILLON-Beyond the Mexican Sierras-Chig-1910-illus-
map-lg8vo-cl-301p (5t2) 4.00
--The Camper's Handbook-NY-(1936)-illus-289p (5c5,ex-libr) 3.50
--Long Labrador Trail-NY-1907-illus-1st ed-Outing Pub Co
(5dd4,cov spots) 4.50 (5tt5) 6.00
--Lure of the Labrador Wild-NY-(1905)-illus-fldg maps-340p-
1st ed (5dd4) 4.50
--same-NY-(1905)-illus-maps-6th ed (5ee2) 2.50
--Packing & Portaging-NY-1916-Outing-illus-133p-ads
(5dd7,f) 4.00
--Saddle & Camp in the Rockies-NY-1911-Outing Pub-1st ed-
302p-illus (5i3) 12.50 (5L0) 6.50
WALLACE,SIR DONALD M-Web of Empire-Lond-1902-4to-504p-
78 plts-map (5a1) 8.50
WALLACE,E-Comanche Lords of the South Plains-(1952)-U Okla-
381p-illus-1st ed (4i7,dj) 10. (4k5,f,dj) 12.50
WALLACE,E R-Descriptive Guide to the Adirondacks-Syracuse-
1894-522p-illus-map-rev&enlrgd ed (5p9) 7.50
WALLACE,E S-Destiny & Glory-1957-illus (5L7) 6.50
WALLACE,EDGAR-Bosambo of the River-Lond-n.d.-Ward Lock-
253p (4t5) 5.00
WALLACE,EDGAR-Thief in the Night-NY-n.d.-World Wide
Pub Co (5ii1,dj) 7.50
WALLACE,EDGAR-Writ in Barracks-Lond-1900-12mo-cl-1st ed
of auth's 1st book (5gg6,f) 25.00
WALLACE,EDW S-The Great Reconnaissance-Bost-(1955)-300p-
map-illus-1st ed (4j6) 5. (4L0,dj) 7.50 (5dd4) 8.50

WALLACE,FREDK WM-Roving Fisherman-Gardenvale,Que-1955-
4to-plts-port-512p   (5s0)   15.00
--Wooden Ships & Iron Men-NY-ca 1925-illus-thk8vo-cl (4b6) 20.00
WALLACE,GEO A-From Taps to Reveille-BowlingGreen-1895-
198p   (4p8,pres) 7.50
WALLACE,GRAHAM-Flight of Sir John Alcock & Sir Arthur
Whitten Brown,Jun 14 to 25,1919-NY-1956-8vo-cl-plts-
1st ed   (5p5)   12.50
WALLACE,HELEN B-Historic Paxton(Pa)....1722 to 1913-1913-
illus   (4m4)   10.00
WALLACE,HENRY A-New Frontiers-NY-1934-12mo-cl-314p-1st ed
                         (5q8,soil) 3.   (5t0)   4.50
--Soviet Asia Mission-NY-c1946-254p-illus-map-cl (5w4,soil) 3.50
--Whose Constitution-NY-1936-12mo-cl-336p (5t0,spots) 4.00
WALLACE,HENRY W-Letters to the Iowa Farm Folk-DesMoines-
1915-8vo-stiff wrps-96p   (5m8,chip) 15.00
--Uncle Henry's Own Story of His Life-DesMoines-1917-Vol 1-
8vo-119p-frontis-8vo-v scarce   (5m8,chip) 25.00
--same-Vol 2, 1859 to 1877-DesMoines-1918-8vo-cl-129p-
v scarce   (5m8)   25.00
WALLACE,HORACE BINNEY-Literary Criticisms....& other papers-
Phila-1856-460p   (5w9,edge wn) 6.50
WALLACE CO,HUGH-Manufacturers of Coats, Gloves,Mitts etc-
Detroit-1913-40p-illus   (5h8)   5.75
WALLACE,IRVING-The Fabulous Originals-NY-1955-Knopf-
8vo-pink bds-cl bk-318p   (5aa2)   4.50
WALLACE,ISABEL-Life & Letters of Gen'l W H L Wallace-Chig-
1909-DonnelleySons-231p-illus-cl   (5r0,pres) 10.00
WALLACE,J N-The Wintering Partners on Peace River-1805-
fldg map   (5w8)   25.00
WALLACE,JOHN-Carpetbag Rule in Florida-Kennesaw-1959-
Continental Book Co   (5x2)   10.00
WALL,JN A-Wall's Hist of Jefferson Co,Ill-Indnpls-1909-618p-
3/4 lea   (5h2)   50.00
WALLACE,JOHN H,JR-A Romance Treating of Disfranchisement
of the Negro etc-NY-1904-8vo-1st ed   (5ss5,pres) 10.00
WALLACE,JOS-Sketch of Life & Public Serv of Edw D Baker-
Springfield-1870-cl-port-144p   (4L8) 15. (5r0)   10.00
WALLACE,LEW-Ben Hur,a Tale of the Christ-(NY,1880)-1st ed,
1st issue(wi dated title pg,lt blu floral cl,prntg error pg 11,
li 37)   (4F0,f,box) 175.00
--same-NY-1880-12mo-dec cl-552p,12p-1st ed
                                  (5m8,cov wn,chip) 35.00
--same-NY-1960-Heritage Pr-486p-illus-boxed (5p7)   10.00
--The Fair God-Bost-1873-12mo-cl-1st ed of auth's 1st book-
1st state(thin papr)(4c4,mint) 65. (5p6) 15. (5gg6,f) 25.00
--same-Bost-1873-12mo-cl   (4c2,autg faded,shaken) 15.00
--same-Bost-1888-586p   (5t4)   5.00
--Lew Wallace,An Autobiography-NY-1906-2 vols-illus
                         (5p0) 7.50   (5x5)   15.00
--Life of Gen'l Ben Harrison-Phila-(1888)-1st ed-illus (5L3,f) 7.50
--Prince of India-NY-1893-Harper-2 vols-12mo-1st ed
                         (4b7) 7.50   (5m2)   6.50
WALLACE,LILY H-The New Amer Etiquette-NY-1941-900p-
illus   (5w7)   2.50
--Rumford Common Sense Cook Book-n.p.-n.d.-64p-illus (5g9) 3.00
--Sea Food Cookery-NY-(1944)-179p   (5c9)   3.50
--Soups,Stews & Chowders-NY-(1945)-248p   (5c9)   4.00
--Woman's World Cook Book-Chig-(1931)-468p-illus-lg4to
                                           (5c9,f)   5.00
WALLACE,MILDRED YOUNG-We Three,papa's ladies-SanAntonio-
(1957)-102p   (5dd4)   3.50
WALLACE,PAUL A W-Blunder Camp-n.p.-1963-10p-map-orig wrps
                                           (5m2)   3.00
--Historic Indian Paths of Penna-n.p.-n.d.-Penna Historical Reprint-
29p-fldg map-orig wrps   (5m2)   3.50
--The Muhlenbergs of Penna-U of Penna-1950-port
                         (5q8,dj) 7.   (5m2)   7.50
--Penna....Seed of a Nation-NY-1962-322p-maps (5w4,dj) 5.00
--White Roots of Peace-1946   (5L7)   3.00
WALLACE,PHILIP B-Colonial Ironwork in Old Philadelphia-NY-
(1930)-photos-lg4to-147p
           (5m5) 45. (5n7) 37.50 (4m4) 35. (4m7)   27.50
WALLACE,SUSAN E-Land of the Pueblos-NY-1888-illus-285p-
1st ed   (4b2,sl shake) 8.50 (5kk7) 15. (5dd1) 7.50
--same-Troy-1889-illus-285p   (5dd4) 6. (4i7)   8.00
WALLACE,W S-The Knight of Dundern-Tor-1960-Rous&MannPr-
22p-illus-dec bds-priv distri only   (5w8)   15.00
--Merchants Clerk in Upper Canada-Tor-1935-26p-stiff wrps
                                           (4b9,sp sl tn) 10.00
--The Pedlars of Quebec,& Other Papers on the Nor'westers-
Tor-(1954)-illus -101p-   (4f9) 7.50   (5w8)   7.50

WALLACE,W S   (continued)
--Ryerson Imprint-Tor-1954-141p   (4b9)   10.00
WALLACE,WADSWORTH-Paul Bunyan & His Great Blue Ox-NY-
1940-238p-illus   (5s4,dj,ex-libr) 5.00
WALLACE,WILLARD M-Traitorous Hero-NY-(1954)-illus-1st ed
                                           (5q8,mint) 5.00
WALLACE,WM-The Battle of Tippecanoe,Triumphs of Science &
Other Poems-Cinn-1837-P McFarlin-(c1837)-mor-106p-
12mo-rare   (4h6,rbnd,rprd) 150.00
WALLACE,WM-Epicureanism-Lond-1880-272p   (5p7)   3.50
WALLACE,WM-Life of Arthur Schopenhauer-1890 (5L7)   3.00
WALLACE,WM-Liszt,Wagner & the Princess-NY-1927-Dutton-
illus   (5p0)   5.00
WALLACE,WM H-Speeches & Writings of-KansCty,Mo-1914-
308p-1st ed-scarce (5p0,pencil) 5. (4L0) 8.50 (5w9) 22.50
WALLACE,WM J-Fair Oaks,1st Annual Reunion of Survivors' Assoc,
23d Penna Vols,Phila,1882-Phila-1883-8vo-orig wrps-54p
                                           (5m6)   8.50
WALLACE,WM KAY-Greater Italy-NY-1917   (5x7)   5.00
WALLACE,WM S-Antoine Robidoux 1794 to 1860-LosAng-1953-
60p-col frontis-Castle Pr-450c prntd-Early Calif Travels Ser,
Vol 14   (5t1)   25.00
WALLACE,WM SWILLING-Journey Through NewMexico's 1st Dist in
1864-LosAng-(1956)-Westernlore Pr-Great West & Indian Ser 6-
12mo-cl-ltd to 350c   (5F5)   12.50
WALLACE'S AMER TROTTING REGISTER-Chig-1893-Vol 12-8vo-
cl-911p   (5t0)   12.00
--same-Vol 15-Chig-1901-8vo-cl-791p   (5t0)   12.00
--same-NY&Chig-1871 thru 1916-Vols 1 thru 21-21 vols-plts
                                (5t7) post extra   300.00
WALLACE'S YEAR BOOK-of Trotting & Pacing-Vols 22 thru 32-
Chig-1907 to 1917-11 vols-8vo-cl   (5t4) ea vol 12.50
WALLACH,S,ed-Narr of Exped of an Amer Squadron to China Seas
& Japan under Command of Perry-NY-1952-305p (5a9)   3.50
WALLACK,LESTER-Memories of 50 Years-NY-1889-Scribner's-cl-
14p plus 232p-ports-facs   (5r0)   7.50
WALLACK-MORRELL,T H-Sketch of the Life of Jas Wm Wallack(sr),
late actor & manager-NY-1865-THMorrell-lg4to-orig wrps-
61p,(1)-ltd 50c,nbrd-lg papr   (5L1,wrps loose)   15.00
WALLANT,EDW L-The Children at the Gate-Harcourt,Brace-
1964-1st ed   (5ss7,vf,dj) 15. (5ss9,f,dj)   10.00
WALLBRIDGE,W G-Desc of Henry Wallbridge-1898-369p (4t2) 22.50
WALLEN,HENRY D-Report,Exped in 1859 from Dalles City to
Great Salt Lake & Back-Wash-1860-fldg map-51p-1st ed
                                           (4n4)   30.00
WALLEN,JAS-From Ox Cart to Aeroplane-Buffalo,NY-(1918)-
50p-ports-plts   (5dd4)   6.00
WALLER,DR ERIC-Bibliotheca Walleriana catalog-1955-2 vols-
comp by H Sallander-4to-buck   (5L7,rbnd) 60.00
WALLER,EDMUND-Works...in Verse & Prose-Lond-1729-Fenton-
4to-frontis-calf   (5b0,rprd) 75.00
WALLER,ELBERT-Illinois Pioneer Days-Litchfld-1918-80p-wrps
                                           (5h1)   5.00
WALLER,GEO-Kidnap,the Story of the Lindbergh Case-NY-1961-
illus-597p   (5q0,dj) 7.50 (5p9)   5.00
WALLER,HORACE,ed-The Last Journals of David Livingstone in
Central Africa-NY-1875-Harper-map-illus-541p (4t5) 10.00
WALLERSTEIN LABORATORIES-Bottle Beer Quality-NY-(1948)-
4to-161p-illus   (5w1)   5.00
WALLICK,EKIN-The Small House for a Moderate Income-NY-1915-
4to-photos-plans-96p   (5w7)   5.00
WALLIHAN,A G-Camera Shots at Big Game-NY-1904-75 photos-
pict cl-1st ed   (5d2)   10.00
--Hoofs,Claws & Antlers of the Rocky Mntns-Denver-1894-(ca 40p)-
folio-photos   (5n4)   25.00
WALLING & GRAY,comp-Official Topographical Atlas of
Massachusetts-(Bost)-1871-calf&cl-folio
           (4c1,lea wn) 25.   (5w0,rub)   32.50
--Penna,New Topographical Atlas wi Descrip Hist,Scientific &
Statistical-1872-folio-hf lea   (4t2)   30.00
WALLING,GEO W-Recollections of a NY Chief of Police...etc-
n.p.-1890-679p plus ads-photos   (4L0,sl wn)   20.00
WALLING,H F-also see WALLING & GRAY
WALLING,H F-Atlas of the State of Michigan-Detroit-(1873)-
col maps-folio   (5r7,ex-libr) 90.00
--Map of the United Counties of Leeds & Grenville,Canada West-
Kingston,C W-1861,62-63x59 inches,on linen-inset illus
                                           (5w8)   150.00
--Official Topographical Atlas of Mass,corr by-(Bost)-1871(4c1) 25.00
WALLING,WM E-Socialists & the War-1915   (5L7)   3.50
--State Socialism,Pro & Con-NY-(1917)-693p (5t4)   7.50
WALLING,WM H,ed-Sexology-Phila-1902   (5x7)   4.75

WALLINGFORD MFG CO-Hand Farming & Garden Tools,
Catalog-Wallingford-1905-8vo-48p-illus-wrps-Catalog C
(5t4)   4.00
WALLINGTON,NELL   U-Historic Churches of America-NY-1907-
259p-illus-1st ed   (5w5) 10.   (5h9)   7.50
WALLIS,FRANK E-How to know architecture-NY&Lond-1910-
326p-plts-4to-cl   (5m5,shake,ex-libr)   9.00
WALLIS,GEO A-Cattle Kings of the Staked Plains-Dallas-(1957)-
photos-180p   (5dd1,mint,dj)   7.50
WALLIS,J-Panorama of England & Wal es-Lond-ca1810-thk16mo-
116p-pict bds-53 hand col maps   (5v0,hng rprd)   25.00
WALLIS,J P R-Fitz-Lond-1955-illus   (5x2,dj)   4.50
--One Man's Hand-Lond-1950-Longmans Green-254p (4t5,dj)   8.00
WALLIS,MRS JONNIE LOCKHART,ed-Sixty Years on Brazos-
LosAng-1930-priv prnt-ltd to 200c,autg   (4c7)   250.00
WALLKILL VALLEY RWY-Articles of Assoc & Laws-Newburgh-
1871-37p-prntd wrps   (5r7,fray)   10.00
WALLMEYER,BRUNO-Pelztragende Tiere...Fur Bearing Animals-
Frankfurt-1951-12mo-215p-5 maps-78 plts-1st ed-Ger & Engl,
text-1st ed   (5w4)   10.00
WALLSTROM,TORD-A Wayfarer in Central Amer-NY-1955-Roy-
192p-illus   (5p0)   5.00
WALMSLEY,H R,ed-The State of Missouri,Its Story-(KansCty,1932)-
photos-495p-1st ed   (5dd1)   7.50
WALMSLEY,LEO-British Ports & Harbours-Lond-1946-48p-
8 col plts   (5s1,dj,warp)   2.50
WALN,ROBT,JR-Life of the Marquis De La Fayette in War of
the Rev-Phila-1825-450p-3 plts-lea-1st ed   (5ee3)   17.50
WALPOLE,F G-Lord Floysham,a novel-Lond-1886-Chapman&Hall-
2 vols-8vo-orig cl-1st ed-errata   (5xx6,f)   30.00
WALPOLE,HORACE-Bibliography of-NewHaven-1948-illus-8vo-cl
(4c1,f)   50.00
--Catalogue of Engravers,Who Have Been Born, or Resided in
England-StrawberryHill-1763-8vo-lea-128p,20p-ports (5t7)   50.00
--same-Lond-1794   (5ii3,lacks port,rbnd,worn)   15.00
--Catalogue of Royal & Noble Authors of England-Lond-1759-
Dodsley-2nd ed-2 vols-calf-frontis   (5u6)   35.00
--Journal of Printing Office at Strawberry Hill-Lond &NY-1923-
Chiswick Pr-4to-bds&lea-ltd to 650c-12 plts (5ee9,box)   30.00
--Letters of-Lond-n.d.(ca 1904)-16mo-frontis-port-849p(thin papr)-
3/4 mor   (5t0)   5.00
--Lord Orford's reminiscences-Lond-1818-for John Sharpe-
12mo-hf calf-port   (5i8)   15.00
--Memoirs of the last 10 Years of Reign of Geo the Second-
Lond-1822-JnMurray-2 vols-4to-calf&bds-extra illus wi
204 ports laid in to size   (5b0,fox)   200.00
WALPOLE,HUGH-The Gateway of Literature-Lond-1934-8vo-
dec orange cl-1022p-plts-Daily Express Publ   (5aa2)   4.50
--Rogue Herries-GardenCty-1930-Doubleday,Doran-1st ed
(5i4,autg,dj)   10.00
--same-Lond-1930-8vo-bds-cl bk papr labls-1st ed-lg papr-
ltd to 200c,autg   (5dd8)   20.00
--The Silver Thorn,a Book of Stories-Lond-1928-lg papr-
ltd to 175c,autg   (5mm2)   15.00
--The Wooden Horse-Lond-1909-12mo-cl-1st ed of auth's 1st book-
2nd issue(with John Murray's imprint on t.p.&at bottom of sp)
(5gg6,vf)   15.00
WALPOLE-BOND,JOHN-History of Sussex Birds-Lond-(1938)-
cl-g.t.-thk8vo-53 col plts-3 vols   (5z9,dj)   30.00
WALSH,BENJ D-First Annual Report on Noxious Insects of State
of Illinois-Chig-1868-Prairie Farmer Co-8vo-104p-plt-wrps
(5j5)   15.00
WALSH,BRANDON-Little Annie Rooney on the Highway to
Adventure-Racine-c1938-Whitman-pic bds-48mo-425p,3p ads-
Big Little Book #1406   (5p1)   5.00
WALSH,E A-Total Power   (5L7)   6.50
WALSH,EDW S-Canal System of NY State-1920(reissue,revised)-
fldg col maps-28p   (4m2,soil)   10.00
WALSH,GEO ETHELBERT-Friend of the Seminole-Elgin-n.d.-(c1911)-
(4a9)   8.00
WALSH,FRANCES-That Eager Zest-Phila&NY-(1961)-Lippincott-
252p-1st ed   (5p1,dj)   3.50
WALSH,HENRY L-Hallowed Were the Gold Dust Trails-SantaClara-
1946-photos-1st ed   (5dd1)   15.00
--same-Univ of SantaClara-(1947)-cl-559p-illus-maps-2nd prntg
(5h5,vf,dj)   10.00
WALSH,JAS J-Our Amer Cardinals-NY-1926-Appleton-352p
(5p0)   7.50
--The 13th,Greatest of Centuries-NY-1924-illus-lg8vo-cl-430p
(5t2)   4.50
WALSH,JOS M-Tea,Its History & Mystery-Phila-1892-priv prnt-
1st ed-illus-265p   (4a9,pres) 20. (4g9,rub)   10.00

WALSH,M C-Brave Ben,or the Brunt of Battle-NY-May 19,1888-
self wrps-23p-War Libr #297   (4h7,sl stns)   7.50
WALSH,MARIE T-The Mission of the Passes-LosAng-1930-illus-
8vo-1st ed   (4g6) 7.50   (5x5)   10.00
WALSH,MICHAEL-New System of Mercantile Arithmetic-
Newburyport,Mass-1806-12mo-lea-274p   (5t0,sp wn)   8.50
--same-Pittsburgh-1812-lea-249p(3)-2nd Pittsburgh ed (5ff7)   20.00
WALSH,R J,ed-Adventures of Marco Polo-NY-1948-4to-col plts
(5yy6)   7.50
WALSH,RICHARD J-The Making of Buffalo Bill-Indnpls-(1928)-
illus-orig cl   (4L0) 8.50   (5m9)   12.50
WALSH,ROBT-Appeal from the Judgements of Great Britain Respecting
the US-Phila-1819-112p-1st ed (5ee3,f) 35. (4m4,rebnd)   25.00
--Amer Register-Vols 1,2(all pub)-1807,08-hf mor-blind stmp
(5L7)   25.00
--Works of The British Poets with Lives,etc-Phila-1819-16mo-
calf-43 vols(of 48?)   (5qq4)   79.00
WALSH,ROBT-Constantinople & Scenery of 7 Churches of Asia
Minor-Lond-ca1840-2 vols-4to-plts-hf calf   (4b6,wn)   45.00
WALSH,SOPHIE-History & Romance of San Juan Islands-Anacortes,
Wash-1932-24p-wrps   (5yy3)   3.00
WALSH,STUART P-13 Years of Scout adventure-Seattle-1923-
174p-priv pub-Lowman&Hanford   (5u3)   3.00
WALSH,W-Secret History of the Oxford Movement-1898-4th ed
(5L7,sp wn)   7.50
WALSH,ZACK-Points in Time-LosAng-1963-Press Baza-orig wrps-
ltd to 500c,nbrd   (5ss9,f)   5.00
WALSINGHAM,CHARLOTTE-Annette,or,chronicles of Bellevue-
Phila-1875-Claxton,Remsen&Haffelfinger-1st ed
(5m2,wn,shake)   5.00
--O'er moor & fen,a novel-Phila-1876-Claxton,Remsen&Haffelfinger-
1st ed   (5m2,rub)   10.00
WALTER,CORNELIA W-Mount Auburn Illustrated-NY-1847-
RMartin-4to-plts-orig mor-floral designs-119p&4p list of
subscr   (5j5,fox)   25.00
WALTER,ELLERY-The World on One Leg-NY-1928-336p-48 illus-
(5dd4,autg,sl stn)   5.00
WALTER,ERICH-Manual For The Essence Industry-NY-1916-
427p   (5w1,hng broke)   8.50
WALTER,FRANK K-Abbrev & Technical Terms Used in Book
Catalogs-Bost-1912-12mo-cl   (4c1,wn)   7.50
WALTER,H-Moses Mendelssohn,Critic & Philosopher-NY-1930-
220p   (5p7)   3.75
WALTER,JAS-Memorials of Wash & of Mary,His Mother & Martha,
His Wife-NY-1887-8vo-ports   (5ss5)   12.50
WALTER,PAUL A F,JR-Race & Culture Relations-NY-1952 (5x7)   7.50
WALTER,RICHARD-Anson's Voyage Around the World 1740 to 44-
Lond-n.d.(ca 1900)-220p-dec cov   (5s1,ex-libr,pres)   3.00
WALTER,WILL-A half century of Nu Sigma Nu, 1882 to 1932-
n.p.-1934-2 vols   (5v6)   15.00
WALTER,WM B-Five Books in One Volume-(FtWayne)-1894
(5ff7)   15.00
WALTER,WM W-The Great Understander-Aurora,Ill-(1931)-12mo-
ports-priv prntd-scarce-1st ed (4L0) 12.50 (5xx5,sl wtrstn)   18.50
WALTERS,LORENZO D-Tombstone's Yesterdays-Tucson-1928-
illus-293p-1st ed
(5dd1,ink) 50. (4L0,wn dj) 75. (5kk4,vf,dj)   60.00
WALTERS,MADGE HARDIN-Early Days & Indian Ways-LosAng-
(1956)-254p-photos-1st ed   (5L0,dj)   7.50
WALTERS,RAYMOND-The Bethlehem Bach Choir-Bost-1918-
t.e.g.-illus-pict g.cl-290p-1st ed   (5w9)   5.00
WALTHER,C F-Resources & advantages of State of Nebraska-n.p.
(Omaha)-n.d.-(1871)-8vo-orig prntd wrps-fldg map-1st ed
(5i0,sp rprd)   40.00
WALTHER,C F W-Die rechte Gestalt einer vom Staate etc-StL-
1864-228p   (5L0,wn)   6.50
WALTHERS,W K-Handbook for Model Railroaders-Wauwatosa-1937-
124p-illus   (5dd4)   3.00
WALTON,ALICE WORTHEN-One woman's life-Atlanta-1900-
Franklin Pr &Pub Co-(rev ed)-illus   (5m2)   10.00
WALTON,AUGUSTUS Q-Hist of Detection,Conviction,Life &
Design of Jn A Murel-Cinn-n.d.-(1850's)-84p-illus-scarce
(5h2,bds) 20. (5L2,wrps)   50.00
WALTON,CLYDE C-Private Smith's Journal,Recollections of the
Late War-Chig-1963-Lakeside Classics   (5x5)   12.50
WALTON,C S-Civil Law in Spain & Spanish America-Wash-1900
(5ff4,rebnd)   25.00
WALTON,E L-Some Desc of Daniel Clark of Windsor,Conn-1913-
278p   (4t2)   12.50
WALTON,EDA LOU-Dawn Boy-NY-(1926)-bds-8vo   (4m8)   12.50
WALTON,FRANCIS,ed-Airman's Almanac-NY-1945-wrps-
512p   (4h4,soil)   5.00

WALTON,FRANK L-Pillars of Yonkers-NY-1951-illus (5tt5) 6.00
--From Tomahawks to Textiles-NY-(1953)-illus-177p
 (5tt5) 5. (5p9) 4. (5e4) 4.75
WALTON, GEO-Flower Finder-Phila-(1916)-394p-col plts-
2nd ed (4g0) 7.50
WALTON, ISAAC-Lives of Dr John Donne;Sir Henry Watton;Mr
Richard Hooker, Mr Geo Herbert & Dr Robt Sanderson-York-
1796-4to-518p-8 ports-calf (5aa0,sl rub) 45.00
--same-Lond-1903-403p-Chiswick Pr (5k0) 6.00
WALTON, IZAAK-The Compleat Angler-Lond-1750-illus-sm8vo-
calf (4c2) 50.00
--same-Lond-1760-(ed by John Hawkins)-16 plts-calf-g. ornaments-
g.e.-1st Hawkins Edition (5b0,f) 125.00
--same-Lond-1784-sm8vo-calf (4c2) 25.00
--same-Lond-1824-(ed by John Major)-14 plts-16 mo
 (5b0,rbkd,f bndg) 65.00
--same-Lond-1824-2 vols-port-Sir John Hawkins ed (5t7) 12.50
--same-NY-1847-2 parts in 1 vol,as issued-12mo-orig cl-g.bk-
g. ornaments on sides-g.e.-Geo Washington Bethune,ed-
1st Amer ed (5gg6,box) 250.00
--same-Lond-1653-prntd by TMaxey-reprntd by Alex Murrary,1869-
3/4 mor (5p6) 15.00
--same-NY-1880-2 vols bnd in 1-green buck-g.lettering-8vo
 (5t5) 22.50
--same-NY-(1880)-2 vols-illus (5t7,libr stmp) 20.00
--same-Bost-1891-2 vols-illus-12mo-cl (5t0) 5.00
--same-Lond-1896-445p-illus-John Major,ed (5t7) 6.50
--same-NY-(ca 1902)-facs of 1st ed-246p (5t7) 6.00
--same-Lond,NY,Tor-(1911)-165p-illus-tip in col illus (5xx7) 12.50
--same-Lond-1925-20 col plts by JasThorpe-sq t8vo-bds-linen sp-
g.lettering (5t8) 15.00
--same-Lond-(1925)-4to-221p-21 col plts by JasThorpe (5p6) 12.50
--same-Bloomsbury-1929-Nonesuch Pr-illus-mor-ltd ed
 (5ii3,f,box) 60.00
WALTON, IZAAK-Waltoniana-Lond-1878-Richard Herne Shepherd,
notes (5rr6) 8.00
WALTON, JOS-Brief Biographies of Some Members of the Soc of
Friends-n.p.(Phila)-n.d.(ca 1900) (5b9) 12.50
WALTON, JOS S-Conrad Weiser & Indian Policy of Colonial
Pennsylvania-Phila-(1900)-illus-420p (4m4) 32.50
WALTON, MRS O F-Little Faith,or Child of the Toy Stall-Lond-
(ca 1880)-sm8vo-96p-illus-cl-Religious Tract Soc (5c8) 4.00
WALTON,PERRY-Story of Textiles-NY-(1925)-274p-illus (5t7) 7.50
--same-NY-1936-274p-illus-new ed (5ww4) 10. (5y2) 5.00
WALTON,R P-Marihuana,American's New Drug Porblem-Phila-
(1933)-R8vo-illus (5t0,libr labl) 4.50
WALTON,THOS-Know Your Own Ship-Lond-1901-336p-illus
 (5s1,ex-libr) 4.00
--same-1909-363p (5s1) 4.00
--Steel Ships,Construction,Maintenance-Lond-1902-290p-
fldg diagrams-scarce (5s1) 20.00
WALTON, W L-Some Descendants of Daniel Clark of Windsor,
Conn-1913-278p (5m2,4t2) 12.50
WALTON,WM M-Life & Adventures of the famous Texan Ben
Thompson-Houston-1954-232p-photos (5r8) 4.00
WALWORTH,ARTHUR-Cape Breton,Isle of Romance-NY-1948-
Longmans-illus-172p (5p9) 4.00
WALWORTH,REV CLARENCE A-Andiatorocte-NY-1888-244p
 (5t4,pres) 10.50
WALWORTH,MRS ELLEN HARDIN-Battles of Saratoga,1777-
Albany-(1891)-Munsell-8vo-illus-orig wrps-191p-1st ed (5m6) 10.00
WALWORTH,JEANNETTE H-An old fogy-NY-(1895)-Merriam-
1st ed (5m2) 12.50
WALWORTH,MANSFIELD TRACY-Warwich,or,the Lost Nationalities
of Amer-1869-NY-1st ed (5x4) 15.00
WALWORTH MFG CO-catalog-Brass & Iron Goods & Tools etc-
Bost-1892-4to-limp lea-303p,interleaved (5m6,wn) 12.50
WALWORTH,R H-Hyde Genealogy-1864-2 vols-1446p (4t2) 75.00
WALZ,JOHN A-German Influence in American Education &
Culture-Phila-(1936)-12mo (5jj3) 5.00
WANAMAKER DIARY,1916-Phila-1916-more than 100p ads-
lg fld in (5b9,mint) 5.00
WANAMAKER,JOHN-Collections of Antiques,Au Quatrieme-NY-
n.d.-JnWanamaker-4 vols-illus-t8vo-25p,21p,21p,19p-
loose as issued in orig prntd papr wrps (5m6) 12.50
--Fall & Winter Catalog,1911,12-NY-(1911)-68p-8vo-pict wrps-
illus (5r7) 25.00
--Flags of America-Phila-(1926)-illus-Sesquicentennial ed-papr-
32p (5q0) 5.00
--Golden Book of the Wanamaker Stores-Phila-1911-318p-illus
 (5w4) 5.50 (5L7) 5. (5hh6) 6.50
--Summer Sale of White-Phila-1906-36p plus covs-illus
 (5b9,pg cut) 4.00

WANAMAKER,R M-Voice of Lincoln-NY-1920-363p-cl (5h2) 3.00
WANDELL,S H-Aaron Burr,a Biography-NY-1927-Putnam-2 vols-
illus (5p0) 15.00
WANDERER,THE-or Female Difficulties-Lond-1814-Longman,Hurst,
Rees,Orme&Brown-5 vols-a.e.g.-calf-1st ed (5d8) 75.00
WANDERING OF A GOLDFINCH-Lond-1816-8vo-lea(g.tooled)-
355p (5t7) 10.50
WANKOWICZ,WITOLD-Sunshine & Storm-Lond-1948-8vo-illus-
cl-1st ed-priv prntd (5p5,pres) 7.50
WANOSTROCHT,N-Grammar of the French Language-Bost-1810-
John West-12mo-orig sheep-lea labl-364p-2nd Amer ed
 (5j5,wn) 12.50
WANSEY,HENRY-An Excursion to the US...1794-Salisbury-1798-
Easton-8vo-mor-port-fldg plt&table-2nd ed,wi additions
 (5n9,sl reprd) 85.00
WAPLES,DOUGLAS-People & Print,Social Aspects of Reading in
Depression-Chig-n.d.-228p (5j4,dj) 8.50
WAPELLO CO,IA,1878-History of-Chig-1878-8vo-hf lea-
illus-map-670p (5m8,bndg fair) 40.00
WAPELLO CO,IOWA-Standard Atlas of,incl plat book-1908-
GAOgle&Co-lg atlas folio-112p (4t2,sl crack) 45.00
WAPLES,R-Treatise on Attachment & Garnishment-Chig-1885-
sheep (5ff4) 6.50
WAR & SLAVERY-or,Victory Only Through Emancipation-
Bost-1861-8p-wrps (5x2) 17.50
WAR BIRDS-Diary of an unknown aviator-NY-(1926)-Doran-
277p-illus-cl (5mm8) 5. (5p0,4a6) 7.50
--same-Lond-1933-WW1-illus (5u7,dj) 4.75
WAR BOOK OF UNIV OF WISC-Madison-1918 (5ww4) 5.00
WAR DEPT-Technical Manual Airplane Structures-Wash-1940-
GPO-132p-illus-TMI 410 (5mm8) 7.50
WAR DEPT TRAINING MANUALS-Training of Pack Animals-
1922 to 1926-self wrps-4 vols (4a6) 25.00
WAR IN DISGUISE-or,Frauds of Neutral Flags-Lond-1805-
2nd ed,enlrgd (5q8) 22.50
--same-Lond-1806-Whittingham-252p-orig wrps-papr labl-4th ed
 (5mm8) 10.00
--same-NY-1806-bds-2nd Amer ed (5g4,wn,ex-libr) 10.00
--same-Lond-1917-from 3rd ed by Sir Francis Piggott (5q8) 7.50
WAR LABOR REPORTS-Wage & Salary Stabilization-Wash-1942 to
45-BNA-Vol 2 thru 28-bnd (5ii7,ex-libr) 150.00
WAR LETTERS-of a Disbanded Volunteer-NY-1864-frontis
 (5s9,cov wn) 5.00
WAR OF THE NATIONS-Portfolio in Roto Graure etchings-NY-
1919-NY Times Co-folio-528p-map (5L3) 15.00
WAR ON ALL FRONTS SERIES-NY-1917-5 vols-illus
 (5w5,sl stns) 8.50
WAR REMIN-By Surgeon of Mosby's Command-Richmond-1890-
236p-errata-cl-(A Monteiro) (5ff7,rbnd) 25. (5xx7) 15.00
WAR SONGS-for Anniversaries & Gatherings of Soldiers etc-
Bost-c1883-Oliver Ditson,publ (5w5) 4.50
WAR WHOOP & TOMAHAWK-NY-1929-illus-1st ed (5m2) 6.00
WAR WITH AMERICA-Lond-1811-72p-8vo-bds-Richard Taylor
 (5L1,rbnd) 45.00
WAR,THE WORLD & WILSON-NY-(1920)-frontis-cl-367p-
1st ed (5t0) 3.75
WARBURG,PAUL M-Federal Reserve System,Its Origin & Growth-
NY-1930-2 vols-cl (5h2) 15.00
WARBURTON,A F-Trial of Officers & Crew of Privateer Savannah
on Charge of Piracy-NY-1862 (5r4,needs rebndg,5s9) 15.00
WARBURTON,EARL CYRUS-Warburtons of Warburton & Arley-
Monterey-1956-sm4to-cl-101p-illus (5hh4,f) 10.00
WARBURTON,ELIOT,ed-Hochelaga,or England in the New World-
Lond-1847-2 vols-frontis-cl-3rd ed (5t2) 25.00
WARBURTON,GEO D-The Conquest of Canada-Lond-1849-2 vols-
2 frontis ports-8vo-1st ed-errata slip in ea vol
 (5m6,fade,rub) 20.00
WARCOLLIER,G-Cidrerie-Paris-1928-484p-12mo-3rd ed (5w1) 6.00
WARD,A B-The Sagebrush Parson-Bost-1906-1st ed (5ee3) 3.00
WARD,A H-Genealogical Hist of Rice Family,Desc of Deacon
Edmund-1858-379p (5t9) 35.00
WARD,A W,ed-Cambridge Modern History-Vols 1 thru 13,incl
index-1934 (5L7,sp sl spots) 95.00
WARD,ANNA A-Dictionary of Quotations in Prose-NY-1889-
701p (5j4) 6.50
WARD,ARTEMUS-also see BROWNE,CHAS F
WARD,ARTEMUS-His Book-Lond-1865 (4j0) 5.00
--Encyclopedia of Food-NY-1923-lg4to-596p-col plts (5c0) 45.00
--Grocers' Hand Book & Directory for 1886-Phila-Phila Grocer
Publ-304p-cl (5hh6) 15.00
WARD,CHAS A-Oracles of Nostradamus-Lond-n.d.-375p,14p
 (5w0) 6.50

WARD,CHAS WILLIS-Humboldt Co,Calif-Eureka-1915-Ward,
Perkins,GillCo-128p-pict wrps-illus-map   (5r0)   7.50
WARD,CHRISTOPHER-The Delaware Continentals,1776 to 1783-
Wilmington-1941-maps-620p   (4m2,dj)   30.00
--Dutch & Swedes on the Delaware,1609 to 64-Phila-1930 (4m2) 17.50
--New Sweden on the Delaware-Phila-1938-map   (4m2)   10.00
--War of Revolution-NY-1952-2 vols
          (5g4,box,5w5) 12.50   (5xx7,box,5p9)   17.50
WARD,E-Time Measurement,Part 1 Historical Review-94p-17 plts-
8vo   (5bb0)   8.00
WARD,EDW-London Spy Compleat in 18 pts-Lond-1924-444p-
port-ltd to 1000c-Casanova Soc   (5aa0)   17.50
WARD,EDWIN-Knapsack Manual for Sportsmen of the Field-
Lond-1872-57p-a.e.g.   (5t7)   5.00
WARD,ELIJAH-True Policy of Government Relative to Conduct of
War-(Wash)-n.d.-(McGill&Witherow)-8p-pamph (5mm8)   12.50
WARD,ELIZ STUART PHELPS-Beyond the Gates-Bost-1883-
Houghton-1st ed   (5m2)   4.00
--14 to 1-Bost-1891-Houghton-1st ed   (5m2)   6.50
--The Gates Ajar-Bost-1869-248p-1st ed-2nd prntng (5x4,scuff) 7.50
WARD,ESTELLE F-The Story of NoWestern Univ-1924-Dodd
                                   (5ww4,dj)   5.00
WARD,F KINGDON-In Farthest Burma-Phila-1921-8vo-311p-
photos-maps   (4a6)   6.00
--Modern Exploration-Lond-(1946)-130p   -illus   (5w3)   4.50
--Mystery Rivers of Tibet-Lond-1923-3 maps-illus-316p,(4)
                                    (5w3,fade)   18.50
--Pilgrimage for Plants-Lond-(1960)-191p-35 plts (5w3)   4.00
--Plant Hunting in the Wilds-Lond-n.d.(ca ?1925)-78p,(1) (5w3) 5.50
--Plant Hunter's Paradise-Lond-(1937)-photos-fldg map-347p
                                      (5w3)   12.50
--A Plant Hunter in Tibet-Lond-(1934)-317p-fldg map-photos
                                      (5w3)   18.50
WARD,FANNY B-Sketch of Battery "I" First Ohio Artillery-
n.p.-n.d.-(1890s?)-95p-wrps   (5ff7)   25.00
WARD,G K-Andrew Warde & His Desc-1910-604p   (5t9)   45.00
WARD,GEO W-Early Development of Chesapeake&Ohio Canal
Project-Balt-1899-fldg bds   (4h8,sp tn)   8.50
WARD,H G-Mexico in 1827-Lond-1828-3/4 calf-g.-mor labls-
2 vols-1st ed-1st issue   (4j7,vf)   165.00
WARD,H W-The Book of the Grape-Lond-(1925)-illus-97p (5w1) 6.50
WARD,HARRY PARKER-Some Amer College Bookplates-Columbus-
1915-Champlin Pr-8vo-482p-12 bkplts & 4 repro(tip in)-dec cl-
typed errata slip tip in-ltd to 500c,autg   (5p1)   42.50
WARD,HERBERT-A Voice from the Congo-NY-1910-Scribner's-
illus   (5x5)   12.50
WARD,MRS H O-Sensible Etiquette of the Best Society-Phila-
(1878)-567p   (5w7)   4.50
WARD,H S-Shakespeare's Town & Times-NY-(1896)-176p-map-
illus-Truslove&Comba   (5p0)   7.50
WARD,MRS HUMPHREY-England's Effort-NY-1916   (5x7)   4.75
--Fenwick's Career-Lond-1906-2 vols-wrps-ltd to 250c,autg (5j2)
                                      (5j2)   90.00
--Robt Elsmere-Lond-1888-3 vols-Smith,Elder&Co-8vo-orig cl-
1st ed   (5xx6,hng weak)   40.00
WARD,HON MRS-The Microscope-Lond-1869-8vo-cl-illus (5p5)12.50
--Microscope Teachings-Lond-1866-g.dec cl-219p-a.e.g.-col plts
                                  (4t7,recased)   27.50
WARD,J O-My Grandpa Went West-Caldwell-1956-130p-col
frontis-1st ed   (5xx5)   4.00
WARD,JAS-Colour Decoration of Architecture-Lond-1913-
Chapman&Hall-136p-12 col plts   (5m5,wn)   12.50
WARD,JOS R C-History of Geo C Meade Post #1,Dept of Penna,
Grand Army of Republic-Phila-1889-horiz8vo-263p-illus
                                      (5w4)   10.00
WARD,JULIUS H-The White Mntns-NY-1890-Appleton-pic cl-
258p-1st ed   (4c5,chip)   27.50
WARD,L R-Nova Scotia,Land of Cooperation-NY-1942-207p-
maps   (4b9,ex-libr) 8. (5q0)   10.00
WARD,LES -40 Years of "Spy"-Lond-1915-351p-port (5t4)   7.50
--Young Ward's Diary-NY-c1935-8vo-Putnam's-321p
                                  (5p1,ex-libr)   10.00
WARD,LYND-The Biggest Bear-Bost-1952-Houghton,Miff-85p-
4to-pict cl-1st ed   (5p1,dj,pres)   25.00
--God's Man-(1929)-Jonathan Cape&Harrison Smith-ltd to 409c,
nbrd,autg   (5F1,f)   27.50
--Madman's Drum,Novel in Woodcuts-NY-(1930)-cl bk bds-
8vo-1st ed   (4m8) 10. (5p6)   12.00
--Prelude to a Million Years-NY-1933-8vo-bds-ltd to 920c,autg
          (5d3,autg) 25. (5m8)   35.00
--Song Without Words-NY-1936-g.bd wi parch sp-ltd ed,autg,
parch box   (4d0) 20. (5d2)   15.00
--Vertigo-NY-1937-Random   (5p7)   6.50

WARD,MAISIE-Gilbert Keith Chesterton-NY-1943-685p-illus
                                     (5m1,dj)   6.50
--Return to Chesterton-NY-1952-1st ed   (5ss9,f,dj)   5.00
WARD,MARCUS-Royal Illuminated Book of Legends-Edinburg-
(ca1875)-Nimmo-1st & 2nd series in 2 vols-40p col plts-
obl 4to-dec cl-scarce   (5cc0)   75.00
WARD,MARGARET-Cimarron Saga-Pampa Print Shop-n.d.(1955)-
8vo-cl-88p-photos   (5g2,autg,mint,dj)   10.00
WARD,MARIA E-Bicycling for Ladies-NY-1896-4to-34 illus-
pict cl-1st ed   (5p5)   17.50
WARD,MARY HUMPHREY-Writings-Bost-1909-16 vols-illus-
hand col frontis-crushed lev mor-Autograph Edition
                                  (5d2,f bndg)   200.00
WARD,MAY ALDEN-Old Colony Days-Bost-1896 (4a9,pres)   10.00
WARD,N LASCELLES-Oriental Missions in B C-Lond-1925-
plts-128p   (5zz8)   12.50
WARD,NANDA-The Black Sombrero-NY-(1952)-Ariel Books-
12mo-(32p)-pict cl-1st ed   (5p1,pres,dj)   10.00
WARD,NATHANIEl-The Simple Cobler of Aggavvam in Amer-
Lond-1647-80p   -sm4to-calf   (5L1)   950.00
WARD,R-Sportsman's Handbook to Collecting,etc-Lond-1906-
9th ed-illus   (5yy6)   6.00
WARD,ROBT PLUMER-An essay on contraband-Lond-1801-Woodfall-
8vo-disbnd-1st ed   (5i8)   15.00
WARD,SAM-In the Gold Rush-Stanford-(1949)-Carvel Collins,ed-
frontis-illus-1st ed   (5dd6)   9.50
WARD,THOS-English Poets,Selections with Critical Intro-NY-
1916 to 21-5 vols   (5qq4,underline)   17.50
WARD,THOS-England's reformation-poem-Lond-1715-for John Baker-
2 vols in 1-12mo-hf calf-2nd ed   (5x3)   30.00
WARD,W H-Architecture of the Renaissance in France...Vol 2,
1640 to 1830-Lond-1926-Batsford-2nd ed-8vo-bds (5m5)   10.00
WARD,WM-Early Schools of Naugatuck From 1730 to 1850-
Naugatuck-c1906-Perry Pr-12mo-cl-95p   (4t1)   10.00
WARD,WM H-Records of Members of Grand Army of Republic wi
complete account of 20th Natl Encampment-SanFran-1886-
frontis-624p-lea   (4b3,wn)   7.50
WARD,WM HAYES-Cylinders & Other Ancient Oriental Seals
in Library of J Pierpont Morgan-NY-1909-priv prntd-4to-
illus-bds-vel bk-t.e.g.-ltd to 250c   (5j2)   30.00
WARD,WM R-Down the Years-Newark-1932-256p-illus(4b8)   6.50
WARD'S QUARTERLY-Vol 1,#1 thru 4-Detroit,1965,66-sml folio
                                     (5y2,vf)   10.00
WARDE,FREDERIC-Bruce Rogers, Designer of Books-Cambr-1926-
Harv U Pr-15 illus-75p-cl   (5tt9,wn,5r5)   15.00
--same-Cambr-1926-cl-pap labl-8vo-2nd impress
                              (4n5,pres,unopened)   15.00
WARDE,FREDK-50 Years of Make Believe-NY-1920-12mo-310p-
ports   (5xx5) 5. (4c9)   6.00
WARDEN,CLIFFORD-Catalogue of Library of US Senate-Wash-
1901-343p   (5j4)   15.00
WARDEN,D B-Statistical,Political & Hist Acct of US of NoAmer-
Edinb-1819-cl-552p-8vo-Vol 1(of 2)   (4p3)   35.00
--same-Edinb-1819-3 vols-lea   (5t4)   17.50
WARDEN,FLORENCE-Ralph Ryder of Brent-Lond-1892-Bentley-
3 vols-8vo-orig cl-1st ed   (5xx6,lend libr labls)   27.50
WARDEN,J-System of Revealed Religion-1769-4to-buck-rev
                                     (5L7,rbnd)   12.50
WARDEN,WM-Letters written on Board His Majesty's Ship
Northumberland & at St Helena,etc-Lond-1816-hf calf-
8vo-port-215p-2nd ed   (4e1)   35.00
--same-Brussels-1817-calf   (5j2,calf wn)   30.00
WARDER,JOHN A-Hedges & Evergreens,Complete Manual-NY-
(1858)-284p-12mo-cl-illus   (5t0,f)   4.50
WARDER,T B-Battle of Young's Branch,or Manassas Plain-Richmond-
1862-Enquirer Book&Job Pr-156p,(1)-maps(2 fld)-lea&cl
                                (5m3,sl crayon)   125.00
WARDLEY,HERBERT O-Education of a Poker Player-NY-1957-
lg8vo-cl   (5p5)   10.00
WARDMAN,GEO-A Trip to Alaska-Bost-1884   (5r7)   15.00
WARDNER,H S-Windsor,Birthplace of Vermont,a Hist of,to 1781-
1927-562p   (5t9)   12.50
WARE COLLECTION-in Botanical Muse of Harv Univ-NY-(1940)-
58p-16 col plts -glass flowers   (5t0) 4. (5s7)   2.50
WARE,EDITH E,ed-Study of Intl Relations in US Survey for 1934-
NY-1934-Columbia U Pr-lg8vo-buck-503p   (5j5,shake)   7.50
WARE,EUGENE F-Indian War of 1864-Topeka-1911-ports-illus-
601p-1st ed   (4L0) 60. (5s9) 90. (4b6,pres)   125.00
--same-NY-1960-St Martin's Pr-483p-illus
                        (5qq8,vf,dj,5k2,dj,5g2)   7.50
WARE,F B-History of Cronyn Mem Church London Ont 1873 to 1949-
n.p.-n.d.-329p-illus   (4b9,autg)   15.00

WARE, MRS HIBBERT-A happy error-Lond-1885-FVWhite&Co-
3 vols-8vo-orig cl-1st ed   (5xx6)   22.50

WARE, J S-Gen Record of Jos Lancaster of Amesbury, Mass-(1933)-
125p   (4t2)   15.00

WARE, JOHN F W-Home Life, What It Is & What It Needs-Bost-
1866-12mo-180p   (5w7)   6.50

WARE, JOS E-Emigrants' Guide to Calif-StLouis-1849-Halsall-
16mo-orig cl-ad inside bk cov-1st ed
          (4h0, facs fldg map, cov loose, Streeter bkplt)   1,000.00
--same-Princeton U-1932-reprint-12mo-cl-63p-fldg map (5h5) 15.00

WARE, NORMAN J-Labor Movement in US, 1860 to 1895-
1929   (5q8, hng rprd)   8.50

WARE, WM-Aurelian, or Rome in the 3rd Century-NY-1848-
CSFrancis-2 vols-12mo-orig cl   (5x1, f)   20.00
--Zenobia-NY, Bost-1838-lea-2 vols-1st ed-rare
          (5x1) 22.50   (5qq4, chip)   25.00

WARE, WM ROTCH, ed-Georgian Period-Bost-1904-folio-
100 plts in fldr   (4b7)   25.00

WARFEL, HARRY R, ed-Letters of Noah Webster-NY-(1953)-
Library Publ   (4p1)   15.00
--Who Killed Grammar?-Gainesville-1952-Univ of Florida Pr-
8vo-87p-prntd wrps   (5p1)   7.50

WARFEL, RUTH FARQUHAR-Poems by Noah Webster-College Park, Md-
1936-Harruth Lefraw-16p-stapled-wrps-Christmas Garland, #1
          (5p1, autgs)   7.50

WARFIELD, B B-2 Studies in History of Doctrine-1897 (5L7, rprd)   5.00

WARFIELD, MRS CATH A-Double Wedding or How She Was Won-
Phila-(1875)-406p   (5t4)   5.00
--The Household of Bouverie, By a Southern Lady-NY-1860-
Derby, etc-2 vols-1st ed of auth's 1st novel (5m2)   7.50
--Lady Ernestine-Phila-(1876)-Peterson-1st ed, 1st state, wi advance
mag advts for '76-thk8vo   (5m2)   8.50
--Sea & Shore-Phila-(1876)-Peterson-1st separate ed (5m2, sl wn) 8.50

WARFIELD, DAVID-Ghetto Silhouettes-NY-Warfield&MAHamm-
1902-189p   (5s2, mint)   10.00

WARFIELD, ETHELBERT DUDLEY-The Kentucky Resolutions of 1798-
NY&Lond-1894-203p-2nd ed   (5t7)   10.00

WARFIELD, WM-Theory & Practice of Cattle breeding-Chig-1890-
386p plus index-Sanders Publ   (4L0)   7.50

WARING, JR, GEO E-The Elements of Agriculture-Montpelier-
1855-SMWalton-bds   (5t4)   5.00
--Waring's Book of the Farm-Phila-c1877-542p-illus (5w0)   7.50
--My Pioneer Past-Bost-(1936)-256p-31 photos
          (5s4, f, pres)   40.00

WARING, I F-Miscellaneous Poems-Indian Hill-1878-12mo-
316p-cl-scarce   (5i4)   15.00

WARING, JOHN B-Examples of Metal Work & Jewellery-Lond-
n.d.-(ca 1850)-Day-17p plts-sml folio (4j1, ex-libr)   15.00

WARING, R N-Short Hist of Warings-1898-60p & gen charts (4t2) 20.00

WARINNER, EMILY-Voyager to Destiny-NY-(1951)-267p
          (5s1, dj, f)   5.00
--same-NY-(1956)-illus-276p   (5t4)   4.00

WARMAN, CY-Weigh of Temagami & other Indian tales-NY-
(1928)-206p-ports-plts   (5xx5, rbnd)   6.75

WARMOTH, H C-War, Politics & Reconstruction-NY-1930-1st ed
          (5x2)   22.50

WARNE, PHILIP S-Patent leather Joe-NY-(1878)-11, (5)p-
7th ed-Beadle's Hf Dime Lib #67-self wrps (5y0)   7.50

WARNEFORD, LT-Adventures of a Naval Officer-NY-(1898)-
219p-g.t.   (5s1)   4.00

WARNER & BEERS-Illinois, Combined Town, County, State, Nat'l
& General Atlas-1872-lg atlas folio-95p-maps (5t9)   65.00

WARNER & SWASEY-Few Astronomical Instruments-Cleve-1900-
folio-36p   (5L7, rub, soil)   15.00

WARNER, ANNA-Gardening by Myself-NY-(1872)-223p-wrps
          (5s7)   7.50

WARNER, ANNA B-Dollars & cents-NY-2 vols-Putnam-1852-
1st ed   (5m2, shelf labl)   7.50

WARNER, CHAS DUDLEY-As We Were Saying-NY-Harper-1891-
219p-24mo-illus-grn cl-g.dec   (5i1)   4.00
--same-NY-1892-219p-illus   (5t7)   5.00
--Back Log Studies-Bost-1873-1st ed (5p6)   10.00
--same-NY-(1914)-281p-cl-21 illus   (5t0)   3.00
--Baddeck & That Sort of Thing-Bost&NY-1901-16mo (5w8, shake) 5.00
--In the Wilderness-Bost-1878-Houghton, Osgood-12mo-cl (5b2) 10.00
--My Summer in a Garden-Bost-1871-12mo-cl-1st ed of auth's
1st book   (5b2, 5gg6, fade)   10.00
--Studies in the South & West With Comments on Canada-NY-1889-
Harper&Bros-8vo-orig bds-1st ed   (5L8, rbkd, libr stmp)   10.00

WARNER, ELISHA-The History of Spanish Fork-Spanish Fork, Utah-
1930-239p-1st ed-scarce   (5L2, f)   20.00

WARNER, ESTHER-New Song in a Strange Land-Bost-1948-
Houghton, Miff-302p-illus   (4t5, 5x2)   2.50

WARNER, FANNIE-Beech Bluff-NY-n.d.-(early 20th century ?)
332p-cl   (5h7)   5.00

WARNER, FRANCES LESTER-Pilgrim Trails-Bost-c1921-pict bds-
cl bkstrp-47p plus illus   (5w9, dj)   5.00
--Surprising the Family-Bost-1926   (5p7)   3.25

WARNER, FRANK W, comp-Montana Territory, History & Business
Directory, 1879-Helena-(1879)-8vo-orig prntd bds-lea bk-
map & illus   (5a3, wn)   200.00

WARNER, H T-Texans & Their State-Houston-ca1919-mor-125 lvs
          (4j7)   35.00

WARNER, J-Walt Disney's Vanishing Prairie-NY-1955-4to-
dec bds-cl bk-photos -1st edition (5p5)   7.50

WARNER, J J-Historical Sketch of Los Angeles Co-LosAng-1876-
88p-wrps-LouisLewin&Co, Mirror Prntng
          (5d6, back wrp in facs) 50.   (5i0)   100.00
--same-LosAng-1936-cl&bds-illus (5dd9) 6.75 (5m9) 10. (5x5) 8.50

WARNER, LANGDON-The Craft of the Japanese Sculptor-NY-
1936-4to-plts-cl-1st ed-Japan Soc of NY-scarce (5p5)   35.00

WARNER, LOUIS H-Archbishop Lamy, an Epoch Maker-SantaFe, NM-
(1936)-316p-1st ed   (4L0)   10.00

WARNER, LUCIEN C-Story of My Life During 70 Eventful Years-
1914-243p   (4t2)   7.50

WARNER, M M-Warner's History of Dakota Co, Nebr-Lyons-1893-
372p-1st ed-v scarce   (5L2, lacks bkstrp)   75.00

WARNER, MATT-Last of the Bandit Riders-Caxton-1940-illus-
337p-1st ed-v scarce (4i7) 27.50 (5kk4, vf, dj)   45.00

WARNER, OLIVER-Trafalgar-Lond-1959-35 illus (5c1)   6.00

WARNER, OPIE L-A Pardoned Lifer, Life of Geo Sontag-
SanBernardino-(1909)-cl-port-211p
          (4L0, wn) 10. (4p2, rprd, wn, 4L0) 15. (4L8)   17.50

WARNER, P R-Peter Willemse Roome Desc-(1883)-348p, 62p
          (5mm3)   17.50

WARNER, R-Antiquitates Culinariae-Lond-1791-137p-folio-illus-
lg papr ed-calf bk-bds   (5c7, sl stn)   75.00

WARNER, REX-The wild goose chase-Lond-1937-Boriswood-8vo-
orig cl-1st ed   (5i8, dj, autg)   12.00

WARNER, RICHARD, Jr-Hampshire-Lond-1789-illus-cl
          (4p2, rbnd, stnd, rprd)   30.00

WARNER, ROBT-The Orchid Album-Lond-1882 to 97-orig dec cl-
g.e.-4to-528 plts-11 vols-1st ed-rare (5z9, vf)   2,000.00

WARNER, SUSAN B-Diana-NY-1877-Putnam-1st ed (5m2, sl wn) 6.50

WARNER, SYDNEY Y-History of the First Presby Church-FtSmith-
1960-167p-cl   (5h0)   8.00

WARNER, SYLVIA TOWNSEND-Lolly Willowes-Lond-1926-
Chatto&Windus-1st ed   (5p9)   6.50

WARNER, W L-Who Shall Be Educated-NY-1944 (5x2)   7.50

WARNER-JENKINSON MFG CO-Ice Cream Carbonated beverages-
StL-(1924)-illus-134p   (5w1)   6.50

WARRACK, JOHN-Greek Sculpture-Lond-n.d.-Kent-30p text-
99 plts-4to-cl   (5m5)   15.00

WARRE, HENRY JAS-Sketches of NoAmer & Oreg Terr-(Lond)-
Dickinson-(1848)-lg folio-20 hand col liths on 16 plts-
1 map-hf orig mor-1st ed   (5hh0)   6,000.00
--same-Barre, Mass-1970-Imprint Soc-ltd for members only-
obl 4to-26p text-71 plts-box as issued (4a8, mint)   50.00

WARREN-An antidote to John Wood's poison-NY-1802-
Southwick&Crooker-8vo-disbnd-1st ed (5i9)   27.50

WARREN&CLARK-Public Libraries in US of Amer, Their History,
Condition & Management-Wash-1876-1187p (5j4, f)   22.50

WARREN, ARTHUR-A Tribute-n.p.-n.d.-Geo Westinghouse-
sm8vo-lea-32p-2 plts   (5e4, sl wn)   4.75

WARREN, B H-Birds of Pennsylvania-Harrisburg-1890-100 col plts-
434p (4p8, rprd) 17.50 (5m2) 22.50 (5L7, rbnd, 4p5, rprd) 25.00
--Report on Birds of Penna-Harrisburg-1888-50 col plts-260p
          (5r5, sl wtrstnd)   20.00

WARREN, C E T-The Admiralty Regrets-Lond-(1958)-photos-248p
          (4h4)   5.00
--The Midget Raiders-NY-1954-8 maps-30 photos (5c1)   6.50

WARREN, CHAS-History of the American Bar-Bost-1911 (5ff4) 12.50
--The Supreme Court in US History-Bost-1923-3 vols-orig cl
          (5m3)   25.00

WARREN, CHAS-Jacobin & Junto, or Early Amer Politics as Viewed
in Diary of Dr Nathan'l Ames-1931-Harvard Univ Pr (5x5, dj) 10.00

WARREN, CHAS MARQUIS-Only the Valiant-Macmillan-1943
          (5F1, f, wn dj)   4.00

WARREN COUNTY, NY-1942-fldg pkt map-WPA-258p (5ff2)   10.00

WARREN, D M-An Elementary Treatise on Physical Geography etc-
Phila-(1873)-folio-pict bds-116p-illus&maps-rev by
A Von Steinwehr   (5t7)   6.50

WARREN, DALE-A Modern Galaxy-Bost-1930-Houghton, Miff-
423p   (5p7)   3.25

USED BOOK PRICE GUIDE

WARREN,EDW R-The Beaver,its work & its ways-Balt-1927-
198p-photos-1st ed-Mono of Amer Soc of Mam,#2
    (4L0) 12.50   (5dd5)   20.00
--The Mammals of Colorado-NY-1910-Putnam's-3 maps-photos
    (5x5)   15.00
WARREN,FRANK S-Moods & Moments in Hawaii-NY-1936-4to-
cl
    (5m9)   7.50
WARREN,G K-Explor in Dacota Country...1855-Wash-1856-
maps-cl-lea labl-illus-79p-1st issues
    (5g4,libr bndg) 35.   (4n4)   65.00
--Prelim Report of Explor in Nebr & Dakota....1855 to 57-Wash-
1875-prntd wrps-125p   (4n4)   30.00
--Profiles of Routes Proposed for a Pac RR to Accompany Report
of Jefferson Davis-1855-lg fldg map   (5a0)   12.50
--Report on Bridging Mississippi River Betw StPaul,Minn & StLouis,
Mo-Wash-1878-29 fldg plts-232p (4j4,fox)   8.50
WARREN,GARNET-The Romance of Design-NY-1926-Dblday,Page-
4to-illus-237p   (5m6,5p0)   10.00
WARREN,GEO WASH-History of the Bunker Hill Monument Assoc
during the 1st Century-Bost-1877-illus-427p (5ss5) 7.50 (5p9) 6.50
WARREN,H L J-Cripple Creek & ColoradoSprngs-ColSprngs-1896-
4to-cl-illus maps-104p (5L5,rbnd,wtr dmgd) 15. (5t2,stnd) 10.00
WARREN,I P-Stanley Families of Amer-1887-352p
    (5t9)   25.00
WARREN,J C-Genealogy of Warren,wi some historical sketches-
1854-114p   (4t2)   45.00
WARREN,JOHN-The Matadors,1879 to 1951-n.p.-1952-sm4to-
mimeo-35p-illus-wrps   (4c7,5n4,2p als)   35.00
WARREN,JOHN B L-Book plates,a Guide to Their Study-NY,Lond-
1900-t8vo-16 plts-scarce   (5t5)   7.50
WARREN,JOHN C-Surgical observations on tumours,wi cases &
operations-Bost-1837-16 hand col plts-orig cl (5g4,f) 50.00
WARREN,JOHN ESAIAS-Para,or Scenes & Adventures on Banks of
Amazon-NY-1851 (4b6,fox,lacks fly,ex-libr) 15.00
WARREN,JOHN H,Jr-30 Yrs Battle with Crime,etc-Poughkeepsie-
1874-illus-8vo-1st ed   (4c8)   15.00
WARREN,GEN JOS-Biographical Sketch of,by a Bostonian-Bost-
1857-12mo-port-orig wrps-1st ed (5ss5)   6.00
WARREN,LOUIS AUSTIN-Lincoln's Parentage & Childhood-
NY&Lond-392p-illus   (5t7)   5.00
--Lincoln's Youth Indiana Years 7 to 21-NY-(1959)-illus-298p
    (5t7,dj)   6.50
WARREN,MRS MERCY-History of the Rise,Progress & Termination
of the Amer Revolution-Bost-1805-3 vols-calf (5w9,wn) 75.00
WARREN,MRS MERCY OTIS-Poems,dramatic & miscellaneous-
Bost-1790-12mo-calf-mor labl-1st ed (5i9,fox) 65.00
WARREN,ORIN-Geneaology of Desc of Jas Warren-1902-138p
    (5t9)   15.00
WARREN,ROBT PENN-All King's Men-NY-(1946)-12mo-cl
    (4c2,sp faded)   17.50
--Eleven Poems on the Same Theme-NY-(1942)-12mo-imprntd wrps-
1st ed   (5ss7,vf)   25.00
--Night Rider-Bost-1939-Houghton,Miff-8vo-cl (5b2,sl stn) 7.50
--Selected Essays-NY-(c1958)-8vo-cl-RandomHse (5b2,f,dj) 7.50
--Selected Poems,New & Old,1923 to 1966-NY-1966-Random-
ltd to 250c,autg,nbrd   (4L4,box,mint)   25.00
--World Enogh & Time-NY-(1950)-RandomHouse-8vo
    (5F0,f) 4.50 (5h6) 4. (4g1,dj)   7.50
--same-NY-(1950)-cl-12mo-nbrd edition for Booksellers of Amer
orig glassine (5F1) 10. (5ss7,f)   17.50
WARREN,S-Experiences of a Barrister & Confessions of an
Attorney-Bost-1856-2 vols in 1 (5r4,shaken) 17.50
WARREN,SIDNEY-Farthest Frontier,the Pacific Northwest-NY-
1949-1st ed   (5xx5)   6.00
WARREN,T ROBINSON-Dust & Foam-NY-1859-397p
    (5s1,ex-libr)   12.50
--Shooting,Boating & Fishing For Young Sportsmen-NY-1871
    (4j1)   12.50
WARREN,W W-History of Ojibway Nation-StPaul-1885-Minn
Hist Soc-535p-frontis (5L2,fray,4i7) 20. (5a0) 32.50
WARREN-REMICK & ALLIED FAMILIES-1949-175p (4t2) 20.00
WARRICK,SPENCER & PERRY COUNTIES-History of Indiana-Chig-
1885-837p-hf lea   (5ji9)   55.00
WARRINER,E-Warriner Family of N E origin-1899-287p (4t2) 15.00
WARRINER,FRANCIS-Cruise of US Frigate Potomac etc-NY-1835-
illus-1st ed-scarce (5yy6,rbnd,bndg wn) 17.50
WARRINGTON,C J S-History of Chemistry in Canada-Tor-1949-
plts-502p   (5nn2,pres)   15.00
WARRNE COUNTY,OHIO-Hist of-Chig-1882-1070p-hf lea
    (5y0,sp wn,crack)   55.00
WARRUM,NOBLE-Utah in the World War-SaltLkCty-1924-Arrow Pr-
8vo-cl-456p-ltd to 1000c   (4t1)   18.50
--Utah Since Statehood-Chig,1919&1920-4 vols-Clarke Publ Co
    (5L2)   35.00

WARSHOW,H T-Representative Industries in US-NY-(1928)-
8vo-illus-1st ed   (5ss5,underline)   7.50
WARSHOW,ROBT IRVING-Alex Hamilton-NY-(1931)-port-
241p   (5L7,5t7)   5.00
WARTHIN,ALDRED S-Old Age,the Major Involution-NY-1929-
Hoeber-8vo-bds-lin bk-papr labl-29 illus-199p-ltd to 230c,
autg   (4d9,f)   12.50
WARTON,JOS,ed-The works of Virgil,in Latin & English-Lond-
1753-for R Dodsley-4 vols-8vo-calf-plts (5x3) 75.00
WAS IT A GHOST?-murders in Bussey's Wood-Bost-(c1868)-
12mo-bds-roan bk-143p   (5g8,rbnd)   15.00
WAS IT INHERITANCE-or,Nannie Grant,a Narr-Phila-1876-
1st ed   (5mm2)   12.50
WASHBURN,A L-Reconn Geology of Portions of Victoria Island etc-
NY-1947-Geol Soc of America-plts-142p-maps (5u6) 7.50
WASHBURN,MAJ ANDREW-Documents In Case of...late of 14th
Reg Mass Volunteers-n.p.-n.d.-(ca 1863)-27p-stitchd (5w5) 6.00
WASHBURN,BRADFORD-Among the Alps with Bradford-NY-1927-
illus   (5b9)   3.00
WASHBURN,CEPHAS-Remin of the Indians-Richmond-(1869)-236p-
1st ed-rare (5L2,wn) 85. (5a3,sl loose) 150.00
WASHBURN,CHAS-Come Into My Parlor-NY-1936-photos-
252p plus index-1st ed   (5dd1)   7.50
WASHBURN,CHAS A-History of Paraguay-Bost,NY-1871-lg8vo-
cl-fldg map-illus-scarce (4a3,sl fade)   65.00
WASHBURN,CHAS G-Interview on Woman Sufrrage from Worcester
Evening Gazette,Oct 16,1915-(Worcester,1915)-4p (5t7) 3.00
--Theodore Roosevelt,Logic of His Career-Bost-1916-plts
    (5qq8,autg)   4.00
WASHBURN,E-Lectures on Study & Practice of the Law-Bost-1876-
5th ed   (5r4)   15.00
WASHBURN,EMORY-Historical Sketches of Leicester-Bost-1860-
467p-illus (5e8) 9.75 (5w9) 7.50 (4t2) 10.00
WASHBURN,G C-Desc of Wm Witter of Swampscott,Mass-(1929)-
394p   (4t2)   17.50
WASHBURN,LOUIS C-Christ Church,Phila-Phila-1925-317p-
illus   (5h9)   8.50
WASHBURN,PETER T-Digest of all the Cases Decided in Supreme
Court of State of Vermont-Woodstock-1845-8vo-calf-823p
    (5t2)   15.00
WASHBURN,ROBT C-Prayer for Profit-NY-1930-1st ed (5m2,dj) 5.00
WASHBURN,ROBT M-Calvin Coolidge,Farmer,Mayor,Gov,Pres,
His Life,Its Lesson-Bost-1924-47p-wrps (5h1) 3.00
WASHBURN,STANLEY-Trails,Trappers & Tenderfeet in New Empire
of Western Canada-NY-1912-350p-fldg map-photos-scarce
    (4L0,fade)   20.00
WASHBURN,SYRENE E-Prospecting for Gold & Other Short Stories-
LosAng-1950-254p-illus (4a8,autg)   10.00
WASHBURN,W WYAN-Brother John's Cannan in Carolina-
Salisbury,NoCar-1958-335p (5u3,autg)   4.00
WASHBURN,WILCOMB E-The Governor & the Rebel-ChapelHill-
(1957)-248p-illus   (5mm8,dj)   5.00
WASHBURN-CROSBY's-Gold Medal Cook Book-Minnpls-1910 & 1917-
lg4to-wrps-74p-illus   (4g0) ea   7.50
WASHBURNE,CARLETON-Remakers of Mankind-NY-c1932 (5x7) 3.75
WASHBURNE,E B-Abraham Lincoln,his personal history &
public record,May 29,1860-(Wash,1860)-8p-disbnd (5g3) 10.00
--Franco German War & Insurrection of the Commune-Wash-
1878-GPO-1st ed-lg8vo-cl   (5p5)   17.50
--History of the English Settlement in Edwards County,Ill-Chig-
1882-402p   (4m2)   17.50
--Sketch of Edw Coles,2nd Gov of Ill-Chig-1882-253p
    (5L7,5j6)   4.50
--Trade with Rebellious States-Wash-1865-HR24-222p (5j6) 4.00
WASHBURNE,H C-Land of Good Shadows-NY-1940-329p-illus
    (4b9,f)   12.00
WASHIAD,THE-or siege of Washington,by an eminent conservative-
n.p.-1858-canto first(all publ?)-12mo-orig prntd wrps-
1st ed   (5i0,sl wn)   17.50
WASHINGTON & KENT COUNTIES(RI)-History of-1889-1,344p-
by Cole   (5q0)   40.00
WASHINGTON & LEE LAW REVIEW-1939 to 71-Vol 1 thru 28
    (5ii7,rbnd)   255.00
--same-cl   (5ii7)ea   11.00
WASHINGTON(DC) ALBUM-n.p.-n.d.-(ca 1890)-accordion fldr
6x9 inches-ca 100 views-cl covs (5w5)   5.00
WASHINGTON & JACKSON-on Negro Soldiers,Gen'l Banks on
Bravery of Negro Troops-Phila-1863-18p-orig wrps-scarce
    (5x5,f)   50.00
WASHINGTON & LEE UNIV-Summer Bulletin,1907-Lexington-
91p-illus-wrps-spec R E Lee nbr (5h6)   4.00
WASHINGTON,BOOKER T-Character Building-NY-1902-illus
    (5x2)   22.50

WASHINGTON, BOOKER T (continued)

--same-NY-1914 (4a9) 5.00
--Frederick Douglass-Phila-1907-365p (5x2) 22.50
--The Future of the Amer Negro-Bost-1899-12mo-cl-g.t.-1st ed
of auth's 1st book-scarce (5gg6,pres) 50.00
--The Man Farthest Down-NY-1912-map (5x2) 25.00
--The Negro in the South-Phila-1907-Jacobs Co-1st ed
(5x2,f bndg,rbnd) 50.00
--A New Negro for New Century-Chig-n.d.-(c1899) (4a9) 9.00
--The Southern Letter-Monthly-Tuskegee Insti, July, Nov, 1896,
Sept, 1897 (5x2) ea 7.50
--The Story of My Life & Work-Naperville, Ill-1900 (5x2) 25.00
--Up from Slavery-NY-1901-frontis-330p (5L7,5ee3) 4.50
--same-Various Printings (5x2) 5.00
--Working with the Hands-NY-1904-illus -1st ed (5x2) 25.00
WASHINGTON, BUSHROD-Reports of Cases Argued & Determined
In Court of Appeals of Virg-Richmond-1798-2 vols
(4j4, fox, rprd) 45.00
WASHINGTON CO, IOWA CENTENNIAL-Evening Journal,
Presenting Progress & Growth etc 1836 to 1936-Washington, Ia-
1936-folio-stiff wrps (5m8) 7.50
WASHINGTON COUNTIES-Official State Pub-Olympia-1943-
80p-sm4to-wrps-illus-dec cov (5s4, bkstrp tn) 4.00
WASHINGTON, DC-City & Capital-Wash-1937-GPO-1141p-
illus-maps in fldr-Amer Guide Ser (5x0) 6.00
WASHINGTON DC-Guide to Nation's Capitol-NY-1942-photos-
pkt map-512p-1st ed-Amer Guide Ser (4L5, dj) 5.00
WASHINGTON, THE EVERGREEN STATE-Scenes World's
Columbian Expos-Chig-1893-JOHestwood-pict wrps (5n4) 12.50
WASHINGTON, GEO-Accounts with the US commencing Jun 1775
& ending Jun 1783-sm folio-hf mor(54p)-(reads 66p)-facs-
n.p.-n.d. (5w0, rub) 17.50
--& Mount Vernon-NY-1889-352p-MDConway, ed-L I Hist Soc,
Vol 4 (5t9) 20.00
--A Circular Letter-Lond-1783-Stockdale-sm4to-hf calf-
1st Engl ed-(same yr as first ed) (5n2) 125.00
--Collection of Papers relative to Half Pay...with Circular Letter-
Bost-1783-Order of General Court-4to-hf mor-tall cpy-
2nd ed(same year as 1st) (5n2) 150.00
--Despedida de Washington al Pueblo de los Estados-Unidos-
Buenos Ayres-(1813)-Ninos Expositos-sm12mo-39p-disbnd-
rare (5L1) 250.00
--Diary...Sept to Dec 1785-Bost-1902-reprnt from Col Soc of
Mass-orig wrps-75p-ltd to 250c (4m0) 5.00
--Epistles Domestic, etc-NY-1796-calf-303p
(4j6) 45. (5m3, hng weak) 65. (5z7) 75.00
--Exhibition of Engraved Portraits of-NY-Dec 14, 1899 to Jan 6,
1900-Grolier Club-51p-12mo-wrps-2 errata sheets (5h9) 6.50
--Geo Washington, Sportsman-n.p.-1928-8vo-bds-cl bk-
100c priv prntd Cosmos Pr, Cambr, Mass (5a3) 50.00
--History of Geo Washington Bicentennial Celebration-Wash-1932-
5 vols-illus-4to (4b7) 50.00
--Journal of ....Sent by the Hon Robt Dinwiddie to the Commandant
of French Forces in Ohio-NY-1865-46p-prntd wrps-fldg map-
(uncut&unopened)-ltd to 200 copies (5r7) 10.00
--The Last Official Address of His Excellency Gen'l....to the
Legis to which is added A Collection of Papers relative to
Half Pay etc-Hartf-1783-Hudson&Goodwin-48p-hf mor-
sm8vo (5L1) 125.00
--Last Will & Testament of...-Bost-Feb, 1800-wrps-24p-sewn
(5g4, f) 17.50 (5z7) 35. (4j1) 32.50
--The Legacy of the Father of His Country-Address of....on
declining Suffrages of his Fellow Citizens for Presidency of the
US (caption title)-8vo-calf-24p (5n2) 85.00
--Letter of Gen'l Washington to Lund Washington, Cambridge,
20 Aug 1775-n.p.-n.d.-8p-stitchd-50c prntd (5g3, unopnd) 12.50
--Letters & Recollections of-being Letters to Tobias Lear & others-
NY-1906-Jared Sparks, ed-8vo-cl-illus (5L1) 10.00
--same-Lond-1906-289p-1st Engl ed (5w9, fade) 12.50
--Letters from His Excell Geo Washington....to Sir John Sinclair
etc-Lond-1800-WBulmer&Co-57p-folio-orig bds
(5L1, pres, loose) 45.00
--Letters from Gen'l Washington in Jun & Jul 1776...Interesting
View of Amer Politics-Phila-1795-(BenjFBache)-Federal Pr-
8vo-bds-44p-(forgeries) (5L1) 35.00
--Life of-Phila-1845-sm4to-cl-juvenile-plts-1st ed (5p5) 25.00
--Official Letters to Amer Congress written during war betw
United Colonies & Great Brit-Bost-1795-2 vols-12mo-mor-
Manning&Loring-1st ed (5n2, vf) 185.00
--same-Lond-1795-2 vols-London ed(without frontis & addi
title pgs) (5g4, wn, broke) 25.00

WASHINGTON, GEORGE (continued)

--same-NY-1796-2 vols-12mo
(5L3, rbnd, lacks port) 50. (5ss5, ex-libr, mismatchd bndg) 12.50
--same-Bost-1796-calf-2 vols (5L3, vg) 65.00
--To the People of the US, Announcing His Intention of Retiring-
Phila-1800-Maxwell-40p-orig bds-(first line on pg 17 ending
"union") (5r7) 25.00
--Tribute to Washington for Febr 22, 1800-Troy-1800-Poem-
RMoffitt-8vo-15p-(John Lovett) (5L1) 25.00
--Washington & Generals of the Amer Revo-Phila-1864-2 vols in 1-
tooled-skiver-336p-illus-wi corr (5w4, edge wn) 7.50
--Washington, His Person As Represented by Artists-Virginia-1873-
R F Walker-23p-wrps-8vo (4a0) 32.50
--Washington und die Nordamerikanische Revolution-Giesen-1807-
12mo-194p-bds-(Sabin & Howes List Later Date) (5L1) 20.00
--Washington's Farewell Address to People of US-NY-1809-
lg16mo-45p-bds&cl-for Wash Benevolent Soc (wi signed
membership lf) (5w5, rub) 10.00
--same-Hudson-1812-sm16mo-47p-orig bds-Wash Benevolent Soc-
signed lf of membership-orig bds-WmENorman
(5L8, lacks frontis, sp def) 10.00
--same-Worcester-1813-Sturtevant-76p-frontis-hf lea (5qq8) 7.50
--same-Springfield-1813-Dickman-narr 12mo-bds-calf sp-port&68p
(5L1, sp wn) 15.00
--same-Hartf-1814-frontis-24mo-70p-hf lea (5L3, f) 15.00
--same-NY-1852-71p-wrps-German transl by FWBogen-Engl&German
(5h7) 5.00
--same-Bost-1913-4to-orig bds-cl bk-ltd to 440c-Riverside Pr
(5m6) 10.00
--Washington's Political Legacies....wi a Biographical Sketch-
NY-1800-Forman-12mo-mor-port inserted-2nd ed(8p list
of subscr) (5n2) 125.00
--Washington's Reception by Ladies of Trenton etc-NY-1903-
Iconophiles Soc-4p facs of the "Chorus"-4to-orig yell prntd wrps-
ltd to 104c-illus (5L1) 20.00
--Will of...to Which is Annexed a Schedule of His Property-
Alexandria-1800-16mo-32p-fragile (5a3, chip) 75.00
--Writings of...wi biog by J Sparks-Bost-1837-12 vols-4to-plts-
maps-lg papr-bds&cl-1st ed (5h9, unopnd, rub) 28.50
--same-Bost-1855-12 vols-illus-maps-plts (5m4) 55.00
--Writings-NY-1889-qtr lea-14 vols-Letterpress Ed-ltd to 750
nbrd sets (4b6, sp lacks) 100.00
WASHINGTON, GUIDE TO EVERGREEN STATE-Portl-(1941)-
photos-maps-pkt map-e.p.map-653p plus index-1st ed-
Amer Guide Ser-WPA (4L5, dj) 15.00
WASHINGTON'S HEADQUARTERS-Historical Sketch of-(NY)-
(1927)-8vo-wrps-(19p)-Wash Hdgtrs Assoc-7th ed (5t7) 4.00
WASHINGTON HISTORICAL QUARTERLY-& Pac NW Qtrly,
Vol 19 #1 to Vol 26, #4-Vol 27, @1 to Vol 45, #4-104 nbrs
(4 issues missng)-(Jan, 1928 thru Oct, 1954) (5s4) 125.00
WASHINGTON, MRS-The Unrivalled Cook Book & Housekeeper's
Guide-NY-1886-640p (5c0) 8.50
WASHINGTON NATIONAL MONUMENT-Its Dedication, Feb 21,
1885-Wash-1885-4to-cl-frontis-priv prntd-1st ed (5p5) 7.50
WASHINGTON, S H L-Early Hist of the Stricklands of Sizergh-
(1942)-100p (5t9) 15.00
WASHINGTON STATE HIST SOC-Building A State, Washington
1889 to 1939-Tacoma-1940-Vol 3-cl-607p, (19)
(5t4) 8. (5r0, dj) 10.00
WASHINGTON ST SUBWAY-Comments on Financial Condition
of Boston Elev Rwy Co-(Bost)-Apr 26, 1902-12mo-16p leaflet,
stapled (5ss5) 12.50
WASHINGTON-Tomb of, at Mount Vernon-Phila-1840-76p-litho-
title pg & 4 plts-8vo-hf mor-(Strickland) (5L1) 35.00
WASHINGTON, Wm-Collection of Relics & Memorabilia of
GWashington-NY-(1920)-illus-priced-Amer Art Assoc (5t4) 10.00
WASHINGTONIAN, THE-for Apr 12, 1813-Windsor(Vt)-1813-4p-
tall folio-weekly (5r7) 25.00
WASHTENAW CO, MICH-Portrait & Biographical Album of-1891-
639p-lea (5mm7, bkstrp loose) 30.00
WASMUTH, GUNTHER-Wasmuth's Lexikon der Baukunst-Berlin-
(1929 to 37)-mor bk-5 vols-4to-col illus-scarce (5jj3, vg) 97.50
WASON, BETTY-Cooking without Cans-NY-(1943)-186p (5c9) 3.00
WASON, J CATHCART-East Africa & Uganda-Lond-1905-12mo-
illus (5j2) 8.00
WASSERMAN, JACOB-Bula Matari, Stanley, Conqueror of a
Continent-NY-1933-Liveright-photos-351p
(4t 5) 3. (5x2) 6. (5t4) 5. (5c6) 5.75
WASSON, ARTHUR LEE-Adventuring with a Purpose-SanAntonio-
(1951)-134p-map-illus (5xx5) 9.50
WASSON, BEN-Devil Beats His Wife-1929 (5L7) 4.00

WASSON,VALENTINA-Mushrooms,Russia & History-NY-1957-
Pantheon-lg4to-buck-g.t.-82 plts(some col)-1st ed-ltd to
512c   (4h0,vf,lacks box)   825.00

WAT TYLER-A dramatic poem,in 3 acts-Lond-1817-12mo-orig
wrps-1st ed,2nd issue   (5x3,box)   30.00

WATANNA,ONOTO-A Japanese Blossom-NY-1906-263p-illus
    (5t7)   8.00

--A Japanese Nightingale-NY&Lond-1901-225p-illus by Yeto
    (5t7)   8.00

WATCH & CLOCK ESCAPEMENTS-Pa-1904-Jewelers Cir,
Keystone-179p-8vo   (5bb0)   15.00

WATER WITCH,THE-Phila-1831-Carey&Lea-1st ed-2 vols-
orig calf&bds   (4b1)   60.00

WATERBURY WOMEN'S CLUB COOK BOOK 1889 to 1939-
Waterbury-1939-317p-stif wrps-spiral bnd   (5c4)   4.00

WATERFIELD,MARGARET H,illus-A Book of Gardens-Lond-(1920)-
131p-8 col illus-12mo-bds   (5s7)   3.00

--Corners of Grey Old Gardens-Lond-(1914,1st ed)-150p-
8 col illus-pict bds   (5s7)   5.00

--Flower Grouping in English,Scotch & Irish Gardens-1907-
JMDent-col illus-237p-4to   (5x0)   17.50

WATERHOUSE,BENJ-Cautions to Young Persons Concerning Health-
Cambridge-1822-5th ed-40p-8vo-wrps   (4c1)   50.00

--Oratio Inauguralis,quam in Academia Harvardiana...(Oct 9,1783)-
4to-orig prntd wrps-(4p),8p-Cambr-1829-1st ed
    (5a3,pres,chip)   60.00

WATERHOUSE,SYLVESTER-Memorial to Congr to Secure Adequate
Approp for Prompt & Thoro Improvement of Mississippi River-
StL-1877-39p-limp cl-front-1st ed   (4dd1,sl ink spot)   12.50

--Resources of Missouri-StL-1867-unbnd-8vo-96p-1st ed
    (4g6) 7.50   (4L0,wrps)   20.00

--Westward Movement of Capital,etc-n.p.-1890-leaflet-12mo-
15p   (5w5,sl stn) 3.50   (4g6)   7.50

WATERLAND,DANIEL-Works-Oxf-1843-calf-g.borders-6 vols-
2nd ed-(Van Mildert,ed)   (4d1)   35.00

WATERLOO,STANLEY-The Story of Ab-Chig-1897-Way&Williams-
12mo-353p-frontis-t.e.g.-bndg designed by Will Bradley-
1st ed   (5p1,spec bndg)   45.00

WATERMAN,ALICE C-Original Recipes & Cooking Help-n.p.-
1907-48p-Nat'l Starch Co-wrps   (5g9,chip)   2.50

WATERMAN,AMY-A Little Preserving Book for a Little Girl-
Bost-1920-frontis-197p   (5c5)   3.00

WATERMAN,CAPT J H-Conquest of the Bison-NY-1945-18p-
illus-8vo-wrps   (5g5)   3.00

WATERMAN,CATHARINE H-Flora's Lexicon-Phila-1850-col frontis-
dec cl-252p   (5t4)   5.00

WATERMAN,N,ed-Ben King's Verse-Bost-1901-12mo   (5x2)   6.00

WATERMAN,THOS-The Dwellings of Colonial America-
ChapelHill-c1950-312p-illus   (5w4)   12.50

--The Mansions of Virginia 1706 to 1776-ChapelHill,NC-(1945)-
456p-illus   (5t7)   12.50

--Native Houses of Western NoAmer-NY-1921-12mo-wrps-97p-
fldg map-illus   (5g5)   3.00

--Whaling Equipment of Makah Indians-Seattle-Jun 1920-
U of W Pub,Vol 1#1-plts-1st ed-67p-wrps   (4b2,soil)   7.50

--Yurok Geography-U C,1920-(UC Pubs in Amer Arch & Eth
Vol 16,#5,pg 177 to 314,plts 1 to 16)-4to-wrps (5h4,f)   15.00

WATERMAN'S-Ideal Fountain Pen-NY-(190?)-catalogue-
photos of 32 models-obl 8vo-17p,(3)-bds   (5hh6)   7.50

WATERS,E-Life in Music- 1955-Macmillan-653p   (5p7)   8.50

WATERS,ETHEL-His Eye is on Sparrow-GardenCty- 1951-1st ed-
278p   (5i3,autg,dj) 12.50 (5x2) 3.   (5L7)   4.50

WATERS,FRANK-The Colorado-NY-(1946)-illus-400p
    (4n1,dj) 8.   (5xx5)   11.00

--same-n.p.-(NY)-c1946-400p-illus-Nat'l Travel Club ed
    (5w0,dj)   4.50

--The Earp Brothers of Tombstone-NY-(1960)-247p-1st ed
  (5ee3,f,dj) 4.   (4L0,f,dj)   5.00

--Leon Gaspard-Flagstaff-1964-Northland Pr-114p-col illus-
cl-ltd ed,autg,box   (5d6)   25.00

--The Man Who Killed the Deer-(1942)-Farrar&Rinehart
    (5F1,vf,dj)   12.50

--Masked Gods,Navaho & Pueblo Ceremonialism-Albuqu-1950-
1st ed-scarce-438p   (5g2) 20. (5L2,dj,4j0)   25.00

--same-Univ of New Mex Pr-1950-ltd to 300c,autg
  (5x5,dj) 20.   (5m9,f,dj)   30.00

--Midas of the Rockies-NY-(1937)-illus-344p-1st ed-scarce
  (5ee3) 12.50 (4m2,dj) 15. (5x5,dj)   17.50

--same-1949-Univ of Denv-Stratton Centennial Ed-cl-347p-
illus   (5m9,crack,dj) 6. (5h5,vf,dj)   10.00

--The Wild Earth's Nobility-NY-1935-8vo-orig cl-454p
    (5F1,dj,mint) 8.50 (5p5)   7.50

WATERS,H F-Genealogical Gleanings in England-1901-1643p-
2 vols   (4t2)   40.00

WATERS,HAROLD-Adventure Unlimited-NY-(1955)-265p-
photos   (5s1,dj)   4.50

WATERS,HENRY F-An Exam of the Engl Ancestry of Geo
Washington-Bost-1889-53p-map-   (5w5,lacks wrps)   4.50

WATERS,L L-Steel Trails to Santa Fe-Lawrence,Ka-1950-493p
plus index-illus-maps-1st ed (5g0,f,dj) 10. (4L0,dj,f)   7.50

WATERS,LAW & ALLIED FAMILIES-Mayflower Ancestry of Geo
Leland Waters-Lincoln-1929-cl-orig wrps bnd in-96p-
(Philomene Jenkins) (4i2,pres) 12.50 (4t2)   7.50

WATERS,NICHOLAS B-System of Surgery from Works of Benj Bell-
Phila-1806-8vo-lea-570p,29p-12 plts-3rd ed (5t0)   15.00

WATERS,R D-Calais,a Treatise on the Town & Vicinity-1852-
31p   (5t9)   15.00

WATERS,R E C-Parish Registers in England-1883-106p (5t9)   7.50

WATERS,RAYMOND-Bethlehem....Long Ago & Today-Bethlehem-
1923-159p-illus   (5w5)   5.00

WATERS,RUSSELL JUDSON-El Estranjero-Chig-1910-illus-8vo-
1st ed   (5dd6) 5. (4g6)   6.00

WATERS,THOS FRANKLIN-Ipswich In the Massachusetts Bay
Colony,1633 to 1700-Ipswich-1905-586p-36 plts&maps-
orig cl bkd bds   (5t9,5m3)   25.00

--A Sketch of the Life of John Winthrop the Younger,Founder
of Ipswich,Mass-(Cambr)-1900-Ipswich Hist Soc #7-t8vo-
illus-2nd ed-ltd to 300c   (5ss5)   8.50

--same-n.p.(Ipswich)-1900-4to-78p (5w0,rbnd,orig wrps bnd in)   8.50

WATERS,WILLARD-Check List of Amer Laws, Charters & Constitu
of 17th & 18th Cent in Huntington Library-SanMarino-1936-
140p-wrps   (5j4)   8.50

WATERS,WM-A Gallery of Western Badmen-(Covington,Ky,
1954)-33p-illus-stiff wrps (5xx5) 4. (5L0,   3.00

WATERSTON,ROBT-Brief Memoir of...a Boston Marchant-Bost-
1869-orig wrps-11p-8vo-(ChasDeane) (5ss5,pres)   10.00

--Catalogue of Library & Collection of Autog Letters,Papers &
Doc...Mass Hist Soc-Bost-1906-t8vo-cl-479p (5j5,ex-libr)   7.50

WATERTON,CHAS-Wanderings in SoAmer,the NW of the US etc
in years 1812,1816,1820 & 1824-Lond-1825-326p-folio-
hf mor   (4t4,wn) 30. (5n4)   45.00

--same-Lond-1828   (5m2)   12.50

--same-Lond-1879-new ed by Wood (5p7,ex-libr)   5.00

--same-Lond-1880-enlrgd-illus   (5r7)   12.50

WATERTOWN LAND & IMPROVEMENT CO-(Watertown,1891)-
obl 8vo-wrps-32p   (5g3,sp tn)   25.00

WATERTOWN LAND & IMPROVEMENT CO-(n.p.,ca 1892)-
4to-wrps-illus-16p   (5g4,corn tn)   25.00

WATERTOWN(MASS)-Military History-1907-281p (4t2,crack)   7.50

WATERY WAR,THE-or,Poetical Descrip of Existing Controversy
betw Pedobaptists & Baptists-by John of Enon-Bost-1808-
34p   (5t7)   15.00

WATKIN,E L-Catholic art & culture-Lond-1947-182p-sm8vo-cl-
illus   (5m5)   10.00

WATKINS,ALBERT,ed-Collections of the Nebr State Historical
Soc..Vol 16-Lincoln-1911-196p-illus (5w0)   10.00

WATKINS,GEO-The Compleat English Brewer or The Whole Art
& Mystery of Brewing-Lond-1768-239p,(4)-12mo-calf
    (5w1,front cov dtchd)   35.00

WATKINS,REV I B-Scripture History, including Lives of most
celebrated Apostles-Lond-1823-sm8vo-2 vols
    (5c8,lacks fldg frontis & title)   15.00

WATKINS,JOHN V-ABC of Orchid Growing-Chig-(1948)-
134p-1st ed   (4g0)   4.50

WATKINS,LURA W-American Glass & Glass Making-NY-1950-
1st ed-illus   (5qq7,dj) 12.50 (5w7)   6.50

--Cambridge Glass 1818 to 1888-Bost-(1930)-12mo-cl-illus (5t7) 10.00

--Development of Amer Glassmaking-Bost-1935-8vo-prntd wrps-
illus-39p   (5t7)   4.50

WATKINS,N J,ed-Pine & Palm Greeting-Balt-1873-131p-ads-cl
  (5h1,soil,rbnd) 5. (5ss5)   17.50

WATKINS,MAJ ROLIN C,ed-History of Monterey & Santa Cruz
Co,Calif-Vol 1(of 2 vols)-Chig-1925-R8vo-504p-port-plts
    (5r8)   20.00

WATKINS,S C G-Remin of Montclair,from 1876-NY-1929-
Barnes&Co-12mo-cl   (4t1,pres)   12.50

WATKINS,SAM R-Co Aytch,Maury Gray's 1st Tenn Regiment-
Jackson,Tenn-1952   (5h6) 20. (5x5,dj)   10.00

WATKINS,SYLVESTER C-Anthology of Amer Negro Literature-
NY-(1944)-The Modern Library- (5j2,dj)   6.50

--Pleasures of Smoking-NY-(1948)-illus-1st ed (4b7)   8.50

WATKINS,W E-Digestion & Mineral Balance Trials on Range
Cattle,etc-Jun,1933-NM Col of Agri Bul #212-32p-wrps
    (5L5)   5.00

WATROUS,ANSEL-Biographical Sketch of Rollin Q Tenney-
(Fort Collins,1918)-(21p)-2 illus-wrps-tied   (4L0)   6.00
WATSON,ALEXANDER WATSON-American Home Garden-NY-
1859-531p-illus   (5xx7)   7.50
WATSON,ARTHUR-Long Harpoon-NewBedford-1929-165p-
illus-1st ed   (5s1,rprd)   15.00
WATSON,AUGUSTA CAMPBELL-Dorothy the Puritan-NY-1893-
frontis-1st ed   (5ee3)   7.50
--Off Lynnport Light,a novel-NY-1895-Dutton-frontis-1st ed
(5m2)   8.50
WATSON,B A-Sportsman's Paradise-Phila-1888-290p-cl-1st ed
(5h2)   8.50
WATSON,B F-Addresses,Reviews & Episodes-NY-1901-8vo-
142p   (4a7,cov soil)   4.50
WATSON,DOUGLAS S-Founding of the First Calif Missions-
SanFran-1934-Nueva Calif Pr-4to-bds   (5h4,f,wn dj)   25.00
--West Wind-LosAng-1934-4to-bds-lea bk-fldg map&ports-
100c prntd by Percy H Booth   (5F5,ex-libr) 45. (5x5)   200.00
WATSON,E H L-Contemporary Comments-Lond-1931-356p-
illus   (5t7,dj)   6.50
WATSON,ELIZABETH ANN-Sketch of Life of George C Yount-
(SanFran-1915?)-16p-wrps   (5tt0)   15.00
WATSON,ELKANAH-Men & Times of the Revolution-NY-1856-
460p   (5w4,edge wn)   25.00
WATSON,ELMO SCOTT-The Professor Goes West-Bloomington-
1954-138p   (4L0,mint) 4.50   (5k0)   6.00
WATSON,ERNEST B-Sheridan to Robertson-Cambridge-1926-
19 illus-8vo-cl-19p,485p-1st ed   (5t0)   7.50
WATSON,ERNEST W-Forty Illustrators & How They Work-NY-
1946-4to-illus   (5jj3)   12.50
WATT,F-Law's Lumber Room-Lond-1895   (5ff4)   7.50
WATSON,FRANCIS-Men & Books,Daniel Defoe-Lond-1952-
Longmans,Green-sm8vo-dec cl-240p,4 facs   (5aa2)   4.50
WATSON,FREDK-A Century of Gunmen-Lond-1931-289(290)p
plus index-1st ed-scarce   (4L0,dj)   15.00
--The Story of the Highland Regiments-Lond-1925-frontis-cl-323p
(5t4)   18.50
WATSON,G-Action for Unity-NY-1937-12mo   (5x2)   5.00
WATSON,GAYLORD,publ-Handbook of the US of Amer & Guide
to Emigration-Chig-1882-Tenney&Weaver-8vo-dec cl-
191p & 5p ads   (5jj5)   20.00
WATSON,HENRY C-Camp Fires of the Revolution-Phila-1863-
448p-plts   (5xx5,fly tn)   5.00
--Heroic Women of History-Phila-1856-496p-illus-g.e. (5xx5)   9.50
WATSON,I-Physicians & Surgeons of America-Concord-1896-
483p-4to-illus   (5ii2)   9.50
WATSON,J -Hand Book of Calisthenics & Gymnastics-NY-1868-
388p-illus   (5ii2)   7.50
WATSON,J-Trial of Jas Watson for High Treason at Bar of
Court of King's Bench-Lond-1817-2 vols-(Gurney) (5ff4)   19.50
WATSON,JAS-The Dog Book-NY-1906-2 vols-4to-746p-photos-
scarce   (4a6)   65.00
WATSON,JAS E-As I Knew Them-Indnpls-(1936)-330p-illus-
1st ed   (5qq8)   5.00
WATSON,JEANNETTE GRACE-Ole Ann & Other Stories-Lond-
1906-cl-126p-illus   (4t7)   8.50
WATSON,JOHN-The Scot of 18th Century-Lond-n.d.-345p (5a1)4.50
WATSON,JOHN-Philosophical Basis of Religion,series of
lectures-1907   (5L7)   6.00
WATSON,JOHN,(MD)-Thermal ventilation & other sanitary
improvements etc-NY-1851-fldng plan-wrps   (5g8)   10.00
WATSON,JOHN F-Annals of Philadelphia-Phila-1830-illus-
calf-1st ed   (5yy6,pg tn,badly fox) 17.50 (4b1,rbnd)   85.00
--same-Phila-1844-illus-2 vols-buck   (5h9,rbnd)   32.50
--same-Phila-1845-orig cl   (5h9)   30.00
--same-Phila-1857-orig cl-609,642p   (5h9)   27.50
--Annals of Phila& Pa,In Olden Time-Phila-1884-illus-1766p-
4to-3 vols   (4m4)   42.50
--same-enlrgd by Willis P Hazard-Phila-1900-3 vols-illus (5w5)   40.00
--Historic Tales of Olden Time-NY-1832-papr labl-sm8vo-10 plts-
1st ed   (4n5,sl fox) 40.00   (5i3,f) 15. (4L8,sl fox)   35.00
--same-Phila-1833-316p-illus   (5m4)   35.00
WATSON,JOHN T-Dictionary of Poetical Quotations-Phila-
1879-frontis-cl-504p   (5t0)   3.75
WATSON,KATE H-Textiles & Clothing-Chig-1911-244p-illus-
Libr of Home Economics   (5n7)   2.50
WATSON,KETTREDGE,BROADWELL & ALLIED FAMILIES-NY-
1961-priv prnt for Mrs Thos J Watson-ports-plts-89p-4to-
g.-mor   (4b6)   25.00
WATSON,L-List of Publications of Dept of Commerce-Wash-1937-
141p-wrps   (5j4)   4.00
WATSON,M M G-Taft Ranch,History of 50 Years of Development-
n.p.-c1920-52p-wrps   (5n4,fox)   25.00

WATSON,MARGARET-Arranging Flowers-NY-n.d.-Studio Pub-
64p-col frontis-photos   (5s7)   2.50
WATSON,N-Round Mystery Mountain-Lond-1935-246p-illus
(4b9)   12.00
WATSON,PAUL BARRON-Tragic Career of Jas Barron,USN-
NY-(1924)-84p-frontis   (5s1,ex-libr)   3.50
WATSON,PETER WM-Dendrologia Brittanica or Trees etc-Lond-
1825-hf calf-8vo-172 col plts-errata lf & last lf Vol 2 misbnd-
illus-2 vols-1st ed   (4n5,rebkd,sl fox)   400.00
WATSON,R-An Apology for the Bible-NY-1796-T&JSwords-
calf -178p   (5q8,ex-libr,wn)   12.50
--same-Phila-Bishop-1796-80p-sewn as issued   (5m2)   15.00
WATSON,RICHARD-The Life of Rev John Wesley-NY-1831-
frontis-12mo-lea-323p   (5t2)   5.00
--same-Cooperstown-1841-328p-lea   (5t7)   7.50
--Observations on Southey's "Life of Wesley"-NY-1821-252p-lea
(5t4)   10.50
WATSON,ROBT-Boy of Great North West-Ottawa-1930-259p-
Graphic Publ-plts   (5s0)   7.50
--Canadas Furbearers-Ottawa-1925-Graphic Publ-card cov (4b9)   8.00
WATSON,ROWLAND-Merry Gentlemen-Lond-1951-sm4to-
frontis-illus-1st ed-237p   (5p0) 6. (5yy6)   10.00
WATSON,S J-Constitutional History of Canada-Tor-1874-157p-
Vol 1(all publ)   (4b9)   10.00
WATSON,REV S L-Remarks on Temperance-Charleston-1859-20p-
disbnd   (5w1,title loose)   4.50
WATSON,THOS A-Exploring Life,the Autobiography of-NY-1926-
315p-illus   (5y2)   7.50
WATSON,VIRGINIA-With Cortes the Conqueror-Phila-1927-
332p-illus   (5w9)   4.50
WATSON,W W -Our Alaskan Trip- Salina-n.d.-(1910 or 1911)-
78p-photos-priv prntd in few copies-rare   (5L0)   15.00
WATSON,WILBUR J-Bridge Architecture-NY-1927-illus-288p-
folio   (5ww3)   15.00
WATSON,WM- Eloping   Angels-Lond-1893-The Bodley Head-
4to-cl-1st ed-ltd to 250c (5p5,rbkd) 10. (5ss3,crack)   25.00
--Epigrams of Art,Life,& Nature-Liverpool-1884-Gilbert G
Walmsley-   12mo-orig cl-sp labl-1st ed-ltd to 50c
(5ss3,labl stnd)   50.00
--Excursions in Criticism-Lond-1893-Elkin Mathews & John Lane-
bds-1st ed-ltd to 50c   (5ss3,crack,sp stn)   35.00
--The Father of the Forest & other poems-Lond-1895-JohnLane-
frontis-cl-1st ed-ltd to 75c   (5ss3,sp stnd)   35.00
--For England-Lond-1904-JohnLane-cl   (5ss3,fade)   10.00
--The Heralds of the Dawn-Lond-1912-The Bodley Head-1st ed
(5ss3,sl chip)   10.00
--The Poems of-Lond-1905-John Lane-2 vols-8vo-orig cl-1st ed
(5ss3,pres,box)   50.00
--Sable & Purple with other peoms-NY-1910-JohnLaneCo-8vo-
cl-1st ed   (5ss3,long pres)   35.00
--The Year of Shame-Lond-1897-JohnLane-cl-1st ed (5ss3,rub) 10.00
WATSON,WINSLOW C-Descriptive & Pict Guide to Champlain
Valley & Adirondacks-(1871?)-144p-12 illus on col papr-
fldg pkt map-resort ads   (4m2,cov blistered)   30.00
WATT,ALEX-The Art of Soap Making-Lond-1907-310p,(16)-illus-
7th ed   (5n7)   5.00
WATT,FRANCIS-The Law's Lumber Room-Lond-1895-JLane (5p9) 5.00
WATT,FREDK-Who Dare to Live-NY-1943-68p poem (5s1,dj)   2.50
WATT,G D-Report of 3 Nights Public Discussion in Bolton betw
Wm Gibson & Rev Woodville Woodman-Liverpool-1851-46p
extract   (5L0)   20.00
WATT,HOMER A-Dictionary of English Literature-NY-1947 (4a1) 6.50
WATT,I-World to Come-Pittsb-1846-563p-calf (5h1,hng rprd)   5.00
WATT,L MACLEAN-The Hills of Home-Lond-(1914)-8vo-cl-260p-
col illus   (5t0)   4.50
WATT,RACHEL STUART-In the Heart of Savagedom-Lond-n.d.-
Pickering & Inglis-photos-422p-4th ed   (4t5)   12.00
WATT,ROBERTA FRYE-Four Wagons West-Portland-(1931)-1st ed
(5jj7) 5. (5s4,ex-libr) 6. (5dd1,f,dj,pres)   8.50
--Story of Seattle-Portland-(1931)-illus-xi,387p (5r0,autg,5cc4)10.00
WATTERS,P-Brunswick-Atlanta-1964-Special report by Southern
Reg Council   (5x2)   7.00
WATTERSON,HENRY-Hist of Spanish Amer War-Chig-(1898)-
662p-cl   (5h7)   7.50
WATTS,EDITH BALLARD-Jesse's Book of Creole & Deep South
Recipes-NY-1954-184p   (5c4) 3.50   (5g9)   5.00
WATTS,FRANKLIN,ed-Voices of History 1943,44-NY-1944(5x7) 4.50
WATTS,GEO-Sermon Preached Before Trustees for Establishing
Colony of Georgia in Amer on Mar 18,1735-Lond-1736-27p-
disbnd   (5x5)   125.00

WATTS,GEO C-The Long Trail-(Oakdale,1949)-port-188p-
  priv prntd   (5xx5,f)   8.50
WATTS,HAMP B-The Babe of the Company-Fayette,Mo-1913-
  33p-photos-wrps-1st ed-rare   (5L5)   175.00
WATTS,ISAAC-Divine & Moral Songs for Children-Bost-1811-
  Armstrong-16mo-72p-frontis-illus-wrps (4F6,sl rprd,fox) 55.00
--same-Lond-1866-illus-dec bndg-bevelled edges (5L0,rprd) 12.50
--Divine Songs...for Use of Children-Lond-(ca1810)-tall 12mo-
  papr bds-frontis-8 illus-70p   (4d1)   15.00
--same-NY-1837-M Day-24mo-47 woodcuts-rare (4F6) 17.50
--Doctrine of Passions Explain'd & Improv'd-Dublin-1737-
  R Reilly-3rd ed   (5aa0,rbnd)   12.50
--Dr Watts' Plain & Easy Catechisms for Children-Newburyport-
  papr bds   (4F6,fox,sl stns)   22.50
--Horae Lyricae-Lond-(1706?)-3 books in 1
    (5v2,lacks t.p.,frontis,1st 3 lvs)   15.00
--same-Lond-1743-frontis-calf-8th ed (4F6) 17.50
--same-Haverhill-1802-port-orig calf (5m1) 7.50
--The Improvement of the Mind -Lond-1804-Rivington-8vo-516p-
  calf   (5rr2,f ox)   15.00
--same-Bennington-1807-Haswell-in 2 parts-24mo-lea-lea labl
    (5p1,sp rprd)   25.00
--Improvement of the Mind-Lond-Rivington-1811-2 pts in 1 vol-
  516p-hf calf   (5a1)   12.50
--same-2 parts in 1 vol-Lond-1821-prntd for Edwards&Knibb-
  calf-3 plts-24mo-lea labl (5p1) 15.00
--Logick,or,the right use of reason-Lond-1745-for Longman&Shewell-
  365p -8th edition   (5v6,rbnd)   10.00
--same-Newburyport-1796-Isaiah Thomas-12mo-285p-calf-
  2nd Amer ed   (5v0)   6.00
--A new Collection of Hymns,including Divine Songs-Liverpool-
  1821-16mo-160p-orig bds-lea sp (5c8) 8.50
--Poetical Works-Stanhope Pr-1807-12mo-calf-g.borders-2 plts-
  2 vols   (5s0)   6.50
--The Psalms of David-Phila-1781-R Aitken-252p -12mo-mor-
  extra,by Stikeman (5L1,broke,lacks 16p music) 15.00
--same-Worcester-1786-Isaiah Thomas-8vo-calf-1st Worcester ed
    (5i9,wn,pres,4 pg def)   125.00
--same-Bost-1791-I Thomas&Andrews-calf-227p(1) (4k9,wn) 17.50
--Psalms,Hymns etc-Bost-(1823-lea labl-496p,15¢ calf(5ss5) 12.50
--Songs Against Faults-NY-n.d.-McLoughlin Bros-24mo-(12p)-
  4 col illus   (5v0)   7.50
--Songs,Divine & Moral-NY-n.d.-Sam'l Wood&Sons-16mo-45p-
  illus wrprs-illus-sewn (5v0,wn) 12.50
--The World to Come-Bost-1758-Rogers&Fowle-2 vols in 1-8vo-
  189p,192p-calf-1st Amer ed (5v2) 60.00
WATTS,MARY ANN-Mystery Revealed-Dayton-1854-62p-wrps
    (5h2,lacks bk wrp,fox)   12.50
WATTS,RICHARD JR-Franco's Black Spain-NY-(1946)-4to-illus-
  by Quintanilla-1st ed (5yy6) 8.00
WATT'S SONGS-Early Religion-NY-(1868)-16mo-pict wrps-col illus-
  (12p)   (5v2,5t7)   6.50
WATT'S SONGS-Praises for Good-(ca 1870s)-McLoughlin,publ-
  12mo-col illus-wrps (5v2,f) 12.50
WATTS-DUNTON,THEODORE-Aylwin-Lond-1899-Hurst&Blackett-
  12mo-cl-1st ed (5ss3,pres,fade) 35.00
--Poetry & the Renascence of Wonder-NY-n.d.(ca 1915)-296p
    (5p6)   7.50
WAUGH,ALEC-Hot Countries-NY-1930-Literary Guild-8vo-
  304p-woodcuts (4a6) 5.00
--In Praise of Wine & Certain Noble Spirits-NY-1959-304p-4to-map
    (4g0)   8.50
--The Lipton Story-GardenCty-1950-277p (5y2) 4.50
--Merchants of Wine-Lond-(1957)-illus-135p (4g0) 8.50
--Unclouded Summer,a Love Story-NY-1948-Farrar,Straus-1st ed
    (4L4,f,dj,autg)   20.00
WAUGH,ARTHUR-Dickensiana-Bloomsbury-1937-Nonesuch Pr-
  lg8vo-cl-1st ed-scarce (5p5) 15.00
--One Man's Road-Lond-1931-389p-illus-1st ed (4b4) 9.50
WAUGH,COULTON-The Comics-NY-1947-Macmillan-illus (5x0)5.00
WAUGH,ELIZ-Collecting Hooked Rugs-NY-(1927)-140p (5n7) 5.00
WAUGH,EVELYN-Love Among the Ruins-Lond-1953-Cr 8vo-illus-
  dec cl-1st ed-orig glassine-ltd to 300c,nbrd,autg (5ss7,mint) 25.00
--The Loved One-Lond-n.d.-8vo-grn cl-t.e.g.-1st ed-ltd to 250c,
  autgs,box (5ee9,2 pres) 100.00
--same-Lond-n.d.-8vo-cl-1st ed (5dd8,dj) 20.00
--Mr Loveday's Little Outing & Other Sad Stories-Lond-1936-
  8vo-cl-1st ed (5dd8,dj,hng rprd) 30.00
--The Ordeal of Gilbert Pinfold-Lond-1957-Cr8vo-cl-1st ed
    (5ss7,vf,dj)   7.50
--Put Out More Flags-Lond-1942-8vo-cl-1st ed (5dd8,dj) 15.00
--Scoop-Lond-1938-8vo-cl-1st ed (5dd8,dj) 50.00

WAUGH,EVELYN (continued)
--Scott's King's Modern Europe-n.p.-1947-Chapman&Hall-
  cl-12mo-1st ed (4g1,dj) 15.00
WAUGH,JULIA-Castro Ville & Henry Castro,Empresario-SanAntonio-
  1934-stiff wrps -100 p (5n4,Streeter copy) 17.50
WAUGH,LORENZO-Autobiography-SanFran-1888-illus-
  4th ed,enlrgd (5m9,fox) 7.50
WAUGH,NORAH-Corsets & Crinolines-Lond-(1954)-115 illus-
  4to-176p (5n7) 7.50
WAVERLEY GALLERY-of Principal Female Characters in Sir
  Walter Scott's Romances-Lond-1841-plts by Heath-R8vo-mor-
    (5tt7,rub,frontis fox)   10.00
WAY,ARTHUR S,trans-The Science of Dining-Lond-1936-174p
    (5g9)   6.00
--The Iliad of Homer-Lond-1910-Macmillan-2 vols-cl-2nd ed
    (5ss3,crack)   15.00
WAY,FREDK,JR-Pilotin' Comes Natural-NY-(1943)-284p-scarce
    (5dd9,autg,sl soil)   16.00
WAY,R P-Antique Dealer-NY-1956-Macmillan-211p (5p0) 4.50
WAY,THOS E-Sgt Fred Platten's 10 Years on the Trail of the
  Redskins-Williams-1959-45p-wrps-illus-1st ed (5g0) 5.00
WAY,T R-The Art of James McNeill Whistler-Lond-1903-53 illus-
  cl-128p (5t2,libr marks) 5.00
--Memories of Jas McNeill Whistler-NY-1912-John Lane-146p-
  4to (4a0) 17.50
--same-Lond&NY-(1912)-illus-150p (5q0) 10.00
WAY TO GET A LESSON-Brookfield-1826-E&G Merriam-32mo-
  31p-illus (5p1,fox) 15.00
WAYGANDT,CORNELIUS-New Hampshire neighbors-NY-1937-
  Holt-1937-368p-illus (5u3) 3.00
WAYLAND,JOHN W-Historic Harrisburg-Staunton-1949-
  ltd to 500c-1st ed (5z5,mint) 30.00
--History of Rockingham Co,Va-Dayton-1912-1st ed
    (5t9,5z5,vg)   25.00
--Men of Mark & Representative Citizens of Harrisonburg &
  Rockingham Co-Staunton-1943-1st ed (5z5,mint) 25.00
--Pathfinder of the Seas-Richmond-1930-191p-illus
    (5ss5) 10. (5c1,4b9) 12.00
--Robert E Lee & His Family-Staunton-1951-illus-1st ed
    (5tt5,f,dj)   6.00
--Scenic & Hist Guide to Shenandoah Valley-Dayton-(1923)-
  106p-cl-2nd ed (5h1) 3.50
--Whispers of the Hills-New Market,Virg-1928-Henkel Pr-
  16mo-104p-pict cl (5p1,pres) 7.50
WAYLEN,MAMES-House of Cromwell & Story of Dunkirk (5t9) 6.50
WAYMAN,DOROTHY G-Edward Sylvester Morse-Cambridge,Mass-
  (1942)-451p-illus (5t4) 5.00
WAYNE,ANTHONY-Ceremonies At Dedication of Equestrian
  Statue of,Valley Forge,Jun,1908-Harrisburg-1909-81p-
  hf mor-illus-fldg,col map (5w4,edge wn) 4.50
WAYNE,ARTHUR T-Birds of SoCarolina-Charleston-1910-fldg map-
  275p-buck (5cc1,rbnd) 16.00
WAYNE,INDIANA,COUNTY OF-Rich-1893-122p-cl-Imperial
  Atlas & Art Folio (5h2,rbkd) 47.50
WAYNE CO,IND-History of-Chig-1884-2 vols (5jj9,rbnd) 55.00
WAYNE CO,MICH-Manual of-1926-300p (4t2) 3.00
WAYNE CO,OHIO-Official Farm Plat Bk & Directory-Madsn-
  n.d.(ca 1958)-76p-wrps (5h2) 7.50
WAYNE,HENRY C-The Sword Exercise,arranged for military
  instruction-Wash-1850,1849,1849-Gideon&Co-cl-23 fldg plts-
  62p & 43p (5L8,chip) 23.50
WAYNE LAW REVIEW-1954 to 70-Vol 1 thru 16 (5ii7,rbnd) 315.00
WAYNE,MARION W-Marguerite Kent-Phila-1870-511p
    (5x4,sp rprd)   10.00
WAYTE,RAYMOND-Coins of the World-NY-(1938)-illus-232p-
  1st ed (5t7) 10.00
WEADOCK,JACK-Dust of the Desert-NY-1936-illus
    (5m9,sl soil,dj)   10.00
WEALE,P B L-The Conflict of Colour-NY-1910-1st ed (5x2) 22.50
WEALE,W H JAS-The Van Eycks & Their Art-Lond-1912-
  Bodley Head-323p-cl-t.e.g.-1st ed-plts (5m5,sl shake) 15.00
WEALTH & BIOGRAPHY-of the wealthy citizens of NY City-
  NY-1845-6th ed (5g4) 15.00
WEALTH OF THE UINTAH BASIN-Vernal,Utah-1914-8vo-76p-
  wrps-ads-promotional-illus (5g5) 7.50
WEAR,BRUCE-Bronze World of Frederic Remington-Tulsa-1966-
  149p-illus (5j4,dj) 8. (5t5) 10.00
WEARE,G E-Cabot's Discovery of NoAmer-Lond-1897-maps-plts-
  256p (5xx5) 8.00
WEATHERBE,K-From the Rideau to the Rhine & Back,6th Field Co
  & Batt Can Engrs,etc-Tor-1928-ports-maps-519p (4d4) 12.50
WEATHERFORD,W D-Amer Churches & the Negro-Bost-1957-
  1st ed (5b9) 5. (5x2) 3.50

WEATHERFORD, W D (continued)
--Negro Life in the South-NY-1918-12mo   (5x2)   15.00
--The Negro From Africa to America-NY-1924-1st ed (5x2)   37.50
--Present Forces in Negro Progress-Wash-1912   (5x2)   27.50
WEATHERHEAD, LESLIE D-Thinking Aloud in War Time-NY-c1940
                                                  (5x7)   3.50
WEATHERLY, FREDK E-Punch & Judy-Lond-(ca 1885)-illus by Patty
    Townsend-col liths-pict bds-MarcusWard (5c8, lacks pref) 10.00
--The Land of Little People-Lond&NY-n.d.-(ca 1887)-12mo-
    48p-cl bk bds-col illus by JMDealy   (5p1, cor wn) 15.00
--Little Miss Marigold-Lond-(ca 1885)-illus by Dealy-23 col plts
                                                  (4F6)   20.00
--Told in the Twilight-NY-n.d.(ca 1883)-illus by MEdwards &
    JCStaples-Dutton-64p-31 col lithos-   pict bds (5p1, wn) 10.00
WEATHERLY, HENRY-A Treatise on the Art of Boiling Sugar-
    Phila-1865-131p, 24p   (5c5, sl wn)   7.50
WEATHERS, JOHN-Beautiful Roses for Garden & Greenhouse-Lond-
    (1903)-152p-33p col plts-pict cov   (5s7, lacks e.p.) 7.50
--The Bulb Book-Lond-1911-cl-8vo   (5z9)   10.00
WEAVER, EMILY P-Canadian History for Boys & Girls-Tor-1905-
    314p-illus-maps   (4a8)   5.00
--Canadian Woman's Annual & Social Service Directory-Tor-
    1915-332p   (5a1)   4.50
--The Counties of Ontario-Tor-1913-Bell&Cockburn-illus-map-
    318p   (5dd7) 9.50 (4b9) 20.00
--Story of Counties of Ontario-Tor-1913-318p-16 plts-map (4d4) 15.00
WEAVER, G S-Lives & Graves of our Presidents-Chig-(1883)-530p-
    cl   (5h1)   5.00
WEATHERSPOON, J B-Sent forth to Preach-1954   (5L7)   4.00
WEAVER, JAS B-Back to the Old Home Farm-DesMoines-1933-
    12mo-wrps-31p   (5m8)   8.50
--A Call to Action-DesMoines-1892   (5x5)   7.50
WEAVER, JOHN V A-Trial Balance-NY-1932-Farrar&Rinehart
                                           (5b2, f, dj, pres) 7.50
WEAVER, LAWRENCE-English Leadwork Its Art & History-Lond-1909-
    268p-4to   (5w7, wn, shake) 7.50
--Story of Royal Scots-Lond-(1915)-272p-16 plts-2 maps (5t0) 5.00
WEAVER, LOUISE BENNETT-Bettina's Best Desserts-NY-(1923)-
    194p-8 col plts   (5g9)   5.00
WEAVER, LUCIUS E-History & Genealogy of a Branch of the
    Weaver Family-Rochester, NY-1928-illus (5tt5, hng split) 17.50
WEAVER, MARTIN G-Mennonites of Lancaster Conference-
    Scottsdale, Pa-1931-1st ed-illus   (5jj3)   15.00
WEAVER, DR R-The Negro & Nat'l Defense-Atlanta-1941-3p-
    wrps-Comm on Interracial Coop   (5x2)   4.00
WEAVER, RAYMOND M-Herman Melville, Mariner & Mystic-
    NY-(1921)-399p-illus   (5m1) 12.50 (5ee3, vf)   15.00
WEAVER, MRS SARAH MARSHALL-Mich Federation Cook Book-
    Charlotte-1909-125p, (39-ads)   (5c4, sl soil) 5.50
WEBB, A P-Bibliography of Works of Thos Hardy-Lond-1916 (4g2) 25.00
WEBB, ADDISON-Beekeeping for Profit & Pleasure-NY-1945-
    illus-116p   (5t7)   5.00
WEBB, ALEX S-The Peninsula, McClellan's Campaign of 1862-
    NY-1881-12mo-231p-1st ed   (5xx5)   4.25
--same-NY-1882   (5xx5)   4.00
WEBB, B J-The Centenary of Catholicity in Kentucky-Louisville-
    1884-ports-594p   (5yy8)   32.50
WEBB, B S-Martin Christopher Randleman, His Kin & Heirs-1965-
    750p   (4t2)   15.00
WEBB, E B-Indian Life at the Old Missions-LosAng-1952-326p-
    52p illus   (5a9, mint, dj) 22.50
WEBB, CHAS-Vagrom Verse-Bost, 1889-1860-12mo-1st ed (5ee3, f) 7.50
WEBB, CHAS HENRY-Liffith Lank, or Lunacy-NY-1866-illus by
    Sol Eytinge, Jr-12mo-prntd wrps-1st ed of auth's 1st book
                                           (5gg6, sl wtrstn) 15.00
--same-NY-1866-Carleton-1st ed-(cl?)   (5m2, wn)   6.50
WEBB, DAN'L-A general history of the Americans, of their customs,
    manners, & colours-Rochdale-1806-TWood-8vo-orig bds-
    papr label-1st ed in Engl   (5i0, f) 90.00
WEBB, EDITH BUCKLAND-Indian Life at Old Missions-LosAng-
    (1952)-Warren F Lewis-326p-illus-cl
                        (5yy3) 30. (5x5, dj) 35. (5h5, vf, dj, box) 25.00
WEBB, EWING T-Strategy in Handling People-Chig-1931-260p-
    illus   (5w4, cov spots) 3.00
WEBB, F R-Manual of Canvas Canoe, Its Construction-NY-1898-
    115p-illus-fldg drwngs in bk plt   (5s1, sl cov stn) 6.00
WEBB, FRANCIS-Somerset, a poem-Lond-1811-4to-orig plain wrps-
    1st ed   -Edward Bentley   (5i8, f, unopnd)
WEBB, MRS G D-Day Dreams in Dixie-Memphis-1924-priv pub
                                                  (5x2)   12.50
WEBB, GEO-A Pima Remembers-Tucson-1959-8vo-126p-cl-1st ed
                                           (5g0, f, dj)   5.00

WEBB, GEO W-Chronological List of Engagements Betw Regular
    Army of US & Various Tribes 1790 to 1898, incl-StJoseph-
    1939-cl-141p   (5F5)   10.00
WEBB, HERSCHEL-An Introduction to Japan-NY-1955-Columbia
    Univ Pr-130p   (5p7)   3.00
WEBB, J WATSON-Speech at Battle Ground of Tippecanoe-
    NY-1856-118p-wrps-3rd ed-"Reprint for Family Circ" (5r7) 12.50
WEBB, JAS M-The Black Man, The Father of Civilization, proven
    by Biblical History-(n.p., n.d.)-(ca 1930)-12mo-illus (5x5) 10.00
WEBB, JAS J-Adventures in the Santa Fe Trade 1844 to 1847-
    Glendale-1931-fldg map-301p-Clark's great SW Hist Ser
    Vol 1   (4L0)   30.00
WEBB, K B-Source Book of Opinion on Human Values-1951 (5L7) 4.00
WEBB, MRS LAURA S-A Requiem for Lee-(NewOrl)-(1870)-16mo-
    32p-port-scarce   (5m4)   50.00
WEBB, SAM'L BLACHLEY-Corres & Journals of-ed by W C Ford-
    NY-1893-3 vols-sm4to-illus-hf mor-ltd to 350 sets (5t0) 50.00
WEBB, SIDNEY-The Decay of Capitalist Civilisation-Westminster-
    1923-t8vo-1st ed   (5r9)   17.50
--The History of Liquor Licensing in England-Lond-1903-
    Michaelmas-special ed prntd by authors for UK Alliance for
    suppr of Liquor Traffic-wrps   (5w1)   25.00
--same-1903-bnd, trade ed   (5w1)   20.00
--Soviet Communism, A New Civilization-NY-1936-2 vols-lg8vo-
    1174p-1st ed   (5p5, box) 25.00
--same-Lond-1937-2 vols in 1-8vl-bnders bds-2nd ed Left Book
    Club Edition Not for Sale   (5t0)   4.50
--same-Lond-(1944)-3rd ed in 1 vol-1007p-postscript (5ss6) 10.00
WEBB, STEPHEN PALFREY-A sketch of causes, operations & results
    of SanFran Vigilance Committee-reprinted from Essex Instit,
    Vol 84, Apr 1948-wrps   (5g4)   7.50
WEBB, THOS H-Information for Kanzas immigrants-Bost-1856-
    stitchd-"11th ed, rev&enlrgd"   (5g4)   15.00
--Organization, Objects & Plan of Operations of Emigrant Aid
    Co, etc-Bost-1854-sewn-24p-3rd ed   (4n4)   40.00
WEBB, THOS S-Freemason's Monitor-Salem-1816-lea-322p (4n9) 15.00
WEBB, TODD-Gold Strikes & Ghost Towns-Dblday&Co-1961-
    1st ed   (5x5) 10. (5k2, dj)   7.50
WEBB, W E-Buffalo Land, etc-Phila-1874-illus-lea labl-503p
                        (5tt0, wn) 15. (4i7, rebnd)   16.00
WEBB, W L-Battles & Biographies of Missourians-KansasCty-1900-
    Hudson Kimberly Pub-404p plus ports-cl-1st ed (5a0)   15.00
--Centennial History of Independence, Mo-n.p.-1927-1st ed-
    294p   (4L0)   30.00
--Champ Clark-NY-1912-NY-1912-photos-256p-1st ed (4L0, dj) 5.00
WEBB, WALTER PRESCOTT-Concerning Mr Dobie & Univ of Texas-
    wrps-Austin-1964-Hertzog Prnt-ltd to 300c   (4c7)   12.50
--Divided We Stand-NY-1937   (5u3) 10. (4a5)   17.50
--The Great Plains-Bost-(1931)-illus-map-525p
                                    (4i7, cov lettering fade) 18.00
--same-(1931)-later imprec(wi errors pg 10 corrected)
                        (4k6) 15. (5h1, rub) 8.50 (5kk4) 12.50
--The Great Plains-Bost-1936-illus-maps-525p (4b6) 25. (5s2) 15.00
--Handbook of Texas-Austin-1952-2 vols   (4i7, mint)   30.00
--An Honest Preface & Other Essays-Bost-1959-216p-1st ed
                                        (4dd1, mint, dj)   6.50
--Story of the Texas Rangers-NY-1957-Eggenhofer, illus-4to-cl-
    True Book-1st ed   (5g6, f, dj)   10.00
--The Texas Rangers-Bost-1935-583p-illus-1st ed
    (4j7) 32.50 (5m9, 5r7) 20. (4i7) 25. (5i3) 22.50 (4L0, dj) 27.50
WEBB, WILFRED M-The Heritage of Dress-Lond-1907-393p-180 illus
                                           (5c3, libr labl) 8.00
WEBB, WM S-Calif & Alaska & over Canadian Pac Rwy-NY-1890-
    R8vo-illus-210p-g.t.-mor-ltd to 500c, nbrd-v scarce
                                           (5dd5, rub)   42.50
--same-Calif & Alaska & Over Canadian Pacific Rwy-NY-1891-
    illus   (4b6)   7.50
WEBBER, C M-Geology Familiarly Illustrated-Lond-1859-
    JBGoodince-orig cl-fold out to 126"-(31 hand col panels)
                                                  (5c8)   35.00
WEBBER, C W-Historical & Revolutionary Incidents of Early Settlers
    of US etc-Phila-1859-416p   (5xx7)   12.50
--The Hunter Naturalist-Phila-1852-col liths-610p
                        (4b3, sp cracked) 25. (4L0)   40.00
--Old Hicks the Guide-NY-1848-1st ed-hf sheep-2 parts in 1
    (5tt6, rub) 50. (5s9, rbkd) 87.50 (5m1, rub)   40.00
--Romance of Natural History-Phila-1852-illus-610p
                        (5ee3, edge wn) 12.50 (5ss8, cov loose) 8.00
--Wild Scenes & Wild Hunters of the World-Phila-1852-illus-lea-
    610p   (5t4, crack)   7.50
WEBBER, HARRY E-12 Months with 8th Mass Infantry in Service
    of US-Salem-1908-frontis-part lea-392p (4p2, rehngd) 12.50

WEBBER, MALCOLM-Medicine Show-Caldwell-1941-8vo-cl-
265p-illus (5m8) 7.50
WEBBER, SAM'L-Mathematics, Compiled from the Best Authors-
Cambr-1808-2 vols-8vo-calf-lea labls-2nd ed (5ss5, rub) 15.00
--A Narrative-n.d.-no publ-April 16, 1807-8vo-tied wi string
(5a0, edges sl rag) 35.00
WEBBER, W L-Books about Books-Bost-1937-1st ed-168p
(5ee3, tn dj) 12.50
WEBER, ALFRED-History of Philosophy-NY-1900-Scribner-630p
(5p7) 5.00
WEBER, BROM-Hart Crane, A Biographical & Critical Study-NY-
(1948)-1st ed (5r9, dj) 10.00
WEBER, CARL J-Hardy in Amer-Waterville-(1946)-8vo-cl-321p
(5t0) 6.50
--Thos Hardy in Maine-Portland-1942-1st ed (5ss3) 5.00
WEBER, F, & CO-Illus Price List of Artist's Materials &
Draughtsmen's Supplies-Phila-(190?)-558p-illus-cl-1 col plt
(5e4) 8.50
WEBER, HARRY F-Centennial History of Mennonites of Illinois-
Scottsdale-1931-illus (5jj3) 15.00
WEBER, HENRY-Metrical Romances of the 13th, 14th & 15th centuries-
Edinb-1810-Vol 1(of 3)-part lea-381p (5p6, cov poor) 10.00
WEBER, HENRY, ed-Popular Romances, Consisting of Imaginary
Voyages & Travels-Edinb-1812-Ballantyne-lg8vo-hf calf-
638p (5aa2) 25.00
WEBER, HERMANN-Spas & Mineral Waters of Europe-Lond-1896-
380p (5w1) 7.50
WEBER, J M ERICH-Praktische Konditorei-Kunst-Dresden-n.d.
(ca 1925?)-90p col plts plus 18p sepia plts plus suppl of
36p-ca sq4to-v scarce (5g9, hng loose) 22.50
WEBER, MAX-Cubist poems-Lond-1914-Elkin Mathews-64p (5v6) 12.00
WEBER, T R-Die Pennsylvanische Choral Harmonie-Hellertown, Pa-
1870-WmHKnauss-sm obl 4to-orig prntd bds-wi 16p manual &
400p, 80p-in Germ & Engl (5L8, sl wn) 20.00
WEBER, THOS-Northern Railroads in the Civil War-NY-1952(5s9) 7.50
WEBER, WM LANDER, ed-Selections from the Southern Poets-NY-
1901-Macmillan-16mo-cl-frontis (5b2) 4.00
WEBSTER, C K, ed-Britain & Independence of Latin Amer 1812 to 1830-
Lond-1938-Oxford U Pr-2 vols-R8vo-cl (4a3) 32.50
--Foreign Policy of Castlereagh 1812 to 15-1931 (5L7) 9.50
WEBSTER, CHAS L-Walt Whitman, Autobiographia or The Story
of a Life-NY-1892-1st issue (5ss9) 20.00
WEBSTER, CLARENCE M-Town Meeting Country-NY-(1945)-256p-
1st ed (5xx5) 4.00
WEBSTER & COMSTOCK MFG CO-Elevating & Conveying
Machinery-Chig-122p, (2)-illus -1888 (5b8) 8.50
WEBSTER, DAN'L-Catalogue of the Private Lirbrary of-to be sold
at auction-Bost-(1875)-wrps (5g4) 10.00
--The Private Correspondence of-Bost-1857-2 vols-ports-1st ed
(5L3, vf) 35. (5q8) 10. (5ii2) 12.50
--Report of (Webster) Concerning Cession of Calif to England-
Wash-1843-1p (4a5) 5.00
--Speech of,...in Great India Rubber Suit-NY-1852-54p
(5h1, rebnd) 10.00
--Speech Upon War With Mexico-Bost-1848-24p (4a5) 10.00
--Speeches & Forensic Arguments-Bost-1830-Perkins&Marvin etc-
8vo-520p-port-hf mor-1st coll ed (5L1, hng wn) 40.00
--The Works of-Bost-1851-6 vols-orig cl (5m2) 15.00
--Works of-Bost-1858-Little, Brown-6 vols (5qq8) 25.00
WEBSTER, E-Phonographic Teacher-NY-(1852)-112p
(5n7) 4. (5ii2) 3.50
WEBSTER, E B-Fishing in the Olympics-Port Angeles, WA-(1923)-
226p-illus (5s4, f, pres) 8.50
--Friendly Mountain-Port Angeles-1921-119p-illus-2nd ed
(5s4, autg) 5.00
--The King of the Olympics-Post Angeles-1920-227p-photos
(5ss1) 15.00
WEBSTER, F B, ed-Shipbuilding Cyclopedia-NY-(1920)-
Simmons Boardman-lg4to-1119p-cl-61 fldg plts
(5ss2, cov wtrstnd) 20.00
WEBSTER, FLETCHER, ed-Private Correspondence of Daniel Webster-
Bost-1857-2 vols (5L3, vf) 35. (5q8) 10. (5ii2) 12.50
WEBSTER, H T-The Best of...-NY-1953-4to-cl&bds-255p-
cartoon collection (5t7) 5. (5w9) 6.00
--The Timid Soul-NY-1931-4to-cl (5t7, autg) 10.50
WEBSTER, HELEN NOYES-Herbs, How to Grow Them & How to
Use Them-Lexington, Mass-(1939)-160p-illus (5s7, pres) 6.50
--same-1942-198p-new ed, rev (5s7, pencil) 3.00
WEBSTER, ISAAC-A Narr of the Captivity of-Metuchen, NJ-
1927-scarce (5dd1) 20.00
WEBSTER, JEAN-Daddy Long Legs-NY-1912-Century-12mo-dec cl-
illus-304p-1st ed (5zz8) 12.50 (5v2, 5p1) 20.00

WEBSTER, JEAN (continued)
--same-NY-n.d.-304p, (8)(ads)-frontis-3 plts-Grosset&Dunlap
(5p1, lacks e.p.) 6.50
WEBSTER, JOHN-The Displaying of Supposed Witchcraft Wherein
Is Affirmed etc-Lond-1677-calf-4to-1st ed (4h5) 250.00
WEBSTER, JOHN-The Duchess of Malfi-Lond-1945-illus-88p-
ltd to 1000c (5t7) 7.50
WEBSTER, JOHN C-Thomas Pichon, "The Spy of Beausejour"-
Sackville, NB-1937-Archives of NS Spec Pub-bds-fldg map-
162p (4a8) 12.50
--Wolfe & The Artists-Tor-1930-30 plts(some col)-74p-ltd to 500c
(5nn2) 12.50
WEBSTER, JOHN W-A Description of the Island of St Michael-Bost-
1821-Williams-244p-illus (5t4) 20.00
--The Parkman Murder, Trial of Prof JnWWebster-Bost-(1850)-64p-
8vo-dbl columns-homemade wrps (5ss5) 10.00
--Trial of Prof...for Murder of Dr Geo Parkman-Bost-1850-
91(3)p-unbnd-stitchd as issued (5w0, lacks port) 12.50
WEBSTER, KIMBALL-Hudson History-1913-648p-GWaldoBrowne, ed
(4t2) 20.00
WEBSTER MFG CO-Machinery for Transmitting Power-Chig-1891-
priced catalogue-178p, (4)-bds-illus (5hh7) 8.50
WEBSTER, MARIE D-Quilts, Their Story & How to Make Them-
NY-1915-Dblday, Page-178p-illus (5x0) 7.50
--same-GardenCty-1916-178p-illus (5t7) 8.50
--same-NY-1943-178p-14 col plts (5n7) 5.00
WEBSTER, NESTA H-Chevalier De Boufflers-NY-1925-441p-illus-
ports (5aa0) 12.50
--same-Lond-1929-441p-ports-facs (5a1) 6.50
WEBSTER, NOAH-An Amer Dictionary of the English Language-
NY-1828-S Converse-calf-2 vols-1st ed-4to-(2500 sets prntd)
(4h5, rebkd) 250. (4k7, vg) 750.00
--same-Springfield-1878-enlrgd by Goodrich&Porter-4to-calf-
lea labl-1840p-65p illus + 3p (4k9, chip) 50.00
--An Amer Selection of Lessons in Reading & Speaking-Bost-1797-
Isaiah Thomas&Ebenezer T Andrews-12mo-orig calf bkd bds-
240p (5ss5, lacks part of front cov) 17.50 (5a0, f) 25.00
--same-Bost-1800-Thomas&Andrews-12mo-papr cov wd bds-lea bk-
240p-Thomas&Andrews 12th ed (5j5, cov wn) 42.50
--same-Bost-1803-12mo-240p-13th ed (5xx7) 15.00
--same-Phila-1807-230p-bds-lea bk-"Hogan's 3rd imprv ed"(5t7)10.00
--The Amer Spelling Book-Brattleborough-(1818)-Holbrook&Fessenden-
blu papr over oak (5jj6, cor chip) 17.50
--same-Middletown-1823-blu papr over oak (5v0, chip) 12.50
--A Compendious Dictionary of the English Language-Hartf-1806-
calf-Webster's 1st Dictionary-1st ed (5v2, sl sp def) 115.00
--Dictionary of The English Language-Hartford-1817-calf-366p
(5i3) 17.50
--The Elementary Spelling Book; being an improvement on the Amer
Spelling Book-WellsRiver, Vt-1831-(White&Wilcox)-frontis-
bds&lea-168p (5t4) 6.50
--same-Pittsbgh-1842-cl bk bds-168p (5jj9, sl wn) 10.00
--same-Albany-1829-1st ed of Webster's revised text-qtr lea (5c8) 22.50
--same-Claremont, NY-(1848)-16mo-prntd bds-168p-Last Revised
Ed (5t7) 6.50
--Elements of Useful Knowledge, Vols 1 & 2-Hartf, 1806-NewHav-
1806-2 vols-12mo-papr cov wd bds-sheep bks (5r7, bndg wn) 35.00
--Philosophical & Practical Grammar of English Language-NewHav-
1807-16mo-lea-250p-1st ed
(5p1, rbkd, rprd) 15. (5t0, crack, lacks fly) 20.00
--Webster Genealogy-1876-9p-wi corrections by Paul L Ford (5t9) 25.00
WEBSTER, PELETIAH-A 7th Essay on Free Trade & Finance, by a
Citizen of Phila-Phila-1785-Eleazer Oswald-38p-disbnd
(5m2) 30.00
WEBSTER, T-The Amer Family Encyclopedia of Useful Knowledge-NY-
1859-1238p (5w7, ex-libr, hng broke) 18.50
WEBSTER'S DICTIONARY-New Int'l Dictionary of the Engl Language-
Springfield, Mass-1926-Merriam Co-2 vols-4to-tan calf-
blind & g.-revised (5b0) 45.00
WECHSBERG, JOS-Blue Trout & Black Truffles-NY-(1953)-285p
(5c5) 4.00
--same-NY-1954-288p (5c9) 4.00
WECTER, DIXON-The Age of the Great Depression, 1929 to 1941-
NY-1948 (4L0) 7.50
--same-NY-1952-Macmillan-362p-illus (5qq8) 6.00
--The hero in America-NY-1941-Scribners-530p-1st ed (5u3) 4.00
--Saga of Amer Society-NY-1937-Scribners-504p-illus-1st ed
(5qq8) 6.75 (5L7, 5q8) 10. (4L0) 7.50
--Sam Clemens of Hannibal-Wash-1952 (5F1, f, tn dj) 7.50
WEDDELL, JAS-A Voyage Towards the South Pole-Lond-1825-
Longman, Hurst-276p-errata slip-8 maps(2 fldg)-8vo-calf-
1st ed (5L7, rbkd) 275.00

WEDECK,HARRY E-Dictionary of Erotic Literature-NY-c1962-
(5x7,dj) 5.00
--Treasury of Witchcraft-NY-(1961)-271p-illus-qtr cl (5c3) 5.00
WEDEL,WALDO-Archeological Remains in Central Kansas & Their
Possible Bearing on Location of Quivira-Wash-1942-10 plts-8vo-
wrps-24p plus plts-1st ed (5g0) 5.00
--Intro to Kansas Archaeology-1959-BAE,B174-maps-97 plts-723p-
hard cov (4b2) 25.00
WEDEMEYER,GEN ALBERT C-Wedemeyer Reports-NY-1959-Holt-
497p (5x9,bkstrp sl tn) 5.50
WEDGWOOD,ETHEL-The Memoirs of The Lord Joinville-Lond-
1906-illus-409p-fldg chart (5m1) 7.50
WEDMORE,FREDK-Whistler & Others-NY-1906-8vo-buck-g.t.
(5p5) 7.50
WEDNT,HERBERT-In Search of Adam-Bost-1956-540p-illus
(5w9,dj) 4.00
WEED,CLARENCE-The Flower Beautiful-Bost-1904-137p-illus
(4g0) 7.50
--Our Trees,How to Know Them-Phila-1908-4to-photos-cl (5t5) 7.50
WEED,HARRIET A-Autobiography of Thurlow Weed-Bost-1883-
2 vols-ports (5q0) 17.50
WEEDEN,H-Old Voices-NY-1904-R8vo-illus-pict cl-1st ed
(5x2) 17.50
WEEDEN,HOWARD-Bandanna Ballads-NY-1899-illus-12mo
(4m8) 7.50 (5x2) 15.00
--same (5L7) 6.00
--Shadows on the Wall-Huntsville-1899-illus-12mo-buck (4c2) 10.00
WEEDEN,WM B-Early Rhode Island-NY-(1910)-1st ed-illus (5tt5)10.00
--Economic & Social History of New England 1620 to 1789-Bost-
(1890)-8vo-cl-2 vols (5t2) 20.00
--same-Bost-1891-2 vols-orig cl-g.t. (5h9) 25.00
WEEDON,GEN'L GEO-Valley Forge Orderly Book of-NY-1902-
323p-maps-t.e.g.-1st ed-ltd to 250c,nbrd (5w4) 40.00
WEEK END BOOKS,THE-Lond-(1955)-Nonesuch Pr-580p
(5ee3,f,dj) 7.50
WEEKES,GEO-of Dorchester,Mass,Genealogy of 1635 to 1650-
in 2 parts-463p,174p (4t2) 40.00
WEEKES,REFINE-Poems,on religious & historical subjects-NY-
1820-JasOram-12mo-hf calf-1st ed (5i9,wn) 22.50
WEEKLY REGISTER-Vol 5 #8-Balt-Oct 23,1813-16p-unbnd as
issued (removed) (5h1) 8.50
WEEKLEY,W M-Denominational Mission Study Course-Dayton-
(1908)-340p-cl (5h7) 7.50
WEEKS,ALVIN G-Massasoit of the Wampanoags-(Fall River,Mass)-
1919-sm8vo-cl-270p-priv prntd (5t2) 5. (5hh3) 7.50
--same-n.p.(Fall Riv)-illus-270p (5w5) 5.00
WEEKS,LORD EDWIN-From the Black Sea Through Persia & India-
NY-1896-Harper-cl-illus-8vo (5v7) 17.50
WEEKS,FRED-Bibliography of NA Geology,Paleontology,
Petrology,& Mineralogy for Years 1892 thru 1900-Wash-1902-
717p (5j4) 12.50
WEEKS,E P-Trial of Rev Joy Hamlet Fairchild on a charge of adultery-
Bost-1845 (5g3) 7.50
WEEKS,J HATTON-The Tin kitchen-NY & Bost-(1896)-Crowell-
photos-1st trade ed (5m2) 8.50
WEEKS,J M-History of Salisbury-1860-362p (5e8) 22.75 (5t9) 17.50
WEEKS,JOHN H-Among the Congo Cannibals-Lond-1913-Seeley,
Service-1 fldg map-photos-351p (4t5,sl loose) 25.00
WEEKS,JOHN M-A Manual, or An Easy Method of Managing Bees-
Brandon,Vt-1839-16mo-orig bds-calf bk-4th ed (5m6,fox) 10.00
WEEKS,MORRIS,JR-Beer & Brewing in Amer-NY-(1949)-75p,(5)-
12mo-illus-wrps (5w1) 3.50
WEEKS,REV S,ed-Life's Retrospect-Autobiog of Moody-Cinn-
(1890)-486p-cl (5h7,rub) 12.50
WEELANDY,PAUL J-Romance of Industry-StLouis-(1933)-1st ed
(5ii3,pres) 20.00
WEEMS,M L-Hymen's Recruiting Sargent-Hartf-1833-Andrus & Judd-
52p (5t4) 10.50
--The Life of Geo Washington-Phila-1809-Carey-228p-calf-labl-
7 plts-9th ed (5m3,chip) 25.00
--Life of William Penn,the Settler of Penna-Phila & Louisville-
1829-Morton & Co-8vo-208p-buck-front is (5rr2,fox,rbnd) 20.00
--The philanthropist-Dumfries,(Va,1799?) (5g4,f) 30.00
--Three Discourses-NY-1929-Intro by Emily E F Skeel-Harbor Pr-
orig cl-bds-ltd ed (5j5,f) 12.50 (5m1) 6.00
WEEMS,MASON-A History of Life & Death, Virtues & Exploits
of Gen Geo Washington-n.p.-n.d.-8vo-374p (5p1,dj) 3.50
WEEN,C L'ESTRANGE-Witch Hunting & Witch Trials-Lond-
1929-frontis-cl-345p (5t2,f,dj) 12.50
WEER,PAUL-Preliminary Notes on the Siouan Family-sep prntng
from Ind Hist Bul Vol 14,#2-Feb,1937-99 to 120p (5L0) 3.00

WEGELIN,OSCAR-Bibliographical List of Literary & Dramatic
Productions & Periodicals by Sam'l Woodworth-NewOrl-1953-
19p-wrps-ltd to200c (5n4) 10.00
--Biblio of Separate Writings of John Esten Cooke-Metuchen-1925-
illus-20p-51c-bds (4h8,lttrs laid in,sl wn,soil) 22.50
--Early Amer Fiction 1774 to 1830-NY-1929-3rd ed (5mm2) 10.00
WEHLE,HARRY B-Amer Miniatures 1730 to 1850-GardenCty-
1927-127p-173 ports-bds-4to (5n7,edge soil) 16.50
WEHLE,HARRY B-Amer Miniatures 1730 to 1850-GardenCty-1937-
GardenCty Pub Co-173 ports-reprnt ed (4a0) 17.50 (4m9,4p7) 12.50
WEHMAN,HENRY J-Confectioner's Guide & Assistant-n.p.-
190?-105p,24p-pict wrps (5c9) 3.50
WEIBEL,ADELE COULIN-Two Thousand Years of Textiles-NY-1952-
illus-folio-169p (5t7,box) 20.00
WEIDMAN,JEROME-The Horse That Could Whistle "Dixie" &
Other Stories-1939-Simon & Schuster (5F1,f,dj) 6.00
--What's In It For Me-1938-Simon & Schuster (5F1,f,dj) 7.50
WEIGALL,ARTHUR-The Life & Times of Akhnaton,Pharaoh of
Egypt-NY-1923-illus-cl-31p,255p (5t2) 8.50
WEIGALL,T H-Boom in Florida-Bodley Head-1931-229p (5u3) 6.50
WEIGERT,HANS W-Compass of the World-NY-1944-maps-466p
(5u6) 8.50 (4b9) 12.00
--same-NY-1945-maps-466p (5ss1,pres) 8.50
WEIGHT,V F-As A Tree Grows-1962-426p-wrps (5t9) 17.50
WEIK,JESSE W-The Real Lincoln, A Portrait-Bost-1923-illus-
cl-314p (5t2) 5. (5t7) 4.50
WEIL,YELLOW KID-Autobiography of America's Master Swindler-
Chig-1948-Brannon,ed-illus-cl-297p-1st ed (5t0) 4.50
WEINREICH,MAX-Hitler's Professors-NY-1946-wrps-291p-8vo
(5yy6) 12.50 (5p1) 15.00
WEINSTEIN,MICHAEL-Precious & Semi Precious Stones-Lond-
1929-138p-illus-cl (5t2) 5.00
WEINSTOCK,MATT-My L A-NY-1947 (4a5) 4.00
WEIR,HARRISON-Animal Stories, Old & New-Lond-(ca 1880)-
illus-sq8vo-pict bds (5c8,rub) 22.50
--Elephant's Feast-Lond-(ca 1860)-Dean & Son-hand col frontis-
dec cl (5c8,sl loose) 10.00
--Every Day in Country-Warne-1883-12mo-dec cl-196p-8 plts-
illus-g.t. (5s0) 5.00
--Shireen & Her Friends-Lond-(1894)-1st ed-8 plts-dec cl (5c8) 6.50
WEIR,JAS-The Winter Lodge-Phila-1854-Lippincott,Grambo-231p-
1st ed (5x4,lacks e.p.) 17.50
WEIR,JOHN F-John Trumbull, Brief Sketch of his Life-NY-1901-80p-
tall 8vo-cl-g.t.-21 plts (4b6,4a0) 25. (4g2) 17.50
WEIR,ROBT-Picture of Embarcation of Pilgrims from Delft Haven-
NY-1843-8vo-wrps-8p-rare (4a0) 32.50
WEIR,WALTER W-A Rating of Calif Soils-Univ of Calif-1936-Bul #599-
8vo-wrps-wi envelope of maps (5h4) 4.50
WEIRS,N H-A Souvenir of-Bost-1897-obl 12mo-orig wrps-
73 illus-orig envelope (5m6,f) 10.00
WEIS,G-Stock Raising in the Northwest,1884-1951-Branding Iron Pr-
12mo-bds-cl bkstrp-ltd to 500c,nbrd,autg (5F5) 15.00
WEISBERGER,BERNARD A-Reporters for the Union-Bost-(1953)-
1st ed (5tt5,dj) 5.00
WEISE,A J-History of City of Troy-Troy-1876-fldg maps & tables-
400p-sheep (4b6) 25. (4t2) 15.00
WEISE,A J-History of City of Albany-1884-illus-fldg maps-
520p (5ff2,rbnd) 12.50 (5Ff2) 15. (5w0) 20.00
WEISEL,GEO F-Men & Trade on the NoWest Frontier as Shown by
the Fort Owen Ledger-Missoula-(1955)-MSU Studies-1st ed-illus-
fldg map (5g4) 10. (5L0) 12.50
WEISER,CONRAD-The Life of-Syracuse,NY-1925-WmMBeauchamp,
ed-125p-frontis-wrps (5h9) 15.00
WEISMANN,ELIZ W-Mexico in Sculpture,1521 to 1821-
Harvard Univ Pr-1950-224p-1st ed (5x5,dj) 15.00
WEISS,CAROLINE D-Collection of Creole Recipes-Mandeville-
(1941)-49,(2)p-spiral bnd wrps (5c4) 2.50
WEISS,GEO-Lighthouse Service-Balt-1926-US Mono #40-158p
(5s1,ex-libr) 6.50
WEISS,HARRY B-Bibliographical,Editorial & Other Activities of
Chas F Heartman-Hattiesburg-1938-24p-wrps-399c
(5n4,fox) 8.50
--Early Amer Naturalist-Springfield-1931-port-frontis-27 illus-
260p,(1) (5w3) 10.00
--The Early Breweries of New Jersey-Trenton-1963-illus-98p-wrps
(5w1) 6.50
--Early Sports & Pastimes in NJ-Trenton-1960-148p-illus-bds
(5w7) 7.50
--An Introduction to Crime & Punishment in NJ-Trenton-1960-
99p-bds (5w7) 7.50
--Thos Say,Early Amer Naturalist-Springfield (5w3) 10. (5m2) 7.50
--They Took to the Waters-Trenton-1962-illus-232p-ltd ed (5w6) 7.50

WEISS, JACOB-The Letter Book of-Allentown-1956-facs-162p-
MJBoyer, ed-Pa Hist Soc, Vol 21 (5w9) 10.00

WEISS, DR J-The Hand Book of Hydropathy-Lond-1844-4to-
438p, (2) (5c5, sp split) 10.00

WEISS, JOHN-Life & Corres of Theodore Parker-NY-1864-2 vols-
478&530p-cl (5h1, sp wn) 15.00

WEISS, SARA-Decimon Huydas-Roch-1906-cl-207p (4h9) 15.00

WEISS, T, ed-Selections from the Note Books of Gerard M Hopkins-
1945-New Directions-bds (5hh1) 7.50

WEISSE, MRS JOHN A-A History of the Bethune Family-NY-
1884-ports-sm4to-gilt mor-54p, 1, 16p mntd, 1, 71p
 (5w4, clippings) 15.00

--same-1884-54p, 39p (4t2) 8.50

WEITENKAMPF, F-Amer Graphic Art-NY-1924-Macmillan-g.e.-
52 illus-8vo-328p (4e0) 25.00

--The Illustrated Book-Cambr-1938-illus-314p-ltd to 210c, box
 (4g2, vf) 35.00

--Quest of Print-NY-1932-illus-286p-8vo (5ww3) 12.50

WELBY, ADLARD-Visit to NoAmer & English Settlements in Illinois,
with a winter residence at Phila-Lond-1821-J Drury-14 plts-
8vo-errata sl-1st ed
 (5s9, cov dtchd) 295. (4h5, f) 275. (5m3, f, f bndg) 325.00

WELBY, HORACE-Mysterie of Life, Death & Futurity-NY-1863-
356p, (2) (5w0, sl wn) 12.50

WELBY, T EARLE-The Cellar Key-Lond-1933-160p (5w1) 5.50

--The Dinner Knell-Lond-(1932)-137p (5g9, pres) 5.00

WELCH, CHRISTOPHER-History of the Boehm Flute-Lond-1892-
8vo-illus (5ss5) 20.00

WELCH, F G-That convention, or 5 days a politician-NY-1872-
Welch-illus-fldg frontis-illus-pict cl-1st ed (5m2) 5.00

WELCH, NELL T-Sunset Flower Arrangement Book-SanFran-1946-
117p (5s7) 2.50

WELCH, P S-Key to Snakes of US, Canada & Lower Calif-NY-1925-
Mich Acad Sci, Vol 5, Pt 2-cl-8vo (4p6, sp tn) 7.50

WELCH, PHILIP H-The Tailor Made Girl, Her Friends, Her Fashions
& Her Follies-NY-1888-Scribner's-illus-52p (5ee3) 6.00

WELCH, SPENCER GLASGOW-A Confederate Surgeon's Letters to
his Wife-Marietta-1954-127p (5j6) 4.00

WELCH, SAML M-Home History, Recoll of Buffalo, 1830 to 1840-
Buffalo-1891-PeterPaul&Bro-8vo-cl-423p
 (4t1) 15. (5m6) 10. (4t2) 12.50

WELD, FRANCIS MINOT, MD-Diaries & Letters of-Bost-1925-
8vo-245p (4a7) 40.00

WELD, ISAAC-Travels Through States of NoAmer & Provinces of
Upper & Lower Canada....1795, 96 & 97-Lond-1799-16 plts-
4to-1st ed (5e2) 300.00

--same-Lond-1799-calf-2 vols-2nd ed(sam year as 1st)-
fldg plts&maps (5r6, f) 175.00

--same-Lond-1800-2 vols-3rd ed-calf-16 fldg maps & illus
 (5tt6, f bndg) 95.00

--same-Lond-1800-orig bds-4 plts-fldg map-4th ed-552p
 (5nn2, rebkd) 50.00

--same-Berlin, Germany-1801-475p-fldg maps-plts-1st German Ed
 (5L3) 37.50

WELDRON FAMILY, THE-or, vicissitudes of fortune, by Maria-
Providence-1848-Weeden&Peck-12mo-modern cl (5x1) 20.00

WELKER, MARTIN-Farm Life in Central Ohio 60 Yrs Ago-n.p.-
(Wooster)-1895-(rprnt from 1892 wi add)-87p-cl-rare
 (5h1, pres) 25.00

WELLARD, JAS HOWARD-Understanding the English-NY-1937
 (5x7) 4.00

WELLCOME, HENRY S-Story of Metlakahtla-Lond-1887-plts-
483p (4a8) 17.50

WELLCOME'S EXCERPTA THERAPEUTICA-Lond-n.d.(1911?)-
Burroughs, Wellcome&Co-USA ed-tall 12mo-400p-col plts-
red cl (4a9) 14.00

WELLER, CHAS E-Yesterday, Chronicle of Early Life in the West-
Indnpls-1921-208p-cl (5dd6, 5h7) 10.00

WELLES, A-Pedigree & Hist of Washington Family-1879-370p
 (5t9) 30.00

WELLES, C M-3 Years' Wanderings of a Connecticut Yankee-NY-
1859-cl-g. (5q8, fade) 10. (5s4, ex-librr, wn) 12.50

WELLES, GIDEON-Diary of-Bost-1911-Houghton, Miff-3 vols-
illus (4a7) 35. (5g3, dj, stmp on t.p.) 25. (5ss5) 17.50

--Lincoln & Seward-NY-1874-8vo-1st ed (5m6, fray) 10.00

WELLES, SUMNER, ed-An Intelligent American's Guide to the
Peace-NY-1945 (5x7) 4.00

--Seven Decisions That Shaped History-NY-c1951-236p-1st ed
 (5w9) 3.75

--The Time for Decision-NY-1944-map (5m2) 6.00

WELLESLEY IN WESTCHESTER-Favorite Recipes of Wellesley
Alumnae-NY-1950-144p-photos inside wrps-spiral bnd
 (5g9, 5c4) 3.00

WELLINGTON, HUBERT-Jacob Epstein-Lond-1925-Benn-4to-
bds-Ser Contemporary British Artists-Rutherston, ed-32p-
36 plts (5m7) 12.50

WELLMAN, FRANCIS L-Day in Court-NY-1910-Macmillan-257p
 (5p9) 5.00

--Gentlemen of the Jury-NY-1924-298p-tip in illus (5w9) 5.00

WELLMAN, KATHERINE-Beauty Begins at Home-NY-1936 (5kk5) 7.50

WELLMAN, MANLY WADE-Rebel Boast-NY-(1956)-317p-cl-
1st ed (5jj9) 4.00

WELLMAN, PAUL I-Bowl of Brass-NY-1944-1st ed (4j0) 7.50

--Broncho Apache, an Indian Novel-NY-1936-8vo-orig cl (5p5) 10.00

--The Comancheros-NY-1952 (4j0) 3.00

--Death in the Desert-NY-1935-279p plus index-photos-fldg map-
1st ed (5kk4, f) 15. (5m9, ex-librr) 6.50 (4L0, f, dj) 20.00

--Death on Horseback-Phila(1947)-484p-maps-plts (5dd1, f, dj) 7.50

--Death on the Prairie-NY-1934-photos-1st ed-scarce
 (5dd1, wn, dj) 15.00

--Glory, God & Gold-NY-1954-402p-1st ed
 (4L0) 7.50 (4i7, dj) 5. (5h9) 6.50

--Indian Wars of the West-1954-Dblday (5kk4, f, dj) 12.50

--same-NY-1956-484p (4i7) 12.00

--The Iron Mistress-GardenCty-1951-410p-map repeated at bk
 (5m9) 3. (5dd6) 6.50

--Jubal Troop-(1939)-Carrick&Evans (5F1, f, dj) 5.00

--Portage Bay-GardenCty-1957-240p-illus (5t7) 6.00

--same-Lond-1957-188p-illus (5dd0) 4.50

--Stuart Symington-GardenCty-1960 (5x7) 3.00

--Trampling Herd-NY-(1939)-illus-453p-1st ed
 (5dd6) 20. (4L0, 4i7, dj rub) 15.00

--same-NY-(1939)-1st ed, 2nd impress (5dd1, dj) 8.50

--same-Doubleday-1952-illus (5jj7, f, dj) 7.50

WELLMAN, THOS B-History of the town of Lynnfield, Mass 1635 to
1895-Bost-n.d.(1895)-268p-illus (5w9) 9. (4t2, wn) 15.00

WELLMAN, WALTER-Aerial Age-NY-1911-illus-1st ed
 (5dd7) 20. (5u7) 12.75

WELLMONT, ADOLE NE-Adolene Wellmont, or the Female
Adventurer....Written by Herself-NY-1853-illus-8vo-orig wrps-
71p-1st ed (4c8, tn) 17.50

WELLS, A J-The Sacramento Valley of Calif-SanFran-1908-97p-
illus-maps-pict wrps-Passenger Dept, SoPac (5r0) 7.50

WELLS, A W-South Africa, A Planned Tour etc-Lond-1949-Dent-
col maps-photos-2nd revision-rprnt-434p (4t5, dj) 8.00

WELLS, AMOS-Social Evenings-Bost-1894-142p -12mo (5w7) 5.50

WELLS, CAROLYN-Best American mystery stories-n.p.-(NY)-
(1931)-Boni (5m2) 6.00

--The Broken O-Phila-(1933)-1st ed (5yy6, dj) 5.00

--Idle Idyls-NY-1900-illus-1st ed (5ee3) 5.00

--A Nonsense Anthology-NY-1902-289p (5t7) 6.00

--Ptomaine Street-Phila-1921-Lippincott-8vo-bds (5b2) 5.00

WELLS, CARVETH-Kapoot-NY-1933-cl-illus-8vo-264p (5v7) 8.50

--Six Years in the Malay Jungle-NY-1925 (5x7) 4.00

--same-GardenCity Publ-n.d.-261p (5x9) 2.00

WELLS, CHAS K-see WELLS, POLK

WELLS, CHAS WESLEY-A Frontier Life, being a Descrip of My
Experience on the Frontier first 42 Years of My Life-Cinn-
(1902)-313p-1st ed-v rare (4L0, sl spots) 50.00

WELLS, DAVID A-Recent Economic Changes & their Effect etc-
NY-1889-cl-12, 493p-1st ed (5t0) 5.00

--The relation of the government to the telegraph-NY-(1873)-
170p-wrps (5g4) 15. (5m3, f) 20.00

--Robinson Crusoe's Money-NY-1876-Harper-illus by Nast-8vo-
pict wrps-118p-plts (5aa2) 12.50

WELLS, DAVID DWIGHT-His lordship's leopard-NY-1900-Holt-
1st ed-pict cl (5m2) 7.50

WELLS, EDW-The Young Gentleman's Trigonometry, Mechanicks,
& Opticks-Lond-1714-prntd for JasKnapton-240p plus 8 plts
(2 fldg), & 172p plus 14 plts-calf (5p1) 50.00

WELLS, EDW L-Hampton & His Cavalry in '64-Richmond-1899-
 (5h6, cov wtrstnd) 22.50

WELLS, EVELYN-Champagne Days of San Francisco-NY-1947-
284p-illus-(not 1st) (5kk4) 5. (5a9, dj) 4.00

--The '49ers-NY-1949 (4a5, 4L0, dj) 6.00

--Fremont Older-NY-1936-illus (5r8) 12. (4n1) 8.50

WELLS, EVELYN K-The Ballad Tree-NY-(1950)-370p (5c3) 6.00

WELLS, F D-The Man in Court-NY-1917 (5ff4) 8.50

WELLS, F P-Hist of Newbury with Gen Records-1902-779p-illus
 (4t2) 25.00

WELLS, FARGO & CO-Express & Banking Official Directory-
SanFran-1895-95p-pamph (5n4) 50.00

WELLS, FARGO & CO'S EXPRESS-Local Tariff from Nicasio
Office-SanFran-1881 to 1882-H S Crocker&Co-35p-orig mrbld
bds&lea (5tt0) 125.00

WELLS, FREDERIC P-Hist of Newbury-1902-779p-illus (5e8) 28.75

WELLS,GABRIEL-The Carter Pollard Disclosures-NY-1934-
13p-orig wrps-1st ed   (5j2)   10.00
WELLS,GEO S-Amer Vacation Book-Bost-1959-221p-illus (5t4) 4.50
WELLS,GERARD-Naval Customs & Traditions-Lond-1930-
12 illus   (5c1)   12.50
WELLS,GOLDIE RUTH-Sila,Song of Congo-StLouis-1945-
Bethany Pr-photos-192p   (4t5)   4.50
WELLS,H G-The Adventures of Tommy-Lond-(1929)-lg4to-45p-
col illus-bds-1st ed   (5v0,f)   10.00
--Die Weltgeschichte in 580 Bildern-Berlin-1930-cl-575p,110p
      (5p6,f)   10.00
--Experiment in Autobiography-NY-1934-1st Amer ed
      (5w5) 5.   (4g1,mint,dj)   8.50
--First & Last Things;a Confession of Faith & Rule of Life-Lond-
1908-1st ed   (5r9)   15.00
--First Men in the Moon-Lond-1901-1st ed-cl-illus (5i3) 12.50
--Floor Games-Bost-1912-sq8vo-94p-plts (5v0,f) 15.00
--The Food of the Gods & How It Came to Earth-NY-1904-
329p-1st Amer ed   (5ee3)   5.00
--The Future in America,a Search after Realities-NY-(1906)-
illus-8vo-cl   (5t2,libr labl)   3.00
--same-Lond-1906-1st ed   (5q8)   6.00
--God the Invisible King-Lond-1917-1st ed (5r9) 12.50
--The Invisible Man-NY-1898-1st Amer ed (5i3) 7.50
--Italy,France & Britain at War-NY-1917-285p-1st ed (5w0) 5.00
--Marriage-Lond-1912-1st ed   (5r9)   8.50
--The New America,the New World-Lond-1935-Cresset Pr-
12mo-96p-1st ed (5q8,sl soil) 5. (4g1,mint,dj) 12.50
--Outline of History-Lond-1919,1920-1st printing-orig 24 pts-
pict wrps (5yy1,f,hf mor box) 185. (5v2,mint) 85.00
--same-NY-(1926)-Macmillan-24 parts-revised-orig wrps (4b5) 50.00
--Select Conversations with an Uncle (Now Extinct) & Two Other
Remin-Lond-1895-16mo-cl-g.t.-1st ed (5gg6,f,autg) 37.50
--The story of a great Schoolmaster-NY-1924-1st Amer ed (5p6) 8.00
--same-Lond-1924-Chatto&Windus-1st ed (4b5,mint,dj) 12.50
--The Time Machine,An Invention-Lond-1895-1st ed
      (5v2,cov stns,lt soil)   20.00
--Univ Corr Coll Tutorial Series-Text Book of Biology-Lond-(1893)-
2 vols-12mo-orig green cl-1st ed of Wells' 1st book-
1st bndg(later issues bnd in brown cl)-Vol 1&2 plus extra
copy of Vol 2 (5gg6) 3 vols   75.00
--War of the Worlds-Lond-1898-303p-orig cl-1st ed (4b4) 27.50
--same-MtVernon-1964-4to-cl-16 col liths-2 vols-Ltd Ed Club
The Time Machine   (5t8)   30.00
--The Work,Wealth & Happiness of Mankind-Lond-1932-8vo-cl-
850p-1st ed   (5t0)   4.00
--The Works of...1887 to 1925-Lond-1926-274p (4g2) 25.00
--World Brain-Lond-1938-1st ed   (4b4)   7.50
WELLS,HARRY L-California-LosAng-n.d.(ca 1932)-12mo-cl-(112p)
      (4t1)   6.50
--History of Nevada Co,Calif-Oakland-1880-Thompson&West-
234p-4to-orig cl-lea back   (5tt0)   175.00
WELLS,HENRY P-The Amer Salmon Fisherman-NY-1886-166p-illus
      (5t7)   5.00
WELLS,J G-Wells' Illus National Handbook-NY-1868-illus-295p
  (5yy8,sl wn) 10. (5j5) 15.00
--Wells' Nat'l Hand Book-NY-1856-JGWells-12mo-cl-144p-
52 wdcuts-1st ed   (5j5)   20.00
WELLS,J W-An Alphabetical List of Battles of the War of the
Rebellion-Wash-1875-81p-yellow wrps (5L3) 17.50
WELLS,JAS M-"With Touch of Elbow" or Death before Dishonor-
Phila-1909-362p-photos-1st ed-scarce (4L0) 30.00
WELLS,JOHN G-Wells' Every Man His Own Lawyer & Business
Form Book-NY-1868-BWHitchcock-thk12mo-prntd bds-
sheep bk-New Ed-rev&enlrgd (5j5,needs rbnd) 10.00
--Wells' Pocket Hand Book of Iowa-NY-(1857)-fldg col map-
136p-1st ed   (4L0,f)   125.00
WELLS,KENNETH McNEIL-Absit Omen-Paris-1927-EdwWTitus-
4to-black papr bds-vel bk & tips-1st ed (5ee9) 15.00
--By Moonstone Creek-Tor-1949-illus-280p (5s0) 4.50
WELLS,LAURA JAY-Jay Family, Colonial Lords of Manors-1938-
Ltd Ed-63p-wrps   (5h9)   5.00
WELLS,POLK-Life & Adventures of Polk Wells...Written by Himself-
(Halls,Mo,1907)-259p-illus-orig cl (4L0) 17.50 (5m3) 20.00
WELLS,RHEA-Andy&Polly-GardenCty-1931-Dblday Doran-(32p)-
oblong-pict bds-1st ed   (5p1)   3.00
WELLS,R W-Law of the State of Missouri-StL-1849-114p-lea cov
  (5s4,ex-libr)   25.00
WELLS,RICHARD A-Manners,Culture & Dress-Springfield-1892-
502p-illus   (5w7)   5.00
WELLS,ROBT-Pleasant Drinks-n.d.(19th Cent)-12mo-93p-wrps
  (5w1)   4.50

WELLS,ROGER HEWES-Amer Local Government-NY-1939-200p
  (5q8,ex-libr) 3.50 (5w4) 5.00
WELLS,ROLLA-Episodes of My Life-(StLouis-1933)-illus-510p-
hf lea (4b3,pres,hng weak) 17.50 (5dd1,rub) 20.00
WELLS,ROSALIE-Covered Bridges in Amer-NY-1931-illus-4to-cl-
135p-1st ed   (5t0,dj)   15.00
--Fans-Wash-1928-42p-photos-bds-12mo (5n7) 3.50
WELLS,SY,ed-Testimonies Concerning Character & Ministry
of Mother Ann Lee-Albany-1827-178p-orig prntd bds-cl sp-
1st ed   (5m3,sp sl tn)   45.00
WELLS,T-Narrative of Life & Adventures of-Biddleford-1874-
204p-photo   (5ii2,fox)   12.50
WELLS,TOM H-Commodore Moore & the Texas Navy-Austin-
1960-218p-illus-1st ed   (5k0,dj)   6.00
WELLS,W-New Theory of Disease-Rochester-1862-144p-
lea&bds   (5ii2)   12.50
WELSBY,W N,ed-Lives of Eminent English Judges of 17th & 18th
Century-Lond-1846   (5r4,rbnd)   13.50
WELLS,WM M-The Desert's Hidden Wealth-n.p.-(1934)-232p-
illus-not 1st prntng (4d6) 5. (4L0,dj) 6.00
WELLS,WM V-Explorations & Adventures in Honduras-NY-1857-
Harper&Bros-maps-illus-588p (4b3) 30.00
WELLS' NEW DESCRIPTIVE CHART-NY-(1869)-56p-ads-wrps
  (5h7)   5.00
WELSH,CHAS-A Book of Nursery Rhymes,Being Mother Goose's
Melodies-Bost,NY&Chig-c1901-Heath-12mo-169p-
170 illus   (5p1)   5.00
WELSH,CHAS-The Language,Sentiment & Poetry of Precious Stones-
NY-1912-128p-bds   (5n7)   4.50
WELSH,CHAS,ed-Chauffeur Chaff or Automobilia-Bost-(1905)-
12mo-1st ed   (5ss5)   10.00
WELSH,HERBERT-The Apache prisoners in Fort Marion,St Augustine,
Flo-Phila-1887-wrps   (5g4)   10.00
--Civilization Among the Sioux Indians-Phila-1893-wrps-58p-
1st ed   (5dd1)   8.50
--Four Weeks Among Some of the Sioux Tribes of Dak & Nebr-
Phila-1882-wrps-31p-1st ed (5dd1,lacks bk wrp) 8.50
--Report of a visit to the Navajo,Pueblo & Hualapais Indians of
New Mexico-Phila-1885-wrps-48p (5m3,vf) 22.50 (5g4,f) 10.00
WELSH,J-A White Baby-NY-1895-16mo (5x2) 15.00
WELSH,COL JAS-Military Remin-Lond-1830-2 vols-views &
fldg maps-sm8vo-mor-2nd ed (5t0) 10.00
WELSTEED,WM-The Dignity & Duty of the Civil Magistrate...a
Sermon-Bost-1751-Kneeland-8vo-mor-1st ed (5n2,lacks hf t.)45.00
WELSH,WM-Report & suppl report of visit to Spotted Tail's tribe of
Brule Sioux Indians etc,Oct 1870-(wrpr title)-Phila-1870
      (5g3)   17.50
--Report of Visit to Sioux & Ponka Indians on the Missouri Rivr-
1872-GPO-36p-blu papr wrps (5dd1,lacks bk wrp) 7.50 (5a0) 10.00
--Sioux & Ponca Indians-Phila-1870-8vo-wrps (4c1) 7.50
WELTMER,SYDNEY A-The Healing Hand-Nevada(Mo)-1925-
lg8vo-cl-scarce   (5p5)   15.00
WELTY,EARL M-The Black Bonanza-NY-1956-243p-cl-illus (5y2) 4.00
WELTY,EUDORA-The Bride of the Innisfallen & Other Stories-
NY-(c 1955)-8vo-cl-Harcourt,Brace
  (5F1,f,dj) 6.75 (5b2,f,dj) 7.50
--The Golden Apples-NY-1949-244p-1st ed
  (4b4,dj) 15. (5b2,f,dj) 7.50
--On Short Stories-NY-1949-bds (5b9,dj) 17.50
--The Ponder Heart-NY-1954-156p-1st ed (4b4) 15.00
--A Sweet Devouring-NY-1968-wrps-papr labl-1st ed-ltd to 150c,
nbrd   (5ss7,autg,mint)   17.50
--Wide Net & Other Stories-NY-1943-1st ed (4b4) 15.00
WELZL,JAN-30 Years in the Golden North-NY-1932-336p-
map   (4L0,dj) 3. (5ss1) 6.00
WEMBRIDGE,E R-Life Among the Lowbrows-Bost-1931 (5x2) 8.50
WEMETT,W M-The Indians of NoDakota-Fargo-1927-frontis-
illus-12mo-256p-scarce   (5dd9)   15.00
--The Story of the Flickertail State-Valley City,NoDak-1923-
16mo-315p-cl   (5p1,rub)   5.00
WEMYSS,STANLEY-General Guide to Rare Americana 1700 to
1943-Phila-1944-172p (5j4) 12.50 (5j5) 7.50 (4g2) 10.00
WENCK,H E-Phantoms of Old Tombstone-Tucson-1951-Ariz
Silhouettes-illus-59p-bnd in cowhide-poetry (5ii1) 25.00
--same-Tucson-1951-cl   (5g5)   7.50
WENDELL & CO-Book of Designs 1924,1925-NY-(1923)-illus-
112p-oblong 8vo   (5t7)   4.50
--same-NY-1920,1-illus-128p   (5e4)   6.75
WENDELL,ARTHUR-Geo Blunt Wendell,Clipper Ship Master-
(Mystic)-1949-207p-hvy wrps-illus (5w0) 8.50
WENDELL,BARRETT-A Literary History of America-NY-1901-
11,574p   (5m1,5t4)   10.00

WENDELL,BARRETT (continued)
--The Privileged Classes-NY-1908 (5q8,ex-libr) 3.50 (5p0) 5.00
--Rankell's remains,an Amer novel-Bost-1887-Ticknor-1st ed(5m2)6.00
--The Temper of the 17th Cent in Engl Literature-NY-1904-
360p (5t7) 5.00
--Traditions of European Literature-NY-1920-669p (5q0) 10.00
WENDELL,EMORY-Wendell's Hist of Banking & Banks & Bankers of
Mich-2 vol-Detr-n.d.-(1902?)-mor (5h1) 20.00
WENDORF,FRED,ed-Salvage Archaeology in the Chama Valley-
SantaFe-1953-School of Amer Research-4to-wrps-124p-illus
(5F5) 8.00
WENDT,LLOYD-Bet A Million-Indnpls 1948 (5a8,dj) 10.00
--Big Bill of Chicago-Indnpls-(1953)-1st ed-384p-cl
(5ff7,f,dj) (5x5) 5.00
--Give Lady What She Wants!-Chig-(1952)-Marshall Field-illus
(5yy6) 5. (5y2) 4.50
--Lords of the Levee-Indnpls-(1943)-8vo-cl-illus-384p (5j5) 6.00
WENGATZ,JOHN C-Miracles in Black-Phila-1938-Blakiston-
photos-177p (4t5) 6.50
WENGER,JOHN C-History of Mennonites of Franconia Conference-
Telford-1937-illus (5jj3) 15.00
WENHAM,EDW-Antique Furniture for Modern Rooms-NY-(1948)-
4to-cl-illus-128p (5t2,f,dj) 5.00
--Collectors Guide to Furniture Design-NY-1928-illus-370p-
4to (5bb0) 12. (5p0) 15.00
--Domestic Silver of Great Britain & Ireland-NY-1931-
Oxford Univ Pr-illus-95 plts (5p0) 15.00
WENNER,GEO U-The Lutherans of NY-NY-1918-illus-1st ed
(5m2) 7.50
WENSLEY,FRED PORTER-40 Years of Scotland Yard-NY-1933-
illus-312p (5p9) 4.50
WENTWORTH,FRANK L-Aspen on the Roaring Fork-Lakewood,Colo-
1950-photos-pkt sketch-1st ed-ltd to 600c-scarce (4L0) 30.00
WENTWORTH,JOHN-Wentworth Genealogy,English & American-
Bost-1878-3 vols-cl (5y0,sp faded) 50. (4t2) 65.00
WENTWORTH,LADY-Thoroughbred Racing Stock & Its Ancestors-
Lond-(1960)-thk4to-illus-rev ed (5j2,dj,box) 45.00
WENTWORTH,M P-Forged in Strong Fires-1948-Caxton Prntrs-
illus-1st ed-ltd ed (4L0,f,dj) 8.50 (5a8,erase,dj) 10.00
WENTZ,A R-The Lutheran Church in Amer History-Phila-1933
(5m2,autg,pencil) 6.50
WENTZ,ABDEL R-Beginnings of German Element in York Co,
Penna-Lancaster-1916-217p-scarce (4m4,autg) 22.50
WENTZ,ROBY-Eleven Western Presses-LosAng-1956-4to-cl over bds-
Int Assn of Printing Hse Craftsmen-scarce
(5m9,autg,spots) 10. (5h4,5j4) 17.50
WEPT OF WISH TON WISH,THE-a Tale-Phila-1829-2 vols-
(Anon)-lea bk-bds-1st ed (5mm2,box) 17.50
WERCK,ALFRED-Stained Glass,A Handbook-NY-1922-167p-
illus-t.e.g. (5w0,dj) 12.50
WERICH,J LORENZO-Pioneer Hunters of Kankakee-n.p.-1920-
197p-cl-scarce (5jj9,f) 25.00
WERNER,CARL A-Tobaccoland-NY-(ca 1900)-8vo-dec buck-illus-
1st ed-scarce (5p5) 10.00
WERNER,E T-Myths & Legends of China-NY-(1922)-454p-
32 col illus (5c3) 10.00
WERNER,HERMAN-On Western Frontier with US Cav 50 Yrs ago-
n.p.-n.d.-(1934)-98p-wrps (5h7) 10.00
WERNER,M R-Barnum-NY-(1923)-illus-8vo-cl-381p
(5w5) 3. (5t2) 4. (5p9) 3.50
--Brigham Young-NY-(1925)-illus-8vo-cl-1st ed (4g6) 7.50
--same-NY-(1925)-2nd printing (4L0) 4.50
--Tammany Hall-GardenCty-1928-Dblday-586p-illus (5qq8) 4.00
WERRY,ADOLPHUS-History of the First Methodist Church,Dallas-
Dallas-1946 (5a8) 8.50
WERTENBAKER,CHAS-Boojum-NY-1928-1st ed (5b9,sl soil) 7.50
WERTENBAKER,T J-American People,a history-NY-1926-486p
(5h9,5L7,ex-libr) 7.50
--Father Knickerbocker Rebels-1948-294p-illus
(5ff2) 8.25 (5m2,dj) 8.50
--Princeton,1746 to 1896-Princeton U-1946 (5a8) 4. (5h9) 7.50
--Torchbearer of the Revolution-Princeton-1940-237p-1st ed
(5w0) 8.75
--Virginia Under Stuarts,1607 to 1688-Princeton-1914-1st ed-
271p-maps (5i3) 17.50
WERTH,ALEX-Moscow War Diary-NY-1942-1st ed (5F0,f) 3.00
WERTH,JOHN J-Dissertation on the Resources and Policy of Calif
Benicia,Calif-1851-8vo-orig prntd wrps (5a3,f) 500.00
WERTHAM,FREDERIC-Seduction of the Innocent-NY&Tor-
c1954-Rinehart-8vo-397p (5p1,fray dj) 7.50
WERTHEIMBER,LOUIS-A Muramasa Blade-Bost-1887-188p-4to-
illus-orig pcit cl (5t2,cov stnd) 3.50
WERTHNER,WM B-Some Amer Trees-NY-1935-illus (4b6) 20.00

WERTSNER,ANNE-Make Your Own Merry Christmas-NY-(1946)-
112p (5c0) 3.50
WESCHER,PAUL-Jean Fouquet &His Time-Basle-1947-
Pleiades Books-111p-4to-cl-plts (5m5) 20.00
WESCOTT,GLENWAY-Apartment in Athens-NY-(1945)-Harper-
1st printing (5m2,dj) 6.50
--Apple of the Eye-NY-1924 (4j0,pres,box) 37.50
--The Babe's Bed-Paris-1930-Harrison-sq8vo-cl-1st ed-
ltd to 375c,autg,box (5d9) 30.00
--The Bitterns,a book of 12 poems-Evanston,III-(1920)-16mo-
orig black & silver wrps-1st ed of Wescott's 1st publication
(5gg6) 50.00
--Calendar of Saints for Unbelievers-NY-1933-12mo-cl (4c2) 20.00
--Good Bye,Wisconsin-NY-1928-12mo-cl bkd bds-Harper&Bros-
1st ed-ltd to 250c,autg (4j0,box) 40. (5ss3) 35.00
--The grandmothers-NY-1927-Harper-1st trade ed-1st prntng
(5b9,vf) 5. (5m2,dj) 7.50
--same-NY-1927-8vo-bds&cl-1st ed-ltd to 250c,autg,box
(5j5) 17.50 (5ee9) 30.00
--Natives of Rock 20 Poems,1921,1922-NY-1925-8vo-bds-
1st ed-ltd to 25c,nbrd for pres & cpyrite-publ's als enclosed
(5ss7,vf) 30.00
WESLEY,C H-The History of Alpha Phi Alpha-50th Anniv Ed-
1906 to 1956-Chig-1959-illus (5x2) 25.00
WESLEY,CHAS-Hymns & Sacred Poems-Lond-1739-sm8vo-1st ed
of Wesley's 1st book (5gg6,calf rprd) 250.00
WESLEY,EDGAR BRUCE-Guarding the Frontier-Univ of Minn Pr-
1935-maps-1st ed (4L0,pres) 35.00
WESLEY,JOHN-A Calm Address to our Amer Colonies-Lond-Hawes-
(1775)-12mo-wrps - 2nd ed (same year as 1st) (5n2) 275.00
--A Calm Address to the Inhabitants of England-Lond-1777-Fry-
12mo-1st ed (5n2) 150.00
--Collection of Hymns for Use of People Called Methodists-Lond-
1814-new ed-543p-mor (5aa0,sl rub) 10.00
--Extract Of the Life of Madam Guion-Lond-1776-230p-12mo-
calf (4p3) 45.00
--A Farther Appeal to Men of Reason & Religion-Lond-1745-
wrps-139p-12mo (4p3) 40.00
--Wesley's Notes upon the New Testament-NY-1841-lea-734p-
1st Amer ed (5t2,rub) 7.50
WESLEYAN-The Doctrines & Discipline of Methodist Church in
Canada-Tor-1859-12mo-lea-248p (5t2) 5.00
WESSEL,BESSIE BLOOM-An Ethnic Survey of Woonsocket,Rhode
Island-Chig-(1931)-fldg charts (5r7,ex-libr) 8.50
WESSELHOEFT,LILY F-Sparrow,the Tramp-Bost-1888-RobertsBros-
16mo-262p(10)(ads)-cl-illus by McDermott (5p1,soil) 3.50
WEST,BENJ-Gallery of Pictures Painted by-1811-16 plts-rare-
Henry Moses,illus (4a0) 85.00
--North American Calendar & Rhode Island Register 1782-
Providence-(1781)-Bennett Wheeler-40p (5yy3,worn) 30.00
--Rhode Island Almanac 1804-Newpt-(1803)-12 lfs-sewed (5h2) 6.50
WEST,CLARENCE-Pulp & Paper Manufacture Bibliography & US
Patents,1942-NY-1943-222p (5j4) 8.50
WEST,EDW W-Historical Sketch of county of StClair from Early
Times to Present-Belleville-1876-wrps-rare-41p-1st ed-
Howes 273 (5j1,chip) 75.00
WEST,EDWARD-Homesteading-Lond-1918-302p-32 plts (5aa0) 12.50
WEST,ELIZABETH H-Calendar of Papers of Martin Van Buren-
1910-663p-index (5zz0) 15.00
WEST,GEO A-Archeological Frauds-Milwkee-Dec,1935-Wis Arch
Vol 15,#3,new series-(22p)-wrps (5L0) 4.00
--Tobacco,Pipes & Smoking Customs of the Amer Indians-Publ Mus
of City of Milwaukee-1934-2 vols-plts-maps (5jj7,f) 75.00
WEST,GOLDSMITH B-The Golden Northwest-Chig-1878-117p plus
ads-1st ed-ex rare (4L0,cov wn,wtrstn) 150.00
WEST,GORDON-By Bus to the Sahara-Lond-n.d.-Travel Book
Club-233p (4t5,f) 5.00
WEST,HERBERT FAULKNER-John Sloan's Last Summer-8vo-wrps-
(IowaCty)-(c1952)-Prairie Pr (5b2) 4.50
--Modern Book Collecting for the Impecunious Amateur-Bost-
1936-8vo-bds&cl-1st ed (5d3,dj) 5.00
--Notes from a Bookman-Hanover-1968-ltd to 399c,autg-rare
)4c7,dj) 45.00
WEST INDIAN DIRECTORY-Vol 1-Lond-1829-H O-lg8vo-
orig wrps-340p,(11)p-lg8vo (5ss2,sl wtrstns) 38.50
WEST INDIAN REPORTS-1958 to 68-Vol 1 thru 12-bnd
(5ii7,ex-libr) 250.00
WEST INDIES PILOT-Wash-1922,29-Hydrogrph Office #128 & #129-
8vo-cl-2 vols-maps-wi suppl 1934 (5t0) 8.00
WEST,J W,ed-Sketches of Our Mountain Pioneers-Lynchb-(1939)-
297p-cl-priv prntd (5h1) 7.50
WEST,JOHN C-Texan in Search of a Fight-Waco-1901-189p-rare
(4j7,pres,leaflet tip in) 85.00

WEST,LEVON-Making An Etching-Lond-1932-Chamberlin-
8vo-79p or mounted illus-How To Do It series   (5ww3)   15.00

WEST,MICHAEL-Clair de Lune & other Troubadour Romances-
Lond-n.d.-(Cheylesmore Pr)-col illus   (4a1)   15.00

WEST,MORRIS L-Tower of Babel-NY-1968-Morrow-1st ed
(4L4,dj,mint,autg)   15.00

WEST,MRS-Letters to a Young Lady-Troy&NY-1806-504p-calf-
lea labl   (5p1,crack)   27.50

WEST,NATH'L-Day of the Locust-NY-1939-1st prntg (4j0,box)   75.00

WEST POINT-A Guide Book to...& Vicinity-NY-1844-
lg fldg map-16mo   (4b6)   20.00

WEST,RAY B,Jr-Kingdom of the Saints-NY-1957
(5x5,dj) 10.   (5m9,dj)   9.50

WEST,REBECCA-Black Lamb & Grey Falcon-NY-1941-lg thk8vo-
cl-1181p-1st ed   (5p5)   8.50
--same-NY-1943-1181p-illus-cl   (5t2)   4.00
--Harriet Hume-Lond-n.d.-Hutchinson   (5x0)   5.00
--Henry James-NY-(1916)-Holt&Co   (5ss9,dj)   6.00
--Selected Poems of Carl Sandburg-NY-1926-1st ed   (4j0)   10.00
--same-NY-1942   (5b9,vf)   3.00
--The Strange Necessity,Essays by-NY-1928-8vo-cl-380p-1st ed
(5t0)   6.00

WEST,RICHARD S,JR-Gideon Welles-Indnpls-(1943)-8vo-379p
(5t7,dj) 6.   (4a7) 10.   (5w4)   8.50

WEST,S H-Life & Times of S H West-Leroy,Ill-(1908)-8vo-298p-
cl-illus   (5h5)   60.00

WEST,SAML E-Cross on the Range-Phila-c1947-Church Hist Soc-
8vo-wrps-105p   (4t1)   6.50

WEST TEXAS HISTORICAL ASSOC YEAR BOOK,Vol 7-Abilene-
Jun,1931-wrps-149p plus index-scarce   (4L5)   10.00

WEST VIRG PULP & PAPER CO-West Virg Inspirations for Printers-
1950,51,52-4to-illus   (5p7)   5.00

WESTBROOK,RICHARD B-The Eliminator-Phila-1892   (5x7)   4.50

WESTBROOK,STILLMAN F-These 18 Months-(Hartf,1934)-8vo-
maps-1st ed   (5ss5,autg)   8.50

WESTBURY,G H-Misadventures of Working Hobo in Canada-Lond-
1930-172p-illus-scarce   (5a1)   6.50

WESTBURY,HUGH-Acte,a novel-Lond-1890Bentley-3 vols-8vo-
orig cl-dec bds-1st ed-v scarce   (5xx6,lend libr labl)   60.00

WESTCOTT,ALLAN-Mahan on Naval Warfare-Bost-1942-
372p-illus-maps   (5s1,pres,ex-libr)   7.00

WESTCOTT,EDW NOYES-David Harum-NY-1898-1st ed,1st issue
(perfect "J" on pg 40)-auth's 1st book
(5v2,vf) 37.50 (5gg6,f) 20.(5ss9)   25.00
--same-NY-1898-1st ed   (5m1) 10.   (4m8,lettrs chip)   8.50
--same-NY-1899-8vo-cl-392p   (5t2)   4.00
--same-NY-(1900)-Appleton-410p-illus ed-special pref (5x4)   7.50
--same-NY-(1900)-8vo-vel-410p-illus-ltd to 750c   (5t7)   15.00

WESTCOTT,FRANK N-Hepsey Burke-NY-(c1915)-illus-8vo-dec cl-
(5b2,f)   4.00

WESTCOTT,THOMPSON-Historic Mansions & Buildings of Phila-
Phila-1895-illus-orig cl-rev'd ed-528p   (4m4,wn)   18.50

WESTERGAARD,W-Danish West Indies under Company Rule 1671 to
1754 with suppl chapter 1755 to 1917-1917-illus   (5L7)   8.50
--Denmark & Hesvig 1848 to 1864-Oxford U Pr-1946-143p-illus
(5a9,dj)   3.50

WESTERMARCK,EDW-History of Human Marriage-Lond-1921-3 vols-
5th ed   (4b7)   37.50
--same-NY-1922-lg8vo-3 vols-5th ed (5t4) 15. (5p5,mint)   25.00
--Origin & Development of Moral Ideas-Lond-1924-2 vols-2nd ed
(4b7)   25.00
--A Short History of Marriage-NY-1930   (5x7)   5.00

WESTERMEIR,CLIFFORD P-Man,Beast,Dust-Denver-(1948)-450p-
1 illus-2nd prntng   (5L2)   5.00

WESTERN ART UNION-Transactions of,for year 1849-Cinn-1849-
Daily Times Prntng Off-8vo-orig pink wrps-plt inserted (5i0) 27.50

WESTERN AUSTRALIA LAW REPORTS-1898 to 1959-Vol 1 thru 60-
bnd   (5ii7,ex-libr) 1,100.00

WESTERN AUSTRALIA REPORTS-1960 to 67-bnd (5ii7,ex-libr) 145.00

WESTERN BAPTIST REVIEW-Frankfort-1845,46-bds-480p-Vol 1,
#1 to #12   (5ff7,wn)   35.00

WESTERN CANADA,DESCRIPTIVE ATLAS OF-n.p.-(1899)-maps-
4to-cl-photos   (4c1)   17.50

WESTERN CARTRIDGE CO-Rifle & Piston Ammunition Hand Book-
East Alton-1934-8vo-64p-illus-wrps   (4a6)   7.50

WESTERN COAL & LUMBER RESOURCES-of Central Coal & Coke
Co of Kansas City,Mo-KansCty,Mo-1902-photos-184p plus
index-1st ed-v scarce   (4t3)   45.00

WESTERN CORRELATOR-Journal of Topeka Industrial & Educa
Inst-May 1902-8p-wrps   (5x2)   20.00

WESTERN FARMER'S ALMANAC FOR 1830-Pittsbrg-(1829)-
18 leaves-sewed as issued   (5jj9)   12.50

WESTERN FEMALE SEMINARY-Memorial,25th Anniv of-Oxford,
Ohio-1881-231p-cl   (5h2)   8.50

WESTERN FRONTIER LIBRARY-Various titles-Norman,Okla,1953 to
1970,all 1st printings of Okla Pr editions-44 vols (5L2)   150.00

WESTERN GALAXY & MONTHLY MAGAZINE-Vol 1,#1 to 4 in 3
issues(all pub)-SaltLkCty-Mar to Jun,1888-ports-views-R8vo-
orig wrps-scarce   (5r8)   32.50

WESTERN HIST CO-History of Boone County,Mo-StLouis-1882-
illus-1144p-1st ed-rare   (4t3,rebnd,4p in facs,sl rprd)   100.00

WESTERN LANCET-Vol 14 #1 to 12-Cinn-1853-763p-wrps-
cl bk   (5h1,lacks July No.,wn)   12.50

WESTERN PATRIOT & CANTON ALMANACK FOR 1847-Canton,
Stark Co,Ohio-(1846)-16 leaves-wrps   (5jj9)   12.50

WESTERN RANGE CATTLE INDUSTRY-(Denver-n.d.)-12p-limp
pict lea   (4c1)   12.50

WESTERN SANITARY COMMISSION-Sketch of Its Origin,History,
etc-StLouis-1864-138p plus index-2 plts-1st ed
(4L0) 7.50   (4c8,rbnd)   20.00

WESTERN SHORE GAZETTEER-& Commercial Directory for State
of Calif-Yolo County-Woodland-(1870)-8vo-hf lea-602p
(5h4,lacks map,chip)   50.00

WESTERN SLOPE COOK BOOK-Eagle,Colo-1912-wrps-
pub by Gymsum M E Church-90p-ads-illus   (4g9,scuff)   10.00

WESTERN TEXAS,IMMIGRANTS GUIDE TO-Sunset Route-n.p.-
(1876)-55p-12mo-prntd wrps-Galv,Harrsbg & SanAnto Rwy Co
(4c1)   25.00

WESTERN WORLD GUIDE BOOK-& Handbook of Useful Info-Chig-
n.d.-(ca 1886)-col maps-256p plus ads   (4L0,wn)   12.50

WESTERN WRITERS OF AMER-Bad Men & Good-NY-1953-8vo-
cl-240p-illus-1st ed   (5g6,autg,f,dj)   7.50

WESTERNERS BRAND BOOK-see LOS ANGELES CORRAL

WESTERVELT,W D-Hawaiian Legends of Volcanoes-Bost-1916-
12mo-illus-Ellis Pr   (5x5)   7.50
--Legends of Ma Ui A,Demi God of Polynesia & of His Mother
Hina-Honolulu-1910-Hawaiian Gazette Co   (5x5)   15.00
--Legends of Old Honolulu-Bost-1916-12mo-illus-Ellis Pr
(5x9) 5.   (5x5)   10.00

WESTFALL,ALFRED-Amer Shakesperian Criticism-NY-1939-305p
(5j4)   8.00

WESTINGHOUSE AIR BRAKE CO-Reference Book-Pittsbg-
Jul 1,1872-4to-147p-illus-fldg charts   (5t4)   20.00

WESTINGHOUSE CO-Threshing Machinery Catalog,1898-illus-
wrps-4to-illus-32p   (4d9)   12.50

WESTLAKE,J WILLIS-How to Write Letters-Phila-1876-12mo-
264p   (5w7,sl stn)   5.00

WESTLICHE "VATERLANDSFREUND" UND CANTONER,DER
CALENDER AUF 1840-Canton-(1839)-13 leaves,sewed-v rare
(5h6,minor rprs)   20.00
--same-..1844-Canton-(1843)-16 leaves including wrps (5h1)   15.00

WESTMAN,E G-The Swedish Element in America-Chig-1931 to
1934-4 vols-illus-lg8vo-cl   (5t2)   25.00

WESTON,CHARIS-Calif & the West-NY-1940-photos-127p-4to-
1st ed-US Camera Book   (5ww3) 50.   (5x5,dj)   25.00
--50 Photographs-NY-1947-ltd to 1500c-4to-initialed by artist
(5ww3)   150.00

WESTON,D C-Wiwigawangapi Kin,Qa Wokiksuye Anpetu Kin
Koya-Madison,SD-1893-wrps-32p   (4L2)   45.00

WESTON,F-The Black Slaves of Prussia-Bost-1918-12mo-23p-
wrps   (5x2)   7.50

WESTON,GEO F-Boston Ways-Bost-(1957)-261p-photos-qtr cl
(5c3)   4.00

WESTON,GEO M-Poor Whites of the South-Wash-1856-wrps-
Buell & Banchard   (4j4)   4.00

WESTON,OTHETO-Mother Lode Album-Stanford-(1948)-sq8vo-
illus   (5r7) 15.   (5h4,tn dj)   20.00
--same-2nd printing   (5h4)   15.00

WESTON,O-Mother Lode Album-Stanford U-(1948)-illus-folio-
178p-1st ed   (4n1,dj) 30.   (5h5,f)   20.00

WESTON,THOS-Hist of Town of Middleboro,Mass-Bost-1906-
724p-cl   (5h7) 12.50   (5m6)   20.00

WESTON,THOS C-Remin Among Rocks in Connection With Geolog
Surv of Canada-Tor-1899-Author-plts-328p   (5zz8)   15.00

WESTON,W-The Yampa Coal Field of Routt Co,Colo-n.p.-n.d.-
(Moffat Road)-(ca 1904)-53p-photos-wrps-pkt map-rare (5L2) 50.00

WESTON,REV WALTER-Mountaineering & Exploration in the
Japanese Alps-Lond-1896-John Murray-346p-illus-hf calf-
fldg maps   (5d7)   10.00

WESTON,WM-Complete Merchant's Clerk-Lond-1754-8vo-calf-
Chas Rivington   (5zz7)   45.00

WESTOVER,ADELE B-Unflinching Courage-JosephCty,Ariz-
n.d.-(ca 1961?)-priv prntd-690p plus index-photos
(4L0,mint)   12.50

USED BOOK PRICE GUIDE

WESTOVER,RUSS-Tillie the Toiler-NY-1927-sq4to-48p-
   pict glazed lmp bds-Cupples-comic strip style   (5aa0)   6.50
WESTPHAL,W-10 Years in SoAfrica-Lond-1892-illus-fldg col map
                                                      (5x2)   17.50
WESTRATE,E V-Those Fatal Generals-1936-illus   (5L7)   4.50
WESTROPP,HODDER-Ancient Symbol Worship-NY-1875-cl-illus-
   98p   (5x7) 6.50   (5p5,mint) 15.00
--Epochs of Painted Vases-Lond-1856-24p-4to-9 plts (5w7) 6.50
WESTWARD HO,A TALE-NY-1832-(J K Paulding)-orig cl-2 vols-
   1st ed   (4g2,fox) 45.   (5b2,box) 100.00
WESTWARD MARCH OF EMIGRATION-in the US considered....
   future of Colo & New Mex-Mar,1874-Lancaster,Pa-1874-
   wrps   (5g3,lacks bk wrp) 25.00
WESTWOOD,T-Bibliotheca Piscatoria-Lond-1883,1901 plus supl in
   orig wrps-2 vols   (5tt5) 25.00
--same-Lond-1883-397p plus ads-t.e.g.-1st ed   (5a9) 30.00
--Chronicle of the "Compleat Angler" of Izaak Walton & Chas
   Cotton-Lond-1864-64p   (5h9,cov wn,pres) 15.00
WETHERBEE,J-A Brief Sketch of Colorado Terr & Gold Mines of
   That Region-Bost-1863-12mo-orig prntd wrps-24p-rare
   (5a3,bk wrp in facs) 250.   (5i9,f,Streeter copy) 650.00
WETHERED,H N-A Short History of Gardens-Lond-(1933)-323p-
   20 plts   (5s7)   7.50
WETHERELL,ELIZ-Queechy-Lond-n.d.-Simpkin,Marshall-frontis-
   calf-bds-16mo-670p-"Author's Complete Edition" (5p1) 12.50
--same-NY-1852-Putnam-2 vols-cl-12mo-10p ads(Vol 1)-1st(5j5) 37.50
WETHERILL,C-History of Religious Soc of Friends,called by some
   Free Quakers-Phila-1894-bds   (5L7,ex-libr,soil) 7.50
WETHILL,CHAS M-The Manufacture of Vinegar-Phila-1860-
   300p,(1)   (5w1,cov dtchd)   8.50
WETMORE,ALEXANDER-Birds-Wash-1931-wrps-166p-69 plts-
   Smi Sci Series   (4p5)   15.00
--Birds of Haiti & Dominican Republic-Wash-1931-Smi Inst #155-
   orig wrps-plts-2 maps-483p   (4p5) 8.   (4a3) 15.00
WETMORE,ALPHONSO-Gazetteer of State of Missouri-StLouis-
   1837-illus-382p-wi appendix-fldg map
   (4g6,lacks map,wn) 22.50 (5ii2,map tn) 75. (4n4) 150.00
WETMORE,CHAS A-Report of...On Mission Indians of SoCalif-
   Wash-1875-17p-wrps   (4a5)   7.50
WETMORE,CLAUDE-Queen Magi's Little People-StLouis-1913-
   Curran Prntng Co-pic cl   (5c8,review copy,sl rpr) 15.00
WETMORE,H-Last of Great Scouts-(1899-Duluth Pr)-267p-
   illus-impr & date on cpyrte pg-(Howes 1st ed)
   (5s4,ex-libr,wn) 8.50 (5ii2) 9.50 (5p7) 7.50 (4L0) 10.00
--same-Chig&Duluth-(1899)-illus-296p
   (4L0) 7.50   (4d9,sl stain) 8.50 (5s4,pres) 12.50
--same-Lond-1903   (4L0)   5.00
--same-NY-1918-illus-G&D   (5m9) 4.   (4L0)   5.00
WETTE,L de-Reise in den Vereinigten Staaten Und Canada in Jahr
   1837-Leipzig-1838-Weidmann-8vo-mor   (4h0,rbnd,vf) 60.00
WETTERGREN,ERIK-Modern Decorative Arts of Sweden-
   Malmo Museum-1926-illus-205p-4to (5ww3,autg by Palm) 30.00
WETTERN,DESMOND-The Lonely Battle-Lond-1960-20 photos
                                    (5c1)   5.00
WETZEL,W A-Benj Franklin As An Economist-John Hopkins Pr-
   1895-pamph-orig wrps   (5qq8)   6.00
WETZELL,MME-Les Petits Enfants,Premieres Lectures-Paris-(c1840)-
   Langlume-t12mo-176p-dec bds-plts-g.t.-frontis
                           (5aa0,sl rub)   12.50
WEWITZER,RALPH-School for Wits-Lond-1815-bds-cl bk
                           (5j2,cov wn)   8.50
WEXLEY,JOHN-Judgment of Julius & Ethel Rosenberg-NY-1955-
   672p   (5w5,dj,box)   5.00
WEY,FRANCIS-Rome-NY-1872-Appleton-thk folio-orig dec lea-
   fldg map-1st US ed   (5m2,rub)   8.50
WEYAND,L R-An Early History of Fayette County-Lagrange-1936-
   383p   (4a5)   37.50
WEYER,EDW-Primitive Peoples Today-NY-(1958)-4to-maps-orig cl-
   photos-14 maps   (5tt5,f)   10.00
WEYER,EDW M,JR,-ed-Strangest Creatures on Earth-NY-(1953)-
   255p-illus   (5p7)   4.50
WEYGANDT,CORNELIUS-The Blue Hills-NY-1936(4m4,dj) 15.00
--The Dutch Country-NY-1939-illus-1st ed
   (5jj3,f,dj) 17.50   (5w5) 16.50
--The Heart of New Hampshire-NY-(1944)   (5m2)   6.00
--A Passing America-NY-(1932)-illus-col frontis-330p-1st ed
   (5m2) 6.   (4m4,autg)   15.00
--Philadelphia Folks-NY-1938-illus   (5m2) 10. (4j9,dj) 15.00
--Plenty of Pennsylvania-NY-1942-illus-319p (5w5,4j9) 15.00
--Red Hills-Phila-1929   (4j9)   15.00
--White Hills-1934-illus   (5L7)   5.00
--Wissahickon Hills-Phila-1930-266p (5ee3,f,dj) 8.50 (4j9) 12.50

WEYL,WALTER-Tired Radicals & Other Papers-NY-1921-1st ed
                                    (5q8)   7.50
WEYL,WALTER E-The End of the War-NY-1918-323p (5w5) 4.50
WEYMAN,STANLEY JOHN-The House of the Wolf-Lond-1890-
   12mo-dec gray cl-1st ed of auth's 1st book-scarce
                           (5gg6,publ pres)   50.00
WEYMOUTH,MASS-Historical Soc Proceedings #1,1879,80-1881-
   127p   (5t9)   10.00
WHALEN,GROVER A-Mr New York-NY-1955-Putnam-312p-illus
                                    (5p9)   5.00
WHALEY,MARCELLUS S-The Old Types Pass-Bost-(1925)-illus-
   8vo-1st ed   (4m8,dj) 8.50   (5x2) 17.50
WHALEY,SAML-History of Township of Mt Pleasant,Wayne Co,Pa-
   NY-1856-v scarce   (4m4) 17.50   (5m2) 13.50
WHALL,W B-Ships,Sea Songs & Shanties-Glasgow-1913-131p-
   illus   (5t4)   12.50
WHALDON,E P-Some Family Records-1934-147p   (5t9) 10.00
WHAREY,JAS BLANTON-The Pilgrim's Progress-Oxford-1928-
   facs   (5v2,mint)   15.00
WHARTON,ANNA H-Colonial Days & Dames-Phila-1895-illus-
   248p   (5e3) 3.50 (5h9) 5.   (5w7) 4.50
--same-Phila-1895-delux ltd to 508c,nbrd-tissue guards-t.e.g.
                           (5w4,fade)   10.00
--Engl Ancestral Homes of Noted Americans-Phila-1915-8vo-
   illus   (5h9) 8.50   (5m6) 12.50
--Heirlooms in Miniature-Phila&Lond-1897-Lippincott-orig dec cl-
   t.e.g.-6th ed   (4m9)   12.50
--same-Phila-1898-259p-illus (5ii2) 12.50 (5n7) 18.50
--same-Phila-1902-259p-plts(some col)   (5xx7) 10.00
--Engl Ancestral Homes of Noted Americans-Phila-1915-314p-
   illus-29 plts-1st ed-g.t.   (5h9,unopnd)   8.50
--Martha Washington-NY-1897-(Scribner's)-12mo-frontis-orig cl-
   g.t.-1st ed   (5h9)   8.50
--Salons,Colonial & Republican-Phila-1900-illus-286p
   (5h9,4p7,fade) 7.50 (5w7)   8.50
--Social Life in the Early Republic-Phila-1902-illus-lea&bds-
   346p   (5t4,scuff)   10.00
--Through Colonial Doorways-Phila-1893-illus-ltd ed 442c
   (5ii3,faded) 15.   (5w4)   10.00
--same-Phila-1893-frontis-237p   (5h9)   6.00
--same-Phila-1898-Lippincott-237p (5w7) 3.50 (5t7,5p5) 5.00
WHARTON,CLARENCE R-El Presidente-Austin-(1926)-197p-port
                                    (5t7)   10.00
--Gail Borden,Pioneer-SanAnt-1941-229p (5n4,Streeter copy) 15.00
--History of Texas-Dallas-1935   (4a5)   9.00
--L'Archeveque-Houston-1941-Anson Jones Pr-wrps (5kk6) 15.00
--Remember Goliad-Houston-1931-ltd to 100c (4c7) 150.00
--San Jacinto,16th Decisive Battle-Houston-1930 (4a5,pres) 27.50
WHARTON,D,ed-Roosevelt Omnibus-NY-1934-sm4to-illus-
   1st ed   (5yy6,dj)   6.00
WHARTON,EDITH-A Backward Glance-1934-Appleton Century
                           (5F1,f,dj)   5.00
--The Book of the Homeless-NY-1916-4to-bds&cl-illus (5d3) 20.00
--The Decoration of Houses-NY-1897-204p-illus
   (5w7,sl chip,5t7,libr labl)   12.50
--NY-1917-cl   (5w7)   8.50
--Ethan Frome-NY-1911-12mo-orig red cl-g.t.-perfect type
   last line of pg 135,1st issue-1st ed
   (4j0) 45. (5yy6,vg) 67.50 (5m1) 35.   (5ee9) 75.00
--same-NY-1922-Scribner-8vo-bds-cl bk-frontis-2000c prntd-
   designed by Bruce Rogers   (5b2)   6.50
--same-Portland(Me)-1939-box-autg-Ltd Ed Club-ltd to 1500c,
   nbrd-sm folio   (5b0)   17.50
--The Gods Arrive-NY-1932-431p-1st ed (4j0) 10. (5b2,rub) 5.00
--House of Mirth-NY-1905-illus-1st ed-1st state (5ii3) 15.(5m1)10.00
--Human Nature-Lond-1933-1st ed-249p   (4b4)   9.50
--In Morocco-NY-1920-lg8vo-cl-290p-illus (5p9) 5. (5t2) 4.00
--Madame de Treymes-NY-1907-12mo-cl-illus-Merrymount Pr-
   1st ed   (5m1) 6.50 (5d3)   5.00
--Motor Flight through France-NY-1908-illus-201p (5q0) 7.50
--The Reef-NY-1912-1st ed   (5m1)   5.00
--Sanctuary-NY-1903-Scribner-1st ed   (5p0)   5.00
--The Writing of Fiction-NY-1925-8vo-bds&cl-178p (5t0) 5.00
WHARTON,F-Digest of the Int'l Law of US-Wash-1886-2nd ed
                           (5r4,needs rebndg)   22.50
WHARTON,FRANCIS,ed-Revolutionary Diplomatic Correspondence
   of the US-Wash-1889-calf-6 vols (4j1,f) 95. (5w4,f bndgs) 75.00
WHARTON,GRACE-The Wits & Beaux of Society-Phila-n.d.-
   (ca 1890)-2 vols-illus-cl   (5t0)   7.50
WHARTON,H M-War Songs & Poems of Southern Confederacy,
   with Personal Remin-n.p.-1904-412p
   (4j4) 27.50   (4j4,rprd) 20. (4b3) 15.00

WHARTON,THOS-"Bobbo" & Other Fancies-NY-1897-
Harper-183p-illus-1st ed   (5m2) 5.   (5x4)   10.00
WHARTON,CAPT W J L-Capt Cook's Journal in H M Bark
"Endeavor", 1768 to 1771-Lond-1893-plts& fldg maps (5c1) 42.50
--Hydrographical Surveying-Lond-1882-360p   (5t7)   6.00
WHAT AMERICA THINKS-Chig-1941-1495p-cartoons   (5i1)   10.00
WHAT'S COOKIN-Hollywood-1944-Children's Hospital-232p
                                                 (4g9)   6.00
WHAT'S COOKING IN WALLA WALLA-WallaW-1954-spir bnd wrps-
144p   (4g9)   5.00
WHAT'S COOKING IN BEVERLY HILLS-n.p.-1957-PTA-122p-
illus-spiral bnd wrps   (5g9)   3.50
WHEAT,CARL I-Books of the Calif Gold Rush-SanFran-1949-
Colt Pr-8vo-bds&cl-Grabhorn Pr-500c prntd   (5d3)   20.00
--First One Hundred Years of Yankee Calif-1949-24p-1st ed-
illus-500c printed   (5r1)   12.50
--Maps of the Calif Gold Region-SanFran-1942-Grabhorn-folio-
cl-ltd to 300c (5h4,pres) 270.   (4h0, libr stmp, vf)   350.00
--same-SanFran-1942-Grabhorn-spec ed of 22c-3/4 lea-folio
                                                 (5x5)   600.00
--Pioneer Press of Calif-Oakland-1948-Grabhorn-30(31)p, 1p-
ltd to 450c,autg   (4L0)   25.00
--The Shirley Letters from the Calif Mines-NY-1949-216p-illus
                                                 (4L0)   7.50
WHEAT,GEO SEAY-The story of the Amer Legion-NY-1919-
Putnams-272p   (5u3)   8.50
WHEAT,JOE BEN-Mogollon Culture Prior to AD 1000-n.p.-
1955-Soc for Amer Arch-wrps   (5L7) 5.   (4L0)   8.50
WHEATLEY,FRANCIS-Cries of Lond-n.d. (1929)-Art Pub-4to-
bds-13 Cries in col-mounted plts-tissue guards   (4k9)   50.00
WHEATLEY,HEWETT-The Rod & Line-Lond-1849-12mo-calf-g.t.-
9 col plts   (4c2)   75.00
WHEATLY,WILKINS W-Square Riggers Before the Wind-NY-
1939-263p-plans in pkt   (5s1,ex-libr) 8.50
WHEATON,ELIZ LEE-Mr George's Joint-NY-1941 (5x2) 5. (5L7) 4.50
WHEATON,EMILY-Russells in Chig-Bost-1902-photos-257p-cl
                                                 (5h2)   7.50
WHEATON,HENRY-Elements of Int'l Law-Phila-1836-1st Amer ed-
375p-cl   (5i3)   15.00
WHEDBEE,T COURTENAY J-Port of Baltimore in the Making,1828
to 1878-Balto-1953-priv prntd-100p-illus   (5p0)   6.00
WHEELER,A C-Iron Trail-NY-1876-46p   (5y0,wrps)   8.50
--Selkirk Mountains-Winnipeg-1912-pict wrps-200p-ports-illus-
fldg maps   (5u6)   4.50
--The Selkirk Range-Ottawa-1905-2 vols in 1-illus (5w8) 10.00
WHEELER,CANDACE-The Development of Embroidery in Amer-
NY-1921-Harper-illus-152p   (5p0)   10.00
--How to Make Rugs-NY-1902-130p-11 plts (5n7,als tip in) 8.50
WHEELER,D E-Writings of Thos Paine-NY-(1908)-V Parke Co-
Centenary Memorial ed-10 vols-ltd to 1550 sets-cl (5p7) 40.00
WHEELER,DAVID H-Our Industrial Utopia & its Unhappy Citizens-
Chig-1895-341p-cl   (5jj9,f)   8.50
WHEELER,E J-Prohibition-NY-1894-227p-5th ed   (5w6)   5.00
WHEELER,EDW L-Deadwood Dick's Device-Cleve-n.d. (early 1900's)-
31,(1)p-pict wrps-(later prntg of Beadle's #104) (5h7)   3.50
--Old Avalanche,the Annihilator-NY-1878-self wrps-18p, (6)p-
Beadles Half Dime Libr   (4h7)   7.50
WHEELER,EDW S-Scheyichbi & the Strand-Phila-1876-116p
                                              (5w0,wn)   15.00
WHEELER,ELIZ ANN-Frugal Housekeepers Kitchen Companion-
NY-1851-Phelps&Fanning-pict wrps-illus (4g9,cov dmgd)   20.00
WHEELER,ELLA-Drops of Water-poems-NY-1872-12mo-cl-
1st ed of auth's 1st book-scarce   (5gg6,f)   25.00
WHEELER,EVERETT-Daniel Webster, Expounder of the Constitution-
NY-1905-port-1st ed   (4b7)   15.00
WHEELER,F R-Book of Cowboys-Bost-(1921)-394p-33 illus-dec cov
                                                 (4i7)   7.00
WHEELER,G D-Old Homes in Stonington-1903-336p-reprinted 1930
                                                 (5t9)   22.50
WHEELER,GEO M-Prelim Report Concerning Explorations & Surveys
Principally in Nev & Ariz-Wash-1872-96p-folio-fldg map
                                          (4L0,ex-libr)   20.00
--Progress Report upon Geograph & Geolog Explor & Surveys-
Wash-1874-lithos-56p-wrps-4to-fldg map (5tt0) 25.(5h5,autg)15.00
--Report on US Geograph Surv West of 100th Meridian-Vol 7,
Archaeology-Wash-1879-4to-496p-plts
                               (5s4,pres,ex-libr,wn)   40.00
WHEELER,GERVASE-Homes for the People-NY-1855 (5w7,sl tn) 10.00
--Rural Homes-NY-(1852)-307p-illus-1st ed   (5t4)   12.50
WHEELER,H F B-Napoleon & the Invasion of England-Lond-1908-
2 vols-illus-8 col illus-g.t.-lev mor   (5d2,f bndg) 20.00
WHEELER,HAROLD-Stirring Deeds of Britain's Sea Dogs in the Great
War-NY-1916-col frontis-17 plts   (5c1)   12.50

WHEELER,HAROLD F B-The Story of Lord Kitchener-Lond-
1916   (5x7)   6.50
WHEELER,HENRY G-History of Congress-NY-1848-orig cl-illus-
2 vols   (5q8,ex-libr, wn) 17.50
WHEELER,HOMER W-Buffalo Days, 40 Yrs in Old West-Indnpls-
(1925)-illus-369p-1st ed-scarce
        (5yy8) 17.50   (4L0) 12.50 (4i7,4n8) 15. (5jj7,f,dj) 13.50
--same-NY-(1925)-reprint   (5dd1)   6.50
--Frontier Trail-LosAng-1923-plts-334p-scarce
             (5L2,sl wn) 17.50   (4L0,autg,4i7)   25.00
WHEELER,JOHN-Treatise of Commerce-NY-GBHotchkiss,ed-
1931-facs ed   (5s1,ex-libr) 5.   (5L7)   10.00
WHEELER,JOHN H-Historical Sketches of North Car 1584 to
1851-Phila-1851-2 vols in 1(as issued (5s9,hng def)   42.50
WHEELER,JOS T-The Maryland Press 1777 to 1790-Balt-1938-
illus-226p   (4g2)   27.50
WHEELER,MARY SPARKES-First Decade of Woman's Foreign
Missionary Soc of Methodist Epis Church-NY-1881-cl-346p-
3 ports   (5r0)   7.50
WHEELER, MONROE-Soutine-MOMA-1950-10 col plts-116p-
8vo   (5ww3)   17.50
--same-Arno Reprint   (5ww3)   9.00
WHEELER,OLIN D-Eastwar Thru the Storied NW-StPaul-(1908)-
tinted photos-wrps-62p   (5dd1)   4.00
--Indianland & Wonderland-StPaul-1894-108p-dec wrps-maps-
1st ed-illus-v scarce   (5j0,fray,sl dmpstns) 17.50
--Sketches of Wonderland-StPaul-1895-110p-maps-illus-wrps
                                                 (5dd9)   5.00
--Trail of Lewis&Clark, 1804 to 1904-NY-(1904)-2 vols-photos-
fldg maps-col frontis   (5s1,wn,lacks Vol 2)15.(5dd1) 25.00
--Wonderland '97-StPaul-1897-2 maps-8vo-111p-wrps
                                    (4g6,lacks wrps)   6.00
--Wonderland 1905 Descriptive of NW-StP-1905-119p-pict wrps-
illus-maps-NP Ry publ   (5h1) 8.50   (5j0)   12.50
--Yellowstone Nat'l Park-StPaul-1901-111p,(1)   (4n9)   7.50
WHEELER,ROBT-Ohio Newspapers, a Living Record-Columbus-
1950-cl-folio-253p   (4t7)   12.50
WHEELER,W O-Ogden Family in Amer-1907-532p with Vol of
37 charts   (4t2)   40.00
WHEELER,W REGINALD-Pine Knots & Bark Peelers-LaJolla-
1960-252p-illus   (5w4,dj)   3.50
WHEELER,WM A-Dictionary of the Noted Names of Fiction-Bost-
1869   (5F0)   3.50
--Mother Goose's Melodies-Bost&NY-(c1878)-8vo-186p-frontis-
17 plts-pict cl -Houghton Mifflin   (5p1,wn)   10.00
WHEELER,WM MORTON-Demons of the Dust-NY-(1930)-Norton-
378p-illus   (5p7)   10.00
WHEELMAN,THE-Magazine of Cycling, Vols 1 thru 5,Oct 1882
thru Mar 1885-5 vols in 4-Bost-1882 to 85-(merged into Outing)
                                                 (5ss5)   30.00
WHEELOCK,JOHN H-Bibliography of Theodore Roosevelt-NY-
1920-ltd to 500c   (5mm2) 10.   (4g2)   15.00
--The Human Fantasy-Bost-1911-1st ed-auth's 1st book (5r9,f) 15.00
--Poems 1911 to 1936-NY-1936-245p (5t7,autg,orig poem)   7.50
WHEELOCK,JULIA S-The Boys in White-NY-1870-274p-a.e.g.-
ports   (5t7)   7.50
WHEELOCK,T B-Journal of Col Dodge's Expedition from Ft Gibson
to the Pawnee Pict Village-Wash-1834-1st issue-scarce-HED
                             (5x5) 45.   (4n4)   50.00
WHEELOCK'S,MRS-Choice Recipes-(StPaul,1904)-147p&ads-
frontis   (5g9,rub)   6.50
WHEELS & WHIMS-Bost-1884-illus-1st ed   (5mm2)   12.50
WHEELWRIGHT,EDITH-The Physick Garden-Lond-(1939)-288p
                                                 (5w3)   12.50
WHEELWRIGHT,EDITH G-Gardening in Stone-NY-n.d.-193p-
photos   (5s7)   5.00
WHEELWRIGHT,JOHN T-Rollo's Journey to Cambridge-Bost&NY-
1926-4to-illus-28p-bds-Memorial Ed   (5p1,wn,dj) 10.00
WHEELWRIGHT'S,MR-Report on steam navigation in the Pacific-
(Lond)-1843-wrpr title   (5g8,lacks bk wrp) 20.00
WHEELWRIGHT,WM B-Lengthening Shadow of One Man-Fitchbrg-
1957-181p-cl-priv prntd   (5h1)   4.00
WHEELWRIGHT,WM BOND-Life & Times of Alvah Crocker-Bost-
1923-4to-priv prntd-14p plus 114p-illus-map-2000c prntd
                                          (5r0, lt stn) 15.00
WHEILDON,W-Letters from Nahant, Historical,Descrip & Misc-
(Bost)-1842-Pr of Bunker Hill Aurora-12mo-orig wrps-
1st ed   (5ss5)   15.00
--Siege & Evacuation of Boston & Charlestown-Bost-1876-8vo-
orig wrps-map & illus-64p   (5ss5)   6.00
WHELAN,CHAS E-Bascom Clarke-Madsn-(1913)-216p-cl (5h7)   5.00

WHELEN,TOWNSEND-Amateur Gunsmithing-Wash-1924-
173p-illus (5t4) 5.00
--The American Rifle-NY-1918-8vo-637p-illus-1st ed
  (5w5,ex-libr) 15. (4a6) 40.00
--same-NY-1920-illus-8vo-cl-637p (5t0) 5.00
--Hunting Big Game-Harrisburg-1946-2 vols-8vo-illus
  (4a6,box,dj) 10. (5ss8) 15.00
--Wilderness Hunting & Wildcraft-Marshalltown-1927-8vo-
338p-photos (4a6) 12.50 (4n9) 7.50
WHELER,GEO-A Journey Into Greece-Lond-1682-in 6 books-R8vo-
483p-bds-lea (5t7) 50.00
WHEN WM AVERY STRATTONG OWNED THE MISSISSIPPI RIVER-
n.p.-n.d.-(1935)-60p-wrps-priv prntd (5h2,pres) 5.00
WHERE MEN ONLY DARE TO GO-Richmond-1885-by an Ex-Boy-
scarce (5h6) 40.00
WHERRY,EDGAR T-Guide to Eastern Ferns-(Lancaster,Pa)-1937-
220p-illus (5s7) 5.50
--Wild Flower Guide,Northeastern & Midland US-GardenCty-
1948-202p-plts-map (5s7) 3.00
--Wild Flowers of Mt Desert Island-1928-164p-illus (5e8) 14.75
WHETHAM,J W B-Across Central Amer-1877-hf mor (5L7) 10.00
WHETMORE,A A-Discussion of subject of Universalism-Colum-
1846-360p-cl (5h7) 15.00
WHIBLEY,LEONARD-A Companion to Greek Studies-Cambr-1905-
672p-illus-1st ed (5w9) 15.00
WHICHER,GEO G-This Was a Poet-NY-1938-illus-1st ed
  (5mm2,dj) 10.00
WHIDDEN,CAPT JOHN D-Ocean Life in the old Sailing Ship
Days-Bost-1908-8vo-illus-314p-1st ed
  (5t2,libr mrks) 3.75 (5ss5) 8.50
WHIFFEN,MARCUS-Stuart & Georgian Churches,Lond,1603 to 1837-
Lond-1947-Batsford-118p-153 plts&plans-8vo-cl
  (5m5,sl soil) 12.00
WHIFFEN,MRS THOS-Keeping Off the Shelf-NY-1928-203p-
illus-1st ed (5w9,dj) 6.50
WHIGS & DEMOCRATS-Richmond-1839-White-80p-orig wrps-
scarce (5ss9,wn) 35.00
WHILLDIN,M-Descrip of Western Texas Publ By Galveston,
Harrisburg & SanAnt Ry Co-Galveston-1876-Sunset Route
map tip in-orig wrps (5r5,f) 100.00
WHIM WHAM,THE-publ 1811 by Johnson&Werner-24mo-buff wrps-
33p -frontis (5p1,lacks t.p.) 50.00
WHIPPLE,A B C-Yankee Whalers in the South Seas-NY-(1954)-
illus-304p (4a1) 7.50 (5e8) 5. (5t4) 6.50 (5p9) 4.50
WHIPPLE,AMIEL W-Report of Explor for a Rwy Route...Missis Riv
to Pac Ocean-Wash-1855-154p (4n4,5tt0,map tn) 30.00
--same-LosAng-1961-ltd to 900c (5h5,f,dj) 5.50
WHIPPLE,C H-Whipple,Wright,Wager,Ward,Pell,McLean Burnet
Families-(LosAng)-1917-ports-117p (5yy8) 15.00
WHIPPLE,H E-Brief Genealogy of the Whipple Families who
settled in RI-1873-63p (4t2) 20.00
WHIPPLE,GEO M-History of Salem Light Infantry from 1805 to
1890-Salem-1890-Essex Inst-148p (5mm8) 6.00
WHIPPLE,GURTH-Fifty Years of Conservation in NY State-1935-
197p-wrps (5zz8) 10.00
WHIPPLE,MAURINE-This is the Place,Utah-NY-1945-Knopf-
1st ed (5s4,f) 6. (5L0,5n4) 5.00
WHIPPLE,WAYNE-The Story Life of Lincoln-Phila-1908-708p
  (5t7) 8.00
WHIST PLAYER'S HAND BOOK-By an Experienced Player-Phila-
1844- 12mo-1st ed of 1st Amer bridge whist rule book (5m6) 17.50
WHISTLER,JAS McNEILL-Catalogue of Exhibition of Port. of...-
Rochester,NY-1915-priv prntd-8 illus(1col)-67p-ltd to 130c,
nbrd (4e0) 37.50
--Eden Versus Whistler-NY-1899-1st Amer ed-sq8vo-dec bds-
  (5nn2) 12.50
--Modern Masters of Etching-Lond-1927-The Studio-illus (5x0) 5.00
--Ten O'Clock,a lecture-Portl,Me-1916-Mosher-54p-4to-
ltd to 450c (4a0,soil,crack) 37.50
--Whistler v Ruskin,Art & Art Critics-Lond-(1878)-12mo-
orig prntd wrps-1st ed of auth's 1st book (5gg6,TRWay's copy) 37.50
WHISTLER,LAWRENCE-Oho-Lond-1946-JnLane-illus-lg8vo-
reversible faces (5c8,dj) 7.50
WHISTON,WM-Genuine Works of Flavius Josephus-Bost-1823-
2 vols-buck (5ww4,libr mrks,rbnd) 15.00
WHITAKER,A P,ed-Documents relating to commercial policy of
Spain in the Floridas-Deland-1931-lg8vo-cl&bds-maps&illus-
Florida State Hist Soc pub (5g4,box) 20.00
WHITAKER,ALEX-Good News from Virginia-Lond-1613-sm4to-
mor.-g.-v rare (4j4,sl worming,f bndg) 1850.
  (4h5,f bndg,marg worm holes) 3,500.00
WHITAKER,ALMA-Baccus Behave-NY-1933-140p (5w6) 3.50

WHITAKER,CHAS H,ed-Bertram Grosvenor Goodhue,Architect
& Master of Many Arts-NY-1925-273 plts-sm folio-AIA (5p7) 35.00
--Architectural Sculpture of State Capitol at Lincoln,Neb-NY-
1926-illus-4to (4b6,sp chip) 12.50
WHITAKER,EPHER-History of Southold,Long Island,Its 1st Century-
Southold-1881-12mo-cl-354p (4t1) 20.00
WHITAKER,FESS-History of F W-(Louisville-1918)-priv prnt-illus
  (4b6) 20.00
WHITAKER,G,DR-Sick Man's Friend-NY-1870-12mo-cl-208p
  (5t0) 5.00
WHITAKER,HERMAN-The Planter-NY-1909-Harper-8vo-pict cl-
frontis (5b2) 7.50
--West Winds,Calif's book of fiction-SanFran-(1914)-frontis-illus
tip in-232p (5dd4) 10.00
WHITAKER,J I S-Birds of Tunisia-Lond-1905-R H Porter-lea&bds-
2 vols-hand col plts-fldg maps-ltd to 250c-v scarce (4p5) 187.75
WHITAKER,JOHN-History of Manchester-1773-buck-2nd ed,corr
  (5L7,rbnd) 15.00
WHITAKER'S PEERAGE-Baronetage,Knightage & Companionage for
1924-Lond-(1924) (5r7) 10.00
WHITBREAD&CO-Inns of Sport-Lond-(1949)-7 col plts-54p-
bds- (5w1) 3.50
--Your Club-Lond-(1950)-7 col plts (5w1) 3.50
WHITBY,CAPT HENRY-Trial of...for Murder of John Pierce-
NY-1812-Gould,Banks&Gould-8vo-95p,(1)-disbnd (5L1) 40.00
WHITCHER,W F-Hist of Haverhill,NHamp-1919-781p (5t9) 17.50
WHITCOMB,C-Whitcomb Family in Amer-1904-621p (4t2) 35.00
WHITCOMB,R P-First History of Bayonne,NJ-Bayonne-1904-illus-
cl (4m4) 10. (4t1) 12.50
WHITE,A R-The Blue & the Gray-KansCty-(1898)-413p-photos
  (5dd1,crude rpr) 5.00
WHITE,ADAM-A Popular History of Mammalia-Lond-1850-16 plts-
scarce-1st ed (5v2) 35.00
--Instructive Picture Book-Edinb-1859-Edmonston&Douglas-folio-
bds-cl bk-frontis-62p-29 dbl pg handcol plts-3rd ed (4d1) 65.00
WHITE,ALMA-Looking Back from Beulah-Zarepath,NJ-1929-illus-
392p (4p8) 7.50
WHITE,ALMIRA LARKIN-Genealogy of Descendants of John White
of Wenham & Lancaster,Mass-Haverhill-1900 to 1909-4 vols-
fldg chart-illus-port (5h9) 45.00
WHITE,AMOS JEROME-Dawn in Bantuland-Bost-1953-
Christopher Pub-297p (4t5,autgs) 15.00
WHITE,ANDREW DICKSON-Autobiography of-NY-1905-2 vols-
1st ed-port (5t4) 8. (5h9) 8.50
--same-NY-1914-ports-2 vols (4j3) 12.50
WHITE&WHITE-A sub treasury of Amer Humor-NY-1941
  (5b9,sl loose) 2.75
WHITE,ANNIE RANDALL-20th Century Etiquette-priv prntd-
4to-col plts-430p- (1900) (5w7,crack) 9.50
WHITE,ARTHUR K-Some White Family Hist-Denv-1948-432p-cl
  (5h1) 10.00
WHITE,ARTHUR V-Long Sault Rapids,St Lawrence River-Ottawa-
1913-Comm of Conserv-384p (5w8,sl shake) 10.00
WHITE,BENJ F-Report of Gov of Montana to Sec of the Int-Wash-
1889-16p-wrps (5n4) 15.00
WHITE,BOUCK-The Book of Dan'l Drew-8vo-NY-1910-1st ed
  (5p9) 4.50 (5ss5) 10.00
WHITE,C A-Artesian Wells Upon the Great Plains-Wash-1882-
37p-wrps (4a5) 5.00
--Bibliogr of NoAmer Invertebrate Paleontology-Wash-1878-132p-
wrps (5i4) 6.00
WHITE,C A-Stray Sweepings-Louisville-1923-12mo (5x2,dj) 22.50
WHITE,C I-Life of Eliza A Seton-Balt-1856-port-462p
  (5yy8,fox,wn) 10.00
WHITE,CAMPBELL P-Gold & Silver Coins-Wash-1832-8vo-71p-
unbnd-House Doc 420 (5m6) 8.50
WHITE,CHAS A,comp-Map of Washington Territory West of Cascade
Mntns-NY-1870-Colton-4 sec,each 2'x2'x9"-fold into cl cov-
rare (5dd0) 150.00
WHITE,CHAS T-Lincoln & prohibition-NY-(c1921)-illus
  (5w0,cor wn) 6.50 (5g3) 12.50
WHITE,DAN'L A-Descendants of Wm White of Haverhill,Mass-
Bost-1889-80p-illus-fldg facs (4t2) 12.50 (5w0) 16.50
WHITE,E B-Charlotte's Web-NY-(1952)-Harper-illus by Garth
Williams-12mo-184p-1st ed (5p1,fray dj) 27.50
--Quo Vadimus?-Harper-1939 (5F1,f,fray dj) 4.00
--Stuart Little-NY-(1945) -illus-12mo-pict cl-Harper
  (5j5,dj) 20. (5v0,mint,dj,4c2,dj) 25.00
WHITE,E N-Norman White,His Anc & Desc-1905-155p (4t2) 10.00
WHITE,E S-Genesis of White Family-1920-346p (4t2,cov loose) 25.00
--Siggins & Other Penna Families-1918-714p (4t2) 15.00
WHITE,E T-Revised Ordinances of City of Yankton-Yankton-1886-
153(154)p plus errata & index-disbnd (5t3) 25.00

WHITE,E V-Choclate Drops from the South-Austin-1932-12mo
        (5x2)   12.50
--Senegambian Sizzles, Negro Stories-Dallas-(1945)-Banks, Upshaw
  && Co-illus   (5x5,dj)   10.00
WHITE,EDW A-Amer Orchid Culture-1939-col plts   (4g0)   20.00
--The Chrysanthemum & its Culture-NY-1930-192p (5s7)   5.00
--Principles of Flower Arrangement-NY-1936-199p-3rd ed-199p
        (5s7)   6.00
WHITE,EDW J-Legal Antiquities-StL-(1913)-349p (5t4)   6.50
WHITE,ELDER JAS-Sketches of Christian Life...of Wm Miller-
  BattleCrk-1875-12mo-416p-frontis-cl (5mm7)   8.50
WHITE,FLORENCE-Flowers as Food-Lond-(1934)-154p (5c5,autg) 7.50
WHITE,FRANCIS S-Story of a Kansas Parish-Atchison-(1911)-
  illus-12mo   (5tt5)   10.00
WHITE,FRANCIS STEWART-Genealogy of Hugh Stewart &
  Descendants-Col-1914-181, 12p-cl (5h7, cov discol) 12.50
WHITE,FREDK-Good & Bad Cats-NY-(1911)-Stokes-(96p)-labels
        (5p1,sl tn)   7.50
WHITE,FREDERIC C-Historical Sketch of South Church, Reformed,
  of NY City-NY-1887-Gilliss Bros-12mo-part cl-57p (4t1) 5.00
WHITE,GEO BRAKELEY-In the Time of Matthias Brakeley of
  Lopatcong-Phila-1888-for priv dist-4to-orig wrps-47p-1st ed
        (5m2)   12.50
WHITE,REV GILBERT-Natural History of Selborne-Lond-1836-
  12mo-323p-15 hand col plts-lea-New ed (5v0)   17.50
--Natural History & Antiquities of Selborne-Lond-1875-illus
        (5ii3)   10.00
--same-& Garden Kalendar-Lond-1900-2 vols-8vo-vellum-g.t.-
  160c, lg papr,autg   (4c2)   50.00
WHITE,GEO S-Memoir of Samuel Slater-Phila-1836-448p & 120p
  (letter from Sec of Tres)-plts (5qq8)   57.50
WHITE,GRACE MILLER-Tess of the Storm Country-NY-(1909)-
  12mo-cl-Illus by Howard C Christy-1st ed of auth's 1st book
        (5gg6,mint,dj,pres)   25.00
WHITE,GWEN-Picture Book of Ancient & Modern Dolls-Lond-
  Black-1928-4to-44p-19 col plts-cl (5a1)   12.50
WHITE,REV HENRY-The Early History of New England-Concord-
  1841-412p-calf-1st ed (5L3)   17.50
--Indian Battles-NY-(1859)-412p (5L3)   15.00
WHITE,HENRY ALEX-Robt E Lee & The Southern Confederacy-
  NY-1897-467p-illus-fldg maps-1st ed (5w5)   12.50
WHITE,HENRY C-Life & Art of Dwight Wm Tryon-Houghton, Miff-
  1930-g. top-227p-illus-crown 4to (4a0,pres)   37.50
WHITE,HOMER-The Norwich Cadets-Northfield, VT-1913-
  illus-8vo   (4m8,pres)   10.00
WHITE HORSE EAGLE, BIG CHIEF-We Indians...as told to
  Edgar von Schmid Pauli-NY-(1931)-256p-1st ed (4b2,dj,f) 10.00
WHITE HOUSE PORCELAIN SERVICE-Designs by an Amer Artist-
  1879-wrps-80p-illus (5t0)   18.50
WHITE,J G-Starling Facts-Chig-1892-224p-cl-3rd ed (5h7)   7.50
WHITE,J M-New Collection of Laws, Charters & Local
  Ordinances of Gov of Gr Britain, France & Spain-Phila-
  1839-sheep-2 vols (5ff4,shake)   37.50
WHITE,JAS,ed-Atlas of Canada-(Toronto)-39 col maps-folio-
        (4b6,rebkd,ex-libr)   75.00
WHITE,JAS-A Compendium of Cattle Medicine-Phila-1823-
  Carey&Lea-sm12mo-233p,2p-calf (5L8,libr stmps,stnd) 7.50
WHITE,JAS-Early Life & Later Exper & Labors of Elder Jos Bates-
  BattleC-1878-320p-cl (5h2)   12.50
WHITE,JAS C-Dermatitis Venenata-Bost-1887-216p (5n7)   6.50
WHITE,JAS DUNDAS-Merchant Shipping Acts, 1894 to 1897-Lond-
  1897-637p   (5s1,rprd)   7.50
WHITE,JAS E-A Life Span & Remin of Railway Mail Serv-Phila-
  (1910)-8vo-1st ed (5ss5)   10.00
WHITE,JOHN-John White's Planters Plea, 1630-Rockport-1930-
  Sandy Bay Hist Soc Vol 1-cl bk bds (5qq8)   12.50
WHITE,JOHN-Amer Drawings of John White, 1577 to 1590-1964-
  Brit Mus & Univ of NC Pr- vols-cl-box (5yy3) 300. (5d9) 350.00
WHITE,JOHN M-The Newer Northwest-StLouis-1894-photos-
  205p   (4b3,lacks wrps)   25.00
WHITE,JOHN r-Sequoia & Kings Canyon Nat'l Parks-Stanford U
  Pr-(1949)-212p-photos-maps-wrps (5s7)   7.50
WHITE,JOS NELSON-Genealogy of-By Himself-Bost-1902-196p-
  ltd to 65c   (4t2)   70.00
WHITE,JOSIAH-Journal of...-n.p.-1946-ltd to 100c (4m4)   25.00
WHITE,K A-A Yankee Trader in the Gold Rush-Riverside Pr-
  1930-294p-illus   (5a9)   7.50
WHITE,LESLIE A-The Evolution of Culture-NY-1959-378p (5c3) 5.00
--Lewis Henry Morgan, The Indian Journals-Univ of Mich Pr-
  (1959)   (5x5,dj)   12.50
--Pioneers in Amer Anthropology,the Bandelier Morgan Letters-
  Albuqu-1940-ports-R8vo-2 vols-ltd to 400c,nbrd
        (5cc4,ex-libr)   60.00

WHITE, LESLIE A (continued)
--The Pueblo of Santa Ana, NM-Amer Anthro Assn-1942 (5qq5) 15.00
WHITE,LYDIA E-Success in Society-Bost-1889-244p, (12) (5w7) 8.50
WHITE,MARGARET E-After Noontide-Bost-1907-frontis-1st ed-
  lg16mo   (5u9)   4.50
WHITE,MARY-The Book of Games-NY-1914(c1896)-191p
        (5w7,wn)   5.00
--How to Make Baskets-NY-1901-194p-illus-Burlap (5s4,soil) 6.00
--same-(and) More Baskets & How to Make Them-NY-1903-
  2 vols-illus   (5t7)   6.00
--How to Make Baskets-NY-1909-194p-illus (5w9)   7.50
--How to Make Baskets-GardenCty-1916-illus-194p (5n7)   3.50
--How to Make Pottery-NY-1904-179p-illus (5n7)   4.50
--More Baskets & How to Make Them-NY-1903-157p (5n7)   3.50
WHITE,MOLLIE ALMA-Looking Back from Beulah-Bound Brook-
  1910-343p-cl   (5y0)   10.00
WHITE MOTOR CO-Operator's Manual for Model 510 Truck-n.d.-
  12mo-illus-wrps (4a6)   10.00
WHITE MOUNTAIN GUIDE BOOK-Concord-1858-E C Eastman-
  1st ed-152p-14p ads-fragile cl (5i3,vg)   20.00
--same-Concord-1866-244p-cl-fldg frontis map-6th ed (5t2) 7.50
WHITE MOUNTAINS-Guide to Path in the, & Adjacent Regions-
  Bost-(1916)-16mo-cl-fldg pkt map (5t7)   4.00
WHITE MNTNS, SOUVENIR OF-Portland-n.d.-Chisholm Bros-
  photogravures & insets fld together in blu papr bds-24mo (5u9)12.50
WHITE MNTNS-Souvenir of the-View book-Portland,Me-n.d.-
  (ca 1880s)-12mo-12 lvs-fld out (5m6)   10.00
WHITE,N-An Easy Guide to the Art of Spelling-Eufield,Mass-
  (1819)-JohnHowe,prntr-1st ed (5t4)   10.00
WHITE,N I-Harry Dexter White, Loyal American-Waban, Mass-
  1956   (5ff4)   6.00
WHITE,NED-Ballads of Tombstone's Yesterdays-Bisbee,Ariz-
  1929 -12mo-pict wrps-EdwPWhite (5g6,f)   17.50
WHITE,NELSON,C-Abbott H Thayer, Painter & Naturalist-
  Conn Printers-1951-277p-illus-4to (4a0,boxed,pres,dj) 45.00
--Life & Art of Frank Currier-n.p.-1936 (4a0)   32.50
WHITE,OWEN P-The Autobiography of a Durable Sinner-Putnam's-
  1942-344p-1st issue(pgs 239 to 244 are an integral part of the
  book)   (5cc5,autg)   35.00
--same-NY-1942-344p -2nd issue(pgs 239 to 242 tip in)
        (4j7) 25.   (5w9)   12.50
--A Frontier Mother-NY-1929-101p-scarce
  (5cc5,f,wn dj) 12.50   (5dd6,5s4,ex-libr,soil,4a5)   15.00
--Lead & Likker-NY-1932-274p-1st ed
  (4j7) 10. (4a5) 20. (5h4,5cc5)   12.50
--Out of Desert-ElPaso-1923-445p (4a5) 45. (4b3)   35.00
--Out of Desert-ElPaso-1924-345p (4a5,5p5)   22.50
--Texas, Informal Biography-NY-1945-267p
  (4a5) 5. (5g5,f) 10. (5dd5) 8.50 (5cc5,f,dj)   6.00
--Them Was The Days-NY-1925-illus-cl
  (4a5) 17.50 (5a8,5g6,5p5)   15.00
--same-Lond-n.d. (ca 1925)-Andrew Melrose Ltd-illus-235p
        (4n8,sp fade)   10.00
--Trigger Fingers-Putnam's-1926-1st ed (5cc5,f)   60.00
WHITE PALFREY, THE-Bost-1829-Cottons&Barnard-16mo-orig prnt
  wrps-20p-scarce chapbook (5rr2)   20.00
WHITE,MRS P A-Kentucky Cookery Book-Chig-1891-316p (5c0) 12.50
WHITE,R H-Development of the Tennessee State Educational
  Organiza 1796 to 1929-Kingsport-1929-Southern Publ
        (5x2,ex-libr)   25.00
WHITE,R E-Padre Junipero Serra & Mission Church of San Carlos
  Del Carmelo-SanFran-1884-PEDougherty-wrps-32p-Steam Pr-
  rare   (5w5,sl tn) 27.50 (4L9)   40.00
WHITE,RICHARD EDW-The Cross of Monterey & other Poems-SanFran-
  1882-Calif Pub-86p plus 3p-cl (5r0,pres)   10.00
WHITE,RICHARD GRANT-Fate of Mansfield Humphreys-Bost-1884-
  446p   (5l1) 6. (5b2) 8.50 (5m2)   6.50
--Poetry....Of The Civil War-NY-1866-334p-1st ed-title in
  red & black (4j4)   9.50
WHITE,RUTH YOUNG-We Too Built Columbus-Columbus-1936-
  cl-480p-1st ed (4h7)   12.50
WHITE,SALLIE JOY-Housekeepers & Homemakers-Bost-1888-260p,
  (1)   (5w7,shake)   5.00
WHITE,SAML-Hist of Amer Troops During Late War-Balt-1830-
  (Roch-1896)-107p-300c,nbrd, autg-rprnt-bds (5h7,sl soil) 15.00
WHITE,SAML S-Catalogue of Dental Materials, Furniture,
  Instruments-Phila-1867-illus-226p-orig cl (5yy3)   50.00
WHITE SEWING MACHINE CO-White Sewing Machines-Cleve-
  1889-sm8vo-8p-self wrps-illus (5b8)   7.50
WHITE,STANFORD-Sketches & Designs-NY-1920-folio-56 plts
        (5ww3,sp repaired)   37.50
WHITE,STEWART EDW-African Camp Fires-NY-1913-illus-378p-
  1st ed   (5yy6,5ss8,broke) 7.50 (5m6)   8.50

WHITE,STEWART EDW (continued)
--Arizona Nights-NY-1907-illus by Wyeth-later ed   (5r7)   7.50
--same-G&D-(1907-illus,N C Wyeth-345p)   (4i7)   5.00
--Blazed Trail Stories-NY-1926-260p   (5s4,sl soil)   3.00
--Camp & Trail-NY-1907-1st ed   (4a1)   10.00
--same-NY-1917-illus-229p   (5s4)   5.00
--The Claim Jumpers-NY-1901-Appleton-1st ed-284p-orig cl-
    auth's 1st book   (5m1) 20.   (5tt6)   20.00
--Danl Boone Wilderness Scout-GardenCty-1922-308p-cl
                (5L7) 5.   (5L7) 3.   (5t4) 5.50(5m8)   4.50
--Folded Hills-GardenCty-1934-(Saga of Andy Burnett)-2 tone cl-
    479p-brown top-"First Edition" on copyrte pg
                (4k6,vg,pres) 7.50   (4k6,f,rprd dj)   10.00
--The Forest-NY-1903-276p-illus by ThosFogarty-
    1st ed   (5ss8) 6.   (4L0) 4.50   (4b3) 6.50   (5ee3,f)   7.50
--Gold-GardenCty-1913-cl-438p-col illus-1st ed
                (5k0,5hh3) 5.   (5r1,5m1,5ee3,f)   6.00
--The Land of Footprints-NY-1916-g.e.-406p   (5ss8)   7.50
--same-Lond-n.d.-illus-462p   (5ss8)   6.00
--Lions in the Path-NY-1926-illus-292p   (5ss8)   8.50
--The Long Rifle-GardenCty-1934-546p   (5r8)   8.00
--The Mountains-NY-1904-illus-1st ed-282p
                (5s4,fade) 6.   (5yy6) 7.50 (5a9) 5.   (5t7)   8.50
--Old Calif,In Picture & Story-1937-Dblday,Doran&Co-4to-
    1st ed   (5m2,dj) 8.50   (5x5,5h5,f,tn dj)   12.50
--The Pass-NY-1906-frontis-illus-1st ed
                (5yy6,5t7,pres) 7.50   (5s4,sl fade)   6.00
--Pole Star-Dblday-1935   (5F1,f,dj)   4.50
--Ranchero-GardenCty-1933-two tone cl-302p-red top-
    "First Edition" on copyrte pg   (4k6,lend libr stmp,dj)   7.50
--The Rediscovered Country-NY-1915-Dblday,Page-fldg map-
    photos-359p   (5yy6) 6.50   (4t5)   7.50
--The Road I Know-NY-1942   (4a1)   5.00
--The Rules of the Game-NY-1910-652p-col illus-illus cl-
    1st ed-"Publ,Oct,1910" on copyrte pg
                (4k6,sl spots) 7.50   (5dd5)   10.00
--The Saga of Andy Burnett-GardenCty-1947-537p,302p,479p,
    & 183p   (5L0,dj)   7.50
--same-GardenCty-(1958)-214p-illus-condensed   (5dd5)   4.50
--Simba-NY-1918-1st ed   (5yy6)   6.00
--Speaking for Myself-NY-1943-245p-1st ed   (5s4,dj,mint)   5.00
--The Story of California-NY-1937-Sun Dial Pr   (5p7)   4.00
--Wild Geese Calling-NY-1940-577p   (4j0,wn)   3.00
WHITE,T H-Mistress Masham's Repose-NY-(c1946)-Putnam's-
    255p-frontis-14 plts-Book club edition   (5p1)   3.50
WHITE,TEN EYCK-Lakeside Musings-Chig-1884-283p-cl
                (5ff7,fade)   10.00
WHITE,TRENTWELL M-Writers of Colonial New England-Bost-
    1929   (5e8) 9.50   (5h9) 10.   (5ss5)   12.50
WHITE,TRUMBULL-Complete Story of the San Francisco Horror-
    n.p.-1906-illus   (5hh3,sl stn)   5.00
--Wizard of Wall Street & His Wealth-Chig-1892-8vo-1st ed
                (5m6,rprd)   7.50
WHITE,W H-The Book of Orchids-Lond-1902-118p-illus (5x0)   4.00
WHITE,W L-They Were Expendable-NY-(1942)-Harcourt,Brace-
    209p   (5mm8,dj,vf) 3.   (5x7)   3.50
WHITE,WALTER-A July holiday in Saxony,Bohemia & Silesia-Lond-
    Champan&Hall-1857-8vo-orig cl-1st ed   (5i8,f)   12.00
WHITE,WALTER-Flight-NY-1926   (5x2)   12.50
--How Far the Promised Land-NY-1955   (5x2,dj)   12.50
--A man called White-NY-1948-Viking-382p
                (5x2) 7.50   (5u3)   7.00
WHITE,WM-Memoirs of Protestant Episcopal Church of the USA-
    1880-Decosta,ed-buck   (5L7,rbnd)   12.50
WHITE,WM ALLEN-The Autobiography of-NY-1946-669p-illus-
    1st prntng   (4L0) 4.   (5L3,mint,dj)   3.50
--Calvin Coolidge,The Man Who is President-1925-MM-252p
                (5e8) 4.   (5t7) 6.   (5x0)   4.50
--Court of Boyville-NY-1899-1st ed   (5v2,mint)   42.50
--same-NY-Dblday&McClure-1900-12mo-358p-pict cl
                (5p1,autg,fade,sl crack)   10.00
--same-NY-McClure,Phillips-12mo-cl-1904   (5ss3,pres)   25.00
--In Our Town-NY-1906-1st ed,2nd impress
                (5ee3,autg,sl crack)   5.00
--Martial Adventures of Henry & Me-NY-1918-Tony Sarg,illus
                (5x7)   5.00
--Old Order Changeth-1910   (5L7)   3.00
--A Puritan in Babylon-NY-1938-460p-port-1st prntng   (5t7)   10.00
--Woodrow Wilson,The Man,his Times & his Task-Bost-1924-8vo-
    cl-port-530p   (5t0)   4.50
WHITE,WM LINDSAY-What People Said-NY-1936-12mo-wrps-
    1st ed of auth's 1st book   (5gg6,advance copy)   10.00

WHITE,WM CHAPMAN-Adirondack Country-NY-(1954)-
    ECaldwell,ed   (5p9) 5.   (5tt5)   7.50
WHITE,WM P-The Presbyterian Church in Phila-Phila-1895-
    311p-illus-t.e.g.   (5w4)   8.50
WHITEBROOK,ROBT BALLARD-Coastal Exploration of Wash-
    PaloAlto-(1959)-t8vo-cl-146p-ltd to 900c   (5h5,f,dj)   15.00
WHITEFIELD,EDWIN-The Home of Our Forefathers-Reading,Mass-
    36 col plts-1st ed-The Author-1886   (5t4)   37.50
--The Homes of Our Forefathers-Bost-1880-33 col plts-3rd ed
                (5t4,rub)   20.00
--Homes of Our Forefathers In Boston,England & Boston,New Engl-
    Bost-1889-138p-4to-orig hf lea-lg papr ed-64 chromoliths
                (5m3,rprd)   40.00
WHITEFIELD,GEO-Journal of a Voyage from Lond to Savannah in
    Georgia-Lond-1739,40,41,43-set of 7 journals bound in 1-lea
                (5s9)   350.00
WHITEHEAD,C-Lives & Exploits of English Highwaymen,Pirates
    & Robbers-Phila&Balt-1835-2 vols-orig bds&labls-1st Amer ed-
    scarce   (5m1)   15.00
WHITEHEAD,CHAS-Richard Savage-Lond-1844-RichardBentley-
    3 vols-12mo-mor-t.e.g.-17 plts-1st ed (5x3,f bndg,sl wn)   50.00
WHITEHEAD,CHAS E-Adventures of Gerard,the Lion Killer-NY-
    1857-sm8vo-432p-illus-cl   (4a6,sl wn)   15.00
--Campfires of Everglades-Edinb-1891-298p-illus
                (5xx7,ex-libr) 17.50(5mm8)   15.00
WHITEHEAD,DON-The FBI Story,a Report to the People-NY-
    (1956)-forward by JEdgarHoover-368p (5dd9) 5.   (5t7,dj)   6.50
WHITEHEAD,JESSUP-Steward's Handbook & Guide to Party
    Catering in 5 parts-Chig-1902(ca 500p)-illus-6th ed (4g9)   10.00
WHITEHEAD,JOHN-Passaic Valley in 3 Centuries-1901-
    469p-scarce-Vol 1(all publ)   (5q0)   20.00
WHITEHEAD,RUSSELL F,ed-White Pine Series of Architectural
    Monogr,Vols 5&6,(Jan 1919 to Dec 1920)-StPaul-c1921-White
    Pine Bur-4to-cl   (4m9)   10.00
WHITEHEAD,WM-The school for lovers, a comedy-Lond-1762-
    Dodsley-8vo-bds-1st ed   (5x3,sl stns)   15.00
WHITEHEAD,WM A,ed-Documents Relating to Colonial History
    of State of N Jersey,1631 to 1737-Newark-1880 to 82-
    Arc of State of NJ,1st Ser,Vol 1 to 5-5 vols-8vo (4c8,rub)   67.50
WHITEHILL,WALTER MUIR-The East India Marine Soc & Peabody
    Mus of Salem-Salem-1949-A sesqui History-243p-illus (5t4)   7.50
WHITEHOUSE,EULA-Texas Flowers in Natural Colors-Austin-
    (1936)-col illus-212p-priv publ-nbrd,autg   (4p8)   17.50
WHITELEY,ISABEL-The Falcon of Langeac-Bost-1897-1st ed
                (5ee3)   5.00
WHITELOCK,D-Anglo Saxon Wills-Cambr-1930-Cambr Studies
    in English Legal History   (5ff4)   17.50
WHITELOCK,JOHN-Authentic Narr of Proceedings of Exped under
    Command of Brig Gen Crawfurd-Lond-1808-hf calf-8vo-
    4 fldg maps-216p-by an Ofcr of the Exped (4p2,vg rprd)   150.00
WHITEMAN,LUTHER H-Glory Roads-NY-(1936)-Crowell (5x5,dj)   5.00
WHITEMAN,MAXWELL-A Century of Fiction by Amer Negroes,
    1853 to 1952-Phila-1955-64p   (5x5,5x2,f)   15.00
WHITEMAN,M M-Damages in Intl Law-Wash-1937 to 43-3 vols
                (5ff4)   47.50
WHITEMAN,PAUL-Jazz-NY-1926-Sears-298p-illus   (5p7)   5.00
WHITFIELD,MILDRED G-The Fine Art of Cooking-Berrien Springs-
    1941-175p   (5c9) 5.   (5c0)   4.50
WHITFIELD,T M-Slavery Agitation in Virginia 1829 to 1832-
    Balt-1930-John Hopkins Pr   (5x2)   27.50
WHITFORD,NOBLE E-Hist of the Canal System of State of NY,
    Vol 2(only)-1906-482p-fldg pkt map-scarce   (4m2)   12.50
--History of Barge Canal of NY State-Albany-1922-610p-illus
                (5zz0,5p7)   10.00
WHITFORD,WM CLARKE-Colorado Volunteers in Civil War,
    NewMex Campaign in 1862-Denver-1906-159p-wrps
                (5j6) 22.50   (4L0,f)   12.50
WHITIN,E STAGG-Factory legislation in Maine-n.p.-1908-
    Columbia Univ thesis   (5g4)   10.00
WHITING,CHAS G-Walks in New England-NY-1903-301p-illus
                (5p9)   4.00
WHITING,F B-Grit,Grief & Gold-Seattle-1933-illus-8vo-1st ed
                (4g6,ex-libr)   15.00
WHITING,GERTRUDE-A Lace Guide for Makers & Collectors-
    NY-1920-fld sampler in rear pkt-photos-415p-in 5 languages
                (5t2,libr mrks) 20.   (5n7,ex-libr,crack)   27.50
WHITING,J L-Shop & Class At Tuskegee-Bost-1940-illus (5x2)   17.50
WHITING,J S-Forts of State of Calif-Longview-1960-1st ed (4a5)   5.50
WHITING,JOHN R-Treasury of Amer Gardening-GardenCty-
    (1955)-272p-col illus-4to   (5s7)   6.00
WHITING,LILIAN-The Land of Enchantment From Pike's Peak to
    the Pac-Bost-1906-illus-347p-1st prntng (4L0) 5.   (5ee3)   7.50

WHITING,PERRY-Autobiography of Perry Whiting-LosAng-
(1930)-334p-illus-fabri   (4L0,5a0,pres) 5.   (5d6)   10.00
WHITING,W-Memoir of Rev Sam'l Whiting & Wife-1873-334p-
2nd ed   37.50
WHITLOCK,BRAND-La Fayette-NY-1924-illus-2 vols
                                  (5t4) 10.   (5w0)   12.50
WHITLOCK,HERBERT-The Story of Jade-NY-1949-illus-222p-
8vo   (5ww3)   20.00
WHITMAN,A A-The Rape of Florida-Poetry-StLouis-1884-
Nixon Jones Printing-1st ed   (5x2)   100.00
--Twasinta's Seminoles-Poetry-StLouis-1885-rev ed   (5x2)   75.00
WHITMAN & TRUE-Maine in the War For the Union-Lewiston-
1865-8vo-637p-buck   (4a7, fox rebnd)   25.00
WHITMAN,ALFRED-Mezzotings of Valentine Green-Lond-1902-
Bullen-Chiswick Pr-g.t.-4to-6 plts-cl-1st ed   (5t5)   10.00
--Print Collector's Handbook-Lond-1902-illus-2nd ed-rev
                                  (5ii3,worn)   10.00
WHITMAN,JASON-The Young Lady's Aid-Portland-1838-
SHColesworthy-hf calf-216p-16mo-a.e.g.   (5p1)   22.50
--Young Man's Assistant-Portl&Bost-1838-sm16mo-emb cl-lea labl-
394p-1st ed   (4k9)   22.50
WHITMAN,SARAH HELEN-Edgar Poe & His Critics-NY-1860-
Rudd&Carleton-8vo-cl   (5m1,chip) 15.   (5b2,f)   20.00
WHITMAN,WALT-After All, Not To Create Only-Bost-1871-
Roberts Bros-24p-1st ed-hf lea (4b1,box,orig cl wrps bnd in)   30.00
--An American Primer-Bost-1904-Horace Traubel,ed-1st ed-
ltd to 500c   (4g2)   30.00
--Calamus-Lond-1897-port-1st ed   (4g2)   40.00
--Complete Prose Works-Bost-1898-Small,Maynard-527p (5p7)   12.50
--Criticism An Essay-Newark-1913-Carteret Book Club-n.p.-
boards-ltd to 100c   (5x4)   20.00
--Democratic Vistas & other papers-Lond-1888-Walter Scott-
Camelot Series-cl-175p   (5p6)   15.00
--The Gathering of the Forces, 1846, 1847-NY-1920-2 vols-
port in ea-bds-lea labl-1st ed-ltd ed, 1250 sets-scarce
                                  (5ee3,f)   25.00
--Good Bye My Fancy-Phila-1891-David McKay-1st ed-port-
66p   (4b1)   35.00
--Grashalme-Leipzig-1904-Diederichs-sq8vo-orig green wrps-
port   (5d3)   15.00
--The Half Breed & Other Stories-Columbia Univ Pr-1927-
illus-1st ed-(155 c prntd on hand made papr,colophon)
                         (5b2,f) 20.   (5m2)   12.50
--I Sit & Look Out-Columbia U-1932-ltd to 1000c (5F1,vf,dj)   17.50
--Leaves of Grass-Brooklyn-1856-20 add poems-2nd ed
                                  (5ee3,rub)   250.00
--same-Bost-Year 85 of the States, (1860,61)-Thayer&Eldridge-
orig cl-g.sp-frontis-1st Bost ed, 1st state-(prntd by Geo C
Rand & Avery on bk of t.pg)   (4g2,sl rub,box,5z7)   75.00
--same-Bost-1860,61-(1879, 188-)-8vo-brown cl-Thayer&Eldridge-
suprious issue of 1860,61 Thayer & Eldridge ed wi same t.pg
& frontis   (5r9)   25.00
--same-Phila-1882-12mo-cl-Rees Welsh   (5ss3,crack)   30.00
--same-Phila-(1900)-frontis-port-cl-526p   (5t0)   5.00
--same-GardenCty-1917-frontis-255p   (5t4)   5.00
--same-Portland,Me-1919-facs of the 1855 ed-prntd by Mosher-
t4to-port-ltd to 250c   (5m4,f)   40.00
--same-NY-1929-sm folio-cl in slipcase-ltd to 1500c,box,nbrd,
Ltd Ed Club   (5b0)   30.00
--same-NY-1931-Dblday,Doran-E Holloway,ed-727p-
inclusive ed   (5p9)   5.00
--same-NY-(1937)-8vo-cl-Rockwell Kent,illus (5cc9,box)   10.00
--same-MtVernon-n.d.-thk folio-Hanna,illus-ltd ed-bds-lea sp
                                  (5yy6,f)   50.00
--same-NY-Heritage Pr-box-RKent,illus   (4a1,Kent pres)   50.00
--Memories of Pres Lincoln & Other Lyrics of the War-Portl-
1912-Mosher-43p-bds-ltd to 950c   (5r7)   10.00
--November Boughs-Phila-1888-David McKay-1st ed-illus-orig cl-
g.t.   (4b1,f)   40.00
--Selected Poems-NY-1892-Webster-1st ed-1st state-port (5m2)   7.50
--Song of the Broad Axe-Phila-1924-Centaur Pr-4to-bds-ltd to 400c
                                  (5m2,dj)   8.50
--Specimen Days in America-Lond-1887-312p
                         (5p6,sl soil) 5.   (5mm2)   7.50
--Two Rivulets,Including Democratic Vistas,Centennial Songs
& Passage to India-Camden-1876-Author "s Ed-1st ed
                                  (5tt6.box,cl dj)   95.00
WHITMAN,WM-The Oto-NY-1937-Columbia U Contb to Anthro-
Vol 28-132p   (5L2)   8.50
WHITMAN, WM,CO-Wool & Cotton in all Forms from Yarn to
Fabric-Bost-1921-177p-cl-4to-fldg plt   (5hh6)   12.50
WHITMAN'S PRINT COLLECTOR'S HANDBOOK-Lond-1921-
rev&enlrgd by Salaman-illus   (4a1,rub)   15.00

WHITMORE,WM H-Abel Bowen, Engraver-Rockwell&Churchill Pr-
1884-wrps-32p-illus-8vo   (4a0)   17.50
--The American Genealogist-Albany-1868-Albany-287p (5t9)   5.00
--Colonial Laws of Massachusetts-Bost-1890-8vo-hf mor(4c1)   20.00
WHITNAH,JOS C-A History of Richmond, Calif-Richmond-c1944-
Chamber of Comm-8vo-cl-128p   (4t1) 15.   (5F5)   10.00
WHITNEY,A-Memorial of-Wash-1846-Sen Doc #161-10p-fldg map-
extracted-v scarce   (5L2)   25.00
WHITNEY,MRS A D T-Real folks-Bost-1872-Osgood-cl-illus-
1st ed   (5i0,f)   10.00
--Sights & Insights-Bost-1876-Osgood-2 vols-cl   (5b2,f)   15.00
--A Summer in Leslie Goldthwaite's Life-Bost-1867-illus (5r7)   10.00
WHITNEY,A R-Descrip Catalogue of Fruits & Ornamental Trees,
Shrubs & Plants-Chig-1855-Demo Pr Steam Pr-8vo-orig wrps-52p-
illus-Franklin Grove Garden-   (5m6)   32.50
WHITNEY,A W-Folk lore from Maryland-NY-1925-Vol 18, Mem
of Amer Folklore Soc-   (5tt5)   10.00
WHITNEY,ASA-Project for RR to Pacific-NY-1849-Geo W Wood-
112p-2 maps-disbnd   (5tt0)   100.00
WHITNEY,CARRIE W-Kansas City, Mo-Chig-1908-illus-3 vols-
lea&cl   (4L0,bkstrp sl wn)   35.00
WHITNEY,CASPAR-The Flowing Road-Phila-1913-over 300p-
g.tooled sp-maps   (5d2,f bndg)   15.00
--Hawaiian America-NY-1899-illus-356p-1st ed
                         (4m2) 10.   (5ee3,5t2)   7.50
--Musk Ox, Bison, Sheep & Goat-NY-1904-illus-284p (5ss8)   7.50
--On Snow Shoes to the Barren Grounds-NY-1896-1st ed-324p-
illus-cl-14p Remington plts
           (5i3) 17.50   (5r6) 24.   (5t7) 15.   (5w8)   25.00
WHITNEY,CHAS S-Bridges-NY-1929-363p-400 plts-cl (5h2)   20.00
WHITNEY,ELINOR-Tyke Y, His book & his mark-NY-1926-
Macmillan-78p-pict cl-12mo-1st ed   (5p1,dj)   5.00
WHITNEY,ERNEST-Pictures & Poems of Pike's Peak Region-
ColoSprngs-(1891)-(ca 26p)-illus-album style   (5s4,rprd)   6.00
WHITNEY,HARRY-Hunting With The Eskimos-NY-1910-453p-illus-
t.e.g.-1st ed   (5w4,rub)   15.00
--same-NY-1911-453p-illus   (5i3,autg) 15.(5ss1,pres,shake)   13.50
WHITNEY,HENRY M,ed-Tourists' Guide thru the Hawaiian Islands-
Honolulu-1890-Gazette Co-maps-plts-cl bk bds
                         (5x5,orig wrps bnd in)   50.00
WHITNEY,J D-California-Bost-1875-16mo-cl-60p(5g4,sp wn)   12.50
--The Climatic Changes of Later Geological Times-Cambr-1882-
4to-cl-14p, 394p   (5t2)   12.50
--Geological Survey of Calif-Cambridge-1880-2 vols-4to
                         (5ii2,hng broken)   12.50
--Names & places-Cambr-1888-239p-100c prntd
printed wrps   (5g8,pres,f,unopnd)   12.50
--Yosemite Guide book-1874-maps-new ed-rev   (5L7)   5.00
WHITNEY,J-Colorado, in the US of Amer-Lond-1867-61p-
2 fldg maps-orig wrps   (5L1,wrps loose) 40.   (5g3,tn)   50.00
WHITNEY,J PARKER-Remin of Sportsman-NY-1906-Forest & Stream)-
1st ed-467p   (5i3)   12.50
WHITNEY,JANET-Abigail Adams-Bost-1947-illus-12mo-cl-357p
                         (5h9) 5.   (5t0)   4.50
WHITNEY, LORENZO H-History of the War for Preservation of
Federal Union-Phila-1863-illus-516p-1 vol(all prntd) (4j4,f)   7.50
WHITNEY MUSEUM OF AMER ART-Century of Amer Landscape
Pulnting 1800 to 1900-Cat,Jan to Feb 1938-16 illus-30p-wrps
                                  (4e0)   12.50
WHITNEY STUD,THE-NY-1902-thk4to-lea&bds-scarce-594p
                                  (5ss5,f)   15.00
WHITNEY,WM D-A Sanskrit Grammar-Bost-1891-cl-551p (5t2)   8.00
WHITON,JOHN M-Sketches of the History of NH-Concord-
1834-222p   (5t7)   17.50
WHITSON,JOHN H-Justin Wingate, Ranchman-Bost-1905-312p-
8vo-orig cl-illus   (5g6)   5.00
--With Fremont the Pathfinder-1903-320p-1st ed-illus (5r1,vg)   10.00
WHITSON,MRS L D-Gilbert St Maurice-Louisvl-1875-12mo-
frontis tip in-cl-2nd ed-scarce   (5b2,chip,pres)   15.00
WHITTAM,GEOFFREY-Whale Hunters-NY-(1925)-182p (5s1,dj,f)   3.00
WHITTAKER,FREDK-The Cadet Button-NY-1878-Sheldon-pict cl-
1st ed   (5m2,lt spot)   10.00
--Complete Life of Gen Geo A Custer-NY-(1876)-648p
               (4a5) 17.50   (5g4,5t7,5ee3)   10.00
--Popular Life of Gen Geo A Custer-NY-1876-648p-illus
                    (5g4) 6.   (5k0)   10.00
WHITTEMORE,EDWIN CAREY-The Centennial History of Waterville,
Me-Waterville-1902-lg8vo-illus-lea&bds (5m6,crack,sl stnd) 15.00
WHITTEMORE,FRANCES-Geo Washington in Sculpture-Bost-1933-
203p-47 illus   (5h9)   6.50
WHITTEMORE,HENRY-Hist of the Adams Family-NY-1893-
McDonald-wrps-84p   (4t1)   10.00

WHITTEMORE,MARGARET-Sketchbook of Kansas Landmarks-
Topeka-c1937-College Pr-8vo-cl-125p   (4t1)   9.50
WHITTEMORE,THOS-Conference Hymns & Tunes-Bost-1843-wrps-
16mo-64p   (5t4)   7.50
WHITTEN,F E-Amer War of Independence-NY-1931-maps-375p
                                               (5m2)   6.00
WHITTIER,JOHN G-Among the Hills-Bost-1869-1st ed(wiout
publisher's monogram on sp)
                (4k9,lt chip) 10. (4j0,fox) 6.50 (5p6)   12.50
--Ballads of New England-Bost-Fields,Osgood-1870-92p-illus
                                          (5t4,5i1)   5.00
--Complete Poetical Works-HM-1881-434p-Household ed (5e8) 3.00
--Home Ballads & Poems-Bost-1860-12mo-orig cl-206p-1st ed(16p
of ads dated "Jul,1860")   (5x4) 15.   (5t0)   7.50
--same-Bost-1861-206p   (5e8)   3.00
--In War Time & Other Poems-Bost-1864-1st ed-1st issue wi 2p
of ads dated Nov 1863,work as "Just Ready"   (5rr6)   25.00
--Jack in the Pulpit-NY-1884-sq8vo-col plt book-8p of floral dec
in oil colors   (5v0)   20.00
--Legends of New Engl-Hartf-1831-12mo-bds-cl-bk-1st ed of
auth's 1st book-3rd state(page iv correctly nbrd)
                        (5gg6,v fox,lack labl,rprd)   75.00
--same-Legends & Lyrics from the Poetic Works of-Bost-1890-
sm12mo-208p   (5t2)   10.00
--Miriam & Other Poems-Bost-Fields Osgood&Co-12mo-1st ed-
1st issue -1871   (5r9) 8.50   (5ss9)   20.00
--Panorama & Other Poems-Bost-1856-1st ed-(no ads,inscrip dated
May)   (5i3,vf)   17.50
--The Penna Pilgrim & Other Poems-Bost-1872-Osgood-cl-frontis-
129p-1st ed   (5j0) 10.   (5x4)   12.50
--Poems-Phila-1838-Jos Healy,pub-orig cl-1st ed
                        (5x4,lea,scuff) 30.   (5z7,fox,chip) 25.00
--Poetical Works-Bost-(1892)-Houghton,Miff-7 vols-cl-vel bk-
ltd to 750 sets   (5ss9,f,orig cl dj)   60.00
--Snow Bound-Chig-c1906-Reilly&Britton-12mo-123p-pict labl-
JohnRNeill,illus-   (5p1)   5.00
--Snow Bound,a winter idyl-NY-1930-ltd to 1500c,nbrd,box-
Ltd Ed Club   (5b0)   15.00
--Whittier's Selected Poems-NY-1949-Heritage Pr-lg8vo-cl-1st ed
                                          (5p5,box)   7.50
WHITTIER WOMEN'S CLUB-Cook Book-Whittier,Ca-1928,29-
ads-wrps-173p   (4g9,chip,stns)   5.00
WHITTINGTON & HIS CAT-NY&Phila-(1835,6)-Solomon King-
pict wrps-Turner&Fisher-32mo chapbook-8 illus pgs (5v0,f) 22.50
WHITTINGTON & HIS CAT-Renowned History of-NewHav-1825-
Sidney Pr-12mo-orig wrps-illus   (5xx9,sl soil)   35.00
WHITTLE,D W-Memoirs of Philip P Bliss-NY-1877-367-illus (5t4)10.00
--same-Chig&NOrl-1878-379p-ports   (5t7)   5.00
WHITTLEBOT,HERNIA-Poems-Lond-(n.d.)-c1927-4to-orig wrps-
errata slip   (5ss9)   15.00
WHITTLESEY,AUSTIN-The Minor Ecclesiastical,Domestic & Garden
Architecture of Southern Spain-NY-1917-lg4to-107 plts (5m2)13.50
WHITTLESEY,CHAS-Contributions to Geology of Ohio-Cleve-
1869-illus-48p-sewed   (4b6)   10.00
--Early History of Cleveland,Ohio-Cleve-1867-8vo-487p-cl-plts-
1st ed   (4n9) 30.   (5ss5,fade)   25.00
--Fugitive Essays-Hudson,O-1852-397p-cl
                (5ff7) 25.   (4m2,rbnd,librr stmp)   35.00
WHITTLESEY,W R-Catalogue of 1st Editions of Stephen C Foster
(1826 to 1864)-Wash-1915-cl   (4j4)   7.50
WHITTOCK,N-Miniature Painter's Manual-Lond-1844-Gilbert &
Piper-sm book-3 hand col plts-76p   (5F9,sl wtrstnd) 10.00
WHITTON,F E-Wolfe in No Amer-Lond-1929-illus-maps-420p
                (5yy8) 6.50   (4b6,4b9)   10.00
WHITTON,JOS-Wags of the Stage-Phila-1902-Rigby-lg papr ed-
illus-ltd to 500c   (5i4,pres)   7.50
WHITTUCK,CHAS-The "Good Man"of 18th Cent-Lond-1901-274p
                                               (5a1)   5.00
WHO'S WHO-in Alabama-Chig-1947-1044p   (5h6)   12.50
--in America,1899,1900-Chig-n.d.-(1899)-Marquis-thk12mo-
orig red cl-1st ed of 1st issue of Who's Who plus next Vol
(1901,2)- v scarce   (5i0) 2 vols 150.00
--in America,1903 to 05-Chig-(1903)-JLeonard,ed (5s4)   12.50
--in America-Vol 12-1922,23   (5q8)   3.00
--in America-Vol 13-1924,25   (5q8)   3.00
--in America-1921; 1926,7; 1930,1; 1932,3; 1934,5; 1936,7
                                          (5t9) ea   2.50
--in Amer Education-Hattiesbury-1968-1st vol-thk sm4to (4b7) 12.00
--in Canada,1925,6-Tor-(1925)-cl-illus   (5w8,crack)   10.00
--in Canada,1940,41-Tor-1941-1480p-ports   (5a1)   8.50
--in Canada-1947,8; 1958,9   (5a1)   7.50
--in Canada-1951,2-Tor   (5w8,crack)   7.50

WHO'S WHO   (continued)
--in Colored Amer-1928,1929-NY-1929-Who's Who in Colored
Amer Publ   (5x2)   37.50
--in the East,Middle Atlantic & Northeastern States-1951 (5L7) 5.00
--in New England-1909-1047p   (5t9)   2.50
--in & From Ohio-Cinn-1910-Vols 1&2-(1258p)-folio-illus-imit lea
                                          (4t7,rprd)   40.00
--in North St Louis-StL-1925-illus-357p-4to   (4b3)   12.50
--in Philadelphia-(Sesquicent)-Vol 3-1776 to 1926-1927-4to
                                               (5L7)   7.50
--in Texas-Dallas-(1931)-334p plus index-photos-embossed-
1st ed   (5L2)   20.00
--in Texas-n.p.-c1957   (5kk6)   15.00
--in World Aviation-Wash-(1955)-Vol 1   (4b7)   10.00
--on the Stage,1908-NY-1908-illus-467p   (5u1,rub)   7.50
WHOLE LIFE &-Strange Surprising Adven or Robinson Crusoe-Lond-
1785-Logographic Pr-2 vols-8vo-hf calf-frontis
                        (5aa2,rbkd,sl wn)   20.00
WHYMPER,CHAS-Egyptian Birds-Lond-1909-orig buck-g.t.-
4to-51 col plts-1st ed-ltd to 100c   (5z9)   20.00
WHYMPER,EDW-Ascent of the Matterhorn-Lond-1880-JnMurray-
8vo-calf-maps-illus-g.   (5b0,rub,lacks e.p.)   17.50
--Travels Amongst Great Andes of the Equator-Lond-1892-maps-456p-
illus-plus Vol of 3 fldg maps-2 vols-Subscr Edition,autg (5t4) 15.00
WHYMPER,FRED-Alaska-(Germ text)-Braunschweig-1869-351p-
fldg map-illus-hf lea   (5L0,cor wtrmrk)   8.50
--Travel & Adventure in Territory of Alaska-Lond-1868-Murray-
illus-fldg map-331p-1st ed   (5dd7,pres) 65.   (5L1) 35.00
WHYTE,MAY-High Class Sweetmaking-England-n.d.-114p-
illus   (5g9,lacks e.p.)   3.00
WHYTE,WM ATHENRY-Land Journey from Asia to Europe-Lond-
1871-cl-fldg map-8vo-336p   (5v7,ex-libr)   18.50
WHYTE-MELVILLE,GEO JOHN-Digby Grand,an Autobiography-
Lond-1853-2 vols-12mo-cl-1st ed-v scarce (5gg6,bndg wn) 50.00
--Contraband-Lond-1871-Chapman&Hall-2 vols-8vo-orig cl-
1st ed   (5xx6,lend calf labl)   20.00
--General Bounce-Lond-1855-Parker-3 vols-8vo-orig cl-1st ed
                                          (5xx6,fade)   30.00
--Holmby House-Lond-1860-Parker-2 vols-8vo-orig cl-1st ed
                                               (5xx6)   27.50
--Horace,Odes,Epodes & Carmen Saeculare-Lond-1850-8vo-cl-
1st ed of auth's 1st book   (5gg6,cl wn)   15.00
--Sarchedon-Lond-1871-Chapman&Hall-3 vols-8vo-orig cl-
1st ed   (5xx3,pres,sl spot)   80.00
WHYTT,ROBT-Essay on Vital & other Involuntary Motions of
Animals-Edinb-1751-calf-8vo-392p-1st ed (4t9,rebkd) 295.00
--Observ on Nature,Causes & Cure of Those Disorders...Called
Nervous Hypochondriac, or Hysteric-Edinb-1765-8vo-orig calf-
520p-1st ed   (4e5,librr stmp,rebkd) 225. (4t9,f) 375.00
--same-Edinb-1765-8vo-calf-2nd ed,corrected
                        (5ee8,rprd,librr stmp)   175.00
WIBERG,FRANK-Printing Ink-NY-1926-illus (4m5,dj)   17.50
WICHER,EDW A-Presbyterian Church in Calif,1849 to 1927-NY-
1927-360p   (5x5,dj,5F5)   10.00
--Summary of History of SanFran Theological Seminary-n.p.-
n.d.-(ca 1921)-R8vo-28p-wrps   (5dd4)   12.50
WICK,BARTHINIUS L-The Amish Mennonites-IowaCty-1894-
(State Hist Soc)-60p   (5L2,lacks wrps)   4.00
WICKERSHAM,GEO W-How I Came to be a Shaker-Mt Lebanon-
n.d.-(1891?)-16p-wrps-v scarce   (5ff7)   8.50
WICKERSHAM,JAS-Bibliography of Alaskan Literature 1724 to
1924-Cordova-1927-635p   (5ss0,autg)   25.00
--Old Yukon-Wash-1938-1st ed-514p-illus-map
        (4L0,5rr0) 12.50   (5i3,rub,5ss1,pres,4g6)   17.50
WICKEY,HARRY-Thus Far,Growth of Amer Artist-NY-1941-
Amer Artists Group-303p-illus   (4a0,dj) 17.50 (5x0) 5.00
WICKHAM,GERTRUDE,ed-Memorial to Pioneer Women of Western
Reserve-n.p.-1896,97-4 vols-wrps as issued-v scarce (4n9) 30.00
--Pioneer Families of Cleveland, 1796 to 1840-Evangelical Publ Hse-
1914-2 vols-4to-cl-maps   (5h4,f)   18.75
WICKHAM,HARVEY-Misbehaviorists-1930   (5L7)   3.50
WICKHAM,ROB S-Friendly Adirondack Peaks-1924-illus-192p
                                               (5p9)   5.00
WICKSON,EDW J-Calif Fruits & How to Grow them-LosAng-1909-
4th ed-4to-pic cl-433p-plts-v scarce (4g0,crack,soil) 10.00
--same-SanFran-1910-604p-5th ed,rev-8vo- (4g0,rub)   8.50
--same-SanFran-8vo-493p-8th ed   (4g0)   8.50
WICKSTROM,GEO W-The Town Crier-RockIsland-(1948)-280p-
cl-2nd prntg   (5ff7)   7.50
WIDDIFIELD'S NEW COOK BOOK-Phila-(1856)-410p,22p (5c0) 18.50
--same-Phila-(1873)   (5c0,fade)   15.00
WIDNEY,JOS P-Race Life of the Aryan People-NY-1907-2 vols
                                               (5x5)   20.00

WIDOW SEYMOR,THE-Phila-1876-632p-illus   (5m1,pres)   10.00
WIEBE,EDW-Paradise of Childhood-Springfield-(1869)-Milton
  Bradley-76p-74 plts-4to-linen-rare   20.00
         (5v2)
WIEDEMANN,THOS-Cheechako Into Sourdough-Portland-(1942)-
  photos-266p   (5ss0,f)   8.00
WIENER,LEO-Mayan & Mexican Origins-Cambr-1926-126 plts-
  300c prntd   (5x5,f)   150.00
WIER,ALBERT E,ed-Ideal Home Music Library-NY-1924-Scribner-
  4to-10 vols & Guide-fab   (5p7)   40.00
--The Piano-NY-Lond&Tor-1941-467p   (5t7)   10.00
--Thesaurus of the Arts-NY-(1943)   (5yy6)   7.50
WIERZBICKI,F P-Calif as it is & as it may be-SanFran-1933-
  Grabhorn Pr-136p-cl bds-Rare Amer Series #8   (5r8)   32.50
WIGGIN,JAS BARTLETT-Wild artist in Boston-Bost-1888-1st ed-
  scarce   (5m2)   10.00
WIGGIN,KATE DOUGLAS-The Birds' Christmas Carol-8vo-cl-
  414th thous   (5d3,dj,pres)   5.00
--same-Bost-Oct 1914-wrps-Dramatic Version-103p   (5c8)   6.00
--same-Bost-(1916)-facs of orig ed-69p-illus   (5ee3)   2.50
--Bluebeard,a Musical Fantasy-NY&Lond-1914-Harper&Bros-
  8vo-58p-cl-col frontis-1st ed-scarce   (5rr2,sl wn)   12.50
--Book of Dorcas Dishes-Maine-1911-96p-frontis-Dorcas Soc of
  Hollis&Burton   (5c4,lacks fly)   7.50
--Children's Rights-Bost&NY-1892-Houghton,Miff-12mo-236p,
  4p ads-1st ed   (5p1,tn dj)   12.50
--Mother Carey's Chickens-Bost-1911-1st ed   (4j0,pres)   15.00
--My Garden of Memory an Autobiography-Bost-(1923,3rd impr)-
  465p-frontis-25 plts   (4h8,sl sp wr)   10.00
--same-Bost-(1924)-Houghton,Miff-465p-illus   (5p9)   5.00
--same-Bost-1926-Houghton,Miff-plts   (4F8)   7.50
--Penelope's Irish Experiences-Bost&NY-1901-Houghton,Miff-
  16mo-(2p)ads,327p-pict cl   (5p1)   5.00
--Penelope's Postscripts-Bost&NY-1915-Houghton,Miff -217p-
  frontis-pict cl-12mo   (5p1)   5.00
--Penelope's Progress-Bost&NY-1898-Houghton,Miff-16mo-
  Scotch plaid cl   (5p1,cor wn) 4.   (5t7)   7.50
--Rebecca of Sunnybrook Farm-Bost-1903-1st ed-1st state(publ
  imprint on sp 1/16") (4j3,rub) 15.   (4F6,vf,dj,autg lttr) 115.00
--same-Bost-1903-Houghton,Miff-8vo-1st ed
    (5b2) 10.   (5rr2) 15.   (5s0,sl wn)   12.50
--same-Lond-1911-8vo-347p-cl-Popular Ed-Gay&Hancock
        (5aa0,pres)   15.00
--same-NY-n.d.-RandomHse-12mo-250p-pict glazed bds-
  illus from motion picture(Shirley Temple)   (5p1)   10.00
--A Summer in a Canon,a Calif story-Bost-(1889)-12mo-278p-
  illus   (5dd6,rbnd)   6.00
--The Writings of-Houghton,Miff-1913 to 23-10 vols- Riverside Pr-
  3/4 mor-t.e.g.-ltd to 500 sets,Autg Ed
    (5ss9,f,pres,extra biog vol) 85.   (5p1)   85.00
WIGGIN,MAURICE-The Passionate Angler-Lond-1949-16 illus-
  calf-t.e.g.-ltd to 300c   (5c1)   17.50
WIGGINS,J R-Freedom or Secrecy-NY-1956   (5ff4)   9.50
WIGGINS,L K-Life & Works of-NY-1907-Paul Laurence Dunbar-
  illus   (5x2)   20.00
WIGHT,CHAS A-The Hatfield Book-(Chicopee Falls,1908)-plts-
  59p   (4d9) 5.   (5t9)   7.50
--Some Old Time Meeting Houses of Conn Valley-ChicopeeFalls-
  1911-144p-illus   (5w4)   8.50
WIGHT,MISS FANNY-Nellie's Christmas Eve-NY-c1908-
  McLoughlinBros-4to-(16p) incl wrps-col illus-mntd on linen-
  stpld-#284   (5p1)   12.50
WIGHT,FREDK S-Milestones of Amer Painting in Our Century-
  NY-1949-Chanticleer Pr-wrps-50 illus(12 col)-4to-135p(4e0) 17.50
WIGHT,SAML F-Adventures in Calif & Nicaragua,in Rhyme-
  Bost-1860-8vo-1st ed   (4m8,rub)   10.00
WIGHT,T-History of Rise & Progress of People Called Quakers,
  in Ireland 1653 to 1700-1811-buck-4th ed   (5L7,rbnd)   12.50
WIGHT,WM WARD-Eleazer Williams,His Forerujners,Himself-
  Milwkee-1896-(71p)-frontis-wrps-Parkman Club Publ #7(4L0) 7.50
WIGHTMAN,F A-Our Canadian Heritage-Tor-1905-287p (4b9) 6.00
WIGHTMAN,FRANCIS P-Little Leather Breeches & other Southern
  Rhymes-NY-1899-4to-orig pict bds   (5c8)   75.00
WIGHTMAN,ORRIN S-Diary of an Amer Physician in Russian
  Revolution of 1917-Brooklyn-1928-lg8vo-cl-52 photos-1st ed-
  v scarce   (5p5,pres)   25.00
WIGHTMAN,WM M-Life of Wm Capers DD-Nashvl-1858-516p-cl
    (5h1,rbnd)   10.00
WIGHTWICK,GEO-Hints to Young Architects-NY-1847-157p-
  1st Amer ed   (5w7,fox,chip)   16.50
WIGLITTLE,JUDGE-10 Years a Police Court Judge-NY-(1884)-
  229p   (5p9)   4.00
WIGNEY,GEO A-Into Treatise on Theory & Practice of Malting
  & Brewing-Brighton-1850-cl-196p   (4n0)   25.00

WIHLFAHRT,JULIUS E-Treatise on Baking-NY-(1935)-4to-468p-
  3rd ed   (5c5)   4.50
WIKOFF,HENRY-My Courtship & Its Consequences-NY-1855-
  8vo-cl-438p   (5i1) 8.   (4c1) 12.50   (5t4)   8.50
WILBARGER,J W-Indian Depredations in Texas-Austin-1889-illus-
  qtr lea-672p   (4L0,sl tn)   125.00
--same-Austin-1890   (5n4,f)   75.00
--same-Austin-1935-672p-illus   (5L3)   32.50
WILBOR,JOHN R-The Story of a Crown-Balt-1924-48p-illus
    (5hh6)   4.50
WILBOUR,CHAS E-Trial of Chas M Jefferds for Murder-NY-1862-
  Ross&Tousey-234p-pamph-removed   (5qq8)   12.50
WILBUR,EARL MORSE-Thos Lamb Eliot 1841 to 1936-Portl-1937-
  139p-illus-cl-priv prntd-fldg tabl   (5a9) 5.   (5r0)   7.50
WILBUR,HOMER-Meliboeus Hipponax,The Biglow Papers-Cambr-
  1848-12mo-First issue(title pg bearing single Cambr imprint &
  12p of ads preceding the title)
    (5r9,cl,sl fray) 30.   (5dd8,mor,f bndg)   37.50
WILBUR,JAS B-Ira Allen,Founder of Vermont,1751 to 1814-Bost-
  1928-illus-2 vols-cl-8vo   (4c1,box) 15.   (4c5,f)   12.50
WILBUR,MARGUERITE E-John Sutter,Rascal & Adventurer-NY-
  (1949)-illus-8vo-1st ed   (5h5,f,dj) 5.   (4g6)   10.00
--Indian Uprising in Lower Calif,1734 to 1737-LosAng-1931-
  Quivira Soc-298p-ltd to 665c (4a5) 35. (4L0,f,unopnd) 50.00
--The Unquenchable Flame-NY-1952-342p   (5t7)   4.50
WILBUR,SIBYL-Life of Mary Baker Eddy-Bost-(1907)-406-illus
    (5t4)   4.00
--same-SC Pub-Bost-(1923)-400p   (5e8)   2.50
WILCOX,EARLEY V-Tropical Agriculture-NY-1916-illus (4g0) 6.00
WILCOX,ELLA W-Custer & Other Poems-n.p.-1896-12mo-134p-cl
    (5mm7)   8.50
--same-Chig-(1896)-Conkey-illus   (4L0) 3.   (5m2)   5.00
--Poems of passion-Chig-1883-Belford,Clarke-1st ed (5m2,sl soil) 10.00
--same-Lond-n.d.-col illus-lg4to-vel-dec edges-ltd,autgs(5p6) 28.00
--Sailing Sunny Seas-Chig-1909-248p-photos-dec cov (5s1) 4.00
--Three Women-Chig&NY-(1897)-Conkey-pict cl   (5m2)   5.00
WILCOX,FRANK-Ohio Indian Trails-Cleve-1933-268p-illus-cl-
  1st ed-ltd,nbrd,autgs   (5y0)   52.50
WILCOX,OWEN N-Wilcox Family History-Cleve-1911-8vo-wrps-
  63p   (4t1)   20.00
WILCOX,R TURNER-The Mode in Costume-NY-(1946)-417p (5t4)10.00
--Mode in Furs-NY-1951-illus-4to-1st Amer ed   (5ii3)   15.00
--Mode in Hats & Headdress-NY-1946-4to-cl-illus-332p-
  188p plts   (5t0,dj)   10.00
WILCOX,VIRGINIA L-Colorado,a Selected Bibliography-Denver-
  (1954)-151p-1st ed   (5L2,dj)   7.50
WILCOX,W D-Camping in Canadian Rockies-1897-2nd ed-map-
  illus-282p-4to   (4b9)   20.00
--Rockies of Canada-1909-3rd ed-300p-illus-pkt map
    (5dd7,locks map) 12. (5r6) 12.50 (4b9,sp fade) 20.00
--same-Revised&Enlrgd ed of "Camping in Canadian Rockies"-
  NY-1916-plts-300p-photos   (5j5,pres) 15.   (4d4)   12.50
WILD BANDITS OF THE BORDER-a Thrilling Story of Adven &
  Exploits of Frank & Jesse James-Chig-(1881)-wrps-313p-
  v scarce-Adams #1138   (5zz5,lacks bk wrp,chip,rprd)   35.00
--same-Chig-n.d.-363p-illus-later ed of above (5zz5,rbnd)   25.00
WILD DICK,INDIAN SLAYER-Garrettsvl-n.d.-(1890's?)-39p-
  wrps-priv prntd-(Elmer Shaw)   (5h1)   15.00
WILD FLOWERS OF AMERICA-NY-1894-(G H Buck&Co)-obl 4to-
  cl-268 col plts   (5q0) 25.   (4j1,sl rub)   22.50
--same-NY-(1894)-obl 8vo   (5p7)   10.00
WILD FLOWERS OF CANADA-Montr-(1894)-Montreal Star-
  obl 4to-mor-a.e.g.-col plts   (5w8)   35.00
WILD OATS,Sown Abroad-Phila-(1853)-227p-cl   (5d6)   10.00
WILD,PAYSON S-The Chig Literary Club-Chig-1947-8vo-bds-
  cl bk-13 ports-143p-Lakeside Pr-g.t.-ltd to 300c
    (5j5,libr strip)   12.50
WILD,ROLAND-Arctic Command...Smellie of Nascopie-Tor-
  1955-194p-port-plts   (4a8)   4.50
--MacNab,Last Laird-Lond-1938-port-plts-256p   (5yy9)   10.00
WILDE,LADY-Driftwood from Scandinavia-Lond-1884-1st ed
    (5yy6,hng split)   15.00
WILDE,OSCAR-The Ballad of Reading Gaol-Lond-1899-331p-
  Chiswick Pr   (5t4,chip)   7.50
--same-NY-Dutton-1928-124p-Vassos illus   (5i1)   5.00
--same-NY-1937-Heritage Pr-R8vo-8 plts-mor   (5p5,box)   10.00
--same-NY-1937-calf-ltd to 1500c,nbrd,box-Ltd Ed Club (5b0) 25.00
--De Profundis-Lond-(1905)-1st ed-Feb 1905 adv
    (5yy6,light fox) 27.50   (5k9,box)   35.00
--The Fisherman & His Soul & other fairy tales-On Murray Hill-
  (1929)-Farrar&Rinehart-212p-15 plts-Nadejen,illus (5p1)   5.00

WILDE,OSCAR (continued)
--For Love of the King-Lond-(1922)-8vo-white buck-1st ed-
ltd ed   (5r9,dj,mint) 25.00
--Happy Prince & Other Tales-D Nutt-1888-sq8vo-(viii),116p-
dec bds-Crane&Hood,illus-1st ed (5dd8,box,5aa0,vg) 75.00
--same-Lond-1910-D Nutt-Crane&Hood,illus-dec bds-7th impres
        (5c8) 13.50
--House of Pomegranates-Lond-1891-McIlvaine-1st ed (4b5) 75.00
--Impressions of America-Sunderland-1906-Keystone Pr-wrps-
500c prntd   (4b4) 15. (5j5,lacks wrps) 12.50
--Lord Arthur Savile's Crime & Other Stories-Lond-1891-prntd bds-
168p   (5ii2,rub) 12.50
--Newdigate Prize Poem,Ravenna-Oxf-1878-12mo-prntd wrps-
1st ed of auth's 1st publ(Univ Arms on title & front wrpr)
        (5gg6) 75.00
--The Picture of Dorian Gray-Lond-Ward,Lock&Co-(1891)-8vo-
orig gray bevelled bds   (5d9,pres,box,broke) 200.00
--same-Carrington,Pais-1908-illus-4to-3/4 vel (5yy6) 15.00
--same-NY-1931-Three Sirens Pr   (4b4,cov fox) 3.50
--Poems-Lond-1881-DavidBogue-8vo-white parch stmpd in g.
wi prunus blossoms-1st bndg-(1st issue 250c prntd) (5d9,box) 100.00
--Salome,a Tragedy in One Act-Grabhorn Pr-1927-col frontis-
bds wi cl bk-ltd to 195c-box (5ee9) 35. (5ss9,f) 30.00
--A Woman of No Importance-Lond-1894-JnLane-sm4to-bds-
500c prntd   (5d3) 75.00
--Works of-NY-1909-LambCo-15 vols-tan buck-ltd to 1000 sets,
nbrd-Sunflower ed   (5p6,sl soil) 35.00
--Writings of-Lond-1907-uniform ed-10 vols-illus-cl-papr labl-
ltd to 800 sets   (5i3,rub) 12.50
WILDE,MRS OSCAR-There Was Once,Grandma's Stories-Lond-
(ca 1888)-ENister-col illus-sq8vo-pict bds (5c8,loose) 12.50
WILDER,DAN'L W-Annals of Kansas-Topeka-1875-691p-1st ed
  (4c1) 12.50 (4p8,rub) 20. (5L2,sp wn) 25. (5tt5) 17.50
WILDER,F L-Picture Prides Current-Vols 1&2 from Sept 1935 thru
Mar 1937-2 vols-Lond-1936,37-8vo (5m6) 12.50
WILDER,LOUISE BEEBE-Colour in My Garden-NY-1927-4to-
illus   (5qq7) 10.00
--same-GardenCty-1930-410p-col illus (5xx7) 7.50
--The Fragrant Path-NY-1932-407p-col frontis (4g0) 10.00
--The Garden in Color-NY-1937-Macmillan-col illus-4to-327p-
    (5x0) 7.50
--The Rock Garden-GardenCty-1935-224p-illus (5s7) 5.00
WILDER, MARSHALL P-Wit & Humor of Amer-(1911)-Funk&Wagnalls-
10 vols-Library Ed   (5ww4) 10.00
WILDER,MITCHELL A-Santos-ColoSprings-(1943)-49p-64 plts-
1st ed-v scarce   (4L0) 25.00
WILDER,THORNTON-The Angel That Troubled the Waters & Other
Plays-Lond&NY-1928-special ed-ltd to 260c,autg,nbrd
    (4j0,sl fox) 20.00
--same-NY-1928-Coward McCann-1st ed-ltd to 778c,autg
    (4b5,f,dj,box) 35.00
--Bridge of San Luis Rey-NY-1927-A&CBoni-illus-235p-1st ed
  (5j5,lend libr) 15. (5cc9,dj) 37.50 (4d4) 20. (5cc9) 22.50
--same-Lond-1927-LongmanGreen-1st Engl ed (4b5,dj,mint) 30.00
--same-NY-1929-illus by Rockwell Kent-8vo-g.t.-1100c,autg,
box   (4c2,sp faded) 25. (5d3) 35.00
--The Cabala-NY-1926-12mo-dec cl-1st ed of auth's 1st book(wi
textual errors)
  (4b5,pres,vg) 50. (5ss7,autg note,f,tn dj) 75. (5gg6,dj,vf) 37.50
--The Eighth Day-NY-1967-Harper-ltd to 500c,autg,nbrd
    (4L4,dj,box,mint) 40.00
--same-NY-(1967)-8vo-cl-1st ed-ltd to 500c,autg,box (5ee9) 35.00
--Heaven's My Destination-Lond-(1934)-1st Engl ed (5i3,dj,f) 12.50
--same-Harper-1935 (4j0) 6. (5F1,tn dj) 3.75
--Ides of March-NY-(1948)-Harper-1st ed (4a1) 5.(5F1,f,dj) 4.00
--James Joyce 1882 to 1941-Aurora,NY-8vo-wrps-1st ed-
150c prntd   (5ss7,vf) 40.00
--The long Christmas dinner & other plays in 1 act-NY-1931-
CowardMcCann-1st trade ed (5m2) 6. (5F1) 7.50
--Woman of Andros-NY-Boni-1930-1st ed
  (4j0,fox) 4.50 (5i1,vg,dj)8. (5w9) 8.50 (4b5,mint,dj) 15.00
WILDER,THEO-Hist of Co C 7th Regmt OVI-Oberlin-1866-83p-
cl-v scarce   (5h2) 35.00
WILDES,HARRY E-Anthony Wayne, Trouble Shooter of the Amer
Revolution-NY-(1941)-8vo-illus-1st ed (5ss5,f,dj) 12.50
--Delaware-1940-illus-Rivers of Amer (5L7) 6.50
--Lonely Midas-NY-1943-illus-1st ed (5w5,dj) 7.50
--Twin Rivers-NY-(1943)-1st ed-illus (5jj3) 8.50
WILDRAKE-Pictorial Gallery of English Race Horses-Lond-1844-
plts-thk t8vo-3/4 mor-g.t. (4b6,rbnd) 50.00
WILDWOOD,W-Thrilling Adventures among Early Settlers-(ca 1870)-
200 illus   (5L7) 7.50

WILEY,HARVEY W-Foods & Their Adulteration-Phila-1907-
illus-1st ed   (5yy6,shaken) 10. (5c5) 12.50
WILEY,JOHN-Correspondence...in Case of-Honolulu-1844-Gov Pr-
8vo-78p(lacks 4 lvs)-errata slip
    (5a3,lacks wrps,2 pgs glued togeth) 75.00
--same-Honolulu-1845-153p-8vo-Gov Pr-stitchd (5a3) 65.00
WILEY,JOHN & CO-Catalogue of Scientific Works-NY-1871
    (5g4) 12.50
WILEY,JOHN L-History of Monrovia-Pasadena,Ca-1927-illus
    (5x5) 12.50
WILEY,RICHARD T-Sim Greene & Tom the Tinker's Men-Phila-
1907-380p-cl   (5h7) 7.50
WILEY,WM H-The Yosemite,Alaska & the Yellowstone-Lond-
(1893)-reprntd from Engrng-maps-illus-4to-230p-scarce
    (5r7,cov dmgd) 15. (4g6) 17.50 (5F5) 25.00
WILHELM,GALE-No Letters for the Dead-RandomHse-(1936)
    (5F1,dj,als) 10.00
WILHELM,R,ed-The Chinese Fairy Book-NY-c1921-Stokes-
8vo-329p-6 col illus-frontis-5 plts-pict cl-1st ed-Fairy Series
    (5p1) 7.50
WILKENS,CLEO GOFF-Index to 1840 Fed Population Census of
Ohio-(FtWayne)-1969 to 1972-cl-4 vols-125 sets prntd (4h7) 100.00
WILKES,BENJ-English Moths & Butterflies...with Plants, Flowers
& Fruits Whereon they feed etc-Lond-(1749?)-BWilkes-
calf-4to-120 handcol plts-rare-(24)p,63p,(4) (5jj8,f) 750.00
WILKES,CHAS-Narr of US Exploring Exped during 1838 thru 1842-
Phila-1845-Lea&Blanchard-5 vols & atlas-cl
    (5tt0,wn) 45. (5t2,bkstrp def) 35. (5tt0,wn) 45.00
--same-Lond-1852-Ingram, Cooke-326p-Vol 2 only(of 2 vols)
    (5x9) 10.00
--US Exploring Exped 1838 to 1842-Phila-1862,1874-
Vol 17(2nd part),Botany-4to-17 folio plts(fld)-bds-cl bk (5g3) 75.00
--Western America,including Calif & Oreg with maps-Phila-
1849-Lea&Blanchard-130p-32p of ads-wrps (5tt0) 200.00
WILKES,GEO-History of Oregon,Geographical & Politicial-NY-
1845-Colyer-8vo-part mor-fldg map-1st ed (4h0,f) 550.00
WILKES,JOHN-North Briton from #1 to #46,incl-Lond-1769-
folio-calf   (5aa0,sl wn,rbkd) 45.00
WILKES,L E-By an Oregon Fireside-1941-144p (4L0) 10.00
WILKESON,FRANK-Recoll of Priv Soldier in Army of Potomac-
NY-1887-Putnam's 246p (5mm8,ex-libr) 6.50 (5j2) 18.00
WILKESON,SAML-Wilkeson's notes on Puget Sound-(NY,1870?)-
47p-stitchd-1st ed   (5g8) 15.00
WILKIE,FRANC B-Davenport,Past & Present-Davenport-1858-
Luse,Lane&Co-8vo-cl-334p (4L0,wn) 15. (5i9) 25. (4t1) 30.00
--35 Yrs of Journalism-Chig-(1891)-324p (5h2) 17.50
WILKIE,F B-The Great Inventions-Phila&Chig-1886-687p-illus-lea
    (5t7) 15.00
--Sketches & notices of the Chicago bar-Chig-1871-3rd ed (5g3) 6.00
WILKIN,W A-Cleverdale Mystery-1882-284p-1st ed (5x4) 15.00
WILKINS,G H-Flying the Arctic-1928-336p-illus
    (5ss1,pres) 17.50 (4b9,lf tn) 10.00
--same-NY-1929-336p-15 plts   (5dd0) 6.00
WILINS,HAROLD T-Capt Kidd & His Skeleton Island-NY-(1937)-
411p-maps-illus   (5s1,ex-libr) 7.50
--Hunting Hidden Treasures-NY-(1929)-266p-plts (5dd9) 7.50
--A Modern Treasure Hunter-Lond-1948 (4a9,vf) 3.50
--Mysteries of Ancient SoAmer-Lond-n.d. (5a8) 8.50
WILKINS,SIR HUBERT-Under the North Pole-Lond-(1931)-347p-
ports-plts-map   (5a1) 6.50
WILKINS,J-Mathematical Magick-Lond-1691-4th ed-295p-
illus-sm8vo-hf lea (4e4,lacks last adv lf,hng weak) 77.50
WILKINS,JAS H-The Great Diamond Hoax-SanFran-1913-283p
    (5x5) 10. (5g6) 12.00
--Glimpse of Old Mexico-(San Rafael)n.p.-1901-8vo-pict cl-illus
    (4a3) 15.00
WILKINS,JOHN-Discovery of New World-Lond-1684-J Rawlins-
2 vols in 1-5th ed   (5yy3) 125.00
WILKINS,MARY E-The Heart's Highway-NY-1900-Dblday-sm8vo-
cl-4 plts-308p-1st ed (5ee3) 5. (5j5) 7.50
--The Jamesons-NY-1899-sm12mo-177p-cl-1st ed (5ee3) 5. (5t0) 4.50
--A New Engl Nun & Other Stories-Lond-1891-468p-cl (5t2) 4.00
--The Pot of Gold & other stories-Bost-(c1892)-Lothrop-12mo-
324p,(10)-illus-1st ed   (5p1) 15.00
WILKINS,PETER-Life & Adventures of-Bost-1847-18mo-pict bds-
improvd ed   (5t7,dmgd) 7.50
WILKINS,WM CLYDE-Chas Dickens in Amer-Lond-1911-
41 plts&ports   (4a8) 5.00
WILKINSON,A-Plantation Stories of Louisiana-Bost-1914-illus-
1st ed   (4m8) 6.50 (5x2) 15.00
WILKINSON,ANNE-Lions in Way-Tor-1956-274p-plts (4a8) 4.50
WILKINSON,DOUG-Land of Long Day-Tor-1955 (5a1) 5. (4F9) 7.50

USED BOOK PRICE GUIDE

WILKINSON,I-Memories of Wilkinson Family in Amer-1869-
585p   (5t9)   30.00
WILKINSON,J B-Annals of Binghamton etc-Bing-1872-12mo
          (5m6) 12.50   (4t2)   17.50
WILKINSON,J GARDNER-On Colour-Lond-1858-4to-
8 col plts   (5n7,crack)   16.50
--Popular Account of Ancient Egyptians-NY-1854-2 vols-12mo-
rev   (5jj3,rub)   12.50
--Topography of Thebes & General View of Egypt-Lond-1835-
hf calf-8vo-11 plts   (4e1,cov loose)   35.00
WILKINSON,JAS-Memoirs of My Own Times-Phila-1816-calf-
charts-3 vols-(laskc atlas)
          (4j4,lacks t.p.) 75.   (5tt0,wn,lacks t.p.)   100.00
WILKINSON,MARGUERITE-Contemporary Poetry-NY-1923-
Macmillan-372p   (5p7)   3.50
WILKINSON,N-The Royal Navy,British Sea Power-Lond-1907-
61 col plts   (5c1)   22.50
WILKINSON,THOS-Tours to British mountains-Lond-1824-8vo-
bds-1st ed   (518)   17.50
WILKINSON,WM C-The Dance of Modern Society-NY-1869-
12mo-77p   (5w7)   6.50
WILKINSON'S GENERAL ATLAS OF THE WORLD-Lond-1809-
2nd ed-sm folio-hf calf-48 col maps(2 dbl pg) (4c1)   60.00
WILLARD,C D-Herald's History of Los Angeles-LosAng-1901-
Kingsley,Barnes&Neuner-54 plts-366p-1st ed (4n1)   18.00
--same-(1911 ed,3rd prntg)-8 added pgs   (4n1)   18.00
WILLARD,CHAS D-Free Harbor Contest of Los Angeles-LosAng-1899-
212p-cl   (5tt0)   7.50
--Herald's Hist of Los Angeles-LosAng-1911(t.p. 1901)-365p-
(Kingsley Barnes)   (4d6)   15.00
WILLARD,DR-Inland Trade with Mexico-Western Monthly Rev,
Apr&May 1829-bds-1st prntd   (4n4)   30.00
WILLARD,MRS EUGENE-Kin da shon's wife, an Alaskan story-
NY-(1892)-Revell-1st ed   (5m2)   8.50
WILLARD,FRANCES E-Glimpses of 50 Yrs-(1889)-Wo Temp Publ
Assoc-698p-illus-1st ed   (5cc6) 5.   (5w1)   6.50
--Occupations for Women-NY-1897-SuccessCo-t8vo-504p-1st ed-
illus   (5ss5)   12.50
--Woman & Temperance-Hartf-1883-653p
          (5ss5) 10.   (5w1,cov loose)   9.50
WILLARD,J W-Simon Willard & His Clocks-Bost-1911-folio-
38 plts-133p-illus-1st ed   (5bb0)   100.00
--same-Mamaroneck-1926-illus-4to-new&corr ed (5j3,f,dj) 35.00
WILLARD,JAS F-English Government at Work 1327 to 1336-
Cambr,Mass-1940-2 vols   (5q0)   17.50
WILLARD,JOS-Willard Memoir-Bost-1858-470p-cl (5a8)   20.00
WILLARD,MARGARET WHEELER-Letters on the Amer Revolution-
Bost-Houghton,Miff-1925-370p-maps-ltd to 1040c
          (5g8) 25.   (5p7)   10.00
WILLARD,S-Plans & Sections of the Obelist on Bunker's Hill-Bost-
1843-sm folio-31p-14 plts-orig qtr sheep-labl
          (5zz7,fox,bkstrp def)   65.00
WILLARD,SAML-A Compleat Body of Divinity-Bost-1726-
Green&Kneeland-folio-calf-port (5L1,broke,lacks frontis) 75.
          (4h0,crack,fox,tn,Streeter bkplt)   285.00
WILLARD STORAGE BATTERY CO-Starting & Lighting Battery-
Cleve-1923-111p   (5y2)   5.00
WILLARD,T A-The City of the Sacred Well-NY-(1926)-illus-8vo
                                            (4g6)   7.50
--Lost Empires of Itzaes & Mayas-Glendale-1933-illus-scarce
          (5ii3) 42.50   (5L0)   25.00
WILLCOX,CORNELIS DEWITT-French English Military Tech
Dictionary-Wash-1917-8vo-582p   (4a6,wn)   5.00
WILLCOX,JN-Approaching Conflict-Chig-1873-254p-cl (5h7) 10.00
WILLERS,DIEDRICH-Town of Fayette-1900-152p (4m2,dj chip) 12.00
WILLETT,EDW-Beadle's Dime Library,Terrapin Dick-1885-29p-
lg mag size   (5ee3,edge wn) 5.00
WILLETT,G-Mammals of Los Angeles Co,CA-LosAng-1944-
wrps-4to-36 illus-34p   (4p5)   5.00
WILLETT,GEO-Birds of the Pacific Slope of Southern Calif-
Hollywood-1912-port   (5x5,autg)   12.50
WILLEY,AUSTIN-History of the Anti Slavery Cause in State &
Nation-Portl,Me-1886-illus-503p
          (4m2,f) 32.50   (5x5) 25.   (5x2)   47.50
WILLEY,B G-History of the White Mountains-Bost-(1870)-12mo-
296p-cl-g.stmpd-frontis-rev by F Thompson (5u9,f)   25.00
--Incidents in White Mntn History-Bost-1856-illus-12mo-321p-
cl-g.stmp-1st ed(3rd thou)   (5u9)   30.00
--same-Bost-1857-307p-illus   (5e8)   34.75
WILLEY,FREEMAN OTIS-The Laborer & the Capitalist-NY-(1896)-
8vo-1st ed   (5m6)   6.50
WILLEY,GEO F-Book of Nutfield,(NH)-1895-367p (5e8)   27.75

WILLEY,SAM'L H-History of College of Calif-SanFran-1887-
Calif Hist Soc, Vol 1,pt 2-440p-wrps   (5tt0)   10.00
WILLIAM OF SWEDEN,PRINCE-Among Pygmies & Gorillas-With
the Swedish Zool Exped to Central Africa 1921-NY-1926-Dutton-
photos-296p-2nd ed   (4t5)   12.50
WILLIAMS,A B-Hampton & His Red Shirts-Charleston-1925 (5x2)27.50
--same-1935-2nd ed   (5x2)   25.00
WILLIAMS,A BRYAN-Game Trails in Brit Col-NY-1925-plts
                                            (5a1)   15.00
WILLIAMS,A M-Studies in Folk Song & Popular Poetry-Bost-1894-
321p   (5ii2)   8.00
WILLIAMS,ARCHIBALD-Conquering the Air-NY-1926-T Nelson-
315p   (5p0)   4.50
--same-NY-1930-rev&enlrgd-illus   (4b7)   8.50
--Romance of Modern Exploration-Phila-1906-384p (4a6)   7.50
WILLIAMS,BEN AMES-All the Brothers were Valiant-NY-1919-
12mo-cl-1st ed of auth's 1st book (5gg6,pic dj,autg,als) 25.00
--Come Spring-1940-Houghton,Miff-1st ed-ltd to 100c,autg
          (5ss9,scuff)   7.50
--It's A Free County-Bost-1945-1st ed   (4j0)   4.50
--"Mr Secretary"-NY-1940-8vo-507p   (4a7)   12.00
WILLIAMS,BENJ S-Orchid Grower's Manual-Lond-1877-orig cl-
12mo-col fldg frontis-38 plts(23 fldg)-5th ed (5z9)   20.00
--same-Lond-1894-7th ed-rev&enlrg-illus   (5tt5)   14.50
WILLIAMS,BLANCHE C-Forever Young-NY-(1943)-Putnam's
          (5p6,f) 7.   (5ss9,dj)   6.50
WILLIAMS,MRS C R-The Neutral French-Provi-(1841)-2 vols in 1-
hf lea-2nd ed   (5x1,cl,wn) 15.   (5w8)   22.50
WILLIAMS,C H C-Williams' New System of Handling & Educating
the Horse etc-Claremont,NH-1878-illus-248p (5t7)   6.50
WILLIAMS,CHAS-Travellers in Africa-Phila-n.d.-Porter&Coates-
340p   (4t5)   6.00
WILLIAMS,CHAS R-Life of Rutherford Birchard Hayes-Col-1928-
2 vols-cl   (5t0,ex-libr) 7.50 (5h1)   15.00
WILLIAMS,CHAUNCEY PRATT-Lone Elk-Denver-1935&1936-wrps-
1st ed of 500c,in 2 parts-Old West Series,#6&7-50p,35p-
v scarce   (5dd1)   25.00
WILLIAMS,C SCOTT-Life & Apostolic Labors of...Junipero Serra-
Pasadena-1913-cl-338p-8vo-   (5F5,pencil) 20.00
WILLIAMS,CLARK-Story of a Grateful Citizen-NY-1934-2 vols-
illus-priv prnt   (4a1,pres) 15. (5w0) 8.50 (4t0)10.00
WILLIAMS,D W-Hist of Jackson Co,Ohio-Vol 1(all publ)-Jackson-
1900-188p-cl-v rare   (5h1)   50.00
WILLIAMS,E-Negro In the Caribbean-Wash-1942 (5x2)   12.50
WILLIAMS,EDWIN-NY Annual Register,1832-NY-1832-12mo-
orig bds-396p-plts-3rd issue   (5m6,rub,cov loose)10.00
WILLIAMS,ELIZ-Child of Sea-HarborSprngs-1905-229p-cl-
1st ed   (5y0,sl rub) 25.00
WILLIAMS,EMILY-Wm Coddington of RI,a sketch-Newport-1941-
                                            (5g4,f)   7.50
WILLIAMS,G C-The Compounder,Williams' Informer,or A Whiskey
Buyer's Guide-StLouis-(1898)-cl-16mo-117p-fldg tables (4t7)12.50
WILLIAMS,GARDNER F-Diamond Mines of SoAfrica-NY-1905-
2 vols-illus   (5yy6,pres,spot)32.50
WILLIAMSON,GEO C-Miniature Collector-NY-1921-308p (5n7)4.50
WILLIAMS,GEO DEE-Maya Spanish Crosses in Yucantan-Cambr-
1931-8vo-245p-plts-wrps-1st ed   (5g6)   15.00
WILLIAMS,GEO F-Memorial War Book-NY-(1894)-4to-illus-cl
          (5x5)   20.00
WILLIAMS,GEO W-History of the Negro Race in Amer...from 1619
to 1880-NY-1883-2 vols   (5w5,ex-libr,stnd) 20. (5x2) 85.00
WILLIAMS,HAROLD A-Western Maryland Rwy Story-Balt-1952-
4to-134p-illus   (5y2)   8.50
WILLIAMS,HARRY-The Steam Navy of England-Lond-1895 (5c1)15.00
WILLIAMS,HARRY-Texas Trails-SanAnt-(1932)-261,(262)p-v scarce
          (4L0)   35.00
WILLIAMS,HARRY L-History of Craighead Co,Ark-LittleRock-
1930-ParkeHarper-8vo-cl-648p   (4t1)   37.50
WILLIAMS,HENRY L-Old Amer Houses-GardenCty-1946-
239p   (5w7,spot)   3.75
WILLIAMS,HENRY-Drugs Against Men-NY-c1935   (5x7)   3.50
--Luther Burbank, His Life & His Work-NY-1915-333p-photos
                                            (5w3)   4.50
WILLIAMS,HENRY T-Beautiful Homes-NY-1878-314p,(6)-illus
                                            (5w7,wn)   7.50
--Pacific Tourist-NY-1877-278p-limp cl   (5tt0,wn)   15.00
--same-NY-1882,3-illus-372p   (4g6)   15.00
--Window Gardening-NY-1878-300p-14th ed   (5s7)   5.00
WILLIAMS,HENRY T-Williams,Tourist Guide & Map of San Juan
Mines-NY-n.d.(1877)-fldg map-wrps-47p,&ads-rare
          (4L0,map split)   300.00

USED BOOK PRICE GUIDE

WILLIAMS, I A-Elements of Book Collecting-NY-1927-Stokes
(5p9,sl stn)   5.00
WILLIAMS, J C-Life in Camp-NH-1864-12mo-cl-167p (5t2)   10.00
WILLIAMS, J D-Amer Illustrated-NY-(1877)-121p-4to-cl
(5t4,wn)   10.50
--same-Bost-(1883)-4to   (5r7,cov stn)   35.00
WILLIAMS, J FLETCHER-History of City of St Paul & Co of Ramsey,
Minn-StPaul-1876-8vo-cl-475p   (4t1,cov dmgd)   25.00
WILLIAMS, J G-I Am Black-Capetown-1949   (5x2)   12.50
WILLIAMS, J H-Yosemite & Its High Sierra-Tacoma&SanFran-1914-
illus-8 col plts-fldg map-limp suede-146p-1st ed   (4n1)   10.00
WILLIAMS, J-Isthmus of Tehuantepec-NY-1852-295p-plts-
fldg map-separate cl vol of maps   (5ii2,4a5,fox)   27.50
--same-NY-1852-errata slip-295p-1st ed
(5a8,ex-libr,cov dtchd) 18.   (5L0,chip)   15.00
WILLIAMS, J W-Big Ranch Country-WichitaFalls-1954 (4c7,dj)   15.00
WILLIAMS, JAS-75 Years on the Border-KansCty,Mo-1912-207p
plus 1p-1st ed   (4L0)   8.50
WILLIAMS, JESSE-Descrip of the US Lands in Iowa-NY-1840-
fldg col map-180p, 1p ads   (4L0)   250.00
WILLIAMS, JESSE LYNCH-The Girl & the Game etc-NY-(c1908)-
12mo-343p,4(ads)-frontis-5 plts-pict cl-t.e.g.-Scribner's
(5p1)   6.50
WILLIAMS, JOHN-A Narrative of Missionary Enterprises in the
South Sea Islands-Lond-1837-589p-col frontis-fldg map
(5x9,wtrstnd)   10.00
WILLIAMS, JOHN-Captivity & Deliverance of..& Mrs Mary
Rowlandson-Brookfield-1811-orig calf-116p,80p(5r6,5m4)   65.00
--Redeemed Captive returning to Zion-Bost-1795-12mo-calf&bds-
132p-6th ed   (5t0)   22.50
--same-Northampton-1853-frontis-192p   (4L0,sl wn)   10.00
WILLIAMS, JOHN A-Thornton, a Kentucky Story-Cinn-1900-cl-
304p-rare   (4b0,sl rub)   17.50
WILLIAMS, JOHN C-Life in Camp, Hist of...14th Vt Reg-
Claremont, NH-1864   (4j4)   12.50
WILLIAMS, JOHN CAMP-An Oneida County Printer Wm Williams-
NY-part vel-ltd to 165c   (4g2)   37.50
WILLIAMS, JOHN G-Adventures of Seventeen Year Old Lad etc-
Bost-1894-Collins Pr-308p-cl   (5tt0)   25.00
WILLIAMS, JOHN H-Guardians of the Columbia-Tacoma-1912-
142p-pict cl-illus(8 col)   (5s4,ex-libr,5m9)   6.50
--same-Tacoma-1912-wros   (5dd1)   4.00
--Mountain That Was God-Tacoma-1910-illus-col plts-R8vo-
112p-hf cl bds   (5cc4)   10.00
--same-1911-142p-rev&enlrgd 2nd ed-illus
(5r1,f,5w5) 8.50   (5a9) 4.   (5s4)   6.50
--Yosemite & its High Sierra-Tacoma&SanFran-1914-145p-illus
(5xx7,autg) 5.   (5r0)   6.00
WILLIAMS, JOHN ROGERS-Handbook of Princeton, NY-1905
(5a8) 4.   (5h9)   7.50
--Philip Vickers Fithian's Journal & Letters, 1767 to 74-
Princeton Univ-1900-1st ed   (5x5)   50.00
WILLIAMS, JN S, ed-American Pioneer, a Monthly Periodical-
Chillicothe-1842 & Cinn-1843-2 vol
(5h7,2nd vol sl clipped short)   100.00
--History of Invasion & Capture of Washington-NY-1857-Harper-
371p-map   (5mm8) 10.   (5l3)   22.50
WILLIAMS, JOS-Narr of a Tour from State of Indiana to Oregon
Terr in years 1841,2-NY-1921-95p-cl   (5d6)   15.00
WILLIAMS, JOS J-Voodoos & Obeahs-NY-1933   (5x2)   17.50
--Whence the Black Irish of Jamaica-NY-1932-illus   (5x2)   17.50
WILLIAMS, KENNETH P-Lincoln Finds A General-Bost-1949-
2 vols-box   (4j4,5t7)   10.00
--same-NY-1949 to 59-5 vols   (5s9)   32.50
WILLIAMS, L S-Family Education & Government in Choctaw
Language-Bost-1835-48p-sewn-wrps-1st ed-scarce
(5t0) 15.   (5L0)   17.50
WILLIAMS, LENORE W-Sandwich Glass-Bridgeport-1922-102p
(5x0)   8.00
WILLIAMS, LEWIS-Chinook by the Sea-Portland-(1924)-136p-scarce
(5s4)   15.00
WILLIAMS, LLEW-The Dalton Brothers in Their Oklahoma Cave-
Chig-n.d.-Donohue-wrps-234p-rare   (4n8,wn)   15.00
WILLIAMS, M B-Heart of Rockies-Saskatoon-n.d.-98p-illus(5aa0)4.50
--Through the Heart of Rockies & Selkirks-Ott-1912-105p-illus-
fldg maps-stiff wrps   (5aa0)   4.50
--same-1924-3rd ed-110p   (5aa0) 4.50   (5w8)   6.00
WILLIAMS, MARGERY-The Velveteen Rabbit-NY-n.d.-(1922?)-
GeoHDoran-12mo-33p-7 inserted col plts(3 dbl pg)-pict bds
(5p1,rub)   17.50
WILLIAMS, MARY FLOYD-History of the San Fran Committee of
Vigilance of 1851-Berkeley-1921-illus-t8vo-1st ed   (4g6)   32.50

WILLIAMS, MEADE C-Early Mackinac-StL-1898-111p-cl-
2nd ed-scarce   (5h2)   10.00
WILLIAMS, MONIER, transl-Sakoontala-NY-1885-calf-ltd ed
(4j3,sp rprd)   22.50
WILLIAMS, MRS-Biography of Revolutionary Heroes-Providence-
1839-312p-frontis-1st ed   (5mm8)   15.00
WILLIAMS, O W-Alsate, the Last of the Chisos Apaches-n.p.-n.d.-
wrps-7(8)p   (5L2)   20.00
--The Big Snow of 1878(captiont.)-n.p.-(1933)-4p-self cov-
1st ed   (4L0)   7.50
--By the Campfire in the SW-n.p.-(1902?)-wrps-26p-1st ed
(4L0)   15.00
--Crusoe or Jack, a Story for Boys-n.p.-n.d.-4p-self cov-v scarce-
1st ed   (4L0)   15.00
--From Dallas to the Site of Lubbock in 1877-n.p.-n.d.-(FtStockton,
1935)-prntd wrps-16p-incl in Myers' Pioneer Surveyor (5g5)   17.50
--In Old Mexico 1879 to 1880-n.p.(FtStockton)-n.d.(1929)-wrps-
48p-v scarce   (5L2) 45.   (5g6)   48.50
--Mendosa, 1684 in Pecos Co, Tex-FtStockton-n.d.-24p-wrps-
scarce-1st ed   (4L0)   20.00
--Muddy Wilson & the Buffalo Stampede-n.p.-1st ed-prntd in
Dallas)-Mar 1938-(7p)-wrps   (4L0)   25.00
--Pecos County, Its History-n.p.-n.d.-24p-self cov-1st ed-
v scarce   (4L0)   35.00
--Pecos Co Panther Hunt Around Livingston Mesa-n.p.-n.d.-(9p)-
wrps-1st ed   (5g0,4L0)   10.00
--Pioneer Surveyor, Frontier Lawyer-ElPaso-1966-photos-336p plus
index-Hertzog-1st ed-maps-o.p.   (5L2, mint)   12.50
WILLIAMS, OSCAR, ed-Little Treasury of Modern Poetry-NY-
1946-Scribner-672p   (5p7)   4.00
WILLIAMS, R E-A Century of Punch, Cartoons-NY-1955-4to-bds&cl-
342p-col plts-1st ed   (5w9)   6.50
WILLIAMS, ROBT-Adventures of an Autograph Collector-NY-1952-
99p   (5j4)   5.00
WILLIAMS, ROGER-Experiments of Spiritual Life & Health & their
preservatives, 1652-(1863)-buck   (5L7,rbnd)   7.50
WILLIAMS, SAML-History of Amer Rev-NewHav-1824   (5t7)   10.00
--Natural & Civil History of Vermont-Walpole-1794-Thos&DCarlisle-
buck-416p-list of subscribers-1st ed-fldg map   (4b1,rbnd)   85.00
WILLIAMS, SAML-City of the Golden Gate-SanFran-1921-
sq8vo-bds-Grabhorn-Book Club of Calif-ltd to 350c, nbrd
(5F5,f)   17.50
WILLIAMS, SAML COLE, ed-Adair's History of the Amer Indians-
JohnsonCty-1930-497p plus index-fldg map-1st ed-ltd to 750c
(5L2,unopnd) 35.   (5h6,box, mint)   45.00
--Early travels in the Tennessee country, 1540 to 1800-JohnsonCty-
1928-illus-maps   (5g8)   30.00
--History of Codification in Tenn-JohnsonCty-1932
(5h6, cov spots)   15.00
--History of Johnson City & Its Environs-JohnsonCty-1940-34p-
bds   (5h6)   4.00
WILLIAMS, SHERWIN-Story of-n.p.-n.d.-bds-64p-illus (5y2)   5.00
WILLIAMS, STANLEY T, ed-Letters from Sunnyside & Spain,
Washington Irving-NewHav-1928-illus-1st ed   (5mm1)   10.00
WILLIAMS, SYDNEY B-Antique Blue & White Spode-Lond-1945-
2nd ed-illus-242p-8vo   (5ww3)   15.00
--same-Lond-1949-rev&enlrgd-3rd ed-248p   (5p0)   12.50
WILLIAMS, THOS BENTON, ed-The Soul of the Red Man-OklaCty-
1937-illus-photos   (4b2, lacks t.p.)   12.50
WILLIAMS, T HARRY-Lincoln & His Generals-NY-1952-Knopf-
(4j4) 5.   (5mm8,5w0)   6.50
WILLIAMS, T J C-History of Frederick Co, Maryland from Earliest
Settlements...contd...to present time by F McKinsey-n.p.-
1910-illus-a.e.g.-lg4to-2 vols-1st ed   (4m2,rbkd)   85.00
--State of Maryland-Balt-1906-Sun Job Prntg-16mo-wrps-168p
(4t1)   7.50
WILLIAMS, TENNESSEE-Baby Doll-Lond-1957-1st Engl ed
(4j0) 6.50   (5b2,f,dj)   7.50
--same-(NY)-(1956)-New Directions-1st ed-script for the film
(5r9,dj)   8.50
--Cat on a Hot Tin Roof-(1955)-New Directions-1st ed (5r9,dj) 12.50
--Hard Candies-New Directions-(1954)-ltd ed, box-1st ed
(5d3) 25.   (4b7,f) 20.   (4b5,sl crack)   22.50
--Le Cri Du Phoenix-La Licorne-1960-orig wrps-4to-ltd to 250c
(4b5,f)   15.00
--Roman Spring of Mrs Stone-NY-(1950)-New Directions-1st ed
(5ss9,dj,vg) 5.   (5b2,f)   6.50
--same-(NY-1950)-New Directions-ltd to 500c, autg, box
(5hh1) 40.   (5d3)   50.00
--Streetcar Named Desire-(NY)-(1947)-New Directions-orig bds-
1st ed   (4b5,rub,fray dj)   20.00

344

WILLIAMS,TENNESSEE (continued)
--The Two Character Play-NY-1969-New Directions-ltd to 350c,
autg,nbrd,box   (4L4,mint) 50.   (5ee9)   40.00
WILLIAMS,VALENTINE-The Man With the Clubfoot-NY-1918-
8vo-1st ed of auth's 1st book   (5i3) 5.   (4m8)   17.50
WILLIAMS,W-Appletons' Southern & Western Travellers' Guide,
With New & Authentic Maps-NY-1850-cl-140p (4j4,ex-libr) 12.50
--NY,Tourist Map of the State-Utica-1830-21x18" fld to 16mo-
cl case   (5t4,rprd)   25.00
--Traveller's & Tourist's Guide thru the US of Amer,Canada etc-
Phila-1853-Lippincott-216p,24p-fldg map 29x24½-12mo-g.cl
                                     (5L1)   60.00
--same-Phila-1855-fldg map-236p plus index (4L0,sl wtrstnd)   50.00
WILLIAMS,W-also see APPLETON'S
WILLIAMS,W R-Instruction Book...for Using Perfection Tailor
System of Dress Cutting-Lawrence-1886-24p-illus-wrps
                                     (5hh7,f)   12.50
WILLIAMS,W W-History of the Fire Lands,Composing Huron & Erie
Co,Ohio-1879-lg4to-illus-524p-v scarce   (4m2,rprd)   40.00
WILLIAMS,WALTER-Missouri, Mother of the West, Illus-Chig-1930-
Amer Hist Soc-lg8vo-cl-5 vols (4t1) 50.   (5h1) 25.   (4t3)   30.00
--State of Missouri,Autobiog-Columbia-1904-591p
                      (5dd6) 6.   (5hh3)   5.00
WILLIAMS,WELLINGTON-Appletons' RR & Steamboat Companion-
NY-1848-313p-orig red cl-30 maps(most fld)-26 illus
                      (5ss5,lacks 1 map) 15.   (5m3)   25.00
WILLIAMS,WM B-Munitions Manufacture in Phila Ordnance Dist-
Phila-1921-674p-illus   (5w5)   5.00
WILLIAMS,WM CARLOS-The Autobiography of-NY-(1951)-
RandomHse-8vo-cl
   (4j0,dj) 15.   (5ss7,vf,wn dj,pres) 65.   (5b2,f,dj)   10.00
--The Build Up-NY-(1952)-RandomHse-1st ed   (5ss9,wn dj)   10.00
--In the Money-(1940)-New Directions-(White Mule-Part 2)
                                     (5F1,dj,def)   10.00
--Kora in Hell,Improvisations-Bost-1920-lg12mo-dec bds-
1st ed   (5ss7,f,dj def)   50.00
--Last Nights of Paris-Macaulay-1929   (5F1,vf,dj)   27.50
--Paterson Book 1 thru 5-NY-1946 to 1958-lg12mo-cl-1st eds-
complete set   (5ss7,vf,dj)   150.00
--Paterson-NY-(1946)-sm12mo-cl-1st ed in New Classics Series
                      (5ss7,pres,f,wn dj)   35.00
--The Pink Church-Columbus-1949-Golden Goose Pr-1st ed-
ltd to 400c,nbrd-144p-orig blue prnt wrps-Chap Book #1
                                     (4b1,f)   40.00
--Selected Letters of-NY-(1957)-348p-1st ed-ltd to 75c,nbrd,
box,autg   (4g2,label wn)   115.00
--A Voyage to Pagany-NY-1928-MacaulayCo-1st ed (5ss9,vg)   20.00
WILLIS,WM L-History of Sacramento Co,Calif...Illus,Complete
in 1 Vol-LosAng-1913-Historic Record-4to-part lea-a.e.g.-
1056p   (4t1)   75.00
WILLIAMSBURG SCRAPBOOK-Richmond,VA-1937-illus
                      (4j4) 7.50   (5w7)   2.00
WILLIAMSON,ADAM-Official Diary-Lond-1912-283p-Camden Soc,
Vol 22   (5a1,fade)   5.00
WILLIAMSON,ALBERT R-An Amer Story-Bloomington-1947-
priv publ-112p-illus   (4b8)   4.50
WILLIAMSON,DAVID BRAINERD-Life & Public Services of
Abraham Lincoln-Phila-(1864)-Peterson-12mo-1st ed (5m6,rub) 22.50
WILLIAMSON,GEO-Memorials of Lineage, Early Life,Education &
Development of Genius of Jas Watt-n.p.-1856-Watt Club-4to-
orig bds-labl   (5j3,rbkd)   20.00
WILLIAMSON,GEO C-Portrait Miniatures-Lond-1897-8vo-illus-
1st ed   (5ss5)   12.50
WILLIAMSON,HAROLD F-Winchester,The Gun That Won the West-
Wash-(1952)-illus-4to-494p-1st ed (5m6,5ss8,mlnt,dj,4p8)   10.00
WILLIAMSON,HENRY-Patriot's Progress-Lond-1930-illus-1st ed
                                     (4j0)   10.00
--The Pathway-Lond-(1928)-JonathanCape-1st ed (5ss9,dj)   7.50
--The Wet Flanders Plain-Lond-1929-8vo-bds-ltd to 80c,autgs
                                     (5ee9)   30.00
WILLIAMSON,J A,ed-Observ of Sir Richard Hawkins-Lond-1933-
Argonaut Pr-4 maps-ltd to 475c   (5c1)   65.00
WILLIAMSON,JAS J-Mosby's Rangers-NY-1896-511p-illus
                                     (5xx7)   20.50
WILLIAMSON,JOHN P-English Dakota Dictionary,Wasicun Ka
Dakota Ieska Wowapi-Yankton,SD-1938   (4k4,f)   12.50
--The Dakota Mission,Past & Present,AD 1886-(Minnpls)-n.d.-
(1886?)-wrps-27p-v rare   (4L0)   150.00
WILLIAMSON,PETER-Life & Curious Adventures of Peter Williamson
Who Was Carried Off From Aberdeen & Sold for a Slave etc-
Aberdeen-1801-144p-papr bds-labl-(not 1st ed)   (5r6)   38.00

WILLIAMSON,PETER (continued)
--Travels of...Among Different Nations & Tribes of Savage
Indians in Amer-by himself-Edinb-1768-12mo-184p-calf-
3 plts(1 fldg)   (4p3,tn,lacks plts) 75.   (5n2)   325.00
WILLIAMSON,R S-Report of His Survey to Ascertain Practicable
Route for RR to Pac Ocean-Wash-1854-6p-SED 52   (4n4)   15.00
--Report Upon Removal of Blossom Rock in SanFran Harbor-Wash-
1871-lg4to-11 maps(1 fldg)-cl   (5g8) 10.   (4a5)   8.50
WILLIAMSON,ROBT W-Ways of the South Sea Savage-Lond-1914-
43 photos-1 fldg map   (5c1,lt fox)   15.00
WILLIAMSON,THAMES-Far North Country-NY-1944-236p-
Amer Folkways   (5L2,5a1) 5.   (5ss1,dj)   6.50
WILLIAMSON,T S-Woope Mowis Owa Kin Dakota Iapi en Pejuta
Wicasta Kaga (also Woope Itakihua)-NY-1872-254p plus 57p
plus 265p dbl col-lea-(wi Psalms & Proverbs(NY, 1871) bnd in)-
rare   (4L2)   100.00
WILLIAMSON,THOS S-Dakota Wowapi Wakan,the Holy Bible,in
Language of Dakotas-NY-1879-Amer Bible Soc-(old Testament)
                                     (4k4,rub)   25.00
--Dakota Wowapi Wakan,the Holy Bible in Language of Dakotas-
NY-1883-(complete Bible)   (4k4,hng wk)   25.00
--same-1900 ed   (4k4,f)   15.00
--same-NY-1914-mor-g.-4to   (4k4,f)   35.00
--Hdinanpapi Wowapi Mowis Owa Inonpa Kin, Dakota Iapi en
Pejuta Wicasta Kaga (also) Lewi Toope-NY-1869-65p & 47p
dbl col-lea-1st ed-rare   (4L2)   100.00
--Josuwa,Qa Wayacopi Kin,Qa Rute,Ohanyanpi Qon Oyakapi
Wowapi Kin-NY-1875-lea-81p,dbl col-1st ed-rare (4L2)   100.00
--Woope Itakihna,Book of Deuteronomy in Dakota Language-NY-
1872-limp cl-57 dbl col pg-rare   (4L2)   100.00
WILLIS,GEO L-Hist of Shelby County,KY-(Louisvl)-1929-illus-
268p   (4p8,pres)   40.00
WILLIS,J,ed-Canadian Boards at Work-Tor-1941-190p (4b9,f)   15.00
WILLIS,J S-John Martin Jr-n.p.-1892-232p   (5m1)   20.00
WILLIS,N P-Amer Scenery-Lond-1840-2 vols-4to-Geo Virtue-
views by WHBartlett-port-map-orig publ "gift" bndg,brown mor-
g.e.   (5L1,sl rub)   225.00
--Canadian Scenery Illustrated-Lond-1842-WHBartlett plts-
orig lea-2 vols   (5dd7,f,f bndg)   470.00
--The Convalescent-NY-1859-456p-orig cl   (4j0,sl stnd)   12.50
--Dashes at life wi a free pencil-Lond-1845-Longman,etc-3 vols-
8vo-orig qtr cl-labls-1st Engl ed   (5i9,cov wn,sp rprd)   25.00
--Famous Persons & Places-NY-1854-Scribner-8vo-cl (5b2)   12.50
--Health Trip to the Tropics-NY-1853-Scribner-1st ed-421p plus
23p   (5L8,libr stmp) 15.   (5l8)   20.00
--Hurry Graphs-NY-1851-2nd ed   (5m1)   8.50
--same-NewOrl-1854-Burnett&Bostwick-364p   (5ee3)   12.50
--Mountain,Lake & River-Bost-1886-4to-96p-25 plts-dec cl
                                     (5t4)   10.00
--People I have Met-NY-1850-357p   (5t4)   4.50
--Pencillings by Way-Auburn-1853-527p-orig cl   (4b4)   15.00
--Summer Cruise in Mediterranean on Board Amer Frigate-Auburn-
1853-396p-cl   (4m8,fade,sig loose) 8.50   (5h2,cov wn)   10.00
--Sketches-Bost-1827-8vo-orig glazed bds-cl bk-papr labl-
1st ed of auth's 1st book   (5gg6)   25.00
--Trenton Falls-NY-1851-Putnam-1st ed-illus-91p-16mo
                      (4b6) 12.50   (5j5)   22.50
--same-NY-1862-16mo-cl-96p-illus   (5t4)   12.50
WILLIS THE PILOT-Sequel to the Swiss Family Robinson-Bost-
1858-Mayhew&Baker-sm8vo-dec grey cl-350p-plts-g.t.(5aa2) 8.50
WILLIS,MRS T F-Housekeeping & Dinner Giving in KansCty,Mo-
KansCty,Mo-1887-290p plus index-1st ed   (5L0,wn)   7.50
WILLIS,WM-Journals of Rev Thos Smith & the Rev Saml Deane-
Portland-1849-hf calf-illus   (5g4,rub,sp nbr) 10.   (5F9)   17.50
WILLISON,CHAS A-Remin of Boy's Service with 76th Ohio-
(Menasha-1908?)-n.d.-127p   (5ff7,pres)   32.50
WILLISON,GEO F-Behold Virginia, the 5th Crown-NY-1951
                      (5x2) 4.   (5h9)   3.00
--Here They Dug Gold-NY-(1946)-308p-3rd ed-enlrg (4L0)   5.00
--Saints & Sinners-1941   (5L7)   4.50
WILLISON,JOHN-The Young Communicant's Catechism-NewHav-
1820-SConverse-24mo-72p-   wrps   (5p1,wtrstnd)   20.00
WILLKIE,H FREDK-A Rebel Yells-NY-(1946)-1st ed (4j3,autg)   15.00
WILKIE,WENDELL L-One World-NY-Ltd Ed Club-4to-lea-
ltd to 500c,autg,box   (5m2)   13.50
--This is Wendell Willkie-NY-1940   (5x7)   3.75
WILLOUGHBY,BARRETT-Alaska Holiday-Bost-1946-296p-plts
                                     (5zz8,lacks fly)   5.00
--Sitka,Portal to Romance-Bost-1930-illus-8vo-1st ed (4g6,dj)   8.50
--The Trail Eater-NY-1929-400p-1st ed   (5ss1)   6.50
WILLOUGHBY,CHAS C-Antiquities of New Engl Indians with
Notes etc-Peabody Mus-1935-314p-illus
                      (5e8,marg notes) 18.75   (5dd1,bkstrp tn)   25.00

WILLOUGHBY,EDWIN E-50 Printers' Marks-Berkeley-1947-
  12mo-cl-153p-Book Arts Club-ltd to 550c   (5tt9,dj)   15.00
--Printing of First Folio of Shakespeare-(Oxford)-1932-illus-
  86p-4to-wrps   (4c1)   6.00
WILLOUGHBY,HAROLD R-Coverdale Psalter etc-Chig-1935-
  Riverside Pr-folio-cl-g.t.-ltd to 225c-Caxton Club
          (4c1,stmpd prntrs sample,box,f)   35.00
WILLOUGHBY,HUGH-Across the Everglades-Phila-1898-8vo-
  1st ed   (5m6)   12.50
WILLOUGHBY-MEADE,G-Chinese ghouls & goblins-Lond-1928-
  8vo-cl-432p   (5m5)   14.00
WILLS,CHAS JAS-John Squire's secret-Lond-1891-3 vols-8vo-
  orig cl-1st ed   (5xx6)   22.50
WILLS,HELEN-Fifteen Thirty-NY-1937-311p-illus (5p0)   5.00
WILLS,J BAXTER-A Mystery Solved-Burlington-(1897)-28p-
  illus-pict wrps-tip in guarantee for Pills (5ee3,lacks bk wrp) 15.00
WILLS,MARY-Winter in Calif-Norristown-1889-150p-white dec cov
         (5s4,cov soil)   5.00
WILLSON,BECKES-Canada-Tor-1907-12 col illus (5w8)   7.50
--The Great Company-Tor-1899-532p plus index-photos-
  maps(1 fldg)   (5dd4) 40.   (5L2,sl spot)   25.00
--same-Lond-1900-2 vols-plts-ports-maps   (5a1)   15.00
--John Slidell & the Confederates in Paris-NY-1932-8vo-296p
         (4a7)   10.00
--Life & Letters of James Wolfe-Lond-1909-illus-522p (5dd7)   14.00
--Life of Lord Strathcona & Mount Royal-1915-632p-illus-map
         (4b9,f)   12.00
--same-Bost&NY-1915-2 vols   (5w8)   15.00
--Lord Strathcona,Story of His Life-Lond-1902-288p-illus (4b9)   8.00
--Province That Has Been Passed By-(1911)-illus-256p-fldg map
         (5q0)   10.00
--Story of Rapid Transit-NY-1903-8vo-37 illus-1st ed (5ss5)   10.00
WILLSON,CLAIR E-Mimes & Miners-Tucson-1935-Bul #1-wrps-
  207p-illus-8vo   (5g0) 5.   (5h5)   8.00
WILLSON,MARCIUS-Amer History-NY-1847-672p-cl-1st ed
        (5ss5,wtrstnd) 10.   (5L1)   20.00
--same-NY-1851-cl-253p   (4b0,rbnd)   10.00
--First Reader of the School & Family Series-NY-(1860)-Harper-
  12mo-(84)p-cl bkd bds-illus   (5p1,wn)   6.50
--School & Family Primer-NY-(c1860)-Harper-12mo-48p-illus-
  cl bkd bds   (5p1,wn)   10.00
WILLSON,RUSSELL-Watch Officer's Guide-Annap-1935-12mo-
  277p-illus-lea   (5s1)   3.00
WILLYS OVERLAND CO-Overland Motor Cars New Models 69 &
  71-Toledo-n.d.(ca 1914)-4to-32p-illus-pic wrps (5xx7)   12.50
WILMER,LAMBERT A-Life,Travels & Advent of Ferdinand de Soto-
  Phila-1858-Lloyd-532p-Sartain,illus-1st ed (5h9)   28.50
--same-Phila-1859-JTLloyd-8vo-cl-Sartain,illus
        (5qq8,rbnd) 10.   (4a3)   20.00
WILMER,MARGARET E-Dumb Traitor-NY-1879-332p-cl (5h7)   7.50
WILMER,RICHARD H-The Recent Past, From a Southern Standpoint-
  NY-1900   (5j5) 7.50   (5r7)   12.50
WILSON,ADRIAN-Printing for Theater-SanFran-1957-folio-cl-
  illus-programs tipped in-ltd to 250c-pkt programs (4n5,vf) 200.00
WILSON,ALEX-American Ornithology-Phila-1808 to 14-orig roan
  & bds-folio-76 handcol plts-9 vols-1st ed-rare
        (5z9,2nd issue Vol 1,fox) 1,000.00
--same-Lond&Edinb-1832-for Chas Scribners-part mor-g.t.-8vo-
  frontis-97 handcol plts-3 vols-Jardine edition (5z9f,sl fox) 100.00
--same-wi notes by Jardine-Bost-1840-mor-g.e.-12mo-col plts-
  Brewer's ed   (5z9,rub,rprd)   45.00
--same-Lond-1876-Chatto&Windus-3 vols-8vo-hf mor-col plts
        (5ss5,rprd)   67.50
WILSON,ANNA M-A Star in a Prison-Elgin-1898-96p-illus
        (5aa0)   8.50
WILSON,ARTHUR B-Charter & Rev Ordinances...of Hannibal, Mo-
  Hannibal-1873-wrps-205p plus index-1st ed
      (4t3,lacks bk wrp) 12.50   (4t3,part lea,rub)   15.00
WILSON,MRS AUGUSTUS,ed-Parsons' Memorial & Historical
  Library Magazine-StLouis-1885-illus-409p-1st ed (4L0)   50.00
WILSON,BARBARA KER-Scottish Folk tales & Legends-Oxford-
  1954-illus-1st ed   (5yy6,dj)   4.50
WILSON,B D-The Indians of Southern Calif in 1852-Caughey,ed-
  SanMarino-1952-190p-hf cl   (5dd6)   15.00
WILSON,BF-The Negro As I Have Known Him-Nashville-
  1946-Parthenon Press   (5x2)   22.50
WILSON,C H-Education for Negroes in Mississippi Since 1910-
  Bost-1947-illus   (5x2)   20.00
WILSON,C W-Picturesque Palestine Sinai & Egypt-NY-(1881)-
  2 vols-folio-lea-illus   (5ii2)   12.50
WILSON,CAROL GREEN -Calif Yankee-Claremont-1946-184p-
  illus   (5r0,pres) 7.50   (5h5,f,dj)   5.00

WILSON,CHAS MORROW-Empire in Green & Gold-(NY,1947)-
  303p-illus   (5s7)   7.50
--Meriwether Lewis of Lewis&Clark-NY-(1934)-photos-maps-1st ed-
  scarce   (5L2)   25.00
--Roots of Amer-NY-1936-316p-photos   (5s4)   6.50
--Trees & Test Tubes-NY-(1943)-352p-illus   (5s7)   8.50
WILSON,DONALD P-My Six Convicts-NY-c1951-369p
        (5p9) 4.   (5w4)   4.50
WILSON,E-Cathedrals of France-NY-1900-208p-folio-cl
        (5m5,tn,rprd)   8.50
WILSON,E N-The White Indian Boy-NY-1919-222p-illus (5ss1)   7.50
WILSON,EARL-Pikes Peak Or Bust-NY-1946-250p   (5s4)   4.50
WILSON,EDITH BOLLING-My Memoir-Indnpla-(1939)-386p
        (5p7) 4.50   (5s9)   3.50
WILSON,EDNA EATON-The Log Cabin Cook Book-Yale,Okla-
  n.d.-wrps-44p   (5h0)   2.50
WILSON,EDMUND-The American Earthquake-NY-1958-
  Dblday Anchor-1st ed   (5ss9)   6.00
--The Amer Jitters-1932-Scribners'   (5F1)   10.00
WILSON,EDWA-Iron Men & Wooden Ships-NY-1924-Frank Shay,ed-
  folio-ltd to 200c,autg,box   (5ee9)   25.00
WILSON,ELIJAH N-Among Shoshones-SaltLkCty-(1910)-illus-
  222p-1st ed   (4L0)   85.00
--same-SaltLkCty-(1910-Skelton Publ-247p-cl-reprnt (5yy3)   15.00
WILSON,EPHRAIM A-Memoirs of the War-Cleve-1893-435p-
  illus-1st ed   (4L0)   20.00
WILSON,ERASMUS-System of Human Anatomy-Phila-1854-
  8vo-23p,576p-lea-4th Amer ed   (5t0)   10.00
WILSON,ERNEST-Amer's Greatest Garden-Bost-1925-123p-
  port-50 plts   (5s7)   7.50
--Aristocrats of the Garden-NY-1917-Dblday,Page-312p-
  ltd to 1200c   (5p7)   12.50
--China,Mother of Gardens-Bost-(1929)-cl-8vo-fldg map-61 plts-
  autg   (5w3) 28.50   (5p7) 25.   (5z9,f)   32.50
--If I Were to Make a Garden-Bost-1931 (5qq7,box) 15. (5xx7,f)10.00
--The Lilies of Eastern Asia-Lond&Bost-(1929)-lg4to-110p-
  16 plts   (5s7,f)   15.00
--Plant Hunter-Bost-1931-197p-photos   (5w3)   9.50
--Plant Hunting-Bost-1927-2 vols-128 photos-autog ed
        (5w3,ex-libr)   25.00
--Rosemary & Rue-Montr-1914-91p   (5w8,pres,sl stn)   12.00
WILSON,F-Crusader in Crinoline-Phila-1941-thk8vo-1st ed-illus
        (5x2,dj)   12.00
WILSON,F A-Annals of Nahant,Mass-Bost-1928-illus-412p
        (4m2) 15.   (5j9)   10.00
WILSON,FRANCIS-Jos Jefferson-NY-1907-354p-illus (5t7)   10.00
--Life of Himself-Bost&NY-1924-463p-illus   (5xx7)   10.00
--John Wilkes Booth-Bost&NY-1929-illus   (5s9,bkstrp tn)   5.00
WILSON,FRAZER E-Around Council Fire-Greenvl-1948-78p-
  wrps-priv prntd-scarce   (5h1)   6.50
--Arthur St Clair-Richmond-1944-253p-illus   (5h9)   8.50
WILSON,G F-Bibliography of Writings of W H Hudson-Lond-1922
        (4g2)   13.50
WILSON,G H-Gone Down the Years-Capetown-1947-Howard
  Timmins-photos-279p-2nd ed   (4t5)   8.00
WILLIAMS,GEO F-Bullet & Shell-NY-1883-454p-illus (5L3)   8.50
WILSON,GEO HERBERT-The History of the Universities' Mission to
  Central Africa-Lond-1936-photos-278p   (4t5)   12.50
WILSON,GRACE E-Robt Browning's Ports,Photos & other Likenesses
  & Their Makers-Baylor Univ-1943-8vo-196p-wrps (5t0)   7.50
WILSON,H-Business Directory of NY City-NY-1852-16mo-ads
        (5yy6)   15.00
--Trow's Directory for the Year Ending May 1,1865-NY-(1865)
        (5t9,rprd)   15.00
WILSON,H W-Ironclads in Action-Lond-1896-2 vols-78 maps,
  plans & illus   (5c1,bndg wn)   35.00
--same-Bost-1896-2 vols-8vo-maps-plans-illus-mor-1st ed (5t2) 15.00
--With the Flag to Pretoria-Lond-1900-2 vols-lg4to-illus-maps-
  4 plts-2 fldg maps   (5c6,water spot)   25.00
WILSON,HAROLD F-The Jersey Shore-NY-1953-3 vols-illus
        (5m2)   25.00
WILSON,HARRIET-Harriet Wilson or memoirs of a woman of fashion
  written by herself-NY-n.d.-(ca 1840?)-JasRameric-12mo-
  orig cl-labl-handcol frontis-v scarce   (5i0)   30.00
WILSON,HARRIETTE-Memoirs of-Lond-n.d.-Navarre Soc-2 vols-
  cl-43 ports   (5i4,sp lt fade)   40.00
WILSON,HARRY LEON-The Boss of Little Arcady-Bost-(1905)-
  Lothrop-371p-1st ed   (5x4)   15.00
--Merton of the movies-GardenCty-1922-Dblday-12mo-orig cl-
  1st ed(so stated on cpyrite pg)   (5i8)   10.00
--Zigzag Tales from the East to the West-NY-1894-12mo-cl-
  1st ed of auth's 1st book   (5gg6)   37.50

WILSON,HENRY-Surveying Improved-Lond-1769-4 parts-
555p-fldg charts-6th ed   (5t4,cov loose) 15.00
WILSON,HENRY-Account of the Pelew Islands....from Journals
of Capt...by Geo Keate-Phila-1789-Jos Crukshank-12mo-
orig calf-256p-1st Amer ed   (5ss2,crack) 45.00
WILSON,HENRY-Wonderful Characters-Lond-1830-illus-calf
                                           (5j2)   15.00
--same-NY-1934-hf calf-plts   (4j1)   15.00
WILSON,HENRY-History of Anti slavery Measures of 37th &
38th US Cong-Bost-1864-384p (5dd4) 6.50   (5t7)   10.00
--History of the Rise & Fall of Slave Power in Amer-Bost-1872-
thk8vo-3 vols   (5x2)   75.00
WILSON,HENRY LANE-Diplomatic Episodes in Mexico,Belgium
& Chile-GardenCty-1927-Dblday,Page-lg8vo-cl-scarce
                  (5p7) 5.   (4a3,hng reprd)   15.00
WILSON,HENRY LOVEJOY-Of Lunar Kingdoms-Caldwell-
1937-1st ed   (5ii3)   12.50
WILSON,HENRY R-Russian Refugee-NY-1887-Knox-610p-
1st ed   (5x4)   12.50
WILSON,HERBERT E-Lore & the Lure of Yosemite-SanFran-1922-
12mo-bds-1st ed   (5dd1,wn) 2.50 (5dd6)   7.00
--same-SanFran-(1923)-photos-133p-autg
                  (5s4,tn) 5.   (5s7,chip)   6.00
--same-LosAng-1929-135p-bds-Wolfer Prntng Co (5s7)   5.00
WILSON,HEWITT-Ceramics,Clay Technology-NY-1927-illus-
1st ed   (5L0,f)   6.50
WILSON,HILL PEEBLES-John Brown,Soldier of Fortune-Lawrence-
1913-437p plus index-photos-1st ed-priv prntd-v scarce
                                           (4L0,pres)   20.00
--same-Bost-1918-1 illus-2nd ed (5L2) 10. (5ss5,ex-libr) 13.50
WILSON,J-Pharmacopoeia Chirurgica-Phila-1818-252p-illus-
bds   (5w3,sp tn,sl wtrstnd) 40.00
WILSON,J-Personal Recoll of War of Reb-NY-1891-391p (5ii2) 7.00
WILSON,J G-Doctrine of Baptism-1871-16mo   (5L7,rbnd)   5.00
WILSON,J G-Appletons' Cyclopedia of Amer Biography-NY-
1888-6 vols   (5j4,loose) 55.00
WILSON,GEN J G-Thackeray in the US-Lond-1904-2 vols-
illus   (5q8,unopnd,dj) 19.50
WILSON,J ALBERT-History of Los Angeles Co-Oakland-1880-
Thompson&West-192p-4to-orig stamp cl   (5tt0,marg stns) 200.00
WILSON,JAS-The Rod & Gun-Edinb-1861-illus-468p-plts
                                           (5i3,f)   17.50
WILSON,CAPT JAS-Missionary Voyage to Southern Pac Ocean...
1796,97,98 in Ship Duff-Lond-1799-4to-395p-calf-illus-
7 fldg maps & charts-1st ed   (5ee3)   125.00
WILSON,JAS A-Life Travels & Adventures,the Greatest Fighter
Living in Texas-Austin-(1927)   (5cc5)   12.50
WILSON,JAS C-Three Wheeling Through Africa-Indnpls-1936-
Bobbs,Merrill-photos   (4t5) 5.   (4a6)   7.50
WILSON,JAS GRANT-Bryant & His Friends-NY-1886-tooled mor-
433p-4to-g.e.-1st ed-ltd to 135c,nbrd   (5p5,f bndg) 35.00
--Mem History of City of NY & Hudson River Valley-1892,1893,-
illus-5 vols   (4m2,rprd,cov wn) 50.00
WILSON,JAS HARRISON-Life & Services of Wm Farrar Smith-
Wilmington-1904-130p-t.e.g.-frontis-1st ed (5w5)   10.00
--Under the Old Flag-NY-1912-2 vols-ports-1st ed (5tt5,crayon)10.00
WILSON,JANE ADELINE-Narr of Sufferings of....During Her
Captivity among Comanche Indians-Hartf,Suppl to the Courant,
Feb 11,1854,complete issue-8p   (4n4)   200.00
WILSON,JOHN-Recreations of Christopher North-Phila-
Cary&Hart-1845-307p-(cheap ed)   (5i1)   5.00
WILSON,JOHN-Dramatic Works of-Edinb-1874-401p-ltd to 450c
                                           (5p6)   15.00
WILSON,JOHN-Importance of the Proof reader-Cambr-1901-
sm4to-orig wrps   (4c1)   15.00
WILSON,JOHN A-Adventures of Alf Wilson-Toledo-1880-cl-
237p-1st ed-rare   (4h7,sl wn) 27.50
WILSON,JOHN E-Russell Co in the War-(Russell,Ka)-1921-
170p-photos-1st ed   (5t3)   10.00
WILSON,JOHN LAIRD-Pictorial History of the Great Civil War-
Phila-1881-976p-4to-illus   (5p0)   7.50
--Story of the War-Phila-(1881)-976p-plts-pic cl-Natl Publ Co
                  (5xx7) 10.   (5s9)   7.50
WILSON,JOHN LYDE-Cupid & Psyche-Charleston,SC-1842-
mor-2 col plts   (5m1,pres)   40.00
WILSON,JOS-Naval Hygiene wi Appendix-Wash-1870-GPO-8vo-
orig hf mor-234p-5 plts(4 col)   (5ss2,cov spots) 15.00
WILSON,L A,ed-Facts About Dallas-Dallas-1911-obl 4to-wrps-
99p-illus   (5a8,chip)   28.50
WILSON,L M-10 Generations from Wm & Mary Dyer-1949-70p-
charts   (5m2)   22.50
WILSON,LOLLIE CAVE-Hard to forget,The Young O Henry-
LosAng-1939   (5a8)   10.00

WILSON,LOU-Meals on Wheels-NY-(1937)-168p (5c0)   3.00
WILSON,LOUIS NG-Stanley Hall,a Sketch-NY-1914-Stechert-
8vo-144p-frontis-7 plts   (5p1)   20.00
WILSON,M C C-John Gibson of Cambridge,Mass & Desc-1900-
542p   (4t2,wn)   28.50
WILSON,MARIAN C-Manuelita,story of San Xavier Del Bac-NY-
Chig-(1891)-US Book-1st ed   (5m2)   10.00
WILSON,MRS MARY A-Mrs Wilson's Cook Book-Phila-(1920)-
502p   (5c0) 6.50 (5c9)   7.50
WILSON,MONA-The Life of Wm Blake-Lond-1927-Nonesuch Pr-
lg4to-illus-397p   (5m1)   30.00
WILSON,NEILL C-Silver Stampede-1937-Macmillan-1st ed
                                           (5x5,f,dj)   20.00
--Southern Pacific-NY-(1952)-266p-illus   (5xx5)   10.00
--Treasure Express-NY-1936-334p-illus-1st ed (5r8,5L2) 12.50
--same-(1936)-3rd printing   (4L0,dj)   8.00
WILSON,P W-Wm Pitt,the Younger-1933   (5L7)   4.00
WILSON,PETER M-Southern Exposure-Univ of NC Pr-1927 (5x5) 15.00
WILSON,R D-Jim Crow Joins Up-NY-1945   (5x2)   25.00
WILSON,RICHARD-35 Sketches & Designs-Lond-1863-35 plts-
4to   (4a2,sp torn) 10.00
WILSON,RICHARD L-Short Ravelings from a Long Yarn-SantaAna-
1936   (5h5,f)   27.50
WILSON,SIR ROBT-Narr of Events during Invasion of Russia by
Napoleon Bonaparte & Retreat of French Army 1812-Lond-1860-
fldg map-t.sp   (5d2,f bndg) 15.00
WILSON,ROBT-Treatise on Steam Boilers-Lond-1879-328p-
fldg chart   (5t4)   5.00
WILSON,ROBT-Half Forgotten By ways of the Old South-Columbia-
1928-321p   (5j6)   4.50
WILSON,ROBT A-Mexico & Its Religion etc-NY-1855-cl
                                           (5a8,sl wn) 18.50
--Mexico,Its Peasants & Its Priests-NY-1856-c1855-new ed
                                           (4h6,hng rprd) 17.50
--New History of Conquest of Mexico-Phila-1859-Challen
                                           (4d9,sp fade) 15.00
WILSON,ROBT F-How to Wine & Dine in Paris-Indnpls-(1930)-
122p   (5g9)   3.50
WILSON,ROBT THOS-Brief remarks on character & composition
of Russian army & a sketch of campaigns in Poland in years
1806&1807-Lond-1810-CRoworth-4to-hf calf-8 handcol maps
(3 fldg)-1st ed   (5i8)   30.00
--History of the British Exped to Egypt-Lond-1803-Roworth-
calf-port-fldg map & plans-2 vols-4th ed   (5v7)   48.50
WILSON,RUFUS ROCKWELL-Historic Long Island-NY-1902-
Berkeley Pr-364p   (5x0)   10.00
--Lincoln in Caricature-NY-1953-4to   (5q8,5t4)   5.00
--same-NY-1935-Pr of Pioneers-ltd to 650c,nbrd,autg (5r0) 17.50
--New England in Letters-NY-1904-384p-1st ed (5ee3)   3.50
--Out of the West-NY-1933-illus-1st ed-Pr of Pioneers-464p
(5yy6,dj) 17.50 (5m9,f,tn dj) 20. (5x5,dj)   30.00
--same-NY-1936-revised (5x5) 17.50 (5m9,sp tn) 7.50 (5dd1,dj) 8.50
--same-NY-1936-ltd to 300c,autg   (5s4)   15.00
--Rambles in Colonial Byways-Phila-1901-2 vols-illus (5r7) 10.00
WILSON,S F-History of the Amer Revolution-Balt-1843-
N Hickman-bds-lea sp-frontis-372,36p-5th ed
                                           (4h8,wn,cov dtchd,ex-libr) 50.00
WILSON,SAML P-Chicago & Its Cess Pools of Infamy-Chig-(1910)-
223p-cl-5th ed   (5h1)   3.50
--Chicago By Gaslight-n.p.-n.d.-(ca1910)-bds-123p (4h7) 5.00
WILSON,SARAH-So African Memories-Lond-1909-12&331p-
19 plts   (5c6)   11.50
WILSON,SARAH A-Visit to Gove Cottage for Entertainment &
Instr of Children-Lond-Harris&Son-1823-sm8vo-156p-5 illus-
1st ed   (5a1,rub)   12.50
WILSON,T L-Sufferings Endured for a Free Government-Wash-
1864-priv prntd   (5x2)   17.50
WILSON,THOS-Arrowpoints,Spearheads & Knives of Prehistoric
Times-extract-(Wash,1897)-Rpt of US Nat'l Mus for 1897-
p815 to 988 plus index-65 plts&figures-lea
                                           (5L2,libr of F E Hodge) 15.00
--Prehistoric Art-(Wash,1896)-extract Nat'l Mus for 1896-
p325 to 664-illus   (4L0,ex-libr) 10.00
--The Swastika-Wash-1896-(254p)-illus-map-Smi Inst pub (5w4) 12.50
WILSON,WM-A Manual of Instruction for Infants' Schools-NY-
1830-Carvill-222p-bds&cl-frontis   (5t7,sp wn) 15.00
WILSON,WM B-Acts & Actors in the Civil War-Phila-1892-114p
                                           (5L3,f)   7.50
WILSON,WM E-Abe Lincoln of Pigeon Creek-NY-(1949)-288p
                                           (5t4)   4.00
WILSON,WM RAE-Travels in Russia-Lond-1828-Longman,etc-2 vols-
8vo-calf-frontis-4 tint plts-1st ed   (5i8)   50.00

WILSON,WOODROW-Case for the League of Nations-Foley,ed-
Princeton Univ Pr-1923-288p   (5L7,dj) 5.   (5p7)   4.75
--Congressional Government-NY-1885-12mo-cl-1st ed of
auth's 1st book   (5gg6,f)   25.00
--same-Bost-(1913)-Houghton,Miff-344p   (5p7)   3.00
--Constitutional Government in the US-NY-1908-Columbia Univ Pr-
236p   (5x0)   4.00
--Division & Reunion, 1829 to 1889-NY-1893-Maps-1st ed
              (5q8,marks)   3.00
--George Washington-NY-1897-illus-1st ed   (5tt5)   10.00
--same-NY-(1924)-illus by Howard Pyle   (5q8)   3.75
--A History of the Amer People-NY-1902-5 vols-ports-maps-
1st ed(Oct 1902 on copyrte pg)   (5m2)   20.00
--same-NY-1931-5 vols-imit lea-ports   (5h9)   12.50
--Mere Literature & Other Essays-Bost-1896-Houghton,Miff-
1st ed   (5ss9)   22.50
--The New Freedom-NY-1913-8vo-1st ed   (5b9,4m8)   4.00
--same-NY-1914   (5x7)   5.00
--On Being Human-NY-c1916-55p-1st ed   (5w0)   5.75
--Public Papers of-NY-(1925 to 27)-6 vols in 3   (5yy6)   12.50
--The State & Federal Governments of the US-Bost-1889-1st separate
ed   (4m8)   4.00
--The State,Elements of Historical & Practical Politics-Bost-
1901-rev ed   (4b7)   7.50
--When a Man Comes to Himself-NY-1915-12mo-cl-1st ed (5dd8)10.00
--Why We Are at War-NY-(1917)-Harper-(1),(4),(79)p
        (5mm8) 6.   (5w0)   5.00
WILSON'S BUSINESS DIRECTORY-NY City,(1855)-1855-420p-
(fldg map laid in)   (5t9)   7.50
WILSON'S ILLUSTRATED TUIDE-to the Hudson River-NY-1849-
24mo-prntd wrps-fldg map-5th ed   (5g8,tn)   5.00
--same-NY-1852-cl-12th ed   (5g8)   5.00
--same-NY-1853-cl   (5g8)   5.00
WILSON'S TALES OF THE BORDERS-& of Scotland-Edinb-
n.d.(1857)-WmNimmo-rev by Leighton-12 vols-lea labls-
calf-raised bands   (5p6,f bndg)   48.00
WILSTACH,FRANK-A Dictionary of Similes-Bost-1916-488p (5j4) 4.00
--same-Bost-1917-cl-488p-8vo   (5t0)   5.00
--same-1924-570p-enlrgd ed   (5j4)   6.00
--Wild Bill Hickok-GardenCty-1926-304p-photos-1st ed
      (5L0,lacks e.p.) 8.50 (5m2)   15.00
--same-GardenCty-(1926)-reprint   (5L0)   4.00
WILSTACH,PAUL-Corres of John Adams & Thos Jefferson-Indnpls-
(1925)-8vo-1st ed   (5ss5)   5.00
--Hudson River Landings-Indnpls-(1933)-311p-illus   (5t4)   8.50
--same-Indnpls-1933-1st ed-ltd ed,autg,box   (5q8)   7.50
--Jefferson & Monticello-GardenCty-1928-8vo-cl-262p-Dblday-
g.t.-2nd ed,rev   (5j5)   6.00
--Mount Vernon,Washington's Home-NY-1916-Dblday,Page-
301p-illus   (5p9) 5.   (5h9)   7.50
--same-Indnpls-(1930)-Bobbs,Merrill-8vo-cl-illus-301p
      (5h9) 6.   (5t9) 10.   (5j5)   7.50
--Patriots off their Pedestals-Indnpls-(1927)-241p (5ee3,f,dj) 5.00
--Potomac Landings-NY-1921-376p-illus-fldg map-Dblday,Page-
(1640c prntd)-1st ed   (5h9)   32.50
--same-Indnpls-1932-Bobbs,Merrill-378p-illus-fldg map (5h9) 12.50
--Richard Mansfield-The Man & the Actor-NY-1908-500p-illus
      (5d2,mor,f bndg) 15.   (5t4)   10.00
--Tidewater Virginia-Indnpls-(1929)-Bobbs,Merrill-lg8vo-cl-
illus-326p   (5j5) 15.   (5h9)   8.50
--same-Tidewater Maryland-Indnpls-(1931)-lg8vo-cl-illus-
383p   (5j5) 15.   (5h9)   10.00
WILTSEE,ERNEST A-The Jos W Gregory Express 1850 to 1853-
Federalsburg-1937-29p-orig stiff wrps-Amer Philatelist Handbook,
ltd to 200c,nbrd   (5m3,pres)   20.00
--The Truth About Fremont,An Inquiry-SanFran-1936-JnHenryNash-
sm4to-54p   (5F5,pres,soil,stnd) 12.50   (5n4)   45.00
WIMER,J-Events in Indian History-Lancaster-1841-633p-fldg engr-
calf   (5ii2,sl tn)   27.50
WIMODAUSIS CLUB COOK BOOK-Tor-1922-256p (5c5)   5.00
WINANS,GEO W-1st Presby Church of Jamaica,NY-Jamaica
on LI-1943-12mo-cl-248p-ltd to 600c   (4t1)   7.50
WINANS,WALTER-The Art of Revolver Shooting-NY-1911-sm4to-
illus-cl-335p   (5t2)   10.00
--Automatic Pistol Shooting-NY-1915-16mo-134p-illus (5xx7) 8.50
--Hints on Revolver Shooting-NY-1904-16mo-130p-illus (5xx7) 8.50
--The Sporting Rifle-NY-1908-217p-illus   (5t4)   16.50
WINANT,CORNELIUS-Soldier's Manuscript-n.p.-1929-priv prnt-
12mo-cl-hf mor   (4c1)   10.00
WINANT,JOHN GILBERT-Letter from Grosvenor Square-Bost-
1947   (5e7) 5.   (5x7) 4.   (5q8)   3.50
WINCH,FRANK-Thrilling Lives of Buffalo Bill & Pawnee Bill-
(NY,1911)-1st ed-rare-cl   (4L0)   20.00

WINCH,FRANK   (continued)
--same-(NY,1911)-3rd ed-224p   (4n9,f)   7.50
WINCHELL,ALEX-Preadamites-Chig-1888-illus (5x2)   20.00
WINCHELL,LILBOURNE A-History of Fresno Co & San Joaquin
Valley-Fresno-c1933-A W Cawston-4to-cl-323p,(100+)
     (4t1) 50.   (5hh4)   27.50
WINCHELL,N H-The aborigines of Minnesota-StPaul-1911-
743p plus index-photos-illus-maps(some fldg)-3/4 lea (5L0) 35.00
--Geology of Minnesota,Final Report-Minnpls-1884 to 1900-maps-
illus-4to-5 vols in 6   (4g6)   **35.00**
--History of Upper Mississippi Valley,Containing Geology of Upper
Mississippi & StLouis Valleys-Minn Hist Co-1881-3/4 lea
     (5t2,lacks e.p.) 12.50   (5x5)   35.00
WINCHESTER,ALICE-Antiques Anniv Book-NY-1916-4to-bds-
165p-illus-Antiques Mag Staff   (5t7)   8.50
--Living with Antiques-NY-(1941)-McBride-illus-153p-4to (5x0) 5.00
WINCHESTER,B-History of the Priesthood-Phila-1843-168p-
1st ed-rare   (5t3)   100.00
WINCHESTER,CLARENCE,ed-Shipping Wonders of the World-Lond-
1936,37-2 vols-30 col plts   (5c1)   25.00
WINCHESTER,MOLLIE C-Oft Told Tales of Lincoln-Chig-(1928)-
190o-cl   (5h7)   5.00
WINCHESTER REPEATING ARMS CO-World Standard Guns &
Ammunition-1932-trade catalog-illus-8vo-127p-wrps (4a6) 7.50
WINCHESTER REPEATING ARMS CO-Snap Shooting by "Ad"
Topperwein-NewHav-1939-8vo-16p-wrps   (4a6)   7.50
WINCHESTER'S-Repeating Fire Arms,Rifled Muskets,Carbines,
& Target Rifles,etc-NewHav-1875-64p-illus-orig illus wrps,
rear with view of plant   (5h8,f)   32.50
WIND ALONG THE WASTE-Oxf-1902-4to-Daniel Pr-orig blu wrps-
ltd to 130c   (5ee9)   50.00
WINDHAM MINING & SMELTING CO-Prospectus of-NewHav-
1881-wrps-8p(Ouray Co,Colo)   (5r5) 35.   (5i9)   22.50
WINDLE,B-The Wessex of Thos Hardy-Lond-1906-illus (5mm2) 5.00
WINDLE,M-Truth & Fancy-Phila-1850-303p-1st ed
     (5ii2) 9.50   (5m1)   7.50
--Life at White Sulphur Springs-Phila-1857-12mo-hf lea-323p
         (5m8,rub)   7.00
WINDLER,BERNARD-Sailing Ships & Barges of Western Mediterranean
& Adriatic Sea-Lond-1926-17 col plts-ltd to 450c (5c1,vf) 40.00
WINDOM,WM OF MINNESOTA-Speech of-NP Rwy-Wash-1869-
60p-wrps   (5h2)   15.00
WINDSOR,DUCHESS OF-Some favorite Southern Recipes of the-
NY-1942-port-180p   (5c0)   5.00
--same-NY-(1952)-180p   (5g9)   3.00
WINECRAFT-Lond-1935-182p-frontis-8 maps   (5w1)   6.50
WINES,E C-2 Years & a Half in the Amer Navy-Lond-1833-2 vols-
hf calf   (5ee3)   25.00
WINES,ENOCH COBB-State of Prisons & of Child Saving Institutions
in the Civilized World-Cambr-1880-708p-orig cl (5m3) 27.50
WINES,FREDC H-Liquor Problem in Its Legislative Aspects-
Bost-1897-342p-cl   (5h7)   10.00
--same-Bost-1899   (5w1)   6.50
WINES OF THE WORLD-Pocket Library-Lond-1949 to 51-
ASimon,ed-8 vols-15p ea-bds-box   (5w1)   10.00
WINFIELD,ARTHUR M-The Rover Boys Series-Grosset&Dunlap-
15 vols   (5ii3,djs)   75.00
WINFIELD,CHAS H-Block House by Bull's Ferry-NY-1904-illus-
map-ltd ed   (4a1)   15.00
--History of Co of Hudson,NJ-NY-1874-1st ed-illus-568p-cl
       (5i3,rbnd)   17.50
WINFREY,DORMAN-Indian Papers of Tex & the SW-Austin-
1966-5 vols-o.p.   (4j7)   75.00
WING,DONALD-Short Title Catalog of Books Printed in Engl,
Scotland,Ireland,Wales & Brit Amer & etc-NY-1945 to 51-
3 vols-scarce   (4j0)   225.00
WING,FRANK-The Fambly Album-Chig-(1917)-drawings-orig bds-
1st ed   (4m8,rub)   5.00
WING,FRANK L-Book of complete info about Pianos-NY-(1904)-
illus-158p-col plts-6th ed   (5t4,cor dmgd)   10.00
--same-NY-1897-in 2 parts-120p-illus-Wing&Son (4g3,vf) 20.00
WING,JACK-The great Union Stock Yards of Chicago-Chig-
1866-8vo-frontis-32p-(10 advts)-rev ed   (5g8)   25.00
WING,JOS E-In Foreign Fields-Chig-1913-549p-photos-map-
1st ed   (4L0,fleck)   6.50
--Sheep Farming in America-Chig-1912-Breeder's Gazette-
new,enlrg (3rd) ed-illus-368p   (4b3,vg)   15.00
WING,VINCENT-Astronomia Instaurata,...In 4 Parts-Lond-1656-
Leybourn,prntr-folio-calf-1st ed (4h0,vg,rprd)   125.00
WINGATE,C E L-Hist of Wingate Family in Engl & Amer-1886-
293p   (5t9)   20.00

WINGATE, EDMOND-Mr Wingate's Arithmetick-Lond-1694-
16mo-544p-lea-9th ed, enlrgd by Dersey
(5p1, lea wn, crude rpr)   50.00
WINGATE, GEO W-Through the Yellowstone Park on Horseback-
NY-1886-251p-pkt map   (5w5, stnd) 6.   (4L0)   10.00
WINGERT, PAUL S-Amer Indian Sculpture-NY-1949-Augustin-144p-
plts   (4a0) 25.   (5ww3)   22.50
WINGET, DAN-Anecdotes of "Buffalo Bill" That Have Never
Appeared in Print-Chig-1927-230p-cl   (5h1, dj)   12.50
WINGFIELD, LEWIS-Notes on Civil Costume in England-Lond-
1884-4to-illus in col   (5j2)   25.00
--same-Lond-n.d. (ca 1885)-24p col illus-34p text-cl-v.e.g.
(5t0)   7.50
WINGRAVE, M M-The May Blossom-NY-(c1880)-Armstrong&Co-
pict bds-prntd in col by Bros Dalziel   (5c8)   25.00
WINGS & STINGS-a Tale for Young People-Lond, etc-1872-Nelson-
159p-by ALOE (C M Tucker)   (4F8)   6.50
WINKELMAN, BARNIE F-John G Johnson, lawyer & art collector-
Phila-1942-Univ of Penna Pr-327p   (5w4) 5.   (5u3)   5.50
--Ten Years of Wall Street-Phila-(1932)-Winston-381p (5qq8)   4.50
WINKLER, E W-Check List of Texas Imprints, 1846 to 1860-Austin-
1949   (5n4)   12.50
--Journal of Secession Convention of Texas, 1861-Austin-1912-
469p   (5n4)   20.00
--Manuscript Letters & Documents of Early Texians 1821 to 45-
Austin-(1937)-Steck Co-4to   (5x5)   37.50
WINKLER, JOHN K-The duPont Dynasty-NY-1935-342p (5y2)   5.50
--Morgan the Magnificent-NY-1930-port   (5m2)   5.00
--Tobacco Tycoon-NY-1941-RandomHse-lg8vo-cl-illus-1st ed-
scarce   (5p5)   12.50
--W R Hearst, An Amer Phenomenon-NY-1928-354p-illus-cl-
1st ed   (5t2)   3.00
WINKLES, The, or Merry Monomaniacs-NY-1855-Appleton-424p-
1st ed   (5x4, sp wn)   15.00
WINN-SMITH, ALICE B-Thrifty Cooking for Wartime-NY-1942-
147p   (5c9)   2.50
WINNEBAGO CO SUMMIT COOK BOOK-ForestCty-1908-
28p-narr8vo-wrps   (5g9)   4.50
WINNIPEG'S EARLY DAYS-Winnipeg-1927-59p-W J Healy-
12 col prints   (5ww4, cov wn)   5.00
WINNIPESAUKEE-& about there-Bost-1886-illus-pict wrps-
2 fldg maps-Boston&Lowell RR   (5g3)   7.50
WINSER, HENRY J-The Great NW, a Guide Book...NoPac RR,
Oreg Rwy&Navig Co etc-NY-1883-pkt map- 276p
(5dd1, 5F5)   17.50
--The Yellowstone Natl Park, a Manual for Tourists-NY-1883-
fldg map-wrps-96p   (4L0, wrp tn)   8.50
WINSHIP, GEO P-Cambridge Press 1638 to 92-Phila-1945-facs-
394p-1st ed   (4g2)   15.00
--Dan'l Berkeley Updike & the Merrymount Press-Rochester-1947-
cl-illus-8vo   (4n5)   7.50
--John Carter Brown Library-Prov-1914-illus-8vo-bds (4c1)   10.00
--The Merrymount Press of Boston-Vienna-1929-hf cl-lea labl-
8vo-60p of illus-deLuxe ed-ltd to 350c   (4n5)   75.00
--Printing Press in SoAmer-Prov-1912-wrps-13p-16mo (4c1)   12.50
--Wilberforce Eames, Bookman-NY-n.d.-4to-wrps   (4c1)   5.00
WINSHIP, GEO PARKER-Coronado Expedition 1540 to 42-Wash-
1896-illus-maps-R8vo   (5dd4, hng broke)   26.00
--The Eliot Indian Tracts-Cambr-1925-wrps-reprntd (5g4) 3. (5L0)   5.00
--Journey of Francisco Vazquez de Coronado-SanFran-1933-
Grabhorn Pr-   illus-R8vo-ltd to 550c
(5r8) 40.   (5b0, dj)   95.00
WINSLOW, ANNA GREEN-Diary of-Bost-1894-Alice Earle, ed-
121p-illus   (5w4, wn)   5.00
WINSLOW, CHAS FREDK-The Cooling Globe-Bost-1865-8vo-
63p   (5L1)   30.00
WINSLOW, HELEN M-Concerning Cats-Bost-(1900)-284p-illus-
cl-1st ed   (5t0)   4.50
WINSLOW, K-Big Pan out-Lond-1952-illus-map-248p-1st ed
(5dd7)   6.00
--same-Lond-1953-248p-plts (5a1, autog) 6.50   (4b9)   6.00
WINSLOW, MIRON-Memoir of Mrs Harriet L Winslow-NY-(1840)-
479p-cl   (5h1)   7.50
WINSON, J W-Wildwood Trails-Vanc-1946-illus-204p
(4a8, 5dd7)   4.50
WINSOR, JUSTIN-Cartier to Frontenac-Bost-1894-379p-illus-
maps-1st ed-t.e.g.   (5w5, wn)   17.50
--Christopher Columbus-Bost-1892-674p-illus-maps-g.t.(5h9, rub)   6.00
--Kohl Collection of maps relating to Amer-Wash-1904-189p
(5j4)   17.50
--Memorial Hist of Bost-Bost-1882, 1881-4 vols-4to-illus-maps-
autogs   (5ii2, autgs) 24.50   (5t9)   20.00

WINSOR, JUSTIN   (continued)
--Mississippi Basin-Bost-1895-484p-cl (5h1, sp wn) 10. (5ee3)   17.50
--Narr & Critical History of Amer-Bost-1889-Houghton, Miff-
8 vols   (5m4, f) 95.   (4b7, sl rub) 87.50
(5ss5, sp tn) 62.50   (5x5, 5w5, 5y0, f, 5qq8, f)   75.00
--Rival Claimants for NoAmer-Worcester-1895-21p-3/4 mor
(4b6)   10.00
--Westward Movement-Bost-(1897)-595p-illus-maps-g.t.-scarce
(5s4, sp sl tn)   12.50
WINSOR, KATHLEEN-Forever Amber-NY-1944-8vo-cl-1st ed
of auth's 1st book   (5gg6, dj)   10.00
WINSOR, M-History of Jewell Co, Kansas-facs of JewellCty, Ka,
1878 ed-(Mankato, Ka)-36 dbl col pg plus ads-wrps
(5L0, mint)   15.00
--Jewell County-(Topeka)-1928-wrps   (4a5) 5.   (5t3)   2.50
WINSTON, R W-It's A Far Cry-NY-1937-illus   (5x2)   7.50
WINSTON, ROBT-USN Aircraft Carrier-NY-1942-4to-88p-
photos   (5s1, ex-libr, pres)   6.00
WINSTON, ROBT W-Robt E Lee, a Biog-NY-1934-428p-illus-maps
(5mm8)   5.00
WINTEMBERG, W J-Roebuck Prehistoric Village Site-Ottawa-
1936-Nat Mus of Can, Bul 83-prntd wrps-178p-plts-fldg amps
(5u6)   6.50
WINTER, ELLA, ed-Letters of Lincoln Steffens-NY-(1938)-
Harcourt, Brace-2 vols-1st ed   (4p1)   35.00
WINTER, GEO-Journals & Indian Paintings of....1837 to 1839-
Indnpls-1948-30 plts(24 col)-208p-4to
(4a9) 35.   (4p8, 4m6, mint) 20.   (5hh4, f)   22.50
WINTER IN THE WEST-NY-1835-Harper-1st ed-2 vols-8vo-
mor(ChasF Hoffman)-auth's 1st book
(5n1, pres, box) 125.   (5gg6, vf)   75.00
WINTER JOURNEY, A-To the Western Islands, Madeira etc-
(Phila)-1909-8vo-illus-1st ed   (5m6, ex-libr)   7.50
WINTER, NEVIN-Hist of NW Ohio-Chig-1917-3 vols-3/4 lea
(5h1)   40.00
--Texas, the Marvelous-Bost-1916-343p-illus-fldg map-1st ed
(5w5) 12.   (5i3)   12.50
WINTER, WM-Life & Art of Edwin Booth-NY-1893-illus-308p
(5qq7, memo tip in) 10.   (5t2)   5.00
--Life & Art of Jos Jefferson-NY-1894-1st ed (5qq7, memo tip in)10.00
--Life & Art of Richard Mansfield-NY-1910-2 vols-lg8vo-1st ed
(5mm2)   7.50
--Old Friends-NY-1909-407p-illus-1st ed   (5ee3)   6.00
--Other days-NY-1908-389p-illus   (5t4)   4.50
--Poems-Bost-1855-12mo-cl-1st ed of auth's 1st book
(5gg6, pres)   37.50
WINTERBOTHAM, W-Hist, Geogr, Commercial, & Philo View of the
US of Amer & etc-NY-1796-Reid-illus-calf-4 vols
(5qq8, hngs broken, lacks atlas)   25.00
--same-of the Chinese Empire-Phila-1796-cl-1st Amer ed
(5p5, rbnd)   45.00
WINTERBURN, JOS & CO-Report of Board of Engineers for Pac
Coast on advantages of Yaquinna Bay as site for harbor of
refuge-SanFran-1879-8vo-orig wrps   (5i9)   15.00
WINTERFIELD, CAPT-Voyages, Distresses & Adventures of, written
by himself-Lond-1802-38p-wrps   (5r6)   15.00
WINTERICH, JOHN T-Another day, another dollar-Phila-1947-
Lippincott-204p   (5u3)   4.00
--Books & The Man-NY-1929-illus   (4m5, f) 15.   (5aa2)   6.50
--Collector's Choice-NY-(1928)-8vo-cl (5p9, sl stn) 4.50 (5d3)   7.50
--Early Amer Books & Printing-Bost-1935-8vo-cl-258p-12 illus-
Riverside Pr-ltd to 300c, autg   (5d3) 25.   (5tt9, f)   22.50
--same-trade edition   (5d3)   5.00
--Primer of Book Collecting-NY-(1926)-Greenberg-200p-2nd prntg
(5e8)   2.50
--same-NY-1927-206p-cl   (5h7)   4.00
--same-1935-265p-12mo-rev&enlrgd   (5ww3)   6.50
WINTERS, ERASTUS-In the 50th Serving Uncle Sam-n.p.-n.d.-
(EWalnut Hills-ca 1905)-188p-cl-scarce   (5h7)   40.00
WINTERS, YVOR-The Proof-NY-1930-12mo-dec bds-1st ed
(5ss7, f, dj)   12.50
--Primitivism & Decadence-NY-(1937)-8vo-cl-146p-1st ed
(5t0, dj)   6.00
WINTHER, OSCAR O-The Great NW, a history-NY-1947-illus-
1st ed-maps   (5r8)   10.00
--Express & Stagecoach Days in Calif-(1936)-Stanford Univ Pr
(5x5, dj, stnd)   5.00
--Old Oregon Country-Blmntn-1950-Ind Univ Soc Sci Ser #7-
348p-plts-wrps   (5a1)   12.50
--Via Western Express & Stagecoach-1945-Stanford U Pr-illus-
cl-158p   (4p7, dj)   7.50

WINTHROP,JOHN-History of New England from 1630 to 1649-
Bost-1825-2 vols-enlrdg 2nd ed-port-hf calf-errata slip
(5i3,sl crack,5m3,ex-libr) 27.50
--Journal of Transactions & Occur in Settlement of Mass-
Hartf-1790-EBabcock-calf-1st ed (5qq8) 100. (5L3,rprd) 90.00
WINTHROP,ROBT C-Life & Letters of John Winthrop-Bost-1864-
452p (5w9,edge wn) 12.50
--Speech on Annexation of Texas-Wash-1845-16p (4a5) 12.50
WINTHROP,THEODORE-Canoe & Saddle-NY-(1862)-375p-
wrps (5s4,cov tn,soil,shake) 4.00
--The Canoe & the Saddle-Bost-1863-375p-16mo
(5a8) 12.50 (5r6) 17. (5L3,f) 17.50 (5s4,bkstrp tn,soil) 13.50
--same-Bost-1864-375p-7th ed (5dd1) 5.00
--same-Bost-1866-375p (5ee3) 7.50
--same-Bost-1871-375p (5w9,sp sl wn) 8.50
--same-NY-1876-375p (4b9,ex-libr) 6.00
--same-Tacoma-1913-hf vel-16 col plts-g.t.-ports
(5s6,editor's pres) 25. (5dd9) 16.50 (5ee3) 17.50
--same-NY-n.d.(ca 1900)-375p (4L0) 5.00
--Edwin Brothertoft-Bost-1862-1st ed (5ee3) 5.00
--John Brent-Bost-1862-359p-1st ed-orig cl (4a5,vg) 60.00
--Life in the Open Air-Bost-1863-mor-4½ x 7"
(5ee3,edge wn) 5. (5d2,f bndg) 20.00
WINTON,JOHN S-Model Factory in a Model City-(NY)-1887-
4to-orig wrps-illus-16p-1st ed (5m6) 15.00
WINTON,W M-Geology of Tarrant County-Austin-1919-fldg map
(4a5) 5.50
WINWAR,FRANCES-The Romantic Rebels-Bost-1935-Little-
507p-illus (5x0) 6.00
WIRKUS,FAUSTIN-White Kings of La Gonave-NY-(1931)-8vo-
333p-photos (4a6) 3.50
WIRT,MRS E W-Flora's Dictionary-Balt-(1855)-LucasBros-
133p,96p-4to-56 col plts-lea (5x0) 85.00
WIRT,LOYAL L-Alaskan Adventures-NY-(1937)-124p-illus
(5ss1,pres) 7.50
WIRT,WM-Letters of the British Spy-NY-1832-Harper-10th ed-
ads-frontis-260p (5qq8,fade) 5.00
--same-NY-1856-Harper-260p-10th ed (5u3) 5.50
--Life of Patrick Henry-Phila-1836-frontis-orig cl-port-468p-
revsd (5h9,rub) 10.00
--Sketches of Life & Character of Patrick Henry-Phila-1817-
Webster-8vo-orig bds-port-1st ed (5n2,cov dtchd,box) 90.00
--same-Phila-1818-Webster-frontis-calf-3rd ed (5qq8) 7.50
--same-NY-1833-443p,19p-port-calf
(5L7,crack,rbk) 6.50 (5i3,f) 17.50
--same-NY-1857-468p (5ee3) 5.00
WISC HISTORICAL SOC COLLECTIONS
--Vols 4 to 14 (5ww4)ea 10.00
--Vols 14 to 20 (5ww4)ea 10.00
--Vol 8-Madison-1876 (5m8,cov wn) 10.00
--Vols 1 to 19-Madison-1903 to 1910-cl (5g4) 50.00
WISC STATE HIST SOC-2nd Annual Rpt & Collections of-Madison-
1856-548p-wrps (5h2) 12.50
WISC HISTORICAL SOC DOMESDAY BOOKS-ed by Jos Schafer-
1922,1937,1927,1932 (5ww4)ea 10.00
WISCONSIN-US Biographical Dictionary & Port Gallery-
Chig-1877-698p-calf-folio-g.e. (4L0,hng rprd) 25. (5n4) 45.00
WISC WILD FLOWERS-n.p.-(1927)-Milwkee Journal Publ Serv
Bur-122p-illus-8vo-pict wrps (5s7) 3.00
WISDOM IN MINIATURE-NY-1824-48mo-orig bds-lea bk-206p-
MDay's 2nd ed (5a3,sl wn) 20.00
WISE,DAN'L-Summer Days on the Hudson-NY-1876-Nelson&
Phillips-288p-pict cl-109 wdcuts-juvenile-1st ed (5j5) 22.50
--The Young Lady's Counsellor-NY-1852-251p-12mo (5w7,fox) 5.00
WISE,DEWITT D-Baker's Island Now & Then-Salem-1940-174p-
illus (5p7) 5.00
WISE ENCYCLOPEDIA OF COOKERY-NY-1953-1329p-32 col plts
(5g9) 10.00
WISE GARDEN ENCYCLOPEDIA-NY-1951-WmHWise-Seymour,ed-
1380p-illus (5p7) 6.00
WISE,GEO-Campaigns & Battles of Army of Northern Virg-NY-
1916-1st ed (5m2) 25.00
WISE,HENRY A-Capt Brand of the "Centipede"-NY-1864-R8vo-
orig pict cl-illus-1st ed (5mm2) 15.00
--Los Gringos-NY-1849-12mo-468p-1st ed
(4g6,sp tn) 12.50 (5dd6) 30.00
--same-Lond-1849-12mo-cl-406p-1st Engl ed (5F5,sp tn) 15.00
--Seven Decades of Union-Phila-1881-illus-frontis-sheep-lea
labls (4b6,sl wn) 20.00
WISE,HERBERT C-Colonial Architecture for Those About to Build-
Phila-1924-207 illus-t8vo (5ss5) 20.00
WISE,ISAAC M-Reminiscences-Cinn-1901-367p-cl (5ff7) 10.00

WISE,J C-Col John Wise of England & Va,His Anc & Desc-
(1918)-355p (5t9) 25.00
WISE,JENNINGS CROPPER-Long Arm of Lee-Lynchburg-1915-
Bell-2 vols-illus (5a0) 30. (5mm8) 27.50
--Red Man in the New World Drama-Wash-(1931)-628p-illus-
1st ed-errata slip (5dd9) 12. (4i7) 20. (5L0) 12.50
--Turn of the Tide-NY-1920-Holt-fldg map-255p(4)
(5mm8) 4. (5x7) 5.00
--Ye Kingdome of Accawmacke,or,the Eastern Shore of Virg-
Richmond-1911-406p (5yy8) 25.00
WISE,JOHN-A System of Aeronautics-Phila-1850-in 3 pts
(5zz4) 100.00
--Thru the Air-Phila-1873-650p-cl-scarce (5h2,rbnd) 25.00
WISE,JOHN S-End of An Era-Bost-(1899)-Houghton,Miff-474p-
t.e.g. (5mm8,ex-libr) 7.50 (5d2,f bndg) 15.00
--Recoll of 13 Presidents-NY-1906-illus-284p-1st ed (5ee3) 5.00
WISE,JOHN SERGEANT-Diomed,the Life,Travels & Observ of
a Dog-Bost-1897-Lamson,Wolffe-sq8vo-illus-mor-1st ed-
330p (5j5) 20.00
WISE SAWS-or Sam Slick in Search of a Wife-NY-n.d.-(ca1855)
(5mm1,sp wn) 7.50
WISE,THOS J-A Bronte Library-Lond-1929-illus-4to-ltd to 120c-
catalog (4g2) 60.00
--Biblio List of Scarcer Works & Uncollected Writings of Algernon
Chas Swinburne-Lond-1897-Priv Subscr-orig cl-ltd to 50c
(5z7,f) 75.00
--Biblio of the Writings of Jos Conrad-Lond-1921-bds-
ltd to 170c-2nd & enlrgd ed (5mm2,unopnd) 35.00
WISE,WM-Silversmith of Old NY-(NY)-(1958)-Myer Myers-180p-
illus (5t7) 5.00
WISEMAN,C M L-Centennial Hist of Lancaster,Ohio & Lancaster
People 1898-Lancaster-1898-407p-cl (5jj9) 25.00
--Pioneer Period & Pioneer People of Fairchild Co,O-Col-1901-
430p (4n9) 28.50
WISEMAN,THEO-Origin & Laws covering Tornadoes,Cyclones,
Thunder Storms & Kansas Twisters-Lawrence,Ks-1885-
Cutler's-8vo-orig prntd wrps-15p (4t9) 150.00
WISLIZENUS,A-Memoir of a Tour to NoMexico,Connected with
Col Doniphan's Exped, in 1846 & 1847-Wash-1848-3 fldg maps-
141p-1st ed (5g8,libr buck) 35. (4j7) 90.00
WISNER,BENJ B-Memoirs of the Late Mrs Susan Huntington of
Boston-Bost-1826-8vo-orig bds-port-1st ed (5m6) 12.50
WISSLER,CLARK-The Amer Indian-NY-1917-435p-illus-fldg map-
1st ed-ex scarce (5L0) 15.00
--same-NY-1922-illus-map-2nd ed (4m9) 10. (4a1) 12.50
--Costumes of the Plains Indians-NY-1915-52p-Anthro Papers-
Vol 17,Part 2 (5L2) 5.00
--Indian Cavalcade,Life on the Old Indian Reservations-NY-
(1938)-351p-20p-illus (4i7) 8. (4L0,dj) 12.50
--Indians of the US-NY-1940-306p plus index-illus-1st ed
(4L0,dj) 10.00
--Masks-1946-Amer Mus of Nat History-4to-32p-1st ed (5g6) 5.00
--Material Culture of the Blackfoot Indians-NY-1910-175p plus
7 plts-wrps-Anthro Papers Vol 5,Part 1-1st ed-scarce (5L2) 8.50
--North American Indians of the Plains-NY-1912-Amer Mus Nat
Hist-147p-illus (4i7) 10.00
WEST,BENJ O-Century of Education in Hawaii-Honolulu-(1940)-
Hawaii Educ Review (5x5) 17.50
WISTAR,CASPAR-A System of Anatomy for the Use of Students of
Medicine-Phil1-1839-2 vols-18 plts(some fldg)-calf-7th ed
(5ee3,vf) 40.00
WISTAR,ISAAC J-Autobiography of Isaac Jones Wistar,1827 to
1905-Phila-1914-2 vols-4to-illus-fldg map-orig bds-papr labls-
1st ed-ltd to 250c-v scarce (5tt6) 125. (4L0) 150.00
--same-Phila-1937-Wistar Inst-6 plts-map-528p
(4L0,f,dj) 8.50 (5m9,dj) 15. (5b0,unopnd,dj) 17.50 (5k0) 12.50
WISTER,FANNY KEMBLE,ed-Owen Wister...Out West,His
Journals & Letters-Chig-(1958)-illus (5ii3) 12.50
WISTER,FRANCIS-25 Years of the Phila Orchestra-(Phila)-c1925-
253p-illus (5w4) 4.00
WISTER,JOHN C-Bulbs for Amer Gardens-Bost-(1930)-278p-
thk8vo (4g0) 12.50
WISTER,JONES-Reminiscences-1920 (5L7) 4.50
WISTER,OWEN-Journey in Search of Christmas-NY-1904-illus by
Remington-pic cl-93p-1st ed
(5m9,f) 15. (5p6) 12.50 (5t2,vf) 20.00
--Lin McLean-NY-1898-illus-1st ed (5ee3) 7.50
--same-NY-1903-illus,Remington (4i7) 6.00
--same-1928-327p-(one of set of 4) (5r1) 6.00
--Members of the Family-NY-1911-1st ed
(5m2,autg tip in) 6. (4a5,dj) 10.00
--same-1928-283p(1 of set of 4) (5r1) 6.00
--Musk Ox,Bison,Sheep & Goat-NY-1904-284p-illus-frontis
(5ss1) 8.00

WISTER,OWEN (continued)
--The New Swiss Family Robinson-Cambr-1882-bds-illus-
 lg8vo-25p,(7)p   (4h8,rebkd,stn,chip)   75.00
--Red Men & White-1896-orig cl-Remington illus-280p-1st ed
       (5kk5) 20.   (5m2,pres)   22.50
--same-NY-1903-280p-Remington,illus   (4b2,shake)   5.00
--same-1928-345p(1 of set of 4)   (5r1)   6.00
--A Straight Deal-NY-1920-287p-1st ed   (4j0) 6.   (5w9)   5.00
--The Virginian-NY-1902-8vo-orig dec cl-illus-1st ed-
 ("Set up & electrotyped Apr 1902" on cpyrte pg)
       (5m1) 25.   (5cc9,4k6) 50.   (5v2,f)   35.00
--same-NY-1911-12mo-cl-illus papr labl-orig illus dj-
 Russell&Remington illus-1st illus ed (5gg4,dj mended) 50.00
--When West Was West-1928-449p   (5s4)   5.00
WITCHELL,CAHS-Evolution of Bird Song-Lond-(1896)253p (5t4) 7.50
WITHER,GER-Juvenilia-Lond-1622-1st ed-sm8vo-blue calf-
 a.e.g.-1st issue-ex rare   (4b1,broke)   100.00
WITHERING,WM-Systematic Arrangement of British Plants,wi
 Easy Intro-Lond-1801-8vo-calf-4 vols-4th ed-32 plts (of 35)
                                         (4e5)   85.00
WITHERS,ALEX S-Chronicles of Border Warfare-Clarksburg,Va-
 1831-Jos Israel-12mo-calf-1st ed   (4L8,4h0,rub,fox) 100.00
WITHERSPOON,HALLIDAY-Men of Illinois-Chig-1902-4to-
 photos-mor-DeLuxe ed   (5m2)   12.50
WITHINGTON,WM-Cutting to the quick,an address-Cambr
 Temperance Soc at Springvlle-Adrian,(Mich)-1838-10p-
 stitchd   (5g3)   25.00
WITHROW,O C J-Romance of Canadian Exhibition-Tor-1936-
 157p-illus   (4b9,vf)   6.00
WITHROW,W H-Barbara Heck-Cinn&NY-1895-8vo-dec cl-illus
                                         (5b2)   6.00
--Native Races of NoAmer-Tor-1895-200p-illus   (4b9)   12.00
--Popular History of Canada-Tor-1885-ports-plts-fldg maps-
 642p   (5s6)   6.50
WITMARK,I-From Ragtime to Swingtime-NY-(1939)-480p-plts
                                         (5c3)   5.00
WITSELL,WM POSTELL-A History of Christ Episc Church,Little
 Rock,Ark-n.p.-n.d.(ca 1914)-333p plus index-photos-1st ed
                                         (4L0)   6.50
WITT,ROBT C-How toLook at Pictures-Lond-1903-illus (4a1) 7.50
WITTE,O A-The Automobile Storage Battery,its Care & Repair-
 Chig-1926-523p-4th ed,rev&enlrgd   (5y2)   4.75
WITTELLE,MARVYN-Pioneer to Commuter-n.p.-c1958-
 Rotary Club,Highland Park-8vo-cl-273p   (4t1)   12.50
WITTEMANN,C & A-Aeronautical Supplies-Brklyn-n.d.(ca 1909)-
 catalog-Aeroplanes,Gliders,Models-17 leaves-pic wrps-
 Albertype Co-oblong   (4b0,brown)   85.00
WITTENBERG,PHILIP-Dangerous Words-NY-(1948)-Col Un Pr-
 335p   (5p9)   5.00
WITTKE,CARL-A History of Canada-NY-1928-8vo-maps
                                         (5w8,dmpstn)   5.00
WITWER,HARRY CHAS-From Baseball to Boches-Bost-(1918)-12mo-
 cl-1st ed of auth's 1st book   (5gg6,f)   15.00
WODEHOUSE,P G-The Pothunters-Lond-1902-12mo-cl-1st ed of
 auth's 1st book-1st state   (5gg6)   25.00
WOFFINGTON,PEG-Choice Receipts By Experienced Housewives-
 NY-1881-74p ads throut-limp cl   (5c0)   7.50
WOLCOTT,IMOGEN-The Yankee Cook Book-NY-1939 ed-398p-
 illus   (5g9)   4.50
WOLCOTT,SAM'L-Memorial of Henry Wolcott of Windsor,Conn-
 1881-439p-ltd to 300c   (5t9)   40.00
WOLCOTT,WILLIAMS-Past & Present of Eaton County-(1915?)-
 663p-illus-red lea-scarce   (5mm7,bkstrp v wn) 40.00
WOLDMAN,ALBERT A-Lincoln & the Russians-Cleve-(1952)-
 311p   (4n9,f,dj) 5.   (5t7)   6.00
WOLF,EDWIN-History of the Jews of Phila from Colonial Times
 to Age of Jackson-Phila-1957   (4m4)   12.50
--Rosenbach,a Biography-1960-1st trade ed-672p-illus-cl
       (4p9,dj,f) 25.   (5kk5,dj)   15.00
WOLF,F E-India Rubber Man-Caldwell-1939-291p-illus (5y2)   6.50
WOLF,GEO A-Blair County's First 100 Years-Altoona-1945-526p
 illus   (5w4)   12.50
WOLF,OTTO C-Breweries & Allied or Auxiliary Buildings-Phila-
 1906-obl 8vo-198p-photos   (5w1,wtrstnd) 25.00
WOLF,SIMON-The Amer Jew as Patriot,Soldier & Citizen-Phila-
 1895-8vo-576p-Louis Edw Levy,ed-1st ed (5ss5,sl cov stn) 10.00
--Presidents I Have Known   -Wash-1918-464p-1st ed (4j4,f) 5.00
WOLF,THEODORE-Geography & Geology of Ecuador-Tor-(1892)-
 684p-59 illus-2 col fldg maps-mor   (5r7,pres)   27.50
--same-Tor-(1933)-Ecuadorian Govt-4to-12 engr- fldg maps-
 684p   (4d9)   7.50
WOLFE,BERTRAM D-Diego Rivera His Life & Times-NY &Lond-
 1939-Knopf-1st ed   (5t5) 10.50 (5x5) 20. (4m9) 12.50

WOLFE,FFRIDA-How to Identify Oriental Rugs-Lond-(1931)-
 4to-cl-col plts   (5t2)   7.50
WOLFE,HAROLD-Herbert Hoover, Public Servant & Leader of
 the Loyal Opposition-NY-1956- cl-507p-1st ed (5m8,dj) 5.00
WOLFE,HUMBERT-Cursory Rhymes-Lond-1927-ErnestBennLtd-
 ltd to 500c,autg   (5ss3,dj) 20.00
--News of the Devil-Lond-1926-1st ed-ltd to 265c,autg (5j2,dj) 10.00
WOLFE,REESE-Yankee Ships-Bobbs Merrill-(1953)-287p-photos-
 1st ed   (5s1,ex-libr) 5.50   (5e8) 5.50 (5h9) 7.50
WOLFE,SAMUEL M-Helper's Impending Crisis Dissected-Phila-
 1860-223p-ads-1st ed-scarce   (5t4) 10.   (5i3)   35.00
WOLFE,THOS-From Death to Morning-NY-1935-1st ed (code A
 on copyrte pg)   (5ss7,mint,advance cpy,pres) 250.
 (5d3,dj,pres) 150. (5d3,f,dj) 15. (5ss9) 10. (5ee3)   12.50
--The Hills Beyond-NY-(1941)-1st ed-HarperBros
       (5F1,dj) 8.   (5yy6,f,dj) 18.50 (4b4) 15. (5ss9) 10.00
--Look Homeward Angel-NY-1929-Scribner emblem on cpyrte pg-
 1st ed-auth's 1st book
       (4b1,uncut) 50. (4n5,pres,cl fade) 125. (5gg6) 35.00
--same-NY-1947-Scribner's-Gorsline,illus   (5ss9,f,dj) 20.00
--Of Time & the River-NY-1935-1st ed
       (4b1,uncut,dj) 32.50 (5p7,dj) 12.50 (5d3,dj)   20.00
--Return of Buck Gavin-NY-1924-illus-Caroline Folk Plays-
 1st ed-pres from editor (5ee3,f) 50.   (4b5,sp fade) 40.00
--same-2nd issue(wiout date on title pg)   (4b5)   10.00
--The Story of a Novel-NY-1936-Scribner-1st ed
       (5p9,dj) 12.50 (5dd8,dj) 25.   (5ee3,dj)   27.50
--The Web & the Rock-NY-1939-Harper-blue cl-1st ed
       (4j0) 22.50 (5yy6,f,dj) 32.50 (5p7,dj,5ss9)   10.00
--same-Lond-1947-641p-1st Engl ed   (4j0)   12.50
--You Can't Go Home Again-NY-(1940)-Harper-8vo-orig cl-
 1st ed   (4h0,vf,dj fade) 25.   (4j0)   22.50
WOLFE,W C-Official Guide & Index,The Post Office SanFran,
 1897-8th Annual Conv,Natl Assoc of Letter Carriers-(SanFran,
 1897)-4to-lea-114p-illus-adv   (5F5,lacks sp) 10.00
WOLFE,WELLINGTON C-Men of Calif 1900 to 1902-SanFran-
 c1901-Pacific Art-8vo-cl-a.e.g.-440p   (4t1)   15.00
WOLFE,WM G-Stories of Guernsey Co,Ohio-Cambr-1943-1093p-
 cl-scarce   (5h1)   32.50
WOLFERT,IRA-Amer Guerilla in the Philippines-NY-1945
                              (5x7) 3.   (5s1)   4.00
--Torpedo 8, Swede Larsen's Bomber Squadron-Bost-(1943)-127p
                                         (5s1)   4.00
--Tucker's People-1943-LBFischer   (5F1,vf,dj)   4.50
WOLFF,FRANCES NATHAN-Four Generations-NY-1939 (5p0) 4.50
WOLFF,JENS-Sketches on a Tour to Copenhagen, through Norway
 & Sweden,etc-Lond-1816-mor-lg4to-plts-2nd ed-140p appendx
                                         (4e1,rprd)   135.00
WOLFF,JOS-Narr of a Mission to Bokhara in Yrs 1843 to 1845,
 etc-NY-1845-cl-384p-plts-8vo   (5v7,fox,ex-libr) 15.00
WOLFF,PAUL-My Experiences in Color Photography-NY-n.d.-
 sm4to-54 col plts   (5yy6)   6.00
WOLFF,WERNER-Island of Death-NY-(1948)-J J Augustin-228p-
 20 plts-cl   (4L0,wn dj) 8.50   (5yy3)   20.00
WOLFORD,LEAH-Play Party in Indiana-Indnpls-1916-cl (4a9) 8.00
WOLLE,MURIEL SIBELL-The Bonanza Trail-Bloomington,Ind-1953-
 510p-illus   (5a0) 7.   (5t4)   10.00
--Stampede to Timberline-Boulder-(1949)-530p plus index-illus-
 maps-errata slip-map e.p.-1st ed (scarce in 1st ed)
                                  (4L0,f,dj,autg)   25.00
--same-(1949)-2nd prntng   (4L0,autg)   10.00
--same-Boulder-(1949)-3rd prntng   (5t2,f,dj) 10.00
WOLLEY,CHAS-Two Year's Journal In New York-Cleve-1902-
 bds-ltd to 250c   (5tt5)   17.50
WOMAN AN ENIGMA-NY-1843-Harper-12mo-1st ed
                                         (5x1,rprd)   55.00
WOMAN'S EXCHANGE COOK BOOK-LaCrosse,Wis-n.d.(ca 1890)-
 110p plus 40p ads   (5g9,wn)   8.50
WOMAN'S HOME COMPANION COOK BOOK-NY-(1942)-
 thk8vo-952p-illus-washable cov   (5c9)   7.50
WOMEN'S MEDICAL COLLEGE OF PENNA-75th Anniv Vol-
 1925   (5L7)   7.50
WOMAN'S RELIQUARY,A-Churchtown Dundrum-1913-The Cuala Pr-
 1st ed   (5ss3,stn) 25.00
WOMEN LAWYERS JOURNAL-1911 to 70-Vol 1 thru 56
                                         (5ii7,rbnd)   595.00
WOMEN OF WYOMING-Casper-(1927)- & Lusk-n.d.(1929)-
 2 vols-photos-Mrs A H Beach,ed-v scarce (5y6)   65.00
WONDERS OF WORLD-Dublin-1825-Brett Smith-12mo-sheep-
 162p-plts   (4a8,rbkd) 5.00

WONDERFUL LIFE-U Surprising Adventurs of That Renowned
    Hero Robinson Crusoe-Lond-1815-WDarton-sm8vo-94p-
    8 plts-orig pict wrps   (5aa2,sl wn)   25.00

WONDERFUL STORIES-of Fuz Buz the Fly and Mother Grabem
    the Spider-Phila-1867-sq8vo-hf mor-1st ed of auth's 1st book-
    ltd to 170c   (5gg6)   50.00

WOOD, A B-50 Years of Yesterdays-Gering,Neb-1945-204p-
    illus-1st ed-ex scarce   (5L2)   75.00

--Pioneer Tales of the NoPlatte Valley & Neb Panhandle-Gering,
    Neb-1938-280p plus index-1st ed-rare   (4L0)   75.00

WOOD,ALLEN H, JR-Grow Them Indoors-Bost-(1939)-221p-illus
                 (5s7)   5.50

WOOD,ALPHONSO-A Class Book of Botany-Bost-1845-
    Crocker&Brewster-8vo-calf-1 vols in 1-1st ed (4h0,fox,rprd)   35.00

WOOD,C,ed-Negro Songs,An Anthology-Little Blue Book #626-
    Girard,Kans-1924-64p-wrps-16mo   (5x2)   6.50

--The Grenwich Village Blues-NY-1926-R8vo   (5x2,dj)   15.00

WOOD CARVING & WHITTLING-NY-1936-handbook-270p
                 (5n7)   4.00

WOOD, CASEY A-Intro to Literature of Vertebrate Zoology-Lond-
    1931-orig cl-4to-col frontis   (4n5,f)   175.00

WOOD,CATHERINE M-Palomar,From Teepee to Telescope-n.p.-
    c1937-8vo-cl-149p   (4t1)   10.00

--same-SanDiego-1937-153p   (5a9,f,autg)   7.00

WOOD,CHAS ERSKINE SCOTT-The Poet in the Desert-Portland,
    Ore-1915-Baltes&Co-8vo-cl bkd bds-1st ed (5ss3,pres,stn)   35.00

WOOD,CLEMENT-Bernarr Macfadden,Study in Success-NY-
    1929-316p-1st ed   (5w0,pres)   6.50

--Complete Book of Games-GardenCty-(1940)-895p-illus (5xx7)   6.00

--Flesh & Other Stories-NY-1929-illus-ltd to 520c,nbrd,autg
              (5ss9,box tn)   12.50

--The Man Who Killed Kitchener-NY-1932   (5x7)   6.50

WOOD CO,OHIO-Plat Book of-Rockford-n.d.-21 leaves-
    fldg map-wrps   (5h1)   5.00

WOOD,DALLAS-History of Palo Alto-PaloAlto-1939,347p-
    photos-deluxe ed   (5s4)   20.00

WOOD,DEAN EARL-Old Santa Fe Trail from Missouri Riv-
    KansCty-(1955)-Panoramic Ed-scarce   (4L0,f)   25.00

WOOD,DE VOLSON-Treatise on Theory of Construction of Bridges
    & Roofs-NY-1873-249p-cl   (5ff7)   12.50

--same-NY-1885-249p-illus-4th ed,rev   (5t4)   5.00

WOOD,EDITH-Middletown's Days & Deeds-Middletown-c1946-
    12mo-cl-281p   (4t1) 10.   (5t9)   7.50

WOOD,EDWIN O-Historic Mackinac-NY-1918-illus-2 vols-
    1st ed   (4m2,ex-libr) 45.   (5ff7)   50.00

WOOD,ELLEN LAMONT-Geo Yount-SanFran-Grabhorn Pr-
    3 plts-fldg chart-ltd to 200c   (5h5,rub)   27.50

WOOD,LADY EMMA CAROLINE-Ruling the roast-Lond-1874-
    Chapman&Hall-3 vols-8vo-orig cl-1st ed   (5xx6,rub)   20.00

--Seadrift-Lond-1871-Chapman&Hall-8vo-cl-1st ed-3 vols
              (5xx6,sp soil)   22.50

WOOD,ERIC FISHER-Note Book of an Intelligence Officer-Ny-
    1917-photos-346p   (4h4)   7.00

WOOD,EUGENE-Back Home-NY-1905-ABFrost,illus-8vo-
    dec cl   (5s 5)   5.00

WOOD,FERNANDO-A biography of-n.p.(NY)-n.d.(1856?)-8vo-
    orig yell wrps-1st ed   (5i9)   15.00

WOOD,GEO-Society of Friends Vindicated-Trenton-1832-
    PJGray-bds-167p,90p-bds-errata slip (5a0,f) 150. (5F9)   60.00

WOOD,GEO B-Dispensatory of the US of Amer-Phila-1833-1073p
              (5t7)   20.00

--same-Phila-1873-1810p   (5w3,wn)   7.50

--Historical & Biogr Memoirs-1872-plt-buck   (5L7,ex-libr)   15.00

WOOD,GEO L-The 7th Regiment,A Record-NY-1865-304p-
    1st ed   (4L0) 20.   (4a7,rbnd)   40.00

WOOD,GRANT-Revolt Against the City-IowaCty-1935-12mo-
    wrps-44p-Clio Pr-#1 of Whirling World Ser (5m8,cov soil)   10.00

WOOD,H P-Homeland-(SanDiego-1900)-illus-12mo-orig wrps-
    36p   (4g6)   12.50

WOOD,HARVEY-Personal Recoll-Pasadena-1955-Dahlstrom-27p-
    illus   (5d6)   15.00

WOOD,HERBERT-The Shores of Lake Aral-Lond-1876-cl-fldg maps-
    8vo-352p   (5v7,fox)   16.50

WOOD,J G-Animate Creation-NY-(1885)-3 vols-col plts-
    rev by Holder   (5t4)   25.00

--same-NY-c1885-col illus-4to-6 vols-rev by Holder (5w0)   30.00

--Common Objects of the Microscope-Lond&NY-n.d.(1864?)-
    bds-12mo-132p-col plts   (4t7,wn)   15.00

--Uncivilized Races,or Natural History of Man,Vol 1,Africa-
    Hartf-1870-Amer Pub-illus-774p   (4t5,fade,wn)   12.50

WOOD,J W-Pasadena,Calif,Historical & Personal-n.p.-1917-
    8vo-cl-565p-illus   (5h4,f)   17.50

WOOD,JAS-The Elements of Optics-Cambr,Engl-1801-
    8vo-calf-2nd ed   (5ss5,ex-libr,crude rbk)   12.50

WOOD,JAS-Memoir of Sylvester Scovel-NewAlbny-(prntd Louisvl)-
    1851-213p-cl   (5h1,libr labl) 15.   (5ss5,pres,sp tn)   17.50

WOOD,JAS P,ed-100 Years Ago-n.p.-Funk&Wagnalls-1947-
    1st ed   (5m2)   5.00

WOOD,JOHN J-Man & His Handiwork-SPCK-1886-8vo-dec cl-
    plts-g.t.-668p   (5s0)   6.50

WOOD,JOHN SEYMOUR-Gramercy Park,a story of NY-NY-
    1892-Appleton-1st ed-bds   (5m2)   6.50

WOOD,L K-Discovery of Humboldt Bay,a narr-(SanFran,1932)-
    lg4to-22p-Soc of Calif Pioneers-ltd to 100c (5r0,sl soil)   7.50

WOOD,L N-Wood Family in England & Amer-1937-130p (5t9)   12.50

WOOD,LESLIE C-Holt,T'Other Way-Middletown-1950-illus
              (5r7)   10.00

WOOD,LOUIS A-War Chief of 6 Nations-Tor-1914-147p-lea(5h7)7.50

WOOD,MORRISON-Fisherman's Wharf Cook Book-SanCarlos-
    1955-244p   (5c0,pres)   3.00

--With a Jug of Wine-NY-(1949)-378p   (5w1)   3.00

WOOD,M E,comp-Hutton,Lawrence & Eleanor,Their Book of
    Association-NY-1905-ltd to 152c,nbrd   (5j3)   18.00

WOOD,M W-History of Alameda Co,Calif-Oakland-1883-
    thk4to-sheep-illus   (5h4,sp dtchd)   30.00

WOOD,NORMAN B-Lives of Famous Indian Chiefs-(1906)-
    771p-illus   (5L2)   12.50

WOOD,O E-West Point Scrap Book-1871   (5L7,sp tn)   7.50

WOOD,R E-Life & Confessions of Jas Gilbert Jenkins-NapaCty-
    1864-56p-frontis-illus-pict wrps-ex rare   (5h5,mint)   50.00

WOOD,ROBT WILLIAMS-How to Tell the Birds from the Flowers
    & other wdcuts-NY-(15th ed,1931)-Duffield-12mo-49p-illus
              (5p1)   5.00

WOOD,RALPH,ed-Pennsylvania Germans-Princeton-1942 (5jj3)10.00

WOOD,RUTH K-Honeymooning in Russia-NY-1911-D,Mead-
    341p-illus   (5p0)   6.00

--Tourist's Calif-NY-1914-395p-illus-fldg,col map
              (5w4,wn) 3.   (5s4)   5.00

--Tourist's NW-NY-1916-photos-528p(5s4,wn) 5. (4g6,ex-libr)   7.50

--same-NY-1917-528p-plts-fldg maps   (5a1)   6.50

WOOD,S-Arithmetical Tables for the Use of Schools-NY-SWood-
    1819-24mo-24p-wrps-v scarce   (4F6)   35.00

WOOD,SAM'L & SONS-The History of Beasts-NY-1821-24mo-
    29p-15 wdcuts   (5jj6,rub)   27.50

--same-NY-n.d.(ca 1822)-flower wrps-sewn-illus   (4F6,vg)   22.50

WOOD,STANLEY-Over the Range to the Golden Gate-Chig-
    1889-351p-illus-1st ed (5s4,wn,ex-libr) 6.(5L3,libr labl)   8.50

--same-1891   (5s4,cov wn)   12.50

--same-Chig-1901-283p-illus(5a0,f) 5.   (5s4,ex-libr,soil)   4.50

--same-Chig-1906-340p-photos   (5s4,sl shake)   7.00

WOOD,SUMNER GILBERT-The Taverns & Turnpikes of Blandford,
    (Mass) 1773 to 1833-(Mass)-1908-329p,(13)-54 illus-priv prntd
              (5w1)   14.50

WOOD,T MARTIN-Whistler-Lond-n.d.-12mo-cl-79p-8 col illus
              (5t0)   3.75

WOOD,THOS-Youth's Biblical & Theological Companion-Lond-
    1827-calf-g. tooled-8vo-504p   (5rr2,f)   15.00

WOOD,W-Gen'l Conchology-Lond-1835-hf lea-246p-
    60 handcol plts-a.e.g.   (5m1,scuff)   65.00

WOOD,WALES W-A History of the 95th Regiment,Illinois Inf Vol,
    1862 to 1865-Chig-1865-Tribune-240p-cl (5d6,wn,soil)   10.00

WOOD,WARREN-Tragedy of the Deserted Isle-Bost-1909-Clark-
    cl-393p   (5tt8)   10.00

WOOD,WM-New England's Prospect-Lond-1639-Dawson-
    sm4to-mor-fldg map-3rd ed   (5n2,trimmed close) 1,500.00

--same-(prntd) Lond-1634-(reprntd Bost,1865)-fldg map-4to-
    ltd to 20c lg papr   (5g4)   60.00

--same-n.p.-(1898)-map-8vo   (5ss5)   10.00

WOOD,WM-Autobiography of-NY-1895-2 vols-illus-scarce
              (5L2)   25.00

WOOD,WM-Select British Documents of the Canadian War 1812-
    Tor-1920 to 28-Champlain Soc-ports-fldg maps-3 vols(in 4)
              (5nn2)   175.00

WOOD,WM B-Personal Recollections of the Stage-Phila-1855-
    477p-frontis (5ii2,lacks bkstrp) 7.50 (5h1,chip) 10. (5w9,wn)   12.50

WOOD,WM R-Past Years in Pickering-Tor-1911-316p-illus-ports
              (5aa0)   12.50

WOOD-MARTIN,WM G-History of Sligo,Co & Town to reign
    of Queen Elizabeth-1882   (5L7)   25.00

WOODARD,D W-Negro Progress In A Mississippi Town,Negro
    Banks of Mississippi-Cheyney,Pa-ca1910-12p-wrps bnd in
              (5x2,libr bds)   20.00

WOODARD,LUKE-Sketches of a Life of 75-Richmond-1907-
    246p-cl   (5y0)   12.50

WOODBERRY,GEO E-History of Wood Engraving-Lond-1883-
illus   (4a1)   15.00
WOODBERRY,GEO G-North Africa & the Desert-NY-1914-
8vo-364p   (4a6)   7.50
WOODBERRY,GEO EDW-Selected Letters of-Walter de la Mare,
ed-Bost&NY-1933-Houghton,Miff-1st ed   (4p1,dj)   10.00
WOODBRIDGE,HENSLEY C-Jack London,A Bibliography-
Georgetwon-1966-o.p. (4t6,mind,dj) 27.50 (4t0,mint,dj) 35.00
WOODBRIDGE,WM C-Modern Atlas,Physica,Political &
Statistical-Hartf-(1843)-sm folio-19 plts(14 col)-fldg bds
                                           (4h8)   12.50
--Rudiments of Geography-Hartf-1822-16mo-208p (5v0) 10.00
WOODBURN,JAS A-Scotch Irish Presbyterians in Monroe Co,
Ind-Indnpls-1910-Vol 4,#8-hvy wrps   (4a9)   5.00
WOODBURY,AUGUSTUS-Maj Gen Ambrose E Burnside & 9th Army
Corps-Prov-1867-Rider-554p-maps-ports   (5mm8,sp wn) 10.00
--2nd RI Regiment-Prov-1875-633p-frontis-map (5mm8) 7.00
WOODBURY,C L-Woodbury Family-1904-251p   (5t9)   17.50
WOODBURY,DAVID O-Beloved Scientist-NY-(1944)-358p-illus
                                  (5p9) 6. (4e4)   7.50
--Builders for Battle-NY-1946-illus   (5tt5)   6.50
--The Colorado Conquest-NY-Dodd Mead-1941-367p-cl
                               (5x5) 15. (5d6)   17.50
--Battlefront of Industry-NY-1948-342p-illus (5y2)   4.50
WOODBURY,ELLEN-Dorothy Quincy,Wife of John Hancock-
Wash-1901-12mo-259p-1st ed   (5h9)   10.00
WOODBURY,FRANK S-Tourist's Guide to Denver-Denver-1882-
74p-map   (5k0,f)   15.00
WOODBURY,GEO-Great Days of Piracy in West Indies-NY-
1951-225p-1st ed   (5h9,f,dj) 6.50
--Story of a Stanley Steamer-NY-(1950)-illus-facs-1st ed (4g3) 12.50
WOODBURY,JOHN-Vermillion Cliffs-n.p.-1933-88p (4L0,pres)25.00
WOODCOCK,H DRYSDALE-Lilies their Culture & Management-
Lond-(1935)-242p-frontis   (4g0)   7.50
WOODCROFT,BENNET-Pneumatics of Hero of Alexandria from
the Orig Greek-Lond-1851-117p-illus-cl-4to (5b8,pres) 47.50
WOOFTER,ANDREW-Jimmie's School Days(cov title)-n.p.-n.d.-
(Spencer-1924?)-68p-cl   (5h7)   8.50
WOODHOUSE,CHAS P-Old English Toby Jugs & their Makers-
Lond-(1949)-sm8vo-bds-48p-1st ed   (5t0,f,dj) 7.50
WOODHULL,VICTORIA C-Origin,Tendencies & Principles of
Govt-NY-1871-247p-cl-1st ed of auth's 1st book
                                      (5h7,5gg6)   15.00
WOODLEY,E C-Canada's Romatnic Heritage-Tor-1940-288p-
plts-ports   (5a1)   5.00
--Untold Tales of Old Quebec-Tor-1949-8vo-cl-illus-216p
                                        (5t0,dj,f)   4.00
WOODLEY,THOS FREDK-Thaddeus Stevens-Harrisburg-1934-
Telegraph Pr-664p-illus (5mm8) 8.50 (5w9,pres) 12.50 (5t0) 7.50
WOODMAN,MISS H J-The Language of Gems-Bost-1846-
160p-16mo   (5w7,chip) 7.50
WOODMAN,H REA-Wichitana,1877 to 97-n.p.-(1948)-282p
                                           (4L0)   15.00
WOODMAN,HENRY-History of Valley Forge-Oaks,Pa-1922-
illus-fldg map-orig wrps-164p   (5mm8)   6.00
WOODMAN,MARY-Cocktails,Ices,Sundaes,Jellies & Amer
Drinks-Lond-ca 1925-155p,(2)-photos   (5w1,hng broke) 5.00
WOODRUFF,C E-Expansion of Races-NY-1909-R8vo (5x2) 20.00
WOODRUFF,H-Trotting Horse of America-NY-1869-412p-frontis
                             (5ii2) 9.50   (5t2)   8.50
WOODRUFF,W-Wing Shooting, by "Chipmunk"-Lond,Ont-
1881-99p-12p adv-pict cl-illus -T G Davey, publ (5w8) 17.50
WOODRUFF,WILFORD-History of His Life & Labors as Recorded
in His Daily Journals-SaltLkCty-1916-Cowley,ed-illus (5r7) 25.00
WOODS,D B-16 Months at the Diggings-NY-1851-199p,8p ads-
1st ed (5L0,wn) 20. (4n1,fox,chip) 35. (5x5,rbnd) 50.00
WOODS,H F-Gods Loaded Dice-Caldwell-1948-298p-illus
                                          (4b9,f)   15.00
WOODS,JOHN-2 Years' Residence in the Settlement on the
Engl Prairie in Illinois Country-Lond-1822-8vo-3 maps(2 fldg)-
old cl&bds   (5a3,cov rprd) 300.00
WOODS,KATHERINE-True Story of Capt John Smith-NY-1901-
illus-maps-1st ed   (5yy8)   5.00
WOODS,NICHOLAS A-Prince of Wales in Canada & the US-
Lond-1861-fldg map-438p   (4d1)   15.00
WOODS,ROBT A-Poor in Great Cities-NY-1895-Scribner's-
cl-400p   (4L9)   10.00
WOODS,S D-Lights & Shadows of Life on Pacific Coast-NY-
1910-474p-1st ed   (4n1) 10.   (5s4,rprd)   9.00
WOODSEON,UREY-The First New Dealer,Wm Goebel-Louisville-
1929-illus   (5yy8,dj) 10.00
WOODSMALL,RUTH F-Eastern Women...Today & Tomorrow-
Bost-1937   (5x7)   4.00

WOODSON,CARTER G-A Century of Negro Migration-Wash-
1918-1st ed   (5x2,ex-libr) 35.00
--Journal of Negro History 1917 to 27-(incomplete run)-orig wrps
                                          (5x5)ea   5.00
--same-July 1920   (5x2)   6.50
--same-Jan,Apr 1948   (5x2)ea   4.50
--The Negro in Our History-Wash-(1922)-illus-393p-1st ed
                                           (4m2)   15.00
--same-Wash-1931-illus-thk8vo   (5x2)   50.00
WOODSON,H M-Hist Gen of Woodsons & Their Connections-
1915-760p   (5t9)   35.00
WOODSON,L H-Amer Negro Slavery In Works of Friedrich
Strubberg,Friedrich Gerstacker, & Otto Ruppius-1949-
Catholic Univ of Amer-1st ed   (5x2)   7.50
WOODSTOCK COOK BOOK-Woodstock,NY-1938-106p-ads-
wrps   (5g9)   3.50
WOODSTOCK(CONN)-Vital Records 1686 to 1854 (5t9)   12.00
WOODSWORTH,JAS S-My Neighbour-Tor-1911-341p-plts (5a1) 5.00
--same-Tor-1913-2nd ed-341p-illus   (4b9,lacks fly) 8.00
WOODWARD,ASHBEL-Life of Gen Natl Lyon-Hartf-1862-
360p-cl   (5F9,vf,5h7,sl chip) 10.00
WOODWARD,ASHBEL-Wampum-Albany-1878-61p-wrps-1st ed
                                           (5L0)   8.50
WOODWARD,ARTHUR-Brief History of Navajo Silversmithing-
1938-78p   (5L7)   4.00
--Feud on the Colorado-LosAng-1955-illus
                             (5h6,autg,wtrstnd) 5.   (5dd5) 9.00
--Lances at San Pascual-SanFran-1948-84p-cl-Calif Hist Soc
                              (5h4,f) 15.   (5d6)   25.00
WOODWARD,E M-History of 3rd Penna Reserve-Trenton-1883-
2 illus-1st ed   (4L0,sp wn)   15.00
--Our Campaigns-Phila-1890-Keystone-362p   (5u3)   10.00
WOODWARD,GEO-Architecture & Rural Art-Vol #1&#2-NY-
1868,9-144p & 132p-   (5w7,crack) 10.00
--Country Homes-NY-(1865)-188p-illus   (5ii2)   9.50
--Woodward's Country Homes-NY-1869-188p-150 illus
                                         (5w7,spots) 7.50
--Woodward's Graperies & Horticultural Buildings-NY-(1865)-
139p-59 illus   (5w6,wn)   5.50
WOODWARD,HENRY-Lyrics of the Umpqua-NY-1889-192p-
1st ed   (4b2,pres)   5.00
WOODWARD,M-Leaves from Gerard's Herbal-Bost-1931 (5w3) 5.00
WOODWARD,P H-Guarding the Mails-Hartf-1876-568p-illus-
1st ed   (5r8,f) 14.   (4L0)   7.50
--same-Hartf-1881-cl-568p   (4n9)   12.50
--Secret Service of the PO Dept-Hartf-1886 (5p5,mint) 35.00
WOODWARD,ROBT P-Trains That Met in the Blizzard-NY-1896-
396p-illus-1st ed   (5m1)   12.50
WOODWARD,S-Adventure in Marine Painting-NY-(1947)-
100p   (5p7)   5.00
WOODWARD,THOS S-Woodward's Remin of the Creek or
Muscogee Indians-(Tuscaloosa-1939)-168p-cl-facs of 1859 ed
                       (5h1) 10.   (4n9,5L7,5L2)   10.00
WOODWARD,W E-Bunk-NY-1923-12mo-cl-1st ed of auth's
1st book   (4n3,f) 15.   (5gg6) 25.00
--Meet General Grant-NY-1928-illus (5h6) 6. (5s9,5p9) 5.00
--Tom Paine,America's Godfather-NY-1945 (5h9) 5. (5w5) 4.50
--Years of Madness-NY-c1951   (5x2) 5.   (5w9)   4.50
WOODWARD,WALTER C-Rise & Early History of Political Parties
in Oregon-Portland-1913-278p-ports   (5s4,ex-libr) 12.50
WOODWORTH,JOHN-Remin of Troy...1790 to 1807...Albany-
1853-Joel Munsell-8vo-wrps-39p   (4t1,lacks frnt cov) 15.00
WOODWORTH,JOHN M-Cholera Epidemic of 1873 in the US-
Wash-1875-1025p-illus   (5t7)   15.00
WOOFTER,T J, JR-Negro Problems in Cities-NY-1928 (5x2) 35.00
--The Basis of Racial Adjustment-Bost-1925-12mo (5x2) 17.50
WOOLACOTT,A P-Mackenzie & His Voyageurs-Lond-1927-
237p-plts   (4b9,sp tn) 6.   (4F9) 12.50
WOOLERY,W K-Bethany Years-Huntington-1941 (5w4,pres) 6.50
WOOLEY,CHAS-2 Years Journal in NY & Part of its Territories
in Amer-NY-1860-reprnt-8vo-cl-97p   (5t0)   7.50
WOOLEY,L H-Calif 1849 to 1913-Glendale-1913-wrps-48p(4n1)12.00
WOOLF,ROSE Y-Robin Hood & His Life in Merry Greenwood-Tuck-
(c1900)-lg sq8vo-pict glaz bds-112p-col plts (5s0)   5.00
WOOLF,VIRGINIA-
--Beau Brummell-NY-1930-Rimington&Hooper-4to-ltd to 550c,
autg   (4b5,vg)   100.00
--Between the Acts-Lond-1941-Hogarth Pr-1st ed (4b5,vg,dj) 20.00
--same-NY-(1041)-1st Amer ed   (5qq4,dj,f) 15.00

WOOLF, VIRGINIA   (continued)
--Captain's Death Bed & Other Essays-NY-(1950)-1st Amer ed
                                    (5hh1)   5.00
--The Common Reader-NY-(1925)-1st ed   (4b5,mint) 17.50
--Death of the Moth & Other Essays-NY-(1942)   (5p9)   4.00
--Flush-Lond-1933-Hogarth Pr-1st ed-lg papr
   (4b5,sp fade,fray dy) 10.   (4b1,dj) 30.   (5i8,dj) 12.00
--same-NY-(1933)-illus   (5ee3,f,dj) 5.   (5ee3,vg)   3.50
--Haunted House & Other Stories-Lond-1943-Hogarth Pr-1st ed
                              (4b5,vg,dj)   20.00
--Hours in a Library-NY-(1957)-16mo-cl (4c2,orig flassine dj) 15.00
--Kew Gardens-Hogarth Pr-n.d.-ltd to 500c,autgs(5F9,sl fade) 25.00
--Letter to a Young Poet-Lond-1932-Hogarth Pr-orig wrps-
   Hogarth Letters #8-1st ed   (4b5)   10.00
--Mr Bennett & Mrs Brown-Lond-1928-Hogarth Pr-wrps-24p-
   2nd impr-orig tissue   (4b5)   7.50
--Moment & Other Essays-Lond-1947-Hogarth Pr-1st ed
   (5ss7,f,dj) 15.   (4b5,sl fade,fray dj)   20.00
--Monday or Tuesday-Lond-1921-12mo-dec bd-cl-bk-1st ed-
   Hogarth Pr   (5cc9)   75.00
--Mrs Dalloway-Lond-1925-8vo-cl-1st ed   (5dd8,sp fade) 40.00
--Orlando-Lond-1928-Leonard&Virginia Woolf-1st Engl ed
   (5ss3,fade,dj) 20.   (4b5,mint,dj)   35.00
--same-NY-(1928)-8vo-cl-illus-333p   (5t0)   4.00
--Reviewing,with note by Leonard Woolf-Lond-1939-
   Hogarth Pr-31p-12mo-wrps-1st ed   (4b5,vg) 15.00
--A Room of One's Own-Lond-1929-1st ed (5ee3)   8.50
--Stravrogin's Confession-Richmond-1922-Hogarth Pr-cl&bds-
   1st ed in Engl   (4i1,vg) 65.00
--Three Guineas-NY-(1938)-Harcourt Brace-1st Amer ed
   (5ss9,fade) 6.50   (5ee3,f)   7.50
--The voyage out-NY-n.d.-(1920)-8vo-cl-1st Amer ed-scarce-
   Doran   (5i8)   15.00
--Walter Sickert-Lond-1934-Hogarth Pr-1st ed-wrps (4b1) 17.50
--The waves-NY-n.d.(1931)-Harcourt,Brace-8vo-cl-1st Amer ed
                                      (5i8)   6.00
--The Years-Lond-1937-Hogarth Pr-1st ed
   (4b1,sl tn dj) 37.50   (4b5,rub)   10.00
WOOLLCOTT,ALEXANDER-War Paintings of Claggett Wilson-
   NY-1928-J H Sears-7p text-24 illus-17x15   (4a0,dj) 45.00
WOOLLEN,W W-Inside Passage to Alaska,1792 to 1920-Cleve-
   1924-Clark-illus-2 vols-1st ed   (5dd7,mint) 64.50
WOOLLEN,WM W-Biog & Hist Sketches of Early Indiana-Indnpls-
   1883-568p-cl-scarce   (5h7)   25.00
WOOLLEY,Edwin C-Reconstruction of Georgia-NY-1901-wrps
                                      (5g4)   15.00
WOOLLEY,JOHN G-Temperance Progress-Lond-1905-517p
                                      (5w1,wn) 5.00
WOOLLEY,L H-Calif 1849 to 1913-Oakl-1913-48p-wrps
   (5tt0) 5.   (5hh4,f)   6.00
WOOLLEY,M-Lida Shaw King-(Bost)-1923-Updike-12p-ltd (5m6)10.00
WOOLMAN,JOHN-The Journal & Essays of-Phila&Lond-1922-
   illus   (5m2)   10.00
--Journal of-Bost-1871-12mo-cl   (5ss3,Whittier pres) 45.00
--same-Phila-1837-12mo-396p   (5h9,rub)   17.50
--Journal of Life & Travels of-Lond-(1901)-16mo-vel-250c prntd
                                      (4c1)   12.50
--Works of-Phila-1774-Crukshank-8vo-orig calf-1st ed
   (5n2) 125.   (5m4)   100.00
--Works of-Burlington-1806-2 parts in 1-423p-calf-4th ed (5m2) 10.00
WOOLSLEY,MRS LOUISA M-Shall Woman Preach?-Caneyvl-
   1891-200p-cl   (5h7)   10.00
WOOLSON,ALVIN M-1st OVHA Co M-(Toledo,1914)-cl-
   95p-rare   (4h7)   35.00
WOOLSON,CONSTANCE-Anne,a Novel-NY-1882-Harper-
   1st ed of auth's 1st novel   (5r7) 10.   (5m2,sl wn) 7.50
WOOLSON,G A-Ferns & How to Grow Them-NY-1910-
   Garden Libr   (4g0)   5.00
WOOLWORTH,JAS M-Nebraska in 1857-OmahaCty,NT-1857-
   12mo-fldg col map-23p adv at end   (5s9,rbnd,map rprd) 295.00
WOOLWORTH,S-Experiences in the Civil War-Newark-1905-
   12mo-orig wrps-79p-3rd prntng   (5ss5)   15.00
--Mississippi Scout-Chig-1867-15p-wrps-v rare (5m3,stnd) 82.50
WOOLWORTH'S-First 75 Years-n.p.-1954-4to-62p   (5y2)   6.50
WOON,BASIL-SanFran & the Golden Empire-NY   (5x5,dj) 12.50
--When It's Cocktail Time in Cuba-NY-1928-284p   (5w1)   3.50
WOOSTER CITY & WAYNE CO-Business Directory-Wooster-
   1900-168p-ads-prntd bds-Lee&Co   (5h1)   10.00
WOOSTER,DAVID-Diseases of the Heart-Bancroft-1867-illus-
   216p   (4p0)   15.00
WOOTEN,DUDLEY G-Complete History of Texas-Dalls-1899-
   498p-illus   (4a5)   22.50

WOOTEN,DUDLEY G   (continued)
--Comprehensive History of Texas,1685 to 1897-Dallas-
   1898-Scharff-2 vols bnd in 4-hf mor-rare (5n4) 175.00
WOOTEN,MATTIE L-Women Tell Story of the SW-SanAnt-1940
                                      (5a8)   12.50
WORCESTER-Atlas of City of-Springfield-1896-L J Richards&Co-
   folio-calf&cl   (4c1,lea wn) 30.00
WORCESTER CO-Atlas of-NY-1870-Beers-folio-cl&calf(4c1) 25.00
WORCESTER CO-Biographical Review-1899-1229p   (5t9) 15.00
WORCESTER,DEAN C-Philippine Islands & Their People-NY-
   1899-529p-fldg map   (5ee3)   5.00
--The Philippines,Past & Present-NY-1914-illus-2 vols-1st ed
                                      (4g3,f)   20.00
WORCESTER,G R G-Junks & Sampans of the Yangtze-Vol 1-
   Shanghai-Misc Ser #53-4to-cl-245p-85 plts & plans(some fldg)-
                                      (5ss2,f) 22.50
--same-Junks & Sampans of the Yangtze-Vol 2-Shanghai-1948-
   4to-cl-(247)p,506p-117 plts-map   (5ss2,f) 22.50
WORCESTER,J D-An Historical Atlas-Bost-c1837-bds-8 dbl pg
   handcol charts -6th edition   (4F6,lt chip) 17.50
WORCESTER,J E-Gazeteer-2 vols-1817-calf-1st ed   (5e1) 15.00
WORCESTER,J F-The Worcester Family-Lynn-1856-111p,(1)
                                      (5w0)   28.50
WORCESTER MAGAZINE & HIST JOURNAL-Worcester-1825,26-
   8vo-bds-Vols 1&2(all publ)   (4c1)   25.00
WORCESTER,NOAH-Friend of Peace-1816-6 nbrs in 2-hf lea
                                      (5L7,wn) 15.00
WORCESTER,S T-Hist of Hollis-1879   (5t9)   15.00
WORCESTER'S ANCIENT ATLAS-Bost-(c1830)-maps-4to-
   5 col maps-stiff bds   (4c1)   25.00
WORCESTER'S MODERN ATLAS-Bost-(c1840)-New ed,rev-4to-
   stiff wrps-12 col maps   (4c1)   20.00
WORD & PHRASEBOOK-for Cinq Semaines en Ballon-Lond-1913-
   Macmillan-16mo-20p-wrps-Siepmann's Elem French Ser (5p1) 5.00
WORDE,WYNKYN DE-The Abbaye of the Holy Ghost-Cambr-
   1907-papr bds-vell sp-prntd by-Facs ed-ltd to 250c (4g2) 40.00
WORDEN,EDW C-Nitrocellulose Industry-NY-1911-2 vols
                                      (5ss5)   17.50
WORDSWORTH,C-Greece,Pict & Descrip etc-Lond-1853-Orr-
   480p-plts-stmpd cl-rev -4to   (5m5)   18.00
WORDSWORTH,WM-The Poetical Works-Edinb-1882-11 vols-
   blue buck-g.-Wm Knight,ed   (5d2)   75.00
--The Prelude-Lond-1850-8vo-cl (4c2,wn,crack) 25. (5i8,sp wn)50.00
--same-NY-1850-1st Amer ed   (5yy6)   10.00
--same-Oxf-1926-Clarendon Pr-Selincourt,ed   (5ss9) 15.00
--The White Doe of Rylstone-Lond-1815-1st ed-bds (5ss9,rbnd) 50.00
WORK,E-Ethiopia,Pawn in European Diplomacy-NY-1935 (5x2) 7.50
WORK,JOHN-Journal of John Work-Vict-1945-illus-98p-
   wrps-scarce   (5dd7,mint,unopened) 15.00
WORK,JOHN W-Amer Negro Songs,A Comprehensive Collection-
   NY-(1940)-Howell,Soskin&Co-sm4to   (5x5) 15.   (5x2) 17.50
--Amer Negro Songs & Spirituals-NY-1940-R8vo   (5x2,dj)   7.50
WORK,M N,ed-Negro Year Book 1921,1922-Tuskegee Inst-1922-
   495p-wrps   (5x2)   30.00
--same-1937,1938-Tuskegee Inst-1937   (5x2)   20.00
WORKING MAN'S GUIDE-&the Laborer's Friend & Advocate,
   The Great Social Question Solved-SanFran-1886-Bacon&Co-
   919p-cl   (5r0)   15.00
WORKMAN,BOYLE-The City That Grew,1840 to 1936-LosAng-1935-
   auth's ed,autg   (4d6) 12.   (5x5)   8.50
--same-LosAng-1936-430p-illus-cl&fab-Southland Publ-DeLuxe ed-
   4th prntng   (5d6,pres) 20.00
WORKMAN,JAS-Essays & Letters on Various Political Subjects-NY-
   1809-165p-l Riley-calf-2nd Amer ed   (5tt8)   400.00
WORKSHOP,THE-NY-n.d.(ca 1870)-WBaumer,ed-4to-Vol 1,
   #1 thru 12-plts-fldg plans-orig wrps as issued (5t4,wrps wn) 25.00
WORLD'S COLUMBIAN EXPOSITION-
-- Chig-1893-16mo-wrps-191p-pkt guide   (5q0)   6.00
--Chig-1893-Rand,McNally-maps-plans-illus-pict wrps-269p-
   Buffalo Bill's ad on bk cov   (5q0)   10.00
--Catalogue of Exhibits of Penna etc-ABFarquhar-(Harrisburg,
   1893)-bds-284p-cl-fldg plts   (5w9)   8.50
--Congress of Women-Chig-1894-2 vols-4to-lea-824p (5t7) 12.50
--Official Catalogue-Part 3-Live stock-Chig-1893-pict wrps
                                      (5g8)   5.00
--Souvenir Book-views-cl-tied   (5a6,vf) 12.50
WORLEY,E D-Iron Horses of Santa Fe Trail-Dallas-1965-oblong 4to-
   spec on permalife papr-ltd to 250c,autg   (4c7,box) 87.50
WORMELEY,MARY E-Our Cousin Veronica-NY-1855-Bunce-
   437p-1st ed   (5x4)   17.50
WORMINGTON,H M-Prehistoric Indians of the SW-Denv-1947-
   8vo-cl-191p   (5h4) 5.   (5L0)   7.50
WORMSER,I-Frankenstein,Inc-NY-1931-8vo-cl-242p (5j5,pres)10.00

WORNER,WM F-Old Lancaster Tales & Traditions-Lancaster-
1927-illus-261p   (4m4)   20.00
WORNUM,RALPH-Lectures on Painting by Royal Academicians-
Lond-1848-Bohn-560p-8vo-cl-plt   (5m5,crack) 30.00
--Some Account of Life & Works of Hans Holbein,Painter-
Lond-1867-sm4to-34 illus-hf lea-426p   (5t0)   17.50
WORSFOLD,T-Staple Inn & Its Story-Lond-(1906)-128p-2nd ed
                                         (5g9)   6.00
WORSLEY,F-Romance of Lloyd's-NY-n.d.-(193-)-36 plts
                               (5L7) 6. (5p0)   7.50
WORSLEY,F A-Under Sail in Frozen North-Phila-1927-2 charts
                                         (5c1)   9.50
WORST,EDW-Foot Power Loom Weaving-Milwkee-1920-277p-
2nd ed,enlrgd   (5n7)   4.00
--same-1924-272p-6th ed   (5n7)   5.00
WORTH,JEAN-A Century of Fashion-Bost-1928-229p-4to (5n7) 6.50
WORTH,JONATHAN-Correspondence-Raleigh-1909-2 vols-
8vo   (5m6,crack)   20.00
WORTHAM,LOUIS-History of Texas-FtWorth-1924-5 vols-8vo-
hf lea   (4j7,f) 75. (5g3) 50. (5dd1) 85.00
WORTHINGTON,ELIZ-How to Cook Husbands-NY-1899-190p
                                    (5c0,shake)   6.50
WORTHINGTON,GEO-Worthington Family Genealogy-1894-
489p   (5t9,lacks t.p.) 75.00
WORTHINGTON CO,GEO-Saddlery Catalog-Cleve-1891-cl-
278p-illus   (4b0)   22.50
WORTHINGTON,W H-Portraits of Sovereigns of England-Lond-
1824-Pickering-plts-4to-   lea   (5t4)   15.00
WORTHINGTON,WM-Fighting Fire,Great Fires of History-Hartf-
1873-fldg plt-1st ed-716p-8vo-illus   (5ss5)   12.50
WORTHY,A N-A Treatise on the Botanic Theory & Practice
of Medicine-Forsyth,Ga-1842-631p,(1) (5w3,wn)   18.50
WORTLEY,EMMELINE S-Travels in the US-Lond-1851-3 vols-
1st ed-orig cl   (4b1)   75.00
--same-NY-1851-463p-cl-1st Amer ed
    (5h1,fox) 10. (5q8,5ee3) 15. (5h1,fox,4b3,sp tn) 10.00
WORTMAN,BILL-Bouncing Down to Baja-LosAng-1954 (5x5) 10.00
WORTMAN,TUNIS-Treatise,concerning political inquiry &
the liberty of the press-NY-1800   (5g4,wn,ex-libr) 25.00
WORTSMAN,GENE-Phenix City-Birmingham-(1955) (5h6,autg) 6.00
WOUK,HERMAN-Aurora Dawn-NY-1947-241p-1st ed-auth's
1st book   (4p4,wn dj) 5.   (4j0)   12.50
--Caine Mutiny-NY-(1951)-494p   (5s1,f,dj)   8.00
--same-NY-1951-494p-1st ed   (4j0,f,dj)   15.00
WPA-see title,state or city
WRANGELL,ADM FERDINAND-Narr of an Exped to the Polar
Sea in 1820 to 23,Commanded by-NY-1841-302p-orig calf-
fldg map   (5m4)   25.00
WRAXALL,C F L-Backwoodsman-Lond-1864-428p-cl-1st Engl ed
                                    (4a5,fox)   85.00
--Black Panther-Bost-1864-Burnham-cl-illus (5cc6) 10.00
WRAXALL,N-Cursory Remarks Made in a Tour Through Some of
the No Parts of Europe,etc-Lond-1775-Cadell-calf-8vo-
412p   (5v7)   65.00
--Tour Through Some of the No Parts of Europe etc-Lond-1771-calf-
8vo-fldg map-3rd ed,corr   (5v7)   50.00
WRAY,J W-South Sea Vagabonds-NY-1941-cl-305p (5t2)   4.00
WREN,C-Study of NoAmer Indian Pottery-WilkesBarre-1914-
101p-wrps   (5w4)   17.50
WRENSCH,FRANK-Horses in Sport-NY-1937-132p-illus-
bds&cl-ltd to 250c,autg,box   (5t7)   15.00
WRIGHT,A H-No American Anura-Wash-1914-Carnegie Inst
#197-buck-98p-21 plts-4to-scarce   (4p6)   28.50
WRIGHT,B C-1st Cavalry Div in World War II-Tokyo-(1947)-
Tappan Pr-(Occupied Japan)-2nd prntg-4to-245p-wrps-
illus   (4a6,dj)   22.50
WRIGHT,CALEB E-On the Lackawanna-Doylestown-1886-
sm12mo-254p-1st ed   (5w4,autg,crack)   10.00
WRIGHT,CHAS-History of Lloyd's-Lond-1928-sm4to-475p-fldg facs-
ports   (5aa0)   20.00
WRIGHT,MRS D G-A Southern Girl in '61-NY-1905-illus-258p-
1st ed   (5h6) 8. (4p8) 12.50
WRIGHT,DUDLEY-Druidism The Ancient Faith Of Britain-Lond-
1924-illus-4to   (5j2)   20.00
WRIGHT,E W,ed-Lewis & Dryden's Marine History of the Pac
NW-Portland-1895-1st   (5x5,sp wn)   125.00
WRIGHT,EDGAR-The Representative Old Time Cowboy-n.p.-
1954-500c published   (5dd1,lacks e.p.) 6.50 (5x5) 10.00
WRIGHT,ESTER C-Saint John River-Tor-1949-plts-maps-254p
                                         (5s0)   7.50
WRIGHT,EUGENE-Great Horn Spoon-NY-(1928)-320p
                               (5s1,ex-libr)   3.50

WRIGHT,F B-Practical Handbook On Distillation of Alcohol
from farm products-(NY-(1907)-Camelot Pr-2nd ed,rev-
271p-cl   (4n0)   5.00
--same-NY-1918-271p-fldg illus   (5w1)   7.50
WRIGHT,F A-Feminism in Greek Literature-Lond&NY-1923 (5t4) 4.00
WRIGHT,FRANK LLOYD-American Architecture-NY-1955-
sm folio-illus-269p   (4b3,f)   12.50
--The Future of Architecture-NY-1953-326p-illus
                          (5t4) 10. (5q0,dj,autg) 12.50
--Genius & Mobocracy-NY-(1949)-sm4to-plts (5tt5) 10.00
WRIGHT,G FREDK-Greenland Icefields & Life in the No Atlantic-
NY-1896-407p-maps-1st ed   (5ee3)   5.00
--Ice Age in NoAmer & Its Bearings upon Antiquity of Man-
NY-1889-lg8vo-illus-pict cl-622p   (5t2) 5. (5L0) 6.00
--Representative Citizens of Ohio-Cleve-1914-542p-mor
                                    (5y0,crack)   50.00
WRIGHT,GEO-The Gentlemen's Miscellany-1st Amer ed-
216p-calf   (5w7,wn)   12.50
WRIGHT,GEO F-History of Sacramento Co,Calif-Oakland-
1880-Thompson&West-294p-folio-cl   (5tt0)   200.00
WRIGHT,HAROLD BELL-Long Ago Told-NY-1929-290p-illus-
1st ed   (5L2)   15.00
--That Printer of Udell's-Chig-1903-Book Supply Co-12mo-
pict cl-illus-1st ed of auth's 1st book
            (5gg6,long als) 75. (4m8,lacks e.p.) 20.00
--The Winning of Barbara Worth-Chig-(1911)-1st ed (5ee3,f) 3.50
WRIGHT,HARRY A,ed-Story of Western Massachusetts-NY-
(1949)-Lewis-illus-4to-4 vols   (4b6) 25. (5e8,f) 32.75
WRIGHT,HARRY B-Witness to Witchcraft-NY-c1957 (5x7) 3.00
WRIGHT,HELEN S-The Great White North-NY-1910-489p-
cl-1st ed   (4m0) 10. (5ee3,f) 8.50
--Old Time Recipes for Home Made Wines,etc-Bost-1919-156p
                                         (5w1)   7.50
WRIGHT,HENDRICK-Hist Sketches of Plymouth,Luzerne Co,Pa-
Phila-(1873)-419p-photos   (5ii2) 9.50 (4m4) 15.00
WRIGHT,HENRIETTA C-Children's Stories in Amer Literature
1861 to 1896-NY-1914-Scribner's-12mo-277p-5 plts-dec cl-
frontis   (5p1)   5.00
WRIGHT,HENRY C-A Kiss for a Blow-Bost-1842-frontis-180p-
1st ed   (5c8,fox)   12.50
WRIGHT,HENRY H-History of 6th Iowa Infantry-IowaCty-1923-
8vo-539p-t.e.g. (4L0) 12.50 (4a7,mint) 30. (5a9) 22.50
WRIGHT,HERBERT EDW-Handy Book for Brewers-Lond-1897-
2nd ed,rev-516p-ads   (4n0) 10. (5w1) 9.50
WRIGHT,HORACE J-Sweet Peas-Lond-n.d.-116p-plts (5s7) 3.50
WRIGHT,J C-Automotive Constr & Operation-NY-1924-446p-
illus   (5y2)   5.00
WRIGHT,J E-With Rifle & Plow-Pittsb-1938-1st ed-illus (5yy6) 6.00
WRIGHT,J O,comp-Cat of Library & Brief List of Engrav &
Etchings Belonging to Theodore Irwin-NY-1887-534p-ltd to
100c,nbrd   (4g2)   47.50
WRIGHT,JAS A-Historical Sketches of the Town of Moravia-
Auburn-1874-289p-plus sketch of 1st Congr Church
                                    (5ff2,rebkd)   15.00
--same-Auburn-(1918)-illus-525p-2nd ed (4d9,hng crack) 14.50
WRIGHT,JOHN-Early Bibles of Amer-NY-1892-ltd ed (5m4) 35.00
WRIGHT,JOHN C-The Crooked Tree-HarborSprngs-n.d.-c1917
                                    (4h6,sl soil) 12.50
WRIGHT,JOHN KIRTLAND-Geographical Lore of Time of Crusade-
NY-1925-(Amer Geogr Soc)   (5yy6) 10. (5w9) 6.50
--Geography in the Making,Amer Geogr Soc-NY-1952-illus-
437p   (4b6)   10.00
WRIGHT,JOHN L-Mr Eagle's USA-Hartf-1898-wrps-224p (4m0) 12.50
WRIGHT,JOHN S-Chicago,Past Present,Future-Chig-1868-
404p-2 maps-1st ed   (5g8) 10. (5ee3,sl wn) 12.50
WRIGHT,JULIA McNAIR-Among the Alaskans-Phila-(1883)-351p-
map-1st ed-scarce   (5L2)   12.50
--The Complete Home-Phila-(1879)-584p   (5w7,broke) 6.50
--Jug or Not-NY-1870-346p-cl-1st ed   (5h7,shake) 7.50
--Mother Goose for Temperance Nurseries-NY-1887-pict wrps-
Nat Temp Soc   (5c8,wrps wn) 17.50
--Mr Gorsvenor's Daughter-NY-(1893)-384p-cl-Amer Tract Soc
                                         (5h7)   5.00
--Secrets of the Convent & Confessional-Cinn&Phila-1873-rprnt-
illus   (5m2)   11.50
WRIGHT,LOUIS B-Atlantic Frontier-NY-1947-354p (5h9) 7.50
--First Gentlemen of Virg-SanMarino-1940 (5d2)   10.00
WRIGHT,LYLE-Sporting Books in the Huntington Libr-SanMarino-
1937-wrps   (5n4)   9.50
WRIGHT,MABEL-Wabeno the Magician-NY&Lond-1899-346p-
cl   (5p1)   5.00
WRIGHT,MARCUS J-Gen'l Scott-NY-1894-cl-Grt Com Ser
                                    (5h7,pres)   8.50

USED BOOK PRICE GUIDE

WRIGHT,MARIE-Mexico-NY-1892-4to-pict wrps-plts-L'Artiste
Pub Co-punchd&tied-1st ed (5g2) 10.00
--Picturesque Mexico-Phila-(1897)-folio-cl-445p (5h4) 20.00
WRIGHT,MARY-Candy Making at Home-Phila-1915-188p (5g9) 4.00
WRIGHT,R R-The Negro in Pennsylvania-(Phila)-n.d.-orig cl-
250p (4m4,spot) 20.00
--Phila Colored Directory,1910-sewn-wrps (5L7,soil) 25.00
WRIGHT,RICHARD-Black Boy-NY-1945-228p (5x2,5j6,5L7) 2.50
--Black Power-NY-1954-Harper-bds (5x2,dj) 6.50 (5b2,dj,f) 7.50
--The Color Curtain-NY-1956-1st ed (5x2,dj) 12.50
--Native Son-NY-1940-8vo-cl-1st ed
(5x2) 6. (5cc9,dj) 17.50 (4j0) 13.50
--The Outsider-NY-1953-1st ed (5x2,dj) 15.00
--Uncle Tom's Children-Cleve&NY-(1943)-250p (5m4,pres) 25.00
--White Man,Listen-NY-1957-1st ed (5ii3) 10.00
WRIGHT,RICHARDSON-The Bed Book of Eating & Drinking-Phila-
(1943)-12mo-320p (5w1,5g9) 5.00
--Forgotten Ladies-Phila-1928-illus (5w7) 5. (5p0) 6. (5tt5) 7.50
--Gardener's Tribute-Phila-1949-256p (5w3) 5.00
--Grandfather was Queer-Phila-(1939)-illus-8vo-cl
(5p0) 6. (4c1) 10.00
--Hawkers & Walkers in Early Amer-Phila-1927-Lippincott-illus-
8vo-cl (5g8,4c1,5qq8) 15.00
--same-1927-2nd ed (4c1) 10.00
--Phila-1927-2nd ed,3rd impress (5m8) 6.00
--Low Cost Suburban Homes-NY-1916-4to-120p (5w7) 5.00
--Practical Book of Garden Flowers-GardenCty-(1941)-319p-illus
(5s7) 3.50
--Practical Book of Outdoor Flowers-GardenCty-(1924)-319p
col plts (5s7,8vo) 5.50 (5s7,lg4to) 6.50
--Revels in Jamaica-NY-1937-illus-1st ed (4b7) 7.50
--Story of Gardening-NY-(1934)-475p-illus (5w3) 6.50
--same-NY-1935 (5s7) 6.50
WRIGHT,ROBT-Life of Gen Jas Oglethorpe-Lond-1867-8vo-430p-
cl-1st ed-scarce (5p5) 17.50
WRIGHT,ROBT M-Dodge City, the Cowboy Capital & Great SW-
(Wichita-1913)-344p-12mo-cl-rare 1st ed(col frontis)
(4n9,rprd) 50. (4c1,box,the Littell copy) 65.
(4L0) 75. (5cc5) 60.00
--same-n.p.-n.d.-342p-2nd prntg (4L0) 17.50
WRIGHT,S A,ed-Spanish Documents Concerning English Voyages
to Caribbean-Hakluyt Soc-1929-2nd Ser,#62-maps-167p (5s6) 7.50
WRIGHT,SOLOMON A-My Rambles as East Texas Cowboy etc-
Austin-1942-159p-cl-Hertzog (5y0,f,dj) 10. (4j0,mint) 17.50
WRIGHT,T D-Technical Horology-Denver-n.d.-318p-8vo-
wrps-reprnt (5bb0) 4.00
WRIGHT,CAPT T J-History of the 8th Regiment Ky Vol Inf during
its 3 Years Campaign-StJoseph-1880-286p-1st ed-ex scarce
(5L5,needs rbndg) 35.00
WRIGHT,THOS-Biographia Britannica Literaria-Anglo Saxon Period-
Lond-1842-8vo-554p-cl (5p6) 30.00
--Caricature History of the Georges-Lond-1898-col frontis-plts-
illus-639p (4d1) 10.00
--History of Caricature & Grotesque in Literature & Art-Lond-
(1864)-494p-hf calf (5c3,edge wn) 4.50
--History of Domestic Manners & Sentiments in England during Middle
Ages-Lond-1862-502p-illus (5c5,rprd) 12.50
--History of France-Lond-(ca1840)-plts-3 vols-4to-tooled mor-
raised bands-1st ed (5p5,f,f bndg) 25.00
--Isaac Watts & Contemporary Hymn Writers-Lond-1914-ports-
plts-279p (5u6) 12.50
--Narratives of Sorcery & Magic-ClintonHall-1852-420p
(5w0,fox) 16.50
WRIGHT,THOS GODDARD-Literary Culture in Early New Engl,
1620 to 1730-NewHav-1920 (5j2) 12.00
WRIGHT,WALTER P-Pictorial Greenhouse Management-Lond-1902-
144p-illus (5s7) 5.00
WRIGHT,WILLARD H,ed-Great detective stories-NY-1928 (5m2) 6.50
WRIGHT,WM-Oil Regions of Penna-NY-1865-275p
(4m4) 12.50 (4i7) 30.00
WRIGHT,WM-Big Bonanza-NY-1947-illus (5m9) 5.00
WRIGHT,WM-The Brontes in Ireland-NY-1893 (5mm2) 6.50
WRIGHT,WM ALDIS,ed-The Cambridge Shakespeare-Lond-1891-
9 vols-t8vo-lg type-buck (5t8,rbnd) 95.00
WRIGHT,WM H-The Grissly Bear-NY-1909-illus-274p
(5i3) 8.50 (5L2) 10. (5s4,soil) 9.50
WRIGHT-DAVIS,MARY-Book of Lincoln-NY-(1919)-399p (5p9) 4.50
WRISTON,JENNIE-A pioneer's odyssey-(Menasha)-1943-map
(5dd1,5g8) 25.00
WRITERS TAKE SIDES-NY-(1938)-12mo-wrps-1st ed (5ss7,vf) 25.00

WRONG,GEO M-Canadian Manor & Its Seigneurs-Tor-1926-
illus-8vo-cl (4c1) 6.00
--The Canadians-NY-1938-illus-t8vo-1st prntg
(4m9) 10. (5t0,dj) 5.00
--Story of Canada-Tor-1931-380p-plts (5a1) 4.50
WROTH,LAWRENCE C-History of the Printed Book Being the
3rd nbr of the Dolphin-NY-1938-lg4to-507p-190 plts-
Ltd Ed Club (5m4) 95.00
--History of printing in Colonial Maryland 1686 to 1776-Balt-
1922-275p-500c prntd-buck (5tt9) 30.00
--Story of Thos Cresap a Maryland Pioneer-Colum-1928-43, (1)p-
wrps (5h7) 3.00
--The Way of a Ship-Portland-1937-8vo-cl-91, (2)p-9 plts
(5ss2,pencil notes) 35.00
WULFING,JOHN MAX-Letters of Gustavus Wulfing-Fulton-
1941-395p-map-2 ports (4L0,mint) 10.00
WUORINEN,JOHN H-Finns on the Delaware, 1638 to 55-NY-
1938-frontis-map-179p (4m2) 15.00
WURLITZER,RUDOLPH,CO-Illus Catalog of Band Instruments,
Drums,Fifes,etc-Cinn-n.d.-(1887)-102p-wrps (5d7) 8.50
WURTTEMBERG,PAUL WILHELM-Erste Reise nach dem Nordlichen
Amerika in den Jahren 1822 bis 1824-Stuttgart und Tubingen-
1835-Cotta-8vo-mor&bds-fldg map-errata lf-2nd ed
(4h0,lt fox) 600.00
WYANDOT CO,OHIO-Hist of-Chig-1884-1065p (4n9,rbnd) 60.00
WYANDOTTE-(anon)-Phila-1843-Lea&Blanchard-2 vols in 1-
1st Amer ed (5x1) 35. (5mm2) 17.50
WYATT,FRANK S-Brief History of Oklahoma-OklahomaCty-(1919)-
maps-illus-(school text) (5L0) 5. (5xx5) 6.25
WYATT,HAROLD F-Passing of Great Fleet-Lond-1909
(5s1,wn) 8.00
WYATT'S-Travel Diary-Chig-1930-fldg maps-1st ed (5L3,f) 25.00
WYCHERLEY,GEO-Buccaneers of Pacific-Indnpls-(1928)-illus
(5tt5) 7.50 (5s1,wn) 6.50
WYCHERLEY,WM-The Country Wife-Lond-1934-4to-col plts-bds
(5t5,autg) 10. (5t8) 12.50
WYCKOFF,WALTER A-The Workers-NY-1897,1901-2 vols (5w5) 10.00
WYETH,ANDREW,illus-1934, 'Twas the Night Before Christmas-
Music by Ann Wyeth-(Needham,Mass,1934)-dec by Andrew
Wyeth-illus opp pg 122-Wyeth's earliest illus (5gg6) 250.00
WYETH,JOHN A-Life of Lt Gen Nathan Bedford Forrest-NY&Lond-
1908-667p-illus (5xx7,autog) 35.00
--Text Book on Surgery-NY-1887-777p-illus-lea (5t7) 15.00
--With Sabre & Scalpel-NY-1914-534p-1st ed (5m2,cov stn) 8.50
WYETH,N C-Boy's King Arthur-NY-1937-9 col plts (4F6) 8.50
--Black Arrow-NY-1933-9 col plts (4F6,f) 8.50
--David Balfour-NY-1933-9 col plts (4F6,f) 8.50
--Merry Adventures of Robin Hood-NY-1935-by HPyle-
Brandywine Ed-frontis&Cov by NCWyeth-headpiece of intro
by Andrew Wyeth (4F6,vg) 60.00
WYETH,NATH J-Corres & Journals,1831 to 36-Eugene-1899-
FGYoungs,ed-wrps-maps-Vol 1,Pts 3 to 6-errata slip
(5g4) 15. (4d4,4L0) 17.50
WYGANDT,C-The Red Hills-Phila-1929-251p-illus-1st ed (5w9) 16.50
WYL,M-Mormon Portraits-SaltLkCty-1886-320p (5dd1,pres) 30.00
WYLIE,ELINOR-Collected Poems of-Knopf-1932
(5p9) 4.50 (5F1,f,dj) 6.50
--Nets to Catch the Wind-NY-(1921)-orig bds-cl bk-1st prntg-
Ltd Ed Club (5tt7) 27.50
--The Orphan Angel-NY-1926-AlfredAKnopf-8vo-bds-1st ed-
ltd to 190c,box,autg (5ss3,sp fade) 25.00
--Trivial Breath-NY-1928-Knopf-8vo-cl-ltd to 100c,autg (5ss3) 45.00
--Venetian Glass Nephew-NY-1925-Doran-1st ed
(4n3,ltd to 250c,autg) 70. (5j5) 15. (5yy6) 7.50
WYLIE,JAS HAMILTON-Reigh of Henry the Fifth-Cambr-1914-
3 vols (5q0) 20.00
WYLIE,PHILIP-An April Afternoon-(1938)-Farrar&Rinehart
(5F1,vf,dj) 7.50
--Essay on Morals-NY-1947-1st ed (4L0) 6.00
WYLIE,W W-Yellowstone Nat'l Park-KansasCty-(188-)-16mo-
99p (5s4,ex-libr,wn) 15.00
WYLER,SEYMOUR B-Book of Sheffield Plate-NY-(1949)-188p-
8vo-illus (5t4) 7.50
--Book of Old Silver-NY-c1937-447p-illus-1st ed (5w0) 18.50
WYLLARD'S WEIRD-Lond-n.d.-(1885)-J&R Maxwell-3 vols-
orig cl-8vo-1st ed-(Mary Braddon) (5xx6,lend libr,soil) 25.00
WYLLYS,RUFUS-Ariz,the History of a Frontier State-Phoenix-
(1950)-1st ed (5t1,5g2,f,dj) 20. (5r8) 26.50 (5s4) 25.00

WYMAN,A L–Los Angeles Times Prize Cook Book–LosAng–
1923–340p–bds   (5c4,bds dtchd) 5.50   (5x5)   10.00

WYMAN,GILBERT,ed–Public Land & Mining Laws of Alaska,
NWT & Brit Col–Fruitvale–1898–1st ed–roan–776p–fldg map
       (5u6,sl wn & stn)   50.00

WYMAN,LILLIE–A Grand Army Man of Rhode Island–Newton,Mass–
1925–thn8vo–ports–ltd ed   (5m6)   8.50

WYMAN,M E T–Desc of Lawrence & Mary Antisell–1908–335p
       (5t9)   45.00

WYMAN,SETH–Life & Adventures of–written by himself–
Manchester,NH–1843–310p–orig cl–labl   (5s2,sp fade)   125.00

WYMAN,W W,prntr–Laws of Wisc Territory,Passed by 4th
Leg Assembly–Madison–WT–1844–114p–orig bds–calf bk (5x5) 85.00

WYMAN,WALKER–Calif Emigrant Letters–NY–(1952)–Bookman–
illus–177p   (4n1,dj) 7.   (5h5,f,dj)   7.50

WYMER,NORMAN–Engl Country Crafts Lond–(1946)–116p (5n7) 6.50

WYNDHAM BIBLE,THE–n.p.–Christmas,1955–4to–vel–bds–g.–
a.e.g.–India papr–ltd to 100c   (5j2)   25.00

WYNDHAM,HORACE–The Magnificent Montez–Lond–(1935)
       (5x5,v stnd)   10.00

WYNDHAM,RICHARD–The Gentle Savage–NY–1936–WmMorrow–
map–photos–287p   (4a6) 10. **(4t5)**   8.00

WYNN,COMMODORE,ed–Negro Who's Who in California–n.p.–
1948–4to–cl–133p   (4t1)   17.50

WYNN,M R–Pioneer Family of Whiskey Flat–LosAng–(1945)–130p–
1st ed   (4n1,dj)   20.00

WYNN,MARCIA–Desert Bonanza–CulverCty–1949–1st ed (5w4) 25.00

WYNN,W T,ed–Southern Literature–NY–1932   (5x2)   17.50

WYNNE,GLADYS–Architecture Shown to the Children–Lond/Edinb–
n.d.–Jack–131p–sm8vo–cl   (5m5,wn)   10.00

WYNNE,JAS,M D–Private Libraries of NY–NY–1860–frontis–
8vo–3/4 mor–472p–1st ed   (5p5) 32.50   (4c8,sl rub)   37.50

WYNNE,JOHN J–Jesuit Martyrs of North Amer–NY–1925–
246p–cl   (5x5) 8.50   (5h1) 7.50   (4b9)   12.00

WYOMING CO,NY–History of–1880–310p (5ff2,rbkd,cov tn) 50.00

WYOMING–A Guide to Its History,Highways & People–NY–(1941)–
WPA–Amer Guide Ser–1st ed–illus–490p–scarce
      (5h7,sl wn dj) 20.   (4b3,dj,vg)   27.50

––same–NY–(1946)–photos–maps–pkt map–468p plus index–
2nd prntg–Amer Guide Ser–WPA   (4L5,dj)   7.50

WYOMING LAW JOURNAL–1946 to 65–Vol 1 thru 19(all publ)
       (5ii7,rbnd)   285.00

WYOMING,POETRY & HISTORY OF–1844–398p(Penna)(4t2)   60.00

WYOMING–Progressive Men of State of...–Chig–1903–
(AWBowen&Co)–dbl col p–illus(1 by Russell)–lea–g.sides–
1st ed–v.scarce   (4t8,f)   125.00

WYOMING–Resources of Wyo,1889–Official Publ–Cheyenne–
1889–Daily Sun Elec Pr–8vo–77p–wrps–rare   (5g6,sp tn)   85.00

WYOMING STOCK GROWERS ASSN–Brand Book for 1884–
Cheyenne–(1884)–12mo–cl–**(64p)**–interleaved–illus–3rd ed
       (5a3)   100.00

WYOMING VALLEY FLOOD SCENES–Mar 2,1902–n.p.–(60)
leaves–cl   (5jj9)   7.50

WYOMING–Wonderful Wyo,the Undeveloped Empire,Cheyenne–
n.p.–n.d.(ca 1912)–12mo–cl–126p–(facs of orig wrps bnd in)
       (4t1,rebnd)   25.00

WYSONG,THOS T–Rocks of Deer Creek,Hartford Co,Maryland–
Balt–1880–Conlon–12mo–cl–123p   (4t1)   12.50

WYSS,J–Le Robinson Suisse....Avec La Suite–Paris–1835–Didier–
2 vols–8vo–ribbed green cl–g.t.–plts–fldg map   (4a8,f)   25.00

––Le Robinson Suisse–Paris–1841–Didier–4th ed–2 vols in 1–
8vo–calf–plts–fldg map   (4a8,f bndg)   12.50

––Swiss Family Robinson–NY–1909–Harper–lg8vo–dec cl–port–
plts–map–602p   (4a8,uncut)   7.50

––same–(Rising Sun Newspaper Co,ca 1950)–398p–frontis–6 plts–
12mo–pict bds–Japanese text   (5p1)   4.50

––same–Ipswich,(U K)–1963–Ltd Ed Club–4to–plts–illus
       (5zz8,box)   35.00

WYTHE,GEO–History of the 90th Div–NY–1920–259p–cl–illus–
maps   (5h0)   8.00

WYTHES,JOS H–Curiosities of the Microscope–Phila–1852–sm4to–
13 plts(5 col)–orig red cl–g.e.   (5L1)   20.00

XANTUS,JANOS–Levelei Ejszakamerikabol–Budapest–1858–
175p,(1)–12 plts–8vo–hf cl   (5L1,Newberry Libr dupl)   250.00

XENOPHON–History of the Affairs of Greece–by Transl of
Thucydides(Wm Smith)–Lond–1770–Benj White–4to–calf–
fldg frontis   (5b0,sl wn)   37.50

XENOPHONS TREATISE OF HOUSEHOLDE–Lond–1537–
Thos Berthelet–8vo–mor–g.–a.e.g.,by Bedford–2nd ed–v rare
       (4i0,f,from Britwell Libr)   1,000.00

XIMENES DE CISNEROS,L–Dissertazione meccanica di due
strumenti che posson–1752–vel   (5L7)   17.50

XIT RANCH–The XIT Brand–Dalhart,Tex–2 issues,Aug 1939 &
Aug 1940–100p & 88p–illus–ads–wrps   (4L0)   12.50

YAGER,WILLARD E,tr–Orite of Adequentaga–Walton,NY–1953–
164p–15 plts   (4m2)   12.50

YAGGY,L W–Museum of Antiquity–NY–1882–944p–illus (5t4) 15.00

YAKIMA GOLDING HOP FARMS–Illustrated Presentation of–
(Wash,1952)–obl 4to–75p photos–80p   (5w1)   10.00

YAKIMA VALLEY,WASH–North Yakima–(1912)–Yakima Comm
Club–63(64)p–wrps–photos   (5L0)   5.00

YAKIMA VALLEY–Stock Raising in...Land of Opportunity–Yakima–
1911–Sunset Homeseeker's Bur–12mo–wrps–16p   (4t1)   10.00

YALE & TOWNE MFG CO–Yale Products–Builders' Locks & Trim–
Catalog #26–Stamford–1929–4to–517p–illus   (5h8)   10.00

YALE BOOK OF STUDENT VERSE 1910 to 1919–1st ed
      (5d3,autg by Howard Buck)   50.00

YALE,CHAS–Outlines of Gen'l History in 3 parts–Rochester–1830–
EPeck&Co–308p–24mo–calf–lea labl–(16p questions) (5p1,fox)20.00

YALE COLLEGE–History of Class of 1918 plus History of Class
of 1918 Forty Yrs on–n.p.–n.d.–2 vols   (5w5)   7.50

YALE COLLEGE–Sketches of–By a Member of that Insti–NY–
1843–Saxton&Miles–18mo–orig cl–192p–illus–1st ed (5j5) 32.50

YALE COLLEGE SUBJECT TO GENERAL ASSEMBLY–NewHav–1784–
44p–sewn–1st ed   (5m3,libr stmp)   27.50

YALE,CYRUS–Life of Rev Jeremiah Hallock–NY–1828–12mo–lea–
316p   (5t2)   6.00

YALE LAW JOURNAL–1891 to 1970–Vols 1 thru 79–bound
      (5rr4,recent rbnd)   1,580.00

––same–single bound volumes   (5rr4)ea   25.00

YALE & CO,T B–#1 Descrip Catalog of Fruits–Rochester–186–?–
Brighton–32p,2p–plts   (5hh6,sl stns)   10.00

––Descriptive Catalogue of Ornamental Trees,Shrubs,Roses–
Rochester–186–?–wrps–32p   (5hh6,sl wn)   10.00

YAMADA,KEICHYU–Scenes from the Life of Buddha–Chig–
1898–8 tipped in col plts   (5x7)   10.00

YAMHILL,CITY OF–& Vic,Oreg–(Portland,1912,SoPac&Yamhill
Devel Club)–31(33)p–photos   (5L0)   5.00

YANCEY,LEWIS A–Aerial Navig & Meteorology–n.p.–1927–cl–
68p   (4a6)   2.00

YANK–Near complete run of 36 issues,starting 7/9/44 to
3/18/45–British ed   (4n6,f)   75.00

YANK,EDITORS OF–The Best From Yank–NY–1945–illus–4to–
1st ed   (5ii3) 10.   (5x7)   6.50

YANKEE,A–The Southwest–NY–1835–Harper–2 vols–12mo–cl–
papr labls–1st ed of Ingraham's 1st book
     (5x1,rbkd) 40.   (5gg6)   175.00

YANKEE COOK BOOK–NY–(1870)–126p–ads–illus–bds
      (5c4,fox,crack hng)   8.50

YANKEE ENTERPRISE–Or the Two Millionaires–Bost–1855–
(Wentworth&Co)–334p–frontis   (5t4)   7.50

YANKS,A BOOK OF AEF VERSE–Publ in France by Stars &
Stripes–1918–(86p)–wrps   (5h1)   7.50

––same–Publ in France by Stars & Stripes–wrps–1st ed (5hh3) 6.00

––same–NY–1919–157p   (5w5,sl cov stn)   6.50

YARD,ROBT S–Book of Nat'l Parks–NY–1919–420p–photos–maps
      (5s4,autg,rprd)   10.00

––Nat'l Parks Portfolio–Wash–1921–266p–photos–maps (5s4,wn) 4.00

––same–Wash–1931–photos–274p–cl (5t2) 4.50 (5s7,5cc1,f)   3.50

––Our federal lands–NY–1928–Scribners–360p   (5u3,ex-libr)   4.50

––The Top of the Continent–NY,Chig&Bost–(c1917)–12mo–
244p–Scribner's–frontis–photos–pict labl   (5p1)   10.00

YARDLEY,HERBERT O–Amer Black Chamber–Lond–(1937)–266p–
Faber   (5p0)   10.00

YARDLEY,J H R–Before the Mayflower–NY–1931–408p–illus (5h9)8.50

YARDLEY,MARGARET,ed–New Jersey Scrap Book of Women
Writers–Newark–1893–illus–2 vols–ltd to 500c   (4b6)   25.00

YARMON,MORTON–Early Amer Antique Furniture–NY–1952–
144p–illus–Sterling Publ   (5x0)   5.00

YARNALL,ELLIS–Wordsworth&Coleridges–NY–1899
      (4a1,pres,bndg stnd)   10.00

YARRELL,WM–History of British Fishes–Lond–(1835)–1835–orig cl–
8vo–woodcuts–2 vols–1st ed   (5z9,vg)   15.00

YARROW,H C–Intro to Study of Mortuary Customs among NoAmer
Indians–Wash–1880–4to–wrps–1 plt–Smi Inst–BAE   (5L1)   10.00

YARROW,WM–Robt Henri,His Life & Works–NY–1921–
Boni&Liveright–115p–plts–ltd to 990c–nbrd (5m7,bkstrp tn) 75.00

YATES,EDMUND H–My Haunts & Their Frequenters–Lond–1854–
16mo–orig illus wrps–1st ed of auth's 1st book–rare (5gg6) 50.00

YATES,JOHN V–History of State of NY–1824–428p–fldg map–
bds–2 parts bnd in 1   (5zz0)   40.00

YATES,LUCY H–Model Kitchen–NY–1905–118p–illus (5w7) 5.00

YATES,RAYMOND F–Hobby Book of Stenciling & Brush Stroke
Painting–NY–1951–131p   (5n7)   5.00

YATES,RAYMOND FRANCIS,ed-Everyman's Guide to Radio-NY-
  1927-Vols 1 to 4-illus   (5b8)   8.50
--same-NY-1926-Vol 4-Contains illus of equipment & wiring diagrams
  not in Vol 4 above   (5b8)   5.00
YATES,ROBT L-When I Was a Harvester-NY-1930-174p
        (5s4) 6.   (5w8)   10.00
YATES,W PAUL-Aviation in Hawaii-Honolulu-(1936)-173p-
  illus-lea-Paradise of Pacific Pr   (5d6,wn)   25.00
YAVAPI CO,ARIZ-Picturesque Gold, Silver & Copper Mining in-
  Prescott-1903-Sappiger-64p   (5n4)   25.00
YAZOO LANDS-Statement of Facts Shewing Right of Certain Co
  to the Lands etc-Phila-1795-stitchd-32 lvs (5r5,fox,unopnd)125.00
YE BOOK OF COPPERHEADS-Phila-1863-24 cartoons-obl 8vo-
  pict wrps   (5g3,sp wn)   20.00
YEAGER,DON G-Bibliogr of Nat'l Parks & Monuments West
  of Mississippi River-Wash-1941-WPA-Part 2,Central States,
  SW States & Terr-mimeo   (5j4)   12.50
YEAKEL,R-Bishop Jos Long Peerless Preacher of Evangelical Assn-
  Cleve-(1897)-261p-cl   (5h1)   8.50
YEARBOOK OF AGRICULTURE-1949-Trees- (5kk7)   7.50
YEARBOOKS -of Amer Pharmaceutical Assoc-Chig-10 vols-
  Vols 4 thru 12,14-1915 thru 23 & 1925   (5w3)   30.00
YEARSLEY,ANN-The royal captives-Phila-1795-WmW Woodward-
  12mo-sheep-labl   (5i0,hng wn)   20.00
YEARSLEY,MACLEOD-Folklore of Fairy Tale-Lond-1924-
  Watts&Co-240p-g. cl   (5c8,dj)   15.00
YEARY,MAMIE-Remin of the Boys in Gray, 1861 to 1865- Dallas
  1912-904p-3/4 mor   (5j6, chip)   100.00
YEATES,W S-Prelim Report on part of Gold Deposits of Georgia-
  Atlanta-1896-542p-maps-illus-orig wrps-Bul #4A
        (5w9,wn,ex-libr)   7.50
YEATS,J B-Letters to his Son W B Yeats & Others 1869 to 1922-
  NY-1946-Dutton-1st ed   (5m2) 7.50   (4p1,dj)   17.50
YEATS,WM BUTLER-Autobiographies,Reveries Over Childhood,
  Youth & Trembling of the Veil-NY-1927-Macmillan-
  1st Amer ed   (5p9) 5.   (5F1,f,dj)   8.00
--Bounty of Sweden-Dublin-1925-Cuala Press-cl bds, lin sp-
  1st ed-ltd to 400c   (5ss7,unopnd,orig glassine) 85. (4g2) 100.00
--The Cat & The Moon & Certain Poems-Dublin-1924-
  Cuala Pr-orig cl bk bds-ltd to 500c   (5ss9,f)   75.00
--The Celtic Twilight-Lond-1902-Cr8vo-cl-frontis-1st ed
        (5ss9,pres,unopnd)   375.00
--Collected Poems-NY-1933-Macmillan   (5m2)   5.00
--Cutting of an Agate-Lond-1919-Macmillan-orig cl-1st Engl ed-
  ltd to 1500c   (4g1) 20.   (5ss3)   30.00
--Death of Synge & Other Passages from an Old Diary-Dublin-
  1928-ltd to 400c   (5a9,f)   72.00
--Deidre-Lond, Dublin-1907-Cr8vo-bds-cl bk-papr labl-1st ed
        (5ss7,autg,sp def)   150.00
--Dramatis Personae-Dublin-1935-Cuala Pr-8vo-bds&cl-
  ltd to 400c-1st ed   (5ee9)   85.00
--same-NY-1936-Macmillan-200p   (5x0)   5.00
--Early Poems & Stories-NY-1925-Macmillan-cl bk bds-ltd to 250c
        (4b5,autg,mint,box)   85.00
--Estrangement-Dublin-1926-Cuala Press-cl bds, lin sp-1st ed-
  ltd to 300c   (5hh1,vg) 65.   (4g2)   100.00
--Fairy & Folk Tales of Irish Peasantry-Lond-1888-1st ed-orig cl-
  ads-6p ads at end-papr labl   (5tt5,f)   120.00
--Four Plays for Dancers-NY-1921-Macmillan-12mo-orig bds-
  1st Amer ed   (5ss9)   10.00
--Four Plays-Churchtown-1921-Cuala Pr-1st ed-ltd to 400c
        (4g1,sl dustsoil)   75.00
--The Hour Glass,Cathleen N Houlihan,the Pot of Broth-Vol 2
  of Plays for Irish Theatre-Lond-1904-Bulen (4g1) 30.00
--If I Were Four and Twenty-Dublin-1940-Cuala Pr-1st ed-
  ltd to 450c,nbrd   (5hh1,vg)   65.00
--The Land of Hearts Desire-Portland-1909-ThosBMosher-12mo-
  orig bds-ltd to 950c   (5ss9,f)   12.50
--same-NY-n.d.-Dodd, Mead-55p-16mo-flex bds (5p7) 3.50
--Letters on Poetry from...to Dorothy Wellesley-Lond, NY, Tor-
  1940-Oxf U Pr-1st ed   (4p1,dj,fox)   15.00
--Michael Robartes & the Dancer-Churchtown-1920-Cuala Pr-
  cl bk bds-ltd to 400c   (4g1,lt dust soil)   75.00
--New Poems-Dublin-1938-Cr8vo-bds-lin bk-papr labls-Cuala Pr-
  1st ed-ltd to 450c,orig glassine   (5ss7)   90.00
--October Blast-Dublin-1927-Cuala Pr-8vo-bds&cl-ltd to 350c-
  1st ed   (5ee9,unopnd)   85.00
--A Packet for Ezra Pound-Dublin-1929-Cuala Pr-8vo-bds&lin-
  ltd to 425c-1st ed   (5ee9,unopnd)   85.00
--Pages from a Diary Written in 1930-Dublin-1944-Cuala Pr-
  8vo-bds&cl-ltd to 280c-1st ed   (5ee9,unopnd)   85.00
--Plays in Prose & Verse-NY-1924-Macmillan-orig cl bk bds-
  spec ed-ltd to 250c,nbrd,autg   (5ss9,wn)   40.00

YEATS,WM BUTLER (continued)
--Poems & Ballads of Young Ireland-Dublin-1888-12mo-orig white
  cl   (5d9,box)   250.00
--Poems of W B Yeats-Lond-1949-Macmillan-2 vols-g.t.-
  ltd to 375 sets-autg   (4b1,mint,box)   450.00
--Poems of Wm Blake-Lond&NY-1893-12mo-orig blue cl-
  g.-t.e.g.-1st ed   (5ee9)   65.00
--The Poetical Works of-NY-1906,07-Macmillan-2 vols-12mo-
  cl-1st ed   (5ss3,fade)   50.00
--Reveries Over Childhood & Youth-Lond-1916-1st trade ed-
  col frontis-2 ports-213p   (5dd0)   30.00
--same-NY-1916-Macmillan-1st Amer ed   (4g1,mint) 35.00
--Samhain,An occasional review-(Dublin)-Sep 1903-4to-
  brown wrps   (5ee9)   35.00
--same-(Dublin)-Nov 1905-4to-brown wrps (5ee9) 25.00
--The secret rose-Lond-1897-Lawrence&Bullen-8vo-orig cl-
  frontis-6 plts-1st ed   (5i8,vf)   80.00
--Selected Poems-NY-1921-Macmillan-1st Amer ed (5ss9) 20.00
--The Shadowy Waters-Lond-1900- -cl-g.t.-1st ed
        (5d9, Wilfrid Gibson's copy)   150.00
--same-NY-n.d.-(1901)-Dodd, Mead-16mo-orig prntd wrps-spec ed
  for Xmas gift-scarce   (5i8,crack)   20.00
--Stories of Red Hanrahan-Dundrum-1904-Dun Emer Pr-8vo-
  orig qtr lin-1st ed-ltd to 500c   (5i8, linen wn) 65.00
--Tower-Lond-1928-8vo-cl dec g.-1st ed (5cc9,dj) 85.00
--Three Things-Lond-1929-#18 of Ariel Poems-orig bds-
  ltd to 500c,autg   (5a9) 50.   (4g1,sp chip) 60.00
--same-n.d.-orig prntd wrps-1st trade ed (4b5,chip) 7.50
--A Vision-Lond-1925-Laurie-8vo-parch bk bds-ltd to 600c,nbrd,
  autg   (4g1,sp fade)   150.00
--Wheels & Butterflies-Lond-1934-Macmillan-1st ed-ltd to 3000c
        (4g1)   20.00
--Where There is Nothing,Being Vol 1 of Plays for an Irish
  Theater-NY&Lond-1903-Macmillan-ltd to 100c on Jap vel
        (4g2)   100.00
--same-Lond-1903-Bullen-cl bk bds-1st Engl ed (4g1) 30.00
--Wild Swans at Coole-Lond-1919-12mo-cl-1st ed
        (5d9,WWGibson's autg)   50.00
--same-NY-1919-Macmillan-1st Amer ed (5d9, mint) 30.00
YEE,CHIANG-Chinese Calligraphy-Cambr,Mass-(1955)-HUP
        (5j3,dj,pres)   12.00
--A Chinese Childhood-NY-(1953)-JnDay-304p-frontis-
  7 col plts-2nd Amer ed (5x0) 6. (5p1,dj tn) 5.00
--The Silent Traveller in Boston-NY-1959-Norton-275p-
  col illus   (5p7)   5.00
--The Silent Traveller in NY-NY-n.d.-JDay-281p-col illus
        (5t7,dj) 5.   (5p0)   6.00
YELLOW BIRD-Life & Adventures of Murieta,Celebrated Calif
  Bandit-Norman-(1955)-210p-bds   (5dd4)   4.50
YELLOW BOOK-An Illus Quarterly-Apr 1894 to 1897-8vo-
  orig yellow bds-Vols 1 thru 13-complete set
        (5m4) 200.   (5ee9)   225.00
YELLOWLEES,JOHN-Yellowless Family-(1931)-54p (4t2) 35.00
YELLOWPLUSH,THE-Correspondence-Phila-1838-12mo-orig bds-
  cl bk-(Thackeray)-1st ed of auth's 1st book (5gg6,hng wn) 250.00
YELLOWSTONE NATL PARK-In Photogravure from Recent Negatives-
  by TW Ingersoll-(StPaul)-c1900-19p   (4a5)   27.50
YELLOWSTONE NATL PARK-1928-Northern Pac-wrps-oblong-
  48p-illus   (5h0)   2.00
YELLOWSTONE NATL PARK,Wyo-US Pub Doc-Wash-1933-
  67p-wrps-illus-maps-stpld   (5s4)   3.50
YELLOWSTONE NATL PARK-US Dept of Int-1935-42p-maps-
  illus   (5ss1)   2.50
YELLOWSTONE RIVER WYO,MONT & NDAK-Wash-1934-
  H Doc #256-176p plus 19 fldg maps   (5L2)   7.50
YENNE,BETTY J-Mercer Co,Ky Census Rec 1789,1800,1820,
  Tax List 1795-FtW-1965-4p,31p,19p,35p-cl-ltd to 100c (5h1)12.50
YENRO,MANUEL-Manual de Cocina Yucateca-Merida De
  Yucatan-1900-107p-wrps-2nd ed,corr&enlrgd (5c5,chip) 22.50
--same-Merida De Yucatan-1903-107p,(3)-bds-3rd ed, corr &enlrgd
        (5c5,wn)   20.00
YEOMAN,R S-Catalog of Modern World Coins-Racine-1957-
  Whitman Pub-509p-illus-fabr-1st ed   (5t7)   7.50
YEOMANS,EDW-Men,Steam & the Driven Wheel-Rutland-
  (1939)-(Tuttle)-173p-illus   (5t7,dj)   5.00
--Shackled Youth-Bost-c1921-Atlantic Monthly Pr-12mo-138p-
  pict cl-t.e.g.   (5p1,sl tn)   10.00
YERBURGH,E R-Some Notes on the Family History-1912-324p
        (4t2)   15.00
YERBURY,F R-Georgian Details of Domestic Architecture-
  1926-lg4to-photos   (4a2,sp tn)   8.50
YERBY,FRANK-The Foxes of Harrow-1946 (5L7) 3.50
--same-NY-1947   (5x2)   2.50

YERKES,JN W-Short Pamphlet Devote to Live Stock Interests of Ky-Danville-1893-29p-wrps (5h1) 8.50

YERKES,R M-Chimpanzees,A Laboratory Colony-NewHav-1943-orig cl-63 plts-321p-v scarce (4p5) 18.50

YERRINGTON,JAS-Rept of Case of Geo C Hersey Indicted for Murder of Betsey Frances Tirrell-Bost-1862-267p (5w0,edge wn) 16.50

YESLAH,M D-A Tenderfoot in Southern Calif-NY-1908-Little&Ives-150p-t8vo-orig buck-autg,nbrd ed (5L8,sl wn) 13.50

YIM,LOUISE-My 40 Year Fight for Korea-Lond-1952-Gollancz-313p (5x9) 3.00

YOAKUM,H-History of Texas from its 1st Settlement in 1685 to Its Annex in 1846-Austin-1936-587p-facs of 1855 ed-2 vols in 1-cl (4j6) 12.50

YOCKEY,FRANCIS P-Imperium-Philosophy of History & Politics-NY-1948 (5x7,dj) 6.50

YOCOM,ERNEST G-High on a Hill-Oberlin-1953-103p-cl-priv publ (5h2,dj) 5.00

YO ANANDA,P-Autobiogr of a Yogi-LosAng-1956-514p-illus-cl (5t2) 4.00

YOHANNAN,JOHN D-A Treasury of Asian Literature-NY-(1956)-487p (5t7) 6.00

YOKLEY,ANN-Grass & Water-1955-280p-illus-1st ed (5k2) 6.50

YOLO COUNTY-Illus Atlas & History of-SanFran-1879-De Pue&Co-folio-lea bkd-illus-ports-maps-scarce (5h4,cov sl wn) 275.00

YONGE,CHARLOTTE M-Aunt Charlotte's Hist of French Hist for Little Ones-Marcus Ward-1884-sm sq8vo-dec cl-a.e.g.-339p-col frontis-plts-7th thous (5s0) 6.50

--A Book of Golden Deeds-Lond-n.d.-4to-g.t.-pict cl-plts (5p5) 10.00

--The Cook & the Captive-n.d.-Nat Soc Depository-8vo-dec cl-plts-g.t.-228p (4a8) 5.00

--Countess Kate-Lond-Faber-1948-8vo-216p-Raverat illus-cl-g. (5a1) 3.50

--The dove in the eagle's nest-Lond-1866-Macmillan-2 vols-8vo-orig cl-1st ed (5xx6) 25.00

--same-NY-1924-315p-col illus (5w9) 6.50

--The Heir of Redclyffe-Lond-1901-8vo-Kate Greenaway,illus- (5p5) 10.00

--The Lances of Lynwood-Lond-1855-JnWParke-8vo-orig cl-frontis-1st ed-7 plts-scarce (5xx6) 35.00

--Love & Life-Lond-1880-Macmillan-2 vols-8vo-orig cl-1st ed (5xx6) 25.00

--Nuttie's father-Lond-1885-Macmillan-2 vols-8vo-orig cl-1st ed (5xx6,f) 45.00

--A reputed changling-Lond-1889-Macmillan-2 vols-8vo-orig cl-1st ed (5xx6) 30.00

--Storehouse of Stories-1870-Macmillan-8vo-cl-g.t.-437p-1st ed (4d1) 15.00

--Story of Easter-Lond-M Ward-(ca1895)-sm8vo-32p-plts&dec padded cl (5a1) 4.50

--Young Folks' History of Greece-Bost-1879-Estes&Lauriat-8vo-dec cl-g.t.-plts-427p (4a8) 5.00

YONGE,SAM'L H-The Site of Old James Towne-Richmond-1904-86p-illus & maps(1 fldg) (5h9) 5. (5r7) 7.50

YONKERS BOARD OF TRADE-Yonkers Illus-(ca 1902)-192p of photos plus list of sights etc (5L3) 3.50

YORICK,MR -A Sentimental Journey Through France & Italy (Laurence Sterne)-Lond-1768-Becket&DeHondt-12mo-calf-2 vols-1st ed (5xx6) 250. (4b5,box) 300.00

--same-Lond-1776-Becket-2 vols-calf (5x3) 10.00

YORK,ALVIN C-Sergeant York-NY-1928-1st ed-illus (4a1,autg) 25.00

YORK,S A,JR,ed-Yale Humor-NewHaven-(1890's?)-94p-illus-10p ads-2nd ed (5i1,cov wn) 4.50

YORKE,DANE-Able Men of Boston-Bost-1950-253p-illus (4b8) 4.50

YORKE,PHILIP-Cassandra-Cambr-1806-Univ Pr-RWatts,prntr-lg4to-leather-a.e.g.-fldg tabl-1st ed (5i8,f,f bndg) 40.00

--The royal tribes of Wales-Wrexham-1799-JohnPainter-hf calf-12 ports-lf of errata-rev (5x3) 20.00

YOSELOFF,T-7 Poets in Search of an Answer-NY-1944 (5x2,dj) 17.50

YOSEMITE NATL PARK,CALIF-SanFran-Pac Novelty Co-handcol illus-sm folio-12 lvs-wrps (4a5) 12.50

YOSEMITE VALLEY THRU THE STEREOSCOPE-NY-(1908)-70p(bnd text)-map-24 slides,in 1 case (5s4,f,dj) 20.00

YOST,KARL-Bibliography of Works of Edna St Vincent Millay-NY-1937-248p-1st ed (4g2) 35.00

--Chas M Russell,Cowboy Artist,a Bibliography-Pasadena-1948-218p-1st ed-ltd to 500c (5yy1) 15. (4a0) 25.00

YOUATT,WM-Cattle,their breeds,management & diseases-Lond-n.d.(ca 1870)-illus-600p (5t4) 5.00

--same-Lond-1864-608p-illus (5dd9,sp wn) 6.00

YOUATT,WM (continued)

--The Dog-NY-1858-Leavitt&Allen-ed wi additions by EJLewis-8vo-pict cl-plts-403p (5j5) 12.50

--same-Phila-(ca 1850)-8vo-403p-illus-EJLewis,ed,wi additions (4a6,hng weak) 10.00

--The Horse,A New Edition wi illus-NY-(ca 1850)-illus-448p (5t7,libr labl) 8.00

--The Pig-Phila-1847-1st ed (5b9,fox) 7.50

YOUELL,GEO-Lower Class-Sea-1938-265p-21 plts (5s1,rprd) 3. (5aa0) 5.00

YOULE,W E-63 Years in the Oilfields-Taft,Calif-1926-8vo-cl-81p&illus-v scarce (5h4,spots,rub) 37.50

YOUMA-Story of West Indian Slave-NY-1890-frontis-orig prnt calico-papr labl-1st ed (5q0) 15.00

YOUMAN,A E-A Dictionary of Every Day Wants-NY-1873-539p,(12)-4to (5w7,sl fray) 8.50

YOUMANS,EDW L-Alcohol & Constitution of Man-NY-1854-142p-wrps (5ff7) 7.50

--Chemical Atlas-NY-1855-folio-106p-13 col plts-1st ed (5v2,fox) 30.00

YOUMANS,ELIZA A,ed-Lessons in Cookery-NY-1878-pic cl-383p-handbook-Natl Training School for Cookery,Lond-(5ww2,chip) 10.00

YOUNG,A-L'Example de la France avis la Grande Bretagne-Quebec-1794-Neilson-calf-149p-2nd ed (5w8,lcaks 16 lvs,close crop) 100.00

YOUNG,A E-The Two Soos,Amer & Canadian-Sault Ste Marie,Ont-(ca 1902)-oblong 8vo-orig wrps-2p of text-52p of illus (5ss5,fray) 12.50

YOUNG,A S"DOC"-Great Negro Baseball Stars-NY-1953-illus (5x2) 6.50

YOUNG,A W-Hist of Warsaw,NY-1869-400p (5t9) 27.50

YOUNG,AGATHA-Women & Crisis-NY-(1959)-389p-cl (5h7,f,dj) 5.00

YOUNG,ALEXANDER-Chronicles of the first planters of Colony of Mass Bay,from 1623 to 1636-Bost-1846-mor-map-port (5g8,libr buck) 20. (5m6) 30.00

YOUNG AMERICAN'S LIBRARY-Phila-(1845 to8)-Lindsay&Blakiston-6 vols-cl-g.spines-illus (5rr2,f) 15.00

YOUNG,ANDREW W-First Lessons in Civil Govt-Cleve-1846-224p-lea (5h1) 7.50 (5h0,rub) 10.00

--History of Chautauqua Co,NY-Buffalo-1875-672p-pt lea (5jj9)35.00

--History of Wayne Co,Indiana-Cinn-1872-RobtClarkeCo-459p plus 1p corr-cl-lea bk-ports-views (5r0) 15.00

YOUNG,ANN ELIZA-Wife #19,or The Story of a life in bondage-Hartf-1877-port-605p (5t4) 10.50

YOUNG,ANNA G-Off Watch-Tor-1957-166p-illus (5a1) 4.50

YOUNG,ART-On my Way-NY-(1928)-illus-ltd ed-bds-vel back (5ii3) 20.00

--Thos Rowlandson-NY-1938-Willey Book Co-54p-illus (5x0) 5.00

YOUNG,BENNETT H-Confederate Wizards of the Saddle-Kennesaw-1958-633p-illus-maps-reprnt(5x2) 15. (4p8) 25.00

--History of Jessamine County,Ky-Louisville-1898-illus-288p (5yy8) 50.00

--The Prehistoric Men of Kentucky-Louisville-1910-329p plus index-maps-photos-cl-1st ed (5LU) 25.00

YOUNG,CHAS ALEX-Historical Documents Advocating Christian Union-Chig-1904 (5x7) 5.00

YOUNG,CHAS E-Dangers of the Trail in 1865-Geneva-1912-map-illus-148p (5dd1,4d9) 10. (5hh3,4a8) 15.00

YOUNG,CHAS L-Wallpaper & Wallpaper Hanging-NY-(1926)-illus-289p (5w7,ex-libr) 5.00

YOUNG,CLIFFORD M,comp-The Young(Jung) Families of Mohawk Valley-Albany-(1947)-2 pts in 1 vol (5jj3) 17.50

YOUNG,DAL-Apologia pro Oscar Wilde-45p-4to-wrps-1st issue (wi "judgment" misspelled on pg14. Imprint on title,cov & beneath last line of text all eradicated (5r9) 17.50

YOUNG,DAVID-Lectures on Science of Astronomy-Morris Town-1821-for Author-108p-12mo-orig sheep (5L1) 25.00

YOUNG,DAVID-Wonderful History of the Morristown Ghost...Revised-Newark-1826-Benj Olds-24mo-orig cl bkd bds-3rd ed (4h0,sp fray) 125.00

--same-Newark-1826-revised-2nd ed (5i0,sp wn) 50.00

YOUNG,DESMOND-Rommel,the Desert Fox-NY-1950-Harper-264p-illus (5p0) 4.50

YOUNG,DONALD-Amer Minority Peoples-NY-1932-621p (5L7) 7.50 (5x2) 15.00

YOUNG,E-SoAmerican Excursion-1940-illus (5L7) 5.00

YOUNG,E G R-Anastasia Arrives-NY-1929-illus (5x2) 7.50

YOUNG,EDWIN-One of Our Submarines-Lond-1952-320p-maps-photos (5s1) 5.00

YOUNG,EGERTON RYERSON-By Canoe & Dog train among the Cree & Salteaux Indiands-Lond-1890-267p-illus (5L0) 6.50

YOUNG, EGERTON RYSERSON (continued)
--same-NY-1891-267p-illus   (4k5,wn) 2.50(4i7) 4. (4L0)   5.00
--same-Lond-1892-262p   (5dd7)   7.50
--same-Tor-n.d.-267p-col plts   (4b9)   5.00
--same-NY-n.d.-267p-illus   (4g7,stnd) 2.50 (5w0)   6.50
--Children of the Forest, A Story of Indian Love-NY-(1904)-
    (Revell)-1st Amer ed   (5ee3,f)   2.50
--On the Indian Trail-NY-(1897)-illus-214p (4b2,sp loose) 6.50
--Oowikapun, or, how the Gospel reached the Nelson River
    Indians-Lond-1895-ChasHKelly-162p-cl   (5d6)   12.50
--same-NY-(1896)-illus-240p   (4b2)   4.00
--Stories from Indian Wigwams & Northern Camp Fires-NY-
    (1892)-illus-dec cov-293p (4b2,rprd,4i7,soil) 4.(5a1,cov spot) 3.50
--same-Lond-1892-plts-293p   (5a1)   4.00
YOUNG EMIGRANTS, THE-A tale designed for young persons-
    Bost-1830-Carter&Hendee-12mo-orig roan & bds-1st ed (5x1) 50.00
YOUNG, ERNEST-West of the Rockies-Lond-1949-220p plus index-
    illus-maps-1st ed   (4L0,dj)   4.00
YOUNG, FILSON-Christopher Columbus & the New World of His
    Discovery-Lond-1906-2 vols-cl-illus-maps (5p5) 20. (5m2) 10.00
--Mastersingers-Lond-(1901)-WmReeves-202p (5p0)   5.00
YOUNG FOLKS'COMPANION-NY-(c1896)-JErskineClarke, ed-
    HMCaldwell-412p-frontis-5 plts-stapld-cl bkd bds
                                         (5p1,edges wn)   12.50
YOUNG, FRANCIS-Every Man His Own Mechanic-Lond-1890-
    Ward, Lock-8th ed-924p plus ads-cl   (5yy3)   15.00
YOUNG, FRANCIS BRETT-Marching on Tanga, With Gen Smuts in
    East Africa-Lond-1917-Collins-fldg map-photos-264p(4t5,fox) 15.00
YOUNG, FRANK-Echoes from Arcadia-Denver-1903-220p-1st ed
    ltd to 200c- v scarce   (5L0)   45.00
YOUNG, FRANK C-Across the Plains in 1865-Denver-1905-224p-
    map-ltd to 200c   (5s2)   65.00
YOUNG, COL G F-The Medici-NY-(1910)-lg&thk8vo-2 vols-
    illus   (5p6,f)   10.00
YOUNG, G GORDON-Voyage of State-Lond-1939-327p-ports-
    plts   (5a1)   5.00
YOUNG, G M-Gibbon-Lond-1932-182p-front   (5a1)   3.50
--Victorian England, portrait of an age-Lond-1936-8vo-cl-213p-
    illus   (5t0)   4.00
YOUNG, G O-Alaskan Trophies Won & Lost-Bost-(1928)-
    illus-248p   (5ss8,autg)   15.00
--same-Hungtinton -1947-plts-273p   (4a8)   12.50
YOUNG, GEOFFREY W-On High Hills-NY-(c 1926)-368p-illus
                                         (5t4)   6.75
YOUNG, GEO, ed-Columbus Memorial etc-Phila-1893-167p-
    frontis-prntd in facs   (4L0)   6.50
YOUNG, GERALD-Witch's Kitchen or the India Rubber Doctor-
    Lond-(ca 1912)-Harrap&Co-8 col plts-dec cl (5c8,lt spot) 15.00
YOUNG, HARRY-Hard Knocks-Portland-1915-242p-25 plts-
    1st ed   (5s4,edges firestnd) 17.50 (4L0)   30.00
--same-Chig-(1915)-242p-cl-2nd ed-17 plts   (5h1)   15.00
YOUNG, HAZEL-The Working Girl Must Eat-Bost-1942-208p
                                         (5c9)   3.00
--The Working Girl's Own Cook Book-Bost-1948-1st ed-227p
                                         (5c9)   3.50
YOUNG HEADS & HAPPY HEARTS-NY-n.d.-McLoughlinBros-
    (10)p-col cov illus-pict wrps   (5ff7)   7.50
YOUNG, HUGH-A Surgeon's Autobiography-1940-Harcourt, Brace-
    3 col prints-2nd ed   (5ww4)   5.00
YOUNG, ISABEL N-The Story of Coffee-NY-(c 1940)-40p-map-
    photos   (5w1)   3.50
YOUNG, J-A Good Man-Indpls-1953-1st ed   (5x2,dj)   7.50
YOUNG, J B-The Battle of Gettysburg-NY-1913-463p-maps-
    illus-1st ed   (5a9)   7.50
YOUNG, J C-Liberia Rediscovered-NY-1934-illus-1st ed (5x2) 4.50
YOUNG, J H-Tourist's Pocket Map of Penna-Phila-1837-col-
    13 x 15"   (5y0)   15.00
YOUNG, J R, ed-Memorial History of City of Phila from its first
    settlement 1895 to 98-4to-plt   (5L7,rbnd)   25.00
YOUNG, REV JACOB-Autobiography of a Pioneer-Cinn-1858-
    port-528p   (5q0)   10.50
--same-Cinn-n.d.-(ca 1890?)-528p-cl-undated Cinn ed (5h1)   6.50
YOUNG, JAS-War With Spain including Battles On Sea & Land-
    Phila-(1898)712p-illus   (5L3)   5.00
YOUNG, JAS C-Harvey S Firestone 1868 to 1938-n.p.-1938-
    bds-82p-frontis-priv prntd   (5y2,sl wn)   5.50
--Liberia Rediscovered-NY-1934-Dblday-photos-211p (4t5)   7.50
YOUNG, JAS WEBB-Ego Biography, Chapt 1, Boyhood-Coapa, NM-
    1955-12mo-priv prntd-ltd to 600c   (5a8)   2.00
YOUNG, JENNIE C-Ceramic Art-1879-4to-illus (5L7,rub)   12.50
YOUNG, JESSE B-Battle of Gettysburg-NY-1913-maps-illus-
    463p   (4m7) 7.50   (5tt5) 10. (5s9) 7.50
--What a Boy Saw In The Army-NY-(1894)-398p-illus-1st ed (5L3) 7.75

YOUNG, JOHN H-Our Deportment-Detroit-1881-424p-
    frontis   (5w4) 5. (5w7,sl fox)   5.50
YOUNG, JOHN P-Journalism in California-SanFran-(1915)-
    illus-8vo-362p   (4g6)   7.50
--San Francisco-SanFran&Chig-(1912)-Clarke-4to-illus-2 vols-
    ltd, autg   (5F5,f)   47.50
YOUNG, JOHN R, ed-Memorial History of City of Phila-NY-
    1895-illus-4to-2 vols   (4m4,rebnd)   30.00
YOUNG, JOHN RUSSELL-Around the World With Gen'l Grant-
    NY-c1879-2 vols-hf lea-illus-4to   (5j6,5h9)   7.50
YOUNG, LIEUT L D-Remin of a Soldier of the Orphan Brigade-
    Paris, Ky-n.d.(1918?)-99p-orig wrps (5x5,marg stn) 7.50 (5L0)15.00
--same-n.p.-n.d.-(Louisvl-1922)-99p-wrps   (5h2)   10.00
YOUNG LADIES'ASTRONOMY-Concise System of Physical,
    Practical & Descrip Astronomy, adapted to Use of Common
    Schools-by M R Bartlett-Utica-1825-bds-195p-4 plts-4to(4p3) 22.50
YOUNG LADIES' TREASURE BOOK-Lond-n.d.(ca 188-)-890p-
    frontis-wdcuts   (5n7)   8.50
YOUNG LADY'S BOOK-Lond-1829-504p, (2)-plts-2nd ed
                                         (5w7, cov sl wn)   5.00
YOUNG, LUCIEN-The "Boston" Man of War at Hawaii-Wash-
    1898-8vo-cl-2 maps(1 fldg)-1st ed-scarce (5p5)   17.50
YOUNG, M-Plantation Bird Legends-NY-1902-illus (5x2)   20.00
YOUNG, M-The Whole Art of Confectionary-NY-1834-1st Amer
    ed from 11th Lond ed-60p-prntd wrps (5c5,rbnd,sl tn,fox) 12.50
YOUNG, M G-The Amer Herb Doctor-Vol 1, 12 issues-1911, 12-
    Seattle-4to-port-frontis-384p, (2),   (5w3,scuff)   20.00
YOUNG MAN'S BOOK OF CLASSICAL LETTERS-Phila-1838-
    12mo-plts-320p   (5w7,fox)   8.50
YOUNG MAN'S LIBRARY-Phila-1835-Desilver, Thomas & Co-
    1st ed-5 vols-t12mo-orig cl-320p ea vol-frontis-g.t. (5u6) 35.00
YOUNG MAN'S OWN BOOK-Phila-1835-16mo-320p-lea
                                         (5w7, scuff)   7.50
YOUNG MAN'S SUNDAY BOOK-NY-1853-Leavitt&Allen-
    320p-32mo-engrv title by Tucker-frontis-pict -a.e.g.(5p1) 12.50
YOUNG MOUNTAINEERS, THE-Short Stories-Bost-1897-
    Houghton, Miff-262p-(Mary N Murfree)-1st ed   (5x4)   25.00
YMCA-Catalogue of library, consti & bylaws of-Richmond-1868-
    Gary&Clemmitt-8vo-stitchd as issued (5i9)   8.00
YOUNG, OTIS-First Military Escort on the Santa Fe Trail-
    Glendale-1952-illus-fldg map-210p plus index (5L0,unopnd) 17.50
YOUNG PEOPLE'S ILLUSTRATED BIBLE HISTORY-Norwich-1873-
    Henry Bill-8vo-frontis-13 plts-4 maps-588p-stampd lea
                                         (5p1,wn)   15.00
YOUNG, ROBT KENNEDY-Tales of Tioga, Penna & Its People-
    Phila-(1916)-12mo-1st ed   (5m6)   8.50
YOUNG, ROBT W-Navajo Language-Phoenix-1943-buck-4to-
    scarce   (4L0,4k5,f)   25.00
--Vocabulary of Coloquial Navaho-Phoenix-1951-cl-12mo
                                         (4k5,f)   12.50
YOUNG, ROGERS W-Robert E Lee & Ft Pulaski-Wash-1941-illus-
    wrps-27p   (4j4)   4.00
YOUNG, ROLAND-Actors & Others -Chig-1925-orig bds-8vo
                                         (4m8)   12.50
--Not for Children-GardenCty-1930-Dblday-thn4to-col pict bds-
    cl bk-unpgd-1st ed   (5j5,dj)   15.00
--This is Congress-NY-1943-1st ed   (5q8,dj)   2.50
YOUNG, S GLENN-Life & Exploits of...Herrin, Ill-n.d.(ca 1924)-
    253p-photos   (5w0,rub,fade) 10. (5L2)   20.00
YOUNG, S HALL-Adventures in Alaska-NY-(1919)-181p-photos-
                                         (5ss1,pres)   10.00
--Alaska Days With John Muir-NY-1915-226p-illus-cl
                         (4b9) 6. (4g7) 3.50 (5a1)   5.00
--Klondike Clan, Tale of the Great Stampede-NY-(1916)-
    Revell-dec cl-393p   (5rr0) 10. (5ss1,pres)   12.50
YOUNG, S P-Wolves of NoAmer-Wash-1944-orig cl-g.-8vo-
    2 parts in 1 vol-131 plts(6 col)-maps-636p   (4p5)   35.00
YOUNG, STANLEY-The Clever Coyote-Harrisburg-1951-photos-
    1st ed   (4L0,f,dj)   8.50
--The Puma, Mysterious Amer Cat-Wash-1946-358p-illus-
    2 parts in 1 vol   (5t7)   7.50
--Sektches of Amer Wild Life-Balt-1946-139p-photos
                                         (5ss1,dj,pres)   8.50
--The Wolf in No Amer History-Caldwell-1946-Caxton-8vo-
    149p-plts-cl (5F5,f,dj) 13.50 (5ss1,pres,5g0,f)   10.00
--The Wolves of NoAmer-Wash-1944-photos-636p-1st ed
                         (5ss1,autg,als) 17.50 (4L0)   25.00
YOUNG, STARK-The Flower in Drama-NY-1923-Scribner-162p
                                         (5x0)   4.50
--Glamour, Essays on the Art of the Theatre-NY-1925-Scribner-
    208p   (5x0)   4.50
--The Theater-NY-(1927)-Doran-182p   (5x0)   4.00
--Theatre Practice-NY-1926-Scribner-illus-208p (5t0,5x0)   5.00

YOUNG,STARK (continued)
--So Red the Rose-NY-1934-8vo-cl-Scribner   (5b2,f)   7.50
YOUNG,THOS-Narr of Residence on the Mosquito Shore-Lond-
1842-illus-12mo-cl   (4c1,v wn)   20.00
--same-1843-3 plts   (5L7,sl stnd,wn)   15.00
YOUNG TRAVELLER'S JOURNAL OF TOUR IN NO & SO AMER-
Lond-1852-illus-16mo-1st ed-(E S Wortley)-scarce (5jj3,sp tn) 75.00
YOUNG,W A-The Silver & Sheffield Plate Collector-Lond-n.d.-
320p-illus   (5w7)   7.50
YOUNG WIFE'S OWN COOK BOOK,THE-NY-1st Baptist Church
Brklyn-special ed-(illus)-124p-ads-(1881,2) (5c0,chip) 12.50
YOUNG WILD WEST & DOUBLE DEUCE-or,Domino Gang of
Denver-By an Old Scout-NY-1917-Wild West Weekly-
col pict wrps   (5k0)   3.50
YOUNG,WM E-Shark Shark-NY-1933-8vo-287p-photos-
cl& shark lea   (4a6,bkstrp tn) 10.00
YWCA COOK BOOK-Nashua-1907-94p,(4) ads
(5c4,lacks wrps,stn)   4.50
YOUNG WOMAN'S GIFT-Of Literature,Science & Morality-
Bost-1851-12mo-192p-col frontis-Pinckney,ed
(5w7,hng weak,sl fox)   5.00
YOUNGBLOOD,CHAS L-A Mighty Hunter-Chig-1890-illus-
362p plus ads-scarce   (4L0)   15.00
YOUNGER,COLE-The Story of Cole Younger-Chig-1903-123p,(124)-
photos-wrps-ex rare-poor grade papr
(5L2,lacks bk wrp,pencil) 100.00
--same-Houston-(1953)-cl-added illus-reprintd   (5L2)   5.00
YOUNGER,EDW-John A Kasson-IowaCty-1955-450p-8vo-cl
(5a9) 5.   (5m8)   7.50
YOUNGMAN,W E-Gleanings from Western Prairies-Cambr,Engl-
1882-214p   (5w5)   10.00
YOUNGS,BENJ S-Testimony of Christ's Second Appearing...
Church of God in this Latter Day-Albany-1810-622p-sheep-
labl-2nd ed,corr   (5m3,labl wn)   40.00
YOUNGSTOWN COOK BK-Women of 1st Presbyterian Church-
Akron-1928-269p   (5c4)   4.00
YOUNGSTOWN SHEET & TUBE CO-50 Years in Steel-Youngstown-
1950-History of the-71p-illus   (5hh6)   4.50
YOUR GARDEN FLOWERS ILLUSTRATED-Lond-(1949)-col plts-
319p-new&rev ed   (5s7)   4.50
YOUR NAVY-Hist-Wash-1946-456p-illus-wrps-dec slbind-stitchd
(5s1,ex-libr)   3.00
YOUTH IN THE GHETTO-NY-1964-R8vo-620p-wrps   (5x2)   17.50
YOUTH'S CABINET,THE-Rev Francis C Woodworth,ed-NY-1846-
illus-8vo-orig cl-384p   (5t0,lacks fly)   4.50
YOUTH'S COMPANION,THE-Bost-1885-Vol 58,#1 to 53-bnd in
1 vol-   folio   (5rr2)   10.00
--same-(1886)-Vol 59(complete)-hf roan-illus   (4a8,rub) 15.00
YOUTH'S FRIEND,THE-Phila-1832-ASSU-
cl spn-12 monthly parts in 1 volume   (5rr2)   10.00
YOUTHS' HISTORY OF THE US IN VERSE-Indnpls-1883-
Carlon&Hollenbeck-12mo-120p-5 plts-bds-lea sp
(5p1,cov wn)   12.50
YOUTH'S INSTRUCTOR & GUARDIAN-Blanchard-1818 to 24-
Vols 2,3,5,8-sm8vo-hf calf-   plts-4 vols
(each vol about 430p)   (5s0,sl stns)   25.00
--same-Lond-Vols 13 & 17-J Mason-2 vols-illus-part lea
(5p6,bndgs poor)   15.00
YOUTH'S INSTRUCTOR IN NATURAL HISTORY-NY-1832-
E Bliss-24mo-36p-20 illus-orange bds -#1   (5p6,chip)   12.50
--same-#7-NY-Bliss-1832-20 illus   (5p6,sp dmgd)   12.50
YOUTH'S NATURAL HISTORY OF ANIMALS,THE-Concord-1832-
Atwood-16mo-16p-illus-wrps   (5v0)   12.50
YOUTH'S NEW DRAWING BOOK-NY-1848-22p-pict bds-
oblong   (5h1)   7.50
YOUTH'S PENNY GAZETTE-ASSU-Phila-(Jan3,1844 to Dec22,
1852)-Vol 2 #1 to Vol 9 #26-part lea-sm folio-illus-in 3 vols-
(unbroken run)   (4h8,sl wn)   87.50
YOXALL,J H-Collecting Old Miniatures-NY-1916-12mo-95p-
illus-(prntd in G B)   (5n7,lt stns)   7.50
YRIARTE,CHAS-Florence-Paris-1881-379p-illus-folio-3/4 lea-
g. tooled   (5t7)   25.00
YUBA COUNTY-History of,Calif-Oakland-1879-Thompson&West-
oblong folio-cl-lea sp-150p-maps in col   (5hh4,sl rub) 225.00
YUBA-SUTTER COUNTIES,CALIF-Soil,water climate,health &
prosperity-Yuba Sutter Co,Calif-(1914)-2p map-illus(2 in col)-
64p-wrps   (5dd9)   3.50
YUKON WORLD,THE-DawsonCty-Oct 2 to Dec 30,1906-Vol 3,
#185 to 261-newspaper-77 nbrs-bnd in heavy brown paper
(5ss4) 175.00
YUMA-From Hell Hole to Haven-by Long&Siciliano-Yuma-1950-
63p-8vo-pict wrps-1st ed   (5g5)   3.00

YURCHAK,PETER-The Slovaks....Their History & Traditions-
Whiting,Ind-1947-rev ed   (5w9)   5.00
YUTANG,LIN-My Country & My People-NY-(1935)-382p-
illus-(11th illus rev ed)   (5t7,autg)   6.00
YZENDOORN,FATHER REGINALD-History of the Catholic
Mission in the Hawaiian Islands-Honolulu-1927-8vo-254p-
illus-   (5h5)   12.50
ZABRISKIE,GEO A-The Bon Vivant's Companion-Ormond Beach,
Fla-"The Doldrums"-1933-t8vo-cl-frontis-82p-Christmas
keepsake   (5w6) 6.50   (5j5)   10.00
--The Pathfinder,Ormond Beach,Fla-1947-Christmas favor-
24p-illus-reprnt NY Hist Qrtrly   (5L2,autg)   7.50
--Ships' Figureheads in & about NY-Ormond Beach,Fla-1946-
21p-illus-Christmas book-rprnt   (5t4,pres)   6.00
ZACCARELLI,JOHN-Pictorial Souvenir Book of the Golden
Northland-DawsonCty,YT-n.d.(1908)-photos-maps-4to
(5dd7,f)   27.50
ZACHARIAH CHANDLER-An outline sketch of His Life & Public
Services-Detroit-1880-Detroit Post & Tribune-illus-cl-a.e.g.
(5q8)   6.00
ZACHARIAS,ELLIS M-Behind Closed Doors-NY-c1950   (5x7)   3.50
ZACHARIE,I-Surgical & Practical Observations on Diseases of the
Human Foot-NY-1860-ChasBNorton-96p-t12mo-orig cl-
6 col plts   (5L8,wn,ex-libr)   18.50
ZAHM,ALBERT F-Aerial Navigation-NY-1911-Appleton   (5p0)   10.00
ZAHN,OTTO-On Art Binding-Memphis-1904-frontis-16mo-
wrps   (4c1,autg)   6.00
ZAHNISER,KATE M-The Zahnisers-Mercer,Pa-1906-218p-cl
(5jj9)   15.00
ZAIDENBERG,ARTHUR-Anyone Can Draw-Cleve-1942-350p-
illus   (5t7)   8.00
--Studies in Figure Drawing-GardenCty-1950-lg8vo-119p-illus-
1st ed   (5w5)   6.50
ZAKRAJSEK,IVANKA-Slovensko Ameriska Kuharica-NY-1945-
495p-in Croatian   (5g9,rub)   4.50
ZALINSKI,E L-Electricity as Used in Sea Coast Defences-NY-
(1888?)-Electric Club-Paper #14-wrps-32p
(5hh7,lacks t.p.&bk wrp,libr stmp)   4.50
ZAMORANO CLUB-A Bookman's View of Los Angeles-LosAng-
1961-108p-cl-for Grolier Club   (5d6)   40.00
ZAMORANO 80-LosAng-1945-ltd to 500c   (4n1,dj)   70.00
ZANGWILL,ISRAEL-The Forcing House,Tragi-Comedy in 4 Acts-
NY-1923-Macmillan-278p   (5p7)   3.00
ZAPF,HERMANN-Manuale Typographicum-NY-1954-Museum Bks
Inc-pamphlets in back cov-German & Engl text-vel&bds
(5tt9,dj,box) 150.00
ZARETZ,CHAS E-Amalgamated Clothing Workers of Amer-NY-
1934-Ancon-8vo-cl-306p   (5j5)   15.00
ZARTMAN,REV RUFUS C-Zartman Family-(1942)-432p-
(rev&enlrgd ed)   (5t9)   20.00
ZATURENSKA,MARY A-Cold Morning Sky-NY-1937-Macmillan-
8vo-cl   (5b2)   5.00
--Threshold & Hearth-NY-1934-Macmillan-8vo-cl-auth's 1st book
(5b2,dj)   12.50
ZAVALA,ADINA DE-History & Legends of the Alamo & Other
Missions In & Around San Antonio-SanAnt-1917-219p (5n4) 15.00
ZEISBERGER,DAVID-Zeisberger's Indian Dictionary-Cambr-
1887-236p-Algonquin & Iroquois   (5m2)   17.50
ZELAYETA,ELENA-Elena's Famous Mexican & Spanish Recipes-
SanFran-1944-127p-spiral bnd wrps   (5g9)   3.00
ZELIA IN THE DESERT-or,The Female Crusoe,written by herself-
Lond-(c1805)-12mo-wrps-36p-frontis-Ann Lemoine&J Rose
(5aa2)   20.00
ZELIE,JOHN SHERIDAN-Bill Pratt,the Saw Buck Philosopher-
Williamstown-1895-157p-Merrymount Pr   (5x0)   4.00
ZEMURRAY,SARAH-100 Unusual Dinners & How to Prepare Them-
(Bost,1938)-156p   (5c9)   3.00
ZENAS,LEONARD-Narr of Adventures of-Chig-1934   (5m9)   7.50
ZENGER,JOHN PETER-The Trial of,of NY,Prntr-Lond-1752-calf
(5q8,cov dtchd)   60.00
ZENZINOV,VLADIMIR-Road to Oblivion-NY-1931-250p-plts
(5aa0)   5.00
ZERAH,THE BELIEVING JEW-NY-1837-1st ed-286p-orig cl
(4b1,sp wrn) 100.00
ZERBE,J S-Automobiles-NY-(c1915)-Cuppples&Leon-12mo-232p-
(8)ads-pict cl-Every Boy's Mechanical Library   (5p1)   25.00
ZERN,ED-To Hell with Hunting-NY-nd.-8vo-99p-illus
(4a6,dj)   2.00
ZERO-Spring Issue-1949-75p-wrps   (5x2)   8.00
ZETA TAU ALPHA COOK BOOK-Alpha Phi Chapt House Fund-
Evanston-n.d.-286p-illus-2nd ed   (5g9)   3.00

ZIEBER,EUGENE-Heraldry in Amer-Phila-1909-orig cl-illus-
427-g.e.-scarce   (5m2) 35.   (5h9,f)   28.50

ZIGROSSER,CARL-The Artist in Amer-NY-1942-207p-illus
                    (5t4) 5.   (5p0)   7.50

--Six Centuries of Fine Prints-NY-(1937)-4to-cl-406p
                    (5m5) 12.   (5t7)   12.50

ZILLIACUS,KONNI-Mirror of the Past-1946
                                   (5L7)   5.00

ZIM,HERBERT-Submarines-NY-(1942)-306p-photos-
                    (5s1,dj,ex-libr)   8.00

ZIMMERMAN,ARTHUR F-Francisco de Toledo,5th Viceroy of Peru-
    Caldwell-1938-307p-v scarce   (4L0)   17.50

ZIMMERMANN,HENRI-Dernier Voyage du Capitaine Cook Autour
    du Monde-Berne-1783-Nouvelle Soc Typogr-2nd French ed-
    rare   (5n9)   575.00

ZIMMERMAN,JAS FULTON-Impressment of American Seamen-
    Columbia Univ Pr-1925-279p-ads   (5qq8)   10.00

ZIMMERN,ALFRED E-The Greek Commonwealth-Oxf-1911-454p
                    (5w9,stnd)   7.50

ZINGG,ROBT MOWRY-A Reconstruction of Uto Aztekan History-
    NY-1939-U of Denv-274p-wrps-scarce   (5L2)   15.00

ZINN,W D-Story of Woodbine Farm-(Buckhannon-1931)-265p-
    cl   (5h1)   8.50

ZINSSER,HANS-As I remember him-Bost-1940-Little,Brown-
    443p   (5v6)   2.00

ZITKALA-SA-American Indian Stories-Wash-1921-wrps-195p-
    frontis   (4L0)   5.00

--Old Indian Legends Retold-Bost-1901-165p-illus-1st ed (4L0)   6.00

ZOE-or the Martel Paper-NY-Sheldon-1865-468p-illus-1st ed
                    (5x4)   15.00

ZOFF,OTTO-The Huguenots,Fighters for God & Human Freedom-
    NY-1942-340p-t8vo-cl-1st ed   (5p5)   10.00

ZOGBAUM,RUFUS F-Horse,Foot & Dragoons-NY-1888-Harper-
    176p-illus-pict cl
    (5mm8) 8.50   (5t2) 10.   (5dd1,sl wn)15.   (5i3)   12.50

ZOLA,EMILE-L'Assommoir-NY-1924-437p-8vo-cl-intro by
    Havelock Ellis   (5t0)   3.75

--same-Lond-1928-Laurie-for Subscr-468p-orig bds-frontis-
    spec ltd ed,autg by A Symons   (5z7)   40.00

--Nana-n.p.-1931-frontis-8vo-cl-517p   (5t0)   4.00

--A Page of Love-Phila-1897-2 vols-illus-Barrie   (5p9)   7.50

--same-Phila-(1897)-2 vols-red mor-extra illus-22 etchings
                    (5ee3,f bndg)   20.00

ZOLOTOW,MAURICE-Marilyn Monroe-NY-1960-340p-illus
                    (5a6,f,dj) 7.50   (5p0)   4.00

ZOLLIKOFER,G J-Sermons on Dignity of Man & Value of objects-
    1802-2 vols-buck   (5L7,rbnd)   12.50

ZOLLERS,GEO D-Thrilling Incidents on Sea & Land-MtMorris-
    1892-400p-cl   (5h2) 10.   (5m2)   15.00

ZOLLINGER,GULIELMA-Maggie McLanehan-Chig-1909-McClurg-
    12mo-311p-Shinn,illus-pict cl   (5p1)   7.50

ZOOLOGY OF CAPT BEECHEY'S VOYAGE-Lond-1839-3 col
    maps(1 fldg)-44 col plts-4to-1st ed   (5z9,f bndg) 1,450.00

ZORN,JOHANNES-Icones Plantarum Medicinalium-336p text-
    5 vols-500 handcol plts-with Amerikanische Gewachse
    nach Linneischer Ordnung-56p text-3 vols-300 col plts-
    Nurnberg,Raspe-1782 to 88-8vo-calf (5jj8) 8 vols 1,850.00

ZORA,LUCIA-Sawdust & Solitude-Bost-1928-illus-230p (5t7)   10.00

ZORNOW,WM FRANK-Lincoln & Party Divided-Norman-
    8vo-264p-1st ed   (4a7,5L0)   8.50

ZUBEK,JOHN P- Doukhobors at War-Tor-1952-250p   (5u6)   7.50

ZUBER,PAUL A-Dans les Mines du Far West,Recits et Aventures-
    Paris-(ca 1913)-illus-lea labl-hf vel (5r7,ex-libr) 20.00

ZUCKER,A E-The Chinese Theatre-Bost-1925-4to-21 plts-dec cl-
    g.t.-1st ed-scarce   (5p5)   35.00

--Ibsen the Master Builder-NY-(1929)-8vo-cl-312p-frontis (5t0) 5.00

--Forty Eighters-NY-1950-illus-1st ed   (5jj3,f,dj)   8.50

ZUEND,JOH JOS-Handbuch der Pferdeund Vieharzney Kune,etc-
    Phila-1832-376,(8)p-lea-fldg frontis (5y0,jnts crack) 15.00

ZUKOR,ADOLPH-The Public is Never Wrong-NY-(1953)-309p
                    (5t7)   6.00

ZUCKER,MORRIS-Philosophy of Amer History,the Historical Field
    Theory-NY-(1945)-694p   (5r7)   10.00

ZUCKERMAN,NATHAN-Wine of Violence-NY-1947-8vo-cl-
    362p   (5t0)   3.50

ZUKOFSKY,LOUIS-Barely & Widely-NY-1958-oblong 12 mo-
    wrps-1st ed-facs of auth's handwritng-ltd to 300c,nbrd,
    autg   (5ss7,unopnd)   35.00

ZUNDEL,WM-History of Old Zion Church-n.p.-n.d.-(c1922)-
    (Westmoreland,Pa)-266p   (4a9,vg)   12.50

ZUVER,LT PAUL E-Short History of Carlisle Barracks-n.p.-n.d.-
    (Carlisle Barracks,1934)-illus-157p-wrps (5u1,cov stn) 15.00

ZWEIG,ARNOLD-The Case of Sergeant Grischa-NY-1928-
    1st Amer ed   (5b9,f,dj)   5.00

ZWEMER,SAM'L M-Childhood in the Moslem World-NY,Chig,
    Tor,Lond&Edinb-(c1915)-8vo-274p,(4)(ads)-40 plts
                    (5p1,lacks frontis)   10.00

ZWEIG,STEFAN-Adepts in Self Portraiture-NY-1928-Viking Pr-
    357p   (5p9)   5.00

--The Invisible Collection-NY-1926-8vo-dec bds-cl bk-illus-
    1st ed-Pynson Prntrs   (5p5)   7.50

--Brazil,Land of the Future-NY-1941-3rd prntg (5q8,sl soil) 5.00

--Story of Magellan,Conqueror of Seas-NY-1938-335p
                    (5dd9) 8.50   (5s1)   4.50

ZYBURA,J D,ed-Present day Thinkers & New Scholasticism-
    1926   (5L7)   5.00

ZYLBERZWEIG,ZALME-Album of the Yiddish Theatre-NY-
    1937-illus-4to-plts   (5yy6,wn,shaken)   12.50

ZYLYFF-The Ponca Chiefs-Bost-1879-146p-1st ed-frontis-
    wrps-v rare   (4L0,lacks part front wrp)   50.00

DEALER-CODE IDENTIFICATION

TO

The USED BOOK PRICE GUIDE

Code 4

(4a1) Biblo & Tannen, #202, 6/72, 63-4th Av., New York 10003
(4a2) Dauber & Pine, #664, 8/70, 66-5th Av., New York 10011
(4a3) Brick Row Book Shop, #95, 6/72, 251 Post, SanFran. 94108
(4a4) J.T.Hickox, #10, 5/72, 4724 Eastman Dr., OklaCty 73122
(4a5) Jenkins Co., #52, 6/72, Box 2085, Austin, Tex., 78767
(4a6) Edw. P. Rich &Co, #1972, 7/72, Box 295, Haverford, 19041
(4a7) D.A.Bulen, #53, 7/72, 301 Randolph, Meadville, Pa. 16335
(4a8) Adelphi Book Shop, #107, 6/72, 822 Fort St, Victoria, B.C.
(4a9) Hoosierland Books, #33, 7/72, Box 932, FtMyers, Fla 33902
(4a0) Olana Gallery, #3, 8/72, 305 E 76 St, NewYork 10021

(4b1) Geo S.MacManus, #212, 7/72, 1317 Irving, Phila. 19107
(4b2) Shorey's, #6(Am Indian), 7/72, 815-3rd, Seattle, Wa 98104
(4b3) Wm.R.Hecht, #101, 7/72, Box 67, Scottsdale, Ariz 85252
(4b4) Jenkins Co, #54, 8/72, Box 2085, Austin, Tex. 78767
(4b5) Heritage Bookshop, #116, 8/72, 6707 HollywdBlvd, 90028
(4b6) Argosy Book Store, #602, 7/72, 116 E 59th, N.Y. 10022
(4b7) Biblo & Tannen, #203, 8/72, 63-4th av, New York 10003
(4b8) Edgar Heyl, #131, 6/72, 11 W.Chase, Baltimore, Md 21201
(4b9) Huronia Canadiana Bks, #22, 7/72, Box 685 Alliston, Ont.
(4b0) Robt G Hayman, #53, 6/73, RFD 1, Carey, Ohio 43316

(4c1) Goodspeed's Bk Shop, #571, 8/72, 18 Beacon, Boston 02108
(4c2) Goodspeed's Bk Shop, #572, 8/72, 18 Beacon, Boston 02108
(4c3) Victoria Book Shop, #17, 7/72, 16 W 36th, NewYork 10018
(4c4) Current Co., #6, 11/72, Box 46, Bristol, R.I. 02809
(4c5) Carry Back Books, #4, 12/72, Franconia, N.H. 03580
(4c6) Cape Cod Books, #7 (Lincoln), 9/71, East Orleans, Ma. 02643
(4c7) Aldredge Book Store, #44, 8/72, 2506 Cedar, Dallas 75201
(4c8) Edw Morrill, #189, 3/73, 25 Kingston St, Boston, Ma, 02111
(4c9) Larry Edmunds Bkshop, #Cinema, 5/73, 6658 Hollywd, 90028
(4c0) Antiquarian Bksellers Cntr, 5/73, 630-5th, N.Y. 10020

(4d1) Adelphi Book Shop, #109, 10/72, 822 Fort, Victoria, B.C.
(4d2) Adelphi Book Shop, #108, 9/72, 822 Fort, Victoria, B.C.
(4d3) Fred A. Berk, #21, 10/72, 7526 Fountain, LosAng, 90046
(4d4) Adelphi Book Shop, #110, 12/72, 822 Fort, Victoria, B.C.
(4d5) Jeff Dykes, #20, 2/73, Box 38, CollegePk, Md. 20740
(4d6) Fred A.Berk, #22, 2/72, 7526 Fountain, LosAng, Ca. 90046
(4d7) W.D.Payton, #1-73, 3/73, 5511 Applegate, Louisv. 40219
(4d8) Adelphi Book Shop, #111, 2/73, 822 Fort, Victoria, B.C.
(4d9) Adrian's, #36, 11/72, 150 N.Brook, Geneva, NY 14456
(4d0) Adelphi Book Shop, #98, 1/71, 822 Fort, Victoria, B.C.

(4e1) Lathrop Harper, #208, 7/72, 22 E. 40th, NewYork 10016
(4e2) Reference Bk Cntr, #106, 8/72, 175-5th Av, NY 10010
(4e3) Witherspoon Bk Shop, Wstrns, 8/72, 12 Nassau, Princeton
(4e4) Edgar Heyl, #130, 6/72, 11 W.Chase, Balt,Md. 21201
(4e5) F.Thos Heller, #139, 308 E. 79th, NY, NY, 10021
(4e6) Huronia Canadiana Bks, #25, 8/72, Box 685, Alliston, Ont.
(4e7) Reference Book Cntr, #1071, 8/72, 175-5th, NY, 10010
(4e8) Reference Book Cntr, #7110, 8/72, 175-5th, NY 10010
(4e9) Huronia Canadiana Bks, #23, 7/72, Alliston, Ontario
(4e0) Olana Gallery, #2, 7/72, 305 E 76th st, NY, NY 10021

(4f1) Current Co, #BW3, 10/72, Box 46, Bristol, RI 02809
(4f2) Whitlock Farm, Spec#7, 1/73, Bethany, Ct. 06525
(4f3) Fairhaven Bk Shop, #723, 8/72, 107 Main, Fairhaven 02719
(4f4) Fairhaven Bk Shop, #724, 10/72, 107 Main, Fairhaven, Ct.
(4f5) F T Heller, #141, 12/72, 308 E 79th st, NY, NY 10021
(4f6) Victoria Bk Shop, #18, 10/72, 16 W 36th, NY, NY 10018
(4f7) Bruce's Books, #5, 7/71, 444 W Margaret, Detroit 48203
(4f8) Anian Books, #101, 5/73, Lantzville, B.C. Canada
(4f9) Anian Books, #11, 5/73, Lantzville, B.C. Canada
(4f0) Jenkins Co, #60, 6/73, Box 2085, Austin, Tex 78767

(4g1) Heritage Bkshop, #118, 5/73, 6707 HollywdBlvd 90028
(4g2) Geo MacManus, #216, 2/73, 1317 Irving, Phila. 19107
(4g3) Nelson Bond, #18, 5/73, 4724 Easthill, Roanoke 24018
(4g4) Adrian's, #37, 7/73, 150 N Brook, Geneva, NY 14456
(4g5) Rudolph Sabbot, #7, 2/73, 5239 Tendilla, WdlandHills, Ca
(4g6) Edw Morrill, #188, 2/73, 25 Kingston, Boston, Ma 02111
(4g7) W D Hall, #117a, 7/72, 99 Maple, E Longmeadow 01028
(4g8) Peter Wolff, #2, 2/73, Box 778, Barrington, Illinois 60010
(4g9) Marian Gore, #1972, 9/72, Box 433, SanGabriel 91775
(4g0) Marian Gore, #1973, 6/73, Box 433, SanGabriel 91775

(4h1) Robt Hayman, #48, 6/72, RFD 1, Carey, O 43316
(4h2) Robt Hayman, #49, 10/72, RFD 1, Carey, O 43316
(4h3) Huronia Canadiana, #26, 10/72, Box 685, Alliston, Ont.
(4h4) Shorey's Bk Store, #1, WW2, 3/73, 815-3rd av, Seattle
(4h5) Heritage Bkshop, #spec Fair, 9/72, 6707 Hollywd 90028
(4h6) Hoosierland Bks, #34, 2/73, Box 932, FtMyers, Fl 33902
(4h7) Robt Hayman, #50, 12/72, RFD 1, Carey, O 43316
(4h8) Edgar Heyl, #132, 10/72, 11 W Chase, Balt, Md 21201
(4h9) Hinkel's Bk Shop, #65, 2/69, Syillwater, Okla 74074
(4h0) John Howell, #42, 7/72, 434 Post, SanFran. Ca 94102

(4i1) Ibis Book Arts, #13, 7/72, Post Sta E, Box 187, HamiltorOnt
(4i2) Antiquity in Books, #1, 10/72, Box 763 MichiganCty, Ind.
(4i3) Ximenes. #29, 3/73, 120 E 85th, NewYork 10028
(4i4) Wm Nash, #36, 3/73, 4265 McClatcheyCi NE, Atlanta Ga
(4i5) Ximenes, #24, 12/71, 120 E 85th, New York 10028
(4i6) B Amtmann, #284, 11/72, 1529 Sherbrooke W, Montreal
(4i7) Heinoldt Bks, #Wstrn, 3/73, South Egg Harbor, NJ 08215
(4i8) Ximenes, #27, 9/72, 120 E 85th, New York 10028
(4i9) Ximenes, #28, 11/72, 120 E 85th, New York 10028
(4i0) Ximenes, #26, 7/72, 120 E 85th, New York 10028

(4j1) Edw Morrill, #190, 5/73, 25 Kingston, Bost 02111
(4j2) Geo MacManus, #215, 1/73, 1317 Irving, Phila 19107
(4j3) Biblo & Tannen, #204, 10/72, 63-4th, NewYork 10003
(4j4) Jenkins Co, #53, 7/72, Box 2085, Austin, Tex 78767
(4j5) F Thos Heller, #140, 10/72, 308 E 79th, NY 10021
(4j6) Jenkins Co, #56, 11/72, Box 2085, Austin, Tex 78767
(4j7) Jenkins Co, #57, 2/73, Box 2085, Austin, Tex 78767
(4j8) Lathrop Harper, #209, 10/72, 22 E 40th, N Y 10016
(4j9) Geo MacManus, #217, 1317 Irving, Phila. 19107 4/73
(4j0) Jenkins Co, #59, 5/73, Box 2085, Austin, Tex 78767

(4k1) J T Hickox, #12, 2/73, 4724 Eastman, OklaCty 73122
(4k2) Robt Hayman, #51, 2/73, RFD 1, Carey, Ohio 43316
(4k3) Wendell Smith, #35, 2/72, Main, Orleans, Ma 02653
(4k4) Ken Crawford, #68, 2/72, 2719 E 16th, NStPaul 55109
(4k5) Ken Crawford, #69, 10/72, 2719 E 16th Av, NStPaul
(4k6) Jeff Dykes, #21, 4/73, Box 38, College Pk, Md 20740
(4k7) Jenkins Co, #58, 3/73, Box 2085, Austin, Tex 78767
(4k8) Laurence Lingle, #42, 4/73, 1415 Eliz blvd, FtWorth, Tex
(4k9) Edw Fales, #15, 5/73, Turnpike rd, Salisbury NH 03268
(4k0) Bibliophile, #731, 5/73, 83 East av, Norwalk, Ct 06851

(4L1) Lathrop Harper, #207, 6/72, 22 E 40th, NewYork 10016
(4L2) T N Luther, #66, 10/72, Box 6083, Shawnee Mission 66206
(4L3) Lawrence Golder, #7, 10/72, Box 144, Collinsville, Conn
(4L4) James Lowe, #3, 11/72, Box 735 Wall St Sta, NY 10005
(4L5) T N Luther, #65, 10/72, Box 6083 ShawneeMission, Kans
(4L6) Incredible Barn, #40, 10/72, Main St, Orleans, Ma 02653
(4L7) Lathrop Harper, #210, 2/73, 22 E 40th, N.Y. 10016
(4L8) Ximenes, #25, 3/72, 120 E 85th, NewYork, NY 10028
(4L9) Lester Roberts, #26, 10/72, 47 GoldenGate av, SF 94102
(4L0) T N Luther, #64, 5/73, Box 6083, ShawneeMission 66206

(4m1) Melvin Marcher, #2, 5/71, Rt 6, Box 589, Tulsa, Ok 74127
(4m2) Geo MacManus, #213, 10/72, 1317 Irving, Phila 19107
(4m3) Robt Merriam, #59, 6/72, 574 Bernardston, Greenfield, Ma
(4m4) Geo MacManus, #214, 12/72, 1317 Irving, Phila 19107
(4m5) Robt Merriam, #60, 6/72, 574 Bernardston, Greenfield, Ma
(4m6) Edw Morrill, #185, 12/72, 25 Kingston, Boston, Ma 02111
(4m7) Edw Morrill, #186, 1/73, 25 Kingston, Bost, Ma 02111
(4m8) Edw Morrill, #187, 1/73, 25 Kingston, Bost, Ma 02111
(4m9) John Makarewich, #57, pt 3, 10/72, Box 395, Tarzana, Ca
(4m0) Edw Morrill, #191, 5/73, 25 Kingston, Bost, Ma 02111

(4n1) Heinoldt Bks, #Calif, 10/72, Central&Buffalo, S EggHarbor NJ
(4n2) Half Moon Bks, #28, 10/72, Box 444, Guilderland, NY 12084
(4n3) Nelson Bond, #16, 2/73, 4724 Easthill dr, Roanoke Va 24018
(4n4) Jenkins Co, #55, 10/72, Box 2085, Austin, Tex 78767
(4n5) John Howell, #43, 10/72, 434 Post, SanFran Ca 94102
(4n6) Nelson Bond, #17, 3/73, 4724 Easthill, Roanoke Va 24018
(4n7) Tom Munnerlyn, #19, 2/73, 8604 Bluedale, Alexandria 22308
(4n8) Thom Munnerlyn, #18, 10/72, 8604 Bluedale, Alexandria, Va
(4n9) Robt Hayman, #52, 3/73, RFD 1, Carey, Ohio 43316
(4n0) Americana Bks, #3.73, 5/73, Box 243, Decatur, Ind 46733

(4p1) Peggy Christian, #9, 10/72, 679 N LaCienega, LA 90069
(4p2) Round-Ups Bk Co, #27, 10/72, 166 Eddy st, SanFran 94102
(4p3) Lee Pritzker, #19, 10/72, Box 293, Oakville, Ont, Canada
(4p4) Fred Wilson, #2, 12/72, Box 561, LenonHillSta, NY 10021
(4p5) Rudolph Sabbot, #5, 10/72, 5239 Tendilla, WoodlandHill, Ca
(4p6) Rudolph Sabbot, #6, 10/72, 5239 Tendilla, WoodlandHills, Ca
(4p7) Pyetell's Bk Shop, #153, 10/72, 333-5th av, Pelham, NY 10803
(4p8) W D Payton, #2-72, 11/72, 511 Applegate, Louisville, Ky 40219
(4p9) John Howell, #44, 5/73, 434 Post St, SanFran, Ca 94102
(4p0) Wayne Pierce, #1, 5/73, Box 240c, Oroville, Ca 95965

(4t1) Saddleback Bk Shop, #12, 11/72, Box 10393, SantaAna 02711
(4t2) Chas Tuttle, #379, 3/73, Rutland, Vt. 05701
(4t3) T N Luther, #67, 12/72, Box 6083, ShawneeMission, Ka 66206
(4t4) Old Mill House Books, #BK, 2/73, Box 77, Stillwater 07875
(4t5) Ottenberg Books, #2, 11/72, 724 Pike, Seattle, Wa 98101
(4t6) Geo Tweney, #London, 7/72, 16660 MarineViewSW, Sea 98166
(4t7) Antiquity in Books, #2, 3/73, Box 763, MichiganCty, Ind 46360
(4t8) T N Luther, #68, 3/73, Box 6083, ShawneeMission, Kans 66206
(4t9) Lathrop Harper, #211, 5/73, 22 E 40th st, NY, NY 10016
(4t0) Geo Tweney, #spec, 5/73, 16660MarineViewSW, Seattle 98166

USED BOOK PRICE GUIDE

DEALER-CODE IDENTIFICATION
TO

The USED BOOK PRICE GUIDE

Code 5

(5a1) Adelphi Book Shop, #91, 10/69, 822 Fort St., Victoria, B.C.
(5a2) Seattle Bookfinders, #725, 5/72, Box 7471, Seattle, 98133
(5a3) Goodspeed's, #553, 4/69, 18 Beacon St., Boston, 02108
(5a4) Anderson Books, #NS-4, 425-18th Av.N.E., StPetersburg 33704
(5a5) Adelphi Book Shop, #96, 8/70, 822 Fort St., Victoria, B.C.
(5a6) Alan Engelhardt, #38, 3/69, Box 603, Canoga Park, Ca. 91305
(5a7) Aldredge Bk Store, #28, 5/67, 2506 CedarSprngs, Dallas 75201
(5a8) Aldredge Bk Store, #31, 11/68, 2506 CedarSprngs, Dallas 75201
(5a9) Americana Exchange, #103, 5/69, 429 Robinson, SanDiego 92103
(5a0) Americana Exchange, #none, 4/70, 429 Robinson, SanD 92103

(5b1) Nelson Bond, #69c, 11/69, 1625 Hampton, Roanoke, Va. 24015
(5b2) Brick Row Bk Shop, #92, 1/71, Box 66186, Houston 77006
(5b3) Blitz Books, #39, 4/70, Box 64, Los Altos, Ca. 94022
(5b4) Blitz Books, #45, 12/70, Box 64, Los Altos, Ca. 94022
(5b5) J.T. Hickox, #5, 3/71, 4724 Eastman Drive, OklahomCty 73122
(5b6) Geo Bryant, #38, 6/69, Box 405, Versailles, Ky. 40383
(5b7) Geo Bryant, #37, 6/69, Box 405, Versailles, Ky. 40383
(5b8) Edgar Heyl, #118, 7/70, 11 W.Chase St., Baltimore 21201
(5b9) Nelson Bond, #69A, 8/69, 1625 Hampton, Roanoke, Va. 24015
(5b0) Bennett&Marshall, #10, 12/70, 8214 Melrose, LosAngles 90046

(5c1) Caravan-Maritime Bks, #181, 6/69, 67-06 168 Pl, Jamaica 11432
(5c2) Victoria Bk Shop, #10, 5/70, 16 W 36 St., New York 10018
(5c3) Cantabrigia Bk Shop, #23, 3/69, 16 Park, Cambridge, Ma 02138
(5c4) Elisabeth Woodburn, #564, 10/70, Hopewell, N.J. 08525
(5c5) Elisabeth Woodburn, #1265, 8/70, Hopewell, N.J. 08525
(5c6) Cellar Book Shop, #Pt.6, 8/70, Box 6, College Pk, Detroit 48221
(5c7) Elisabeth Woodburn, #267, 10/70, Hopewell, N.J. 08525
(5c8) Justin Schiller, #21, 10/68, 2038 E 64 St., Brooklyn 11234
(5c9) Marian L Gore, #none, 8/70, Box 433 SanGabriel, Ca. 91775
(5c0) Elisabeth Woodburn, #968, 8/70, Hopewell, N.J. 08525

(5d1) Philip Duschnes, #191, 10/70, 699 Madison, New York 10021
(5d2) Dawson's Bk Shop, #392, 1/70, 535 N Larchmont, LA, Ca. 90004
(5d3) Philip Duschnes, #183, 6/68, 699 Madison, New York 10021
(5d4) Denning House, #27, 3/71, Box 42, Salisbury Mills, NY 12577
(5d5) Philip Duschnes, #188, 5/69, 699 Madison, New York 10021
(5d6) Dawson's Bk Shop, #396, 8/70, 535 N Larchmont, LA, Ca 90004
(5d7) Dawson's Bk Shop, #391, 11/69, 535 N Larchmont, LA 90004
(5d8) Philip Duschnes, #189, 5/69, 699 Madison, New York 10021
(5d9) Philip Duschnes, #187, 1/69, 699 Madison, New York 10021
(5d0) Americana Books, #1.71, 8/71, Decatur, Ind. 46733

(5e1) Claude Held, #5, 3/71, Box 140, Buffalo, N.Y. 14225
(5e2) I Ehrlich, #none, 6/69, Box 994 Sta B, Montreal, Canada
(5e3) Larry Geraghty, #8, 10/69, 1 Pope Rd, Westbrook, Me 04092
(5e4) Edgar Heyl, #114, 11/69, 11 W Chase St, Baltimore 21201
(5e5) F Thos Heller, #130, 7/69, 308 E 79 St, New York 10021
(5e6) F Thos Heller, #133, 5/70, 308 E 79 St., New York 10021
(5e7) El Cascajero, #17, 10/70, 506 W Broadway, New York 10012
(5e8) New England Books, #41, 3/68, Petersham, Mass. 01366
(5e9) Edith Hall, #none, 1/69, 14 Roosevelt, Roseland, N.J. 07068
(5e0) Min-Ree Shop, #16, 5/72, 8442 Grand Av, Elmhurst 11373

(5f1) Holmes Book Co, #41, 4/71, 274-14 St., Oakland, Ca. 94612
(5f2) Family Book Shop, #9, 6/70, 1367 E Colorado, Glendale 91205
(5f3) American Fragments, #233, 10/70, Box 128, DelMar, Ca. 92014
(5f4) American Fragments, #234, 11/70, Box 128, DelMar, Ca 92014
(5f5) Holmes Book Co, #96, 1/71, 274-14th St, Oakland, Ca 94612
(5f6) Geo A Foster, Jr, #4, 1/71, 2218 E Jackson Blvd, Elkhart 46514
(5f7) Family Book Shop, #11, 8/70, 1367 E Colorado, Glendale 91205
(5f8) John W Caler, #none, 11/68, 7506 Clybourn, SunValley 91352
(5f9) American Fragments, #23, 8/69, Box 273, Del Mar, Ca 92014
(5f0) Hillside Book Shop, #9, 1/70, Franklin, N.H., 03235

(5g1) Larry Golder, #1, 4/70, P.O.Box 144, Collinsville, Ct 06022
(5g2) L E Gay, #26, 7/70, Box 548, Lordsburg, N.M. 88045
(5g3) Goodspeed's Book Shop, #549, 8/68, 18 Beacon, Boston 02108
(5g4) Goodspeed's Book Shop, #554, 4/69, 18 Beacon, Boston 02108
(5g5) L E Gay, #25, 3/70, Box 548, Lordsburg, N.M. 88045
(5g6) L E Gay, #24, 3/70, Box 548, Lordsburg, N.M. 88045
(5g7) L E Gay, #20, 3/69, Box 548, Lordsburg, N.M. 88045
(5g8) Goodspeed's Book Shop, #551, 10/68, 18 Beacon, Boston02108
(5g9) Marian L Gore, #none, 10/69, Box 433, SanGabriel, Ca 91775
(5g0) L E Gay, #23, 1/70, Box 548, Lordsburg, N.M. 88045

(5h1) Robt G Hayman, #37, 1/70, RFD 1, Carey, Ohio 43316
(5h2) Robt G Hayman, #38, 3/70, RFD 1, Carey, Ohio 43316
(5h3) Robt G Hayman, #39, 6/70, RFD 1, Carey, Ohio 43316
(5h4) Holmes Book Co, #93, 11/68, 274-14 St, Oakland, Ca 94612
(5h5) Holmes Book Co, #95, 4/70, 274-14 St, Oakland, Ca 94612
(5h6) F M Hill, #16A, 11/69, Box 1037, Kingsport, Tenn 37662
(5h7) Robt G Hayman, #40, 9/70, RFD 1, Carey, Ohio 43316
(5h8) Edgar Heyl, #107, 6/69, 11 W Chase, Baltimore, Md 21201
(5h9) Hale House, #69, 4/69, Box 181, Wynnewood, Pa 19096
(5h0) Hinkel's Book Shop, #69, 4/70, Stillwater, Okla. 74074

(5i1) Incredible Books, #21, 4/70, Main St., Orleans, Ma. 02653
(5i2) Int'l Bookfinders, #180, 5/69, Box 3003, BeverlyHills, 90212
(5i3) Edw Myers, #5, 2/72, Box 47, Collinsville, Ct 06022
(5i4) Edw P Rich, #none, 2/72, Box 295, Haverford Pa, 19041
(5i5) American Fragments, #235, 12/70, Box 128, DelMar 92014
(5i6) Bernard Amtmann, #282, 2/72, 1176 Sherbrooke W, Montreal
(5i7) Ximenes, #19, 2/71, 120 E 85 St, New York 10028
(5i8) Ximenes, #18, 12/70, 120 E 85 St, New York 10028
(5i9) Ximenes, #11, 10/69, 120 E 85 St, New York 10028
(5i0) Ximenes, #14, 4/70, 120 E 85 St, New York 10028

(5j1) T N Luther, #59, 4/71, Box 6083, Shawnee Mission 66206
(5j2) Douglas M Jacobs, #21, 9/70, Box 625, Ridgefield, 06877
(5j3) Douglas M Jacobs, #20, 9/69, Box 625, Ridgefield, 06877
(5j4) Jenkins Co, #34, 7/70, Box 2085, Austin, Tex 78767
(5j5) Jas F Carr, #54, 12/70, 227 E 81 St, New York 10028
(5j6) Jenkins Co, #42, 3/71, Box 2085, Austin Tex 78767
(5j7) Jenkins Co, #37, 10/71, Box 2085, Austin, Tex 78767
(5j8) J & J Hanrahan, #2, 3/69, Box 406, Durham, NH 03824
(5j9) J & J Hanrahan, #3, 4/69, Box 406, Durham, NH 03824
(5j0) Jeff Dykes, #16, 8/71, Box 38, College Park, Md 20740

(5k1) J T Hickox, #4, 1/71, 4724 Eastman, OklahomaCty 73122
(5k2) J T Hickox, #2, 9/70, 4724 Eastman, OklahomaCity 73122
(5k3) Incredible Barn, #22, 10/70, Main St, Orleans, Mass 02653
(5k4) Ken Crawford, #64A, 2/71, 2719 E 16 Av, N StPaul 55109
(5k5) Int'l House Books, #K,L,M, 10/70, 88 Elm, Brewer, Me 04412
(5k6) F M Hill, #14, 1/68, Box 1037, Kingsport, Tenn 37662
(5k7) Jenkins Co, #39, 1/71, Box 2085, Austin, Tex 78767
(5k8) Jenkins Co, #38, 12/70, Box 2085, Austin, Tex 78767
(5k9) Douglas Jacobs, #19, 11/68, Box 625, Ridgefield, Ct 06877
(5k0) J. T. Hickox, #1, 7/70, 4724 Eastman, OklahomaCity 73122

(5L1) Lathrop Harper, #201, 3/70, 22 E 40 St, New York 10016
(5L2) T N Luther, #58, 12/70, Box 6083, ShawneeMission, Ks 66206
(5L3) Lawrence Golder, #3, 9/70, Box 144, Collinsville, Ct 06022
(5L4) Lawrence Golder, #4, 2/71, Box 144, Collinsville, Ct 06022
(5L5) T N Luther, #55, 9/70, Box 6083, ShawneeMission, Ks 66206
(5L6) Incredible Barn, #25, 3/71, Main St, Orleans, Mass 02653
(5L7) Wm H Allen, #201, 11/70, 2031 Walnut, Philadelphia 19103
(5L8) Leamington Bk Shop, #33, 9/68, 623 Caroline, Fredksbg 22401
(5L9) Lester Roberts Bk Shop, #19, 3/68, 47 GoldenGate, SF 94102
(5L0) T N Luther, #54, 5/70, Box 6083, ShawneeMission, Ks 66206

(5m1) Geo S MacManus, #198, 11/69, 1317 Irving, Phila. 19107
(5m2) Geo S MacManus, #196, 4/69, 1317 Irving, Phila. 19107
(5m3) M & S Rare Books, #3, 12/70, Weston, Mass 02193
(5m4) Geo S MacManus, #204, 5/71, 1317 Irving, Phila. 19107
(5m5) Arthur Minters, #29, 1/71, 84 University Pl, N.Y. 10003
(5m6) Edw Morrill, #166, 1/71, 25 Kingston, Boston Ma 02111
(5m7) Arthur Minters, #30, 2/71, 84 University Pl, N.Y. 10003
(5m8) Pauline Millen, #2, 10/68, 3325 CrescentDr, DesMoines 50312
(5m9) John Makarewich, #10, 1/69, Box 395, Tarzana, Ca 91356
(5m0) Geo Milkey, #none, 7/70, 252 Portsmouth, Greenland 03840

(5n1) Kenneth Nebenzahl, #21, 10/68, 333 N Michigan, Chicago
(5n2) Kenneth Nebenzahl, #22, 5/69, 333 N Mich., Chicago 60601
(5n3) Denning House, #24, 11/70, Box 42, SalisburyMills, NY 12577
(5n4) Jenkins Co, #41, 2/71, Box 2085, Austin, Tex 78767
(5n5) John Howell, #39, 4/70, 434 Post, SanFrancisco 94102
(5n6) Kenneth Nebenzahl, #20, 12/67, 333 N Mich., Chicago 60601
(5n7) Elisabeth Woodburn, #867, 10/70, Hopewell, N.J. 08525
(5n8) G A Bibby, #102, 2/71, 714 Pleasant, Roseville, Ca 95678
(5n9) Kenneth Nebenzahl, #23, 10/69, 333 N Mich., Chicago60601
(5n0) Incredible Barn, #30, 6/71, Main St, Orleans, Mass 02653

(5p1) Peggy Christian, #7, 2/71, 769 N LaCienega, LA, Ca 90069
(5p2) Health Research, #4-A, 12/70, Mokelumne Hill, Ca 95245
(5p3) Maggie DuPriest's, #4, 8/68, 1544 S Dixie Hwy, CoralGables
(5p4) Put man Bookshop, #115, 1/69, 304 W Jeff, Bloomington 61701
(5p5) Out-of-Print Bk Cntr, #105, 1/71, 25-09 36 Av, L.I.C., N.Y.
(5p6) Putman Bookshop, #116, 5/69, 304 W Jeff, Bloomington, Ill.
(5p7) Pyetell's Bk Shop, #147, 4/70, 333 5thAv, Pelham, NY 10803
(5p8) Plantation Book Shop, #88, 7/69, 301 S Wall, Natchez 39120
(5p9) Pyetell's Bk Shop, #149, 4/70, 333 5 Av, Pelham, NY 10803
(5p0) Pyetell's Bk Shop, #151, 9/70, 333 5 Av, Pelham, NY 10803

(5q1) Ken Hottle, #19, 3/71, Box 714, Allentown, Pa 18105
(5q2) Hillcrest House, #82, 1/71, Drw 279, Old Greenwich 06870
(5q3) Geo Loukides, #AV, 10/70, Box 77, Stillwater, NJ 07875
(5q4) John Makarewich, #11, 2/69, Box 395, Tarzana, Ca 91356
(5q5) Otto Penzler, #1, 6/69, 2771 Bainbridge, New York 10458
(5q6) Pyetell's Bk Shop, #144, 4/70, 333 5 Av, Pelham, NY 10803
(5q7) Lorraine Smith, #none, 10/70, 73 Wash. St., Reno, Nev 89503
(5q8) Durham Bk Serv, #19, 11/68, Haddam Qtr Rd, Durham, Conn.
(5q9) Wendell A Ross, #none, 8/69, 23 SanJano, Goleta, Ca 93017
(5q0) Chas E Tuttle, #378, 1/72, Rutland, Vt. 05701

(5r1) Rose Tree Inn Bk Shop, #210, 1/71, Tombstone, Ariz 85638
(5r2) Frank E Reynolds, #47, 2/70, 599 Middle St. Portsmouth, N.H.
(5r3) Leona Rostenberg, #48, 5/69, Box 188, Gracie Sta, NY 10028
(5r4) Fred Rothman, #77, 4/71, 57 Leuning, S Hackensack, 07606
(5r5) M & R Books, #none, 10/70, Box 933, Waynesboro, Va 22980
(5r6) Mrs. Reid Carlson, #none, 8/70, 1000 Chew, RD 5, Mansfld, O
(5r7) Argosy Bk Stores, #577, 1/71, 116 E 59, New York 10022
(5r8) Arthur H Clark, #553, 5/70, 1264 S Central, Glendale, Ca.
(5r9) Argosy Bk Stores, #579, 1/71, 116 E 59 St, New York 10022
(5r0) Lester Roberts Bk Shop, #23, 1/70, 47 Golden Gate, SF 94102

(5s1) Shorey's Bk Store, #1, 11/70, 815-3 Av, Seattle, Wa 98104
(5s2) Stinson House, #none, 1/71, Rumney, N.H. 03266
(5s3) Adelphi Bk Shop, #100, 4/71, 822 Fort, Victoria, BC, Canada
(5s4) Shorey's Bk Store, #24, 11/70, 815-3 Av, Seattle, Wa 98104
(5s5) Seattle Bookfinders, #722, #2/72, Box 7174, Seattle, 98133
(5s6) Adelphi Bk Shop, #95, 6/70, 822 Fort, Victoria, BC, Canada
(5s7) Marian Gore, #10070, 7/70, Box 433, SanGabriel, Ca 91775
(5s8) Adelphi Bk Shop, #81, 2/68, 822 Fort, Victoria, BC, Canada
(5s9) Stechert-Hainer, #383, 10/69, 31 E 10, New York 10003
(5s0) Adelphi Bk Shop, #99, 2/71, 822 Fort, Victoria, BC, Canada

(5t1) Int'l Bkfinders, #185, 10/69, Box 3003, BeverlyHills, 90212
(5t2) Chas E Tuttle, #369, 1/69, Rutland, Vt. 05701
(5t3) T N Luther, #53, 3/70, Box 6083, ShawneeMission, Ks 66206
(5t4) Chas E Tuttle, #374, 9/70, Rutland, Vt. 05701
(5t5) Leo Weitz, #84, 1/70, 1377 Lexington, New York 10028
(5t6) Geo H Tweney, 10/70, 16660 MarineView SW, Seattle 98166
(5t7) Chas Tuttle, #375, 1/71, Rutland, Vt. 05701
(5t8) Leo Weitz, #85, 3/71, 1377 Lexington, New York 10028
(5t9) Chas E Tuttle, #373, 8/69, Rutland, Vt. 05701
(5t0) Chas E Tuttle, #372, 1/70, Rutland, Vt. 05701

(5u1) Thos Munnerlyn, #15, 1/71, 1018 Stowe, Abilene, Tex 79605
(5u2) Robt Shuhi, #22, 3/71, Box 136, Bantam, Conn. 06750
(5u3) Urban Books, #13, 9/70, 295 Grizzly Peak, Berkeley 94708
(5u4) T N Luther, #57, 11/70, Box 6083, ShawneeMission, Ks 66206
(5u5) Philip Duschnes, #195, 3/71, 699 Madison, New York 10021
(5u6) Adelphi Bk Shop, #105, 2/72, 822 Fort, Victoria, BC, Canada
(5u7) Roger H Hunt, #none, 1/71, 1709 Camus Ln, Madison 53705
(5u8) T N Luther, #56, 10/70, Box 6083, ShawneeMission, Ks 66206
(5u9) Carry Back Books, #3, 2/72, Franconia, NH 03580
(5u0) Min-Ree Shop, #14, 5/70, 8442 Grand Av, Elmhurst, NY

(5v1) Victoria Bk Shop, #13, 2/71, 16 W 36 St, New York 10018
(5v2) Victoria Bk Shop, #12, 10/70, 16 W 36th, NewYork 10018
(5v3) Appleland Books, #none, 12/70, Box 966, Winchester, Va.
(5v4) Geo E Milkey, #none, 10/70, Box 30, Greenland, NH 03840
(5v5) Mid-West Bk Serv, #127, 8/70, 4301 Kensington, Detroit
(5v6) Urban Books, #16, 9/70, 295 Grizzly Peak, Berkeley, Calif.
(5v7) Alex Hertz, #TV70, 4/70, 88-28 43 Av, Elmhurst, NY 11373
(5v8) Cardinal Bk Serv, #68-2, 3/68, Box 190, Hampton, Va 23369
(5v9) Alex Zaretsky, #none, 11/68, 2217 Victory Pkwy, Cincinnati
(5v0) Victoria Bk Shop, #9, 3/70, 16 W 36 St, New York 10018

(5w1) Elisabeth Woodburn, #970, 2/71, Hopewell, NJ 08525
(5w2) Jeff Wilson, #32, 2/69, 3549 Rhoads, NewtownSq, Pa. 19073
(5w3) Elisabeth Woodburn, #168, 10/70, Hopewell, NJ 08525
(5w4) Jeff Wilson, #30, 9/68, 3549 Rhoads, NewtownSq, Pa. 19073
(5w5) Jeff Wilson, #34, 9/69, 3549 Rhoads, NewtownSq, Pa. 19073
(5w6) Elisabeth Woodburn, #966, 8/70, Hopewell, NJ 08525
(5w7) Elisabeth Woodburn, #767, 8/70, Hopewell, NJ 08525
(5w8) Wm P Wolfe, #26, 6/68, 222 rue de 'Hopital, Montreal 1
(5w9) Jeff Wilson, #33, 4/69, 3549 Rhoads, NewtownSq, Pa. 19073
(5w0) Jeff Wilson, #38, 5/70, 3549 Rhoads, NewtownSq, Pa. 19073

(5x1) Ximenes, #15,6/70,24 W 45th St,New York 10036
(5x2) Universal Books, #121,8/70,6258 Hollywood,Hollywd 90028
(5x3) Ximenes, #13,3/70, 24 W 45th St, New York 10036
(5x4) Paulette Greene, #70-1,4/70,140 Princeton,RockvilleCntr,NY
(5x5) Heritage Bkshop, #105,11/69,6707 Hollywd,Hollywd 90028
(5x6) L E Gay, #19,2/69, Box 548, Lordsburg, NM 88045
(5x7) Jeff Wilson, #35,11/69,3549 Rhoads,NewtownSq,Pa. 19073
(5x8) Blitz Books, #24,1/68, Box 64, Los Altos,Ca. 94022
(5x9) Urban Bks, #10,6/69,295 GrizzlyPeak,Berkeley,Ca. 94708
(5x0) Pyetell's Bk Shop, #150,4/70, 333 -5th Av, Pelham, NY

(5y1) Thos Munnerlvn, #14,10/70,1018 Stowe,Abilene,Tx 79605
(5y2) Edgar Heyl, #120, 10/70, 11 W Chase, Baltimore, Md 21201
(5y3) Edgar Heyl, #111,7/69, 11 W Chase, Baltimore, Md 21201
(5y4) Edgar Heyl, #110,6/69, 11 W Chase, Baltimore, Md 21201
(5y5) T N Luther, #52,10/69,ShawneeMission,Ks. 66206
(5y6) T N Luther, #51, 9/69, ShawneeMission, Ks 66206
(5y7) T N Luther, #50, 3/69, Shawnee Mission, Ks 66206
(5y8) Thos Munnerlyn, #13,9/70,1018 Stowe,Abilene,Tx 79605
(5y9) T N Luther, #49, 2/69, Box 6083,ShawneeMission,Kans.
(5y0) Robt Hayman, #43,6/71, RFD1, Carey,Ohio 43316

(5z1) Arthur Clark, #575,5/71,1264 S Central Av, Glendale,Ca.
(5z2) Zeitlin & VerBrugge, #227,3/71,815 N LaCienega, LA,Ca.
(5z3) Carry Back Books, #1,6/71, Franconia, NH, 03580
(5z4) Victoria Bk Shop, #14,6/71,16 W 36 St, New York 10018
(5z5) Nelson Bond, #10,6/71,1625 Hampton,Roanoke,Va.24015
(5z6) T N Luther, #46,5/68, Box 6083, ShawneeMission, Ks 66206
(5z7) Jenkins Co, #45,7/71, Box 2085, Austin,Tex. 78767
(5z8) M & R Books, #7,4/68, Box 933, Waynesboro, Va. 22980
(5z9) John Howell, #38,5/69,434 Post, SanFran.,Ca 94102
(5z0) Jenkins Co, #44,7/71,Box 2085,Austin,Tex 78767

(5aa1) Hugh Anson-Cartwright, #1,1/70,229College,Toronto 2B
(5aa2) Adelphi Bk Shop, #250,1970, 822 Fort, Victoria,B.C.
(5aa3) Robt Hayman, #36,9/69, RFD 1, Carey,Ohio 43316
(5aa4) Robt Hayman, #32, 9/68, RFD 1,Carey,Ohio 43316
(5aa5) Robt Hayman, #35, 6/69, RFD 1, Carey, Ohio 43316
(5aa6) R R Allen, #16,1/71,5300 Bluefield, Knoxville,Tn.37921
(5aa7) Adelphi Bk Shop, #97,10/70, 822 Fort, Victoria, B.C.
(5aa8) Robt Hayman, #33, 1/69, RFD 1, Carey, Ohio 43316
(5aa9) Robt Hayman, #31, 6/68, RFD 1, Carey, Ohio 43316
(5aa0) Adelphi Bk Shop, #101,7/71, 822 Fort, Victoria, B.C.

(5bb1) Bibliophile, #711,1/71,83 East Av, Norwalk,Ct. 06851
(5bb2) Bibliophile, #692,9/70,83 East Av, Norwalk,Ct. 06851
(5bb3) G A Bibby, #104,6/71,714 Pleasant, Roseville,Ca. 95678
(5bb4) T N Luther, #62,1/72, Box 6083, ShawneeMission,Ks.66206
(5bb5) G A Bibby, #101,12/70,714 Pleasant,Roseville,Ca. 95678
(5bb6) G A Bibby, #100,11/70,714 Pleasant,Roseville,Ca. 95678
(5bb7) G A Bibby, #97,11/70,714 Pleasant, Roseville,Ca. 95678
(5bb8) G A Bibby, #98,11/70,714 Pleasant, Roseville,Ca 95678
(5bb9) G A Bibby, #99,11/70,714 Pleasant, Roseville,Ca 95678
(5bb0) Adams Brown, #94D,9/71, Box 399, Exeter, NH 03833

(5cc1) Pierce Bk Co, #55,7/71, Winthrop, Iowa 50682
(5cc2) Dauber & Pine Bkshop, #663,10/70,66-5 Av, New York
(5cc3) Dauber & Pine, #662,10/70, 66-5 Av, New York 10011
(5cc4) Arthur H Clark, #573,5/71,1264 S Central, Glendale,Ca.
(5cc5) Ken Crawford, #64B,5/71,2719 E 16 av, N.StPaul 55109
(5cc6) Edw P Rich, #none,5/71, Box 295, Haverford, Pa. 19041
(5cc7) Edgar Heyl, #123,5/71,11 W Chase st, Baltimore 21201
(5cc8) Jenkins Co, #43,5/71,Box 2085, Austin,Tx 78767
(5cc9) Philip Duschnes, #196,5/71,699 Madison,N Y 10021
(5cc0) Justin Schiller, #23,7/69,2038 E 64, Brooklyn, NY 11234

(5dd1) T N Luther, #63,2/72, Box 6083, ShawneeMission, Ks 66206
(5dd2) Western Hemisphere #2,8/70,1613 Central, Sroughton,Ma.
(5dd3) Western Hemisphere, #3, 9/70,1613 Central,Sroughton,Ma.
(5dd4) Arthur H Clark, #563,4/71,1264 S Central, Glendale, Ca.
(5dd5) Arthur H Clark, #555,12/70,1264 S Central, Glendale, Ca.
(5dd6) Arthur H Clark, #557,1/71, 1264 S Central, Glendale, Ca.
(5dd7) Haunted Bookshop, #8,12/70,845 Fort, Victoria, B.C.
(5dd8) Philip Duschnes, #186,6/68,699 Madison,NewYork 10021
(5dd9) Arthur H Clark, #511,8/70,1264 S Central, Glendale 91204
(5dd0) Adelphi Bk Shop, #102, 8/71,822 Fort, Victoria, B.C.

(5ee1) F Thos Heller, #135,5/71,308 E 79, New York 10021
(5ee2) Edw Myers, #18,2/71,Box 47, Collinsville,Ct. 06002
(5ee3) Edw Myers, #3, 11/70, Box 47, Collinsville, Ct 06002
(5ee4) F Thos Heller, #none, 12/70, 308 E 79 St, NewYork 10021
(5ee5) F Thos Heller, #134(2),10/70,308 E 79, New York 10021
(5ee6) F Thos Heller, #134,7/70,308 E 79 St, NewYork 10021
(5ee7) F Thos Heller, #129,5/69,308 E 79 St, NewYork 10021
(5ee8) F.Thos Heller, #129(2),5/69,308 E 79, NewYork 10021
(5ee9) Philip Duschnes, #193,10/70,699 Madison, New York
(5ee0) Edw Myers, #4,9/71,Box 47, Collinsville, Ct. 06022

(5ff1) Current Co, #3,1/72, Box 46, Bristol,R.I. 02809
(5ff2) Half Moon Books, #27, 1/72, Box 444, Guilderland, N.Y.
(5ff3) T N Luther, #45,9/67,Box 6083, ShawneeMission, 66206
(5ff4) Fred Rothman, #79,12/71,57 Leuning, S Hackensack,n.j.
(5ff5) Pat T Conley, #1,8/71,1100 Pontiac, Cranston,R.I. 02920
(5ff6) Lathrop Harper, #205,11/71,22 E 40, New York 10016
(5ff7) Robt Hayman, #46,1/72, RFD 1, Carey,Ohio 43316
(5ff8) T N Luther, #48,10/68,Box 6083, ShawneeMission, 66206
(5ff9) Goodspeed's Bk Shop, #546,4/68,18 Beacon, Boston 02108
(5ff0) Norman Clayton, #1,9/71,79 Lakeshore Cir, Sacramento,Ca

(5gg1) Robt J Drake, #none,11/68,682 Miller, Richmond, B.C.
(5gg2) Robt J Drake, #none,11/68, 682 Miller, Richmond,B.C.
(5gg3) Robt J Drake, #none,3/69, 682 Miller, Richmond,B.C.
(5gg4) Goodspeed's Bk Shop, #547,18 Beacon, Boston 4/68
(5gg5) L E Gay, #21,1/70,Box 548, Lordsburg, NM 88045
(5gg6) Goodspeed's Bk Shop, #566,1/71, 18 Beacon, Boston,Ma.
(5gg7) L E Gay, #27,1/71,Box 548, Lordsburg, NM 88045
(5gg8) L E Gay, #28, 1/71, Box 548, Lordsburg, NM 88045
(5gg9) L E Gay, #29, 2/71, Box 548, Lordsburg, N.M. 88045
(5gg0) Incredible Barn, #32, 10/71, Main St, Orleans,Ma.02653

(5hh1) Heritage Bkshop, #107,9/70,6707 Hollywood, Hollywd,Ca
(5hh2) Adelphi Bk Shop, #88,4/69,822 Fort, Victoria, B.C.
(5hh3) J T Hickox, #3,10/70,4724 Eastman, OklahomaCty, Okla.
(5hh4) Holmes Book Co, #94,1/70,274-14th, Oakland, Ca.94612
(5hh5) Robt Hayman, #34,3/69, RFD 1, Carey, Ohio 43316
(5hh6) Edgar Heyl, #116,4/70,11 W Chase, Baltimore,Md 21201
(5hh7) Edgar Heyl, #117,5/70,11 W Chase, Baltimore,Md.21201
(5hh8) Adelphi Bk Shop, #94,4/70, 822 Fort, Victoria, B.C.
(5hh9) Adelphi Bk Shop, #93, 2/70, 822 Fort St, Victoria, B.C.
(5hh0) John Howell, #40,9/70,434 Post, SanFrancisco 94102

(5ii1) J T Hickox, #9, 3/72, 4724 Eastman, OklahomaCty 73122
(5ii2) Ken Hottle, #23,5/72, Box 714, Allentown, Pa. 18105
(5ii3) Biblo & Tannen, #201,5/72, 63-4th Av, New York 10003
(5ii4) Edw C Fales, #14,5/72, Turnpike rd, Salisbury, NH 03268
(5ii5) Jenkins Co, #51,5/72, Box 2085, Austin, Tex. 78767
(5ii6) Goodspeeds Bk Shop, #544,11/67,18 Beacon, Boston,Ma.
(5ii7) Fred B Rothman, #80,4/72,57 Leuning St, S Hackensack,NJ
(5ii8) Geo MacManus, #211,5/72,1317 Irving, Philadelphia,Pa.
(5ii9) Edgar Heyl, #129,4/72,11 W Chase st, Baltimore 21201
(5ii0) F Thos Heller, #138,4/72, 308 E 79 St, NewYork 10021

(5jj1) Lyrebird Bksellers, #1,3/72, Box 1252, SanRafael 94902
(5jj2) Geo MacManus, #209, 1/72, 1317 Irving, Philadelphia, Pa
(5jj3) Biblo & Tannen, #199, 3/72, 63-4th av, NewYork 10003
(5jj4) Book Center, #371, 10/7, 207 N Main, SantaAna 92701
(5jj5) F Thos Heller, #136, 7/71, 308 E 79 St, NewYork 10021
(5jj6) Victoria Bk Shop, #16, 16 W 36th st, New York, 10018
(5jj7) Ken Crawford, #67, 4/72, 2719 E 16th av, StPaul 55109
(5jj8) Lathrop Harper, #206, 4/72, 22 E 40th st, NewYork 10016
(5jj9) Robt Hayman, #47, 7/72, RFD 1, Carey, Ohio 43316
(5jj0) Geo MacManus, #210, 4/72, 1317 Irving, Phila. 19017

(5kk1) Gary Woolson, #46, 11/71, Box 1051, Bangor, Me 04401
(5kk2) Robt Hayman, #30, 4/68, RFD 1, Carey, Ohio 43316
(5kk3) Min-Ree Shop, #15, 10/71, 8442 Grand, Elmhurst 11373
(5kk4) Ken Crawford, #65, 8/71, 2719 E 16 av, N.StPaul 55109
(5kk5) J T Hickox, #8, 10/71, 4724 Eastman Dr. , Okla.City
(5kk6) Jenkins Co, #46, 9/71, Box 2085, Austin, Tex. 78767
(5kk7) Hickox, #7, 7/71, 4724 Eastman Drive, OklahomaCty
(5kk8) Hale House, #71B, 9/71, Box 818, Wynnewood, Pa.
(5kk9) Hale House, #71C, 9/71, Box 818, Wynnewood 19096
(5kk0) Bibliophile, #713, 4/71, 83 East Av, Norwalk 06851

(5mm1) Geo MacManus, #206, 6/71, 1317 Irving, Phila 19107
(5mm2) Geo MacManus, #202, 10/70, 1317 Irving, Phila 19107
(5mm3) Chas E. Tuttle, #376, 7/71, Rutland, Vt. 05701
(5mm4) Jenkins Co, #48, 3/72, Box 2085, Austin, Tex 78767
(5mm5) Rouse's Bookhouse, #35, 3/69, Box 13, Charlevoix, Mi.
(5mm6) Rouse's Bookhouse, #41, 7/70, Box 13, Charlevoix, Mi.
(5mm7) Rouse's Bkhouse, #37, 10/69, Box 13, Charlevoix 49720
(5mm8) Bucklins Books, #63, 5/71, Ipswich, Mass 01938
(5mm9) Aries Bookseach, #703, 8/70, Box 2428, VanNuys, Ca.
(5mm0) Pauline Millen, #4, 9/71, 3325 Crescent, DesMoines

(5nn1) Heinoldt Books, #none, 10/71, SoEggHarbor, NJ 08215
(5nn2) Adelphi Bk Shop, #104, 1/72, 822 Fort st, Victoria, B C
(5nn3) Denning House, #33, 10/71, Box 42, SallisburyMills, NY
(5nn4) Jenkins Co, #47, 11/71, Box 2085, Austin, Tex. 78767
(5nn5) Blitz Books, #50, 1/72, Box 64, Los Altos, Ca. 94022
(5nn6) Biblo & Tannen, #198, 1/72, 63-4th av, N.Y. 10003
(5nn7) Heritage Bkshop, #115, 1/72, 6707 Hollywd, Hollywood
(5nn8) Bernard Amtmann, #280, 1/72, 1176 Sherbrooke, Mntrl
(5nn9) Wendell Smith, #34, 1/72, Main st, Orleans, Ma 02653
(5nn0) Wendell Smith, #33, 12/71, Main st, Orleans, Ma 02653

(5qq1) Banquette Bk Shop, #10, 2/68. 55 Sutter, SF, Ca. 94102
(5qq2) Chas Apfelbaum, 11/71, 39 Flower, ValleyStream 11581
(5qq3) Americana Books, #2.71, 10/71, Box 243, Decatur 46733
(5qq4) Putman Bkshop, #121, 7/71, 304 W Jeff, Bloomington, Ill
(5qq5) Ottenberg Books, #1, 7/70, 724 Pine, Seattle 98101
(5qq6) Owens' Rare Books, #5, 12/71, Box 4173, Madison 53711
(5qq7) Carry Back Bks, #2, 11/71, Franconia, N.H. 03580
(5qq8) Bucklins Books, #64, 10/71, Ipswich, Mass. 01938
(5qq9) Apfelbaum, #none, 12/71, 39 Flower, ValleyStream, N.Y.
(5qq0) Justin Schiller, #19, 6/68, 2038 E 64th st, Bklyn 11234

(5rr1) R Devonshire, #1, 1/72, RD2, GenungGdns, Ithaca 148 50
(5rr2) Edw P Rich, #none, 9/71, Box 295, Haverford, Pa 19041
(5rr3) Geo MacManus, #208, 11/71, 1317 Irving, Phila. 19107
(5rr4) Fred Rothman, #78, 4/71, 57 Leuning, S Hackensack, NJ
(5rr5) Family Book Store, #23, 11/71, 1367 EColo, Glendale, Ca
(5rr6) Seattle Bkfinders, #721, 1/72, Box 7471, Seattle 98133
(5rr7) Victoria Bk Shop, #15, 11/71, 16 W 36th St, NewYork, NY
(5rr8) Lathrop Harper, #3, 2/68, 22 E 40th , NewYork 100 16
(5rr9) York County Bks, #10, 11/71, 25 Gerrard W, Toronto, Ont
(5rr0) Lester Roberts, #25, 9/71, 47 GoldenGate, SF, Ca 94102

(5ss1) Shorey Book Store, #11, 11/70, 815-3rd av, Seattle 98104
(5ss2) Alfred Paine, #72, 1/71, Wolefits rd, Bethel, Ct. 06801
(5ss3) Scribner Rare Bk Shop, #173, 12/70, 597-5 av, NY 10017
(5ss4) Shorey's, #1, 12/70, 815 - 3rd Av, Seattle, Wa. 98104
(5ss5) Edw Morrill, #165, 12/70, 25 Kingston, Boston, Ma 02111
(5ss6) Shorey's, #1(Russian), 1/71, 815-3rd av, Seattle 98104
(5ss7) House of Books, #none, 1/71, 667 Madison, N.Y. 10021
(5ss8) Shorey's, #1(Hunting), 11/70, 815-3rd av, Seattle 98104
(5ss9) Heritage Bkshop, #109, 1/71, 6707 Hollywd, Hollywd, Ca.
(5ss0) Shorey's, #13, 8/71, 815 - 3rd Av., Seattle , Wa. 98104

(5tt1) Laurence Lingle, #25, 1/72, 1415 Elizabeth, FtWorth, Tx.
(5tt2) Heritage Bkshop, #114, 9/71, 6707 Hollywd, Hollywood, Ca
(5tt3) T N Luther, #60, 9/71, Box 6083, ShawneeMission, 66206
(5tt4) Robt Hayman, #44, 9/71, RFD 1, Varey, Ohio 43316
(5tt5) Biblo & Tannen, #196, 9/71, 63-4thAv, NewYork 10003
(5tt6) Geo MacManus, #207, 9/71, 1317 Irving, Phila., 19017
(5tt7) Carnegie Bk Shop, #319, 9/71, 140 E 59th st, N.Y. 10022
(5tt8) Dawson's Bk Shop, #404, 10/71, 535 N Larchmont, LA, Ca
(5tt9) Dawson's Bk Shop, #403, 10/71, 535 N Larchmont, LA, Ca
(5tt0) Dawson's Bk Shop, #379, 10/71, 535 N Larchmont, LA, Ca

(5ww1) Hale House, #72A, 1/72, Box 181, Wynnewood, Pa 19096
(5ww2) Marian Gore, #none, 5/71, Box 433, SanGarbiel, 91775
(5ww3) Book Gallery, #9, 10/71, 512 Mamaroneck, White Plns, NY
(5ww4) Owens' Books, #4, 8/70, Box 4173, Madison, Wis 53711
(5ww5) Wstrn Hemisphere, #5, 10/70, 1613Central, Stoughton, Ma.
(5ww6) Wstrn Hemisphere, #6, 10/70, 1613Central, Stoughton, Ma.
(5ww7) Wstrn Hemisphere, #7, 10/70, 1613Central, Stoughton, Ma.
(5ww8) Wstrn Hemisphere, #8, 10/70, 1613Central, Stoughton, Ma.
(5ww9) T N Luther, #47, 5/68, Box 6083, ShawneeMission, Ks 66206
(5ww0) Marian Gore, #none, 1/68, Box 433, SanGabriel, Ca 91775

(5xx1) Adrian's, #36, 5/71, 150 N Brook, Geneva , NY 14456
(5xx2) Nicholas Sysyn, #4, 5/71, Pleasant St, Antrim, NH 03440
(5xx3) L E Gay, #30, 3/71, Box 548, Lordsburg, NM 88045
(5xx4) Heritage Bookshop, #list, 1/71, 6707 Hollywd, Hollywd, Ca.
(5xx5) Arthur H Clark, #561, 1/71, 1264 S Central, Glendale, Ca.
(5xx6) Ximenes, #16, 10/70, 120 E 85th St, NewYork 10028
(5xx7) Chas E Tuttle, #377, 5/71, Rutland, Vt. 05701
(5xx8) J T Hickox, #6, 5/71, 4724 Eastman Drive, OklaCty 73122
(5xx9) Ximenes, #21, 7/71, 120 E 85th St, NewYork 10028
(5xx0) Richard Ramer, #1, 8/71, 45 Martense, Brklyn, NY 11226

(5yy1) Jenkins Co, #49, 4/72, Box 2085, Austin, Tex 78767
(5yy2) R Devonshire, #2, 4/72, RD2, GenungGdns, Ithaca 14850
(5yy3) Dawson's Bk Shop, #408, 4/72, 535 N Larchmont, LA 90004
(5yy4) Jenkins Co, #51, 4/72, Box 2085, Austin, Tex. 78767
(5yy5) Incredible Barn, #38, 5/72, Main st, Orleans, Ma 02653
(5yy6) Biblo & Tannen, #200, 4/72, 63-4th av, NewYork 10003
(5yy7) T N Luther, #64, 4/72, Box 6083, ShawneeMission, Ks 66206
(5yy8) W D Payton, #1-72, 5/72, 5511 Applegate, Louisville 40219
(5yy9) Adelphi Bk Shop, #106, 5/72, 822 Fort, Victoria, B.C.
(5yy0) Ken Hottle, #22, 3/72, Box 714, Allentown, Pa 18105

(5zz1) Arthur Clark, #577, 9/71, 1264 S Central, Glendale 91204
(5zz2) Current Co, 9/71, Box 46, Bristol, R.I. 02809
(5zz3) Old Mill House Bks, #BB, 8/71, Box 77, Stillwater, 07875
(5zz4) Zion Book Store, #list, 9/71, 254 S Main, SaltLakeCity, U
(5zz5) T N Luther, #61, 10/71, Box 6083, ShawneeMission, Kans
(5zz6) Edgar Heyl, #127, 10/71, 11 W Chase, Baltimore, 21201
(5zz7) Alta Calif Bkstore, #48, 10/71, 1407 Solano, Albany, Cal.
(5zz8) Adelphi Bk Shop, #103, 10/71, 822 Fort, Victoria, B.C.
(5zz9) Robt Hayman, #45, 10/71, RFD 1, Carey, Ohio 43316
(5zz0) Half Moon Bks, #26, 9/71, Box 444, Guilderland, NY